1986 TEXAS ALMANAC
AND STATE INDUSTRIAL GUIDE

P9-ECA-612

SESQUICENTENNIAL EDITION

With Gratitude

With the 1986-87 Texas Almanac, Miss Ruth Harris, associate editor, completes a 49-year career with The Dallas Morning News. This book is the 21st Almanac that Miss Harris has helped prepare, and she has worked on more Almanacs than anyone else in the publication's 129-year history. Few people in Texas can equal Miss Harris' knowledge of the state. The management of The Dallas Morning News, the A.H. Belo Corp. and her co-workers extend their sincere appreciation for her tireless, exacting and dedicated work. Miss Harris has helped make the Texas Almanac the respected institution it is today.

ISBN 0-914511-02-5 (Hardbound)
ISBN 0-914511-03-3 (Paperbound)
Copyright 1985, A. H. Belo Corp., Communications Center, Dallas, Tx. 75265
Library of Congress Card No. 10-3390

TABLE OF CONTENTS

MIKE KINGSTON, *Editor*
RUTH HARRIS, *Associate Editor*
MARY G. CRAWFORD, *Editorial Assistant*
ERMA BAILEY, *Artist* DAVID DEAL, *Artist*

Horseshoe Bay...

...Discover it!

ESCAPE to the Texas Hill Country. PLAY the courses that are part of the largest Robert Trent Jones designed golf complex in the nation . . . the 54 holes of Horseshoe Bay. ENJOY all the incredible amenities of this truly international residential resort.

YES! Own a part of this peaceful place . . . created for pleasure. Choose property on the golf course, by the water, in the hills. A lot; an existing home, townhome or condo; one of the "Homes of Horseshoe Bay" to be built on your site. Primary or vacation home. Investment opportunity. Make what you want of Horseshoe Bay. The decision is yours.

A special video presentation is available for viewing in the privacy of your own home. For more information, call (512) 598-2553.

23-mile long, constant-level Lake LBJ, limitless watersports . . . full-service marina.

Spectacular tennis center highlighted by oriental water gardens . . . outdoor and covered courts.

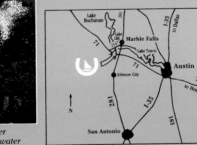

Private airport with 6,000-ft. lighted runway capable of landing a DC-9.

In Texas, Call Toll-Free:
800-292-1545

HORSESHOE BAY CORP
P.O. Box 7752 • Horseshoe Bay, TX 78654

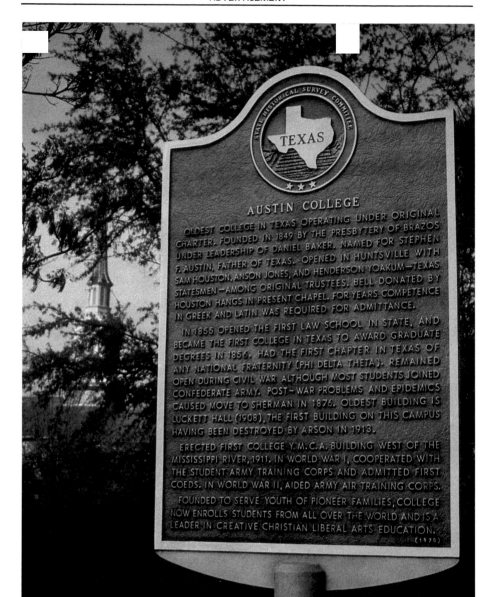

TEXAS ENVIRONMENT

Once common throughout most of the state, the black bear now is found only in isolated pockets in East Texas and the Trans-Pecos. (Almanac photo of exhibit at the Dallas Museum of Natural History.)

Texas Wildlife at the Sesquicentennial

This article was compiled and edited by the staff of the Dallas Museum of Natural History and Aquarium, Louis Gorr, director. Contributors included: Larry Calvin, aquarium director; Vicki Davis, curator of live animals; Charles E. Finsley, curator of earth science and botany (editor); Dr. Richard Fullington, curator of collections and invertebrates; Steve Robertson, aquatic biologist; Steve R. Runnels, curator of ornithology; Dr. David M. Schleser, freshwater aquarist; and William Wilson, curator of mammals.

The Dallas Museum of Natural History and Aquarium were founded in 1936 as part of the Texas Centennial celebration. Their purpose was to tell the story of the animal specimens they housed, as that story was known in 1936. Today, many of the exhibits and the wildlife have changed. What are some of the animal winners and losers as we have moved from 1936 most of the way through the 20th century? What will be the "natural habitat" of the next century?

As people who work with nature, the staff of the institution offers the following perspective on wildlife at the Sesquicentennial.

The Birds

Texas bird life was first brought to the attention of the scientific world in 1837 when John James Audubon, bird artist and naturalist, came to the Republic. As is the case today, Audubon found the Texas coast an excellent place for observing birds. Many that he saw — like the blue-winged teal, snowy egret and great blue heron — are still abundant. But Audubon also found **brown pelicans** everywhere. The 1936 Texas Centennial visitors also would have found abundant brown pelicans had they visited the coast. But after World War II, pesticides washing down our rivers changed the picture. Brown pelican reproduction declined. The once-numerous birds faced total extinction in Texas in the 1960s. Conservation efforts were successful, and the brown pelicans are making a slow comeback. Time travelers from 1936 would be surprised to find the coast so devoid of these big brown birds that once stole fishermen's bait.

A different kind of story follows from an observation of Audubon's on May 9, 1837, on a trip up Buffalo Bayou to Houston: "It was here today that I found the **ivory-billed woodpecker** in abundance." Ornithologists today probably have the final story of this largest North American woodpecker. In 1936 a few remained in the dense woods of Southeast Texas. The ivory-bill was last reliably photographed in Louisiana in 1937. Rumors of the bird's survival persist, but it is now probably extinct.

Other Texas birds, like the **greater prairie chicken**, the **passenger pigeon** and the **Carolina parakeet**, were only a memory by 1936.

The **house sparrow** was unknown in Texas until 1867 when a small flock was imported into Galveston. They are now one of the most common Texas birds. Some birds, however, have invaded our state without the deliberate help of man. At the turn of the century, the **great-tailed grackle** was found only along the South Texas border. These invaders from tropical America have advanced across the state, reaching Dallas in 1947. They can be seen today in Fair Park in Dallas, but they were not guests at the 1936 Centennial.

Another famous invader is the **cattle egret**. As recently as 1958, it first appeared along Mustang Island east of Corpus Christi. Thus began a phenomenally successful range extension throughout the state. There are over 2 million cattle egrets in Texas today.

Texas heads toward its bicentennial as the No. 1 bird state. More than 550 species are found here (two-thirds of the kinds of birds in the entire United States). The loss of wild habitat has been and continues to be the biggest problem for Texas birds. Birds facing the biggest threat include the **whooping crane** (which shows improvement), the **golden-cheeked warbler**, red-cockaded woodpecker, Attwater's prairie chicken, peregrine falcon and Southern bald eagle.

The Mammals

The larger the wild animal, the less it has been able to coexist with man in Texas. In 1936, a few people were still alive who knew something about the last **black bear**

The pronghorn antelope's (above) habitat extends from the Davis Mountains in Southwest Texas north to the Panhandle, but shrinkage of the bald eagle's (left) habitat threatens its existence (exhibits at the Dallas Museum of Natural History).

Great blue herons (right) and brown pelicans (below) were both abundant at the time of the Texas Centennial. But pelicans recently faced extinction because of pesticide runoff. Their numbers are now increasing due to conservation efforts (exhibits at the Dallas Museum of Natural History).

killed in Dallas or Houston. The German geologist, Ferdinand Roemer, reports that, in 1847, the newly founded town of Fredericksburg lighted lamps and cooked with plentiful bear oil supplied by enterprising Indians. In 1936, people were closer to such memories, but the great large mammals of Texas were fast disappearing from even the remote areas of the state. However, some large mammals remain.

Vernon Bailey in his 1905 biological survey of Texas (a survey the Dallas Museum of Natural History used as a "Bible" for exhibit labels in 1936) stated, "No part of the United States affords more perfect conditions for deer than southern Texas . . . all that is required for their maintenance and rapid increase is efficient protection."

Whitetail deer are today the most important game animal in Texas. There are about 2.5 million deer in the state, with about 1.4 million on the Edward's Plateau of Central Texas. The largest whitetails occur, as Bailey predicted, on the South Texas plains. Hunters harvest less than 10 percent of the deer population each year, while the **coyote** ranks first and the **bobcat** second as nature's predators of Texas deer.

Landowners have helped maintain a healthy deer population in Texas. Ranchers often find revenues from deer hunting to be an important source of income, more probably than ranchers earned 50 years ago, before the modern demand for hunting leases from the growing urban population.

In 1890, naturalist Clark P. Streator reported the **armadillo** as a rare animal on Raglan's ranch near Eagle Pass, where he reported two had been taken in 10 years. In 1891, the animals were reported as common north of Brownsville and much sought after for food. In 1904, baskets made of armadillo shells began to show up in curio shops in San Antonio. In 1936, they were still considered a South Texas animal, associated in the art of the Centennial with cacti and yucca. The range of the nine-banded armadillo continued to move northward so that it is universal throughout East Texas today. Armadillo popularity in song and story also has grown. The armadillo probably will play a large part in the symbolism of the Sesquicentennial.

It is impossible to detail the ups and downs of all the mammals of Texas during the past 50 years, but here are a few examples.

When the Dallas Museum of Natural History was built in 1936, one of the first habitat groups was the **pronghorn "antelope."** The label spoke of the animal's near extinction. Careful state protection and controlled hunting have literally saved the pronghorn. Similarly, the once-plentiful **Texas river otter** was in 1936 a very much endangered animal. By 1945, all trapping of otter was prohibited. However, by 1950, the population had recovered to the point that an open season was allowed. In all the United States, nowhere do otter have a better chance of survival than in Texas.

To the surprise of many, **mink** still live in Texas as it heads for the 21st century. In the large cities, such as Dallas and Houston, mink are often found dead on highways near streams or ponds. Mink are found today in all of East Texas and as far south as Corpus Christi. In 1936, there were many Texans who trapped for a living; today, the number has greatly diminished. So there is a sort of modern respite for some animals.

In general, today's Texans have a different relationship with animals, especially mammals, than did early-day residents. We keep fewer household domestic food animals, especially in our cities. The dirt and grime of professions like trapping or meat hunting are treated as peculiar. Consequently, we worry less about the fox in the hen house or other threats from wild animals. To some extent, things are easier for some wildlife. The past is recalled when a beaver chews down a favorite tree, perhaps right in Downtown Dallas.

The Invertebrates

Invertebrates are animals with no internal skeleton, like insects, spiders and worms. Few people worry about their extinction. Many are considered to be pests to be eradicated rather than a valued part of our environment. Others, like the **oysters**, have given much benefit and profit. Seven out of 10 species of animals on earth are invertebrates.

It was not until 1983 that the World Wildlife Fund published the first Red Data Book on the world's endangered insects. There were 582 species listed. The Centennial visitors of 1936 probably had no conception that such creatures would ever be written about in this way. But invertebrates are important because they are the "grease" that makes the natural world go round. They are the major food source for most higher forms of life

and most invertebrates are beneficial to us in one form or another.

Early Texas settlers would ride in the family wagon from San Antonio to the San Marcos River to catch a very special kind of once-plentiful freshwater **shrimp**, the Macrobrachium. They had a picnic feeding on this five-pound prawn. This delicacy is now extinct. Dams along the river prevented the young from getting to the coastal bays where they must be to properly mature and later return far upstream to spawn.

As Texas streams and rivers became polluted, much of our aquatic fauna diminished. Texas once had the leading pearl button industry in the nation. As an illustration of the timing of this stream pollution, in 1935, six different species of colorful freshwater sponges lived in the streams around Dallas. Today, there is but one species.

Many native Texas invertebrates are losing ground to imported invertebrates. The most notorious example is the imported fire ant. Fire ants devour any living thing within a 50-foot radius of their nest.

Texas in the 1980s is more urbanized than in the past, and some invertebrates have responded to the challenge. Termites from Formosa, more insidious than natives, are spreading northward from Houston. Species of wasps never found before in Dallas are finding suitable nesting sites under eaves and around housing developments. The fiddle spider, or brown recluse, with a poisonous bite is finding an excellent new home in seldom-used corners of urban buildings. As we have lost some wild habitats, a vast new habitat is emerging, inviting a new flora and fauna — "urbana." It is doubtful that this new environment will be plowed under soon, as have been so many natural habitats. Our modern age is one of increasing awareness of invertebrates.

Rocks, Minerals and Fossils

Development of knowledge about the mineral wealth was one of the first scientific endeavors in Texas. The early interest was a mixture of dreams of gold and silver and a very practical concern for fertile land and solid building stone. In the end, it was the industrial minerals that became the most valuable resources. Texas **granite**, **marble** and **limestone** have far outstripped in total value the relatively small amount of **gold**, **silver** and **mercury** that was mined in Texas.

In 1936, Texans had seen the high-grade ores in gold, silver and mercury depleted. Oil was still going strong from the shallow fields of the early discoveries. Today high technology is needed to produce ores of lower grade or oil from greater depths or more unyielding source rocks.

Yet some echoes of 1936 remain. Texas quarries at Cedar Park near Austin has cut and carved the unique **Cordova creme** and **Cordova shell** stone for many years. It contains one of the world's most beautiful conglomerates of fossil shells. This distinctive Texas stone has been used in buildings throughout the world. It was utilized in many of the buildings in Fair Park in Dallas for the Texas Centennial. Structures such as the **San Jacinto Monument** in Houston and **Texas Memorial Museum** in Austin are other examples. Despite extensive use for 50 years, the deposits are still plentiful, and its acceptance by artists and architects is growing.

Not all Texas traditions are based in the first 100 years of Texas history. Since the Centennial, the Legislature has recognized an official **Texas gemstone** — **Texas blue topaz** from Mason County. The lawmakers also have dignified **fossil palm wood** from East Texas as the official **Texas rock or fossil**. At the same time, ranchers like Frank Woodward Sr. and Jr. have spent these last 50 years earning worldwide recognition for the beautiful Texas **agates** of West Texas. So-called red plume and pom-pom agates are found nowhere else in the world. The area around Balmorhea has become famous for magnificent blue agates.

Although several "dinosaur hunters" like Jacob Boll of Dallas prowled Texas, sending large reptilian specimens back to eastern museums in the late 1800s, modern paleontology began largely with the government-funded excavations of the Great Depression. The thousands of fossils excavated during the Depression provided excellent collections for the **Panhandle-Plains Museum** in Canyon and **Texas Memorial Museum** in Austin. Fifty years later the scientific importance of many of these discoveries is still being researched.

Fossil discoveries of note are made frequently today. University of Texas scientists found a giant flying reptile in the Big Bend. Its wingspread was larger than many small airplanes. Researchers from Texas Tech University in Lubbock have made numerous discover-

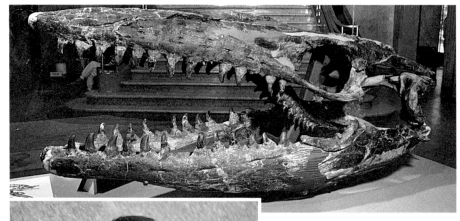

This mosasaur skull (above), which belonged to a dinosaur-age swimming reptile as long as a school bus, was found near Dallas (exhibit at Dallas Museum of Natural History). Beaver (left) are abundant along Texas streams, even in large cities (photo courtesy Dallas Museum of Natural History).

Once thought to be a South Texas animal, the armor-plated armadillo (right) now ranges throughout much of the state (photo courtesy Dallas Museum of Natural History). Alligators, (below) endangered at the time of the Texas Centennial because of hunting and urban growth, have made a strong comeback since 1969 (exhibit at Dallas Museum of Natural History).

ies of fossils and early artifacts at the **Lubbock Lake** site. Also their vertebrate paleontologist, Dr. Sankar Chatterjee, has discovered an important new dinosaur-like creature, which he named after Post, Texas — the **Postosuchus.** The **Strecker Museum** in Waco is still working on a site containing more than a dozen prehistoric elephants. Dr. Walter W. Dalquest at Midwestern University in Wichita Falls, Dr. Ernest L. Lundelius at UT-Austin and Professor Bob Slaughter at Southern Methodist University are all independently discovering new types of fossil mammals, including camels, rhinoceros and unusual rodents millions of years old. The Dallas Museum of Natural History, among many finds, is reconstructing a large mosasaur, a swimming reptile from the age of dinosaurs, that was as long as a school bus.

Without doubt, 50 years after the many excavations of the Depression, Texas fossil beds have only begun to yield the profusion of their treasures.

Plant Life

Plant life has always been varied and abundant in Texas. The Spanish explorers rode through dense woodlands in East Texas. Early American colonists, such as Stephen F. Austin, did not see Texas as a desert but as rich farm land. The common expression is that the prairie grasses were as tall as the belly of a horse. Thousands of years of slow, fragile soil formation had even established grass on much of what is today the desert land of far West Texas. Geological studies show that all of Texas was wetter and cooler several thousand years ago than in recent centuries. Central Texas, being on the edge of the great woodlands to the east, was a savannah land of wildflower meadows interspersed with trees. Extraordinary herds of bison aided in keeping the trees from overgrowing the land by grazing and browsing back the woody vegetation. Regular prairie fires also controlled trees.

By 1936, much land had been cleared and worn out by overgrazing by cattle or by growing crops like cotton. We are so used to seeing great areas of mesquite trees and brush that we consider it natural. Mesquite is actually an invader into areas that have been abused to an extent that the soil cannot crowd out with native grasses such invading plants. Texas has regained very little native vegetation in the last 50 years, while the use of fertilizer and herbicides has created a productive but unnatural agriculture. Probably in plants more than in any other form of nature, today's Texans are like the people of 1936. They have continued the reduction of the eastern woodlands and put cattle or crops on all the other land possible. This is not necessarily wrong, but it has created an urgency to conservation efforts — what is to be preserved must be actively set aside. Texans cannot merely assume, as did the pioneers, that wild, native lands will always be there without special conservation efforts.

One of the most pressing conservation efforts at the time of the Sesquicentennial is an interest on behalf of many groups in the native prairies of Texas. Areas that reportedly have never seen a plow and that generally bear good stands of Bluestem grass are the subject of conservation efforts and will continue to be. Great park lands today preserve the desert of the Big Bend in West Texas and the Big Thicket of East Texas. The future should bring similar preservation to the native grasslands.

Reptiles

Many people have characterized Texas as the land of the **rattlesnake**, so it will come as no surprise that the state has a very interesting reptile population. Only in recent years has there been any effort to assess the effects that destruction of habitat and hobby or scientific collecting have had on such animals. The **American alligator**, one of Texas' most impressive reptiles, is a case in point.

The alligator has led a very interesting existence the last 50 years. This large predator has suffered the problems typical of many native animal species in Texas since 1936. Habitat reduction and drainage of wetlands due to urban growth have had serious effects on the alligator population. These factors resulted in nest destruction and loss of suitable reproductive sites. There has also been pressure from the leather industry. Overharvesting of skins brought the alligator population to a dangerously low level in the 1960s. Although trade in alligator leather had been thriving since the 1870s — more than 2 million were killed in the 1800s — improved technology through the 1930s and 1940s hastened the decline. By the late 1950s, populations in Louisiana had dropped 90 percent. Such statistics prompted the federal government to list the alligator as endangered in 1967.

Poaching of alligators then became the problem. This was controlled when the federal government regulated the interstate shipment of hides, thus eliminating the illegal leather trade.

Since 1969, alligator populations have recovered in all areas of their range. In 1974, Texas had 26,784 alligators in 74 counties. Ten years later, estimates for Texas stand at 100,000 coastal and 100,000 inland alligators — a total of 200,000.

The alligator's rapid recovery suggests that it will continue to survive if managed. In fact, its recovery has caused a new problem to face the species. Can the alligator coexist with man? Urbanization of the wetlands has already brought the alligator too close for comfort in some areas in Florida. That state has had a nuisance alligator program in operation since 1980. The managed harvest of skins has been in progress in Louisiana for several years, and several Southeast Texas counties allow a seasonal harvest as well.

Allowing some harvest of alligators makes it possible for owners of wetlands to see some profit from the reptiles, encouraging landowners to retain their wetlands instead of draining them for other uses. This may ensure the continuance of suitable habitat for the alligators.

It will be interesting to watch the progress of the alligator. The case, along with those of the **pronghorn** and the **brown pelican**, proves what can be done to conserve endangered species if the danger is realized in time.

Texas Marine Fish

Texas has one of the longest coastlines in the United States. One-twelfth of coastal America borders the state. Including the bays, there are 624 miles of beachfront extending from the Sabine River to the Rio Grande. Long, narrow barrier islands protect most of the coastline from the open Gulf of Mexico. Strategically placed along the vast coastline is a network of man-made jetties. The jetties, composed of granite rock from Central Texas, were built by the U.S. Army Corps of Engineers. The jetties provide safe, navigable waters for ocean-going vessels entering Texas ports. These artificial reefs soon became home for a variety of marine life, some of it quite new to Texas. These important alterations increase and stabilize fish populations by providing permanent features on an otherwise sandy, shifting coastline.

The embayments along the coast are important because they provide the nursery grounds for economically important species. These two topographic features, along with the semitropical climate moderated by Gulf breezes, provide the necessary ingredients to support a large and diverse population of marine fish.

In the 1830s and 1840s, the Galveston Bay area was an epicenter of commerce and population. Early naturalists came to Galveston to document the diverse flora and fauna of Texas shores. From 1836 to 1880, several naturalists made surveys of the marine fish of the Texas coast. These lists were sketchy and incomplete at best. In 1880, the state government embarked on a program to gather landing data from commercial fish dealers. The data were needed to monitor one of our fastest growing early industries. Two fish were targeted in this study — the plentiful red drum and the spotted sea trout. Between 1880 and 1927, the survey was conducted about every five years. From 1927 to 1956, annual surveys were made. Since 1956, economic activity has been so great as to require monthly surveys from dealers. These records show us what our forefathers experienced, a coast rich and abundant in food from the sea.

Statistically the harvests increased in poundage each year until the 1980s, when the catches diminished and prices increased per pound.

The reasons for the decline in coastal commercial fish harvests are many and diverse. Commercially valuable marine fish are dependent on coastal water conditions for all or part of their life cycle. Man's influence on the Gulf Coast estuaries of Texas is the most important factor in the decline of marine fish populations. Complex changes occurred when the waterways were developed for transportation and shipping. Marshes and shallow bays were filled in by land developers, eliminating important nurseries for larval fish. Also, significant changes have occurred in Texas coastal waters by the dumping of millions of pounds of industrial and domestic sewage into Galveston Bay each day. Over-fishing and the destruction of larval fish pulled up inadvertently in shrimp nets account for innumerable losses. Probably the most significant industry to affect the ecology of the Texas coast is the oil business. The quality of our multimillion-dollar fishing industry will

The macrobrachium (above), a large freshwater shrimp which can weigh up to five pounds, was once abundant in the San Marcos River (exhibit at the Fort Worth Zoo Aquarium). Man-made jetties along the Gulf Coast are home to many species of small fish (left) (exhibit at Dallas Museum of Natural History and Aquarium).

The poisonous brown recluse spider (right) is making itself at home in cities and towns across Texas (photo courtesy Dallas Museum of Natural History and Aquarium). The alligator gar (below) which can weigh up to 250 pounds, is the largest Texas freshwater fish (exhibit at Dallas Museum of Natural History and Aquarium).

depend on how carefully oil resources are removed from the Gulf.

Yet to come will be the generating plants which use vast amounts of bay waters for cooling and in turn heat the bay environment to unnatural levels.

Just as habitat destruction has caused drops in commercial marine fish harvests, man-made jetties have brought a variety of non-commercial, tropical marine fish to the shores of Texas. By extending these granite structures out into the Gulf, permanent homes have been provided for a diverse population of fish from the Caribbean and Sargasso Seas. Over 50 new species of fish call the Texas jetties home.

Aquaculture, a form of marine agriculture, and resource management will be the keys to the future success of native population of marine fish. But man is not solely responsible for the success or failure of our coastal fish. Environmental factors such as rainfall, hurricanes and climatic changes all play a role in the future of our marine fish.

If our founding fathers were to walk the Texas shores today, not knowing the challenges the years of civilization have brought (oil rigs, high rise apartments, pollution), they would feel confident that our marine fish resources were being well conserved and managed.

Freshwater Fishes

Texas has more than 200 species of freshwater fish. The fish range in size from the primitive Texas-sized 250-pound **alligator gar** (with scales hard enough to be used as arrowheads) to the one-inch **pygmy sunfish**, a tiny relative of the largemouth bass.

Many fish living in the state are also found over a large area of the United States, while others are found nowhere else but in Texas (so-called endemic species). Among the endemic Texas species, a few, such as the guadalupe bass, have a fairly large distribution occurring in large numbers. Others are limited to a single spring or subterranean water system and are on the endangered lists.

Since the Texas Centennial, many large lakes, stock tanks and other impoundments have been constructed for flood control, water storage and recreational purposes. These man-made bodies of water have greatly increased the aquatic habitat available for fish, especially those fish preferring non-flowing, warmer waters. On the other hand, dam construction has prevented the upstream migration and spawning runs of many fish species, such as the unique and increasingly rare **paddlefish** and **shovelnose sturgeon**.

The rising water in **Lake Amistad** on the Rio Grande has totally inundated **Goodenough Spring**, the sole habitat of the Goodenough gambusia, a small, guppy-like, live-bearing Texas endemic species. So this fish was exterminated in the wild.

Some other species of Texas fish have done very well indeed and actually have extended their ranges over the last 50 years. Most of these can be included in the categories of deliberately stocked game fish or bait fish accidentally released by fishermen. **Channel catfish**, various **sunfish** (often called "bream"), **black bass**, **grass carp** and **red-horse shiners** can be included in such categories.

Although most fish found in Texas are native, many are introductions from elsewhere. Some introductions were accidental, like the widespread **goldfish**. Most, however, were deliberately introduced. The carp originally came from Europe — where it had been formerly introduced from Asia. It is now found statewide. Its desirability is still hotly debated. On the positive side, it grows to a large size, fights well when hooked and will survive in waters that are too poor to support more desirable species. Anti-carp forces remind us that it out-competes other species, clouds the water by rummaging through the bottom muck and eats fish spawn and the aquatic plants that serve as retreats for game fish fry. No matter what we may think of the lowly carp, one thing is certain: It is here to stay.

A more recent and favorably received introduction is the **striped bass**. This species was introduced for its potential as a game fish. This hope has been more than realized. Not only does it grow to over 30 pounds, but it is a most vigorous fighter when hooked and an excellent food fish when properly prepared. It is generally fished for with heavy tackle reminiscent of deep-sea fishing. The "striper" is an Atlantic Ocean marine species, normally ascending rivers only to spawn. When it became landlocked in fresh water, the same striped bass was found not only to thrive but also to reproduce in its new environment. What effect this voracious, large, schooling fish will have on our native species remains to be seen. At present, it is a welcome addition to the fish fauna of our large lakes.

Found in abundance near Buffalo Bayou in 1837, the ivory-billed woodpecker is believed by most ornithologists to be extinct. (Almanac photo of exhibit at the Dallas Museum of Natural History.)

Fishery biologists have recently created a fish previously unknown to science by artificially crossing a striped bass with our native sand bass (white bass). These hybrids are sterile and will not overpopulate the waters into which they are introduced, yet grow at a phenomenal rate, reaching three pounds in 18 months.

Another man-made species widely introduced is the hybrid **sunfish**, a sterile cross between the bluegill and the red-eared sunfish, which reaches four pounds in weight. It has become popular in stocking smaller lakes and farm ponds.

Many of Texas' most fascinating fish live their lives underground in the caves of the Edward's aquifer, an underground body of water between five and 40 miles wide and 175 miles long. The water moves through the caverns of the Texas Hill Country and emerges only as springs. It serves as the source of drinking water for San Antonio and is tapped for irrigation. Amazing as it seems, some of the fish and other animals of this aquifer are limited to its cavernous underground portion. Two of these are the toothless blind catfish and the wide-mouthed blind catfish. These small, bizarre fish, living in conditions of perpetual darkness, have lost their eyes and all pigment, appearing pale, ghostly, pinkish-white in color. Their lack of eyes is more than compensated for by their other senses. The toothless blind catfish has a highly developed sense of smell and taste buds located all over its body. The predacious, wide-mouthed blind catfish possesses a sensory system so acute it can detect the pressure waves created by the swimming motions of the almost microscopic blind shrimp and other tiny aquatic life it feeds upon.

Although living underground and away from man, the future of these amazing animals is not secure. The heavy pumping from the Edward's aquifer is removing water faster than it is being replaced by percolating rainwater from above. There is danger of its being pumped dry within the next 100 years. Such a disaster would not only destroy the unique fish species inhabiting this water, but would be a major calamity for the people, farms and industries dependent upon it.

The State of Texas is very aware of the precious nature of its water reserves, and much research and study is now in progress to assure a plentiful supply of water in the future to satisfy the needs of both the human population and all the diverse and wonderful plants and animals inhabiting Texas in 1986.

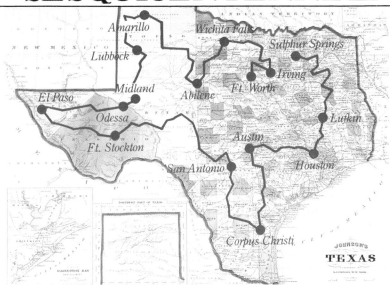

HOLD TEXAS HISTORY IN YOUR HAND

The Colt Walker Black Powder Revolver

140 years ago Captain Samuel H. Walker asked the legendary Sam Colt to build an issue of "horse pistols" for the U.S. Mounted Rifles. These great guns helped win Texas and remained the most powerful handgun in the world for almost 100 years.

Now this magnificent handgun can be yours. The Texas Sesquicentennial Commission has authorized a limited historical issue of 5,000 to honor the state's 150th year of independence. This pistol is an exact reproduction of the original Colt Walker Revolver. Although perfectly capable of firing, it is exempt from federal firearms regulations and can be shipped directly to your home.

The craftsmanship in this commemorative is superb. The decorative work and etching is done in the finest 22 karat gold and pure silver (etched in Texas by Aurum Etchings of Garland). All accoutrements are case color hardened or 22 karat gold finish. This Walker issue comes to you in its own presentation case, hand crafted by Rosborg Case Co. using the finest oak, velvet and brass.

This unique issue is sure to be subscribed soon so order yours today. See it at your favorite firearms dealer or call the Texas Wagon Train Association direct for a free color brochure. Ordering instructions are on the next page.

Price $1,995.00 delivered.
Order today. Call 1-800-441-0028 (Texas) or 1-800-255-1986 (US).

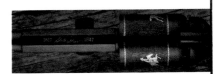

TEXAS WAGON TRAIN ASSOC.

Approved and sanctioned as the only Official Sesquicentennial Black Powder Revolver.

REMEMBER THE ALAMO WITH JIM BOWIE'S FAMOUS BOWIE KNIFE

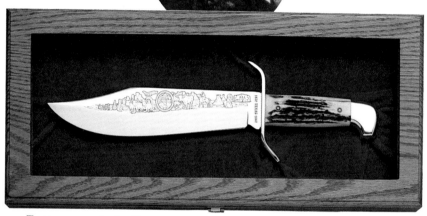

To commemorate the Texas Sesquicentennial, the Texas Wagon Train Association is offering a limited issue of the knife carried by Jim Bowie, defender of the Alamo.

The blade of this great knife is made from finest quality stainless and is etched in 22 carat gold with scenes from Texas history. On one side are scenes from the Alamo to the Space Shuttle and on the reverse The Texas Wagon Train, centerpiece of the Texas Sesquicentennial. The handles are of finest hand-gathered Sambar stag and this unique Texas Commemorative comes in its own oak presentation case with glass top.

This instant heirloom is a must for the experienced knife collector and the first-time buyer. Guaranteed 100 years, this limited issue "Bowie" will surely be a sell-out so order yours today. See the order form on following page for ordering information or see your favorite dealer.

TEXAS
WAGON
TRAIN
ASSOC.

HAPPY BIRTHDAY, TEXAS!

1836 – 1986

TEXAS SESQUICENTENNIAL COMMEMORATIVE POSTER

Own a piece of Texas history with this B. Herd montage. This is the only B. Herd original ever offered in poster form. This painting portrays scenes of Texas history from the Alamo to the Space Shuttle. Great for giving.

About the artist — B. Herd is a native Texan currently working and living in Dallas. Sharp detail, vivid color, variety of subject matter and unique style describe Mr. Herd's oil paintings. Self-taught, his style has not taken on a similarity of any other artist but is clearly the "B. Herd" style. Mr. Herd's work is owned by collectors throughout the U.S.

$6.95 postpaid
Approximate size 24"x36"

- -

TEXAS WILDLIFE

Texas has many native animals and birds, plus species introduced on game preserves.

More than 540 species of **birds** — about three fourths of all different species found in the United States — have been identified in Texas.

Some 142 species of **animals**, including some that today are extremely rare, are found in Texas.

Through efforts of the **Texas Parks and Wildlife Department** and many individual landowners involved in conservation practices, our wildlife should be a permanent resource.

Hunting, Fishing Licenses

The Texas Legislature in 1985 passed a bill increasing most license fees. The non-resident **general hunting license** was raised to $200. This is valid for taking all legal species of wildlife in Texas including deer, turkey, javelina, antelope, aoudad sheep and all small game and migratory game birds.

In addition, the nonresident small game hunting license was raised to $75 and allows out-of-state hunters to take quail, dove, squirrel, pheasant, waterfowl, sandhill cranes and other legal small game in the state. However, special stamps are required in addition to a hunting license for all hunters taking waterfowl or white-winged doves. An archery stamp is required for taking deer, turkey or javelina during the special archery season only.

Fees for resident sport fishing licenses stayed at $8, for nonresidents, $15. Resident combination hunting and fishing licenses are priced at $15; resident hunting fees, $10; resident hunting exempt, $6; temporary nonresident fishing, $8. All hunting and fishing licenses are valid from Sept. 1 of one year through Aug. 31 of the following year.

The Parks and Wildlife Department reported revenue of $24.6 million from sales of all licenses during 1983-84, an increase of some $7 million over 1982-83.

Sales of resident combination hunting and fishing licenses decreased during the 2-year period, but revenue was increased by $1.4 million. Numbers of resident hunting licenses also decreased, but revenue climbed by approximately $538,000. Resident fishing license sales increased by 131,146 licenses and $3.1 million in revenue.

In the state fiscal year 1983-84, the Parks and Wildlife Department sold 681,802 resident combination hunting and fishing licenses and 1,057,246 resident fishing licenses were sold. Visiting hunters to Texas bought 25,726 non-resident licenses, which include small game, during the period. There were sales of 30,560 non-resident fishing licenses and 67,388 5-day non-resident fishing licenses.

Trappers' licenses sold totaled 30,963, and the department sold over 41,000 archery stamps. White-winged dove stamp sales totaled 46,913.

There were 373,000 whitetail **deer** killed in the 1983-84 hunting season, the most killed in 10 years and up 17 percent over the 1982-83 season. Wild **turkey** killed in 1983-84 estimated at 34,396 down from record high harvest of 54,624 in 1982-83. There were 4,411 mule **deer** killed in 1983-84, compared to 4,741 the year before. The **javelina** harvest also dropped, from 24,549 in 1982-83, to 20,636 in 1983-84.

Hunting and Fishing

Texas offers a wide variety of hunting and fishing and ranks among the leading states in this form of recreation.

In the federal fiscal year of 1983, 1,453,978 hunters held licenses in Texas, exceeded only by Pennsylvania with 2,207,919; and there were 1,789,298 fishing licenses issued, exceeded only by California with 6,626,510.

In 1982, there were 1,408,528 hunting licenses issued in Texas; 1,909,503 fishing licenses.

Freshwater Fishing

During the 1983-84 fiscal year, an estimated three million Texas fishermen spent more than 9 million days fishing on our 1½ million acres of lakes and 80,000 miles of rivers, streams and bayous.

These Texans fished for sport and for food avidly seeking such longtime favorites as **largemouth bass, crappie, sunfish, white bass** and the various species of **catfish**. They did not neglect the introduced **smallmouth bass, striped bass, hybrid stripers** and **walleye,** which had

been stocked by the Texas Parks and Wildlife Department.

Texas lakes proved to be extremely attractive to freshwater fishermen and recreationists. Texans and visitors spent several hundred million dollars vitalizing the state's economy with their purchases of goods and services relating to fishing and outdoor recreation.

Increasing human population is putting a severe strain on some fishery resources. A careful analysis is being made of more restrictive regulations, which may be implemented soon.

But the streams and rivers which once supplied vast numbers of these native fishes in the years since World War II have been slowed in their rush to the Gulf of Mexico by hundreds of major and smaller impoundments. The reservoirs dammed along the waterways still contain great populations of native species along shorelines, in the coves and throughout the shallow upper reaches of their tributaries. But the vast open and deep waters of most reservoirs provide a natural habitat mostly for less desirable species such as **carp** and **shad.** Unfortunately, pollution problems are increasing in some rivers.

In recent years, the Texas Parks and Wildlife Department's Fisheries Division has been working toward a balance of fish populations which would increase popular fishing in all areas of reservoirs. The most promising answer has been in providing **predator** species which are also desired by sport fishermen.

Among the most successful introductions of non-native species are:

Walleye are a northern U.S. native which inhabit open and deep waters not normally frequented by native Texas fish. Noted as spirited gamefish and delicious on the table, walleyes are also voracious predators of rough fish. They reach 12 to 15 pounds and have been stocked in a number of Texas lakes.

Striped bass are saltwater fish which spawn in rivers but can live and reproduce entirely in fresh water when landlocked. They have been successfully propagated and stocked in Texas reservoirs. Reproducing populations have now been established in **Lakes Whitney** and **Texoma,** and possibly in **Amistad** and **Livingston Reservoirs.** Adults reach 25 to 40 pounds in lakes.

A hybrid cross of **striped bass** with Texas **white bass** has also been developed. They reach three pounds and more in 18 months and get up to 20 pounds.

In order to continue an effort to fill every lake with fish, the department is also upgrading production of native species with these programs:

Red drum, hybrid red drum and **hybrid corvina** are thriving in some lakes.

Florida bass, a largemouth which grows heavier than Texas bass, are being stocked in every new reservoir as it fills, along with older lakes. The Florida species has proved it can thrive very successfully, and catches of 12-pound fish are not uncommon.

Smallmouth bass, rugged fish ordinarily found in running streams, are being stocked in several older but steep-sided, deep and rocky lakes and are reproducing.

Additional help for these bass are programs for improving lake habitat with brush shelters and other fish attractors which improve spawning conditions and provide better fishing; seeking the stabilization of lake levels during the critical spawning season and through the period when baby bass need shoreline protection, and establishing secluded, protected nursery coves where brood bass may spawn and the offspring thrive without danger from predators in the main lake.

In addition, **rainbow trout** are stocked regularly on a put-and-take basis in the Guadalupe River below Canyon Dam, the Brazos River below Possum Kingdom, in Foster County Park near San Angelo, at Boykin Springs near Lufkin, the San Gabriel River below Lake Georgetown dam, and in a number of small state park lakes.

Saltwater Fishing

Sport fishing in both the inshore waters of the Texas coast and offshore in the Gulf of Mexico has long been a favorite recreation of both Texans and visitors. In 1984 the Texas Parks and Wildlife Department continued finfish population studies and recreational harvest studies.

There were three major projects during fiscal year 1984 dealing with finfish resources. These included: (1)

monitoring the availability of adult and juvenile fin-fishes; (2) monitoring the recreational harvest of finfish and (3) the enhancement of **red drum** in Texas bays.

Monitoring of the relative abundance of adult finfishes in eight Texas bay systems continued using 600-foot-long gill nets with individual 150-foot sections of 3-, 4-, 5- and 6-inch stretched mesh. Bag seines (60 feet long) and 20- or 40-foot trawls were used to determine the abundance of juvenile finfishes. Assessment of the success of HB 1000 (67th Texas Legislature) in reducing overfishing on red drum and **spotted seatrout** is continuing through routine monitoring and special studies.

The devastating freeze of December 1983-January 1984 on the Texas coast resulted in the death of over 15 million aquatic animals, including 567,000 spotted seatrout, 225,000 black drum and 90,000 red drum. Sampling after the freeze indicated that spotted seatrout populations were down by over 50 percent from that measured in 1983.

A cooperative agreement between the National Marine Fisheries Service (NMFS) and the Texas Parks and Wildlife Department (TPWD) provided for the gathering of complementary catch rate and harvest information of the recreational fisheries. TPWD obtained sport boat and charter fleet catch rate and harvest data, and NMFS obtained wade bank, pier, surf and jetty catch rate and harvest data. When these data are combined, it will be possible to estimate the total harvest of the sport fishery.

The **John Wilson Marine Fish Hatchery**, a cooperative venture by the Central Power and Light Company, the Gulf Coast Conservation Association and the Texas Parks and Wildlife Department started operation in 1983. Over seven million red drum fingerlings were stocked in each of two bays in 1983 and 1984 in an effort to rebuild population levels.

The shellfish program consisted of four major projects including: (1) shrimp population monitoring in bays for availability, size and movement; (2) shrimp population monitoring in the Gulf of Mexico; (3) oyster population monitoring; (4) blue crab population monitoring. About 36,000 shrimp were tagged to determine the feasibility of estimating shrimp mortality in bays. Population monitoring of valuable commercial and sport species was carried out to determine trends in relative abundance, and to determine the factors that affect abundance in order to recommend closed seasons and other management options. **Shrimp, crabs** and associated organisms were monitored with bag seines along shorelines; with 20-foot wide otter trawls in deeper (+3 feet) portions of bays and passes leading from the bays to the Gulf of Mexico and with 40-foot otter trawls in the Gulf of Mexico.

For many years Texas has closed its Gulf territorial waters (9 nautical miles) in the Gulf of Mexico to shrimping during June 1-July 15 to allow small shrimp leaving the bays to grow to a larger size before harvest and minimize waste from discarding. These season dates may be changed if biologists find that there may be an earlier, later or prolonged emigration of brown shrimp. In 1984 an early emigration occurred and the season was set for 30 minutes after sunset on May 16 to 30 minutes after sunset July 6.

Biological monitoring of oyster reefs in Galveston Bay in 1982 indicated that preseason abundance of market **oysters** was the highest in recent years. The harvest in 1983 was a record high. In 1978, biological samples revealed the lowest oyster abundance in Galveston Bay since 1956 and the Parks and Wildlife Commission closed the Nov. 1-April 30 season on Dec. 15. Recovery of oysters in 1982 is attributed to favorable weather conditions and the spreading of oyster shell for cultch over approximately 700 acres of bay bottom. It is estimated that spat setting was increased by 1.5 million per acre.

Commercial Fisheries

Shrimp made up 79 percent of the pounds landed and 91 percent of the value of all reported commercial marine products during 1983. Over 8.8 million pounds of blue crabs valued at $3.2 million and 7.9 million pounds of oysters valued at $11.3 million demonstrate the increasing importance of these species in the commercial fishery.

Commercial Landings*
(Jan. 1, 1983 to Dec. 31, 1983)
Source: Texas Parks and Wildlife Department

Species		
Finfish	Pounds	Value
Drum, Black	1,492,800	$ 971,000
Flounder	474,300	445,600
Sheepshead	275,900	66,000
Snapper, Red	261,900	383,500
Other	425,600	118,500
Total Finfish	2,930,500	$ 1,984,600
Shellfish		
Shrimp (Heads On):		
Brown and Pink	50,707,300	$125,430,400
White	20,369,500	45,682,800
Other	916,900	330,600
Crabs	8,829,100	3,250,300
Oysters	7,940,700	11,336,700
Squid	7,800	3,200
Total Shellfish	88,771,300	$186,034,000
Grand Total	91,701,800	$188,018,600

*Preliminary data.

National Wildlife Refuges

In addition to the many state and national parks that can be reached from most major cities in Texas, there are 10 national wildlife refuges that may be visited at different times of the year for bird watching and wildlife viewing. It is best to write before visiting to check on facilities available and to be sure the refuge is open to visitors at that time. Addresses are given at the end of the description of each refuge.

Texas has more than 177,500 acres set aside in its 10 national wildlife refuges. Short sketches of each are given below:

Anahuac

The 24,293 acres of this refuge are managed primarily for migrating and wintering waterfowl, but the threatened **American alligator** also resides in its boundaries. As many as 30 species of **ducks** and **geese** have been sighted; in fact, waterfowl may be observed there year around. Of the 253 species listed in the refuge checklist, birders will find 42 species that actually nest at Anahuac. Many shorebirds also enjoy sanctuary here. Visitors may observe wildlife, sightsee, take photographs or engage in crabbing, fishing and floundering. Overnight camping permitted only along bay shore and is limited to three days. Write directly to refuge for information concerning public recreational uses and regulations. Address: P.O. Box 278, Anahuac, Tx. 77514. Phone (409)267-3337.

Aransas

The 54,829 acres of this refuge furnish a home for **whooping cranes** in Texas. Its primary function is to provide a wintering area for waterfowl, wading birds and the endangered whoopers but many other birds and mammals live in its diverse habitats. An archery hunt is held each year to help control the deer herd. More than 350 species of birds have been observed at Aransas. Birding is enhanced by a U.S. Fish and Wildlife leaflet that describes the birding spots and tells what to look for and when. **Deer, raccoons, armadillos,** and **opossums** and many kinds of birds can be seen throughout the day. November through March most popular time to visit Aransas because many migratory waterfowl and the whoopers are present. Address: P.O. Box 100, Austwell, Tx. 77950. Phone (512) 286-3559.

Attwater Prairie Chicken

The refuge was established on July 1, 1972, to preserve habitat for the endangered Attwater's Prairie Chicken. The refuge is comprised of 7,980 acres of land. Ninety percent of the land is native prairie, and the remainder is comprised of cultivated croplands and a narrow strip of riparian woodlands. The refuge is open to the public from dawn to dusk daily, except during the period from Feb. 15 until May 1, when entrance is authorized by reservations only. The refuge is open to the public for wildlife/wildlands observations, photography and wildlife research. During the winter, large numbers of ducks, geese and sandhill cranes concentrate on the refuge fields and marshes to feed and rest. For more information write to: Refuge Manager, P.O. Box 518, Eagle Lake, Tx. 77434, or phone (409) 234-3021.

Brazoria

The 11,000 acres of this refuge serve as nesting area for mottled ducks and its coastal salt marshes are part of ancestral wintering grounds of the **snow goose.** Fishing, crabbing and oystering allowed in public waters on and around refuge and waterfowl hunting permitted in specified areas. Access for these sports by boat only. Since established in 1966, 247 species of birds have been identified here. **Freeport Christmas Bird Count** always records one of highest number of species observed in nation. Prospective birders should check on refuge conditions in advance of planning trip because access is poor and roads often muddy. Address: P.O. Drawer 1088, Angleton, TX. 77515. Phone (409) 849-6062.

Buffalo Lake

Known originally as **Tierra Blanca Water Conservation Project,** this is one of major waterfowl refuges in the Central Flyway. Its 7,677 acres is winter refuge for 1 million ducks and 80,000 geese and summer refuge for 500,000 people when water is available. At present the lake is dry with the dam and spillway needing major rehabilitation. Portions of refuge are open from March through October for picnicking, sightseeing, birding, nature study, photography and camping. Checklist indicates 275 species of birds sighted at Buffalo Lake with 44 species nesting. Write for information. Address: P.O. Box 228, Umbarger, Tx. 79091. Phone (806) 499-3382.

Hagerman

When **Denison Dam** was built creating **Lake Texoma,** 11,000 acres were set aside to provide food and safe resting place for migrating waterfowl and assure survival of all plant and animal species using area. Serves as winter home for several thousand ducks and geese. The 3,000-acre marsh and water area hosts large numbers of **Canada geese** and lesser flights of **snow** and white-fronted **geese.** Open meadows to dense stands of pecan, oak, ash and juniper comprise refuge's upland habitat and provide homes for songbirds, **quail, doves, squirrels, foxes, opossums, skunks, armadillos, rabbits, deer** and many other animals. **Beavers, raccoons** and **mink** favor stream and marsh banks.

Oil was discovered on refuge lands in 1951 and about 160 producing wells are presently operating. More than 35,000 people visit Hagerman each year to enjoy birding, sightseeing, nature study, photography, fishing and frogging. Hunting is restricted to dove and is closely regulated. Fishing permitted from April 1 to Sept. 30. Overnight camping not allowed. Write for information: Route 3, Box 123, Sherman, Tx. 75090. Phone (214) 786-2826.

Laguna Atascosa

Established 1946 as southernmost waterfowl refuge in Central Flyway, this refuge contains 46,000 acres, 7,000 of which are marsh and open water. It supports substantial numbers of wintering ducks, including one of larger concentrations of **redheads** and also home for rare **ocelot** and **jaguarundi.** Winter months most popular for visitors. Birding popular year around because of migratory birds in fall and winter, and exotic Mexican birds in summer. There are 354 bird species and 31 mammal species considered part of the refuge fauna. Walking trails and auto tours provided and fishing permitted in Harlingen Ship Channel. Archery deer season and controlled gun hunt held most years on 27,000 acres. No other hunting allowed. Write for information: P.O. Box 450, Rio Hondo, Tx. 78583. Phone (512) 748-3607.

Muleshoe

Oldest of national refuges in Texas, more than 5,000 acres of the 5,809 acres are composed of short-grass rangeland with scattered mesquite. As many as 700,000 migrating waterfowl in residence by end of December. Also serves as roosting area for **sandhill cranes.** Birding is best during October and November when 213 species are present. Five miles of road suitable for automobile travel reveal **rabbits, scaled quail, prairie dogs, burrowing owls** and occasionally **coyote, badger** or **skunk.** Visitor activities limited to birding, nature study, photography and sightseeing. Write for information: P.O. Box 549, Muleshoe, Tx. 79347. Phone (806)946-3341.

San Bernard

More than 80,000 **snow** and **blue geese** use the 24,000 acres as wintering area; **mottled ducks** nest here. **Shorebirds, gulls** and **terns** use mud flats and **herons, egrets** and **ibis** are common on lower marsh area ponds. Bird checklist contains 245 species. Waterfowl hunting allowed and temporary blinds may be used in public hunting areas. No permits necessary for public hunting areas, but "Special Permit Waterfowl Hunt" held on refuge with participating hunters phoning in reservations just prior to the season. Information about special permit hunt should be obtained from refuge manager. Write P.O. Drawer 1088, Angleton, Tx. 77515. Phone (409) 849-6062.

Santa Ana

Established in 1943 and referred to as **"gem of the National Wildlife Refuge System,"** this 2,080 acre subtropical forest and native brushland provides habitat for more than 300 species of birds, 30 species of mammals, 50 species of reptiles and amphibians and 450 plant species. The refuge benefits more endangered and threatened species than any other refuge in the system. Bird watchers come from all over the United States and many foreign countries to view many Mexican bird species that reach the northern edge of their ranges in South Texas. Five trees on the refuge are classified as national champions: **Berlandier ash, brazil, honey mesquite, guayacan** and **Texas ebony.** This credits them as being the largest of their species in the United States. A Texas ebony natural area is set aside for scientific and educational purposes. Public facilities include Visitor Center, over 14 miles of foot trails, photography blinds and a 6.7-mile one-way tour road. Tour road is closed to private vehicles during winter months and an interpretive tram is available. Foot access is permitted from sunrise to sunset; vehicles permitted on tour road from 9:00 a.m. to 4:30 p.m. when tram is not operating. For information write: Refuge Manager, Route 1, Box 202A, Alamo, Tx. 78516. Phone (512) 787-3079.

State Wildlife Management Areas

In addition to the above national refuges in Texas, there are **23 wildlife management areas** administered by the Texas Parks and Wildlife Department. A brief description of each is given below. Research concerning the preservation, management and wise use of wildlife and our other natural resources is conducted on these study areas. Many of the wildlife management areas are open to the public for nature study, hiking, camping, hunting and fishing. Hunting is regulated by permit systems administered by either self-registration, first-come-first-served, or computer selection.

Alabama Creek Wildlife Management Area (Trinity County)—Approximately 14,500 acres of national forest land south of Apple Springs. Cooperative management program with U.S. Forest Service. Camping permitted at Forest Service campground on Neches River Feb. 1 through Sept. 30; from Oct. 1 to Jan. 31, camping limited to designated campsites. Deer gun hunting participants selected by computer drawing. Other hunting allowed by self-registration.

Angelina-Neches Scientific Area (Combined with Dam B Unit. See listing below.)

Bannister WMA (San Augustine County)—Contains 20,700 acres of national forest land east of Lufkin managed in a cooperative program with the U.S. Forest Service. Camping permitted anywhere on area from Feb. 1 through Sept. 30; from Oct. 1 to Jan. 31, camping limited to designated campsites. Deer gun hunting participants selected by computer drawing. Other hunting allowed by self-registration.

Black Gap WMA (Brewster County along Rio Grande)—Contains 77,805 acres owned plus 23,073 acres leased from General Land Office. Research conducted on desert mule deer, desert bighorn sheep, javelina, cougar and scaled quail. Black bear occasionally present. Primitive camping along river for fishermen and at designated sites for hunters. Fishing permitted from March 15 through June 15. Javelina hunting participants selected by computer drawing. Other hunting allowed by self-registration.

Caddo WMA (Fannin County)—Contains 16,140 acres of national forest land east of Bonham managed in a cooperative program with the U.S. Forest Service. The 13,360-acre **Bois d'Arc Unit** offers fishing and designated campsites on **Coffee Mill Lake** and **Lake Davy Crockett** Feb. 1 through Sept. 30; from Oct. 1 to Jan. 31, camping limited to designated campsites. This WMA is predominantly hardwood and pine forest. The 2,780-acre **Ladonia Unit** contains grassland prairie. Deer gun hunting participants selected by computer drawing. Other hunting by self-registration.

Chaparral WMA (La Salle and Dimmit Counties)— Research on brush country vegetation and wildlife conducted on 15,200 acres enclosed by high fence west of Artesia Wells. No public use facilities. Deer and javelina hunting participants selected by computer drawing. Other hunting on first-come-first-served basis.

Dam B-Angelina Neches Unit of Eastern WMA (Jasper and Tyler Counties)—Access only by boat to 13,445 acres west of Jasper adjacent to **B. A. Steinhagen Lake** at confluence of Angelina and Neches Rivers. Hunting for deer, feral hog and other legal wildlife species by self-registration. Permit from U.S. Corps of Engineers required for camping.

Gene Howe WMA (Hemphill County)—Research conducted on wildlife management on 5,821 acres of upper and rolling plains habitat east of Canadian on the south fork of the Canadian River. Contains remnant population of lesser prairie chicken. Deer and turkey hunters selected by computer drawing. Other hunting by self-registration.

Granger Unit of Eastern WMA (Williamson County)—Contains 6,716 acres of land and 4,400 acres of water on **Lake Granger** northeast of Taylor. Pheasant hunters selected by computer drawing. Other hunting by self-registration.

Guadalupe Delta WMA (Calhoun County)—Contains 1,580 acres of coastal delta marsh along the perimeter of **Mission Lake** northwest of Seadrift used as a waterfowl refuge and for wildlife management research. Area is in initial phases of development and no public use facilities are present. Hunting on first-come-first-served basis.

Gus Engeling WMA (Anderson County)—Contains 10,941 acres of woodland west of Palestine used for wildlife management research. Fishing available on Catfish Creek and two small impoundments. Public use facilities include two nature trails and designated campsites. Deer, feral hog and turkey hunters selected by computer drawing. Other hunting on first-come-first-served basis.

James E. Daughtrey WMA (Live Oak and McMullen Counties)—Contains approximately 25,000 acres located on perimeter of **Choke Canyon Reservoir** northwest of Three Rivers. Park and recreation facilities being developed on a portion of the area. Deer, javelina and turkey hunters selected by computer drawing. Other hunting on first-come-first-served basis.

J.D. Murphree WMA (Jefferson County)—Contains 12,389 acres of coastal marsh on Taylor's Bayou southwest of Port Arthur used as a waterfowl refuge for wildlife management research. Free access for fishing. Boat ramps available for use during public hunts. Alligators are numerous. Hunting for waterfowl and other legal wildlife species is on first-come-first-served basis.

Kerr WMA (Kerr County)—Research conducted on wildlife management and habitat development on 6,493 acres of Edwards Plateau juniper-oak habitat under high fence west of Kerrville. Intensive studies conducted on white-tailed deer genetics. Free fishing access to north fork of Guadalupe River. **Golden-cheeked warbler** is summer resident. Computer selection of hunters for deer and turkey hunts. Area open to public on scheduled field days with demonstration of habitat management procedures.

Las Palomas WMA (Cameron, Hidalgo, Presidio, Starr, and Willacy Counties)—Thirteen tracts comprised of 3,129 acres in the Rio Grande Valley of south and west Texas. Primary use is to provide nesting habitat for white-winged dove. Ocelot, jaguarundi and cougar are present. Computer selection of hunters for white-winged dove and chachalaca hunts.

Matador WMA (Cottle County) — Contains 28,183 acres of upper and rolling plains northwest of Paducah. Research conducted on wildlife habitat development and upland game bird management. Small population of pronghorn antelope present on area. Turkey hunters selected by computer drawing. Production of both bobwhite and scaled quail is generally high and draws much hunter interest. Hunting for quail is on first-come-first-served basis. Mourning dove hunting allowed by self-registration.

Matagorda Island WMA (Calhoun County)—Approximately 36,568 acres of marsh and island uplands south of Port O'Connor and accessible only by boat. Operated under cooperative agreement with the U.S. Fish and Wildlife Service and the General Land Office. Primary objective is to conserve habitats for endangered species and other migratory and resident wildlife species. **Whooping cranes** winter in the area and regularly utilize the southern portion of the island. Free access for marine fishing, nature study, hiking and beachcombing. Camping only in designated areas. Deer hunters selected by computer drawing. Hunting for waterfowl, quail and mourning dove on first-come-first-served basis.

Moore Plantation WMA (Sabine County)—Includes 22,800 acres of national forest land east of Pineland under cooperative management agreement with U.S. Forest Service. Also contains 2,100 acres leased from Temple-Eastex, Inc. Camping permitted anywhere Feb. 1 through Sept. 30; from Oct. 1 to Jan. 31, camping limited to designated campsites. Deer gun hunting partici-

pants selected by computer drawing. Other hunting by self-registration.

North Toledo Bend Unit of Eastern WMA (Shelby County)—Composed of 3,600 acres of land and water along the Sabine River east of Center. Primary use is as a waterfowl management area and refuge. No camping permitted on area. No regular gun season for deer. Other hunting by self-registration.

Pat Mayse Unit of Eastern WMA (Lamar County)—Contains approximately 8,925 acres of land and water adjacent to Pat Mayse Reservoir northwest of Paris. Contains wooded uplands and bottomland hardwood habitats. No camping on area, but allowed on designated campsite at adjacent U.S. Corps of Engineers facility at Lamar Point. Fishing allowed by self-registration. Participants for deer gun hunts selected by computer drawing. Other hunting by self-registration.

Sheldon WMA (Harris County)—Contains 2,503 acres on **Carpenter's Bayou** east of Houston utilized primarily as a waterfowl and shorebird sanctuary. Composed largely of **Sheldon Reservoir** with adjacent levees and shoreline marsh. Cropland areas managed for production of wildlife foods. Public use facilities include two boat ramps with parking areas, five T-head fishing piers and 5.5 miles of levees. Free access for fishing. No hunting permitted.

Sierra Diablo WMA (Culberson County)—Includes 7,791 acres in the Sierra Diablo Mountains northwest of Van Horn. Utilized primarily for research concerning reintroduction of desert bighorn sheep to native ranges and management of desert mule deer. Mule deer hunt participants selected by computer drawing. Area closed to public except for mule deer hunts.

Somerville Unit of Eastern WMA (Burleson and Lee Counties)—Approximately 3,500 acres in two units, the **Yegua Creek Unit** and the **Nails Creek Unit**, near **Lake Somerville** south of Caldwell. No camping on the area. Public use facilites are available nearby at U.S. Army Corps of Engineers Recreation Areas and at Lake Somerville State Recreation Areas. Deer gun hunt participants selected by computer drawing. Other hunting and fishing by self-registration.

Walter Buck WMA (Kimble County)—Contains approximately 2,200 acres of juniper-oak habitat in limestone escarpment southwest of Junction. Adjacent to the **South Llano River State Park** which is in initial phase of development. Participants in deer and javelina hunts selected by computer drawing. Area not open to the public except for public hunts.

RESEARCH FACILITIES, FISH HATCHERIES

The **Texas Parks and Wildlife Department** operates a number of fish hatcheries and research facilities in Texas for studying exotic fish.

In the list below, the fish hatcheries have no public facilities, but scheduled tours are available, by letter request for groups of 20 or more, in May or June. There are no rates or charges. Write to individual hatchery for information.

Research Facilities

Heart of the Hills—Junction Star Route, Box 62, Ingram. Research is primarily culture-oriented with emphasis on intensive indoor culturing techniques. Studies primarily deal with exotic fish such as Nile perch, peacock, bass and various forage fish.

Fort Worth Research Unit—6200 Hatchery Road, Fort Worth. Research concentrates on ecological evaluation of management procedures. Primary work deals with evaluation of Florida large mouth bass and native largemouths in reservoirs and stream fisheries.

Fish Hatcheries

Dundee Fish Hatchery—Archer County on Big Wichita River. Total acreage 141; pond acreage 78. Consists of 94 earthen ponds; fishes raised include striped bass, largemouth bass, channel catfish, flathead catfish (during some years) and hybrid sunfish.

Eagle Mountain—Tarrant County below Eagle Mountain Reservoir Dam. Total acreage 70; pond acreage 46.1. Consists of 30 earthen ponds; fishes raised consist of largemouth bass, channel catfish, hybrid sunfish and other sunfish species.

Fort Worth—Tarrant County south of Lake Worth. Total acreage 66; pond acreage 35.5. Consists of 22 earthen ponds; fishes raised include bass, catfish, sunfish and other species in certain years.

Huntsville—Walker County, off State 19. Total acreage 247; pond acreage 32.51. Consists of 39 earthen ponds; fishes raised are largemouth bass, channel catfish, occasionally flathead catfish and various sunfish species.

Jasper—Jasper County off State 63. Total acreage 227; pond acreage 64. Consists of 63 earthen ponds;

fishes raised include largemouth bass, blue catfish, channel catfish and various species of sunfish.

John Wilson Marine—Nueces County, near Corpus Christi. Total area 30 acres with 20 acres of pond. Red drum fish fingerlings reared for stocking in Texas bays. Facility only one of its kind in world, resulted from cooperative effort by TP&WD, Gulf Coast Conservation Association and Central Power & Light Co. of Corpus Christi.

Lewisville—Denton County, below Garza-Little Elm Reservoir Dam off State 121. Total acreage 125; pond acreage 42.31. Consists of 55 earthen ponds. Oldest state hatchery, although relocated three times. First on State Fair Grounds in Dallas in 1911. In 1935 moved to White Rock Hatchery (Dallas). In 1938, moved to new location. In 1952 U.S. Army Corps of Engineers exchanged property for new location below **Garza-Little Elm Dam** since **Lake Dallas** site would be inundated. Fishes raised include largemouth bass, channel catfish, sunfish species and, occasionally, flathead catfish. Experimental work being done in sunfish hybridization.

Possum Kingdom—Palo Pinto County, below Possum Kingdom Reservoir Dam on State 16. Total acreage 103; pond acreage 28.98. Consists of 44 earthen ponds; fishes raised are largemouth bass, channel catfish, hybrid sunfish and striped bass.

San Angelo No. 1—Tom Green County on US 87 at South Concho River. Total acreage 160; pond acreage 40. Consists of 40 earthen ponds; fishes raised are largemouth bass, channel catfish, warmouth bass and sunfish species.

San Angelo No. 2—Tom Green County off US 277 at Lake Nasworthy. Total acreage 170; pond acreage 42. Consists of 31 earthen ponds. Originally constructed and operated by U.S. Fish and Wildlife Service until 1955; Texas Game and Fish Commission (predecessor of State Parks and Wildlife Department) took over in 1957. Fishes raised include largemouth bass, channel catfish and sunfish; also primary striped bass rearing area.

San Marcos—Hays County south of San Marcos. Total acreage 118; pond acreage 59.26. Consists of 92 earthen ponds; fishes raised include largemouth bass, smallmouth bass, Florida largemouth bass, channel catfish, hybrid sunfish and striped bass.

Tyler—Smith County off State 31. Total acreage 42; pond acreage 15. Consists of 35 earthen ponds; fishes produced are largemouth bass, Florida bass, channel catfish, flathead catfish, hybrid sunfish and other sunfish species.

Coastal Fisheries Branch

These facilities are mainly rented from private owners for office space and boat dockage. There are no public facilities.

Arroyo Colorado Marine Field Station—Cameron County on Arroyo Colorado in Lower Laguna Madre.

Flour Bluff Marine Field Station—Nueces County on waterfront in Upper Laguna Madre near Flour Bluff.

Marine Fishery Research Station—Calhoun County, off State 35 on Well Point Road. Total acreage 40; pond acreage 22.8. Experimental marine research; station tours not regularly scheduled but available by letter request. No rates or charges. Has 21 ponds; serves as headquarters for Coastal Fisheries personnel in Matagorda Bay area.

Port Aransas Marine Laboratory—Nueces County, at Port Aransas. Owned by National Marine Fisheries Service, leased to University of Texas, Parks and Wildlife Department joint occupancy; used for spawning saltwater fish, principally red drum. No public use facilities available.

Rockport Marine Laboratory—Aransas County, on Rockport Boat Basin. Total acreage 0.25. Free marine aquarium and display open to public, 8-5 every day; display contains exhibit of plants and animals including extensive shell collection. Headquarters for Coastal Fisheries research; large marine library; complete marine way and repair shop for department vessels; home port for research vessel, Western Gulf.

Seabrook Marine Field Laboratory—Harris County on Seabrook waterfront. Headquarters for Coastal Fisheries research on Galveston Bay system; licenses sold and public information leaflets available. No rates or charges. Lab contains facilities for biological research and chemical analysis.

Seadrift Marine Field Station—Calhoun County. No public use facilities, but personnel will discuss ongoing projects of San Antonio and Espiritu Santo Bays.

Swan Point Fisherman Access Area—Calhoun County, south of Seadrift at end of Swan Point Road on San Antonio Bay. Total acreage 9. Facilities include boat ramp and parking. No rates or charges. To be devel-

oped as fishermen's access area to San Antonio Bay; presently provides access to bay for wade fishing and boating. Oyster reef extending from end of Swan Point provides unique wade fishing area.

Other Facilities

Management and Research Station—Smith County, five miles E. of Tyler on FM 848. Total acreage 87. No public use facilities. Experiment research, serves as headquarters for turkey and pheasant hatching programs; serves as headquarters for Region 3 wildlife staff and inland fisheries state biologist and crew.

Mammals

A few of the leading native mammals of Texas are described here. More complete information is found in "The Mammals of Texas," by William B. Davis, Bulletin 41 of the Texas Parks and Wildlife Department, Austin.

ANTELOPE. — The **American antelope** (Antilocarpa americana Ord), or **Pronghorn antelope**, is primarily a plains animal. It almost became extinct, but a continuous closed season and sound management program raised its numbers and there have been limited open seasons since 1944. Specifically, these animals inhabit the plains and basin regions of Brewster, Presidio, Jeff Davis, Culberson and Hudspeth Counties. They have also sufficiently increased in numbers in the Permian Basin and Panhandle to permit open seasons in recent years.

ARMADILLO. — The **nine-banded armadillo** (Dasypus novemcinctus, Linnaeus) is one of Texas' most interesting mammals. It has migrated north and east and is now common as far north and east as Oklahoma and Mississippi. There has been limited commercialization of the armadillo's shell in the manufacture of curios.

BADGER. — The badger (Taxidea taxus, Schreber) is found through West Texas, but in greatly reduced numbers since wholesale eradication of the prairie dog on which the badger preyed. It is a predator, but its pelt is valuable. The range of the badger includes the Texas Panhandle and South Texas, where it is common.

BAT. — Twenty-nine species of these winged mammals have been found in Texas, but most of them are rare. The **Brazilian bat** (Tadarida, brasiliensis) and the **cave myotis** (Myotis velifer, Allen) constitute most of the bat population of the caves of Southwest and West Texas. They have some economic value for their deposits of **guano**. Some commercial guano has been produced from Mason Bat Cave, Mason County; Beaver Creek Cavern, Burnet County; and from large deposits in other caves including Devil's Sink Hole in Edwards County, Blowout Cave in Blanco County and Bandera Bat Cave, Bandera County. The **big brown bat** (Eptesicus fuscus, Beauvois), the **red bat** (Lasiurus borealis, Muller) and the **evening bat** (Nycticeius humeralis Rafinesque) are found in East and Southeast Texas. The evening and big brown bats are forest and woodland dwelling mammals. Most of the rarer species of Texas bats have been found along the Rio Grande and in the Trans-Pecos.

BEAR. — The **black bear** (Ursus americanus Pallas) was formerly common throughout most of the state. It is now almost extinct with only small pockets of animals surviving in the inaccessible river bottoms of Eastern Texas and in the higher portions of the Trans-Pecos.

BEAVER. — Two subspecies of beaver are found in Texas, the **Mexican beaver** (Castor canadensis mexicanus) ranging along the Rio Grande and Devils River and the **Texas beaver** (Castor canadensis texensis) which has been brought back from the verge of extinction to abundance through restocking.

BIGHORN. — (See **Sheep.**)

BISON. — The largest of native terrestrial wild mammals of North America, the **American bison**, or **buffalo** (Bison bison, Linnaeus) is found today on a few ranches and in zoos. This fine animal became rare about 1885 as the result of slaughter for hides, reaching a peak about the year 1875. Estimates of the number of buffalo killed vary, but as many as 200,000 hides were sold in Fort Worth at a two-day sale. Except for the interest of the late **Col. Charles Goodnight** and a few other forevisioned men, the bison might be extinct.

CAT. — The **jaguar** (Felis onca Linnaeus) is probably now extinct in Texas and, along with the **ocelot**, **jaguarundi and margay**, is listed as rare and endangered by both federal and state wildlife agencies. The **cougar** (Felis concolor, Linnaeus), which is also known as **mountain lion, puma, panther, Mexican cougar**, etc., is found occasionally in the broken country of the Edwards Plateau and in the Trans-Pecos Mountains and the South Texas brush country. The former **panther** of the East Texas forest, which was closely related, may be extinct in Texas but still exists in a few areas of Southeastern U.S. The **ocelot** (Felis pardalis Linnaeus), also known as the **leopard cat**, is found usually along the border. The **red-and-gray cat**, or **jaguarundi** (Felis yagouaroundi Geoffroy) is found in extreme South Texas. The **margay** (Felis Wiedii Schinz) was reported in 1884 near Eagle Pass. The **bobcat** (Felis rufus Schreber) is found over the state in large numbers. The **feral housecat** has become a destroyer of game in many parts of Texas.

COATI. — The **coati** (Nasua narica Linnaeus), a relative of the raccoon, is occasionally found in southern Texas. It inhabits woodland areas and feeds both on the ground and in trees. The species is also found occasionally in Big Bend National Park.

COYOTE. — The **coyote** (Canis latrans Say), great in number, is the most destructive Texas predator of livestock. On the other hand, it is probably the most valuable predator in the balance of nature. It is a protection to crops and range lands by its control of rodents, rabbits, etc. It is found throughout the state, but is most numerous in the brush country of Southwest Texas.

CHIPMUNK. — The **gray-footed chipmunk** (Tamias canipes, Bailey) is found at high altitudes in the Guadalupe and Sierra Diablo ranges of the Trans-Pecos. (See "Ground Squirrel" with which it is often confused in public reference.)

DEER. — The **white-tailed deer** (Odocoileus virginianus Boddaert) is an important Texas game animal. Its number in Texas is estimated at 3 million. It thrives best in the wooded and broken areas of the Edwards Plateau and south of San Antonio where it often competes for feed with domestic animals. Texas Parks and Wildlife Department has had success in transplanting deer to East Texas, the timbered sections of North Central Texas, and even in the thinly populated areas of Northwest Texas the white-tailed deer population has increased greatly. The **mule deer**, (Odocoileus heminous Rafinesque) is found principally in the Trans-Pecos and in smaller numbers in the less thickly settled parts of the Staked Plains. It has increased in number in recent years. The little **Del Carmen deer** (white-tailed subspecies) is found in limited numbers in the high valleys of the Chisos Mountains in the Big Bend. The **American elk** (Cervus canadensis Erxleben), though not the original subspecies found in Texas, has been introduced into the Guadalupe and Davis Mountains.

FERRET. — The **black-footed ferret** (Mustela nigripes, Audubon and Bachman) was formerly found widely ranging through the West Texas country of the prairie dog on which it preyed. It is now considered extinct in Texas. It is of the same genus as the weasel and mink.

FOX. — Most common is the **gray fox** (Uro (Urocyon cinereoargenteus Schreber) found in the forested area of East Texas and throughout most of the state where there is cover, notably in the broken parts of the Edwards Plateau and the rough country at the foot of the Staked Plains. The **kit** or **Swift fox** (Vulpes velox Say) is found in the plains country of Northwest Texas. The **kit fox** (Vulpes macrotis Merriam) is found in the Trans-Pecos and is fairly numerous in some localities. The **red fox** (Vulpes vulpes) is not a native but was introduced for sport.

GOPHER. — Six species of pocket gophers occur in Texas. The **Botta's pocket gopher** (Thomomys bottae, Eydoux and Gervais) is found in West Texas south of the High Plains, notably along the Rio Grande. The **Plains pocket gopher** (Geomys bursarius, Shaw) is found in the Panhandle and throughout North Central and East Texas. The **desert pocket gopher** (Geomys arenarius Merriam) and the **yellow-faced pocket gopher** (Pappogeomys castanops Baird) are found in the Trans-Pecos. The **Texas pocket gopher** (Geomys personatus True) is found in the sandy soils of the lower coastal region.

GROUND SQUIRREL. — There are five or more species, living usually in the western part of the state. The **rock squirrel** (Spermophilus variegatus) is found throughout the Edwards Plateau and Trans-Pecos. The **Mexican ground squirrel** (Spermophilus mexicanus) is found in the Mexican border country from Brownsville to the Davis Mountains. The **spotted ground squirrel** (Spermophilus spilosoma) is found generally in favorable localities throughout the western half of the state. The **thirteen-lined ground squirrel** (Spermophilus tridecemlineatus Mitchill) is found in the Panhandle and in a narrow strip from Red River to the Gulf between Dallas

and Corpus Christi. The **Texas antelope squirrel** (Ammospermophilus interpres Merriam) is found along the Rio Grande from El Paso to Val Verde County.

JAVELINA. — The **javelina** or **collared peccary** (Tayassu tajacu, Dicotyles) is found in the border country of Southwest Texas. It is fairly numerous. Its meat is edible if properly prepared, and there is limited use of its hide for the manufacture of gloves and other leather articles. Hunting it with dogs is a favorite sport of that region. A scrappy animal, it is the subject of many tall tales.

MINK. — The **mink** (Mustela vison Schreber) is found in East Texas and along the Coastal Belt, usually in forested river bottoms. It yields a considerable fur crop. It is akin to the otter and weasel. Mink farming, partly with native and partly with introduced species, is found on a limited scale, usually in East Texas.

MOLE. — The **mole** (Scalopus aquaticus Linnaeus) is found generally throughout the eastern half of the state.

MUSKRAT. — There are three subspecies of muskrat in Texas, the **muskrat** (Ondatra zibethica rivalicia Bangs) which is found in Southeast Texas near Beaumont where it is commercially produced on muskrat ranges; the **Pecos River muskrat** (Ondatra zibethica ripensis) of Western Texas and the **Great Plains muskrat** (Ondatra zibethica cinnamonia) of the Panhandle region. The muskrat is one of the most valuable of Texas' fur-bearing animals. Production of pelts comes largely from the coastal area near Beaumont.

NUTRIA. — This introduced species (Myocastor coypus, Molina) is found in Texas, except the Panhandle and extreme western portions. The fur is not valued too highly and, since they are in competition with muskrats, their spread is discouraged. They are used widely in Texas as a cure-all for ponds choked with vegetation.

OPOSSUM. — This Texas marsupial, the Virginia opossum (Didelphis virginiana) is found in nearly all parts of the state. The opossum has economic value for its pelt, and its meat is considered a delicacy by some. It is one of the chief contributors to the Texas fur crop.

OTTER. — A few **river otter** (Lutra canadensis Schreber) are found along East Texas rivers and coastal marshes. Although it is a prized fur-bearing animal, there is no evidence that the river otter can be considered either rare or endangered. The species is numerous in Liberty County where biologists have determined that its numbers have increased in recent years. While excess populations of this species, like other forms of wildlife, can be harvested with no danger to the species, loss of habitat through encroaching civilization presents the most formidable threat to its continued existence.

PORCUPINE. — The **yellow-haired porcupine** (Erethizon dorsatum, Linnaeus) is found in small numbers in higher mountain ranges of the Trans-Pecos and has recently moved into the eastern portion of the Panhandle along the Caprock.

PRAIRIE DOG. — Until recent years probably no sight was so universal in West Texas as the **black-tailed prairie dog** (Cynomys ludovicianus Ord) and its burrow. Naturalists estimated its population in the hundreds of millions. Its destruction of range grasses, plus its peculiar susceptibility to eradication (usually by the introduction of the fumes of carbon disulphide into its burrow) have caused a great reduction of its numbers over its past range. However, it is making a comeback. **Prairie dog towns** often covered many acres with thickly spaced burrows or **prairie dog holes**. It is being propagated in several public zoos, notably in the prairie dog town in **Mackenzie Park** at Lubbock. It has been accorded its monument in Texas in the name of the **Prairie Dog Town Fork** of the Red River along one segment of which is located the beautiful Palo Duro Canyon.

RABBIT. — The **black-tailed jack rabbit** (Lepus californicus Gray) is found throughout Texas except in the East Texas forest area. It breeds rapidly, and its long hind legs make it one of the world's faster-running animals. The **Eastern cottontail** (Sylvilagus floridanus Allen) is found throughout Texas except in Trans-Pecos region. The **desert cottontail** (Sylvilagus auduboni Baird) is found in South and West Texas, usually on the open range. The **swamp rabbit** (Sylvilagus aquaticus Bachman) is found in East Texas and the coastal area.

RACCOON. — The **raccoon** (Procyon lotor, Linnaeus) is found along streams throughout Texas.

RATS AND MICE. — There are forty or fifty species of rats and mice in Texas of varying characteristics, habitats and economic destructiveness. The **Norway rat** (Rattus norvegicus, Berkenhout) and the **black rat**

(Rattus rattus, Linnaeus) are probably the most common and the most destructive. Some of the species are native, and others, notably the Norway rat, are invaders. The common **house mouse** (Mus musculis Linnaeus) is estimated in the hundreds of millions annually. The rare **Guadalupe Mountain vole** (Microtus mexicanus guadalupensis Bailey) is found only in the **Guadalupe Mountains National Park** and just over the border into New Mexico.

RINGTAIL.—The **ringtail**, (Bassariscus astutus Lichtenstein) is found generally in wooded areas west of the Trinity and in the broken sections of the Edwards Plateau. It is a valuable fur-bearing mammal.

SHEEP.—The **barbary**, or **Aoudad, sheep** (Ammotragus lervia Pallas), first introduced to the Palo Duro Canyon area in 1957-58, have become firmly established. Barbary sheep have been introduced into many areas of Texas, but are designated as game animals in only eight counties of the Panhandle surrounding Palo Duro Canyon. Efforts are now under way by the Texas Parks and Wildlife Department to establish the **desert bighorn** (Ovis canadensis Shaw) in range formerly occupied.

SHREW.—Three species are found in Texas, the **northern short-tailed shrew** (Blarina brevicauda Say), the **least shrew** (Cryptotis parva Say) and the **desert shrew** (Notiosorex crawfordi Coues). The first-mentioned is rarer, occurring in the Big Thicket. The least shrew is found generally in South Central and East Texas. The gray shrew is found in very limited numbers in the semiarid areas of West Texas and along the border.

SKUNK.—There are six species of skunk in Texas. The **Eastern spotted skunk** (Spilogale putorius Rafinesque) is found throughout North Texas. A small skunk, it is often erroneously called civet cat. This skunk also is found in East Texas and the Gulf area. The **Western spotted skunk** (Spilogale gracilis Merriam) is found in the central, western and southern parts of the state. The **long-tailed**, or **broad-striped skunk** (Mephitis mephitis Schreber) is found in many parts of the state, usually along streams or in wooded areas. The **hooded skunk** (Mephitis macroura Lichtenstein) is found in limited numbers in the Trans-Pecos mountains. The **Gulf Coast hog-nosed skunk** (Conepatus leuconotus Lichtenstein), found in the Brownsville area, ranges southward into Mexico. The **mountain hog-nosed skunk** (Conepatus mesoleucus Lichtenstein) is found in sparsely timbered areas of Edwards Plateau, Central Texas, Trans-Pecos.

SQUIRREL.—The **fox squirrel** (Sciurus niger Linnaeus) is found throughout East, Central and West Central Texas. The **gray**, or **cat squirrel** (Sciurus carolinensis Gmelin) is found generally in the eastern third of the state. The **flying squirrel** (Glaucomys volans Linnaeus) is widely distributed in the Piney Woods and the East Texas Post Oak Belt.

WEASEL.—The **brindled** or **long-tailed weasel** (Mustela frenata Lichtenstein), akin to the mink, is found in the Panhandle-Plains and South Texas.

WOLF.—The **red wolf** (Canis rufus Audubon) was once found over a wide range in Eastern and Central Texas. It is now considered extirpated from the wild with the only known remnants of the population now in captive propagation. The **gray wolf** (Canis lupus Linnaeus) once had a wide range over Central, Southern and Western Texas. It has been reduced almost to extinction. The **red wolf** and **gray wolf** are listed on the federal and state rare and endangered species lists; the few **gray wolves** which may be encountered in Texas are believed to be occasional individuals crossing over from Mexico.

Reptiles

Most of the more than 100 species of **snakes** found in Texas are beneficial as also are other reptiles. There are **15 poisonous species** and subspecies and there are more cases of snakebite reported in Texas than any other state. Principal **poisonous reptiles** include three kinds of **copperheads** (Southern, Broadbanded and Trans-Pecos); one kind of **cottonmouth**; 10 kinds of **rattlesnakes** (western massasauga, desert massasauga, western pigmy, western diamondback, timber, banded rock, mottled rock, blacktailed, Mojave and prairie); and the **Texas coral snake**.

Also noteworthy are the **horned lizard; the vinegarroon**, a type of **whip scorpion**, also harmless; **tarantulas**, a hairy spider; and **alligators**.

LAKES AND RESERVOIRS

The large increase in the number of reservoirs in Texas during the past half-century has greatly improved water conservation and supplies. As late as 1913, Texas had only eight major reservoirs with a total storage capacity of 376,000 acre-feet. Most of this capacity was in **Medina Lake**, with 254,000 acre-feet capacity, created by a dam completed in May, 1913.

By 1920, Texas had 11 major reservoirs with combined storage capacity of 449,710 acre-feet. The state water agency reported 32 reservoirs and 1,284,520 acre-feet capacity in 1930; 47 reservoirs with 5,369,550 acre-feet capacity in 1940; 66 with 9,623,870 acre-feet capacity by 1950; 105 with total capacity of 22,746,200 in 1960; 149 with total capacity of 51,086,200 in 1970; 168 with total capacity of 53,302,400 in 1980. In January, 1983, Texas had 189 major reservoirs existing or under construction, with a total capacity near 58.6 million acre-feet, of which 38.4 million acre-feet was conservation storage, 17.8 million acre-feet was flood control storage and 2.4 million acre-feet was considered inactive.

The following table lists reservoirs in Texas having more than 5,000 acre-feet capacity. A few locally significant reservoirs of less capacity are not included. With few exceptions, the listed reservoirs are those that were completed by Jan. 1, 1985 and in use. An asterisk (*) indicates those that are under construction.

There are about 5,700 reservoirs in Texas with the surface areas of 10 acres or larger; however, conservation water storage capacity in the listed reservoirs represents about 97 percent of total conservation water storage capacity in all Texas reservoirs.

Conservation storage capacity is used in the table below; the **surface area** used is that area at conservation elevation only. (Different methods of computing capacity are used; detailed information may be obtained from Texas Department of Water Resources, Austin; U.S. Army Corps of Engineers, or local sources.) Also, it should be noted that boundary reservoir capacities include water designated for Texas use and non-Texas water.

In the list below, information is given in the following order: (1) Name of lake or reservoir; (2) county or counties in which located; (3) river or creek on which located; (4) location with respect to some city or town; (5) purpose of reservoir; (6) owner of reservoir. Some of these items, when not listed, are not available. For the larger lakes and reservoirs, the dam impounding water to form the lake bears the same name, unless otherwise indicated. Abbreviations in list below are as follows: L., lake; R., river; Co., county; Cr., creek; (C) conservation; (FC) flood control; (R) recreation; (P) power; (M) municipal; (D) domestic; (Ir.) irrigation; (In.) industry; (Mi.) mining including oil production; (FH) fish hatchery; USAE, United States Army Corps of Engineers; WC&ID, Water Control and Improvement District; WID, Water Improvement District; USBR, United States Bureau of Reclamation.

Lakes and Reservoirs	Conservation Surface Area (Acres)	Conservation Storage Capacity (Acre-Ft.)
Abilene L.—Taylor Co.; Elm Cr.; 6 mi. NW Tuscola; (M-In.-R); City of Abilene	595	7,900
Addicks Reservoir.—Harris Co.; S. Mayde and Langham Crs.; 1 mi. E. Addicks; (for flood control only); USAE	0	0
Alcoa L.—Milam Co.; Sandy Cr.; 7 mi. SW Rockdale; (In.-R); Aluminum Co. of America .	880	14,750
Amistad Reservoir.—Val Verde Co.; Rio Grande, dam between Del Rio and confluence of Rio Grande and Devils River; an international project of the U.S. and Mexico; 12 mi. NW Del Rio; (C-R-Ir.-P-FC); International Boundary and Water Com. (Texas' share of conservation capacity is 56.2 percent.)	64,900	3,383,900

Lakes and Reservoirs — (continued)

	Conservation Surface Area (Acres)	Conservation Storage Capacity (Acre-Ft.)
Amon G. Carter, L.—Montague Co.; Big Sandy Cr.; 6 mi. S Bowie; (M-In.); City of Bowie	1,540	20,050
Anahuac L.—Chambers Co.; Turtle Bayou; near Anahuac; (Ir.-In.-Mi.); Chambers-Liberty Counties Navigation District.	5,300	35,300
Aquilla L.—Hill Co.; Aquilla Cr.; 10.2 mi. SW of Hillsboro; (FC-M-Ir.-In.-R); USAE-Brazos R. Auth.	3,280	52,400
Arlington L.—Tarrant Co.; Village Cr.; 7 mi. W Arlington; (M-In.); City of Arlington	2,275	45,710
Arrowhead, L.—Clay Co.; Little Wichita R.; 13 mi. SE Wichita Falls; (M); City of Wichita Falls.	16,200	262,100
Athens, L.—Henderson Co.; 8 mi. E Athens; (M-FC-R); Athens Mun. Water Authority (formerly **Flat Creek Reservoir**).	1,520	32,690
Aubrey L.—(See **Ray Roberts L.**)		
Austin, L.—Travis Co.; Colorado R.; W Austin city limits; (M-In.-P); City of Austin, leased to LCRA (impounded by **Tom Miller Dam**).	1,830	21,000
Balmorhea, L.—Reeves Co.; Sandia Cr.; 3 mi. SE Balmorhea; (Ir.); Reeves Co. WID No. 1	573	6,350
Bardwell L.—Ellis Co.; Waxahachie Cr.; 3 mi. SE Bardwell; (FC-C-R); USAE.	3,570	53,580
Barker R.—Harris-Fort Bend Counties; Buffalo Bayou; 1 mi. S Addicks; (for flood control only); USAE	0	0
Barney M. Davis Cooling Reservoir.—Nueces Co.; off-channel storage reservoir of Laguna Madre arm of Gulf; 14 mi. SE Corpus Christi; (In.); Central Power & Light Co. . . .	1,100	6,600
Bastrop, L.—Bastrop Co.; Spicer Cr.; 3 mi. NE Bastrop; (In.); LCRA	906	16,590
Baylor Creek Reservoir.—Childress Co.; 10 mi. NW Childress; (M-R); City of Childress . . .	610	9,220
Belton L.—Bell-Coryell Counties; Leon R.; 3 mi. N. Belton; (M-FC-In.-Ir.); USAE-Brazos R. Auth	12,300	457,300
Benbrook L.—Tarrant Co.; Clear Fk. Trinity R.; 10 mi. SW Fort Worth; (FC-R); USAE . . .	3,770	88,200
Big Brown Creek Reservoir.—Freestone Co. (See **Fairfield L.**)		
Big Hill Reservoir.—Jefferson Co. (See **J. D. Murphree Area Impoundments**.)		
Bivins L.—Randall Co.; Palo Duro Cr.; 8 mi. NW Canyon; (M); Amarillo (also known as **Amarillo City Lake**); City of Amarillo	379	5,120
Blackburn Crossing L.—(See **Lake Palestine**.)		
Bonham, L.—Fannin Co.; Timber Cr.; 5 mi. NE Bonham; (M); Bonham Mun. Water Auth..	1,020	12,000
Bowie L.—(See **Amon G. Carter, L.**).		
Brady Creek Reservoir.—McCulloch Co.; Brady Cr.; 3 mi. W Brady; (M-In.); City of Brady	2,020	29,110
Brandy Branch Reservoir.—Harrison Co.; Brandy Br.; 10 mi. SW Marshall; (In.); Southwestern Electric Power Co.	1,240	29,500
Brazoria Reservoir.—Brazoria Co.; off-channel reservoir; 1 mi. NE Brazoria; (In.); Dow Chemical Co..	1,865	21,970
Bridgeport R.—Wise-Jack Counties; W. Fk. of Trinity R.; 4 mi. W Bridgeport; (M-In.-FC-R); Tarrant Co. WC&ID Dist. No. 1	13,000	386,420
Brownwood, L.—Brown Co.; Pecan Bayou; 8 mi. N Brownwood; (M-In.-Ir.); Brown Co. WC&ID No. 1.	7,300	143,400
Brushy Creek Reservoir.—(See **Valley L.**).		
Bryan Utilities L.—Brazos Co.; unnamed stream; 6 mi. NW Bryan; (R-In.); City of Bryan	829	15,227
Buchanan, L.—Burnet-Llano-San Saba Counties; Colorado R.; 13 mi. W Burnet; (M-Ir.-Mi.-P); LCRA	23,060	955,200
Buffalo Springs L.—Lubbock Co.; Double Mtn.Fk. Brazos R.; 9 mi. SE Lubbock; (M-In.-R); Lubbock Co. WC & ID No. 1; (impounded by **W. G. McMillan Sr. Dam**)	200	3,950
Buffalo L.—Randall Co.; Tierra Blanca Cr.; 2 mi. S Umbarger; (R); U.S. Fish & Wildlife Service (impounded by **Umbarger Dam**).	1,900	18,150
Caddo L.—Harrison-Marion Counties, Texas and Caddo Parish, La. An original natural lake, whose surface and capacity were increased by the construction of a dam on Cypress Creek near Mooringsport, La..	25,400	59,800
Calaveras L.—Bexar Co.; Calaveras Cr.; 15 mi. SE San Antonio; (In.); City Public Service Bd. of San Antonio	3,450	61,800
Camp Creek L.—Robertson Co.; 13 mi. E Franklin; (R); Camp Creek Water Co.	750	8,550
Canyon L.—Comal Co.; Guadalupe R.; 12 mi. NW New Braunfels; (M-In.-P-FC); Guadalupe-Blanco R. Authority & USAE.	8,240	385,600
Casa Blanca L.—Webb Co.; Chacon Cr.; 3 mi. NE Laredo; (R); Webb County (impounded by **Country Club Dam**)	1,656	20,000
Cedar Bayou Cooling Reservoir.—Chambers Co.; Cedar Bayou; 15 mi. SW Anahuac; (In.); Houston Lighting & Power Co.	2,600	20,000
Cedar Creek Reservoir.—Henderson-Kaufman Counties; Cedar Cr.; 3 mi. NE Trinidad; (sometimes called **Joe B. Hogsett L.**); (M-R); Tarrant Co. WC&ID No. 1.	33,750	679,200
Cedar Creek Reservoir.—Fayette Co.; Cedar Cr.; 8.5 mi. E. La Grange; (In.); LCRA.	2,420	71,400
Champion Creek Reservoir.—Mitchell Co.; 7 mi. S. Colorado City; (M-In.); Tex. Elec. Service Co.	1,560	41,600
Cherokee L.—Gregg-Rusk Counties; Cherokee Bayou; 12 mi. SE Longview; (M-In.-R); Cherokee Water Co..	3,987	46,700
Choke Canyon Reservoir.—Live Oak-McMullen Counties; Frio R.; 4 mi. W Three Rivers; (M-In.-R-FC); City of Corpus Christi-USBR	26,000	690,400
Cisco, L.—Eastland Co.; Sandy Cr.; 4 mi. N. Cisco; (M); City of Cisco (impounded by **Williamson Dam**)	445	8,800
Cleburne, L. Pat.—Johnson Co.; Nolan R.; 4 mi. S. Cleburne; (M); City of Cleburne	1,550	25,300
Clyde, L.—Callahan Co.; N. Prong Pecan Bayou; 6 mi. S. Clyde; (M); City of Clyde and USDA Soil Conservation Service.	449	5,748
Coffee Mill L.—Fannin Co.; Coffee Mill Cr.; 12 mi. NW Honey Grove; (R); U.S. Forest Service	650	8,000
Coleman L.—Coleman Co.; Jim Ned Cr.; 14 mi. N. Coleman; (M-In.); City of Coleman . . .	2,000	40,000
Coleto Creek Reservoir.—Goliad-Victoria Counties; Coleto Cr.; 12 mi. SW Victoria; (In); Guadalupe-Blanco River Auth..	3,100	35,080
Colorado City, L.—Mitchell Co.; Morgan Cr.; 4 mi. SW Colorado City; (M-In.-P); Texas Elec. Service Co.	1,612	30,800

Lakes and Reservoirs— (continued)

	Conservation Surface Area (Acres)	Conservation Storage Capacity (Acre-Ft.)
Conroe, L.—Montgomery-Walker Counties; W. Fk. San Jacinto R.; 7 mi. NW Conroe; (M-In.-Mi.); San Jacinto River Authority, City of Houston and Texas Water Dev. Bd. .	20,985	429,900
*****Cooper L.**—Delta-Hopkins Counties; Sulphur R.; 3 mi. SE Cooper; (FC-M-R); USAE . . .	19,305	310,000
Corpus Christi, L.—Live Oak-San Patricio-Jim Wells Counties; Nueces R.; 4 mi. SW Mathis; (P-M-In.-Ir.-Mi.-R.); Lower Nueces River WSD (impounded by **Wesley E. Seale Dam**)	19,336	269,900
Crook, L.—Lamar Co.; Pine Cr.; 5 Mi. N. Paris; (M); City of Paris.	1,226	9,964
Cypress Springs, L.—Franklin Co.; Big Cypress Cr.; 8 mi. SE Mount Vernon; (In-M); Franklin Co. WD and Texas Water Development Board (formerly **Franklin Co. L**); impounded by **Franklin Co. Dam**	3,400	66,800
Dallas L.—(See **Lewisville L.**)		
Dam B Reservoir.—(See **Steinhagen L., B.A.**)		
Daniel, L.—Stephens Co.; Gunsolus Cr.; 7 mi. S Breckenridge; (M-In.); City of Breckenridge; (impounded by **Gunsolus Creek Dam**)	924	9,515
Davis L.—Knox Co.; Double Dutchman Cr.; 5 mi. SE Benjamin; (Ir); League Ranch	585	5,395
DeCordova Bend Reservoir.—(See **Lake Granbury**)		
Decker L.—(See **Walter E. Long, Lake**)		
Delta Lake Res. Units 1 and 2.—Hidalgo Co.; Rio Grande (off channel); 4 mi. N. Monte Alto; (Ir.); Hidalgo-Willacy Counties WC&ID No. 1 (formerly **Monte Alto Reservoir**) . . .	2,371	25,000
Diable Reservoir.—(See **Amistad Reservoir**.)		
Diversion, L.—Archer-Baylor Counties; Wichita R.; 14 mi. W Holliday; (M-In.); City of Wichita Falls and Wichita Co. WID No. 2	3,419	40,000
Dunlap, L.—Guadalupe Co.; Guadalupe R.; 9 mi. NW Seguin; (P); Guadalupe-Blanco R. Authority; (impounded by **TP-1 Dam**)	410	3,550
Eagle L.—Colorado Co.; Colorado R. (off channel); in Eagle Lake; (Ir.); Lakeside Irrigation Co.	1,200	9,600
Eagle Mountain Reservoir.—Tarrant-Wise Counties; W. Fk. Trinity R.; 14 mi. NW Fort Worth; (M-In.-Ir.); Tarrant Co. WC&ID No. 1.	9,200	190,300
East L.—(See **Victor Braunig Lake**.)		
Eddleman L.—(See **Lake Graham**.)		
Electra City L.—Wilbarger Co.; Camp Cr. and Beaver Cr.; 7 mi. SW Electra; (In.-M); City of Electra	660	8,055
Ellison Creek Reservoir.—Morris Co.; Ellison Cr.; 8 mi. S. Daingerfield; (P-In.); Lone Star Steel	1,516	24,700
Fairfield L.—Freestone Co.; Big Brown Cr.; 11 mi. NE Fairfield; (In.); TP&L, Fairfield Rec. Service Co., DP&L and Industrial Generating Co. (formerly **Big Brown Creek Reservoir**)	2,350	50,600
Falcon Reservoir.—Starr-Zapata Counties; Rio Grande; (International—U.S.-Mexico); 3 mi. W Falcon Heights; (M-In.-Ir.-FC-P-R); International Boundary and Water Com.; (Texas' share of total conservation capacity is 58.6 per cent)	87,210	2,667,600
Farmers Creek Reservoir.—Montague Co.; 8 mi. NE Nocona; (M-In.-Mi.) N Montague County Water Supply District (also known as **Lake Nocona**)	1,470	25,400
Ferrell's Bridge Dam Reservoir.—(See **Lake O' the Pines**.)		
Flat Creek Reservoir.—(See **Athens Lake**.)		
Forest Grove Reservoir.—Henderson Co.; Caney Cr.; 7 mi. NW Athens; (In.); Texas Utilities Services, Inc., Agent	1,502	20,038
Forney Reservoir.—(See **Ray Hubbard Lake**.)		
Fort Phantom Hill Reservoir.—Jones Co.; Elm Cr.; 5 mi. S. Nugent; (M-R); City of Abilene	4,246	74,300
Franklin County L.—(See **Cypress Springs Lake**.)		
Galveston County Industrial Water Reservoir.—Galveston Co.; off-channel storage Dickinson Bayou; 16 mi. S La Porte; (In.-M.); Galveston Co. Water Auth.	812	7,308
Garza-Little Elm.—(See **Lewisville L.**)		
Georgetown L.—Williamson Co.; N. Fk. San Gabriel R.; 3.5 mi. W Georgetown; (FC-M-In.); USAE (formerly **North Fork L.**)	1,310	37,050
Gibbons Creek Reservoir.—Grimes Co.; Gibbons Cr.; 9.5 mi NW Anderson; (In.); Texas Mun. Power Agency	2,490	26,824
Gladewater, L.—Upshur Co.; Glade Cr.; in Gladewater; (M-R); City of Gladewater	800	6,950
Graham L.—Young Co.; Flint and Salt Creeks; 2 mi. NW Graham; (M-In.); City of Graham	2,550	45,000
Granbury L.—Hood-Parker Counties; Brazos R.; 8 mi. SE Granbury; (M-In.-Ir.-P); Brazos River Authority (impounded by **DeCordova Bend Dam**)	8,700	151,300
Granger L.—Williamson Co.; San Gabriel R.; 10 mi. NE Taylor; (FC-M-In.); USAE (formerly **Laneport Lake**)	4,400	64,540
Granite Shoals L.—(See **Johnson L.**)		
Grapevine L.—Tarrant-Denton Counties; Denton Cr.; 2 mi. NE Grapevine; (M-FC-In.-R.); USAE	7,380	187,700
Greenbelt L.—Donley Co.; Salt Fk. Red R.; 5 mi. N Clarendon; (M-In.); Greenbelt M&I Water Auth.	1,990	58,200
H-4 Reservoir.—Gonzales Co.; Guadalupe R.; 4.5 mi. SE Belmont; (P); Guadalupe-Blanco R. Auth. (also called **Guadalupe Reservoir H-4**)	696	5,200
Halbert, L.—Navarro Co.; Elm Cr.; 4 mi. SE Corsicana; (M-In-R); City of Corsicana	650	7,420
Harris Reservoir.—Brazoria Co.; off-channel between Brazos R. and Oyster Cr.; 8 mi. NW Angleton; (In.); Dow Chemical Co.	1,663	12,000
Hawkins, L.—Wood Co.; Little Sandy Cr.; 3 mi. NW Hawkins; (FC-R); Wood County; (impounded by **Wood Co. Dam No. 3**)	776	11,570
Holbrook L.—Wood Co.; Keys Cr.; 4 mi. NW Mineola; (FC-R); Wood County; (impounded by **Wood Co. Dam No. 2**)	653	7,770
Honea Reservoir.—(See **Conroe Lake**.)		
Hords Creek L.—Coleman Co.; Hords Cr.; 5 mi. NW Valera; (M-FC); City of Coleman and USAE	510	8,600
Houston County L.—Houston Co.; Little Elkhart Cr.; 10 mi. NW Crockett; (M-In.); Houston Co. WC&ID No. 1.	1,282	19,500
Houston, L.—Harris Co.; San Jacinto R.; 4 mi. N Sheldon; (M-In.-Ir.-Mi.-R.); City of Houston; (impounded by **Lake Houston Dam**)	12,240	140,500

	Conservation Surface Area (Acres)	Conservation Storage Capacity (Acre-Ft.)
Hubbard Creek Reservoir.—Stephens Co.; 6 mi. NW Breckenridge; (M-In.-Mi.); West Central Texas Mun. Water Authority	15,250	317,800
Imperial Reservoir.—Reeves-Pecos Counties; Pecos R.; 35 mi. N Fort Stockton; (Ir.); Pecos County WC&ID No. 2.	1,530	6,000
Inks L.—Burnet-Llano Counties; Colorado R.; 12 mi. W Burnet; (M-Ir.-Mi.-P); Lower Colorado River Authority	803	17,540
Iron Bridge Dam L.—(See **Lake Tawakoni**.)		
Jacksonville, L.—Cherokee Co.; Gum Cr.; 5 mi. SW Jacksonville; (M-R); City of Jacksonville; (impounded by **Buckner Dam**)	1,320	30,500
J. B. Thomas, L.—Scurry-Borden Counties; Colorado R.; 16 mi. SW Snyder; (M-In.-R); Colorado River Mun. Water Dist.; (impounded by **Colorado R. Dam**)	7,820	202,300
J. D. Murphree Wildlife Management Area Impoundments.—Jefferson Co.; off-channel reservoirs between Big Hill and Taylor Bayous; at Port Acres; (FH-R); State Park & Wildlife Dept. (formerly **Big Hill Reservoir**)	6,881	13,500
Joe B. Hogsett, L.—(See **Cedar Creek Reservoir.**).		
*Joe Pool Reservoir.**—Dallas-Tarrant-Ellis Counties; Mountain Cr.; 14 mi. SW Dallas; (FC-M-R); USAE-Trinity River Auth.	7,470	176,900
Johnson Creek Reservoir.—Marion Co.; 13 mi. NW Jefferson; (In.); Southwestern Electric Co.	650	10,100
Johnson L., Lyndon B.—Burnet-Llano Counties; (formerly **Granite Shoals L.**); Colorado R.; 5 mi. SW Marble Falls; (P); LCRA; (impounded by **Alvin Wirtz Dam**)	6,375	138,500
Kemp, L.—Baylor Co.; Wichita R.; 6 mi. N Mabelle; (M-P-Ir.); City of Wichita Falls; Wichita Co. WID No. 2	16,540	319,600
Kemp Diversion Dam.—(See **Diversion Lake.**).		
Kickapoo, L.—Archer Co.; N. Fk. Little Wichita R.; 10 mi. NW Archer City; (M); City of Wichita Falls	6,200	106,000
Kiowa, L.—Cooke Co.; Indian Cr.; 8 mi. SE Gainesville; (R); Lake Kiowa, Inc.	560	7,000
Kirby L.—Taylor Co.; Cedar Cr.; 5 mi. S. Abilene; (M); City of Abilene	740	7,620
Kurth, L.—Angelina Co.; off-channel reservoir; 8 mi. N Lufkin; (In.); Southland Paper Mills, Inc.	770	16,200
Lake Creek L.—McLennan Co.; Manos Cr.; 4 mi. SW Riesel; (In.); Texas P&L Co.	550	8,400
Lake Fork Reservoir.—Wood-Rains Counties; Lake Fork Cr.; 5 mi. W Quitman; (M-In.); SRA	27,690	635,200
Lake O' the Pines.—Marion-Upshur-Harrison-Morris-Camp Counties; Cypress Cr.; 9 mi. W Jefferson; (FC-R-In.-M); USAE. (Lake impounded by **Ferrell's Bridge Dam**).	18,700	252,000
*Lakeview L.**—(See **Joe Pool Reservoir.**).		
Lampasas Reservoir.—(See **Stillhouse Hollow Reservoir.**).		
Laneport L.—(See **Granger Lake.**).		
Lavon L. (Enlargement).—Collin Co.; East Fk. Trinity R.; 2 mi. W Lavon; (M-FC-In.); USAE	21,400	443,800
Leon Reservoir.—Eastland Co.; Leon R.; 7 mi. S Ranger; (M-In.); Eastland Co. Water Supply Dist	1,590	26,420
Lewis Creek Reservoir.—Montgomery Co.; Lewis Cr.; 10 mi. NW Conroe; (In.) Gulf States Utilities Co.	1,010	16,400
Lewisville L.—Denton Co.; Elm Fk. Trinity R.; 2 mi. NE Lewisville; (M-FC-In.-R); USAE; (called also **Lake Dallas** and **Garza-Little Elm**)	23,280	464,500
Limestone, L.—Leon-Limestone-Robertson Counties; Navasota R.; 7 mi. NW Marquez; (M-In.-Ir.); BRA	14,200	225,400
Livingston L.—Polk-San Jacinto-Trinity-Walker Counties; Trinity R.; 6 mi. SW Livingston; (M-In.-Ir.); City of Houston and Trinity River Authority	82,600	1,750,000
Loma Alta Reservoir.—Cameron Co.; off-channel Rio Grande; 8 mi. NE Brownsville; (M-In.); Brownsville Navigation Dist.	2,490	26,500
Lone Star Reservoir.—(See **Ellison Creek Lake.**).		
Los Fresnos, Resaca de.—(See **Resacas.**.)		
McGee Bend Reservoir.—(See **Sam Rayburn Reservoir.**)		
McQueeney, L.—Guadalupe Co.; Guadalupe R.; 5 mi. W Seguin; (P); Guadalupe-Blanco R. Authority; (impounded by **Abbott Dam**)	396	5,000
Mackenzie Reservoir.—Briscoe Co.; Tule Cr.; 9 mi. NW Silverton; (M); Mackenzie Mun. Water Auth	910	46,250
Marble Falls L.—Burnet County; Colorado R.; (impounded by **Max Starcke Dam**); 1.25 mi. SE Marble Falls; (P); LCRA	780	8,760
Martin L.—Rusk-Panola Counties; Martin Cr.; 17 mi. NE Henderson; (P); Texas Utilities Service Co., Inc.	5,020	77,620
Max Starcke Dam.—(See **Marble Falls Lake.**).		
Medina L.—Medina-Bandera Counties; Medina R.; 8 mi. W Rio Medina; (Ir.); Bexar-Medina-Atascosa Co. WID No. 1.	5,575	254,000
Meredith, L.—Moore-Potter-Hutchinson Counties; Canadian R.; 10 mi. NW Borger; (M-In.-FC-R); cooperative project for municipal water supply by Amarillo, Lubbock and other High Plains Cities. Canadian R. Municipal Water Authority-USBR; (impounded by **Sanford Dam**)	16,504	821,300
Mexia, L.—Limestone Co.; Navasota R.; 7 mi. SW Mexia; (M-In); Bistone Mun. Water Dist.; (impounded by **Bistone Dam**)	1,200	10,000
Millers Creek Reservoir.—Baylor Co.; Millers Cr.; 9 mi. SE Goree; (M); No. Central Tex. Mun. Water Auth. and Texas Water Development Board	2,350	30,700
Mineral Wells L.—Parker Co.; Rock Cr.; 4 mi. E Mineral Wells; (M); Palo Pinto Co. Mun. WD No. 1	646	6,760
Monte Alto Reservoir.—(See **Delta Lake Res. Units 1 and 2.**)		
Monticello Reservoir.—Titus Co.; Blundell Cr.; 2.5 mi. E. Monticello; (In.); Industrial Generating Co.	2,000	40,100
Moss L., Hubert H.—Cooke Co.; Fish Cr.; 10 mi. NW Gainesville; (M-In.); City of Gainesville	1,125	23,210
Mountain Creek L.—Dallas Co.; Mountain Cr.; 4 mi. SE Grand Prairie; (In.); Dallas P&L Co.	2,710	22,840
Mud Creek Dam L.—(See **Tyler Lake, East.**)		

Lakes and Reservoirs— (continued)

	Conservation Surface Area (Acres)	Conservation Storage Capacity (Acre-Ft.)
Murphree, J. D. Area Impoundments. —(See J. D. Murphree.)		
Murvaul L.—Panola Co.; Murvaul Bayou; 10 mi. SW Carthage; (M-In.-R); Panola Co. Fresh Water Supply Dist. No. 1	3,820	45,815
Nacogdoches, L.—Nacogdoches Co.; Bayo Loco Cr.; 10 mi. W Nacogdoches; (M); City of Nacogdoches	2,210	41,140
Nasworthy, L.—Tom Green Co.; S Concho R.; 6 mi. SW San Angelo; (M-In.-Ir.); City of San Angelo	1,596	12,390
Navarro Mills L.—Navarro-Hill Counties; Richland Cr.; 16 mi. SW Corsicana; (M-FC); USAE	5,070	60,900
Nacona L. — (See **Farmers Creek Reservoir.**)		
North Fk. Buffalo Creek Reservoir.—Wichita Co.; 5 mi. NW Iowa Park; (M); Wichita Co. WC&ID No. 3	1,500	15,400
North Fork L.—(See **Georgetown L.**)		
North L.—Dallas Co.; S. Fork Grapevine Cr.; 2 mi. SE Coppell; (In.); Dallas P&L Co.	800	17,000
Oak Creek Reservoir.—Coke Co.; 5 mi. SE Blackwell; (M-In.); City of Sweetwater	2,375	39,360
O. C. Fisher L.—Tom Green Co.; N. Concho R.; 3 mi. NW San Angelo; (M-FC-C-Ir.-R-In.-Mi); USAE — Upper Colo. Auth. (formerly **San Angelo L.**)	5,440	119,200
Olmos Reservoir.—Bexar Co.; Olmos Cr.; in San Antonio city limits; (exclusively for flood control); maximum capacity 12,600 acre-feet; City of San Antonio	0	0
Palestine, L.—Anderson-Cherokee-Henderson-Smith Counties; Neches R.; 4 mi. E Frankston; (M-In.-R); Upper Neches R. MWA (impounded by **Blackburn Crossing Dam**)	25,560	411,300
Palmetto Bend Reservoir. — (See **Texana, L.**).		
Palo Alto Resaca. — (See **Resacas** in this list.)		
Palo Pinto, L.—Palo Pinto Co.; 15 mi. SW Mineral Wells; (M-In.); Palo Pinto Co. Municipal Water Dist. No. 1	2,661	42,200
Panola L.—(See **Murvaul L.**)		
Pat Mayse L.—Lamar Co.; Sanders Cr.; 2 mi. SW Arthur City; (M-In.-FC); USAE.	5,993	124,500
Pinkston Reservoir.—Shelby Co.; Sandy Cr.; 12.5 mi. SW Center; (M); City of Center; (formerly **Sandy Creek Reservoir**)	523	7,380
Possum Kingdom L.—Palo Pinto-Young-Stephens-Jack Counties; Brazos R.; 11 mi. SW Graford; (M-In.-Ir.-Mi.-P-R); Brazos R. Authority; (impounded by **Morris Sheppard Dam**)	17,700	569,380
Proctor L.—Comanche Co.; Leon R.; 9 mi. NE Comanche; (M-In.-Ir.-FC); USAE-Brazos River Authority	4,610	59,300
Quarters Resaca.—(See **Resacas.**)		
Quitman, L.—Wood Co.; Dry Cr.; 4 mi. N Quitman; (FC-R); Wood County (impounded by **Wood Co. Dam No. 1**)	814	7,440
Randall, L.—Grayson Co.; Shawnee Cr.; 4 mi. NW Denison; (M); City of Denison	311	6,290
Ray Hubbard, L.—Collin-Dallas-Kaufman-Rockwall Counties; (formerly called **Forney Reservoir**); E. Fk. Trinity R.; 15 mi. E Dallas; (M); City of Dallas	22,745	490,000
***Ray Roberts L.**—Denton-Cooke-Grayson Counties; Elm Fk. Trinity R.; 11 mi. NE Denton; (FC-M-D); City of Denton, Dallas, USAE; (also known as **Aubrey Reservoir**)	29,350	799,600
Red Bluff Reservoir.—Loving-Reeves Counties, Texas; and Eddy Co., N.M.; Pecos R.; 5 mi. N Orla; (Ir.-P); Red Bluff Water Power Control District	11,700	307,000
Resacas.—Cameron-Hidalgo-Willacy Counties; Rio Grande; these reservoirs are primarily for storage of water during periods of normal or above-normal flow in the river for use when the river's current is low. Some of these are old loops and bends in the river that have been isolated by the river changing its channel. They are known by the Spanish name as resacas. Also a number of reservoirs have been constructed and connected with the main channel of the river by ditches through which the reservoirs are filled either by gravity flow or by pumping. This is reserve irrigation water for use during periods of low flow in the river channel. Most of these reservoirs are near the main channel of the river, but some of them are 20 or 25 miles distant.		
Reservoir No. 1 & No. 2.—Cameron Co.; off-channel Rio Grande R.; 7 mi. SW San Benito; (Ir.-M-In.); Cameron Co. WID No. 2	900	14,200
***Richland Creek Reservoir.**—Freestone-Navarro Counties; Richland Cr.; 23 mi. SE Corsicana; (M); Tarrant Co. WCID No. 1.	38,850	1,135,000
Rita Blanca L.—Hartley Co.; Rita Blanca Cr.; 2 mi. S Dalhart; (R); City of Dalhart	524	12,100
River Crest L.—Red River County; off-channel reservoir; 7 mi. SE Bogata; (In.); Texas P&L	555	7,000
Robert Lee Reservoir.—(See **Spence Reservoir.**)		
Salt Creek L.—(See **Graham L.**)		
Sam Rayburn Reservoir.—Jasper-Angelina-Sabine-Nacogdoches-San Augustine Counties; Angelina R.; (formerly **McGee Bend**); (FC-P-M-In.-Ir.-R); USAE	114,500	2,876,300
San Angelo L.—(See **O. C. Fisher L.**)		
Sandlin, L. Bob.—Titus-Wood-Camp-Franklin Counties; Big Cypress Cr.; 5 mi. SW Mount Pleasant; (In.-M-R); Titus Co. FWSD No. 1 (impounded by **Fort Sherman Dam**)	9,460	202,300
Sandy Creek Reservoir.—(See **Pinkston Reservoir.**)		
Sandow L.—(See **Alcoa Lake.**)		
San Esteban L.—Presidio Co.; Alamito Cr.; 10 mi. S Marfa; (R); Wm. B. Blakemore	762	18,770
Sanford Reservoir.—(See **Meredith Lake.**)		
Santa Rosa L.—Wilbarger Co.; Beaver Cr.; 15 mi. S Vernon; (Mi.); W. T. Waggoner Estate	1,500	11,570
Sheldon Reservoir.—Harris Co.; Carpenters Bayou; 2 mi. SW Sheldon; (R-FH); State Parks & Wildlife Dept.	1,700	5,420
Smithers L.—Fort Bend Co.; Dry Creek; 10 mi. SE Richmond; (In.); Houston Lighting & Power Co.	2,480	18,700
Somerville L.—Burleson-Washington Counties; Yegua Cr.; 2 mi. S Somerville; (M-In.-Ir.-FC); USAE-Brazos River Authority	11,460	160,100
Southland Paper Mills Reservoir.—(See **Kurth Lake.**)		
South Texas Project Reservoir.—Matagorda Co.; off-channel Colorado R.; 16 mi. S Bay City; (In.); Houston Lighting & Power.	7,000	187,000

Lakes and Reservoirs— (continued)

	Conservation Surface Area (Acres)	Conservation Storage Capacity (Acre-Ft.)
Spence Reservoir, E.V.—Coke Co.; Colorado R.; 2 mi. W. Robert Lee; (M-In.-Mi); Colorado R. Mun. Water Dist.; (impounded by **Robert Lee Dam**)	14,950	484,800
Squaw Creek Reservoir.—Somervell-Hood Counties; Squaw Cr.; 4.5 mi. N Glen Rose; (In.); Texas Utilities Services, Inc.	3,228	151,047
Stamford, L.—Haskell Co.; Paint Cr.; 10 mi. SE Haskell; (M-In.); City of Stamford	4,690	52,700
Steinhagen L., B. A.—(Also called **Town Bluff Reservoir** and **Dam B. Reservoir**); Tyler-Jasper Counties; Neches R.; ½ mi. N Town Bluff; (FC-R-C); (impounded by **Town Bluff Dam**)	13,700	94,200
Stillhouse Hollow L.—Bell Co.; Lampasas R.; 5 mi. SW Belton; (M-In.-Ir.-FC); USAE-Brazos R. Authority; (sometimes called **Lampasas Reservoir**)	6,430	234,900
Striker Creek Reservoir.—Rusk-Cherokee Counties; Striker Cr.; 18 mi. SW Henderson; (M-In.); Angelina-Nacogdoches WC&ID No. 1	2,400	26,960
Sulphur Springs L.—Hopkins Co.; White Oak Cr.; 2 mi. N Sulphur Springs; (M); Sulphur Springs WD; (impounded by **Lake Sulphur Springs Dam** and formerly called **White Oak Creek Reservoir**)	1,910	17,710
Swauano Creek Reservoir.—(See **Welsh Reservoir.**)		
Sweetwater L.—Nolan Co.; Bitter and Cottonwood Creeks; 6 mi. SE Sweetwater; (M-In.); City of Sweetwater.	630	11,900
Tawakoni, L.—Rains-Van Zandt-Hunt Counties; Sabine R.; 9 mi. NE Wills Point; (M-In.-Ir.-R); Sabine River Authority; (impounded by **Iron Bridge Dam**)	36,700	936,200
Terrell City L., New.—Kaufman Co.; Muddy Cedar Cr.; 6 mi. E Terrell; (M-R); City of Terrell	830	8,712
Texana, L.—Jackson Co.; Navidad R. and Sandy Cr.; 6.8 mi. SE Edna; (M-Ir); USBR, Lavaca-Navidad R. Auth., Texas Water Dev. Bd.; (formerly **Palmetto Bend Reservoir**)	11,000	157,900
Texarkana L.—(See **Wright Patman Lake.**).		
Texoma L.—Grayson-Cooke Counties, Texas; Bryan-Marshall-Love Counties, Okla.; impounded by **Denison Dam** on Red R. short distance below confluence of Red and Washita Rivers; (P-FC-C-R); USAE	89,000	2,722,000
Thomas L.—(See **J. B. Thomas L.**)		
Toledo Bend Reservoir.—Newton-Panola-Sabine-Shelby Counties; Sabine R.; 14 mi. NE Burkeville; (M-In.-Ir.-P-R); Sabine River Authority. (Texas' share of capacity is half amount shown.)	181,600	4,472,900
Town Bluff Reservoir.—(See **Steinhagen, Lake B. A.**)		
Tradinghouse Creek Reservoir.—McLennan Co.; Tradinghouse Cr.; 9 mi. E Waco; (In.); Texas P&L	2,010	35,124
Travis, L.—Travis-Burnet Counties; Colorado R.; 13 mi. NW Austin; (M-In.-Ir.-Mi.-P-FC-R); LCRA; (impounded by **Mansfield Dam**)	18,930	1,144,100
Trinidad L.—Henderson Co.; off-channel reservoir Trinity R.; 2 mi. S Trinidad; (P); Texas P&L Co.	740	7,450
Truscott Brine L.—Knox Co.; Bluff Cr.; 26 mi. NNW Knox City; (Chlorine Control); Red River Auth. of Texas	2,978	107,000
Turtle Bayou Reservoir.—(See **Anahuac Lake.**).		
Twin Buttes Reservoir.—Tom Green Co.; Concho R.; 8 mi. SW San Angelo; (M-In.-FC-Ir.-R.); City of San Angelo-USBR-Tom Green Co. WC&ID No. 1	9,080	177,800
Twin Oaks Reservoir.—Robertson Co.; Duck Cr.; 12 mi. N Franklin; (In); Texas P&L.	2,300	30,319
Tyler L.—Smith Co.; Prairie and Mud Crs.; 12 mi. SE Tyler; (M-In); City of Tyler; (impounded by **Whitehouse** and **Mud Creek Dams**)	4,800	73,700
Upper Nueces Reservoir.—Zavala Co.; Nueces R.; 6 mi. N Crystal City; (Ir.); Zavala-Dimmit Co. WID No. 1.	316	7,590
Valley Acres Reservoir.—Hidalgo Co.; off-channel Rio Grande; 7 mi. N Mercedes; (Ir-M-FC); Valley Acres Water Dist.	906	7,840
Valley L.—Fannin-Grayson Counties; 2.5 mi. N Savoy; (P); TP&L; (formerly **Brushy Creek Reservoir**)	1,080	16,400
Victor Braunig L.—Bexar Co.; Arroyo Seco; 15 mi. SE San Antonio; (In.); City Public Service Bd. of San Antonio	1,350	26,500
Waco L.—McLennan Co.; Bosque R.; 2 mi. W Waco; (M-FC-C-R); City of Waco-USAE-Brazos River Authority	7,270	151,900
***Wallisville L.**—Liberty-Chambers Counties; Trinity R.; 2 mi. S Wallisville; (M-In.-Ir.); USAE	19,700	58,000
Walter E. Long L.—Travis Co.; Decker Cr.; 9 mi. E of capital, Austin; (M-In.-R); City of Austin; (formerly **Decker Lake**)	1,269	33,940
Waxahachie L.—Ellis Co.; S Prong Waxahachie Cr.; 4 mi. SE Waxahachie; (M-In); Ellis County WC&ID No. 1; (impounded by **S. Prong Dam**)	690	13,500
Weatherford L.—Parker Co.; Clear Fork Trinity River; 7 mi. E Weatherford; (M-In.); City of Weatherford	1,210	19,470
Welsh Reservoir.—Titus Co.; Swauano Cr.; 11 mi. SE Mount Pleasant; (R-In.); Southwestern Electric Power Co.; (formerly **Swauano Creek Reservoir.**)	1,365	23,587
White Oak Creek Reservoir.—(See **Sulphur Springs Lake.**)		
White River L.—Crosby Co.; 16 mi. SE Crosbyton; (M-In.-Mi.); White River Municipal Water Dist.	2,020	44,300
White Rock L.—Dallas Co.; White Rock Cr.; within NE Dallas city limits; (R); City of Dallas.	1,119	10,740
Whitney L.—Hill-Bosque-Johnson Counties; Brazos R.; 5.5 mi. SW Whitney; (FC-P); USAE	23,560	622,800
Wichita, L.—Wichita Co.; Holliday Cr.; 6 mi. SW Wichita Falls; (M-P-R); City of Wichita Falls.	2,200	9,000
Winnsboro, L.—Wood Co.; Big Sandy Cr.; 6 mi. SW Winnsboro; (FC-R); Wood County; (impounded by **Wood Co. Dam No. 4**)	806	8,100
Winters L.—Runnels Co.; Elm Cr.; 4.5 mi. E. Winters; (M); City of Winters	640	8,370
Worth, L.—Tarrant Co.; W. Fk. Trinity R.; in NW Fort Worth; (M); City of Fort Worth	3,560	38,130
Wright Patman L.—Bowie-Cass-Morris-Titus-Red River Counties; Sulphur R.; 8 mi. SW Texarkana; (FC-M); USAE; (formerly **Texarkana Lake**)	20,300	142,700

*Reservoir under construction.

WATER SUPPLIES AND NEEDS

The 65th Legislature combined the functions of three state water agencies — those of the **Water Development Board**, the **Water Quality Board** and the **Water Rights Commission** — into a single agency, the **Texas Department of Water Resources**. The action abolished the Texas Water Quality Board and provided for a 3-member **Texas Water Commission** to handle judical matters, a 6-member **Texas Water Development Board** to establish policy for the department and an executive director to manage the department.

Texas, through its river authorities, municipalities, water districts and state-level agencies, exercises the dominant role in development of municipal and industrial water supplies. Approximately 80 percent of the money invested in the state's water projects has been provided by Texas entities of government.

Ground-Water Supplies and Use

Aquifers underlie more than half of the area of Texas. This ground water has long been the principal source of municipal supplies, but cities now increasingly depend upon surface reservoirs due to depletion of water in aquifer storage. More than half of Texas' total agricultural crop value is produced utilizing **ground water** for irrigation, mainly from the **High Plains (Ogallala) aquifer** on the High Plains.

Declining water levels, mining and exhaustion of ground water, coupled with increasing energy costs, are major problems facing the state's water managers today.

Major aquifers in Texas follow (see map):

High Plains (Ogallala) — This formation furnishes practically the only usable quality water on the High Plains. It is composed of unconsolidated, fine- to coarse-grained, gray to red sand, clay, silt and gravel. Effective recharge from precipitation is small, averaging less than one-quarter inch yearly; whereas pumping is heavy, averaging about five million acre-feet

yearly. Depletion at the present pumping rate threatens this as a water source for irrigation. The High Plains aquifer supplies Texas' largest irrigated farming region, which produces most of the cotton, grain sorghum and other crops.

Alluvium and Bolson Deposits — These water-bearing deposits are scattered throughout many areas in the state. They include the **Hueco and Mesilla Bolsons**, the **Cenozoic Alluvium** of West Texas, the alluviums of North Central Texas, the **Leona Alluvium** of Tom Green County and the **Brazos River Alluvium** of Southeast Texas. These deposits consist generally of sand, gravel, silt and clay. The quality of the water can range from fresh to saline.

In the westernmost Texas region, the Mesilla and Hueco Bolsons are the primary source of water supply for the **El Paso area** where serious problems exist regarding ground-water depletion and quality degradation. Other sources of ground-water supply are from the **Salt Bolson (Wildhorse Draw, Michigan Flat, Lobo Flat** and **Ryan Flat** areas), the **Red Light Draw Bolson,** the

MAJOR AQUIFERS

EXPLANATION

MAJOR AQUIFERS
Yields large quantities of water in large areas of the State

High Plains (Ogallala)

Alluvium and Bolson Deposits

Edwards—Trinity (Plateau)

Edwards (Balcones Fault Zone)

OUTCROP
DOWNDIP   Trinity Group

Carrizo—Wilcox

Gulf Coast

STATE OF TEXAS
Texas Department of Water Resources
Austin, Texas

Scale in Miles

Scale in Kilometers
February 1979

Green River Valley Bolson and the **Presidio** and **Redford Bolsons.** In the Cenozoic Alluvium region, the **Pecos-Coyonosa** area and northeastern **Ward County** are the most productive areas of usable quality ground water. Supplies are produced from the **Seymour aquifer** in North Central Texas.

Edwards-Trinity (Plateau) — This aquifer underlies the **Edwards Plateau region** of Southwest Texas. It consists of saturated sediments of the **Lower Cretaceous Comanchean Series** made up of sand, sandstone, gravel and conglomerate of the **Trinity Group (Antlers Sand)**; and cherty, gypseous, argillaceous, cavernous limestones and dolomites of the **Comanche Peak, Edwards and Georgetown Formations.** The ground water generally flows southeasterly, and near the edge of the Plateau, movement is toward the main streams where the water issues from springs. The water ranges in quality from fresh to slightly saline and is hard. Most of the municipalities on the Plateau depend on this aquifer for their water supply. Where the land is arable and yield from wells is sufficient, irrigated farming is possible. Problems exist in those areas where development has exceeded the capabilities of the aquifer.

Edwards (Balcones Fault Zone) — Ground water occurs in fractures, honeycomb zones and solution channels in this aquifer that underlies an area along the **Balcones Fault Zone** from **Kinney County** on the west through **Bexar County** to **Bell County** on the north. Geologically, it is made up of the **Edwards and associated limestones** of Cretaceous age and consists of massive to thin-bedded, nodular, cherty, gypseous, argillaceous, white to gray limestone and dolomite of the **Comanche Peak, Edwards** and **Georgetown Formations,** which have been downset from the Edwards Plateau due to faulting. The aquifer is recharged rapidly by water discharged from springs along the edge of the Edwards Plateau which then flows in streams that traverse the many faults along the Balcones. The ground water moves through the aquifer generally in an easterly, northeasterly direction to points of discharge, notable of which are **Leona, San Antonio, San Pedro, Comal, San Marcos, Barton** and **Salado Springs,** plus numerous smaller springs. In **Bexar County,** wells pumping from this aquifer are among the world's largest. The water is generally of good quality and it is used for public supply, irrigation, industrial, domestic and livestock watering purposes. Hydrologically, the aquifer is unique and is one of the state's most valuable natural resources. In the past, the aquifer was adequate to meet **San Antonio's** water needs, but increased growth and development in this area necessitate additional surface water supplies.

Trinity Group — These basal Cretaceous-age rocks extend over a large area of North and Central Texas and are composed primarily of sand with interbedded clays, limestone, dolomite, gravel and conglomerates. The Trinity Group is made up of the **Twin Mountains, Glen Rose** and **Paluxy Formations;** however, to the west and north where the Glen Rose Formation thins or pinches out, the **Twin Mountains** and **Paluxy Formations** coalesce and are called the **Antlers Formation.** The water quality is acceptable for most municipal and industrial purposes. Extensive irrigation occurs in **Comanche, Eastland** and **Erath Counties.** The aquifer has been overdeveloped in the **Dallas-Fort Worth** metropolitan area and in the vicinity of **Waco** where water levels have declined to as much as 1,200 feet below the land surface.

Carrizo-Wilcox — This aquifer of Eocene age is one of the most extensive water-bearing formations in Texas geograpically, and it furnishes water to wells in a wide belt extending from the Rio Grande northeastward into Arkansas and Louisiana. It consists of hydrologically connected ferruginous, cross-bedded sand with clay, sandstone, silt, lignite and gravel of the **Wilcox Group** and overlying **Carrizo Formation.** Throughout most of Texas, the Carrizo-Wilcox aquifer yields fresh to slightly saline water which is acceptable for most irrigation, public supply and industrial uses. Because of excessive pumping, the water levels have been significantly lowered particularly in the **Winter Garden District** of Dimmit and Zavala Counties and in the municipal and industrial areas located north of **Lufkin** in **Angelina** and **Nacogdoches Counties.**

Gulf Coast Aquifer — Geologically, the Gulf Coast aquifer ranges in age from Miocene to Holocene, and it is collectively composed of the **Catahoula, Oakville, Lagarto, Goliad, Willis, Lissie** and **Beaumont Formations.** Lithologically, it consists of alternating beds of clay, silt, sand and gravel which are hydrologically connected. The principal water-bearing units are the **Goliad, Willis** and **Lissie Formations.** It parallels the Texas Gulf

Coast from Mexico to Louisiana. Normally, fresh to slightly saline ground water occurs in the aquifer from the San Antonio River basin northeastward to Louisiana. In this area, large quantities are pumped for municipal, industrial and irrigation use. Ground-water quality tends to deteriorate in the San Antonio River basin and southwestward to Mexico where there are areas in which no appreciable amounts of fresh to slightly saline water can be found. Problems of land-surface subsidence in the Houston area are well documented. Additionally, withdrawal of ground water from the Gulf Coast aquifer can cause increased chloride content, especially in the southwest portion, and salt-water encroachment along the coast. Therefore, management of future withdrawals from the aquifer is necessary in order to alleviate serious ground-water problems.

Minor aquifers occur in Texas as shown on the accompanying map and, in certain areas, are a significant source of water supply.

Water Budget

Average annual precipitation in Texas is estimated at 413,000,000 acre-feet. (One acre-foot is 325,851 gallons.) The **Average Yearly Water Budget for Texas,** which follows, was compiled by the **Texas Department of Water Resources.**

This shows that more water is lost through evaporation, consumption by useless weeds and brush and discharge into the Gulf of Mexico than is used by Texas municipalities, industries and agriculture. In addition to these losses, precipitation is very unevenly distributed in Texas, with abundant supplies in the eastern half of the state contrasting with scarcities in the western portion. Also, it shows that the total outgo exceeds the income, which is the result of mining ground water.

AVERAGE ANNUAL WATER BUDGET FOR TEXAS

	Million Acre-Ft.	Per Cent
INCOME		
All precipitation	413	100.0
OUTGO		
Evaporation	174	42.0
From plant cover	52	12.5
From soil surface	122	29.5
Transpiration	193	47.0
From non-economic plants	154	37.5
Cultivated crops	16	4.0
Range and pasture plants	13	3.0
Commercial forests	10	2.5
Addition to ground-water storage	5	1.0
Surface Runoff	49	12.0
Industrial, municipal and irrigation consumption	2	0.5
Evaporation from water surface	8	2.0
Discharged into sea	39	9.5
Total Outgo	421	102.0

Streams and Drainage Basins

Some 3,700 streams are identified in the **U.S. Geological Survey Gazetteer of Texas Streams.** Their combined length is about 80,000 miles, and they drain 263,513 square miles within Texas. The following discussion describes 13 major rivers in its first part, with a later description of secondary streams.

Rio Grande

The Pueblo Indians called this river **Posoge,** "river of great water." In 1582, Antonio de Espejo of Nueva Vizcaya, Mexico, followed the course of the Rio Conchos to its confluence with a great river, which Espejo named **Rio de Norte** (River of the North). The name **Rio Grande** was first given the stream apparently by the explorer Juan de Oñate, who arrived on its banks near present day El Paso in 1598.

Thereafter the names were often consolidated, as **Rio Grande del Norte.** (It has its counterpart in the Portuguese Rio Grande do Sul in the state of that name in Brazil.) It was shown also on early Spanish maps as **Rio San Buenaventura** and **Rio Ganapetuan.** In its lower course it early acquired the name **Rio Bravo,** and it is called by that name today by many Mexicans living in its valley. At times it has also been known as **Rio Turbio,** probably because of its appearance during its frequent rises.

From source to mouth, the Rio Grande drops 12,000 feet to sea level as a snow-fed mountain torrent, carver of canyons, desert stream and meandering coastal river. Along its banks and in its valley Indian civilizations developed, and the white man made some of his first North American settlements.

This river rises in Colorado, flows the north-south length of New Mexico and forms the boundary of Texas and international U.S.-Mexican boundary for 889 to 1,248 miles, depending upon method of measurement. (See Texas Boundary Line.) The length of the Rio Grande, as of other rivers, depends on method of measurement and varies yearly as its course changes. Latest International Boundary and Water Commission figure is 1,896 miles, which is considerably below the 2,200-mile figure often used. Depending upon methods of measurement, the Rio Grande is the fourth- or fifth-longest North American river, exceeded only by the Missouri-Mississippi, McKenzie-Peace, St. Lawrence and possibly Yukon. Since all of these except the Missouri-Mississippi are partly in Canada, the Rio Grande is the second-longest river entirely within or bordering the United States. It is Texas' longest river.

The snow-fed flow of the Rio Grande is used for irrigation in Colorado below the San Juan Mountains where the river rises at the Continental Divide. Turning south, it flows through a canyon in northern New Mexico and again irrigates a broad valley of central New Mexico. Dating from the 1600s, this is the oldest irrigated area of the United States, where Spanish missionaries encouraged Indian irrigation. Southern New Mexico impounds Rio Grande waters in Elephant Butte Reservoir for irrigation for 150 miles of valley above and below El Paso. Here is the oldest irrigated area in Texas and one of the oldest in the United States. Extensive irrigation practically exhausts the water supply. In this valley are situated the three oldest towns in Texas — Ysleta, Socorro and San Elizario. At the lower end of the El Paso irrigated valley, the upper Rio Grande, a snow-fed mountain stream, virtually ends except in seasons of above-normal flow.

It starts as a perennially flowing stream again where the Rio Conchos of Mexico flows into it at Presidio-Ojinaga. Through the Big Bend the Rio Grande flows through three successive canyons, the **Santa Elena**, the **Mariscal** and the **Boquillas**. The Santa Elena has a river bed elevation of 2,145 feet and a canyon rim elevation of 3,661. Corresponding figures for the Mariscal are 1,925 and 3,625, those for the Boquillas, 1,850 and 3,490. The river here flows around the base of the great Chisos Mountains. For about 100 miles the river is the southern boundary of the **Big Bend National Park**.

Below the Big Bend, the Rio Grande gradually emerges from mountains onto the Coastal Plains. At the confluence of the Rio Grande and Devils River, the U.S. and Mexico have built **Amistad Dam**, to impound 3,383,900 acre-feet of water, of which Texas' share is 56.2 per cent; and **Falcon Reservoir**, also an international project, impounds 2,667,600 acre-feet of water, of which Texas' share in Zapata and Starr Counties is 58.6 per cent. Finally, the Rio Grande has created a fertile delta where it joins the Gulf of Mexico, called the **Lower Rio Grande Valley**, that is a major vegetable-fruit area.

The Rio Grande drains over 40,000 square miles of Texas.

Principal tributaries flowing from the Texas side of the Rio Grande are the Pecos and the Devils Rivers. On the Mexican side are the **Rio Conchos**, the **Rio Salado** and the **Rio San Juan**. About three-fourths of the water running into the Rio Grande below El Paso comes from the Mexican side.

Nueces River

The Nueces River rises in Edwards County and flows 315 miles to Nueces Bay on the Gulf near Corpus Christi. Draining 17,000 square miles, it is a beautiful spring-fed stream flowing through canyons until it issues from the Balcones Escarpment onto the Coastal Plain in northern Uvalde County. Alonso de Leon, in 1689, gave it its name. (Nueces, plural of nuez, means nuts in Spanish.) Much earlier Cabeza de Vaca referred to a Rio de las Nueces in this region, probably the same stream. Its original Indian name seems to have been Chotilapacquen. Crossing Texas in 1691, Teran de los Rios named the river San Diego. The Nueces was the boundary line between the Spanish provinces of Texas and Nuevo Santander. After the Revolution of 1836 both Texas and Mexico claimed the territory between the Nueces and the Rio Grande, a dispute which was settled by the Treaty of Guadalupe Hidalgo in 1848 which fixed the international boundary at the Rio Grande. Nueces runoff is about 620,000 acre-feet a year in its lower course. Principal water conservation project is **Lake Corpus Christi**. Principal tributaries of the Nueces are the **Frio** and the **Atascosa**.

San Antonio River

The San Antonio River has its source in large springs within and near the corporate limits of San Antonio. It flows 180 miles across the Coastal Plain to a junction with the Guadalupe near the Gulf Coast. Its channel through San Antonio has been developed into a parkway. Its principal tributaries are the **Medina River** and **Cibolo Creek**, both spring-fed streams and this, with its own origin in springs, gives it a remarkably steady flow of clear water.

This stream was first named the Leon by Alonso de Leon during his trip across Texas in 1689. (De Leon was not naming the stream for himself, but called it "lion" because its channel was filled with a rampaging flood.)

Because of its limited and relatively arid drainage area (4,200 square miles) the average runoff of the San Antonio River is relatively small, about 350,000 acre-feet annually near its mouth, but its flow, because of its springs, is one of the steadiest of Texas rivers.

Guadalupe River

The Guadalupe rises in its north and south prongs in the west central part of Kerr County. A spring-fed stream, it flows eastward through the Hill Country until it issues from the Balcones Escarpment near New Braunfels. It then meanders across the Coastal Plain to San Antonio Bay. Its total length is about 250 miles, and its drainage area about 6,000 square miles. Its principal tributaries are the **San Marcos**, another spring-fed stream which flows into it in Gonzales County, the **San Antonio** which flows into it just above its mouth on San Antonio Bay and the **Comal** which joins it at New Braunfels. The **Comal River** has its source in large springs within the city limits of New Braunfels and flows only about 2.5 miles to the Guadalupe. It is the **shortest river in Texas** and also the shortest river in the United States carrying an equivalent amount of water. There has been power development on the Guadalupe near Gonzales and Cuero for many years. Because of its springs, and its considerable drainage area, it has an annual runoff of more than 1,000,000 acre-feet in its lower course.

The name Guadalupe is derived from Nuestra Senora de Guadalupe, the name given the stream by Alonso de Leon.

Lavaca River

The Lavaca River is considered a primary stream in the Texas Basin because it flows directly into the Gulf, through Lavaca Bay. Without a spring water source and with only a small watershed, including that of its principal tributary, the **Navidad**, its flow is intermittent. The Spanish called it the Lavaca (cow) River because of the numerous bison they found. It is the principal stream running into the Gulf between the Guadalupe and the Colorado. Runoff averages about 600,000 acre-feet yearly into the Gulf.

Colorado River

Measured by length and drainage area, the Colorado is the largest river wholly in Texas. (This comparison excludes the Brazos whose drainage basin extends into New Mexico.) Rising in Dawson County, the Colorado flows about 600 miles to Matagorda Bay on the Gulf. Its drainage area is 39,900 square miles. Its runoff reaches a volume of more than 2,000,000 acre-feet near the Gulf. Its name is a Spanish word meaning "reddish." There is evidence that the name, Colorado, was given originally by Spanish explorers to the muddy Brazos and Spanish mapmakers later transposed the two names. The river flows through a rolling, usually prairie terrain to the vicinity of San Saba County where it enters the rugged Hill Country and Burnet-Llano Basin. It passes through a picturesque series of canyons until it issues from the Balcones Escarpment at Austin and flows across the Coastal Plain to the Gulf. In this area the most remarkable series of reservoirs in Texas has been built. There are two large reservoirs, **Lake Buchanan** in Burnet-Llano Counties and **Lake Travis** in Travis County. Between these, in Burnet County, are three smaller reservoirs: **Inks**, **Johnson** (formerly **Granite Shoals**) and **Marble Falls**, built to aid power production from water running over the Buchanan Lake Spillway. Below Lake Travis is the older **Lake Austin**, largely filled with silt, whose dam maintains a head for production of power from waters flowing down from the lakes above. Town Lake is in the City of Austin. This area is known as the **Highland Lakes Country**.

As early as the 1820s Anglo-Americans settled on the banks of the lower Colorado, and in 1839 the **Capital Commission** of the Republic of Texas chose the picturesque area where the river flows from the Balcones Escarpment as the site of a new capital of the Republic — now **Austin**, capital of the state. The early colonists encouraged navigation along the lower channel with some success and boats occasionally ventured as far up stream as Austin. However, a natural log "raft" in the channel near the Gulf blocked river traffic. Conservation and utilization of the waters of the Colorado are under jurisdiction of three agencies created by the state Legislature, the **Lower, Central** and **Upper Colorado River Authorities.**

The principal tributaries of the Colorado are the several prongs of the **Concho River** on its upper course, the **Pecan Bayou (farthest west "bayou" in the United States)** and the Llano, San Saba and Pedernales Rivers. All except the Pecan Bayou flow into the Colorado from the Edwards Plateau and are spring-fed, perennially flowing. In the numerous mussels found along these streams occasional pearls have been found. The Middle Concho was designated on early Spanish maps as **Rio de las Perlas.**

Brazos River

The Brazos is the largest river between the Rio Grande and the Red River and third in size of all rivers in Texas. It rises in three upper forks, the **Double Mountain, Salt** and **Clear Forks** of the Brazos. The Brazos River proper is considered as beginning where the Double Mountain and Salt Forks flow together in Stonewall County. The Clear Fork joins this main stream in Young County, just above Lake Possum Kingdom. The Brazos crosses most of the main physiographic regions of Texas — High Plains, West Texas Lower Rolling Plains, West Cross Timbers, Grand Prairie and Gulf Coastal Plain.

The total length from the source of its longest upper prong, the Double Mountain Fork, to the mouth of the main stream at the Gulf, is about 840 miles and the drainage area is about 42,800 square miles.

It flows directly into the Gulf near Freeport. Its annual runoff at places along its lower channel exceeds 5,000,000 acre-feet.

The original name of this river was **Brazos de Dios,** meaning "Arms of God." There are several legends as to why. One is that the Coronado expedition wandering on the trackless Llano Estacado exhausted its water and was threatened with death from thirst. Arriving at the bank of the river they gave it the name of Brazos de Dios in thankfulness. Another is that a ship exhausted its water supply and its crew was saved when they found the mouth of the Brazos. Still another story is that miners on the San Saba were forced by drouth to seek water near present-day Waco and called it Brazos de Dios in thankfulness. There is also the theory that the early Spanish cartographers called the river "Arms of God" because of the great spread of its tributaries.

Much early Anglo-American colonization of Texas took place in the Brazos Valley. On its channel were **San Felipe de Austin,** capital of Austin's colony, **Washington-on-the-Brazos,** where Texans declared independence, and other historic settlements. There was some navigation of the lower channel of the Brazos in this period. Near its mouth it intersects the Gulf Intracoastal Waterway which provides connection with the commerce on the Mississippi.

Most of the Brazos Valley lies within the boundaries of the **Brazos River Authority** which conducts a multi-purpose program for development. A large reservoir on the Brazos is **Lake Whitney** (622,800 acre-feet capacity) on the main channel where it is the boundary line between Hill and Bosque Counties. Another large reservoir is **Lake Possum Kingdom** in Palo Pinto, Stephens, Young and Jack Counties. **Lake Waco** on the Bosque and **Belton Lake** on the Leon are among the principal reservoirs on its tributaries. In addition to its three upper forks, other chief tributaries are the **Paluxy, Little** and **Navasota Rivers.**

San Jacinto River

A short river with a drainage basin of 3,976 square miles and nearly 2,000,000 acre-feet runoff, the San Jacinto runs directly to the Gulf through Galveston Bay. It is formed by the junction of its East and West Forks in the northeastern part of Harris County. Its total length, including the East Fork, is about 85 miles. There are two stories of the origin of its name. One is that when early explorers discovered it, its channel was choked with hyacinth. The other is that it was discovered on Aug. 17, St. Hyacinth's Day. Through the lower course of the San Jacinto and its tributary, Buffalo Bayou, runs the Houston Ship Channel connecting the Port of Houston with the Gulf. On the shore of the San Jacinto was fought the **Battle of San Jacinto,** April 21, 1836, in which Texas won its independence from Mexico. The **San Jacinto State Park and monument** are there.

Trinity River

The Trinity rises in its East Fork, Elm Fork, West Fork and Clear Fork in Grayson, Montague, Archer and Parker Counties, respectively. The main stream begins with the junction of the Elm and West Forks at Dallas. Its length is 550 river miles and its drainage area, 17,969 square miles. Because of moderate to heavy rainfall over its drainage area, it has a flow of 5,800,000 acre-feet near its mouth on the Gulf, exceeded only by the Neches, Red and the Sabine River Basins.

The Trinity derives its name from the Spanish "Trinidad." Alonso de Leon named it **La Santisima Trinidad** (the Most Holy Trinity).

Navigation was developed along its lower course with several river port towns, such as **Sebastopol,** in Trinity County. For many years there has been a basin-wide movement for navigation, conservation and utilization of its water. The **Trinity River Authority** is a state agency and the **Trinity Improvement Association** is a publicly supported nonprofit organization advocating its development.

The Trinity has in its valley more large cities and population and greater industrial development than any other river basin in Texas. On the Lower Coastal Plain there is large use of its waters for rice irrigation. Largest reservoir on the Elm Fork is **Lewisville Lake** (formerly **Garza-Little Elm** and **Lake Dallas**). There are four reservoirs above Fort Worth — **Lake Worth, Eagle Mountain** and **Bridgeport** on the West Fork and **Lake Benbrook** on the Clear Fork. **Lake Lavon** in southeast Collin County and **Lake Ray Hubbard** in Collin-Dallas-Kaufman-Rockwall Counties are on the East Fork.

Neches River

The Neches is in East Texas with total length of about 416 miles and drainage area of 10,011 square miles. Abundant rainfall over its entire basin gives it a flow near the Gulf of about 6,000,000 acre-feet a year. The river takes its name from the Neches Indians that the early Spanish explorers found living along its banks. Principal tributary of the Neches, and comparable with the Neches in length and flow above their confluence, is the **Angelina River,** so named from **Angelina (Little Angel),** a **Hainai Indian girl** who converted to Christianity and played an important role in the early development of this region.

Both the Neches and the Angelina run most of their courses in the Piney Woods and there was much settlement along them as early as the 1820s. **Sam Rayburn (McGee Bend)** Reservoir, near Jasper on the Angelina River, was completed and dedicated in 1965.

Sabine River

The Sabine River is formed by three forks rising in Collin and Hunt Counties. From its sources to its mouth on **Sabine Lake,** it flows approximately 360 miles and drains 9,733 square miles. Sabine comes from the Spanish word for cypress, as does the name of the Sabinal River, which flows into the Frio in Southwest Texas. The Sabine has the largest water discharge (6,800,000 acre-feet) at its mouth of any Texas river. Throughout most of Texas history the lower Sabine has been the eastern Texas boundary line though for a while there was doubt as to whether the Sabine or the Arroyo Hondo, east of the Sabine in Louisiana, was the boundary. For a number of years the outlaw-infested neutral ground lay between them. There was also a boundary dispute in which it was alleged that the Neches was really the Sabine and, therefore, the boundary.

Travelers over the Camino Real or Old San Antonio Road crossed the Sabine at the famous Gaines Ferry and there were famous crossings for the Atascosito Road and other travel and trade routes of that day.

Two of Texas' larger man-made reservoirs have been created by dams constructed on the Sabine River. The first of these was **Lake Tawakoni,** in Hunt, Rains and Van Zandt Counties, with a capacity of 936,200 acre-feet. **Toledo Bend Reservoir** impounds 4,472,900 acre-feet of water on the Sabine in Newton, Panola, Sabine and Shelby Counties. This is a joint project of Texas and Louisiana, through the Sabine River Authority.

Red River

The Red River (1,360 miles) is exceeded in length only by the Rio Grande among rivers associated with Texas. Its original source is water in Curry County, New Mexico, near the Texas boundary, forming a definite channel as it crosses Deaf Smith County, Texas, in tributaries that flow into **Prairie Dog Town Fork of the Red River**. These waters carve the spectacular **Palo Duro Canyon** of the High Plains before the Red River leaves the Cap Rock Escarpment, flowing eastward.

Where the Red River crosses the 100th meridian, the river becomes the Texas-Oklahoma boundary and is soon joined by the **Salt Fork** to form the main channel. Its length across the Panhandle is about 200 miles and, from the Panhandle east, it is the Texas-Oklahoma boundary line for 440 miles and thereafter the Texas-Arkansas boundary for 40 miles before it flows into Arkansas where it swings south to flow through Louisiana. The Red River is a part of the Mississippi drainage basin, and at one time it emptied all of its water into the Mississippi. In recent years, however, part of its water, especially at flood stage, has flowed to the Gulf via the Atchafalaya. The Red River takes its name from the red color of the current. This caused every explorer who came to its banks to call it "red" regardless of the language he spoke — **Rio Rojo** or **Rio Roxo** in Spanish, **Riviere Rouge** in French and Red River in English. The Spanish and French names were often found on maps until the middle of the last century when the English, Red River, came to be generally accepted. At an early date the river became the axis for French advance from Louisiana northwestward as far as present-day Montague County. There was consistent early navigation of the river from its mouth on the Mississippi to Shreveport, above which navigation was blocked by a natural **log raft**. A number of important gateways into Texas from the North were established along the stream such as **Pecan Point** and **Jonesborough** in Red River County, **Colbert Ferry** and **Preston** in Grayson County and, later, **Doan's Store Crossing** in Wilbarger County. The river was a menace to the early traveler because of both its variable current and its **quicksands** which brought disaster to many a trail herd cow as well as ox team and covered wagon.

The largest water conservation project on the Red River is **Lake Texoma** which is the largest lake lying wholly or partly in Texas and the tenth largest reservoir (in capacity) in the United States. Its capacity is 5,382,000 acre feet. Texas' share is 2,722,000.

Red River water's high content of salt and other minerals limits its usefulness along its upper reaches. Ten salt springs and tributaries in Texas and Oklahoma contribute most of these minerals.

The uppermost tributary of the Red River in Texas is the Tierra Blanca Creek, which rises in Curry County, N.M., and flows easterly across Deaf Smith and Randall Counties to become the Prairie Dog Town Fork a few miles east of Canyon. Other principal tributaries in Texas are the Pease and the Wichita in North Central Texas and the Sulphur in Northeast Texas, which flows into the Red River after it has crossed the boundary line into Arkansas. From Oklahoma the principal tributary is the **Washita**. The **Ouachita**, a river with the same pronunciation of its name, though spelled differently, is the principal tributary to its lower course.

Canadian River

The Canadian River heads near Raton Pass in northern New Mexico near the Colorado boundary line and flows into Texas on the west line of Oldham County. It crosses the Texas Panhandle into Oklahoma and there flows into the Arkansas. Most of its course across the Panhandle is in a deep gorge. A tributary dips into Texas' North Panhandle and then flows to a confluence with the main channel in Oklahoma. Among several theories as to how the Canadian got its name, one is that some early explorers thought it flowed into Canada. **Lake Meredith**, formed by **Sanford Dam** on the Canadian, provides water for 11 Panhandle cities.

Because of the deep gorge and the **quicksand** at many places, the Canadian has been a peculiarly difficult stream to bridge. It is known especially in its lower course in Oklahoma as outstanding among the streams of the country for great amount of quicksand in its channel.

Texas Forest Resources

This information was compiled and prepared by Sam D. Logan, director of Information and Education for the Texas Forest Service in the Texas A&M University System.

Texas harvested more timber than it grew in 1983, a surprising increase in harvest volume considering the relatively low profits of the forest products industry. The recession of the early 1980s slowed the demand for timber products and gave the forests a breather. Most experts, however, predict that more timber will be harvested than grown during the latter part of this decade.

Perhaps the greatest economic gain of the 20th century since the 1930s has been reforestation, both in protecting existing timber and in planting new forests. This reforestation commitment has been even more intensely renewed in recent years as most experts agree that the "nation's woodbasket" is shifting from the Pacific Northwest to the Southern forests, which extend from East Texas to the Atlantic Ocean. While both public and private cooperation has reduced fires and pests and has increased tree planting and fostered natural regrowth, the resource is still hard-pressed to keep pace with increasing demands.

The 11.5 million acres of East Texas — an area larger than the states of Massachusetts and Vermont combined — are the land base for the important renewable resource which translates into "commercial grade timber."

Estimated market value of harvested timber (delivered value) was approximately $487.1 million in late 1983. At the same time, recreational opportunities among forests have been expanded. The **Texas Forestry Association Woodlands Trails** program provides public hiking through designated scenic portions of privately owned timberland. (Information is available from Texas Forestry Association, P.O. Box 1488, Lufkin, Tx 75901; Texas Highway Department and other sources.) State and national forests in East Texas also are improving recreational facilities and provide habitat and forage for wildlife. Trees are also valuable for control of stream flow and prevention of pollution and erosion.

The following information was supplied largely by Texas Forest Service, Texas Forestry Association and federal agencies. Texas' forested area, including some secondary woodland and forest areas, totals an estimated 23.4 million acres. The principal forest and woodlands regions are: pine-hardwood, 10,901,500 acres; post oak, 2,993,600; East and West Cross Timbers, 2,226,310; cedar brakes, 4,561,053; coastal forests, 575,071, and miscellaneous, 774,442.

The most important forest area of the state, producing nearly all of the commercial timber, is the East Texas pine-hardwood region known as the **Piney Woods**. It extends over all or part of 43 counties.

Forest Conservation

Many agencies, companies, associations and others cooperate in the **conservation of Texas forest resources**. Among them are federal and state agencies, district and city and county governments, timber producers, processors and wood products manufacturers. Only a few major programs can be listed here.

Texas Reforestation Foundation

One of the most successful new programs is the Texas Reforestation Foundation (TRe), which is a landowner-assistance, forestry-incentives program designed to help regenerate and improve Texas' timberlands. Unlike other assistance programs, TRe is wholly financed by private interests through voluntary contributions. The money is distributed to private nonindustrial Texas landowners on a matching basis with operations directed from the TFA office in Lufkin, with technical assistance from the Texas Forest Service. TRe is a nonprofit foundation, operating with its own elected board of directors.

Since TRe began in 1980, more than $1 million in cost-share funds from the foundation have helped to regenerate nearly 25,000 acres of Texas land. These figures represent an outlay of about $43.98 per acre, or roughly half the total cost of acres treated.

Tree Farms

A tree farm is a privately owned, taxpaying woodland dedicated to continuing growth of forest crops and officially recognized by the **Texas Forestry Association** in cooperation with **American Forest Institute**, the national sponsor, and **Southern Forest Institute**, the regional sponsor. Tree farmers agree to manage their timber for the growth and harvest of forest products, and to protect their timber from fires, insects, disease and destructive overgrazing. Any landowner with 10 or more acres of forest land on which the trees are more than one year of age or land with a stand of viable tree seedlings may qualify.

On Jan. 1, 1984, there were 2,510 officially recognized tree farms in Texas, according to the Texas Forestry Association. Total area was 4,162,127 acres. **Texas ranked sixth** in the nation in number of tree farms and tenth in number of acres in them.

Texas Forest Service

In 1915, the Legislature created a **State Department of Forestry** and placed it under the direction of the **Agricultural & Mechanical College of Texas.**

In 1926, it was reorganized as the **Texas Forest Service (TFS)** under the board of the A&M College. Today the office of the director, the **Forest Management Department, Reforestation Department, Forest Genetics Laboratory** and the **Information and Education Section** are located on the campus of Texas A&M University in College Station.

The **Forest Fire Control Department, Forest Products Laboratory** and **Forest Pest Control Section** are located in the **Cudlipp Forestry Center** at Lufkin. Five area offices and 13 districts are located throughout East Texas, with area offices headquartered at Linden, Henderson, Lufkin, Woodville and Conroe.

In 1971, a staff silviculturist was stationed in Lubbock to assist landowners in establishing and maintaining windbreaks to protect their homesteads and fields from the high, drying winds in that region. In 1973, an urban forestry program was established to assist the public and city governments with developing land to maintain the urban forests, with TFS foresters in Fort Worth and San Antonio.

Forest Protection From Pests

Insects and diseases affecting forest trees cost landowners millions of dollars annually. The **TFS Pest Control Section**, established in 1962, is responsible for monitoring pest activity on 12 million acres of state and private forest lands in East Texas. The section also conducts applied research on major insect and disease pests of pine seed orchards, plantations and natural forest stands. The major insect pest of Texas forests is the **southern pine beetle.** Other important insect pests include seed and cone destroying insects, leaf-cutting ants, pine tip moths and pine sawflies. The most important disease in East Texas pine forests is fusiform rust. In Central Texas, oak diseases are causing considerable concern.

In the South southern pine beetles kill more timber annually than forest fires. The Texas Forest Service coordinates all beetle control activity in Texas, which includes detecting infestations from the air, notifying landowners and assisting them in controlling the infestations. The most severe outbreak of southern pine beetles known in Texas occurred in 1976 when an estimated 51 million cubic feet of timber was killed.

Valuable seeds carrying superior genetic qualities must be protected from insect pests in southern pine seed orchards. Without control measures insects will usually reduce potential seed crops by more than 50 percent. **Coneworms** and **seedbugs** are the major insect pests in southern pine seed orchards. The TFS is involved in a research program directed toward developing improved measures for controlling these insect pests.

Pests of young pine plantations are increasing in importance with the acceleration of reforestation in East Texas. Texas leaf-cutting ants often cause serious mortality when present in or near newly planted pine plantations. These ants prefer deep, sandy soils and damage pine seedlings by removing needles and buds, particularly in the winter when other green vegetation is unavailable. This insect pest must be controlled in new plantations to prevent economic losses. Other pests in pine plantations include **pine tip moth, pine sawflies, gophers** and **rabbits.**

Fusiform rust has been recognized for many years as a severe problem on both slash and loblolly pines in the southeastern United States. The disease has its greatest impact in nurseries, seed orchards and young pine plantations. The TFS has been involved in periodic surveys, initiated in Texas in 1969, which have indicated that fusiform rust is most severe in slash pine plantations in Southeast Texas. Loblolly pine is not seriously damaged. The severity of the disease has increased dramatically in recent years. The TFS also is evaluating forest management practices and rust-resistant growing stock that will reduce losses caused by this disease.

Extensive mortality of oaks in the hill country of Central Texas is creating increasing public concern. Two vascular wilt organisms, "oak decline" and more recently "oak wilt," have been cited as the major causal agents of live oak disease in Central Texas. Although at least two different organisms are involved, the incidence and severity of each disease is poorly understood. Oak wilt appears to be responsible for much of the live oak mortality.

In an 11.3 million-acre area of Central Texas, the TFS is actively involved in a cooperative project to estimate the amount of total oak mortality, determine the relative incidence and severity of the various oak diseases, identify causal organisms associated with oak mortality, pilot test available prevention/suppression methods and develop procedures for reforesting the area of tree mortality. Without a better understanding of the oak diseases involved, the future of live oak as a landscape or forest tree in Central Texas may be threatened.

Texas Forest Service entomologists are also asked to evaluate insect and disease problems in other areas of the state. Assistance has been provided regarding windbreak trees in the High Plains area and problems in coniferous forests in the mountains of West Texas.

The **gypsy moth** has been a serious defoliator of hardwood trees in the Northeast United States for many years. In the past decade this insect pest has been transported to many other areas of the country, including California, Florida, Michigan and Washington. During the summer of 1984, male gypsy moths were trapped for the first time in Texas. Although no established gypsy moth populations are known to occur in Texas, more intensive monitoring with moth traps will be conducted in 1985 and beyond. A task force of leading entomologists in the state has been formed, and trapping and control plans are being formulated to prevent gypsy moth from becoming a serious tree pest in Texas.

Forest Fire Protection

Organized fire protection is provided by the TFS with some financial assistance from the federal government and from landowners. Texas first qualified for federal assistance in protection against forest fires in 1916. A division of forest protection, now the **Forest Fire Control Department,** was established at Lufkin in 1925.

From 1925 through 1984, **162,246 forest fires** were reported and suppressed in East Texas by TFS. In 1984, 2,172 fires burned 35,958 acres, averaging 16.6 acres per fire. For the past 10 years, the average annual acreage loss to wildfire was 0.13 percent of the area protected.

Causes of the 2,172 fires in 1984 were: debris burning, 62 percent; incendiary, 18 percent; smokers, 4 per-

Forest Pests, by Rank

Table below shows by rank the leading insect and disease problems afflicting the forests of Texas in 1983.

Rank, Pest	Rank, Pest	Rank, Pest
1. Southern pine beetle	5. Terminal & shoot insects	8. Reproduction weevils
2. Fusiform rust	6. Annosus root rot	9. Oak wilt/decline
3. Town ants	7. Pine defoliators	10. Hardwood defoliators
4. Other pine bark beetles		

cent; campfires, 2 percent; and miscellaneous, equipment use, railroads and children amounted to 13 percent. Lightning caused 1 percent of all forest fires.

For 57 years, from 1916 to 1975, basic rural fire fighting responsibility was confined to 48 counties, or the commercial forest area of East Texas.

The backbone of the TFS fire operations is a two-man fire crew with a crawler tractor equipped with a fire plow. This unit and its transport vehicle are both equipped with two-way radios. There are 85 such units in the 48-county area. These crewmen are trained at the **Texas Forest Service Ground Cover Training Facility** in Lufkin.

In 1973, the TFS was given the responsibility by State legislation for rural wildland fire defense in the whole state. The law authorized the TFS to develop rural fire protection plans and to provide training and equipment to organized groups throughout the state. It did not expand the operational area of the TFS fire units beyond the 48 counties of East Texas.

Rural Fire Protection In Texas

Of the huge loss annually caused by fire in the United States, much occurs in towns and villages with fewer than 10,000 residents. In general, most of these towns can ill afford fire equipment necessary for their protection. The **Rural Community Fire Protection Program (RCFP)**, administered in Texas through the Texas Forest Service, is helping meet this need.

Since fewer than half the towns have fire protection, TFS began a uniform fire reporting system on Jan. 1, 1976. Fire departments from 250 towns of fewer than 10,000 population cooperate in the computerized system. Unfortunately, some towns have not been consistent in providing data. In view of the adoption of the national reporting system in 1981, TFS scaled down the project to avoid duplication.

Some counties have received increased requests for operating funds from local communities whose main fire business has been in areas outside of corporate limits. There is an understandable but unfortunate tendency for city fire departments to refuse to make rural runs, and the smaller communities with established, well-organized departments are finding it increasingly expensive to take up the slack.

TFS began, in September 1973, an equipment development and testing program to assist rural communities in acquiring basic fire trucks at affordable prices. Testimony to the unqualified popularity of this equipment phase is that TFS has, through 1984, modified and delivered more than 700 complete rural fire trucks to small communities all over the state — with more than 100 active requests on hand at all times.

TFS is field-testing a new type of suppression equipment that may well evolve into a family of systems with wide applicability and effectiveness. The system is basically an air-injection, foam-generating unit that combines a foaming agent in water under pressure. Expansion rates vary from 5-to-1 to as high as 20-to-1, depending upon equipment and operating characteristics. The equipment has practical use on standard tractor-plow units for safety and tractor operator protection. On pumper units used by volunteer fire departments, it greatly extends pumping time.

The TFS established courses to provide basic, intermediate and advanced training to VFD cooperators and to other interested groups. The courses comprise segments on equipment operation and maintenance, fire behavior, tactics and ground fire organization.

In 1976, the original training team included a chief training officer and two assistants. Inordinate travel costs and difficult scheduling problems for the team quickly necessitated a different approach. Contractual arrangements have been made with 10 certified fire trainers in various regions of Texas to deliver the standard courses to local volunteers. All Texas Forest Service training is certified by the **Texas Firemen's and Fire Marshal's Association** and counts toward fireman certification.

As of December 1984, the Texas Forest Service trainers have conducted more than 2,000 classes and trained 29,545 firefighters. Plans are to continue to offer the course at the request of local fire departments. All trainer expense is paid by the Texas Forest Service.

Tree Seedlings

Pine seedlings are required for reforestation where natural seeding is delayed or unavailable. The **Indian Mound Nursery**, near Alto, Cherokee County, with an area of 120 acres, has a capacity for producing 40 million pine seedlings annually. Seedlings are sold at cost. Applications for seedlings are obtained from the TFS,

county agricultural agents and Soil Conservation Service district supervisors.

A major proportion of the seedlings are raised from genetically improved seed produced by the TFS seed orchard. Varieties available include loblolly pine selected for growth rate and form, loblolly pine selected for drought resistance and slash pine selected for resistance to fusiform rust.

Conifer and hardwood seedlings for the High Plains are grown at the West Texas Nursery in Lubbock. Two crops of conifer seedlings are grown in a climate-controlled greenhouse and shipped in styrofoam containers to planters in about 60 counties each spring. A variety of bare-root hardwood seedlings is also produced. Distribution is made through Soil and Water Conservation Districts.

State Forests

The first state forest, now known as the **E. O. Siecke State Forest** in Newton County, was purchased by the state in 1924. It contains 1,722 acres of pine land. An additional 100 acres were added by a 99-year lease in 1946.

The **W. Goodrich Jones State Forest**, south of Conroe in Montgomery County, containing 1,725 acres, was purchased in 1926. A 20-acre adjunct was given to the state in 1969.

The **I. D. Fairchild State Forest**, Texas' largest, is located west of Rusk in Cherokee County. This forest was transferred from the state prison system in 1925. An additional 536 acres were added to the original 2,360 acres in 1963 from the Texas State Hospitals and Special Schools, bringing the combined acreage total to 2,896.

ESTIMATED TIMBER INCOME EAST TEXAS, 1983

Because of rounding of odd cents, columns don't add up.

County—	Total value paid for delivered timber products (Dollars)	Industrial private nonfarm and public timberlands (Dollars)	Farm and misc. timberlands (Dollars)
Anderson . . .	$9,169,930	$2,659,280	$6,510,650
Angelina . . .	20,956,098	13,411,903	7,544,195
Bowie	9,370,049	2,342,512	7,027,537
Camp	2,984,771	29,848	2,954,923
Cass	22,471,688	5,842,639	16,629,049
Chambers . . .	468,608	60,919	407,689
Cherokee . . .	21,018,901	6,515,859	14,503,042
Franklin	257,289	2,573	254,716
Gregg	2,398,556	23,986	2,374,570
Grimes	3,635,995	2,108,877	1,527,118
Hardin	21,207,851	14,845,495	6,362,355
Harris	1,758,943	140,715	1,618,228
Harrison	13,013,238	1,171,191	11,842,047
Houston	13,690,860	4,791,801	8,899,059
Jasper	19,651,382	14,738,537	4,912,846
Jefferson . . .	297,416	0	297,416
Leon	1,114,651	222,930	891,721
Liberty	9,273,959	4,173,282	5,100,678
Marion	14,859,983	2,971,997	11,887,987
Montgomery.	18,917,318	3,026,771	15,890,547
Morris	5,708,990	57,090	5,651,900
Nacogdoches	18,750,267	6,375,091	12,375,176
Newton	22,499,132	17,324,332	5,174,800
Orange	1,506,716	647,888	858,828
Panola	16,505,142	2,805,874	13,699,268
Polk	43,792,788	35,034,231	8,758,558
Red River . . .	2,744,872	631,321	2,113,552
Rusk	14,258,473	998,093	13,260,380
Sabine	18,076,664	13,195,965	4,880,699
San Augustine	17,426,726	12,721,510	4,705,216
San Jacinto . .	10,955,750	5,149,202	5,806,547
Shelby	19,549,055	5,864,716	13,684,338
Smith	8,465,846	84,658	8,381,188
Titus	1,877,850	18,778	1,859,071
Trinity	16,428,284	11,664,082	4,764,202
Tyler	32,894,089	24,341,626	8,552,463
Upshur	8,480,319	84,803	8,395,516
Walker	15,580,818	3,583,588	11,997,230
Waller	1,102,417	407,894	694,523
Wood	2,649,451	79,484	2,569,968
Other counties. . .	1,366,420	1,052,144	314,277
State Totals . .	$487,137,557	$221,203,485	$265,934,072

The **John Henry Kirby State Forest** of 626 acres was donated by the late lumberman, **John Henry Kirby**, in 1929, and later donors. Revenue from this forest is given to the Association of Former Students of Texas A&M University for student loan purposes. All of the state forests are used primarily for demonstration and research.

The newest state forest, the **Paul N. Masterson Memorial Forest** of 520 acres, was donated in the fall of 1984. Mrs. Leonora O'Neal Masterson of Beaumont donated the land in Jasper County in honor of her husband, an active member of the Texas Forestry Association and a tree farmer.

Forest Industry And Harvest Trends

The commercial timber-producing region of Texas, known as the Piney Woods, is in the eastern part of the state. There are about 40 East Texas counties from which large amounts of timber are harvested. About four of every five trees harvested are pine. These trees are principally used to make paper products, lumber and plywood.

The 1983 Harvest

The 1983 Texas timber harvest totaled 638 million cubic feet, an increase of 31 percent from the 1982 harvest and was the highest level reported since the TFS surveys have been published. The top three producing counties in the state were Polk, Cass and Tyler. The pine harvest of 490 million cubic feet was up 23 percent, and the hardwood harvest of 148 million feet was up 66 percent. The total **sawlog harvest** was increased by 37 percent to 969.6 million board feet. The pine portion of this cut increased 47 percent to 802 million board feet, whereas the hardwood sawlog cut only increased 4 percent to 167.5 million board feet.

Veneer logs demonstrated a modest 1 percent increase over the harvest rate set in 1982. The amount of **pulpwood** harvested in Texas showed a very significant increase. The total harvest was up 49 percent, or 1,173,088 cords. Both pine and hardwood pulpwood har-

vests were higher in 1983; however, hardwood pulpwood demonstrated an astounding 127 percent increase to 1,123,902 cords. Total pulpwood production in 1983 was 5.6 million cords, a new Texas record.

Poles and pilings were the only two products to decline in 1983, registering reductions of 7 percent and 45 percent. Post production was up 2 percent to 1.19 million posts. With **exports** of 92.2 million cubic feet and imports of 85.9 million cubic feet, Texas once again became a net exporter of wood products. While total imports increased 24 percent, this was not enough to offset the 92 percent increase in wood fiber exports.

Primary Forest Products

Pine lumber production came close to matching the previous record set in 1978 by attaining a level of 862.4 million board feet. This was an increase of 15 percent over the 1982 production mark. Hardwood lumber production, on the other hand, declined for the third straight year to a level of 152.4 million board feet, a drop of 5 percent from 1982. Hardwood **crosstie** production dropped 11 percent in 1982. Texas **plywood and waferboard production** reached a level of 1.9 billion square feet, an increase of 18 percent over the previous record set in 1982. Texas plywood production represented about 9 percent of total U.S. softwood plywood production. Total **paper and paperboard production** in Texas increased 4 percent in 1983. There were changes in the relative amounts of each product. Paper declined 8 percent, whereas paperboard increased 14 percent. Total Texas production of 2.5 million tons represented about 4 percent of total U.S. paper and paperboard production.

Total production of **treated wood** increased 35 percent to 39.2 million cubic feet. This was due to a fairly significant increase in the volume of **switch ties, cross arms and lumber**. There have been fairly dramatic changes in the relative composition of lumber and plywood in the various treated products. The combined volume of treated lumber and plywood represented 20

TEXAS LUMBER PRODUCTION, 1975-1983

Year—	*Lumber production Pine	Hardwood	Tie production Pine	Hardwood
	Thd. bd. ft.		Thd. pieces	
1975	704,572	147,359	352	978
1976	844,253	146,333	502	878
1977	848,253	191,686	259	1,366
1978	867,759	214,118	297	1,314
1979	845,830	204,536	305	1,214
1980	755,078	292,221	173	1,475
1981	707,311	275,591	172	1,756
1982	752,727	160,235	154	971
1983	862,378	152,350	155	866

*Includes tie volumes.

TEXAS PLYWOOD PRODUCTION, 1975-1983

Year—	Pine	Year—	Pine
	Thd. sq. ft.		Thd. sq. ft.
1975	959,649	1980	1,481,944
1976	1,225,513	1981	1,553,345
1977	1,352,527	1982	1,604,102
1978	1,455,139	1983	1,898,556
1979	1,299,282		

TEXAS PULPWOOD PRODUCTION, 1975-1983

Year	Roundwood Pine	Hardwood	Chips & Sawdust Pine	Hardwood	All Species Total Pulpwood Production
	Thousand cords				
1975	2,051	295	1,114	89	3,549
1976	1,982	404	1,088	111	3,585
1977	2,028	401	1,115	86	3,630
1978	2,068	458	1,118	185	3,829
1979	2,128	453	1,131	128	3,868
1980	2,196	473	1,378	183	4,230
1981	2,114	395	1,329	177	4,016
1982	1,900	495	1,445	135	3,975
1983	2,444	1,124	1,772	262	5,602

PRIMARY FOREST PRODUCTS BY SPECIES GROUP, 1953-83

Year	*Pulpwood Production Softwood	*Pulpwood Production Hardwood	Lumber Production Softwood	Lumber Production Hardwood	Plywood Production Softwood	**Paper & Paperboard Production Softwood
	(Cords)		(Thd. bd. ft.)		(Thd. sq. ft.)	(Thd. tons)
1953	1,159,261	51,443	...	...	...	...
1954	1,003,561	50,772	...	...	...	...
1955	1,119,486	84,289	798,200	359,200	...	...
1956	1,339,239	119,776	625,500	314,200	...	...
1957	1,260,390	160,528	569,900	266,600	...	...
1958	1,208,400	177,600	499,000	218,000	...	...
1959	1,185,300	230,300	465,800	283,500	...	...
1960	1,192,700	233,700	454,800	302,800	...	...
1961	1,195,700	245,800	430,200	275,000	...	...
1962	1,162,900	266,700	497,000	260,640	...	...
1963	1,172,500	271,100	567,800	271,440	...	...
1964	1,294,695	281,345	676,982	251,286	...	...
1965	1,294,535	362,087	700,250	355,190	93,000	...
1966	1,495,090	397,080	701,000	331,030	120,000	...
1967	1,657,495	319,669	632,353	160,447	120,000	...
1968	1,831,204	288,987	682,097	148,343	193,300	...
1969	1,996,144	331,781	788,471	183,027	221,300	...
1970	2,046,056	302,779	746,408	152,154	248,676	...
1971	2,215,913	306,033	805,989	149,370	447,003	...
1972	2,814,025	387,131	842,865	148,660	690,808	...
1973	3,081,143	412,355	807,995	120,879	767,688	...
1974	3,294,200	553,100	684,602	171,093	782,615	...
1975	3,164,200	384,100	704,572	147,359	959,649	...
1976	3,070,000	515,000	844,095	146,366	1,225,513	...
1977	3,143,045	486,845	848,253	191,686	1,352,527	...
1978	3,216,900	643,776	867,759	214,118	1,455,139	...
1979	3,286,800	582,013	845,830	204,536	1,299,282	...
1980	3,574,000	656,000	755,078	292,221	1,481,944	...
1981	3,443,000	572,000	707,311	275,591	1,553,345	2,339
1982	3,345,000	630,000	752,727	160,235	1,604,102	2,405
1983	4,216,000	1,386,000	862,378	152,350	1,898,556	2,497

*Includes both roundwood and residues.
**Reporting change made this information available starting in 1981.

Annual Growth and Annual Harvest of Growing Stock in East Texas 1975-1983

Year	Species	Growth (Millions Cu. Ft.)	Harvest (Millions Cu. Ft.)	Harvest Per Cent of Growth
1975	Pine	458.4	389.3	85
	Hardwood	208.5	72.6	35
1976	Pine	461.2	432.8	94
	Hardwood	215.7	80.6	37
1977	Pine	461.9	453.9	98
	Hardwood	222.7	89.1	40
1978	Pine	461.6	475.4	103
	Hardwood	229.1	103.1	45
1979	Pine	461.3	465.1	100
	Hardwood	236.4	102.4	43
1980	Pine	461.5	446.8	97
	Hardwood	243.5	109.6	45
1981	Pine	463.2	418.3	90
	Hardwood	251.1	99.6	40
1982	Pine	466.5	397.9	85
	Hardwood	259.5	89.2	34
1983	Pine	467.8	490.1	105
	Hardwood	267.2	148.3	56

percent of the total treated volume in 1979. By 1983 treated lumber and plywood increased to over 58 percent of the total volume.

Due to the dramatic increase in harvest, 1983 saw Texas return once again to a growth/harvest deficit situation. In Texas more wood was cut in 1983 than was grown. The marked increase in the pine harvest rate to about 105 percent of growth is indicative of how readily the Texas forest products industry can react to improving economic conditions.

A total 226,613 acres were planted with pine seedlings in 1983. About 146,376 acres were planted on forest industry land, 52,664 acres on public land and 27,573 acres on nonindustrial private land. Most nonindustrial private reforestation and timber stand improvement (TSI) activities were funded by the cost-sharing programs available to Texas forest landowners. The federally funded **Forestry Incentives Program (FIP)** provided cost shares of $717,030, which helped defray the expense of 15,624 acres of tree planting and 3,570 acres of TSI. The **Texas Reforestation Foundation, Inc.** (TRe) is a nonprofit corporation funded by all of the major forest products companies in Texas and several in Oklahoma, Arkansas and Louisiana. TRe provided cost shares of $342,677, which helped fund 8,894 acres of tree planting and 1,033 acres of TSI. There were 3,915 acres of tree planting and 2,256 acres of TSI accomplished by nonindustrial private forest landowners with no cost-share assistance.

National Forests in Texas

Four national forests and two national grasslands, administered as the national forests in Texas, have a total net acreage of 703,193 and a gross area within the proclaimed boundaries of 1,915,036 acres. They cover part of 15 Texas counties, as follows:

ANGELINA NATIONAL FOREST—Angelina County, 58,842 acres; Jasper, 19,733; Nacogdoches, 9,542; San Augustine, 66,799. Total, 154,916.

DAVY CROCKETT NATIONAL FOREST—Houston County, 93,583 acres; Trinity, 67,910. Total, 161,493.

SABINE NATIONAL FOREST—Jasper County, 64 acres; Sabine, 114,498; San Augustine, 4,317; Shelby, 67,762; Newton, 1,579. Total, 188,220.

SAM HOUSTON NATIONAL FOREST—Montgomery County, 47,358 acres; San Jacinto, 59,596; Walker, 53,490. Total, 160,444.

CADDO NATIONAL GRASSLAND—Fannin County, 17,796 acres. Total, 17,796.

LYNDON B. JOHNSON NATIONAL GRASSLAND—Montague County, 61 acres; Wise, 20,263. Total, 20,324.

Administrative Units

Administration is by the Forest Service, U. S. Department of Agriculture, with the Forest Supervisor's headquarters in Lufkin. There are eight ranger districts administered by District Forest Rangers as follows:

Angelina National Forest, Angelina District, at Lufkin. Sabine National Forest, Tenaha District at San Augustine; Yellowpine District at Hemphill. Davy Crockett National Forest, Neches Ranger District at Crockett; Trinity District at Apple Springs. Sam Houston National Forest, Raven District at New Waverly; San Jacinto District at Cleveland. National Grasslands, Caddo-Lyndon B. Johnson District at Decatur.

National Forests in Texas were established by invitation of the Texas Legislature by an Act of 1933, authorizing the purchase of lands in Texas for the establishment of national forests. President Franklin D. Roosevelt proclaimed these purchases of national forests on Oct. 15, 1936.

Timber Management

Each national forest constitutes a timber management working circle. All work is done under a detailed prescription prepared by a trained forester. Over 80,000 acres have been reforested artificially and thousands of additional acres have been treated to increase the quantity and quality of the timber.

Sales of sawtimber, pulpwood and other forest products are made at regular intervals.

The estimated net growth is over 200 million board feet per year and is valued at $20 million. About one-third of this growth is removed by cutting. The balance is left to grow. By the year 2000, growth is expected to exceed 300 million board feet per year.

Fire Protection

U.S. Forest Service cooperates with the Texas Forest Service in the protection of private and forest service lands inside the national forest boundaries. Detection of forest fires is done from airplanes.

Grazing Permits

Permits to graze cattle on national forests and national grasslands are granted to local residents for an annual fee. In calendar year 1984, approximately 4,700 head of cattle were grazed on national forests and 2,000 head of cattle were grazed on the Caddo-Lyndon B. Johnson area.

There are many lake areas in the national forests in Texas. This is Bouton Lake in Angelina National Forest.

Hunting and Fishing

The Forest Service manages the home of many varieties of wildlife.

State hunting and fishing laws and regulations apply to all national forest land. Game law enforcement is carried out by Texas Parks and Wildlife Department.

The **Angelina, Sabine, Neches** and **San Jacinto Rivers, Sam Rayburn** and **Toledo Bend Reservoirs, Lake Conroe** and many small streams provide a wide variety of fishing opportunities.

Recreation Facilities

An estimated 2 million people visited the national forests in Texas for recreation in 1984. Many of these used established recreation areas. These areas are primarily for the purpose of picnicking, swimming, fishing, camping, boating and nature enjoyment and are: **Ratcliff Lake**, 25 miles west of Lufkin on Highway 7, has a 45-acre lake and facilities for picnicking, swimming, boating, fishing, camping and a 250-seat capacity campfire theater. **Double Lake**, 3 miles south of Coldspring on FM Road 2025, has a 30-acre lake and facilities for picnicking, camping, swimming and fishing. **Stubblefield Lake**, 15 miles northwest of New Waverly on the shores of **Lake Conroe**, has facilities for camping, picnicking and fishing. **Scotts Ridge Boat Ramp**, 8 miles west of Willis, provides a boat ramp and parking lot on **Lake Conroe**. **Boykin Springs**, 15 miles southwest of Zavalla, has a 6-acre lake and facilities for swimming, picnicking, fishing and camping. **Red Hills Lake**, 4 miles north of Milam on Highway 87, has a 17-acre lake and facilities for fishing, swimming, camping and picnicking. **Bouton Lake**, 7 miles southeast of Zavalla off Texas Highway 63, has a 9-acre natural lake with facilities for camping, picnicking and fishing.

Several areas have been built on the shores of **Sam Rayburn** Reservoir, which has 100 miles of national forest shoreline. These areas provide camping, picnicking, nature enjoyment, boating and fishing. Recreation areas are: **Sandy Creek** on Forest Service Road 333, 25 miles northwest of Jasper; **Letney**, 22 miles northwest of Jasper off FM 255; **Caney Creek**, 10 miles southeast of Zavalla off FM 2743, in addition to the facilities mentioned above, has a 500-seat capacity campfire theater for evening campfire programs; **Harvey Creek**, 10 miles south of Broaddus on FM 2390, and **Townsend**, 7 miles north off FM 1277.

Willow Oak Recreation Area was the first public outdoor recreation area to be completed on the Texas side of **Toledo Bend Reservoir**. It consists of 15 picnic sites, 122 camping sites, four group camping sites, a boat ramp, a fish cleaning house, a sanitary dumping station, a nature trail and a 500-seat capacity campfire theater. Willow Oak is located 14 miles south of Hemphill off State Highway 87.

Indian Mounds Recreation Area is on Toledo Bend Reservoir. It is accessible by FM 83 and Forest Service Road 115 a total distance of 15 miles east of Hemphill. The area has camping facilities and a boat launch ramp.

Ragtown is 25 miles southeast of Center, accessible by State Highways 87 and 139, County Highway 3184 and Forest Service Road 132. It is on **Toledo Bend Reservoir** and has facilities for camping and boat launching. **Lakeview** is a primitive campground on **Toledo Bend Reservoir** located 12 miles southeast of Hemphill, accessible by State Highway 87, County Highway 2928 and Forest Service Road 120.

Recreation on the National Grasslands

Lake Davy Crockett Recreation Area is 11 miles north of Honey Grove on FM 100. This area is operated by a concessioner who charges fees for certain facilities and services. There is a lodge, rental cabin, marina, boat launch ramp, small cafe and camping sites on a 450-acre lake. **Coffee Mill Lake Recreation Area** has picnic facilities on a 750-acre lake. This area is 4 miles west of Lake Davy Crockett Recreation Area. **Black Creek Lake Picnic Area** is located 8 miles southeast of Alvord. It has picnic facilities and a boat launch ramp. This site is on a 30-acre lake.

Roads and Improvements

There are approximately 1,700 miles of roads on these public lands of which 799 miles are maintained by the Forest Service as all-weather roads.

Hiking Trails on National Forests

The **Lone Star Hiking Trail** is approximately 140 miles long and is located on the **Sam Houston National Forest** in Montgomery, Walker and San Jacinto Counties. Twenty-six miles of the trail in San Jacinto County has been designated as **national recreation trail**.

The **4Cs National Recreation Trail** is 19 miles long and goes from **Ratcliff Recreation Area** to the Neches Bluff overlook on the **Davy Crockett National Forest**.

The **Saw Mill Trail** is 5½ miles long and goes from the old Aldrich Saw Mill site to **Boykin Springs Recreation Area** on the **Angelina National Forest**.

National Grasslands

The submarginal Dust Bowl project lands, purchased by the federal government under the Bankhead-Jones Farm Tenant Act, are today well covered with grasses and native shrubs. They are administered much like the national forests under a policy of multiple use for range, watershed, recreation and wildlife.

Lake McClellan in Gray County and **Lake Marvin** in Hemphill County, created for flood control and recreation, receive over 178,000 recreation visitors annually. These lake areas provide camping, picnicking, fishing and boating facilities. A limited amount of wildlife provides for public hunting under state game laws.

The **Rita Blanca National Grassland** is located in Cimarron County, Okla., and in Dallam County, Texas. Headquarters for this district is at Texline, Texas. Headquarters for the **Black Kettle** and **Lake McClellan National Grasslands** is at Cheyenne, Okla. This ranger administers grasslands in Roger Mills County, Okla., and in Hemphill and Gray Counties in Texas.

Responsibility for administration in the **Caddo-Lyndon B. Johnson National Grasslands**, located in small scattered tracts in North Texas, was transferred to the Forest Supervisor, National Forests in Texas at Lufkin, July 1, 1970. These grasslands were formerly administered by the Southwestern Region of the U.S. Forest Service with headquarters at Amarillo.

VEGETATIONAL AREAS

Difference in amount and frequency of rainfall, in soils and in frost-free days, gives Texas a great variety of vegetation. From the forests of East Texas to the deserts of West Texas, from the grassy plains of North Texas to the semi-arid brushlands of South Texas, plant species change continuously.

The following discussion of Texas' 10 vegetational areas (see map) and rangeland resources was prepared for the Texas Almanac by authorities at Texas A&M University. Plant species of the state are listed in Texas A&M publication MP 585.

Sideoats grama, which occurs on more different soils in Texas than any other native grass, was officially designated as the **state grass of Texas** by the Texas Legislature in 1971.

The 10 principal plant life areas of Texas, starting in the east, are:

1. **Piney Woods.** Most of this area of some 16 million acres ranges from about 50 to 500 feet above sea level and receives 40 to 60 inches of rain yearly. Many rivers, creeks and bayous drain the region. Nearly all of Texas' commercial timber comes from this area. Pine is the principal timber. There are three native species — the **longleaf, shortleaf** and **loblolly pine**. An introduced species, the **slash pine**, also is widely grown. Hardwoods include a variety of **oaks, elm, hickory, magnolia, sweet and black gum, tupelo** and others.

The area is interspersed with native and improved grasslands. Cattle are the primary grazing animals. Deer and quail are abundant in properly managed localities. Primary forage plants, under proper grazing management, include species of the **bluestems, rossettegrass, panicums, paspalums, beaked needlegrass, Canada and Virginia wildryes, purpletop, broadleaf and spike woodoats, switchcane, lovegrasses, Indiangrass** and **legume** species.

Highly disturbed areas have understory and overstory of undesirable woody plants that suppress growth of pine and desirable grasses. The primary forage grasses have been reduced and the grasslands invaded by **threeawns, annual grasses, weeds, broomsedge bluestem, red lovegrass** and shrubby woody species.

2. **Gulf Prairies and Marshes.** The gulf prairies and marshes cover approximately 10 million acres. There are two subunits: (a) The **marsh** and **salt grasses** immediately at tidewater, and (b) a little farther inland, a strip of **bluestems** and **tall grasses**, with some **gramas** in the western part. These grasses, except **salt** and **marsh grasses**, make excellent grazing. **Oaks, elm** and other hardwoods grow to some extent, especially along streams, and the area has some **post oak** and brushy extensions along its borders. Much of the Gulf Prairies is fertile farmland. The area is well suited for cattle.

Principal grasses of the Gulf Prairies are **tall bunchgrasses**, including **big bluestem, little bluestem, seacoast bluestem, Indiangrass, eastern gamagrass, Texas wintergrass, switchgrass** and **gulf cordgrass**. Seashore saltgrass occurs on moist saline sites. Heavy grazing has changed the range vegetation in many cases so that the predominant grasses are the less desirable **broomsedge bluestem, smutgrass, threeawns, tumblegrass** and many other inferior grasses. The other plants that have invaded the productive grasslands include **oak underbrush, macartney rose, huisache, mesquite, prickly pear, ragweed, bitter sneezeweed, broomweed** and others.

Vegetation of the Gulf Marshes consists primarily of **sedges, bullrush, flat-sedges, beakrush**, and other rushes, **smooth cordgrass, marshhay cordgrass, marsh millet** and **maidencane**. The marshes are grazed best during winter.

3. **Post Oak Savannah.** This secondary forest region, also called the **Post Oak Belt**, covers some 9 million acres. It is immediately west of the primary forest region, and with less annual rainfall and a little higher elevation. Principal trees are **post oak, blackjack oak** and **elm**. Along streams are growths of **pecans, walnuts** and other kinds of water-demanding trees. The southwestern extension of this belt is often poorly defined with large areas of prairie.

The upland soils are sandy and sandy loam, while the bottomlands are sandy loams and clays.

The original vegetation consisted mainly of **little bluestem, big bluestem, Indiangrass, switchgrass, purpletop, silver bluestem, Texas wintergrass, spike woodoats, longleaf woodoats, post oak** and **blackjack oak.** The area is still largely native or improved grasslands, with small farms located throughout. Intensive grazing has

caused much of this area to degenerate to dense stands of a woody understory of **yaupon, greenbriar** and **oak brush.** Mesquite has become a serious problem. Good forage plants have been replaced by such inferior plants as **splitbeard bluestem, red lovegrass, broomsedge bluestem, broomweed, bullnettle** and **western ragweed.**

4. **Blackland Prairies.** This area of about 11 million acres, while called a "prairie," has much timber along the streams, including a variety of **oaks, pecan, elm, bois d'arc** and **mesquite.** In its native state it was largely a grassy plain — the first native grassland in the westward extension of the Southern Forest Region.

Most of this fertile area has been cultivated, and only small acreages of meadowland remain in original vegetation. In heavily grazed pastures, the **tall bunchgrass** has been replaced by **buffalograss, Texas grama** and other less productive grasses. **Mesquite, lotebush** and other woody plants have invaded the grasslands.

The original grass vegetation includes **big** and **little bluestem, Indiangrass, switchgrass, sideoats grama, hairy grama, tall dropseed, Texas wintergrass** and **buffalograss.** Nongrass vegetation is largely legumes and composites.

5. **Cross Timbers and Prairies.** Approximately 16.5 million acres of alternating woodlands, often called the West Cross Timbers, and prairies constitute this region. Sharp changes in the vegetational cover are associated with different soils and topography, but the grass composition is rather uniform.

The prairie-type grasses are **big bluestem, little bluestem, Indiangrass, switchgrass, Canada wildrye, sideoats grama, hairy grama, tall grama, tall dropseed, Texas wintergrass, blue grama** and **buffalograss.**

On the Cross Timbers soils, the grasses are composed of **big bluestem, little bluestem, hooded windmillgrass, sand lovegrass, Indiangrass, switchgrass** and many species of **legumes.** The woody vegetation includes **shinnery, blackjack, post** and **live oaks.**

The entire area has been invaded heavily by woody brush plants of **oaks, mesquite, juniper** and other unpalatable plants that furnish little forage for livestock.

6. **South Texas Plains.** South of San Antonio, between the coast and the Rio Grande, are some 20 million acres of subtropical dryland vegetation, consisting of small trees, shrubs, cactus, weeds and grasses. The area is noteworthy for extensive brushlands, known as the **brush country**, or the Spanish equivalents of **chaparral** or **monte.** Principal plants are **mesquite, small live oak, post oak, prickly pear** (Opuntia) **cactus, catclaw, blackbrush, whitebrush, huajillo, huisache, cenizo** and others which often grow very densely. The original vegetation was mainly perennial warm-season **bunchgrasses** in post oak, live oak and mesquite savannahs. Other brush species form dense thickets on the ridges and along streams. Long-continued grazing caused the region to be densely covered with a mixture of brush. Most of the desirable grasses have persisted under the protection of brush and cacti.

There are distinct differences in the original plant communities on various soils. Dominant grasses on the sandy loam soils are **seacoast bluestem, bristlegrass, paspalum, windmillgrass, trichloris, silver bluestem, big sandbur** and **tanglehead.** Dominant grasses on the clay and clay loams are **silver bluestem, Arizona cottontop, buffalograss, common curlymesquite, bristlegrass, pappusgrass, gramas, plains lovegrass, Texas cupgrass, vinemesquite,** other panicums and **Texas wintergrass.** Low saline areas are characterized by **gulf cordgrass, seashore saltgrass, alkali sacaton** and **switchgrass.** In the post oak and live oak savannahs, the grasses are mainly **seacoast bluestem, Indiangrass, switchgrass, crinkleawn, paspalums** and **panicums.** Today much of the area has been reseeded to **buffelgrass.**

7. **Edwards Plateau.** These 24 million acres are rolling to mountainous, with woodlands in the eastern part and grassy prairies in the west. There is a good deal of brushy growth in the central and eastern parts. The combination of grasses, weeds and small trees is ideal for cattle, sheep, goats, deer and wild turkey.

This limestone-based area is characterized by the large number of springfed, perennially flowing streams which originate in its interior and flow across the **Balcones Escarpment** which bounds it on the south and east. The soils are shallow, ranging from sands to clays and are calcareous in reaction. This area is predominantly rangeland, with cultivation confined to the deeper soils.

In the east central portion is the well marked **Central Basin** centering in Mason, Llano and Burnet Counties, with a mixture of granitic and sandy soils. The western portion of the area is comprised of the semiarid **Stockton Plateau.**

Noteworthy is the growth of **cypress** along the perennially flowing streams. Separated by many miles from cypress growth of the moist Southern Forest Belt, they constitute one of Texas' several "**Islands**" **of vegetation.** These trees grow to stately proportions and, in the past, have been commercialized.

The principal grasses of the clay soils are **cane bluestem, silver bluestem, little bluestem, sideoats grama, hairy grama, Indiangrass, common curlymesquite, buffalograss, fall witchgrass, plains lovegrass, wildryes** and **Texas wintergrass.**

The rocky areas support tall or mid-grasses with an overstory of **live oak, shinnery oak, cedar** and **mesquite.** The heavy clay soils have a mixture of **tobosagrass, buffalograss, sideoats grama** and **mesquite.**

Throughout the **Edwards Plateau, live oak, shinnery oak, mesquite** and **cedar** dominate the woody vegetation. Woody plants have invaded to the degree that they should be controlled before range forage plants can re-establish.

8. Rolling Plains. This is a region of approximately 24 million acres of alternating woodlands and prairies. The area is half mesquite woodland and half prairie. **Mesquite trees** have advanced steadily over former grasslands for many years, despite constant control efforts.

Soils range from coarse sands along outwash terraces adjacent to streams to tight or compact clays on redbed clays and shales. Rough broken lands on steep slopes are found in the western portion. About two-thirds of the area is rangeland. But cultivation is important in certain localities.

The original vegetation includes **big, little, sand** and **silver bluestems, Texas wintergrass, Indiangrass, switchgrass, sideoats** and **blue gramas, wildryes, tobosa** and **buffalograss** on the clay soils.

The sandy soils support **tall bunchgrasses,** mainly **sand bluestem. Sand shinnery oak, sand sagebrush** and **mesquite** are the dominant woody plants.

Continued heavy grazing causes increase in woody plants, low-value grasses such as **red grama, red lovegrass, tumblegrass, gummy lovegrass, Texas grama, sand dropseed** and **sand bur;** and **western ragweed, croton** and many other weeds. **Yucca** is a problem plant on certain rangelands.

9. High Plains. The High Plains, some 20 million treeless acres, are an extension of the **Great Plains** to the north. The level nature and porous soils prevent drainage over wide areas. The relatively light rainfall flows into the numerous shallow "playa" lakes or sinks into the ground to feed the great underground aquifer that is the source of water for the countless wells that irrigate the surface of the plains. A large part of this area is under irrigated farming, but native grassland remains in about one half of the High Plains.

Blue grama and **buffalograss** comprise the principal vegetation on the clay and clay loam "hardland" soils. Important grasses on the sandy loam "sandy land" soils are **little bluestem, western wheatgrass, Indiangrass, switchgrass** and **sand reedgrass. Sand shinnery oak, sand sagebrush, mesquite** and **yucca** are conspicuous invading brushy plants.

10. Trans-Pecos, Mountains and Basins. With as little as 8 inches of annual rainfall, long hot summers and usually cloudless skies to encourage evaporation, this

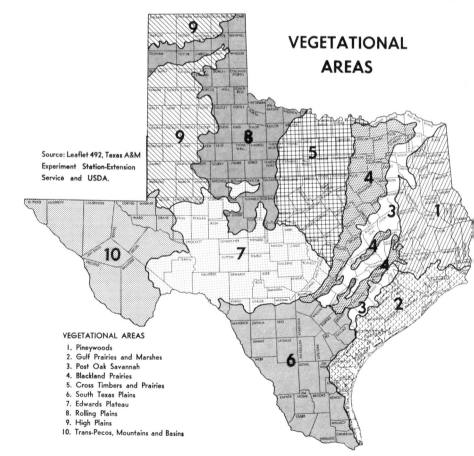

VEGETATIONAL AREAS

Source: Leaflet 492, Texas A&M Experiment Station-Extension Service and USDA.

VEGETATIONAL AREAS

1. Pineywoods
2. Gulf Prairies and Marshes
3. Post Oak Savannah
4. Blackland Prairies
5. Cross Timbers and Prairies
6. South Texas Plains
7. Edwards Plateau
8. Rolling Plains
9. High Plains
10. Trans-Pecos, Mountains and Basins

18-million-acre area produces only drouth-resistant vegetation without irrigation. Grass is usually short and sparse. The principal growth consists of such shrubs as **lechuguilla, ocotillo, yucca, cenizo** and other arid land plants. In the more arid areas, **yeso, chino** and **tobosa grasses** prevail. There is some **mesquite**. The vegetation includes creosote-tarbush, desert shrub, grama grassland, yucca and juniper savannahs, pine oak forest and saline flats.

The mountains are 3,000 to 8,000 feet in elevation and support **pinon pine, juniper** and some **ponderosa pine** and other forest vegetation on a few of the higher slopes.

The grass vegetation, especially on the higher mountain slopes, includes many southwestern and Rocky Mountain species not present elsewhere in Texas. On the desert flats, **black grama, burrograss** and **fluffgrass** are frequent. More productive sites have numerous species of **grama, muhly, Arizona cottontop, dropseed** and **perennial threeawn grasses**. At the higher elevations, **plains bristlegrass, little bluestem, Texas bluestem, sideoats grama, chino grama, blue grama**, pinon ricegrass, **wolftail** and several species of needlegrass are frequent.

The common invaders on all depleted ranges are woody plants, burrograss, **fluffgrass, hairy tridens, ear muhly, sand muhly, red grama, broom snakeweed, croton, cacti** and several poisonous plants.

Range Resources

More than 100 million acres of Texas are devoted to providing grazing for domestic and wild animals. This is the largest single use for land in the state. Primary range uses include: Watershed for streams, springs, lakes, food and cover for wildlife, forage for domestic livestock and recreation for man.

The **Piney Woods**, primarily valued for timber, also provide significant grazing. More than 80 per cent of the acreage is devoted to range in the **Edwards Plateau, Cross Timbers and Prairies, South Texas Plains** and **Trans-Pecos Mountains and Basins.**

Because it is perennial, range is a renewable resource. Range management seeks to perpetuate plants and methods which yield maximum returns, while controlling or eliminating competitive, undesirable plants.

SOIL CONSERVATION AND USE

The following discussion was prepared especially for the Texas Almanac by the **Soil Conservation Service**, U. S. Department of Agriculture, Temple, Texas. Additional information may be obtained from that source.

The vast expanse of Texas soils encouraged wasteful use of soil and water throughout much of the state's history. Some **1,000 different soils series** are recognized in the state. Settlers were attracted by these rich soils and the abundant water of the eastern half of the region, used them to build an agriculture and agribusiness of vast proportions, then found their abuse had created critical problems.

In the 1930s, interest in soil and water conservation began to mount. In 1935, the Soil Conservation Service was created in the U. S. Department of Agriculture. In 1939, the **Texas Soil Conservation Law** made it possible for landowners to organize local soil and water conservation districts.

The state as of Jan. 1, 1983, had **201 conservation districts** which manage the various conservation functions within the district. A subdivision of state government, each district is governed by a board of 5 elected landowners. Technical assistance in planning and applying conservation work is provided through the USDA Soil Conservation Service. State funds for districts are administered through the **Texas State Soil and Water Conservation Board.** (See Index.)

A recent national erosion inventory showed that more than twice as much soil is being lost to wind erosion each year than to sheet and rill erosion. The inventory also showed that about one-fourth of all land in Texas is "prime farmland."

The 1982 National Resources Inventory showed this breakdown of land use:

Use	Acres
Non-Federal	
Cropland	33,319,600
Pasture land	17,042,800
Range land	95,353,100
Forest land	9,323,600
Other land	2,391,700
Urban and Built-up land	4,387,500
Rural Transportation	2,233,500
Small Water Areas (Less than 40 acres)	713,500
Federal	
All Land Uses	2,998,300
Total Land Area	167,763,600
Census Water (More than 40 acres)	2,992,700
*Total Surface Area	170,756,300

*This figure for total area differs from that given in the Physiography Chapter; also, it differs from that given by the State Land Office in Chapter on State Government.

Soil Subdivisions

Most authorities divide Texas into 20 major subdivisions that have similar or related soils, vegetation, topography, climate and land uses. These are called Major Land Resource Areas. Brief descriptions of these subdivisions follow.

1. TRANS-PECOS SOILS

The 18 million acres of the Trans-Pecos, mostly west of the Pecos River, are diverse plains and valleys intermixed with mountains — quite different from other Texas areas. (See also section on physiography.)

Upland soils are light reddish brown to brown clay loams, clays and sands, (mostly high in lime, some saline) and many areas of shallow soils and rock lands. Main series: Hoban, Reeves, Reagan (lower basins); Brewster, Lozier, Verhalen, Musquiz (mountains and valleys); Hueco, Wink, Kermit (sandy soils); Orla (gypsic soils). Bottomland soils are dark grayish brown to reddish brown, silt loams to clayey, alluvial soils (some saline). Main series: Harkey, Glendale, Saneli (Rio Grande); Pecos, Arno (Pecos River).

Rainfall is sparse, and vegetative cover is as thin and as variable as the topography, soils and drainage conditions. In general it is of two types: short grasses and shrubs on the flat soils of the basins and valleys, and a mixture of mid and short grasses and species of oak, pine, juniper and semiarid plants and shrubs on the rough and mountainous lands. Alkali sacaton and other salt tolerant plants occur in the basin.

2. HIGH PLAINS SOILS

The High Plains area comprises the vast high plateau of more than 19 million acres in Northwestern Texas. It lies in the southern part of the Great Plains province that includes large similar areas in Oklahoma and New Mexico. The flat, nearly level surface of very large areas has few streams of any dissection to cause local relief. However, several major rivers originate in the High Plains or cross the area. The largest is the Canadian River which has cut a deep valley across the Panhandle section.

Playas, small intermittent lakes scattered through the area, lie up to 20 feet below the surrounding flat plains. Early estimates were that playas numbered 37,000; a 1965 survey indicated more than 19,000 in 44 counties, occupying some 340,000 acres. They received most of the runoff, with less than 10 percent of this water percolating back to the aquifer. In 1969 there were only limited numbers being utilized for recharge wells to return water to aquifers.

Soils are brown to reddish, mostly deep, clay loams, sandy loams and sands. Free lime is present under many soils at various depths. Main series: Pullman, Olton, Sherm (hardlands); Amarillo, Portales (mixed lands); Brownfield, Tivoli (sandy lands); Potter (loamy soils, shallow over caliche). The Guadalupe, Spur and Bippus series are the main soils of bottomlands, but are minor in extent.

The soils are moderately productive and the flat surface encourages irrigation and mechanization. Limited rainfall and constant danger of wind erosion are handicaps; but the region is Texas' leading producer of three most important crops — cotton, grain sorghums and wheat.

The native vegetation is of three distinct kinds. In the northern part and on the fine-textured soils south of the Canadian River, the vegetation is short grasses, mainly **buffalo** with some **grama**. In the southern part on the sandy loam soils it is largely **grama** and **threeawn**. On the deep sandy soils it is mainly **little bluestem, sand dropseed, sideoats grama** and **threeawn grasses**. In places these sands support a thick growth of **shinoak** and **sand sage** (Artemisia).

3. ROLLING PLAINS SOILS

The Rolling Plains comprise an eastern section of the Great Plains in Northwestern Texas. The area lies west of the North Central Prairies and extends from the edge of the Edwards Plateau in Tom Green County northward into Oklahoma. It includes about 23 million acres. The **Red Beds** and associated reddish soils led to use of the name **Red Plains** by some.

Upland soils are pale brown through reddish brown to dark grayish brown; sandy loams, clay loams and clays. Most soils have free lime in the lower part and are saline in places; some are shallow and stony; some are deep sands. Main series: Miles, Woodward, Springer, Vernon, Tillman (northern two-thirds); Abilene, Rowena, Mereta, Lueders (southern one-third).

Bottomland soils include minor areas of reddish brown, sandy to clayey, alluvial soils. Main series: Lincoln, Yahola, Guadalupe, Clairemont, Spur, Bippus and Mangum.

The native vegetation varies with soils and surface conditions. On the finer textured soils **curly mesquite, buffalo** and **grama grasses** are dominant with some scattered shrubs in places. On the coarser-textured soils the principal grasses are **little bluestem, sideoats grama** and **threeawn grasses** with **sand sage** and **shinnery** on areas of deep sand.

4. ROLLING RED PRAIRIES SOILS

The Rolling Red Prairies occupy about 1 million acres in North Central Texas adjoining Oklahoma. The area is dominantly prairie. The principal soils are of the Anocon, Bluegrove, Kamay, Kirkland and Stoneburg series. Bottomland soils are of the Gaddy, Yomont and Mangum.

Native vegetation is mainly **little bluestrem, sideoats, hairy** and **blue grama, Indian** and **buffalo grass.** The area is mainly used for cattle ranching and growing small grains.

5. NORTH CENTRAL PRAIRIE SOILS

The North Central Prairies occupy about 5 million acres in Central North Texas. The area lies between the Western Cross Timbers and Rolling Plains and was heretofore often referred to as the Reddish Prairie. The area is dominantly prairie, but numerous small wooded areas are intermixed. The principal soils are of the Truce, Thurber, Bonti, and Owens series. Narrow strips of alluvial soils, mainly of the Elandco and Frio series, occur in the flood plains of local streams. Small areas of other soils similar to those of the West Cross Timbers and Grand Prairie are intermixed. They are best suited for growing small grains and native grasses.

Native vegetation is mainly **little bluestem, sideoats, hairy** and **blue grama, Indian** and **buffalo grass.** Scrubby trees and shrubs, mainly **post oak** and **mesquite,** and **cacti** grow rather thickly in places.

6. EDWARDS PLATEAU SOILS

The 23 million acres of the Edwards Plateau are on an extensive tableland of Southwest Texas. Many of the soils are shallow over limestone, and streams have cut many valleys and canyons. Upland soils are dark, calcareous clays and clay loams, mostly gravelly and stony. Some deeper, less stony soils occur on the flat divides. Main series: Tarrant, Eckrant, Brackett and Tobosa (eastern two-thirds); Ector, Upton, Reagan (western one-third). Bottomland soils include minor areas of dark, calcareous, clayey alluvial soils. Main series: Frio, Oakalla and Dev.

This is principally a livestock, ranching region, the center of Texas' and the nation's mohair and wool production. Except where there is limited irrigation, cropping is largely confined to such drought-resistant crops as grain sorghums and grasses. Grasses, shrubs and scrubby trees dominate the native vegetation. There are many **cedar brakes.**

7. CENTRAL BASIN SOILS

The Central Basin, also known as the **Llano Basin,** occupies a relatively small area in Central Texas. It includes parts or all of Llano, Mason, Gillespie and adjoining counties. The total area is about 1.5 million acres.

Upland soils are reddish brown to brown, mostly gravelly and stony, sandy loams shallow over granite, limestone, gneiss and schist; deeper, less stony, sandy loam soils in the valleys. Main series: Pontotoc, Pedernales, Ligon, Castell, Katemcy, Hensley and Voca. Bottomland soils are minor areas of dark gray, alluvial soils. Main series: Frio, Gowen and Oakalla.

The native vegetation is grass and small **oak** and **mesquite trees.** On some rocky slopes, **juniper** forms the principal growth. Ranching is the main enterprise, with some farms producing peaches, grain sorghum and wheat.

8. NORTHERN RIO GRANDE PLAIN SOILS

The Northern Rio Grande Plain comprises about 5 million acres in an area of Southern Texas extending from Uvalde to Beeville. The main soils are deep, reddish brown or dark grayish brown, loamy, and of the Clareville, Elmendorf, Floresville, Miguel and Webb series in the eastern part. Native range is grassland, thorny brush and cacti. Most of the area is range grazed by beef cattle. Grain sorghum, cotton, corn, flax and small grain are grown in the eastern part. Irrigated cropland is in the Winter Garden area of the western part and produces corn, cotton, grain sorghum, and truck crops such as spinach, carrots and cabbage.

9. WESTERN RIO GRANDE PLAIN SOILS

The Western Rio Grande Plain comprises about 6 million acres in an area of Southwestern Texas from Del Rio to Rio Grande City. The main upland soils are clayey, saline and of the Catarina and Montell series. The vegetation is mid and short grasses with low thorny brush and **cacti.** Soils along the Rio Grande are mainly the Laredo, Rio Grande and Zalla series. Most of the soils along the river are used for growing vegetables and sorghums. The upland soils are used for grazing beef cattle.

10. CENTRAL RIO GRANDE PLAIN SOILS

The Central Rio Grande Plain comprises about 6 million acres in an area of Southern Texas from Live Oak to Hidalgo County. The main soils are Nueces and Sarita series (sandy); Delfina, Delmita and Duval (loamy); Randado and Zapata series (shallow). The vegetation is tall and mid grasses with scattered trees and shrubs. Much of the area is in large ranches used for raising beef cattle. A few areas are used for growing grain sorghum, cotton and small grain.

11. LOWER RIO GRANDE VALLEY SOILS

The Lower Rio Grande Valley comprises about 1.5 million acres in extreme Southern Texas. The main soils are deep, loamy and clayey, and of the Brennan, Hidalgo, Harlingen, Raymondville and Rio Grande series. Most of the soils are used for growing irrigated vegetables and citrus, along with cotton, grain sorghum and sugar cane. Some areas are in range and used for growing beef cattle.

12. WEST CROSS TIMBERS SOILS

The West Cross Timbers comprises a total of about 2.7 million acres. The area includes the wooded section west of the Grand Prairie and extends from the Red River southward to the north edge of Brown County. Small areas also occur intermixed or interlaced with soils of the western part of the Grand Prairie. The principal series are Windthorst, Nimrod and Duffau. Narrow areas of alluvial soils, mainly of the Gowen series, occur in the flood plains of local streams. Soils of the Ships, Yahola and Weswood series occur in the flood plains of the through-flowing rivers.

The native vegetation is mainly **shinnery oak** and **post oak** trees and a few other hardwoods. The trees are scrubby, of small size and unsuited for most uses other than **firewood** or **fence posts.** In places, grasses, including **little bluestem, grama** and **threeawn,** and scattered **mesquite** trees form a thick ground cover where the oak overstory is thin. Rangeland and pastures are used for grazing beef and dairy cattle. Crops are peanuts, grain sorghum, small grains, peaches, pecans and vegetables.

13. EAST CROSS TIMBERS SOILS

The East Cross Timbers includes a long narrow strip of wooded soils that separates the northern parts of the Blackland Prairie and Grand Prairie. This strip is only a few miles wide and extends from the Red River southward into Hill County and includes a total area of about 1 million acres. The soils are mainly of the Callisburg, Crosstell, Silstid and Gasil series.

The native vegetation is mainly **post oak** trees and a few other hardwoods. The trees are scrubby, of small size and unsuited for most uses other than firewood or fence posts. In places, grasses, including **little bluestem, grama** and **threeawn,** and scattered **mesquite** trees form a thick ground cover where the oak overstory is thin. Rangelands and pastures are used for grazing beef and dairy cattle. Crops are peanuts, grain sorghums, small grains, peaches, pecans and vegetables.

14. GRAND PRAIRIE SOILS

The Grand Prairie includes the prairie just west of the Blackland Prairie in North Central Texas. It extends south from the Red River to about the Colorado River and comprises about 7 million acres.

The principal soils of the Grand Prairie are of the Eckrant, Slidell and Denton series. Small areas of soils of the Crawford, Brackett, Krum and Lewisville series occur also on the uplands. Alluvial soils, mainly of the Frio and Bosque series, occur in the flood plains of streams.

The native vegetation is mainly short grasses with some mid and tall grasses on the deeper soils. **Buffalo** and **grama grasses**, **little bluestem** and **Indian grass** are the most widespread. In many places, especially on rocky slopes of shallow soils, small **oak** and **juniper trees** form a thick cover, and scattered **mesquite trees** occur throughout the area. The area is mainly used for growing beef cattle. Some small grain, grain sorghum and corn are grown.

15. BLACKLAND PRAIRIE SOILS

An almost treeless area, the Blackland Prairies consist of about 13 million acres of East Central Texas extending southwesterly from the Red River to Bexar County. There are smaller, similar areas to the southeast.

The soils of the greater portion of the Blackland Prairie proper are mainly of the Houston Black, Heiden and Austin series with smaller areas of Lewisville, Altoga and Eddy soils. Bottomland soils are mainly Tinn and Trinity clays.

The native vegetation consists of bunch and short grasses. The main species are little and big **bluestems**, **grama**, **Indian**, **buffalo** and **threeawn grasses**. In places, scattered **mesquite trees**, **cacti** and other shrubs form a rather thick cover. Hardwood trees — mainly **elm**, **hackberry** and **pecan** — occur in stream bottoms. The main crops are grain sorghum, wheat, cotton, corn and hay. Pastures are used for beef and dairy cattle.

16. CLAYPAN AREA SOILS

The Claypan Area is a level to gently rolling moderately dissected woodland savannah to brushy area (**Post Oak Belt**) with moderate surface drainage. The area is more than 3.5 million acres.

Upland soils are sandy loams, commonly thin over gray, mottled or red, firm, clayey subsoils. Some deep, sandy soils with less clayey subsoils exist. Main series: Lufkin, Axtell, Tabor (thin-surface claypan soils); Freestone and Padina (thick-surface sandy and loamy soils). Bottomlands are reddish brown to dark gray, to loamy to clayey alluvial soils. Main series: Ships, Weswood (Brazos and Colorado Rivers); Kaufman, Trinity, Gladewater, Nahatche (Trinity River and other smaller streams).

Vegetation consists of scattered stands of **post oak** and **blackjack oak** with tall bunch grasses in the uplands; **yaupon** and other underbrush prevalent in places. In the bottomlands, hardwoods are predominant but **pecans** occur in some areas. The land is woodland and brushy range. A few areas are used for tame pasture and cool-season forage crops.

17. EAST TEXAS TIMBERLAND SOILS

The East Texas Timberlands comprise the forested eastern part of the state, about 14 million acres.

The principal soil series are the Woodtell, Kirvin, Cuthbert, Bowie, Lilbert and Tonkawa soils in the northern and central parts; Nacogdoches and Elrose soils in the "Redland" section; and Diboll, Kisatche, Rayburn, Tehran, Doucette, Pinetucky and Shankler soils in the southern part of the area. Alluvial soils, mainly Mantachie, Iuka, Severn, Oklared and Urbo are on flood plains of streams.

The native vegetation is a pine-hardwood forest. It is mainly **loblolly pine**, **shortleaf pine**, **sweetgum** and **red oak trees** with an understory of grasses and shrubs. Forestry and pastures are the main uses.

18. COAST PRAIRIE SOILS

The Coast Prairie includes the nearly flat strip that is near the Gulf Coast in Southeast Texas in the humid and subhumid zones. It ranges from 30 to 80 miles in width and parallels the coast from the Sabine River in Orange County to Baffin Bay in Kleberg County. Total area of the Coast Prairie is about 9 million acres. The principal soils in the eastern portion from about the San Antonio River to the Sabine River are Lake Charles, Bernard, Edna, Morey and Beaumont soils near the coast, comprising more than 4 million acres.

The more inland soils in the eastern section are Hockley, Katy and Crowley series, comprising nearly 2 million acres. The portions west and south of the San Antonio River are Victoria, Orelia, Papalote and Clareville soils, comprising some 2 million acres. Other important soils, which occur in the bottomlands, are Brazoria, Norwood, Pledger, Kaman and Urbo. The nearly level topography and productive soils encourage farming. Rice, grain sorghum, cotton and soybeans are main crops. The native vegetation is tall prairie grasses, mainly species of **andropogon**, **paspalum** and **panicum**, with a narrow fringe of trees along the streams.

19. COAST SALINE PRAIRIES SOILS

The Coast Saline Prairies include a narrow strip of wet lowlands adjacent to the coast and the barrier islands that extend from Mexico to Louisiana. The surface is at or only a few feet above sea level and it ranges from 3 to 20 miles wide. The total area is about 3 million acres. Important soil series are the Harris, Tatton, Veston and Galveston series in the eastern part, and the Mustang, Aransas, Placedo, Francitas, Barrada and Galveston in the southern part. Cattle grazing is the chief economic use of the various salt tolerant **cordgrasses** and **sedges**. Recreation is an important use of the barrier islands.

20. FLATWOODS SOILS

The Flatwoods area includes the flat, rather poorly drained forested area in humid Southeast Texas. Total area is about 2.5 million acres. Most soils have a water table near the surface at least part of the year. Soils are mainly fine sandy loam with loamy or clayey subsoils. Important soil series are the Segno, Sorter, Splendora, Kirbyville, Malbis and Evadale.

The land is mainly used for forest. The typical vegetation is a pine-hardwood forest that is **longleaf pine**, **loblolly pine**, **sweetgum** and various **oak** species.

PHYSICAL FEATURES, GEOLOGY

Geologically, Texas is a crossroads, where four major physiographic subdivisions of North America come together: the **Rocky Mountain Region**, the **Great Western High Plains**, **Great Western Lower Plains** and the **Gulf Coastal Forested Plains**.

The highest point in Texas is **Guadalupe Peak**, 8,749 feet above sea level. Guadalupe and its twin, **El Capitan** (8,085 feet) are in West Texas near the New Mexico boundary. A plateau, most of it 2,600 to 4,300 feet above sea level, extends across West Texas above the Cap Rock. Below that escarpment the surface slopes downward to sea level along the Gulf of Mexico.

All of the true mountains and most of the spectacular physical features are found in the western half of Texas. These include the canyons of the **Big Bend** of the Rio Grande and tributaries in the southwest, the Edwards Plateau with its hills, spring-fed streams and lakes, the **Cap Rock Escarpment** and **Palo Duro Canyon**.

Peaks, Canyons and Caves

In addition to Guadalupe and El Capitan, other known, named peaks more than 8,000 feet higher than sea level include **Shumard**, 8,615 feet; **Bartlett**, 8,508; **Bush Mountain**, 8,631; and, about three miles to the east, **Pine Top Mountain**, 8,676. There may be other eminences above 8,000 feet in the area; but the preceding list includes all of the known, named "peaks" above this elevation.

In 1966 and 1967, federal and state legislation authorized the creation of **Guadalupe Mountains National Park** of 77,000 acres in Culberson and Hudspeth Counties. The area includes not only Texas' highest mountain but also scenic **McKittrick Canyon**.

Mount Emory in the Chisos Mountains, 7,825 feet, is another well-known elevation and there are numerous other identifiable peaks of over 7,000 feet in the Trans-Pecos area. An accompanying table gives the elevations of many Texas cities and towns. Ranges of elevations within counties appear in the county discussions. **Fort Davis**, officially 5,050 feet high, is the **highest town** of size in Texas and its county, **Jeff Davis**, has the **highest average county elevation**. Highest railway point is **Paisano**, 5,078 feet, on the Southern Pacific in Presidio County. **Texas highways reach a peak point of 6,791 feet** at the end of a tap from State Highway 118 to McDonald Observatory on Mount Locke.

Most of the canyons of Texas are found in the Trans-Pecos, Staked Plains, Burnet-Llano and Edwards Plateau regions. The Big Bend of the Rio Grande has the famed **Santa Elena** gorge, with a rim elevation of 3,661 feet, and the **Boquillas** and **Mariscal Canyons**. Tributaries of the Rio Grande form other canyons, such as the **Maravillas**. Other Trans-Pecos canyons include **Capote, McKittrick, Pine, Limpia, Musquiz, Cherry** and **Madera**, and the **Box Canyon**.

Along the edges of the Edwards Plateau are attractive canyons on such rivers as the **Frio, Nueces, Sabinal, Guadalupe, Medina** and **Devils**. The **Colorado River** forms some interesting gorges above Austin.

Palo Duro and **Tule Canyons** are striking features of the Staked Plains.

Several hundred **caves** of the Edwards Plateau and other rugged areas of Texas are known. Many are listed in the Texas Cave Survey and Index. A few noteworthy caves include, by counties: **Longhorn Cavern** in Burnet; **Wonder Cave** in Hays (name changed to **Wonder World** to include park area); **Natural Bridge Cavern** in Comal; **Devil's Sinkhole, Palace, Dragool, Kickapoo** and **Green Caves** in Edwards; **Caverns of Sonora** and **Felton Cave** in Sutton; **Cascade Caverns** and the **Century Caverns** in Kendall; **Indian Creek, Rambies's** and **Frio Bat Caves** in Uvalde; **Fern, Diablo, Fawcett** and **Lead Caves** in Val Verde; **Marathon Cave** in Brewster; 0-9 **Water Well Cave** in Crockett, and Menard County's **Jack Pit Cave**, with 19,000 feet of passage, the longest officially mapped Texas cave. **Inner Space Cave** near Georgetown, was discovered in the 1960s.

Physical Regions

Principal physical regions of Texas usually are listed as follows: (See also Plant Life and Soils.)

THE GULF COASTAL PLAINS

Texas' Gulf Coastal Plains are the western extension of the coastal plain extending from the Atlantic to beyond the Rio Grande. Its characteristic rolling to hilly surface covered with a heavy growth of pine and hardwoods extends into East Texas, but in the increasingly arid west its forests become secondary in nature, consisting largely of post oaks and, farther west, prairies and brush lands.

The western limit of the Gulf Coastal Plains in Texas is the line of the **Balcones Fault** and **Escarpment**. This geologic fault or shearing of underground strata extends eastward from a point on the Rio Grande near Del Rio. It extends to the northwestern part of Bexar County where it turns northeastward and extends through Comal, Hays and Travis Counties, intersecting the Colorado River immediately above Austin. The fault line is a single, definite geologic feature, accompanied by a line of southward- and eastward-facing hills. The resemblance of the hills to balconies when viewed from the plain below accounts for the Spanish name, balcones. North of Travis County the subterranean fault line and the surface line of hills become less distinct, the fault itself breaking into several irregularly parallel lines which extend all the way to the Red River. This northern subterranean extension of the Balcones fault line is approximately along the western margin of the Blackland Belt.

This fault line is usually accepted as the boundary between lowland and upland Texas. Below this fault line the surface is characteristically soil brought down from above and deposited as new earth. Above the Balcones fault the surface is characteristically eroded.

Pine Belt or "Piney Woods"

The Pine Belt (often called locally the "Piney Woods") extends into Texas from the east 75 to 125 miles. From north to south it extends from the Red River to within about 25 miles of the Gulf Coast. Interspersed among the pines are some hardwood timbers, usually in valleys of rivers and creeks. This area is the source of practically all of Texas' large commercial timber production. (See index for chapter on forest resources.) It was settled early in Texas history and is an older farming area of the state. This area's soils and climate are adaptable to production of a variety of fruit and vegetable crops. Cattle raising has increased greatly, accompanied by the development of pastures planted to improved grasses. Lumber production is the principal manufacturing industry. There is a large iron and steel industry near Daingerfield in Morris County based on nearby iron deposits. Iron deposits are also worked in Rusk and one or two other counties.

A great oil field discovered in Gregg, Rusk and Smith Counties in 1931 has done more than anything else to contribute to the economic growth of the area. This area has a variety of clays, lignite, and other minerals as potentials for development.

Post Oak Belt

The main Post Oak Belt of Texas is wedged between the Pine Belt on the east, Blacklands on the west, and the Coastal Prairies on the south, covering a considerable area in East Central Texas. Principal industry is diversified farming and livestock raising.

Throughout, it is spotty in character with some insular areas of blackland soil, and some that closely resemble those of the Pine Belt. There is a small isolated area of pines in Bastrop County known as the **Lost Pines**. The Post Oak Belt has lignite, commercial clays and some other minerals.

Blackland Belt

The Blackland Belt stretches from the Rio Grande to the Red River, lying just below the line of the Balcones Fault, and varying in width from 15 to 70 miles. It is narrowest below the segment of the Balcones Fault from the Rio Grande to Bexar County and gradually widens as it runs northeast to the Red River. Its rolling prairie, easily turned by the plow, developed rapidly as a farming area until the 1930s and was the principal cotton-producing area of Texas. Now, however, other Texas irrigated, mechanized areas lead in farming. Because of the early growth, the Blackland Belt is still the most thickly populated area in the state and contains within it and along its border more of the state's large and middle-sized cities than any other area. Primarily because of this concentration of population, this belt has the most diversified manufacturing industry of the state.

Coastal Prairies

The Texas Coastal Prairies extend westward along the coast from the Sabine River, reaching inland 30 to 60 miles. Between the Sabine and Galveston Bay the line of demarcation between the prairies and the Pine Belt forests to the north is very distinct. The Coastal Prairie in varying character extends along the Gulf from the Sabine to the Lower Rio Grande Valley. The eastern half is covered with a heavy growth of grass; the western half, in a more arid area, is covered with short grass, and in some places with small timber and brush. The soil is heavy alluvial. Grass supports the densest cattle population in Texas, and cattle ranching is the principal agricultural industry. Rice is a major crop, grown under irrigation from wells and rivers. Cotton and truck crops are grown.

Coastal Prairie areas have seen the greatest industrial development in Texas history since World War II. Chief concentration has been from Orange and Beaumont to Houston, and much of the development has been in **petrochemicals**, or chemicals derived from petroleum.

Corpus Christi, and the surrounding **Coastal Bend** region, and Brownsville, with its adjacent **Lower Rio Grande Valley** area, are rapidly developing seaports, agricultural and industrial sections. Cotton, grain, vegetables and citrus fruits are the principal crops. Cattle production is significant, with the famed **King Ranch** and other large ranches located here.

Lower Rio Grande Valley

The deep alluvial soils and distinctive economy cause the Lower Rio Grande Valley to be classified as a subregion of the Gulf Coastal Plain. Here is concentrated Texas' greatest citrus-winter vegetable area because of the normal absence of freezing weather and the rich delta soils of the Rio Grande. Despite occasional **damaging freezes**, as in 1951 and 1961, the Lower Valley ranks high among the nation's intensified fruit-and-truck regions. Much of the acreage is irrigated from the Rio Grande, although dryland farming also is practiced.

Rio Grande Plain

This may be roughly defined as lying south of San Antonio and between the Rio Grande and the Gulf Coast. The Rio Grande Plain shows characteristics of both the Texas Gulf Coastal Plain and the North Mexico Plains because there is similarity of topography, climate and plant life all the way from the Balcones Escarpment in Texas to the Sierra Madre Oriental in Mexico which runs past Monterrey about 160 miles south of Laredo.

The Rio Grande Plain is part prairie but much of it is covered with a dense growth of **prickly pear, cactus, mesquite, dwarf oak, catclaw, huajillo, huisache, blackbrush, cenizo** and other wild shrubs. This country is devoted primarily to raising cattle, sheep and goats. The Texas Angora goat and mohair industry centers in this area and on the Edwards Plateau which borders it on the north. San Antonio and Laredo are its chief commercial centers, with San Antonio dominating trade.

There is some dryland farming and the **Winter Garden**, centering in Dimmit and Zavala Counties north of Laredo, irrigates from wells and streams to produce vegetables in late winter and early spring. Primarily, however, the central and western part of the Rio Grande Plain is devoted to livestock raising. The rainfall is generally between 20 and 25 inches annually and the hot summers bring heavy evaporation so that cultivation without irrigation is limited. Over a large area in the central and western parts of the Rio Grande Plain, the growth of **small oaks, mesquite, prickly pear (Opuntia) cactus** and a variety of wild shrubs is very dense and it is often called the **Brush Country**. It is also referred to as the **Chaparral** and the **monte**. (Monte is a Spanish word meaning mountain, also heavy forest or dense brush.)

NORTH CENTRAL PLAINS

The North Central Plains of Texas are an extension into Texas of the lower level of the Great Plains which extend northward to the Canadian border, paralleling the Great High Plains to the west. The North Central Plains of Texas extend from the Blackland Belt on the east to the **Cap Rock Escarpment** on the west. From north to south they extend from the Red River to the Colorado.

West Texas Rolling Prairies

The West Texas Rolling Prairies, approximately the western two-thirds of the North Central Plains in Texas, rise from east to west in altitude from about 750 feet to 2,500 feet at the base of the Cap Rock Escarpment. Annual rainfall ranges from about 30 inches on the east to 20 on the west. Temperature varies rather widely between summer's heat and winter's cold.

This area still has a large cattle-raising industry with many of the state's largest ranches. However, there is much level cultivable land.

Grand Prairie

Near the eastern edge of the North Central Plains is the Grand Prairie, extending south from the Red River in an irregular band through Cooke, Montague, Wise, Denton, Tarrant, Parker, Hood, Johnson, Coryell and some adjacent counties. It is a limestone-based area, usually treeless except along the numerous streams, and adapted primarily to livestock raising and staple crop growing.

It is sometimes called the **Fort Worth Prairie**, and has an agricultural economy and largely rural population with no large cities except Fort Worth on its eastern boundary.

East and West Cross Timbers

Hanging over the top of the Grand Prairie and dropping down on each side are the East and West Cross Timbers. The two southward extending bands are connected by a narrow strip along the Red River. The East Cross Timbers extend southward from the Red River through eastern Denton County and along the Dallas-Tarrant County boundary, thence spottily through Johnson County into Hill County. The much larger **West Cross Timbers** extend from the Red River south through Clay, Montague, Jack, Wise, Parker, Palo Pinto, Hood, Erath, Eastland, Comanche, Brown

MAJOR NATURAL REGIONS

Map shows four great physiographic regions that extend into Texas — Gulf Coastal Plains, Low Western Plains, High Western Plains, Western Mountain Region — and subdivisions in Texas.

and Mills Counties to the Colorado, where they meet the Edwards Plateau. Their soils are adapted to fruit and vegetable crops which reach considerable commercial production in some areas as in Parker, Erath, Eastland and Comanche Counties.

STAKED PLAINS OR LLANO ESTACADO

The Great High Plains which lie to the east of the base of the Rocky Mountains extend into Northwest Texas. This Texas area is known as the **Staked Plains** or the Spanish equivalent *Llano Estacado.

*Historians differ as to the origin of this name. Some think that it came from the fact that the Coronado expedition, crossing the trackless sea of grass, staked its route so that it would be guided on its return trip. Others think that the "estacado" refers to the palisaded appearance of the Cap Rock in many places, especially the west-facing escarpment in New Mexico.

The **Cap Rock Escarpment** is the dividing line between the High Plains and the Lower Rolling Plains of West Texas. Like the Balcones Escarpment, the Cap Rock Escarpment is an outstanding natural boundary line. Unlike the Balcones Escarpment, the Cap Rock Escarpment is caused by surface erosion. In many places this escarpment is a striking physical feature, rising abruptly 200, 500 and in some places almost 1,000 feet above the plains at its base. Where rivers issue from the eastern face of this escarpment there frequently are notable canyons such as the **Palo Duro Canyon** on the Prairie Dog Town Fork (main channel) of the Red River and the gorge along the Canadian as it crosses the Panhandle north of Amarillo.

Along the eastern edge of the Panhandle there is a gradual descent of the earth's surface from high to low plains, but at the Red River the Cap Rock Escarpment becomes a striking surface feature. It continues as an east-facing mountain wall south through Briscoe, Floyd, Motley, Dickens, Crosby, Garza and Borden Counties, gradually decreasing in elevation. South of Borden County the escarpment turns west to the vicinity of Winkler County, then turns north through the eastern part of New Mexico.

Stretching over the largest level plain of its kind in the United States, the Great High Plains rise gradually from about 2,700 feet on the east to more than 4,000 in spots along the New Mexico border.

Chiefly because of climate and the resultant agriculture, subdivisions are called the **North Plains** and **South Plains.** The North Plains, from Hale County north, has primarily wheat and grain sorghum farming, but with significant ranching and petroleum developments. Amarillo is the largest city, with Plainview, Borger and others as important commercial centers. The South Plains, also a leading grain sorghum region, leads Texas in cotton production. Lubbock is the principal city, and Lubbock County the state's largest cotton producer. Irrigation, centered around Lubbock and Plainview, from underground reservoirs, waters much of the crop acreage.

Edwards Plateau

Geographers usually consider that the great plains at the foot of the Rocky Mountains actually continue southeastward from the High Plains of Northwest Texas to the Rio Grande and the line of the Balcones Escarpment. This southern and lower extension of the Great Plains in Texas is known as the Edwards Plateau.

It lies between the Rio Grande and the Colorado River. Its southeastern border is the Balcones Escarpment from the Rio Grande at Del Rio eastward to San Antonio and thence to Austin on the Colorado. Its upper boundary is the Pecos River, though the **Stockton Plateau** in the Trans-Pecos region is geologically and topographically classed with the Edwards Plateau. The Edwards Plateau varies from about 750 feet high at its southern and eastern borders to about 2,700 feet in places. Almost the entire surface is a thin, limestone-based soil covered with a medium to thick growth of cedar, small oak and mesquite with a varying growth of prickly pear. Grass for cattle, weeds for sheep and tree foliage for the browsing goats, support three industries—cattle, goat and sheep raising—upon which the area's economy depends. It is the nation's leading Angora goat and mohair producing region and one of the nation's leading sheep and wool areas. A few crops are grown.

The Hill Country

The Hill Country is a popular name for an area of hills and spring-fed streams along the edge of the Bal-

cones Escarpment. It is popular with tourists who visit the dude ranches and other attractions. Notable large springs include **Barton Springs** at Austin, **San Marcos Springs** at San Marcos, **Comal Springs** at New Braunfels, several springs at San Antonio, and a number of others.

The Burnet-Llano Basin

The Burnet-Llano Basin lies at the junction of the Colorado and Llano Rivers in Burnet and Llano Counties. Earlier this was known as the "Central Mineral Region," because of the evidence there of a large number of minerals.

On the Colorado River in this area a succession of dams impounds two large and four small reservoirs. Uppermost is **Lake Buchanan,** one of the two large reservoirs, between Burnet and Llano Counties. Below it in the western part of Travis County is **Lake Travis.** Between these two large reservoirs are three smaller ones, **Inks, L. B. Johnson** (formerly **Granite Shoals**) and **Marble Falls** reservoirs, used primarily for maintaining heads to produce electric power from the overflow from Lake Buchanan. **Lake Austin** is just above the City of Austin. Still another small lake is formed by a low-water dam in Austin.

A name for this recreational area is the **Highland Lakes Country.** Geologically this is the most interesting area in Texas, some of the world's oldest rocks being found at the surface.

TRANS-PECOS TEXAS

The triangular "panhandle" of Texas west of the Pecos River, bounded on the north by New Mexico and on the south by the Republic of Mexico, is distinctive in its physical and economic conditions. Traversed from north to south by an eastern range of the Rockies it contains all of Texas' true mountains.

Pecos Valley-Stockton Plateau

The eastern third of the Trans-Pecos is a rolling to rough country lying in the valley of the Pecos River and on the Stockton Plateau at the eastern base of the Davis Mountains. With only 10 to 12 inches of rainfall annually this was exclusively ranching country until two decades ago when the discovery of great quantities of groundwater brought irrigation of cotton, alfalfa and other crops.

Highest of the Trans-Pecos Mountains is the **Guadalupe Range,** which enters the state from New Mexico. It comes to an abrupt end about 20 miles south of the boundary line where are situated **Guadalupe Peak,** (8,749 feet, highest in Texas) and **El Capitan** (8,085 feet), which, because of perspective, appears to the observer on the plain below to be higher than Guadalupe and was for many years thought to be the highest mountain in Texas. Lying just west of the Guadalupe range and extending to the **Hueco Mountains** a short distance east of El Paso is the **Diablo Plateau** or basin. It has no drainage outlet to the sea. The runoff from the scant rain that falls on its surface drains into a series of salt lakes that lie just west of the Guadalupe Mountains. These lakes are entirely dry during periods of low rainfall exposing bottoms of solid salt and for years they were a source of commercial salt. Conflicting claims to this natural resource caused the **Salt War** of the 1870s. (See index, "Salt War.")

Davis Mountains

The **Davis Mountains** are principally in Jeff Davis County. The highest peak, **Mount Livermore,** (8,206 feet) is one of the highest in Texas. There are a number of mountains more than 7,000 feet high. These mountains intercept the moisture-bearing winds and cause more precipitation than elsewhere in the Trans-Pecos. They are greener with the growth of grass and forest trees than the other Trans-Pecos mountains. Noteworthy are the **San Solomon Springs** at the northern base of these mountains.

Big Bend

South of the Davis Mountains lies the **Big Bend** country, so called because it is encompassed on three sides by a great southward swing of the Rio Grande. It is a mountainous country of scant rainfall and sparse population. Its principal mountains, the **Chisos,** rise to 7,825 feet in **Mount Emory.** Along the Rio Grande are the **Santa Elena, Mariscal** and **Boquillas Canyons** with rim elevations of 3,500 to 3,775 feet. They are among the noteworthy canyons of the North American continent. Because of its remarkable topography, and plant and animal life, the United States Government maintains in the southern part of this region along the Rio Grande the Big Bend National Park with headquarters in a deep valley in the Chisos Mountains. It is a favorite recreation area.

Upper Rio Grande Valley

The Upper Rio Grande (El Paso) Valley is a narrow strip of irrigated land running down the river from El Paso for a distance of 75 miles or more. In this area are the historic towns and missions of **Ysleta, Socorro** and **San Elizario**, oldest in Texas. Cotton is the chief product of the valley, much of it long-staple variety. This limited area has a dense urban and rural population in marked contrast to the territory surrounding it.

Area of Texas

Texas occupies about 7 per cent of the total water and land area of the United States. **Second in size** among the states, Texas, according to the revised 1980 U.S. Census Bureau figures, has a land and water area of 266,807 square miles as compared with Alaska's 591,004 square miles. California, third largest state, has 158,706 square miles. Texas is as large as all of New England, New York, Pennsylvania, Ohio and Illinois combined.

The state's area consists of 262,017 square miles of land and 4,790 square miles of inland water, or 167,690,880 acres of land area and 3,065,600 acres of inland water.

The area given here differs from that given by the State Land Office in the Chapter on State Government.

LENGTH AND BREADTH

The longest straight-line distance in a general north-south direction is 801 miles from the northwest corner of the Panhandle to the extreme southern tip of Texas on the Rio Grande below Brownsville. The greatest east-west distance is 773 miles from the extreme eastward bend in the Sabine River in Newton County to the extreme western bulge of the Rio Grande just above El Paso. The **geographic center** of Texas is southwest of Mercury in the northern portion of McCulloch County.

LATITUDE, LONGITUDE—ELEVATION

The extremes of latitude and longitude are as follows: From Latitude 25° 50′ N. at the extreme southern turn of the Rio Grande on the south line of Cameron County to Latitude 36° 30′ N. along the north line of the Panhandle, and from Longitude 93° 31′ W. at the extreme eastern point on the Sabine River on the east line of Newton County to Longitude 106° 38′ W. on the extreme westward point on the Rio Grande above El Paso.

In elevation the surface of the state varies from sea level along the Gulf Coast to 8,749 feet at the summit of Guadalupe Mountain in Culberson County.

TEXAS BOUNDARY LINE

The boundary of Texas by segments, including only larger river bends and only the great arc of the coast line, is as follows:

	Miles
Rio Grande	889.0
Coast line	367.0
Sabine River, Lake and Pass	180.0
Sabine River to Red River	106.5
Red River	480.0
East Panhandle line	133.6
North Panhandle line	167.0
West Panhandle line	310.2
Along 32nd parallel	209.0
Total	2,842.3

Following the smaller meanderings of the rivers and the tidewater coast line, the following are the boundary measurements:

Rio Grande	1,248
Coast line (tidewater)	624
Sabine River, Lake and Pass	292
Red River	726
The five line segments given above	926
Total, including line segments given in table above	3,816

WEATHER HIGHLIGHTS, 1983 and 1984

The following summary was prepared for this edition by John F. Griffiths and Janine M. Bryan, Office of State Climatologist, Meteorology Department, Texas A&M University, College Station.

Jan. 20-21, 1983: A severe snowstorm dumped snow in excess of 8 inches over a wide area, including the Panhandle and the South Plains. **Snowfall records** were shattered in Lubbock, as 25.3 inches of snow fell breaking the old record of 21.4 inches for any given month; 16.8 inches of snow fell in one storm replacing the 14.8 inch record.

Feb. 3-4, 1983: A snowstorm in the Texas Panhandle brought heavy snowfall, totaling 14 inches in Amarillo and 15 inches in Dumas and Borger.

March 15, 1983: The strongest documented **tornado** ever to occur in the **Lower Rio Grande Valley** struck **Cameron County**, causing damage rated up to F3 in force (158-206 mph winds).

April 1, 1983: High winds in North Texas caused three fatalities and 16 injuries. Peak winds of 60 to 70 mph at Weather Service offices and airports were common, with an 89 mph gust reported by a Wichita Falls TV station.

April 5-7, 1983: The largest **snowstorm** in **El Paso's** history ended after dumping 16.5 inches on the area.

May 20, 1983: Three deaths in Harris County and one death each in Washington and Jefferson counties resulted from tornadoes, as severe weather invaded those areas. Thunderstorms and hail were responsible for 13 other deaths in southern Texas.

May, 1983: Numerous reports of flash flooding, especially in the Hill Country, were common. Eight deaths were attributed to the flooding.

Aug. 15-21, 1983: **Hurricane Alicia** was the first hurricane to make landfall in the continental U.S. in three years (Aug. 18), and one of the costliest in Texas history ($3 billion). Alicia caused widespread damage to a large section of Southeast Texas, including coastal areas near **Galveston** and the entire **Houston** area. Alicia spawned 22 tornadoes, and highest winds were estimated near 130 mph. In all, 18 people in South Texas were killed and 1,800 injured as a result of the tropical storm.

Sept. 18-20, 1983: Heavy rains over South Central Texas, the Upper Coast and Southeast Texas were responsible for widespread flooding, claiming four lives during the period.

Oct. 9, 1983: In Burnet County, two lives were lost as a result of flash flooding.

Oct. 18-20, 1983: Remnants of **Hurricane Tico** dumped heavy rains in North and South Central Texas as it pushed northeastward across Texas from the Big Bend region to near Wichita Falls. Several rainfall stations reached or surpassed the 7 inch rain mark, while others measured 5-7 inches. A record crest of 37 feet for the Red River was set in Northern Cooke County. This **flood** will be known as one of the largest in the history of the South Plains.

Dec. 18-30, 1983: A frigid arctic air mass persisted over the entire state during the latter part of the month, making it the **coldest December on record**. (See 1983 review.)

Jun. 5, 1984: One man was killed when a tornado struck the mobile home he was housed in near the town of Orient in Tom Green County.

Aug. 8-9, 1984: A record amount of rainfall for El Paso, (2.30 inches in a 24-hour period), was set during August.

Oct. 18, 1984: Near the town of Argo, one woman was killed and another seriously injured when a tornado destroyed the house they were occupying.

In 1983 there were 186 tornadoes. Of these, 8 were killer tornadoes causing 1 death each.

In 1984, 95 tornadoes were reported in Texas; May and June reported the most.

Weather Summary—1983

The year 1983 featured the cold snap of December that set new low temperature records across the state. It was the coldest month ever for most areas of Texas. Departures from the mean ranged from -2.7°F in the Trans-Pecos region to an incredible -13°F in the Panhandle. An all-time record low for San Angelo was set (-1°F) and record December lows were broken in other localities. The **greatest total snowfall** occurred in **Follett** with 16.5 inches. To contrast the first and second halves of the month, the **highest temperature recorded** in Texas was 92°F in Benavides on Dec. 10, and the **lowest** was -16°F in Lipscomb on Dec. 30. Another interesting comparison was in College Station, where the difference in mean temperature between Dec. 1-15 and Dec. 16-31 was 26.2°F.

January brought cooler-than-average temperatures throughout Texas, with slightly above expected precipitation in the Panhandle, Edwards Plateau and Trans-Pecos areas, and below-expected precipitation in the rest of the state. In February, precipitation was above average for all of Texas, especially in the Southern and Lower Valley regions. March and April began a cooling trend, dropping temperatures to well below the mean throughout the state, with extreme departures from average of nearly -6°F in the Panhandle. March brought above-average precipitation for all but the High Plains area, while nearly all of Texas experienced a very dry April, with only the Trans-Pecos area receiving its mean amount. Temperatures in May and June were also cooler than usual across the state, except for slightly above-average temperatures in the Lower Valley. May was also drier than average for the Southern, Lower Valley and Trans-Pecos areas, while East Texas and the North Central regions received above-average precipitation. The rest of the state received expected amounts. The Lower Valley and Trans-Pecos areas remained dry through June, while most of Texas had average precipitation. July brought dry conditions in the north and well-above-average precipitation in the south, with extremes of only 0.60 inches in the High Plains to over 9 inches in the Upper Coast. August and September were very hot and dry in the Panhandle, Trans-Pecos and Edwards Plateau regions, while average temperatures and precipitation amounts prevailed over the rest of the state. October's temperatures were above the mean throughout the state, but the Panhandle, Trans-Pecos and Edwards Plateau areas felt relief from the dry summer as much above-average precipitation occurred. Only East Texas experienced a relatively dry October. November saw above-average temperatures throughout the state, as departures ranged from +1.5°F in East Texas to +4.0°F in the Southern Region. A reversal occurred in December with cold spells causing temperatures to plummet across the state, ending 1983 with one of the coldest months on record.

Weather Summary—1984

The October rains of 1984 broke **greatest precipitation** records for the month in many localities including Houston (16.05 inches) and Waco (10.51 inches). The departure for the Upper Coast area was +9.60 inches, and in East Texas precipitation was 8.87 inches above the mean. The greatest total precipitation for the month was 27.16 inches in Midway and the greatest amount for one day officially was 12.20 inches in Port O'Connor on Oct. 20. However, an unofficial observer in Odem measured 25 inches of rain in a 3.5 hour period on Oct. 19.

As a continuation of the cold spell in December, 1983, January of 1984 began with well-below-average temperatures throughout the state, with a departure of -5.4°F in East Texas. Precipitation was well below the

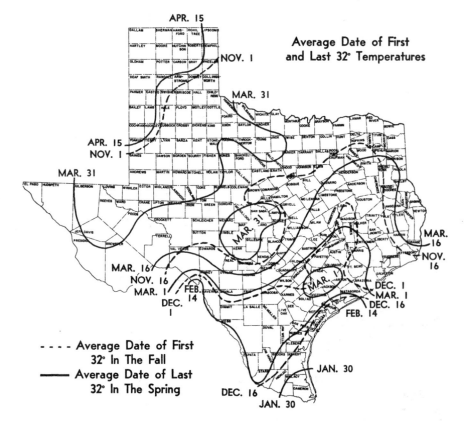

Average Date of First and Last 32° Temperatures

- - - - Average Date of First 32° In The Fall

—— Average Date of Last 32° In The Spring

mean in the north, while the south experienced above-average amounts (over 300% of the mean in the Lower Valley). February brought average temperatures to most of the state, with warmer-than-usual temperatures in the north. Precipitation was average for the Low Rolling Plains through North Central and East Texas, while below-average amounts were recorded over the rest of the state. Temperatures in March and April showed a slight cooling trend in the north, while above-average temperatures were observed in the south. March was very dry for the Trans-Pecos, Edwards Plateau and the Lower Valley regions, while the rest of Texas enjoyed average or above-average precipitation. April was a very dry month for all of Texas, especially in the Trans-Pecos area and in the south. El Paso received 0.01 inches of rain and Brownsville reported only a trace. In May, above-average temperatures prevailed in the north, and the south had temperatures near the mean. Precipitation was below the expected amounts in the north and in the South Central region, while average amounts prevailed in the rest of the state. June saw above-average temperatures in the Low Rolling Plains and Edwards Plateau areas, while most of Texas experienced temperatures near the mean. Above-average precipitation occurred in the High Plains and Trans-Pecos areas, while the rest of Texas observed below the expected amount. July brought below-average temperatures for all of Texas, with precipitation below the mean in the north, and average precipitation amounts in the south. In August, above-average precipitation prevailed in the Panhandle and Trans-Pecos areas, while the rest of the state had amounts below the mean. September was a cool, dry month for Texas, although the Lower Valley had a moisture surplus of over 7 inches of rain. A reversal occurred in October, with well-above-average precipitation in all areas except the Lower Valley, which received less than half of its mean. Above-average temperatures were observed in the south and in East Texas, while the rest of the state experienced temperatures below the mean. November began a warming trend throughout the state, and it continued into December. December departures ranged from +1.5°F in the High Plains to +8.3°F in the Upper Valley area. The dry spell continued in the Lower Valley in November, and precipitation was slightly below the expected amount in neighboring southern Texas. Above-average precipitation persisted in the north. In December, below-average precipitation occurred in East Texas and the the Upper Coast, while the rest of the state experienced well-above-average precipitation (over 400 percent from the mean in the Low Rolling Plains).

McAllen and Presidio ranked in the top five cities for having reported the greatest number of national daily highest temperatures in both 1983 and 1984.

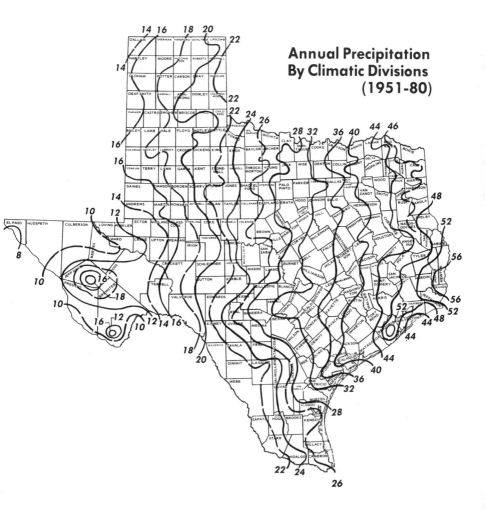

Annual Precipitation By Climatic Divisions (1951-80)

Destructive Storms

This list of exceptionally destructive storms in Texas since 1766 is compiled from ESSA-Weather Bureau information:

Sept., 4, 1766: Hurricane. Galveston Bay. A mission destroyed.

Sept. 12, 1818: Hurricane. Galveston Island. Salt water flowed four feet deep. Only six buildings remained habitable. Of the six vessels and two barges in the harbor, even the two not seriously damaged were reduced to dismasted hulks. Pirate **Jean Lafitte** moved to one hulk so his **Red House** might serve as a hospital.

Aug. 6, 1844: Hurricane. Mouth of Rio Grande. All houses destroyed at the mouth of the river and at **Brazos Santiago,** 8 miles north; 70 lives lost.

Sept. 19, 1854: Hurricane. After striking near **Matagorda,** the hurricane moved inland northwestward over **Columbus.** The main impact fell in Matagorda and Lavaca Bays. Almost all buildings in Matagorda were destroyed. Four lives were lost in the town; more lives were lost on the peninsula.

Oct. 3, 1867: Hurricane. This hurricane moved inland south of **Galveston,** but raked the entire Texas coast from the Rio Grande to the Sabine. **Bagdad** and **Clarksville,** towns at the mouth of the Rio Grande, were destroyed. Much of **Galveston** was flooded and property damage there was estimated at $1,000,000.

Sept. 16, 1875: Hurricane. Struck **Indianola,** Calhoun County. Three fourths of town swept away; 176 lives lost. Flooding from the bay caused nearly all destruction.

Aug. 13, 1880: Hurricane. Center struck **Matamoras, Mexico;** lower Texas coast affected.

Oct. 12-13, 1880: Hurricane. Brownsville. City nearly destroyed, many lives lost.

Aug. 19-21, 1886: Hurricane. Indianola. Every house destroyed or damaged. Indianola never rebuilt.

Oct. 12, 1886: Hurricane. Sabine, Jefferson County. Hurricane passed over Sabine. The inundation extended 20 miles inland and nearly every house in the vicinity was moved from its foundation; 150 persons were drowned.

April 28, 1893: Tornado. Cisco, Eastland County; 23 killed, 93 injured; damage $400,000.

May 15, 1896: Tornadoes, Sherman, Grayson County; **Justin,** Denton County; **Gribble Springs,** Cooke County; 76 killed; damage $225,000.

Sept. 12, 1897: Hurricane. Many houses in **Port Arthur** were demolished; 13 killed, damage $150,000.

May 1, 1898: Tornado. Mobeetie, Wheeler County. Four killed, several injured; damage $35,000.

June 27-July 1, 1899: Rainstorm. A storm, centered over the Brazos River watershed, precipitated an average of 17 inches over an area of 7,000 square miles. At **Hearne** the gage overflowed at 24 inches and there was an estimated total rainfall of 30 inches. At **Turnersville,** Coryell County, 33 inches were recorded in three days. This rain caused the worst **Brazos River** flood on record. Between 30 and 35 lives were lost. Property damage was estimated at $9,000,000.

April 5-8, 1900: Rainstorm. This storm began in two centers, over Val Verde County on the Rio Grande, and over Swisher County on the High Plains, and converged in the vicinity of Travis County, causing disastrous floods in the Colorado, Brazos and Guadalupe Rivers. **McDonald Dam** on the Colorado River at Austin crumbled suddenly. A wall of water swept through the city taking at least 23 lives. Damage was estimated at $1,250,000.

Sept. 8-9, 1900: Hurricane. Galveston. The **Great Galveston Storm** was the worst natural disaster in U.S. history. Loss of life at Galveston has been estimated at 6,000 to 8,000, but the exact number has never been definitely ascertained. The island was completely inundated, and not a single structure escaped damage. Most of the loss of life was due to drowning by storm tides that reached 15 feet or more. The anemometer blew away when the wind reached 100 miles per hour at 6:15 p.m. on

METEOROLOGICAL DATA

Source: NOAA, Environmental Data Service, Local Climatological Data.

Additional data for these locations are listed in the table of Texas temperature, freeze, growing season, and precipitation records, by counties.

	Temperature						Precipitation					Relative Humidity		Wind			
	Record Highest	Month and Yr.	Record Lowest	Month and Yr.	No. Days Max. 90° and Above	No. Days Min. 32° and Below	Maximum in 24 Hours	Month and Year	Max. Snowfall in 24 Hours	Month and Year	6:00 A.M. CST	Noon CST	Speed, MPH Mean Annual	Highest Miles Per Hour	Month and Year	Per Cent Possible Sunshine
Abilene	111	8-43	—9	†1-47	96	55	6.78	5-08	4.3	8.0	†1-19	74	50	12.2	109	6-51	71
Amarillo	108	6-53	—16	2-99	65	110	6.75	5-51	13.9	20.6	3-34	72	45	13.7	84	5-49	73
Austin	109	†7-54	—2	1-49	104	23	19.03	9-21	1.2	9.7	11-37	83	56	9.3	57	2-47	61
Brownsville	106	3-84	12	2-99	117	2	12.19	9-67	‡‡	‡‡	†11-76	88	60	11.6	106	9-33	61
Corpus Christi	105	7-34	11	2-99	102	7	8.92	8-80	0.1	5.0	1-97	90	63	12.0	161	8-70	63
Dallas-Fort Worth	113	6-80	—8	†2-99	95	41	9.57	9-32	2.9	12.1	1-64	82	56	10.8	77	7-36	66
Del Rio	111	†7-60	11	2-51	125	18	8.88	6-35	0.8	4.7	1-26	79	54	9.9	62	3-35	70
El Paso	112	7-79	—8	1-62	106	62	6.50	7-1881	4.4	8.4	11-06	55	35	9.2	70	†5-50	83
Galveston	101	7-32	8	2-99	12	4	14.35	7-00	0.2	15.4	2-95	83	72	11.0	*100	9-00	63
***Houston	108	8-09	5	†1-40	92	24	15.65	8-45	0.4	4.4	2-60	91	60	7.8	84	3-26	56
Lubbock	109	†7-40	—17	2-33	79	96	5.82	10-83	8.8	16.3	1-83	74	46	12.5	70	5-52	73
Midland-Odessa	109	6-51	—11	2-33	97	63	5.99	7-61	3.4	6.8	1-74	73	42	11.1	67	2-60	75
Prt. Arthur-Beaumont	107	8-62	11	1-30	82	17	17.76	7-43	0.5	††20.0	2-95	91	64	10.0	91	8-40	58
San Angelo	111	†7-60	—1	12-83	108	53	11.75	9-36	3.0	7.4	1-78	78	49	10.5	75	4-69	70
San Antonio	107	8-09	0	1-49	111	23	7.28	9-73	0.5	5.0	1-40	83	55	9.4	74	8-42	60
Victoria	110	7-39	9	1-30	102	13	9.30	6-77	‡‡	1.2	1-73	89	60	10.0	§150	9-61	62
Waco	112	8-69	—5	1-49	106	35	7.18	5-53	1.5	7.0	1-49	83	57	11.3	69	6-61	63
Wichita Falls	117	6-80	—12	1-47	107	69	6.22	9-80	5.7	5.9	1-66	82	51	11.7	92	6-45	68
**Shreveport, La.	110	8-09	—5	2-99	88	37	7.17	4-53	1.3	5.6	1-82	87	58	8.6	52	4-75	63

*100 mph recorded at 6:15 p.m. Sept. 8 just before anemometer blew away. Maximum velocity estimated 120 mph from NE between 7:30 p.m. and 8:30 p.m.

†Also recorded on earlier dates, months or years.

‡Anemometer damaged.

§Highest sustained wind estimated 110 mph. Highest gust estimated 150 mph at 5:55 p.m., Sept. 11, 1961.

**These stations are included because they are near the boundary line and their data can be considered representative of the eastern border of Texas.

††Measured at Orange, Texas, near Port Arthur.

‡‡Trace, an amount too small to measure.

***The official Houston station was moved from near downtown to Intercontinental Airport, located 12 miles north of the old station.

the 8th. Wind reached an estimated maximum velocity of 120 miles per hour between 7:30 and 8:30 p.m. Property damage has been estimated at $30 to $40 million.

May 18, 1902: Tornado. A large part of Goliad destroyed. 114 Killed; more than 230 injured; damage $50,000. One of two most disastrous tornadoes to occur in Texas.

April 26, 1906: Tornado. Bellevue, Clay County, demolished; considerable damage done at Stoneburg, 7 miles east; 17 killed, 20 injured; damage $300,000.

May 6, 1907: Tornado. North of Sulphur Springs, Hopkins County; 5 killed, 19 injured.

May 13, 1908: Tornado. Linden, Cass County. Four killed, 7 injured; damage $75,000.

May 22-25, 1908: Rainstorm; unique because it originated on the Pacific Coast. It moved first into North Texas and southern Oklahoma and thence to Central Texas, precipitating as much as 10 inches. Heaviest floods were in the upper Trinity basin, but flooding was general as far south as the Nueces. Property damage exceeded $5,000,000, and 11 lives were lost in the Dallas vicinity.

March 23, 1909: Tornado. Slidell, Wise County; 11 killed, 10 injured; damage $30,000.

May 30, 1909: Tornado. Zephyr, Brown County; 28 killed, many injured; damage $90,000.

July 21, 1909: Hurricane. Velasco, Brazoria County. One half of town destroyed, 41 lives lost; damage $2,000,000.

Dec. 1-5, 1913: Rainstorm. This caused the second major Brazos River flood, and caused more deaths than the storm of 1899. It formed over Central Texas and spread both southwest and northeast with precipitation of 15 inches at San Marcos and 11 inches at Kaufman. Floods caused loss of 177 lives and $8,541,000 damage.

April 20-26, 1915: Rainstorm. Originated over Central Texas and spread into North and East Texas with precipitation up to 17 inches, causing floods in Trinity, Brazos, Colorado, and Guadalupe Rivers. More than 40 lives lost and $2,330,000 damage.

Aug. 16-19, 1915: Hurricane. Galveston. Peak wind gusts of 120 miles recorded at Galveston; tide ranged 9.5 to 14.3 feet above mean sea level in the city, and up to 16.1 feet near the causeway. Business section flooded with 5 to 6 feet of water. At least 275 lives lost, damage $56,000,000. A new seawall prevented a repetition of the 1900 disaster.

Aug. 18, 1916: Hurricane. Corpus Christi. Maximum wind speed 100 miles per hour. 20 Lives lost; damage $1,600,000.

Jan. 10-12, 1918: Blizzard. This was the most severe since that of February, 1899; it gave zero weather in North Texas and temperatures from 7° to 12° below freezing along the lower coast.

April 9, 1919: Tornado. Leonard, Ector and Ravenna in Fannin County; 20 killed, 45 injured; damage $125,000.

April 9, 1919: Tornado. Henderson, Van Zandt, Wood, Camp, and Red River Counties, 42 killed, 150 injured; damage $450,000.

May 7, 1919: Windstorms. Starr, Hidalgo, Willacy and Cameron Counties. Violent thunderstorms with high winds, hail and rain occurred between Rio Grande City and the coast, killing 10 persons. Damage to property and crops was $500,000. Seven were killed at Mission.

Sept. 14, 1919: Hurricane. Near Corpus Christi. Center moved inland south of Corpus Christi; tides 16 feet above normal in that area and 8.8 feet above normal at Galveston. Extreme wind at Corpus Christi measured at 110 miles per hour; 284 lives lost; damage $20,272,000.

April 13, 1921: Tornado. Melissa, Collin County, and Petty, Lamar County. Melissa was practically destroyed; 12 killed, 80 injured; damage $500,000.

April 15, 1921: Tornado. Wood, Cass and Bowie Counties; 10 killed, 50 injured; damage $85,000.

Sept. 8-10, 1921: Rainstorm. Probably the greatest rainstorm in Texas history, it entered Mexico as a hurricane from the Gulf. Torrential rains fell as the storm moved northeasterly across Texas. Record floods occurred in Bexar, Travis, Williamson, Bell and Milam Counties, killing 215 persons, with property losses over $19,000,000. Five to nine feet of water stood in downtown San Antonio. A total of 23.98 inches was measured at the U.S. Weather Bureau station at Taylor during a period of 35 hours, with a 24-hour maximum of 23.11 on September 9-10. The greatest rainfall recorded in United States history occurred during 18 consecutive hours fell at Thrall, Williamson County, 36.40 inches fell on Sept. 9.

April 8, 1922: Tornado. Rowena, Runnels County. Seven killed, 52 injured; damage $55,000.

April 8, 1922: Tornado. Oplin, Callahan County. Five killed, 30 injured; damage $15,000.

April 23-28, 1922: Rainstorm. An exceptional storm that entered Texas from the west and moved from the Panhandle to North Central and East Texas. Rains up to 12.6 inches over Parker, Tarrant, and Dallas Counties caused severe floods in the Upper Trinity at Fort Worth; 11 lives were lost; damage was estimated at $1,000,000.

May 4, 1922: Tornado. Austin, Travis County; 12 killed, 50 injured; damage $500,000.

May 14, 1923: Tornado. Howard and **Mitchell Counties;** 23 killed, 100 injured; damage $50,000.

April 12, 1927: Tornado. Edwards, Real and Uvalde Counties; 74 killed, 205 injured; damage $1,230,000. Most of damage was in Rocksprings where 72 deaths occurred and town was practically destroyed.

May 9, 1927: Tornado. Garland; Eleven killed; damage $100,000.

May 9, 1927: Tornado. Nevada, Collin County; Wolfe City, Hunt County; and Tigertown, Lamar County; 28 killed, over 200 injured; damage $900,000.

Jan. 4, 1929: Tornado. Near Bay City, Matagorda County. Five killed, 14 injured.

April 24, 1929: Tornado. Slocum, Anderson County; 7 killed, 20 injured; damage $200,000.

May 24-31, 1929: Rainstorm. Beginning over Caldwell County, a storm spread over much of Central and Coastal Texas with maximum rainfall of 12.9 inches, causing floods in Colorado, Guadalupe, Brazos, Trinity, Neches and Sabine Rivers. Much damage at Houston from overflow of bayous. Damage estimated at $6,000,000.

May 6, 1930: Tornado. Bynum, Irene and Mertens in Hill County; Ennis, Ellis County; and Frost, Navarro County; 41 killed; damage $2,100,000.

May 6, 1930: Tornado. Kenedy and Runge in Karnes County; Nordheim, DeWitt County; 36 killed, 34 injured; damage $127,000.

June 30-July 2, 1932: Rainstorm. Torrential rains fell over the upper watersheds of the Nueces and Guadalupe Rivers, causing destructive floods. Seven persons drowned; property losses exceeded $500,000.

Aug. 13, 1932: Hurricane. Near Freeport, Brazoria County. Wind speed at East Columbia estimated at 100 miles per hour; 40 lives lost, 200 injured; damage $7,500,000.

March 30, 1933: Tornado. Angelina, Nacogdoches and San Augustine Counties; 10 killed, 56 injured; damage $200,000.

April 26, 1933: Tornado. Bowie County near Texarkana. Five killed, 38 injured; damage $14,000.

May 10, 1933: Tornado. Near Brownwood, Brown County. Four killed, seven injured; damage $250,000.

July 22-25, 1933: Tropical Storm. One of the greatest U.S. storms in area and general rainfall. The storm reached the vicinity of Freeport late on July 22 and moved very slowly overland into eastern Texas, July 22-25. The storm center moved onto northern Louisiana on the 25th. Rainfall averaged 12.50 inches over an area of about 25,000 square miles. Twenty inches or more fell in a small area of eastern Texas and western Louisiana

1983 WEATHER EXTREMES

Lowest Temp.—Lipscomb, Lipscomb County,
Dec. 30 . . . . −16°F
Highest Temp.—Boquillas Ranger Station,
Brewster County, June 19 . . . . 113°F
Presidio, Presidio County,
July 5 . . . . 113°F
Robstown, Nueces County,
Aug. 31 . . . . 113°F
24-hr. Precip.—Newgulf, Wharton County,
Oct. 17 . . . . 13.47″
Monthly Precip.—Sugar Land, Fort Bend
County,
Sept. . . . . 17.47″
Least Annual Precip.—Grandfalls, Ward
County . . . . . . 5.42″
Greatest Annual Precip.—Liberty, Liberty
County . . . . . 83.62″

1984 WEATHER EXTREMES

Lowest Temp.—Dalhart, Dalham County, Jan. 19 −14°F
Stratford, Sherman County,
Jan. 19 . . . . −14°F
Highest Temp.—Glen Rose, Somervell County,
Aug. 19 . . . . 115°F
24-hr. Precip.—Port O'Connor, Calhoun
County,
Oct. 20 . . . . 12.20″
Monthly Precip.—Midway, Madison County,
October . . . . 27.16″
(Least and Greatest Annual Precipitation for 1984 not available when this section went to press.)

surrounding **Logansport, La.** The 4-day total at Logansport was 22.30 inches. Property damage was estimated at $1,114,790.

July 30, 1933: **Tornado.** Oak Cliff section of **Dallas,** Dallas County. Five killed, 30 injured; damage $500,000.

Sept. 4-5, 1933: **Hurricane.** Near **Brownsville.** Center passed inland a short distance north of Brownsville where an extreme wind of 106 miles per hour was measured before the anemometer blew away. Peak wind gusts were estimated at 120 to 125 miles per hour. 40 known dead, 500 injured; damage $16,903,100. About 90 per cent of the citrus crop in the Lower Rio Grande Valley was destroyed.

July 25, 1934: **Hurricane.** Near **Seadrift,** Calhoun County, 19 lives lost, many minor injuries; damage $4,500,000. About 85 per cent of damage was in crops.

Sept. 15-18, 1936: **Rainstorm.** Excessive rains over the North Concho and Middle Concho Rivers caused a sharp rise in the Concho River which overflowed **San Angelo;** much of the business district and 500 homes were flooded. Four persons drowned and property losses estimated at $5,000,000. Four-day storm rainfall at San Angelo measured 25.19 inches, of which 11.75 inches fell on the 15th.

June 10, 1938: **Tornado.** Clyde, Callahan County; 14 killed, 9 injured; damage $85,000.

Sept. 23, 1941: **Hurricane.** Near **Matagorda.** Center moved inland near Matagorda, and passed over **Houston** about midnight. Extremely high tides along coast in the **Matagorda** to **Galveston** area. Heaviest property and crop losses were in counties from Matagorda County to the Sabine River. Four lives lost. Damage was $6,503,300.

April 28, 1942: **Tornado.** Crowell, Foard County; 11 killed, 250 injured; damage $1,500,000.

Aug. 30, 1942: **Hurricane. Matagorda Bay.** Highest wind estimated 115 miles per hour at **Seadrift.** Tide at **Matagorda,** 14.7 feet. Storm moved west-north-westward and finally diminished over the Edwards Plateau; 8 lives lost, property damage estimated at $11,500,000, and crop damage estimated at $15,000,000.

May 10, 1943: **Tornado. Laird Hill,** Rusk County, and **Kilgore,** Gregg County. Four killed, 25 injured; damage $1,000,000.

July 27, 1943: **Hurricane.** Near **Galveston.** Center moved inland across Bolivar Peninsula and Trinity Bay. A wind gust of 104 miles per hour was recorded at **Texas City;** 19 lives lost; damage estimated at $16,550,000.

Aug. 26-27, 1945: **Hurricane.** Aransas-San Antonio Bay area. At **Port O'Connor,** the wind reached 105 miles per hour when the cups were torn from the anemometer. Peak gusts of 135 miles per hour were estimated at **Seadrift, Port O'Connor** and **Port Lavaca;** 3 killed, 25 injured; damage $20,133,000.

Jan. 4, 1946: **Tornado.** Near **Lufkin,** Angelina County and **Nacogdoches,** Nacogdoches County; 13 killed, 250 injured; damage $2,050,000.

Jan. 4, 1946: **Tornado.** Near **Palestine,** Anderson County; 15 killed, 60 injured; damage $500,000.

May 18, 1946: **Tornado. Clay, Montague** and **Denton** Counties. Four killed, damage $112,000.

April 9, 1947: **Tornado, White Deer,** Carson County; **Glazier,** Hemphill County; and **Higgins,** Lipscomb County; 68 killed, 201 injured; damage $1,550,000. Glazier completely destroyed. One of the largest tornadoes on record. Width of path, 1½ miles at Higgins; length of path, 221 miles across portions of Texas, Oklahoma and Kansas. This tornado also struck **Woodward, Okla.**

EXTREME TEXAS WEATHER RECORDS

NOAA Environmental Data Service lists the following recorded extremes of weather in Texas:

TEMPERATURE

Lowest—Tulia, February 12, 1899			−23° F
Seminole, February 8, 1933.			−23° F
Highest—Seymour, August 12, 1936.			120° F
Coldest Winter			1898-1899

RAINFALL

Wettest year—entire state	1941	42.62 in.
Driest year—entire state	1917	14.30 in.
Greatest annual—Clarksville	1873	109.38 in.
Least annual—Wink	1956	1.76 in.
†Greatest in 24 hours—Thrall		
September 9-10, 1921		38.20 in.

SNOWFALL

Greatest seasonal—Romero 1923-1924.	65.0 in.
Greatest monthly—Hale Center	
February, 1956	36.0 in.
Greatest single storm—Hale Center	
Feb. 2-5, 1956	33.0 in.
Greatest in 24 Hours—Plainview	
Feb. 3-4, 1956	24.0 in.
Maximum depth on ground—Hale Center	
Feb. 5, 1956	33.0 in.

WIND VELOCITY

Highest sustained wind (fastest mile)			
*Matagorda—Sept. 11, 1961	SE	145 mph
*Port Lavaca—Sept. 11, 1961	NE	145 mph
Highest peak gust (instantaneous velocity)			
*Aransas Pass—Aug. 3, 1970 (est.)	SW	180 mph
*Robstown—Aug. 3, 1970 (est.)	WSW	180 mph

*These velocities occurred during hurricanes. Theoretically, much higher velocities are possible within the vortex of a tornado, but no measurement with an anemometer has ever been made. The U.S. Weather Bureau's experimental Doppler radar equipment, a device which permits direct measurement of the high speeds in a spinning tornado funnel, received its first big test in the Wichita Falls tornado of April 2, 1958. This was the first tornado tracked by the Doppler radar, and for the first time in history, rotating winds up to 280 mph were clocked.

†Greatest 24-hour rainfall ever recorded in Texas at an official observing site occurred at Albany (Shackelford County) on Aug. 4, 1978 — 29.05 inches.

TEXAS ANNUAL AVERAGE PRECIPITATION, 1892-1984

Source: State Climatologist for Texas

Year—	Inches	Year—	Inches
1892	26.32	1938	25.35
1893	18.50	1939	23.52
1894	25.61	1940	32.70
1895	29.83	**1941	42.62
1896	25.15	1942	30.68
1897	24.21	1943	24.28
1898	24.56	1944	34.08
1899	27.57	1945	30.06
1900	36.87	1946	35.16
1901	20.13	1947	24.75
1902	28.28	1948	21.79
1903	29.64	1949	35.08
1904	26.78	1950	24.48
1905	35.98	1951	21.99
1906	29.19	1952	23.27
1907	28.51	1953	24.76
1908	29.06	1954	19.03
1909	21.58	1955	23.59
1910	19.52	1956	16.17
1911	26.83	1957	36.93
1912	24.92	1958	32.71
1913	33.25	1959	31.29
1914	35.19	1960	33.78
1915	28.79	1961	30.20
1916	23.05	1962	24.05
*1917	14.30	1963	20.95
1918	26.03	1964	24.11
1919	42.15	1965	27.55
1920	29.90	1966	28.68
1921	25.18	1967	28.44
1922	29.83	1968	34.54
1923	37.24	1969	29.85
1924	22.32	1970	26.36
1925	25.37	1971	29.58
1926	32.97	1972	28.73
1927	24.32	1973	38.37
1928	27.56	1974	32.78
1929	29.47	1975	29.07
1930	28.44	1976	33.37
1931	28.37	1977	24.04
1932	32.76	1978	27.00
1933	26.15	1979	31.43
1934	25.59	1980	24.49
1935	35.80	1981	32.65
1936	30.32	1982	26.97
1937	25.89	1983	25.75
		1984	26.08

93-year mean 28.09 inches.
*Driest year, 1917.
**Wettest year, 1941.

May 3, 1948: **Tornado, McKinney,** Collin County; 3 killed, 43 injured; $2,000,000 damage.

May 15, 1949: **Tornado, Amarillo** and vicinity. Six killed, 83 injured. Total damage from tornado, wind and hail, $5,310,000. Total destrucion over one block by three block area in southern part of city; airport and 45 airplanes damaged; 28 railroad boxcars blown off track.

Oct. 3-4, 1949: **Hurricane, Freeport.** Maximum wind speed at Freeport estimated at 135 miles per hour. Maximum wind measured at the **Houston** airport, 90 miles per hour. Tide at Freeport reached 11.5 feet mean sea level; 2 killed; damage in Texas $6,500,000.

Sept. 8-10, 1952: **Rainstorm.** Heavy rains over the Colorado and Guadalupe River watersheds in southwestern Texas caused major flooding. From 23 to 26 inches fell between **Kerrville, Blanco** and **Boerne.** Highest stages ever known occurred in the Pedernales River; 5 lives lost, 3 injured; 17 homes destroyed, 454 damaged. Property loss several million dollars.

March 13, 1953: **Tornado. Jud** and **O'Brien,** Haskell County; and **Knox City,** Knox County; 17 killed, 25 injured; damage $600,000.

May 11, 1953: **Tornado.** Near **San Angelo,** Tom Green County. Eleven killed, 159 injured; damage $3,239,000.

May 11, 1953: **Tornado. Waco,** McLennan County; 114 killed, 597 injured; damage $41,150,000. One of two most disastrous tornadoes; 150 homes destroyed, 900 homes damaged; 185 other buildings destroyed; 500 other buildings damaged.

June 26-28, 1954: **Tropical Storm.** Hurricane Alice moved in from the Gulf south of **Brownsville** up the Rio Grande. Heaviest rains were in the **Langtry-Sheffield-Ozona** area, where as much as 27.10 inches of rain fell in 48 hours near **Pandale.** This resulted in the **greatest flood on the middle Rio Grande** since June, 1865. Rises of 50 to 60 feet, or 30 to 40 feet above flood stage, within 48 hours, occurred at **Eagle Pass** and at **Laredo.** An 86-foot wall of water in the Pecos River canyon washed out the highway bridge that had been erected 50 feet above the river. The international bridge at Laredo also was washed out. Most of the deaths and severe property damage were in Mexico.

Feb. 1-5, 1956: **Blizzard.** Northwestern Texas. On Feb. 1, a blizzard moved into the Panhandle and South Plains, disrupting all transportation. Snow and wind continued through Feb. 5. The snowfall was the heaviest on record in Texas. **Hale Center** received a total of 33.0 inches, Feb. 2-5, the greatest for a single storm. Twenty deaths.

March 22-25, 1957: **Blizzard.** Texas Panhandle. The storm caused heavy livestock losses. All transportation facilities halted and about 4,000 persons were marooned. Ten persons died.

April 2, 1957: **Tornado. Dallas,** Dallas County; 10 killed, 200 injured; damage $4,000,000. Moving through Oak Cliff and West Dallas, it damaged 574 buildings, largely homes.

April-May, 1957: **Torrential Rains.** Excessive flooding occurred throughout the area east of the Pecos River to the Sabine River during the last 10 days of April; 17 lives were lost, and several hundred homes were destroyed. During May, more than 4,000 persons were evacuated from unprotected lowlands on the West Fork of the Trinity above **Fort Worth** and along creeks in Fort Worth. Twenty-nine houses at **Christoval** were damaged or destroyed and 83 houses and furnishings at **San Angelo** were damaged. Five persons were drowned in floods in South Central Texas.

May 15, 1957: **Tornado. Silverton,** Briscoe County; 21 killed, 80 injured; damage $500,000.

June 27, 1957: **Hurricane Audrey.** Center crossed the Gulf coast near the Texas-Louisiana line. **Orange** was in the western portion of the eye between 9 and 10 a.m. In Texas, nine lives were lost, 450 persons injured; property damage was $8,000,000. Damage was extensive in Jefferson and Orange Counties, with less in Chambers and Galveston Counties. Maximum wind reported in Texas, 85 m.p.h. at Sabine Pass, with gusts to 100 m.p.h.

March 31, 1959: **Tornado. Vaughan** and **Bynum,** Hill County. Six killed, 31 injured; Vaughan was almost completely destroyed.

Oct. 28, 1960: **Rainstorm.** Rains of 7-10 inches fell in South Central Texas; 11 died from drowning in flash floods. In Austin about 300 families were driven from their homes. Damage in Austin was estimated at $2,500,000.

Sept. 8-14, 1961: **Hurricane Carla.** Port O'Connor; maximum wind gust at **Port Lavaca** estimated at 175 miles per hour. Highest tide was 18.5 feet at **Port Lavaca.**

Most damage was to coastal counties between **Corpus Christi** and **Port Arthur** and inland Jackson, Harris and Wharton Counties. In Texas, 34 persons died; 7 in a tornado that swept across Galveston Island; 465 persons were injured. Property and crop damage conservatively estimated at $300,000,000. The evacuation of an estimated 250,000 persons kept loss of life low. Hurricane Carla was the **largest hurricane** of record.

TEXAS DROUGHTS, 1892-1984

The following table shows the duration and extent of Texas droughts by major areas, 1892-1984. For this purpose, droughts are arbitrarily defined as when the division has less than 75 per cent of the 1931-1960 average precipitation. The 1931-60 average precipitation is shown at the bottom of the table for each area, in inches. A short table which follows shows the frequency of droughts in each area and the total years of droughts in the area. No climatic subdivision had less than 75 per cent of average rainfall in 1965, 1966, 1967, 1968, 1969, 1971, 1972, 1973, 1974, 1975, 1976, 1977, 1978, 1979, 1980, 1981, 1982, 1983 or 1984.

Year	High Plains	Low Rolling Plains	North Central	East Texas	Trans-Pecos	Edwards Plateau	South Central	Upper Coast	Southern	Lower Valley
1892					68			73		
1893			67	70		49	56	64	53	59
1894					68					
1897							73		72	
1898									69	51
1901		71	70			60	62	70	44	
1902									65	73
1907										65
1909			72	68	67	74	70			
1910	59	59	64	69	43	65	69	74	59	
1911										70
1916		73		74	70		73	69		
1917	58	50	63	59	44	46	42	50	32	48
1920										71
1921					72					73
1922					68					
1924			73	73		71		72		
1925			72				72			
1927									74	74
1933	72				62	68				
1934	66				46	69				
1937									72	
1939						69				72
1943			72							
1948			73	74	62		73	67		
1950						68			74	64
1951					61	53				
1952	68	66			73				56	70
1953	69				49	73				
1954	70	71	68	73		50	50	57	71	
1956	51	57	61	68	44	43	55	62	53	53
1962						68			67	65
1963			63	68		65	61	73		
1964	74				69					63
1970	65	63								

1931-1960 Normal (inches) — 18.51, 22.99, 32.93, 45.96, 12.03, 25.91, 33.24, 46.19, 22.33, 24.27.

1941-1970 Normal (inches) — 18.59, 23.18, 32.94, 45.37, 11.57, 23.94, 33.03, 46.43, 21.95, 23.44.

1951-1980 Normal (inches) — 17.73, 22.80, 32.14, 44.65, 11.65, 23.52, 34.03, 45.93, 22.91, 24.73.

DROUGHT FREQUENCY

This table shows the number of years of drought and the number of separate droughts. For example, the High Plains has had 10 drought years, consisting of five 1-year droughts, one 2-year drought and one 3-year drought, for a total of seven droughts.

Years	High Plains	Low Rolling Plains	North Central	East Texas	Trans-Pecos	Edwards Plateau	South Central	Upper Coast	Southern	Lower Valley
1	5	6	8	6	5	7	10	8	9	13
2	1	1	2	2	4	4	2	2	2	1
3	1				1					
Total Droughts	7	7	10	8	10	11	12	10	11	14
Drought Years	10	8	12	10	16	15	14	12	13	15

Sept. 7, 1962: **Rainstorm. Fort Worth.** Rains fell over the Big Fossil and Denton Creek watersheds ranging up to 11 inches of fall in three hours. Extensive damage from flash flooding occurred in **Richland Hills** and **Haltom City.**

Sept. 16-20, 1963: **Hurricane.** Rains of 15 to 23.5 inches fell in portions of Jefferson, Newton and Orange Counties when **Hurricane Cindy** became stationary west of **Port Arthur.** Flooding from the excessive rainfall resulted in total property damage of $11,600,000 and agricultural losses of $500,000.

April 3, 1964: **Tornado. Wichita Falls.** Seven killed, 111 injured; damage $15,000,000; 225 homes destroyed, 50 with major damage, and 200 with minor damage. Sixteen other buildings received major damage.

Sept. 21-23, 1964: **Rainstorm.** Collin, Dallas and Tarrant Counties. Rains of more than 12 inches fell during the first eight hours of the 21st. Flash flooding of tributaries of the Trinity River and smaller creeks and streams resulted in two drownings and an estimated $3,000,000 property damage. Flooding of homes occurred in all sections of **McKinney.** In **Fort Worth,** there was considerable damage to residences along Big Fossil and White Rock Creeks. Expensive homes in North Dallas were heavily damaged.

Jan. 25, 1965: **Duststorm.** West Texas. The worst duststorm since February, 1956, developed on the southern High Plains. Winds, gusting up to 75 miles per hour at **Lubbock,** sent dust billowing to 31,000 feet in the area from the Texas-New Mexico border eastward to a line from **Tulia** to **Abilene.** Ground visibility was reduced to about 100 yards in many sections. The worst hit was the **Muleshoe, Seminole, Plains, Morton** area on the South Plains. The rain gage at Reese Air Force Base, Lubbock, contained 3½ inches of fine sand.

June 2, 1965: **Tornado. Hale Center,** Hale County. Four killed, 76 injured; damage $8,000,000.

June 11, 1965: **Rainstorm. Sanderson,** Terrell County. Torrential rains of up to 8 inches in two hours near Sanderson caused a major flash flood that swept through the town. As a result, 26 persons drowned and property losses were estimated at $2,715,000.

April 22-29, 1966. Northeast Texas. Twenty to 26 inches of rain fell in portions of Wood, Smith, Morris, Upshur, Gregg, Marion and Harrison Counties. Nineteen persons drowned in the rampaging rivers and creeks that swept away bridges, roads and dams, and caused an estimated $12,000,000 damage.

April 28, 1966. Dallas County. Flash flooding from torrential rains in Dallas County resulted in 14 persons drowned and property losses estimated at $15,000,000.

Sept. 18-23, 1967. **Hurricane Beulah.** Near Brownsville. The third largest hurricane of record, Hurricane Beulah moved inland near the mouth of the Rio Grande on the 20th. Wind gusts of 136 miles per hour were reported during Beulah's passage. Rains 10 to 20 inches over much of the area south of San Antonio resulted in record-breaking floods. An unofficial gaging station at Falfurrias registered the highest accumulated rainfall, 36 inches. The resultant stream overflow and surface runoff inundated 1.4 million acres. Beulah spawned 115 tornadoes, all in Texas; the greatest number on record for any hurricane. Hurricane Beulah caused 13 deaths and 37 injuries, of which five deaths and 34 injuries were attributed to tornadoes. Property losses were estimated at $100 million and crop losses at $50 million.

There were no exceptionally destructive storms in Texas in 1968 and 1969.

April 18, 1970: **Tornado.** Near **Clarendon,** Donley County. Seventeen killed, 42 injured; damage $2,100,000. Fourteen persons were killed at a resort community at Green Belt Reservoir, 7½ miles north of Clarendon.

May 11, 1970: **Tornado. Lubbock,** Lubbock County. Twenty-six killed, 500 injured; damage $135,000,000, the costliest tornado in Texas history. Fifteen square miles, almost one-quarter of the city of Lubbock, suffered damage.

Aug. 3-5, 1970: **Hurricane Celia.** Corpus Christi. Hurricane Celia was a unique but severe storm. Measured in dollars, it was the costliest in the state's history. Sustained wind speeds reached 130 miles per hour, but it was great bursts of kinetic energy of short duration that appeared to cause the severe damage. Wind gusts of 161 miles per hour were measured at the Corpus Christi National Weather Service Office. At Aransas Pass, peak wind gusts were estimated as high as 180 miles per hour, after the wind equipment had been blown away. Celia caused 11 deaths in Texas, at least 466 injuries, and total property and crop damage in Texas estimated at $453,773,000. Hurricane Celia crossed the Texas coastline midway between Corpus Christi and Aransas Pass

about 3:30 p.m. CST on Aug. 3. Hardest hit was the metropolitan area of Corpus Christi, including Robstown, Aransas Pass, Port Aransas and small towns on the north side of Corpus Christi Bay.

Feb. 20-22, 1971. **Blizzard.** Panhandle. Paralyzing blizzard, worst since March 22-25, 1957, storm transformed Panhandle into one vast snowfield as 6 to 26 inches of snow were whipped by 40 to 60 miles per hour winds into drifts up to 12 feet high. At **Follett,** 3-day snowfall was 26 inches. Three persons killed; property and livestock losses were $3,100,000.

Sept. 9-13, 1971. **Hurricane Fern.** Coastal Bend. Ten to 26 inches of rain resulted in some of worst flooding since **Hurricane Beulah** in 1967. Two persons killed; losses were $30,231,000.

May 11-12, 1972. **Rainstorm.** South Central Texas. Seventeen drowned at New Braunfels, one at McQueeney. New Braunfels and Seguin hardest hit. Property damage $17,500,000.

June 12-13, 1973. **Rainstorm.** Southeastern Texas. Ten drowned. Over $50,000,000 in property and crop damage. From 10-15 inches of rain recorded.

Nov. 23-24, 1974. **Flash Flooding.** Central Texas. Over $1,000,000 in property damage. Thirteen people killed, ten in Travis County.

Jan. 31-Feb. 1, 1975: **Flooding.** Nacogdoches County. Widespread heavy rain caused flash flooding here, resulting in 3 deaths; damage over $5,500,000.

May 23, 1975: **Rainstorm.** Austin area. Heavy rains, high winds, and hail resulted in over $5,000,000 property damage; 40 people injured. Four deaths were caused by drowning.

June 15, 1976: **Rainstorm.** Harris County. Rains in excess of 13 inches caused damage estimated at near $25,000,000. Eight deaths were storm-related, including 3 drownings.

Jan. 8-9, 1977: **Icestorm.** North Central and Northeast Texas. Up to three inches of ice caused six deaths and extensive damage.

Mar. 27, 1977: **Flooding:** Tarrant, Somervell and Dallas Counties. Heavy rains were responsible for five drownings and over $1,000,000 damage.

Feb. 7-8, 1978: **Snow and icestorm:** Johnson, Ellis, Hill and Navarro Counties. Snow and ice-covered roads caused three traffic fatalities and widespread damage. Thousands of motorists were stranded on I-35 near Hillsboro.

April 22, 1978: **Hailstorm.** Texarkana. Hail up to 2¼ inches in diameter pelted Bowie County and accounted for over $15,000,000 damage to homes, businesses and vehicles.

May 26, 1978: **Flooding.** Canyon. Four people drowned and 15 others were injured as 10 inches of rain fell in less than two hours west of Canyon, sending a wall of water through **Palo Duro Canyon.**

July 2-19, 1978: **Heatwave.** Dallas and Tarrant Counties. Eighteen consecutive afternoons with temperatures of 100 degrees were responsible for 21 deaths and 53 injuries.

Aug. 1-4, 1978: **Heavy rains, flooding:** Edwards Plateau, Low Rolling Plain. Remnants of **Tropical Storm Amelia** caused some of the worst flooding of this century. As much as 30 inches of rain fell near **Albany** in Shackelford County, where six drownings were reported. **Bandera, Kerr, Kendall** and **Gillespie Counties** were hit hard, as 27 people drowned and the damage total was at least $50,000,000.

Dec. 30-31, 1978: **Icestorm.** North Central Texas. Possibly the worst **icestorm** in 30 years hit Dallas County particularly hard. Damage estimates reached $14,000,000 and six deaths were storm-related.

April 10, 1979: The worst single **tornado** in Texas' history hit **Wichita Falls.** Earlier on the same day, several tornadoes hit farther west. The destruction in Wichita Falls resulted in 42 dead, 1,740 injured, over 3,000 homes destroyed and damage of approximately $400 million. An estimated 20,000 persons were left homeless by this storm.

In all, the tornadoes on April 10 killed 53 people, injured 1,812 and caused over $500 million damages.

May 3, 1979: **Dallas County** was hit with a wave of the most destructive thunderstorms in many years; 37 injuries and $5 million in damages resulted.

July 24-25, 1979: Tropical storm **Claudette** caused over $750,000,000 in property and crop damage, but fortunately only few injuries. Near **Alvin,** 43 inches of rain fell, a new state record for 24 hours.

Aug. 24, 1979: One of the worst **hailstorms** in West Texas in the past 100 years; $200,000,000 in crops, mostly cotton, destroyed.

Sept. 18-20, 1979: Coastal flooding from heavy rain, 18 inches in 24 hours at **Aransas Pass**, and 13 inches at **Rockport**.

Aug. 9-11, 1980: **Hurricane Allen** hit South Texas and left 3 dead, causing $650,000,000-$750,000,000 in property and crop damages. Over 250,000 coastal residents had to be evacuated. The worst damage occurred along **Padre Island** and in **Corpus Christi**. Over 20 inches of rain fell in extreme South Texas, and 29 tornadoes occurred; one of the worst hurricane-related outbreaks.

Summer 1980: One of the hottest summers in Texas history.

Sept. 5-8, 1980: **Hurricane Danielle** brought rain and flooding both to Southeast and Central Texas. Seventeen inches of rain fell at **Port Arthur**, and 25 inches near **Junction**.

May 8, 1981: The **most destructive thunderstorm** ever in the United States occurred in Tarrant, Dallas and surrounding counties. Hail damage was estimated at $200 million.

May 24-25, 1981: Severe flooding in Austin claimed 13 lives, injured about 100 and caused $40 million in damages. Up to 5.5 inches of rain fell in one hour just west of the city.

Oct. 11-14, 1981: Record rains in North Central Texas caused by the remains of Pacific **Hurricane Norma**. Over 20 inches fell in some locations.

April 2, 1982: A tornado outbreak in Northeast Texas. The most severe **tornado struck Paris**; 10 people were killed, 170 injured and 1,000 left homeless. Over $50 million in damages resulted. A total of 7 tornadoes that day left 11 dead and 174 injured.

May 25, 1982: Golf ball-sized hail in **Monahans** did $8 million in damages.

May, 1982: Texas recorded 123 tornadoes, the most ever in May, and one less than the most recorded in any single month in the state. One death of 23 injuries occurred.

Tornadoes take a toll in human life and property damage in Texas during April and May.

Sept. 11, 1982: **Tropical Storm Chris**. The year's only tropical storm in Texas hit the coast near Port Arthur with 55 mph winds. Rainfall was minimal.

Dec. 24, 1982: Rains of up to 15 inches occurred in Southeast Texas.

Dec. 1982: **El Paso** recorded 18.2 inches of snow, the most in any month there.

Note: 1983/1984 destructive storms are given in Weather Highlights, 1983 and 1984.

PRECIPITATION (INCHES) 1983

	High Plains	Low Rolling Plains	North Central	East Texas	Trans-Pecos	Edwards Plateau	South Central	Upper Coast	Southern	Lower Valley
Jan	1.55	2.10	1.40	1.48	.84	1.55	1.88	3.21	.85	.80
Feb	1.07	.92	2.58	5.45	.47	1.36	3.22	5.64	2.52	4.63
Mar	.72	1.59	3.59	4.79	.46	1.93	4.49	4.01	1.36	1.10
Apr	.83	1.19	.65	1.01	.43	.38	.13	.39	.02	.00
May	2.13	3.13	5.81	8.12	.75	2.53	4.43	4.72	1.66	1.75
Jun	2.24	2.56	3.05	4.12	.90	3.34	3.10	4.69	2.68	2.14
July	.60	.86	1.63	2.43	.70	1.14	5.17	9.06	2.31	5.20
Aug	.54	.42	2.56	4.54	.90	1.24	2.97	8.14	1.98	1.94
Sept	.74	.69	1.15	2.72	1.11	.90	4.80	9.85	2.52	4.33
Oct	3.82	6.75	2.79	1.97	2.74	3.81	3.48	3.29	2.49	2.14
Nov	.79	1.36	2.22	3.81	.89	1.83	2.33	3.58	1.16	1.26
Dec.	.56	.63	.92	4.53	.09	.19	.90	2.98	.38	.70
Ann	15.59	22.20	28.35	44.92	10.28	20.20	36.90	59.56	19.93	25.99

TEMPERATURES 1983

	High Plains	Low Rolling Plains	North Central	East Texas	Trans-Pecos	Edwards Plateau	South Central	Upper Coast	Southern	Lower Valley
Jan	35.2	40.2	43.4	44.6	44.3	45.4	50.2	51.3	52.5	57.4
Feb	39.8	44.6	47.7	48.8	49.7	49.9	53.5	54.3	56.7	62.0
Mar	47.8	52.1	54.1	54.8	56.4	57.1	59.9	59.4	63.6	68.0
April	52.6	57.9	60.5	60.3	60.4	63.5	66.1	64.9	70.7	72.4
May	64.0	68.7	69.8	69.8	72.1	73.3	74.4	73.7	79.0	79.0
June	72.1	74.9	76.0	76.3	78.8	77.4	79.6	79.4	82.7	83.6
July	80.5	83.2	82.4	81.2	82.7	82.6	82.6	82.5	85.1	84.5
Aug	81.2	85.2	84.3	82.6	81.7	83.2	83.8	83.0	86.3	85.3
Sept	74.1	77.3	77.0	75.5	77.8	78.0	78.4	77.3	81.2	81.6
Oct	62.0	66.3	67.9	67.0	67.4	69.2	71.7	71.3	74.2	75.8
Nov	50.1	54.9	57.9	57.6	56.0	58.9	64.3	64.3	66.7	70.7
Dec	28.4	31.4	35.3	38.6	43.5	39.5	45.2	47.5	47.9	53.3
Ann	57.3	61.4	63.0	63.1	64.2	64.8	67.5	67.4	70.6	72.8

PRECIPITATION (INCHES) 1984

	High Plains	Low Rolling Plains	North Central	East Texas	Trans-Pecos	Edwards Plateau	South Central	Upper Coast	Southern	Lower Valley
Jan	.31	.48	1.14	2.06	.65	1.56	3.15	4.39	2.18	4.00
Feb	.33	.81	1.89	4.26	.04	.37	1.29	2.42	.41	.80
Mar	.95	.86	3.58	3.96	.11	.61	1.52	1.53	.43	.13
Apr	.93	.48	.99	1.22	.00	.24	.27	.37	.14	.05
May	1.06	.82	2.47	3.98	1.69	1.42	2.24	4.78	2.59	3.18
Jun	3.64	2.01	2.68	2.96	3.47	1.60	1.55	1.51	1.05	1.38
July	1.49	1.35	1.46	2.28	.97	1.38	2.05	3.69	1.10	1.61
Aug	3.32	2.73	1.61	1.96	2.04	0.77	1.54	3.76	.69	.99
Sept	.98	1.43	1.47	2.55	1.45	2.06	1.99	5.46	2.05	12.65
Oct	2.86	3.23	8.18	12.25	2.69	4.88	8.02	13.33	4.70	1.37
Nov	1.43	2.48	2.67	3.95	1.16	1.69	1.84	3.08	1.01	.19
Dec	1.51	3.41	4.80	3.48	1.28	3.74	3.29	2.66	1.86	1.85
Ann	18.81	20.09	32.94	44.91	15.55	20.32	28.75	46.98	18.21	28.20

TEMPERATURES 1984

	High Plains	Low Rolling Plains	North Central	East Texas	Trans-Pecos	Edwards Plateau	South Central	Upper Coast	Southern	Lower Valley
Jan	34.7	38.5	40.0	40.9	43.0	42.3	48.0	48.1	50.0	53.6
Feb	43.1	47.9	50.7	50.7	48.7	51.1	55.8	55.7	58.9	62.0
Mar	46.8	52.2	56.8	57.1	56.9	59.6	63.7	62.3	68.2	69.9
April	54.7	60.6	64.1	64.6	64.6	67.0	70.9	69.4	75.7	76.8
May	68.3	73.4	74.2	72.8	74.9	76.0	76.6	75.5	79.7	79.1
June	76.2	82.0	81.2	79.3	78.6	81.5	81.6	80.5	84.0	82.8
July	78.1	83.1	84.0	82.0	80.4	82.6	83.9	82.6	85.7	84.2
Aug	77.3	82.4	84.4	82.5	80.0	83.0	84.0	82.5	86.1	84.8
Sept	68.4	72.4	75.1	75.0	72.8	74.7	78.0	77.1	79.7	78.9
Oct	56.9	61.7	66.1	68.3	62.9	66.3	72.8	74.0	74.6	78.1
Nov	47.7	51.8	54.5	55.3	52.9	55.2	61.3	61.8	63.0	67.9
Dec	41.6	46.2	52.5	57.4	49.8	54.1	61.7	63.6	63.1	68.3
Ann	57.8	62.7	65.3	65.5	63.8	66.1	69.9	69.4	72.4	73.9

Texas' Record Cold Wave

The "Winter of '99" was long remembered by Texans. It brought the most intense cold wave on record throughout the state on Feb. 11-12-13, 1899.

Minimum temperatures ranged from 6 to 23 degrees below zero over the northern portion of the state to about 12 above over the southern portion. Lowest temperatures occurred on the morning of Feb. 12 except at a few locations where the minimum was observed the next day. The Weather Bureau Office at Galveston recorded a temperature of 7.5 degrees, the lowest of record since the opening of this station in 1871. The next morning, Galveston Bay was covered over with thin ice except in the main channel or tide current.

The lowest temperature ever recorded in Texas (−23 degrees) occurred at Tulia on Feb. 12 — a record which was later equalled at Seminole on Feb. 8, 1933.

Winter weather hit Texas early in February, 1899. Cold Polar Canadian air entered Texas Feb. 4, reaching Central Texas on Feb. 6. Temperatures moderated a little, in advance of a second surge of cold air that entered the Texas Panhandle during the early morning of Feb. 8. As this mass of cold air reached Brownsville at about 6 a.m. on Feb. 10, the third and most frigid mass of Polar Canadian air was poised over Alberta and Saskatchewan ready to plunge southward. This chilling outbreak reached Texas very early in the morning of Feb. 11, and by 7 a.m. the next day, was centered over portions of Northwest Texas, Oklahoma and Kansas. By now, the leading edge of the air mass had plunged as far south as the Isthmus of Tehuantepec in southern Mexico. By Feb. 13, the air mass was centered over the Texas coast, while the cold front (the leading edge of the air mass) had reached San Salvador in Central America. The highest barometric pressure (reduced to sea level) recorded in Texas during the cold wave was 31.06 inches of mercury (1051.8 millibars) at Abilene. At Galveston, the highest barometric pressure recorded was 30.73 inches (1040.6 millibars).

Minimum temperatures recorded at existing stations in Texas counties on Feb. 12, 1899, included: −16 degrees in Potter County, −23 in Swisher, −14 in Crosby, −10 in Knox, −12 in Cooke, Montague, Denton and Fisher Counties; −10 in Dallas and Hopkins, −11 in Collin and Parker, −9 in Harrison, Ellis and Erath, −8 in Hale and Tarrant.

Temperatures of zero or several degrees below were registered through Central Texas, while Feb. 13 brought such readings as 11 above zero in Nueces County, 5 in Webb County, 8 in Jefferson County and 12 at the tip of Texas in Cameron County.

HOW COLD DOES IT FEEL?

Many factors enter into the feeling of coolness or extreme cold, the temperature and wind speed being most important. The following simplified table is based upon more complex "Wind-Chill" indexes available from the U.S. Army and National Oceanic and Atmospheric Administration (National Weather Service).

Thermometer readings are listed in the figures across the top of the chart; the wind speeds are shown down the left side. To determine how chilly it really is, get the proper column for each. Note the figure where they cross.

Thus, a 20-degree temperature with a 20-mile-an-hour wind is equal in chill to 10 degrees below zero. A temperature of 10 degrees with a 15 mph wind is equal to 18 below.

A 10-mile-an-hour wind sets twigs dancing in the trees. A 25-mile-an-hour wind sets big branches moving, and if the temperature is even cool, it sets teeth chattering.

A chill-effect of anything below 25 below zero creates the danger of freezing for persons not properly clothed.

Estimated Wind Speed MPH	ACTUAL THERMOMETER READING						
	50	40	30	20	10	0	−10
	EQUIVALENT TEMPERATURE						
Calm	50	40	30	20	10	0	−10
5	48	37	27	16	6	−5	−15
10	40	28	16	4	−9	−21	−33
15	36	22	9	−5	−18	−36	−45
20	32	18	4	−10	−25	−39	−53
25	30	16	0	−15	−29	−44	−59
30	28	13	−2	−18	−33	−48	−63
35	27	11	−4	−20	−35	−49	−67
40	26	10	−6	−21	−37	−53	−69

Tornadoes

An average of 109 tornadoes touch Texas soil each year. The annual total varies considerably, and certain areas are struck more often than others. Tornadoes occur with greatest frequency in the Red River Valley.

While tornadoes may occur in any month, and at any hour of the day, they occur with greatest frequency during the late spring and early summer months, and between the hours of 4 p.m. and 8 p.m. In the period 1951-1984, nearly 39 percent of all Texas tornadoes occurred within the 3-month period of April, May and June. Slightly more than one-fourth of the total occurred in May.

Partly due to the state's size, more tornadoes have been recorded in Texas than in any other state. Between 1951 and 1984, 4,031 funnel clouds reached the ground, thus becoming tornadoes. In the density of tornadoes, Texas ranks eleventh among the 50 states, with an average of 3.9 tornadoes per 10,000 square miles per year during this period.

The greatest outbreak of tornadoes on record in Texas was associated with Hurricane Beulah in September 1967; 115 tornadoes, all in Texas, are known to have occurred with this great hurricane within a 5-day period, Sept. 19-23. Sixty-seven occurred on Sept. 20, a Texas record for a single day. As a result of Hurricane Beulah, September 1967, had 124 tornadoes, a Texas record for a single month. The greatest number in Texas in a single year was 232, also in 1967. The second-highest number in a single year was in 1982, when 203 tornadoes occurred in Texas, 123 of them in May, making it the worst outbreak of spring tornadoes in Texas.

An accompanying table, compiled by Environmental Data Service, National Oceanic and Atmospheric Administration, lists tornado occurrences in Texas, by months, for the period 1951-1984.

NUMBER TEXAS TORNADOES 1951-1984

Source: State Climatologist for Texas

Year	Jan.	Feb.	Mar.	April	May	June	July	Aug.	Sept.	Oct.	Nov.	Dec.	Annual
1951...	0	0	1	1	5	7	1	0	0	0	0	0	15
1952...	0	1	3	4	2	1	0	1	0	0	0	1	13
1953...	0	2	2	3	6	2	3	5	0	2	1	6	32
1954...	0	3	1	23	21	14	5	1	4	5	0	0	77
1955...	0	0	7	15	42	32	1	5	2	0	0	0	104
1956...	0	3	5	3	17	5	6	4	2	9	2	0	56
1957...	0	1	21	69	33	5	0	3	2	6	5	0	145
1958...	2	0	7	12	15	13	10	7	0	0	8	0	74
1959...	0	0	8	4	32	14	10	3	4	5	6	0	86
1960...	4	1	0	8	29	14	3	4	2	11	1	0	77
1961...	0	1	21	15	24	30	9	2	12	0	10	0	124
1962...	0	4	12	9	25	56	12	15	7	2	0	1	143
1963...	0	0	3	9	19	24	8	4	6	4	5	0	82
1964...	0	1	6	22	15	11	9	7	3	1	3	0	78
1965...	2	5	3	7	43	24	2	9	4	6	0	3	108
1966...	0	4	1	21	22	15	3	8	3	0	0	0	77
1967...	0	2	11	17	34	22	10	5	124	2	0	5	232
1968...	2	1	3	13	47	21	4	8	5	8	11	16	139
1969...	0	1	1	16	65	16	6	7	6	8	1	0	127
1970...	1	3	5	23	23	9	5	20	9	20	0	3	121
1971...	0	20	10	24	27	33	7	20	7	16	4	23	191
1972...	1	0	19	13	43	12	19	13	8	9	7	0	144
1973...	14	1	29	25	21	24	4	8	5	3	9	4	147
1974...	2	1	8	19	18	26	3	9	6	22	2	0	116
1975...	5	2	9	12	50	18	10	3	3	3	1	1	117
1976...	1	1	8	53	63	11	16	6	13	4	0	0	176
1977...	0	0	3	34	50	4	5	5	12	0	6	4	123
1978...	0	0	0	34	65	10	13	6	6	1	2	0	137
1979...	1	2	24	33	39	14	12	10	4	15	3	0	157
1980...	0	2	7	26	44	21	2	34	10	5	0	2	153
1981...	0	7	7	9	71	26	5	20	5	23	3	0	176
1982...	0	0	6	27	123	36	4	0	3	0	3	1	203
1983...	5	7	24	1	62	35	4	22	5	0	7	14	186
1984...	0	13	9	18	19	19	0	4	1	5	2	5	95
Total..	40	89	284	622	1,214	624	211	278	283	195	102	89	4,031

TEXAS TEMPERATURE, FREEZE, GROWING SEASON AND PRECIPITATION RECORDS, BY COUNTIES

Data in the table below are from the office of the State Climatologist for Texas, College Station. Because of the small change in averages, data are revised only at intervals of several years. Data below are the latest compilations, as of Jan. 1, 1985.

Table shows temperature, freeze, growing season and precipitation for each county in Texas. Data for counties where a National Weather Service Station has not been maintained long enough to establish a reliable mean are interpolated from isoline charts prepared from mean values from stations with long-established records. Mean maximum temperature for July is computed from the sum of the daily maxima. Mean minimum January is computed from the sum of the daily minima. Mean monthly temperature for July is the sum of mean maximum and mean minimum (for July) divided by 2. For stations where precipitation "Length of Record" has been left blank, data are based on the 30-year normal period 1941-70. Stations which have a specified precipitation "Length of Record" are based on data mainly from the period 1931-60.

County and Station	Temperature — Length of record (Yr.)	July Mean Max (°F.)	January Mean Min. (°F.)	Record Highest (°F.)	Record Lowest (°F.)	Avg. Freeze — Last in Spring	First in Fall	Growing Season (Days)	Precip. Length of Record (Yr.)	Jan. (In.)	Feb. (In.)	Mar. (In.)	Apr. (In.)	May (In.)	June (In.)	July (In.)	Aug. (In.)	Sept. (In.)	Oct. (In.)	Nov. (In.)	Dec. (In.)	Annual (In.)
Anderson, Palestine	82	94	37	114	-6	Mar. 8	Nov. 27	264	11	3.32	3.16	3.42	4.31	5.09	3.36	1.96	2.51	3.34	3.16	3.26	3.62	40.51
‡Andrews, Andrews	14	96	30	106	0	Apr. 6	Nov. 5	213	11	0.70	0.49	0.42	0.89	2.15	1.40	1.90	1.50	1.82	2.05	0.44	0.61	14.37
Angelina, Lufkin	65	94	39	110	-2	Mar. 14	Nov. 13	244	14	3.73	3.64	3.65	4.53	5.09	3.24	3.00	2.53	4.80	2.97	1.85	4.04	42.99
Aransas, Rockport	17	90	48	100	10	Feb. 7	Dec. 16	312	14	3.00	2.12	1.87	2.90	3.20	2.60	3.00	3.50	4.80	2.90	1.85	2.35	33.19
‡Archer, Archer City	12	98	28	112	4	Mar. 31	Dec. 16	220	31	1.24	1.48	1.87	2.12	3.20	2.87	1.94	1.58	2.93	2.93	1.47	1.49	25.26
‡Armstrong, Claude	14	97	19	105	-9	Apr. 6	Nov. 5	213	8	0.68	0.64	0.83	1.45	3.50	2.90	2.40	2.45	1.85	1.85	0.83	0.10	19.98
Atascosa, Poteet	34	97	42	110	-1	Feb. 26	Dec. 3	282	—	1.53	2.12	2.49	2.74	3.50	2.69	2.40	1.83	3.88	2.52	1.61	1.38	26.58
Austin, Sealy	50	95	44	110	-2	Feb. 26	Dec. 6	282	—	3.10	3.34	2.49	3.80	4.65	4.21	3.00	3.31	3.88	3.75	3.00	3.51	47.04
Bailey, Muleshoe	48	92	20	105	-21	Apr. 22	Oct. 20	181	—	0.55	0.47	0.47	0.93	2.42	2.65	3.00	2.10	2.91	1.67	0.52	0.52	17.29
‡Bandera, Medina	11	94	32	105	9	Mar. 26	Nov. 16	235	10	1.69	1.77	1.68	2.65	4.20	3.02	2.35	2.00	3.70	2.60	1.28	1.88	28.82
Bastrop, Smithville	52	96	40	111	-14	Mar. 6	Nov. 29	268	—	2.54	3.01	2.16	4.12	4.07	3.66	2.18	2.59	4.37	2.94	2.78	2.40	36.82
Baylor, Seymour	50	98	28	120	-14	Apr. 3	Nov. 3	214	—	1.11	1.31	1.31	2.38	3.40	3.40	2.56	2.04	3.11	2.67	1.29	1.15	26.36
Bee, Beeville	78	95	45	111	-4	Feb. 22	Dec. 4	285	—	1.67	2.01	1.40	2.57	3.53	2.76	2.33	2.32	4.12	2.76	1.79	1.64	28.90
Bell, Temple	84	96	37	112	-1	Mar. 11	Nov. 24	258	—	2.39	2.82	2.01	3.94	4.87	2.98	2.22	2.21	4.26	2.89	1.79	2.42	34.00
‡Bexar, San Antonio	91	94	42	107	0	Mar. 6	Nov. 26	265	—	1.66	2.06	1.54	2.54	4.20	3.07	1.69	2.41	3.71	2.84	1.77	1.46	27.54
Blanco, Blanco	74	96	36	110	-6	Mar. 26	Nov. 15	234	—	2.12	3.00	1.54	3.55	3.98	2.90	1.99	2.21	4.65	3.60	2.09	2.20	34.39
‡Borden, Gail	13	96	36	106	-3	Apr. 6	Nov. 6	214	37	0.75	0.67	0.67	1.38	2.85	3.02	2.40	1.60	2.15	2.05	0.78	0.82	18.20
Bosque, Whitney Dam	26	96	36	111	-3	Mar. 23	Nov. 21	243	25	2.43	2.57	2.57	4.08	3.00	3.00	2.20	1.70	2.95	2.51	2.31	2.71	33.20
Bowie, Texarkana Dam	13	95	35	107	10	Mar. 21	Nov. 11	235	25	4.50	4.04	4.50	5.20	5.00	3.45	3.55	3.05	2.95	3.00	2.71	4.50	47.59
Brazoria, Angleton	61	91	46	110	10	Mar. 5	Nov. 28	268	—	3.66	3.93	3.18	3.31	4.48	5.01	4.96	5.20	5.98	4.02	3.89	4.55	52.17
Brazos, College Station	24	95	42	110	-3	Mar. 1	Nov. 30	274	—	2.56	3.13	2.62	4.15	4.37	3.64	2.75	2.63	2.80	3.02	3.15	3.23	39.21
‡Brewster, Alpine	45	89	32	106	-9	Mar. 31	Nov. 9	223	—	0.74	0.38	0.35	0.49	1.18	2.59	2.72	2.50	2.23	1.33	0.52	0.52	15.53
‡Briscoe, Silverton	14	94	26	103	-9	Apr. 6	Nov. 6	214	—	0.72	0.58	0.58	1.46	3.16	3.67	2.62	2.42	2.23	1.67	0.61	0.75	20.50
Brooks, Falfurrias	68	96	48	112	-2	Feb. 10	Dec. 10	303	—	1.46	1.44	0.81	1.68	3.16	2.51	1.17	2.48	4.93	2.40	0.98	1.16	24.18
Brown, Brownwood	82	96	33	113	-2	Mar. 22	Nov. 19	242	—	1.69	1.88	1.68	3.05	4.20	3.13	1.60	1.48	3.70	2.83	1.38	1.39	27.42
‡Burleson, Somerville	11	94	38	105	11	Mar. 1	Dec. 1	275	7	3.00	3.05	2.62	3.58	4.20	3.25	2.75	2.60	2.80	2.80	3.30	3.50	37.45
Burnet, Burnet	81	96	37	114	-3	Mar. 29	Nov. 14	230	—	1.87	2.16	1.91	3.48	3.99	2.61	1.46	1.78	3.61	3.25	1.89	1.80	29.81
‡Caldwell, Luling	88	96	41	110	-3	Feb. 27	Nov. 29	275	—	2.03	2.62	1.97	3.73	3.56	3.91	1.78	2.08	4.50	2.88	2.28	1.91	32.65
Calhoun, Port Lavaca	35	92	47	107	3	Feb. 19	Dec. 16	300	32	2.90	2.65	2.35	3.20	3.45	2.75	1.81	3.00	4.50	3.35	2.38	2.80	36.83
‡Callahan, Putnam	13	96	33	110	3	Mar. 28	Nov. 11	228	—	1.34	1.15	1.30	2.72	4.48	2.68	1.64	1.99	5.98	2.74	1.45	1.10	24.92
Cameron, Harlingen	60	95	51	108	21	Feb. 4	Dec. 12	341	—	1.44	1.37	0.84	1.51	2.99	2.38	1.40	2.99	4.67	2.95	1.47	1.12	25.13
‡Camp, Pittsburg (near)	55	95	36	—	—	Mar. 21	Nov. 14	238	33	4.00	3.70	4.00	4.85	4.25	3.25	2.82	2.55	1.86	3.10	4.40	4.40	45.25
‡Carson, Panhandle	14	93	21	109	-10	Apr. 17	Oct. 25	191	—	0.61	0.66	0.90	1.18	3.20	3.67	2.82	2.72	1.86	1.90	0.64	0.76	20.92
‡Cass, Linden	7	92	31	103	0	Apr. 10	Nov. 11	237	32	4.40	4.00	4.50	5.00	3.63	3.25	2.95	2.95	4.93	4.30	4.60	4.60	46.90
‡Castro, Dimmitt	14	93	22	104	-8	Apr. 16	Oct. 26	193	—	0.46	0.47	0.66	1.04	2.17	3.11	2.78	2.08	1.83	1.95	0.53	0.64	17.72
Chambers, Anahuac (near)	44	91	44	110	11	Mar. 5	Nov. 21	261	30	3.94	3.85	2.83	4.15	4.62	4.67	5.87	5.32	5.27	4.04	4.13	4.65	52.84
Cherokee, Rusk	33	94	38	107	-11	Mar. 8	Nov. 21	258	—	4.00	3.79	4.31	4.30	5.00	3.00	5.00	2.80	4.64	3.10	4.70	4.70	44.26
Childress, Childress	60	98	26	115	-13	Apr. 3	Nov. 6	217	—	0.78	0.82	1.07	1.95	3.54	3.06	1.78	1.89	3.57	2.06	0.70	0.85	20.67
Clay, Henrietta	78	98	30	116	-6	Apr. 27	Nov. 14	232	—	1.37	1.59	1.30	3.35	4.87	3.73	2.13	2.00	2.33	3.33	1.72	1.61	31.40
‡Cochran, Morton	14	92	23	105	-12	Apr. 18	Oct. 24	189	26	0.60	0.39	0.40	0.89	2.45	1.90	2.37	2.00	2.10	1.85	0.30	0.37	15.62

*Growing Season

Texas Temperature, Frost, Growing Season and Precipitation Records, by Counties. — (continued.)

County and Station	Length of Record (Temp) Yr.	July Mean Max °F.	January Mean Min °F.	Record Highest °F.	Record Lowest °F.	Last in Spring	First in Fall	Growing Season Days	Length of Record (Precip) Yr.	January In.	February In.	March In.	April In.	May In.	June In.	July In.	August In.	September In.	October In.	November In.	December In.	Annual In.
Coke, Robert Lee	14	97	29	109	5	Mar. 31	Nov. 12	226	32	0.94	0.92	1.05	1.92	3.45	2.10	2.00	1.38	2.60	2.10	0.90	1.12	20.48
Coleman, Coleman	84	96	34	114	-6	Mar. 26	Nov. 16	235		1.62	1.26	1.26	2.86	4.27	2.89	1.86	2.09	3.35	2.54	1.51	1.27	26.82
Collin, McKinney	59	96	34	118	-7	Mar. 26	Nov. 11	230	25	2.15	2.61	3.16	4.82	5.17	3.68	2.54	2.18	3.99	3.01	2.64	2.15	38.10
Collingsworth, Wellington	16	96	34	110	3	Apr. 1	Nov. 3	212		0.77	1.05	1.05	2.05	4.30	3.05	2.10	2.05	2.10	2.15	0.63	0.99	22.03
Colorado, Columbus	14	86	39	106	13	Mar. 1	Dec. 6	280		2.78	3.55	2.53	4.24	4.58	4.01	2.59	3.14	4.43	3.23	3.02	3.22	41.32
Comal, New Braunfels	89	96	40	110	2	Mar. 6	Nov. 26	265	12	2.13	2.73	1.91	3.00	3.92	3.29	1.83	2.47	3.93	3.50	2.42	2.42	33.19
Comanche, Proctor Reservoir	95	95	33	108	0	Mar. 27	Nov. 20	238		1.90	1.68	1.68	3.12	4.45	1.95	2.09	1.44	2.74	2.73	1.74	1.80	28.45
Concho, Paint Rock	13	96	35	109	9	Mar. 29	Nov. 12	228		1.31	1.07	1.21	2.40	3.69	1.95	1.42	1.93	2.97	2.23	1.09	1.01	22.28
Cooke, Gainesville	85	96	36	112	5	Mar. 27	Nov. 8	226		1.78	2.58	2.58	3.90	4.76	3.82	2.12	2.34	3.59	2.95	2.05	1.80	33.88
Coryell, Gatesville	59	96	36	112	-6	Mar. 25	Nov. 21	241		2.12	2.73	2.22	3.65	4.62	2.94	1.55	2.09	3.30	3.02	2.17	2.11	32.58
Cottle, Paducah	14	97	27	111	-4	Apr. 2	Nov. 7	219	11	0.76	0.58	1.00	1.96	3.68	1.39	2.13	1.83	2.27	1.50	0.85	0.98	22.12
Crane, Crane	25	96	27	112	1	Mar. 31	Nov. 1	225		0.85	0.80	0.36	0.80	1.83	1.50	1.70	1.20	1.65	1.60	0.35	0.65	12.97
Crockett, Ozona	64	95	38	108	-8	Mar. 26	Nov. 14	233	32	0.82	0.80	0.46	1.12	2.50	2.00	1.55	1.10	1.60	2.55	0.56	0.72	14.90
Crosby, Crosbyton	33	95	26	108	-14	Apr. 10	Nov. 2	206		0.73	0.29	0.99	1.47	3.33	2.63	2.55	1.93	2.44	0.97	0.82	0.86	21.01
Culberson, Van Horn		93	30	108	-17	Apr. 1	Nov. 11	224		0.54	0.29	0.24	0.35	0.59	0.92	1.75	1.82	1.70	0.97	0.54	0.51	10.22
Dallam, Dalhart	28	95	19	107	-21	Apr. 23	Oct. 18	178		0.36	0.48	0.73	1.44	2.78	3.24	3.24	2.53	1.48	3.18	0.40	0.45	17.38
Dallas, Dallas	95	95	36	115	-10	Mar. 23	Nov. 13	235		1.96	2.57	3.04	4.72	4.85	3.27	1.80	2.36	3.25	1.94	2.60	2.34	35.94
Dawson, Lamesa	48	94	22	111	-6	Apr. 20	Nov. 6	212		0.65	0.38	0.78	1.00	2.39	2.07	2.07	2.22	2.33	1.94	0.67	0.59	16.09
Deaf Smith, Hereford	44	94	22	111	-17	Apr. 25	Oct. 22	185		0.46	0.49	0.60	1.13	2.35	2.86	2.65	2.25	1.63	2.52	0.45	0.59	17.37
Delta, Cooper		96	34			Mar. 27	Nov. 13	233	28	3.20	3.40	3.70	4.80	5.40	4.10	3.30	3.22	3.05	3.30	3.55	3.40	43.67
Denton, Denton	61	96	34	109	-3	Mar. 27	Nov. 8	226		1.57	2.35	2.55	3.12	4.90	3.30	1.88	1.99	3.79	2.52	2.19	2.01	33.29
De Witt, Cuero	22	95	44	109	5	Mar. 3	Nov. 29	270		2.05	2.46	1.52	3.12	4.07	3.28	2.34	2.62	4.25	3.30	2.29	2.07	33.37
Dickens, Dickens	20	96	30	114	9	Apr. 4	Nov. 7	217	11	0.69	1.16	0.71	1.91	3.03	2.60	2.22	2.60	2.53	2.52	0.84	0.91	20.24
Dimmit, Carrizo Springs	49	96	42	110	13	Feb. 19	Dec. 6	290		0.86	0.79	0.79	1.91	3.41	2.18	1.21	2.34	3.32	2.15	0.94	0.86	21.50
Donley, Clarendon	20	97	26	117	-11	Apr. 9	Nov. 1	206	21	0.72	0.86	0.86	1.85	3.85	1.63	2.30	3.00	1.95	2.15	0.58	0.90	20.74
Duval, Freer	14	96	42	109	12	Feb. 16	Dec. 11	298	32	1.40	1.35	1.00	1.85	3.05	2.44	1.62	2.10	3.65	2.20	0.99	1.50	23.15
Eastland, Eastland	66	96	30	115	-5	Mar. 27	Nov. 11	229		1.58	1.52	1.51	3.09	4.05	2.64	1.86	2.11	2.78	2.94	1.62	1.39	27.09
Ector, Penwell	13	96	38	107	3	Apr. 1	Nov. 6	217	31	0.80	0.34	0.34	0.83	2.00	1.55	1.85	1.45	1.75	2.15	0.40	0.65	13.77
Edwards, Rocksprings	37	96	33	107	-9	Mar. 16	Nov. 21	250	40	0.99	1.12	1.00	1.85	3.13	2.80	1.88	1.80	2.62	2.15	0.80	1.05	21.19
Ellis, Waxahachie	21	94	42			Mar. 20	Nov. 21	246		2.02	2.38	2.38	4.36	4.83	3.33	1.94	3.11	3.60	2.88	2.53	2.53	35.95
El Paso, El Paso	98	96	32	109	-8	Mar. 9	Nov. 12	248		0.39	0.42	0.39	0.24	0.32	0.60	1.53	1.12	1.16	0.78	0.32	0.50	7.77
Erath, Dublin	74	96	34	114	9	Mar. 27	Nov. 19	238		1.89	2.09	1.78	3.12	4.79	3.16	2.12	2.13	3.47	2.93	1.99	1.64	31.24
Falls, Marlin	31	94	38	112	7	Mar. 13	Nov. 25	257		2.42	2.73	2.60	3.99	5.62	4.54	1.47	2.13	3.18	2.93	2.96	2.81	35.34
Fannin, Bonham	31	96	33	112	-7	Mar. 27	Nov. 10	228		2.11	3.06	3.52	5.26	4.93	3.80	3.01	2.17	4.52	2.88	2.92	2.53	43.62
Fayette, Flatonia	67	98	42	111	4	Mar. 2	Dec. 2	277	25	2.11	3.06	1.94	4.90	4.03	3.45	2.09	2.17	4.53	2.88	2.58	2.53	35.67
Fisher, Rotan	36	94	31	111	3	Apr. 2	Nov. 6	218		0.89	0.90	0.96	1.86	3.79	2.71	1.91	1.56	2.36	2.35	1.01	0.91	21.21
Floyd, Floydada	26	98	26	109	-9	Apr. 7	Nov. 9	213	7	0.85	1.05	0.76	2.12	3.35	2.83	2.50	1.78	2.25	2.71	0.60	0.88	20.18
Foard, Crowell	70	94	28		6	Apr. 14	Nov. 7	219		0.96	1.25	1.06	2.63	4.33	2.83	2.50	1.78	2.63	2.71	1.09	0.98	23.93
Fort Bend, Sugar Land	10	94	35	108	10	Feb. 23	Dec. 14	296	31	3.33	3.61	2.47	3.83	4.69	3.71	3.71	3.98	4.27	3.20	3.96	3.63	45.07
Franklin, Mount Vernon		94	36	105		Mar. 23	Nov. 12	234	49	3.70	3.58	3.90	4.90	5.25	3.45	3.50	2.60	3.20	3.20	3.90	3.90	44.78
Freestone, Fairfield	58	98	36	109	8	Mar. 11	Dec. 11	263		3.20	3.13	3.05	4.24	4.90	3.10	2.20	2.25	3.10	2.75	3.35	3.60	38.53
Frio, Dilley	42	98	42	111		Feb. 23	Dec. 8	281		1.23	0.89	0.89	2.30	3.37	2.73	1.41	3.45	2.99	2.35	1.25	1.18	23.36
Gaines, Seminole	104	94	26	113	8	Apr. 8	Nov. 8	210		0.55	0.60	0.59	1.07	2.40	1.62	1.91	1.90	2.04	2.00	0.54	0.61	15.83
Galveston, Galveston	14	87	49	101	24	Jan. 24	Dec. 25	335		3.02	2.60	2.60	1.44	3.16	4.41	4.41	1.68	5.60	2.83	3.16	3.67	42.20
Garza, Post	67	94	28	109	0	Apr. 5	Nov. 5	216		0.68	0.65	0.81	1.44	3.06	2.71	2.36	1.68	1.94	2.11	0.74	0.73	18.91
Gillespie, Fredericksburg		95	36	109	-5	Apr. 1	Nov. 6	219	7	1.38	1.81	1.55	2.88	3.33	2.88	1.38	2.60	3.72	3.04	1.54	1.32	27.45

Texas Temperature, Frost, Growing Season and Precipitation Records, by Counties.— (continued.)

County and Station	Temp. Length of record (Yr.)	Mean Max July (°F)	Mean Min January (°F)	Record Highest (°F)	Record Lowest (°F)	Last in Spring	First in Fall	Growing Season (Days)	Precip. Length of Record (Yr.)	January (In.)	February (In.)	March (In.)	April (In.)	May (In.)	June (In.)	July (In.)	August (In.)	September (In.)	October (In.)	November (In.)	December (In.)	Annual (In.)
‡Glasscock, Garden City	12	94	22	110	-7	Apr. 2	Nov. 10	222	—	0.66	0.60	0.69	1.24	2.38	1.67	2.04	1.41	1.87	1.80	0.64	0.81	15.81
Goliad, Goliad	37	94	46	112	7	Feb. 24	Dec. 7	285	—	1.92	2.62	1.74	2.60	4.40	3.55	2.53	2.88	4.22	3.60	2.14	1.95	33.79
Gonzales, Gonzales	11	96	42	104	18	Feb. 28	Dec. 7	276	—	1.93	1.41	1.74	1.83	3.46	3.55	1.76	2.37	4.16	3.10	2.14	2.03	32.07
Gray, Pampa	40	94	23	109	-12	Feb. 15	Oct. 27	195	—	0.47	0.71	0.83	1.83	3.12	3.47	2.74	2.40	1.88	1.97	0.58	0.69	20.14
Grayson, Sherman	87	96	32	113	-2	Mar. 27	Nov. 9	227	—	1.92	3.03	2.99	4.89	5.76	3.85	2.51	2.63	4.18	3.07	2.68	2.32	39.83
Gregg, Longview	87	96	38	113	-7	Mar. 14	Nov. 16	247	—	3.92	3.75	3.84	5.63	6.07	3.62	3.14	2.51	3.70	3.09	3.84	4.07	47.18
‡Grimes, Anderson	77	96	42	110	4	Mar. 1	Dec. 4	278	—	3.12	3.33	2.86	4.31	4.32	2.94	2.45	2.45	4.10	3.10	3.39	3.36	40.52
Guadalupe, Seguin	47	96	42	110	0	Mar. 1	Nov. 28	267	—	1.80	2.46	1.77	3.21	3.49	2.94	1.78	2.13	4.09	3.37	2.08	1.64	30.67
Hale, Plainview	77	93	26	108	-8	Apr. 10	Nov. 6	211	—	0.71	0.60	0.75	1.38	3.10	3.10	2.63	1.89	2.14	1.76	0.76	0.76	19.34
Hall, Memphis	68	98	26	117	-11	Apr. 4	Nov. 4	213	—	0.75	0.83	0.83	1.86	3.82	2.98	1.97	1.96	2.27	1.92	0.60	0.74	20.53
Hamilton, Hamilton	14	96	34	109	-6	Mar. 27	Nov. 27	239	—	1.82	1.98	1.86	3.53	4.34	2.58	1.42	2.36	3.22	3.15	1.77	1.58	29.61
Hansford, Spearman	63	92	20	111	-22	Apr. 22	Oct. 25	186	—	0.56	0.72	1.49	1.49	3.29	2.79	3.58	2.79	1.94	1.86	0.76	0.68	22.16
Hardeman, Quanah (near)	111	99	28	119	-1	Mar. 31	Nov. 7	221	—	0.77	0.93	1.29	2.39	3.92	3.10	2.15	2.11	2.98	2.70	0.97	1.01	24.32
Hardin, Kountze	—	93	42	—	—	Mar. 13	Nov. 14	246	6	4.75	4.45	4.45	4.50	4.25	4.25	5.30	5.20	3.75	3.20	4.50	5.40	53.00
Harris, Houston	51	93	45	108	-5	Feb. 14	Dec. 11	300	64	3.57	3.54	2.68	3.54	5.10	4.52	4.12	4.35	4.65	4.05	4.03	4.04	48.19
Harrison, Marshall	71	95	37	109	-9	Mar. 16	Nov. 19	245	—	4.16	3.84	3.84	5.27	5.32	3.25	3.05	2.62	3.46	3.14	3.66	4.18	46.19
Hartley, Channing	9	92	20	104	-3	Apr. 22	Oct. 19	180	—	0.58	0.50	0.68	1.35	2.88	2.30	2.55	2.75	1.53	2.62	1.30	0.66	18.00
Haskell, Haskell	21	97	30	111	-3	Apr. 28	Nov. 15	232	—	0.93	1.21	1.10	2.26	3.92	2.73	2.38	2.13	2.65	2.46	1.23	1.07	24.14
Hays, San Marcos	82	96	40	109	-14	Mar. 14	Nov. 23	254	—	2.00	2.93	3.29	3.29	2.70	3.68	1.77	1.77	4.52	3.00	2.23	2.01	33.75
Hemphill, Canadian	65	95	40	108	-14	Apr. 9	Oct. 30	204	—	0.62	0.70	0.90	1.57	4.09	3.05	2.44	2.17	1.84	1.78	0.59	0.75	20.50
Henderson, Athens	22	95	37	109	2	Mar. 11	Nov. 26	260	24	3.10	3.30	3.25	4.40	5.25	3.20	2.25	2.25	3.10	3.10	3.50	3.80	40.40
Hidalgo, Mission	58	97	49	110	18	Feb. 7	Dec. 8	327	—	1.22	1.13	0.68	1.66	2.30	2.51	0.81	1.68	3.62	2.62	0.94	0.73	19.90
Hill, Hillsboro	71	96	30	110	-11	Mar. 19	Nov. 21	247	—	2.16	2.74	2.34	4.36	3.92	3.31	1.80	1.79	3.71	3.31	2.46	2.28	34.47
Hockley, Levelland	35	93	24	109	-16	Apr. 15	Oct. 28	196	32	0.61	0.47	0.52	1.00	2.70	2.10	2.05	1.70	2.31	2.00	0.50	0.50	16.60
Hood, Granbury	32	96	34	—	-6	Mar. 26	Nov. 13	232	29	2.36	2.35	1.05	3.55	5.20	2.90	2.05	1.75	2.78	2.75	1.95	2.30	31.78
Hopkins, Sulphur Springs	47	94	34	114	-10	Mar. 23	Nov. 16	238	21	2.76	3.47	3.89	5.48	4.75	3.67	2.88	2.57	2.85	4.02	3.45	3.15	45.29
Houston, Crockett	21	95	38	117	7	Feb. 6	Nov. 26	265	—	3.58	3.35	2.82	4.38	4.75	3.37	2.94	2.57	3.71	3.33	3.91	3.61	41.72
Howard, Big Spring	73	95	30	102	0	Apr. 4	Nov. 7	217	—	0.60	0.58	1.42	1.22	2.57	1.58	1.25	1.49	1.63	1.83	0.74	0.74	15.88
‡Hudspeth, Sierra Blanca	14	93	27	107	-7	Apr. 26	Nov. 12	231	—	0.46	0.26	0.53	0.30	0.53	0.60	1.25	1.30	1.25	0.97	0.33	0.41	7.86
Hunt, Greenville (near)	74	94	34	107	-4	Mar. 21	Nov. 13	237	11	2.36	3.21	3.68	3.68	5.20	3.97	3.04	3.04	3.75	2.75	3.20	2.88	43.08
Hutchinson, Borger	27	93	32	107	-12	Apr. 20	Oct. 24	187	—	0.64	0.62	0.90	1.40	3.35	2.87	2.55	2.62	1.75	1.75	0.65	0.81	19.91
Irion, Mertzon	13	96	32	108	2	Mar. 27	Nov. 14	232	—	1.08	1.14	0.98	2.37	2.92	2.23	1.31	2.02	3.33	2.08	1.04	0.83	21.33
Jack, Jacksboro	34	97	42	112	-3	Apr. 1	Nov. 5	218	—	1.64	1.55	2.24	3.76	3.02	3.02	2.35	2.01	3.09	3.92	1.90	1.45	29.78
Jackson, Edna	8	96	40	105	18	Feb. 19	Dec. 6	290	—	2.40	2.92	2.24	2.98	4.47	4.35	2.71	3.31	5.20	3.92	2.69	2.46	39.65
Jasper, Jasper	20	93	40	107	-4	Mar. 23	Nov. 6	229	21	4.94	4.50	4.56	4.56	5.42	4.37	3.43	3.43	3.63	3.63	4.39	4.69	51.03
Jeff Davis, Mount Locke	40	82	31	97	-10	—	—	—	—	0.83	0.48	0.48	0.46	1.49	2.47	3.77	3.42	2.75	1.51	0.56	0.54	18.74
Jefferson, Port Arthur	31	91	44	97	7	Mar. 11	Nov. 16	250	65	4.06	4.24	4.05	4.19	4.94	4.81	5.89	3.11	5.34	3.71	4.26	4.26	55.07
‡Jim Hogg, Hebbronville	15	99	47	109	11	Feb. 15	Dec. 4	303	—	1.35	1.15	0.90	1.70	2.55	2.28	1.40	1.88	3.45	1.90	0.92	1.30	20.78
Jim Wells, Alice	22	96	47	107	12	Feb. 18	Dec. 15	289	15	1.61	1.61	1.07	1.97	4.75	2.96	1.66	2.52	4.93	2.84	1.61	1.29	27.04
Johnson, Cleburne	68	96	35	114	-3	Mar. 25	Nov. 14	233	25	1.80	2.57	2.28	4.07	4.75	3.33	2.57	2.57	2.99	2.93	0.96	2.04	33.04
Jones, Anson	18	97	30	110	0	Mar. 31	Nov. 9	223	15	0.90	1.28	0.92	1.89	4.15	2.96	1.97	1.55	2.55	2.54	1.34	1.32	23.37
Karnes, Kenedy	26	96	44	112	7	Feb. 24	Dec. 2	281	25	2.05	1.89	1.89	2.50	2.50	2.99	3.11	2.80	4.32	2.82	2.11	2.20	31.93
Kaufman, Kaufman	76	94	35	113	-3	Mar. 18	Nov. 21	248	—	2.46	3.06	2.91	5.00	5.32	3.45	2.62	2.13	3.43	3.53	2.95	2.93	39.82
Kendall, Boerne	83	94	38	110	4	Mar. 25	Nov. 11	231	14	1.76	2.49	3.84	2.88	3.84	2.57	2.13	2.47	4.35	3.09	1.76	1.82	30.39
Kenedy, Armstrong	17	95	48	108	14	Feb. 2	Dec. 18	319	14	1.91	1.62	1.42	1.68	3.21	2.18	2.01	2.50	5.16	2.31	1.12	1.49	26.61
Kent, Jayton	14	97	28	110	-2	Apr. 4	Nov. 6	216	8	0.84	0.93	0.79	1.75	3.50	2.38	2.10	2.10	2.25	2.20	0.96	0.95	20.75

Texas Temperature, Frost, Growing Season and Precipitation Records, by Counties. — (continued.)

County and Station	Temperature Length of Record (Yr.)	Mean Max. July (°F.)	Mean Min. January (°F.)	Record Highest (°F.)	Record Lowest (°F.)	Last in Spring	First in Fall	Growing Season Days	Precip. Length of Record (Yr.)	January (In.)	February (In.)	March (In.)	April (In.)	May (In.)	June (In.)	July (In.)	August (In.)	September (In.)	October (In.)	November (In.)	December (In.)	Annual (In.)
Kerr, Kerrville	78	94	34	110	-7	Apr. 7	Nov. 7	216	—	1.57	2.24	1.98	3.08	3.75	2.61	1.66	2.05	4.05	3.54	1.66	1.66	29.75
!Kimble, Junction	7	97	33	110	-11	Apr. 3	Nov. 3	213	—	1.24	1.37	1.13	2.22	2.82	2.53	1.71	2.50	2.89	1.90	1.03	0.99	22.33
!King, Guthrie	12	99	27	114	2	Apr. 3	Nov. 8	219	26	0.89	0.95	0.90	1.88	3.55	2.60	1.95	2.12	2.53	2.25	0.98	1.00	21.60
!Kinney, Brackettville	18	94	39	108	8	Apr. 1	Nov. 26	270	—	0.92	1.28	0.92	1.99	3.16	3.09	1.07	1.83	4.71	2.25	0.75	0.79	20.85
Kleberg, Kingsville	26	96	48	108	11	Feb. 5	Dec. 16	314	23	1.65	1.50	1.30	2.05	3.00	2.30	2.00	2.50	4.75	2.45	1.38	1.62	26.50
Knox, Munday	37	98	28	116	-6	Apr. 11	Nov. 6	237	—	0.95	1.13	1.29	2.43	3.76	2.85	2.93	2.05	2.93	3.43	1.17	1.17	24.64
Lamar, Paris	87	95	34	115	-13	Mar. 25	Oct. 27	235	—	2.60	3.54	3.61	5.43	5.52	3.90	3.54	2.99	4.13	3.43	3.33	3.15	45.17
Lamb, Littlefield	22	93	24	110	-14	Apr. 16	Nov. 1	194	—	0.57	0.47	1.22	1.43	3.80	3.07	1.37	1.96	3.27	1.84	0.42	0.51	18.04
Lampasas, Lampasas	83	96	36	112	-7	Apr. 2	Nov. 10	223	—	1.73	2.14	1.95	3.46	4.21	2.70	1.05	2.30	3.27	2.71	1.55	1.95	29.80
La Salle, Cotulla	20	99	43	116	12	Feb. 20	Dec. 6	288	—	1.00	1.40	0.82	2.05	2.80	2.24	3.23	1.80	2.21	2.21	1.06	1.06	20.72
Lavaca, Hallettsville	83	95	44	111	5	Mar. 1	Dec. 6	280	11	2.38	2.86	2.17	3.36	4.67	3.55	2.35	2.79	4.07	2.89	3.00	2.60	36.27
!Lee, Lexington	14	94	38	105	12	Mar. 12	Nov. 29	273	—	2.75	2.90	2.40	3.75	4.00	3.65	2.50	2.38	3.72	2.55	3.04	3.04	35.88
Leon, Centerville	36	95	43	111	-3	Mar. 1	Dec. 1	270	—	3.39	3.39	2.85	4.45	4.56	3.19	2.00	2.65	3.22	3.54	3.24	3.25	39.48
Liberty, Liberty	72	92	43	108	8	Mar. 6	Nov. 19	261	—	3.91	4.25	2.73	4.29	4.84	4.18	4.61	3.87	4.45	3.97	2.99	4.73	49.75
Limestone, Mexia	70	96	37	108	-2	Mar. 3	Nov. 26	255	—	2.96	2.99	2.99	4.44	4.87	3.25	1.69	2.10	3.58	3.58	2.81	2.81	37.59
Lipscomb, Follett	40	95	23	110	-12	Apr. 10	Oct. 29	202	—	0.58	0.87	1.26	1.62	3.43	3.29	3.38	2.50	1.84	1.94	0.68	0.68	22.16
Live Oak, George West	—	97	45	—	—	Feb. 6	Dec. 6	289	—	1.43	1.82	1.47	2.05	3.80	2.50	2.68	2.17	3.72	2.57	1.65	1.43	25.64
Llano, Llano	83	98	41	115	-7	Mar. 29	Nov. 13	229	—	1.37	1.92	2.36	2.59	3.16	2.14	1.20	1.91	3.79	1.50	1.50	1.37	26.20
Loving, Mentone	11	96	19	109	-2	Mar. 3	Nov. 8	222	26	0.50	0.28	0.50	0.65	1.05	1.10	1.51	1.51	2.19	2.05	0.33	0.38	10.31
Lubbock, Lubbock	61	92	25	109	-17	Apr. 9	Nov. 3	208	—	0.55	0.50	0.89	1.08	3.17	2.78	2.23	1.87	2.19	2.05	0.49	0.61	18.41
Lynn, Tahoka	47	94	27	109	-15	Apr. 15	Nov. 9	217	—	0.62	0.59	0.81	1.72	3.09	2.33	2.29	1.52	2.35	1.93	1.14	0.65	17.88
McCulloch, Brady	47	96	38	108	0	Mar. 31	Nov. 12	226	—	1.36	1.49	1.21	2.59	3.54	2.34	1.61	1.81	3.29	2.34	1.14	1.14	23.46
McLennan, Waco	93	98	38	111	-5	Mar. 16	Nov. 24	253	14	1.87	2.38	2.36	4.02	4.60	2.73	1.47	2.10	3.19	2.55	2.01	2.27	31.26
McMullen, Tilden	17	97	40	110	9	Feb. 19	Dec. 1	291	41	3.50	1.54	1.15	2.15	3.25	2.75	1.90	2.60	3.60	2.80	1.80	3.90	25.27
Madison, Madisonville	33	94	34	110	6	Mar. 1	Dec. 6	272	—	3.78	3.74	3.93	5.29	4.60	3.19	2.90	2.57	3.37	3.06	3.70	4.05	41.50
Marion, Jefferson	—	94	36	—	—	Mar. 18	Nov. 9	236	31	3.78	3.74	3.93	4.49	4.60	3.19	2.35	2.57	3.37	3.06	3.78	4.05	44.83
Martin, Lenorah	19	95	34	109	8	Apr. 8	Nov. 6	215	—	0.75	0.64	0.57	1.05	2.35	1.70	1.61	1.50	1.95	1.70	0.70	0.76	15.72
Mason, Mason	48	94	34	103	11	Apr. 1	Nov. 6	217	—	1.51	1.65	1.34	2.54	3.82	2.46	1.65	2.17	3.05	2.26	1.26	1.15	24.68
Matagorda, Matagorda	82	100	40	115	7	Feb. 7	Dec. 10	296	—	3.05	3.04	2.23	3.31	3.82	3.56	1.58	4.49	6.03	3.69	2.97	3.06	42.29
Maverick, Eagle Pass	—	100	40	—	—	Feb. 21	Dec. 3	285	—	0.95	1.04	1.91	1.91	3.25	1.59	1.32	2.21	3.13	1.92	0.69	0.74	19.74
Medina, Hondo	72	96	42	109	4	Mar. 6	Nov. 6	263	—	1.67	2.25	1.48	2.77	3.66	2.72	1.65	2.43	3.89	3.00	1.41	1.50	28.43
!Menard, Menard	14	96	30	109	-11	Mar. 31	Nov. 9	220	—	1.08	1.14	0.98	2.37	2.92	2.23	1.31	2.02	3.33	2.08	1.04	0.83	21.33
Midland, Midland	21	95	30	109	-7	Apr. 3	Nov. 3	218	—	0.59	0.56	0.59	0.85	2.16	1.49	1.32	1.52	1.54	1.38	0.49	0.52	13.51
Milam, Cameron	64	96	40	114	-7	Mar. 13	Nov. 24	256	—	2.49	2.82	2.31	4.20	3.72	2.88	1.88	1.95	3.67	3.03	2.79	2.77	33.87
!Mills, Goldthwaite	15	87	34	107	4	Mar. 31	Nov. 16	230	—	1.63	1.78	1.10	3.22	3.48	2.47	1.32	1.88	3.12	2.89	1.92	1.57	27.52
Mitchell, Colorado City	55	96	30	115	-7	Apr. 3	Nov. 6	217	—	0.77	0.88	0.87	1.83	3.16	2.09	2.19	1.68	2.37	1.98	1.00	0.94	19.68
Montague, Bowie	20	96	34	112	-3	Mar. 27	Nov. 11	229	17	3.63	1.88	3.05	4.67	4.86	3.20	3.29	3.61	3.78	2.85	3.82	4.05	39.39
Montgomery, Conroe	55	94	40	109	-18	Mar. 1	Nov. 26	270	—	3.63	3.54	2.65	4.20	5.35	3.68	3.29	2.62	3.55	3.64	3.89	4.05	45.53
Moore, Dumas	36	93	20	109	-4	Apr. 27	Oct. 22	185	35	0.60	0.54	0.54	1.30	5.35	2.45	3.25	2.67	2.60	3.15	0.64	0.70	18.33
!Morris, Daingerfield (near)	16	95	30	110	—	Mar. 21	Nov. 12	236	28	0.63	4.20	0.81	4.83	4.69	4.66	1.88	—	4.90	2.77	1.63	4.55	46.12
Motley, Matador	28	96	26	112	-4	Apr. 1	Nov. 7	218	—	0.63	0.67	0.81	1.67	3.30	2.94	3.29	1.86	2.16	2.32	0.76	0.89	20.35
Nacogdoches, Nacogdoches	75	94	36	114	14	Mar. 15	Nov. 23	243	—	4.20	3.92	4.73	4.83	5.45	3.97	3.29	2.53	3.78	3.53	3.82	4.68	47.53
Navarro, Corsicana	96	95	36	110	-7	Mar. 13	Nov. 27	259	—	2.56	2.94	2.81	4.69	5.45	3.00	1.75	2.21	3.20	3.53	2.79	2.81	37.74
Newton, Kirbyville	46	93	30	107	11	Mar. 23	Nov. 9	228	—	4.73	4.57	4.65	4.66	5.55	4.31	2.27	3.78	2.86	2.51	2.86	4.58	54.16
Nolan, Roscoe	38	96	30	110	-11	Apr. 20	Nov. 9	221	—	0.91	0.97	1.05	2.16	2.92	2.72	2.35	1.53	2.91	2.77	1.14	1.02	22.19
Nueces, Corpus Christi	88	94	37	105	11	Feb. 9	Dec. 15	309	—	1.58	1.95	1.10	2.15	3.17	2.67	1.88	3.20	4.90	—	1.63	1.53	28.53

Texas Temperature, Frost, Growing Season and Precipitation Records, by Counties. — (continued.)

County and Station	+Length of Record (Yr.)	Mean Max. July (°F.)	Mean Min. January (°F.)	Highest Record (°F.)	Lowest Record (°F.)	Last in Spring	First in Fall	Growing Season (Days)	+Length of Record (Yr.)	Jan. (In.)	Feb. (In.)	March (In.)	April (In.)	May (In.)	June (In.)	July (In.)	August (In.)	September (In.)	October (In.)	November (In.)	December (In.)	Annual (In.)
‡Ochiltree, Perryton	12	93	18	106	−12	Apr. 18	Oct. 26	191	—	0.54	0.70	1.09	1.33	3.03	3.05	3.33	2.43	1.90	1.66	0.70	0.72	20.48
Oldham, Vega	52	91	22	108	−17	Apr. 16	Oct. 21	186	—	0.55	0.66	0.82	1.29	2.56	3.04	3.17	2.85	1.76	1.54	0.56	0.75	19.54
‡Orange, Orange	24	91	41	99	19	Mar. 16	Nov. 11	240	18	4.28	4.94	3.47	4.91	5.15	5.04	6.70	5.43	6.76	3.70	5.60	4.24	59.92
Palo Pinto, Mineral Wells	24	95	33	112	7	Mar. 31	Nov. 7	221	18	1.80	2.05	2.00	3.20	5.15	3.00	1.88	1.70	2.75	3.75	1.80	2.05	30.13
Panola, Carthage	24	95	38	108	3	Mar. 16	Nov. 11	240	21	4.50	4.15	4.00	3.40	5.45	3.50	3.50	2.78	2.75	3.15	4.45	5.10	48.08
Parker, Weatherford	86	96	34	113	−11	Mar. 29	Nov. 20	225	—	1.89	2.39	2.16	4.08	4.90	3.06	1.99	1.94	3.44	3.05	1.72	1.75	32.37
Parmer, Friona	14	96	31	108	−15	Apr. 20	Oct. 26	183	42	0.61	0.45	0.80	1.10	2.80	2.38	2.20	2.20	2.56	1.85	0.63	0.47	17.50
Pecos, Fort Stockton	21	93	33	114	−7	Mar. 31	Nov. 10	224	—	0.65	0.57	0.42	0.78	1.57	1.47	1.39	1.26	1.38	1.31	0.58	0.58	11.85
Polk, Livingston	38	93	39	111	1	Mar. 11	Nov. 16	250	—	4.04	4.04	3.77	4.70	4.77	3.31	3.73	3.33	3.73	4.04	4.17	4.17	47.19
Potter, Amarillo	83	92	24	108	−16	Apr. 17	Oct. 24	190	—	0.54	0.56	0.77	1.23	2.83	3.45	2.95	2.93	1.93	1.83	0.53	0.73	20.28
Presidio, Presidio	48	100	34	117	4	Mar. 20	Nov. 13	238	—	0.41	0.20	0.61	0.21	0.60	1.24	1.35	1.23	1.51	0.89	0.34	0.33	8.47
Rains, Emory	13	96	35	110	3	Mar. 22	Nov. 18	242	26	3.10	3.40	3.60	4.70	5.50	3.60	1.59	2.50	2.85	3.25	3.65	3.65	42.95
Randall, Canyon	21	93	39	107	−10	Apr. 15	Oct. 27	195	—	0.62	0.52	0.67	1.36	2.74	3.45	3.01	2.77	1.82	1.93	0.55	0.72	20.16
Reagan, Big Lake	13	96	36	106	6	Mar. 28	Nov. 12	229	7	0.85	0.70	1.08	1.08	1.50	1.80	1.80	1.13	2.30	1.62	0.56	0.78	14.72
Real, Prade Ranch	19	94	38	104	−5	Mar. 26	Nov. 17	236	17	1.25	1.30	1.30	2.20	3.50	2.87	2.00	1.85	2.88	2.35	1.00	1.38	23.88
Red River, Clarksville	72	94	34	115	−7	Mar. 22	Nov. 12	234	—	2.97	3.52	3.20	5.73	1.50	3.43	4.27	2.76	3.50	3.47	2.75	3.31	45.29
Reeves, Balmorhea	52	94	32	112	−9	Apr. 1	Nov. 15	226	25	0.63	0.49	0.44	0.59	1.50	1.47	1.59	1.37	1.64	1.25	1.14	0.53	11.99
‡Refugio, Refugio	18	94	42	106	8	Feb. 14	Dec. 14	304	—	2.03	2.06	1.60	2.97	3.66	2.75	1.83	3.50	2.11	2.91	1.90	2.37	33.76
Roberts, Miami	67	94	23	114	−15	Apr. 16	Oct. 16	192	11	0.58	0.77	0.93	1.47	3.96	3.35	2.90	2.61	2.11	2.03	0.68	0.82	21.91
Robertson, Franklin	14	96	40	110	6	Mar. 6	Nov. 20	268	—	2.85	2.94	2.94	3.88	5.45	3.02	2.48	2.16	3.16	3.03	3.16	3.19	35.80
Rockwall, Rockwall	7	96	34	109	11	Mar. 23	Nov. 14	236	—	2.29	2.92	3.14	5.16	5.45	3.86	2.16	2.18	3.16	3.18	2.75	2.43	38.68
Runnels, Ballinger	78	96	38	116	−9	Mar. 30	Nov. 17	228	—	1.23	1.04	1.05	2.19	3.84	1.41	1.41	2.02	2.66	2.26	1.14	0.97	21.85
Rusk, Henderson	33	96	38	108	2	Mar. 11	Nov. 16	250	—	3.77	3.82	2.81	4.94	5.60	3.53	2.81	2.82	2.90	3.34	3.65	4.15	46.22
Sabine, Bronson	29	93	35	114	6	Apr. 16	Nov. 12	236	48	5.50	4.40	4.00	4.80	5.40	3.65	4.10	3.00	2.90	3.24	4.95	5.45	51.94
‡San Augustine, Jackson Hill	14	94	38	106	6	Mar. 19	Nov. 12	238	30	5.20	4.40	3.75	4.80	5.40	4.00	4.00	2.88	2.90	3.20	4.80	5.25	50.23
‡San Jacinto, Coldspring (near)	13	95	38	104	12	Mar. 5	Nov. 21	261	18	4.40	4.05	3.20	4.50	4.70	2.60	4.15	3.00	3.45	3.45	4.50	4.70	48.25
‡San Patricio, Sinton	18	95	38	107	6	Feb. 1	Dec. 14	303	49	1.85	1.80	1.60	3.25	3.25	2.60	2.50	3.80	4.65	2.85	3.96	2.20	30.60
‡San Saba, San Saba	13	96	40	108	8	Apr. 1	Nov. 12	227	—	1.49	0.91	1.59	3.00	3.68	2.07	1.37	2.51	3.29	3.40	1.64	1.42	26.19
‡Schleicher, Eldorado (near)	9	96	30	107	−10	Mar. 28	Nov. 12	229	—	0.87	0.60	0.81	1.78	2.07	2.07	1.50	1.65	2.78	1.86	0.81	0.73	18.19
Scurry, Snyder	63	96	28	115	−10	Apr. 4	Nov. 4	214	—	0.63	0.60	0.75	1.61	3.50	2.57	2.22	1.61	1.95	2.22	0.91	0.75	19.32
Shackelford, Albany	92	97	38	114	−8	Mar. 30	Nov. 9	224	—	1.29	1.50	1.18	2.99	4.08	2.57	2.38	3.00	3.21	2.59	1.42	1.20	26.57
Shelby, Center	35	98	31	110	0	Mar. 17	Nov. 12	240	—	4.15	4.30	1.60	5.06	5.51	3.96	2.16	3.80	3.63	3.40	3.96	4.56	49.94
Sherman, Stratford	55	93	37	108	−20	Apr. 23	Oct. 21	182	18	0.36	0.45	0.83	1.36	2.81	2.47	3.57	2.51	1.57	1.42	0.54	0.47	18.36
Smith, Tyler	21	98	30	108	8	Mar. 21	Nov. 21	259	10	3.88	3.67	1.18	4.89	5.45	3.27	2.12	2.91	2.74	3.23	4.77	4.77	46.19
‡Somervell, Glen Rose	13	98	38	110	−7	Mar. 25	Nov. 16	236	—	2.15	2.40	2.13	3.75	5.00	2.90	2.12	2.00	3.97	2.75	2.05	2.04	32.65
Starr, Rio Grande City	92	98	48	114	16	Feb. 16	Dec. 7	314	—	0.90	0.96	1.29	1.69	4.08	2.06	2.06	1.84	3.21	2.14	1.42	0.62	18.87
Stephens, Breckenridge	49	98	31	114	−9	Mar. 31	Nov. 11	222	—	1.41	0.72	0.97	2.98	3.96	2.16	2.16	1.95	3.05	2.46	1.62	1.26	26.33
Sterling, Sterling City	13	99	37	108	5	Apr. 1	Nov. 10	224	22	0.83	0.97	1.07	1.80	2.81	1.85	2.14	1.86	1.57	1.96	0.87	0.94	19.00
‡Stonewall, Aspermont	14	99	30	112	2	Mar. 24	Nov. 16	220	—	0.68	0.95	1.07	2.18	3.60	2.89	2.07	1.91	2.61	2.43	1.11	0.84	22.36
Sutton, Sonora	27	94	38	105	0	Mar. 26	Nov. 16	235	43	0.90	0.64	0.64	1.54	5.00	2.35	1.43	1.76	1.75	1.95	0.67	0.78	17.59
Swisher, Tulia	21	93	24	109	−23	Apr. 10	Nov. 1	205	18	0.70	0.61	0.69	1.50	3.12	2.75	2.40	2.10	1.95	1.75	0.58	0.79	18.94
Tarrant, Fort Worth	76	96	33	112	−8	Mar. 26	Nov. 11	230	—	1.80	2.36	2.54	4.30	4.47	3.05	1.84	2.26	3.15	2.68	2.03	1.82	32.30
Taylor, Abilene	89	96	33	109	−8	Mar. 31	Nov. 11	225	22	1.02	0.97	1.07	2.47	3.63	2.82	2.05	2.05	1.94	2.60	1.02	1.02	23.59
‡Terrell, Sanderson	14	93	26	110	8	Mar. 21	Nov. 13	237	—	0.62	0.44	0.27	0.73	1.63	2.34	1.19	2.05	1.32	1.20	0.35	0.51	17.21
Terry, Brownfield	22	93	29	111	−8	Apr. 10	Nov. 10	206	—	0.59	0.50	0.73	1.08	2.53	2.41	1.81	1.81	1.32	1.99	0.35	0.49	17.21
Throckmorton, Throckmorton	50	98	29	119	−9	Mar. 31	Nov. 6	220	—	1.16	1.34	1.33	2.95	4.05	2.98	2.05	2.05	3.11	2.70	1.23	1.16	25.82

Texas Temperature, Frost, Growing Season and Precipitation Records, by Counties. — (continued.)

County and Station	†Length of Record (Yr.)	Temperature Mean Max July (°F)	Mean Min January (°F)	Record Highest (°F)	Record Lowest (°F)	Average Freeze Dates Last in Spring	First in Fall	*Growing Season Days	†Length of Record (Yr.)	Jan. (In.)	Feb. (In.)	Mar. (In.)	Apr. (In.)	May (In.)	June (In.)	July (In.)	Aug. (In.)	Sept. (In.)	Oct. (In.)	Nov. (In.)	Dec. (In.)	Annual (In.)
Titus, Mount Pleasant	59	95	35	118	-51	Mar. 23	Nov. 12	233	—	3.26	3.62	3.97	5.32	5.58	3.45	2.86	3.05	3.95	3.61	3.78	3.54	45.99
Tom Green, San Angelo	65	98	34	111	1	Mar. 25	Nov. 15	235	—	0.81	0.79	0.87	1.66	2.70	1.88	1.23	1.44	2.74	1.86	0.85	0.70	17.53
Travis, Austin	79	95	41	109	-2	Mar. 3	Nov. 28	270	—	1.88	3.09	1.89	3.49	3.97	3.13	1.88	2.20	3.68	3.02	2.04	2.22	32.49
Trinity, Groveton	9	94	39	102	17	Mar. 6	Nov. 21	260	29	4.20	4.00	3.40	4.50	4.80	3.75	3.50	2.80	3.00	3.00	4.50	4.34	45.95
Tyler, Rockland	11	94	38	106	7	Mar. 16	Nov. 12	241	—	4.50	4.17	3.33	4.53	5.70	4.19	3.58	2.79	3.70	3.61	3.93	4.34	48.37
Upshur, Gilmer	59	96	37	114	-4	Mar. 16	Nov. 16	245	—	3.30	3.62	3.84	6.03	5.47	3.56	2.68	2.70	3.49	3.06	3.85	4.14	45.74
Upton, McCamey	43	96	33	113	1	Mar. 26	Nov. 12	232	—	0.64	0.51	0.48	0.77	1.91	1.64	1.64	2.40	1.34	1.39	0.53	0.58	12.70
Uvalde, Uvalde	72	96	40	114	0	Mar. 10	Nov. 21	255	—	1.20	1.55	1.15	2.06	2.96	2.53	1.63	2.30	3.10	2.84	0.98	0.93	23.23
Val Verde, Del Rio	71	94	41	111	12	Feb. 12	Dec. 9	300	—	0.60	0.57	0.72	1.57	2.41	2.03	1.02	1.02	3.05	2.07	0.65	0.52	16.88
Van Zandt, Wills Point	52	94	35	115	-1	Mar. 16	Nov. 21	250	—	2.92	3.31	3.35	5.86	5.76	3.53	2.27	2.10	3.41	3.71	3.53	3.34	43.09
Victoria, Victoria	30	92	46	110	9	Feb. 19	Dec. 6	290	—	1.76	2.65	1.89	3.96	3.96	3.31	2.79	3.63	4.61	3.63	2.31	1.95	34.29
Walker, Huntsville	91	94	46	107	-2	Mar. 7	Nov. 27	265	67	3.51	3.73	3.12	4.63	4.61	4.05	3.24	3.01	4.15	3.39	3.62	3.93	44.99
‡Waller, Hempstead	13	95	39	107	13	Feb. 24	Nov. 23	283	—	3.50	3.30	2.87	4.35	4.30	3.45	3.45	2.95	3.40	3.45	3.45	4.00	41.67
Ward, Monahans	16	96	30	108	-9	Apr. 1	Nov. 10	223	13	0.80	0.40	0.33	0.76	1.60	1.20	1.75	1.40	1.38	1.50	0.35	0.57	12.04
Washington, Brenham	91	95	43	111	-1	Mar. 3	Dec. 4	277	—	2.84	3.23	2.70	3.87	4.41	3.53	2.31	2.96	3.85	3.20	3.82	3.22	39.94
Webb, Laredo	40	99	47	115	5	Feb. 1	Dec. 26	322	—	0.81	1.05	0.50	2.25	2.25	2.03	0.94	1.63	3.14	3.06	1.02	0.87	17.87
Wharton, Pierce	68	93	44	108	4	Feb. 5	Nov. 26	266	—	2.77	3.11	2.49	3.06	4.09	4.45	3.28	3.63	4.37	4.32	2.96	2.93	41.46
‡Wheeler, Shamrock	12	97	26	106	-14	Apr. 27	Nov. 11	208	—	0.65	0.97	1.09	2.03	3.95	3.62	2.57	2.23	2.37	2.36	0.70	0.83	23.70
Wichita, Wichita Falls	57	97	33	113	-12	Mar. 27	Nov. 7	229	—	1.07	1.16	1.62	3.16	4.58	3.39	2.16	1.77	3.00	2.68	1.35	1.28	27.22
Wilbarger, Vernon	42	98	29	119	-7	Mar. 31	Nov. 7	221	—	0.96	1.27	1.41	2.40	4.68	3.22	2.12	1.60	2.73	3.02	1.18	1.06	25.65
‡Willacy, Raymondville	60	96	52	107	19	Feb. 8	Dec. 11	331	—	1.60	1.68	0.50	3.73	3.73	3.35	1.30	2.23	5.13	2.66	1.37	0.95	25.80
Williamson, Taylor	73	96	39	112	-5	Mar. 11	Nov. 24	258	—	2.25	2.94	2.10	3.61	3.63	3.25	1.56	2.23	4.01	3.21	2.47	2.72	33.98
Wilson, Floresville	14	96	42	106	14	Feb. 24	Dec. 1	280	—	1.83	2.27	1.33	2.66	3.60	2.72	1.64	2.56	3.79	2.67	1.91	1.58	28.68
Winkler, Wink	35	96	29	114	-14	Apr. 3	Nov. 8	219	—	0.54	0.33	0.40	0.75	1.27	1.21	1.62	1.51	1.27	1.18	0.36	0.37	10.81
Wise, Bridgeport	40	96	33	115	-1	Mar. 31	Nov. 6	220	—	1.67	1.83	2.19	3.73	4.19	3.08	1.79	1.84	3.04	2.86	1.75	1.77	29.74
Wood, Mineola	10	96	36	107	9	Mar. 17	Nov. 18	246	7	3.50	3.75	3.75	4.75	5.40	3.35	3.20	2.70	2.75	3.25	4.00	4.10	44.30
Yoakum, Plains	20	92	24	108	-12	Apr. 15	Oct. 31	199	32	0.58	0.39	0.40	0.80	2.30	1.81	2.25	1.75	2.13	2.13	0.28	0.30	14.99
Young, Graham	69	98	31	117	-8	Apr. 2	Nov. 4	216	11	1.37	1.62	1.73	3.47	4.12	2.97	1.85	1.25	3.35	2.67	1.64	1.33	28.03
‡Zapata, Zapata	14	100	46	112	21	Feb. 14	Dec. 15	304	11	0.94	0.80	0.68	1.50	2.25	1.95	1.30	1.65	2.90	1.60	0.76	0.90	17.23
Zavala, Crystal City	21	99	41	109	11	Feb. 24	Dec. 1	280	—	0.93	1.28	0.88	1.67	3.46	2.27	1.19	2.44	3.21	2.48	0.93	0.80	21.54

*Average interval between the last 32°F temperature in spring and the first 32°F temperature in the fall.

†Significant moves of location of Weather Bureau stations may cause records at a town not to be comparable. This accounts for short records listed at some points; e.g., Groveton has many years of weather records but a short-time record is used because of changes in locations that make comparisons inaccurate.

‡Stations with newly revised temperature data.

Weather Reduces Pollution

Urbanization, industrialization and agribusiness practices are increasing air pollution problems in Texas, as in other states. But frequent changes in air mass and regional-scale weather disturbances in Texas do not favor objectionable concentrations of air pollutants much of the time.

There are significant seasonal and geographical variations. Statewide, most serious pollution is likely to occur in December and January (also in November in the Northeast). Conditions in warmer months are less conducive to pollution.

On a yearly basis, West Texas has less potential for air pollution than East Texas. The frequency of light winds and temperature inversions at night tend to create pollution problems.

Few high-pressure systems stagnate over Texas for any length of time; therefore, the meteorological situation most favorable for serious air-pollution episodes rarely is present. In Texas stagnation is more likely to occur over the East Texas Pine Belt and in the El Paso area than elsewhere.

Happy Birthday from a native son.

The Lone Star.

*For a hundred and fifty years now
it has shined.*

*A solid anchor
at the base of America.
Texas.*

*There's no place else
we'd rather call home.*

*And home it's been
since the day we were born.*

Just say when.^{SM}

CALENDAR FOR 1986 AND 1987

The subsequent calendars were calculated principally from basic data in the U.S. Naval Observatory's publication, the **American Ephemeris and Nautical Almanac.** Data were adapted for use in Texas on the basis of **Central Standard Time,** except for the period from 2 a.m. on the last Sunday in April until 2 a.m. on the last Sunday in October, when **Daylight Saving Time,** which is one hour earlier than Central Standard Time, is in effect.

All of Texas is in the CST zone except El Paso and Hudspeth Counties and the northwest corner of Culberson County which observe **Mountain Standard Time.** See accompanying map. MST is one hour earlier than CST.

All times here are figured for the intersection of meridian 98° West and parallel 32° 30′ North which is about nine miles northwest of Tolar, Hood County. This point is chosen because of its central location with respect to Texas and the Southwestern States.

To get Central Standard Time of sunrise or sunset, moonrise or moonset for any point in Texas apply the following rules: Add to the time given in this calendar four minutes for each degree of longitude that any given place lies west of the 98th meridian, and subtract four minutes for each degree of longitude such place lies east of the 98th meridian.

At times there will also be considerable variation for distances north and south of the line of latitude 32 degrees 30 minutes north, but the rule for calculating it would be complicated. Procedure given above will get sufficiently close results.

An accompanying map shows the intersection for which all time is calculated, with some Texas major cities and their longitude. These make it convenient to calculate time at any given point.

Planetary Configurations and Phenomena

In the center column of the calendar on following pages are given the phenomena and planetary configurations of heavens for 1986 and 1987. Below is an explanation of the signs of the Sun, Moon and planets, and symbols used in the tables:

☉ The Sun.	⊕ The Earth.	♅ Uranus.
☾ The Moon.	♂ Mars.	♆ Neptune.
☿ Mercury.	♃ Jupiter.	♇ Pluto.
♀ Venus.	♄ Saturn.	

Aspects

☌ This symbol appearing before the symbols for heavenly bodies means they are "in conjunction," that is having the same longitude as applies to the sky and appearing near each other.

☍ This symbol means that the two heavenly bodies are in "opposition," or differ by 180 degrees of longitude.

Common Astronomical Terms

Aphelion — Point at which a planet's orbit is farthest from the sun.

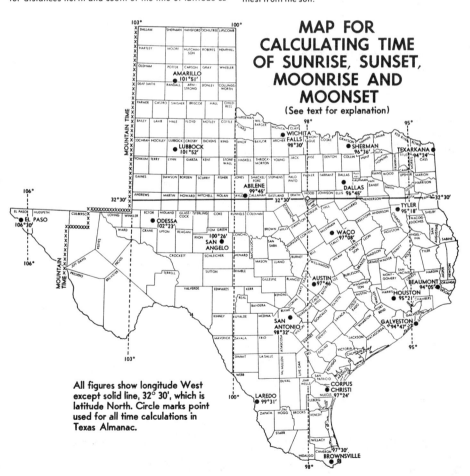

MAP FOR CALCULATING TIME OF SUNRISE, SUNSET, MOONRISE AND MOONSET
(See text for explanation)

All figures show longitude West except solid line, 32° 30′, which is latitude North. Circle marks point used for all time calculations in Texas Almanac.

Perihelion — Point at which a planet's orbit is nearest the sun.

Apogee — That point of the moon's orbit farthest from the earth.

Perigee — That point of the moon's orbit nearest the earth.

Aspect — Apparent situation of a planet with respect to another body.

Eclipses: 1986 and 1987

There will be four eclipses during 1986, two of the Sun and two of the Moon, as follows:

April 9—Partial eclipse of the Sun, visible part of Indonesia, Australia, New Guinea, south New Zealand and part of Antarctica.

April 24—Total eclipse of the Moon, beginning visible in western half of North America, Pacific Ocean, eastern U.S.S.R. and Asia, southeast Asia, Australia, New Zealand, eastern Indian Ocean and Antarctica except Atlantic coast; end visible in western Alaska, Pacific Ocean, Indian Ocean except eastern edge, Antarctica except Palmer Peninsula and Princess Margaret Coast, Australia, New Zealand and central, eastern and southeast Asia.

Oct. 3—Annular eclipse of the Sun, visible extreme northeast Asia, North America except extreme southwest, arctic regions, Greenland, Iceland, north of South America.

Oct. 17—Total eclipse of the Moon, beginning visible in New Zealand, Australia, western Pacific Ocean, eastern Antarctica, Asia, Europe except extreme west, Africa except western extremity; end visible in extreme western Australia, eastern Antarctica, Indian Ocean, Asia except extreme eastern parts, Europe, Africa, Greenland, extreme northeastern North America, eastern South America and Atlantic Ocean.

On Nov. 13, a Transit of Mercury will occur over the disk of the Sun.

1987

There will be four eclipses during 1987, two of the Sun and two of the Moon, as follows:

March 29—Annular total eclipse of the Sun, visible southern South America, part of Antarctica, Africa except northwest, extreme southeast Europe and southwest Asia.

April 14—Penumbral eclipse of the Moon, beginning visible eastern North America, South America, Antarctica, Africa, Europe, eastern South Pacific Ocean; end visible North America except Alaska, Central and South America, Antarctica, western Africa, western Europe, southern Greenland, Atlantic Ocean and eastern Pacific Ocean.

Sept. 23—Annular eclipse of the Sun, visible Asia, except northeast and southwestern parts, Japan, Philippine Islands, Indonesia except southwestern part, New Guinea, northeast Australia, New Zealand except extreme southern part.

Oct. 7—Penumbral eclipse of the Moon, beginning visible in North America except Alaska, Central and South America, Africa, Europe, eastern Asia, Greenland, Atlantic Ocean and eastern half of the South Pacific Ocean; end visible in North, Central and South America, Antarctica toward South America, western North Africa, western Europe, Greenland, Atlantic Ocean and eastern Pacific Ocean.

Chronological Eras and Cycles, 1986 and 1987

The year 1986 of the Christian era comprises the latter part of the 210th and the beginning of the 211th year of the independence of the United States of America, and corresponds to the year 6699 of the Julian period.

Jan. 1, 1986, Julian calendar, corresponds to Jan. 14, 1986, Gregorian calendar.

The year 7495 of the Byzantine era begins on Sept. 14, 1986, Gregorian calendar.

The year 5747 of the Jewish era begins at sunset on Oct. 3, 1986, Gregorian calendar.

The year 4623 of the Chinese era begins Feb. 9, 1986.

The year 2739 since the foundation of Rome, according to VARRO, begins on Jan. 14, 1986, Gregorian calendar.

The year 2735 of the era of NABONASSAR begins on April 27, 1986, Gregorian calendar.

The year 2298 of the Grecian era, or the era of the SELEUCIDAE, begins in the present-day usage of the Syrians on Oct. 14, 1986, or on Sept. 14, 1986, Gregorian calendar, according to different sects.

The year 1703 of the era of DIOCLETIAN begins on Sept. 11, 1986, Gregorian calendar.

The year 1407 of the Islamic era, or the era of the Hegira, begins at sunset on Sept. 5, 1986, Gregorian calendar.

The year 1908 of the Saka era begins on March 22, 1986, Gregorian calendar, in the reformed Indian calendar.

The year 2646 of the Japanese era begins on Jan. 1, 1986, Gregorian calendar.

CHRONOLOGICAL CYCLES, 1986

Dominical Letter	E	Julian Period	6699
Epact	19	Roman Indiction	9
Golden Number or		Solar Cycle	7
Lunar Cycle	XI		

CHRONOLOGICAL ERAS, 1987

The year 1987 of the Christian era comprises the latter part of the 211th and the beginning of the 212th year of the independence of the United States of America, and corresponds to the year 6700 of the Julian period.

Jan. 1, 1987, Julian calendar, corresponds to Jan. 14, 1987, Gregorian calendar.

The year 7496 of the Byzantine era begins on Sept. 14, 1987, Gregorian calendar.

The year 5748 of the Jewish era begins at sunset on Sept. 23, 1987, Gregorian calendar.

The year 4624 of the Chinese era begins Jan. 29, 1987.

The year 2740 since the foundation of Rome, according to VARRO, begins on Jan. 14, 1987, Gregorian calendar.

The year 2736 of the era of NABONASSAR begins on April 27, 1987, Gregorian calendar.

The year 2299 of the Grecian era, or the era of the SELEUCIDAE, begins in the present-day usage of the Syrians on Sept. 14 (or Oct. 14), Gregorian calendar, according to different sects.

The year 1704 of the era of DIOCLETIAN begins on Sept. 12, 1987, Gregorian calendar.

The year 1408 of the Islamic era, or the era of the Hegira, begins at sunset on Aug. 25, 1987, Gregorian calendar.

The year 1909 of the Saka era begins on March 22, 1987, Gregorian calendar, in the reformed Indian calendar.

The year 2647 of the Japanese era begins on Jan. 1, 1987, Gregorian calendar.

CHRONOLOGICAL CYCLES, 1987

Dominical Letter	D	Julian Period	6700
Epact	30	Roman Indiction	10
Golden Number or		Solar Cycle	8
Lunar Cycle	XII		

The Seasons, 1986 and 1987

The seasons of 1986 begin as follows, **Central Standard Time** (Daylight Saving Time, April 27-Oct. 30): **Spring**, March 20, 4:03 p.m.; **Summer**, June 21, 11:30 a.m.; **Fall**, Sept. 23, 2:59 a.m.; **Winter**, Dec. 21, 10:02 p.m.

1987

The seasons of 1987 begin as follows, **Central Standard Time** (Daylight Saving Time, April 26-Oct. 25): **Spring**, March 20, 9:52 p.m.; **Summer**, June 21, 5:11 p.m.; **Fall**, Sept. 23, 8:45 a.m.; **Winter**, Dec. 22, 3:46 a.m.

Morning and Evening Stars, 1986

Morning Stars, 1986

Venus—Nov. 12-Dec. 31.

Mars—Jan. 1-July 10.

Jupiter—March 4-Sept. 10.

Saturn—Jan. 1-May 28; Dec. 22-Dec. 31.

Evening Stars, 1986

Venus—March 2-Oct. 31.

Mars—July 10-Dec. 31.

Jupiter—Jan. 1-Feb. 5; Sept. 10-Dec. 31.

Saturn—May 28-Nov. 17.

(Data for 1987 not available when this section went to press.)

THE HOMESTEAD AT WELLS BRANCH
by
PROVIDENT DEVELOPMENT COMPANY

At the heart of Wells Branch, a 1,053 acre master-planned community by Provident Development Company, lies the heritage of Texas. Wild Indians, tepees and pioneers might be considered tales of the past, but the Wells Branch Homestead of Captain Nelson Merrell, legendary Indian fighter and Texas Ranger, brings them to life.

The Wells Branch Homestead stands as a working pioneer museum built in 1937 for Captain Nelson Merrell. Centered in Katherine Fleischer Park, the log cabin of cedar and elm began Merrelltown, a settlement reborn as Wells Branch.

Provident stumbled upon the almost 150 year old cabin while building the Wells Branch community. Rather than bulldoze this remnant of Texas' past, the company chose to incorporate its historic value into the new community. Provident financed the Homestead's restoration in 1982 and established a trust fund for its upkeep.

O. T. Baker, a former director of the Institute of Texas Cultures, restored the cabin and constructed its surrounding smoke house, corn crib, syrup mill, wash shed and three-hole outhouse, using only original material found on the grounds.

"Today the cry is that so many people are moving into Austin that developers are destroying all of this natural habitat and pioneer look," said Baker. To help Provident preserve Texas' past, Baker not only skillfully restored the Homestead, but he also holds tours through it on Tuesdays and Thursdays. Assisted by Provident employee Bill Todd, they demonstrate how Indian and frontier lifestyles developed during the pioneer days, and fascinate listeners with tales of the past.

To get to Wells Branch, take the Pflugerville/1825 exit off IH 35 in north Austin, and go west onto Wells Branch Parkway. To find the Homestead, turn right on Wellsport Drive and left on Klattenhoff to Katherine Fleischer Park. For more information on the Homestead, call Cheri Warfield, Provident Development Company.

Holidays, Anniversaries and Festivals, 1986 and 1987

Bank Holidays — By act of the Sixty-second Legislature, 1971, legally prescribed (compulsory) bank holidays in Texas, in addition to Sundays, are New Year's Day, Washington's Birthday, Memorial Day, Independence Day, Labor Day, Columbus Day, Veterans Day, Thanksgiving and Christmas. Should New Year's Day, Independence Day or Christmas fall on Saturday, banks close the preceding Friday. Should any of the three fall on Sunday banks close the next Monday. At their option, banks may close one day a week besides Sunday, usually Saturday, but on any day selected by individual banks. Prior to this act, permitting a 5-day banking week, bank holidays included all holidays in the list below marked with asterisk (*), double asterisk (**) or dagger (†).

1986		1987	
*New Year's Day	Wednesday, Jan. 1	*New Year's Day	Thursday, Jan. 1
Epiphany	Monday, Jan. 6	Epiphany	Tuesday, Jan. 6
§Arbor Day (Third Friday in January)	Friday, Jan. 17	§Arbor Day (Third Friday in January)	Friday, Jan. 16
**Confederate Heroes Day	Sunday, Jan. 19	**Confederate Heroes Day	Monday, Jan. 19
‡‡Martin Luther King's Birthday	Monday, Jan. 20	‡‡Martin Luther King's Birthday	Monday, Jan. 19
*Lincoln's Birthday	Wednesday, Feb. 12	*Lincoln's Birthday	Thursday, Feb. 12
Ash Wednesday	Wednesday, Feb. 12	‡‡Washington's Birthday	Monday, Feb. 16
‡‡Washington's Birthday	Monday, Feb. 17	†Texas Independence Day	Monday, March 2
†Texas Independence Day	Monday, March 2	‡Sam Houston Day	Monday, March 2
‡Sam Houston Day	Sunday, March 2	‡Texas Flag Day	Monday, March 2
‡Texas Flag Day	Sunday, March 2	Ash Wednesday	Wednesday, March 4
Palm Sunday	Sunday, March 23	Palm Sunday	Sunday, April 12
Good Friday	Friday, March 28	First Day of Passover (Pesach)	Tuesday, April 14
Easter Sunday	Sunday, March 30	Good Friday	Friday, April 17
†San Jacinto Day	Monday, April 21	Easter Sunday	Sunday, April 19
†Texas Sesquicentennial Day	Monday, April 21	†San Jacinto Day	Tuesday, April 21
First Day of Passover (Pesach)	Thursday, April 24	First Day of Ramadan (Tabular)	Thursday, April 30
Ascension Day	Thursday, May 8	‡‡Memorial Day	Monday, May 25
First Day of Ramadan (Tabular)	Saturday, May 10	Ascension Day	Thursday, May 28
Whit Sunday — Pentecost	Sunday, May 18	Feast of Weeks (Shebuoth)	Wednesday, June 3
Trinity Sunday	Sunday, May 25	Whit Sunday — Pentecost	Sunday, June 7
‡‡Memorial Day	Monday, May 26	Trinity Sunday	Sunday, June 14
Feast of Weeks (Shavuot)	Friday, June 13	U.S. Flag Day	Sunday, June 14
U.S. Flag Day	Saturday, June 14	†Emancipation Day	Friday, June 19
†Emancipation Day	Thursday, June 19	*Independence Day	Saturday, July 4
*Independence Day	Friday, July 4	‡Texas Pioneers' Day	Wednesday, Aug. 12
‡Texas Pioneers' Day	Tuesday, Aug. 12	Islamic New Year (Tabular)	Wednesday, Aug. 26
†Lyndon B. Johnson's Birthday	Wednesday, Aug. 27	†Lyndon B. Johnson's Birthday	Thursday, Aug. 27
*Labor Day	Monday, Sept. 1	*Labor Day	Monday, Sept. 7
Islamic New Year (Tabular)	Saturday, Sept. 6	Jewish New Year (Rosh Hashanah)	Thursday, Sept. 24
‡Casimir Pulaski Day	Saturday, Oct. 11	Day of Atonement (Yom Kippur)	Saturday, Oct. 3
‡‡Columbus Day	Monday, Oct. 13	First Day of Tabernacles (Succoth)	Thursday, Oct. 8
Day of Atonement (Yom Kippur)	Monday, Oct. 13	‡Casimir Pulaski Day	Sunday, Oct. 11
‡§Poetry Day	Wednesday, Oct. 15	‡‡Columbus Day	Monday, Oct. 12
First Day of Tabernacles (Succoth)	Saturday, Oct. 18	‡§Poetry Day	Thursday, Oct. 15
‡Father of Texas Day	Monday, Nov. 3	*General Election Day	Tuesday, Nov. 3
*General Election Day	Tuesday, Nov. 4	‡Father of Texas Day	Tuesday, Nov. 3
*Veterans Day	Tuesday, Nov. 11	*Veterans Day	Wednesday, Nov. 11
*Thanksgiving Day †† (Fourth Thursday)	Thursday, Nov. 27	*Thanksgiving Day †† (Fourth Thursday)	Thursday, Nov. 26
First Sunday in Advent	Sunday, Nov. 30	First Sunday in Advent	Sunday, Nov. 29
Hanukkah (Feast of Lights)	Friday, Dec. 19	*Christmas Day	Friday, Dec. 25
*Christmas Day	Thursday, Dec. 25		

*National holidays which are also state holidays by act of the Texas Legislature, except Lincoln's Birthday, Feb. 12, which was exclusively a bank holiday, until the number of bank holidays was restricted by state law in 1955, providing a 5-day week and restricting the number of bank holidays.

†Legal holiday in Texas only.

‡"Special observance days," set aside by Texas Legislature. They are not legal holidays, though two of them fall on March 2, which is otherwise designated as a state legal holiday, except for bank closing.

§A "special observance day" by resolution of the Texas Legislature but also observed by legislative enactment in many other states.

In 1973, the Texas Legislature made Lyndon B. Johnson's Birthday, Aug. 27, a state holiday and made Jan. 19 **Confederate Heroes Day, combining the birthdays of Robert E. Lee (Jan. 19) and Jefferson Davis (June 3).

††**THANKSGIVING DAY IN TEXAS** was designated as the "fourth Thursday in November" by the Fifty-fifth Legislature, 1957. This made the state Thanksgiving coincide with the national holiday in all years. Prior to that Texas had, beginning with 1939, celebrated separate national and state Thanksgiving Days in all Novembers having five Thursdays. Texas, first by governor's proclamation, and by legislative resolution after 1951, continued to observe the last Thursday, until changed in 1957 to coincide in all years with the national holiday.

‡‡Starting in 1971, these changes were made in official holidays by the U.S. and Texas governments to give employees 3-day holiday weekends: Columbus Day made national holiday and set for second Monday in October; Washington's Birthday will be observed on third Monday in February; Memorial Day will be observed on last Monday in May.

TEXAS SESQUICENTENNIAL, 1986

Since the state will be observing its sesquicentennial in 1986, the Sixty-ninth Legislature in 1985 set aside Monday, April 21, 1986, as Texas Sesquicentennial Day. It is also San Jacinto Day. The sesquicentennial observance will be for 1986 only.

Texas Special Observance Weeks, 1986 and 1987

Texas Week in 1986 will be the week of Saturday, March 1 to Friday, March 7, inclusive; in 1987, it will be observed the week of Sunday, March 1 to Saturday, March 7, inclusive. This week includes **Texas Independence Day**, March 2.

Texas Conservation and Beautification Week includes the period beginning two days before **San Jacinto Day**, April 21, and ending two days after **National Wildflower Day**, April 24.

WE'RE BLAZING TRAILS FOR A BETTER TEXAS.

Triland developments bring a new concept to Texas living. Total environments that give Texans the convenience of living where they work where they shop where they play. Like our 2500-acre Valley Ranch with its adjoining 700-acre Cowboys Center. And now we're getting another new perspective on Texas lands, from the back of a covered wagon.

———— ★ ————

BLAZING A TRAIL ON THE TEXAS WAGON TRAIN.

This January, Triland's Valley Ranch and Cowboys Center hitch up to the Texas Wagon Train in celebration of the Lone Star's sesquicentennial year. As Wagon Train sponsors, we'll help get the 3000-mile show on the road for its tour of Texas. 200,000 people will be waiting for the wagons as we roll from town to town. It's a six-month journey that ends with an Independencce Day party as big as the state.

———— ★ ————

BLAZING A TRAIL FOR TEXAS LAND USE.

Of course Triland isn't in it just for fun. We're in it to see the lay of the land. To view our state from a perspective as fresh as when our forebears first set sight on their new home. After all, this is our home too. We're a Texas-based company intent on working in harmony with the land to bring better living concepts to the people. So that when we reach the Texas bicentennial in 2035, we'll still have just as much to celebrate.

CALENDAR FOR 1986

(Time given in this calendar is according to **Central Standard Time.** See page 81 for explanation of how to get exact time at any certain Texas point. Boldface figures indicate p.m.)

1st Month JANUARY, 1986 31 Days

Moon's Phases.—Last Qr., Jan. 3, 1:47 p.m.; New, Jan. 10, 6:22 a.m.; First Qr., Jan. 17, 4:13 p.m.; Full, Jan. 25, 6:31 p.m.

Day of Year	Day of Month	Day of Week	Planetary Configurations —Phenomena	*Hour of Sunrise	*Hour of Sunset	*Hour of Moonrise	*Hour of Moonset
1	1	We.	⊕ at Perihelion...	7:34	5:37	**11:02**	11:22
2	2	Th.		7:34	5:38	...	11:51
3	3	Fr.		7:34	5:39	12:05	**12:20**
4	4	Sa.		7:34	5:39	1:10	**12:51**
5	5	Sun.	♂☌☾	7:34	5:40	2:17	**1:24**
6	6	Mo.		7:35	5:41	3:27	**2:04**
7	7	Tu.	♄☌☾	7:35	5:42	4:40	**2:51**
8	8	We.	♀☌♆	7:35	5:43	5:53	**3:46**
9	9	Th.		7:35	5:44	7:02	**4:50**
10	10	Fr.		7:35	5:45	8:02	**5:59**
11	11	Sa.		7:35	5:46	8:52	**7:10**
12	12	Su.	♃☌☾	7:35	5:47	9:34	**8:18**
13	13	Mo.		7:35	5:48	10:09	**9:22**
14	14	Tu.		7:35	5:48	10:38	**10:23**
15	15	We.		7:35	5:49	11:06	**11:21**
16	16	Th.		7:34	5:50	11:31	...
17	17	Fr.		7:34	5:51	11:57	12:17
18	18	Sa.		7:34	5:52	**12:24**	1:13
19	19	Su.	♀ Superior	7:33	5:53	**12:54**	2:09
20	20	Mo.		7:33	5:54	**1:28**	3:06
21	21	Tu.		7:33	5:54	**2:07**	4:04
22	22	We.		7:33	5:55	**2:52**	5:02
23	23	Th.		7:32	5:56	**3:44**	5:58
24	24	Fr.		7:32	5:57	**4:42**	6:49
25	25	Sa.		7:31	5:58	**5:44**	7:35
26	26	Su.		7:31	5:59	**6:48**	8:16
27	27	Mo.		7:31	6:00	**7:52**	8:52
28	28	Tu.		7:30	6:01	**8:56**	9:24
29	29	We.		7:29	6:02	**10:00**	9:54
30	30	Th.		7:28	6:03	**11:03**	10:23
31	31	Fr.	☿ Superior	7:28	6:04	...	10:53

2nd Month FEBRUARY, 1986 28 Days

Moon's Phases.—Last Qr., Feb. 1, 10:41 p.m.; New, Feb. 8, 6:55 p.m.; First Qr., Feb. 16, 1:55 p.m.; Full, Feb. 24, 9:02 a.m.

Day of Year	Day of Month	Day of Week	Planetary Configurations —Phenomena	*Hour of Sunrise	*Hour of Sunset	*Hour of Moonrise	*Hour of Moonset
32	1	Sa.		7:27	6:05	12:09	11:25
33	2	Su.		7:27	6:06	1:17	**12:01**
34	3	Mo.	♂☌☾	7:26	6:07	2:27	**12:43**
35	4	Tu.	♅☌☾	7:25	6:08	3:37	**1:34**
36	5	We.	♆☌☾	7:24	6:08	4:46	**2:33**
37	6	Th.		7:24	6:09	5:48	**3:39**
38	7	Fr.		7:23	6:10	6:41	**4:49**
39	8	Sa.		7:22	6:11	7:26	**5:58**
40	9	Su.		7:21	6:12	8:04	**7:04**
41	10	Mo.		7:21	6:13	8:36	**8:06**
42	11	Tu.		7:20	6:14	9:05	**9:06**
43	12	We.		7:19	6:15	9:31	**10:04**
44	13	Th.	♇ Stationary	7:18	6:15	9:58	**11:01**
45	14	Fr.		7:17	6:16	10:24	**11:58**
46	15	Sa.		7:16	6:17	10:52	...
47	16	Su.	☾ at Apogee	7:15	6:18	11:24	12:55
48	17	Mo.	♂☌♄	7:14	6:19	**12:00**	1:53
49	18	Tu.	♃☌☉	7:13	6:20	**12:43**	2:51
50	19	We.		7:12	6:20	**1:32**	3:47
51	20	Th.		7:11	6:21	**2:27**	4:40
52	21	Fr.		7:10	6:22	**3:28**	5:28
53	22	Sa.		7:09	6:23	**4:32**	6:11
54	23	Su.		7:08	6:24	**5:37**	6:49
55	24	Mo.		7:07	6:25	**6:43**	7:24
56	25	Tu.		7:05	6:26	**7:48**	7:55
57	26	We.		7:04	6:27	**8:54**	8:24
58	27	Th.		7:03	6:28	**10:01**	8:55
59	28	Fr.	☿ Gr. elong. E.	7:02	6:28	**11:09**	9:27

3rd Month MARCH, 1986 31 Days

Moon's Phases.—Last. Qr., March 3, 6:17 a.m.; New, March 10, 8:52 a.m.; First Qr., March 18, 10:39 a.m.; Full, March 25, 9:02 p.m.

Day of Year	Day of Month	Day of Week	Planetary Configurations —Phenomena	*Hour of Sunrise	*Hour of Sunset	*Hour of Moonrise	*Hour of Moonset
60	1	Sa.	☾ at Perigee	7:00	6:29	...	10:02
61	2	Su.		6:59	6:30	12:19	10:43
62	3	Mo.	♄☌☾	6:58	6:31	1:30	11:30
63	4	Tu.	♆☌☾	6:57	6:32	2:38	**12:25**
64	5	We.		6:55	6:32	3:41	**1:28**
65	6	Th.	☿ Stationary	6:53	6:33	4:37	**2:35**
66	7	Fr.		6:51	6:34	5:23	**3:43**
67	8	Sa.	☿☌♀	6:49	6:35	6:02	**4:49**
68	9	Su.		6:48	6:36	6:35	**5:52**
69	10	Mo.		6:47	6:37	7:05	**6:52**
70	11	Tu.	♀☌☾	6:46	6:38	7:31	**7:51**
71	12	We.		6:44	6:39	7:58	**8:49**
72	13	Th.	♂☌♅	6:43	6:39	8:24	**9:46**
73	14	Fr.		6:42	6:40	8:51	**10:43**
74	15	Sa.		6:42	6:40	9:22	**11:42**
75	16	Su.	☾ at Apogee	6:40	6:41	9:57	...
76	17	Mo.		6:40	6:41	10:36	12:40
77	18	Tu.		6:39	6:42	11:22	1:36
78	19	We.	♄ Stationary	6:38	6:43	**12:14**	2:30
79	20	Th.	Spring Begins	6:37	6:43	**1:12**	3:20
80	21	Fr.		6:35	6:44	**2:14**	4:05
81	22	Sa.		6:34	6:45	**3:18**	4:44
82	23	Su.		6:32	6:46	**4:23**	5:20
83	24	Mo.		6:31	6:47	**5:29**	5:52
84	25	Tu.		6:30	6:47	**6:36**	6:22
85	26	We.		6:28	6:48	**7:44**	6:53
86	27	Th.	♅ Stationary	6:27	6:48	**8:54**	7:25
87	28	Fr.	☾ at Perigee	6:26	6:49	**10:06**	7:59
88	29	Sa.	☿ Stationary	6:25	6:50	**11:19**	8:39
89	30	Su.	♄☌☾	6:24	6:51	...	9:26
90	31	Mo.	♅☌☾	6:22	6:52	12:30	10:20

4th Month APRIL, 1986 30 Days

Moon's Phases.—Last Qr., April 1, 1:30 p.m.; New, April 9, 12:08 a.m.; First Qr., April 17, 4:35 a.m.; Full, April 24, 6:46 a.m.; Last Qr., April 30, 10:22 p.m.

Day of Year	Day of Month	Day of Week	Planetary Configurations —Phenomena	*Hour of Sunrise	*Hour of Sunset	*Hour of Moonrise	*Hour of Moonset
91	1	Tu.	♆☌☾	6:21	6:53	1:36	11:20
92	2	We.		6:20	6:53	2:34	**12:27**
93	3	Th.		6:19	6:54	3:23	**1:34**
94	4	Fr.		6:18	6:54	4:03	**2:40**
95	5	Sa.	♃☌☾	6:16	6:55	4:37	**3:43**
96	6	Su.	☿☌☾	6:14	6:55	5:07	**4:43**
97	7	Mo.	♆ Stationary	6:13	6:56	5:34	**5:42**
98	8	Tu.	♂☌♆	6:12	6:57	6:00	**6:39**
99	9	We.	Eclipse ☉	6:11	6:57	6:26	**7:36**
100	10	Th.	♀☌☾	6:10	6:58	6:53	**8:34**
101	11	Fr.		6:08	6:59	7:22	**9:31**
102	12	Sa.		6:07	6:59	7:55	**10:30**
103	13	Su.	☿ Gr. elong. W.	6:06	7:00	8:32	**11:27**
104	14	Mo.		6:04	7:01	9:15	...
105	15	Tu.		6:03	7:01	10:05	12:22
106	16	We.		6:02	7:02	10:59	1:13
107	17	Th.		6:01	7:03	11:58	1:59
108	18	Fr.		6:00	7:04	**1:00**	2:39
109	19	Sa.		5:59	7:05	**2:04**	3:16
110	20	Su.		5:58	7:05	**3:08**	3:49
111	21	Mo.		5:57	7:06	**4:14**	4:19
112	22	Tu.		5:56	7:07	**5:21**	4:49
113	23	We.		5:55	7:08	**6:31**	5:20
114	24	Th.	Eclipse ☾	5:53	7:08	**7:44**	5:53
115	25	Fr.	☾ at Perigee	5:52	7:09	**8:58**	6:32
116	26	Sa.	♄☌☾	5:51	7:10	**10:13**	7:16
117	27	†Su.	♅☌☾	6:50	8:11	...	9:09
118	28	Mo.	♆☌☾	6:49	8:11	12:25	10:10
119	29	Tu.	♂☌☾	6:48	8:12	1:28	11:16
120	30	We.		6:47	8:13	2:21	**12:25**

†Daylight Saving Time began at 2 a.m.

CALENDAR FOR 1986

5th Month MAY, 1986 31 Days

Moon's Phases.—New, May 8, 5:10 p.m.; First Qr., May 16, 8:00 p.m.; Full, May 23, 3:45 p.m.; Last Qr., May 30, 7:55 a.m.

Day of Year	Day of Month	Day of Week	Planetary Configurations —Phenomena	*Hour of Sunrise	Sunset	Moonrise	Moonset
121	1	Th.		6:46	8:13	3:04	**1:32**
122	2	Fr.		6:45	8:14	3:40	**2:36**
123	3	Sa.	♃☌☾	6:44	8:15	4:11	**3:37**
124	4	Su.		6:43	8:15	4:38	**4:36**
125	5	Mo.		6:42	8:16	5:04	**5:33**
126	6	Tu.		6:41	8:17	5:29	**6:29**
127	7	We.	☿☌☾	6:40	8:18	5:56	**7:26**
128	8	Th.		6:39	8:18	6:25	**8:24**
129	9	Fr.		6:38	8:19	6:55	**9:22**
130	10	Sa.	☾ at Apogee	6:37	8:20	7:30	**10:20**
131	11	Su.	♀☌☾	6:37	8:21	8:12	**11:16**
132	12	Mo.		6:36	8:22	8:59	...
133	13	Tu.		6:35	8:23	9:52	12:08
134	14	We.		6:34	8:23	10:49	12:55
135	15	Th.		6:33	8:24	11:49	1:38
136	16	Fr.		6:33	8:24	**12:50**	2:14
137	17	Sa.		6:32	8:25	**1:52**	2:47
138	18	Su.		6:32	8:25	**2:56**	3:18
139	19	Mo.		6:32	8:26	**3:59**	3:46
140	20	Tu.	☿ Superior	6:31	8:26	**5:06**	4:16
141	21	We.		6:31	8:27	**6:16**	4:48
142	22	Th.		6:31	8:28	**7:30**	5:23
143	23	Fr.	☾ at Perigee	6:30	8:29	**8:46**	6:03
144	24	Sa.	♄☌☾	6:29	8:30	**10:02**	6:54
145	25	Su.	♆☌☾	6:29	8:30	**11:12**	7:52
146	26	Mo.	♂☌☾	6:28	8:31	...	8:59
147	27	Tu.		6:28	8:32	12:11	10:10
148	28	We.		6:28	8:32	1:01	11:20
149	29	Th.		6:27	8:33	1:40	**12:28**
150	30	Fr.		6:27	8:33	2:13	**1:31**
151	31	Sa.	♃☌☾	6:26	8:34	2:42	**2:30**

6th Month JUNE, 1986 30 Days

Moon's Phases.—New, June 7, 9:00 a.m.; First Qr., June 15, 7:00 a.m.; Full, June 21, 10:42 p.m.; Last Qr., June 28, 7:53 p.m.

Day of Year	Day of Month	Day of Week	Planetary Configurations —Phenomena	*Hour of Sunrise	Sunset	Moonrise	Moonset
152	1	Su.		6:26	8:34	3:09	**3:29**
153	2	Mo.		6:25	8:35	3:34	**4:25**
154	3	Tu.		6:25	8:35	4:00	**5:21**
155	4	We.		6:24	8:36	4:27	**6:18**
156	5	Th.		6:24	8:36	4:57	**7:16**
157	6	Fr.	☾ at Apogee	6:24	8:37	5:32	**8:14**
158	7	Sa.		6:23	8:37	6:11	**9:10**
159	8	Su.		6:23	8:38	6:57	**10:04**
160	9	Mo.	☿☌☾	6:23	8:38	7:47	**10:53**
161	10	Tu.	♀☌☾	6:23	8:39	8:43	**11:36**
162	11	We.		6:23	8:39	9:43	...
163	12	Th.		6:23	8:40	10:43	12:15
164	13	Fr.		6:23	8:40	11:43	12:48
165	14	Sa.		6:23	8:41	**12:44**	1:18
166	15	Su.		6:23	8:41	**1:45**	1:48
167	16	Mo.		6:23	8:42	**2:49**	2:15
168	17	Tu.		6:23	8:42	**3:55**	2:45
169	18	We.		6:24	8:42	**5:05**	3:17
170	19	Th.		6:24	8:43	**6:19**	3:54
171	20	Fr.	♄☌☾	6:24	8:43	**7:35**	4:38
172	21	Sa.	Summer Begins	6:24	8:43	**8:48**	5:32
173	22	Su.	♆☌☾	6:25	8:44	**9:54**	6:35
174	23	Mo.	♂☌☾	6:25	8:44	**10:49**	7:46
175	24	Tu.		6:25	8:44	**11:35**	8:59
176	25	We.	☿ Gr. elong. E.	6:25	8:44	...	10:10
177	26	Th.		6:26	8:45	12:11	11:18
178	27	Fr.	♃☌☾	6:26	8:45	12:43	**12:21**
179	28	Sa.		6:27	8:45	1:11	**1:20**
180	29	Su.		6:27	8:45	1:37	**2:18**
181	30	Mo.		6:28	8:45	2:03	**3:15**

7th Month JULY, 1986 31 Days

Moon's Phases.—New, July 6, 11:55 p.m.; First Qr., July 14, 3:10 p.m.; Full, July 21, 5:40 a.m.; Last Qr., July 28, 10:34 a.m.

Day of Year	Day of Month	Day of Week	Planetary Configurations —Phenomena	*Hour of Sunrise	Sunset	Moonrise	Moonset
182	1	Tu.		6:28	8:44	2:30	**4:12**
183	2	We.		6:29	8:44	2:59	**5:09**
184	3	Th.		6:29	8:44	3:32	**6:07**
185	4	Fr.	☾ at Apogee	6:30	8:44	4:10	**7:04**
186	5	Sa.	⊕ at Aphelion	6:30	8:44	4:53	**8:00**
187	6	Su.		6:31	8:43	5:43	**8:50**
188	7	Mo.		6:31	8:43	6:38	**9:36**
189	8	Tu.	☿☌☾	6:31	8:43	7:36	**10:15**
190	9	We.		6:32	8:43	8:37	**10:50**
191	10	Th.	♀☌☾	6:32	8:42	9:38	**11:21**
192	11	Fr.		6:33	8:42	10:38	**11:50**
193	12	Sa.		6:33	8:42	11:39	...
194	13	Su.	♃ Stationary	6:34	8:42	**12:40**	12:18
195	14	Mo.		6:34	8:41	**1:43**	12:45
196	15	Tu.		6:35	8:41	**2:50**	1:15
197	16	We.		6:35	8:41	**4:00**	1:49
198	17	Th.	♄☌☾	6:36	8:40	**5:13**	2:29
199	18	Fr.	♅☌☾	6:37	8:40	**6:26**	3:17
200	19	Sa.	♆☌☾	6:38	8:39	**7:33**	4:15
201	20	Su.	♂☌☾	6:38	8:39	**8:34**	5:21
202	21	Mo.	♇ Stationary	6:39	8:38	**9:24**	6:34
203	22	Tu.		6:39	8:38	**10:05**	7:47
204	23	We.		6:40	8:37	**10:40**	8:58
205	24	Th.		6:40	8:37	**11:10**	10:05
206	25	Fr.	♃☌☾	6:41	8:36	**11:37**	11:07
207	26	Sa.		6:41	8:36	...	**12:07**
208	27	Su.		6:42	8:35	12:04	**1:06**
209	28	Mo.		6:42	8:34	12:31	**2:03**
210	29	Tu.		6:43	8:33	1:00	**3:01**
211	30	We.		6:44	8:32	1:31	**3:59**
212	31	Th.	☾ at Apogee	6:44	8:31	2:07	**4:57**

8th Month AUGUST, 1986 31 Days

Moon's Phases.—New, Aug. 5, 1:36 p.m.; First Qr., Aug. 12, 9:21 p.m.; Full, Aug. 19, 1:54 p.m.; Last Qr., Aug. 27, 3:38 a.m.

Day of Year	Day of Month	Day of Week	Planetary Configurations —Phenomena	*Hour of Sunrise	Sunset	Moonrise	Moonset
213	1	Fr.		6:45	8:31	2:49	**5:53**
214	2	Sa.	☿ Stationary	6:46	8:30	3:36	**6:46**
215	3	Su.		6:47	8:29	4:30	**7:33**
216	4	Mo.	☿☌☾	6:48	8:28	5:28	**8:15**
217	5	Tu.		6:49	8:27	6:29	**8:52**
218	6	We.		6:50	8:26	7:30	**9:24**
219	7	Th.	♄ Stationary	6:50	8:25	8:32	**9:54**
220	8	Fr.		6:51	8:25	9:33	**10:21**
221	9	Sa.	♀☌☾	6:51	8:24	10:34	**10:49**
222	10	Su.		6:52	8:23	11:37	**11:17**
223	11	Mo.	☿ Gr. elong. W.	6:53	8:22	**12:41**	**11:49**
224	12	Tu.	♂ Stationary	6:53	8:21	**1:49**	...
225	13	We.	♄☌☾	6:54	8:20	**2:59**	12:26
226	14	Th.	♅☌☾	6:54	8:19	**4:11**	1:10
227	15	Fr.	♆☌☾	6:55	8:18	**5:19**	2:02
228	16	Sa.	♂☌☾	6:56	8:17	**6:21**	3:04
229	17	Su.		6:57	8:15	**7:14**	4:13
230	18	Mo.		6:58	8:14	**7:59**	5:25
231	19	Tu.		6:58	8:13	**8:35**	6:36
232	20	We.		6:59	8:12	**9:07**	7:45
233	21	Th.	♃☌☾	6:59	8:11	**9:36**	8:50
234	22	Fr.		7:00	8:10	**10:03**	9:52
235	23	Sa.		7:01	8:09	**10:31**	10:52
236	24	Su.		7:01	8:07	**10:58**	11:51
237	25	Mo.		7:02	8:06	**11:29**	**12:50**
238	26	Tu.		7:02	8:05	...	**1:49**
239	27	We.	♀ Gr. elong. E.	7:03	8:04	12:04	**2:48**
240	28	Th.	☾ at Apogee	7:03	8:03	12:43	**3:44**
241	29	Fr.		7:04	8:02	1:29	**4:38**
242	30	Sa.		7:05	8:01	2:20	**5:28**
243	31	Su.		7:06	8:00	3:17	**6:11**

CALENDAR FOR 1986

9th Month **SEPTEMBER, 1986** **30 Days**

Moon's Phases.—New, Sept. 4, 2:10 a.m.; First Qr., Sept. 11, 2:41 a.m.; Full, Sept. 18, 12:34 a.m.; Last Qr., Sept. 25, 10:17 p.m.

Day of Year	Day of Month	Day of Week	Planetary Configurations —Phenomena	*Hour of Sunrise	*Hour of Sunset	*Hour of Moonrise	*Hour of Moonset
244	1	Mo.		7:07	7:58	4:17	**6:50**
245	2	Tu.		7:07	7:57	5:18	**7:23**
246	3	We.		7:08	7:55	6:21	**7:55**
247	4	Th.		7:09	7:54	7:23	**8:24**
248	5	Fr.	☿Superior	7:09	7:52	8:25	**8:52**
249	6	Sa.		7:10	7:51	9:29	**9:20**
250	7	Su.	♀☌☾	7:10	7:49	10:34	**9:51**
251	8	Mo.		7:11	7:48	11:41	**10:26**
252	9	Tu.		7:12	7:47	**12:51**	**11:07**
253	10	We.	♄☌☾	7:12	7:46	**2:02**	**11:56**
254	11	Th.	♅☌☾	7:13	7:45	**3:10**	...
255	12	Fr.	♆☌☾	7:13	7:43	**4:13**	12:54
256	13	Sa.	♂☌☾	7:14	7:42	**5:08**	1:59
257	14	Su.	♆ Stationary	7:14	7:41	**5:54**	3:09
258	15	Mo.		7:15	7:40	**6:32**	4:19
259	16	Tu.		7:16	7:38	**7:06**	5:28
260	17	We.	♃☌☾	7:16	7:37	**7:35**	6:34
261	18	Th.		7:17	7:35	**8:03**	7:36
262	19	Fr.		7:18	7:34	**8:30**	8:37
263	20	Sa.		7:18	7:32	**8:57**	9:37
264	21	Su.		7:19	7:31	**9:27**	10:37
265	22	Mo.		7:19	7:29	**10:00**	11:37
266	23	Tu.	Autumn Begins	7:20	7:28	**10:39**	**12:36**
267	24	We.		7:20	7:27	**11:21**	**1:34**
268	25	Th.	☾at Apogee	7:21	7:25	...	**2:29**
269	26	Fr.		7:21	7:24	12:09	**3:20**
270	27	Sa.		7:22	7:23	1:04	**4:06**
271	28	Su.		7:23	7:22	2:03	**4:46**
272	29	Mo.		7:23	7:21	3:03	**5:22**
273	30	Tu.		7:24	7:19	4:05	**5:53**

10th Month **OCTOBER, 1986** **31 Days**

Moon's Phases.—New, Oct. 3, 1:55 p.m.; First Qr., Oct. 10, 8:28 a.m.; Full, Oct. 17, 2:22 p.m.; Last Qr., Oct. 25, 5:26 p.m.

Day of Year	Day of Month	Day of Week	Planetary Configurations —Phenomena	*Hour of Sunrise	*Hour of Sunset	*Hour of Moonrise	*Hour of Moonset
274	1	We.	♀Gr. brilliancy	7:25	7:18	5:08	**6:23**
275	2	Th.		7:26	7:17	6:10	**6:52**
276	3	Fr.	Eclipse☉	7:27	7:15	7:14	**7:20**
277	4	Sa.		7:28	7:14	8:20	**7:51**
278	5	Su.	☿☌☾	7:28	7:14	9:29	**8:26**
279	6	Mo.	♀☌☾	7:29	7:11	10:39	**9:05**
280	7	Tu.	♄☌☾	7:29	7:10	11:52	**9:52**
281	8	We.	♅☌☾	7:30	7:09	**1:03**	**10:48**
282	9	Th.	♆☌☾	7:31	7:08	**2:08**	**11:51**
283	10	Fr.		7:32	7:07	**3:06**	...
284	11	Sa.	♂☌☾	7:33	7:06	**3:53**	1:00
285	12	Su.	♃☌☾	7:33	7:05	**4:33**	2:09
286	13	Mo.		7:34	7:03	**5:07**	3:17
287	14	Tu.		7:35	7:02	**5:37**	4:22
288	15	We.	♀Stationary	7:36	7:01	**6:05**	5:25
289	16	Th.		7:37	7:00	**6:31**	6:26
290	17	Fr.	Eclipse☾	7:38	6:59	**6:58**	7:25
291	18	Sa.	☿☌♀	7:38	6:57	**7:27**	8:24
292	19	Su.		7:39	6:56	**7:58**	9:24
293	20	Mo.		7:40	6:55	**8:34**	10:24
294	21	Tu.	☿Gr. elong E.	7:41	6:54	**9:15**	11:33
295	22	We.		7:41	6:52	**10:02**	**12:20**
296	23	Th.	☾at Apogee	7:42	6:51	**10:54**	**1:13**
297	24	Fr.		7:43	6:50	**11:51**	**2:00**
298	25	Sa.		7:43	6:49	...	**2:42**
299	26	†Su.		6:44	5:47	12:49	**2:19**
300	27	Mo.		6:45	5:47	12:50	**2:52**
301	28	Tu.		6:46	5:46	1:50	**3:21**
302	29	We.		6:47	5:46	2:52	**3:50**
303	30	Th.	♇☌☉	6:48	5:45	3:55	**4:18**
304	31	Fr.		6:48	5:44	5:00	**4:48**

†Daylight Saving Time ended at 2 a.m.

11th Month **NOVEMBER, 1986** **30 Days**

Moon's Phases.—New, Nov. 2, 12:02 a.m.; First Qr., Nov. 8, 3:11 p.m.; Full, Nov. 16, 6:12 a.m.; Last Qr., Nov. 24, 10:50 a.m.

Day of Year	Day of Month	Day of Week	Planetary Configurations —Phenomena	*Hour of Sunrise	*Hour of Sunset	*Hour of Moonrise	*Hour of Moonset
305	1	Sa.		6:49	5:43	6:08	**5:20**
306	2	Su.	☿Stationary	6:50	5:42	7:19	**5:59**
307	3	Mo.	☿☌☾	6:51	5:41	8:33	**6:43**
308	4	Tu.	♄☌☾	6:52	5:40	9:47	**7:38**
309	5	We.	♆☌☾	6:53	5:39	10:57	**8:41**
310	6	Th.		6:53	5:38	11:59	**9:50**
311	7	Fr.		6:54	5:37	**12:51**	**11:00**
312	8	Sa.	♂☌☾	6:55	5:36	**1:34**	...
313	9	Su.		6:56	5:35	**2:10**	12:10
314	10	Mo.	♃☌☾	6:57	5:35	**2:41**	1:16
315	11	Tu.		6:58	5:34	**3:08**	2:18
316	12	We.	Transit of Mercury	6:59	5:34	**3:34**	3:18
317	13	Th.		6:59	5:33	**4:01**	4:17
318	14	Fr.		7:00	5:33	**4:28**	5:15
319	15	Sa.		7:01	5:32	**4:58**	6:14
320	16	Su.		7:02	5:32	**5:33**	7:14
321	17	Mo.		7:03	5:31	**6:12**	8:13
322	18	Tu.		7:04	5:31	**6:56**	9:11
323	19	We.	☾at Apogee	7:05	5:30	**7:46**	10:05
324	20	Th.		7:06	5:30	**8:41**	10:55
325	21	Fr.	☿Stationary	7:07	5:29	**9:38**	11:39
326	22	Sa.		7:08	5:29	**10:38**	**12:17**
327	23	Su.	♀Stationary	7:09	5:28	**11:38**	**12:51**
328	24	Mo.		7:10	5:28	...	**1:21**
329	25	Tu.		7:11	5:28	12:37	**1:49**
330	26	We.		7:12	5:27	1:37	**2:16**
331	27	Th.		7:13	5:27	2:39	**2:43**
332	28	Fr.		7:14	5:27	3:44	**3:14**
333	29	Sa.	♀☌☾	7:15	5:26	4:52	**3:49**
334	30	Su.	☿☌☾	7:16	5:26	6:05	**4:31**

12th Month **DECEMBER, 1986** **31 Days**

Moon's Phases.—New, Dec. 1, 10:43 a.m.; First Qr., Dec. 8, 2:01 a.m.; Full, Dec. 16, 1:04 a.m.; Last Qr., Dec. 24, 3:17 a.m.; New, Dec. 30, 9:10 p.m.

Day of Year	Day of Month	Day of Week	Planetary Configurations —Phenomena	*Hour of Sunrise	*Hour of Sunset	*Hour of Moonrise	*Hour of Moonset
335	1	Mo.		7:16	5:26	7:21	**5:21**
336	2	Tu.	☾at Perigee	7:17	5:26	8:36	**6:22**
337	3	We.	♆☌☾	7:18	5:26	9:44	**7:32**
338	4	Th.	♄☌☾	7:19	5:26	10:43	**8:45**
339	5	Fr.		7:20	5:26	11:31	**9:58**
340	6	Sa.		7:20	5:26	**12:10**	**11:06**
341	7	Su.	♂☌☾	7:21	5:26	**12:42**	...
342	8	Mo.		7:21	5:27	**1:12**	12:11
343	9	Tu.		7:22	5:27	**1:38**	1:12
344	10	We.		7:23	5:27	**2:05**	2:11
345	11	Th.	♀Gr. Brilliancy	7:24	5:27	**2:32**	3:10
346	12	Fr.		7:24	5:27	**3:01**	4:08
347	13	Sa.		7:25	5:28	**3:33**	5:07
348	14	Su.	♅☌☉	7:26	5:28	**4:11**	6:06
349	15	Mo.		7:26	5:28	**4:53**	7:04
350	16	Tu.	☾at Apogee	7:27	5:28	**5:42**	8:00
351	17	We.		7:28	5:29	**6:35**	8:51
352	18	Th.		7:28	5:29	**7:32**	9:36
353	19	Fr.	♂☌♃	7:29	5:30	**8:30**	10:16
354	20	Sa.		7:29	5:30	**9:29**	10:51
355	21	Su.	Winter Begins	7:30	5:31	**10:28**	11:21
356	22	Mo.		7:30	5:31	**11:26**	11:49
357	23	Tu.		7:30	5:32	...	**12:16**
358	24	We.		7:31	5:32	12:25	**12:43**
359	25	Th.	☿☌♅	7:31	5:33	1:27	**1:10**
360	26	Fr.		7:32	5:33	2:31	**1:42**
361	27	Sa.	♆☌☉	7:32	5:34	3:39	**2:19**
362	28	Su.		7:33	5:34	4:52	**3:04**
363	29	Mo.	♄☌☾	7:33	5:35	6:07	**3:59**
364	30	Tu.	☾at Perigee	7:34	5:36	7:19	**5:04**
365	31	We.		7:34	5:37	8:24	**6:18**

CALENDAR FOR 1987

(Time given in this calendar is according to **Central Standard Time**. See page 81 for explanation of how to get exact time at any certain Texas point. Boldface figures indicate p.m.)

1st Month **JANUARY, 1987** **31 Days**

Moon's Phases.—First Qr., Jan. 6, 4:34 p.m.; Full, Jan. 14, 8:30 p.m.; Last Qr., Jan. 22, 4:45 p.m.; New, Jan. 29, 7:44 a.m.

Day of Year	Day of Month	Day of Week	Planetary Configurations—Phenomena	*Hour of Sunrise	Sunset	Moonrise	Moonset
1	1	Th.		7:34	5:37	9:19	**7:34**
2	2	Fr.		7:34	5:38	10:04	**8:48**
3	3	Sa.		7:34	5:39	10.40	**9:56**
4	4	Su.	⊕ at Perihelion	7:34	5:39	11:11	**11:02**
5	5	Mo.	♂☌☾	7:34	5:40	11:40	...
6	6	Tu.		7:35	5:41	**12:07**	12:04
7	7	We.		7:35	5:42	**12:34**	1:04
8	8	Th.		7:35	5:43	**1:03**	2:02
9	9	Fr.		7:35	5:44	**1:34**	3:01
10	10	Sa.		7:35	5:45	**2:10**	4:00
11	11	Su.		7:35	5:46	**2:50**	4:58
12	12	Mo.	☿ Superior	7:35	5:47	**3:37**	5:55
13	13	Tu.		7:35	5:48	**4:30**	6:47
14	14	We.		7:35	5:48	**5:26**	7:35
15	15	Th.	♀ Gr. elong. W.	7:35	5:49	**6:25**	8:16
16	16	Fr.		7:34	5:50	**7:24**	8:52
17	17	Sa.		7:34	5:51	**8:22**	9:24
18	18	Su.		7:34	5:52	**9:20**	9:53
19	19	Mo.		7:33	5:53	**10:18**	10:19
20	20	Tu.		7:33	5:54	**11:18**	10:45
21	21	We.		7:33	5:54	...	11:12
22	22	Th.		7:33	5:55	12:19	11:41
23	23	Fr.		7:32	5:56	1:24	**12:14**
24	24	Sa.	♀☌♄	7:32	5:57	2:32	**12:53**
25	25	Su.	♄☌☾	7:31	5:58	3:43	**1:41**
26	26	Mo.	♀☌☾	7:31	5:59	4:55	**2:40**
27	27	Tu.	♆☌☾	7:31	6:00	6:03	**3:50**
28	28	We.	☾ at Perigee	7:30	6:01	7:02	**4:04**
29	29	Th.		7:29	6:02	7:52	**6:20**
30	30	Fr.		7:28	6:03	8:33	**7:33**
31	31	Sa.	♀☌♂	7:28	6:04	9:08	**8:42**

2nd Month **FEBRUARY, 1987** **28 Days**

Moon's Phases.—First Qr., Feb. 5, 10:21 a.m.; Full, Feb. 13, 2:58 p.m.; Last Qr., Feb. 21, 2:56 a.m.; New, Feb. 27, 6:51 p.m.

Day of Year	Day of Month	Day of Week	Planetary Configurations—Phenomena	*Hour of Sunrise	Sunset	Moonrise	Moonset
32	1	Su.	♃☌☾	7:27	6:05	9:38	**9:48**
33	2	Mo.		7:27	6:06	10:06	**10:50**
34	3	Tu.	♂☌☾	7:26	6:07	10:34	**11:51**
35	4	We.		7:25	6:08	11:03	...
36	5	Th.		7:24	6:08	11:33	12:52
37	6	Fr.		7:24	6:09	**12:08**	1:52
38	7	Sa.		7:23	6:10	**12:47**	2:51
39	8	Su.		7:22	6:11	**1:32**	3:48
40	9	Mo.	☾ at Apogee	7:21	6:12	**2:22**	4:42
41	10	Tu.		7:21	6:13	**3:18**	5:32
42	11	We.	☿ Gr. elong. E.	7:20	6:14	**4:16**	6:15
43	12	Th.		7:19	6:15	**5:16**	6:53
44	13	Fr.		7:18	6:15	**6:15**	7:26
45	14	Sa.		7:17	6:16	**7:14**	7:56
46	15	Su.		7:16	6:17	**8:13**	8:23
47	16	Mo.	♇ Sta. in R.A.	7:15	6:18	**9:12**	8:49
48	17	Tu.	☿ Sta. in R.A.	7:14	6:19	**10:13**	9:16
49	18	We.		7:13	6:20	**11:16**	9:43
50	19	Th.		7:12	6:20	...	10:15
51	20	Fr.		7:11	6:21	12:22	10:51
52	21	Sa.		7:10	6:22	1:30	11:35
53	22	Su.	♄☌☾	7:09	6:23	2:40	**12:35**
54	23	Mo.	♆☌☾	7:08	6:24	3:48	**1:37**
55	24	Tu.	♀☌☾	7:07	6:25	4:48	**2:41**
56	25	We.	☾ at Perigee	7:05	6:26	5:41	**3:55**
57	26	Th.		7:04	6:27	6:25	**5:08**
58	27	Fr.		7:03	6:28	7:01	**6:18**
59	28	Sa.		7:02	6:28	7:33	**7:26**

3rd Month **MARCH, 1987** **31 Days**

Moon's Phases.—First Qr., March 7, 5:58 a.m.; Full, March 15, 7:13 a.m.; Last Qr., March 22, 10:22 a.m.; New, March 29, 6:46 a.m.

Day of Year	Day of Month	Day of Week	Planetary Configurations—Phenomena	*Hour of Sunrise	Sunset	Moonrise	Moonset
60	1	Su.	♃☌☾	7:00	6:29	8:03	**8:31**
61	2	Mo.		6:59	6:30	8:32	**9:34**
62	3	Tu.		6:58	6:31	9:01	**10:36**
63	4	We.	♂☌☾	6:57	6:32	9:31	**11:38**
64	5	Th.		6:55	6:32	10:04	...
65	6	Fr.		6:53	6:33	10:43	12:40
66	7	Sa.		6:51	6:34	11:26	1:39
67	8	Su.		6:49	6:35	**12:14**	2:35
68	9	Mo.	☾ at Apogee	6:48	6:36	**1:08**	3:26
69	10	Tu.		6:47	6:37	**2:06**	4:11
70	11	We.	☿ Sta. in R.A.	6:46	6:38	**3:05**	4:51
71	12	Th.		6:44	6:39	**4:04**	5:26
72	13	Fr.		6:43	6:39	**5:03**	5:57
73	14	Sa.		6:42	6:40	**6:03**	6:25
74	15	Su.		6:42	6:40	**7:03**	6:52
75	16	Mo.		6:40	6:41	**8:04**	7:19
76	17	Tu.		6:40	6:41	**9:08**	7:46
77	18	We.		6:39	6:42	**10:14**	8:17
78	19	Th.		6:38	6:43	**11:23**	8:52
79	20	Fr.	Spring Begins	6:37	6:43	...	9:33
80	21	Sa.	♄☌☾	6:35	6:44	12:32	10:23
81	22	Su.	♂☌☾	6:34	6:45	1:40	11:21
82	23	Mo.		6:32	6:46	2:42	**12:28**
83	24	Tu.	☾ at Perigee	6:31	6:47	3:35	**1:38**
84	25	We.		6:30	6:47	4:20	**2:50**
85	26	Th.	☿ Gr. elong. W.	6:28	6:48	4:59	**4:00**
86	27	Fr.	☿☌☾	6:27	6:48	5:32	**5:07**
87	28	Sa.		6:26	6:49	6:02	**6:13**
88	29	Su.		6:25	6:50	6:30	**7:16**
89	30	Mo.		6:24	6:51	6:58	**8:19**
90	31	Tu.	♄ Sta. in R.A.	6:22	6:52	7:28	**9:22**

4th Month **APRIL, 1987** **30 Days**

Moon's Phases.—First Qr., April 6, 1:48 a.m.; Full, April 13, 8:31 p.m.; Last Qr., April 20, 4:15 p.m.; New, April 27, 8:34 p.m.

Day of Year	Day of Month	Day of Week	Planetary Configurations—Phenomena	*Hour of Sunrise	Sunset	Moonrise	Moonset
91	1	We.		6:21	6:53	8:01	**10:25**
92	2	Th.	♂☌☾	6:20	6:53	8:37	**11:26**
93	3	Fr.		6:19	6:54	9:18	...
94	4	Sa.		6:18	6:54	10:05	12:24
95	5	Su.		6:16	6:55	10:57	1:18
96	6	Mo.	☾ at Apogee	6:14	6:55	11:53	2:06
97	7	Tu.		6:13	6:56	**12:52**	2:48
98	8	We.		6:12	6:57	**1:51**	3:24
99	9	Th.	♆ Sta. in R.A.	6:11	6:57	**2:50**	3:56
100	10	Fr.		6:10	6:58	**3:50**	4:26
101	11	Sa.		6:08	6:59	**4:50**	4:52
102	12	Su.		6:07	6:59	**5:50**	5:19
103	13	Mo.		6:06	7:00	**6:55**	5:47
104	14	Tu.		6:04	7:01	**8:01**	6:16
105	15	We.		6:03	7:01	**9:10**	6:50
106	16	Th.		6:02	7:02	**10:22**	7:30
107	17	Fr.		6:01	7:03	**11:32**	8:18
108	18	Sa.	☾ at Perigee	6:00	7:04	...	9:15
109	19	Su.	☿☌♃	5:59	7:05	12:36	10:20
110	20	Mo.		5:58	7:05	1:33	11:30
111	21	Tu.		5:57	7:06	2:20	**12:40**
112	22	We.		5:56	7:07	3:00	**1:50**
113	23	Th.		5:55	7:08	3:34	**2:57**
114	24	Fr.		5:53	7:08	4:04	**4:00**
115	25	Sa.	♀☌☾	5:52	7:09	4:31	**5:03**
116	26	†Su.	♃☌☾	6:51	8:10	5:59	**7:05**
117	27	Mo.		6:50	8:11	6:27	**8:07**
118	28	Tu.		6:49	8:11	6:58	**9:10**
119	29	We.		6:48	8:12	7:34	**10:12**
120	30	Th.		6:47	8:13	8:13	**11:12**

†Daylight Saving Time began at 2 a.m.

CALENDAR FOR 1987

5th Month **MAY, 1987** **31 Days**

Moon's Phases.—First Qr., May 5, 9:26 p.m.; Full, May 13, 7:50 a.m.; Last Qr., May 19, 11:02 p.m.; New, May 27, 10:13 a.m.

Day of Year	Day of Month	Day of Week	Planetary Configurations —Phenomena	*Hour of Sunrise	Sunset	Moonrise	Moonset
121	1	Fr.	♂☌☾	6:46	8:13	8:58	...
122	2	Sa.		6:45	8:14	9:48	12:08
123	3	Su.	☾ at Apogee	6:44	8:15	10:43	12:59
124	4	Mo.	♀☌♃	6:43	8:15	11:40	1:43
125	5	Tu.		6:42	8:16	**12:39**	2:21
126	6	We.		6:41	8:17	**1:37**	2:55
127	7	Th.	☿ Superior	6:40	8:18	**2:35**	3:25
128	8	Fr.		6:39	8:18	**3:35**	3:53
129	9	Sa.		6:38	8:19	**4:34**	4:18
130	10	Su.		6:37	8:20	**5:36**	4:45
131	11	Mo.		6:37	8:21	**6:41**	5:14
132	12	Tu.		6:36	8:22	**7:50**	5:46
133	13	We.		6:35	8:23	**9:02**	6:23
134	14	Th.		6:34	8:23	**10:16**	7:10
135	15	Fr.	☾ at Perigee	6:33	8:24	**11:25**	8:04
136	16	Sa.	♆☌☾	6:33	8:24	...	9:08
137	17	Su.		6:32	8:25	12:26	10:19
138	18	Mo.		6:32	8:25	1:18	11:31
139	19	Tu.		6:32	8:26	2:00	**12:42**
140	20	We.		6:31	8:26	2:36	**1:49**
141	21	Th.		6:31	8:27	3:06	**2:53**
142	22	Fr.		6:31	8:28	3:35	**3:56**
143	23	Sa.	♃☌☾	6:30	8:29	4:02	**4:57**
144	24	Su.		6:29	8:30	4:30	**5:58**
145	25	Mo.	♀☌☾	6:29	8:30	5:00	**7:00**
146	26	Tu.		6:28	8:31	5:32	**8:01**
147	27	We.		6:28	8:32	6:09	**9:01**
148	28	Th.		6:28	8:32	6:52	**9:59**
149	29	Fr.	♂☌☾	6:27	8:33	7:41	**10:52**
150	30	Sa.		6:27	8:33	8:34	**11:39**
151	31	Su.	☾ at Apogee	6:26	8:34	9:31	...

6th Month **JUNE, 1987** **30 Days**

Moon's Phases.—First Qr., June 4, 1:53 p.m.; Full, June 11, 3:49 p.m.; Last Qr., June 18, 6:02 a.m.; New, June 26, 12:37 a.m.

Day of Year	Day of Month	Day of Week	Planetary Configurations —Phenomena	*Hour of Sunrise	Sunset	Moonrise	Moonset
152	1	Mo.		6:26	8:34	10:29	12:19
153	2	Tu.		6:25	8:35	11:27	12:55
154	3	We.		6:25	8:35	**12:25**	1:25
155	4	Th.		6:24	8:36	**1:22**	1:53
156	5	Fr.		6:24	8:36	**2:20**	2:19
157	6	Sa.		6:24	8:37	**3:19**	2:44
158	7	Su.	☿ Gr. elong. E.	6:23	8:37	**4:21**	3:11
159	8	Mo.		6:23	8:38	**5:28**	3:41
160	9	Tu.		6:23	8:38	**6:38**	4:15
161	10	We.		6:23	8:39	**7:52**	4:57
162	11	Th.	♄☌☾	6:23	8:39	**9:04**	5:47
163	12	Fr.	☾ at Perigee	6:23	8:40	**10:11**	6:49
164	13	Sa.		6:23	8:40	**11:09**	8:00
165	14	Su.		6:23	8:41	**11:57**	9:14
166	15	Mo.		6:23	8:41	...	10:29
167	16	Tu.		6:23	8:42	12:36	11:40
168	17	We.		6:23	8:42	1:09	**12:46**
169	18	Th.		6:24	8:42	1:38	**1:50**
170	19	Fr.		6:24	8:43	2:06	**2:52**
171	20	Sa.	☿ Sta. in R.A.	6:24	8:43	2:33	**3:53**
172	21	Su.		6:24	8:43	3:02	**4:53**
173	22	Mo.	Summer Begins	6:25	8:44	3:34	**5:55**
174	23	Tu.		6:25	8:44	4:09	**6:55**
175	24	We.	♀☌☾	6:25	8:44	4:50	**7:53**
176	25	Th.		6:25	8:44	5:36	**8:47**
177	26	Fr.		6:26	8:45	6:28	**9:36**
178	27	Sa.	☾ at Apogee	6:26	8:45	7:24	**10:18**
179	28	Su.		6:27	8:45	8:22	**10:54**
180	29	Mo.		6:27	8:45	9:20	**11:26**
181	30	Tu.		6:28	8:45	10:17	**11:55**

7th Month **JULY, 1987** **31 Days**

Moon's Phases.—First Qr., July 4, 3:34 a.m.; Full, July 10, 10:33 p.m.; Last Qr., July 17, 3:17 p.m.; New, July 25, 3:37 p.m.

Day of Year	Day of Month	Day of Week	Planetary Configurations —Phenomena	*Hour of Sunrise	Sunset	Moonrise	Moonset
182	1	We.		6:28	8:44	11:15	...
183	2	Th.		6:29	8:44	**12:11**	12:21
184	3	Fr.	⊕ at Aphelion	6:29	8:44	**1:08**	12:46
185	4	Sa.		6:30	8:44	**2:07**	1:12
186	5	Su.		6:30	8:44	**3:09**	1:39
187	6	Mo.		6:31	8:43	**4:16**	2:10
188	7	Tu.		6:31	8:43	**5:27**	2:47
189	8	We.	♄☌☾	6:31	8:43	**6:40**	3:33
190	9	Th.	♂☌☾	6:32	8:43	**7:49**	4:28
191	10	Fr.	♆☌☾	6:32	8:42	**8:53**	5:34
192	11	Sa.	☾ at Perigee	6:33	8:42	**9:46**	6:49
193	12	Su.		6:33	8:42	**10:30**	8:06
194	13	Mo.		6:34	8:42	**11:06**	9:21
195	14	Tu.		6:34	8:41	**11:38**	10:32
196	15	We.	☿ Sta. in R.A.	6:35	8:41	...	11:39
197	16	Th.		6:35	8:41	12:07	**12:42**
198	17	Fr.		6:36	8:40	12:35	**1:45**
199	18	Sa.	♃☌☾	6:37	8:40	1:05	**2:47**
200	19	Su.		6:38	8:39	1:35	**3:48**
201	20	Mo.		6:38	8:39	2:10	**4:49**
202	21	Tu.		6:39	8:38	2:49	**5:48**
203	22	We.		6:39	8:38	3:33	**6:43**
204	23	Th.	♇ Sta. in R.A.	6:40	8:37	4:23	**7:34**
205	24	Fr.		6:40	8:37	5:18	**8:18**
206	25	Sa.	☿ Gr. elong. W.	6:41	8:36	6:15	**8:56**
207	26	Su.		6:41	8:36	7:14	**9:28**
208	27	Mo.		6:42	8:35	8:12	**9:58**
209	28	Tu.		6:42	8:34	9:09	**10:24**
210	29	We.		6:43	8:33	10:05	**10:50**
211	30	Th.		6:44	8:32	11:01	**11:14**
212	31	Fr.		6:44	8:31	11:59	**11:41**

8th Month **AUGUST, 1987** **31 Days**

Moon's Phases.—First Qr., Aug. 2, 2:24 p.m.; Full, Aug. 9, 5:17 a.m.; Last Qr., Aug. 16, 3:25 a.m.; New, Aug. 24, 6:59 a.m.; First Qr., Aug. 31, 10:48 p.m.

Day of Year	Day of Month	Day of Week	Planetary Configurations —Phenomena	*Hour of Sunrise	Sunset	Moonrise	Moonset
213	1	Sa.		6:45	8:31	**12:59**	...
214	2	Su.		6:46	8:30	**2:02**	12:09
215	3	Mo.		6:47	8:29	**3:09**	12:42
216	4	Tu.		6:48	8:28	**4:19**	1:22
217	5	We.	♄☌☾	6:49	8:27	**5:29**	2:12
218	6	Th.	♆☌☾	6:50	8:26	**6:34**	3:11
219	7	Fr.		6:50	8:25	**7:31**	4:21
220	8	Sa.	☾ at Perigee	6:51	8:25	**8:20**	5:37
221	9	Su.		6:51	8:24	**9:00**	6:54
222	10	Mo.		6:52	8:23	**9:35**	8:08
223	11	Tu.		6:53	8:22	**10:05**	9:19
224	12	We.		6:53	8:21	**10:34**	10:27
225	13	Th.		6:54	8:20	**11:04**	11:32
226	14	Fr.	♃☌☾	6:54	8:19	**11:35**	**12:36**
227	15	Sa.		6:55	8:18	...	**1:39**
228	16	Su.		6:56	8:17	12:08	**2:41**
229	17	Mo.		6:57	8:15	12:46	**3:41**
230	18	Tu.		6:58	8:14	1:30	**4:39**
231	19	We.	♄ Sta. in R.A.	6:58	8:13	2:19	**5:30**
232	20	Th.	☿ Superior	6:59	8:12	3:12	**6:17**
233	21	Fr.	☾ at Apogee	6:59	8:11	4:09	**6:57**
234	22	Sa.		7:00	8:10	5:07	**7:31**
235	23	Su.	♀ Superior	7:01	8:09	6:05	**8:01**
236	24	Mo.		7:01	8:07	7:03	**8:28**
237	25	Tu.	♂☌☉	7:02	8:06	8:00	**8:54**
238	26	We.		7:02	8:05	8:57	**9:19**
239	27	Th.		7:03	8:04	9:54	**9:45**
240	28	Fr.		7:03	8:03	10:53	**10:12**
241	29	Sa.		7:04	8:02	11:55	**10:43**
242	30	Su.		7:05	8:01	**12:59**	**11:20**
243	31	Mo.		7:06	8:00	**2:07**	...

CALENDAR FOR 1987

9th Month **SEPTEMBER, 1987** **30 Days**

Moon's Phases.—Full, Sept. 7, 1:13 p.m.; Last Qr., Sept. 14, 6:44 p.m.; New, Sept. 22, 10:08 p.m.; First Qr., Sept. 30, 5:39 a.m.

Day of Year	Day of Month	Day of Week	Planetary Configurations —Phenomena	*Hour of Sunrise	Sunset	Moonrise	Moonset
244	1	Mo.	♅ Sta. in R.A.	7:07	7:58	**3:15**	12:04
245	2	We.	♆☌☾	7:07	7:57	**4:20**	12:58
246	3	Th.	. . . .	7:08	7:55	**5:19**	2:02
247	4	Fr.	. . . .	7:09	7:54	**6:09**	3:13
248	5	Sa.	☾ at Perigee	7:09	7:52	**6:52**	4:28
249	6	Su.	. . . .	7:10	7:51	**7:29**	5:42
250	7	Mo.	. . . .	7:10	7:49	**8:02**	6:55
251	8	Tu.	. . . .	7:11	7:48	**8:31**	8:04
252	9	We.	. . . .	7:12	7:47	**9:02**	9:11
253	10	Th.	♃☌☾	7:12	7:46	**9:32**	10:17
254	11	Fr.	. . . .	7:13	7:45	**10:05**	11:23
255	12	Sa.	. . . .	7:13	7:43	**10:42**	**12:28**
256	13	Su.	. . . .	7:14	7:42	**11:24**	**1:31**
257	14	Mo.	. . . .	7:14	7:41	. . .	**2:31**
258	15	Tu.	. . . .	7:15	7:40	12:11	**3:25**
259	16	We.	. . . .	7:16	7:38	1:04	**4:13**
260	17	Th.	☾ at Apogee	7:16	7:37	2:00	**4:56**
261	18	Fr.	. . . .	7:17	7:35	2:58	**5:31**
262	19	Sa.	. . . .	7:18	7:34	3:57	**6:03**
263	20	Su.	. . . .	7:18	7:32	4:55	**6:32**
264	21	Mo.	. . . .	7:19	7:31	5:53	**6:58**
265	22	Tu.	. . . .	7:19	7:29	6:49	**7:23**
266	23	We.	Fall Begins	7:20	7:28	7:47	**7:48**
267	24	Th.	. . . .	7:20	7:27	8:46	**8:15**
268	25	Fr.	☿☌☾	7:21	7:25	9:48	**8:45**
269	26	Sa.	. . . .	7:21	7:24	10:52	**9:20**
270	27	Su.	. . . .	7:22	7:23	11:59	**10:02**
271	28	Mo.	♄☌☾	7:23	7:22	**1:06**	**10:53**
272	29	Tu.	♅☌☾	7:23	7:21	**2:11**	**11:51**
273	30	We.	♆☌☾	7:24	7:19	**3:11**	. . .

10th Month **OCTOBER, 1987** **31 Days**

Moon's Phases.—Full, Oct. 6, 11:12 p.m.; Last Qr., Oct. 14, 1:06 p.m.; New, Oct. 22, 12:28 p.m.; First Qr., Oct. 29, 11:10 a.m.

Day of Year	Day of Month	Day of Week	Planetary Configurations —Phenomena	*Hour of Sunrise	Sunset	Moonrise	Moonset
274	1	Th.	. . . .	7:25	7:18	**4:04**	12:59
275	2	Fr.	. . . .	7:26	7:17	**4:48**	2:10
276	3	Sa.	☾ at Perigee	7:27	7:15	**5:26**	3:23
277	4	Su.	☿ Gr. elong. E.	7:28	7:14	**5:59**	4:34
278	5	Mo.	. . . .	7:28	7:14	**6:29**	5:43
279	6	Tu.	. . . .	7:29	7:11	**6:58**	6:50
280	7	We.	. . . .	7:29	7:10	**7:28**	7:56
281	8	Th.	♃☌☾	7:30	7:09	**8:00**	9:03
282	9	Fr.	. . . .	7:31	7:08	**8:36**	10:10
283	10	Sa.	. . . .	7:32	7:07	**9:17**	11:15
284	11	Su.	. . . .	7:33	7:06	**10:03**	**12:17**
285	12	Mo.	. . . .	7:33	7:05	**10:54**	**1:15**
286	13	Tu.	. . . .	7:34	7:03	**11:50**	**2:07**
287	14	We.	. . . .	7:35	7:02	. . .	**2:52**
288	15	Th.	☾ at Apogee	7:36	7:01	12:47	**3:31**
289	16	Fr.	☿ Sta. in R.A.	7:37	7:00	1:45	**4:04**
290	17	Sa.	. . . .	7:38	6:59	2:44	**4:33**
291	18	Su.	. . . .	7:38	6:57	3:41	**5:00**
292	19	Mo.	☿☌♀	7:39	6:56	4:39	**5:25**
293	20	Tu.	♂☌☾	7:40	6:55	5:36	**5:50**
294	21	We.	. . . .	7:41	6:54	6:35	**6:17**
295	22	Th.	. . . .	7:41	6:52	7:37	**6:46**
296	23	Fr.	♀☌☾	7:42	6:51	8:40	**7:20**
297	24	Sa.	. . . .	7:43	6:50	9:48	**8:00**
298	25	†Su.	. . . .	6:43	5:49	9:57	**7:48**
299	26	Mo.	♅☌☾	6:44	5:47	11:05	**8:46**
300	27	Tu.	♆☌☾	6:45	5:47	**12:07**	**9:51**
301	28	We.	. . . .	6:46	5:46	**1:01**	**11:01**
302	29	Th.	☾ at Perigee	6:47	5:46	**1:47**	. . .
303	30	Fr.	. . . .	6:48	5:45	**2:26**	12:13
304	31	Sa.	. . . .	6:48	5:44	**2:59**	1:22

†Daylight Saving Time ended at 2 a.m.

11th Month **NOVEMBER, 1987** **30 Days**

Moon's Phases.—Full, Nov. 5, 10:46 a.m.; Last Qr., Nov. 13, 8:38 a.m.; New, Nov. 21, 12:33 a.m.; First Qr., Nov. 27, 6:37 p.m.

Day of Year	Day of Month	Day of Week	Planetary Configurations —Phenomena	*Hour of Sunrise	Sunset	Moonrise	Moonset
305	1	Su.	. . . .	6:49	5:43	**3:29**	2:29
306	2	Mo.	♇☌☉	6:50	5:42	**3:58**	3:35
307	3	Tu.	. . . .	6:51	5:41	**4:27**	4:41
308	4	We.	♃☌☾	6:52	5:40	**4:57**	5:45
309	5	Th.	☿ Sta. in R.A.	6:53	5:39	**5:31**	6:51
310	6	Fr.	. . . .	6:53	5:38	**6:10**	7:57
311	7	Sa.	. . . .	6:54	5:37	**6:54**	9:00
312	8	Su.	. . . .	6:55	5:36	**7:43**	10:02
313	9	Mo.	. . . .	6:56	5:35	**8:38**	10:57
314	10	Tu.	. . . .	6:57	5:35	**9:35**	11:45
315	11	We.	. . . .	6:58	5:34	**10:34**	**12:27**
316	12	Th.	☾ at Apogee	6:59	5:34	**11:32**	**1:02**
317	13	Fr.	☿ Gr. elong. W.	6:59	5:33	. . .	**1:32**
318	14	Sa.	. . . .	7:00	5:33	12:30	**2:00**
319	15	Su.	. . . .	7:01	5:32	1:26	**2:26**
320	16	Mo.	. . . .	7:02	5:32	2:23	**2:51**
321	17	Tu.	. . . .	7:03	5:31	3:20	**3:17**
322	18	We.	♂☌☾	7:04	5:31	4:20	**3:44**
323	19	Th.	☿☌☾	7:05	5:30	5:23	**4:16**
324	20	Fr.	♀☌♄	7:06	5:30	6:31	**4:54**
325	21	Sa.	. . . .	7:07	5:29	7:41	**5:41**
326	22	Su.	♀☌☾	7:08	5:29	8:51	**6:35**
327	23	Mo.	♆☌☾	7:09	5:28	9:57	**7:41**
328	24	Tu.	☾ at Perigee	7:10	5:28	10:55	**8:51**
329	25	We.	. . . .	7:11	5:28	11:45	**10:03**
330	26	Th.	. . . .	7:12	5:27	**12:26**	**11:14**
331	27	Fr.	. . . .	7:13	5:27	**1:01**	. . .
332	28	Sa.	. . . .	7:14	5:27	**1:32**	12:22
333	29	Su.	. . . .	7:15	5:26	**2:00**	1:28
334	30	Mo.	. . . .	7:16	5:26	**2:29**	2:31

12th Month **DECEMBER, 1987** **31 Days**

Moon's Phases.—Full, Dec. 5, 2:01 a.m.; Last Qr., Dec. 13, 5:41 a.m.; New, Dec. 20, 12:25 p.m.; First Qr., Dec. 27, 4:01 a.m.

Day of Year	Day of Month	Day of Week	Planetary Configurations —Phenomena	*Hour of Sunrise	Sunset	Moonrise	Moonset
335	1	Tu.	♃☌☾	7:16	5:26	**2:58**	3:35
336	2	We.	. . . .	7:17	5:26	**3:30**	4:39
337	3	Th.	♀☌♆	7:18	5:26	**4:06**	5:43
338	4	Fr..	. . . .	7:19	5:26	**4:48**	6:48
339	5	Sa.	. . . .	7:20	5:26	**5:35**	7:49
340	6	Su.	. . . .	7:20	5:26	**6:28**	8:47
341	7	Mo.	. . . .	7:21	5:26	**7:25**	9:38
342	8	Tu.	. . . .	7:21	5:27	**8:23**	10:22
343	9	We.	. . . .	7:22	5:27	**9:22**	10:59
344	10	Th.	☾ at Apogee	7:23	5:27	**10:19**	11:31
345	11	Fr.	. . . .	7:24	5:27	**11:15**	**12:00**
346	12	Sa.	. . . .	7:24	5:27	. . .	**12:26**
347	13	Su.	. . . .	7:25	5:28	12:11	**12:51**
348	14	Mo.	. . . .	7:26	5:28	1:07	**1:15**
349	15	Tu.	♄☌☉	7:26	5:28	2:04	**1:42**
350	16	We.	. . . .	7:27	5:28	3:04	**2:11**
351	17	Th.	♂☌☾	7:28	5:29	4:09	**2:46**
352	18	Fr.	. . . .	7:28	5:29	5:17	**3:28**
353	19	Sa.	♅☌☉	7:29	5:30	6:28	**4:20**
354	20	Su.	. . . .	7:29	5:30	7:37	**5:21**
355	21	Mo.	. . . .	7:30	5:31	8:41	**6:32**
356	22	Tu.	Winter Begins . . .	7:30	5:31	9:37	**7:47**
357	23	We.	☿ Superior	7:30	5:32	10:23	**9:01**
358	24	Th.	. . . .	7:31	5:32	11:00	**10:12**
359	25	Fr.	. . . .	7:31	5:33	11:34	**11:20**
360	26	Sa.	. . . .	7:32	5:33	**12:04**	. . .
361	27	Su.	. . . .	7:32	5:34	**12:32**	12:26
362	28	Mo.	♃☌☾	7:33	5:34	**1:01**	1:29
363	29	Tu.	♆☌☉	7:33	5:35	**1:32**	2:32
364	30	We.	. . . .	7:34	5:36	**2:06**	3:36
365	31	Th.	. . . .	7:34	5:37	**2:45**	4:39

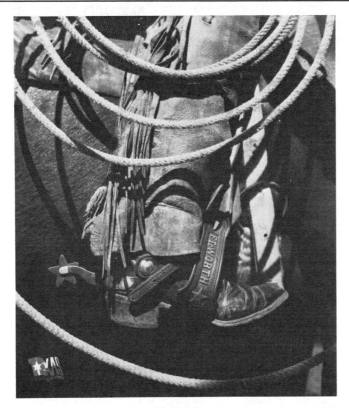

THE 150th YEAR
1836-1986

TEXAS

THE TEXAS DRIFTER

Selected to represent the State of Texas by the Texas 1986 Sesqui-centennial Commission, this rich full-color rendition of a Texas Cowboy has become the most popular Texas poster ever printed. It has been exhibited in 5 museums including an exhibition at the Metropolitan Museum of Art in NYC.

The focal point of the 20″×26″ classic "Drifter" is a stirrup which was hand-made by a Fort Worth harness co. for the local Texas Rangers in 1888.

Expect delivery of this outstanding addition to home or office within one week after receipt of your order.

Send your check or money order for $16.00 plus $.84 state and local taxes, Visa or MasterCard No. to:

> HAVARD DESIGN
> 6720 WELCH
> FORT WORTH, TEXAS
> 76133

Orders accepted by calling 817-294-5588

Produced by Gary Havard, Kay Huckabee & J. Dalton.
© copyright 1981 by Identity Arts, Fort Worth, Texas.

249-YEAR CALENDAR, 1752-2000, A.D., INCLUSIVE

By this calendar one may ascertain the day of week for any day of month and year for the period 1752-2000, inclusive. The calendar covers the period beginning with †1752, the year of the adoption by England of the New Style, or Gregorian calendar.

To ascertain any day of the week, first look in the table for the year required, and under the months are figures which refer to the corresponding figures at the head of the columns of days below. For example: To know on what day of the week Aug. 4 fell in the year 1914, in the table of years look for 1914, and in a parallel line under Aug., is Fig. 6, which directs to Col. 6, in which it will be seen that Aug. 4 fell on Tuesday.

COMMON YEARS, 1753 TO 1999

					Jan.	Feb.	Mar.	Apr.	May	June	July	Aug.	Sept.	Oct.	Nov.	Dec.
1761	1767	1778	1789	1795	....	....	....	....	....	....						
1801	1807	1818	1829	1835	1846	1857	1863	1874	1885	1891	4	7	7	3	5	1	3	6	2	4	7	2
1903	1914	1925	1931	1942	1953	1959	1970	1981	1987	1998						
1762	1773	1779	1790	....	....	....	....	....	....	....						
1802	1813	1819	1830	1841	1847	1858	1869	1875	1886	1897	5	1	1	4	6	2	4	7	3	5	1	3
1909	1915	1926	1937	1943	1954	1965	1971	1982	1993	1999						
1757	1763	1774	1785	1791	....	....	....	....	....	....						
1803	1814	1825	1831	1842	1853	1859	1870	1881	1887	1898	6	2	2	5	7	3	5	1	4	6	2	4
1910	1921	1927	1938	1949	1955	1966	1977	1983	1994	....						
1754	1765	1771	1782	1793	1799	....	....	....	....	....						
1805	1811	1822	1833	1839	1850	1861	1867	1878	1889	1895	2	5	5	1	3	6	1	4	7	2	5	7
1901	1907	1918	1929	1935	1946	1957	1963	1974	1985	1991						
1755	1766	1777	1783	1794	1800	....	....	....	....	....						
1806	1817	1823	1834	1845	1851	1862	1873	1879	1890	....	3	6	6	2	4	7	2	5	1	3	6	1
1902	1913	1919	1930	1941	1947	1958	1969	1975	1986	1997						
1758	1769	1775	1786	1797	....	....	....	....	....	....						
1809	1815	1826	1837	1843	1854	1865	1871	1882	1893	1899	7	3	3	6	1	4	6	2	5	7	3	5
1905	1911	1922	1933	1939	1950	1961	1967	1978	1989	1995						
1753	1759	1770	1781	1787	1798	....	....	....	....	....						
1810	1821	1827	1838	1849	1855	1866	1877	1883	1894	1900	1	4	4	7	2	5	7	3	6	1	4	6
1906	1917	1923	1934	1945	1951	1962	1973	1979	1990	....						

LEAP YEARS, 1976 TO 2000

										Jan.	Feb.	Mar.	Apr.	May	June	July	Aug.	Sept.	Oct.	Nov.	Dec.
											29										
1764	1792	1804	1832	1860	1888	....	1928	1956	1984	7	3	4	7	2	5	7	3	6	1	4	6
1768	1796	1808	1836	1864	1892	1904	1932	1960	1988	5	1	2	5	7	3	5	1	4	6	2	4
1772	....	1812	1840	1868	1896	1908	1936	1964	1992	3	6	7	3	5	1	3	6	2	4	7	2
1776	....	1816	1844	1872	....	1912	1940	1968	1996	1	4	5	1	3	6	1	4	7	2	5	7
1780	....	1820	1848	1876	....	1916	1944	1972	2000	6	2	3	6	1	4	6	2	5	7	3	5
1756	1784	1824	1852	1880	....	1920	1948	1976	....	4	7	1	4	6	2	4	7	3	5	1	3
1760	1788	1828	1856	1884	....	1924	1952	1980	....	2	5	6	2	4	7	2	5	1	3	6	1

1	2	3	4	5	6	7
Mon. 1	Tues. 1	Wed. 1	Thurs. 1	Fri. 1	Sat. 1	SUN. 1
Tues. 2	Wed. 2	Thurs. 2	Fri. 2	Sat. 2	SUN. 2	Mon. 2
Wed. 3	Thurs. 3	Fri. 3	Sat. 3	SUN. 3	Mon. 3	Tues. 3
Thurs. 4	Fri. 4	Sat. 4	SUN. 4	Mon. 4	Tues. 4	Wed. 4
Fri. 5	Sat. 5	SUN. 5	Mon. 5	Tues. 5	Wed. 5	Thurs. 5
Sat. 6	SUN. 6	Mon. 6	Tues. 6	Wed. 6	Thurs. 6	Fri. 6
SUN. 7	Mon. 7	Tues. 7	Wed. 7	Thurs. 7	Fri. 7	Sat. 7
Mon. 8	Tues. 8	Wed. 8	Thurs. 8	Fri. 8	Sat. 8	SUN. 8
Tues. 9	Wed. 9	Thurs. 9	Fri 9	Sat. 9	SUN. 9	Mon. 9
Wed. 10	Thurs. 10	Fri. 10	Sat. 10	SUN. 10	Mon. 10	Tues. 10
Thurs. . . . 11	Fri. 11	Sat. 11	SUN. 11	Mon. 11	Tues. 11	Wed. 11
Fri. 12	Sat. 12	SUN. 12	Mon. 12	Tues. 12	Wed. 12	Thurs. . . . 12
Sat. 13	SUN. 13	Mon. 13	Tues. 13	Wed. 13	Thurs. . . . 13	Fri. 13
SUN. 14	Mon. 14	Tues. 14	Wed. 14	Thurs. . . . 14	Fri. 14	Sat. 14
Mon. 15	Tues. . . . 15	Wed. 15	Thurs. . . . 15	Fri. 15	Sat. 15	SUN. 15
Tues. 16	Wed. 16	Thurs. . . . 16	Fri. 16	Sat. 16	SUN. 16	Mon. 16
Wed. 17	Thurs. . . . 17	Fri. 17	Sat. 17	SUN. 17	Mon. 17	Tues. 17
Thurs. . . . 18	Fri 18	Sat. 18	SUN. 18	Mon. 18	Tues. 18	Wed. 18
Fri. 19	Sat. 19	SUN. 19	Mon. 19	Tues. 19	Wed. 19	Thurs. . . . 19
Sat. 20	SUN. 20	Mon. 20	Tues. 20	Wed. 20	Thurs. . . . 20	Fri. 20
SUN. 21	Mon. 21	Tues. 21	Wed. 21	Thurs. . . . 21	Fri. 21	Sat. 21
Mon. 22	Tues. 22	Wed. 22	Thurs. . . . 22	Fri. 22	Sat. 22	SUN. 22
Tues. 23	Wed. 23	Thurs. . . . 23	Fri. 23	Sat. 23	SUN. 23	Mon. 23
Wed. 24	Thurs. . . . 24	Fri. 24	Sat. 24	SUN. 24	Mon. 24	Tues. 24
Thurs. . . . 25	Fri. 25	Sat. 25	SUN. 25	Mon. 25	Tues. . . . 25	Wed. 25
Fri. 26	Sat. 26	SUN. 26	Mon. 26	Tues. 26	Wed. 26	Thurs. . . . 26
Sat. 27	SUN. 27	Mon. 27	Tues. 27	Wed. 27	Thurs. . . . 27	Fri. 27
SUN. 28	Mon. 28	Tues. 28	Wed. 28	Thurs. . . . 28	Fri. 28	Sat. 28
Mon. 29	Tues. 29	Wed. 29	Thurs. . . . 29	Fri. 29	Sat. 29	SUN. 29
Tues. 30	Wed. 30	Thurs. . . . 30	Fri. 30	Sat. 30	SUN. 30	Mon. 30
Wed. 31	Thurs. . . . 31	Fri. 31	Sat. 31	SUN. 31	Mon. 31	Tues. 31

†Days of the week can be calculated for 1752 as follows: 1752 is the same as 1772 from Jan. 1 to Sept. 2, inclusive. It is the same as 1780 from Sept. 14 to Dec. 31. (Note that 1752, 1772 and 1780 are leap years.) Sept. 3 to 13, inclusive, were omitted in the change from Old Style to New Style (Julian to Gregorian) calendar.

BEGINNING OF YEAR

The Athenians began the year in June, the Macedonians in September, the Romans first in March and afterward in January, the Persians on Aug. 11, the ancient Mexicans on Feb. 23. The Chinese year, which begins late in January or early in February, is similar to the Mohammedan year in having twelve months of twenty-nine and thirty days alternating, while in every nineteen years there are seven years which have thirteen months. This is not quite commensurate with planetary movements, hence the Chinese have formed a cycle of sixty years in which period twenty-two intercalary months occur.

TEXAS RECREATION

A storm brews over the Chihuahuan Desert in the Big Bend area of Texas.

Texas State Parks

Texas' expanding system of state parks attracted **18,617,465 visitors** in fiscal 1984. The parks offer contrasting attractions, mountains and canyons, forests, spring-fed streams, sandy dunes and saltwater surf.

Most of these parks are listed here. **Texas Parks and Wildlife Department** provided the information. Additional information is available from the Department's Austin headquarters, personnel at individual parks or other sources of tourist information.

Abilene State Recreational Area, 19 miles southwest of Abilene in Taylor County, 621 acres. The land was deeded by the City of Abilene in 1933. A part of the official **Texas longhorn herd** is located in the park. In addition to **Lake Abilene, Buffalo Gap**, the original Taylor County seat (1878) and one of the early frontier settlements through which passed the **Butterfield Stage Route** (also called the **Southern Overland Mail Route**), is nearby. Buffalo Gap was on the **Western**, or **Dodge City, Trail** over which pioneer Texas cattlemen drove herds to Kansas.

Acton State Historic Site, is a .006-acre cemetery plot where **Davy Crockett's** second wife, Elizabeth, was buried in 1860. It is six miles east of Granbury in Hood County.

Adm. Nimitz Museum Historical Park is 9.1 acres in Fredericksburg featuring **Nimitz Steamboat Hotel**, which is now museum; named for **Adm. Chester W. Nimitz** of World War II fame. Nearby is **Kerrville State Park**.

Atlanta State Recreation Area is 1,475 acres located 11 miles northwest of Atlanta in Cass County; adjacent to **Wright Patman Dam and Lake**. Texas acquired the land from the U.S. Army in 1954.

Balmorhea State Recreation Area is 45.9 acres four miles southwest of Balmorhea in Reeves County, deeded in 1935 by private owners. Swimming pool fed by natural spring (**San Solomon Springs**); also provides water to **pupfish refuge** located in park. Nearby are city of **Pecos, Fort Davis National Historic Site**, scenic loop drive through **Davis Mountains** and **Davis Mountains State Park**.

Bastrop State Park is 3,503.7 acres. The park was acquired by deeds from the City of Bastrop and private owners during 1933 to 1935. Site of famous "Lost Pines," isolated timbered region of loblolly pine and hardwoods. Nearby **Lake Bastrop** offers good fishing. **State capitol** at Austin 30 miles away; 13-mile drive through forest leads to **Buescher State Park**.

Bentsen-Rio Grande State Park, a scenic park, is along the Rio Grande in Hidalgo County. The 587 acres were acquired from private owners in 1944. Park is excellent base from which to tour Rio Grande Valley of Texas and adjacent Mexico; most attractions within 1½ hours' drive. Three miles of hiking trail lead to Rio Grande; provides chance to study unique plants, animals and birds of park. Many species of birds unique to southern United States found here, including **Lichenstein's oriole, pauraque, groove-billed ani, green jay, Kiskadee flycatcher, red-billed pigeon, elf owl** and **chachalaca**. Park also one of last natural refuges in Texas for cats such as **ocelot** and **jaguarundi**.

Battleship Texas State Historic Site, located in Harris County, eight miles southeast of Houston on U.S. 78 and IH-45 to Texas 225, then east on Texas 225 for 12 miles to Texas 134 for three miles to Park Road 1836. The U.S.S. Texas was moored in the Houston Ship Channel at the **San Jacinto Battleground** on San Jacinto Day, 1948, and is the only survivor of the dreadnought class, a veteran of two world wars and many campaigns. The Battleship is open every day, June 1-Aug. 31, 10:00 a.m.-6:00 p.m.; Sept. 1-May 31, 10:00 a.m.-5:00 p.m. Admission charges: Ages 12 and over, $2.00; 6 to 11, $1.00; under 6, free.

Big Spring State Recreation Area is 370 acres located in Howard County. It was named for a natural spring which was replaced by an artifical spring. The park was deeded by the City of Big Spring in 1934 and 1935. Drive to top of Scenic Mountain provides panoramic view of surrounding country. The "big spring" nearby provided watering place for herds of buffalo, antelope and wild horses. Used extensively also as campsite for early Indians, explorers and settlers. **Prairie dog colony** on mountain.

Blanco State Recreation Area is 104.6 acres, along the Blanco River in Blanco County. The land was deeded in 1936 by private owners. Park was used as campsite by early explorers and settlers. **LBJ Ranch** and **LBJ State Historical Park** located less then 30 miles away.

(Continued on p. 104.)

99

We're Filling a Building
With User-Friendliness

"User-friendly" usually means that a computer or computer program is easy to learn, easy to use, and helpful.

We feel the user-friendly concept should extend to the whole process of learning about computerware, and learning what it can do for a business, and talking with companies that produce it, and finally deciding what's best to buy.

So we took that concept, wrapped a building around it, and called it INFOMART*.

It's the world's first international trade center devoted exclusively to information processing products and services. It's just five minutes from downtown. It's open for you Monday through Friday, 8:30 - 5:30. And there's no admission fee.

At INFOMART, you can define your needs with the help of our Resource Center, visit permanent showrooms of leading computerware producers, and attend specialized conferences and trade shows. INFOMART co-sponsors INDEX* Events (for INformation and Data EXchange), where experienced professionals in many fields help both new and knowledgeable computer users to learn how they can increase productivity.

We can't explain 1.5 million square feet of user-friendliness here. Why don't you come to INFOMART and see for yourself.

For General INFOMART Information: **(214) 746-3500**
For INDEX Event Information: **(800) 367-7100 or (214) 746-INFO**

*THE WORLD'S FIRST INFORMATION
PROCESSING MARKET CENTER*
1950 Stemmons Freeway
Dallas, Texas 75207

*INFOMART AND INDEX are registered trademarks of Dallas Market Center

TEXAS STATE PARKS

	CAMPING	SCREENED SHELTERS	GROUP FACILITY	CAMPSITES ELEC./SEWAGE	CAMPSITES WATER/ELEC.	RESTROOMS	SHOWERS	CABINS	PICNICKING	GROCERIES	FISHING	SWIMMING	WATER SKIING	BOAT RAMP	MUSEUM/EXHIBIT	HISTORIC STRUCTURE	DAY USE ONLY	GROUP TRAILER	TRAILER DUMP STATION	NATURE HIKING TRAILS	MISCELLANEOUS
STATE RECREATION AREAS																					
ABILENE	•	•	P	•	•	•	•		•		•			•					•	•	L
ARROYO COLORADO	AREA PRESENTLY CLOSED TO PUBLIC PENDING DEVELOPMENT																				
ATLANTA	•		P	•	•	•	•		•		○	○	○	•					•	•	
BALMORHEA (SAN SOLOMON SPRINGS COURTS)	•				•	•	•	•	•			•							•		
BIG SPRING					•				•						•	•		•		•	D
BLANCO	•	•	P	•	•	•	•		•		○	○		•					•	•	Z
BONHAM	•		P/GB	•	•	•	•		•		•	•		•					•		B
BRAZOS ISLAND * UNDEVELOPED GULF BEACH	○								○	○	○										
BRAZOS BEND/HALE RANCH PARK SITE	•	•	S	•	•	•	•		•		•								•	•	P,Z
BRYAN BEACH UNDEVELOPED GULF BEACH	○								○		○	○									
CASSELLS BOYKIN	•				•				•	○	○	○	•								
CLEBURNE	•	•	GB	•	•	•	•		•	•	○	•		•					•	•	
EISENHOWER MARINA	•	•	S	•	•	•	•		•	•	•	•	○	•				•	•	•	
FAIRFIELD LAKE	•				•	•	•		•	•	•	•	•	○	•				•	•	Z
FALCON AIRSTRIP	•	•	S	•	•	•	•		•		○	○	○	•					•		
FORT PARKER	•	•	GB	•	•	•	•		•		○	○	○	•					•	•	Z
GOOSE ISLAND	•	•	S	•	•	•	•		•		○	○	○	•					•	•	
JEFF DAVIS*																					
KERRVILLE	•	•	SP	•	•	•	•		•		○	○		•					•	•	
LAKE ARROWHEAD	•		P	•	•	•	•		•	•	•	•	•	○	•				•		E
LAKE BOB SANDLIN	AREA PRESENTLY CLOSED TO PUBLIC PENDING DEVELOPMENT																				
LAKE BROWNWOOD	•	•	P	•	•	•	•		•	•	•	•	•	○	•				•	•	
LAKE COLORADO CITY	•		S,P	•	•	•	•		•		•	•	•	○	•				•		
LAKE CORPUS CHRISTI	•	•	P	•	•	•	•		•	•	•	•	○	○	•				•		
LAKE LIVINGSTON	•	•			•	•	•		•	•	•	•	•	○	•			•	•	•	
LAKE SOMERVILLE	•		P	•	•	•	•		•		•	○	○	•				•	•	•	C,E,Z
LAKE WHITNEY AIRSTRIPS	•	•	C	•	•	•	•		•		○	•	○	•					•	•	
LOCKHART	•		S	•	•	•	•		•		•			•							G
MACKENZIE*	•				•				•		•	•	•								G
MARTIN CREEK PARK SITE**	•	•	C	•	•	•	•		•	•	○	○	○	•		•			•	•	Z
MERIDIAN	•	•	C	•	•	•	•		•		○	○		•					•	•	Z
LAKE MINERALS WELLS	•	•	•	•	•	•	•		•	•	•	•		•					•	•	B,Z,E
LAKE TEXANA	•		P	•	•	•	•		•		•	○		•					•	•	
POSSUM KINGDOM	•	•			•	•	•		•		•	○	○	•					•	•	LB
PURTIS CREEK PARK SITE**	AREA PRESENTLY CLOSED TO PUBLIC PENDING DEVELOPMENT																				
RUSK/PALESTINE	•		P	•	•	•	•		•		○								•		
TIPS*	•		P	•	•	•	•		•		○										
VILLAGE CREEK PARK SITE**	AREA PRESENTLY CLOSED TO PUBLIC PENDING DEVELOPMENT																				
STATE PARKS																					
BASTROP	•		H/GB	•	•	•	•	•	•		○	•								•	Z,GD
BENTSEN-RIO GRANDE	•		P	•		•	•		•		○								•	•	
SOUTH LLANO RIVER PARK SITE**	AREA PRESENTLY CLOSED TO PUBLIC PENDING DEVELOPMENT																				
BUESCHER	•	•	S	•	•	•	•		•		•								•	•	P
CADDO LAKE	•	•	S	•	•	•	•	•	•	•	•		○	○	○				•	•	
CAPROCK CANYONS	•		P	•	•	•	•		•	•	•				•	•			•	•	E,Z
COPPER BREAKS	•		P	•	•	•	•		•		•	•	•	•		•			•	•	L,E,Z
DAINGERFIELD	•		P	•	•	•	•		•		•	•		•					•	•	
DAVIS MOUNTAINS (INDIAN LODGE)	•		P	•	•	•	•	•	•						•				•	•	D
DINOSAUR VALLEY DINOSAUR FOOTPRINTS	•		P	•	•	•	•		•		○	○		•					•	•	L
GALVESTON ISLAND SUMMER DRAMA "The Lone Star"	•	•			•	•	•		•		○	○						•	•	•	
GARNER	•		CS	•	•	•	•	•	•	•	○	○							•		M
GUADALUPE RIVER	•				•	•	•		•		○	○							•	•	Z
HUNTSVILLE	•	•	P	•	•	•	•		•	•	•	○		•	•				•	•	BM
INKS LAKE	•	•	P	•	•	•	•		•	•	•	•	•	○	•			•	•	•	C,Z/GB
LAKE LEWISVILLE					•				•		○	○	○	•			•				
LAKE MINERAL WELLS	•	•	•		•	•	•		•	•	•	•		•					•	•	B,Z
LONGHORN CAVERN* DAILY CAVERN TOURS	•					•			•						•	•	•				E
MARTIN DIES JR.	•	•	S	•	•	•	•		•		•	•	○	•					•	•	
McKINNEY FALLS	•	•	•	C,S	•	•	•		•		○				•	•			•	•	
MONAHANS SANDHILLS	•				•	•	•		•						•	•			•	•	
MOTHER NEFF	•		X		•	•	•		•		○								•	•	

TEXAS STATE PARKS

	CAMPING	SCREENED SHELTERS	GROUP FACILITY	CAMPSITES ELEC./SEWAGE	CAMPSITES WATER/ELEC.	RESTROOMS	SHOWERS	CABINS	PICNICKING	GROCERIES	FISHING	SWIMMING	WATER SKIING	BOAT RAMP	MUSEUM/EXHIBIT	HISTORIC STRUCTURE	DAY USE ONLY	GROUP TRAILER	TRAILER DUMP STATION	NATURE HIKING TRAILS	MISCELLANEOUS
MUSTANG ISLAND	●				●	●	●		●		○	○							●	●	C,Z
PALMETTO	●				●	●	●		●		○	○							●	●	X
PALO DURO CANYON SUMMER DRAMA "Texas"	●			●	●	●	●		●	●	●					●			●	●	RE LD
PEDERNALES FALLS	●				●	●	●		●		○	○							●	●	C,Z
RESACA DE LA PALMA SITE**	AREA PRESENTLY CLOSED TO PUBLIC PENDING DEVELOPMENT																				
SEA RIM	●				●	●	●		●		○	○		●	●				●	●	C,Z
TYLER	●	●	PC	●	●	●	●		●	●	●	●		●					●	●	B
STATE HISTORICAL PARKS																					
ADMIRAL NIMITZ									●						●	●	●				A
FORT GRIFFIN	●		P		●	●	●		●		○				●	●				●	L
FORT RICHARDSON	●		P		●	●	●		●		○				●	●				●	Z
GOLIAD	●	●	S	●	●	●	●		●		○	●			●	●		●	●	●	P Z
GOVERNOR HOGG SHRINE			P			●			●						●	●	●				
HUECO TANKS INDIAN PICTOGRAPHS	●				●	●	●		●							●			●	●	
JIM HOGG						●			●						●	●	●				
LYNDON B. JOHNSON			S			●			●		○	○			●	●	●			●	LA
MISSION TEJAS	●		P	●	●	●	●		●		○	○				●			●	●	
SABINE PASS BATTLEGROUND						●			●		○			●		●					
SAN JACINTO BATTLEGROUND BATTLESHIP TEXAS			P			●			●						●	●	●				
SEMINOLE CANYON INDIAN PICTOGRAPHS	●				●	●	●		●							●			●	●	
STEPHEN F. AUSTIN	●	●	S	●		●	●		●		○	●			●	●			●	●	G
TEXAS STATE RAILROAD CONTACT PARK FOR SCHEDULE OF RUNS						●			●							●	●				
VARNER-HOGG GUIDED TOURS			P			●			●						●	●	●				
WASHINGTON-ON-THE-BRAZOS						●			●						●	●	●				A,X
STATE NATURAL AREAS/FISHING PIERS																					
COPANO BAY*						●					●			●							
ENCHANTED ROCK	●		P		●	●	●		●										●	●	C,Z
LOST MAPLES	●					●			●		○	○		●				●	●	●	C,Z
HILL COUNTRY	○																				E,Z
PORT LAVACA*						●					●			●							
QUEEN ISABELLA*						●					●										
STATE HISTORIC SITES/STRUCTURES																					
ACTON BURIAL SITE OF DAVY CROCKETT'S WIFE																●					
CADDOAN MOUNDS						●			●						●	●	●				
CONFEDERATE REUNION GROUNDS			P			●			●		○	○				●	●				
EISENHOWER BIRTHPLACE						●			●						●	●	●				
FANNIN BATTLEGROUND			P			●			●							●	●				
FANTHORP INN**	AREA PRESENTLY CLOSED TO PUBLIC PENDING DEVELOPMENT																				
FORT LANCASTER						●			●						●	●	●				
FORT LEATON						●			●		●				●	●	●				
FORT McKAVETT						●			●						●	●	●				
FULTON MANSION															●	●	●				
LANDMARK INN (HOTEL ROOMS)						●			●		●				●	●				●	
LIPANTITLAN*	○								●												
MAGOFFIN HOME						●			●						●	●	●				
MATAGORDA ISLAND	Q		CT							○	○	○				●		●		●	C,Z
MONUMENT HILL / KREISCHE COMPLEX						●			●		●				●	●	●			●	
JOSE ANTONIO NAVARRO						●			●						●	●	●				
OLD FORT PARKER						●			●						●	●	●				
PORT ISABEL LIGHTHOUSE															●	●	●				
RANCHO DE LAS CABRAS**	AREA PRESENTLY CLOSED TO PUBLIC PENDING DEVELOPMENT																				
SAN JOSE MISSION *						●									●	●	●				
SAM BELL MAXEY HOUSE															●	●	●				
SEBASTOPOL HOUSE	AREA PRESENTLY CLOSED TO PUBLIC PENDING DEVELOPMENT																				
STARR MANSION**	AREA PRESENTLY CLOSED TO PUBLIC PENDING DEVELOPMENT																				

FACILITIES

* FACILITIES NOT OPERATED BY PARKS AND WILDLIFE
** SITES ARE NOT OFFICIALLY NAMED
○ PERMITTED BUT FACILITIES NOT PROVIDED
● FACILITIES OR SERVICES PROVIDED FOR ACTIVITY

A AUDITORIUM
B BOATS FOR RENT
C GROUP CAMP
CT CHEMICAL TOILETS
D SCENIC DRIVE
E EQUESTRIAN TRAIL
G GOLF
H GROUP HALL

L TEXAS LONGHORN HERD
M MINIATURE GOLF
P GROUP PICNIC
R RENTAL HORSES
S RECREATION HALL
X OPEN SHELTERS
GB GROUP BARRACKS
Z PRIMITIVE CAMPING

For information on those park facilities accessible to and usable by the handicapped, ask for park brochure on handicapped facilities.

Heritage Park in Corpus Christi is a favorite tourist attraction in that city.

Bonham State Recreation Area is a 261-acre park located near Bonham in Fannin County. It includes a 65-acre lake. The land was acquired in 1933 and 1934 from the City of Bonham. **Sam Rayburn Memorial Library** in Bonham. **Sam Rayburn Home** and **Brushy Creek Reservoir** nearby.

Brazos Bend State Park (formerly **Big Creek Park Site**) in Fort Bend County, seven miles west of Rosharon on FM 762 (approximately 28 miles south of Houston). Total acreage, 4,897. Acquired from private landowners in 1976.

Brazos Island State Recreation Area is 216.6 acres 23 miles northeast of Brownsville in Cameron County. A scenic park, the land was acquired from the Texas General Land Office in 1957. Brownsville, Mexico, **Port Isabel Lighthouse State Historic Structure** and South Padre Island within hour's driving distance; slightly longer drive leads into heart of Rio Grande Valley. Historical spots of surrounding area include two battle sites (**Palo Alto** and **Resaca de la Palma**) from Mexican War, 1846, and battle site of **Palmito Ranch, last land engagement of Civil War**, May 1865. (No development as of 1985.)

Bryan Beach State Recreation Area, is 878 acres near Freeport. Acquired by purchase in 1973 from private sources. (No developed facilities in 1985.)

Buescher State Park, a scenic area, is 1,012 acres near Smithville in Bastrop County. The state was deeded the park by the City of Smithville between 1933 and 1936. **El Camino Real** (King's Highway) once ran near park; road connected **San Antonio de Bexar** with Spanish missions in East Texas and generally followed present-day Texas State Highway 21 and **Old San Antonio Road**. Parkland included in Stephen F. Austin's colonial grant. Scenic park road connects **Buescher State Park** with **Bastrop State Park**.

Caddo Lake State Park, one mile west of Karnack in Harrison County, consists of 480 acres along the 25,400 surface-acre **Caddo Lake**. A scenic area, it was acquired from private owners in 1933-37. Nearby Karnack is childhood home of **Mrs. Lyndon B. Johnson**. Close by is old city of **Jefferson**, famous as commercial center of Northeast Texas during last half of 19th century. Caddo Indian legend attributes formation of **Caddo Lake** to earthquake. Lake originally a natural lake, but dam added in 1914 for flood control; new dam replaced old one in 1971.

Caddoan Mounds State Historic Site in Cherokee County near Alto. Total of 93.5 acres acquired in 1975 by condemnation.

Caprock Canyons State Park, 3.5 miles north of Quitaque off Texas 86 in Briscoe County, has 13,960.6 acres. Purchased in 1975.

Cassells-Boykin State Park, Angelina County, seven miles northeast of Zavalla on **Lake Sam Rayburn**. Total acreage, 265. Acquired in October, 1982, by lease from the Department of the Army. Facilities include boat ramp, two-pit toilets, 20 picnic sites, 10 campsites, water well and dump station. No fees are charged.

Cleburne State Recreation Area is a 528-acre park located in Johnson County; 75 acres are designated a **wildlife refuge**; **116-acre lake**; acquired from the City of Cleburne, Johnson County and private owners in 1935 and 1938. Glen Rose **dinosaur tracks** may be seen at nearby **Dinosaur Valley State Park**.

Confederate Reunion Grounds State Historical Park, located in Limestone County on the Navasota River where it is joined by Jack's Creek, and is 78.5 acres in size. The park may be reached by going 6 miles south of Mexia on State Highway 14, then 2.5 miles west on FM 2705.

Copano Bay State Fishing Pier, a 6-acre park with restaurant and fishing pier, located five miles north of Rockport in Aransas County. Jurisdiction transferred from the Texas Highway Department in 1967; operated by leased concession.

Copper Breaks State Park, 12 miles south of Quanah on Texas 6, was acquired in 1970. Recreation park features rugged scenic beauty on 1,888.7 acres, and has a 70-acre lake. Medicine Mounds were important ceremonial sites of Comanche Indians. Nearby **Pease River** was site of battle, 1860, in which **Cynthia Ann Parker** was recovered from Comanches. Portion of official Texas longhorn herd maintained at park.

Daingerfield State Park in Morris County is a 551-acre recreational area which includes an 80-surface-acre lake; deeded in 1935 by private owners. This area center of iron industry in Texas; nearby is **Lone Star Steel Co.** On grounds of company is old blast furnace that helped in manufacturing guns and other metal objects for Civil War.

Dwight D. Eisenhower Birthplace State Park in Denison is site of his home.

Davis Mountains State Park is 1,869 acres in Jeff Davis County. The scenic area, near Fort Davis, was deeded over many years by private owners. First European, **Antonio de Espejo**, came to area in 1583. Nearby points of interest include **Fort Davis National Historic Site, McDonald Observatory** and scenic loop through **Davis Mountains. Davis Mountains State Park** located halfway between **Carlsbad Caverns** and **Big Bend National Park.** Nearby are scenic **Limpia, Madera, Musquiz** and **Keesey Canyons; Camino del Rio**; ghost town of **Shafter; Capote Falls, Sul Ross State University** in Alpine and **Fort Leaton State Historic Site.**

Dinosaur Valley State Park, located near Glen Rose in Somervell County, is a 1,523-acre scenic park. Land was acquired from private owners in 1969 and 1973. Dinosaur tracks and two full-scale dinosaur models on display. There is longhorn herd in park.

Eisenhower State Recreation Area, 457 acres located in Grayson County, was acquired by an Army lease in 1954 and named for the 34th President, Dwight David Eisenhower. Park located on shores of **Lake Texoma.** First Anglo settlers came to area in 1835 and 1836; **Fort Johnson** was established in area in 1840; **Colbert's Ferry** established on Red River in 1853 and operated until 1931.

Eisenhower Birthplace State Park, a Historic Site, is 3 acres, including the birthplace of **Dwight David Eisenhower,** in Denison, Grayson County. The property was acquired in 1958 from the Sid Richardson Foundation. Restoration of home complete, with furnishings of period and some personal effects of Gen. Eisenhower. His history of World Wars I and II is here. Also crank-type telephone with personal greetings from "Ike." Town of **Denison** established on **Butterfield Mail Route** in 1858.

Enchanted Rock State Natural Area is 1,643 acres on Big Sandy Creek 18 miles north of Fredericksburg on FM 965. Acquired in 1978 from Nature Conservancy of Texas, Inc. **Enchanted Rock** is huge granite boulder rising 500 feet above ground and covering 640 acres. Indians believed ghost fires flickered at top and were awed by weird creaking and groaning geologists now say resulted from rock's heating by day and contracting in cool night.

Fairfield Lake State Recreation Area is 1,460 acres, six miles northeast of the City of Fairfield in Freestone County. Now open for overnight use, the park is leased

from Texas Utilities. Surrounding woods predominantly oak and offer sanctuary for many species of birds and wildlife.

Falcon State Recreation Area is 573 acres located at southern end of **Falcon Lake** at Falcon Heights in Starr and Zapata Counties. The park was leased from the International Boundary and Water Commission in 1954. Nearby are Mexico and **Fort Ringgold** in Rio Grande City; **Bentsen-Rio Grande Valley State Park** is 65 miles away.

Fannin Battleground State Historic Site, 9 miles east of Goliad in Goliad County. The park was acquired by legislative enactment in 1965. At this site on March 20, 1836, **Col. J. W. Fannin** surrendered to Mexican **Gen. Jose Urrea** after **Battle of Coleto;** 342 massacred and 28 escaped near what is now **Goliad State Historical Park.** Near Fannin site is **Gen. Zaragoza's Birthplace** and partially restored **Mission Nuestra Senora del Espiritu Santo de Zuniga.** (See also **Goliad State Historical Park** in this list.)

Fanthorp Inn State Historic Site 1.4 acres in Anderson and Grimes Counties; acquired by purchase in 1977 from Edward Buffington. Closed to public in 1985.

Fort Griffin State Historical Park is 506 acres 15 miles north of Albany in Shackelford County. The state was deeded the land by the county in 1935. A herd of Texas longhorns resides on the park range. On bluff overlooking townsite of Fort Griffin and Clear Fork of Brazos River valley are ruins of **Old Fort Griffin,** restored bakery, replicas of enlisted men's huts. (Townsite is not in park boundaries.) Fort constructed in 1867, deactivated 1881; crumbling ruins of various structures still may be seen. Albany annually holds "**Fandangle**" in commemoration of frontier times.

Fort Lancaster State Historic Site, 81.6-acres located about 33 miles west of Ozona on U.S. 290 in Crockett County, acquired in 1968 by deed from Crockett County; Henry Meadows donated 41 acres in 1975. **Fort Lancaster** established Aug. 20, 1855, to guard San Antonio-El Paso Road and protect movement of supplies and immigrants from Indian hostilities; fort abandoned March 19, 1861, after Texas seceded from Union.

Fort Leaton State Historic Site, four miles east of Presidio in Presidio County on FM 170, was acquired in 1967 from private owners. Consists of 16.5 acres, 5 of

which are on site of pioneer trading post. In 1848 **Ben Leaton** built fortified trading post known as **Fort Leaton** near present Presidio, Texas. Ben Leaton died in 1851. Partial reconstruction of fort begun in early 1930s and in 1936 Texas Centennial Commission placed marker at site.

Fort McKavett State Historic Site, 80.8 acres acquired in 1967 and 1968 in part from the Fort McKavett Restoration, Inc., and Menard County, is located 17 miles west of Menard. Fort built for protection of settlers against Indians in 1852. Originally called **Camp San Saba**, built by War Department as protection for frontier settlers. Camp later renamed for **Capt. Henry McKavett**, killed at Battle of Monterrey, Sept. 21, 1846. Fort abandoned March 1859; reoccupied April 1, 1868; after **Gen. Ranald S. Mackenzie** subdued Indians, fort no longer needed, abandoned June 30, 1883.

Fort Parker State Recreation Area includes 1,485.2 acres south of Mexia in Limestone County. Named for the former fort located near the present park, the site was acquired by deeds from private owners between 1935 and 1937. Nearby point of interest is **Old Fort Parker State Historic Site**, replica of fort erected in 1834 for protection from Indians. Daughter of founder, **Cynthia Ann Parker**, captured by Indians May 19, 1836. She married **Chief Peta Nocona** and mothered **Quanah Parker**, last great Comanche chief, involved in **Battle of Palo Duro**.

Fort Richardson State Historical Park, located one-half mile south of Jacksboro in Jack County, is 396.1 acres. Acquired in 1968 from City of Jacksboro. Fort founded in summer of 1866; named **Fort Jacksboro** at that time. April 1867 it was abandoned for site 20 miles farther north; on Nov. 19, 1867, made permanent post at Jacksboro and named for **Israel Richardson**. **Fort Richardson** part of defensive system against Indians. Expeditions sent from Fort Richardson arrested Indians responsible for **Salt Creek Massacre** in 1871 and fought Comanches in Palo Duro Canyon. Fort abandoned again in May 1878.

Fulton Mansion State Historic Structure 3.4 miles north of Rockport in Aransas County. Total acreage of 2.3 acquired by purchase from private owner in 1976. Three-story wooden structure, built in 1871-1876, was home of George W. Fulton, prominent in South Texas for economic and commercial influence; mansion derives significance from its innovative construction and Victorian design.

Galveston Island State Park, located approximately 6 miles southwest of Galveston on FM 3005, is a 1,944-acre site acquired in 1970 from private owners. Offers camping, nature study and fishing amid sand dunes and grassland.

Garner State Park is 1,419.8 acres of recreational facilities in northern Uvalde County. Named for **John Nance Garner**, U.S. Vice-President, 1933-1941, the park was deeded in 1934 by private owners. Nearby is **John Nance "Cactus Jack" Garner Museum** in Uvalde. Nearby also are historic ruins of **Mission Nuestra de la Candelaria del Canon**, founded in 1749; **Camp Sabinal** (a U.S. Cavalry post and later Texas Ranger camp) established 1856; **Fort Inge**, established 1849.

Goliad State Historical Park is 186.6 acres along the San Antonio River in Goliad County. The land was deeded in 1931 by the City and County of Goliad. Nearby are the sites of several battles in the Texas fight for independence from Mexico. The park includes a replica of **Mission Nuestra Senora del Espiritu Santo de Zuniga**, originally established 1722 and settled at its present site in 1749. Park unit contains **Gen. Zaragoza's Birthplace** which is located at **Presidio la Bahia**. He was Mexican national hero who led troops against French at historic Battle of Puebla. Park property also contains ruins of **Mission Nuestra Senora del Rosario**, established 1754, located four miles west of Goliad on U.S. 59. Other nearby points of historical interest are restored **Presidio Nuestra Senora de Loreto de la Bahia**, established 1722 and settled on site in 1749; it is located ¼ mile south of **Goliad State Historical Park** on U.S. 183. Goliad memorial shaft marking common burial site of **Fannin** and victims of **Goliad massacre** (1836) is near Presidio la Bahia. (See also write-up under **Fannin Battleground State Historic Site**, above.)

Goose Island State Recreation Area in Aransas County is 307 acres; it was deeded by private owners in 1931-1935. Located here is the tree estimated to be 2,000 years old and listed by American Forestry Association as the **national co-champion live oak**; certified largest live oak in Texas in 1969. **Aransas Wildlife Refuge**, wintering ground for rare and endangered **whooping cranes**, just across St. Charles Bay.

Gov. Hogg Shrine State Historical Park is a 26.7-acre tract in Quitman, Wood County. Named for **James Stephen Hogg**, first native-born Governor of Texas, the park includes a museum housing items which belonged to Hogg. Seventeen acres deeded by the Wood County Old Settlers Reunion Association in 1946; 4.74 acres gift of Miss Ima Hogg in 1970; 3 acres purchased. Old Settlers Reunion held annually in August in this park. **Gov. James Stephen Hogg Memorial Shrine** created in 1941. Gov. Hogg's wedding held in **Stinson Home; Miss Ima Hogg Museum** houses both park headquarters and display of representative history of entire Northeast Texas area.

Guadalupe River State Park in Kendall and Comal Counties, 13 miles east of Boerne on Texas 46. Total acreage 1,937.7 on Guadalupe River. Acquired by deed from private owners in 1975. Park has four miles of river frontage with several white-water rapids and is located in middle of 20-mile stretch of Guadalupe River noted for canoeing. It has picnic and camp sites with restroom and shower facilities.

Hale Ranch Park Site. (See **Brazos Bend State Park**.)
Hardeman County State Park. (See **Copper Breaks State Park**.)

Hill Country State Natural Area (Louise Merrick Unit) in Bandera and Medina Counties, nine miles west of Bandera on FM 1077. Total acreage 4,753 acquired by gift from Louise Merrick in 1976. Park is located in typical Texas Hill Country on West Verde Creek and contains several spring-fed streams.

Hueco Tanks State Historical Park, located 32 miles northeast of El Paso in El Paso County, was obtained from the county in 1969. Featured in this 860.3-acre park are large natural cisterns and site of last great Indian battle in county. Apaches, Kiowas, Comanches and earlier Indian tribesmen camped here and left behind **pictographs** telling of their adventures. Tanks served as watering place for **Butterfield Overland Mail Route**.

Huntsville State Park is 2,083.2-acre recreational area in Walker County, acquired by deeds from private owners in 1934. **Sam Houston State University** located at nearby Huntsville. **Texas Department of Corrections** also located in Huntsville, home of **Huntsville Prison Rodeo** held each Sunday in October. At Huntsville is old homestead of Sam Houston (**Steamboat House**) and his grave; homestead contains personal effects of Houston. Park adjoins **Sam Houston National Forest** and encloses **Lake Raven**. Approximately 50 miles away is **Alabama-Coushatta Indian Reservation** in Polk County.

Inks Lake State Park is 1,200.7 acres of recreational facilities along Inks Lake, on the Colorado River, in Burnet County. The park was acquired by deeds from the Lower Colorado River Authority and private owners in 1940. Nearby are **Longhorn Cavern State Park, LBJ Ranch, LBJ State Historical Park, Pedernales Falls State Park** and **Enchanted Rock State Natural Area**. Granite **Mountain** and quarry at nearby Marble Falls furnished material for Texas **state capitol**. Deer, turkey and other wildlife abundant. **Buchanan Dam**, largest multi-arch dam in world, located six miles from park.

Jeff Davis State Recreation Area is 37.9 acres southeast of Hillsboro in Hill County. The state acquired the land in 1924 from the Veterans' Administration and leased it to the American Legion until the year 2043. (No park development.)

Jim Hogg State Historical Park is 177.4 acres in **East Texas Piney Woods** in Cherokee County. A memorial to the state's first native-born governor, **James Stephen Hogg**, the property was deeded by the City of Rusk in 1941.

Jose Antonio Navarro State Historic Site on .6 acre in downtown San Antonio was acquired by donation from San Antonio Conservation Society Foundation in 1975. Has furnished Navarro House complex built about 1848.

Kerrville State Recreation Area is a 517.2-acre area along the Guadalupe River in Kerr County. The land was deeded by the City of Kerrville in 1934. Near the park is the site of **Camp Verde**, scene of an experiment involving the use of **camels** for transportation; the camp was active from 1855 to 1869. **Bandera Pass**, 12 miles south of Kerrville, noted gap in chain of mountains through which passed **camel caravans**, wagon trains, Spanish conquistadores, immigrant trains. In nearby Fredericksburg is atmosphere of old country of Germany and famous **Nimitz Hotel**. (See **Admiral Nimitz Museum Historical Area**.)

Kreische Complex Park Site located adjacent to **Monument Hill State Historic Site** in LaGrange, Fayette County, is 35.98 acres, acquired by purchase from private owners. Contains Kreische Brewery and house complex built between 1850-1855 on Colorado River;

WHAT BUSINESS IS COMING TO IN TEXAS.

Caddoan Indian hut at State Historic Site in East Texas.

probably first commercial brewery in state. Brewery closed in 1888; it now consists of several intact structures surrounded by ruins in various stages of deterioration. Various out-buildings located on site were associated with brewery and family.

Lake Arrowhead State Recreation Area, south of Wichita Falls in Clay County; this 524-acre park was acquired from City of Wichita Falls in 1970.

Lake Brownwood State Recreation Area in Brown County is 537.5 acres acquired from the Brown County Water Improvement District No. 1 in 1934. Park situated on **Lake Brownwood** near **geographical center** of Texas.

Lake Colorado City State Recreation Area, 500 acres leased for 50 years from a utility company. It is located in Mitchell County 11 miles southwest of Colorado City.

Lake Corpus Christi State Recreation Area, a 365 land-acre park located in San Patricio, Jim Wells and Live Oak Counties, was leased from City of Corpus Christi in 1934. Lake noted for big blue, channel and yellow catfish. Sunfish, bass and crappie also taken. City of Corpus Christi and **Padre Island National Seashore** are nearby.

Lake Livingston State Recreation Area, in Polk County, six miles southwest of Livingston on FM 3126, contains 635.5 acres along Lake Livingston. Acquired by deed from private landowners in 1971. Near ghost town of **Swartwout,** steamboat landing on Trinity River in 1830s and 1840s. Polk County's first Commissioners Court met there before voters selected Livingston as county seat.

Lake Lewisville State Park is 721 acres north of Lewisville. (Closed for development.)

Lake Mineral Wells State Park, located four miles east of the City of Mineral Wells on Highway 180 in Parker County, consists of 2,865 acres encompassing **Lake Mineral Wells.** The City of Mineral Wells donated 1,095 acres and the 646-acre lake to Texas Parks and Wildlife Department in 1976. The remaining 1,102 acres resulted from a transfer of a portion of **Fort Wolters Army Post** by the U.S. Government to the State of Texas for use as park land.

Lake Somerville State Recreation Area, in Lee and Burleson Counties, was leased from the federal government in 1969. The 5,200-acre park includes many recreational facilities. Many species of wild game observed at park; white-tailed deer, fox, coyote, raccoon, rabbit and quail abundant. Various park areas feature sandy or grassy shallow shorelines ideal for wading or swimming.

Lake Texana State Park (formerly Palmetto Bend State Park Site) is 575 acres, seven miles east of Edna on State Highway 111, with camping, boating, fishing, picnicking facilities.

Lake Whitney State Recreation Area is 955 acres along the east shore of **Lake Whitney** in Hill County. Acquired in 1954 by a Department of the Army lease, the state has control until 2003. Located on **Lake Whitney** near ruins of **Towash,** early Texas settlement inundated by Lake Whitney. Towash Village named for chief of Hainai Indians that moved into area in 1835. Park noted for bluebonnets in spring.

Landmark Inn State Historic Site 4.7 acres in Castroville acquired through donation by Miss Ruth Lawler in 1974. **Castroville,** known as **Little Alsace of Texas,** headquarters for group of Alsatian farmers settled there in 1840s. **Landmark Inn** built about 1844 as residence and store for Caesar Monad, mayor of Castroville 1851-1864.

Lipantitlan State Historic Site is five acres east of Orange Grove in Nueces County. The property was deeded by private owners in 1937. Fort constructed here in 1833 by Mexican government; fort fell to Texas forces in 1835. **Lake Corpus Christi State Recreation Area** is nearby.

Lockhart State Recreation Area is 263.7 acres near Lockhart in Caldwell County. The land was deeded by private owners between 1934 and 1937. **Emanuel Episcopal Church** in Lockhart one of oldest Protestant churches in continuous use in Texas. After Comanche **raid at Linnville, Battle of Plum Creek** (1840) was fought in area.

Longhorn Cavern State Park in Burnet County is 639 acres classified as a scenic park. It was acquired in 1932-1937 from private owners. The cave has been used as a shelter since prehistoric times. Among legends about the cave is one that the outlaw Sam Bass hid a $2 million cache of stolen money. Another legend is that the defenders of the Confederacy made gunpowder in the cave during the Civil War, and another story states Gen. Robert E. Lee, while stationed in Texas before the Civil War, chased some Indians into the cave but lost their trail. **Inks Lake State Park** and federal fish hatchery located nearby. Park operated by concession agreement.

Lost Maples State Natural Area consists of 2,174.2 scenic acres in Bandera County, four miles north of Vanderpool on Ranch Road 187. (Formerly **Sabinal Canyon State Park.**) Acquired by purchase from private owners in 1973. Outstanding example of Edwards Plateau flora and fauna, features isolated stand of uncommon Uvalde **bigtooth maple. Golden-cheeked warbler** and **black-capped vireo** have been sighted in park.

Lyndon B. Johnson State Historical Park, in Gillespie County near Stonewall, is 717.8-acre park. Acquired in 1967 with private donations. Statue of **Johnson** unveiled in 1974 ceremonies. Home of **Lyndon B. Johnson** located north bank of Pedernales River across Ranch Road 1 from park; portion of official Texas **longhorn herd** maintained at park. Wildlife exhibit includes turkey, deer and buffalo. Living history demonstrations in progress at restored **Sauer-Beckmann house.** Reconstruction of **Johnson birthplace,** located east of ranch house at end of Park Road 49, open to public. Nearby is family cemetery where former president and relatives buried. In Johnson City is boyhood home of President Johnson. Near outskirts of Johnson City is cluster of stone barns and buildings constructed by his grandfather, Sam Ealy Johnson Sr., and his brother Tom. (See also **National Parks.**)

McKinney Falls State Park in Travis County east of Interstate 35 and near Bergstrom AFB is a 632.7-acre park acquired in 1970 from private donation. The headquarters of the **Parks and Wildlife Department** are at this location.

Mackenzie State Recreation Area in Lubbock County is a 542.2-acre park acquired in 1935 from the City of Lubbock, then leased to that city until 2037. The park was named for Gen. Ranald S. Mackenzie, famous for his campaigns against Indians in West Texas. One of the main features is a colony of native Texas **prairie dogs;** a section is called "**Prairie Dog Town.**" (Not operated by parks department.)

Magoffin Home State Historic Site, in El Paso County in the City of El Paso; total acreage, 1.5. Purchased jointly by the State of Texas and the City of El Paso in 1976, it is operated by the Texas Parks and Wildlife Department. The Magoffin Home was built in 1875 by pioneer El Pasoan Joseph Magoffin and displays a regional architectural style developed in the Southwest between 1865 and 1880.

Martin Creek Lake State Recreation Area, in Rusk County, 4 miles south of Tatum off State Highway 43. Total acreage 216.4 acres, deeded to the Parks and Wildlife Department by the Texas Utilities Generating Company in 1976. Pending development, approximately 15 acres immediately adjacent to the boat ramp is available for public use. The site is being operated by a concession contract at this time and provides boat ramps and parking area, fishing and picnic supplies

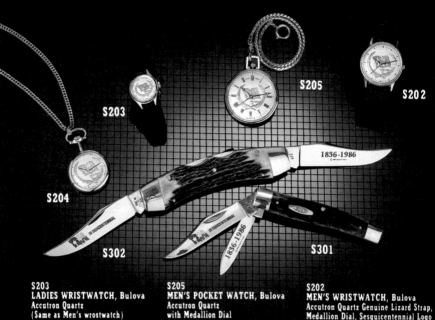

and limited picnic sites for day use visitors. The primary use of the Martin Creek Lake State Park Site is to provide boat ramp access to the reservoir for fishermen.

Martin Dies Jr. State Park, until 1965 the Dam B State Park, is 705-acre recreational area in Jasper and Tyler Counties. The land was acquired from the U.S. Army Corps of Engineers by lease in 1964. Park located at edge of **Big Thicket.** In spring, Dogwood Festival is held at Woodville. Park approximately 30 miles from **Alabama-Coushatta Indian Reservation.**

Matagorda Island Wildlife Conservation/Park Area, separated from the mainland by San Antonio and Espiritu Santo Bays, Matagorda Island is one of the barrier islands that border the Gulf and protect the mainland from the great tides and strong wave action of the open ocean. The southwestern tip of the island, consisting of 11,500 acres, is privately owned and the remainder, which extends approximately 24 miles northeastwardly, consists of 24,893 acres of state land and 19,000 acres of federal land. Under a cooperative agreement between the U.S. Department of the Interior and the State of Texas approved in 1983, the entire area of public lands is managed by the Texas Parks and Wildlife Department.

Meridian State Recreation Area in Bosque County is a 502.4-acre park including a 73-acre lake. The land was acquired from private owners in 1933-1935. **Tonkawa Indians** lived in surrounding area before coming of white man; **Tawakoni Indians** also occupied area prior to 1841. **Texas-Santa Fe expedition** of 1841 passed through Bosque County near present site of park. Park located on Bee Creek in Bosque Valley is very popular for bream, crappie, catfish and bass fishing. **Golden-cheeked warblers** nest here annually.

Mission Tejas State Historical Park is a 118-acre park in Houston County. Situated in the **Davy Crockett National Forest,** the park was acquired from the Texas Forest Service in 1957 by legislative enactment. In the park is a replica of the **Mission San Francisco de los Tejas,** which was established in 1690; was first mission in East Texas; abandoned due to Indians; re-established 1716 but again abandoned 1719. In 1721, third attempt made and was successful for a while but was abandoned for third and final time in 1730 and moved to San Antonio; renamed **San Francisco de la Espada** and is today one of San Antonio's four historic mission sites.

Monahans Sandhills State Park consists of 3,840 acres of sand dunes in Ward and Winkler Counties. The land is leased by the state until 2056. Because water was readily available, dunes used as meeting place by raiding Indians. Burial site of prehistoric Indians in exhibit building adjacent to interpretive center. **Odessa meteor crater** is nearby.

Monument Hill State Historic Site consists of 4.4 acres southwest of La Grange in Fayette County. The land was acquired in two parcels — monument and tomb area transferred from Board of Control in 1949; the rest from the Archbishop of San Antonio in 1956. The hill, a historical site, bears a memorial shaft dedicated to **Capt. Nicholas Dawson** and his men, who fought at **Salado Creek** in 1842, in Mexican Gen. Woll's invasion of Texas, and to the men of the ''**black bean lottery**'' (1843) of the **Mier Expedition.** Bodies of these heroes were brought to Monument Hill for reburial in 1848. In La-Grange, old tree under which Captain Dawson recruited ill-fated expedition still stands.

Mother Neff State Park was the **first official state park** in Texas. It originated with six acres designated for park purposes by the will of Mrs. I.E. Neff, mother of **Pat M. Neff,** Governor of Texas from 1921 to 1925. The park now contains 259 acres along the Leon River in Coryell County and is classified a historical park. The additional land was deeded to the state in 1934 by private owners.

Mustang Island State Park is 3,703.6 acres on Gulf of Mexico in Nueces County, 14 miles south of Port Aransas; acquired from private owners in 1972.

Old Fort Parker State Historic Site, an 11-acre park in Limestone County, was deeded by private owners in 1933. In the park is a replica of **Fort Parker** stockade, built in 1834 and was site of abduction of **Cynthia Ann Parker** on May 19, 1836, by Comanche and Kiowa Indians.

Palmetto State Park, a scenic park, is 263.6 acres along the San Marcos River in Gonzales County. The land was deeded in 1934-1937 by private owners. Artesian wells produce distinctive, sulphur-laden water. Nearby Gonzales and Ottine important in early Texas history. Gonzales settled 1825 as center of **Green DeWitt's colonies.** Nearby is site of **Elks' Hospital** and

Texas Rehabilitation Center.

Palmetto Bend State Park, in Jackson County. (See **Lake Texana State Park.**)

Palo Duro Canyon State Park, the state's largest, consists of 16,402 acres in Armstrong and Randall Counties. The land was deeded by private owners in 1933 and is the scene of the annual production of the drama, **Texas.** Scenic canyon one million years old and exposes rocks spanning about 200 million years of geological time. **Coronado** may have visited canyon in 1541. Canyon officially discovered by **Capt. R. B. Marcy** in 1852. Scene of decisive battle in 1874 between Comanche and Kiowa Indians and U.S. Army troops under **Gen. Ranald Mackenzie.** Also scene of early ranch undertaking started by **Charles Goodnight** in 1876.

Pedernales Falls State Park, 4,860 acres in Blanco County about 14 miles east of Johnson City. Acquired from private owners in 1970 along banks of scenic Pedernales River. This area, formerly Circle Bar Ranch, typifies Edwards Plateau with live oaks, deer, turkey and stone hills. **Golden-cheeked warbler** nests here.

Port Isabel Lighthouse State Historic Structure consists of .6 acre in Port Isabel in Cameron County. It was acquired by purchase from private owners in 1950 and includes a **lighthouse** constructed in 1852; near battle site of **Palmito Ranch** (1865); lighthouse remodeled 1952 and is still used. Resort facilities available across Queen Isabella Causeway at **South Padre Island.**

Port Lavaca State Fishing Pier is a recreational area, acquired by transfer of authority from Texas Highway Department in 1963. It is 1.8 acres on Lavaca Bay in Calhoun County. Main attraction is a 3,200-foot fishing pier made from the former causeway across the bay. Port Lavaca City Park is at base of the pier and offers a boat ramp, camping and picnicking facilities. Operated by leased concession.

Possum Kingdom State Recreation Area in Palo Pinto County is 1,528.7 acres adjacent to **Possum Kingdom Lake,** in Palo Pinto Mountains and Brazos River Valley. Numerous deer, other wildlife and some cattle of official **Texas longhorn herd** live in park. The area was acquired from the Brazos River Authority in 1940.

Purtis Creek Park Site in Henderson and Van Zandt Counties, three miles north of Eustace on FM 316. Total acreage 1,582.4 acquired in 1976 from private owners. (Closed pending development.)

Queen Isabella State Fishing Pier in Cameron County was transferred from the Texas State Highway Department in 1973. It is a 5,100-foot lighted fishing pier on seven acres, which connects Port Isabel with South Padre Island. Operated by leased concession.

Rancho de las Cabras State Park Site located in Wilson County. Acquired in 1977 and consists of 99.2 acres. Consists of chapel and three rooms facing walled patio. (Site closed to public.)

Resaca de la Palma State Park Site in Cameron County, three miles northwest of Brownsville, consists of 1,100 acres. Acquired by purchase from private owners in 1978. (Closed to public pending development.)

Rusk/Palestine State Park. Rusk unit located adjacent to Texas State Railroad Rusk Depot with total acreage of 110. Palestine unit located adjacent to Texas State Railroad Palestine Depot with 26 acres.

Sabine Pass Battleground State Historical Park in Jefferson County, southeast of Sabine Pass, contains 56.3 acres, acquired by deed from Kountze County Trust in 1971. **Richard W. Dowling,** with small Confederate force, repelled an attempted 1863 invasion of Texas by Union naval gunboats during Civil War.

Sam Bell Maxey House State Historic Structure in Paris, Lamar County, donated by City of Paris in 1976. Consists of .4 acre. Most of furnishings accumulated by Maxey family included. In March 1971, the Maxey House was officially listed on the National Register of Historical Places.

San Jacinto Battleground State Historical Park is 329.9 acres on which is situated the 570-foot-tall monument erected in honor of Texans who defeated Mexican **Gen. Antonio Lopez de Santa Anna** on April 21, 1836. The site, classified a historical park, is in east Harris County. The 59th Legislature transferred the park to the Texas Parks and Wildlife Department. The **U.S.S. Texas,** another state historical shrine, is moored in the park.

San Jose Mission National Park. Transferred to National Park Service in April 1983.

Sea Rim State Park in Jefferson County, 10 miles west of Sabine Pass, contains 15,109.1 acres of marshland with five miles of Gulf beach shoreline, acquired from private owners in 1972. It is prime wintering area for waterfowl; also home of endangered **red wolf,** American alligator, rare river **otter** and **muskrat.**

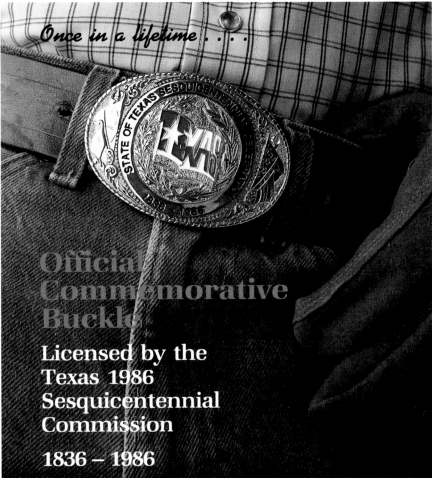

The clocktower in the quadrangle at historic Fort Sam Houston is a favorite tourist attraction.

Sebastopol House State Historic Structure in Seguin, Guadalupe County, was acquired by purchase in 1976 from Seguin Conservation Society, approximately 2.2 acres. Period furnishing on display in the residence. Pending facility repair and development, not open to public.

Seminole Canyon State Historic Site in Val Verde County, nine miles west of Comstock, contains 2,172.5 acres; acquired by purchase from private owners in 1973. Canyon area contains several important prehistoric **Indian pictograph sites**. Historic interpretive center open.

Sheldon Wildlife Management Area and Park Site, Harris County on Carpenter's Bayou 20 miles northeast of downtown Houston just north of US 90. Total acreage, 2,503. Acquired by purchase in 1952 from the City of Houston. Facilities include 2 boat ramps with parking areas and restrooms; 5 T-head fishing piers and 5.5 miles of levees. Activities include nature study of coastal marshland habitat; bird watching of primarily waterfowl and marsh birds, and fishing with free access to all public facilities during the prescribed mid-February through September fishing season. No rates or charges.

Starr Mansion State Historic Site 3.1 acres in Marshall, Harrison County, not open to the public in 1985.

Stephen F. Austin State Historical Park, is 667.4 acres along the Brazos River in Austin County, named for the "**Father of Texas**." The area was deeded by the San Felipe de Austin Corporation and the San Felipe Park Association in 1940. Site of township of **San Felipe** was seat of government where conventions of 1832 and 1833 and **Consultation of 1835** held. These led to **Texas Declaration of Independence**. San Felipe was home of **Stephen F. Austin** and other famous early Texans; home of Texas' first Anglo newspaper (the **Texas Gazette**) founded in 1829; postal system of Texas originated here; beginning of **Texas Rangers**.

Texas State Railroad State Historical Park, Anderson and Cherokee Counties, between the cities of Palestine and Rusk, adjacent to US 84. Total acreage, 488.7. Acquired by Legislative Act in 1971. Opened for limited runs in summer. See local Parks and Wildlife office for schedules. The railroad was built by the State of Texas to support the state-owned iron works at Rusk. Begun in 1896, the railroad was gradually extended until it reached Palestine in 1909 and established regular rail service between the towns.

Tips State Recreation Area, 31.3 acres of recreational facilities, is on the Frio River in Live Oak County. The park, a mile west of Three Rivers, was deeded by private owners in 1925 and then leased for 99 years to Three Rivers. Park near site of **first glass factory** in Texas. Privately operated.

Tyler State Park is 985.5 acres, classified as recreational, north of Tyler in Smith County. Included is a 64-acre lake. The land was deeded by private owners in 1934 and 1935. Nearby Tyler famous as **rose capital of world**; there is located **Tyler Junior College** and planetarium, **Tyler Rose Garden, Caldwell Children's Zoo** and the **Goodman Museum**. Tyler is home of the **Tyler Rose Festival** each fall. **Morton salt mines** in Grand Saline, 40 miles from park.

Varner-Hogg Plantation State Historical Park is 65.7 acres along Varner Creek east of West Columbia in Brazoria County. The land originally was owned by Martin Varner, a member of **Stephen F. Austin's** "**Old Three Hundred**" colony, but became a later home of Texas governor, **James Stephen Hogg**. The state acquired the property in 1956 by a deed from Miss Ima Hogg, daughter of the former governor. First rum distillery in Texas established in 1829 by Varner.

Washington-on-the-Brazos State Historical Park, consists of 154.1 acres southwest of Navasota in Washington County. The land was deeded by private owners in 1916. The land includes the site of the signing in 1836 of the Texas **Declaration of Independence** from Mexico, as well as the site of the later signing of the **Constitution of the Republic of Texas**. In 1842 and 1845, the land included the capitol of the Republic; it also included the home of **Anson Jones, last president of the Republic of Texas**.

Future Parks

The following parks were in the planning stage when this edition of the Texas Almanac went to press:

Choke Canyon; Franklin Mountains; Lake Houston; South Llano River; Village Creek Park; Arroyo Colorado; Eagle Mountain Lake; Lake Bob Sandlin; Lakeview Park; Davis Hill; Lake Tawakoni; and Gorman Falls.

National Parks, Historical Sites, Recreation Areas in Texas

Texas has two national parks, a national seashore, a biological preserve, several historic sites, memorials and recreation areas and 10 national wildlife refuges under supervision of the U.S. Department of Interior. In addition, the state has four national forests (see index) under jurisdiction of U.S. Department of Agriculture.

The **number of visitors** to national park sites in Texas has fluctuated during the last seven years, partly due to gasoline rationing during 1980 and 1981. The number of visitors to national parks in Texas since 1978: 4,831,200; 4,760,400; 4,170,700; 3,968,200; 4,747,800; 4,664,800 and 4,800,795.

Alibates Flint Quarries National Monument consists of 1,079 acres in Potter County. For more than 10,000 years, pre-Columbian Indians dug agatized limestone from the quarries to make projectile points, knives, scrapers and other tools. The area is presently undeveloped and access is by guided tours only. There were 1,900 daily visits made to the area in 1983, and 120,875 overnight stays.

Amistad Recreation Area contains the U.S. portion of **Amistad Reservoir** on the Rio Grande. Of 65,000 acres in the area, 43,250 acres are in United States. Limited camping space, and camping from boats permitted on

shore. Commercial campgrounds, motels, hotels in area. Open year round. In 1983, there were 120,875 overnight stays reported, and 1,221,400 daily visits.

Big Bend National Park, established in 1944, has spectacular mountain and desert scenery, a variety of unusual geological structures. Located in the great bend of the **Rio Grande**, the **international boundary** between United States and Mexico. Park contains 740,118 acres. Numerous camp sites are located in park, and the Chisos Mountain Lodge has accommodations for approximately 150 guests. Write for reservations to National Park Concessions, Inc., Big Bend National Park, Texas 79834. Park open year round. There were 220,119 overnight stays in 1983, and 164,900 daily visits.

Big Thicket National Preserve, set at 84,550 acres in Polk, Hardin, Liberty, Tyler, Jasper, Orange and Jefferson Counties, was authorized Oct. 11, 1974, to protect biological crossroads of the flora and fauna of the north, south, east and west. Five of the 12 units authorized have developments open to the public as follows: **Turkey Creek Unit**, 7,800 acres, with double loop self-guiding nature trail and accessible public information station located on FM 420, 2½ miles east of Highway 69. Also a 9-mile hiking trail with accessible ½-mile long

San Antonio is noted for its many missions in the San Antonio Missions National Historical Park.

spur into a pitcher plant savannah. **Beech Creek Unit**, 4,856 acres, has 1-mile loop trail through beech forest. **Hickory Creek Savannah Unit**, 668 acres, with 1-mile self-guiding nature trail and ½-mile accessible loop. **Beaumont Unit**, 6,218 acres, has a marked canoe trail available. Waterway corridors open to visitors are: **Little Pine Island Bayou** connecting Lance Rosier Unit to Beaumont Unit. **Menard Creek Corridor** south and west of Big Sandy Unit to Trinity River. **Neches River** from Dam B south to Beaumont. There were only 289 overnight stays recorded in 1983, and 33,400 daily visits.

Chamizal National Memorial, established in 1973, consists of 54.9 acres dedicated to the peaceful settlement of a 99-year-old boundary dispute between the United States and Mexico. Located in the south-central part of El Paso, the park is open year-round from 8:00 a.m. to 5:00 p.m., and from 7:00 p.m. to 11:00 p.m. during performances. It hosts a variety of programs throughout the year, some of which include: The Border Folk Festival (first weekend in October); The Siglo de Oro "Spanish Golden Age Presentation" (February-March); The Fourth of July — Fiesta of the Arts Celebration; The Sixteenth of September "Grito" Celebration. All programs are held in the park's quest to commemorate the signing of the Chamizal Treaty, through the promotion of intercultural communication, understanding and harmony. There were 119,600 daily visits in 1983.

Fort Davis National Historic Site in Jeff Davis County was a key post in the West Texas defense system, guarding immigrants on the San Antonio-El Paso Road. The 460-acre historic site was established in 1963. Lodging at Alpine, Marfa or Indian Lodge in **Davis Mountains State Park**. Open year round; 71,300 daily visits in 1983.

Guadalupe Mountains National Park, established 1972, consists of 76,293 acres in Hudspeth and Culberson Counties. A mountain mass of Permian limestone rises abruptly from the surrounding desert and contains one

of the most extensive fossil reefs on record. Deep canyons cut through this exposed fossil reef and provide a rare opportunity for geologic study. Special points of interest are **McKittrick Canyon** and **Guadalupe Peak**, the **highest in Texas**. Campground near Pine Springs Headquarters area has 24 tent sites plus RV parking, and is hub for 80 miles of trails. Dog Canyon area located one mile south of Texas-New Mexico state line, at end of NM State Road 137 and County Road 414, contains 18 tent spaces equipped with tables, grills, new comfort station and parking spaces for five self-contained recreational vehicles. Also a new visitor contact station and visitor horse corral. Open year round. Lodging at Van Horn, Texas; White's City or Carlsbad, N.M. There were 21,533 overnight stays in 1983; and 142,700 daily visits.

Lake Meredith Recreation Area, about 35 miles northeast of Amarillo, consists of a reservoir behind **Sanford Dam** on the Canadian River, in Moore, Hutchinson and Potter Counties. Occupies 44,951 acres; popular for water-based activities. Marine launching ramps, picnic areas, unimproved campsites. Commercial lodging and trailer hookups available in nearby towns. Open year round. There were 196,864 recorded overnight stays in 1983, and 1,844,900 daily visits.

Lyndon B. Johnson National Historical Park includes the boyhood home of the 36th President of United States, and the Johnson Settlement in Johnson City; free bus tour starting at the **LBJ State Park** includes the **LBJ Birthplace, old school, cemetery** and close-up exterior look at the **Texas White House**. Site in Blanco and Gillespie Counties was established Dec. 2, 1969, and contains 250 acres. Open year round. No camping on site; commercial campground, motels in area. There were 299,500 daily visits in 1983.

Padre Island National Seashore consists of a 67.5-mile stretch of a barrier island along the Gulf Coast; noted for its wide sand beaches, excellent fishing and abundant bird and marine life. Contains 130,355 acres in Kleberg, Willacy and Kenedy Counties. Open year round. One paved campground (fee charged) located north of Malaquite Beach, unpaved (primitive) campground area south of beach. Commercial lodging available outside boundaries of National Seashore. There were 78,895 recorded overnight stays in 1983, and 630,200 daily visits.

Palo Alto Battlefield National Historic Site, Brownsville, contains the site of the first of two important **Mexican War** battles fought on American soil. **Gen. Zachary Taylor's** victory here made invasion of Mexico possible. There are no federal facilities available at this time. No data available on daily visits.

Rio Grande Wild and Scenic River, care Big Bend National Park, is a 191.2-mile strip on the American shore of the Rio Grande in the Chihuahuan Desert that protects the river. It begins in Big Bend National Park and continues downstream to the Terrell-Val Verde County line. There are federal facilities in **Big Bend National Park** only. No data available on daily visits.

San Antonio Missions National Historical Park consists of four Spanish Colonial Missions and two acequias, or irrigation systems, including **Espada Dam** and aqueduct. Each of the four missions — **Concepcion, San Jose, San Juan** and **Espada** — are open 8-5 MST and 9-6 DST. The park includes 475 acres and is located within the city of San Antonio. Each of the church structures continues to be used as an active parish. For more information, contact San Antonio Missions National Historical Park, 727 E. Durango, Room A 612, San Antonio, Tx. 78206; 512/229-6000. There were 134,900 visits in 1983.

RECREATIONAL VISITS TO NATIONAL PARKS IN TEXAS

Below is given information on National Parks in Texas. This was furnished by the **National Park Service**. Recreation visits to National Park Service Areas in Texas, by years, numbered 4,760,400 in 1979; 4,170,700 in 1980; 3,968,200 in 1981; 4,747,800 in 1982; 4,664,800 in 1983 and 4,800,795 in 1984. Because of rounding, totals may not add up.

There were 97 trails in the National Park Areas in Texas and 409 miles of trails.

Name of Facility—	1981	1982	1983	1984
Alibates Flint Quarries National Monument, Potter County	2,400	2,400	1,900	2,265
Amistad Recreational Area, Rio Grande	976,400	1,259,700	1,221,400	1,164,360
Big Bend National Park	167,300	180,100	164,900	167,670
Big Thicket National Recreation Area	22,800	43,800	33,400	81,550
Chamizal National Monument, El Paso County	104,700	114,800	119,600	125,750
Fort Davis National Historic Site, Jeff Davis County	71,200	75,000	71,300	69,010
Guadalupe Mountains National Park, Hudspeth & Culberson Counties	142,600	140,600	142,700	151,850
Lake Meredith National Recreational Area, Amarillo	1,559,300	1,909,700	1,844,900	1,944,650
Lyndon B. Johnson National Historic Park, Johnson City	300,700	290,500	299,500	276,420
Padre Island National Seashore	620,800	731,200	630,200	613,400
**San Antonio Missions National Historical Park	0	0	134,900	205,100

**1984 was first full year of visits to this park.

Performers are on stage for production of Paul Green's "Texas" in Palo Duro Canyon State Park.

Recreational Special Events

Fairs, festivals and other special events provide year-round recreation in Texas. Some are of national interest and many attract attendance from over the state. Most of them are primarily of local and regional interest.

In addition to those listed here, the recreational paragraph in the county descriptions and the Standard Metropolitan Statistical Areas pages refer to numerous events. Texas Department of Highways and Public Transportation, Austin 78701, Texas Tourist Development Agency, Austin, and local and regional chambers of commerce can supply more information and dates.

The list of fairs and expositions below was compiled by the **Texas Association of Fairs and Expositions,** 411 W. Front, Tyler 75702. Specific dates may be obtained from local managers.

Folklife Festival
The University of Texas Institute of Texan Cultures presents an annual Texas Folklife Festival in August. For further information, write Texas Folklife Festival, P.O. Box 1226, San Antonio, Texas 78294.

Texas Arts and Crafts Fair
The Texas Arts and Crafts Foundation at Kerrville sponsors an arts and crafts fair in May each year. For further information, write to TACF, P.O. Box 1527, Kerrville 78028.

Sports and Vacation Show
The **Southwest Sports, RV and Vacation Show** is presented annually at Dallas Convention Center. The oldest and largest outdoor-living exposition in the South, it has been sponsored throughout its 37 years by The Dallas Morning News. Featured are exhibits of vactionlands from throughout North America, recreational vehicles, fishing tackle, hunting equipment, boats and accessories and a stage, tank and aerial show.

Sports Show dates will be March 5 through 9, 1986 and March 4 through 8, 1987.

Fairs and Expositions
City—Name of Event, Date, Executive, Address
Abilene—West Texas Fair; Sept.; Sid Saverance, Box 5527 (79608).

Alvarado—Pioneers and Old Settlers Reunion; Aug.; Otis A. Lane, Box 577 (76009).

Amarillo—Tri-State Fair; Sept.; Lynn M. Griffin, Box 31087 (79120).

Angleton—Brazoria Co. Fair; Oct.; Box 818 (77515).

Athens—Black-eyed Pea Jamboree; July; Sandra D. Weir, Box 608 (75751).

Bay City—Bay City Rice Festival; Oct.; Box 262 (77414).

Bay City—Matagorda Co. Fair; March; Michael J. Pruett, Box 1803 (77414).

Beaumont—South Texas State Fair; Oct.; Joe Goetschius, Box 3207 (77704).

Bellville—Austin Co. Fair; Oct.; C. W. Brandes, Box 141 (77418).

Belton—Belton Rodeo and Celebration; July; Clarence Griggs, Box 659 (76513).

Big Spring—Howard Co. Fair; Sept.; Geraldene Posey, Box 2356 (79720).

Boerne—Boerne Berges Fest; June; Tim Kloss, Box 748 (78006).

Boerne—Kendall Co. Fair; Sept.; Jerry Collins, Box 954 (78006).

Brenham—Washington Co. Fair; Sept.; Douglas Borchardt, Box 105 (77833).

Caldwell—Burleson Co. Fair; June; John Vallentine, Box 634 (77836).

Clifton—Central Texas Fair & Rodeo; Aug.; Jimmy Burch, Box 562 (76634).

Columbus—Colorado Co. Fair; Sept.; Tom Northrup, Box 506 (78934).

Conroe—Montgomery Co. Fair; March; Stuart Traylor, Box 2347 (77305).

Corpus Christi—Buccaneer Days; April-May; Bob Tucker, Box 30404 (78404).

Dallas—State Fair of Texas; Sept.-Oct., 1986; Oct., 1987; Wayne H. Gallagher, Box 26010 (75226).

Decatur—Wise Co. Old Settlers Reunion; July; Don Niblett, Box 549 (76234).

DeLeon—DeLeon Peach & Melon Festival; Aug.; Betty Terrill, Box 44 (76444).

Denton—North Texas State Fair; Aug.; James Roden, Box 1695 (76202).

Edna—Jackson Co. Fair; Sept.-Oct.; Milton Bain, Box 788 (77957).

Fairfield—Freestone Co. Fair; Aug.; Gene Chavers, Box 900 (75840).

Fredericksburg—Gillespie Co. Fair; Aug.; Bernice Seipp, Box 526 (78624).

Freer—Freer Rattlesnake Roundup; April; Jesse Hammack, Box 717 (78357).

Greenville—Hunt Co. Fair; Aug.; Bobby F. Harris, Box 1071 (75401).

Hallettsville—Lavaca Co. Fair; Oct.-Nov.; Mrs. Debra Garner, Box 69 (77964).

Hearne—Robertson Co. Fair; March; O. L. Harris Jr., Rt. 2, Box 98 (77859).

Hempstead—Waller Co. Fair; Sept.; Roy Wiesner, Box 911 (77445).

Hico—Old Settlers Reunion; July; Milton Rainwater, Rt. 3 (76457).

Hondo—Medina Co. Fair; Sept.; Bonnie Moos, Box 4 (78861).

Houston—Houston-Harris Co. Fair; Sept.; Mark Soper, Box 41048 (77240).

Hughes Springs—Wildflower Trails of Texas; April; Bill McKinney, Rt. 1, Box 178 (75656).

Huntsville—Walker Co. Fair; April; Spencer L. Karr, Box 1817 (77340).

Johnson City—Blanco Co. Fair; Aug.; Camille Coleman, Box 262 (78636).

Kenedy—Bluebonnet Days; May; Rhonda Lineburg, Box 724 (78119).

Killeen—Central Texas Exposition; March-April; John R. Cowsert, Box 878 (76541).

La Grange—Fayette Co. Fair; Aug.; R. J. Edwards, Box 544 (78945).

Lamesa—Dawson Co. Fair; Sept.; John J. Hegi, Box 301 (79331).

Laredo—Laredo Frontier Days & Rattlesnack Roundup; May; Elsa Rairie, Box 2245 (78041).

Laredo—Laredo International Fair & Expo.; March; Ruben M. Garcia, Box 1770 (78044).

Lubbock—Panhandle-South Plains Fair; Sept.; Steve Lewis, Box 208 (79408).

Marshall—Central E. Tex. Fair; Sept.; Jerry A. Martez, Drawer BB (75670).

Nacogdoches—Piney Woods Fair; Oct.; Becky Boren, Box 368 (75963).

Navasota—Grimes Co. Fair; June; John J. Patout, 217 E. Washington (77868).

New Braunfels—Comal Co. Fair; Sept.; Jan Jochec, Box 223 (78130).

Odessa—Permian Basin Fair & Expo.; Sept.; Donald D. Thorn, Box 4812 (79760).

Palestine—Anderson Co. Fair; May; W. K. Spaith, Box 228 (75801).

Paris—Red River Valley Expo.; Sept.; Ronnie A. Nutt, Box 964 (75460).

Port Lavaca—Calhoun Co. Fair; Oct.; Chas. L. Ward, 501 Sunnydale (77979).

Refugio—Refugio Co. Fair; Oct.; Glenn Naylor, Box 88 (78377).

Rosenberg—Fort Bend Co. Fair; Sept.-Oct.; Lawrence Elkins, Box 428 (77471).

Sante Fe—Galveston Co. Fair & Rodeo; April-May; Velma Acree, Box 889 (77510).

Snyder—Scurry Co. Fair; Sept.; Max Van Roeder, 2605 Ave. M. (79549).

Stamford—Texas Cowboy Reunion; July; E. C. Swenson, Box 551 (79553).

Sulphur Springs—Hopkins Co. Fall Festival; Sept.; Sharon Helm, Box 177 (75482).

Tourism in Texas

Tourism has retained its place as a major industry in Texas. In 1983 (the latest full year for which information is available), visitors spent $13.7 billion, according to the U.S. Travel Data Center in Washington, D.C. Vacations and other pleasure trips still rank far ahead of business and conventions as reasons for visiting Texas. The state ranked behind only California and Florida, although New York was running a strong fourth.

In economic terms, every county in the state except Kenedy and Loving shared in travel-related income. There were 278,095 travel-related jobs in the state, generating a payroll of $2,943,772,000. Travel produced state tax receipts of $309,694,000 and local revenues of $164,822,000.

The top 10 counties in total travel-related expenditures were: Harris, 3,321,574,000; Dallas, $3,153,516,000; Tarrant, $1,282,581,000; Bexar, $795,125,000; Travis, $349,715,000; El Paso, $344,043,000; Cameron, $293,272,000; Nueces, $266,672,000; Galveston, $211,730,000; and Hidalgo, $182,761,000.

A year-end origin study by the Texas Tourist Development Agency found that 37.6 million persons visited the state in 1984. Business traffic accounted for 13.1 million of the visitors, or 35 percent, and represented an increase of 22.4 percent over 1983. Ninety-one percent of the visitors were from the United States with the remaining nine percent from foreign countries. California again supplied the most visitors with 4.2 million; Oklahoma moved ahead of Louisiana with 3.7 million, and Louisiana was third with 2.9 million. France supplied the most foreign visitors to Texas with 541,000, slightly ahead of second-place Britian with 538,000. Mexico, which usually supplies the most foreign visitors to the state, slipped to third with 461,000 visitors, and Germany was fourth with 424,000.

In 1984, 36 percent of the visitors took lodging in Texas' hotels and motor inns, with the remainder staying with friends and relatives in private homes. The average size of the visitor party staying in public accommodations was 1.5 persons. In private homes, the average size of the visiting party was 2.6 persons. The average stay was 2.3 nights in public accommodations and 5.9 nights in private homes.

This study is conducted for TTDA by Pannell Kerr Foster, a national hotel consulting firm. It surveys private households, as well as hotel registrations, to determine the extent of out-of-state visitation.

These figures do not reflect the travel and tourism of Texans within their home state.

Recreation Facilities and Visitation Data Corps of Engineers' Lakes Texas 1984

Facilities available for visitors at U.S. Army Corps of Engineers' lakes in Texas, in 1984, are listed below. Since facilities change often, it is best to check at the time of visit.

Nearly 57 million visitors in 1984 enjoyed the recreational facilities at lakes in Texas under the management of the U.S. Army Corps of Engineers. Lake Texoma, with more than 8 million visitors, led in attendance in Texas and ranked second in the U.S. among Corps lakes.

Name of Reservoir and Stream—	Swim Areas	Launch Ramps	Picnic Sites	Camp Sites	Rental Units	Visitation
Addicks & Barker..	...	...	650	...	...	1,573,000
Aquilla	...	2	...	...	...	38,100
Bardwell	2	7	56	128	...	945,100
Belton	3	19	387	232	7	2,293,000
Benbrook	2	16	151	117	...	3,067,500
Canyon	6	25	195	690	33	2,342,200
Georgetown.......	1	3	124	228	...	931,900
Granger	2	5	130	168	...	321,600
Grapevine........	2	17	118	207	...	4,649,800
Hords Creek	1	10	5	163	...	831,100
Lake O' The Pines .	12	29	179	522	91	2,768,200
Lavon	5	25	416	151	...	3,202,800
Lewisville	7	36	279	360	...	5,899,600
Navarro Mills	2	6	...	246	...	1,428,900
Pat Mayse	8	11	10	349	...	379,000
O. C. Fisher	1	16	138	147	...	1,293,900
Proctor..........	...	6	44	190	...	873,700
Sam Rayburn	8	32	89	790	96	3,132,300
Somerville........	2	12	266	799	16	2,011,300
Stillhouse Hollow ..	2	5	45	122	...	1,011,100
Texoma..........	10	65	389	2,123	438	8,324,300
Town Bluff........	2	14	70	364	46	615,300
Waco............	1	9	60	347	...	4,630,400
Whitney..........	3	29	48	547	...	2,220,000
Wright Patman ...	9	19	350	494	...	2,056,100
Total	87	418	4,199	9,484	727	56,840,200

The French Legation Museum, a diplomat's legacy to Texas, is located in Austin.

Texarkana—Four States Fair; Sept.-Oct.; Marion Reed, Box 1915 (75504).

Tyler—East Texas Fair; Sept.; Bob Murdoch, 411 W. Front (75702).

Waco—Heart O'Texas Fair; Oct.; Leon Dollens, Box 7581 (76710).

Wharton—Wharton Co. Fair & Expo.; April; John Joyce, Rt. 2, Box 232 (77488).

Livestock Shows

Austin—Austin-Travis Co. Livestock Show; March; Kenneth Hees, Box 15703 (78761).

Donna—South Texas Lamb & Sheep Expo.; Jan.; Jas. C. McQueen, Box 794 (78537).

El Paso—Southwestern International Livestock Show & Rodeo; Feb.; Bernie Ricono, Box 10239 (79993).

Fort Worth—Southwestern Expo. & Fat Stock Show; Jan.-Feb.; W. R. Watt Jr., Box 150 (76101).

Giddings—Lee Co. Jr. Livestock Show; March; Ruby Weiser, Box 599 (78942).

Houston—Houston Livestock Show & Rodeo; Feb.-March; Dan A. Gattis, Box 20070 (77225).

Mercedes—Rio Grande Valley Livestock Show; March; Frances Cooper, Box 867 (78570).

San Angelo—San Angelo Stock Show & Rodeo; March; Sheila H. Rathmell, Box 2450 (76902).

San Antonio—San Antonio Livestock Expo.; Feb.; Mary Nan West, Box 20228 (78220).

STATE PARK NATURE/INTERPRETIVE AND HIKING TRAILS

Trails in state parks are designated as nature/interpretive trails or hiking trails, and many parks have both. Nature trails usually are less than a mile long with informational stops to explain points of interest. Hiking trails are longer, with some hikes requiring more stamina than others. Only those hiking trails of at least one mile in length are included in the following list. All designated nature trails are included. All trails are through flora native to the area.

Nature/Interpretive Trails

Abilene State Recreation Area: Elm Creek Nature Trail in Taylor County; guide posts and trail brochures available at park identify particular points of interest. Parts of trail are accessible to the handicapped.

Atlanta State Recreation Area: This 2.4-mile nature trail in Cass County winds through an undeveloped area of the park.

Bentsen-Rio Grande Valley State Park: Singing Chaparral Nature Trail in Hidalgo County has informational stops that correspond to park brochure; trail is 1.5 miles long.

Caddo Lake State Park: Forest Nature Trail in Harrison County is a little less than one mile long; numbered stops correspond to brochure explaining features of diversified vegetation.

Copper Breaks State Park: Juniper Ridge Nature Trail in Hardeman County is .5-mile long and a self-guided interpretive route through a portion of rugged breaks of Pease River. Many areas off trail are loose, unstable rock, and users are asked to remain on trail to avoid possible personal injury and to prevent creating further erosion.

Galveston Island State Park: Clapper Rail Nature Trail in Galveston County is a 3-mile trail through salt meadows and marsh; freshwater ponds located in meadows. Trail terminates with observation point overlooking surf and sea. Special features include bird blinds for photography and 1,000-foot boardwalk over marsh. Boardwalk accessible to handicapped.

Goliad State Historical Park: Two trails—the River Trail along San Antonio River, and Aranama Trail through subtropical woodland in Goliad County. Parts of trails are accessible to handicapped. Goliad is located on meeting ground of Gulf Coast Prairie and South Texas Brush Country.

Huntsville State Park: Big Chinquapin Nature Trail in Walker County is 1.3 miles long; bridges and boardwalks have not yet been constructed across marsh, so some wet or muddy spots may be encountered; also must cross a creek or two.

Lake Brownwood State Recreation Area: Texas Oaks Nature Trail in Brown County is just under a mile in length and portions are accessible to handicapped.

Lyndon B. Johnson State Historical Park: This is a 1.4-mile nature trail in Gillespie County, along which are informational stops where recordings of late President Johnson's voice convey message of the trail; trail accessible to the handicapped and passes through a living history exhibit of early 1900 farm life.

McKinney Falls State Park: Smith Rock Shelter Nature Trail in Travis County is just under a mile long; passes Smith Rock Shelter, an Indian campsite, and the remains of the McKinney homestead and mill.

Mission Tejas State Historical Park: Mile-long Tejas Timber Trail in Houston County.

Monahans Sandhills State Park: Short nature trail in Ward and Winkler Counties; tracks in sand tell of activity in foreboding, seemingly barren sand dunes.

Palmetto State Park: Palmetto and River Nature Trails in Gonzales County total about one mile; at one time, this area was called Ottine Swamp; rare plant profusion found in park.

Pedernales Falls State Park: Hill Country Nature Trail in Blanco County .5-mile long; numbered trail markers correspond to interpretive booklet.

Sea Rim State Park: Gambusia Nature Trail in Jefferson County just under mile in length; consists of ele-

This 1856 hand-drawn Howe tub pumper was once used to fight fires in Texas.

Mason Lankford displays newest addition to Fire Museum of Texas collection, an 1856 hand-drawn Howe tub pumper.

vated boardwalk two feet above marsh. Numbered trail markers correspond to interpretive booklet.

Seminole Canyon State Historical Park: A 1.5-mile trail in Val Verde County goes to **Fate Bell Shelter Cave** where visitors can see ancient **Indian** pictographs; climb back up from canyon floor strenuous.

Tyler State Park: Whispering Pines Nature Trail in Smith County is short trail with numbered stops that correspond to interpretive booklet; walk especially beautiful in spring when redbuds and dogwoods bloom.

Hiking Trails

Bastrop State Park: Several miles of undeveloped trails in Bastrop County through **Lost Pines** and other geographically isolated members of plant species.

Bentsen-Rio Grande Valley State Park: A 1.8-mile hiking trail in Hidalgo County lets hikers experience South Texas brushland, Rio Grande and old oxbow lake or resaca.

Caddo Lake State Park: There are 3.2 miles of hiking trails in Harrison County through scenic East Texas forests.

Copper Breaks State Park: Bull Canyon Hiking Trail in Hardeman County is pleasant, fairly easy hike about two miles long.

Daingerfield State Park: Scenic 2.5-mile hiking trail in Morris County; portions of trail are accessible to handicapped.

Davis Mountains State Park: Trail in Jeff Davis County is more than 4 miles long, one-way; begins at park's interpretive center, passes two overlooks on highest ridge and connects with trail leading to **Fort Davis National Historic Site.** Could be several-hour venture.

Dinosaur Valley State Park: Trail in Somervell County is 1.5-miles and goes near best-preserved dinosaur fossil footprints in Texas.

Eisenhower State Recreation Area: Trail 4.2 miles long in Grayson County, traverses entire length of park on Lake Texoma; passes through rugged ravines and grasslands.

Enchanted Rock State Natural Area (Gillespie County): No formally developed trails, but ample opportunity for both hiking and rock climbing.

Fairfield Lake State Recreation Area: Seven-mile hiking trail in Freestone County around **Big Brown Creek Primitive Camping Area.** An out-and-back trail, not a loop.

Garner State Park: Numerous undeveloped hiking trails in Uvalde County; short paved hike-and-bike trail runs along entrance road from park headquarters to main concession area.

Hueco Tanks State Historical Park: Few limited-access trails in El Paso County but many opportunities for climbing and hiking among boulders; **Chihuahuan Desert** scrub vegetation; caves and rock formations displaying **Indian rock art** main attractions.

Huntsville State Park: This 8.5-mile trail in Walker County takes about four hours to hike entire length; five miles are designated for bicyclists and one mile designated for handicapped users.

Inks Lake State Park: Loop trails total about seven miles in Burnet County; primitive camping area available for backpackers.

Jim Hogg State Historical Park: One-mile trail and 3-mile trail through typical East Texas Piney Woods in Cherokee County.

Kerrville State Recreation Area: Two trails—.5-mile trail along shore of Flat Rock Lake on Guadalupe River; 2-mile developed trail in Hill Country Unit in Kerr County; several miles of primitive trails where white-tailed deer and wild turkey are common.

Lake Brownwood State Recreation Area (Brown County): System of trails totals 3.5 miles; portions accessible to handicapped recreationists.

Lake Livingston State Recreation Area: System of interconnecting trails in Polk County totals about 4.5 miles along shoreline of Lake Livingston and in East Texas Piney Woods.

Lake Mineral Wells State Park: Five-mile hiking trail in Parker County; some parts require stamina and endurance; others designed primarily for short nature walks.

Lake Somerville State Recreation Area: Somerville Trailway 21-mile system in Lee and Burleson Counties; longest single trail in any state park; connects Birch Creek Unit on north with Nails Creek Unit on south; backpacking and equestrian camping. Area open to public, but visitors should be aware of oil and gas exploration in area. Shorter trails loop through post oak woodlands and along lakeshore; each unit has segments designated for the handicapped.

Lost Maples State Natural Area: Ten-mile hiking trail in Bandera County well marked and color coded for easy orientation; several trail loops offer option for distance and degree of difficulty. Eight primitive camping areas with four portable toilets located along trails.

McKinney Falls State Park: Three-mile, surfaced hike and bike trail in Travis County passes along creek through upland woods and back to visitor center.

Meridian State Recreation Area (Bosque County): Several small trails interconnecting to form loop around Meridian Lake; 6-mile trail passes interesting features, including scenic overlook of lake and a bee cave. **Juniper** dominant vegetation furnishing nesting area for **Golden-cheeked warbler.**

Mustang Island State Park: One-mile loop through marsh grass and dunes in Nueces County; trail head located on Park Road 53, just south of park entrance.

Palo Duro Canyon State Park: Trail 4.5 miles up Sunday Canyon past Sleeping Indian, Satanta's Face and turnaround at Lighthouse landmark in Armstrong and Randall Counties.

Pedernales Falls State Park: Wolf Mountain Hiking Trail in Blanco County is 7 miles with primitive camping available; trail rugged; hilly terrain along Pedernales River yet easy enough for people in reasonably good physical shape to hike.

Seminole Canyon State Historical Park: Six-mile trail gives hikers look at hot and dry **Chihuahuan Desert** in Val Verde County.

Stephen F. Austin State Historical Park: Two separate trails totaling 2.5 miles in Austin County.

Tyler State Park: Hiking trail 2.5 miles long in Smith County; portions of trail are accessible to handicapped.

Equestrian Trails

Lake Arrowhead State Recreation Area: This is an 80-acre area in Clay and Archer Counties designated for horseback riding; visitors must bring own horses.

Lake Mineral Wells State Park: Has 8.5-mile equestrian trail in Parker County; camping available and adequate parking for 20 horse trailers.

Lake Somerville State Recreation Area: Somerville Trailway in Lee and Burleson Counties permits horseback riding and equestrian camping.

Palo Duro Canyon State Park: Has 4.5-mile equestrian trail in Armstrong and Randall Counties; rental horses are available, or visitors may bring their own.

WOODLAND TRAILS

Below is given brief description of the fifteen Texas Forestry Association's Woodland Trails. For further information, write Texas Forestry Assn., P.O. Box 1488, Lufkin, Texas 75901, or phone (713) 634-5523.

Four-C's Trail.—Eastern Houston County, 18 miles east of Crockett on Texas 7. Follows old rail tram line along Neches River bottom. Length, 19 miles.

Bull Creek Trail.—Northwestern Polk County, 8.5 miles west of Corrigan on U.S. 287. Winds along banks of Bull Creek. Noted for its large magnolias, oaks, gums and pines. Length, 1½ miles.

Griff Ross Trail.—Southern Rusk County, 2.2 miles east of Mount Enterprise on U.S. 84. Follows gentle slope of hill to edge of a forest stream. Donated to TFA by Dr. and Mrs. William F. Ross, Dallas, in memory of his parents, Dr. and Mrs. Griff Ross, Mount Enterprise. Length, ½ mile.

Dogwood Trail.—Central Tyler County, 3 miles east of Woodville off U.S. 190. Winding along banks of Theuvenin Creek, trail is noted for dogwood blooms in spring. Length, 1½ miles.

Longleaf Pine Trail.—Northeastern Polk County, 3 miles east of Camden on Farm Road 62. Noted for large longleaf pines, many 100 years or older. Features nesting holes of rare red-cockaded woodpecker. Length, 2 miles.

Angelina Trail.—Located in Angelina County, 10 miles west of Lufkin on Texas 103. Trail winds through mixed pine-hardwood forest. Portions of trail follow course of Wise Branch, rocky, spring-fed stream. Length, 1½ miles.

Big Creek Trail.—East Central San Jacinto County, west of Shepherd on Forest Service Road 217. Three loops, partially following Big Creek, clear running stream. Longest loop, 4½ miles.

Moscow Trail.—Northern Polk County, 1 mile south of Moscow on U.S. 59. Meanders along banks of Long King Creek, and is noted for tall pines and large variety of other forest growth. Length, 2 trails, ½ mile and 1½ miles.

New Birmingham Trail.—Cherokee County, beside Farm Road 343 South of Rusk. Winds through part of old

New Birmingham, site of a ghost town of 1880s. Noted for hills and rugged hiking terrain. Now owned and operated by City of Rusk. Length, 2½ miles.

Apolonia Trail.—Southeast Grimes County, 8 miles east of Anderson on FM 2819. Three loops provide scene changes from pine forest to post oaks to blackland prairie. Lengths, ¼ mile, 1.1 miles and 1.9 miles.

Sawmill Trail.—North Jasper County, off Texas 63 south of Zavalla. Three trailheads, one at Aldridge, one at Boykin Springs campground and one at Bouton Lake campground. Maintained by U.S. Forest Service. Length, 5½ miles.

Old River Trail.—Western Jasper County, 2.9 miles on unpaved road off Farm Road 1747. Follows abandoned railroad into swampy Angelina River bottom land noted for bog flowers, hardwood and other growth. Historic river port of Bevilport is nearby. Length, 1½ miles.

Sylvan Trail.—Central Newton County, opposite roadside park on U.S. 190, 4 miles southeast of Newton. Meanders through area noted for picturesque loblolly pines. Location of two old logging railroads. Length, ½ mile.

Yellow Poplar Trail.—Northern Marion County, 8.5 miles north of Jefferson on U.S. 59 opposite roadside park. Winds through only stand of yellow poplar in Texas, and includes state champion tree. Nearby historical marker commemorates life of pioneer physician-legislator M. D. Taylor. Length, 1 mile.

Wild Azalea Canyons Trail.—Northern Newton County, 4.4 miles north of Newton on Texas 87, then 6.7 miles east on Farm Road 1414, then 1.8 miles on unpaved roads. Inside pocket wilderness noted for longleaf forest, rock cliffs and wild azaleas that bloom each spring. Maintained by Temple EastTexas Inc. in conjunction with Magnolia Garden Club, Beaumont. Several trails of varying lengths; trail open only during bloom season, March-April.

TEXAS
SESQUICENTENNIAL

The 25 Most Important Figures in Texas History

Thousands of men and women have contributed to the development of Texas in the 150 years since independence from Mexico was achieved. As the Sesquicentennial celebration developed, the Texas Almanac and the Texas State Historical Association conceived the idea of asking knowledgeable people to consider the figures who through their careers and leadership have contributed the most to the development of Texas.

Nominations were solicited from the public at large and the memberships of several history and heritage organizations. The membership of the TSHA then was asked to take an advisory vote from the long list of persons submitted for consideration. The criteria required that the nominee have been a resident of the state, the Republic of Texas or the area within the present geographical boundaries of Texas; that the individual's impact on Texas came before 1970; and that no living Texans were to be nominated.

The advisory vote was taken in early 1984, and a 16-member screening committee selected by the TSHA made the selection of the top 25 figures in the state's history. Essays on each of the final 25 appear on the following pages.

Members of the screening committee included: Dr. Lewis L. Gould, University of Texas at Austin, chairman; Miss Llerena Friend, retired historian, UT-Austin, Wichita Falls, vice-chairman; Dr. Felix D. Almaraz Jr., University of Texas at San Antonio; Dr. Alwyn Barr, Texas Tech University; J. P. Bryan Jr., TSHA past president, Houston; J. Conrad Dunagan, historian, Monahans; Dr. Archie McDonald, Stephen F. Austin University; H. Stanley Marcus, businessman and civic leader, Dallas; Ben E. Pingenot, TSHA past president, Eagle Pass; Dr. Rupert N. Richardson, past president TSHA and Hardin-Simmons University; Dr. A. Ray Stephens, North Texas State University; Maj. J. R. Parten, historian, Houston; Dr. Marilyn M. Sibley, TSHA past president, Houston; Dr. W. H. Timmons, University of Texas at El Paso; Robert S. Weddle, historian, Bonham; and Dr. L. Tuffly Ellis, executive director, TSHA.

As might be expected, the selection of the final 25 figures was difficult. Several important figures received general support but did not make the final list. The advisory committee has asked that these men be cited as worthy of honorable mention. This list includes George W. Brackenridge, James Bowie, Will L. Clayton, Henry Cohen, Norris W. Cuney, Edward M. House, George W. Littlefield, William S. Porter and Sid Richardson.

While this project was undertaken to honor those persons whose contributions have significantly contributed to the development of today's Texas, it also is hoped that the exercise will provoke all Texans to consider the contributions of all our forebears.

Each of the following biographical essays was written by an authority on the subject. The Texas Almanac wishes to thank everyone who participated in the selection of the 25 individuals whose brief biographies follow. These figures truly have left an indelible mark on Texas.

—Mike Kingston, editor of the Texas Almanac.

Stephen F. Austin

This article was written by Dr. Joseph McKnight, Professor of Law, Southern Methodist University.

No individual's name is more closely linked to the history of modern Texas than Stephen Fuller Austin. The colonizer was a man of courage, integrity and vision whose leadership guided the Anglo-American settlement of the region. He is properly known as the "father of Texas."

The elder son of Moses and Maria (Brown) Austin was born Nov. 3, 1793, in Wythe County, Va. His father had achieved some success in lead mining. In 1798, the Austins moved to the town of St. Genevieve, Mo., then in the Spanish province of Louisiana. The elder Austin wanted to take advantage of the generous land-grant policy of the Spanish and to mine the rich lead deposits on the Mississippi.

At St. Genevieve, Moses Austin obtained a grant of land along with permission to settle 30 families in the region. Thus, from his early youth, Stephen Austin participated in a wilderness settlement project and learned by his father's example the skills that would prove useful in dealing with frontier ways and men of different cultures.

Stephen attended the Bacon Academy in Connecticut and Transylvania University at Lexington, Ky. Though he did not receive a degree, he was very well educated by the standards of the time.

At age 16, Stephen rejoined his family in Missouri Territory and began to work with his father. Moses' business prospered for a time, but the War of 1812 and its aftermath, along with some instances of poor business judgment, plunged it to the brink of financial ruin.

In 1814, Stephen was elected to the lower house of the Missouri Territorial Legislature and was twice reelected. For the most part, he maintained a tactful silence as far as the public record reveals.

In June 1819, Stephen moved to the newly created Arkansas Territory to try to restore the family fortunes. Land speculation seemed to be the key to success. After an unsuccessful campaign for territorial delegate to Congress, young Austin was appointed to a vacancy on an Arkansas circuit court, which was soon abolished.

In November 1820, Stephen moved to New Orleans, where he renewed an acquaintance with Joseph H. Hawkins, an attorney from Kentucky, who offered to take him into his office to study law. Stephen accepted this offer, and, to provide for his expenses, worked as a newspaper editor. But fate cut this career short.

Stephen F. Austin

Still intrigued by Spain's generous land-grant policy for foreign settlers, Moses Austin received permission to bring 300 families to settle in Texas. Stephen was on his way to join his father in the venture when he received word of Moses' death.

Young Austin took up his father's task with enthusiasm, despite early reservations. At San Antonio, Stephen was acknowledged as the successor to his father's interest, and he returned to New Orleans to make final preparations for moving permanently to Texas. With the financial backing of Joseph Hawkins, he returned to Texas in January 1822 with the first group of immigrants who settled on the banks of the Brazos River.

Austin learned, however, that Mexico's break with Spain had destroyed his authority to settle colonists and

137

distribute land. So he went to Mexico City to settle the matter. The government was in turmoil. A general colonization law was under consideration, but many pressures directed attention away from the needs of frontier colonists. Austin remained in Mexico for more than a year. He took an indirect role in preparing the federal Constitution of 1824, which created a form of government similar to the United States'. After receiving approval for his colonization project, Austin returned to Texas with authority to work with a land commissioner to issue land titles to his colonists. In 1825, 1827 and 1828, he was granted further contracts to bring 900 additional colonists to Texas, along with another contract in partnership with Samuel M. Williams.

Austin held broad judicial and administrative authority in his colony until local self-government was organized under the state Constitution of 1827. He used his power wisely for the benefit of his colonists, though there was some friction in the distribution of lands. On the whole, however, the colonists accepted his authority without complaint. He served as chief judge of the colony, acting as a court of appeals in civil matters. Serious criminal complaints were reviewed in Monterrey or Saltillo.

Since most colonists were unable to speak or read Spanish, Austin was practically the sole authority on existing law. He promulgated civil and criminal codes for his colonists in 1825 and, in 1829, a translation of the colonization law was published under his supervision.

He proved himself a loyal citizen of Mexico, and in 1827, Austin and some of his colonists helped put down a rebellion of Anglo-Americans at Nacogdoches.

Austin's personal governing of his settlers ended in 1827, but he continued to supervise land grants, to meet the constant Indian threats and to further the general welfare. His efforts toward the 1829 enactment of a state law granting a 12-year moratorium on prior debts and exemption of land grants and tools of trade from debt thereafter is illustrative of his concern. In 1830-32, Austin served in the state Legislature.

Though the Constitution forbade the importation of slaves, Austin helped arrange legislation to evade that prohibition. Even after the Mexican national government prohibited further American immigration into Texas in April 1830, Austin convinced authorities to allow him to continue to introduce colonists. Nonetheless, the settlers in Austin's colonies were deeply concerned by the immigration act, which, like the official attitude toward slavery, they felt was directed toward them.

Though under Spanish rule Texas had been a separate province, the region was joined with Coahuila under the Mexican Constitution of 1824 with the understanding that Texas might become a separate state when its population warranted. Austin was the president of a convention that met in June 1832 with separate statehood as one of its principal objectives. Since Hispanic Texans did not participate in this meeting, Austin spent much of the next year urging their cooperation so that a united petition on statehood might be presented

to the national government. A second convention was held in San Felipe in April 1833, a petition for statehood was again proposed and a constitution for Texas as a state was drafted. Austin was entrusted with the task of taking the petition to Mexico City.

Austin was successful in negotiating the repeal of the 1830 law against immigration but failed in getting more than encouragement toward separate statehood. In exasperation with the Mexican authorities' attitude on the issue of statehood, Austin wrote a letter in October 1833 to the city council in San Antonio. The message was interpreted as rebellious in tone and was turned over to the federal authorities. On his way back to Texas, Austin was arrested in Saltillo and was returned to Mexico City as a prisoner. Though no charges were made against him, he was not released on bond until December 1834. Even then he was not allowed to leave the federal district. Though elected to the state Legislature for the session of 1835, Austin was not released until July, after the Legislature had adjourned. Austin returned to Texas by way of New Orleans. His detention in Mexico City caused great concern among his colonists and heightened their antagonisms toward the Mexican authorities.

On his return in August 1835, Austin found Texas in a state of great unrest as a result of the suppression of the federal Constitution of 1824 by the national centralist government. Austin supported a convention held in October but opposed a movement for independence then being advocated by many. The convention set up a separate state government under the 1824 Constitution.

Though Austin was elected by the armed volunteers who gathered at Gonzales to lead them to San Antonio, he was called upon by the convention to serve as one of three commissioners to the United States. He arrived in New Orleans in January 1836 and began work to procure supplies and munitions and to convince the United States to annex Texas if it should declare independence. President Andrew Jackson and congressional leaders were not prepared to give assurances regarding annexation though independence was declared in March 1836. But the commissioners' efforts in encouraging support for Texas were otherwise generally successful.

Austin returned to Texas in June 1836 and was persuaded to seek the presidency of the Republic. But Sam Houston, the hero of San Jacinto, won, and Austin accepted appointment as the new Republic's secretary of state.

Austin had given his youth and health to Texas and had forgone the pleasures of home and family. When he died on Dec. 16, 1836, after a short illness, Austin's financial situation was little better than it had been when he arrived in Texas. To Austin's patience, caution and conciliation can be attributed much of the success of the early Anglo-American colonization of Texas that laid the foundation for American statehood nine years after his death.

Eugene C. Barker

This article was written by Dr. William Pool,
Professor of History,
Southwest Texas State University.

When Lester G. Bugbee and George Pierce Garrison finished their life spans in the early 20th century, Eugene C. Barker was on hand to take up the unfinished task of his two former teachers and friends. A student and faculty member at the University of Texas from 1896 until 1952, the venerable Barker won universal recognition as the greatest of all Texas and southwestern historians.

He was born near Riverside, Walker County, on Nov. 10, 1874, the son of Joseph and Fannie Holland Barker. Shortly after Joseph Barker's untimely death in 1888, Fannie Barker moved her family to Palestine, where 14-year-old Eugene found employment in the railroad shops. In the months that followed, young Barker became an expert blacksmith and attended evening school in the home of Miss Shirley Green. Determined to secure a university education, Barker entered the University of Texas in September 1896. Despite financial hardship, he earned the B.A. degree in 1899 and the M.A. in 1900. He served as a tutor in history at the university from 1899 to 1901; instructor from 1901 to 1908; adjunct professor from 1908 to 1911; associate professor, 1911-1913; professor from 1913 until his retire-

ment in 1951; and professor emeritus from 1951 until his death in 1956. When the title of Distinguished Professor was created in 1937, Dr. Barker was among the first three chosen for this position.

On May 6, 1903, Dr. Barker married Matilda LeGrand Weeden, a woman of great charm and culture who provided an ideal background and atmosphere for the historian's future work. In 1906, Barker took a leave of absence and went north for graduate work. He studied first at the University of Pennsylvania and later at Harvard. In 1908, Barker completed his Ph.D. at Pennsylvania and returned to the University of Texas. He was promoted to associate professor in 1911 and named chairman of the department of history in 1913.

It was during the 32 years of his full professorship that Dr. Barker did his scholarly work. When he returned from Pennsylvania in 1908 he found the field of Texas and southwestern history open and inviting. With the rare judgment that was characteristic of so much that he did, Barker selected this field of study as his own. As first major project — one which Barker stated was inherited from Bugbee and Garrison — he chose the life of Stephen F. Austin. Before writing the biography, Barker collected, edited and published *The Austin Papers.* These papers covered the period from 1765 to 1836 and were published by the American Historical Association (1924-1928). Barker's *Life of Stephen F. Austin* was published in 1925. This work has frequently been described as a classic and has been called the finest single piece of historical writing done in Texas. Barker's other major publications included *Mexico and Texas, 1821-1835* (1928), *Readings in Texas History* (1929), *The Father of Texas* (1935) and *The Writings of Sam Houston*, edited in collaboration with Miss Amelia Williams and published in eight volumes (1938-1941). In the meantime, Dr. Barker served as managing editor of the *Southwestern Historical Quarterly* from 1910 to 1937. In 1911, aided by suggestions from his friend, Herbert Eugene Bolton, the scope of the publication was expanded and the name changed from *The Quarterly of the Texas State Historical Association*. For 27 years, Barker not only edited the publication, but he also contributed many articles. Through these writings, he showed the influence of the Texas question and of Texas history on general American history — especially the history of the American West. It has been said that in this connection he exploded some of the early myths that had gained wide acceptance among historians. One was that the westward expansion of the United States, the annexation of Texas and the Mexican War resulted from a conspiracy of southerners to expand territory; another was the idea that in the Texas revolution and the Mexican War all of the fault was on the Mexican side.

Instrumental in building the Littlefield collection of sources of the history of the South, Dr. Barker's greatest contribution to the university was the building of the department of history, which, during his active career, came to rank among the best in the state universities of the nation. In the late years of his life, Dr. George P. Garrison had managed to add Charles William Ramsdell and Frederic Duncalf to the small departmental faculty. As a result, one of Barker's first priorities was to expand a growing history department. Within a few months Thad Weed Riker, Frank Burr Marsh, William R. Manning and Augustus Charles Krey were added to the faculty of what was called the School of History. Two years later Milton R. Gutsch moved to Austin to join Barker's staff. The department was later strengthened with the addition of Walter Prescott Webb (1918), Charles Wilson Hackett (1919) and Rudolph L. Biesele (1925). With the exception of Manning and Krey, all of these men spent their entire academic careers at the university — a remarkable group of historians.

In a memorial resolution, three of Dr. Barker's fellow professors said that "It is when we come to his character that language to describe him is hard to come by. Great as his scholarship, sound as his teaching, both were equalled or surpassed by his strength of character. Physically he was tall and angular, rugged is the word for him. His eyes were keen, his nose aquiline, his forehead high. He had about him an unconscious austerity, the sort found in generals and in Indian chiefs." Dr. Walter P. Webb once remarked that at times Dr. Barker had reminded him "In his combination of power and kindliness of a great Newfoundland dog moving a little awkwardly and with tolerance among the nimbler breeds around him. I have seen him at other times as an Indian chief. If he could be induced to don a Sioux war bonnet he would pass for an Indian chief anywhere." The late Roy Bedichek, who knew Barker as a student in the late 1890s, remembered "a face already grim but kindly." Milton R. Gutsch, a colleague, summarized the significance of Barker's leadership by calling attention to the fact that "If there is one characteristic that stands out more predominantly than others, it is courage — the courage of his convictions. He has always been willing to fight for his beliefs and when he does he fights hard and does not pull his punches . . . More than once when the university's very existence seemed to be threatened by politics, and a courageous and forceful leader was needed, the faculty turned to this man; and he did not fail them." Of course, Gutsch is referring to the Ferguson controversy of 1916-17 when Barker and his friends in the Ex-Students Association led the fight that resulted in the ultimate impeachment of Gov. James E. Ferguson; the battle to prevent Gov. Pat M. Neff from being appointed president of the university in 1924; and the dismissal of Dr. Homer P. Rainey from the university presidency in 1944-45.

Barker once described the ideal "historian" as one who approached his investigations without preconceived opinions, who collected all the evidence available and formed his conclusions with a critical mind, free of bias of all sorts. Barker's "historian" tried to present a picture of conditions and events as they actually were, together with their causes and consequences. In other words, the "historian" tried to be honest. On another occasion Barker explained the ideal "teacher": "Perhaps one teaches as an act of faith, hoping to contribute to habits of straight thinking, intellectual honesty, good judgment, tolerance and independence, while imparting some knowledge of the culture and experience of the past which has helped to make the present and which in some form will undoubtedly help to shape the future."

The death of Barker on Oct. 22, 1956, marked the end of an era in the history of the University of Texas. For many years after the Ferguson controversy of 1916-17, Barker exercised a remarkable influence as a leader of the university faculty. Led by him and a few others, the faculty followed policies that determined university affairs for a quarter of a century. These leaders were all men of character and integrity, and, while they did not lay the foundations of the University of Texas, they did build a university on the earlier labor of others; to a large extent, they made the institution what it is today.

Gail Borden

This article was written by Dr. Joe B. Frantz, Professor of History, University of Texas at Austin.

Gail Borden was an illustration of the premise that there is no way to defeat a creature that keeps on coming. A product of the eastern side of the Mississippi River frontier, he moved with the frequency of pioneers; had little formal education (a year and a half); rose to prominence as a surveyor, minor statesman, publisher, government official and land developer. He failed miserably as an inventor, kept on inventing, failed some more and, in the end, became an internationally acclaimed inventor and founder of a company that today belongs among the aristocratic corporations listed in the *Fortune* 500, sporting a multibillion dollar yearly income.

Borden was born in Norwich, N. Y., west of the Catskills, on Nov. 9, 1801, a descendant of English settlers who arrived in New England in the 1630s. The Bordens birthed descendants with such regularity that by 1900, 6,000 of them could trace their ancestry directly to the first Borden in America. Among the collateral descendants are Lizzie Borden, whose alleged murder of her father and mother in New England intrigues mystery buffs to this day; and A. P. Borden, generally credited with having introduced Brahman cattle into Texas.

When Gail Borden was barely into his teens, his father took his family to Kentucky, where young Gail helped survey the future city of Covington, opposite Cincinnati. In 1816, Borden was living in New London, Ind., now a ghost town, where he obtained his scant schooling. In the early 1820s, he moved to Amite County in southwestern Mississippi as official county surveyor and deputy federal surveyor. While he was there, his next younger brother, Thomas H., joined Stephen F. Austin's colony as one of the Old Three Hundred. Gail Borden's father-in-law, Eli Mercer, also gave $2,500 to help sustain the first Baptist missionary in Texas.

With this sort of prelude Borden also decided to seek his fortune in Texas, arriving at Galveston Island on the day before Christmas, 1829. Although officially a farmer and stock raiser in upper Fort Bend County, he continued his surveying activities and within two months had succeeded Thomas H. Borden as Austin's official surveyor. He sometimes doubled as colonial secretary for Austin whenever Samuel May Williams was absent. Meanwhile, he had represented San Felipe at the Convention of 1833, at which the first Texas constitution was drawn up on the supposition that Texas was about to be separated from the jurisdiction of the province of Coahuila y Texas.

Nine days after the first shots were fired at Gonzales to begin the Texas Revolution against Mexico,

Gail Borden published the *Telegraph and Texas Register* in San Felipe, with his brother Thomas and a printer named Joseph Baker as his partners. This would become Texas' first permanent newspaper despite the inauspicious timing of its beginning. While Borden was preparing for his new venture, he also served as a member of San Felipe's committee of correspondence and prepared the first topographical map of Texas. Idleness was not one of his faults.

As other newspapers fell by the wayside under the deprivations of war, Borden's *Telegraph and Texas Register* became the only publication remaining in Texas and the official organ of the new Texas government. Much of the official documentation of the Texas government can be found only in the surviving copies of the paper. When Gen. Santa Anna captured Harrisburg on his way to San Jacinto, he dumped Borden's press into Buffalo Bayou, tumid with spring rains, thereby silencing for a period the last free voice in Texas. But eight copies of the *Telegraph* had been run off and were salvaged so that Texans could learn what had happened since the previous issue.

The *Telegraph and Texas Register* was published in four Texas towns—San Felipe, Harrisburg, Columbia and Houston—and in all but San Felipe it was the first newspaper in each town's history. It lasted until the late 1870s, having spent approximately 40 years in Houston. In a tenuous way it was the predecessor of the *Houston Post*, as one of Borden's sons-in-law helped found that long-lasting newspaper. Borden's connection with the *Telegraph* ended, though, in June 1837, when he sold out to Jacob W. Cruger, another transplanted New Yorker.

No longer a newspaper publisher, Borden moved to Galveston Island to become the first collector of customs for the port under the Republic of Texas. As a devoted supporter of Sam Houston, Borden was removed from office when Mirabeau B. Lamar became the Republic's second president. When Houston became president a second time, he reappointed Borden, only to remove him after 16 months in a dispute over evaluation of Texas exchequers.

Borden next turned to real estate as secretary and agent of the Galveston City Company, which owned most of Galveston Island. From 1839 to 1851, Borden helped sell 2,500 island lots as Galveston began its growth as Texas' largest city. Meanwhile he invented a "locomotive bath house" for women who wished to bathe in the Gulf of Mexico, and he served as alderman, during which term his council rid the island of gamblers, a temporary measure repeated with regularity over the past century and a half.

In the mid-1840s, Borden began experimenting with various inventions. He supposedly tinkered with a huge refrigerator in which he intended to isolate Galvestonians during yellow fever season. He also invented a "terraqueous machine," a forerunner of amphibious craft that could go equally well on land or water. The census of 1850 shows him worth $100,000, a considerable sum for that era in Texas.

Borden blew his small fortune on a meat biscuit, a dehydrated meat mixed with flour, which he hoped to sell to sailors and to travelers heading overland for the gold fields in California. The invention won him a gold medal at London's Crystal Palace world's fair in 1851. Encouraged, he moved his operation that same year to be near major purchasing centers. But sales were few, and about all he accomplished was to go bankrupt and scatter his children among relatives. His second wife left him during this period of loss.

At the nadir of his inventing-marketing phase, Borden received in 1853 a patent for condensing milk in vacuum, but he had a three-year fight to certify his patent in both the United States and England. He opened a milk condensing factory in Connecticut, but quickly failed during the Panic of 1857. Through a chance meeting with Jeremiah Milbank, a New York financier, he received new backing, opened another Connecticut factory, but again seemed doomed to failure until the Civil War brought a demand for portable milk that would not sour for the use of Union soldiers. With the army satisfied with Borden's product, sales soared, and he opened another factory in Connecticut, two in New York and one in Illinois, while licensing other concerns in Pennsylvania and Maine. Altogether, Borden's plants and licensees dominated the markets in New York, Chicago, Philadelphia and Boston, four of the principal outlets in the northern United States.

After the Civil War, Borden returned to Texas, where Texans apparently bore him no ill will for serving the Union, possibly because Texans admire successful people. He established a meat packing plant at Borden, Texas, west of Columbus, and a sawmill and cooperware factory at Bastrop. None of them was particularly successful. He also occupied himself with various philanthropies, including a freedmen's school, a white children's school, a day school and a Sunday school for black children, five churches, maintenance of two missionaries and various poorly paid teachers, ministers and students.

When Borden died in Borden, Texas, on Jan. 11, 1874, his body was shipped in a private car to New York, where he was buried in Woodlawn Cemetery. There a gravestone marks his grave with the inscription:—"I fried and failed,—I fried again and again, and succeeded."

Those two lines sum up the life of Gail Borden, Texas' first major inventor.

Borden County in West Texas and its county seat, Gail, are named in this Texan's honor.

Tom Connally

This article was written by Dr. Frank H. Smyrl, Professor of History, University of Texas at Tyler.

One of the most influential members of the United States Senate during the crucial decades of the Great Depression, World War II and the opening of the Cold War was Thomas Terry Connally. Indeed, of all Texans who have served in that body only Lyndon B. Johnson in his days as majority leader could claim a more significant role in Senate affairs. With concerns almost as broad as those of the Senate itself, Connally came to symbolize the membership of the Senate even to the point of being the model for caricatures of a senator.

Tom Connally was the only son who survived to adulthood in the family of Jones and Mary Ellen Terry Connally. His mother, first the wife of Jones Connally's brother, was left a widow with one daughter during the Civil War. Upon their marriage, Connally's parents settled in McLennan County. Tom, the last of nine children, was born Aug. 19, 1877, on a cotton farm near Hewitt. His father prospered, and when Tom was five years old, the family moved to a larger farm and home near Eddy, where young Connally grew to manhood.

While life was not without its pleasures, the Connally household was subject to the stern discipline of the Baptist denomination. (In later life he joined the Methodist Episcopal Church.) Both father and mother contributed a great deal to the upbringing of the children, but there is little doubt that his mother's was the great-er influence, as she relentlessly encouraged him to educate himself. After graduating from nearby Baylor University in 1896 with a B.A. degree, he earned a law degree from the University of Texas at Austin in 1898. Attracted by the popular Spanish-American War, his efforts to join the Rough Riders met with rejection. He nevertheless joined the army and rose to the rank of sergeant major. His unit was still training in Florida when the war ended.

Returning home, Connally entered law practice in Marlin, county seat of Falls County. Finding the transition to politics easy, the young lawyer was elected to the state Legislature in 1900 and 1902, where he followed a "progressive" path within the Democratic Party. Successful both in law and politics, Connally married Louise Clarkson on Nov. 16, 1904.

Connally's law practice continued to prosper, giving him an even greater opportunity for political involvement. He won races for county attorney of Falls County in 1906 and 1908. Then, in 1916, he won election to Congress from the 11th District, an office to which he was re-elected six times.

In Congress, Connally was named to the normally insignificant House Foreign Affairs Committee just as that body prepared in special session a declaration of war against Germany. Already 40 years of age, the freshman congressman soon resigned his seat and accepted a commission as captain in the U. S. Army. His toughest battle was with influenza, and he was still at Fort Meade, Va., when the armistice came.

After serving 12 years in the U.S. House, Connally announced for the Senate in the Democratic primary of 1928. It was the most difficult race of his long political career. Campaigning with unceasing confidence and energy, Connally achieved a runoff with incumbent Sen. Earle B. Mayfield, whose connection with the Ku Klux Klan was a definite factor in Connally's nomination. For his own part, Connally focused positively on more fundamental issues affecting his agriculturally based state, making a positive effort to become known outside his home district. In the general election, he won an easy victory.

Connally was the only Democrat to enter the Senate in 1929, giving him significant seniority over the many Democrats swept into office in 1932. Largely because of his previous service on the House Foreign Affairs Committee, Connally was named to the highly influential Senate Foreign Relations Committee in his freshman term. Reflecting the main concerns of his constituents, however, Connally spent most of his effort dealing with matters related to agriculture and oil. He contributed a feature to the Agricultural Adjustment Act of 1933 reducing the gold content of the dollar. Although not actually its author, he was perhaps best known in the 1930s for the law popularly known as the Connally Hot Oil Act, an effective check on the illegal production of oil that threatened to negate one of the few bright spots in the dismal economy.

Other major national legislation of special importance to Texas that Connally helped shape and enact included the Jones-Connally Act and the Agricultural Adjustment Act of 1935. A strong party man who usually supported New Deal proposals in Congress, he considered the National Industrial Recovery Act unconstitutional and became a leader of opposition to Roosevelt's court reorganization plan. Connally apparently pleased a majority of the voters of Texas by his actions, winning a second term in the Senate in a hard-fought race in 1934 against Joe Bailey Jr. As World War II approached, Connally moved suddenly up the seniority ladder to the chairmanship of the Senate Foreign Relations Committee. Then, the unexpected death of senior Sen. Morris Sheppard placed Connally even higher in the echelons of Texas politics and influence in Washington.

In his private life, Connally was stunned in 1935 by the death of his wife, Louise. Their son, Ben, born in 1910, finished law school and became a federal judge in Texas. For a number of years, Connally shared a bachelor's apartment in Washington with a favorite colleague, Sen. Kenneth McKellar of Tennessee. Later, following the death of Sen. Morris Sheppard, Connally began courting his widow, Lucile Sanderson Sheppard, whom he married in 1942.

While wartime concerns occupied much of Connally's time for the next few years, he quickly became associated with the effort to establish a peace that would be more lasting than that which ended World War I. Sponsoring what is popularly known as the Connally Resolution, he worked diligently to make the United States a leading participant in the United Nations. President Harry S. Truman named him to the delegation that represented the United States in San Francisco at the 1945 organizational meeting of the United Nations.

Re-elected to the Senate in 1940 and 1946 with little opposition, Connally spent the postwar years primarily tending to matters of the Senate Foreign Relations Committee. He teamed with isolationist-turned-internationalist Arthur Vandenberg to work closely with Secretary of State Dean Acheson in hammering out what became the bipartisan foreign policy of the Truman administration.

During his 36 years in Congress, Connally became widely known for his debating skills, wit and parliamentary ability. A man of integrity, he was respected by friend and foe. Approaching 75 years of age as the elections of 1952 neared, Connally decided to retire. He had not run a seriously contested political race since 1934, had maintained virtually no political organization in Texas, was closely associated with what conservative Texas voters referred to as "the mess in Washington" and recognized the strength and popularity of the younger challenger, Texas Atty. Gen. Price Daniel.

During the last decade of his life, Connally enjoyed a quiet retirement in Washington. He took advantage of his privileges in the Senate barber shop but seldom made a public pronouncement. A rare exception was a statement in support of John F. Kennedy, Democratic candidate for president in 1960. He died of pneumonia Oct. 28, 1963, and was buried beside his first wife in Marlin's Calvary Cemetery.

J. Frank Dobie

This article was written by Dr. Don B. Graham, Professor of English, University of Texas at Austin.

From his arrival on the national scene in 1931, until his death in 1964, J. Frank Dobie was the dominant figure in Texas literature. Given his roots, this might seem to have been an unlikely destiny for a youth nurtured in the ranching country of southwest Texas. Born on Sept. 26, 1888, in Live Oak County, Dobie attended ranch schools and early in life evidenced an equal interest in the practices of ranching culture and reading. His family, members of a patrician class, though of relatively modest financial means, valued education highly and sent all six of the Dobie children to college.

Dobie attended Southwestern University at Georgetown where he added to his already keen love of reading a devotion to Romantic poetry. Following his graduation in 1910, he worked for a summer as a reporter on the *San Antonio Express* before accepting a position as high school principal and teacher in Alpine. In 1913, he continued his education and acquired valuable experience outside the state, taking an M.A. degree at Columbia University in 1914. After another brief stint in newspaper work, with the *Galveston Tribune,* Dobie joined the faculty of the University of Texas in 1914.

The war interrupted this appointment, and Dobie served in an artillery division in France, an experience of which he remained very proud for the rest of his life. After the war, he returned to the University, taking time off in 1920-21 to oversee his uncle's ranch. Then, from 1923 to 1925, he served as chairman of the English Department at Oklahoma A&M University (now Oklahoma State), returning to the University of Texas in 1925, where he remained until 1947.

In the 1920s Dobie began to play a very active role in the study and recognition of literary culture in the Southwest. One sphere of activity was the Texas Folklore Society, which Dobie helped reorganize in 1922. He was editor and secretary of the organization for the next 20 years. Dobie also advanced the cause of southwestern literature through his teaching. In 1929, he persuaded the Department of English to let him offer a course called Life and Literature of the Southwest. Through this course, Dobie touched hundreds of students, inspiring them with his love of literature and folklore and challenging them with his rigorous intellectual standards. This course eventually resulted in 1943 in one of Dobie's most valuable publications, *Guide to Life and Literature of the Southwest.*

More importantly, Dobie also was instrumental in creating regional literature in his own right. Calling himself a "teller of tall tales," he set out to record the legends and customs of the cattle country. In 1929, he published *A Vaquero of the Brush Country* and in 1931, *Coronado's Children,* the two books that gave him national recognition. Over the years, many books followed: *Tongues of the Monte* (1935), *Apache Gold and Yaqui Silver* (1939), *The Longhorns* (1941), *The Ben Lilly Legend* (1950), *The Mustangs* (1952), *Cow People* (1964) and the posthumous *Some Part of Myself* (1967). With these and other books, Dobie lay claim to being the state's most important writer. However, his standing as an author has fallen steadily since his death in 1964. Larry McMurtry and Greg Curtis (of *Texas Monthly*) have deprecated Dobie's literary abilities. Still, Dobie has his admirers, and the fact remains that, 20 years after his death, most of his books are still in print.

Whatever the final verdict on Dobie's literary merit, his importance to the cultural life of Texas in the 20th century remains large. In the late 1930s, Dobie underwent a political conversion, becoming a New Dealer and repudiating the political conservatism of his heritage. This change marked a turning point in his career, though he continued to write popular books out of the old rock, as he might have said. He became a notable defender of intellectual freedom and civil rights at a time when Texas was beset with a kind of provincial chauvinism that found its national equivalent in Mc-Carthyism. And indeed, Dobie himself became a victim of the era when the University instituted a rule to force Dobie's return from successive leaves. When Dobie refused, the University fired him in 1947. Though officially no longer a part of the University, Dobie continued to play an active part in the intellectual life of the University community until his death.

During the 1950s, Dobie entered fully into the role for which he seemed so well fitted — that of "Mr. Texas," as his friend and biographer Lon Tinkle dubbed him. Dobie was famous throughout the state, thanks to his books, his colorful and outspoken public persona, and the fact that since 1939 his writings had appeared regularly in Texas newspapers. In addition, he was a leading figure in the Texas Institute of Letters, an organization founded in the Centennial year to recognize the literary accomplishments of Texas writers. During this period, Dobie, along with his old friends Walter Prescott Webb and Roy Bedichek, ruled supreme as the Texas triumvirate, three men in Texas who cared about ideas, literature and the life of the mind.

National and international honors came to Dobie over the years. In 1944, he received an honorary master of arts from Cambridge University, England, for his service there as a lecturer in American history. In 1945-46, he was appointed a member of the United States National Commission, UNESCO, and, in 1964, as a consultant to the Library of Congress. He also received, just a few days before his death, the Medal of Freedom from President Lyndon B. Johnson.

In death as in life, Dobie continued to exert positive influences upon the cultural life of Texas. His extensive library of more than 11,000 volumes, all dealing with range life, was bequeathed to the University of Texas for the benefit of future scholars. Funds from the Dobie estate are used each year to improve the holdings of small public libraries around the state. Also Dobie's beloved Paisano Ranch, southwest of Austin, provides a haven for writers and artists selected each year to spend six months at the site. Many Texas writers, such as Billy Lee Brammer, have attested to the importance J. Frank Dobie made in their lives, showing them that it was possible to think of the Southwest as a fit subject for literature.

Clara Driscoll

This article was written by Dr. Dorothy DeMoss, Professor of History, Texas Woman's University.

Clara Driscoll was quite a woman, even by Texas standards. Historic preservationist, philanthropist, author, business executive, club leader, rancher, politician and rugged individualist, she was an outstanding participant whatever the activity.

Born April 2, 1881, in St. Mary's on Copano Bay, she was the second child and only daughter of Robert and Julia (Fox) Driscoll. Her Irish Catholic forebears had helped settle the area between the Nueces and Guadalupe Rivers in South Texas, and both of her grandfathers fought in the Texas Revolution. By 1890, Driscoll's father was one of the most innovative and successful cattlemen in Texas and had amassed a multimillion-dollar empire in land, banking and commercial developments centered in the Corpus Christi area. For her education he urged his daughter to attend the private Miss Peebles and Thompson's School in New York City and the convent Chateau Dieudonne near Paris, France.

After almost a decade of study and travel abroad, Clara Driscoll returned to Texas at age 18, imbued with an appreciation of the past and the importance of preserving historic monuments and sites in Texas for the benefit of future generations. She was aghast to discover the severe dilapidation of what she considered the "Grandest Monument in the History of the World," the Mission of San Antonio de Valero, familiarly called the Alamo, location of the most illustrious battle of the Texas Revolution in 1836.

Although the state had purchased the mission's chapel in 1883, the adjoining three-acre plaza and barracks area, where much of the siege and final struggle had taken place, had been sold to private interests and allowed to fall into decay and disrepair. The Daughters of the Republic of Texas, led by Adina de Zavala, already had sought to purchase the property and preserve it as a shrine. In 1903, Driscoll joined with the Daughters in an effort to raise $75,000 to prevent the conversion of the site into a hotel facility. When the public response to the appeal for funds fell short, Miss Driscoll presented her own certified check for the major portion of the purchase cost. Two years later, the state accepted clear title and deed to the property and conveyed the entire Alamo site to the Daughters for safekeeping. As a result of her leadership in the crusade the attractive, 22-year-old philanthropist received extensive national publicity and was hailed as the "Savior of the Alamo" by the press.

After the successful completion of the Alamo project, Driscoll embarked upon a writing career. Her novel, *The Girl of LaGloria*, in 1905 and a collection of short stories, *In the Shadow of the Alamo*, in 1906 both emphasized romantic images of ranch life on the Texas frontier. She also wrote a comic opera, "Mexicana," and financed its elaborate production on Broadway in 1906 in collaboration with the well-known producers, Sam and Lee Schubert.

On the last day of July 1906, Clara Driscoll married Henry Hulme "Hal" Sevier in a private ceremony at St. Patrick's Cathedral in New York City. She had met him several years earlier in Austin, when he was serving in the Texas Legislature. A journalist by training, Sevier had taken a position as financial editor of the *New York Sun*. The couple built an opulent villa at Oyster Bay, Long Island, and entertained extensively. Mrs. Sevier soon became involved in the New York City Texas Club and served as its president.

In 1914, Robert Driscoll Sr. died and the Seviers decided to return to Austin to be nearer her family's financial interests. Hal Sevier established a daily newspaper, the *Austin American*, and his wife became active in the Austin Garden Club, Daughters of the Republic of Texas and Pan American Round Table. At the same time, she directed the construction of a magnificent Italianate-style mansion, which she named Laguna Gloria. Located on the Colorado River, the villa occupied a site once owned by Stephen F. Austin and contained a rose window modeled on the one at Mission San Jose in San Antonio. In keeping with her appreciation of Texas history, Mrs. Sevier located and purchased for the mansion two wrought iron gates that at one time had stood at the south entrance of the state capitol grounds to keep out wandering cattle.

At the death of her brother, Robert Driscoll Jr., in 1929, Clara Sevier closed Laguna Gloria and moved with her husband to her family's Palo Alto ranch headquarters to manage extensive land and petroleum properties and to become president of the Corpus Christi Bank and Trust Company. Under her astute leadership, the dominion almost doubled in value. In 1933, President Franklin D. Roosevelt appointed Hal Sevier to be the U.S. ambassador to Chile. For the next two years, Clara D. Sevier actively assisted her husband in carrying out diplomatic activities at the embassy in Santiago.

Upon their return to Texas in 1935, the Seviers legally separated and two years later the 31-year marriage was dissolved. After the divorce, she took legal action to resume her maiden name and was thereafter officially known as Mrs. Clara Driscoll.

During the next several years, much of Driscoll's time, energy and money were devoted to historic preservation, civic betterment and club activity. She generously assisted the Texas Federation of Women's Clubs by donating $92,000 to liquidate the mortgage on its Austin clubhouse. Earlier she had purchased the last remaining plot of land in the block adjacent to the Alamo and given it to the Daughters of the Republic of Texas. In 1936, she served as vice chairman of the Texas State Centennial Exposition's executive board. In 1943, she presented Laguna Gloria to the Texas Fine Arts Association to be used as a museum. As a memorial to her brother and to improve the economic life of Corpus Christi, she constructed the lavish 20-story Hotel Robert Driscoll, where she resided in the large penthouse apartment.

Colorful, outspoken and independent minded, Driscoll was at her best in the political arena. A loyal Democrat, she was elected as the party's national committeewoman from Texas in 1928 and served in that position for an unprecedented 16 years. In 1939, she promoted the candidacy of her friend John Nance Garner for president. After Franklin Roosevelt was renominated, she remained loyal to what she considered the best interests of her party and supported the president's fourth-term efforts during a bitter battle at the 1944 state convention. *The Dallas Morning News* later commented regarding her political importance that "she moved with distinction in Texas and national political hierarchies" and that "political potentates and Texas voters knew her equally well."

She died suddenly on July 17, 1945, in Corpus Christi. After her body had lain in state at the Alamo chapel, she was interred at the Masonic Cemetery in San Antonio. She bequeathed the bulk of her multimil-

lion-dollar family fortune to establish the Driscoll Foundation Children's Hospital in Corpus Christi to provide free medical care to underprivileged children.

Clara Driscoll deserves to be remembered as an outstanding Texan because of her philanthropy, business acumen, political savvy and achievements in historic preservation. More significantly, she should be recognized for imparting to all citizens of the state her keen belief that the traditions and culture of Texas must be fostered and cherished so that future generations might share in the pride and accomplishment.

John Nance Garner

This article was written by Dr. Evan Anders, Associate Professor of History, University of Texas at Arlington.

John Nance Garner of Uvalde, held the office of Speaker of the U.S. House of Representatives from 1931 into 1933 and then served as Franklin Roosevelt's vice president for two terms from 1933 into 1941. Although Garner played an important role in initially promoting Roosevelt's far-reaching New Deal policies and in later obstructing the program, the native Texan is most commonly remembered for the humor and forthrightness of his political observations.

Garner's penchant for blunt talk neatly complemented his striking physical appearance and his provincial life-style. He self-consciously projected the image of a common man, and a parsimonious one at that. By the time he assumed the speakership, however, he had served in Congress for 28 years and had accumulated a sizable fortune. As the owner of two banks and extensive real estate, ranching and farm holdings, he was the richest man in Uvalde. Appearances were deceptive, however. For three decades, he was a force to be reckoned with in national politics.

From the very start of his life, Garner showed political promise. He was actually born in a log cabin on Nov. 22, 1868, on a small farm in Northeastern Texas 20 miles south of the Red River. To be sure, the log cabin was a two-story structure containing seven rooms, a carved, winding staircase and fireplaces on both floors. Garner attended Vanderbilt University and returned home to study law under a local attorney. He passed the state bar examination shortly before his 21st birthday. When a doctor diagnosed his failing health as tuberculosis and prescribed recuperation in a dry climate, Garner moved to Uvalde. From the time of his arrival in 1892, he was clearly a man on the make. He quickly recovered his health and joined an established law firm. For payment for his legal services, he collected land, livestock and corporate stock. Garner also engaged in land speculation and assumed control of a small newspaper. He married Mariette Rheiner, the daughter of an influential rancher. By 1898, the young lawyer started his successful political career with election as a Democratic representative to the Texas Legislature.

Garner embraced the traditional, 19th-century Democratic concepts of limited government, states rights and white supremacy. Nevertheless, he was not uncompromising. During the 1890s, a serious economic depression generated a farm protest movement and gave rise to both the Populist Party and a reform-minded faction within the Texas Democratic Party. By the time Garner arrived in Austin, conservative Democrats had reasserted their dominance over state politics, but the Uvalde lawmaker pursued a middle-of-the-road course grounded in opportunism and conviction. As an ambitious small-town entrepreneur, he shared the reformers' resentment of huge interstate corporations and combinations, and he was willing to use governmental authority to police big business. He voted for antitrust laws, proposed the regulation of the insurance industry and sponsored an ambitious tax reform package.

Ideology and specific policy commitments, however, were never Garner's overriding concerns. Instead, he was preoccupied with political advancement and the mechanics of the legislative process. With a goal of serving in the U.S. Congress in mind, he formed close ties with the Democratic bosses of South Texas and used his position on the House Committee on Congressional Districts to draw up a new district that included his power base in Uvalde. The competition for the congressional seat was still surprisingly strong, but the support of James B. Wells and the other machine leaders of the Lower Rio Grande Valley carried Garner to victory and Washington in 1902.

As a freshman congressman, Garner quietly looked after the interests of his constituents, especially the South Texas bosses, concentrated on learning the techniques of exercising congressional influence and faithfully followed the directions of the Democratic leadership. Success followed. In 1909, Garner became the Democratic whip, and four years later, he received a seat on the House Ways and Means Committee, which controls tariff and tax legislation. Garner supported President Woodrow Wilson's New Freedom reform program, which included tariff reductions and the creation of the Federal Reserve System and the Federal Trade Commission. The Texas congressman even sponsored the inclusion of the graduated income provision in the Underwood-Simmons Tariff, a measure that marked the beginning of the permanent income tax system in this country. During America's involvement in World War I, Garner emerged as the leading congressional proponent of Wilson's tax and bond proposals for financing the war effort.

So long as a strong and thoughtful Democratic leader like Woodrow Wilson defined the commitment of the national party, Garner's growing mastery of legislative skills produced impressive results. Without strong leadership, Garner and his fellow congressional Democrats foundered. Faced with conservative Republican domination of the national government throughout the 1920s, Garner failed to use his influence as the ranking Democrat on the Ways and Means Committee and later as the House Minority Leader to develop a coherent set of alternative Democratic policies.

With the Democratic triumphs in the congressional election of 1930, Garner became the Speaker of the House. Unfortunately, he proved to be no more resourceful than the Republicans in coping with the economic collapse.

Despite his failure to provide effective congressional leadership in the face of the Depression, Garner gained the support of the Hearst newspaper chain in the race for the 1932 Democratic presidential nomination and scored an impressive victory in the California primary. When a deadlocked national Democratic convention was threatened, Garner threw his support behind the front-runner, Franklin Roosevelt, and insured the New York governor's nomination. Although Garner had no desire to trade his powerful position in the House for the office of vice president, he agreed to serve as Roosevelt's running mate for the sake of enhancing party unity. With the Roosevelt landslide of 1932, Garner became the 33rd vice president of the United States and only the second person to hold both the speakership and the vice presidency.

Despite his lingering conservatism, Garner loyally supported Roosevelt during his first term in office. The vice president used his friendships in Congress and his complete understanding of the legislative process to help promote the New Deal. As the Depression-ravaged economy began to improve, however, Garner and other conservative Democrats resisted further change. When the defeat of Roosevelt's court-packing plan in 1937 revealed the president's unexpected political vulnerability, Garner joined a number of Southern Democratic and Republican congressional leaders to form a conservative coalition, which greatly reduced the output of relief and reform legislation during Roosevelt's second term.

The president deeply resented what he considered Garner's betrayal. The break between the two men became complete when Roosevelt decided to run for a third term in 1940 and thereby thwarted Garner's own presidential ambitions. Without Garner on the ticket, Roosevelt again swept to victory, and the veteran Texas politician returned to Uvalde, where he lived in peaceful retirement until his death in 1967.

Always a superb legislative tactician, Garner

served his country well when he was acting under the strong leadership of Woodrow Wilson and Franklin Roosevelt. Yet Garner lacked the political vision necessary to leave his own lasting imprint on American politics. Never able to completely transcend his small-town provincialism, he failed to develop imaginative solutions for the problems and crises besetting American society during the first half of the 20th century. Through all the vacillations of his career, only his commitment to party regularity appeared consistent. In the end, he violated even this principle when he joined the revolt against Franklin Roosevelt's leadership in 1937.

Ima Hogg

This article was written by Mr. Lonn N. Taylor, Deputy Director Collection and Research, Museum of New Mexico.

Ima Hogg, the only daughter of James Stephen Hogg and Sarah Ann Stinson Hogg, was born in Mineola on July 10, 1882. Her father, an attorney and newspaper editor, named her after the heroine of an epic poem, *The Fate of Marvin*, written by his brother. In 1886, James Stephen Hogg was elected attorney general of Texas, and four years later, he became the state's first native-born governor. He was a progressive Democrat whose administration was marked by legislation that limited the power of private corporations and improved the quality of public education in Texas. Gov. Hogg's populist philosophy had a strong effect on his daughter's social thought and, to a great extent, determined the civic causes to which she devoted the latter part of her life.

Ima Hogg was thrown into close contact with her father's political associates at an early age. Her mother died in 1895 when Ima was 13, and after spending a year at Coronal Institute in San Marcos, she returned to Austin to help manage her father's household and care for her younger brothers, Mike and Tom. An older brother, Will, was at the University of Texas. During the late 1890s, Ima accompanied her father on business and political trips and became acquainted with the leading Texas political thinkers of the period, including ex-Confederates John H. Reagan, Francis Lubbock and A. W. Terrell, and younger men such as Horace Chilton, Charles Culberson and Edward M. House. These associations produced a lifelong interest in politics and a high standard of political integrity by which she judged Texas and national politicians until her death.

Miss Hogg entered the University of Texas in 1899, but did not graduate, moving instead to New York in 1901 to study at the National Conservatory of Music. She remained there until 1907, when she went to Europe to study with pianists Franz Schwarenka and Martin Krause. She traveled for two years in Germany and Austria-Hungary, developing a strong taste for German literature and music. During those years, Ima Hogg decided not to follow a professional career as a concert pianist, but to return to Texas. Her father's death in 1906 had left her with independent means, and in 1909, she returned to Houston to teach piano and, with her brother Will, to play an active role in that city's civic life.

In 1902, Gov. Hogg had helped to form the Texas Company (now Texaco) to produce and transport oil from the Spindletop, Sour Lake and Humble oil fields. After Hogg's death, Will became the head of the family's business interests, and Will soon began a career of private and public philanthropy that was to distinguish the family throughout the greater part of this century. The Hogg business enterprises and philanthropies were family affairs. From 1909 until Will Hogg died in 1930, he and his sister shared a series of residences in Houston; they were joined from 1915 to 1929 by their brother Mike. Will Hogg once had stationery printed for the family firm, Hogg Brothers, Inc., that read "Miss Ima and Hogg Brothers, Inc." The family business operations and philanthropies were greatly expanded by the discovery of oil on family property at West Columbia in 1919.

In 1911, Will Hogg established Texas' first statewide educational foundation, the Organization for the Enlargement by the State of Texas of Its Institutions of Higher Learning. In the following years, he worked to create the Houston YMCA and the Houston Museum of Fine Arts, organized the Houston Forum of Civics and served as chairman of the Houston City Planning Commission, using his own money liberally to further all of these causes. "The government," he once said, "made a mistake originally in not reserving for its own use all wealth below the soil. What I don't pay back in taxes on the oil that should not have been mine, I'm glad to give away for the public welfare."

Ima Hogg's early interests centered on the Houston Symphony, which she helped to found in 1913. She served as vice president from 1913 to 1917 and as president from 1917 to 1921, and she was active in every aspect of the organization during its fledgling years, from selling advertising in the program to selecting musicians. Miss Hogg remained one of the moving spirits of the symphony all of her life, serving 10 more terms as president between 1946 and 1956, and she was as concerned with the details of its daily operations when she was in her late eighties as she had been in 1913.

In 1920, on a visit to New York, she became interested in American antique furniture and decorative arts and decided to build a private collection that would eventually enrich a Texas museum. During the next three decades, Ima became one of the most prominent collectors in the field, traveling in the East and buying through New York dealers and auction houses to bring to Houston some of the finest examples of 18th century American furniture in the world. In 1948, she was made honorary curator for American art at the Houston Museum of Fine Arts; 10 years later, she decided to give the River Oaks home, Bayou Bend, that she and her brothers had built 30 years before to the museum along with her decorative arts collection. In 1966, the Bayou Bend Collection of the Houston Museum of Fine Arts was opened to the public, endowed with an initial gift of $750,000 from Ima Hogg.

After Will Hogg's death in 1930, Ima Hogg began to shoulder some of his civic responsibilities. In 1929, she had founded the Houston Child Guidance Clinic, a pioneering institution in child psychiatry. Her interest in mental health continued to grow, and in 1940, she and Robert Sutherland, a sociologist at the University of Texas, used a bequest from the estate of Will Hogg to create the Hogg Foundation for Mental Health. Under Ima Hogg's guidance, the foundation adopted a broad, pluralistic definition of mental health, emphasizing general public education as well as the treatment of specific mental illnesses. Three years later, she was elected to her first and only public office, the Houston School Board, and held the position until 1949. During those years, she was also active in the Texas Welfare Association, the League of Women Voters, the Daughters of the Republic of Texas and the Texas State Historical Association. In 1948, she became the first woman president of the Philosophical Society of Texas.

Ima Hogg had an abiding interest in the history of Texas that went beyond the writing of history. She encouraged Robert Cotner of the University of Texas Department of History to write his monumental biography of her father, and she became a prime mover in the historic preservation movement in Texas. In the early 1950s, she restored her father's home, Varner Plantation, at West Columbia, presenting it and its furnishings to the state in 1958 as Varner-Hogg State Park. In 1953, she helped to create and became a charter member of the Texas State Historical Survey Committee (now the Texas Historical Commission), the state's first preservation agency and its official link with the federal government on preservation matters. In 1963, she purchased a 180-acre historic farmstead at Winedale in Fayette County, restored a number of structures there dating from the 1840s and presented it to the University of Texas at Austin for use as a center for the study of historic preservation. She formed an important collection of Texas furniture and regional decorative arts at Winedale and encouraged research and publication in this field. She also restored her parents' home at Quitman and had it moved to Jim Hogg State Park. Her contributions to the preservation movement were recognized by awards from the Texas Heritage Foundation, the National Society of Interior Designers, the American Association for State and Local History and the National Trust for Historic Preservation.

Ima Hogg was motivated by the conviction that much is expected of those with wealth and talent. She was intolerant of selfishness and egotism and scornful of the self-indulgence and public ostentation associated with many oil-rich Texans. Her greatest contribution to the state was to set an example of thoughtful civic leadership for Texans with new-found wealth and to quietly, but persistently, encourage others to follow that example. She died in her 93rd year, while on vacation in London, England, on August 19, 1975, and was buried with her parents and brothers in Oakwood Cemetery, Austin.

Eugene C. Barker

Gail Borden

J. Frank Dobie

Tom Connally

Photo Credits

Photographs of Barker, and James Hogg from Texas State Archives, Austin; Connally, Dobie, Garner and Ima Hogg from Dallas Morning News files; Driscoll and Borden are courtesy of the Eugene C. Barker Texas History Center, University of Texas at Austin.

Clara Driscoll

John Nance Garner

Ima Hogg

James S. Hogg

James Stephen Hogg

This article was written by Dr. James Tinsley,
Professor of History,
University of Houston.

James Stephen Hogg, often called "the people's governor," was the first native Texan elected to the state's highest office, serving two terms, 1891-1895. Born near Rusk in Cherokee County on March 24, 1851, Hogg was the son of a politically prominent lawyer, planter and Confederate general who died of illness in 1862. Thereafter, economic misfortune beset the family, and young Hogg had to forgo a formal education, learning instead while working as a printer's devil in Rusk. Later, he edited newspapers in Longview and Quitman, beginning his political career in Wood County as justice of the peace in 1873.

Hogg became a licensed attorney in 1875, was defeated in a race for the state Legislature in 1876, but won election as Wood County Attorney in 1878. Two years later, he became district attorney for the six-county Seventh Judicial District, which encompassed Smith County and the politically important city of Tyler.

As a local prosecutor, Hogg established a reputation for enforcing the law in defense of consumer rights as well as for felony prosecutions. In Wood County, the phrase "a Hogg quart" meant a full measure of goods or services whether one referred to a bottle of kerosene or the quality of passenger service on the railroad. He was also an excellent campaigner, establishing rapport with rural audiences by occasionally drinking water from the bucket rather than a dipper or glass and by punctuating his remarks with an expressive "by gatlings."

From 1884 to 1886, Hogg engaged in private law practice in Tyler, preparing to run for state attorney general in 1886. He possessed excellent qualifications for a statewide political campaign. His aristocratic birth and early childhood afforded him the confidence and self-assurance needed to contest on an equal plane the economic royalists of the day. On the other hand, the poverty of his youth gave him something in common with the plain people, an identification he cultivated and maintained throughout his political career. Hogg also represented the first generation of Texans to achieve political maturity after the Civil War and Reconstruction era. New names, new faces and the enthusiasm of youth were invading the councils of the Democratic Party, sweeping away time-honored and well-worn politicos and the issues of the past.

Hogg was a crusading attorney general from 1877 to 1891. He closed down the Texas Traffic Association by which railroad managers avoided competition in setting rates and pooling traffic — a hollow victory as the managers simply moved their base of operations to St. Louis. But Hogg also forced the railroads to return six million acres of the land the state gave to subsidize construction of main line track when his "sidings and switching case" revealed the railroads took land for auxiliary track as well. He had a hand in drafting the state's first antitrust law in 1889 and his "circular letter" to district attorneys around the state exposed the fraudulent activities of some 40 insurance companies. Finally, Hogg fought with Charles Goodnight and other West Texas cattlemen over their abuse of the leasing provisions of state school lands. In victory or defeat, the portly attorney general appeared to be on the side of the masses against corporate power and personal greed.

Hogg announced for governor in 1890 with a strong endorsement from the Farmers' Alliance, the agrarian organization whose chief demands were stringent control of corporate wealth and better rural credit facilities. Hogg and the Alliance also campaigned for ratification of a constitutional amendment authorizing the creation of a state railroad commission. The victory of Hogg and the commission marked the triumph of agrarian reform over the conservative Bourbon Democrats who had ruled Texas since 1874.

As governor, Hogg worked with the Legislature in drafting the railroad commission bill and then persuaded the venerable John H. Reagan to give up his seat in the United States Senate to chair the three-man commission. Hogg's other two appointments (commissioners were later elected) were worthy individuals but neither was a man the Farmers' Alliance had endorsed.

The Alliance's disenchantment with Hogg turned to dismay in October 1891, when Hogg read out of the Democratic Party persons who endorsed the subtreasury plan touted by the Alliance as the answer to credit problems cotton farmers in Texas faced. By 1892, Alliancemen in droves deserted the Democratic Party and Hogg in favor of the new Populist Party.

While Hogg in his first term did not go far enough to satisfy the Alliance, he went too far in the view of conservatives who complained that his reforms were driving capital out of the state. Under the leadership of George Clark of Waco, the conservatives attempted to block Hogg's renomination in 1892, but failing in that, Clark announced against him in the general election.

Hogg's re-election in 1892 was a watershed event in Texas politics. In "the fight of his life," Hogg stood off the Populists on the left and the Clark forces on the right. Among those who came to his aid was a young Houstonian, Edward M. House, upon whom Hogg bestowed the honorary title of colonel, an appellation House carried throughout the remainder of his long career as a political adviser to other Texas governors and to President Woodrow Wilson.

During his second term of office, Hogg pushed through four more reform measures: An act regulating the sale of railroad stocks and bonds, an alien land law, a bill requiring land corporations to sell holdings within 15 years and a measure restricting the indebtedness of cities and counties. During his last year in office, Hogg made political peace with the conservatives of his party, agreeing to retire from public office in 1895 if the conservatives would pledge not to repeal the "Hogg laws."

Claiming he left office "with only $50 in his pocket," Hogg resumed the practice of law in Austin, later moving to Houston after the turn of the century. Though out of office, Hogg was seldom out of the public eye. His law practice flourished, and with the discovery of oil at Spindletop in 1901, he and James Swayne formed a syndicate that dealt extensively in oil leases. The Hogg-Swayne syndicate then became a part of the new Texas Company (now Texaco) that Joseph S. Cullinan organized in 1902. Profits from his law practice and business ventures allowed Hogg to buy the Varner Plantation in Brazoria County in 1901, where he moved from Austin and resided until the time of his death.

As an elder statesman, Hogg also continued to be one of the most articulate voices for political reform in Texas. The three governors who followed him in office over the next 12 years — Charles A. Culberson, Joseph D. Sayers and Samuel W.T. Lanham — were influenced more by Col. House's moderate to conservative coalition than by Hogg, but in 1905, shortly before his death, Hogg strongly endorsed progressive Thomas M. Campbell whose tenure as governor from 1907 to 1911 revived many of Hogg's policies. When illness prevented his appearing in person, Hogg recorded a speech to be played at a statewide gathering of political leaders in Dallas in November 1905. In what could be called his last political manifesto, Hogg called for "rotation in office permanently established; nepotism forbidden; equality of taxation a fact; organized lobbying at Austin suppressed; the free pass system honestly, effectively abolished; oil pipelines placed under the commission's control; insolvent corporations put out of business; all bonds and stocks of every class of transportation limited by law; corporate control of Texas made impossible; and public records disclose every official act and be open to all, to the end that everyone shall know that, in Texas, public office is the center of public conscience, and that no graft, no crime, no public wrong, shall ever stain or corrupt our State."

On Jan. 26, 1905, Hogg was injured in a train wreck returning to Houston from Varner Plantation. Though he recovered enough to make occasional public appearances, complications from the injury resulted in his death on March 3, 1906.

Hogg and his wife, Sarah Ann Stinson Hogg, who preceded him in death in 1895, had four children who later became prominent in their own right; a daughter, Ima, and three sons, William Clifford, Michael and Thomas Elisha.

Sam Houston

This article was written by Dr. Thomas Kreneck,
Associate Director,
Houston Metropolitan Research Center

Sam Houston, a quintessential Jacksonian, was the dominant political figure in Texas from the mid-1830s until his death in 1863. Active in public affairs as a young man in his home state of Tennessee, he relocated to Texas in late 1832, where he became immediately involved in the politics of rebellion and was as responsible as any other individual for Texas' separation from Mexico in 1836. Thereafter, he remained prominently positioned in Texas affairs as president of the Texas Republic, United States senator after annexation and as a one-term governor before he was deposed by the Texas secessionists in 1861.

Houston's early life was representative of the restless spirit of the American westward movement. Born in Rockbridge County, Va., on March 2, 1793, into a family of minor gentry, he was the fifth of nine children of Samuel and Elizabeth Paxton Houston. Following his father's death in 1807, young Sam migrated with his mother and siblings to Blount County, Tenn., then a part of North Carolina, where the family had purchased land near the town of Maryville. Not finding these new surroundings to his liking, Sam left home and went to live with a band of local Cherokee Indians. There he was adopted into the tribe and learned the ways of the native Americans. He spent the majority of his late adolescence with the Cherokees under Chief Oolooteka and from that time became an avid defender of the rights of Indians.

In 1813, Houston joined the United States Army in its effort against the British. He participated in the crucial Battle of Horseshoe Bend against the Creek Indian allies of England. Gravely wounded in that engagement, Houston's bravery won the admiration of Gen. Andrew Jackson, and the two men developed a close personal friendship. Jackson became Houston's mentor and in return received the younger man's undying loyalty. It was through Jackson's patronage that Houston became an Indian agent in Tennessee in 1817 after recovering from his battlefield injuries. In that position he assisted in Cherokee removal to Indian territory in the West.

Sam Houston entered the Tennessee political arena in late 1818 after reading law in the offices of a local attorney. In October of that year he was elected district attorney of the Nashville district. His meteoric rise continued when he became adjutant general of the Tennessee Militia. By 1823, Houston was elected to the United States Congress from Tennessee and won re-election in 1825. Firmly within the Jackson political junta, Sam Houston was elected governor of the state as an internal improvements candidate. As congressman and governor, he worked mightily for Jackson's election to the presidency and could well have been seen as Jackson's political heir apparent.

In 1829, however, Houston's fortunes rapidly vanished when he quit the governorship and left Tennessee. He had married Eliza H. Allen on Jan. 1, 1829, but in April they separated. She returned to the home of her parents, while the distraught governor resigned his position and fled to Indian territory in Arkansas where he took up residence in the new home of his old friend Oolooteka. From 1829 until 1832, he was involved in Indian politics and business ventures.

Having numerous friends and associates already settled and active in Texas, Houston decided by late 1832 to seek his fortune in that troubled Mexican province. He attended the Convention of 1833 as a representative from Nacogdoches where he had taken up residence. From the beginning of his association with Texas, Houston was concerned with two principal activities: politics and land speculation. His experience,

ability and commanding physical stature ensured him an early prominent role in Texas affairs. He was aligned from the start with those individuals who chafed under Mexican rule. Indeed, there has been lingering suspicion that Houston was Jackson's personal agent in Texas to foment American acquisition of that rich area. By the fall of 1835, Houston represented Nacogdoches at the Consultation, and in November was elected major general of the Texas army by the General Council as the Anglo-Texans prepared to resist what they considered to be arbitrary rule from Mexico City.

Gen. Houston was a powerful member of the Convention of 1836, which met at Washington-on-the-Brazos in early March. There, on March 2, he added his signature to the Texas Declaration of Independence and became, by vote of the convention delegates, commander in chief of the army of the new republic. He then joined his small army at Gonzales where he proceeded to train the volunteers as a fighting force.

As disaster befell the Texas rebels at the Alamo and Goliad, Houston led his men in a retreat into East Texas as the army of Gen. Antonio Lopez de Santa Anna pursued its victorious course. On April 21, 1836, however, Houston and his force won the Battle of San Jacinto where in addition to capturing a large portion of Santa Anna's army, they also took the dictator prisoner. With Santa Anna in their custody, the Texas rebels obtained a cessation of hostilities and withdrawal of enemy forces across the Rio Grande. Sam Houston emerged from the revolution as the leading figure in Texas, forever linked with its struggle for independence.

Houston was twice elected president of the Texas Republic during its decade of existence. As its first regularly elected president, he served from December 1836 to December 1838, and then from December 1841 to December 1844. Between these two terms, from late 1838 to late 1841, he led the congressional opposition to his political adversary, President Mirabeau B. Lamar. Between December 1844 and the formal transfer of Texas to the United States in early 1846, Houston served as adviser to the last chief executive of the Republic, Anson Jones. In 1840, Sam Houston married Margaret Lea of Alabama. They eventually had eight healthy children, all of whom lived to adulthood.

Sam Houston favored the annexation of Texas, and was elected by the Texas Legislature to the United States Senate along with Thomas Jefferson Rusk. He served in that position until 1859. During his tenure in the Senate, Houston was an articulate spokesman for the rights of Indians and for preservation of the Union. Indeed, he came under increasing criticism from his Southern colleagues for his rigid adherence to the Union over so-called Southern rights. His belief in Unionism had its origins in his Jacksonian loyalties. He was an avid supporter of the Compromise of 1850 and against repeal of the Missouri Compromise.

His defense of the Union was one of the most dramatic periods in Houston's career; but it was so unpopular in his home state that the Texas Legislature elected John Hemphill to replace him. Houston showed remarkable resiliency, a lifelong trait, by seeking and winning the Texas governorship in 1859. Gov. Houston opposed the secessionists as vehemently as he had done in the Senate, and correctly predicted Southern defeat in a civil war. As part of his effort to protect the Union he was mentioned as a presidential candidate on several occasions. When Texas seceded in 1861, Houston was removed from office for declining to take the oath of allegiance to the Confederacy. Thereafter, he retired with his wife and children to Huntsville where he died of pneumonia on July 26, 1863, passing into Texas history as one of its most colorful and controversial figures.

Lyndon Baines Johnson

This article was written by Dr. Emmette S. Redford,
Professor of Government, University of Texas at Austin.

Lyndon Baines Johnson, 36th president of the United States, was born on Aug. 27, 1908, near Stonewall, Texas, the son of Sam Ealy Jr. and Rebecca Baines Johnson. His paternal grandfather had been a trail driver to Kansas and his maternal grandfather a lawyer and state official. His father was a farmer, real estate salesman and a member of the Texas House of Repre-

sentatives for 12 years.

The family lived in Johnson City, Texas, for periods of Lyndon's childhood and youth. He graduated from the 11-grade Johnson City High School at 15 years of age. For a time his life appeared aimless as he joined a group for casual labor in California and then worked on a road gang in his home county.

On the advice of his parents, he enrolled at San Marcos State Teachers College, where he graduated in 1930. He taught in the Cotulla and Houston public schools, and in 1932 moved to Washington, D. C. to serve as secretary for Congressman Richard Kleberg. In 1935, he was appointed State Director for Texas of the National Youth Administration (NYA), whose purpose was creation of job opportunities for unemployed youth.

In 1934, he met an East Texas girl. After a whirlwind courtship of two months, they were married on Nov. 17, 1934. Ten and 13 years later, their two daughters, Lynda Bird and Luci Baines, were born. In the meantime, Lady Bird's talents and avidity for political assistance and counsel to her husband became evident.

Johnson moved abruptly from administrative responsibility to electoral politics in 1937. The death of Congressman James Buchanan created a vacancy in the 10th Congressional District. Johnson leaped into the race and defeated eight other candidates in a plurality election. Johnson was the only candidate to back President Franklin Roosevelt's so-called "court-packing" proposal and other New Deal measures.

The young Texas congressman began his service with virtually 100 percent support of President Roosevelt's New Deal and almost instantly developed a close affiliation with the president. He supported the Fair Labor Standards Act of 1938, which set minimum wages and maximum hours, and other New Deal measures such as rural electrification, public works, agricultural supports and public housing. Also, he supported the development of the nation's military preparedness prior to World War II.

Four days after Pearl Harbor, Johnson reported for duty in the Navy, retaining his seat in Congress. He returned to Washington in July 1942 after President Roosevelt ordered congressmen in military service back to their legislative responsibilities.

The New Deal programs provided Johnson with unusual opportunities for constituency service. He ardently worked for local action and federal appropriations for rural electrification and for completion of the dam construction program in his district. He also supported federal aid to public housing in Austin and earned a reputation for service to his constituency.

In 1940, when U.S. Sen. Morris Sheppard of Texas died, Johnson became a candidate for the seat and lost by a narrow margin to Gov. Lee O'Daniel. In 1948, Johnson ran again, this time facing Gov. Coke Stevenson in the Democratic runoff primary. As the results were reported late from voting precincts, Johnson became the apparent victor by 87 votes. Following contests in the state Democratic convention and the courts, he became the Democratic candidate. Johnson won the November election and was re-elected overwhelmingly in 1954, eventually serving as senator for 12 years.

Johnson was appointed a member of the Armed Services Committee and designated chairman of the Preparedness Subcommittee, serving on both to the end of his tenure. He was also a member successively of the Interstate and Foreign Commerce Committee (1949-55), the Finance Committee (1955-57) and the Appropriations Committee (1957-61). He was chairman of the Committee on Aeronautical and Space Sciences (1957-61).

He moved quickly into a leadership position in the Senate, becoming party whip in 1951, minority leader in 1953 and majority leader in 1955. He gained renown as one of the strongest legislative leaders in national history, and especially for talents in persuasion and construction of majority coalitions. Serving with a Republican president, he proclaimed a stance of constructive but selective cooperation with the chief executive.

Plagued by several illnesses in his life, Johnson suffered a severe heart attack July 2, 1955. After recuperating at his home, he returned to service in Washington the following January.

As senator, Johnson supported strong national defense, foreign assistance and other measures of international cooperation and backed the oil and agricultural interests of his state. He voted for civil rights legislation passed in 1957, and his leadership contributed to the compromise that ensured its passage. He maneuvered a solid vote of Democratic senators for the censorship of Sen. Joseph McCarthy. Near the end of his service as chairman of the Committee on Aeronautical and Space Sciences, he sponsored legislation for space exploration.

During his tenure as senator there was intense intraparty conflict among Democrats in his state. Johnson led his party to the Democratic convention and was favorite son candidate for president in 1956, supported his party's ticket in national elections and placed himself in a middle position between liberal and conservative factions of the state party.

In 1960, after defeat at the Democratic convention in his effort to win his party's nomination for president, Johnson became John F. Kennedy's running mate and was elected vice president. In that office, he attended meetings of the cabinet and the National Security Council, was chairman of the National Aeronautics and Space Council, the President's Committee on Equal Employment Opportunity and of the Peace Corps Advisory Council. President Kennedy sent him on a number of missions to various nations.

Catapulted into the presidency by the assassination of President Kennedy on Nov. 22, 1963, Johnson moved immediately to numerous conferences and addresses to demonstrate to the nation and the world his mastery of his new responsibilities. His theme was continuity of the government and of the Kennedy program. He succeeded in gaining congressional enactment of major parts of that program, including anti-poverty legislation and the Civil Rights Act of 1964.

He was continued in the presidency by election in 1964, winning by the largest popular percentage (61.1) received by any 20th century candidate for the office. He had announced a "Great Society" program. Backed by his large electoral victory, he gained legislative approval of a domestic program that exhibited three features.

—First, it was the most sweeping national legislative agenda enacted since the New Deal, including aid to education, urban renewal, Medicare and Medicaid, removal of obstacles to the right to vote, conservation of resources, beautification of highways and assault on crime and delinquency.

—Second, it was more largely planned and directed from the White House than previous legislative programs.

—Third, in contrast to the emphasis in New Deal legislation on salvaging the economy and assistance to those in need, the Great Society program was directed in the main toward broadening opportunity of individuals in the American society.

While successful in his legislative program, Johnson led the nation more deeply into the Vietnam quagmire. The bombing of North Vietnam positions and an enormous increase of American ground forces in Vietnam after July 1965 did not prevent deterioration of the American effort. Rioting against the war, particularly by youths, spread through American cities.

To the surprise of the nation, Johnson, whether from anguish over the course of the war or his health or other reasons, announced on March 31, 1968, that he would not be a candidate for re-election. He retired, after 36 years in the national government, on Jan. 20, 1969, to his ranch home near Stonewall, Texas. He died on Jan. 22, 1973, and was buried in the family cemetery a short distance from his birthplace.

Anson Jones

This article was written by Dr. Marilyn Sibley, Professor of History, Houston Baptist University.

President Anson Jones, M.D., gave the main address at the ceremony that ended the Republic of Texas. "The final act in this great drama is now performed," he told an assembly of dignitaries and citizens in Austin on Feb. 19, 1846. "The Republic of Texas is no more." Then he stepped forward to lower with his own hands the lone star flag of Texas.

The act marked the high point of Jones' life. The Republic had endured for 10 years, and for almost that long, he had wrestled with the question of annexation to

the United States. As congressman, minister, senator, secretary of state and president, he dealt with the issue, using diplomacy, direct and indirect, and, on occasion, dissimulation and bluff. More than once he saw his prospects of success vanish in thin air. Thus, he could watch with a sense of personal accomplishment as the flag of the United States replaced the lone star. He cherished the idea that history would award him the title "Architect of Annexation."

For all his preoccupation with annexation, Anson Jones had not come to Texas with that thought in mind. Like many others, he had drifted to the area because life had not gone well for him elsewhere. Born at Great

Barrington, Ma., on Jan. 20, 1798, he was the 13th child of poor tenant farmers, Solomon and Sarah Jones. Jones could well feel from time to time that the number was unlucky, for he had trouble finding his niche in life. At the insistence of his family, he studied medicine, but his efforts to establish a practice were unsuccessful. For a time he taught school. For two years, he visited Venezuela. In 1832, he became a commission merchant in New Orleans. The mercantile venture ended quickly in unqualified failure, and Anson Jones — alone and 35 years old — found himself in a strange city without means of a livelihood. He had $32 in his pocket, a small stock of medicine and a debt of $2,000.

Expecting little but with little to lose, Jones booked passage to the Mexican state of Texas in October 1833. There he found the success and recognition that had eluded him elsewhere. In short order, he established a thriving medical practice. He met Mary Smith McCrory, a young widow whom he married in 1840. With four other men, he organized the first Masonic lodge in Texas. He also took part in public affairs, making the acquaintance of men who had laid the groundwork for the Texas Revolution. When the discontent of the Texans reached the crisis point, Jones stood among the first to ask for independence. When the call to arms came, he volunteered as a private and doubled as a surgeon. Thus it was that he came to the field of San Jacinto on April 21, 1836, in company with the two other men, Sam Houston and Mirabeau B. Lamar, whom the Texans would elect as their presidents.

During the decade of the Republic, Jones rose through the ranks to the presidency, focusing his attention on foreign relations. In the first election of the Republic — the same election that gave Sam Houston his first term as president — Texans almost unanimously requested annexation to the United States. The mother country rejected that request, whereupon Anson Jones as a member of the Texas Congress set forth a policy of alternatives that characterized his approach. Since the United States had rejected annexation, he submitted, Texas should withdraw the offer and maintain independence by seeking friends in Europe.

When Houston began his second term as president in 1841, Jones was appointed secretary of state, and the pair pursued together a policy of alternatives. Both understood the expansionist spirit that ran rife in the United States and the desire of England and France to block that expansion. The Texans played the continents against each other. On the one hand, they courted European friendship to whet the interest of the United

States; on the other, they hinted that annexation was imminent to whip up European determination to block it. Later an unseemly quarrel developed between Jones and Houston over who originated the policy of alternatives, but at the time, they worked so closely together that neither could claim the policy exclusively.

The policy came to fruition after Jones succeeded Houston as president. By the summer of 1845, Jones had two firm choices to offer Texans — annexation to the United States or independence guaranteed by England and France. A seasoned negotiator by this time, Jones saw opportunity for yet another round of the diplomatic game to obtain better terms of annexation. But his fellow Texans would have none of that. They failed to understand the intricacies of diplomacy, and, eager for annexation and fearful of losing the chance, they rose in fury to denounce Jones for stalling. They accused him of being a tool of the British, hanged him in effigy and even launched an effort to remove him from office. He came to the end of the Republic the most vilified man in Texas.

Because of public sentiment, Jones ended his public career at the same time he ended the Republic. He retired to his plantation in early 1846, confident, as he said, that "history and posterity will do me no wrong." But as the years passed and Texans tended to forget him along with the annexation controversy, he brooded over his neglect. An accident caused one of his arms to wither, and with much spare time, he prepared his papers for publication, adding bitter comments about his former colleagues, especially Sam Houston, that tarnished his historical reputation more than theirs.

Texans seemed to remember Jones once more in 1857, when the Legislature faced the task of choosing two new senators. Jones anticipated emerging from retirement to accept one of the positions. When the Legislature acted, he received not a single vote. The rebuff plunged him into despondency. He made a sentimental trip to Houston, and in the building where he began his public career in 1837, he ended his life on Jan. 9, 1858.

Belatedly, history and posterity gave Jones his due. Shortly after his death, the Legislature named a county for him, stipulating that the county seat be named Anson. A noted historian, Herbert Gambrell, wrote a biography that lifted the shadow cast by Jones' own book and refurbished his reputation.

If Anson Jones was not the "Architect of Annexation," as he hoped to be recalled, he was assuredly the "Co-architect."

Jesse Holman Jones

This article was written by Dr. Don E. Carleton, Director, Eugene C. Barker Texas History Center.

To his closest colleagues, he was "Mr. Jesse"; to many Texans, he was "Mr. Houston," civic leader and philanthropist; to his employees, he was "Mr. Jones," captain of a vast business empire; and to his critics he was "Jesus H. Jones," wielder of enormous financial power during the presidency of Franklin D. Roosevelt. By whatever name, Jesse Holman Jones ranks among those few Texans whose fame and influence have significantly transcended the state's boundaries.

Jesse Jones was born in Robertson County, Tn., on April 5, 1874, one of five children of William Hasque Jones and Laura Holman Jones. When Jesse was nine years old, his father sold their 100-acre farm and moved the family to Dallas. After three years in Dallas, Jesse's father purchased a farm on the Kentucky-Tennessee state line, where the family relocated. In 1891, Jones returned to Dallas, took courses at Hill's Business College and worked as an itinerant laborer and salesman. After his father's death in 1893, Jones returned to Kentucky to settle the estate and to help with the tobacco crop. During that summer, Jones took a break from his farm work to see the Columbian Exposition World's Fair in Chicago, an experience that would remain with him for the rest of his life. He later stated that "Seeing Chicago, the tall buildings . . . and the World's Fair gave me an ambition to get out into the big world."

Jones decided that his fortune could be made in the rapidly developing cities of Texas, so he began his business career working for the M. T. Jones Lumber Company in Dallas and Hillsboro, a company owned by his uncle. After his uncle's death in 1898, Jones became general manager of the company and moved to Houston, where the business was headquartered. By 1902,

Jones had become a prosperous young Houston businessman. He retained his position at M. T. Jones but also organized his own firm, the South Texas Lumber Company. These businesses survived the financial panic of 1907, and Jones emerged as one of the city's dominant business leaders. Jones soon diversified into building and banking. He built the 10-story Bristol Hotel in 1908 to begin a construction program that would produce more than 30 major buildings in downtown Houston by the 1920s. These included the 18-story Rice Hotel and the Houston Chronicle, Bankers' Mortgage and Gulf buildings. The 34-story Gulf Building, which Jones built in 1928, remained the tallest building in Texas for more than 25 years. Jones also built office buildings in other cities, including Fort Worth and New York City. As a banker, Jones developed the National Bank of Commerce (later Texas Commerce Bank) into one of the state's leading financial institutions.

Jones played a key role in the creation of the Houston Ship Channel and the Port of Houston. In 1914, he persuaded his fellow Houston bankers to buy enough bonds to match federal funds to dredge the ship canal. He subsequently served as the first chairman of the Houston Harbor Board, which planned the construction of the Port of Houston.

Jones was an enthusiastic supporter of Woodrow Wilson in the 1912 presidential campaign. Although Wilson sought unsuccessfully to involve Jones in the administration, Jones accepted Wilson's invitation to serve as the director of General Military Relief for the American Red Cross after the United States entered World War I. After two years in Washington, Jones returned to Houston in 1919. One year later he married Mary Gibbs.

In 1924, after serving as a Texas delegate to the

Democratic National Convention in New York, Jones became director of finance for the presidential campaign of John W. Davis. After Davis' defeat, Jones remained as finance chairman and kept the party solvent until he relinquished the position in 1928. While finance director, Jones succeeded in bringing the 1918 National Democratic Convention to Houston. Two years earlier, Jones had become sole owner of the *Houston Chronicle*. The newspaper became Jones' editorial voice and enhanced his political influence in the state. The Texas delegation made Jones its favorite son candidate for the presidential nomination at the convention in Houston, but New York Gov. Al Smith easily won the nomination.

Although Jones was a significant figure in Texas political and business circles by the end of the 1920s, he did not become a truly powerful national figure until the Depression. In January 1932, Speaker of the House of Representatives John Nance Garner and Sen. Carter Glass persuaded President Herbert Hoover to appoint Jones to the board of directors of the Reconstruction Finance Corporation (RFC). Congress had created the RFC to provide government loans to businesses threatened by the Depression. In 1933, newly elected President Franklin D. Roosevelt appointed Jones RFC chairman.

Jones played an important role during Roosevelt's first two terms in office (1933-1941). Under his direction, the RFC encouraged credit expansion, lessened Wall Street's dominance over the nation's banks and provided crucial financial support to Depression-weakened railroads. The RFC became the nation's largest bank and its biggest investor. Despite impressive achievements, Jones had his critics. Congress also had intended for the RFC to provide loan relief to small businesses. Jones' insistence, however, that borrowers have strong collateral and a lengthy record of financial responsibility made most small business enterprises ineligible for help. One critic claimed that if a business was strong enough to meet Jones' criteria, "It was ordinarily easier to borrow privately."

Nevertheless, because of his fiscal competence and powerful conservative Democratic political support, FDR expanded Jones' responsibilities. In 1939, Roosevelt placed Jones in charge of the Federal Loan Agency, which included the Federal Housing Administration, the Home Owners' Loan Corporation and the Export-Import Bank. Jones relinquished the chairmanship of the RFC but retained control over its activities. Jones joined Roosevelt's cabinet in 1940 as Secretary of Commerce. In an impressive demonstration of confidence in Jesse Jones' integrity, Congress passed special legislation allowing Jones to retain his authority over the RFC and the Federal Loan Agency. Rarely in American history has an individual other than the president been granted supervision over as much of the nation's public money as was Jesse Jones. After the United States entered World War II, Jones also became a member of the War Production Board and played a significant role in mobilizing the industrial war effort.

Jones was a leader among those in the New Deal who advocated a conservative role for the federal government in the social and economic affairs of the nation. As a result, he feuded openly with such New Deal liberals as Henry Wallace and Harold L. Ickes. The liberals eventually dominated, and Jones lost influence with the president. Jones' public feud with Vice President Wallace and the suspicion that Jones had secretly encouraged the anti-Roosevelt Texas Regulars at the Democratic State Convention in 1944 eventually led Roosevelt to remove Jones from his Commerce Department post. Jones was further humiliated by Roosevelt's appointment of Wallace to replace him. After 13 years in Washington, Jones returned to Houston. Although semi-retired, he remained active politically. Bitter about his dismissal, Jones attracted national attention in 1948 when he published a front-page editorial in the *Chronicle* announcing support for the Republican Party's presidential ticket of Thomas E. Dewey and Earl Warren. In 1951, Jones published an account of his RFC years in the book, *Fifty Billion Dollars*.

In his remaining years, Jones concentrated his attention on philanthropic activities. He and his wife established the Houston Endowment in 1937 to support a variety of charitable and educational endeavors. Jesse Jones died in Houston on June 1, 1956.

Mirabeau B. Lamar

This article was written by Dr. Dorman Winfrey, Director, Texas State Library.

Texans pride themselves on being hard-headed, practical people, but visionaries too played a role in the state's history. One of these figures centered attention on education and ambitions of empire. Mirabeau Buonaparte Lamar, the son of John and Rebecca (Lamar) Lamar, was born on a plantation near Louisville, Jefferson County, Ga., on Aug. 16, 1798.

His parents were first cousins and were descended from French Huguenots who immigrated to the United States in the 17th century. When Mirabeau was 10 years of age, the family moved to a location near the new state capital of Milledgeville. For a short period, the boy attended academies in the capital city and nearby Eatonton. His formal education was rudimentary, but interests in history and literature were nurtured by private study.

In 1819, Lamar traveled to the newly admitted state of Alabama, and for a time, he was engaged in a general mercantile business at Cahawba. He soon sold his interest to a partner and became co-publisher of the *Cahawba Press*. During this period, Lamar became closely allied with the States' Rights and Nullification movements. He left Alabama in 1823 and assumed the position of private secretary to Georgia's new governor, George M. Troup. Lamar married Tabitha Jordan on Jan. 1, 1826, and 10 months later, a daughter, Rebecca Ann, was born. In 1828, Lamar moved his family to Columbus, a new trading town established on Indian lands in Muscogee County. He established the town's first newspaper, the *Columbus Enquirer*, which was a political organ as well as an outlet for Lamar's earliest literary efforts. His views on states' rights won the young editor considerable renown, and in 1829, he ran successfully for a seat in the Georgia Senate. His political career was interrupted in 1830 by a series of personal tragedies. His wife died that year of tuberculosis, and shortly thereafter, his brother committed suicide. Lamar was overwhelmed with despondency. He withdrew from politics and journeyed to the insurgent Mexican province of Texas, ostensibly to write and convalesce.

Lamar intended to compile a history of Texas, but was soon caught up in the turmoil of the Texas Revolution. He served conspicuously as a commander of cavalry at the Battle of San Jacinto, and within a short time, Lamar held a succession of appointed offices, including Secretary of War and Commander-in-Chief of the Army. In the summer of 1836, he retired to civilian life at Brazoria, but was encouraged to seek the vice presidency in Texas' first general election that following September. He won and thus became the understudy and heir apparent to the chief executive, Sam Houston, who was prohibited from seeking a second term by the Republic Constitution. The duties of the vice president were not demanding, and Lamar spent most of this time traveling and collecting the papers and reminiscences of early Texas pioneers, including Stephen F. Austin.

In April 1838, Lamar was nominated for the presidency, sharing the ticket with David G. Burnet. During his term as vice president, Lamar had become a bitter opponent of President Houston, whom he considered an irresponsible inebriate. Houston's supporters nominated two candidates, both of whom committed suicide before the general election. Although another candidate announced during the closing days of the contest, Lamar won the office by a greater margin of votes than had Houston two years earlier.

To stabilize Texas' rapidly depreciating currency, President Lamar advocated the establishment of a national bank, and he simultaneously solicited recognition and commercial treaties from foreign nations. He opposed Texas' resettlement of Indians removed from the United States and severely chastised native hostiles who committed depredations against the western settlements. During the first year of Lamar's administration, Texas became the first country in the world to ensure that a man's home and means of livelihood could not be taken away for debt. This liberal property law was embodied in the Homestead Act, passed by Congress on Jan. 26, 1839.

Lamar sought peace with Mexico, initially through

Sam Houston

Lyndon B. Johnson

Anson Jones

Jesse Jones

Photo Credits

Photos of Houston, Anson Jones, Lamar, Navarro, Ney and Nimitz from Texas State Archives, Austin; Johnson and Jesse Jones from Dallas Morning News files.

Mirabeau B. Lamar

Jose Navarro

Elisabet Ney

Chester Nimitz

the good offices of the United States and Great Britain, and later by direct negotiation. When these efforts failed, he made an alliance with the rebellious state of Yucatan, leasing the Texas Navy to the insurgents and providing the personnel to man the vessels. President Lamar also launched an unsuccessful military expedition against the New Mexican trading center of Santa Fe. Perhaps the greatest and most enduring accomplishment of Lamar's presidency was the establishment of a system of public education endowed entirely from the public domain. The success of Lamar's work for education provided his title as the "Father of Education" in Texas.

The improvident Santa Fe Expedition and the Republic's continued financial troubles overshadowed the positive aspects of Lamar's administration, and he left office as unpopular as his predecessor, Sam Houston. Houston recovered from his unpopularity to succeed Lamar, who withdrew to his home outside Richmond in Fort Bend County at the end of 1841 and began a self-imposed retirement. Lamar entered public service only twice during the remainder of his life. In the course of the Mexican War, he served in the Second Legislature as state representative for the internationally disputed counties of Nueces and San Patricio. Fol-

lowing the cessation of hostilities, he once again turned his attentions to writing and collecting historical manuscripts. In 1851, he married Henrietta Maffitt of Galveston. This union produced a second daughter, Loretto Evalina, in 1852. Financial difficulties troubled the Lamar household, and in 1857, Lamar accepted a joint diplomatic mission to Nicaragua and Costa Rica, to relieve his debts. For 20 months, Lamar attempted to stabilize relations with those countries in the wake of the William Walker adventure and American and French designs to establish an isthmian transit route. He resigned in the spring of 1859 and returned to his Richmond plantation. His health was failing, and on Dec. 18, 1859, while friends and relatives gathered at his home for the holidays, Mirabeau Lamar suffered a massive heart attack and died the following day.

Many contemporaries considered Lamar an impractical romantic. Anson Jones wrote: "Texas is too small for a man of such wild, visionary and vaulting ambition." Lamar was a dreamer, but the Republic of Texas was built on dreams and aspirations and sustained itself with them when the treasury was empty and the future uncertain. He played a vital role in holding before the people of Texas a vision of the future that gave them a unifying goal even when their fate seemed darkest.

Jose Antonio Navarro

This article was written by Dr. Stanley Siegel, Professor of History, University of Houston.

Jose Antonio Navarro was born in San Antonio on Feb. 27, 1795, the son of Angel and Maria Josefa Navarro. His father, a native of the island of Corsica, resigned a commission in the Spanish military to emigrate to Mexico. In Mexico City, he married Maria Josefa Ruiz y Pena, daughter of a noble family, and later moved to San Antonio on the Texas frontier. Because Texas had no such educational institutions, 10-year-old Navarro was sent to school in Saltillo for a year and began preparations for a commercial career.

Navarro was caught up early in Mexico's struggle against Spain for independence. Along with other members of his family, he fled across the Sabine in 1813, following Spanish Royalist Gen. Joaquin Arredondo's reconquest of Texas at the battle of the Medina River. After three years of exile in the United States, his mother obtained a royal grant of clemency, and Navarro returned to Texas. Managing a general store and studying law in San Antonio, the young man rejoiced in Mexico's attaining nationhood in 1821. Recognition of his abilities came that year when he was elected a member of the Coahuila y Texas legislature. While a legislator at Saltillo and later as a delegate to the federal congress at Mexico City, Navarro advocated the colonization of Texas through the award of empresario contracts.

While Navarro initially remained aloof from the developing political controversy in Texas, by the winter of 1835, Navarro counted himself among the adherents of Texas independence. Thus, although elected as a representative from Coahuila y Texas to the national congress at Mexico City, he feigned illness and refused to attend. Adamantly opposed to Santa Anna's assumption of unbridled power, Navarro saw in the Texas "Declaration of Causes" a true reflection of Mexican liberty and devotion to the Constitution of 1824.

When it became apparent that Santa Anna would not countenance Texas statehood, Navarro proclaimed for independence. One of four delegates from Bexar to the Independence Convention at Washington-on-the-Brazos, he joined with his uncle, Francisco Ruiz, and Lorenzo de Zavala as Latin signers of the Declaration. Navarro was then assigned a seat on the committee entrusted with drafting the Republic of Texas Constitution. Later he took pride in the fact that no official distinction was made in that document between the civil and voting rights of Anglos and Mexican-Texans.

As a member of the Texas Congress from Bexar County, Navarro generally supported the policies of President Mirabeau B. Lamar. In this capacity, he was designated as one of four commissioners to accompany the men of the Santa Fe expedition. Despite much evidence to the contrary, Lamar preferred to believe that the inhabitants of Santa Fe would welcome Texas rule. Therefore, the choice of Navarro, a native Mexican, as a Texas representative was a sensible move. Texas history records few more ill-advised ventures than Lamar's Santa Fe campaign. Due to Indian attack and the

ravages of hunger and thirst, many of the original volunteers perished before reaching their destination. The remainder, perhaps betrayed by one of their own guides, tamely surrendered outside the walls of the city. Gen. Manuel Armijo, the governor of the Mexican state of New Mexico, then offered Navarro his freedom if he would attest his loyalty to Mexico once again. Upon his refusal, the Texas commissioner set out on the march to Mexico City with the rest of the prisoners.

Incarcerated under extremely harsh conditions in Mexico City, Navarro was held for two months and then brought to trial on a charge equivalent to treason. Sentenced to death, the verdict was set aside on appeal to a higher court and reduced to life imprisonment. This finding so angered Santa Anna that he had Navarro transferred to Mexico's most brutal dungeon prison, San Juan de Ulloa at Veracruz. Held for 14 months and, on occasion, near death, Navarro was ultimately paroled upon condition that he remain in the vicinity of Veracruz. He then escaped by taking passage on a British ship bound for Havana. From there, he made his way to New Orleans and to Texas, returning to a hero's welcome.

Virtually from the time of independence, Navarro had been a strong proponent of annexation to the United States. He was aware of the military shortcomings of the Republic as demonstrated in the failures of the Santa Fe and Mier episodes and also of the persistent financial problems that beset Texas. As a state in the Union, the defense of the frontier against Indian attack would be improved, and new economic opportunities were expected to come after annexation. While he did not campaign actively, his sentiments were well known, and Navarro was selected as the only native Mexican delegate to the convention of July 1845 held at Austin. There he voted for annexation and remained to help write the first state constitution.

Despite protests that he wished to return to private life, Navarro was elected a senator from the 18th district to the First and Second state Legislatures. As a testimony to his service to Texas over many years, in April 1846, the Legislature created Navarro County. The infant community of Corsicana was designated as the county seat and named for Navarro's father's birthplace, the island of Corsica. In 1849, Navarro declined to run again for the state Legislature and, returning to San Antonio, devoted himself to his varied interests. Maintaining a general store, practicing law and speculating in land filled his days. His marriage, contracted in 1825 to Margarita de la Garza, had proved a constant source of happiness to him. Seven children were born to their union, and Navarro easily turned from politics to the rearing and educating of his family.

During the decade of the 1850s, Texans found themselves increasingly preoccupied with their relation to the federal Union. In 1854, Navarro joined in the general condemnation of Sen. Sam Houston's vote against the Kansas-Nebraska Act. As a Roman Catholic, he also was opposed to Houston's association with the Know-Nothing Party in Texas. Then the implications for the

South of John Brown's raid at Harper's Ferry edged him further along the path of state sovereignty. Navarro supported John Breckinridge in the presidential election of 1860 while dissenting from Gov. Houston's position that he would not advocate secession. Navarro was an enthusiastic defender of secession, and all four of his sons fought for the Confederate army.

Navarro passed away of natural causes on Jan. 13, 1871. His wife had preceded him in death, and in 1936 the Texas Centennial Commission placed a joint monument at their graves in the San Fernando Cemetery, No. 1, San Antonio. His career spanned a half-century of Texas history commencing with the Mexican Revolution of 1810 and culminating with disunion in 1861. As a signer of the Declaration of Independence, and an architect of the Republic and state constitutions, Navarro left a record of accomplishments rarely matched.

Elisabet Ney

This article was written by Mrs. Emily F. Cutrer, Assistant Instructor of American Studies, University of Texas at Austin.

During the fall of 1892, the German-born sculptor Elisabet Ney built and moved into a studio named Formosa on the outskirts of Austin. That move, her friend, supporter and early biographer Bride Neill Taylor would later claim, marked "a new era in the development of the state," one which saw the emergence of Texas from a cultural frontier with little need or appreciation for the visual arts to a society increasingly aware of painting and sculpture and their importance to the community.

When Ney opened her Austin studio, only a handful of professional artists made their homes in Texas. But upon her death in 1907, a number of prominent painters and sculptors lived and worked in the state, several cities had the beginnings of museums, and public places, as well as private homes, displayed the work of artists who called themselves Texans.

Elisabet Ney was hardly the sole, or even main, cause of this blossoming of artistic activity, yet her biography is a significant chapter in the story of the state's cultural development. Not only did her presence in the state help nurture an interest in public art and raise the aesthetic value of that work, but her life and career are representative of the problems and concerns faced by Texas' first professional artists.

As were a number of other early artists in the state — Richard Petri, Hermann Lungkwitz and Theodore Gentilz, for example — Elisabet Ney was European by birth and training. Born in Munster, Westphalia, on Jan. 26, 1833, into the family of a prosperous stonecarver, Ney decided at an early age to become a sculptor. With only the grudging consent of her parents, she left home at the age of 19 and became one of the first women to enroll in the prestigious Munich Academy of Art. Two years later, she moved to Berlin to study with one of the most famous sculptors of the time, Christian Daniel Rauch. Her sculpture clearly shows the effect of this mentor's training. In general, it combines a neoclassic approach to form, scale and material with naturalistic detail, and thus is typical of academic work produced throughout the 19th century.

No one has been able to document exactly why Ney left Europe in 1870. She may have been involved in the political intrigue surrounding Bismarck's attempts to unify Germany under Prussian domination and was forced to flee or, influenced by Utopian thinking, she may have wanted to try a new and simpler lifestyle. Perhaps both precipitated the move. After two years in Georgia, her first home in the New World, however, she and her husband of eight years, a physician named Edmund Montgomery, purchased Liendo Plantation near Hempstead, Texas, in 1873. For more than 10 years, Ney made little attempt to resume her career. Instead she devoted her time to running the plantation and raising her one surviving son, Lorne Ney Montgomery.

When Ney did try to resume her work in the 1880s, she found that the state was not a promising market for a professional sculptor. What demands existed usually were filled by the stonemasons in the larger cities who could provide polished marble and granite, precast figures to serve any number of purposes and the minimum of carving needed for gravestones and small monuments.

Ney did not receive a commission until 1892 when a group of women decided not only that Texas must have a building at the World's Columbian Exposition, which was scheduled to open in Chicago the following year, but also that this structure should be decorated with portraits of the state's heroes. Thanks to her friend, former Gov. Oran Roberts, Ney was asked to produce two statues, one of Sam Houston, the other of Stephen F. Austin, for the Texas Building at the World's Fair.

That commission marked the beginning of a prolific, new career for Ney. She built her Austin studio, and after completing the statues of Houston and Austin, she began producing numerous portrait busts of great Texans, among them Lawrence Sullivan Ross, Francis R. Lubbock, John H. Reagan and Joseph D. Sayers. She worked with women's organizations, such as the Daughters of the Republic of Texas, to see that her statues of Austin and Houston were placed in both the state and national capitols where they remain today. Thanks to the effort of the United Daughters of the Confederacy, she obtained from the state Legislature a commission for a memorial to Albert Sidney Johnston erected over his grave in the State Cemetery at Austin. Although she was unsuccessful in her attempts to obtain commissions for major public monuments or to establish an art department at the University of Texas, two of her fondest hopes, Ney's studio was a mecca for that part of the Austin community that enjoyed good art and conversation.

Ney attracted attention, however, as much for her seemingly eccentric lifestyle as for her art. Using her maiden name, wearing unusual artist's attire and living in a simple, classically inspired studio among ornate Victorian homes, she was a source of gossip for those who were not among her small circle of friends and supporters. The public's misunderstanding of her lifestyle caused her great distress. "Except for my few friends," she wrote one of her supporters in disgust, "I might have fancied myself to have been drifted among the . . . Bushmen while I was in Austin."

Nevertheless, she remained committed to Texas and the development of its cultural institutions. On a return voyage from Europe she wrote, "Though I am truly void of what one would call patriotism . . . the appellation of *Texas* has a charm of a peculiar kind, such as the name of no other part of the wide earth."

Ney died in Austin on June 29, 1907, and was buried at Liendo. Shortly after her death, Ella Dancy Dibrell of Seguin, an active supporter and patron of Ney during the final years of her life, purchased the Austin studio and part of its surrounding grounds in order to establish an Elisabet Ney Museum. She also gathered together many of Ney's friends and supporters to found the Texas Fine Arts Association whose purpose was not only to maintain the museum, but also to promote the growth of fine arts in the state. Although the TFAA and the Elisabet Ney Museum are no longer associated, they both are active contributors to the development of the arts in Texas.

Chester W. Nimitz

This article was written by Mr. Robert S. Weddle, M.A., Author of four books, Bonham, Texas.

Chester William Nimitz, who led Allied forces to victory in the Pacific in World War II, was born at Fredericksburg, on Feb. 24, 1885, the son of Chester Bernard and Anna Henke Nimitz. His father died before he was born. During his early years, his grandfather Charles H. Nimitz—a German immigrant, former seaman and owner of the Nimitz Hotel—served as the father figure whom Nimitz often credited with shaping his character and values.

In 1890, Chester's mother married her late husband's younger brother, William Nimitz, and they moved to Kerrville, where the stepfather-uncle managed the St. Charles Hotel. Chester, in doing the numerous hotel chores demanded of him, acquired the discipline that served him throughout his career as a naval officer.

The hotel business was not lucrative, and young Nimitz saw little opportunity for college. At age 15, he planned to become, through apprenticeship, a surveyor, but a suggestion that he seek appointment to the

U.S. Military Academy changed his direction. On learning that no such appointment would be available for several years, he applied for the U.S. Naval Academy instead. He graduated seventh in his class of 114 at Annapolis on Jan. 30, 1905.

After two years' training as a passed midshipman aboard the *U.S.S. Ohio*, he was commissioned an ensign and given his first command, the old Spanish gunboat *Panay* in the Philippines. Soon transferred to the *Decatur*, Nimitz ran the old four-stack destroyer aground in Batangas Bay (Philippines), bringing upon himself court-martial and reprimand. Under the shadow of the incident, he was denied his request for battleship duty and was assigned instead to a submarine. Though disappointed, the young officer built in four consecutive undersea commands a reservoir of experience that proved invaluable in both world wars, when submarines were crucial to the defense effort. By age 27, Nimitz had earned command of the entire Atlantic submarine force and was becoming a leading "pigboat" authority.

In 1913, he married Miss Catherine Vance Freeman of Wollaston, Ma. The couple was to have three daughters and a son. Shortly after the honeymoon, they left for Europe, where he studied diesel engines in Germany and Belgium. Nimitz returned to Brooklyn Navy Yard to supervise the building and installation of the first diesel engine to power a U.S. Navy vessel.

With the rank of commander in World War I, the Texan served as chief of staff to Adm. Samuel S. Robison, who commanded the Atlantic Submarine Force. Later he was executive officer of the U.S. battleship *South Carolina*, transporting troops back to the United States. Afterward, he went to Pearl Harbor to build the submarine base and command Submarine Division 14.

Between wars, Nimitz progressed through the various steps prescribed by the Navy for training its commanders. At the Navy War College, 1922-1923, he dealt with a theoretical Pacific war, developing the plan that eventually was put to practical use. The next three years, he served again as chief of staff to Adm. Robison, who during that time became commander-in-chief of the U.S. Fleet.

In what appeared to be a "backwater" assignment, he went to the University of California at Berkeley in 1926 to develop the prototype for the Naval Reserve Officers Training Corps. The model was duplicated in 52 colleges and universities. In June 1927, 22 years after leaving the academy, Nimitz was promoted to the rank of captain.

Leaving Berkeley in 1929, he commanded Submarine Division 20 at San Diego. Then came command of the *U.S.S. Rigel* and the San Diego destroyer base and, in 1933, the cruiser *Augusta*, flagship of the Asiatic Fleet. After service in Washington as assistant chief of the Navy's Bureau of Navigation, he at last acquired flag rank (rear admiral) and took command first of a cruiser division then a battleship division of the Battle Force. In 1939, he became chief of the Bureau of Navigation. Had he not been committed to the four-year assignment, Nimitz probably would have been chosen instead of Adm. Husband E. Kimmel as commander-in-chief of the Pacific Fleet (CinCPac); it might have been the Texan's career that ended with Japan's surprise attack on Pearl Harbor on

Dec. 7, 1941, instead of Kimmel's.

As the United States geared for war, Nimitz traveled incognito from Washington to arrive at Pearl Harbor on Christmas Day 1941 as Kimmel's replacement. In their unavoidably painful meeting, Nimitz was sympathetic, telling Kimmel, "The same thing could have happened to me." On taking command with the five-star rank of fleet admiral, he recognized his major task as combatting the tendency of both public and military to reflect on American mistakes that had permitted the disaster and brought the United States into World War II. He focused instead on the mistakes of the enemy and the positive aspects of the American position: The Pearl Harbor submarine base remained intact, and the aircraft carriers, which had been at sea on Dec. 7, had been spared.

From the nerve center at CinCPac headquarters, Nimitz directed these forces to action. With the carrier-based Doolittle raid on Japanese cities in April 1942 and victories in the Coral Sea and at Midway Island, confidence was restored, and allied forces seized the initiative. Nimitz was named commander-in-chief of Pacific Ocean Areas (CinCPOA), in addition to his Pacific Fleet command. With authority over the entire Pacific theater except for Gen. Douglas MacArthur's Southwest Pacific sector and the inactive southeast, he contributed the leadership and coordinated the offensive that brought the Japanese to unconditional surrender. Nimitz signed the peace treaty for the United States aboard the battleship *Missouri* in Tokyo Bay on Sept. 2, 1945.

Given a hero's welcome in the United States, the wartime leader was awarded numerous medals and commendations by foreign governments. From his own, he wore both the Army and Navy Distinguished Service medals.

On Dec. 15, 1945, Nimitz succeeded Adm. Ernest J. King as commander-in-chief of the U.S. Fleet and withdrew after two years. Never officially retired, he was assigned to "duty as directed by the Secretary of Navy." Among other activities, he served the United Nations as roving ambassador, was a regent of the University of California, and, by appointment of President Harry Truman, became chairman of the Presidential Commission on Internal Security and Individual Rights. He also worked to re-establish good will between the United States and Japan, raising funds to restore Adm. Heihachiro Togo's flagship.

After being injured in a severe fall in 1963, the admiral moved with his wife from their house in Berkeley to naval quarters on Treasure Island in San Francisco Bay. In January 1966, he suffered a stroke and died on Feb. 20. He was buried in Golden Gate National Cemetery, San Bruno, Ca.

In 1964, a local citizen group established the Fleet Admiral Chester W. Nimitz Memorial Naval Museum in the old Nimitz Hotel at Fredericksburg. The project evolved into the state-supported Admiral Nimitz Center and thence into the Admiral Nimitz State Historical Park. Besides the memorabilia and multimedia displays pertaining to World War II, the park includes the Japanese Peace Garden, a Bicentennial gift from Japan in 1976.

Sam Rayburn

This article was written by Dr. Edward Phillips Professor Emeritus of History, Austin College.

Texas has sent many capable legislators and statesmen to Washington. None carved a more enviable record for vision, integrity and leadership than Samuel Taliaferro Rayburn.

This statesman-to-be was born Jan. 30, 1882, near Lenoir, Roane County, Tn., the eighth of 11 children born to William Marion and Martha Waller Rayburn. His father, a poor, illiterate farmer, had served four years in the Confederate Army. His mother was from a more prestigious, politically active family from Virginia and Tennessee.

In 1887, Will Rayburn sold his 40-acre farm and moved his family to Fannin County, Texas, where he purchased 40 acres of cotton land at Flag Springs, south of Windom. Here young Sam grew up, worked hard at farm chores and got the basics of a sound education from the local one-room school.

In 1900, young Rayburn entered East Texas Normal College, left the next year to teach, then returned to

finish his degree in 1903. He taught at Greenwood, Dial and Lannius in East Texas before starting a new career in politics. In 1906, he was elected to the state Legislature from Fannin County and served through 1912. While serving in the Legislature he attended the University of Texas Law School, leaving for lack of funds in 1908 but completing his studies in the law office of Thurmond and Steger in Bonham.

Though admitted to the bar, Rayburn practiced little law, for his heart was in politics. In 1911, he was elected Speaker of the 32nd Legislature and presided ably over one of the most turbulent sessions since Reconstruction. In 1912, he ran for Congress to fill the seat vacated by Choice B. Randell. He was victor in the primary despite getting just 23 percent of the vote but won handily in November.

On April 7, 1913, Sam Rayburn was sworn in as a member of the House of Representatives and continued to serve in that body until his death 48 years later. Though somewhat a Populist, he supported much of Woodrow Wilson's domestic and foreign programs. Appointed early to the House Committee on Interstate and Foreign Commerce, he won the president's praise by authoring a bill to regulate the stocks and bonds of railroads. He also sponsored the War Risk Insurance Act that provided death benefits to survivors of servicemen lost in World War I. Never an isolationist, Rayburn supported Wilson's League of Nations but watched its defeat and with fellow Democrats had to endure Republican ascendancy throughout the 1920s.

The Great Depression brought the Democrats back into power. In 1931, Rayburn became chairman of the Interstate and Foreign Commerce Committee. After swinging the support of delegates pledged to fellow-Texan John Nance Garner to Franklin Roosevelt at the 1932 national Democratic convention, Rayburn became a leading power in the New Deal. In 1933, he sponsored the Truth-in-Securities Act and the Railroad Rehabilitation Act, and, two years later, guided through the House the acts that established the Securities and Exchange Commission and the Federal Communications Commission. In 1935, he got passage of the vital Rural Electrification Act and the Public Utility Holding Company Act, both strongly contested by the utilities lobby.

Rayburn was recognized for his leadership in January 1937 by being selected Majority Leader in the House. Three years later, Sept. 16, 1940, he succeeded to the speakership at the death of William Bankhead. For the next 21 years, Sam Rayburn held the post of Speaker except for the 80th and 83rd Congresses (1947-1949 and 1953-1955) when the Republicans controlled the House.

As Speaker, Rayburn exercised much power, and his influence increased with each session. As World War II approached, the Texan gave strong support to the defense program and boldly gaveled down an attempt to defeat the extension of Selective Service shortly before Pearl Harbor. During the war, he made every effort to provide the servicemen (and women) with all the material resources they needed to win the conflict in the shortest time. He got sufficient funds from the House for the Manhattan (atomic bomb) project even though he could not tell the members what the funds were for. His reputation for integrity was assurance enough.

He encouraged the establishment of the United Nations and strongly supported assistance to countries resisting communist aggression. When Republican Dwight D. Eisenhower occupied the White House, Sam Rayburn supported the administration's foreign policy and made bi-partisanship a reality in that field. In 1948, 1952 and 1956, he chaired the Democratic National Convention and won acclaim from the new television audiences. In 1960, he relinquished this role to work for the nomination of his protege, Lyndon B. Johnson. When Johnson lost the nomination, Rayburn unhesitatingly supported young John F. Kennedy, campaigned strongly for him and worked hard for his New Frontier programs in the 87th Congress.

In September 1961, illness forced the Speaker to return to Bonham where he died of cancer on Nov. 16. His death was marked with unprecedented tributes. Presidents Truman, Eisenhower and Kennedy and President-to-be Johnson attended the funeral in Bonham along with a great delegation from Congress and the nation.

A moderate and pragmatist, Sam Rayburn believed in compromise and common sense. He was ever loyal to the Democratic Party, strongly opposing the Dixiecrats and Shivercrats who bolted the party in presidential elections. Except for a three-month marriage in 1928, he was a lifelong bachelor. Rayburn retained close ties with his brothers and sisters and their children, and he never outgrew his attachment to Bonham, returning there whenever Congress was in recess and disdaining to go on junkets or travel abroad. Compiling no fortune, he lived frugally though comfortably and gained an enviable reputation for honesty and integrity. He guarded special Texas interests, particularly the Tidelands and the oil depletion allowance, and he was ever considerate of the needs of the farmer, sponsoring REA and farm-to-market roads and promoting crop subsidies. His vision, however, was remarkably national and international. One of the nation's most powerful legislators, he must also rank as one of its best.

John Henninger Reagan

This article was written by Dr. Ben Procter, Professor of History, Texas Christian University.

Born on Oct. 8, 1818, in the shadow of the Smoky Mountains in Sevier County, Tn., John Henninger Reagan was the eldest son of Timothy Richard and Elizabeth Reagan. His early life was not unlike that of many young men who grew to maturity in early 19th century frontier America.

But in 1834, Reagan, whose desire for education and learning permeated his life, decided to follow his ambitions. After a year of "hiring out" to a local planter, he attended Boyd's Creek Academy for 15 months. When funds ran low, he worked so that in 1837 he could study for a year at Southwestern Seminary in Maryville.

In 1838, Reagan left Tennessee to seek greater monetary gain. Briefly he managed a plantation near Natchez before being lured to Texas where a job, supposedly at Nacogdoches, awaited him. Soon after arrival, however, he became involved in the Cherokee War.

For the next two years, Reagan worked as a deputy surveyor and frontier scout before being elected a justice of the peace and captain of a militia company in Nacogdoches. After studying law for several years, he procured a temporary law license in 1846 and opened an office at Buffalo on the Trinity River.

In April 1846, he was elected the first county judge of Henderson County. The next year he became a member of the Second Legislature of Texas. Reagan lost a legislative election in 1849, but in 1852, he won a special election for a district judgeship.

After 1855, Reagan became more prominent. In East Texas, he helped the Democratic Party defeat the surging Know-Nothing Party, thereby contributing to his re-election as judge in 1856, as well as to his own personal popularity. Consequently in the summer of 1857, the Democrats nominated and elected him congressman from the Eastern District of Texas. In Washington he attended to his constituents' needs and dealt with the disruptive forces loosed by "Bleeding Kansas." He soon became fearful for the safety of the Union and in 1859, together with Sam Houston who was running for governor, campaigned for the principles of Union against Southern firebrand opponents. Both men

won impressive victories.

After John Brown attacked the federal arsenal at Harper's Ferry, Va., on Oct. 16, 1859, all hope of Union vanished, at least as far as Reagan was concerned. With Republicans in the House inexorably opposed to Southerners no matter what the issue — and in control — and with Southern Rights men equally adamant, any hope of compromise was remote. Then with the election of Abraham Lincoln in November 1860, the breakup of the Union began. On Jan. 15, 1861, Reagan resigned his congressional seat.

Two weeks later, Reagan returned to Texas and for the next four years served the Confederate States of America. In Austin on Jan. 30, 1861, he attended the Texas Secession Convention, met specifically with Gov. Houston, and persuaded him to "submit to the will of the people" and recognize the convention. As a result, Texas withdrew from the Union on Feb. 2, and two days later, delegates elected Reagan as one of the state's seven representatives to the Secession Convention in Montgomery, Ala. Within a month, Reagan was appointed Postmaster General of the Confederacy, whereupon he raided the United States Post Office of its documents and Southern personnel. Upon the transfer of the Confederate capital to Richmond, Va., late in the spring of 1861, he sought ways to make his department self-sufficient by March 1, 1863, as prescribed by the Confederate Constitution. He therefore abolished the franking privilege and raised postal rates. He also cut expenses to the bare minimum by eliminating costly routes, inducing competition for mail runs and employing a smaller but efficient staff. He was even able to persuade railroad executives to cut transportation charges in half and accept Confederate bonds in whole or partial payment. Although such stringent measures were necessary, the public became dissatisfied, harshly and abusively criticizing Reagan, despite the fact that Union armies had disrupted routes, had demolished postal facilities and had interrupted mail with increasing frequency.

On April 2, 1865, the end of the Confederacy was at hand. President Jefferson Davis and his cabinet were forced to flee southward from Richmond. For five weeks the Confederate government eluded Union patrols in both North and South Carolina. After Secretary of the Treasury George A. Trenholm resigned on April 27, Reagan was thereafter entrusted with the duties of the Treasury Department — but not for long. On May 9, near Abbeville, Ga., Jefferson Davis, former Texas Gov. Francis R. Lubbock and Reagan were captured.

The harsh realities of losing awaited the Confederate leaders. On May 25, 1865, Reagan, along with Vice President Alexander H. Stephens of Georgia, was sent to Fort Warren in Boston harbor. For the next 22 weeks, Reagan was imprisoned in solitary confinement. After reading Northern journals and newspapers, which revealed the depth of animosity and bitterness for the South, he wrote an open communication to the people of Texas on Aug. 11. In this Fort Warren letter, he appealed to Texans, as conquered people, to recognize the authority of the United States, renounce immediately both secession and slavery (which had been decided by force of arms), and, if demanded by the federal government, extend the "elective franchise" to former slaves; otherwise, he predicted, Texas would face the "twin disasters" of military despotism and universal Negro suffrage. After obtaining release from Fort Warren and returning to Texas early in December 1865, Reagan discovered that most Texans had politically disinherited him because of the Fort Warren letter. He therefore retired to Fort Houston, his family home at Palestine, and farmed his neglected fields.

But when the First Reconstruction Act of March 2, 1867, went into effect and thereby confirmed his prophecies of military rule and Negro suffrage, Reagan became known as the "Old Roman," a modern-day Cincinnatus who had sacrificed popularity and political power in behalf of his fellow Texans. Consequently he once again assumed a position as a state leader. And although Republican E. J. Davis became governor in 1870, Reagan and other Democrats worked to regain power and restore political harmony to the state. On Jan. 19, 1874, they forced Davis to surrender the governorship. In the meantime, Reagan was granted amnesty by the federal government and had full citizenship restored. In 1874, he received the Democratic nomination for the First Congressional District and was easily elected.

From 1875 to 1887, Reagan served in Congress but also participated in state politics. In 1875, he was a delegate to the Texas Constitutional Convention, which framed the Constitution of 1876. But, more importantly, he led a 12-year fight in Congress to regulate railroads. Despite formidable opposition from these powerful corporations, he enacted into law the Interstate Commerce Act of 1887.

As further appreciation for his legislative record, the Legislature elevated Reagan to the U. S. Senate in January 1887. But before the end of his term he changed jobs. Because good friend Gov. James Stephen Hogg had run on a platform of state regulation of railroads, Reagan was persuaded to resign his Senate seat and accept the chairmanship of the newly formed Texas Railroad Commission. Although attempting unsuccessfully to obtain the Democratic nomination for governor in 1894, Reagan remained chairman of the Railroad Commission until his retirement in January 1903. His tenure provided the leadership and prestige so necessary to the early years of this extremely powerful state regulatory body.

In the latter part of his life Reagan was much concerned about preserving history as well as his heritage. In 1897, he helped found the Texas State Historical Association. On a number of occasions he attended meetings of the Confederate veterans throughout the state. And after retirement in 1903, he worked for two years to complete his *Memoirs*.

On March 6, 1905, the "Old Roman" of Texas died of pneumonia and was buried in Palestine. Throughout his life he had remained true to his convictions; he had fought for the people of Texas, despite personal or political consequences. To Texas and the South, such actions made him a statesman, even a prophet; and even in his own country, in death as in life, he was not without honor.

Thomas Jefferson Rusk

This article was written by Dr. J. Milton Nance, Professor of History, Texas A&M University.

One of the most popular, effective and patriotic leaders of the Republic and during the early statehood of Texas was Thomas Jefferson Rusk. Of Scotch-Irish ancestry, he was born Dec. 5, 1803, in the Pendleton District of South Carolina, the first son of John and Mary (Sterritt) Rusk.

One of seven children, Rusk's formal education was limited to the little country school in the area. But the schooling laid the foundation for self-education and development of an excellent command of the English language as reflected later in his speeches and writings.

John C. Calhoun, a family friend upon whose land the Rusk's lived, took great interest in young Rusk, urging him to study law. Calhoun even let Rusk work in his law office, where the youngster trained under one of the best lawyers in the country. After obtaining his law license, Rusk in 1825 moved to Habersham County, Ga., where he soon developed a successful law practice.

Rusk married Mary F. "Polly" Cleveland in 1827. She had very little education, but proved to be a wonderful, understanding wife and devoted mother. Her father, John Cleveland, was a prominent merchant, landowner and member for 20 years of the Georgia legislature. Rusk soon became a partner with his father-in-law in the mercantile business.

Rusk came to Texas in 1834 in pursuit of two swindlers who had taken money from him and his in-laws, leaving him in dire financial straits. At Nacogdoches he met Sam Houston. The two quickly developed a lasting friendship, although they sometimes publicly and bitterly criticized each other. Houston took Rusk before the local alcalde on Feb. 11, 1835, where the newcomer took an oath of allegiance to Mexico, became a citizen and declared that his occupation was farming and stock raising. As a citizen and man of family, he was entitled to receive a league and a labor of land. A few days later, he wrote to his wife that he intended to move to Texas to live. He believed that there was a wonderful opportunity in Texas for the practice of law since there were so few men of legal talent in the area. He urged his brother, David, to bring Polly and the children to Texas as soon as possible.

Rusk soon became embroiled in Texas-Mexican politics. On one occasion, the alcalde invited those attending a meeting to speak freely. Rusk did so, and after the meeting, the alcalde ordered him arrested. But the Americans prevented the alcalde from carrying out the order. Thereafter, Rusk was identified with the liberal element critical of Mexican rule in Texas. Rusk served in the Texas army during the revolution and was a member of the Convention of 1836 and signed the document that declared Texas' independence from Mexico. Interim President David Burnet appointed Rusk Secretary of War, and he joined Houston during the latter days of the Runaway Scrape. When Houston was wounded during the Battle of San Jacinto, Rusk assumed field command of the troops, and many historians thought that he was the true hero of the battle.

During the next two decades, Rusk assumed a range of responsibilities for the Republic and the early state of Texas. Among many other duties, he served as a member of the Second Congress of the Republic, was Chief Justice of the Supreme Court of Texas and was president of the Convention of 1845 that accepted annexation and drafted the first state constitution of Texas. The Legislature twice elected Rusk to the U. S. Senate, where he represented Texas well from 1846 to 1857.

While in the Senate, Rusk secured incorporation of Texas naval officers and equipment into the U. S. Navy, obtained a large appropriation to explore for artesian wells on the plains of Texas, worked to secure a wagon road from El Paso to California, and a railroad across Texas from the Dallas-Fort Worth area to El Paso; and to improve mail lines, mail stages, fortifications, roads, river navigation and telegraph communications in Texas. Rusk was urged to be a Democratic candidate for president in 1852 and 1856 and was offered the position of Postmaster General by President James Buchanan in March 1857. In the same month, he was elected President pro tempore of the U.S. Senate, and for a short time presided over the upper house.

But Rusk suffered from personal problems. Upon return home to Nacogdoches in April 1857, he was not in the best of health. He missed his wife Polly who died on April 23, 1856. Rusk had been a heavy drinker but had moderated while in Washington. A distressed state of mind developed. The only public office that he had ever held for any length of time, which paid a reasonably good and

Sam Rayburn

John H. Reagan

Thomas J. Rusk

Ashbel Smith

Photo Credits

Photos of Reagan, Rusk, Smith, Travis and Zavala from Texas State Archives, Austin; Rayburn, Webb and Zaharias from Dallas Morning News files.

William B. Travis

Walter P. Webb

Babe Zaharias

Lorenzo de Zavala

regular salary, was that of U.S. Senator. Most others he had accepted and then resigned after a short time. One could not blame a family man of modest means for not holding office long in the Republic when the pay was low and uncertain. He brooded and kept much to himself. Then like several other Texas leaders before him, Rusk committed suicide on July 29, 1857, at age 53, and was buried beside his wife in Oak Grove Cemetery, Nacogdoches.

In the untimely death of this great man, Texas and the United States both suffered a heavy loss. He was simple in manner, generous, courageous, republican in tastes, candid, fair, just and honest in all things. He was a soldier from a sense of duty, fearless and strong in battle. He was a man of great intellect without ambition and pride, but one who was always ready to serve his country when needed. Rusk was an affectionate father and noble husband. His greatest weakness was drinking to excess.

During his lifetime he became a universally popular figure in Texas. Rusk stood at the top among the great men of the Republic of Texas and pre-Civil War Texas. On the national scene he was a man of great promise. In a decade at the nation's capital, he had grown in favor and wisdom, and had become one of the most popular Senators in Washington. As John S. Ford wrote, "(Rusk) was an acknowledged power in the land — a ruler of Israel. The lawyer, the statesman, the general, the patriotic citizen, the steadfast friend, had the heart-felt esteem of all who knew him. He was the only man in Texas who could show the shadow of a claim as the peer of General Houston in the esteem, admiration and love of the people."

Ashbel Smith

This article was written by Ms. Elizabeth Silverthorne, free-lance writer and author, Salado, Texas.

Ashbel Smith has been called the "Father of Texas medicine" and the "Father of the University of Texas." During the almost half-century he lived in Texas, he made valuable contributions to his adopted state not only in the fields of medicine and education, but also in politics, agriculture, stock raising, warfare, finance, transportation, immigration and as a writer.

When Smith arrived in Texas in 1837, expecting to practice medicine and perhaps to speculate in land, he was better trained than most doctors in the 19th century. Born in Hartford, Conn., he attended the excellent public schools there and then went on to obtain three degrees from Yale. He had an additional year of medical training in Paris, which was the mecca for the most brilliant scientists in the world at that time.

During the disastrous cholera epidemic of 1832 in Paris, Smith helped treat the victims. When the epidemic subsided, he wrote a pamphlet on the disease. His ideas were well-received by medical experts, and he was considered an authority on cholera.

In Texas, Smith soon numbered among his patients most of the leaders of the Republic, including Sam Houston, David Burnet, James Pinckney Henderson, Mirabeau B. Lamar — and their families. He was appointed surgeon general of the Texas Army by the Texas Congress. In this capacity, he set up an efficient system of operation for the medical branch of the army and established the first hospital in Houston.

During the terrible 1839 epidemic of yellow fever in Galveston, Smith treated victims and published factual reports of the progress of the disease with advice to the public on how to take care of their health during the plague. From his case notes and observations, he wrote the first treatise on yellow fever in Texas.

To fight medical quackery in Texas, Ashbel Smith worked to establish a Board of Medical Censors and served as its first chairman. In 1848, he met with 10 other Galveston doctors to form the Medical and Surgical Society of Galveston. For five years, he worked within this group and on his own to organize the Texas Medical Association. He was chairman of the committee that drafted the constitution and bylaws of the TMA, and in 1882, he served as its president. When the Texas Medical College and Hospital was organized in 1873, he was elected president of the board of trustees.

Politics always fascinated Smith. Before he came to Texas, he had been involved in politics in North Carolina, where he was practicing medicine. On his arrival in Texas, Smith became Sam Houston's roommate and close friend. Recognizing his friend's diplomatic ability, Sam Houston used him as a commissioner to negotiate peace treaties with Texas Indians.

In 1842, Houston sent Smith to Europe as the Republic's charge d'affaires to England and France, where his fluency in French was invaluable. During the two years he served in this position, Smith represented Texas ably.

When Anson Jones became president of the Republic, he appointed Smith as his secretary of state. Smith worked with Jones to give Texans a choice between remaining independent or joining the United States. To this end, he negotiated an agreement, called the Smith-Cuervas Treaty, with Mexico by which that country finally recognized the independence of Texas.

After Texas became a state, Smith served in the state Legislature three times as a representative from Harris County. As a lawmaker, he worked on measures to encourage railroad building in Texas, to encourage immigration, to improve common schools and to pay off the public debt.

Smith was one of the founders of the Democratic Party in Texas. He held offices at the county and state levels and went as a delegate to several national Democratic conventions.

In addition to serving as surgeon general of the army, Smith served Texas twice more in military roles. During the Mexican War, he was on active duty with Gen. Zachary Taylor in Mexico. When the Civil War began, despite his northern heritage and his age (56), he entered the Confederate service. At Galveston Bay, he organized a company, which included one of Sam Houston's sons and two of Anson Jones'. As captain, he drilled and trained this company, the Bayland Guards, and led them into battle at Shiloh. During this fight, he was seriously wounded. Cited for bravery and promoted to full colonel, he was named commander of the Second Texas Infantry. He led this group in several engagements in Mississippi. During the siege of Vicksburg, he was in command of one of the most vulnerable forts, located at the entrance to the city. Following the surrender of Vicksburg, he was in charge of several positions on the Gulf Coast of Texas in the vicinity of Matagorda Peninsula and was credited with preventing union invasions in that area. Toward the end of the war, he was put in charge of the defenses of Galveston. When the war ended, Gov. Pendleton Murrah sent him as one of the two commissioners from Texas to negotiate peace terms for Texas with Union officials in New Orleans.

From the day he arrived in Texas, Smith began observing and writing letters and articles about the climate, topography, soil, vegetation and wildlife. Soon after his arrival, he established a plantation, Evergreen, on Galveston Bay, and became an experimenter and innovator in raising crops and livestock. He was interested in cross-breeding cattle and in discovering which kinds of sheep did best on the Gulf Coast. He grew different varieties of cotton; raised sugar cane from which he made sugar and molasses; and he tried growing various kinds of grapes, from which he made wine.

He was superintendent of the first Texas state fair, held in Corpus Christi in 1852. And he was elected the first president of the Texas State Agricultural Society when it was formed in 1853.

Smith's ability in judging agricultural products and livestock was recognized internationally. In 1851, he was a Texas delegate to the Great London Exhibition at the Crystal Palace. In 1876, he was a judge at the Great International Exhibition in Philadelphia. In 1878, he was named by President Rutherford B. Hayes to be one of the two honorary commissioners from Texas to represent the United States at the Paris International Exposition, where he served as a judge.

Of Smith's many interests, education was the cause closest to his heart. He often urged that Texas should underwrite the education of every one of its children. He also championed education for Negroes and for women. He was an organizer and charter member of many groups, such as the Philosophical Society of Texas and the Texas Literary Institute, whose aims were to promote public eduction in Texas. He served as the superintendent of the Houston Academy and as the trustee on a number of school boards in Houston, Galveston and Austin. He was one of three commissioners appointed by Gov. Richard Coke to establish an "Agricultural and Mechanical College of Texas, for the benefit of the Colored Youths," near Hempstead.

Smith's last years were spent in a tremendous burst of energy and a sustained effort to establish a great state university with a first class medical branch. As president of the first board of regents of the University of Texas, he worked sometimes against strenuous opposition to recruit the best professors available and to set up a curriculum worthy of a first-rate school.

He was a powerful orator and an indefatigable writer. His speeches and writings were published as chapters in books and in scientific, agricultural, educational and general magazines, journals and newspapers in the United States and in Europe.

Smith never married, although he had many romances in his life. When he died on Jan. 21, 1886, at Evergreen, he was given a state funeral and buried in the State Cemetery in Austin, with all the honors his adopted state could confer.

William B. Travis

This article was written by Dr. Archie P. McDonald, Professor of History, Stephen F. Austin State University.

When a handful of Texas patriots died at the Alamo, their commander was William B. Travis, one of the most courageous and enigmatic figures in the state's history.

Travis, born Aug. 9, 1809, was the eldest of 11 children of Mark and Jemima Stallworth Travis of Saluda County, S. C. His boyhood centered around the work of the family farm, attendance at the Red Bank Church, home schooling and play with area children. James Butler Bonham, who also served in the defense of the Alamo, was one of these. The Travis family moved to Conecuh County, Alabama, in 1818. There they helped found the communities of Sparta and Evergreen. After attending local schools, Travis read law under James Dellet and became a practicing attorney in Claiborne, Ala.

On Oct. 26, 1828, Travis married Rosanna Cato, one of his former students. Their first child, Charles Edward, was born in August 1829. For a year, young Travis appeared to intend to remain in Claiborne. But he abruptly abandoned his wife, son and unborn daughter (Susan Isabella) and departed. Travis' motives for leaving are obscure, but a story persisted that he killed a man before his departure.

Travis arrived in Texas in the summer of 1831 after the Mexican Law of April 6, 1830, made his immigration illegal. He visited San Felipe de Austin on May 21 and obtained land from Stephen F. Austin. Travis also established a legal practice in Anahuac, a significant port of entry on Galveston Bay. He traveled the country doing legal work and became associated with a group of militants who opposed the Law of April 6, 1830. Eventually this group would be known as the War Party as tension increased between the Mexican government and American settlers in Texas.

Travis had many occasions to be on opposite sides in legal matters with the commander of the Mexican garrison at Anahuac, Col. Juan (John) Davis Bradburn, a Kentuckian in the service of Mexico. Bradburn enforced the Law of April 6, 1830 against immigration, refused to allow state officials to alienate land to American settlers arriving after the passage of the law and allegedly used materials and slaves belonging to the settlers to build his camp.

The principal dispute at Anahuac occurred in 1832 when William Logan of Louisiana engaged Travis to secure the return of runaway slaves being harbored by Bradburn. Logan returned to Louisiana for proof of ownership and threatened Bradburn that he also would return with help. Travis alarmed Bradburn with a note passed to a sentry that Logan had returned with a large force. Bradburn turned out his entire garrison to chase shadows. Suspecting Travis as the perpetrator of the prank, Bradburn sent soldiers to his law office to arrest Travis and his partner, Patrick Jack. They were held in a guard house and later in two brick kilns.

Word of their arrest spread and men assembled to demand their release. They drafted the Turtle Bayou Resolutions, which pledged their loyalty to the states' rights constitution of 1824 but not to the present centralist regime, and demanded the release of the prisoners. John Austin traveled to Velasco to obtain a cannon to force Bradburn to comply. Col. Jose de las Piedras, commander at Nacogdoches, hurried to Anahuac. Although in sympathy with Bradburn, he realized that the Mexican forces were outnumbered. He ordered Travis and Jack released to civil authorities, who soon released them altogether. This began the disturbances of 1832 that resulted in armed clashes at Velasco and Nacog-

doches later that summer and produced the conventions of 1832 and 1833 with their petitions for repeal of the Law of April 6, 1830 and separate statehood.

Travis moved his legal practice to San Felipe in the aftermath of the clash at Anahuac. He was elected secretary of the *ayuntiemento* there and was accepted, despite his youth, into the councils of government. He also met Rebeca Cummins, who lived at Mill Creek, and began a courtship that resulted in an understanding that they would marry once Travis was divorced. Rosanna Travis began divorce proceedings against her husband in 1834, charging him with desertion. She had permitted their son, Charles Edward, to move to Texas.

After Stephen F. Austin carried the petition of the Convention of 1833 to the government in Mexico City and was incarcerated, fears for his safety cooled politics in Texas until the summer of 1835. By then Antonio Lopez de Santa Anna had asserted full centralist authority in the Mexican government and reestablished a customs house and military garrison at Anahuac. In late June, Travis, leading about 25 men, captured the Mexican soldiers easily. The action alarmed the Peace Party, and for several months Travis was regarded by many Texans as a troublemaker.

Gen. Martin Perfecto de Cos, Mexican military commander in the north, moved his command to San Antonio. He branded Travis and others as outlaws and demanded that the Texans surrender them for military trial.

Travis served briefly in the action surrounding the beginning of the Texas Revolution at Gonzales and San Antonio in late 1835, advised officials on the organization of a cavalry unit and then became the army's chief recruiting officer. Gov. Henry Smith ordered Travis to recruit 100 men and reinforce Col. James C. Neill at San Antonio in January 1836.

Travis was able to recruit only 29 men, and he requested to be relieved from embarrassment. But Smith insisted he report to Neill. Within a few days, Travis found himself in command of about 50 men when Neill took leave. James Bowie arrived with 100 volunteers, and he and Travis quarreled over command. They were able to effect an uneasy truce of joint command until Bowie's illness and injury from a fall forced him to bed. Travis then took full command of the Texas forces.

Travis directed the preparation of the Mission San Antonio de Valero, known as the Alamo, for the anticipated arrival of Santa Anna and the main command of the Mexican army. With engineer Green Jamison, he had walls strengthened, palaisades constructed to fill gaps in the wall, mounted cannon and stored provisions inside the fortress. He also wrote letters to every official in Texas requesting reinforcements, but only the 35 male residents of Gonzales came to his relief, raising the number of the Alamo's defenders to approximately 183. His letter addressed, "To the People of Texas and All Americans in the World," which was written on Feb. 24, two days after Santa Anna's advance arrived in San Antonio to begin a 13-day siege, brought more than enough help to Texas from the United States if they had arrived in time.

When Santa Anna had his forces ready, he ordered an assault on the Alamo just before dawn on March 6, 1836. The Mexicans overpowered the Texans within a few hours. Travis died early in the battle from a single bullet wound in the head. His body and those of the other defenders were burned. Only 27 years of age at his death, the nature of Travis' passing elevated him from being a mere commander of an obscure garrison to become a genuine hero of the American and Texas frontier.

Walter Prescott Webb

This article was written by Dr. Jim B. Pearson, Professor of History, North Texas State University.

His manners were those of a Southern gentleman; his face was marked from days of farming on the plains of West Texas; his mind was that of a world intellectual. Graduate students laughed at his sense of humor and marveled at his pure joy in examining an idea from every angle possible. It was apparent to all who knew him that Arnold J. Toynbee correctly wrote: "Walter Prescott Webb was a scholar whose mind went on growing all through his life . . .''

Webb's ancestors were southerners. In 1883, his parents, Casner and Mary Webb, followed other southerners from Mississippi seeking land in East Texas. In 1888, Walter was born in the Piney Woods of Panola County, in a house surrounded by cotton fields.

When Webb was four, the family moved to Wayland community in Stephens County. Surrounded by blackjacks and scrub oaks, Webb experienced the struggle that marked frontier life in a plains environment. Older neighbors still talked about Indian raids, buffalo hunts and cattle rustlers. The environment marked him, and Webb learned his lessons well.

While his father taught at several rural schools or farmed, Walter did the chores at home. With only eight years of intermittent public education, 18-year-old Walter Webb earned a teaching certificate and began teaching at various one-teacher schools.

In January 1909, Webb received a letter from William E. Hinds of New York offering to loan him $500 to attend college. Hinds had replied to a letter Webb had written to a magazine asking for assistance in getting an education to become a writer. Webb was enrolled at the University of Texas in the fall of 1909. Until his death in 1912, Hinds, whom Webb never met, continued to support the young Texan's education. In 1915, at the age of 27, Webb completed his degree.

On Sept. 16, 1916, Walter Webb married Jane Elizabeth Oliphant of Austin. Webb taught in San Antonio schools. But he was working as a bookkeeper when the University of Texas history department invited him to teach a course for prospective public school history instructors. Webb began a 45-year association with the school that fall.

In 1920, Webb earned the M.A. degree at the University of Texas and decided to expand his research topic, "The Texas Rangers in the Mexican War," into a comprehensive history of the Texas Rangers. In the midst of this research, Webb had the insight that crystallized his early years' experience, the Rangers' success in fighting plains Indians and a concept of his favorite professor, Lindley Miller Keasbey, that geography caused people to adjust to their environment. Webb theorized that the plains environment modified the way people behaved.

When his book, The Great Plains, was published in 1931, the history faculty suggested that it be used as his doctoral dissertation. The University of Texas granted the 44-year-old Webb the Ph.D. in 1932. In December 1958, the University of Chicago granted him an honorary doctor of laws degree.

The Great Plains was well acclaimed. The New York Times called the book "a new interpretation of the American West." Columbia University chose it for the Loubat Prize. Scholars and lay reviewers alike lauded Webb's style and originality. In 1939, the Social Science Research Council selected The Great Plains as the most outstanding contribution to American history since World War I. In 1956, the Mississippi Valley Historical Association voted it the best book by a living historian in the first half of the 20th century.

Webb became a full professor in 1933 and returned to his original research. In 1935, he published The Texas Rangers, which received popular acclaim. Paramount Pictures chose the book to feature as its Texas Centennial film. Two years later, his book, Divided We Stand: The Crisis of a Frontierless Democracy, prompted President Franklin D. Roosevelt to declare the South to be the nation's No. 1 economic problem.

Meanwhile, Webb added to his reputation as a teacher. He accepted invitations to serve as a visiting professor at Duke University, Harvard, the University of West Virginia and the University of Wyoming. In 1938, he accepted an eight-month appointment as Harkness Lecturer at the University of London.

On his return to Austin, Webb served as director of the Texas State Historical Association. He initiated the

Handbook of Texas, a unique two-volume encyclopedia about Texas, and founded a junior historian branch of the association in 1939. Webb finally took a break from his duties in 1942, when he accepted an offer to serve as the Harmsworth Professor of American History at Oxford.

While working on Divided We Stand, Webb was struck with the impact on Europe of the opening of North America, South America, Australia and the southern half of Africa. With the research of his doctoral seminar students, he finally published The Great Frontier in 1952. His hypothesis was that the opening of these lands sparked a 400-year boom. During this boom, the institutions of Western civilization — capitalism, individualism and democracy — developed. By 1900, the world faced a frontierless society. Thus, the boom institutions were changing and would continue to be modified by this new environment.

Many historians and writers regarded The Great Frontier highly, but others considered such gloomspreading un-American. The book was nominated for the Pulitzer Prize but did not win. Webb did receive the Texas Institute of Letters Award of $10,000. Although heartened by Arnold J. Toynbee's praise, he was generally disappointed in the reception of what he considered to be his greatest contribution to his profession. The University of Texas recognized his contribution, however, and, in 1952, named him a Distinguished Professor of History. In 1958, the Second International Congress of Historians of the United States and Mexico focused on his hypothesis.

In 1958, at age 70, Webb had reached retirement, but he continued to write and lecture. His list of honors grew. The Mississippi Valley Historical Association (now the Organization of American Historians) elected him president in 1954-55. In 1957-58, he served as president of the American Historical Association. The American Council of Learned Societies gave him a $10,000 cash award for a lifetime of distinguished scholarship. The Ex-Students Association at the University of Texas named him as one of their four most distinguished alumni. During 1959, while teaching as a visiting professor three days a week at Rice, he accepted a position as a part-time special consultant to U.S. Senate Majority Leader Lyndon B. Johnson.

On June 28, 1960, Jane, his wife of 43 years, died. He resigned himself to his work and his friends. But an old friend, Terrell Maverick, the widow of Congressman and former Mayor of San Antonio Maury Maverick, began to play a larger role in his life. They were married Dec. 14, 1961.

Terrell uncovered a manuscript that her first husband had inherited from his aunt, Ellen Slayden. This lady had written her impressions of Washington personalities and events while her husband served as congressman from 1897 to 1919. Webb and Terrell edited the work and published it as Washington Wife: The Journal of Ellen Maury Slayden.

On March 8, 1963, Webb was killed in an automobile accident, in which Terrell also was seriously injured.

The State of Texas paid tribute to Webb by granting permission for him to be buried in the State Cemetery in Austin. He is honored by an endowed Webb chair at the University of Texas at Austin, a faculty office building and center and the Walter Prescott Webb Society sponsored by the Texas State Historical Association. A lecture series was established in his name at the University of Texas at Arlington.

Webb wrote or edited more than 20 books and wrote many articles and essays. He was a charter member and later a fellow of the Texas Institute of Letters. But he was a teacher first, and from the time he entered his first one-teacher school until his death, Walter Prescott Webb never lost his love of teaching. Perhaps his greatest contribution was his impact on the lives of his students, who remember him with respect and affection.

Babe Zaharias

This article was written by Dr. Margaret Henson, Professor of History, University of Houston at Clear Lake.

Texans admire Mildred Ella "Babe" Didrikson Zaharias for three reasons: her athletic prowess, her easy, informal good humor and her gritty fight against cancer that finally ended her life in 1953. She also was one of

the world's outstanding women athletes.

At age 20, she broke two women's records at the 1932 Los Angeles Olympics in the javelin and the 80-meter hurdles and came in second in the high jump. Turning to golf in 1934, Babe won every available title by 1950, both amateur and professional, including the world and national open tournaments. In 1950, the Associated Press named her the outstanding woman athlete of the first half of the 20th century. There was no sport, except table tennis, in which the well-coordinated Texan did not excel, and she performed them all with a zest that assured the wise-cracking young woman a large following.

Babe was the sixth of seven children of Hanna Marie Olsen, a former Norwegian figure skater, and Ole Didrikson, an immigrant ship's carpenter who had sailed around Cape Horn 19 times. Born in Port Arthur on June 26, 1912, Babe grew up in Beaumont where she played on the high school girls' basketball team. Called "Baby" by her family, the nickname changed to "Babe" in the 1920s when she became proficient at hitting home runs while playing with the neighborhood boys. Her father built a high jump in the backyard for his children and also a weight-lifting device created from broomsticks and some old flatirons. Thus encouraged to develop athletic abilities, Babe also achieved the necessary competitive drive to overcome and defeat both male and female schoolmates.

At age 16, she became a member of the Golden Cyclone Athletic Club's basketball team and was placed on the payroll, a necessary requirement of the Employers Casualty Company of Dallas, the club's sponsor. A senior in high school, Babe received special permission from her school to play ball with the Cyclones in February 1930, with the understanding that she would return in June to take her final examinations and graduate with her class.

After two years with the Golden Cyclone squad, Babe was twice chosen All-American basketball forward in addition to winning awards in lifesaving and figure skating. She also acquired 92 medals and 17 loving cups as a member of the company's track team. By 1932 when she entered the Olympics, she already held the Southern Amateur Athletic Union record for every track and field event that she had entered and had been named the world's greatest woman athlete by the publication *Famous American Athletes of Today*.

Bumptious and cocky, Babe attracted almost as much attention for her looks and attitude as her athletic prowess at Los Angeles in 1932. Scorning makeup and with her short straight hair plastered back, her boyish figure gave no promise of the attractive woman she later became. Reporters seeking colorful stories described her body as whippy as a fly rod, with piano wire muscles. They noted her doorstop jaw and the pale slit mouth, adding that the Texas twang emerged from the side of the wide mouth. The joking and boasting that became her trademark were, of course, a protective shell to hide her vulnerable feminine side.

Needing money, Babe willingly accepted bizarre engagements exploiting her athletic ability and fame. She barnstormed with the Babe Didrikson All-American Basketball Team, the only female on the squad. She also played with the bearded House of David five and pitched a baseball game against them for exhibition. One week she played the Palace Theater in New York City, where she sang, played her mouth organ, told jokes and demonstrated her athletic talents by running on a treadmill, jumping hurdles and flying over a high jump. She even toured the country with another woman playing billiards. Ignoring critics who assailed her as a sideshow freak, Babe managed to save several thousand dollars to underwrite her goal to become the world's greatest golfer.

She entered her first golf tournament in 1934 and the next year won the Texas Women's Golf Association championship. But her brash attitude and her recent tour on the entertainment circuit caused the U.S. Golf Association to bar her from future amateur contests. Thereupon she turned professional for the next four and one-half years. Any longer would have made her permanently ineligible for the amateur golf tournaments. She signed with a sporting goods company for a salary and royalties while she perfected her golf.

Babe met George Zaharias, a 300-pound wrestler, during a publicity stunt in 1938. She posed for photographs perched on his shoulder and also was the victim while he showed her a "neck hold." Soon afterward they married, and he became a devoted promoter of her golfing career. He owned a tailor shop in Beverly Hills, and Babe opened a women's sportswear shop next door. For a number of years, she had made her own sports outfits and even had won a prize in the 1931 Texas State Fair. Through her example and influence, women golfers abandoned the traditional conservative skirts and adopted culottes and slacks.

In 1944 after several years of petitioning, Babe was reinstated as an amateur by the golfing association. For the next three years, Babe won trophy after trophy, but she always turned down money prizes in order to maintain her amateur status. In 1945, the Associated Press voted her the best woman athlete of the year. After seventeen consecutive victories including the British Ladies Amateur title in 1947, which no American had previously won, the *New York Times* said, "There's never been anyone quite like her." She was the first woman to make the long, hard-hitting drives like men, and her example changed women's golfing when younger golfers copied her style. Texas golfing great Byron Nelson remarked that her 284-yard brassie drive from tee to green was one only eight men professionals could accomplish. Her record drives were over 315 yards.

Having won every major amateur title, Babe turned professional in August 1947. The years had modified her appearance and no one could mistake her for a boy. Five feet, six inches tall and weighing 145 pounds, Babe had a trim, but full, figure. Her grey-green eyes lighted with pleasure when reporters noted the change, and she bragged about her home permanents, makeup and skill as a seamstress. Residing in Denver, and later Tampa, Fl., Babe supervised a small business making sportswear, co-authored her biography and decorated the home that she and her husband built on their own golf course near Tampa. She played in tournaments 10 months each year and earned over $100,000 annually in prize money, exhibition tournaments and endorsements.

During the summer of 1952, Babe failed to be a top money winner for the first time in her career. She quietly dropped from sight, had a hernia operation and returned to tournament play the following year. But she was often tired, and her game was off. Finally she was diagnosed as having cancer of the colon and quick surgery was required.

While most sports writers decided her career was over, Babe was well enough to resume playing golf in 1953, and on July 3, 1954, she defeated 52 of her colleagues to win the U.S. Women's Open by 12 strokes.

But the victory was short-lived. She continued to play exhibition tournaments over the next three years to raise money to establish a cancer research fund. In 1953, she was elected to the recently established Texas Sports Hall of Fame, but her health deteriorated and she died at John Sealy Hospital in Galveston on Sept. 27, 1956. She was buried at Beaumont and a Texas historical marker placed in 1968 marks her grave.

Lorenzo de Zavala

This article was written by Dr. Raymond Estep, Professor Emeritus of History, The Air University, Montgomery, Ala.

Of the 59 men who wrote the Constitution of the Republic of Texas none equalled the diminutive 48-year-old Mexican, Lorenzo de Zavala, in education, linguistic ability, political experience or diplomatic service. Few, if any, of his fellow delegates had seen as much of North America, and even fewer had traveled as widely in Europe. The skills he had acquired during two turbulent decades of service in political institutions in Merida, Mexico City, Madrid and Paris uniquely qualified him for the role he was to play in helping to draft the constitution and in serving as vice president of the new republic.

Manuel Lorenzo Justiniano de Zavala y Saenz, the fifth of nine children of Anastasio de Zavala y Velazquez and Maria Barbara Saenz y Castro, was born on Oct. 3, 1788 in Tecoh, a small village located near Merida, Yucatan. After graduating from the Tridentine Seminary of San Ildefonso in Merida in 1807, he founded and edited several newspapers and became a forceful advocate of liberal reforms. His political activities led to his arrest and confinement in 1814 in the prison fortress of San Juan de Ulloa in the harbor of Veracruz. Already thoroughly trained in Spanish and Latin, and self-taught in French, he quickly learned to read English without a tutor. Most of his time, however, was devoted to the study of medical textbooks, which prepared him to enter the practice of medicine upon his release from imprisonment in 1817. In 1820, he was elected to the Provincial Assembly of Yucatan. In the following year, he served as a deputy to the Cortes in Madrid, before returning to Yucatan by way of Paris, London and New Orleans.

During the remainder of his life Zavala was one of Mexico's more active political leaders. From 1822 to 1824, he served as a deputy from Yucatan in both the First and Second Constituent Congresses in Mexico City, and from 1824 to 1826, he represented his native state in the Mexican Senate. During this period, he became one of the leaders of the newly formed Federalist Party and also took an active role in promoting the cause of York Rite Masonry, which came to be closely linked with the fortunes of that party.

From 1827 to 1829, Zavala was governor of the State of Mexico, a post he gave up to serve President Guerrero as secretary of the treasury from April to October 1829. Forced out of politics by the newly installed Centralist regime, he left Mexico in May 1830. Traveling by steamboat from New Orleans to Pittsburgh, he then visited Niagara Falls, Montreal, Quebec, Albany, New York City, Boston, Philadelphia and Washington. In the capital, he had dinner with President Jackson and Vice President Van Buren at the White House. In New York, on Oct. 16, 1830, he transferred his interest in the empresario grant of several thousand acres of land in southeastern Texas, which he and two partners had received from the State of Coahuila y Texas on March 12, 1829.

After spending most of 1831 in France and England, Zavala resided in New York City from November 1831 until his return to Mexico in the summer of 1832. In December, he was installed for a second time as governor of the State of Mexico, an office he vacated in October 1833 to become once again a deputy from Yucatan in the Chamber of Deputies in Mexico City. At the end of November, he was named as the first minister plenipotentiary of the Mexican legation in Paris. He was officially received by King Louis Philippe on April 26, 1834.

Angered by President Santa Anna's defection to the Centralist opposition, Zavala renounced his diplomatic post on Aug. 30, 1834, but remained in Paris until his successor arrived in March 1835. Although he had been ordered to return to Mexico City, Zavala feared to do so while Santa Anna remained in power. Shortly after arriving in New York City in May 1835, he informed the Mexican foreign office that he planned to settle in Texas, where he could remain aloof from Mexico's political struggles, and where he hoped to regain some of his personal fortune.

He arrived in Texas early in July and immediately began discussions with local leaders on the political future of the state, at first in the Permanent Council, and later in the Consultation, which he attended as a delegate from the municipality of Harrisburg. In the Convention that met at Washington-on-the-Brazos on March 1, 1836, he joined the other delegates in drafting and signing the Declaration of Independence and the Constitution. On March 17, his fellow delegates named him the ad interim vice president of the Republic of Texas, which they had just created.

On the day that the Convention adjourned, Zavala and many of the other delegates fled to Harrisburg, and later to Galveston Island, in their efforts to escape capture by Santa Anna's army as it swept eastward across Texas in the days after the fall of the Alamo. Following the defeat of Santa Anna on April 21 at San Jacinto, some of the wounded — both Texans and Mexicans — were treated at Zavala's home, which was located a few miles north of the battlefield on the north side of Buffalo Bayou. In the days after the battle, Zavala interviewed Santa Anna and many of his officers, and, as vice president, participated in the negotiations that produced the Treaties of Velasco. On May 27 he was named one of the commissioners to accompany Santa Anna to Mexico City. After this plan was aborted, Zavala returned to his home and took no further active role in the government. His resignation as vice president became effective on Oct. 17, 1836.

Less than four weeks later a norther overturned the rowboat in which Zavala was crossing Buffalo Bayou. He and his son Augustine survived the accident, but exposure to the cold wind and water caused him to develop pneumonia. He died on Nov. 15, 1836, and was buried near his home. In 1931, the State of Texas erected a marker at the site, which is now part of San Jacinto State Park.

Zavala was married twice. His first wife, Teresa Correa y Correa, whom he married about 1807, bore him three children: Manuela, Lorenzo Jr. and a second daughter who died in infancy. After her death in 1831, he married Emily West in New York City on Nov. 12, 1831. To this marriage were born three children: Augustine, Emily and Ricardo, all of whom grew to maturity in Texas.

Zavala County, created in 1858, the village of Zavala (c. 1834-1878) in Jasper County and the rural settlement of Zavala in Angelina County all perpetuate the memory of the first vice president of the Republic of Texas.

Location of the Capitals of Texas

There have been many different **capitals** of the area that is Texas, including a number that served only briefly.

Capitals of the six nations which have ruled Texas have been Madrid, Spain; Paris, France; Mexico, D.F., Mexico; San Felipe de Austin, Washington-on-the-Brazos, Harrisburg, Galveston Island, Velasco, Columbia, Houston and Austin, of the Republic of Texas; Washington, D.C., United States; Montgomery, Al., and Richmond, Va., Confederate States of America.

While Texas was associated with Spain and the Republic of Mexico, its government was administered largely from Coahuila, which alternately had **Monclova** and **Saltillo** as its state capital.

In 1721-22 **Marquis de Aguayo**, governor of Coahuila including Texas, led an expedition north of the Rio Grande and established the presidio of **Los Adaes** a short distance east of the Sabine River on the site of present-day Robeline, La. **Los Adaes** became the capital of Texas and remained so for half a century. After the ceding of Louisiana to Spain by France in 1762, the eastern Texas and western Louisiana posts were gradually abandoned, including Los Adaes, and the seat of government was moved to **San Antonio**, which was the capital of Texas from 1772 until 1824. After Mexico became independent of Spain, Texas was again united with Coahuila of which **Saltillo** was then the capital. The first state congress convened there Aug. 15, 1824. The capital of **Coahuila-Texas** was moved to **Monclova**, March 9, 1833. A heated controversy between Saltillo and Monclova ensued. When the issue was placed before President Santa Anna, he favored Monclova.

The first Anglo-American capital of Texas was **San Felipe de Austin**. The Consultation of 1835, at which the various municipalities of Texas were represented, met at this place, which continued to be the official headquarters until March 1, 1836.

The provisional government of Texas met at **Washington-on-the-Brazos** March 1, 1836. This convention, in which all powers of sovereignty were claimed and exercised, adopted the Declaration of Independence, wrote a constitution and inaugurated executive officers, March 2. Because of the movement of Santa Anna's troops, President Burnet selected **Harrisburg** on Buffalo Bayou as the temporary capital.

At the approach of Santa Anna, President Burnet, with a part of his Cabinet, took refuge on **Galveston Island**. After the Battle of San Jacinto, the Treaty of Velasco was signed at **Velasco**, temporary seat of government.

In October, 1836, the first permanent government of the Republic of Texas went into operation at **Columbia**.

President Houston, on Dec. 15, 1836, ordered the seat of government removed to **Houston**, where it remained from April 10, 1837, until the meeting of Congress in 1840.

President Lamar in 1839 had approved a bill naming the Capital Commission, which selected the "site of the town of **Waterloo**, on the north bank of the Colorado," as the permanent capital. This was confirmed by the Texas Congress Jan. 19, 1840, and the place was named **Austin** in honor of Stephen F. Austin.

No trace is left of most of the early buildings in which the seat of government was housed. The **Spanish Governors' palace** still stands at San Antonio. A one-story frame building that served as the Capitol at Columbia has been restored. A frame structure at present site of the Rice Hotel was the Capitol at **Houston**. When **Austin** was selected as the capital, several log buildings were used until the first permanent structure was erected. This burned Nov. 9, 1881, and a temporary Capitol located off the Capitol grounds at the head of Congress Avenue served until completion of the present structure, which was opened May 16, 1888.

Five Days
of Destiny
in Texas

This article was written by Mike Kingston, editor of the Texas Almanac.

More than 54,750 days have passed since Texas declared its independence from Mexico. Though there have been wars and Indian raids, political debates and elections, most of the days since March 2, 1836, have been uneventful. Texans went about the mundane business of transforming a wilderness into a modern society. But among those thousands of days, a handful harbored events that transformed Texas, in some cases, and, in other instances, had a great impact on United States and world history.

The following are brief accounts of these "five days of destiny" in Texas history and their impact.

April 21, 1836

In the late afternoon of this spring day on the plains of San Jacinto in present-day Houston, Gen. Sam Houston and a small band of Texans defeated a troop of Mexican soldiers in a short battle. The following day, Gen. Antonio Lopez de Santa Anna, dictator of Mexico and commander of the troops, was captured while trying to escape the field of battle.

With Santa Anna's capture, the Texans affirmed the independence that they had declared from Mexico on March 2, less than two months before. Although the two nations remained belligerent for the next nine years, Texas stood as a republic, a member of the family of the world's nations, until its annexation to the United States in 1845. Texas' claim to the entire watershed of the Rio Grande to its source in Colorado was accepted by the United States, which went to war with Mexico to back it up. As a result of the war with Mexico, the United States acquired the present-day Southwest and California and became a truly continental nation. Harbors acquired on the West Coast allowed American merchants to open trade with the Orient, and the U.S. role in world affairs was greatly expanded. The fact that Texas existed gave the United States the opportunity to contest Mexico for the large territory that Spain had claimed, but not developed, for more than two centuries.

Without Houston's victory over Santa Anna at San Jacinto, how different would the face of the United States be today? No one knows, of course. Most historians feel that the power of Manifest Destiny would have pushed the United States westward into the Mexican territories regardless of the excuses necessary to justify the movement. Texas' existence allowed the United States to claim purity of motive in its war with Mexico and to demand the large territory as indemnity for the expense of the war and the loss of American life.

On the other hand, if Santa Anna had prevailed, Mexican history might have been much different. The nation was in constant turmoil from 1828 until 1855. Centralists and republicans battled for control of the government, and the Mexican presidency changed hands 36 times during these turbulent years. Two major problems included continuing recriminations over the loss of half the Mexican state to the United States in the War of 1846 and the lack of a single leader who by force of personality could unify the country.

A victory over the Anglo-Texans at San Jacinto would have allowed Santa Anna to return to Mexico City a national hero. With that prestige, the government could have been stabilized — albeit under the centralists. Serious attention could have been given to coloniz-

Spindletop blew out of control for several days in 1910. Its discovery near Beaumont opened the oil age. Photo courtesy of Mid-Continent Oil and Gas Association.

163

A wounded Sam Houston accepts the surrender of Mexican President Antonio Lopez de Santa Anna the day after the battle of San Jacinto. This painting by William H. Huddle hangs in the State Capitol in Austin. Photo courtesy of the Texas Department of Highways and Public Transportation.

ing Texas with Europeans and Mexican citizens, as had been planned but never accomplished by both Spain and Mexico. A stable Mexican government might have attracted more serious support from England and France in case of hostilities with the United States. And the face of North America might be much different today.

But the victory of the Texas army, made up mostly of "Old Texans" who had established homes and families in the Mexican state, opened the door for Anglo-American colonization of the Southwest and California.

January 10, 1901

Anthony Lucas was not a fly-by-night wildcatter. An experienced oil man and engineer, he was convinced that there was oil around the salt domes near Beaumont in Southeast Texas. On Jan. 10, 1901, Lucas' faith was richly rewarded. Legendary Spindletop, which opened the world's largest oil boom at that time, blew in on the evening of that winter day. And with it, the oil age opened for the world.

Within days, Spindletop exceeded Texas' previous annual oil production of 836,000 barrels, and by the end of the first year, the well gushed forth 3.2 million barrels of oil.

Lucas was not the only person who felt that there was oil near the salt domes. Patillo Higgins drilled wells in the area around Spindletop for a decade before his money ran out, but no oil was discovered. Higgins leased to Lucas the land on which Spindletop was located.

Oil had been produced at Corsicana for many years before Spindletop blew in, but never in the quantities reached after Lucas' discovery. Indians had used oil from seeps for medicine, and Spanish explorers caulked boats with the tar-like substance. During the 19th century, oil discovered near Nacogdoches was used on roads to keep down the dust and occasionally as a lubricant.

The staggering volume of oil unleashed by Spindletop and subsequent discoveries gave U.S. industry a cheap and plentiful source of energy. Railroads soon converted from coal to oil, and steamship companies were not far behind. With such a cheap and ready supply of energy, personal automobiles were within the reach of many Americans. The increased use of automobiles and trucks for transportation required an improvement of the nation's highway systems.

Texas became the nation's undisputed leader in oil production in 1930 with the discovery of the East Texas

oil field by C. M. "Dad" Joiner. The glut of oil caused by this find drove oil prices down to ruinous levels, and the state stepped in to control production as a conservation measure. The conservation also allowed the Texas Railroad Commission to set the world price of oil from the 1930s until the Arab oil crisis of the 1970s.

Texas, the nation and the world were never the same after Anthony Lucas' historic discovery opened the gates to the oil age, which has brought both great prosperity and problems.

March 2, 1910

No military establishment had a more inauspicious beginning than the United States Air Force. On March 2, 1910, Lt. Benjamin D. Foulois was catapulted into the air for a seven and one-half minute flight around a drill field at Fort Sam Houston in San Antonio. A second flight that day resulted in a crash that damaged the plane and delayed Lt. Foulois' "training" for 10 days.

These flights capped the entrance of the United States Army into the air age. Shortly after the Wright brothers' successful flight at Kitty Hawk, N.C., in 1903, the military application of the new airplanes was recognized. In 1908, the army and the Wright brothers, Orville and Wilbur, entered into a contract to provide the first military airplane. The contract called for the machine to pass a series of speed and cross-country tests and for two military pilots to be trained by the inventors. Lt. Foulois was a member of the Aeronautics Board that supervised the tests.

An accident that killed an officer and injured Orville Wright at the Fort Myers, Va., proving grounds delayed the tests until June 1909. A month later, the plane passed the required tests, and two officers were trained to fly it at College Park, Md. Lt. Foulois was scheduled for flight training but received only three hours of in-the-air instruction from Wilbur Wright and another pilot before being ordered to another assignment. The young lieutenant did not solo until he reached San Antonio.

In November 1909, Lt. Foulois was called to the office of Gen. James Allen, Chief Signal Officer of the Army, and was asked how long it would take to crate the army's only airplane for shipment to San Antonio. "Twenty-four hours," Foulois replied. Also present at the meeting was James L. Slayden, congressman from San Antonio and chairman of the U.S. House Committee on Military Affairs. Foulois was ordered to "take plenty of spare parts" and to "teach yourself to fly" in San Antonio.

The ground crew surrounds Old No. 1, the airplane in which Lt. Benjamin Foulois launched American military aviation in 1910. Photo courtesy of the Fort Sam Houston Museum.

Fort Sam Houston had two advantages: The weather was good enough for year-round operations, and there was room enough to keep the flight training from interfering with regular troop operations.

Lt. Foulois arrived in San Antonio with nine-man ground crew on Feb. 5, 1910. In less than a month, the biplane — called "Old No. 1" — was assembled. On March 2, 1910, the young army officer soloed. As Foulois trained himself to fly, the need for improvements in the plane became obvious. First, Foulois saw that he needed to stay with the plane, and a safety harness to keep him in his seat was developed. Because the catapult system used to launch the aircraft was so unwieldy, Foulois and his ground team designed a landing gear, which was successfully tested in August 1910.

With a civilian pilot, Foulois also flew on the first operational flight in March 1911. Covering the distance between Laredo and Eagle Pass in a record time of about two hours, Foulois called the flight the first military air reconnaissance made with U.S. Army troops on the ground.

The flight training operations moved to College Park, Md., for a brief time but returned to Texas during World War I. From then until 1938, all U.S. military pilots were trained in Texas, and today the state remains a center for military aviation and for military aviation contractors. Foulois rose to the rank of major general and was Chief of Air Corps upon his retirement in 1935.

September 12, 1958

Today hundreds of devices use integrated circuits, those tiny pieces of silicon on which minute electronic circuits are printed. The use of these chips has created a "second industrial revolution." Without them, homes would be without computers; man might still have never walked on the moon or sent probes to nearby planets; and hundreds of conveniences that are taken for granted today might not exist.

In the late 1950s, however, the electronic industry was frustrated. Bell Laboratories had introduced the transistor in 1948, a great advance at the time. No longer were vacuum tubes needed in electric circuits, and this allowed for miniaturization of electronic devices. But the industry faced a numbers barrier: Engineers could design intricate circuits with 1,000, 100,000 or more components. But the human hand could not wire the components together. Even if it could have, the labor costs would have been astronomical. The technology simply was not available to bring to life the grand designs that were on many drawing boards.

Jack S. Kilby of Texas Instruments in Dallas provided the breakthrough that revolutionized the world.

Kilby joined TI in April 1958 to work on the "tyranny of numbers," as the problem was called. The solution being considered was to devise a method to fit components together without wiring. Kilby did not think the idea would work.

At the time, all TI employees took their vacation time at once in July. Kilby had not been with the company long enough for a vacation, so he spent the time alone at the office. It was time well spent. TI engineers had designed a silicon transistor, and Kilby realized that the company was committed to using the material.

Kilby began to consider what could be made of silicon. It was already known that the parts of standard semiconductor devices, diodes and transistors, could be made from silicon. The material simply was doped with the proper impurities to make it conduct electric current. The silicon products were not as good as those made with other materials, but they would work. And what has been called the "Monolithic Idea" was born. If you could make any component from one material, the components of an entire circuit could be placed in a monolithic block of that material. With all the components in a single chip, no wiring would be necessary.

After TI's vacation period ended, Kilby got approval from his supervisor to build a prototype integrated

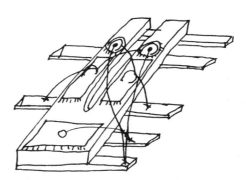

This is Jack S. Kilby's sketch of an integrated circuit taken from his notebooks. The successful testing of the concept in 1958 was the first step into the "second industrial revolution." Sketch courtesy of Texas Instruments.

This classic picture in 1963 captured the swearing in of Lyndon B. Johnson of Texas as the 36th President of the United States after the assassination of John F. Kennedy in Dallas. U.S. District Judge Sarah T. Hughes administered the oath, and Lady Bird Johnson and Jackie Kennedy looked on. Associated Press Photo.

circuit. On Sept. 12, 1958, the device was successfully tested at the TI laboratories, and the "tyranny of numbers" was overthrown.

In California, Robert Noyce reached the same conclusion from a different direction. Kilby and Noyce are credited jointly for the Monolithic Idea, and both received the National Medal of Science for the work. Kilby, who holds several other patents, also is a member of the National Inventors' Hall of Fame.

The "second industrial revolution" got its big push forward in a Texas laboratory.

November 22, 1963

John F. Kennedy, the 35th president of the United States, was assassinated while riding in a motorcade in Downtown Dallas on Nov. 22, 1963. He was the first president to be killed in office since William McKinley died at an assassin's hand in 1901. A Texan, Vice President Lyndon B. Johnson, took office shortly after Kennedy was pronounced dead at Parkland Hospital in Dallas.

Historians have yet to write a final evaluation of the administrations of either Kennedy or Johnson. But Kennedy's death introduced a dual age of accomplishment and turbulence into American history.

Johnson, considered a master politician by most contemporary observers, received a great deal of cooperation and support from a guilt-ridden nation during the early days of his administration. Opposition to controversial portions of Kennedy's legislative program in the U.S. Congress evaporated. Under Johnson's guidance, civil rights legislation and sweeping social programs, like Medicare, were passed. Contemporaries have credited Johnson's legislative skill and the contrite attitude of the Congress with the success of the program.

Johnson also easily won a full presidential term in the election of 1964, and shortly thereafter, his administration ran into serious problems in the conduct of the war in Vietnam.

The death of Kennedy, which reintroduced violence into the political dialogue of the period, has been called the end of America's "age of innocence." As Johnson committed more U.S. troops to the fighting in Vietnam, opposition became increasingly violent. Riots over Vietnam and civil rights issues became common. In 1968, violence became more intense and spread to all phases of politics. Civil rights leader Martin Luther King Jr. and Sen. Robert F. Kennedy, a presidential candidate, were assassinated.

Republican Richard M. Nixon won a narrow victory over Hubert H. Humphrey in 1968, when a bitterly divided Democratic Party could not unite. Nixon's election marked the end of the legacy of the Kennedy assassination. The Republican's resignation during the Watergate scandal was unrelated. But it continued the instability in national leadership and fostered a feeling of insecurity.

In Dallas, the assassination prompted a lengthy period of introspection. A great deal of criticism — much of it unwarranted — focused on the city. In the two decades after the death, Dallas evolved a more mature, cosmopolitan attitude, while retaining its basic political conservatism.

Kennedy's death ended a period of normalcy for the nation. The turbulence and controversy in the years that followed caused a great many Americans to reevaluate their country.

The elapsed time from the assassination is still too short for a final historical assessment of the post-Kennedy years. For those Americans who lived through it, however, the world has not been the same — nor is it likely to be again.

A Concise History of Texas

THIS short history of Texas from prehistoric times to the present was prepared especially for the Sesquicentennial by Mike Kingston, editor of the Texas Almanac. As in any project of this magnitude, Kingston had the help of many people. He particularly wants to thank Ruth Harris, Mary Crawford and Paula LaRocque of The Dallas Morning News for proofreading and editing the material.

Several professionals critiqued the manuscript, and their comments and suggestions were invaluable. Included among these were: Dr. Alan Skinner, an independent professional archaeologist of Dallas; Bob Forrester, an amateur archaeologist of Fort Worth; Dr. David Weber, chairman of the Department of History, Southern Methodist University; Dr. Archie P. McDonald, professor of history, Stephen F. Austin University; Dr. Fane Downs, professor of history, McMurry College; Dr. Paul Lack, professor of history, McMurry College; Dr. Alwyn Barr, chairman of the Department of History, Texas Tech University; and Dr. Adrian N. Anderson, chairman of the Department of History, Lamar University; and Dr. Ernest Wallace, Horn Professor, Emeritus, Texas Tech University. Any errors, of course, are those of the author alone.

Table of Contents

Prehistoric Texas

MANY factors make the once-simple picture of early humanity in Texas a much more complex and interesting problem. More than 30,000 archaeological sites have been registered with the state, and new ones are discovered regularly. Archaeologists, with the aid of scientists from other disciplines, are bringing more sophisticated techniques to bear on the studies of the clues that prehistoric Texans left. New discoveries and more detailed information open additional dimensions to our knowledge of early man in the state.

The picture of early humans in Texas will not be brought into final focus for decades. But indications are that these first human inhabitants of the state were probably more intelligent, more resourceful and more culturally developed than the often conveyed image of the "squatting savage."

One basic theory remains unchallenged — how these people got to the New World. Early Texans were descendants of those Asian groups that migrated across the Bering Strait during the Ice Ages of the past 50,000 years. At intermittent periods, enough water would accumulate in the massive glaciers worldwide to lower the sealevel several hundred feet. During these periods, the Bering Strait would become a 1,300-mile-wide land bridge between North America and Asia. These early adventurers worked their way southward for thousands of years, eventually getting as far as Tierra del Fuego in Argentina 10,000 years ago. These migrations populated both North and South America in a relatively short time. It is generally accepted that these people walked to the New World, although some scientists suggest that groups may have come by sea.

By land or sea, they brought a paleolithic technology. Their primitive tool kit contained projectile points, scrapers and other simple stone tools. Atlatls, or spear-throwing sticks, were used to launch projectiles. Basically these people were big game hunters and may have followed their prey across the land bridge.

Biologically they were completely modern homo sapiens. No evidence has been found to indicate that any evolutionary change occurred in the New World. Dressed in modern attire, scientists say, these early Texans would be indistinguishable from those of today.

Four basic periods reflecting cultural advancement of early inhabitants are used by archaeologists in classifying evidence. These periods are the Paleo-Indian (20,000 years ago to 7,000 years ago); Archaic (7,000 years ago to about the time of Christ); Woodland (time of Christ to 800-1,000 years ago), and Neo-American, or Late Prehistoric, (800-1,000 years ago until European contact). Not all early people advanced through all these stages in Texas. Much cultural change was made in adaptation to changes in climate. The Caddo Indians of East Texas, for example, reached the Neo-American stage before French and Spanish explorers made contact in the 16th and 17th centuries. Others, such as the Karankawas of the Gulf Coast, advanced no further than the Archaic at the same time. Still others advanced and then regressed in the face of a changing climate.

The earliest confirmed evidence indicates that these humans were in Texas between 10,000 and 13,000 years ago. "Midland Minnie," which was identified from only a few pieces of skull, was discovered in Midland County in 1953. Dated by chemical techniques, the remains were determined to be 10,000 years old. In 1983, the discoveries of two burial sites dating to about the same period or earlier were announced. Archaeologists with the Texas Department of Highways and Public Transportation uncovered the complete skeleton of a woman in the excavation on a farm-to-market road project near Leander, north of Austin in Central Texas. Material found in the grave site was radiocarbon dated at 10,000 to 13,000 years old. The site also was a well-preserved ceremonial burial with artifacts such as a grinding stone and beads found with the skeleton. A rock, which could have been a primitive headstone, also was found in the grave.

Shortly after the Leander discovery was announced, amateur archaeologists working an excavation near Waco reported the discovery of a double burial of a man and child. Material from this grave site was radiocarbon dated at 10,000 years, too. In addition, the two skeletons were covered with several large stones, which, along with other evidence, indicated a ceremonial burial. Artifacts — apparently from the High Plains and the Gulf Coast — were found in the grave, indicating the people participated in a wide trade territory.

Paleo-Indians have long been considered successful big game hunters. Artifacts from this period are found across the state but not in great number, indicating they were a small, nomadic population. Some of the artifacts have been found in conjunction with kill sites of large animals. Texas' climate was cooler and much wetter during this period, providing lush grasslands to be grazed by large animals. Early Texans hunted prehistoric bison, which were seven feet tall at the shoulder, and small horses. Although the horse evolved to its modern state in the New World, it had become extinct and had to be returned to the New World in the 16th century by European explorers.

PREHISTORIC Texans used the same hunting tactics for thousands of years. In one area on the Rio Grande in Val Verde County, sites ranging in age from Paleo to Archaic to Pre-Historic indicate that bison were driven over the edge of a cliff to their deaths and then butchered. The ages of the sites vary from hundreds to thousands of years.

Archaeological studies came relatively late to Texas, and the delay probably cost the state a place in the terminology of science. In 1924, a man and a boy walking down the dry bed of Lone Wolf Creek near Colorado City in Mitchell County found the skeleton of an ancient bison eroding from the bank. Within the rib cage of the skeleton were found three projectile points that are described today as "Clovis" points. Large and with a characteristic design, Clovis points are now benchmarks for dating the earliest evidence of man in North America. The Texas discovery could not be dated to the satisfaction of scientists of the day. In 1936, similar points found at a kill site near Clovis, N.M., could be scientifically dated. The New Mexico city is now honored as the namesake of the points. Folsom points, which are smaller and fluted, also are named for a New Mexico community near which the first of these points was found and dated in 1926.

Prior to the discoveries near Leander and Waco, only four or five complete skeletons of Paleo-Indians had been discovered in the New World. These people had long been considered to be nomads with an egalitarian society. With evidence of ceremonial burials and artifacts indicating broad trade territories, new dimensions will be added to the cultural assessment of these early Texans.

For example, the projectile points and other artifacts found in the Paleo sites of Texas differ significantly from those excavated in Northern Mexico sites, indicating two distinct cultural traditions within a narrow geographical range.

A S Texas' climate changed at the end of the Ice Age about 7,000 years ago, inhabitants adapted. Apparently the state experienced an extended period of warming and drying and a population increase. Archaic Indians accommodated the change by broadening cyclical hunting and gathering patterns and by becoming less selective in game. They stalked smaller animals, as well as large beasts, as indicated by the reduced size of the projectile points found at these sites. Their tool kit was expanded to include stone drills, axes and knives used to work bone and wood. And these Texans began to harvest fruits and nuts when in season and exploited rivers for food, as indicated by the fresh-water mussel shells in ancient garbage heaps. Archaic Indians also had broad trade territories. Flint from the Alibates quarry in the Panhandle was transported throughout a territory thousands of square miles wide, and chert from the Edwards Plateau was used to make projectile points and other artifacts found in North and East Texas.

Several burial sites from this period also have been excavated. The bodies were buried with tools and sometimes dogs. A site near Houston contained dozens of burials, indicating that these early people had returned to the same area over hundreds of years to bury the dead. Dating between 5,000 and 6,000 years old, the site produced artifacts made of chert from near Little Rock, Ark., and sea shells possibly from Florida.

The people were involved in a much wider trade territory than previously thought. At about the time of Christ, the Woodland stage began to emerge in parts of Texas. This period is distinguished by the development of complex, settled societies. The people were less nomadic. While they still ranged widely in search of game, crops and local wild plants provided much of their diets. And the first evidence of social stratification is found. The bow and arrow came into use, and the first pottery is associated with this period. Between 750-800 A.D., Pre-Caddoan Indians in East Texas had formed primitive villages and were building distinctive mounds for burials and for rituals.

Some Indians reached this stage and then reverted when the climate changed, as it did in the Texas Panhandle and along the Rio Grande. In these areas, evidence has been found of agriculture-based communities that ceased to exist.

The Neo-American period, which is best exemplified by the highly civilized Caddos of East Texas, is dated between 800-1000 A.D. and the time of the European contact with New World natives. Early Texans that reached this stage had very complex cultures with well-defined social stratification. They were fully agricultural and participated in exotic trade over wide areas.

When the Europeans arrived, they found people in Texas living in cultures that ranged from the very primitive to the highly complex.

Archaeologists often are frustrated by the theories propounded by amateurs and speculators who propose that similarities between cultures in different areas indicate a contact. Other questions are raised that simply cannot be answered by the present stage of research and understanding. Some of those will be reviewed here.

One of the most enduring, but unresolved, theories is that Prehistoric Texas was on the route that colonists of the Olmec or Toltec civilizations in early Mexico fol-

lowed to the Mississippi Valley and the Southeast United States. There are many similarities between the early Mexican civilizations and the Mississippi cultures. Both built large ceremonial mounds, had similar social organizations and shared other cultural traits. In Mexico, these early tendencies evolved into the massive pyramids also characterizing the Maya and Aztec civilizations that greeted early Spaniards. Although some amateurs have found tantalizing evidence of an overland migration between these New World cultures, acceptable scientific proof has not been established.

The earliest evidence of the presence of humans in Texas also has been clouded by enigmatic finds. In the 1950s, for example, amateur archaeologist R. King Harris and other members of the Dallas Archeological Society found a Clovis projectile point along the shoreline of Lake Lewisville in Denton County before the dam was completed. Radiocarbon dating of material found in the hearths associated with the point ran off the scale of the day. According to these tests, the points were associated with material that was almost 40,000 years old — much before early humans were in the New World, according to conventional wisdom. Subsequent investigations in the early 1980s found that the dated samples were contaminated with lignite, a hydrocarbon that would throw the dating far askew. The final evaluation of the hearths, which were restudied when a drought lowered the water level in the lake, was that they were about 10,000 years old. But the sites do represent the first use of a fuel other than wood for a fire in the New World.

Another question not so easily answered is the case of the Malakoff-Trinidad heads found in Henderson County in the 1920s and 1930s. These are three largest ones that have apparent hand-carved human features. They were found in the bottom of a gravel stratum over an eight-year period. And with the exception of the final stone, no scientific archaeological surveys were made of the discovery sites. If the heads were deposited in the bottom of the stratum in which they were found, they indicate that humanity was in Texas — and the New World — 40,000 to 50,000 years ago, again far earlier than thought by many of today's scientists. Because of the lack of a professional survey at the time of discovery, this question may never be answered.

Other mysteries also exist. On a West Central Texas hillside, a series of vertical and horizontal lines firmly engraved in sandstone have been deciphered as a form of ancient Celtic line writing in a Celtiberian language. Epigrapher Barry Fell, a marine biologist turned epigrapher, has been criticized by professional archaeologists for errors and misinterpretation of engravings in rock in other sections of the country. But he holds fast to the theory that these inscriptions were left by Celtic adventurers and traders, giving travel instructions to others. The inscriptions are examples, Fell contends, of a well-developed trade between Europe and the New World long before Columbus or even the Vikings and Irish monks ventured westward.

In another case, a plaque bearing what was interpreted as ancient Libyan writing was found in the Big Bend in the early 1960s. The plaque itself was lost, but pictures of it have been deciphered by Fell. These, too, verified his contention that even African peoples were trading in the New World long before the usually accepted discoverers of North and South America took to the sea.

T HIS curiosity is compounded by an incident mentioned by Spanish colonizer Jose de Escandon in the middle 18th century when he came upon a tribe of black Indians near the mouth of the Rio Grande. These "Indians" told the explorer that their ancestors had come to the New World by boat from a homeland that must have been Africa. They were identified as negroids, and the blacks fought with spears and shields unlike those used by other Indians in the area. Escandon speculated that the blacks were survivors of the wreck of a slave boat or that they had escaped from a slave colony on an island in the Gulf of Mexico. No further mention is made of this tribe by later colonizers or explorers. But the blacks had intermarried with local Indian women, and chances are that they were absorbed by other bands in the area. Nevertheless, in recent years, there has been speculation, based on the Negroid features on some Olmec and Toltec statues, that blacks from Africa visited the New World — and possibly Texas — long before Columbus opened the New World for European colonization.

No definitive answers to these puzzles are expected or obtainable. They stand outside the usual realm of archaeological research. But they still present questions about the prehistory of Texas that should be borne in mind. Studies have found that legends often have a basis in fact. Other enigmas are based on enough evidence to put them a degree beyond rank speculation. But these ideas have yet to rest on the foundation of solid scientific evidence necessary to make them a part of the state's prehistory.

The Spanish Period

SPAIN'S conquest of the New World was one of the first acts of a vigorous, emerging nation. For 700 years, the Spanish fought to oust the Moorish invaders from the Iberian Peninsula. Regional and ethnic divisions hampered the effort, but the marriage of Isabella of Castile and Ferdinand of Aragon unified the country under a single monarchy.

Under Ferdinand's leadership in early 1492, the Spanish army conquered the province of Granada, completing the reconquista. Later in the year, Ferdinand and Isabella took a major stride toward shaping world history by commissioning Christopher Columbus to find a western route to the Far East.

Some historians characterize this voyage and subsequent subjugation of the New World as an extension of the Christian crusades against the Muslims. From the beginning, Columbus' exploration had religious, as well as economic, goals. In a papal bull in 1493, Pope Alexander VI gave Spain the right to develop any new lands that might be discovered west of the longitude 100 leagues west of the Azores and Cape Verde. But the assignment was conditioned on the Spanish making "God's name known there." The ultimate goal of Columbus' voyage was to establish contact with the Great Khan, a mythical figure as it turned out, in the Far East. Initially trade was to be developed, and Christianity was to be taken to the pagans. Ultimately, however, the Spaniards hoped to form an alliance with the powers of the Far East to put the Muslims in pincers and to break their control of the rich overland trade routes through the Middle East and to secure Christian dominance of the Holy Land.

From Columbus' first contact with New World natives, missionaries were in the forefront of the exploration. Early in the conquest, the Spanish crown decreed that the pagans must submit to Christian authority and receive religious instruction. If the natives refused, a "just war" could be initiated against them with enslavement to follow. And the Spanish conquest of Mexico and Central America was accomplished with astonishing speed. Between 1519-21, Hernan Cortez conquered the Aztecs in the Valley of Mexico and partially transformed the sophisticated Indian culture into the image of Christian Spain. The Aztecs of Central Mexico and the Mayans of the Yucatan and Central America, however, were settled, civilized people, much accustomed to following hierarchical leadership and to paying tribute or taxes. Although they stubbornly resisted the Spanish, the ultimate conquest was relatively simple.

Unlike Anglo-Americans, the Spanish had little racial prejudice in the modern sense. Throughout the long struggle with the Moors, the great gulf was between Christians and infidels, not between races. However, dark-skinned people were considered inferior, for most were thought to be infidels. From the initial contact, Spaniards intermixed with Indian women. The only social or religious limitation was the qualification that the women accept Christianity.

Spanish monarchs and religious leaders agonized over the treatment of New World natives. The conquest was bloody, as might be expected in a war. And afterward, other natives resisted conversion to Christianity. Spanish occupation policy also produced atrocities. Throughout the reconquest of the Iberian Peninsula, the Spanish required tribute from the conquered peoples. To reward the conquistadors for the perilous adventure in the New World, an encomienda system was established, in keeping with the practice used throughout the reconquista. The Spaniards were granted land and the use of natives. For this, the grantee was required to protect the Indians, to provide for their needs and to see that they were taught the faith. Too often the system was abused and degenerated into a form of slavery.

By 1540 the concern about treatment of the New World natives became so serious that Charles V suspended expeditions while a junta considered arguments about the proper policy toward treatment of the Indians. Pope Paul III in 1537 issued a papal bull asserting that the Indians were not "dumb brutes" and should not be enslaved. Bartolome de las Casas, a Dominican missionary with many years of experience in the New World, urged a humane policy. He suggested that priests be given strict parental control while the natives received religious instruction. The mission system that developed reflected some of Las Casas' suggestions. Others disagreed with this argument and harked back to Aristotle's theory of natural slavery. The argument held that some segments of mankind were born to serve a leisure class. The Spaniards, of course, were to be the leisure class.

Official policy of Spanish kings and popes was to treat the New World natives as reasoning human beings. They believed that all humans could be improved with patient instruction. In 1573, an ordinance was promulgated decreeing that "pacification," not "conquest," of the New World was Spain's goal. But policies and pronouncements often did not survive the trip across the Atlantic. The king's policy might always be obeyed, it was said, but it was not always enforced.

Humane treatment of the Indians had more practical sides, too. While England and France had excess populations to colonize the New World, Spain was a relatively sparsely settled nation. Therefore the crown's policy incorporated the Indians as an integral part of the colonization effort. They would be turned into good Spanish citizens. To this end, the mission system was developed with two basic goals: To convert the Indians to Christianity and to make them economically productive citizens. With the protection of the military, the aborigines in an untamed area who expressed a willingness to receive instruction would be congregated at a mission to be taught the faith and a trade as well. When the Indians' training was completed, the mission would be secularized as a church. The missionaries would move to another area. The system worked with varying degrees of success, although the zeal of the Franciscan, Dominican and Jesuit missionaries seldom waned.

"Pacification" of the New World became more difficult as the Spaniards moved north of the Valley of Mexico. The fierce Chichimecas resisted the Spanish yoke as vigorously as they had the Aztecs. These were nomadic Indians whose culture had little resemblance to that of the Aztecs or Mayans. In 1528, two expeditions launched by Cortez from the Rio Panuco crossed the Rio Grande but did not stay. No doubt other explorers briefly probed the region north of the Great River.

AS early as 1519, Alonso Alvarez de Pineda, a captain in the service of Francisco Garay, governor of Jamaica, mapped the coast of Texas. Early historians credited Alvarez de Pineda with exploring the Rio Grande from its mouth to the Brownsville area and with referring to the river as the "Rio de las Palmas." But recent research questions this interpretation. The first recorded exploration of today's Texas was made in the 1530s by Alvar Nunez Cabeza de Vaca, two other Spaniards and a Moorish black slave named "Esteban." They were members of the expedition commanded by Panfilo de Narvaez that left Cuba in 1528 to explore Florida — which included most of the southeastern United States and all the land westward to the Rio Grande at the time. Ill-fated from the beginning, many members of the expedition lost their lives, and others, including Cabeza de Vaca, were shipwrecked on the Texas coast. Cabeza de Vaca and his companions, although separated at intervals, survived and lived with a series of Indian tribes that inhabited much of southwestern and far western Texas. Through a combination of good luck and skill, Cabeza de Vaca gained a reputation as a healer, and after a time he was held in great esteem by many Indian groups. At one point in his wanderings, the Spaniard performed the first recorded medical surgery in the state by removing an arrow head from a man's chest. Wherever the little band of Spaniards went, however, stories circulated about the lands of great wealth to the north — the Seven (Golden) Cities of Cibola. When Cabeza de Vaca was reunited with his countrymen in Mexico in 1536, these tales excited the interest of authorities.

In 1540, Francisco Vazquez de Coronado, governor of New Galicia, was commissioned to lead an exploration of the American Southwest. The quest took him to the land of the Pueblo Indians in New Mexico. Here his interest in riches was further enhanced with tales of Gran Quivira, a land rumored to be even richer than Cibola. Native Americans learned it was best to keep the Europeans away from their homes, so they would suggest vast riches could be found in other areas. So Coronado pursued a fruitless search for the riches across the High Plains of Texas, Oklahoma and Kansas. Missionaries on the expedition found the number of potential souls to save overwhelming and stayed in the upper Rio Grande valley.

While Coronado was investigating Texas' High Plains from the west, Luis Moscoso de Alvarado assumed leadership of Hernando de Soto's expedition when the commander died on the banks of the Mississippi River. In 1542, Moscoso's group ventured as far west as Central Texas before returning to the Mississippi. While sailing for Mexico, the group was shipwrecked for a time at the mouth of the Sabine River. Here they used oil from seeps to caulk their boats, ignoring the claims of local Indians that the petroleum had great medicinal properties. This was the first recorded use of the mineral in the state — the mineral that has become synonymous with Texas.

But an era was ending. Cortez had found great riches that could be easily reaped in the Aztec and Mayan kingdoms. Other conquistadors had been equally successful, and even lesser adventurers had profited within the encomienda system. These vigorous, ambitious men who had fought first to free Spain from the Moors and then to conquer the New World were aging. The Coronado expedition is considered by some historians as the last of the old regime. Certainly the makeup was different. More non-Spaniards participated, and the men were younger, without the battle experience of the older warrior-explorers. And the northern territories were unlike central Mexico in climate, culture and economic potential. Quick wealth was not to be found. A new generation of explorers and settlers would be required to venture into the harsh northern territories.

One of this new breed was Luis de Carvajal, a member of a Jewish family that converted to Christianity. He was given a huge land grant stretching from the Rio Panuco in Mexico to an area near present-day San Antonio. As part of the bargain, he agreed to introduce cattle into the region. Though it is not known if Carvajal ever visited Texas, cattle that he brought into Mexico are thought to have migrated north of the Rio Grande. Carvajal died while imprisoned during the Inquisition for failing to denounce his sister as a Jew.

Spain had no precedents from which to develop an administrative system for the New World colonies. What evolved was cumbersome procedure that stifled initiative and action. The Council of the Indes administered New Spain, as Mexico was called, and viceroys supervised regional affairs. Philip II completely centralized the system upon taking the throne in 1556, however. Several administrative councils became only consulting bodies. Philip made all final decisions on affairs of state, down to the most inconsequential details. Consequently, decisions had to filter through a bureaucracy that stretched across the Atlantic. The process could — and did in some cases — take years. Philip's successors delegated authority to ministers after his death in 1598, but the system remained cumbersome and troublesome.

FORTY years passed after the Coronado and Moscoso expeditions before Fray Agustin Rodriguez, a Franciscan missionary, and Francisco Sanchez Chamuscado, a soldier, led an expedition to Texas and New Mexico. Following the Rio Conchos in Mexico to its confluence with the Rio Grande near present-day Presidio and then turning northwestward in the Great River's valley, the explorers passed through the El Paso area in 1581. Among the Pueblo Indians great material wealth was not found, but the missionary was satisfied with the spiritual potential of the pagans. Father Rodriguez died a martyr. The following year, Antonio de Espejo led a relief expedition up the Pecos

River from the Rio Grande to the Pueblo Indian area only to learn of the missionary's fate.

Permanent colonization of the upper Rio Grande valley was accomplished as the 16th century drew to a close. Juan de Onate was granted the right to develop the area in which the Pueblo Indians lived. In 1598, he blazed a trail across the desert from Santa Barbara, Chihuahua, to intersect the Rio Grande at the Pass of the North — today's El Paso. For the next 200 years, this was the supply route from the interior of Mexico that served the northern colonies. And the El Paso-Juarez area developed as a way station. The first permanent settlement in Texas was established in 1681 after the Pueblo Indians rebelled and drove the Spanish settlers southward. The colonists retreated to the El Paso area, where the missions of Ysleta del Sur and Socorro del Sur — each named for a community in New Mexico — were established. Ysleta pueblo originally was located on the south side of the Rio Grande, but as the river changed course, it ended up on the north bank. Now part of El Paso, the community is considered the oldest European settlement in Texas.

TEXAS was attractive to the Spanish in the 16th and 17th centuries. Small expeditions found trade possibilities, and missionaries had ventured into the territory to instruct the Indians. Frays Juan de Salas and Diego Lopez responded to a request by the Jumano Indians for religious instruction in 1629, and for a brief time the priests lived with the Indians near present-day San Angelo.

Missionary efforts also were made north of the Rio Grande. In 1675, Fernando del Bosque and Fray Juan Larios led an expedition to gain insight into the Coahuiltecan bands in the region. Capt. Juan Dominguez led an expedition that established a mission among the Jumano Indians at the La Junta — the confluence of the Rio Grande and the Rio Conchos. This mission was closed in 1688, and a priest blamed its problems on the military and others who enslaved many Indians to work in the north Mexico mines. But the Spanish crown was preoccupied with affairs in Europe. The colonial wealth also was diverted to these activities — and to extravagant living at court — rather than to investment in development of the New World. Ironically, it was affairs of state in Europe, rather than the resources and natural attractiveness of the territory, that first riveted Spain's attention on Texas. From 1681 to 1697, Spain and France were at war on the Continent, as they had been for much of the 17th century.

Spain's claim to the vast stretch of the New World from Florida to the Pacific Ocean rankled the French. In 1682, an ambitious and courageous Rene Robert Cavalier, Sieur de la Salle, explored the Mississippi to its mouth at the Gulf of Mexico. LaSalle claimed the vast territory for France, cutting the heart out of Spain's North American territories. Two years later, LaSalle returned to the New World with four ships and enough colonists to establish his country's claim in this segment of Spanish America. Some historians think that LaSalle's expedition was blown past the mouth of the Mississippi by a Gulf storm and ended up on the Texas coast by mistake; others think Texas was his planned destination. Nevertheless, though short of supplies because of the loss of two ships, the French colonists established Fort Saint Louis at the head of Lavaca Bay. Hostile Indians, bad weather and disease took their toll on the small enclave, although LaSalle managed three expeditions into the surrounding countryside. Based on these explorations, the French made a weak claim that the Rio Grande was the western boundary of Louisiana Territory. In 1687, LaSalle and a group of soldiers began an overland trip to find French outposts on the Mississippi. Somewhere near present-day Navasota in Grimes County, the great explorer was murdered by one of his men. His grave has never been found.

When Spanish officials heard from Indians about the French colony, a frenzied search for LaSalle was launched. Five sea expeditions combed the Gulf Coast from the Rio Grande to today's Florida. And six land expeditions into Texas' interior provided Spanish officials with the first detailed information about the territory. Finally, in 1689, Capt. Alonso de Leon, governor of Coahuila, re-entered Texas at a ford near present-day Eagle Pass and headed eastward. He found the charred remains of Fort Saint Louis at the head of Lavaca Bay. Indians had destroyed the settlement and killed many colonists. DeLeon continued tracking survivors of the ill-fated colony into East Texas.

On this journey, Father Damian Massanet accompanied the official. The priest was fascinated with tales about the "Tejas" Indians of the region. "Tejas" meant friendly, but at the time the term was considered a tribal name. Actually these Indians were members of the Caddo Confederacy that controlled parts of four present states — Texas, Louisiana, Arkansas and Oklahoma. They were the most culturally developed of all Texas Indians. They farmed, had a well-developed leadership structure and traded across a broad area. Unlike other Indians, they had judicial and diplomatic procedures to settle disputes between groups within the confederacy. The Caddo religion also acknowledged one supreme god, which the Spanish felt made them prime candidates for conversion to Christianity. For years, the Tejas had been brought to the attention of the Spanish by the Jumano Indians who traded with them and with the Pueblo Indians of New Mexico.

Usually the Caddos did not let strangers enter their territory. Trade usually was carried on at annual fairs that were held on the periphery of their settlements. But with the French trading with the Caddos' enemies, the East Texas Indians were anxious to develop contacts with Europeans to obtain trade goods, guns and horses. Hence the Spanish were quite welcome.

When a Tejas chief asked Father Massanet to stay and instruct his people in religion, the Spaniards quickly promised to return and establish a mission. The pledge was redeemed in 1690 when the mission San Francisco de las Tejas was founded near present-day Weches in Houston County. A few months later, a second mission, Santisimo Nombre de Maria, was established nearby, only to be washed away by a flood in a few months.

Twin disasters struck this missionary effort. Spanish officials soon lost interest in the French threat. And as was the case with many New World Indians who had no resistance to European diseases, the Tejas soon were felled by an epidemic that killed many. Some Indians blamed the illness on the holy water used for baptism by the priests. Soon the mission languished. It was difficult to supply, being so far from the other Spanish outposts in northern Mexico, and the Caddos remained committed to their native religion. Also the priests often insulted the Indians' leaders and medicine men, and the soldiers were troublesome.

In addition to being the first European settlements in East Texas, the missions also brought ranching to the region. The herds of cattle driven to the area by De Leon were the first organized movement of livestock in Texas.

In 1693, Spanish officials closed the missions, however, leaving the Tejas to the stealthful ministrations of French traders for two decades.

Europeans and Indians

ALTHOUGH Spain had not made a determined effort to settle Texas, great changes were coming to the territory. The French had opened trade with Indians along the Mississippi River and its tributaries and had made contact with Indians on the High Plains. French guns and horses were changing the nature of warfare among the Indians.

Spain introduced horses into Texas and the Southwest. No one is sure when or how the Comanches got mounts. But in the late 17th century they began moving on to the Plains from their Rocky Mountain homelands. On foot, the Comanches were not intimidating. They were short and stocky and somewhat awkward in appearance. They were among the best horsemen in the world, however, and were fierce warriors, spreading terror wherever they went.

The southward movement of the Comanches and their allies on the Great Plains played havoc with the established homelands of several groups of Indians. The Apaches were the first to be displaced. And the Apaches were the first of the fierce Plains Indians to worry the Spanish. In the 1720s, the Apaches moved onto the lower Texas Plains, taking the traditional hunting grounds of the Jumanos and others. The nomadic Coahuiltecan bands were particularly hard hit. Attempts by these Indians to gain Spanish support against the Apaches were fruitless until the late 1720s, and by that time, many of the Apaches' enemies, like the Jumanos, had joined the raiders. As early as 1707, the El Paso area was under siege by the Apaches.

Although the Spanish stayed out of the Indian wars in the beginning of their excursions into Texas, they were soon drawn into the fray. In 1699, the French established a colony on the Mississippi River in Louisiana and began trading with the Indians in East Texas. The Spanish had to respond to the challenge to protect their interests.

Spanish officials became committed to opening Texas for trade and colonization. In 1700, the mission San Juan Bautista was moved to a site on the south side of the Rio Grande near present-day Eagle Pass where two excellent fords provided access across the river. The mission became the gateway to colonial Texas from Mexico, and many figures who shaped the territory's future passed through this portal.

In Europe, Philip V, the grandson of the French king with aspirations to the French throne, ascended to the Spanish throne in 1701, becoming the first of the Bourbon kings. He instituted reforms in the clumsy administrative system, but it remained an impediment to development of the New World frontier.

In 1709, Fray Antonio de San Buenaventura y Olivares made an initial request to establish a mission at San Pedro Springs (today's San Antonio) to minister to the Coahuiltecans, who were suffering at the hands of the Apaches. The request was denied. But the Spanish were xenophobic about the French, and quickly responded to any threat, real or perceived, by their European enemies.

Religious intrigue involving the French spurred the Spanish into action that led to the establishment of permanent missions and the colonization of Texas. Father Francisco Hidalgo had served at the Tejas missions in East Texas in the early 1690s and longed to return. When Spanish officials turned a deaf ear to his request, the priest secretly wrote the French governor of Louisiana in New Orleans seeking help in establishing a mission among the Tejas. Always anxious to open trade with the Spanish, the governor dispatched Louis Juchereau de Saint Denis, an adventurer and explorer, to find the priest and to enter into trade negotiations. While crossing Texas, Saint Denis was impressed with the number of wild cattle that roamed the region. These no doubt were the offspring of the cattle left at the East Texas missions, and the result of De Leon's practice of leaving a cow and a calf at each river crossing while traveling to East Texas in 1689. When Saint Denis arrived at San Juan Bautista, the Spanish were aghast at his temerity. Fears of new French incursions into Texas were fanned. Though Saint Denis vowed he wanted only to open trade — which was strictly forbidden by Spanish colonial policy — he was sent to Mexico City for questioning. Upon release by Spanish authorities, Saint Denis returned to San Juan Bautista, married the commandant's granddaughter and served as a guide for the expedition that established the second set of missions in East Texas.

FATHER Hidalgo's dream of returning to the Tejas was realized when he accompanied Capt. Diego Ramon on the expedition. The mission San Francisco de los Neches was established in 1716 near the site of the old San Francisco de los Tejas mission. Nuestra Senora de Guadalupe was located at the present-day site of Nacogdoches, and Nuestra Senora de los Dolores was placed near present-day San Augustine. Two other missions were located in the area, and another was built across the Sabine River in Louisiana. The East Texas missions did little better on the second try. Saint Denis, who was well-liked by the Indians, planned to stay in the area to set up a trading post. But the suspicious Spanish forced him to leave, to the distress of the Indians. Supplying the missions also was a problem, as it had been in the 1690s. The Indians were unhappy with the trade goods and the delays in receiving supplies. Soon it became apparent that a way station between northern Mexico and the East Texas missions was needed.

In 1718, Spanish officials consented to Fray Olivares' request to found a mission at San Pedro Springs.

Because the Indians of the region often did not get along with each other, other missions soon were established to serve each group. And for a time these missions flourished and each became an early ranching center. But the missions' large herds of cattle and horses soon attracted trouble.

About 1720, the Apaches made their first appearance in the San Antonio area. One settler was killed and scalped and raids on the missions' herds began. Punitive retaliation by the Spanish only outraged the Apaches, and religious authorities opposed the military operations. Attempts to negotiate a peace with the Apaches failed, but the raids subsided between 1726 and 1731.

War broke out between the French and Spanish in Europe, and the East Texas missions were temporarily abandoned a second time in 1717 after a comic-opera incident in which the mission at Nacogdoches was engaged by French soldiers from Natchitoches in present-day Louisiana.

The expulsion from East Texas prompted the Spanish to return with the largest military operation of the period. The Marquis San Miguel de Aguayo, a nobleman of Coahuila, was ordered to launch a retaliatory offensive, but the orders were soon changed. Texas' defenses were to be strengthened. Because of the time lag in receiving orders, Aguayo's expedition did not get into the field until 1721. With 500 men, 4,000 horses and large herds of livestock, he reached San Antonio in April 1721, and after strengthening the presidio there he headed for East Texas.

UNKNOWN to the Spanish in Texas, the French had suffered a financial disaster. John Law, a Scottish banker, had launched an investment scheme that involved the issuance of paper money in France to finance the development of colonies on the Mississippi River. The bubble broke in 1720, and the French government all but abandoned the colonization effort while retrenching to repair the damage to the nation's economy. In some cases, Indians in the Mississippi valley attacked French traders in rebellion against the diminished trade. But Saint Denis had been given command of French troops in Louisiana and tried to arrange a truce with Aguayo to prevent the remanning of Spanish missions and presidios in the region. The ploy did not work. Forts and missions were reestablished, and a presidio was built at Los Adaes to keep an eye on the French at Natchitoches. This presidio, which was located near present-day Robeline, La., became the capital of the province of Texas for the next half century.

Aguayo was successful in strengthening the defenses in Texas. He reestablished six missions, founded three more. Two new presidios were established, one reestablished and a fourth strengthened. When Aguayo left Texas, 269 soldiers were on duty in a territory that previously was defended by only 60 to 70. He also separated the province of Texas from Coahuila for the first time, drawing the boundary along the San Antonio and Medina rivers.

While Texas' eastern frontier was threatened by the French in the 18th century, the greatest problem for the Spanish existed in the thinly populated areas of western Texas. The Comanches began their southward movement from the Northern Plains at the beginning of the century, relentlessly pushing the Apaches and others before them. The Apaches moved westward and southward. Attempts by the Jumano Indians to have missions established in the Big Bend near the junction of the Rio Grande and the Rio Conchos — the Junta de los Rios — were thwarted by hostiles in 1717-18. A mission built near present-day Del Rio suffered a similar fate. And San Juan Bautista, built unfortunately close to one prong of the Comanche trail crossing the Rio Grande, was under constant threat. Only the most adventuresome Spaniard or Mexican braved the hazards of this frontier to attempt colonization, and often the price paid for a display of courage was the settler's life. By the middle 1730s, the Apaches were raiding mercilessly south of the Rio Grande. Monclova and Saltillo were endangered, and the province of Sonora was on the brink of destruction. The Spanish concentrated their defensive efforts south of the river to protect the silver mines and ranches in northern Mexico. The province of Texas was actually "behind enemy lines" for much of the time.

The San Antonio missions felt the Apache wrath. The mission system, which attempted to convert the Indians to Christianity and to "civilize" them, was partially successful in subduing minor tribes. But the Spanish realized that more stable colonization efforts must be made. Mexican Indians, such as the Tlascalans who fought with Cortez against the Aztecs, were brought into Texas to serve as examples of "good" Indians for the wayward natives. In 1731, descendants of the colonists of the Canary Islands were brought to Texas and founded the Villa of San Fernando de Bexar, the first civil jurisdiction in the province and today's San Antonio. But the province remained thinly populated, much to the despair of Spanish officials.

As desperate as was the plight of Texas, the Spanish were more concerned about another area. One of Spain's most successful colonization efforts in the New World came in the Lower Rio Grande Valley. But the history of the effort underscores the lengthy process of decision-making in Spanish Texas. In the late 1730s, officials became concerned over the vulnerability of Seno Mexico — the large area between the Sierra Madre Oriental and the Gulf Coast in Northern Mexico. The area was unsettled, a haven for runaway Indian slaves and marauders, and it was a wide-open pathway for the English or French from the Gulf to the rich silver mines in Durango.

For seven years the search for the right colonizer went on before Jose de Escandon was selected in 1746. A professional military man and successful administrator, Escandon earned a high reputation by subduing Indians in Central Mexico. On receiving the assignment, he launched a broad land survey of the area running from the mountains to the Gulf and from the Rio Panuco in Tamaulipas, Mexico, to the Nueces River in Texas. In 1747, he began placing colonists in settlements throughout the area. Tomas Sanchez received a land grant on the Rio Grande in 1755 from which Laredo developed. And other small Texas communities along the river sprang up as a result of Escandon's well-executed plan. Many old Mexican families in Texas hold title to their land based on grants in this period.

Escandon's colony became the state of Nuevo Santander, named for the founder's home province in Spain. The boundaries extended to the Nueces River, placing the Lower Rio Grande Valley outside of Texas.

Escandon also contributed to the early development of ranching in South Texas. In 1753 he granted Capt. Jose Vasquiz Borrego 433,800 acres of land to develop a ranch. The headquarters was located near the present-day town of San Ygnacio in Zapata County. Other large land grants also helped establish large-scale ranching in the area, although Texas never developed the hacienda concept that was used in Mexico. Ranching helped the economy, but the livestock also attracted Indians.

AS devastating as the Apaches were to Spanish settlements, they were getting the worst of their fight with the Comanches and their allies. By 1747, the Apaches around San Antonio were ready to make peace and said they were ready to enter missions. Attempts to gather them in existing missions failed because other Indians feared and hated them after many years of bloody warfare. In 1757, officials established the mission of San Saba de la Santa Cruz in present-day Menard County. Two years later, the Spanish encountered the Comanches in Texas for the first time. The Comanches, with their allies from the Plains, devastated the mission, killing several priests and Indians. Spanish officials were irate. After much debate they launched a punitive expedition to punish the raiders. Col. Diego Ortiz Parrilla led a mixed army of Mexican Indians, Lipan Apaches and Spanish soldiers. The force engaged a mixed group of Plains Indians at Spanish Fort on a bend of the Red River in present-day Montague County. Entrenched in a stockade with a crude moat, the Indians fought with French weapons and used disciplined tactics in the field. Abandoned by their allies, the Spanish suffered a humiliating loss, the worst inflicted on them by Texas Indians during the colonial period.

The battle of Spanish Fort was a turning point in Indian warfare. The Plains Indians proved they could adapt to European field tactics. And for a time, they had set aside tribal animosities to present a united front against the colonizers. The Spanish had easily defeated sedentary Indians in Mexico, but the Plains Indians were a different breed, as the defeat of the Spanish proved. Obviously, new tactics were needed if the Spanish were to stay in Texas.

LaSalle's Landing

More than 2,000 people gathered in Port Lavaca to witness the tricentennial re-enactment of the landing of Rene Robert Cavalier, Sieur de la Salle, in Lavaca Bay. LaSalle established a French claim to the territory of Texas that was not finally reconciled until the United States annexed the region in 1845. Above, LaSalle (light coat), portrayed by Paul Hammerschmidt, and his party, (l-r) Brian Weiss, Joe Survovik and Nathan Mallison, are shown staking a claim to the territory upon which they would settle for a short time. At right, the approach of the French explorer and his crew is enacted with a replica of his ship, designed on the lines of a Chinese junk, in the background. The French colony did not last long, as weather, Indians and disease took their toll. LaSalle was killed by his men when on an overland trip to make contact with French outposts on the Mississippi River. LaSalle's adventure brought the second of Texas' six flags to the territory and set the stage for the claim of Texans to the Rio Grande as the boundary of the Republic in 1836.

On this gently sloping hillside near Robeline, La., stood the governor's mansion that served as the capitol of the Spanish province of Texas from 1721 to 1773. The site of the presidio was preserved by the citizens of Robeline, and the state now operates it as a commemorative site. Texas Almanac Photo.

Texas' Capital in Louisiana

Many archaeological sites are lost to vandals long before they can be preserved for future generations. Texas can thank the residents of Robeline, La., for the preservation of the site of one of the Lone Star State's colonial capitals: The Los Adaes presidio.

A local historian, J. Fair Hardin, researched the location of the presidio and, on his recommendation in 1931, the Colonial Dames of the XVII Century provided Natchitoches Parish with funds to buy the site. Although little was done to excavate the presidio, the site was protected. In 1972, Robeline residents organized the Los Adaes Foundation and, in 1978, got the mission and presidio placed on the National Register of Historic Places. A year later, the 12-acre tract of land on which the presidio is located was deeded to the state with the understanding that a commemorative site would be developed. In 1985, the site was designated a National Historic Landmark.

History Highlights

The mission, San Miguel, at Los Adaes was established by the Spanish in 1716 to serve the Adaes tribe of the Caddo Indians. Three years later, French troops from Fort St. Jean Baptiste in present-day Natchitoches ousted the Spanish. But the Marquis de Aguayo in 1721 re-established the mission and built a fort nearby to offset the French influence in what was then a border area. From 1721 to 1773, Los Adaes served as the provincial capital of Texas.

H. F. "Pete" Gregory, professor of anthropology at Northwestern Louisiana State University at Natchitoches, began small excavations of the presidio site in 1964 and, in the next 20 years, established the parameters of the fort. Dr. Gregory says the presidio site is unique in that no city has grown up around it. Therefore the undisturbed location is a treasure chest of 18th century history for both Texas and Louisiana.

Though through much of Los Adaes' history, trade between the Spanish and nearby French was prohibited, Gregory has uncovered evidence of a well-developed trade between the adversaries.

French-made artifacts are almost as common as Spanish. Pieces of English and French tableware, Indian pottery, European trade beads, weapons and other artifacts turned up in the excavations reflect strong cultural contact between the many peoples who lived and traded in the area.

Although drawings with dimensions were available, archaeologists were surprised at the size of the fort because of the quirk of the Spanish engineers. A common unit of measurement for the colonial Spanish was the vara, which is usually defined as a length of about 33 and one-third inches. At the Los Adaes presidio, however, a 40-inch vara was used, a full 20 percent longer than usual. The longer unit of measurement apparently also was used at some Spanish facilities in present-day Texas.

The hexagonal fort had three bulwarks and was surrounded by moats. Two four-pounder cannons were located in each bulwark. The facility, complete with a governor's mansion, chapel, barracks, stables and other amenities, was large enough to house 300 soldiers. That was a large establishment for the day.

Untouched in the current excavations is the nearby mission site and cemetery, which are on private land. The state has been in negotiations to acquire the 25-acre tract that should prove to be another treasure trove of 18th century Spanish-French colonial history.

Despite the amount of work that already has been done at the site, archaeologist Gregory indicates than another 20 years of excavation are needed to fully explore these historic sites. Work proceeds as funds are made available by the state government.

The State of Louisiana has built an archaeological laboratory on the site to house the hundreds of artifacts that already have been recovered from the presidio and homes sites surrounding it. A museum and interpretive center are planned to make the site an even more exciting tourist attraction.

Los Adaes is the only capital of Texas to be located outside the present-day boundaries of Texas or Mexico. And it may be the best preserved for archaeologists of all the previous capitals. If so, it is a tribute to the pride and foresight of the residents of Robeline and to the State of Louisiana.

The Demise of Spain

SPAIN'S final 60 years of control of the province of Texas were marked with a few successes and a multitude of failures, all of which could be attributed to a breakdown in the administrative system. Charles III, the fourth of the Bourbon line of kings and generally recognized as an enlightened despot, took the throne in 1759. Soon he launched a series of reforms in the New World. The king's choice of administrators was excellent. In 1765, Jose de Galvez was dispatched to New Spain (an area that then included all of modern Mexico and much of today's American West) with instructions to improve both the economy and the defense.

Galvez initially toured parts of the vast region, gaining first-hand insight into the practical problems of the colony. And there were many that could be traced to Spain's basic concepts of colonial government. Texas, in particular, suffered from the mercantilist economic system that attempted to funnel all colonial trade through ports in Mexico.

In a typical trip, trade goods bound for Texas would enter New Spain at the port of Veracruz. From there they would be shipped to Mexico City and then Saltillo before reaching Texas. At each stop, charges would be added. By the time the goods reached Texas, they would be prohibitively expensive. Texas' economy was limited. Ranching was its foundation, and there were few markets for Texas cattle and horses. The mines in northern Mexico were serviced by haciendas in that region. Texas' market was limited to the army, the missions and the few colonists who lived in the province.

Also, because of the mercantilist approach, trade with the French in Louisiana Territory was strictly forbidden. But Spanish Texans were practical people. When a demand for Texas cattle and horses developed in Louisiana, a healthy smuggling trade arose. Texas' livestock became a medium of exchange for low-cost trade goods provided by French traders. And government officials in Texas often were bribed to look the other way.

Problems with the Comanches, Apaches and "Nortenos," as the Spanish called some tribes, continued to plague the province, too. The Marquis de Rubi was commissioned to inspect the defenses of the entire northern New Spain frontier from California to Louisiana. Rubi reached Texas in 1767 and was appalled by the deplorable condition of the province's defenses. At San Saba mission, there were not enough horses for each soldier, although each should have had four or five mounts to be properly equipped. Soldiers at Los Adaes had only two guns and two shields for the entire 60-man contingent. Morale was low throughout the province. In some cases, officers were selling equipment and uniforms to soldiers at greatly inflated prices. Rubi recommended sweeping reforms in the defense system. But some changes were based on faulty assumptions.

In 1762, France ceded the Louisiana Territory to Spain in compensation for Spain's help in the losing effort in the Seven Years War in Europe. The politics of the day convinced the French that it was better that this huge — and largely undefined — area be in the hands of the Spanish than the British. For the Spanish in Texas, the cession was a mixed blessing, however. True, the French were no longer an immediate threat on the province's eastern boundary. But the fact lulled Rubi into a false sense of security.

With the need to defend East Texas from the French diminished, Rubi moved to construct Texas' defenses around the needs of the mining and ranching areas in northern Mexico. This meant closing the East Texas missions and presidios and moving the soldiers and colonists to San Antonio to bolster defenses against the Indians. In addition, Rubi moved the presidio San Elizario north of the Rio Grande to defend the El Paso area and abandoned the San Saba mission and presidio, which were inactive anyway. Presidio La Bahia was strengthened, and a military way station was established at Arroyo del Cibola to protect the road between San Antonio and La Bahia. As a practical matter, however, much of Texas was not to be defended; it was, in a sense, "behind enemy lines."

Charles III's well-intentioned reorganization of New Spain took almost a decade. And in the interim, conflicting policies took their toll on good will and attempts to pacify the various Indian groups in Texas.

When Spain undertook the administration of Louisiana Territory, one of the terms of the cession by France was that the region would enjoy certain trading privileges denied to other Spanish dependencies. So although Texas and Louisiana were neighbors, trade between the two provinces was banned. The crown further complicated matters by placing the administration of Louisiana under authorities in Cuba, while Texas remained under the authorities in Mexico City. Officials often acted as if the two Spanish provinces were actually warring foreign countries. This was an intolerable burden on Spanish settlers in East Texas and on French traders who were being integrated into the effort to control the Nortenos, a term which covered a number of Plains Indians in Texas.

The Nortenos, who for a time were allied with the Comanches, warred intermittently against the Spanish after their victory at Spanish Fort in 1759. Nortenos resented treaties between the Spanish and their enemies, the Apaches. Punitive expeditions by the Spanish military only deepened the hostility and prompted retaliation. By the early 1770s, the Osage Indians were encouraged by renegade French traders and the British to raid the Nortenos, who in turn recouped losses of horses and livestock by sacking Spanish settlements.

Several attempts were made by Spanish officials in Texas to make peace with the Nortenos, but the prohibition of trade with Louisiana stymied the efforts. Often the Spanish were not able to produce annual gifts that were promised, and a strict ban on supplying the Indians with guns and munitions hurt the effort. The peace overtures to the Nortenos also damaged relations with the mission Apaches. Rubi's order to close the East Texas missions and forts was not executed until 1773, when Indian depredations again increased around San Antonio. On just a few days' notice, the settlers were ordered to gather up their personal belongings and leave. Many died on the trip across Texas to the new capital at San Antonio. Others were bankrupted when they had to leave behind many possessions acquired during a lifetime. And the incident emphasized another weakness in the Spanish colonial system: Unlike later American settlers, the Spaniards did not have control of their destinies. Too often geopolitical considerations were paramount in the government's colonial policy.

Although the East Texans were offered their choice of unsettled land around San Antonio, the good property had long ago been taken by early colonists. What good land was available was too exposed to Indian raids. The settlers, led by Antonio Gil Y'barbo and Gil Flores, petitioned officials for permission to move back to East Texas. They got approval to go as far as the Trinity River, where in 1774 they set up a fortified village, named Bucareli in honor of the viceroy, on the present-day Walker County line where the Camino Real crossed the river.

WITHOUT a listening post in Louisiana and with communications with the sister colony often officially banned, Texas officials were hard-pressed to keep up with the activities of the Nortenos. When settlers at Bucareli were frightened by Comanche raids in 1778 and 1779 and discouraged by continuing floods that washed away crops, they moved farther east to set up a community at the site of the old Nacogdoches mission. This marked the founding of present-day Nacogdoches. Although the move was not sanctioned initially, Y'barbo later was named lieutenant governor of the province at the settlement and established a clandestine trade and intelligence network with the French traders in Louisiana.

Jose de Galvez' survey of New Spain bore fruit in 1776, when as minister of the Indes he established the Internal Provinces to administer the defense of the northern frontier of New Spain. Under the new arrangement, Texas and Louisiana were ordered to cooperate, which temporarily eased many of the problems.

Not all the changes were welcome, however. Upon becoming commandant general of the Internal Provinces in 1776, Teodoro de Croix decreed that all unbranded livestock in Texas was the property of the crown. Ranchers and missionaries were furious. They complained that they had been unable to conduct semi-annual roundups of their stock for years because of the Indian hostilities. De Croix relented to the extent of giving the stockmen four months to brand and mark their cattle and horses, and thereafter they were required to pay fees on their animals. Texas' cattle and horse market improved in 1780 when a concession was granted by the king to allow legal livestock trade with Louisiana.

Bernardo de Galvez, the nephew of Jose and the namesake of Galveston County, was named acting governor of Louisiana in 1777. He had experience as an Indian fighter along the Rio Grande and had an insight into the colonial situation. During the American War for Independence, the younger Galvez occupied the British in Florida, preventing them from concentrating attention on the American revolutionaries. And Galvez had cattle driven from the Gulf Plains and South Texas to supply the Americans along the Mississippi River. The cattle drives were the forerunners of the later livestock movements that played so great a role in the development of Texas after the American Civil War.

During the last two decades of the 18th century, Spain reached the zenith of its power in the northern provinces of New Spain. Operating within Jose de Galvez' recommendations, Charles III reformed the administration of New Spain. Talented, experienced leaders were given control of the new provinces and improvements were made. Although maintaining amicable relations with the various Indian groups in Texas was difficult, the Spanish made accommodations with most of the aborigines. Some of the Apaches remained intractable, and groups within the Comanches sometimes failed to honor treaties made by other Comanche leaders. In 1791, Juan de Ugalde defeated Lipan and Mescalero Apaches in the Lower Rio Grande Valley and brought peace for many years to that region. (Despite the difference in spelling, Uvalde County in South Texas is named for this soldier.)

ONE of the tragedies of the period was the untimely death of the promising young administrator, Bernardo de Galvez. His family had a long record of service to the Spanish crown, and Bernardo in 1785 succeeded his father, Matias, as viceroy of New Spain. Such was the crown's confidence in the new administrator that he retained control of Cuba, the Floridas and Louisiana and gained authority over the Internal Provinces in addition to his other responsibilities. Galvez conceived a policy that maintained peace with the Indians until the turn of the century. Very simply, he gave the Indians the choice between war and peace. Those that chose peace were given annual gifts and, in some cases, old firearms. Indians that chose war were mercilessly pursued. As long as the gifts were forthcoming and frontier-wise administrators were kept in the provinces, relative peace was maintained. But young Galvez died in an epidemic in 1786, and the great promise of his early administration was not fulfilled.

The death of Charles III in 1788 and the beginning of the French Revolution a year later also weakened Spain's hold of the New World dominions. Charles IV was not as good a sovereign as his predecessor, and his choice of ministers was poor. The quality of frontier administrators declined, and relations with Indians soured.

Charles IV's major blunder, however, was to side with French royalty during the revolution, earning Spain the enmity of Napoleon Bonaparte when he assumed control of the government. Spain also allied with England in an effort to thwart Napoleon, and in this losing cause, the Spanish were forced to cede Louisiana back to France. In 1803, Napoleon broke a promise to retain the territory and sold it to the United States. Spain's problems in the New World thereby took on an altogether different dimension. Anglo-Americans cast longing eyes on the vast undeveloped territory of Texas. The available land east of the Mississippi River was being quickly developed as the Americans drove the Indians of the American Southeast westward from their historic homelands.

With certain exceptions for royalists who left the American colonies during the revolution, Spain had maintained a strict prohibition against Anglo or other non-Spanish settlers in their New World territories. But they were unprepared to police the eastern border of Texas after removing the presidios in the 1760s. What had been a provincial line became virtually overnight an international boundary, and an ill-defined one at that.

Spain and France had never set a specific boundary between Texas and Louisiana, and during the colonial period from 1762 to 1803, only a general line was acknowledged. Thomas Jefferson initially tried to claim all of Texas to the Rio Grande as part of the Louisiana Purchase, based on weak French claims tied to LaSalle's explorations. For a period of time, Spanish and American authorities created a no-man's-land between the Sabine River and Arroyo Hondo, which became a refuge for renegades from both nations.

Anglo-Americans began to probe the Spanish frontier. Some settled in East Texas and were tolerated by authorities. Others, however, were thought to have more nefarious designs. Philip Nolan was the first of the American filibusters to test Spanish resolve. Several times, both authorized and unauthorized, he entered Texas to capture wild horses to sell in the United States. But in 1801, the Spanish perceived an attempted armed uprising by Nolan and his followers. He was killed in a battle near present-day Waco, and his company was taken captive to work in the mines of northern Mexico.

In 1806, Anglo-Americans were showing up in the El Paso area. Lt. Zebulon Pike, commissioned by President Jefferson to survey the newly acquired lands of the Louisiana Purchase, was taken into custody in the upper Rio Grande Valley. After a journey into the interior of Mexico, however, he was released and returned to the United States through Texas, becoming the first Anglo-American to write of the geographic features and economic potential of the region.

Spanish officials were beginning to realize that the economic potential of Texas must be developed if the Anglo-Americans were to be neutralized. In the late 18th and early 19th centuries, several attempts were made to find a short route to Sante Fe to open trade with that sister province. Later Moses Austin and Mirabeau Lamar would see the same economic potential in Texas-Santa Fe trade, although it was never realized.

On the continent, Spain's fortunes were at a low ebb. Napoleon was pressuring Charles IV, whose abdication in 1808 the French ruler refused to accept. Ferdinand VII claimed the crown, and Napoleon in the same year placed his brother, Joseph Bonaparte, on the throne. Spain rebelled against this foreign intrusion, and the War for Independence on the Iberian Peninsula was on.

Resistance to Spanish rule had developed in the New World colonies. Liberal ideas from the American and French revolutions had grown popular, despite the crown's attempts to prevent their dissemination. And chaos reigned in the colonies. From the time of Philip II, Spain had been a tightly centralized monarchy with the crown making most decisions. But during the war on the peninsula, three sovereigns — Charles IV, Ferdinand VII and Joseph Bonaparte — often issued edicts simultaneously. The colonials rebelled. Father Miguel Hidalgo ignited the Mexican war for independence on Sept. 16, 1810. And a bloody, decade-long conflict ensued, taking on the trappings of a civil war in many respects. Native Spaniards were fought by Spaniards of Mexican birth. Mestizos — mixed-blood Mexicans — and Indians also joined in the fight for control of the government.

The French control of Spain reached its peak in 1810-1811. England entered the fray on the side of the Spanish, and in 1811, the Spanish parliament — the Cortes — wrote a liberal constitution providing for self-government once control of the peninsula was regained. But Spain was not ready for the liberal government designed by the Cortes, and more disturbances followed as Ferdinand VII regained the throne and dissolved the Cortes.

MEXICO'S war for independence was savage and bloody in the interior provinces, and Texas suffered, as well. In 1811, Capt. Juan Bautista Casas briefly seized Gov. Manuel de Salcedo and military commander Simon de Herrera in the name of King Ferdinand. But the revolt was quickly and bloodily repressed. Later that year, Jose Bernardo Gutierrez de Lara of Revilla (now Guerrero south of Laredo on the Rio Grande) was appointed the diplomatic agent of the Mexican revolutionaries and journeyed to Washington to seek recognition of the newly proclaimed nation. While Gutierrez was warmly received by U.S. officials, he received no formal recognition and no money or arms. In early 1812, the Mexican patriot traveled to Natchitoches, La., where, with the help of U.S. agents, an expedition was organized. Augustus W. Magee, a West Point graduate who had served in the neutral zone between the Sabine and Arroyo Hondo, commanded the troop, which entered Texas in August 1812. This "Republican Army of the North" easily took Nacogdoches, where it gathered recruits, and La Bahia. After withstanding a siege at La Bahia, the army took San Antonio and proclaimed the first Republic of Texas in April 1813. A few months later, the republican forces were bloodily subdued at the Battle of the Medina River. Royalist Gen. Joaquin de Arredondo executed a staggering number of more than 300 republicans, including some Americans, at San Antonio, and a young lieutenant, Antonio Lopez de Santa Anna, was recognized for valor under fire. The Green Flag of the first republic was never recognized by any foreign government. Thinly populated Texas was devastated, however.

Republican furor waned after Ferdinand VII regained the throne, and while Spanish officials in Texas accepted a return to the old order, they knew that more trouble would be forthcoming if the province continued to be neglected. Spain and the United States reached agreement on the eastern boundary of Texas in 1819 in a treaty that provided for the U.S. purchase of Spanish claims to Florida. But the relinquishing of claims to Texas was considered treasonous by some Americans who took matters into their own hands. Dr. James Long led two expeditions into Texas to claim the territory for Americans. The first was successful in capturing Nacogdoches, where many Anglo settlers joined his rebellion. The filibuster returned to the United States briefly, and reentered Texas to complete his conquest. But while attempting to take La Bahia, he was captured by Mexicans, who had gained independence from Spain in 1821. Dr. Long was taken to Mexico City where he died under mysterious circumstances. His wife, Jane, accompanied him on the second expedition and bore the first Anglo-American child to be born in the province, folklore holds. She was a popular figure in the early days of Anglo-American immigration into Texas.

Ferdinand VII was forced to re-assemble the Spanish Cortes in 1820, and a colonization law was passed that welcomed foreigners into Texas, if they pledged loyalty to the Spanish monarchy and to the constitution.

But Spain's role in the history of Texas was over. The Mexicans had gained their independence and would repel an attempted invasion by the king. After almost 300 years, the Spanish had changed the face of Texas, and the Latin nation's culture remains affixed to the state's history. The Anglo-American tide that would sweep across the Southwest was poised at the province's eastern boundary. In only a few years, it would surge across the former Spanish territory.

The Mexican Period

A S Spain's grip on the New World slipped between 1790 and 1820, Texas was almost forgotten, an internal province of little importance. Colonization was ignored, and the Spanish government had larger problems in Europe and in Mexico.

Spain's mercantile economic policy penalized colonists in the area, working to charge them high prices for trade goods and paying low prices for products sent to markets in the interior of New Spain. As a result, settlers had no incentives to come to Texas. Indeed, men of ambition in the province often turned to illegal trade with Louisiana or to smuggling to prosper.

On the positive side, however, Indians of the province had been mollified through annual gifts and by developing a dependence on Spain for trade goods. Ranching flourished. A census in 1803 indicated that there were 100,000 head of cattle in Texas; in 1795, a census also found 69 families living on 45 ranches in the San Antonio area. But aside from a few additional families in Nacogdoches and La Bahia, the province was thinly populated.

When Spain returned the Louisiana Territory to France in the secret treaty of San Ildefonso in 1800, the vulnerability of Texas as a border province again became a concern. In Louisiana, Spain had relaxed its colonization policies. No attempt was made to use the mission system along the Mississippi River. Instead, an immigration policy was adopted that resembled later approaches in Texas. It provided for land grants, commercial privileges and religious toleration for colonists in exchange for a loyalty oath and actual settlement of land.

After Spain gave up Louisiana, Gen. Nemesio Salcedo, commandant-general of the Internal Provinces, allowed former Spanish subjects in Louisiana to settle in Texas. After 1805, other foreigners, under threat of death, were banned.

Several unsuccessful attempts also were made to attract colonists from the interior of Mexico. Gen. Salcedo improved the border defenses when the United States tried to press claims to the Rio Grande as the western boundary of Louisiana.

Texas' major problem was its isolation. Except for the threat of foreign immigration, the province was far removed from the political passions in Spain and Mexico City. The Spanish Cortes, for example, opened colonies to limited self-government in 1812, but the liberalization had little impact in Texas. Federalists and royalists battled for power in Mexico City, but except for a brief flirtation with republicanism after the Magee-Gutierrez expedition in 1813, Texas was unchanged and stagnated. But Spanish and Mexican officials knew that the province must be populated or lost.

Even worse, as the Spanish colonial government declined, Indians recognized its weakness. Annual gifts no longer were distributed. And as important, the Indians found an independent source of weapons and ammunition after American traders in Louisiana Territory began supplying guns and goods in exchange for horses and cattle. Frontier dangers were compounded after Father Hidalgo's 1810 uprising. The private ownership of firearms was prohibited. Indians stepped up raids, and settlers had fewer means of defense.

Therefore, Texas was in a state of suspension, only indirectly by the forces of political and social change that were gripping not only Europe and Mexico, but the North American continent as well. In the United States, currents of dissatisfaction were generated that made Texas very attractive. Federal land policy, agricultural practices and economic disruptions, along with population pressures, were steadily moving the Anglo-Americans westward.

Land policy was a long-standing point of contention between Eastern industrialists and frontiersmen. The industrialists favored high prices and tight credit policies on federal land sold to pioneers. The businessmen feared a reduction in their work force if land policies made settlement of the western lands too inviting. Until 1820, the government opened bidding on land at $2 an acre with a minimum purchase of 640 acres. The purchaser was required to pay down one-quarter of the price in cash, and the balance was due in four annual payments. And cash was scarce on the frontier.

Early in the 19th century, state banks began issuing scrip that was accepted by government land offices for purchases. With the financial panic of 1819, the nation's first major economic depression, these banks were among the first to fail. Many businessmen were ruined, and farmers saw prices drop below the cost of raising crops. The frontier was particularly hard hit.

After 1820, the federal government reduced land prices to $1.25 an acre with an 80-acre minimum purchase and credit policies were relaxed somewhat. Even in those days, Congress "primed the pump" of the nation's economy with a more lenient land policy that would stimulate financial growth. But the price was still high and the required cash was hard to come by.

T HE unstable economy made restless Americans look for fresh opportunities. The U.S.-Spanish boundary between the Americans and the rich agricultural lands of East Texas was no barrier to the energetic, nomadic pioneers. Early in the 19th century, they began to filter across the invisible dividing line to squat on New Spain's eastern frontier. Because the boundary was ill-defined until the Adams-Onis treaty of 1819, many Americans thought they were settling in the newly acquired Louisiana Territory of the United States. In 1815, for example, founders of the settlement of Jonesborough in present-day Red River County thought they were in Arkansas. (In fact, in 1824, the community was designated the seat of government of Miller County, Ark., and it was not until Texas attained statehood that the matter of jurisdiction was resolved.) Individual Anglos settled in Southeast Texas and were not disturbed by Spanish authorities. Nacogdoches attracted an undesirable element from the United States, in part because of its proximity to the neutral zone, the no-man's-land between the Sabine River and the Arroyo Hondo before the boundary settlement. As early as 1801 American traders had infiltrated East Texas. By 1804, Anglo families had become numerous enough around Nacogdoches for the Spanish military commander to attempt to expel non-Catholics.

East Texas was particularly attractive to farmers. Over the centuries the Caddo Indians — called Tejas by the Spanish — had cultivated hundreds of acres of land. When the Indians were hit hard by epidemics in the late 18th century, the rich farmland fell into disuse. But it was still cleared, and the open fields between the Sabine and Angelina rivers were quickly settled.

Texas' Spanish Heritage

More than a century and a half have passed since Spain completed its 300-year occupation of Texas. Yet Spanish influence perhaps is stronger today than while the Europeans were inhabiting the state. This heritage is so ingrained in the culture that often Texans do not realize its influence. Spain's presence in Texas is revealed in religion, law, the professions, architecture, language and place names. Roman Catholicism was brought to Texas by Spanish missionaries, who tried to convert the region's aborigines to Christianity and to make them productive Spanish citizens. About one Texan in five adheres to this faith.

The Spanish language is the mother tongue of about 20 percent of the state's population. And elements of the language are plentiful in everyday useage. Many place names — such as El Paso, San Antonio, Hidalgo, San Angelo and others — are Spanish, and most of the major rivers in the state — Rio Grande, Brazos, Colorado, San Antonio and Palacios — are either outright Spanish names, or some, like the Trinity River, are anglicized versions of Spanish names. One historian has found that 41 of 254 county names are of Spanish origin, and countless other Texas landmarks have Spanish names.

Perhaps the greatest economic impact of the Spanish was the introduction of horses, cattle and sheep into Texas. Although the horse had evolved in North America, the animal had become extinct by the time the first Spanish conquistadors reached Texas. North American natives had no domestic livestock, living instead on the buffalo. So it was from Spanish cattle that the legendary Texas Longhorn developed, and the first cattle probably were brought to the Lower Rio Grande Valley early in the 16th century. The large herds of wild mustangs that greeted Anglo-American settlers in the early 19th century developed from horses that strayed from the early Spanish explorers.

The Spanish also introduced cattle ranching methods into the state, although in recent years scholars have pointed out that much of the ranching tradition could have come from the Southeastern United States as well. Certainly Spain's colonial policies, which allowed large grants of land in leagues (more than 4,000 acres each), fostered cattle ranching in Texas. Much of the terminology of the cowboy, as well as the actual techniques of handling, breeding and caring for cattle, also had origins in the Spanish language.

Much architecture in Texas has a distinctive Spanish flavor and incorporates Spanish techniques designed to keep buildings cool in the torrid Southwestern sun. Missions and other colonial religious structures give the state's architecture a unique flavor.

Texas' legal system also owes a great debt to Spanish law. Although the Republic of Texas adopted English common law as the basic legal system in 1840, many elements of Spanish law were retained. These are seen largely in court procedures, but there are some elements that Texans consider basic rights that were adopted from Spanish law.

Titles to about one-seventh of Texas' land area can be traced back to old Spanish land grants. When a country assumes jurisdiction of an area from another country, the laws of the original ruler are maintained and honored until changed. Consequently, many Texans can trace their land titles to these grants.

Until 1869, Texas, unlike the other states, retained the mineral rights of land granted to colonists. For almost 30 years after the writing of the Constitution of 1869, mineral rights were granted with the land. But the policy was changed in the 1890s, and the state now has mineral rights in about 8 percent of the land in Texas.

Three other elements of law — women's rights, adoption and homestead protection — also had their origins in Spanish law. Under English common law, women had few property rights with their husbands.

History Highlights

As one legal critic noted, husband and wife were recognized as one under the common law, but the husband was the one. Spanish law gave women full rights of ownership and laid the basis for Texas' community property law.

English law also did not have provisions for bringing an outsider into the family through adoption. Even a child born out of wedlock could not be legitimatized even if the father and mother married. Spanish law provided for adoption, and Texas brought the principle into its law.

Stephen F. Austin also got Spanish officials to broaden a concept of Roman law to include homestead exemptions. Many pioneer Texans left debts in the United States when they immigrated. Austin thought it unfair for creditors to take land that settlers had cleared and cultivated. Roman and Spanish laws protected the tools of a craftsman from confiscation because of debt. The theory was that the debt could never be paid if the artist did not have his tools. The same principle was applied to homesteads in colonial Texas.

Wags point out that the Spanish influence even extends to high school football. The cheer that some older Texans recall — "Two-bits, four-bits, six-bits, a dollar; all for the Cowboys stand up and holler"— is based on the Spanish monetary system, which also was adopted by the United States. The "bits" refer to pieces of eight, which were the standard money of colonial Texas and the Republic.

Without the strong heritage left by Spain, the face of Texas would be much different than that to which most Texans are accustomed.

The largest group of early immigrants from the United States was not Anglo, but Indian. As early as 1818, Cherokees from the Southeast United States came to Texas, settling north of Nacogdoches on lands between the Trinity and Sabine rivers. The Cherokees had been among the first U.S. Indians to accept the federal government's offers of resettlement. As American pioneers entered the newly acquired lands of Georgia, Alabama and other areas of the Southeast, the Indians were systematically removed, through legal means or otherwise. The early U.S. policy of attempting to "civilize" and assimilate the Native Americans was changing. Pioneers wanted the Indians' land, and that meant that the native peoples must be moved. Some settled on land provided in Arkansas Territory, but others, like groups of Cherokees, came to Texas, seeking to escape the hostility of the Anglos. And these Cherokees were among the "Five Civilized Tribes" that had adopted agriculture and many Anglo customs in an unsuccessful attempt to get along with their new neighbors.

Alabama and Coushatta tribes had exercised squatters' rights in present Sabine County in the early 1800s, and soon after the Cherokees arrived, groups of Shawnee, Delaware and Kickapoo Indians came from the United States. All sought from the Spanish and Mexican governments title to some of the prime farmland in the region. The presence of the Indians became a factor in the Anglos' disputes with the Mexican government, which attempted, by promising land titles to the Indians, to play the two groups of U.S. immigrants against each other.

After 1820, the second wave of immigrants arrived, larger than the first and of different character. These Anglos were not so interested in agricultural opportunities as in other schemes to quickly recoup their fortunes.

The only group of immigrants expelled by Spanish authorities were Napoleonic exiles who in 1818 attempted to set up the French colony of Champ d'Asile on the present site of Liberty in Liberty County.

Spain, and later Mexico, recognized the danger represented by the unregulated, informal colonization by Americans. The Spanish Cortes' colonization law of 1813 attempted to build a buffer between the eastern frontier and Northern Mexico. The act served as the basis for later Mexican immigration policy through which it was hoped that European and Mexican colonists could be attracted to Texas to dilute the Anglo population. To prevent smuggling, which flourished because of a lack of legal ports, colonies were prohibited within 26 miles — or 10 leagues — of the coast. Also, special permission was required for Americans to settle within 52 miles of the international boundary, although this prohibition often was ignored. As initially envisioned, Americans would be allowed to settle the interior of the vast territory. European and Mexican colonists would be placed along the eastern frontier to limit contact between the Americans and the United States. The Americans already in Texas illegally would be stable if given a stake in the province through land ownership, officials felt.

MOSES Austin, a former Spanish subject who had suffered a severe financial setback in the panic of 1819, applied for the first empresario grant from the Spanish government. With the intercession of Baron de Bastrop, a friend of Austin's from Missouri Territory, Gov. Antonio Maria Martinez approved the request in January 1821. Austin agreed to settle 300 families on land bounded by the Brazos and Colorado rivers on the east and west, by the El Camino Real (the old military road running from San Antonio to Nacogdoches) on the north and by the Gulf Coast, since his grant came before settlement in the area was prohibited. But Austin died in June 1821, leaving the work to his son, Stephen F. Austin.

The younger Austin was uniquely qualified for leadership of the colonial enterprise. Although born in Virginia in 1793, he moved with his parents to Missouri Territory at the age of five. Austin's experiences as a youth gave him an understanding of the disposition of the Spanish and Mexican administrators with whom he dealt. The 27-year-old empresario also was well educated, had served in the Missouri legislature and was appointed judge in Arkansas Territory before coming to Texas. Austin's problems began immediately upon entering Texas when he learned that Mexico had gained independence from Spain. Although his first colonists arrived in December 1821, Austin was told by Gov. Martinez that the provisional government would not recognize the Spanish grant. The new government had to approve the colonization program, Austin learned. So he spent a year in Mexico City, observing the organization of the new government and lobbying for his colonial authorization. On occasion he advised Mexican leaders on the creation of a federal system of government. Finally in January 1823 the Spanish grant was affirmed by the Mexican government.

Mexico's land policy, like Spain's, differed from the U.S. approach. Whereas the United States sold land directly to settlers or to speculators who dealt with the pioneers, the Mexicans retained tight control of the property transfer until predetermined agreements for development were fulfilled. But a 4,428-acre sitio — a square league — and a 177-acre labor could be obtained for only surveying costs and administrative fees as low as $50. The empresario was rewarded with grants of large tracts of land — but only when he fulfilled his quota of families to be brought to the colonies. Considering the prices the U.S. government charged, Texas' land was indeed a bargain — and a major attraction to those Anglo-Americans looking for a new start.

Austin had almost complete civil and military responsibility for his colony. He set up stringent requirements for his colonists, including requiring presentation of affidavits from community leaders at their previous home vouching for their good character and sober work habits. On several occasions, Austin had disreputable characters forcibly removed from his colony. As a consequence of these high standards, Austin attracted many financially stable colonists. And he made some enemies.

Austin was scrupulous in following the terms of his grant. He knew that Mexican officials, like the Spanish, distrusted the intentions of Americans, and the young empresario wanted to give no cause for suspicion. But despite Austin's efforts, the mistrust by officials persisted. They knew that whenever U.S. and Spanish boundaries had met, the Spanish boundaries receded. Florida had been lost in the agreement that set Texas' eastern boundary. Rights in Oregon Territory also had been given to the United States in the same treaty.

Under the Constitution of 1824, Mexicans reversed the U.S. approach to land distribution. The federalist government gave the states responsibility for developing public lands. And colonization policy became even more liberal as the government of Coahuila y Texas, which was the poorest of all the new Mexican states, sought to exploit the economic potential of the region and to build a buffer between Northern Mexico and both the United States and the Plains Indians. The state colonization law of 1825 brought explosive growth to Texas. More than 25 empresarios were commissioned to settle colonists. By 1830, Texas boasted an estimated population of 15,000, with Anglos outnumbering Mexicans by a margin of four to one.

Austin was easily the most successful empresario. After his initial success, Austin was authorized in 1825 to bring 900 more families to Texas, and in 1831, he and his partner, Samuel Williams, received another concession to bring 800 Mexican and European families. Through Austin's efforts, 1,540 land titles were issued to settlers, and the population of his colonies in 1831 was 5,665. The next two most successful empresarios were Green DeWitt and Martin De Leon.

Green DeWitt was authorized in April 1825 to bring 400 families to Texas in an area west of Austin's colony. Mexican officials felt that establishment of towns was important, and in 1825, Gonzales, in present-day Gonzales County, was laid out by surveyor James Kerr. The community was named in honor of Coahuila y Texas Gov. Rafael Gonzales. Because of the danger of Indian raids many of DeWitt's colonists stayed in a small community called Old Station on the Lavaca River near the coast until 1827, when a peace treaty with the Karankawas was signed after a military campaign by joint American and Mexican forces.

DeWitt's colony suffered from other Indian attacks. First the Tonkawas raided because they were being pressed by the Comanches and Wichitas, who had moved into the South Plains. Later the Plains Indians found the horse and cattle herds of the colony lucrative sources of plunder.

DeWitt did not bring 400 families to the province, as he had contracted, but 166 land titles were issued to settlers who came to Texas through his efforts.

South and west of DeWitt's colony, Martin de Leon, a rancher in Tamaulipas who admired the region during a cattle drive, received a grant from the provincial delegation of San Fernando de Bexar for another colony. Because the Coahuila y Texas legislature was unaware of De Leon's grant, DeWitt's grant overlapped, and there were problems when the two empresarios tried to colonize the same region. De Leon won the dispute because his grant pre-dated DeWitt's and because Mexican citizens were given preference in colonization.

Forty-one Mexican families were settled in the region by De Leon, who in 1824 also founded the city of Guadalupe Victoria, named for the first Mexican president. By 1833, the city had a population of 200.

AUSTIN'S colony flourished, in part because of his understanding of the Mexican character and the necessity for strict adherence to Mexican law. Other empresarios were not so diligent.

In the early years of colonization, the settlers busied themselves by clearing lands, planting crops, building homes and fighting Indians. Many were successful in establishing a subsistence economy. One weakness of the Mexican colonial policy was that it did not provide the factors for a market economy. While towns were established, credit, banks and good roads were not provided by the government. Ports were established at Galveston and Matagorda bays after Mexican independence, but the colonists felt they needed more, particularly one at the mouth of the Brazos. And foreign ships were barred from coastwise trade, which posed a particular hardship since Mexico had few merchant ships.

One attempt to establish a bank failed. When Jose Felix Trespalacios was appointed the political and military chief of Texas in 1822, there was a limited amount of money in circulation in the province. Soldiers and officials were paid irregularly. So Trespalacios set up the Banco Nacional de Texas in San Antonio, which in November 1822 issued to soldiers and officials notes that could be redeemed at face value. Trespalacios had not received prior approval of the central government, which liked the idea. But in late 1822, the government decreed that only two-thirds of the face value of the notes would be redeemed in gold; the rest would be paid in government notes. The value of the Texas bank notes dropped, and the bank failed, leaving, in part, a residual distrust of banks that remained a part of the Texas heritage until the early 20th century.

In eastern Texas and the Austin colony, cotton was planted almost immediately by the new colonists. Four cotton gins were in operation in East Texas by 1826. In 1828, 500 bales of cotton were produced in the Austin colony alone. But in DeWitt colony, the basic crop was corn. Many settlers also raised cattle, hogs and goats for milk.

Although there were complaints about the administration of government, the colonists concentrated on establishing themselves in a new land. Most of the unrest was brought about through a lack of understanding of the Spanish language and an unfamiliarity with the institutions of the government of the fledgling Republic.

MEXICAN officials, however, distrusted the intentions of the colonists. Most disputes were settled amicably enough, although there undoubtedly was discontent. DeWitt's Old Station near Lavaca Bay was interpreted by some officials as an attempt to develop a way station for smugglers. In fact, James Kerr had misunderstood the 10-league setback requirement for settlements near the coast; he thought the distance began at the outer islands, not on the coast itself.

The first major conflict between the Mexican government and Anglo settlers arose through a misunderstanding. Hayden Edwards received a large land grant around Nacogdoches to be distributed to new colonists. But Edwards misunderstood his charter. He first tried to set himself up as a military commander for the area, which was interpreted by Mexican officials as an attempted revolt. Then the empresario attempted to take land away from long-time Mexican settlers who could not prove title to their property. Many of the families held land under informal grants made by Gil Y'barbo almost a half-century earlier, and others had not fulfilled the tedious requirements of Spanish land law to get full title. Others had simply lost the documents, of which there was no record in the Spanish archives. Acts more attributable to ignorance than guile were interpreted by Mexican officials as steps toward insurrection. Finally while Hayden Edwards was in the United States on business in 1826, his brother, Benjamin, declared the independence of the Republic of Fredonia and ejected a group of Mexican soldiers from the area.

Most Anglos did not support the revolt. So the Fredonians made a pact with a group of Cherokees to give the Indians the northern half of Texas in exchange for their support in the rebellion. The Mexican army, aided by a contingent of Austin's colonists, quickly put down the revolt. The rebellious leaders fled to the United States. But the insurgency sowed seeds of distrust with Mexican officials. As important in the long run, Anglos from the previously isolated colonies opened communication.

Mexican officials' hope of attracting large numbers of European immigrants never materialized.

Government instability, stagnant economy and religious intolerance outweighed whatever attractions Europeans might find in Mexico, and the United States was a more popular place to relocate. Nevertheless, two small colonies of Europeans were settled. James Power and James Hewetson got a special concession to settle an area on the coast between the Lavaca and Nueces rivers. Despite many problems, the town of Refugio, located on the site of the old mission by the same name, was established and almost 200 land titles were issued under this grant. John McMullen and James McGloin got a grant just north of the Power-Hewetson concession and had 84 grants issued to their colonists, most of whom were from Ireland. San Patricio was settled in the McMullen-McGloin colony.

In late 1827, Gen. Manuel Mier y Teran, a soldier, statesman and intellectual, was dispatched by President Victoria on an apparent mission to locate the actual boundary line between the United States and Mexico. In fact, however, Teran was taking the pulse of Texas. Mexican officials could not ignore the nagging threat of American intentions in their northern state.

Although he found no overt rebellion, the tour only reinforced Teran's concern about the developing American influence in Texas. The farther east he traveled, the less Mexican influence he found in the society. In East Texas, only a few long-time Mexican settlers remained, and he noted they were of the poorest classes. From this review of Texas, Teran made three major recommendations: A military occupation of Texas, to provide protection from Indians, but also to isolate the Anglo-American colonies; a counter-colonization program aimed at attracting European and Mexican settlers; and the opening of coastwise trade to develop closer economic ties with the interior of Mexico.

Austin had advocated more coastwise trade to Teran. Most Texas trade went through New Orleans, and Austin, along with Teran, understood that that could become a major problem.

In 1829, Gen. Teran became commandant general of the Eastern Interior Provinces and began to carry out his program, much of which was incorporated in the Law of April 6, 1830, which was obnoxious to most American colonists in Texas. The law went beyond Teran's recommendations by in essence barring further Anglo-American immigration into Texas. Also, it provided for Mexican convict-soldiers, and their families, to be sent to the area, with an option to stay at the end of their terms under favorable circumstances provided by the government.

TERAN reinforced garrisons at San Antonio, La Bahia, Nacogdoches and Velasco. And five new garrisons, three with Nahuatl names to reinforce their Mexican character, were established: Anahuac on Galveston Bay, Tenoxtitlan on the Brazos, Lipantitlan on the Nueces River, Lavaca on the river of the same name, and Teran on the Neches River.

The moving of additional armed forces into Texas concerned the Anglo-Americans, and it was unrest caused by the 1828 election and the military occupation of the state a year later that led to revolution.

Frontier Racial Attitudes

So much of the history of 19th century Texas is written in blood that one would think that there was a special meanness and intolerance exhibited by Americans who colonized the vast territory. Mexicans and Indians were victims of random and often deadly violence, and blacks were first enslaved and after emancipation were victims of gross discrimination that often was expressed in mortal force.

To understand the atmosphere of this period, two European colonization policies must be examined. The Spanish approach to developing Mexico and the American Southwest relates directly to the expression of Anglo-Saxonism that marked the American experience in 19th century Texas.

Spain's great adventure in the New World began as a religious, as well as an economic, crusade. When Isabel and Ferdinand commissioned Christopher Columbus to find a new route to the Far East, the idea was to develop trade and to enter into an alliance with the rulers of the region against the Muslims who

ruled Africa and the Middle East. From the beginning, however, the westward thrust was a manifestation of an effort to spread Christianity — first to the Far East and eventually to the remainder of the pagan world. Spanish missionary efforts began with the

History Highlights

first contact with natives of the New World. Pope Paul III legitimatized the effort by granting Spain the right to develop all new lands discovered west of a line 100 leagues west of the Canary Islands, providing the Spanish spread the Christian faith.

Violence characterized Spain's initial contact with New World natives, justified on the grounds that the Indians resisted Christianity. Compounding the problem was the desire of the conquistadors to obtain wealth. Gold was more attractive to many European settlers than spreading the faith of the Spanish kings. This gulf between the temporal and spiritual marked the Spanish policy in the New World. From the beginning, Spanish monarchs were concerned about the treatment of the natives. Throughout the reconquest of the Iberian peninsula, the Spanish required conquered territories to pay tribute. Spanish numbers were few, and the Spanish leaders understood that expulsion of the conquered peoples would destroy the economy. Similar strategy was pursued in the New World. Spanish settlers in some cases were given encomiendas, in which use of the land and the natives was authorized by the crown. In exchange, the settlers went to instruct the natives in the faith, provide for their upkeep and defend them. Too often, the system degenerated into a form of slavery.

The early abuses of the system and the general mistreatment of the aborigines prompted a great debate in Spain. What was the proper policy to protect the natives? The Church and its missionaries urged a humane policy. But others advocated the Aristotelian theory of natural slavery: that some segments of mankind were born to slavery and to serve those whose lives should be devoted to virtue and leisure. Spaniards felt that they had sacrificed too much while regaining the peninsula from the Moors to do manual labor in the New World. The more tolerant view prevailed in the debates of the 16th century. Both Spanish kings and the popes officially mandated humane treatment for the natives and prohibited their enslavement. The uncertainty about how to regard the natives slowed the development of the New World. The 40-year delay before Coronado's exploration of the upper Rio Grande valley and the first settlement by Juan Onate in 1598, in part, was caused by the debate. In 1573, the king of Spain issued an ordinance changing the nation's goal in the New World from one of "conquest" to "pacification." However, policies conceived in Spain and in Rome often were radically altered on the voyage across the Atlantic. The king's policy shall be obeyed, it was said, but the policy will not be executed. Consequently, the New World natives continued to be abused throughout most of the Spanish dominance.

But the Indians also had a role in the Spanish scheme for developing the New World. Racial prejudice was not a factor. In the 16th century, the great division was between Christians and infidels, not races. From the first days of Spanish colonization, colonizers intermarried with native women. The Indians also were looked upon as potential Spanish citizens. Unlike England and France, which had an excess of populations to develop the New World, Spain was thinly populated. Consequently, Spain had to use the New World natives to "colonize" the new lands. The mission system was a response to this need. Basically, missionaries gathered willing Indians to a church. The natives were schooled in the faith, taught trades and were protected by the military during the training period. When indoctrination was complete, the missionaries moved on. The goals were simple: The Indians would be conquered, converted, exploited and assimilated. In short, they would become productive Spanish citizens. Courageous missionaries braved the hazards of Northern Mexico and the American Southwest to establish the mission strategy. The success varied, but the system left a mark on the Southwest. Texas historian Elizabeth A. H. John evaluated the Spanish experience with the natives like this:

". . . Contrary to the Black Legend, and notwithstanding flagrant violations of Indian rights, it is on the Spanish frontier that one finds the earliest commitment to due process for Indians and the only consistent efforts to foster self-governance of Indian communities."

Historian Ronald Sanders commented:

". . . But Spaniards were never bothered by the physical manifestations of race differences as northern Europeans have tended to be; it was doctrinal divergence, and the possibility of the taint of heresy being carried into the bloodstream, that primarily worked to arouse racism in them."

And Sanders observed that the ethnic diversity of Spanish history made the Spaniards instinctual anthropologists:

". . . Spaniards were foremost among those in the 16th century who could find alien racial traditions to be interesting and significant as long as they were not dangerous."

When Anglo-Americans encountered the frontier culture of Spain, they found a mixed race — Spanish and Indian — with a strong Roman Catholic affiliation. Both conflicted with the social attitudes of the Americans, who were predominantly Southerners.

A racial philosophy had gained strength in the United States, especially the South, in the early 19th century. The culture American colonists found in Spanish-Mexican Texas was both foreign and unacceptable to their racial concepts.

When the English embarked on their colonization of the New World, their attitudes toward the natives and the goals of the effort were little different from the Spanish. The letters of patent setting up the Virginia companies in London and Plymouth in 1606 stressed the conversion and civilization of the natives as the prime motive of settlement. But economic considerations later predominated.

Initially the English considered the natives "brutes." But by the 18th century, the idea of the "noble savage," free of the corruption of civilization, took hold. Throughout the early colonial period, the English pursued an officially humane policy. The church, Anglican and Roman, had long held that mankind came from a single creation by a supreme being. Therefore, although some segments of the human family might have greater advantages or better developed talents, all peoples were capable of improvement — infinitely perfectible. Many efforts were made to convert the Indians. In the 17th century, Protestants started schools and pursued a range of missionary activities among the natives. After 1622, when Indians in Virginia revolted and killed several hundred English colonists, attitudes began to change.

The British government pursued a legalistic policy, however, insisting that the natives be reimbursed when they gave up the right to use the land. Perhaps the one major difference in the Spanish and English attitudes concerned the Indians' relation to the land — or at least the use of the lands. While the Spanish usurped the natives' land for the crown, the English felt that the Indians were using the soil under the concept of usufruct. This meant that the natives did not own the land, but they were entitled to its use. When Indians "sold" land, they were giving up only a secondary right. The English crown, like the Spanish monarch, owned the land.

German Romanticists, however, began a movement that would completely change the attitudes of the English and Americans toward other peoples. The Germans developed an interest in uniqueness in language and in national and racial origins. Not surprisingly, they proposed that Indo-Europeans had exhibited special talents that spread civilization to the West. These special people had migrated from Central Asia, established a society based on democratic principles in Northern Europe and had brought civilization to the western world.

The English embraced the racial concept. But they emphasized the development of their "Anglo-Saxon" nation, founded by a race that expanded the special talents for self-government originally practiced in the forests of ancient Germany. While the attitude was embraced in England, it often was manifested in a policy that asserted that as a special people the English had special responsibilities to primitive people, not special privileges.

Americans were influenced by the English attitudes, and the concept of special responsibilities toward native peoples directed early expansionist policy after the American Revolution. But as the westward movement across the North American continent gained momentum, attitudes changed. Success begot confidence and then arrogance. The attitude of special responsibility was replaced with a concept that Americans had special privileges. Until 1829, the federal government held that native peoples could be trained in democratic principles and led to civilization. Thereafter, the direction of the national policy was simply to get the Indians out of the way of the advance of the Anglo-Saxon civilization. In the 1830s,

Georgia made it clear that no Indians were wanted in the state, either on reservations or on private land. Room had to be made in the state for the Anglo-Saxons who would properly develop the rich agricultural land. It was made clear that Indians who remained would not be candidates for assimilation and citizenship; they would be second-class citizens like the free blacks. And many Indians were enslaved, a practice that began not long after the first English settlements were established.

Frontier attitudes in America generally reflected a hatred for Indians and their desire to retain their native lands. Every effort, legal and otherwise, was made to remove the aborigines. By the 1830s, the attitude finally forced the federal government to remove thousands of natives from the Deep South to Indian Territory. Thousands died on the infamous Trail of Tears and others unsuccessfully resisted. Blood was spilled, as Americans prosecuted their ill-disguised policy of racial superiority.

Between 1820 and 1850, the concept of the racial superiority of Anglo-Saxons gained popularity, although some observers criticized it. One asserted, "The allegations of superiority of race and destiny neither require nor deserve any answer; they are but pretences under which to disguise ambition, cupidity, or silly vanity." Abolitionists' agitation in the North beginning in the 1830s also forced Southerners to defend slavery on the basis of racial superiority. Scientific and pseudoscientific arguments that allegedly found traits of racial inferiority in blacks and Indians also became popular. Basically, if the South was to defend slavery, the institution must be blamed on the blacks. Conventional wisdom in the South held that blacks deserved to be slaves because they were racially inferior. The argument was not unlike that used by 16th century Spaniards who invoked Aristotle's concept of natural slavery to defend mistreatment of Mexican Indians.

Early Anglo colonists in Texas no doubt harbored many of these attitudes, although during the early days of the Austin Colony, little evidence suggests that the Americans planned to be anything but good Mexican citizens. In other parts of the state, Americans were not so docile. The Fredonian Rebellion in 1827 grew out of an attempt by Anglos to divest old Spanish settlers of their land in East Texas.

The Anglo experience in Texas between 1821 and 1836 also raised questions in the settlers' minds regarding the Mexican's ability to operate a democratic government. Mexico, of course, was experiencing many difficulties establishing an administration after gaining independence from Spain. Internal feuds and a state of almost constant revolution impeded efforts. Nevertheless, Anglo-Texans were disgruntled by several governmental shortcomings.

Whatever latent attitudes toward Mexicans early Texas colonists might have held were reinforced and charged with emotion during the war for Texas independence in 1836. Wartime passions are exaggerated when the conflict involves peoples of different religions and of different races. The Mexicans, faced by the predominantly Protestant Texans, were Catholics, were a mixed race and were still associated with the Spanish. English propagandists promoted the idea of leyenda negra — the Black Legend. This concept held that the Spanish abused their New World charges and committed abominable outrages. Therefore they were to be hated. And this long-held belief added a third strike to Anglo-Texans' attitudes toward the Mexicans.

After Texas gained independence from Mexico, migration from the Southern states increased greatly. And the new settlers brought their racial attitudes with them. Indians had been removed from the South, and that policy was often pursued by Texans. Ironically, most Texas Indians welcomed the coming of the Anglo-Americans. But the attitudes of the newcomers assured conflict. Anglo officials at Nacogdoches complained in 1832, for example, that the Mexican military commander, Col. Jose de las Piedras, "has insulted us while in the exercise of our functions by saying that Americans and Indians are by him held in the same estimation, and as colonists on the same footing . . ."

Official government policy swung to extremes after Texas gained independence from Mexico.

President Sam Houston, a friend of Indians since his youth in Tennessee, tried to reconcile the Indians and the Anglos and succeeded in maintaining an uneasy peace between the groups. But his successor, Mirabeau B. Lamar, waged relentless war against Indians and expelled several tribes from Texas in 1839.

German settlers in Central Texas in 1847 made a treaty with the Comanches, and both sides abided by the agreement. It had the distinction of being the only treaty that was kept with Indians in the state. Anglo settlers were not anxious to cooperate with the Indians and, possibly blinded by their racial attitudes, seriously misunderstood and underestimated the Indians. In 1841 Texan-Indian relations deteriorated after the ill-fated Council House Fight in San Antonio. Texans had asked to meet with Comanche leaders to discuss an exchange of prisoners. The Texans were outraged when the Indians brought only one white prisoner to the meeting. The Indians were locked in the Council House and were to be kept until more prisoners were released. But Comanches would fight to the death before being taken prisoner, and several of the chiefs did in San Antonio on that day. Anglo credibility suffered, and the Indian troubles escalated.

The experience of blacks in Texas was little different from that suffered elsewhere in the South. Under the Spanish and Mexican governments, free blacks had full rights of citizenship. Some were landowners and leaders in their communities. But after independence, free blacks were encouraged — subtly or otherwise — to leave. Unlike Mexicans and Indians, however, blacks had economic value, both as chattel and through the work they performed. After emancipation, blacks were tolerated in the state because they were needed as field workers. But the attitude that blacks being an inferior race lasted well into the 20th century.

Some Anglo-Texans seemed to consider it manly to abuse a Mexican, Indian or black. Resistance by the minority groups was considered brutality and another characteristic of inferior peoples. And resistance also invited massive retaliation.

Early Texans reflected the Southern culture from which most of them emerged. They held the same social attitudes and embraced the same concept of the racial superiority of the so-called Anglo-Saxon race. The violence of the times and the brutal discrimination against peoples of color in Texas probably can be explained, in part, by the absence of mediating institutions on the frontier. Society put few reins on individual behavior, and such institutions as were available were manned by officials who held the same attitudes toward the victims of frontier violence as did the perpetrators of the acts.

Peer pressure also entered into the actions of some early settlers. Noah Smithwick recalled a pitched battle in which runaway slaves courageously fought off an attempt by settlers to recapture them:

"That was unquestionably the worst fight I ever got into. I think now, looking back over a life of ninety years, that that was about the meanest thing I ever did. Though having been all my life accustomed to such things I did not then take that view of it. The capture of fugitive slaves was a necessity of the institution (of slavery)."

This frontier conduct was not unique to Anglo-Americans in Texas. The conquistadors and early Spanish colonists in the New World also reacted violently to frontier conditions. Historian Louis Bertrand had this observation about these 16th century forerunners to the Anglos:

". . . As always happens in colonial countries, the character of the colonist was strengthened by the contradiction, or the hostility, of his surroundings. When he was subjected to the influence of foreign customs and new environment, some of his racial feelings and prejudices, some of his ideas, acquired fresh vigour. It happened also that, as the colonist was no longer in contact with the motherland, where national characteristics were in course of evolution, his own remained stationary. . . . The feelings, the instincts, the prejudices which he had brought with him from his native environment became intensified or exaggerated without being transformed."

And so it was on the Texas frontier. While Anglo-Texans carved a dynamic state out of a wilderness, they wrote a sad and tragic chapter in race relations.

Prelude to Revolution

MEXICO'S war for independence had achieved little more than separation from Spain. Sensing that liberal reforms in Spain would reduce the authority of royalists in the New World, Mexican conservatives led the revolt against the mother country. And they achieved early victories in the debate over the form of government the newly independent Mexico should adopt.

The majority of Mexicans had little concept of self-government. The Spanish Constitution of 1812 had provided for election of local officials, but it was not universally implemented. Offsetting this brief experience was a 300-year tradition of authoritarian, centralized colonial government. Since the reign of Phillip II, administration of the Spanish colonies was tightly controlled and slow-moving.

An independent Mexico was torn between advocates of centralist and republican forms of government. Centralists wanted a strong central government with appointed officials at the state and local level who would be under the direction of Mexico City. Federalists supported the election of officials at lower levels, who would run their own administrations. The former royalists won the opening debates, setting Emperor Agustin de Iturbide on the new Mexican throne. But he soon was overthrown and the Constitution of 1824 adopted. Constructing a federal framework of government and making it function smoothly, however, are difficult for a people inexperienced in self-government. The fiercely independent character of the Mexican people often prohibited the acquiescence so necessary to democratic government.

The turbulence experienced in Texas as the Mexicans attempted to set up a representative government was not an isolated experience in the period. Within months after the rebellion in Texas, federalists in California and New Mexico also revolted. But the central government's reaction was not so harsh. Santa Anna's ruthless attempt to crush the Anglo-led rebellion in Texas was motivated as much by the fear of losing the colony to the United States as by the desire to punish the political dissidents. The uprisings in California and New Mexico were settled diplomatically, not with the sword as in Texas.

Friction between the two cultures was inevitable. To settle in Texas, pioneers had to become Mexican citizens and to embrace Roman Catholicism. Most of the Americans were Protestants, if they adhered to any religion, and they were fiercely defensive of the right to religious freedom enjoyed in the United States. Although no more than one-fourth of the Americans ever swore allegiance to the Catholic church, the requirement was a long-standing irritation. Compounding the problem was the fact that to be legal, marriages had to be blessed by a priest. For a decade after the founding of the Austin colony, no priest regularly ministered to the people. A system of contract marriages evolved in which couples took out a bond to have their union blessed by a priest when one was available. Occasionally, couples who found they could not live together would simply destroy the bond to dissolve the marriage if no priest had blessed the union.

Slavery, too, was a point of contention. Mexico prohibited the introduction of slavery after December 1827. Nevertheless, many slaveholders in Austin's colony became nervous at the official rhetoric. Several efforts were made to evade the government policy. Austin got the state legislature to recognize labor contracts under which slaves were technically free but bound themselves to their masters for life. Often entire families were covered by a single contract. While many early Anglo colonists were not slaveholders, they were Southerners, and the ownership of slaves was a cultural institution that they supported. The problem was never settled during the colonial period despite the tensions it generated.

There also was a long delay in getting land titles after the settlers had made the required improvements. And the Mexican court system was cumbersome. Appeals in civil cases and pleadings in criminal cases had to go 700 miles to Saltillo for adjudication, causing interminable and expensive delays in the administration of justice.

Balancing these complaints, however, were many advantages. Taxes, tithes and excises were suspended for several years. Farm implements and household goods could be brought into the colony with no duty charged. Good land was cheap and available for those willing to turn a wilderness into productive farmland.

Austin kept attuned to the settlers' problems, seeking relief from the Mexican government when possible. Many Austin colonists left the United States with a burden of debt brought about by the economic recession. Austin sought relief from the legislature of Coahuila y Texas with the enactment in 1828 of a homestead law that prohibited a person's property from being taken for debt accrued outside Mexico. Based on early Roman and Spanish law, this statute was the forerunner of the homestead protection enjoyed by Texans today.

Mistrust was mutual between Mexican officials and the colonists. As the population grew, the settlers' complaints intensified. Mexican officials' alarm grew in proportion to the population. Hopes of attracting European and Mexican colonists to dilute the burgeoning number of Anglos were not realized. Only a few Irish settlers had been attracted to the San Patricio grant on the Gulf Coast.

Andrew Jackson's election to the American presidency in 1828 further fanned Mexican fears. Jackson was known to covet Texas. The new president reportedly once told a Mexican diplomat that "the United States should never have lost the opportunity to obtain Texas, and that the way to obtain a territory was first to occupy it and, after having possession, treat for it, as had been done in Florida." Indeed, several informal offers to purchase Texas were made by U.S. officials before and after Jackson's election.

The Mexican election of 1828 also was a turning point in the history of the young republic. Self-government had been in effect in parts of Mexico since 1812. Mexico had begun the difficult transition from being an appendage of an absolutist monarchy to a federal republic. Mexicans were transformed from subjects of a crown into citizens in a republic. But the transformation was incomplete. Democracy requires an acquiescence of strongly held individual opinions to the results of the ballot box. But the orderly transfer of power in Mexico was dealt a death blow in 1828 when the legally elected administration of Manuel Gomez Pedraza was overthrown by supporters of Vicente Guerrero, who in turn was ousted by his own vice president Anastasio Bustamante. Mexico's most chaotic political period followed. The pattern of military intervention, coup and countercoup would last a century. Between May 1833 and August 1855, the Mexican presidency changed hands 36 times. The average length of term was only seven and one-half months. As government replaced government and revolt followed rebellion, many Mexicans became disenchanted with the republican experiment. They understood their quality of life had declined without a strong, well-organized colonial administrative system. The centralist form of government eventually won out.

BUT the Americans who came to Texas were republicans to the core. On his tour of the state in 1827 and 1828, Gen. Manuel Mier y Teran noted that they "carried their constitutions in their pockets." And he feared the Americans' desire for more rights and liberties than the government was prepared to offer would lead to rebellion.

Most of the early Anglo colonists in Texas, however, intended to fulfill their pledge to become good Mexican citizens. But they had made the commitment with the understanding that they would live under a republican form of government as set forth in the Constitution of 1824. The political turmoil following the 1828 presidential election raised doubts in the Americans' minds about the ability of Mexicans to make that form of government function properly.

Unrest increased in Texas when Gen. Teran began reinforcing existing garrisons and establishing new ones. But a major factor in the discontent of Americans came with the decree of April 6, 1830, when the Mexican government in essence banned further Anglo-American immigration into Texas and tried to control slavery.

Austin protested that the prohibition against American immigration would not stop the flow of Anglos into Texas; it would stop only the stable, prosperous Americans from coming to the region. The great empresario had a firm image of the type of colonist he wanted — a Southern gentleman. Austin feared another type of settler: Those " . . . ardent, inexperienced, hot-headed youths piping from college, or ignorant, self-willed 'mobbish' mountaineers and frontiersmen who 'hold to lynch law' and damning those who are in office merely because they are in office would totally ruin us forever.''

Austin's predictions about immigration were fulfilled. Legal immigration may have been barred, but illegal entry was not. By 1834, when the law was repealed, it was estimated that the number of Americans and their slaves in Texas totaled 20,700, double the number of four years earlier. By 1836, that number had reached 35,000.

THE first two incidents that inflamed Anglo-American colonists, ironically, were instigated by Americans in the service of the Mexican government. George Fisher, a Serbian by birth but a naturalized American, was ordered by Gen. Teran to set up a customs house at Anahuac on Galveston Bay and to appoint a deputy to a house at Brazoria at the mouth of the Brazos. Fisher tried to require ships leaving the Brazos to stop at Anahuac to pay duties, and in one case, a soldier was wounded when a ship failed to heed the order. In retaliation, Fisher tried to impound goods shipped into the Austin Colony until duties were paid. But Teran removed Fisher from office before further incident. Austin argued that the Americans were not being disloyal or attempting to avoid duties; Fisher's order was simply impractical. Nevertheless, the government abandoned attempts to collect duties in September 1832 and did not resume collection until the spring of 1835.

Col. John Davis Bradburn's problems were more serious. Teran gave him command of the newly established garrison of Anahuac, which was located near the settlement of Atascosito. The small community was one of many settled illegally by Anglo-Americans early in the 19th century. But Mexican authorities had promised to provide the settlers legal titles to their land. In 1831, Francisco Madero was appointed land commissioner to issue the titles. Bradburn detained Madero, arguing that his actions were illegal. The settlement, Bradburn asserted, was too close to the coast. The officer also disbanded a new ayuntamiento established by Madero at Liberty. Madero argued that the Americans settled the land before the Law of April 6, 1830, and the statute did not apply to them. Madero was freed and the titles issued, but complaints about Bradburn continued. He was charged with using the settlers' slaves without compensation to build military structures, with enticing slaves to escape and with arresting colonists and holding them for military trial. William B. Travis was jailed when he tried to represent the claims of a Louisiana slaveholder. An armed revolt ensued that resulted in Bradburn's removal from office. Mexican officials felt that Bradburn's actions had prompted the rebellion, and some ayuntamientos criticized the actions of the insurgents. Although Bradburn was removed from office as a gesture of appeasement, the incidents further kindled the emotions of the settlers — and deepened the concern of the Mexican government.

Thereafter, the colonists began a campaign to drive the Mexican soldiers from Texas, and except for the adroitness of Austin, the settlers would have brought upon themselves severe retribution from the government.

Events in 1830 ended the Texans' usual aloofness to the political maneuverings in Mexico. Gen. Bustamante had replaced Guererro as president and made himself dictator. Troops rebelled in Veracruz in January 1832, and, led by Santa Anna, were fighting to replace the dictator. Santa Anna, ever an opportunist, declared himself a friend of the republican cause, and Texans backed him. During the engagement at Anahuac, the insurgents who sought release of Travis and other prisoners had declared for Santa Anna. While the revolt at Anahuac was bloodless, Mexican soldiers were killed and injured at Velasco when Texans ran a blockade in an attempt to get aid to the other insurgents. Mexican troops at Nacogdoches also were ousted, although many soldiers were anxious to return to Mexico to fight with Santa Anna and the republic.

Upon hearing the reports of the insurgency in Texas in 1832, Gen. Jose Antonio Mexia brought 400 troops to the state by sea. He was lavishly feted by the Texans and was convinced that there was no rebellion against the government. A supporter of Santa Anna, Mexia returned to Mexico.

Heady with success and with Santa Anna's federalist campaign in Mexico going so well, the Texans felt it was time to petition the government for reforms and to explain their actions. A convention was called in San Felipe, the capital of Austin's colony, in October 1832. With Austin serving as president of the convention, several concerns were expressed to the government. Delegates wanted Texas separated from Coahuila, titles for land in East Texas, encroachments on Indian lands stopped, a militia to defend against Indian attacks, and government-donated land for schools. Mexican officials condemned the meeting, explaining that it was not the proper way to express grievances. Therefore, the concerns were not presented to the government.

Mexican officials, however, were concerned about the "illegal" convention. The proper method of addressing the government, under their system, was to function through the legally constituted ayuntamiento in each colony. For the Americans, the conventions were simply their traditional method of petitioning the government.

Despite the objections of the government, a second convention was called in April of 1833 at San Felipe. This time the radical faction of the colonists controlled, with William H. Wharton serving as president. Nevertheless, the requests of the delegates were essentially the same. They wanted the Law of April 6, 1830, repealed, and they wanted a separation from Coahuila. Serving in his first official capacity in Texas, Sam Houston, a former governor of Tennessee and former congressman, chaired the committee that wrote a sample state constitution. It was based on the Massachusetts' constitution and incorporated few of the features usually found in the constitutions of Mexican states. Austin and two other delegates were selected to present the pleadings to the newly elected Mexican president, Santa Anna.

Austin alone reached Mexico City in October 1833 and presented the petition to Vice President Gomez Farias, who was running the government in the absence of President Santa Anna. A cholera epidemic swept Mexico City — and Texas — at the time, and Austin got no response from Farias. The acting president was preoccupied with other problems and also disagreed with the proposal that Texas be given independent statehood. Distressed by the delay, Austin wrote the ayuntamiento in San Antonio advising it to set up a state government. Upon his resumption of office, Santa Anna met with Austin and agreed with most of the reforms the Texans had requested, except the separation from Coahuila. On the return trip to Texas in December, Austin stopped in Saltillo, where he was arrested. The letter he had written in a huff to San Antonio was interpreted as a call for revolution. Austin was returned to Mexico City and imprisoned.

UNDER Farias' instructions, Col. Juan Nepomuceno Almonte toured Texas in 1834 with a twofold purpose: To assure settlers that the government was moving to implement reforms and to determine the attitude of the colonists. Almonte found no unrest in Texas and advocated most of the reforms that Austin had requested in Mexico City.

Indeed, despite the turmoil, Texas was prospering. By 1834, some 7,000 bales of cotton with a value of $315,000 were shipped to New Orleans. In the middle of the decade, Texas exports, including cotton and beaver, otter and deer skins, amounted to $500,000. Trade ratios were out of balance, however, because $630,000 in manufactured goods were imported. Almonte also found that there was little currency in Texas. Ninety percent of the business transactions were conducted in barter or credit, "which gives the country, in its trading relations, the appearance of a continued fair,'' he observed.

In 1833 and 1834, the Coahuila y Texas legislature also was diligently trying to respond to the complaints of the Texas colonists. The English language was recognized for official purposes. Religious toleration was approved (Gen. Teran in 1828 had noted that freedom of religion was better than no religion at all, which was the case in Texas at the time). And the court system was revised, providing Texas with an appellate court and trial by jury. Previously, the legislature had approved schools for the colonists, but this measure was not fully implemented because of a lack of funds and low population density. Texas also was divided into three departments, Bexar, Nacogdoches and Brazos, to facilitate administration.

In Mexico City, however, a different scenario was developing. Santa Anna had in essence shared the presidency with Farias, allowing the vice president to enact many federalist reforms that proved unpopular with the church, the wealthy and the military. Santa Anna assumed supreme authority in April 1834, exiled the vice president and began a program of dismantling the federalist government. By October 1835, a centralist government had replaced the federalist, and the Congress was subservient to Santa Anna.

Among the most offensive changes dictated by Santa Anna was the reduction of the militia to one man per each 500 population. The intent was to eliminate possible armed opposition to the emerging centralist government. But liberals in the state of Zacatecas in Central Mexico rebelled. Santa Anna's response was particularly brutal, as he tried to make an example of the rebels. Troops were allowed to sack the state capital after the victory over the insurgents.

Trouble also was brewing closer to the Texans. In March 1833, the Coahuila y Texas legislature moved the state capital from Saltillo to Monclova. The Monclova legislature in 1834 gave the governor authority to sell 400 sitios — or 1.77 million acres of land — to finance the government and to provide for protection. Land speculators jumped at the opportunity to obtain land so cheap.

A year later, the lawmakers criticized Santa Anna's repudiation of federalism. Seeing a chance to regain lost prestige, Saltillo declared for Santa Anna and set up an opposition government. But in the spring of 1835, Santa Anna sent his brother-in-law, Martin Perfecto de Cos, to break up the state government at Monclova.

Texans were appalled by the breakdown in state government, coming on the heels of so many assurances that the political situation was to improve. Texas politics were polarizing. A "war party" advocated breaking away from Mexico altogether, while a "peace party" urged calm and riding out the political storm. Most of the settlers, however, aligned with neither group. And it is said that the passion for rebellion was directly proportional to the stake the individual had in Texas. The long-time settlers wanted to maintain a status quo; newcomers favored revolt.

In January 1835, Santa Anna sent a detachment of soldiers to Anahuac to reinforce the customs office. But duties were being charged irregularly at various ports on the coast. William B. Travis, in an act not supported by all colonists, led a contingent of armed colonists against the Mexican soldiers, who withdrew without a fight.

Although some members of the peace party wrote Gen. Cos, stationed at Matamoros, apologizing for the action, he was not compromising. Cos demanded that members of the group be arrested and turned over to him. The Texans refused.

The committees of correspondence, organized at the Convention of 1832, began organizing another meeting. Because the term "convention" aroused visions of revolution in the eyes of Mexican officials, the gathering at Washington-on-the-Brazos in October 1835 was called a "consultation." But with the break-down of the state government and with Santa Anna's repeal of the Constitution of 1824, the American settlers felt well within their rights to provide a new framework within which to govern Texas.

Help also came from an unexpected source. Austin was released from prison and arrived in Texas in September 1835. He immediately began agitation for a representative convention to deal with the developing crisis. Austin's long-standing support for patience was at an end. He urged war to protect Texas' rights in the Mexican confederation under the Constitution of 1824.

Fresh from brutally putting down the rebellion in Zacatecas, Santa Anna turned his attention to Texas. Gen. Cos was determined to regarrison the state, and the settlers were equally adamant about keeping soldiers out.

COL. Domingo Ugartechea, headquartered at San Antonio, became concerned about armed rebellion when he heard of the incident at Anahuac. And he recalled a six-pound cannon that had been given DeWitt colonists to fight Indians. Ugartechea ordered Cpl. Casimira de Leon with five men to Gonzales to retrieve the weapon. No problems were expected. But officials at Gonzales refused to surrender the weapon. When the Mexicans reinforced Cpl. De Leon's forces, a call was sent out for volunteers to help the Texans. Dozens responded. On Oct. 2, 1835, the Texans challenged the Mexicans with a "come-and-take-it" flag over the cannon. After a brief skirmish, the Mexicans withdrew, but the first rounds in the Texas Revolution had been fired.

Gen. Cos had entered San Antonio while the Texans were occupied with the affair in Gonzales. When the Mexicans left Gonzales, the volunteer force followed them to San Antonio.

The consultation in Washington-on-the-Brazos created a provisional government with Henry Smith as governor and with an executive council. Austin, despite a lack of military experience, was named commander-in-chief of the army. He immediately went to San Antonio.

Capt. George Collinsworth had captured Goliad and a large store of supplies, which was taken to the Texans besieging San Antonio. Austin remained at the head of the "Army of the People" until mid November when he was sent to the United States to plead the Texans' cause for aid. Edward Burleson assumed command. In early December, a special force of Texans — led by Ben Milam, who died in the battle — assaulted the city, and five days later, Gen. Cos capitulated. The Mexican leader and his troops were furloughed with the understanding they would not fight against the cause of the Constitution of 1824 again, a pledge that Cos broke.

The Texans were euphoric with the string of victories over Mexican forces. It was a euphoria born of overconfidence, it turned out, and led to mistakes that claimed hundreds of lives.

But the Texas Revolution was under way.

End of the Beginning

AS 1836 opened, Texans felt in control of their destiny. The Mexican army had been driven from their soil. Winter was at hand. And the settlers were secure in their land and their liberties.

But tragedy loomed. Easy victories over Mexican forces at Anahuac, Nacogdoches, Goliad, Gonzales and San Antonio in the fall of 1835 had given them a false sense of security. Their frontier independence had served well in forcing Mexicans from their soil. Texans proved their unwillingness to take orders from the Mexican military, but they were not in a mood to take orders from each other either. That independent mood was their undoing, for no government worth the name coordinated the defense of Texas. Consequently, as the Mexican counterattack developed, no one was in charge. In November 1835, the Consultation failed to outline the duties and responsibilities of the provisional government it created. Henry Smith was named governor, and he and the provisional council — one representative from each of the 12 municipalities — were to run the administration. They were antagonists from the beginning. By mid-January the arrangement collapsed, but in the interim much damage was done. With the Mexican military out of Texas, the settlers' primary concern was relieved; the "war" was over.

They had won. The victory's consolidation, however, was a point of contention. Smith supported complete independence for Texas. The council wanted to link up with Mexican liberals to restore the Constitution of 1824. Gen. Jose A. Mexia was to lead a rebellion against the dictator Antonio Lopez de Santa Anna at Tampico. If the Texans could attract the support of the liberal rebels, there was a chance to restore constitutional government in Mexico.

That was the sense of a resolution passed by the Consultation. And the council tried to implement the goal with disastrous results. Sam Houston was commander-in-chief of the Texas forces, but he had little authority. The council, pursuing its intention of gaining Mexican liberal support, conceived the idea of a campaign against Matamoros, the port city across the Rio Grande from present-day Brownsville. Dr. James Grant promoted the plan. He owned property in northern Mexico that had been confiscated by the government. If the dictator were overthrown, Grant could reclaim the land.

The so-called old settlers, however, had lost interest in the conflict. After Gen. Martin Perfecto de Cos had been driven from San Antonio in December 1835, the Texan army had dwindled. Texas volunteers returned home to prepare for spring planting. Their places in the ranks were taken by Americans who flocked to Texas to fight Mexico. On Christmas Day, about 750 men, mostly American volunteers, made up the Texas army. Four hundred men were at San Antonio, 70 at Washington-on-the-Brazos, 80 at Goliad and 200 at Velasco. The provisional government's attempt to establish a regular army failed. It never had more than 80 soldiers, leaving most of the fighting to volunteers.

In late December, the provisional council authorized the Matamoros expedition with a round of comic-opera appointments. First Frank W. Johnson was appointed commander, and when he declined, James W. Fannin was named. Dr. Grant was given the post of commander of the volunteers. Shortly thereafter, Johnson changed his mind, and the council made him commander of the expedition again. Fannin retained his authority, however. Houston was not informed of any of the changes. So the Texas army had four commanders in chief.

DR. Grant and Johnson soon took 300 men and supplies from San Antonio, heading south to set up a command post near Refugio. By Jan. 6, Col. James C. Neill had only 104 men — none Texans — and no clothing or supplies under his command at San Antonio. Fannin, one of the few Texas officers with West Point training, declined to participate in the Matamoros expedition after occupying the old fort at Goliad.

Houston initially planned a line of defense along the San Antonio River, which had strongly fortified positions at Goliad and San Antonio. But with the command split and none of the other three "command-ers" willing to take orders, Houston's hands were tied. He visited Refugio but failed to convince Grant and Johnson to abandon plans for attacking Matamoros. Houston was successful in keeping many men from participating. When he left, Grant and Johnson had only about 150 men remaining under their command.

The status of the strongholds along the San Antonio River also was of concern. In mid-January, Houston sent James Bowie to San Antonio to determine if the Alamo was defensible. If not, Bowie had orders to destroy it and withdraw the men and artillery to Gonzales and Copano.

Houston took a furlough to travel to East Texas and meet with the Cherokees. Settlers were concerned about the Indians' intentions. Several chiefs of the Cherokees had met in September 1835 with Mexican officers in San Antonio. The Consultation had approved a "solemn declaration" to recognize Indian claims to ownership of land north of the San Antonio Road and between the Angelina and Sabine rivers. This pledge was repeated in the treaty Houston negotiated in exchange for the Indians' neutrality in the conflict with Mexico. (After the revolution, the treaty was rejected by the Texas Senate, and the Indians later were driven from the land.)

If the Texans' defense was disorganized, few settlers worried. Some thought the Mexicans would not try to re-enter Texas. Others felt the Mexican army would not mount an offensive until spring. The reasons were logical, if wrong. Mexico was experiencing financial problems, and the army was weakened by the continuing civil war between federalists and central-ists. The government was disorganized. And the rich buffalo grass on the South Texas prairies was dead, denying fodder for invaders' horses and livestock.

Few Texans counted on the energy and determina-tion of Gen. Antonio Lopez de Santa Anna, the dictator of Mexico. In August 1835, he proclaimed his intention of driving Anglo-American settlers from Texas and of executing any Americans found taking up arms or supporting the rebellion against Mexico. The cam-paign would be financed through the confiscation of the settlers' property. Preparations for the invasion began in the fall at San Luis Potosi. The army's depleted ranks were filled with conscripts. Forced loans were obtained from the church and other sources, and lenders were given outrageously benefi-cial terms for some funds. But arrangements were hurried and incomplete. Many of the soldiers were not properly clothed for the march in the cold winter weather. Mayan Indian recruits from the Yucatan, unaccustomed to the northers and other conditions in Northern Mexico, suffered pitiably, for example. Also the army, including officers, was put on half rations from the beginning. And no provision was made for physicans and field hospitals. Nevertheless, about 6,000 men were under arms as the army marched toward Texas.

Racial overtones permeated both sides of the developing conflict. Texans did not trust Mexican-Texans and usually stayed aloof from them. At Refugio, Mexican-Texans complained about abuse from Grant's and Johnson's men. And the Mexican-Texans were dubious about the motives of the Anglos. Many Mexican-Texans were willing to fight for restora-tion of the Constitution of 1824, but refused to take up arms for an independent Anglo Texas in which they would be a minority. Santa Anna held Anglo frontiers-men in contempt for many years.

As a 19-year-old lieutenant in the Royal Spanish Army, Santa Anna had served in Gen. Joaquin de Arredondo's campaign against republicans after the Gutierrez-Magee rebellion in 1813, which created the first Republic of Texas. Arredondo had been merciless in his retribution, killing more than 300 republicans at San Antonio alone. Santa Anna was revolted by the crude attempts of the Anglo frontiersmen to defend themselves against the best European tactics of the day. And he boasted that he would plant the eagles of Mexico on the banks of the Sabine River and even march to Washington, D.C., to teach the Anglos a lesson in the upcoming campaign.

If Santa Anna had been determined to punish Texas when he began the campaign, he became fanatical when his brother-in-law, Gen. Cos, crossed the Rio Grande with the remnants of his command, which was defeated at San Antonio. Santa Anna ordered Cos to ignore his pledge not to enter Texas again to fight against the Constitution of 1824.

On Feb. 12, Santa Anna's main force crossed the Rio Grande headed for San Antonio. The Mexican battle plan has been debated. But Mexico's national pride had been bruised by the series of defeats the nation's army had suffered in 1835, capped by Gen. Cos' ouster from San Antonio in December. The main body of the army moved northward on San Antonio, but Gen. Jose Urrea was ordered along the coast. Few Texans thought San Antonio — or Bexar as it was generally called — was worth defending. The direct route to the rich Anglo-Texan colonies on the Brazos and Colorado rivers was along the coast. Many strategists anticipat-ed a quick thrust at San Felipe de Austin, the capital of Austin's colony and of Anglo Texas. Mexican strate-gists, however, did not want to leave a well-defended outpost to their rear during the campaign. And Santa Anna could not leave a pocket of Anglo-Americans behind him when he had pledged to sweep them all from Texas.

The grueling march took Santa Anna 11 days and cost many lives. The weather turned brutal and northers and rain took a heavy toll among the soldiers and animals. Texan scouts also had made the trek more difficult by burning large areas of grassland that the Mexicans had counted on as forage.

WHILE the Mexicans prepared for war through the fall and early winter, the Texans' defensive preparations floundered. On Feb. 11, Gov. Smith sent Col. William Barret Travis to San Antonio to relieve Col. Neill. Immediately a split in command arose. Most of the American defenders were volun-teers, who looked to Bowie as their leader. Travis had only a handful of Texas army regulars. So Bowie and Travis agreed to share the command. Almost immedi-ately, Travis began asking for reinforcements. Only 150 men were available to fight, and Travis sought aid from Fannin, from Gov. Smith, from Houston, from the provisional council and from the citizens of the United States. Only a plea to Gonzales was answered.

Aside from the pleas for help, however, activity around San Antonio was leisurely. Discipline was lax, and work on improving the fortifications of the Alamo moved slowly. Indeed, the defenders of San Antonio were fortunate not to have suffered a successful surprise attack on Feb. 22. Santa Anna ordered a surprise attack by Gen. Ramirez y Sesma's cavalry, but a rain-swollen creek scuttled the plan. The Texans would have had their hands full for they were enjoying a fandango celebrating George Washington's birthday at the time, and only 10 men guarded the Alamo. The following morning, however, the forward elements of the Mexican army were spotted by guards at San Antonio and their presence was confirmed by scouts. Quickly the Texans and Americans retreated to the Alamo, which soon was under siege by hundreds of Mexican soldiers whose ranks were being reinforced daily.

Santa Anna left no doubt regarding his attitude toward the Anglo defenders of the Alamo. Upon arrival, he had hoisted a blood-red flag, the traditional Mexican symbol of no quarter, no surrender, no mercy. Travis and Bowie defiantly answered the display with a cannon shot.

Immediately the Mexicans began surrounding the Alamo and bombarding it. Throughout the first night and nights to come, Santa Anna kept up a continual din to destroy the defenders' morale.

On Feb. 24, Bowie took ill and relinquished his share of command to Travis. That evening, Travis penned one of the most stirring appeals for help in the annals of history:

Commandancy of the Alamo—
Bejar, Feby. 24th, 1836
To the people of Texas & all Americans in the world—

Fellow citizens & compatriots—

I am besieged, by a thousand or more of the Mexicans under Santa Anna — I have sustained a continual Bombardment & cannonade for 24 hours & have not lost a man — The enemy has demanded a surrender at discretion, otherwise, the garrison are to be put to the sword, if the fort is taken — I have answered the demand with a cannon shot, & our flag still waves proudly from the walls — I shall never surrender or retreat. Then I call on you in the name of Liberty, of patriotism & everything dear to the American character, to come to our aid, with all dispatch — The enemy is receiving reinforcements daily & will no doubt increase to three or four thousand in four or five days. If this call is neglected, I am determined to sustain myself as long as possible & and die like a soldier who never forgets what is due to his own honor & that of his country — VICTORY OR DEATH.

William Barret Travis,
Lt. Col. comdt.

P.S. The Lord is on our side — When the enemy appeared in sight we had not three bushels of corn — We have since found in deserted houses 80 or 90 bushels and got into the walls 20 or 30 head of Beeves.

Travis.

Within weeks, the plea for help was circulated up the Mississippi Valley and along the eastern seaboard of the United States. It is credited with generating hundreds of volunteers for the Texas cause. But they came far too late to help Travis and his little band of heroes at the Alamo.

The closest garrison of any size to the Alamo was at Goliad under Fannin's command. But Fannin refused several requests from Travis for aid. On Feb. 26, however, he began a relief march, only to have a wagon break down less than a mile from his fort. After a night's reflection on the tactical situation, he turned back.

Near Refugio on Feb. 28, Gen. Urrea fought with remnants of the Matamoros expedition under Johnson, killing several and taking 21 prisoners. The prisoners later were executed by Santa Anna's orders. Johnson escaped to carry word of the engagement to Fannin at Goliad. When news of this battle reached San Antonio, however, Mexican morale soared. The army had suffered nothing but losses, embarrassment and humiliation at the hands of the Texans for a year. Urrea's conquest was seen as a turning point. And on March 3, the general's troops ambushed another remnant of the Matamoros expedition at Agua Dulce Creek, and Dr. Grant and 15 others were killed.

Although the Mexican bombardment of the Alamo continued daily, none of the defenders was killed. In fact, they conducted several successful forays outside the fortress to burn buildings that were providing cover for the Mexican gunners and to gather firewood. Messengers also successfully moved through the Mexican lines at will, and 32 reinforcements from Gonzales under George Kimball and Albert Martin made it into the Alamo without a loss on March 1. But Santa Anna was tightening the perimeter. The last messenger got out on March 3, carrying, among other items, a letter to Jesse Grimes in which Travis asserted to the convention meeting at Washington-on-the-Brazos: "If independence is not declared, I shall lay down my arms, and so will the men under my command. But under the flag of independence, we are ready to peril our lives 100 times a day . . ."

Travis was unaware that the convention had declared Texas' independence from Mexico on March 2 and was engaged in writing a constitution and forming a government for the new republic. Historians disagree over which flag flew over the defenders of the Alamo. Mexican sources have said that Santa Anna was outraged when he saw flying over the fortress a Mexican tri-color, identical to the ones carried by his troops except with the numbers "1 8 2 4" emblazoned upon it. Texas historians have accepted this version because the defenders of the Alamo could not have known that independence had been declared. To the knowledge of the Alamo's defenders, the last official government position taken by Texans was in support of the Constitution of 1824, which the flag symbolized. But the only flag found after the battle, according to historian Walter Lord, was one flown by the New Orleans Grays.

BY March 5 Santa Anna had 4,000 men in camp, a force he felt sufficient to subdue the Alamo. Mexican sources said he was furious that the Texans had held out through 12 days of bombardment and siege. The longer the small band held off the Mexicans, the less would be his glory. Other Mexican commanders felt that major losses in life were not necessary to take the fortress; the defenders could have been starved out eventually. But Santa Anna would not hear of it. His confidence rested in his troops' courage and their training in the best of Napoleonic military tactics. Crude frontiersmen, El Presidente thought, had little chance against this sort of sophisticated armed might.

Santa Anna overlooked the marksmanship of the frontiersmen behind the walls of the Alamo. To a man they had been raised with weapons and trained to hunt. With their long rifles, Davy Crockett and his Tennesseans prided themselves on regularly hitting targets at 200 yards or more. Mexican smooth-bore muskets could carry only 70 yards, and not accurately at that. Faced with the Mexicans' give-no-quarter policy, the defenders of the Alamo would be doubly lethal.

Historians disagree on the date, and in some cases whether the event took place. But legend holds that on March 3 or March 5, Col. Travis called his command together and explained the bleak outlook. He apologized if he had misled them into believing that reinforcements were on the way. But he explained that he had told them that in good faith; he had thought help was coming. Then the young colonel drew a line in the dirt and asked those willing to die for freedom to cross with him. Jim Bowie had his sick bed carried across. Only Louis Rose, a veteran of Napoleon's bitter retreat from Moscow, chose to fight another day. He slipped out of the Alamo that night.

Mexican troops were up well before dawn on March 6 preparing for the final assault on the Alamo. When reminded that there were no doctors or hospital facilities available, Santa Anna reportedly snapped that that was all the better. The troops would know, he said, that it was "not as bad to die as to come out wounded." Twenty-five hundred men in perfect formation surrounded the fortress and on command commenced their attack. During the action, the Mexican bands struck up the deguello, a traditional Spanish march dating back to the battles against the Moors. It signified a no-quarter, throat-cutting, merciless death. The first troops were cut down by the murderous cannon fire from the Alamo's guns and by the precision marksmanship of the frontiersmen's long rifles. Cannon loaded with scrap iron mowed down the Mexican regulars by the squad. There is no doubting the courage of the Mexican soldiers as they faced the lethal fire. At first they would fall back, regroup and attack again. Although the Mexicans were executing perfect Napoleonic maneuvers, they lacked the cannon to give the fortress an appropriate initial bombardment. Also, Mexican commanders were unaware that British army instructions at the time warned that frontal assaults on frontier riflemen behind breastworks could be conducted only with unacceptable casualties. Attempt after attempt at placing scaling ladders was thwarted by the Alamo's cannon and riflemen. But Mexican artillery finally began to have its effect. A wall was breached. The first few Mexican soldiers through the opening were killed. The number of skirmishers soon became too great. The Alamo's huge courtyard was

Texas Declaration of Independence

On March 2, 1836, Texas' Declaration of Independence from Mexico was adopted at Washington-on-the-Brazos. **Richard Ellis** served as president of this convention of delegates chosen by Texans. Ellis appointed five on a committee to write the document but **George C. Childress** wrote it with little help from the others. He is known as the **author of the declaration.**

The following text contains the exact wording and punctuation of the original Texas Declaration of Independence and the names of signers are exactly as written on the original document.

When a government has ceased to protect the lives, liberty and property of the people from whom its legitimate powers are derived, and for the advancement of whose happiness it was instituted; and so far from being a guarantee for the enjoyment of those inestimable and inalienable rights, becomes an instrument in the hands of evil rulers for their oppression; when the Federal Republican Constitution of their country, which they have sworn to support, no longer has a substantial existence, and the whole nature of their government has been forcibly changed without their consent, from a restricted federative republic, composed of sovereign states, to a consolidated central military despotism, in which every interest is disregarded but that of the army and the priesthood — both the eternal enemies of civil liberty, and the ever-ready minions of power, and the usual instruments of tyrants; When, long after the spirit of the constitution has departed, moderation is at length, so far lost, by those in power that even the semblance of freedom is removed, and the forms, themselves, of the constitution discontinued; and so far from their petitions and remonstrances being regarded, the agents who bear them are thrown into dungeons; and mercenary armies sent forth to force a new government upon them at the point of the bayonet; When in consequence of such acts of malfeasance and abdication, on the part of the government, anarchy prevails, and civil society is dissolved into its original elements; In such a crisis, the first law of nature, the right of self-preservation — the inherent and inalienable right of the people to appeal to first principles and take their political affairs into their own hands in extreme cases — enjoins it as a right towards themselves and a sacred obligation to their posterity, to abolish such government and create another in its stead, calculated to rescue them from impending dangers, and to secure their future welfare and happiness.

Nations, as well as individuals, are amenable for their acts to the public opinion of mankind. A statement of a part of our grievances is, therefore, submitted to an impartial world, in justification of the hazardous but unavoidable step now taken of severing our political connection with the Mexican people, and assuming an independent attitude among the nations of the earth.

The Mexican government, by its colonization laws, invited and induced the Anglo-American population of Texas to colonize its wilderness under the pledged faith of a written constitution, that they should continue to enjoy that constitutional liberty and republican government to which they had been habituated in the land of their birth, the United States of America. In this expectation they have been cruelly disappointed, inasmuch as the Mexican nation has acquiesced in the late changes made in the government by General Antonio Lopez de Santa Anna, who, having overturned the constitution of his country, now offers us the cruel alternative either to

---

filled with desperate hand-to-hand fighting. Mexicans were armed with bayonets; the defenders used rifle butts and Bowie knives. So frenzied had the Mexican soldiers become that the corpses of defenders were mutilated. Travis died of a bullet wound to the head. Bowie was killed in his sick bed, selling his life dearly with a brace of pistols left for his defense. Crockett's fate is still debated. Some sources say he died in a pile of Mexican soldiers, victims of his rifle and knife. One Mexican officer, Enrique De La Pena, held that Crockett was captured with a few other defenders and executed by Santa Anna.

When the fighting stopped between 8:30 and 9 a.m., all the defenders were dead. Only a few women, children and black slaves survived the assault.

But Travis and his men placed a heavy price indeed on the victory. Almost one-third of the attack force was killed or wounded. And these were the flower of the Mexican army, veterans for the most part. Their deaths in such number set back Santa Anna's timetable. Although recruits were available from the ranks of Mexican-Texans, they had to be trained. The Napoleonic tactics used by the army required highly trained soldiers, and training took time. The fall of the Alamo also brutally shook the old Texans out of their lethargy, and no doubt shamed them, too, for ignoring Travis' appeals for help.

Sam Houston, finally given command of all Texas' army, left the convention at Washington-on-the-Brazos on the day of the fall of the Alamo. On March 11, he arrived at Gonzales to begin organizing the troops. He found just over 370 men at the town, many of whom had been on their way to aid Travis. Two days later, Mrs. Dickinson, the wife of one of the victims of the Alamo, and two slaves arrived with the news of the fall of the fortress. Houston immediately began an evacuation of Gonzales, taking the inhabitants and leaving the town in flames to deny it to the Mexican forces he thought were close behind.

Houston ordered Fannin to abandon the old presidio La Bahia at Goliad and to retreat to Victoria. Fannin had arrived at the fort in late January with more than 400 men. As a former West Pointer, he had a background in military planning. Troops were drilled, and fortifications were improved. But Fannin had been indecisive. Travis' pleas for help were refused, and after receiving Houston's orders, Fannin waited for scouting parties to return. Finally, on March 19, he left, but too late. Forward elements of Gen. Urrea's troops caught Fannin's command on an open prairie

near a wooded area. After a short battle, Fannin fortified his position around a broken-down ammunition wagon. Through the night, the Mexican troops were reinforced. After a brief skirmish the following morning, Fannin surrendered.

A controversy surrounded the capitulation. Survivors of Fannin's command later argued that they surrendered with the understanding they would be treated as prisoners of war. Documents indicate, however, that the surrender was unconditional, and the troops were thrown on the mercy of the Mexican commanders. The prisoners were marched to Goliad where they were kept under light restraint. So unconcerned were they that it is said that not one violated the pledge not to attempt an escape. Santa Anna was furious, however, when Gen. Urrea appealed for clemency for the captives. The Mexican leader issued the orders in triplicate for their execution. On March 27, a Palm Sunday, most of the prisoners were divided into groups and marched out of Goliad, thinking they were being transferred to other facilities. When the executions began, many escaped. But about 350 were killed.

In less than a month, Texas' military forces had lost almost 700 men in battle or by execution. Fewer than one in five of these were old settlers, most being American volunteers who had not been in Texas when hostilities began the previous fall. Houston spent almost two weeks on the Colorado River, and on March 26 began a retreat to the Brazos.

Santa Anna had not left San Antonio, but word of the losses soon reached the settlers who began leaving their homes, often in haste. When the Mexican army began pursuit of Houston's forces, Jose Enrique de la Pena, a young staff officer, lamented the fear that the war generated. He blamed the war on a group of promoters. These promoters, the young officer observed, "painted us as savages, as men more ferocious than beasts, to which belief the events of the Alamo, La Bahia and the mission at Refugio unfortunately contributed. No one will disagree with me that provisions should have been made to prevent the war, or that once begun in order to vindicate an injured nation, it should have been carried out in a less disastrous fashion."

But the old Texans finally faced the reality of the conflict. While many ran for safety, others joined Houston for the defense of the Republic. As one soldier noted, "We ask nor expect no quarter in the future." The Texans were on their way to San Jacinto.

abandon our homes, acquired by so many privations, or submit to the most intolerable of all tyranny, the combined despotism of the sword and the priesthood.

It has sacrificed our welfare to the state of Coahuila, by which our interests have been continually depressed, through a jealous and partial course of legislation carried on at a far distant seat of government, by a hostile majority, in an unknown tongue; and this too, notwithstanding we have petitioned in the humblest terms, for the establishment of a separate state government, and have, in accordance with the provisions of the national constitution, presented to the general Congress, a republican constitution which was without just cause contemptuously rejected.

It incarcerated in a dungeon, for a long time, one of our citizens, for no other cause but a zealous endeavor to procure the acceptance of our constitution and the establishment of a state government.

It has failed and refused to secure on a firm basis, the right of trial by jury; that palladium of civil liberty, and only safe guarantee for the life, liberty, and property of the citizen.

It has failed to establish any public system of education, although possessed of almost boundless resources (the public domain) and although, it is an axiom, in political science, that unless a people are educated and enlightened it is idle to expect the continuance of civil liberty, or the capacity for self-government.

It has suffered the military commandants stationed among us to exercise arbitrary acts of oppression and tyranny; thus trampling upon the most sacred rights of the citizen and rendering the military superior to the civil power.

It has dissolved by force of arms, the state Congress of Coahuila and Texas, and obliged our representatives to fly for their lives from the seat of government; thus depriving us of the fundamental political right of representation.

It has demanded the surrender of a number of our citizens, and ordered military detachments to seize and carry them into the interior for trial; in contempt of the civil authorities, and in defiance of the laws and the constitution.

It has made piratical attacks upon our commerce; by commissioning foreign desperadoes, and authorizing them to seize our vessels, and convey the property of our citizens to far distant ports of confiscation.

It denies us the right of worshiping the Almighty according to the dictates of our own consciences, by the support of a national religion calculated to promote the temporal interests of its human functionaries rather than the glory of the true and living God.

It has demanded us to deliver up our arms; which are essential to our defense, the rightful property of freemen, and formidable only to tyrannical governments.

It has invaded our country, both by sea and by land, with intent to lay waste our territory and drive us from our homes; and has now a large mercenary army advancing to carry on against us a war of extermination.

It has, through its emissaries, incited the merciless savage, with the tomahawk and scalping knife, to massacre the inhabitants of our defenseless frontiers.

It hath been, during the whole time of our connection with it, the contemptible sport and victim of successive military revolutions and hath continually exhibited every characteristic of a weak, corrupt, and tyrannical government.

These, and other grievances, were patiently borne by the people of Texas until they reached that point at which forbearance ceases to be a virtue. We then took up arms in defense of the national constitution. We appealed to our Mexican brethren for assistance. Our appeal has been made in vain. Though months have lapsed, no sympathetic response has yet been heard from the Interior. We are, therefore, forced to the melancholy conclusion that the Mexican people have acquiesced in the destruction of their liberty, and the substitution therefor of a military government — that they are unfit to be free and incapable of self-government.

The necessity of self-preservation, therefore, now decrees our eternal political separation.

We, therefore, the delegates, with plenary powers, of the people of Texas, in solemn convention assembled, appealing to a candid world for the necessities of our condition, do hereby resolve and declare that our political connection with the Mexican nation has forever ended; and that the people of Texas do now constitute a free, sovereign and independent republic, and are fully invested with all the rights and attributes which properly belong to the independent nations; and conscious of the rectitude of our intentions, we fearlessly and confidently commit the issue to the decision of the Supreme Arbiter of the destinies of nations.

RICHARD ELLIS, president of the convention and Delegate from Red River.

Charles B. Stewart	JB Woods	Thos. Barnet	Thomas Jefferson Rusk
John S. D. Byrom	Chas. S. Taylor	Franco Ruiz	John S. Roberts
J. Antonio Navarro	Robert Hamilton	Jesse B. Badgett	Collin McKinney
Wm. D. Lacey	Albert H Latimer	William Menefee	James Power
Jno. Fisher	Sam Houston	Mathew Caldwell	David Thomas
William Mottley	Edwd. Conrad	Lorenzo de Zavala	Martin Parmer
Stephen H. Everitt	Edwin O. LeGrand	Geo W Smyth	Stephen W. Blount
Elijah Stapp	Jas. Gaines	Claiborne West	Wm. Clark, Jr
Wm. B Scates	Sydney O. Penington	M. B. Menard	Wm. Carrol Crawford
A. B. Hardin	Jno Turner	J. W. Bunton	Benj. Briggs Goodrich
Thos. J. Gazley	G. M. Barnett	R M Coleman	James G. Swisher
Sterling C. Robertson	Jesse Grimes	Jas Collinsworth	S Rhoads Fisher
Edwin Waller	John W. Moore	Asa Brigham	John W. Bower
Geo. C. Childress	Saml. A Maverick	Bailey Hardeman	(from Bejar)
Rob.Potter	Sam P. Carson	A. Briscoe	

Test. H. S. Kemble Secretary

San Jacinto and Beyond

SAM Houston spent only a short time at the convention that met March 1, 1836, at Washington-on-the-Brazos. But he may have been the most important man there, for he insisted that the Texans form a coherent government. The Alamo was besieged and in danger, he argued, because there had been no government in Texas.

Attempts to adjourn the convention so the delegates could rush to San Antonio were defeated. Long-winded oratory was discouraged. The convention quickly got down to the business of forming a government. Richard Ellis was named president, and a committee chaired by George Childress wrote a Declaration of Independence, patterned on the one that separated the United States from Great Britain. The declaration was adopted on March 2, and on March 6, the day the Alamo fell, Houston left the convention with full command of all the armed forces in Texas.

Upon arrival at Gonzales, Houston had quickly discerned the Texans' position was untenable. He had only a handful of men, the Alamo had fallen, the settlers were in chaos, and the position was far

THE MORRISON MILLING COMPANY
P.O. BOX 719 · DENTON, TEXAS 76201 · (817) 387-6111

1986 Texas Sesquicentennial Wagon Train Sponsor.

removed from the Anglo population that was so necessary for supplies and reinforcements. Near midnight, he began the long march to San Jacinto.

By March 17, Houston had reached Burnam's Crossing on the Colorado River, near the present city of LaGrange. Two days later, the small army crossed the river and moved south to Beason's Ford near present-day Columbus. There he began to receive reinforcements. Within a week, the small force had become almost respectable with 1,200-1,400 men in camp.

AT the same time Houston reached the Colorado, the convention at Washington-on-the-Brazos was completing work on a constitution for the new Republic. Only slightly did it differ from the U.S. Constitution. The Texas charter called for a unitary government, rather than dividing the territory into states. And from the Mexican constitution, it prohibited the president from succeeding himself after one three-year term. Ministers of the gospel also were prohibited from holding public office. David Burnet was named interim president of the new government and Lorenzo de Zavala was vice president. Thomas J. Rusk was secretary of war. Upon completion of the work, the new government moved to Harrisburg.

In the excitement of the period, however, important steps were not taken. Stephen F. Austin, serving as Texas' agent in the United States, complained the group was never informed that independence had been declared. William Wharton and Branch T. Archer also were Texas' agents.

Close on Houston's heels was Gen. Joaquin de Ramirez y Sesma who had been dispatched from San Antonio by Santa Anna on March 11 to follow the Texans. Seven hundred and twenty-five men were in Ramirez y Sesma's command, and he sought reinforcements as soon as the Texans were spotted. Heavy rains swelled the river, preventing the Mexicans from crossing.

Houston was criticized for not fighting at this point. But the Texans' commander explained that he would have inevitably suffered casualties and had no means to transport them. Also, the Mexicans could easily be reinforced with numbers far exceeding the small Texan contingent. In addition, word of Fannin's loss had reached the area, and settlers were in full flight. On March 27, Houston moved his men to San Felipe on the Brazos, and left on the following day for Groce's Crossing 20 miles up river, which he reached March 31. The Texans were getting restless for a fight. Moseley Baker and Wylie Martin and their men, however, refused to follow Houston to Groce's, so they were ordered to defend the river crossings at San Felipe and at Fort Bend.

At Groce's Crossing, the Texans had a respite, offering Houston an opportunity to organize and drill his forces. Most of the volunteers had no military experience. In a battle against well-drilled forces, they would have been at a disadvantage. So Houston attempted to instill military discipline. Up to this point, one of the army's major responsibilities had been the protection of settlers involved in the Runaway Scrape, as the retreat was called. To reinforce discipline, Houston hanged four men accused of raping women and robbing settlers.

Santa Anna had divided his forces after the fall of the Alamo. Gen. Gaona had been ordered to Nacogdoches along a northern route, but he soon was diverted to San Felipe. Ramirez y Sesma had been in pursuit of the main force of the Texas army, and Gen. Jose Urrea was following a path along the coast from Goliad to Brazoria.

Santa Anna initially considered returning to Mexico City after the Alamo fell. The war was over in his mind, and the dictator, fully aware of the fickle political tides that rocked the Mexican government, wanted to consolidate politically his victories on the battlefield. But his general staff talked him out of leaving.

So Santa Anna joined Ramirez y Sesma on April 7, and the Mexicans entered San Felipe on that day. Mexican intelligence informed the dictator that the Texas government was in Harrisburg, and Santa Anna immediately conceived a plan of capturing the rebel leadership to end the war. But he could not cross the Brazos until April 10, when his troops finally gained control of the Fort Bend crossing from Texan sharpshooters. Three days later Ramirez y Sesma arrived, and the Mexicans reached Harrisburg on April 15. But the Texas government was gone, barely escaping advance units of Mexicans who watched them row to a schooner bound for Galveston. Settlers, however, told the Mexicans that Houston was marching toward Lynch's ferry on the San Jacinto River in an attempt to escape to Louisiana. Santa Anna burned Harrisburg and headed toward the ferry.

At Groce's Crossing, Houston was successful in organizing the army. On April 13, using the steamboat Yellow Stone, the army crossed the river, and orders were sent to outlying units to gather at Donoho's. Martin, who had refused to leave the Brazos, again ignored Houston's command to march and took his troops to Nacogdoches to defend against a feared Indian uprising.

The Texas army was impatient for a fight, and there was talk in the ranks that, if action did not develop soon, a new commander should be elected. So prevalent were the rumblings that Houston posted warnings that he would shoot any man who tried to mutiny. But the Texas government also was distressed with the commander-in-chief's tactics. On April 13, Houston received a message from President Burnet:

"This country expects something from you; the government looks to you for action. The time has arrived to determine whether we are to give up the country and make the best of our way out of it or to meet the enemy and make at least one struggle for our boasted independence."

Fifteen miles east of Donoho's was a fork in the road; one leg went to Nacogdoches and the other to Harrisburg. Here one of the great mysteries of the San Jacinto campaign rests. Critics long said that Houston had no intention of fighting the Mexicans, that his plan was to cross into Louisiana where protection of the U.S. Army was available.

Indeed, Gen. Edmund P. Gaines, commander of Fort Jessup near Natchitoches, La., had moved a large body of U.S. troops to the Sabine River by April 1836. Settlers in East Texas feared an Indian uprising while so many men were away fighting the Mexican army. The United States was under a treaty obligation to Mexico to maintain peaceful relations with the Indians. But Gen. Gaines' investigation found the Cherokees and others "more interested in planting corn" than in fighting. Nevertheless the U.S. troops remained on the Sabine until the fall of 1836.

When the Texas army reached the fork in the road, it marched toward Harrisburg, as Houston had indicated he planned to do in a letter written the previous night. Along the road, two Mexican couriers were captured and gave Houston the information he had hoped for. Santa Anna was leading the small Mexican force that in its haste had moved in front of Houston. Now the Texans had an opportunity to win the war. Throughout the war, Houston's intelligence system had operated efficiently. Scouts, commanded by Erastus "Deaf" Smith, kept the Texans informed of Mexican troop movements. Hendrick Arnold, a free black, was a valuable spy, posing as a runaway slave to enter Mexican camps to gain information.

On April 19, the Texans crossed Buffalo Bayou and made contact with an advance force of Mexican cavalry on April 20. A brief skirmish ensued, and the Texans were ready for more action. But Houston waited. So impressive was the performance of one private, Mirabeau B. Lamar, that Houston promoted him to colonel of the cavalry the next day.

EARLY on April 21, Gen. Martin Perfecto de Cos reinforced Santa Anna's troop with more than 500 men. Santa Anna complained later that they were recruits and not "picked" veterans that he had requested from Gen. Vicente Filisola, his second in command. Nevertheless, the new troops, who had marched all night, disrupted the camp's routine for a time, but soon all the soldiers and officers settled down for a mid-day rest. Curiously, no sentries were posted, although the Mexicans knew that the small Texas army was no more than a mile away across Peggy McCormick's ranch on the San Jacinto plain.

Houston held a council of war at noon on April 21, with the consensus being that the Texans should attack early the next day. But the men wanted to fight, so about 3 p.m., Houston ordered them to parade and the battle was launched at 4:30 p.m.

A company of Mexican-Texans, commanded by Juan Seguin, had served as the army's rear guard through much of the retreat across Texas and had fought many skirmishes with the Mexican army in the process. Perhaps fearing the Mexican-Texans would be mistaken for Mexican soldiers, Houston had assigned the company to guard duty as the battle approached. But after the men protested, they fought in the battle of San Jacinto.

Historians disagree widely on the number of troops on each side. Houston probably had about 900 while Santa Anna had between 1,100 and 1,300. But the Texans had the decided psychological advantage. Two-thirds of the fledgling Republic's army were "old Texans" who had family and land to defend. They had an investment of years of toil in building their homes. And they were just plain fighting mad about the massacre of men at the Alamo and Goliad. In less than 20 minutes — with strains of "Won't You Come to the Bower" and "Yankee Doodle" mingling with outraged cries of "Remember the Alamo" and "Remember Goliad" — they set the Mexican army to rout. More than 600 Mexicans were killed and hundreds more wounded or captured. Only nine of the Texans died in the fight. The killing frenzy of the Texans lasted until almost sunset.

C RITICS claimed that Houston tried to call a retreat and was guilty of other unworthy conduct during the battle. But the commander had two horses shot from under him and was severely wounded in the encounter. Thomas J. Rusk, secretary of war, however, probably was the most outstanding commander on the field.

But it was not until the following day that Santa Anna, who fled from his forces early in the fight, was captured. Houston had given patrols prophetic advice: "You will find the hero of Tampico, if you find him at all, making his retreat on all fours, and he will be dressed as bad at least as a common soldier." And that was the case. One Texan noticed that a grubby soldier his patrol found in the high grass had a silk shirt under his filthy jacket. Although denying he was an officer, the Mexican was taken back to camp by the patrol, where he was welcomed with cries of "El Presidente! El Presidente!" by other prisoners. Santa Anna introduced himself when taken to the wounded Houston.

Houston quickly got the Mexican dictator to agree to a truce and to order his armies to cease hostilities and withdraw to San Antonio and Victoria. Texas soldiers were ready to execute Santa Anna on the spot for the atrocities at the Alamo and Goliad. But Houston had no intention of killing him. Seeing the Texans' hostility, Santa Anna made quick conciliations, even offering to negotiate an immediate treaty with Houston. But the Texas commander refused, leaving that responsibility to the civil government. Houston soon left for New Orleans to have his wounded ankle treated.

Mexican critics of Gen. Filisola, Santa Anna's second in command, have argued that he should have ignored the dictator's orders, since they were given under duress, and attacked the Texans. The Italian-born officer had little choice, however, because he was almost out of supplies. The four-ship Texas navy, commanded by Charles E. Hawkins, kept the Gulf clear of Mexican shipping. Supply lines therefore were stretched hundreds of miles overland, and Houston's scorched-earth policy in retreat had denied the Mexicans forage from the land.

President Burnet took charge of Santa Anna, and on May 14 the dictator signed two treaties at Velasco, a public document and a secret one. The public agreement declared that hostilities would cease, that the Mexican army would withdraw to south of the Rio Grande, that prisoners would be released and that Santa Anna would be shipped to Veracruz as soon as possible. In the secret treaty, Santa Anna agreed to recognize Texas' independence, to give diplomatic recognition, to negotiate a commercial treaty and to set the Rio Grande as the new Republic's southern boundary.

Historian Eugene Barker has noted that "The Texas Revolution was not a spontaneous outburst of patriotic indignation against Mexican oppression. Few of the colonists were satisfied with all features of Mexican rule but few were also ready to go to the length of armed rebellion . . ." Some Texas settlers went so far as to oppose the rebellion. Gen. Urrea received almost an enthusiastic welcome when he entered Columbia on April 21. He observed that the settlers felt that many of the rebels were adventurers and were a greater threat to the colonists than the Mexican army. Houston found the names of many Texas Tories among Santa Anna's papers after San Jacinto. He never released the names, but a company of men commanded by Capt. James Kokernot was sent to inform the Tories that they were then supporting a lost cause.

Texas soon faced another military threat, this one from its own army. One historian noted that the disagreement between the military and civilian government over policy and procedure after the revolution brought Texas near the establishment of the very type of military domination that it fought to avoid.

The character of the Texas army was changing rapidly after San Jacinto. Again, the old settlers, who provided two-thirds of the manpower for the fighting force at the time, were ready to go home. Almost immediately, some began drifting off to plant crops or to defend against anticipated Indian raids. These were not professional fighting men, but farmers and shopkeepers who had taken up arms in defense of family and home.

Rusk assumed command of the army when Houston left, and he was detailed to follow the Mexican army out of Texas. Further hostilities were to be avoided, however. But the army soon began to melt away, and neither reinforcements nor supplies were forthcoming. Rusk complained that between the Colorado River and Goliad and San Antonio "There is not a particle of corn or a hoof of cattle." Rusk's officers accused the government of neglecting the army. Burnet was informed by officers that he was to drop all other matters and give "particular attention" to the army or the army might find it necessary "to pursue at home our most sacred rights."

Burnet denied the charges of neglect and objected to the threat. "When the civil government of a country is compelled to receive a prescription of its duties from an armed force, that government is, if not virtually dissolved, in great danger of being lost in the blazonry of military misrule."

The government's problems deepened in early June when it attempted to release Santa Anna in compliance with the Velasco treaty. Gen. Thomas J. Green, a Texas agent in the United States, arrived with a group of volunteers he had raised. He took the Mexican leader off the ship and held him in army custody despite objections by President Burnet and the cabinet.

By July, the character of the army, and its attitude, changed substantially. Almost three-quarters of the 2,500 men under arms had not been in Texas when the battle of San Jacinto was fought. Most were American volunteers who came to Texas to seek vengeance against the Mexicans for atrocities at Goliad and the Alamo and to take advantage of the large land grants the Republic was giving for military service. But the new army was outraged that the Mexican leaders had not been hanged, although Burnet courageously pointed out that there was no precedent to try or punish a commander for official acts performed during war.

Because of the problems with the new army, Burnet ordered agents in New Orleans to send no more volunteers from the United States. Matters continued to deteriorate, however. Word was received that the Mexican Senate had repudiated Santa Anna's agreements in the treaty of Velasco. Texas agents sent to Matamoros were taken into custody, and it was rumored that Gen. Jose Urrea was marching into Texas with a new army.

I N early July, Gen. Rusk sent Col. Henry Millard to Velasco to discuss various military matters with the president and the cabinet. While in the capital, Millard ordered Maj. Amasa Turner to arrest Burnet and to confiscate the cabinet's archives. Turner instead told Burnet of the order. The outraged president ordered Rusk to dismiss Millard from the rolls of the military and declared "the good people of Texas have been insulted and outraged in the person of the Chief Magistrate; a violent revolution has been attempted, involving the overthrow of the civil authorities and evidently intended to create a military supremacy in the government."

The crisis eased somewhat when attention became riveted on the rumored invasion by Urrea. Burnet ordered the army to prepare for an expedition against Matamoros, and that pacified the officers and men.

But Texas was in deep financial trouble. Debts from the revolution totaled $1,250,000 by the end of August 1836. So in July, Burnet called for an election on the first Monday in September.

Texas had won its independence from Mexico and from a threatened military dictatorship within its own army. But its future was far from assured.

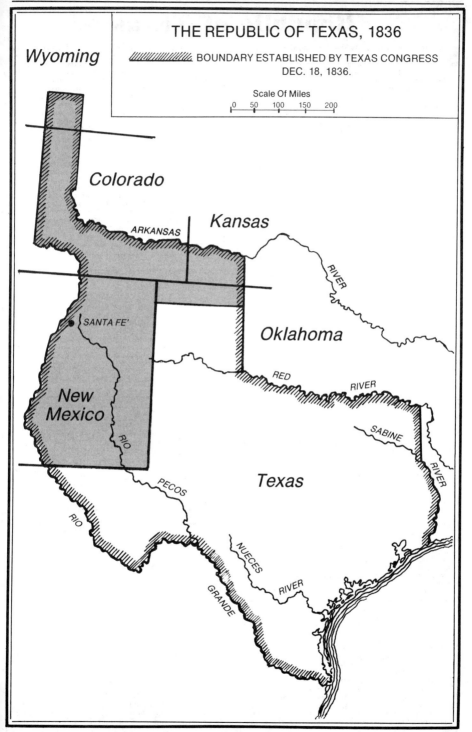

THE REPUBLIC OF TEXAS, 1836

BOUNDARY ESTABLISHED BY TEXAS CONGRESS DEC. 18, 1836.

Scale Of Miles

0   50   100   150   200

Wyoming

Colorado

Kansas

ARKANSAS

Oklahoma

SANTA FE'

New Mexico

RIO

Texas

PECOS

RED RIVER

SABINE RIVER

NUECES RIVER

RIO GRANDE

Republic of Texas

SAM Houston was easily the most dominant figure through the nearly 10-year history of the Republic of Texas. While he was roundly criticized for the retreat across Texas during the revolution, the victory at San Jacinto endeared him to most of the new nation's inhabitants.

Houston handily defeated Henry Smith and Stephen F. Austin in the election called in September 1836 by President David G. Burnet and the interim government. Mirabeau B. Lamar was elected vice president, and voters approved the Republic's constitution and overwhelmingly expressed a desire for annexation to the United States.

Houston was inaugurated on Oct. 22 at the capital in Columbia, which was little more than a frontier village. The first cabinet appointed by the new president represented an attempt to heal old political wounds. Austin was named secretary of state; former provisional governor Henry Smith was secretary of treasury; Thomas J. Rusk, secretary of war; J. Pinckney Henderson, attorney general; Robert Barr, postmaster general, and J. Rhoads Fisher, secretary of navy. The First Congress of Texas, which convened Oct. 3, named James Collinsworth the chief justice of the Supreme Court.

A host of problems faced the new government. Gen. Santa Anna was still in custody, and public opinion favored his execution. Texas' leadership wisely kept Santa Anna alive, first to keep from giving the Mexicans an emotional rallying point for launching another invasion, which the leader's death would have represented. And second, the Texas leaders hoped that the dictator would keep his promise to work for recognition of Texas, as he promised in the secret Treaty of Velasco. Santa Anna was released in November 1836 and made his way to Washington, D.C. Houston hoped the dictator could convince President Jackson to recognize Texas. Jackson refused to see Santa Anna, who returned to Mexico where he had fallen from power.

Texas suffered a major tragedy in late December 1836 when Austin, the acknowledged "Father of Texas," died of pneumonia after working long hours at the drafty capital at Columbia. The steamboat Yellow Stone ferried his body to Peach Point on the Brazos for burial. This historic steamboat played a major role in Texas history. In April the craft had been used to ferry Houston's army across the Brazos at Groce's Crossing; later the boat transported President Burnet and his cabinet to San Jacinto and carried the government and Santa Anna to Velasco for treaty negotiations. The historic ship sank in Buffalo Bayou in late 1837.

Houston's second major challenge was even more vexing than the problem with Santa Anna. Felix Huston had assumed command of the Texas army when Rusk resigned to take a cabinet post. Huston favored an invasion of Mexico, and the army, made up now mostly of American volunteers, who came to Texas after the battle of San Jacinto, was rebellious and ready to fight. Houston tried to replace Huston as commander with Albert Sidney Johnston, but Huston seriously wounded Johnston in a duel. In May 1837, Huston was asked to Columbia to discuss the invasion. While Huston was away from the troops, Houston sent Rusk to furlough the army without pay — but with generous land grants. Only 600 men were retained in the army.

The Republic's other problems were less tractable. The economy needed attention; Indians still represented a menace; Mexico remained warlike; foreign relations had to be developed, and relations with the United States had to be firmed up.

The economy proved to be the most troublesome. Texas began its experience as a Republic in a boom atmosphere. While most Texans existed in a subsistence economy, raising only enough crops to feed themselves, independence attracted land speculators. Everyone wanted to be in on the beginning of the new nation. But there was little currency in Texas. Some gold and silver Mexican coins were in circulation, but the principal medium of exchange was bank notes from the United States. These notes were in all denominations with no common base. Only the strength of the

'Unredeemed Texas'

Until the admission of Alaska into the Union in 1958, Texas was in land area the largest of the United States. More than 267,000 square miles are within its boundaries. But early Texas was not nearly as large, and present-day Texas is only a shadow of the "empire" envisioned by the state's early leaders.

As a Spanish province in 1681, the original Texas was located between the Trinity and Sabine rivers. The East Texas mission, San Francisco de los Tejas, was an unofficial capital because it was so far removed from the Spanish colonies in Northern Mexico. In 1693, this mission was abandoned.

For many reasons, the Spanish provinces in Northern Mexico had ill-defined boundaries. The southern, eastern and western limits would be well located. But the northern boundaries were obscure because, as a practical matter, they were determined by where the Plains Indians would allow colonists to settle.

When missions were established in the San Antonio area in 1718, the Medina River was considered the boundary between Texas and Coahuila. Jose de Escandon's colony of Nuevo Santander (today's Tamaulipas) was bounded on the north by the Nueces River in the mid-18th century. A description of the course of the Rio Grande in 1744 never mentioned the river's touching Texas. Indeed, the Rio Grande had never been a boundary except between the provinces of Nuevo Vizcaya (Chihuahua) and Nuevo Mexico in the early 18th century.

In 1685 and again in 1712, the French tried to set the Rio Grande as the western limits of the Louisiana Territory. But these claims were based on LaSalle's explorations, and Spain had a better case by virtue of its limited occupation of the area. President Thomas Jefferson tried unsuccessfully to press the French argument when the United States purchased the Louisiana Territory in 1803.

When Anglo-American colonization began, Texas' southwestern boundary with Nuevo Santander and Coahuila was the Nueces River. After Mexico gained its independence from Spain, Coahuila and Texas were combined into a single state in the Constitution of 1824.

History Highlights

The United States had a long-standing interest in acquiring Texas. Efforts were made to purchase the territory from Mexico, first by President John Quincy Adams and later by Andrew Jackson. Commercial interests in the United States also wanted a port on the Pacific coast, and in 1835, President Jackson broadened an offer to include purchase of Texas and a route to the area of San Francisco Bay in California.

When Texans won their independence in 1836, Mexico was stunned at the declaration that the entire Rio Grande valley to its headwaters in Colorado was claimed as the new republic's western boundary. In the Treaty of Velasco, Gen. Santa Anna agreed to withdraw Mexican troops to the south side of the Rio Grande. On this basis, the First Texas Congress claimed to the Rio Grande watershed as the Republic's south and west boundary.

There were probably several reasons for this precedent-setting claim. First, Sam Houston was a close friend and confidant of President Jackson, bank from which they were issued guaranteed the notes.

At the same time the United States also was experiencing an economic boom, but one based on speculation in canals, railroads and land. Foreigners invested heavily in these schemes. In the period 1835-37, nearly 40 million acres of federal land were sold, mostly to speculators, who borrowed from banks to make payments. The number of bank loans soared 500 percent between 1830 and 1837, and many of the institutions made loans without regard to reserves.

By 1836, revenue from federal land sales reached $24 million, and the U.S. Congress opted to distribute the federal surplus among the states on a population basis. The drain of cash from "pet banks" caused a hardship that was intensified when President Andrew Jackson in 1836 required that land payments be made only in hard currency or in notes from banks that paid specie (cash) for their outstanding notes. In May 1837, New York banks stopped paying hard money for their notes or other obligations, and this action precipitated a crisis that resulted in the failure of hundreds of banks. For the next five years, the United States was thrown into the worst economic depression in its history. The economic decline was aggravated when foreign investors withdrew their cash, and a series of crop failures reduced the purchasing power of the major segment of the agricultural economy.

Texas was not affected by the initial decline. But when the depression finally hit the new Republic, it was as devastating as in the United States and lasted longer.

Houston's first administration was plagued by a lack of money. Land was Texas' only asset, and conflicting policies were adopted for use of land. On one hand, land was to be used to back notes issued by the government. On the other hand, generous land grants were to be used to attract immigrants. But when vast amounts of land were given away, the resource was of little use as collateral because it would not hold its value. During the life of the Republic, more than 36.8 million acres of land were alienated by the congresses of Texas. The Republic's Constitution specified that white heads of families living in Texas on March 2, 1836, could receive a First Class headright of a league and a labor — 4,605 acres — of land. Single men could get 1,476 acres. Subsequent headrights were approved for new-

comers, and additional grants were available for men who served in the army.

During his first administration, Houston issued $650,000 in interest-bearing notes — so-called "Star Money," because the star of Texas was printed on the backs of the notes — that held their value when redeemed in late 1838. This issue, redeemed before the Panic of 1837 reached Texas, was the only specie issued by the Republic that did not devalue immediately.

The Texas Congress tried to levy some direct taxes, but these were easily evaded. And the taxes were difficult to collect because there simply was little hard cash in Texas. The only source of real revenue was customs collections, and these were paid grudgingly by Texans. The tariffs ranged from one percent on breadstuffs to 50 percent on silk, and custom revenues represented between 50 and 80 percent of the government's income throughout the life of the Republic.

Standing armies are expensive to maintain, so to keep the cost of government down, Houston sought to maintain peaceful relations with the Indians and with Mexico. Frontier defense was to be maintained by local militia. The Congress authorized a line of block houses and trading posts along the frontier, and Houston met personally with the chiefs of several tribes in an effort to maintain peace. But the Texas Senate declined to ratify the treaty Houston had made with the Cherokees and other Indians in East Texas during the revolution, and this hurt the peace efforts. Also many of the trading posts promised to the Indians in agreements were never opened, damaging the government's credibility in the eyes of the Indians.

H OUSTON'S policy of frontier defense relied on ranging companies — the Texas Rangers. Since Stephen F. Austin personally financed a group of 10 men to protect his small colony in 1823, these organizations had been active in Texas. Before the Revolution in 1835, small groups of men had been commissioned to guard the frontier against Indians while other Texans were occupied with the Mexican army. The service of the historic Texas Rangers has been well-documented, and during this period, Capt. Jack Hays was the best-known of these frontier defenders. Also during this era, the six-shooter, one of the most important innovations in weaponry, was introduced into Texas.

Relations with Mexico were stagnant. Mexicans were too involved with internal politics to be concerned

and he knew of the designs Jackson had on expansion. The Rio Grande also was a natural, defendable boundary. And one early dream of Moses and Stephen F. Austin was to divert the lucrative trade between Missouri and Santa Fe from the Santa Fe Trail to ports in Texas, which were much closer to Santa Fe than the Mississippi River.

Thus the boundaries of the Republic of Texas had a much different configuration than that of the present state, as the map on the preceding page indicates. The Republic had a land area almost 105,000 square miles larger than today's Texas, and it included land that is in the present states of New Mexico, Colorado, Wyoming, Kansas and Oklahoma.

Leaders of the Republic soon learned that claiming land and possessing it were entirely different matters. Efforts to extend the Republic's jurisdiction beyond the boundaries of the old Spanish province of Texas were usually unsuccessful. Between the Nueces River and the Rio Grande, an area known as the Nueces Strip, there was nothing but desert. Some early Texans favored leaving it that way to maintain a buffer against Mexican attacks on the settled area of the Republic. Governors of the northern Mexican states asked President Mirabeau B. Lamar to allow trade in the region, and the Texas Congress in 1839 authorized the chief executive to do so. Trade relations soon cooled, however, when Mexican agents were discovered among the traders. These agents used the cover to incite Indians to violence against the Texans, and the trade was soon curtailed.

Texas was too thinly populated to send its own citizens to colonize the Nueces Strip. For a time, the Republic toyed with the idea of giving the Franco-Texienne Co. a grant of 3 million acres of land to establish a series of military colonies along the western frontier, including colonies in the infamous Strip. But the Texas Congress rejected the idea

in 1840, fearing that the foreign company would bring in too many French colonists. France then would have too great a foothold in the fledgling Republic. In 1842, empresario grants were given to several individuals to colonize the region, but only Henri Castro settled a successful colony.

President Lamar then turned his attention to Santa Fe. During Lamar's administration, the Republic's finances were severely strained. The Panic of 1837 in the United States had dried up credit sources, and the money issued by the Republic had depreciated in value to only a few cents on the dollar. The dream of diverting the trade from Santa Fe to Texas' ports was a great attraction to Lamar. Not only would the Republic's economy be improved, but the trade would generate much-needed customs revenues. Not all Texans agreed, however. When the Congress failed to approve the scheme, Lamar launched an expedition based on the 1839 authorization to open trade along the Rio Grande. In 1841, the Santa Fe Expedition left with orders to open trade. Based on unofficial reports of discontent with Mexican officials in Santa Fe, Lamar was confident of the success of the enterprise. Almost 300 soldiers and traders made up the Texas contingent. Little was known about the route from near Austin to Santa Fe, and the expedition exhausted its supplies and suffered many hardships before reaching its destination.

The Santa Fe Expedition ended in disaster. Mexican officials learned of its coming and stirred up the populace against the "invasion" by Texas. Members of the expedition were taken into custody and, after undergoing many hardships on a lengthy march, were imprisoned in Mexico City.

Houston had replaced Lamar as president when word of the disaster reached Austin in 1842. Texans were outraged at the stories of mistreatment of the prisoners. The Texas Congress reacted

with Texas. But they also were adamant about refusing to recognize the independence of the Republic of Texas and about accepting the Rio Grande as any sort of boundary line.

EARLY attempts to gain recognition from England, France and other European countries also were stymied, as the nations waited to see if Texas could remain independent from Mexico.

The greatest disappointment in Houston's first term was the failure to have the Republic annexed to the United States. Henry Morfit, President Jackson's agent, toured the new Republic in the summer of 1836. Although impressed, Morfit reported that Texas' best chance at continued independence lay in the "stupidity of the rulers of Mexico and the financial embarrassment of the Mexican government." He recommended that annexation be delayed. Though U.S. Secretary of State John Forsyth recommended that diplomatic recognition be withheld until others nations led the way, U.S. recognition of Texas' independence came in March 1837, President Jackson's last official act in office. But in June 1837, John Quincy Adams led off the abolitionists' campaign against Texas by denouncing annexation on the floor of the U.S. House. Late that year, Houston withdrew the formal request for annexation. Texas' pride had suffered a severe blow.

Although immigrants were attracted to Texas, the Republic's economy was slow in developing. Almost all manufactured goods had to be imported throughout the history of the Republic, throwing foreign trade out of balance and aggravating the shortage of currency. Most Texans were farmers, eking out an existence for their families. Any surplus crops had to be sold in the immediate neighborhood because transportation facilities were nonexistent. The Republic left most road construction and maintenance to local government. And most of the roads were only cleared trails, muddy to the extent of impassability in wet weather and dusty in dry seasons. Goods had to be hauled by oxcarts or by horse, and fees were high.

The Republic's major rivers never fulfilled the promise of transportation arteries that early explorers expected. Although the Sabine, Red, Trinity and Brazos rivers had steamboat traffic at times, the waterways defied navigation very far inland. The water flow in most of the rivers was seasonal, and at many times,

there was simply not enough water to float a craft. Snags, sharp meandering routes along with other obstacles also thwarted navigation, and sand bars at the rivers' mouths were hazardous.

In inland Texas, Preston located on the Red River in present-day Grayson County and Jefferson located near Cypress Bayou in Marion County were major points for river traffic, though much of it was seasonal. Several smaller communities on the lower reaches of other rivers also had water service. The Brazos with heavy cotton farming along its lower reaches was one of the most accessible rivers for water traffic. A small lumbering industry was developing on the rivers, too, with several sawmills in operation around Buffalo Bayou. The lumber was provided for local needs.

In addition to farming, cattle raising already was established in the Republic, and the animals were driven overland to markets in Louisiana. The Coastal Prairies, the Piney Woods and Northeast Texas were the principal centers of cattle ranching in the Republic, as well as South Texas.

San Antonio was the largest town in the Republic, but it was on the frontier and too near Mexico to play a leading role in affairs. The eastern rivers and the coast were the Anglo-American population centers. In April 1837, the capital of the Republic was moved from Columbia to the new city of Houston on Buffalo Bayou. The new capital was named for the hero of San Jacinto and was developed by the brothers A. C. and J. K. Allen near the previous capital of Harrisburg, which was burned by the Mexican army.

Houston's foreign policy achieved initial success when J. Pinckney Henderson negotiated a trade treaty with Great Britain. Although the agreement was short of outright diplomatic recognition, it was progress. In the next few years, France, Belgium, The Netherlands and some German states recognized the new Republic.

Under the constitution, Houston's first term lasted only two years, and he could not succeed himself. The Republic's politics already were dividing along lines of personalities. Houston was a controversial figure, and opponents roundly criticized his drinking habits, along with his policies as president. Lamar, an outspoken opponent of the first president, was the leading candidate to succeed Houston. And Lamar won the

by passing a bill annexing the northern states of Mexico, which included California. Houston vetoed the bill because, he argued, it would hold the Republic up to ridicule in the eyes of the world's nations. The disaster of the Santa Fe Expedition hurt the Republic's financial standing with European nations because it indicated that the government could not control the territory it claimed. And the affair raised doubts about the Republic's maintaining its independence.

Passions remained strong, however, as the citizens of the Republic demanded revenge against Mexico for the mistreatment of the members of the expedition who were taken prisoner. In December of 1842, a military contingent of 750 men was authorized to mount raids along the Rio Grande in retaliation for Gen. Adrian Woll's brief capture of San Antonio in September. Under Thomas Somervell, the party raided Laredo. But when Somervell could find no objectives of military value to pursue, he tried to disband the unit. Five companies of men wanted to continue the raids, and they elected William S. Fisher commander. This group attacked Mier in Mexico, was defeated and taken prisoner. These prisoners also were marched to Mexico City under great hardship, giving Texans another disastrous military operation to digest.

Upon learning of the Mier operation, officials in the United States, who were trying to mediate a settlement between Texas and Mexico, warned Texans to restrict military operations to territory claimed by Texas and to forgo any further incursions into Mexico. Two attempts by Texans to disrupt trade on the Santa Fe Trail in 1842 and 1843 also were unsuccessful and drew criticism from the United States.

Thereafter, the leadership of the Republic of Texas concentrated on the numerous other problems afflicting the young nation and continued to pursue the annexation of Texas to the United States.

In Washington, efforts were made by President James Polk to negotiate purchase of Texas and what is now the Southwest and California. But Mexico rejected the proposals. The United States was concerned with English and French interest in the Pacific coast. Mexico was warned that while the United States would not take action against Mexican development of California, it would take steps to prohibit California from becoming a French or English colony.

Despite warnings from Mexico, the United States and Texas reached an agreement on annexation in 1845. In anticipation of the agreement, President Polk sent Gen. Zachary Taylor with a military force to Corpus Christi in August of 1845. When the annexation was approved, Taylor was ordered in early 1846 to move to the mouth of the Rio Grande. The Mexicans were outraged that U.S. forces were moving into the disputed Nueces Strip while negotiations over Texas' sovereignty over the area were still under way. But with the approval of annexation, the United States was bound to defend Texas' claim to the territory.

When hostilities between the United States and Mexico broke out in the Lower Rio Grande Valley, Brig. Gen. Stephen Kearny was dispatched to occupy Santa Fe, which he took without resistance. But the action was providential for Texas' future claims to the territory. Kearny set up a civil government backed by the military. When Texas Gov. J. Pinckney Henderson learned of the action, he protested to President Polk against any action that would affect Texas' claims to the territory. Polk assured the Texan that the state's claims were secure, but he added that the matter should be considered by the U.S. Congress.

In March of 1848, Gov. George T. Wood informed the Legislature that the failure of the state to organize the Santa Fe territory could result in the loss of claims to it. So in 1848 Santa Fe County, Texas, was established by the Legislature.

election handily when two opponents recruited by Houston's partisans committed suicide.

Lamar brought a different style of government to the Republic of Texas. He was a dreamer, a visionary. Texas, he felt, was in competition with the United States to see which would control the North American continent.

While Houston had been passive, partly out of frugality, in relations with Mexico and Indians, Lamar was more active. He thought Mexico could be forced to accept Texas' independence, and that the borders of the new Republic could be drawn with a sword. Lamar foresaw a Texas empire controlling all the territory to the Pacific Ocean and much of northern Mexico. Indians, the Republic's second president thought, were simply tenants in residence on the land they occupied and had no right to title if white settlers coveted the area.

While Lamar's visions may have been in keeping with those held by many Texans, his administration suffered from economic malaise. Houston was frugal, Lamar a spendthrift. Houston's first term cost Texas only about $500,000, while Lamar and the Congress spent $5 million in the next three years. During Lamar's administration, Texas became afflicted with the so-called "original sin of Americans," as one economist noted — the paper money disease. The government issued paper bills totaling more than $3.5 million in the next three years, leaving a debt of almost $6 million. The notes issued by the government during this period — called "Redbacks" because of the color of the back of the bill — carried no interest and soon depreciated. By the end of Lamar's administration the money was worth only two to three cents on the dollar.

Early in 1839, Lamar gained recognition as the "father of education" in Texas when the Congress granted each of the existing 23 counties three leagues of land to be used for education. Later the allotment was increased to four leagues. Fifty leagues of land also were set aside for development of a university. Despite the lip service paid to education, the government did not have the money for several years to set up a school system. Most education during the Republic was provided by private schools and churches.

Lamar's Indian policies, however, were the most dramatic departure from Houston's. One difference lay in the men's experience. Houston had lived with Cherokees as a child, was adopted as a member of a tribe and advocated Indian rights long before coming to Texas. He was one of the few Anglos who tried to give Indians title to their land rather than place them on reservations. Lamar more accurately reflected the frontier attitude toward the native Americans. His first experience in public life was as secretary to Gov. George Troup of Georgia who successfully opposed the federal government's policy of assimilation of Indians at the time. Indians were simply removed from Georgia.

Texans' concern about Indian's intentions was raised in 1838 when Vicente Cordova, a former official at Nacogdoches, led an uprising of dissident Mexican-Texans, Anglos and Indians in East Texas. Cordova escaped, but Manuel Flores, a Mexican trader, was killed near Austin in 1839. Found on Flores' body were letters urging the Cherokees and other East Texas Indians to take up arms against the white settlers. Texans first tried to negotiate the Cherokees' removal from the region, but in July 1839, the Indians were forcibly ejected from Texas at the battle of the Neches River. Houston's close friend, the aging Cherokee chief Philip Bowles, was killed in the battle while Houston was visiting former President Jackson in Tennessee.

THE most tragic miscalculation in Lamar policy came in March 1840 when a group of Comanches was invited to San Antonio to exchange prisoners. Chief Maguara led 12 other chiefs and dozens of warriors and their families to the city. But they brought only one white girl, who told of harsh treatment at the hands of the Indians. Texas' commissioners, Hugh McLeod and William G. Cooke, and militia commander, William S. Fisher, decided to hold the chiefs until more prisoners were returned. But the Comanches would not be taken prisoner, and the so-called Council House Fight ensued. Many chiefs and warriors were killed and their families captured. Word spread among the Indians of this treachery. In August 1840, an estimated 600 Indians raided Linnville and Victoria near the Gulf Coast in retaliation. Texas' militia under Ranger Ben McCulloch ambushed the raiding party at Plum Creek, killing several of the raiders and recovering horses, livestock and plunder. Later in the year, John H. Moore led a successful campaign against Comanches camped near the present town of Colorado City. The Comanches were Texans' implacable enemies until finally defeated in 1875.

Worth County, which included southern New Mexico, and El Paso and Presidio Counties in Texas were created in 1849.

New Mexicans resisted, however. In a convention in October of 1848, they declared their opposition to slavery, which was allowed in Texas, and to having their territory dismembered. New Mexico had been a Spanish province since Juan de Onate established a colony near Santa Fe in 1598, almost a century before the first development in Texas. For many years, it was a self-governing province with no connection whatsoever to the Spanish activities in Texas. And the 19th century New Mexicans wanted to keep their independence from Austin.

Robert S. Neighbors, an Indian agent, was commissioned in January of 1850 by Gov. Peter H. Bell to organize the territories claimed by Texas in New Mexico. Neighbors was successful in setting up a Texas government in El Paso County, thereby saving that region for Texas. But he was unsuccessful elsewhere.

In Washington, the question of Texas' boundaries had become entwined in the debate over slavery, and the new state was in danger of losing a great deal of the territory it claimed. The New York legislature, for example, became so concerned that it instructed the state's congressmen to oppose even Texas' claim to the Nueces Strip because no civil jurisdiction had been set up there prior to the Mexican War.

Texans were infuriated by the failure of the U.S. government to back up Texas' claims to New Mexico. Many felt that President Polk had assured Texas its claims would be honored and that Texans had voted for annexation on that basis. If the claims were not to be honored, some Texans felt, the whole question of annexation should be reconsidered.

But Texas' poor financial condition led to a compromise. As a Republic, Texas had acquired substantial debt. Repayment was pledged on the basis of customs receipts and on land sales. When annexed to the United States, Texas retained its public lands, but lost its customs revenues to the United States, which also refused to assume the public debt. Since Texas would lose part of its ability to service the outstanding debt if its land claims were not honored, it was decided that the U.S. government should pay the state $10 million in lieu of the claims. Knowing the passions of his citizens, Gov. Bell called a referendum to determine if Texans thought the compromise was satisfactory. They did by a count of 4,473 "for" and 1,988 "against." And thereby, they accepted the present boundaries of the State of Texas.

But there was one more chapter in the story of "Unredeemed Texas." At the beginning of the Civil War in 1862, Confederate Gen. Henry H. Sibley launched a campaign from El Paso to take the upper Rio Grande valley to cut off a possible invasion of Texas from New Mexico. After early successes, Gen. Sibley's supply train was captured by Union forces at Glorietta Pass and the Texans were forced to retreat.

Certainly, Sibley did not think the effort was worth the money and lives expended. But other historians argue that if Sibley had been successful, the United States would have been cut off from California during the Civil War. With a Confederate California, the South would have had access to gold mines, timber for ships and ports that could not be blockaded by the United States, three elements that cost them the war.

So the loss of Unredeemed Texas may have been bad news for the Lone Star State — but a boon for the United States.

Historians point out that while Lamar's Indian policy was expensive and of questionable morality, it was effective. Large regions of the Republic were cleared of native Americans for immigrants.

To demonstrate his intention to expand the boundaries of the Republic, Lamar wanted the capital moved from Houston. In early 1839, a commission was appointed to select a site to be located near the frontier and named for Stephen F. Austin. Lamar supported the selection of a site on the Colorado River the previous year while on a buffalo hunt. (Historian Eugene C. Barker also noted that Austin had once selected a site in the immediate area for a permanent home that was never built, although this was not connected to Lamar's choice.) Construction of government buildings began in the spring of 1839, and on Oct. 17, 1839, Lamar arrived with an official cavalcade to occupy Austin, the new capital of the Republic. Sam Houston and others never liked the site, feeling it was too vulnerable to attacks by Indians and the Mexican army.

Lamar's foreign policy bore fruit. In 1839, France became the first Europen nation to extend diplomatic recognition to the newest North American republic. Holland, The Netherlands and Great Britain followed suit in 1840, and Belgium joined the others in 1841. In exchange for Texas' promise to suppress the importation of slaves, Great Britain agreed to mediate Texas' discussions with Mexico. Lamar attempted to bludgeon Mexico into negotiations with the second Texas navy, which took to the seas under the command of Edwin Ward Moore, the "port captain of the Navy." The navy raided Mexican ports and shipping, and for a time it was "rented" to republican rebels in Yucatan, another Mexican state in revolt against the centralist government.

While Lamar was dreaming of empire, Texas' fragile economy collapsed. By the fall of 1840, the boom spirit had completely evaporated, and the economic depression that had swept the United States in 1837 was fully felt in the Republic. Its currency was almost worthless and its credit nonexistent. Lamar had long hoped for a major loan with which to establish a national bank to smooth Texas' economic problems. But most of the world was still gripped by the depression, and Texas could not obtain loans from either the United States or Europe.

Texas also was not attracting as many settlers as was hoped when generous land grants were offered to newcomers. The Fifth Congress revived the empresario program that had been successful for the Mexican government. Immigration companies would be chartered to bring colonists to the Republic. The newcomers would be given free land, and the company would receive blocks of land when immigration quotas were filled.

Several bills chartering companies were considered. The Peters Colony bill was passed in February 1841, setting aside large tracts of land in North Central Texas, running from about the present Dallas-Fort Worth area to the Red River. The Franco-Texiene bill, which would have brought several thousand European immigrants to the Republic, was defeated when concern arose about the impact on the country of such a conclave. Fear of the pro-abolitionist leanings of foreign colonists also may have been a factor.

In 1842, a general colonization law was passed. Henri Castro, a Frenchman, received two grants for settling 600 Europeans, and Henry Francis Fisher and Burchard Miller contracted to bring 1,000 settlers. In 1844, the Fisher-Miller grants were sold to the Adelsverein, a society for promoting German immigration.

LAMAR'S hopes for a $5 million loan were dashed in an incident that would be comical, if not so serious. The French charge d'affaires to Texas, Count Alphonse de Saligny, had many difficulties adjusting to life in frontier Austin. When he refused to pay his hotel bill, innkeeper Richard Bullock cursed him roundly. Saligny was offended, and to placate him, the Texas Congress passed a law against verbally abusing foreign emissaries. Troubles between the count and the innkeeper deepened when Saligny's servant killed some of Bullock's pigs, which were eating grain at the Frenchman's stable. When authorities failed to prosecute Bullock for again cursing him, Saligny demanded his credentials and left Texas. After that, a $5 million loan to Texas by the French government was cancelled. Saligny's brother-in-law was France's minister of finance.

Lamar tried several means of improving the government's finances. In 1839, the Congress autho-

rized the opening of trade with Mexican merchants along the Rio Grande, but this soon soured because Texans were afraid that Mexican agents among the traders were stirring up trouble for settlers with the Indians. Lamar used the authority given in 1839 to launch the Santa Fe expedition in 1841. But this effort ended in disaster.

Lamar tried to reopen negotiations with Mexico. But Bernard Bee in 1839 was not allowed to land in Mexico. James Treat was received by Mexican officials in 1839, probably as a move to keep Texas from backing dissidents in Northern Mexico. In 1841, the Mexican government refused to accept James Webb. This region was almost forgotten by the Mexican government in the political chaos following the Texas Revolution. And the state of limbo was not acceptable to residents near the Rio Grande. In 1839, Antonio Canales, an attorney from Revilla (today's Guerrero), gained support for an independence movement. Canales envisioned a Republic of the Rio Grande separate from Mexico and composed of all the northern Mexican states. Cols. Jose Maria Gonzales of Laredo and Antonio Zapata of Revilla were prominent in the early military successes of Canales. In January 1840, the Republic of the Rio Grande was declared and Laredo was the capital. The movement was short-lived as Mexican centralists defeated its army. Canales capitulated to offers of a commission in the Mexican army, and Gonzales and Zapata, for whom Zapata County in the Lower Rio Grande Valley is named, were executed. The Texas government stayed out of the fight, although many Texans fought in the independence movement.

FROM his seat in Congress, Houston had been a vocal critic of Lamar's administration. Texas' first president became the Republic's third chief executive when Lamar supporters, backing David G. Burnet, could not mount a serious campaign against the hero of San Jacinto.

Houston's second administration was even more frugal than his first. Government expenses were cut to the bone, and by late 1844, income almost matched expenditures. In 1842, Houston had to suspend — not repudiate — the Republic's debt, and he re-entered negotiations with Indian tribes in an attempt to quell the raids on settlements. A series of trading posts were opened along the frontier to pacify the native Americans.

War fever reached a high pitch in Texas in 1842, however, and Houston grew increasingly unpopular because he would not launch an offensive war against Mexico. Texans were irate at the mistreatment of the members of the Santa Fe Expedition who had been captured and marched to Mexico City. In retaliation for the expedition, Mexico, too, caused trouble. In March 1842, Gen. Rafael Vasquez launched guerrilla raids on San Antonio, Victoria and Goliad, but quickly left the Republic. Thirty-five hundred Texas volunteers quickly gathered at San Antonio, demanding that Mexico be punished. Houston urged calm, but the clamor increased when Gen. Adrian Woll with 1,400 men took San Antonio in September 1842. He raised the Mexican flag and declared the reconquest of Texas. Ranger Capt. Jack Hays was camped nearby and within days 600 volunteers had joined him, anxious to drive the Mexican invaders from Texas soil. Gen. Woll withdrew after the Battle of Salado.

Alexander Somervell was commanded by Houston to follow with 700 troops and harass the Mexican army, but Somervell was warned to observe the rules of civilized warfare. Houston wanted no retaliatory raids into Mexico. Somervell reached Laredo in early December 1842 and found no Mexican troops. The Texans sacked Laredo, but Somervell ordered them to return the plunder. Two hundred soldiers were sent home from Laredo, and Somervell continued the expedition, crossing the Rio Grande to find military targets. A few days later, the commander returned home, but 300 soldiers decided to continue the raid under the command of William S. Fisher. On Christmas day, this group attacked the village of Mier, only to be defeated by a Mexican force that outnumbered them 10-to-one.

After an attempted mass escape, the survivors of the Mier expedition were marched to Mexico City where Santa Anna, again in political power, ordered their execution. When officers refused to carry out the order, it was amended to require execution of one of every 10 Texans. The prisoners drew beans to determine who would be shot; bearers of black beans were executed. Texans again were outraged by the treatment of prisoners, but the war fever soon subsided. Two major defeats within a year were humiliating enough without attempting a poorly financed offensive war.

Never a fan of the new capital at Austin, Houston took the occasion of the Woll invasion of San Antonio to move the seat of government to Washington-on-the-Brazos where the Seventh Congress convened in November 1842. Houston wanted to permanently move the capital away from the exposed frontier and he gave confidential orders to Col. Thomas I. Smith and Capt. Eli Chandler to remove the Republic's records from Austin. The records were taken at night, but when Austin residents were alerted to the removal by a warning shot from a cannon fired by Mrs. Angelina Eberly, a party led by Mark B. Lewis caught the ox train on Brushy Creek in Williamson County. The so-called Archives War ended without a shot fired, and the records were returned to Austin.

Houston also had problems with the Texas Navy. His recall orders were ignored by Commodore Moore, and finally, Houston asked for international help in returning the "pirates" to Texas. Moore returned voluntarily and asked for a court-martial to clear his name. He was convicted on only two minor charges.

Many free blacks lived in Texas, and some fought in the revolution. The First Texas Congress had provided land grants for them, but in 1840, the Congress passed a punitive law designed to force free blacks to leave Texas. The law was not vigorously enforced, and the Congress approved many exemptions in individual bills. Houston went a step further in his second administration by issuing pardons in advance for free blacks convicted under the law.

While the Republic left most road construction to local government, the Congress did authorize construction of the Central National Road to tie Preston on the Red River in Grayson County to Austin. The road crossed the Trinity River near the confluence of its three forks, and a thriving community grew around a trading post opened by John Neely Bryan. The city is today's Dallas.

Galveston was the Republic's major port of entry, although the new community of Houston was making a bid for leadership. Many public works were considered by the Congresses of Texas to facilitate trade and transportation. None was more bizarre than the suggestion of Houston's aggressive promoters to change the route of the Brazos River to empty into Buffalo Bayou. The bayou was Houston's lifeline to the Gulf, but it periodically ran low. Houston's leadership felt that rerouting the Brazos was reasonable, since the waterway had in ages past emptied into the bayou. The Congress rejected the idea.

As Houston completed his second term, the United States was becoming more interested in annexation. Texas had seriously flirted with Great Britain and France, and the Americans did not want a rival republic with close foreign ties on the North American continent. Houston orchestrated the early stages of the final step toward annexation. But his successor, Anson Jones, completed the process.

The Republic of Texas' main claim to fame is simply endurance. Its settlers, unlike other Americans who had military help, had cleared a large region of Indians by themselves, had established farms and communities and had persevered through extreme economic hardship. Adroit political leadership had gained the Republic recognition from many foreign countries. And although dreams of empire may have dimmed, Texans had firmly established an identity on a major portion of the North American continent. As Texas prepared to enter the United States, the frontier had been pushed to a line running from Corpus Christi through San Antonio, New Braunfels, Austin, Belton, Waco and Dallas to Preston.

The U.S. presidential campaign of 1844 was to make Texas a part of the Union.

Annexation

ANNEXATION to the United States was not a foregone conclusion for Texans once independence from Mexico was gained in 1836. American volunteers had shed much blood in the Texas Revolution, and patriotic passions flamed high as the Anglo-Texans battled the Mexican army across Texas.

Once the gun smoke settled and negotiations between Texas and the United States began, the road was not smooth. Indeed, on occasion, the Texans resorted to guile. Sam Houston noted that Texas "was more coy than forward" as the negotiations reached a climax.

William H. Wharton was Texas' first representative in Washington. His instructions were to gain diplomatic recognition of the new Republic's independence. After some squabbles, Congress appropriated funds for a minister in Texas, and President Andrew Jackson recognized the new country in one of his last acts in office in March 1837. Later that year, Memucan Hunt replaced Wharton, and although he pursued annexation, President Martin Van Buren rejected the appeal in September 1837. The president noted that annexation of an independent nation was of doubtful constitutionality and that Texas still was nominally at war with Mexico. Annexation could lead to a war between the United States and Mexico with Great Britain possibly siding with the Mexicans.

John Quincy Adams in 1837 argued that annexation was unconstitutional. The congressman mounted a campaign against annexation in the U.S. House in June and July 1838. He claimed the issue was a plan by the Southern slaveholders to strengthen their hand by annexing Texas and dividing it into several states. Texans revolted in 1836, Adams claimed, when Mexico tried to abolish slavery. In late 1838, Houston instructed Texas' minister in Washington to withdraw the annexation proposal, and the Texas Senate approved this action in 1839.

Annexation was in limbo during the presidential term of Mirabeau B. Lamar. He felt that the loss of freedom and independence as a nation was too high a price to pay for Texas to join the United States. Lamar held visions of empire in which Texas would rival the United States for supremacy on the North American continent. However, when Lamar was successful in gaining recognition for Texas by several European countries, the United States' interest in annexation was rekindled.

Great Britain maintained a close relationship with Texas and Mexico and made strenuous efforts to get Mexico to recognize Texas' independence and to develop normal diplomatic relations. This close relationship between Great Britain and Texas raised fears in the United States. Some Americans were concerned that Great Britain might attempt to make Texas part of its empire. Southerners feared for the future of slavery in Texas, which had renounced the importation of slaves as a concession to get a trade treaty with Great Britain. Newspapers noted that U.S. trade with Texas had suffered after the Republic received diplomatic recognition from European nations.

In Houston's second term, Texas began playing coy. Early, Houston suggested to the Texas minister in Washington that negotiations on annexation could be reopened if chances for success were good. Issac Van Zandt, Texas' minister to Washington, wrote that President John Tyler and the cabinet were anxious to annex Texas but worried about ratification in the U.S. Senate. Houston then suggested dropping the matter, hoping that he would be able to settle matters with Mexico.

U.S. Secretary of State Abel P. Upshur tried to reopen negotiations in October 1843, but Van Zandt said he had no instructions on the question. Texas wanted military protection while negotiations were under way, and this was not forthcoming. Upshur was killed in an accident, and John C. Calhoun replaced him. In the meantime, J. Pinckney Henderson was sent to Washington to help Van Zandt with the negotiations.

In January 1844, Houston again gave Van Zandt instructions to open negotiations, if chances of success were good. The president did not want another failure that could damage negotiations with other countries. Calhoun ordered a naval force to the Gulf and moved U.S. troops to the southwest border, which was the best he could do to provide Texas protection while negotiations were in progress.

On April 11, 1844, Texas and the United States signed a treaty for annexation. Texas would enter the Union as a territory, not a state, under terms of the treaty. The United States would assume Texas' debt up to $10 million and would negotiate with Mexico Texas' southwestern boundary. The treaty was sent to the U.S. Senate for ratification on April 22.

National politics intervened, however. The Whigs came down solidly against annexation and westward expansion. Abolitionists in the party apparently were more afraid of the slavery issue than expansion. The Senate rejected the annexation treaty on June 8 by a vote of 35-16. At least 15 of the opposition votes came from Southern Whig senators who had been counted on for support. Houston suggested to British agents that he was done with annexation after the rejection.

But the annexation of Texas and westward expansion became major issues in the 1844 presidential campaign. Through eight ballots at the Democratic convention, Van Buren failed to receive the necessary two-thirds majority for nomination. On the ninth ballot, his name was withdrawn from consideration, and the convention stampeded to James K. Polk, a supporter of expansion and the party's first "dark horse" nominee. In addition, the Democratic platform included a strong expansion plank, calling for the reoccupation of Oregon and the reannexation of Texas. Polk was elected president in November but would not take office until March 1845.

Great Britain and France increased pressure on Mexico to recognize Texas in hopes that independence would be more attractive to Texans than annexation. But Mexico delayed the decision.

In December 1844, President Tyler declared that the people had spoken on the issue of annexation and resubmitted it to Congress. Several bills were introduced in the U.S. House representing various proposals for annexation. In February 1845, the Congress approved a resolution that would bring Texas into the Union as a state. Texas would cede its public property — such as forts, barracks and custom houses — to the United States, but it could keep its public lands and must retain its public debt. The territory could be divided into four new states in addition to the original Texas. And the United States would negotiate the Rio Grande boundary claim. Texas had to present a state constitution for congressional approval by Jan. 1, 1846. These terms were much more beneficial to Texas than had been those of the treaty that the Senate rejected in 1844.

Political parties did not develop in the Republic of Texas, and annexiation was not a partisan issue. But annexation did set the tone of Texas' politics for more than a century. One editor noted in January 1845, "We are all Democrats in Texas, since the glorious victory of that party, who fearlessly espoused our cause and nailed the 'Lone Star' to the top mast of their noble ship."

British officials asked the Texas government to delay consideration of the U.S. offer for 90 days to attempt to get Mexico to recognize the Republic. The delay did no good. Texans' minds were made up.

President Anson Jones, who succeeded Houston, called the Texas Congress into special session on June 16 and called a convention to write a state constitution into session in Austin on July 4. Mexico finally recognized Texas' independence, but the recognition was rejected. Texas voters overwhelmingly accepted the U.S. proposal and approved the new constitution in a referendum.

On Dec. 29, 1845, the U.S. Congress accepted the state constitution and Texas became a part of the United States.

State officials were elected in December 1845, and on Feb. 19, 1846, the flag of the Republic of Texas was lowered for the last time in Austin and was replaced by the stars and stripes of the United States. J. Pinckney Henderson was sworn in as the first governor of Texas by the speaker of the Texas House.

In an eloquent speech, President Jones reviewed the life of the Republic:

"The lone star of Texas, which ten years since arose amid cloud, over fields of carnage, and obscurely shone for a while, has culminated, and, following an inscrutable destiny, has passed on and become fixed forever in that glorious constellation which all freemen and lovers of freedom in the world must reverence and adore — the American Union. Blending its rays with its sister stars, long may it continue to shine, and may a gracious heaven smile upon this consummation of the wishes of the two republics, now joined together in one. 'May the union be perpetual, and may it be the means of conferring benefits and blessings upon the people of all the States' is my ardent prayer. The final act of this great drama is now performed. The Republic of Texas is no more."

Early Statehood

THE entry of Texas into the Union touched off the War with Mexico, a war that some historians now think was planned by President James K. Polk to obtain the vast American Southwest from Mexico.

Between J. Pinckney Henderson's 1845 election and inauguration as Texas' first governor, U.S. agents tried to get Republic of Texas President Anson Jones to send troops into the contested area between the Nueces River and the Rio Grande — the so-called Nueces Strip. The Republic had claimed the Rio Grande as its southern boundary, but no civil administration was established south of the Nueces River.

Many Texans supported the move, but President Jones flatly refused to initiate any military action after Mexico's attempted recognition of Texas as a nation. Jones was proud of the fact that at the end of his term Texas was at peace with its traditional enemies — the Mexicans and Indians. Jones also argued that if there was to be war with Mexico ". . . the United States Government must take all the responsibility, and all the expense and all the labour of hostile movements upon Mexico . . . Somebody else must break up the state of peace. It shall not be me."

U.S. Gen. Zachary Taylor was sent to Corpus Christi just above the Nueces River in July 1845. In February 1846, just after Texas formally entered the Union, the general was ordered to move troops into the disputed Nueces Strip and to the mouth of the Rio Grande. A month later, Gen. Taylor marched. Mexican officials protested the entry of U.S. troops into the territory, claiming that its status was under negotiation. But Gen. Taylor proceeded to set up a camp at Point Isabel (now Port Isabel) near Brazos Santiago and to fortify a position, under the command of Maj. Jacob Brown, across the Rio Grande from Matamoros. The young officer was killed in a bombardment of the facility in May 1846, and Brownsville is named in his honor.

The U.S. army was in a state of transition at the time. It had last engaged another organized army more

than 30 years before during the War of 1812. The military's principal duties in the interim had been to move Indians from the eastern United States to new lands in the west and to fight Indians if they resisted the move. West Point had been under attack in the U.S. Senate, in which the question of the compatibility of a standing army with democratic freedom was debated. The performance of West Point graduates in the ranks of junior officers during the war may have saved the institution.

After Gen. Taylor refused to leave the disputed territory, Mexican President Mariano Paredes declared the opening of a defensive war against the Americans on April 24, 1846. Gen. Anastasio Torrejon crossed the Rio Grande above Matamoros and defeated a small force of U.S. dragoons shortly thereafter. The war with Mexico was under way.

On May 8, U.S. troops moving to relieve Maj. Brown's fort encountered a Mexican force under Gen. Mariano Arista at Palo Alto, about 12 miles from today's Brownsville. Although the Mexican contingent was twice as large as the American, the light artillery tactics of the West Point graduates gave the U.S. forces a victory. The next day the Mexican army was badly mauled at Resaca de la Palma and retreated across the river. Gen. Taylor waited two weeks before crossing the Rio Grande and occupying Matamoros. In the interim, however, he sent news of the military encounters to Washington, and President Polk persuaded Congress to declare war against Mexico on May 13, arguing that American blood had been spilled on American soil. After the initial encounters, the war was fought south of the Rio Grande.

President Polk devised a plan to raise 50,000 volunteers from every section of the United States to fight the war. Texans had long dreamed of carrying a war into the interior of Mexico, and more than 8,000 volunteered for service. About 5,000 Texans actually saw action in Mexico — including Gov. Henderson, who got permission from the Legislature to join the U.S. army during the war. When the Texas Rangers volunteered, they introduced the U.S. army to a new weapon — the six-shooter. The revolvers had been used for several years on the Texas frontier, and the Rangers demanded to be equipped with Colt revolvers when they joined the army. The initial contract to manufacture 1,000 of the weapons rescued Samuel Colt from bankruptcy, and he became a successful gun manufacturer.

Although the actual fighting took place in Mexico, some military activity continued along the lower Rio Grande as the army secured transportation points across the river. In July 1846, Capt. Richard A. Gillespie passed through Laredo and asserted Texas and U.S. sovereignty. For the first time, the American flag flew over the city. A few months later, Mirabeau B. Lamar, serving as a captain in the U.S. forces, established civil administration in Laredo, and for a time the city was in a huge Nueces County that included all of the Lower Rio Grande Valley with Corpus Christi the county seat. In July 1847, the first election in Laredo attracted 40 voters, 37 of whom were Mexicans. Lamar maintained discipline among his 150 troops by banning liquor sales, and regular patrols helped curb Indian activities in the region where 700 persons reportedly had been killed in the previous 20 years.

Steamboat transportation returned to the Rio Grande for the first time since 1831, when Henry Austin left with his ship Ariel. The paddlewheelers provided an important supply link for U.S. forces along the river and in Northern Mexico throughout the war. And important historical figures like Richard King, founder of the King Ranch, and Mifflin Kenedy, another regional rancher, businessman and leader, first came to the Lower Rio Grande Valley as steamboat operators during the war.

Much farther up the Rio Grande, the war was hardly noticed. Alexander Doniphan led U.S. forces south from Sante Fe, which had been secured by Brig. Gen. Stephen Kearny, in December 1846. After a minor skirmish with Mexican forces just north of present-day El Paso, Doniphan established American jurisdiction in this part of Texas.

U.S. Gen. Winfield Scott brought the war to a close in March 1847 with the capture of Mexico City. When the Treaty of Guadalupe Hidalgo was signed on Feb. 2, 1848, the United States had acquired the American Southwest for development. And in Texas, the Rio Grande became an international boundary, and the borderlands entered a turbulent period. One agreement required the United States to prohibit raids by Plains Indians — primarily the Comanches and Apaches— into the interior of Mexico.

Texas faced many old problems and a few new ones while embarking on the early days of statehood. George T. Wood was elected governor in 1847, succeeding J. Pinckney Henderson who did not seek re-election. The state government, like the Republic, was short of cash. Although Texas kept its public lands, the United States got the customs receipts, which had been the Republic's major source of hard cash. And the state's claim to more than 105,000 square miles of land that included territory in New Mexico, Colorado, Wyoming, Kansas and Oklahoma was under attack in Congress. Wood threatened to go to war with the United States over the disputed land, and he also supported removal of all Indians from Texas' territory.

At the end of the Mexican War, most of Texas north and west of a line drawn from Preston on the Red River through Dallas, Austin and San Antonio to Laredo on the Rio Grande was unexplored territory controlled by Indians. One of the first orders of business in the new state was to explore the vast unknown territory.

THE face of Far West Texas was to change rapidly. In early 1848, gold was discovered at Sutter's Mill in California and within a few months a gold rush across the continent was on. Jack Coffee Hays and a group of Texas Rangers tried to blaze a trail from San Antonio to El Paso in early 1848, but they got lost and almost died of thirst before returning to civilization.

In March 1849, Robert S. Neighbors, John S. Ford and Indian guides set out from Torrey's trading post near today's Waco to find an accessible route to El Paso. They blazed what was called the Upper Trail, which crossed the Pecos River at Horsehead Crossing, and reached El Paso on May 2. On returning along the estimated 500-mile trip, they met wagons already moving west. At the same time, U.S. Army Capt. William Henry Chase Whiting in late May opened the lower El Paso-San Antonio route that ran to the south of Neighbors' trail. Whiting also is the first writer to use the

term "Big Bend" for that region of the state. Lt. Francis T. Bryan surveyed both trails.

Ports such as Galveston and Indianola, which was established in 1849 on the west shore of Matagorda Bay, dispatched pioneers along the western trails to California. Many went through San Antonio. By the end of the year, 4,000 people had traveled along the trails through El Paso, which was to develop into a way station for goldseekers and other adventurers. For centuries, the El Paso region had been a major point along the trade route from the interior of Mexico to Santa Fe. The California gold rush established the area along two major trade routes.

U.S. Army Capt. Randolph B. Marcy led a third expedition through unexplored Texas in 1849, covering most of West Central Texas and tying into previously established routes. Marcy's trail later was used by the Butterfield Stage Line. Also during that year, the U.S. War Department established a string of frontier forts running from Fort Duncan at Eagle Pass on the south to Fort Worth on the north. Inexperience in fighting mounted Plains Indians led the army to station infantry at the forts. One Texas editor noted that "The idea of repelling mounted Indians, the most expert horsemen in the world, with a force of foot soldiers, is ridiculous."

ONE group of German settlers had little trouble with the Comanches, however. John O. Meusebach became leader of the German immigration movement in Texas in 1846. He led a wagon train of some 120 settlers to the site of today's Fredericksburg in May 1846, and a year later, Meusebach made a treaty with Comanche leaders on the San Saba River, which both sides kept. This was the only successful compact between white men and Indians in the state's history.

Germans, rather than Anglos, were the first whites to push into this frontier region after annexation. Germans also migrated to the major cities, like San Antonio and Galveston, and by 1850 there were more people of German birth or parentage in Texas than there were Mexican-Texans.

The eastern part of Texas was flourishing under statehood, as had been expected. The estimated population of 150,000 at annexation grew to 212,592, including 58,161 slaves, at the first U.S. census in 1850. Large plantations were blossoming in the valleys of the Brazos and Trinity Rivers where steamboat transportation to Galveston and Houston was available. Leaders in these areas, however, were worried about the lack of railroad transportation and about a labor shortage. Texas was exporting 500,000 bales of cotton a year in the 1850s, but it was felt that the land could produce three million to five million bales if adequate labor — slave labor — was available.

Although Galveston was the state's major port, Jefferson in Marion County also was a shipping center. A huge log raft on the Red River backed water into Big Cypress Bayou, making Jefferson accessible by steamship. Goods from this northeast Texas city could be shipped to markets along the Mississippi River and to New Orleans.

As the state's population grew, the regions developed distinct population characteristics. The southeast and eastern sections attracted immigrants from the Lower South, the major slaveholding states. Major plantations developed in these areas. North Texas got more Upper Southerners and Midwesterners. These immigrants were mostly small farmers and few owned slaves.

Mexican-Texans had difficulty with the Anglo immigrants. The so-called "cart war" broke out in 1857. Mexican teamsters controlled the transportation of goods from the Gulf coast to San Antonio and could charge much lower rates than their competition. But a campaign of terror was launched by Anglo haulers, especially around Goliad, in an attempt to drive the Mexican-Texans out of business. Intervention by the U.S. and Mexican governments finally brought the situation under control, but it stands as an example of the attitudes held by Anglos toward Mexican-Texans.

Cotton was by far the state's largest money crop. But corn, sweet potatoes, wheat and sugar also were produced. Saw milling and grain milling became the major industries, employing 40 percent of the manufacturing workers.

In the 1849 election, Peter H. Bell defeated incumbent George Wood. Bell's administration was distinguished by settling the land disputes with the federal government. In the Compromise of 1850, Texas gave up claims to lands that are located outside the present borders in exchange for $10 million. The total settlement with the United States, including interest on some delayed funds and compensation for fighting some Indians, amounted to $12 million. That sum was used to pay off the debt of the Republic. Most of the state taxes for several years were remitted to local governments for constructing public buildings, and $2 million was set aside for a school fund during Gov. Elisha M. Pease's administration.

Gov. Bell was the first Texas governor to be elected to a second term, and he resigned in November 1853 to take a seat in Congress. Lt. Gov. James W. Henderson served as chief executive for less than a month before Gov. Pease took office. Henderson's tenure is the shortest of any Texas governor.

Although most Texans probably could be classified as Democrats, political parties were weak during the period of early statehood. Personalities dominated most elections, and Sam Houston was the state's major political figure. Candidates were judged as to whether they were pro-Houston or anti-Houston. Early attempts to formally organize the Democrats failed, and the party had no formal structure on the local level. Statewide conventions were held only to select delegates to national conventions.

After the mid-1850s, however, opposition party victories, particularly the Know-Nothing Party, in local elections prompted Democrats to organize a more formal party structure. The Know-Nothings were a nativist group that arose during the decade. By 1859, the party had disappeared. For most Texans, however, politics were unimportant. Voter turnouts were low. National events began to bear more heavily on the state in the 1850s, and the movement toward support for secession from the Union gained strength.

Secession

TEXAS was far removed from the centers of authority and civilization in the 1850s. Settlers in the new state were more concerned with daily problems, but as the decade passed, the national debate over slavery became a factor in Texas' politics and economic and cultural lives.

Slavery had been a major issue in American politics for decades. The issue cooled somewhat by the Missouri Compromise of 1820 that barred slavery in territory north of a line drawn by the law. But the fear of slavery spreading into the Southwest was used by opponents of Texas' initial efforts to be annexed to the United States. The issue flared anew during the Mexican War. Rep. David Wilmot added a proviso to various fiscal bills in 1846 and 1847 in the U.S. House. It would have barred slavery in any territory gained by the United States by virtue of the Mexican War. Although the House approved the Wilmot Proviso, the Senate never did. Thereafter, however, slavery began to dominate almost all the actions of Congress.

In 1854, Sen. Stephen Douglas, D-Ill., sponsored legislation that in essence repealed the Missouri Compromise by allowing the residents of the territories of Kansas and Nebraska to decide whether they wanted slavery. Since both territories were north of the line drawn against involuntary servitude, abolitionists bitterly opposed the measure. Sam Houston, serving as one of the state's first U.S. Senators, won the undying hatred of Southern Democrats and many Texans by opposing Douglas' legislation. Always a strong Unionist, Houston's vote against the Kansas-Nebraska Act in 1854 cost him any chance of being reappointed to the Senate by the Texas Legislature five years later.

In addition, Texas' population almost tripled in the decade between 1850 and 1860 when 604,215 people were counted, including 182,921 slaves. (Indians were not counted.) Many of these new settlers came from the Lower South and had strong ties to the institution of slavery, even if they were not slaveholders. Population studies indicate that three-quarters of the Texas population and two-thirds of the farmers did not own slaves. But slaveowners controlled 60 to 70 percent of the wealth of the state and produced 90 percent of the cotton. The slaveowning farmers also tightened their grip on state politics during the decade. Studies indicate that in 1850, 41.4 percent of the state's officeholders were from the slaveholding class; a decade later, 51.1 percent of the officeholders also were slaveholders. Politics in antebellum Texas was a mix of democracy and aristocracy. But despite the lack of economic restrictions on free male suffrage, the slaveowning elite dominated politics.

In addition to the political power of the slaveholders, they also provided role models for new immigrants to the state. Land was cheap or free in Texas, as it always had been, and since land ownership was an element of social status, the state represented economic opportunity to newcomers. These new Texans saw slave ownership as another step up the economic ladder, regardless of whether they owned slaves or not. Slave ownership was an economic goal, for with slaves more land could be cultivated and more cotton grown. The attitude was prevalent in areas of Texas where slaveholding was not widespread or even practical. Against this background were the politics of Texas played and the passions for secession from the Union fanned through the 1850s.

Much of the decade of the 1850s was tranquil as Texans went about the business of developing the vast state. Even the frontier areas were relatively peaceful as the U.S. Army became more expert at handling the mounted Plains Indians. With more than 3,000 troops stationed in Texas by 1853, the Indians were quiet. The Texas Legislature even agreed to provide the U.S. government with up to 50,000 acres of land to set up reservations to pacify the state's Indian tribes. Two reservations were set up on the Clear Fork of the Brazos River in West Central Texas. One in Throckmorton County was set aside for the Comanches, and the other in Young County was to accommodate Indians from various other groups. By 1855, these reservations were in operation under the direction of Indian Agent Robert S. Neighbors. Camp Cooper was established near the Comanche Reservation and the Second Cavalry kept peace in the area. Several well-known officers commanded the small post, including Albert Sidney Johnston, Robert E. Lee and John B. Hood. When established, these reservations were in advance of the frontier settlement line. But the surrounding country soon was settled. Anglo hostility toward the Indians was fanned when raiding parties began to prey on settlers. Although there was no evidence that reservation Indians were involved, the frontier settlers began to demand removal of the Indians from Texas. By 1858, Neighbors was convinced that the move was necessary, and in August 1859, the reservations were closed and the Indians moved north of the Red River. Settlers quickly claimed the reservation land. The move did not end the Indian raids. Many of the transported Indians felt that the government had acted in bad faith and joined the attacks on settlements in Texas. As the decade drew to a close, the army became less effective in combatting the guerrilla tactics of the Indians, and the breakdown in defense had political repercussions.

In addition to the constant Indian problem, another fact of life was becoming apparent to settlers along the frontier. By 1860, the Texas frontier had moved westward to a line that ran irregularly from Henrietta on the north to Fort Belknap in Young County, Palo Pinto, Brownwood, Llano, Kerrville and Uvalde to Laredo. West of this line was a new land for the settlers from the woodlands of the South and the eastern United States. The treeless prairies and the marked reduction in rainfall posed a new barrier. New farming techniques would be needed to cope with the different environment, and the Indians must be subdued. Cattle ranching would prosper on the prairies, but the industry was in its infancy at the time. The frontier settlers found markets at the military forts and the communities around them. But development of the region had stalled.

In Austin, the 1850s were a relatively progressive period. Relieved of public debt, the state government began to debate economic issues. One of the most important was the development of railroads. One plan that was seriously considered would have made railroad construction a state responsibility. But in 1856, the Legislature decided that private corporations would build the railroad lines with generous state aid. Grants of money were used, or the railway lines would be given 16 alternate sections of land (10,240 acres) for each mile of track built. Construction of the first railroad to move cotton and sugar to Galveston — the Buffalo Bayou, Brazos and Colorado Railway — began in

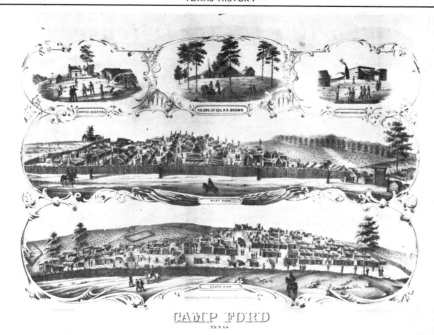

Camp Ford (above), in Smith County near Tyler, was used to house federal prisoners during the Civil War. At one time the 10-acre stockaded enclosure held more than 6,000 internees. Confederate munitions were manufactured in the Yarbrough building (3-story white building at right below) on the square in Tyler, while harness was made for the Confederate army in the adjoining Boren building (to left of Yarbrough building). Photos courtesy Smith County Historical Society.

'Forting Up' for Defense

The frontier of West Texas was a particularly precarious place to live during the Civil War. During the 1850s, many Plains Indians had been placed on reservations in Young and Throckmorton counties. Settlers demanded their removal, however, and after the Indians were taken to present-day Oklahoma, many joined with other hostiles to raid the frontier. Federal troops, which had defended the frontier were withdrawn at the beginning of the Civil War, and Confederate attention was concentrated on the war in the east. There were a few state troops and a loosely organized militia, but most frontiersmen depended on themselves for defense.

On Oct. 13, 1864, occurred one of the bloodiest Indian raids in Texas history. Near Elm Creek in Young County, a band of between 500 and 1,000 Comanches and Kiowas went on a daylong rampage, moving from ranch to ranch scalping, killing, looting, burning and driving off cattle. When they finally retreated, 12 settlers were dead and 13 homes destroyed. Two women and four children were taken captive.

The frontier families, horrified by the wholesale slaughter of the Elm Creek Raid, "forted up." Some families simply fortified their existing homes. But others gathered together and built clusters of temporary picket houses surrounded by picket stockade fences. In most cases, the houses were built along the sides of a large square, with one wall of each house serving as part of the stockade fence. Pickets were set into the gaps between the houses, creating a solid fortification. There may have been as many as 100 such forts along the entire Texas frontier. Since they were not intended for permanent occupation, there are few ruins to mark their sites.

History Highlights

One of the largest of these family installations was Fort Davis, located in Stephens County on the north bank of the Clear Fork of the Brazos River just east of the Shackelford County line (not to be confused with the military Fort Davis in Jeff Davis County). Fort Davis was begun a scant week after the Elm Creek Raid. A 24-year-old resident, Samuel Pierce Newcomb, and his wife, Susan, both kept diaries of life in the fort. Newcomb wrote that Fort Davis was 300 feet by 325 feet, bisected by a 25-foot alley. Unlike most of these temporary shelters, Fort Davis contained a stone building, an existing house, which served as one corner of the fort's perimeter. Women and children hid there when Indians were reported nearby. The ruins of that structure have been made usable as a hunting lodge in recent years.

By Jan. 1, 1865, when Newcomb began to keep his diary, about 120 people were living in Fort Davis, with more planning to move in. By summer of 1865, the little settlement also included a smokehouse, a schoolhouse and a blacksmith shop.

The men of the fort spent much time traveling to and from the mill in Parker County for flour, a risky, Indian-plagued round-trip journey of 200 miles taking four to six weeks in an ox-drawn wagon.

Obtaining salt took less time, but it was no less dangerous, since Ledbetter's Salt Works was about 25 miles from Fort Davis near present-day Albany.

Because most supplies had to be hauled in from quite a distance, the residents of Fort Davis made their own candles, soap and furniture. Since all the fabric mills were in the North, and the South was blockaded during the war, cloth was also made at home from necessity, if not from thrift. Substitutes were found for many items: Coffee was replaced by parched okra or sweet potatoes. Honey and syrup took the place of scarce sugar.

A severe drought that began in 1864 limited agriculture at Fort Davis. Food for frontier families included beef, milk and butter from their own cattle, buffalo meat, deer, antelope, prairie chickens, wild turkeys, wild plums and pecans. Some families kept

This stone building, which stood at one corner of the Fort Davis stockade, sheltered women and children when Indians were nearby.

chickens. Roasted, cured buffalo tongue was a particular treat.

Cattle raising, scouting for Indians and buffalo hunting occupied most of the men's time, when they were not going for flour or salt. While the men were away on roundups, scouting trips or hunts, life for the women was almost unbearably lonely. And the extreme heat, the blue northers, the dust storms and the ever-present threat of Indian attack made life miserable as well.

Life in Fort Davis was not entirely grim, however. Any excuse was used for holding a party. All new houses were dedicated with a dance. Young people turned pecan and wild plum hunts into picnics. And a wedding was cause for a full-scale celebration. The bride's family invited everyone in Fort Davis and the neighboring forts to as elaborate a wedding feast as could be managed on the frontier. There were usually dancing for adults and a candy pull for children.

One of the most welcome visitors to Fort Davis was Parson George Webb Slaughter, a Baptist preacher who lived in Palo Pinto. On each of the two recorded trips he made to the fort, Parson Slaughter stayed several days, preaching several times a day and performing numerous baptisms. Weddings that had been awaiting his arrival were held. On the day before Christmas 1865, Newcomb wrote, ". . . I understand that there were a few grown persons in this place that never had heard the word of God preached until today."

The dedication of a hand-made Confederate flag was cause for a community celebration on March 2, 1865. Visitors came from neighboring forts for the ceremony, which included a pot luck dinner and a dance.

When a blue norther froze the Clear Fork of the Brazos in December 1865, Newcomb, a native of Connecticut, provided the frontiersmen great amusement when he hauled out his long-unused ice skates and took a turn on the ice.

Sam and Susan Newcomb moved to Throckmorton County in the spring of 1866. Many other residents had already left Fort Davis for other fortifications or to return to their own ranches. Fort Davis was pretty well abandoned by 1867, and it slowly disintegrated. Only the rebuilt stone building is still standing to mark the site of this once-bustling community on the Texas frontier — and to serve as a monument to the heroism of frontier Texans.

—*MARY G. CRAWFORD*

1851, and by 1853, 20 miles of track had been built. By 1860, almost 404 miles of railroad existed, mostly in the Houston-Galveston area.

IN addition, other transportation was available. In North Texas, ox carts were the primary source of transportation for commerce. Although slow, the animals were reliable, especially in dry weather. By 1860, 31 stagecoach lines were operating in Texas, including some tied into intercontinental travel. The Butterfield Line began operation in the state in 1858 running from St. Louis and Memphis through Texas to San Francisco. Mail service between San Antonio and San Diego, Calif., commenced in 1857.

One economic problem that the state government could not and the federal government would not solve was the labor shortage. Cotton raising at the time was labor intensive, and in the minds of the plantation owners, that meant slave labor. Importation of African slaves had been prohibited in the United States in 1808 and in the early days of the Texas Republic. An illegal trade flourished in Texas, however, and hundreds, if not thousands, of the slaves in the state had been imported through this system. But some of the state's leadership saw the reopening of the slave trade as a solution to the labor shortage. More slaves also would bring the price down, and small landowners could afford to acquire involuntary labor. The view was hardly universal, however, because free laborers among the European immigrants saw it as a move to eliminate their jobs or to keep wages low. Support for reopening the slave trade also was light among the small farmers of North Texas and the settlers along the frontier.

An outgrowth of the labor problem was strong private support in Texas for the filibuster expeditions to Cuba and Central America in the 1850s. Proponents of slavery thought it would be advantageous to have slave colonies in these areas to supply the labor needs of the state.

Politics quickened in the mid-1850s with the appearance of the Know-Nothing Party, which based its platform on a pro-American, anti-immigrant foundation. Because of the large number of foreign-born settlers, the party attracted many Anglo voters. In 1854, the Know-Nothings elected candidates to city offices in San Antonio, and a year later, the mayor of Galveston was elected with the party's backing. Also in 1855, the Know-Nothings elected 20 representatives and five senators to the Legislature. The successes spurred the Democrats to serious party organization. For the first time, the party nominated statewide candidates at a convention in 1857. Hardin Runnels, a former lieutenant governor and speaker of the Texas House, got the nomination at the convention held in Waco. Sam Houston returned to Texas to seek the governorship as an independent, but he also got Know-Nothing backing. Democrats were organized, however, and Houston was dealt his only election defeat in his political career.

Runnels was a strong states-rights Democrat and irritated many Texans during his administration by advocating reopening the slave trade. His popularity on the frontier also dropped when Indian raids became more severe, and neither the state nor federal governments could stop them.

Most Texans still were ambivalent about secession. The Union was seen as a protector of physical and economic stability. No threats to person or property were perceived in remaining attached to the United States. In 1859, Houston again challenged Runnels and based his campaign on Unionism. Combined with Houston's personal popularity, his position on the secession issue apparently satisfied most voters, for they gave him a solid victory over the more radical Runnels. In addition, Unionists A.J. Hamilton and John H. Reagan won the state's two congressional seats. Texans gave the states-rights Democrats a sound whipping at the polls. Within a few months, however, events were to

change radically the political atmosphere in the state. The defense of slavery was the major concern. But other issues arose that secessionists could use in their arguments for withdrawal from the Union. Shortly after Houston's election, word of John Brown's raid on Harper's Ferry in Virginia reached Texas. States-rights proponents pointed out that it was an example of militant Northerners willing to resort to violence to impose their views on the South. On the frontier, the army could not control Indian raids, and with the later refusal of a Republican-controlled Congress to provide essential aid in fighting Indians, the federal government fell into disrepute. On the Texas border, Juan Cortina, a Mexican hero-bandit, captured Brownsville for a time, and rumor had it that he was backed by abolitionists.

Each breakdown in order or failure to provide adequate services, like frontier defense, threw the efficacy of the Union into doubt. Secessionists played on the growing distrust. Then in the summer of 1860, a series of fires in cities around the state aroused fears that an abolitionist plot was afoot and that a slave uprising might be at hand — a traditional concern in a slaveholding society. Vigilantes lynched blacks and Northerners across Texas, and a siege mentality developed. Texans who once viewed the Union as a beneficent protector now wondered if the institution was obsolete. When the election of Republican Abraham Lincoln — though he was not on the ballot in Texas — as president became apparent, secessionists went to work in earnest. Pleas were made to Gov. Houston to call the Legislature into session to consider a secession ordinance. Houston refused, hoping the passions would cool. They did not. Finally, Oran M. Roberts and other secessionist leaders issued a call to the counties to hold elections and send delegates to a convention in Austin to consider the secession ordinance. Ninety-two of 122 counties responded, and on Jan. 28, 1861, the convention convened. Houston called the Legislature into session to try to thwart the convention, but the lawmakers legalized the meeting, noting that the state constitution delegated to the citizens the power to "alter, reform or abolish" their government in any manner they felt expedient. Houston then insisted that any action of the convention must be ratified by voters.

ROBERTS chaired the secession convention, and it quickly passed the secession ordinance on Feb. 1. Only eight delegates voted against it, while 166 supported secession. An election was called for Feb. 23, 1861, and the ensuing campaign was marked by intimidation, intolerance and violence. Opponents of secession were often intimidated — except Gov. Houston, who courageously stumped the state opposing withdrawal from the Union. Houston argued that the convention had overstepped its authority by joining Texas to the Confederacy. The governor declared that if Texas was to leave the Union, it should revert to its status as an independent republic. Only one-fourth of the state's population had been in Texas during the days of independence and the argument carried no weight. On election day, 76 percent of 61,000 voters approved secession, which would become official March 2, 1861, exactly 25 years after Texas had proclaimed its independence from Mexico. However, only Edwin Waller had the distinction of signing both the secession ordinance in 1861 and the Declaration of Independence in 1836.

President Lincoln reportedly sent Gov. Houston a letter offering 50,000 federal troops to keep Texas in the Union. But after a meeting with other Unionists, Houston declined the offer. "I love Texas too well to bring strife and bloodshed upon her," the governor declared. On March 16, Houston refused to take an oath of loyalty to the Confederacy and was replaced in office by Lt. Gov. Edward Clark.

Texas then embarked on one of the darkest periods in its history.

Civil War

TEXAS fared fairly well through the Civil War. The state did not suffer the devastation of its Southern colleagues. Only on a few occasions did Union troops occupy territory in Texas, except in the El Paso area. A manpower shortage did develop as so many men joined the Confederate army or served in the ranks of state troops.

Texas' cotton was important to the Confederate war effort, for it could be transported from Gulf ports

when other Southern shipping lanes were blockaded. Some goods became difficult to buy, but unlike other Southern states, Texas still received consumer goods because of the trade that was carried on through Mexico during the war. Public order did break down particularly during the latter part of the war. Army deserters often passed through on the way to Mexico, and with so many men in military service, some communities were left poorly defended or policed. These hardships hardly compared to the damage done by military operations and by the complete social disruption in other states. Texas was virtually without manufacturing facilities prior to the war, however. Several small munitions factories were set up in the state. Bullets were made at the State Land Office in Austin, for example. And the state penitentiary became a major manufacturer of cloth for the Confederacy.

After the secession ordinance was approved by voters, the convention reconvened on March 2, 1861, in Austin. Although the question of joining the Confederacy was not on the ballot, most Texans felt approval was implied. So the convention accepted the provisional government of the Confederacy, and delegates to Montgomery were instructed to apply for statehood. The action was unnecessary since the Confederate Congress already had passed a law admitting Texas as a state.

Military operations began in Texas even before voters approved the secession ordinance. The secession convention appointed a public safety committee to see to preparations for war. The initial goal was to take charge of U.S. army facilities in the state.

Ben McCulloch led a contingent of Texas troops to San Antonio. After brief negotiations, U.S. Maj. Gen. David E. Twiggs surrendered U.S. forces — about 2,700 men scattered across the state — and facilities to the Texans on Feb. 15, 1861. Twiggs was later court-martialed for his action. Like many U.S. army officers, the commander of the Department of Texas was a southern sympathizer and later was given a commission in the Confederate army. On the other hand, Col. Robert E. Lee refused to take an oath of allegiance to the Confederacy before leaving Texas and did not leave the U.S. army until he reached Washington and properly resigned.

Col. William C. Young and Lt. Col. James W. Throckmorton secured three federal posts north of the Red River in May 1861 without firing a shot. Throckmorton, a future governor, was one of many Unionists who opposed secession but fought for Texas in the Confederacy.

Secessionists had argued that the North would not contest the dissolution of the Union. They felt that the great commercial nations of Europe would not allow the North to disrupt the important cotton trade. Therefore early in the war, the Confederate government did not think a large army would be needed. Even if hostilities broke out, it was felt that any war would be short. Most of these arguments were overturned shortly after the firing on Fort Sumter, South Carolina.

Thousands of Texans volunteered for service in the Confederate army as soon as hostilities broke out between the North and South. And after Francis R. Lubbock was elected governor in 1861, he worked to see that the state also fulfilled its manpower quotas under the Confederate conscription law of April 1862. Texans fought in every Confederate campaign in the war. Confederate President Jefferson Davis was highly complimentary of the prowess of Texas soldiers in an address to the troops in Virginia, noting that "The troops from other states have their reputations to gain. The sons of the defenders of the Alamo have theirs to maintain." Units like Hood's Brigade and Terry's Texas Rangers became legendary. Sul Ross, a future governor, fought in more than 130 battles, entering the war a private and emerging as an officer. Although accurate figures are not available, historians estimate that between 70,000 and 90,000 Texans fought for the Confederacy, and between 2,000 and 3,000, including some former slaves, saw service in the Union army.

TEXAS was important to the Confederacy for several reasons. It had a great reservoir of men with some military experience. With more than 400 miles of shoreline, the state could provide important ports, and as the most westerly of the Southern states, Texas held the key to Confederate expansion to the west.

Texas also had some unique problems. It had to defend three of its borders from hostile forces: From the Union on the Gulf coast, from the Mexicans in the borderlands, and from the Indians on the frontier, including along the Red River. Consequently there were tensions between the state and Confederate governments at times during the war. Some Texas governors, like Pendleton Murrah, felt that more manpower should be devoted to frontier defense, and consequently he was not always cooperative with demands from Richmond for additional troops.

Texas' coastline was completely without defenses when the Civil War broke out. Slave labor was used to fortify Sabine Pass, Galveston, Matagorda Island, Aransas Pass and Port Isabel. The work was speeded up when the Union blockade of the Gulf ports reached Texas in July 1861.

On land, Texans participated in one of the war's most ambitious early campaigns. Col. John R. Baylor had taken Union posts in southern New Mexico soon after thewar broke out. In late 1861, Gen. Henry H. Sibley was ordered to conduct in the upper Rio Grande Valley a major campaign designed to cut the Union off from California. With 3,000 men, Sibley captured Santa Fe and Albuquerque in early 1862. But the campaign failed when Union soldiers captured the Texans' supply train during the battle of Glorietta Pass in northern New Mexico. Sibley's forces left New Mexico in complete disarray. After the Texans straggled through the El Paso area, Union Col. E.E. Eyre, leading the California Column, occupied the Far West Texas outpost for the remainder of the war. If Gen. Sibley had been successful, the Civil War might have turned out differently. Subsequent campaigns against Union forces in California would have been necessary, but there was support for the Confederate cause in Southern California. And defenses against counterattacks by the Union would have had to be maintained. But with Confederates in control of California's gold, lumber and ports, many of the South's difficulties could have been avoided. The gold would have supported Confederate money; the lumber would have provided ships, and the ports would have opened trade, since the Union could not have blockaded ports on both the Gulf and Pacific coasts. With Sibley's defeat, these opportunities were lost.

ONE of the most important unsung battles of the Civil War may not have been fought by Americans at all, but by Mexican troops under the command of a native of Texas, Ignacio Zaragoza, at Puebla near Mexico City on May 5, 1862. The French were attempting to place Maximilian on the throne of Mexico. But Gen. Zaragoza defeated the French army at Puebla, delaying the conquest of Mexico for more than a year. Some historians think the French would have supported the Confederate cause if they had gained full control of Mexico at the time. If so, more ports would have been open to Confederate trading, and the character of the Civil War might have changed. Mexico's annual Cinco de Mayo celebration commemorates Zaragoza's victory. He was born near Goliad in 1829.

Texans became disenchanted with the Confederate government early in the war. Gov. Lubbock had to levy direct state taxes for the first time since the Compromise of 1850, and by war's end, the Confederacy had collected more than $37 million in the state. But most of the complaints about the government centered on Brig. Gen. Paul O. Hebert, the Confederate commander of the Department of Texas. In April 1862, Gen. Hebert declared martial law without notifying state officials. Opposition to the South's new conscription law, which exempted persons owning more than 15 slaves among other categories of exemptions, prompted the action. In November 1862, the commander prohibited the export of cotton except under government control, and this proved a disastrous policy. And the final blow came when Gen. Hebert failed to defend Galveston and it fell into Union hands in the fall of 1862.

Maj. Gen. John B. Magruder replaced Hebert and was much more popular. The new commander's first actions were to combat the Union offensive against Texas ports. Sabine Pass had been closed in September 1862 by the Union blockade and Galveston was in Northern hands. On Jan. 1, 1863, Magruder retook Galveston with the help of two "cotton clad" gunboats, the Bayou City and Neptune. Decks of the two steamboats were lined with cotton bales for protection, and sharpshooters proved devastating in battles against the Union fleet. Three weeks later, Magruder used two other cotton clad steamboats to break the Union blockade of Sabine Pass, and two of the state's major ports were reopened.

Late in 1863, the Union launched a major offensive against the Texas coast that was partly successful. On Sept. 8, however, Texas Lt. Dick Dowling and 42 men fought off a 1,500-man Union invasion force at Sabine Pass. In a brief battle, Dowling's command sank two Union gunboats and put the other invasion ships to flight.

Gen. N.J.T. Dana was more successful at the mouth of the Rio Grande. On Nov. 1, 1863, he landed 7,000 troops at Brazos Santiago, and five days later, Union forces entered Brownsville, which had been set on fire by the retreating Confederate Gen. Hamilton Bee.

Union control of Brownsville and the Lower Rio Grande Valley forced the rerouting of the cotton trail across Texas. Brownsville and Matamoros were major shipping points for Southern cotton. The Rio Grande was declared an international river in the Treaty of Guadalupe Hidalgo in 1848, and it could not be legally blockaded by the Union. Texas shippers operated under the Mexican flag, and the region boomed economically from the trade. After the Union took the mouth of the Rio Grande, the cotton trail was shifted up river to Laredo and Eagle Pass where the river could be crossed. Then the cotton was transported overland to Matamoros.

Texas Unionists led by E.J. Davis were active in the Valley, including as far upriver as Rio Grande City. Col. John S. "Rip" Ford, commanding state troops, finally pushed the Union soldiers out of Brownsville in July 1864, reopening the important port for the Confederacy. Most of the Union troops were withdrawn, however, to be used in an invasion of Texas along the Red River through Louisiana.

Union Maj. Gen. Nathaniel Banks conceived the invasion, planning to mass troops in Louisiana to march into Texas. The plan was thwarted with Confederate victories at the battles of Mansfield, La., and Pleasant Hill, La., in April 1864. Most of Texas never saw a Union soldier during the war. And the ones they might have seen were in the prisoner of war camps operated in Kerr County, at Hempstead or the largest, Camp Ford, near Tyler, which could accommodate 5,000 prisoners.

There was considerable fighting, however, on the Texas frontier. Early in the war, the Confederates tried to man some frontier forts, but the troops were transferred to East Texas in 1864. State attempts to patrol the frontier were not successful in stopping Indian raids. As the defenses grew weaker, the Indians became bolder, raiding in groups numbering in the hundreds rather than in the traditional small bands. Many settlers moved to more secure areas, and the state's frontier receded up to 100 miles eastward in some areas. In many cases, the settlers who remained on the frontier "forted up" in private facilities. Several families would band together for protection, and crude stockades and other breastworks were constructed. Probably the largest of these private forts was Fort Davis in northwest Stephens County where more than 100 people gathered.

As the war dragged on, the mood of Texas changed. Despite the lack of devastation, many families had sacrificed on the home front. With the manpower shortage, many women had to operate plantations and farms with little help. There also was a shortage of consumer goods and prices were greatly inflated. Slaveholders had been exempt from service in many cases, and the homefolks began to feel that they were sacrificing loved ones and suffering hardship so cotton speculators could profit. Public order broke down as refugees flocked to Texas. And slaves from other states were sent to Texas for safekeeping. When the war ended, there were an estimated 400,000 slaves in Texas, more than double the number counted in the 1860 census.

Morale was low in Texas in early 1865. Soldiers at Galveston and Houston began to mutiny. At Austin, Confederate soldiers raided the state treasury in March, and found only $5,000 in specie. Units broke up, and the army simply dissolved before Gen. Lee surrendered at Appomattox in April 1865.

A month earlier, Texas had an opportunity to enter into a separate peace. U.S. Maj. Gen. Lew Wallace, an unofficial representative of Gen. Ulysses S. Grant, met with Confederate Brig. Gen. John E. Slaughter and Col. John S. Ford at Port Isabel on March 10, 1865. Gen. Wallace offered Texas and the Trans-Mississippi Department a separate peace, so Union and Confederate forces could unite in a show of force to the French in Mexico. The offer was presented to the Confederate command in Houston, where it was rejected. U.S. officials were concerned that they would have to enforce the Monroe Doctrine in Mexico, where both the French and English had interests. If the offer had been accepted, Texas possibly could have been spared the agonies of Reconstruction.

The last battle of the Civil War was fought more than a month after Lee's surrender. Col. Ford led a troop of Confederates in the battle of Palmito Ranch near Brownsville on May 11, 1865. After the victory, the troops learned of the surrender.

On June 19, 1865, Gen. Gordon Granger, under the command of Gen. Philip M. Sheridan, arrived in Galveston with 1,800 men to begin the Union occupation of Texas. Gen. Granger proclaimed the emancipation of the slaves. And A.J. Hamilton, a Unionist and former Texas congressman, was named provisional governor of Texas by President Andrew Johnson. Gov. Pendleton Murrah, elected in 1863, fled to Mexico with other Confederate officials, who feared prosecution for their part in the rebellion. Texas was embarked on Reconstruction.

Reconstruction

TEXAS was in turmoil when the Civil War ended. Although thousands of the state's men had died in the conflict, the state was hardly touched by the war. Indian raids had caused as much damage as the skirmishes with the Union army along the Gulf coast and in the Lower Rio Grande Valley.

Even worse, confusion reigned. No one knew what to expect from the conquering Union army. Gov. Pendleton Murrah had tried to call the Legislature into special session to repeal the secession ordinance and to ease Texas' reentry into the Union. But it became apparent that federal authorities would not accept the actions of the Confederate government as legitimate.

As the Confederate army dissolved in April and May 1865, lawlessness prevailed across the state. Confusion seemed to paralyze authorities.

Upon landing at Galveston on June 19, 1865, Union Gen. Gordon Granger dispatched troops to the population centers of the state to restore civil authority. But only a handful of the 50,000 federal troops that came to Texas was stationed in the interior. Most were sent to the Rio Grande as a show of force against the French in Mexico. Clandestine aid was supplied to Mexican President Benito Juarez in his fight against the French and the Mexican royalists.

Texas' frontier, which had suffered an increasing number of Indian raids at the end of the war, got no relief. The federal government banned local militia, fearing that the Confederates would continue to fight a guerrilla war. But the frontier forts were not remanned, and the prohibition against a militia denied settlers a means of self-defense. Provisional Gov. A.J. Hamilton, however, did allow some counties to organize local police forces to work with the military.

The emancipation proclamation issued by Gen. Granger added to the confusion. Thousands of former black slaves were freed. The Union had no plan for providing direction for the freed men. Some stayed on the plantations, but others left immediately, eager to exercise their new freedom. Many blacks migrated to the cities where they felt the federal soldiers would provide protection. Still others traveled the countryside, seeking family members and loved ones from whom they had been separated during the war. Unaccustomed to free blacks, white Texans feared a breakdown in law and order. The status of the newly freed slaves in society also was not defined. And not the least of the problems was the failure of slaveholders to plan for emancipation.

The Freedman's Bureau, authorized by Congress in March 1865, began operation in September 1865 under Gen. E.M. Gregory. It had the responsibility to provide education, relief aid, labor supervision and judicial protection for the newly freed slaves. The bureau was most successful in opening schools for blacks. Education was a priority because 95 percent of the freed slaves were illiterate. The agency also was partially successful in getting blacks back to work on plantations under reasonable labor contracts. But because it was perceived as being involved in partisan politics, many Texans disliked the bureau. It was disbanded in 1870 when President Ulysses S. Grant declared Reconstruction at an end.

Some plantation owners harbored hopes that they would be paid for their property loss when the slaves were freed. In some cases, the slaves were not released from plantations for up to a year. To add to the confusion, some former slaves had the false notion that the federal government was going to parcel out the plantation lands to them. These blacks simply bided their time, waiting for the division of land.

In Washington, President Andrew Johnson tried to

pursue Lincoln's ideas for reconstruction. The rebellious states would be brought back into the Union as quickly as possible. As Johnson executed the plan, Congress became enraged. Public opinion in the North required the rebels to be punished for secession.

A.J. Hamilton assumed the provisional governorship on June 22, 1865. He planned to restore civil government as quickly as possible, and soon a series of meetings were held with unionists. Then Hamilton set up a statewide system of voter registration. Prospective voters had to take loyalty oaths to the Union, and former Confederate officials and wealthy planters had to get presidential pardons to regain full civil rights.

Voter registration went slowly, and violence was common. Hamilton interpreted these actions as acts of disloyalty to the Union and delayed calling a constitutional convention as long as possible.

Adding to the confusion was the fact that unionists were split over how the state should be readmitted to the Union. Some unionists who had stayed in Texas during the war had suffered discrimination and intimidation from Confederates, and they wanted revenge. Other unionists had fought for the Confederacy and wanted Reconstruction to be as quick as possible. And a third group had been forced to leave and live in the North. This group had a good idea of what the victors had in mind for the South and Texas.

Under pressure from President Johnson, Hamilton called for an election of delegates to a constitutional convention in January 1866, and the convention convened on Feb. 6, 1866. Hamilton told the parley what was expected: Former slaves were to be given civil rights; the secession ordinance had to be repealed; Civil War debt had to be repudiated, and slavery was to be abolished with the ratification of the Thirteenth Amendment.

Many delegates to the convention were former secessionists, and there was little support for compromise. J.W. Throckmorton, a unionist and one of eight men who had opposed secession in the convention of 1861, was elected chairman of the convention. But a coalition of conservative unionists and Democrats controlled the convention. As a consequence, Texas took limited steps toward appeasing the victorious North. Slavery was abolished, and blacks were given some civil rights. But they still could not vote and were barred from testifying in trials against whites. No action was taken on the Thirteenth Amendment, which abolished slavery, because, the argument went, it already had been ratified. Otherwise the constitution written by the convention followed closely the Constitution of 1845. President Johnson in August 1866 accepted the constitution and declared insurrection over in Texas, the last of the Southern states so accepted under Presidential Reconstruction.

Throckmorton was elected governor in June, when other state and local officials were selected by voters under the new constitution. However, Texans had not learned a lesson from the war. When the Legislature met, a series of laws limiting the rights of blacks were passed. In labor disputes, for example, the employers were to be the final arbitrators. The codes also bound an entire family's labor, not just the head of the household, to an employer. Many of the laws later were overturned by the Freedman's Bureau or military authorities. Funding for black education would be limited to what could be provided by black taxpayers. Since few blacks owned land or had jobs, that provision effectively denied education to black children. The thrust of the laws and the attitude of the lawmakers was clear, however: Blacks simply were not to be considered full citizens.

In addition, the Legislature appointed O.M. Roberts and David G. Burnet, both ardent secessionists, to the U.S. Senate. Neither was seated by Radical Republicans in the upper house.

RADICAL unionists, led by Hamilton, felt that the constitutional convention had not gone far enough in providing full rights of citizenship to blacks. They appealed to federal authorities in Washington, and the Congress in March 1867 responded with a Reconstruction plan of its own. The Southern states were declared to have no legal government, and the former Confederacy was divided into districts to be administered by the military until satisfactory Reconstruction was effected. Texas and Louisiana made up the Fifth Military District under the command of Gen. Philip H. Sheridan.

The freeing of the slaves threw the Texas economy into a crisis. Plantation owners were hard-pressed to attract adequate field labor, especially for harvesting.

And since the state's cash economy depended on cotton production, a recession resulted. But in South and West Texas a new industry was developing. In 1866, an estimated 260,000 head of cattle were driven to market outside the state, primarily to Sedalia, Mo. Cattle raising had been basically a hide and tallow industry before the war. But the North and Midwest had developed a taste for beef, and there were thousands of head of wild cattle in Texas for the taking. During the war, herds had not been tended, and unbranded cattle were common across the state. South Texas and the coastal prairies had a long tradition of cattle raising, dating from the Spanish colonial period. Other traditions had come to Northeast Texas and the Piney Woods of East Texas from the eastern United States. And West Central Texas was among the major source areas for cattle for the emerging business.

THE great trail drives moved northward to Kansas in 1867 after Texas drovers encountered resistance from farmers in Missouri and Kansas. "Texas fever," which afflicted cattle in these areas, became a problem, killing the native animals although not affecting Texas cattle. The opening of railheads at Abilene, Kan., and other locations gave Texans alternate markets for their herds. But growth of the cattle industry helped offset some of the problems brought on by the labor shortage in the cotton industry.

Gov. Throckmorton clashed often with Gen. Sheridan and Gen. Charles Griffin, commander of the Texas subdistrict of the military district. The governor thought the state had gone far enough in establishing rights for the newly freed slaves and other matters. One federal official noted that Texas resisted Reconstruction so strenuously because it "had not been whipped" in the war. Finally in August 1867, Throckmorton and other state officials were removed from office by Sheridan because they were considered an "impediment to the reconstruction." E.M. Pease, the former two-term governor and a unionist, was named provisional governor by the military authorities.

A new constitutional convention was called by Gen. Winfield S. Hancock, who replaced Sheridan in November 1867. For the first time, blacks were allowed to participate in the elections selecting delegates. Stricter regulations also disenfranchised between 7,000-10,000 former Confederates. A total of 59,633 whites and 49,497 blacks, however, registered for the election. Many whites stayed away from the polls on election day, but the convention call was approved. Delegates gathered on June 1, 1868. The Constitution of 1869 granted full rights of citizenship to blacks, created a system of education, delegated broad powers to the governor and generally reflected the views of the state's unionists. Deliberations got bogged down on partisan political matters, however, and the convention spent $200,000, an unheard-of sum. At one point, Radical Republicans, arguing that parts of Texas were ungovernable because of the continuing violence, tried to create a State of West Texas, west of the Colorado River, but Congress would not accept dividing the state.

Gov. Pease, disgusted with the convention and the military authorities, resigned in September 1869, and Texas had no chief executive until January 1870, when E.J. Davis took office. The new constitution was approved by voters in November 1869, and Davis was elected governor.

The Republican Party formally organized in Texas in April 1867. Despite internal problems, Radical Republicans, with almost 100 percent support from black voters, controlled the Legislature. Meeting in February 1870, the Legislature passed a series of so-called "obnoxious acts." These created a state militia under the governor's control; created a state police force, also controlled by the governor; postponed the 1870 general election to 1872; enabled the governor to appoint more than 8,500 local officeholders, and granted subsidized bonds for railroad construction at a rate of $10,000 a mile. For the first time, however, a system of public education was created. The law required compulsory attendance of school for four months a year, set aside one-quarter of the state's annual revenue for education and levied a poll tax to support education. Schools also were to be integrated, which enraged many white Texans.

Heavy-handed tactics were used by Radical Republicans in the Senate, where they held only a slim majority. When Democrats and some moderates walked out to break a quorum while considering the militia bill, the Senate leadership had them arrested. Four senators were returned to the capital to give the Senate a quorum, and 10 were jailed for several days while the upper house considered many of the controversial parts of Gov. Davis' program.

Violence was rampant in Texas. One study found that between the close of the Civil War in 1865 and June 1868, 1,035 were murdered in Texas, including 486 blacks, mostly the victims of white violence. Gov. Davis argued that he needed broad police powers to restore order. And despite their unpopularity, the state police and militia — blacks made up 40 percent of the police and a majority of the militia — brought the lawlessness under control in many areas.

The Davis administration was the most unpopular in Texas' history. In fairness, historians have noted that Davis did not feel that whites could be trusted to assure the rights of the newly freed blacks. Therefore many of the governor's actions that have been interpreted as abuses of power were, in the governor's view, his constitutional responsibility. Davis personally was a man of integrity. But he made some bad appointments. His adjutant general, James Davidson, absconded with $37,000 in state funds in 1872, and other officials and legislators were accused of corruption.

State taxes also skyrocketed during the Davis administration and gave moderate Republicans and Democrats a major issue to use against him. E.M. Pease chaired a taxpayers' convention that met in Austin in September 1871 to protest the levies. A.J. Hamilton pointed out that in 1866, state taxes had amounted to 15 cents per $100 worth of property; by 1871, the tax rate had risen to $2.175 per $100 evaluation. Local taxes also rose because communities would offer grants to attract railroads.

Democrats, aided by moderate Republicans, regained control of the Legislature in the 1872 elections — at which Austin also was designated the permanent capital of Texas. In 1873, the lawmakers set about stripping the governor of many of the powers the Radical Republicans had given him.

Through the turbulent period, Texas' economy rebounded. Cotton production had dropped more than 80,000 bales between 1859 and 1869 to 350,629 bales. But by 1873, Texas re-emerged as the leading cotton-producing state. Manufacturing increased with production at 2,399 plants increasing to $11.5 million in 1870 from $6.6 million at 983 plants in 1860. The cattle business that sprang up after the war moved 700,000 head to Kansas in 1871 in the greatest drive in history. So despite the political dissension, Texas was progressing economically.

Gov. Davis also was a champion of frontier defense, which was often neglected by the federal government. Ranger companies were authorized for patrol, but when that proved too expensive, local militia were used

by the state. The federal government was slow to re-establish frontier forts. One reason was that Congress was working on a new Indian policy. Another apparently was that federal authorities did not know the situation on the frontier. Gen. Sheridan once answered critics of frontier defense with the charge that more unionists and blacks were being killed by Confederates than were dying at the hands of Indians. He may have been right. An incomplete report from county judges found that between May 1865 and July 1867, 163 persons had been killed by Indians on the frontier, 43 carried into captivity and 24 wounded.

But attempts to pacify Indians on reservations did not ease Texas' plight. The Comanches and Kiowas in particular did not look on Texans as Americans. Texas was a place apart from the rest of the United States in their minds. One Comanche chief insolently told an Indian agent that, if the Great Father did not want the young reservation Indians raiding Texas, Texas should be moved.

THE ferocity of the raids was vividly brought home to Gen. William T. Sherman, general in chief of the army, in May 1871. He and a small party were inspecting frontier facilities and traveled from Fort Belknap to Fort Richardson. Shortly after reaching Fort Richardson, survivors of a wagon train that had followed the military party reached the fort. They told a story of brutal murder and torture during an Indian attack at Salt Creek in Young County. Gen. Sherman immediately ordered Col. Ranald Mackenzie to launch a vigorous campaign against the Indians. Three Kiowa chiefs, Santank, Satanta and Big Tree, were arrested on the reservation for the crime, and Satanta and Big Tree were tried in state court. At the request of Indian authorities, Gov. Davis pardoned them after a short time in prison.

Cols. Mackenzie and Nelson A. Miles conducted a vigorous campaign against the Comanche and Kiowa, breaking their backs in the Red River campaign. For the first time, the army pursued the Indians to their previous sanctuaries on the Texas Plains. And in a September 1874 engagement in Palo Duro Canyon, the Indians' horses were killed. Without the animals for transportation, the braves soon reported to the reservations. Texas' Indian problems were at an end.

The political turmoil also ended with the gubernatorial election of 1873 when Richard Coke easily defeated Davis. Davis tried to get federal authorities to keep him in office until April, but President Grant refused to intervene. And in January of 1874, Democrats were in control of state government again. The end of Reconstruction concluded the turbulent Civil War era, although the attitudes that developed during the period lasted well into the 20th century.

Retrenchment

WHEN Gov. Richard Coke and conservative Democrats regained control of state government in 1874, they had power but little else. Texas' economy, unlike that of the rest of the defeated South, was not in ruins. Although there were labor problems, railroads expanded, manufacturing grew and cotton production returned to pre-war levels by 1873. But the economic Panic of 1873 slowed recovery.

Pre-Civil War Texas' economy was based on two factors: slaves and land. After the war, the slaves were free, and land values dropped precipitously. And little hard currency was to be had. Confederate money was worthless, and few Texans had acquired much gold during the war.

Gov. E.J. Davis' administration also was accused of extravagance. But Texans bore a tax burden much lighter than other Southern states.

Railroad construction had resumed after the war, and the total mileage tripled to almost 1,500 miles before the economic panic curtailed work in 1873.

Coke and the Legislature therefore had little choice in financing state government. The Democrats chose to cut state spending dramatically. Although the Davis administration was accused of profligate spending, many Democrats had supported the appropriations. With Davis out of office, however, public education was cut to the bone, the prison system was put on a pay-as-you-go basis by continuing a tragic policy initiated under Davis of leasing convicts to private contractors.

A constitutional convention was called in 1875 to rewrite the state constitution, a hated vestige of Radical Republican rule. Again, every avenue to cutting spending at any level of government was explored. Salaries of public officials were slashed. The number of offices was reduced. Judgeships, along with most other offices, were made elective rather than appointive. The Legislature was prohibited from assuming debt beyond $200,000 without a statewide vote. The state road program was curtailed, and the immigration bureau was eliminated. State chartered banks also were prohibited, as they had been in every Texas constitution but one since 1836. Perhaps the worst change was the destruction of the statewide school system. The new charter created a "community system" without a power of taxation, and schools were segregated by race. The constitution, which was approved by voters on Feb. 15, 1876, reflected the public attitudes of the day. Almost half the delegates to the convention were members of the Grange, a new organization that had come to Texas in 1873 to relieve the plight of the farmer. Under Reconstruction, Texans felt they had experienced what government could do to them, not for them. They had borne what they considered a burden of heavy taxation for programs that they neither supported nor approved. And they wanted no repeat performances. Though the United States was in the middle of the Industrial Revolution, the basic law of Texas reflected a world view more in line with 1836.

Despite the basic reactionary character, the charter also was visionary. Following the lead of several other states, the Democrats declared railroads to be common carriers and subject to regulation. But consistent with the desire for keeping government at a minimum, no method for regulation of railroads was provided, and the omission was to fire political debates for a decade and a half.

Another major challenge was the re-establishment of law and order across the state. Since before the Civil War, respect for civil authority had been on the decline in Texas. After the war, the situation deteriorated as thousands of disillusioned and embittered soldiers returned home to suffer under Reconstruction. Indians remained a problem, although the U.S. Army was making progress in taming the frontier. And in the long troublesome Nueces Strip — the land between the Nueces River and the Rio Grande — the Mexican bandit-hero Juan Cortina was again causing trouble. The enigmatic Cortina had served both the Union and Confederacy during the Civil War, and at one time, the Texas Senate approved a pardon for him before the House bowed to a public outcry and let the matter drop. While serving as an official of the Mexican government, however, Cortina also operated a thriving cattle theft business north of the Rio Grande, stealing stock to fulfill meat contracts with Cuba. Anglo ranchers were not safe from the marauders, and many settlers took the law into their own hands, victimizing Mexican-Texans in the process.

TO meet the dual challenge of lawlessness and Indian insurrection, Gov. Coke in 1874 re-established the Texas Rangers. Major L. H. McNelly was to lead the Special Force to clean up the borderlands, and Maj. John B. Jones commanded the Frontier Battalion, consisting of six companies of 75 Rangers each.

McNelly's force of only 40 men was controversial because it took few prisoners. The Rangers were ordered to kill captives if any attempt was made to free them. But McNelly also developed an excellent intelligence system that kept him a step ahead of the bandits. One of his first acts was to remove the Anglo posses from the field, for many had been used as cover for individuals to settle personal grievances. After a few months in the field, McNelly's force killed 13 Mexican bandits in a running gun battle, and the bodies were displayed on the square at Brownsville as an example for future cattle thieves. Soon the situation was under control, and McNelly moved his operations farther up the Rio Grande to clean out American outlaws operating around Eagle Pass.

Major Jones' task was more difficult. His Frontier Battalion was divided into small groups that continually patrolled the edges of settled Texas to discourage Indian raids. The U.S. Army also put a severe crimp in raids. Cavalry units, under Ranald Mackenzie, relentlessly pursued Indians across the plains. Jones and a group of Rangers fought the last battle against Indians in northern Texas in June 1875 at Lost Valley on the Jack-Young County line. Twenty-seven Rangers, commanded by Jones, engaged 100 Indians for a full day before getting help from Fort Richardson.

Thereafter most Indian raids were concentrated in Far West Texas where U.S. Army Lt. John Bullis and his Negro Seminole Indian Scouts waged a relentless campaign against the Apaches. The last Indian battle in Texas was fought in January 1881 when Capt. George Baylor and a group of Rangers ambushed the remnants of Chief Victorio's Apaches in the Sierra Diablo Mountains.

Also by 1881, every part of Texas had felt the presence of the Rangers. The day of the professional outlaw was coming to an end. Major Jones had quelled feuds in several counties and had reduced the list of wanted criminals in the state. Rampant lawlessness had been reduced to mere sporadic outbursts.

Gov. Coke was re-elected in 1876, but he left office in December of that year for a seat in the U.S. Senate. Lt. Gov. Richard Hubbard replaced him.

Though Texas' population grew substantially after Reconstruction, transportation remained a major problem. The state's rivers were not navigable except for a few miles from the Gulf. Counties were given responsibility for creating and maintaining a road system, and in East Texas, the most populous part of the state, a "firstclass road" was one in which tree stumps were no more than six inches in height. To facilitate construction of much-needed railroads, the Legislature in 1876 established a land-grant system. Railroad companies got 16 alternate sections of land for each mile of track completed, with payment beginning after completion of 10 miles of track. Between 1875 and 1885, one-half of the total railroad mileage built in the 19th century in Texas was completed. In 1877, Texas led all states in railroad construction, and the following year, the construction in Texas exceeded the aggregate for

all other states and territories combined. But embarrassed state officials discovered in 1881 that the Legislature had given away eight million more acres of land than was available, and the land-grant law was repealed. More than 32 million acres of land were granted to railroads during the period, however.

As railroads extended across the state, the character of the economy began to change. Farmers began to move from self-contained subsistence agriculture to commercial production. But this meant that they had to purchase many household goods and supplies that they once provided by their own labor. Cash, rather than barter, became the medium of exchange, and in the war-ravaged Confederacy, the need for hard money compounded many problems.

In addition, the construction of railroads spurred other industries. In 1880, Texas & Pacific Railroad alone purchased 500,000 crossties to stimulate lumbering, which became the state's largest manufacturing industry.

Emancipation of the slaves brought about a major realignment of the division of labor in the state. Many owners of large plantations were financially ruined by the loss of slaves and by the drop in land prices. At first, landowners feared there would be a labor shortage, because it was felt that the former slaves would not work for wages. Within a decade, however, most blacks were either employed on farms, had entered into share-cropping agreements or had acquired land. White landowners often would not sell land to blacks or would charge high interest rates for the purchase. Like all small farmers, blacks also got caught in the crop-lien system in which they had to mortgage future crops to buy supplies on credit. Often they still owed money after selling their crops, and a cycle of permanent indebtedness developed. Wage demands of the blacks and a basic prejudice against the former slaves also prompted efforts to attract immigrants into the state. The effort was successful, but landowners also found that many new immigrants worked for others only briefly before acquiring land for themselves. By 1876, 62 percent of the workers were white, with blacks making up only 38 percent. Unlike some other states, Texas did not develop a class of black artisans during the slavery period, so after the war, those blacks not engaged in agricultural work held only menial jobs in either rural or urban areas. A class of independent black businessmen developed only slowly, and most were in service industries like cafes, barbershops and funeral parlors.

Conservative Democrats maintained a firm grip on state politics for almost 20 years after Reconstruction, although dissident political groups arose periodically. The thrust of the Democratic administrations was economy in government and white supremacy. Despite heroic efforts, the state government remained in debt, which served as a continual reminder of the failure of the Confederacy. Texans could not divide the quest of blacks for full civil rights from full social equality. And most white Texans continued to expect subservience from blacks. Efforts had been made to legally discriminate against blacks after the Civil War. In 1866, the Legislature required railroads to provide separate accommodations for black passengers, and the law was not repealed until 1871. Later the lawmakers eliminated state licensing for many businesses in an effort to avoid the antidiscrimination thrust of the federal Civil Rights law of 1875.

IN statewide politics, race was not a major question because the percentage of blacks in the population was declining, although the number of blacks in the state grew. In local politics, however, particularly in East Texas, race was a major factor. Blacks were in the majority in several counties in the so-called Black Belt. Here blacks, along with white Republicans, often controlled local offices. Often white Democrats would use intimidation and violence to discourage black voter participation. As often, black politicians would bend the law. In some counties, specially colored ballots were used for black-supported slates of candidates so illiterate voters could more easily vote a straight ticket. The practice was ended by an 1879 law that required certain types of ballots. As early as 1874 some local Democratic clubs conceived the all-white primary as an instrument for denying blacks participation in local government. Although initial efforts were unsuccessful, the approach continued and finally became state Democratic policy after the turn of the century.

Violence against blacks often was fatal. One source estimates that 500 blacks died in mob violence between 1870 and 1900. Many were victims of lynching after being accused of crimes. On occasion, the victims proved to be innocent.

For 15 years after Reconstruction ended, Texas Democrats could campaign against the Civil War and expect success. During this period, most statewide officeholders and local officials were Confederate veterans. O. M. Roberts, chief justice of the state supreme court, became a compromise candidate for governor when the Democratic convention deadlocked. Roberts, who chaired the secession convention of 1861, was elected for the first of two terms in 1878 and pursued a strict policy of fiscal austerity. He cut spending for public education from one-quarter to one-seventh of state revenues one year and supported a law providing for the sale of stateland at 50-cents an acre. Despite the intent of providing cheap land for immigrants, the law actually encouraged widespread speculation, driving land prices up for farmers.

John Ireland succeeded Roberts as governor and continued the tight fiscal policies. Ireland opposed the liberal land policies of his predecessors and is credited with saving much public land for the state schoolchildren. But cracks were developing in the Democratic dominance of state politics. G. W. (Wash) Jones, a former Democratic lieutenant governor, contested Ireland as an independent in 1882 and polled more than 100,000 votes. It was an impressive showing by a dissident candidate against the entrenched Democrats.

Economic and social problems that began in the 1870s became the major political issues in the 1880s. Democrats were hard-pressed to maintain control of the state government in the turbulent final 20 years of the 19th century.

Economy in Transition

HOLLYWOOD distorted the picture of the Texas economy. While the cowboy and cattle drives are romantic subjects, the fact is that the simple cotton farmer was the backbone of the state's economy well into the 20th century.

But neither the farmer nor the cattleman prospered throughout the last quarter of the 19th century. At the root of their problems was federal monetary policy and the lingering effects of the Civil War.

To finance the war, the Union had gone off the gold standard and had issued paper money — or greenbacks. Throughout the war, paper money could not be redeemed for specie from the national government. The prevailing monetary theory, however, held that this paper was only fiat money without real value. Only a gold-backed currency had intrinsic value. At the end of the war, there were almost $500 million in national bank notes in circulation. Northeastern bankers began to lobby for a return to the gold standard and to hard money. Although the issuance of paper money had brought about a business boom in the Union during the war, inflation also increased. Silver was demonetized in 1873. Congress passed the Specie Resumption Act in 1875 that returned the nation to the gold standard in 1879. Almost immediately a contraction in currency began. Between 1873 and 1891, the amount of national bank notes in circulation declined from $339 million to $168 million.

The reduction in the money supply was devastating in the defeated South. Of the region's major fiscal assets, slaves had been lost altogether and, because of the lack of money, land values plummeted. In 1870, Texas land was valued at an average of $2.62 an acre, compared with the national average of $18.26 an acre. Confederate money was worthless, and gold was scarce. Massachusetts alone had five times more national bank currency in circulation than the entire South.

With the money supply declining and the national economy growing, farm prices dropped. In 1870, a bushel of wheat brought $1, but by 1885, it had dropped to 80 cents. And in the 1890s, wheat was 60 cents a bushel. Except for a brief spurt in the early 1880s, cattle prices followed those of agricultural products.

Credit became an important commodity. And Texas was ill-equipped to meet the challenge. State-chartered banks were prohibited by the constitution, and there were hardly enough national banks to service the state's growing population. To compound the farmers' problems, national banks would not loan money with land as a collateral. The credit problem was exacerbated in Texas by growth. In 1870, there were 61,125 farms in the state; 30 years later, the number spiraled to 352,190.

The transition from a self-sufficient agricultural economy to commercial agriculture that the state experienced also strained the farmers' need for credit. Efficient commercial farms needed more land and mechanized equipment. Both were expensive. The war had stripped Texas of its farm implements, and it took time to replace them. In 1860, the value of Texas farm implements per farm was $24 above the national average. For the remainder of the century, however, Texas' average per farm was $50-$60 below the national average, and other regions surpassed the state. Bad weather and poor prices often forced land-owning farmers into tenancy. Between 1880 and 1890, the number of farms in Texas doubled, but the number of tenants tripled. By 1900, almost half the state's farmers were tenants.

The much-criticized crop-lien system was developed following the Civil War to meet the credit needs of small farmers. Merchants would extend credit to farmers throughout the year in exchange for liens on their crops. In most cases cotton was the major cash crop. Critics have blamed the creditors for prohibiting farmers from diversifying. But that is only partly true. Many farmers faithfully planted cotton because it seldom had a complete failure. Through almost any type of bad weather, some cotton would be produced when other crops failed completely. But the result of the crop-lien system, particularly when small farmers did not have enough acreage to operate efficiently, was a state of continual debt and despair.

Furnishing merchants also have been criticized for charging high interest rates for goods that carried premium prices when sold on credit. But many small farmers were not good businessmen, and the merchant's risks were high.

Cotton was a physically demanding crop to raise. One estimate was that it took 168 man-hours of labor to raise one acre of cotton a year. But many small farmers toiled long hours and then found at the end of the year that their labor had yielded no return. In some cases, they had gone further in debt to the furnishing merchant.

The work ethic held that a man would benefit from his toil. When this apparently failed, farmers looked to the monetary system and the railroads as the causes. Their discontent hence became the source of the agrarian revolt that developed in the 1880s and 1890s.

Farmers, on the other hand, were criticized for thinking of themselves as laborers, rather than investors or capitalists. Across the South, land traditionally had been looked on as a tool, not an investment. Once a piece of land was worn out, the farmer discarded it by moving to the next frontier. But in Texas the familiar land use pattern broke down as the frontier reached the arid plains. Farmers were slow in understanding that new techniques would be needed for dry-land farming, and the periodic droughts, originally thought to be aberrations in the weather, wrought considerable misery before settlers solved the problems of successfully farming land beyond the 98th meridian.

WITH the defeat of the Indians and the buffalo kill that began in 1874-75, West Texas was opened first to cattlemen and later to farmers. Cattlemen traditionally practiced open-range grazing from Spanish colonial days until the early 1880s. Livestock was allowed to roam over wide areas and was rounded up twice a year. Huge cattle drives following the war had proved successful, and when the High Plains of Texas were cleared of Indians and buffalo, cattle thrived on the rich grasses. Large cattle operations developed. Charles Goodnight established the JA Ranch in the Palo Duro Canyon in the Panhandle in the 1870s, and others soon followed. The huge cattle drives ended about the same time that many states quarantined Texas cattle because of the "Texas Fever" they carried — which was fatal to other domestic livestock. Railroads snaked across Texas in the 1880s, establishing shipping points and eliminating the need for the long drives to out-of-state markets.

Cattle prices improved between 1880 and 1885, but other problems faced stockraisers. In 1883, the Legislature required that stockmen pay grazing fees for state land that their cattle used. Previously this grazing had been free, and many cattleraisers ignored the law or circumvented it by fixing bids to keep fees low. Attempts to prosecute ranchers for conspiring against the law failed because most public officials and jurors in western Texas were either cattlemen or employees of the ranches.

The introduction of barbed wire in the early 1880s brought a revolution to ranching. Texas had long needed a cheap form of fencing. Stone and wooden fences were expensive, and in West Texas the materials simply were not available. Without fences, however, the quality of cattle herds could not be improved. Farmers also needed fences in cattle-raising regions to keep stock from ruining their fields. The new wire was introduced into Texas at Denison in the late 1870s, and in less than 10 years, it had spread across the state. John W. "Bet a Million" Gates, one of the most successful barbed-wire salesmen, dramatically demonstrated the new product by building a corral in downtown San Antonio and wagering that a steer could not break out. The animal didn't, and ranchers bought the wire.

SMALL range wars developed between open-range cattlemen and fencers as barbed wire moved across the state. Often landowners would block public roads and seal off water holes with their new fences. Fence-cutters would simply snip the wire to remove the barriers. The battles became particularly bitter during droughts when cattle were cut off from water. Finally, Gov. John Ireland called a special session of the Legislature in 1883 to make fence-cutting and the fencing of public lands illegal. Estimates are that more than $20 million in property damage was done by fence-cutters, and the adverse publicity surrounding the battles discouraged immigration and land development for a time.

The cattle boom of the 1880s also attracted foreign investment to the state. Thirteen British corporations — five from England and eight from Scotland — invested an estimated $25 million in Texas and controlled between them 15 million to 20 million acres of land, primarily on the High Plains and the Rolling Plains. The operations proved generally unprofitable for investors when cattle prices dropped. Drought, bitter winters, cattle thieves and public animosity also took their toll. But the foreign investors are credited with introducing barbed-wire on a large scale, bringing windmills to the region and with improving cattle herds.

One of the largest ranches was created after a disaster in Austin. The state capitol burned in 1881, and the following year, the Legislature gave the Capitol Syndicate three million acres of land to construct a new building. The project was completed in 1888. With the land, the XIT Ranch in the Panhandle was established in 1885, covering parts of nine counties: Dallam, Hartley, Oldham, Deaf Smith, Parmer, Castro, Bailey, Lamb and Hockley. More than 1,500 miles of fence enclosed the ranch, which was operated until 1901 when tracts were sold by the syndicate.

The breakup of the large ranches began in the 1880s and continued after the turn of the century. Small farmers entered the region and purchased the large estates piecemeal. The immigration proved more profitable to the large ranches than cattleraising.

As bleak as the picture was, there were bright spots. After 1860, cottonseed, which had been a waste and a nuisance, developed commercial value. Previously it had been burned or dumped into streams and rivers to the dismay of other Texans. But it was discovered that cottonseed cake could be sold to stock raisers for feed, and the oil became valuable. Cotton presses could be easily moved, and a thriving industry developed. By 1900, cottonseed processing became the second largest industry in Texas, behind lumbering.

Lumbering continued to grow, and by 1890 became the state's largest industry. Improved transportation also allowed wood products to be shipped outside the state as well as to be used within Texas.

In December 1887, the Texas League of Professional Baseball Clubs was organized, and in its inaugural season, Austin, Dallas, Fort Worth, Galveston, Houston and San Antonio fielded teams.

Railroad expansion also continued at a brisk pace. In 1880, there were 3,025 miles of track in operation, and a decade later, the mileage more than doubled to 8,667. In hand with railroad expansion, coal production was initiated in the late 1870s. A mine in Stephens County in West Central Texas produced coal for Fort Griffin and shipped to Fort Worth at a price of $11 a ton, $2 below the eastern price. As coal became available in quantity, the railroads abandoned wood as fuel. In the 1880s, commercial coal production began in Palo Pinto County, and Thurber, near the Palo Pinto-Erath county line, became a major coal production center for the Texas &

Pacific Railroad. On the border, Eagle Pass became a coal production center for the Southern Pacific.

Galveston and San Antonio were important trade centers in the last quarter of the century. Galveston was a major cotton-shipping center, and San Antonio was a supply center for the frontier forts. Along the border, El Paso and Laredo became major international trade centers. The Southern Pacific reached El Paso from the west in 1881, and shortly thereafter a northern railroad tied into the Mexican system. Maintenance shops were established at El Paso, and nearby coal mines provided fuel for trains visiting the trade center. Entrepreneur Uriah Lott completed a rail line to Laredo in November 1881, and a few days later, Jay Gould's International and Great Northern Railroad arrived, tying the border community to San Antonio and northern markets. Laredo and its sister city, Nuevo Laredo, marked the arrival of the railroads with a month-long celebration.

Railroad towns blossomed in the wake of construction. Many grew from crew camps. As Jay Gould's Texas & Pacific Railroad moved west from Fort Worth, the cities of Gordon, Eastland, Baird and Abilene were laid out in 1880, and the following year, Sweetwater, Colorado City and Big Spring were established along the route. T&P and Southern Pacific met at Sierra Blanca about 90 miles east of El Paso on Jan.1, 1882, completing connections with the East and West coasts for Texas.

In 1887, the Fort Worth and Denver City Railroad began a diagonal extension across West Texas and the Panhandle. It crossed Childress, Donley, Armstrong, Potter, Hartley and Dallam Counties in the Panhandle and reached Texline on the New Mexico-Texas state line in 1888. The cities of Childress, Clarendon, Amarillo and Dalhart became terminal points for farmers and ranchers. With this extension, most areas of Texas had railroads. But Lubbock on the South Plains and the Lower Rio Grande Valley did not receive rail service until after the turn of the century.

The entry of the Texas & Pacific and the Missouri-Kansas-Texas railroads from the northeast changed trade patterns in the state. Since the days of the Republic, trade generally had flowed to Gulf ports and primarily at Galveston. Jefferson in Northeast Texas served as a gateway to the Mississippi River, but it never carried the volume of trade that was common at Galveston. The earliest railroad systems in the state also were centered around Houston and Galveston, again directing trade southward. With the T&P and Katy lines, North Texas had direct access to markets in St. Louis and the East.

Some problems developed with the railroads, however. In 1882, Jay Gould and Collis P. Huntington, owner of the Southern Pacific, entered into a secret agreement that amounted to creation of a monopoly of rail service in Texas. They agreed to stop competitive track extensions, to divide under a pooling arrangement freight moving from New Orleans and El Paso, to purchase all competing railroads in Texas, and to share the track between Sierra Blanca and El Paso. Railroads owned by the pair soon organized the Texas Traffic Association with its goals of increasing revenues and doing away with abuses and losses. When the courts ordered the association dissolved, the railroads simply reorganized associations based outside Texas.

THE Legislature made weak attempts to regulate railroads, as provided by the state constitution. Gov. Coke had recommended creation of a railroad commission in 1876, but was ignored. Gould thwarted an attempt to create a commission in 1881 with a visit to the state during the Legislative debate. The railroad tycoon subdued the lawmakers' interest with thinly disguised threats that capital would abandon Texas if the state interfered with railroad business. In 1879, the lawmakers did set a maximum rate that railroads could charge for freight and made it unlawful for a rail carrier to discriminate against any person or place. But the laws were loosely enforced.

With the railroads came Texas' first militant labor organizations. The state's traditional agrarian society had little need for unions. Some workers had organized during the days of the Republic. Journeyman printers struck a Houston newspaper in 1839, and groups of artisans organized loosely to seek legislation. Texas' mechanics lien law of 1839 was one of the first protections for workers of its type in North America. Workingmen's associations organized occasionally prior to the Civil War, but they were weak and often did not last long. Only two unions existed in Galveston at the outbreak of the war. Prior to 1870, no outside unions provided aid to Texas workers. In the self-sustaining agricultural economy, unions also were looked upon as "Yankee innovations" and "abominations." After the Civil War, unions became more numerous. The Screwmen's Benevolent Association of Galveston organized in 1866 and lasted into the 20th century after affiliation with a national union. Black dock workers also organized in Galveston, and skilled workers, such as carpenters and bricklayers, struck in major cities.

With the railroads, however, came the militant Knights of Labor. In 1885, the union struck and gained concessions from T&P Railroad, but a year later, another strike turned violent. Troops were called out to protect railroad property, and the strike failed. The unions were heavily criticized for the job action, and the labor movement in Texas remained weak until the state's industrial base developed in the 20th century.

As the 19th century closed, Texas remained an agricultural state, albeit commercial agriculture and not family farms. But the industrial base was growing. Between 1870 and 1900, the per capita value of manufactured goods in the United States rose from $109 to $171. In Texas, these per capita values increased from $14 to $39. But manufacturing values in Texas industry still were only one-half of the annual agricultural values.

But Texas was definitely a state in transition, and there was no better evidence than the tumultuous political upheavals of the last quarter of the 19th century.

The Agrarian Revolt

CONSERVATIVE Texas Democrats maintained control of the state government throughout most of the last quarter of the 19th century. Their ascendancy was based on white supremacy and on the strong emotional rejection of the Radical Republican Reconstruction era. As across most of the United States, Texans had no attraction to burning national issues. Regional and local interests prevailed.

But as the plight of the farmers worsened, strong passions were unleashed that overrode the issues of secession and the Civil War on the national level. A series of third parties with national affiliations arose in Texas that seriously threatened to break the Democrats' grip on the state house and the Legislature.

Texas farmers were not alone in their poverty. The entire South suffered, and the condition was noted by O.H. Kelley, a clerk in the Agricultural Bureau in Washington, on a trip through the region. He was appalled by the Southern farmers' poverty and apathy. To give voice to their plight, he organized the National Grange — the Patrons of Husbandry — in the nation's capital in 1867. The first Texas Grange was established in 1872 at Salado in Bell County. At its peak membership in 1877, the state organization claimed 45,000 members, including 6,000 women, in more than 1,200 local chapters. It had a threefold purpose: To improve the home life of its members; to foster social intercourse to the mutual benefit of all, and to provide economic benefits in dealing with the business world. Grangers were encouraged to participate in politics as citizens, but the organization was not directly involved. Many local Granges and the state organization petitioned the Legislature on various issues, and members felt they had a voice in government through the organization. About half of the 90 delegates to the state constitutional convention of 1875 were Grangers, and they left their mark on the state charter that provided for limited government, restrictions on taxation and debt, and provided a framework for railroad regulation.

The Grange's lasting contribution came through its educational programs. Many of the local meetings were agricultural schools, teaching farmers how to be more efficient. The founding of Texas Agricultural & Mechanical College (now University) in 1876 received strong support from the organization.

But the Grange foundered on two issues. First, it established the Texas Cooperative Association in an effort to circumvent the furnishing merchant who held so many farmers in debt. The goal was to eliminate the middle man and to provide merchandise wholesale to farmers. The state cooperative was to be associated with local cooperatives sponsored by the organization. And this effort attracted many members. Unfortunately, it did not work. The cash-only Grange stores were of no help to farmers who had no cash. And in 1883 and 1884 both the state and local cooperatives suffered severe financial losses because of bad crops and many closed their doors. In addition, as time passed, farmers became more militant and wanted an organization that was more directly involved in politics. State Grange leaders would not abandon the original nonpolitical policy. While most farmers were emotionally tied to the Democratic Party and wanted to work within its framework, others were becoming disenchanted with the "party of the fathers." The Grange's membership began to fall.

The Greenback Party was attractive to many farmers, although the Grange leadership remained loyal to the Democratic Party. The monetary devaluation that was damaging farmers also took its toll on the wages of workers in the industrialized parts of the nation. On the national level, the Greenback Party began activity in 1876 and reached Texas two years later. Although the party supported issues like women's suffrage and an income tax, its basic goal was to provide a greater money supply. Greenbackers opposed the return to the gold standard, supported remonetization of silver and demanded repeal of the national bank law. First and foremost, the party supported an expansion of the currency to eliminate the growing economic hardship of many Americans. In four gubernatorial elections between 1878 and 1884, Greenbackers supplanted Republicans as runners-up to the winning Democrats. In 1882, Greenbacker G.W. "Wash" Jones polled 102,501 votes, the most ever attracted by a dissident party in the state up to that time. In local races, Greenbackers occasionally were successful, as in the case of the party candidate who was elected mayor of Dallas. The Greenback movement failed, however, when the Democrats usurped some of its platform planks. Farmers also became uncomfortable with some of the radical socialists who gained control of the national party. There was little cultural affinity between the farmers and the socialists of the industrial world. Farmers looked elsewhere for a political champion.

In 1877, another farm organization was established. On the J.R. Allen farm in Lampasas County, a group of farmers banded together in the Knights of Alliance with its purpose "to assist the civil officers in maintaining law and order." This group was primarily concerned with curbing livestock thefts. But it had a simple ritual, and its literary program was borrowed from the Grange. The Alliance was reorganized in 1879 in Poolville in Parker County, and in the next few years, it provided the impetus for the radical politics of the 1890s.

By 1886, the Alliance, led by S.O. Daws and William Lamb, became more radical. At a meeting in Cleburne, the organization issued a list of 17 "demands" — in contrast to the Grange's simple petitions — addressed to the state and federal governments. These included demands for fiscal reform, railroad regulation, changes in land policy and the recognition of labor unions. Though some conservative Alliance members were distressed at the apparent split with the Democratic Party, the organization's membership grew tremendously after the meeting. By the time a second meeting was held in Waco in January 1887 to heal the rift that developed, the Alliance claimed 200,000 members in 3,000 chartered suballiances in Texas.

In Waco, Dr. Charles W. Macune struck a compromise between the divergent elements and took a major step toward spreading the Alliance's influence. He proposed a national system of cooperatives to market farm products and to serve as a purchasing medium for farmers. Within five weeks, Texas lecturers were sent to other states throughout the South. When a national convention was held in Shreveport, La., in October 1887, 10 states that had been organized in eight months were represented.

Democrats easily weathered the early third-party challenges in Texas. Democratic governors continued their policies of fiscal austerity. John Ireland successfully coped with the fence-cutting wars and reversed some of the liberal land policies that were fueling speculation. Lawrence S. "Sul" Ross, elected in 1888, was a popular Confederate veteran who benefited from a large monetary settlement with the federal government. Texas was compensated for its costs in fighting Indians and guarding the Mexican border. Ross cut taxes and improved state services.

In 1886, a new breed of Texas politician appeared. James Stephen Hogg was not a Confederate veteran, although his father was, and he was not tied to the party policies of the past. As a reform-minded attorney general, Hogg had actively enforced the state's few railroad regulatory laws. Through the experience, he became convinced that the state must have a railroad commission. With farmers' support, Hogg was elected governor in 1890, and at the same time, a debate on the constitutionality of a railroad commission was settled when voters amended the constitution to provide for one. Hogg led a group of young Democrats who were a step removed from Reconstruction and ties with the Confederate past. These young Democrats launched a brief reform era in state government.

Nationally, the growing power of the emerging corporate interests had become a major political issue. In 1887, Congressman John Reagan of Texas won a 10-year fight to establish the Interstate Commerce Commission to regulate railroads. Two years later, the Texas Legislature passed an anti-trust law, just weeks after Kansas had approved the first such statute in the nation.

Hogg was bitterly opposed in his campaign, but the reform mood of the state was evident. Voters returned only 22 of the 106 members of the Texas House in 1890. The Legislature created the Railroad Commission of Texas in 1891 after an extended debate. A compromise was reached that allowed the first commission to be appointed by the governor, but beginning in 1894, the panel would be elected. Hogg accomplished one of the great political moves of the century by luring Reagan out of the U.S. Senate to serve as the first chairman of the commission, along with commissioners L.L. Foster and William P. McLean. Reagan's long battle to create the ICC gave him an intimate knowledge of railroad operations, and, as the former postmaster general of the Confederacy, he was well-respected by all Texans.

Despite his reputation as a reformer, Hogg accepted the growing use of Jim Crow laws to limit minority access to public services. In 1891, the Legislature responded to public demands and required railroads to provide separate accommodations for blacks and whites.

The stage was being set for one of the major political campaigns in Texas history, however. Farmers did not think that Hogg had gone far enough in his reform program, and they were distressed that Hogg had not appointed a farmer to the railroad commission.

In 1889, Charles Macune, now editor of the Farmers Alliance's national newspaper, the National Economist in Washington, had proposed a radical new monetary system. Under his plan, the federal government would eliminate the farmers' credit pinch, underwriting cooperatives by issuing greenbacks to provide credit for farmers' crops. A more flexible national currency would be created in the process. In addition, the government would store the crops until time for sale and issue "subtreasury" certificates that would serve as legal tender. While the plan contained elements of a modern crop insurance program, it was wildly radical at the time. Texas Democrats had refused to endorse either the subtreasury plan or free silver in their 1890 platform, and to many farmers this was a signal of the party's insensitivity to their plight. Many began to look elsewhere for the solutions to their problems.

The Kansas Farmers Alliance provided the answer in 1888: direct political action through sponsoring slates of candidates. Kansas' success prompted the formation of the People's Party in Texas in August 1891.

The 1892 general election was one of the most spirited in the state's history. Conservative Democrats, after Gov. Hogg's supporters shut them out of the so-called roundhouse convention in Houston, bolted and nominated railroad attorney George Clark for the governorship. Populists for the first time had a presidential candidate, James Weaver, and a gubernatorial candidate, T.L. Nugent.

Texas Republicans also broke ranks. The party's strength centered in the black vote. After the death of former Gov. E.J. Davis in 1883, Norris Wright Cuney, a black, was the party leader. Cuney was considered one of the most astute politicians of the period, and he controlled federal patronage. White Republicans revolted against the black leadership, and these so-called "Lily-whites" nominated Andrew Jackson Houston, son of Sam Houston, for governor. Black Republicans recognized that, alone, their strength was limited, and throughout the latter part of the 19th century, they practiced fusion politics, backing candidates of third parties when they deemed it appropriate. Cuney led the Republicans into a coalition with the conservative Democrats in 1892, backing George Clark.

THE election also marked the first time that major Democratic candidates courted the black vote. Gov. Hogg's supporters organized black voter clubs, and the governor got about one-half of the black vote. Black farmers were in a quandary. Their financial problems were the same as those small farmers who backed the Populists. White Populists varied in their sympathy with the racial concerns of the blacks. On the local level, some whites showed sympathy with black concerns about education, voting and law enforcement. Minority farmers also were reluctant to abandon the Republican Party because it was their only political base in Texas.

Hogg was re-elected in 1892 with a 43 percent plurality in a field of four candidates.

During his second term, Hogg continued to try to correct abuses by the railroads. Transportation rates were based in part on railroads' investments. The governor charged during the campaign that railroads had watered their stock, meaning more was sold than necessary for operation. In the previous seven years, Hogg argued, railroad construction had been negligible, but railroad obligations had increased at a rate of $30 million a year. In addition, for rate purposes, railroads claimed outstanding stocks and bonds valued at $455,520,744, while for tax purposes, these same properties were valued at $63,000,000. In 1893, the Legislature gave the railroad commission authority to review new stock sales and to regulate the sales.

Populists continued to run well in state races until 1898. But historians have placed the beginning of the party's demise in the 1896 presidential election in which national Populists fused with the Democrats and supported William Jennings Bryan. This fusion weakened the demand for Macune's subtreasury plan, which would have created a new monetary system, in favor of the Democrats' "free silver" platform plank. Although the Populist philosophy lived on, the party declined in importance after the 1898 elections. Following a depression in the early 1890s, farm prices began to rise after a European crop failure in 1897, and gold discoveries in South Africa, Australia and Alaska helped relieve the currency shortage. Farmers remained active in politics, but most returned to the Democratic Party, which usurped many of the Populists' issues.

But Texas was on the brink of another revolution — an economic revolution that would forever change the face of the state.

Spindletop

SELDOM can a people's history be traced to a single event on a single day. But Texas' entrance into the industrial age can be linked directly to the discovery of oil at Spindletop, three miles from Beaumont, on Jan. 10, 1901. From that day, Texas' progress from a rural, agricultural state to a modern industrial giant has been steady.

The presence of oil near the salt domes along Texas' Gulf Coast had been suspected for many years. Patillo Higgins drilled wells near Spindletop for a decade before his resources were exhausted. In 1900, Higgins leased land to Anthony Lucas to prospect for oil.

Quicksand in the area presented a serious engineering problem to Higgins and to Lucas. But Lucas had experience with similar problems in Louisiana before coming to Texas. A telescoping system of casing, ranging from 12-inch pipe at the surface to four-inch pipe at the bottom of the hole was devised to keep the sand from filling the hole as it was dug. The Lucas No. 1 was spudded-in with a rotary rig in October 1900, and on the afternoon of Jan. 10, blew in. Initial production was estimated between 75,000 and 80,000 barrels of oil per day. Lucas was hardly prepared for the quantity of oil the well produced, and for several days, the oil flowed freely before the drilling crew could bring it under control. Oil was stored in earthen tanks when possible, but much simply was wasted.

Within days, the area was engulfed in Texas' first oil boom. Investors and con men from across the nation descended to enrich themselves in the hysterical activity that followed. Land values skyrocketed. Hundreds of wells were drilled as close together as possible. Little effort was made to stem the flow of oil until a disastrous fire struck the field in March 1901.

Spindletop was not the first oil strike in Texas. Even before Europeans came to the area, oil from seeps had been used by Indians for medicinal purposes. Early Spanish explorers used it as a lubricant and to caulk boats.

Lyne Barret drilled the first commercial well near Nacogdoches in 1866. But there were few uses for his product. Oil also was used to settle dust on public roads. But it was principally used as a lubricant and occasionally as a fuel. Barret's well at Oil Springs was 106 feet deep and produced 10 barrels of oil a day. The field was abandoned and reopened in 1887, though it was never commercially profitable.

Wells also were made in Brown County in 1878 and in Bexar County in 1886 before the first major commercial well was completed at Corsicana in 1894, when oil was struck while the city was drilling a water well. The first well was abandoned, but others soon were drilled. By 1898, Corsicana had 342 wells producing 500,000 barrels of oil a year. Joseph S. Cullinan, a former employee of Standard Oil, arrived in Corsicana in 1897 and developed an integrated oil operation. He constructed the state's first pipeline to serve a refinery he also built. Cullinan also was a champion of conservation, supporting an 1899 law that required abandoned wells to be plugged. He also demonstrated the value of petroleum as a locomotive fuel.

With the development of the Corsicana wells, Texas' oil production in 1900 was 836,000 barrels a year, about one-nineteenth of the total U.S. production.

Spindletop exceeded that production within a few days. In its first year of operation, the well produced 3.2 million barrels of oil. But the price also dropped to three cents a barrel. Desperately needed new markets for oil were soon forthcoming. Railroads were the first to recognize the advantage of the new, inexpensive resource. They soon began converting locomotives from coal to oil. Steamship lines followed suit, and many industries found great cost-saving advantages in fueling boilers with inexpensive oil rather than more expensive coal. Cattlemen even experimented with oil as a possi-

ble dip to rid cattle of the ticks that carried so-called Texas Fever, although it caused the animals to get too hot in the summer. These customers supported the industry until automobiles were in widespread use.

Railroad tank cars at first were used to haul oil, but by January 1902, a pipeline had been completed from Spindletop to the Neches River. Soon lines were constructed to points on the Gulf.

Several major oil companies also got their start with Spindletop. Cullinan came from Corsicana and with partners organized the Texas Fuel Co. in 1902 and erected a refinery at Port Arthur. The company grew into Texaco. Likewise, Gulf and Mobil also trace their beginnings to Texas' first major oil strike.

Oil strikes soon followed at Sour Lake and Humble, near Houston. In North Texas, W.T. Waggoner discovered oil in 1904 while drilling for water in Wichita County. The Petrolia Field also opened in 1904, and a few years later, the Electra Field was opened. In 1917, oil was discovered at Ranger in Eastland County. The boom days of Ranger were depicted in the movie "Boom Town," and it is probably the best known of the boom towns. Discoveries followed at Burkburnett, Breckenridge, Mexia and in West Texas.

Texas' oil production grew steadily until it reached 28 million in 1905 and then declined until 1910. Thereafter the growth resumed.

Until 1928, Texas vied with California and Oklahoma for oil production leadership in the United States. But Texas gained a lead that was never relinquished after the discovery of the East Texas Field by C.M. "Dad" Joiner in October 1930. Joiner's Daisy Bradford No. 3, drilled near Kilgore, was the first of 1,000 wells drilled in the field in a six-month period. In the first year, the East Texas Field yielded 100 million barrels of oil. When it was finally defined, the field proved to be 42 miles long, four to eight miles wide and covered 200 square miles. Virtually every acre produced oil.

Natural gas, which was often considered a nuisance and wasted, also was recognized as an important resource. In 1909, Lone Star Gas was organized and ran a pipeline to carry natural gas to Dallas and Fort Worth a year later. Within a few years, the state's major cities had access to this important fuel.

Progressivism

AFTER Jim Hogg left the governor's office in 1895, the reform movement waned. The flurry of passionate political activity during the late 1880s and early 1890s left Texans ready for a respite. Hogg's successor, Charles A. Culberson, was moderately progressive, but the character of the Legislature was changing. In 1890, about half the members were farmers, but by the turn of the century, two-thirds of the lawmakers were lawyers and businessmen. Also, the reform movement had almost brought the railroads to heel, and these were the most obvious extensions of growing corporate power in Texas.

Gov. Culberson's successors, Joseph D. Sayers and S.W.T. Lanham, the last Confederate veteran to serve as governor, were more conservative than Culberson. In 1901, Sayers had to cope with the tragic hurricane that destroyed Galveston in September, killing 6,000 people. In rebuilding from that disaster, Galveston's civic leaders fashioned the commission form of municipal government that was widely copied nationally. Amarillo later refined the system into the council-manager organization that is widely used today. And the great Galveston storm also reinforced arguments by Houston's leadership that an inland port should be built for protection against such tragedies and disruptions of trade. The Houston Ship Channel was soon to be a reality.

The reform spirit in government was not completely dead, however. In 1901, the Legislature prohibited the issuing of railroad passes to public officials. More than 270,000 passes were issued to officials that year, and farmers claimed that the free rides increased their freight rates and influenced public policy as well. In 1903, State Sen. A.W. Terrell got a major election reform law approved, a measure that was further modified two years later. A primary system was established to replace a hodge-podge of practices for nominating candidates that had led to charges of irregularities after each election. And the state, for the first time, imposed the

poll tax as a requisite for voting. Historians differ on whether the levy was designed to keep blacks or poor whites from voting. Certainly the poll tax cut election turnouts. Black voter participation dropped from about 100,000 in the 1890s to an estimated 5,000 in 1906. The Democratic State Executive Committee also recommended that county committees limit participation in primaries to whites only, and most accepted the suggestion.

Also in the reform spirit, the Legislature in 1903 prohibited abuse of child labor and set minimum ages at which children could work in certain industries. The action preceded federal child-labor laws by 13 years.

The election of Thomas M. Campbell as governor in 1906 introduced the progressive period in Texas politics. Interest revived in controlling corporate influence. Under Campbell, the state's anti-trust laws were strengthened and a pure food and drug law was passed. Texas took the lead of states with similar statutes, and the Robertson Insurance Law of 1907 also had a major impact. Life insurance companies were required to invest in Texas 75 percent of their reserves on policies in effect in the state. Less than one percent of the reserves had been invested in Texas prior to the law. Some companies left Texas. But the law was beneficial in the capital-starved economy. Texas' officials also vigorously prosecuted anti-trust cases, notably the Waters-Pierce Oil Co. suit, and the state was developing an anti-business reputation.

In 1904, voters amended the constitution to allow the state to charter banks for the first time in history, and this eased some of the farmers' credit problems. And in 1909, the Legislature approved a bank deposit insurance plan that predated the federal program of the 1930s.

The discovery of oil sparked an economic revolution. And other industries flourished. Lumbering entered a period of exceptional growth. In 1901, John H. Kirby organized the Kirby Lumber Co., capitalized with $10 million. The firm's mills developed a capacity to process more than 300 million board-feet of lumber a year. By 1900, Texas mills processed one billion board-feet of lumber a year, and three times in the next 20 years production topped two billion board-feet annually. The peak year was 1907 when almost 2.2 billion board feet were produced. By 1930, 18 million acres of Texas pineland had produced 60 billion board-feet of lumber over a 50-year period.

THE growth in lumber production, however, brought problems. Conservationists warned of overcutting as early as the 1880s. W. Goodrich Jones, called the "Father of Texas Forestry," organized the Texas Arbor Day and Forestry Association in 1889, and in 1914, Jones founded the Texas Forestry Association. Its successor, the Texas Forest Service, today is operated by Texas A&M University. After a boom during World War I, lumbering declined in Texas. Only 354 million board-feet were produced in 1932. The state's 14 million to 16 million acre virgin pine forests had been depleted to one million acres.

In addition, lumber companies also operated much like feudal barons. Isolated company towns were built around mills, and workers, about 40 percent of whom were black, were paid in merchandise checks that could be redeemed only at company stores. Union attempts to organize lumber workers were thwarted until the 1930s. Because lumbering was far removed from most of the state's population centers, little interest was aroused by the companies' practices.

With Campbell's election, the progressive era in Texas government was underway. The era is characterized by the attempt to improve both individuals and society through government action. In Texas, with the small corporate influence under acceptable control, attention turned to the moral issue of prohibition. Progressives and prohibitionists joined forces against the conservative establishment to exert a major influence in state government for the next two decades. The period also was dominated by the personality of Joseph W. Bailey, who served as U.S. Senator from 1901 to 1913. Bailey's ethics were called into question when he served as a counsel for oil companies while in the Senate. Although he was cleared of wrongdoing by a legislative investigation, Bailey did not seek re-election in 1912. And voters split along pro-Bailey and anti-Bailey lines for many years thereafter, depending on which side of a political issue the former senator took.

Prohibitionists had long been active in Texas. They had the local-option clause written into the Constitution of 1876, which allowed counties or their subdivisions to be voted dry. In 1887, a prohibition amendment to the constitution had been defeated by a two-to-one margin, and public attention had been turned to other problems. In the early 20th century, the movement gathered strength. Most of Texas already was dry because of local option. When voters rejected a prohibition amendment to the constitution by a slim margin in 1911, the state had 167 dry counties, 61 partially wet ones and 21 totally wet counties. The heavily populated counties, however, were wet. But prohibition continued to be a major issue.

In 1910, Oscar Colquitt, a wet, won a hard-fought campaign. His administration was progressive, but turbulent.

A quiet but significant event also occurred when Lt. Benjamin D. Foulois arrived in San Antonio in 1910 with a crated biplane. The young officer had three orders: assemble the plane; learn to fly it, and teach others to fly the machine. Foulois' arrival in the Texas city marks the beginning of American military aviation. In 1911, he flew the first military mission from Laredo to Eagle Pass in record time, and by 1919, regular patrols of the border were flown.

Problems along the U.S.-Mexico border escalated in 1911. The regime of Mexican President Porfirio Diaz became increasingly unpopular. Francisco Madero challenged Diaz for the presidency in 1910 and was imprisoned for a time during the campaign. He decided that only revolution would remove the unpopular dictator from office. Madero plotted his revolution from hideouts in San Antonio and Dallas and launched his rebellion in early 1911. Soon the revolutionaries controlled some northern Mexican states, including Chihuahua. Juarez and El Paso were major contact points. El Paso residents would stand on rooftops to observe the fighting between revolutionaries and government troops. And some Americans were killed.

A thin line often divided the true revolutionaries and outright bandits. The Lower Rio Grande Valley was particularly hard hit by renegades. After pleas to the federal government got no action, Gov. Colquitt sent state militia and Texas Rangers into the Valley in 1913 to protect Texans after Matamoros fell to the rebels. Unfortunately, the Rangers killed many innocent Mexican-Texans during the operation. In addition to problems caused by the fighting and raids, thousands of Mexican refugees flooded Texas border towns to escape the violence of the revolution.

Texas progressives became prominent nationally in the presidential election of 1912. Several Texans had quietly urged New Jersey Gov. Woodrow Wilson to seek the presidency, and in the precinct caucuses of 1912, progressives gained control of the party. Texas' delegation to the national Democratic convention in Baltimore was instructed to vote for Wilson as long as his name was in nomination. Through 46 ballots, the "Immortal Forty" stuck with Wilson until he received the Democratic nomination. And Texas overwhelmingly supported Wilson at the polls. E. M. House, who had been active behind the scenes in Texas politics since Jim Hogg's second campaign in 1892, became a close personal adviser to President Wilson, and three Texans served in the cabinet: Postmaster Albert Sidney Burleson, Attorney General Thomas Watt Gregory and Secretary of Agriculture David Houston.

Also in 1912, Texans selected a U.S. Senator at the ballot box for the first time. The Terrell Election Law required a preferential primary for all offices, although the Legislature still officially appointed U.S. Senators. In 1906 and 1910, incumbents had not been opposed. But when Joseph Bailey declined to seek re-election in 1912, Morris Sheppard received a plurality of the popular vote. Runoffs were not required at the time. In early 1913, Gov. Colquitt recommended that the Legislature honor R.M.Johnson, a newspaper publisher and long-time conservative Democrat, by appointing him to Sen. Bailey's unserved term. Johnson was appointed senator, but served only 26 days. Sheppard's supporters argued that he should get the early appointment to gain valuable seniority over other freshmen senators, and the Legislature agreed.

In 1914, James E. Ferguson entered Texas politics, and for the next three decades, "Farmer Jim" was one of the most dominating and colorful figures on the political stage. A banker in Temple, Ferguson entered the 1914 gubernatorial campaign after a friend turned down the race. Ferguson skirted the prohibition issue by pledging to veto any legislation pertaining to alcoholic beverages. His strength was in the farming community, however. Sixty-two percent of Texas' farmers were tenants, and the candidate pledged to back legislation to limit tenant rents. Ferguson also was a dynamic orator. He easily won the primary and rolled over three opponents in the general election.

Ferguson's first administration was successful. The Legislature passed the law limiting tenants' rents, although it was poorly enforced. And aid to rural schools was improved. In early 1915, the border problems heated up. A Mexican national was arrested in Cameron County carrying a so-called "Plan of San Diego." The document outlined plans to create a rebellion of Mexican-Americans, Indians, Japanese and blacks in Texas and the Southwest. Once all Anglo males over age 16 were eliminated, a new republic controlled by blacks would be created to serve as a buffer between the United States and Mexico. Authorship of the plan has never been determined, but whatever its intent, it started a bloodbath in the Lower Rio Grande Valley. Mexican soldiers participated in raids across the Rio Grande, and Gov. Ferguson sent in the Rangers. Historians differ on the number of people who lost their lives, but a safe assessment would be "hundreds." Tensions were raised so high that Gov. Ferguson and Mexican President Venustiano Carranza met at Nuevo Laredo in November 1915 to improve relations. But the raids continued.

PANCHO Villa raided Columbus, N.M., in early 1916, and two small Texas villages in the Big Bend, Glenn Springs and Bouquillas, also were attacked. In July, President Wilson determined the hostilities were critical and activated the National Guard. Soon 100,000 American troops were stationed along the border. Fort Bliss in El Paso housed 60,000 men, and Fort Duncan near Eagle Pass was home to 16,000 more.

With the exception of Gen. John J. Pershing's pursuit of Villa into Northern Mexico, few American troops crossed into Mexico. But the service along the border gave soldiers basic training that was put to use when the United States entered World War I in 1917.

An era ended when these veterans of the Battle of San Jacinto met in Goliad in 1906, 70 years after the historical clash with Mexican troops. The following year there were not enough survivors to hold a reunion.

All of Texas responded with aid when Galveston was hit by a hurricane in 1900. More than 6,000 people were killed in this disaster, which was one of the worst in the history of the United States.

These pictures represent two periods in Texas history. Above (l-r) C. M. "Dad" Joiner shakes hands with geologist A. D. Lloyd after the discovery of the giant East Texas oil field in 1930. Photo from Mid-Continent Oil and Gas Association. Below, the fruits of a raid on a still in Gonzales County are on display. Such raids and results were common in Texas during the Prohibition era that began in 1919.

Gov. Ferguson was easily re-elected in 1916, and he worked well with the Legislature the following year. But after the Legislature adjourned, the governor got into a dispute with the board of regents of the University of Texas. The disagreement culminated with the governor vetoing all appropriations for the school. As the controversy swirled, the Travis County grand jury indicted Gov. Ferguson for misappropriation of funds and for embezzlement. In July 1917, Speaker of the Texas House F. O. Fuller called a special session of the Legislature to consider impeachment of the governor. Although the state constitution provides that only the governor can call special sessions, the attorney general said that it was appropriate for the speaker to call a session on impeachment. The Texas House voted 21 articles of impeachment, and the Senate in August 1917 convicted Ferguson on 10 of the charges. The Senate's judgment not only removed Ferguson from office, but barred him from seeking office again. Ferguson resigned the day before the Senate rendered the decision in an attempt to avoid the prohibition against seeking further office.

Lt. Gov. Will Hobby of Houston became governor. His first order of business was to mobilize Texas to fight in World War I.

War and Reaction

WILL Hobby immediately turned his attention to Texas' war effort after assuming the governorship following Ferguson's removal. Ferguson had appointed a Council of Defense to guide the state's war activities. It helped the Red Cross, conducted war-bond drives and aided in drought relief. The council also became involved in some anti-German and anti-pacifist activities that developed.

Texas participated actively in the war. Almost 200,000 young Texans, including 31,000 blacks, volunteered for military service, and 450 Texas women served in the nurses' corps. Five thousand lost their lives overseas, either fighting or in the influenza epidemics that swept the military. Texas also was a major training ground during the conflict, with 250,000 soldiers getting basic training in the state.

On the negative side, the war frenzy opened a period of intolerance and nativism in the state. German-Texans were suspect because of their national ancestry. A law was passed to prohibit speaking against the war effort. Persons who failed to participate in patriotic activities often were punished. Gov. Hobby even vetoed the appropriation for the German department at the University of Texas.

Ferguson's removal from office was a devastating blow to the state's antiprohibitionists. It was learned that the former governor had received a $156,000 loan from members of the brewers' association while in office. And this provided ammunition for the progressives. Here was an industry that had not been brought under control. With so many young men receiving military training in the state, prohibitionists proposed to prohibit saloons within a 10-mile radius of military posts to protect the soldiers from the temptations of alcohol and vice. One critic said that step alone would dry up 90 percent of the state. The measure was approved in a special session in February 1918, and at the same time, the national prohibition amendment, which had been introduced in Congress by Texas Sen. Morris Sheppard, was ratified by the lawmakers. Women also were given the right to vote in the state primaries at the same session.

Hobby easily won election to a full term as governor in 1918, and progressives and prohibitionists gained control of the Legislature.

Although national prohibition was to become effective in early 1920, the Legislature presented a prohibition amendment to voters in May 1919, and it was approved, bringing prohibition to Texas earlier than to the rest of the nation. At the same time, a women's suffrage amendment was defeated.

Although World War I ended in November 1918, it brought many changes to Texas. Rising prices during the war had increased the militancy of labor unions. Open Shop Associations were organized in many cities. And in 1921, Gov. Hobby declared martial law and called out state troops to end a dock strike in Galveston. Blacks also became more militant after the war. Discrimination against black soldiers led in 1917 to a riot in Houston in which several people were killed.

Federal courts stripped the Texas Railroad Commission of its authority to regulate interstate rates in the "Shreveport case" in 1914. The commission had set up a rate structure for goods entering Texas from Louisiana that had been detrimental to Shreveport merchants. The commission was given additional regulatory responsibility with the approval of a constitutional amendment in 1917 authorizing the state to regulate natural resources. The state also changed a long-standing policy that prohibited companies from operating in more than one field in their industry. Major oil companies needed integrated operations in which they could produce, transport, refine and sell petroleum products, and they lobbied to have the restrictive laws repealed. Finally the lawmakers agreed, and in another move, the Legislature in 1919 also prohibited the waste of natural resources, especially oil, and authorized the railroad commission to regulate pipelines, which carried petroleum. Although the commission approved a rule in 1920 that regulated the spacing of oil wells (Rule 37), little more was done. The oil industry was doing well in Texas, and everyone concerned left well enough alone.

With the election of Mexican President Alvaro Obregon in 1920, the fighting along the U.S.-Mexican border subsided. Although mistrust between the Mexicans and Texans remained for many years, a cohesive social intercourse developed. In 1919, State Rep. J. T. Canales of Brownsville instigated an investigation of the Texas Rangers' role in the border problems. As a result of the study, the Rangers' manpower was reduced from 1,000 members to 76, and stringent limitations were placed on the agency's activities. Standards for members of the force also were upgraded. Later the Rangers were merged with the highway patrol to form the Department of Public Safety.

Pat M. Neff won the gubernatorial election of 1920, beating former Sen. Bailey. Neff visited 152 counties and made 850 speeches in his campaign. As a former prosecuting attorney in McLennan County, Neff made law and order the major thrust of his administration. Like many governors of the period, Neff was more progressive than the Legislature, and his program often fared poorly. During his administration, however, the state took full responsibility for developing a highway system. And a gasoline tax was imposed. A state park board also was established, and Neff's mother donated 10 acres of land near McGregor for the state's first park. In 1921, a group of West Texans threatened to form a new state because Neff vetoed the creation of a new college in their area. Two years later, Texas Tech College was authorized in Lubbock and opened its doors in 1925.

NEFF had problems with the Legislature. Since 1907, it had become the lawmakers' practice not to pass an appropriations bill in the regular session. They were paid $5 a day for the first 60 days of the session, and only $2 a day thereafter. But they received $5 a day in special sessions. In addition, they got travel allowances when returning home between sessions. Neff called the lawmakers into special session the day after the regular session ended in March 1923, but the lawmakers met for only one hour and adjourned, ending what may have been the shortest legislative session anywhere.

Although still predominantly a rural state, Texas cities were growing. In 1900, only 17 percent of the population lived in urban areas; by 1920, that figure had almost doubled to 32 percent. A discontent developed with the growth of the cities. Rural Texans had long seen cities as hotbeds of vice and immorality. Simple rural values were cherished, and it seemed that these values were threatened in a changing world. After World War I, this transition accelerated. In addition, "foreigners" in the state became suspect; nativism reasserted itself. The German-Texans were associated with the enemy in the war, and Mexican-Texans were mostly of the Roman Catholic religion and likened to the troublemakers along the border. Texas was a fertile ground for the new Ku Klux Klan that entered the state in late 1920. The Klan's philosophy was a mixture of patriotism, law-and-order, nativism, white supremacy and Victorian morals. Its influence spread quickly across the state, and reports of Klan violence and murder were rampant.

Prohibition had brought a widespread disrespect for law. Peace officers and other officials often ignored speakeasies, gambling and other vice. The Klan seemed to many Texans to be an appropriate instrument for restoring law and order and for maintaining Victorian morality in towns and cities. By 1922, many of the state's large communities were under direct Klan influence. Between 1922 and 1924 in Dallas, for example, the Klan controlled every public office in city and county government. Opposition was raised, but it was ineffective in the early stages of the development of the Klan.

In 1922, a Klan-backed candidate, Earle Mayfield, was elected to the U.S. Senate from Texas, and the state gained the reputation as the most powerful Klan bastion in the Union. Hiram Wesley Evans of Dallas also was elected imperial wizard of the national Klan in that year.

Gov. Neff never denounced the Klan by name, although he did deplore violence in any form. Once when the governor was out of the state, Lt. Gov. T. Whitfield Davidson ordered the Rangers to investigate a Klan murder. Neff concurred in the order, but soon the investigation was dropped.

After 1922, the Klan became more directly involved in politics and planned to elect the next governor in 1924. Judge Felix Robertson of Dallas got the organization's backing in the Democratic primary. Former governor Ferguson filed to run for the office, but the Texas Supreme Court ruled that he could not because of the impeachment conviction. So Ferguson placed his wife, Miriam A. Ferguson, on the ballot. Several other prominent Democrats also entered the race.

As soon as Mrs. Ferguson entered the race, she was dubbed "Ma" from the initials of her first and middle names. And she ran a vigorous campaign, although it was her husband's oratory that attracted the crowds, particularly in rural areas. The Fergusons made no secret that Jim would have a big influence on his wife's administration. One campaign slogan was, "Two governors for the price of one." Mrs. Ferguson surprised most observers by finishing second to Robertson in the first primary. And she easily won the runoff when many Texans decided that "Fergusonism" was preferable to the Klan in the governor's office.

Minorities began organizing in Texas to seek their civil rights. The National Association for the Advancement of Colored People opened a Texas chapter in 1912, and by 1919, there were chapters in 31 Texas communities. Similarly, Mexican-Texans formed Orden Hijos de America in 1921, and in 1927, the League of Latin-American Citizens was organized.

The Klan also dominated the Legislature in 1923, and a law passed that year barring blacks from participation in the Democratic primary had been passed. Although blacks had in fact been barred from voting in primaries for years, this law gave Dr. Lawrence A. Nixon, a black dentist from El Paso, the opportunity to go to court to fight the all-white primary. In 1927, the U.S. Supreme Court overturned the statute, but that was only the beginning of several court battles — which were not resolved until 1944, when blacks were finally accorded the right to vote in Democratic primaries.

Disgruntled Democrats and Klansmen tried to beat Mrs. Ferguson in the general election, but although George Butte, the Republican nominee, did better than any other candidate running against a Democrat in many years, Ma Ferguson became governor of Texas. Voters also sent 91 new members to the Texas House, purging it of many of the Klan-backed representatives. After the 1924 election, the Klan's power ebbed rapidly in Texas.

Mrs. Ferguson named Emma Grigsby Meharg as Texas' first woman secretary of state in 1925. The governors Ferguson administration was stormy. Jim was accused of cronyism in awarding highway contracts and in other matters. And "Ma" returned to her husband's practice of liberal clemency for prisoners. In two years, Mrs. Ferguson extended clemency to 3,595 inmates.

Although Jim Ferguson was at his bombastic best in the 1926 Democratic primary, young Attorney General Dan Moody had little trouble winning the nomination and the general election. Texas Republicans in a unique twist held their first primary in 1926 because of Butte's showing against Mrs. Ferguson two years earlier. Political parties were required to hold primaries if they polled more than 100,000 votes in the previous general election.

At age 33, Moody was the youngest person ever to become governor of Texas. Like many of the state's governors, he was more progressive than the Legislature, and much of his program did not pass. Moody was successful in some government reorganization. He also cleaned up the highway department, which had been criticized under the Fergusons, and abandoned the liberal clemency policy for prisoners. And Moody worked at changing Texas' image as an anti-business state. "The day of the political trust-buster is gone," he told one Eastern journalist.

PROGRESSIVES and prohibitionists still had a major influence on the Democratic Party, and 1928 was a watershed year for them. Moody easily won re-nomination and re-election. But the state party was drifting away from the direction of national Democrats. Big-city politicians and political machines controlled by recent immigrants gained influence in the national party. Their political positions and apparent values were foreign to many Texans. When Al Smith, a wet and a Roman Catholic, won the presidential nomination at the national Democratic convention in Houston, Texans were hard-pressed to remain faithful to the "party of the fathers." Moody, who had been considered a potential national figure, ruined his political career trying to straddle the fence, angering both wets and drys, Catholics and Protestants. Former governor Colquitt led an exodus of so-called "Hoovercrats" from the state Democratic convention in 1928, and for the first time in its history, Texas gave its electoral votes to a Republican, Herbert Hoover, in the general election.

Through the 1920s, oil continued to increase in importance in Texas' economy. New discoveries were made at Mexia in 1920, Luling in 1922, Big Lake in Reagan County in 1923, in the Wortham Field in 1924 and in Borger in 1926. But oil still did not dominate the state's economic life.

As late as 1929, meat packing, cottonseed processing and various milling operations exceeded the added value of petroleum refining. And as the 1920s ended, lumbering and food processing shared major economic roles with the petroleum industry. During the decade, Texas grew between 35-42 percent of U.S. cotton and 20-30 percent of the world crop. Irrigation and mechanization opened new areas of Texas to cotton production. In 1918, the U.S. Department of Agriculture reported 50,588 bales of cotton grown on the Texas Plains. Eight years later, more than 1.1 million bales were grown in the region, mostly around Lubbock.

But Texas with the rest of the nation was on the threshhold of a major economic disaster that would have irreversible consequences. The Great Depression was at hand.

Depression and War

TEXAS suffered with the rest of the nation through the Great Depression of the 1930s. Historians have noted that the state's economic collapse was not as severe, however, as that which struck the industrialized states. Texas' economy had sputtered through the decade of the 1920s, primarily because of the fluctuation of the price of cotton and other agricultural products. But agricultural prices were improving toward the end of the decade.

The Fergusons attempted a political comeback in the gubernatorial election of 1930. But Texans elected Ross S. Sterling, the founder of Humble Oil Co. and a successful businessman. Early in the Depression, Texans remained optimistic that the economic problems were temporary, another of the cyclical downturns the nation experienced periodically. Indeed, some Texans even felt that the hardships would be beneficial, ridding the economy of speculators and poor businessmen. Those attitudes gave way to increasing concern as the poor business conditions dragged on.

A piece of good luck turned into a near economic disaster for the state in late 1930. C. M. "Dad" Joiner struck oil near Kilgore, and soon the East Texas oil boom was in full swing. Thousands of wells were drilled. Millions of barrels of new oil flooded the market, making producers and small landowners wealthy. The major oil companies had been caught by surprise by the large discovery. They owned only 20 percent of the producing leases in the region. Independent oil operators discovered the field and did most of the development. Soon the glut of new oil drove market prices down from $1.10 a barrel in 1930 to 10 cents in 1931. Around the state many wells had to be shut in because they could not produce oil profitably at the low prices. The major companies also saw their reserves in other parts of the state losing value because of the declining prices.

THE railroad commission attempted to control production through proration, which assigned production quotas to each well. The first proration order limited each well to about 1,000 barrels a day of production. Proration had two goals: To protect reserves through conservation and to maintain prices by limiting production. In August 1931, the Legislature approved a statute prohibiting the commission from prorating production to market demand. For several months, the railroad commission was hard-pressed to control production, facing resistance from producers as well as adverse court rulings. In February 1931, Gov. Sterling sent state troops into the East Texas Field to maintain order and to force compliance with the proration orders. A federal court later ruled the governor's actions illegal. Gov. Sterling was roundly criticized for sending troops into East Texas. Opponents said the action was taken to aid the major oil companies to the disadvantage of independent producers. Finally, in April 1933, the railroad commission prorated production on the basis, in part, of bottom-hole pressure in each well, and the courts upheld this approach. In Washington, Texas Sen. Tom Connally authored the Hot Oil Act, which involved the federal government in regulation by prohibiting oil produced in violation of state law from being sold in interstate commerce. Thereafter, Texas' producers accepted the concept of proration. Since Texas was the nation's largest oil producer, the railroad commission could set the national price of oil through proration for several decades thereafter.

Despite the problems, the oil boom helped East Texas weather the Depression better than other sections of the state. Farmers were hit particularly hard by 1931. Bumper crops had produced the familiar reduction in prices. Cotton dropped from 18 cents per pound in 1928 to six cents in 1931. That year Louisiana Gov. Huey Long proposed a ban on growing cotton in 1932 to eliminate the surplus. The Louisiana legislature enacted the ban, but Texas was the key state to the plan since it led the nation in cotton production. Gov. Sterling was cool to the idea, but responded to public support of it by calling a special session of the Legislature. The lawmakers passed a cotton acreage limitation bill in 1931, but the law was declared unconstitutional the following year.

Government statistics on unemployment in the period are incomplete, but in February 1932, Gov. Sterling estimated that 300,000 Texans were out of work. Many of them were destitute. One feature of the Depression had become the number of transients drifting from city to city looking for work. Local governments and private agencies tried to provide relief for the unemployed, but the effort was soon overwhelmed by the number of persons needing help. In Houston, blacks and Mexican-Texans were warned not to apply for relief because there was not enough money to take care of whites, and many Hispanics returned to Mexico voluntarily and otherwise. To relieve the local governments, Gov. Sterling proposed a bond program to repay counties for highways they had built and to start a public works program. Texans' long-held faith in self-reliance and rugged individualism was put to a severe test. As optimism faded, attempts were made to find a scapegoat. President Hoover and the Republican Party were the likely choices. The party had taken credit for the economic prosperity that the nation had enjoyed in the 1920s; but it had to assume responsibility for the collapse as well. Many Texans felt guilty about abandoning the Democratic Party in 1928. By 1932, many were looking to the federal government to provide relief from the effects of the Depression.

Texas Congressman John Nance Garner was a presidential candidate when the Democrats held their national convention. To avoid a deadlocked convention, Garner maneuvered the Texans to change strategy. On the fourth ballot, the Texas delegation voted for the eventual nominee, New York Gov. Franklin D. Roosevelt. Garner got the second place on the ticket that swept into office in the general election.

In Texas, Miriam Ferguson was successful in unseating Gov. Sterling in the Democratic primary, winning by about 4,000 votes. Her second administration was less turbulent than the first. State government costs were reduced, and voters approved $20 million in so-called "bread bonds" to help provide relief. In 1933, horse-racing came to the state, authorized through a rider on an appropriations bill. The law was repealed in 1937. Prohibition also was repealed in 1933, although much of Texas remained dry under the local-option laws and the prohibition against open saloons. State government faced a series of financial problems during Mrs. Ferguson's second term. The annual deficit climbed to $14 million, and the state had to default on the interest payments on some bonds. Voters aggravated the situation by approving a $3,000 homestead exemption. Many property owners were losing their homes because they could not pay taxes. And while the exemption saved their homesteads, it worsened the state's financial problems.

Many Texas banks failed during the Depression, as did banks nationally. One of Roosevelt's first actions was to declare a national bank holiday in 1933. Gov. Ferguson closed state banks at the same time, although she had to "assume" authority that was not in the law.

In Washington, Texans played an important role in shaping Roosevelt's New Deal. As vice president, Garner presided over the Senate and maneuvered legislation through the upper house. Texans also chaired six major committees in the House: Sam Rayburn, Interstate and Foreign Commerce; Hatton W. Sumners, Judiciary; Fritz G. Lanham, Public Buildings and Grounds; J.J. Mansfield, Rivers and Harbors, and James P. Buchanan, Appropriations. With this influence, the Texas delegation supported the president's early social programs. In addition, Jesse Jones of Houston served as director of the Reconstruction Finance Corporation, the Federal Loan Administration and as Secretary of Commerce. Jones was one of the most influential men in Washington and second only to Roosevelt in wielding financial power to effect recovery.

As the New Deal developed, Texas benefited. Almost $1.5 billion was pumped into the state's economy in the early years of President Roosevelt's program. Farmers benefited from higher incomes, though they had restrictions placed on production. Ironically, the Agricultural Adjustment Act fulfilled many of the Populists' demands of a half-century earlier by providing price protection, an expanded money supply and easy farm credit. The Federal Emergency Relief Administration, created in 1933, provided aid for up to 298,000 people a year between 1933 and 1935. And the lumber industry, which had deteriorated in the late 1920s, rebounded, as the Civilian Conservation Corps, created to provide jobs for young people, aided in replanting many acres of depleted forest lands. By 1939, the industry was producing one billion board feet of lumber again, after dropping to almost one-third that volume in 1932.

The aid to farmers and cattlemen was particularly timely because the state began to experience another cycle of drought. Poor conservation practices had left many of the state's farmlands open to erosion. During the Dust Bowl days of the early- and mid-1930s, for example, the weather bureau in Amarillo reported 192 dust storms within a three-year period. Cooperation between state and federal agencies helped improve farmers' conservation efforts and reduced the erosion problem by the end of the decade.

Although the New Deal provided economic relief for many Texans, the state became divided politically over the thrust of the program late in the 1930s. In 1937, the break became most apparent. Frustrated that the U.S. Supreme Court had declared many of the New Deal programs to be unconstitutional, President Roosevelt proposed that the membership of the court be enlarged to allow him to appoint a new majority. Vice-President Garner adamantly opposed the so-called "court-packing" plan, as did many elected officials in Texas. Although public officials' criticism became vitriolic, Roosevelt remained popular with voters, carrying the state in 1940, after Garner left the vice presidency, and in 1944.

MRS. Ferguson did not seek re-election in 1934, and Attorney General James V. Allred was elected. Under his administration, several social welfare programs were initiated, including old-age pensions, teachers' retirement and workmen's compensation. Allred also signed legislation that created the Texas Centennial celebration, marking a century of independence from Mexico. It was hoped that the Centennial would generate jobs and money. Allred was re-elected in 1936.

Some of the New Deal's luster also dimmed when the nation was struck by another recession in 1937. Although Texas' economic condition improved toward the end of the decade, a full recovery was not realized until the beginning of World War II — when the state went through another industrial revolution.

In 1938, voters elected one of the most colorful figures in the state's political history to the governor's office. W. Lee "Pappy" O'Daniel, a flour salesman and leader of a radio hillbilly band, came from nowhere to defeat a field of much better known candidates in the Democratic primary and to easily win the general election. When re-elected two years later, O'Daniel became the first candidate to poll more than one million votes in a Texas election.

But O'Daniel's skills of state did not equal his campaigning ability, and throughout his administration, the governor and the Legislature were in conflict. In early 1941, long-time U.S. Senator Morris Sheppard died, and O'Daniel wanted the office. He appointed Andrew Jackson Houston, Sam Houston's aged son, to fill the vacancy. Houston died after only 24 days in office. O'Daniel won the special election for the post and was elected to a full term in 1942 in a close race with a young congressman, Lyndon B. Johnson.

Lt. Gov. Coke R. Stevenson succeeded O'Daniel and brought a broad knowledge of government to the office. Stevenson was elected to two full terms as governor. Thanks to frugal management and greatly increasing revenues during the war years, he left the state treasury with a surplus in 1947. Voters also solved the continuing deficit problem by approving a pay-as-you-go amendment to the constitution in 1942. It requires the state comptroller to certify that tax revenues will be available to support appropriations. Otherwise the money cannot be spent.

After the Japanese bombed Pearl Harbor on Dec. 7, 1941, Texans were in the forefront of the World War II effort. Texas Sen. Tom Connally, chairman of the Foreign Relations Committee, introduced the resolution declaring war on Japan on Dec. 8.

As in every war fought by the United States after Texas entered the Union, young Texans flocked to military service. More than 750,000 served, including 12,000 women in the auxiliary services. In December 1942, U.S. Secretary of the Navy Frank Knox said Texas contributed the largest percentage of its male population to the armed forces of any state. Thirty Texans won Congressional Medals of Honor in the fighting, and Audie Murphy, a young farm boy from Farmersville, was the most decorated soldier in the war.

Important contributions also were made at home. Texas was the site of 15 training posts, at which more than one and a quarter million men were trained, and of several prisoner-of-war camps.

Texas industry also flourished. Between mid-1940 and the peak of wartime production activity in November 1943, the number of manufacturing workers in Texas rose from 185,000 to 443,000. New industries that started up during the period included aircraft construction, ordnance and primary metals. Shipbuilders on the Texas Gulf coast employed 96,000 workers, and the aircraft industries employed 82,000. The state's petrochemical industry also expanded.

Between 1919 and 1939, Texas' manufacturing grew at a rate of 4.06 percent a year; in the next 15 years, the growth rate would accelerate to 9.38 percent annually. World War II changed the face of the world, but probably no region was affected more than Texas. The state was on the threshhold of becoming one of the nation's industrial giants.

Post-War Texas

WORLD War II irrevocably changed the face of Texas. During the decade of the 1940s, the state's population switched from predominantly rural to 60 percent urban. The number of manufacturing workers almost doubled. And as had been the dream of Texas leaders for more than a century, the state began to attract outside investment and new industry.

The state's politics became increasingly controlled by conservative Democrats after Gov. Allred left office. In 1946, Beauford H. Jester, a member of the railroad commission, gained the governorship. Under Jester in 1947, the Legislature passed the state's right-to-work law, prohibiting mandatory union membership, and reorganized public education with passage of the Gilmer-Aikin Act.

In 1948, Sen. W. Lee O'Daniel did not seek re-election. Congressman Lyndon Johnson and former Gov. Coke Stevenson vied for the Democratic nomination. In the runoff, Johnson won by a mere 87 votes in the closest — and most hotly disputed — statewide election in Texas' history. Johnson quickly rose to a leadership position in the U.S. Senate, and, with House Speaker Sam Rayburn, gave Texas substantial influence in national political affairs.

Although re-elected in 1948, Jester died in July 1949, the only Texas governor to die in office, and Lt. Gov. Allan Shivers succeeded him. During Shivers' administration, state spending more than doubled, reaching $805.7 million in 1956, as the governor increased appropriations for eleemosynary institutions, school salaries, retirement benefits, highways and old-age pensions. The 51st Legislature met for a total of 177 days in regular and special sessions in 1947, a record at the time.

Shivers broke with tradition, successfully winning three full terms as governor after completing Jester's unexpired term. Shivers also led a revolt by Texas Democrats against the national party in 1952. The governor, who gained both the Democratic and Republican nominations for the office under the law that allowed cross-filing that year, supported Republican Dwight Eisenhower for the presidency. Many Texas Democrats broke with the national party over the so-called "Tidelands issue." Texas claimed land 12 miles out into the Gulf as state lands. The issue was important because revenue from oil and natural gas production from the area supported public education in the state. Major oil companies also backed Texas' position because state royalties on minerals produced from the land were much lower than federal royalties. President Harry S.

Truman vetoed legislation that would have given Texas title to the land. Democratic presidential nominee Adlai Stevenson was no more sympathetic to the issue, and Texas gave its electoral votes to Republican Dwight Eisenhower in an election that attracted a two million-vote turnout for the first time in Texas. President Eisenhower signed a measure into law guaranteeing Texas' tidelands.

Scandal struck state government in 1954 when irregularities were discovered in the handling of funds in the veterans' land program in the General Land Office. Land Commissioner Bascom Giles was convicted of several charges and sent to prison. Several insurance companies also went bankrupt in the mid-1950s, prompting a reorganization of the State Board of Insurance in 1957.

In 1954, the U.S. Supreme Court ruled unconstitutional the segregation of schools, and for the next quarter-century, school integration became a major political issue. By the late 1960s, most institutions were integrated, but the state's major cities continued to wage court battles against forced busing of students to attain racial balance. Blacks and Mexican-Texans also made gains in voting rights during the 1950s.

Shivers had easily defeated Ralph W. Yarborough in the Democratic primary in 1952, but the divisions between the party's loyalists and those who bolted ranks to join Republicans in presidential races were growing. Shivers barely led the first 1954 primary over Yarborough and won the nomination with 53 percent of the vote in the runoff. Yarborough ran an equally close race against Price Daniel, a U.S. Senator who sought the governorship in 1956. Upon election as governor, Daniel left the Senate, and Yarborough won a special election to fill the vacancy in 1957. William A. Blakley, whom Yarborough defeated, had been appointed to the Senate seat by Shivers. In 1961, Blakley also was appointed to fill the vacancy created by Sen. Lyndon B. Johnson's election to the vice presidency. Blakley has the distinction of serving in both the Rusk and Houston successions in the Senate. Yarborough beat Blakley for a full term in 1958 and won re-election in 1964 before losing to Lloyd Bentsen in 1970 in the Democratic primary. Although a liberal, Yarborough proved to be unusually durable in Texas' conservative political climate.

The state budget topped $1 billion for the first time in 1958. A year later, a financial crisis gripped state government. Three special sessions were needed for the lawmakers to agree on a record appropriations bill. In 1960, voters approved a constitutional amendment that limited regular sessions to 140 days. The Legislature met for 205 days in regular and special sessions in 1961-62 and levied, over Gov. Daniel's opposition, the state's first broad-based sales tax in 1962.

THROUGH the 1950s and 1960s, Texas' industrial base had expanded and diversified. Petroleum exploration, production, transportation and refining remained the cornerstones, but other industries grew. Attracted by cheap electricity, the aluminum industry came to Texas after World War II. Starting from the base developed during World War II, defense industries and associated high-tech firms, specializing in electronics and computers, centered on the Dallas-Fort Worth area and Houston. One of the most important scientific breakthroughs of the century came in 1959 in Dallas. Jack Kilby, an engineer at Texas Instruments, developed and patented the microchip that became the central part of the computers of the 1980s.

Sen. Lyndon Johnson unsuccessfully sought the Democratic presidential nomination in 1960, and John F. Kennedy subsequently selected the Texan as his running mate. Johnson is credited with keeping several Southern states, including Texas, in the Democratic column in the close election. Kennedy was a Roman Catholic and a liberal, a combination normally rejected by the Southern states. When Johnson left the Senate to assume his new office in 1961, John Tower won a special election that attracted more than 70 candidates and became the first Republican since Reconstruction to serve as a Texas Senator.

During the early 1960s, Harris County was chosen as the site for the National Aeronautics and Space Administration's manned spacecraft center, now the Lyndon B. Johnson Space Center. The acquisition of the facility further diversified Texas' industrial base.

In 1962, John B. Connally, a former aide to Vice President Johnson and Secretary of the Navy under Kennedy, returned to Texas to seek the governorship. Gov. Daniel sought an unprecedented fourth term and was defeated in the Democratic primary. Connally won a close Democratic runoff over Don Yarborough and was elected easily. As governor, Connally concentrated on improving public education and state services and water development. He was re-elected in 1964 and 1966.

One of the major tragedies in the nation's history occurred in Dallas on Nov. 22, 1963, when President Kennedy was assassinated while riding in a motorcade. Gov. Connally also was seriously wounded. Lyndon B. Johnson was administered the oath of the presidency by Federal Judge Sarah T. Hughes of Dallas aboard Air Force One at Love Field. Lee Harvey Oswald was arrested for the murder of the president on the afternoon of the assassination, but Oswald was killed by Dallas nightclub operator Jack Ruby the following day. An extensive investigation into the assassination of President Kennedy was conducted by the Warren Commission. The panel concluded that Oswald was the killer and that he acted alone. Ruby, who was convicted of killing Oswald, died of cancer in the Dallas County jail in 1967 while the case was being appealed.

The assassination damaged the Republican Party in Texas, however. Building strength in Texas' conservative political atmosphere in 1962, eight Republicans, the most in decades, had been elected to the Texas House. And two Republicans — Ed Foreman of Odessa and Bruce Alger of Dallas — served in Congress. All were defeated in the 1964 general election.

In the emotional aftermath of the tragedy, Johnson, who won the presidency outright in a landslide election in 1964, persuaded the Congress to pass a series of civil rights and social welfare programs that changed the face of the nation. Texas was particularly hard hit by the civil rights legislation and a series of lawsuits challenging election practices. During the 1960s, the state constitutional limitation of urban representation in the Legislature was overturned. The poll tax was declared unconstitutional, and the practice of electing officials from at-large districts fell to the so-called "one-man, one-vote" ruling. As a result, more Republican, minority and liberal officials were elected, particularly from urban areas. In 1966, Curtis Graves and Barbara Jordan of Houston and Joe Lockridge of Dallas became the first blacks to serve in the Texas Legislature since 1898.

Lyndon Johnson did not seek re-election in 1968. The nation had become involved in an unpopular war in South Vietnam, and Johnson bowed out of the race in the interest of national unity. Democrats, however, stayed firmly in control of state government. Preston Smith was elected governor, and Ben Barnes gained the

lieutenant governorship. Both also were re-elected in 1970. Although state spending continued to increase, particularly on education, the Legislature otherwise was quiet. A minimum-wage law was approved, and public kindergartens were authorized in 1969. At a special session, one of the state's major scandals developed. Gov. Smith allowed the lawmakers to consider special banking legislation supported by Houston banker Frank Sharp. Several public officials were implicated in receiving favors from the banker for seeing that the legislation passed. Texas House Speaker Gus Mutscher and Rep. Tommy Shannon were convicted of conspiracy to accept bribes in a trial held in Abilene. Mutscher subsequently completed his probation, had his rights restored and was elected county judge of Washington County.

But voters in 1972 demanded a new leadership in the state capital. Smith and Barnes were defeated in the Democratic primary, and Dolph Briscoe was elected governor. William P. Hobby Jr., son of the former governor, was elected lieutenant governor. In the fall, Texans gave presidential candidate Richard Nixon the state's electoral votes. Nixon carried 246 counties over Democrat George McGovern and received more than 65 percent of the popular vote, the largest recorded by a Republican in Texas.

The Legislature in 1973 was dominated by a reform atmosphere in the wake of the Sharpstown scandal. Price Daniel Jr., son of the former governor, was selected speaker of the House, and several laws concerning ethics and disclosure of campaign donations and spending were passed. Open meetings and open records statutes also were approved.

By 1970, Texas had become an even more urban state. The census found almost 11.2 million people in the state, ranking it sixth nationally. Three Texas cities, Houston, Dallas and San Antonio, were among the 10 largest in the nation.

Through the first half of the 1970s, several major changes were made in state policy. Liquor-by-the-drink had become legal, the age of majority had been lowered from 20 to 18, giving young people the right to vote, and the state's first Public Utilities Commission was created, hearing its initial case in September 1976.

Texas entered a period of unparalleled prosperity in 1973 when the Organization of Petroleum Exporting Countries boycotted the American market. Severe energy shortages resulted, and the price of oil and natural gas skyrocketed. The federal government had allowed foreign oil to be imported through the 1960s, severely reducing the incentives to find and produce domestic oil. Consequently, domestic producers could not compensate for the loss in foreign oil as a result of the boycott. The Texas Railroad Commission had long complained about the importation of foreign oil, and in 1972, the panel had removed proration controls from wells in the state, allowing 100 percent production. For the rest of the decade, domestic producers mounted a major exploration effort, drilling thousands of wells. Nevertheless, Texas' oil and gas production peaked in 1970 and has been declining since. Newly discovered oil and gas have not replaced the declining reserves. While Texans suffered from the inflation that followed, the state prospered. Tax revenues at all levels of government increased, and state revenues, basically derived from oil and gas taxes, spiraled, as did the state budget.

WITH the new revenue from inflation and petroleum taxes, state spending rose from $2.95 billion in 1970 to $8.6 billion in 1979, and education led the advance, moving from 42 percent of the budget to 51.5 percent. But there was no increase in state tax rates.

It was no surprise that education was one of the major beneficiaries of increased state spending. After World War II, more emphasis was placed on education across the state. Community colleges sprang up in many cities, and a total of 109 colleges were established between the end of the war and 1980. Quantity did not assure quality, however, and Texas' public and higher education seldom were ranked among national leaders.

In 1972, voters approved an amendment authorizing the Legislature to sit as a Constitutional Convention to rewrite the 1876 charter. Judge Robert W. Calvert, former chief justice of the Texas Supreme Court, served as chairman of the Texas Constitutional Revision Commission that held hearings around the state and proposed a new constitution to the Legislature in 1974. But the lawmakers met for several months, spent $5 million and failed to propose anything to be considered by voters. The public was outraged, and in 1975, the Legislature presented the work of the convention to voters in the form of eight constitutional amendments. All were defeated in a special election in November 1975.

Texas voters participated in their first presidential primary in 1976. Jimmy Carter of Georgia won the Democratic primary, and eventually the presidency, and Ronald Reagan carried the state's Republicans, but lost the party's nomination to President Gerald Ford.

In 1977, Texas farmers joined a national farm protest movement against price levels for their products, which, they said, were being sold below the cost of production.

The state proved politically volatile in 1978. First, Attorney General John Hill defeated Gov. Dolph Briscoe in the Democratic primary. A political newcomer, William P. Clements, upset Hill in the general election, giving Texas its first Republican governor since Reconstruction. And also for the first time since Reconstruction, state officials were elected for four-year terms. And a major shakeup occurred in the state's congressional delegation when six members of the U.S. House retired and three more were defeated at the polls. Texas, which usually had strong, experienced representation in Washington, included nine freshmen congressmen in its 24-member delegation.

Bibliography
Books

Adams, Frank Carter, **Texas Democracy: A Centennial History of Politics and Personalities of the Democratic Party 1836-1936, Vol. I**; Democratic Historical Association, Austin, 1936.

Adams, Willena C., editor, **Texas Cities and the Great Depression**; Texas Memorial Museum, Austin, 1973.

Ashcraft, Allan C., **Texas in the Civil War**; Texas Civil War Centennial Commission, Austin, 1962.

Ashford, Gerald, **Spanish Texas: Yesterday and Today**; Jenkins Publishing Co., The Pemberton Press, Austin, 1971.

Barker, Eugene C., editor, **Readings in Texas History**; Southwest Press, Dallas, 1929.

Barker, Eugene C., **The Life of Stephen F. Austin, Founder of Texas, 1793-1836**; Cokesbury Press, Dallas, 1926.

Barksdale, E.C., **The Genesis of the Aviation Industry in North Texas**; Bureau of Business Research, University of Texas, Austin, 1958.

Barnhill, J. Herschel, **From Surplus to Substitution: Energy in Texas**; American Press, Boston, 1983.

Barr, Alwyn, **Black Texans: A History of Negroes in Texas 1528-1971**; Jenkins Publishing Co., The Pemberton Press, Austin, 1973.

Barr, Alwyn, **Reconstruction to Reform: Texas Politics, 1876-1906**; University of Texas Press, Austin, 1971.

Becerra, Francisco, **A Mexican Sergeant's Recollections of the Alamo and San Jacinto**; Jenkins Publishing Co., Austin, 1980.

Bertrand, Louis, and Sir Charles Petrie, **The History of Spain: From the Musulmans to Franco**; Collier Books, New York, 1971.

Binkley, William C., **The Expansionist Movement in Texas 1836-1850**; University of California Publications in History, Vol. 13, University of California Press, Berkeley, 1925.

Binkley, William C., **The Texas Revolution**; Louisiana State University Press, Baton Rouge, 1952 (rpt. Texas State Historical Association, Austin, 1979).

Brown, Norman D., **Hood, Bonnet, and Little Brown Jug**; Texas A&M University Press, College Station, 1984.

Buenger, Walter L., **Secession and the Union in Texas**; University of Texas Press, Austin, 1984.

Campbell, Randolph B., and Richard G. Lowe, **Wealth and Power in Antebellum Texas**; Texas A&M University Press, College Station, 1977.

Casdorph, Paul, **The Republican Party in Texas, 1865-1965**; Jenkins Publishing Co.,The Pemberton Press, Austin, 1965.

Castaneda, Carlos E., editor, **The Mexican Side of the Texas Revolution**; P.L. Turner Co., Austin, 1928 (rpt. Graphic Ideas, Inc., Austin, 1970).

Castaneda, Carlos E., **Our Catholic Heritage in Texas, Vols. 1-3**; Von Boeckmann-Jones Co., Austin, 1933-38.

Clarke, Mary Whatley, **Thomas J. Rusk: Soldier, Statesman, Jurist**; Jenkins Publishing Co., The Pemberton Press, Austin, 1971.

Connor, Seymour V., **Adventure in Glory: The Saga of Texas, 1836-1849**; Steck-Vaughn Co., Austin, 1965.

Cotner, Robert C., **James Stephen Hogg: A Biography**; University of Texas Press, Austin, 1959.

Crocket, G.L., **Two Centuries in East Texas**; Southwest Press, Dallas, 1932.

Davis, Ronald L., **Twentieth Century Cultural Life in Texas**; American Press, Boston, 1981.

De la Pena, Jose Enrique, **With Santa Anna in Texas: A Personal Narrative of the Revolution**, Trans. Carmen Perry; Texas A&M University Press, College Station, 1975.

DeLeon, Arnoldo, **The Mexican Image in Nineteenth Century Texas**; American Press, Boston, 1982.

DeLeon, Arnoldo, **The Tejano Community, 1836-1900**; University of New Mexico Press, Albuquerque, 1982.

DeLeon, Arnoldo, **They Called Them Greasers: Anglo Attitudes Toward Mexicans in Texas, 1821-1900**; University of Texas Press, Austin, 1983.

DeVoto, Bernard, **The Year of Decision: 1846**; Little, Brown and Co., Boston, 1943.

Dixon, Sam Houston, and Louis Wiltz Kemp, **The Heroes of San Jacinto**; Anson Jones Press, Houston, 1932.

Dodge, Bertha S., **Cotton: The Plant That Would Be King**; University of Texas Press, Austin, 1984.

Drinnon, Richard, **Facing West: The Metaphysics of Indian-Hating and Empire-Building**; New American Library, New York, 1980.

Durham, George, **Taming the Nueces Strip**; University of Texas Press, Austin, 1982.

Easterlin, Richard A., David Ward, William Bernard, and Reed Ueda, **Immigration**; Belknap Press of Harvard University Press, Cambridge, 1982.

Farber, James, **Texas, C.S.A.: A Spotlight on Disaster**; The Jackson Co., New York, 1947.

Fehrenbach, T.R., **Comanches: The Destruction of a People**; Alfred A. Knopf Co.,New York, 1976.

Fehrenbach, T.R., **Lone Star: A History of Texas and the Texans**; MacMillan Co., New York, 1968.

Foner, Eric, **Nothing But Freedom: Emancipation and Its Legacy**; Louisiana State University Press, Baton Rouge, 1983.

Fornell, Earl Wesley, **The Galveston Era: The Texas Crescent on the Eve of Secession**; University of Texas Press, Austin, 1961.

Frantz, Joe B., **Texas: A Bicentennial History**; W. W. Norton & Co., New York, 1976.

Friend, Llerena B., **Sam Houston: The Great Designer**; University of Texas Press, Austin, 1954.

Gambrell, Herbert, **Anson Jones: The Last President of Texas**; Doubleday and Co., Inc., Garden City, N.J., 1948.

Gard, Wayne, **The Chisholm Trail**; University of Oklahoma Press, Norman, 1954.

Goodwyn, Lawrence, **The Populist Moment: A Short History of the Agrarian Revolt in America**; Oxford University Press, New York, 1978.

Gouge, William M., **The Fiscal History of Texas**; Lippincott, Grambo, and Co., Philadelphia, 1852.

Gould, Lewis L., **Progressives and Prohibitionists: Texas Democrats in the Wilson Era**; University of Texas Press, Austin, 1973.

Graham, Philip, **The Life and Poems of Mirabeau Buonaparte Lamar**; University of North Carolina Press, Chapel Hill, 1938.

Grant, Joseph M., and Lawrence L. Crum, **The Development of State Chartered Banking in Texas**; Bureau of Business Research, University of Texas at Austin, 1978.

Green, George Norris, **A Liberal's View of Texas Politics, 1890s-1930s**; American Press, Boston, 1981.

Green, George Norris, **A Liberal View of Texas Politics Since the 1930s**; American Press, Boston, 1981.

Green, George Norris, **The Establishment in Texas Politics: The Primitive Years, 1938-1957**; Greenwood Press, Westport, Conn., 1979.

Gregory, Jack, and Rennard Strickland, **Sam Houston with the Cherokees 1829-1833;** University of Texas Press, Austin, 1967.

Haley, J. Evetts, **The XIT Ranch of Texas and the Early Days of the Llano Estacado;** University of Oklahoma Press, Norman, 1954.

Hanke, Lewis, **Aristotle and the American Indian: A Study of Race Prejudice in the Modern World;** University of Indiana Press, Bloomington, 1959.

Harper, William G., **The Texas Blue Laws;** Exposition Press, Hicksville, N.Y., 1974.

Hawkins, Wallace, **El Sal Del Rey;** Texas State Historical Association, 1947.

Henson, Margaret S., **Anglo American Women in Texas, 1820-1850;** American Press, Boston, 1982.

Hewitt, W. Phil, **Land and Community: European Migration to Rural Texas in the 19th Century;** American Press, Boston, 1981.

Hinkle, Stacy C., **Wings Over the Border: The Army Air Service Armed Patrol of the United States-Mexico Border 1919-1921;** Southwestern Studies, Texas Western Press, El Paso, 1970.

Hogan, William Ransom, **The Texas Republic;** University of Texas Press, Austin, 1969.

Horgan, Paul, **The Great River, Vols. 1-2;** Rinehart & Co., Inc., New York, 1954.

Horsman, Reginald, **Race and Manifest Destiny: The Origins of American Racial Anglo-Saxonism;** Harvard University Press, Cambridge, 1981.

Innes, Hammond, **The Conquistadors;** Alfred A. Knopf, New York, 1969.

Institute of Texan Cultures, **The Indian Texans;** University of Texas at San Antonio, 1970.

Institute of Texan Cultures, **The Spanish Texans;** University of Texas at San Antonio, 1972.

Irby, James A., **Backdoor at Bagdad;** Southwestern Series, Texas Western Press, El Paso, 1968.

James, Marquis, **The Raven: A Biography of Sam Houston;** Blue Ribbon Books, Inc., New York City, 1929.

John, Elizabeth A.H., **Storms Brewed In Other Men's Worlds: The Confrontation of Indians, Spanish and French in the Southwest, 1540-1795;** Texas A&M University Press, College Station, 1975.

Jones, Billy M., **The Search for Maturity: Saga of Texas, 1875-1900;** Steck-Vaughn Co., Austin, 1965.

Jordan, Terry G., **Environment and Environmental Perceptions in Texas;** American Press, Boston, 1980.

Jordan, Terry G., **Immigration to Texas;** American Press, Boston, 1980.

Jordan, Terry G., **Trails to Texas: Southern Roots of Western Cattle Ranching;** University of Nebraska Press, Lincoln, 1981.

Leckie, William H., **The Buffalo Soldiers: A Narrative of the Negro Cavalry in the West;** University of Oklahoma Press, Norman, 1967.

Lindheim, Milton, **The Republic of the Rio Grande;** W.M. Morrison, Bookseller, Waco, 1964.

Lockhart, James, and Stuart B. Schwartz, **Early Latin America: A History of Colonial Spanish America and Brazil;** Cambridge University Press, Cambridge, 1983.

Lord, Walter, **A Time to Stand: The Epic of the Alamo;** Harpers & Row, New York, 1961 (rpt. University of Nebraska Press, Lincoln, 1978).

Lukes, Edward A., **DeWitt Colony of Texas;** Jenkins Publishing Co., The Pemberton Press, Austin, 1976.

Malone, Dumas, **Jefferson the President: First Term 1801-1805;** Little, Brown and Co., Boston, 1970.

Malone, Dumas, **Jefferson the President: Second Term 1805-1809;** Little, Brown and Co., New York, 1974.

Martin, Roscoe, **The People's Party in Texas: A Study in Third Party Politics;** University of Texas Press, Austin, 1970.

Maxwell, Robert S., and Robert D. Baker, **Sawdust Empire: The Texas Lumber Industry, 1830-1940;** Texas A&M University Press, College Station, 1983.

Maxwell, Robert S., **Texas Economic Growth, 1890 to World War II: From Frontier to Industrial Giant;** American Press, Boston, 1981.

McDonald, Archie P., **Texas: All Hail the Mighty State;** Eakin Press, Austin, 1983.

McDonald, Archie P., **The Trail to San Jacinto;** American Press, Boston, 1981.

McDonald, Archie P., **Travis;** Jenkins Publishing Co., The Pemberton Press, Austin, 1976.

McDonald, Archie P., **The Republic of Texas;** American Press, Boston, 1981.

McKay, Seth S., and Odie B. Faulk, **Texas After Spindletop: Saga of Texas, 1901-1965;** Steck-Vaughn Co., Austin, 1965.

Meinig, D.W., **Imperial Texas: An Interpretive Essay in Cultural Geography;** University of Texas Press, Austin, 1969.

Merk, Frederick, **The History of the Westward Movement;** Alfred E. Knopf, New York, 1978.

Meyer, Michael C., and Sherman, William L., **The Course of Mexican History;** Oxford University Press, New York, 1979.

Miller, Hurbert J., **Jose de Escandon, Colonizer of Nuevo Santander;** New Santander Press, Edinburg, 1980.

Miller, Thomas L., **The Public Lands of Texas, 1519-1970;** University of Oklahoma Press, Norman, 1972.

Moneyhon, Carl H., **Republicanism in Reconstruction Texas;** University of Texas Press, Austin, 1980.

Myres, John Myres, **The Alamo;** E.P. Dutton and Co., 1948 (rpt. University of Nebraska Press, Lincoln, 1973).

Myres, Sandra L., **Native Americans of Texas;** American Press, Boston, 1981.

Newcomb, W.W. Jr., **The Indians of Texas;** University of Texas Press, Austin, 1961.

Norman, Mary Anne, **The Texas Economy Since World War II;** American Press, Boston, 1983.

Nunn, W.C., **Texas Under the Carpetbaggers;** University of Texas Press, Austin, 1962.

Pettigrew, Thomas E., George M. Fredrickson, Dale T. Knobel, Nathan Glazer and Reed Ueda, **Prejudice;** Belknap Press of Harvard University Press, Cambridge, 1982.

Pilkington, William T., **Imaging Texas: The Literature of the Lone Star State;** American Press, Boston, 1981.

Price, Glenn W., **Origins of the War with Mexico: Polk-Stockton Intrigue;** University of Texas Press, Austin, 1967.

Prindle, David F., **Petroleum Politics and the Texas Railroad Commission;** University of Texas Press, Austin, 1981.

Procter, Ben H., **Not Without Honor: The Life of John H. Reagan;** University of Texas Press, Austin, 1962.

Puryear, Pamela A., and Nath Winfield Jr., **Sandbars and Sternwheelers: Navagation on the Brazos;** Texas A&M University Press, College Station, 1976.

Raat, W. Dirk, editor, **Mexico: From Independence to Revolution, 1810-1910;** University of Nebraska Press, Lincoln, 1982.

Raat, W. Dirk, **Revoltosos;** Texas A&M University Press, College Station, 1981.

Ramsdell, Charles William, **Reconstruction in Texas;** Columbia University Press, New York, 1910 (rpt. University of Texas Press, Austin, 1970).

Red, William Stuart, **The Texas Colonists and Religion 1821-1836;** E. L. Shettles, Publisher, Austin, 1924.

Reed, S.G., **A History of the Texas Railroads;** St. Clair Publishing Co., Houston, 1941.

Rice, Lawrence D., **The Negro in Texas 1874-1900;** Louisiana State University Press, Baton Rouge, 1971.

Richardson, Rupert N., **Colonel House: The Texas Years;** Hardin-Simmons University Publications in History, Abilene, 1964.

Richardson, Rupert N., Ernest Wallace and Adrian N. Anderson, **Texas: The Lone Star State;** Prentice-Hall, Inc., Englewood Cliffs, N.J., 1970.

Richardson, Rupert N., **The Frontier of Northwest Texas, 1846-1876;** The Arthur H. Clark Co., Glendale, Calif., 1963.

Rodriguez, Louis J., **Dynamics of Growth: An Economic Profile of Texas;** Madrona Press, Austin, 1978.

Rosenbaum, Robert J., **Mexican Resistance in the Southwest;** University of Texas Press, Austin, 1981.

Rosenbaum, Robert J., **The History of Mexican Americans in Texas;** American Press, Boston, 1980.

Rutherford, Bruce, **Ferguson: The Impeachment of Jim Ferguson;** Eakin Press, Austin, 1983.

Samora, Julian, Joe Bernal and Albert Pena, **Gunpowder Justice: A Reassessment of the Texas Rangers;** Notre Dame Press, South Bend, 1979.

Sibley, Marilyn McAdams, **The Port of Houston, A History;** University of Texas Press, Austin, 1968.

Sierra, Justo, **The Political Evolution of the Mexican People,** trans. Charles Ramsdell; University of Texas Press, Austin, 1969.

Silverthorne, Elizabeth, **Ashbel Smith of Texas: Pioneer, Patriot, Statesman, 1805-1886;** Texas A&M University Press, College Station, 1982.

Smallwood, James, **The Great Recovery: The New Deal in Texas;** American Press, Boston, 1983.

Smallwood, James, **The Struggle for Equality: Blacks in Texas;** American Press, Boston, 1983.

Smithwick, Noah, **The Evolution of a State or Recol-**

lections of Old Texas Days; H.P.N. Gammell, Austin, 1900 (rpt. University of Texas Press, Austin, 1983).

Smyrl, Frank H., **Texas in Gray: The Civil War Years, 1861-1865**; American Press, Boston, 1983.

Smyrl, Frank H., **The Twenty-Eighth Star: Texas During the Period of Early Statehood, 1846-1861**; American Press, Boston, 1983.

Sonnichsen, C.L., **Pass of the North: Four Centuries on the Rio Grande, Vol.** I -1529-1917; Texas Western Press, UT-El Paso, 1968.

Spratt, John Stricklin, **The Road to Spindletop: Economic Change in Texas, 1875-1901**; SMU Press, Dallas, 1955 (rpt. University of Texas Press, Austin, 1983).

Stambaugh, J. Lee, and Lillian J., **The Lower Rio Grande Valley of Texas: Its Colonization and Industrialization, 1518-1953**; The Jenkins Co., San Felipe Press, Austin, 1974.

Syers, Ed, **Texas: The Beginning 1519-1834**; Texian Press, Waco, 1978.

Taylor, Virginia H., **The Franco-Texan Land Co.**; University of Texas Press, Austin, 1969.

Timmons, W.H., **The Anglo-American Advance Into Texas, 1810-1830**; American Press, Boston, 1981.

Tinkle, Lon, **The Alamo (13 Days to Glory**, McGraw-Hill Book Co., New York, 1958); New American Library, New York.

Tolbert, Frank, **The Day of San Jacinto**; McGraw-Hill Book Co., Inc., New York, 1959.

Utley, Robert M., **The Indian Frontier of the American West 1846-1890**; University of New Mexico Press, Albuquerque, 1984.

Vigness, David M., **The Revolutionary Decades: The Saga of Texas, 1810-1836**; Steck-Vaughn Co., Austin, 1965.

Vigness, David M., **Spanish Texas, 1519-1810**; American Press, Boston, 1983.

Wallace, Ernest, **Charles DeMorse: Pioneer Editor and Statesman**; Texas Tech Press, Lubbock, 1943.

Wallace, Ernest, and David M. Vigness, **Documents of Texas History**; The Steck Co., Austin, 1963.

Wallace, Ernest, and E. Adamson Hoebel, **The Comanches: Lords of the South Plains**; University of Oklahoma Press, Norman, 1952.

Wallace, Ernest, **The Howling of Coyotes: Reconstruction Efforts to Divide Texas**; Texas A&M University Press, College Station, 1979.

Wallace, Ernest, **Ranald S. Mackenzie on the Texas Frontier**; West Texas Museum Association, Lubbock, 1965.

Wallace, Ernest, **Texas in Turmoil: The Saga of Texas: 1849-1875**; Steck-Vaughn Co., Austin, 1965.

Webb, Walter Prescott, and H. Bailey Carroll, editors, **Handbook of Texas, Vols. 1-3**; Texas State Historical Association, Austin, 1952 and 1976.

Webb, Walter Prescott, **The Great Frontier**; University of Texas Press, Austin, 1964.

Webb, Walter Prescott, **The Great Plains**; University of Nebraska Press, Lincoln, 1981.

Webb, Walter Prescott, **The Texas Rangers: A Century of Frontier Defense**; Houghton Mifflin, Boston, 1935 (rpt.University of Texas Press, Austin, 1980).

Weber, David J., **The Mexican Frontier, 1821-1846: The American Southwest Under Mexico**; University of New Mexico Press, Albuquerque, 1982.

Weber, David J., editor, **New Spain's Far Northern Frontier**; University of New Mexico Press, Albuquerque, 1979.

Weddle, Robert S., **San Juan Bautista: Gateway to Spanish Texas**; University of Texas Press, Austin, 1968.

Weddle, Robert S., **Wilderness Manhunt: The Spanish Search for LaSalle**; University of Texas Press, Austin, 1973.

Whisenhunt, Donald W., editor, **Texas: A Sesquicentennial Celebration**; Eakin Press, Austin, 1984.

Whisenhunt, Donald W., editor, **The Depression in the Southwest**; Kennikat Press, Port Washington, N.Y., 1980.

Whisenhunt, Donald W., **The Depression in Texas**; American Press, Boston, 1982.

Whisenhunt, Donald W., **The Depression in Texas: The Hoover Years**; Garland Publishing, Inc., New York, 1983.

Whisenhunt, Donald W., **The Development of Higher Education in Texas**; American Press, Boston, 1983.

White, Dabney, editor, and T. C. Richardson, author, **East Texas: Its History and Its Makers, Vols. I-IV**; Lewis Historical Publishing Co., New York.

Wilkinson, J. B., **Laredo and the Rio Grande Frontier**; Jenkins Publishing Co., Austin, 1975.

Williams, Clayton W. (Ernest Wallace, editor), **Texas' Last Frontier: Fort Stockton and the Trans-Pecos, 1861-1895**; Texas A&M University Press, College Station, 1982.

Williams, Lyle W., **Ranches and Ranching in Spanish Texas**; American Press, Boston, 1982.

Williams, T. Harry, Richard N. Current and Frank Freidel, **A History of the United States (to 1876)**; Alfred A. Knopf, Inc., New York, 1959.

Wilson, James A., **Hide & Horn in Texas: The Spread of Cattle Ranching 1836-1900**; American Press, Boston, 1983.

Wintz, Cary D., **Reconstruction in Texas**; American Press, Boston, 1983.

Wintz, Cary D., **Texas Politics in the Gilded Age, 1873-1890**; American Press, Boston, 1983.

Wright, J. Leitch Jr., **The Only Land They Knew: The Tragic Story of the American Indian in the South**; The Free Press (Division of MacMillan Publishing Co.), New York, 1981.

Wyatt-Brown, Bertram, **Southern Honor: Ethics and Behavior in the Old South**; Oxford University Press, New York, 1982.

Articles

Barker, Eugene C., "The Annexation of Texas"; Southwestern Historical Quarterly(SWHQ), Vol. L, No. 1, July 1946.

Barker, Eugene C., "Land Speculation as a Cause of the Texas Revolution"; Texas State Historical Quarterly (SWHQ), Vol. X, No. 1, July 1906.

Barker, Eugene C., "The San Jacinto Campaign"; SWHQ, Vol. IV, No. 4, April 1901.

Barker, Eugene C., "The Texan Revolutionary Army"; SWHQ, Vol. IX, No. 4, April 1906.

Bender, A.B., "Opening Routes Across West Texas, 1848-1850"; SWHQ, Vol. XXXVII,No. 2, October 1933.

Bender, A.B., "The Texas Frontier, 1848-1861, Part II"; SWHQ Vol. XVI, No. 1, July 1912.

Binkley, William C., "The Activities of the Texan Revolutionary Army after San Jacinto"; Journal of Southern History, Vol. VI, August 1940.

Bolton, H.E., "The Spanish Occupation of Texas, 1519-1690"; SWHQ, Vol. XVI, No. 1, July 1912.

Caldwell, Edwin L., "Highlights of the Development of Manufacturing in Texas,1900-1960"; SWHQ, Vol. LXVIII, No. 4, April 1965.

Calvert, Robert A., "Nineteenth-Century Farmers, Cotton, and Prosperity"; SWHQ,Vol. LXXIII, No. 4, April 1970.

Casdorf, Paul D., "Norris Wright Cuney and Texas Republican Politics, 1883-1896"; SWHQ, Vol. LXVIII, No. 4, April 1965.

Cohen, Barry M., "The Texas-Mexico Border, 1858-1867"; Texana, Vol. VI, No. 2, Summer 1968.

Cox, Isaac Joslin, "The Louisiana Texas Frontier"; SWHQ, Vol. X, No. 1, July 1906.

Crane, M.M., "Recollections of the Establishment of the Texas Railroad Commission"; SWHQ, Vol. L, No. 4, April 1947.

Davenport, Harbert, "Notes on Early Steamboating on the Rio Grande"; SWHQ, Vol. XLIX, No. 2, October 1945.

Elliott, Claude, "Union Sentiment in Texas, 1861-65"; SWHQ, Vol. L, No. 4, April 1947.

Ellis, L. Tuffly, "Maritime Commerce on the Far Western Gulf, 1861-1865"; SWHQ, Vol. LXXVII, No. 2, October 1973.

Foner, Eric, "The New view of Reconstruction"; American Heritage Magazine, Oct./Nov. 1983, Vol. 34, No. 6.

Gard, Wayne, "The Fence-Cutters"; SWHQ, Vol. LI, No. 1, July 1947.

Havins, T.R., "Texas Fever"; SWHQ, Vol. LII, No. 2, October 1948.

Holt, R.D., "The Introduction of Barbed Wire Into Texas and the Fence Cutting War"; West Texas Historical Association Yearbook (WTHA Yearbook), Vol. VI, June 1930.

Houston, Sam, "Houston's Last Speech in the United States Senate"; Texas Almanac of 1860, Galveston News, Galveston, 1860.

Inglis, G. Douglas, "The Men of Cibola: New Investigations on the Francisco Vazquez de Coronado Expedition"; Panhandle-Plains Historical Review, Vol. LV, 1982.

Kilgore, Dan, "Texas Cattle Origins"; The Cattleman Magazine, January, 1983.

Kingston, Mike, "Archaeology: A Slow Start in Texas"; Texas Almanac, 1984-85, Dallas Morning News, Dallas, 1984.

Kingston, Mike, "**A History of the Texas Border-lands**"; Texas Almanac, 1984-85, Dallas Morning News, Dallas, 1984.

Koch, Lena Clara, "**The Federal Indian Policy in Texas, 1845-60**"; SWHQ, Vol. XXVIII, No. 2, April 1925.

Labadie, N.D., "**San Jacinto Campaign**"; Texas Almanac of 1859, Galveston News, Galveston, 1859.

Marshall, Ray, "**Some Reflections on Labor History**"; SWHQ, Vol. LXXV, No. 2, October 1971.

Marshall, Thomas Maitland, "**The Southwestern Boundary of Texas, 1821-1840**"; SWHQ, Vol. XIV, No. 4, April 1911.

Martin, Roscoe C., "**The Grange as a Political Factor in Texas**"; Southwestern Political and Social Science Quarterly, Vol. VI, June 1925-March 1926.

Martin, Roscoe C., "**The Greenback Party in Texas**"; SWHQ, Vol. XXX, No. 3, January 1927.

Myres, Sandra, "**Spanish Cattle Kingdom**"; Texana, Vol. IV, No. 3, Fall 1966.

Neighbours, Kenneth F., "**The Expedition of Maj. Robert S. Neighbors to El Paso in 1849**"; SWHQ, Vol. LVIII, No. 1, July 1954.

Neighbours, Kenneth F., "**Indian Exodus out of Texas in 1859**"; WTHA Yearbook, Vol. XXXVI, 1960.

Neighbours, Kenneth F., "**The Struggle Over the Upper Rio Grande Region in 1850**"; SWHQ, Vol. LXI, No. 4, April 1958.

Norvell, James R., "**The Railroad Commission of Texas, Its Origin and History**"; SWHQ, Vol. LXVIII, No. 4, April 1965.

Parvin, Bob, "**In Search of the First Texans**"; Texas Parks and Wildlife Magazine, October 1983.

Peterson, Robert L., "**Jay Gould and the Texas Railroad Commission**"; SWHQ, Vol. LVIII, No. 3., January 1955.

Porter, Kenneth Wiggins, "**The Seminole Negro-Indian Scouts, 1870-81**"; SWHQ, Vol. LV, No. 3, January 1952.

Reese, James V., "**The Early History of Labor Organizations in Texas, 1838-1876**"; SWHQ, Vol. LXXII, No. 1, July 1968.

Reese, James V., "**The Evolution of an Early Texas Union: The Screwmans' Benevolent Association of Galveston, 1866-1891**"; SWHQ, Vol. LXXV, No. 2, October 1971.

Rippy, J. Fred, "**British Investments in Texas Land and Livestock**"; SWHQ, Vol. LVIII, No. 3, January 1955.

Smith, Ralph A., "**The Farmers' Alliance in Texas**"; SWHQ, Vol. XLVIII, No. 3, January 1945.

Smith, Ralp h A., "**The Grange Movement in Texas, 1873-1900**"; SWHQ, Vol. XLII, No.4, April 1939.

Smyrl, Frank H., "**Texans in the Union Army, 1861-65**"; SWHQ, Vol. LXV, No. 2, October 1961.

Spillman, W.J., "**Adjustment of the Texas Boundary in 1850**"; SWHQ, Vol. VII, No. 3, January 1904.

Steiner, Stan, "**Jewish Conquistadors: America's First Cowboys?**"; American West Magazine, Sept./Oct. 1983.

Vigness, David M., "**Indian Raids on the Lower Rio Grande, 1836-37**"; SWHQ, Vol. LIX, No. 1, July 1955.

Walker, Ralph, "**Long's Lone Star Republic: The death of James Long and the Texas filibustering era**"; American History Illustrated, Vol XVIII, No. 10, February 1984.

Watford, W.H., "**Confederate Western Ambitions**"; SWHQ, Vol. XLIV, No. 2, October 1938.

Weddle, Robert S., "**San Juan Bautista: Mother of Texas Missions**"; SWHQ, Vol. LXXI, No. 4, April 1968.

Wilcox, Seb S., "**Laredo During the Texas Republic**"; SWHQ, Vol. XLII, No. 2, October 1938.

State Flags and Other Symbols

Texas often is called the **Lone Star State** because of its state flag with a single star; this also was the **flag of the Republic of Texas**. The following information about the flag and other Texas symbols may be supplemented by information available from the Texas State Library, Austin.

At the Convention of 1836, at Washington-on-the-Brazos, **Lorenzo de Zavala** is reported to have designed a flag for the Republic — a blue field with a white star of five points central, with the letters T E X A S, one letter between each star point. Probably because of the hasty dispersion of the Convention and loss of part of the Convention notes, nothing further was done with the De Zavala recommendation.

The **first official flag of the Republic**, known as **David G. Burnet's flag**, was adopted on Dec. 10, 1836, as the national standard, "the conformation of which shall be an azure ground with a large golden star central." A new national standard was worked out and approved by Mirabeau B. Lamar on Jan. 25, 1839. This flag consisted of a blue perpendicular stripe of the width of one-third of the whole length of the flag with a white star of five points in the center thereof; and two horizontal stripes of equal breadth, the upper stripe white, the lower red, of the length of two-thirds of the whole flag. This is the **Lone Star Flag.**

Six Flags of Texas

Six different flags have flown over Texas during eight changes of sovereignty. The accepted sequence of these flags follows:

Spanish — 1519-1685.
French — 1685-1690.
Spanish — 1690-1821.
Mexican — 1821-1836.
Republic of Texas — 1836-1845.
United States — 1845-1861.
Confederate States — 1861-1865.
United States — 1865 to the present.

State Flag

The **Lone Star Flag** consists of a blue field with a single white star and white and red horizontal stripes, with white uppermost. This flag was adopted by the Third Congress of the Republic, Jan. 25, 1839, at Houston. Although generally used, the state flag was not officially described and usage rules adopted until 1933. These rules are from Acts of Forty-third Legislature (p. 186, ch. 187).

Flown out-of-doors, the Texas flag must be on flagpole or staff at least two and one half times as long as the flag. It should not be unfurled earlier than sunrise

and should not be left out in rain, snow or other inclement weather. It should be flown with the white stripe uppermost except in case of distress. When the flag is displayed against a wall, the blue field should be at the flag's own right (observer's left). The Texas flag should be displayed on all state memorial days; it should fly at every school on every regular school day.

The Texas flag should be on the marching left in a procession in which the flag of the United States is carried; its staff should be behind the staff of the flag of the United States when the two are displayed with crossed staffs. The Texas flag should be underneath the national flag when the two are flown from the same halyard. When flown from separate, adjacent flagpoles, the United States flag and the Texas flag should be approximately the same size and on flagpoles of equal length, and the United States flag should be on "the flag's own right," i.e., to the observer's left. The Texas flag should never be used for any utilitarian or strictly decorative purpose. No advertising should be placed upon the flag or flagstaff, and no picture of the flag be used in an advertisement. When the Texas flag is in such condition that it is no longer a suitable emblem for display, it should be destroyed, preferably by burning, "with the spirit of respect and reverence which all Texans owe the emblem."

Texas Flag Pledge

A pledge to the Texas flag also was adopted by the Forty-third Legislature and from 1933 until 1965 that pledge was used. It contained a phrase, "Flag of 1836," which was historically incorrect, as Texas did not have a flag in 1836. On April 3, 1965, Gov. John Connally signed an act of the Fifty-ninth Legislature officially designating the pledge to the Texas flag as follows:

"Honor the Texas Flag.
I pledge allegiance to thee,
Texas, one and indivisible."

Other Symbols

State Seal. — The seal of the State of Texas consists of "a star of five points, encircled by olive and live oak branches, and the words, 'the State of Texas'." (State Constitution, Art. IV, Sec. 19.) The state seal is a slight modification of the Great Seal of the Republic of Texas, adopted by the Congress of the Republic, Dec. 10, 1836, and readopted with modifications in 1839.

State Citizenship Designation. — The people of Texas usually call themselves **Texans**. However, **Texian** was generally used in the early period of history.

State Motto. — The state motto of Texas is "**Friendship.**" The word, Texas, or Tejas, was the Spanish pronunciation of a Caddo Indian word meaning "friends"

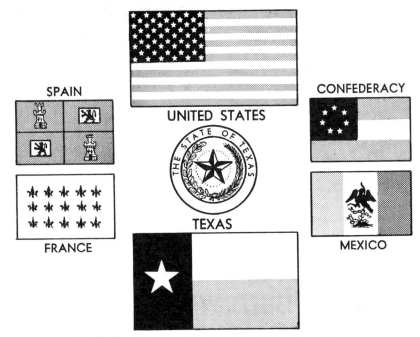

SPAIN

UNITED STATES

CONFEDERACY

FRANCE

TEXAS

MEXICO

The Six Flags of Texas and the Texas State Seal are shown here.

or "allies." (Acts of 1930, fourth called session of Forty-first Legislature, p. 105.)

State Tree. — The **pecan** is the state tree of Texas. The sentiment that led to its official adoption probably grew out of the request of Gov. James Stephen Hogg that a pecan tree be planted at his grave. (Acts of 1919, Thirty-sixth Legislature, regular session, p. 155; also Acts of 1927, Fortieth Legislature, p. 234.)

State Stone. — **Palmwood.**

State Flower. — The state flower of Texas is the **bluebonnet**, also called **buffalo clover, wolf flower, "el conejo"** (the rabbit). The bluebonnet was adopted as the State Flower, on request of the Society of Colonial Dames in Texas, by the Twenty-seventh Legislature, 1901. (See acts of regular session, p. 232.) The original resolution designated Lupinus subcarnosus as the **state flower,** but a resolution (HCR 44) signed March 8, 1971, by Gov. Preston Smith provided legal status as the state flower of Texas for "Lupinus Texensis and any other variety of bluebonnet."

State Bird. — The **mockingbird** (Mimus Polyglottos) is the state bird of Texas, adopted by the Legislature at the request of the Texas Federation of Women's Clubs. (Acts of 1927, Fortieth Legislature, regular session, p. 486.)

State Dish. — **Chili** was proclaimed the Texas state dish by the Texas Legislature in 1977.

State Gem. — **Topaz** is the official Texas gem, found in Llano uplift area, especially west to northwest of Mason.

State Grass. — **Sideoats grama,** a native grass found on many different soils, was designated by the Legislature as the **state grass of Texas.**

State Holidays. — Texas has two state holidays and several special observance days. The two holidays are **Texas Independence Day,** March 2, and **San Jacinto Day,** April 21. (See index for list of Texas holidays and special observances.)

State Song. — The state song of Texas is "**Texas, Our Texas.**" The music was written by the late William J. Marsh (who died Feb. 1, 1971, in Fort Worth at age 90), and the words by Marsh and Gladys Yoakum Wright, both of Fort Worth. It was adopted as the result of an award offered by the Legislature. (Acts of 1929, first called session, Forty-first Legislature, p. 286.) Its text follows:

TEXAS, OUR TEXAS

Texas, our Texas! All hail the mighty State!
Texas, our Texas! So wonderful, so great!
Boldest and grandest, withstanding every test;
O empire wide and glorious, you stand supremely blest.

Chorus

God bless you, Texas! And keep you brave and strong.
That you may grow in power and worth, throughout the ages long.

Refrain

Texas, O Texas! Your freeborn single star,
Sends out its radiance to nations near and far.
Emblem of freedom! It sets our hearts aglow.
With thoughts of San Jacinto and glorious Alamo.
Texas, dear Texas! From tyrant grip now free,
Shines forth in splendor your star of destiny!
Mother of Heroes! We come your children true.
Proclaiming our allegiance, our faith, our love for you.
— Words by Gladys Yoakum Wright and William J. Marsh. Music by William J. Marsh.

The adopted song of the University of Texas, "**The Eyes of Texas,**" is also frequently sung at public gatherings. It is usually sung by a standing audience and has a measure of recognition as a state song. Origin of this song is as follows: William Lamdin Prather, president of the University of Texas, 1899-1906, frequently said to the students, "The eyes of Texas are upon you." A university minstrel, as a prank when President Prather was present, sang a song, using this phrase, which had been written by a student, John Lang Sinclair, to the tune of "I've Been Working on the Railroad (Levee)." Gradually it became the adopted song of the University and is popular throughout Texas.

THE EYES OF TEXAS

The eyes of Texas are upon you
All the livelong day.
The eyes of Texas are upon you
You cannot get away.
Do not think you can escape them,
At night or early in the morn,
The eyes of Texas are upon you
Till Gabriel blows his horn.

Women in Texas History

This article on women in Texas history was prepared by Ruthe Winegarten of Austin and Frieda Werden of Washington, D.C.

Texas women have always been active participants in the development of the state, though their significant contributions have not always been documented in the history books. They have worked to protect and support their tribes and families. They have built tepees and founded cities, done housework and field work and labored without pay as slaves. They have worked for pay in offices, in homes, on farms and in factories; they have owned and managed small businesses and giant corporations; they have taught school and practiced law and medicine. As wives, mothers and single women they have cared for their children and those of others. Their nurturing has extended beyond their families and neighbors to include the broader community. As individuals and through their organizations they have founded schools, libraries, hospitals, churches, synagogues, museums and symphony orchestras. They have enriched society with their art, literature and music. And they have fought for their legal and civil rights, for social reforms and for peace.

Texas women come from many different ethnic groups, each with its own distinctive story—native Americans, Hispanics, Anglos, blacks and immigrants. The particular experiences of rural and urban women and women of different social and economic classes have often been dissimilar, and yet most Texas women have shared many common experiences—marriage, motherhood, family care, healing, hard work and community building.

When the Spanish arrived in Texas in 1528, they found Indian women working, and sometimes fighting, alongside the men of their tribes. The very survival of the tribes depended on women's labor, which included hunting small game, gathering and preparing food, hauling wood and water, fashioning baskets and pottery, caring for the children, acting as midwives and growing beans, corn and squash. Comanche and Kiowa women of the 18th and 19th centuries could be considered Texas' earliest engineers and architects: They built 300-pound, buffalo-hide tepees of ingenious design and transported them on travois attached to their two-horned work saddles. Women working in teams could set up or strike a camp in 30 minutes. Kiowa Apache women, who made their own tools, were expert hide tanners, skinners and butchers of bison.

We know the names of only two Texas Indian women leaders, both of them of the matrilineal Caddo tribe: Angelina, who attended the College of Zacatecas in the late 1600s and served as translator for the French and Spanish about 1700, and Santa Adiva, a tribal leader in the 1760s. Santa Adiva was described by Spanish missionary Fray Gasper de Solis as "like a queen," having many men and women "like priests and captains at her service."

During the 1600s and 1700s, Spanish missionaries and soldiers arrived in Texas to establish missions and presidios, resulting in intermarriage and mingling among Spanish, Indians and mestizos. Sometimes these unions were voluntary; sometimes Indian women were enslaved by Spanish soldiers. Hispanic women were housewives, midwives, colonizers, curanderas (healers), shepherds, laundresses, dressmakers, cooks, peddlers, innkeepers, farm workers, butchers and animal skinners.

Beginning in the 1700s, women colonists arrived in Texas. Although most were subservient to men, some were women of property and influence. When a group of Canary Islanders came to San Antonio in 1731 to form the first permanent Spanish settlement in Texas, their official leader was Maria Betancour, a widow. More than 60 Spanish or Mexican land grants were awarded directly to women; other women inherited land from their husbands or fathers, such as Dona Rosa Hinojosa de Balli, a skillful businesswoman and Texas' first cattle queen, who owned one-third of the Lower Rio Grande Valley. Dona Maria Calvillo of Wilson County inherited her father's ranch in 1790 and scandalized the countryside by riding on horseback with her ranch-hands. Maria Cassiano, wife of the Spanish governor of Texas in 1808, conducted all affairs of state when her husband was away.

There were black women living in Texas as early as 1792, when the Spanish census counted 186 free mulatta and Negro women. When Mexico outlawed slavery in 1830, other free black women migrated to the Texas territory. A few, like Galveston nurse Mary Madison, petitioned the Texas Congress to remain free. Black women slaves were being sold in the Galveston slave market by 1818, while more arrived with Stephen F. Austin's Old 300 Colony in the 1820s.

As in most wars, women's help was vital to the Texas cause in its struggle for independence from Mexico in the 1830s. Notable among these was Dona Patricia de la Garza de Leon, widowed cofounder of Victoria, who gave the Texans financial aid, and Madame Andrea Candelaria, one of 15 survivors of Santa Anna's siege of the Alamo, who received a state pension for her work as a nurse.

Continuing Mexican incursions into central Texas in 1842 led Sam Houston to order the Texas Archives moved to Houston. The citizens of Austin protested, fearing that, once the government records were gone, Houston would attempt to move the seat of government there permanently. In December 1842, when Houston sent a company of rangers to move the archives, innkeeper Angelina Eberly fired a cannon to warn the Austin vigilance committee, which overtook the rangers and regained the archives. Eberly stored the archives until the government returned to Austin.

During the continuing troubles with Mexico, journalist Jane McManus Cazneau wrote articles for Eastern newspapers favoring Texas' annexation to the United States. Secretary of State Buchanan sent her on a secret mission to Mexico in 1847.

Sarah Borginnis, known as "The Great Western," traveled with Gen. Zachary Taylor's army during the war with Mexico in 1846-48, cooking, washing, loading cartridges and dressing wounds, as women did on both sides of that war. For her many acts of heroism, she was buried with full military honors and was awarded a medal posthumously.

Women entrepreneurs were already active in Texas by this time. Among the early small businesswomen of Texas was Jane Long, who, during the Texas Revolution, ran an inn at Brazoria, with the help of her slave Kian, where the revolutionists were said to have stored their gunpowder. Two innkeepers of that same era were Pamelia Mann, who ran the Mansion Hotel in Houston in the late 1830s, and Mrs. Erastus "Deaf" Smith, who operated a boarding house in San Antonio in the 1840s.

Although it was a woman, Mary Austin Holley, the cousin of Stephen F. Austin, who in 1833 wrote the first book in English about Texas, educational opportunities for women in early Texas were scarce. With the founding by Frances Trask of Texas' first academy for white girls in Independence in 1834 and the establishing of Ursuline Academy in Galveston in 1847, a slow improvement in the availability of education began.

Though politically turbulent, the mid-1800s were not devoid of entertainment and culture: The first theatrical company toured the state in 1838. The hit of the 1850s was a ballet company starring Adah Menken, who later earned the title "The Naked Lady of Nacogdoches" for her performances wearing a flesh-colored body stocking. Amelia Barr, who lived in Texas from 1856 to 1868, wrote and published 81 novels.

Slavery played a vital role in the economic development of Texas' agricultural industry from the 1840s into the 1860s. Without either pay or the hope of freedom, women field hands cleared land, chopped and picked cotton and built fences. They butchered hogs, constructed roads and dug wells. House slaves cooked and cleaned, washed and ironed, spun yarn and wove it into cloth, cared for children and wet-nursed.

A few women slaves, among them Tomas Morgan, were able to purchase their freedom with the proceeds of their own labor. The daughter of Elizabeth Ramsey of Matagorda raised funds in Ohio to buy her mother out of slavery. Other slaves resisted by running away, arson, and even mudering their masters.

The same backbreaking chores as the slaves performed were being done by many white women alongside their husbands on farms and ranches, where most Texans lived until the mid-20th century.

A few white women of this period, such as Norwegian immigrant Elise Waerenskjold, spoke out courageously against slavery. Melinda Rankin, who founded the Rio Grande Female Seminary in Brownsville in 1854, lost her job in 1862 because of her pro-Union senti-

In 1984, the Governor's Commission for Women inducted 12 honorees into the first Texas Women's Hall of Fame. These women are listed on the following pages. Above are (l-r) Arts and Humanities: Dr. Amy Freeman Lee, artist and lecturer; Business and Finance: Oveta Culp Hobby, daily newspaper publisher, U.S. Cabinet member and commander, WACs in World War II; Civic and Volunteer Involvement: Christia Adair, teacher and civil rights activist.

ments. In New Braunfels, Helen Landa stayed and ran the family business when her husband was forced to flee from neighbors enraged because he had freed his slaves. Chipita Rodriguez, an elderly and respected innkeeper in San Patricio, was hanged in 1863 for a murder she did not commit, possibly framed because she had gathered information for the Union.

On the Confederate side during the Civil War were, among others, Sally Skull, a gunrunner, and Sophia Coffee Porter, who got a troop of Yankees drunk, then forded the Red River on a mule to warn Confederate troops.

Education for blacks was practically nonexistent during slavery, and after emancipation, black educational opportunities lagged far behind those for whites, but they were beginning to improve. In freedmen's communities, ex-slaves set up their own schools, and the Freedmen's Bureau established schools as well, taught by black and white women from both the North and the South.

Texas took a giant educational step ahead in 1875 by establishing a public school system, followed by a giant step backward in 1876, when a new state constitution required "separate but equal" facilities for black and white students.

Not only was secondary education available statewide, higher education also was becoming steadily more accessible to both black and white women. Prairie View State Normal School, a state-supported school for training black teachers, was founded in 1879, becoming coeducational in 1880. Texas also established Sam Houston Normal College, a coeducational teacher-training facility for white students, in 1879. Around 1900, Hispanic women organized escuelitas to provide bilingual education for children.

In the 1870s, women with education or specialized training were blazing trails for those to follow. The first state botanist, in 1872, and author of the state's first botany textbook was Maud Jeannie Young. During the 1870s, Nettie Houston Power Bringhurst and Lizzie Johnson sold their writings to magazines back East, and in 1879, Lydia Starr McPherson founded and published the *Sherman Democrat*, the only woman at that time to own and edit a newspaper.

Dallas' first capitalist was Sarah Cockrell, who invested in real estate and flour mills and, in 1872, built the first iron bridge over the Trinity River.

By 1880, 12 percent of Texas women over the age of 10 worked for wages, the 10 jobs most often held by women being agricultural laborer, domestic, laundress, laborer, farmer, dressmaker, teacher, hotel and restaurant worker, boarding house keeper and music teacher. Wages were unconscionably low; the first organized action by Texas women toward obtaining fair pay was probably taken in Galveston in 1877 when black laundry workers staged a strike, demanding $1.50 a day.

The availability of better-paying jobs often follows better education. And Texas improved the educational

opportunities for women once more in 1883 by opening the coeducational, state-supported University of Texas at Austin.

The 1880s and 1890s saw an increasing interest by Texas women in culture and entertainment. Prior to that, the domestic arts and entertainment—music, handwork, home decorating, and quilting—were the most common. But literary, social and cultural clubs began forming in the early 1880s, creating an atmosphere which encouraged individual artists and entertainers. One of the first of these clubs was the Women's Art Exchange in Austin. The Texas Women's World's Fair Association created the award-winning Texas pavilion for the World's Columbian Exhibition in Chicago in 1893, featuring the work of Texas' first eminent sculptor, Elisabet Ney.

During the last half of the 19th century, Texas women were building their communities by organizing churches, founding schools and libraries, museums and churches. Galveston in 1856 was the site of the first Jewish religious service in Texas, arranged by Rosanna Osterman, who provided funds in her will for hospitals, synagogues and homes for widows and orphans.

Delilah Harris, an ex-slave and pioneer, donated land for the Smith Chapel African Methodist Episcopal Church in Bethlehem, Texas. Fannie Breedlove Davis and Dr. Maud A. B. Fuller were the founders of white and black women's Baptist missionary societies, respectively. In 1883, Rebecca Williams founded the Methodist Church of Childress in her West Texas dugout home. The Sisters of Charity of the Incarnate Word founded the largest Catholic hospital in the United States—the Santa Rosa Hospital—in San Antonio in 1869. Religious orders eventually founded 42 Texas hospitals.

Beginning in the 1890s, the Texas Federation of Women's Clubs established 85 percent of the public libraries in the state. By 1899, most women's clubs had shifted their focus from culture to social reform. They worked to improve jails, parks and schools, and promoted conservation and preservation, public health and sanitation and laws protecting women and children. The National Council of Jewish Women founded night schools in several cities. Around 1900, Methodist women organized YWCAs to help young women make the transition from rural to urban life. Various women's clubs lobbied successfully for laws for compulsory school attendance, school lunches and sanitary drinking fountains. In 1905, the Texas Association of Colored Women's Clubs was organized to provide cultural enrichment for its members and to improve conditions for young people. In 1926, the San Antonio Conservation Society saved the San Antonio River from being paved as a drainage ditch.

The late 1800s also saw Texas women making places for themselves in the medical professions. Henrietta Cunningham became the first registered woman pharmacist in 1888. The first class of professional nurses in Texas graduated from John Sealy Hospital in Galveston

Texas Women's Hall of Fame honorees — (l-r) Communications: Vivian Castleberry, women's editor of a daily newspaper and award-winning journalist; Community Leadership: Lila Cockrell, former mayor of San Antonio; Education: Dr. Mary Evelyn Blagg Huey, first woman president, Texas Woman's University.

in 1895. Although women doctors trained in the East and abroad were practicing in Texas as early as 1876, Dr. Daisy Emery Allen and Dr. Maria Delalondre defied prejudice to become, in 1897, the first two women to graduate from Texas medical schools, and in the following year, Dr. Mary Lou Shelman was certified by examination to practice dentistry. By 1909, the Texas Graduate Nurses Association had persuaded the Texas Legislature to establish licensing standards.

The first organized political movement of Texas women was the Women's Christian Temperance Union (WCTU), founded in 1882 in Paris, Texas. Organized to fight alcohol abuse, the WCTU was to have influence beyond its original purpose. Not only did the WCTU work for adoption of the 18th Amendment (prohibition), which took effect in 1920, it also taught Texas women how to organize and to speak effectively. These skills were expanded and honed to a cutting edge in the suffrage movement, utilizing as it did a press campaign, grass-roots organization, mass meetings, petitions, suffrage schools and booths at department stores and the State Fair.

It took over 50 years of hard work for Texas women to free themselves from their political classification with "idiots, imbeciles, aliens and the insane" and win the right to vote. The Texas suffrage movement began with the introduction of the first suffrage resolution at the Reconstruction Convention in 1868. With the founding of the Texas Equal Suffrage Association, the movement gained momentum under leaders such as Rebecca Hayes of Galveston (1893-95) and Annette Finnigan of Houston (1903-05), culminating in the final push to victory (1913-19) led by Eleanor Brackenridge of San Antonio, Minnie Fisher Cunningham of Galveston and Jane Y. McCallum of Austin.

Texas women won an interim victory in 1918 when they were granted the right, only 17 days before the election, to vote in the Texas Democratic primary. 386,000 women registered in time to vote.

The Texas Legislature led the South in ratifying the 19th Amendment in special session on June 23, 1919, and was the ninth nationally to do so. Woman suffrage became a reality nationwide in 1920.

The early 1900s saw many political firsts among Texas women and an increase in their political participation. As early as 1908, Mrs. E. P. Turner and Mrs. P. P. Tucker of Dallas became the first women elected to a local school board in Texas. Dr. Annie Webb Blanton was elected in 1918 to the first statewide office ever held by a woman—State Superintendent of Public Instruction. In 1922, Edith Wilmans of Dallas became the first woman elected to the Texas House of Representatives, followed in 1926 by Margie Neal's election to the Texas Senate. Texas had two women secretaries of state in the 1920s: Emma Meharg and Jane Y. McCallum. Texas elected a woman governor, Miriam A. "Ma" Ferguson, in 1925 and elected her for a second term in 1933. By 1930, almost half the county treasurers were women.

Higher education became more accessible to Texas

women in 1903 with the opening of the Texas Industrial Institute and College for the Education of White Girls of the State of Texas in Arts and Sciences (now Texas Woman's University).

Around 1900, women began entering the workplace in larger numbers. Already more than half of public schoolteachers were women. The fields of nursing, social work, library science and home economics also welcomed women. The first director of Houston's Carnegie Library was Julia Ideson. The legal profession, which had been barely cracked by Frances Cox Henderson in the mid-1800s, was further opened to women by Hortense Sparks Ward, who is believed to have been the first woman licensed to practice law in Texas (1910). She wrote the Married Women's Property Rights Bill in 1913 and in 1925, was appointed Chief Justice of a special all-woman Supreme Court.

Women entrepreneurs were also active in the early 1900s. In 1907, Carrie Marcus Neiman, a marketing expert, cofounded internationally famous Neiman-Marcus specialty department store, at the same time that Mrs. A. W. Rysinger supplied hand-tailored clothing to Austin's fashionable black women.

During World War I, Texas women played important roles. Marjorie Stinson and her sister Katherine, among America's first flyers, founded a flying school in San Antonio in 1915 and trained Canadian pilots for the war. Katherine raised $2 million in a series of fundraising flights for the Red Cross. Her request to serve as a war pilot was denied, but she later volunteered as an ambulance driver in France.

Along the border around 1910, Hispanic women founded groups such as La Cruz Blanca to aid refugees and wounded during the Mexican Revolution. Hispanic women writers, among them journalist Jovita Idar and poet Sara Estela Ramirez, supported the Mexican Revolution with their writings.

The League of Women Voters, founded in the days of the final effort to ratify the 19th Amendment, registered voters and made wide-ranging studies of the issues. In the 1920s, the Texas Association of Colored Women's Clubs was assisted by League president Jessie Daniel Ames in obtaining funds for a state training school for black girls.

From 1922 to 1927, the Women's Joint Legislative Council, popularly known as the Petticoat Lobby, used its newly acquired lobbying skills to persuade the 28th and 29th Legislatures to enact legislation on behalf of maternal and infant health, schools, prison reform, prohibition and prevention of child labor. The Petticoat Lobby was a coalition of women's organizations led by Jane Y. McCallum.

After the war, the Texas Federation of Women's Clubs backed American entry into the League of Nations. Anna Pennybacker, who served as president of the club in 1901, was a pacifist, author of the first Texas history textbook (1888) and president of the General Federation of Women's Clubs from 1902 to 1908, represented three Texas newspapers from 1925 to 1931 at the

Texas Women's Hall of Fame honorees — (l-r) Education: Dr. Kate Atkinson Bell, teacher and public school administrator; Health Professions: Dr. Clotilde P. Garcia, physician, author and civic leader; Legal: Sarah T. Hughes, legislator, state and federal district judge.

League of Nations in Geneva and toured as a speaker on behalf of world peace.

Children's health was the concern of nurse Mae Smith, who borrowed Red Cross tents in 1913 to establish a "baby camp" for sick children in Dallas. By 1929, she had raised funds for a proper children's hospital, the Bradford Hospital of the Children's Medical Center. In Corpus Christi, Clara Driscoll left her fortune to establish a children's hospital.

Answering a desperate but long-ignored need, Edna Gladney ran the Texas Children's Home in Fort Worth from 1925 to 1960. Later called the Edna Gladney Home, it was Texas' first agency to provide services for unwed mothers and adoptive homes for children. Gladney's lobbying forced the Texas Legislature to pass laws erasing the word "illegitimate" from birth certificates. Another, related need was met when Kate Ripley and her husband established Texas' first planned parenthood clinic in Dallas in 1935, although dissemination of birth control information and devices was a violation of federal law at the time.

Opportunities for women in the workplace were steadily increasing through increased access to education and changes in the economy. Low wages, however, were still a problem. Telephone workers in San Antonio struck in 1900 to protest 13-hour days and seven-day work weeks. Hispanic laundry workers in El Paso won weekly wages of $5.50 to $7 in a strike in 1919, which, in turn, pushed up domestic workers' earnings. Thirteen Dallas factories were organized by the International Ladies Garment Workers Union (ILGWU) in 1935. Led by 22-year-old Emma Tenayuca, 12,000 pecan shellers in San Antonio walked out in 1938 in protest of wages of three to five cents an hour.

In 1924, Dr. Mary Gearing, the first woman on the University of Texas at Austin's Faculty Building Committee, oversaw the design of 15 buildings. Black educator Dr. Mary Elizabeth Blanton was named president of Tillotson College in Austin in 1930, becoming the first woman to head a Texas college. She held that post until 1944.

Sarah T. Hughes of Dallas was the first woman appointed to a district judgeship (1935); she was re-elected seven times. In 1961, President John F. Kennedy appointed her Texas' first female federal judge, and she swore in Lyndon Baines Johnson as president in 1963 in Dallas.

The only woman working for a state geological survey in 1938 was Helen Plummer, a consulting paleontologist for the Texas Bureau of Economic Geology.

Dallas entrepreneurs Elsie Frankfurt and Edna F. Ravkind founded Page Boy Maternity Fashions in 1938, appropriately staging their first style show at New York's Stork Club.

Grace Noll Crowell increased the recognition of Texas women's contributions to the arts when she served as Texas' third Poet Laureate during the 1930s. Gwendolyn Bennett's poems were published in a number of anthologies of the works of Negro poets.

Women's sports gained respect through Tad Lucas' championship trick riding every year from 1925 to 1931. Babe Didrikson Zaharias' mastery of a wide variety of sports, including golf, track, basketball, high jump and decathlon, was rewarded with two Olympic gold medals in 1932.

World War II marked the first major military involvement of Texas women in a war effort. More than 8,000 Texas women served in the Women's Army Corps (WACs), and Houston's Oveta Culp Hobby went to Washington as the first WAC director, becoming the first woman to hold the rank of colonel. Hobby had begun working for the Houston Post in 1931, and she became its publisher in 1964. She was the first woman director of the American Society of Newspaper Editors and the first cabinet secretary of the Dept. of Health, Education and Welfare.

Another 4,200 Texans served in the WAVES (Women Appointed for Voluntary Emergency Service). Civilian job opportunities for women also increased during the war years, and wages began to rise. A civilian job that required military risks and military discipline was flying for the WASPs, the Women's Airforce Service Pilots. Avenger Field, the WASP headquarters in Sweetwater, was the only all-woman air base in history. Some 25,000 women pilots applied for training, but only 1,074 passed all the tests. WASPs ferried all types of aircraft, tested disabled and newly repaired planes and flew targets for antiaircraft practice. Thirty-eight died in this service to their country. In 1979, 34 years after the war ended, the U. S. Congress finally awarded these women their military benefits.

Many more women served on the home front, filling jobs vacated by servicemen in plants converted from peacetime to wartime manufacturing. Women served as air raid wardens, rollers of bandages, collectors of scrap metal and sellers of war bonds. The war effort further broke down sex barriers to some traditionally male occupations. One barrier-breaker was Dr. Dora Strother, a former WASP who became Chief of Human Factors Engineering at Bell Helicopter Textron.

Once considered a provincial backwater in matters artistic, Texas and Dallas received national acclaim as the home of the Margo Jones Theatre from 1947 to 1959. Margo Jones established her theatre in the State Fair grounds soon after codirecting the original production of Tennessee Williams' The Glass Menagerie on Broadway. Pioneering in arena staging, Jones produced the premieres of Williams' Summer and Smoke and Jerome Lawrence and Robert E. Lee's Inherit the Wind. Katherine Ann Porter won the Pulitzer Prize for her novel Ship of Fools.

Houston's black children benefitted from the donation by Anna Dupree, a hairdresser, and her husband of funds for the Anna Dupree Cottage of the Negro Child Center in 1944. And black women benefitted from the opening in 1947 of Texas State University for Negroes (later Texas Southern University), also in Houston.

Texas Women's Hall of Fame honorees— (l-r) Public Service: Lady Bird Johnson, beautification, wildflower research and educational programs for children, and Barbara Jordan, Texas state senator, U.S. congresswoman and professor of public affairs; Science and Technology: Dr. Jeane Porter Hester, internist and cancer researcher.

The struggles of black women in the 1940s contributed to the giant strides made by blacks, both in Texas and nationally, in the 1950s. The Supreme Court decision in 1950 that blacks must be admitted to graduate programs at the University of Texas was followed closely by the decision in 1954 known as *Brown vs. Board of Education*—the decision which mandated desegregation of all public schools.

Charlye O. Farris led Texas black women into the legal profession, becoming, in 1954, the first black woman admitted to the Texas Bar. In 1958, Mrs. Charles B. White was elected to the Houston School Board, becoming the first black elected to office in Texas since Reconstruction.

All women benefitted in 1954 when, largely through the work of the League of Women Voters and the Texas Federation of Business and Professional Women's Clubs, women won the right to serve on juries.

From the end of the 1950s into the 1980s, women entrepreneurs have continued to break new ground. In 1958, a secretary, Bette Graham, developed Liquid Paper typing correction fluid in her kitchen and launched a corporation. In 1963, Mary Kay Ash founded the cosmetics empire that bears her name. In 1974, Lucille Bishop Smith, a black home economist who had developed the first hot roll mix in the United States, founded her own family corporation at the age of 82. Ninfa Laurenzo launched the multimillion-dollar restaurant chain, Ninfa's.

In the 1950s and 1960s, National Association for the Advancement of Colored People leader Christia Adair organized campaigns in Houston to end violence against blacks and to integrate public facilities, such as libraries, airports, restaurants and department stores. Juanita Craft, a statewide NAACP leader, was elected to the Dallas City Council in the 1970s. La Raza Unida was headed by Virginia Musquiz.

Although the legal and scientific communities were slow to accept women (In 1970, only eight percent of the students at the University of Texas at Austin Law School were women), progress was being made. In 1974, Dr. Lorene Rogers was appointed president of the University of Texas at Austin, becoming the first woman president of a major publicly supported U.S. university. In 1976, Dr. Mary Evelyn Blagg Huey became the first woman president of Texas Woman's University. Dr. Pauline Mack, a national expert in the fields of textiles and nutrition, served as director of Texas Woman's University's Research Institute from 1962 until 1983 and won an award for her studies in bone density for the National Aeronautics and Space Administration's Skylab Program. There are eight women astronauts in the space program in Houston, including Dr. Sally Ride, first American woman in space, and Dr. Katherine Sullivan, first American woman to walk in space. By 1984, 28 percent of the medical students at the University of Texas Medical School at Galveston were female.

The labor movement of the 1960s and 1970s concentrated on previous gains in working conditions and wages. Farm workers marched from the Rio Grande to Austin in 1966, demanding a minimum wage of $1.25 per hour. International Ladies Garment Workers' Union members struck in Laredo in 1967, and a prolonged strike in 1972-74 by 9,500 Amalgamated Clothing workers, bolstered by a national boycott, was successful. These gains were important to the 51 percent of Texas women over 16 who were in the labor force by 1978.

Under the leadership of Hermine Tobolowsky, the Business and Professional Women's Clubs lobbied for 25 years to achieve the 1972 Equal Legal Rights Amendment (ELRA) to the Texas Constitution. It was endorsed by Texas voters by a margin of four-to-one. In 1973, the Texas Legislature ratified the national Equal Rights Amendment, becoming the first Southern state to do so.

Despite previous gains, "firsts" for women were still occurring: In 1974, Dr. Lorene Rogers was appointed president of the University of Texas at Austin, becoming the first woman president of a major publicly supported U. S. university. Gabrielle McDonald of Houston became, in 1979, the first black woman ever appointed to a federal judgeship. The first Hispanic woman judge in Texas, Elma Salinas, was appointed by Gov. Mark White in 1983 and was elected to a full term in 1984.

With the advent of the civil rights and women's liberation movements of the 1960s and 1970s, a new wave of women officeholders, both elected and appointed, appeared.

In 1976, Barbara Jordan of Houston became the first black elected to the Texas Senate since Reconstruction, and in 1972 was elected to the U.S. Congress. That same year, Irma Rangel of Kingsville was the first Mexican-American woman elected to the Texas House.

The 1970s saw various presidential appointments of Texas women. President Gerald Ford appointed Anne Armstrong U.S. Ambassador to Great Britain and President Jimmy Carter appointed Sarah Weddington, a state legislator, as his assistant for women's issues. He also appointed Gabrielle McDonald of Houston as the nation's first black female federal judge.

During that same decade, Texas cities elected women mayors: Carole McLellan in Austin, Lila Cockrell in San Antonio and Kathy Whitmire in Houston. Adlene Harrison served as Dallas Mayor Pro Tem.

The 1980s saw the first woman in fifty years elected to a statewide office—State Treasurer Ann Richards (1982). In 1983, Mark White appointed Elma Salinas as Texas' first Mexican-American female judge, and she was elected to a full term in 1984. In 1984, White appointed Myra McDaniel as Secretary of State, the first black to hold a statewide appointive position, and only the third woman ever to hold that office.

To those who examine women's history, a trend is clearly visible: Women have been a major force for culture, for community and for survival in every ethnic group and across the bounds of race, religion and tribe. Only when women's history is thoroughly understood as co-equal and interwoven with histories left by men will the history of Texas be accurately represented.

Texas Women's Time Line

1848—Treaty of Guadalupe Hidalgo guarantees property rights of nonresident Mexican male and female landowners.

1865—Slaves are freed, men and women.

1868—First women's suffrage petition is submitted to the Texas Legislature.

1887—Women's Christian Temperance Union endorses suffrage.

1893—The Texas Equal Rights Association is founded in Dallas by Rebecca Hayes; lasts until 1895.

1902—The Texas Legislature passes a law requiring the payment of a poll tax to register to vote.

1903—The Texas Equal Suffrage Association is founded by Annette Finnigan of Houston; it lasts until 1905.

1906-10—The Texas Legislature passes reform legislation, such as the Pure Foods Act, largely through women's efforts.

1911—Jovita Idar of Laredo founds La Liga Femenil Mexicanista (League of Mexican Women).

1913—The Texas Equal Suffrage Association is revitalized, largely through the efforts of Eleanor Brackenridge.

1913—The Married Women's Property Act gives married women the right to manage their separate property.

1915—A child labor law and a compulsory school attendance law are passed.

1918—The Texas Equal Suffrage Association helps to impeach Gov. Jim Ferguson.

1918—Texas women gain the right to vote in state primary elections; they register 386,000 voters in 17 days and help elect Dr. Annie Webb Blanton to the office of State Superintendent of Instruction.

1919—The Texas Legislature ratifies the 19th (suffrage) amendment to the federal constitution.

1920—The National Prohibition (18th) and Suffrage (19th) Amendments take effect.

1921—The Texas Legislature passes a maternal and infant health program.

1922—Edith Wilmans of Dallas becomes the first woman elected to the Texas House of Representatives.

1922-27—The Women's Joint Legislative Council, a coalition of groups known as the Petticoat Lobby, gets its entire legislative program adopted.

1924—Miriam Amanda "Ma" Ferguson is elected Texas governor on an anti-Ku Klux Klan platform.

1925—Texas' All-Woman Supreme Court, appointed by outgoing governor Pat Neff, is composed of Hortense Ward, Hattie Henenberg and Ruth Brazzil.

1925—Gov. Ma Ferguson appoints Emma Meharg Texas' first female Secretary of State.

1926—Publisher Margie Neal of Carthage is the first woman elected to the Texas Senate.

1927—Jane Y. McCallum is appointed Secretary of State and serves two terms, until 1933.

1928—Clara Driscoll is the first Texas woman elected to the Democratic National Committee; serves until 1944.

1935—Sarah T. Hughes of Dallas is appointed Texas' first female state judge.

1944—The White Primary Law is declared unconstitutional by the U.S. Supreme Court.

1954—Texas women obtain the right to serve on juries.

1960s—La Raza Unida is founded and the civil rights movement is active; both involve women.

1964—The U.S. Civil Rights Act is passed.

1965—The U.S. Voting Rights Act is passed.

1966—The poll tax is declared unconstitutional.

1966—Barbara Jordan becomes the first black since Reconstruction elected to the Texas Senate .

1967—The Matrimonial Property Act gives married women the general power to contract.

1971—The Texas Women's Political Caucus is organized, and Chicanas hold their first statewide meeting.

1972—Sarah Weddington of Austin wins a landmark case (Roe v. Wade) before the U.S. Supreme Court, establishing a woman's right to seek an abortion.

1972—Barbara Jordan is elected to Congress, becoming the first black from Texas to serve.

1972—Texas voters approve the Texas Equal Legal Rights Amendment by a margin of 4 to 1.

1972—Irma Rangel of Kingsville becomes the first Mexican-American woman elected to the Texas Legislature.

1973—The Texas Legislature endorses the national Equal Rights Amendment.

1975—The Voting Rights Act of 1965 is strengthened to include Texas and to require bilingual voter assistance.

1970s—Austin, Houston and San Antonio elect women mayors: Carole McLellan, Kathy Whitmire and Lila Cockrell.

1973-1979—The number of women in the Legislature increases from 2 to 13.

1982—The Voting Rights Act is strengthened to foster single-member districts.

1982—Ann Richards is elected State Treasurer, the first woman to hold that office and the first woman in 50 years elected to statewide office.

1984—A special session of the Legislature passes a law covering farm workers under workers' compensation.

1984—Myra McDaniel is appointed Secretary of State by Gov. Mark White, becoming the first black to hold a statewide appointive position of cabinet stature.

1984—Leslie Benitez is appointed as Gov. Mark White's chief legal counsel, becoming the highest Hispanic officeholder in the state.

Selected Bibliography

Barr, Alwyn, **Black Texans: A History of Negroes in Texas, 1528-1971**; Jenkins Press, Austin, 1973.

Branda, Eldon, editor, **Handbook of of Texas, Volume Three**; Texas State Historical Assn., Austin, 1976.

Cotera, Martha, **Diosa y Hembra. The History and Heritage of Chicanas in the U.S.**; Information Systems Dev., Austin, 1976.

Crawford, Ann Fears, and Crystal Sasse Ragsdale, **Women in Texas, their Lives, their Experiences, their Accomplishments**; Eakin Press, Burnet, 1982.

Malone, Ann Patton, **Women on the Texas Frontier, a Cross-Cultural Perspective**; Texas Western Press, El Paso, 1983.

Newcombe, W. W., Jr., **The Indians of Texas**; UT Press, Austin, 1961.

Pickrell, Mrs. Annie Doom, **Pioneer Women in Texas**; Steck, Austin, 1929.

Rogers, Mary Beth, **Texas Women: A Celebration of History Exhibit Catalog**; Texas Foundation for Women's Resources, Austin, 1981.

Rogers, Mary Beth, Sherry Smith, and Janelle Scott, **We Can Fly, Stories of Katherine Stinson and Other**

Gutsy Texas Women; Ellen C. Temple, Austin, 1983.

"Texas Women: A Celebration of History" Exhibit Narrative, unpublished; Texas Foundation for Women's Resources, Austin, 1981.

Texas Foundation for Women's Resources, unpublished concept papers, 1978-1980 by Brewer, Rose; Chapa, Evey; Cotera, Martha; Fleming, Nancy; Hield, Melissa; Scott, Janelle; Smith, Sherry; Werden, Frieda; and Winegarten, Ruthe.

Webb, Walter Prescott, editor, **The Handbook of Texas in Two Volumes**; Texas State Historical Assn., Austin, 1952.

Weddington, Sarah, Jane Hickie, Deanna Fitzgerald, Elizabeth W. Fernea and Marilyn P. Duncan, **Texas Women in Politics**; Foundation for Women's Resources, Austin, 1977.

Winegarten, Ruthe, editor, **Finder's Guide to the Texas Women: A Celebration of History Exhibit Archives**; Texas Woman's University, Denton, 1984.

Winegarten, Ruthe, editor, **Texas Women's History Project Bibliography**; Texas Foundation for Women's Resources, Austin, 1980.

Map provided by the
Texas General Land Office

TEXAS COUNTIES AND TOWNS

These pages describe Texas' 254 counties and hundreds of towns. Descriptions are based on reports from chambers of commerce, Texas Agricultural Extension Service, federal and state agencies and many others. Note also pages devoted to the metropolitan areas beginning on Page 385. Consult the index for other county information.

County maps are based on those of the Texas Highway Department and are copyrighted, 1985, as are the entire contents.

LETTER-NUMBER COMBINATIONS in parentheses with each county denote location on the map on this page. For example, Anderson County (J-19) means that Anderson County can be found near the intersection of lines J and 19 on the larger map.

AREA: Revised 1980 U.S. Census land area; excludes land submerged by water.

TOPOGRAPHY: Descriptions are from U.S. Geological Survey and local sources.

HISTORY, ORGANIZATION, COUNTY NAMES: From Texas Statutes, Fulmore's History and Geography of Texas as Told in County Names, WPA Historical Records Survey and Texas Centennial Commission Report.

COURTS, CONGRESSIONAL DISTRICTS, ETC.: The following abbreviations are used: Cong. Dist., Congressional District; St. Sen. Dist., State Senatorial District; St. Rep. Dist., State Representative District; St. Dist. Cts., State District Courts; U.S. Jud. Dist., U.S. Judicial District; Ct. Appeals, Court of Appeals; Admin. Jud. Dist., Administrative Judicial District.

The designations used in the following counties were districts as constituted for the 1984 elections.

Texas is divided into four U.S. Judicial Districts: Northern, Southern, Eastern and Western. The following abbreviations are used to designate the city in which the court sits: N-Ab: Abilene; N-Am: Amarillo; N-DI: Dallas; N-FW: Fort Worth; N-Lb: Lubbock; N-SAng: San Angelo; N-WF: Wichita Falls; S-Br: Brownsville; S-CC: Corpus Christi; S-Gn: Galveston; S-Hn: Houston; S-La: Laredo; S-Va: Victoria; E-Bt: Beaumont; E-Ml: Marshall; E-Ps: Paris; E-Sh: Sherman; E-Tx: Texarkana; E-Ty: Tyler; W-An: Austin; W-DR: Del Rio; W-EP: El Paso; W-Pe: Pecos; W-SAnt; San Antonio; W-Wa: Waco; W-M-O: Midland-Odessa.

AGRICULTURE: 1982 Census of Agriculture; County Agents' reports for 1985 are included when available.

Much additional Texas agricultural information will be found in the Texas Almanac section devoted to crops and livestock. This includes total cash receipts and production of major livestock and their products, and crops; along with discussions of leading commodities.

That information was obtained largely from Texas Crop and Livestock Reporting Service of the Texas Department of Agriculture and U.S. Department of Agriculture. Annual information for each Texas county, based upon surveys, may be obtained from this source; write to P.O. Box 70, Austin 78767.

POPULATION: Revised July 1, 1982, U.S. Census figures are used for counties; revised April 1, 1980 Census figures are used for incorporated cities and towns. Texas Almanac estimates, based on reports from county agents, chambers of commerce and others, used where no official Census figures available. In some cases late adjustments in county totals will cause breakdowns not to add up.

ALTITUDES: U.S. Geological Survey, Texas Department of Highways and Public Transportation and Texas Railroad Commission.

WEATHER: From NOAA State Climatologist, College Station.

MINERALS: Oil value, 1984, State Comptroller.

MANUFACTURING: Preliminary U.S. Census of Manufactures, 1982. Product value figure contains some duplication; data not available for Value Added by Manufacture, a more accurate figure. *Symbol indicates data withheld to avoid disclosing individual operations.

SOILS: Texas Agricultural Experiment Station, U.S. Soil Conservation Service.

HIGHWAYS: Texas Department of Highways and Public Transportation.

EMPLOYMENT, WAGES: Texas Employment Commission; employment in first quarter, 1984; annual wages are four times first-quarter wages. Includes firms with four or more on payroll, excludes owners and other nonsalaried persons.

TAX VALUE: 1984 Total assessed valuation, (before exemptions), State Property Tax Board. N.A. indicates information not available July 1, 1985.

FEDERAL EXPENDITURES: U.S. Census for Office of Management and Budget, 1983.

VOTER REGISTRATION: Voters eligible on Nov. 2, 1984, office of Secretary of State's Election Division.

INCOME: Effective Buying Income, 1985, Sales Management Magazine, (further reproduction prohibited without written permission from Sales Management).

TAXABLE SALES: Amount subject to 4.125 percent state sales tax in 1984; Comptroller of Public Accounts.

RAILROADS: Texas Railroad Commission records as of 1984 used on county maps.

CRIME INDEX: Information for 1984 covers murder, rape, robbery, aggravated assault, burglary, theft and motor vehicle theft; furnished by Texas Department of Corrections.

TDC POPULATION: No. inmates per county, April 1, 1985; furnished by TDC.

SERVICE INDUSTRIES: 1982 U.S. Census of Service Industries.

†Where this symbol appears, it refers to Value of Land and Buildings per farm in 1982.

*Where this symbol appears in the following counties, it indicates that data were withheld to avoid disclosure of individual operations.

LEGEND FOR MAPS

Following is explanation of signs and symbols used:

▬▬▬ Paved road of all types.

▬╫▬ Indicates divided roads.

▬▭▭▭ Surfaced roads—all-weather gravel, shell, etc.

= = =: Roads under construction.

(With few exceptions roads shown on these maps are state and federal highways. Local roads of all types of improvement thread the counties of Texas.)

▬▩ Incorporated towns.

▬○ Unincorporated towns.

▬◉ County seats.

▬⬡20⬡ Interstate highway numbers.

▬⬠2⬠ U.S. highway numbers.

▬⬡2A⬡ Alternate U.S. highway numbers.

▬⬡2⬡ State highway numbers.

▬⬜2⬜ Farm to market roads.

▬⬡2⬡ Park roads, temporary designations.

▬⬜LR⬜ County or local roads.

+-+-+-+ Railroads.

🌲✈ Airports.

Notable parks.

Anderson

LOCATION: East Texas (J-19).
HISTORY: First settled in 1830s; created from Houston County and organized in 1846; named for **K. L. Anderson**, last vice-president, Texas Republic.

Cong. Dist. 2	U.S. Jud. Dist. . . E-Tyler
St. Sen. Dist. 3	Ct. Appeals 12
St. Rep. Dist 11	Admin. Jud. Dist. 1
St. Dist. Cts. . . . 3, 87, 349	

PHYSICAL FEATURES: Hilly, slopes to Trinity and Neches Rivers; sandy, clay, black soils; pines, hardwoods used commercially.

RECREATION. Fishing, hunting, many streams, lakes; **Dogwood Trails;** historic sites; **Engeling Wildlife Refuge; Texas State Railroad Park** for tourists; civic auditorium; county fair; arts, crafts festival; tour of old homes. Tourist information center in restored 1890 depot.

MINERALS: Oil and gas.

1982 Pop. 42,200	Voters reg.	20,785
Area (sq. mi.) 1,077	Whlsle. sales $190,033,000	
Altitude (ft.) 300-800	Oil value $57,936,844	
Ann. rainfall (in.) . 40.51	No. employed 12,941	
Jan. temp. min. 37	Wages paid . $213,062,948	
July temp. max. 94	Tax value . $1,324,071,647	
Growing season (da.) 264	Income $336,708,000	
No. farms, 1982 . . . 1,356	Taxable sales $161,369,340	
No. acres in farms 320,075	Fed. expend. . $79,184,000	
†Value per farm $188,456	Crime Index 1,495	
Cropland harvested 31,047	TDC Pop. 48	

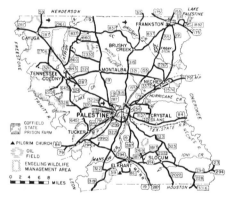

AGRICULTURE: Annual agricultural receipts average about $25.7 million, 87% from livestock and products. Hay, peas, watermelon and peanuts principal crops; over 50% of land in forests and $3 million worth of timber products sold.

BUSINESS: Manufacturing, distribution, agribusiness, tourism; hunting and fishing leases; Texas Department of Corrections units.

MANUFACTURING: 43 Plants; 1,700 Employees; Payroll, $26,100,000; Product Value, $167,600,000.

SERVICE INDUSTRIES: 178 Establishments; Receipts, $40,862,000; Annual Payroll, $11,349,000; No. employees, 1,068.

PALESTINE (15,948) county seat; wholesale meats, automotive parts, clothing, metal, wood products manufactured; large aluminum smelting plant; transportation center; agribusiness center; shipping center; **Scientific Balloon Station;** hospital; library; vocational-technical facilities; Anderson College Center, branch of **Henderson County Junior College.**

Other towns include **Frankston** (1,255), **Elkhart** (1,317), **Tennessee Colony,** which is site of **Coffield** and **Beto Units, Texas Department of Corrections.**

Andrews

LOCATION: Borders New Mexico (I-7).
HISTORY: Created 1876 from Bexar Territory; organized 1910; named for Texas Revolutionary soldier, **Richard Andrews.**

Cong. Dist. 19	U.S. Jud. Dist . . . W:M-O
St. Sen. Dist. 28	Ct. Appeals 8
St. Rep. Dist. 77	Admin. Jud. Dist. 7
St. Dist. Cts. 109	

PHYSICAL FEATURES: Plains, drain to playas; grass, mesquite, shin oak; red clay, sandy soils.

RECREATION: Prairie dog town, oil museum, local events, tourist trailer facilities.

MINERALS: A leading producer of oil and gas.

1982 Pop. 15,000	Voters reg. 6,797	
Area (sq. mi.) 1,501	Whlsle. sales . $27,059,000	
Altitude (ft.) . 3,000-3,400	Oil value $763,220,503	
Ann. rainfall (in.) . 14.37	No. employed . . . 6,803	
Jan. temp. min. 30	Wages paid . $142,497,216	
July temp. max. 96	Tax value . $3,001,161,426	
Growing season (da.) 213	Income $153,049,000	
No. farms, 1982 . . . 128	Taxable sales $56,915,920	
No. acres in farms 746,354	Fed. expend. . $24,941,000	
†Value per farm $1,064,664	Crime Index 441	
Cropland harvested 39,679	TDC Pop. 23	

AGRICULTURE: Income averages $11.8 million, 65% from cattle, remainder cotton, sorghums; small grains, corn, hay; 12,000 acres irrigated.

BUSINESS: Chiefly oil related; vacuum cleaner manufacturing; agribusiness.

MANUFACTURING: None noted in census report.

SERVICE INDUSTRIES: 60 Establishments; Receipts, $19,515,000; Annual Payroll, $6,051,000; No. Employees, 399.

ANDREWS (11,061) county seat; oil marketing center; hospitals, rest home, mental health center; parks.

Angelina

LOCATION: In east (K-21).
HISTORY: Created, organized 1846, from Nacogdoches County; named for **Angelina River.**

Cong. Dist. 2	U.S. Jud. Dist. . . E.-Tyler
St. Sen. Dist. 3	Ct. Appeals 9
St. Rep. Dist. 17	Admin. Jud. Dist. 2
St. Dist. Cts. 159, 217	

PHYSICAL FEATURES: Rolling, hilly; black, red, gray soils; **Angelina National Forest;** much lumbering.

RECREATION: **Lake Sam Rayburn;** national, state forests, parks; historic sites; Texas Forest Festival third Saturday in May; Forestry Association Museum and historical locomotive exhibit; historical and creative arts museum; woodland trails; Ellen Trout Park and Zoo; county rodeo.

MINERALS: Limited output natural gas, oil.

1982 Pop. 67,600	Voters reg. 35,985	
Area (sq. mi.) 807	Whlsle. sales $237,342,000	
Altitude (ft.) 200-380	Oil value $2,078,109	
Ann. rainfall (in.) . 42.99	No. employed . . . 25,325	
Jan. temp. min. 39	Wages paid . $413,784,944	
July temp. max. 94	Tax value . $1,851,931,766	
Growing season (da.) 244	Income $573,252,000	
No. farms, 1982 . . . 723	Taxable sales $324,978,502	
No. acres in farms 118,536	Fed. expend. $100,430,000	
†Value per farm $174,646	Crime Index 2,449	
Cropland harvested 9,307	TDC Pop. 190	

AGRICULTURE: Leading timber-producing county with 70% of land in commercial forests; more than $12 million average annual income from beef cattle, poultry; some hay, vegetables marketed.

BUSINESS: Many plants make oil field pumping units, newsprint, other paper products; wood products,

Angelina County (Cont'd.)

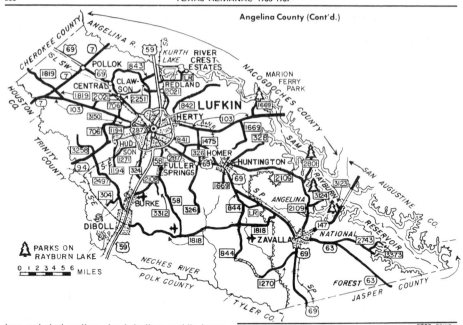

iron and steel castings, truck trailers; mobile home units, horse stables.

MANUFACTURING: 122 Plants; 8,000 Employees; Payroll, $142,600,000; Product Value, $807,500,000.

SERVICE INDUSTRIES: 350 Establishments; Receipts; $71,238,000; Annual Payroll, $25,307,000; No. employees, 2,043.

LUFKIN (28,562) county seat, a leading manufacturing center; **Angelina College**; two hospitals; **Lufkin State School** (mentally retarded); **Texas Forest Service Cudlipp Forestry Center; U.S. Forest Service; Ellen Trout Park Zoo; Historical and Creative Arts Center.** Other towns include **Diboll** (5,227), **Huntington** (1,672), **Burke** (322), **Fuller Springs** (1,470), **Hudson** (1,659), **Zavalla** (762), **Herty.**

Aransas

LOCATION: On Coast (Q-17).

HISTORY: Created, organized, 1871, from Refugio County; named for **Rio Nuestra Senora de Aranzazu**, derived from a Spanish palace.

Cong. Dist. 14	U.S. Jud. Dist. . . . . S-CC
St. Sen. Dist. 18	Ct. Appeals 13
St. Rep. Dist. 36	Admin. Jud. Dist. 4
St. Dist. Cts. . . 36, 156, 343	

PHYSICAL FEATURES: Flat; sandy loam, coastal clay soils; many bays, inlets; mesquites, live oaks.

RECREATION: Many fishing, hunting, tourist facilities: **Fulton Mansion; Goose Island State Park; Aransas National Wildlife Refuge; State Marine Lab;** marine aquarium; many resort homes, Rockport Art Center.

MINERALS: Oil and gas produced.

1982 Pop. 16,000	Voters reg. 8,167
Area (sq. mi.) 280	Whlsle. sales . $10,739,000
Altitude (ft.) 50	Oil value . . . $14,324,497
Ann. rainfall (in.) . 33.19	No. employed 4,937
Jan. temp. min. 48	Wages paid . . $79,633,824
July temp. max. 92	Tax value . . $870,157,270
Growing season (da.) 312	Income $168,657,000
No. farms, 1982 61	Taxable sales $65,797,185
No. acres in farms. 27,883	Fed. expend. $200,731,000
†Value per farm $375,033	Crime Index 739
Cropland harvested 2,763	TDC Pop. 37

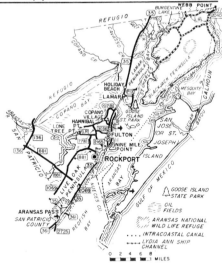

AGRICULTURE: Average income of $1.5 million from livestock, chiefly beef cattle; grains.

BUSINESS: Tourism, fishing and shrimping; oil production; refining; shipbuilding, offshore equipment fabricated; carbon plant.

MANUFACTURING: None noted in census report.

SERVICE INDUSTRIES: 70 Establishments; Receipts, $10,495,000; Annual Payroll, $2,833,000; No. employees, 286.

ROCKPORT (3,686) county seat; fishing; tourist center; art festival; oyster fest; sea fair in October; library.

Aransas Pass (7,173 in Aransas, Nueces and San Patricio Counties) deepwater port on **Intracoastal Canal,** oil producing; refining; industrial plants; shrimping, fishing, tourism; hospital, nursing home; art festival in July, Shrimporee in October. Other towns include **Fulton** (725), **Lamar.**

Archer

LOCATION: North Central (F-14).

HISTORY: Created from Fannin Land District, 1858; organized, 1880. Named for **Dr. B. T. Archer,** Republic of Texas commissioner to U.S.

Cong. Dist.	13	U.S. Jud. Dist.	N-WF
St. Sen. Dist.	30	Ct. Appeals	2
St. Rep. Dist.	80	Admin. Jud. Dist.	8
St. Dist. Cts.	97		

PHYSICAL FEATURES: Rolling, hilly, drained by Wichita River forks; black, red loams, sandy soils; mesquites, post oaks.

RECREATION: Lakes Arrowhead, Kickapoo, Diversion; rattlesnake roundup in spring; local events; quail hunting.

MINERALS: Oil, gas, stone produced.

1982 Pop.	7,500	Voters reg.	4,772
Area (sq. mi.)	907	Whlsle. sales	$37,959,000
Altitude (ft.)	900-1,400	Oil value	$121,058,034
Ann. rainfall (in.)	25.26	No. employed	2,000
Jan. temp. min.	28	Wages paid	$32,101,388
July temp. max.	98	Tax value	$605,729,366
Growing season (da.)	220	Income	$63,651,000
No. farms, 1982	465	Taxable sales	$27,656,296
No. acres in farms	544,170	Fed. expend.	$33,617,000
†Value per farm	$486,222	Crime Index	123
Cropland harvested	59,118	TDC Pop.	6

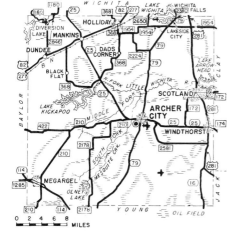

AGRICULTURE: Income averages $39 million, 80% from beef and dairy cattle; wheat, other grains.

BUSINESS: Cattle and oil field services.

MANUFACTURING: None noted in census report.

SERVICE INDUSTRIES: 18 Establishments; Receipts, $2,956,000; Annual Payroll, $938,000; No. employees, 107.

ARCHER CITY: (1,862) county seat; hospital, nursing home, library, County Museum. Other towns include **Holliday** (1,349), **Windthorst** (409), **Megargel** (381), **Lakeside City**(515), **Scotland** (367) and part of **Wichita Falls.**

Armstrong

LOCATION: Northwest, in Panhandle (D-9).

HISTORY: Created from Bexar District, 1876; organized 1890. Name honors pioneer family.

Cong. Dist.	13	U.S. Jud. Dist.	N-Am.
St. Sen. Dist.	31	Ct. Appeals	7
St. Rep. Dist.	84	Admin. Jud. Dist.	9
St. Dist. Cts.	47		

PHYSICAL FEATURES: Plain, broken by **Palo Duro Canyon, Cap Rock.** Chocolate loam, gray soils.

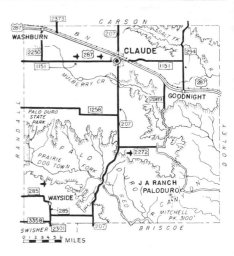

MINERALS: Sand, gravel produced.

RECREATION: Palo Duro Canyon State Park; pioneer **Goodnight Ranch home and townsite;** Caprock Celebration in July.

1982 Pop.	1,900	Voters reg.	1,334
Area (sq. mi.)	910	Whlsle. sales	$*
Altitude (ft.)	2,400-3,500	Oil value	0
Ann. rainfall (in.)	19.98	No. employed	787
Jan. temp. min.	19	Wages paid	$22,807,664
July temp. max.	92	Tax value	$163,251,340
Growing season (da.)	213	Income	$22,772,000
No. farms, 1982	240	Taxable sales	$2,369,355
No. acres in farms	552,856	Fed. expend.	$15,290,000
†Value per farm	$546,845	Crime Index	23
Cropland harv.	100,434	TDC Pop.	3

AGRICULTURE: $15.5 million average income, 50% from beef cattle; wheat, sorghums, chief crops. 15,000 acres irrigated.

BUSINESS: Agribusiness center.

MANUFACTURING: None noted in census report.

SERVICE INDUSTRIES: 3 Establishments; Receipts, NA. Annual Payroll, NA; No. Employees, NA.

CLAUDE (1,112) county seat; ranching, farming supplies; plow manufacturing; medical center; convalescent home; Spring trade fair.

Atascosa

LOCATION: South, near San Antonio (P-14).

HISTORY: Created, organized from Bexar District, 1856. **Atascosa** is boggy in Spanish.

Cong. Dist.	15	U.S. Jud. Dist.	W-SAnt.
St. Sen. Dist.	21	Ct. Appeals	4
St. Rep. Dist.	45	Admin. Jud. Dist.	4
St. Dist. Cts.	81, 218		

PHYSICAL FEATURES: Grassy prairie, drained by Atascosa River, tributaries. Mesquites, other brush.

RECREATION: Local events; quail, deer hunting; Longhorn Museum; river park; little theater group; county fair; strawberry festival at Poteet in April; home of the cowboy festival in August.

MINERALS: Oil, gas, lignite.

1982 Pop.	26,100	Voters reg.	14,079
Area (sq. mi.)	1,218	Whlsle. sales	$108,563,000
Altitude (ft.)	300-700	Oil value	$48,598,465
Ann. rainfall (in.)	26.58	No. employed	5,917
Jan. temp. min.	42	Wages paid	$84,645,028
July temp. max.	97	Tax value	$1,325,325,906
Growing season (da.)	282	Income	$202,254,000
No. farms, 1982	1,256	Taxable sales	$78,089,695
No. acres in farms	754,587	Fed. expend.	$40,159,000
†Value per farm	$374,018	Crime Index	481
Cropland harvested	70,257	TDC Pop.	56

AGRICULTURE: About $50 million average income, 60% from cattle, dairy products, hogs; peanuts, grain, hay; pecans, strawberries; 40,000 acres irrigated.

Atascosa County (Cont'd.)

1982 Pop.	19,300	Voters reg.	9,640
Area (sq. mi.)	656	Whlsle. sales	$74,603,000
Altitude (ft.)	150-400	Oil value	$2,828,004
Ann. rainfall (in.)	42.04	No. employed	6,069
Jan. temp. min.	44	Wages paid	$94,288,296
July temp. max.	95	Tax value	$1,197,387,314
Growing season (da.)	282	Income	$202,552,000
No. farms, 1982	1,677	Taxable sales	$70,540,533
No. acres in farms	312,414	Fed. expend.	$38,802,000
†Value per farm	$323,304	Crime Index	379
Cropland harvested	47,932	TDC Pop.	38

BUSINESS: Agribusiness center, steel, other manufacturing.

MANUFACTURING: 31 Plants; 1,400 Employees; Payroll, $27,700,000; Product Value, $173,500,000.

SERVICE INDUSTRIES: 76 Establishments; Receipts, $11,222,000; Annual Payroll, $3,895,000; No. Employees, 495.

BELLVILLE (2,860) county seat; clothing, furniture, trailers, tubing, food products manufactured; oil production; hospital. Other towns include **Sealy** (3,875) oil field manufacturing, picturesque downtown; **Wallis** (1,138); **San Felipe** (532) colonial capital of Texas.

BUSINESS: Agribusinesses, oil well supplies, services; coal plant; light manufacturing; shipping.

MANUFACTURING: None noted in census report.

SERVICE INDUSTRIES: 77 Establishments; Receipts, $14,725,000; Annual Payroll, $3,952,000; No. Employees, 529.

JOURDANTON (2,743) county seat; hospital, rest home. **Pleasanton** (6,346) hospitals, nursing homes; "home of the cowboy"; peanut processing; power plant. Other towns include **Poteet** (3,086) "strawberry capital"; **Lytle** (1,920), **Christine** (392), **Charlotte** (1,443).

Austin

LOCATION: Southeast (N-18).

HISTORY: Birthplace of Anglo-American colonization, named for **Stephen F. Austin**, colonists' leader; county created, organized 1837.

Cong. Dist.	14	U.S. Jud. Dist.	S-Hn.
St. Sen. Dist.	5	Ct. Appeals	1, 14
St. Rep. Dist.	30	Admin. Jud. Dist.	3
St. Dist. Cts.	155		

PHYSICAL FEATURES: Level to hilly, drained by San Bernard, Brazos Rivers. Black prairie to sandy upland soils.

RECREATION: Fishing, hunting, local events; **Stephen F. Austin State Park**, other historic sites; bluebonnet trails in spring.

MINERALS: Oil, gas.

AGRICULTURE: About $38 million average yearly income, 80% from livestock, poultry; sorghums, small grains, rice, corn, peanuts, cotton.

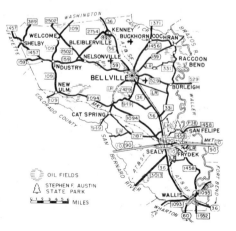

Bailey

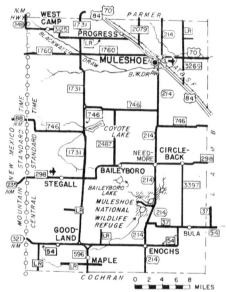

LOCATION: Northwest (E-7).

HISTORY: Created from Bexar District, 1876, organized 1917. Named for Alamo hero, **Peter J. Bailey.**

Cong. Dist.	19	U.S. Jud. Dist.	N-Lb.
St. Sen. Dist.	31	Ct. Appeals	7
St. Rep. Dist.	85	Admin. Jud. Dist.	9
St. Dist. Cts.	287		

PHYSICAL FEATURES: Plain; mostly sandy loam soils; mesquite brush; drains to Brazos, playas.

RECREATION: Muleshoe National Wildlife Refuge; local events; hunting.

MINERALS: Insignificant.

1982 Pop.	8,300	Voters reg.	3,679
Area (sq. mi.)	827	Whlsle. sales	$83,094,000
Altitude (ft.)	3,800-4,400	Oil value	0
Ann. rainfall (in.)	17.29	No. employed	1,766
Jan. temp. min.	20	Wages paid	$22,819,384
July temp. max.	92	Tax value	$309,745,284
Growing season (da.)	181	Income	$51,277,000
No. farms, 1982	442	Taxable sales	$18,654,805
No. acres in farms	451,460	Fed. expend.	$48,841,000
†Value per farm	$495,894	Crime Index	190
Cropland harv.	230,760	TDC Pop.	13

AGRICULTURE: About $61 million farm receipts annually, 60% from crops, 40% from livestock; crops include sorghums, corn, cotton, wheat, alfalfa, vegetables, sunflowers; about 165,000 acres irrigated; cattle, hogs, sheep; feedlots.

BUSINESS: Farm supply manufacturing, food processing plants, other agribusinesses.

MANUFACTURING: None noted in census report.

SERVICE INDUSTRIES: 41 Establishments; Receipts, $4,294,000; Annual Payroll, $1,131,000; No. employees, 156.

MULESHOE (4,842) county seat; feed processing, farm tools manufacturing; hospital; **National Mule Memorial.**

Bandera

LOCATION: Southwest (N-13.)

HISTORY: Created, organized from Bexar, Uvalde Counties, 1856; named for Bandera (flag) Mts.

Cong. Dist.	21	U.S. Jud. Dist.	W-SAnt.
St. Sen. Dist.	25	Ct. Appeals	4
St. Rep. Dist.	45	Admin. Jud. Dist.	6
St. Dist. Cts.	216		

PHYSICAL FEATURES: Hilly, plateau; Medina River, Lake; limestone, sandy soils; dominated by various species of oaks, walnuts, native cherry and Uvalde maple.

RECREATION: Dude and resort ranches, RV parks; hunting, leases, fishing; **Frontier Times Museum; Lost Maples State Park;** Fun-tier Days celebration, youth rodeo.

MINERALS: Not significant.

1982 Pop.	7,500	Voters reg.	5,259
Area (sq. mi.)	793	Whlsle. sales	$438,000
Altitude (ft.)	1,200-2,400	Oil value	0
Ann. rainfall (in.)	28.82	No. employed	1,866
Jan. temp. min.	32	Wages paid	$28,738,072
July temp. max.	94	Tax value	$507,503,233
Growing season (da.)	235	Income	$76,088,000
No. farms, 1982	475	Taxable sales	$17,463,196
No. acres in farms	339,087	Fed. expend.	$26,612,000
†Value per farm	$458,221	Crime Index	150
Cropland harvested	5,916	TDC Pop.	8

AGRICULTURE: Over 95% of $6.8 million yearly agricultural income from beef cattle, sheep, goats, poultry and post cedar.

BUSINESS: Tourism, hunting, fishing, purse factory, ranching supplies, marketing.

MANUFACTURING: None noted in census report.

SERVICE INDUSTRIES: 30 Establishments; Receipts, $4,399,000; Annual Payroll, $1,104,000; No. Employees, 132.

BANDERA (947) county seat; cedar mill, cedar shingle factory, purse factory; hunting, guest ranching center; girls camp; museums; local events; nursing home. Other towns include **Medina, Lake Hills, Pipe Creek, Vanderpool** and **Tarpley.**

Bastrop

LOCATION: Near Austin (M-16).

HISTORY: First settled 1829; county created 1836, organized 1837; named for **Baron de Bastrop,** who aided colonists.

Cong. Dist.	10	U.S. Jud. Dist.	W-An.
St. Sen. Dist.	18	Ct. Appeals	3
St. Rep. Dist.	30	Admin. Jud. Dist.	2
St. Dist. Cts.	21, 335		

PHYSICAL FEATURES: Rolling; alluvial, sandy, loam soils; varied timber, "**Lost Pines**"; bisected by Colorado River.

RECREATION: Center of "Lost Pines" region; fishing, hunting; **Bastrop, Buescher State Parks; Lake Bas-**

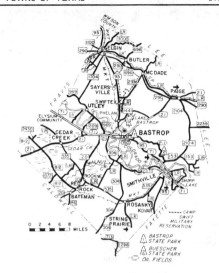

trop; historic sites; museum; Elgin Western Days in July; Smithville Jamboree in April; Texas State Championship BBQ Cookoff in July.

MINERALS: Clay, oil, gas and lignite.

1982 Pop.	28,200	Voters reg.	17,386
Area (sq. mi.)	895	Whlsle. sales	$17,369,000
Altitude (ft.)	400-600	Oil value	$5,799,251
Ann. rainfall (in.)	36-82	No. employed	4,523
Jan. temp. min.	40	Wages paid	$55,127,272
July temp. max.	96	Tax value	$1,009,323,502
Growing season (da.)	268	Income	$242,473,000
No. farms, 1982	1,507	Taxable sales	$59,460,835
No. acres in farms	377,258	Fed. expend.	$56,159,000
†Value per farm	$267,721	Crime Index	839
Cropland harvested	33,150	TDC Pop.	38

AGRICULTURE: Average farm income $28 million, 90% from beef, dairy cattle, hogs, poultry. Crops include grain sorghums, pecans, corn, wheat, oats; fruit production beginning.

BUSINESS: Agribusiness, brick, electronic equipment, other manufacturing; tourism attracting residents from Austin.

MANUFACTURING: 28 Plants; 700 Employees; Payroll, $9,600,000; Product Value, $39,400,000.

SERVICE INDUSTRIES: 66 Establishments; Receipts, $10,827,000; Annual Payroll, $3,472,000; No. Employees, 313.

BASTROP (3,789) county seat; oil well supply, agribusinesses, furniture manufacturing; hospital; **University of Texas Cancer research center;** federal correctional center. **Elgin** (4,535) famous for sausages; brick plants, cottonseed mill, food processing, furniture plant, agribusinesses; research instruments; leather works; hospital, nursing home. **Smithville** (3,470) cedar products, manufacturing, trading center; Environmental Science Park for Cancer Research; hospital, nursing home, medical clinics.

Baylor

LOCATION: North central (F-13).

HISTORY: Created from Fannin County, 1858; organized 1879. Named for **H. W. Baylor, Texas Ranger** surgeon.

Cong. Dist.	13	U.S. Jud. Dist.	N-WF
St. Sen. Dist.	30	Ct. Appeals	11
St. Rep. Dist.	80	Admin. Jud. Dist.	9
St. Dist. Cts.	50		

PHYSICAL FEATURES: Level to hilly; drains to Brazos, Wichita Rivers; sandy, loam, red soils; grassy, mesquites, cedars.

RECREATION: Lake Kemp; Millers Creek Reservoir; Fish Day in May, Settlers reunion and rodeo in July; hunting and fishing.

MINERALS: Oil, gas produced.

This structure on St. James Street in London housed ministers from the Republic of Texas from 1842-1845. Photo courtesy John Bennett, member Texas Historical Commission.

1982 Pop. 5,200	Voters reg. 3,437
Area (sq. mi.) 862	Whlsle. sales . $28,895,000
Altitude (ft.) 1,250	Oil value $13,548,749
Ann. rainfall (in.) . 26.36	No. employed . . . 1,519
Jan. temp. min. 28	Wages paid . . $17,919,376
July temp. max. 98	Tax value . . $315,002,172
Growing season (da.) 214	Income $43,021,000
No. farms, 1982 351	Taxable sales $14,177,919
No. acres in farms 401,373	Fed. expend. . $25,247,000
†Value per farm $392,248	Crime Index 127
Cropland harv. . . 112,789	TDC Pop. 5

AGRICULTURE: About $16 million average annual income; livestock, mainly stocker cattle; wheat, cotton, grain sorghums.

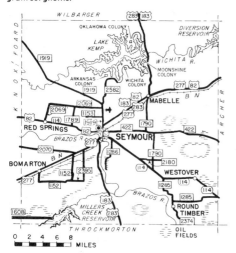

BUSINESS: Chiefly agribusiness; oil, gas production; light manufacturing.

MANUFACTURING: None noted in census report.

SERVICE INDUSTRIES: 38 Establishments; Receipts, $6,466,000; Annual Payroll, $1,638,000; No. Employees, 191.

SEYMOUR (3,657) county seat; agribusiness center; clothes manufacturing; metal works; hospital, nursing home; city park.

Bee

LOCATION: Southeast (P-15).

HISTORY: Created from Karnes, Live Oak, Goliad, Refugio, San Patricio Counties, 1857; organized 1858; named for **Gen. Barnard Bee.**

Cong. Dist. 14		U.S. Jud. Dist. . . . . S-CC
St. Sen. Dist. 21		Ct. Appeals 13
St. Rep. Dist. 33		Admin. Jud. Dist. 4
St. Dist. Cts. . 36, 156, 343		

PHYSICAL FEATURES: Level to rolling; black clay, sandy, loam soils; brushy.

RECREATION: Hunting leases, camping, historical sites, western week in October, junior livestock show.

MINERALS: Considerable oil, gas produced.

1982 Pop. 27,200	Voters reg. 14,433
Area (sq. mi.) 880	Whlsle. sales . $75,151,000
Altitude (ft.) 100-400	Oil value $29,282,867
Ann. rainfall (in.) . 28.90	No. employed 6,514
Jan. temp. min. 45	Wages paid . . $90,004,896
July temp. max. 95	Tax value . . $902,525,781
Growing season (da.) 285	Income $221,615,000
No. farms, 1982 688	Taxable sales $94,087,511
No. acres in farms 414,241	Fed. expend. . $91,585,000
†Value per farm $382,257	Crime Index 650
Cropland harvested 85,248	TDC Pop. 52

AGRICULTURE: More than $28 million average income, from beef cattle, hogs, grain sorghums, small grains, cotton; some irrigation.

BUSINESS: Oil supplies, bottling plant, agribusiness; military installations provide major income source.

MANUFACTURING: None noted in census report.
SERVICE INDUSTRIES: 98 Establishments; Receipts, $24,319,000; Annual Payroll, $7,498,000; No. Employees, 62.

BEEVILLE (14,574) county seat; **Naval Air Station**; oil field services; agribusiness center; community college, hospital, nursing homes.

Bell

LOCATION: Central (K-16).
HISTORY: Created from Milam County and organized, 1850; named for **Gov. P. H. Bell.**

Cong. Dist. 11	U.S. Jud. Dist. . . W-Waco
St. Sen. Dist. 24	Ct. Appeals 3
St. Rep. Dist. 53, 54	Admin. Jud. Dist. 3
St. Dist. Cts. 27, 146, 169, 264	

PHYSICAL FEATURES: Level to hilly; black to light soils; mixed timber.

RECREATION: Fishing, hunting; **Belton, Stillhouse Hollow Lakes;** historic sites include **Stagecoach Inn** at Salado; rattlesnake roundup at Belton in March; Salado art fair in August.
MINERALS: Stone, sand, gravel.

1982 Pop. 164,100		Voters reg. 63,873
Area (sq. mi.) 1,055		Whlsle. sales $556,268,000
Altitude (ft.) 400-1,200		Oil value $5,139
Ann. rainfall (in.) . 34.00		No. employed 47,258
Jan. temp. min. 37		Wages paid . $676,354,228
July temp. max. 96		Tax value . $3,166,727,696
Growing season (da.) 258		Income . . . $1,391,795,000
No. farms, 1982 . . . 1,667		Taxable sales $672,543,791
No. acres in farms 449,648		Fed. exp. . . $1,124,994,000
†Value per farm $225,416		Crime Index 7,976
Cropland harv. . . 158,627		TDC Pop. 478

AGRICULTURE: About $37 million average farm income; 60% from cattle, sheep, goats, hogs, horses, poultry; a leading turkey-producing county; grain sorghums, cotton, hay, pecans, wheat, corn and cedar.
BUSINESS: Diversified manufacturers include computer equipment, plastic goods, furniture, clothing, agribusiness; distribution center; **Fort Hood;** tourism.
MANUFACTURING: 121 Plants; 7,000 Employees; Payroll, $107,000,000; Product Value, $616,300,000.
SERVICE INDUSTRIES: 651 Establishments; Receipts, $216,199,000; Annual Payroll, $65,716,000; No. Employees, 5,017.

BELTON (10,660) county seat; **Mary Hardin-Baylor University;** school furniture, insulation, mobile home manufacturing; clinics, nursing home.

Killeen (46,296); see metro area page; site of **Fort Hood** military installation; **Central Texas College** and **American Technological University;** varied manufacturing; medical center.

Temple (42,354); see metro area page; hub of one of nation's fastest growing urban areas; diversified industries; rail center; marketing and distribution center; market for large area; county zoo; **Temple Junior College;** one of nation's leading medical centers, **Scott and White Clinic and Hospital.**

Other towns include **Harker Heights** (7,345), **Rogers** (1,242), **Nolanville** (1,308), **Bartlett** (1,567, mostly Williamson County) leading soil conservation center; **Holland** (863), **Troy** (1,353), **Little River Academy** (1,155), **Morgans Point Resort** (1,082). **Salado** is historic town with **Central Texas Area Museum, Stagecoach Inn,** and arts, crafts and antique shops.

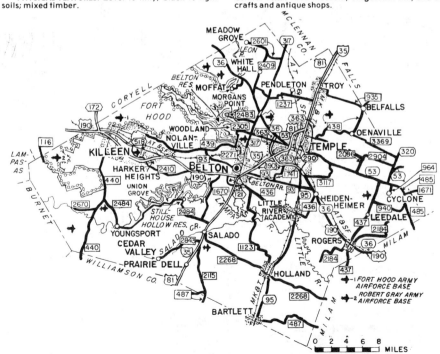

Bexar

LOCATION: South (N-14).

HISTORY: Created 1836, organized 1837, from Spanish municipality named for **Duke de Bexar**; many historic sites.

Cong. Dist. 20, 21, 23	U.S. Jud. Dist. . . . W-SAnt.
St. Sen. Dist. . . . 19, 21, 26	Ct. Appeals 4
St. Rep. Dist. . . . 115-124	Admin. Jud. Dist. 4
St. Dist. Cts. 37, 45, 57, 73, 131, 144, 150, 166, 175, 186, 187, 224, 225, 226, 227, 285, 288, 289, 290	

PHYSICAL FEATURES: Hilly; heavy black to thin limestone soils; springfed streams; underground water; mesquite, other brush.

1982 Pop. 1,052,100	Voters reg. 495,000
Area (sq. mi.) 1,248	Whlsle. sales $7,000,384,000
Altitude (ft.) . . . 500-1,500	Oil value $32,599,236
Ann. rainfall (in.) . 27.54	No. employed . . . 379,720
Jan. temp. min. 42	Wages paid $6,010,117,500
July temp. max. 94	Tax value $25,068,919,735
Growing season (da.) 265	Income . . . $9,498,103,000
No. farms, 1982 . . . 2,007	Tax.sales . $5,725,383,699
No. acres in farms 500,467	Fed. exp. . . $3,839,915,000
†Value per farm $339,050	Crime Index 86,535
Cropland harvested 79,133	TDC Pop. 2,119

RECREATION: Major tourist and retirement area; **Alamo**, missions, other historic sites; river walk; Hertzberg circus collection; Brackenridge Park; zoo; symphony orchestra; HemisFair Plaza; Folk Festival; many military posts; parks; museums; deer, turkey, other hunting; fishing; many special events; major livestock show.

MINERALS: Cement, stone, oil, gas, sand and gravel, lime, clays.

EDUCATION: San Antonio College, St. Philips College, junior colleges; senior, **Incarnate Word College, Our Lady of the Lake University**, St. Mary's University, Trinity University, University of Texas at San Antonio, UT Institute of Texan Cultures, UT Health Science Center at San Antonio (five divisions), **University of Mexico at San Antonio, Oblate School of Theology and Texas Lutheran College.**

AGRICULTURE: About $63 million yearly farm income, 56% from beef, dairy cattle, poultry, sheep, goats; sorghums, vegetables, hay, corn, nursery plant production, peanuts; about 20,000 acres irrigated.

BUSINESS: Large federal payrolls; federal expenditure a major factor; tourist business; varied manufactures; distribution center for large area; education center.

MANUFACTURING: 920 Plants; 44,700 Employees, Payroll, $698,000,000; Product Value, $3,271,900,000.

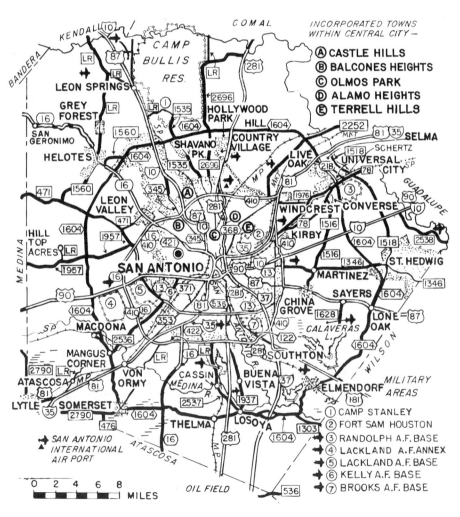

SERVICE INDUSTRIES: 5,846 Establishments; Receipts, $1,843,462,000; Annual Payroll, $692,226,000; No. Employees, 54,540.

SAN ANTONIO (786,023) county seat; Texas' third largest city (see metro area page); state's largest military center; varied manufacturing with emphasis on high-tech industries, construction equipment, concrete, dairy products, soft drinks, clothing, aircraft; mild climate; Alamo, other historic sites attract many tourists; HemisFair Plaza; Folk Festival; popular retirement area; **Institute of Texan Cultures.**

Other towns include **Balcones Heights** (2,511), **Alamo Heights,** (6,252), **Castle Hills** (4,773), **China Grove** (434), **Converse** (5,150), **Elmendorf** (492), **Grey Forest** (442), **Helotes** (1,409), **Hill Country Village** (972), **Hollywood Park** (3,231), **Kirby** (6,435), **Leon Valley** (9,088), **Live Oak** (8,183), **Olmos Park** (2,069), **Saint Hedwig** (970), **Schertz** (7,262 mostly Guadalupe County), **Selma** (528), **Shavano Park** (1,448), **Somerset** (1,102), **Terrell Hills** (4,644), **Universal City** (10,720), **Windcrest** (5,332).

Blanco

LOCATION: Central (M-14).
HISTORY: Created, organized, 1858, from Burnet, Comal, Gillespie, Hays Counties; named for **Blanco** (white) **River.**

Cong. Dist.	10	U.S. Jud. Dist.	W-An.
St. Sen. Dist.	14	Ct. Appeals	3
St. Rep. Dist.	45	Admin. Jud. Dist.	3
St. Dist. Cts.	33		

PHYSICAL FEATURES: Hilly; Blanco, Pedernales Rivers; cedars, pecans, other trees.
RECREATION: President Lyndon B. Johnson boyhood home. **Blanco State Park; Pedernales Falls State Park;** hunting, fishing; scenic drives.
MINERALS: Insignificant.

1982 Pop.	4,900	Voters reg.	3,548
Area (sq. mi.)	714	Whlsle. sales	$20,099,000
Altitude (ft.)	800-1,850	Oil value	0
Ann. rainfall (in.)	34.39	No. employed	1,291
Jan. temp. min.	36	Wages paid	$15,234,012
July temp. max.	96	Tax value	$419,713,901
Growing season (da.)	234	Income	$49,174,000
No. farms, 1982	488	Taxable sales	$19,784,215
No. acres in farms	370,830	Fed. expend.	$13,095,000
†Value per farm	$735,223	Crime Index	62
Cropland harvested	6,762	TDC Pop.	3

AGRICULTURE: About $11 million yearly income, mostly from cattle, sheep, goats, hogs, hunting leases;

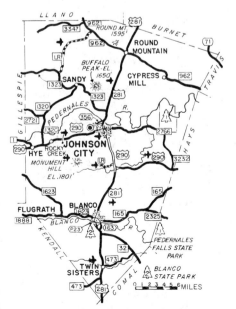

peaches, grapes, hay.
BUSINESS: Trailer manufacturing, tourism, ranch supplies, marketing.
MANUFACTURING: None noted in census report.
SERVICE INDUSTRIES: 13 Establishments; Receipts, $2,102,000; Annual Payroll, $606,000; No. Employees, 84.
JOHNSON CITY (872) county seat; tourist center. **Blanco** (1,179) ranch supply center.

Borden

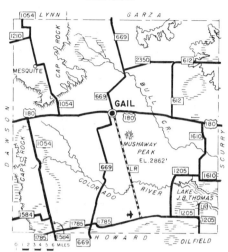

LOCATION: West (H-9).
HISTORY: Created, 1876, from Bexar District, organized, 1891; named for **Gail Borden,** pioneer patriot, inventor, editor.

Cong. Dist.	17	U.S. Jud. Dist.	N-Lb.
St. Sen. Dist.	28	Ct. Appeals	11
St. Rep. Dist.	69	Admin. Jud. Dist.	7
St. Dist. Cts.	132		

PHYSICAL FEATURES: Rolling, broken by **Cap Rock Escarpment;** drains to Colorado River, **Lake J. B. Thomas;** sandy loam, clay soils.
RECREATION: Fishing; hunting; Lake J. B. Thomas; museum; junior livestock show and rodeo.
MINERALS: Oil, gas, sand and gravel.

1982 Pop.	1,000	Voters reg.	572
Area (sq. mi.)	900	Whlsle. sales	0
Altitude (ft.)	2,400-3,000	Oil value	$153,468,225
Ann. rainfall (in.)	18.20	No. employed	428
Jan. temp. min.	32	Wages paid	$6,469,040
July temp. max.	96	Tax value	$611,636,085
Growing season (da.)	214	Income	$5,449,000
No. farms, 1982	135	Taxable sales	$95,950
No. acres in farms	576,202	Fed. expend.	$10,681,000
†Value per farm	$963,519	Crime Index	11
Cropland harvested	33,045	TDC Pop.	0

AGRICULTURE: About $9 million annual income mostly from beef cattle, sheep, horses; cotton, wheat, sorghums, hay.
BUSINESS: Oil, agribusiness.
MANUFACTURING: None noted in censes report.
SERVICE INDUSTRIES: None in Borden Co.
GAIL (est. 189) county seat; county museum.

Bosque

LOCATION: Central (J-15).
HISTORY: Created, organized, 1854, from Milam District, McLennan County; named for **Bosque** (woods) **River.**

Cong. Dist.	11	U.S. Jud. Dist.	W-Waco
St. Sen. Dist.	22	Ct. Appeals	10
St. Rep. Dist.	57	Admin. Jud. Dist.	3
St. Dist. Cts.	220		

Bosque County
(Cont'd.)

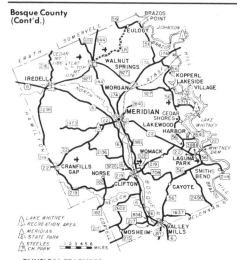

PHYSICAL FEATURES: Hilly, broken by Bosque, Brazos Rivers; limestone to alluvial soils; cedars, oaks, mesquites.

RECREATION: Lake Whitney, Meridian State Park, Bosque Memorial Museum at Clifton; fishing, hunting; scenic routes, golf course, **Norwegian** smorgasbord at Norse community in November, Central Texas Youth Fair in Clifton in August; **Texas Safari** wildlife park in Clifton.

MINERALS: Lime, stone.

1982 Pop.	13,600	Voters reg.	7,978
Area (sq. mi.)	989	Whlsle. sales	$33,814,000
Altitude (ft.)	500-1,200	Oil value	$814,972
Ann. rainfall (in.)	33.20	No. employed	3,009
Jan. temp. min.	36	Wages paid	$38,971,968
July temp. max.	96	Tax value	$558,157,388
Growing season (da.)	243	Income	$130,079,000
No. farms, 1982	1,004	Taxable sales	$31,129,629
No. acres in farms 551,965		Fed. expend.	$36,645,000
†Value per farm $347,264		Crime Index	318
Cropland harvested 61,966		TDC Pop.	11

AGRICULTURE: About $33 million average annual income, nearly all from cattle, goats, sheep, poultry, hogs; peanuts, cotton, pecans, wheat, sorghums; cedar for posts.

BUSINESS: Agribusiness, tourism, small industries.

MANUFACTURING: 24 Plants; 900 Employees; Payroll, $12,500,000; Product Value, $64,300,000.

SERVICE INDUSTRIES: 41 Establishments; Receipts, $6,007,000; Annual Payroll, $2,291,000; No. Employees, 168.

MERIDIAN (1,330) county seat; distribution center; varied manufacturing.

Clifton (3,063) area trade center; light manufacturing; hospital, rest home.

Other towns include **Valley Mills** (1,236, part McLennan County) with several small industries; **Iredell** (407), **Cranfills Gap** (341), **Morgan** (485) and **Walnut Springs** (613).

Bowie

LOCATION: Northeast (F-21).

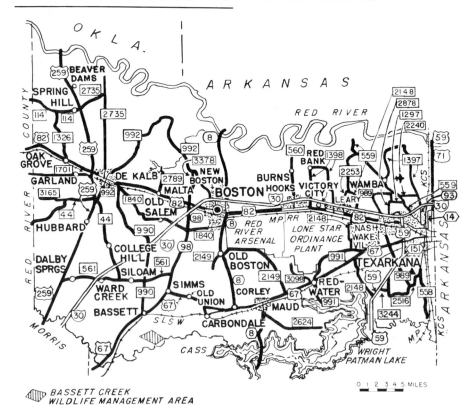

BASSETT CREEK
WILDLIFE MANAGEMENT AREA
▲ FEDERAL CORRECTIONAL INSTITUTION

0 1 2 3 4 5 MILES

HISTORY: Created 1840 from Red River County, organized 1841; named for Alamo hero, **James Bowie.**

Cong. Dist. 1	U.S. Jud. Dist. . . . . E-Tx.
St. Sen. Dist. 1	Ct. Appeals 6
St. Rep. Dist. 1	Admin. Jud. Dist. 1
St. Dist. Cts. . . 5, 102, 202	

PHYSICAL FEATURES: Hilly, forested; clay, sandy, alluvial soils; drained by Red and Sulphur Rivers.

RECREATION: Lake Wright Patman, other lakes; hunting, fishing, historic sites, pioneer days.

MINERALS: Oil, gas, sand, gravel.

1982 Pop. 76,500	Voters reg. 43,596
Area (sq. mi.) 891	Whlsle. sales $355,607,000
Altitude (ft.) 200-450	Oil value $406,496
Ann. rainfall (in.) . 47.59	No. employed 22,797
Jan. temp. min. 35	Wages paid . $320,815,536
July temp. max. 95	Tax value . $1,602,367,283
Growing season (da.) 235	Income $647,733,000
No. farms, 1982 . . . 1,130	Taxable sales $338,206,251
No. acres in farms 253,880	Fed. expend. $462,964,000
†Value per farm $176,125	Crime Index 3,553
Cropland harvested 60,080	TDC Pop. 180

AGRICULTURE: About $31 million annual income mostly from beef, dairy cattle, poultry, swine; crops include wheat, soybeans, hay; timber harvested.

BUSINESS: Manufacturing, agribusiness, government employment, tourism, **U.S. Army Depot,** ordnance plant.

MANUFACTURING: 83 Plants; 4,400 Employees; Payroll, $79,600,000; Product Value, $454,300,000.

SERVICE INDUSTRIES: 415 Establishments; Receipts, $101,264,000; Annual Payroll, $38,683,000; No. Employees, 2,891.

BOSTON (est. 200) county seat.

Texarkana (est. 78,813 in Texas-Arkansas; 31,271 in Texas; see metro page); distribution, **Red River Army Depot,** manufacturing center; medical center; **Texarkana Community College, East Texas State University at Texarkana;** hospitals; federal correctional unit; state line tourist attractions; Four States Fair in October and Piney Woods Rendezvous in April.

New Boston (4,628) paper mill.

Other towns include **De Kalb** (2,217), **Hooks** (2,507), **Leary** (253), **Maud** (1,059), **Nash** (2,022), **Wake Village** (3,865).

Brazoria

LOCATION: On coast (O-20).

HISTORY: Created 1836, organized 1837 from Municipality of Brazoria, name derived from Brazos River. Settled by **Stephen F. Austin** colonists.

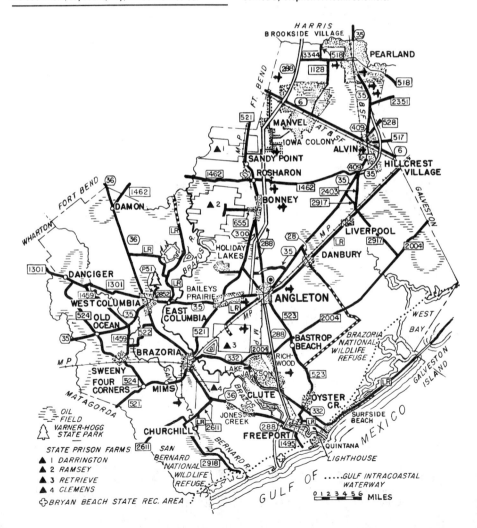

Cong. Dist. 14, 22
St. Sen. Dist. 17, 18
St. Rep. Dist. . . . 27, 28, 29
St. Dist. Cts. . . 23, 149, 239, 300
U.S. Jud. Dist. . . . . S-Gn.
Ct. Appeals 1, 14
Admin. Jud. Dist. 2

PHYSICAL FEATURES: Flat, coastal soils, drained by Brazos and San Bernard Rivers.

RECREATION: Water sports, 20 miles natural beach; fishing, hunting; many historic sites; **Varner-Hogg State Park;** replica of first capitol of Republic of Texas at **West Columbia;** San Jacinto Day festival.

MINERALS: Oil, gas, magnesium, salt, sand and gravel.

1982 Pop. 178,400	Voters reg. 83,673
Area (sq. mi.) 1,407	Whlsle. sales $403,311,000
Altitude (ft.) . . . . . . -60	Oil value . . . $44,360,184
Ann. rainfall (in.) . . 52.17	No. employed 57,441
Jan. temp. min. 46	Wages paid $1,260,328,224
July temp. max. 91	Tax value . $8,733,891,110
Growing season (da.) 268	Income . . . $2,148,430,000
No. farms, 1982 . . . 1,316	Taxable sales $678,606,617
No. acres in farms 630,791	Fed. exp. . . $1,491,072,000
†Value per farm $686,244	Crime Index 6,461
Cropland harv. . . 120,932	TDC Pop. 244

AGRICULTURE: About $45 million average annual income, 66% from rice, cotton, commercial turf, soybeans; 34% from livestock.

BUSINESS: Extensive petroleum and chemical industry; fishing; tourism; agribusiness.

MANUFACTURING: 186 Plants; 17,800 Employees; Payroll, $505,300,000; Product Value, $6,441,700,000.

SERVICE INDUSTRIES: 751 Establishments; Receipts, $245,984,000; Annual Payroll, $90,250,000; No. Employees, 5,639.

ANGLETON (13,929) county seat; banking and distribution center for large oil, chemical, agricultural area, rice, livestock operations; state's largest county fair; hospital, nursing home.

Brazosport: A community of nine cities. Community has world's largest basic chemical complex, shrimp and other commercial fishing; port facilities; tourism; **Brazosport College;** hospital; school district. Brazosport cities include:

Brazoria (3,025), **Clute City** (9,577), **Freeport** (13,444), **Jones Creek** (2,634), **Lake Jackson** (19,102), **Oyster Creek** (1,473), **Quintana** (30), **Richwood** (2,591), **Surfside Beach** (577).

Other county towns include **Alvin** (16,515) chemical plants, rice farming center, hospital, nursing home, **Alvin Community College; Pearland** (13,248), **West Columbia** (4,109) with replica of first state capitol; **Sweeny** (3,538), **Baileys Prairie** (353), **Bonney** (94), **Brookside** (1,453), **Danbury** (1,357), **Hillcrest** (771), **Iowa Colony** (585), **Liverpool** (602), **Manvel** (3,549); **Holiday Lakes** (583).

Brazos

LOCATION: Southeast (L-18).

HISTORY: Created 1841 from Robertson, Washington Counties, named **Navasota;** renamed for Brazos River in 1842, organized 1843; fastest growing SMSA in state in 1980 census.

Cong. Dist. 6	U.S. Jud. Dist. . . . . S-Hn.
St. Sen. Dist. 5	Ct. Appeals 1, 10, 14
St. Rep. Dist. 14	Admin. Jud. Dist. 2
St. Dist. Cts. 85, 272	

PHYSICAL FEATURES: Between Brazos, Navasota Rivers; rich bottom soils, sandy, clays on rolling uplands; mostly oak trees.

1982 Pop. 112,100	Voters reg. 62,507
Area (sq. mi.) 588	Whlsle. sales $283,643,000
Altitude (ft.) 200-400	Oil value . . . $193,092,184
Ann. rainfall (in.) . 39.21	No. employed 45,934
Jan. temp. min. 42	Wages paid . $694,985,932
July temp. max. 95	Tax value . $3,182,436,454
Growing season (da.) 274	Income . . . $1,054,959,000
No. farms, 1982 . . . 874	Taxable sales $563,041,345
No. acres in farms 256,837	Fed. expend. $214,708,000
†Value per farm $317,878	Crime Index 7,095
Cropland harvested 40,845	TDC Pop. 211

RECREATION: Fishing, hunting; Texas World Speedway, many springtime festivals, Texas A&M events.

MINERALS: Sand and gravel, lignite, gas, oil.

AGRICULTURE: About 75% of over $35 million annual income from cattle, hogs; sorghums, corn, cotton, wheat, oats, pecans chief crops.

BUSINESS: Agribusiness center; computers, research and development; offshore technology; four industrial parks. **Texas A&M University** enterprises major economic factor.

MANUFACTURING: 72 Plants; 3,200 Employees; Payroll, $48,900,000; Product Value, $272,500,000.

SERVICE INDUSTRIES: 568 Establishments; Receipts, $150,749,000; Annual Payroll, $51,839,000; No. Employees, 4,225.

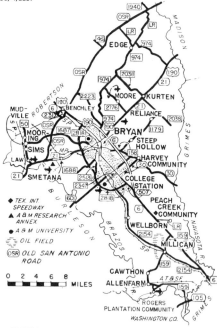

BRYAN (44,337) county seat; (see metro page); university enterprises; business forms, defense electronics, aluminum buildings, furniture, shoe products, other varied manufacturing; agribusiness center; hospitals.

College Station (37,272); home of **Texas A&M University System;** mini-computers; offshore technology; other research and development.

Brewster

LOCATION: In Rio Grande's Big Bend (N-6).

HISTORY: Created, organized, 1887, from Presidio County; named for **Henry P. Brewster,** Texas Republic Secretary of War.

Cong. Dist. 21	U.S. Jud. Dist. . . . W-Pe.
St. Sen. Dist. 25	Ct. Appeals 8
St. Rep. Dist. 68	Admin. Jud. Dist. 6
St. Dist. Cts. 83	

PHYSICAL FEATURES: Largest Texas county, area equal to Connecticut plus Rhode Island; mountains and deep canyons, distinctive geology, plant life, animals.

RECREATION: Many tourist attractions; **Big Bend National Park;** ghost mining towns; scenic drives, canyons, mountains; among last U.S. unspoiled "frontier" areas; **Museum of the Big Bend at Sul Ross State U.;**

annual **Chili Cook-Off at Terlingua**; retirement area; Big Bend summer theater at Alpine; Cavalry post at Lajitas; hunting leases.

MINERALS: Sand and gravel, fluorspar.

1982 Pop.	7,700	Voters reg.	4,971
Area (sq. mi.)	6,169	Whlsle. sales	$19,321,000
Altitude (ft.)	1,700-7,835	Oil value	$36,536
Ann. rainfall (in.)	15.53	No. employed	2,633
Jan. temp. min.	32	Wages paid	$31,123,736
July temp. max.	89	Tax value	$198,649,089
Growing season (da.)	223	Income	$51,956,000
No. farms, 1982	110	Taxable sales	$25,961,170
No. ac. in farms	2,551,747	Fed. expend.	$25,596,000
†Value per farm	$3,089,964	Crime Index	172
Cropland harvested.	N.A.	TDC Pop.	8

AGRICULTURE: About $12 million average income, nearly all from cattle, sheep, goats; pecans.

BUSINESS: Sul Ross State University; ranching; tourism; retirement developments; hunting leases; some curio manufacturing.

MANUFACTURING: None noted in census report.

SERVICE INDUSTRIES: 43 Establishments; Receipts, $8,974,000; Annual Payroll, $3,020,000; No. Employees, 435.

ALPINE (5,465) county seat; center for ranch trade, tourism; **Sul Ross State University;** hospital; local events; varied manufacturing.

Marathon, ranching center, tourism, gateway to **Big Bend National Park.**

Briscoe

LOCATION: Northwest (D-9).

HISTORY: Created from Bexar District, 1876, organized 1892; named for **Andrew Briscoe,** Texas Republic soldier.

Cong. Dist.	13	U.S. Jud. Dist.	N-Am.
St. Sen. Dist.	31	Ct. Appeals	7
St. Rep. Dist.	84	Admin. Jud. Dist.	9
St. Dist. Cts.	110		

PHYSICAL FEATURES: Partly on High Plains, broken by **Cap Rock Escarpment,** fork of Red River; sandy, loam soils.

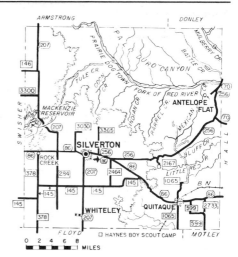

RECREATION: Hunting, fishing; scenic drives; local events; **Briscoe County Museum; Caprock Canyon State Park, Mackenzie Reservoir.**

MINERALS: Insignificant.

1982 Pop.	2,500	Voters reg.	1,532
Area (sq. mi.)	887	Whlsle. sales	$7,072,000
Altitude (ft.)	2,100-3,300	Oil value	$152,525
Ann. rainfall (in.)	20.50	No. employed	304
Jan. temp. min.	26	Wages paid	$3,247,004
July temp. max.	94	Tax value	$126,511,183
Growing season (da.)	214	Income	$15,734,000
No. farms, 1982	251	Taxable sales	$6,198,954
No. acres in farms	397,057	Fed. expend.	$16,028,000
†Value per farm	$630,797	Crime Index	27
Cropland harvested	83,014	TDC Pop.	1

AGRICULTURE: About $14 million average annual income from wheat, grain sorghums, cotton; beef cattle, cattle feeding increasing; over 43,000 acres irrigated.

BUSINESS: Agribusinesses.

MANUFACTURING: None noted in census report.

SERVICE INDUSTRIES: 6 Establishments; Receipts, $176,000; Annual Payroll, $75,000; No. Employees, 8.

SILVERTON (918) county seat; agribusiness center; irrigation supplies manufactured; county clinic.

Quitaque (696), trade center.

Brooks

LOCATION: South (S-15).

HISTORY: Created from Hidalgo, Starr, Zapata Counties, 1911, organized same year. Named for **J. A. Brooks,** Ranger-legislator.

Cong. Dist.	15	U.S. Jud. Dist.	S-CC
St. Sen. Dist.	20	Ct. Appeals	4
St. Rep. Dist.	37	Admin. Jud. Dist.	5
St. Dist. Cts.	79		

PHYSICAL FEATURES: Level to rolling; brushy; light to dark sandy loam soils.

MINERALS: Oil, gas production.

1982 Pop.	8,800	Voters reg.	6,071
Area (sq. mi.)	942	Whlsle. sales	$16,746,000
Altitude (ft.)	100-400	Oil value	$8,557,062
Ann. rainfall (in.)	24.18	No. employed	2,338
Jan. temp. min.	48	Wages paid	$30,215,080
July temp. max.	98	Tax value	$787,098,670
Growing season (da.)	303	Income	$50,540,000
No. farms, 1982	331	Taxable sales	$19,583,341
No. acres in farms	484,104	Fed. expend.	$18,231,000
†Value per farm	$535,535	Crime Index	144
Cropland harvested	14,852	TDC Pop.	18

RECREATION: Hunting, fishing; **Texas Ranger Museum, Don Pedrito Shrine.**

AGRICULTURE: Over $16.5 million average annual income mostly from beef, dairy cattle; grain, corn, hay, watermelons, vegetables.

Brooks County (Cont'd.)

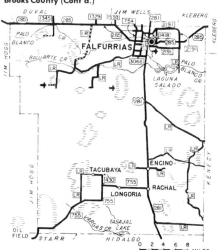

BUSINESS: Chiefly oil, gas, cattle raising.
MANUFACTURING: None noted in census report.
SERVICE INDUSTRIES: 25 Establishments; Receipts, $3,557,000; Annual Payroll, $1,218,000; No. Employees, 126.

FALFURRIAS (6,103) county seat; retail center; agribusinesses, dairy center; hospital, nursing home, museum, library.

Brown

LOCATION: Central (J-13).
HISTORY: Named for Indian fighter, **Henry S. Brown;** created 1856 from Comanche, Travis Counties, organized 1857.

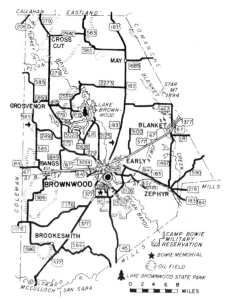

Cong. Dist.	11	U.S. Jud. Dist.	N-SAng.
St. Sen. Dist.	24	Ct. Appeals	11
St. Rep. Dist.	65	Admin. Jud. Dist.	7
St. Dist. Cts.	35		

PHYSICAL FEATURES: Rolling, hilly; drains to Colorado River; varied soils, timber.
RECREATION: Lake Brownwood State Park; MacArthur Academy of Freedom; fishing, hunting; Brown County Youth Festival in January; other local events.
MINERALS: Stone, oil, gas, clays.

1982 Pop.	34,500	Voters reg.	17,662
Area (sq. mi.)	936	Whlsle. sales	$93,500,000
Altitude (ft.)	1,200-2,000	Oil value	$16,984,978
Ann. rainfall (in.)	27.42	No. employed	11,256
Jan. temp. min.	33	Wages paid	$165,202,868
July temp. max.	96	Tax value	$1,034,023,917
Growing season (da.)	242	Income	$309,308,000
No. farms, 1982	1,181	Taxable sales	$133,015,098
No. acres in farms	524,387	Fed. expend.	$81,082,000
†Value per farm	$231,419	Crime Index	1,437
Cropland harvested	47,548	TDC Pop.	91

AGRICULTURE: About 80% of $32 million average income from beef cattle, sheep, goats, hogs; wheat, grain sorghums, peanuts chief crops; about 6,000 acres irrigated.
BUSINESS: Agribusinesses, general and oil field value manufacturing plants.
MANUFACTURING: 39 Plants; 2,700 Employees; Payroll, $42,500,000; Product Value, $318,600,000.
SERVICE INDUSTRIES: 182 Establishments; Receipts, $31,566,000; Annual Payroll, $11,591,000; No. Employees, 1,171.

BROWNWOOD (19,396) county seat; varied industries; **Howard Payne University, MacArthur Academy of Freedom; State Home and School;** State 4-H club center; hospitals.

Other towns include **Bangs** (1,716), **Blanket** (388), **Early** (2,313).

Burleson

LOCATION: East central (L-17).
HISTORY: Created, organized, 1846, from Milam, Washington Counties; named for **Edward Burleson** of Texas Revolution.

Cong. Dist.	14	U.S. Jud. Dist.	W-An.
St. Sen. Dist.	5	Ct. Appeals	1, 14
St. Rep. Dist.	13	Admin. Jud. Dist.	2
St. Dist. Cts.	21, 335		

MINERALS: Oil, gas, sand and gravel.

1982 Pop.	14,700	Voters reg.	8,229
Area (sq. mi.)	668	Whlsle. sales	$50,952,000
Altitude (ft.)	225-475	Oil value	$254,238,298
Ann. rainfall (in.)	34.45	No. employed	3,013
Jan. temp. min.	38	Wages paid	$43,081,448
July temp. max.	94	Tax value	$1,256,059,748
Growing season (da.)	275	Income	$113,318,000
No. farms, 1982	1,260	Taxable sales	$47,890,533
No. acres in farms	332,765	Fed. expend.	$27,783,000
†Value per farm	$243,765	Crime Index	332
Cropland harvested	50,525	TDC Pop.	41

PHYSICAL FEATURES: Rolling to hilly; drains to Brazos, Yegua Creek, **Somerville Lake;** loam and heavy bottom soils; oaks, other trees.

RECREATION: Fishing, limited hunting; **Somerville Lake** recreation; Birch Creek Park; historic sites.

AGRICULTURE: About $25 million average annual income, about 85% from beef cattle, hogs, horses. Cotton, grain major crops; soybeans, watermelons, vegetables; about 8,500 acres irrigated.

BUSINESS: Agribusiness, significant oil and gas discoveries since 1979; varied manufacturing.

MANUFACTURING: None noted in census report.

SERVICE INDUSTRIES: 44 Establishments; Receipts, $9,561,000; Annual Payroll, $3,625,000; No. Employees, 328.

CALDWELL (2,953) county seat; plants make aluminum furniture, other products; oil field tool and servicing; hospital, nursing home; Burleson County Fair in September.

Somerville (1,814) has furniture factory; museum, heritage park, local events. Other towns are **Snook** (408) and **Clay.**

Burnet

LOCATION: Central (L-15).

HISTORY: Created from Bell, Travis, Williamson Counties, 1852; organized 1854; named for **David G. Burnet**, provisional president, Texas Republic.

Cong. Dist.	10	U.S. Jud. Dist.	W-An.
St. Sen. Dist.	24	Ct. Appeals	3
St. Rep. Dist.	52	Admin. Jud. Dist.	3
St. Dist. Cts.	33		

PHYSICAL FEATURES: Many lakes; hilly; caves; sandy, red, black waxy soils; cedars, other trees.

RECREATION: Water sports on lakes; sites of historic forts; **Granite Mt.** furnished stone for **Texas Capitol**; deer, other hunting; major tourist center; **Longhorn Cavern** and **Inks Lake State Parks; Bluebonnet Trail** in spring.

MINERALS: Stone, graphite, sand and gravel

1982 Pop.	19,200	Voters reg. 12,398
Area (sq. mi.)	994	Whlsle. sales $18,041,000
Altitude (ft.)	600-1,600	Oil value 0
Ann. rainfall (in.)	29.81	No. employed 4,860
Jan. temp. min.	37	Wages paid $65,040,232
July temp. max.	96	Tax value $964,517,859
Growing season (da.)	230	Income $197,451,000
No. farms, 1982	827	Taxable sales $95,131,606
No. acres in farms	530,039	Fed. expend. $71,450,000
†Value per farm	$534,464	Crime Index 499
Cropland harvested	14,759	TDC Pop. 13

AGRICULTURE: About 85% of $15.8 million average income from cattle, sheep, goats; income from cedar posts, pecans, hay; some grains.

BUSINESS: Stone processing, manufacturing, agri-

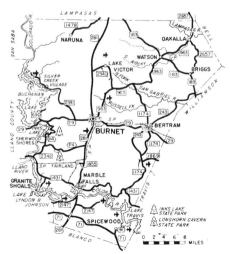

businesses, tourist trade, hunting leases.

MANUFACTURING: 28 Plants; 700 Employees; Payroll, $9,400,000; Product Value, $35,400,000.

SERVICE INDUSTRIES: 100 Establishments; Receipts, $24,759,000; Annual Payroll, $8,490,000; No. Employees, 931.

BURNET (3,410) county seat; stone, graphite products; agribusiness; tourism; 2 hospitals, nursing homes.

Marble Falls (3,252) ranching, manufacturing of precision instruments, sporting goods; stone quarrying and tourist center; nursing home. Other towns are **Bertram** (824) ranching center; rest home; **Granite Shoals** (634).

Caldwell

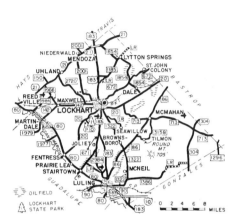

LOCATION: South Central (N-16).

HISTORY: Created, organized from Bastrop, Gonzales Counties, 1848. Named for Indian fighter, **Mathew Caldwell.**

Cong. Dist.	10	U.S. Jud. Dist.	W-An.
St. Sen. Dist.	18	Ct. Appeals	3
St. Rep. Dist.	31	Admin. Jud. Dist.	3
St. Dist. Cts.	22, 207, 274		

PHYSICAL FEATURES: Varied soils ranging from black clay to waxy; level, draining to San Marcos River.

RECREATION: Fishing, hunting; **Lockhart State Park; Luling Watermelon Thump;** Chisholm Trail roundup at Lockhart; Plum Creek battle reenactment; oldest library in Texas, museums, nature trails; rodeo.

MINERALS: Oil, gas, gravel.

1982 Pop.	24,800	Voters reg. 11,938
Area (sq. mi.)	546	Whlsle. sales $46,535,000
Altitude (ft.)	375-750	Oil value $79,177,576
Ann. rainfall (in.)	32.65	No. employed 5,137
Jan. temp. min.	41	Wages paid $70,842,448
July temp. max.	96	Tax value $627,345,806
Growing season (da.)	275	Income $178,184,000
No. farms, 1982	977	Taxable sales $70,321,032
No. acres in farms	255,504	Fed. expend. $42,647,000
†Value per farm	$263,471	Crime Index 449
Cropland harvested	38,542	TDC Pop. 72

AGRICULTURE: More than $30 million average annual income, mostly from beef cattle, hogs, poultry; cotton, sorghums, wheat, corn, watermelons are leading crops.

BUSINESS: Petroleum, agribusiness, varied manufacturing.

MANUFACTURING: None noted in census report.

SERVICE INDUSTRIES: 82 Establishments; Receipts, $10,359,000; Annual Payroll, $3,466,000; No. Employees, 416.

LOCKHART (7,953) county seat; varied manufacturing plants, tourism; hospital, rest home.

Luling (5,039) oil industry center; concrete, poultry processing plants, iron works; other manufacturing; **Luling Foundation;** hospital, nursing homes.

Calhoun

LOCATION: On coast (P-18).

HISTORY: Created, organized from Jackson, Matagorda, Victoria Counties, 1846. Named for **John C. Calhoun**, U.S. statesman.

Cong. Dist.	14	U.S. Jud. Dist.	S-Va.
St. Sen. Dist.	18	Ct. Appeals	13
St. Rep. Dist.	32	Admin. Jud. Dist.	4
St. Dist. Cts.	24, 135, 267		

PHYSICAL FEATURES: Sandy, broken by bays; partly on Matagorda Island.

RECREATION: Beaches, fishing, water sports, historic sites, **Indianola State Park**, county park, **Matagorda Island, Green Lake**; Labor Day aircraft show and fishing festival, LaSalle Days in April, county fair.

MINERALS: Gas, oil.

1982 Pop.	21,300	Voters reg.	10,891
Area (sq. mi.)	540	Whlsle. sales	$70,230,000
Altitude (ft.) sea level-50		Oil value	$36,200,648
Ann. rainfall (in.)	36.83	No. employed	8,271
Jan. temp. min.	47	Wages paid	$186,937,608
July temp. max.	92	Tax value	$197,332,105
Growing season (da.)	300	Income	$193,355,000
No. farms, 1982	273	Taxable sales	$82,207,194
No. acres in farms	197,292	Fed. expend.	$161,757,000
†Value per farm	$517,663	Crime Index	695
Crops harvested	57,341	TDC Pop.	42

AGRICULTURE: About 65% of $18 million average income from rice, grain sorghum, soybeans, corn; 6,000 acres irrigated; beef cattle.

BUSINESS: Manufacturing, agribusiness; petroleum, tourism, fishing and fish processing.

MANUFACTURING: 21 Plants; *Employees; Payroll, N.A.; Product Value, N.A.

SERVICE INDUSTRIES: 78 Establishments; Receipts, $13,830,000; Annual Payroll $4,608,000; No. Employees, 513.

PORT LAVACA (10,911) county seat; commercial seafood operations, shipping, tourist center, chemical, offshore drilling rig, other manufacturing; hospital, nursing home.

Point Comfort (1,125) aluminum and plastic plants, deepwater port. Other towns include **Seadrift** (1,277), **Port O'Connor** which is a fishing and resort center and offshore drilling supply base.

Callahan

LOCATION: West central (I-13).

HISTORY: Created 1858 from Bexar, Bosque, Travis Counties; organized 1877; named for Texas Ranger, **J. H. Callahan**.

Cong. Dist.	17	U.S. Jud. Dist.	N-Ab.
St. Sen. Dist.	30	Ct. Appeals	11
St. Rep. Dist.	64	Admin. Jud. Dist.	7
St. Dist. Cts.	42		

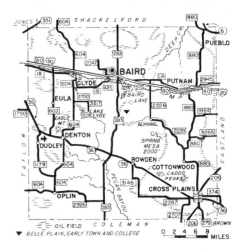

Legend: OIL FIELD · BELLE PLAIN, EARLY TOWN AND COLLEGE · 0 2 4 6 8 MILES

PHYSICAL FEATURES: On divide between Brazos, Colorado River watersheds; level to rolling.

RECREATION: Hunting, local events, **Clyde Lake**, county museum, old settler reunion in July.

MINERALS: Oil and gas.

1982 Pop.	11,700	Voters reg.	7,051
Area (sq. mi.)	899	Whlsle. sales	$14,331,000
Altitude (ft.)	1,500-2,100	Oil value	$43,847,754
Ann. rainfall (in.)	24.92	No. employed	1,471
Jan. temp. min.	33	Wages paid	$19,802,476
July temp. max.	96	Tax value	$451,512,777
Growing season (da.)	228	Income	$98,107,000
No. farms, 1982	800	Taxable sales	$17,913,927
†Value per farm	$276,976	Fed. expend.	$23,252,000
Cropland harvested 53,409		Crime Index	115
		TDC Pop.	16

AGRICULTURE: About 75% of $18 million average income from beef cattle, sheep and hogs; wheat, peanuts, grain sorghums chief crops.

BUSINESS: Oil field services, agribusiness; county in Abilene SMSA.

MANUFACTURING: None noted in census report.

SERVICE INDUSTRIES: 26 Establishments; Receipts, $3,087,000; Annual Payroll, $1,129,000; No. Employees, 175.

BAIRD (1,696) county seat; center for ranching, oil field supplies; window manufacturer and candy packing, shipping; county hospital, clinic, nursing home.

Other towns include **Clyde** (2,562) metal products, helicopter parts, other small manufacturing; many work in Abilene; **Cross Plains** (1,240), **Putnam** (116).

Cameron

LOCATION: Southern tip (U-16).

HISTORY: Created, organized from Nueces County, 1848; named for **Capt. Ewen Cameron** of Mier Expedition.

Cong. Dist.	15	U.S. Jud. Dist.	S-Br.
St. Sen. Dist.	27	Ct. Appeals	13
St. Rep. Dist.	37, 38, 39	Admin. Jud. Dist.	5
St. Dist. Cts. 103, 107, 138, 197, 357			

PHYSICAL FEATURES: Rich Rio Grande Valley soils; flat; semitropical climate.

RECREATION: Year-round resort; fishing, hunting, water sports; historical sites; Mexican gateway; **Padre Island; Laguna-Atascosa Wildlife Refuge**; numerous local events; recreational vehicle center; Confederate Air Force Museum, air shows at Harlingen; Iwo Jima Monument.

MINERALS: Natural gas, oil.

AGRICULTURE: One of state's leading counties in total farm income amounting to about $91 million annually; cotton, sorghums, citrus, vegetables, sugarcane; some cattle, hogs, goats; over 168,000 acres irrigated.

BUSINESS: Fruit, vegetables, seafood processing;

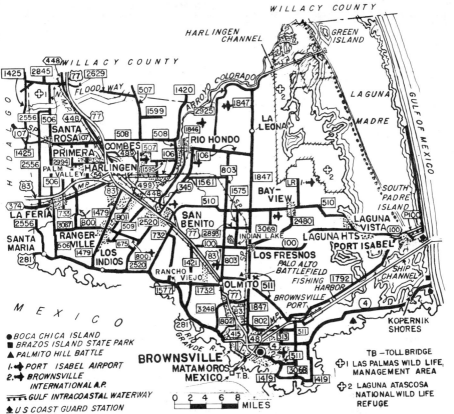

- ● BOCA CHICA ISLAND
- ■ BRAZOS ISLAND STATE PARK
- ▲ PALMITO HILL BATTLE
- I-← PORT ISABEL AIRPORT
- 2.← BROWNSVILLE INTERNATIONAL A.P.
- ↟↟↟ GULF INTRACOASTAL WATERWAY
- ⚓ U S COAST GUARD STATION

TB – TOLL BRIDGE
✢1 LAS PALMAS WILD LIFE, MANAGEMENT AREA
✢2 LAGUNA ATASCOSA NATIONAL WILD LIFE REFUGE

1982 Pop. 230,500	Voters reg. 95,780
Area (sq. mi.) 905	Whlsle. sales $829,626,000
Altitude (ft.) sea level-60	Oil value $146,604
Ann. rainfall (in.) . 25.13	No. employed 62,059
Jan. temp. min. 51	Wages paid . $776,668,436
July temp. max. 95	Tax value . $4,152,034,714
Growing season (da.) 341	Income . . . $1,429,019,000
No. farms, 1982 . . . 1,173	Taxable sales $768,856,217
No. acres in farms 386,129	Fed. expend. $560,207,000
†Value per farm $546,272	Crime Index 13,934
Cropland harv. . . 228,224	TDC Pop. 315

fishing, shipping, tourism; agribusiness; manufacturing.

MANUFACTURING: 187 Plants; 11,400 Employees; Payroll, $146,700,000; Product Value, $867,000,000.

SERVICE INDUSTRIES: 948 Establishments; Receipts, $249,054,000; Annual Payroll; $77,917,000; No. Employees, 7,299.

BROWNSVILLE (84,997) county seat (see metro page); varied industries, shipping, Port of Brownsville, fishing, extensive tourism, agribusiness; Texas Southmost College; hospitals, nursing homes, crippled children health center; Gladys Porter Zoo for endangered species.

Harlingen (43,543) agribusiness and tourist center; varied manufacturing; port; wholesale and distribution center; recreational vehicle rally and pads; Texas State Technical Institute; Valley Baptist Medical Center; Mental Health, Retardation Center; State Tuberculosis Hospital; Confederate Air Force Flying Museum.

San Benito (17,988) agribusiness, tourism, varied manufacturing; hospital.

Other towns include **Bayview** (291), **Combes** (1,488), **Indian Lake** (190), **La Feria** (3,495), **Laguna Vista** (632), **Los Fresnos** (2,173), **Palm Valley** (798), **Rancho Viejo** (208), **Port Isabel** (3,769), **Primera** (1,380), **Rio Hondo** (1,673), **Santa Rosa** (1,889) and **South Padre Island** (791) shipyard.

Camp

LOCATION: Northeast (G-20).
HISTORY: Created, organized from Upshur County, 1874; named for jurist-legislator, J. L. Camp.

Cong. Dist. 1	U.S. Jud. Dist. . . . . E-MI.
St. Sen. Dist. 1	Ct. Appeals 6
St. Rep. Dist. 8	Admin. Jud. Dist. 1
St. Dist. Cts. 76, 276	

PHYSICAL FEATURES: Hilly, forested; drains to Cypress Creek on north; Lake O' the Pines, Lake Bob Sandlin.
RECREATION: Water sports, fishing on six lakes within 20 miles of Pittsburg; local events.
MINERALS: Oil, gas, clays.
AGRICULTURE: Over $47 million annual income,

1982 Pop.	9,800	Voters reg.	5,640
Area (sq. mi.)	203	Whlsle. sales	$17,896,000
Altitude (ft.)	300-500	Oil value	$7,515,680
Ann. rainfall (in.)	45.25	No. employed	2,638
Jan. temp. min.	36	Wages paid	$33,816,808
July temp. max.	95	Tax value	$315,037,236
Growing season (da.)	238	Income	$94,158,000
No. farms, 1982	413	Taxable sales	$26,734,498
No. acres in farms	69,666	Fed. expend.	$17,539,000
†Value per farm	$145,245	Crime Index	184
Cropland harvested	10,500	TDC Pop.	24

more than 90% from livestock, dairy, poultry; peaches, vegetables, hay chief crops; timber harvest estimated at $1.7 million.

BUSINESS: Agribusiness, timber industries; light manufacturing, food processing; retirement center.

MANUFACTURING: None noted in census report.

SERVICE INDUSTRIES: 39 Establishments; Receipts, $4,630,000; Annual Payroll, $1,565,000; No. Employees, 179.

PITTSBURG (4,245) county seat; several industries manufacture furniture, clothing, oil field products, metal buildings, air filters, steel castings, brick, process feed; hospital, nursing homes; community college under construction.

Carson

LOCATION: Northwestern (C-9).

HISTORY: Created from Bexar District, 1876; organized 1888; named for Republic of Texas Secretary of State, **S. P. Carson.**

Cong. Dist.	13	U.S. Jud. Dist.	N-Am.
St. Sen. Dist.	31	Ct. Appeals	7
St. Rep. Dist.	88	Admin. Jud. Dist.	9
St. Dist. Cts.	100		

PHYSICAL FEATURES: Level, some broken land; loam soils.

RECREATION: Museum, local events, sausage festivals.

MINERALS: Oil, gas production.

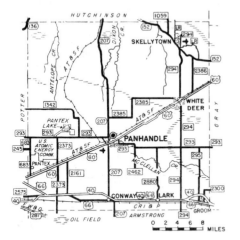

1982 Pop.	7,100	Voters reg.	4,362
Area (sq. mi.)	924	Whlsle. sales	$30,373,000
Altitude (ft.)	3,200-3,500	Oil value	$40,650,739
Ann. rainfall (in.)	20.92	No. employed	3,884
Jan. temp. min.	21	Wages paid	$85,329,552
July temp. max.	93	Tax value	$976,488,626
Growing season (da.)	191	Income	$68,148,000
No. farms, 1982	352	Taxable sales	$10,121,484
No. acres in farms	728,673	Fed. expend.	$40,472,000
†Value per farm	$784,963	Crime Index	74
Cropland harv.	191,154	TDC Pop.	13

AGRICULTURE: $35 million average annual income from milo, wheat, corn, beef cattle; 113,000 acres irrigated.

BUSINESS: Agribusinesses, oil field services.

MANUFACTURING: None noted in census report.

SERVICE INDUSTRIES: 14 Establishments; Receipts, $1,440,000; Annual Payroll, $253,000; No. Employees, 38.

PANHANDLE (2,226) county seat; agribusiness, petroleum center; nursing homes; airport; varied manufacturing.

Other towns include **White Deer** (1,210), **Skellytown** (899), **Groom** (736).

Cass

LOCATION: Northeast (G-21).

HISTORY: Named for **U. S. Sen. Lewis Cass**; created, organized 1846 from Bowie County.

Cong. Dist.	1	U.S. Jud. Dist.	E-Ml.
St. Sen. Dist.	1	Ct. Appeals	6
St. Rep. Dist.	8	Admin. Jud. Dist.	1
St. Dist. Cts.	5		

PHYSICAL FEATURES: Rolling, forested; timber produced; drained by Cypress Bayou, Sulphur River.

RECREATION: Fishing, water sports, weekly rodeo; **Lake Wright Patman, Atlanta State Park,** Wildflower Trails in spring, forest festival.

MINERALS: Gas, oil, iron ore.

1982 Pop.	30,600	Voters reg.	17,970
Area (sq. mi.)	937	Whlsle. sales	$39,196,000
Altitude (ft.)	200-500	Oil value	$36,594,421
Ann. rainfall (in.)	46.90	No. employed	6,445
Jan. temp. min.	31	Wages paid	$101,735,008
July temp. max.	92	Tax value	$1,292,259,119
Growing season (da.)	237	Income	$266,153,000
No. farms, 1982	894	Taxable sales	$68,523,737
No. acres in farms	195,528	Fed. expend.	$57,583,000
†Value per farm	$172,365	Crime Index	353
Cropland harvested	25,415	TDC Pop.	40

AGRICULTURE: More than $14 million average income with 75% from beef cattle, hogs; hay, watermelons, fruits and vegetables; timber income significant.

BUSINESS: Paper mill, wood products, steel products, varied manufacturing; agribusinesses.

MANUFACTURING: 41 Plants; 700 Employees; Payroll, $8,400,000; Product Value, $59,100,000.

SERVICE INDUSTRIES: 96 Establishments; Receipts, $16,130,000; Annual Payroll, $5,828,000; No. Employees, 614.

LINDEN (2,443) county seat; oil tank manufacturing, wood treating plant, boat factory, garment manufacturing, other small plants; hospital, nursing home.

Atlanta (6,272) paper mill, clothing, computer terminals, trailer factories, other varied manufacturing; oil field servicing; agribusinesses; hospitals.

Other towns include **Avinger** (671), **Bloomburg** (419), **Domino** (249), **Douglassville** (228), **Hughes Springs** (2,196) near steel mill, **Marietta** (169), **Queen City** (1,748).

Castro

LOCATION: Northwest (D-8).

HISTORY: Created 1876 from Bexar District, organized 1891. Named for **Henri Castro,** Texas colonizer.

Cong. Dist. . . . . 19 U.S. Jud. Dist. . . . N-Am.
St. Sen. Dist. . . . . . . 31 Ct. Appeals 7
St. Rep. Dist. . . . . . . 85 Admin. Jud. Dist. 9
St. Dist. Cts. 64, 242

PHYSICAL FEATURES: Flat, drains to creeks, draws and playas; underground water.
RECREATION: Local events; pheasant hunting.
MINERALS: Not significant.

1982 Pop.	10,600	Voters reg.	4,737
Area (sq. mi.)	899	Whlsle. sales	$87,102,000
Altitude (ft.)	3,500-4,000	Oil value	0
Ann. rainfall (in.)	17.72	No. employed	2,050
Jan. temp. min.	22	Wages paid . .	$28,646,388
July temp. max.	93	Tax value . .	$498,223,441
Growing season (da.)	193	Income	$60,933,000
No. farms, 1982	483	Taxable sales	$19,932,587
No. acres in farms	548,529	Fed. expend. .	$84,864,000
†Value per farm	$708,600	Crime Index	194
Cropland harv. . .	276,577	TDC Pop.	9

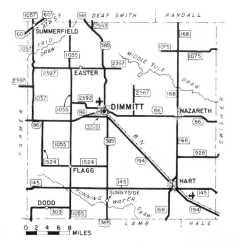

AGRICULTURE: More than $152 million average annual income makes county one of state's leading agricultural producers; major crops are corn, wheat, sorghums, cotton, vegetables; more than 300,000 acres irrigated; feedlots with 225,000 head capacity.
BUSINESS: Varied agribusinesses.
MANUFACTURING: None noted in census report.
SERVICE INDUSTRIES: 40 Establishments; Receipts, $4,235,000; Annual Payroll, $1,091,000; No. Employees, 128.
DIMMITT (5,019) county seat; corn-milling and starch plants; farm equipment, fertilizer manufacturing, food processing, other agribusinesses; library; hospital. Other towns are Hart (1,008) and Nazareth (299).

Chambers

LOCATION: On Galveston, other bays (M-21).
HISTORY: Named for **Gen. T. J. Chambers** surveyor; created, organized 1858 from Liberty, Jefferson Counties.
Cong. Dist. . . . . 9 U.S. Jud. Dist. . . . . S-Gn.
St. Sen. Dist. . . . . . . 4 Ct. Appeals 1, 14
St. Rep. Dist. . . . . . . 21 Admin. Jud. Dist. 2
St. Dist. Cts. . . . 253, 344
MINERALS: Oil, gas, salt, clays, sand and gravel.

1982 Pop.	19,100	Voters reg.	10,801
Area (sq. mi.)	616	Whlsle. sales	$271,722,000
Altitude (ft.)	sea level-50	Oil value	$69,167,989
Ann. rainfall (in.) .	52.84	No. employed	6,210
Jan. temp. min.	44	Wages paid .	$137,146,928
July temp. max.	91	Tax value . $3,651,444,665
Growing season (da.)	261	Income	$181,410,000
No. farms, 1982	332	Taxable sales	$69,018,433
No. acres in farms	312,966	Fed. expend. .	$75,255,000
†Value per farm	$1,030,764	Crime Index	651
Cropland harvested	92,944	TDC Pop.	53

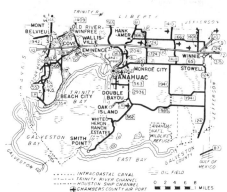

- - - - INTRACOASTAL CANAL — — OIL FIELD
------ TRINITY RIVER CHANNEL
—•—•— HOUSTON SHIP CHANNEL
⊕ CHAMBERS COUNTY AIR PORT

0 2 4 6 8
MILES

PHYSICAL FEATURES: Level, coastal soils; some forests.
RECREATION: Fishing, hunting; all water sports; camping facilities; 10 county parks; **Anahuac National Wildlife Refuge**; historic sites; **Texas Rice Festival.**
AGRICULTURE: About $30 million income; about 85% from rice, soybeans; beef cattle; 44,000 acres irrigated; 15,000 acres timber.
BUSINESS: Petroleum, chemicals, steel plants, agribusinesses, varied manufacturing, tourism.
MANUFACTURING: None noted in census report.
SERVICE INDUSTRIES: 60 Establishments; Receipts, $10,869,000; Annual Payroll, $4,550,000; No. Employees, 336.
ANAHUAC: (1,840) county seat; canal connects with Houston Ship Channel; agribusiness; hospital.
Other towns include **Mont Belvieu**, (1,730), **Beach City** (977), **Cove** (645), **Old River-Winfree** (1,058).

Cherokee

LOCATION: East (J-20).
HISTORY: Named for Indians; created, organized 1846 from Nacogdoches County.
Cong. Dist. . . . . 1 U.S. Jud. Dist. . . . E-Ty.
St. Sen. Dist. . . . . . . 3 Ct. Appeals 12
St. Rep. Dist. . . . . . . 11 Admin. Jud. Dis. 1
St. Dist. Cts. 2
PHYSICAL FEATURES: Hilly, partly forested; drains to Angelina, Neches Rivers; many streams, lakes; sandy, clay soils.
RECREATION: Water activities; fishing, hunting on many lakes; numerous historical sites, homes; Texas State Railroad excursion train; state parks.
Among points of interest are **Love's Lookout Park, Jim Hogg State Park,** birthplace of **first native Texan to become Governor; Caddo Mounds State Park** near Alto; site of ghost town of **New Birmingham;** Nature Trails through forests; and several lakes.
MINERALS: Oil, gas, clays.

1982 Pop.	38,500	Voters reg.	20,040
Area (sq. mi.)	1,052	Whlsle. sales	$100,108,000
Altitude (ft.)	250-570	Oil value	$6,025,426
Ann. rainfall (in.) .	44.26	No. employed	11,941
Jan. temp. min.	38	Wages paid .	$160,791,368
July temp. max.	94	Tax value . $1,334,172,942
Growing season (da.)	258	Income	$312,370,000
No. farms, 1982	1,439	Taxable sales $108,280,568
No. acres in farms	248,735	Fed. expend. .	$66,117,000
†Value per farm	$196,983	Crime Index	952
Cropland harvested	30,551	TDC Pop.	64

AGRICULTURE: More than $55 million average income, about 65% from cattle, poultry; greenhouse plants, hay, vegetables, fruits; timber production including Christmas trees.
BUSINESS: Wood and plastics industries, other factories; agribusiness.
MANUFACTURING: 96 Plants; 3,300 Employees; Payroll, $37,700,000; Product Value, $161,400,000.
SERVICE INDUSTRIES: 138 Establishments; Receipts, $24,830,000; Annual Payroll, $9,409,000; No. Employees, 837.

Cherokee County (Cont'd.)

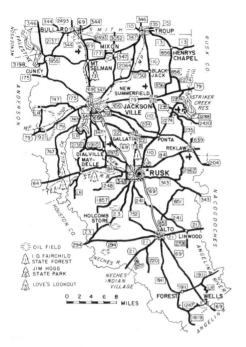

RUSK (4,681) county seat; pulpwood shipping center; woodworking plants; milk processor; other factories; **Rusk State Hospital**, other hospitals; state railroad, Rusk state park with camping.

Jacksonville (12,264), more than 60 industrial firms make wood, plastic products, metal buildings, baskets; vegetable and hothouse floral production; hospitals, clinic; **Lon Morris College, Jacksonville College, Baptist M.A. Theological Seminary.**

Other towns include **Wells** (926), **Troup** (1,911, partly in Smith County), **Bullard** (681, partly in Smith County), **Alto** (1,203), **New Summerfield** (319), **Reklaw** (305, part Rusk County), **Gallatin** (230).

Childress

LOCATION: Northwest (D-11).

HISTORY: Created 1876 from Bexar, Young Districts; organized 1887; named for **author of Texas Declaration of Independence, George C. Childress.**

Cong. Dist.	13	U.S. Jud. Dist.	N-Am.
St. Sen. Dist.	30	Ct. Appeals	7
St. Rep. Dist.	84	Admin. Jud. Dist.	9
St. Dist. Cts.	100		

PHYSICAL FEATURES: Rolling prairie, draining to Prairie Dog Fork of Red River; mixed soils.

RECREATION: Water recreation on **Lakes Childress** and **Baylor**, fishing, hunting; parks; county museum; July 4th ice cream freeze, other events.

MINERALS: Small production oil, gas.

1982 Pop.	6,900	Voters reg.	3,631
Area (sq. mi.)	707	Whlsle. sales	$16,049,000
Altitude (ft.)	1,600-1,900	Oil value	$269,890
Ann. rainfall (in.)	20.67	No. employed	1,963
Jan. temp. min.	26	Wages paid	$23,295,540
July temp. max.	99	Tax value	$152,083,495
Growing season (da.)	217	Income	$48,007,000
No. farms, 1982	323	Taxable sales	$18,441,993
No. acres in farms	342,181	Fed. expend.	$27,051,000
†Value per farm	$308,337	Crime Index	162
Cropland harvested	93,197	TDC Pop.	8

AGRICULTURE: About $17 million average income from cotton, wheat, sorghums, cattle; 6,000 acres irrigated.

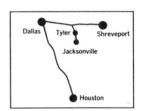

BUSINESS: Agribusinesses; varied manufacturing.
MANUFACTURING: 8 Plants; *Employees; Payroll, N.A.; Product Value, N.A.
SERVICE INDUSTRIES: 37 Establishments; Receipts, $6,023,000; Annual Payroll, $1,769,000; No. Employees, 208.

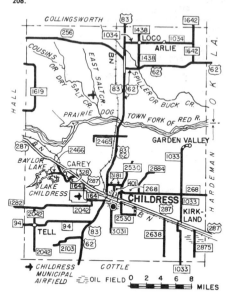

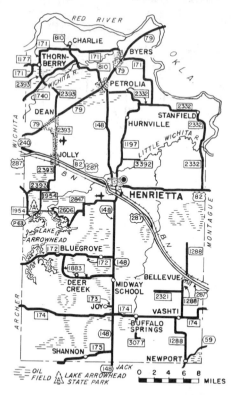

CHILDRESS (5,817) county seat; has more than 80% of county's population; plants make apparel, mobile homes, fences, wood products; hospital, nursing homes; home of Greenbelt Bowl, high school football all-star game.

Clay

LOCATION: North central (F-14).
HISTORY: Created, organized from Cooke County, 1857; Indians forced disorganization, 1862; reorganized, 1873; named for **Henry Clay**, U.S. statesman.

Cong. Dist.	13	U.S. Jud. Dist.	N-WF
St. Sen. Dist.	30	Ct. Appeals	2
St. Rep. Dist.	80	Admin. Jud. Dist.	8
St. Dist. Cts.	97		

PHYSICAL FEATURES: Hilly, rolling; drains to Red, Trinity Rivers, Lake Arrowhead; sandy loam, chocolate soils; mesquites, post oaks.
RECREATION: Fishing, water sports at **Lake Arrowhead;** local events.
MINERALS: Oil and gas, stone.

1982 Pop.	9,700	Voters reg.	6,425
Area (sq. mi.)	1,085	Whlse. sales	$12,838,000
Altitude (ft.)	900-1,100	Oil value	$81,599,079
Ann. rainfall (in.)	31.40	No. employed	1,382
Jan. temp. min.	30	Wages paid	$18,865,688
July temp. max.	98	Tax value	$603,727,644
Growing season (da.)	232	Income	$93,807,000
No. farms, 1982	813	Taxable sales	$15,190,123
No. acres in farms	582,620	Fed. expend.	$20,511,000
†Value per farm	$288,600	Crime Index	273
Cropland harvested	68,014	TDC Pop.	5

AGRICULTURE: Most of $38 million average income from livestock, chiefly beef and dairy cattle, swine; wheat, cotton, grain sorghums.
BUSINESS: Oil; agribusinesses; varied manufacturing.
MANUFACTURING: None noted in census report.
SERVICE INDUSTRIES: 16 Establishments; Receipts, $3,255,000; Annual Payroll, $1,405,000; No. Employees, 122.

HENRIETTA (3,149) county seat; plants make trophies, flatbed and livestock trailers, mobile homes, other products; hospital, rest homes; Pioneer Reunion and rodeo in September.
Other towns include **Petrolia** (755), **Bellevue** (352), **Byers** (556), **Jolly** (174), **Dean** (212).

Cochran

LOCATION: Adjoins New Mexico (F-7).
HISTORY: Created from Bexar, Young Districts, 1876; organized 1924; named for **Robert Cochran**, who died in Alamo.

Cong. Dist.	19	U.S. Jud. Dist.	N-Lb.
St. Sen. Dist.	28	Ct. Appeals	7
St. Rep. Dist.	77	Admin. Jud. Dist.	9
St. Dist. Cts.	286		

PHYSICAL FEATURES: Many small lakes (playas); level prairie; underground water; loam, sandy loam soils.
RECREATION: Rodeo, county fair, museum.
MINERALS: Oil, gas.

1982 Pop.	4,900	Voters reg.	2,487
Area (sq. mi.)	775	Whlse. sales	$8,168,000
Altitude (ft.)	3,500-3,800	Oil value	$265,457,512
Ann. rainfall (in.)	15.62	No. employed	1,040
Jan. temp. min.	23	Wages paid	$13,376,632
July temp. max.	92	Tax value	$996,108,355
Growing season (da.)	189	Income	$31,161,000
No. farms, 1982	279	Taxable sales	$5,516,669
No. acres in farms	375,319	Fed. expend.	$29,298,000
†Value per farm	$347,172	Crime Index	99
Cropland harv.	219,133	TDC Pop.	5

AGRICULTURE: More than $40 million average income from cotton, sorghums, wheat; cattle, extensive cattle feeding; 108,000 acres irrigated.
BUSINESS: Agribusinesses; feedlots.
MANUFACTURING: None noted in census report.
SERVICE INDUSTRIES: 12 Establishments; Receipts,

Cochran County (Cont'd.)

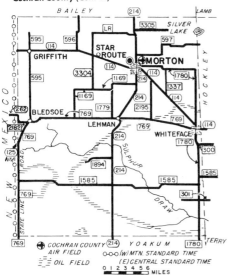

COCHRAN COUNTY AIR FIELD
OIL FIELD
(W) MTN. STANDARD TIME
(E) CENTRAL STANDARD TIME
0 1 2 3 4 5 6 MILES

$2,851,000; Annual Payroll, $1,732,000; No. Employees, 138.

MORTON (2,674) county seat; hospital, center for oil, agricultural trade, meat packing; **Whiteface** (463).

Coke

LOCATION: West central (J-11).

HISTORY: Created, organized 1889 from Tom Green County; named for Gov. **Richard Coke.**

Cong. Dist.	17	U.S. Jud. Dist.	N-SAng.
St. Sen. Dist.	25	Ct. Appeals	3
St. Rep. Dist.	66	Admin. Jud. Dist.	7
St. Dist. Cts	51		

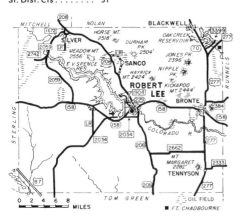

1982 Pop.	3,500	Voters reg.	2,297
Area (sq. mi.)	908	Whlsle. sales	$6,551,000
Altitude (ft.)	1,800-2,600	Oil value	$51,570,765
Ann. rainfall (in.)	20.48	No. employed	843
Jan. temp. min.	29	Wages paid	$13,473,888
July temp. max.	97	Tax value	$339,267,253
Growing season (da.)	226	Income	$31,260,000
No. farms, 1982	357	Taxable sales	$5,252,942
No. acres in farms	500,398	Fed. expend.	$8,052,000
†Value per farm	$452,801	Crime Index	49
Cropland harvested	10,464	TDC Pop.	3

PHYSICAL FEATURES: Prairie, hills, Colorado River valley; sandy loam, red soils. E. V. Spence Reservoir (formerly Robert Lee).

RECREATION: Hunting, fishing; **Lake Spence, Oak Creek Reservoir;** historic sites, county museum, local events.

MINERALS: Oil, gas, sand and gravel.

AGRICULTURE: More than 90% of $10.8 million annual farm income from cattle, sheep, goats and horses; cotton, sorghums, small grains, hay leading crops.

BUSINESS: Oil well supplies, agribusinesses, tourism.

MANUFACTURING: None noted in census report.

SERVICE INDUSTRIES: 6 Establishments; Receipts, $650,000; Annual Payroll, $109,000; No. Employees, 12.

ROBERT LEE (1,202) county seat; ranching; oil, gas center; hospital, nursing home; **Bronte** (983) and **Blackwell** (286, partly in Nolan County).

Coleman

LOCATION: West central (J-12).

HISTORY: Created 1858 from Brown, Travis Counties; organization began 1862, completed 1864; named for Houston's aide, **R. M. Coleman.**

Cong. Dist.	17	U.S. Jud. Dist.	N-SAng.
St. Sen. Dist.	24	Ct. Appeals	11
St. Rep. Dist.	65	Admin. Jud. Dist.	7
St. Dist. Cts.	42		

PHYSICAL FEATURES: Hilly, rolling; drains to Colorado River, Pecan Bayou; lakes; some mesquite, oaks.

RECREATION: Fishing, hunting; water sports; local events; historic sites; **Lake Coleman, Lake Scarborough, Hord's Creek Reservoir, other lakes; Santa Anna Peak.**

MINERALS: Oil, gas, coal, stone, clays.

1982 Pop.	10,500	Voters reg.	6,305
Area (sq. mi.)	1,277	Whlsle. sales	$27,099,000
Altitude (ft.)	1,500-2,250	Oil value	$47,198,879
Ann. rainfall (in.)	26.52	No. employed	2,474
Jan. temp. min.	34	Wages paid	$29,769,456
July temp. max.	96	Tax value	$436,616,230
Growing season (da.)	235	Income	$88,604,000
No. farms, 1982	837	Taxable sales	$34,702,953
No. acres in farms	749,613	Fed. expend.	$29,335,000
†Value per farm	$415,676	Crime Index	134
Cropland harv.	106,080	TDC Pop.	18

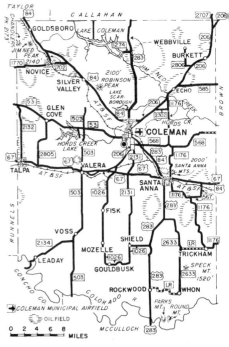

COLEMAN MUNICIPAL AIRFIELD
OIL FIELD
0 2 4 6 8 MILES

AGRICULTURE: In excess of 80% of $21 million average annual income from cattle, sheep, hogs; wheat, oats, grain sorghums, cotton.

BUSINESS: Agribusinesses, petroleum, tile, brick plants, other manufacturers.

MANUFACTURING: None noted in census report.

SERVICE INDUSTRIES: 47 Establishments; Receipts, $6,979,000; Annual Payroll, $1,918,000; No. Employees, 251.

COLEMAN (5,960) county seat; varied manufacturing and agribusinesses; hospital, nursing home. **Santa Anna** (1,535), clay industry; **Novice** (201) and **Talpa** (122).

Collin

LOCATION: North central (G-17).

HISTORY: Created from Fannin County and organized, 1846. Named for pioneer there, **Collin McKinney.**

Cong. Dist. 3, 4, 26	U.S. Jud. Dist. . . . . E-Sh.
St. Sen. Dist. 2, 8	Ct. Appeals 5
St. Rep. Dist. . . . 60, 61, 62	Admin. Jud. Dist. 1
St. Dist. Cts. . 199, 219, 296	

MINERALS: Limited stone production.

1982 Pop. 160,900	Voters reg. 98,624
Area (sq. mi.) 851	Whlse. sales $708,532,000
Altitude (ft.) 450-700	Oil value 0
Ann. rainfall (in.) . 38.10	No. employed 41,642
Jan. temp. min. 34	Wages paid . . $722,770,088
July temp. max. 96	Tax value $11,831,624,528
Growing season (da.) 230	Income . . $2,102,494,000
No. farms, 1982 . . . 1,543	Taxable sales $893,748,307
No. acres in farms 354,799	Fed. expend. $265,608,000
†Value per farm $459,767	Crime Index 7,146
Cropland harv. . . 165,657	TDC Pop. 208

PHYSICAL FEATURES: Heavy, black clay soil; level to rolling; drains to Trinity, Lake Lavon.

RECREATION: Fishing, water sports on **Lavon,** other lakes; historic sites; old homes restoration, tours; Heard Natural Science Museum, McKinney Historical District, Old Collin County Post Office, Bolin Wildlife Exhibit; South Fork Ranch of Dallas TV series near Wylie; local events in Plano.

AGRICULTURE: More than $43 million average annual income equally divided between crops, livestock; sorghums, wheat, hay, cotton, chief crops; beef cattle, horses.

BUSINESS: Varied manufacturing plants, agribusinesses, retail and wholesale center. Many work in Dallas (part of Dallas-Fort Worth SMSA, see metro page).

MANUFACTURING: 168 Plants, 6,100 Employees; Payroll, $102,700,000; Product Value, $582,900,000.

SERVICE INDUSTRIES: 718 Establishments; Receipts, $164,636,000; Annual Payroll, $60,067,000; No. Employees, 4,579.

McKINNEY (16,256) county seat; agribusiness, trade center; varied industries; hospitals, nursing homes; fashion outlet; three museums.

Plano (72,331), one of nation's fastest growing cities; boat, metals; newspaper printing, computer forms, satellite communications, bakery equipment, other manufacturing; research center, growing commercial and financial center; hospital, nursing homes.

Other towns include **Addison** (5,553, mostly in Dallas County), **Allen** (8,314), **Altoga** (269), **Anna** (855), **Blue Ridge** (442), **Celina** (1,520), **Dallas** (904,078, mostly Dallas County), **Fairview** (180), **Farmersville** (2,360), **Frisco** (3,499), **Josephine** (416), **Lavon** (185), **Lowry Crossing** (443), **Lucas** (1,371), **Melissa** (604), **Murphy** (1,150), **New Hope** (331), **Parker** (1,098), **Princeton** (3,408), **Prosper** (675), **Richardson** (72,496, mostly Dallas County), **Royse City** (1,566, part Rockwall County), **Sachse** (1,640, partly Dallas County), **Saint Paul** (363), **Westminster** (278), **Weston** (405) and **Wylie** (3,152).

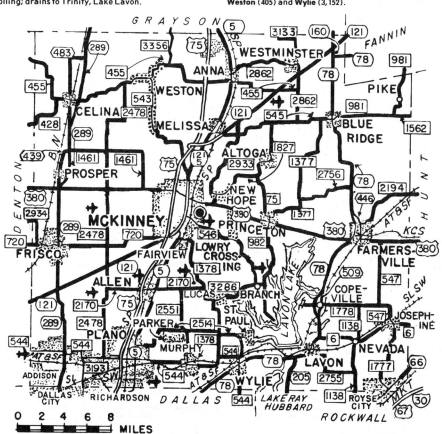

0 2 4 6 8
MILES

Collingsworth

LOCATION: In Panhandle (D-11).

HISTORY: Created, 1876, from Bexar and Young Districts, organized 1890. Named for Republic of Texas' first Chief Justice, **James Collinsworth**; name misspelled in law.

Cong. Dist. 13	U.S. Jud. Dist. . . . N-Am.
St. Sen. Dist. 31	Ct. Appeals 7
St. Rep. Dist. 84	Admin. Jud. Dist. 9
St. Dist. Cts. 100	

PHYSICAL FEATURES: Rolling, broken terrain, draining to Red River forks; sandy and loam soils.

RECREATION: Children's camp, county museum, Pioneer park.

MINERALS: Gas, oil production.

1982 Pop.	4,500	Voters reg.	2,523
Area (sq. mi.)	909	Whlsle. sales . .	$7,399,000
Altitude (ft.) .	1,800-2,600	Oil value	$334,192
Ann. rainfall (in.) .	22.03	No. employed	1,046
Jan. temp. min.	26	Wages paid . .	$13,001,388
July temp. max.	99	Tax value . .	$156,436,746
Growing season (da.)	212	Income	$35,619,000
No. farms, 1982	388	Taxable sales .	$7,102,747
No. acres in farms	459,678	Fed. expend. .	$19,615,000
†Value per farm	$341,067	Crime Index	92
Cropland harvested	86,337	TDC Pop.	9

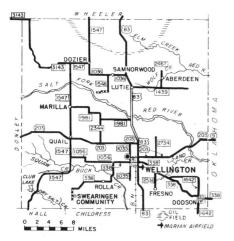

AGRICULTURE: About $20 million average income from cotton, grains, beef cattle; 10,000 acres irrigated.

BUSINESS: Chiefly agribusinesses, railroad manufacturing, light industry.

MANUFACTURING: None noted in census report.

SERVICE INDUSTRIES: 20 Establishments; Receipts, $1,652,000; Annual Payroll $584,000; No. Employees, 70.

WELLINGTON (3,043) county seat; feedlots, other agribusinesses; rail spike factory; hospital; **Dodson** (185).

Colorado

LOCATION: Southeast (N-18).

HISTORY: Created 1836, an original county, organized 1837. Named for **Colorado River.**

Cong. Dist. 14	U.S. Jud. Dist. . . . . S-Hn.
St. Sen. Dist. 5	Ct. Appeals 1, 14
St. Rep. Dist. 30	Admin. Jud. Dist. 3
St. Dist. Cts. 25, 2D25	

PHYSICAL FEATURES: 3 soil types; level to rolling; bisected by Colorado River; oaks leading timber.

RECREATION: Hunting, many historic sites, homes; **Attwater's Prairie Chicken Preserve**, local events.

MINERALS: Gas, oil, sand and gravel, stone.

AGRICULTURE: About $53 million average income from beef, dairy cattle, poultry, hogs, rice, corn, grains, cotton, hay, soybeans; 50,000 acres irrigated, mostly rice.

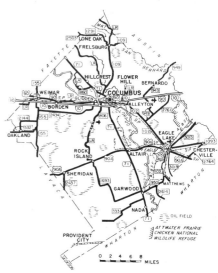

1982 Pop.	19,500	Voters reg.	10,194
Area (sq. mi.)	964	Whlsle. sales .	$71,454,000
Altitude (ft.)	150-400	Oil value	$15,981,146
Ann. rainfall (in.) .	41.32	No. employed	5,920
Jan. temp. min.	39	Wages paid . .	$87,829,828
July temp. max.	86	Tax value .	$1,317,957,593
Growing season (da.)	280	Income	$172,573,000
No. farms, 1982 . . .	1,424	Taxable sales	$76,921,321
No. acres in farms	596,786	Fed. expend. .	$46,502,000
†Value per farm	$433,035	Crime Index	254
Cropland harv. . .	101,244	TDC Pop.	22

BUSINESS: Agribusinesses; oil field services and equipment manufacturing. Plants process minerals.

MANUFACTURING: 24 Plants; 800 Employees; Payroll, $13,000,000; Product Value, $59,900,000.

SERVICE INDUSTRIES: 101 Establishments; Receipts, $13,329,000; Annual Payroll, $4,473,000; No. employees, 479.

COLUMBUS (3,923) county seat; agribusiness center; sand, gravel industries; oil, gas servicing, processing; oil field and clothing manufacturing; hospital, nursing home, many historical sites, old homes. Art show and antique sale in **May.**

Other towns include **Eagle Lake**, (3,921) farming center; concrete products; **Weimar** (2,128) varied manufacturing; hospital, nursing home.

Comal

LOCATION: South central (N-14).

HISTORY: Created and organized from Bexar, Gonzales, Travis Counties, 1846; named for **Comal River.**

Cong. Dist. 21	U.S. Jud. Dist. . . . W-SAnt.
St. Sen. Dist. 21	Ct. Appeals 3
St. Rep. Dist. 46	Admin. Jud. Dist. 3
St. Dist. Cts. . . 22, 207, 274	

PHYSICAL FEATURES: Hilly, spring-fed streams; 2½-mile-long Comal called "shortest U.S. river"; Guadalupe River; Canyon Lake.

1982 Pop.	39,400	Voters reg.	24,053
Area (sq. mi.)	555	Whlsle. sales .	$53,375,000
Altitude (ft.) . . .	650-1,700	Oil value	0
Ann. rainfall (in.) .	33.19	No. employed	12,403
Jan. temp. min.	40	Wages paid .	$178,932,456
July temp. max.	96	Tax value .	$1,794,845,074
Growing season (da.)	265	Income	$440,242,000
No. farms, 1982 . . .	584	Taxable sales	$184,853,168
No. acres in farms	195,271	Fed. expend.	$105,599,000
†Value per farm	$340,930	Crime Index	1,507
Cropland harvested	11,969	TDC Pop.	54

RECREATION: Tourist center; fishing, hunting; historic sites, museum; scenic drives; **Canyon Lake** facilities; **Landa Park, Prince Solms Park**, other county parks; **Natural Bridge Cavern**; river resorts, lodges, river sports; Wurstfest in November, other local events, old homes.

MINERALS: Stone, lime, sand and gravel.

AGRICULTURE: About 85% of $8 million farm income from beef cattle; some sorghum, wheat, oats.

BUSINESS: Plants make textiles, apparel, furniture, metal products, mineral, electrical manufacturing, concrete products; tourist business; county in San Antonio SMSA, see metro page.

MANUFACTURING: 50 Plants; 2,800 Employees; Payroll, $40,800,000; Product Value, $188,300,000.

SERVICE INDUSTRIES: 253 Establishments; Receipts, $41,839,000; Annual Payroll, $14,673,000; No. Employees, 1,456.

NEW BRAUNFELS (22,402) county seat; textile, furniture, metal products factories; tourist center; hospital, nursing homes, center for retarded.

Other towns include **Garden Ridge** (647) and **Schertz** (7,262) mostly in Guadalupe County.

Comanche

LOCATION: Central (J-14).

HISTORY: Created, organized, 1856, from Bosque, Coryell Counties; named for **Indians.**

Cong. Dist. 17	U.S. Jud. Dist. . . . . N-FW
St. Sen. Dist. 22	Ct. Appeals 11
St. Rep. Dist. 65	Admin Jud. Dist. 3
St. Dist. Cts. 220	

PHYSICAL FEATURES: Rolling, hilly; sandy, loam,

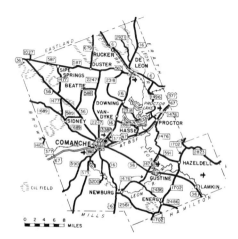

waxy soils; drains to Leon River, Proctor Reservoir; pecans, oaks, mesquites, cedars.

RECREATION: Hunting, fishing, **Lake Proctor;** local parks, museums, local events.

MINERALS: Limited gas, oil, stone, clay.

1982 Pop. 12,900	Voters reg. 7,751
Area (sq. mi.) 930	Whlsle. sales . $97,484,000
Altitude (ft.) . . . 650-1,700	Oil value $3,238,947
Ann. rainfall (in.) . 28.45	No. employed 2,842
Jan. temp. min. 32	Wages paid . . $33,570,180
July temp. max. 95	Tax value . . $470,964,945
Growing season (da.) 238	Income $98,363,000
No. farms, 1982 . . 1,350	Taxable sales $31,456,111
No. acres in farms 494,533	Fed. expend. . $39,507,000
†Value per farm $247,362	Crime Index 161
Cropland harvested 94,748	TDC Pop. 18

AGRICULTURE: $72 million average annual income, 75% from beef, dairy cattle, swine, sheep and goats; peanuts, grains, hay leading crops; pecans, fruit also produced; 30,000 acres irrigated, mostly peanuts.

BUSINESS: Peanut and pecan shelling plants; other agribusinesses; food processing; leather factory, pottery, clothing, varied other plants.

MANUFACTURING: 18 Plants; 500 Employees; Payroll, $5,700,000; Product Value, $69,800,000.

SERVICE INDUSTRIES: 55 Establishments; Receipts, $8,556,000; Annual Payroll, $2,854,000; No. Employees, 358.

COMANCHE (4,075) county seat; plants make clothing, leather, ceramic goods; agribusinesses; hospital, nursing home; public library.

DeLeon (2,478), marketing center for peanuts, pecans, peaches; **Gustine** (416).

Concho

LOCATION: Central (K-12).

HISTORY: Created from Bexar District, 1858, organized 1879. Named for **Concho River.**

Cong. Dist. 17	U.S. Jud. Dist. . . N-SAng.
St. Sen. Dist. 24	Ct. Appeals 3
St. Rep. Dist. 67	Admin. Jud. Dist. 7
St. Dist. Cts. . . . 119, 198	

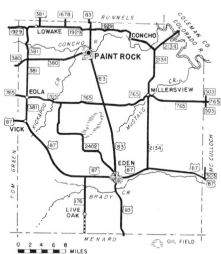

1982 Pop. 3,000	Voters reg. 2,006
Area (sq. mi.) 992	Whlsle. sales . . $1,647,000
Altitude (ft.) . . 1,600-2,100	Oil value $8,505,283
Ann. rainfall (in.) . 22.28	No. employed 532
Jan. temp. min. 35	Wages paid . . $6,021,708
July temp. max. 96	Tax value . . $289,623,089
Growing season (da.) 228	Income $26,014,000
No. farms, 1982 . . . 376	Taxable sales . $3,508,745
No. acres in farms 604,432	Fed. expend. . $12,614,000
†Value per farm $566,210	Crime Index 37
Cropland harv. . . . 92,941	TDC Pop. 2

PHYSICAL FEATURES: Rough, broken area to south; level in north; sandy, loam and dark soils; drains to creeks and Colorado River.

RECREATION: Famed for 1,500 Indian **pictographs,** largest collection known; local events.

MINERALS: Oil, gas, stone produced.

AGRICULTURE: More than $19 million farm income, 60% from sheep, cattle, goats; leading sheep producing county; grains, cotton chief crops.

BUSINESS: Chiefly agribusinesses.

MANUFACTURING: None noted in census report.

SERVICE INDUSTRIES: 6 Establishments; Receipts, $1,129,000; Annual Payroll, $323,000; No. Employees, 44.

PAINT ROCK (256) county seat; named for **Indian pictographs;** ranching, farming center. **Eden** (1,294), is largest town, hospital, nursing home.

MANUFACTURING: 57 Plants; 3,100 Employees; Payroll, $55,600,000; Product Value, $294,700,000.

SERVICE INDUSTRIES: 135 Establishments; Receipts, $23,976,000; Annual Payroll, $7,894,000; No. Employees, 701.

GAINESVILLE (14,081) county seat; factories make pipe, garments, boots, fishing lures, metal products, aircraft equipment; agribusinesses; **Cooke County College;** hospitals, nursing homes; **Gainesville State School; Camp Sweeney** for diabetic children.

Muenster (1,408) is a dairy center with Associated Milk Producers plant, cheese factory, REA headquarters, oil production center, feed processing, dress factory, other industries; hospital.

Other towns include **Callisburg** (281), **Lindsay** (581) and **Valley View** (514).

Cooke

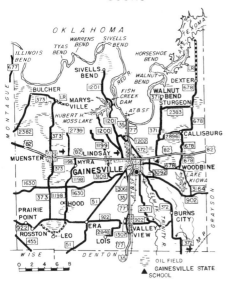

LOCATION: North central, adjoins Oklahoma (F-16).

HISTORY: Created, organized, 1848, from Fannin County; named for **Capt. W. G. Cooke** of Texas Revolution.

Cong. Dist. . . . . . . 17, 26   U.S. Jud. Dist. . . . . E-Sh.
St. Sen. Dist. 30   Ct. Appeals 2
St. Rep. Dist. 63   Admin. Jud. Dist. 8
St. Dist. Cts. 235

PHYSICAL FEATURES: Drains to Red, Trinity Rivers; **Lake Texoma** in northeast corner; sandy, red, loam soils.

RECREATION: Water sports; **Lake Ray Roberts** under construction; hunting, fishing; **Frank Buck Zoo;** museum; park; local events.

MINERALS: Oil, gas, sand and gravel.

1982 Pop. 28,600	Voters reg. 15,921
Area (sq. mi.) 893	Whlsle. sales $152,369,000
Altitude (ft.) . . . 700-1,100	Oil value $86,112,848
Ann. rainfall (in.) . . 33.88	No. employed 9,569
Jan. temp. min. 32	Wages paid . $140,202,384
July temp. max. 96	Tax value . . $1,125,300,231
Growing season (da.) 226	Income $260,278,000
No. farms, 1982 . . . 1,230	Taxable sales $119,345,525
No. acres in farms 411,978	Fed. expend. . $59,359,000
†Value per farm $222,808	Crime Index 820
Cropland harvested 93,191	TDC Pop. 54

AGRICULTURE: About 80% of $43 million average annual income from beef, dairy cattle, poultry, hogs, horses; crops include wheat, oats, grain sorghum, peanuts, hay; some irrigation.

BUSINESS: Agribusinesses, oil industries, varied manufacturing.

Coryell

LOCATION: Central (K-15).

HISTORY: Created from Bell County, organized, 1854; named for local pioneer, **James Coryell.**

Cong. Dist. 11   U.S. Jud. Dist. . . . . W-Wa.
St. Sen. Dist. 24   Ct. Appeals 10
St. Rep. Dist. 57   Admin. Jud. Dist. 3
St. Dist. Cts. 52

PHYSICAL FEATURES: Leon Valley in center, remainder rolling, hilly.

RECREATION: Mother Neff State Park; hunting; nearby lakes and Leon River. **Fort Hood** brings many visitors; historic homes; log jail; local events.

MINERALS: Small stone, sand and gravel production.

1982 Pop. 58,900	Voters reg. 17,168
Area (sq. mi.) 1,057	Whlsle. sales . $30,056,000
Altitude (ft.) . . . 650-1,300	Oil value 0
Ann. rainfall (in.) . . 32.58	No. employed 5,886
Jan. temp. min. 36	Wages paid . . $75,186,480
July temp. max. 96	Tax value . . $777,668,702
Growing season (da.) 241	Income $539,920,000
No. farms, 1982 . . . 991	Taxable sales $79,810,282
No. acres in farms 621,577	Fed. expend. . $77,163,000
†Value per farm $290,742	Crime Index 1,079
Cropland harvested 66,850	TDC Pop. 46

AGRICULTURE: About 75% of $34 million average annual income from beef cattle, horses, sheep, goats; grains, hay, pecans produced; cedar posts.

BUSINESS: Fort Hood military business, agribusinesses, plastics and other manufacturing. Part of Killeen-Temple SMSA.

MANUFACTURING: None noted in census report.

SERVICE INDUSTRIES: 104 Establishments; Receipts, $13,367,000; Annual Payroll, $5,371,000; No. Employees, 851.

GATESVILLE (6,260) county seat; agribusinesses; plants make boats, trailers, clothing, furniture, plastic medical products, other products; **Mountain View and Gatesville** prisons for women; hospitals.

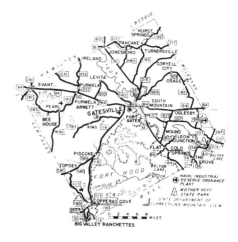

Copperas Cove (19,469), business center for **Fort Hood**, apparel, varied manufacturing; **Central Texas College**; hospital. Other towns include **Evant** (425), **Fort Gates** (777) and **Oglesby** (443).

Cottle

LOCATION: Northwest (E-11).

HISTORY: Created, 1876, from Fannin County; organized 1892; named for **George W. Cottle**, Alamo hero.

Cong. Dist.	13	U.S. Jud. Dist.	N-WF
St. Sen. Dist.	30	Ct. Appeals	7
St. Rep. Dist.	78	Admin. Jud. Dist.	9
St. Dist. Cts.	50		

PHYSICAL FEATURES: Rough in west, level in east; gray, black, sandy and loam soils; drains to Pease River.

RECREATION: Settlers reunion in April; hunting; Matador Wildlife Management Area.

MINERALS: Not significant.

1982 Pop.	2,800	Voters reg.	1,831
Area (sq. mi.)	895	Whlsle. sales	$3,424,000
Altitude (ft.)	1,600-2,100	Oil value	$2,937,033
Ann. rainfall (in.)	22.12	No. employed	846
Jan. temp. min.	27	Wages paid	$12,796,724
July temp. max.	97	Tax value	$135,572,496
Growing season (da.)	219	Income	$25,881,000
No. farms, 1982	235	Taxable sales	$4,079,572
No. acres in farms	488,882	Fed. expend.	$20,187,000
†Value per farm	$589,706	Crime Index	14
Cropland harvested	92,574	TDC Pop.	4

AGRICULTURE: In excess of $15 million average income, from cotton, grains, guar, beef cattle, alfalfa; 6,000 acres irrigated.

BUSINESS: Chiefly agribusinesses and gasoline manufacturing.

MANUFACTURING: None noted in census report.

SERVICE INDUSTRIES: 16 Establishments; Receipts, $1,764,000; Annual Payroll, $606,000; No. Employees, 88.

PADUCAH (2,216) county seat; farm and ranch trading center; gasoline manufacturing; hospital.

Crane

LOCATION: Southwest (J-7).

HISTORY: Created from Tom Green County, 1887, organized 1927; named for Baylor U. President **W. C. Crane**.

Cong. Dist.	21	U.S. Jud. Dist.	W-MO
St. Sen. Dist.	25	Ct. Appeals	8
St. Rep. Dist.	69	Admin. Jud. Dist.	7
St. Dist. Cts.	109		

PHYSICAL FEATURES: Rolling prairie, Pecos Valley, some hills; sandy, loam soils; **Juan Cordona Lake**.

RECREATION: Local events; sites of pioneer trails and historic Horsehead Crossing on Pecos River; Castle Gap Park, camping park.

MINERALS: Among county leaders in oil, gas production.

AGRICULTURE: Cattle ranching brings about $2.5 million yearly; very little farming.

Crockett

LOCATION: Southwest (L-9).

HISTORY: Created 1875, from Bexar, organized 1891; named for Alamo hero, **David Crockett**.

Cong. Dist.	21
St. Sen. Dist.	25
St. Rep. Dist.	67
St. Dist. Cts.	112
U.S. Jud. Dist.	N-SAng.
Ct. Appeals	8
Admin. Jud. Dist.	6

PHYSICAL FEATURES: Level to rough, hilly terrain; drains to Pecos River on south; rocky soils.

RECREATION: Hunting; historic site, **Fort Lancaster State Park**; county museum; Davy Crockett statue in park.

MINERALS: Oil, gas, stone production.

1982 Pop.	5,100	Voters reg.	2,758
Area (sq. mi.)	2,806	Whlsle. sales	$2,969,000
Altitude (ft.)	1,500-2,800	Oil value	$134,800,527
Ann. rainfall (in.)	14,90	No. employed	1,700
Jan. temp. min.	38	Wages paid	$27,277,788
July temp. max.	95	Tax value	$905,169,632
Growing season (da.)	233	Income	$44,200,000
No. farms, 1982	154	Taxable sales	$13,338,180
No. ac. in farms.	1,749,913	Fed. expend.	$6,495,000
†Value per farm	$2,094,961	Crime Index	94
Cropland harvested.	526	TDC Pop.	10

AGRICULTURE: A major sheep producing county; more than $16 million average income from cattle, sheep, goats, horses.

BUSINESS: Oil, ranching businesses.

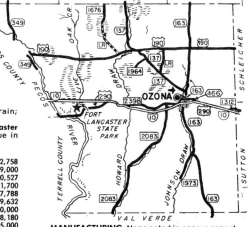

MANUFACTURING: None noted in census report.

SERVICE INDUSTRIES: 21 Establishments; Receipts, $6,342,000; Annual Payroll, $1,522,000; No. Employees, 136.

OZONA (est. 3,500) county seat; trade center for large ranching area; hunting leases; tourism; hospital; nursing home.

Fort Lancaster, once home of camels in Texas, is now a ruin. Associated Press Photo.

1982 Pop.	5,000	Voters reg.	2,883
Area (sq. mi.)	782	Whlsle. sales	$5,852,000
Altitude (ft.)	2,400-3,000	Oil value	$237,374,724
Ann. rainfall (in.)	12.97	No. employed	2,134
Jan. temp. min.	29	Wages paid	$47,169,096
July temp. max.	96	Tax value	$2,273,148,342
Growing season (da.)	225	Income	$52,134,000
No. farms, 1982	30	Taxable sales	$13,834,970
No. acres in farms	306,422	Fed. expend.	$4,913,000
†Value per farm	$1,041,733	Crime Index	84
Cropland harvested.	N.A.	TDC Pop.	7

CRANE (3,622) county seat; oil well servicing, production; steel foundry, concrete products; hospital, nursing home.

BUSINESS: Oil-based economy.
MANUFACTURING: None noted in census report.
SERVICE INDUSTRIES: 19 Establishments; Receipts, $2,593,000; Annual Payroll, $737,000; No. Employees, 86.

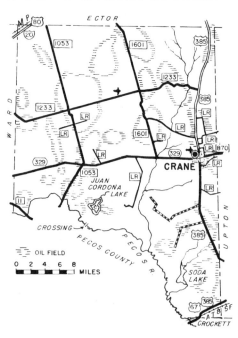

Crosby

LOCATION: Northwest (F-9).
HISTORY: Created from Bexar District, 1876, organized 1886; named for Texas Land Commissioner Stephen Crosby.

Cong. Dist.	17	U.S. Jud. Dist.	N-Lb.
St. Sen. Dist.	28	Ct. Appeals	7
St. Rep. Dist.	84	Admin. Jud. Dist.	9
St. Dist. Cts.	72		

PHYSICAL FEATURES: Flat, rich soil above Cap Rock, broken below; drains into Brazos forks and playas.
RECREATION: White River Reservoir; Silver Falls Park; **Crosby County Pioneer Museum** at Crosbyton and Ralls Historical Museum have many Indian artifacts; Crosbyton Solar Power Plant; settlers reunion in August.
MINERALS: Sand, gravel, oil, gas.

1982 Pop.	8,700	Voters reg.	4,188
Area (sq. mi.)	898	Whlsle. sales	$28,267,000
Altitude (ft.)	2,100-3,200	Oil value	$30,419,436
Ann. rainfall (in.)	21.01	No. employed	1,692
Jan. temp. min.	26	Wages paid	$21,364,976
July temp. max.	94	Tax value	$338,100,659
Growing season (da.)	206	Income	$52,019,000
No. farms, 1982	430	Taxable sales	$9,761,250
No. acres in farms	477,303	Fed. expend.	$55,645,000
†Value per farm	$844,892	Crime Index	71
Cropland harv.	213,320	TDC Pop.	7

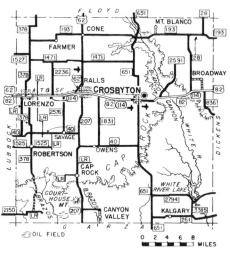

AGRICULTURE: About $42 million annual average income from cotton, sorghums, wheat, soybeans, sunflowers, cattle, hogs, poultry; 125,000 acres irrigated.
BUSINESS: Agribusinesses, manufacturing, gasohol and solar plants; tourism; drug and alcohol treatment center.
MANUFACTURING: None noted in census report.
SERVICE INDUSTRIES: 24 Establishments; Receipts, $2,222,000; Annual Payroll, $696,000; No. Employees, 126.
CROSBYTON (2,289) county seat; agribusiness, trade center; hospital, rehabilitation center.
Other towns include **Ralls** (2,422), **Lorenzo** (1,394).

Culberson

LOCATION: Far west (J-4).

HISTORY: Created from El Paso County, 1911, organized 1912; named for **D. B. Culberson**, Texas congressman.

Cong. Dist.	16	U.S. Jud. Dist.	W-Pe.
St. Sen. Dist.	25	Ct. Appeals	8
St. Rep. Dist.	69	Admin. Jud. Dist.	6
St. Dist. Cts.	34, 205, 210		

PHYSICAL FEATURES: Texas' highest mountains, entire county over 3,000 feet; slopes toward Pecos Valley on east, Diablo Bolson on west; salt lakes; unique vegetation in canyons.

RECREATION: Guadalupe Mountains National Park; Guadalupe and **El Capitan,** twin peaks; scenic canyons and mountains; historical museum at Van Horn; historical salt deposits.

MINERALS: Oil, gas, marble, stone.

1982 Pop.	3,400	Voters reg.	1,707
Area (sq. mi.)	3,815	Whlsle. sales	$1,469,000
Altitude (ft.)	3,000-8,751	Oil value	$7,418,278
Ann. rainfall (in.)	10.22	No. employed	1,374
Jan. temp. min.	30	Wages paid	$21,943,340
July temp. max.	95	Tax value	$372,993,686
Growing season (da.)	224	Income	$15,415,000
No. farms, 1982	70	Taxable sales	$9,428,898
No. ac. in farms	1,909,817	Fed. expend.	$10,388,000
†Value per farm	$3,558,629	Crime Index	32
Cropland harvested.	N.A.	TDC Pop.	14

AGRICULTURE: Almost $8 million average income from cattle, cotton, grains, pecans, vegetables; 20,000 acres irrigated.

BUSINESS: Agribusinesses, tourism, some mineral processing, oil production.

MANUFACTURING: None noted in census report.

SERVICE INDUSTRIES: 24 Establishments; Receipts, $3,766,000; Annual Payroll, $1,005,000; No. Employees, 151.

VAN HORN (2,772) county seat; ranching center; rock crushing; hospital.

Dallam

LOCATION: Northwestern corner (A-7).

HISTORY: Created from Bexar District, 1876, organized 1891. Named for lawyer-editor **James W. Dallam.**

Cong. Dist.	13	U.S. Jud. Dist.	N-Am.
St. Sen. Dist.	31	Ct. Appeals	7
St. Rep. Dist.	88	Admin. Jud. Dist.	9
St. Dist. Cts.	69		

PHYSICAL FEATURES: Prairie, over 3,800 ft. elevation, broken by creeks; playas; sandy, loam soils. Rita Blanca National Grasslands.

RECREATION: Local events, **XIT Museum; XIT Rodeo,** and **Reunion** in August; **Lake Rita Blanca,** in Hartley County.

MINERALS: Not significant.

1982 Pop.	6,700	Voters reg.	3,148
Area (sq. mi.)	1,505	Whlsle. sales	$98,399,000
Altitude (ft.)	3,800-4,600	Oil value	0
Ann. rainfall (in.)	17.38	No. employed	2,557
Jan. temp. min.	19	Wages paid	$37,474,792
July temp. max.	92	Tax value	$257,395,723
Growing season (da.)	178	Income	$41,439,000
No. farms, 1982	378	Taxable sales	$26,891,842
No. acres in farms	841,456	Fed. expend.	$55,120,000
†Value per farm	$917,204	Crime Index	164
Cropland harv.	261,412	TDC Pop.	21

Dallam County (Cont'd.)

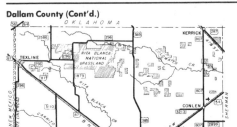

AGRICULTURE: About $59 million annual average income from beef cattle; corn, wheat, sorghums, alfalfa; 158,400 acres irrigated.

BUSINESS: Agribusinesses, tourism.

MANUFACTURING: None noted in census report.

SERVICE INDUSTRIES: 49 Establishments; Receipts, $8,818,000; Annual Payroll, $2,460,000; No. Employees, 336.

DALHART (6,854, in Dallam and Hartley) county seat; agribusiness center for wide area of Texas, Oklahoma, New Mexico; railroad; cattle feedlots, small manufacturing; bottling plant; hospital, nursing home; **Texline** (477).

Dallas

LOCATION: North central (H-17).

HISTORY: Created, organized, 1846, from Nacogdoches, Robertson Counties; named for U.S. Vice-President **George Mifflin Dallas.**

Cong. Dist. 3, 5, 6, 24	St. Dist. Cts. . .	14, 44, 68,
St. Sen. Dist. . . 2, 8, 9, 10,		95, 101, 116, 134, 160, 162,
16, 23		191, 192, 193, 194, 195, 203,
Rep. Dist. 98-114		204, 254, 255, 256, 265, 282,
U.S. Jud. Dist. . . . . N-Dl.		283, 291, 292, 298, 301, 302,
Ct. Appeals 5		303, 304, 305, 330, Cr.,
Admin. Jud. Dist. 1		Cr. 2, Cr. 3, Cr. 4, Cr. 5

PHYSICAL FEATURES: Mostly flat, heavy Blackland soils, sandy clays in west; drains to Trinity River, tributaries.

Lone Star Cadillac is rolling.

For 50 years Lone Star Cadillac has served Dallas in the heart of downtown.

In summer 1985, we drive to Jupiter and Northwest Highway. For your convenience and so we may continue to provide the same quality service our reputation was built upon.

In our new state-of-the-art facility, we will continue to grow with Dallas at an accelerated pace that forces our competition to take a back seat.

Come see us. See our Cadillacs. Experience our service. And see what's rolling. For us. And for you.

★ Lone Star Cadillac

Texas' Star Cadillac Dealer
11501 East Northwest Highway
Dallas, Texas 75218
214/348-2211

RECREATION: Dallas County leads all other Texas recreation points as a destination for visitors. Its major attractions include cultural, athletic and special events, the **State Fair of Texas**, conventions and trade shows. Year-round attractions include the **Hall of State, Museum of Fine Arts, Health Museum, Museum of Natural History, SMU Owen Fine Arts Center, Biblical Arts Center; Dallas Zoo, Dallas Theater Center, Wax World, Dallas News Sports and Vacation Show;** also symphonies, professional and amateur sports, dinner playhouses, Texas broadcast museum; many restored historical buildings; special shows, and many lakes with full recreational facilities in the vicinity. (See also Tarrant County.)

MINERALS: Production of sand, gravel, cement, stone, clays.

EDUCATION: Within Dallas County are the following colleges and universities: **Southern Methodist University** (University Park), **University of Dallas** (Irving), **Dallas Baptist College, University of Texas at Dallas** (Richardson), **University of Texas Health Science Center at Dallas,** with three schools — **Southwestern Medical School,** **School of Allied Health Sciences and Graduate School of Bio-Medical Sciences** — **Wadley Research Institute, Baylor University Dental College, Texas Woman's University** — **Dallas Center** with two campuses, **Bishop College,** with seven colleges; **Northwood Institute,** (Cedar Hill), **Amber University** (Garland), **East Texas State University Metroplex Commuter Facility** (Garland), **Dallas County Community College System,** with seven colleges; **Northwood Institute,** (Cedar Hill), **Amber University** (Garland), **Dallas Bible College, Dallas Christian College, Dallas Theological Seminary** and others.

1982 Pop.	1,641,400	Voters reg.	884,653
Area (sq. mi.)	880	Whlsle. sls.	$45,073,370,000
Altitude (ft.)	450-750	Oil value	$93,327
Ann. rainfall (in.)	35.94	No. employed	1,041,617
Jan. temp. min.	36	Wages paid	$22,410,460,224
July temp. max.	95	Tax value	$84,832,904,460
Growing season (da.)	235	Income	$19,590,239,000
No. farms, 1982	1,046	Taxable sls.	$16,788,557,595
No. acres in farms	191,547	Fed. expd.	$4,563,473,000
†Value per farm	$336,602	Crime Index	161,004
Cropland harvested	47,186	TDC Pop.	6,696

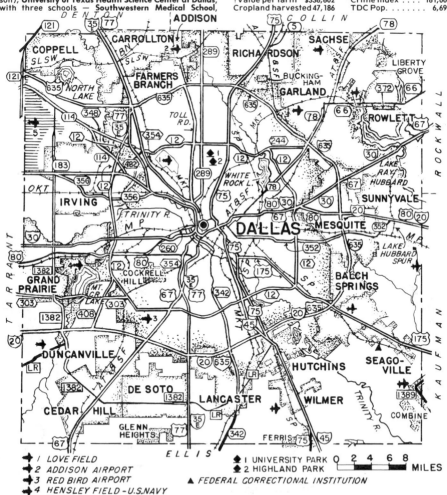

+ 1 LOVE FIELD
+ 2 ADDISON AIRPORT
+ 3 RED BIRD AIRPORT
+ 4 HENSLEY FIELD – U.S. NAVY
≡+ 5 DALLAS-FORT WORTH INTERNATIONAL AIRPORT

♠ 1 UNIVERSITY PARK
♠ 2 HIGHLAND PARK
▲ FEDERAL CORRECTIONAL INSTITUTION

0 2 4 6 8 MILES

AGRICULTURE: More than $35 million average annual farm income from beef cattle, horses, hogs and dairy products; nursery crops, cotton, wheat, oats, sorghums. Dallas is a leading center for agribusinesses, agricultural publications and trade associations.

BUSINESS: A national center for insurance, banking, transportation, electronics manufacturing, data processing, conventions and trade shows. More than 3,000 manufacturing plants make apparel, building material, food, oil field supply, electronic and many other products. Tourism is a major industry.

MANUFACTURING: 3,501 Plants; 192,800 Employees; Payroll, $3,913,800,000; Product Value, $15,696,000,000.

SERVICE INDUSTRIES: 12,785 Establishments; Receipts, $6,239,556,000; Annual Payroll, $2,231,055,000; No. Employees, 140,764.

DALLAS (904,078, partly Collin County) county seat; second largest city in Texas, seventh largest in U.S.; (see metro page). Center for commerce, transportation, banking, insurance, retail and wholesale trade,

manufacturing, distribution, data processing; conventions and trade shows. A favorite destination for tourists. Large banks; one of nation's busiest transportation hubs; headquarters of 657 firms with net worth of $1 million or more, ranking third nationally in this category; served by nation's largest airport; Dallas has home offices of more insurance firms than any other U.S. city; world headquarters for **U.S. Army and Air Force Exchange Service; Naval Air Station;** a leading cotton market and center for farm implements, trade associations, graphic arts and motion picture production; one of nation's leading fashion and computer centers; outstanding medical centers; **American Heart Association** headquarters; **Boy Scouts of America** headquarters; consular offices of many countries; plants make or process electronic, food, apparel, paper, chemical, furniture, plastic, stone, clay and glass, metal products; scientific goods and controlling instruments made.

Dallas ranked as one of the nation's top three cities in numbers of conventions, trade and market shows in

HURST
PRINTING
COMPANY

A company built
on integrity, craftsmanship
and quality . . .
resulting in outstanding service
to the most discriminating
printing buyers.

11070 N. STEMMONS FREEWAY • DALLAS, TEXAS 75229 • TELEPHONE (214) 247-1234

1984-85 with 2,070, attended by over 2 million visitors to city, spending half a billion dollars. **Dallas Convention Center**, located in the downtown area, has 1.9 million square feet under one roof with more than 600,000 square feet of exhibit space and 75 meeting rooms; **Dallas Market Hall** offers 202,000 square feet of exhibit space, 17 meeting rooms and a seating capacity of approximately 27,000. Facilities also at State Fair grounds. **World Trade Center** is international market center with 1.4 million square feet. **Infomart**, a giant computer sales complex, recently opened. **Reunion Arena** has up to 30,000 square feet of space, seats up to 20,000, and has parking space for 5,000 cars.

Other cities of Dallas County, where much growth has occurred in recent years, include: **Garland** (138,857) county's second largest city; center for industry and agriculture; more than 300 industrial plants; attractive residential areas; near lakes; **Amber University** and **East Texas State University** branch; medical centers.

Irving (109,943) manufacturing and distribution; service industries; leading residential center; **University of Dallas**; **North Lake College**, unit of community college system; **Texas Stadium**, home of **Dallas Cowboys** professional football team; hospitals; parks; adjacent to Dallas-Fort Worth International Airport.

Mesquite (67,053) residential city with varied industries and distribution center; popular rodeo; **Eastfield College** of community college system.

Richardson (72,496, partly Collin County) extensive electronic manufacturing, varied other science-oriented manufacturing, research firms; corporate and division headquarters of major firms; residential city; University of Texas at Dallas; near Texas A&M Research Center; parks; hospitals.

Grand Prairie (71,462, partly in Tarrant) aircraft, aerospace, concrete, chemical manufacturing; other plants; distribution center; major recreation center with wax museum; **Traders Village; Texas Sports Hall of Fame**; wildlife park; go-cart racing; **Joe Pool Lake** nearing completion; other attractions; medical center, nursing homes.

Farmers Branch (24,863) distribution center, varied manufacturing; residential city; **Brookhaven College** of community college system.

Carrollton (40,595, partly Denton County) residential city with many plants, distribution center.

Duncanville (27,781) varied manufacturing; residential city; industrial development; recreation with **Joe Pool Lake** nearing completion.

Lancaster (14,807) industrial and agricultural center; plants make hydraulic and plumbing equipment, swimming pools, chemicals, many other products; warehouse and distribution facilities; rebuilt old town area; **Cedar Valley College**, a campus of community college system; a residential city.

DeSoto (15,538) rapidly growing residential city for many employed in metro area.

Other towns include **Highland Park** (8,909) residential city; **University Park** (22,254) residential city with **Southern Methodist University; Balch Springs** (13,746).

Also **Addison** (5,553, partly Collin County) retail and restaurant city; **Buckingham** (159), **Cedar Hill** (6,849), **Cockrell Hill** (3,262), **Combine** (688, mostly Kaufman County), **Coppell** (3,826), **Ferris** (2,228, mostly Ellis Coun-

The Dallas Farmers Market is a busy scene during vegetable season. Here two women select produce.

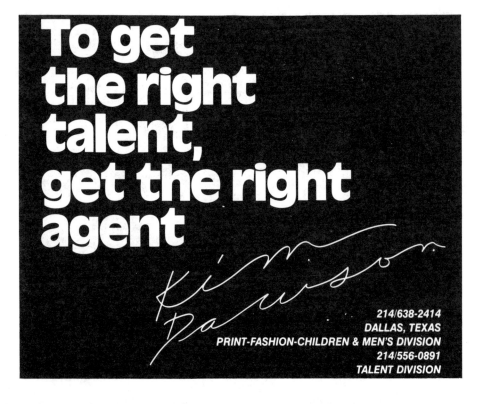

ty), **Glenn Heights** (1,033), **Grapevine** (11,801, mostly Tarrant County), **Hutchins** (2,837), **Rowlett** (7,522, partly Rockwall County), **Sachse** (1,640, partly Collin County), **Seagoville** (7,304), **Sunnyvale** (1,404), **Wilmer** (2,367).

Dawson

LOCATION: West (H-8).

HISTORY: Created from Bexar District, 1876, organized 1905; named for **Nicholas M. Dawson**, San Jacinto veteran.

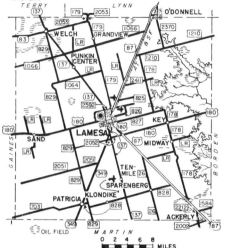

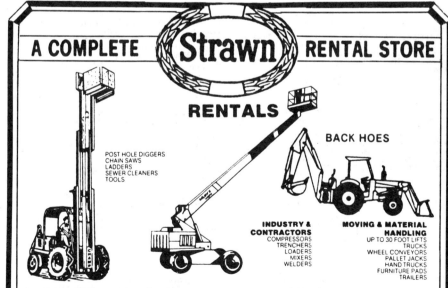

Cong. Dist.	19	U.S. Jud. Dist.	N-Lb.
St. Sen. Dist.	28	Ct. Appeals	11
St. Rep. Dist.	77	Admin. Jud. Dist.	7
St. Dist. Cts.	106		

PHYSICAL FEATURES: Rolling prairie, broken on east; drains to playas; sandy and loam soils.

RECREATION: Local parks, Dawson County Museum; campground; local events.

MINERALS: Production of gas, oil.

1982 Pop.	16,700	Voters reg.	8,451
Area (sq. mi.)	903	Whlsle. sales	$85,876,000
Altitude (ft.)	2,600-3,200	Oil value	$218,055,551
Ann. rainfall (in.)	16.09	No. employed	3,668
Jan. temp. min.	28	Wages paid	$51,825,944
July temp. max.	94	Tax value	$1,108,530,509
Growing season (da.)	212	Income	$119,329,000
No. farms, 1982	581	Taxable sales	$49,417,962
No. acres in farms	584,492	Fed. expend.	$71,875,000
†Value per farm	$643,093	Crime Index	638
Cropland harv.	278,169	TDC Pop.	52

AGRICULTURE: About $45 million average annual income, 90% from crops; a major cotton producing county; also sorghums, wheat, other grains; cattle, hogs; 15,000 acres irrigated for cotton.

BUSINESS: Agribusinesses, oil industries; manufacturing.

MANUFACTURING: None noted in census report.

SERVICE INDUSTRIES: 66 Establishments; Receipts, $10,734,000; Annual Payroll, $3,140,000; No. Employees, 383.

LAMESA (11,790) county seat; agribusinesses, food processing, oil field services, textiles, clothing, farm and gin equipment manufactured, new computerized cotton classing office; hospital, nursing homes; library, museum, campus of **Howard County Junior College.**

Other towns include **Ackerly** (317, partly in Martin County) and **O'Donnell** (1,200, partly in Lynn County).

Deaf Smith

LOCATION: Northwest (C-7).

HISTORY: Created, 1876, from Bexar District; organized 1890. Named for famed scout, **Erastus (Deaf) Smith.**

Cong. Dist.	19	U.S. Jud. Dist.	N-Am.
St. Sen. Dist.	31	Ct. Appeals	7
St. Rep. Dist.	86	Admin. Jud. Dist.	9
St. Dist. Cts.	222		

PHYSICAL FEATURES: Level plain, partly broken; chocolate and sandy loam soils; drains to playas, **Palo Duro** and **Tierra Blanca Creeks.**

RECREATION: Local events, museum, tours; National Cowgirl Hall of Fame.

MINERALS: Not significant.

1982 Pop.	20,400	Voters reg.	9,887
Area (sq. mi.)	1,497	Whlsle. sales	$139,643,000
Altitude (ft.)	3,200-4,200	Oil value	$28,613
Ann. rainfall (in.)	17.37	No. employed	5,788
Jan. temp. min.	22	Wages paid	$80,558,244
July temp. max.	93	Tax value	$424,452,523
Growing season (da.)	185	Income	$135,982,000
No. farms, 1982	655	Taxable sales	$56,543,243
No. acres in farms	820,095	Fed. expend.	$89,074,000
†Value per farm	$572,406	Crime Index	932
Cropland harv.	332,085	TDC Pop.	46

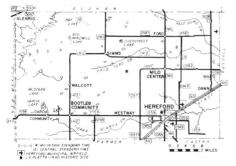

AGRICULTURE: One of state's leading farm-producing counties with more than $240 million annual average income, 80% from livestock; large feedlot operations; crops include sorghums, wheat, oats, barley, sugar beets, corn, cotton, onions, other vegetables, sunflowers; 250,000 acres irrigated.

BUSINESS: Sugar refinery; meat packers; offset printing; other varied industries, mostly agribusinesses.

MANUFACTURING: 24 Plants; 1,100 Employees; Payroll, $18,100,000; Product Value, 272,500,000.

SERVICE INDUSTRIES: 90 Establishments; Receipts, $20,622,000; Annual Payroll, $7,209,000; No. Employees, 673.

HEREFORD (15,853) county seat; agribusinesses, sugar refining, food processing, varied manufacturing; hospital, nursing home.

Delta

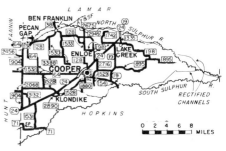

LOCATION: Northeast (F-19).

HISTORY: Created from Lamar, Hopkins Counties, and organized, 1870. Greek letter **delta** origin of name, because of shape.

Cong. Dist.	1	U.S. Jud. Dist.	E-Ps.
St. Sen. Dist.	1	Ct. Appeals	6
St. Rep. Dist.	2	Admin. Jud. Dist.	1
St. Dist. Cts.	8, 62		

PHYSICAL FEATURES: Between two forks of Sulphur River; black, sandy, loam soils.

RECREATION: Fishing, hunting, local events; **Lake Cooper** under construction.

MINERALS: Not significant.

1982 Pop.	4,800	Voters reg.	3,084
Area (sq. mi.)	278	Whlsle. sales	$2,147,000
Altitude (ft.)	450-550	Oil value	$591,507
Ann. rainfall (in.)	43.67	No. employed	689
Jan. temp. min.	34	Wages paid	$7,519,808
July temp. max.	94	Tax value	$148,701,362
Growing season (da.)	233	Income	$33,104,000
No. farms, 1982	446	Taxable sales	$2,984,102
No. acres in farms	150,156	Fed. expend.	$25,399,000
†Value per farm	$244,011	Crime Index	102
Cropland harvested	55,073	TDC Pop.	17

AGRICULTURE: In excess of $18 million annual average income from beef, dairy cattle, cotton, wheat, sorghums, other grains; some firewood.

BUSINESS: Agribusinesses, tourism, manufacturing.

MANUFACTURING: None noted in census report.

SERVICE INDUSTRIES: 11 Establishments; Receipts, $1,602,000; Annual Payroll, $630,000; No. Employees, 99.

COOPER (2,338) county seat; industrial park; manufacturing, agribusinesses; county museum. **Pecan Gap** (250, partly Fannin County).

Denton

LOCATION: North central (G-16).

HISTORY: Created, organized out of Fannin County, 1846; named for **John B. Denton,** pioneer preacher.

Cong. Dist.	26	U.S. Jud. Dist.	E-Sh.
St. Sen. Dist.	10, 22, 30	Ct. Appeals	2
St. Rep. Dist.	59, 61	Admin. Jud. Dist.	8
St. Dist. Cts.	16, 158, 211		

PHYSICAL FEATURES: Partly hilly, draining to Trinity River, two lakes; Blackland and Grand Prairie soils.

RECREATION: Water activities at **Lewisville, Grapevine Lakes,** seven U.S. Corps of Engineers' parks; **Lake Ray Roberts** under construction; universities' cultural, athletic activities including "Texas Women: a Celebration of History" exhibit in the TWU library; State D.A.R. Museum "First Ladies of Texas" collection of gowns and memorabilia, Little Chapel-in-the-Woods, Botanical Gardens and other events; local events; (see also Dallas, Tarrant Counties).

MINERALS: Limited output oil, sand, gravel, gas, clay.

1982 Pop.	157,300	Voters reg.	97,758
Area (sq. mi.)	911	Whlsle. sales	$427,645,000
Altitude (ft.)	500-900	Oil value	$1,034,340
Ann. rainfall (in.)	33.29	No. employed	47,641
Jan. temp. min.	34	Wages paid	$761,277,900
July temp. max.	96	Tax value	$5,390,377,054
Growing season (da.)	226	Income	$2,121,539,000
No. farms, 1982	1,417	Taxable sales	$826,931,805
No. acres in farms	384,284	Fed. expend.	$365,818,000
†Value per farm	$371,441	Crime Index	8,586
Cropland harv.	115,322	TDC Pop.	210

AGRICULTURE: About $50 million average farm income, 75% from horses, cattle, poultry, dairy products; grains, cotton, hay, peanuts principal crops.

BUSINESS: Varied industries, colleges, tourism; part of Dallas-Fort Worth SMSA.

MANUFACTURING: 164 Plants; 8,300 Employees; Payroll, $144,300,000; Product Value, $592,600,000.

SERVICE INDUSTRIES: 670 Establishments; Receipts, $140,706,000; Annual Payroll, $50,548,000; No. Employees, 4,427.

DENTON (48,063) county seat; (see Dallas, Fort Worth metro pages); **North Texas State University, Texas Woman's University, Denton State School** (for mentally retarded); civil defense center; plants make food products, apparel, brick, trucks, oil tools, heating and cooling equipment, many other products; hospital, nursing homes; women's museum.

Lewisville (24,273), varied industries, near **Dallas-Fort Worth Airport, Lake Lewisville.**

Other towns include **Carrollton** (40,591, part Dallas), **Pilot Point** (2,211) with varied manufacturing and antique shops; **Flower Mound** (4,402), **Argyle** (1,111), **Aubrey** (948), **Bartonville** (441), **Copper Canyon** (465), **Cor-**

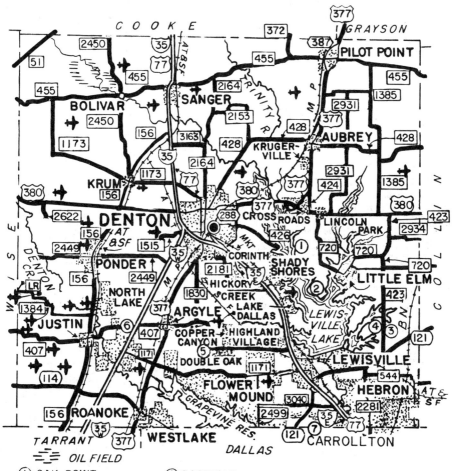

① OAK POINT
② LAKEWOOD VILLAGE
③ THE COLONY
④ EASTVALE
⑤ BARTONVILLE
⑥ CORRAL CITY
⑦ COPPELL

OIL FIELD

0 2 4 6 8 MILES

inth (1,264), **Corral City** (85), **Cross Roads** (302), **Dallas** (904,078, mostly Dallas County), **Double Oak** (836), **Eastvale** (503), **Hebron** (385), **Hickory Creek** (1,422), **Highland Village** (3,246), **Justin** (920), **Krugerville** (469), **Krum** (917), **Lake Dallas** (3,177), **Lakewood Village** (165), **Lincoln Park** (39), **Little Elm** (926), **Northlake** (143), **Oak Point** (387), **Ponder** (297), **Roanoke** (910), **Sanger** (2,574) varied manufacturing, hospital; **Shady Shores** (813), **Southlake** (2,808, mostly Tarrant County), **The Colony** (11,586) and **Westlake** (214, partly Tarrant).

De Witt

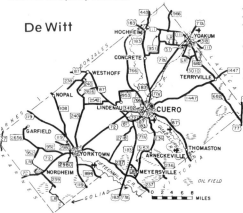

LOCATION: South (O-16).

HISTORY: Created from Gonzales, Goliad, Victoria Counties and organized, 1846; named for **Green De Witt**, colonizer.

Cong. Dist.	14	U.S. Jud. Dist.	S-Va.
St. Sen. Dist.	18	Ct. Appeals	13
St. Rep. Dist.	31	Admin. Jud. Dist.	4
St. Dist. Cts.	24, 135, 267		

PHYSICAL FEATURES: Drained by Guadalupe and tributaries; rolling to level; waxy, loam, sandy soils.

RECREATION: Hunting, fishing, local events; historic homes, museum.

MINERALS: Production of oil and gas.

1982 Pop.	20,000	Voters reg.	9,381
Area (sq. mi.)	910	Whlsle. sales	$201,942,000
Altitude (ft.)	150-400	Oil value	$11,606,008
Ann. rainfall (in.)	33.37	No. employed	5,724
Jan. temp. min.	44	Wages paid	$73,136,520
July temp. max.	96	Tax value	$794,014,170
Growing season (da.)	270	Income	$151,961,000
No. farms, 1982	1,619	Taxable sales	$52,882,373
No. acres in farms	523,285	Fed. expend.	$36,996,000
†Value per farm	$228,673	Crime Index	216
Cropland harvested	40,653	TDC Pop.	59

AGRICULTURE: About $38 million annual farm income, mostly from beef cattle, dairy products, hogs, poultry; crops include sorghums, corn, oats, wheat, pecans.

BUSINESS: Wood, furniture plants, textile mill, varied manufacturing, agribusinesses.

MANUFACTURING: 23 Plants; 1,100 Employees; Payroll, $14,300,000; Product Value, $70,200,000.

SERVICE INDUSTRIES: 72 Establishments; Receipts, $14,629,000; Annual Payroll, $4,555,000; No. Employees, 613.

CUERO (7,124) county seat; turkey hatcheries, furniture, wood products, other manufacturing; agribusinesses, soft drink bottling; hospital, nursing homes; annual Turkeyfest. Other towns include **Yoakum** (6,148, part Lavaca), **Yorktown** (2,498) hospital, nursing home, historical museum, oil well servicing; **Nordheim** (369).

Dickens

LOCATION: Northwest (F-10).

HISTORY: Created, 1876, from Bexar District; organized 1891; named for Alamo hero who is variously listed as **James R. Dimkins**, **James R. Dimpkins** and **J. Dickens.** (According to noted authority Dr. Amelia Williams, writing in the Southwestern Historical Quarterly.)

Cong. Dist.	13	U.S. Jud. Dist.	N-Lb.
St. Sen. Dist.	30	Ct. Appeals	7
St. Rep. Dist.	84	Admin. Jud. Dist.	9
St. Dist. Cts.	110		

PHYSICAL FEATURES: Broken land, Cap Rock in northwest; sandy, chocolate, red soils; drains to Croton, Duck Creeks.

RECREATION: Hunting, fishing, local events.

MINERALS: Small oil, gas output.

1982 Pop.	3,300	Voters reg.	2,081
Area (sq. mi.)	907	Whlsle. sales	$3,848,000
Altitude (ft.)	2,000-3,000	Oil value	$1,342,158
Ann. rainfall (in.)	20.24	No. employed	558
Jan. temp. min.	28	Wages paid	$6,838,960
July temp. max.	95	Tax value	$98,070,201
Growing season (da.)	217	Income	$18,758,000
No. farms, 1982	330	Taxable sales	$5,458,077
No. acres in farms	513,862	Fed. expend.	$24,354,000
†Value per farm	$488,861	Crime Index	78
Cropland harvested	74,585	TDC Pop.	5

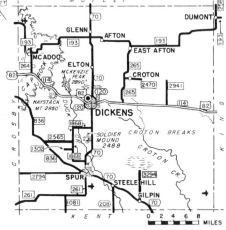

AGRICULTURE: Crop-livestock income averages about $21.5 million, mostly from beef cattle, cotton, wheat, sorghums; 14,000 acres irrigated.

BUSINESS: Chiefly ranching, farming supplies, some manufacturing.

MANUFACTURING: None noted in census report.

SERVICE INDUSTRIES: 9 Establishments; Receipts, $1,419,000; Annual Payroll, $374,000; No. Employees, 75.

DICKENS (409) county seat.

Spur (1,690) principal agribusiness center; site of **Texas A&M Research Station.**

Dimmit

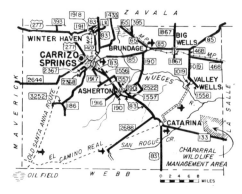

LOCATION: Southwest (Q-12).

HISTORY: Named for **Philip Dimitt** of Texas Revolution; law misspelled name; created 1858 from Bexar, Maverick, Uvalde, Webb Counties; organized 1880.

Cong. Dist.	23	U.S. Jud. Dist.	W-SAnt.
St. Sen. Dist.	21	Ct. Appeals	4
St. Rep. Dist.	44	Admin. Jud. Dist.	4
St. Dist. Cts.	293		

PHYSICAL FEATURES: Level to rolling; much brush; sandy, loam, red soils; drained by Nueces and tributaries.

RECREATION: Hunting, fishing, lake campsites; local events; mild climate makes area "Winter Garden" for tourists.

MINERALS: Oil, gas production.

1982 Pop.	11,800	Voters reg.	6,910
Area (sq. mi.)	1,307	Whsle. sales	$18,568,000
Altitude (ft.)	500-800	Oil value	$72,762,405
Ann. rainfall (in.)	21.50	No. employed	2,975
Jan. temp. min.	42	Wages paid	$36,895,612
July temp. max.	99	Tax value	$808,226,408
Growing season (da.)	290	Income	$56,984,000
No. farms, 1982	224	Taxable sales	$25,757,367
No. acres in farms	743,105	Fed. expend.	$12,918,000
†Value per farm	$1,167,049	Crime Index	42
Cropland harvested	13,578	TDC Pop.	16

AGRICULTURE: About $20 million annual average income from vegetables, livestock, 50,000 pecan trees; among leading irrigated vegetable growing counties since early in century; 10,000 acres irrigated.

BUSINESS: Agribusinesses, petroleum products, other varied manufacturing; tourism.

MANUFACTURING: None noted in census report.

SERVICE INDUSTRIES: 36 Establishments; Receipts, $7,583,000; Annual Payroll, $2,652,000; No. Employees, 225.

CARRIZO SPRINGS (6,886) county seat; agribusiness center, feedlot, food processing, garment manufacturing; oil and gas processing; hunting center; pecan shelling plant; hospitals, nursing home. Other towns include **Asherton** (1,574), **Big Wells** (939).

Donley

LOCATION: Northwest (D-10).

HISTORY: Created, 1876, organized 1882, out of Bexar District; named for Texas Supreme Court Justice **S. P. Donley.**

Cong. Dist.	13	U.S. Jud. Dist.	N-Am.
St. Sen. Dist.	31	Ct. Appeals	7
St. Rep. Dist.	84	Admin. Jud. Dist.	9
St. Dist. Cts.	100		

PHYSICAL FEATURES: Bisected by Red River Salt Fork; rolling to level; clay, loam, sandy soils.

RECREATION: **Greenbelt Lake,** hunting, fishing, camping, water sports; local events.

MINERALS: Small amount natural gas.

1982 Pop.	4,200	Voters reg.	2,444
Area (sq. mi.)	929	Whsle. sales	$3,696,000
Altitude (ft.)	2,200-3,200	Oil value	0
Ann. rainfall (in.)	20.74	No. employed	743
Jan. temp. min.	26	Wages paid	$9,461,196
July temp. max.	96	Tax value	$165,671,168
Growing season (da.)	206	Income	$29,712,000
No. farms, 1982	365	Taxable sales	$8,235,122
No. acres in farms	590,639	Fed. expend.	$15,358,000
†Value per farm	$394,929	Crime Index	100
Cropland harvested	57,784	TDC Pop.	18

AGRICULTURE: About $15 million average annual income, 66% from beef cattle, hogs, horses; cotton, corn, sorghums, wheat, alfalfa chief crops; 12,000 acres irrigated.

BUSINESS: Agribusinesses; distribution; varied manufacturing.

MANUFACTURING: None noted in census report.

SERVICE INDUSTRIES: 15 Establishments; Receipts, $1,184,000; Annual Payroll, $219,000; No. Employees, 33.

CLARENDON (2,220) county seat; **Clarendon Junior College; Burton Memorial Library;** agribusinesses, farm, road equipment, leather goods manufacturing, tourism; other towns include **Hedley** (380) and **Howardwick** (165).

Duval

LOCATION: South (R-15).

HISTORY: Created from Live Oak, Nueces, Starr Counties, 1858, organized 1876; named for **B. H. Duval,** Goliad martyr.

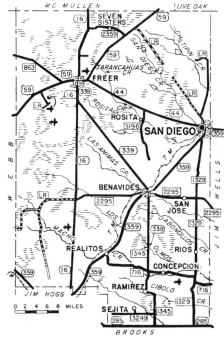

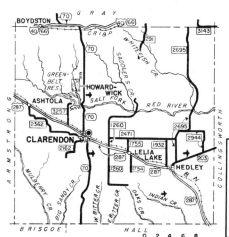

Drive 3 blocks off highway 287 in Clarendon to visit Martin-Lowe House, the carefully restored Queen Anne Victorian house at 507 W. 5th, a 1904 landmark of Panhandle ranching heritage. Sanctioned by Texas Historical Commission marker, National Register nomination.

Call Dr. Zell R. SoRelle (806) 874-3332 for appointment. Hours: 10-5 throughout Sesquicentennial year. May thru Aug. in 1987. Adults $3.50, children $2.00.

Cong. Dist.	15	U.S. Jud. Dist.	S-CC
St. Sen. Dist.	21	Ct. Appeals	4
St. Rep. Dist.	44	Admin. Jud. Dist.	5
St. Dist. Cts.	229		

PHYSICAL FEATURES: Level to hilly, brushy in most areas; varied soils.

RECREATION: Hunting, tourist crossroads, rattlesnake roundup, local events.

MINERALS: Production of oil, gas, salt, uranium, sand and gravel.

1982 Pop.	12,900	Voters reg.	8,707
Area (sq. mi.)	1,795	Whlsle. sales	$17,955,000
Altitude (ft.)	250-800	Oil value	$85,731,763
Ann. rainfall (in.)	23.15	No. employed	3,141
Jan. temp. min.	42	Wages paid	$46,152,792
July temp. max.	97	Tax value	$1,393,900,473
Growing season (da.)	298	Income	$87,458,000
No. farms, 1982	1,074	Taxable sales	$20,688,347
No. acres in farms	970,827	Fed. expend.	$22,220,000
†Value per farm	$393,529	Crime Index	195
Cropland harvested	58,744	TDC Pop.	13

AGRICULTURE: About $28 million annual average income, 75% from beef cattle, remainder from grains, cotton, vegetables, hay.

BUSINESS: Ranching, petroleum, tourism.

MANUFACTURING: None noted in census report.

SERVICE INDUSTRIES: 27 Establishments; Receipts, $3,480,000; Annual Payroll, $843,000; No. Employees, 147.

SAN DIEGO (5,225, part in Jim Wells) county seat; ranching, oil field, tourist center; hospital. Other towns include **Benavides** (1,978), **Freer** (3,213) U.S. Border Patrol Station.

Eastland

LOCATION: Central (I-13).

HISTORY: Created from Bosque, Coryell, Travis Counties, 1858, organized 1873; named for **W. M. Eastland,** Mier Expedition martyr.

Cong. Dist.	17	U.S. Jud. Dist.	N-Ab.
St. Sen. Dist.	22	Ct. Appeals	11
St. Rep. Dist.	65	Admin. Jud. Dist.	8
St. Dist. Cts.	91		

PHYSICAL FEATURES: Hilly, rolling; sandy, loam soils; drained to Leon River forks.

RECREATION: Fishing, **Lake Leon, Lake Cisco;** water sports; hunting; festivals; historic sites and displays.

MINERALS: Production of oil, gas, stone, clays, sand and gravel.

1982 Pop.	20,700	Voters reg.	11,274
Area (sq. mi.)	924	Whlsle. sales	$224,808,000
Altitude (ft.)	1,200-1,800	Oil value	$71,180,696
Ann. rainfall (in.)	27.09	No. employed	5,254
Jan. temp. min.	32	Wages paid	$69,119,604
July temp. max.	96	Tax value	$687,607,818
Growing season (da.)	229	Income	$164,830,000
No. farms, 1982	1,111	Taxable sales	$68,760,566
No. acres in farms	469,113	Fed. expend.	$66,105,000
†Value per farm	$222,055	Crime Index	438
Cropland harvested	57,106	TDC Pop.	43

AGRICULTURE: $28 million average annual income

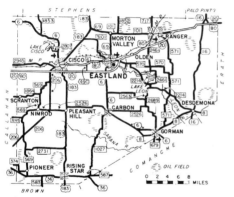

with 60% from beef cattle, sheep, horses; peanuts, wheat, sorghums major crops; 10,000 acres irrigated.

BUSINESS: Agribusinesses, petroleum industries, varied manufacturing.

MANUFACTURING: 43 Plants; 800 Employees; Payroll, $9,800,000; Product Value, $49,000,000.

SERVICE INDUSTRIES: 93 Establishments; Receipts, $14,040,000; Annual Payroll, $5,081,000; No. Employees, 556.

EASTLAND (3,747) county seat; plants make clothing, building stones, steel tanks, portable buildings, oilfield equipment; agribusinesses; printing; mental health center, hospital, nursing homes.

Cisco (4,517) plants make clothing, steel tanks, oilfield equipment, other products; **Cisco Junior College;** hospitals.

Ranger (3,142) agribusinesses, athletic clothing, sportswear, aerospace components manufacturing, oil field center; **Ranger Junior College;** hospital, nursing home. Other towns include **Gorman** (1,258) peanut processing, other agribusinesses; hospital, nursing home; **Rising Star** (1,204) farming center; **Carbon** (281).

Ector

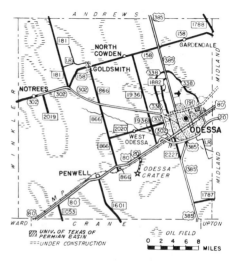

LOCATION: West (J-7).

HISTORY: Created from Tom Green County, 1887; organized, 1891; named for Texas legislator-jurist, **M. D. Ector.**

Cong. Dist.	16, 19	U.S. Jud. Dist.	W: M-O
St. Sen. Dist.	28	Ct. Appeals	8
St. Rep. Dist.	69, 73	Admin. Jud. Dist.	7
St. Dist. Cts.	70, 161, 244		

PHYSICAL FEATURES: Level to rolling, some sand dunes; **meteor crater;** limited vegetation.

RECREATION: Metropolitan cultural events; 2nd largest **U.S. meteor crater; Globe Theatre replica; Odessa College Museum.**

MINERALS: Leading oil-producing county with more than 2 billion barrels since 1926; gas, cement, stone.

1982 Pop.	134,200	Voters reg.	57,983
Area (sq. mi.)	903	Whlsle. sales	$1,679,140,000
Altitude (ft.)	2,500-3,300	Oil value	$959,915,222
Ann. rainfall (in.)	13.77	No. employed	50,373
Jan. temp. min.	30	Wages paid	$990,619,824
July temp. max.	96	Tax value	$6,027,131,751
Growing season (da.)	217	Income	$1,439,774,000
No. farms, 1982	214	Taxable sales	$944,305,197
No. acres in farms	584,766	Fed. expend.	$124,830,000
†Value per farm	$419,736	Crime Index	10,441
Cropland harvested	1,003	TDC Pop.	349

AGRICULTURE: Average farm income more than $4.5 million, from beef cattle, poultry; pecans, hay.

BUSINESS: Oil-based economy. Center for Permian Basin oil field operations.

MANUFACTURING: 323 Plants; 8,600 Employees; Payroll, $182,300,000; Product Value, $1,561,500,000.

SERVICE INDUSTRIES: 871 Establishments; Receipts, $368,461,000; Annual Payroll, $115,479,000; No. Employees, 6,975.

ODESSA (90,027) county seat (see metro page); **Odessa College, University of Texas of Permian Basin;** hospital; cultural center; oil field services, supplies; large petrochemical complex; other industries; **Goldsmith** (409).

Edwards

LOCATION: Southwest (M-11).

HISTORY: Created from Bexar District, 1858; organized 1883; named for Nacogdoches empresario, **Hayden Edwards.**

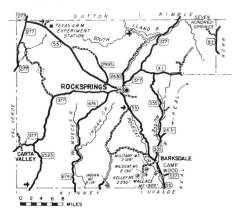

PHYSICAL FEATURES: Rolling, hilly; caves; spring-fed streams; rocky, thin soils; drained by Llano, Nueces Rivers; varied timber.

RECREATION: Leading deer, turkey hunting area; fishing; scenic drives; local events.

MINERALS: Oil, gas.

1982 Pop.	2,100	Voters reg.	1,245
Area (sq. mi.)	2,120	Whlsle. sales	$5,528,000
Altitude (ft.)	1,500-2,500	Oil value	$411,409
Ann. rainfall (in.)	21.19	No. employed	364
Jan. temp. min.	38	Wages paid	$4,840,324
July temp. max.	94	Tax value	$521,101,667
Growing season (da.)	250	Income	$12,546,000
No. farms, 1982	226	Taxable sales	$2,854,659
No. acs. in farms	1,025,318	Fed. expend.	$6,061,000
†Value per farm	$1,272,589	Crime Index	8
Cropland harvested	1,049	TDC Pop.	3

AGRICULTURE: More than $13 million average income, almost entirely from Angora goats, sheep, cattle, horses, hogs; some hay; center of nation's goat-mohair production.

BUSINESS: Ranching economy; revenue also from hunting leases, tourism, oil, gas production.

MANUFACTURING: None noted in census report.

SERVICE INDUSTRIES: 5 Establishments; Receipts, $382,000; Annual Payroll, $85,000; No. Employees, 6.

ROCKSPRINGS (1,317) county seat; ranching, hunting center; tourism; hospital.

Cong. Dist.	21	U.S. Jud. Dist.	W-Del Rio
St. Sen. Dist.	25	Ct. Appeals	4
St. Rep. Dist.	67	Admin. Jud. Dist.	6
St. Dist. Cts.	63		

Ellis

LOCATION: Central (I-17).

HISTORY: Created 1849, organized 1850, from Navarro County. Named for **Richard Ellis**, president of Convention of 1836.

Cong. Dist.	6	U.S. Jud. Dist.	N-Dallas
St. Sen. Dist.	9	Ct. Appeals	10
St. Rep. Dist.	4	Admin. Jud. Dist.	1
St. Dist. Cts.	40		

Ellis County (Cont'd.)

PHYSICAL FEATURES: Rich Blackland soils; level to rolling; Chambers Creek, Trinity River.

RECREATION: National polka festival at Ennis; Gingerbread Trail homes tour and medieval fair at Waxahachie; cabrito cookoff; Italian Festival in Italy; Bluebonnet Trails; hunting.

MINERALS: Cement, stone, clay, oil, gas.

1982 Pop.	62,500	Voters reg.	36,082
Area (sq. mi.)	939	Whlsle. sales	$136,735,000
Altitude (ft.)	300-700	Oil value	$322,485
Ann. rainfall (in.)	35.95	No. employed	18,177
Jan. temp. min.	35	Wages paid	$274,345,388
July temp. max.	96	Tax value	$2,108,183,573
Growing season (da.)	246	Income	$586,945,000
No. farms, 1982	1,608	Taxable sales	$265,506,860
No. acres in farms	445,380	Fed. expend.	$116,061,000
†Value per farm	$255,581	Crime Index	2,355
Cropland harv.	190,868	TDC Pop.	110

AGRICULTURE: About $50 million average annual income, evenly split between crops, including cotton, sorghums, other grains, nursery operations; and cattle, horses, hogs, dairy production, poultry; honey production.

BUSINESS: Varied manufacturing, agribusinesses; many employed in Dallas (see metro page.)

MANUFACTURING: 107 Plants; 6,600 Employees; Payroll $113,800,000; Product Value, $835,700,000.

SERVICE INDUSTRIES: 203 Establishments; Receipts, $39,988,000; Annual Payroll, $14,301,000; No. Employees, 1,320.

WAXAHACHIE (14,624) county seat; varied manufacturing includes furniture, oil field equipment, apparel, commercial refrigeration, cottonseed products, millwork, fiberglass insulation, glass containers, monuments, business stationery, plastic piping, fertilizers, concrete and other products; **Southwestern Assemblies of God College** and branch of **Navarro Junior College;** motion picture production; hospital, nursing homes.

Ennis (12,110) agribusinesses; plants produce business forms, apparel, roofing, mobile homes, other items; hospitals, nursing home; national polka festival in May.

Midlothian (3,219) cement plants, clothing, other factories.

Ferris (2,228, part in Dallas) large brick plant; other industries. Other towns include **Italy** (1,306) garment factory and varied manufacturing; **Palmer** (1,187), **Red Oak** (1,882), **Alma** (171), **Bardwell** (335), **Garrett** (220), **Maypearl** (626), **Milford** (681), **Ovilla** (1,067).

El Paso

LOCATION: Most western county (J-1).

HISTORY: Created from Bexar District, 1849; organized 1850; named for historic northern pass (**Paso del Norte**).

PHYSICAL FEATURES: Fertile Rio Grande Valley; 7,000-ft. mountains; desert vegetation except where irrigated.

Cong. Dist.	16	U.S. Jud. Dist.	W-El Paso
St. Sen. Dist.	25, 29	Ct. Appeals	8
St. Rep. Dist.	70-74	Admin. Jud. Dist.	6
St. Dist. Cts.	34, 41, 65, 120, 168, 171, 205, 210, 243, 327		

RECREATION: Gateway to Mexico; varied U.S.-Mexican metropolitan events, **Chamizal Museum;** major tourist center; December **Sun Carnival** with annual Sun Bowl football game; El Paso Festival in July; missions and other historic sites; near Carlsbad Caverns, White Sands, bullfighting, horse racing.

MINERALS: Production of cement, stone, sand and gravel.

1982 Pop.	513,400	Voters reg.	191,313
Area (sq. mi.)	1,014	Whlsle. sales	$2,830,211,000
Altitude (ft.)	3,500-7,100	Oil value	0
Ann. rainfall (in.)	7.77	No. employed	156,649
Jan. temp. min.	32	Wages paid	$2,208,729,908
July temp. max.	94	Tax value	$8,707,515,749
Growing season (da.)	248	Income	$3,767,474,000
No. farms, 1982	452	Tax. sales	$1,839,034,195
No. acres in farms	299,665	Fed. expd.	$1,305,587,000
†Value per farm	$569,002	Crime Index	31,954
Cropland harvested	47,577	TDC Pop.	748

AGRICULTURE: About $48 million average annual income from dairy and beef cattle, hogs; cotton, grain, pecans, hay; 50,000 acres irrigated, mostly cotton.

BUSINESS: Government is major economic factor with wages and salaries exceeding $138.7 million annually; wholesale, retail distribution center; tourism; varied manufacturers; ore smelting, refining, cotton, food processing.

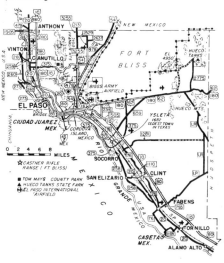

MANUFACTURING: 471 Plants; 38,300 Employees; Payroll, $465,900,000; Product Value, $4,221,000,000.

SERVICE INDUSTRIES: 2,292 Establishments; Receipts, $600,182,000; Annual Payroll, $220,796,000; No. Employees, 17,909.

EL PASO (425,259) county seat (see metro page); fourth-largest Texas city; lowest altitude all-weather pass through Rocky Mountains; a center for government operations, manufacturing, trade and distribution; refining and processing of ore, oil, food, cotton and other farm and ranch products; plants make apparel, electronics products, footwear, building materials, other products; **University of Texas at El Paso; El Paso Community College;** home of **U.S. Army Air Defense Command;** 16 hospitals; museums. Numerous tourist attractions, convention, civic center, community theater, symphony orchestra, gateway to Mexico and largest U.S. city on Mexican border.

Federal installations include **Fort Bliss, Wm. Beaumont General Hospital** and **La Tuna** correction institution.

Ysleta, oldest Texas town, now in El Paso. Other towns include **Anthony** (2,640), **Clint** (1,314), **Vinton** (372), **Canutillo, Fabens, San Elizario.**

Erath

LOCATION: North central (I-14).

HISTORY: Created from Bosque, Coryell Counties, 1856, organized same year; named for **George B. Erath**, Texas Revolution figure.

Cong. Dist.	17	U.S. Jud. Dist.	N-FW
St. Sen. Dist.	22	Ct. Appeals	11
St. Rep. Dist.	58	Admin. Jud. Dist.	8
St. Dist. Cts.	266		

PHYSICAL FEATURES: Hilly, rolling plains; clay loam, sandy soils; drains to Bosque River, Paluxy Creek.

RECREATION: Tarleton State University of Texas A&M with fine arts center; Historical House museum; old courthouse; log cabins; Thurber, ghost town; museums; nearby lakes, Bosque River Park; Dublin Community Fall Fair.

MINERALS: Gas, oil, coal.

1982 Pop.	23,500	Voters reg.	13,584
Area (sq. mi.)	1,080	Whlsle. sales	$69,769,000
Altitude (ft.)	900-1,750	Oil value	$291,100
Ann. rainfall (in.)	31.24	No. employed	7,548
Jan. temp. min.	34	Wages paid	$99,327,512
July temp. max.	96	Tax value	$912,010,772
Growing season (da.)	238	Income	$234,534,000
No. farms, 1982	1,564	Taxable sales	$85,965,430
No. acres in farms	553,935	Fed. expend.	$54,756,000
†Value per farm	$251,881	Crime Index	498
Cropland harvested	58,212	TDC Pop.	33

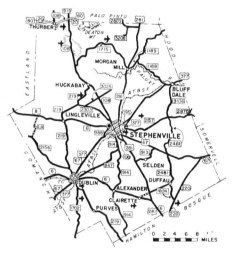

AGRICULTURE: Over 80% of $100 million average annual income from dairy, beef cattle, other livestock, poultry; state's second leading county in milk production; peanuts, the major cash crop, small grains, fruit, sorghums chief crops; 5,000 acres irrigated, mostly peanuts.

BUSINESS: Agricultural, industrial and educational enterprises.

MANUFACTURING: 30 Plants; 1,100 Employees; Payroll, $15,100,000; Product Value, $90,800,000.

SERVICE INDUSTRIES: 113 Establishments; Receipts, $21,569,000; Annual Payroll, $6,696,000; No. Employees, 811.

STEPHENVILLE (11,881) county seat; Tarleton State University of Texas A&M; plants make coated abrasives, automotive parts, clothing, gratings and fasteners, mobile homes, steel products, feeds; electrical products; hospital, clinics, mental health-mental retardation center; Texas A&M research and extension center.

Dublin (2,723) agribusiness center; clothing; food products manufactured; hospital, nursing home.

Falls

LOCATION: Central (K-17).

HISTORY: Created and organized, 1850 from Limestone, Milam Counties; named for Brazos River falls.

Cong. Dist.	11	U.S. Jud. Dist.	W-Wa.
St. Sen. Dist.	9	Ct. Appeals	10
St. Rep. Dist.	55	Admin. Jud. Dist.	3
St. Dist. Cts.	82		

PHYSICAL FEATURES: Level to rolling; bisected by Brazos; Blackland, red, sandy loam soils; mineral springs.

RECREATION: Fishing, camping, mineral baths attract visitors; Falls County Youth Fair at Marlin.

MINERALS: Gas, small oil output; stone.

1982 Pop.	18,200	Voters reg.	10,095
Area (sq. mi.)	770	Whlsle. sales	$110,005,000
Altitude (ft.)	300-500	Oil value	$793,175
Ann. rainfall (in.)	35.34	No. employed	3,356
Jan. temp. min.	38	Wages paid	$38,744,116
July temp. max.	96	Tax value	$502,911,881
Growing season (da.)	257	Income	$135,843,000
No. farms, 1982	1,117	Taxable sales	$41,594,608
No. acres in farms	386,285	Fed. expend.	$68,987,000
†Value per farm	$250,124	Crime Index	254
Cropland harv.	126,210	TDC Pop.	37

AGRICULTURE: More than $34 million average annual income; 75% from beef cattle, hogs, turkeys, eggs; crops include sorghums, hay, cotton, wheat, oats; 4,000 acres of cotton irrigated.

BUSINESS: Varied manufacturing; agribusinesses.

MANUFACTURING: 13 Plants; 500 Employees; Payroll, $5,700,000; Product Value, $27,900,000.

SERVICE INDUSTRIES: 46 Establishments; Receipts, $9,481,000; Annual Payroll, $4,032,000; No. Employees, 433.

MARLIN (7,099) county seat; agribusinesses; small industries; noted for mineral water and spas; geothermally heated hospital; apparel, rug manufacturing; printing; veterans hospital.

Rosebud (2,076), **Lott** (865), **Bruceville-Eddy** (1,038, mostly McLennan County) and **Golinda** (335, partly McLennan County) are other towns.

Fannin

LOCATION: Borders Oklahoma (F-18).

HISTORY: Created from Red River County, 1837, organized, 1838; named for **James W. Fannin**, Goliad martyr.

Cong. Dist.	4	U.S. Jud. Dist	E-Paris
St. Sen. Dist.	2	Ct. Appeals	6
St. Rep. Dist.	2	Admin. Jud. Dist.	1
St. Dist. Cts.	6,336		

MINERALS: Not significant.

1982 Pop.	24,100	Voters reg.	15,161
Area (sq. mi.)	895	Whlsle. sales	$109,069,000
Altitude (ft.)	500-700	Oil value	0
Ann. rainfall (in.)	43.62	No. employed	4,911
Jan. temp. min.	33	Wages paid	$65,633,956
July temp. max.	94	Tax value	$654,039,199
Growing season (da.)	228	Income	$196,709,000
No. farms, 1982	1,576	Taxable sales	$47,320,037
No. acres in farms	432,564	Fed. expend.	$104,127,000
†Value per farm	$196,789	Crime Index	464
Cropland harv.	162,957	TDC Pop.	33

Fannin County (Cont'd.)

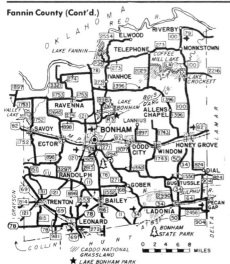

PHYSICAL FEATURES: Rolling prairie, drained by Red River, Bois d'Arc Creek; mostly Blackland soils. **Caddo National Grassland.**

RECREATION: Sam Rayburn home, Sam Rayburn Memorial Library; Bonham State Park; lake activities on several area lakes; hunting; Ivanhoe Winery.

AGRICULTURE: About $40 million average annual income from beef cattle, hogs, sorghums, small grains, soybeans, peanuts, hay, cotton, grapes; 3,900 acres irrigated.

BUSINESS: Varied manufacturing, agribusinesses, distribution, meat packing, timber.

MANUFACTURING: 36 Plants; 1,500 Employees; Payroll, $23,500,000; Product Value, $155,800,000.

SERVICE INDUSTRIES: 63 Establishments; Receipts, $9,427,000; Annual Payroll, $3,300,000; No. Employees, 402.

BONHAM (7,338) county seat; plants make clothing, mobile homes, fertilizers, other products; hospitals.

Other towns include **Bailey** (185), **Dodd City** (286), **Ector** (573), **Honey Grove** (1,973), **Ladonia** (761), **Leonard** (1,421), **Pecan Gap** (250, mostly Delta County), **Savoy** (855), **Trenton** (691) and **Windom** (276).

Fayette

LOCATION: South (N-17).

HISTORY: Created from Bastrop, Colorado Counties, 1837; organized, 1838; named for French hero of U.S. Revolution, **Marquis de Lafayette.**

Cong. Dist.	14	U.S. Jud. Dist.	S-Hn.
St. Sen. Dist.	18	Ct. Appeals	3
St. Rep. Dist.	30	Admin. Jud. Dist. . . .	3
St. Dist. Cts.	155		

PHYSICAL FEATURES: Rolling to level, bisected by Colorado River; sandy loam, black waxy soils.

RECREATION: Many historical restorations at **Round Top** and **Winedale,** including **Winedale Inn;** museums; **Monument Hill State Park, Faison Home Museum,** other historic sites; hunting, fishing, Fayette Power Project Lake; piano festival at **Round Top;** Czech chili cookoff at **Flatonia;** Fayette County Fair and Heritage Days at LaGrange.

MINERALS: Oil, gas, clays, sand and gravel.

1982 Pop.	20,500	Voters reg.	11,729
Area (sq. mi.)	950	Whlsle. sales .	$94,251,000
Altitude (ft.)	200-500	Oil value . . .	$162,248,713
Ann. rainfall (in.) .	35.67	No. employed	6,297
Jan. temp. min.	42	Wages paid . .	$84,374,336
July temp. max.	96	Tax value .	$1,921,957,738
Growing season (da.)	277	Income . .	$182,116,000
No. farms, 1982 . . .	2,610	Taxable sales	$83,115,863
No. acres in farms	467,736	Fed. expend. .	$47,586,000
†Value per farm	$255,016	Crime Index	89
Cropland harvested	64,261	TDC Pop.	14

AGRICULTURE: About $52 million annual average income, about 80% from beef, dairy cattle, hogs, poultry; crops include corn, sorghums, hay, peanuts, pecans.

BUSINESS: Agribusinesses, oil production, manufacturing includes steel fencing; and tourism.

MANUFACTURING: 32 Plants; 500 Employees; Payroll, $7,700,000; Product Value, $52,200,000.

SERVICE INDUSTRIES: 120 Establishments; Receipts, $19,647,000; Annual Payroll, $6,508,000; No. Employees, 735.

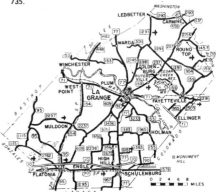

LA GRANGE (3,768) county seat; plants make metal fences, laminated timber, monuments; wholesale nursery, other products; feed processing; power generation; hospital, rest home, clinics.

Schulenburg (2,469), steel, aluminum products, oilfield equipment, toys, feeds, fertilizers, dairy products, meat processing; rest home, clinics.

Other towns include **Round Top** (87) of historical interest; **Flatonia** (1,070), varied manufacturing including machine parts, refining, oil field gaskets; **Fayetteville** (356) and **Carmine** (239).

Fisher

LOCATION: West central (H-11).

HISTORY: Created from Bexar District, 1876; organized, 1886; named for **S. R. Fisher,** Texas Republic Secretary of Navy.

Cong. Dist.	17	U.S. Jud. Dist.	N-Ab.
St. Sen. Dist.	30	Ct. Appeals	11
St. Rep. Dist.	78	Admin. Jud. Dist. . . .	7
St. Dist. Cts.	32		

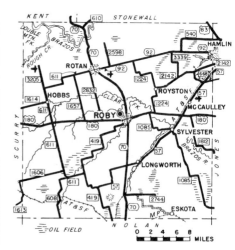

PHYSICAL FEATURES: Rolling; red, sandy loam soils; drains to forks of Brazos River.
RECREATION: Hunting, fishing; local events.
MINERALS: Production of oil, gas, gypsum, clays.

1982 Pop.	5,900	Voters reg.	3,299
Area (sq. mi.)	897	Whlsle. sales	$5,556,000
Altitude (ft.)	1,600-2,300	Oil value	$76,305,899
Ann. rainfall (in.)	21.21	No. employed	1,229
Jan. temp. min.	31	Wages paid	$18,967,072
July temp. max.	98	Tax value	$381,351,872
Growing season (da.)	218	Income	$43,939,000
No. farms, 1982	688	Taxable sales	$7,706,790
No. acres in farms	507,523	Fed. expend.	$34,402,000
†Value per farm	$258,785	Crime Index	59
Cropland harv.	135,108	TDC Pop.	10

AGRICULTURE: The $32 million average income is from cattle, hogs, dairy products, sheep, cotton, grains, soybeans, hay.
BUSINESS: Oil, gypsum, agribusinesses, electric co-op.
MANUFACTURING: None noted in census report.
SERVICE INDUSTRIES: 21 Establishments; Receipts, $2,855,000; Annual Payroll, $894,000; No. Employees, 133.
ROBY (814) county seat; agribusinesses; electric co-op headquarters; hospital, rest home.
Rotan (2,284) gypsum plant, oil mill, agribusinesses.
Hamlin (3,248, mostly in Jones County) is farming center.

Floyd

LOCATION: Northwest (E-9).
HISTORY: Created from Bexar District, 1876; organized 1890. Named for **D. W. Floyd**, Alamo martyr.

Cong. Dist.	13	U.S. Jud. Dist. . . . N-Lb.
St. Sen. Dist.	30	Ct. Appeals 7
St. Rep. Dist.	84	Admin. Jud. Dist. 9
St. Dist. Cts.	110	

PHYSICAL FEATURES: Flat, broken by Cap Rock on east and by White River on south; many playas; red, black loam soils.
RECREATION: Hunting, fishing; museum; local events; county fair at Lockney.
MINERALS: Not significant.

1982 Pop.	9,500	Voters reg.	4,997
Area (sq. mi.)	992	Whlsle. sales	$81,498,000
Altitude (ft.)	2,400-3,300	Oil value	$3,314
Ann. rainfall (in.)	20.18	No. employed	1,853
Jan. temp. min.	26	Wages paid	$21,931,380
July temp. max.	94	Tax value	$351,323,204
Growing season (da.)	213	Income	$54,299,000
No. farms, 1982	590	Taxable sales	$11,989,429
No. acres in farms	617,911	Fed. expend.	$100,108,000
†Value per farm	$563,694	Crime Index	99
Cropland harv.	314,848	TDC Pop.	11

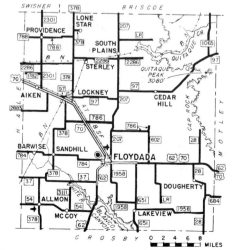

AGRICULTURE: More than $75 million average annual income from cotton, wheat, vegetables, soybeans, corn, sunflowers; beef cattle, hogs; 220,000 acres irrigated.
BUSINESS: Livestock feeds, farm machinery and oilfield manufacturing; other agribusinesses; metal products; printing.
MANUFACTURING: None noted in census report.
SERVICE INDUSTRIES: 31 Establishments; Receipts, $3,521,000; Annual Payroll, $1,135,000; No. Employees, 129.
FLOYDADA (4,193) county seat; plants make farm products, race cars, sheet metal goods, oilfield equipment; meat and vegetable processing; trade, distribution, medical center; **Texas A&M Engineering Extension Service.**
Lockney (2,334) agribusiness center; plants make farm, oilfield equipment, bird houses; hospital, nursing home.

Foard

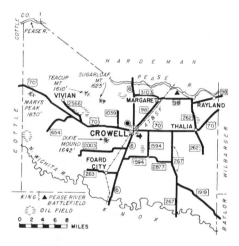

LOCATION: Northwest (E-12).
HISTORY: Created out of Cottle, Hardeman, King, Knox Counties, 1891, and organized same year. Named for **Maj. Robert L. Foard** of Confederacy.

Cong. Dist.	13	U.S. Jud. Dist. . . . . N-WF
St. Sen. Dist.	30	Ct. Appeals 7
St. Rep. Dist.	80	Admin. Jud. Dist. 9
St. Dist. Cts.	46	

PHYSICAL FEATURES: Drains to N. Wichita, Pease Rivers; sandy, loam soils, rolling surface.
RECREATION: Copper Breaks State Park across county line 8 miles north of Crowell; local events.
MINERALS: Oil, gas.

1982 Pop.	2,000	Voters reg.	1,412
Area (sq. mi.)	703	Whlsle. sales	$2,193,000
Altitude (ft.)	1,400-1,700	Oil value	$10,480,628
Ann. rainfall (in.)	23.93	No. employed	459
Jan. temp. min.	28	Wages paid	$4,560,108
July temp. max.	98	Tax value	$134,099,052
Growing season (da.)	219	Income	$15,550,000
No. farms, 1982	250	Taxable sales	$1,990,542
No. acres in farms	342,617	Fed. expend.	$15,291,000
†Value per farm	$421,984	Crime Index	50
Cropland harvested	95,368	TDC Pop.	1

AGRICULTURE: $11.5 million average farm income from grains, cotton; beef cattle, hogs; more than 4,000 acres irrigated.
BUSINESS: Agribusiness, oil economy.
MANUFACTURING: None noted in census report.
SERVICE INDUSTRIES: 6 Establishments; Receipts, $742,000; Annual Payroll, $228,000; No. Employees, 37.
CROWELL (1,509) county seat; agribusiness center, factories make sporting goods; hospital, nursing home.

Fort Bend

LOCATION: Southeast (N-19).

HISTORY: Named for river bend where Austin's colonists settled, among state's more historic counties; created 1837 from Austin County, organized 1838; scene of early **Jaybird-Woodpecker War.**

Cong. Dist. 22	U.S. Jud. Dist. . . . . S-Hn.
St. Sen. Dist. . . 7, 13, 17,18	Ct. Appeals 1, 14
St. Rep. Dist. 26, 27	Admin. Jud. Dist. 2
St. Dist. Cts. . 240, 268, 328	

PHYSICAL FEATURES: Drained by Brazos, San Bernard Rivers; level to rolling; rich alluvial soils; some loams, clays.

RECREATION: Many historic sites, museum, memorials; fishing, hunting; Czech Fest at Rosenberg first weekend in May, county fair in October.

MINERALS: Production of oil, gas, sulphur, salt, clays, sand and gravel.

1982 Pop. 154,500	Voters reg. 82,449
Area (sq. mi.) 876	Whlsle. sales $962,987,000
Altitude (ft.) 80-250	Oil value $45,342,918
Ann. rainfall (in.) . 45.07	No. employed 35,208
Jan. temp. min. 44	Wages paid . . $694,274,152
July temp. max. 94	Tax value . $8,239,310,033
Growing season (da.) 296	Income . . . $2,034,741,000
No. farms, 1982 . . . 1,179	Taxable sales $537,183,994
No. acres in farms 401,711	Fed. expd. . $3,526,695,000
†Value per farm $569,168	Crime Index 5,769
Cropland harv. . . 143,309	TDC Pop. 123

AGRICULTURE: More than $67 million average annual income, about 75% from rice, cotton, sorghums, soybeans, corn; cattle, poultry, hogs; vegetables produced; 28,000 acres irrigated, mostly rice, nursery crops.

BUSINESS: Petrochemicals, sulphur, sugar refinery; many residents work in Houston plants; county is part of Houston metro area.

MANUFACTURING: 127 Plants; 12,200 Employees; Payroll, $279,700,000; Product Value, $1,081,500,000.

SERVICE INDUSTRIES: 507 Establishments; Receipts, $138,596,000; Annual Payroll, $50,904,000; No. Employees, 3,607.

RICHMOND (9,692) county seat; **Richmond State School** (for mentally retarded); adjoins larger **Rosenberg** (17,840) which has varied industries including food processing; annual Czech festival; **Wharton County Junior College** Annex.

Sugar Land (8,826) has sugar refinery, prison farm. Other towns include **Katy** (5,660, part Harris and Waller Counties), **Missouri City** (24,423, part Harris), **Stafford** (4,755, part Harris), **Needville** (1,417), **Houston** (1,595,138, mostly Harris County), **Beasley** (410), **Kendleton** (606), **Orchard** (408), **Fulshear** (594), **Pleak** (619), **Arcola** (661), **Simonton** (603) and **Thompsons** (240).

Franklin

LOCATION: Northeast (C-21).

HISTORY: Created, organized 1875 from Titus County; named for **Judge B. C. Franklin** of Texas.

Cong. Dist. 1	U.S. Jud. Dist. . . . . E-Tx.
St. Sen. Dist. 1	Ct. Appeals 6
St. Rep. Dist. 8	Admin. Jud. Dist. 1
St. Dist. Cts. 8, 62	

MINERALS: Oil, gas and lignite produced.

AGRICULTURE: About 90% of $30 million average annual income from dairy and beef cattle, poultry; hay is principal crop; timber marketed for estimated $500,000.

BUSINESS: Agribusinesses, oil, tourism.

MANUFACTURING: None noted in census report.

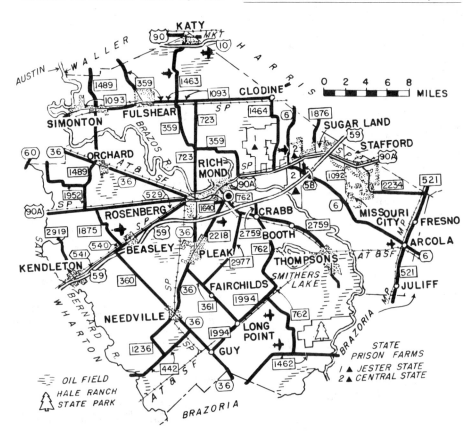

PHYSICAL FEATURES: Many wooded hills; drained by numerous streams; alluvial to sandy clay soils. **Cypress Springs Lake.**

RECREATION: Fishing, water sports on **Cypress Springs Lake**; local events, county fair.

1982 Pop.	7,100
Area (sq. mi.)	294
Altitude (ft.)	300-500
Ann. rainfall (in.)	44.78
Jan. temp. min.	35
July temp. max.	94
Growing season (da.)	234
No. farms, 1982	478
No. acres in farms	117,175
†Value per farm	$204,630
Cropland harvested	16,182
Voters reg.	4,223
Whlsle. sales	$6,377,000
Oil value	$24,061,816
No. employed	1,183
Wages paid	$12,083,816
Tax value	$446,917,520
Income	$67,024,000
Taxable sales	$10,913,340
Fed. expend.	$11,954,000
Crime Index	186
TDC Pop.	23

SERVICE INDUSTRIES: 19 Establishments; Receipts, $3,877,000; Annual Payroll, $1,530,000; No. Employees, 182.

MOUNT VERNON (2,025) county seat; furniture, clothing factories, beef packing; livestock market, supply center; hospital; psychiatric hospital under construction; **Winnsboro** (3,458, mostly in Wood, also Hopkins).

Freestone

LOCATION: East central (J-18).

HISTORY: Named for indigenous stone; created 1850 from Limestone County, organized 1851.

Cong. Dist.	6	U.S. Jud. Dist.	W-Wa.
St. Sen. Dist.	9	Ct. Appeals	10
St. Rep. Dist.	11	Admin. Jud. Dist.	2
St. Dist. Cts.	77, 87		

PHYSICAL FEATURES: Rolling, drains to Trinity River; Blackland, sandy, loam soils.

RECREATION: Fishing, hunting; **Fairfield Lake** recreation area; local events; historic sites, railroad museum at Teague; Coon Hunters championship in September.

▲ COFFIELD STATE PRISON FARM
● FAIRFIELD LAKE STATE PARK

MINERALS: Stone, gas, coal, oil, iron ore.

1982 Pop.	15,800	Voters reg.	9,031
Area (sq. mi.)	888	Whlsle. sales	$27,891,000
Altitude (ft.)	300-500	Oil value	$9,729,996
Ann. rainfall (in.)	38.53	No. employed	4,435
Jan. temp. min.	36	Wages paid	$75,234,196
July temp. max.	94	Tax value	$1,178,534,098
Growing season (da.)	263	Income	$134,793,000
No. farms, 1982	1,101	Taxable sales	$146,719,993
No. acres in farms	381,248	Fed. expend.	$29,849,000
†Value per farm	$266,325	Crime Index	417
Cropland harvested	25,490	TDC Pop.	44

AGRICULTURE: About $21 million average annual income, mostly from cattle, hogs, poultry; hardwood timber; peaches, berries, pecans; oats for grazing.

BUSINESS: Mining, stone quarry, brick plant, varied manufacturing plants, agribusinesses; new electricity generating station.

MANUFACTURING: None noted in census report.

SERVICE INDUSTRIES: 53 Establishments; Receipts, $8,705,000; Annual Payroll, $2,725,000; No. Employees, 335.

FAIRFIELD (3,505) county seat; headquarters Continental Telephone Co.; lignite mining; sewing factory; stone quarry; trading center; hospital, nursing home; Freestone County Museum.

Teague (3,390), has brick plant, railroad museum; hospital, nursing home.

Other towns include **Wortham** (1,187), **Streetman** (415, part Navarro), **Kirvin** (107).

Frio

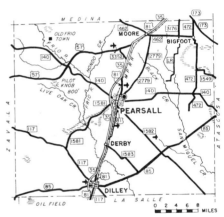

LOCATION: South (P-13).

HISTORY: Created, organized, 1871, from Atascosa, Bexar, Uvalde Counties; named for **Frio** (cold) **River.**

Cong. Dist.	15	U.S. Jud. Dist.	W-SAnt.
St. Sen. Dist.	21	Ct. Appeals	4
St. Rep. Dist.	45	Admin. Jud. Dist.	4
St. Dist. Cts.	81, 218		

PHYSICAL FEATURES: Rolling, much brush; bisected by Frio River; sandy, red sandy loam soils.

RECREATION: Hunting; local events; Big Foot Wallace Museum, other museums; in Winter Garden area.

MINERALS: Production of oil, gas, stone.

1982 Pop.	14,300	Voters reg.	7,728
Area (sq. mi.)	1,133	Whlsle. sales	$56,692,000
Altitude (ft.)	400-700	Oil value	$73,204,333
Ann. rainfall (in.)	23.36	No. employed	2,763
Jan. temp. min.	42	Wages paid	$32,369,024
July temp. max.	98	Tax value	$706,375,305
Growing season (da.)	281	Income	$77,597,000
No. farms, 1982	526	Taxable sales	$27,517,585
No. acres in farms	671,340	Fed. expend.	$21,547,000
†Value per farm	$716,606	Crime Index	211
Cropland harvested	97,936	TDC Pop.	36

AGRICULTURE: $55 million average annual income; leading county for peanut production with over 50 million pounds grown yearly; also grain sorghums, small grains, cotton, melons, vegetables, pecans, peaches;

about 50,000 acres irrigated; beef cattle, swine; revenue from hunting leases.

BUSINESS: Chiefly agribusinesses, oil field services.

MANUFACTURING: None noted in census report.

SERVICE INDUSTRIES: 46 Establishments; Receipts, $8,086,000; Annual Payroll, $2,228,000; No. Employees, 239.

PEARSALL (7,383) county seat; oil, ranching center; food processing; melon, vegetable, livestock shipping; hospital, rest homes. Other towns include Dilly (2,579), **Moore.**

Gaines

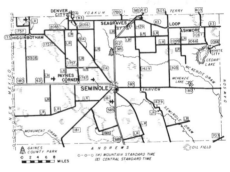

LOCATION: Adjoins New Mexico (H-7).

HISTORY: Created from Bexar District, 1876, organized 1905; named for **James Gaines,** signer of Texas Declaration of Independence.

Cong. Dist.	19	U.S. Jud. Dist.	N-Lb.
St. Sen. Dist.	28	Ct. Appeals	8
St. Rep. Dist.	77	Admin. Jud. Dist.	7
St. Dist. Cts.	106		

PHYSICAL FEATURES: Flat, drains to playas and draws; underground water supply.

RECREATION: Local events.

MINERALS: Production of oil, gas, sodium sulphate; one of leading oil-producing counties.

1982 Pop.	13,700	Voters reg.	5,800
Area (sq. mi.)	1,504	Whlsle. sales	0
Altitude (ft.)	3,000-3,600	Oil value	$976,673,553
Ann. rainfall (in.)	15.83	No. employed	4,756
Jan. temp. min.	26	Wages paid	$82,709,648
July temp. max.	94	Tax value	$3,988,577,978
Growing season (da.)	210	Income	$104,938,000
No. farms, 1982	619	Taxable sales	$33,488,303
No. acres in farms	765,551	Fed. expend.	$75,594,000
†Value per farm	$785,341	Crime Index	343
Cropland harv.	421,054	TDC Pop.	21

AGRICULTURE: State's second largest cotton-producing county; more than $105 million average annual income from cotton, sorghums, wheat, vegetables, peanuts, sunflowers, peaches, pecans; cattle, sheep, hogs; 400,000 acres irrigated.

BUSINESS: Major oil-producing county; oil field activities, agribusinesses, varied manufacturing.

MANUFACTURING: None noted in census report.

SERVICE INDUSTDRIES: 46 Establishments; Receipts, $6,317,000; Annual Payroll, $2,031,000; No. Employees, 209.

SEMINOLE (6,080) county seat; market for farmers, oil field workers; petrochemical plants; clothing; cotton delinting plant; hospital. **Seagraves** (2,596), is market for 3-county area; carbon black plant; sewing factory; state mental health clinic.

Galveston

LOCATION: On coast, island (N-21).

HISTORY: Among most historic counties; created from Brazoria County, 1838; organized, 1839; named for Spanish governor of Louisiana, **Count Bernardo de Galvez.**

Cong. Dist.	9	U.S. Jud. Dist.	S-Gn.
St. Sen. Dist.	4, 11, 17	Ct. Appeals	1, 14
St. Rep. Dist.	24, 25	Admin. Jud. Dist.	2
St. Dist. Cts.	10, 56, 122, 212, 306		

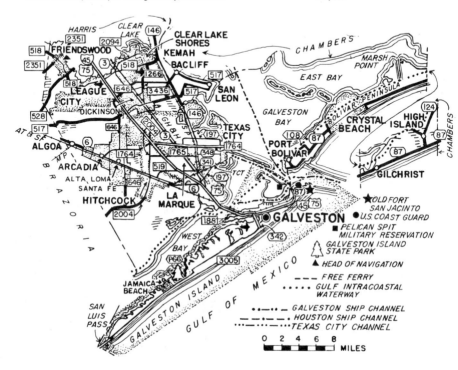

PHYSICAL FEATURES: Partly island, partly coastal; flat, artificial drainage; sandy, loam, clay soils; broken by bays.

RECREATION: Popular tourist and convention center; fishing, surfing, boating, sailing and other water sports on 32-mile Gulf beach, bay, tributaries; mild climate; Spring Historical District tour includes many homes, sites; **Sea-Arama; Rosenberg Library; Salt Water Fishing Hall of Fame;** museums; Shrimp Festival; strawberry festival at Dickinson; drama "Lone Star" presented in outdoor amphitheater in summer; restored sailing ship, railroad museum and many other events.

MINERALS: Production of oil, gas, clays, sand and gravel.

1982 Pop.	207,600	Voters reg.	112,456
Area (sq. mi.)	399	Whlsle. sales	$448,819,000
Altitude (ft.) sea level	-50	Oil value	$68,223,717
Ann. rainfall (in.)	42.20	No. employed	68,155
Jan. temp. min.	49	Wages paid	$1,282,567,432
July temp. max.	87	Tax value	$8,012,065,750
Growing season (da.)	335	Income	$2,287,447,000
No. farms, 1982	438	Taxable sales	$974,884,375
†Value per farm	$280,689	Fed. expd.	$2,612,297,000
Cropland harvested	17,085	Crime Index	12,710
		TDC Pop.	492

AGRICULTURE: About $6 million average annual income from rice, beef cattle, horses, soybeans, grain sorghums, corn, honey.

BUSINESS: Port activities dominate economy; varied manufacturing; tourism; medical education center; oceanographic research center; ship building; fishing.

MANUFACTURING: 134 Plants; 11,200 Employees; Payroll, $317,000,000; Product Value, $11,426,300,000.

SERVICE INDUSTRIES: 962 Establishments; Receipts, $263,285,000; Annual Payroll, $95,739,000; No. Employees, 7,174.

GALVESTON (61,902) county seat (see metro page); shipping; tourist business; shipyard; other industries; port container facility; **University of Texas Medical Branch; National Maritime Research Center; Texas A&M Maritime Academy; Galveston College;** hospitals.

Texas City (41,201) refining, petrochemical plants; seaport; **College of the Mainland;** hospitals; varied local events.

Other towns include **LaMarque** (15,372), **League City** (16,578), **Clear Lake Shores** (755), **Crystal Beach** (776), **Friendswood** (10,719), **Hitchcock** (6,103) hospital; **Jamaica Beach** (365), **Kemah** (1,304), **Dickinson** (7,505) with mineral oil plant, hospitals; **Santa Fe** (6,172) and **Tiki Island** (183).

Garza

LOCATION: Northwest (G-9).

HISTORY: Created from Bexar District, 1876; organized 1907; named for early Texas family.

Cong. Dist.	17	U.S. Jud. Dist.	N-Lb.
St. Sen. Dist.	28	Ct. Appeals	7
St. Rep. Dist.	78	Admin. Jud. Dist.	7
St. Dist. Cts.	106		

PHYSICAL FEATURES: Rough, broken land, with playas, gullies, canyons, Brazos River forks; sandy, loam, clay soils; Cap Rock on West.

RECREATION: Local events; historical markers; scenic areas; Post-Garza Museum; White River Lake.

MINERALS: Production of oil, gas.

1982 Pop.	5,600	Voters reg.	2,692
Area (sq. mi.)	895	Whlsle. sales	$5,691,000
Altitude (ft.)	2,100-3,000	Oil value	$193,136,866
Ann. rainfall (in.)	18.91	No. employed	1,472
Jan. temp. min.	28	Wages paid	$22,421,500
July temp. max.	95	Tax value	$635,536,641
Growing season (da.)	216	Income	$42,732,000
No. farms, 1982	240	Taxable sales	$15,557,293
No. acres in farms	570,986	Fed. expend.	$14,468,000
†Value per farm	$559,004	Crime Index	48
Cropland harvested	47,500	TDC Pop.	11

AGRICULTURE: $16 million average annual income, 60% from crops, mostly from cotton, grains; remainder from cattle, some hogs; 8,000 acres irrigated.

BUSINESS: Economy based on oil, farming, textile mill employment.

MANUFACTURING: None noted in census report.

SERVICE INDUSTRIES: 17 Establishments; Receipts, $3,566,000; Annual Payroll, $1,147,000; No. Employees, 89.

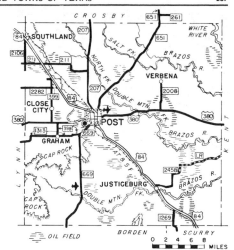

POST (3,961) county seat; founded by **C. W. Post,** cereal manufacturer; has had textile mill since 1912; hospital, nursing home.

Gillespie

LOCATION: West central (M-13).

HISTORY: Created and organized, 1848, from Bexar, Travis Counties; named for **Texas Ranger Capt. R. A. Gillespie;** historic German settlement in heart of Comanche country, birthplace of **President Lyndon B. Johnson** and **Fleet Admiral Chester W. Nimitz.**

Cong. Dist.	21	U.S. Jud. Dist.	W-An.
St. Sen. Dist.	25	Ct. Appeals	4
St. Rep. Dist.	67	Admin. Jud. Dist.	6
St. Dist. Cts.	216		

PHYSICAL FEATURES: Plateau and hills, broken by spring-fed streams.

RECREATION: Among leading deer hunting areas; fishing; numerous historic sites and tourist attractions include **Lyndon B. Johnson National Historic Park, LBJ Ranch** and **Lyndon B. Johnson State Park, Admiral Nimitz State Historical Park; Pioneer Museum Complex, Enchanted Rock State Park;** many festivals and celebrations including Oktoberfest in October.

MINERALS: Sand, gravel, granite, gypsum.

1982 Pop.	14,200	Voters reg.	8,894
Area (sq. mi.)	1,061	Whlsle. sales	$69,648,000
Altitude (ft.)	1,100-2,250	Oil value	0
Ann. rainfall (in.)	27.45	No. employed	4,052
Jan. temp. min.	36	Wages paid	$46,538,004
July temp. max.	95	Tax value	$1,007,856,638
Growing season (da.)	219	Income	$124,396,000
No. farms, 1982	1,285	Taxable sales	$61,997,093
No. acres in farms	634,710	Fed. expend.	$40,167,000
†Value per farm	$443,203	Crime Index	272
Cropland harvested	37,862	TDC Pop.	12

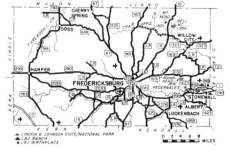

LYNDON B. JOHNSON STATE/NATIONAL PARK
LBJ RANCH
LBJ BIRTHPLACE

AGRICULTURE: About $32 million average annual income, 90% from cattle, sheep, goats, hogs, turkeys; crops include hay, sorghums, oats, wheat; largest peach producing county in state.

BUSINESS: Agribusinesses, tourism, food processing, hunting leases, small manufacturing; granite for markers.

MANUFACTURING: 25 Plants; 500 Employees; Payroll, $5,600,000; Product Value, $32,000,000.

SERVICE INDUSTRIES: 100 Establishments; Receipts, $16,621,000; Annual Payroll, $5,814,000; No. Employees, 562.

FREDERICKSBURG (6,412) county seat; plants make leather goods, trailers; food processing, foundry, agribusinesses; apparel manufacturing; limited wine production; museum, tourist attractions; hospital.

Other towns include **Harper, Stonewall.**

Glasscock

LOCATION: West (J-9).

HISTORY: Created, 1887, from Tom Green County; organized, 1893; named for Texas pioneer, **George W. Glasscock.**

Cong. Dist.	17	U.S. Jud. Dist.	N-SAng.
St. Sen. Dist.	25	Ct. Appeals	8
St. Rep. Dist.	69	Admin. Jud. Dist.	7
St. Dist. Cts.	118		

PHYSICAL FEATURES: Level, broken by several small streams; sandy, loam soils.

RECREATION: Local events.

MINERALS: Production of oil, gas.

1982 Pop.	1,200	Voters reg.	715
Area (sq. mi.)	900	Whlsle. sales	$*
Altitude (ft.)	2,300-2,750	Oil value	$143,144,073
Ann. rainfall (in.)	15.81	No. employed	226
Jan. temp. min.	22	Wages paid	$3,527,820
July temp. max.	94	Tax value	$444,130,963
Growing season (da.)	222	Income	$8,216,000
No. farms, 1982	200	Taxable sales	$672,705
No. acres in farms	503,851	Fed. expend.	$18,277,000
†Value per farm	$820,025	Crime Index	24
Cropland harvested	71,915	TDC Pop.	0

AGRICULTURE: About $23.7 million average income chiefly from cotton, grain sorghums, wheat, beef cattle, sheep; 38,000 acres irrigated.

BUSINESS: Economy based on oil, farming and ranching.

MANUFACTURING: None noted in census report.

SERVICE INDUSTRIES: 2 Establishments; Receipts, N.A.; Annual Payroll, N.A.; No. Employees, N.A.

GARDEN CITY (pop. est. 293) county seat; serves sparsely settled ranching, oil area.

Goliad

LOCATION: South (P-16).

HISTORY: Among most historic areas; created 1836 from Spanish municipality, organized 1837; name is anagram of (H)idalgo.

Cong. Dist.	14	U.S. Jud. Dist.	S-Va.
St. Sen. Dist.	18	Ct. Appeals	13
St. Rep. Dist.	31	Admin. Jud. Dist.	4
St. Dist. Cts.	24, 135, 267		

PHYSICAL FEATURES: Rolling, brushy; bisected by San Antonio River; sandy, loam, alluvial soils.

RECREATION: Many historic sites including missions, restored **Presidio La Bahia, Fannin Battleground; Goliad State Park;** Gen. **Ignacio Zaragoza** statue, **Mission Espiritu Santo de Zuniga; Old Market House** museum; fishing, hunting, camping; horse races.

MINERALS: Production of oil, gas.

1982 Pop.	5,400	Voters reg.	3,502
Area (sq. mi.)	859	Whlsle. sales	$3,337,000
Altitude (ft.)	-350	Oil value	$22,638,707
Ann. rainfall (in.)	33.79	No. employed	1,120
Jan. temp. min.	46	Wages paid	$16,075,200
July temp. max.	94	Tax value	$869,929,620
Growing season (da.)	285	Income	$43,359,000
No. farms, 1982	674	Taxable sales	$8,097,155
No. acres in farms	438,706	Fed. expend.	$11,799,000
†Value per farm	$352,545	Crime Index	113
Cropland harvested	26,220	TDC Pop.	11

AGRICULTURE: $27 million average annual income, more than 90% from cattle, hogs, sheep, poultry, horses; crops include sorghums, corn.

BUSINESS: Primarily based on oil; agribusiness, tourist income, electricity generating plant.

MANUFACTURING: None noted in census report.

SERVICE INDUSTRIES: 24 Establishments; Receipts, $2,907,000; Annual Payroll, $909,000; No. Employees, 120.

GOLIAD (1,990) county seat; many historic sites; tourism; oil; agribusinesses; hospital; library.

Gonzales

LOCATION: South central (N-16).

HISTORY: Among most historic areas and first Anglo-American settlements; original county, created 1836, organized 1837; named for Texas and Coahuila Gov. **Rafael Gonzales.**

Cong. Dist.	14, 15	U.S. Jud. Dist.	W-SAnt.
St. Sen. Dist.	18	Ct. Appeals	13
St. Rep. Dist.	31	Admin. Jud. Dist.	3
St. Dist. Cts.	25, 2D25		

PHYSICAL FEATURES: Rolling, rich bottom soils along Guadalupe and its tributaries; some sandy areas; many oaks, pecans.

RECREATION: Historic sites, homes; 86 officially recognized homes or historical markers; **Palmetto State Park, Gonzales Museum, Gonzales County jail** and museum, **Independence Park;** other historical attractions. "Come and Take It" festival in Gonzales.

MINERALS: Production of gas, oil, clay, gravel.

1982 Pop.	18,500	Voters reg.	10,247
Area (sq. mi.)	1,068	Whlsle. sales	$118,390,000
Altitude (ft.)	250-400	Oil value	$70,881,653
Ann. rainfall (in.)	32.07	No. employed	5,295
Jan. temp. min.	42	Wages paid	$61,050,004
July temp. max.	96	Tax value	$593,895,770
Growing season (da.)	276	Income	$128,690,000
No. farms, 1982	1,632	Taxable sales	$49,812,343
No. acres in farms	625,730	Fed. expend.	$40,717,000
†Value per farm	$347,374	Crime Index	478
Cropland harvested	39,460	TDC Pop.	30

AGRICULTURE: More than $162 million average annual income. Top poultry and egg producing county in state; cattle; crops include grain, corn, peanuts, melons, pecans.

BUSINESS: Agribusinesses, poultry processing; feed plants; tile, clay plants.

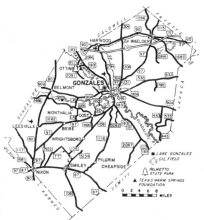

MANUFACTURING: 18 Plants; 700 Employees; Payroll, $6,400,000; Product Value, $95,300,000.

SERVICE INDUSTRIES: 89 Establishments; Receipts, $14,030,000; Annual Payroll, $4,645,000; No. Employees, 469.

GONZALES (7,152) county seat; "**Lexington of Texas,**" poultry shipping, processing center; feed mills, clay products plant; ornamental tile plant; pipe fabrication; hospital; nursing home; museum; Texas Rehabilitation Hospital.

Ottine has **Palmetto State Park, Elks Crippled Children's Hospital; Gonzales Warm Springs Foundation Hospital.**

Other towns include **Waelder** (942), **Nixon** (2,008) poultry processing and livestock center, and **Smiley** (505).

Gray

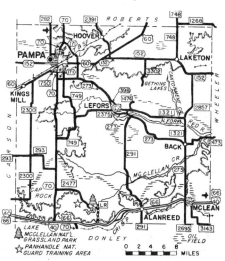

LOCATION: In Panhandle (C-10).

HISTORY: Created, 1876, from Bexar District; organized, 1902; named for **Peter W. Gray,** member first State Legislature.

Cong. Dist.	13	U.S. Jud. Dist.	N-Am.
St. Sen. Dist.	31	Ct. Appeals	7
St. Rep. Dist.	84	Admin. Jud. Dist.	9
St. Dist. Cts.	31, 223		

PHYSICAL FEATURES: Level, broken by Red River forks, tributaries; sandy loam, waxy soils.

RECREATION: Water sports, **Lake McClellan National Grasslands Park; White Deer Land Museum;** golf tournaments, rodeos, other local events.

MINERALS: Production of oil, gas, sand, gravel.

1982 Pop.	27,700	Voters reg.	14,802
Area (sq. mi.)	921	Whlsle. sales	$325,225,000
Altitude (ft.)	2,500-3,300	Oil value	$88,739,183
Ann. rainfall (in.)	20.14	No. employed	9,620
Jan. temp. min.	23	Wages paid	$177,960,976
July temp. max.	94	Tax value	$1,396,549,851
Growing season (da.)	195	Income	$271,151,000
No. farms, 1982	350	Taxable sales	$191,480,621
No. acres in farms	495,937	Fed. expend.	$54,876,000
†Value per farm	$503,050	Crime Index	1,272
Cropland harv.	105,053	TDC Pop.	53

AGRICULTURE: About $40 million average annual income, over 80% from feed and stocker cattle, hogs; sorghums, wheat, corn, hay chief crops; 22,000 acres irrigated; large feedlots.

BUSINESS: Economy based on petroleum, agriculture, feed lot operations, chemical plant, other manufacturing.

MANUFACTURING: 36 Plants; 2,200 Employees; Payroll, $50,400,000; Product Value, $360,300,000.

SERVICE INDUSTRIES: 182 Establishments; Receipts, $40,214,000; Annual Payroll, $11,823,000; No. Employees, 1,022.

PAMPA (21,396) county seat; chemical plants; petroleum processing; feedlots; meat packers; apparel, furniture plants, laminated windshields and tempered window glass manufactured; other industries; hospitals, nursing homes.

Other towns include **McLean** (1,160) and **Lefors** (829).

Grayson

LOCATION: North; adjoins Oklahoma (F-17).

HISTORY: Created, organized, 1846, from Fannin County; named for Republic of Texas **Atty. Gen. Peter W. Grayson.**

Cong. Dist. 4	U.S. Jud. Dist. . . . . E-Sh.
St. Sen. Dist. 30	Ct. Appeals 5
St. Rep. Dist. 62	Admin. Jud. Dist. 1
St. Dist. Cts. . . 15, 59, 336	

PHYSICAL FEATURES: Level, some low hills; sandy loam, Blackland soils; drains to Red River on north and to tributaries of the Trinity River on the south.

RECREATION: Lake Texoma is a leading fishing, tourist attraction; annual striper fishing derby on lake and Red River; **Lake Ray Roberts** under construction; Western Week; **Pres. Dwight D. Eisenhower birthplace; Eisenhower State Park;** varied cultural activities; **Hagerman Wildlife Refuge;** many local events.

MINERALS: Production of oil, gas, stone.

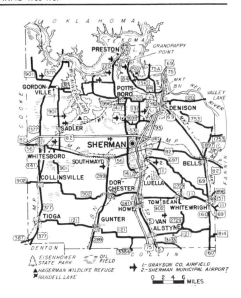

1982 Pop. 92,300	Voters reg. 49,980
Area (sq. mi.) 934	Whlsle. sales $273,523,000
Altitude (ft.) 500-800	Oil value . . . $116,892,545
Ann. rainfall (in.) . 39.83	No. employed 32,874
Jan. temp. min. 32	Wages paid . $547,149,688
July temp. max. 96	Tax value . $2,468,550,899
Growing season (da.) 227	Income $896,153,000
No. farms, 1982 . . . 1,765	Taxable sales $433,139,067
No. acres in farms 406,171	Fed. expend. $273,464,000
†Value per farm $223,687	Crime Index 5,503
Cropland harv. . . 130,332	TDC Pop. 114

AGRICULTURE: About $35 million average annual income, 65% beef, dairy cattle, hogs, horses, poultry; crops include wheat, oats, sorghums, peanuts, hay; 4,000 acres irrigated.

BUSINESS: Primarily a manufacturing, distribution and trade center for northern Texas and southern Oklahoma; tourism, minerals, agribusinesses significant.

MANUFACTURING: 127 Plants; 11,100 Employees; Payroll, $223,000,000; Product Value, $1,490,700,000.

SERVICE INDUSTRIES: 501 Establishments; Receipts, $106,902,000; Annual Payroll, $41,652,000; No. Employees, 3,426.

SHERMAN (30,413) county seat; plants manufacture foods, meat products, livestock trailers, clothing, fishing lures, electronic products, ferrous and aluminum castings, truck bodies, conveyors, office equipment, surgical supplies, other products; many processors and distributors for major companies; **Austin College;** hospitals.

Denison (23,884); electronics manufacturing, transportation center; plants process foods, make clothing, furniture, plastics, many other products; tourist center; hospitals.

Grayson County College between Sherman-Denison.
Whitewright (1,760) clothing, sausage manufacturing; clinics, nursing home.

Other towns include **Bells** (846), **Collinsville** (860), **Dorchester** (205), **Gunter** (849), **Howe** (2,072), **Luella** (371), **Pottsboro** (895), **Sadler** (329), **Southmayd** (318), **Tioga** (511), **Tom Bean** (811), **Van Alstyne** (1,860), and **Whitesboro** (3,197).

Gregg

LOCATION: Northeast (H-20).
HISTORY: Created, organized, 1873, from Rusk, Upshur Counties; named for **Confederate Gen. John Gregg.**

Cong. Dist. 4   U.S. Jud. Dist. . . . . E-Ty.
St. Sen. Dist. 1   Ct. Appeals 6, 12
St. Rep. Dist. 7   Admin. Jud. Dist. 1
St. Dist. Cts. . 124, 188, 307

PHYSICAL FEATURES: Hilly, timbered; some commercial lumbering; sandy, clay, alluvial soils; bisected by Sabine River.
RECREATION: Water activities on area lakes; hunting; varied cultural events; East Texas Oil Museum, tourism.
MINERALS: Leading oil producing county with over 2.5 billion bbl. production since 1931; mostly from East Texas field; gas, sand and gravel.

1982 Pop.	109,700	Voters reg.	58,106
Area (sq. mi.)	273	Whlsle. sales	$917,633,000
Altitude (ft.)	300-500	Oil value . . .	$695,947,456
Ann. rainfall (in.) .	47.18	No. employed	46,502
Jan. temp. min.	38	Wages paid . . .	$781,240,700
July temp. max.	96	Tax value .	$6,800,048,801
Growing season (da.)	247	Income . . .	$1,111,239,000
No. farms, 1982	378	Taxable sales	$858,147,727
No. acres in farms .	64,156	Fed. expend.	$251,337,000
†Value per farm	$159,931	Crime Index	6,206
Cropland harvested	6,108	TDC Pop.	247

AGRICULTURE: About $4.5 million average income from beef cattle, hay production, race horse breeding, timber, Christmas tree production; crops negligible.
BUSINESS: Oil-based economy, but with significant other manufacturing; tourism; conventions; agribusinesses and lignite coal production.
MANUFACTURING: 202 Plants; 11,300 Employees; Payroll, $253,700,000; Product Value, $1,784,800,000.
SERVICE INDUSTRIES: 807 Establishments; Receipts, $251,688,000; Annual Payroll, $78,676,000; No. Employees, 6,655.

LONGVIEW (62,762, partly Harrison County) county seat; center for East Texas oil industry; plants make aircraft components, plastics, chemicals, heavy equipment, recreational vehicles, metal cans, metal buildings, brewery products, paints, hats, steel products, mobile homes, railway equipment; many other products; convention center; **LeTourneau College;** and **Kilgore College Longview Center;** hospitals.

Kilgore (11,331, in Gregg and Rusk Counties) oil center; plants make ceramic products, clothing, boats, valves, other products; **Kilgore College;** hospitals; **East Texas Treatment Center.**

Other towns include **Gladewater** (6,548, part Upshur) with apparel, boat, oil field equipment manufacturers; hospital. **White Oak** (4,415), **Clarksville City** (525), **Easton** (333, partly Rusk), **Lakeport** (835), **Liberty City** (1,121), **Rolling Meadows** (252) and **Warren City** (281, partly Upshur).

Grimes

LOCATION: Southeast (L-18).
HISTORY: Created from Montgomery County and organized, 1846; named for **Jesse Grimes,** who signed Texas Declaration of Independence.
PHYSICAL FEATURES: Rich bottom soils along Brazos, Navasota Rivers; remainder hilly, partly forested.
RECREATION: Hunting, fishing; historic sites; renaissance festival in October; county fair.
AGRICULTURE: About $40 million average annual income; over 90% from beef, dairy cattle, hogs; crops include grains, corn, soybeans, watermelons, Christmas trees, some timber.
BUSINESS: Varied manufacturing, agribusinesses.
MANUFACTURING: 27 Plants; 1,400 Employees; Payroll, $23,900,000; Product Value, $178,600,000.
SERVICE INDUSTRIES: 59 Establishments; Receipts, $8,522,000; Annual Payroll, $3,257,000; No. Employees, 336.

Grimes County (Cont'd.)

Cong. Dist.	6
St. Sen. Dist.	5
St. Rep. Dist.	15
St. Dist. Cts.	12, 278
U.S. Jud. Dist.	S-Hn.
Ct. Appeals	1, 14
Admin. Jud. Dist.	2

MINERALS: Some oil, gas, coal production.

1982 Pop.	15,500
Area (sq. mi.)	799
Altitude (ft.)	200-400
Ann. rainfall (in.)	40.52
Jan. temp. min.	40
July temp. max.	96
Growing season (da.)	278
No. farms, 1982	1,196
No. acres in farms	350,998
†Value per farm	$348,661
Cropland harvested	25,645
Voters reg.	8,695
Whlsle. sales	$63,230,000
Oil value	$21,369,572
No. employed	3,868
Wages paid	$62,487,944
Tax value	$1,168,742,450
Income	$112,930,000
Taxable sales	$48,531,522
Fed. expend.	$30,724,000
Crime Index	495
TDC Pop.	28

ANDERSON (est. 320) county seat; rural center.

Navasota (5,971) agribusiness center for parts of three counties; plants make steel products, mobile homes, cheese, furniture, oil field supplies; food, wood processing; hospitals. **Todd Mission** (65) home of Texas Renaissance Festival in October.

Guadalupe

LOCATION: South central (N-15).

HISTORY: Created, organized, 1846, from Bexar, Gonzales Counties; named for river.

Cong. Dist.	14
St. Sen. Dist.	21
St. Rep. Dist.	46
St. Dist. Cts.	25, 2D25
U.S. Jud. Dist.	W-SAnt.
Ct. Appeals	4
Admin. Jud. Dist.	3

PHYSICAL FEATURES: Bisected by Guadalupe River; level to slightly rolling surface; sandy, loam, Blackland soils.

RECREATION: Fishing, hunting; historic sites; high school rodeo, festivals, other local events.

MINERALS: Production of oil, gas, sand and gravel, clays.

1982 Pop.	49,400
Area (sq. mi.)	713
Altitude (ft.)	450-700
Ann. rainfall (in.)	30.67
Jan. temp. min.	42
July temp. max.	96
Growing season (da.)	267
No. farms, 1982	1,702
No. acres in farms	344,880
†Value per farm	$231,092
Cropland harvested	85,547
Voters reg.	26,850
Whlsle. sales	$159,644,000
Oil value	$42,953,577
No. employed	12,875
Wages paid	$180,227,560
Tax value	$1,359,245,580
Income	$472,462,000
Taxable sales	$187,237,180
Fed. expend.	$130,225,000
Crime Index	1,827
TDC Pop.	49

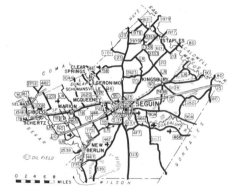

AGRICULTURE: About $28 million average annual income, 65% from beef, dairy cattle, hogs, poultry; crops include sorghums, corn, wheat, oats, cotton, peanuts, pecans.

BUSINESS: Agribusinesses, varied manufacturing, many employed in San Antonio; county in San Antonio metro area.

MANUFACTURING: 54 Plants; 3,200 Employees; Payroll, $47,400,000; Product Value, $299,100,000.

SERVICE INDUSTRIES: 187 Establishments; Receipts, $33,988,000; Annual Payroll, $12,099,000; No. Employees, 1,140.

SEGUIN (17,854) county seat; plants make aircraft parts, car radios, livestock feed, furniture, sporting guns, telescopic mounts, millwork, steel, fiberglass products, cotton goods, other products; **Texas Lutheran College;** hospital, clinics, nursing home.

Other towns include **Schertz** (7,262, part Bexar), **Cibolo** (549), **Marion** (674), **New Berlin** (253).

Hale

LOCATION: Northwest (E-8).

HISTORY: Created from Bexar District, 1876; organized 1888; named for **Lt. J. C. Hale,** who died at San Jacinto.

Cong. Dist.	19
St. Sen. Dist.	31
St. Rep. Dist.	85
St. Dist. Cts.	64, 242
U.S. Jud. Dist.	N-Lb.
Ct. Appeals	7
Admin. Jud. Dist.	9

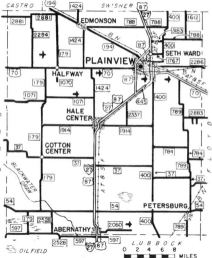

PHYSICAL FEATURES: Level; fertile sandy, loam soils; many playas; large underground water supply.

RECREATION: Local events; Llano Estacado Museum; Panhandle Parade of Breeds.

MINERALS: Production of oil, gas.

1982 Pop.	38,000
Area (sq. mi.)	1,005
Altitude (ft.)	3,200-3,600
Ann. rainfall (in.)	19.34
Jan. temp. min.	26
July temp. max.	93
Growing season (da.)	211
No. farms, 1982	832
No. acres in farms	610,359
†Value per farm	$531,148
Cropland harv.	419,856
Voters reg.	15,928
Whlsle. sales	$277,832,000
Oil value	$11,485,754
No. employed	11,420
Wages paid	$151,712,972
Tax value	$1,257,529,584
Income	$260,176,000
Taxable sales	$106,021,009
Fed. expend.	$156,422,000
Crime Index	1,850
TDC Pop.	91

AGRICULTURE: About $123 million average annual income, one of leading farm-producing counties; 80% from crops including cotton, corn, soybeans, sorghums, wheat, vegetables; beef cattle, swine, sheep; 468,000 acres irrigated.

BUSINESS: Many agribusinesses, food processing plants, manufacturing.

MANUFACTURING: 48 Plants; 2,100 Employees; Payroll, $33,600,000; Product Value, $698,500,000.

SERVICE INDUSTRIES: 191 Establishments; Receipts, $28,006,000; Annual Payroll, $7,887,000; No. Employees, 841.

PLAINVIEW (22,187) county seat; meat packing plants, other industries; **Wayland Baptist University;** hospitals, international occupational center.

Other towns include **Abernathy** (2,904, part Lubbock), textile mill; **Hale Center** (2,297), **Petersburg** (1,633), **Seth Ward, Edmonson** (291).

Hall

LOCATION: Northwest (D-10).

HISTORY: Created 1876, from Bexar, Young Districts; organized 1890; named for Republic of Texas **Secretary of War W. D. C. Hall.**

Cong. Dist. 13
St. Sen. Dist. 31
St. Rep. Dist. 84
St. Dist. Cts. 100

U.S. Jud. Dist. . . . N-Am.
Ct. Appeals 7
Admin. Jud. Dist. 9

MINERALS: Not significant.

PHYSICAL FEATURES: Rolling to hilly, broken by Red River forks, tributaries; red and black sandy loam soils.

RECREATION: Fishing, hunting; museum; local events.

1982 Pop.	5,200	Voters reg.	3,075
Area (sq. mi.)	876	Whlsle. sales .	$11,320,000
Altitude (ft.) .	1,750-2,400	Oil value.	0
Ann. rainfall (in.) .	20.53	No. employed	1,076
Jan. temp. min. . . .	26	Wages paid .	$12,083,928
July temp. max. . . .	98	Tax value .	$189,645,313
Growing season (da.)	213	Income	$28,979,000
No. farms, 1982 . . .	341	Taxable sales	$9,158,034
No. acres in farms	458,988	Fed. expend. .	$28,861,000
†Value per farm	$346,065	Crime Index	96
Cropland harv. . .	105,052	TDC Pop.	9

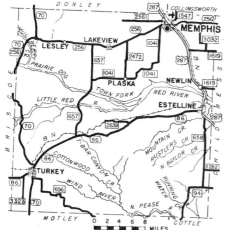

AGRICULTURE: About $24 million average annual income, 80% from crops including cotton, sorghums, peanuts, wheat, vegetables; also beef cattle, hogs; 20,000 acres irrigated.

BUSINESS: Textiles; grain, cotton processing; farm, ranch supplies, marketing for large rural area.

MANUFACTURING: None noted in census report.

SERVICE INDUSTRIES: 21 Establishments; Receipts, $2,564,000; Annual Payroll, $699,000; No. Employees, 89.

MEMPHIS (3,352) county seat; bed sheet manufacturing plant, foundry, cotton gins, food processing, compresses; grain elevators, irrigation equipment; hospital, nursing home.

Other towns include **Estelline** (258), **Lakeview** (244), **Turkey** (644).

Hamilton

LOCATION: Central (J-14).

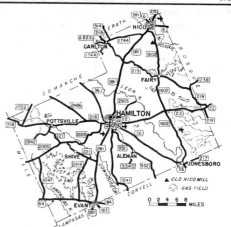

HISTORY: Created 1842; then re-created, organized, 1858, from Bosque, Comanche, Lampasas Counties; named for South Carolinian, **Gov. James Hamilton,** who aided Texas Revolution and Republic.

Cong. Dist. 11
St. Sen. Dist. 22
St. Rep. Dist. 54
St. Dist. Cts. 220

U.S. Jud. Dist. . . . W-Wa.
Ct. Appeals 10
Admin. Jud. Dist. 3

PHYSICAL FEATURES: Hilly, broken by scenic valleys; loam soils.

RECREATION: Deer, quail, dove, duck hunting; dove festival in September; Old Settlers Reunion in Hico.

MINERALS: Limited gas, oil, gravel.

1982 Pop.	8,100	Voters reg.	4,743
Area (sq. mi.)	836	Whlsle. sales .	$30,864,000
Altitude (ft.) . .	900-1,600	Oil value	$47,195
Ann. rainfall (in.) .	29.61	No. employed	1,781
Jan. temp. min. . . .	34	Wages paid . .	$20,370,688
July temp. max. . . .	96	Tax value .	$350,075,971
Growing season (da.)	239	Income	$72,578,000
No. farms, 1982 . . .	956	Taxable sales	$18,873,897
No. acres in farms	438,290	Fed. expend. .	$25,076,000
†Value per farm	$301,178	Crime Index	188
Cropland harvested	56,474	TDC Pop.	10

AGRICULTURE: More than $34 million average annual production; 90% from cattle, hogs, sheep, goats, poultry; crops include sorghums, small grains, cotton, hay, pecans.

BUSINESS: Agribusiness including more than 40 dairies; varied manufacturing; hunting leases, many residents commute to cities to work.

MANUFACTURING: None noted in census report.

SERVICE INDUSTRIES: 44 Establishments; Receipts, $7,143,000; Annual Payroll, $2,555,000; No. Employees, 312.

HAMILTON (3,189) county seat; plants make garments, wood molding, steel products, machine parts; hospital, nursing homes; library. **Hico** (1,375) is other principal town.

Hansford

LOCATION: Top of Panhandle (A-9).

HISTORY: Created, 1876, from Bexar, Young Districts; organized 1889; named for **Judge J. M. Hansford.**

Cong. Dist. 13
St. Sen. Dist. 31
St. Rep. Dist. 88
St. Dist. Cts. 84

U.S. Jud. Dist. . . . N-Am.
Ct. Appeals 7
Admin. Jud. Dist. 9

1982 Pop.	6,400	Voters reg.	3,288
Area (sq. mi.)	921	Whlsle. sales	$228,428,000
Altitude (ft.) .	2,950-3,300	Oil value . .	$14,533,916
Ann. rainfall (in.) .	22.16	No. employed	1,735
Jan. temp. min. . . .	20	Wages paid . .	$30,139,412
July temp. max. . . .	94	Tax value . .	$499,332,180
Growing season (da.)	186	Income	$55,737,000
No. farms, 1982 . . .	315	Taxable sales	$19,721,463
No. acres in farms	584,953	Fed. expend. .	$52,340,000
†Value per farm	$926,511	Crime Index	102
Cropland harv. . .	203,607	TDC Pop.	6

Hansford County (Cont'd.)

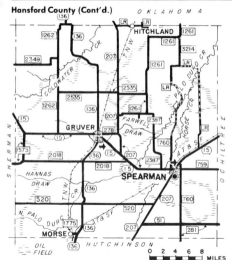

PHYSICAL FEATURES: Level, drains to playas, creeks, draws; sandy, loam, black soils; underground water.

RECREATION: Stationmasters House Museum, hunting, local events.

MINERALS: Production of gas, oil, stone, helium.

AGRICULTURE: $104 million average annual income, 65% from livestock; large cattle feeding operations; crops include sorghums, wheat, corn; 200,000 acres irrigated.

BUSINESS: Agribusinesses; mineral operations.

MANUFACTURING: None noted in census report.

SERVICE INDUSTRIES: 33 Establishments; Receipts, $3,907,000; Annual Payroll, $1,257,000; No. Employees, 92.

SPEARMAN (3,413) county seat; feedlots; center for grain marketing, storage; gas processing; hospital, retirement center; municipal airport. **Gruver** (1,216) is other principal town.

Hardeman

LOCATION: Borders Oklahoma (E-12).

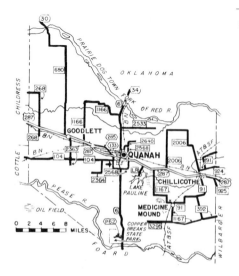

1982 Pop.	42,100	Voters reg.	26,255
Area (sq. mi.)	898	Whlsle. sales	$166,324,000
Altitude (ft.)	30-200	Oil value	$74,259,824
Ann. rainfall (in.)	53.00	No. employed	7,301
Jan. temp. min.	42	Wages paid	$110,391,636
July temp. max.	93	Tax value	$1,453,718,506
Growing season (da.)	246	Income	$409,029,000
No. farms, 1982	331	Taxable sales	$103,229,733
No. acres in farms	70,142	Fed. expend.	$89,964,000
†Value per farm	$204,798	Crime Index	712
Cropland harvested	3,725	TDC Pop.	42

HISTORY: Created, 1858, from Fannin; re-created, 1876, organized, 1884; named for pioneer Texas brothers, **Bailey** and **T. J. Hardeman.**

Cong. Dist.	13	U.S. Jud. Dist.	N-WF
St. Sen. Dist.	30	Ct. Appeals	7
St. Rep. Dist.	80	Admin. Jud. Dist.	9
St. Dist. Cts.	46		

PHYSICAL FEATURES: Rolling, broken area on divide between Pease, Red River forks; sandy, sandy loam soils.

RECREATION: Copper Breaks State Park; Lake Pauline activities; museum; local events.

MINERALS: Production of oil, gas, gypsum.

1982 Pop.	6,500	Voters reg.	3,348
Area (sq. mi.)	688	Whlsle. sales	$15,864,000
Altitude (ft.)	1,300-1,600	Oil value	$78,608,989
Ann. rainfall (in.)	24.32	No. employed	1,839
Jan. temp. min.	28	Wages paid	$26,722,212
July temp. max.	99	Tax value	$341,526,112
Growing season (da.)	221	Income	$50,801,000
No. farms, 1982	362	Taxable sales	$15,328,013
No. acres in farms	322,723	Fed. expend.	$28,885,000
†Value per farm	$401,110	Crime Index	117
Cropland harv.	133,953	TDC Pop.	7

AGRICULTURE: About $20 million average annual income, 65% from wheat, cotton, other crops; beef cattle, horses, hogs; about 6,000 acres irrigated, mostly cotton.

BUSINESS: Agribusinesses, some manufacturing.

MANUFACTURING: None noted in census report.

SERVICE INDUSTRIES: 30 Establishments; Receipts, $3,412,000; Annual Payroll, $1,096,000; No. Employees, 154.

QUANAH (3,890) county seat; agribusinesses, gypsum plant makes wall board; cotton oil mill, sheet metal works, other plants; hospital, rest homes. **Chillicothe** (1,052) is other principal town.

Hardin

LOCATION: Southeast (L-21).

HISTORY: Created, organized, 1858, from Jefferson, Liberty Counties. Named for Texas Revolutionist **William Hardin.**

Cong. Dist.	2	U.S. Jud. Dist.	E-Bt.
St. Sen. Dist.	3	Ct. Appeals	9
St. Rep. Dist.	20	Admin. Jud. Dist.	2
St. Dist. Cts.	88, 356		

PHYSICAL FEATURES: Heavily timbered; many streams; sandy, loam soils; **Big Thicket** covers much of area.

RECREATION: Big Thicket with rare plant, animal life; part of **Big Thicket National Preserve; Big Thicket Museum** at Saratoga; hunting, fishing; local events.

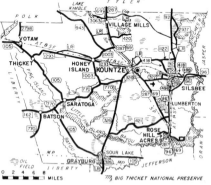

MINERALS: Poduction of oil, gas, sand and gravel.

AGRICULTURE: Almost $4.8 million average annual income, most of it from forestry products; over 85% of county forested; beef cattle, hogs, horses, goats; crops include soybeans, rice, hay; timber harvested, Christmas tree production increasing.

BUSINESS: Paper making, wood processing, minerals, food processing; county in Beaumont-Port Arthur-Orange SMSA (see metro page).

MANUFACTURING: 36 Plants; Employees, N.A.; Payroll, N.A.; Product Value, N.A.

SERVICE INDUSTRIES: 99 Establishments; Receipts, $15,629,000; Annual Payroll, $5,125,000; No. Employees, 560.

KOUNTZE (2,716) county seat; tourism.

Silsbee (7,684) is trade, manufacturing center; lumber, paper, particle board, sawmills; rubber plant; oil, gas processing; rail division point; hospital, nursing home. Other towns include **Lumberton** (2,480) hospital; **Rose Hill Acres** (460), **Sour Lake** (1,807), **Saratoga** and **Grayburg** (194).

Harris

LOCATION: Southeast (M-20).

HISTORY: Created, 1836, organized, 1837; named for **John R. Harris,** 1824 founder of Harrisburg.

PHYSICAL FEATURES: Level; typically coastal surface and soils; many bayous, lakes, canals for artificial drainage; partly forested.

Cong. Dist. 7, 8, 9, 18, 22, 25	St. Dist. Cts. . . 11, 55, 61,
St. Sen.	80, 113, 125, 127, 129, 133,
Dist. 4, 5, 6, 7, 11, 13, 15, 17	151, 152, 157, 164, 165, 174,
St. Rep. Dist. 125-150	176, 177, 178, 179, 180, 182,
U.S. Jud. Dist. . . . . . S-Hn.	183, 184, 185, 189, 190, 208,
Ct. Appeals 1, 14	209, 215, 228, 230, 232, 234,
Admin. Jud. Dist. 2	245, 246, 247, 248, 257, 262,
	263, 269, 270, 280, 281, 295,
	308, 309, 310, 311, 312, 313,
	314, 315, 333, 334, 337, 338,
	339, 351

MINERALS: Among leading oil, gas, petrochemical areas; production of petroleum, cement, natural gas liquids, natural gas, salt, lime, sand and gravel, clays, stone; approximately 1 billion bbls. oil produced since 1905; center of multicounty petrochemicals developments that are the world's largest (see Minerals section).

RECREATION: Fishing, boating, other freshwater and saltwater activities; **Astroworld** and **Waterworld** amusement parks and adjacent domed stadium; numerous athletic and cultural events associated with universities and colleges; professional baseball, football, basketball, other sports; **Jones Hall for the Performing Arts, Nina Vance Alley Theatre, Houston Theatre Center, Music Hall, coliseum, Convention Center, The Summit** — a 17,000-seat sports and entertainment center, **Sam Houston Park** with restored early Houston homes, church, stores; **Museum of Fine Arts, Contemporary Arts Museum, Rice Museum; Sarah Campbell Blaffer Gallery** at University of Houston; museum of natural science, planetarium, zoological gardens in Hermann Park; **San Jacinto Battleground State Park** with museum, Battleship Texas; **Lyndon B. Johnson Space Center;** annual **Livestock Show and Rodeo;** Houston Festival in spring; Azalea Trail, numerous art shows, cultural events, other tourist attractions. (Consult chambers of commerce or Greater Houston Convention and Visitors Council for details and dates.)

EDUCATION: Houston is a university center: more than 140,000 students are enrolled in 28 colleges and universities in Harris County. Senior colleges and universities: **Rice University, University of Houston** (three branches in Harris County), **Texas Southern University, University of St. Thomas, Houston Baptist University, Houston Baptist University Nursing School, South Texas College of Law, Hispanic International University.** Junior colleges: **Houston Community College System, Lee College, San Jacinto College, North Harris County Junior College.** Medical schools and colleges: **University of St. Thomas Nursing School, University of Texas Health Science Center at Houston** (seven branches. See index for Universities and Colleges for individual schools therein), **Baylor College of Medicine, Institute of Religion and Human Development, Texas Chiropractic College, Texas Woman's University-Houston Center.** Theological schools: **Gulf Coast Bible College, St. Mary's Seminary, Texas Bible College.** Houston also has many business, technical and trade schools.

1982 Pop. 2,684,100	Voters reg. 1,295,381
Area (sq. mi.) 1,734	Whlsle. sls. $96,567,531,000
Altitude (ft.) sea level-310	Oil value $58,948,682
Ann. rainfall (in.) . 48.19	No. employed . . 1,318,891
Jan. temp. min. 45	Wages paid $29,716,422,856
July temp. max. 93	Tax value . . . . N.A.
Growing season (da.) 300	Income . . $32,346,727,000
No. farms, 1982 . . . 1,943	Taxable sls.$19,601,907,489
No. acres in farms 388,660	Fed. expd. $10,802,774,000
†Value per farm $474,525	Crime Index 204,121
Cropland harvested 86,123	TDC Pop. 9,054

AGRICULTURE: $72.1 million annual income, about 25% from cattle, hogs, horses, poultry, dairy products; crops include rice, nursery crops, soybeans, grains, hay, corn, vegetables; some 50,000 acres irrigated, mostly rice.

BUSINESS: Highly industrialized county, with more than 3,800 manufacturing plants; corporate management center; nation's largest concentration of petrochemical plants; largest U.S. wheat-exporting port, the 2nd largest U.S. port in value of foreign trade and 3rd largest U.S. port in total tonnage; petroleum refining, chemicals, food and kindred products, fabricated metal products, non-electrical machinery, primary metals, scientific instruments; paper and allied products, printing and publishing, numerous other products manufactured; center of energy, space and medical research; center of international business, with 64 foreign banks and 5th largest consular corps in U.S.; increasing convention, tourist business; see Houston metro page for data on metropolitan area; see also sections on minerals, manufacturing, etc.

MANUFACTURING: 4,417 Plants; 229,100 Employees; Payroll, $5,621,200,000; Product Value, $43,804,200,000.

SERVICE INDUSTRIES: 18,832 Establishments; Receipts, $10,837,370,000; Annual Payroll, $3,956,456,000; No. Employees, 226,334.

HOUSTON (1,595,138, in Harris, Fort Bend, Montgomery Counties, largest Texas city, 4th largest in U.S.); see also Houston metro page; county seat; ranks first in manufacture of petroleum equipment, agricultural chemicals, fertilizers, pesticides, oil and gas pipeline transmission; ranks high in commercial bank demand deposits, wholesale sales, retail sales, value added by manufacture and manufacturing payrolls; 64 foreign bank branches; 54 foreign consular offices; 27 foreign trade, investment and tourism offices; a leading scientific center; ranks fifth in manufacture of machinery, sixth in fabricated metals; a major distribution and shipping center; engineering and research center; food processing, textile mills; plants make apparel, lumber and wood products, furniture, paper, publications, chemical, petroleum and coal products, stone, clay and glass products, electrical and electronic products, many others; major medical and educational center; 7th largest public school system in U.S.; prominent corporate center, with more than 200 firms locating corporate headquarters, divisions or subsidiaries since 1970.

Pasadena (112,560) residential city with large industrial area; civic center; retail mall; **San Jacinto College, Texas Chiropractic College;** 4 hospitals; historical museum; strawberry festival; Gilley's, the famous Western nightspot.

Bellaire (14,950) residential city, with several major office buildings; manufacturing plants; hospitals.

Other towns are **Seabrook** (4,670), **Nassau Bay** (4,526), **El Lago** (3,129), **Webster** (2,405), **Taylor Lake Village** (3,669), **Clear Lake,** an unincorporated town, computer-related industry; hospital; **Lyndon B. Johnson Space Center, University of Houston-Clear Lake.** Bayport industrial complex includes Port of Bayport; 12 major marinas; 2 hospitals.

Baytown (56,923) refining, petrochemical center; steel manufacturing; **Lee College;** major shopping mall; hospital center; historical homes tour.

Tomball (3,996) petrochemicals; retail center; hospital, sports medicine center.

Humble (6,729) manufactures oil field equipment, gaskets; retail center; hospital.

Other towns include **Bunker Hill Village** (3,750), **Deer Park** (22,648), **Galena Park** (9,879), **Hedwig Village** (2,506), **Hilshire Village** (621), **Jersey Village** (4,084), **Hunters Creek Village** (4,215), **Jacinto City** (8,953), **Katy** (5,660, part Waller and Fort Bend), **La Porte** (14,062), **Lomax** (2,991), **Morgan's Point** (428), **Missouri City** (24,423, part Fort Bend), **Piney Point Village** (2,958), **Shore Acres** (1,260), **South Houston** (13,293), **Southside Place** (1,366), **Spring Valley** (3,353), **Stafford** (4,755, mostly Fort Bend), **Waller** (1,241, mostly Waller) and **West University Place** (12,010). (See also information on Fort Bend, Montgomery, Waller and Liberty Counties; also see Galveston County.)

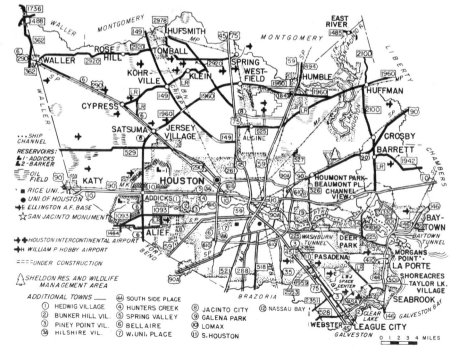

ADDITIONAL TOWNS
① HEDWIG VILLAGE
② BUNKER HILL VIL.
③ PINEY POINT VIL.
㉞ HILSHIRE VIL.
④ SOUTH SIDE PLACE
⑤ HUNTERS CREEK
⑤ SPRING VALLEY
⑥ BELLAIRE
⑦ W. UNI. PLACE
⑧ JACINTO CITY
⑨ GALENA PARK
⑩ LOMAX
⑪ S. HOUSTON
⑫ NASSAU BAY

0 1 2 3 4 MILES

Harrison

LOCATION: Northeast (H-21).

HISTORY: Created, 1839, from Shelby County; organized, 1842; named for eloquent advocate of Texas Revolution, **Jonas Harrison.**

Cong. Dist. 1	U.S. Jud. Dist. . . . . E-MI.
St. Sen. Dist. 1	Ct. Appeals 6
St. Rep. Dist. 9	Admin. Jud. Dist. 1
St. Dist. Cts. 71	

PHYSICAL FEATURES: Hilly, rolling; over half forested; Sabine River; **Caddo Lake.**

★ LONGHORN ORDNANCE WORKS
△ CADDO LAKE STATE PARK

1982 Pop. 55,500	Voters reg. 32,531
Area (sq. mi.) 908	Whlsle. sales $251,149,000
Altitude (ft.) 200-400	Oil value $32,947,890
Ann. rainfall (in.) . 46.19	No. employed . . . 18,487
Jan. temp. min. 37	Wages paid . $357,370,408
July temp. max. 95	Tax value . $2,487,055,479
Growing season (da.) 245	Income $496,359,000
No. farms, 1982 . . . 1,031	Taxable sales $165,823,845
No. acres in farms 197,646	Fed. expend. $136,499,000
†Value per farm $208,386	Crime Index 2,172
Cropland harvested 18,559	TDC Pop. 111

RECREATION: Fishing, other water activities; hunting; many plantation homes, historic sites; Stagecoach Days in May; Old Courthouse Museum; Old World Store; **Caddo Lake** and **State Park, Lake O' The Pines,** Pirkey Lake.

MINERALS: Production of oil, gas, coal, clays, sand and gravel.

AGRICULTURE: About $18 million average annual income, 90% from cattle, hogs, poultry; crops include wheat, oats, grains, corn, hay; timber.

BUSINESS: Oil, gas processing; lumbering; pottery manufacturing; varied manufacturing.

MANUFACTURING: 84 Plants; 4,700 Employees; Payroll, $82,600,000; Product Value, $420,100,000.

SERVICE INDUSTRIES: 191 Establishments; Receipts, $59,016,000; Annual Payroll, $19,279,000; No. Employees, 1,391.

MARSHALL (24,921) county seat; petroleum, lumber processing; chemicals, steel products; tile, pottery, aluminum products; plants make bus frames, apparel, other products; civic center; **Wiley College; East Texas Baptist College;** historic sites.

Other towns include **Hallsville** (1,556), power plant, **Longview** (62,762, mostly Gregg County), **Nesbitt** (129), **Scottsville** (245), **Uncertain** (176) and **Waskom** (1,821).

Hartley

LOCATION: Borders New Mexico (B-8).

HISTORY: Created, 1876, from Bexar, Young Districts; organized, 1891; named for Texas pioneers, **O. C.** and **R. K. Hartley.**

Cong. Dist. 13	U.S. Jud. Dist. . . . N-Am.
St. Sen. Dist. 31	Ct. Appeals 7
St. Rep. Dist. 88	Admin. Jud. Dist. 9
St. Dist. Cts. 69	

PHYSICAL FEATURES: Level; drains to playas, Canadian River, tributaries; sandy, loam, chocolate soils; **Lake Rita Blanca.**

RECREATION: **Lake Rita Blanca** activities; ranch museum; local events; XIT Rodeo and Reunion at Dalhart.

MINERALS: Natural gas.

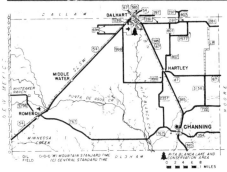

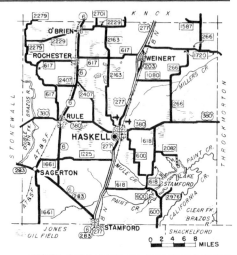

1982 Pop.	3,700	Voters reg.	2,295
Area (sq. mi.)	1,462	Whlse. sales	$6,033,000
Altitude (ft.)	3,400-4,200	Oil value	$445,366
Ann. rainfall (in.)	18.00	No. employed	378
Jan. temp. min.	20	Wages paid	$4,785,096
July temp. max.	92	Tax value	$175,609,265
Growing season (da.)	180	Income	$33,429,000
No. farms, 1982	208	Taxable sales	$2,646,203
No. acres in farms	879,814	Fed. expend.	$25,089,000
†Value per farm	$1,327,986	Crime Index	19
Cropland harv.	157,962	TDC Pop.	2

AGRICULTURE: About $81 million average annual income from sorghums, wheat, corn, cattle; about 90,000 acres irrigated.

BUSINESS: Economy based on agriculture, gas production; varied manufacturing.

MANUFACTURING: None noted in census report.

SERVICE INDUSTRIES: 10 Establishments; Receipts, $788,000; Annual Payroll, $177,000; No. Employees, 20.

CHANNING (304) county seat.

Dalhart (6,854, in Dallam and Hartley Counties) has feedlots, feed and meat processing plants, other industries.

Haskell

LOCATION: West central (G-12).

HISTORY: Created, 1858, from Milam, Fannin Counties; re-created, 1876; organized, 1885; named for Goliad martyr, **C. R. Haskell.**

Cong. Dist.	17	U.S. Jud. Dist.	N-Ab.
St. Sen. Dist.	30	Ct. Appeals	11
St. Rep. Dist.	64	Admin. Jud. Dist.	7
St. Dist. Cts.	39		

PHYSICAL FEATURES: Rolling; broken areas; drained by Brazos tributaries; **Lake Stamford;** sandy loam, gray, black soils.

RECREATION: Lake Stamford activities; local events; hunting.

MINERALS: Production of oil and gas.

1982 Pop.	7,600	Voters reg.	4,722
Area (sq. mi.)	901	Whlse. sales	$15,164,000
Altitude (ft.)	1,400-1,800	Oil value	$38,800,695
Ann. rainfall (in.)	24.14	No. employed	1,546
Jan. temp. min.	30	Wages paid	$20,142,944
July temp. max.	97	Tax value	$440,808,905
Growing season (da.)	232	Income	$49,451,000
No. farms, 1982	670	Taxable sales	$18,491,809
No. acres in farms	453,623	Fed. expend.	$39,436,000
†Value per farm	$334,979	Crime Index	103
Cropland harv.	203,912	TDC Pop.	8

AGRICULTURE: About $30 million average annual income, 85% from cotton, grains; remainder from beef cattle, hogs; about 15,000 acres irrigated cropland, 5,000 pasture.

BUSINESS: Agribusinesses, oil field operations.

MANUFACTURING: None noted in census report.

SERVICE INDUSTRIES: 30 Establishments; Receipts, $4,111,000; Annual Payroll, $1,174,000; No. Employees, 175.

HASKELL (3,782) county seat; farm trading center. **O'Brien** (212), **Rochester** (492), **Rule** (1,015) **Stamford** (4,542, mostly Jones County) and **Weinert** (253) other principal towns.

Hays

LOCATION: South central (M-15).

HISTORY: Created 1843 from Travis County; organized same year; named for **Capt. Jack Hays,** famous Texas Ranger.

Cong. Dist.	10	U.S. Jud. Dist.	W-An.
St. Sen. Dist.	14	Ct. Appeals	3
St. Rep. Dist.	47	Admin. Jud. Dist.	3
St. Dist. Cts.	22, 207, 274		

PHYSICAL FEATURES: Partly hilly, partly Blackland; spring-fed streams; canyons; caves.

RECREATION: Major tourist center; retirement area; fine fishing, hunting; **Aquarena; Pioneer Town; Wonder World;** university cultural, athletic events, Cypress Creek and Blanco River resorts and recreation,

guest ranches; antique shops at Wimberley; "Chilympiad" men's cookoff in September.

MINERALS: Sand and gravel, cement produced.

1982 Pop.	43,700	Voters reg.	27,113
Area (sq. mi.)	678	Whlsle. sales	$90,652,000
Altitude (ft.)	600-1,600	Oil value	0
Ann. rainfall (in.)	33.75	No. employed	14,287
Jan. temp. min.	40	Wages paid	$186,209,204
July temp. max.	96	Tax value	$1,567,199,809
No. farms, 1982	643	Income	$378,865,000
No. acres in farms	210,668	Taxable sales	$200,918,339
†Value per farm	$432,160	Fed. expend.	$91,575,000
Cropland harvested	24,888	Crime Index	2,836
		TDC Pop.	65

AGRICULTURE: About $13 million average annual income, 85% from cattle, hogs, sheep; crops include sorghums, hay, wheat, corn, cotton, some peaches and cedar posts.

BUSINESS: Tourism, education, retirement village, some manufacturing; county part of Austin SMSA, see metro page.

MANUFACTURING: 27 Plants; 1,300 Employees; Payroll, $20,900,000; Product Value, $90,400,000.

SERVICE INDUSTRIES: 211 Establishments; Receipts; $50,307,000; Annual Payroll, $16,361,000; No. Employees, 1,848.

SAN MARCOS (23,420) county seat; recreational-educational center; **Southwest Texas State University, San Marcos Baptist Academy, Gary job training center; Scheib center** for mentally handicapped; **Aquarena, Wonder World;** varied manufacturing, printing and distribution center; hospital. "Chilympiad" and "Cinco de Mayo" cookoffs.

Wimberley (3,065), river resorts, recreation, retirement area; antique shops; cement plant; "First Saturday" market days April-November, Hillaceous 10,000 Run in April; country crafts fair in May. Other towns include **Buda** (597), **Hays** (286), **Kyle** (2,093) and **Dripping Springs** (606).

Hemphill

LOCATION: Eastern Panhandle (B-11).

HISTORY: Created from Bexar, Young Districts, 1876; organized 1887; named for Republic of Texas Justice **John Hemphill.**

Cong. Dist.	13
St. Sen. Dist.	31
St. Rep. Dist.	88
St. Dist. Cts.	31
U.S. Jud. Dist.	N-Am.
Ct. Appeals	7
Admin. Jud. Dist.	9

PHYSICAL FEATURES: Sloping surface, broken by Canadian, Washita Rivers, Lake Marvin; sandy, red, dark soils.

RECREATION: Lake Marvin activities; foliage tours; hunting, fishing; **Buffalo Wallow Indian Battleground, Gene Howe Wildlife Management Area,** golf course.

MINERALS: Production of oil and gas.

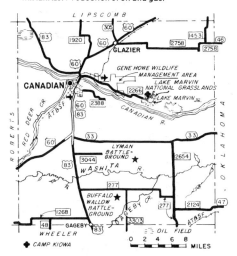

1982 Pop.	6,300	Voters reg.	2,748
Area (sq. mi.)	903	Whlsle. sales	$39,371,000
Altitude (ft.)	2,200-2,800	Oil value	$15,706,842
Ann. rainfall (in.)	20.50	No. employed	1,605
Jan. temp. min.	23	Wages paid	$30,244,256
July temp. max.	95	Tax value	$1,402,400,660
Growing season (da.)	204	Income	$54,643,000
No. farms, 1982	221	Taxable sales	$30,043,283
No. acres in farms	618,105	Fed. expend.	$7,315,000
†Value per farm	$642,104	Crime Index	124
Cropland harvested	44,703	TDC Pop.	5

AGRICULTURE: More than 85% of $28 million average farm income from beef cattle, hogs; wheat, hay, sorghums principal crops; 4,600 acres irrigated for hay, forages.

BUSINESS: Economy based on petroleum production and refining, livestock production.

MANUFACTURING: None noted in census report.

SERVICE INDUSTRIES: 34 Establishments; Receipts, $16,211,000; Annual Payroll, $3,665,000; No. Employees, 224.

CANADIAN (3,491) county seat; oil and gas production; feedlot; hospital, nursing home; golf course.

Henderson

LOCATION: East (I-19).

HISTORY: Created and organized, 1846, from Houston, Nacogdoches Counties; named for **Gov. J. Pinckney Henderson.**

Cong. Dist.	1
St. Sen. Dist.	9
St. Rep. Dist.	12
St. Dist. Cts.	3, 173
U.S. Jud. Dist.	E-Ty.
Ct. Appeals	12
Admin. Jud. Dist.	1

PHYSICAL FEATURES: Hilly, rolling; one-third forested; bounded by Neches, Trinity Rivers; sandy, loam, clay soils; commercial timber; **Cedar Creek,** other lakes.

RECREATION: Cedar Creek Reservoir, Lake Palestine, other public, private lakes; hunting, fishing; annual Black-eyed Pea festival, fiddlers' reunion.

MINERALS: Production of oil, gas, clays, lignite, sulphur, sand and gravel.

1982 Pop.	45,600	Voters reg.	29,820
Area (sq. mi.)	888	Whlsle. sales	$103,922,000
Altitude (ft.)	300-600	Oil value	$101,218,433
Ann. rainfall (in.)	40.40	No. employed	9,300
Jan. temp. min.	37	Wages paid	$136,381,800
July temp. max.	95	Tax value	$2,325,227,348
Growing season (da.)	260	Income	$462,218,000
No. farms, 1982	1,509	Taxable sales	$168,471,590
No. acres in farms	323,887	Fed. expend.	$71,655,000
†Value per farm	$182,056	Crime Index	1,429
Cropland harvested	41,185	TDC Pop.	68

AGRICULTURE: About 85% of almost $41 million income from cattle, hogs, horses, poultry; crops include grain, hay, fruits, vegetables, melons, nursery crops; hardwood timber marketed.

BUSINESS: Varied manufacturing; agribusinesses; minerals; recreation.

MANUFACTURING: 45 Plants; 2,000 Employees; Payroll, $25,400,000; Product Value, $168,000,000.

SERVICE INDUSTRIES: 138 Establishments; Receipts; $22,344,000; Annual Payroll, $8,019,000; No. Employees, 825.

ATHENS (10,197) county seat; plants make TV sets, furniture, picture frames, mobile homes, clothing, brick, clay products, boats, electronic, apparel, medical and other products; **Henderson County Junior College;** hospital.

Trinidad (1,130) has methane, power plants. **Malakoff** (2,082) has brick factory. **Seven Points** (647) center of lake activity. Other towns include **Chandler** (1,308), **Eustace** (541) gas producing plant; **Murchison** (513), **Tool** (1,464), **Berryville** (513), **Brownsboro** (582), **Caney City** (312), **Coffee City** (254), **Enchanted Oaks** (212), **Gun Barrel City** (2,118), **Moore Station** (335), **Payne Springs** (422), **Poynor** (272), and **Star Harbor** (310).

Hidalgo

LOCATION: Extreme south (U-15).

HISTORY: Settled early by Spaniards; created, organized, 1852, from Cameron, Starr Counties; named for Mexican leader, **Miguel Hidalgo y Costillo.**

Cong. Dist. 15	U.S. Jud. Dist. . . . . S-Br.
St. Sen. Dist. 20, 27	Ct. Appeals 13
St. Rep. Dist 40-42,	Admin. Jud. Dist. 5
St. Dist. Cts. . . 92, 93, 139,	
206,275,332	

PHYSICAL FEATURES: Rich alluvial soils along Rio Grande; sandy, loam soils in north; semitropical vegetation.

RECREATION: Winter resort, retirement area; fishing, hunting; gateway to Mexico; historical sites; live steam museum at Alamo, Weslaso Bi-cultural museum, other museums; many attractions; Rio Grande Valley livestock show at Mercedes; South Texas Lamb and Sheep show at Donna, Citrus Fiesta at Mission; Fiesta Hidalgo in March and annual Spring Arts and Plant Sale in April at Edinburg; consult chambers of commerce for special events.

MINERALS: Production of oil, gas, sand and gravel, stone.

1982 Pop.	315,100	Voters reg.	137,302
Area (sq. mi.)	1,569	Whlsle. sales	$1,357,790,000
Altitude (ft.)	40-275	Oil value	$4,878,863
Ann. rainfall (in.) . .	19.90	No. employed	83,964
Jan. temp. min.	49	Wages paid .	$998,861,568
July temp. max.	97	Tax value .	$5,410,067,991
Growing season (da.)	327	Income . . .	$1,743,422,000
No. farms, 1982 . .	2,310	Taxable sls.	$1,014,857,685
No. acres in farms	833,565	Fed. expend.	$558,691,000
†Value per farm	$627,402	Crime Index . . .	15,893
Cropland harv. . .	432,482	TDC Pop.	271

AGRICULTURE: $320 million average annual income makes county a leader in farm product sales; 90% of farm cash receipts from crops, principally from cotton,

citrus, grain, vegetables, sugar cane; livestock includes cattle, dairy products, hogs, poultry, horses; 350,000 acres irrigated.

BUSINESS: Food processing, shipping; other agribusinesses; tourism; mineral operations; diversified metro area, see McAllen-Pharr-Edinburg metro page.

MANUFACTURING: 171 Plants; 7,100 Employees; Payroll, $79,200,000; Product Value, $547,000,000.

SERVICE INDUSTRIES: 1,051 Establishments; Receipts, $249,063,000; Annual Payroll, $75,233,000; No. Employees, 6,850.

EDINBURG (24,075) county seat celebrated 75th anniversary in 1983; fruit and vegetable processors, packers; agribusinesses; petroleum operations; clothing, metal products, other manufacturing; tourist center; **Pan American University;** planetarium; hospitals; South Texas High School for special education, **Tropical Texas Center for Mental Health-Mental Retardation;** museum, fiestas.

McAllen (66,281) is a popular tourist center and has numerous agribusinesses; petroleum processing, plants make rubber products, medical equipment, hospital furniture, electronics, food equipment, apparel, other products; food processing, packing and shipping; trade center; major port of entry into Mexico; foreign trade zone.

Pharr (21,381) is an agribusiness and trading center.

Mission (22,653) is center for Valley citrus industry; candle manufacturer; Screwworm Eradication Center; fiberglass auto parts; agribusiness, tourism center.

Weslaco (19,331) is a food processing center; numerous other agribusinesses; clothing manufacturing; steel fabricator; tourist center; bi-cultural museum; citrus and vegetable research; hospital, nursing home; sugar cane festival in February.

Donna (9,952) agribusiness center; canning plants; furniture factory; tourism. Numerous other trading centers include **Alamo** (5,831), **Edcouch** (3,092), **Elsa** (5,061), **Hidalgo** (2,288), **La Joya** (2,018), **La Villa** (1,442), **Mercedes** (11,851), **Palmhurst** (364), **Palmview** (683), **Alton** (2,732), **San Juan** (7,608), and **Progreso Lakes** (197).

Hill

LOCATION: Central (I-16).

HISTORY: Created from Navarro County, organized, 1853; named for **G. W. Hill,** Republic of Texas official.

Cong. Dist. 6	U.S. Jud. Dist. . . . . W-Wa.
St. Sen. Dist. 9	Ct. Appeals 10
St. Rep. Dist. 57	Admin. Jud. Dist. 3
St. Dist. Cts. 66	

PHYSICAL FEATURES: Level to rolling; Blackland soils, some sandy loams; drains to Brazos; Lake Whitney, Navarro Mills Reservoir.

RECREATION: Lake Whitney, Navarro Mills Reservoir activities; excursion boat on Lake Whitney; **Hill Junior College; Confederate Museum,** historic structures; art festival in June; motorcycle track, varied activities.

MINERALS: Lime, stone, gas, oil.

1982 Pop.......... 25,800	Voters reg....... 14,030
Area (sq. mi.)...... 968	Whlsle. sales . $42,610,000
Altitude (ft.).... 400-900	Oil value...... $234,009
Ann. rainfall (in.) . 34.47	No. employed 5,596
Jan. temp. min...... 36	Wages paid .. $72,499,880
July temp. max. 96	Tax value . . $751,508,662
Growing season (da.) 247	Income $213,793,000
No. farms, 1982 ... 1,544	Taxable sales $62,267,812
No. acres in farms 463,927	Fed. expend.. $66,005,000
†Value per farm $193,701	Crime Index 833
Cropland harv... 214,495	TDC Pop. 42

AGRICULTURE: About $57 million average annual income, 60% from crops including cotton, grains, peanuts; beef and dairy cattle, hogs, horses, poultry.

BUSINESS: Agribusinesses, varied manufacturing, tourism.

MANUFACTURING: 35 Plants; 1,200 Employees; Payroll, $16,400,000; Product Value, $87,500,000.

SERVICE INDUSTRIES: 83 Establishments; Receipts, $10,789,000; Annual Payroll, $3,657,000; No. Employees, 348.

HILLSBORO (7,397) county seat; gins, grain processors; plants make apparel, pipe, tubing, fertilizers, steel, mobile homes, sheetmetal, insulation, wood products, rubber and plastic products. **Hill Junior College,** hospital, old courthouse and depot restoration; **Aquilla Lake.**

Whitney (1,631) is tourist center; varied manufacturing; hospital, nursing homes. Other towns include **Abbott** (359), **Aquilla** (130), **Blum** (357), **Bynum** (232), **Covington** (259), **Hubbard** (1,676), **Itasca** (1,600), **Malone** (315), **Mertens** (133), **Mount Calm** (393) and **Penelope** (235).

Hockley

LOCATION: Northwest (F-7).

HISTORY: Created, 1876, from Bexar, Young Districts; organized 1921; named for Republic of Texas Secretary of War, **Gen. G. W. Hockley.**

Cong. Dist. 19	U.S. Jud. Dist..... N-Lb.
St. Sen. Dist. 31	Ct. Appeals 7
St. Rep. Dist....... 77	Admin. Jud. Dist. 9
St. Dist. Cts. 286	

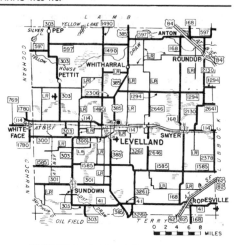

MINERALS: Production of oil, gas, stone; one of leading oil-producing counties with more than 1 billion barrels produced.

1982 Pop.......... 24,100	Voters reg....... 11,875
Area (sq. mi.)...... 908	Whlsle. sales . $89,429,000
Altitude (ft.). 3,300-3,650	Oil value... $454,755,517
Ann. rainfall (in.) . 16.60	No. employed 7,251
Jan. temp. min...... 24	Wages paid . $126,641,280
July temp. max. 93	Tax value . $3,220,331,401
Growing season (da.) 196	Income $192,058,000
No. farms, 1982 633	Taxable sales $81,114,054
No. acres in farms 525,853	Fed. expend. $106,300,000
†Value per farm $387,561	Crime Index 868
Cropland harv. . 317,976	TDC Pop. 34

Presidio County Courthouse in Marfa was built in 1886.

PHYSICAL FEATURES: Flat, draining to numerous playas, **Yellow House River, Lake;** loam, sandy loam soils.

RECREATION: Local events, Early Settlers' Day in July.

AGRICULTURE: More than 70% of $49 million income from crops, principally cotton, sorghums, wheat, soybeans, corn, hay, sunflowers; livestock includes cattle, hogs, sheep; 190,000 acres irrigated.

BUSINESS: Economy based on extensive oil, gas production and services, manufacturing, varied agribusinesses.

MANUFACTURING: None noted in census report.

SERVICE INDUSTRIES: 86 Establishments; Receipts, $19,252,000; Annual Payroll, $5,890,000; No. Employees, 476.

LEVELLAND (13,809) county seat; petroleum processing; oilfield equipment made; agribusinesses include vegetable oil mill, cattle feeding, other enterprises; cotton gins; **South Plains College;** hospital; art museum.

Other towns include **Anton** (1,180) with rabbit processing plant; **Sundown** (1,511), **Smyer** (455) and **Ropesville** (489).

Hood

LOCATION: Central (I-15).

HISTORY: Created, organized, 1866, from Johnson County; named for **Confederate Gen. John B. Hood.**

Cong. Dist. 6	U.S. Jud. Dist. . . . . N-FW
St. Sen. Dist. 22	Ct. Appeals 2
St. Rep. Dist. 64	Admin. Jud. Dist. 8
St. Dist. Cts. 355	

PHYSICAL FEATURES: Hilly; broken by Paluxy, Brazos Rivers; sandy, sandy loam soils.

RECREATION: Fishing; scenic areas; summer theater; **Lake Granbury; Acton State Park.**

MINERALS: Gas, stone, oil.

1982 Pop. 19,900	Voters reg. 13,663
Area (sq. mi.) 425	Whlsle. sales . $27,252,000
Altitude (ft.) . . . 600-1,200	Oil value 0
Ann. rainfall (in.) . 31.78	No. employed 4,263
Jan. temp. min. 34	Wages paid . . $70,823,472
July temp. max. 96	Tax value . . $817,077,960
Growing season (da.) 232	Income $280,363,000
No. farms, 1982 593	Taxable sales $76,716,281
No. acres in farms 238,234	Fed. expend. . $43,022,000
†Value per farm $307,872	Crime Index 630
Cropland harvested 21,837	TDC Pop. 39

AGRICULTURE: About $17.5 million average annual income, 60% from beef cattle; crops include peanuts, grains, pecans; 3,000 acres irrigated.

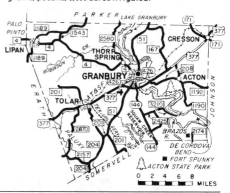

BUSINESS: Agribusinesses; tourism, gas production, county part of Dallas-Fort Worth SMSA, see metro page.

MANUFACTURING: None noted in census report.

SERVICE INDUSTRIES: 78 Establishments; Receipts, $13,409,000; Annual Payroll, $4,178,000; No. Employees, 434.

GRANBURY (3,332) county seat; nuclear power plant; agribusinesses; tourism; historic buildings; hospital, nursing homes. Other towns are **Lipan** (435), **Tolar** (415), **Cresson** and **Acton**.

Houston

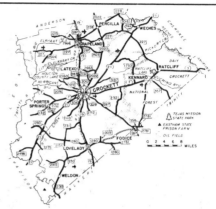

LOCATION: East (K-19).

HISTORY: Created, organized, 1837 from Nacogdoches County, by Republic of Texas; named for **Sam Houston.**

Cong. Dist. 2	U.S. Jud. Dist. . . . . E-Ty.
St. Sen. Dist. 5	Ct. Appeals 12
St. Rep. Dist. 15	Admin. Jud. Dist. 1
St. Dist. Cts. 3, 349	

PHYSICAL FEATURES: Rolling, draining to Neches, Trinity Rivers; over half forested; commercial timber production.

RECREATION: Fishing, hunting; **Davy Crockett National Forest; Tejas Mission State Park;** 75 historical markers; **Houston County Lake;** many local events.

MINERALS: Production of oil, gas, sand and gravel.

1982 Pop.	23,700	Voters reg.	12,180
Area (sq. mi.)	1,234	Whlsle. sales .	$41,295,000
Altitude (ft.)	200-500	Oil value	$20,622,204
Ann. rainfall (in.) .	41.72	No. employed . . .	9,580
Jan. temp. min.	38	Wages paid . .	$204,672,804
July temp. max.	95	Tax value . .	$947,778,297
Growing season (da.)	265	Income . . .	$170,546,000
No. farms, 1982 . . .	1,387	Taxable sales	$54,403,049
No. acres in farms	450,995	Fed. expend..	$44,215,000
†Value per farm	$303,771	Crime Index	533
Cropland harvested	45,497	TDC Pop.	27

AGRICULTURE: About $40 million average annual income, 80% from cattle, poultry; crops include cotton, peanuts, coastal hay; also timber sales.

BUSINESS: Economy based on livestock, timber, manufacturing, tourism.

MANUFACTURING: 41 Plants; 1,200 Employees; Payroll, $20,300,000; Product Value, $135,900,000.

SERVICE INDUSTRIES: 79 Establishments; Receipts, $16,261,000; Annual Payroll, $5,147,000; No. Employees, 568.

CROCKETT (7,405) county seat; plants make concrete, wood products, steel joists, plastics, woodworks, furniture, clothing, mobile homes, process foods; hospitals, nursing homes; **Crockett State School and Wilderness Program;** 5th oldest Texas town; many historic sites. **Grapeland** (1,634), **Kennard** (424), **Latexo** (312), **Lovelady** (509) other principal towns.

Hopkins

LOCATION: Northeast (G-19).

HISTORY: Created, organized, 1846, from Lamar,

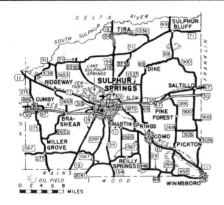

1982 Pop. 26,300
Area (sq. mi.) 789
Altitude (ft.) 350-650
Ann. rainfall (in.) . 45.29
Jan. temp. min. 34
July temp. max. 94
Growing season (da.) 238
No. farms, 1982 . . . 1,673
No. acres in farms 355,622
†Value per farm $248,128
Cropland harvested 60,254

Voters reg. 13,735
Whlsle. sales $258,824,000
Oil value $30,624,434
No. employed 8,177
Wages paid . $114,695,828
Tax value . $1,116,652,759
Income $218,032,000
Taxable sales $88,126,539
Fed. expend. . $50,457,000
Crime Index 1,019
TDC Pop. 60

AGRICULTURE: Leading dairy county in Texas and U.S.; about 490 Grade A dairies; also leader in beef cattle production; 95% of $139 million average annual farm income from cattle, hogs; hay, grains, soybeans leading crops; timber.

BUSINESS: Dairies, large milk processing plants; agribusinesses; varied manufacturing.

MANUFACTURING: 31 Plants; 2,300 Employees; Payroll, $37,000,000; Product Value, $293,700,000.

SERVICE INDUSTRIES: 103 Establishments; Receipts, $15,807,000; Annual Payroll, $5,241,000; No. Employees, 594.

SULPHUR SPRINGS (12,804) county seat; milk plants; factories make candy, clothing, brick, valves, paints, plastics, motor homes, other products; trading center; hospital, nursing homes; heritage museum. Other towns are **Como** (554), **Cumby** (647) and **Tira** (249).

Nacogdoches Counties; named for pioneer settlers, **David Hopkins Family.**

Cong. Dist. 1
St. Sen. Dist. 1
St. Rep. Dist. 2
St. Dist. Cts. 8, 62

U.S. Jud. Dist. . . . . E-Ps.
Ct. Appeals 6, 12
Admin. Jud. Dist. 1

PHYSICAL FEATURES: Drains northward to S. Sulphur River; light, sandy to heavier black soils; varied timber, including pines.

RECREATION: Fishing, hunting; **Sulphur Springs Lake** activities; museum; indoor rodeo, dairy festival.

MINERALS: Production of oil, gas and lignite.

Howard

LOCATION: West (I-9).

HISTORY: Named for **V. E. Howard**, Texas legislator; created, 1876, from Bexar, Young Districts; organized, 1882.

Cong. Dist. 17
St. Sen. Dist. 28
St. Rep. Dist. 69
St. Dist. Cts. 118

U.S. Jud. Dist. . . . . N-Ab.
Ct. Appeals 11
Admin. Jud. Dist. 7

PHYSICAL FEATURES: On southern edge Llano Estacado; sandy, sandy loam soils.

RECREATION: Big Spring State Park; campground in **Comanche Trail Park;** several small parks; **Moss Creek Lake;** various other area lakes; museum; historical sites; county fair.

MINERALS: Production of oil, gas, sand, gravel and stone.

1982 Pop. 36,500	Voters reg. 17,229
Area (sq. mi.) 901	Whlsle. sales $119,974,000
Altitude (ft.) . 2,200-2,700	Oil value . . . $337,166,210
Ann. rainfall (in.) . 15.88	No. employed . . . 11,340
Jan. temp. min. 30	Wages paid . $183,332,848
July temp. max. 95	Tax value . $1,744,078,361
Growing season (da.) 217	Income $308,673,000
No. farms, 1982 398	Taxable sales $165,035,633
No. acres in farms 460,561	Fed. expend. $119,739,000
†Value per farm $416,593	Crime Index 2,068
Cropland harvested 98,569	TDC Pop. 94

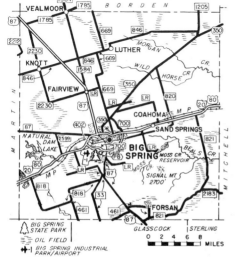

AGRICULTURE: $29.1 million average annual income, 90% from crops, principally cotton, wheat and sorghum; beef cattle; some 4,000 acres of irrigated land.

BUSINESS: Oil, gas operations; agribusinesses; varied manufacturing, including clothing.

MANUFACTURING: 33 Plants; Employees, N.A.; Payroll, N.A.; Product Value, N.A.

SERVICE INDUSTRIES: 177 Establishments; Receipts, $36,623,000; Annual Payroll, $13,120,000; No. Employees, 1,084.

BIG SPRING (24,804) county seat; plants make petrochemicals, carbon black, fiberglass pipe, plastics, teaching aids, clothing; medical center with 6 hospitals; **Howard College; school for the deaf; federal prison unit.**

Other principal towns are **Coahoma** (1,069) a farming center; **Forsan** (239).

Hudspeth

LOCATION: Far west (K-2).

HISTORY: Named for Texas political leader, **Claude B. Hudspeth;** created, organized, 1917, from El Paso County.

Cong. Dist. 16
St. Sen. Dist. 25
St. Rep. Dist. 69
St. Dist. Cts. . . 34,205,210

U.S. Jud. Dist. . . . . W-Pe.
Ct. Appeals 8
Admin. Jud. Dist. 6

PHYSICAL FEATURES: Plateau, basin terrain, draining to salt lakes, Rio Grande; mostly rocky, alkaline, clay soils, except alluvial along Rio Grande; desert, mountain vegetation.

RECREATION: Part of Guadalupe Mountains Nation-

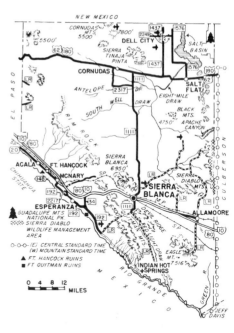

al **Park** containing unique plant life, canyons; scenic drives; fort ruins; hot springs; salt basin; white sands; hunting; many local events.

MINERALS: Talc, stone, gypsum produced.

1982 Pop. 2,900	Voters reg. 1,272
Area (sq. mi.) 4,566	Whlsle. sales . $1,529,000
Altitude (ft.) . 3,200-7,500	Oil value 0
Ann. rainfall (in.) . . . 7.86	No. employed 529
Jan. temp. min. 27	Wages paid . . . $6,928,960
July temp. max. 93	Tax value . . $297,454,910
Growing season (da.) 231	Income $14,333,000
No. farms, 1982 139	Taxable sales . $1,440,858
No. acs. in farms 2,136,639	Fed. expend. . $13,449,000
†Value per farm $1,943,698	Crime Index 19
Cropland harvested 30,486	TDC Pop. 9

AGRICULTURE: About $18 million average annual income from cotton, alfalfa, vegetables, pecans; 25,000 acres irrigated; feed lot; cattle, hogs.

BUSINESS: Agribusiness, mining, tourism, hunting leases.

MANUFACTURING: None noted in census report.

SERVICE INDUSTRIES: 7 Establishments; Receipts, $315,000; Annual Payroll, $59,000; No. Employees, 13.

SIERRA BLANCA (est. 700) county seat; ranching center; tourist stop on interstate highway; land development. **Dell City** (495) feed lots; clinic, trading center.

Hunt

LOCATION: North (G-18).

HISTORY: Named for **Memucan Hunt,** Republic of Texas Secretary of Navy; created, organized, 1846, from Fannin, Nacogdoches Counties.

Cong. Dist. 1, 4
St. Sen. Dist. 2
St. Rep. Dist. 3
St. Dist. Cts. . . 196, 354

U.S. Jud. Dist. . . . . N-Di.
Ct. Appeals 5, 6
Admin. Jud. Dist. 1

PHYSICAL FEATURES: Mostly heavy Blackland soil, some loam, sandy loams; level to rolling; Sabine, Sulphur Rivers; **Lake Tawakoni.**

RECREATION: Lake Tawakoni; **East Texas State University** events; local events; county fair.

MINERALS: Gas, oil, sand.

AGRICULTURE: $37 million average annual income, 60% from cattle, horses, dairy products; hay, cotton, sorghums, wheat, oats; some timber.

1982 Pop.	59,300	Voters reg.	31,968
Area (sq. mi.)	840	Whlsle. sales	$105,880,000
Altitude (ft.)	400-700	Oil value	$610,403
Ann. rainfall (in.)	43.08	No. employed	19,290
Jan. temp. min.	34	Wages paid	$309,243,368
July temp. max.	94	Tax value	$1,350,507,445
Growing season (da.)	237	Income	$552,536,000
No. farms, 1982	1,864	Taxable sales	$207,228,537
No. acres in farms	360,609	Fed. expend.	$381,798,000
†Value per farm	$149,273	Crime Index	3,370
Cropland harv.	113,269	TDC Pop.	93

BUSINESS: Agribusinesses, education, varied manufacturing; many residents employed in Dallas metro area.

MANUFACTURING: 71 Plants; 7,200 Employees; Payroll, $137,700,000; Product Value, $536,100,000.

SERVICE INDUSTRIES: 236 Establishments; Receipts, $38,491,000; Annual Payroll, $13,702,000; No. Employees, 1,266.

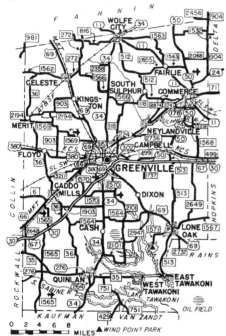

GREENVILLE (22,161) county seat; plants process foods, make electronic parts, clothing, plastics, drill bits, aircraft modification; hospital, nursing homes.

Commerce (8,136) East Texas State University major economic factor; plants make wood products, mobile homes, medical products; hospital, nursing homes. Other towns include **Caddo Mills** (1,060), **Campbell**(549), **Celeste** (716), **Lone Oak** (467), **Neylandville** (168), **Quinlan** (1,002), **West Tawakoni** (840), and **Wolfe City** (1,594), cottonseed milling, printing, sweaters and cheerleading supplies.

Hutchinson

LOCATION: North Panhandle (B-9).

HISTORY: Created, 1876, from Bexar Territory; organized 1901; named for pioneer jurist, **Anderson Hutchinson.**

Cong. Dist.	13	U.S. Jud. Dist.	N-Am.
St. Sen. Dist.	31	Ct. Appeals	7
St. Rep. Dist.	88	Admin. Jud. Dist.	9
St. Dist. Cts.	84, 316		

PHYSICAL FEATURES: Plain, broken by Canadian River and tributaries, **Lake Meredith;** many fertile valleys along streams.

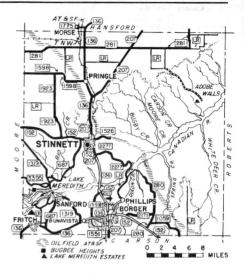

RECREATION: Lake **Meredith** activities; fishing, camping, boating; **Alibates Flint Quarries** (in nearby Potter County); **Adobe Walls,** historic Indian battle site, "world's largest" fish fry in June.

MINERALS: Production of gas, oil, salt, sand and gravel.

1982 Pop.	29,200	Voters reg.	15,301
Area (sq. mi.)	871	Whlsle. sales	$267,499,000
Altitude (ft.)	2,750-3,400	Oil value	$73,620,820
Ann. rainfall (in.)	19.91	No. employed	10,998
Jan. temp. min.	22	Wages paid	$253,797,168
July temp. max.	93	Tax value	$1,703,594,456
Growing season (da.)	187	Income	$318,833,000
No. farms, 1982	157	Taxable sales	$115,686,608
No. acres in farms	471,424	Fed. expend.	$51,663,000
†Value per farm	$734,331	Crime Index	820
Cropland harv.	60,335	TDC Pop.	50

AGRICULTURE: About $15 million average annual income from wheat, corn, alfalfa, sorghums; beef cattle, hogs, poultry; over 40,000 acres irrigated.

BUSINESS: Oil, gas, petrochemicals; agribusiness; varied manufacturing; tourism.

MANUFACTURING: 33 Plants; N.A. Employees; Payroll, N.A.; Product Value, N.A.

SERVICE INDUSTRIES: 126 Establishments; Receipts, $45,042,000; Annual Payroll, $16,285,000; No. Employees, 1,099.

STINNETT (2,222) county seat; petroleum, gas refining, farm center; drilling rig manufacturing; rubber production. **Borger** (15,837) petroleum operating center; petrochemical plants; varied manufacturing, tourism; machine, welding shops, petroleum show; **Frank Phillips College;** hospital, nursing homes.

Other towns are **Bunavista, Fritch** (2,299 part Moore), **Phillips** and **Sanford** (249).

Irion

LOCATION: Southwest (K-10).

HISTORY: Named for Republic of Texas leader, **R. A. Irion;** created, organized, 1889, from Tom Green County.

Cong. Dist.	21	U.S. Jud. Dist.	N-SAng.
St. Sen. Dist.	25	Ct. Appeals	3
St. Rep. Dist.	67	Admin. Jud. Dist.	7
St. Dist. Cts.	51		

PHYSICAL FEATURES: Hilly, broken by Middle Concho, tributaries; clay, sandy soils.

RECREATION: Hunting; historic sites; old Sherwood courthouse established in 1860; county fair, horse show.

MINERALS: Production of oil, gas.

AGRICULTURE: About $7.5 million annual average income, about 90% from cattle, sheep, goats; crops include pecans, sorghums, small grains, cotton.

Irion County (Cont'd.)

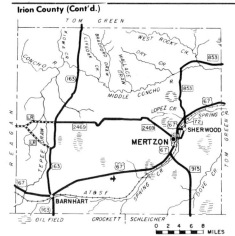

1982 Pop.	1,600	Voters reg.	1,009
Area (sq. mi.)	1,052	Whlsle. sales	$9,555,000
Altitude (ft.)	2,000-2,800	Oil value	$97,167,565
Ann. rainfall (in.)	21.33	No. employed	407
Jan. temp. min.	32	Wages paid	$8,062,880
July temp. max.	96	Tax value	$391,249,737
Growing season (da.)	232	Income	$11,751,000
No. farms, 1982	127	Taxable sales	$7,150,804
No. acres in farms	792,872	Fed. expend.	$2,944,000
†Value per farm	$1,237,153	Crime Index	0
Cropland harvested	1,265	TDC Pop.	2

BUSINESS: Ranching; oil, gas production.
MANUFACTURING: None nonted in census report.
SERVICE INDUSTRIES: 1 Establishment; Receipts, N.A.; Annual Payroll, N.A.; No. Employees, N.A.
MERTZON (687) county seat; ranching and wool warehouse center.

Jack

LOCATION: North (G-14).
HISTORY: Named for brothers, **P.C.** and **W. H. Jack,** leaders in Texas' independence effort; created 1856, from Cooke County; organized, 1857.

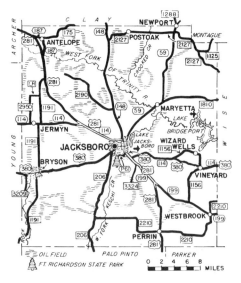

Cong. Dist.	17	U.S. Jud. Dist.	N-FW
St. Sen. Dist.	30	Ct. Appeals	2
St. Rep. Dist.	80	Admin. Jud. Dist.	8
St. Dist. Cts.	271		

PHYSICAL FEATURES: Rolling, broken by West Fork of the Trinity, other streams; sandy, dark brown, loam soils; **Lake Bridgeport; Lake Jacksboro.**
RECREATION: Lake activities; **Fort Richardson State Park,** other historic sites; rattlesnake hunt, rodeo, golf tournaments.
MINERALS: Production of oil, gas, stone.

1982 Pop.	7,800	Voters reg.	4,383
Area (sq. mi.)	920	Whlsle. sales	$56,748,000
Altitude (ft.)	800-1,350	Oil value	$98,132,957
Ann. rainfall (in.)	29.78	No. employed	2,036
Jan. temp. min.	32	Wages paid	$34,600,480
July temp. max.	97	Tax value	$838,815,740
Growing season (da.)	218	Income	$68,102,000
No. farms, 1982	644	Taxable sales	$32,220,884
No. acres in farms	508,649	Fed. expend.	$15,519,000
†Value per farm	$316,852	Crime Index	151
Cropland harvested	13,160	TDC Pop.	17

AGRICULTURE: About $12 million average annual income, over 90% from beef cattle, horses; crops include wheat, oats, hay; firewood.
BUSINESS: Economy based on petroleum production, oil field services, livestock, manufacturing, tourism and recreation.
MANUFACTURING: None noted in census report.
SERVICE INDUSTRIES: 30 Establishments; Receipts, $4,309,000; Annual Payroll, $1,287,000; No. Employees, 151.
JACKSBORO (4,000) county seat; agribusinesses; plants make garments; oil well servicing, supplies; hospital, nursing home.
Bryson (579) other leading town.

Jackson

LOCATION: On coast (O-18).
HISTORY: Mexican municipality, created 1835, became original county next year; named for **U.S. President Andrew Jackson.**

Cong. Dist.	14	U.S. Jud. Dist.	S-Va.
St. Sen. Dist.	18	Ct. Appeals	13
St. Rep. Dist.	31	Admin. Jud. Dist.	4
St. Dist. Cts.	24, 135, 267		

PHYSICAL FEATURES: Loam, clay, black soils; drains to creek, rivers, bays; prairie and motts of trees.
RECREATION: Hunting, fishing; historic sites; Texana Museum; Lake Texana activities; county fair.
MINERALS: Production of oil, gas.
AGRICULTURE: $43 million average annual income, 85% from rice, sorghums, corn, cotton, other crops; a leading rice county; 32,000 acres irrigated for rice; beef cattle.

1982 Pop.	13,700	Voters reg.	7,836
Area (sq. mi.)	844	Whlsle. sales	$95,510,000
Altitude (ft.) sea level	-150	Oil value	$138,756,728
Ann. rainfall (in.)	39.65	No. employed	3,192
Jan. temp. min.	42	Wages paid	$46,551,568
July temp. max.	94	Tax value	$1,260,018,939
Growing season (da.)	290	Income	$117,010,000
No. farms, 1982	801	Taxable sales	$33,175,764
No. acres in farms	443,346	Fed. expend.	$46,950,000
†Value per farm	$565,266	Crime Index	171
Cropland harv.	146,935	TDC Pop.	55

BUSINESS: Petroleum production and operation; metal fabrication and tooling, sheet metal works, other manufacturing; agribusinesses; lake recreation.

MANUFACTURING: None noted in census report.

SERVICE INDUSTRIES: 65 Establishments; Receipts, $11,299,000; Annual Payroll, $3,834,000; No. Employees, 400.

EDNA (5,650) county seat; oil industry and agribusiness center; hospitals, nursing homes. **Ganado** (1,770) and **La Ward** (218) are other principal towns.

Jasper

LOCATION: Southeast (L-22).

HISTORY: Created, 1836, organized, 1837, from Mexican municipality; named for **Sgt. William Jasper** of U.S. Revolution.

1982 Pop.	31,200	Voters reg.	18,972
Area (sq. mi.)	921	Whlsle. sales	$53,209,000
Altitude (ft.)	30-200	Oil value	$25,739,144
Ann. rainfall (in.)	51.03	No. employed	8,541
Jan. temp. min.	40	Wages paid	$134,285,608
July temp. max.	93	Tax value	$1,269,840,811
Growing season (da.)	229	Income	$274,419,000
No. farms, 1982	659	Taxable sales	$156,288,774
No. acres in farms	76,097	Fed. expend.	$49,647,000
†Value per farm	$151,593	Crime Index	687
Cropland harvested	7,731	TDC Pop.	44

BUSINESS: Economy based on timber industries, oil, tourism, fishing, agriculture.

Jeff Davis

LOCATION: Southwest (I-5).

HISTORY: Named for **Jefferson Davis**, U.S. War Secretary, Confederate president; created, organized, 1887, from Presidio County.

PHYSICAL FEATURES: Highest average elevation in Texas, one mile or higher; peaks, canyons, plateaus; intermountain wash, clay, loam soils; cedars, oaks in highlands.

Cong. Dist.	2	U.S. Jud. Dist.	E-Bt.
St. Sen. Dist.	3	Ct. Appeals	9
St. Rep. Dist.	20	Admin. Jud. Dist.	2
St. Dist. Cts.	1, 1A		

PHYSICAL FEATURES: Angelina and Sabine National Forests; Sam Rayburn, Steinhagen Lakes; Neches River.

RECREATION: Lake activities; hunting; **Martin Dies State Park;** azalea trail in spring; rodeo.

MINERALS: Oil, gas produced.

AGRICULTURE: $25 million average annual income, about 90% from cattle, hogs, poultry, horses; crops include vegetables, fruit, pecans, 87% of area forested, timber is major income producer with annual sale of $13 million.

MANUFACTURING: 42 Plants; 2,600 Employees; Payroll, $57,000,000; Product Value, $400,800,000.

SERVICE INDUSTRIES: 118 Establishments; Receipts, $20,396,000; Annual Payroll, $5,402,000; No. Employees, 485.

JASPER (6,959) county seat; wood industries; plywood mill, sawmills, poultry processing plants, feed mills.

Other towns include **Buna, Browndell** (228), **Kirbyville** (1,972).

MINERALS: Not significant.

AGRICULTURE: Large ranches make this a leading county for range production of cattle, with an annual value of about $8.2 million; hunting leases significant; wine grapes, feed grains, alfalfa; about 3,000 acres irrigated.

BUSINESS: Ranching, tourism.

MANUFACTURING: None noted in census report.

Cong. Dist.	16	St. Dist. Cts.	83
St. Sen. Dist.	25	U.S. Jud. Dist.	W-Pe.
St. Rep. Dist.	69	Ct. Appeals	8
		Admin. Jud. Dist.	6

1982 Pop.	1,600
Area (sq. mi.)	2,258
Altitude (ft.)	3,800-5,200
Ann. rainfall (in.)	18.74
Jan. temp. min.	31
July temp. max.	82
Growing season (da.)	209
No. farms, 1982	78
No. acs. in farms	1,621,940
†Value per farm	$2,471,333
Cropland harvested.	N.A.
Voters reg.	1,130
Whlsle. sales	$0
Oil value	$0
No. employed	387
Wages paid	$5,099,768
Tax value	$140,437,177
Income	$11,397,000
Taxable sales	$2,596,356
Fed. expend.	$4,670,000
Crime Index	0
TDC Pop.	0

RECREATION: Scenic drives; hunting; **Fort Davis** National Historic site; **Davis Mountains State Park; McDonald Observatory; Harvard Radio Astronomy Station; Prude Ranch** summer camp.

SERVICE INDUSTRIES: 5 Establishments; Receipts, $1,190,000; Annual Payroll, $196,000; No. Employees, 27.

FORT DAVIS (est. 900) county seat; trade, scenic tourist center. **Valentine** (328) other town.

Jefferson

LOCATION: Southeast (M-22).

HISTORY: Created, 1836, from Mexican municipality; organized, 1837; named for **U.S. President Thomas Jefferson.**

Cong. Dist. 9	U.S. Jud. Dist. . . . . E-Bt.	
St. Sen. Dist. 4	Ct. Appeals 9	
St. Rep. Dist. 20-23	Admin. Jud. Dist. 2	
St. Dist. Cts. . . 58, 60, 136,		
172, 252, 279, 317, Cr. 1		

PHYSICAL FEATURES: Grassy plain, with timber in northwest; beach sands, sandy loams, black clay soils; drains to Neches River, Gulf of Mexico.

MINERALS: Large producer of oil, gas, sulphur, salt, sand and gravel; **Spindletop,** first major Texas oil field; large petrochemical industry.

RECREATION: Beaches, fresh and saltwater fishing; duck, goose hunting; water activities; **Dick Dowling Monument and Park; Spindletop** site and boom town restoration; museum; saltwater lake; **Murphree Wildlife Refuge; Lamar University;** other events; historic sites; CavOILcade at Port Arthur, South Texas Fair, "Tall Ships" Sesquicentennial event, many festivals; **"Tex" Ritter** memorial and park at Nederland, also Dutch and French museums.

1982 Pop. 257,400	Voters reg. 145,290
Area (sq. mi.) 937	Whlsle. sales $2,494,072,000
Altitude (ft.) sea level-50	Oil value $85,011,515
Ann. rainfall (in.) . 55.07	No. employed . . . 107,432
Jan. temp. min. 44	Wages paid $2,215,827,068
July temp. max. 91	Tax value $10,946,902,738
Growing season (da.) 250	Income . . . $2,737,280,000
No. farms, 1982 502	Taxable sls. $1,310,545,536
No. acres in farms 368,391	Fed. expd.. $1,806,886,000
†Value per farm $623,195	Crime Index 14,379
Cropland harvested 73,167	TDC Pop. 1,041

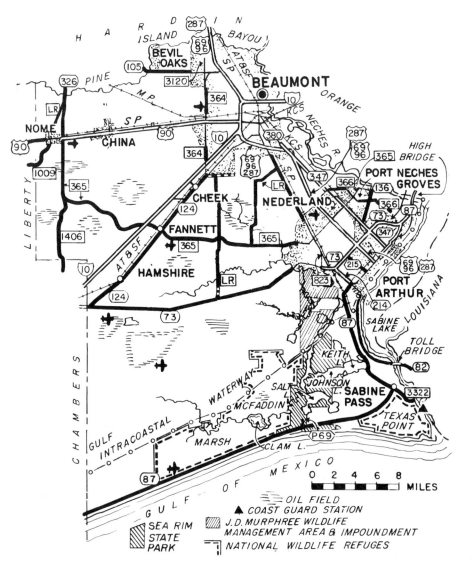

AGRICULTURE: About $25 million average income, over 80% from crops, chiefly rice and soybeans; beef cattle; 38,000 acres irrigated, mostly rice; timber.

BUSINESS: Petrochemicals, other chemical plants; shipbuilding; steel mill; port activity; oil field supplies dominate economy.

MANUFACTURING: 235 Plants; 27,100 Employees; Payroll, $729,100,000; Product Value, $17,438,500,000.

SERVICE INDUSTRIES: 1,570 Establishments; Receipts, $521,484,000; Annual Payroll, $192,622,000; No. Employees, 12,785.

BEAUMONT (118,102) county seat; see also metro page; varied chemical, petrochemical plants; oil refinery; shipbuilding; extensive port activities; rice milling center; steel mill; **Lamar University;** many hospitals, nursing homes; South Texas State Fair.

Port Arthur (61,251) center for oil, chemical activities; shipping, drydock; food processing; rice milling; tourism; **Lamar University** branch.

Nederland (16,855) oil and chemical plants; hospital. **Groves** (17,090) oil and chemical industry, engine service; hospital; library; tourism. Other towns include **Bevil Oaks** (1,306), **China** (1,351), **Griffing Park** (consolidated with Port Arthur in 1983), **Nome** (550), **Port Neches** (13,944) and **Sabine Pass.**

Jim Hogg

LOCATION: South (S-14).

HISTORY: Named for **Texas Gov. James Stephen Hogg;** created, organized, 1913, from Brooks, Duval Counties.

Cong. Dist.	15	U.S. Jud. Dist.	S-La.
St. Sen. Dist.	21	Ct. Appeals	4
St. Rep. Dist.	44	Admin. Jud. Dist.	4
St. Dist. Cts.	229		

PHYSICAL FEATURES: Rolling plain, with heavy brush cover; white blow soil and sandy loam; parts hilly, broken.

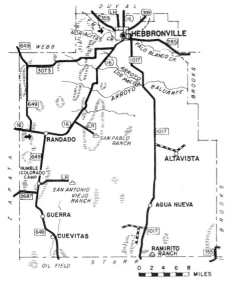

1982 Pop.	5,500	Voters reg.	3,999
Area (sq. mi.)	1,136	Whlsle. sales	$*
Altitude (ft.)	300-800	Oil value	$15,047,567
Ann. rainfall (in.)	20.78	No. employed	1,289
Jan. temp. min.	47	Wages paid	$14,691,712
July temp. max.	99	Tax value	$407,693,494
Growing season (da.)	303	Income	$32,755,000
No. farms, 1982	206	Taxable sales	$16,266,972
No. acres in farms	849,098	Fed. expend.	$8,175,000
†Value per farm	$924,063	Crime Index	49
Cropland harvested	5,083	TDC Pop.	5

RECREATION: Center of whitetail deer and bobwhite quail hunting; local events.

MINERALS: Oil, gas.

AGRICULTURE: More than $15 million average annual income, 80% from cattle ranching; sorghum principal crop; 2,000 acres irrigated.

BUSINESS: Oil, cattle operations.

MANUFACTURING: None noted in census report.

SERVICE INDUSTRIES: 19 Establishments; Receipts, $3,199,000; Annual Payroll, $849,000; No. Employees, 85.

HEBBRONVILLE (est. 4,050) county seat; center for ranching, oil field activities.

Jim Wells

LOCATION: South (R-5).

Cong. Dist.	15
St. Sen. Dist.	20
St. Rep. Dist.	44
St. Dist. Cts.	79
U.S. Jud. Dist.	S-CC
Ct. Appeals	4
Admin. Jud. Dist.	5

HISTORY: Created, 1911, from Nueces County; organized 1912; named for developer, J. B. Wells Jr.

PHYSICAL FEATURES: Level to rolling; sandy to dark soils; grassy, mesquite brush.

RECREATION: Hunting; fiestas, other local events, wildflower tour at Premont in March; oil and gas exposition in April.

MINERALS: Production of oil, gas, caliche.

1982 Pop.	38,200		
Area (sq. mi.)	867		
Altitude (ft.)	100-400		
Ann. rainfall (in.)	27.04		
Jan. temp. min.	47	Oil value	$15,524,271
July temp. max.	97	No. employed	11,538
Growing season (da.)	289	Wages paid	$178,196,664
No. farms, 1982	785	Tax value	$1,424,479,451
No. acres in farms	461,689	Income	$252,706,000
†Value per farm	$425,530	Taxable sales	$182,595,299
Cropland harv.	129,276	Fed. expend.	$64,477,000
Voters reg.	22,498	Crime Index	1,640
Whlsle. sales	$241,962,000	TDC Pop.	72

AGRICULTURE: About $33 million average annual income from beef, dairy cattle, hogs, poultry; cotton, sorghums, wheat, corn, vegetables, watermelons; estimated 9,000 acres irrigated.

BUSINESS: Oil, gas production, cotton and cattle dominate economy.

MANUFACTURING: None noted in census report.

SERVICE INDUSTRIES: 207 Establishments; Receipts, $110,904,000; Annual Payroll, $27,180,000; No. Employees, 1,920.

ALICE (20,961) county seat; oil field servicing center; agribusinesses; hospital, nursing home; Fiesta Bandana; **Bee County Junior College** branch.

Other towns include **Alice Southwest, Orange Grove** (1,212), **Premont** (2,984) hunting center, watermelon shipping, petroleum recycling plant; **San Diego** (5,225, part Duval).

Johnson

LOCATION: North (I-16).

HISTORY: Named for **Col. M. T. Johnson** of Mexican War, Confederacy; created, organized, 1854, out of Ellis, Hill, Navarro Counties.

Cong. Dist.	6	U.S. Jud. Dist.	N-DI.
St. Sen. Dist.	22	Ct. Appeals	10
St. Rep. Dist.	58	Admin. Jud. Dist.	3
St. Dist. Cts.	18, 249		

PHYSICAL FEATURES: Hilly, rolling, many soil types; Brazos, Trinity Rivers; **Lake Pat Cleburne.**

RECREATION: Excellent bird, deer hunting; water activities on **Lake Pat Cleburne, Lake Whitney** and at **Cleburne State Recreation Area;** museum; local events.

MINERALS: Lime, stone, sand, gravel.

1982 Pop.	73,200	Voters reg.	38,959
Area (sq. mi.)	731	Whlsle. sales	$133,404,000
Altitude (ft.)	600-1,000	Oil value	0
Ann. rainfall (in.)	33.04	No. employed	16,576
Jan. temp. min.	35	Wages paid	$226,699,796
July temp. max.	96	Tax value	$1,654,199,918
Growing season (da.)	233	Income	$766,335,000
No. farms, 1982	1,798	Taxable sales	$230,461,862
No. acres in farms	322,150	Fed. expend.	$135,084,000
†Value per farm	$215,991	Crime Index	2,556
Cropland harvested	84,262	TDC Pop.	103

AGRICULTURE: A leading dairy county; 85% of an estimated $52 million annual income from cattle, horses, hogs and dairy products; crops include sorghums, cotton, peanuts, oats, wheat, hay, corn, truck crops, horticultural crops.

BUSINESS: Agribusinesses; railroad shops; manufacturing; distribution; lake activities; employment in Fort Worth and other parts of its metro area (see metro page).

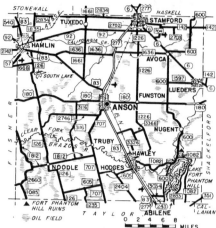

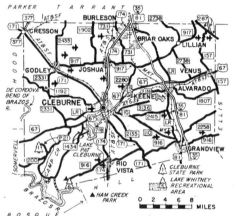

MANUFACTURING: 124 Plants; 4,000 Employees; Payroll, $57,700,000; Product Value, $312,800,000.

SERVICE INDUSTRIES: 261 Establishments; Receipts, $46,567,000; Annual Payroll, $15,555,000; No. Employees, 1,568.

CLEBURNE (19,218) county seat; dairy center; rail shipping terminal; railroad shops; varied manufacturing including wall components, detention hardware, pre-fab siding and trusses; agribusinesses; hospital.

Burleson (11,734, part Tarrant), plants make feed mixers, mobile homes, other products. Other towns include **Alvarado** (2,701), **Briaroaks** (592), **Godley** (614), **Grandview** (1,205), **Joshua** (1,470), **Keene** (3,013), **Mansfield** (8,102 mostly Tarrant), **Rio Vista** (509) and **Venus** (518).

Jones

LOCATION: West Central (H-12).

HISTORY: Named for last Republic of Texas president, **Anson Jones;** created 1858, from Bexar, Bosque Counties; re-created, 1876; organized, 1881.

Cong. Dist.	17	U.S. Jud. Dist.	N-Ab.
St. Sen. Dist.	30	Ct. Appeals	11
St. Rep. Dist.	78	Admin. Jud. Dist.	7
St. Dist. Cts.	259		

PHYSICAL FEATURES: Level to rolling prairie; drained by Brazos River fork, tributaries; **Lake Stamford.**

RECREATION: Lake activities; **Ft. Phantom Hill** site; **Cowboys Christmas Ball; Cowboy Reunion** July 4th weekend; old courthouse, art show.

MINERALS: Oil, gas, sand and gravel, stone.

1982 Pop.	17,600	Voters reg.	9,940
Area (sq. mi.)	931	Whlsle. sales	$51,783,000
Altitude (ft.)	1,600-2,000	Oil value	$78,471,546
Ann. rainfall (in.)	23.37	No. employed	4,008
Jan. temp. min.	30	Wages paid	$57,220,608
July temp. max.	97	Tax value	$623,407,134
Growing season (da.)	223	Income	$135,140,000
No. farms, 1982	948	Taxable sales	$55,374,059
No. acres in farms	533,875	Fed. expend.	$80,199,000
†Value per farm	$284,757	Crime Index	278
Cropland harv.	216,587	TDC Pop.	25

AGRICULTURE: $36 million annual income, 75% from cotton, wheat, milo; beef cattle, hogs, horses, sheep.

BUSINESS: Agribusinesses; clothing manufacturing; plants make a variety of products.

MANUFACTURING: None nonted in census report.

SERVICE INDUSTRIES: 67 Establishments; Receipts, $10,293,000; Annual Payroll, $3,743,000; No. Employees, 460.

ANSON (2,831) county seat; farming center, trailer manufacturing, apparel factory; hospital, rest home.

Stamford (4,542 part Haskell), agribusinesses; apparel manufacturing, cotton gin and compress; hospital, mental health center, rest homes. **Hamlin** (3,248, part in Fisher), farming center; varied manufacturing. Other towns include **Hawley** (679), **Lueders** (420) limestone quarry. Also includes part of **Abilene.**

Karnes

LOCATION: South (O-15).

HISTORY: Created, organized, 1854, from Bexar, Goliad, San Patricio Counties; named for Texas Revolutionary figure, **Henry W. Karnes.**

Cong. Dist.	15	U.S. Jud. Dist.	W-SAnt.
St. Sen. Dist.	18	Ct. Appeals	4
St. Rep. Dist.	33	Admin. Jud. Dist.	4
St. Dist. Cts.	81, 218		

PHYSICAL FEATURES: Sandy loam, dark clay, alluvial soils in rolling terrain, traversed by San Antonio River; mesquite, oak trees.

RECREATION: Historic sites include **Old Helena; Panna Maria,** Texas' oldest Polish settlement; bird hunting; local events, golf course and tennis courts; Bluebonnet Days at Kenedy in April; restored courthouse and museum at Helena.

1982 Pop.	13,700	Voters reg.	7,379
Area (sq. mi.)	753	Whlsle. sales	$85,936,000
Altitude (ft.)	180,500	Oil value	$11,175,273
Ann. rainfall (in.)	31.93	No. employed	3,850
Jan. temp. min.	44	Wages paid	$56,823,844
July temp. max.	96	Tax value	$580,810,551
Growing season (da.)	281	Income	$107,290,000
No. farms, 1982	1,075	Taxable sales	$36,194,812
No. acres in farms	420,688	Fed. expend.	$27,423,000
†Value per farm	$252,515	Crime Index	75
Cropland harvested	64,216	TDC Pop.	34

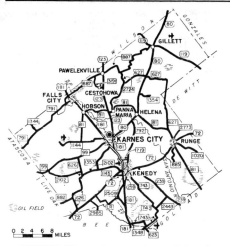

MINERALS: Oil, gas, stone; **uranium producing plant** at Falls City.

AGRICULTURE: $35 million average income, 80% from beef, dairy cattle, hogs; crops include sorghums, wheat, oats, corn, flax.

BUSINESS: Agribusiness, mineral production, tourism; varied manufacturing.

MANUFACTURING: None noted in census report.

SERVICE INDUSTRIES: 59 Establishments; Receipts, $7,320,000; Annual Payroll, $2,348,000; No. Employees, 264.

KARNES CITY (3,296) county seat; farm-trading, processing center; oil producing and servicing; plants make furniture, fiberglass products; barbed wire, farm, oil field equipment, other products; uranium ore processing; hospitals, nursing homes, library.

Kenedy (4,356), livestock sales, food processing, other agribusinesses; varied manufacturing; hunting center; rest homes, library.

Other towns include **Runge** (1,244), **Falls City** (580).

Kendall

LOCATION: South central (M-14).

HISTORY: Created, organized from Blanco, Kerr Counties, 1862; named for pioneer journalist-sheepman, contributor to Texas Almanac, **George W. Kendall.**

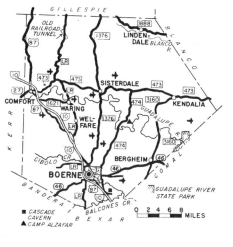

Cong. Dist.	21	U.S. Jud. Dist.	W.-SAnt.
St. Sen. Dist.	25	Ct. Appeals	4
St. Rep. Dist.	46	Admin. Jud. Dist.	6
St. Dist. Cts.	216		

PHYSICAL FEATURES: Hilly, plateau, with springfed streams, caves, scenic drives.

RECREATION: Hunting, fishing, Guadalupe River; tourist center; **Cascade Caverns;** historic sites; festival, other local celebrations.

MINERALS: Natural gas discovered.

1982 Pop.	11,800	Voters reg.	7,124
Area (sq. mi.)	663	Whlsle. sales	$26,852,000
Altitude (ft.)	1,000-2,000	Oil value	0
Ann. rainfall (in.)	30.39	No. employed	2,880
Jan. temp. min.	38	Wages paid	$32,783,168
July temp. max.	94	Tax value	$661,224,518
Growing season (da.)	231	Income	$115,532,000
No. farms, 1982	586	Taxable sales	$38,914,520
No. acres in farms 347,388		Fed. expend.	$30,219,000
†Value per farm $553,420		Crime Index	242
Cropland harvested 10,477		TDC Pop.	13

AGRICULTURE: More than $10 million average income, 90% from cattle, sheep, Angora goats, horses; some sorghums, wheat, oats.

BUSINESS: Agribusinesses, some manufacturing.

MANUFACTURING: None noted in census report.

SERVICE INDUSTRIES: 61 Establishments; Receipts, $12,480,000; Annual Payroll, $4,699,000; No. Employees, 462.

BOERNE (3,229) county seat; livestock, tourism, varied manufacturing; nursing homes. **Comfort** has "True to the Union" Civil War monument; hospital. **Sisterdale** is other principal town.

Kaufman

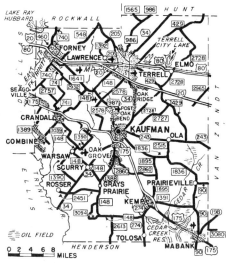

LOCATION: North (H-18).

HISTORY: Created from Henderson County and organized, 1848; named for member of Texas and U.S. Congresses, **D. S. Kaufman.**

Cong. Dist.	4	U.S. Jud. Dist.	N-Dl.
St. Sen. Dist.	2	Ct. Appeals	5, 12
St. Rep. Dist.	4	Admin. Jud. Dist.	1
St. Dist. Cts.	86		

1982 Pop.	42,300	Voters reg.	22,909
Area (sq. mi.)	788	Whlsle. sales	$112,458,000
Altitude (ft.)	300-550	Oil value	$6,002,526
Ann. rainfall (in.)	39.82	No. employed	11,846
Jan. temp. min.	35	Wages paid	$165,197,468
July temp. max.	95	Tax value	$1,108,440,075
Growing season (da.)	248	Income	$379,083,000
No. farms, 1982	1,505	Taxable sales	$157,611,820
No. acres in farms 391,886		Fed. expend.	$94,742,000
†Value per farm $238,866		Crime Index	1,477
Cropland harvested 68,924		TDC Pop.	112

PHYSICAL FEATURES: Largely Blackland prairie, draining to Trinity River, Cedar Creek and Lake.

RECREATION: Activities at **Cedar Creek** and **Ray Hubbard Lakes; Porter Farm** near Terrell is historic site of origin of **U.S.-Texas Agricultural Extension program;** historical homes at Terrell.

MINERALS: Oil, stone, gas.

AGRICULTURE: $45 million average annual income, 80% from cattle, hogs, poultry, horses, crawfish; crops include cotton, grain, hay, oats, wheat.

BUSINESS: Varied manufacturing; trade center; part of Dallas metro area.

MANUFACTURING: 72 Plants; 2,500 Employees; Payroll, $35,300,000; Product Value, $212,400,000.

SERVICE INDUSTRIES: 153 Establishments; Receipts, $23,028,000; Annual Payroll, $8,123,000; No. Employees, 964.

KAUFMAN (4,658) county seat; plants make steel products, furniture, clothing, other products.

Terrell (13,269), agribusinesses; plants make athletic uniforms, dresses, plastic goods, school supplies, machine parts, other products; **Terrell State Hospital; Southwestern Christian College.**

Other towns include **Forney** (2,483), **Mabank** (1,443), **Kemp** (1,035), **Combine** (688, partly Dallas County), **Crandall** (831), **Heath** (1,459, mostly Rockwall County), **Oak Grove** (319), **Oak Ridge** (183), **Post Oak Bend** (266), and **Grays Prairie** (171).

Kenedy

LOCATION: Southern, coastal (S-16).

HISTORY: Among last counties created, organized, 1921, from Cameron, Hidalgo, Willacy; named for pioneer ranchman, **Capt. Mifflin Kenedy.**

Cong. Dist. 27	U.S. Jud. Dist. . . . . S-CC
St. Sen. Dist. 20	Ct. Appeals 13
St. Rep. Dist. 37	Admin. Jud. Dist. 5
St. Dist. Cts. 28, 105	

PHYSICAL FEATURES: Typical coastal flat, sandy terrain, some loam soils; motts of live oaks.

MINERALS: Oil, gas.

1982 Pop. 500	Voters reg. 329
Area (sq. mi.) 1,389	Whlsle. sales . . . . . . $*
Altitude (ft.) sea level-100	Oil value $2,521,181
Ann. rainfall (in.) . 26.61	No. employed 333
Jan. temp. min. 48	Wages paid . . . $4,663,876
July temp. max. 95	Tax value . . $941,402,875
Growing season (da.) 319	Income $7,132,000
No. farms, 1982 25	Taxable sales . . $226,976
No. acres in farms 569,640	Fed. expend. . . . $733,000
†Value per farm $5,090,240	Crime Index 11
Cropland harvested 1,800	TDC Pop. 0

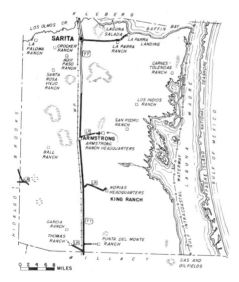

AGRICULTURE: About $16 million average income, nearly all from cattle on large ranches.

BUSINESS: Oil-ranching economy.

MANUFACTURING: None noted in census report.

SERVICE INDUSTRIES: None noted in census report.

SARITA (est. 185) county seat of one of the state's least populated counties; cattle shipping point; headquarters for large ranch enterprises; gas processing. Other town is **Armstrong.**

Kent

LOCATION: West (G-10).

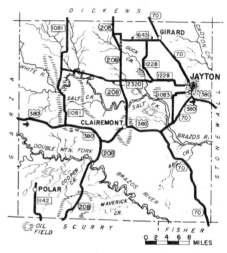

HISTORY: Created, 1876, from Bexar, Young Territories; organized 1892. Name honors **Andrew Kent,** one of "**Immortal 32**" from Gonzales who died in Alamo.

Cong. Dist. 13	U.S. Jud. Dist. . . . . N-Lb.
St. Sen. Dist. 30	Ct. Appeals 7
St. Rep. Dist. 78	Admin. Jud. Dist. 7
St. Dist. Cts. 39	

PHYSICAL FEATURES: Rolling, broken terrain; drains to Salt and Double Mountain Forks Brazos River; sandy, loam soils.

RECREATION: Hunting, local events; scenic croton breaks and salt flat.

MINERALS: Oil, gas, sand and gravel.

1982 Pop. 1,200	Voters reg. 890
Area (sq. mi.) 878	Whlsle. sales . . . . . . $*
Altitude (ft.) . 1,900-2,400	Oil value . . . $240,120,180
Ann. rainfall (in.) . 20.75	No. employed 239
Jan. temp. min. 28	Wages paid . . . $2,936,076
July temp. max. 97	Tax value . . $835,957,395
Growing season (da.) 216	Income $6,260,000
No. farms, 1982 177	Taxable sales . . $746,751
No. acres in farms 580,407	Fed. expend. . . $5,483,000
†Value per farm $666,308	Crime Index 3
Cropland harvested 26,291	TDC Pop. 0

AGRICULTURE: About $8 million average income, largely from cattle, sheep; cotton, wheat, sorghums, peanuts, grain produced; about 500 acres irrigated.

BUSINESS: Agribusinesses, oil field operations.

MANUFACTURING: None noted in census report.

SERVICE INDUSTRIES: 1 Establishments; Receipts, N.A.; Annual Payroll, N.A.; No. Employees, N.A.

JAYTON (638) county seat; oil field services, farm trade center.

Kerr

LOCATION: Southwest central (M-13).

HISTORY: Created, organized, 1856, from Bexar County; named for member of Austin's Colony, **James Kerr.**

Kerr County (Cont'd.)

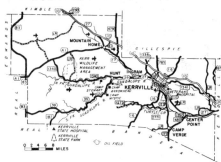

Cong. Dist.	21	U.S. Jud. Dist.	W-SAnt.
St. Sen. Dist.	25	Ct. Appeals	4
St. Rep. Dist.	67	Admin. Jud. Dist.	6
St. Dist. Cts.	198, 216		

PHYSICAL FEATURES: Hills, spring-fed streams are scenic attractions. New dam and lake on Guadalupe River.

RECREATION: Very popular area for tourists, hunters, fishermen; dude ranches; **Kerrville State Park**; wildlife management area; hatchery; Texas Arts and Crafts Fair in Kerrville; Experimental aircraft fly-in; Cowboy Artists Museum.

MINERALS: Limited sand, gravel.

1982 Pop.	30,200	Voters reg.	19,385
Area (sq. mi.)	1,107	Whlsle. sales	$32,929,000
Altitude (ft.)	1,400-2,400	Oil value	$284,120
Ann. rainfall (in.)	29.75	No. employed	9,242
Jan. temp. min.	34	Wages paid	$124,430,912
July temp. max.	94	Tax value	$1,236,544,978
Growing season (da.)	216	Income	$362,468,000
No. farms, 1982	529	Taxable sales	$157,778,991
No. acres in farms	589,223	Fed. expend.	$110,547,000
†Value per farm	$620,890	Crime Index	1,063
Cropland harvested	7,967	TDC Pop.	45

AGRICULTURE: An estimated $9 million average income, 90% from cattle, sheep, goats; cedar posts sold; hay, oats, milo, wheat, pecans.

BUSINESS: Tourism; agribusinesses; manufacturing.

MANUFACTURING: 33 Plants; 1,100 Employees; Payroll, $15,200,000; Product Value, $67,600,000.

SERVICE INDUSTRIES: 221 Establishments; Receipts, $41,036,000; Annual Payroll, $13,290,000; No. Employees, 1,283.

KERRVILLE (15,276) county seat; tourist center; many camps for recreation nearby; plants make aircraft, boats, recreational equipment, jewelry, glass; **Schreiner College**, now a 4-year school; **Kerrville State Hospital; Veterans Hospital**, also local hospital. Other major town, **Ingram** (1,235).

Kimble

LOCATION: Central southwest (L-12).

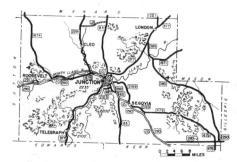

HISTORY: Created from Bexar County, 1858; organized 1876; named for **George C. Kimble**, among Gonzales' "**Immortal 32**" who died in Alamo.

Cong. Dist.	21	U.S. Jud. Dist.	W-An.
St. Sen. Dist.	25	Ct. Appeals	4
St. Rep. Dist.	67	Admin. Jud. Dist.	6
St. Dist. Cts.	198		

PHYSICAL FEATURES: Broken, rolling plain; drains to Llano River; sandy, gray, chocolate loam soils.

RECREATION: Hunting, fishing in spring-fed streams; among leading deer counties; **Lake Junction**; Kimble Kow Kick, other local events; state park under development.

MINERALS: Limited sand, gravel, gas, oil.

1982 Pop.	4,200	Voters reg.	2,535
Area (sq. mi.)	1,250	Whlsle. sales	$13,001,000
Altitude (ft.)	1,400-2,400	Oil value	$52,289
Ann. rainfall (in.)	22.33	No. employed	1,018
Jan. temp. min.	33	Wages paid	$12,233,412
July temp. max.	97	Tax value	$370,799,891
Growing season (da.)	213	Income	$28,723,000
No. farms, 1982	423	Taxable sales	$12,253,956
No. acres in farms	720,012	Fed. expend.	$10,995,000
†Value per farm	$688,480	Crime Index	6
Cropland harvested	6,097	TDC Pop.	8

AGRICULTURE: About $10 million average income, 90% from sheep, goats, cattle, hogs, horses; crops include pecans, fruit.

BUSINESS: Livestock producing, wool, mohair, tourism, hunting, fishing dominate economy. Cedar oil and wood products sold.

MANUFACTURING: None noted in census report.

SERVICE INDUSTRIES: 27 Establishments; Receipts, $2,850,000; Annual Payroll, $676,000; No. Employees, 132.

JUNCTION (2,593) county seat; cedar oil plant; pecan processing; ranching; tourism center; **Texas Tech University Center**; hospital, nursing home.

King

LOCATION: Northwest (F-11).

HISTORY: Created, 1876, from Bexar District; organized 1891; named for **William P. King** of "**Immortal 32**" from Gonzales who died in Alamo.

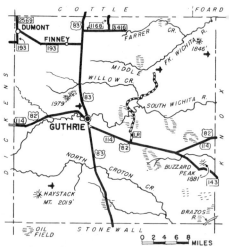

1982 Pop.	400	Voters reg.	282
Area (sq. mi.)	914	Whlsle. sales	$*
Altitude (ft.)	1,500-2,000	Oil value	$110,046,092
Ann. rainfall (in.)	21.60	No. employed	218
Jan. temp. min.	27	Wages paid	$4,461,764
July temp. max.	99	Tax value	$256,926,095
Growing season (da.)	219	Income	$3,185,000
No. farms, 1982	45	Taxable sales	$704,611
No. acres in farms	418,003	Fed. expend.	$2,489,000
†Value per farm	$964,867	Crime Index	1
Cropland harvested	11,811	TDC Pop.	0

Cong. Dist.	13	U.S. Jud. Dist.	N-WF
St. Sen. Dist.	30	Ct. Appeals	7
St. Rep. Dist.	78	Admin. Jud. Dist.	9
St. Dist. Cts.	50		

PHYSICAL FEATURES: Hilly, broken by Wichita and Brazos tributaries; extensive grassland; dark loam to red soils.

RECREATION: Local events.

MINERALS: Oil, gas.

AGRICULTURE: $10 million average income, over 90 percent from beef cattle; cotton, grains produced.

BUSINESS: Minerals, ranching provide most income.

MANUFACTURING: None noted in census report.

SERVICE INDUSTRIES: None noted in census report.

GUTHRIE (est. 140) county seat; ranch supply center.

Kinney

LOCATION: Southwest (O-11).

HISTORY: Created from Bexar County, 1850; organized, 1874; named for **H. L. Kinney**, founder of Corpus Christi.

Cong. Dist.	23	U.S. Jud. Dist.	W-DR
St. Sen. Dist.	25	Ct. Appeals	4
St. Rep. Dist.	68	Admin. Jud. Dist.	6
St. Dist. Cts.	63		

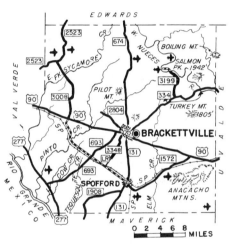

PHYSICAL FEATURES: Hilly, broken by many Rio Grande tributaries; **Anacacho Mountains; Nueces Canyon.**

RECREATION: Hunting; **Alamo Village guest ranch; Seminole Cemetery; Fort Clark Springs;** frontier fair in March.

MINERALS: Not significant.

1982 Pop.	2,300	Voters reg.	1,812
Area (sq. mi.)	1,359	Whlsle. sales	$*
Altitude (ft.)	1,000-2,000	Oil value	$371,675
Ann. rainfall (in.)	20.85	No. employed	440
Jan. temp. min.	39	Wages paid	$4,768,724
July temp. max.	94	Tax value	$256,584,425
Growing season (da.)	270	Income	$14,683,000
No. farms, 1982	108	Taxable sales	$3,320,362
No. acres in farms	704,467	Fed. expend.	$18,338,000
†Value per farm	$2,163,694	Crime Index	37
Cropland harvested	3,025	TDC Pop.	0

AGRICULTURE: About $9.8 million average income, 85% from cattle, sheep, goats; grains, corn, onions produced. About 5,000 acres irrigated for grass, sorghums, vegetables.

BUSINESS: Agribusinesses; tourist trade.

MANUFACTURING: None noted in census report.

SERVICE INDUSTRIES: 6 Establishments; Receipts, $1,561,000; Annual Payroll, $521,000; No. Employees, 89.

BRACKETTVILLE (1,676) county seat; tourist center; local market; clinic; **Spofford** (77).

Kleberg

LOCATION: Southern coast (R-16).

HISTORY: Created, organized, 1913, from Nueces County; named for San Jacinto veteran-rancher, **Robert Kleberg.**

Cong. Dist.	27	U.S. Jud. Dist.	S-CC
St. Sen. Dist.	20	Ct. Appeals	13
St. Rep. Dist.	37	Admin. Jud. Dist.	5
St. Dist. Cts.	28, 105		

PHYSICAL FEATURES: Coastal plain, broken by bays; sandy, loam, clay soils; tree motts.

RECREATION: Fishing, water activities, park on Baffin Bay; wildlife sanctuary; **Texas A&I** events, museum; **King Ranch** headquarters; livestock show.

MINERALS: Production of oil, gas; stone.

1982 Pop.	34,400	Voters reg.	14,955
Area (sq. mi.)	853	Whlsle. sales	$40,857,000
Altitude (ft.) sea level-150		Oil value	$12,130,568
Ann. rainfall (in.)	26.50	No. employed	9,212
Jan. temp. min.	48	Wages paid	$124,236,060
July temp. max.	96	Tax value	$2,881,204,432
Growing season (da.)	314	Income	$249,132,000
No. farms, 1982	255	Taxable sales	$101,324,256
No. acres in farms	919,233	Fed. expend.	$227,073,000
†Value per farm	$687,200	Crime Index	1,706
Cropland harvested	89,905	TDC Pop.	59

AGRICULTURE: An estimated $40 million average annual income, 65% from cattle, hogs, poultry, horses; wheat, sorghums, cotton, corn, vegetables grown.

BUSINESS: Economy based on petroleum, cattle ranching; some manufacturing.

MANUFACTURING: None noted in census report.

SERVICE INDUSTRIES: 133 Establishments; Receipts, $25,817,000; Annual Payroll, $8,802,000; No. Employees, 918.

KINGSVILLE (28,808) county seat; industrial plants; petroleum processing; **Texas A&I University;** headquarters of **King Ranch, Santa Gertrudis Breeders International; Naval Air Station;** hospital.

Knox

LOCATION: Northwest (F-12).

HISTORY: Created from Bexar, Young Territories, 1858; re-created, 1876; organized 1886, named for U.S. Secretary of War, **Gen. Henry Knox.**

Cong. Dist.	13	U.S. Jud. Dist.	N-WF
St. Sen. Dist.	30	Ct. Appeals	11
St. Rep. Dist.	78	Admin. Jud. Dist.	9
St. Dist. Cts.	50		

PHYSICAL FEATURES: Eroded breaks on rolling plains; Brazos, Wichita Rivers; sandy, loam soils.

RECREATION: Lake activities, local events; centennial celebration during Sesquicentennial.

MINERALS: Oil, gas.

1982 Pop.	5,600	Voters reg.	3,102
Area (sq. mi.)	845	Whlsle. sales	$26,042,000
Altitude (ft.)	1,300-1,700	Oil value	$44,731,947
Ann. rainfall (in.)	24.64	No. employed	1,142
Jan. temp. min.	28	Wages paid	$15,036,960
July temp. max.	98	Tax value	$231,612,722
Growing season (da.)	217	Income	$32,197,000
No. farms, 1982	403	Taxable sales	$11,150,424
No. acres in farms	476,930	Fed. expend.	$36,460,000
†Value per farm	$487,620	Crime Index	81
Cropland harv.	146,184	TDC Pop.	3

AGRICULTURE: About $31 million average income, 70% from crops that include cotton, wheat, sorghums, guar, corn, potatoes; beef cattle, sheep; about 33,000 acres irrigated.

BUSINESS: Agribusinesses, petroleum operations.

MANUFACTURING: None noted in census report.

SERVICE INDUSTRIES: 22 Establishments; Receipts, $3,835,000; Annual Payroll, $1,320,000; No. Employees, 151.

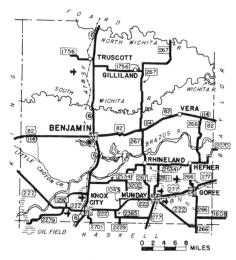

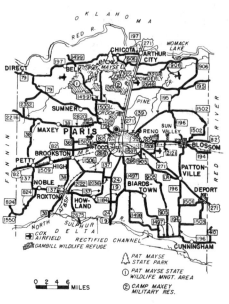

BENJAMIN (257) county seat; trade, market center; hospital, nursing home.

Munday (1,738) vegetable shipping center; portable offices, buildings manufactured; vegetable festival; **Texas A&M Experiment Vegetable Research Station;** center of irrigation from Seymour aquifer; library, nursing home.

Knox City (1,546) agribusiness, petroleum center; county hospital, nursing home; cap company; plant materials research center. **Goree** (524).

Lamar

LOCATION: Northeast (F-19).

HISTORY: Created, 1840, from Red River County; organized, 1841; named for Republic of Texas president, **Mirabeau B. Lamar.**

Cong. Dist.	1	U.S. Jud. Dist.	E-Ps.
St. Sen. Dist.	1	Ct. Appeals	6
St. Rep. Dist.	2	Admin. Jud. Dist.	1
St. Dist. Cts.	6, 62		

PHYSICAL FEATURES: On divide between Red, Sulphur Rivers; soils chiefly Blackland, except along Red; pines, hardwoods.

RECREATION: Pat Mayse Lake activities; **Gambill** goose refuge; hunting, fishing; Flying Tigers Air Museum, A.M. Aikin Archives; other museums; arts fair; Red River Valley Exposition; antique auto rally; other local events.

MINERALS: Negligible.

1982 Pop.	43,000	Voters reg.	22,398
Area (sq. mi.)	919	Whlsle. sales	$133,581,000
Altitude (ft.)	400-611	Oil value	0
Ann. rainfall (in.)	45.17	No. employed	15,157
Jan. temp. min.	34	Wages paid	$232,709,144
July temp. max.	94	Tax value	$811,232,481
Growing season (da.)	235	Income	$365,977,000
No. farms, 1982	1,432	Taxable sales	$193,078,386
No. acres in farms	388,214	Fed. expend.	$109,919,000
†Value per farm	$204,056	Crime Index	3,928
Cropland harv.	125,945	TDC Pop.	131

AGRICULTURE: About $40 million average income, 80% from beef, dairy cattle; chief crops are wheat, peanuts, sorghums, soybeans, cotton; a leading hay-producing county; timber marketed.

BUSINESS: Varied manufacturing; agribusinesses; tourism.

MANUFACTURING: 50 Plants; 4,800 Employees; Payroll, $80,800,000; Product Value, $728,900,000.

SERVICE INDUSTRIES: 251 Establishments; Receipts, $43,693,000; Annual Payroll, $16,569,000; No. Employees, 1,364.

PARIS (25,498) county seat; plants make canned soups, steam generating equipment, apparel, food products, farm supplies, other products; medical center, nursing homes; **Paris Junior College.**

Other towns include **Blossom** (1,487), **Deport** (724, part Red River), **Reno** (1,059), **Roxton** (735), **Sun Valley** (76) and **Toco** (164).

Lamb

LOCATION: Northwest (E-8).

HISTORY: Created 1876, from Bexar District; organized, 1908; named for San Jacinto Battle victim, **Lt. G. A. Lamb.**

Cong. Dist.	19	U.S. Jud. Dist.	N-Lb.
St. Sen. Dist.	31	Ct. Appeals	7
St. Rep. Dist.	85	Admin. Jud. Dist.	9
St. Dist. Cts.	154		

PHYSICAL FEATURES: Rich, red, brown soils on plain; some hills; drains to numerous playas, Brazos Double Mountain Fork.

RECREATION: Local events; Sandhills celebration.

MINERALS: Production oil, stone, gas.

1982 Pop.	18,500	Voters reg.	9,269
Area (sq. mi.)	1,013	Whlsle. sales	$70,574,000
Altitude (ft.)	3,400-3,800	Oil value	$1,826,757
Ann. rainfall (in.)	18.04	No. employed	4,657
Jan. temp. min.	24	Wages paid	$67,662,972
July temp. max.	93	Tax value	$986,930,207
Growing season (da.)	194	Income	$124,599,000
No. farms, 1982	823	Taxable sales	$30,517,855
No. acres in farms	558,260	Fed. expend.	$99,412,000
†Value per farm	$412,696	Crime Index	373
Cropland harv.	353,804	TDC Pop.	13

AGRICULTURE: Nearly $113 million average income, evenly split among sorghums, cotton, corn, soybeans, wheat, other crops and cattle, hogs, sheep, horses; 300,000 acres irrigated.

BUSINESS: Agribusinesses.

MANUFACTURING: 12 Plants; Employees, N.A.; Payroll, N.A.; Product Value, N.A.

SERVICE INDUSTRIES: 68 Establishments; Receipts,

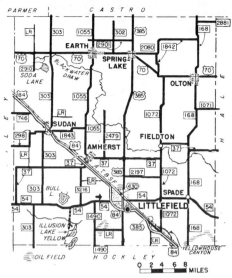

1982 Pop.	12,700	Voters reg.	6,770
Area (sq. mi.)	714	Whlsle. sales	$38,306,000
Altitude (ft.)	800-1,700	Oil value	0
Ann. rainfall (in.)	29.80	No. employed	2,424
Jan. temp. min.	36	Wages paid	$28,517,144
July temp. max.	96	Tax value	$295,839,650
Growing season (da.)	223	Income	$104,440,000
No. farms, 1982	611	Taxable sales	$31,432,842
No. acres in farms	431,276	Fed. expend.	$37,471,000
†Value per farm	$441,525	Crime Index	336
Cropland harvested	22,389	TDC Pop.	37

MANUFACTURING: None noted in census report.

SERVICE INDUSTRIES: 53 Establishments; Receipts, $7,059,000; Annual Payroll, $2,497,000; No. Employees, 272.

LAMPASAS (6,165) county seat; ranching, hunting center; plants make feeds, tacos, egg products, plastics, western boots, apparel, nut harvesters, building trusses, rubber products, brooms, mops; hospital, nursing homes. **Lometa** (666) other principal town.

La Salle

LOCATION: South (Q-13).

HISTORY: Created from Bexar County, 1858; organized 1880; named for **Robert Cavelier Sieur de la Salle**, French explorer who died in Texas.

Cong. Dist.	15	U.S. Jud. Dist.	S-La.
St. Sen. Dist.	21	Ct. Appeals	4
St. Rep. Dist.	44	Admin. Jud. Dist.	4
St. Dist. Cts.	81, 218		

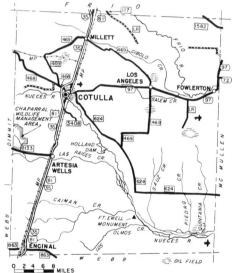

PHYSICAL FEATURES: Brushy plain, broken by Nueces, Frio and their tributary streams; chocolate, dark gray, sandy loam soils.

RECREATION: Nature trails; **Chaparral Wildlife Management Area**; deer, bird, javelina hunting; wild hog cookoff; fishing; Cotulla school where the late **Pres. Lyndon B. Johnson** taught attracts tourists.

MINERALS: Production of oil, gas.

1982 Pop.	5,800	Voters reg.	3,686
Area (sq. mi.)	1,517	Whlsle. sales	$18,346,000
Altitude (ft.)	300-600	Oil value	$14,061,060
Ann. rainfall (in.)	20.72	No. employed	991
Jan. temp. min.	43	Wages paid	$11,634,268
July temp. max.	99	Tax value	$329,042,815
Growing season (da.)	288	Income	$31,981,000
No. farms, 1982	256	Taxable sales	$8,393,047
No. acres in farms	808,081	Fed. expend.	$8,996,000
†Value per farm	$1,238,961	Crime Index	52
Cropland harvested	21,174	TDC Pop.	9

AGRICULTURE: An estimated $23 million average income, 90% from beef and stocker cattle; crops include

$8,662,000; Annual Payroll, $2,526,000; No. Employees, 297.

LITTLEFIELD (7,409) county seat; agribusinesses, trade center; textile mill; plants make fertilizer, irrigation, other farm products; hospitals, nursing homes; airport.

Other towns include **Earth** (1,512) grain, cotton center, **Olton** (2,235) farm and feed lot center, **Sudan** (1,091), **Amherst** (971) and **Springlake** (222).

Lampasas

LOCATION: Central (K-14).

HISTORY: Name is Spanish for lilies, found in nearby streams; county created, organized, 1856, from Bell, Travis.

Cong. Dist.	11	U.S. Jud. Dist.	W-An.
St. Sen. Dist.	24	Ct. Appeals	3
St. Rep. Dist.	54	Admin. Jud. Dist.	3
St. Dist. Cts.	27		

PHYSICAL FEATURES: Rolling, hilly; Colorado, Lampasas Rivers; cedars, oaks, pecans.

RECREATION: Hunting, fishing in streams; local events.

MINERALS: Sand and gravel.

AGRICULTURE: About $16 million average income, 90% from cattle, hogs, sheep, goats; crops include oats, wheat, fruit, pecans.

BUSINESS: Many employed at **Fort Hood**; several industrial plants; tourism; agribusinesses.

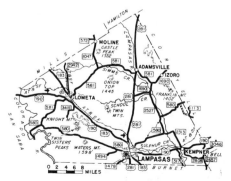

guar, sorghums, cotton, wheat, oats, peanuts, vegetables, melons; less than 4,000 acres irrigated.

BUSINESS: Agribusinesses, hunting leases, oil and gas production.

MANFUACTURING: None noted in census report.

SERVICE INDUSTRIES: 15 Establishments; Receipts, $2,174,000; Annual Payroll, $652,000; No. Employees, 56.

COTULLA (3,912) county seat; welding and steel fabrication; agribusiness center; clinic; **Encinal** (704) other major town.

Lavaca

LOCATION: South (N-17).

HISTORY: Named for Spanish word for cow, la vaca, from name of river; created, organized, 1846, from Colorado, Jackson, Gonzales, Victoria Counties.

Cong. Dist.	14	U.S. Jud. Dist. S-Va.
St. Sen. Dist.	18	Ct. Appeals	13
St. Rep. Dist.	31	Admin. Jud. Dist.	3
St. Dist. Cts.	25, 2D25		

PHYSICAL FEATURES: North rolling, south plains; sandy loam, black waxy soils; drains to Lavaca, Navidad Rivers.

RECREATION: Deer, other hunting, fishing; **Yoakum Tom-Tom** June celebration; spring flower trails, fiddlers frolic, domino tournaments; other events.

MINERALS: Oil, gas.

1982 Pop.	18,400	Voters reg.	10,888
Area (sq. mi.)	971	Whlsle. sales	$67,226,000
Altitude (ft.)	100-300	Oil value	$19,198,644
Ann. rainfall (in.)	36.27	No. employed	4,838
Jan. temp. min.	44	Wages paid	$59,172,920
July temp. max.	95	Tax value	$1,232,328,503
Growing season (da.)	280	Income	$159,881,000
No. farms, 1982	2,315	Taxable sales	$52,350,731
No. acres in farms	491,530	Fed. expend.	$50,951,000
†Value per farm	$193,986	Crime Index	286
Cropland harvested	47,796	TDC Pop.	14

AGRICULTURE: About $43 million average income, 80% from cattle, hogs, poultry; crops include sorghums, small grains, corn, rice, hay, peaches, pecans, legumes. Nearly 5,000 acres irrigated, mostly rice.

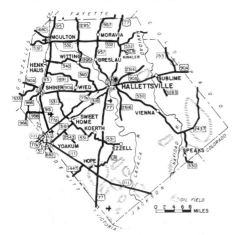

BUSINESS: Varied manufacturing; leather goods center; agribusinesses; oil and gas production.

MANUFACTURING: 35 Plants; 1,600 Employees; Payroll, $18,900,000; Product Value, $101,900,000.

SERVICE INDUSTRIES: 87 Establishments; Receipts, $12,846,000; Annual Payroll, $4,523,000; No. Employees, 541.

HALLETTSVILLE (2,865) county seat; plants make plastic products, furniture, portable buildings, other products; Lavaca Medical Center, nursing home.

Yoakum (6,148, part in De Witt County) plants make leather goods, furniture, process foods; hospital, nursing homes.

Shiner (2,213) brewery, wire products, saddle factory; hospital, nursing home.

Moulton (1,009) plants make boots, other leather products; feed mills, machine shop; other agribusinesses; clinic, nursing home; Czech, German polka, waltz fest.

Lee

LOCATION: Southeast (M-17).

HISTORY: Created from Bastrop, Burleson, Fayette, Washington Counties and organized in 1874; named for **Confederate Gen. Robert E. Lee.**

Cong. Dist.	14	U.S. Jud. Dist.	W-An.
St. Sen. Dist.	18	Ct. Appeals	3
St. Rep. Dist.	30	Admin. Jud. Dist.	2
St. Dist. Cts.	21, 335		

RECREATION: Fishing, hunting; pioneer village, historical museum and structures; new motels; local events; historic sites.

MINERALS: Oil, gas, lignite.

PHYSICAL FEATURES: Rolling, broken by Yegua and its tributaries; red to black soils, sandy to heavy loams.

1982 Pop.	13,700	Voters reg.	6,764
Area (sq. mi.)	631	Whlsle. sales	$115,600,000
Altitude (ft.)	270-790	Oil value	$210,763,778
Ann. rainfall (in.)	35.88	No. employed	4,371
Jan. temp. min.	38	Wages paid	$68,188,528
July temp. max.	94	Tax value	$1,062,174,636
Growing season (da.)	273	Income	$101,076,000
No. farms, 1982	1,447	Taxable sales	$79,280,936
No. acres in farms	291,929	Fed. expend.	$17,614,000
†Value per farm	$220,518	Crime Index	262
Cropland harvested	32,535	TDC Pop.	20

AGRICULTURE: Nearly $32 million average income, 85% from cattle, hogs, poultry; peanuts, wheat, oats, cotton, corn, hay.

BUSINESS: Varied manufacturing; agribusinesses; oil and gas operations.

MANUFACTURING: None noted in census report.

SERVICE INDUSTRIES: 70 Establishments; Receipts, $19,541,000; Annual Payroll, $5,490,000; No. Employees, 554.

GIDDINGS (3,950) county seat; oil field services and trucking; plants make boots, furniture, plastic products; livestock auctions; process meats; hospital, nursing homes; historical museum; **Blinn College** extension; **Giddings State School and Home;** Geburtstag celebration.

Other towns include **Lexington** (1,065) livestock marketing center, nursery, peanut drying plant, many work at aluminum plant; **Serbin,** Wendish museum.

Leon

LOCATION: East central (K-18).

HISTORY: Created, organized, 1846, from Robertson County; named for Spanish founder of Victoria, **Martin de Leon.**

Cong. Dist.	6	U.S. Jud. Dist.	W-Wa.
St. Sen. Dist.	5	Ct. Appeals	10
St. Rep. Dist.	15	Admin. Jud. Dist.	2
St. Dist. Cts.	12, 87, 278		

PHYSICAL FEATURES: Hilly, rolling, almost half covered by timber; drains to Navasota, Trinity and tributaries; sandy, dark, alluvial soils.

RECREATION: Hilltop Lakes resort area; sites of **Camino Real, Fort Boggy;** deer hunting.

MINERALS: Oil, gas, iron ore, lignite.

1982 Pop. 10,500	Voters reg. 7,664
Area (sq. mi.) 1,078	Whlsle. sales . $36,045,000
Altitude (ft.) 150-500	Oil value $11,989,669
Ann. rainfall (in.) . 39.48	No. employed 2,835
Jan. temp. min. 38	Wages paid . . $48,355,980
July temp. max. 95	Tax value . $1,012,864,788
Growing season (da.) 270	Income $86,623,000
No. farms, 1982 . . 1,227	Taxable sales $28,822,633
No. acres in farms 442,387	Fed. expend. . $27,417,000
†Value per farm $370,121	Crime Index 154
Cropland harvested 34,454	TDC Pop. 13

AGRICULTURE: About $34 million average income, over 90% from livestock, principally beef cattle, hogs, poultry, horses; crops include hay, corn, sorghum, vegetables; timber estimated $2 million.

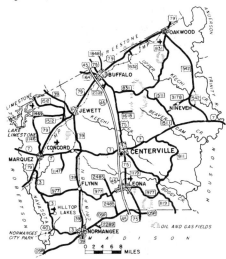

BUSINESS: Agribusinesses, oil production.

MANUFACTURING: 13 Plants; Employees, N.A.; Payroll, N.A.; Product Value, N.A.

SERVICE INDUSTRIES: 33 Establishments; Receipts, $4,444,000; Annual Payroll, $1,256,000; No. Employees, 179.

CENTERVILLE (799) county seat; steel products; farming center; clinic, nursing home.

Buffalo (1,507) farming center; electricity generating plant; hospital, nursing home.

Other towns include **Normangee** (636, partly Madison County), **Oakwood** (606), **Jewett** (597), **Leona** (165), **Marquez** (231).

Liberty

LOCATION: Southeast (M-20).

HISTORY: Named for Spanish municipality, **Libertad,** from which it was created in 1836; organized, 1837.

Cong. Dist. 2	U.S. Jud. Dist. . . . . E-Bt.
St. Sen. Dist. 4	Ct. Appeals 9
St. Rep. Dist. 21	Admin. Jud. Dist. 2
St. Dist. Cts. 75, 253	

1982 Pop. 51,400	Voters reg. 25,066
Area (sq. mi.) 1,174	Whlsle. sales $144,711,000
Altitude (ft.) 20-200	Oil value $79,021,575
Ann. rainfall (in.) . 49.75	No. employed . . . 12,074
Jan. temp. min. 43	Wages paid . $189,717,216
July temp. max. 93	Tax value . $1,765,169,943
Growing season (da.) 261	Income $507,242,000
No. farms, 1982 . . 1,209	Taxable sales $242,603,050
No. acres in farms 373,954	Fed. expend. $109,135,000
†Value per farm $449,003	Crime Index 1,988
Cropland harv. . . 133,912	TDC Pop. 119

PHYSICAL FEATURES: Rolling; 60 percent in pine, hardwood timber; bisected by Trinity River; sandy, loam, black soils; Wallisville Reservoir; Big Thicket.

RECREATION: Big Thicket; hunting, fishing; historic sites; Trinity Valley exposition in October.

MINERALS: Oil, gas, sulphur, sand and gravel.

AGRICULTURE: About $32 million average income, ¾ from crops, principally rice, soybeans; beef cattle; timber marketed; 32,000 acres irrigated for rice; pulpwood, lumber, Christmas trees.

BUSINESS: Agribusinesses; chemical plants; varied manufacturing; tourism; forest industries; many work in Houston.

MANUFACTURING: 64 Plants; 1,700 Employees; Payroll, $32,200,000; Product Value, $189,200,000.

SERVICE INDUSTRIES: 187 Establishments; Receipts, $42,022,000; Annual Payroll, $13,480,000; No. Employees, 1,229.

LIBERTY (7,945) county seat; port on barge canal; sulphur, oil, chemicals, timber, steel processed, shipped; farm products processed, shipped; hospital, nursing homes; library, museum; regional historical resources depository; oil pipe manufacturing and oil field services; liberty bell tower and plaza.

Other towns include **Cleveland** (5,977) forest products processed, shipped; farm, petroleum products shipped; tourism; library, museum; hospital; **Dayton** (4,908); **Daisetta** (1,177) manufacturing; oil, food processing; **Ames** (1,155), **Devers** (507), **Hardin** (779), **Kenefick** (763), **North Cleveland** (259) and **Plum Grove** (455).

Limestone

LOCATION: East central (J-17).

HISTORY: Created from Robertson County and organized, 1846; named for indigenous rock.

Cong. Dist. 6	U.S. Jud. Dist. . . . W-Wa.
St. Sen. Dist. 9	Ct. Appeals 10
St. Rep. Dist. 12	Admin. Jud. Dist. 2
St. Dist. Cts. 77, 87	

PHYSICAL FEATURES: Borders Blacklands, level to rolling; drained by Navasota and tributaries; on divide between Brazos and Trinity; **Lake Mexia, Lake Springfield, Lake Limestone.**

MINERALS: Production of oil, gas, sand and gravel, clay, stone, lignite.

1982 Pop. 20,300	Voters reg. 12,771
Area (sq. mi.) 931	Whlsle. sales . $74,944,000
Altitude (ft.) 350-600	Oil value $6,281,874
Ann. rainfall (in.) . 37.59	No. employed 7,692
Jan. temp. min. 37	Wages paid . $114,095,496
July temp. max. 96	Tax value . $1,029,080,301
Growing season (da.) 255	Income $160,396,000
No. farms, 1982 . . . 1,209	Taxable sales $64,557,276
No. acres in farms 460,183	Fed. expend. . $48,541,000
†Value per farm $233,304	Crime Index 658
Cropland harvested 57,993	TDC Pop. 77

Limestone County (Cont'd.)

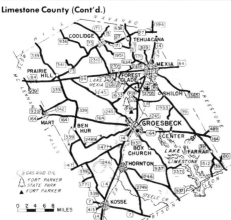

RECREATION: Fishing, water activities; restored **Fort Parker, Fort Parker State Park**; Confederate reunion ground, other historic sites; museum; hunting; Red Stocking Follies, fiddle festival, arts and crafts, other events.

AGRICULTURE: About $37 million average annual income, 90% from cattle, hogs, horses; crops include sorghums, cotton, hay, peaches, oats, wheat, corn, peanuts, pecans.

BUSINESS: Varied manufacturing; agribusinesses; tourism; mineral operations.

MANUFACTURING: 19 Plants; 600 Employees; Payroll, $7,200,000; Product Value, $25,600,000.

SERVICE INDUSTRIES: 60 Establishments; Receipts, $8,695,000; Annual Payroll, $3,022,000; No. Employees, 354.

GROESBECK (3,373) county seat; livestock market; plants make fiber material, trailers, concrete brick, ladies' garments, industrial products; food processing; hospital, nursing home.

Mexia (7,094) agribusiness center; wholesale grocery distribution; furniture, sportswear, other products; **Mexia State School**; hospital.

Other towns include **Coolidge** (810), **Kosse** (484), **Tehuacana** (265) and **Thornton** (498).

Lipscomb

LOCATION: Northeast corner of Panhandle (A-11).

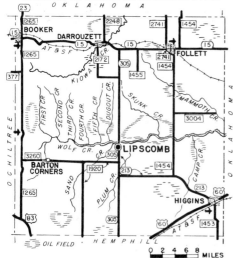

HISTORY: Created, 1876, from Bexar District; organized, 1887; named for **A. S. Lipscomb**, Republic of Texas leader.

Cong. Dist.	13	U.S. Jud. Dist.	N-Am.
St. Sen. Dist.	31	Ct. Appeals	7
St. Rep. Dist.	88	Admin. Jud. Dist.	9
St. Dist. Cts.	31		

PHYSICAL FEATURES: Plain, broken in east; drains to tributaries of Canadian, Wolf Creek; sandy loam, black soils.

RECREATION: Local events.

MINERALS: Production of oil, gas.

1982 Pop.	4,300	Voters reg.	2,247
Area (sq. mi.)	933	Whlsle. sales	$27,277,000
Altitude (ft.)	2,350-2,850	Oil value	$76,781,233
Ann. rainfall (in.)	22.16	No. employed	1,063
Jan. temp. min.	23	Wages paid	$17,936,260
July temp. max.	95	Tax value	$949,424,716
Growing season (da.)	202	Income	$37,206,000
No. farms, 1982	294	Taxable sales	$15,383,781
No. acres in farms	539,793	Fed. income	$12,528,000
†Value per farm	$581,241	Crime Index	50
Cropland harvested	89,262	TDC Pop.	5

AGRICULTURE: About $19 million average annual income, 65% from beef cattle, hogs; crops include wheat, sorghums, corn, alfalfa; about 17,000 acres irrigated.

BUSINESS: Agribusinesses; oil, gas operations.

MANUFACTURING: None noted in census report.

SERVICE INDUSTRIES: 19 Establishments; Receipts, $1,840,000; Annual Payroll, $421,000; No. Employees, 33.

LIPSCOMB (est. 190) county seat.

Other towns include **Booker** (1,219), **Darrouzett** (444), **Follett** (547) and **Higgins** (702).

Live Oak

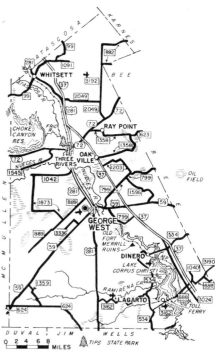

LOCATION: South (Q-15).

HISTORY: Named for predominant tree; created, organized, 1856, from Nueces, San Patricio Counties.

Cong. Dist.	15	U.S. Jud. Dist.	S-CC
St. Sen. Dist.	21	Ct. Appeals	13
St. Rep. Dist.	45	Admin. Jud. Dist.	4
St. Dist. Cts.	36, 156, 343		

PHYSICAL FEATURES: Brushy plains, partly broken

by Nueces and tributaries; black waxy, gray sandy, other soils.

RECREATION: Lake Corpus Christi activities; **Choke Canyon Reservoir Dam;** hunting; Tips State Park, county fair.

MINERALS: Production of gas, oil, sand and gravel, uranium.

1982 Pop.	9,900	Voters reg.	6,790
Area (sq. mi.)	1,057	Whlsle. sales	$36,169,000
Altitude (ft.)	70-400	Oil value	$19,207,007
Ann. rainfall (in.)	25.64	No. employed	2,239
Jan. temp. min.	45	Wages paid	$35,061,816
July temp. max.	97	Tax value	$1,493,498,268
Growing season (da.)	289	Income	$77,437,000
No. farms, 1982	770	Taxable sales	$21,588,376
No. acres in farms	520,959	Fed. expend.	$26,439,000
†Value per farm	$413,955	Crime Index	140
Cropland harvested	71,950	TDC Pop.	20

AGRICULTURE: Some $25 million average yearly income, 70% from beef cattle, hogs; crops include sorghums, cotton, corn, wheat, hay.

BUSINESS: Oil activities, agribusinesses dominate economy.

MANUFACTURING: None noted in census report.

SERVICE INDUSTRIES: 42 Establishments; Receipts, $5,406,000; Annual Payroll, $1,659,000; No. Employees, 177.

GEORGE WEST (2,627) county seat; agribusinesses; petroleum refineries; uranium mining. **Three Rivers** (2,133) has refineries, boat factory.

Llano

LOCATION: West Central (L-14).

HISTORY: Name is Spanish for plains; created, organized, 1856, from Bexar District, Gillespie County.

Cong. Dist.	21	U.S. Jud. Dist.	W-An.
St. Sen. Dist.	24	Ct. Appeals	3
St. Rep. Dist.	47	Admin. Jud. Dist.	3
St. Dist. Cts.	33		

PHYSICAL FEATURES: Drains to Colorado, Llano Rivers; rolling to hilly; **Buchanan, Inks, Lyndon B. Johnson Lakes.**

RECREATION: No. 1 deer hunting county; fishing, **Highland Lakes** activities; major tourist area; **Enchanted Rock State Park;** Spring Bluebonnet festival.

MINERALS: Stone, vermiculite.

1982 Pop.	10,600	Voters reg.	8,261
Area (sq. mi.)	939	Whlsle. sales	$85,529,000
Altitude (ft.)	800-2,000	Oil value	0
Ann. rainfall (in.)	26.20	No. employed	2,030
Jan. temp. min.	34	Wages paid	$24,994,948
July temp. max.	98	Tax value	$963,593,603
Growing season (da.)	229	Income	$107,288,000
No. farms, 1982	520	Taxable sales	$36,400,634
No. acres in farms	532,196	Fed. expend.	$34,683,000
†Value per farm	$706,637	Crime Index	128
Cropland harvested	4,781	TDC Pop.	6

AGRICULTURE: An estimated $18.5 million average yearly income, more than 90% from beef cattle, hogs, goats, turkeys; crops include peanuts, oats, hay.

BUSINESS: Tourism; ranch trading center; granite mined.

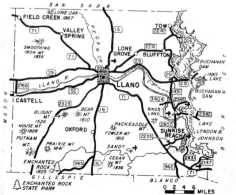

MANUFACTURING: None noted in census report.

SERVICE INDUSTRIES: 55 Establishments; Receipts, $8,152,000; Annual Payroll, $2,250,000; No. Employees, 357.

LLANO (3,071) county seat; tourist, hunting center; granite processing, rock crushing, winery, feed processing; hospital, nursing home. **Kingsland**, tourism, light manufacturing, nursing home. Other towns include **Buchanan Dam, Sunrise Beach** (420).

Loving

LOCATION: New Mexico line (J-6).

HISTORY: Last county organized; created 1887 from Tom Green; organized 1931; named for **Oliver Loving**, trail driver.

Cong. Dist.	16	U.S. Jud. Dist.	W-Pe.
St. Sen. Dist.	25	Ct. Appeals	8
St. Rep. Dist.	69	Admin. Jud. Dist.	7
St. Dist. Cts.	143		

PHYSICAL FEATURES: Rolling prairies drain to Pecos River; **Red Bluff Lake;** sandy, loam, clay soils.

MINERALS: Production of oil, gas.

1982 Pop.	100	Voters reg.	96
Area (sq. mi.)	671	Whlsle. sales	$*
Altitude (ft.)	2,700-3,100	Oil value	$40,168,529
Ann. rainfall (in.)	10.31	No. employed	89
Jan. temp. min.	29	Wages paid	$1,979,000
July temp. max.	96	Tax value	$372,627,243
Growing season (da.)	222	Income	$1,845,000
No. farms, 1982	15	Taxable sales	$87,530
No. acres in farms	350,350	Fed. expend.	$148,000
†Value per farm	$4,056,667	Crime Index	7
Cropland harvested	N.A.	TDC Pop.	0

AGRICULTURE: About $500,000 income from beef cattle; no crops.

BUSINESS: Petroleum operations.

MANUFACTURING: None noted in census report.

SERVICE INDUSTRIES: 1 Establishment; Receipts, N.A.; Annual Payroll, N.A.; No. Employees, N.A.

MENTONE (est. 50) county seat; supply center for oil fields; only town.

Lubbock

LOCATION: Northwest (F-8).

HISTORY: Named for **Col. Tom S. Lubbock**, an organizer of **Confederate Terry's Rangers;** county created, 1876, from Bexar District; organized, 1891.

Cong. Dist.	19	U.S. Jud. Dist.	N-Lb.
St. Sen. Dist.	28	Ct. Appeals	7
St. Rep. Dist.	82-84	Admin. Jud. Dist.	9
St. Dist. Cts.	72, 99, 137, 140, 237		

1982 Pop.	216,700	Voters reg.	105,535
Area (sq. mi.)	900	Whlsle. sales	$2,714,813,000
Altitude (ft.)	2,900-3,400	Oil value	$44,767,369
Ann. rainfall (in.)	18.41	No. employed	85,077
Jan. temp. min.	25	Wages paid	$1,314,983,872
July temp. max.	96	Tax value	$4,908,604,123
Growing season (da.)	208	Income	$2,037,771,000
No. farms, 1982	1,029	Taxable sales	$1,210,250,147
No. acres in farms	551,441	Fed. expend.	$678,438,000
†Value per farm	$463,444	Crime Index	20,443
Crops harvested	301,709	TDC Pop.	562

PHYSICAL FEATURES: Level plains, broken by 1,500 playas, Yellow House River; rich soils, with underground water.

RECREATION: Lubbock Lake archaeological site; lake activities; **Texas Tech** events; Lubbock Civic Center, **Museum of Texas Tech** and **Moody Planetarium**; **Mackenzie State Park; Ranching Heritage Center; Panhandle-South Plains Fair; Lubbock Arts Festival** in April; **Buffalo Springs Lake.**

MINERALS: Oil, gas, stone, sand and gravel.

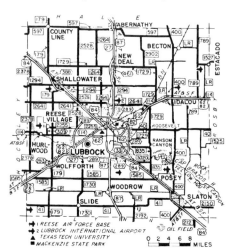

1 REESE AIR FORCE BASE
2 LUBBOCK INTERNATIONAL AIRPORT
▲ TEXAS TECH UNIVERSITY
■ MACKENZIE STATE PARK

0 2 4 6 8 MILES

AGRICULTURE: $100 million average yearly income, about 75% from crops, including cotton, wine grapes, sorghums, wheat, corn, sunflowers, soybeans; 225,000 acres irrigated; feedlot cattle, poultry, hogs.

BUSINESS: World's largest cottonseed processing center; Texas' leading agribusiness center; headquarters for large cotton cooperative; cattle feedlots; manufacturing. See metro page.

MANUFACTURING: 292 Plants; 11,700 Employees; Payroll, $197,700,000; Product Value, $949,500,000.

SERVICE INDUSTRIES: 1,373 Establishments; Receipts, $388,487,000; Annual Payroll, $135,378,000; No. Employees, 11,141.

LUBBOCK (173,979) county seat; center for large agricultural area; major electronics company's consumer products headquarters for making, servicing calculators; other large plants process oilseeds, make earthmoving equipment, mobile homes, food containers, fire protection equipment, clothing, other products; distribution center for South Plains; large feedlots; medical center, psychiatric hospital; museum; **Texas Tech University** with law and medical schools; **Lubbock Christian College, South Plains College, Wayland Baptist College** campus; **Reese Air Force Base;** numerous hospitals, nursing homes; state school for mentally retarded.

Other towns include **Abernathy** (2,904, part Hale County) cotton spinning mill; **Idalou** (2,348), **Shallowater** (1,932), **Slaton** (6,804) cotton, rail, manufacturing center; **Wolfforth** (1,701), **Ransom Canyon** (561) and **New Deal** (637).

Lynn

LOCATION: Northwest (G-8).

HISTORY: Created, 1876, from Bexar District; organized, 1903; named for Alamo martyr, **W. Lynn** (or Linn).

Cong. Dist.	17	U.S. Jud. Dist.	N-Lb.
St. Sen. Dist.	28	Ct. Appeals	7
St. Rep. Dist.	78	Admin. Jud. Dist.	7
St. Dist. Cts.	106		

PHYSICAL FEATURES: Plain, broken by Cap Rock Escarpment, playas and draws; sandy loam, black, gray soils.

RECREATION: Local events.

MINERALS: Oil, gas, stone.

1982 Pop.	8,300	Voters reg.	4,285
Area (sq. mi.)	888	Whlsle. sales	$21,564,000
Altitude (ft.)	2,650-3,300	Oil value	$14,464,660
Ann. rainfall (in.)	17.88	No. employed	1,172
Jan. temp. min.	27	Wages paid	$16,273,052
July temp. max.	94	Tax value	$291,845,785
Growing season (da.)	217	Income	$44,951,000
No. farms, 1982	556	Taxable sales	$7,611,919
No. acres in farms	518,590	Fed. expend.	$52,874,000
†Value per farm	$537,455	Crime Index	136
Cropland harv.	267,741	TDC Pop.	7

AGRICULTURE: About $50 million average income, 90% from cotton, sorghums, wheat; cattle, hogs, sheep; 60,000 acres irrigated.

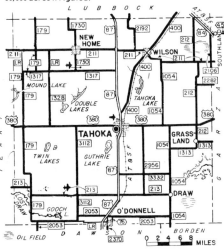

0 2 4 6 8 MILES

BUSINESS: Cotton, grain sorghum industries.

MANUFACTURING: None noted in census report.

SERVICE INDUSTRIES: 18 Establishments; Receipts, $1,704,000; Annual Payroll, $374,000; No. Employees, 44.

TAHOKA (3,262) county seat; cotton center; cotton compress; farm equipment manufacturing; hospital, nursing home. Other towns include O'Donnell (1,200, part Dawson County), Wilson (578), New Home (274).

McMullen

LOCATION: South (Q-14).

HISTORY: Created from Atascosa, Bexar, Live Oak Counties, 1858; organized, 1862, reorganized, 1877; named for Irish empresario, John McMullen.

MINERALS: Production of gas, oil, stone and coal.

RECREATION: Deer hunting; Lions Club Rodeo, August-September; 4-H Livestock show and sale in April; Choke Canyon Reservoir and wildlife management area.

AGRICULTURE: About $9 million average annual income, more than 90% from beef cattle; crops are sorghums, hay, corn.

BUSINESS: Oil, gas production, cattle raising dominate economy.

MANUFACTURING: None noted in census report.

SERVICE INDUSTRIES: 1 Establishment; Receipts, N.A.; Annual Payroll, N.A.; No. Employees, N.A.

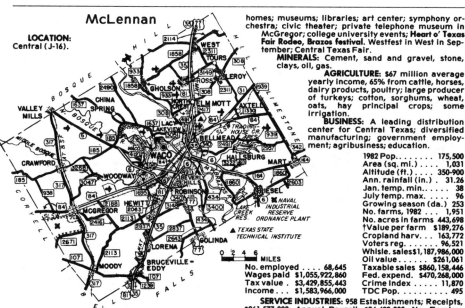

Cong. Dist.		15
St. Sen. Dist.		21
St. Rep. Dist.		44
St. Dist. Cts.	36, 156, 343	
U.S. Jud. Dist.		S-La.
Ct. Appeals		4
Admin. Jud. Dist.		7

PHYSICAL FEATURES: Brushy plain, sloping to Frio, Nueces and tributaries; saline clay soils.

1982 Pop.	800		
Area (sq. mi.)	1,163		
Altitude (ft.)	150-500		
Ann. rainfall (in.)	25.27		
Jan. temp. min.	44		
July temp. max.	98		
Growing season (da.)	291		
No. farms, 1982	208		
No. acres in farms	530,958		
†Value per farm	$1,325,971		
Cropland harvested	11,308		
Voters reg.	622		
Whlsle. sales	$*	Income	$7,504,000
Oil value	$78,650,607	Taxable sales	$878,646
No. employed	322	Fed. expend.	$3,043,000
Wages paid	$5,386,180	Crime index	13
Tax value	$371,330,834	TDC Pop.	4

TILDEN (est. 500) county seat; ranching, oil, gas center.

McLennan

LOCATION: Central (J-16).

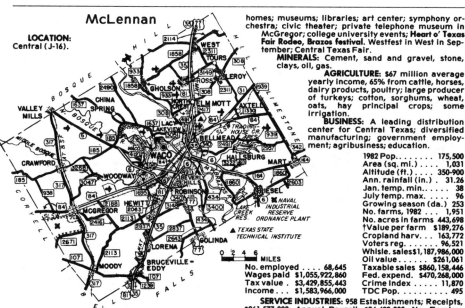

HISTORY: Created from Milam County and organized in 1850; named for an original settler, Neil McLennan Sr.

PHYSICAL FEATURES: Mostly Blackland prairie, but rolling hills in west; drains to Bosque, Brazos Rivers and Lake Waco; heavy, loam, sandy soils.

Cong. Dist.	11	U.S. Jud. Dist. W-Wa.
St. Sen. Dist.	9	Ct. Appeals 10
St. Rep. Dist.	55, 56	Admin. Jud. Dist. 1
St. Dist Cts.	19, 54, 74, 170	

MANUFACTURING: 261 Plants; 14,900 Employees; Payroll, $237,100,000; Product Value, $1,328,100,000.

RECREATION: Varied metropolitan activities (see chamber of commerce for dates); Fort Fisher Park with camping facilities; Homer Garrison Jr. Texas Ranger Museum; Texas Ranger Hall of Fame; Cameron Park; Lake Waco; Brazos River events; zoo; historic sites and homes; museums; libraries; art center; symphony orchestra; civic theater; private telephone museum in McGregor; college university events; Heart o' Texas Fair Rodeo, Brazos festival. Westfest in West in September; Central Texas Fair.

MINERALS: Cement, sand and gravel, stone, clays, oil, gas.

AGRICULTURE: $67 million average yearly income, 65% from cattle, horses, dairy products, poultry; large producer of turkeys; cotton, sorghums, wheat, oats, hay principal crops; some irrigation.

BUSINESS: A leading distribution center for Central Texas; diversified manufacturing; government employment; agribusiness; education.

1982 Pop.	175,500
Area (sq. mi.)	1,031
Altitude (ft.)	350-900
Ann. rainfall (in.)	31.26
Jan. temp. min.	38
July temp. max.	96
Growing season (da.)	253
No. farms, 1982	1,951
No. acres in farms	443,698
†Value per farm	$189,276
Cropland harv.	163,772
Voters reg.	96,521
Whlsle. sales	$1,187,986,000
Oil value	$261,061
Taxable sales	$860,158,446
Fed. expend.	$470,268,000
Crime index	11,870
TDC Pop.	495

No. employed	68,645
Wages paid	$1,055,922,860
Tax value	$3,429,855,443
Income	$1,583,966,000

SERVICE INDUSTRIES: 958 Establishments; Receipts, $261,577,000; Annual Payroll, $94,428,000; No. Employees, 8,025.

WACO (101,261) county seat; see metro page; center for manufacturing, tourism, conventions, agribusinesses; plants make tires, glass products, health care products, food products, lumber, batteries, apparel, steel products, many other products; Baylor University; Paul Quinn College; McLennan Community College; Texas State Technical Institute; Veterans Administration regional office and hospital; other hospitals.

Other towns include Bellmead (7,569), Beverly Hills (2,083), Bruceville-Eddy (1,038, partly Falls County), Crawford (610), Gholson (263), Golinda (335, partly Falls County), Hallsburg (455), Hewitt (5,247), Lacy-Lakeview (2,752), Leroy (253), Lorena (619), McGregor (4,513) rocket motors, fuel devices, other products manufactured, nursing home; Mart (2,324) plastics, concrete services; Moody (1,385), Northcrest (1,944), Riesel (691), Robinson (6,074), Ross (200), Valley Mills (1,236, mostly Bosque County), West (2,485) and Woodway (7,091).

McCulloch

LOCATION: Texas' **geographical center** in county (K-13).

HISTORY: Created from Bexar District, 1856; organized, 1876; named for Texas pioneer, **Gen. Ben McCulloch.**

Cong. Dist. 21	U.S. Jud. Dist. . . . W-An.
St. Sen. Dist. 24	Ct. Appeals 3
St. Rep. Dist. 65	Admin. Jud. Dist. 2
St. Dist. Cts. 198	

PHYSICAL FEATURES: Hilly and rolling; drains to Colorado, Brady Creek and lake, San Saba River; black loams to sandy soils.

RECREATION: Hunting; **Brady Lake** activities; muzzle loading rifle association state championship, horse racing, world championship barbecue goat cook-off; other local events.

MINERALS: Production oil, sand, gravel, stone, gas.

1982 Pop.	8,800	Voters reg.	5,106
Area (sq. mi.)	1,071	Whlsle. sales .	$43,542,000
Altitude (ft.) .	1,300-2,000	Oil value	$120,760
Ann. rainfall (in.) .	23.46	No. employed . . .	2,465
Jan. temp. min.	34	Wages paid . .	$29,346,920
July temp. max. . . .	96	Tax value . .	$443,533,097
Growing season (da.)	226	Income	$67,573,000
No. farms, 1982	520	Taxable sales	$27,436,680
No. acres in farms 679,225		Fed. expend. .	$26,491,000
†Value per farm	$604,466	Crime Index	185
Cropland harvested 62,547		TDC Pop.	12

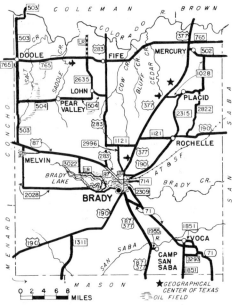

★ GEOGRAPHICAL
CENTER OF TEXAS

≡ OIL FIELD

AGRICULTURE: About $21 million average income, 80% from beef cattle, sheep, goats, hogs; crops include oats, wheat, sorghums, cotton, peanuts, hay. About 2,000 acres irrigated.

BUSINESS: Agribusinesses, manufacturing, tourism, hunting leases.

MANUFACTURING: None noted in census report.

SERVICE INDUSTRIES: 45 Establishments; Receipts, $8,035,000; Annual Payroll, $2,358,000; No. Employees, 314.

BRADY (5,969) county seat; ranching and tourist headquarters; plants process mohair and wool, peanuts, sand, make trailers, farm equipment, other products; hospital, nursing homes; **Central Texas College. Melvin** (202) other principal town.

Madison

LOCATION: East Central (K-18).

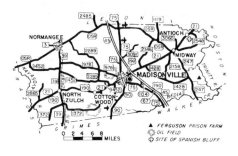

▲ FERGUSON PRISON FARM
≡ OIL FIELD
✛ SITE OF SPANISH BLUFF

HISTORY: Named for **U.S. President James Madison;** created from Grimes, Leon, Walker Counties, 1853; organized, 1854.

Cong. Dist. 6	U.S. Jud. Dist. . . . . S-Hn.
St. Sen. Dist. 5	Ct. Appeals 10
St. Rep. Dist. 15	Admin. Jud. Dist. 3
St. Dist. Cts. 12, 278	

PHYSICAL FEATURES: Hilly, draining to Trinity, Navasota Rivers, Bedias Creek on boundaries; fifth of area timbered; alluvial, loam, sandy soils.

RECREATION: Fishing, hunting; water activities at **Lake Madison;** Madisonville **Sidewalk Cattlemen's** celebration in June; historic sites.

MINERALS: Production of oil, gas and gravel.

1982 Pop.	11,500	Voters reg.	5,309
Area (sq. mi.)	473	Whlsle. sales .	$39,858,000
Altitude (ft.) . . .	200-370	Oil value . . .	$63,725,980
Ann. rainfall (in.) .	41.50	No. employed . . .	2,749
Jan. temp. min.	40	Wages paid . .	$41,221,988
July temp. max. . . .	94	Tax value . .	$566,855,020
Growing season (da.)	272	Income	$87,994,000
No. farms, 1982	708	Taxable sales	$24,659,550
No. acres in farms 196,322		Fed. expend. .	$16,094,000
†Value per farm	$281,347	Crime Index	316
Cropland harvested 13,709		TDC Pop.	13

AGRICULTURE: Over $36 million average annual income, about evenly split between cattle, horses, hogs and sorghums, oats, pecans; mushroom production.

BUSINESS: Agribusinesses, oil production, manufacturing.

MANUFACTURING: None noted in census report.

SERVICE INDUSTRIES: 42 Establishments; Receipts, $5,986,000; Annual Payroll, $1,951,000; No. Employees, 194.

MADISONVILLE (3,660) county seat; farm trading center; mushroom processing; plants make clothes, fiberglass products; hospital, nursing home, library; **Normangee** (636, mostly Leon County).

Marion

LOCATION: Northeast (G-21).

HISTORY: Created, organized, 1860, from Cass County; named for **U.S. Gen. Francis Marion.**

Cong. Dist. 1	U.S. Jud. Dist. . . . . E-Mi.
St. Sen. Dist. 1	Ct. Appeals 6
St. Rep. Dist. 8	Admin. Jud. Dist. 2
St. Dist. Cts. 115, 276	

PHYSICAL FEATURES: Hilly, three-fourths forested with pines, hardwoods; drains to **Caddo Lake, Lake O' the Pines, Cypress Bayou.**

RECREATION: Lake O' the Pines, Caddo activities; hunting; **Excelsior Hotel;** 84 medallions on historic sites including **Jay Gould railroad car, House of Four Seasons; Freeman plantation;** historical museum; historical pilgrimage in May.

MINERALS: Oil, gas, clays, lignite.

1982 Pop.	10,700	Voters reg.	7,035
Area (sq. mi.)	385	Whlsle. sales	$*
Altitude (ft.) . . .	200-500	Oil value	$7,600,141
Ann. rainfall (in.) .	44.83	No. employed . . .	1,611
Jan. temp. min.	36	Wages paid . .	$20,503,780
July temp. max. . . .	94	Tax value . .	$390,129,116
Growing season (da.)	236	Income	$77,379,000
No. farms, 1982	207	Taxable sales	$13,689,464
No. acres in farms .	49,081	Fed. expend. .	$19,360,000
†Value per farm	$148,217	Crime Index	229
Cropland harvested 5,388		TDC Pop.	27

AGRICULTURE: About $4.5 million average income, 90% from beef cattle and some poultry, swine and horses; hay, horticulture, fruit, vegetables are top crops; estimated $7.7 million in timber sales.

BUSINESS: Oil, timber industries; recreation; syrup plant.

MANUFACTURING: None noted in census report.

SERVICE INDUSTRIES: 31 Establishments; Receipts, $3,444,000; Annual Payroll, $1,019,000; No. Employees, 150.

JEFFERSON (2,643) county seat; one of state's oldest towns and once a major river port; sawmills; plants make syrup, reels, glass, oil field equipment and other products; antique shops; hospitals, nursing homes; historic pilgrimage each May, festival in October.

Martin

LOCATION: West (I-8).

HISTORY: Created from Bexar District, 1876; organized, 1884; named for **Republic of Texas Sen. Wylie Martin.**

Cong. Dist.	17	U.S. Jud. Dist.	W:M-O
St. Sen. Dist.	28	Ct. Appeals	8
St. Rep. Dist.	77	Admin. Jud. Dist.	6
St. Dist. Cts.	118		

PHYSICAL FEATURES: Sandy, loam soils on plain, broken by playas, creeks.

RECREATION: Museum, local events.

MINERALS: Oil, gas.

1982 Pop.	5,200	Voters reg.	2,623
Area (sq. mi.)	914	Whlsle. sales	$21,592,000
Altitude (ft.)	2,550-3,000	Oil value	$231,064,289
Ann. rainfall (in.)	15.72	No. employed	897
Jan. temp. min.	30	Wages paid	$14,894,272
July temp. max.	95	Tax value	$873,341,163
Growing season (da.)	215	Income	$37,336,000
No. farms, 1982	390	Taxable sales	$6,502,328
No. acres in farms	564,710	Fed. expend.	$47,548,000
†Value per farm	$716,969	Crime Index	93
Cropland harv.	157,866	TDC Pop.	3

AGRICULTURE: About $35 million average annual income, 90% from cotton, small grains, remainder from cattle; 11,000 acres irrigated.

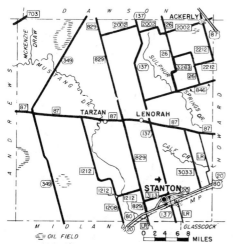

BUSINESS: Petroleum production, agribusinesses dominate economy.

MANUFACTURING: None noted in census report.

SERVICE INDUSTRIES: 16 Establishments; Receipts, $1,073,000; Annual Payroll, $390,000; No. Employees, 31.

STANTON (2,314) county seat; center for oil, ranching business; cotton compress; county hospital. **Ackerly** (317, partly Dawson County).

Mason

LOCATION: Central (L-13).

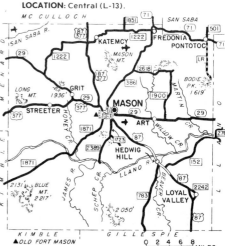

HISTORY: Created from Bexar, Gillespie Counties, organized, 1858; named for Mexican War victim, **Lt. G. T. Mason.**

Cong. Dist.	21	U.S. Jud. Dist.	W-An.
St. Sen. Dist.	25	Ct. Appeals	4
St. Rep. Dist.	67	Admin. Jud. Dist.	7
St. Dist. Cts.	33		

PHYSICAL FEATURES: Hilly, draining to Llano, San Saba and tributaries; limestone, red soils; varied timber.

RECREATION: Major tourist area; outstanding deer, turkey hunting, river fishing; camping; bluebonnet trails; historic homes; Ft. Mason Museum; local events.

MINERALS: Not significant.

1982 Pop.	3,600	Voters reg.	2,380
Area (sq. mi.)	934	Whlsle. sales	$26,659,000
Altitude (ft.)	1,300-2,200	Oil value	$320,169
Ann. rainfall (in.)	24.68	No. employed	737
Jan. temp. min.	34	Wages paid	$7,015,944
July temp. max.	95	Tax value	$371,037,466
Growing season (da.)	217	Income	$23,905,000
No. farms, 1982	567	Taxable sales	$7,366,242
No. acres in farms	559,836	Fed. expend.	$9,498,000
†Value per farm	$596,843	Crime Index	15
Cropland harvested	11,181	TDC Pop.	2

AGRICULTURE: Some $21 million average yearly income, 80% from cattle, hogs, sheep, goats; peanuts, hay, coastal bermuda grass, wheat, oats, watermelon produced. Some 8,000 acres irrigated, mostly peanuts, hay.

BUSINESS: Ranching, hunting, tourism, soft drink bottling.

MANUFACTURING: None noted in census report.

SERVICE INDUSTRIES: 15 Establishments; Receipts, $1,731,000; Annual Payroll, $567,000; No. Employees, 86.

MASON (2,153) county seat; tourist, ranching center; candy manufacturing; museum.

Matagorda

LOCATION: On coast (O-19).

HISTORY: An original county, created 1836 from Spanish municipality, named for canebrake; organized 1837; settled by Stephen F. Austin colonists.

Cong. Dist. 14
St. Sen. Dist. 18
St. Rep. Dist. 29
St. Dist. Cts. 23, 130

U.S. Jud. Dist. . . . . S-Gn.
Ct. Appeals 13
Admin. Jud. Dist. 3

PHYSICAL FEATURES: Flat, broken by bays; contains part of **Matagorda Island;** many different soils; drains to Colorado River, creeks, coast.

RECREATION: Coastal activities, including fishing, water sports, hunting; historic sites, museums; Rice Festival, local events.

MINERALS: Production of gas, oil, salt.

1982 Pop. 37,200	Voters reg. 20,199
Area (sq. mi.) 1,127	Whlsle. sales $241,619,000
Altitude (ft.) sea level-70	Oil value $43,688,615
Ann. rainfall (in.) . 42.29	No. employed . . . 10,696
Jan. temp. min. 48	Wages paid . $198,673,348
July temp. max. 90	Tax value . $2,941,257,607
Growing season (da.) 296	Income $376,401,000
No. farms, 1982 703	Taxable sales $153,703,601
No. acres in farms 572,911	Fed. expend. $203,411,000
†Value per farm $845,861	Crime Index 2,085
Cropland harv. . . 188,927	TDC Pop. 75

AGRICULTURE: A $68 million average annual income, 80% from rice, cotton, sorghums, soybeans, other crops; beef cattle produced. Estimated 5,000 acres irrigated for rice.

BUSINESS: Petroleum operations, petrochemicals, agribusinesses dominate the economy; varied manufacturing; tourism significant.

MANUFACTURING: 24 Plants; Employees, N.A.; Payroll, N.A.; Product Value, N.A.

SERVICE INDUSTIRES: 183 Establishments; Receipts, $44,505,000; Annual Payroll, $12,848,000; No. Employees, 1,057.

BAY CITY (17,837) county seat; petrochemical, plastics, fertilizer plants, nuclear power plant; gas, oil processing, commercial fishing; tourist center; hospital, nursing homes; rice festival in October, fair and rodeo in March. Other towns include **Palacios** (4,667) tourism, seafood processing, petrochemical; hospital, library, airport. Other towns are **Van Vleck, Matagorda, Markham** and **Blessing.**

Maverick

LOCATION: On Rio Grande (P-11).

HISTORY: Named for pioneer, **Sam A. Maverick,** whose name is synonym for unbranded cattle; created 1856, from Kinney County; organized 1871.

Cong. Dist. 23
St. Sen. Dist. 21
St. Rep. Dist. 68
St. Dist. Cts. 293

U.S. Jud. Dist. . . . . W-DR
Ct. Appeals 4
Admin. Jud. Dist. 4

PHYSICAL FEATURES: Broken, rolling surface, with dense brush; clay, sandy, alluvial soils.

RECREATION: Tourist gateway to Mexico; whitetail deer, bird hunting; fishing; International Friendship Festival at Eagle Pass; annual events.

MINERALS: Production of oil, gas, sand and gravel.

AGRICULTURE: A $39.3 million average annual income, 90% from beef cattle, feedlots; crops include oats, sorghums, wheat, pecans, vegetables. About 16,000 acres irrigated from Rio Grande.

BUSINESS: Oil production, operations; agribusinesses; feedlots; tourist trade with Mexico.

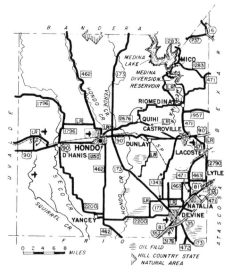

1982 Pop. 34,200	Voters reg. 10,683
Area (sq. mi.) 1,287	Whlsle. sales . $33,588,000
Altitude (ft.) . . . 550-1,000	Oil value $11,319,238
Ann. rainfall (in.) . 19.74	No. employed 6,310
Jan. temp. min. 40	Wages paid . . $69,647,720
July temp. max. 100	Tax value . . $988,082,817
Growing season (da.) 285	Income $153,666,000
No. farms, 1982 176	Taxable sales $88,788,921
No. acres in farms 718,297	Fed. expend. . $31,600,000
†Value per farm $1,386,074	Crime Index 1,547
Cropland harvested 15,725	TDC Pop. 19

MANUFACTURING: 14 Plants; 1,000 Employees; Payroll, $7,600,000; Product Value, $65,500,000.

SERVICE INDUSTRIES: 81 Establishments; Receipts, $11,345,000; Annual Payroll, $3,233,000; No. Employees, 426.

EAGLE PASS (21,407) county seat; varied manufacturing; tourism center; major rail and highway entry point into Mexico; hospital.

Medina

LOCATION: Southwest (O-13).

HISTORY: Created, organized, 1848, from Bexar; settled by Alsatians led by **Henri Castro;** named for river, probably for Spanish engineer, **Pedro Medina.**

Cong. Dist.	23	U.S. Jud. Dist.	W-SAnt.
St. Sen. Dist.	25	Ct. Appeals	4
St. Rep. Dist.	45	Admin. Jud. Dist.	6
St. Dist. Cts.	38		

PHYSICAL FEATURES: Scenic hills in north; south has fertile valleys, rolling surface; Medina River, lake.

RECREATION: A leading deer area; scenic drives; camping; fishing; historic sites, museum; **Landmark Inn** at Castroville; special tourist events; county fair.

MINERALS: Oil, gas, clay, sand, gravel.

1982 Pop.	23,600	Voters reg.	13,160
Area (sq. mi.)	1,331	Whlsle. sales	$72,657,000
Altitude (ft.)	600-1,900	Oil value	$7,462,007
Ann. rainfall (in.)	28.43	No. employed	4,957
Jan. temp. min.	42	Wages paid	$59,221,104
July temp. max.	96	Tax value	$721,004,580
Growing season (da.)	263	Income	$177,621,000
No. farms, 1982	1,480	Taxable sales	$54,905,772
No. acres in farms	710,419	Fed. expend.	$62,102,000
†Value per farm	$391,189	Crime Index	516
Cropland harv.	110,400	TDC Pop.	22

AGRICULTURE: $45 million average yearly income, 60% from cattle, hogs, sheep; crops include sorghum, small grains, corn, peanuts, hay, soybeans, guar, cotton, vegetables; 32,000 acres irrigated.

BUSINESS: Agribusinesses, tourism, varied manufacturing.

MANUFACTURING: 21 Plants; 600 Employees; Payroll, $7,200,000; Product Value, $26,700,000.

SERVICE INDUSTRIES: 88 Establishments; Receipts, $15,861,000; Annual Payroll, $4,585,000; No Employees, 576.

HONDO (6,057) county seat; plants make bathroom fixtures, brick and tile, metal buildings, oil field tanks, aircraft parts and accessories, other products; hospital, nursing homes; U.S. Air Force flight screening center.

Devine (3,756) peanut storage, shipping center; tire testing; 2 cattle feedlots; clothing factory; nurseries; nursing homes. Other towns include **Castroville** (1,821) Alsatian events, bakery; **Natalia** (1,264) carpet underlaying manufactured, **La Coste** (862).

Menard

LOCATION: Central (L-12).

HISTORY: Created from Bexar, 1858, organized, 1871; named for Galveston's founder, **Michel B. Menard**.

Cong. Dist.	21	U.S. Jud. Dist.	N-SAng.
St. Sen. Dist.	25	Ct. Appeals	4
St. Rep. Dist.	67	Admin. Jud. Dist.	3
St. Dist. Cts.	198		

PHYSICAL FEATURES: Rolling, draining to San Saba and tributaries; limestone soils.

1982 Pop.	2,300	Voters reg.	1,672
Area (sq. mi.)	902	Whlsle. sales	$*
Altitude (ft.)	1,700-2,400	Oil value	$4,297,295
Ann. rainfall (in.)	21.33	No. employed	412
Jan. temp. min.	30	Wages paid	$4,550,872
July temp. max.	96	Tax value	$260,297,940
Growing season (da.)	220	Income	$11,427,000
No. farms, 1982	58	Taxable sales	$3,559,422
No. acres in farms	463,848	Fed. expend.	$8,273,000
†Value per farm	$606,578	Crime Index	18
Cropland harvested	4,867	TDC Pop.	2

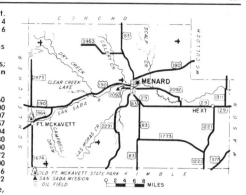

RECREATION: Hunting, fishing; historic sites include **Real Presidio de San Saba, Ft. McKavett State Park;** museum, country store, **San Saba River.**

MINERALS: Oil, gas.

AGRICULTURE: About $13 million average annual income, 90% from beef cattle, sheep, goats; crops include grains, pecans; 2,000 acres irrigated.

BUSINESS: Agribusinesses, tourism, oil and gas production.

MANUFACTURING: None noted in census report.

SERVICE INDUSTRIES: 8 Establishments; Receipts, N.A.; Annual Payroll, N.A.; No. Employees, N.A.

MENARD (1,697) county seat; ranching center; hospital.

Midland

LOCATION: West (J-8).

HISTORY: Created from Tom Green, organized, 1885; name came from midway location on railroad between El Paso and Fort Worth.

Cong. Dist.	21	U.S. Jud. Dist.	W:M-O
St. Sen. Dist.	25	Ct. Appeals	8
St. Rep. Dist.	76	Admin. Jud. Dist.	7
St. Dist. Cts.	142, 238, 318		

PHYSICAL FEATURES: Flat, broken by draws; sandy, loam soils.

1982 Pop.	97,400	Voters reg.	54,638
Area (sq. mi.)	902	Whlsle. sales	$2,334,324,000
Altitude (ft.)	2,550-2,900	Oil value	$253,063,131
Ann. rainfall (in.)	13.51	No. employed	49,445
Jan. temp. min.	31	Wages paid	$1,084,018,088
July temp. max.	95	Tax value	$5,294,730,140
Growing season (da.)	218	Income	$1,288,353,000
No. farms, 1982	335	Taxable sales	$891,927,029
No. acres in farms	822,053	Fed. expend.	$122,804,000
†Value per farm	$740,661	Crime Index	5,171
Cropland harvested	41,571	TDC Pop.	313

RECREATION: Permian Basin Petroleum Museum, Library and Hall of Fame; Museum of the Southwest; Pliska Aviation Museum; zoo; polo, golf, tennis; professional

Midland County (Cont'd.)

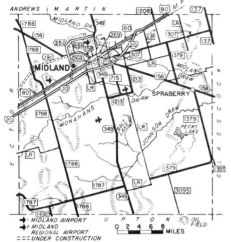

MIDLAND AIRPORT
MIDLAND REGIONAL AIRPORT
UNDER CONSTRUCTION

baseball, community theater, metropolitan events (ask chamber of commerce for dates).

MINERALS: Production of oil, gas, stone.

AGRICULTURE: About $15 million average annual income from beef cattle, horses, sheep; cotton, sorghums, small grains; over 12,000 acres irrigated.

BUSINESS: Among leading petroleum-producing counties; distributing, administrative center for oil industry; manufacturing including computer and telecommunications (see metro page).

MANUFACTURING: 139 Plants; 4,300 Employees; Payroll, $92,300,000; Product Value, $427,700,000.

SERVICE INDUSTRIES: 774 Establishments; Receipts, $328,985,000; Annual Payroll, $119,588,000; No. Employees, 8,051.

MIDLAND (70,525) county seat; center for petroleum, petrochemical operations; plants make clothing, oil field and other petroleum-related equipment, plastics, electronic calculators, other products; livestock sale center; **Midland College**; hospitals.

Milam

LOCATION: East central (L-16).

HISTORY: Created, 1836, from municipality named for **Ben Milam**, 1835 leader in capture of San Antonio; organized, 1837.

LOCATION: Central (J-14).

HISTORY: Created, organized, 1887, from Brown, Comanche, Hamilton, Lampasas Counties; named for pioneer jurist, **John T. Mills.**

Cong. Dist.	11	U.S. Jud. Dist.	N-SAng.
St. Sen. Dist.	24	Ct. Appeals	3
St. Rep. Dist.	54	Admin. Jud. Dist.	3
St. Dist. Cts.	35		

PHYSICAL FEATURES: Hills, plateau draining to Colorado River on southwest; sandy, loam soils.

1982 Pop.	4,500	Voters reg.	2,977
Area (sq. mi.)	748	Whlse. sales .	$9,851,000
Altitude (ft.) .	1,100-1,700	Oil value	0
Ann. rainfall (in.)	27.52	No. employed	1,248
Jan. temp. min.	34	Wages paid	$17,559,460
July temp. max.	87	Tax value	$255,881,170
Growing season (da.)	230	Income	$38,525,000
No. farms, 1982	677	Taxable sales	$9,903,273
No. acres in farms	391,933	Fed. expend.	$16,881,000
†Value per farm	$323,214	Crime Index	5
Cropland harvested	27,570	TDC Pop.	2

Cong. Dist.	11	U.S. Jud. Dist.	W-Wa.
St. Sen. Dist.	5	Ct. Appeals	3
St. Rep. Dist.	13	Admin. Jud. Dist.	3
St. Dist. Cts.	20		

PHYSICAL FEATURES: Partly level Blackland; southeast rolling; Brazos, Little Rivers.

RECREATION: Fishing, hunting; historic sites include Ft. Sullivan, Indian battlegrounds, mission sites; Milam County Museum in old jail at Cameron; festivals, other local events; **Alcoa Lake.**

MINERALS: Large lignite deposits; limited oil, gas.

1982 Pop.	23,000	Voters reg.	12,299
Area (sq. mi.)	1,019	Whlse. sales .	$34,248,000
Altitude (ft.)	250-600	Oil value	$10,499,295
Ann. rainfall (in.)	33.87	No. employed	6,555
Jan. temp. min.	39	Wages paid	$135,333,988
July temp. max.	96	Tax value .	$1,463,003,915
Growing season (da.)	256	Income	$193,392,000
No. farms, 1982	1,583	Taxable sales	$51,581,144
No. acres in farms	516,077	Fed. expend.	$50,593,000
†Value per farm	$244,065	Crime Index	537
Cropland harv.	114,566	TDC Pop.	48

AGRICULTURE: $52 million average annual income, 70% from cattle, hogs, poultry; crops include sorghums, cotton, wheat, hay, corn.

BUSINESS: Many employed at aluminum plant; varied manufacturing; lignite mining; agribusinesses.

MANUFACTURING: 20 Plants; Employees, N.A.; Payroll, N.A.; Product Value, N.A.

SERVICE INDUSTRIES: 87 Establishments; Receipts, $11,166,000; Annual Payroll, $4,127,000; No Employees, 585.

CAMERON (5,721) county seat; plants make doors, furniture, apparel, steel products, pipe and fertilizer; power generation; other products; hospitals, nursing homes.

Rockdale (5,611) has large aluminum plant; lignite mining center; hospital, nursing homes. **Thorndale** (1,300) has cotton oil mill; **Buckholts** (388), **Milano** (468).

Mills

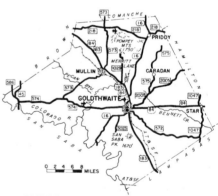

RECREATION: Fishing, deer hunting; historic suspension bridge.

MINERALS: Not significant.

AGRICULTURE: About $23 million average yearly income, 90% from sheep, beef cattle, goats, hogs, horses; crops principally small grains, sorghums, forage crops, pecans, peanuts.

BUSINESS: Chiefly agribusiness, hunting leases.

MANUFACTURING: None noted in census report.

SERVICE INDUSTRIES: 17 Establishments; Receipts, $3,044,000; Annual Payroll, $1,204,000; No. Employees, 154.

GOLDTHWAITE (1,783) county seat; center for farming, ranching activity; plants make farming equipment; hospital, nursing homes. **Mullin** (213).

Mitchell

LOCATION: West (I-10).

HISTORY: Created, 1876, from Bexar District; organized, 1881; named for pioneer brothers, **Asa and Eli Mitchell.**

Cong. Dist.	17	U.S. Jud. Dist.	N-Ab.
St. Sen. Dist.	30	Ct. Appeals	11
St. Rep. Dist.	66	Admin. Jud. Dist.	7
St. Dist. Cts.	32		

PHYSICAL FEATURES: Rolling, draining to Colorado and tributaries; sandy, red, dark soils; **Colorado City** and **Champion Creek Lakes.**

RECREATION: Lake activities; **Lake Colorado City State Park**; museum, playhouse; hunting; local events.

MINERALS: Production of oil, gas.

1982 Pop.	9,500	Voters reg.	4,779
Area (sq. mi.)	912	Whlsle. sales	$21,534,000
Altitude (ft.)	1,900-2,400	Oil value	$132,971,203
Ann. rainfall (in.)	19.68	No. employed	2,227
Jan. temp. min.	30	Wages paid	$30,206,400
July temp. max.	96	Tax value	$726,463,257
Growing season (da.)	217	Income	$66,908,000
No. farms, 1982	406	Taxable sales	$25,912,937
No. acres in farms	677,541	Fed. expend.	$26,446,000
†Value per farm	$564,372	Crime Index	255
Cropland harvested	70,848	TDC Pop.	16

AGRICULTURE: Some $18 million annual average income from beef cattle, hogs, sheep, horses, dairy products; poultry; cotton, sorghums, small grains; 4,000 acres irrigated.

BUSINESS: Chiefly oil, agribusinesses; some manufacturing.

MANUFACTURING: None noted in census report.

SERVICE INDUSTRIES: 41 Establishments; Receipts, $4,663,000; Annual Payroll, $1,571,000; No. Employees, 217.

COLORADO CITY (5,405) county seat; plants make clothing, farm implements, carpet pads, process cotton, cottonseed, furs; electric service center; hospital, nursing homes. Other towns include **Loraine** (929) retirement center, and **Westbrook** (298).

Montague

LOCATION: North (F-15).

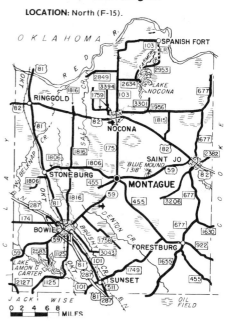

HISTORY: Created from Cooke, 1857, organized, 1858; named for pioneer, **Daniel Montague.**

Cong. Dist.	17	U.S. Jud. Dist.	N-WF
St. Sen. Dist.	30	Ct. Appeals	2
St. Rep. Dist.	80	Admin. Jud. Dist.	8
St. Dist. Cts.	97		

PHYSICAL FEATURES: Rolling, draining to tributaries of Trinity, Red Rivers; sandy loams, red, black soils; **Lake Nocona, Lake Amon G. Carter; Lyndon B. Johnson National Grasslands.**

RECREATION: Lake activities; scenic drives, museums; historical sites; Jim Bowie Days, "Chism Trail" scenic drive; other local events.

MINERALS: Production of oil, gas, stone.

1982 Pop.	18,500	Voters reg.	10,658
Area (sq. mi.)	928	Whlsle. sales	$54,793,000
Altitude (ft.)	800-1,250	Oil value	$77,345,155
Ann. rainfall (in.)	29.39	No. employed	4,460
Jan. temp. min.	32	Wages paid	$56,961,028
July temp. max.	96	Tax value	$647,440,869
Growing season (da.)	229	Income	$144,142,000
No. farms, 1982	1,065	Taxable sales	$56,954,534
No. acres in farms	434,642	Fed. expend.	$42,301,000
†Value per farm	$212,711	Crime Index	380
Cropland harvested	37,951	TDC Pop.	19

AGRICULTURE: $26 million average annual income, 80% from livestock, chiefly beef, dairy cattle; crops include wheat, sorghums, peanuts, pasture grasses, peaches, apples, grapes, pecans, vegetables.

BUSINESS: Agribusinesses; oil production; varied manufacturing.

MANUFACTURING: 28 Plants; 900 Employees; Payroll, $10,200,000; Product Value, $54,800,000.

SERVICE INDUSTRIES: 85 Establishments; Receipts, $13,568,000; Annual Payroll, $4,804,000; No. Employees, 623.

MONTAGUE (est. 400) county seat; farm trade center.

Bowie (5,610) agribusiness center; apparel, boats, farm equipment, insulation, business uniforms, metal products manufactured; livestock sales; hospital, nursing home; library; Jim Bowie Days in June; historical

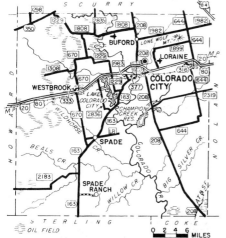

museum. **Nocona** (2,992) is a major boot and leather goods, sporting goods, clothing manufacturing center; also uniforms, helicopter parts; hospital. **Saint Jo** (1,071) is farm trade center.

Montgomery

LOCATION: Southeast (M-19).
HISTORY: Created, organized, 1837, from Washington County; named for **U.S. Revolutionary Gen. Richard Montgomery.**

Cong. Dist.	2, 6, 8	U.S. Jud. Dist.	S-Hn.
St. Sen. Dist.	3, 4, 5	Ct. Appeals	9
St. Rep. Dist.	15, 16	Admin. Jud. Dist.	2
St. Dist. Cts.9, 2D9, 221,284			

PHYSICAL FEATURES: Rolling, over three-fourths timbered; **Sam Houston National Forest** over large area; loam, sandy, alluvial soils.
RECREATION: Hunting, fishing; **Lake Conroe** activities; **Sam Houston National Forest; W. G. Jones State Forest;** Texas Renaissance Festival; county fair.
MINERALS: Production of oil, gas, sand and gravel.

1982 Pop.	148,700	Voters reg.	73,066
Area (sq. mi.)	1,047	Whlsle. sales	$565,738,000
Altitude (ft.)	150-400	Oil value	$95,454,776
Ann. rainfall (in.)	45.53	No. employed	32,193
Jan. temp. min.	40	Wages paid	$565,952,536
July temp. max.	94	Tax value	$6,670,835,780
Growing season (da.)	270	Income	$1,711,662,000
No. farms, 1982	797	Taxable sales	$648,094,265
No. acres in farms 165,277		Fed. expend.	$296,250,000
†Value per farm	$265,952	Crime Index	6,236
Cropland harvested 6,239		TDC Pop.	267

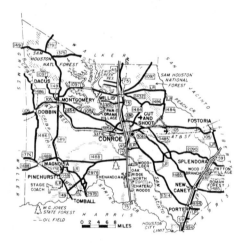

AGRICULTURE: About $18 million average annual income from beef, dairy cattle, hogs, horses; hay, nursery and greenhouse products, vegetables; substantial income from timber products.
BUSINESS: Many people work in Houston; center for lumber, oil production.
MANUFACTURING: 183 Plants; 4,500 Employees; Payroll, $76,000,000; Product Value, $435,200,000.
SERVICE INDUSTRIES: 575 Establishments; Receipts, $163,204,000; Annual Payroll, $58,065,000; No. Employees, 4,194.
CONROE (18,034) county seat; many residential communities; workers employed in Houston; distribution center; plants make oil, wood, helicopters, oil field equipment, other products; new hospital, nursing home; **Conroe College.**
Other towns include **Chateau Woods** (590), **Cut and Shoot** (568), **Magnolia** (867), **Montgomery** (258), **Oak Ridge** (2,504), **Panorama Village** (1,186), **Patton** (1,050), **Roman Forest** (929), **Shenandoah** (1,793), **Splendora** (721), **Stagecoach** (349), **Woodloch** (351), **Willis** (1,674), **Woodbranch** (720) and small part of Houston.

Morris

LOCATION: Northeast (G-20).
HISTORY: Named for legislator-jurist **W. W. Morris;** created from Titus County and organized in 1875.

Cong. Dist.	1
St. Sen. Dist.	1
St. Rep. Dist.	8
St. Dist. Cts.	76, 276
U.S. Jud. Dist.	E-Ml.
Ct. Appeals.	6
Admin. Jud. Dist.	1

MINERALS: Iron ore.

1982 Pop.	15,400		
Area (sq. mi.)	256		
Altitude (ft.)	250-600		
Ann. rainfall (in.)	46.12		
Jan. temp. min.	30		
July temp. max.	95		
Growing season (da.)	236		
No. farms, 1982	380		
No. acres in farms 74,136			
†Value per farm	$161,926		
Cropland harvested 10,374			
Voters reg.	9,053		
Whlsle. sales	$83,917,000		
Oil value	0		
No. employed	7,188	Wages paid.	$138,558,560
Tax value	$1,012,718,047	Income	$127,114,000
Taxable sales $77,914,402		Fed. Expd.	$25,175,000
Crime index	306	TDC Pop.	23

PHYSICAL FEATURES: Rolling, forested hills; drains to streams, **Lone Star** and **Daingerfield Lakes.**
RECREATION: Activities on **Lake O' The Pines,** many small lakes; fishing, hunting; **Daingerfield State Park;** museum in Daingerfield; local events.
AGRICULTURE: An estimated $10 million average yearly income, 70% from beef cattle; crops include peanuts, sweet potatoes, corn, sorghums, vegetables; pine and hardwood timber sales.
BUSINESS: Steel mill; manufacturing; tourism; livestock, timber production.
MANUFACTURING: 26 Plants; Employees, N.A.; Payroll, N.A.; Product Value, N.A.
SERVICE INDUSTRIES: 50 Establishments; Receipts, $14,299,000; Annual Payroll, $4,561,000; No. Employees, 416.
DAINGERFIELD (3,030) county seat; plants make garments, chemicals, roofing products; process pipe, other steel products; many work in steel mill; hospital, clinics, nursing home, library.
Other towns include **Lone Star** (2,036) site of steel mill; **Naples** (1,908) and **Omaha** (960).

Moore

LOCATION: Northwest (B-8).
HISTORY: Created, 1876, from Bexar District; organized 1892; named for Republic of Texas Navy Commander, **E. W. Moore.**

Cong. Dist.	13	U.S. Jud. Dist.	N-Am.
St. Sen. Dist.	31	Ct. Appeals.	7
St. Rep. Dist.	88	Admin. Jud. Dist.	9
St. Dist. Cts.	69		

PHYSICAL FEATURES: Flat to rolling, broken by creeks; sandy loams; **Lake Meredith.**
RECREATION: Lake Meredith activities; Dumas Dogie Days in June; historical museum; local events, art exhibits.
MINERALS: Production of natural gas, helium, oil.

1982 Pop.	17,200	Voters reg.	8,211
Area (sq. mi.)	905	Whlsle. sales	$76,144,000
Altitude (ft.)	2,900-3,700	Oil value	$26,136,142
Ann. rainfall (in.)	18.33	No. employed	6,219
Jan. temp. min.	20	Wages paid	$118,425,908
July temp. max.	93	Tax value	$1,361,698,451
Growing season (da.)	195	Income	$154,500,000
No. farms, 1982	270	Taxable sales	$59,976,895
No. acres in farms 535,362		Fed. expend.	$61,385,000
†Value per farm	$906,522	Crime Index	360
Cropland harv.	169,202	TDC Pop.	33

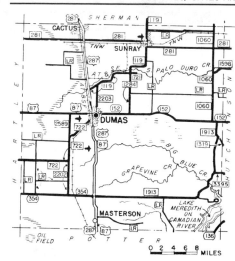

AGRICULTURE: About $100 million average annual income, 75% from cattle; custom feedlots; crops include sorghums, wheat, corn; 200,000 acres irrigated.

BUSINESS: Extensive petroleum operations; major natural gas producing county; beef processing, sorghum seed production, other agribusinesses.

MANUFACTURING: 18 Plants; Employees, N.A.; Payroll, N.A.; Product Value, N.A.

SERVICE INDUSTRIES: 80 Establishments; Receipts, $13,569,000; Annual Payroll, $4,442,000; No. Employees, 381.

DUMAS (12,194) county seat; tourism; petrochemical, refining, gas processing plants; feedlots; grain elevators; beef packers; fertilizer plants, leather tannery; hospital, nursing home.

Other towns include **Fritch** (2,299, part Hutchinson County), **Sunray** (1,952), **Cactus** (898) large beef packing facility.

Motley

LOCATION: Northwest (E-10).

HISTORY: Created out of Bexar District, 1876; organ-

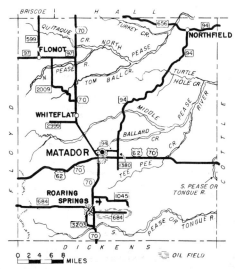

ized 1891; named for **Dr. J. W. Mottley,** Texas Declaration of Independence signer, but name misspelled in law.

Cong. Dist.	13	U.S. Jud. Dist.	N-Lb.
St. Sen. Dist.	30	Ct. Appeals	7
St. Rep. Dist.	84	Admin. Jud. Dist.	9
St. Dist. Cts.	110		

PHYSICAL FEATURES: Rough terrain, broken by Pease tributaries; sandy to red clay soils.

RECREATION: Local events; some hunting; Matador Ranch headquarters; spring-fed pool at Roaring Springs; settlers reunion.

MINERALS: Oil, sand and gravel, gas.

1982 Pop.	1,900	Voters reg.	1,189
Area (sq. mi.)	959	Whlsle. sales	$*
Altitude (ft.)	1,900-3,000	Oil value	$4,388,350
Ann. rainfall (in.)	20.35	No. employed	231
Jan. temp. min.	26	Wages paid	$2,484,672
July temp. max.	96	Tax value	$125,619,964
Growing season (da.)	218	Income	$11,651,000
No. farms, 1982	233	Taxable sales	$2,617,525
No. acres in farms	512,458	Fed. expend.	$10,868,000
†Value per farm	$523,124	Crime Index	12
Cropland harvested	54,964	TDC Pop.	2

AGRICULTURE: About $16 million average yearly income, ½ from beef cattle, horses; crops include cotton, peanuts, wheat, guar, other grains.

BUSINESS: Economy based on livestock, oil production.

MANUFACTURING: None noted in census report.

SERVICE INDUSTRIES: 4 Establishments; Receipts, $135,000; Annual Payroll, $19,000; No. Employees, 2.

MATADOR (1,052) county seat; farm trading center; **Roaring Springs** (315) cotton gin, jewelry manufacturing.

Nacogdoches

LOCATION: East (J-21).

HISTORY: Original county; created, 1836, organized, 1837; named for Indians; one of most historic areas.

Cong. Dist.	2	U.S. Jud. Dist.	E-Ty.
St. Sen. Dist.	3	Ct. Appeals	12
St. Rep. Dist.	10	Admin. Jud. Dist.	1
St. Dist. Cts.	145		

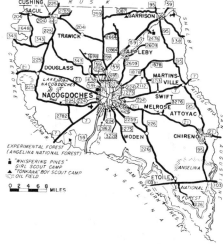

1982 Pop.	48,700	Voters reg.	28,112
Area (sq. mi.)	939	Whlsle. sales	$126,086,000
Altitude (ft.)	150-600	Oil value	$4,062,727
Ann. rainfall (in.)	47.53	No. employed	16,896
Jan. temp. min.	39	Wages paid	$217,248,000
July temp. max.	94	Tax value	$1,265,639,816
Growing season (da.)	243	Income	$390,377,000
No. farms, 1982	1,237	Taxable sales	$193,001,884
No. acres in farms	234,565	Fed. expend.	$81,994,000
†Value per farm	$199,064	Crime Index	1,733
Cropland harvested	22,170	TDC Pop.	112

PHYSICAL FEATURES: On divide between streams; hilly; two-thirds forested; red, gray, sandy soils; **Sam Rayburn Lake.**

RECREATION: Lake, river activities; **Stephen F. Austin University events; Angelina National Forest;** historic sites major tourist attraction, including **Old Stone Fort,** pioneer homes, museums.

MINERALS: First Texas oil found here, 1866; production of gas, oil, clay, stone.

AGRICULTURE: About $112 million average annual income, 90% from cattle, poultry, dairy products; leading broiler producing county; timber sales an estimated $12 million.

BUSINESS: Agribusinesses, manufacturing, education and tourism are leading economic factors.

MANUFACTURING: 69 Plants; 3,800 Employees; Payroll, $48,600,000; Product Value, $357,900,000.

SERVICE INDUSTRIES: 238 Establishments; Receipts, $44,230,000; Annual Payroll, $13,074,000; No. Employees, 1,319.

NACOGDOCHES (27,149) county seat; plants make valves, feed, fertilizers, aluminum furniture, wood products, business forms, transformers, candy, dresses, motor homes; poultry processing center, other agribusinesses; trade, tourism center; **Stephen F. Austin University;** hospitals, nursing homes; many historic sites, homes; museum.

Other towns include **Garrison** (1,059), **Cushing** (518), **Appleby** (453), **Chireno** (371).

Navarro

LOCATION: North central (I-17).

HISTORY: Created from Robertson County, organized in 1846; named for Republic of Texas leader, **Jose Antonio Navarro.**

Cong. Dist.	6	U.S. Jud. Dist.	N-DI.
St. Sen. Dist.	9	Ct. Appeals	10
St. Rep. Dist.	12	Admin. Jud. Dist.	3
St. Dist. Cts.	13		

PHYSICAL FEATURES: Level Blackland, some rolling; Chambers, Richland Creeks, Trinity River; **Navarro Mills Lake.**

RECREATION: Navarro Mills Lake activities; Pioneer Village; historic sites, homes; new reservoir under construction.

MINERALS: Longest continuous Texas oil flow; over 200 million bbls. since 1895; production of oil, gas, sand and gravel.

1982 Pop.	36,700	Voters reg.	20,695
Area (sq. mi.)	1,068	Whlsle. sales	$126,916,000
Altitude (ft.)	270-600	Oil value	$22,788,025
Ann. rainfall (in.)	37.74	No. employed	11,768
Jan. temp. min.	36	Wages paid	$177,918,004
July temp. max.	96	Tax value	$1,222,460,543
Growing season (da.)	259	Income	$324,222,000
No. farms, 1982	1,464	Taxable sales	$144,865,836
No. acres in farms	501,179	Fed. expend.	$81,845,000
†Value per farm	$212,316	Crime Index	1,695
Cropland harv.	108,610	TDC Pop.	130

AGRICULTURE: About $38 million average yearly income, 2/3 from beef, dairy cattle, hogs, horses; crops include cotton, sorghums, wheat, oats, hay, corn; salvage lumber and firewood sold.

BUSINESS: Diversified manufacturing, agribusinesses, oil field operations, distribution.

MANUFACTURING: 50 Plants; 2,700 Employees; Payroll, $46,500,000; Product Value, $259,200,000.

SERVICE INDUSTRIES: 152 Establishments; Receipts, $39,440,000; Annual Payroll, $14,355,000; No. Employees, 1,125.

CORSICANA (21,712) county seat; major industrial growth; large bakery; plants make hats, clothing, bottles, flat glass; oil field specialties, chemicals, plastic pipe, architectural metal products, railroad products, insulation; meat packing; other products; distribution center; **Navarro College;** new hospital.

Kerens (1,582) has fertilizer and petrochemical complex, other manufacturing; nursing home.

Other towns include **Angus** (244), **Barry** (192), **Blooming Grove** (823), **Dawson** (747), **Emhouse** (197), **Frost** (564), **Goodlow** (343), **Mustang** (12), **Powell** (111), **Retreat** (255), **Rice** (439), **Richland** (260) and **Streetman** (415, mostly Freestone County).

Newton

LOCATION: Easternmost county (L-22).

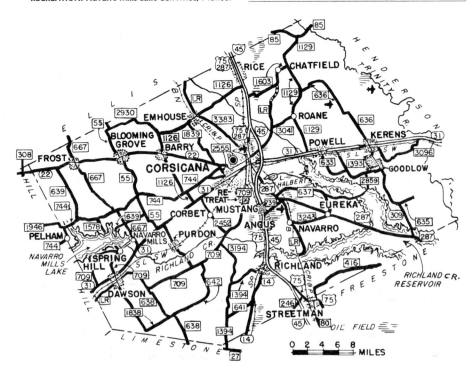

HISTORY: Created, organized, 1846, from Jasper County; was named for **U.S. Revolutionary Corp. John Newton.**

RECREATION: Water sports; fishing, hunting, tourism, **E. O. Siecke State Forest.**

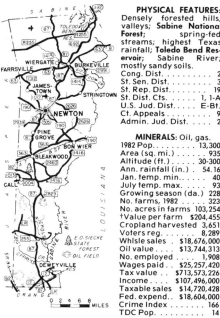

PHYSICAL FEATURES: Densely forested hills, valleys; **Sabine National Forest;** spring-fed streams; highest Texas rainfall; **Toledo Bend Reservoir;** Sabine River; mostly sandy soils.

Cong. Dist.	2
St. Sen. Dist.	3
St. Rep. Dist.	19
St. Dist. Cts.	1, 1-A
U.S. Jud. Dist.	E-Bt.
Ct. Appeals	9
Admin. Jud. Dist.	2

MINERALS: Oil, gas.

1982 Pop.	13,300
Area (sq. mi.)	935
Altitude (ft.)	30-300
Ann. rainfall (in.)	54.16
Jan. temp. min.	40
July temp. max.	93
Growing season (da.)	228
No. farms, 1982	323
No. acres in farms	103,254
†Value per farm	$204,455
Cropland harvested	3,651
Voters reg.	8,289
Whlsle sales	$18,676,000
Oil value	$13,744,313
No. employed	1,908
Wages paid	$25,257,420
Tax value	$713,573,226
Income	$107,496,000
Taxable sales	$14,720,428
Fed. expend.	$18,604,000
Crime Index	166
TDC Pop.	14

AGRICULTURE: About $3.8 million average yearly income from beef cattle, poultry, peaches, vegetables. Timber income estimated at $15 million.

MANUFACTURING: 25 Plants; 700 Employees; Payroll, $8,400,000; Product Value, $50,700,000.

SERVICE INDUSTRIES: 18 Establishments; Receipts, $1,772,000; Annual Payroll, $458,000; No. Employees, 52.

BUSINESS: Forestry activities, beef cattle production, tourism main economic factors. Crawfish production beginning.

NEWTON (1,620) county seat; lumber manufacturing; plywood mill; hospital; tourism.

Nolan

LOCATION: West central (I-11).

HISTORY: Created from Bexar, Young Districts, 1876; organized 1881; named for adventurer **Philip Nolan.**

Cong. Dist.	17	U.S. Jud. Dist.	N-Ab.
St. Sen. Dist.	24	Ct. Appeals	11
St. Rep. Dist.	78	Admin. Jud. Dist.	7
St. Dist. Cts.	32		

PHYSICAL FEATURES: On divide between Brazos, Colorado watersheds; mostly red sandy loams, some waxy, sandy soils; **Sweetwater, Trammell, Oak Creek Lakes.**

RECREATION: Sweetwater and Oak Creek Lakes; hunting; rattlesnake roundup in March; rodeos, other local events.

MINERALS: Production of oil, gas, cement, gypsum, stone, sand and gravel, clays.

1982 Pop.	18,100	Voters reg.	8,843
Area (sq. mi.)	915	Whlsle. sales	$102,860,000
Altitude (ft.)	2,000-2,700	Oil value	$80,942,515
Ann. rainfall (in.)	22.19	No. employed	5,741
Jan. temp. min.	30	Wages paid	$85,981,460
July temp. max.	96	Tax value	$630,969,737
Growing season (da.)	221	Income	$156,796,000
No. farms, 1982	452	Taxable sales	$65,957,554
No. acres in farms	472,843	Fed. expend.	$44,229,000
†Value per farm	$379,465	Crime Index	818
Cropland harvested	71,642	TDC Pop.	73

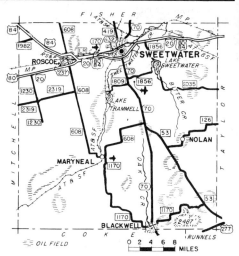

AGRICULTURE: An estimated $25 million average annual income from cattle, hogs, sheep and cotton, grains; about 4,000 acres irrigated for cotton.

BUSINESS: Varied manufacturing; agribusinesses; oil and gas production.

MANUFACTURING: 19 Plants; 1,300 Employees; Payroll, $22,100,000; Product Value, $131,900,000.

SERVICE INDUSTRIES: 79 Establishments; Receipts, $14,591,000; Annual Payroll, $4,962,000; No. Employees, 523.

SWEETWATER (12,242) county seat; plants make gypsum products, cement, cotton oil products, apparel, metal detectors; **Texas State Technical Institute;** hospital, nursing homes.

Roscoe (1,628) is trade center; **Blackwell** (286, partly Coke County).

Nueces

LOCATION: Southern coast (R-16).

HISTORY: Name is Spanish for nuts, from river; created, organized, 1846, out of San Patricio County.

Cong. Dist.	15, 27	U.S. Jud. Dist.	S-CC
St. Sen. Dist.	20	Ct. Appeals	13
St. Rep. Dist.	34-36	Admin. Jud. Dist.	5
St. Dist. Cts.	28, 94,		
105, 117, 148, 214, 319, 347			

RECREATION: Major resort area; fishing, water sports; **Padre Island National Seashore; Mustang Island State Park; Art Museum of South Texas, Corpus Christi Museum; Buccaneer Days,** jazz festival, deep sea roundup, other metropolitan events.

MINERALS: Production of oil, gas, cement, lime, sand and gravel.

PHYSICAL FEATURES: Flat, rich soils, broken by bays, Nueces River, Petronila Creek; includes **Mustang Island,** north tip of **Padre Island.**

1982 Pop.	283,100	Voters reg.	149,137
Area (sq. mi.)	847	Whlsle. sales	$1,889,109,000
Altitude (ft.) sea-level-180		Oil value	$58,326,120
Ann. rainfall (in.)	28.53	No. employed	110,475
Jan. temp. min.	47	Wages paid	$1,911,887,248
July temp. max.	94	Tax value	$11,128,963,398
Growing season (da.)	309	Income	$2,568,762,000
No. farms, 1982	735	Tax. sales	$1,858,251,264
No. acres in farms	458,844	Fed. exp.	$1,080,121,000
†Value per farm	$743,083	Crime Index	21,185
Cropland harv.	317,513	TDC Pop.	584

AGRICULTURE: About $60 million average annual income, over 80% from grain sorghums, corn, cotton; leading sorghum county; livestock includes beef, dairy cattle, horses.

BUSINESS: Diversified economy includes petroleum, agriculture, tourism, coastal shipping, manufacturing; military complex; see metro page.

MANUFACTURING: 244 Plants; 12,300 Employees; Payroll, $260,000,000; Product Value, $8,575,200,000.

Nueces County (Cont'd.)

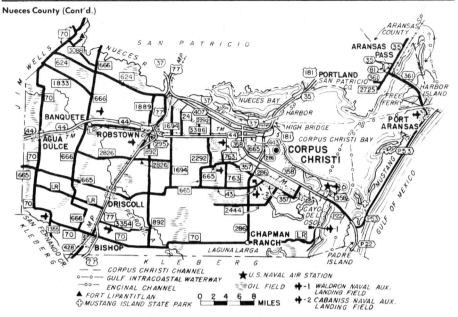

CORPUS CHRISTI CHANNEL
GULF INTRACOASTAL WATERWAY
ENCINAL CHANNEL
▲ FORT LIPANTITLAN
⊕ MUSTANG ISLAND STATE PARK

★ U.S. NAVAL AIR STATION
◆ OIL FIELD
✈-1 WALDRON NAVAL AUX. LANDING FIELD
✈-2 CABANISS NAVAL AUX. LANDING FIELD

0 2 4 6 8 MILES

SERVICE INDUSTRIES: 1,977 Establishments; Receipts, $622,374,000; Annual Payroll, $221,513,000; No. Employees, 15,302.

CORPUS CHRISTI (232,134) county seat; major seaport; petrochemical, aluminum plants; clothing manufacturing; seafood processing, electronics, telecommunications; offshore drilling equipment, zinc processing, corn products, other plants; **Naval Air Station; Army depot; Corpus Christi State University; Del Mar College;** hospitals; museums; recreation centers; gateway to **Padre Island National Seashore;** near **Aransas Wildlife Refuge.**

Other towns include **Agua Dulce** (934), **Aransas Pass** (7,173, part Aransas, San Patricio counties), **Bishop** (3,706) chemical plants, **Driscoll** (648), **Port Aransas** (1,968), **Portland** (12,023, mostly San Patricio), **Robstown** (12,100) clothing plant, hospital, agribusiness; **San Patricio** (241, mostly San Patricio County).

Ochiltree

LOCATION: Extreme Northwest (A-10).

HISTORY: Created from Bexar District, 1876, organized, 1889; named for Republic of Texas leader, **W. B. Ochiltree.**

Cong. Dist.	13	U.S. Jud. Dist.	N-Am.
St. Sen. Dist.	31	Ct. Appeals	7
St. Rep. Dist.	88	Admin. Jud. Dist.	9
St. Dist. Cts.	84		

PHYSICAL FEATURES: Level, broken by creeks; deep loam, clay soils.

RECREATION: Local events; Wolf Creek Park; Indian "Buried City" site.

MINERALS: Oil, gas.

1982 Pop.	10,800	Voters reg.	5,249
Area (sq. mi.)	919	Whlse. sales	$128,434,000
Altitude (ft.)	2,500-3,100	Oil value	$100,953,441
Ann. rainfall (in.)	20.48	No. employed	4,299
Jan. temp. min.	18	Wages paid	$80,093,960
July temp. max.	93	Tax value	$832,745,286
Growing season (da.)	191	Income	$107,606,000
No. farms, 1982	394	Taxable sales	$63,539,790
No. acres in farms	612,836	Fed. expend.	$44,553,000
†Value per farm	$733,551	Crime Index	336
Cropland harv.	267,989	TDC Pop.	30

AGRICULTURE: About $50.5 million average annual income, from beef cattle; crops include wheat, sorghums, corn, alfalfa. About 60,000 acres irrigated for wheat and sorghum.

BUSINESS: Oil, agribusinesses, center of large feedlot operations.

MANUFACTURING: None quoted in census report.

SERVICE INDUSTRIES: 70 Establishments; Receipts, $16,203,000; Annual Payroll, $5,104,000; No. Employees, 435.

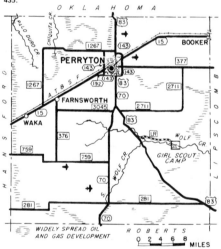

WIDELY SPREAD OIL AND GAS DEVELOPMENT

0 2 4 6 8 MILES

PERRYTON (7,991) county seat; oil field services and equipment manufacturing, cattle feeding, grain center; plastic fittings made; hospital, nursing home.

Oldham

LOCATION: Northwest (C-7).

HISTORY: Created 1876, from Bexar District, organized, 1880; named for editor-Confederate Senator, **W. S. Oldham.**

Cong. Dist.	13	U.S. Jud. Dist.	N-Am.
St. Sen. Dist.	31	Ct. Appeals	7
St. Rep. Dist.	88	Admin. Jud. Dist.	9
St. Dist. Cts.	222		

PHYSICAL FEATURES: Level, broken by Canadian River and tributaries.

RECREATION: Old Tascosa, with **Boot Hill Cemetery,** pioneer cowboy towns.

MINERALS: Sand and gravel, oil, gas, stone.

1982 Pop.	2,300	Voters reg.	1,341
Area (sq. mi.)	1,485	Whsle. sales	$12,842,000
Altitude (ft.)	3,200-4,200	Oil value	$31,736,221
Ann. rainfall (in.)	19.54	No. employed	595
Jan. temp. min.	22	Wages paid	$8,009,008
July temp. max.	92	Tax value	$226,623,106
Growing season (da.)	186	Income	$12,972,000
No. farms, 1982	150	Taxable sales	$10,647,252
No. acs. in farms	1,116,543	Fed. expend.	$10,619,000
†Value per farm	$2,029,327	Crime Index	44
Cropland harvested	72,739	TDC Pop.	7

AGRICULTURE: About $27.5 million average yearly income, 80% from beef cattle; crops include sorghums, wheat; 25,000 acres irrigated.

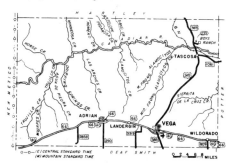

BUSINESS: Ranching center.

MANUFACTURING: None noted in census report.

SERVICE INDUSTRIES: 8 Establishments; Receipts, $1,659,000; Annual Payroll, $356,000; No. Employees, N.A.

VEGA (900) county seat; ranching trade center; **Cal Farley's Boys Ranch** on U.S. Highway 385; **Adrian (222).**

Orange

LOCATION: Extreme Southeast (M-22).

HISTORY: Created from Jefferson County, organized in 1852; named for early orange grove.

Cong. Dist.	2	U.S. Jud. Dist.	E-B
St. Sen. Dist.	4	Ct. Appeals	9
St. Rep. Dist.	19	Admin. Jud. Dist.	2
St. Dist. Cts.	128, 163, 260		

PHYSICAL FEATURES: Bounded by Sabine, Neches, **Sabine Lake;** coastal soils; two-thirds timbered.

RECREATION: Fishing, hunting; other water sports; county park, museums, historical homes, crawfish promotion day, metropolitan area events.

MINERALS: Production of oil, gas, clays, sand and gravel.

1982 Pop.	88,200	Voters reg.	44,920
Area (sq. mi.)	362	Whsle. sales	$88,064,000
Altitude (ft.)	sea level-31	Oil value	$21,988,695
Ann. rainfall (in.)	59.92	No. employed	21,261
Jan. temp. min.	41	Wages paid	$454,473,720
July temp. max.	91	Tax value	$2,910,020,574
Growing season (da.)	240	Income	$929,151,000
No. farms, 1982	315	Taxable sales	$254,773,967
No. acres in farms	59,534	Fed. expend.	$253,799,000
†Value per farm	$343,981	Crime Index	3,784
Cropland harvested	8,578	TDC Pop.	187

AGRICULTURE: About $5.5 million from forest products, including Christmas trees; rice, soybeans, nursery stock, cattle; crawfish production.

BUSINESS: Petrochemicals; shipbuilding, shipping, agribusinesses, tourism; lumber processing; see Beaumont-Port Arthur metro page.

MANUFACTURING: 82 Plants; Employees, N.A.; Payroll, N.A.; Product Value, N.A.

SERVICE INDUSTRIES: 258 Establishments; Receipts, $67,563,000; Annual Payroll, $20,528,000; No. Employees, 1,938.

ORANGE: (23,628) county seat; seaport; plants make petrochemicals, container board, ships, cement, carbon black, steel, plastics, marble products; rice, soy-

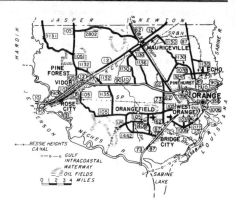

bean, timber processing and shipping; **Lamar University** branch, hospital, theater, museum.

Other towns include **Bridge City (7,667), Pinehurst (2,928), Vidor (11,834), West Orange (4,610), Pine Forest (639), Rose City (663).**

Palo Pinto

LOCATION: North central (H-14).

HISTORY: Created, 1856, from Bosque, Navarro Counties; organized, 1857; named for creek, Spanish for painted stick.

Cong. Dist.	17	U.S. Jud. Dist.	N-FW
St. Sen. Dist.	22	Ct. Appeals	11
St. Rep. Dist.	64	Admin. Jud. Dist.	8
St. Dist. Cts.	29		

PHYSICAL FEATURES: Broken, hilly, wooded in parts; **Possum Kingdom Lake; Palo Pinto Creek Reservoir;** sandy, gray, black soils.

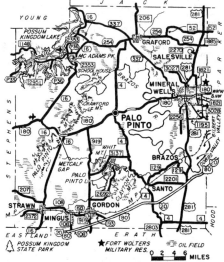

1982 Pop.	25,700	Voters reg.	13,632
Area (sq. mi.)	949	Whsle. sales	$69,442,000
Altitude (ft.)	800-1,450	Oil value	$7,514,207
Ann. rainfall (in.)	30.13	No. employed	7,403
Jan. temp. min.	33	Wages paid	$109,575,724
July temp. max.	96	Tax value	$821,014,110
Growing season (da.)	221	Income	$202,679,000
No. farms, 1982	655	Taxable sales	$111,748,597
No. acres in farms	478,296	Fed. expend.	$52,301,000
†Value per farm	$337,928	Crime Index	1,152
Cropland harvested	20,010	TDC Pop.	64

RECREATION: Tourist center; lake activities; hunting, fishing, water sports; **Possum Kingdom State Park; Mineral Wells State Park; Lake Palo Pinto.**

MINERALS: Oil, gas, clays, sand and gravel.

AGRICULTURE: About $12 million average annual income, more than 90% from beef cattle, hogs, goats, sheep, horses; some pecans, peaches and vegetables, grains, hay; hunting, fishing leases; firewood, cedar fence posts marketed.

BUSINESS: Varied manufacturing, tourism, agribusinesses.

MANUFACTURING: 44 Plants; 2,400 Employees; Payroll, $33,300,000; Product Value, $137,600,000.

SERVICE INDUSTRIES: 116 Establishments; Receipts, $19,122,000; Annual Payroll, $6,335,000; No Employees, 612.

PALO PINTO (est. 350) county seat (unincorporated community); annual old settlers reunion; farm trade center.

Mineral Wells (14,468, partly in Parker) plants make clay pipe, aircraft systems, plastics, electronic products, brick, feeds, clothes, many other products; county hospital; tourist center.

Other towns include **Strawn** (694), **Graford** (495), **Gordon** (516), **Mingus** (212).

Panola

LOCATION: On Louisiana line (I-21).

HISTORY: Name is Indian word for cotton; created from Harrison, Shelby Counties and organized, 1846.

Cong. Dist. 1	U.S. Jud. Dist. . . . . E-Ty.
St. Sen. Dist. 1	Ct. Appeals 6, 12
St. Rep. Dist. 10	Admin. Jud. Dist. 1
St. Dist. Cts. 123	

PHYSICAL FEATURES: Three-fifths forested, rolling plain; broken by Sabine, **Murvaul Creek and Reservoir, Toledo Bend Lake.**

RECREATION: Lake Murvaul fishing, other water activities; hunting; scenic drives; Jim Reeves memorial; historic sites, homes; museum; **Pirtle Boy Scout Reservation.**

MINERALS: Gas, oil, coal.

1982 Pop. 22,000	Voters reg. 12,816
Area (sq. mi.) 812	Whlsle. sales . $32,587,000
Altitude (ft.) 200-500	Oil value $16,542,919
Ann. rainfall (in.) . . 48.08	No. employed 5,170
Jan. temp. min. 38	Wages paid . . $62,431,432
July temp. max. 95	Tax value . $2,027,540,324
Growing season (da.) 240	Income $190,778,000
No. farms, 1982 934	Taxable sales $47,667,508
No. acres in farms 207,134	Fed. expend. . $33,498,000
†Value per farm $218,422	Crime Index 527
Cropland harvested 17,600	TDC Pop. 36

AGRICULTURE: About $35 million average yearly income, 90% from cattle, hogs, poultry; among leading broiler counties; timber sales significant.

BUSINESS: Agribusinesses; varied manufacturing; forest industries; gas processing, oil field operation.

MANUFACTURING: 19 Plants; 600 Employees; Payroll, $9,000,000; Product Value, $51,000,000.

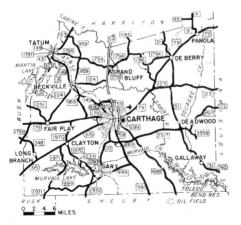

SERVICE INDUSTRIES: 74 Establishments; Receipts, $13,749,000; Annual Payroll, $3,945,000; No. Employees, 435.

CARTHAGE (6,447) county seat; plants process petroleum, make oil field equipment; poultry processing, supplies; sawmills; **Panola Junior College;** county hospital, clinics, nursing homes. **Beckville** (945), **Gary** (322), **Tatum** (1,339, mostly Rusk County) other principal towns.

Parker

LOCATION: North central (H-15).

HISTORY: Named for pioneer legislator, **Isaac Parker;** created, organized, 1855, from Bosque, Navarro Counties.

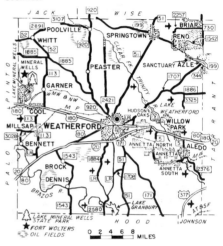

Cong. Dist. 17	U.S. Jud. Dist. . . . . N-FW
St. Sen. Dist. 22	Ct. Appeals 2
St. Rep. Dist. 63	Admin. Jud. Dist. 8
St. Dist. Cts. 43	

PHYSICAL FEATURES: Hilly, broken by Brazos, Trinity tributaries; varied soils; **Lake Weatherford** and **Lake Granbury.**

RECREATION: Railroad museum; park; water sports; nature trails; hunting; homes tour; festival in spring.

MINERALS: Production of gas, oil, stone, sand and gravel, clays.

1982 Pop. 47,900	Voters reg. 26,937
Area (sq. mi.) 902	Whlsle. sales . $94,125,000
Altitude (ft.) 700-1,400	Oil value $1,921,448
Ann. rainfall (in.) . . 32,37	No. employed 9,175
Jan. temp. min. 34	Wages paid . . $122,776,708
July temp. max. 96	Tax value . $1,189,030,484
Growing season (da.) 225	Income $492,917,000
No. farms, 1982 . . . 1,751	Taxable sales $137,119,857
No. acres in farms 374,611	Fed. expend. . $73,310,000
†Value per farm $282,370	Crime Index 1,490
Cropland harvested 39,114	TDC Pop. 66

AGRICULTURE: About $41 million average yearly income, 80% from beef, dairy cattle, hogs, horses; crops chiefly peanuts, peaches, melons, hay; firewood marketed.

BUSINESS: Primarily agribusinesses; varied manufacturing; many work in Fort Worth; county part of Dallas-Fort Worth SMSA. See metro page.

MANUFACTURING: 73 Plants; 1,400 Employees; Payroll, $19,100,000; Product Value, $111,500,000.

SERVICE INDUSTRIES: 158 Establishments; Receipts, $22,622,000; Annual Payroll, $6,768,000; No. Employees, 702.

WEATHERFORD (12,049) county seat; agribusiness center; plants make plastics, rubber products, oil field equipment; **Weatherford College;** hospital, nursing homes.

Other towns include **Azle** (5,822, mostly Tarrant County), **Springtown** (1,658), **Mineral Wells** (14,468, mostly Palo Pinto County), **Aledo** (1,027), **Reno** (1,174), **Briar** (1,810, mostly Wise County), **Cool** (202), **Willow Park** (1,107), **Anneta** (454), **Anneta North** (197), **Anneta South** (249), **Hudson Oaks** (309) and **Millsap** (439).

nesses; hospital, nursing home. **Bovina** (1,499) is farm trade center.

Parmer

LOCATION: Northwest (D-7).
HISTORY: Named for Republic of Texas figure, **Martin Parmer;** created from Bexar District, 1876, organized, 1907.

Cong. Dist.	19	U.S. Jud. Dist.	N-Am.
St. Sen. Dist.	31	Ct. Appeals	7
St. Rep. Dist.	85	Admin. Jud. Dist.	9
St. Dist. Cts.	287		

PHYSICAL FEATURES: Level, broken by draws, playas; sandy, clay, loam soils.
RECREATION: Maize Days in September; other local events.
MINERALS: Not significant.

1982 Pop.	11,100	Voters reg.	4,346
Area (sq. mi.)	885	Whlsle. sales	$160,908,000
Altitude (ft.)	3,800-4,100	Oil value	$45,620
Ann. rainfall (in.)	17.50	No. employed	3,132
Jan. temp. min.	21	Wages paid	$47,864,140
July temp. max.	92	Tax value	$392,673,884
Growing season (da.)	183	Income	$62,493,000
No. farms, 1982	661	Taxable sales	$15,401,327
No. acres in farms	544,890	Fed. expend.	$92,000,000
†Value per farm	$548,368	Crime Index	216
Cropland harv.	321,588	TDC Pop.	17

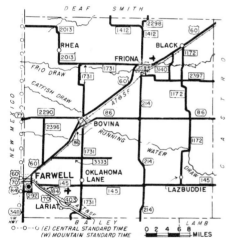

AGRICULTURE: About $163 million average yearly income from cattle, hogs, sheep, crops; among leading counties in total farm income; large cattle feeding operations; a leading producer of cattle, cattle on feed, corn, sugar beets, sunflowers, potatoes; crops also include sorghums, cotton, wheat, barley, vegetables, soybeans; 260,000 acres irrigated.
BUSINESS: Cattle feeding; grain elevators; meat packing plant, varied other agribusinesses.
MANUFACTURING: 11 Plants; Employees, N.A.; Payroll, N.A.; Product Value, N.A.
SERVICE INDUSTRIES: 31 Establishments; Receipts, $5,271,000; Annual Payroll, $1,768,000; No. Employees, 158.
FARWELL (1,354) county seat, agribusiness and trade center on New Mexico line; grain elevators; well drilling services; plants make farm and irrigation equipment, cattle feed, apparel, other products.
Friona (3,809) grain elevators; fertilizer processing; meat packing plant; large feedlots; other agribusi-

Polk

LOCATION: Southeast (K-20).

HISTORY: Named for **U.S. President James K. Polk;** created from Liberty County, organized, 1846.

Cong. Dist.	2	U.S. Jud. Dist.	S-Hn.
St. Sen. Dist.	3	Ct. Appeals	9
St. Rep. Dist.	18	Admin. Jud. Dist.	2
St. Dist. Cts.	9, 2D9, 258		

PHYSICAL FEATURES: Rolling; densely forested, with Big Thicket, unique plant, animal-life area; Neches, Trinity River, tributaries.
RECREATION: Tourist center; **Lake Livingston** fishing, other water activities; hunting; **Alabama-Coushatta Indian Reservation, Museum; Big Thicket;** woodlands trails, champion trees; historic homes; local events.
MINERALS: Oil, gas, sand and gravel.

1982 Pop.	26,200	Voters reg.	15,921
Area (sq. mi.)	1,061	Whlsle. sales	$62,066,000
Altitude (ft.)	100-300	Oil value	$23,375,635
Ann. rainfall (in.)	47.19	No. employed	6,599
Jan. temp. min.	39	Wages paid	$92,237,884
July temp. max.	93	Tax value	$1,079,866,848
Growing season (da.)	250	Income	$225,503,000
No. farms, 1982	530	Taxable sales	$101,330,087
No. acres in farms	161,772	Fed. expend.	$62,942,000
†Value per farm	$264,994	Crime Index	985
Cropland harvested	7,564	TDC Pop.	49

AGRICULTURE: Leading Texas county in timber products delivered to mill and rail sidings, Christmas trees; $10 million from livestock, poultry; crops include peaches, blueberries, vegetables, soybeans.
BUSINESS: Timber, lumber production, tourism, oil.
MANUFACTURING: 37 Plants; 1,200 Employees; Payroll, $21,000,000; Product Value, $115,100,000.
SERVICE INDUSTRIES: 92 Establishments; Receipts, $18,860,000; Annual Payroll, $6,871,000; No. Employees, 601.
LIVINGSTON (4,928) county seat; center for lumbering, tourism, oil.
Corrigan (1,770) plywood plant; **Goodrich** (350); **Onalaska** (386), **Seven Oaks** (300) other towns.

Pecos

LOCATION: West (L-7).

HISTORY: Second-largest county; created from Presidio, 1871; organized, 1872; named for **Pecos River,** name origin uncertain.

PHYSICAL FEATURES: High, broken plateau; draining to Pecos and tributaries; sandy, clay, loam soils.

MINERALS: A leading petroleum producing county; gas, oil.

AGRICULTURE: $27 million average yearly income, 75% from cattle, sheep, goats; crops include cotton, grains, vegetables, alfalfa, pecans; 20,000 acres irrigated.

BUSINESS: Oil, gas chief factor in economy; agribusiness center; some manufacturing; tourism.

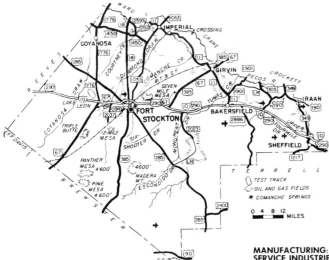

Cong. Dist.	21
St. Sen Dist	25
St. Rep. Dist	68
St. Dist. Cts.	83, 112
U.S. Jud. Dist	W-Pe.
Ct. Appeals	8
Admin. Jud. Dist	6

1982 Pop.	16,900
Area (sq. mi.)	4,776
Altitude (ft.)	2,000-5,200
Ann. rainfall (in.)	11.85
Jan. temp. min.	33
July temp. max.	94
Growing season (da.)	224
No. farms, 1982	284
No. ac. in farms.	2,616,740
†Value per farm	$1,078,817
Cropland harvested	18,482
Voters Reg.	7,791
Whlsle. sales	$55,804,000
Oil value	$1,133,265,343
No. employed	5,403
Wages paid	$101,835,656
Tax value	$7,830,182,655
Income	$113,120,000
Taxable sales	$58,821,974
Fed. Exp.	$16,134,000
Crime index	459
TDC Pop.	35

MANUFACTURING: None noted in Census report.

SERVICE INDUSTRIES: 76 Establishments; Receipts, $17,170,000; Annual Payroll, $4,689,000; No. Employees, 512.

FORT STOCKTON (8,688) county seat; distribution center for petroleum industry; tire test center; oil, gas processing; sulphur production; garment plant, varied manufacturing; hospital, nursing home; water carnival in July.

Iraan (1,358) is oil, gas center with ranching, tourist business; hospital.

RECREATION: A major tourist area for recreational, scenic, historical attractions; **Old Fort Stockton, Annie Riggs Museum,** stage coach stop; scenic drives; **Dinosaur Track Roadside Park;** cattle trail sites; **Alley Oop Park** at Iraan; archaeological museum with oil, ranch heritage collections.

Potter

LOCATION: Northwest (C-8).

HISTORY: Named for **Robert Potter,** Republic of Texas leader; created, 1876, from Bexar District; organized, 1887.

Cong. Dist.	13	U.S. Jud. Dist.	N-Am.
St. Sen. Dist.	31	Ct. Appeals	7
St. Rep. Dist.	87	Admin. Jud. Dist.	9
St. Dist. Cts.	47, 108, 181, 251, 320		

PHYSICAL FEATURES: Mostly level, part rolling; broken by Canadian River and tributaries; sandy, sandy loam, chocolate loam, clay soils; **Lake Meredith.**

RECREATION: Metropolitan events (ask chamber of commerce); **Lake Meredith** activities; **Alibates Flint Quarry National Monument;** hunting, fishing; Tri-State Fair.

MINERALS: Gas, oil, cement, stone, clays, sand and gravel.

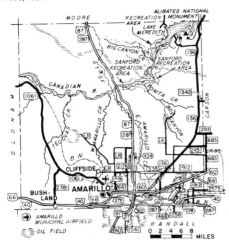

1982 Pop.	103,300	Voters reg.	40,566
Area (sq. mi.)	902	Whlsle. sales	$1,717,559,000
Altitude (ft.)	3,000-3,800	Oil value	$10,229,360
Ann. rainfall (in.)	20.28	No. employed	60,636
Jan. temp. min.	24	Wages paid	$1,031,702,636
July temp. max.	92	Tax value	$3,001,444,675
Growing season (da.)	190	Income	$892,910,000
No. farms, 1982	178	Taxable sales	$967,863,727
No. acres in farms	490,937	Fed. acres	$405,048,000
†Value per farm	$688,230	Crime Index	10,254
Cropland harvested	21,878	TDC Pop.	332

AGRICULTURE: About $10 million average yearly income, 80% from beef cattle; wheat, sorghums, chief crops. More than 20,000 acres irrigated.

BUSINESS: Transportation, distribution hub for large area; feedlot operations; petrochemicals; gas processing; agribusinesses; see metro page.

MANUFACTURING: 163 Plants; 11,600 Employees; Payroll, $213,700,000; Product Value, $2,596,900,000.

SERVICE INDUSTRIES: 872 Establishments; Receipts, $296,005,000; Annual Payroll, $100,366,000; No. Employees, 7,207.

AMARILLO (149,230, part in Randall County) county seat; urban hub for North Panhandle oil, ranching area; distribution, marketing center for portions of five states; plants make many products; food processing; copper refinery; **Amarillo College; Northwest Hospital School of Nursing; Texas State Technical Institute** branch; nine hospitals, nursing homes; airport; museum; varied cultural, athletic and other recreational events.

Presidio

LOCATION: Extreme Southwest (M-5).
HISTORY: Created, 1850, from Bexar District; organized, 1875; now 4th largest county; named for Spanish **Presidio del Norte** (fort of the north).

Cong. Dist.	21	U.S. Jud. Dist.	W-Pe.
St. Sen. Dist.	25	Ct. Appeals	8
St. Rep. Dist.	68	Admin. Jud. Dist.	6
St. Dist. Cts.	83		

PHYSICAL FEATURES: Rugged, mountainous; some of Texas' tallest mountains; many scenic drives; clays, loams, sandy loams on uplands; intermountain wash; timber sparse; **Capote Falls**, state's highest.
RECREATION: Tourist center; near **Big Bend National Park;** mild climate and scenic surroundings; extensive hunting; scenic drives along Rio Grande in mountains; ghost towns, **Fort D. A. Russell; Fort Leaton State Park;** gateway to Mexico West Coast by rail; large ranches; ask chamber of commerce, Marfa.
MINERALS: Sand and gravel.

1982 Pop.	5,500	Voters reg.	2,854
Area (sq. mi.)	3,857	Whlsle. sales	$2,917,000
Altitude (ft.)	2,400-7,730	Oil value	0
Ann. rainfall (in.)	8.47	No. employed	801
Jan. temp. min.	33	Wages paid	$9,282,656
July temp. max.	100	Tax value	$255,353,322
Growing season (da.)	238	Income	$23,596,000
No. farms, 1982	137	Taxable sales	$10,507,540
No. ac. in farms	1,981,461	Fed. expend.	$12,915,000
†Value per farm	$2,847,686	Crime Index	42
Cropland harvested	N.A.	TDC Pop.	4

AGRICULTURE: About 65% of $18 million average farm income from cattle, sheep, goat ranching; cantaloupes, onions, alfalfa chief crops; 10,000 acres irrigated.
BUSINESS: Ranching, income from hunting leases, tourism major economic factors.
MANUFACTURING: None noted in census report.
SERVICE INDUSTRIES: 14 Establishments; Receipts,

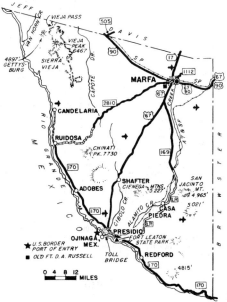

$758,000; Annual Payroll, $243,000; No. Employees, 51.
MARFA (2,466) county seat; ranching supply and tourist center for large area; major gateway to mountainous area on Rio Grande in Texas and Mexico; many nearby tourist attractions, including scenic rail route to Mexican West Coast; U.S. Border Patrol sector headquarters.
Presidio (1,603) international bridge to open in 1985.

Rains

LOCATION: Northeast (G-18).

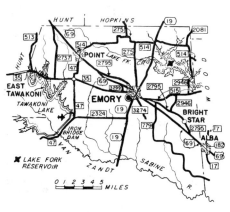

HISTORY: County, county seat named for **Emory Rains,** Republic of Texas leader; county created, organized, 1870, from Hopkins, Hunt, Wood.
PHYSICAL FEATURES: Rolling; partly Blackland, sandy loams, sandy soils; Sabine River, **Lake Tawakoni.**
RECREATION: Lake Tawakoni and **Lake Fork Reservoir** activities, local events.
Minerals: Gas, oil, coal.

Cong. Dist.	4	U.S. Jud. Dist.	E-Ty.
St. Sen. Dist.	2	Ct. Appeals	12
St. Rep. Dist.	3	Admin. Jud. Dist.	1
St. Dist. Cts.	8, 354		

1982 Pop.	5,200	Voters reg.	3,674
Area (sq. mi.)	243	Whlsle. sales	$11,581,000
Altitude (ft.)	350-550	Oil value	0
Ann. rainfall (in.)	42.95	No. employed	929
Jan. temp. min.	35	Wages paid	$11,686,244
July temp. max.	94	Tax value	$183,349,566
Growing season (da.)	242	Income	$44,381,000
No. farms, 1982	438	Taxable sales	$8,823,831
No. acres in farms	94,123	Fed. expend.	$9,868,000
†Value per farm	$155,897	Crime Index	141
Cropland harvested	15,997	TDC Pop.	8

AGRICULTURE: About $15 million average yearly income, 90% from cattle, hogs; wheat, cotton, hay chief crops.
BUSINESS: Economy based upon oil, tourism, agribusinesses, some manufacturing.
MANUFACTURING: None noted in census report.
SERVICE INDUSTRIES: 11 Establishments; Receipts, $885,000; Annual Payroll, $241,000; No. Employees, 19.
EMORY (813) county seat; center for local trade, tourism; some manufacturing including clothing factory and cabinet shop; clinic. **East Tawakoni** (404) and **Point** (468) are centers for **Lake Tawakoni** tourist activities; **Alba** (568, part Wood County).

Randall

LOCATION: Northwest (C-8).
HISTORY: Created, 1876, from Bexar District; organized, 1889; named for **Confederate Gen. Horace Randal** (county name misspelled when created).

Cong. Dist.	13	U.S. Jud. Dist.	N-Am.
St. Sen. Dist.	31	Ct. Appeals	7
St. Rep. Dist.	86	Admin. Jud. Dist.	9
St. Dist. Cts.	47,181, 251		

Randall County (Cont'd.)

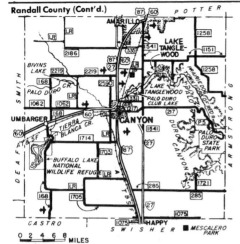

PHYSICAL FEATURES: Level, but broken by scenic Palo Duro Canyon, Tierra Blanca (Buffalo) Lake; silty clay, loam soils.

MINERALS: Not significant.

1982 Pop. 79,300	Voters reg. 46,564
Area (sq. mi.) 917	Whlsle. sales $525,166,000
Altitude (ft.) . 3,000-3,800	Oil value 0
Ann. rainfall (in.) . 20.16	No. employed 15,303
Jan. temp. min. 23	Wages paid . . $220,465,968
July temp. max. 93	Tax value . $1,948,239,902
Growing season (da.) 195	Income . . . $1,084,922,000
No. farms, 1982 575	Taxable sales $177,949,221
No. acres in farms 481,896	Fed. expend. . $89,844,000
†Value per farm $396,023	Crime Index 411
Cropland harv. . . 161,471	TDC Pop. 94

T·E·X·A·S

A MUSICAL ROMANCE OF PANHANDLE HISTORY
By PAUL GREEN

1986
21st Season

For
Reservations
or Information
Write:
Box 268
Canyon, Texas
79015
Or Call
655-2181

June 11-August 23
Monday thru Saturday Nights
PALO DURO CANYON STATE PARK

RECREATION: Palo Duro Canyon State Park, with "Texas" drama, "A Day in the Old West" celebration, major tourist attraction (ask chamber of commerce for dates); Panhandle-Plains Historical Museum; West Texas State University events; Aoudad sheep, migratory water fowl hunting in season; Buffalo Lake National Wildlife Refuge.

AGRICULTURE: About $65 million average yearly income, 75% from cattle, hogs; wheat, sorghums, corn, principal crops; more than 70,000 acres irrigated.

BUSINESS: Agribusinesses, education, some manufacturing, tourism; part of Amarillo metro area (see metro page).

MANUFACTURING: 32 Plants; 1,000 Employees; Payroll, $16,400,000; Product Value, $88,500,000.

SERVICE INDUSTRIES: 264 Establishments; Receipts, $46,601,000; Annual Payroll, $15,668,000; No. Employees, 1,403.

CANYON (10,724) county seat; West Texas State University major economic influence; Amarillo College; ranching, feedlots, farming center; gateway to Palo Duro Canyon State Park (see recreation, above); hospital. Amarillo is partly in Randall County (see Potter County). Happy (674, mostly Swisher County), Lake Tanglewood (485) other towns.

Reagan

LOCATION: Southwest (K-9).

HISTORY: Named for Sen. John H. Reagan, first chairman, Texas Railroad Commission; county created, organized, 1903, from Tom Green.

PHYSICAL FEATURES: Level to hilly, broken by draws, Big Lake; sandy, loam, clay soils.

RECREATION: Lake fishing, local events.

MINERALS: Gas oil.

Cong. Dist. 21	U.S. Jud. Dist. . . N-SAng.
St. Sen. Dist. 25	Ct. Appeals 8
St. Rep. Dist. 69	Admin. Jud. Dist. 6
St. Dist. Cts. 83, 112	
1982 Pop. 4,700	Voters reg. 2,073
Area (sq. mi.) 1,173	Whlsle. sales . $15,504,000
Altitude (ft.) . 2,400-2,700	Oil value . . . $281,799,597
Ann. rainfall (in.) . 14.72	No. employed 1,826
Jan. temp. min. 36	Wages paid . . $35,389,376
July temp. max. 96	Tax value . $736,069,480
Growing season (da.) 229	Income $35,380,000
No. farms, 1982 123	Taxable sales $20,652,746
No. acres in farms 636,780	Fed. expend. . . $8,754,000
†Value per farm $924,114	Crime Index 83
Cropland harvested 30,053	TDC Pop. 3

AGRICULTURE: About $9.5 million average annual income, 65% from beef cattle, sheep; cotton, grains principal crops; 22,600 acres irrigated.

BUSINESS: Economy based on large oil production, natural gas, ranching.

MANUFACTURING: None noted in census reports.

SERVICE INDUSTRIES: 18 Establishments; Receipts, $3,351,000; Annual Payroll, $923,000; No. Employees, 85.

BIG LAKE (3,404) county seat; center for oil activities, ranching trade; Hickman Library and Museum; Texon Reunion in June; hospital.

Real

LOCATION: Southwest central (N-12).

Cong. Dist.	21	U.S. Jud. Dist.	W-SAnt.
St. Sen. Dist.	25	Ct. Appeals	4
St. Rep. Dist.	67	Admin. Jud. Dist.	6
St. Dist. Cts.	38		

MINERALS: Not significant.

1982 Pop.	2,600	Voters reg.	2,074
Area (sq. mi.)	697	Whlsle. sales	$*
Altitude (ft.)	1,500-2,400	Oil value	0
Ann. rainfall (in.)	23.88	No. employed	314
Jan. temp. min.	38	Wages paid	$3,147,164
July temp. max.	94	Tax value	$219,023,241
Growing season (da.)	236	Income	$13,685,000
No. farms, 1982	177	Taxable sales	$3,792,872
No. acres in farms	311,411	Fed. expend.	$5,956,000
†Value per farm	$1,062,475	Crime Index	25
Cropland harvested	1,801	TDC Pop.	1

HISTORY:
Created, organized, 1913, from Bandera, Edwards, Kerr Counties; named for legislator-ranchman Julius Real.

PHYSICAL FEATURES: Hilly, spring-fed streams, scenic canyons; Frio River; Nueces River; cedars, pecans, many live-oak, including second largest oak in state; walnut trees, other vegetation.

RECREATION: Major tourist, hunting center; many deer killed each season; fishing; Frio River; Nueces River; camping; artists' haven; Spanish mission site, **Camp Wood;** scenic drives.

AGRICULTURE: A leading mohair-producing county; cattle, sheep, goats produce practically all of $5.3 million average farm income; income from hunting leases.

BUSINESS: Tourism, hunting leases major source of income; ranch supplies; cedar sales; popular area for artists, recreational "second homes."

MANUFACTURING: None noted in census report.

SERVICE INDUSTRIES: 1 Establishment; Receipts, N.A.; Annual Payroll, N.A.; No. Employees, N.A.

LEAKEY (468) county seat; center for ranching, tourism; medical facilities; cedar mill and log manufacturing; **Camp Wood** (728) serves as tourist, ranching hub for parts of 3 counties.

Red River

LOCATION: Northeast (F-20).

HISTORY: Created 1836, as original county; organized, 1837; named for **Red River,** its northern boundary.

Cong. Dist.	1	U.S. Jud. Dist.	E-Ps.
St. Sen. Dist.	1	Ct. Appeals	6
St. Rep. Dist.	1	Admin. Jud. Dist.	1
St. Dist. Cts.	6, 102		

PHYSICAL FEATURES: On Red River-Sulphur divide; 39 different soil types; half timbered.

RECREATION: Historical sites; water activities; hunting; local events.

MINERALS: Small oil flow, gas.

1982 Pop.	15,800	Voters reg.	8,917
Area (sq. mi.)	1,054	Whlsle. sales	$20,870,000
Altitude (ft.)	250-500	Oil value	$1,477,136
Ann. rainfall (in.)	45.29	No. employed	3,382
Jan. temp. min.	34	Wages paid	$36,927,684
July temp. max.	94	Tax value	$498,486,456
Growing season (da.)	234	Income	$106,868,000
No. farms, 1982	1,027	Taxable sales	22,117,906
No. acres in farms	358,081	Fed. expend.	$53,349,000
†Value per farm	$233,485	Crime Index	351
Cropland harvested	88,640	TDC Pop.	38

AGRICULTURE: About $28.7 million average yearly

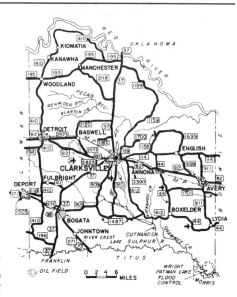

income, 65% from cattle, hogs, poultry; crops include soybeans, cotton, sorghums, wheat; timber sales estimated at $3.5 million.

BUSINESS: Agribusinesses; lumbering; manufacturing.

MANUFACTURING: 24 Plants; 1,300 Employees; Payroll, $12,600,000; Product Value, $63,700,000.

SERVICE INDUSTRIES: 44 Establishments; Receipts, $6,686,000; Annual Payroll, $2,717,000; No. Employees, 321.

CLARKSVILLE (4,917) county seat; plants make wood, aluminum products, boats, brushes, furniture, other products; hospital, nursing home, library, vocational school.

Other towns include **Bogata** (1,508), **Detroit** (805), **Deport** (724, mostly Lamar County), **Annona** (471), **Avery** (520).

Reeves

LOCATION: Southwest (K-6).

HISTORY: Created, 1883, from Pecos County; organized, 1884; named for **Confederate Col. George R. Reeves.**

Cong. Dist.	16	U.S. Jud. Dist.	W-Pe.
St. Sen. Dist.	25	Ct. Appeals	8
St. Rep. Dist.	69	Admin. Jud. Dist.	7
St. Dist. Cts.	143		

PHYSICAL FEATURES: Rolling plains, broken by many draws, Pecos River tributaries, **Balmorhea, Toyah, Red Bluff Lakes; Davis Mountains** on south; chocolate loam, clay, sandy, mountain wash soils.

RECREATION: A major "western" tourist area; replica of **Judge Roy Bean Store,** "**Law West of Pecos**"; western museum; park with javelina, prairie dogs, other animals; scenic drives; annual rodeo (celebrated centennial of first rodeo in 1983); water activities; **Balmorhea State Park** and lake.

MINERALS: Production of oil, gas, sand, gravel.

1982 Pop.	16,600	Voters reg.	8,375
Area (sq. mi.)	2,626	Whlsle. sales	$37,354,000
Altitude (ft.)	2,500-5,000	Oil value	$36,258,963
Ann. rainfall (in.)	11.99	No. employed	4,120
Jan. temp. min.	32	Wages paid	$61,861,832
July temp. max.	94	Tax value	$576,715,492
Growing season (da.)	226	Income	$103,888,000
No. farms, 1982	149	Taxable sales	$49,694,645
No. acs. in farms	1,247,396	Fed. expend.	$22,309,000
†Value per farm	$1,060,490	Crime Index	722
Cropland harvested	N.A.	TDC Pop.	42

AGRICULTURE: About $40 million average annual in-

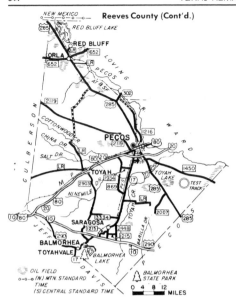

Reeves County (Cont'd.)

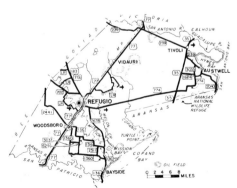

come, 80% from beef, dairy cattle; crops include cotton, grains, alfalfa, pecans; 29,000 acres irrigated.

BUSINESS: Petroleum production; agribusinesses; tourism; feedlots; some manufacturing

MANUFACTURING: None noted in census report.

SERVICE INDUSTRIES: 75 Establishments; Receipts, $17,315,000; Annual Payroll, $4,611,000; No. Employees, 474.

PECOS (12,855) county seat; ranching, oil industry center; vegetables, pecans, cotton marketing, shipping, other agribusinesses; automotive proving grounds; hospital, nursing home; tourism.

Other towns include **Balmorhea** (568), **Toyah** (165).

Refugio

LOCATION: Southern coast (Q-17).

HISTORY: Original county, created 1836, organized, 1837; named for **Mission Our Lady of Refuge.**

Cong. Dist. 14	U.S. Jud. Dist. . . . . S-Va.
St. Sen. Dist. 18	Ct. Appeals 13
St. Rep. Dist. 32	Admin. Jud. Dist. 4
St. Dist. Cts. . 24, 135, 267	

PHYSICAL FEATURES: Coastal plain, broken by streams, bays; sandy, loam, black soils; mesquite, oak, huisache motts.

RECREATION: Water activities; hunting, fishing; historic sites; **Aransas National Wildlife Refuge**, "home of the whooping crane."

MINERALS: Production of oil, gas.

1982 Pop.	9,200	Voters reg.	5,700
Area (sq. mi.)	771	Whlsle. sales .	$32,706,000
Altitude (ft.) sea level-100		Oil value . . .	$634,893,170
Ann. rainfall (in.) .	33.76	No. employed . . .	2,724
Jan. temp. min.	44	Wages paid . .	$44,882,040
July temp. max.	94	Tax value .	$1,969,341,780
Growing season (da.)	304	Income . . .	$80,375,000
No. farms, 1982	262	Taxable sales	$27,719,225
No. acres in farms 524,439		Fed. expend. .	$29,727,000
†Value per farm	$843,740	Crime Index	148
Cropland harvested 84,271		TDC Pop.	17

AGRICULTURE: About $23.5 million average yearly income from sorghums, cotton, corn, wheat; beef cattle, horses.

BUSINESS: Petroleum, petrochemical production, agribusinesses, tourism main economic factors.

MANUFACTURING: None noted in census report.

SERVICE INDUSTRIES: 34 Establishments; Receipts, $6,607,000; Annual Payroll, $2,480,000; No. Employees, 165.

REFUGIO (3,898) county seat; center for petroleum producing, agribusiness activities; hospital, nursing home.

Other towns include **Woodsboro** (1,974), **Austwell** (280) and **Bayside** (381).

Roberts

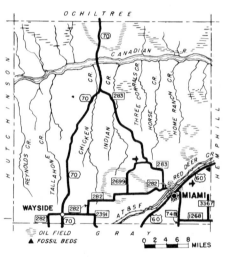

LOCATION: Northwestern Panhandle (B-10).

HISTORY: Created, 1876, from Bexar District; organized, 1889; named for Texas leaders, **John S. Roberts** and **Gov. O. M. Roberts.**

Cong. Dist. 13	U.S. Jud. Dist. . . . . N-Am.
St. Sen. Dist. 31	Ct. Appeals 7
St. Rep. Dist. 88	Admin. Jud. Dist. 9
St. Dist. Cts. 31	

PHYSICAL FEATURES: Rolling, broken by Canadian and many tributaries; Red Deer Creek; black, sandy loam, alluvial soils.

RECREATION: National cow-calling contest; scenic drives; county museum.

MINERALS: Production of gas, oil.

1982 Pop.	1,200	Voters reg.	799
Area (sq. mi.)	915	Whlsle. sales . .	$3,113,000
Altitude (ft.) .	2,500-3,200	Oil value	$14,999,287
Ann. rainfall (in.) .	21.91	No. employed . . .	375
Jan. temp. min.	23	Wages paid . . .	$7,083,576
July temp. max.	94	Tax value . .	$476,713,495
Growing season (da.)	192	Income	$9,364,000
No. farms, 1982	103	Taxable sales .	$2,139,454
No. acres in farms 565,608		Fed. expend. . .	$4,769,000
†Value per farm $1,160,356		Crime Index	13
Cropland harvested 24,906		TDC Pop.	2

AGRICULTURE: About $9 million average yearly income, 75% from beef cattle; crops include wheat, milo, corn; about 6,700 acres irrigated for grains.

BUSINESS: Agribusinesses, oil field operations.

MANUFACTURING: None noted in census report.

SERVICE INDUSTRIES: 2 Establishments; Receipts, N.A.; Annual Payroll, N.A.; No. Employees, N.A.

MIAMI (813) county seat; center for ranching, oil industry activities; some oil field equipment manufacturing.

Robertson

LOCATION: East central (K-17).

HISTORY: Among first counties, created 1837, organized 1838, subdivided into many others later; named for pioneer, **Sterling Clack Robertson.**

Cong. Dist.	6	U.S. Jud. Dist.	W-Wa.
St. Sen. Dist.	5	Ct. Appeals	10
St. Rep. Dist.	13	Admin Jud. Dist.	2
St. Dist. Cts.	82		

PHYSICAL FEATURES: Drains to Brazos, Navasota Rivers; sandy soils, heavy in bottoms.

RECREATION: Hunting, fishing; historic sites; historic homes tour; Country Music Jamboree; county fair at Hearne; dogwood trails.

MINERALS: Gas, oil, lignite.

1982 Pop.	15,300	Voters reg.	9,315
Area (sq. mi.)	864	Whlsle. sales	$97,774,000
Altitude (ft.)	250-500	Oil value	$2,457,437
Ann. rainfall (in.)	35.80	No. employed	2,824
Jan. temp. min.	40	Wages paid	$35,886,344
July temp. max.	96	Tax value	$660,263,401
Growing season (da.)	268	Income	$108,106,000
No. farms, 1982	1,100	Taxable sales	$29,438,531
No. acres in farms	385,786	Fed. expend.	$39,434,000
†Value per farm	$308,890	Crime Index	675
Cropland harvested	52,931	TDC Pop.	38

AGRICULTURE: About $38 million average yearly income, 75% from beef cattle, dairy products, hogs, horses, poultry; crops include cotton, sorghums, small grains, watermelons, corn; 15,000 acres irrigated, mostly cotton.

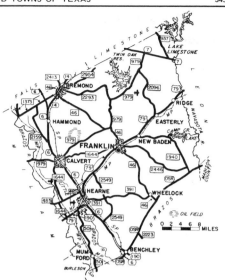

BUSINESS: Agribusinesses, brick manufacturing, electricity generating plant under construction.

MANUFACTURING: None noted in census report.

SERVICE INDUSTRIES: 37 Establishments; Receipts, $6,841,000; Annual Payroll, $2,483,000; No. Employees, 261.

FRANKLIN (1,349) county seat; farm trade center.

Other towns include **Hearne** (5,418), some manufacturing; hospital, nursing home; library. **Bremond** (1,025), **Calvert** (1,732) antique shops; annual pilgrimage in April.

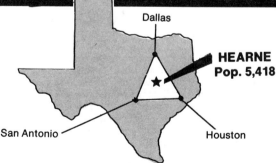

Rockwall

LOCATION: North central (G-17).

HISTORY: Created, organized, 1873, from Kaufman; smallest county; named for wall-like rock formation.

PHYSICAL FEATURES: Rolling prairie, mostly Blackland soil; Trinity River; Lake Ray Hubbard.

MINERALS: Not significant.

Cong. Dist.	4	U.S. Jud. Dist.	N-DI.
St. Sen. Dist.	2	Ct. Appeals	5
St. Rep. Dist.	3	Admin. Jud. Dist.	1
St. Dist. Cts.	86		

RECREATION: Lake Ray Hubbard activities (also see Dallas County); unusual rock outcropping.

1982 Pop.	16,700	Voters reg.	11,449
Area (sq. mi.)	128	Whlsle. sales	$17,308,000
Altitude (ft.)	400-550	Oil value	$8,641
Ann. rainfall (in.)	38.68	No. employed	3,517
Jan. temp. min.	34	Wages paid	$54,582,476
July temp. max.	96	Tax value	$828,272,634
Growing season (da.)	236	Income	$238,598,000
No. farms, 1982	191	Taxable sales	$70,056,558
No. acres in farms	50,570	Fed. expend.	$23,351,000
†Value per farm	$459,550	Crime Index	442
Cropland harvested	18,870	TDC Pop.	16

AGRICULTURE: About $6 million average yearly farm income from beef cattle, horses; crops including wheat, cotton, sorghums; tree farms.

BUSINESS: Industrial employment in local plants, Dallas; in Dallas metro area; tourist and residential business around **Lake Ray Hubbard;** varied manufacturing.

MANUFACTURING: 27 Plants; 700 Employees; Payroll, $11,500,000; Product Value, $65,500,000.

SERVICE INDUSTRIES: 67 Establishments; Receipts, $12,446,000; Annual Payroll, $4,186,000; No. Employees, 305.

ROCKWALL (5,939) county seat; plants make aluminum, leather goods, windows; apparel, steel products; hospital, clinics, nursing home.

Royse City (1,566, part in Collin County), plants produce typewriter ribbons, elevators, clothing. Other towns include **Heath** (1,459, part Kaufman County), **Fate** (263), **McLendon-Chisholm** (403), **Rowlett** (7,522, part Dallas County), and small part of **Dallas.**

Runnels

LOCATION: Central (J-11).

HISTORY: Named for planter-legislator, **H. G. Runnels;** created, 1858, from Bexar, Travis Counties; organized, 1880.

Cong. Dist.	17	U.S. Jud. Dist.	N-SAng.
St. Sen. Dist.	24	Ct. Appeals	3
St. Rep. Dist.	65	Admin. Jud. Dist.	7
St. Dist. Cts.	119		

PHYSICAL FEATURES: Level to rolling, bisected by Colorado and tributaries; sandy loam, black waxy soils.

RECREATION: Hunting, fishing; Festival of Ethnic Cultures of Ballinger in April; 47 historical markers in county.

MINERALS: Production of oil, gas, sand and gravel.

1982 Pop.	12,100	Voters reg.	6,522
Area (sq. mi.)	1,056	Whlsle. sales	$70,011,000
Altitude (ft.)	1,500-2,100	Oil value	$74,890,403
Ann. rainfall (in.)	21.85	No. employed	3,320
Jan. temp. min.	34	Wages paid	$46,398,284
July temp. max.	96	Tax value	$578,620,726
Growing season (da.)	228	Income	$97,370,000
No. farms, 1982	867	Taxable sales	$51,918,038
No. acres in farms	602,788	Fed. expend.	$35,204,000
†Value per farm	$357,698	Crime Index	97
Cropland harv.	202,185	TDC Pop.	19

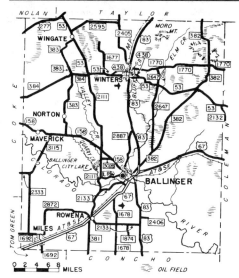

AGRICULTURE: About $40 million average yearly income, 60% from cattle, sheep, poultry; crops include cotton, sorghums, wheat.

BUSINESS: Agribusinesses, oil activity, manufacturing.

MANUFACTURING: 14 Plants; 700 Employees; Payroll, $7,500,000; Product Value, $34,100,000.

SERVICE INDUSTRIES: 47 Establishments; Receipts, $5,222,000; Annual Payroll, $1,523,000; No. Employees, 222.

BALLINGER (4,207) county seat; Carnegie Library; plants make garments, communications equipment, bumpers, livestock feed, cotton compress; metal products; oil field services; meat processor; hospital; **Western Texas College** extension. **Winters** (3,061), varied manufacturing; museum; nursing home, hospital; **Miles** (720) other major towns.

Rusk

LOCATION: East (I-20)

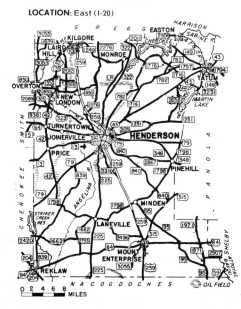

HISTORY: Named for Republic of Texas, state leader, **T. J. Rusk**; created from Nacogdoches County and organized, 1843.

New London, March 18, 1937, was site of one of Texas' worst disasters, when a school explosion killed 293 students and faculty.

Cong. Dist. 1	U.S. Jud. Dist. . . . . E-Ty.
St. Sen. Dist. 3	Ct. Appeals 6, 12
St. Rep. Dist. 9	Admin. Jud. Dist. 1
St. Dist. Cts. 4	

PHYSICAL FEATURES: On Sabine-Angelina divide; varied deep, sandy soils; over half in pines, hardwoods; **Striker Creek Reservoir; Lake Cherokee.**

RECREATION: Water sports; historic homes, sites; scenic drives; marked site of East Texas Field discovery oil well; golf tournaments.

MINERALS: A leading oil county; over 1.5 billion bbls. since 1930; part of East Texas field; gas, lignite, clays also produced.

1982 Pop. 42,600	Voters reg. 26,663
Area (sq. mi.) 932	Whlsle. sales . $84,029,000
Altitude (ft.) 250-750	Oil value . . . $195,405,294
Ann. rainfall (in.) . . 46.22	No. employed 12,723
Jan. temp. min. 38	Wages paid . . $237,763,088
July temp. max. 94	Tax value . $2,996,823,422
Growing season (da.) 250	Income $413,984,000
No. farms, 1982 . . . 1,372	Taxable sales $105,385,878
No. acres in farms 281,569	Fed. expend. . $73,924,000
†Value per farm $160,504	Crime Index 1,003
Cropland harvested 28,243	TDC Pop. 82

AGRICULTURE: About $27 million average annual income, 90% from cattle, dairy products, hogs, poultry, horses; crops include watermelons, vegetables, hay, grains, corn; timber income estimated at $3 million.

BUSINESS: Economy based on oil, lumbering, agribusinesses, tourism.

MANUFACTURING: 56 Plants; 1,800 Employees; Payroll, $24,300,000; Product Value, $101,100,000.

SERVICE INDUSTRIES: 139 Establishments; Receipts, $34,799,000; Annual Payroll, $10,084,000; No. Employees, 987.

HENDERSON (11,473) county seat; center for agribusiness, oil industry activities; plants make bricks, clothing, fiberglass, other products; hospital.

Overton (2,430, part Smith County) oil, lumbering center; petroleum production, processing; crosstie milling, dress factory; **Texas A&M Research and Extension Center**; hospital, nursing home. Other towns are **Kilgore** (11,006 part Gregg County), **New London** (942), **Tatum** (1,339, part Panola County), **Easton** (333, part Gregg County), **Mount Enterprise** (485), **Reklaw** (305, part Cherokee County).

Sabine

LOCATION: Borders Louisiana (J-22).

HISTORY: An original county, created 1836; organized, 1837; name is cypress in Spanish.

Cong. Dist. 2	U.S. Jud. Dist. . . . . E-Bt.
St. Sen. Dist. 3	Ct. Appeals 12
St. Rep. Dist. 17	Admin. Jud. Dist. 2
St. Dist. Cts. 1, 273	

PHYSICAL FEATURES: Four-fifths forested; 114,498 acres in **Sabine National Forest; Sabine River, Toledo Bend Reservoir** on east; **Sam Rayburn Reservoir** on southwest.

RECREATION: Toledo Bend, Sam Rayburn Lake activities; many camp sites, marinas; **McMahan's Chapel**, pioneer Protestant Church; **Sabine National Forest**; hunting.

MINERALS: Not significant.

1982 Pop. 9,000	Voters reg. 9,011
Area (sq. mi.) 486	Whlsle. sales . . $5,007,000
Altitude (ft.) 150-350	Oil value $2,616,385
Ann. rainfall (in.) . . 51.94	No. employed 1,554
Jan. temp. min. 38	Wages paid . . $19,794,276
July temp. max. 94	Tax value . . $265,417,617
Growing season (da.) 236	Income $65,515,000
No. farms, 1982 . . . 256	Taxable sales $19,275,710
No. acres in farms . 37,160	Fed. expend. . $21,543,000
†Value per farm $124,957	Crime Index 107
Cropland harvested 2,609	TDC Pop. 9

AGRICULTURE: About $10 million average yearly income from beef cattle, poultry; vegetables; among leading broiler producers; significant timber marketing.

Sabine County (Cont'd.)

BAY OF SAM RAYBURN RESERVOIR
▲ MC MAHAN CHAPEL

1982 Pop.	9,000	Voters reg.	6,329
Area (sq. mi.)	524	Whlsle. sales	$11,588,000
Altitude (ft.)	100-400	Oil value	$5,328
Ann. rainfall (in.)	50.23	No. employed	1,439
Jan. temp. min.	35	Wages paid	$16,702,924
July temp. max.	93	Tax value	$288,231,444
Growing season (da.)	238	Income	$66,574,000
No. farms, 1982	355	Taxable sales	$17,267,376
No. acres in farms	60,462	Fed. expend.	$15,872,000
†Value per farm	$140,225	Crime Index	316
Cropland harvested	6,152	TDC Pop.	14

BUSINESS: Economy based on tourism, broilers, timber industries.

MANUFACTURING: None noted in census report.

SERVICE INDUSTRIES: 18 Establishments; Receipts, $2,789,000; Annual Payroll, $645,000; No. Employees, 72.

HEMPHILL (1,353) county seat; center for timber, poultry industries. **Pineland** (1,111) has plywood mill, other timber industries; **Bronson** (254).

San Augustine

LOCATION: East (J-21).

HISTORY: Among most historic counties; created and named for Mexican municipality in 1836, an original county; organized 1837.

PHYSICAL FEATURES: Hilly; four-fifths forested, with 66,799 acres in **Angelina National Forest**, 4,317 in **Sabine National Forest**; **Sam Rayburn Reservoir**; varied soils, sandy to black alluvial.

RECREATION: Lake activities; annual tour of antiques, arts, crafts show; annual forestry day; many historic homes; **McMahan's Chapel**, pioneer Protestant Church in nearby Sabine County; tourist facilities in national forests.

MINERALS: Small amount oil.

Cong. Dist.	1	U.S. Jud. Dist.	E-Bt.
St. Sen. Dist.	3	Ct. Appeals	12
St. Rep. Dist.	17	Admin. Jud. Dist.	2
St. Dist. Cts.	1, 273		

AGRICULTURE: About $15 million average annual income, mostly from beef cattle, poultry; a leading broiler producing county; timber sales estimated at $12.5 million.

BUSINESS: Lumbering; poultry processing, shipping; varied manufacturing.

MANUFACTURING: None noted in census report.

SERVICE INDUSTRIES: 31 Establishments; Receipts, $4,317,000; Annual Payroll, $1,358,000; No. Employees, 160.

SAN AUGUSTINE (2,930) county seat; tourism; livestock, plants process poultry, make fiberglass products, lumber and other wood products, metal fabrication, transformers and meters. Deep East Texas Electric Cooperative; feed mills; lumbering; hospital; "Oldest Anglo-Saxon Town in Texas" with many historic homes; **Broaddus** (225).

San Jacinto

LOCATION: Southeast (L-20).

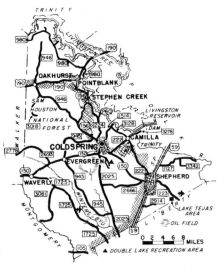

▲ DOUBLE LAKE RECREATION AREA

HISTORY: Created from Liberty, Montgomery, Polk, Walker Counties, 1869; re-created, organized, 1870; named for **Battle of San Jacinto**.

Cong. Dist.	2	U.S. Jud. Dist.	S-Hn.
St. Sen. Dist.	3	Ct. Appeals	9
St. Rep. Dist.	18	Admin. Jud. Dist.	2
St. Dist. Cts.	9, 2D9, 258		

PHYSICAL FEATURES: Rolling hills; four-fifths forested; 58,625 acres in **Sam Houston National Forest**; Trinity, San Jacinto Rivers.

RECREATION: **Lake Livingston** water activities; Double Lake; Wolf Creek Park; hunting; county fair; **Sam Houston National Forest**; old courthouse and jail are tourist attractions. Approximatey 60% of county in national forest.

MINERALS: Oil, gas and iron ore.

1982 Pop.	11,900	Voters reg.	8,704
Area (sq. mi.)	572	Whlsle. sales	$2,081,000
Altitude (ft.)	100-300	Oil value	$2,447,912
Ann. rainfall (in.)	48.25	No. employed	1,078
Jan. temp. min.	38	Wages paid	$12,856,896
July temp. max.	94	Tax value	$843,625,885
Growing season (da.)	261	Income	$107,076,000
No. farms, 1982	315	Taxable sales	$14,149,443
No. acres in farms	77,585	Fed. expend.	$17,586,000
†Value per farm	$244,272	Crime Index	400
Cropland harvested	3,622	TDC Pop.	20

AGRICULTURE: Some $6.5 million average annual income from beef cattle, horses, soybeans, hay; timber sales.

BUSINESS: Economy based on timber and oil.
MANUFACTURING: 15 Plants; Employees, N.A.; Payroll, N.A.; Product Value, N.A.
SERVICE INDUSTRIES: 20 Establishments; Receipts, $4,106,000; Annual Payroll, $1,618,000; No. Employees, 164.

COLDSPRING (569) county seat; center for lumbering, farm trade; historic sites. **Shepherd** (1,674), **Pointblank** (325), **Oakhurst** (214) other towns.

San Patricio

LOCATION: Southern coast (Q-16).
HISTORY: Created from, named for earlier municipality in 1836; organized, 1837, reorganized, 1847.

Cong. Dist.	15	U.S. Jud. Dist.	S-CC
St. Sen. Dist.	20	Ct. Appeals	13
St. Rep. Dist.	33	Admin. Jud. Dist.	4
St. Dist. Cts.	36, 156, 343		

PHYSICAL FEATURES: Between Aransas, Nueces Rivers, draining to them and bays; sandy loam, clay, black loam soils; **Lake Corpus Christi.**
RECREATION: Water activities; hunting; Corpus Christi Bay; **Lake Corpus Christi State Park; Welder Wildlife Refuge; Welder Park;** festivals, fishing tournament at Mathis; shrimporee in October; local events.
MINERALS: Production of oil, gas, stone, clays.

1982 Pop.	61,100	Voters reg.	31,768
Area (sq. mi.)	693	Whlsle. sales	$89,754,000
Altitude (ft.) sea level-150		Oil value	$63,418,383
Ann. rainfall (in.)	30.60	No. employed	12,312
Jan. temp. min.	44	Wages paid	$202,996,256
July temp. max.	95	Tax value	$2,115,023,492
Growing season (da.)	303	Income	$486,204,000
No. farms, 1982	605	Taxable sales	$135,395,095
No. acres in farms 382,323		Fed. expend.	$197,171,000
†Value per farm $720,479		Crime Index	1,979
Cropland harv.	217,479	TDC Pop.	125

AGRICULTURE: About $65 million average annual income from sorghums, cotton, vegetables, corn, hay; beef cattle, hogs, goats, horses, poultry; cattle feedlots; 5,000 acres irrigated.
BUSINESS: Oil center; petrochemicals; agribusinesses; manufacturing; tourism; in Corpus Christi metro area.
MANUFACTURING: 32 Plants; 2,600 Employees; Payroll, $72,000,000; Product Value, $511,900,000.
SERVICE INDUSTRIES: 209 Establishments; Receipts, $36,016,000; Annual Payroll, $12,534,000; No. Employees, 1,127.

SINTON (6,044) county seat; oil, agribusiness center; zoo, fiddlers' festival; 18-hole golf course.

Aransas Pass (7,173, part in Aransas, Nueces Counties) shrimping and tourist center; offshore well servicing; aluminum and chemical plants; hospitals.

Other towns include **Gregory** (2,739), **Ingleside** (5,436) offshore oil services; **Lake City** (431), **Lakeside** (276), **Mathis** (5,667) varied manufacturing; medical clinics. **Odem** (2,363) petroleum processing, steel fabrication; **Portland** (12,023, part Nueces County), **Taft** (3,686) **Blackland Museum; San Patricio** (241, part Nueces County) and **Taft Southwest.**

San Saba

LOCATION: Central (K-14).
HISTORY: Created from Bexar and organized, 1856; named for river.

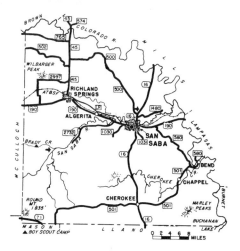

Cong. Dist.	11	U.S. Jud. Dist.	W-An.
St. Sen. Dist.	24	Ct. Appeals	3
St. Rep. Dist.	54	Admin. Jud. Dist.	3
St. Dist. Cts.	33		

PHYSICAL FEATURES: Hilly, rolling; bisected by San Saba River; Colorado River on east; black, gray sandy loam, alluvial soils.
RECREATION: A leading deer hunting area; annual rodeos, tractor pull, pecan festival; historic sites; fishing; scenic drives; Gorman Falls.
MINERALS: Limited stone production.

1982 Pop.	6,000	Voters reg.	3,471
Area (sq. mi.)	1,136	Whlsle. sales	$33,205,000
Altitude (ft.)	1,100-1,800	Oil value	0
Ann. rainfall (in.)	26.19	No. employed	1,362
Jan. temp. min.	34	Wages paid	$15,575,584
July temp. max.	96	Tax value	$387,211,534
Growing season (da.) 227		Income	$46,641,000
No. farms, 1982	643	Taxable sales $12,339,679	
No. acres in farms 708,937		Fed. expend.	$16,062,000
†Value per farm $636,476		Crime Index	60
Cropland harvested 32,436		TDC Pop.	7

AGRICULTURE: About 80% of $28 million average farm income from cattle, hogs, sheep, goats, turkeys; crops include oats, wheat, peanuts, hay; about 7,200 acres irrigated.
BUSINESS: Agribusinesses; pecans; stone processing; tourist and hunting lease income.
MANUFACTURING: None noted in census report.
SERVICE INDUSTRIES: 25 Establishments; Receipts, $4,169,000; Annual Payroll, $1,250,000; No. Employees, 236.

SAN SABA (2,847) county seat; "Pecan capital of the world," agribusinesses; stone quarries, rock crushing plant; manufacturing includes caps, feed, fertilizer; hospital, nursing homes; **Richland Springs** (420) another town.

Schleicher

LOCATION: Southwest (L-11).
HISTORY: Named for **Gustav Schleicher,** founder of German colony; county created from Crockett, 1887, organized, 1901.

Cong. Dist.	21	U.S. Jud. Dist.	N-SAng.
St. Sen. Dist.	25	Ct. Appeals	3
St. Rep. Dist.	67	Admin. Jud. Dist.	7
St. Dist. Cts.	51		

PHYSICAL FEATURES: Plateau, broken by Devils River, Concho, San Saba tributaries; part hilly; black soils.
RECREATION: Hunting; livestock show in January; youth rodeo in April, open rodeo in August.
MINERALS: Production of oil, gas.

Schleicher County (Cont'd.)

1982 Pop.	3,100	Voters reg.	1,609
Area (sq. mi.)	1,309	Whlsle. sales	$8,321,000
Altitude (ft.)	2,100-2,450	Oil value	$32,808,666
Ann. rainfall (in.)	18.19	No. employed	894
Jan. temp. min.	30	Wages paid	$17,026,832
July temp. max.	94	Tax value	$418,692,790
Growing season (da.)	229	Income	$24,894,000
No. farms, 1982	265	Taxable sales	$4,711,358
No. acres in farms	802,055	Fed. expend.	$11,290,000
†Value per farm	$1,036,498	Crime Index	40
Cropland harvested	19,086	TDC Pop.	3

AGRICULTURE: An estimated $14 million average annual income, 80% from cattle, sheep, goats; crops include cotton, small grains, hay; 1,000 acres irrigated, mostly cotton.

BUSINESS: Oil and ranching economy.

MANUFACTURING: None noted in census report.

SERVICE INDUSTRIES: 7 Establishments; Receipts, $1,455,000; Annual Payroll, $312,000; No. Employees, 35.

ELDORADO (2,061) county seat; center for livestock, woolen mill, mohair marketing; oil activities; medical center.

Scurry

LOCATION: West (H-10).

HISTORY: Created from Bexar, 1876; organized 1884; named for **Confederate Gen. W. R. Scurry.**

Cong. Dist.	17	U.S. Jud. Dist.	N-Lb.
St. Sen. Dist.	30	Ct. Appeals	11
St. Rep. Dist.	78	Admin. Jud. Dist.	7
St. Dist. Cts.	132		

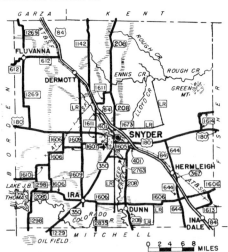

PHYSICAL FEATURES: Drained by Colorado, Brazos tributaries; **Lake J. B. Thomas;** prairie, some hills; sandy, loam soils.

RECREATION: Lake J. B. Thomas water recreation; **Sandstone Canyon Indian pictographs; Towle Memorial Park;** museums.

MINERALS: Nation's leading oil-producing county; also gas, stone.

1982 Pop.	19,500	Voters reg.	9,322
Area (sq. mi.)	900	Whlsle. sales	$96,748,000
Altitude (ft.)	2,000-2,700	Oil value	$430,097,894
Ann. rainfall (in.)	19.32	No. employed	6,756
Jan. temp. min.	28	Wages paid	$122,526,748
July temp. max.	96	Tax value	$2,651,574,590
Growing season (da.)	214	Income	$198,535,000
No. farms, 1982	614	Taxable sales	$96,968,263
No. acres in farms	484,387	Fed. expend.	$36,506,000
†Value per farm	$313,914	Crime Index	454
Cropland harvested	84,398	TDC Pop.	75

AGRICULTURE: Some $24.6 million average annual income from cattle, hogs, sheep, cotton, sorghums, small grains; 2,000 acres irrigated for cotton, pastures.

BUSINESS: Oil production major economic factor; agribusinesses; manufacturing.

MANUFACTURING: None noted in census report.

SERVICE INDUSTRIES: 102 Establishments; Receipts, $20,983,000; Annual Payroll, $6,112,000; No. Employees, 647.

SNYDER (12,705) county seat; plants process oil, gas, magnesium; make apparel, wax, brick, other products; **Western Texas College;** hospital, nursing home.

Shackelford

LOCATION: Central (H-13).

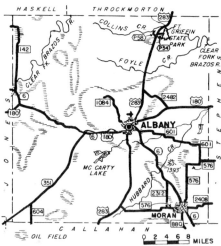

HISTORY: Created from Bosque County, 1858; organized, 1874; named for **Dr. John Shackelford,** Texas Revolutionary hero.

Cong. Dist.	17	U.S. Jud. Dist.	N-Ab.
St. Sen. Dist.	30	Ct. Appeals	11
St. Rep. Dist.	64	Admin. Jud. Dist.	7
St. Dist. Cts.	259		

PHYSICAL FEATURES: Rolling, hilly, numerous tributaries of Brazos; sandy and chocolate loam soils; **McCarty Lake.**

RECREATION: Fort Griffin State Park (in National Register of Historic Places), June **Fandangle** major tourist attractions; courthouse historical district; lake activities; hunting.

MINERALS: Production of oil, gas.

1982 Pop.	4,100
Area (sq. mi.)	915
Altitude (ft.).	1,200-2,000
Ann. rainfall (in.)	26.57
Jan. temp. min.	31
July temp. max.	97
Growing season (da.)	224
No. farms, 1982	258
No. acres in farms	573,238
†Value per farm	$566,705
Cropland harvested	28,752

Voters reg.	2,463
Whlsle. sales	$5,376,000
Oil value	$73,346,935
No. employed	1,187
Wages paid	$20,803,544
Tax value	$356,550,477
Income	$41,784,000
Taxable sales	$16,940,442
Fed. expend.	$8,811,000
Crime Index	42
TDC Pop.	9

AGRICULTURE: About $12 million average annual income, 85% from cattle, sheep, horses, hogs; crops include cotton, wheat.

BUSINESS: Oil and ranching economy; some manufacturing; June "**Fandangle**" is tourist attraction.

MANUFACTURING: None noted in census report.

SERVICE INDUSTRIES: 15 Establishments; Receipts, $5,858,000; Annual Payroll, $3,614,000; No. Employees, 175.

ALBANY (2,450) county seat; oil and agribusiness center; plants make oil field equipment; quarter-horse breeding, training; historical district; hospital; **Lueders** (420, part Jones County), **Moran** (344) major towns.

Shelby

LOCATION: Borders Louisiana (I-21).

HISTORY: Original county, created 1836; organized, 1837; named for **Isaac Shelby** of American Revolution.

Cong. Dist.	1
St. Sen. Dist.	3
St. Rep. Dist.	10
St. Dist. Cts.	123, 273

U.S. Jud. Dist.	E-Ty.
Ct. Appeals	12
Admin. Jud. Dist.	1

PHYSICAL FEATURES: Partly hills, much bottomland; much timber; 67,762 acres in **Sabine National Forest**; **Toledo Bend Lake**; Sabine, Attoyac, other streams; sandy, clay, alluvial soils.

RECREATION: Toledo Bend Reservoir activities; **Sabine National Forest**; hunting, fishing; camping; historic sites; poultry festival in October.

MINERALS: Gas, oil.

1982 Pop.	23,700
Area (sq. mi.)	791
Altitude (ft.)	150-400
Ann. rainfall (in.)	49.94
Jan. temp. min.	38
July temp. max.	94
Growing season (da.)	240
No. farms, 1982	1,117
No. acres in farms	199,827
†Value per farm	$169,318
Cropland harvested	16,595

Voters reg.	13,741
Whlsle. sales	$67,695,000
Oil value	$632,961
No. employed	5,120
Wages paid	$65,414,036
Tax value	$643,881,708
Income	$182,535,000
Taxable sales	$59,321,940
Fed. expend.	$46,740,000
Crime Index	452
TDC Pop.	42

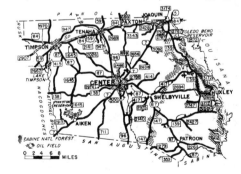

AGRICULTURE: A leader in broiler and egg production; most of $79 million average yearly income from poultry, beef cattle, hogs, hay, sweet potatoes; timber sales estimated $9 million.

BUSINESS: Broiler, egg production, cattle, timber leading economic factors; tourism.

MANUFACTURING: 51 Plants; 1,800 Employees; Payroll, $19,300,000; Product Value, $139,400,000.

SERVICE INDUSTRIES: 58 Establishments; Receipts, $10,001,000; Annual Payroll, $2,675,000; No. Employees, 385.

CENTER (5,827) county seat; plants process poultry,

timber, feeds; hospitals, nursing homes; **Shelby College Center.**

Other towns include **Tenaha** (1,005), **Timpson** (1,164) food processing, feed mill; **Joaquin** (917), **Huxley** (341).

Sherman

LOCATION: Top of Panhandle (A-8).

HISTORY: Named for Texas **Gen. Sidney Sherman**; county created from Bexar District, 1876; organized 1889.

Cong. Dist.	13
St. Sen. Dist.	31
St. Rep. Dist.	88
St. Dist. Cts.	69

U.S. Jud. Dist.	N-Am.
Ct. Appeals	7
Admin. Jud. Dist.	9

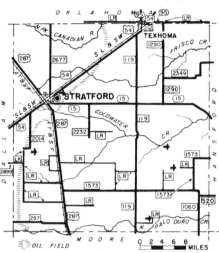

PHYSICAL FEATURES: Level, broken by creeks, playas; sandy to dark loam soils; underground water.

RECREATION: Local events; pheasant hunting.

MINERALS: Production of gas, oil.

1982 Pop.	3,200
Area (sq. mi.)	923
Altitude (ft.)	3,300-3,800
Ann. rainfall (in.)	18.36
Jan. temp. min.	19
July temp. max.	93
Growing season (da.)	182
No. farms, 1982	279
No. acres in farms	567,918
†Value per farm	$909,125
Cropland harv.	194,465

Voters reg.	1,928
Whlsle. sales	$23,112,000
Oil value	$322,991
No. employed	1,288
Wages paid	$21,989,632
Tax value	$478,797,094
Income	$38,840,000
Taxable sales	$4,560,840
Fed. expend.	$40,722,000
Crime Index	2
TDC Pop.	1

AGRICULTURE: An estimated $83 million average annual income, 65% from beef and stocker cattle, hogs; much cattle feeding; crops chiefly wheat, sorghums; 110,000 acres irrigated.

BUSINESS: Agribusinesses, large feedlot operations.

MANUFACTURING: None noted in census report.

SERVICE INDUSTRIES: 10 Establishments; Receipts, $1,277,000; Annual Payroll, $372,000; No. Employees, 34.

STRATFORD (1,917) county seat; agribusiness center; large feedlots and feed production; steel fabrication; tannery; industrial authority; nursing home. **Texhoma** (358) other principal town.

Smith

LOCATION: Northeast (H-19).

HISTORY: Named for Texas Revolutionary **Gen. James Smith**; county created, organized, 1846, from Nacogdoches.

Con. Dist.	4
St. Sen. Dist.	2
St. Rep. Dist.	5, 6
St. Dist. Cts.	7, 114, 241,321

U.S. Jud. Dist.	E-Ty.
Ct. Appeals	12
Admin. Jud. Dist.	1

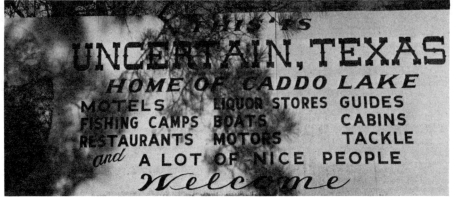

The sign in Uncertain, Texas, shows that visitors are welcome.

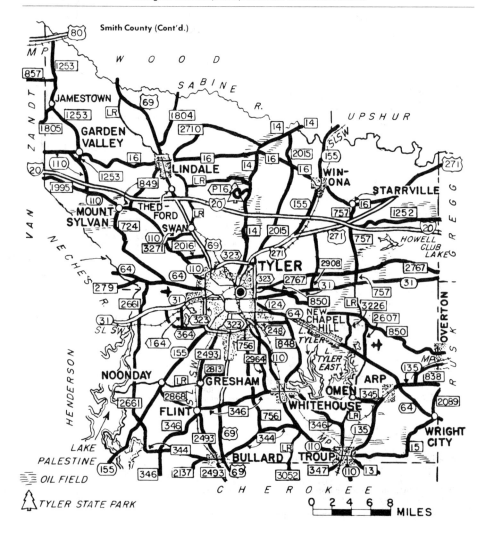

PHYSICAL FEATURES: Rolling hills, many timbered; Sabine, Neches, other streams; **Lakes Tyler, Palestine;** alluvial, gray, sandy loam, clay soils.

RECREATION: Activities on **Lakes Palestine, Tyler,** other lakes; famed **Tyler Rose Garden;** Texas Rose Festival in October; Azalea Trail in spring; **Tyler State Park;** Goodman Museum; East Texas Fair; collegiate events.

MINERALS: Production of oil, gas, clays, sand and gravel, stone.

1982 Pop. 136,700	Voters reg. 77,345
Area (sq. mi.) 932	Whlsle. sales$1,051,782,000
Altitude (ft.) 300-600	Oil value . . . $111,098,245
Ann. rainfall (in.) . 46.19	No. employed 59,761
Jan. temp. min. 37	Wages paid $1,037,516,684
July temp. max. 94	Tax value . $3,797,333,467
Growing season (da.) 259	Income . . . $1,482,102,000
No. farms, 1982 . . . 1,689	Taxable sales $857,819,280
No. acres in farms 246,909	Fed. expend. $235,515,000
†Value per farm $168,527	Crime Index 8,464
Cropland harvested 33,436	TDC Pop. 323

AGRICULTURE: A major producer of rose bushes and horticultural crops with sales of over $78 million annually. Livestock include beef, dairy cattle, horses, poultry; blueberries, peaches, pecans, vegetables; timber sales estimated at $2.5 million.

BUSINESS: Varied manufacturing; agribusinesses; rose production center; oil production; tourism. See metro page.

MANUFACTURING: 168 Plants; 12,300 Employees; Payroll, $221,500,000; Product Value, $1,632,700,000.

SERVICE INDUSTRIES: 935 Establishments; Receipts, $332,927,000; Annual Payroll, $97,387,000; No. Employees, 6,634.

TYLER (70,508) county seat; "Rose Capital of the World"; administrative, operations center for oil production; manufacturers and processors make tires, pipe, heating and cooling systems, refrigeration equipment, clothing, boxes, gas compressors, fertilizers, other products; **Texas College, University of Texas at Tyler, Tyler Junior College; University of Texas Health Center;** medical center; school of nursing.

Other towns include **Lindale** (2,180), **Troup** (1,911, part Cherokee County), **Whitehouse** (2,172), **New Chap**el **Hill** (618), **Arp** (939), **Bullard** (681, part Cherokee County), **Overton** (2,430, part Rusk County), **Winona** (443), **Noonday** (385).

Somervell

LOCATION: North central (I-15).

HISTORY: 3rd smallest county; created, organized as **Somerville County,** 1875, from Hood, Bosque; name changed to proper spelling 1876; named for Texas Republic **Gen. Alexander Somervell.**

Cong. Dist. 17	U.S. Jud. Dist. . . . . W-Wa.
St. Sen. Dist. 22	Ct. Appeals 10
St. Rep. Dist. 58	Admin. Jud. Dist. 3
St. Dist. Cts. 18, 249	

PHYSICAL FEATURES: Hilly; Brazos, Paluxy Rivers; gray, dark, alluvial soils.

RECREATION: Fishing, hunting; unique geological formations; **Dinosaur Valley State Park;** Glen Rose Big Rock Park; nature trails, museum.

MINERALS: Limited sand, gravel.

1982 Pop. 4,200	Voters reg. 2,832
Area (sq. mi.) 188	Whlsle. sales . . $3,173,000
Altitude (ft.) . . . 600-1,300	Oil value 0
Ann. rainfall (in.) . 32.65	No. employed 5,612
Jan. temp. min. 32	Wages paid . $141,946,492
July temp. max. 98	Tax value . $1,798,741,071
Growing season (da.) 236	Income $47,302,000
No. farms, 1982 234	Taxable sales $10,089,875
No. acres in farms . 62,614	Fed. expend. . $7,157,000
†Value per farm $140,585	Crime Index 98
Cropland harvested 5,874	TDC Pop. 4

AGRICULTURE: About $3 million average yearly income, ¾ from beef cattle, hogs; crops include hay, peanuts, small grains, pecans.

Miss Tyler, 1985, Natalie Evetts

BUSINESS: Tourism, agribusinesses.
MANUFACTURING: None noted in census report.
SERVICE INDUSTRIES: 12 Establishments; Receipts, $1,737,000; Annual Payroll, $609,000; No. Employees, 65.
GLEN ROSE (2,075) county seat; tourist, farm trade center; hospital, nursing home; nuclear plant under construction.

SERVICE INDUSTRIES: 42 Establishments; Receipts, $4,885,000; Annual Payroll, $1,264,000; No. Employees, 206.
RIO GRANDE CITY (est. 5,720) county seat; agribusiness center; brick factory; exports to Mexico; hospital.
Other towns include **La Grulla** (1,442), **Roma-Los Saenz** (3,384).

Starr

LOCATION: Far south (U-14).
HISTORY: Named for **Dr. J. H. Starr** of Republic of Texas; county created from Nueces, organized 1848.

Cong. Dist.	15	U.S. Jud. Dist.	S-Br.
St. Sen. Dist.	21	Ct. Appeals	4
St. Rep. Dist.	37	Admin. Jud. Dist.	5
St. Dist. Cts.	229		

PHYSICAL FEATURES: Rolling, some hills; dense brush; clay, loam, sandy soils; alluvial on Rio Grande; **Falcon Reservoir**.
RECREATION: Falcon Reservoir activities; deer, white wing dove hunting; access to Mexico; historic houses; grotto at Rio Grande City.
MINERALS: Production of oil, gas, sand and gravel.

1982 Pop.	30,000	Voters reg.	15,678
Area (sq. mi.)	1,226	Whlsle. sales	$26,320,000
Altitude (ft.)	150-500	Oil value	$23,590,214
Ann. rainfall (in.)	18.87	No. employed	5,120
Jan. temp. min.	48	Wages paid	$53,749,400
July temp. max.	98	Tax value	$949,227,222
Growing season (da.)	314	Income	$128,593,000
No. farms, 1982	830	Taxable sales	$41,241,160
No. acres in farms	556,079	Fed. expend.	$39,747,000
†Value per farm	$393,745	Crime Index	429
Cropland harvested	87,731	TDC Pop.	13

AGRICULTURE: $63 million average annual income, 66% from crops, including sorghums, cotton, vegetables; beef cattle, hogs, sheep, horses; 20,000 acres irrigated for vegetables.
BUSINESS: Vegetable packing, shipping, other agribusinesses; oil processing; tourism.
MANUFACTURING: None noted in census report.

Stephens

LOCATION: North central (H-13).

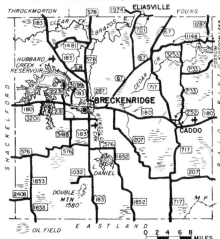

HISTORY: Created as **Buchanan**, 1858, from Bosque; renamed, 1861, for Confederate Vice President, **Alexander H. Stephens**; organized 1876.

Cong. Dist.	17	U.S. Jud. Dist	N-Ab.
St. Sen. Dist.	22	Ct. Appeals	11
St. Rep. Dist	64	Admin. Jud. Dist	8
St. Dist. Cts.	90		

PHYSICAL FEATURES: Broken, hilly; **Hubbard Creek, Possum Kingdom, Daniel Lakes;** Brazos River; loam, sandy soils.
RECREATION: Lake activities; hunting; camp sites; historical points; **Swenson Museum;** Sandefer Oil Museum; Aviation museum; local events.

1982 Pop.	10,900	Voters reg.	6,077
Area (sq. mi.)	894	Whlsle. sales	$43,513,000
Altitude (ft.)	1,000-1,600	Oil value	$113,618,083
Ann. rainfall (in.)	26.33	No. employed	3,224
Jan. temp. min.	31	Wages paid	$47,790,616
July temp. max.	98	Tax value	$787,153,569
Growing season (da.)	222	Income	$97,312,000
No. farms, 1982	431	Taxable sales	$47,603,200
No. acres in farms	533,494	Fed. expend.	$21,447,000
†Value per farm	$402,480	Crime Index	227
Cropland harvested	14,499	TDC Pop.	13

MINERALS: Oil, gas, stone.

AGRICULTURE: $12 million average annual income, 90% from beef cattle, horses, hogs, sheep; crops include wheat, oats, hay, peanuts, sorghums, cotton.

BUSINESS: Oil, agribusinesses, recreation, manufacturing of mobil homes, furniture, aircraft parts, petrochemicals, oil field equipment.

MANUFACTURING: 16 Plants; 500 Employees; Payroll, $7,500,000; Product Value, $31,000,000.

SERVICE INDUSTRIES: 68 Establishments; Receipts; $9,766,000; Annual Payroll, $2,745,000; No. Employees, 276.

BRECKENRIDGE (6,921) county seat; oil and agribusiness center; plants make clothing, petrochemicals, mobile homes, furniture, oil field equipment, aircraft parts, plaques and trophies, other products; hospital, nursing homes; airport; arts center and library.

Sterling

LOCATION: Southwest (J-10).

HISTORY: Named for buffalo hunter, **W. S. Sterling;** created, organized, 1891, from Tom Green County.

PHYSICAL FEATURES: Central prairie, surrounded by hills, broken by Concho and tributaries; sandy to black soils.

RECREATION: Hunting; local events.

MINERALS: Oil, gas.

AGRICULTURE: Some $6.5 million average annual income, nearly all from beef cattle, sheep, goats.

Cong. Dist.	17	U.S. Jud. Dist.	N-SAng.
St. Sen. Dist.	25	Ct. Appeals	3
St. Rep. Dist	66	Admin. Jud. Dist	7
St. Dist. Cts.	51		

1982 Pop.	1,400	Voters reg.	897
Area (sq. mi.)	923	Whsle. sales	$2,076,000
Altitude (ft.)	2,200-2,600	Oil value	$78,821,553
Ann. rainfall (in.)	19.00	No. employed	386
Jan. temp. min.	33	Wages paid	$6,457,036
July temp. max.	95	Tax value	$538,243,960
Growing season (da.)	224	Income	$8,135,000
No. farms, 1982	78	Taxable sales	$4,219,906
†Value per farm	$1,968,551	Fed. expend.	$2,401,000
Cropland harvested.	N.A.	TDC Pop.	1

BUSINESS: Oil and ranching economy; hunting leases.

MANUFACTURING: None noted in census report.

SERVICE INDUSTRIES: 3 Establishments; Receipts, $149,000; Annual Payroll, $43,000; No. Employees, 9.

STERLING CITY (915) county seat; ranching trade center; oil field services; hospital, nursing home.

Stonewall

LOCATION: Northwest, below Cap Rock (G-11).

HISTORY: Named for **Confederate Gen. T. J. (Stonewall) Jackson;** created from Bexar, 1876, organized 1888.

Cong. Dist.	17	U.S. Jud. Dist.	N-Ab.
St. Sen. Dist.	30	Ct. Appeals	11
St. Rep. Dist	78	Admin. Jud. Dist	7
St. Dist. Cts	39		

PHYSICAL FEATURES: Level, bisected by Brazos forks; sandy loam, sandy, other soils; some hills.

RECREATION: Local events.

MINERALS: Production of oil, gas, gypsum.

AGRICULTURE: An estimated $12 million average yearly income from beef cattle, hogs; cotton, sorghums, small grains, peanuts; 5,000 acres irrigated.

BUSINESS: Oil, agribusinesses leading economic factors.

MANUFACTURING: None noted in census report.

1982 Pop.	2,400	Voters reg.	1,702
Area (sq. mi.)	925	Whsle. sales	$4,112,000
Altitude (ft.)	1,500-2,400	Oil value	$115,136,240
Ann. rainfall (in.)	22.36	No. employed	666
Jan. temp. min.	30	Wages paid	$10,347,316
July temp. max.	99	Tax value	$324,739,155
Growing season (da.)	220	Income	$21,570,000
No. farms, 1982	337	Taxable sales	$5,648,102
No. acres in farms	530,306	Fed. expend.	$7,866,000
†Value per farm	$445,833	Crime Index	29
Cropland harvested	54,118	TDC Pop.	6

SERVICE INDUSTRIES: 5 Establishments; Receipts, $1,614,000; Annual Payroll, $500,000; No. Employees, 58.

ASPERMONT (1,357) county seat; center for oil field, ranching operations.

Sutton

LOCATION: Southwest (L-11).

HISTORY: Created from Crockett, 1887; organized, 1890; named for Confederate soldier, **Col. John S. Sutton.**

Cong. Dist.	21	U.S. Jud. Dist.	N-SAng.
St. Sen. Dist.	25	Ct. Appeals	4
St. Rep. Dist.	67	Admin. Jud. Dist	6
St. Dist. Cts.	112		

▲ CAVERNS OF SONORA

1982 Pop.	5,700	Voters reg.	2,642
Area (sq. mi.)	1,455	Whsle. sales	$22,369,000
Altitude (ft.)	1,900-2,300	Oil value	$1,867,158
Ann. rainfall (in.)	17.59	No. employed	1,752
Jan. temp. min.	38	Wages paid	$29,977,176
July temp. max.	94	Tax value	$770,398,430
Growing season (da.)	235	Income	$50,818,000
No. farms, 1982	177	Taxable sales	$23,870,954
No. acres in farms	919,359	Fed. expend.	$8,565,000
†Value per farm	$1,382,661	Crime Index	101
Cropland harvested	1,042	TDC Pop.	13

PHYSICAL FEATURES: Level, broken by tributaries of Devils, Llano Rivers; black, red loam soils.

RECREATION: Among leading hunting counties; **Caverns of Sonora;** local events.

MINERALS: Production of oil, gas, stone.

AGRICULTURE: About $13 million average annual income, almost all from cattle, sheep, goats.

BUSINESS: Agribusinesses, oil, tourism; hunting leases.

MANUFACTURING: None noted in census report.

SERVICE INDUSTRIES: 26 Establishments; Receipts, $8,425,000; Annual Payroll, $2,067,000; No. Employees, 181.

SONORA (3,856) county seat; oil field services; cattle, wool, mohair marketing center; **Texas A&M Agricultural Research Substation;** hospital, nursing homes.

Swisher

LOCATION: Northwest (D-8).

HISTORY: Named for **J. G. Swisher** of Texas Revolution; county created from Bexar, Young Territories, 1876; organized, 1890; among last Indian strongholds.

Cong. Dist. 13	U.S. Jud. Dist . . . N-Am.
St. Sen. Dist. 31	Ct. Appeals 7
St. Rep. Dist 85	Admin. Jud. Dist 9
St. Dist. Cts. 64, 242	

PHYSICAL FEATURES: Level, broken by Tule Canyon and Creek; playas; large underground water supply; rich soils.

RECREATION: Mackenzie Reservoir, Tule Lake activities; museum; local events.

MINERALS: Not significant.

1982 Pop. 9,200	Voters reg. 4,786
Area (sq. mi.) 902	Whlse. sales . $87,359,000
Altitude (ft.) . 3,000-3,600	Oil value 0
Ann. rainfall (in.) . 18.94	No. employed 2,039
Jan. temp. min. 24	Wages paid . . $25,493,252
July temp. max. 93	Tax value . . $325,246,227
Growing season (da.) 205	Income $57,360,000
No. farms, 1982 551	Taxable sales $15,407,159
No. acres in farms 546,460	Fed. expend. . $55,854,000
†Value per farm $573,946	Crime Index 280
Cropland harv. . . 277,549	TDC Pop. 11

AGRICULTURE: Among leading counties in farm income; about $125 million average annual income, 60% fed cattle; crops include sorghums, wheat, cotton, corn, soybeans; 189,000 acres irrigated.

BUSINESS: Large feedlots, grain storage, other agribusinesses; varied manufacturing; tourism.

MANUFACTURING: None noted in census report.

SERVICE INDUSTRIES: 45 Establishments; Receipts, $8,687,000; Annual Payroll, $3,463,000; No. Employees, 239.

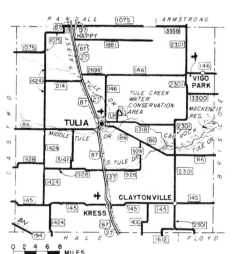

The Fort Worth Stockyard area has undergone a facelift. The Livestock Exchange is shown here.

TULIA (5,033) county seat; center for farming activities; plants make a variety of products; grain storage; meat processors; hospital, nursing home; library, museum.

Other towns include **Happy** (674, part Randall County), **Kress** (783).

Tarrant

LOCATION: North (H-16).

HISTORY: Named for **Gen. Edward H. Tarrant,** who helped drive Indians from area; county created, 1849, from Navarro County; organized 1850.

Cong. Dist. 12, 24, 26	U.S. Jud. Dist . . . . N-FW
St. Sen. Dist. . 10, 12, 22, 23	Ct. Appeals 2
St. Rep. Dist 89-97	St. Dist. Cts. . . . 17, 48, 67,
Admin. Jud. Dist. 8	96, 141, 153, 213, 231, 233,
	236, 297, 322, 323, 324, 325,
	342, 348, 352, 360,
	Cr. 1, Cr. 2, Cr. 3, Cr. 4

PHYSICAL FEATURES: Part Blackland, level to rolling; drains to Trinity; **Worth, Grapevine, Eagle Mountain, Benbrook Lakes.**

RECREATION: Numerous metropolitan events (ask chambers of commerce); **Scott Theatre; Amon G. Carter Museum; Kimbell Art Museum; Fort Worth Art Museum; Museum of Science and History; Casa Manana;** famed **Botanic Gardens; Forest Park Zoo; Log Cabin Village; Six Flags Over Texas** at Arlington; **Southwestern Exposition, Fat Stock show;** Convention center; **Stockyards Historical District; Colonial National Golf Tournament; Texas Rangers** baseball at Arlington, other major athletic events.

Wide range of Sesquicentennial activities planned (check with Fort Worth Texas Sesquicentennial Committee for details).

MINERALS: Production of cement, sand, gravel, stone, gas.

EDUCATION: Among leading educational centers; schools include **Texas Christian University, Texas Wesleyan College, Southwestern Baptist Theological Seminary, Tarrant County Junior College System** (three campuses), **Texas College of Osteopathic Medicine** (merged with North Texas State University in 1975) all in Fort Worth; **University of Texas at Arlington, Arlington Baptist College, Bauder Fashion College** in Arlington.

1982 Pop........ 929,000	Voters reg...... 508,870
Area (sq. mi.)...... 868	Whlsle. sls. $10,103,133,000
Altitude (ft.)... 500-1,000	Oil value........... 0
Ann. rainfall (in.). 32.30	No. employed... 410,924
Jan. temp. min...... 35	Wages paid $7,757,424,888
July temp. max..... 96	Tax value $33,557,219,759
Growing season (da.) 230	Income.. $10,226,503,000
No. farms, 1982... 1,227	Taxable sls. $6,582,720,037
No. acres in farms 202,052	Fed. expd.. $4,671,555,000
†Value per farm $382,286	Crime Index..... 85,549
Cropland harvested 44,023	TDC Pop........ 2,169

AGRICULTURE: $24 million average farm income; dairy and beef cattle, hogs and poultry; headquarters for large dairy producers' organization at Arlington; large production eggs, milk; horses; major nursery stock production; crops include grain sorghums, small grains, cotton, pecans, vegetables.

BUSINESS: Diversified urban economy (see Fort Worth metro page); planes, helicopters, foods, mobile homes, electronic equipment, chemicals, plastics among products of more than 1,100 factories; large federal expenditure due to defense industries; **Dallas-Fort Worth Airport** nation's largest; 4th most-populous Texas county; economy closely associated with Dallas urban area; in 1973 the Fort Worth and Dallas PMSAs were combined to form the most populous metro area in Texas and the 10th ranking nationally, see metro page.

MANUFACTURING: 1,841 Plants; 100,700 Employees; Payroll, $2,097,200,000; Product Value, $11,325,000,000.

SERVICE INDUSTRIES: 5,638 Establishments; Receipts, $1,851,786,000; Annual Payroll, $683,511,000; No. Employees, 50,306.

FORT WORTH (385,164) county seat; mercantile, commercial, banking and finance, insurance, manufacturing and wholesale trade center for much of West Texas; a leader in aerospace activities with large plane, helicopter and other plants; educational center (see Education, above); outstanding cultural center; museums; many conventions, other activities; serves as distribution center for wide area; agribusiness center for large area of state with large grain storage facilities,

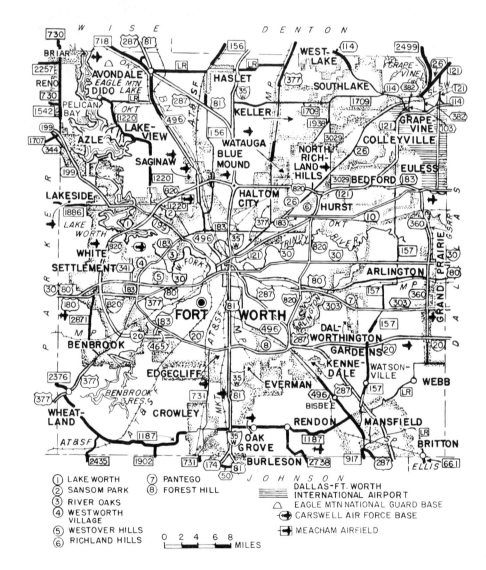

① LAKE WORTH	⑦ PANTEGO		
② SANSOM PARK	⑧ FOREST HILL		
③ RIVER OAKS			DALLAS-FT. WORTH INTERNATIONAL AIRPORT
④ WESTWORTH VILLAGE			EAGLE MTN NATIONAL GUARD BASE
⑤ WESTOVER HILLS			CARSWELL AIR FORCE BASE
⑥ RICHLAND HILLS			MEACHAM AIRFIELD

0 2 4 6 8 MILES

Dallas-Fort Worth International Airport. Billy Bob's Texas night club, Johnnie High's Music Revue; hospitals, nursing homes; **Log Cabin Village.**

Arlington (160,113) 350 firms in large industrial district; industries make and distribute autos, food products, farm, oil field equipment, electronic components, aircraft and parts, rubber and plastic products; many other products; **University of Texas at Arlington; Arlington Baptist College; Bauder Fashion College;** medical and psychiatric hospitals, nursing homes; a leading recreation center with **Six Flags Over Texas** amusement park, other attractions; **Texas Rangers** baseball club.

Grand Prairie (71,462, mostly in Dallas County).

Grapevine (11,801, partly Dallas County) has light manufacturing plants, Grapevine Lake-oriented tourist trade, air freight handling; **Grapevine Opry;** hospital; near **Dallas-Fort Worth Airport.**

White Settlement (13,508) adjacent to large plane plant, **Carswell Air Force Base;** hospital, nursing homes.

Mansfield (8,102, partly Johnson County) industrial parks; plants make various products; hospital.

Other towns include Azle (5,822, partly in Parker County), **Bedford** (20,821), **Benbrook** (13,579) **Blue Mound** (2,169), **Briar** (1,810 partly Parker and Wise Counties), **Burleson** (11,734, partly in Johnson County), **Colleyville** (6,700), **Crowley** (5,852), **Dalworthington Gardens** (1,100), **Edgecliff** (2,695), **Euless** (24,002), **Everman** (5,387), **Forest Hill** (11,684), **Haltom City** (29,014), **Haslet** (262), **Hurst** (31,420), **Keller** (4,156), **Kennedale** (2,594), **Lakeside** (957), **Lake Worth** (4,394), **North Richland Hills** (30,592), **Pantego** (2,431), **Pelican Bay** (518), **Richland Hills** (7,977), **River Oaks** (6,890), **Saginaw** (5,736), **Sansom Park Village** (3,921), **Southlake** (2,808 partly in Denton County), **Watauga** (10,284), **Westlake** (214, partly in Denton County), **Westover Hills** (671), **Westworth** (3,651).

Taylor

LOCATION: Central (I-12).

HISTORY: Named for Alamo heroes, **Edward, James, George Taylor,** brothers; county created from Bexar, Travis, 1858; organized 1878.

Cong. Dist.	17	U.S. Jud. Dist.	N-Ab.
St. Sen. Dist.	24	Ct. Appeals	11
St. Rep. Dist.	78, 79	Admin. Jud. Dist.	7
St. Dist. Cts.	42, 104, 326, 350		

PHYSICAL FEATURES: Prairies, with **Callahan Divide,** draining to Colorado tributaries, Brazos forks; **Lakes Abilene, Kirby, Fort Phantom Hill;** mostly loam soils.

RECREATION: Metropolitan, school events (ask chambers of commerce); **Abilene State Park;** lake activities; Nelson Park Zoo; Texas Cowboy Reunion, West Texas Fair; **Fort Phantom Hill; Buffalo Gap** historical tour and art festival; rodeo, other events.

MINERALS: Production of oil, gas, stone, clays, sand and gravel.

1982 Pop. 118,600	Voters reg. 60,732
Area (sq. mi.) 917	Whlsle. sales$1,533,562,000
Altitude (ft.) . 1,700-2,400	Oil value $63,889,114
Ann. rainfall (in.) . 23.59	No. employed . . . 48,802
Jan. temp. min. 33	Wages paid . $776,211,052
July temp. max. 94	Tax value . $3,655,057,066
Growing season (da.) 225	Income . . . $1,088,362,000
No. farms, 1982 911	Taxable sales $809,081,359
No. acres in farms 435,628	Fed. expend. $535,111,000
†Value per farm $223,707	Crime Index 6,164
Cropland harv. . . 114,719	TDC Pop. 317

AGRICULTURE: About $43 million average annual income, 80% from cattle, hogs, sheep, horses; crops chiefly are cotton, sorghums, wheat; 5,000 acres irrigated, mostly pasture.

BUSINESS: Major economic factors include **Dyess Air Force Base**, feedlots, agribusiness, diversified manufacturing; education; see metro page.

MANUFACTURING: 145 Plants; 5,800 Employees; Payroll, $91,200,000; Product Value, $1,515,800,000.

SERVICE INDUSTRIES: 804 Establishments; Receipts, $223,847,000; Annual Payroll, $78,879,000; No. Employees, 6,066.

ABILENE (98,315, partly in Jones County) county seat; distribution center for large area; plants make apparel, trailers, building materials, aircraft parts, consumer electronics, plumbing fixtures, musical instruments, uniforms, beverage cans, other products; process cottonseed, meats, dairy products; oil field service center; **Abilene Christian University, Hardin-Simmons University, McMurry College; Cisco Junior College** branch; medical center; **Abilene State School; West Texas Rehabilitation Center.**

Merkel (2,493) manufacturing; oil field services; feedlot; nursing home. **Tye** (1,394), **Tuscola** (660), **Buffalo Gap** (387), **Impact** (54), **Lawn** (390), **Trent** (313) other principal towns.

Terrell

LOCATION: Borders Mexico (M-8).

HISTORY: Named for **Confederate Gen. A. W. Terrell;** county created, organized 1905, from Pecos.

Cong. Dist. 21	U.S. Jud. Dist. . . . W-DR
St. Sen. Dist. 25	Ct. Appeals 8
St. Rep. Dist. 68	Admin. Jud. Dist. 6
St. Dist. Cts. 63	

PHYSICAL FEATURES: Semimountainous, many canyons; rocky, limestone soils.

RECREATION: Hunting; lower canyons of Rio Grande accessible by boat; local events.

MINERALS: Production of gas, oil.

1982 Pop. 1,500	Voters reg. 978
Area (sq. mi.) 2,357	Whlsle. sales . . . . . . $*
Altitude (ft.) . 1,200-3,600	Oil value $3,001,289
Ann. rainfall (in.) . 11.21	No. employed . . . 371
Jan. temp. min. 30	Wages paid . . $5,177,020
July temp. max. 93	Tax value . . $302,551,065
Growing season (da.) 237	Income $12,949,000
No. farms, 1982 77	Taxable sales . $2,251,891
No. acs. in farms 1,246,506	Fed. expend. . $6,401,000
†Value per farm $2,587,935	Crime Index 10
Cropland harvested. N.A.	TDC Pop. 1

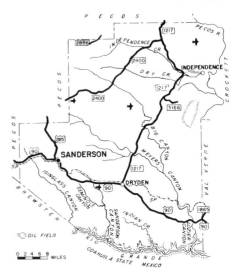

OIL FIELD

0 2 4 6 8 MILES

AGRICULTURE: Some $9 million average annual income, nearly all from sheep, goats, beef cattle; among leading counties in sheep, goat production.

BUSINESS: Ranching economy; oil and natural gas exploration increasing.

MANUFACTURING: None noted in census report.

SERVICE INDUSTRIES: 3 Establishments; Receipts, $188,000; Annual Payroll, $28,000; No. Employees, 5.

SANDERSON (est. 1,500) county seat; center for ranching, petroleum operations; rail terminal.

Terry

LOCATION: West (G-7).

HISTORY: Named for head of famed Texas Ranger troop, **Col. B. F. Terry.** County created from Bexar District, 1876; organized, 1904.

Cong. Dist. 19	U.S. Jud. Dist. . . . . N-Lb.
St. Sen. Dist. 28	Ct. Appeals 7
St. Rep. Dist. 77	Admin. Jud. Dist. 9
St. Dist. Cts. 121	

PHYSICAL FEATURES: Level, broken by draws, playas; sandy, sandy loam, loam soils.

RECREATION: Local events; Terry County Heritage Museum, fall harvest festival.

MINERALS: Production of oil, gas, sodium sulphate.

AGRICULTURE: Among leading cotton counties; about $75 million average annual income, 90% from cotton, sorghums, wheat; some cattle, hogs; 115,000 acres irrigated, mostly cotton.

BUSINESS: Petroleum, agribusinesses.

MANUFACTURING: None noted in census report.

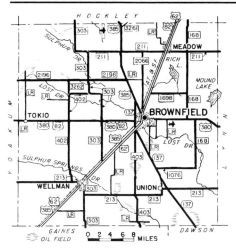

1982 Pop.	15,100	Voters reg.	7,887
Area (sq. mi.)	886	Whlsle. sales	$217,358,000
Altitude (ft.)	3,100-3,600	Oil value	$341,739,505
Ann. rainfall (in.)	17.21	No. employed	4,241
Jan. temp. min.	26	Wages paid	$71,045,212
July temp. max.	93	Tax value	$1,386,339,820
Growing season (da.)	206	Income	$108,536,000
No. farms, 1982	532	Taxable sales	$43,176,930
No. acres in farms	511,578	Fed. expend.	$84,288,000
†Value per farm	$471,572	Crime Index	711
Cropland harv.	337,626	TDC Pop.	49

SERVICE INDUSTRIES: 67 Establishments; Receipts, $13,221,000; Annual Payroll, $3,859,000; No. Employees, 348.

BROWNFIELD (10,387) county seat; oil field services; plants make irrigation equipment, fertilizers, cotton module systems, process minerals; hospital, clinics, nursing homes.

Other towns include **Meadow** (571) and **Wellman** (239).

Throckmorton

LOCATION: North central (G-13).
HISTORY: Named for **Dr. W. E. Throckmorton**, father of Gov. J. W. Throckmorton; county created from Fannin, 1858; organized, 1879.

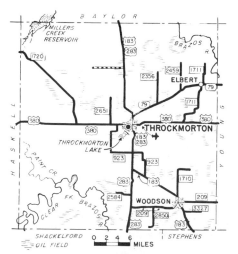

Cong. Dist.	17	U.S. Jud. Dist.	N-Ab.
St. Sen. Dist.	30	Ct. Appeals	11
St. Rep. Dist.	64	Admin. Jud. Dist.	7
St. Dist. Cts.	39		

PHYSICAL FEATURES: Rolling, between Brazos forks; red to black soils.
RECREATION: Hunting, fishing; historic sites include **Camp Cooper, Camp Wilson**, site of former Comanche reservation; restored ranch home.
MINERALS: Production of gas, oil.

1982 Pop.	2,200	Voters reg.	1,419
Area (sq. mi.)	912	Whlsle. sales	$*
Altitude (ft.)	1,200-2,000	Oil value	$64,386,714
Ann. rainfall (in.)	25.82	No. employed	517
Jan. temp. min.	29	Wages paid	$6,826,352
July temp. max.	98	Tax value	$198,655,193
Growing season (da.)	220	Income	$13,662,000
No. farms, 1982	306	Taxable sales	$4,615,200
No. acres in farms	504,472	Fed. expend.	$9,086,000
†Value per farm	$576,222	Crime Index	17
Cropland harvested	60,268	TDC Pop.	0

AGRICULTURE: About $17 million average annual income, 75% from cattle, sheep, horses; crops include wheat, oats, cotton, sorghums, hay.
BUSINESS: Oil and agribusiness economy.
MANUFACTURING: None noted in census report.
SERVICE INDUSTRIES: 11 Establishments; Receipts, $1,385,000; Annual Payroll, $526,000; No. Employees, 51.
THROCKMORTON (1,174) county seat; plants make oil field equipment, other products; hospital, nursing home; oil field services. **Woodson** (291) other principal town.

Titus

LOCATION: Northeast (G-20).
HISTORY: Named for pioneer settler, **A. J. Titus**; county created from Bowie, Red River and organized 1846.
PHYSICAL FEATURES: Small and hilly; drains to Big Cypress Creek, Sulphur River; timbered.
RECREATION: Fishing, hunting; activities on **Monticello Reservoir, Lake Bob Sandlin, Welsh Reservoir**, other area lakes; railroad museum; riverboat; local events.
MINERALS: Production of oil, gas, lignite.

Cong. Dist.	1	U.S. Jud. Dist.	E-Tx.
St. Sen. Dist.	1	Ct. Appeals	6
St. Rep. Dist.	8	Admin. Jud. Dist.	1
St. Dist. Cts.	76, 276		

1982 Pop.	22,300	Voters reg.	12,387
Area (sq. mi.)	412	Whlsle. sales	$76,574,000
Altitude (ft.)	250-450	Oil value	$27,053,991
Ann. rainfall (in.)	45.99	No. employed	8,328
Jan. temp. min.	35	Wages paid	$148,800,536
July temp. max.	95	Tax value	$1,611,947,869
Growing season (da.)	233	Income	$212,210,000
No. farms, 1982	778	Taxable sales	$102,602,910
No. acres in farms	190,385	Fed. expend.	$41,398,000
†Value per farm	$165,098	Crime Index	616
Cropland harvested	21,064	TDC Pop.	43

AGRICULTURE: About $30 million average annual income, over 90% from cattle, dairy products, poultry; among leading counties in broilers; crops include corn, watermelons, sorghums, hay, peanuts.
BUSINESS: Economy based largely on oil, agribusinesses, tourism; lignite mining and power generation.
MANUFACTURING: 31 Plants; 1,500 Employees; Payroll, $20,500,000; Product Value, $358,100,000.
SERVICE INDUSTRIES: 129 Establishments; Receipts, $27,476,000; Annual Payroll, $8,407,000; No. Employees, 849.

MOUNT PLEASANT (11,003) county seat; tourism; plants make cables, furniture, other products; beef, poultry processing plants; hospital, nursing homes; Cyprus Basin Community College (branch Paris Junior College).

Talco (751), **Monticello** (43), **Winfield** (349), **Miller's Cove** (61) other principal towns.

Trinity

LOCATION: Southeast (K-20).

HISTORY: Named for river; county created, organized, 1850, out of Houston County.

Cong. Dist. 2	U.S. Jud. Dist . . . . S-Hn.
St. Sen. Dist. 5	Ct. Appeals 1, 14
St. Rep. Dist 17	Admin. Jud. Dist. 2
St. Dist. Cts. . . . 2D9, 258	

MINERALS: Limited oil, gas, lignite, sand and gravel.

PHYSICAL FEATURES: Heavily forested hills, between Neches and Trinity; rich alluvial soils, sandy upland; 67,910 acres in **Davy Crockett National Forest.**

RECREATION: Lake Livingston activities; fishing, hiking, hunting; **Davy Crockett National Forest**; historic sites.

1982 Pop. 10,400	Voters reg. 8,087
Area (sq. mi.) 692	Whlsle. sales . $16,430,000
Altitude (ft.) 150-400	Oil value. $46,185
Ann. rainfall (in.) . 45.95	No. employed . . . 1,643
Jan. temp. min. 39	Wages paid . . $20,417,092
July temp. max. 94	Tax value . . $523,558,007
Growing season (da.) 260	Income $79,229,000
No. farms, 1982 . . . 520	Taxable sales $23,234,035
No. acres in farms 144,019	Fed. expend.. $22,311,000
†Value per farm $207,727	Crime Index 170
Cropland harvested 9,010	TDC Pop. 29

AGRICULTURE: Timber sales produce income of more than $6.2 million; more than $11 million other farm income from beef cattle, hogs; hay, sweet potatoes, peaches, pecans.

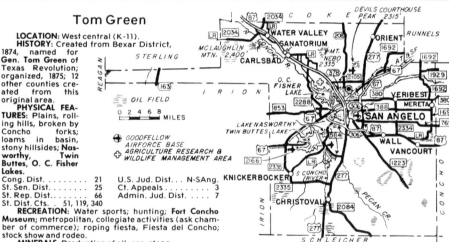

BUSINESS: Forestry, tourism, cattle chief sources income.

MANUFACTURING: None noted in census report.

SERVICE INDUSTRIES: 28 Establishments; Receipts, $3,406,000; Annual Payroll; $749,000; No. Employees, 84.

GROVETON (1,262) county seat; gateway to Davy Crockett National Forest recreation areas; lumbering center; clothing and oil field chemical manufacturing; hospital, nursing home; airport.

Other principal town is **Trinity** (2,620) steel fabrication; hospital, nursing home; a forest industries center near **Lake Livingston.**

Tom Green

LOCATION: West central (K-11).

HISTORY: Created from Bexar District, 1874, named for **Gen. Tom Green** of Texas Revolution; organized, 1875; 12 other counties created from this original area.

PHYSICAL FEATURES: Plains, rolling hills, broken by Concho forks; loams in basin, stony hillsides; **Nasworthy**, **Twin Buttes, O. C. Fisher Lakes.**

Cong. Dist. 21	U.S. Jud. Dist. . . N-SAng.
St. Sen. Dist. 25	Ct. Appeals 3
St. Rep. Dist. 66	Admin. Jud. Dist. 7
St. Dist. Cts. . . 51, 119, 340	

RECREATION: Water sports; hunting; **Fort Concho Museum**; metropolitan, collegiate activities (ask chamber of commerce); roping fiesta, Fiesta del Concho; stock show and rodeo.

MINERALS: Production of oil, gas, stone.

1982 Pop. 90,700	Voters reg. 47,124
Area (sq. mi.) 1,515	Whlsle. sales $621,333,000
Altitude (ft.) . 1,700-2,600	Oil value. . . . $44,914,703
Ann. rainfall (in.) . 17.53	No. employed . . . 36,092
Jan. temp. min. 34	Wages paid . $547,891,304
July temp. max. 98	Tax value . . $996,468,220
Growing season (da.) 235	Income $933,267,000
No. farms, 1982 806	Taxable sales $493,980,231
No. acres in farms 968,035	Fed. expend. $228,872,000
†Value per farm $553,559	Crime Index 5,206
Cropland harv. . 142,189	TDC Pop. 255

AGRICULTURE: An estimated $52 million average annual income from beef, dairy cattle, sheep, goats; a leading producer of wool, mohair; cotton, wheat, oats, sorghums; 15,000 acres irrigated.

BUSINESS: "**Sheep and Wool Capital**"; economy based on varied agribusinesses, manufacturing; trade center for large area, educational center, medical center; see San Angelo metro page.

MANUFACTURING: 101 Plants; 5,100 Employees; Payroll, $70,200,000; Product Value, $363,100,000.

SERVICE INDUSTRIES: 542 Establishments; Receipts; $163,165,000; Annual Payroll, $56,390,000; No. Employees, 4,094.

SAN ANGELO (73,240) county seat; varied agribusinesses; livestock feeding, packing center; plants make sportswear, footwear, surgical supplies, millwork, aircraft parts, oilfield equipment, other products; hospital; **Angelo State University; Texas A&M Research and Extension Center.**

Travis

LOCATION: Central (M-15).

HISTORY: Created, 1840, when Austin became Texas Capital, from Bastrop County; organized, 1843; named for Alamo commander, **Col. Wm. B. Travis**; many other counties created from original area.

Cong. Dist. 10	U. S. Jud. Dist . . . W-An.
St. Sen. Dist. 14	Ct. Appeals 3
St. Rep. Dist 47-51	Admin. Jud. Dist 3
St. Dist. Cts. . . 53, 98, 126,	
147, 167, 200, 201, 250,	
261, 299, 331, 345, 353	

PHYSICAL FEATURES: Scenic hills, broken by Colorado River and lakes; cedars, pecans, other trees; diverse soils, mineral deposits.

RECREATION: Major tourist center; 95 miles of Colorado River lakes from Austin northwestward; hunting, fishing; Austin Aqua Festival; livestock exposition; many collegiate, metropolitan, governmental events; (ask chamber of commerce, Texas Highway Department, Tourist Development Agency).

1982 Pop. 447,600	Voters reg. 299,027
Area (sq. mi.) 989	Whlsle. sales $1,889,983,000
Altitude (ft.) . . . 400-1,400	Oil value $165,949
Ann. rainfall (in.) . 32.49	No. employed . . . 263,758
Jan. temp. min. 41	Wages paid $4,639,132,452
July temp. max. 95	Tax value $23,013,109,894
Growing season (da.) 270	Income . . . $5,155,261,000
No. farms, 1982 . . . 1,061	Taxable sls. $4,041,116,763
No. acres in farms 362,502	Fed. exp. . $5,215,955,000
†Value per farm $461,971	Crime Index 36,672
Cropland harvested 66,140	TDC Pop. 1,086

MINERALS: Production of lime, stone, sand, gravel, oil and gas.

EDUCATION: **University of Texas** main campus, South's largest university; **St. Edward's University, Maryhill College, Concordia Lutheran College, Huston-Tillotson College, Austin Community College;** many state eleemosynary schools, institutions.

AGRICULTURE: Almost $44 million average annual income from beef, dairy cattle, hogs; crops include sorghums, cotton, small grains, pecans.

BUSINESS: Urbanized area (see Austin metro page) with economy based on education, state government, tourism, research and industry; many conventions.

MANUFACTURING: 537 Plants; 29,000 Employees; Payroll, $589,900,000; Product Value, $2,353,900,000.

SERVICE INDUSTRIES: 3,529 Establishments; Receipts, $1,320,824,000; Annual Payroll, $513,496,000; No. Employees, 35,190.

AUSTIN: (345,890) county seat and state capital; large state and federal payrolls; **University of Texas, Austin Community College,** other schools (see **Education** above); a leading convention, tourism city; **Lyndon B. Johnson Presidential Library;** many research and science-oriented industries; hospitals, including state institutions; popular retirement area; **Bergstrom Air Force Base,** other federal activities; plants make electronic, business equipment, boats, many other products.

Other growing suburban towns include **West Lake Hills** (2,166), **Lakeway** (790), **Manor** (1,044), **Pflugerville** (745), **Rollingwood** (1,027), **San Leanna** (290), **Sunset Valley** (420) and **Lago Vista** (2,500) resort community on **Lake Travis.**

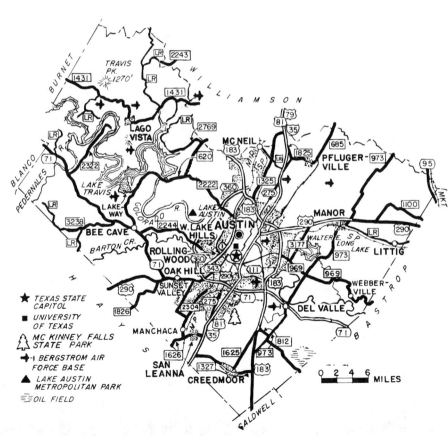

★ *TEXAS STATE CAPITOL*

■ *UNIVERSITY OF TEXAS*

⋀ *MC KINNEY FALLS STATE PARK*

✦⊣ *BERGSTROM AIR FORCE BASE*

▲ *LAKE AUSTIN METROPOLITAN PARK*

≋ *OIL FIELD*

0 2 4 6 MILES

Tyler

LOCATION: Southeast (K-21).

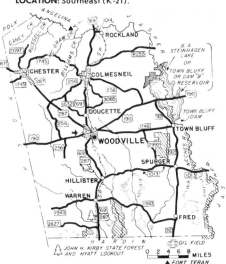

////// STATE WILDLIFE SCIENTIFIC AREA
\\\\ BIG THICKET NATIONAL PRESERVE

HISTORY: Named for U.S. president, **John Tyler;** county created, organized, 1846, from Liberty.

Cong. Dist. 2   U.S. Jud. Dist . . . . E-Bt.
St. Sen. Dist. 3   Ct. Appeals 9
St. Rep. Dist 18   Admin. Jud. Dist. 2
St. Dist. Cts. 88, 1-A

PHYSICAL FEATURES: Hilly, densely timbered; drains to Neches, Angelina, other streams; **Lake B. A. Steinhagen** (formerly **Town Bluff and Dam B**); **Big Thicket** is unique plant-animal area.

RECREATION: Big Thicket National Preserve; guest ranch; **Heritage Village;** lake activities; **Allan Shivers Museum; John Henry Kirby State Forest;** historic sites; near **Alabama-Coushatta Indian Reservation;** dogwood festival in spring; rodeo, arts and crafts fair, other local events.

MINERALS: Production of oil, gas.

1982 Pop.	16,600	Voters reg.	10,488
Area (sq. mi.)	922	Whlsle. sales . .	$6,218,000
Altitude (ft.)	50-400	Oil value	$7,061,033
Ann. rainfall (in.) .	48.37	No. employed . .	2,903
Jan. temp. min.	38	Wages paid . .	$36,178,592
July temp. max.	94	Tax value . .	$747,599,566
Growing season (da.)	241	Income	$149,708,000
No. farms, 1982	496	Taxable sales	$31,681,476
No. acres in farms	100,403	Fed. expend. .	$35,682,000
†Value per farm	$215,958	Crime Index	260
Cropland harvested	6,869	TDC Pop.	31

AGRICULTURE: Timber sales major income source, with over 500,000 forest acres including Christmas trees; $7 million additional annual average farming income from cattle, hogs, poultry, goats, vegetables, soybeans.

BUSINESS: Lumbering, poultry processing, some manufacturing; tourism, catfish production.

MANUFACTURING: 39 Plants; 600 Employees; Payroll, $6,400,000; Product Value, $41,900,000.

SERVICE INDUSTRIES: 36 Establishments; Receipts, $5,355,000; Annual Payroll, $1,926,000; No. Employees, 284.

WOODVILLE (2,821) county seat; center for lumber manufacturing, livestock marketing; plants make aluminum products, portable buildings, wood products,

industrial products; tourist center; hospital, nursing homes, rehabilitation center.

Other towns include **Chester** (305) and **Colmesneil** (553).

Upshur

LOCATION: Northeast (H-20).

HISTORY: Created from Harrison, Nacogdoches Counties, 1846; organized same year; named for U.S. Secretary of State, **A. P. Upshur.**

Cong. Dist. 1   U.S. Jud. Dist. . . . E-MI.
St. Sen. Dist. 1   Ct. Appeals 6, 12
St. Rep. Dist. 5   Admin. Jud. Dist. 1
St. Dist. Cts. 115

PHYSICAL FEATURES: Rolling to hilly, over half forested; drains to Sabine, Cypress Creek, **Lake O' the Pines, Lake Gladewater.**

RECREATION: Scenic trails; hunting, fishing; East Texas October "Yamboree"; rodeo, other local events.

MINERALS: Production of oil, gas, sand and gravel.

1982 Pop.	31,100	Voters reg.	17,997
Area (sq. mi.)	587	Whlsle. sales .	$24,999,000
Altitude (ft.)	225-600	Oil value . . .	$13,212,130
Ann. rainfall (in.) .	45.74	No. employed	4,385
Jan. temp. min.	37	Wages paid . .	$52,027,468
July temp. max.	96	Tax value .	$1,056,047,863
Growing season (da.)	245	Income	$274,239,000
No. farms, 1982 . . .	1,022	Taxable sales	$51,266,472
No. acres in farms	156,828	Fed. expend. .	$45,981,000
†Value per farm	$146,219	Crime Index	952
Cropland harvested	20,273	TDC Pop.	33

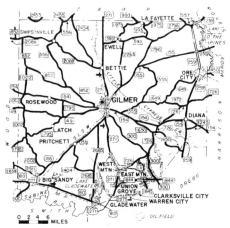

AGRICULTURE: More than $40 million average yearly income, 90% from beef, dairy cattle, hogs, poultry; among leading broiler and dairy producing counties; timber, vegetable crops, hay, peaches.

BUSINESS: Manufacturing, agribusinesses, petroleum production and lumber mill are leading economic factors; many work at nearby steel mills and other area plants.

MANUFACTURING: 31 Plants; 500 Employees; Payroll, $5,800,000; Product Value, $35,400,000.

SERVICE INDUSTRIES: 57 Establishments; Receipts, $6,917,000; Annual Payroll, $2,024,000; No. Employees, 198.

GILMER (5,167) county seat; plants make electrical conduits and fittings, ceramic bathroom accessories, dresses, other products; process meat, vegetables, lumber; hospital, nursing homes.

Big Sandy (1,258) **Ambassador College; Gladewater** (6,548, mostly in Gregg County), **Ore City** (1,050), **War-**

ren City (281, mostly Gregg County), East Mountain (855), Union Grove (344) and West Mountain (395) are other principal towns.

Upton

LOCATION: West (K-8).

HISTORY: Created in 1887 from Tom Green County, not organized until 1910; name honors brothers, **John** and **William Upton**, Confederate colonels.

PHYSICAL FEATURES: North flat, south rolling, hilly; limestone, sandy loam soils, drains to creeks.

RECREATION: Historic sites, **Mendoza Trail Museum**; scenic areas; local events.

MINERALS: Production of oil, gas.

Cong. Dist. 21	U.S. Jud. Dist . . . W:M-0
St. Sen. Dist. 25	Ct. Appeals 8
St. Rep. Dist. 69	Admin. Jud. Dist 6
St. Dist. Cts. 83, 112	

1982 Pop. 5,300	Voters reg. 2,834
Area (sq. mi.) 1,243	Whlsle. sales . $20,134,000
Altitude (ft.) . . 2,400-3,150	Oil value . . . $206,418,155
Ann. rainfall (in.) . 12.70	No. employed 1,674
Jan. temp. min. 33	Wages paid . . $34,690,392
July temp. max. 96	Tax value . $1,023,199,715
Growing season (da.) 232	Income $39,129,000
No. farms, 1982 89	Taxable sales $23,337,109
No. acres in farms 750,403	Fed. expend. . $8,348,000
†Value per farm$1,231,888	Crime Index 76
Cropland harvested 21,604	TDC Pop. 4

AGRICULTURE: About $5.3 million average yearly income equally divided among sheep, goats, cattle and cotton; wheat, pecan production; 10,000 acres irrigated for cotton, pecans.

BUSINESS: Petroleum production, ranching, tourism.

MANUFACTURING: None noted in census report.

SERVICE INDUSTRIES: 12 Establishments; Receipts, $1,170,000; Annual Payroll, $220,000; No. Employees, 21.

RANKIN (1,216) county seat, and **McCamey** (2,436) are centers for oil and ranching activities; hospitals, nursing home; annual pecan show.

Uvalde

LOCATION: Southwest (O-12).

HISTORY: Created from Bexar, 1850; organized, 1853; re-created, organized, 1856; named for **Gov. Juan de Ugalde** of Coahuila, with name Anglicized.

Cong. Dist. 23	U.S. Jud. Dist . . . W-DR
St. Sen. Dist. 25	Ct. Appeals 4
St. Rep. Dist. 67	Admin. Jud. Dist 6
St. Dist. Cts. 38	

PHYSICAL FEATURES: Part on Edwards Plateau, most is rolling hills below escarpment; spring-fed Sabinal, Frio, Leona, Nueces Rivers; cypress, cedar, other trees; unique **maple groves**.

RECREATION: Major deer, turkey hunting area; **Garner State Park**; water activities on scenic rivers; **John N. Garner Museum**; Uvalde Memorial Park; scenic trails; historic sites; local events; recreational homes.

MINERALS: Production asphalt, stone, sand and gravel, oil.

AGRICULTURE: About $53 million average annual income, from beef cattle, hogs, sheep, goats; crops include wheat, corn, oats, grain sorghums, cotton, vegetables; 56,000 acres irrigated.

1982 Pop. 23,000	Voters reg. 12,092
Area (sq. mi.) 1,564	Whlsle. sales $233,091,000
Altitude (ft.) . . . 700-2,000	Oil value 0
Ann. rainfall (in.) . 23.23	No. employed 6,329
Jan. temp. min. 40	Wages paid . . $78,400,624
July temp. max. 96	Tax value . . $724,211,831
Growing season (da.) 255	Income . . . $165,999,000
No. farms, 1982 531	Taxable sales $76,950,045
No. acres in farms 850,002	Fed. expend. . $41,802,000
†Value per farm $924,793	Crime Index 622
Cropland harvested 76,966	TDC Pop. 22

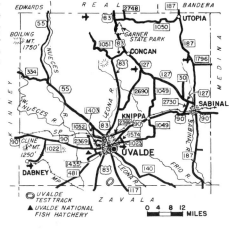

BUSINESS: Agribusinesses; light manufacturing; tourism; hunting leases.

MANUFACTURING: None noted in census report.

SERVICE INDUSTRIES: 115 Establishments; Receipts, $20,644,000; Annual Payroll, $6,223,000; No. Employees, 663.

UVALDE (14,178) county seat; plants make clothes, asphalt products, pipe, process vegetables, wool, mohair; **Southwest Texas Junior College; Texas A&M Research and Extension Center;** hospital.

Sabinal (1,827) center for ranching, farming area; gateway to **Frio** and **Sabinal Canyons;** tourist, recreational, retirement areas.

Val Verde

LOCATION: Southwest (N-10).

HISTORY: Named for Civil War battle, **Val Verde** (green valley); county created, organized, 1885, from Crockett, Kinney, Pecos Counties.

Cong. Dist. 21	U.S. Jud. Dist. . . . W-DR
St. Sen. Dist. 25	Ct. Appeals 4
St. Rep. Dist. 68	Admin. Jud. Dist 6
St. Dist. Cts. 63	

PHYSICAL FEATURES: Rolling, hilly; brushy; Devils, Pecos Rivers, **Amistad Lake;** limestone, alluvial soils.

MINERALS: Production sand and gravel, gas, oil.

1982 Pop. 37,900	Voters reg. 14,366
Area (sq. mi.) 3,150	Whlsle. sales . $65,328,000
Altitude (ft.) . . . 900-2,200	Oil value $32,279
Ann. rainfall (in.) . 16.88	No. employed 7,530
Jan. temp. min. 40	Wages paid . . $86,260,996
July temp. max. 94	Tax value . . $875,160,502
Growing season (da.) 300	Income $245,409,000
No. farms, 1982 253	Taxable sales $101,575,373
No. acs. in farms 1,834,214	Fed. expend. $132,615,000
†Value per farm$1,379,700	Crime Index 1,558
Cropland harvested. N.A.	TDC Pop. 56

Val Verde County (Cont'd.)

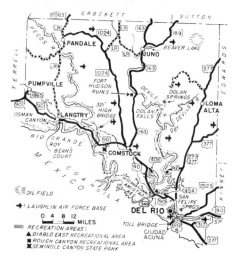

RECREATION: Mexican gateway; deer hunting; Amistad Lake activities; Langtry restoration of Judge Roy Bean's saloon; San Felipe Springs.

AGRICULTURE: Some $16 million average yearly income, nearly all from sheep, Angora goats, cattle.

BUSINESS: Agribusiness; tourism; area trade center; large military, other U.S. expenditures.

MANUFACTURING: 20 Plants; 800 Employees; Payroll, $8,400,000; Product Value, $46,000,000.

SERVICE INDUSTRIES: 148 Establishments; Receipts, $23,370,000; Annual Payroll, $7,628,000; No. Employees, 808.

DEL RIO (30,034) county seat; center for tourism and trade with Mexico; plants make clothing, electronic equipment; hospital; nursing homes.

Van Zandt

LOCATION: Northeast (H-18).

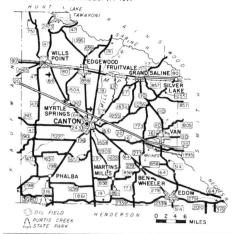

HISTORY: Named for Republic of Texas leader, Isaac Van Zandt; county created, organized from Henderson, 1848.

Cong. Dist.	4	U.S. Jud. Dist.	E-Ty.
St. Sen. Dist.	2	Ct. Appeals	5, 12
St. Rep. Dist.	5	Admin. Jud. Dist.	1
St. Dist. Cts.	294		

PHYSICAL FEATURES: In three soil belts; level to rolling; Sabine, Neches Rivers; Lake Tawakoni; partly forested.

RECREATION: Lake activities; historic sites; Canton "First Monday" trades day, county fair, salt festival.

MINERALS: Production of oil, gas, salt, clays.

1982 Pop.	33,000	Voters reg.	20,063
Area (sq. mi.)	855	Whlsle. sales	$34,805,000
Altitude (ft.)	400-600	Oil value	$32,562,009
Ann. rainfall (in.)	43.09	No. employed	5,146
Jan. temp. min.	35	Wages paid	$66,059,100
July temp. max.	94	Tax value	$1,126,691,543
Growing season (da.)	250	Income	$317,049,000
No. farms, 1982	2,328	Taxable sales	$56,084,264
No. acres in farms	375,685	Fed. expend.	$64,368,000
†Value per farm	$156,113	Crime Index	825
Cropland harvested	54,754	TDC Pop.	55

AGRICULTURE: An estimated $51 million average annual income, 70% from cattle, hogs, dairy products; a leading county in beef cows and calves; crops include nursery stock, vegetables, grains, cotton, hay.

BUSINESS: Economy based on oil, tourism, agribusinesses, light manufacturing; many commute to jobs in Dallas.

MANUFACTURING: 31 Plants; 1,000 Employees; Payroll, $12,800,000; Product Value, $61,600,000.

SERVICE INDUSTRIES: 97 Establishments; Receipts, $16,579,000; Annual Payroll, $5,960,000; No. Employees, 678.

CANTON (2,845) county seat; popular "Trades Day" each first Monday; agribusiness center; apparel factory, trailer plants; nursing homes.

Wills Point (2,631) plants make clothing, mobile homes, aluminum products, other products; nurseries; many work in Dallas, Greenville; livestock marketing center; clinic, nursing home.

Van (1,881) oil activity center; agribusinesses; concrete mixing plant; nursing homes, clinic.

Grand Saline (2,709) salt plant; oil field equipment and apparel manufacturers; steel sinks made; hospital; salt festival in June.

Edgewood (1,413) has oil, gas refineries, hat, rope manufacturing; steel fabrication.

Other towns include **Edom** (250) and **Fruitvale** (367).

Victoria

LOCATION: South (P-17).

HISTORY: An original county, created 1836 from Mexican municipality named for Mexican president, Guadalupe Victoria.

Cong. Dist.	14	U.S. Jud. Dist.	S-Va.
St. Sen. Dist.	18	Ct. Appeals	13
St. Rep. Dist.	32	Admin. Jud. Dist.	4
St. Dist. Cts.	24, 135, 267		

PHYSICAL FEATURES: Rolling, intersected by many streams; sandy loams, clays, alluvial soils.

RECREATION: Fishing, hunting; saltwater activities; many historic homes, sites; recreational park; zoo; Bach Festival in May, Armadillo Festival in August, Super Bowl of Chili, International Food Fair, oil and gas show; ask chamber of commerce.

MINERALS: Production of oil, gas, sand and gravel.

1982 Pop.	72,900	Voters reg.	38,524
Area (sq. mi.)	887	Whlsle. sales	$979,738,000
Altitude (ft.)	-200	Oil value	$57,449,254
Ann. rainfall (in.)	34.29	No. employed	27,836
Jan. temp. min.	46	Wages paid	$479,251,400
July temp. max.	92	Tax value	$3,215,139,973
Growing season (da.)	290	Income	$769,376,000
No. farms, 1982	1,057	Taxable sales	$469,213,397
No. ac. in farms	493,008	Fed. expend.	$159,681,000
†Value per farm	$376,216	Crime Index	4,212
Cropland harvested	90,466	TDC Pop.	174

AGRICULTURE: $33.5 million average farm income from sorghums, rice, corn, beef cattle, hogs, poultry; 5,000 acres irrigated, mostly rice.

BUSINESS: Income from oil, manufacturing, petrochemical plants, agribusiness, tourism.

MANUFACTURING: 62 Plants; 3,600 Employees; Payroll, $85,100,000; Product Value, $644,200,000.

SERVICE INDUSTRIES: 504 Establishments; Receipts, $144,915,000; Annual Payroll, $49,348,000; No. Employees, 3,348.

VICTORIA (50,695) county seat; tourism, agribusiness center; on barge canal; plants make petrochemicals, aluminum, steel products, oil field equipment; foundry equipment; **Victoria College, University of Houston at Victoria;** Community Theater, Symphony; hospitals.

Bloomington is other principal town.

Walker

LOCATION: Southeast (L-19).

HISTORY: Created, organized 1846, from Montgomery County; first named for U.S. Secretary of Treasury, **R. J. Walker;** renamed, 1863, for Texas Ranger **Capt. S. H. Walker.**

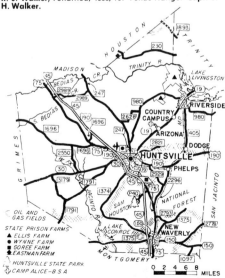

Cong. Dist. 2	U.S. Jud. Dist. . . . . S-Hn.
St. Sen. Dist. 5	Ct. Appeals 1, 14
St. Rep. Dist. 18	Admin. Jud. Dist. 2
St. Dist. Cts. 12, 278	

PHYSICAL FEATURES: Rolling hills; over 70 percent forested; **Sam Houston National Forest;** San Jacinto, Trinity Rivers; large Texas prison farm units.

RECREATION: Fishing, hunting; **Lake Livingston** activities; **Sam Houston museum, homes, grave;** other historic sites; **Huntsville State Park; Sam Houston National Forest;** October Texas prison rodeo; county fair.

MINERALS: Clays, gas, oil, sand and gravel, stone.

1982 Pop. 46,300	Voters reg. 18,921
Area (sq. mi.) 786	Whlsle. sales . $52,840,000
Altitude (ft.) 150-450	Oil value $141,531
Ann. rainfall (in.) . 44.99	No. employed . . . 15,887
Jan. temp. min. 41	Wages paid . $240,611,896
July temp. max. 94	Tax value . . $871,088,842
Growing season (da.) 265	Income . . . $388,486,000
No. farms, 1982 624	Taxable sales $145,949,077
No. acres in farms 259,682	Fed. expend. . $52,092,000
†Value per farm $441,173	Crime Index 1,630
Cropland harvested 14,653	TDC Pop. 88

AGRICULTURE: About $18.5 million average yearly income, 60% from cattle, hogs; crops include hay, vegetables, some cotton, grains; estimated $20 million from timber sales.

BUSINESS: Economy based on education, state employment, agribusiness, lumbering, tourism.

MANUFACTURING: 36 Plants; 2,100 Employees; Payroll, $47,000,000; Product Value, $268,400,000.

SERVICE INDUSTRIES: 163 Establishments; Receipts, $37,873,000; Annual Payroll, $12,649,000; No. Employees, 1,099.

HUNTSVILLE (23,936) county seat; Texas Department of Corrections headquarters; **Sam Houston State University** and adjoining museum; plants make wood products, valves, tools; oil, gas, lignite exploration; hospital.

Other towns include **New Waverly** (824) and **Riverside** (425).

Waller

LOCATION: Southeast (M-18).

Cong. Dist. 14	
St. Sen. Dist. 5	
St. Rep. Dist. 13	
St. Dist. Cts. 9, 155	
U.S. Jud. Dist. . . . . S-Hn.	
Ct. Appeals 1, 14	
Admin. Jud. Dist. 2	

HISTORY: Named for **Edwin Waller,** Republic of Texas leader; county created, organized, 1873, from Austin, Grimes.

PHYSICAL FEATURES: Rolling prairie; drains to Brazos and San Jacinto Rivers; alluvial soils; almost one-fifth forested.

RECREATION: Fishing, hunting; historic sites; historical museum; county fair.

MINERALS: Oil, gas, sand and gravel.

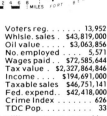

1982 Pop. 21,700	Voters reg. 13,952
Area (sq. mi.) 514	Whlsle. sales . $43,819,000
Altitude (ft.) 100-300	Oil value $3,063,856
Ann. rainfall (in.) . 41.67	No. employed 5,571
Jan. temp. min. 39	Wages paid . . $72,585,644
July temp. max. 95	Tax value . $2,327,864,846
Growing season (da.) 283	Income . . . $194,691,000
No. farms, 1982 809	Taxable sales $46,751,141
No. acres in farms 238,315	Fed. expend. . $42,418,000
†Value per farm $498,786	Crime Index 626
Cropland harvested 63,574	TDC Pop. 33

AGRICULTURE: About $35 million average annual income from beef cattle, hogs, goats, sheep; rice, corn, peanuts, soybeans, vegetables; 14,000 acres irrigated for rice; timber marketed.

BUSINESS: Economy based on oil, agribusiness,

Houston area growth; manufacturing; county part of Houston PMSA, see metro page.

MANUFACTURING: 28 Plants; 1,000 Employees; Payroll, $23,600,000; Product Value, $95,300,000.

SERVICE INDUSTRIES: 63 Establishments; Receipts, $9,004,000; Annual Payroll, $3,249,000; No. Employees, 343.

HEMPSTEAD (3,456) county seat; agribusiness center; varied manufacturing; hospital, clinic, nursing home.

Prairie View (3,993) site of **Prairie View A&M University.** Other towns include **Katy** (5,660, partly in Fort Bend, Harris Counties); **Waller** (1,241, part in Harris County); **Brookshire** (2,175); **Pattison** (318).

Ward

LOCATION: Far west (J-6).

HISTORY: Named for Republic of Texas leader, **Thomas W. Ward;** county created from Tom Green, 1887; organized, 1892.

Cong. Dist.	16	U.S. Jud. Dist.	W-Pe.
St. Sen. Dist.	25	Ct. Appeals	8
St. Rep. Dist.	69	Admin. Jud. Dist.	7
St. Dist. Cts.	143		

PHYSICAL FEATURES: Plain, sloping to Pecos River; sandy, loam soils.

RECREATION: Sandhills State Park, Museum; Pyote Rattlesnake Museum; county park; local events.

MINERALS: Production of oil, gas, sand and gravel.

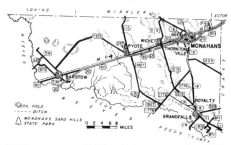

1982 Pop.	16,000	Voters reg.	6,766
Area (sq. mi.)	836	Whlsle. sales	$176,155,000
Altitude (ft.)	2,300-2,800	Oil value	$151,992,847
Ann. rainfall (in.)	12.04	No. employed	5,104
Jan. temp. min.	30	Wages paid	$101,186,940
July temp. max.	96	Tax value	$1,575,912,291
Growing season (da.)	223	Income	$133,243,000
No. farms, 1982	80	Taxable sales	$66,549,025
No. acres in farms	445,406	Fed. expend.	$17,584,000
†Value per farm	$538,275	Crime Index	566
Cropland harvested	332	TDC Pop.	31

AGRICULTURE: About $2.7 million average annual income, more than 95% from beef cattle; alfalfa, hay; 300 acres of alfalfa irrigated.

BUSINESS: Oil, gas, other minerals dominate economy.

MANUFACTURING: None noted in census report.

SERVICE INDUSTRIES: 73 Establishments; Receipts, $21,162,000; Annual Payroll, $6,094,000; No. Employees, 405.

MONAHANS (8,397) county seat; center for oil, agribusiness activities; oil field equipment; gasoline plant; pecan shelling; county hospital, **West Texas Children's Home,** nursing home.

Other towns include **Barstow** (637), **Grandfalls** (635), **Pyote** (382) **Odessa Junior College** extension; **Thornton-ville** (717) and **Wickett** (689).

Washington

LOCATION: Southeast (M-18).

HISTORY: Named for **George Washington;** an original county created in 1836; organized, 1837.

Cong. Dist.	10	U.S. Jud. Dist.	W-An.
St. Sen. Dist.	5	Ct. Appeals	1, 14
St. Rep. Dist.	13	Admin. Jud. Dist.	2
St. Dist. Cts.	21,335		

PHYSICAL FEATURES: Rolling prairie of sandy loam, alluvial soils; Brazos and tributaries.

RECREATION: Many historic sites; **Washington-on-the-Brazos State Park; Texas Baptist Historical Museum; Star of Republic Museum; Lake Somerville;** fishing, hunting; old homes; bluebonnet trails in spring; Maifest.

MINERALS: Oil, gas and stone.

1982 Pop.	23,600	Voters reg.	13,095
Area (sq. mi.)	610	Whlsle. sales	$156,400,000
Altitude (ft.)	150-500	Oil value	$15,658,393
Ann. rainfall (in.)	39.94	No. employed	9,465
Jan. temp. min.	43	Wages paid	$143,787,588
July temp. max.	95	Tax value	$1,250,390,000
Growing season (da.)	277	Income	$229,463,000
No. farms, 1982	1,839	Taxable sales	$113,038,500
No. acres in farms	305,119	Fed. expend.	$42,263,000
†Value per farm	$359,778	Crime Index	517
Cropland harvested	39,024	TDC Pop.	41

AGRICULTURE: Over $35 million average annual income, 90% from cattle, hogs, horses, dairy products, poultry; crops chiefly sorghums, corn, oats, hay, nursery stock, vegetables, pecans.

BUSINESS: Agribusinesses, oil, tourism, manufacturing.

MANUFACTURING: 32 Plants; 1,600 Employees; Payroll, $23,500,000; Product Value, $175,600,000.

SERVICE INDUSTRIES: 124 Establishments; Receipts, $28,598,000; Annual Payroll, $10,725,000; No. Employees, 883.

BRENHAM (10,966) county seat; plants process cotton, make furniture, other products; **Blinn College;** hospitals; **Brenham State School. Burton** (325) another principal town.

Webb

LOCATION: Southwest (R-13).

HISTORY: Named for Republic of Texas leader, **James Webb;** created, organized, 1848, from Nueces and Bexar.

Cong. Dist.	23	U.S. Jud. Dist.	S-La.
St. Sen. Dist.	21	Ct. Appeals	4
St. Rep. Dist.	43	Admin. Jud. Dist.	4
St. Dist. Cts.	49, 111,341		

PHYSICAL FEATURES: Rolling, some hills; much brush; sandy, gray soils; alluvial along Rio Grande.

1982 Pop.	109,900	Voters reg.	41,050
Area (sq. mi.)	3,363	Whlsle. sales	$399,066,000
Altitude (ft.)	400-700	Oil value	$23,468,558
Ann. rainfall (in.)	17.87	No. employed	29,888
Jan. temp. min.	47	Wages paid	$371,820,792
July temp. max.	99	Tax value	$4,158,649,606
Growing season (da.)	322	Income	$586,873,000
No. farms, 1982	422	Taxable sales	$452,409,955
No. acs. in farms	1,644,342	Fed. expend.	$144,053,000
†Value per farm	$1,784,287	Crime Index	7,556
Cropland harvested	6,198	TDC Pop.	79

Lines like this form in populous cities for everything from tickets to concerts, to waiting to vote, to waiting for food at concession stands.

RECREATION: Major tourist gateway to Mexico; hunting, fishing; water recreation, golf; **Border Olympics** in March; Rio Grande art festival in April; Washington Birthday celebration; historic sites; museum.

MINERALS: Production of gas, oil, sand and gravel, stone.

AGRICULTURE: Among leading beef cattle counties; more than $37.5 million average annual income, mostly from calf production, horses, goats; crops include vegetables, sorghums, small grains, cotton.

BUSINESS: International trade, tourism, oil and gas operations, government center; manufacturing, agribusinesses; a major gateway for trade and tourism with Mexico; see Laredo metro page.

MANUFACTURING: 56 Plants; 1,500 Employees; Payroll, $16,800,000; Product Value, $74,800,000.

SERVICE INDUSTRIES: 424 Establishments; Receipts; $107,953,000; Annual Payroll, $30,340,000; No. Employees, 2,804.

LAREDO (91,449) county seat; town founded in 1755; plants make brick, clothing, shoes, electronics, other products; meat packing; major rail and highway gateway to Mexico; **Laredo Junior College; Laredo State University;** mental health-retardation center, hospitals, nursing homes; many tourist accommodations.

Wharton

LOCATION: Southeast (O-18).

HISTORY: Named for **John A., William H. Wharton,** brothers active in Texas Revolution; county created, organized, 1846, from Jackson, Matagorda.

MINERALS: Production of oil, gas, sulphur.

1982 Pop.	40,900	Voters reg.	21,059
Area (sq. mi.)	1,086	Whlsle. sales	$218,169,000
Altitude (ft.)	50-200	Oil value	$42,827,522
Ann. rainfall (in.)	41.46	No. employed	10,913
Jan. temp. min.	44	Wages paid	$164,150,380
July temp. max.	93	Tax value	$2,416,884,602
Growing season (da.)	266	Income	$355,872,000
No. farms, 1982	1,258	Taxable sales	$196,196,171
No. acres in farms	643,339	Fed. expend.	$95,987,000
†Value per farm	$587,073	Crime Index	1,387
Cropland harv.	327,010	TDC Pop.	83

Ancient bones, stone spear tips and other reminders of the past are part of Bissell Collection of artifacts donated to Museum of the Southwest in Midland.

PHYSICAL FEATURES: Prairie; bisected by Colorado River; alluvial, black, sandy loam soils.

Cong. Dist. 14	U.S. Jud. Dist. . . . . S-Hn.
St. Sen. Dist. 5	Ct. Appeals 13
St. Rep. Dist. 29	Admin. Jud. Dist. 2
St. Dist. Cts. 23, 329	

RECREATION: Hunting, fishing; big game trophy, art and historical museums; historic sites; festivals.

AGRICULTURE: About $114 million average annual income, 80% from crops; leading rice-producing county; other crops are sorghums, cotton, peaches, soybeans; beef cattle, hogs, poultry; about 87,000 acres irrigated.

BUSINESS: Economy based on oil, sulphur, other minerals; agribusinesses, varied manufacturing.

MANUFACTURING: 51 Plants; 1,000 Employees; Payroll, $15,000,000; Product Value, $76,700,000.

SERVICE INDUSTRIES: 197 Establishments; Receipts, $39,929,000; Annual Payroll, $15,341,000; No. Employees, 1,296.

WHARTON (9,033) county seat; plants process minerals, rice, hides, pipe, farm equipment, beverage packing; **Wharton County Junior College**; hospitals, clinics, nursing homes.

El Campo (10,462) plants process aluminum, make plastic and metal products, clothing; rice drying, storage; hospital, nursing homes; **East Bernard** has agribusinesses, varied manufacturing.

Wheeler

LOCATION: Eastern Panhandle (C-11).

HISTORY: Named for pioneer jurist, **R. T. Wheeler**; county created from Bexar, Young Districts, 1876; organized 1879.

Cong. Dist. 13	U.S. Jud. Dist. . . . . N-Am.
St. Sen. Dist. 31	Ct. Appeals 7
St. Rep. Dist. 88	Admin. Jud. Dist. 9
St. Dist. Cts. 31	

PHYSICAL FEATURES: Plain, on edge of Cap Rock; Red River, Sweetwater Creek; some canyons; red sandy loam, black clay soils.

RECREATION: Shamrock St. Patrick's Day event, Pioneer West museum at Shamrock; historic sites, **Old Mobeetie, Fort Elliott.**

1982 Pop. 7,800		Voters reg. 4,589
Area (sq. mi.) 905		Whlsle. sales . $23,969,000
Altitude (ft.) . 2,000-2,800		Oil value $16,932,896
Ann. rainfall (in.) . 23.70		No. employed 1,860
Jan. temp. min. 26		Wages paid . . $28,070,280
July temp. max. 97		Tax value . $1,185,351,436
Growing season (da.) 208		Income $76,909,000
No. farms, 1982 507		Taxable sales $17,993,095
No. acres in farms 492,597		Fed. expend. . $18,407,000
†Value per farm $294,603		Crime Index 101
Cropland harvested 91,421		TDC Pop. 10

MINERALS: Production of oil, gas.

AGRICULTURE: About $34 million average annual income, 90% from beef and stocker cattle, hogs; crops

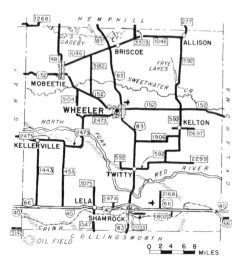

include wheat, sorghums, cotton, alfalfa; 13,000 acres irrigated, mostly wheat, grain sorghum.

BUSINESS: Oil-agribusiness economy.

MANUFACTURING: None noted in census report.

SERVICE INDUSTRIES: 36 Establishments; Receipts, $5,458,000; Annual Payroll, $1,670,000; No. Employees, 185.

WHEELER (1,584) county seat; large feedlots; agribusiness petroleum center; hospital, nursing home.

Shamrock (2,834) agribusiness, oil, gas processing plants; chemical plant; tourist center; hospital, nursing home. **Mobeetie** (291) other principal town.

Wichita

LOCATION: North (E-14).

HISTORY: Named for Indian tribe; county created from Young Territory, 1858; organized, 1882.

Cong. Dist. 13	U.S. Jud. Dist. . . . . N-WF
St. Sen. Dist. 30	Ct. Appeals 2
St. Rep. Dist. 80, 81	Admin. Jud. Dist. 8
St. Dist. Cts. . . . 30, 78, 89	

PHYSICAL FEATURES: Prairie; Red, Wichita Rivers; **N.Fork Buffalo Creek, Wichita Lakes;** sandy, loam soils.

RECREATION: Metropolitan events (ask chamber of commerce); museums; historic Kell House, historic tour; Oil Bowl football game in August; collegiate activities; water sports on several lakes; **Lake Arrowhead State Park.**

AGRICULTURE: Some $23 million average yearly income from beef cattle, hogs, horses, dairy products; cotton, sorghum, wheat, other grains, hay; 22,000 acres irrigated for cotton and coastal bermuda pastures.

BUSINESS: Economy based on retail trade for large area, government, manufacturing, oil and agribusinesses; vocational training center. See Wichita Falls metro page.

MINERALS: Production of oil, gas, sand, gravel, stone.

1982 Pop.	125,500	Voters reg.	62,432
Area (sq. mi.)	606	Whlse. sales	$576,384,000
Altitude (ft.) . . .	900-1,200	Oil value . . .	$135,261,404
Ann. rainfall (in.) .	27.22	No. employed	47,532
Jan. temp. min.	31	Wages paid .	$784,641,788
July temp. max.	97	Tax value .	$3,298,362,618
Growing season (da.)	229	Income . . .	$1,166,930,000
No. farms, 1982	583	Taxable sales	$643,161,361
No. acres in farms	316,877	Fed. expend.	$507,987,000
†Value per farm	$296,600	Crime Index	7,929
Cropland harvested	91,498	TDC Pop.	217

MANUFACTURING: 173 Plants; Employees, N.A.; Payroll, N.A.; Product Value, N.A.

SERVICE INDUSTRIES: 722 Establishments; Receipts, $231,277,000; Annual Payroll, $75,786,000; No. Employees, 6,580.

WICHITA FALLS (94,201, partly in Archer and Clay Counties) county seat; centennial in 1982; distribution center for large area of Texas, Oklahoma; plants make fiberglass products, clothing, electric components, mechanical parts, aircraft turbine components, hand tools, other products; oil field services; **Midwestern State University; Vernon Regional Junior College** nearby; vocational technical training center; **Sheppard Air Force Base; Wichita Falls State Hospital,** other hospitals.

Burkburnett (10,668) plants make chemical products, plastics, rodeo equipment, machinery, other products; nursing home.

Iowa Park (6,184) plants make fertilizers, oil field equipment; clinic, nursing home.

Electra (3,755) agribusiness, oil center; varied manufacturing; hospital, clinic, nursing home.

Pleasant Valley (335) another town, **Lakeside City** (515).

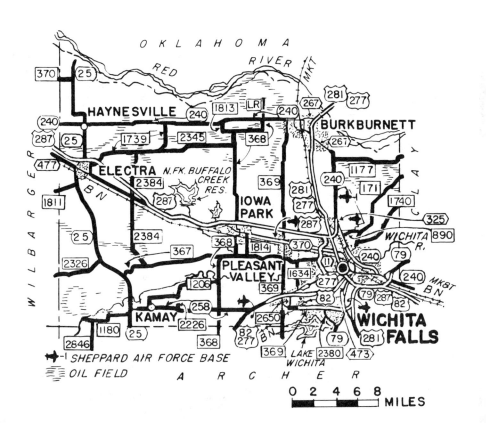

Wilbarger

LOCATION: North (E-13).

HISTORY: Named for pioneers **Josiah, Mathias Wilbarger;** created from Bexar District, 1858; organized 1881.

PHYSICAL FEATURES: Rolling; Red, Pease Rivers, tributaries; sandy, loam, waxy soils; **Santa Rosa Lake.**

Cong. Dist.	13	U.S. Jud. Dist.	N-WF
St. Sen. Dist.	30	Ct. Appeals	7
St. Rep. Dist.	80	Admin. Jud. Dist.	9
St. Dist. Cts.	46		

RECREATION: Santa Rosa Roundup, rodeo, parade in late spring, Green Belt Fair in fall; **Doan's Crossing,** site of cattle drive; other historic sites; Red River Valley Museum; Moore bird egg collection; hunting, fishing.

MINERALS: Production of oil, gas.

1982 Pop.	16,300	Voters reg.	8,116
Area (sq. mi.)	947	Whlsle. sales	$53,420,000
Altitude (ft.)	1,050-1,400	Oil value	$52,487,311
Ann. rainfall (in.)	25.65	No. employed	5,988
Jan. temp. min.	29	Wages paid	$86,059,204
July temp. max.	98	Tax value	$558,784,892
Growing season (da.)	221	Income	$136,293,000
No. farms, 1982	557	Taxable sales	$57,970,935
No. acres in farms	881,429	Fed. expend.	$54,020,000
†Value per farm	$482,822	Crime Index	645
Cropland harv.	195,510	TDC Pop.	21

AGRICULTURE: About $38 million average farm income from cotton, wheat, hay, guar, sorghums, other grains; cattle, hogs, horses; 25,000 acres irrigated for alfalfa.

BUSINESS: Agribusinesses and oil.

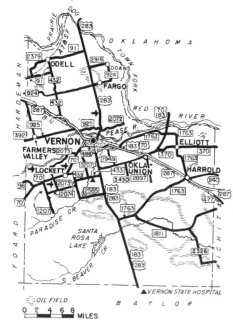

MANUFACTURING: 14 Plants; Employees, N.A.; Payroll, N.A.; Product Value, N.A.

SERVICE INDUSTRIES: 88 Establishments; Receipts, $13,376,000; Annual Payroll, $4,119,000; No. Employees, 399.

VERNON (12,695) county seat; agribusiness and oil center; plants make boots, clothes, guar products, meat processing; new electricity generating plant; Vernon **Regional Junior College;** mental health center, hospital. **Lockett** is site of **Texas A&M Research and Extension Center.**

Willacy

LOCATION: South (T-16).

HISTORY: Named for Texas legislator, John G. Willacy; county created, organized, 1911 from Cameron, Hidalgo; reorganized 1921.

Cong. Dist.	27	U.S. Jud. Dist.	S-Br.
St. Sen. Dist.	20	Ct. Appeals	13
St. Rep. Dist.	37	Admin. Jud. Dist.	5
St. Dist. Cts.	103, 107, 138, 197, 357		

PHYSICAL FEATURES: Flat, sloping to Laguna Madre; alluvial, sandy, marshy soils; **Padre Island; La Sal Vieja, salt lake; Laguna Atascosa Wildlife Refuge.**

RECREATION: Fresh and salt water fishing, hunting; local events; mild climate attracts many winter tourists; Port Mansfield fishing tournament in July; winter fun festival.

MINERALS: Production of oil, gas.

1982 Pop.	18,200	Voters reg.	9,155
Area (sq. mi.)	589	Whlsle. sales	$26,212,000
Altitude (ft.)	sea level-50	Oil value	$36,146,442
Ann. rainfall (in.)	25.80	No. employed	3,289
Jan. temp. min.	50	Wages paid	$35,390,876
July temp. max.	96	Tax value	$627,877,130
Growing season (da.)	331	Income	$87,911,000
No. farms, 1982	322	Taxable sales	$22,087,796
No. acres in farms	234,422	Fed. expend.	$52,103,000
†Value per farm	$754,882	Crime Index	441
Cropland harv.	177,619	TDC Pop.	36

AGRICULTURE: About $44 million average yearly income, 90% from crops, chiefly cotton, sorghums, sugarcane, corn, vegetables, citrus; cattle, hog production; 38,000 acres irrigated.

BUSINESS: Primarily oil, agribusinesses; tourism; shipping from **Port Mansfield.**

MANUFACTURING: None noted in census report.

SERVICE INDUSTRIES: 48 Establishments; Receipts, $4,604,000; Annual Payroll, $1,208,000; No. Employees, 195.

RAYMONDVILLE (9,493) county seat; agribusiness and oil center; clothing, fiberglass products manufactured; vegetables, seafood processed, shipped; tourist center; hospital. **Lyford** (1,618), **San Perlita** (475) other principal towns. **Port Mansfield** is popular Gulf Coast fishing port; shrimp processing.

Williamson

LOCATION: Central (L-16).

HISTORY: Named for **Robert M. Williamson,** pioneer leader; county created from Milam, County 1848.

Cong. Dist.	11, 14	U.S. Jud. Dist.	W-An.
St. Sen. Dist.	5, 18	Ct. Appeals	3
St. Rep. Dist.	52	Admin. Jud. Dist.	3
St. Dist. Cts.	26, 277		

1982 Pop.	85,700	Voters reg.	50,614
Area (sq. mi.)	1,137	Whlsle. sales	$144,262,000
Altitude (ft.)	425-1,200	Oil value	$239,201
Ann. rainfall (in.)	33.98	No. employed	20,197
Jan. temp. min.	39	Wages paid	$282,181,232
July temp. max.	96	Tax value	$3,070,711,953
Growing season (da.)	258	Income	$922,318,000
No. farms, 1982	1,558	Taxable sales	$368,465,474
No. acres in farms	515,596	Fed. expend.	$157,627,000
†Value per farm	$300,480	Crime Index	2,882
Cropland harv.	200,920	TDC Pop.	153

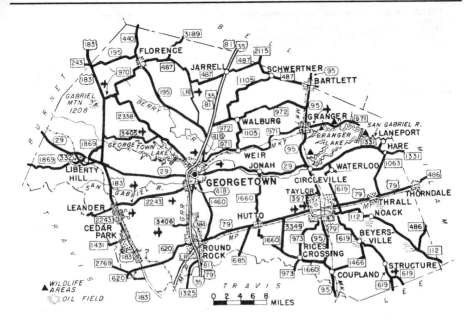

PHYSICAL FEATURES: Level to rolling; mostly Black-land soil, some loam, sand; drained by San Gabriel, tributaries.

RECREATION: San Gabriel Park; water recreation on lakes; Inner Space Cavern; historic sites; hunting; Dan Moody Museum at Taylor; rattlesnake sacking; barbecue cookoff.

MINERALS: Building stone, sand and gravel, oil.

AGRICULTURE: More than $60 million average yearly income, divided among sorghums, wheat, corn, cotton; cattle, hogs, poultry, sheep, goats; income from deer leases, cedar posts.

BUSINESS: Agribusinesses, varied manufacturing, education are main economic factors.

MANUFACTURING: 117 Plants; 4,200 Employees; Payroll, $67,500,000; Product Value, $397,900,000.

SERVICE INDUSTRIES: 331 Establishments; Receipts, $51,207,000; Annual Payroll, $17,227,000; No. Employees, 1,714.

GEORGETOWN (9,468) county seat; agribusiness center; Southwestern University; Inner Space Cavern; plants make electric motors, structural products, electronic products, many other products; hospital, nursing homes. See Austin metro page.

Taylor (10,619) rapidly growing industrial, agribusiness and publishing center; Granger Lake; plants make furniture, clothing, bedding, machine shop products, fertilizers, many other products; process cottonseed, meats; barbecue catering; central newspaper printing plant; hospital, nursing homes; Temple Junior College extension.

Round Rock (12,740) plants make electronic equipment, generators, electric motors, lime, tools; Texas Baptist Children's Home; hospital, nursing homes. Other towns include Bartlett (1,567, part Bell County) first rural electrification in nation in 1933; clinic, rest home, library; Granger (1,236), Cedar Park (3,474), Florence (744), Hutto (659), Thrall (573) and Leander (2,179).

Wilson

LOCATION: South (O-15).

HISTORY: Created from Bexar, Karnes Counties and organized, 1860; named for James C. Wilson, member of Mier Expedition.

Cong. Dist. 15	U.S. Jud. Dist. . . W-SAnt.
St. Sen. Dist. 21	Ct. Appeals 4
St. Rep. Dist. 45	Admin. Jud. Dist. 4
St. Dist. Cts. 81, 218	

PHYSICAL FEATURES: Rolling plains; mostly sandy soils, some heavier; San Antonio River, Cibolo Creek.

1982 Pop. 17,300		Voters reg. 11,655
Area (sq. mi.) 807		Whlsle. sales . $22,168,000
Altitude (ft.) 300-600		Oil value. . . . $41,942,579
Ann. rainfall (in.) . 28.68		No. employed 2,340
Jan. temp. min. 42		Wages paid . . $27,402,144
July temp. max. 96		Tax value . . $752,913,170
Growing season (da.) 280		Income $128,641,000
No. farms, 1982 . . . 1,672		Taxable sales $35,746,338
No. acres in farms 442,931		Fed. expend. . $28,223,000
†Value per farm $258,833		Crime Index 315
Cropland harvested 90,093		TDC Pop. 25

RECREATION: Stockdale watermelon festival in June; Floresville peanut festival in October; Wilson County Junior Livestock Show in January; arts, craft show in May.

MINERALS: Production of oil, gas, clays.

AGRICULTURE: About $48 million average annual income, 60% from beef, dairy cattle, hogs, poultry; crops include peanuts, sorghums, corn, small grains, vegetables, melons, fruit; 10,000 acres irrigated.

BUSINESS: Chiefly agribusinesses; some employed in San Antonio.

MANUFACTURING: None noted in census report.

SERVICE INDUSTRIES: 42 Establishments; Receipts, $4,763,000; Annual Payroll, $1,812,000; No. Employees, 233.

FLORESVILLE (4,381) county seat; agribusiness center; hospital, nursing home; shopping mall.

Stockdale (1,265) peanut drying plant, meat processing; medical center, nursing home, city park, pool. Other towns include **Poth** (1,461) and **La Vernia** (632).

Winkler

LOCATION: West (J-7).

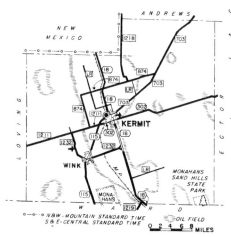

° ° — ° N & W - MOUNTAIN STANDARD TIME
S & E - CENTRAL STANDARD TIME   OIL FIELD

HISTORY: Named for **Confederate Col. C. M. Winkler;** county created from Tom Green, 1887; organized, 1910.

Cong. Dist. 16	U.S. Jud. Dist. . . . . W-Pe.
St. Sen. Dist. 25	Ct. Appeals 8
St. Rep. Dist. 69	Admin. Jud. Dist. 7
St. Dist. Cts. 109	

PHYSICAL FEATURES: Plains, partly sandy hills.

RECREATION: Monahans Sandhills State Park in nearby Ward County; museum; zoo; wooden oil derrick; local events.

MINERALS: A leading petroleum producing county; gas, salt also produced.

1982 Pop. 11,400	Voters reg. 4,714
Area (sq. mi.) 840	Whlsle. sales . $28,440,000
Altitude (ft.) . 2,700-3,500	Oil value . . . $167,607,444
Ann. rainfall (in.) . 10.81	No. employed 2,595
Jan. temp. min. 29	Wages paid . . $47,106,044
July temp. max. 96	Tax value . $1,198,102,110
Growing season (da.) 219	Income $92,840,000
No. farms, 1982 . . . 32	Taxable sales $32,446,406
No. acres in farms 480,010	Fed. expend. . $11,795,000
†Value per farm $2,935,781	Crime Index 262
Cropland harvested. N.A.	TDC Pop. 15

AGRICULTURE: About $1.9 million average yearly income, nearly all from beef cattle; 1,000 acres irrigated pasture.

BUSINESS: Oil economy, among leading petroleum producing counties.

MANUFACTURING: None noted in census report.

SERVICE INDUSTRIES: 54 Establishments; Receipts, $10,511,000; Annual Payroll, $3,112,000; No. Employees, 261.

KERMIT (8,015) county seat, and **Wink** (1,182) are oil activity centers; hospital, nursing homes.

Wise

LOCATION: North (G-15).

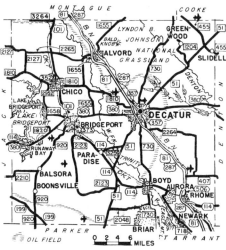

HISTORY: Created, organized, 1856, from Cooke County; named for Virginian, **U.S. Sen. Henry A. Wise,** who favored Texas annexation.

Cong. Dist. 17	U.S. Jud. Dist. . . . . N-FW
St. Sen. Dist. 22	Ct. Appeals 2
St. Rep. Dist. 63	Admin. Jud. Dist. 8
St. Dist. Cts. 271	

PHYSICAL FEATURES: Rolling, hilly; clay, loam, sandy soils; **Lake Bridgeport; Eagle Mountain Lake.**

RECREATION: Lake Bridgeport activities; hunting; exotic deer preserve; historical sites; **Lyndon B. Johnson National Grasslands;** museum, little theater; Chisholm Trail Days in June; Sheriff's Posse rodeo; old courthouse; old settlers reunion; Butterfield Stage days, rodeo in July.

MINERALS: Production of gas, oil, stone, clays, sand, gravel.

1982 Pop. 28,500	Voters reg. 15,878
Area (sq. mi.) 902	Whlsle. sales $198,364,000
Altitude (ft.) . . . 650-1,300	Oil value . . . $51,145,763
Ann. rainfall (in.) . 29.74	No. employed 5,942
Jan. temp. min. 33	Wages paid . . $98,662,728
July temp. max. 96	Tax value . $1,771,978,592
Growing season (da.) 220	Income $285,650,000
No. farms, 1982 . . . 1,561	Taxable sales $88,058,308
No. acres in farms 406,292	Fed. expend. . $42,356,000
†Value per farm $208,113	Crime Index 604
Cropland harvested 51,664	TDC Pop. 35

AGRICULTURE: More than $52.5 million average annual income, 85% from dairy, beef cattle, horses, sheep, poultry; a leading dairy county; crops include sorghums, small grains, peanuts, vegetables, cantaloupes, watermelons, pecans.

BUSINESS: Agribusinesses, petroleum, recreation leading economic factors. Many work in Fort Worth.

MANUFACTURING: 32 Plants; 6,000 Employees; Payroll, $10,100,000; Product Value, $112,000,000.

SERVICE INDUSTRIES: 72 Establishments; Receipts, $13,659,000; Annual Payroll, $5,066,000; No. Employees, 456.

DECATUR (4,104) county seat; center for petroleum production, dairying, cattle marketing; plants make clothing, glass, graphite, other products; hospital, nursing homes.

Bridgeport (3,737) trade center for lake resort; gas,

oil production; agribusinesses; plants make brick, crushed limestone, metal fabrication, other products; hospital, rest home.

Other towns include **Alvord** (874), **Aurora** (376), **Boyd** (889), **Briar** (1,810, partly Parker and Tarrant Counties), **Chico** (890), **Fairview** (180), **Lake Bridgeport** (271), **Newark** (466), **Rhome** (478), **Runaway Bay** (504).

Wood

LOCATION: Northeast (G-19).

HISTORY: Created from Van Zandt County and organized, 1850; named for **Gov. George T. Wood.**

Cong. Dist.	4	U.S. Jud. Dist.	E-Ty.
St. Sen. Dist.	2	Ct. Appeals	6, 12
St. Rep. Dist.	3	Admin. Jud. Dist.	1
St. Dist. Cts.	114, 294		

PHYSICAL FEATURES: Hilly, almost half forested; sandy to alluvial soils; drained by Sabine and tributaries; 4 county lakes; many private lakes.

RECREATION: Activities at **Lake Fork Reservoir;** hunting; **Gov. Hogg Shrine State Park and museum;** historic sites; scenic drives; annual Autumn Trails, dogwood fiesta, wildflower trail, other local events.

MINERALS: A leading petroleum producing county; gas, sand, gravel, clays also produced.

1982 Pop.	25,600	Voters reg.	15,025
Area (sq. mi.)	689	Whlsle. sales	$175,532,000
Altitude (ft.)	250-600	Oil value	$150,037,946
Ann. rainfall (in.)	44.30	No. employed	6,148
Jan. temp. min.	36	Wages paid	$83,707,912
July temp. max.	94	Tax value	$1,749,743,509
Growing season (da.)	246	Income	$248,001,000
No. farms, 1982	1,277	Taxable sales	$86,473,692
†Value per farm	$179,499	Fed. expend.	$67,416,000
Cropland harvested	31,233	Crime Index	512
		TDC Pop.	58

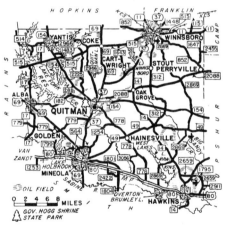

0 2 4 6 8 MILES
△ GOV. HOGG SHRINE STATE PARK

AGRICULTURE: About $40 million average yearly income, more than 80% from dairy, beef cattle, hogs; watermelons, sweet potatoes, other vegetables, hay, corn, small grains; some Christmas trees, timber sold.

BUSINESS: Minerals, agribusinesses, tourism.

MANUFACTURING: 30 Plants; 800 Employees; Payroll, $8,000,000; Product Value, $74,200,000.

SERVICE INDUSTRIES: 94 Establishments; Receipts, $15,153,000; Annual Payroll, $5,508,000; No. Employees, 780.

QUITMAN (1,893) county seat; agribusiness center; plants make boats, fence posts, fishing lines; hospital, nursing homes; dogwood fiesta in spring.

Mineola (4,346) farm trade, tourism center; railroad center; plants make clothing, camping, boating equipment; livestock feeds, other farm products; manufacturing includes precision machinery, electronics, metal finishing; hospital, nursing home.

Other towns include **Winnsboro** (3,458, part Franklin), **Hawkins** (1,302), **Alba** (568), **Yantis** (210).

Yoakum

LOCATION: Borders New Mexico (G-7).

HISTORY: Named for **Henderson Yoakum,** pioneer historian; created from Bexar District, 1876; organized, 1907.

PHYSICAL FEATURES: Level to rolling; playas, draws; sandy, loam, chocolate soils.

RECREATION: Local events; Tsa Mo Ga Museum at Plains.

MINERALS: Production of oil, gas, salt makes this a leading minerals producing county.

Cong. Dist.	19	U.S. Jud. Dist.	N-Lb.
St. Sen. Dist.	28	Ct. Civil Appeals	7
St. Rep. Dist.	77	Admin. Jud. Dist.	9
St. Dist. Cts.	121		
1982 Pop.	8,500	Voters reg.	3,819
Area (sq. mi.)	800	Whlsle. sales	$37,137,000
Altitude (ft.)	3,400-3,900	Oil value	$1,330,731,117
Ann. rainfall (in.)	14.99	No. employed	3,336
Jan. temp. min.	24	Wages paid	$66,898,912
July temp. max.	92	Tax value	$3,363,106,870
Growing season (da.)	199	Income	$84,004,000
No. farms, 1982	296	Taxable sales	$31,378,190
No. acres in farms	345,280	Fed. expend.	$42,821,000
†Value per farm	$450,334	Crime Index	283
Cropland harv.	175,900	TDC Pop.	13

AGRICULTURE: About $38 million average yearly income, 90% from grains, cotton, sorghums, alfalfa, corn; beef cattle, hogs, horses, sheep; 131,000 acres irrigated.

BUSINESS: Oil, agriculture dominate economy.

MANUFACTURING: None noted in census report.

SERVICE INDUSTRIES: 49 Establishments; Receipts, $12,410,000; Annual Payroll, $3,074,000; No. Employees, 241.

PLAINS (1,457) county seat; oil and agribusiness center.

Denver City (4,704) center for oil, farming activities in two counties; hospital, library.

Young

LOCATION: North (G-14).

HISTORY: Named for early Texan, **Col. W. C. Young;** county created, organized from Bosque, Fannin, 1856; reorganized, 1874.

Cong. Dist.	17	U.S. Jud. Dist.	N-WF
St. Sen. Dist.	30	Ct. Appeals	2
St. Rep. Dist.	64	Admin. Jud. Dist.	8
St. Dist. Cts.	90		

MINERALS: Production of oil, gas, sand and gravel.

1982 Pop.	19,700	Voters reg.	10,576
Area (sq. mi.)	919	Whlsle. sales	$104,032,000
Altitude (ft.)	1,000-1,300	Oil value	$124,185,857
Ann. rainfall (in.)	28.03	No. employed	7,427
Jan. temp. min.	31	Wages paid	$122,205,816
July temp. max.	98	Tax value	$807,262,220
Growing season (da.)	216	Income	$217,868,000
No. farms, 1982	710	Taxable sales	$110,456,703
No. acres in farms	550,517	Fed. expend.	$45,754,000
†Value per farm	$255,924	Crime Index	286
Cropland harvested	68,055	TDC Pop.	38

Young County (Cont'd.)

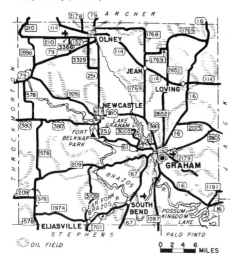

OIL FIELD — 0 2 4 6 MILES

PHYSICAL FEATURES: Hilly, broken; drained by Brazos and tributaries; **Possum Kingdom, Lake Graham.**

RECREATION: Fishing, boating and water sports at **Possum Kingdom** and **Lake Graham; Fort Belknap State Park;** site of former large **Indian reservation;** marker at oak tree in Graham where ranchmen formed forerunner of **Texas and Southwestern Cattle Raisers' Association;** one-arm dove hunt at Olney.

AGRICULTURE: About 60% of $20 million average farm income from beef cattle, hogs, sheep, goats; wheat chief crop; oats, cotton, hay; hunting leases.

BUSINESS: Oil, agribusinesses, tourism.

MANUFACTURING: 27 Plants; 1,400 Employees; Payroll, $24,300,000; Product Value, $130,600,000.

SERVICE INDUSTRIES: 115 Establishments; Receipts, $23,270,000; Annual Payroll, $7,647,000; No. Employees, 730.

GRAHAM (9,170) county seat; plants make computer products, apparel, fences, fiberglass products, aluminum, floral products; hospital, nursing homes, mental health clinic, **Ranger Junior College** extension.

Olney (4,060) agribusiness center; plants make apparel, recreational vehicles, aluminum products, rubber hose, agricultural airplanes, other products; hospital, nursing homes.

Newcastle (688) other principal town.

Zapata

LOCATION: South (S-13).

HISTORY: Named for **Col. Antonio Zapata,** pioneer Mexican rancher; county created, organized, 1858, from Starr, Webb.

PHYSICAL FEATURES: Rolling; brushy; broken by tributaries of Rio Grande; **Falcon Lake.**

AGRICULTURE: About $18 million average yearly income, 90% from beef cattle; sorghums, cotton, vegetables produced, some irrigated.

RECREATION: Falcon Lake is tourist attraction; historic sites; winter tourist center.

MINERALS: Production of gas, oil.

OIL FIELD — 0 2 4 6 MILES

Cong. Dist.	15	U.S. Jud. Dist.	S-La.
St. Sen. Dist.	21	Ct. Appeals	4
St. Rep. Dist.	44	Admin. Jud. Dist.	4
St. Dist. Cts.	49		

1982 Pop.	7,600	Voters reg.	4,914
Area (sq. mi.)	999	Whlsle. sales	$*
Altitude (ft.)	200-800	Oil value	$4,019,145
Ann. rainfall (in.)	17.23	No. employed	1,281
Jan. temp. min.	46	Wages paid	$16,072,440
July temp. max.	100	Tax value	$1,214,029,374
Growing season (da.)	304	Income	$38,666,000
No. farms, 1982	313	Taxable sales	$10,694,422
No. acres in farms	384,120	Fed. expend.	$11,682,000
†Value per farm	$421,246	Crime Index	51
Cropland harvested	2,070	TDC Pop.	5

BUSINESS: Economy based on oil, ranching, **Falcon Lake** activities.

MANUFACTURING: None noted in census report.

SERVICE INDUSTRIES: 15 Establishments; Receipts, $2,281,000; Annual Payroll, $785,000; No. Employees, 251.

ZAPATA (est. 3,500) county seat; tourist, agribusiness, oil center, developing as a retirement center; clinic.

Zavala

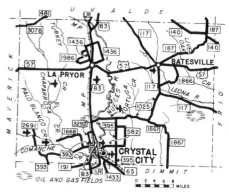

OIL AND GAS FIELDS — 0 2 4 6 8 MILES

LOCATION: Southwest (P-12).

HISTORY: Created from Maverick, Uvalde Counties, 1858; organized, 1884; named for Texas Revolutionary leader, **Lorenzo de Zavala.**

Cong. Dist.	23	U.S. Jud. Dist.	W-DR
St. Sen. Dist.	21	Ct. Appeals	4
St. Rep. Dist.	44	Admin. Jud. Dist.	6
St. Dist. Cts	293		

PHYSICAL FEATURES: Level to rolling; much brush; Nueces, Leona, other streams.

RECREATION: Hunting, fishing; annual spinach festival; local events.

MINERALS: Production of oil, gas.

1982 Pop.	12,000	Voters reg.	7,220
Area (sq. mi.)	1,298	Whlsle. sales	$11,307,000
Altitude (ft.)	550-900	Oil value	$23,132,952
Ann. rainfall (in.)	21.54	No. employed	2,632
Jan. temp. min.	41	Wages paid	$26,168,296
July temp. max.	99	Tax value	$568,853,124
Growing season (da.)	280	Income	$51,953,000
No. farms, 1982	264	Taxable sales	$13,647,659
No. acres in farms	764,132	Fed. expend.	$18,729,000
†Value per farm	$1,340,386	Crime Index	223
Cropland harvested	63,822	TDC Pop.	9

AGRICULTURE: About $42 million average annual income from cotton, sorghums, small grains, corn, pecans, vegetables; beef, dairy cattle, sheep, goats, poultry; 38,000 acres irrigated.

BUSINESS: Chiefly agribusinesses, leading county in Winter Garden truck area; oil, gas, hunting income.

MANUFACTURING: 6 Plants; Employees, N.A.; Payroll, N.A.; Product Value, N.A.

SERVICE INDUSTRIES: 18 Establishments; Receipts, $2,617,000; Annual Payroll, $532,000; No. Employees, 60.

CRYSTAL CITY (8,334) county seat; varied agribusinesses including packing plants for vegetables; oil field services; cotton gin; hospital; spinach capital, "Home of Popeye."

TEXAS
CULTURE

The Nutcracker ballet, which includes the Arabian Dance shown here, was presented by the Lone Star Ballet and the Amarillo Symphony as part of Amarillo's celebration of Christmas 1983. Photo courtesy Lone Star Ballet.

THE FINE ARTS IN TEXAS

The following information on the fine arts in Texas was prepared for the Texas Almanac by Patrice Walker and J. Brown of the Texas Commission on the Arts.

Culture in Texas, as in any market, is a mixture of activity generated by both the commercial and the non-profit sectors.

The commercial sector encompasses Texas-based profit-making businesses including commercial recording artists (such as the legendary Willie Nelson), nightclubs, record companies, private galleries, assorted boutiques which carry fine art collectibles and private dance and music halls. In addition, Texas is becoming an important media center, with Texas-based publications, television and film companies gaining national recognition.

Texas also has extensive cultural resources offered by non-profit organizations that are engaged in charitable, educational and/or humanitarian activities.

The Texas Legislature has authorized five state agencies to administer cultural services and funds for the public good. The five agencies, listed below, fall under the auspices of the Texas Legislature's Cultural and Historical Resources Committee. They are:

Texas Commission on the Arts, Box 13406, Capitol Sta., Austin 78711; **Texas Film Commission,** Box 12428, Austin 78711; **Texas Historical Commission,** Box 12276, Austin 78711; **Texas State Library and Archives Commission,** Box 12927, Austin 78711, and the **State Preservation Board,** Box 13286, Austin 78711.

In 1985, the 69th Legislature authorized the formation of the **Texas Sesquicentennial Commission,** Box 1986, Austin 78767, to provide oversight responsibility for official products and activities related to the year-long celebration. Although not a state agency, another organization which provides cultural services to the citizens of Texas is the **Texas Committee on the Humanities,** 1604 Nueces, Austin 78701.

The **Texas Commission on the Arts** was established in 1965 to develop a receptive climate for the arts in Texas, to attract outstanding artists to Texas, to serve as a source of arts information to state government and Texas at large and to expand and enhance the cultural opportunities for all Texans. The commission accomplishes these goals by providing financial, informational and technical assistance.

The agency is headed by an executive director and is organized into four divisions: Administrative, Performing Arts, Visual Arts/Communication Arts and Special Projects/Local Arts Agencies.

The Texas Commission on the Arts provides services and financial assistance to a wide range of nonprofit arts organizations. Its clientele includes theaters (professional, civic, children's, ethnic), media (radio, television, film, publications), festivals, music (folk, symphonic, chamber, choral, jazz, opera and new music), visual arts (sculpture, crafts, photography, painting, environmental), dance (modern, ballet, folkloric), schools, presenters of cultural events and services organizations.

Texas' major arts institutions — orchestras, museums, dance companies, theaters and cultural centers — are listed below. These and others can also be found under the subhead, "Recreation," in the county reports and in metropolitan area discussions.

Amarillo — Amarillo Symphony Orchestra, Box 2552 (79105).

Austin — Austin Symphony Orchestra, 1101 Red River (78701); Laguna Gloria Art Museum, Box 5568 (78763); Paramount Theatre for the Performing Arts, Box 1205 (78767).

Corpus Christi — Art Museum of South Texas, 1902 N. Shoreline Dr. (78401); Corpus Christi Symphony Orchestra, Box 495 (78403).

Dallas — Dallas Ballet, 1925 Elm (75201); Dallas Opera, 3000 Turtle Creek Blvd., Ste. 100 (75219); Dallas Museum of Art, 1717 N. Harwood (75201); Dallas Symphony Orchestra, Box 26207 (75226); Dallas Theatre Center, 3636 Turtle Creek Blvd. (75219); Theatre Three, 2800 Routh (75201).

El Paso — El Paso Museum Of Arts, 1211 Montana Ave. (79902); El Paso Symphony Orchestra, Box 180 (79942).

Fort Worth — Amon Carter Museum Of Western Art, Box 2365 (76101); Fort Worth Art Museum, 1309 Montgomery (76107); Fort Worth Ballet Assn., 6841B Green Oaks Rd. (76116); Fort Worth Opera, 4401 Trail Lake Dr. (76109); Fort Worth Symphony Orchestra, 4401 Trail Lake Dr. (76109); Kimbell Art Museum, Box 9440 (76107).

Houston — Contemporary Arts Museum, 5216 Montrose Blvd. (77006); Houston Ballet, 615 Louisiana (77002); Houston Grand Opera, 615 Louisiana (77002); Houston Museum of Fine Arts, Box 6828 (77265); Houston Symphony Orchestra, 615 Louisiana (77002); Nina Vance Alley Theatre, 615 Texas (77002); Society for the

Performing Arts, 615 Louisiana (77002); Texas Opera Theatre, 401 Louisiana, 8th Floor (77002); Theatre Under the Stars, 1999 W. Gray (77019).

Midland/Odessa — Midland/Odessa Symphony and Chorale, Box 6266 (79701).

Round Top — James Dick Foundation for the Performing Arts, Box 89 (78954).

San Antonio — Carver Cultural Center, 226 N. Hackberry (78202); Guadalupe Cultural Arts Center, 1300 Guadalupe (78207); McNay Art Institute, 6000 N. New Braunfels (78209); San Antonio Art Institute, 6000 N. New Braunfels (78209); San Antonio Museum Association, Box 2601 (78299-2601); San Antonio Performing Arts Assn., 201 N. St. Mary's, Ste. 618 (78205); San Antonio Symphony Orchestra, 109 Lexington Ave., Ste. 207 (78205).

The **Texas Assembly of Arts Councils**, 121 E. 8th, Austin 78701, promotes, develops and supports local arts agencies. Listed below are the members as of mid-1985:

Abilene—Abilene Cultural Affairs Council, Box 2281 (79604).

Albany—The Old Jail Foundation, Rt. 1, Box 1 (76430).

Amarillo—Convention & Visitors Council, 1000 S. Polk (79101).

Arlington—Arlington Fine Arts Council, Box 13741 (76013).

Austin—Austin Arts Commission — PARD, Box 1088 (78767).

Beaumont—South East Texas Arts Council, Box 3925 (77704).

Bellaire—Arts Council of Bellaire, Box 862 (77401).

Big Spring—Big Spring Cultural Affairs Council, Box 1391 (79720).

Bonham—FUN, Inc., 407 Jo Aynn Circle (75418).

Borger—Magic Plains Arts Council, Box 12 (79007).

Brenham—Arts Council of Washington County, Box 2063 (77833).

Brownwood—Cultural Affairs Commission, Box 880 (76801).

Bryan/College Station—Arts Council of Brazos Valley, 111 University Dr., #217 (77840).

Burkburnett—Community Education Fine Arts Council, Box 1028 (76354).

Calvert—Robertson County Arts Council, Box 211 (77837).

Carrizo Springs—Arts Council of Dimmit County, 414 Pena (78834).

Childress—Arts Council of Childress, 1104 Ave. F NW (79201).

Clear Lake—Cultural Affairs Council, 1201 Nasa Rd. 1 (77058).

Clifton—Bosque Conservatory of Fine Arts, Box 123 (76634).

Corpus Christi—Corpus Christi Arts Council, 1521 N. Chaparral (78401).

Corsicana—Navarro Council of the Arts, Box 2224 (75110).

Dalhart—Dalhart Independent School District, Box 152 (79022).

Dallas—Dallas City Arts Program, Majestic Theatre, 1925 Elm (75201).

Deer Park—Deer Park Cultural Arts Council, Box 857-B (77536).

Del Rio—Del Rio Council for the Arts, Box 178 (78841).

Denison—Convention & Tourist Bureau, Denison Arts Council, 313 W. Woodward (75020).

Denton—Greater Denton Arts Council, Box 1194 (76202).

DeSoto—DeSoto Council of Cultural Arts, 321 Woodhaven Dr. (75115).

Duncanville—Duncanville Regional Arts Assn., 1313 Greenhills Ct. (75137).

Eagle Pass—Arts Council of Eagle Pass, 1910 Olive (78852).

El Paso—El Paso Arts Alliance, 333 E. Missouri (79901); El Paso Arts Resource Department, City of El Paso, 2 Civic Center Plaza (79901).

Floydada—Floyd County Arts Association, Box 304 (79235).

Fort Stockton—Fort Stockton Fine Arts Association, Box 1353 (79735).

Fort Worth—Arts Council of Fort Worth and Tarrant County, Tandy Center One, Ste. 150 (76102).

Gainesville—Cooke County Arts Council, Box 251 (76240).

Galveston—Galveston Arts, Box 1105 (77553).

Garland—Garland Arts Council, Box 401889 (75040).

Gonzales—Gonzales Arts Council, Box 1818 (78629).

Granbury—Hood County Arts Council, Box 595 (76048).

Grand Prairie—Grand Prairie Arts Council, Box 531613 (75053).

Hillsboro—Hillsboro Arts Council, Hillsboro Chamber of Commerce, Box 734 (76645).

Houston—Cultural Arts Council of Houston, 1950 W. Gray, Ste. 6 (77019).

Huntsville—Huntsville Arts Commission, 1212 Ave. M (77340).

Hurst/Euless/Bedford—Trinity Arts Council, Box 18345, Fort Worth (76118).

Irving—City of Irving Arts Board, 3501 N. McArthur, #324 (75062).

Jacksonville—Cultural Affairs Committee, Box 1231 (75766).

Kerrville—Kerrville Area Council for the Arts, Box 790 (78028).

Lake Jackson—Brazosport Fine Arts Council, 400 College Dr. (77566).

Laredo—Laredo Council for the Arts, Box 790 (78040).

Levelland—Fine Arts Council of Levelland, Box 8084 (79338).

Lewisville—Greater Lewisville Arts Council, 217 S. Stemmons, #215 (75067).

Liberty Hill—Cultural Affairs Council, Box 255 (78642).

Longview—Longview Arts Council, 519 E. Young (75602).

Lubbock—Lubbock Cultural Affairs Council, Box 561 (79408).

Lufkin—Angelina Co. Cultural Affairs Council, Rt. 1, Box 75, Pollok (75969).

Marshall—Marshall Cultural Affairs Council, Box 520 (75760).

Mesquite—Mesquite Performing Arts Council, Eastfield Community College, 3737 Motley (75150).

Midland—Midland Arts Assembly, Box 3494 (79702).

Monahans—Ward County Activities Council, 1509 S. Kenneth (79756).

Munday—Munday Entertainment Team, Rt. 1 (76731).

Nacogdoches—SFA/Nacogdoches Arts, Box 13022, SFA Sta. (75962).

New Braunfels—Greater New Braunfels Arts Council, 105 Briarwood (78130).

Odessa—Odessa Cultural Council, Box 7195 (79760).

Pampa—Pampa Fine Arts Association, Box 818 (79065).

Paris—Arts Development Council, 1260 20th N.E. (75460).

Pasadena—Pasadena Area Cultural Arts Council, Box 672 (77501).

Pittsburg—Pittsburg/Camp County Arts Council, Box 72 (75686).

Plainview—Plainview Cultural Council, Box 627 (79072).

Plano—Cultural Arts Council of Plano, 1076 Collin Creek Mall, 811 N. Central Expwy. (75075).

Port Lavaca—Calhoun Arts Council, Box 31 (77979).

Post—Caprock Cultural Association, 201 E. Main (79356).

Richardson—Richardson Arts Commission, Box 309 (75080).

Rio Grande Valley—R. G. Valley Council for the Arts, 714 McKee, Edinburg (78539); Upper Valley Arts Council, 714 McKee, Edinburg (78539).

Rockwall—Rockwall Cultural Arts Council, 307 Greenhill Ln. (75087).

San Angelo—Concho Valley Arts Council, 500 Rio Concho Dr. (76903).

San Antonio—Arts Council of San Antonio, 225 S. Presa (78205).

Seagoville—Seagoville Fine Arts Council, 301 Shadywood Ln. (75159).

Seguin—Seguin Council for the Arts, Box 852 (78155).

Sherman—Council for the Arts & Humanities, Box 1029 (75090).

Stephenville—Cross Timbers Fine Arts Council, Box 1172 (76401).

Sweetwater—Sweetwater Auditorium Comm., Box 1148 (79556).

Temple—Cultural Activities Center, Box 3292 (76501).

Texarkana—Texarkana Regional Arts & Humanities Council, Box 1171 (75504).

Texas City—Arts Council Development Committee, 8001 Palmer Hwy. (77591).

The Woodlands—The Woodlands Living Arts Council, Box 7411 (77380).

Uvalde—Uvalde Arts Council, Box 1451 (78801).

Vernon—Vernon Council of the Arts, Box 1765 (76384).

Victoria—Victoria Arts Council, Box 1758 (77902).

Waco—Cultural Development Committee, 3115 Pine, #202 (76708).

Waxahachie—Waxahachie Arts Council, Rt. 3, Box 282 (75165).

Weatherford—Weatherford Performing Arts, 110 Oriole, (76086).

Wichita Falls—Wichita Falls Arts Commission, 710 Fillmore (76301).

Public Libraries

The following information on Texas public libraries was furnished by Jim Scheppke and Mitchell Gidseg of the Library Development Division, Texas State Library, Austin.

Texas public libraries continue to improve in their efforts to meet the educational, informational and recreational needs of the state's citizens. Perhaps no other public-supported institution directly serves as many Texans, young and old, as does the public library. The latest statistics, for 1983, reported to the Texas State Library by 425 public libraries across Texas bear this fact out. They show:

• A total of 46,407,080 books were checked out to Texans in 1983, a figure equivalent to approximately 3.3 books for every person in the state.

• A total of 4,124,988 items other than books were checked out to Texans in 1983. These items include records, cassettes, magazines, 16 mm films, videocassettes and art prints.

• A total of 5,214,689 answers to reference questions were provided by public libraries, both in the library and over the telephone.

• A total of 4,226,699 persons attended programs at the public library, including "story hour" programs and summer reading club programs for children, as well as cultural, entertainment and adult education programs for adults.

• Audiences totaling 9,985,442 persons viewed films and videocassettes provided by the public library in 1983.

The growth in these services has been considerable over the past five years. During this period, from 1979 to 1983, book circulation has increased by 13.3 percent. Circulation of materials other than books had a dramatic increase of 102.9 percent. The number of reference questions handled by library reference staffs has increased by 32.1 percent. And the number of persons attending programs in the library has risen by 43.8 percent in the past five years.

All of these services were provided by public libraries in 1983 with very modest support from tax sources. Total city and county tax support of public libraries in 1983 amounted to only $7.28 per capita, about half the price of an average hardback book. The State of Texas expended approximately 27 cents per capita in 1983 to finance 10 cooperative public library systems, which undertook various projects to develop and improve public library services. The total breakdown of public library funding, by source of funds, was as follows in 1983:

Source	Amount	Percent
Cities	$ 77,935,669	75%
Counties	17,877,113	17%
State	3,870,086	4%
Federal	1,110,125	1%
Other (Private, etc.)	3,097,086	3%
TOTAL	$103,900,079	100%

There is considerable data that suggest that this level of support is inadequate to meet the needs of Texas citizens for public library services. Out of the 425 libraries reporting for 1983 to the Texas State Library, 67 failed to meet the minimum standards for adequacy of budget, staff, book collection and hours of operation set by the state. Statistics for these 67 libraries show that the typical library in this category serves just under 6,500 population, with a budget from tax sources of less than $14,000 annually and a paid staff consisting of one person. Clearly, much remains to be done, particularly in less populated areas of the state, to bring library services up to adequate standards. Libraries in urban Texas face a different, but no less critical, problem of coping with rapid population growth and consequent demands for service by new residents. As the major Texas cities grow in size and population, there is a need for new library facilities in outlying suburban areas, along with new library collections and staff to provide service at these facilities.

The following table lists all 425 public libraries in Texas, along with statistics on two of the most important services provided to Texas citizens — circulation of library materials (books as well as audiovisual and other materials), and information, provided by library staff to persons asking reference questions at the library, as well as over the telephone. Some of the libraries were unable to report the number of reference questions received in 1983. These are listed as "N.A." The following abbreviations are also used in the chart below: L., library; P.L., public library; C.L., county library; Mem. L., memorial library; Mun. L., municipal library, and Com. L., community library.

Library, County—	Number Volumes Circulated	Inquiries Handled
Abernathy C.L., Hale	5,853	1,429
Abilene P.L., Taylor	625,227	176,590
Alamo P.L., Hidalgo	— 12,102	1,392
Albany, Shackelford C.L., Shackelford	4,200	0
Alice P.L., Jim Wells	247,493	16,207
Allen P.L., Collin	45,245	N.A.
Alpine P.L., Brewster	53,595	N.A.
Alto, Stella Hill Mem. L., Cherokee	2,945	227
Amarillo P.L., Potter	794,934	253,149
Anahuac, Chambers C.L., Chambers	111,066	3,545
Andrews C. L., Andrews	37,056	3,526
Angleton, Brazoria C.L., Brazoria	668,614	41,370
Anna Com. L., Collin	413	N.A.
Anson P.L., Jones	6,029	0
Aransas Pass P.L., San Patricio	28,536	802
Archer City, Archer C.L., Archer	N.A.	0
Arlington P.L., Tarrant	814,840	333,551
Aspermont, Stonewall C.L., Stonewall	18,192	319
Athens, Henderson C. Mem. L., Henderson	69,760	N.A.
Atlanta Mem. L., Cass	19,224	N.A.
Austin P.L., Travis	1,975,626	221,600
Azle P.L., Tarrant	31,037	1,698
Baird, Callahan C.L., Callahan	7,691	75
Balch Springs P.L., Dallas	15,228	N.A.
Ballinger, Carnegie L., Runnels	11,494	N.A.
Bandera C.L., Bandera	21,112	1,120
Barksdale, Nueces Canyon P.L., Edwards	9,777	103
Bartlett, Teinert Mem. P.L., Bell	4,908	1,250
Bastrop P.L., Bastrop	48,193	1,656
Bay City P.L., Matagorda	29,585	535
Baytown, Sterling Mun. L., Harris	545,017	32,859
Beaumont P.L., Jefferson	392,086	30,429
Bedford P.L., Tarrant	208,647	N.A.
Beeville, Bee C. P.L., Bee	58,688	N.A.
Bellaire City L., Harris	143,649	4,483
Bellville P.L., Austin	36,780	1,769
Belton City L., Bell	70,921	2,832
Big Lake, Reagan C.L., Reagan	15,671	800
Big Spring, Howard C.L., Howard	113,178	12,290
Blanco L., Blanco	3,127	0
Blue Mound Com. L., Tarrant	N.A.	250
Boerne P.L., Kendall	53,565	4,977
Bonham P.L., Fannin	54,976	3,240
Borger, Hutchinson C.L., Hutchinson	96,609	2,571
Bowie P.L., Montague	46,045	6,850
Brackettville, Kinney C.P.L., Kinney	8,811	373
Brady, F.M. (Buck) Richards Mem. L., McCulloch	55,212	4,500
Breckenridge P.L., Stephens	3,029	N.A.
Brenham, Nancy Carol Roberts Mem. L., Washington	75,517	2,500
Bridgeport P.L., Wise	30,562	898
Brownfield, Kendrick Mem. L., Terry	43,829	3,192
Brownsville, Arnulfo L. Oliveira Mem. L., Cameron	114,463	10,782
Brownwood P.L., Brown	93,999	5,000
Bryan P.L., Brazos	314,345	15,355
Buda P.L., Hays	*N.A.	†0
Buffalo P.L., Leon	2,006	48
Bullard Com. L., Smith	N.A.	95
Buna P.L., Jasper	3,667	25
Burkburnett L., Wichita	40,073	4,563
Burleson P.L., Johnson	59,183	N.A.
Burnet, Herman Brown Free L., Burnet	101,173	11,565
Caldwell, Harrie P. Woodson Mem. L., Burleson	18,320	445
Cameron P.L., Milam	24,108	120
Canadian, Hemphill C.L., Hemphill	55,704	2,557
Canton, Van Zandt C.L., Van Zandt	29,173	N.A.
Canyon P.L., Randall	23,941	507
Canyon Lake, Tye Preston Mem. L., Comal	20,433	860
Carrizo Springs, Dimmit C.P.L., Dimmit	18,346	1,050
Carrollton P.L., Dallas	244,541	N.A.
Carthage, Service League L., Panola	N.A.	245
Castroville P.L., Medina	13,198	1,344
Cedar Park P.L., Williamson	16,292	208
Center, Fannie Brown Booth Mem. L., Shelby	20,183	1,300
Chico P.L., Wise	2,951	28
Childress P.L., Childress	23,598	1,096
Cisco P.L., Eastland	5,640	0
Clarendon, Gabie Betts Burton Mem. L., Donley	13,829	N.A.
Clarksville, Red River C.P.L., Red River	24,769	N.A.
Claude P.L., Armstrong	N.A.	0
Cleburne P.L., Johnson	131,900	N.A.
Cleveland, Austin Mem. L., Liberty	31,684	2,010
Clifton, Nellie Pederson Civic L., Bosque	N.A.	N.A.
Clyde P.L., Callahan	5,889	450
Coleman P.L., Coleman	18,932	617
Colorado City, Mitchell C.P.L., Mitchell	37,590	N.A.
Columbus, Nesbitt Mem. L., Colorado	32,739	5,000
Comanche P.L., Comanche	24,423	N.A.
Comfort P.L., Kendall	21,250	1,101
Commerce P.L., Hunt	19,497	1,080
Conroe, Montgomery C.L., Montgomery	366,172	46,902
Cooper, Delta C.P.L., Delta	*0	†0
Copperas Cove P.L., Coryell	64,619	1,524
Corpus Christi, LaRetama P.L., Nueces	688,743	165,743
Corrigan P.L., Polk	12,982	600
Corsicana P.L., Navarro	115,612	3,422
Cotulla, Alexander Mem. L., La Salle	9,567	450
Crane C.L., Crane	39,808	4,000
Crockett P.L., Houston	48,568	525
Crosbyton, Crosby C.L., Crosby	28,544	1,745
Cross Plains L., Callahan	6,052	100
Crystal City Mem. L., Zavala	4,236	780
Cuero P.L., DeWitt	16,564	178
Cushing L., Nacogdoches	*N.A.	†500
Daingerfield P.L., Morris	17,444	256
Dalhart, Dallam C.L., Dallam	23,407	500
Dallas County P.L., Dallas	193,878	14,264
Dallas P.L., Dallas	3,948,338	3,250,634
Dayton P.L., Liberty	11,529	N.A.
Decatur P.L., Wise	23,864	0
Deer Park P.L., Harris	127,670	8,335
DeLeon P.L., Comanche	N.A.	75
Dell City, G. Grebing P.L., Hudspeth	15,996	10
Del Rio, Val Verde C.L., Val Verde	79,132	8,330
Denison P.L., Grayson	133,608	21,555
Denton P.L., Denton	242,583	10,422
Denver City, Yoakum C.L., Yoakum	32,892	3,000
Devine P.L., Medina	7,561	442
Diboll, T.L.L. Temple Mem. L., Angelina	32,525	6,635
Dickinson P.L., Galveston	32,596	1,841
Dimmitt, Rhoads Mem. L., Castro	21,660	2,061
Donna P.L., Hidalgo	17,692	5,482
Dublin P.L., Erath	3,555	25
Dumas, Killgore Mem. L., Moore	86,502	6,358
Duncanville P.L., Dallas	134,687	N.A.
Eagle Lake, Eula & David Wintermann L., Colorado	16,927	1,782

Library, County—	Number Volumes Circulated	Inquiries Handled
Eagle Lake, Eula & David		
Wintermann L., Colorado	16,927	1,782
Eagle Pass P.L., Maverick	33,830	N.A.
Eastland, Centennial Mem. L.,		
Eastland	4,190	32
Eden P.L., Concho	3,540	390
Edinburg P.L., Hidalgo	94,005	5,753
Edna, Jackson C.L., Jackson	17,662	0
Eldorado P.L., Schleicher	7,421	250
Electra P.L., Wichita	34,890	1,400
El Paso P.L., El Paso	1,184,157	102,314
Elsa P.L., Hidalgo	16,688	200
Emory, Rains C.P.L., Rains	7,232	67
Ennis P.L., Ellis	25,067	N.A.
Euless P.L., Tarrant	112,902	9,714
Fabens, El Paso C.L., El Paso	54,812	4,300
Fairfield L., Freestone	19,153	5,047
Falfurrias, Ed Rachal Mem. L.,		
Brooks	74,701	1,823
Farmers Branch P.L., Dallas	150,328	N.A.
Farmersville, Charles J. Rike		
Mem. L., Collin	8,267	75
Ferris P.L, Ellis	2,328	730
Florence P.L., Williamson	3,856	200
Floresville, Wilson C.P.L., Wilson	44,381	N.A.
Floydada C.L., Floyd	17,595	1,800
Fort Davis, Jeff Davis C.L.,		
Jeff Davis	4,695	253
Fort Stockton P.L., Pecos	141,022	13,940
Fort Worth P.L., Tarrant	2,920,351	395,545
Franklin, Robertson C.L.,		
Robertson	3,032	15
Fredericksburg, Pioneer Mem. L.,		
Gillespie	85,241	1,427
Friendswood P.L., Galveston	99,059	N.A.
Friona P.L., Parmer.	18,946	950
Gainesville, Cooke C.L., Cooke	67,682	2,318
Galveston, Rosenberg L.,		
Galveston	238,232	46,307
Garland, Nicholson Mem. L.,		
Dallas	595,251	59,936
Garwood, Veterans Mem. L.,		
Colorado.	N.A.	0
Gatesville P.L., Coryell.	30,767	750
Georgetown P.L., Williamson	89,757	N.A.
George West, Live Oak C.L.,		
Live Oak	63,290	1,500
Giddings, Rufus Young King L.,		
Lee	28,994	315
Gilmer, Upshur C.L., Upshur	29,297	660
Gladewater, Lee P.L., Gregg	39,983	330
Glen Rose, Glen Rose-Somervell L.,		
Somervell	14,743	1,075
Gonzales P.L., Gonzales	31,978	4,800
Graham P.L., Young	99,465	4,992
Granbury, Hood C.L., Hood	55,511	6,240
Grand Prairie Mem. L., Dallas	192,435	10,682
Grand Saline P.L., Van Zandt	10,180	265
Grapevine P.L., Tarrant.	75,622	1,842
Greenville, W. Walworth Harrison		
P.L., Hunt	77,623	10,000
Groesbeck, Maffett Mem. L.,		
Limestone	17,047	250
Groves P.L., Jefferson	32,813	6,432
Groveton, Ethel R. Reese P. L.,		
Trinity	6,705	0
Gruver City L., Hansford	2,824	0
Hale Center P.L., Hale	6,751	113
Hallettsville, Friench Simpson		
Mem. L., Lavaca	20,269	1,200
Haltom City P.L., Tarrant.	188,190	25,000
Hamilton P.L., Hamilton	18,999	423
Harker Heights P.L., Bell	10,665	231
Harlingen P.L., Cameron	148,925	4,000
Haskell C.L., Haskell	17,729	N.A.
Hearne, Smith-Welch Mem. L.,		
Robertson.	11,219	109
Hebbronville, Jim Hogg C.P.L.,		
Jim Hogg	7,267	N.A.
Hempstead, Waller C.L., Waller	15,659	2,000
Henderson, Rusk C. Mem. L.,		
Rusk.	135,139	3,557
Henrietta, Edwards P.L., Clay	38,303	N.A.
Hereford, Deaf Smith C.L.,		
Deaf Smith	161,164	2,094
Highland Park L., Dallas	69,394	N.A.
Hillsboro City L., Hill	28,774	11,700
Hitchcock P.L., Galveston	10,682	N.A.

Library, County—	Number Volumes Circulated	Inquiries Handled
Hondo P.L., Medina	15,831	30
Honey Grove Mem. L., Fannin	10,717	948
Houston, Harris C.P.L., Harris	2,701,561	266,677
Houston P.L., Harris.	6,331,119	2,868,328
Howe P.L., Grayson	2,252	0
Huntsville P.L., Walker	64,342	9,986
Hurst P.L., Tarrant	331,840	N.A.
Imperial P.L., Pecos.	9,554	900
Ingleside P.L., San Patricio	19,205	1,050
Iowa Park L., Wichita	17,323	N.A.
Iraan P.L., Pecos	11,923	4
Irving P.L., Dallas	469,353	110,730
Jacksboro P.L., Jack	19,868	1,150
Jacksonville P.L., Cherokee	58,795	N.A.
Jasper P.L., Jasper	22,080	N.A.
Jayton, Kent C.L., Kent	1,724	N.A.
Jefferson, Carnegie L., Marion.	N.A.	0
Johnson City L., Blanco	8,382	N.A.
Jourdanton Com. L., Atascosa	11,674	1,323
Junction, Kimble C.L., Kimble	31,544	788
Kaufman C.L., Kaufman	23,482	50
Keller P.L., Tarrant	18,708	N.A.
Kendalia P.L., Kendall	2,736	24
Kenedy, Karnes C.L., Karnes	118,682	2,338
Kermit, Winkler C.L., Winkler	77,470	7,525
Kerrville, Butt-Holdsworth		
Mem. L., Kerr	128,136	6,870
Kilgore P.L., Gregg	56,075	2,182
Killeen P.L., Bell	95,572	20,500
Kingsville, Robert J. Kleberg P.L.,		
Kleberg	169,834	N.A.
Kirbyville P.L., Jasper	9,583	N.A.
Kountze P.L., Hardin	17,648	3,743
Kyle Com. L., Hays	10,179	N.A.
La Feria, Bailey H. Dunlap		
Mem. L., Cameron	14,869	3,669
La Grange, Fayette P.L.,		
Fayette	29,204	642
Laguna Vista P.L., Cameron	2,041	0
Lake Dallas, Lake Cities L.,		
Denton	4,152	278
Lake Worth P.L., Tarrant	15,684	N.A.
La Marque P.L., Galveston	48,964	1,974
Lamesa, Dawson C.P.L., Dawson	66,412	N.A.
Lampasas P.L., Lampasas	39,554	2,200
Laredo P.L., Webb	78,645	N.A.
League City P.L., Galveston	132,574	N.A.
Leon Valley, Northwest		
Com. L., Bexar	30,237	1,824
Levelland, Hockley C. Mem. L.,		
Hockley	29,676	633
Lewisville P.L., Denton	238,885	N.A.
Liberty Mun. L., Liberty.	67,367	3,049
Littlefield, Lamb C.L., Lamb	24,861	921
Livingston, Murphy Mem. L.,		
Polk	55,228	N.A.
Llano C.P.L., Llano	60,435	N.A.
Lockhart, Dr. Eugene Clark L.,		
Caldwell	41,007	N.A.
Longview, Nicholson Mem. L.,		
Gregg	128,185	5,763
Los Fresnos, Ethel Whipple		
Mem. L., Cameron	20,102	N.A.
Lubbock, City-County L.,		
Lubbock	514,540	74,453
Lufkin, Kurth Mem. L., Angelina	155,558	17,651
Luling P.L., Caldwell	31,964	940
Lytle P.L., Atascosa	6,482	347
McAllen Mem. L., Hidalgo	317,253	30,427
McCamey, Upton C.P.L., Upton	21,752	525
McKinney Mem. P.L., Collin.	85,609	1,200
McLean, Lovett Mem. L., Gray.	15,291	186
Madisonville C.L., Madison	25,096	309
Malakoff P.L., Henderson	16,476	150
Mansfield P.L., Tarrant	40,715	5,839
Marfa P.L., Presidio	35,018	980
Marlin P.L., Falls.	12,504	N.A.
Marshall P.L., Harrison	73,776	7,554
Mason C. Free L., Mason	9,969	31
Matador, Motley C.L., Motley.	8,702	1,243
Mathis P.L., San Patricio	8,370	250
Memphis P.L., Hall	14,731	702
Menard P.L., Menard.	16,020	0
Mercedes Mem. L., Hidalgo	74,388	3,378
Mertzon, Irion C.L., Irion	N.A.	0
Mesquite P.L., Dallas.	250,578	35,443
Mexia, Gibbs Mem. L., Limestone	35,237	5,000
Midland C.P.L., Midland	365,639	38,174

Library, County—	Number Volumes Circulated	Inquiries Handled
Midlothian, A. H. Meadows L., Ellis	8,469	305
Mineola Mem. L., Wood	17,825	N.A.
Mineral Wells, Boyce Ditto Mun. L., Palo Pinto	57,872	21,400
Mission, Speer Mem. L., Hidalgo	90,929	5,044
Monahans, Ward C.L., Ward	99,528	7,888
Morgan's Point L., Bell	932	0
Morton, Cochran C.L., Cochran	4,953	40
Mount Calm Regional L., Hill	4,570	400
Mount Pleasant Mun. L., Titus	57,224	3,500
Mt. Vernon, Franklin C.L., Franklin	31,509	1,550
Muenster P.L., Cooke	13,391	150
Muleshoe Area P.L., Bailey	51,514	1,500
Munday, City-County L., Knox	10,059	N.A.
Nacogdoches P.L., Nacogdoches	101,292	14,400
Navasota, Grimes C.L., Grimes	30,127	1,427
Nederland, D. Bob Henson Mem. L., Jefferson	87,984	8,793
Nederland, Jefferson C.L., Jefferson	86,354	3,443
New Boston P.L., Bowie	18,101	910
New Braunfels, Dittlinger Mem. L., Comal	95,713	1,407
Newton C.P.L., Newton	6,601	N.A.
Nixon P.L., Gonzales	9,721	42
Nocona P.L., Montague	9,047	2,280
North Richland Hills P.L., Tarrant	159,519	12,170
Odem P.L., San Patricio	2,516	10
Odessa, Ector C.L., Ector	620,353	53,126
Olney Com.L., Young	48,906	N.A.
Orange P.L., Orange	145,613	N.A.
Ozona, Crockett C.L., Crockett	1,751	N.A.
Paducah, Bicentennial City-County L., Cottle	4,546	40
Paint Rock, H. B. Crozier Mem. L., Concho	1,941	38
Palacios L., Matagorda	22,868	N.A.
Palestine, Carnegie L., Anderson	98,133	N.A.
Pampa, Lovett Mem. L., Gray	118,170	7,150
Panhandle, Carson C.L., Carson	6,449	N.A.
Paris P.L., Lamar	141,630	23,070
Pasadena P.L., Harris	356,964	41,414
Pearsall, Frio P.L., Frio	51,532	800
Pecos, Reeves C.L., Reeves	24,394	N.A.
Perryton, Perry Mem. L., Ochiltree	44,096	4,042
Petersburg P.L., Hale	8,475	N.A.
Pflugerville Com. L., Travis	3,763	N.A.
Pharr Mem. L., Hidalgo	93,658	3,926
Pilot Point Com. L., Denton	7,441	N.A.
Pineland, Arthur Temple Sr. Mem. L., Sabine	15,320	190
Pittsburg-Camp C.L., Camp	40,587	1,150
Plains, Yoakum C.L., Yoakum	26,234	508
Plainview, Unger Mem. L., Hale	52,417	N.A.
Plano P.L., Collin	484,918	28,294
Pleasanton P.L., Atascosa	41,112	6,800
Port Aransas P.L., Nueces	13,018	1,280
Port Arthur P.L., Jefferson	206,324	40,136
Port Isabel P.L., Cameron	12,399	N.A.
Portland, Bell-Whittington P.L., San Patricio	62,233	3,851
Port Lavaca, Calhoun C.L., Calhoun	73,957	N.A.
Port Neches, Effie & Wilton Herbert P.L., Jefferson	55,588	N.A.
Post P.L., Garza	10,580	645
Poteet P.L., Atascosa	10,601	578
Presidio, City of, L., Presidio	569	5
Quanah, Hardeman C.P.L., Hardeman	23,783	1,200
Quemado P.L., Maverick	10,325	206
Quitman P.L., Wood	18,932	3,000
Rankin P.L., Upton	17,361	200
Raymondville, Reber Mem. L., Willacy	46,974	3,077
Refugio C.P.L., Refugio	17,791	N.A.
Richardson P.L., Dallas	496,290	46,081
Richland Hills P.L., Tarrant	65,997	7,500
Richmond, Fort Bend C.L., Fort Bend	356,386	15,386
Rio Hondo P.L., Cameron	3,026	400
River Oaks P.L., Tarrant	77,028	101
Roanoke P.L., Denton	5,762	N.A.
Robert Lee, Coke C.L., Coke	9,179	N.A.
Robstown, Nueces C.L., Nueces	48,402	N.A.
Rockdale, Lucy Hill Patterson Mem. L., Milam	22,461	2,076
Rockport, Aransas C.P.L., Aransas	35,061	866
Rocksprings, Edwards C. Mem. L., Edwards	2,010	12
Rockwall C.L., Rockwall	28,940	2,600
Rotan P.L., Fisher	9,674	271
Round Rock P.L., Williamson	84,862	1,500
Rusk, Singletary Mem. L., Cherokee	16,896	775
Saginaw P.L., Tarrant	18,684	1,438
San Angelo, Tom Green C.L., Tom Green	529,718	33,753
San Antonio P.L., Bexar	2,331,918	†200,520
San Augustine P.L., San Augustine	28,017	903
San Benito P.L., Cameron	57,296	6,588
Sanderson, Terrell C.P.L., Terrell	23,574	430
San Juan P.L., Hidalgo	4,803	0
San Marcos P.L., Hays	119,311	5,253
San Saba, Rylander Mem.L., San Saba	27,716	N.A.
Santa Anna City L., Coleman	N.A.	N.A.
Santa Fe Com. L., Galveston	12,192	210
Schertz P.L., Guadalupe	28,967	1,740
Schulenburg P.L., Fayette	13,760	750
Sealy, Virgil & Josephine Gordon Mem.L., Austin	23,322	802
Seguin, Seguin-Guadalupe C.P.L., Guadalupe	66,030	6,514
Seminole, Gaines C.L., Gaines	57,464	2,483
Seymour, Baylor County Free L., Baylor	13,700	1,200
Shamrock P.L., Wheeler	19,177	N.A.
Shepherd, Roland Tisinger Mem. L., San Jacinto	7,968	0
Sheridan Youth Mem. L., Colorado	985	0
Sherman P.L., Grayson	211,796	N.A.
Silsbee P.L., Hardin	110,332	7,014
Sinton, San Patricio C.L., San Patricio	0	0
Sinton P.L., San Patricio	28,092	2,335
Smiley, Stella Ellis Hart Mem. L., Gonzales	4,539	147
Smithville P.L., Bastrop	25,941	500
Snyder, Scurry C.L., Scurry	61,766	5,700
Sonora, Sutton C.L., Sutton	15,193	200
Sour Lake, Alma M. Carpenter P.L., Hardin	10,314	25
Spearman, Hansford C.L., Hansford	21,579	710
Splendora City L., Montgomery	14,508	1,000
Spur, Dickens C. Spur P.L., Dickens	5,000	200
Stamford, Carnegie L., Jones	9,328	539
Stanton, Martin C.L., Martin	5,637	0
Stephenville P.L., Erath	58,496	N.A.
Stratford, Sherman C.L., Sherman	7,210	300
Sulphur Springs P.L., Hopkins	50,949	N.A.
Sweetwater County-City L., Nolan	104,552	7,000
Taft P.L., San Patricio	17,635	764
Tahoka City-County L., Lynn	4,037	N.A.
Taylor P.L., Williamson	25,000	N.A.
Teague L., Freestone	13,085	600
Temple P.L., Bell	183,921	34,389
Terrell P.L., Kaufman	73,364	3,263
Texarkana P.L., Bowie	153,569	N.A.
Texas City, Moore Mem. P.L., Galveston	154,804	6,853
The Colony P.L., Denton	25,126	3,503
Trinity, Blanche K. Werner P.L., Trinity	15,885	300
Tulia, Swisher C.L., Swisher	20,532	695
Tyler P.L., Smith	317,851	62,314
Uvalde, El Progreso Mem. L., Uvalde	94,063	N.A.
Van Alstyne P.L., Grayson	8,133	96
Van Horn City-County L., Culberson	15,764	510
Vernon, Carnegie City-County L., Wilbarger	38,881	N.A.
Victoria P.L., Victoria	287,336	60,244
Vidor P.L., Orange	24,514	720
Waco-McLennan C.L., McLennan	510,320	135,000
Waelder P.L., Gonzales	560	0
Wallis, Austin C.L., Austin	10,148	244
Warrenton, Fayette C. Bookmobile, Fayette	3,233	125

Library, County—	Number Volumes Circulated	Inquiries Handled
Waxahachie, Nicholas P. Sims L., Ellis	161,342	N.A.
Weatherford P.L., Parker	97,439	N.A.
Weimar P.L., Colorado	14,607	825
Wellington, Collingsworth C.L., Collingsworth	11,591	44
Wells, Rube Sessions Mem. L., Cherokee	6,150	450
Weslaco P.L, Hidalgo	94,108	1,791
Wharton C.L., Wharton	202,547	5,585
Wheeler P.L., Wheeler	17,698	840
Whitesboro P.L., Grayson	22,606	N.A.
White Settlement P.L., Tarrant	58,623	7,769
Whitewright P.L., Grayson	10,367	N.A.
Wichita Falls, Kemp P.L., Wichita	198,587	8,009
Wimberley, Village L., Hays	9,192	N.A.
Winters P.L., Runnels	5,470	30
Wolfe City P.L., Hunt	5,046	N.A.
Woodville, Allan Shivers L., Tyler	36,744	9,625
Wylie P.L., Collin	12,676	1,078
Yoakum P.L., De Witt	18,790	N.A.
Yorktown P.L., De Witt	11,424	251
Zapata C.P.L., Zapata	4,350	12

*Newly established library in 1983.
†Figure represents reference questions answered at the central library facility only.

Poets Laureate

Texas Legislature designates Texas Poets Laureate and alternates. Poetry Society of Texas and Secretary of Senate's office, Austin, supplied this list for recent years.

1971-1972 Dr. Terry Fontenot, Port Arthur; Faye Carr Adams, Dallas, alternate.
1972-1973 Mrs. Clark Gresham, Burkburnett; Marion McDaniel, Sidney, alternate.
1973-1974 Mrs. Violette Newton, Beaumont; Mrs. Stella Woodall, San Antonio, alternate.
1974-1975 Mrs. Lila Todd O'Niell, Port Arthur; C. W. Miller, San Antonio, alternate.
1975-1976 Mrs. Ethel Osborn Hill, Port Arthur; Dr. Gene Shuford, Denton, alternate.
1976-1977 Mrs. Florice Stripling Jeffers, Burkburnett; Mrs. Vera L. Eckert, San Angelo, alternate.
1977-1978 Mrs. Ruth Carruth, Vernon; Mrs. Joy Gresham Hagstrom, Burkburnett, alternate.
1978-1979 Patsy Stodghill, Dallas; Dorothy B. Elfstroman, Galveston, alternate.
1979-1980 Dorothy B. Elfstroman, Galveston; Ruth Carruth, Vernon, alternate.
1980-1981 Weems S. Dykes, McCamey; Mildred Crabtree Speer, Amarillo, alternate.
1981-1982 No appointment made.
1982-1983 William D. Barney, Fort Worth; Vassar Miller, Houston, alternate.
No appointment made for 1983-84, 1984-85 or 1985-86.

Texas Institute of Letters

Since 1939, the **Texas Institute of Letters** has chosen each year outstanding books which are either by Texans or about Texas subjects. Awards have been made for fiction, nonfiction, Southwest history, general information, children's books, poetry and book design. These awards for recent years are listed below:

Year—Author — **Title**
1980 Michael Mewshaw . . . . Life for Death
Laura Furman . . . . The Glass House
Joel Warren Barna (co-winner)
. . . Inbetween and Houston City Magazine article
Bryan Woolley (co-winner)
. . . . Dallas Times Herald Column
Naomi Shihab Nye . . . . . . Different Ways to Pray
David Hall . . . . The Smell in Bertha's House
Myra Livingston . . . . No Way of Knowing
Tom Lea . . . . . . (First "Career in Texas Letters" Award)
The Guadalupe Mountains of Texas (best book design award; most important contribution to knowledge)
1981 Phillip Lopate . . . . . . Bachelorhood: Tales of the Metropolis
Beverly Lowry . . . . Daddy's Girl
John Ettling . . . . Ther Germ of Laziness
Michael Berryhill . . . . The Death of a Poet
Doug Crowell . . . . Work
Pattiann Rogers . . . . . The Expectations of Light
Book Design Award: Sidney Feinberg and Jean Paul Tremblay for "On the Border," by Tom Miller
Frank J. Mangan for "Fort Bliss: An Illustrated History," by Leon C. Metz
Larry Smitherman for "Texas Folk Art," by Cecelia Steinfeldt
1982 Robert A. Caro . The Path to Power: The Years of Lyndon Johnson
Allen Hannay . Love and Other Natural Disasters
David J. Weber . The Mexican Frontier, 1821-1846; The American Southwest Under Mexico
Paul Burka . . . . The King of the Forest
Jack Kent (co-winner) . . The Once-Upon-a-Time Dragon
Ouida Sebestyen (co-winner) . . . . IOU's
Roland E. Sodowsky . . . . Landlady
Naomi Shihab Nye (co-winner) . . . . Hugging the Jukebox
Thomas Whitbread (co-winner) . . . . . Whomp and Moonshiver
Book Design Award: Barbara and Fred Whitehead for "Journey to Pleasant Hill: The Civil War Letters of Captain Elijah P. Petty, Walker's Texas Division, C.S.A."
In 1982, a special award honoring the late Barbara McCombs and the late Lon Tinkle was given John Graves of Glen Rose for continuing excellence in Texas letters.

Year—Author — **Title**
1983 Michael Mewshaw . . . . Short Circuit
Joe Coomer . . . . The Decatur Road
Lawrence C. Kelly . . . The Assault on Assimilation
Albert Goldbarth . . . . . . Original Light: New and Selected Poems, 1973-1983
Bryan Woolley . . . . . Where Texas Meets the Sea
Jack Kent . . . . Silly Goose
Tom Zigal . . . . Curios
Book Design Award: Barbara and Fred Whitehead for "Clem Maverick," written by R. G. Vliet.
The special Barbara McCombs/Lon Tinkle Award for continuing excellence in Texas Letters: William Owens, originally of Pin Hook, Texas.
A special citation for an important contribution to knowledge was presented to the Texas Almanac.
1984 Max Apple . . . . Free Agents
Celia Morris Eckhardt (co-winner) Fanny Wright
John Bloom and Jim Atkinson (co-winners)
. . . . Evidence of Love
William Roger Louis . . . The British Empire in the Middle East, 1945-1951
Rosemary Catacalos . . . Again for the First Time
Beverly Lowry . . So Far From the Road, So Long Until Morning
Judith MacBain Alter . . . Luke and the Van Zandt County War
Jeff Unger (co-winner) . . . . Huck at 100
John Davidson (co-winner) . . . . . . The Man Who Dreamed Luckenbach
Drew Jubera (co-winner) To Find A Mockingbird: The Search for Harper Lee
Book Design Award: George Lenox . . . The Other Texas Frontier
The special Barbara McCombs/Lon Tinkle Award for continuing excellence in Texas Letters: Larry McMurtry, Washington, D.C.

TEXAS WRITER RECOGNITION AWARDS

The first **Texas Writer Recognition Awards** were offered in 1981 to 10 Texas writers. The awards are administered by the **Texas Institute of Letters** on behalf of the **Texas Commission on the Arts** and are designed to aid writers in completion of works in progress. Each received $2,000.

1981 Lee Merrill of El Paso, short story; Annette Sanford of Ganado, short story; Estela Portillo of El Paso, novel; Ken Harrison of Dallas, screenplay; Glenn Hardin of Austin, poetry; Joyce Pounds Hardy of Houston, poetry; Timothy Green of Austin, poetry; Jackie Simon of Houston, short story; Jan Reid of Kingsbury, novel; and James Applegate Wood of Austin, poetry.

This award is not an annual event; no awards have been made since 1981. It is hoped that it will be given again some time in the future.

TEXAS
POPULATION

Metropolitan Areas of Texas

The federal government, effective June 30, 1983, redefined the geographic units it uses to gather statistics in metropolitan areas in the United States. The **Standard Metropolitan Statistical Area (SMSA)** and the **Standard Consolidated Statistical Area (SCSA)** were abandoned in favor of a 3-tier system. SMSAs included one or more counties, and SCSAs covered two or more adjoining SMSAs.

Under the new definitions used by the U.S. Office of Management and Budget, there are three methods of classifying metropolitan areas. The **Metropolitan Statistical Areas (MSA)** are free-standing metropolitan areas composed of one or more counties. **Primary Metropolitan Statistical Areas (PMSA)** are sub-units of a larger classification, **Consolidated Metropolitan Statistical Areas (CMSA)**. CMSAs are metropolitan areas with more than 1 million population and are made up of two or more PMSAs.

With the new system, Texas now has 28 PMSAs and MSAs rather than the 26 SMSAs it had under the old classification. The major change is that **Brazoria County** is now considered a sub-unit of the Houston-Galveston-Brazoria County CMSA, rather than a part of the old Houston SMSA. And **Dallas and Fort Worth-Arlington** are considered separate PMSAs, as well as being combined in the **Dallas-Fort Worth CMSA**.

Various demographic data reflecting the new alignments have been published and some of these are given in accompanying write-ups of individual areas.

New Metropolitan Statistical Areas (MSA) In Texas

	July 1, 1982 Population
Consolidated Metropolitan Statistical Areas (CMSA):	
Houston-Galveston-Brazoria CMSA	
(Houston PMSA, Galveston-Texas City PMSA and Brazoria PMSA)	3,446,500
Dallas-Fort Worth CMSA (Dallas PMSA and Fort Worth-Arlington PMSA)	3,131,200
Metropolitan Statistical Areas (MSA) and Primary Metropolitan Statistical Areas (PMSA):	
Level A — Population 1,000,000 or More	
Houston PMSA (Fort Bend, Harris, Liberty, Montgomery and Waller Counties)	3,060,500
Dallas PMSA (Collin, Dallas, Denton, Ellis, Kaufman and Rockwall Counties)	2,081,200
San Antonio MSA (Bexar, Comal and Guadalupe Counties)	1,141,000
Fort Worth-Arlington PMSA (Johnson, Parker and Tarrant Counties)	1,050,000
Level B — Population 250,000 to 1,000,000	
Austin MSA (Hays, Travis and Williamson Counties)	577,100
El Paso MSA (El Paso County)	513,400
Beaumont-Port Arthur MSA (Hardin, Jefferson and Orange Counties)	387,700
Corpus Christi MSA (Nueces and San Patricio Counties)	344,100
McAllen-Edinburg-Mission MSA (Hidalgo County)	315,100
Level C — Population 100,000 to 250,000	
Brownsville-Harlingen MSA (Cameron County)	230,500
Killeen-Temple MSA (Bell and Coryell Counties)	223,000
Lubbock MSA (Lubbock County)	216,700
Galveston-Texas City PMSA (Galveston County)	207,600
Amarillo MSA (Potter and Randall Counties)	182,600
Brazoria PMSA (Brazoria County)	178,400
Waco MSA (McLennan County)	175,500
Longview-Marshall MSA (Gregg and Harrison Counties)	165,200
Tyler MSA (Smith County)	136,700
Odessa MSA (Ector County)	134,200
Wichita Falls MSA (Wichita County)	125,500
Abilene MSA (Taylor County)	118,600
Bryan-College Station MSA (Brazos County)	112,100
Laredo MSA (Webb County)	109,900
*Texarkana MSA (Bowie County, Tx. and Miller County, Ark.)	76,500
Level D — Population Under 100,000	
Midland MSA (Midland County)	97,400
Sherman-Denison MSA (Grayson County)	92,300
San Angelo MSA (Tom Green County)	90,700
Victoria MSA (Victoria County)	72,900
*Figures for Bowie County, Texas only.	

Nelson Park Zoo in Abilene is a popular tourist attraction for hometown folks as well as visitors.

Abilene

The Abilene MSA, which encompasses Taylor County, had a 1982 population of 118,600, according to the U.S. Census. Established in 1881 by the Texas & Pacific Railroad and a group of cattlemen, Abilene initially was a shipping center for cattle, wool and buffalo bones. A few years later, agricultural products were added. Although petroleum production and oil field services are the cornerstones of the economy, Abilene is diversifying. It is a major retail center for a 22-county area and a major health care center for the region. In 1982, 145 manufacturers employed 5,800 persons to produce a variety of goods ranging from oil field equipment to military electronics to musical instruments. Manufacturing payroll was $91,200,000. Value of manufactured shipments was $1,515,800,000. Retail sales amounted to $804,342,000; wholesale sales brought in $1,533,562,000 and service industries contributed more than $223,847,000 to the economy. The area had a per capita personal income of $11,777 in 1983. Its location on several major highways and rail lines plus scheduled air service make Abilene a travel center. Dyess Air Force Base is also a major economic factor in the region. The Abilene Civic Center offers convention facilities, and there is a broad range of cultural activities. Institutions of higher learning in Abilene include Abilene Christian University, Hardin-Simmons University and McMurry College. There are also branches of Cisco Junior College and the Texas State Technical Institute. Recreational attractions in the Abilene area include Fort Phantom Hill, Nelson Park Zoo, Abilene State Park and several lakes.

Because of the wide-open spaces around Amarillo, cowboys and related activities are an integral part of their culture. Shown here is a rodeo arena with a pen of bulls perhaps used in riding or roping contests.

Amarillo

The center of a 5-state marketing and distribution area, Amarillo is the central city of a metropolitan area that includes Randall and Potter Counties. The MSA population in 1982 was 182,600. Amarillo was established as a cattle shipping center in 1887, as the railroads moved across the Texas Panhandle. Significant oil and natural gas discoveries near the city in 1918 expanded the dimensions of its economy. In 1982, Amarillo was home to 195 manufacturing establishments that employed 12,600 people with a payroll of $94,300,000. Value of manufactured shipments was $2,685,400,000. Retail sales amounted to $1,220,497,000; wholesale sales brought in $2,242,725,000 and service industries contributed more than $342,606,000 to the economy. The area had a per capita personal income of $11,924 in 1983. Amarillo is a medical and education center for the High Plains region. Amarillo College is a comprehensive community college, and West Texas State University is located in Canyon in Randall County. Many recreational and tourist attractions make the region an ideal vacation area. Amarillo has golf courses, a civic center, art galleries and other facilities. Palo Duro Canyon State Park, one of the state's most popular tourist attractions, features a summer musical, "Texas," which is presented in the outdoor Pioneer Amphitheatre. Alibates Flint Quarries and Texas Panhandle Pueblo Culture National Monument are located in Potter County, and the Panhandle-Plains Museum in Canyon is considered one of the state's finest facilities.

This field of Texas bluebonnets, the state flower of Texas, is just one of the many acres of wildflowers that grace the Texas countryside in the spring.

Austin

The Austin MSA — comprising Travis, Hays and Williamson Counties — had a population in 1982 of 577,100. Austin, the state capital, is the central city and one of the most vibrant communities in the state. Austin is a center for state government, education and tourism. In recent years, it has diversified its economic base further through the attraction of "21st century" industries, such as computers and semiconductors. In 1982, 681 manufacturing establishments employed 34,400 people with a payroll of $678,200,000. Value of manufactured shipments was $2,842,200,000. Retail sales amounted to $3,399,672,000; wholesale sales brought in $2,124,897,000 and service industries contributed more than $1,422,338,000 to the economy. The area had a per capita personal income in 1983 of $11,937, a 13.3 percent increase over 1982, which earned it the ranking of 91st nationally, according to the U.S. Department of Commerce. The central campus of the University of Texas is located in Austin, as are St. Edwards University, Austin Community College, Maryhill College, Concordia Lutheran College and Huston-Tillotson College. Many of the state's eleemosynary schools and institutions also are located in the capital. Cultural, educational and historical attractions bring thousands of visitors to Austin and the area each year. The State Capitol, the Governor's Mansion and the Lyndon B. Johnson Presidential Library, located on the campus of the University of Texas, are primary tourist destinations. In the vicinity of the 3-county MSA are President Johnson's boyhood home, the LBJ Ranch and State Park, the picturesque Texas Hill Country and numerous Colorado River lakes. Living conditions in Austin earned the capital city the rank of first among the largest 52 Texas cities in a 1985 University of Texas at Arlington "quality of life" survey. Other major cities in the metropolitan area are Taylor, a manufacturing, publishing and agribusiness center; Georgetown, home of Southwestern University; San Marcos, a recreation and education center with Southwest Texas State University and San Marcos Baptist Academy, and Round Rock, a manufacturing and residential center.

San Angelo's annual Fiesta del Concho (right) brings crowds to the banks of the Concho River each June.

New construction in dynamic Houston causes constant changes in its skyline (left). Dallas' I.M. Pei-designed City Hall (below) is not only the seat of city government, it is also a tourist attraction because of its dramatic architectural style.

Beaumont-Port Arthur

The Beaumont-Port Arthur MSA comprises Jefferson, Hardin and Orange Counties and is one of the most heavily industrialized areas in Texas. It had a population of 387,700 in 1982, according to the U.S. Census Bureau. In addition to the industrialization, the area also is the cradle of the modern oil business in Texas. Beaumont was the state's first oil boom town. On Jan. 10, 1901, Anthony Francis Lucas brought in the first well in the Spindletop Field near the city. Much of the industry in the region is petroleum related. Beaumont and Port Arthur have many petrochemical plants and refineries. Shipbuilding and oil field equipment manufacturing also are major industries. In 1982, 353 manufacturing establishments employed 37,300 people with a payroll of $992,200,000. Value of manufactured shipments was $19,708,900,000. Retail sales amounted to $2,093,311,000; wholesale sales brought in $2,748,460,000 and the service industries contributed more than $604,676,000 to the economy. The area had a per capita personal income of $12,013 in 1983. Nearby Orange is a center for rice milling, petroleum processing and shipping enterprises and is a center for processing timber harvested in East Texas. Lamar University's main campus is located at Beaumont and branch campuses are in Port Arthur and Orange. Proximity to the Gulf also provides numerous recreation opportunities. Sea Rim Park offers 10 miles of protected sand beach.

Brazoria

Brazoria is the state's newest PMSA, having been deleted from the Houston PMSA in June 1983. The Brazoria PMSA, which encompasses Brazoria County, had a population of 178,400 in July 1982, according to the Bureau of the Census. Settled by Stephen F. Austin's colonists in 1821, Brazoria County played a vital role in the struggle for independence from Mexico. Columbia (now West Columbia) served as the first capital of the Republic, and Texas' first Congress met there on Oct. 22, 1836. Brazoria County claims the world's largest basic chemical complex at Brazosport, a nine-city community anchored by Freeport and Lake Jackson. In 1982, 186 manufacturers in Brazoria County employed more than 17,800 people in plants producing primarily petrochemical products. The manufacturing payroll was $505,300,000. Value of manufactured shipments was $6,441,700,000. Retail sales amounted to $795,628,000; wholesale sales brought in $403,311,000 and service industries contributed more than $245,984,000 to the economy. The area had a per capita personal income of $11,860 in 1983. The Brazosport area is also home to a sizable shrimp and commercial fishing fleet. Tourists flock to Brazoria County's 20 miles of sandy beach. They also are attracted by the historic Varner-Hogg Plantation, formerly the home of Gov. James Stephen Hogg, and a replica of the first capitol of the Republic of Texas.

★ ORANGE ★
A GREAT TASTE OF TEXAS!

Has Everything To Offer!

- Historical Homes
- Stark House (1894)
- Presbyterian Church (1912)
- Stark Museum of Art
- Heritage House Museum
- Brown Mansion
- Lutcher Theater of Performing Arts
- Claiborne West Park
- Hunting & Salt or Fresh Water Fishing
- Natatorium
- Lamar University at Orange
- Delta Downs Race Track

Home of International Gumbo Cookoff 1st Saturday in May

Nowhere in our nation does Texas, Mexican and Cajun French culture and cuisine come together and blend so well. Generations of men have searched the banks of Sabine River for Jean LaFitte's hidden treasures. Cypress swamps, western and Indian art, Cajun and TexMex flavor greets visitors to Orange.

Birthday Party Homecoming March 1-2, 1986

Join us for celebrations throughout the sesquicentennial year! Orange will begin by dedicating a star shaped flower bed, designed by logo designer Tim Finnel on January 1st. Heritage arts festivals, a reinactment of the first settlers landing along the banks of the Sabine River, parades, reunions, square dancing, historical home tours are just a few events you won't want to miss.

International Gumbo Cook-Off, boat tours, Star Spangled 4th, suntan contests, ski shows, Bridge City Bayou Bash Days create fun filled weekends just for you.

History will repeat itself during a weekend of "War Between the States" highlighting 1861-1865. Hot air balloon tours, art shows, quilt festival, Vidor Bar-b-que Cookoff, Miss Orange County Beauty Pageant, Trace of Old Lace Style Show, the play "Texas" and a concert by George Straight await you and your homecoming to Orange!

Orange Convention Visitors Bureau • P.O. Box 218 • Orange TX, 77630 • (409)883-3536

The dramatic lighting of the Fort Worth skyline at night (above) lends an air of sophistication to the city "Where the West Begins." Corpus Christi (left) combines business with recreation, to the delight of residents and visitors alike, while Abilene is the site of two major universities (Hardin-Simmons is shown below) as well as one four-year college and a junior college.

Brownsville-Harlingen

At the southernmost tip of Texas is the Brownsville-Harlingen MSA, which comprises Cameron County. The region is one of the fastest growing metropolitan areas in the nation. In 1980, the U.S. Census Bureau reported a population of 209,727. By 1982, the figure had grown to 230,500. With a semi-tropical climate that provides a 341-day growing season, the area is one of the nation's leading producers of citrus fruits and winter vegetables. In addition, seafood processing, fishing, shipping and varied manufacturing are major economic factors. Three major ports and several industrial parks serve as a lure for new industry. In 1982, 187 manufacturing establishments employed 11,400 people with a payroll of $146,700,000. Value of manufactured shipments was $867,000,000. Retail sales amounted to $1,025,512,000; wholesale sales brought in $829,626,000 and the service industries contributed more than $249,054,000 to the economy. In 1983, the area had a per capita personal income of $6,654. Located on the Gulf, with easy access to Mexico and with a mean temperature of 74 degrees, the area has become a major year-round tourist center. Attractions include the Gladys Porter Zoo for endangered species and the Confederate Air Force Museum. Several major events are held each year, including Charro Days in Brownsville each February, RioFest in Harlingen each March and the Cameron County Fair in San Benito each January. Many "snowbirds," residents of northern states, make the area their winter home. Educational facilities include Texas Southmost College in Brownsville and the Rio Grande Campus of Texas State Technical Institute in Harlingen.

Bryan-College Station

The Bryan-College Station MSA is built around Texas A&M University. Encompassing all of Brazos County, the area had a population of 112,100, according to 1982 figures from the Bureau of the Census. That represented a 19.7 percent increase since 1980. The university is located in College Station. Texas A&M's schools of agriculture and engineering are the largest in the nation, and it is one of the nation's leading research centers. In addition to agricultural research, projects in particle physics and development of hydrogen as a fuel are in progress. Bryan is a center of agribusiness for the thriving farm and livestock region. Light manufacturing has been attracted to the community in recent years. In 1982, 72 manufacturing establishments employed 3,200 people with a payroll of $48,900,000. Value of manufactured shipments was $272,500,000. Retail sales amounted to $591,693,000; wholesale sales brought in $283,643,000 and the service industries contributed more than $150,749,000 to the economy. The area had a per capita personal income of $9,085 in 1983. The future for the MSA seems bright, particularly in light of Texas A&M's drive for excellence in many academic disciplines. Additional impetus for development is provided by its location near other major metropolitan areas in Texas, the picturesque countryside and the cultural and athletic events available at the university. The community offers numerous special events as diverse as a kite-flying contest, livestock show, rodeo, jazz festival, Bohemian festival and historic homes tour. More than 200 sanctioned events are planned in celebration of the Sesquicentennial.

The sailboats gracing the Corpus Christi shoreline are just one of the many tourist-related activities that make Corpus Christi one of the favorite playgrounds for Texans and out-of-staters as well.

Corpus Christi

Nueces and San Patricio Counties make up the Corpus Christi MSA. The 2-county area had a population of 344,100, according to the 1982 census figures. The mild climate and the waters of both Corpus Christi Bay and the Gulf of Mexico attract tourists year round. Corpus Christi has become a winter home for many people from other states who come to enjoy the fishing, sailing, surfing, swimming and other water recreation. In addition to being the gateway to Padre Island National Seashore and a major tourist area, Corpus Christi is a major port, a retail center and a center for coastal petrochemical production. Oil and natural gas are produced in the region, and farming and ranching are major economic activities. In addition, a naval air station and an army depot are located in the city. The battleship USS Wisconsin, an aircraft carrier and three support ships will be stationed in Corpus Christi by 1990, creating an annual payroll of more than $50 million with the relocation of 7,500 naval personnel into the area and the creation of 3,000 permanent civilian jobs. In 1982, the Corpus Christi MSA's 276 manufacturing establishments employed 14,900 people with a payroll of $332,000,000. Value of manufactured shipments was $9,087,200,000. Retail sales amounted to $1,844,288,000; wholesale sales brought in $1,978,863,000 and the service industries contributed more than $658,390,000 to the economy. The area had a per capita personal income of $10,503 in 1983. Educational and cultural activities also are available. Corpus Christi State University (part of the University System of South Texas) and Del Mar College are in the city, which also has recreationnal facilities, museums, parks and wildlife refuges.

Dallas' historic West End District shown above has revitalized that part of Dallas with the introduction of cafes of various cultures. The Dallas skyline in its nighttime splendor is shown below.

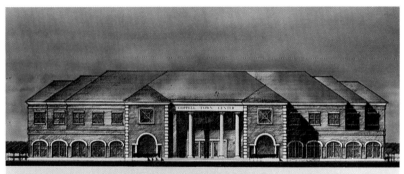

The new downtown Dallas Museum of Art houses many interesting collections.

Dallas

The second largest city in Texas, and seventh in the nation, Dallas had a 1980 population of 904,078, according to census figures. Per capita income in 1983 was $14,222, ranking it 21st in the nation. The backbone of Dallas' industry includes banking, insurance, transportation and data processing, plus such "clean" manufacturing as electronic components. Dallas is a distribution and marketing center for a large part of the Southwest, with many large exhibit facilities, among them the Dallas Market Center, the World Trade Center, and the new Infomart, a computer and computer equipment center. More than 650 firms with a net worth of $1 million or more have their headquarters in Dallas, and it is the home office of more insurance firms than any other U.S. city. In 1982, almost 2,000 conventions were held in Dallas, and conventions and tourism bring in more than 1,640,000 visitors who spend half a billion dollars per year. Dallas ranks third in Texas in spending by the U.S. Department of Defense-- $1.2 billion in fiscal year 1984. Dallas has a world-class symphony, ballet company and opera company, along with several professional and semi-professional theatrical companies. The Dallas Museum of Art is nationally praised, and there are several museums, an aquarium and a garden center on the grounds of Fair Park, which also boasts the largest collection of art deco buildings still standing in the U.S. The quality of life in Dallas earned it a ranking of third in Texas in a survey conducted in 1985 by the University of Texas at Arlington.

Old City Park is shown above. Dallasites have incorporated buildings from different areas of interest into a fascinating park-like atmosphere to show the early history of Dallas. Union Terminal Building, shown below, once served as the railroad terminal for the Dallas area. It now houses cafes and restaurants catering to office workers in the area, as well as serving Amtrak passengers and business.

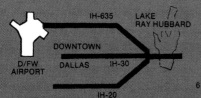

Dallas/Fort Worth

Dallas and Fort Worth are the central cities of a Consolidated Metropolitan Statistical Area that includes nine counties: Dallas, Tarrant, Denton, Collin, Rockwall, Kaufman, Ellis, Johnson and Parker. The CMSA had a population in 1982 of 3,131,200, second in population to the Houston CMSA. A 1985 report from the Census Bureau revealed that between 1980 and 1984, the Dallas/Fort Worth CMSA was the second-fastest-growing MSA in the nation at 14.2 percent, second only to Houston. Although Dallas and Fort Worth dominate the region in population and economic and cultural activities, several of the suburban communities are becoming important cities in their own right. Arlington, with a population of 160,113, has a diverse economy based on manufacturing and warehousing, education and entertainment. The Six Flags amusement park and Arlington Stadium, home of professional baseball's Texas Rangers, are in the city, along with a water recreation park. Garland had 138,857 population in 1980 and has a solid industrial base. Irving, which abuts the D/FW Airport, is the site of Las Colinas, one of the nation's most rapidly growing business districts. Texas Stadium, home of the Dallas Cowboys, is also in Irving, which had a 1980 population of 109,943. Grand Prairie, which along with Richardson and Plano had a 1980 population in excess of 70,000, also is becoming an entertainment center with Traders' Village, a huge flea market, a wild-

The Livestock Exchange Building pictured above is part of the historical restoration of this Fort Worth area.

The Tarrant County Courthouse shown here in downtown Fort Worth houses many of the local government activities of the city.

life park, three museums and a water recreation park. A major economic factor in the region is the D/FW Airport, which was built by Dallas and Fort Worth. One of the major airports in the nation, it makes the region virtually a crossroad for national and world travel. Many firms have moved to the area in recent years because of the travel and shipping convenience afforded by the airpoort. The highly diversified economy of the area includes worldwide petroleum operations, trade and distribution, government, banking, insurance, communications and manufacturing. In 1982, 6,122 manufacturing establishments in the region employed 324,000 people with a payroll of $6,507,200,000. Value of manufactured shipments was $29,856,100,000. Retail sales amounted to $19,189,241,000; wholesale sales brought in $56,806,710,000 and service industries contributed more than $8,541,335,000 to the economy. The area had a per capita personal income of $13,846. More than 1,100 companies with assets of at least $1 million call the Dallas/Fort Worth region home, as do more than 250 insurance companies and more than 80 corporations with stocks on the New York or American exchanges. The area leads the state in the number of visitors and is one of the nation's leading convention centers. Dallas ranks high nationally in the number of attractions it hosts. For more detailed information on the specific counties, see the Texas Counties section of the Almanac, pages 235-376.

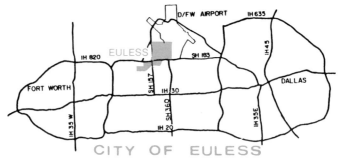

Sundance Square shown above is part of the Fort Worth historical preservation work being done to bring visitors, and hometown folks as well, part of the early history of "Cowtown." The Water Gardens shown below are a restful change of pace in the bustling city of Fort Worth.

The hub of the METROPLEX

This is the year to rediscover the fun of a Texas Vacation. Come to the "Entertainment Capitol" of the state and enjoy Six Flags Over Texas, the most popular attraction in the Southwest. See American League Baseball in Arlington Stadium with the Texas Rangers. Experience Wet 'n Wild, the world's largest water fun theme park. Other local attractions include Traders Village, Wax Museum of the Southwest, Texas Sports Hall of Fame, White Water and International Wildlife Park. Call or write for complete details.

Arlington...a great place, a great vacation and a great price!

Arlington Convention & Visitors Bureau
P.O. Box A / Arlington, TX 76010 / (817) 265-7721

The growth of Fort Worth from a thriving frontier outpost to a bustling, dynamic city is shown by the downtown skyline that greets the eye today.

Fort Worth/Arlington

Fast-growing Fort Worth had a population in 1982 of 385,164 housed in 156,031 housing units. Known by its motto, ''Where the West Begins,'' Fort Worth has a diverse business and industrial community that includes state-of-the-art aerospace activities and the gigantic, Western-themed nightclub, Billy Bob's Texas. It has ultramodern electronic banking and the historic Fort Worth Stockyards. There is also a major agribusiness complex, including large grain storage facilities. Seven major railroads interconnect in Fort Worth, making it a shipping hub for the southwest. The U.S. Department of Defense spent more money in Fort Worth in fiscal year 1984, $3.1 billion, than in any other area in Texas. Eight colleges and universities, with a combined enrollment of 63,000 students, call Fort Worth home. Prominent among these are Texas Christian University and Texas Wesleyan College. Fort Worth's cultural community is enhanced by a large number of excellent museums, among them the Kimbell Art Museum, the Amon Carter Museum of Western Art and the Museum of Science and History. The downtown area is a visually interesting mix of modern and historic buildings. Many sesquicentennial events and celebrations are planned during 1986. For details, contact the chamber of commerce or the sesquicentennial committee. Medical care in Fort Worth is furnished by 41 hospitals and 50 private convalescent homes. Arlington, just east of Fort Worth, has a large and diverse industrial district, where plants make automobiles, food products, farm and oil field equipment, electronic components, medical supplies, concrete products, rubber and plastic products, among others. Institutions of higher learning in Arlington include the University of Texas at Arlington, Arlington Baptist College and Bauder Fashion College. The health needs of Arlington residents are met by medical and psychiatric hospitals and several nursing homes. The Arlington amusement park, Six Flags Over Texas, is a favorite destination of visitors to North Texas. The major league baseball club, the Texas Rangers, also calls Arlington home.

Three aspects of Fort Worth are illustrated here: The always bustling Amon G. Carter Jr. Exhibits Hall houses many varied events (above left); the tranquil Trinity River (above right) as it flows near Fort Worth; and the Omni Theatre (below), which offers spectacular "wrap-around" movies.

El Paso

The El Paso MSA comprises El Paso County, and it is the westernmost MSA in Texas, serving a trade area that extends into large parts of West Texas, Mexico and New Mexico. In 1982, it had a population of 513,400, according to census figures. Government, education, tourism and manufacturing are the cornerstones of the region's economy. Refining, ore processing, oil production and agricultural products also contribute significantly. In 1982, 471 manufacturing establishments employed 38,300 people with a payroll of $465,900,000. Value of manufactured shipments was $4,221,000,000. Retail sales amounted to $2,120,722,000; wholesale sales brought in $2,830,211,000 and service industries contributed more than $600,182,000 to the economy. The area had a per capita personal income in 1983 of $8,290. As a center for government in the Southwest, El Paso County also benefits from federal expenditures of more than $1 billion a year. Government installations include Fort Bliss, William Beaumont Army Medical Center and the U.S. Army Air Defense Command. With its twin city of Ciudad Juarez just across the Rio Grande, the El Paso area is part of the largest urban area on the U.S.-Mexico border. With strong Spanish influence, El Paso has diverse cultural and recreational attractions. The oldest missions in Texas are located in the city, and museums, art galleries and splendid shopping opportunities on both sides of the border attract many visitors. The annual Sun Carnival is held in December. Educational facilities include the University of Texas at El Paso and El Paso Community College.

Killeen-Temple

Bell and Coryell Counties comprise the Killeen-Temple MSA, which was among the fastest growing areas in the nation in the 1970s. In 1982, the Bureau of the Census reported an area population of 223,000. Military payrolls are a cornerstone of the local economy. Killeen is located at the main entrance to Fort Hood, and the military base extends over parts of Bell and Coryell Counties. In 1984, 41,951 soldiers were stationed there. Health services and manufacturing are also important to the region's economy. In 1982, 139 manufacturing establishments employed 7,300 people with a payroll of $111,100,000. Value of manufactured shipments was $629,200,000. Retail sales amounted to $892,169,000; wholesale sales brought in $586,342,000, and service industries contributed more than $229,566,000 to the economy. The area had a per capita personal income of $9,930 in 1983. Temple is internationally known as a medical center with hospitals that are among the world's finest. Texas A&M University College of Medicine students receive part of their clinical training at Scott and White Memorial Hospital and the Olin E. Teague Veterans' Medical Center in Temple, which also is affiliated with other college programs in health science training. Other schools in the area are Temple Junior College, the University of Mary Hardin-Baylor in Belton and the American Technological University and Central Texas College in Killeen. In addition, recreational facilities are available in the region, and picturesque Salado has long been a favorite tourist destination.

Hundreds of miles of white sand beach (above) and a mild climate lure thousands of visitors to Texas' Gulf Coast each year. The stage of Houston's Jones Hall for the Performing Arts (below) showcases some of the world's greatest performances.

The remodeled Galvez Hotel shown above is one of many modern hotels and motels that line the seawall of this popular vacation spot.

Galveston-Texas City

Some 207,600 people lived in the Galveston-Texas City MSA, according to 1982 census figures. The area covers Galveston County, which also is part of the larger Houston-Galveston-Brazoria CMSA. The CMSA increased 15 percent in population between 1980 and 1984, according to a 1985 Census Bureau report, due largely to the growth in Galveston. Galveston has been important since before Texas gained its independence from Mexico. Pirates once used the island as a base from which to raid in the Gulf. The port, the state's oldest and one of the most modern, ranks as one of the world's largest cotton ports. Texas City's deepwater port serves the community's large industrial complex that includes oil refineries and petrochemical plants. Port-related services in the area include ship repair and offshore oil and gas activities. In 1982, 134 manufacturing establishments employed 11,200 people with a payroll of $317,000,000 to produce a variety of goods including copper products, pipe, oil well drilling fluids, chemicals and paper products. Value of manufactured shipments was $11,426,300,000. Retail sales amounted to $1,042,954,000; wholesale sales brought in $448,819,000 and service industries contributed more than $263,285,000 to the economy. The area had a per capita personal income of $12,323 in 1983. The University of Texas Medical Branch is located in Galveston, as is the world-famous Shriners Burn Institute. Institutions of higher learning include Galveston College, the National Maritime Research Center and Texas A&M University at Galveston. College of the Mainland is located at Texas City. One of the most historic cities in Texas, Galveston is a favorite of tourists. The historical drama, "Lone Star," is presented during the summer at the Mary Moody Northen Amphitheater in Galveston Island State Park. Museums and art galleries are of interest, as are the many historic buildings in the city. Scenic beaches along the Gulf of Mexico and the warm climate have also helped attract Texans and others to the island community.

The thriving Port of Houston shown above ranks second or third among U.S. ports in the export of various items.

Houston

Houston is Texas' largest metropolitan area and one of the most dynamic cities in the nation. In 1982, Houston ranked fifth nationally in population behind New York, Chicago, Los Angeles and Philadelphia, with a population of 1,595,138. The Houston-Galveston-Brazoria Consolidated Metropolitan Statistical Area, which includes the old Galveston-Texas City SMSA, had a population in 1982 of 3,446,500. A 1985 report from the Census Bureau revealed that this area increased 15 percent in population between 1980 and 1984, more than any other MSA. This increase pulled them from ninth to eighth place among the nation's metropolitan areas. Houston is highly industrialized, with more than 3,800 manufacturing plants and the nation's largest concentration of petrochemical plants. In addition, the Port of Houston is one of the busiest in the nation, ranking among the top ports in the tonnage handled and in the amount of foreign trade that passes through it. In 1982, the CMSA boasted 5,139 manufacturing establishments employing 277,400 people with a payroll of $6,855,000,000. Value of manufactured shipments in the CMSA was $63,473,400,000. Retail sales amounted to $20,662,251,000; wholesale sales brought in $99,136,916,000 and service industries contributed more than $11,699,465,000 to the economy. In 1983, the city of Houston had a per capita personal income of $13,655. The international nature of Houston's economy is reflected in the fact that the city has 64 foreign bank branches, 27 foreign trade, investment and tourism offices and the fifth largest consular corps in the U.S. With 62 hospitals, Houston is a major medical research and treatment center. The city is the home of Rice University, the University Houston and several other schools. Houston's cultural attractions include world-class ballet, symphony and opera as well as art and science museums and several excellent theaters. Tourism and conventions are also major segments of the region's economy. Points of interest include the Astrodome, home of professional football and baseball teams, the Lyndon B. Johnson Space Center, the San Jacinto Battleground State Park, the Houston Convention Center and many other attractions. Numerous towns in the region plan many varied events for the Sesquicentennial. Check with chambers of commerce for details. For more information, see Harris County under the Counties section in the Almanac.

Visitors line up outside the capital of the Republic of the Rio Grande at Laredo.

Laredo

Laredo is the central city of the MSA that covers Webb County. The area, which borders on the Rio Grande, had a population of 109,900 in 1982, according to the U.S. Census Bureau. Laredo is one of the oldest cities in Texas, having been established by Tomas Sanchez in 1755 on a land grant issued by the great Spanish colonizer Jose de Escandon. From its earliest history, Laredo was a transportation hub, at one time having one of the first ferries operating across the river. For many years, Laredo was a major point on the Camino Real between Mexico City and San Antonio de Bexar. Today it is a major link in trade between the United States and Mexico, which includes warehousing and import and export activities. In addition, Laredo is a trade center for a large agricultural production region, which is based on the region's 322-day growing season. Manufacturing also provides a part of Laredo's economy. In 1982, 56 manufacturing plants employed 1,500 people with a payroll of $16,800,000; value of manufactured shipments was $74,800,000. Retail sales amounted to $701,337,000; wholesale sales brought in $399,066,000, and service industries contributed more than $107,953,000 to the economy. In 1983, the area had a per capita personal income of $6,017. Tourism also is a major activity. Points of historical interest, plus the markets in both Laredo and its sister city of Nuevo Laredo, provide visitors many attractions. Many meetings and conventions are held in Laredo. Laredo Junior College and Laredo State University are located in the city.

Longview-Marshall

The Longview-Marshall MSA comprises Gregg and Harrison Counties, with a 1982 population of 165,200, according to the U.S. Census Bureau. The scenic Piney Woods of Northeast Texas are the backdrop for the region. While tourism and recreation are not the major economic factors, they are growing in importance. There are several area lakes, and Kilgore has an outstanding oil industry museum. Discovery of oil and natural gas in the area in the 1930s changed the rural character of the region. Longview became a petroleum production center. Manufacturing grew in importance. Kilgore is in the heart of the famous East Texas oil field. Marshall is a growing community with varied industrial development and recreational facilities, including nearby Caddo Lake and Lake O' The Pines. It was named an All American city for the Bicentennial year. These communities have experienced major industrial growth in the past three decades, and their manufacturing plants produce a wide variety of products. In 1982, the area had 286 manufacturing plants employing 16,000 people with a payroll of $336,300,000. Value of manufactured shipments that year was $2,204,900,000. Retail sales amounted to $1,064,402,000; wholesale sales brought in $1,168,782,000, and service industries contributed more than $310,704,000 to the economy. The area had a per capita personal income of $11,008 in 1983. LeTourneau College is located at Longview, and Kilgore is the home of Kilgore College and the famous Kilgore Rangerettes. Educational facilities at Marshall include Wiley College and East Texas Baptist College.

Lubbock

The Lubbock MSA encompasses Lubbock County, which by the 1982 Census had a population of 216,700. The area's early history was one of Plains Indians, buffalo hunters and ranchers. The rich grasses of the South Plains were ideal for cattle. Farmers replaced cattlemen around the turn of the century, and cotton was soon the region's leading crop. With the development of irrigation, Lubbock became the center of one of the world's leading cotton and grain producing regions. Lubbock is the world's largest cottonseed processing center and is headquarters for a large cotton cooperative. The city of Lubbock is the center of a large trade and distribution area. In 1982, 292 manufacturing establishments in the Lubbock MSA employed 11,700 people with a payroll of $197,700,000. Value of manufactured shipments was $949,500,000. Retail sales amounted to $1,344,799,000; wholesale sales brought in another $2,714,813,000, and service industries contributed more than $388,487,000 to the economy. The area had a per capita personal income of $11,123 in 1983. Two institutions of higher learning—Texas Tech University and Health Science Center and Lubbock Christian College—are located in the city. There are a number of tourist attractions. A Ranching Heritage Center on the Texas Tech campus preserves structures and the culture of the settlers of the High Plains. Mackenzie State Park is located nearby, and the Lubbock Lake archaeological site is one of the most interesting in the state.

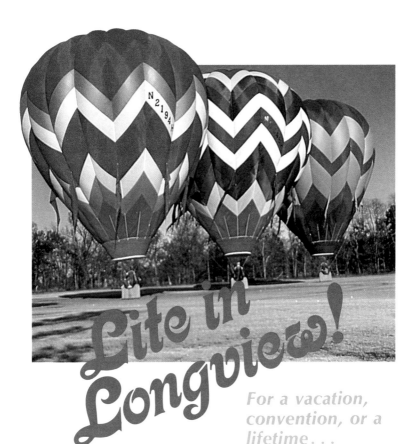

The old and the modern exist comfortably together in Longview: the Rempert Bank Building (above), site of the infamous Dalton gang's last raid, and the Student Memorial Building (below) at Le Tourneau College.

McAllen-Edinburg-Mission

The cities of McAllen, Edinburg and Mission are centers of a metropolitan area that covers Hidalgo County in the Lower Rio Grande Valley. The region's population in 1982 was 315,100, according to the U.S. Census Bureau. It is one of the fastest-growing MSAs in the nation and ranks among the highest foreign trade zones. This area has a longer history than much of Texas, having been settled by the Spanish colonizer Jose de Escandon in the mid-1700s. Cattle raising was the first major industry. When railroad development reached the Lower Rio Grande Valley after 1900, land developers began attracting farmers to take advantage of the rich soil through irrigation. The area now is a winter garden with a growing season of 327 days each year. Production, processing and shipping of citrus fruits, vegetables, cotton and livestock are major economic factors. In 1982, there were 171 manufacturing plants in the MSA employing 7,100 people with a payroll of $79,200,000; value of manufactured shipments was $547,000,000. Retail sales amounted to $1,352,119,000; wholesale sales brought in $1,357,790,000, and service industries contributed more than $249,063,000 to the economy. The area had a per capita personal income of $6,012 in 1983.

With a 327-day growing season, Hidalgo County produces a wide variety of vegetables (top) and citrus fruits, as well as the decorative palm trees that line many highways throughout the Lower Rio Grande Valley (below).

Midland

Midland is the hub of a metropolitan area covering Midland County. The 1982 population was 97,400, according to the U.S. Census Bureau. The city ranked fourth in a University of Texas at Arlington survey on the quality of life in Texas' 52 largest cities. The petroleum industry dominates the area's economy. Midland is an administrative and operations center for production in the Permian Basin, which for much of the 20th century has been the nation's most productive petroleum reservoir. Midland was established in the 1870s. Originally, the area was a farming and ranching community. But with the discovery of oil in the Permian Basin in 1923, exploration, production and processing became the major economic enterprises. Plants manufacturing electronic components have been opened recently in the area. In 1982, a total of 139 manufacturing plants employed 4,300 people with a payroll of $92,300,000; value of manufactured shipments was $427,700,000. Retail sales amounted to $713,358,000; wholesale sales brought in $2,334,324,000, and service industries contributed more than $328,985,000 to the economy. The area had a per capita personal income of $15,507. In 1983, the city of Midland ranked eighth nationally in per capita income, with $15,507, and ranked first in Texas.

Odessa

Odessa is the central city of a metropolitan area covering Ector County. The Census Bureau's 1982 population count for the area was 134,200. Odessa is one of the West Texas cities that owes much of its development to the discovery of oil. Established by the Texas & Pacific Railroad in 1886, it was initially a cow town with some agriculture. When oil was discovered in 1929, the character of the community soon changed. Petroleum production and associated services dominated the economy. Odessa is now the operations center for many oil companies in the rich Permian Basin. It continues to be a service and supply center for petroleum production, and a large petrochemical complex is located in the area. Many manufacturing plants have located near Odessa. In 1982, 323 manufacturing plants employed 8,600 people with a payroll of $182,300,000. Value of manufactured shipments was $1,561,500,000. Retail sales amounted to $993,340,000; wholesale sales brought in $1,679,140,000, and service industries contributed more than $368,461,000 to the economy. In 1983, the area had a per capita personal income of $11,512. Odessa's per capita income the same year was $11,512. Educational and cultural activities are available in the city. The University of Texas of the Permian Basin and Odessa College are located in Odessa, as is the Texas Tech Academic Health Center. The famous Globe Theatre, an authentic replica of Shakespeare's 16th century Globe Theatre in London, is a major attraction. Odessa has many museums, the Prairie Dog Park and nearby Meteor Crater. In addition, many fairs and festivals make this a favorite tourist area.

Midland is shown on this page in varying aspects from the skyscraper looming in the downtown area, on the left, to the night scene of the skyline shown immediately below, to the buildings, fountains and strolling area shown in the bottom photo.

San Angelo

San Angelo is the central city of the metropolitan area that comprises Tom Green County in West Texas. The 1982 census figures report a population of 90,700 for the county. San Angelo was established as a trading post near Fort Concho on the West Texas frontier in 1867. When the railroads arrived in the late 1880s, the city became a shipping point and distribution center for a wide area. Today the city is a center for petroleum production, as well as for cattle, sheep, goats and other agricultural products. San Angelo has long been recognized as the "Sheep and Wool Capital of the World." It is the nation's largest primary wool market and is a leading center for producing, processing and shipping wool and mohair. Manufacturing also plays a role in San Angelo's economy. In 1982, 101 manufacturing plants employed 5,100 people with a payroll of $70,200,000; value of manufactured shipments was $363,100,000. Retail sales amounted to $571,448,000; wholesale sales brought in $621,333,000, and service industries contributed more than $163,165,000 to the economy. The area had a per capita personal income of $11,580 in 1983. Angelo State University and a Texas A&M University Research and Extension Center are located in the community. Tourist attractions include three lakes, the Fort Concho Museum, Fiesta del Concho and other events.

San Antonio

San Antonio is the 11th largest city in the nation and the third largest in Texas, according to the 1980 census. It is the core city for a metropolitan area that includes Bexar, Comal and Guadalupe Counties, which in 1982 had a population of 1,141,000. San Antonio was rated the second best place in Texas to live by a study made by the University of Texas at Arlington in 1985. San Antonio is one of Texas' most picturesque and historic cities. In the mid-18th century, it was the capital of the Spanish province of Texas. A major tourist destination, San Antonio is home of one of Texas' most revered shrines, the Alamo. Other major attractions include four Spanish missions located in the city, the Paseo del Rio (river walk), the Tower of the Americas and HemisFair Plaza, the Institute of Texan Cultures and Brackenridge Park. The Folklife Festival in July-August draws many visitors. San Antonio has long been a military center and was the site at which much of the development of the nation's early military aviation took place. Fort Sam Houston, Brooke Army Medical Center and Brooks, Kelly, Lackland and Randolph Air Force bases are located in the area. The metropolitan area serves as a wholesale, retail, financial and distribution center for a wide area and has varied manufacturing plants. In 1982, 1,024 manufacturing establishments employed 50,600 people with a payroll of $786,200,000; value of manufactured shipments was $3,759,300,000. Retail sales amounted to $5,553,729,000; wholesale sales brought in $7,213,403,000, and service industries contributed more than $1,919,289,000 to the economy. San Antonio's per capita income was $10,569 in 1983. Education facilities include the University of Texas at San Antonio, San Antonio College, St. Philip's College, Incarnate Word College, Our Lady of the Lake University, St. Mary's University and Trinity University.

The historic Alamo in San Antonio is shown at right, while below left a calf roping contest is held in San Angelo.

The San Antonio river walk is shown in photo above right, while the historic Fort Concho Museum in San Angelo is shown to the left.

The municipal rose garden at Tyler is shown above. Tyler is known worldwide for its roses and is known as the "Rose Capital." Below is a home in Tyler with beautiful azaleas in bloom. Tyler sponsors an Azalea Trail each spring.

Texarkana

The Texarkana metropolitan area—which had a population of 126,904 in the 1980 census—consists of Bowie County, Texas, and Miller County, Ark. In 1982, the Texas population was 76,500. Texarkana, the central city in the MSA, sits astride the Texas-Arkansas state line. The city serves as a trade and transportation center for a region that also includes parts of Oklahoma and Louisiana. The fertile Red River Valley bisects the region, and Texarkana is the agribusiness center for rich farming, livestock and timber enterprises. A U.S. Army depot and ordnance plant near Texarkana, Texas, are major economic factors in the region. Manufacturing plants also produce a wide variety of goods. In 1982, there were 127 manufacturing establishments employing 8,400 people with a payroll of $178,100,000. Value of manufactured shipments was $1,025,500,000. Retail sales amounted to $622,158,000; wholesale sales brought in $486,726,000, and service industries contributed more than $145,119,000 to the economy. The area had a per capita personal income of $9,557 in 1983. Texarkana Community College and East Texas State University at Texarkana provide excellent educational opportunities for residents of the region. Superb recreational opportunities also exist at several large lakes in the region, including Wright Patman and Caddo, and at Crystal Springs Beach at Maud.

Tyler

Tyler is the central city of a metropolitan area that covers Smith County. The area's population, according to the 1982 census, was 136,700. Tyler is an administrative and operations center for petroleum production throughout the rich East Texas oil field. In addition, manufacturing and processing play an important role in the Tyler MSA's economy. In 1982, 168 manufacturing establishments employed 12,300 people with a payroll of $221,500,000. Value of manufactured shipments was $1,632,700,000. Retail sales amounted to $801,304,000; wholesale sales brought in $1,051,782,000, and service industries contributed more than $332,927,000 to the economy. The area had a per capita personal income of $12,188 in 1983. Tyler is famous for its production of field-grown rose bushes. It is the nation's largest rose bush growing area, producing an estimated 20 million bushes a year, which is about half the national supply. It is also a rich crop and livestock area. Visitors by the thousands come each year to Tyler to the Azalea Trails in the spring and to the autumn Rose Festival. Many also visit the municipal rose garden. In addition, the city boasts museums, a planetarium, a children's zoo and other attractions. Many lakes and the Tyler State Park are nearby. Tyler also is a major medical center, and its educational facilities include the University of Texas at Tyler, Tyler Junior College and Texas College.

Victoria

Victoria was designated an MSA as a result of 1980 census figures. The metropolitan area, which encompasses Victoria county, had a population of 72,900 in 1982. Mexican colonizer Martin de Leon founded Victoria in 1824, which makes it the second oldest city in Texas. The entire region has a rich and colorful history. With a barge canal that connects to the nation's super-highway system of waterways via the Gulf Intracoastal Waterway, the Victoria metropolitan area is a center for industrial expansion. In 1982, an estimated 62 plants employing 3,600 persons earning $85,100,000, manufactured goods, including steel products, oil field and foundry equipment, aluminum and petro-chemicals, with a manufactured value of $644,200,000. Retail sales amounted to $492,936,000; wholesale sales brought in $1,051,782,000 and service industries contributed $17,756,000 to the economy. The area had a per capita personal income of $11,928 in 1983. Victoria is also an agribusiness center, with grain sorghum and beef cattle the major revenue producers. Attractions in Victoria include the Victoria Symphony Orchestra, the Fine Arts Association, historic homes and a nationally recognized Bach Festival. Whether one prefers hunting and fishing, visiting museums or basking in the sun on a sandy beach, all this and more can be found within a two-hour drive of Victoria. Victoria is the medical center for a seven-county area, with the newest and most advanced equipment available. Victoria College and the Victoria branch of the University of Houston offer two-year, four-year and post-graduate degrees, and their evening courses continue to be very popular in the community.

The charming Old Courthouse in Victoria is but one of the many historic buildings and sites in the city.

VICTORIA!

Just a two-hour drive from Austin, Houston and San Antonio, Victoria enjoys the warm, mild climate of the Texas Gulf Coast…and worker productivity 50% above the national average. Victoria, ranked 16th nationwide in terms of business economics.

Victoria offers the components that make a business operation competitive: excellent accessibility to supplies and materials via 3 U.S. highways, rail service, a modern barge canal and commercial air transportation. Plus low housing costs, no labor unions, and short commuting times to work.

VICTORIA…shouldn't you be here?

Victoria Economic Development Corporation (512) 575-0241

Sherman-Denison

Sherman and Denison, situated near Lake Texoma and the Red River, are the principal cities of a metropolitan area that covers Grayson County. In 1982, the U.S. Census Bureau reported a population of 92,300. North Texas and Southern Oklahoma are served by the trade and distribution centers located in the two cities. This is a rich farming and livestock section of the state, and both communities have food processing plants. Manufacturing also has been attracted to the area, and the plants produce a variety of goods. In 1982, 127 manufacturing establishments employed 11,100 people with a payroll of $223,000,000; value of manufactured shipments was $1,490,700,000. Retail sales amounted to $488,622,000; wholesale sales brought in $273,523,000, and service industries contributed more than $106,902,000 to the economy. The area had a per capita personal income of $11,148 in 1983. A growing number of people who work in the Dallas-Fort Worth area commute from Sherman-Denison. Excellent educational facilities are available to residents of both cities. Austin College is located in Sherman, and Grayson County College is located midway between the two communities. Tourist attractions in the area include President Dwight Eisenhower's birthplace in Denison, Lake Texoma, Eisenhower State Park and Grayson County Frontier Village.

One of the largest lakes in Texas, Lake Texoma (left) near Sherman and Denison, offers a full range of water-related activities.

Since 1849, Austin College in Sherman (right) has offered excellent educational opportunities to students throughout the state.

Waco

Waco is the major city of a metropolitan area that covers McLennan County. The U.S. Census Bureau's 1982 population count for the area was 175,500. Built on the site of an ancient Waco Indian village, the first Anglo settlement occurred in 1837 when the Texas Rangers established a camp by the springs that flowed in the area. The camp became Fort Fisher. Waco has long been a major banking, transportation and retail trade center for a large segment of the state. It began as an agribusiness center when Central Texas was one of the world's largest cotton producing regions. It continues to serve the fertile Blacklands farm belt, which produces grains, grasses for livestock and other crops as well as cotton. Numerous manufacturing plants have located in Waco because of the city's central location among the major metropolitan areas of Texas. In 1982, there were 261 manufacturing establishments in the Waco MSA employing 14,900 people with a payroll of $237,100,000. Value of manufactured shipments was $1,328,100,000. Retail sales amounted to $943,336,000; wholesale sales brought in $1,187,986,000, and service industries contributed more than $261,577,000 to the economy. The area had a per capita personal income of $10,958 in 1983. Educational institutions include Baylor University, McLennan County Community College, Texas State Technical Institute and Paul Quinn College. Tourist attractions include Cameron Park, a beauty spot on the banks of the Brazos River, which flows through the city, and the Texas Ranger Hall of Fame. Special events like the Brazos River Festival and Cotton Palace Pageant lure visitors. A hall of fame for Texas high school football, basketball and tennis stars also is open.

Wichita Falls

Wichita Falls is the central city of a metropolitan area that comprises Wichita County. In 1982, the U.S. Census Bureau listed 125,500 people living in the Wichita Falls MSA. The area was a favorite Indian hunting ground until the 1870s. With the arrival of the railroads in 1882, Wichita Falls became a transportation center; the first cargo was a load of buffalo bones. The region has since become an important manufacturing, wholesale and retail and distribution center for a large section of North Texas and southern Oklahoma. Wichita County was one of the state's earliest petroleum-producing areas, and today it is a leading operations center for North Texas oil production. Agribusiness is an important economic factor, and manufacturing plants within the area produce a variety of goods. In 1982, 179 manufacturing establishments had manufactured shipments valued at approximately $865 million. Retail sales amounted to $782,703,000; wholesale sales brought in $576,384,000, and service industries contributed more than $231,277,000. The 1983 per capita income was $11,970. Sheppard Air Force Base makes a major contribution to the area's economy. Cultural, athletic and recreational events are offered at Midwestern University, and Vernon Regional Junior College is nearby in Wilbarger County. Lakes Wichita, Kemp, Kickapoo and Arrowhead provide important recreational facilities for the region.

San Antonio, one of Texas' most picturesque and historic cities, is also the third largest city in the state and eleventh largest in the nation.

Population Characteristics of Texas

The following article was written especially for this edition of the Texas Almanac by R. L. Skrabanek, professor emeritus, Department of Sociology, Texas A&M University, College Station.

Population Growth

The **U. S. Bureau of the Census** estimated Texas' population for July 1, 1984, at 15,989,000. This is an increase of 1,759,000 over the 14,229,000 people counted in the April 1, 1980, census. More people have been added to the state's population since 1980 than during any comparable period in the history of the state and this follows on the heels of Texas' previous all-time high in population growth of more than 3 million in the 1970s. Thus, about 30 percent of the state's total number of people in 1984 have been added only in the last 14 years. Only one state — California — added more people since 1970.

The state's population growth rate between 1980 and 1984 (12.4 percent) was three times higher than the nation as a whole (4.2 percent). It outstripped the nation's population growth rate by the widest margin ever. Furthermore, Texas added more than twice the total number of people as all of the combined northern states in the last four years.

Texas currently ranks third among states in total population as compared with sixth in 1960, having passed Ohio and Illinois in the 1960s and Pennsylvania in the 1970s. California's estimated population of 25,622,000 and New York's 17,735,000 exceeded Texas' 15,989,000 people by fairly wide margins in 1984. But if New York and Texas population growth patterns continue at the same pace as between 1980 and 1984, Texas will pass New York to become the nation's second most populous state before 1990.

Migration from other states and regions is playing a much larger role in Texas' population growth in the 1980s than in the past. Census Bureau estimates indicate a total of 630,000 births and 246,000 deaths in Texas during the first 27 months following the national census of April 1, 1980, for a natural increase of 384,000 persons. During this same period, the state attracted 667,000 more residents through migration than left the state. In some ways, Texas can be compared to a giant human

magnet pulling in increasingly larger numbers of people. The state had approximately 300,000 net in-migrants in each of the first two years of the 1980s. This far outstrips an estimated net in-migration of approximately 177,000 per year in the 1970s and an annual average of only 21,400 in the 1960s and 11,400 in the 1950s.

In the 1950s net migration accounted for only 6 percent of Texas' total population growth. This figure jumped to 13 percent of all additional Texans in the 1960s and took a quantum leap in the 1970s, when migration accounted for 58 percent of Texas' total population growth. In the first two years of the 1980s, 63 percent of Texas' population growth came from net migration.

In spite of the number of people almost doubling since 1950, Texas is still one of the less densely populated states in the nation. In 1980, the state contained 54.3 persons per square mile of land area, a population density exceeded by 29 other states. Texas was well below the national average of 64 persons per square mile in 1980.

Population densities vary greatly in different parts of the state, with East Texas being more densely populated than other areas. In 1980, population densities ranged from 1,769 persons per square mile in **Dallas County** to 0.1 per square mile in **Loving County.** Only four of the state's 254 counties had over 500 persons per square mile (Bexar, Dallas, Harris and Tarrant), while at the other extreme seven had less than one person per square mile (Culberson, Hudspeth, Jeff Davis, Kenedy, Loving, McMullen and Terrell). All of these are in the western and southern portions of the state.

Although Texas is experiencing record-breaking population growth, the state's 254 counties have wide disparities in their increases and losses. There also is a wide range in the number of people living in different counties. Harris County had the largest number of people in 1982 — 2,684,000 — followed by Dallas County with 1,641,000, and Bexar County with 1,052,000. Harris County had 18 percent of the state's population in 1982 and Dallas County 11 percent. The six counties with the largest populations — Harris, Dallas, Bexar, Tarrant, El Paso and Travis — had almost one-half (48 percent) of the state's people.

At the other extreme, Loving County had the fewest people — 100 — in 1982. Three other counties, all of which are in West or South Texas, had less than 1,000. These were King (400), Kenedy (500) and McMullen (800).

A much larger proportion of counties are experiencing population gains than in past years. For example, 222 of the state's 254 counties had increases between 1980 and 1982, but between 1970 and 1980 only 210 registered population gains.

Harris County recorded the largest increase (274,000) between 1980 and 1982, followed by Dallas County (85,000). Four others — Bexar, Tarrant, Travis and El Paso — each had population increases of over 25,000. These six counties with the largest population gains accounted for 52 percent of the state's additional people between 1980 and 1982, with Harris County alone accounting for 26 percent of the state's total population increase.

Residential Composition

Just 45 years ago, Texas had more rural residents than urban. By 1970, however, 80 percent of the state's people lived in urban places. Since the proportionate share that urban residents make up of the state's population remained unchanged during the last decade, four out of five Texans lived in urban areas in 1980. Texas ranks 11th among all states with the highest proportion of urban population and is above the national level, which has 74 percent of its residents classified as urban. The state's urban population increased by 2,411,000 between 1970 and 1980. This growth has been so rapid that Texas had three cities listed in the top 10 most populous cities in the United States in 1982. Houston ranked fourth with 1,726,000. Dallas was seventh with 944,000 and San Antonio ranked tenth with 819,000.

The rural population of Texas peaked in 1940 at 3,503,000 but declined steadily until 1970 when over 2,267,000 people lived in rural areas. However, the 1970s saw a turnaround after three consecutive decades of population losses in rural parts of Texas, with the number jumping back up to 2,897,000 in 1980. Thus, in spite of an increase of 630,000 in the 1970s, rural areas of the state still have approximately 600,000 fewer people than they had in 1940.

Although rural areas have only one-fifth of the state's people, Texas still has a large rural population

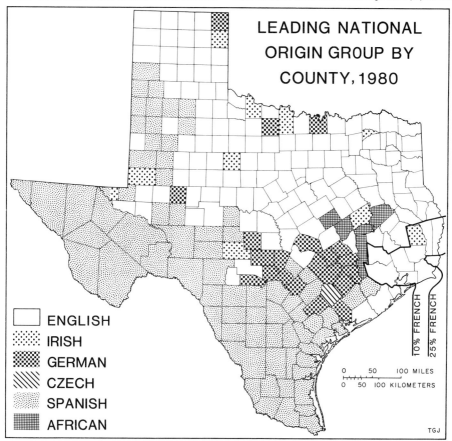

LEADING NATIONAL ORIGIN GROUP BY COUNTY, 1980

ENGLISH
IRISH
GERMAN
CZECH
SPANISH
AFRICAN

10% FRENCH
25% FRENCH

0   50   100 MILES
0 50 100 KILOMETERS

TGJ

This map was prepared by Terry G. Jordan, professor of Geography at The University of Texas at Austin. It is based on computer tapes of the 1980 census of the United States, the first to include a question about remote national ancestry. For each Texas county, the shadings indicate the largest national origin group, including persons wholly or partially of that ancestry. French ancestry was in no county the largest, but the population reported as fully or partially French is shown for southeastern Texas. The English and Irish counties should be regarded as part of a single ancestral region, since both involve British ancestry dating back, in most cases, to colonial times. "English" seems to have been exaggerated in numbers and used by many as synonymous with "British." Preparation of this map was funded by the endowment of the Walter Prescott Webb Chair in History and Ideas, of which Professor Jordan is the present holder.

Famous statewide, the Fort Worth Botanic Garden offers a peaceful respite from the daily rush of business.

based on several standards. For example, 23 of the 50 states that make up the nation have total populations that are smaller than the rural population of Texas. Only two states (Pennsylvania and North Carolina) had more rural residents than Texas in 1980. Moreover, half of Texas' counties had more rural people than urban in 1980, and the entire populations of 52 counties were classified as rural in 1980.

Not only is Texas an urban state but it also is made up largely of metropolitan residents. A new classification for metropolitan residence was adopted in June, 1983. The previous term, Standard Metropolitan Statistical Area (SMSA) was replaced by Metropolitan Statistical Area (MSA). In 1983, 80 percent of the state's people lived in MSAs, which is a higher proportion than the nation as a whole, where 76 percent resided in MSAs.

The six-county Houston-Galveston-Brazoria Consolidated Metropolitan Statistical Area (CMSA) had the largest number of people (3,458,000) in 1982 and ranked 8th in population among all of the nation's metropolitan areas. At the same time, the 9-county Dallas-Fort Worth CMSA had the second largest population (3,143,000) and ranked 10th nationally. The San Antonio MSA, which consists of three counties, was the state's only other metropolitan area with over one million people — (1,135,000 in 1982) — and ranked 33rd nationally. Thus the Houston-Galveston-Brazoria CMSA had 22.6 percent of the state's people in 1982, followed by Dallas-Fort Worth CSMA's 20.6 percent and San Antonio MSA's 7.4 percent. These three combined metropolitan areas had one-half of the state's residents in 1982.

Sex Composition

Females in Texas outnumbered males by 230,000 in 1980. In the 1800s men predominated in numbers by a wide margin, but a steady trend took place from male to female predominance that lasted through the 1960-70 decade.

In 1920, there were approximately 155,000 more males than females in the state. The margin by which males outnumbered females decreased with each succeeding census until in 1960, for the first time, Texas had approximately 90,000 more women than men. And the margin increased to 234,000 in 1970. But this margin declined slightly to 232,000 in 1980.

Expressed in terms of the number of males for each 100 females, the state index was 115 in 1850. By 1900, it had been reduced to 107 and by 1940 to 101. In 1950, the numbers of females and males were almost equally bal-

anced. But by 1960 the sex ratio fell to 98.1, and in 1970, there were only 95.9 males per 100 females. In 1980, Texas had 96.8 males per 100 females. The sex ratio in 1980 was slightly lower in the nation as a whole than in Texas; the national ratio was 94.5 males per 100 females.

The trend toward female predominance in numbers may be viewed as an indication of the stage of population maturity Texas has reached. Most areas in the early stages of settlement usually attract more men than women. Then, as the area develops, females tend to increase in numbers at a faster rate than males. A part of this population maturity is explained by life expectancy differences. Not only have women always lived longer than men, but the difference in their life expectancies has been widening. For example, at birth in 1900, females could expect to outlive males by about two years. Among babies born in 1983, the girls can expect to outlive the boys by about eight years. The fact that the margin by which females outnumber males did not continue to widen in the 1970s is explained by migration differences of the two sexes. In the 1960s, approximately 135,000 more females moved into the state than migrated out while there were only 71,000 net male in-migrants. This situation was reversed in the 1970s when 930,000 more males moved into Texas than left while there were 850,000 net female in-migrants.

Age Composition

Texas has been shifting from a younger population to an older. The average Texan today is eight years older than the average resident in 1900. The median age of the state's people increased from 26.4 years in 1970 to 28.2 years in 1980. This increase occurred at about the same rate as it did in the nation, where the median age increased from 28.1 to 30 years. Thus, the average Texan is about two years younger than the average U.S. resident.

Substantial differences exist in the age distributions of the populations of Texas counties. The range in median ages in 1980 was 22.3 years for Maverick County to 55.4 years for Llano County. An additional four counties — Brazos, Coryell, Hays and Starr — all have unusually young populations, with median ages of less than 23. At the other extreme, three other counties — Hamilton, **Loving** and Mills — have populations whose median ages are more than 45 years.

Another way of gauging changes in age composition is to divide the state's people into three broad age groups that correspond roughly to the major stages of an individual's life cycle.

These are the young (persons under 20 years of age); the adults (younger and middle-aged adults 20-64 years of age), and the aged (65 years of age and older). The proportion of young persons under 20 years of age has declined from slightly more than one-half of all Texans in 1900 to only one of three in 1980. Their proportionate share continued to drop between 1970 and 1980 — from 39.5 to 34.2 percent.

The proportion of persons 20-64 years of age increased from 44.9 percent in 1900 to 56.2 percent in 1980.

The aged population has had the most spectacular growth. As a consequence, persons 65 years of age and older increased their proportionate share from 1 of every 67 Texans in 1870 to 1 of every 40 in 1900, and 1 of every 10 in 1980. Older people continued to increase their numbers at a more rapid rate than the remainder of the state's population between 1970 and 1980, when they comprised 8.9 and 9.6 percent of the state's people, respectively. At the same time, Texas has a lower proportion of older persons than the nation as a whole. In 1980, 11.3 percent of the United States population was 65 years of age or older.

Racial and Ethnic Composition

While Texas always has had a predominantly white population, the people are from a broad variety of racial, ethnic and nationality groups. The two major racial groups are whites and blacks, and the three major ethnic groups are anglos, blacks and Hispanics, or Spanish origin.

Whites made up 80 percent of the Texas population in 1980. Anglos (all whites minus Hispanics) comprised 66 percent of the total population; Hispanics 21 percent; blacks 12 percent; and all other nonwhites, 1 percent. The comparable percentages in the nation as a whole are 83 percent whites, 80 percent anglos, 6 percent Hispanics, 12 percent blacks and 2 percent for other nonwhites. Thus, the biggest difference in the ethnic composition of Texas and the United States is the number of Hispanics. Texas had one-fifth of the nation's

This suspension bridge, modeled after the famous Brooklyn Bridge, is a leading tourist attraction in Waco.

TEXAS POPULATION—TOTAL, URBAN, RURAL 1850-1980

Data in this table are from the U.S. Bureau of Census for each decennial census, 1850 to 1980. Minus (—) sign denotes decrease.

Census Year—	Rank Among States	The State Population	Increase Over Preceding Census Number	Per Cent	Pop. Per Sq. Mi.	*Urban Places Population	Increase Over Preceding Census Number	Per Cent	*†Rural Territory Population	Change From Preceding Census Number	Per Cent	Per Cent of Total Urban	Rural
1980.	3	14,229,191	3,030,536	27.1	54.3	11,331,577	2,410,631	27.0	2,897,614	621,830	27.3	79.6	20.4
‡1970.	4	11,198,655	1,618,978	16.9	42.7	8,920,946	1,734,935	24.1	2,275,784	—117,882	—4.9	79.7	20.3
1960.	6	9,579,677	1,868,483	24.2	36.4	7,186,011	2,347,951	48.5	2,393,666	—479,468	—16.7	75.0	25.0
*1950.	6	7,711,194	1,296,370	20.2	29.3	4,838,060	1,926,671	66.2	2,873,134	—630,301	—18.0	62.7	37.3
*1950.	6	7,711,194	1,296,370	20.2	29.3	4,612,666	1,701,277	58.4	3,098,528	—404,907	—11.6	59.8	40.2
1940.	6	6,414,824	590,109	10.1	24.3	2,911,389	522,041	21.8	3,503,435	68,068	2.0	45.4	54.6
1930.	5	5,824,715	1,161,487	24.9	22.1	2,339,348	876,659	58.0	3,435,367	284,828	9.0	41.0	59.0
1920.	5	4,663,228	766,686	19.7	17.8	1,512,689	574,585	61.2	3,150,539	192,101	6.5	32.4	67.6
1910.	5	3,896,542	847,832	27.8	14.8	938,104	417,345	80.1	2,958,438	430,487	17.0	24.1	75.9
1900.	6	3,048,710	813,183	36.4	11.6	520,759	171,248	49.0	2,527,951	641,935	34.0	17.1	82.9
1890.	7	2,235,527	643,778	40.4	8.5	349,511	202,716	138.1	1,886,016	441,062	30.5	15.6	84.4
1880.	11	1,591,749	773,170	94.5	6.1	146,795	92,274	169.2	1,444,954	680,896	89.1	9.2	90.8
1870.	19	818,579	214,364	35.5	3.1	54,521	27,906	104.9	764,058	186,458	32.3	6.7	93.3
1860.	23	604,215	391,623	184.2	2.3	26,615	18,950	274.2	577,600	372,673	181.9	4.4	95.6
1850.	25	212,592			0.8	7,665			204,927			3.6	96.4

*Two lines of data are given for 1950. The top line shows "urban" and "rural" population data, according to the new method of classifying population adopted for the 1950 census. The second line shows the 1950 population figures broken down according to the old method of classification used prior to 1950. (Prior to 1950 "urban" population included that living in incorporated places of 2,500 or more. All other was placed in "rural." In the census of 1950, the new method classed as "urban" all population in both incorporated and unincorporated places of 2,500 or more, and also the unincorporated suburban population of cities of 50,000 or more. Approximately the same classifications were used in subsequent censuses.)

†Rural population is divided by the United States Bureau of the Census into that actually living on farms and that living in rural areas but not on farms, principally in incorporated and unincorporated towns and villages of less than 2,500 population.

‡1970 total figure revised; no later data available for urban and rural breakdown.

These ruins are all that remain of Fort Phantom Hill near Abilene, which was built in 1851 and served as a military post and as a stop on the Butterfield Overland Mail stagecoach line.

Hispanics — 2,985,643 — in 1980 and ranked second among all states. But California exceeded Texas in Hispanics by a wide margin. These two states had 52 percent of the nation's Hispanic population in 1980.

Although Hispanics tend to be more evenly distributed throughout different areas of the state than blacks, with the exception of the larger East Texas cities, they are concentrated more in South and West Texas. There is not a single county that does not have some Hispanics. Bexar County had the largest number (461,000) in 1980, followed by Harris, El Paso, Hidalgo, Cameron and Dallas, all with more than 150,000 Hispanics. At the other extreme, 13 counties had fewer than 100 Hispanics. Hispanics comprised more than 90 percent of the total populations in four Texas counties in 1980 — Starr, Webb, Jim Hogg and Maverick Counties. An additional 10 counties had more than 75 percent Hispanics. All of the counties with the highest proportions of Hispanics are in South and West Texas. These counties border Mexico or are a fairly short distance from the Texas-Mexico border.

Texas had the third largest black population in the nation in 1980 — 1,710,250. Only New York and California had more black residents. Over time, the black population of Texas has increased in numbers but declined as a proportion of the total population. In 1870, blacks made up 31.1 percent of the state's people but declined to 12.5 percent by 1970 and 12.0 percent in 1980. Although data are lacking for Hispanics for past years, they are clearly the most rapidly growing minority in Texas as well as the United States. Hispanics increased their proportionate share of the state's population from 18.4 percent in 1970 to 21.0 percent in 1980.

The overall distribution of blacks and Hispanics among the separate sections of the state is quite different. In 1980, blacks were heavily concentrated in East Texas where about 80 percent resided. Two counties with the state's largest cities had the largest number of blacks. Harris County had 474,000 and Dallas County 288,000. These two counties had about 45 percent of Texas' total black population. Counties with highest proportions of blacks in 1980 were Waller with 42 percent and Harrison, Houston, Marion and Robertson, all with more than 30 percent. At the other extreme, 67 counties, all located in West and South Texas, had black populations of fewer than 100, and 10 of these had no blacks.

POPULATION OF CITIES AND TOWNS

The Census enumerates all incorporated places, regardless of size. These places are indicated in the list below by the use of lightface capital letters.

In the case of smaller, unincorporated places, the figure is an estimate of the number of persons considered locally as living in that community because of business, school or church association.

Metropolitan Statistical Area population for 1982 is from U.S. Census Bureau.

Population of cities and towns in this list are from the revised U.S. Census for 1980.

Other information in the following table includes:

Incorporated Places: Places that were incorporated in 1980, and included in the census of that year, are printed in lightface capitals, e.g., "ABBOTT."

Unincorporated Places: Unincorporated places that were not enumerated by the 1980 Census are printed in lightface type, e.g., "Acton." The population figure is an estimate.

Places incorporated since the 1980 Census are printed in **boldface** type. The population figure is an estimate.

Post Offices: Places with post offices are marked with an asterisk (*) e.g., "*Ace."

Banking Towns: Towns with one or more banks are marked with a dagger, e.g., "†ALAMO." (This includes national, state and private banking institutions.) Information from Federal Reserve Bank, Dallas.

Number of Business establishments: The number following the name of the county, in the list below, indicates the number of rated business establishments in the given town, or city, e.g., "Adamsville, Lampasas, 1" means that Adamsville in Lampasas has 1 business establishment given a credit rating by Dun & Bradstreet.

Location: County in which town is located immediately follows name of town, e.g., "Aberfoyle, Hunt," meaning Aberfoyle in Hunt County.

Town and County—	Pop.	Town and County—	Pop.	Town and County—	Pop.
A		Acworth, Red River	20	Aiken, Shelby	33
*ABBOTT, HILL, 3	359	Adams Gardens, Cameron	200	Aikin Grove, Red River	26
Aberfoyle, Hunt	35	Adamsville, Lampasas, 1	28	Airport City, Bexar	106
*†ABERNATHY, Hale-		*†Addicks, Harris	150	Airville, Bell	10
Lubbock, 45	2,904	Addielou, Red River	31	*†ALAMO, Hidalgo, 70	5,831
*†ABILENE, Jones-		*†ADDISON, Collin-		Alamo Alto, El Paso	25
Taylor, 1,837	98,315	Dallas, 190	5,553	†ALAMO HEIGHTS, Bexar	
1982 metro. pop.	118,600	*Adkins, Bexar, 27	241	(San Antonio suburb)	6,252
Academy, Bell	60	Admiral, Callahan	18	*Alanreed, Gray	60
Acala, Hudspeth	25	*ADRIAN, Oldham, 6	222	*ALBA, Rains-Wood, 13	568
*Ace, Polk	40	*Afton, Dickens, 4	100	*†ALBANY, Shackelford, 83	2,450
*ACKERLY, Dawson-		*AGUA DULCE, Nueces, 14	934	*Albert, Gillespie, 2	25
Martin, 7	317	Agua Nueva, Jim Hogg	20	†Aldine, Harris	12,623
Acme, Hardeman	14	Aguilares, Webb	25	*†ALEDO, Parker, 28	1,027
Acton, Hood	130	*Aiken, Floyd	140	Aleman, Hamilton	60
Acuff, Lubbock	30			Alexander, Erath	40

Town and County—	Pop.
BONNEY, Brazoria	94
Bonus, Wharton	42
*Bon Wier, Newton, 7	475
*†BOOKER, Lipscomb-Ochiltree, 48	1,219
Boonsville, Wise	52
*Booth, Fort Bend	40
†BORGER, Hutchinson, 398	15,837
Bosqueville, McLennan	72
*Boston, Bowie, 1	200
*†BOVINA, Parmer, 25	1,499
*†BOWIE, Montague, 153	5,610
Box Church, Limestone	45
Boxelder, Red River	75
Boyce, Ellis	75
*†BOYD, Wise, 37	889
*Boys' Ranch, Oldham	410
Boz, Ellis	15
Brachfield, Rusk	30
Bracken, Comal	76
*†BRACKETTVILLE, Kinney, 28	1,676
Brad, Palo Pinto	26
Bradford, Anderson	22
Bradshaw, Taylor	61
*†BRADY, McCulloch, 130	5,969
Branch, Collin	447
Branchville, Milam	196
*Brandon, Hill	80
*Brashear, Hopkins, 1	280
*†BRAZORIA, Brazoria, 50	3,025
Brazos, Palo Pinto	47

Brazosport, Brazoria.—This is the group city name applied to the industrial and port area including Freeport, Clute, Quintana, Richwood, Brazoria, Lake Jackson, Jones Creek, Oyster Creek and Surfside and having a joint Brazosport Independent School District and joint Brazosport Chamber of Commerce. Total pop. 52,453.

*†BRECKENRIDGE, Stephens, 155	6,921
*†BREMOND, Robertson, 15	1,025
*†BRENHAM, Washington, 393	10,966
Breslau, Lavaca	65
BRIAR, Parker-Tarrant-Wise	1,810
BRIAROAKS, Johnson	592
Brice, Hall	37
*†BRIDGE CITY, Orange, 105	7,667
*†BRIDGEPORT, Wise, 153	3,737
*Briggs, Burnet, 1	92
Bright Star, Rains	45
*Briscoe, Wheeler, 5	210
Bristol, Ellis	94
Britton, Ellis	30
*BROADDUS, San Augustine, 7	225
Broadway, Lamar	25
Brock, Parker	51
Bronco, Yoakum	30
*BRONSON, Sabine, 2	254
*†BRONTE, Coke, 17	983
*Brookeland, Sabine, 6	220
*Brookesmith, Brown, 3	61
Brooks, Panola	40
*†BROOKSHIRE, Waller, 67	2,175
BROOKSIDE, Brazoria	1,453
*Brookston, Lamar, 2	70
Broome, Panola	21
Broome, Sterling	18
BROWNDELL, Jasper	228
*†BROWNFIELD, Terry, 188	10,387
Browning, Smith	25
*†BROWNSBORO, Henderson, 13	582
*†BROWNSVILLE, Cameron, 1,151	84,997
Brownsville-Harlingen 1982 metro. pop.	230,500
*†BROWNWOOD, Brown, 450	19,396
*BRUCEVILLE, Falls-McLennan, 2	1,038
(Bruceville-Eddy share city government)	

Town and County—	Pop.
Brundage, Dimmit	50
*Bruni, Webb, 12	214
Brunswick, Cherokee	50
Brushy Creek, Anderson	50
*†BRYAN, Brazos, 955	44,337
Bryan-College Station—1982 metro. pop.	112,100
Bryans Mill, Cass	71
Bryarly, Red River	32
*†BRYSON, Jack, 8	579
*Buchanan Dam, Llano, 23	1,011
Buck Creek, Cottle	69
Buckeye, Matagorda	25
*†BUCKHOLTS, Milam, 5	388
Buckhorn, Austin	20
BUCKINGHAM, Dallas	159
*†BUDA, Hays, 54	597
*†BUFFALO, Leon, 52	1,507
*BUFFALO GAP, Taylor, 9	387
Buffalo Springs, Clay	51
Buford, Mitchell	25
Bug Tussle, Fannin	30
*Bula, Bailey, 5	105
Bulcher, Cooke	60
*†BULLARD, Cherokee-Smith, 22	681
Bulverde, Comal	25
*†Buna, Jasper, 44	1,669
Bunavista, Hutchinson	1,410
Buncombe, Panola	87
Bunger, Young	26
BUNKER HILL VILLAGE, Harris	3,750
Bunyan, Erath	20
*†BURKBURNETT, Wichita, 128	10,668
BURKE, Angelina	322
*Burkett, Coleman, 3	30
*Burkeville, Newton, 3	515
Burleigh, Austin	69
*†BURLESON, Johnson-Tarrant, 147	11,734
*Burlington, Milam, 1	125
*†BURNET, Burnet, 127	3,410
Burns City, Cooke	61
*†BURTON, Washington, 16	325
Busby, Fisher	12
*Bushland, Potter, 6	130
Bustamante, Zapata	25
Butler, Freestone	67
*†BYERS, Clay, 12	556
*BYNUM, Hill	232
Byrd, Ellis	15

C

*CACTUS, Moore, 12	898
*Caddo, Stephens, 2	40
*†CADDO MILLS, Hunt, 15	1,060
Cadiz, Bee	15
Calallen, Nueces (annexed by Corpus Christi)	
Calaveras, Wilson	70
*†CALDWELL, Burleson, 143	2,953
Calf Creek, McCulloch	23
*Call, Jasper-Newton, 7	170
*Calliham, McMullen	25
CALLISBURG, Cooke	281
Call Junction, Jasper	50
*†CALVERT, Robertson, 20	1,732
*Camden, Polk, 2	1,200
*†CAMERON, Milam, 83	5,721
Camilla, San Jacinto	70
*CAMPBELL, Hunt, 5	549
*Campbellton, Atascosa, 3	275
Camp Air, Mason	31
Camp Creek Lake, Robertson	241
Camp Ruby, Polk	35
Camp San Saba, McCulloch	36
Camp Springs, Scurry	10
Camp Switch, Gregg	70
Camp Verde, Kerr, 1	41
*CAMP WOOD, Real, 13	728
*†CANADIAN, Hemphill, 110	3,491
Candelaria, Presidio	55
Caney, Matagorda	296
CANEY CITY, Henderson	312
Cannon, Grayson	75
*†CANTON, Van Zandt, 83	2,845
*Canutillo, El Paso, 27	1,800
*†CANYON, Randall, 137	10,724

Town and County—	Pop.
Canyon City, Comal	100
†Canyon Lake, Comal	100
Caplen, Galveston	30
Caps, Taylor	100
Caradan, Mills	20
*CARBON, Eastland, 3	281
Carbondale, Bowie	30
*Carey, Childress	57
Carlisle (P.O. Price), Rusk	161
Carlisle, Trinity	95
*Carlsbad, Tom Green, 4	100
Carlson, Travis	61
*Carlton, Hamilton, 1	70
*†CARMINE, Fayette, 6	239
Carmona, Polk	50
Caro, Nacogdoches	113
Carricitos, Cameron	25
*†CARRIZO SPRINGS, Dimmit, 114	6,886
Carroll, Smith	60
*†CARROLLTON, Dallas-Denton, 915	40,595
Carson, Fannin	22
Carta Valley, Edwards	20
Carterville, Cass	25
*†CARTHAGE, Panola, 156	6,447
Cartwright, Wood	61
Casa Piedra, Presidio	21
Casey, El Paso	115
Cash, Hunt	56
*Cason, Morris, 4	165
Cass, Cass	50
*Castell, Llano, 1	72
Castle Heights, McLennan	80
†CASTLE HILLS, Bexar	4,773
*†CASTROVILLE, Medina, 45	1,821
*Catarina, Dimmit, 4	45
*Cat Spring, Austin, 3	76
Caviness, Lamar	80
Cawthon, Brazos	75
Cayote, Bosque	75
*Cayuga, Anderson, 2	56
Cedar Bayou-Stewart Heights, Chambers-Harris	1,000
*Cedar Creek, Bastrop, 8	145
*†CEDAR HILL, Dallas, 83	6,849
Cedar Lake, Matagorda	148
*Cedar Lane, Matagorda	85
*†CEDAR PARK, Williamson, 100	3,474
Cedar Shores Estates, Bosque	170
Cedar Springs, Falls	90
Cedar Valley, Travis	70
*Cee Vee, Cottle, 1	71
Cego, Falls	98
*†CELESTE, Hunt, 5	716
*†CELINA, Collin, 30	1,520
Center, Limestone	76
*†CENTER, Shelby, 170	5,827
Center City, Mills	15
*Center Point, Kerr, 14	566
*†CENTERVILLE, Leon, 23	799
Central, Angelina	105
*Centralia, Trinity	26
Cestohowa, Karnes	110
*Chalk, Cottle	45
Chalk Mountain, Erath	25
Chambersville, Collin	40
Chambliss, Collin	25
Champion, Nolan	16
Chance-Loeb, Hardin (see Lumberton)	
*†CHANDLER, Henderson, 26	1,308
Chaney, Eastland	35
*†Channelview, Harris, 248	8,227
*CHANNING, Hartley, 8	304
Chapman, Rusk	20
*Chapman Ranch, Nueces, 2	100
Chappel, San Saba	25
*†Chappell Hill, Washington, 9	310
Charco, Goliad	61
Charleston, Delta	48
Charlie, Clay	65
*†CHARLOTTE, Atascosa, 22	1,443
Chase Field, Bee	1,221
*Chatfield, Navarro, 1	40

Town and County—	Pop.	Town and County—	Pop.	Town and County—	Pop.
CHATEAU WOODS, Montgomery	590	*†COLMESNEIL, Tyler, 12	553	*†Crosby, Harris, 108	2,500
*Cheapside, Gonzales	31	Cologne, Goliad	35	*†CROSBYTON, Crosby, 30	2,289
Cheek, Jefferson	62	Colorado, Jim Hogg	23	Cross, Grimes	49
*Cherokee, San Saba, 6	175	*†COLORADO CITY, Mitchell, 95	5,405	Cross Cut, Brown	45
Cherry Spring, Gillespie	75	Colton, Travis	50	*†CROSS PLAINS, Callahan, 37	1,240
*†CHESTER, Tyler, 4	305	*†COLUMBUS, Colorado, 113	3,923	CROSS ROADS, Denton	302
*†CHICO, Wise, 25	890	Comal, Comal	40	Cross Roads, Henderson	135
*Chicota, Lamar	125	*†COMANCHE, Comanche, 94	4,075	Crow, Wood	25
*†CHILDRESS, Childress, 106	5,817	*COMBES, Cameron, 12	1,488	*†CROWELL, Foard, 25	1,509
*†CHILLICOTHE, Hardeman, 20	1,052	COMBINE, Kaufman-Dallas	688	*†CROWLEY, Tarrant, 79	5,852
*†Chilton, Falls, 10	310	*†Comfort, Kendall, 40	1,460	Cryer Creek, Navarro	15
*CHINA, Jefferson, 8	1,351	*†COMMERCE, Hunt, 90	8,136	CRYSTAL BEACH, Galveston	1,600
CHINA GROVE, Bexar	434	*COMO, Hopkins, 10	554	*†CRYSTAL CITY, Zavala, 62	8,334
*China Spring, McLennan, 8	181	*Comstock, Val Verde, 2	375	Crystal Falls, Stephens	10
*†CHIRENO, Nacogdoches, 4	371	Comyn, Comanche	27	*†CUERO, DeWitt, 120	7,124
Chisholm, Rockwall (See McLendon-Chisholm)		*Concan, Uvalde, 5	71	Cuevitas, Jim Hogg	12
Chita, Trinity	75	*Concepcion, Duval, 1	25	*CUMBY, Hopkins, 11	647
Chocolate Bayou, Brazoria	60	Concord, Hunt	30	*Cuney, Cherokee	75
*Choice, Shelby	21	*Concord, Leon	28	*Cunningham, Lamar	110
*Chriesman, Burleson	30	Concord, Liberty	26	Currie, Navarro	25
*CHRISTINE, Atascosa, 1	392	Concord, Rusk	23	*†CUSHING, Nacogdoches, 25	518
*Christoval, Tom Green, 8	216	Concrete, DeWitt	46	Cusseta, Cass	30
Church Hill, Rusk	15	*Cone, Crosby	110	Cuthand, Red River	32
*†CIBOLO, Guadalupe, 27	549	Conlen, Dallam	61	CUT AND SHOOT, Montgomery	568
Cipres, Hidalgo	20	*†CONROE, Montgomery, 1,070	18,034	Cyclone, Bell	55
Circleback, Bailey	45	*CONVERSE, Bexar, 65	5,150	Cypress, Franklin	20
Circleville, Williamson	42	Conway, Carson	50	*†Cypress, Harris, 143	260
*†CISCO, Eastland, 105	4,517	Cooks Point, Burleson	60	Cypress Mill, Blanco	56
Cistern, Fayette	75	*Cookville, Titus, 1	105	**D**	
Clairemont, Kent	35	COOL, Parker	202	Dabney, Uvalde	30
Clairette, Erath	55	*†COOLIDGE, Limestone, 12	810	Dacosta, Victoria	89
Clara-Fairview, Wichita	100	*†COOPER, Delta, 31	2,338	Dacus, Montgomery	161
*†CLARENDON, Donley, 40	2,220	*Copeville, Collin, 7	106	*†DAINGERFIELD, Morris, 73	3,030
*†Claraville, Bee	23	*†COPPELL, Dallas-Denton, 52	3,826	*DAISETTA, Liberty, 15	1,177
*†CLARKSVILLE, Red River, 86	4,917	*†COPPERAS COVE, Coryell, 132	19,469	Dalby Springs, Bowie	60
CLARKSVILLE CITY, Gregg	525	COPPER CANYON, Denton	465	*Dale, Caldwell, 3	126
Clarkwood, Nueces (Annexed by Corpus Christi)		Corbet, Navarro	80	*†DALHART, Dallam-Hartley, 155	6,854
*†CLAUDE, Armstrong, 13	1,112	Cordele, Jackson	74	*Dallardsville, Polk	350
Clauene, Hockley	24	CORINTH, Denton	1,264	*†DALLAS, Dallas, 20,872	904,078
Clawson, Angelina	195	Corinth, Jones	25	Dallas-Fort Worth 1982 CMSA pop.	3,131,200
Clay, Burleson	61	Corley, Bowie	35	DALWORTHINGTON GARDENS, Tarrant	1,100
*Clayton, Panola, 1	79	Cornett, Cass	30	Dam B (Dogwood Station), Tyler	56
Claytonville, Fisher	21	*†CORPUS CHRISTI, Nueces, 3,887	232,134	*Damon, Brazoria, 16	375
Claytonville, Swisher	116	1982 metro. pop.	344,100	*†DANBURY, Brazoria, 12	1,357
Clear Lake, Collin	50	CORRAL CITY, Denton	54	*Danciger, Brazoria, 1	314
Clear Lake, Harris	22,000	*†CORRIGAN, Polk, 30	1,770	*Danevang, Wharton, 1	61
CLEAR LAKE SHORES, Galveston	755	*†CORSICANA, Navarro, 437	21,712	Darco, Harrison	85
Clear Spring, Guadalupe	60	Coryell City, Coryell	125	*DARROUZETT, Lipscomb, 11	444
*†CLEBURNE, Johnson, 360	19,218	*Cost, Gonzales, 5	62	*Davilla, Milam	72
Clegg, Live Oak	25	*Cotton Center, Hale, 9	260	*Dawn, Deaf Smith, 4	94
Clemville, Matagorda	54	Cotton Gin, Freestone	28	*†DAWSON, Navarro, 1	747
Cleo, Kimble	81	Cottonwood, Callahan	65	*†DAYTON, Liberty, 130	4,908
Cleveland, Austin	78	Cottonwood, Erath	23	Deadwood, Panola	106
*†CLEVELAND, Liberty, 235	5,977	Cottonwood-Concord, Freestone	61	DEAN, Clay	212
Cliffside, Potter	206	Cottonwood, Kaufman	90	Dean, Lubbock	18
*†CLIFTON, Bosque, 83	3,063	Cottonwood, Madison	40	*†Deanville, Burleson, 7	130
Climax, Collin	40	Cottonwood, Somervell	24	*De Berry, Panola, 9	191
Cline, Uvalde	10	*†COTULLA, La Salle, 52	3,912	*†DECATUR, Wise, 112	4,104
*CLINT, El Paso, 13	1,314	County Line, Hale-Lubbock	30	*†DEER PARK, Harris, 265	22,648
Clodine, Fort Bend	31	Country Campus, Walker	60	*†DE KALB, Bowie, 48	2,217
Clopton, Franklin	15	*†Coupland, Williamson, 7	135	Delaware Bend, Cooke	40
*†CLUTE, Brazoria, 207	9,577	Courtney, Grimes	55	*†DE LEON, Comanche, 64	2,478
*†CLYDE, Caliahan, 45	2,562	COVE, Chambers	645	DELL CITY, Hudspeth, 11	495
*†COAHOMA, Howard, 20	1,069	Cove City, Orange (annexed by Orange)		*Delmita, Starr, 1	99
Cochran, Austin	116	*COVINGTON, Hill, 1	259	*DEL RIO, Val Verde, 345	30,034
COCKRELL HILL, Dallas	3,262	Cow Creek, Erath	14	*Del Valle, Travis, 37	300
COFFEE CITY, Henderson	254	*Coyanosa, Pecos, 1	270	Delwin, Cottle	70
Coffeeville, Upshur	50	Coy City, Karnes	30	Denhawken, Wilson	10
Coke, Wood	105	Crabb, Fort Bend	41	*†DENISON, Grayson, 360	23,884
*†COLDSPRING, San Jacinto, 27	569	Craft, Cherokee	21	Sherman-Denison 1982 metro. pop.	92,300
*†COLEMAN, Coleman, 107	5,960	Crafton, Wise	20	Denning, San Augustine	361
Colfax, Van Zandt	35	*†CRANDALL, Kaufman, 15	831	*Dennis, Parker	86
*Collegeport, Matagorda	91	*†CRANE, Crane, 75	3,622	*†DENTON, Denton, 575	48,063
*†COLLEGE STATION, Brazos, 438	37,272	*†CRANFILLS GAP, Bosque, 7	341	*†DENVER CITY, Yoakum, 135	4,704
Bryan-College Station— 1982 metro. pop.	112,100	*CRAWFORD, McLennan, 12	610	*†DEPORT, Lamar-Red River, 8	724
*†COLLEYVILLE, Tarrant, 101	6,700	Creedmoor, Travis, 3	75	Derby, Frio	50
*†COLLINSVILLE, Grayson, 14	860	*Cresson, Hood, 9	208	*Dermott, Scurry	50
		Crisp, Ellis	90		
		*†CROCKETT, Houston, 165	7,405		

Town and County—	Pop.
*Desdemona, Eastland, 3	180
Desert, Collin	25
*†DESOTO, Dallas, 200	15,538
*DETROIT, Red River, 8	805
*DEVERS, Liberty, 12	507
*†DEVINE, Medina, 75	3,756
Dew, Freestone	71
Dewalt, Fort Bend	40
DeWees, Wilson	10
*Deweyville, Newton, 13	850
Dewville, Gonzales	15
Dexter, Cooke	70
*†D'Hanis, Medina, 5	506
Dial, Hutchinson	20
Dial, Fannin	76
*Dialville, Cherokee	200
*Diana, Upshur, 7	200
*†DIBOLL, Angelina, 37	5,227
*DICKENS, Dickens, 8	409
*†DICKINSON, Galveston, 118	7,505
*Dike, Hopkins, 6	170
*†DILLEY, Frio, 51	2,579
Dilworth, Gonzales	15
*†Dime Box, Lee, 15	313
*†DIMMITT, Castro, 93	5,019
Dimple, Red River	25
Dinero, Live Oak, 2	35
Direct, Lamar	70
Dirgin, Rusk	12
Dittlinger, Comal	171
Divot, Frio	28
Dixie, Grayson	25
Dixon, Hunt	31
Doans, Wilbarger	20
*Dobbin, Montgomery, 5	170
Dobrowolski, Atascosa	10
Dodd, Castro	35
*DODD CITY, Fannin, 2	286
*Dodge, Walker, 1	150
*DODSON, Collingsworth, 1	185
Dog Ridge, Bell	125
Dolores, Webb	20
DOMINO, Cass	249
*†Donie, Freestone, 4	206
*†DONNA, Hidalgo, 81	9,952
Donnybrook Place, Harris	392
*Doole, McCulloch, 3	74
*DORCHESTER, Grayson, 7	205
*Doss, Gillespie, 1	75
Dot, Falls	21
Dothan, Eastland	20
DOUBLE OAK, Denton	836
*Doucette, Tyler	131
*Dougherty, Floyd, 3	135
Dougherty, Rains	75
*Douglass, Nacogdoches, 1	75
*DOUGLASSVILLE, Cass, 5	228
Downing, Comanche	20
Downsville, McLennan	35
Dozier, Collingsworth	30
Drane, Navarro	16
Draw, Lynn	39
Dresden, Navarro	25
*Driftwood, Hays, 2	21
*†Dripping Springs, Hays, 26	606
*DRISCOLL, Nueces, 4	648
*Dryden, Terrell	45
Dryer, Gonzales	20
*†DUBLIN, Erath, 58	2,723
Dudley, Callahan	25
*Duffau, Erath	76
*†DUMAS, Moore, 128	12,194
*Dumont, King, 1	95
*†DUNCANVILLE, Dallas, 337	27,781
Dundee, Archer	40
Dunlap, Cottle	30
Dunlap, Travis	80
Dunlay, Medina, 2	110
*Dunn, Scurry	75
Duplex, Fannin	25
Durango, Falls	54
E	
Eagle, Chambers	50
*†EAGLE LAKE, Colorado, 70	3,921
*†EAGLE PASS, Maverick, 275	21,407
†EARLY, Brown	2,313
*†EARTH, Lamb, 23	1,512
Easeville, Atascosa	20
*†East Bernard, Wharton, 51	1,500
East Columbia, Brazoria	95
Easter, Castro	91
Easterly, Robertson	61
*†EASTLAND, Eastland, 130	3,747
EAST MOUNTAIN, Upshur	855
*EASTON, Gregg-Rusk	333
EAST TAWAKONI, Rains	404
EASTVALE, Denton	670
Ebenezer, Camp	55
Echo, Coleman	16
Echo, Orange	25
Ecleto, Karnes	22
*ECTOR, Fannin, 2	573
*EDCOUCH, Hidalgo, 12	3,092
*EDDY, Falls-McLennan, 8	1,038
(Bruceville-Eddy share city government)	
*†EDEN, Concho, 23	1,294
Edge, Brazos	100
EDGECLIFF, Tarrant	2,695
*†EDGEWOOD, Van Zandt, 23	1,413
*†EDINBURG, Hidalgo, 333	24,075
McAllen-Mission-Edinburg 1982 metro. pop.	315,100
*EDMONSON, Hale, 5	291
*†EDNA, Jackson, 110	5,650
Edna Hill, Erath	32
EDOM, Van Zandt, 2	250
*Edroy, San Patricio, 8	200
Egan, Johnson	21
*Egypt, Wharton, 1	26
*Elbert, Throckmorton, 3	150
*EL CAMPO, Wharton, 290	10,462
El Campo South, Wharton	1,111
*†ELDORADO, Schleicher, 37	2,061
*†ELECTRA, Wichita, 78	3,755
*†ELGIN, Bastrop, 55	4,535
*Eliasville, Young, 2	116
*El Indio, Maverick, 2	148
Elk, McLennan (See Hallsburg)	
*ELKHART, Anderson, 22	1,317
*EL LAGO, Harris	3,129
*Ellinger, Fayette, 3	200
Elliott, Wilbarger	50
*Elmaton, Matagorda	165
*ELMENDORF, Bexar, 15	492
Elm Grove Camp, Guadalupe	100
*Elm Mott, McLennan, 17	190
*Elmo, Kaufman, 2	90
Elmont, Grayson	41
Elmwood, Anderson	20
Eloise, Falls	47
*†EL PASO, El Paso, 3,977	425,259
1982 metro. pop.	513,400
Elroy, Travis	55
*†ELSA, Hidalgo, 30	5,061
*El Sauz, Starr	85
Elwood, Fannin	31
*†Elysian Fields, Harrison, 1	300
Emberson, Lamar	80
Emblem, Hopkins	52
EMHOUSE, Navarro, 1	197
Emmett, Navarro	100
*EMORY, Rains, 33	813
ENCHANTED OAKS, Henderson	212
*ENCINAL, La Salle, 7	704
*Encino, Brooks, 4	110
*Energy, Comanche	65
Engle, Fayette	106
English, Red River	92
*†Enloe, Delta, 2	150
*†ENNIS, Ellis, 235	12,110
*Enochs, Bailey, 1	164
Ensign, Ellis	10
Enterprise, Van Zandt	90
Eolian, Stephens	20
*Eola, Concho, 3	218
*Era, Cooke, 3	200
Erath, McLennan	50
Erin, Jasper	40
Escobares, Starr	216
Escobas, Zapata	25
Esperanza, Hudspeth	75
Esseville, Atascosa	25
Estacado, Lubbock	80
*ESTELLINE, Hall, 5	258
Ethel, Grayson	25
*Etoile, Nacogdoches, 2	70
Etter, Moore	160
Eula, Callahan	125
*†EULESS, Tarrant, 332	24,002
Eulogy, Bosque	45
Eureka, Navarro	75
*†EUSTACE, Henderson, 10	541
*Evadale, Jasper, 13	715
*†EVANT, Coryell-Hamilton-Lampasas, 12	425
Evergreen, San Jacinto	50
†EVERMAN, Tarrant (See Fort Worth)	5,387
Ewell, Upshur	100
Exell, Moore-Potter	200
Ezzell, Lavaca	55
F	
*†Fabens, El Paso, 33	3,400
Fairbanks, Harris	1,050
Fairchilds, Fort Bend	95
*†FAIRFIELD, Freestone, 95	3,505
Fairlie, Hunt	80
Fair Oaks, Freestone	23
Fair Play, Panola	80
FAIRVIEW, Collin	893
Fairview, Wilson	112
Fairview, Howard	85
FAIRVIEW, Wise	180
Fairy, Hamilton	31
Falcon, Zapata	50
*Falcon Heights, Starr, 1	361
*†FALFURRIAS, Brooks, 73	6,103
*†FALLS CITY, Karnes, 23	580
Fannett, Jefferson	105
*Fannin, Goliad	94
Fargo, Wilbarger	161
Farmer, Crosby	49
†FARMERS BRANCH, Dallas (See Dallas)	24,863
Farmers Valley, Wilbarger	50
*†FARMERSVILLE, Collin, 47	2,360
Farmington, Grayson	20
*Farnsworth, Ochiltree, 6	149
Farrar, Limestone	51
Farrsville, Newton	150
*†FARWELL, Parmer, 33	1,354
*Fashing, Atascosa	50
*FATE, Rockwall, 2	263
Faught, Lamar	25
Faulkner, Lamar	48
*†FAYETTEVILLE, Fayette, 13	356
Faysville, Hidalgo	300
Fedor, Lee	76
*Fentress, Caldwell, 1	85
*†FERRIS, Dallas-Ellis, 32	2,228
Field Creek, Llano	32
*Fieldton, Lamb, 3	126
Field Schoolhouse, Erath	12
*Fife, McCulloch	32
Files Valley, Hill	50
Fink, Grayson	25
Finney, Hale	15
Finney, King	70
*Fischer, Comal, 3	20
Fisk, Coleman	50
Flagg, Castro	50
*Flat, Coryell, 2	210
Flatwoods, Eastland	56
*†FLATONIA, Fayette, 48	1,070
*Flint, Smith, 20	150
Flo, Leon	20
*Flomot, Motley, 1	181
*†FLORENCE, Williamson, 12	744
*†FLORESVILLE, Wilson, 75	4,381
Florey, Andrews	25
†FLOWER MOUND, Denton	4,402
Floyd, Hunt	220
*†FLOYDADA, Floyd, 70	4,193
*Fluvanna, Scurry, 6	180
*Flynn, Leon, 4	81
Foard City, Foard	10
Fodice, Houston	49

Town and County—	Pop.	Town and County—	Pop.	Town and County—	Pop.
*†FOLLETT, Lipscomb, 23	547	Garner, Parker	98	*GRAYBURG, Hardin	194
Foncine, Collin	20	Garner Park, Uvalde	40	Grays Prairie, Kaufman	171
Foot, Collin	20	GARRETT, Ellis	220	Graytown, Wilson	21
Fordtran, Victoria	18	Garretts Bluff, Lamar	20	Green, Karnes	35
*Forest, Cherokee	85	*†GARRISON, Nacogdoches,		Green Creek, Erath	75
*Forestburg, Montague, 1	200	32.	1,059	Green Lake, Calhoun	51
Forest Glade, Limestone	340	*Garwood, Colorado, 22	975	*†GREENVILLE, Hunt, 355	22,161
Forest Grove, Collin	20	*GARY, Panola, 10	322	Greenvine, Washington	35
Forest Grove, Milam	40	Gastonia, Kaufman	30	Greenwood, Hopkins	35
†FOREST HILL, Tarrant	11,684	*†GATESVILLE, Coryell, 87.	6,260	Greenwood, Midland	32
*†FORNEY, Kaufman, 62	2,483	*Gause, Milam, 2.	210	*Greenwood, Wise	76
*Forreston, Ellis, 11	300	Gay Hill, Washington	145	*GREGORY, San Patricio,	
*FORSAN, Howard, 11	239	*Geneva, Sabine	100	20.	2,739
Fort Bliss, El Paso	13,288	George's Creek, Somervell	66	Gresham, Smith	100
*†Fort Davis, Jeff Davis, 13	900	*†GEORGETOWN, Williamson,		GREY FOREST, Bexar	442
FORT GATES, Coryell	777	250.	9,468	Grice, Upshur	20
Fort Griffin, Shackelford	96	*†GEORGE WEST, Live Oak,		Griffin, Cherokee	21
*Fort Hancock, Hudspeth, 4	400	59.	2,627	Griffing Park, Jefferson	
†Fort Hood, Bell-Coryell, 9	32,597	Germania, Midland	27	(Consolidated with	
*Fort McKavett, Menard	103	*Geronimo, Guadalupe, 5	150	Port Arthur in 1983.)	
Fort Sam Houston, Bexar	10,553	GHOLSON, McLennan	263	Grit, Mason	63
Fort Spunky, Hood	15	*†GIDDINGS, Lee, 215	3,950	*†GROESBECK, Limestone,	
*†FORT STOCKTON, Pecos,		*Gilchrist, Galveston, 2	750	56.	3,373
197.	8,688	Giles, Donley	12	*†GROOM, Carson, 25	736
Fort Wolters, Palo Pinto-		*Gillett, Karnes	120	Grosvenor, Brown	31
Parker.	3,743	Gilliland, Knox	103	*GROVES, Jefferson, 145	17,090
*†FORT WORTH, Tarrant-		*†GILMER, Upshur, 113.	5,167	*†GROVETON, Trinity, 26	1,262
Johnson, 8,148	385,164	Ginger, Rains	96	Grow, King	85
1982 metro. pop.	1,050,000	*Girard, Kent, 1	125	Gruene, Comal	20
*Fowlerton, La Salle, 1	100	*Girvin, Pecos	30	*GRULLA, Starr,	
Frame Switch, Williamson	20	Givins, Lamar	135	(See La Grulla)	
*Francitas, Jackson	30	Glade, Tarrant	20	*†GRUVER, Hansford, 31	1,216
*Frankel City, Andrews	1,344	*†GLADEWATER, Gregg-		Guadalupe, Victoria	106
*†FRANKLIN, Robertson, 24	1,349	Upshur, 113	6,548	Guadalupe Station, Culberson	80
*†FRANKSTON, Anderson,		Glaze City, Gonzales	10	*Guerra, Jim Hogg	75
50.	1,255	*Glazier, Hemphill	20	Guion, Taylor	18
*Fred, Tyler, 2.	239	Glen Cove, Coleman	40	Gulf Dial, Hutchinson	80
*†FREDERICKSBURG, Gillespie,		Glendale, Trinity	78	Gulf Park (and Jones Creek),	
238.	6,412	Glenfawn, Rusk	16	Brazoria	2,150
*Fredonia, Mason, 1	74	*Glen Flora, Wharton, 1	210	GUN BARREL CITY,	
*†FREEPORT, Brazoria,		Glenn, Dickens	12	Henderson	2,118
390.	13,444	GLENN HEIGHTS, Dallas	1,033	Gunsight, Stephens	6
*†FREER, Duval, 81	3,213	*†GLEN ROSE, Somervell,		*GUNTER, Grayson, 9	849
Freestone, Freestone	35	33.	2,075	*†GUSTINE, Comanche, 8	416
Frelsburg, Colorado	75	Glidden, Colorado	55	*Guthrie, King, 4.	140
*Fresno, Fort Bend, 23	161	Glory, Lamar	30	*Guy, Fort Bend, 5.	25
Freyburg, Fayette	45	*Gober, Fannin, 1	146	**H**	
Friday, Trinity	41	*GODLEY, Johnson, 12	614	Hackberry, Cottle	26
Friendship, Williamson	48	*Golden, Wood, 5.	156	Hagansport, Franklin	40
*†FRIENDSWOOD, Galveston,		Goldfinch, Frio	35	Hail, Fannin	30
244.	10,719	*Goldsboro, Coleman	30	Hainesville, Wood	74
Frio, Castro	60	*GOLDSMITH, Ector, 17	409	*†HALE CENTER, Hale, 37	2,297
*†FRIONA, Parmer, 77	3,809	*GOLDTHWAITE, Mills, 46.	1,783	Halfway, Hale	70
Frio Town, Frio	38	*†GOLIAD, Goliad, 37	1,990	*†HALLETTSVILLE, Lavaca,	
*†FRISCO, Collin, 76	4,400	GOLINDA, Falls-McLennan	335	110.	2,865
*FRITCH, Hutchinson-Moore,		*GONZALES, Gonzales, 187	7,152	HALLSBURG, McLennan	455
31.	2,299	*Goodland, Bailey, 2	65	*†HALLSVILLE, Harrison, 34.	1,556
*Fronton, Starr	110	Goodlett, Hardeman	205	Halsted, Fayette	46
*†FROST, Navarro, 9.	564	GOODLOW, Navarro	343	†HALTOM CITY, Tarrant	29,014
Fruitland, Montague	20	Goodnight, Armstrong	25	Hamby, Taylor	100
*FRUITVALE, Van Zandt, 6.	367	*GOODRICH, Polk, 7	350	*†HAMILTON, Hamilton, 71.	3,189
Frydek, Austin	150	Goodsprings, Rusk	21	*†HAMLIN, Jones-Fisher, 55	3,248
Fulbright, Red River	200	*GORDON, Palo Pinto, 14.	516	Hammond, Robertson	15
FULLER SPRINGS, Angelina	1,470	*Gordonville, Grayson, 28	220	Hamon, Gonzales	44
*†FULSHEAR, Fort Bend, 15	594	*GOREE, Knox, 5	524	*Hamshire, Jefferson, 6.	350
*FULTON, Aransas, 37.	725	*†GORMAN, Eastland, 25	1,258	*Hankamer, Chambers, 4	189
Funston, Jones	76	*Gouldbusk, Coleman	70	*†HAPPY, Swisher-Randall, 15.	674
		Gourdneck, Panola	62	Happy Union, Hale	15
G		Grace, King	70	Harbin, Erath	21
*Gail, Borden, 4.	189	Graceton, Upshur	40	*HARDIN, Liberty, 11	779
*†GAINESVILLE, Cooke,		*†GRAFORD, Palo Pinto, 16.	495	Hare, Williamson	70
323.	14,081	*†GRAHAM, Young, 367.	9,170	*Hargill, Hidalgo, 4	550
*†GALENA PARK, Harris,		Graham Chapel, Garza	82	†HARKER HEIGHTS, Bell	7,345
116.	9,879	Grand Bluff, Panola	97	Harkeyville, San Saba	12
*GALLATIN, Cherokee, 1	230	*†GRANBURY, Hood, 270	3,332	*Harleton, Harrison, 5	260
Galloway, Panola	71	*GRANDFALLS, Ward, 13	635	*†HARLINGEN, Cameron,	
*†GALVESTON, Galveston,		*†GRAND PRAIRIE, Dallas-		781.	43,543
955.	61,902	Tarrant, 1,239.	71,462	Brownsville-Harlingen	
Galveston-Texas City—		*†GRAND SALINE, Van Zandt,		1982 metro. pop.	230,500
1982 metro. pop.	207,600	57.	2,709	Harmon, Lamar	35
*†GANADO, Jackson, 27	1,770	*GRANDVIEW, Johnson, 38	1,205	*†Harper, Gillespie, 15.	383
Garceno, Starr	45	*†GRANGER, Williamson, 12.	1,236	Harris Chapel, Panola	180
*Garciasville, Starr, 2	104	GRANITE SHOALS, Burnet	634	Harrison, McLennan	25
*Garden City, Glasscock, 6.	293	*†GRAPELAND, Houston, 29	1,634	*Harrold, Wilbarger, 4.	320
*Gardendale, Ector, 12	40	*†GRAPEVINE, Tarrant-Dallas		*†HART, Castro, 34	1,008
Gardendale, La Salle	59	287.	11,801	Hartburg, Newton	275
GARDEN RIDGE, Comal.	647	Grassland, Lynn	61	*Hartley, Hartley, 5	370
Garden Valley, Smith	150	Grassyville, Bastrop	50	Harvey, Brazos	310
*†GARLAND, Dallas, 1,770.	138,857	Grayback, Wilbarger	25	*Harwood, Gonzales, 2.	112

Town and County—	Pop.	Town and County—	Pop.	Town and County—	Pop.
†Kingwood, Harris	50	*†LAMPASAS, Lampasas, 125	6,165	*Lissie, Wharton, 3	70
Kinkler, Lavaca	75			Littig, Travis	37
Kiomatia, Red River	61	*†LANCASTER, Dallas, 229	14,807	*LITTLE ELM, Denton, 7	926
†KIRBY, Bexar	6,435			*†LITTLEFIELD, Lamb, 103	7,409
*†KIRBYVILLE, Jasper, 70	1,972	Landrum Station, Cameron	125	Little New York, Gonzales	20
*Kirkland, Childress	100	*Lane City, Wharton, 3	111	*LITTLE RIVER-ACADEMY,	
Kirtley, Fayette	43	Laneport, Williamson	60	Bell, 7	1,155
*KIRVIN, Freestone	107	*Laneville, Rusk, 6	200	LIVE OAK, Bexar	8,183
Kleberg, Dallas, 1	4,961	*Langtry, Val Verde	145	*LIVERPOOL, Brazoria, 6	602
*Klondike, Delta	135	Lanier, Cass	40	*†LIVINGSTON, Polk, 245	4,928
*Knickerbocker, Tom Green	50	Lanley, Freestone	27	*†LLANO, Llano, 76	3,071
*Knippa, Uvalde, 10	360	Lannius, Fannin	79	Lobo, Culberson	40
*Knott, Howard, 2	685	La Paloma, Cameron	110	Locker, San Saba	16
*KNOX CITY, Knox, 28	1,546	*†LA PORTE, Harris, 315	14,062	Lockett, Wilbarger	200
Koerth, Lavaca	45	*†La Pryor, Zavala, 18	550	Lockettville, Hockley	20
Kokomo, Eastland	25	*†LAREDO, Webb, 1,273	91,449	*†LOCKHART, Caldwell, 103	7,953
Kopernik Shores, Cameron	26	1982 metro. pop.	109,900	*†LOCKNEY, Floyd, 41	2,334
*Kopperl, Bosque, 1	225	La Reforma, Starr	45	*Lodi, Marion, 2	164
Kosciusko, Wilson	81	*Lariat, Parmer, 2	200	*Lohn, McCulloch, 2	149
*†KOSSE, Limestone, 12	484	Lark, Carson	26	Lois, Cooke	60
*†KOUNTZE, Hardin, 56	2,716	*Larue, Henderson, 7	160	*Lolita, Jackson, 7	300
*†KRESS, Swisher, 20	783	*La Salle, Jackson	75	Loma Alta, Val Verde	30
KRUGERVILLE, Denton	469	*Lasara, Willacy, 3	100	LOMAX, Harris	2,991
*†KRUM, Denton, 13	917	Lassater, Marion	48	*†LOMETA, Lampasas, 16	666
*Kurten, Brazos, 8	150	Latch, Upshur	50	*London, Kimble, 2	180
*†KYLE, Hays, 35	2,093	*LATEXO, Houston, 3	312	Lone Camp, Palo Pinto	32
Kyote, Atascosa	25	Latium, Washington	30	Lone Cedar, Ellis	18
L		Laughlin, Val Verde	3,458	Lone Elm, Ellis	20
*La Blanca, Hidalgo	150	La Union, Cameron	20	*Lone Grove, Llano	50
Lackland, Bexar	19,141	Laurel, Newton	125	*†LONE OAK, Hunt, 6	467
*†LACOSTE, Medina, 14	862	Laureles, Cameron	20	Lone Star, Floyd	125
LACY-LAKEVIEW, McLennan		*†LA VERNIA, Wilson, 23	632	*†LONE STAR, Morris, 69	2,036
	2,752	*LA VILLA, Hidalgo, 3	1,442	*Long Branch, Panola, 1	181
Lacy, Trinity	24	*LAVON, Collin, 1	185	*Long Mott, Calhoun, 6	76
*†LADONIA, Fannin, 8	761	*LA WARD, Jackson, 6	218	Longpoint, Washington	80
LaFayette, Upshur	80	*Lawn, Taylor, 6	390	*†LONGVIEW, Gregg, 1,665	62,762
*†LA FERIA, Cameron, 32	3,495	Lawrence, Kaufman	113	1982 metro. pop.	165,200
Lagarto, Live Oak	80	Lazare, Cottle	26	Longworth, Fisher	65
La Gloria, Starr	102	*Lazbuddie, Parmer, 9	248	*Loop, Gaines, 9	315
†Lago Vista, Travis	2,500	*Leaday, Coleman	55	*Lopeno, Zapata, 1	100
*†LA GRANGE, Fayette, 199	3,768	*†LEAGUE CITY, Galveston-		*†LORAINE, Mitchell, 6	929
LA GRULLA, Starr, 2	1,442	Harris, 184	16,578	*LORENA, McLennan, 30	619
Laguna Heights, Cameron	740	*†LEAKEY, Real, 15	468	*†LORENZO, Crosby, 15	1,394
Laguna Park, Bosque	550	*LEANDER, Williamson, 90	2,179	*Los Angeles, La Salle	140
LAGUNA VISTA, Cameron	632	LEARY, Bowie	253	Los Barreras, Starr	125
*Laird Hill, Rusk, 1	405	Lebanon, Collin	50	*Los Ebanos, Hidalgo	100
La Isla, El Paso	29	*Ledbetter, Fayette, 3	76	*†LOS FRESNOS, Cameron,	
Lajitas, Brewster	6	Leedale, Bell	20	29	2,173
*LA JOYA, Hidalgo, 11	2,018	*Leesburg, Camp, 3	115	*Los Indios, Cameron	206
Lake Arrowhead, Clay	75	*Leesville, Gonzales, 5	150	Losoya, Bexar	322
Lake Barbara, Brazoria		*LEFORS, Gray, 10	829	Los Saenz, Starr (Incorporated	
(Consolidated with Clute)		*Leggett, Polk, 6	375	with Roma; census enumerated	
LAKE BRIDGEPORT, Wise	271	Leigh, Harrison	100	as Roma-Los Saenz).	
Lake Cisco, Eastland	105	Lela, Wheeler	135	*†LOTT, Falls, 11	865
LAKE CITY, San Patricio	431	*Lelia Lake, Donley, 2	125	Lotta, Harrison	10
*Lake Creek, Delta, 2	60	*Leming, Atascosa, 3	250	*†Louise, Wharton, 15	310
*†LAKE DALLAS, Denton, 49	3,177	*Lenorah, Martin, 3	70	*†LOVELADY, Houston, 10	509
Lake Dunlap, Guadalupe	200	Lenz, Karnes	20	*Loving, Young, 9	240
Lake Hills, Bandera	300	Leo, Cooke	80	*Lowake, Concho	40
*†LAKE JACKSON, Brazoria, 195	19,102	*LEONA, Leon	165	LOWRY CROSSING, Collin	443
Lake Leon, Eastland	75	*†LEONARD, Fannin, 26	1,421	Loyal Valley, Mason	150
Lake Nueces, Uvalde	15	*Leon Junction, Coryell	25	*Lozano, Cameron	200
Lake Placid, Guadalupe	300	Leon Springs, Bexar	137	*†LUBBOCK, Lubbock,	
LAKEPORT, Gregg	835	LEON VALLEY, Bexar	9,088	3,165	173,979
LAKE RANSOM CANYON,		*†LEROY, McLennan, 3	253	1982 metro. pop.	216,700
Lubbock	561	Lesley, Hall	39	LUCAS, Collin	2,000
LAKESIDE CITY,		*†LEVELLAND, Hockley,		Luckenbach, Gillespie	25
Archer-Wichita	515	295	13,809	*†LUEDERS, Jones, 6	420
Lakeside, San Patricio	276	Leverett's Chapel, Rusk	450	LUELLA, Grayson	371
LAKESIDE, Tarrant	957	Levi, McLennan	50	*†LUFKIN, Angelina, 693	28,562
Lakeside Village, Bosque	226	Levita, Coryell	70	*†LULING, Caldwell, 142	5,039
LAKE TANGLEWOOD, Randall	485	*†LEWISVILLE, Denton, 517	24,273	†LUMBERTON, Hardin	2,480
Laketon, Gray	12	*LEXINGTON, Lee, 21	1,065	Lund, Travis	50
Lake Victor, Burnet	215	Liberty, Freestone	75	Luther, Howard	335
Lakeview, Floyd	45	*†LIBERTY, Liberty, 260	7,945	Lutie, Collingsworth	35
*LAKEVIEW, Hall, 2	244	†LIBERTY CITY, Gregg	1,121	Lydia, Red River	58
Lakeview (Merged		*Liberty Hill, Williamson, 15	300	*LYFORD, Willacy, 13	1,618
with Port Arthur)		*Lillian, Johnson, 3	105	Lynchburg, Harris	100
LAKEWAY, Travis	790	*Lincoln, Lee, 4	276	*Lyons, Burleson, 3	360
LAKEWOOD VILLAGE, Denton	165	LINCOLN PARK, Denton	39	*†LYTLE, Atascosa, 15	1,920
†LAKE WORTH, Tarrant	4,394	*†LINDALE, Smith, 67	2,180	Lytton Springs, Caldwell	76
Lamar, Aransas	150	*†LINDEN, Cass, 37	2,443	**Mc**	
*LA MARQUE, Galveston, 163	15,372	Lindenau, DeWitt	50	*McAdoo, Dickens, 1	169
Lamasco, Fannin	32	*LINDSAY, Cooke, 6	581	*†McALLEN, Hidalgo, 66,281	
*†LAMESA, Dawson, 217	11,790	*Lingleville, Erath	100	McAllen-Mission-Edinburg	
Lamkin, Comanche	88	*Linn, Hidalgo, 5	450	1982 metro. pop.	315,100
		Linwood, Cherokee	40	*†McCAMEY, Upton, 51	2,436
		*†LIPAN, Hood, 11	435	*McCaulley, Fisher, 1	96
		*Lipscomb, Lipscomb, 2	190	McClanahan, Falls	60

Town and County—	Pop.
Nelta, Hopkins	36
*Nemo, Somervell, 2	56
NESBITT, Harrison	129
Neuville, Shelby	43
*Nevada, Collin, 4	400
*NEWARK, Wise, 8	466
*New Baden, Robertson, 1	105
NEW BERLIN, Guadalupe	253
*†NEW BOSTON, Bowie, 46	4,628
*†NEW BRAUNFELS, Comal, 558	22,402
Newburg, Comanche	35
Newby, Leon	40
*†New Caney, Montgomery, 81	2,771
*†NEWCASTLE, Young, 4	688
NEW CHAPEL HILL, Smith	618
*NEW DEAL, Lubbock, 7	637
*Newgulf, Wharton, 2	963
NEW HOME, Lynn, 5	274
NEW HOPE, Collin	331
New Hope, Jones	25
New Hope, Freestone	85
Newlin, Hall	31
*NEW LONDON, Rusk, 13	942
New Lynn, Lynn	18
Newman, El Paso	60
*Newport, Clay	70
New Salem, Rusk	31
Newsome, Camp	100
*NEW SUMMERFIELD, Cherokee, 2	319
New Sweden, Travis	60
*†NEWTON, Newton, 45	1,620
*New Ulm, Austin, 7	650
*†NEW WAVERLY, Walker, 28	824
New Wehdem, Austin	100
New Willard, Polk	160
NEYLANDVILLE, Hunt	168
Nickel Creek, Culberson	16
Niederwald, Hays	79
Nigton, Trinity	34
Nimrod, Eastland	85
Nineveh, Leon	101
*†NIXON, Gonzales, 26	2,008
Noack, Williamson	60
Nobility, Fannin	21
Noble, Lamar	40
*†NOCONA, Montague, 84	2,992
Nogalus Prairie, Trinity	41
*Nolan, Nolan	131
*NOLANVILLE, Bell, 5	1,308
*NOME, Jefferson, 16	550
Noodle, Jones	
Noonday, Smith	385
Nopal, DeWitt	25
*†NORDHEIM, DeWitt, 7	369
Norman, Williamson	20
Normandy, Maverick	98
*†NORMANGEE, Leon-Madison, 12	636
*Normanna, Bee, 2	75
Norse, Bosque	110
NORTH CLEVELAND, Liberty	259
North Cowden, Ector	80
NORTHCREST, McLennan	1,944
*Northfield, Motley	25
NORTHLAKE, Denton	143
†NORTH RICHLAND HILLS, Tarrant	30,592
Northrup, Lee	71
North San Pedro, Nueces	2,229
*North Zulch, Madison, 2	100
*Norton, Runnels	76
Notla, Ochiltree	20
*Notrees, Ector, 1	338
*NOVICE, Coleman, 1	201
Novohrad, Lavaca	35
Noxville, Kimble	75
Nugent, Jones	41
*Nursery, Victoria, 4	106
O	
Oakalla, Burnet	45
Oak Forest, Gonzales	25
Oak Grove, Bowie	60
OAK GROVE, Kaufman	319
Oak Grove, Wood	74
Oak Hill, Rusk	24

Town and County—	Pop.
Oak Hill, Travis	425
*Oakhurst, San Jacinto, 4	214
Oaklake, McLennan	60
*Oakland, Colorado, 1	80
Oakland, Van Zandt	26
OAK POINT, Denton	387
Oak Ridge, Fannin	90
OAK RIDGE, Kaufman	183
OAK RIDGE NORTH, Montgomery	2,504
Oakville, Live Oak, 1	260
*†OAKWOOD, Leon, 6	606
*O'BRIEN, Haskell, 1	212
Ocee, McLennan	35
*Odell, Wilbarger	131
*†ODEM, San Patricio, 27	2,363
*†ODESSA, Ector, 2,675	90,027
1982 metro. pop.	134,200
*†O'DONNELL, Lynn-Dawson, 20	1,200
Oenaville, Bell	140
O'Farrell, Cass	20
Ogden, Comal	20
*†OGLESBY, Coryell, 1	470
*Oilton, Webb	150
Oklahoma Lane, Parmer	64
*Oklaunion, Wilbarger, 1	138
Okra, Eastland	20
Ola, Kaufman	50
*Olden, Eastland, 1	110
Old Center, Panola	83
Oldenburg, Fayette	54
*Old Glory, Stonewall	125
*Old Ocean, Brazoria, 12	915
OLD RIVER, Chambers	1,058
Old Salem, Newton	85
Olin, Hamilton	12
Olivia, Calhoun	215
*Olmito, Cameron, 11	200
OLMOS PARK, Bexar	2,069
*†OLNEY, Young, 95	4,060
*†OLTON, Lamb, 41	2,235
*†OMAHA, Morris, 15	960
Omen, Smith	150
*†ONALASKA, Polk, 43	386
Oplin, Callahan	75
O'Quinn, Fayette	25
*†ORANGE, Orange, 521	23,628
*Orangefield, Orange, 11	725
*†ORANGE GROVE, Jim Wells, 27	1,212
Orangeville, Fannin	23
*ORCHARD, Fort Bend, 7	408
*ORE CITY, Upshur, 33	1,050
Orient, Tom Green	40
*Orla, Reeves, 4	183
Osage, Coryell	30
Oscar, Bell	10
Osceola, Hill	90
Otey, Brazoria	318
Otis Chalk, Howard	79
*Ottine, Gonzales	90
*Otto, Falls	85
*Ovalo, Taylor	225
*†OVERTON, Rusk-Smith, 39	2,430
OVILLA, Dallas-Ellis	1,067
Owens, Crosby	75
Oxford, Llano	33
OYSTER CREEK, Brazoria	1,473
*†Ozona, Crockett, 72	3,500
P	
Padgett, Young	23
*†PADUCAH, Cottle, 48	2,216
*Paige, Bastrop, 4	275
*†PAINT ROCK, Concho, 5	256
*†PALACIOS, Matagorda, 49	4,667
Palava, Fisher	12
*†PALESTINE, Anderson, 345	15,948
Palito Blanco, Jim Wells	35
*†PALMER, Ellis, 14	1,187
PALMHURST, Hidalgo	364
PALM VALLEY, Cameron	798
PALMVIEW, Hidalgo	683
Paloduro, Armstrong (See JA Ranch)	
*Palo Pinto, Palo Pinto, 6	350
*Paluxy, Hood	76

Town and County—	Pop.
*†PAMPA, Gray, 489	21,396
Pandale, Val Verde	20
*Pandora, Wilson	57
*†PANHANDLE, Carson, 27	2,226
*Panna Maria, Karnes, 1	96
*Panola, Panola, 3	296
PANORAMA VILLAGE, Montgomery	1,186
PANTEGO, Tarrant	2,431
Pantex, Carson	115
Papalote, Bee	70
*Paradise, Wise, 9	275
*†PARIS, Lamar, 445	25,498
Park, Fayette	22
Park Community, Navarro	160
PARKER, Collin	1,250
Parker, Johnson	21
Parkview Estates, Guadalupe	400
Parnell, Hall	43
Parsley Hill, Wilbarger	40
Parvin, Denton	44
*†PASADENA, Harris, 1,130	112,560
Patilo, Erath	10
Patricia, Dawson	60
Patroon, Shelby	55
*PATTISON, Waller, 5	318
PATTON, Montgomery	1,050
*Pattonville, Lamar, 2	180
Pawelekville, Karnes	105
*Pawnee, Bee, 2	249
Paxton, Shelby	161
PAYNE SPRINGS, Henderson	422
*Peacock, Stonewall, 1	125
Pearl, Coryell	125
*†PEARLAND, Brazoria, 340	13,248
Pear Ridge, Jefferson (Consolidated with Port Arthur.)	
*†PEARSALL, Frio, 140	7,383
*Pear Valley, McCulloch	37
*Peaster, Parker, 1	80
*PECAN GAP, Delta-Fannin, 6	250
*†PECOS, Reeves, 185	12,855
Peden, Tarrant	40
*Peggy, Atascosa, 2	20
Pelham, Navarro	75
Pelican Bay, Tarrant	518
*Pendleton, Bell	65
*PENELOPE, Hill, 1	235
*Penitas, Hidalgo, 1	150
*Pennington, Trinity, 1	100
*Penwell, Ector, 3	74
Peoria, Hill	81
*Pep, Hockley, 2	50
Percilla, Houston	95
Perrin, Grayson	1,709
*Perrin, Jack, 2	300
*Perry, Falls	96
*†PERRYTON, Ochiltree, 220	7,991
Perryville, Wood	52
Peters, Austin	25
*†PETERSBURG, Hale, 31	1,633
Peter's Prairie, Red River	40
Petroleum, Jim Hogg	15
*PETROLIA, Clay, 6	755
Petteway, Robertson	25
*Pettit, Hockley, 1	26
*Pettus, Bee, 12	400
*Petty, Lamar	100
Petty, Lynn	24
Petty's Chapel, Navarro	25
*†PFLUGERVILLE, Travis, 35	745
Phalba, Van Zandt	58
*†PHARR, Hidalgo, 282	21,381
*Phelps, Walker	98
Phillips, Hutchinson, 1	2,515
Phillipsburg, Washington	40
*Pickton, Hopkins, 2	90
Pidcoke, Coryell	30
Piedmont, Grimes	46
*Pierce, Wharton	49
Pike, Collin	80
Pilgrim, Gonzales	60
Pilgrim Rest, Rains	72
Pilotgrove, Grayson	75
*†PILOT POINT, Denton, 43	2,211

Town and County—	Pop.	Town and County—	Pop.	Town and County—	Pop.
Pine, Camp	78	PRIMERA, Cameron	1,380	Rhineland, Knox	196
Pine Forest, Hopkins	51	Primrose, Van Zandt	24	*†RHOME, Wise, 15	478
PINE FOREST, Orange	639	*†PRINCETON, Collin, 28	2,450	Rhonesboro, Upshur	40
Pine Grove, Newton	160	Pringle, Hutchinson	40	Ricardo, Kleberg	120
Pinehill, Rusk	49	Pritchett, Upshur	125	*†RICE, Navarro, 4	439
*Pinehurst, Montgomery, 32	290	*Proctor, Comanche, 3	220	Rices Crossing, Williamson	100
†PINEHURST, Orange	2,928	*Progreso, Hidalgo, 12	185	*Richards, Grimes, 2	296
*†PINELAND, Sabine, 18	1,111	Progreso Lakes, Hidalgo	197	*†RICHARDSON, Dallas-Collin,	
Pine Mills, Wood	2	Progress, Bailey	49	1,545.	72,496
Pine Springs, Culberson	20	*†PROSPER, Collin, 11	675	*RICHLAND, Navarro, 1	260
PINEY POINT VILLAGE,		Providence, Angelina	103	RICHLAND HILLS, Tarrant	7,977
Harris	2,958	Pueblo, Eastland	46	*RICHLAND SPRINGS,	
Pioneer, Eastland	40	Puerto Rico, Hidalgo	91	San Saba, 8	420
*Pipecreek, Bandera, 11	66	Pullman, Potter	31	*†RICHMOND, Fort Bend, 157	9,692
*†PITTSBURG, Camp, 80	4,245	Pumpville, Val Verde	21	†RICHWOOD, Brazoria	2,591
*Placedo, Victoria, 6	515	Punkin Center, Eastland	12	*Ridge, Robertson	67
Placid, McCulloch	32	*Purdon, Navarro, 2	133	Ridgeway, Hopkins	54
*†PLAINS, Yoakum, 15	1,457	Purley, Franklin	81	*†RIESEL, McLennan, 5	691
*†PLAINVIEW, Hale, 395	22,187	*Purmela, Coryell, 1	61	*Ringgold, Montague	100
Plank, Hardin	205	Pursley, Navarro	40	*Rio Frio, Real	50
*†PLANO, Collin, 1,175.	99,100	Purves, Erath	50	*†Rio Grande City, Starr,	
*Plantersville, Grimes, 5	212	*PUTNAM, Callahan, 7	116	94.	5,720
Plaska, Hall	21	*PYOTE, Ward	382	*RIO HONDO, Cameron, 24	1,673
Plateau, Culberson	5			*Riomedina, Medina	49
PLEAK, Fort Bend	619	**Q**		Rios, Duval	75
Pleasant Grove, Falls	35	*Quail, Collingsworth	92	*†RIO VISTA, Johnson, 6	509
Pleasant Hill, Eastland	15	*†QUANAH, Hardeman, 77	3,890	*†RISING STAR, Eastland,	
*†PLEASANTON, Atascosa,		Quarterway, Hale	5	23.	1,204
115.	6,346	*QUEEN CITY, Cass, 21	1,748	Rita, Burleson	50
PLEASANT VALLEY, Wichita	335	*Quemado, Maverick, 5	426	Riverby, Fannin	15
*Pledger, Matagorda, 2	159	Quihi, Medina	96	RIVER OAKS, Tarrant	6,890
*Plum, Fayette, 3	95	*†QUINLAN, Hunt, 51	1,002	*RIVERSIDE, Walker, 6	425
PLUM GROVE, Liberty	455	QUINTANA, Brazoria	30	*Riviera, Kleberg, 14	550
*†POINT, Rains, 14	468	*†QUITAQUE, Briscoe, 11	696	Roane, Navarro	120
*POINTBLANK, San Jacinto, 11	325	*†QUITMAN, Wood, 75.	1,893	*†ROANOKE, Denton, 63	910
*†POINT COMFORT, Calhoun,				Roans Prairie, Grimes, 2	56
12.	1,125	**R**		*ROARING SPRINGS, Motley,	
Point Enterprise, Limestone	200	Rabbs Prairie, Fayette	31	6	315
Polar, Kent	20	Rachal, Brooks	36	*†ROBERT LEE, Coke, 25	1,202
*Pollok, Angelina, 4	300	Radium, Jones	26	Robertson, Crosby	35
*PONDER, Denton, 3.	297	Ragtown, Lamar	25	†ROBINSON, McLennan	6,074
Ponta, Cherokee	50	*Rainbow, Somervell, 5	76	*†ROBSTOWN, Nueces, 146	12,100
*Pontotoc, Mason	206	Raisin, Victoria	40	*†ROBY, Fisher, 9	814
*Poolville, Parker, 7	230	*†RALLS, Crosby, 37	2,422	*Rochelle, McCulloch, 4	163
*†PORT ARANSAS, Nueces,		Ramirez, Duval	40	*†ROCHESTER, Haskell, 10	492
73.	1,968	RANCHO VIEJO, Cameron	208	Rock Creek, McLennan	25
*†PORT ARTHUR, Jefferson,		Randado, Jim Hogg	15	Rock Creek, Somervell	36
631.	61,251	Randolph, Bexar	5,329	*†ROCKDALE, Milam, 105.	5,611
Beaumont-Port Arthur		*Randolph, Fannin, 1	70	Rockett, Ellis	124
1982 metro. pop.	387,700	*†RANGER, Eastland, 56	3,142	Rockhill, Collin	25
*Port Bolivar, Galveston, 22	1,200	Rangerville, Cameron	80	Rock Hill, Wood	21
*†Porter, Montgomery, 114	2,146	Rankin, Ellis	12	*Rock Island, Colorado, 8.	160
Porter Springs, Houston	50	*†RANKIN, Upton, 16.	1,216	*Rockland, Tyler	105
*†PORT ISABEL, Cameron,		Ransom Canyon, Lubbock	581	Rockne, Bastrop	400
98.	3,769	*Ratcliff, Houston	106	*†ROCKPORT, Aransas, 232	3,686
*†PORTLAND, Nueces-		Ratibor, Bell	10	*†ROCKSPRINGS, Edwards,	
San Patricio, 104.	12,023	*Ravenna, Fannin, 1	186	26.	1,317
*†PORT LAVACA, Calhoun,		Rayburn, Liberty	30	*†ROCKWALL, Rockwall, 175	5,939
185.	10,911	Rayland, Foard	30	*Rockwood, Coleman	80
Port Mansfield, Willacy, 8	731	*†RAYMONDVILLE, Willacy,		Rocky Branch, Morris	120
*†PORT NECHES, Jefferson,		90.	9,493	ROCKY MOUND, Camp	123
117.	13,944	Ray Point, Live Oak	75	*Roganville, Jasper	100
*Port O'Connor, Calhoun,		*Raywood, Liberty, 16	231	*†ROGERS, Bell, 15	1,242
15.	810	Razor, Lamar	15	ROLLING MEADOWS, Gregg	252
Posey, Lubbock	125	*Reagan, Falls, 2	200	ROLLINGWOOD, Travis	1,027
*†POST, Garza, 76	3,961	Reagan Wells, Uvalde	20	*†ROMA-LOS SAENZ, Starr,	
Postoak, Jack	79	Reagor Springs, Ellis	45	35.	3,384
POST OAK BEND, Kaufman	266	*Realitos, Duval, 1	250	(Roma and Los Saenz are inde-	
*†POTEET, Atascosa, 28	3,086	Red Bluff, Reeves	40	pendent towns but are incorpo-	
*†POTH, Wilson, 20	1,461	Red Cut Heights, Bowie	563	rated together.)	
Potosi, Taylor	149	*Redford, Presidio	107	ROMAN FOREST, Montgomery	929
*†POTTSBORO, Grayson, 35	895	Red Hill, Cass	20	*Romayor, Liberty	96
*Pottsville, Hamilton, 2	312	*†RED OAK, Ellis, 61	1,882	*Romero, Hartley	25
*Powderly, Lamar, 9	185	Red Ranger, Bell	15	Romney, Eastland	12
*†POWELL, Navarro, 3	111	*Red Rock, Bastrop, 1	100	*Roosevelt, Kimble, 2	98
*POYNOR, Henderson, 5	272	*Red Springs, Baylor, 2	100	Roosevelt, Lubbock	3,500
Praesel, Milam	115	*†Redwater, Bowie, 5	460	*ROPESVILLE, Hockley, 7	489
Praha, Fayette	25	Redwood, Guadalupe	40	*Rosanky, Bastrop, 4	210
Prairie Dell, Bell	20	Reese, Cherokee	75	*†ROSCOE, Nolan, 20.	1,628
*Prairie Hill, Limestone	150	Reese Village, Lubbock	2,600	*†ROSEBUD, Falls, 29	2,076
*Prairie Lea, Caldwell	100	*†REFUGIO, Refugio, 89	3,898	ROSE CITY, Orange	663
Prairie Point, Cooke	30	Regency, Mills	25	ROSE HILL ACRES, Hardin	460
PRAIRIE VIEW, Waller, 3	3,993	Reilly Springs, Hopkins	44	*†ROSENBERG, Fort Bend,	
Prairieville, Kaufman	50	*REKLAW, Cherokee-Rusk, 4	305	319.	17,840
*†PREMONT, Jim Wells, 42	2,984	Rendon, Tarrant	90	Rosenthal, McLennan	55
*†Presidio, Presidio, 21	1,603	RENO, Lamar	1,059	Rosevine, Sabine	50
Preston, Grayson	250	RENO, Parker	1,174	Rosewood, Upshur	100
*Price, Rusk, 3	275	RETREAT, Navarro	255	*Rosharon, Brazoria, 27.	435
*Priddy, Mills, 6	215	Rhea, Parmer	98	Rosita, Starr	220
		Rhea Mills, Collin	47		

Town and County—	Pop.
*ROSS, McLennan, 3	200
Ross City, Howard	81
*Rosser, Kaufman, 2	255
*Rosston, Cooke	110
Rossville, Atascosa	47
*†ROTAN, Fisher, 27	2,284
*Round Mountain, Blanco, 3	73
Round Prairie, Navarro	40
*†ROUND ROCK, Williamson, 335	12,740
Round Timber, Baylor	10
*†ROUND TOP, Fayette, 4	87
Roundup, Hockley	27
Rowden, Callahan	30
*†Rowena, Runnels, 7	466
*†ROWLETT, Dallas-Rockwall, 147	7,522
*†ROXTON, Lamar, 4	735
*Royalty, Ward, 3	196
*†ROYSE CITY, Rockwall-Collin, 27	1,566
Royston, Fisher	30
Rucker's Bridge, Lamar	20
Rugby, Red River	24
Ruidosa, Presidio	43
*†RULE, Haskell, 21	1,015
RUNAWAY BAY, Wise	504
*†RUNGE, Karnes, 11	1,244
Rural Shade, Navarro	30
*†RUSK, Cherokee, 62	4,681
Russell, Leon	27
Rutersville, Fayette	72
*Rye, Liberty, 9	76
S	
Sabanna, Eastland	12
*†SABINAL, Uvalde, 24	1,827
Sabine, Jefferson	75
Sabine, Gregg	750
*Sabine Pass, Jefferson, 32	1,500
*SACHSE, Collin-Dallas	1,640
†Sacul, Nacogdoches, 1	170
*SADLER, Grayson, 3	329
Sagerton, Haskell, 1	115
†SAGINAW, Tarrant, 2	5,736
Saint Francis, Potter	30
*Saint Hedwig, Bexar, 4	970
*†SAINT JO, Montague, 18	1,071
SAINT PAUL, Collin	400
Saint Paul, San Patricio	180
*†Salado, Bell, 27	400
Salem, Victoria	25
Salesville, Palo Pinto	40
*Salineno, Starr, 1	155
Salmon, Anderson	20
*Salt Flat, Hudspeth	35
Salt Gap, McCulloch	25
*Saltillo, Hopkins, 1	200
Samfordyce, Hidalgo	85
*Samnorwood, Collingsworth	110
Sample, Gonzales	25
*†SAN ANGELO, Tom Green, 1,149	73,240
1982 metro. pop.	90,700
*†SAN ANTONIO, Bexar, 12,326	786,023
1982 metro. pop.	1,141,000
Sanatorium, Tom Green	450
*†SAN AUGUSTINE, San Augustine, 55	2,930
*†SAN BENITO, Cameron, 152	17,988
San Carlos, Hidalgo	100
Sanco, Coke	30
Sanctuary, Parker	215
Sand, Dawson	30
*†Sanderson, Terrell, 12	1,500
Sand Springs, Howard	903
*Sandia, Jim Wells, 11	215
*†SAN DIEGO, Duval-Jim Wells, 25	5,225
Sandoval, Williamson	50
*Sandy, Blanco, 2	25
Sandy Harbor, Llano	85
Sandy Hill, Washington	50
Sandy Point, Brazoria	30
*San Elizario, El Paso, 1	1,100
*SAN FELIPE, Austin, 4	532
*SANFORD, Hutchinson, 4	249
San Gabriel, Milam, 1	96
*†SANGER, Denton, 36	2,574
*San Isidro, Starr, 7	130
San Jacinto Monument, Harris	50
*†SAN JUAN, Hidalgo, 53	7,608
SAN LEANNA, Travis	290
San Leon, Galveston	100
*†SAN MARCOS, Hays, 395	23,420
SAN PATRICIO, Nueces-San Patricio	241
San Pedro, Zapata	25
*SAN PERLITA, Willacy, 1	475
*†SAN SABA, San Saba, 62	2,847
SANSOM PARK VILLAGE, Tarrant	3,921
*†SANTA ANNA, Coleman, 26	1,535
Santa Anna, Starr	30
Santa Catarina, Starr	48
*Santa Elena, Starr, 1	64
*SANTA FE, Galveston, 57	6,172
*Santa Maria, Cameron, 1	210
*SANTA ROSA, Cameron, 21	1,889
*†Santo, Palo Pinto, 14	312
*San Ygnacio, Zapata, 3	895
*Saragosa, Reeves	185
*Saratoga, Hardin, 3	1,000
Sarco, Goliad	50
Sardis, Fisher	12
Sargent, Matagorda	76
*Sarita, Kenedy	185
*Saspamco, Wilson, 2	262
*Satin, Falls, 1	138
Sattler, Comal	30
Saturn, Gonzales	15
*SAVOY, Fannin, 7	855
Scharbauer City, Ector	20
Schattel, Frio	130
*†SCHERTZ, Bexar-Comal-Guadalupe, 63	7,262
School Hill, Erath	22
Schroeder, Goliad	208
*†SCHULENBURG, Fayette, 69	2,469
Schumannsville, Guadalupe	400
*†Schwertner, Williamson, 3	150
*SCOTLAND, Archer, 3	367
*SCOTTSVILLE, Harrison, 13	245
Scranton, Eastland	40
*Scroggins, Franklin, 4	125
*Scurry, Kaufman, 7	315
Scyene, Dallas	155
*†SEABROOK, Harris, 197	4,670
*†SEADRIFT, Calhoun, 15	1,277
*†SEAGOVILLE, Dallas, 75	7,304
*†SEAGRAVES, Gaines, 39	2,596
Seale, Robertson	26
*†SEALY, Austin, 122	3,875
Seaton, Bell	50
Sebastopol, Trinity	31
*Sebastian, Willacy, 7	404
Security, Montgomery	24
Sedalia, Collin	25
*Segno, Polk	80
Segovia, Kimble	101
*†SEGUIN, Guadalupe, 431	17,854
Selden, Erath	71
Selfs, Fannin	30
SELMA, Bexar	528
*Selman City, Rusk, 9	271
*†SEMINOLE, Gaines, 155	6,080
Serbin, Lee	90
Seth Ward, Hale	1,600
SEVEN OAKS, Polk	300
†SEVEN POINTS, Henderson	647
Seven Sisters, Duval	60
Sexton, Sabine	27
*†SEYMOUR, Baylor, 88	3,657
Shady Grove, Cherokee	20
SHADY SHORES, Denton	813
*Shafter, Presidio	31
*†SHALLOWATER, Lubbock, 12	1,932
*†SHAMROCK, Wheeler, 65	2,834
Shannon, Clay	23
Sharp, Milam	60
SHAVANO PARK, Bexar	1,448
*Sheffield, Pecos, 6	300
Shelby, Austin	175
*Shelbyville, Shelby, 8	215
Sheldon, Harris	1,665
Shell Camp, Gregg	225
SHENANDOAH, Montgomery	1,793
Shep, Taylor	60
*†SHEPHERD, San Jacinto, 17	1,674
*Sheridan, Colorado, 7	225
*†SHERMAN, Grayson, 545	30,413
Sherman-Denison— 1982 metro. pop.	92,300
Sherwood, Irion	47
Shield, Coleman	13
Shiloh, Denton	55
Shiloh, Limestone	110
*†SHINER, Lavaca, 42	2,213
Shire, Rusk	200
*†Shiro, Grimes, 2	205
Shive, Hamilton	61
SHOREACRES, Harris	1,260
*Sidney, Comanche, 2	196
*†Sierra Blanca, Hudspeth, 11	700
Siloam, Bowie	50
*†SILSBEE, Hardin, 177	7,684
*Silver, Coke, 2	60
Silver Lake, Van Zandt	42
*†SILVERTON, Briscoe, 13	918
Silver Valley, Coleman	20
Simmons, Live Oak	35
*Simms, Bowie, 3	240
*SIMONTON, Fort Bend, 11	603
Simpsonville, Upshur	100
*Singleton, Grimes	44
*†SINTON, San Patricio, 102	6,044
Sipe Springs, Comanche	110
Sisterdale, Kendall, 4	63
Sivells Bend, Cooke	100
*SKELLYTOWN, Carson, 11	899
*Skidmore, Bee, 10	150
*†SLATON, Lubbock, 81	6,804
Slayden, Gonzales	15
Slide, Lubbock	44
*Slidell, Wise, 2	175
Slocum, Anderson	125
Smetana, Brazos	80
*†SMILEY, Gonzales, 13	505
Smithfield, Tarrant, 2	1,000
*Smithland, Marion	179
Smith Oaks, Grayson	50
Smithson Valley, Comal	15
*†SMITHVILLE, Bastrop, 63	3,470
*SMYER, Hockley, 3	455
Snipe, Brazoria	78
*†SNOOK, Burleson, 7	408
Snow Hill, Collin	20
*†SNYDER, Scurry, 310	12,705
Socorro, El Paso	350
Sodville, San Patricio	40
Solms, Comal	40
*†SOMERSET, Bexar, 15	1,102
*†SOMERVILLE, Burleson, 19	1,814
Sonoma, Ellis (Consolidated with Ennis)	
*†SONORA, Sutton, 95	3,856
*†SOUR LAKE, Hardin, 35	1,807
*South Bend, Young, 1	100
South Bosque, McLennan	80
South Camp, King	35
South Franklin, Franklin	30
South Groveton, Trinity	175
*†SOUTH HOUSTON, Harris, 262	13,293
SOUTHLAKE, Denton-Tarrant, 47	2,808
Southland, Garza, 1	168
*SOUTHMAYD, Grayson, 2	318
†SOUTH PADRE ISLAND, Cameron, 77	791
*South Plains, Floyd, 5	120
South San Pedro, Nueces	3,065
SOUTHSIDE PLACE, Harris	1,366
South Sulphur, Hunt	60
South Texarkana, Bowie	370
Southton, Bexar	113
*Spade, Lamb, 3	174
Spanish Fort, Montague	50
Sparenberg, Dawson	20
Sparks, Bell	30
*Speaks, Lavaca	60

Town and County—	Pop.	Town and County—	Pop.	Town and County—	Pop.
Utley, Bastrop	30	*Wayside, Armstrong, 4	40	Wilcox, Burleson	40
*Utopia, Uvalde, 8	360	*†WEATHERFORD, Parker,		Wilderville, Falls	45
*†UVALDE, Uvalde, 260	14,178	330	12,049	Wildhorse, Culberson	35
V		Weaver, Hopkins	35	*Wildorado, Oldham, 12	180
Valdasta, Collin	40	Webb, Tarrant	43	Wilkinson, Titus	39
*VALENTINE, Jeff Davis, 3	328	Webb, Webb	40	William Penn, Washington	100
*Valera, Coleman, 1	80	Webberville, Travis	50	Williamson Settlement, Orange	175
*†VALLEY MILLS, Bosque-		Webbville, Coleman	50	*†WILLIS, Montgomery, 61	1,674
McLennan, 22	1,236	*†WEBSTER, Harris, 245	2,405	*Willow City, Gillespie	75
*Valley Spring, Llano, 1	50	Weches, Houston	26	Willow Grove, McLennan	50
*†VALLEY VIEW, Cooke, 11	514	*Weesatche, Goliad, 3	516	WILLOW PARK, Parker	1,107
Valley View, Cottle	20	*†WEIMAR, Colorado, 73	2,128	*†WILLS POINT, Van Zandt,	
Valley Wells, Dimmit	25	*WEINERT, Haskell, 5	253	88	2,631
*VAN, Van Zandt, 28	1,881	*Weir, Williamson, 1	100	*WILMER, Dallas, 15	2,367
*†VAN ALSTYNE, Grayson,		*Welch, Dawson, 8	110	*†WILSON, Lynn, 10	578
26	1,860	Welcome, Austin	150	*†Wimberley, Hays, 70	3,065
Vance, Real	20	Weldon, Houston	131	*Winchester, Fayette, 4	50
*Vancourt, Tom Green, 3	125	Welfare, Kendall, 1	36	WINDCREST, Bexar	5,332
*Vanderbilt, Jackson, 11	667	*Wellborn, Brazos, 1	100	*†WINDOM, Fannin, 1	276
*Vanderpool, Bandera, 3	20	*†WELLINGTON, Collingsworth,		*WINDTHORST, Archer, 17	409
Vandyke, Comanche	20	59	3,043	*WINFIELD, Titus, 6	349
*†VAN HORN, Culberson,		*WELLMAN, Terry, 1	239	Winfree, Chambers	30
62	2,772	*†WELLS, Cherokee, 6	926	*†Wingate, Runnels, 3	216
*Van Vleck, Matagorda, 12	1,051	Wentworth, Van Zandt	32	*†WINK, Winkler, 5	1,182
Vashti, Clay	140	Weser, Goliad	48	Winkler, Freestone-	
Vaughan, Hill	70	*†WESLACO, Hidalgo, 220	19,331	Navarro	26
Vealmoor, Howard, 2	179	Wesley, Washington	60	*†Winnie, Chambers, 96	5,512
*†VEGA, Oldham, 22	900	*†WEST, McLennan, 50	2,485	*†WINNSBORO, Wood-Franklin,	
*VENUS, Johnson, 9	518	*WESTBROOK, Mitchell, 5	298	117	3,458
*Vera, Knox, 2	276	West Camp, Bailey	50	*WINONA, Smith, 11	443
*Veribest, Tom Green, 3	40	*†WEST COLUMBIA,		Winter Haven, Dimmit	112
*†VERNON, Wilbarger, 205	12,695	Brazoria, 81	4,109	*†WINTERS, Runnels, 68	3,061
*Viboras, Starr	22	Westfield, Harris, 4	275	Wise, Van Zandt	29
Vick, Concho	20	*†Westhoff, DeWitt, 1	410	Witting, Lavaca	90
Victoria, Limestone	50	WESTLAKE, Denton-Tarrant	214	Wizard Wells, Jack	69
*†VICTORIA, Victoria, 1,095.	50,695	†WEST LAKE HILLS, Travis	2,166	*Woden, Nacogdoches	70
1982 metro. pop.	72,900	*WESTMINSTER, Collin, 1	278	*†WOLFE CITY, Hunt, 21	1,594
Vidauri, Refugio	85	WEST MOUNTAIN, Upshur	395	*WOLFFORTH, Lubbock, 24	1,701
*†VIDOR, Orange, 184	11,834	*WESTON, Collin, 2	50	Womack, Bosque	25
Vienna, Lavaca	40	WEST ORANGE, Orange	4,610	Woodbine, Cooke	246
View, Taylor, 1	75	Westover, Baylor	61	WOODBRANCH, Montgomery	720
Vigo Park, Swisher	31	WESTOVER HILLS, Tarrant	671	Woodbury, Hill	40
*Village Mills, Hardin, 6	300	Westphalia, Falls	324	Wood Hi, Victoria	35
Vincent, Howard	500	*West Point, Fayette	205	*Woodlake, Grayson	60
*Vineyard, Jack	37	WEST TAWAKONI, Hunt	840	Woodland, Trinity	301
Vinton, El Paso	372	†WEST UNIVERSITY PLACE,		Woodland, Red River	50
Violet, Nueces	160	Harris	12,010	Woodland Hills, Dallas	
*Voca, McCulloch, 1	56	WESTWORTH, Tarrant	3,651	(Consolidated with	
*Von Ormy, Bexar, 20	264	*Wetmore, Bexar, 29	175	De Soto)	
*Voss, Coleman	20	*†WHARTON, Wharton, 177	9,033	*Woodlawn, Harrison, 3	370
*Votaw, Hardin, 1	160	*†WHEELER, Wheeler, 41	1,584	WOODLOCH, Montgomery	351
W		*Wheelock, Robertson, 1	125	Woodrow, Lubbock	85
*†WACO, McLennan, 1,720.	101,261	WHISPERING OAKS, Montgomery		Woods, Panola	65
1982 metro. pop.	175,500	(Name changed to WOODLOCH)		*WOODSBORO, Refugio, 27	1,974
*Wadsworth, Matagorda, 3	152	White City, San Augustine	20	*†WOODSON, Throckmorton,	
*WAELDER, Gonzales, 5	942	*White City, Wilbarger	40	10	291
*Waka, Ochiltree, 4	145	White City, Wise	50	*†WOODVILLE, Tyler, 92	2,821
Wake, Crosby	50	*†WHITE DEER, Carson, 16	1,210	Woodward, La Salle	20
WAKE VILLAGE, Bowie	3,865	*WHITEFACE, Cochran, 6	463	†WOODWAY, McLennan	7,091
*†Walburg, Williamson, 4	250	Whiteflat, Motley	20	Woosley, Rains	47
Waldeck, Fayette	35	White Hall, Bell	45	*†WORTHAM, Freestone,	
Walhalla, Fayette	37	*†WHITEHOUSE, Smith,		17	1,187
*Wall, Tom Green, 8	200	61	2,172	Worthing, Lavaca	55
*†WALLER, Harris-Waller,		*WHITE OAK, Gregg, 57	4,415	Wright City, Smith	172
80	1,241	White Rock, Hunt	73	*Wrightsboro, Gonzales	76
*†WALLIS, Austin, 15	1,138	White Rock, Red River	40	*†WYLIE, Collin, 105	4,100
*Wallisville, Chambers	25	*†WHITESBORO, Grayson,		**Y**	
Walnut Grove, Collin	200	53	3,197	*Yancey, Medina, 2	186
*WALNUT SPRINGS,		†WHITE SETTLEMENT,		*YANTIS, Wood, 6	210
Bosque, 8	613	Tarrant	13,508	Yard, Anderson	18
Walton, Van Zandt	35	*†WHITEWRIGHT, Grayson,		Yellowpine, Sabine	74
Wamba, Bowie	70	26	1,760	*†YOAKUM, Lavaca-DeWitt,	
*Warda, Fayette, 4	67	*Whitharral, Hockley, 2	111	110	6,148
*Waring, Kendall, 2	73	Whitman, Washington	25	*†YORKTOWN, DeWitt, 49	2,498
*Warren, Tyler, 4	304	*†WHITNEY, Hill, 47	1,631	Young, Freestone	27
WARREN CITY, Gregg-		*Whitsett, Live Oak, 2	350	Youngsport, Bell	30
Upshur	281	Whitson, Coryell	30	Ysleta (now in El Paso)	
Warrenton, Fayette, 2	50	*Whitt, Parker	38	**Z**	
Warsaw, Kaufman	58	Whittenburg, Hutchinson		Zabcikville, Bell	28
Washburn, Armstrong	70	(See Phillips)		*†Zapata, Zapata, 70	3,500
*Washington, Washington, 6	265	*Whon, Coleman	15	*ZAVALLA, Angelina, 10	762
*†WASKOM, Harrison, 29	1,821	*†WICHITA FALLS, Wichita-		*Zephyr, Brown, 2	198
Wastella, Nolan	13	Archer-Clay, 1,755	94,201	Zippville, Guadalupe	98
WATAUGA, Tarrant	10,284	1982 metro. pop.	125,500	Zorn, Guadalupe	26
Waterloo, Williamson	60	*WICKETT, Ward, 26	689	Zuehl, Guadalupe	49
*Water Valley, Tom Green	120	Wied, Lavaca	65	*†For meanings of asterisk, dag-	
Waverly, San Jacinto	50	*Wiergate, Newton, 4	461	ger, capital letters, figures and oth-	
*†WAXAHACHIE, Ellis, 247	14,624	Wiggins, McLennan	28	er reference marks, see notes at be-	
Wayland, Stephens	15			ginning of table.	

Dallas Morning News' 100th-year birthday cake is cut by Jeremy Halbreich, executive vice president. It was presented by the Dallas Historical Society.

Belo Becomes a Publicly Held Corporation

A. H. Belo Corporation, the publisher of **The Dallas Morning News** and the **Texas Almanac**, has a history parallel to that of Texas itself. Pioneered in 1842 as the 1-page **Galveston News**, A. H. Belo has grown to become a leading southwestern media company, encompassing both newspaper publishing and broadcasting operations in this rapidly growing region.

A. H. Belo is the **oldest continuously operating business in Texas.** Founded by **Samuel Bangs**, a transplanted publisher from Boston, the company was in the publishing business three years before the Republic of Texas achieved statehood. Bangs had a long history of business failures and, recognizing that his fledgling Texas newspaper business was working out no better than his previous endeavors, sold the business to **Wilbur F. Cherry** and **Michael Cronican** less than a year later. Cronican, in turn, found himself less than adept in the publishing business and soon sold his interest in the company to Cherry.

Another Massachusetts emigre, **Willard Richardson**, became editor of the paper a few years later. He campaigned editorially for annexation, fiscal responsibility and railroads. Soon after his campaign began, Texas was annexed to the United States. In 1857, Richardson conceived and founded the Texas Almanac, which he hoped would help attract settlers to the new state. Eight years later, he hired **A. H. Belo**, for whom the company was eventually renamed. Belo, a former Confederate colonel from North Carolina, joined the company as bookkeeper. Belo was made a full partner in the growing company after only three months, and he carved out a new life for himself in the Southwest.

Nine years later, **George Bannerman Dealey**, a 15-year-old English emigrant, was hired as an office boy. Dealey, like Belo, was full of enthusiasm and energy. He, too, quickly moved up in the company. Working tirelessly, Dealey made his way up from office boy to business manager and then to publisher of **The Dallas Morning News.** It was Dealey who chose the then-small settlement of Dallas as a better site for the newspaper venture. Dealey and other members of the Galveston News staff relocated in Dallas and the company prospered and grew.

The Dallas Morning News began publication on Oct. 1, 1885, with a circulation of 5,000 subscribers. After being in operation only two months, The Dallas Morning News acquired its first competitor, the **Dallas Herald** (not to be confused with the current **Dallas Times Herald**). Rather than compete with each other for subscribers, the two newspapers combined, keeping the name of The Dallas Morning News, but dating itself with the volume number of the former Dallas Herald.

In 1906, on the 21st anniversary of The Dallas Morning News, Dealey gave a speech that soon became the motto for the company: "Build The News upon the rock of truth and righteousness. Conduct it always upon the lines of fairness and integrity. Acknowledge the right of the people to get from the newspaper both sides of every important question." Today these words are carved in a 3-story-high space above the entrance to The Dallas Morning News. The News building, a long-standing dream of Dealey, was completed in 1949, three years after his death.

December 1981 marked the beginning of a new era in A. H. Belo Corporation's history. In that month, the company became a publicly held entity, and its common stock started trading in the over-the-counter market. The company then broadened its long-term growth plans to include the emerging Southwest and Mid-South regions.

While A. H. Belo has grown into a multi-faceted media entity, The Dallas Morning News remains the flagship of its newspaper business. Growing from that original 1-page newspaper in Galveston, The Dallas Morning News now has a total daily circulation of more than 368,600. It is the leading newspaper in the Dallas-Fort Worth area and its growth is evident in the opening in 1985 of its $57 million satellite printing plant in Plano, Texas.

In 1963, A. H. Belo purchased the News Texan organization that published 6 daily newspapers — the Arlington Daily News, Garland Daily News, Grand Prairie Daily News, Irving Daily News, Mid-Cities Daily News and Richardson Daily News — and the weekly Suburban News, serving the rapidly growing suburban communities of Dallas and Fort Worth.

Belo entered the television broadcasting business in 1950 with the acquisition of its principal station, **WFAA-TV**, Channel 8, the ABC affiliate in Dallas-Fort Worth. The station had begun broadcasting five months earlier as **KBTV-TV. Belo Broadcasting Corporation**, a wholly owned subsidiary of A. H. Belo, manages WFAA-TV and other broadcasting interests.

In June 1983, Belo Broadcasting entered an agreement with Dun & Bradstreet to purchase four television stations for $501 million. The company acquired VHF stations **KHOU-TV** in Houston, **KXTV** in Sacramento, **KOTV** in Tulsa and **WVEC-TV** in Hampton-Norfolk, VA.

Belo also was a pioneer in radio in Texas. It began operating a 50-watt **WFAA-AM** on June 26, 1922, which was the first network station in the state. In addition to WFAA-AM — the call letters were changed to **KRQX-AM** in 1983 — the company also owns **KZEW-FM** in Dallas/Fort Worth and **KOA-AM** and **KOAQ-FM** in Denver, CO.

The Dallas Morning News Celebrated 100th Year

The Dallas Morning News celebrated its 100th anniversary in October 1985.

The newspaper was founded on Oct. 1, 1885, by G. B. Dealey after an extensive survey of cities in North Texas. Dealey was an agent of the Galveston News, a publication of the A. H. Belo Corporation.

In 1923, the corporation sold the Galveston News. Three years later, Dealey and associates purchased the Belo Corporation, which publishes the News, the Texas Almanac and other periodicals.

OFFICERS AND DIRECTORS

Officers of **A. H. Belo Corporation** are: James M. Moroney Jr., chairman of the board/chief executive officer; Robert W. Decherd, president/chief operating officer; James P. Sheehan, executive vice president/chief financial officer; Robert G. Norvell, vice president/treasurer/secretary; Michael D. Perry, vice president/controller; and, Walter G. Mullins, vice president/administration.

Officers of **The Dallas Morning News** are: John A. Rector Jr., publisher; Burl Osborne, president and editor; Jeremy L. Halbreich, executive vice president; Harry M. Stanley Jr., senior vice president; J. William Cox, senior vice president/administration and finance; James A. Keeley, vice president/operations.

The following are members of the A. H. Belo Corporation board of directors: John W. Bassett Jr., Lloyd S. Bowles Sr., Joe M. Dealey, Robert W. Decherd, Ward L. Huey Jr., Lester A. Levy, James M. Moroney Jr., Reece A. Overcash Jr., John A. Rector Jr., William H. Seay, James P. Sheehan, William T. Solomon, Thomas B. Walker Jr. and J. McDonald Williams.

Officers of **Belo Broadcasting** are: Ward L. Huey Jr., president/chief executive officer; Lee R. Salzberger, vice president, administration; Frank B. Davis, vice president, engineering/operations; David T. Lane, president, WFAA-TV; Terrence S. Ford, president, KHOU-TV; Allan Howard Espeseth, vice president, KXTV; J. William Beindorf, vice president, WVEC-TV; John Irvin, vice president, KOTV; Gene Boivin, vice president, KRQX-AM, KZEW-FM; and Lee Larsen, vice president, KOA-AM, KOAQ-FM. Also, Herman M. Haag Jr., vice president and executive news director, WFAA-TV; and Denson F. Walker Jr., vice president, administration, WFAA-TV.

Below are brief biographical sketches of the members of the board of directors.

Robert W. Decherd

Robert W. Decherd is president and chief operating officer of A.H. Belo Corporation, and has been a member of the company's board of directors since 1976. He is the son of the late H. Ben Decherd, who served as chairman of the board until his death in 1972.

After graduating from St. Mark's School of Texas in Dallas, Mr. Decherd entered Harvard University. While at Harvard, he became the first Texan to be elected president of the Harvard Crimson, the university's daily student newspaper. Mr. Decherd had worked previously at News-Texan Inc. and was a stringer for the New York Times. He graduated cum laude from Harvard in 1973.

Returning to Dallas, Mr. Decherd joined the management training program at The News in September 1973. He spent the next three years moving through each department of the newspaper. He was named assistant to the executive editor in September 1976. In 1978, he became corporate assistant of Belo and in March 1979, he was elected vice president, corporate administration.

In February 1980, Mr. Decherd was elected executive vice president of The News, a position he held until January 1982. Subsequently he assumed the additional titles of executive vice president of A. H. Belo Corporation (May 1981) and chief operating officer of A. H. Belo Corporation (January 1984). In January 1985, Mr. Decherd was elected president and chief operating officer. In March 1980, Mr. Decherd was also elected a director of Belo Broadcasting Corporation.

John A. Rector Jr.

John A. Rector Jr., publisher of The Dallas Morning News, was elected to the board of directors of the A. H. Belo Corporation in January 1983.

A graduate of the University of Oklahoma, Mr. Rector joined The News in September 1947, after a three-and-one-half year tour of duty in the U.S. Army as a staff sergeant in ordnance in both the European and Pacific theaters in World War II. He worked as a member of the advertising staff and progressed steadily through management ranks to executive vice president in 1980.

Mr. Rector serves on the board of directors of the Dallas County Red Cross, the Better Business Bureau, the Dallas Opera, and the Dallas Zoological Society. He also serves on the board for Metropolitan Sunday Newspapers and the advisory committee for the University of Texas College of Communications.

James M. Moroney Jr.

James M. Moroney Jr., chairman and chief executive officer of A. H. Belo Corporation, is the son of the late James M. Moroney and the late Maidie Dealey Moroney. He was born in Dallas, attended Highland Park School and St. John's Military Academy in Delafield, Wis. He graduated from the University of Texas at Austin in 1943. During summer vacations, he worked part-time at radio and television stations WFAA and The Dallas Morning News.

During World War II, he entered the U.S. Navy, rising to the rank of lieutenant (jg). He saw much action, including the D-Day landing in Normandy. He was released from active duty in 1946.

Mr. Moroney joined The News as a reporter, served as an advertising salesman and worked in the promotion and circulation departments before becoming assistant to the business manager in 1950. He also spent a year at the radio and television stations.

He progressed to assistant treasurer of the corporation and was elected to the board of directors in 1952. In 1955, he was named treasurer, elevated to vice president and treasurer in 1960 and became executive vice president in 1970. In 1973, Mr. Moroney was named president and chief executive officer of Belo Broadcasting Corporation and in 1974 became chairman of the board of that corporation, a title he retains.

In 1980, he was elected to president and chief executive officer of The Dallas Morning News and president and chief operating officer of A. H. Belo Corporation.

He was promoted to the position of president and chief executive officer of A. H. Belo Corporation in January 1983. In April 1984 he was elected to the additional position of chairman of the board. In January 1985 he relinquished the title of president.

Joe M. Dealey

Joe M. Dealey, past chairman of the board of the A. H. Belo Corporation, is the son of the late E. M. (Ted) Dealey and the late Clara MacDonald Dealey. A native of Dallas, he was graduated from Highland Park High School and, in 1941, from the University of Texas at Austin. By attending the Southwest School of Printing, he learned to operate mechanical equipment in the printing industry. He also worked in the mailing room and photographic laboratory of The News. His permanent employment began Jan. 4, 1942, as a reporter.

In May of 1942, Mr. Dealey joined the U.S. Air Force, serving two years as an aircraft mechanic. After attending Officers Training School, he was graduated in 1944 as a second lieutenant. He served as aircraft maintenance officer in the United States and in Berlin until his discharge from service in 1946.

Returning to his previous job as a reporter on The News, Mr. Dealey later served as assistant business news editor and assistant to the managing editor. He joined the executive department as assistant secretary in 1950, being elected to the board of directors in 1952. From 1955 until 1960, he was secretary of the corporation and was president until 1980 when he was named chairman and chief executive officer following an internal reorganization of the company, a post he held until Dec. 31, 1982, when he became chairman of the board.

Ward L. Huey Jr.

Ward L. Huey Jr., president and chief executive officer of Belo Broadcasting Corporation, has an extensive background in broadcast operations and management.

A graduate of Southern Methodist University, Huey joined the WFAA-TV production department in 1960 after working as an account executive for Glenn Advertising in Dallas. In 1961, he became sales service manager for WFAA-TV. The following year he was named an account executive and in 1965 was promoted to regional sales manager. Two years later, Huey became general sales manager directing all sales and marketing for the station on both local and national levels.

In 1971 Huey was named director of sales for WFAA-TV and Belo's CBS TV affiliate in Beaumont, KFDM-TV. In late 1972, he was promoted to WFAA-TV station manager, responsible for all phases of station operations, and in 1973 was elected a vice president.

Jan. 1, 1975, Huey was named vice president and general manager of Belo Broadcasting Corporation with management responsibilities for all Belo radio and television properties and was also elected to its board of directors. March 21, 1978, he was elected executive vice president and in May, 1980, became chief operating officer for the Corporation. Most recently, Huey became president and chief executive officer of Belo Broadcasting Corporation April 27, 1981, and was elected to the board of directors of A.H. Belo Corporation on April 20, 1982. He serves on the A.H. Belo Corporation management committee.

A native of Dallas, Huey is a past chairman of the ABC Television Affiliates Board of Governors, a present member of the board of directors of the Television Bureau of Advertising, the board of directors of the Maximum Service Telecasters and the board of directors of the Television Operators Caucus. His civic activities include the board of directors of the Salesmanship Club of Dallas, the board of trustees of Children's Medical Center, the advisory board of Goodwill Industries and active membership in the Dallas Assembly. He has previously served on the boards of the Association of Broadcast Executives of Texas, the Dallas Advertising League and the SMU Alumni Association.

John W. Bassett Jr.

John W. Bassett Jr. is a native of Roswell, N.M., where he practices law. After graduating from Roswell High School, he attended Stanford University where he majored in economics and received a bachelor's degree in 1960.

Following graduation, he was commissioned as a second lieutenant in the Army and entered active duty at Fort Benning, Ga. He served in the Second Infantry Division there and in the Army Reserves where he was advanced to first lieutenant.

Mr. Bassett attended the University of Texas School of Law and became an associate editor of The Texas Law Review. Upon graduating with honors in June 1964, he was awarded a Bachelor of Law degree and became a member of the Order of the Coif, a legal honorary organization.

After passing the Texas and New Mexico Bar examinations in 1964, he practiced law in Roswell.

In 1966, Mr. Bassett was selected as a White House Fellow and for a year served as a special assistant to the attorney general of the United States.

In October 1967, Mr. Bassett returned to private practice with the law firm of Atwood, Malone, Mann and Turner, P.A. in Roswell.

Mr. Bassett was elected to the board of directors of A. H. Belo Corporation in 1979. He also serves as chairman of the board of Southwest Bank of Roswell and is chairman of the board of St. Mary's Hospital in Roswell.

Lloyd S. Bowles Sr.

Lloyd S. Bowles Sr., chairman of the board and chief executive officer of Dallas Federal Savings and Loan Association, was elected a director of A. H. Belo Corporation on March 27, 1973.

Born in Oklahoma, the son of a Baptist minister, he attended SMU and Marshall College in Huntington, W. Va., before serving as finance officer in the Army from 1943 to 1946. After his discharge, he joined Dallas Federal. He is a director of a number of local and national businesses and has served in cultural, educational, civic and religious activities, from leading the United Way drive, to working on behalf of the State Fair of Texas and the Dallas Symphony Association and as deacon of Park Cities Baptist Church.

Mr. Bowles has held virtually every top savings and loan industry post, including chairman of the Federal Savings and Loan Advisory Council of Washington for an unprecedented five terms, president of the U.S. League of Savings Associations, member of the executive committee and chairman of the legislative committee of the U.S. League, president and director of the Southwestern Savings and Loan Conference and the Texas Savings and Loan League, and director of the Federal Home Loan Bank of Little Rock.

Lester A. Levy

Lester A. Levy was born and educated in Dallas. He attended the University of Texas at Austin until early 1943 at which time he entered the Air Force. He received his license to practice law during 1943 while in the service. After an honorable discharge in 1946, he joined his father's company, now known as NCH Corporation, while awaiting a semester change in order to take refresher courses at the University of Texas. His father's untimely death caused him to remain with the company where he is presently chairman of the board of directors.

Mr. Levy serves as a director of NCH Corporation, InterFirst Corporation and A.H. Belo Corporation. He has served on the boards of the University of Dallas, Greenhill School, Baylor College of Dentistry, the Lamplighter School, and was a co-founder and director of the Winston School. He has also served as a trustee for Temple Emanu-El, Golden Acres Home for the Aged and Special Care and Career Center (formerly Special Care School for Handicapped Children).

Reece A. Overcash Jr.

Reece A. Overcash Jr. is chairman and chief executive officer of Associates Corporation of North America, one of the nation's largest independent financial services organizations. He also is senior executive vice president of Gulf + Western Industries, Inc., and president of that firm's financial services group. The Associates is a G + W company.

Mr. Overcash was born and reared in Charlotte, N.C., where he was named as "Man of the Year" in 1972. He earned a degree in commerce from the University of North Carolina and served in the infantry during World War II.

From 1950 to 1952, he was an accountant with a CPA firm in Charlotte. He joined Home Finance Group in 1952 (a predecessor company of American Credit Corp.). Mr. Overcash was named president of American Credit in 1970 and became that company's chief executive officer in 1974. In 1975, he joined The Associates as president and chief operating officer.

He was elected chief executive officer of The Associates in August 1978, and chairman of the board in August 1979. In March 1983, he also was elected to the G + W offices.

Mr. Overcash is active in many professional, civic and community organizations and serves as director of InterFirst Bank of Dallas, Duke Power Company, Chilton Corporation and a number of other organizations. He was elected to the board of directors of A. H. Belo Corporation on April 19, 1983.

William H. Seay

William H. Seay is retired chairman and chief executive officer of the board of Southwestern Life Insurance Company, which is one of the nation's 10 largest stock life insurance companies, and Southwestern General Life Insurance Company.

Mr. Seay was born and reared in Dallas. He holds a degree in business administration from the University of Texas and served during World War II as an infantry captain in the Army.

In 1948 he became a partner in the Dallas investment banking firm of Henry, Seay and Black. Eleven years later he joined Universal Life and Accident Insurance Company as vice president, advancing in 1961 to president.

Universal was acquired by Southwestern Life Insurance Company in September 1968, and four months later Mr. Seay was named president and chief executive officer of the parent firm. He continued in that capacity until the transition to a holding-company concept in late 1972.

Mr. Seay is active in many professional, civic and community organizations, and serves as director of numerous Dallas-based business firms. He was elected to the board of directors of A. H. Belo Corporation on March 27, 1973.

James P. Sheehan

James P. Sheehan joined A. H. Belo Corporation as senior vice president, and chief financial officer in February 1982, and was elected to the Board of Directors in April 1982. He became executive vice president of Belo in 1984.

Prior to joining Belo, he spent eight years with United Technologies Corporation and most recently was vice president and controller of the Pratt and Whitney Manufacturing Division.

He also held the positions of director of manufacturing for Otis Elevator North America and controller for Otis Elevator, and served on the UTC corporate staff.

Before joining United Technologies, Mr. Sheehan was a financial analyst with Ford Motor Company and accounting manager for Audits and Surveys, Inc.

He received a B.S. in accounting from Seton Hall University, and an M.B.A. in finance from Wayne State University. From 1967 to 1969 he served in the U.S. Navy.

William T. Solomon

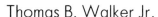

William T. Solomon is the president and chief executive officer of Austin Industries Inc., which is one of the five largest general contracting organizations based in the southern half of the United States.

Mr. Solomon was born and reared in Dallas. He holds a civil engineering degree from Southern Methodist University and a masters in business administration from Harvard Graduate School of Business.

He joined Austin full-time in 1967, immediately upon completion of his formal education. He became president and chief executive officer in 1970.

Mr. Solomon was formerly chairman of the board of the Dallas Chamber of Commerce and is a member of the board of directors of A. H. Belo Corporation (since April 1983) and Republic Bank Dallas as well as numerous civic and community organizations.

Thomas B. Walker Jr.

Thomas B. Walker Jr. is a native of Nashville, Tenn. and is a Phi Beta Kappa graduate of Vanderbilt University. During World War II he served as a lieutenant in the U.S. Navy operating in the Mediterranean, Atlantic and South Pacific areas.

After the war, Mr. Walker joined the Equitable Securities Corporation and moved to Dallas in 1950. He served as senior vice president and director, Equitable Securities (American Express Company) until 1968.

In 1968, he became a partner of Goldman, Sachs & Co. and is a member of the management committee of that firm.

In addition, Mr. Walker is a director of A. H. Belo, Intermedics, Inc., Sysco Corporation and Transatlantic Fund, Inc., and he is vice chairman of the Board of Trustees of Vanderbilt University. He also is a member of the executive and investment committees of Vanderbilt and is a trustee and member of the investment committee of the Dallas Museum of Fine Arts.

J. McDonald Williams

J. McDonald (Don) Williams is a native of Roswell, N. M. He graduated from Abilene Christian University in 1963 and from George Washington University Law School in 1966, both with honors.

He practiced law in Dallas seven years until he joined the Trammell Crow Company in May 1973. He entered the firm as the partner responsible for overseas developments and then was named managing partner in 1977.

Mr. Williams was elected to the board of directors of A. H. Belo Corporation in 1985. He also serves on the boards of InterFirst Bank, Dallas, Abilene Christian University, George Washington University and Southwestern Christian College. He currently serves as the chairman of the board of both Dallas Challenge, Inc., a non-profit organization assisting youths with chemical dependency problems, and the National Realty Committee.

Many television and news services covered the Republican Convention in Dallas in August 1984 at the Dallas Convention Center.

Radio and Television

In 1985, Standard Rate and Data Service, Inc., reported **76 television stations** in Texas and **570 radio stations,** including **AM** and **FM** stations.

First radio broadcasting in Texas was that by **Station WRR,** owned by the City of Dallas, in the fall of 1920. Texas' first television station, **WBAP-TV,** owned by the Fort Worth Star-Telegram, started telecasts on Sept. 29, 1948.

A. H. Belo Corporation, publishers of The Dallas Morning News and Texas Almanac, began operating radio station **WFAA-AM** (now **KRQX-AM**) on June 26, 1922. Five years later this station was the first in Texas to join a national network. Television operations of WFAA started in February, 1950. In 1960, **WFAA-FM** was added to Belo's radio properties, changing its call letters to **KZEW-FM** on Sept. 25, 1973.

A separate corporation for the broadcast properties of A. H. Belo, **Belo Broadcasting Corporation,** was formed on May 24, 1973. This wholly owned subsidiary of A. H. Belo Corporation now controls operations of **WFAA-AM** Radio (now **KRQX-AM**), **KZEW-FM** Radio and **WFAA** Television in Dallas, **KHOU-TV** in Houston; **KXTV** in Sacramento, Ca.; **KOTV** in Tulsa, Ok.; **WVEC-TV** in Hampton-Norfolk, Va., and radio stations **KOA** and **KOAQ** in Denver, Co.

Newspapers

Newspaper publishing in Texas is 170 years old. The first newspaper known to have been published in Texas, the **Gaceta de Texas,** came out in May, 1813, at Nacogdoches. It consisted of one sheet, 7 by 13 inches, printed on both sides in Spanish. Editors William Shaler and Jose Alvarez de Toledo may have published only one issue. A month later they edited **El Mejicano** in Louisiana. Both papers were organs of the **Gutierrez-Magee Expedition.**

While efforts were made to publish a number of newspapers, the only noteworthy paper at the time of the Texas Revolution was the **Telegraph and Texas Register,** which started Oct. 10, 1835, at San Felipe de Austin and became the official newspaper of the Texas Republic. **Gail Borden Jr., Thomas Borden** and **Joseph Baker** were publishers.

Texas newspapers founded between 1813 and 1846 are listed in "Gaceta to Gazette," by John Melton Wallace.

Sixty newspapers were listed in the first edition of the Texas Almanac, published in 1857. Among these was **The Galveston News,** first published on April 11, 1842, and the predecessor of **The Dallas Morning News** which the Galveston firm established in Dallas on Oct. 1, 1885. (See page 458 for history of The Dallas Morning News, Texas Almanac and associated enterprises.)

The Texas Daily Newspaper Association in May, 1985, listed **113 daily newspapers** in Texas with 3,940,593 daily and 4,315,102 Sunday circulation. Of this, 1,904,806 was for morning papers; 1,163,082 for evening papers, and 872,705 for all-day papers.

The **469 weekly newspapers** had 1.3 million circulation, according to the Texas Press Association.

Twelve Texas newspapers have won a coveted Pulitzer Prize, as follows:

The Alice Echo won a Pulitzer in 1955 for General/Spot Reporting; Cuero Record, 1955, Investigative Reporting; Amarillo Globe-Times, 1961, Meritorious Public Service; Pecos Enterprise, 1963, Special Reporting; Dallas Times-Herald, 1964, Spot News Photography; The Houston Post, 1965, Special Reporting; Lufkin News, 1977, Meritorious Public Service; Dallas Times-Herald, 1980, Feature Photography; Fort Worth Star-Telegram, 1981, Spot News Photography; Austin American-Statesman, 1982, Editorial Cartooning; Dallas Times-Herald, 1983, Feature Photography; Fort Worth Star Telegram, 1985, Meritorious Public Service.

Newspapers, Radio and Television Stations

The radio and television stations in the list below are those with valid current operating licenses. Not included are those with only construction permits or with applications pending.

Abernathy—Newspaper: Weekly Review.

Abilene—Newspapers: Reporter-News (D); Wylie Journal. **Radio-AM:** KEAN, 1280 Khz; KORQ, 1340; KFOX, 1470; KFMN, 1560. **Radio-FM:** KGNZ, 88.1; KORQ, 100.7; KEAN, 105.1; KFMN, 107.9. **TV:** KRBC-Ch. 9; KTAB-Ch. 32.

Alamo—Radio-FM: KJAV, 104.9.

Alamo Heights—Radio-AM: KDRY, 1100 Khz.

Albany—Newspaper: News.

Alice—Newspaper: Echo-News (D). **Radio-AM:** KOPY, 1070 Khz. **Radio-FM:** KDSI, 92.1; KBIC, 102.3.

Allen—Newspaper: American.

Allison—Newspaper: Allison/Wheeler Capitol Review.

Alpine—Newspaper: Avalanche. **Radio-AM:** KVLF, 1240 Khz.

Alto—Newspaper: Herald.

Alvarado—Newspaper: Bulletin.

Alvin—Newspaper: Sun. **Radio-AM:** KTEK, 1110 Khz. **Radio-FM:** KACC, 91.3.

Alvord—Newspaper: News.

Amarillo—Newspaper: News & Globe Times (D). **Radio-AM:** KGMC, 710 Khz.; KIXZ, 940; KDJM, 1010; KZIP, 1310; KQIZ, 1360; KPUR, 1440. **Radio-FM:** KACV, 89.9; KQIZ, 93.1; KBUY, 94.1; KGNC, 97.9; KMML, 98.7; KWAS, 101.9. **TV:** KAMR-Ch. 4; KVII-Ch. 7; KFDA-Ch. 10; KJTV-Ch. 14.

Amherst—Newspaper: Press.

Anahuac—Newspaper: Chambers County Progress.

Andrews—Newspaper: Andrews County News. **Radio-AM:** KACT, 1360 Khz. **Radio-FM:** KACT, 105.5.

Angleton—Newspaper: Times (D).

Anson—Newspaper: Western Observer. **Radio-FM:** KTCE, 98.3.

Aransas Pass—Newspaper: Progress.

Archer City—Newspaper: Archer County News.

Arlington—Newspaper: Daily News (D). **Radio-FM:** KJIM, 94.9.

Aspermont—Newspaper: News.

Athens—Newspapers: Daily Review (D); Weekly Review. **Radio-AM:** KBUD, 1410 Khz.

Atlanta—Newspapers: Citizens Journal; Times. **Radio-AM:** KALT, 990 Khz. **Radio-FM:** KPYN, 99.3.

Austin—Newspapers: American-Statesman (D); Westlake Picayune. **Radio-AM:** KLBJ, 590 Khz.; KVET, 1300; KMMM, 1370; KNCW, 1490. **Radio-FM:** KAZI, 88.7; KMFA, 89.5; KUT, 90.5; KLBJ, 93.7; KOKE, 95.5; KHFI, 98.3; KASE, 100.7; KPEZ, 102.3. **TV:** KTBC-Ch. 7; KLRU-Ch. 18; KVUE-Ch. 24; KTVV-Ch. 36; KBYO-Ch. 42.

Azle—Newspaper: News-Advertiser.

Baird—Newspaper: Callahan County Star.

Balch Springs—Newspaper: News.

Ballinger—Newspaper: Ledger. **Radio-AM:** KRUN, 1400 Khz. **Radio-FM:** KRUN, 103.1.

Bandera—Newspaper: Bulletin. **Radio-FM:** KNLC, 98.3.

Bangs—Newspaper: Brown County Gazette.

Bartlett—Newspaper: Tribune Progress.

Bastrop—Newspaper: Advertiser.

Bay City—Newspaper: Daily Tribune (D). **Radio-AM:** KIOX, 1270 Khz. **Radio-FM:** KMKS, 92.1.

Baytown—Newspaper: Sun (D). **Radio-AM:** KBUK, 1360 Khz.

Beaumont—Newspaper: Enterprise (D). **Radio-AM:** KLVI, 560 Khz.; KTRM, 990; KIEZ, 1380; KAYC, 1450. **Radio-FM:** KVLU, 91.3; KAYC, 91.5; KZZB, 95.1; KAYD, 97.5; KWIC, 107.7. **TV:** KFDN-Ch. 6; KBMT-Ch. 12.

Beeville—Newspaper: Bee-Picayune. **Radio-AM:** KIBL, 1490 Khz. **Radio-FM:** KIBL, 104.9.

Bellevue—Newspaper: News.

Bellville—Newspaper: Times. **Radio-AM:** KACO, 1090 Khz.

Belton—Newspaper: Journal. **Radio-AM:** KTON, 940 Khz. **Radio-FM:** KTQN, 106.3. **TV:** KNCT-Ch. 46.

Big Lake—Newspaper: Wildcat. **Radio-AM:** KWGH, 1290 Khz. **Radio-FM:** K272AO, 102.3.

Big Sandy—Newspaper: Big S & H Journal.

Big Spring—Newspaper: Herald (D). **Radio-AM:** KKIK, 1270 Khz.; KBYG, 1400; KBST, 1490. **Radio-FM:** KWKI, 95.3, K280BP, 103.9. **TV:** KWAB-Ch. 4.

Bishop—Radio-FM: KFLZ, 107.1.

Blanco—Newspaper: Blanco County News.

Blossom—Newspaper: Times.

Boerne—Newspaper: Star. **Radio-AM:** KBRN, 1500 Khz.

Bogata—Newspaper: News.

Bonham—Newspaper: Daily Favorite (D). **Radio-AM:** KFYN, 1420 Khz. **Radio-FM:** KFYZ, 98.3.

Booker—Newspaper: News.

Borger—Newspaper: News-Herald (D). **Radio-AM:** KQTY, 1490 Khz.; KBBB, 1600. **Radio-FM:** KDXR, 104.3.

Bovina—Newspaper: Blade.

Bowie—Newspaper: News. **Radio-AM:** KBAN, 1410 Khz.

Brackettville—Newspaper: The Kinney Cavalryman.

Brady—Newspapers: Herald; Standard. **Radio-AM:** KNEL, 1490 Khz. **Radio-FM:** KIXV, 95.3.

Breckenridge—Newspaper: American. **Radio-AM:** KSTB, 1430 Khz. **Radio-FM:** KROO, 93.5.

Bremond—Newspaper: Press.

Brenham—Newspaper: Banner-Press (D). **Radio-AM:** KTTX, 1280 Khz. **Radio-FM:** KWHI, 106.3.

Bridgeport—Newspaper: Index. **Radio-FM:** KWCS, 96.7.

Brookshire—Newspaper: Banner.

Brownfield—Newspaper: News. **Radio-AM:** KKUB, 1300 Khz. **Radio-FM:** KKTC, 103.9.

Brownsboro—Newspaper: Chandler & Brownsboro Statesman.

Brownsville—Newspapers: Herald (D); Times. **Radio-AM:** KBOR, 1600 Khz. **Radio-FM:** KBNR, 88.3; KRIX, 99.5; KTXF, 100.3; K280AY, 103.9. **TV:** KVEO-Ch. 23.

Brownwood—Newspaper: Bulletin (D). **Radio-AM:** KXYL, 1240 Khz.; KBWB, 1380. **Radio-FM:** KPSN, 99.3; KOXE, 101.5; KXYL, 104.1.

Bryan—Newspaper: Eagle (D). **Radio-AM:** KTAM, 1240 Khz.; KAGC, 1510. **Radio-FM:** KORA, 98.3; KKYS, 104.9. **TV:** KBTX-Ch. 3.

Buda—Newspaper: Onion Creek Free Press.

Buffalo—Newspaper: Press.

Buna—Newspaper: East Texas News.

Burkburnett—Newspaper: Informer-Star.

Burleson—Newspapers: Dispatcher; Star.

Burnet—Newspaper: Bulletin. **Radio-AM:** KMLB, 1340 Khz. **Radio-FM:** KMRB, 107.1.

Caldwell—Newspaper: Burleson County Citizen-Tribune.

Cameron—Newspaper: Herald; Chronicle. **Radio-AM:** KMIL, 1330 Khz.

Canadian—Newspaper: Record. **Radio-FM:** KEZP, 103.1.

Canton—Newspaper: Herald.

Canyon—Newspaper: News. **Radio-AM:** KHBJ, 1550 Khz. **Radio-FM:** KWTS, 91.1; KHBQ, 107.1.

Carlisle—Radio-AM: KTLK, 1460 Khz.

Carrizo Springs—Newspaper: Javelin. **Radio-AM:** KBEN, 1450 Khz.

Carrollton—Newspaper: Chronicle (D).

Carthage—Newspapers: Panola County Post; Panola Watchman. **Radio-AM:** KGAS, 1590 Khz.

Castroville—Newspaper: News Bulletin.

Cedar Hill—Newspaper: Chronicle.

Cedar Park—Newspaper: Hill Country News.

Celina—Newspaper: Record.

Center—Newspaper: Light & Champion. **Radio-AM:** KDET, 930 Khz. **Radio-FM:** KLCR, 102.3.

Centerville—Newspaper: News.

Chico—Newspaper: Texan.

Childress—Newspaper: Index. **Radio-AM:** KCTX, 1510 Khz. **Radio-FM:** KQAI, 95.9.

Chillicothe—Newspaper: Valley News.

Cisco—Newspaper: Press.

Clarendon—Newspaper: Press.

Clarksville—Newspaper: Times. **Radio-AM:** KCAR, 1350 Khz.

Claude—Newspaper: News.

Clear Lake City—Newspaper: Citizen (D).

Cleburne—Newspapers: Times-Review (D); Johnson County News. **Radio-AM:** K CLE, 1120 K hz.

Cleveland—Newspaper: Advocate. **Radio-AM:** KLEV, 1410 K hz.

Clifton—Newspaper: Record.

Clute—Newspaper: Brazosport Facts (D).

Clyde—Newspaper: Journal.

Coleman—Newspapers: Coleman County Chronicle; Democrat-Voice. **Radio-AM:** KSTA, 1000 K hz. **Radio-FM:** KSTA, 107.1.

College Station—Newspaper: Battalion (D). **Radio-AM:** WTAM, 1150 K hz. **Radio-FM:** KAMU, 90.9; KTAW, 92.1. **TV:** KAMU-Ch. 15.

Colorado City—Newspaper: Record. **Radio-AM:** KVMC, 1320 K hz.

Columbus—Newspaper: Colorado County Citizen. **Radio-FM:** KULM, 98.3.

Comanche—Newspaper: Chief. **Radio-AM:** KCOM, 1550 K hz.

Comfort—Newspaper: News.

Commerce—Newspaper: Journal. **Radio-FM:** KETR, 88.9; KEMM, 92.1.

Conroe—Newspaper: The Courier (D). **Radio-AM:** KIKR, 880 K hz.; KMUV, 1140. **Radio-FM:** KJOJ, 106.9.

Cooper—Newspaper: Review.

Copperas Cove—Newspaper: Leader Press. **Radio-FM:** KOOV, 103.1.

Corpus Christi—Newspapers: Caller-Times (D); Coastal Bend Legal & Business News (D); South Texas Catholic. **Radio-AM:** KCTA, 1030 K hz.; KCCT, 1150; KSIX, 1230; KRYS, 1360; KUMO, 1400; KEYS, 1440. **Radio-FM:** KKED, 90.3; KEXX, 93.9; KZFM, 95.5; KIOU, 96.5; KRYS, 99.1. **TV:** KIII-Ch. 3; KRIS-Ch. 6; KZTV-Ch. 10; KEDT-Ch. 16; KORO-Ch. 28.

Corrigan—Newspaper: Times.

Corsicana—Newspaper: Daily Sun (D). **Radio-AM:** KAND, 1340 K hz. **Radio-FM:** KAND, 107.9.

Cotulla—Newspaper: Record.

Crane—Newspaper: News. **Radio-AM:** KXOI, 810 K hz.

Crockett—Newspaper: Houston County Courier. **Radio-AM:** KIVY, 1290 K hz. **Radio-FM:** KIVY, 92.7.

Crosbyton—Newspaper: Review.

Cross Plains—Newspaper: Review.

Crowell—Newspaper: Foard County News.

Crowley—Newspaper: Crowley Beacon.

Crystal City—Newspaper: Zavala County Sentinel.

Cuero—Newspaper: Record. **Radio-AM:** KQRO, 1600 K hz.

Cushing—Newspaper: News.

Daingerfield—Newspaper: Steel Country Bee. **Radio-AM:** KEGG, 1560 K hz.

Dalhart—Newspaper: Texan (D). **Radio-AM:** KXIT, 1240 K hz. **Radio-FM:** KXIT, 95.9.

Dallas—Newspapers: Daily Commercial Record (D); Dallas Morning News (D); Dallas Times Herald (D); Dallas/Fort Worth Business Journal; Oak Cliff Tribune; Park Cities News; Post Tribune; Suburban Tribune; Dallas/Fort Worth Texas Jewish Post; White Rocker News. **Radio-AM:** KRQX, 570 K hz.; KSKY, 660; KPBC, 1040; KRLD, 1080; KLIF, 1190; KAAM, 1310; KMEZ, 1480. **Radio-FM:** KRSM, 88.5; KCBI, 89.3; KERA, 90.1; KNON, 90.9; KVTT, 91.7; KAFM, 92.5; KZEW, 97.9; KLUV, 98.7; KMEZ, 100.3; WRR, 101.1; KMGC, 102.9; KKDA, 104.5; KQZY, 105.3; K292BV, 106.3. **TV:** KDFW-Ch. 4; WFAA-Ch. 8; KERA-Ch. 13; KDFI-Ch. 27; KRLD-Ch. 33; KXTX-Ch. 39.

Decatur—Newspapers: Wise County Messenger; Wise Times.

Deer Park—Newspaper: Progress.

De Kalb—Newspaper: News.

DeLeon—Newspaper: Free Press.

Dell City—Newspaper: Hudspeth County Herald.

Del Rio—Newspaper: News-Herald (D). **Radio-AM:** KDLK, 1230 K hz.; KWMC, 1490. **Radio-FM:** KLKE, 94.3.

Del Valle—**Radio-AM:** KIXL, 970 K hz.

Denison—Newspaper: Herald (D). **Radio-AM:** KDSX, 950 K hz. (Denison-Sherman). **Radio-FM:** KDSQ, 101.7; KLAK, 104.9.

Denton—Newspapers: Record-Chronicle (D); Denton County Enterprise. **Radio-AM:** KDNT, 1440 K hz. **Radio-FM:** KNTU, 88.5; KTKS, 106.1.

Denver City—Newspaper: Press.

Deport—Newspaper: Times.

DeSoto—Newspaper: News-Advertiser.

Devine—Newspaper: Medina Valley Times; News. **Radio-FM:** KDCI, 92.1.

Diboll—Newspaper: Free Press. **Radio-AM:** KIPR, 1260 K hz. **Radio-FM:** KIPR, 95.5.

Dilley—Newspaper: Herald.

Dimmitt—Newspaper: Castro County News. **Radio-AM:** KDHN, 1470 K hz.

Donna—Newspaper: Events.

Dripping Springs—Newspaper: Dispatch.

Dublin—Newspaper: Progress.

Dumas—Newspaper: Moore County News-Press. **Radio-AM:** KDDD, 800 K hz. **Radio-FM:** KMRE, 95.3.

Duncanville—Newspaper: Suburban.

Eagle Lake—Newspaper: Headlight.

Eagle Pass—Newspaper: News-Guide. **Radio-AM:** KEPS, 1270 K hz. **Radio-FM:** KINL, 92.7.

Earth—Newspaper: News-Sun.

East Bernard—Newspaper: Tribune.

Eastland—Newspaper: Telegram. **Radio-AM:** KEAS, 1590 K hz. **Radio-FM:** KVMX, 96.7.

Eden—Newspaper: Echo.

Edgewood—Newspaper: Enterprise.

Edinburg—Newspaper: Daily Review (D). **Radio-AM:** KURV, 710 K hz. **Radio-FM:** KOIR, 88.5; KBFM, 104.1; KVLY, 107.9.

Edna—Newspaper: Herald. **Radio-AM:** KVOJ, 1130 K hz.

El Campo—Newspaper: Leader-News. **Radio-AM:** KULP, 1390 K hz. **Radio-FM:** KXGC, 96.9.

Eldorado—Newspaper: Schleicher County Leader. **Radio-FM:** K272AS, 102.3.

Electra—Newspaper: Star News.

Elgin—Newspaper: Courier. **Radio-AM:** KELG, 1440 K hz.

El Paso—Newspapers: Herald-Post (D); Times (D). **Radio-AM:** KROD, 600 K hz.; KHEY, 690; KEPB, 750; KYSR, 920; KAMA, 1060; KKMJ, 1150; KALY, 1340; KTSM, 1380; KELP, 1590. **Radio-FM:** KTEP, 88.5; KFIM, 92.3; KAMZ, 93.1; KEZB, 93.9; KSET, 94.7; KLAQ, 95.5; KHEY, 96.3; KYSR, 97.5; KTSM, 99.9; KLOZ, 102.1. **TV:** KDBC-Ch. 4; KVIA-Ch. 7; KTSN-Ch. 9; KCOS-Ch. 13; KCIK-Ch. 14; KINT-Ch. 26.

Emory—Newspaper: Rains County Leader.

Ennis—Newspapers: Daily News (D); Weekly Local; Press.

Everman—Newspaper: Times.

Fabens—**Radio-FM:** KPAS, 103.1.

Fairfield—Newspaper: Recorder.

Falfurrias—Newspaper: Facts. **Radio-AM:** KPSO, 1260 K hz. **Radio-FM:** KPSO, 106.3.

Farmersville—Newspaper: Times.

Farwell—Newspaper: State Line Tribune. **Radio-AM:** KIJN, 1060 K hz.

Flatonia—Newspaper: Argus.

Floresville—Newspaper: Chronicle-Journal. **Radio-FM:** KWCB, 94.3.

Floydada—Newspaper: Floyd County Hesperian. **Radio-AM:** KKAP, 900 K hz.

Follett—Newspaper: Lipscomb County Limelight.

Forney—Newspaper: Messenger.

Fort Stockton—Newspaper: Pioneer. **Radio-AM:** KFST, 860 K hz. **Radio-FM:** KPJH, 94.3.

Fort Worth—Newspapers: Commercial Recorder (D); Star-Telegram (D); Eastside News; News-Tribune; Weekly Livestock Reporter. **Radio-AM:** WBAP, 820 K hz.; KFJZ, 870; KHVN, 970; KSSA, 1270; KXOL, 1360; KUQQ, 1540. **Radio-FM:** KTCU, 88.7; KESS, 94.1; KSCS, 96.3; KPLX, 99.5; KNOK, 107.5; KEGL, 97.1; KTXQ, 102.1. **TV:** KXAS-Ch. 5; KTVT-Ch. 11; KTXA-Ch. 21.

Franklin—Newspaper: News Weekly.

Frankston—Newspaper: Citizen.

Fredericksburg—Newspaper: Standard/Radio Post. **Radio-AM:** KMAF, 910 K hz. **Radio-FM:** KFAN, 101.1.

Freeport—**Radio-AM:** KBRZ, 1460 K hz.

Freer—Newspaper: Free Press. **Radio-FM:** KOBR, 95.9.

Friendswood—Newspaper: Journal.

Friona—Newspaper: Star.

Frisco—Newspaper: Enterprise.

Gail—Newspaper: The Borden Star.

Gainesville—Newspaper: Daily Register (D). **Radio-AM:** KGAF, 1580 K hz. **Radio-FM:** KDNT, 94.5.

Galveston—Newspaper: Daily News (D). **Radio-AM:** KILE, 1400 K hz.; KGBC, 1540. **Radio-FM:** KXKX, 106.5.

Ganado—Newspaper: Tribune.

Garland—Newspaper: Daily News (D). **TV:** KIAB-Ch. 23.

Garrison—Newspaper: News.

Gatesville—Newspaper: Messenger & Star-Forum. **Radio-FM:** KPEP, 98.3.

Georgetown—Newspapers: Sunday Sun; Williamson County Sun. **Radio-AM:** KGTN, 1530 K hz. **Radio-FM:** KGTN, 96.7.

Giddings—Newspaper: Times & News. **Radio-FM:** KGID, 101.7

Gilmer—Newspaper: Mirror. **Radio-AM:** KHYM, 1060 Khz. **Radio-FM:** KNIF, 95.3.

Gladewater—Newspaper: Mirror. **Radio-AM:** KEES, 1430 Khz.

Glen Rose—Newspaper: Reporter.

Goldthwaite—Newspaper: Eagle.

Goliad—Newspapers: Advance Guard; Texas Express.

Gonzales—Newspapers: Daily Inquirer (D); Weekly Inquirer. **Radio-AM:** KCTI, 1450 Khz.

Gorman—Newspaper: Progress.

Graham—Newspaper: Leader-Reporter. **Radio-AM:** KSWA, 1330 Khz. **Radio-FM:** KWKQ, 107.1.

Granbury—Newspaper: Hood County News. **Radio-AM:** KPAR, 1420 Khz.

Grand Prairie—Newspaper: Daily News (D). **Radio-AM:** KKDA, 730 Khz.

Grand Saline—Newspaper: Sun.

Grandview—Newspaper: Tribune.

Granger—Newspaper: News.

Grapeland—Newspaper: Messenger.

Greenville—Newspaper: Herald-Banner (D). **Radio-AM:** KGVL, 1400 Khz. **Radio-FM:** KIKT, 93.5.

Groesbeck—Newspaper: Journal.

Groom—Newspaper: News.

Groveton—Newspaper: News.

Gruver—Newspaper: Statesman.

Hale Center—Newspaper: American.

Hallettsville—Newspaper: Tribune-Herald. **Radio-AM:** KRJH, 1520 Khz.

Hallsville—Newspaper: Herald.

Hamilton—Newspaper: Herald-News. **Radio-AM:** KCLW, 900 Khz.

Hamlin—Newspaper: Herald.

Harlingen—Newspaper: Valley Morning Star (D). **Radio-AM:** KGBT, 1530 Khz. **Radio-FM:** KELT, 94.5; KIWW, 96.1. **TV:** KGBT-Ch. 4; KMBN-Ch. 60.

Harper—Newspaper: Herald.

Hart—Newspaper: Beat.

Haskell—Newspaper: Free Press. **Radio-FM:** KVRP, 95.5.

Hawley—Newspaper: Jones County Journal.

Hearne—Newspaper: Democrat.

Hebbronville—Newspaper: Enterprise.

Helotes—Radio-AM: KXAM, 1440 Khz.

Hemphill—Newspaper: Sabine County Reporter. **Radio-AM:** KAWS, 1240 Khz.

Hempstead—Newspaper: Waller County News-Citizen.

Henderson—Newspaper: Daily News (D). **Radio-AM:** KGRI, 1000 Khz.; KWRD, 1470. **Radio-FM:** KGRI, 100.1.

Henrietta—Newspaper: Clay County Leader.

Hereford—Newspaper: Brand (D). **Radio-AM:** KPAN, 860 Khz. **Radio-FM:** KPAN, 106.3.

Hico—Newspaper: News-Review.

Highland Park (Dallas)—Radio-AM: KVIL, 1150 Khz. **Radio-FM:** KVIL, 103.7.

Highlands—Newspaper: Star.

Hillsboro—Newspaper: Reporter. **Radio-AM:** KHBR, 1560 Khz. **Radio-FM:** KJNE, 102.5.

Hondo—Newspaper: Anvil Herald. **Radio-AM:** KRME, 1460 Khz.

Honey Grove—Newspaper: Signal-Citizen.

Houston—Newspapers: Chronicle (D); Daily Court Review (D); Post (D); Business Journal; Forward Times; Informer; Jewish Herald Voice. **Radio-AM:** KILT, 610 Khz.; KTRH, 740; KKBQ, 790; KEYH, 850; KPRC, 950; KLAT, 1010; KRBE, 1070; KNUZ, 1230; KXYZ, 1320; KCON, 1430; KYOK, 1590. **Radio-FM:** KUHF, 88.7; KPFT, 90.1; KTSU, 90.9; KTRU, 91.7; KLTR, 93.7; KLEF, 94.5; KIKK, 95.7; KSRR, 96.5; KFMK, 97.9; KODA, 99.1; KILT, 100.3; KLOL, 101.1; KMJQ, 102.1; KQUE, 102.9; KRBE, 104.1; KHCB, 105.7. **TV:** KPRC-Ch. 2; KUHT-Ch. 8; KHOU-Ch. 11; KTRK-Ch. 13; KTXN-Ch. 20; KRIV-Ch. 26; KHTV-Ch. 39.

Howe—Newspaper: Enterprise.

Hubbard—Newspaper: City News.

Humble—Radio-AM: KTUN, 1180 Khz.

Huntington—Radio-AM: KIPR, 1260 Khz.

Huntsville—Newspaper: Item (D). **Radio-AM:** KKMX, 1400 Khz.; KSAM, 1490. **Radio-FM:** KSHU, 89.3; KHUN, 101.7.

Hurst—Newspaper: Mid-Cities Daily News (D).

Idalou—Newspapers: Beacon; Country Press.

Ingleside—Newspaper: Index.

Ingram—Newspaper: News.

Iowa Park—Newspaper: Leader.

Iraan—Newspaper: News.

Irving—Newspaper: Daily News (D). **TV:** KLTJ-Ch. 49.

Italy—Newspaper: Press.

Itasca—Newspaper: Item.

Jacksboro—Newspapers: Gazette-News; Jack County Herald.

Jacksonville—Newspaper: Daily Progress (D). **Radio-AM:** KEBE, 1400 Khz. **Radio-FM:** KOOI, 106.5.

Jasper—Newspaper: News-Boy. **Radio-AM:** KTXJ, 1350 Khz. **Radio-FM:** KWYX, 102.3.

Jayton—Newspaper: Chronicle.

Jefferson—Newspaper: Jimplecute.

Jewett—Newspaper: Messenger.

Johnson City—Newspaper: Record-Courier.

Joshua—Newspaper: Tribune.

Junction—Newspaper: Eagle. **Radio-AM:** KMBL, 1450 Khz. **Raido-FM:** K272AU, 102.3.

Karnes City—Newspaper: Karnes Citation.

Katy—Newspaper: Times.

Kaufman—Newspaper: Herald.

Keene—Radio-FM: KJCR, 88.3.

Kemp—Newspaper: Cedar Creek Pilot.

Kenedy—Newspaper: Advance Times. **Radio-AM:** KAML, 990 Khz. **Radio-FM:** KTNR, 92.1.

Kennedale—Newspaper: News.

Kerens—Newspaper: Tribune.

Kermit—Newspaper: Winkler County News. **Radio-AM:** KERB, 600 Khz.

Kerrville—Newspapers: Daily Times (D); Mountain Sun. **Radio-AM:** KERV, 1230 Khz. **Radio-FM:** KRVL, 94.3.

Kilgore—Newspaper: News Herald (D). **Radio-AM:** KOCA, 1240 Khz. **Radio-FM:** KKTX, 95.9.

Killeen—Newspaper: Daily Herald (D). **Radio-AM:** KIIZ, 1050 Khz. **Radio-FM:** KNCT, 91.3; KIXS, 93.3.

Kingsville—Newspaper: Record. **Radio-AM:** KINE, 1330 Khz. **Radio-FM:** KTAI, 91.1; KODK, 92.7; KDUV, 97.7.

Kirbyville—Newspaper: Banner.

Knox City—Newspaper: Knox County News.

Kountze—Newspaper: News-Visitor.

Kress—Newspaper: Chronicle.

Ladonia—Newspaper: News.

La Feria—Newspaper: News.

La Grange—Newspapers: Fayette County Record; Journal. **Radio-AM:** KVLG, 1570 Khz. **Radio-FM:** KMUZ, 104.9.

Lake Dallas—Newspaper: Lake Cities Sun.

Lake Jackson—Newspaper: Brazorian News. **Radio-FM:** KGOL, 107.5.

LaMarque—Newspaper: Times.

Lamesa—Newspaper: Press-Reporter. **Radio-AM:** KPET, 690 Khz. **Radio-FM:** KIOF, 104.7.

Lampasas—Newspaper: Dispatch Record. **Radio-AM:** KCYL, 1450 Khz. **Radio-FM:** KLTD, 99.3.

Lancaster—Newspapers: Leader; News.

La Porte—Newspaper: Bayshore Sun.

Laredo—Newspapers: News (D); Morning Times (D). **Radio-AM:** KLAR, 1300 Khz.; KVOZ, 1490. **Radio-FM:** KFIX, 92.7; KOYE, 94.9. **TV:** KGNS-Ch. 8; KVTV-Ch. 13.

La Vernia—Newspaper: News.

Leakey—Newspaper: Real County American.

Leonard—Newspaper: Graphic.

Levelland—Newspapers: Hockley County News-Press; Leader. **Radio-AM:** KLVT, 1230 Khz. **Radio-FM:** KHOC, 105.5.

Lewisville—Newspaper: Daily Leader (D).

Liberty—Newspaper: Vindicator. **Radio-AM:** KPXE, 1050 Khz.

Lindale—Newspaper: News.

Linden—Newspaper: Cass County Sun.

Little Elm—Newspaper: Colony Courier.

Littlefield—Newspaper: Lamb County Leader-News. **Radio-AM:** KZZN, 1490 Khz.

Livingston—Newspapers: Lake Livingston Progress; Polk County Enterprise. **Radio-AM:** KETX, 1440 Khz. **Radio-FM:** KETX, 92.1.

Llano—Newspaper: News.

Lockhart—Newspaper: Post-Register. **Radio-AM:** KHJK, 1060 Khz.

Lockney—Newspaper: Beacon

Longview—Newspaper: News-Journal (D). **Radio-AM:** KLUE, 1280 Khz.; KFRO, 1370. **Radio-FM:** KYKX, 105.7. **TV:** KLMG-Ch. 51.

Lorenzo—Newspaper: Leader.

Lubbock—Newspaper: Avalanche-Journal (D). **Radio-AM:** KRLB, 580 Khz.; KFYO, 790; KSEL, 950; KFMX, 1340; KLFB, 1420; KTLK, 1460; KEND, 1590. **Radio-FM:** KTXT, 88.1; KOHM, 91.1; KSEL, 93.7; KFMX, 94.5; KLLL, 96.3; KRLB, 99.5; KTEZ, 101.1; KFYO, 102.5. **TV:** KTXT-Ch. 5; KCBD-Ch. 11; KLBK-Ch. 13; KAMC-Ch. 28; KJAA-Ch. 34.

Rosebud—Newspaper: News.
Rosenberg-Richmond—Newspaper: Fort Bend Herald-Coaster (D). Radio-AM: KFRD, 980 Khz. Radio-FM: KFRD, 104.9.
Rotan—Newspaper: Advance-Star-Record.
Round Rock—Newspaper: Leader. Radio-FM: KNCS, 88.1.
Rowena—Newspaper: Press.
Rowlett—Newspaper: Lakeside Record American.
Rusk—Newspapers: Cherokee County Banner; Cherokeean. Radio-AM: KTLU, 1580 Khz. Radio-FM: KWRW, 97.7.
Saint Jo—Newspaper: Tribune.
San Angelo—Newspaper: Standard-Times (D). Radio-AM: KGKL, 960 Khz.; KQSA, 1260; KTEO, 1340; KBIL, 1420. Radio-FM: KBIL, 92.9; KWLW, 93.9; KIXY, 94.7; KGKL, 97.5. TV: KACB-Ch. 3; KIDV-Ch. 6; KLST-Ch. 8.
San Antonio—Newspapers: Commercial Recorder (D); Express & News (D); Light (D); North San Antonio Times; Texas Farm & Ranch News. Radio-AM: KTSA, 550 Khz.; KSLR, 630; KKYX, 680; KSJL, 760; KONO, 860; KFHN, 1150; WOAI, 1200; KXET, 1250; KBUC, 1310; KCOR, 1350; KAPE, 1480; KEDA, 1540. Radio-FM: KUKU, 89.1; KSYM, 90.1; KPAC, 90.9; KRTU, 91.7; KITY, 92.9; K237AS, 95.3; KSAQ, 96.1; KAJA, 97.3; KISS, 99.5; KLLS, 100.3; KQXT, 101.9; KTFM, 102.7; KXZL, 104.5; KBUC, 107.5. TV: KMOL-Ch. 4; KENS-Ch. 5; KLRN-Ch. 9; KSAT-Ch. 12; KWEX-Ch. 41.
San Augustine—Newspapers: Rambler; Tribune.
San Benito—Newspaper: News.
Sanderson—Newspaper: Times.
Sanger—Newspaper: Courier.
San Juan—Newspaper: San Juan/Pharr/Alamo Advance News.
San Marcos—Newspapers: Daily Record (D); News. Radio-AM: KCNY, 1470 Khz. Radio-FM: KEYI, 103.5.
San Saba—Newspaper: News & Star. Radio-AM: KDAL, 1410 Khz.
Santa Anna—Newspaper: News.
Schulenburg—Newspaper: Sticker.
Seabrook—Radio-FM: KZRQ, 92.1.
Seagoville—Newspaper: Suburbia News.
Seagraves—Newspaper: Gaines County News.
Sealy—Newspaper: News.
Seguin—Newspapers: Gazette-Enterprise (D); Citizen. Radio-AM: KWED, 1580 Khz. Radio-FM: KSMG, 105.3.
Seminole—Newspaper: Sentinel. Radio-AM: KIKZ, 1250 Khz.
Seymour—Newspaper: Baylor County Banner. Radio-AM: KSEY, 1230 Khz. Radio-FM: KSEY, 94.3.
Shamrock—Newspaper: Texan. Radio-AM: KBYP, 1580 Khz.
Shepherd—Newspaper: San Jacinto News-Times.
Sherman—Newspaper: Democrat (D). Radio-AM: KIKM, 910 Khz.; KTXO, 1500. Radio-FM: KZXL, 96.7.
Shiner—Newspaper: Gazette.
Silsbee—Newspaper: Bee. Radio-AM: KKAS, 1300 Khz. Radio-FM: KWDX, 101.7.
Silverton—Newspaper: Briscoe County News.
Sinton—Newspaper: San Patricio County News. Radio-AM: KDAE, 1590 Khz. Radio-FM: KNCN, 101.3; KOUL, 103.3.
Slaton—Newspaper: Slatonite. Radio-AM: KCAS, 1050 Khz. Radio-FM: KJAK, 92.7.
Smithville—Newspaper: Bastrop County Times.
Snyder—Newspaper: Daily News (D). Radio-AM: KSNY, 1430 Khz. Radio-FM: KSNY, 101.7.
Somerville—Newspaper: Tribune.
Sonora—Newspaper: Devil's River News. Radio-AM: KVRN, 980 Khz. Radio-FM: KHOS, 92.1.
Spearman—Newspapers: Hansford Plainsman; Reporter. Radio-FM: KRDF, 98.3.
Springtown—Newspaper: Epigraph.
Spur—Newspaper: Texas Spur.
Stamford—Newspaper: American. Radio-AM: KDWT, 1400 Khz.
Stephenville—Newspaper: Empire-Tribune (D). Radio-AM: KSTV, 1510 Khz. Radio-FM: KSTV, 98.3.
Sterling City—Newspaper: News-Record.
Stockdale—Newspaper: Star.
Stratford—Newspaper: Star.
Sudan—Newspaper: Beacon-News.
Sulphur Springs—Newspaper: Daily News-Telegram (D). Radio-AM: KSST, 1230 Khz. Radio-FM: KDXE, 95.9.
Sweetwater—Newspaper: Reporter (D). Radio-AM: KXOX, 1240 Khz. Radio-FM: KXOX, 96.7. TV: KTXS-Ch. 12.

Taft—Newspaper: Tribune.
Tahoka—Newspaper: Lynn County News.
Talco—Newspaper: Times.
Tatum—Newspaper: Trammel Trace Tribune.
Taylor—Newspaper: Daily Press (D). Radio-AM: KTAE, 1260 Khz. Radio-FM: KRGT, 92.1.
Teague—Newspaper: Chronicle.
Temple—Newspaper: Daily Telegram (D). Radio-AM: KTEM, 1400 Khz. Radio-FM: KPLE, 104.9. TV: KCEN-Ch. 6.
Terrell—Newspaper: Tribune (D). Radio-AM: KTER, 1570 Khz. Radio-FM: KTLR, 107.1.
Terrell Hills—Radio-AM: KRNN, 930 Khz. Radio-FM: KESI, 106.3.
Texarkana—Newspaper: Gazette (D). Radio-AM: KCMC, 740 Khz; KADO, 940; KTFS, 1400. Radio-FM: KTAL, 98.1; KOSY, 102.5. TV: KTAL-Ch. 6.
Texas City—Newspaper: Sun (D). Radio-AM: KYST, 920 Khz.
Thorndale—Newspaper: Champion.
Three Rivers—Newspaper: Progress.
Throckmorton—Newspaper: Tribune.
Trenton—Newspaper: Tribune.
Trinity—Newspaper: Standard.
Troup—Newspaper: Times Banner.
Tulia—Newspaper: Herald. Radio-AM: KTUE, 1260 Khz.
Tye—Radio-FM: KTYE, 99.3.
Tyler—Newspaper: Courier-Times-Telegraph (D). Radio-AM: KTBB, 600 Khz.; KZEV, 690; KTYL, 1330; KDOK, 1490. Radio-FM: KVNE, 89.5; KROZ, 92.1; KTYL, 93.1; KNUE, 101.5. TV: KLTV-Ch. 7.
Uvalde—Newspaper: Leader-News. Radio-AM: KVOU, 1400 Khz. Radio-FM: KLXQ, 102.3; KYUF, 104.9.
Valley Mills—Newspaper: Tribune.
Van—Newspaper: Progress.
Van Alstyne—Newspaper: Leader.
Van Horn—Newspaper: Advocate.
Vega—Newspaper: Enterprise.
Vernon—Newspaper: Daily Record (D). Radio-AM: KVWC, 1490 Khz. Radio-FM: KVWC, 102.3.
Victoria—Newspapers: Advocate (D); Business Journal. Radio-AM: KCWM, 1340 Khz.; KMAL, 1410. Radio-FM: KVIC, 95.1; KTXN, 98.7; K288BY, 105.5; KZEU, 107.9. TV: KVCT-Ch. 19; KAVU-Ch. 25.
Vidor—Newspaper: Vidorian.
Waco—Newspapers: Tribune-Herald (D); Citizen; Messenger. Radio-AM: KWTX, 1230 Khz.; WACO, 1460; KRZI, 1580; KBBW, 1010. Radio-FM: KNFO, 95.5; KWTX, 97.5; KHOO, 99.9; KWBU, 107.1. TV: KWTX-Ch. 10.
Wallis—Newspaper: News Review.
Waskom—Newspaper: Weekly.
Waxahachie—Newspaper: Daily Light (D). Radio-AM: KBEC, 1390 Khz.
Weatherford—Newspaper: Democrat (D). Radio-AM: KZEE, 1220 Khz.
Weimar—Newspaper: Mercury.
Wellington—Newspaper: Leader.
Weslaco—Newspaper: News. Radio-AM: KRGV, 1290 Khz. TV: KRGV-Ch. 5.
West—Newspaper: News.
West Lake Hills—Radio-AM: KTXZ, 1560 Khz.
Wharton—Newspaper: Journal-Spectator. Radio-AM: KANI, 1500 Khz.
Wheeler—Newspaper: Times.
White Deer—Newspaper: News.
Whitehouse—Radio-FM: KEYP, 99.3.
Whitesboro—Newspaper: News-Record.
Whitewright—Newspaper: Sun.
Whitney—Newspapers: Messenger; Lake Whitney Star.
Wichita Falls—Newspaper: Times-Record-News (D). Radio-AM: KWFT, 620 Khz.; KGTN, 990; KLLF, 1290. Radio-FM: KNIN, 92.9; KLUR, 99.9; KKQV, 103.3; KTLT, 106.3. TV: KFDX-Ch. 3; KAUZ-Ch. 6.
Wills Point—Newspapers: Chronicle; Van Zandt News.
Wimberley—Newspaper: View.
Wink—Newspaper: Bulletin.
Winnsboro—Newspaper: News.
Winters—Newspaper: Enterprise.
Wolfe City—Newspaper: Mirror.
Woodville—Newspapers: Tyler County Booster; Woodsman. Radio-AM: KVLL, 1490 Khz.
Wylie—Newspaper: News.
Yoakum—Newspaper: Herald Times.
Yorktown—Newspapers: De Witt County View; News.
Zapata—Newspaper: Zapata County News.

STATEWIDE CIVIC ORGANIZATIONS

Listed below are privately supported civic, commercial and other nonprofit statewide organizations in Texas which provided information on questionnaires sent out by the Texas Almanac. Organizations which did not return questionnaires by June 15, 1985, are not included. In some cases regional organizations are included.

Zip codes are given for executive officers or office addresses, where available.

Listing of organizations is alphabetical, according to the key word in the title.

Advertising Agencies, S. W. Assn. of.—Pres., Jim Rice, 3623 N. W. 36th, Oklahoma City, OK; Exec. Dir., Bob Burke. Office Address: 8700 Stemmons Frwy., Ste. 303, Dallas 74247.

AFL-CIO, Texas.—Pres., Harry Hubbard, Box 12727, Austin. Office Address: 1106 Lavaca, Austin 78701.

Aging, Texas Assn. of Homes for the.—Pres., Sandra B. Derrow, 9417 Great Hills Tr., Apt. 3044, Austin; Exec. Dir., Mike Sims, Box 1909, Waco. Office Address: 6225 Hwy. 290 E, Ste. 204, Austin 78723.

AGRICULTURAL ORGANIZATIONS

Agents Assn., Texas County.—Pres., Don D. Cowan, County Bldg., San Benito; Sec., Charles Moss, Rt. 2, Armory, Angleton 77515.

Aviation Assn., Texas.—Pres., Harold Hardcastle; Exec. Dir., Harry P. Whitworth. Office Address: 1000 Brazos, Ste. 200, Austin 78701.

Cooperative Council, Texas.—Pres., Vernon Lewis, 7115 Gainsborough, Amarillo; Exec. Vice Pres., Billy L. Conner. Office Address: Box 9527, Autin 78766.

Teachers Assn. of Texas, Vocational.—Pres., Terry A. Phillips, Box 1251, Seagraves; Exec. Dir., W. H. Meischen. Office Address: 614 E. 12th, Austin 78701.

Workers of Texas, Professional.—Pres., Dr. Johnny Johnston, Ag. Ed. Dept., Tarleton St. Univ., Stephenville 76402.

Airport Executives, Assn. of Texas.—Pres., Carlos Gonzales, Laredo Internatl. Airport, Box 579, Laredo; Exec. Dir., Ted Willis. Office Address 211 E. 7th, Ste. 1020, Austin 78701.

American Legion, Dept. of Texas.—Dept. Cmdr., John D. Morris; Dept. Adjt., W. H. McGregor. Office Address: 709 E. 10th, Austin 78701.

American Legion Auxiliary, Dept. of Texas.—Pres., Jane Shultz, 3501 Tanglewood Dr., Bryan; Exec. Dir., Mae Paust. Office Address: 709 E. 10th, Austin 78701.

Amusement and Music Operators of Texas.—Pres., Byron Cook, Box 692, Corsicana; Exec. Dir., Pat Miller. Office Address: 4302 Airport Blvd., Austin 78722.

Anesthesiologists, Texas Society of.—Pres., Dr. John A. Jenicek, Anes. Dept., UTMB, Galveston; Exec. Dir., Mary Jones. Office Address: 1905 N. Lamar Blvd., Suite 107, Austin 78705.

Angus Assn. of America, Texas Red.—Pres., George W. Baechtle, Box 235, Emhouse; Exec. Dir., Harrison Walker. Office Address: Box 793, Eagle Lake 77434.

Angus Assn., Texas.—Pres., J. V. Heyser, Rt. 2, Cisco; Exec. Dir., Wendell Berry. Office Address: 233 N. Judkins, Fort Worth 76111.

Apartment Assn., Texas.—Pres., Clinton Wolf, 4706 Alabama, El Paso; Exec. Dir., Jerry Adams. Office Address: 1005 Congress, Ste. 420, Austin 78701.

Apparel Manufacturers Assn., S.W. (SAMA) Div. of Am. Apparel Manufacturers Assn. (AAMA).—Exec. Vice Pres., Gene M. Grounds, 3000 Irving Blvd., Dallas; Exec. Dir., Jane Stanton. Office Address: Box 585931, Dallas 75258.

Archaeology, Institute of Nautical.—Pres., Dr. Donald A. Frey; Exec. Dir., Dr. George F. Bass. Office Address: Drawer AU, College Station 77840.

Archeological Society, The Texas.—Pres., C. K. Chandler, 13719 Brook Hollow, San Antonio. Office Address: Center for Archaeological Research, Univ. of Tex. at San Antonio, San Antonio 78285.

Architects, Am. Institute of (Dallas Chapter).—Pres., Jim Meyers; Exec. Dir., Loretta Thomas. Office Address: 2800 Routh, Ste. 141, Dallas 75201.

Architects, Texas Society of.—Pres., Jim Foster, 7007 St. Mary's, Ste. 1600, San Antonio; Exec. Dir., Des Taylor. Office Address: 1400 Norwood Tower, Austin 78701.

Art Education Assn., Texas.—Pres. James M. Clarke, Aldine Independent School Dist., 14910 Aldine-Westfield Rd., Houston 77032.

Assessing Officers, Texas Assn. of.—Pres., Kelley Utley, Box 120, Belton; Exec. Dir., Martha Noble Carmean. Office Address: Box 26550, Austin 78755.

Association Executives, Texas Society of.—Pres., John N. Kemp, Drawer 4679, Austin; Exec. Dir., Marilyn Monroe, 2550 S. IH-35, Ste. 200, Austin 78704.

Attorneys Assn., Texas City.—Pres., Merrill Nunn, Box 1971, Amarillo; Exec. Dir., Ted Willis. Office Address: 211 E. 7th, Ste. 1020, Austin 78701.

Austin College Alumni Assn.—Pres., Dr. Harry E. Smith, Campus Box P, Sherman; Exec. Dir., Dr. Howard A. Starr. Office Address: Campus Box H, Sherman 75090.

Auto and Truck Parts Assn., Texas.—Pres., Dave Head, 7311 Scott, Houston; Exec. Dir., Michael T. Marks. Office Address: 506 W. 12th, Austin 78701.

Automobile Dealers Assn., Texas.—Pres., Gene Fondren, 1108 Lavaca, Austin; Chmn. of Board, Don Buckalew. Office Address: Box 1028, Austin 78767.

Automotive Service Assn., Independent.—Pres., Jerry Bellot, 2301 Memorial, Port Arthur; Exec. Dir., Allen Richey. Office Address: 1904 Airport Frwy., Ste. 100, Bedford 76021.

Automotive Wholesalers of Texas.—Chmn., G. C. Morris, 1505 S. IH-35, Austin. Office Address: Box 788, Austin 78767.

Bakers Assn., Inc., Texas.—Pres., David Brown, Box 1039, San Antonio; Exec. Vice Pres., Alva M. Burger. Office Address: 5743 Marquita, Dallas 75206.

Bank Counsel, Texas Assn. of.—Pres., Ben Munson, Box 1099, Denison; Secy.-Treas., Jim Lederer. Office Address: 203 W. Tenth, Austin 78701.

Bankers Assn. of Texas, Independent.—Pres., John Shivers, Box 16400, Ft. Worth; Exec. Dir., F. Hagen McMahon. Office Address: 700 United Bank Tower, Austin 78701.

Baptist General Convention of Texas.—Pres., Dr. W. Winfred Moore, 1st Baptist Church, Tyler & 13th, Amarillo; Exec. Dir., Dr. Wm. M. Pinson Jr. Office Address: 511 N. Akard, Dallas 75201-3355.

Bar of Texas, State.—Pres., Charles Smith; Exec. Dir., Edward O. Coultas. Office Address: Box 12487, Austin 78711.

Baylor Alumni Assn.—Pres., Robert L. Morrison, 1212 S. University Parks Dr., Waco; Exec. Vice Pres., Dr. James F. Cole. Office Address: Campus Box 378, Waco 76798.

Beefmaster Breeders Universal.—Exec. Dir., Gene Kuykendall, 6800 Park Ten Blvd., Ste. 290W, San Antonio 78213.

Big Bend Natural History Association, Inc.—Exec. Dir., John R. Pearson, Box 68, Big Bend National Park 79834.

Blindness, Texas Society to Prevent (See Prevent Blindness.)

B'nai B'rith Women, (S.W. Region).—Pres., Phyllis Kalmin, 8210 Frontenac, Houston; Reg. Dir., Mrs. Marvin Green. Office Address: 4660 Beechnut, Apt. 246, Houston 77096.

Boating Trades Assn. of Texas.—Pres., Pat Helton, 3134 Old Spanish Tr., Houston; Exec. Dir., Julian O. Read. Office Address: 411 Adolphus Tower, Dallas 75202.

Bowling Proprietors' Assn. of America, Inc.—Pres., James A. Brooks, 1212 N. Roberson, Conroe; Exec. Dir., V. A. Wapensky. Office Address: Box 5802, Arlington 76011.

Brahman Breeders Assn., Am.—Pres., Sloan Williams, Hungerford; Exec. Vice Pres., Wendell E. Schronk. Office Address: 1313 La Concha Ln., Houston 77054.

Brangus Assn., American Red.—Pres., John Sosnowy. Office Address: 7801 N. Lamar, Suite D-92, Austin 78752.

Brangus Breeders Assn., Internatl.—Pres., Reese Woodling, 5970 E. San Leandro, Tucson, AZ; Exec. Vice Pres., J D. Morrow. Office Address: 9500 Tioga Dr., San Antonio 78230.

Brangus Breeders Assn., Texas.—Pres., Kermit Wendland, Rt. 2, Box 160, Miles; Exec. Sec., Michael Sturgess. Office Address: 505 E. University, Ste. 603, College Station 77840.

Broadcasters, Texas Assn. of.—Pres., Don Chaney, Box 7935, Tyler; Exec. Vice Pres., Bonner McLane. Office Address: Box 14787, Austin 78761.

Broiler Council, Texas. (See Poultry Associations.)

Building and Construction Trade Council, Texas.—Pres., R. Harold White, Box 4477, Wichita Falls; Exec. Sec.-Treas., Jackie W. St. Clair. Office Address: 1106 Lavaca, Ste. 204, Austin 78701.

Building Officials Association of Texas.—Pres., H. T. Hardy, Box 729, Grapevine; Exec. Dir., Ted Willis. Office Address: 211 E. 7th, Ste. 1020, Austin 78701.

Business, Natl. Fed. of Independent/Texas—St. Dir. of Govt. Relations, Robert A. Sfluka Jr. Office Address: 815 Brazos, Ste. 400L, Austin 78701.

Business, Texas Association of.—Pres., L. W. Gray. Office Address: 6900 Fannin, Ste. 240, Houston 77030.

Cancer Society, American (Texas Div., Inc.).—Pres., Dr. Charles A. Coltman Jr., 4450 Medical Dr., San Antonio; Exec. Dir., Jack M. Hardison. Office Address: 3834 Spicewood Springs Rd., Austin 78759.

Carpet Cleaners Assn., Texas Professional.—Pres. Dan Hudson, 305 E. Austin, Marshall; Exec. Dir., Jeff D. Martin. Office Address: 4302 Airport Blvd., Austin 78722.

Cattle Raisers Assn., Inc., Texas and Southwestern.—Pres., John M. Shelton III, Box 430, Amarillo; Sec.-Gen. Mgr., Don C. King. Office Address: 1301 W. Seventh, Fort Worth 76102.

Cement Assn., Portland (S. Central Region).—Reg. Mgr., Warren G. Burres. Office Address: 10300 N. Central Expwy., Ste. 452V, Dallas 75231.

Cerebral Palsy Assn. of Texas, Inc., United.—Pres., Wallace Pellerin, 7952 Anderson Sq., Austin; Exec. Dir., E. Dianne Bisig. Office Address: 7801 N. Lamar, Ste. 39, Austin 78752.

CHAMBERS OF COMMERCE ASSNS.

East Texas.—Pres., Billy Bob Crim, Box 1250, Kilgore; Exec. Dir., James F. McAuley. Office Address: Box 1592, Longview 75606.

Executives, Texas.—Pres. Jimmy Lyles, Box 640, Corpus Christi; Exec. Sec., Flo Brister. Office Address: 408 Vaughn Bldg., Austin 78701.

Managers and Secretaries Assn. of East Texas.—Pres., Tracey S. Wheeler, Box 330, Baytown. Office Address: Box 1592, Longview 75606.

Rio Grande Valley.—Pres., H. W. Card Jr.; Exec. Vice Pres., C. F. Giles. Office Address: Box 1499, Weslaco 78596.

Texas State.—Pres., Tom Champion Jr., Box 2062, Brownsville. Office Address: 1012 Perry-Brooks Bldg., Austin 78701.

Christian Church (Disciples of Christ) in the Southwest.—Moderator, Jerrell J. Cosby, 2404-A Garden Park Ct., Arlington; Reg. Minister & Pres., James C. Suggs. Office Address: 2909 Lubbock, Fort Worth 76109.

Christmas Tree Growers Assn., Texas.—Pres., Don Kachtik, Orange; Exec. Sec.-Treas., E. R. Wagoner. Office Address: 1003 Markus, Lufkin 75901.

Churches, Texas Conference of.—Pres., Bishop Ernest T. Dixon Jr., Box 28509, San Antonio; Exec. Dir., Rev. Dr. Frank H. Dietz. Office Address: 2704 Rio Grande, Apt. 9, Austin 78705.

Church Women United in Texas.—Pres., Mrs. Mickey Gergeni. Office Address: 3917 Doris, Amarillo 79109.

Circulation Management Assn., Texas.—Pres., Vince Fusco, Box 2171, San Antonio. Office Address: Box 1870, Fort Worth 76101.

Citrus and Vegetable Assn., Texas.—Pres., Heino Brausch, Box 1187, LaFeria; Exec. Dir., William Weeks. Office Address: Box 671, Harlingen 78550.

City Management Assn., Texas.—Pres., George Patterson; Exec. Dir., Ted Willis. Office Address: 211 E. 7th, Ste. 1020, Austin 78701.

City Personnel and Civil Service Officials of Texas, Assn. of.—(Name changed; see **Municipal Personnel Assn., Texas.**)

City Planners Assn. of Texas.—Pres., H. David Jones, Box 2000, Lubbock; Exec. Dir., Ted Willis. Office Address: 211 E. 7th, Ste. 1020, Austin 78701.

Clerks and Secretaries of Texas, Assn. of City.—Pres., June Krause, P.O. Drawer 1, Schertz; Exec. Dir., Ted Willis. Office Address: 211 E. 7th, Ste. 1020, Austin 78701.

Colleges and Universities, Assn. of Texas.—Pres., Dr. Billy J. Franklin, Lamar Univ., Beaumont; Exec. Dir., Dr. J. R. Woolf. Office Address: UTA Box 19023, Arlington 76019.

Colleges and Universities of Texas, Council of Presidents of the Public Senior.—Chmn., Dr. C. Robert Kemble, Lamar Univ. System, Lamar Stn., Box 11900, Beaumont; Exec. Dir., Wanda J. Mills. Office Address: 2609 Coatbridge, Austin 78745-3423.

Communication Assn., Internatl.—Pres., Dr. Brenda Dervin, Seattle, WA.; Exec. Dir., Robert L. Cox. Office Address: 8140 Burnet Rd., Austin 78758.

Community Services, Inc.—(See **United Way of Texas.**)

Conservation Districts, Assn. of Texas Soil and Water.—Pres., Waldo Smith, Box 1252, Brenham. Office Address: Box 658, Temple 76503.

Consumer Assn., Texas.—Pres., Brad Wiewel, Box 50057, Austin; Exec. Dir., Jeaneen McMaster, Box 12513, Austin. Office Address: 1300 Guadalupe, Austin 78701.

CONTRACTORS ASSOCIATIONS

Southwest Association of Building Service.—Pres., Walt Kattengell, New Orleans, LA; Exec. Dir., Jeff D. Martin. Office Address: 4302 Airport Blvd., Austin 78722.

Association of Drilled Shaft (Contractors), Inc.—Dir., Scot Litke. Office Address: Box 280379, Dallas 75228.

Associated General of Texas—Highway, Heavy, Utilities & Industrial Branch—Pres., Keith Keller, Box 393, Fredericksburg; Exec. Dir., Thomas L. Johnson, 3402 Westledge Cir., Austin. Office Address: 300 Barton Springs Rd., Austin 78704.

Texas Association of Landscape.—Pres., Gordon Domaschk, 9811 Bee Caves Rd., Austin; Exec. Dir., Jeff D. Martin. Office Address: 4302 Airport Blvd., Austin 78722.

Texas Council Painting and Decorating (Contractors) Assn.—Pres., M. E. Murphy, Box 10072, Amarillo; Exec. Dir., Pat Miller. Office Address: 4302 Airport Blvd., Austin 78722.

Associated Plumbing, Heating and Cooling of Texas, Inc.—Pres., Stanley Brooks, 4340 Verone, Bellaire; Exec. Dir., Pat Miller. Office Address: 4302 Airport Blvd., Austin 78722.

Urethane Foam (Contractors) Assn.—Pres., Hubert Coon, Box 17504, San Antonio; Exec. Dir., Don R. McCullough. Office Address: 4302 Airport Blvd., Austin 78722.

Convention and Visitor Bureaus, Texas Assn. of.—Pres., John R. Mosty, Box 2277, San Antonio; Exec. Dir., David Ferguson. Office Address: 100 Washington, Box 1370, Waco 76702.

Corrections Assn., Texas.—Pres., David Myers, Rt. 1, Box 16, Lovelady; Exec. Dir., Jeff D. Martin. Office Address: 4302 Airport Blvd., Austin 78722.

COTTON ASSOCIATIONS

Cotton Assn., Texas.—Pres., George Clay; Exec. Vice Pres., H. A. Poteet. Office Address: 811 Cotton Exchange Bldg., Dallas 75201.

Cotton Ginners Assn., Texas.—Pres., J. O. Williams, Frost; Exec. Vice Pres., J. H. Price. Office Address: Box 814080, Dallas 75381.

Cotton Growers, Inc., Plains.—Pres., Tommy D. Fondren, Box 308, Lorenzo; Exec. Vice Pres., Donald A. Johnson. Office Address: Box 3640, Lubbock 79452.

Cotton Growers Co-operative Assn., Texas.—Pres., Paul Underwood, Itasca; Exec. Dir., A. E. Schmidt. Office Address: Box 391, Taylor 76574.

Cotton Growers Assn., Rolling Plains.—Pres., Edward Ekdahl, Rt. 1, Avoca; Exec. Dir., Mark Lundgren. Office Address: 113 Wetherbee, Stamford 79553.

Cottonseed Crushers Assn., Inc., Texas.—Pres., Wayne Martin, Box 1889, Lubbock; Exec. Vice Pres., Jack Whetstone. Office Address: 1004 Cotton Exchange Bldg., Dallas 75201.

Counselor Educator and Supervision, Texas Assn. of.—Pres., Margaret Etchison, 324 Fairfax, Brownsville; Exec. Sec., Charlotte McKay. Office Address: 316 W. 12th, Ste. 402, Austin 78701.

Counties, Texas Assn. of (TAC).—Pres., Norman Troy, Beaumont; Exec. Dir., Sam E. Clonts, Box 2131, Austin. Office Address: 604 United Bank Tower, 400 W. 15th, Austin 78701.

CREDIT ASSOCIATIONS

Credit Management Assn. of Texas.—Pres., Lane Donaldson, Box 950, Waco; Exec. Dir., Pat Miller. Office Address: 4302 Airport Blvd., Austin 78722.

Credit Union Management Assn., Inc., Natl.—Pres., Paul Deaton, Dayton, OH; Treas., L. Phil Davis. Office Address: Box 140099, Dallas 75214.

Credit Union League and Affiliates, Texas.—Pres., Jack L. Eaker; Chmn. of Board, Paul A. Mitchell, 333 Lockwood Dr., Houston. Office Address: Box 225147, Dallas 75265.

DAUGHTERS ASSOCIATIONS

Of American Colonists, Texas Society.—Pres., Mrs. Walter K. Henry, 1202 Caudill, College Station 77840.

Of the Confederacy, Texas Div. of the United.—Pres., Mrs. S. C. Bell, Box 129, Pattison, TX. Office Address: 112 E. 11th, Austin 78701.

Of 1812, Texas Society, United States.—Pres., Mrs. P. M. McKee, 4065 Ligustrum, Abilene 79605.

Of the Republic of Texas.—Pres. Gen., Mrs. Grady Dennis Rash Jr., 1 Soapberry Ln., Rockwall. Office Address: 112 E. 11th, Austin 78701.

Dermatological Society, Texas.—Pres., R. A. Stevenson, 2806 N. Navarro, Victoria; Exec. Dir., Iris Wenzel. Office Address: 1801 N. Lamar Blvd., Austin 78701.

Diabetes and Endocrine Assn., Texas.—Exec. Dir., Dr. Eric A. Orzeck. Office Address: 8181 N. Stadium Dr., Ste. 200, Houston 77054.

Diabetes Assn., Inc., American (Texas Affiliate, Inc.).—Pres., Dr. Brian R. Tulloch; Exec. Dir., Phillip L. Fry. Office Address: 6201 Middle Fiskville, Ste. C, Austin 78752.

Discover Texas Assn.—Chmn., Gary Dalton, 9001 Kirby Dr., Houston; Exec. Dir., Jim Battersby. Office Address: 8500 Village Dr., San Antonio 78217.

Donkey and Mule Society, Inc., Am.— Pres., Paul A. Hutchins; Member Services Officer, Betsy Hutchins. Office Address: Rt. 5, Box 65, Denton 76201.

Earth Scientists, Society of Independent Professional.—Pres., A. Scott Ritchie, 125 N. Market, Ste. 950, Wichita, KS; Exec. Sec., Diane Finstrom. Office Address: 4925 Greenville Ave., Ste. 170, Dallas 75206.

Egg Council, Texas.—Pres., Jimmie Wall, Linn; Exec. Vice Pres., Bill Powers. Office Address: Box 9589, Austin 78766.

Electric Cooperatives, Inc., Texas.—Exec. Dir., James A. Morriss. Office Address: Box 9589, Austin 78766.

Electronics Assn., Inc., Texas.—Pres., Freeman Douglas, 15230 Hwy. 2 N., Webster; Exec. Dir., Clyde Nabors. Office Address: 2708 W. Berry, Ft. Worth 76109.

ENGINEERS ASSOCIATIONS

American Society of Civil (Texas Sec.).—Pres., H. Cecil Allen, Box 13089, Houston; Exec. Sec., Dr. Fred P. Wagner Jr. Office Address: Box 4250, Lubbock 79409.

Council of Texas, Inc., Consulting.—Pres., Conrad S. Hinshaw, 6161 Savoy, Ste. 1199, Houston; Exec. Dir., J. P. Word. Office Address: Suite 420, San Jacinto Bldg., Austin 78701.

Environmental Health Assn., Texas.—Pres., Jim Dunaway, Box 1114, Henderson; Exec. Dir., R. L. Minnich. Office Address: Box 349, Longview 75606.

Fair Assn., East Texas.—Pres., Don Blasingame, Rt. 5, Box 180, Tyler; Secy.-Mgr., Bob Murdoch. Office Address: 411 W. Front, Tyler 75702.

Fair, State of Texas.—Pres., Joe H. Dealey, Dallas; Exec. Vice Pres. & Gen. Mgr., Wayne H. Gallagher. Office Address: Box 26010, Dallas 75226.

Fairs and Expositions, Texas Assn. of.—Pres., Don Clark, State Fair of Texas, Box 26010, Dallas; Sec.-Treas., Ms. Frances Cooper. Office Address: Box 867, Mercedes 78570.

Family Physicians, Texas Academy of.—Pres., Dr. Rafael Garza, McAllen; Exec. Dir., James M. White. Office Address: 8301 MoPac, Ste. 309A, Austin 78759.

Farm and Ranch Club, East Texas.—Pres., Bernard Mask; Sec.-Treas., Bob Murdoch. Office Address: 411 W. Front, Tyler 75702.

Farm Bureau, Texas.—Pres., S. M. True Jr., Plainview; Exec. Dir., Warren Newberry, Box 489, Waco. Office Address: 7420 Fish Pond Rd., Waco 76710.

Farmers Union, Texas.—Pres., Mike Moeller. Office Address: Box 7276, Waco 76714-7276.

Fashion Assn., Inc., American.—Pres., Sam Nohra; Exec. Sec., Bette Hamilton, Box AM586454, Dallas. Office Address: Suite M5F18, Menswear Mart, Dallas 75258.

Finance Officers Assn., Texas Chapter of Municipal.—Pres., Dan Parker, Box 830309, Richardson; Exec. Dir., Ted Willis. Office Address: 211 E. 7th, Ste. 1020, Austin 78701.

Fire Chiefs Assn., Texas.—Pres., Jim Harrington, Box 758, Port Neches; Exec. Dir., Ted Willis. Office Address: 211 E. 7th, Ste. 1020, Austin 78701.

Firemen's and Fire Marshals' Assn., State.—Pres., Robert Stubblefield, 709 Alexander, Killeen; Exec. Mgr., Ed Kirkham. Office Address: Box 13326, Austin 78711.

Folklore Society, Texas.—Pres., Melvin R. Mason, Dept. of English, SHSU, Huntsville; Exec. Dir., F. E. Abernethy. Office Address: Box 13007 SFA Sta., Nacogdoches 75962.

Food Industry Assn., N. Central Texas.—Pres., Clyde Stricklin, Box 6452, Ft. Worth; Exec. Dir., Daisy Fern Nelson, 4334 Harvest Hill Rd., Dallas. Office Address:

1515 W. Mockingbird Ln., Ste. 113, Dallas 75235.

Food Processors Assn., Texas.—Pres., Bill Renfro, Box 321, Fort Worth; Exec. Dir., Al B. Wagner Jr. Office Address: Box 341, College Station 77841.

Foresters, Texas Society of American.—Pres., Charles Walker, Texas Forest Service, 508 Pan American Dr., Livingston; Business Mgr., E. R. Wagoner. Office Address: Box 3625, Lufkin 75903.

Forestry Assn., Texas.—Pres., Gene M. Meyers, Box 3107, Conroe; Exec. Vice Pres., Ron Hufford. Office Address: 1903 Atkinson Dr., Lufkin 75901.

Funeral Directors Assn., Inc., Texas.—Pres., Leo T. Metcalf III, Box 2925, Conroe; Exec. Dir., Edward A. McGuire. Office Address: 1513 S. IH-35, Austin 78741.

Future Farmers of America, Texas Assn. of.—Pres., Coby Shorter III, 1204 Seaholm, Eagle Lake; Exec. Dir., Durwin Hill. Office Address: Box 14925, Austin 78761.

Gas Assn., Southern.—Chmn. of the Board, James E. Tyree, Box 871, Tulsa, OK; Chief Staff Officer, Roger H. Reid. Office Address: 4230 LBJ Frwy., Ste. 414, Dallas 75244.

Genealogical Society, Texas State.—Pres., Trevia Wooster Beverly, 2507 Tannehill, Houston 77008-3052.

Geological Society, West Texas.—Pres., F. Dan Kozak, Box 1595, Midland; Exec. Dir., Marie D. Bellomy. Office Address: 119 N. Colorado, Ste. 109, Midland 79701.

Geophysical Society, Dallas.—Pres., James D. Robertson, ARCO Resources Technology, 2300 W. Plano Pkwy., Plano. Office Address: Box 402306, Dallas 75240.

Ginners Assn., Texas Independent.—Pres., Larry Nelson, Tule Creek Gin, Rt. 1, Tulia; Exec. Dir., Donald G. Smith. Office Address: 5010 University, Ste. 350, Lubbock 79413.

Goat Breeders Assn., Am. Angora.—Pres., S. J. Shanklin, Rocksprings 78880.

Grain and Feed Assn., Texas.—Pres., Larry Alley, Box 40, Temple; Exec. Vice Pres., Raymond R. Nolen. Office Address: 1107 Sinclair Bldg., Fort Worth 76102.

Grange, Texas State.—Pres., Clifton Lampman, Rt. 17, Box 126AX, San Antonio; Exec. Dir., James H. Kiles, Luckenbach Rt., Box 6A, Fredericksbury 78624.

Health, Physical Education, Recreation and Dance, Texas Assn. for.—Pres., Mrs. Jean Dudney, Rt. 1, Box 1850, Boerne; Exec. Dir., Quentin A. Christian. Office Address: Box 7578, University Sta., Austin 78713.

Heart Assn., American, Texas Affiliate.—Pres., Dr. James M. Atkins, 5323 Harry Hines Blvd., Dallas; Exec. Dir., Sam Inman, Box 15186, Austin. Office Address: 1700 Rutherford Ln., Austin 78754.

Highway 67 Assn., U.S.—Pres., Willard Robertson, Box 463, Alvarado; Sec.-Treas., George R. Jordan. Office Address: 401 Rio Concho Dr., San Angelo 76903.

HISTORICAL ASSOCIATIONS

East Texas.—Pres., William J. Brophy; Exec. Dir., Archie P. McDonald. Office Address: Box 6223, SFA Sta., Nacogdoches 75962.

Oral History Assn.—Pres., Martha Ross, Univ. of Maryland, College Park, MD; Exec. Dir., Ronald E. Marcello. Office Address: Box 13734, NTSU, Denton 76203.

History Assn., Texas Oral.—Pres., Mary Faye Barnes, Galveston; Sec.-Treas., Rebecca S. Jimenez. Office Address: CSB Box 401, Baylor U, Waco 76798.

Panhandle-Plains Society.—Pres., Richard D. Palmer; Exec. Vice Pres., B. Byron Price Jr. Office Address: Box 967 W.T. Station, Canyon 79016.

Texas State.—Pres., Dr. Archie P. McDonald, Dept. of History, Stephen F. Austin St. Univ., Nacogdoches; Exec. Dir., vacancy. Office Address: 2.306 Sid Richardson Hall, UT Sta., Austin 78712.

West Texas.—Pres., Dr. Fane Downs, McMurry College, Abilene; Exec. Dir., Dr. B. W. Aston. Office Address: Box 152, HSU, Abilene 79698.

Historical Foundation, The Texas.—Pres., J. P. Bryan, 1300 Main, Ste. 1520, Houston; Exec. Dir., Leon M. Lurie. Office Address: Box 12243, Austin 78711.

Home Economics Assn., Texas.—Pres., Dr. Catherine B. Crawford, Rt. 3, Box 213AA, Lubbock; Exec. Dir., Margaret J. Sloan. Office Address: Box 831, Hurst 76053.

Home Fashions League, Inc., Natl.—Pres., Loretta Miles, 4401 S. Willoway Estate Ct., Bloomfield Hills, MI; Exec. Dir., Marilyn J. Miller. Office Address: Box 58045, Dallas 75258.

Homefurnishings Assn., Southwest.—Pres., Harold Leon, 116 W. Juan Linn, Victoria; Exec. Dir., Al Stillman. Office Address: Box 581207, Dallas 75258.

HORSE ASSOCIATIONS

Appaloosa (Horse) Club, Texas.—Pres., Bob Kuehner, Rt. 1, Box 213-A, Converse; Exec. Sec., Cheryl Palmer. Office Address: Box 1449, Burleson 76028.

National Cutting (Horse) Assn.—Pres., Tom Lyons, Rt. 4, Box 163, Grandview; Exec. Dir., Zack T. Wood Jr. Office Address: Box 12155, Fort Worth 76121.

Miniature (Horse) Assn., Inc., Internatl. Am.—Pres., Lee Martin, Rt. 3, Box 290, Edmond, OK; Exec. Sec., Jim Summers, 171 Moonlight Dr., Plano. Office Address: Box 129, Burleson 76028.

American Paint.—Pres., Bill Bryan, Rt. 8, Box 238, Edmond, OK; Exec. Sec., Ed Roberts, 313 Oak Haven, Keller. Office Address: Box 18519, Fort Worth 76118-0519.

American Quarter.—Pres., Stephen Kleberg, King Ranch, Kingsville; Exec. Dir., Ronald Blackwell. Office Address: 2701 IH-40 East, Amarillo 79168.

HOSPITAL ASSOCIATIONS (Office Address of each one is 6225 U.S. Highway 290 E., Austin 78761.)

Accountants, Texas Assn. of.—(See Financial Administration below.)

Assn., Texas.—Chmn., James J. Farnsworth, 1935 Amelia St., Dallas; Pres., O. Ray Hurst.

Auxiliaries, Texas Assn. of.—Pres., Mrs. Morris S. Buchanan, 2420 N. McCullough, Apt. 101, San Antonio; Vice Pres., Kay Dunlap.

Educators, Texas Society for.—Pres., Paula Dodson, Box 31, Ft. Worth; Exec. Dir., Nancy Ebert.

Engineers, Texas Assn. of.—Pres., David McCormack, 4110 Guadalupe St., Austin; Exec. Dir., Thomas M. Brush.

Executive Housekeepers, Texas Society of.—Pres., Anna Rodriguez, Box 3710, Brownsville; Exec. Dir., Robert J. Zamen.

Financial Administration, Texas Assn. of.—Pres., Marshall Chamness Jr., 8200 Walnut Hill Ln., Dallas; Exec. Dir., Burnham B. Jones.

Food Service Directors, Texas Society of.—Pres., Nancy Karcis, 7600 Beechnut, Houston; Exec. Dir., Roy Ayers Jr.

Governing Boards, Texas Assn. of.—Pres., Jud A. Cramer, Box 2920, Ft. Worth; Exec. Dir., Kenneth W. Peters.

Infection Control Practitioners, Texas Society of.—Pres., Ona Baker, Box 1110, Amarillo; Exec. Dir., Linda N. Broussard.

Information Systems Society, Texas.—Pres., Richard Searle, Box 2068, Laredo; Exec. Dir., David B. Dildy.

Medical Staff Services, Texas Society for.—Pres., Gail Cooper, Box 55227, Houston; Exec. Dir., Tracy L. Wilson.

Nurses, Texas Assn. of Operating Room.—Pres., Juanita Carrell, 1100 W. 49th, Austin; Exec. Dir., Joan Houston.

Nurses, Texas Society of Professional.—Pres., Winnie Lockhart, 1635 North Loop W, Houston; Exec. Dir., Joan Houston.

Nursing Service Administrators, Texas Society for.—Pres., Opal Bevil, 7600 Beechnut, Houston; Exec. Dir., Joan Houston.

Patient Representatives, Texas Society of.—Pres., Ginny Gremillion, 1203 Ross Sterling, Houston; Exec. Dir., Thomas English.

Personnel Administration, Texas Society for.—Pres., Randall Baker, Box 2588, Harlingen; Exec. Dir., Gordon L. Wright.

Personnel, Texas Society of Central Service.—Pres., John M. Johnson, Box 2756, Texas City; Exec. Dir., Roy Ayers Jr.

Public Relations, Texas Society for.—Pres., Ann Ward Rogers, Drawer 5741, San Angelo; Exec. Dir., Thomas English.

Purchasing and Materials Management, Texas Society of.—Pres., Tom L. Lawson, 2001 N. Oregon, El Paso; Exec. Dir., Eric L. MacEwan Jr.

Quality Assurance, Texas Society for.—Pres., Ann Schmitt, Box 20269, Houston; Exec. Dir., Kenneth W. Peters. Office Address: Box 15587, Austin 78761.

Social Work Directors, Texas Society for.—Pres., Jerry Humble, Box 125, Round Rock; Exec. Dir., Sharon J. Bettis.

Volunteer Services, Texas Assn., Directors of.—Pres., Martha Page Lawson, 6723 Bertner Ave., Houston; Exec. Dir., Kay Dunlap.

Industrial Arts Assn., Texas.—Exec. Sec., W. A. Mayfield. Office Address: Rt. 25, Box 744, Tyler 75707.

INSURANCE ASSOCIATIONS

Advisory Assn., Texas.—Chmn. of Exec. Comm., J.

D. White, Box 1502, Houston; Gen. Mgr., Roy E. Hoga. Office Address: Box 15, Austin 78782.

Independent Agents of Texas.—Pres., Richard E. Marks; Exec. Dir., Ernest Stromberger. Office Address: Box 1663, Austin 78767.

General Agents and Managers Assn., Texas.—Pres., Robert L. Grant, 7322 Southwest Freeway, Ste. 555, Houston; Exec. Dir., E. Kenneth Tooley. Office Address: 1920 S. IH-35, Austin 78704.

Information Service, Inc., S.W.—Pres., Jerry F. Johns; Sec.-Treas., Howard Howell. Office Address: 8705 Shoal Creek Blvd., Ste. 212, , Austin 78758.

Legal Reserve Officials Assn., Texas.—Pres., Walter B. Smith Jr., Box 1530, Dallas; Exec. Dir., Dave Smith. Office Address: 3724 Jefferson, Ste. 113, Austin 78731.

Life Underwriters, Texas Assn. of.—Pres., Rosalie L. Kuntz, Box 3147, Pasadena; Exec. Dir., E. Kenneth Tooley. Office Address: 1920 S. IH-35, Austin 78704.

Interior Designers, Texas Chapter of American Society of.—Pres., Tom Berry. Office Address: Box 58525, Dallas 75258.

Internal Medicine, Texas Society of.—Pres., Marshall McCabe, 606 Commodore Way, Houston; Exec. Dir., Iris Wenzel. Office Address: 1801 N. Lamar Blvd., Austin 78701.

Jewelers Assn., Inc., Texas.—Pres., Charles Payne, 4950 S. Loop 289, Lubbock; Exec. Dir., Michael R. Moore. Office Address: 504 W. 12th, Austin 78701.

Journalism Assn., Community College.—Pres., Mary Hires, Randolph, NJ; Exec. Dir., Ralph L. Sellmeyer, 3600 W. Garfield, Midland 79705.

Judges Assn., Texas Municipal Court.—Pres., Elinor Walters, Box 539, Seabrook; Exec. Dir., Ted Willis. Office Address: 211 E. 7th, Ste. 1020, Austin 78701.

Knights of Columbus, Texas State Council.—State Deputy, Dee Simon, Drawer S, Groves; State Exec. Sec., Charles Emery. Office Address: 2500 Columbus Dr., Austin 78746.

Knights of the Order of San Jacinto.—Knight Comdr., T. Talmage Main Jr., 4564 Arcady, Dallas 75205

Knights of Pythias, Grand Lodge of Texas.—Grand Chancellor, Roland Fiedler, 3713 Charlton Ave., Waco Grand Sec., Max Williams, 1103 Reel Rd., Longview Office Address: Box 10071, Longview 75604.

Land & Royalty Owners Assn., West Texas.—Pres., Billy McCormick, 200 36th Pl., Snyder; Exec. Dir., Dor R. McCullough. Office Address: 4302 Airport Blvd., Austin 78722.

Land Title Assn., Texas.—Exec. Dir., Catherine Lancaster. Office Address: 220 W. 7th, Ste. 201, Austin 78701.

Language Assn., South Central Modern.—Pres., John I. Fischer, Baton Rouge, LA; Exec. Dir., Paul A Parrish. Office Address: Dept. of English, Texas A&M Univ., College Station 77843.

Lawyers Assn., Texas Young (Formerly State Junior Bar of Texas).—Pres. David Seidler, 430 S. Commercial Aransas Pass; Coordinator, Sherrie Lacy. Office Address: Box 12487, Austin 78711.

League of Women Voters of Texas.—Pres., Lois Carpenter; Exec. Dir., Joann Lovelace. Office Address: 1212 Guadalupe, Ste. 107, Austin 78701.

Letters, Texas Institute of.—Pres., Stephen Harrigan, Box 1569, Austin; Exec. Dir., John Edward Weems. Office Address: Box 8594, Waco 76714-8594.

Libertarian Party of Texas.—Chmn., Roger Gary, 72 Aganier, San Antonio. Office Address: 7887 Katy Frwy. Ste. 386, Houston 77024.

Library Directors Assn., Texas Municipal.—Pres., Patricia L. Doyle, Box 517, McKinney; Exec. Dir., Ted Willis. Office Address: 211 E. 7th, Ste. 1020, Austin 78701.

Lung Assn. of Texas, Am. (formerly Texas TB&RD Assn.).—Pres., Mrs. Una Grace Nash, 2429 Robinson Way, Huntsville; Mgng. Dir., Wendell Teltow. Office Address: 7701 N. Lamar Blvd., Ste. 104, Austin 78752 1088.

Lutheran Church in America, Texas-La. Synod.—Pres., Philip L. Wahlberg. Office Address: Box 4362 Austin 78765.

Manufactured Housing Assn., Texas.—Pres., Wi Ehrle. Office Address: Box 14428, Austin 78761.

Marine Retailers Assn. of America.—Pres., Gordo Peterson, Minneapolis, MN; Exec. Dir., B. J. Fergusor 2600 Southwest Frwy., Ste. 305, Houston. Office Address 11511 Katy Frwy., Ste., 335, Houston 77079.

Mayors, Councilmembers and Commissioners, Assn of.—1st Vice Pres., Tom Reid, Pearland; Exec. Dir., Te Willis. Office Address: 211 E. 7th, Ste. 1020, Austin 78701.

Meat Packers Assn., S.W.—Pres., Ron Loggins; Exe Dir., Leon N. Kothmann. Office Address: 1333 Corpora Dr., Ste. 103, Irving 75062.

MEDICAL ASSOCIATIONS

Assistants-State of Texas, American Assn. of.—Pres., Donna Papagno, 2304 Deadwood Dr., Austin; Exec. Dir., Iris Wenzel. Office Address: 1801 N. Lamar Blvd., Austin 78701.

Association, Texas.—Pres., Dr. D. Clifford Burross, No. 6 Eureka Cir., Wichita Falls; Exec. Dir., C. Lincoln Williston. Office Address: 1801 N. Lamar Blvd., Austin 78701.

Association Auxiliary, Texas.—Pres., Mrs. C. B. Bruner, 3700 Autumn Dr., Fort Worth; Adm. Dir., Amy Wilson. Office Address: 1801 N. Lamar Blvd., Austin 78701.

Osteopathic Assn., Texas.—Pres., Dr. Donald M. Peterson, Fort Worth; Exec. Dir., Tex Roberts. Office Address: 226 Bailey, Fort Worth 76101.

Podiatric Medical Assn., Texas.—Pres., Sheldon P. Goren, 17215 Red Oak, Ste. 102, Houston; Exec. Dir., Sally B. Yaryan. Office Address: 5017 Bull Creek Rd., Austin 78731.

Association, Texas Veterinary.—Pres., Dr. John A. Wood; Exec. Dir., David P. Lancaster. Office Address: 612 Scarbrough Bldg., Austin 78701.

Mental Health Assn. in Texas.—Pres., Helen J. Farabee; Exec. Dir., Stella L. Mullins. Office Address: 1111 W. 24th, Austin 78705.

Mesquite, Los Amigos del.—Pres., Ms. Rozan Reed Williams, Box 202029, Dallas; Treas.-Memb. Chmn., Jim Lee, Reagan Wells Rt., Box 122, Uvalde. Office Address: Box 15551, Austin 78761.

Military Order of The Stars and Bars, Tex. Div.—Cmdr., James A. York, 505 Merrill, Houston 77009.

Military Order of the World Wars.—Chief Admin. Officer, George E. Loikow, Sgt.-Maj. (Ret.), 435 N. Lee, Alexandria, VA. 22314.

Moose Assn., Texas.—Pres., Larry Cardwell, 5640 Brookside Dr., Ft. Worth; Exec. Dir., Chester Smith. Office Address: Box 6424, Odessa 79767.

Motorcycle Dealers Assn., Texas.—Pres., Darryl Hurst, 1117 Bingle Rd., Houston; Exec. Dir., Michael T. Marks. Office Address: 506 W. 12th, Austin 78701.

Motor Transportation Assn., Texas.—Pres., Terry Townsend, 4200 North Hills Dr., Austin; Chmn., W. K. Barnett, 1611 Ave. M., Lubbock. Office Address: 700 E. 11th, Austin 78767.

Municipal Advisory Council of Texas.—Chmn., Bd. of Trustees, Lewis W. Pollok III; Exec. Dir., Danny Burger. Office Address: Box 2968, Austin 78769-2968.

Municipal League, Texas.—Exec. Dir., Ted Willis. Office Address: 211 E. 7th, Ste. 1020, Austin 78701.

Municipal Personnel Assn., Texas.—Pres., Nancy Carney, Box 469002, Garland; Exec. Dir., Ted Willis. Office Address: 211 E. 7th, Ste. 1020, Austin 78701.

Music Educators Assn., Inc., Texas.—Pres., Jim Van Zandt, 7705 N. Briarridge Ct., Ft. Worth; Exec. Dir., Bill Cormack, Box 49469, Austin. Office Address: 807 Stark, Austin 78756.

Music Schools, Texas Assn. of.—Pres., Dr. Marceau Myers, School of Music, NTSU, Denton; Exec. Dir., Dr. Robert Blocker. Office Address: School of Music, Baylor Univ., Waco 76798.

Names Institute, S. Central.—Dir., Fred Tarpley, Dept. of Literature and Languages, ETSU, Commerce 75428.

National Guard Assn. of Texas.—Pres., Col. Walter J. Dingler; Exec. Dir., CW4 (Ret) Len Tallas. Office Address: Box 10045, Austin 78766.

Neuropsychiatric Assn., Texas.—(Succeeded by Texas Dist. Branch of the American Psychiatric Assn.)

New England Women, Tex. Colony #121, Natl. Society of.—Pres., Mrs. Ansel J. Syphers, 5106 W. Stanford, Dallas 75209; Historian and Sesquicent. Chmn., Mrs. William H. Tabb, 6458 Lavendale, Dallas.

Newspaper Assn., Texas Daily.—Pres., John Roberts, Box 1518, Victoria; Exec. Vice Pres., Philip A. Berkebile. Office Address: 1005 Congress, Ste. 495, Austin 78701.

Nurserymen, Texas Assn. of.—Pres., Floyd E. Ireland, 11820 High Star, Houston; Exec. Vice Pres., Bill R. Fullingim, 302 Leisurewood Dr., Buda. Office Address: 512 E. Riverside Dr., Ste. 207, Austin 78704.

Nursing, Texas League for.—Pres., Barbara Lust, 4922 Tiffany Ln., Cibolo; Exec. Dir., Edith C. Ayers. Office Address: 6225 U.S. Hwy. 290-E., Austin 78723.

Obstetricians and Gynecologists, Texas Assn. of.—Pres., George Sullivan, 526 W. Seminary, Fort Worth; Exec. Dir., Iris Wenzel. Office Address: 1801 N. Lamar Blvd., Austin 78701.

Many organizations, such as this Southern Baptist Convention, hold their annual meetings in the Dallas Convention Center.

Office Product Dealers Assn. of Greater Austin.—Pres., Eldore Urban, 8409 N. Lamar, Austin; Exec. Dir., Don R. McCullough. Office Address: 4302 Airport Blvd., Austin 78722.

OIL AND GAS ASSOCIATIONS

Crude Oil Reclaimers Assn., Texas.—Pres., Philip Kimmel; Exec. Dir., Don R. McCullough. Office Address: 4302 Airport Blvd., Austin 78722.

North Texas.—Pres., Ed S. Spragins, 720 Hamilton Bldg., Wichita Falls; Exec. Vice Pres., Tom Haywood. Office Address: 1106 City National Bldg., Wichita Falls 76301.

Texas Mid-Continent.—Pres., William H. Abington; Chmn., J. C. Walter Jr., 240 The Main Bldg., 1212 Main, Houston. Office Address: 400 W. 15th, Ste. 500, Austin 78701.

West Central Texas.—Pres., Dan Fergus, Box 1479, Abilene; Exec. Dir., Alex Mills. Office Address: Box 2332, Abilene 79604.

Ophthalmological Assn., Texas.—Pres., John Eisenlohr, 2811 Lemmon Ave. E., Dallas; Exec. Dir., Iris Wenzel. Office Address: 1801 N. Lamar Blvd., Austin 78701.

Optometric Assn., Texas.—Pres., Dr. Floyd L. Thornton, 1616 10th, Wichita Falls; Exec. Dir., Stanley Boysen. Office Address: 1016 LaPosada, Ste. 174, Austin 78752.

Optometric Assn., Aux. to the Texas.—Exec. Dir., Sandra Rosen. Office Address: 8014 Duffield, Houston 77071.

Orthopedic Assn., Texas.—Pres., Jerry Julian, 3100 Red River, Austin; Exec. Dir., Iris Wenzel. Office Address: 1801 N. Lamar Blvd., Austin 78701.

Parents and Teachers, Texas Congress of.—Pres., Mary Tippin; Exec. Dir., Bob Keck. Office Address: 408 W. 11th, Austin 78701.

Parks and Recreation Assn., Texas Municipal.—Pres., Sharon Prete, 214 E. Main, Round Rock; Exec. Dir., Ted Willis. Office Address: 211 E. 7th, Ste. 1020, Austin 78701.

Parliamentarians, Texas State Assn. of.—Pres., Mrs. Donna Reed, 9318 Faircrest, Dallas 75238.

Pathologists, Inc., Texas Society of.—Pres., Thomas McConnell, 3434 Swiss Ave., Dallas; Exec. Dir., Iris Wenzel. Office Address: 1801 N. Lamar Blvd., Austin 78701.

Peanut Growers' Assn., S.W.—Pres., Johnnie Rollins, Rt. 2, Box 17 B, Granbury; Mgr., Ross Wilson. Office Address: Box 338, Gorman 76454.

Pecan Growers Assn., Inc.—Pres., Kenneth Pape, Box 1281, Seguin; Exec. Dir., Norman Winter. Office Address: P. O. Drawer CC, College Station 77841.

Pediatric Society, Texas.—Pres., Milam Tharo, 8215 Westchester, Dallas; Adm. Asst., Mary Greene. Office Address: 1801 N. Lamar Blvd., Austin 78701.

Pediatrics, Am. Academy of (Texas Chapter).—Chmn., L. Leighton Hill, 1200 Morrison Ave., Houston; Adm. Asst., Mary Greene. Office Address: 1801 N. Lamar Blvd., Austin 78701.

Personnel Consultants, Texas Assn. of.—Pres., Joy Perkins, 15400 Knoll Trail Dr., Apt. 212, Dallas; Exec. Dir., Janice E. Meador. Office Address: 722 Fairmont Pkwy., Pasadena 77504.

Pest Control Assn., Inc., Texas.—Pres., James Boren, Box 8118, Corpus Christi; Exec. Dir., Don R. McCullough. Office Address: 4302 Airport Blvd., Austin 78722.

PETROLEUM ASSOCIATIONS

Engineers, Society of.—Pres. Kenneth Robbins; Exec. Dir., Dan K. Adamson. Office Address: Box 833836, Richardson 75083-3836.

Equipment Suppliers Assn.—Pres., E. C. Broun Jr., 6500 Texas Commerce Tower, Houston; Exec. Dir., William J. Sallans. Office Address: 9225 Katy Frwy, Ste. 401, Houston 77024.

Pharmaceutical Assn., Texas.—Pres., Barbara T. Slover, 7824 S. Frwy., Ft. Worth; Exec. Dir., Luther R. Parker, Box 14709, Austin. Office Address: 1624 E. Anderson Ln., Austin 78752.

Philosophical Society of Texas.—Pres. Joe Greenhill, 1410 United Bank Tower, 400 W. 15th, Austin; Sec., Dorman H. Winfrey. Office Address: Box 12927, Capitol Sta., Austin 78711.

Physical Therapy Assn., Texas (Chap. of Am. Physical Therapy Assn.).—Pres., Susan McPhail, 8299 Cambridge, Apt. 2004, Houston; Exec. Dir., Cathy Greene. Office Address: 211 E. 7th, Ste. 714, Austin 78701.

Physicians in Nuclear Medicine, Texas Assn. of.—Pres., David McMurray, 7700 Floyd Curl Dr., San Antonio; Exec. Dir., Iris Wenzel. Office Address: 1801 N. Lamar Blvd., Austin 78701.

Plant Food Inst., Texas.—Pres., Bill Barton Jr., Box 1725, Bay City; Exec. Dir., Pat Miller. Office Address: 4302 Airport Blvd., Austin 78722.

Plastic Surgeons, Texas Society of.—Pres., Francis Burton, 8601 Village Dr., San Antonio; Exec. Dir., Iris Wenzel. Office Address: 1801 N. Lamar Blvd., Austin 78701.

Podiatry Assn., Texas.—(See Texas Podiatric Medical Assn. under Medical Associations.)

Poetry Society of Texas.—Pres., John Vaughan, Marshall; Cor. Sec., Faye Carr Adams. Office Address: 4244 Skillman, Dallas 75206.

Police Assn., Texas.—Pres., Kenneth Rosenquest, Victoria; Exec. Dir., Glen H. McLaughlin. Office Address: Box 4247, Austin 78765.

Police Chiefs Assn., Texas.—Pres., David N. Beidelman, Box 8005, Dallas; Exec. Dir., Ted Willis. Office Address: 211 E. 7th, Ste. 1020, Austin 78701.

POULTRY ASSOCIATIONS (Office Address of each one is Box 9589, Austin 78766.)

Texas Allied Assn.—Pres., Charles Yarbrough, Godley; Exec. Vice Pres., Bill Powers.

Texas Broiler Council.—Pres., Elray Woods, Pluss-Tex., Lufkin; Exec. Vice Pres., Bill Powers.

Texas Federation.—Pres., Joe Conerly, Indian River Internatl., Nacogdoches; Exec. Vice Pres., Bill Powers.

Texas Improvement Assn.—Pres., Bob Sellers, Indian River Internatl., Nacogdoches; Exec. Vice Pres: Bill Powers.

Texas Turkey Federation.—Pres., Dick Taylor, Plantation Foods, Waco; Exec. Vice Pres., Bill Powers.

PRESS ASSOCIATIONS

South Texas.—Pres., Fred Barbee, El Campo; Exec. Dir., Chester Evans. Office Address: 605 S. Wells, Edna 77957.

Texas.—Pres., Frank Baker, Ft. Stockton Pioneer, 210 N. Nelson, Ft. Stockton; Exec. Vice Pres., Lyndell Williams. Office Address: 718 W. 5th, Austin 78701.

Texas High School.—Dir., Dr. Mary K. Sparks, Dept. of Journalism, TWU, Denton. Office Address: Box 23866, TWU, Denton 76204.

West Texas.—Pres., David Werst, Big Lake Wildcat, Big Lake; Exec. Dir., Barbara Craig Kelly. Office Address: 2502 Ivanhoe, Abilene 79605.

Prevent Blindness, Texas Society to (Dallas Br.).—Pres., Edward G. Maier, 1201 Elm, Ste. 2200, Dallas; Exec. Dir., Judith M. Todd. Office Address: 3610 Fairmount, Dallas 75219.

Producers & Royalty Owners Assn., Texas Ind. (TIPRO).—Pres., Bruce Anderson, 900 Allied Bank Plaza, Houston; Exec. Vice Pres., Julian G. Martin. Office Address: 1910 InterFirst Tower, Austin 78701.

Property Owners, Natl. Assn. of (NAPO).—Pres., Ben Wallis; Exec. Dir., Cynthia Portfolio. Office Address: 2400 Tower Life Bldg., San Antonio 78205.

Psychiatric Society Assn., Texas (Dist. Br. of the Am. Psychiatric Assn.).—Pres., Spencer Bayles, 7500 Beechnut, Houston; Adm. Asst., Carrie Laymon. Office Address: 1801 N. Lamar Blvd., Austin 78701.

Public Works Assn., Texas.—Pres., Clarence T. Daugherty, Collin County Courthouse, McKinney; Exec. Dir., Ted Willis. Office Address: 211 E. 7th, Ste. 1020, Austin 78701.

Purchasing Institute, Inc., Natl.—Pres., Kenneth Davis, Rock Hill, SC; Exec. Dir., J. Nelson Slater. Office Address: 433 Westcliff Prof. Bldg., Dallas 75224.

Purchasing Managers Assn., Texas Municipal.—Pres., Mary Etta Jackson, Box 1562, Houston; Exec. Dir., Ted Willis. Office Address: 211 E. 7th, Ste. 1020, Austin 78701.

Pythias, Knights of, Grand Lodge of Texas.—(See Knights of Pythias.)

Radiological Society, Texas.—Pres., Wayne Ramsey, 1101 N. 19th, Abilene; Exec. Dir., Iris Wenzel. Office Address: 1801 N. Lamar Blvd., Austin 78701.

Ranching Heritage Assn.—Pres., J. D. Cage, Rt. 3, Box 415, Muleshoe; Exec. Vice Pres. & Gen. Mgr., Alvin G. Davis. Office Address: Box 4040, Lubbock 79409.

Range Management, Texas Sec. of the Society for.—Pres., Patrick Reardon, 6 El Norte Cir., Uvalde 78801.

Recreational Vehicle Assn., Texas.—Pres., Ed Blain, 3509 Forest Ln., Garland; Exec. Dir., Cliff Houy. Office Address: 3355 Bee Caves Rd., Austin 78746.

Research League, Texas.—Pres., Dr. Jared E. Hazleton, Box 12456, Austin; Exec. Dir., T. Boone Pickens Jr., Mesa Petroleum Co., Box 2009, Amarillo. Office Address: 1117 Red River, Austin 78701.

Respiratory Therapy, Texas Society for.—Pres., John Hiser, Tarrant Co. Jr. College, 828 Harwood Rd., Hurst; Exec. Dir., Michael T. Marks. Office Address: 506 W. 12th, Austin 78701.

Retailers Assn., Texas.—Pres., J. V. Johnson, 3110 Alamo Creek Cir., San Antonio; Exec. Vice Pres., Michael R. Moore. Office Address: 504 W. 12th, Austin 78701.

Roads/Transportation Assn., Texas Good.—Chmn., Oliver Thomas, Box 2071, Lubbock; Exec. Dir., Eugene W. Robbins. Office Address: 408 Vaughn Bldg., Austin 78701.

Safety Assn., Inc., Texas.—Pres. B. Gawain Bonner, Rt. 3, Box 458, Huntsville; Exec. Vice Pres., George R. Gustafson. Office Address: Box 9345, Austin 78786.

Santa Gertrudis Breeders Internatl.—Pres., Bob Wasson; Exec. Dir., W. M. Warren. Office Address: Box 1257, Kingsville 78363.

Savings and Loan League, Texas.—Pres., William E. Brady, Box 1308, Denton; Exec. Dir., Tom S. King. Office Address: 408 W. 14th, Austin 78701.

SCHOOL ASSOCIATIONS

Boards, Texas Assn. of.—Pres., John Quisenberry, 2613 E. 21st, Odessa; Exec. Dir., Orbry D. Holden. Office Address: Box 400, Austin 78767-0400.

Food Service Assn., Texas.—Pres., Elizabeth Rouse, 6100 Guadalupe, Austin; Exec. Dir., Carole Pfennig. Office Address: 316 W. 12th, Austin 78701.

Private, Texas Assn. of.—Pres., Carolyn S. Willard, 2829 W. Northwest Hwy., Dallas; Exec. Dir., Vernon Stewart. Office Address: Box 13481, Austin 75006.

Public Relations Assn., Texas Chapter, Natl.—Pres., Susan Dacus; Exec. Sec., Don Agnew. Office Address: Box 8615, Tyler 75711.

Science, Texas Academy of.—Pres., Dr. William J. Clark, Wildlife & Fisheries Sciences Dept., Texas A&M Univ., College Station; Exec. Dir., Drawer H6, College Station 77844.

Secretaries Assn., Texas Educational.—Pres., Mrs. Sarah Hargrove, 5921 Trail Lake, Ft. Worth. Office Address: 1101 Trinity, Austin 78701.

Sheep Breeders' Assn., Am. Rambouillet.—Pres., Leonard Chapman, Bison, SD; Exec. Dir., Mrs. LaVerne McDonald, 3409 Oxford Av., San Angelo. Office Address: 2709 Sherwood Way, San Angelo 76901.

Sheriffs' Assn. of Texas, Inc.—Pres., Sheriff Rick Thompson, Presidio Co., Drawer V, Marfa; Exec. Dir., Gordon Johnson. Office Address: 1106 Clayton Ln, Ste. 103E, Austin 78765.

Shorthand Reporters Assn., Texas.—Pres., Joe Belton, 1509 Main, Ste. 509, Dallas; Exec. Dir., Jeff D. Martin. Office Address: 4302 Airport Blvd., Austin 78722.

Shrimp Assn., The Texas.—Pres., David Eymard, Star Rt., Box 20, Shrimp Basin, Brownsville; Exec. Dir., Ralph Rayburn. Office Address: 403 Vaughn Bldg., 807 Brazos, Austin 78701.

Shrine Assn., Texas.—Pres., Kerry L. Linley, 3109 Ivanhoe, Abilene; Sec.-Treas., W. A. Spoonts. Office Address: Box 1950, Wichita Falls 76307.

Sign Manufacturers Assn., Texas.—Pres., Albert Santa Maria, Box 8188, Houston; Exec. Dir., Marcie Mayo. Office Address: Box 165041, Irving 75061.

Skeet Shooters Assn., Texas.—Sec.-Treas., Ms. Ruby E. Welch. Office Address: Drawer 141108, Dallas 75214-1108.

Skeet Shooting Assn., Natl.—Pres., Dr. Ted C. Hatfield, Lousiville, KY; Exec. Dir., Ann Myers. Office Address: Box 28188, San Antonio 78228.

Social Welfare Assn., Texas.—(Name changed to Texas United Community Services, Inc.; now United Way of Texas.)

Social Workers, Texas Chapter of the Natl. Assn. of.—Pres., Ann Milnor; Exec. Dir., Susan E. Negreen. Office Address: 2512 IH-35 S., Ste. 310, Austin 78704.

Soft Drink Assn., Texas.—Pres., E. T. Summers III, Coca-Cola Bottling Co., Box 30, Cuero; Exec. Dir., Virgil Musick. Office Address: Box 2258, Abilene 79604.

SONS ASSOCIATIONS

Of American Revolution (Texas Society).—Pres., William R. Eddleman, 3232 Republic Natl. Bank Tower, Dallas; Sec.-Treas., Col. Joe M. Hill. Office Address: Box 670768, Dallas 75367-0768.

Of Confederate Veterans (Texas Div.).—Cmdr., Denis Fluker, 8911 Springview Ln., Houston; Adjt., S. C. Bell, Box 129, Pattison. Office Address: Box 619, Hillsboro 76645.

Of Hermann in the State of Texas, Grand Lodge of the Order of the.—Pres., Louis B. Engelke, 515 S. St. Mary's, San Antonio; Exec. Dir., Louis R. Hoog Jr. Office Address: Box 1941, San Antonio 78297.

Of Republic of Texas.—Pres. Gen., Abe San Miguel, 145 E. Magnolia, San Antonio; Sec.-Gen., La Von Tindall, Rt. 3 Box 91, San Augustine. Office Address: 519 Hyannis Port N., Crosby 77532.

Southern Methodist University Alumni Assn.—Pres., Dr. Bobby B. Lyle; Exec. Dir., Dr. Gary A. Ransdell. Office Address: 3000 Dallas, Dallas 75205.

Soybean Assn., Texas.—Pres., Robert Ledbetter; Exec. Dir., Alan Krob, 3504 E. Louisville, Broken Arrow, OK. Office Address: Box 161, Dallas 75221.

Speech-Language-Hearing Assn., Texas.—Pres., Dr. Joseph W. Helmick, TCU, Fort Worth; Exec. Sec., Dr. Richard W. Stream. Office Address: Div. of Communication Disorders, NTSU, Box 5008, Denton 76203.

Sportsmen's Clubs of Texas (SCOT).—Pres., William B. LeBlanc, Box 1737, Fulton; Exec. Dir., Alan Allen, 3622 Peregrine Falcon, Austin. Office Address: 311 Vaughn Bldg., 807 Brazos, Austin 78701.

State Song Assn., Texas.—Pres., Mrs. Charles A. Stephens, 3405 Hemphill, Ft. Worth 76110.

Stock and Bond Dealers Assn., The Texas.—Pres., Raymond Wooldridge, 2001 Bryan Tower, Ste. 2300, Dallas; Exec. Sec., C. W. Houser. Office Address: Box 1727, Austin 78767.

Surgeons (N. Tex. Chap.), Am. College of.—Pres., Dr. Bohn Dixon Allen, 801 Rd. to Six Flags W., Ste. 101, Arlington; Sec., Dr. Michael S. McArthur, 214 E. Houston, Tyler. Office Address: Dallas Co. Med. Soc., Box 4680, Sta. A, Dallas 75208.

Surveyors Assn., Texas.—Pres., Ralph Harris, 1406 Hether, Austin; Exec. Dir., Don R. McCullough. Office Address: 4302 Airport Blvd., Austin 78722.

Tax Administrators, Texas Assn. of Municipal.—Pres., Bobby R. Forshage, Box 591, Seguin; Exec. Dir., Ted Willis. Office Address: 211 E. 7th, Ste. 1020, Austin 78701.

Taxpayers, Inc., Texas Assn. of.—Pres., C. Ivan Wilson, Box 4666, Corpus Christi; Exec. Vice Pres., Robert W. Strauser. Office Address: 711 MBank Tower, Austin 78701.

TCU Alumni Assn.—Pres., Tom E. Hill, One Tandy Center, Ste. 606, Fort Worth; Exec. Dir., DeVonna Tinney. Office Address: Box 32921, Fort Worth 76129.

TEACHERS ASSOCIATIONS

Texas Classroom—Pres., Thomasine Sparks; Exec. Dir., Jeri Stone. Office Address: Box 1489, Austin 78767.

Texas Assn. of College.—Pres., Dr. Nelson Thornton, Mktg. & Mgmt., Sam Houston St. Univ., Huntsville; Exec. Dir., Nancy A. Bene. Office Address: 316 W. 12th, Ste. 212, Austin 78741.

Dancing, Inc., Texas Assn. of (Teachers of).—Pres., Sara Harvey, 1119 Hill City, Duncanville 75116.

English, Texas Joint Council (Teachers of).—Pres., Karen Kutiper, Alief ISD, Box 68, Alief; Exec. Dir., Dr. Marvin Harris. Office Address: East Tex. Baptist Univ., Marshall 75670.

Texas Federation of.—Pres., John Cole, Box 776, Austin. Office Address: 2003 N. Lamar, Austin 78705.

Junior College (Teachers) Assn., Texas.—Pres., Michael M. Looney, 1300 San Pedro Ave., San Antonio; Exec. Sec., Charles L. Burnside, 5424 Highway 290 West, Ste. 101, Austin 78735.

Texas State.—Pres., Charles N. Beard; Exec. Sec., James T. Butler. Office Address: 316 W. 12th, Austin 78701.

Technical Society, Texas.—Pres., Dr. Lu McClellen, Eastfield College, 3737 Motley, Mesquite. Office Address: TSTI, Waco 76705.

Telephone Pioneers of America (Lone Star Chap. No. 22).—Pres., C. J. McAnally, 308 S. Akard, Rm. 1714, Dallas. Office Address: 311 S. Akard, Dallas 75202.

Texas Rangers Assn., Former.—Pres., J. J. Klevenhagen, 3805 Broadway, San Antonio; Chmn. of Bd., Mrs. Katie Welder. Office Address: Box 6354, San Antonio 78209

Theatre Owners of Texas, Natl. Assn. of.—Pres., Ed Kershaw; Exec. Dir., Bernie Palmer. Office Address: 10300 N. Central Expwy., Bldg. 5, Ste. 210, Dallas 75231.

Thoracic Society, Texas (Med. Sec. of Am. Lung Assn. of Texas).—Pres., Dr. Gary D. Harris, 7402 Bridgewater, San Antonio; Managing Dir., Ed Carter. Office Address: 7701 N. Lamar Blvd., Ste. 104, Austin 78752.

Tobacco and Candy Distributors, Inc., Texas Assn. of.—Pres., Hale Ham, 910 E. Southcross, San Antonio; Exec. Vice Pres., Joe Ratcliff. Office Address: 3636 Executive Center Dr., Ste. 208, Austin 78731.

Travelers Protective Assn. of America (Texas Div.).—Pres., Joe Perricone, 245 W. Sunset, Vidor; Exec. Dir., John J. Turner, R.R. 2, Cushing. Office Address: Box 3383, Waco 76707.

Turkey Federation, Texas.—(See **Poultry Associations**.)

United Way of Texas (formerly Texas United Community Services.)—Pres., Phil Strickland, 511 N. Akard Bldg., Rm. 735, Dallas; Exec. Vice Pres., William S. Link. Office Address: Box 15164, Austin 78761.

University Professors, Am. Assn. of (Tex. Conference).—Pres., Dr. Charlie Nichols, Texas Wesleyan College, Ft. Worth; Exec. Dir., Dr. Frances K. Sage. Office Address: 316 W. 12th, Austin 78701.

University Women, Am. Assn. of (Texas Div.).—Pres., Rema Lou Brown, 731 Buoy Rd., Houston 77062.

Urological Society, Texas.—Pres., Jan Ogletree, 1313 Red River, Austin; Exec. Dir., Iris Wenzel. Office Address: 1801 N. Lamar Blvd., Austin 78701.

Utility Assn., Texas Municipal.—Pres., Bob Derrington, Box 4398, Odessa; Exec. Dir., Ted Willis. Office Address: 211 E. 7th, Ste. 1020, Austin 78701.

Value Engineers, Inc., Society of Am.—Pres., John A. Jonelis. Office Address: 220 N. Story Rd., Ste. 114, Irving 75061.

Veterans of Foreign Wars of U.S., Dept. of Texas.—Adjt. Qm., Glen M. Gardner Jr. Office Address: 8503 N. IH-35, Austin 78753.

War of 1812 in the State of Texas, Gen. Society of the.—Pres., Lloyd D. Bockstruck, 3955-C Buena Vista, Dallas; Sec.-Treas., Thomas F. Bresnehen Jr. Office Address: 3207 Top Hill Rd., San Antonio 78209.

Wars in Texas, The Society of Colonial.—Pres., Richard Gentry Paxton, 2023 Northridge Dr., Austin; Exec. Dir., Thomas F. Bresnehen Jr. Office Address: 3207 Top Hill Rd., San Antonio 78209.

Water Conservation Assn., Texas.—Pres., Duncan Ellison, Water, Inc., Lubbock; Exec. Dir., Leroy Goodson. Office Address: 206 San Jacinto Bldg., Austin 78701.

Wheat Producers Assn., Texas.—Pres., Robert Graves, Rt. 2, Box 52, Perryton; Exec. Dir., D. G. Nelson. Office Address: 624 Texas Commerce Bank Bldg., Amarillo 79109.

Women's Clubs, Texas Fed. of.—Pres., Mrs. Harold Green, Box 1305, Tahoka; Exec. Dir., Mrs. Margie L. Brown, 2504 Cockburn Dr., Austin. Office Address: 2312 San Gabriel, Austin 78705.

CONSTITUTION OF TEXAS

Following is the complete text of the Constitution of Texas. It includes the original document which was adopted on Feb. 15, 1876, plus the 269 amendments approved through the election of Nov. 6, 1984.

Each amendment is accompanied by a footnote explaining when it was adopted. This text, with footnotes, of the Constitution is copyrighted by the A. H. Belo Corporation and may not be reprinted without written permission from the publisher.

Amendment of the Texas Constitution requires a two-thirds favorable vote by both the Texas House of Representatives and the Senate, followed by a majority vote of approval by voters in a statewide election.

Prior to 1973, amendments to the constitution could not be submitted by a special session of the Legislature. But the constitution was amended in 1972 to allow submission of amendments if the special session were opened to the subject by the governor.

Constitutional amendments are not subject to a gubernatorial veto. Once submitted, voters have the final decision on whether to change the constitution as proposed.

The following table lists the total number of amendments submitted to voters by the Texas Legislature and shows the year in which the Legislature approved them for submission to voters; e.g., the Sixty-ninth Legislature in 1985 approved 16 amendments to be submitted to voters — 13 in 1985 and three in 1986.

Year	No.	Year	No.	Year	No.
1879	1	1917	3	1953	11
1881	2	1919	13	1955	9
1883	5	1921	5	1957	12
1887	6	1923	2	1959	4
1889	2	1925	4	1961	14
1891	5	1927	8	1963	7
1893	2	1929	7	1965	27
1895	2	1931	9	1967	20
1897	5	1933	12	1969	16
1899	1	1935	13	1971	18
1901	1	1937	7	1973	9
1903	3	1939	4	1975	12
1905	3	1941	5	1977	15
1907	9	1943	3	1978	1
1909	4	1945	8	1979	12
1911	5	1947	9	1981	10
1913	7	1949	10	1982	3
1915	7	1951	7	1983	19
				1985	16

Amendments, 1983

Eleven amendments were voted on Nov. 8, 1983, as follows:

HJR 1 — Allowing for the assignment of income for the enforcement of court-ordered child support payments. Approved 607,219 to 157,826.

HJR 30 — Authorizing statutory provisions for succession of public office during disasters caused by enemy attack. Approved 449,631 to 280,790.

HJR 70 — Providing for assignment of judges of certain courts with probate jurisdiction. Approved 485,540 to 222,275.

HJR 91 — Authorizing fewer justice of the peace and constable precincts in certain counties. Approved 570,347 to 170,910.

HJR 105 — Replacing the limitation on the value of an urban homestead with a limitation based on size. Approved 434,332 to 281,819.

SJR 1 — Authorizing the exemption from taxation of property of certain veterans organizations. Defeated 388,197 to 346,337.

SJR 12 — Authorizing use of the permanent school fund to guarantee school bonds. Approved 457,590 to 269,037.

SJR 13 — Establishing the Board of Pardons and Paroles as a statutory agency and giving the board the power to revoke paroles. Approved 498,998 to 235,344.

SJR 14 — Relating to financial assistance to veterans and authorizing the issuance of bonds to finance the Veterans' Land Program and the Veterans' Housing Assistance Program. Approved 533,509 to 219,342.

SJR 17 — Permitting a city or town to expend public funds and levy assessments for the relocation or replacement of sanitation sewer laterals on private property. Approved 380,448 to 345,149.

SJR 1 (SS) — Relating to the associations of producers of agricultural commodities. Approved 463,357 to 255,468.

Amendments, 1984

Eight amendments were voted on Nov. 6, 1984, as follows:

HJR 4 — Relating to the Commission on Judicial Conduct and the authority to discipline active judges, certain retired and former judges, and certain masters and magistrates of the courts. Approved 2,858,130 to 854,655.

HJR 19 — Providing funds for the support of higher education and restructuring the permanent university fund. Approved 2,926,392 to 1,145,819.

HJR 22 — Resetting the per diem for members of the Legislature. Defeated 2,504,733 to 1,233,314.

HJR 29 — Relating to the powers of state-chartered banks. Approved 2,967,984 to 994,084.

HJR 65 — Relating to payment of assistance to dependent survivors of certain public servants killed on duty. Approved 2,559,892 to 1,469,551.

HJR 73 — Permitting the use of public funds and credit for payment of premiums on certain insurance contracts of mutual insurance companies. Defeated 2,406,003 to 1,301,880.

SJR 20 — Abolishing the office of county treasurer in Bexar and Collin Counties. Approved 2,291,452 to 1,091,186.

SJR 22 — Relating to the manner in which a vacancy in the office of lieutenant governor is to be filled. Approved 2,377,602 to 1,426,217.

Amendments, 1985

Thirteen amendments were to be voted on Nov. 5, 1985, as follows:

HJR 6 — Authorizing issuance of additional Texas water development bonds to create special water funds for conservation and development.

HJR 19 — Authorizing issuance of general obligation bonds to provide financing assistance for purchase of farm and ranch land.

HJR 27 — Relating to number of precincts in Chambers County.

HJR 54 — Authorizing Legislature to enact laws permitting a city or town to spend public funds and levy assessments for relocation or replacement of water laterals on private property.

HJR 72 — Authorizing Legislature to require prior approval of expenditure or emergency transfer of other appropriated funds.

HJR 89 — Relating to authority of Legislature to regulate provision of health care by hospital districts.

SJR 6 — Relating to placement of state inmates in penal or correctional facilities of other states.

SJR 9 — Providing additional bonding authority for veterans' housing assistance program and changing definition of those veterans eligible to participate.

SJR 10 — Granting Supreme Court and Court of Criminal Appeals jurisdiction to answer questions of state law certified from federal appellate courts.

SJR 14 — Creating Judicial Districts Board and providing for reapportionment of judicial districts by that board or by the Legislative Redistricting Board.

SJR 16 — Relating to manner in which a person is charged with criminal offense and to jurisdiction of courts in criminal cases.

SJR 21 — Authorizing use of proceeds from sale of permanent school fund land to acquire other land as part of permanent school fund.

SJR 27 — Abolishing office of county treasurer in Andrews and El Paso Counties and abolishing office of county surveyor in Collin, Dallas, Denton, El Paso, Henderson and Randall Counties.

Amendments, 1986

Three amendments were to be voted on Nov. 4, 1986, as follows:

HJR 73 — Allowing political subdivisions to purchase certain mutual insurance.

SJR 15 — Relating to apportionment of value of railroad rolling stock among counties for purpose of property taxation.

SJR 33 — Relating to statutory revision and to requirement that each bill have a title expressing subject of bill.

Text of Texas Constitution

The following is a complete text of the Constitution of Texas, containing all amendments adopted through Nov. 2, 1982, with explanatory footnotes:

Preamble

Humbly invoking the blessings of Almighty God, the people of the State of Texas do ordain and establish this Constitution.

ARTICLE I. — BILL OF RIGHTS

That the general, great and essential principles of liberty and free government may be recognized and established, we declare:

Sec. 1. Texas Free and Independent. — Texas is a free and independent State, subject only to the Constitution of the United States, and the maintenance of our free institutions and the perpetuity of the Union depend upon the preservation of the right of local self-government, unimpaired to all the states.

Sec. 2. All Political Power Is Inherent in the People. — All political power is inherent in the people, and all free governments are founded on their authority, and instituted for their benefit. The faith of the people of Texas stands pledged to the preservation of a republican form of government, and subject to this limitation only, they have at all times the inalienable right to alter, reform or abolish their government in such manner as they may think expedient.

Sec. 3. All Free Men Have Equal Rights. — All free men, when they form a social compact, have equal rights, and no man, or set of men, is entitled to exclusive separate public emoluments or privileges but in consideration of public services.

Sec. 3-a. Equality under the law shall not be denied or abridged because of sex, race, color, creed or national origin. This amendment is self-operative.

[Note. — Sec. 3-a of Art. I is an added amendment setting forth civil rights for all. Submitted by the Sixtysecond Legislature (1971) and adopted in an election Nov. 7, 1972.]

Sec. 4. There Shall Be No Religious Test for Office. — No religious test shall ever be required as a qualification to any office or public trust in this State; nor shall anyone be excluded from holding office on account of his religious sentiments, provided he acknowledge the existence of a Supreme Being.

Sec. 5. How Oaths Shall Be Administered. — No person shall be disqualified to give evidence in any of the courts of this State on account of his religious opinions, or for want of any religious belief, but all oaths or affirmations shall be administered in the mode most binding upon the conscience, and shall be taken subject to the pains and penalties of perjury.

Sec. 6. Freedom in Religious Worship Guaranteed. — All men have a natural and indefeasible right to worship Almighty God according to the dictates of their own consciences. No man shall be compelled to attend, erect or support any place of worship, or to maintain any ministry against his consent. No human authority ought, in any case whatever, to control or interfere with the rights of conscience in matters of religion, and no preference shall ever be given by law to any religious society or mode of worship. But it shall be the duty of the Legislature to pass such laws as may be necessary to protect equally every religious denomination in the peaceable enjoyment of its own mode of public worship.

Sec. 7. No Appropriation for Sectarian Purposes. — No money shall be appropriated or drawn from the Treasury for the benefit of any sect, or religious society, theological or religious seminary, nor shall property belonging to the State be appropriated for any such purposes.

Sec. 8. Liberty of Speech and Press Guaranteed; Libel. Every person shall be at liberty to speak, write or publish his opinions, on any subject, being responsible for the abuse of that privilege; and no law shall ever be passed curtailing the liberty of speech or of the press. In prosecutions for the publication of papers, investigating the conduct of officers or men in public capacity, or when the matter published is proper for public information, the truth thereof may be given in evidence. And in all indictments for libels, the jury shall have the right to determine the law and the facts, under the direction of the court, as in other cases.

Sec. 9. No Unreasonable Seizures and Searches Allowed. — The people shall be secure in their persons, houses, papers and possessions from all unreasonable seizures or searches, and no warrant to search any place, or to seize any person or thing, shall issue with out describing them as near as may be, or without probable cause, supported by oath or affirmation.

Sec. 10. Rights of Accused Persons in Criminal Prosecutions. — In all criminal prosecutions the accused shall have a speedy public trial by an impartial jury. He shall have the right to demand the nature and cause of the accusation against him, and to have a copy thereof. He shall not be compelled to give evidence against himself and shall have the right of being heard by himself or counsel, or both; shall be confronted by the witnesses against him and shall have compulsory process for obtaining witnesses in his favor, except that when the witness resides out of the State and the offense charged is a violation of any of the antitrust laws of this State, the defendant and the State shall have the right to produce and have the evidence admitted by deposition, under such rules and laws as the Legislature may hereafter provide; and no person shall be held to answer for a criminal offense, unless on an indictment of a grand jury, except in cases in which the punishment is by fine or imprisonment, otherwise than in the penitentiary; in cases of impeachment and in cases arising in the army or navy, or in the militia, when in actual service in time of war or public danger.

[Note. — The foregoing is an amended section, the amendment consisting of the addition of that clause relating to depositions of witnesses resident outside of the State in antitrust suits. Submitted by the Thirty-fifth Legislature (1917) and adopted at election on Nov. 5, 1918.]

Sec. 11. Bail. — All prisoners shall be bailable by sufficient sureties, unless for capital offenses, when the proof is evident; but this provision shall not be so construed as to prevent bail after indictment found upon examination of the evidence, in such manner as may be prescribed by law.

Sec. 11-a. Multiple Convictions; Denial of Bail. — Any person (1) accused of a felony less than capital in this State, who has been theretofore twice convicted of a felony, the second conviction being subsequent to the first, both in point of time of commission of the offense and conviction therefor, (2) accused of a felony less than capital in this State, committed while on bail for a prior felony for which he has been indicted, or (3) accused of a felony less than capital in this State involving the use of a deadly weapon after being convicted of a prior felony, after a hearing, and upon evidence substantially showing the guilt of the accused of the offense in (1) or (3) above or of the offense committed while on bail in (2) above, may be denied bail pending trial, by a district judge in this State, if said order denying bail pending trial is issued within seven calendar days subsequent to the time of incarceration of the accused; provided, however, that if the accused is not accorded a trial upon the accusation under (1) or (3) above or the accusation and indictment used under (2) above within sixty (60) days from the time of his incarceration upon the accusation, the order denying bail shall be automatically set aside, unless a continuance is obtained upon the motion or request of the accused; provided, further, that the right of appeal to the Court of Criminal Appeals of this State is expressly accorded the accused for a review of any judgment or order made hereunder, and said appeal shall be given preference by the Court of Criminal Appeals.

[Note.—Sec. 11-a of Art. I is an added amendment permitting denial of bail to a person charged with a felony less than capital who has been theretofore twice convicted of a felony. Submitted by the Fifty-fourth Legislature (1955) and adopted in election Nov. 6, 1956. This section was amended to provide for further denial of bail under circumstances (2) and (3) above, and providing for 60-day limit to that person's incarceration without trial; and providing for that person's right of appeal. Submitted by the Sixty-fifth Legislature (1977) and adopted in election Nov. 8, 1977.]

Sec. 12. The Writ of Habeas Corpus. — The writ of habeas corpus is a writ of right, and shall never be suspended. The Legislature shall enact laws to render the remedy speedy and effectual.

Sec. 13. Excessive Bail and Fine and Unusual Punishment Prohibited; Courts Open. — Excessive bail shall not be required, nor excessive fines imposed, nor cruel or unusual punishment inflicted. All courts shall be open, and every person for an injury done him in his lands, goods, person or reputation, shall have due course of law.

Sec. 14. No Person Shall Be Put Twice in Jeopardy. — No person, for the same offense, shall be twice put in jeopardy of life or liberty, nor shall a person be again put upon trial for the same offense after a verdict of not guilty in a court of competent jurisdiction.

Sec. 15. Right of Trial by Jury. — The right of trial by jury shall remain inviolate. The Legislature shall pass such laws as may be needed to regulate the same, and to maintain its purity and efficiency. Provided, that the Legislature may provide for the temporary commitment, for observation and/or treatment, of mentally ill persons not charged with a criminal offense, for a period of time not to exceed ninety (90) days, by order of the County Court without the necessity of a trial by jury.

[Note. — The original Sec. 15 of Art. I was amended to add the last sentence. Submitted by the Forty-fourth Legislature (1935) and adopted in an election Aug. 24, 1935.]

Section 15-a. No person shall be committed as a person of unsound mind except on competent medical or psychiatric testimony. The Legislature may enact all laws necessary

Article I — (Cont'd.); Article II and III

to provide for the trial, adjudication of insanity and commitment of persons of unsound mind and to provide for a method of appeal from judgments rendered in such cases. Such laws may provide for a waiver of trial by jury. In cases where the person under inquiry has not been charged with the commission of a criminal offense, by the concurrence of the person under inquiry, or his next of kin, and an attorney ad litem appointed by a judge of either the County or Probate Court of the county where the trial is being held, and shall provide for a method of service of notice of such trial upon the person under inquiry and of his right to demand a trial by jury.

[Note. — Sec. 15-a of Art. I is an added amendment relating to requiring medical or psychiatric testimony for commitment of persons of unsound mind and authorizing Legislature to provide for trial and commitment of such persons and for waiver of trial by jury where the person under inquiry has not been charged with commission of a criminal offense. Submitted by the Fiftyfourth Legislature (1955) and adopted in election Nov. 6, 1956.]

Sec. 16. There Shall Be No Bill of Attainder or Ex-Post Facto Laws. — No bill of attainder or ex post facto law, retroactive law, or any other law impairing the obligation of contracts shall be made.

Sec. 17. Privileges and Franchises: Eminent Domain. — No person's property shall be taken, damaged or destroyed for or applied to public use without adequate compensation being made, unless by the consent of such person; and when taken, except for the use of the State, such compensation shall be first made or secured by a deposit of money; and no irrevocable or uncontrollable grant of special privileges or immunities shall be made; but all privileges and franchises granted by the Legislature, or created under its authority, shall be subject to the control thereof.

Sec. 18. No Imprisonment for Debt. — No person shall ever be imprisoned for debt.

Sec. 19. Due Course of Law. — No citizen of this State shall be deprived of life, liberty, property, privileges or immunities, or in any manner disfranchised, except by the due course of the law of the land.

Sec. 20. No Outlawry or Deportations. — No citizen shall be outlawed, nor shall any person be transported out of the State for any offense committed within the same.

Sec. 21. Corruption of Blood, Forfeiture; Suicide. — No conviction shall work corruption of blood or forfeiture of estate, and the estates of those who destroy their own lives shall descend or vest as in the case of natural death.

Sec. 22. Treason. — Treason against the State shall consist only in levying war against it, or adhering to its enemies, giving them aid and comfort; and no person shall be convicted of treason except on the testimony of two witnesses to the same overt act or on confession in open court.

Sec. 23. Right to Bear Arms. — Every citizen shall have the right to keep and bear arms in the lawful defense of himself or the State; but the Legislature shall have power, by law, to regulate the wearing of arms, with a view to prevent crime.

Sec. 24. Military Subordinate to Civil Authority. — The military shall at all times be subordinate to the civil authority.

Sec. 25. Quartering Soldiers. — No soldier shall in time of peace be quartered in the house of any citizen without the consent of the owner, nor in time of war but in a manner prescribed by law.

Sec. 26. Perpetuities; Monopolies; Primogeniture; Entailments. — Perpetuities and monopolies are contrary to the genius of a free government, and shall never be allowed, nor shall the law of primogeniture or entailments ever be in force in this State.

Sec. 27. Right of Petition Guaranteed. — The citizens shall have the right, in a peaceable manner, to assemble together for their common good and apply to those invested with the powers of government for redress of grievances or other purposes, by petition, address or remonstrance.

Sec. 28. Power to Suspend Laws. — No power of suspending laws in this State shall be exercised except by the Legislature.

Sec. 29. "Bill of Rights" Inviolate. — To guard against transgressions of the high powers being delegated, we declare that everything in this "Bill of Rights" is excepted out of the general powers of government, and shall forever remain inviolate, and all laws contrary thereto, or to the following provisions, shall be void.

ARTICLE II. — THE POWERS OF GOVERNMENT

Sec. 1. Departments of Government to Be Kept Distinct. — The powers of the government of the State of Texas shall be divided into three distinct departments, each of which shall be confined to a separate body of magistracy, to wit: Those which are legislative to one, those which are executive to another, and those which are judicial to another; and no person, or collection of persons, being of one of these departments shall exercise any power properly attached to either of the others, except in the instances herein expressly permitted.

ARTICLE III. — LEGISLATIVE DEPARTMENT

Sec. 1. The Legislature: House and Senate. — The legislative power of this State shall be vested in a Senate and House of Representatives, which together shall be styled "The Legislature of the State of Texas."

Sec. 2. Number of Members Limited. — The Senate shall consist of thirty-one members, and shall never be increased above this number. The House of Representatives shall consist of ninety-three members until the first apportionment after the adoption of this Constitution, when or at any apportionment thereafter the number of Representatives may be increased by the Legislature, upon the ratio of not more than one Representative for every 15,000 inhabitants; provided, the number of Representatives shall never exceed 150.

Sec. 3. Election of Senators; New Apportionment. — The Senators shall be chosen by the qualified electors for the term of four years; but a new Senate shall be chosen after every apportionment, and the Senators elected after each apportionment shall be divided by lot into two classes. The seats of the Senators of the first class shall be vacated at the expiration of the first two years, and those of the second class at the expiration of four years, so that one half of the Senators shall be chosen biennially thereafter. Senators shall take office following their election, on the day set by law for the convening of the regular session of the Legislature, and shall serve thereafter for the full term of years to which elected and until their successors shall have been elected and qualified.

[Note. — The foregoing Sec. 3 of Art. III was amended to establish the date on which newly elected members of the Senate shall qualify and take office. Submitted by the Fifty-ninth Legislature (1965) and adopted in election Nov. 8, 1966.]

Sec. 4. Election of Representatives; Term of Office. — The members of the House of Representatives shall be chosen by the qualified electors for the term of two years. Representatives shall take office following their election, on the day set by law for the convening of the regular session of the Legislature, and shall serve thereafter for the full term of years to which elected and until their successors shall have been elected and qualified.

[Note.—The foregoing Sec. 4 of Art. III was amended to provide for the date on which newly elected members of the House of Representatives shall qualify and take office. Submitted by the Fifty-ninth Legislature (1965) and adopted in an election Nov. 8, 1966.]

Sec. 5. Time of Meeting; Method of Procedure. — The Legislature shall meet every two years at such time as may be provided by law and at other times when convened by the Governor. When convened in regular session, the first thirty days thereof shall be devoted to the introduction of bills and resolutions, acting upon emergency appropriations, passing upon the confirmation of the recess appointees of the Governor and such emergency matters as may be submitted by the Governor in special messages to the Legislature; provided, that during the succeeding thirty days of the regular session of the Legislature the various committees of each house shall hold hearings to consider all bills and resolutions and other matters then pending; and such emergency matters as may be submitted by the Governor; provided, further that during the following sixty days the Legislature shall act upon such bills and resolutions as may be then pending and upon such emergency matters as may be submitted by the Governor in special messages to the Legislature; provided, however, either house may otherwise determine its order of business by an affirmative vote of four fifths of its membership.

[Note. — Sec. 5 of Art. III has been amended once, to provide for a 120-day session. It was submitted together with the amendment of Sec. 24 of Art. III. Submitted by the Forty-first Legislature (1929); ratified Nov. 4, 1930.]

Sec. 6. Qualifications of Senators. — No person shall be a Senator unless he be a citizen of the United States, and at the time of his election, a qualified elector of this State, and shall have been a resident of this State five years next preceding his election and the last year thereof a resident of the district for which he shall be chosen, and shall have attained the age of twenty-six years.

Sec. 7. Qualifications of Representatives. — No person shall be a Representative unless he be a citizen of the United States, and, at the time of his election, a qualified elector of this State, and shall have been a resident of this State two years preceding his election, the last year thereof a resident of the district for which he shall be chosen, and shall have attained the age of twenty-one years.

Sec. 8. Each House to Judge Qualifications of Its Own Members. — Each house shall be the judge of the qualifications and election of its own members; but contested elections shall be determined in such manner as shall be provided by law.

Sec. 9. President Pro Tem of the Senate; Speaker of the

Article III — (Cont'd.)

House; Officers. — (a) The Senate shall, at the beginning and close of each session, and at such other times as may be necessary, elect one of its members President pro tempore, who shall perform the duties of the Lieutenant Governor in any case of absence or disability of that officer. If the said office of Lieutenant Governor becomes vacant, the President pro tempore of the Senate shall convene the Committee of the Whole Senate within 30 days after the vacancy occurs. The Committee of the Whole shall elect one of its members to perform the duties of the Lieutenant Governor in addition to his duties as Senator until the next general election. If the Senator so elected ceases to be a Senator before the election of a new Lieutenant Governor, another Senator shall be elected in the same manner to perform the duties of the Lieutenant Governor until the next general election. Until the Committee of the Whole elects one of its members for this purpose, the President pro tempore shall perform the duties of the Lieutenant Governor as provided by this subsection.

(b) The House of Representatives shall, when it first assembles, organize temporarily, and thereupon proceed to the election of a Speaker from its own members.

(c) Each House shall choose its other officers.

[Note. — Sec. 9 of Art. III was amended to provide for method of filling a vacancy in the office of Lieutenant Governor. Submitted by the Sixty-eighth Legislature (1983) and approved in election Nov. 6, 1984.]

Sec. 10. Quorum. — Two thirds of each house shall constitute a quorum to do business, but a smaller number may adjourn from day to day and compel the attendance of absent members, in such manner and under such penalties as each house may provide.

Sec. 11. Rules: Power to Punish and Expel. — Each house may determine the rules of its own proceedings, punish members for disorderly conduct, and, with the consent of two thirds, expel a member, but not a second time for the same offense.

Sec. 12. Journal: Yeas and Nays. — Each house shall keep a journal of its proceedings, and publish the same; and the yeas and nays of the members of either house on any question shall, at the desire of any three members present, be entered on the journals.

Sec. 13. Vacancies, How Filled. — When vacancies occur in either house, the Governor, or the person exercising the power of the Governor, shall issue writs of election to fill such vacancies; and should the Governor fail to issue a writ of election to fill any such vacancy within twenty days after it occurs, the returning officer of the district in which such vacancy may have happened shall be authorized to order an election for that purpose.

Sec. 14. Members of Legislature Privileged From Arrest. — Senators and Representatives shall, except in cases of treason, felony or breach of the peace, be privileged from arrest during the session of the Legislature, and in going to or returning from the same, allowing one day for every twenty miles such member may reside from the place at which the Legislature is convened.

Sec. 15. Each House May Punish Disorderly Conduct. — Each house may punish, by imprisonment, during its sessions, any person not a member for disrespectful or disorderly conduct in its presence, or for obstructing any of its proceedings; provided, such imprisonment shall not, at any one time, exceed forty-eight hours.

Sec. 16. Sessions to Be Open. — The sessions of each house shall be open, except the Senate when in executive session.

Sec. 17. Adjournments. — Neither house shall, without the consent of the other, adjourn for more than three days, nor to any other place than that where the Legislature may be sitting.

Sec. 18. Ineligibility of Members to Certain Offices; Not to Be Interested in Contracts. — No Senator or Representative shall, during the term for which he was elected, be eligible to (1) any civil office of profit under this State which shall have been created, or the emoluments of which may have been increased, during such term, or (2) any office or place, the appointment to which may be made, in whole or in part, by either branch of the Legislature; provided, however, the fact that the term of office of Senators and Representatives does not end precisely on the last day of December but extends a few days into January of the succeeding year shall be considered as de minimis, and the ineligibility herein created shall terminate on the last day in December of the last full calendar year of the term for which he was elected. No member of either House shall vote for any other member for any office whatever, which may be filled by a vote of the Legislature, except in such cases as are in this Constitution provided, nor shall any member of the Legislature be interested, either directly or indirectly, in any contract with the State, or any county thereof, authorized by any law passed during the term for which he was elected.

[Note.—Sec. 18 of Art. III was amended to fix the time during which members of Legislature shall be ineligible to hold other office. Submitted by the Sixtieth Legislature (1967) and adopted in election Nov. 5, 1968.]

Sec. 19. What Officers Ineligible to Membership in Legislature. — No judge of any court, Secretary of State, Attorney General, clerk of any court of record, or any person holding a lucrative office under the United States, or this State, or any foreign government, shall, during the term for which he is elected or appointed, be eligible to the Legislature.

Sec. 20. Receivers or Disbursers of Public Funds Not Eligible to Membership in the Legislature Until Discharge Received. — No person who at any time may have been a collector of taxes or who may have been otherwise entrusted with public money, shall be eligible to the Legislature, or to any office of profit or trust under the State Government, until he shall have obtained a discharge for the amount of such collections, or for all public moneys with which he may have been entrusted.

Sec. 21. Freedom in Debate. — No member shall be questioned in any other place for words spoken in debate in either house.

Sec. 22. Personal Interest in Measure or Bill. — A member who has a personal or private interest in any measure or bill, proposed or pending before the Legislature, shall disclose the fact to the house of which he is a member, and shall not vote thereon.

Sec. 23. Removal Vacates Office. — If any Senator or Representative remove his residence from the district or county for which he was elected, his office shall thereby become vacant, and the vacancy shall be filled as provided in Sec. 13 of this article.

Sec. 23-a. John Tarleton Contract Validated. — The Legislature is authorized to appropriate so much money as may be necessary, not to exceed seventy-five thousand ($75,000) dollars, to pay claims incurred by John Tarleton Agricultural College for the construction of a building on the campus of such college pursuant to deficiency authorization by the Governor of Texas on Aug. 31, 1937.

[Note. — Sec. 23-a. of Art. III is an added amendment to provide for payment of a contractor whose contract had been annulled. Submitted by the Forty-ninth Legislature (1945) and ratified in election Nov. 5, 1946.]

Sec. 24. Mileage and Per Diem. — Members of the Legislature shall receive from the Public Treasury a salary of Six Hundred Dollars ($600) per month. Each member shall also receive a per diem of Thirty Dollars ($30) for each day during each Regular and Special Session of the Legislature. No Regular Session shall be of longer duration than one hundred and forty (140) days.

In addition to the per diem the Members of each House shall be entitled to mileage at the same rate as prescribed by law for employees of the State of Texas. This amendment takes effect on April 22, 1975.

[Note. — Sec. 24 of Art. III has been amended four times, first raising the per diem and decreasing the mileage. It was submitted with the amendment of Sec. 5 of Art. III. Submitted by Forty-first Legislature (1929); ratified Nov. 4, 1930. Further amended to raise per diem to $25 for first 120 days only. Submitted by Fifty-third Legislature (1953) and adopted in election Nov. 2, 1954. Further amended to fix the salary at $4,800 per year and setting the per diem at $12 per day for first 120 days of regular session and 30 days of each special session. Submitted by Fifty-sixth Legislature (1959) and adopted in election Nov. 8, 1960. It was amended to set salaries of members of Legislature at $600 per month and set per diem of $30 per day during legislative sessions and a mileage allowance at the same rate provided by law for state employees. Submitted by Sixty-fourth Legislature (1975) and adopted in election April 22, 1975.]

Sec. 25. Senatorial Districts, How Apportioned. — The State shall be divided into senatorial districts of contiguous territory according to the number of qualified electors, as nearly as may be, and each district shall be entitled to elect one Senator; and no single county shall be entitled to more than one Senator.

Sec. 26. Representative Districts, How Apportioned. — The members of the House of Representatives shall be apportioned among the several counties, according to the number of population in each, as nearly as may be, on a ratio obtained by dividing the population of the State, by the number of members of which the House is composed; provided that whenever a single county has sufficient population to be entitled to a Representative, such county shall be formed into a separate representative district, and when two or more counties are required to make up the ratio of representation, such counties shall be contiguous to each other; and when any one county has more than sufficient population to be entitled to one or more Representatives, such Representative or Representatives shall be apportioned to such county, and for any surplus of population it may be joined in a representative district with any other contiguous county or counties.

Article III — (Cont'd.)

Sec. 26-a. Redistricting According to Population. — Provided, however, that no county shall be entitled to or have under any apportionment more than seven (7) Representatives unless the population of such county shall exceed seven hundred thousand (700,000) people as ascertained by the most recent United States census, in which event such county shall be entitled to one additional Representative for each one hundred thousand (100,000) population in excess of seven hundred thousand (700,000) population as shown by the latest United States census; nor shall any district be created which would permit any county to have more than seven (7) Representatives except under the conditions set forth above.

[Note.—Sec. 26-a of Art. III is an added amendment, to place limitation on representation of counties with large population. Adopted in election Nov. 3, 1936.]

Sec. 27. Election of Members. — Elections for Senators and Representatives shall be general throughout the State, and shall be regulated by law.

Sec. 28. Reapportionment After Each Census. — The Legislature shall, at its first regular session after the publication of each United States decennial census, apportion the State into senatorial and representative districts, agreeable to the provisions of Sections 25, 26 and 26-a of this Article. In the event the Legislature shall at any such first regular session following the publication of a United States decennial census, fail to make such apportionment, same shall be done by the Legislative Redistricting Board of Texas, which is hereby created, and shall be composed of five (5) members, as follows: The Lieutenant Governor, the Speaker of the House of Representatives, the Attorney General, the Comptroller of Public Accounts and the Commissioner of the General Land Office, a majority of whom shall constitute a quorum. Said board shall assemble in the City of Austin within ninety (90) days after the final adjournment of such regular session. The board shall, within sixty (60) days after assembling, apportion the State into senatorial and representative districts, or into senatorial or representative districts, as the failure of action of such Legislature may make necessary. Such apportionment shall be in writing and signed by three (3) or more of the members of the board duly acknowledged as the act and deed of such board, and when so executed and filed with the Secretary of State, shall have force and effect of law. Such apportionment shall become effective at the next succeeding statewide general election. The Supreme Court of Texas shall have jurisdiction to compel such commission to perform its duties in accordance with the provisions of this section by writ of mandamus or other extraordinary writs conformable to the usages of law. The Legislature shall provide necessary funds for clerical and technical aid and for other expenses incidental to the work of the board, and the Lieutenant Governor and the Speaker of the House of Representatives shall be entitled to receive per diem and travel expense during the board's session in the same manner and amount as they would receive while attending a special session of the Legislature. This amendment shall become effective Jan. 1, 1951.

[Note. — The foregoing Section 28 of Art. III was amended to provide for the Legislative Redistricting Board of Texas, this action being taken because of failure of past Legislatures to obey the mandate in the original Sec. 28 to redistrict the state after each decennial census. Submitted by the Fiftieth Legislature (1947) and adopted Nov. 2, 1948.]

Proceedings

Sec. 29. Enacting Clause. — The enacting clause of all laws shall be: "Be it enacted by the Legislature of the State of Texas."

Sec. 30. Laws to Be Passed by Bill: Amendments. — No law shall be passed, except by bill, and no bill shall be so amended in its passage through either house as to change its original purpose.

Sec. 31. Bills May Originate in Either House and May Be Amended or Rejected by the Other House. — Bills may originate in either house, and when passed by such house may be amended, altered or rejected by the other.

Sec. 32. Bills to Be Read on Three Several Days: Suspension of Rule. — No bill shall have the force of a law until it has been read on three several days in each house, and free discussion allowed thereon; but in cases of imperative public necessity (which necessity shall be stated in a preamble or in the body of the bill) four fifths of the house in which the bill may be pending may suspend this rule, the yeas and nays being taken on the question of suspension and entered upon the journals.

Sec. 33. Bills for Raising Revenue. — All bills for raising revenue shall originate in the House of Representatives, but the Senate may amend or reject them as other bills.

Sec. 34. Bill or Resolution Defeated, Not to Be Considered Again. — After a bill has been considered and defeated by either house of the Legislature, no bill containing the same substance shall be passed into a law during the same session. After a resolution has been acted on and defeated, no resolution containing the same substance shall be considered at the same session.

Sec. 35. Bills to Contain but One Subject, Which Must Be Expressed in Title. — No bill (except general appropriation bills, which may embrace the various subjects and accounts for and on account of which moneys are appropriated) shall contain more than one subject, which shall be expressed in its title. But if any subject shall be embraced in an act which shall not be expressed in the title such act shall be void only as to so much thereof as shall not be so expressed.

Sec. 36. Reviving or Amending Laws. — No law shall be revived or amended by reference to its title; but in such case the act revived, or the section or sections amended, shall be re-enacted and published at length.

Sec. 37. Reference to Committees. — No bill shall be considered unless it has been first referred to a committee and reported thereon, and no bill shall be passed which has not been presented and referred to and reported from a committee at least three days before the final adjournment of the Legislature.

Sec. 38. Signing Bills. — The presiding officer of each house shall, in the presence of the house over which he presides, sign all bills and joint resolutions passed by the Legislature, after their titles have been publicly read before signing, and the fact of signing shall be entered on the journals.

Sec. 39. When Laws Take Effect. — No law passed by the Legislature, except the general appropriation act, shall take effect or go into force until ninety days after the adjournment of the session at which it was enacted, unless in case of an emergency, which emergency must be expressed in a preamble or in the body of the act, the Legislature shall, by a vote of two thirds of all the members elected to each house, otherwise direct; said vote to be taken by yeas and nays, and entered upon the journals.

Sec. 40. Business and Duration of Special Sessions. — When the Legislature shall be convened in special session, there shall be no legislation upon subjects other than those designated in the proclamation of the Governor calling such session, or presented to them by the Governor; and no such session shall be of longer duration than thirty days.

Sec. 41. Elections: Votes, How Taken. — In all elections by the Senate and House of Representatives, jointly or separately, the vote shall be given viva voce, except in the election of their officers.

[Note. — Sec. 42 of Art. III, relating to passage of laws, was deleted by constitutional amendment in election Aug. 5, 1969.]

Requirements and Limitations

Sec. 43. Revision and Publication of Laws. — The first session of the Legislature under this Constitution shall provide for revising, digesting and publishing the laws, civil and criminal; and a like revision, digest and publication may be made every ten years thereafter; provided, that in the adoption of and giving effect to any such digest or revision the Legislature shall not be limited by Secs. 35 and 36 of this article.

Sec. 44. Compensation of Officers: Payment of Claims. — The Legislature shall provide by law for the compensation of all officers, servants, agents and public contractors, not provided for in this Constitution, but shall not grant extra compensation to any officer, agent, servant or public contractors, after such public service shall have been performed or contract entered into for the performance of the same; nor grant, by appropriation or otherwise, any amount of money out of the Treasury of the State, to any individual, on a claim, real or pretended, when the same shall not have been provided for by pre-existing law; nor employ anyone in the name of the State, unless authorized by pre-existing law.

Sec. 45. Change of Venue. — The power to change the venue in civil and criminal cases shall be vested in the courts, to be exercised in such manner as shall be provided by law; and the Legislature shall pass laws for that purpose.

[Note. — Sec. 46 of Art. III, relating to vagrant laws, was deleted by constitutional amendment in election Aug. 5, 1969.]

Sec. 47. Lotteries Shall Be Prohibited. — (a) The Legislature shall pass laws prohibiting lotteries and gift enterprises in this State.

(b) The Legislature by law may authorize and regulate bingo games conducted by a church, synagogue, religious society, volunteer fire department, nonprofit veterans organization, fraternal organization, or nonprofit organization supporting medical research or treatment programs. A law enacted under this subsection must permit the qualified voters of any county, justice precinct, or incorporated city or town to determine from time to time by a majority vote of the qualified voters voting on the question at an election whether bingo games may be held in the county, justice precinct, or city or town. The law must also require that:

Article III — (Cont'd.)

(1) all proceeds from the games are spent in Texas for charitable purposes of the organizations;

(2) the games are limited to one location as defined by law on property owned or leased by the church, synagogue, religious society, volunteer fire department, nonprofit veterans organization, fraternal organization, or nonprofit organization supporting medical research or treatment programs; and

(3) the games are conducted, promoted, and administered by members of the church, synagogue, religious society, volunteer fire department, nonprofit veterans organization, fraternal organization, or nonprofit organization supporting medical research or treatment programs.

(c) The law enacted by the Legislature authorizing bingo games must include:

(1) a requirement that the entities conducting the games report quarterly to the Comptroller of Public Accounts about the amount of proceeds that the entities collect from the games and the purposes for which the proceeds are spent; and

(2) criminal or civil penalties to enforce the reporting requirement.

[Note. — The foregoing Sec. 47 of Art. III was amended to authorize bingo games on local option basis if games are conducted by religious society or other charitable society and proceeds are to be spent in Texas for charitable purposes of the organization. Submitted by the Sixty-sixth Legislature (1979) and adopted in election Nov. 4, 1980.]

[Note. — Sec. 48 of Art. III, relating to power to levy taxes, was deleted by constitutional amendment in election Aug. 5, 1969.]

[Note. — Sec. 48a and Sec. 48b, relating to the Teachers' Retirement Fund and Teachers' Retirement System, respectively, were deleted by constitutional amendment in an election April 22, 1975. See also note under Art. III, Sec. 51e and Sec. 51f; Art. XVI, Sec. 62 and Sec. 63. See also Art. XVI, Sec. 67, which replaces the foregoing Sections.]

Sec. 48-d. Rural Fire Prevention Districts. — The Legislature shall have the power to provide for the establishment and creation of rural fire-prevention districts and to authorize a tax on the ad valorem property situated in said districts not to exceed three (3c) cents on the one hundred ($100) dollars valuation for the support thereof; provided that no tax shall be levied in support of said districts until approved by vote of the people residing therein.

[Note—The foregoing Sec. 48-d of Art. III was submitted as an amendment by the Fifty-first Legislature (1949) and ratified in an election Nov. 8, 1949. The absence of Section 48-c is explained by the fact that such section was proposed as an amendment but failed to carry.]

Sec. 49. Purpose for Which Debts May Be Created. — No debt shall be created by or on behalf of the State, except to supply casual deficiencies of revenue, repel invasion, suppress insurrection, defend the State in war or pay existing debt; and the debt created to supply deficiencies in the revenue shall never exceed in the aggregate at any one time $200,000.

Sec. 49-a. Limiting Appropriations to Anticipated Revenue; Comptroller's Certification Required; Issuance of Certain General Revenue Bonds Authorized. — It shall be the duty of the Comptroller of Public Accounts in advance of each regular session of the Legislature to prepare and submit to the Governor and to the Legislature upon its convening a statement under oath showing fully the financial condition of the State Treasury at the close of the last fiscal period and an estimate of the probable receipts and disbursements for the then current fiscal year. There shall also be contained in said statement an itemized estimate of the anticipated revenue based on the laws then in effect that will be received by and for the State from all sources showing the fund accounts to be credited during the succeeding biennium and said statement shall contain such other information as may be required by law. Supplemental statements shall be submitted at any special session of the Legislature and at such other times as may be necessary to show probable changes.

From and after Jan. 1, 1945, save in the case of emergency and imperative public necessity and with a four-fifths vote of the total membership of each house, no appropriation in excess of the cash and anticipated revenue of the funds from which such appropriation is to be made shall be valid. From and after Jan. 1, 1945, no bill containing an appropriation shall be considered as passed or be sent to the Governor for consideration until and less the Comptroller of Public Accounts endorses his certificate thereon showing that the amount appropriated is within the amount estimated to be available in the affected funds. When the Comptroller finds an appropriation bill exceeds the estimated revenue he shall endorse such finding thereon and return to the house in which same originated. Such infor-

mation shall be immediately made known to both the House of Representatives and the Senate, and the necessary steps shall be taken to bring such appropriation to within the revenue, either by providing additional revenue or reducing the appropriation.

For the purpose of financing the outstanding obligations of the general revenue fund of the State and placing its current accounts on a cash basis the Legislature of the State of Texas is hereby authorized to provide for the issuance, sale and retirement of serial bonds equal in principal to the total outstanding, valid and approved obligations owing by said fund on Sept. 1, 1943, provided such bonds shall not draw interest in excess of 2 per cent per annum and shall mature within twenty years from date.

[Note. — The foregoing Sec. 49-a of Art. III is an amendment added to provide for Comptroller's estimates of receipts and disbursements and limit legislative appropriations, as stated. Adopted in an election Nov. 3, 1942.]

Sec. 49-b. Veterans' Land Board: Bonds Authorized for Creation of Veterans' Land Fund; Purchase of Land by State and Sales to Veterans. — By virtue of prior amendments to this Constitution, there has been created a governmental agency of the State of Texas performing governmental duties which has been designated the Veterans' Land Board. Said Board shall continue to function for the purposes specified in all of the prior Constitutional Amendments except as modified herein. Said Board shall be composed of the Commissioner of the General Land Office and two (2) citizens of the State of Texas, one (1) of whom shall be well versed in veterans' affairs and one (1) of whom shall be well versed in finances. One (1) such citizen member shall, with the advice and consent of the Senate, be appointed biennially by the Governor to serve for a term of four (4) years; but the members serving on said Board on the date of adoption hereof shall complete the terms to which they were appointed. In the event of the resignation or death of any such citizen member, the Governor shall appoint a replacement to serve for the unexpired portion of the term to which the deceased or resigning member had been appointed. The compensation for said citizen members shall be as is now or may hereafter be fixed by the Legislature; and each shall make bond in such amount as is now or may hereafter be prescribed by the Legislature.

The Commissioner of the General Land Office shall act as Chairman of said Board and shall be the administrator of the Veterans' Land Program under such terms and restrictions as are now or may hereafter be provided by law. In the absence or illness of said Commissioner, the Chief Clerk of the General Land Office shall be the Acting Chairman of said Board with the same duties and powers that said Commissioner would have if present.

The Veterans' Land Board may provide for, issue and sell not to exceed Nine Hundred and Fifty Million Dollars ($950,000,000) in bonds or obligations of the State of Texas for the purpose of creating a fund to be known as the Veterans' Land Fund, Seven Hundred Million Dollars ($700,000,000) of which have heretofore been authorized. Such bonds or obligations shall be sold for not less than par value and accrued interest; shall be issued in such forms, denominations, and upon such terms as are now or may hereafter be provided by law; shall be issued and sold at such times, at such places, and in such installments as may be determined by said Board; and shall bear a rate or rates of interest as may be fixed by said Board but the weighted average annual interest rate, as that phrase is commonly and ordinarily used and understood in the municipal-bond market, of all the bonds issued and sold in any installment of any bonds may not exceed the rate specified in Sec. 65 of this article. All bonds or obligations issued and sold hereunder shall, after execution by the Board, approval by the Attorney General of Texas, registration by the Comptroller of Public Accounts of the State of Texas, and delivery to the purchaser or purchasers, be incontestable and shall constitute general obligations of the State of Texas under the Constitution of Texas; and all bonds heretofore issued and sold by said Board are hereby in all respects validated and declared to be general obligations of the State of Texas. In order to prevent default in the payment of principal or interest on any such bonds, the Legislature shall appropriate a sufficient amount to pay the same.

In the sale of any such bonds or obligations, a preferential right of purchase shall be given to the administrators of the various Teacher Retirement Funds, the Permanent University Funds, and the Permanent School Funds.

Said Veterans' Land Fund shall consist of any lands heretofore or hereafter purchased by said Board, until the sale price therefor, together with any interest and penalties due, have been received by said Board (although nothing herein shall be construed to prevent said Board from accepting full payment for a portion of any tract), and of the moneys attributable to any bonds heretofore or hereafter issued and sold by said Board which moneys so attributable shall include but shall not be limited to the proceeds from the issuance and sale of such bonds; the moneys received from the sale or resale of any lands, or rights therein, pur-

Article III — (Cont'd.)

chased with such proceeds; the moneys received from the sale or resale of any lands, or rights therein, purchased with other moneys attributable to such bonds; the interest and penalties received from the sale or resale of such lands, or rights therein; the bonuses, income, rents, royalties, and any other pecuniary benefit received by said Board from any such lands; sums received by way of indemnity or forfeiture for the failure of any bidder for the purchase of any such bonds to comply with his bid and accept and pay for such bonds or for the failure of any bidder for the purchase of any lands comprising a part of said Fund to comply with his bid and accept and pay for any such lands; and interest received from investments of any such moneys. The principal and interest on the bonds heretofore and hereafter issued by said Board shall be paid out of the moneys of said Fund in comformance with the Constitutional provisions authorizing such bonds; but the moneys of said Fund which are not immediately committed to the payment of principal and interest on such bonds, the purchase of lands as herein provided, or the payment of expenses as herein provided may be invested in bonds or obligations of the United States until such funds are needed for such purposes.

All moneys comprising a part of said Fund and not expended for the purposes herein provided shall be a part of said Fund until there are sufficient moneys therein to retire fully all of the bonds heretofore or hereafter issued and sold by said Board, at which time all such moneys remaining in said Fund, except such portion thereof as may be necessary to retire all such bonds which portion shall be set aside and retained in said Fund for the purpose of retiring all such bonds, shall be deposited to the credit of the General Revenue Fund to be appropriated to such purposes as may be prescribed by law. All moneys becoming a part of said Fund thereafter shall likewise be deposited to the credit of the General Revenue Fund.

When a Division of said Fund (each Division consisting of the moneys attributable to the bonds issue and sold pursuant to a single Constitutional authorization, and the lands purchased therewith) contains sufficient moneys to retire all of the bonds secured by such Division, the moneys thereof, except such portion as may be needed to retire all of the bonds secured by such Division which portion shall be set aside and remain a part of such Division for the purpose of retiring all such bonds, may be used for the purpose of paying the principal and the interest thereon, together with the expenses herein authorized, or any other bonds heretofore or hereafter issued and sold by said Board. Such use shall be a matter for the discretion and direction of said Board; but there may be no such use of any such moneys contrary to the rights of any holder of any of the bonds issued and sold by said Board or violative of any contract to which said Board is a party.

The Veterans' Land Fund shall be used by said Board for the purpose of purchasing lands situated in the State of Texas owned by the United States or any governmental agency thereof, owned by the Texas Prison System or any other governmental agency of the State of Texas, or owned by any person, firm, or corporation. All lands thus purchased shall be acquired at the lowest price obtainable, to be paid for in cash, and shall be a part of such Fund. Such lands heretofore or hereafter purchased and comprising a part of said Fund are hereby declared to be held for a governmental purpose, although the individual purchasers thereof shall be subject to taxation to the same extent and in the same manner as are purchasers of lands dedicated to the Permanent Free Public School Fund.

The lands of the Veterans' Land Fund shall be sold by said Board in such quantities, on such terms, at such prices, at such rates of interest and under such rules and regulations as are now or may hereafter be provided by law to veterans who served not less than ninety (90) continuous days, unless sooner discharged by reason of a service-connected disability, on active duty in the Army, Navy, Air Force, Coast Guard or Marine Corps of the United States after September 16, 1940, and who, upon the date of filing his or her application to purchase any such land is a citizen of the United States, is a bona fide resident of the State of Texas, and has not been dishonorably discharged from any branch of the Armed Forces above-named and who at the time of his or her enlistment, induction, commissioning, or drafting was a bona fide resident of the State of Texas, or who has resided in Texas at least five (5) years prior to the date of filing his or her application, and provided that in the event of the death of an eligible Texas veteran after the veteran has filed with the Board an application and contract of sale to purchase through the Board the tract selected by him or her and before the purchase has been completed, then the surviving spouse may complete the transaction. The unmarried surviving spouses of veterans who died in the line of duty may also apply to purchase a tract through the Board provided the deceased veterans meet the requirements set out in this Article with the exception that the deceased veterans need not have served ninety (90) continuous days and provided further that the deceased veterans were bona fide residents of the State of Texas at the time of enlistment, induction, commissioning, or drafting. The foregoing notwithstanding, any lands in the Veterans' Land Fund which have been first offered for sale to veterans and which have not been sold may be sold or resold to such purchasers, in such quantities, and on such terms, and at such prices and rates of interest, and under such rules and regulations as are now or may hereafter be provided by law.

Said Veterans' Land Fund, to the extent of the moneys attributable to any bonds hereafter issued and sold by said Board may be used by said Board, as is now or may hereafter be provided by law, for the purpose of paying the expenses of surveying, monumenting, road construction, legal fees, recordation fees, advertising and other like costs necessary or incidental to the purchase and sale, or resale, of any lands purchased with any of the moneys attributable to such additional bonds, such expenses to be added to the price of such lands when sold, or resold, by said Board; for the purpose of paying the expenses of issuing, selling, and delivering any such additional bonds; and for the purpose of meeting the expenses of paying the interest or principal due or to become due on any such additional bonds.

All of the moneys attributable to any series of bonds hereafter issued and sold by said Board (a 'series of bonds' being all of the bonds issued and sold in a single transaction as a single installment of bonds) may be used for the purchase of lands as herein provided, to be sold as herein provided, for a period ending eight (8) years after the date of sale of such series of bonds; provided, however, that so much of such moneys as may be necessary to pay interest on bonds hereafter issued and sold shall be set aside for that purpose in accordance with the resolution adopted by said Board authorizing the issuance and sale of such series of bonds. After such eight (8) year period, all of such moneys shall be set aside for the retirement of any bonds hereafter issued and sold and to pay interest thereon, together with any expenses as provided herein, in accordance with the resolution or resolutions authorizing the issuance and sale of such additional bonds, until there are sufficient moneys to retire all of the bonds hereafter issued and sold, at which time all such moneys then remaining a part of said Veterans' Land Fund and thereafter becoming a part of said Fund shall be governed as elsewhere provided herein.

This amendment being intended only to establish a basic framework and not to be a comprehensive treatment of the Veterans' Land Program, there is hereby reposed in the Legislature full power to implement and effectuate the design and objects of this amendment, including the power to delegate such duties, responsibilities, functions, and authority to the Veterans' Land Board as it believes necessary.

Should the Legislature enact any enabling laws in anticipation of this amendment, no such law shall be void by reason of its anticipatory nature.

[Note. — The foregoing Sec. 49-b of Art. III has been amended nine times: First, for the purpose of aiding war veterans in land purchases. Submitted by Forty-ninth Legislature (1945), and ratified in a special election Nov. 7, 1946. (It was by error that the date was set as Nov. 7 instead of Nov. 5, which was the general election date.) Second, it was amended to increase the authorized bond issue from $25,000,000 to $100,000,000 and to make minor changes. Submitted by Fifty-second Legislature (1951), and ratified in an election Nov. 13, 1951. Third, it was amended to change membership of the Veterans' Land Board and to raise the total of bonds authorized to $200,000,000. Submitted by Fifty-fourth Legislature (1955) and adopted in election Nov. 6, 1956. Fourth, it was amended to fix the rate of interest not to exceed 3½ per cent per annum. Submitted by Fifty-sixth Legislature (1959) and adopted in election Nov. 8, 1960. Fifth, it was amended to provide for offering land in the Veterans' Land Fund to nonveteran purchasers after land has first been offered to veterans. Submitted by Fifty-seventh Legislature (1961) and adopted in election Nov. 6, 1962. Sixth, to extend Veterans' Land Program by authorizing sale of bonds to increase Veterans' Land Fund for purchasing land to be sold to Texas veterans who served between Sept. 16, 1940, and date of formal withdrawal of U.S. troops from Viet Nam; and providing for additional $200,000,000 in bonds for this program. Submitted by Sixtieth Legislature (1967) and adopted in election Nov. 11, 1967. Seventh, to provide for additional $100 million in bonds for the Veterans' Land Fund and to make all veterans eligible to participate who served in armed forces after Sept. 16, 1940. Submitted by Sixty-third Legislature (1973) and adopted in election Nov. 6, 1973. Eighth, to provide for additional $200 million in bonds for the Veterans' Land Fund and to extend the right to apply to purchase land to unmarried surviving spouses of veterans who meet requirements set out herein. Submitted by Sixty-fifth Legislature (1977) and adopted in election Nov. 8, 1977. Ninth, to raise to $950 million the amount of bonds authorized for the Veterans' Land Fund. Submitted by Sixty-seventh Legislature (1981) and adopted in election Nov. 3, 1981.]

Sec. 49-b-1. Bonds Authorized to Finance Veterans' Land

Article III — (Cont'd.)

Program and Veterans' Housing Assistance Program. — (a) In addition to the general obligation bonds authorized to be issued and to be sold by the Veterans' Land Board by Sec. 49-b of this article, the Veterans' Land Board may provide for, issue, and sell not to exceed $800 million in bonds of the State of Texas to provide financing to veterans of the state in recognition of their service to their state and country.

(b) For purposes of this section, "veteran" means a person who served not less than 90 continuous days, unless sooner discharged by reason of a service connected disability, on active duty in the Army, Navy, Air Force, Coast Guard, or Marine Corps of the United States after Sept. 16, 1940, and who, upon the date of filing his or her application for financial assistance under this section is a citizen of the United States, is a bona fide resident of the State of Texas, and was discharged from military service under honorable conditions from any branch of the above-named Armed Forces and who at the time of his or her enlistment, induction, commissioning, or drafting was a bona fide resident of the State of Texas or who has resided in Texas at least five years immediately before the date of filing his or her application. In the event of the death of an eligible Texas veteran after the veteran has filed an application, the veteran's surviving spouse may complete the transaction. The term veteran also includes the unmarried surviving spouse of a veteran who died in the line of duty, if the deceased veteran meets the requirements set out in this section with the exception that the deceased veteran need not have served 90 continuous days and if the deceased veteran was a bona fide resident of the State of Texas at the time of enlistment, induction, commissioning, or drafting.

(c) The bonds shall be sold for not less than par value and accrued interest; shall be issued in such forms and denominations, upon such terms, at such times and places, and in such installments as may be determined by the board; and, notwithstanding the rate of interest specified by any other provision of this Constitution, shall bear a rate or rates of interest fixed by the board. All bonds issued and sold pursuant to Subsections (a) through (f) of this section shall, after execution by the board, approval by the Attorney General of Texas, registration by the Comptroller of Public Accounts of the State of Texas, and delivery to the purchaser or purchasers, be incontestable and shall constitute general obligations of the state under the Constitution of Texas.

(d) Three hundred million dollars of the state bonds authorized by this section shall be used to augment the Veterans' Land Fund. The Veterans' Land Fund shall be used by the board for the purpose of purchasing lands situated in the State of Texas owned by the United States government or any agency thereof, the State of Texas or any subdivision or agency thereof, or any person, firm, or corporation. The lands shall be sold to veterans in such quantities, on such terms, at such prices, at such rates of interest, and under such rules and regulations as may be authorized by law. The expenses of the board in connection with the issuance of the bonds and the purchase and sale of the lands may be paid from money in the fund. The Veterans' Land Fund shall continue to consist of any lands purchased by the board until the sale price therefor, together with any interest and penalties due, have been received by the board (although nothing herein shall prevent the board from accepting full payment for a portion of any tract) and of the money attributable to any bonds issued and sold by the board for the Veterans' Land Fund, which money so attributable shall include but shall not be limited to the proceeds from the issuance and sale of such bonds; the money received from the sale or resale of any lands, or rights therein, purchased from such proceeds; the money received from the sale or resale of any lands, or rights therein, purchased with other money attributable to such bonds; the interest and penalties received from the sale or resale of such lands, or rights therein; the bonuses, income, rents, royalties, and any other pecuniary benefit received by the board from any such lands; sums received by way of indemnity or forfeiture for the failure of any bidder for the purchase of any such lands to comply with his bid and accept and pay for such lands or for the failure of any bidder for the purchase of any lands comprising a part of the fund to comply with his bid and accept and pay for any such lands; and interest received from investments of any such money. The principal of and interest on the general obligation bonds previously authorized by Sec. 49-b of this Constitution shall be paid out of the money of the fund in conformance with the constitutional provisions authorizing such bonds. The principal of and interest on the general obligation bonds authorized by this section for the benefit of the Veterans' Land Fund shall be paid out of the money of the fund, but the money of the fund which is not immediately committed to the payment of principal and interest on such bonds, the purchase of lands as herein provided, or the payment of expenses as herein provided may be invested in bonds or obligations of the United States until the money is needed for such purposes.

(e) The Veterans' Housing Assistance Fund is created,

and $500 million of the state bonds authorized by this section shall be used for the Veterans' Housing Assistance Fund. Money in the Veterans' Housing Assistance Fund shall be administered by the Veterans' Land Board and shall be used for the purpose of making home mortgage loans to veterans for housing within the State of Texas in such quantities, on such terms, at such rates of interest, and under such rules and regulations as may be authorized by law. The expenses of the board in connection with the issuance of the bonds and the making of the loans may be paid from money in the fund. The Veterans' Housing Assistance Fund shall consist of any interest of the board in all home mortgage loans made to veterans by the board pursuant to a Veterans' Housing Assistance Program which the Legislature may establish by appropriate legislation until, with respect to any such home mortgage loan, the principal amount, together with any interest and penalties due, have been received by the board; the money attributable to any bonds issued and sold by the board to provide money for the fund, which money so attributable shall include but shall not be limited to the proceeds from the issuance and sale of such bonds; income, rents, and any other pecuniary benefit received by the board as a result of making such loans; sums received by way of indemnity or forfeiture for the failure of any bidder for the purchase of any such bonds to comply with his bid and accept and pay for such bonds; and interest received from investments of any such money. The principal of and interest on the general obligation bonds authorized by this section for the benefit of the Veterans' Housing Assistance Fund shall be paid out of the money of the fund, but the money of the fund which is not immediately committed to the payment of principal and interest on such bonds, the making of home mortgage loans as herein provided, or the payment of expenses as herein provided may be invested in bonds or obligations of the United States until the money is needed for such purposes.

(f) To the extent there is not money in either the Veterans' Land Fund or the Veterans' Housing Assistance Fund, as the case may be, available for payment of principal of and interest on the general obligation bonds authorized by this section to provide money for either of the funds, there is hereby appropriated out of the first money coming into the treasury in each fiscal year, not otherwise appropriated by this Constitution, an amount which is sufficient to pay the principal of and interest on such general obligation bonds that mature or become due during that fiscal year.

(g) Receipt of all kinds of the funds determined by the board not to be required for the payment of principal of and interest on the general obligation bonds herein authorized, heretofore authorized, or hereafter authorized by this Constitution to be issued by the board to provide money for either of the funds may be used by the board, to the extent not inconsistent with the proceedings authorizing such bonds, to pay the principal of and interest on general obligation bonds issued to provide money for the other fund, or to pay the principal of and interest on revenue bonds of the board issued for the purposes of providing funds for the purchasing of lands and making the sale thereof to veterans or making home mortgage loans to veterans as provided by this section. The revenue bonds shall be special obligations and payable only from the receipt of the funds and shall not constitute indebtedness of the state or the Veterans' Land Board. The board is authorized to issue such revenue bonds from time to time which shall not exceed an aggregate principal amount that can be fully retired from the receipts of the funds and other revenues pledged to the retirement of the revenue bonds. The revenue bonds shall be issued in such forms and denominations, upon such terms, at such times and places, and in such installments as may be determined by the board; and, notwithstanding the rate of interest specified by any other provision of the Constitution, shall bear a rate or rates of interest fixed by the board.

[Note. — The foregoing Sec. 49-b-1 of Art. III, an amendment, was added to provide financial assistance to veterans and to authorize issuance of bonds to finance the Veterans' Land Program and the Veterans' Housing Assistance Program. Submitted by Sixty-eighth Legislature (1983) and adopted in election Nov. 8, 1983.]

Sec. 49-c. Texas Water Development Board, Fund; Purpose. — There is hereby created as an agency of the State of Texas the Water Development Board to exercise such powers as necessary under this provision together with such other duties and restrictions as may be prescribed by law. The qualifications, compensation and number of members of said Board shall be determined by law. They shall be appointed by the Governor with the advice and consent of the Senate in the manner and for such terms as may be prescribed by law.

The Texas Water Development Board shall have the authority to provide for, issue and sell general obligation bonds of the State of Texas in an amount not to exceed One Hundred Million Dollars ($100,000,000). The Legislature of Texas, upon two-thirds (⅔) vote of the elected Members of each House, may authorize the Board to issue additional bonds in an amount not exceeding One Hundred Million

Article III — (Cont'd.)

Dollars ($100,000,000). The bonds authorized herein or permitted to be authorized by the Legislature shall be called "Texas Water Development Bonds," shall be executed in such form, denominations and upon such terms as may be prescribed by law, provided, however, such that the bonds shall not bear more than four percent (4%) interest per annum; they may be issued in such installments as the Board finds feasible and practical in accomplishing the purpose set forth herein.

All moneys received from the sale of State bonds shall be deposited in a fund hereby created in the State Treasury to be known as the Texas Water Development Fund to be administered (without further appropriation) by the Texas Water Development Board in such manner as prescribed by law.

Such fund shall be used only for the purpose of aiding or making funds available upon such terms and conditions as the Legislature may prescribe, to the various political subdivisions or bodies politic and corporate of the State of Texas including river authorities, conservation and reclamation districts and districts created or organized or authorized to be created or organized under Article XVI, Section 59 or Article III, Section 52, of this Constitution, interstate compact commissions to which the State of Texas is a party and municipal corporations, in the conservation and development of the water resources of this State, including the control, storing and preservation of its storm and flood waters and the waters of its rivers and streams, for all useful and lawful purposes by the acquisition, improvement, extension, or construction of dams, reservoirs and other water storage projects, including any system necessary for the transportation of water from storage to points of treatment and or distribution, including facilities for transporting water therefrom to wholesale purchasers, or for any one or more of such purposes or methods.

Any or all financial assistance as provided herein shall be repaid with interest upon such terms, conditions and manner of repayment as may be provided by law.

While any of the bonds authorized by this provision or while any of the bonds that may be authorized by the Legislature under this provision, or any interest on any of such bonds, is outstanding and unpaid, there is hereby appropriated out of the first moneys coming into the Treasury in each fiscal year, not otherwise appropriated by this Constitution, an amount which is sufficient to pay the principal and interest on such bonds that mature or become due during such fiscal year, less the amount in the sinking fund at the close of the prior fiscal year.

The Legislature may provide for the investment of moneys available in the Texas Water Development Fund, and the interest and sinking funds established for the payment of bonds issued by the Texas Water Development Board. Income from such investment shall be used for the purposes prescribed by the Legislature. The Legislature may also make appropriations from the General Revenue Fund for paying administrative expenses of the Board.

From the moneys received by the Texas Water Development Board as repayment of principal for financial assistance or as interest thereon, there shall be deposited in the interest and sinking fund for the bonds authorized by this Section sufficient moneys to pay the interest and principal to become due during the ensuing year and sufficient to establish and maintain a reserve in said fund equal to the average annual principal and interest requirements on all outstanding bonds issued under this Section. If any year prior to December 31, 1982 moneys are received in excess of the foregoing requirements then such excess shall be deposited to the Texas Water Development Fund, and may be used for administrative expenses of the Board and for the same purposes and upon the same terms and conditions prescribed for the proceeds derived from the sale of such State bonds. No grant of financial assistance shall be made under the provisions of this Section after December 31, 1982, and all moneys thereafter received as repayment of principal for financial assistance or as interest thereon shall be deposited in the interest and sinking fund for the State bonds; except that such amount as may be required to meet the administrative expenses of the Board may be annually set aside; and provided, that after all State bonds have been fully paid with interest, or after there are on deposit in the interest and sinking fund sufficient moneys to pay all future maturities of principal and interest, additional moneys so received shall be deposited to the General Revenue Fund.

All bonds issued hereunder shall after approval by the Attorney General, registration by the Comptroller of Public Accounts of the State of Texas, and delivery to the purchasers, be incontestable and shall constitute general obligations of the State of Texas under the Constitution of Texas.

[Note. — The foregoing Sec. 49-c of Art. III, an amendment, was added, setting up the Texas Water Development Board and Fund and providing for supervision thereof. Submitted by the Fifty-fifth Legislature (1957) and adopted in election Nov. 5, 1957.]

Sec. 49-d. Development and Conservation of Public Waters.

— It is hereby declared to be the policy of the State of Texas to encourage the optimum development of the limited number of feasible sites available for the construction or enlargement of dams and reservoirs for the conservation of the public waters of the state, which waters are held in trust for the use and benefit of the public. The proceeds from the sale of the additional bonds authorized hereunder deposited in the Texas Water Development Fund and the proceeds of bonds previously authorized by Art. III, Sec. 49-c of this Constitution, may be used by the Texas Water Development Board, under such provisions as the Legislature may prescribe by general law, including the requirement of a permit for storage or beneficial use, for the additional purposes of acquiring and developing storage facilities, and any system or works necessary for the filtration, treatment and transportation of water from storage to points of treatment, filtration and/or distribution, including facilities for transporting water therefrom to wholesale purchasers, or for any one or more of such purposes or methods; provided however, the Texas Water Development Fund or any other state fund provided for water development, transmission, transfer or filtration shall not be used to finance any project which contemplates or results in the removal from the basin of origin of any surface water necessary to supply the reasonably foreseeable future water requirements for the next ensuing fifty-year period within the river basin of origin, except on a temporary, interim basis.

Under such provisions as the Legislature may prescribe by general law the Texas Water Development Fund may be used for the conservation and development of water for useful purposes by construction or reconstruction or enlargement of reservoirs constructed or to be constructed or enlarged within the State of Texas or on any stream constituting a boundary of the State of Texas, together with any system or works necessary for the filtration, treatment and/or transportation of water, by any one or more of the following governmental agencies; by the United States of America or any agency, department or instrumentality thereof; by the State of Texas or any agency, department or instrumentality thereof; by political subdivisions or bodies politic and corporate of the state; by interstate compact commissions to which the State of Texas is a party; and by municipal corporations. The Legislature shall provide terms and conditions under which the Texas Water Development Board may sell, transfer or lease, in whole or in part, any reservoir and associated system or works which the Texas Water Development Board has financed in whole or in part.

Under such provisions as the Legislature may prescribe by general law, the Texas Water Development Board may also execute long-term contracts with the United States or any of its agencies for the acquisition and development of storage facilities in reservoirs constructed or to be constructed by the Federal Government. Such contracts when executed shall constitute general obligations of the State of Texas in the same manner and with the same effect as state bonds issued under the authority of the preceding Sec. 49-c of this Constitution, and the provisions in said Sec. 49-c with respect to payment of principal and interest on state bonds issued shall likewise apply with respect to payment of principal and interest required to be paid by such contracts. If storage facilities are acquired for a term of years, such contracts shall contain provisions for renewal that will protect the state's investment.

The aggregate of the bonds authorized hereunder shall not exceed $200,000,000 and shall be in addition to the aggregate of the bonds previously authorized by said Sec. 49-c of Art. III of this Constitution. The Legislature upon two-thirds (2/3) vote of the elected members of each House, may authorize the board to issue all or any portion of such $200,000,000 in additional bonds herein authorized.

The Legislature shall provide terms and conditions for the Texas Water Development Board to sell, transfer or lease, in whole or in part, any acquired storage facilities or the right to use such storage facilities together with any associated system or works necessary for the filtration, treatment or transportation of water at a price not less than the direct cost of the board in acquiring same; and the Legislature may provide terms and conditions for the board to sell any unappropriated public waters of the state that might be stored in such facilities. As a prerequisite to the purchase of such storage or water, the applicant therefor shall have secured a valid permit from the Texas Water Commission or its successor authorizing the acquisition of such storage facilities or the water impounded therein. The money received from any sale, transfer or lease of storage facilities or associated system or works shall be used to pay principal and interest on state bonds issued or contractual obligations incurred by the Texas Water Development Board, provided that when moneys are sufficient to pay the full amount of indebtedness then outstanding and the full amount of interest to accrue thereon, any further sums received from the sale, transfer or lease of such storage facilities or associated system or works may be used for the acquisition of additional storage facilities or associated system or works or for providing financial assistance as author-

Article III — (Cont'd.)

ized by said Sec. 49-c. Money received from the sale of water, which shall include standby service, may be used for the operation and maintenance of acquired facilities, and for the payment of principal and interest on debt incurred.

Should the Legislature enact enabling laws in anticipation of the adoption of this amendment, such acts shall not be void by reason of their anticipatory character.

[Note. — The foregoing Sec. 49-d of Art. III, an amendment, was added to authorize the Texas Water Development Board to acquire and develop storage facilities in reservoirs and to dispose of such storage facilities and water upon such terms as Legislature shall prescribe. Submitted by the Fifty-seventh Legislature (1961) and adopted in election Nov. 6, 1962. It was further amended to provide for optimum development of water reservoirs and investment of the Texas Water Development Fund. Submitted by the Fifty-ninth Legislature (1965) and adopted in an election Nov. 8, 1966.]

Sec. 49-d-1. **Water Development Bonds.** — (a) The Texas Water Development Board shall upon direction of the Texas Water Quality Board, or any successor agency designated by the Legislature, issue additional Texas Water Development Bonds up to an additional aggregate principal amount of Two Hundred Million Dollars ($200,000,000) to provide grants, loans, or any combination of grants and loans for water quality enhancement purposes as established by the Legislature. The Texas Water Quality Board or any successor agency designated by the Legislature may make such grants and loans to political subdivisions or bodies politic and corporate of the State of Texas, including municipal corporations, river authorities, conservation and reclamation districts, and districts created or organized or authorized to be created or organized under Art. XVI, Sec. 59, or Art. III, Sec. 52, of this Constitution, State agencies, and interstate agencies and compact commissions to which the State of Texas is a party, and upon such terms and conditions as the Legislature may authorize by general law. The bonds shall be issued for such terms, in such denominations, form and installments, and upon such conditions as the Legislature may authorize.

(b) The proceeds from the sale of such bonds shall be deposited in the Texas Water Development Fund to be invested and administered as prescribed by law.

(c) The bonds authorized in this Sec. 49-d-1 and all bonds authorized by Sections 49-c and 49-d of Art. III shall bear interest at not more than 6 percent per annum and mature as the Texas Water Development Board shall prescribe, subject to the limitations as may be imposed by the Legislature.

(d) The Texas Water Development Fund shall be used for the purposes heretofore permitted by, and subject to the limitations in Sections 49-c, 49-d and 49-d-1; provided, however, that the financial assistance may be made pursuant to the provisions of Sections 49-c, 49-d and 49-d-1 subject only to the availability of funds and without regard to the provisions in Sec. 49-c that such financial assistance shall terminate after Dec. 31, 1982.

(e) Texas Water Development Bonds are secured by the general credit of the State and shall after approval by the Attorney General, registration by the Comptroller of Public Accounts of the State of Texas, and delivery to the purchasers, be incontestable and shall constitute general obligations of the State of Texas under the Constitution of Texas.

(f) Should the Legislature enact enabling laws in anticipation of the adoption of this amendment, such acts shall not be void by reason of their anticipatory character.

[Note. — The foregoing Sec. 49-d-1, an amendment, was added to provide for an additional $100,000,000 for grants and loans for water improvement; also to raise the interest rate on water bonds to 6 per cent. Submitted by the Sixty-second Legislature (1971) and adopted in an election May 18, 1971. It was amended to increase to $200,000,000 the amount available for water quality enhancement. Submitted by the Sixty-fourth Legislature (1975) and adopted in an election Nov. 2, 1976.]

Sec. 49-e. **Texas Park Development Bonds.** — The Parks and Wildlife Department, or its successor vested with the powers, duties, and authority which deals with the operation, maintenance, and improvement of State Parks, shall have the authority to provide for, issue and sell general obligation bonds of the State of Texas in an amount not to exceed Seventy-Five Million Dollars ($75,000,000). The bonds authorized herein shall be called "Texas Park Development Bond," shall be executed in such form, denominations, and upon such terms as may be prescribed by law, provided, however, that the bonds shall bear a rate or rates of interest as may be fixed by the Parks and Wildlife Department or its successor, but the weighted average annual interest rate, as that phrase is commonly and ordinarily used and understood in the municipal bond market, of all the bonds issued and sold in any installment of any bonds,

shall not exceed four and one-half percent (4½%) interest per annum; they may be issued in such installments as said Parks and Wildlife Department, or its said successor, finds feasible and practical in accomplishing the purpose set forth herein.

All moneys received from the sale of said bonds shall be deposited in a fund hereby created with the State Treasurer to be known as the Texas Park Development Fund to be administered (without further appropriation) by the said Parks and Wildlife Department, or its said successor, in such manner as prescribed by law.

Such fund shall be used by said Parks and Wildlife Department, or its said successor, under such provisions as the Legislature may prescribe by general law, for the purposes of acquiring lands from the United States, or any governmental agency thereof, from any governmental agency of the State of Texas, or from any person, firm, or corporation, for State Park Sites and for developing said sites as State Parks.

While any of the bonds authorized by this provision, or any interest on any such bonds, is outstanding and unpaid, there is hereby appropriated out of the first moneys coming into the Treasury in each fiscal year, not otherwise appropriated by this Constitution, an amount which is sufficient to pay the principal and interest on such bonds that mature or become due during such fiscal year, less the amount in the interest and sinking fund at the close of the prior fiscal year, which includes any receipts derived during the prior fiscal year by said Parks and Wildlife Department, or its said successor, from admission charges to State Parks, as the Legislature may prescribe by general law.

The Legislature may provide for the investment of moneys available in the Texas Park Development Fund and the interest and sinking fund established for the payment of bonds issued by said Parks and Wildlife Department, or its said successor. Income from such investment shall be used for the purposes prescribed by the Legislature.

From the moneys received by said Parks and Wildlife Department, or its said successor, from the sale of the bonds issued hereunder, there shall be deposited in the interest and sinking fund for the bonds authorized by this section sufficient moneys to pay the interest to become due during the State fiscal year in which the bonds were issued. After all bonds have been fully paid with interest, or after there are on deposit in the interest and sinking fund sufficient moneys to pay all future maturities of principal and interest, additional moneys received from admission charges to State Parks shall be deposited to the State Parks Fund, or any successor fund which may be established by the Legislature as a depository for Park revenue earned by said Parks and Wildlife Department, or its said successor.

All bonds issued hereunder shall after approval by the Attorney General, registration by the Comptroller of Public Accounts of the State of Texas, and delivery to the purchasers, be incontestable and shall constitute general obligations of the State of Texas under the Constitution of Texas.

Should the Legislature enact enabling laws in anticipation of the adoption of this amendment, such acts shall not be void by reason of their anticipatory nature.

[Note. — The foregoing Sec. 49-e of Art. III, an amendment, was added to authorize issuance and sale of $75,000,000 in bonds to create the Texas Park Development Fund to acquire lands for State Park sites and to develop State Parks. Submitted by the Sixtieth Legislature (1967) and adopted in election Nov. 11, 1967.]

Sec. 50. **Credit of State Not to Be Pledged.** — The Legislature shall have no power to give or to lend or to authorize the giving or lending of the credit of the State in aid of, or to any person, association or corporation, whether municipal or other, or to pledge the credit of the State in any manner whatsoever, for the payment of the liabilities, present or prospective, of any individual, association of individuals, municipal or other corporation whatsoever.

Sec. 50-a. **State Medical Education Board; Fund; Purpose.** — The Legislature shall create a State Medical Education Board to be composed of not more than six (6) members whose qualifications, duties and terms of office shall be prescribed by law. The Legislature shall also establish a State Medical Education Fund and make adequate appropriations thereto to be used by the State Medical Education Board to provide grants, loans or scholarships to students desiring to study medicine and agreeing to practice in the rural areas of this State, upon such terms and conditions as shall be prescribed by law. The term "rural areas" as used in this section shall be defined by law.

[Note. — The foregoing Sec. 50-a of Art. III, an amendment, was added for the stated purpose of providing scholarships and to set up a State Medical Education Board. Submitted by the Fifty-second Legislature and adopted in an election Nov. 4, 1952.]

Sec. 50-b. **Student Loans.** — (a) The Legislature may provide that the Coordinating Board, Texas College and University System, or its successor or successors, shall

Article III — (Cont'd.)

have the authority to provide for, issue and sell general obligation bonds of the State of Texas in an amount not to exceed Eighty-five Million Dollars ($85,000,000). The bonds authorized herein, shall be called "Texas College Student Loan Bonds," shall be executed in such form, denominations and upon such terms as may be prescribed by law, provided, however, that the bonds shall not bear more than four per cent (4%) interest per annum; they may be issued in such installments as the Board finds feasible and practical in accomplishing the purposes of this section.

(b) All moneys received from the sale of such bonds shall be deposited in a fund hereby created in the State Treasury to be known as the Texas Opportunity Plan Fund to be administered by the Coordinating Board, Texas College and University System, or its successor or successors to make loans to students who have been admitted to attend any institution of higher education within the State of Texas, public or private, including Junior Colleges, which are recognized or accredited under terms and conditions prescribed by the Legislature, and to pay interest and principal on such bonds and provide a sinking fund therefor under such conditions as the Legislature may prescribe.

(c) While any of the bonds, or interest on said bonds authorized by this section is outstanding and unpaid, there is hereby appropriated out of the first moneys coming into the Treasury in each fiscal year, not otherwise appropriated by this Constitution, an amount sufficient to pay the principal and interest on such bonds that mature or become due during such fiscal year, less the amount in the sinking fund at the close of the prior fiscal year.

(d) The Legislature may provide for the investment of moneys available in the Texas Opportunity Plan Fund, and the interest and sinking funds established for the payment of bonds issued by the Coordinating Board, Texas College and University System, or its successor or successors. Income from such investment shall be used for the purposes prescribed by the Legislature.

(e) All bonds issued hereunder shall, after approval by the Attorney General, registration by the Comptroller of Public Accounts of the State of Texas, and delivery to the purchasers, be incontestable and shall constitute general obligations of the State of Texas under this Constitution.

(f) Should the Legislature enact enabling laws in anticipation of the adoption of this amendment, such acts shall not be void because of their anticipatory nature.

[Note. — The foregoing Sec. 50-b of Art. III, an amendment, was added to provide a system of student loans at institutions of higher education and to provide for creation of the Texas Opportunity Plan Fund. Submitted by the Fifty-ninth Legislature (1965) and adopted in an election Nov. 2, 1965.]

Sec. 50-b-1. (a) The Legislature may provide that the Coordinating Board, Texas College and University System, or its successor or successors, shall have authority to provide for, issue and sell general obligation bonds of the State of Texas in an amount not to exceed Two Hundred Million Dollars ($200,000,000) in addition to those heretofore authorized to be issued pursuant to Sec. 50-b of the Constitution. The bonds authorized herein shall be executed in such form, upon such terms and be in such denomination as may be prescribed by law and shall bear interest, and be issued in such installments as shall be prescribed by the Board provided that the maximum net effective interest rate to be borne by such bonds may be fixed by law.

(b) The moneys received from the sale of such bonds shall be deposited to the credit of the Texas Opportunity Plan Fund created by Sec. 50-b of the Constitution and shall otherwise be handled as provided in Sec. 50-b of the Constitution and the laws enacted pursuant thereto.

(c) The said bonds shall be general obligations of the state and shall be payable in the same manner and from the same sources as bonds heretofore authorized pursuant to Sec. 50-b.

(d) All bonds issued hereunder shall, after approval by the Attorney General, registration by the Comptroller of Public Accounts of the State of Texas, and delivery to the purchasers, be incontestable and shall constitute general obligations of the State of Texas under this Constitution.

(e) Should the Legislature enact enabling laws in anticipation of the adoption of this amendment such acts shall not be void because of their anticipatory nature.

[Note.—The foregoing Sec. 50-b-1 of Art. III, an amendment, was added to provide for additional loans to students at higher educational institutions under the Texas Opportunity Plan. Submitted by the Sixty-first Legislature (1969) and adopted in election Aug. 5, 1969.]

Sec. 50-c. Farm and Ranch Loan Security Fund. — (a) The Legislature may provide that the commissioner of agriculture shall have the authority to provide for, issue, and sell general obligation bonds of the State of Texas in an amount not to exceed $10 million. The bonds shall be called "Farm and Ranch Loan Security Bonds" and shall be executed in

such form, denominations, and on such terms as may be prescribed by law. The bonds shall bear interest rates fixed by the Legislature of the State of Texas.

(b) All money received from the sale of Farm and Ranch Loan Security Bonds shall be deposited in a fund hereby created with the State Treasurer to be known as the "Farm and Ranch Loan Security Fund." This fund shall be administered without further appropriation by the commissioner of agriculture in the manner prescribed by law.

(c) The Farm and Ranch Loan Security Fund shall be used by the commissioner of agriculture under provisions prescribed by the Legislature for the purpose of guaranteeing loans used for the purchase of farm and ranch real estate, for acquiring real estate mortgages or deeds of trust on lands purchased with guaranteed loans, and to advance to the borrower a percentage of the principal and interest due on those loans; provided that the commissioner shall require at least six percent interest be paid by the borrower on any advance of principal and interest. The Legislature may authorize the commissioner to sell at foreclosure any land acquired in this manner, and proceeds from that sale shall be deposited in the Farm and Ranch Loan Security Fund.

(d) The Legislature may provide for the investment of money available in the Farm and Ranch Loan Security Fund and the interest and sinking fund established for the payment of bonds issued by the commissioner of agriculture. Income from the investment shall be used for purposes prescribed by the Legislature.

(e) While any of the bonds authorized by this section or any interest on those bonds is outstanding and unpaid, there is hereby appropriated out of the first money coming into the treasury in each fiscal year not otherwise appropriated by this constitution an amount that is sufficient to pay the principal and interest on the bonds that mature or become due during the fiscal year less the amount in the interest and sinking fund at the close of the prior fiscal year.

[Note. — Sec. 50-c of Art. III, an amendment, was added to provide for the guarantee of loans for purchase of farm and ranch real estate for qualified borrowers by the sale of general obligation bonds of the State of Texas. Submitted by the Sixty-sixth Legislature (1979) and adopted in election Nov. 6, 1979.]

Sec. 51. Tax Levy Authorized for Confederate Soldiers and Sailors and Their Widows. — The Legislature shall have no power to make any grant or authorize the making of any grant of public moneys to any individual, association of individuals, municipal or other corporations whatsoever; provided, however, the Legislature may grant aid to indigent and disabled Confederate soldiers and sailors under such regulations and limitations as may be deemed by the Legislature as expedient, and to their widows in indigent circumstances under such regulations and limitations as may be deemed by the Legislature as expedient; provided that the provisions of this Section shall not be construed so as to prevent the grant of aid in cases of public calamity.

[Note.—The foregoing Sec. 51 of Art. III, in its present form, is the result of much amendment. The original Sec. 51, which prohibited all grants of public money to individuals, associations, etc., with the single exception of cases of "public calamity," has been amended nine times, as follows: (1) Establishing Confederate Home. Submitted by Twenty-third Legislature (1893) and ratified at election, Nov. 6, 1894, and proclaimed adopted Dec. 21, 1894. (2) Providing for pensions for Confederate veterans from appropriations not to exceed $250,000 annually. Submitted by Twenty-fifth Legislature (1897), adopted at election, Nov. 1, 1898, and proclaimed Dec. 22, 1898. (3) Raising amount that might be appropriated for Confederate pensions from $250,000 to $500,000 annually. Submitted by Twenty-eighth Legislature (1903), adopted in election, Nov. 8, 1904, and proclaimed Dec. 29, 1904. (4) Increasing authorized maximum appropriations for Confederate Home from $100,000 to $150,000 annually. Submitted by Thirty-first Legislature (1909), adopted in election, Nov. 8, 1910, and declared adopted Dec. 31, 1910. (5) Authorizing 5c ad valorem tax for Confederate pension fund—also omitting "public calamity" clause. Submitted by Thirty-second Legislature (1911), adopted Nov. 3, 1912, and proclaimed Dec. 30, 1912. (6) Authorizing 7c ad valorem tax for Confederate pension fund —also reinstating "public calamity" clause. Submitted by Thirty-eighth Legislature (1923) and adopted Nov. 4, 1924. (7) Eliminating specific restrictions upon grants of aid to Confederate soldiers, sailors and others with respect to date of removal to Texas, etc.; and conferring such authority upon the Legislature. Submitted by Fortieth Legislature (1927); ratified Nov. 6, 1928; proclaimed Feb. 6, 1929. (8) Cutting tax from 7c to 2c by addition of Sec. 17 of Art. VII, which was deleted by Constitutional amendment in 1982. (9) Further amended to provide for abolition of the two cents ad valorem tax for this purpose by Dec. 31, 1976, but making provision for aiding these veterans and their widows. (See also Art. VIII, Sec. 1-e.) Submitted by Sixtieth Legislature (1967) and adopted in election Nov. 5, 1968.]

Article III — (Cont'd.)

Sec. 51-a.—Assistance and Medical Care to Needy Aged, Needy Blind, Needy Children and Totally Disabled; Limitation on Expenditures for Same. — The Legislature shall have the power, by General Laws, to provide, subject to limitations herein contained, and such other limitations, restrictions and regulations as may by the Legislature be deemed expedient, for assistance grants to dependent children and the caretakers of such children, needy persons who are totally and permanently disabled because of a mental or physical handicap, needy aged persons and needy blind persons.

The Legislature may provide by General Law for medical care, rehabilitation and other similar services for needy persons. The Legislature may prescribe such other eligibility requirements for participation in these programs as it deems appropriate and may make appropriations out of state funds for such purposes. The maximum amount paid out of state funds for assistance grants to or on behalf of needy dependent children and their caretakers shall not exceed the amount of Eighty Million Dollars ($80,000,000) during any fiscal year, except that the limit shall be One Hundred Sixty Million Dollars ($160,000,000) for the two years of the 1982-1983 biennium. For the two years of each subsequent biennium, the maximum amount shall not exceed one percent of the state budget. The Legislature by general statute shall provide for the means for determining the state budget amounts, including state and other funds appropriated by the Legislature, to be used in establishing the biennial limit.

Provided further, that if the limitations and restrictions herein contained are found to be in conflict with the provisions of appropriate federal statutes, as they now are or as they may be amended to the extent that federal matching money is not available to the state for these purposes, then and in that event the Legislature is specifically authorized and empowered to prescribe such limitations and restrictions and enact such laws as may be necessary in order that such federal matching money will be available for assistance and or medical care for or on behalf of needy persons.

Nothing in this section shall be construed to amend, modify or repeal Sec. 31 of Art. XVI of this Constitution; provided further, however, that such medical care, services or assistance shall also include the employment of objective or subjective means, without the use of drugs, for the purpose of ascertaining and measuring the powers of vision of the human eye, and fitting lenses or prisms to correct or remedy any defect or abnormal condition of vision. Nothing herein shall be construed to permit optometrists to treat the eyes for any defect whatsoever in any manner nor to administer nor to prescribe any drug or physical treatment whatsoever, unless such optometrist is a regularly licensed physician or surgeon under the laws of this state.

[Note.—The foregoing Sec. 51-a of Art. III, an amendment, was first submitted by Forty-ninth Legislature and adopted in an election Aug. 25, 1945. It supplanted four earlier amendments, as follows: An original Sec. 51-a which provided for issuance of $20,000,000 in state bonds for relief (the so-called "Bread bonds") this amendment having been submitted by Forty-third Legislature and adopted Aug. 26, 1933; and also Secs. 51-b, 51-c and 51-d, which originally provided for old-age pensions and other welfare measures, adopted in elections Aug. 24, 1935 and Aug. 23, 1937. Because of this consolidation, the Constitution did skip from Sec. 51-a to Sec. 51-e until a Sec. 51-b was added in election Nov. 2, 1954, and a Subsection 51-a was added in election Nov. 5, 1957. It was further amended to raise the limit from $35,000,000 to $42,000,000. Submitted by Fifty-third Legislature (1953) and adopted in election Nov. 2, 1954. It was again amended to raise the limit from $42,000,000 to $47,000,000 and authorizing legislative appropriations to raise the needed money. Submitted by Fifty-fifth Legislature (1957) and adopted in election Nov. 5, 1957. It was further amended to raise the total amount of assistance to $52,000,000 per year. Submitted by Fifty-seventh Legislature (1961) and adopted in election Nov. 6, 1962. It was further amended to combine the former Sections 51-a and 51-b-1 of Art. III into one section to be known as Sec. 51-a; further raising the total amount of assistance to $60,000,000 per year and providing that Legislature shall prescribe the residence requirements. Submitted by Fifty-eighth Legislature (1963) and adopted in election Nov. 9, 1963. It was further amended in 1965 to create a new Sec. 51-a which consolidates the old Sec. 51-a and Subsections 51-a-1 and 51-a-2. The new Sec. 51-a enables the State of Texas to cooperate with the U.S. government in providing assistance and medical care for the needy aged, needy blind, needy children and needy totally disabled; expands age categories of those eligible for blind assistance and of needy children; and extends eligibility for the aged to citizens of the U.S. or noncitizens who have resided in the U.S. for 25 years. Submitted by Fifty-ninth Legislature (1965) and adopted in election Nov. 2, 1965. It was again amended to raise the limit on amount to be expended from $60,000,000 to $80,000,000 a year. It further pro-

vided that certain amounts be allocated out of the Omnibus Tax Clearance Fund for aid to permanently and totally disabled, families with dependent children and for old-age assistance. Submitted by Sixty-first Legislature (1969) and adopted in an election Aug. 5, 1969. The regular session of the Sixty-seventh Legislature (1981) submitted an amendment to raise the amount to be expended on Aid for Dependent Children in the 1982-1983 biennium to a maximum of $160 million and, for each subsequent biennium, the maximum amount would not exceed one percent of the state budget. This proposed amendment inadvertently cut out other needy recipients and SJR 10 of the Called Session of the Sixty-seventh Legislature (1982) amended the proposed amendment to include other needy recipients in this fund. Adopted in election Nov. 2, 1982.]

[Note. — Sec. 51-b of Art. III, creating the State Building Commission and the State Building Fund, was eliminated by a constitutional amendment in an election Nov. 7, 1978.]

Sec. 51-c. False Imprisonment. — The Legislature may grant aid and compensation to any person who has heretofore paid a fine or served a sentence in prison, or who may hereafter pay a fine or serve a sentence in prison, under the laws of this State for an offense for which he or she is not guilty, under such regulations and limitations as the Legislature may deem expedient.

[Note. — Sec. 51-c of Art. III was added to provide that Legislature may grant aid and compensation to persons who have been fined or imprisoned under laws of this state for offenses of which they are not guilty. Submitted by the Fifty-fourth Legislature (1955) and adopted in election Nov. 6, 1956.]

Sec. 51-d. Assistance to Survivors of Law Enforcement Officers Killed on Duty. — The Legislature shall have the power, by general law, to provide for the payment of assistance by the State of Texas to the surviving spouse, minor children, and surviving dependent parents, brothers, and sisters of officers, employees and agents, including members of organized volunteer fire departments and members of organized police reserve or auxiliary units with authority to make an arrest, of the state or of any city, county, district, or other political subdivision who, because of the hazardous nature of their duties, suffer death in the course of the performance of those official duties. Should the Legislature enact any enabling laws in anticipation of this amendment, no such law shall be void by reason of its anticipatory nature.

[Note. — The foregoing Sec. 51-d, an amendment, was added to provide assistance for survivors of law enforcement officers killed in performance of their duty. Submitted by the Fifty-ninth Legislature (1965), and adopted in election Nov. 8, 1966. It was further amended to provide for assistance to survivors of members of volunteer fire departments and organized police reserve, or auxiliary units with authority to make arrests, of political subdivisions of the state. Submitted by the Sixty-first Legislature (1969) and adopted in election Aug. 5, 1969. It was again amended to provide compensation for dependent parents, brothers and sisters of officers killed in performing their duties. Submitted by the Sixty-eighth Legislature (1983) and adopted in election Nov. 6, 1984.]

[Note. — Sec. 51e and Sec. 51f, relating to City and Town Pension System and Local Pension Plans, respectively, were deleted by a constitutional amendment election April 22, 1975. See also note under Art. III, Sec. 48a and Sec. 48b; Art. XVI, Sec. 62 and Sec. 63. See also Art. XVI, Sec. 67, which replaces the foregoing Sections.]

Sec. 51-g. Social Security Coverage for Municipal Employees. — The Legislature shall have the power to pass such laws as may be necessary to enable the State to enter into agreements with the Federal Government to obtain for proprietary employees of its political subdivisions coverage under the old-age and survivors insurance provisions of Title II of the Federal Social Security Act as amended. The Legislature shall have the power to make appropriations and authorize all obligations necessary to the establishment of such Social Security coverage program.

[Note. — The foregoing Sec. 51-g of Art.III, an amendment, was added for the stated purpose of extending Social Security coverage to municipal employees. Submitted by the Fifty-third Legislature (1953) and adopted in an election Nov. 2, 1954.]

Sec. 52. Counties, Cities, Etc., Not Authorized to Grant Money or Become Stockholders; Exceptions. — (a) Except as otherwise provided by this section, the Legislature shall have no power to authorize any county, city, town or other political corporation or subdivision of the State to lend its credit or to grant public money or thing of value in aid of, or to any individual, association or corporation whatsoever, or to become a stockholder in such corporation, association or company.

Article III — (Cont'd.)

(b) Under legislative provision any county, any political subdivision of a county, any number of adjoining counties or any political subdivision of the State or any defined district now or hereafter to be described and defined within the State of Texas, and which may or may not include towns, villages or municipal corporations, upon a vote of a two-thirds majority of the resident property taxpayers voting thereon who are qualified electors of such district or territory, to be affected thereby, in addition to all other debts, may issue bonds or otherwise lend its credit in any amount not to exceed one fourth of the assessed valuation of the real property of such district or territory, except that the total bonded indebtedness of any city or town shall never exceed the limits imposed by other provisions of this Constitution, and levy and collect taxes to pay the interest thereon and provide a sinking fund for the redemption thereof, as the Legislature may authorize, and in such manner as it may authorize the same, for the following purposes, to wit:

(1) The improvement of rivers, creeks and streams to prevent overflows and to permit of navigation thereof or irrigation thereof, or in aid of such purposes.

(2) The construction and maintenance of pools, lakes, reservoirs, dams, canals and waterways for the purposes of irrigation, drainage or navigation, or in aid thereof.

(3) The construction, maintenance and operation of macadamized, graveled or paved roads and turnpikes or in aid thereof.

(c) Notwithstanding the provisions of Subsection (b) of this section, bonds may be issued by any county in an amount not to exceed one fourth of the assessed valuation of the real property in the county, for the construction, maintenance, and operation of macadamized, graveled, or paved roads and turnpikes, or in aid thereof, upon a vote of a majority of the resident property taxpayers voting thereon who are qualified electors of the county, and without the necessity of further or amendatory legislation. The county may levy and collect taxes to pay the interest on the bonds as it becomes due and to provide a sinking fund for redemption of the bonds.

(d) Any defined district created under this section that is authorized to issue bonds or otherwise lend its credit for the purposes stated in Subdivisions (1) and (2) of Subsection (b) of this section may engage in fire-fighting activities and may issue bonds or otherwise lend its credit for fire-fighting purposes as provided by law and this constitution.

[Note. — The foregoing Sec. 52 of Art. III, is an amended section, the amendment authorizing formation of districts for issuance of bonds for leveeing, drainage, irrigation, highway construction and other public improvements. Submitted by the Twenty-eighth Legislature (1903), adopted in election, Nov. 8, 1904, and proclaimed Dec. 29, 1904. It was further amended to permit any county, on vote of a majority of qualified property taxpaying electors, to issue road bonds in an amount not exceeding one fourth of assessed valuation of the real property in the county. Submitted by the Sixty-first Legislature (1969) and adopted in election Nov. 3, 1970. It was further amended by adding Subsection (d) to authorize certain districts to engage in firefighting activities and to issue bonds or otherwise lend their credit for fire-fighting purposes. (See also Subsection (f) of Sec. 59, Art. XVI.) Submitted by the Sixty-fifth Legislature (1977) and adopted in election Nov. 7, 1978.]

Sec. 52-b. Legislature Prohibited to Lend Credit of State in Building or Maintaining Toll Roads and Turnpikes. — The Legislature shall have no power or authority to in any manner lend the credit of the State or grant any public money to, or assume any indebtedness, present or future, bonded or otherwise, of any individual, person, firm, partnership, association, corporation, public corporation, public agency, or political subdivision of the State, or anyone else, which is now or hereafter authorized to construct, maintain or operate toll roads and turnpikes within this State.

[Note. — The foregoing Sec. 52-b of Art. III, an amendment, was added for the stated purpose of prohibiting Legislature from lending credit of State in building or maintaining toll roads and turnpikes. Submitted by the Fifty-third Legislature (1953) and adopted in an election Nov. 2, 1954.]

Sec. 52-d. Harris County Road Districts. — Upon the vote of a majority of the resident qualified electors owning rendered taxable property therein so authorizing, a county or road district may collect an annual tax for a period not exceeding five (5) years to create a fund for constructing lasting and permanent roads and bridges or both. No contract involving the expenditure of any of such fund shall be valid unless, when it is made, money shall be on hand in such fund.

At such election, the Commissioners Court shall submit for adoption a road plan and designate the amount of special tax to be levied; the number of years said tax is to be levied; the location, description and character of the roads and bridges; and the estimated cost thereof. The funds raised by such taxes shall not be used for purposes other than those specified in the plan submitted to the voters. Elections may be held from time to time to extend or discontinue said plan or to increase or diminish said tax. The Legislature shall enact laws prescribing the procedure hereunder.

The provisions of this section shall apply only to Harris County and road districts therein.

[Note. — The foregoing Sec. 52-d of Art. III, an amendment, was added for the stated purpose of giving special local tax powers to Harris County. Adopted in an election Aug. 23, 1937.]

Note that Secs. 52-a and 52-c are omitted. Such sections never existed. The Fifty-third Legislature (1953) submitted an amendment to be numbered 52-b, and same was adopted in an election Nov. 2, 1954. Obviously, the designation, "Sec. 52-d," in Senate Joint Resolution No. 16 of the Forty-fifth Legislature resulted from confusion of a new section number with the sequence of paragraphs "a, b and c" under section 52 immediately above. Some published texts of the State Constitution give this as "Paragraph d," under Sec. 52, as it might properly have been designated, but SJR No. 16 of the Fifty-third Legislature definitely gave it as a separate "Sec. 52-d." Since Sec. 52-b was added in 1954, Secs. 52-a and 52-c are still missing.

Sec. 52-e. Dallas County Road Bonds. — Bonds to be issued by Dallas County under Sec. 52 of Art. III of this Constitution for the construction, maintenance and operation of macadamized, graveled or paved roads and turnpikes, or in aid thereof, may, without the necessity of further or amendatory legislation, be issued upon a vote of a majority of the resident property taxpayers voting thereon who are qualified electors of said county, and bonds heretofore or hereafter issued under Subsections (a) and (b) of said Sec. 52 shall not be included in determining the debt limit prescribed in said Section.

[Note. — The foregoing Sec. 52-e of Art. III, an amendment, was added to allow Dallas County to issue bonds for construction of roads upon majority vote of resident property taxpayers. Submitted by the Sixtieth Legislature (1967) and adopted in election Nov. 5, 1968.]

Note: As in the case of Sec. 52-d above, this section might more properly have been designated as paragraph "e" under Sec. 52, but the Sixtieth Legislature designated it as Sec. 52-e, which resulted in there being two Sections 52-e, as they also designated the section below, relating to payment of medical expenses for county and precinct officials, as Sec. 52-e.

Sec. 52-e. Payment of Medical Expenses for County and Precinct Officials. — Each county in the State of Texas is hereby authorized to pay all medical expenses, all doctor bills and all hospital bills for Sheriffs, Deputy Sheriffs, Constables, Deputy Constables and other county and precinct law enforcement officials who are injured in the course of their official duties; providing that while said Sheriff, Deputy Sheriff, Constable, Deputy Constable or other county or precinct law enforcement official is hospitalized or incapacitated that the county shall continue to pay his maximum salary; providing, however, that said payment of salary shall cease on the expiration of the term of office to which such official was elected or appointed. Provided, however, that no provision contained herein shall be construed to amend, modify, repeal or nullify Art. XVI, Sec. 31, of the Constitution of the State of Texas.

[Note. — The foregoing Sec. 52-e of Art. III, an amendment, was added to authorize counties to pay medical bills for county and precinct law enforcement officials who are injured in line of duty; and the county shall continue to pay maximum salary for duration of term to which they were elected or appointed. Submitted by the Sixtieth Legislature (1967) and adopted in election Nov. 11, 1967.]

Sec. 52-f. Private Roads in County. — A county with a population of 5,000 or less, according to the most recent federal census, may construct and maintain private roads if it imposes a reasonable charge for the work. The Legislature by general law may limit this authority. Revenue received from private road work may be used only for the construction, including right-of-way acquisition, or maintenance of public roads.

[Note. — Sec. 52-f of Art. III, an amendment, was added to authorize counties with population of 5,000 or less to perform private road work. Submitted by the Sixty-sixth Legislature (1979) and adopted in election Nov. 4, 1980.]

Sec. 53. Extra Compensation by Municipal Corporations. — The Legislature shall have no power to grant or to authorize any county or municipal authority to grant any extra compensation, fee or allowance to a public officer, agent,

Article III — (Cont'd.)

servant or contractor, after service has been rendered or a contract has been entered into and performed in whole or in part; nor pay, nor authorize the payment of any claim created against any county or municipality of the State under any agreement or contract made without authority of law.

Sec. 54. **Liens on Railroads.** — The Legislature shall have no power to release or alienate any lien held by the State upon any railroad, or in anywise change the tenor or meaning or pass any act explanatory thereof; but the same shall be enforced in accordance with the original terms upon which it was acquired.

Sec. 55. **Power of Legislature to Release Debt.** — The Legislature shall have no power to release or extinguish, or to authorize the releasing or extinguishing, in whole or in part, the indebtedness, liability or obligation of any corporation or individual, to this State or to any county or defined subdivision thereof, or other municipal corporation therein, except delinquent taxes which have been due for a period of at least ten years.

[Note—The foregoing Sec. 55 of Art. III is an amendment of an original section, the amendment having been adopted to include the clause "except delinquent taxes which have been due for a period of at least ten years." Submitted by the Forty-second Legislature (1931) and adopted in an election Nov. 8, 1932. Proclaimed Jan. 9, 1933.]

Sec. 56. **Special Laws; Limitations.** — The Legislature shall not, except as otherwise provided in this Constitution, pass any local or special law authorizing:

The creation, extension or impairing of liens;

Regulating the affairs of counties, cities, towns, wards or school districts;

Changing the names of persons or places;

Changing the venue in civil or criminal cases;

Authorizing the laying out, opening, altering or maintaining of roads, highways, streets or alleys;

Relating to ferries or bridges, or incorporating ferry or bridge companies, except for the erection of bridges crossing streams which form boundaries between this and any other State;

Vacating roads, town plats, streets or alleys;

Relating to cemeteries, graveyards or public grounds not of the states;

Authorizing the adoption or legitimation of children;

Locating or changing county seats;

Incorporating cities, towns or villages, or changing their charter;

For the opening and conducting of election or fixing or changing the places of voting;

Granting divorces;

Creating offices, or prescribing the powers and duties of officers in counties, cities, towns, election or school districts;

Changing the law of descent or succession;

Regulating the practice or jurisdiction of, or changing the rules of evidence in any judicial proceeding or inquiry before courts, justices of the peace, sheriffs, commissioners, arbitrators or other tribunals, or providing or changing methods for the collection of debts or the enforcing of judgments or prescribing the effect of judicial sales of real estate;

Regulating the fees or extending the powers and duties of aldermen, justices of the peace, magistrates or constables;

Regulating the management of public schools, the building or repairing of schoolhouses, and the raising of money for such purposes;

Fixing the rate of interest;

Affecting the estates of minors or persons under disability;

Remitting fines, penalties and forfeitures and refunding moneys legally paid into the Treasury;

Exempting property from taxation;

Regulating labor, trade, mining and manufacturing;

Declaring any named person of age;

Extending the time for the assessment or collection of taxes, or otherwise relieving any assessor or collector of taxes from the due performance of his official duties or his securities from liability;

Giving effect to informal or invalid wills or deeds;

Summoning or impaneling grand or petit juries;

For limitation of civil or criminal actions;

For incorporating railroads or other works of internal improvements;

And in all other cases where a general law can be made applicable no local or special law shall be enacted; provided, that nothing herein contained shall be construed to prohibit the Legislature from passing special laws for the preservation of the game and fish of this State in certain localities.

Sec. 57. **Notice of Local or Special Laws.** — No local or special law shall be passed unless notice of the intention to apply therefor shall have been published in the locality where the matter or thing to be affected may be situated, which notice shall state the substance of the contemplated law, and shall be published at least thirty days prior to the introduction into the Legislature of such bill and in the manner to be provided by law. The evidence of such notice having been published shall be exhibited in the Legislature before such act shall be passed.

Sec. 58. **Sessions to Be Held at Austin, Seat of Government.** — The Legislature shall hold its sessions at the City of Austin, which is hereby declared to be the seat of government.

Sec. 59. **Workmen's Compensation for State Employees.** — The Legislature shall have power to pass such laws as may be necessary to provide for workmen's compensation insurance for such State employees, as in its judgment is necessary or required; and to provide for the payment of all costs, charges and premiums on such policies of insurance; providing, the state shall never be required to purchase insurance for any employee.

[Note. — The foregoing Sec. 59 of Art. III, an amendment, was added for the stated purpose of providing for workmen's compensation for state employees. Adopted in an election, Nov. 3, 1936.]

Sec. 60. **Workmen's Compensation Insurance for County Employees.** — The Legislature shall have the power to pass such laws as may be necessary to enable all counties and other political subdivisions of this State to provide Workmen's Compensation insurance, including the right to provide its own insurance risk, for all employees of the county or political subdivision as in its judgment is necessary or required; and the Legislature shall provide suitable laws for the administration of such insurance in the counties or political subdivisions of this State and for the payment of the costs, charges and premiums on such policies of insurance and the benefits to be paid thereunder.

[Note. — The foregoing Sec. 60 of Art. III was first added for the stated purpose of providing workmen's compensation insurance for county employees. Adopted in election Nov. 2, 1948. Further amended to include all political subdivisions. Submitted by the Fifty-seventh Legislature (1961) and adopted in election Nov. 6, 1962.]

Sec. 61. The Legislature shall have the power to enact laws to enable cities, towns and villages of this state to provide Workmen's Compensation Insurance, including the right to provide their own insurance risk for all employees; and the Legislature shall provide suitable laws for the administration of such insurance in the said municipalities and for payment of the costs, charges, and premiums on policies of insurance and the benefits to be paid thereunder.

[Note. — The foregoing Sec. 61 of Art. III, an amendment, was added for the stated purpose of providing workmen's compensation insurance for municipal employees. Submitted by the Fifty-second Legislature and adopted in an election Nov. 4, 1952.]

Sec. 61-a. **Salary of Governor, Attorney General, Comptroller of Public Accounts, Treasurer, Commissioner of General Land Office and Secretary of State.** — The Legislature shall not fix the salary of the Governor, Attorney General, Comptroller of Public Accounts, the Treasurer, Commissioner of the General Land Office or Secretary of State at a sum less than that fixed for such officials in the Constitution on Jan. 1, 1953.

[Note. — The foregoing Sec. 61-a of Art. III, an amendment, was added to fix the salaries of the aforementioned officials. Submitted by the Fifty-third Legislature (1953) and adopted in an election Nov. 2, 1954; as submitted in SJR 5, this amendment was designated merely as "Section 61" duplicating the number of an existing section. To distinguish between the two, it is here designated as "Section 61-a."]

Sec. 62. **Continuity of State and Local Governmental Operations.** — (a) The Legislature, in order to insure continuity of state and local governmental operations in periods of emergency resulting from disasters caused by enemy attack, shall have the power and the immediate duty to provide for prompt and temporary succession to the powers and duties of public offices, of whatever nature and whether filled by election or appointment, the incumbents of which may become unavailable for carrying on the powers and duties of such offices. Provided, however, that Article I of the Constitution of Texas, known as the "Bill of Rights" shall not be in any manner affected, amended, impaired, suspended, repealed or suspended hereby.

(b) When such a period of emergency or the immediate threat of enemy attack exists, the Legislature may suspend procedural rules imposed by this Constitution that relate to:

(1) the order of business of the Legislature;

(2) the percentage of each house of the Legislature necessary to constitute a quorum;

Article III — (Cont'd.); Article IV

(3) the requirement that a bill must be read on three days in each house before it has the force of law;

(4) the requirement that a bill must be referred to and reported from committee before its consideration; and

(5) the date on which laws passed by the Legislature take effect.

(c) When such a period of emergency or the immediate threat of enemy attack exists, the Governor, after consulting with the Lieutenant Governor and the Speaker of the House of Representatives, may suspend the constitutional requirement that the Legislature hold its sessions in Austin, the seat of government. When this requirement has been suspended, the Governor shall determine a place other than Austin at which the Legislature will hold its sessions during such period of emergency or immediate threat of enemy attack. The Governor shall notify the Lieutenant Governor and the Speaker of the House of Representatives of the place and time at which the Legislature will meet. The Governor may take security precautions, consistent with the state of emergency, in determining the extent to which that information may be released.

(d) To suspend the constitutional rules specified by Subsection (b) of this section, the Governor must issue a proclamation and the House of Representatives and the Senate must concur in the proclamation as provided by this section.

(e) The Governor's proclamation must declare that a period of emergency resulting from disasters caused by enemy attack exists, or that the immediate threat of enemy attack exists, and that suspension of constitutional rules relating to legislative procedure is necessary to assure continuity of state government. The proclamation must specify the period, not to exceed two years, during which the constitutional rules specified by Subsection (b) of this section are suspended.

(f) The House of Representatives and the Senate, by concurrent resolution approved by the majority of the members present, must concur in the Governor's proclamation. A resolution of the House of Representatives and the Senate concurring in the Governor's proclamation suspends the constitutional rules specified by Subsection (b) of this section for the period of time specified by the Governor's proclamation.

(g) The constitutional rules specified by Subsection (b) of this section may not be suspended for more than two years under a single proclamation. A suspension may be renewed, however, if the Governor issues another proclamation as provided by Subsection (e) of this section and the House of Representatives and the Senate, by concurrent resolution, concur in that proclamation.

[Note. — The foregoing Sec. 62 of Art. III, an amendment, was added to provide for temporary succession to powers and duties of public offices in periods of emergency resulting from disaster caused by enemy attack. Submitted by the Fifty-seventh Legislature (1961) and adopted in election Nov. 6, 1962. It was further amended to authorize suspension of certain constitutional rules relating to legislative procedure during disasters or during immediate threat of enemy attack. Submitted by Sixty-eighth Legislature (1983) and adopted in election Nov. 8, 1983.]

Sec. 63. Consolidation of Governmental Functions in Counties of 1,200,000 or More Inhabitants. — (1) The Legislature may by statute provide for the consolidation of some functions of government of any one or more political subdivisions comprising or located within any county in this state having one million, two hundred thousand (1,200,000) or more inhabitants. Any such statute shall require an election to be held within the political subdivisions affected thereby with approval by a majority of the voters in each of these political subdivisions, under such terms and conditions as the Legislature may require.

(2) The county government, or any political subdivision(s) comprising or located therein, may contract one with another for the performance of governmental functions required or authorized by this Constitution or the laws of this state, under such terms and conditions as the Legislature may prescribe. The term "governmental functions," as it relates to counties, includes all duties, activities and operations of statewide importance in which the county acts for the state, as well as of local importance, whether required or authorized by this Constitution or the laws of this state.

[Note. — The foregoing Sec. 63 of Art. III, an amendment, was added to provide for consolidation of governmental functions between political subdivisions within counties of 1,200,000 or more inhabitants. Submitted by the Fifty-ninth Legislature (1965) and adopted in election Nov. 8, 1966.]

Sec. 64. Consolidation of Governmental Offices and Functions in Counties. — (a) The Legislature may by general statute provide for consolidation of governmental offices and functions of government of any one or more political

subdivisions comprising or located within any county. Any such statute shall require an election to be held within the political subdivisions affected thereby with approval by a majority of the voters in each of these subdivisions, under such terms and conditions as the Legislature may require.

(b) The county government, or any political subdivision(s) comprising or located therein, may contract one with another for the performance of governmental functions required or authorized by this Constitution or the Laws of this State, under such terms and conditions as the Legislature may prescribe. No person acting under a contract made pursuant to this Subsection (b) shall be deemed to hold more than one office of honor, trust or profit or more than one civil office of emolument. The term "governmental functions," as it relates to counties, includes all duties, activities and operations of statewide importance in which the county acts for the State, as well as of local importance, whether required or authorized by this Constitution or the Laws of this State.

[Note. — The foregoing Sec. 64 of Art. III, an amendment, was first added to provide for consolidation of governmental functions in El Paso and Tarrant Counties. Submitted by the Sixtieth Legislature (1967) and adopted in election Nov. 5, 1968. It was further amended to provide for consolidation of governmental functions in any county. Submitted by the Sixty-first Legislature (1969) and adopted in election Nov. 3, 1970.]

Sec. 65. Interest Rate on State Bonds. — (a) Wherever the Constitution authorizes an agency, instrumentality, or subdivision of the State to issue bonds and specifies the maximum rate of interest which may be paid on such bonds issued pursuant to such constitutional authority, such bonds may bear interest at rates not to exceed a weighted average annual interest rate of 12 percent unless otherwise provided by Subsection (b) of this section. All Constitutional provisions specifically setting rates in conflict with this provision are hereby repealed.

(b) Bonds issued by the Veterans' Land Board after the effective date of this subsection bear interest at a rate or rates determined by the board, but the rate or rates may not exceed a net effective interest rate of 10 percent per year unless otherwise provided by law. A statute that is in effect on the effective date of this subsection and that sets as a maximum interest rate payable on bonds issued by the Veterans' Land Board a rate different from the maximum rate provided by this subsection is ineffective unless reenacted by the Legislature after that date.

[Note. — Sec. 65 of Art. III is an added amendment to set the interest rate on state bonds not to exceed a weighted average annual interest of 6 per cent. Submitted by the Sixty-second Legislature (1971) and adopted in an election Nov. 7, 1972. The interest rate was raised to 12 percent in an amendment submitted by a special session of the Sixty-seventh Legislature (1982) and adopted in election Nov. 2, 1982.]

ARTICLE IV. — EXECUTIVE DEPARTMENT

Sec. 1. Officers of Executive Department. — The executive department of the State shall consist of a Governor, who shall be the chief executive officer of the State; a Lieutenant Governor, Secretary of State, Comptroller of Public Accounts, Treasurer, Commissioner of the General Land Office and Attorney General.

Sec. 2. Election of Executive Officers. — All the above officers of the executive department (except Secretary of State) shall be elected by the qualified voters of the State at the time and places of election for members of the Legislature.

Sec. 3. Election Results; Ties; Contests. — The returns of every election for said executive officers, until otherwise provided by law, shall be made out, sealed up and transmitted by the returning officers prescribed by law, to the seat of government, directed to the Secretary of State, who shall deliver the same to the Speaker of the House of Representatives as soon as the Speaker shall be chosen, and the said Speaker shall, during the first week of the session of the Legislature, open and publish them in the presence of both houses of the Legislature. The person voted for at said election having the highest number of votes for each of said offices, respectively, and being constitutionally eligible, shall be declared by the Speaker, under sanction of the Legislature, to be elected to said office. But if two or more persons shall have the highest and an equal number of votes for either of said offices, one of them shall be immediately chosen to such office by a joint vote of both houses of the Legislature. Contested elections for either of said offices shall be determined by both houses of the Legislature in joint session.

Sec. 3-a. Gubernatorial Succession. — If, at the time the Legislature shall canvass the election returns for the offices of Governor and Lieutenant Governor, the person receiving the highest number of votes for the office of Governor, as declared by the Speaker, has died, then the person having the highest number of votes for the office of Lieutenant

Article IV — (Cont'd.)

Governor shall act as Governor until after the next general election. It is further provided that in the event the person with the highest number of votes for the Office of Governor as declared by the Speaker, shall become disabled, or fail to qualify, then the Lieutenant Governor shall act as Governor until a person has qualified for the office of Governor or until after the next general election. Any succession to the governorship not otherwise provided for in this Constitution may be provided for by law; provided, however, that any person succeeding to the office of Governor shall be qualified as otherwise provided in this Constitution, and shall, during the entire term to which he may succeed, be under all the restrictions and inhibitions imposed in this Constitution on the Governor.

[Note. — An added amendment, for the purpose stated therein. Submitted by the Fiftieth Legislature (1947) and adopted in election, Nov. 2, 1948.]

Sec. 4. **Governor, When Installed; Term; Qualifications.** — The Governor elected at the general election in 1974, and thereafter, shall be installed on the first Tuesday after the organization of the Legislature, or as soon thereafter as practicable, and shall hold his office for the term of four years, or until his successor shall be duly installed. He shall be at least thirty years of age, a citizen of the United States, and shall have resided in this State at least five years immediately preceding his election.

[Note. — Sec. 4 of Art. IV was amended to raise to four years the term of office of Governor. Submitted by the Sixty-second Legislature (1971) and adopted in an election Nov. 7, 1972.]

Sec. 5. **Governor's Salary and Mansion.** — The Governor shall, at stated times, receive as compensation for his service an annual salary in an amount to be fixed by the Legislature, and shall have the use and occupation of the Governor's Mansion, fixtures and furniture.

[Note. — The foregoing Sec. 5 of Art. IV was first amended to raise Governor's salary from $4,000 to $12,000. Adopted in an election Nov. 3, 1936. Further amended to give Legislature authority to fix salary. Submitted by the Fifty-third Legislature (1953) and adopted in election Nov. 2, 1954.]

Sec. 6. **Governor to Hold No Other Office, Etc.** — During the time he holds the office of Governor he shall not hold any other office, civil, military or corporate; nor shall he practice any profession or receive compensation, reward, fee or the promise thereof for the same; nor receive any salary, reward or compensation or the promise thereof from any person or corporation for any service rendered or performed during the time he is Governor or to be thereafter rendered or performed.

Sec. 7. **Commander in Chief; May Call Out Militia.** — He shall be commander in chief of the military forces of the State, except when they are called into actual service of the United States. He shall have power to call forth the militia to execute the laws of the State, to suppress insurrections, repel invasions and protect the frontier from hostile incursions by Indians or other predatory bands.

Sec. 8. **Governor May Convene Legislature.** — The Governor may, on extraordinary occasions, convene the Legislature at the seat of government or at a different place in case that should be in possession of the public enemy, or in case of the prevalence of disease threat. His proclamation therefor shall state specifically the purpose for which the Legislature is convened.

Sec. 9. **Governor's Message; to Account for Moneys; Present Estimates, Etc.** — The Governor shall, at the commencement of each session of the Legislature, and at the close of his term of office, give to the Legislature information, by message, of the condition of the State; and he shall recommend to the Legislature such measures as he may deem expedient. He shall account to the Legislature for all public moneys received and paid out by him from any funds subject to his order, with vouchers; and shall accompany his message with a statement of the same. And at the commencement of each regular session he shall present estimates of the amount of money required to be raised by taxation for all purposes.

Sec. 10. **Governor Shall Cause the Laws to Be Executed; Intercourse With Other States.** — He shall cause the laws to be faithfully executed and shall conduct, in person, or in such manner as shall be prescribed by law, all intercourse and business of the State with other States and with the United States.

Sec. 11. **Board of Pardons and Paroles: Advisory Authority to Governor in Granting Reprieves, Paroles, Pardons, Etc.** — The Legislature shall by law establish a Board of Pardons and Paroles and shall require it to keep record of its actions and the reasons for its actions. The Legislature shall have authority to enact parole laws.

In all criminal cases, except treason and impeachment, the Governor shall have power, after conviction, on the written signed recommendation and advice of the Board of Pardons and Paroles, or a majority thereof, to grant reprieves and commutations of punishment and pardons; and under such rules as the Legislature may prescribe, and upon the written recommendation and advice of a majority of the Board of Pardons and Paroles, he shall have the power to remit fines and forfeitures. The Governor shall have the power to grant one reprieve in any capital case for a period not to exceed thirty (30) days; and he shall have the power to revoke conditional pardons. With the advice and consent of the Legislature, he may grant reprieves, commutations of punishment and pardons in cases of treason.

[Note. — The foregoing Sec. 11 of Art. IV was amended from the original to establish the stated procedure for granting pardons and paroles, which was originally vested exclusively in the Governor's office. Submitted by the Forty-fourth Legislature (1935) and adopted in an election Nov. 3, 1936. It was again amended to make the Board of Pardons and Paroles a statutory agency and to give the board power to revoke paroles. Submitted by the Sixty-eighth Legislature (1983) and adopted in election Nov. 8, 1983.]

Sec. 11-a. **Suspension of Sentences; Probation.** — The courts of the State of Texas having original jurisdiction of criminal actions shall have the power, after conviction, to suspend the imposition or execution of sentence and to place the defendant upon probation and to reimpose such sentence, under such conditions as the Legislature may prescribe.

[Note. — The foregoing Sec. 11-a of Art. IV, an amendment, was added for the stated purpose of providing suspended sentences. Submitted by the Fortyfourth Legislature (1935) and adopted in election Aug. 24, 1935.]

Sec. 12. **Governor to Fill Vacancies in State and District Offices.** — All vacancies in State or district offices, except members of the Legislature, shall be filled, unless otherwise provided by law, by appointment of the Governor, which appointment, if made during its session, shall be with the advice and consent of two thirds of the Senate present. If made during the recess of the Senate, the said appointee, or some other person to fill such vacancy, shall be nominated to the Senate during the first ten days of its session. If rejected, said office shall immediately become vacant, and the Governor shall, without delay, make further nominations until a confirmation takes place. But should there be no confirmation during the session of the Senate, the Governor shall not thereafter appoint any person to fill such vacancy who has been rejected by the Senate, but may appoint some other person to fill the vacancy until the next session of the Senate or until the regular election to said office, should it sooner occur. Appointments to vacancies in offices elective by the people shall only continue until the first general election thereafter.

Sec. 13. **Where Governor Shall Reside.** — During the session of the Legislature the Governor shall reside where its sessions are held and at all other times at the seat of government, except when, by act of the Legislature, he may be required or authorized to reside elsewhere.

Sec. 14. **Approval of Bills; Veto Bill Not Returned to Become a Law.** — Every bill which shall have passed both houses of the Legislature shall be presented to the Governor for his approval. If he approve, he shall sign it, but if he disapprove it, he shall return it with his objections to the house in which it originated, which house shall enter the objections at large upon its journal, and proceed to reconsider it. If, after such reconsideration, two thirds of the members present agree to pass the bill, it shall be sent, with the objections, to the other house, by which likewise it shall be reconsidered, and if approved by two thirds of the members of that house, it shall become a law; but in such cases the votes of both houses shall be determined by yeas and nays; and the names of the members voting for and against the bill shall be entered on the journal of each house, respectively. If any bill shall not be returned by the Governor with his objections within ten days (Sundays excepted) after it shall have been presented to him, the same shall be a law in like manner as if he had signed it, unless the Legislature, by its adjournment, prevent its return, in which case it shall be a law, unless he shall file the same, with his objections, in the office of the Secretary of State and give notice thereof by public proclamation within twenty days after such adjournment. If any bill presented to the Governor contains several items of appropriation he may object to one or more of such items, and approve the other portion of the bill. In such case he shall append to the bill, at the time of signing it, a statement of the items to which he objects, and no item so objected to shall take effect. If the Legislature be in session he shall transmit to the house in which the bill originated a copy of such statement, and the items objected to shall be separately considered. If, on reconsideration, one or more of such items be approved by two thirds of the members present, of each house, the same shall be part of the law, notwithstanding the objections of the Gov-

Article IV — (Cont'd.)

ernor. If any such bill containing several items of appropriation not having been presented to the Governor ten days (Sundays excepted) prior to adjournment, be in the hands of the Governor at the time of adjournment, he shall have twenty days from such adjournment within which to file objections to any items thereof and make proclamation of the same, and such item or items shall not take effect.

Sec. 15. **What to Be Presented for Approval.** — Every order, resolution or vote to which the concurrence of both houses of the Legislature may be necessary except on questions of adjournment shall be presented to the Governor, and before it shall take effect shall be approved by him; or, being disapproved, shall be repassed by both houses, and all the rules, provisions and limitations shall apply thereto as prescribed in the last preceding section in the case of a bill.

Sec. 16. **Lieutenant Governor; Election; Term; Powers and Duties.** — There shall also be a Lieutenant Governor, who shall be chosen at every election for Governor by the same electors, in the same manner, continue in office for the same time and possess the same qualifications. The electors shall distinguish for whom they vote as Governor and for whom as Lieutenant Governor. The Lieutenant Governor shall, by virtue of his office, be President of the Senate and shall have, when in committee of the whole, a right to debate, and vote on all questions; and when the Senate is equally divided, to give the casting vote. In case of the death, resignation, removal from office, inability or refusal of the Governor to serve, or of his impeachment or absence from the State, the Lieutenant Governor shall exercise the powers and authority appertaining to the office of Governor until another be chosen at the periodical election, and be duly qualified; or until the Governor, impeached, absent or disabled, shall be acquitted, return or his disability be removed.

Sec. 17. **Vacancy in Office; Compensation.** — If, during the vacancy in the office of Governor, the Lieutenant Governor should die, resign, refuse to serve or be removed from office or be unable to serve; or if he shall be impeached or absent from the State, the President of the Senate, for the time being, shall, in like manner, administer the government until he shall be superseded by a Governor or Lieutenant Governor. The Lieutenant Governor shall, while he acts as President of the Senate, receive for his services the same compensation and mileage which shall be allowed to the members of the Senate, and no more; and during the time he administers the government as Governor, he shall receive in like manner the same compensation which the Governor would have received had he been employed in the duties of his office, and no more. The President, for the time being, of the Senate, shall, during the time he administers the government, receive in like manner the same compensation which the Governor would have received had he been employed in the duties of his office.

Sec. 18. **Succession to Governorship.** — The Lieutenant Governor, or President of the Senate, succeeding to the office of Governor shall, during the entire terms to which he may succeed, be under all the restrictions and inhibitions imposed in this Constitution on the Governor.

Sec. 19. **Seal of State; Secretary of State to Keep, Etc.** — There shall be a seal of the State which shall be kept by the Secretary of State and used by him officially under the direction of the Governor. The seal of the State shall be a star of five points, encircled by olive and live oak branches, and the words "The State of Texas."

Sec. 20. **Commissions to Be Signed and Sealed.** — All commissions shall be in the name and by the authority of the State of Texas, sealed with the State seal, signed by the Governor, and attested by the Secretary of State.

Sec. 21. **Secretary of State; Term; Duties; Compensation.** — There shall be a Secretary of State, who shall be appointed by the Governor, by and with the advice and consent of the Senate, and who shall continue in office during the term of service of the Governor. He shall authenticate the publication of the laws and keep a fair register of all official acts and proceedings of the Governor, and shall, when required, lay the same and all papers, minutes and vouchers relative thereto, before the Legislature or either house thereof, and shall perform such other duties as may be required of him by law. He shall receive for his services an annual salary in an amount to be fixed by the Legislature.

[Note. — The foregoing Sec. 21 of Art. IV was first amended from the original to raise the salary of the secretary of State from $2,000 to $6,000 a year. Amendment adopted in an election Nov. 3, 1936. Further amended to give Legislature authority to fix salary. Submitted by the Fifty-third Legislature (1953) and adopted in election Nov. 2, 1954.]

Sec. 22. **Attorney General; Term; Duties; Residence; Salary.** — The Attorney General elected at the general election in 1974, and thereafter, shall hold his office for four years and until his successor is duly qualified. He shall represent the State in all suits and pleas in the Supreme Court of the State in which the state may be a party, and shall especially

inquire into the charter rights of all private corporations, and from time to time in the name of the State, take such action in the courts as may be proper and necessary to prevent any private corporation from exercising any power or demanding or collecting any species of taxes, tolls, freight or wharfage not authorized by law. He shall whenever sufficient cause exists, seek a judicial forfeiture of such charters, unless otherwise expressly directed by law, and give legal advice in writing to the Governor and other executive officers, when requested by them, and perform such other duties as may be required by law. He shall reside at the seat of government during his continuance in office. He shall receive for his services an annual salary in an amount to be fixed by the Legislature.

[Note. — The foregoing Sec. 22 of Art. IV was amended from the original to raise the Attorney General's fixed salary from $2,000 to $10,000 a year and to eliminate provisions for fees not to exceed $2,000 a year. Amendment adopted in an election Nov. 3, 1936. Further amended to give Legislature authority to fix salary. Submitted by the Fifty-third Legislature (1953) and adopted in election Nov. 2, 1954. It was further amended to lengthen the term of office from two to four years. Submitted by the Sixty-second Legislature (1971) and adopted in an election Nov. 7, 1972.]

Sec. 23. **Comptroller; Treasurer, and Commissioner of the General Land Office; Terms; Salaries; Residence; Fees.** — The Comptroller of Public Accounts, the Treasurer and the Commissioner of the General Land Office and any statutory state officer who is elected by the electorate of Texas at large, unless a term of office is otherwise specifically provided in this Constitution, shall each hold office for the term of four years and until his successor is qualified. The four-year term applies to these officers who are elected at the general election in 1974 or thereafter. Each shall receive an annual salary in an amount to be fixed by Legislature; reside at the capital of the State during his continuance in office, and perform such duties as are or may be required by law. They and the Secretary of State shall not receive to their own use any fees, costs or perquisites of office. All fees that may be payable by law for any service performed by any officer specified in this section, or in his office, shall be paid, when received into the State Treasury.

[Note. — The foregoing Sec. 23 of Art. IV was first amended from the original to raise salaries of three state officials mentioned from $2,500 each to $6,000 each annually. Amendment adopted in an election Nov. 3, 1936. Further amended to give Legislature authority to fix salary. Submitted by the Fifty-third Legislature (1953) and adopted in election Nov. 2, 1954. It was further amended to raise to four years the term of office of the above-named officials. Submitted by the Sixty-second Legislature (1971) and adopted in an election Nov. 7, 1972.]

Sec. 24. **Officers to Account to the Governor; Duty of Governor; False Reports.** — An account shall be kept by the officers of the executive department and by all officers and managers of State institutions of all moneys and choses in action received and disbursed or otherwise disposed of by them, severally, from all sources, and for every service performed; and a semi-annual report thereof shall be made to the Governor, under oath. The Governor may, at any time, require information in writing from any and all of said officers or managers upon any subject relating to the duties, conditions, management and expenses of their respective offices and institutions, which information shall be required by the Governor under oath, and the Governor may also inspect their books, accounts, vouchers and public funds; and any officer or manager who, at any time shall willfully make a false report or give false information, shall be guilty of perjury and so adjudged and punished accordingly and removed from office.

Sec. 25. **Laws for Investigation of Breaches of Trust.** — The Legislature shall pass efficient laws facilitating the investigation of breaches of trust and duty by all custodians of public funds and providing for their suspensions from office on reasonable cause shown, and for the appointment of temporary incumbents of their offices during such suspensions.

Sec. 26. **Notaries Public.** — (a) The Secretary of State shall appoint a convenient number of notaries public for the state who shall perform such duties as now are or may be prescribed by law. The qualifications of notaries public shall be prescribed by law.

(b) The terms of office of notaries public shall not be less than two years nor more than four years as provided by law.

TEMPORARY PROVISION. (a) This temporary provision applies to the constitutional amendment proposed by HJR No. 108, 66th Legislature, Regular Session, 1979.

(b) The constitutional amendment takes effect Jan. 1, 1980.

(c) Each person who was appointed a notary public before Jan. 1, 1980, continues to serve as a notary public for the term for which the person was appointed.

Article IV — (Cont'd.); Article V

(d) This temporary provision expires Jan. 1, 1982.

[Note. — The foregoing Sec. 26 of Art. IV was amended from the original to give the Secretary of State the authority, formerly held by the Governor, to appoint notaries public, and to include the stated contents of paragraphs (b) and (c). Submitted by the Forty-sixth Legislature (1939), and adopted in an election Nov. 5, 1940. It was further amended to establish terms of notaries public for not less than two years nor more than four years; did away with old sections (b) and (c) and provided for temporary terms of office for those notaries already serving. Submitted by the Sixty-sixth Legislature, 1979, and adopted in election Nov. 6, 1979.]

ARTICLE V. — JUDICIAL DEPARTMENT

Sec. 1. **The Several Courts; Criminal Courts.** — The judicial power of this State shall be vested in one Supreme Court, in one Court of Criminal Appeals, in Courts of Appeals, in District Courts, in County Courts, in Commissioners' Courts, in courts of Justices of the Peace and in such other courts as may be provided by law.

The Legislature may establish such other courts as it may deem necessary and prescribe the jurisdiction and organization thereof and may conform the jurisdiction of the district and other inferior courts thereto.

[Note. — The foregoing Sec. 1 of Art. V is an amended section, being a general revision of the original, to provide for "Courts of Civil Appeals" and a "Court of Criminal Appeals" in place of the old "Court of Appeals," making minor changes. Submitted by the Twenty-second Legislature (1891), ratified at an election Aug. 11, 1891, and declared adopted Sept. 22, 1891. It was amended to provide for a Court of Criminal Appeals with nine judges and to permit the court to sit in panels of three judges. (See also note under Sec. 4 below.) Submitted by the Sixty-fifth Legislature (1977) and adopted in election Nov. 8, 1977. It was further amended to change Courts of Civil Appeals to Courts of Appeal. Submitted by the Sixty-sixth Legislature (1979) and adopted in election Nov. 4, 1980.]

Sec. 1-a. **Retirement and Compensation of Judges.** — (1) Subject to the further provisions of this section, the Legislature shall provide for the retirement and compensation of justices and judges of the Appellate Courts and District and Criminal District Courts on account of length of service, age and disability, and for their reassignment to active duty where and when needed. The office of every such justice and judge shall become vacant when the incumbent reaches the age of seventy-five (75) years or such earlier age, not less than seventy (70) years, as the Legislature may prescribe; but, in the case of an incumbent whose term of office includes the effective date of this Amendment, this provision shall not prevent him from serving the remainder of said term nor be applicable to him before his period or periods of judicial service shall have reached a total of ten (10) years.

(2) The name of the State Judicial Qualifications Commission is changed to the State Commission on Judicial Conduct. The Commission consists of eleven (11) members, to wit: (i) one (1) Justice of a Court of Appeals; (ii) one (1) District Judge; (iii) two (2) members of the State Bar, who have respectively practiced as such for over ten (10) consecutive years next preceding their selection; (iiii) four (4) citizens, at least thirty (30) years of age, not licensed to practice law nor holding any salaried public office or employment; (v) one (1) Justice of the Peace; (vi) one (1) Judge of a Municipal Court; and, (vii) one (1) Judge of a County Court at Law; provided that no person shall be or remain a member of the Commission, who does not maintain physical residence within this state, or who resides in, or holds a judgeship within or for, the same Supreme Judicial District as another member of the Commission, or who shall have ceased to retain the qualifications above specified for his respective class of membership, except that the Justice of the Peace and the Judges of a Municipal Court and or a County Court at Law shall be selected at large without regard to whether they reside or hold a judgeship in the same Supreme Judicial District as another member of the Commission. Commissioners of classes (i), (ii), and (vii) above shall be chosen by the Supreme Court with advice and consent of the Senate, those of class (iii) by the Board of Directors of the State Bar under regulations to be prescribed by the Supreme Court with advice and consent of the Senate, those of class (iiii) by appointment of the Governor with advice and consent of the Senate, and the commissioners of classes (v) and (vi) by appointment of the Supreme Court as provided by law, with the advice and consent of the Senate.

(3) The regular term of office of Commissioners shall be six (6) years; but the initial members of each of classes (i), (ii) and (iii) shall respectively be chosen for terms of four (4) and six (6) years, and the initial members of class (iiii) for respective terms of two (2), four (4) and six (6) years. Interim vacancies shall be filled in the same manner as vacancies due to expiration of a full term, but only for the unexpired portion of the term in question. Commissioners may succeed themselves in office only if having served less than three (3) consecutive years.

(4) Commissioners shall receive no compensation for their services as such. The Legislature shall provide for the payment of the necessary expense for the operation of the Commission.

(5) The Commission may hold its meetings, hearings and other proceedings at such times and places as it shall determine but shall meet at Austin at least once each year. It shall annually select one of its members as chairman. A quorum shall consist of six (6) members. Proceedings shall be by majority vote of those present, except that recommendations for retirement, censure, suspension, or removal of any person holding an office named in paragraph A of Subsection (6) of this section shall be by affirmative vote of at least six (6) members.

(6) A. Any justice or judge of the courts established by this Constitution or created by the Legislature as provided in Sec. 1, Art. V, of this Constitution, may, subject to the other provisions hereof, be removed from office for willful or persistent violation of rules promulgated by the Supreme Court of Texas, incompetence in performing the duties of the office, willful violation of the Code of Judicial Conduct, or willful or persistent conduct that is clearly inconsistent with the proper performance of his duties or casts public discredit upon the judiciary or administration of justice. Any person holding such office may be disciplined or censured, in lieu of removal from office, as provided by this section. Any person holding an office specified in this subsection may be suspended from office with or without pay by the Commission immediately on being indicted by a State or Federal grand jury for a felony offense or charged with a misdemeanor involving official misconduct. On the filing of a sworn complaint charging a person holding such office with willful or persistent violation of rules promulgated by the Supreme Court of Texas, incompetence in performing the duties of the office, willful violation of the Code of Judicial Conduct, or willful and persistent conduct that is clearly inconsistent with the proper performance of his duties or casts public discredit on the judiciary or on the administration of justice, the Commission, after giving the person notice and an opportunity to appear and be heard before the Commission, may recommend to the Supreme Court the suspension of such person from office. The Supreme Court, after considering the record of such appearance and the recommendation of the Commission, may suspend the person from office with or without pay, pending final disposition of the charge.

B. Any person holding an office named in paragraph A of this subsection who is eligible for retirement benefits under the laws of this state providing for judicial retirement may be involuntarily retired, and any person holding an office named in that paragraph who is not eligible for retirement benefits under such laws may be removed from office, for disability seriously interfering with the performance of his duties, which is, or is likely to become, permanent in nature.

C. The law relating to the removal, discipline, suspension, or censure of a Justice or Judge of the courts established by this Constitution or created by the Legislature as provided in this Constitution applies to a master or magistrate appointed as provided by law to serve a trial court of this State and to a retired or former Judge who continues as a judicial officer subject to an assignment to sit on a court of this State. Under the law relating to the removal of an active Justice or Judge, the Commission and the review tribunal may prohibit a retired or former Judge from holding judicial office in the future or from sitting on a court of this State by assignment.

(7) The Commission shall keep itself informed as fully as may be of circumstances relating to the misconduct or disability of particular persons holding an office named in paragraph A of Subsection (6) of this section, receive complaints or reports, formal or informal, from any source in this behalf and make such preliminary investigations as it may determine. Its orders for the attendance or testimony of witnesses or for the production of documents at any hearing or investigation shall be enforceable by contempt proceedings in the District Court or by a Master.

(8) After such investigation as it deems necessary, the Commission may in its discretion issue a private or public admonition, warning, reprimand, or requirement that the person obtain additional training or education, or if the Commission determines that the situation merits such action, it may institute formal proceedings and order a formal hearing to be held before it concerning the public censure, removal, or retirement of a person holding an office or position specified in Subsection (6) of this section, or it may in its discretion request the Supreme Court to appoint an active or retired District Judge or Justice of a Court of Appeals, or retired Judge or Justice of the Court of Criminal Appeals or the Supreme Court, as a Master to hear and take evidence in any such matter, and to report thereon to the Commission. The Master shall have all the power of a District Judge in the enforcement of orders pertaining to witnesses, evidence, and procedure. If, after formal hear-

Article V — (Cont'd.)

ing, or after considering the record and report of a Master, the Commission finds good cause therefor, it shall issue an order of public censure or it shall recommend to a review tribunal the removal or retirement, as the case may be, of the person in question holding an office or position specified in Subsection (6) of this section and shall thereupon file with the tribunal the entire record before the Commission.

(9) A tribunal to review the Commission's recommendation for the removal or retirement of a person holding an office or position specified in Subsection (6) of this section is composed of seven (7) Justices or Judges of the Courts of Appeals who are selected by lot by the Chief Justice of the Supreme Court. Each Court of Appeals shall designate one of its members for inclusion in the list from which the selection is made. Service on the tribunal shall be considered part of the official duties of a judge, and no additional compensation may be paid for such service. The review tribunal shall review the record of the proceedings on the law and facts and in its discretion may, for good cause shown, permit the introduction of additional evidence. Within 90 days after the date on which the record is filed with the review tribunal, it shall order public censure, retirement or removal, as it finds just and proper, or wholly reject the recommendation. A Justice, Judge, Master, or Magistrate may appeal a decision of the review tribunal to the Supreme Court under the substantial evidence rule. Upon an order for involuntary retirement for disability or an order for removal, the office in question shall become vacant. The review tribunal, in an order for involuntary retirement for disability or an order for removal, may prohibit such person from holding judicial office in the future. The rights of an incumbent so retired to retirement benefits shall be the same as if his retirement had been voluntary.

(10) All papers filed with and proceedings before the Commission or a Master shall be confidential, unless otherwise provided by law, and the filing of papers with, and the giving of testimony before the Commission or a Master shall be privileged, unless otherwise provided by law. However, the Commission may issue a public statement through its executive director or its Chairman at any time during any of its proceedings under this Section when sources other than the Commission cause notoriety concerning a Judge or the Commission itself and the Commission determines that the best interests of a Judge or of the public will be served by issuing the statement.

(11) The Supreme Court shall by rule provide for the procedure before the Commission, Masters, review tribunal, and the Supreme Court. Such rule shall provide the right of discovery of evidence to a Justice, Judge, Master, or Magistrate after formal proceedings are instituted and shall afford to any person holding an office or position specified in Subsection (6) of this section, against whom a proceeding is instituted to cause his retirement or removal, due process of law for the procedure before the Commission, Masters, review tribunal, and the Supreme Court in the same manner that any person whose property rights are in jeopardy in an adjudicatory proceeding is entitled to due process of law, regardless of whether or not the interest of the person holding an office or position specified in Subsection (6) of this section in remaining in active status is considered to be a right or a privilege. Due process shall include the right to notice, counsel, hearing, confrontation of his accusers, and all such other incidents of due process as are ordinarily available in proceedings whether or not misfeasance is charged, upon proof of which a penalty may be imposed.

(12) No person holding an office specified in Subsection (6) of this section shall sit as a member of the Commission in any proceeding involving his own suspension, discipline, censure, retirement or removal.

(13) This Sec. 1-a is alternative to and cumulative of, the methods of removal of persons holding an office named in paragraph A of Subsection (6) of this section provided elsewhere in this Constitution.

(14) The Legislature may promulgate laws in furtherance of this Section that are not inconsistent with its provisions.

TEMPORARY PROVISION. (a) This temporary provision applies to the constitutional amendment proposed by H.J.R. No. 4, Sixty-eighth Legislature, Regular Session, 1983, and expires Jan. 1, 1988.

(b) The constitutional amendment takes effect Jan. 1, 1985.

(c) The initial term of the commissioner of class (v) added by amendment in 1977 expired on Nov. 19, 1979. The initial term of the commissioner of class (vi) and (vii) expires on Nov. 19, 1985.

(d) Each person holding office as a member of the Commission on Judicial Conduct on Jan. 1, 1985, continues to hold the office for the term for which he was appointed.

(e) The offices of the first commissioner of class (i) and the first commissioner of class (ii) whose terms expire after Jan. 1, 1985, are abolished on the expiration of the terms.

(f) Changes made in the constitution by this amend-

ment do not apply to investigations and formal proceedings where the investigation of judicial conduct by the commission began before Jan. 1, 1985.

[Note. — The foregoing Sec. 1-a was added to provide for retirement and compensation of judges. Submitted by Fiftieth Legislature (1947) and adopted in election, Nov. 2, 1948. It was amended to provide for automatic retirement of district and appellate judges for old age; to create the State Judicial Qualifications Commission and defining its functions; and empowering the Supreme Court to remove district and appellate judges for misconduct and to retire such judges in cases of disability. Submitted by Fifty-ninth Legislature (1965) and adopted in election Nov. 2, 1965. It was further amended to specifically name those offices under the jurisdiction of the Commission and to broaden the Commission's duties and powers. Submitted by Sixty-first Legislature (1969) and adopted in election Nov. 3, 1970. It was further amended to change the name of the State Judicial Qualifications Commission to the State Commission on Judicial Conduct; raise the number of members of the Commission to eleven; set out specific qualifications for membership; and provide for the suspension, censure, removal or involuntary retirement of a justice under certain circumstances. Submitted by Sixty-fifth Legislature (1977) and adopted in election Nov. 8, 1977. It was again amended to specify ways to discipline active judges, certain retired and former judges, and certain masters and magistrates of courts. Submitted by Sixty-eighth Legislature (1983) and adopted in election Nov. 6, 1984.]

Sec. 2. **Supreme Court; Quorum; Qualifications; Election; Salary; Vacancy.** — The Supreme Court shall consist of the Chief Justice and eight Justices, any five of whom shall constitute a quorum, and the concurrence of five shall be necessary to a decision of a case; provided, that when the business of the court may require, the court may sit in sections as designated by the court to hear argument of causes and to consider applications for writs of error or other preliminary matters. No person shall be eligible to serve in the office of Chief Justice or Justice of the Supreme Court unless the person is licensed to practice law in this state and is, at the time of election, a citizen of the United States and of this State and has attained the age of thirty-five years and has been a practicing lawyer or a lawyer and judge of a court of record together at least ten years. Said Justices shall be elected (three of them each two years) by the qualified voters of the State at a general election; shall hold their offices six years or until their successors are elected and qualified; and shall each receive such compensation as shall be provided by law. In case of a vacancy in the office of the Chief Justice or any Justice of the Supreme Court, the Governor shall fill the vacancy until the next general election for State officers, and at such general election the vacancy for the unexpired term shall be filled by election by the qualified voters of the State. The Justices of the Supreme Court who may be in office at the time this amendment takes effect shall continue in office until the expiration of their terms of office under the present Constitution and until their successors are elected and qualified.

[Note. — The foregoing Sec. 2 of Art. V has been thrice amended: (1) To raise salaries and make minor adjustments, by amendment submitted by the Twenty-second Legislature, ratified in an election Aug. 11, 1891, and declared adopted Sept. 22, 1891; (2) to raise the number of justices on the Supreme Court from three to nine and make other adjustments, by amendment submitted by the Forty-ninth Legislature and adopted in an election Aug. 25, 1945; and (3) to change name of Commission of Appeals and qualifications of Supreme Court Justices. Submitted by the Sixty-sixth Legislature (1979) and adopted in election Nov. 4, 1980.]

Sec. 3. **Jurisdiction; Terms of Court.** — The Supreme Court shall exercise the judicial power of the state except as otherwise provided in this Constitution. Its jurisdiction shall be co-extensive with the limits of the State and its determinations shall be final except in criminal law matters. Its appellate jurisdiction shall be final and shall extend to all cases except in criminal law matters and as otherwise provided in this Constitution or by law. The Supreme Court and the Justices thereof shall have power to issue writs of habeas corpus, as may be prescribed by law; and under such regulations as may be prescribed by law, the said courts and the Justices thereof may issue the writs of mandamus, procedendo, certiorari and such other writs as may be necessary to enforce its jurisdiction. The Legislature may confer original jurisdiction on the Supreme Court to issue writs of quo warranto and mandamus in such cases as may be specified, except as against the Governor of the State.

The Supreme Court shall also have power, upon affidavit or otherwise as by the court may be determined to ascertain such matters of fact as may be necessary to the proper exercise of its jurisdiction.

The Supreme Court shall appoint a clerk, who shall give bond in such manner as is now or may hereafter be re-

Article V — (Cont'd.)

quired by law, and he may hold his office for four years and shall be subject to removal by said court for good cause entered of record on the minutes of said court, who shall receive such compensation as the Legislature may provide.

[Note.—The foregoing Sec. 3 of Art. V has been thrice amended, as follows: (1) To readjust jurisdiction of the Supreme Court to that of the Courts of Civil Appeals which were established by amendment of the same date, and also to consolidate the original Sec. 4, providing for a clerk of the court, with Sec. 3, by amendment submitted by the Twenty-second Legislature (1891), ratified Aug. 11, 1891, and proclaimed Sept. 22, 1891; (2) to eliminate provisions that the Supreme Court "sit from first Monday in October of each year until the last Saturday in June of the next year," by amendment submitted as part of the amendment, which added Sec. 3-a. See note of that section; and (3) redefining the jurisdiction of the Supreme Court. Submitted by the Sixtysixth Legislature (1979) and adopted in election Nov. 4, 1980.]

Sec. 3-a. **Time of Sitting.** — The Supreme Court may sit at any time during the year at the seat of government for the transaction of business and each term thereof shall begin and end with each calendar year.

[Note.—The foregoing Sec. 3-a of Art. V was added to make the time of sitting of the Supreme Court discretionary with that court. It was substituted for a provision formerly incorporated in Sec. 3. (See note on Sec. 3.) Submitted by the Forty-first Legislature (1929), ratified in an election Nov. 4, 1930, and proclaimed Dec. 17, 1930.]

Sec. 3-b. **Direct Appeal.** — The Legislature shall have the power to provide by law, for an appeal direct to the Supreme Court of this State from an order of any trial court granting or denying an interlocutory or permanent injunction on the grounds of the constitutionality or unconstitutionality of any statute of this State, or on the validity or invalidity of any administrative order issued by any state agency under any statute of this State.

[Note.—The foregoing Sec. 3-b of Art. V was added for the stated purpose of providing for direct appeals. Submitted by the Forty-sixth Legislature and adopted in an election Nov. 5, 1940.]

Sec. 4. **Court of Criminal Appeals.** — The Court of Criminal Appeals shall consist of eight Judges and one Presiding Judge. The Judges shall have the same qualifications and receive the same salaries as the Associate Justices of the Supreme Court, and the Presiding Judge shall have the same qualifications and receive the same salary as the Chief Justice of the Supreme Court. The Presiding Judge and the Judges shall be elected by the qualified voters of the state at a general election and shall hold their offices for a term of six years. In case of a vacancy in the office of a Judge of the Court of Criminal Appeals, the Governor shall, with the advice and consent of the Senate, fill said vacancy by appointment until the next succeeding general election.

For the purpose of hearing cases, the Court of Criminal Appeals may sit in panels of three Judges, the designation thereof to be under rules established by the court. In a panel of three Judges, two Judges shall constitute a quorum and the concurrence of two Judges shall be necessary for a decision. The Presiding Judge, under rules established by the court, shall convene the court en banc for the transaction of all other business and may convene the court en banc for the purpose of hearing cases. The court must sit en banc during proceedings involving capital punishment and other cases as required by law. When convened en banc, five Judges shall constitute a quorum and the concurrence of five Judges shall be necessary for a decision. The Court of Criminal Appeals may appoint Commissioners in aid of the Court of Criminal Appeals as provided by law.

[Note.—The foregoing Sec. 4 of Art. V is an amendment, superseding, in part, the original Sec. 5 which provided for the former "Court of Appeals." The original Sec. 4 provided for the appointment of Supreme Court clerks, and was absorbed in the amended Sec. 3. Submitted by the Twenty-second Legislature (1891); ratified Aug. 11, 1891, and adopted Sept. 22, 1891. It was further amended to raise number of judges from three to five and define their terms of office. Submitted by the Fifty-ninth Legislature (1965) and adopted in election Nov. 8, 1966. It was again amended to raise the number of judges from five to nine and to provide that the Court of Criminal Appeals may sit in panels of three judges. Submitted by the Sixty-fifth Legislature (1977) and adopted in election Nov. 8, 1977.]

Sec. 5. **Jurisdiction; Power; Terms; Clerk, Etc.** — The Court of Criminal Appeals shall have final appellate jurisdiction coextensive with the limits of the State and its determinations shall be final in all criminal cases of whatever grade, with such exceptions and under such regulations as may be provided in this Constitution or as prescribed by law.

The appeal of all cases in which the death penalty has been assessed shall be to the Court of Criminal Appeals. The appeal of all other criminal cases shall be to the Courts of Appeal as prescribed by law. In addition, the Court of Criminal Appeals may, on its own motion, review a decision of a Court of Appeals in a criminal case as provided by law. Discretionary review by the Court of Criminal Appeals is not a matter of right, but of sound judicial discretion.

Subject to such regulations as may be prescribed by law, the Court of Criminal Appeals and the Judges thereof shall have the power to issue the writ of habeas corpus, and in criminal law matters, the writs of mandamus, procedendo, prohibition, and certiorari. The court and the judges thereof shall have the power to issue such other writs as may be necessary to protect its jurisdiction or enforce its judgments. The court shall have the power upon affidavit or otherwise to ascertain such matters of fact as may be necessary to the exercise of its jurisdiction.

The Court of Criminal Appeals may sit for the transaction of business at any time during the year and each term shall begin and end with each calendar year. The Court of Criminal Appeals shall appoint a clerk of the court who shall give bond in such manner as is now or may hereafter be required by law, and who shall hold his office for a term of four years unless sooner removed by the court for good cause entered of record on the minutes of said court.

The clerk of the Court of Criminal Appeals who may be in office at the time when this amendment takes effect shall continue in office for the term of his appointment.

[Note.—The foregoing Sec. 5 of Art. V is an amendment, superseding primarily the original Sec. 6, which defined jurisdiction, powers, etc. of the old "Court of Appeals." (See also note on Sec. 6 below.) Submitted by Twenty-second Legislature (1891); ratified at an election Aug. 11, 1891, and declared adopted Sept. 22, 1891. It was further amended to redefine jurisdiction, powers and terms of office. Submitted by Fifty-ninth Legislature (1965) and adopted in election Nov. 8, 1966. (See note under Sec. 4 above.) It was again amended to enlarge the court's jurisdiction and to redefine its term of office. Submitted by Sixty-fifth Legislature (1977) and adopted in election Nov. 8, 1977. It was again amended to redefine jurisdiction of Courts of Criminal Appeals. Submitted by Sixty-sixth Legislature (1979) and adopted in election Nov. 4, 1980.]

Sec. 6. **Supreme Judicial Districts; Courts of Civil Appeals; Jurisdiction; Term; Justices; Election; Salary; Clerk.** — The Legislature shall divide the State into such supreme judicial districts as the population and business may require, and shall establish a Court of Appeals in each of said districts, which shall consist of a Chief Justice and at least two Associate Justices, who shall have the qualifications as herein prescribed for Justices of the Supreme Court. The Court of Appeals may sit in sections as authorized by law. The concurrence of a majority of the judges sitting in a section is necessary to decide a case. Said Court of Appeals shall have appellate jurisdiction coextensive with the limits of their respective districts, which shall extend to all cases of which the District Courts or County Courts have original or appellate jurisdiction under such restrictions and regulations as may be prescribed by law. Provided, that the decisions of said courts shall be conclusive on all questions of fact brought before them on appeal or error. Said courts shall have such other jurisdiction, original and appellate, as may be prescribed by law.

Each of said Courts of Appeals shall hold its sessions at a place in its district to be designated by the Legislature and at such time as may be prescribed by law. Said justices shall be elected by the qualified voters of their respective districts at a general election for a term of six years and shall receive for their services the sum provided by law. Each Court of Appeals shall appoint a clerk in the same manner as the clerk of the Supreme Court, which clerk shall receive such compensation as may be fixed by law.

On the effective date of this amendment the Justices of the present Courts of Civil Appeals become the Justices of the Courts of Appeals for the term of office to which elected or appointed as Justices of the Courts of Civil Appeals, and the Supreme Judicial Districts become the Supreme Judicial Districts for the Courts of Appeals. All constitutional and statutory references to the Courts of Civil Appeals shall be construed to mean the Courts of Appeals.

[Note.—The foregoing Sec. 6 of Art. V, establishing the Courts of Civil Appeals, is an amendment, superseding parts of the original Secs. 5 and 6, which provided for the old "Court of Appeals," and defined its jurisdiction, powers, etc. Submitted by the Twenty-second Legislature (1891), ratified at an election Aug. 11, 1891, and declared adopted Sept. 22, 1891. It was further amended to increase the number of justices on a Court of Civil Appeals, permitting a Court of Civil Appeals to sit in sections and requiring a concurrence of a majority of justices to decide a case. Submitted by the Sixty-fifth Legislature (1977) and adopted in election Nov. 7, 1978. It was again amended to change the name of the Courts of Civil Appeals to the Courts of Appeal

Article V — (Cont'd.)

and to redefine the jurisdiction of said courts. Submitted by the Sixty-sixth Legislature (1979) and adopted in election Nov. 4, 1980.]

Sec. 7. **Judicial Districts; Judges; Their Qualifications; Residence; Term of Office; Salary; Terms of Court.** — The State shall be divided into as many judicial districts as may now or hereafter be provided by law, which may be increased or diminished by law. For each district there shall be elected by the qualified voters thereof, at a General Election, a Judge, who shall be a citizen of the United States and of this State, who shall be licensed to practice law in this State and shall have been a practicing lawyer or a Judge of a Court in this State, or both combined, for four (4) years next preceding his election, who shall have resided in the district in which he was elected for two (2) years next preceding his election, who shall reside in his district during his term of office, who shall hold his office for the period of four (4) years, and shall receive for his services an annual salary to be fixed by the Legislature. The Court shall conduct its proceedings at the county seat of the county in which the case is pending, except as otherwise provided by law. He shall hold the regular terms of his Court at the County seat of each County in his district at least twice in each year in such manner as may be prescribed by law. The Legislature shall have power by General and Special Laws to make such provisions concerning the terms or sessions of each Court as it may deem necessary.

The Legislature shall also provide for the holding of District Court when the Judge thereof is absent, or is from any cause disabled or disqualified from presiding.

The District Judges who may be in office when this Amendment takes effect shall hold their offices until their respective terms shall expire under their present election or appointment.

[Note.—The foregoing Sec. 7 of Art. V has been twice amended: (1) Effecting a general revision of the original Sec. 7 to eliminate specification that judge must be "twenty-five years of age" and making minor changes. Submitted by the Twenty-second Legislature (1891) and ratified in election Aug. 11, 1891. (2) Providing that the District Court shall conduct its proceedings in the county seat of the county in which the case is pending "except as otherwise provided by law." Submitted by the Fifty-first Legislature (1949) and adopted in election Nov. 8, 1949.]

Sec. 8. **Jurisdiction and Powers of the District Courts.** — The District Court shall have original jurisdiction of all criminal cases of the grade of felony; in all suits in behalf of the State to recover penalties, forfeitures and escheats; of all cases of divorce; of all misdemeanors involving official misconduct; of all suits to recover damages for slander or defamation of character; of all suits for trial of titles of land and for the enforcement of liens thereon; of all suits for the trial of the right of property levied upon by virtue of any writ of execution, sequestration or attachment when the property levied on shall be equal to or exceed in value $500; of all suits, complaints or pleas whatever, without regard to any distinction between law and equity, when the matter in controversy shall be valued at or amount to $500, exclusive of interest; of contested elections; and said court and the judges thereof shall have power to issue writs of habeas corpus, mandamus, injunction and certiorari, and all writs necessary to enforce their jurisdiction.

The District Court shall have appellate jurisdiction and general control in probate matters over the County Court established in each county for appointing guardians, granting letters testamentary and of administration, probating wills, for settling the accounts of executors, administrators, guardians, and for the transaction of all business appertaining to estates; and original jurisdiction and general control over executors, administrators, guardians and minors, under such regulations as may be prescribed by law. The District Court shall have appellate jurisdiction and general supervisory control over the County Commissioners' Court with such exceptions and under such regulations as may be prescribed by law; and shall have general original jurisdiction over all causes of action whatever for which a remedy or jurisdiction is not provided by law or this Constitution, and such other jurisdiction, original and appellate, as may be provided by law.

The District Court, concurrently with the County Court, shall have the general jurisdiction of a Probate Court. It shall probate wills, appoint guardians of minors, idiots, lunatics, persons non compos mentis and common drunkards, grant letters testamentary and of administration, settle accounts of executors, transact all business appertaining to deceased persons, minors, idiots, lunatics, persons non compos mentis and common drunkards, including the settlement, partition and distribution of estates of deceased persons and to apprentice minors, as provided by law. In any proceeding involving the general jurisdiction of a Probate Court, including such specified proceedings, the District Court shall also have all other jurisdiction conferred upon the District Court by law. The Legislature, how-

ever, shall have the power, by local or general law, Sec. 16 of Art. V of this Constitution notwithstanding, to increase, diminish or eliminate the jurisdiction of either the District Court or the County Court in probate matters, and in cases of any such change of jurisdiction, the Legislature shall also conform the jurisdiction of the other courts to such change. The Legislature shall have power to adopt rules governing the filing, distribution and transfer of all such cases and proceedings as between District Courts, County Courts, and other courts having jurisdiction thereof, and may provide that all appeals in such matters shall be to the Courts of (Civil) Appeals.

[Note.—The foregoing Sec. 8 of Art. V is an amendment of the original Sec. 8, including the words "of contested elections" in the first paragraph and adding the last sentence in the second paragraph. Submitted by the Twenty-second Legislature (1891), ratified at an election Aug. 11, 1891, and declared adopted Sept. 22, 1891. It was further amended to give District and County Courts general jurisdiction over probate matters; and further provided that Legislature may increase, diminish or eliminate jurisdiction of District Court or County Court in probate matters; and further provided that Legislature may provide that all appeals in such matters be to Courts of Civil Appeals. Submitted by the Sixty-third Legislature (1973) and adopted in election Nov. 6, 1973.]

Sec. 9. **Clerk of the District Court; Term of Office; How Removed; How Vacancy Is Filled.** — There shall be a Clerk for the District Court of each county, who shall be elected by the qualified voters for state and county officers, and who shall hold his office for four years, subject to removal by information, or by indictment of a grand jury and conviction by a petit jury. In case of vacancy the judge of a District Court shall have the power to appoint a Clerk, who shall hold until the office can be filled by election.

[Note.—The foregoing Sec. 9 of Art. V has been amended to change the term of office from two to four years. Submitted by the Fifty-third Legislature (1953) and adopted in election Nov. 2, 1954.]

Sec. 10. **Jury Trial; by Whom Fee Is to Be Paid.** — In the trial of all cases in the District Courts, the plaintiff or defendant shall, upon application made in open court, have the right of trial by jury; but no jury shall be impaneled in any civil case unless demanded by a party to the case, and a jury fee be paid by the party demanding a jury, for such sum and with such exceptions as may be prescribed by the Legislature.

Sec. 11. **Disqualification of Judges; Special Judges; Exchange of Districts; Vacancies.** — No judge shall sit in any case wherein he may be interested, or where either of the parties may be connected with him either by affinity or consanguinity, within such a degree as may be prescribed by law, or when he shall have been counsel in the case. When the Supreme Court, the Court of Civil Appeals, the Court of Criminal Appeals, or any member of either, shall be thus disqualified to hear and determine any case or cases in said court, the same shall be certified to the Governor of the State, who shall immediately commission the requisite number of persons, learned in the law, for the trial and determination of such cause or causes. When a Judge of the District Court is disqualified by any of the causes above stated, the parties may, by consent, appoint a proper person to try said case; or, upon their failing to do so, a competent person may be appointed to try the same in the county where it is pending in such manner as may be prescribed by law.

And the District Judges may exchange districts or hold courts for each other when they may deem it expedient, and shall do so when required by law. This disqualification of Judges of inferior tribunals shall be remedied, and vacancies in their offices filled, as may be prescribed by law.

[Note. — The foregoing Sec. II of Art. V is an amended section, having been amended to use correct references to courts as established in amended Secs. 1, 3, 4, 5 and 6. Submitted by the Twenty-second Legislature (1891), ratified at an election Aug. 11, 1891, and declared adopted Sept. 22, 1891.]

Sec. 12. **Judges Conservators of Peace; Style of Writs; Prosecution by State.** — All judges of courts of this State, by virtue of their office *(shall) be conservators of the peace throughout the State. The style of all writs and processes shall be "The State of Texas." All prosecutions shall be carried on in the name and by the authority of the State of Texas, and shall conclude "against the peace and dignity of the State."

*The word "shall," was omitted, apparently by error, from the resolution proposing this amended section.

[Note. — The foregoing Sec. 12 of Art. V has been amended from the original to substitute "Courts of the State" for enumeration of kinds of courts contained in

Article V — (Cont'd.)

original sections and applying to courts before general revision of judiciary in 1891. Submitted by the Twenty-second Legislature (1891), ratified at an election Aug. 11, 1891, and declared adopted Sept. 22, 1891.]

Sec. 13. Jurors, Grand and Petit; Number Required to Return Verdict. — Grand and petit juries in the District Courts shall be composed of twelve men; but nine members of a grand jury shall be a quorum to transact business and present bills. In trials of civil cases and in trials of criminal cases below the grade of felony in the District Courts, nine members of the jury concurring may render a verdict, but when the verdict shall be rendered by less than the whole number, it shall be signed by every member of the jury concurring in it. When, pending the trial of any case, one or more jurors, not exceeding three, may die, or be disabled from sitting, the remainder of the jury shall have the power to render the verdict; provided, that the Legislature may change or modify the rule authorizing less than the whole number of the jury to render a verdict.

Sec. 14. Districts Fixed by Ordinance. — The judicial districts in this State and the time of holding the courts therein are fixed by ordinance forming part of this Constitution until otherwise provided by law.

Sec. 15. County Court; Election; Term of Office of County Judges; Fees. — There shall be established in each county in this State, a County Court, which shall be a court of record; and there shall be elected in each county by the qualified voters a County Judge, who shall be well informed in the law of the state, shall be a conservator of the peace, and shall hold his office for four years and until his successor shall be elected and qualified. He shall receive as compensation for his services such fees and perquisites as may be prescribed by law.

[Note. — The foregoing Sec. 15 of Art. V has been amended to change the term of office from two to four years. Submitted by the Fifty-third Legislature (1953) and adopted in election Nov. 2, 1954.]

Sec. 16. Jurisdiction of County Court; Appeals; Probate Jurisdiction; May Issue Writs; Judge Disqualified, When. — The County Courts shall have original jurisdiction of all misdemeanors of which exclusive original jurisdiction is not given to the Justices Courts as the same is now or may hereafter be prescribed by law, and when the fine to be imposed shall exceed $200; and they shall have concurrent jurisdiction with the Justice Court in all civil cases when the matter in controversy shall exceed in value $200 and not exceed $500, exclusive of interest, unless otherwise provided by law; and concurrent jurisdiction with the District Court when the matter in controversy shall exceed $500 and not exceed $1,000, exclusive of interest, but shall not have jurisdiction of suits for recovery of land. They shall have appellate jurisdiction in cases, civil and criminal, of which Justices Courts have original jurisdiction, but of such civil cases only when the judgment of the court appealed from shall exceed $20, exclusive of costs, under such regulations as may be prescribed by law. In all appeals from Justices Courts there shall be a trial de novo in the County Court, and appeals may be prosecuted from the final judgment rendered in such cases by the County Court, as well as in all cases, civil and criminal, of which the County Court has exclusive or concurrent or original jurisdiction as may be prescribed by law and this Constitution.

The County Court shall have the general jurisdiction of a Probate Court; they shall probate wills, appoint guardians of minors, idiots, lunatics, persons non compos mentis, and common drunkards; grant letters testamentary and of administration; settle accounts of executors; transact all business appertaining to deceased persons, minors, idiots, lunatics, persons non compos mentis, and common drunkards, including the settlement, partition and distribution of estates of deceased persons; and to apprentice minors as provided by law; and the County Court or Judge thereof shall have power to issue writs of injunctions, mandamus, and all writs necessary to the enforcement of the jurisdiction of said court, and to issue writs of habeas corpus in cases where the offense charged is within the jurisdiction of the County Court, or any other court or tribunal inferior to said court. The County Court shall not have criminal jurisdiction in any county where there is a Criminal District Court unless expressly conferred by law and in such counties appeals from Justices Courts and other inferior courts and tribunals in criminal cases shall be to the Criminal District Court, under such regulations as may be prescribed by law; and in all such cases an appeal shall lie from such District Court as may be prescribed by law and this Constitution. When the Judge of the County Court is disqualified in any case pending in the County Court the parties interested may, by consent, appoint a proper person to try said case, or upon their failing to do so, a competent person may be appointed to try the same in the county where it is pending in such manner as may be prescribed by law.

[Note. — The foregoing Sec. 16 of Art. V is an amendment from the original to make changes relating to appeals to the county court, relating to disqualification of the judge, and minor changes. Submitted by the Twenty-second Legislature (1891), ratified at an election Aug. 11, 1891, and declared adopted Sept. 22, 1891. It was further amended to extend jurisdiction of Justices of Peace in civil cases. (See also Sec. 19 of Art. V.) Submitted by the Sixty-fifth Legislature (1977) and adopted in election Nov. 7, 1978. It was amended again to redefine jurisdiction of appellate courts. Submitted by the Sixty-sixth Legislature (1979) and adopted in election Nov. 4, 1980.]

Sec. 16-a. The Legislature, by local or general law, may provide a system for judges of statutory courts with probate jurisdiction to hold court in any county in this state for any other statutory court judge with probate jurisdiction or for a judge of a constitutional county court.

[Note. — The foregoing Sec. 16-a of Art. V, an amendment, was added to provide for assignment of judges of certain courts with probate jurisdiction to other county courts with probate jurisdiction, and to county courts. Submitted by Sixty-eighth Legislature (1983) and adopted in election Nov. 8, 1983.]

Sec. 17. Terms of County Court for Criminal Business; Prosecution Commenced by Information; Grand Jury to Inquire Into Misdemeanors; Quashing of Grand Jury Indictments; Jury. — The County Court shall hold a term for civil business at least once in every two months, and shall dispose of probate business, either in term time or vacation, as may be provided by law, and said court shall hold a term for criminal business once in every month, as may be provided by law. Prosecutions may be commenced in said court by information filed by the County Attorney, or by affidavit, as may be provided by law. Grand juries impaneled in the District Courts shall inquire into misdemeanors, and all indictments therefor returned into the District Courts shall forthwith be certified to the County Courts, or other inferior courts having jurisdiction to try them, for trial; and if such indictment be quashed in the county, or other inferior court, the person charged shall not be discharged if there is probable cause of guilt, but may be held by such court or magistrate to answer an information or affidavit. A jury in the County Court shall consist of six men; but no jury shall be impaneled to try a civil case, unless demanded by one of the parties, who shall pay such jury fee therefor in advance as may be prescribed by law, unless he makes affidavit that he is unable to pay the same.

Sec. 18. Terms of Justices of the Peace; County Commissioners and Commissioners' Court. — (a) Each county in the state, with a population of 30,000 or more, according to the most recent federal census, from time to time, for the convenience of the people, shall be divided into not less than four and not more than eight precincts. Each county in the State with a population of 18,000 or more but less than 30,000 according to the most recent federal census, from time to time, for the convenience of the people, shall be divided into not less than two and not more than five precincts. Each county in the State with a population of less than 18,000, according to the most recent federal census, from time to time, for the convenience of the people, shall be designated as a single precinct or, if the Commissioners Court determines that the county needs more than one precinct, shall be divided into not more than four precincts. The division or designation shall be made by the Commissioners Court provided for by this Constitution. In each such precinct there shall be elected one Justice of the Peace and one Constable, each of whom shall hold his office for four years and until his successor shall be elected and qualified; provided that in any precinct in which there may be a city of 18,000 or more inhabitants, there shall be elected two Justices of the Peace.

(b) Each county shall, in the manner provided for justice of the peace and constable precincts, be divided into four Commissioners' precincts in each of which there shall be elected by the qualified voters thereof one County Commissioner, who shall hold his office for four years and until his successor shall be elected and qualified. The County Commissioners so chosen, with the County Judge as presiding officer, shall compose the County Commissioners Court, which shall exercise such powers and jurisdiction over all county business as is conferred by this Constitution and the laws of the state, or as may be hereafter prescribed.

(c) When the boundaries of justice of the peace and constable precincts are changed, each Justice and Constable in office on the effective date of the change, or elected to a term of office beginning on or after the effective date of the change, shall serve in the precinct in which the person resides for the term to which each was elected or appointed, even though the change in boundaries places the person's residence outside the precinct for which he was elected or appointed, abolishes the precinct for which he was elected or appointed, or temporarily results in extra Justices or Constables serving in a precinct. When, as a result of a change of precinct boundaries, a vacancy occurs in the of-

Article V — (Cont'd.)

fice of Justice of the Peace or Constable, the Commissioners' Court shall fill the vacancy by appointment until the next general election.

(d) When the boundaries of commissioners precincts are changed, each commissioner in office on the effective date of the change, or elected to a term of office beginning on or after the effective date of the change, shall serve in the precinct to which each was elected or appointed for the entire term to which each was elected or appointed, even though the change in boundaries places the person's residence outside the precinct for which he was elected or appointed.

Temporary Provision. (a) The amendment of Art. V, Sec. 18, of the Texas Constitution proposed by the Sixty-eighth Legislature, Regular Session, authorizing fewer justice of the peace and constable precincts in certain counties, takes effect Jan. 1, 1984.

(b) A county that has a population of less than 30,000, according to the 1980 federal census, and that has more than four justice of the peace and constable precincts on Jan. 1, 1984, may keep that number of precincts until Jan. 1, 1987. On and after Jan. 1, 1987, the county must have a number of justice of the peace and constable precincts authorized by Art. V, Sec. 18, of the Texas Constitution.

(c) This provision expires Jan. 2, 1987.

[Note. — The foregoing Sec. 18 of Art. V was first amended to change the term of office for Justices of the Peace and Constables from two to four years. Submitted by the Fifty-third Legislature (1953) and adopted in election Nov. 2, 1954. It was again amended to authorize fewer justice of the peace and constable precincts in counties with populations of less than 30,000 and to provide for continuous service by Justices of Peace, Constables and County Commissioners when precinct boundaries are changed. Submitted by Sixty-eighth Legislature (1983) and adopted in election Nov. 8, 1983.]

Sec. 19. **Criminal Jurisdiction of Justices of the Peace; Appeals; Justices of the Peace ex-Officio Notaries.** — Justices of the Peace shall have jurisdiction in criminal matters of all cases where the penalty or fine to be imposed by law may not be more than for two hundred dollars, and exclusive jurisdiction in civil matters of all cases where the amount in controversy is two hundred dollars or less, exclusive of interest, unless exclusive original jurisdiction is given to the District or County Courts; and concurrent jurisdiction with the County Courts when the matter in controversy exceeds two hundred dollars and does not exceed five hundred dollars, exclusive of interest, unless exclusive jurisdiction is given to the County Courts, and, as provided by law, when the matter in controversy exceeds five hundred dollars, concurrent jurisdiction with both the County Courts and the District Courts in an amount not to exceed one thousand dollars exclusive of interest, unless exclusive jurisdiction is given to the County Courts or the District Courts; and such other jurisdiction, criminal and civil, as may be provided by law, under such regulations as may be prescribed by law; and appeals to the County Courts shall be allowed in all cases decided in Justices' Courts where the judgment is for more than twenty dollars exclusive of costs; and in all criminal cases under such regulations as may be prescribed by law. And the justices of the peace shall be ex officio notaries public. And they shall hold their courts at such times and places as may be provided by law.

[Note. — The foregoing Sec. 19 of Art. V was amended to extend jurisdiction of Justices of Peace and to give them jurisdiction in civil matters involving $200 or less. (See also Sec. 16 of Art. V.) Submitted by the Sixtyfifth Legislature (1977) and adopted in election Nov. 7, 1978.]

Sec. 20. **County Clerk; Election; Terms; Duties; Vacancies.** — There shall be elected for each county, by the qualified voters, a County Clerk, who shall hold his office for four years, who shall be clerk of the County and Commissioners' Courts and recorder of the county, whose duties, perquisites and fees of office shall be prescribed by the Legislature, and a vacancy in whose office shall be filled by the Commissioners' Court until the next general election; provided, that in counties having a population of less than 8,000 persons there may be an election of a single clerk, who shall perform the duties of District and County Clerks.

[Note. — The foregoing Sec. 20 of Art. V has been amended to change the term of office from two to four years. Submitted by the Fifty-third Legislature (1953) and adopted in election Nov. 2, 1954.]

Sec. 21. **County and District Attorneys; Duties; Vacancies; Fees.** — A County Attorney, for counties in which there is not a resident Criminal District Attorney, shall be elected by the qualified voters of each county, who shall be commissioned by the Governor and hold his office for the term of four years. In case of vacancy the Commissioners' Court of the county shall have power to appoint a County Attorney

until the next general election. The County Attorneys shall represent the State in all cases in the District and inferior courts in their respective counties; but if any county shall be included in a district in which there shall be a District Attorney, the respective duties of District Attorneys and County Attorneys shall, in such counties, be regulated by the Legislature. The Legislature may provide for the election of District Attorneys in such districts as may be deemed necessary, and make provisions for the compensation of District Attorneys and County Attorneys. District Attorneys shall hold office for a term of four years, and until their successors have qualified.

[Note. — The foregoing Sec. 21 of Art. V has been amended to change the term of office from two to four years; also leaves solely to Legislature provision for annual salary to be paid by State to District and County Attorneys. Submitted by the Fifty-third Legislature (1953) and adopted in election Nov. 2, 1954.]

Sec. 22. **Jurisdiction of Courts May Be Changed by Legislature.** — The Legislature shall have power, by local or general law, to increase, diminish or change the civil and criminal jurisdiction of County Courts; and in cases of any such change of jurisdiction the Legislature shall also conform the jurisdiction of the other courts to such change.

Sec. 23. **Sheriff; Term of Office; Vacancy.** — There shall be elected by the qualified voters of each county a Sheriff, who shall hold his office for the term of four years, whose duties and perquisites and fees of office shall be prescribed by the Legislature, and vacancies in whose office shall be filled by the Commissioners' Court until the next general election.

[Note. — The foregoing Sec. 23 of Art. V has been amended to change the term of office from two to four years. Submitted by the Fifty-third Legislature (1953) and adopted in election Nov. 2, 1954.]

Sec. 24. **Certain Officers Removed by District Courts for Drunkenness, Incompetency, Official Misconduct, Etc.** — County Judges, County Attorneys, Clerks of the District and County Courts, Justices of the Peace, Constables and other county officers may be removed by the Judges of the District Courts for incompetency, official misconduct, habitual drunkenness or other causes defined by law, upon the cause therefor being set forth in writing, and the finding of its truth by a jury.

Sec. 25. **Supreme Court to Regulate Practice.** — The Supreme Court shall have power to make and establish rules of procedure not inconsistent with the laws of the State for the government of said court and the other courts of this State, to expedite the dispatch of business therein.

[Note. — The foregoing Sec. 25 of Art V was amended from the original to add the phrase "not inconsistent with the laws of the State." Submitted by the Twenty-second Legislature (1891), ratified at an election Aug. 11, 1891, and declared adopted Sept. 22, 1891.]

Sec. 26. **No Appeal in Criminal Cases by the State.** — The State shall have no right of appeal in criminal cases.

Sec. 27. **Transfer of Cases by the Legislature.** — The Legislature shall, at its first session provide for the transfer of all business, civil and criminal, pending in District Courts, over which jurisdiction is given by this Constitution to the County Courts or other inferior courts, to such county or inferior courts, and for the trial or disposition of all such causes by such county or other inferior courts.

Sec. 28. **Vacancies in Offices of Judges of Superior Courts to Be Filled by the Governor.** — Vacancies in the office of the Judges of the Supreme Court, the Court of Criminal Appeals, the Court of Civil Appeals and District Courts shall be filled by the Governor until the next succeeding general election, and vacancies in the office of County Judge and Justices of the Peace shall be filled by the Commissioners' Court until the next succeeding general election.

[Note. — The foregoing Sec. 28 of Art. V has been amended from the original to make names of courts harmonize with names in amended Secs. 1, 3, 4, 5 and 6. Submitted by the Twenty-second Legislature (1891), ratified in an election Aug. 11, 1891, and declared adopted Sept. 22, 1891. This section was again amended to provide that appointments to the offices of County Judge and Justice of the Peace should be filled only to the next succeeding general election instead of for the full elected term. Submitted by the Fiftyfifth Legislature (1957) and adopted in election Nov. 4, 1958.]

Sec. 29. **Terms of County Courts; Probate Business; Prosecutions.** — The County Court shall hold at least four terms for both civil and criminal business annually, as may be provided by the Legislature, or by the Commissioners' Court of the county under authority of law, and such other terms each year as may be fixed by the Commissioners' Court; provided, the Commissioners' Court of any county having fixed the times and number of terms of the County Court shall not change the same again until the expiration

Article V — (Cont'd.); Article VI

of one year. Said court shall dispose of probate business either in term time or vacation, under such regulations as may be prescribed by law. Prosecutions may be commenced in said courts in such manner as is or may be provided by law, and a jury therein shall consist of six men. Until otherwise provided, the terms of the County Court shall be held on the first Mondays in February, May, August and November, and may remain in session three weeks.

[Note. — Sec. 29 of Art. V, an amendment, was added for stated purpose of prescribing county court terms. Submitted by the Eighteenth Legislature (1883), ratified in an election Aug. 14, 1883, and proclaimed Sept. 25, 1883.]

Sec. 30. **County Judges and Criminal District Attorneys; Terms.** — The Judges of all courts of county-wide jurisdiction heretofore or hereafter created by the Legislature of this State, and all Criminal District Attorneys now or hereafter authorized by the laws of this State, shall be elected for a term of four years, and shall serve until their successors have qualified.

[Note. — Sec. 30 of Art. V, an amendment, was added for purpose of prescribing term of office of County Judges and Criminal District Attorneys. Submitted by the Fifty-third Legislature (1953) and adopted in election Nov. 2, 1954.]

ARTICLE VI. — SUFFRAGE

Sec. 1. **Persons Who Cannot Vote.** — The following classes of persons shall not be allowed to vote in this State, to wit:

*First: Persons under eighteen (18) years of age.

Second: Idiots and lunatics.

Third: All paupers supported by any county.

Fourth: All persons convicted of any felony, subject to such exceptions as the Legislature may make.

[Note. — The foregoing Sec. 1 of Art. VI has been twice amended from the original to give privilege of ballot to officers and enlisted men of National Guard, National Guard Reserves, Officers Reserve Corps, Organized Reserves and retired officers and enlisted men of Army, Navy and Marine Corps. Submitted by the Forty-second Legislature (1931) and adopted in an election Nov. 8, 1932. Proclaimed Jan. 9, 1933. It was further amended by HJR 10 submitted by the Fifty-third Legislature (1953) and adopted in an election Nov. 2, 1954, to remove restrictions against members of the Armed Forces. This amendment also repealed the original Sec. 2-a of Art. VI which provided for poll tax exemption for war veterans. See also note under Sec. 2 and new Sec. 2-a.* Texas on April 27, 1971, became the twenty-first state to ratify an amendment to the U.S. Constitution lowering the voting age to 18 from 21. When Ohio ratified the amendment in July, 1971, it was the 38th state to do so, the number required to change the voting age.]

Sec. 2. **Annual Registration; Absentee Voting.** — Every person subject to none of the foregoing disqualifications, who shall have attained the age of *21 years and who shall be a citizen of the United States and who shall have resided in this State one year next preceding an election and the last six months within the district or county in which such person offers to vote, shall be deemed a qualified elector; provided, however, that before offering to vote at an election a voter shall have registered annually, but such requirement for registration shall not be considered a qualification of an elector within the meaning of the term "qualified elector" as used in any other Article of this Constitution in respect to any matter except qualification and eligibility to vote at an election. Any legislation enacted in anticipation of the adoption of this Amendment shall not be invalid because of its anticipatory nature. The Legislature may authorize absentee voting. And this provision of the Constitution shall be self-enacting without the necessity of further legislation.

[Note. — The foregoing Sec. 2 of Art. VI has been amended six times, as follows: (1) To include provision that declaration of foreigner must be filed at least six months before election to enable him to vote in such election. Submitted by Twenty-fourth Legislature (1895), ratified in an election Nov. 3, 1896, and declared adopted Dec. 18, 1896. (2) To make poll tax receipt certificate of registration for voting. Submitted by Twenty-seventh Legislature (1901), ratified in an election Nov. 4, 1902, and declared adopted Dec. 26, 1902. (3) To limit suffrage to citizens; allowing husband or wife to pay poll tax for other; authorizing absentee voting. Submitted by Thirty-seventh Legislature (1921) and ratified in election July 23, 1921. (4) To extend suffrage to members of the Armed Forces of the United States. Submitted by Fifty-third Legislature (1953) and adopted in an election Nov. 2, 1954. (5) To omit the requirement that members of armed services may vote only in county in which they resided at time of entering the service. Submitted by Fifty-ninth Legislature (1965) and adopted in election Nov. 8, 1966. (6) To repeal the poll tax as a voting requirement and substituting therefor annual registration. Submitted by Fifty-ninth Legislature (1965), adopted in election Nov. 8, 1966. *See also note under Sec. 1 above.]

Sec. 2-a. **Vote for Electors for President and Vice President and Statewide Offices.** — (a) Notwithstanding any other provision of this Constitution, the Legislature may enact laws and provide a method of registration, including the time of such registration, permitting any person who is qualified to vote in this state except for the residence requirements within a county or district, as set forth in Sec. 2 of this article, to vote for (1) electors for president and vice president of the United States and (2) all offices, questions or propositions to be voted on by all electors throughout this state.

(b) Notwithstanding any other provision of this Constitution, the Legislature may enact laws and provide for a method of registration, including the time for such registration, permitting any person (1) who is qualified to vote in this state except for the residence requirements of Sec. 2 of this article, and (2) who shall have resided anywhere within this state at least thirty (30) days next preceding a general election in a presidential election year, and (3) who shall have been a qualified elector in another state immediately prior to his removal to this state or would have been eligible to vote in such other state had he remained there until such election, to vote for electors for president and vice president of the United States in that election.

(c) Notwithstanding any other provision of this Constitution, the Legislature may enact laws and provide for a method of registration, including the time for such registration, permitting absentee voting for electors for president and vice president of the United States in this state by former residents of this state (1) who have removed to another state, and (2) who meet all qualifications, except residence requirements, for voting for electors for president and vice president in this state at the time of the election, but the privileges of suffrage as so granted shall be only for such period of time as would permit a former resident of this state to meet the residence requirements for voting in his new state of residence, and in no case for more than twenty-four (24) months.

[Note. — The foregoing Sec. 2-a, an amendment, was added to provide for voting on electors for president and vice president and on all statewide offices. Submitted by the Fifty-ninth Legislature (1965) and adopted in election Nov. 8, 1966.]

Sec. 3. **Electors in Towns and Cities; Only Property Taxpayers to Vote in Certain Instances.** — All qualified electors of the State, as herein described, who shall have resided for six months immediately preceding an election within the limits of any city or corporate town, shall have the right to vote for Mayor and all other elective officers; but in all elections to determine expenditure of money or assumption of debt, only those shall be qualified to vote who pay taxes on property in said city or incorporated town; provided, that no poll tax for the payment of debts thus incurred shall be levied upon the persons debarred from voting in relation thereto.

Sec. 3-a. **Only Those Who Have Rendered Property for Taxation May Vote in Bond Elections.** — When an election is held by any county, or any number of counties, or any political subdivision of the State, or any political subdivision of a county, or any defined district now or hereafter to be described and defined within the State and which may or may not include towns, villages or municipal corporations, or any city, town or village, for the purpose of issuing bonds or otherwise lending credit, or expending money or assuming any debt, only qualified electors who own taxable property in the State, county, political subdivision, district, city, town or village where such election is held, and who have duly rendered the same for taxation, shall be qualified to vote and all electors shall vote in the election precinct of their residence.

[Note. — The foregoing Sec. 3-a of Art. VI, an amendment, was added for the purpose of limiting voters participating in bond elections to those who have rendered property for taxation. Submitted by the Forty-second Legislature (1931) and adopted in an election Nov. 8, 1932; proclaimed Jan. 9, 1933.]

Sec. 4. **Voter Registration.** — In all elections by the people the vote shall be by ballot, and the Legislature shall provide for the numbering of tickets and make such other regulations as may be necessary to detect and punish fraud and preserve the purity of the ballot box; and the Legislature shall provide by law for the registration of all voters.

[Note. — The foregoing Sec. 4 of Art. VI has been amended twice as follows: A provision for the registration of voters in cities of 10,000 or more population was added by amendment submitted by the Twenty-second Legislature (1891), ratified in election Aug. 11, 1891, and declared adopted Sept. 22, 1891. It was further amended to delete this provision for registration of voters in cities of 10,000 or more

Article VI — (Cont'd.); Article VII

population. (See also note under Sec. 2, Art. VI.) Submitted by the Fifty-ninth Legislature (1965) and adopted in election Nov. 8, 1966.]

Sec. 5. **Voters Privileged From Arrest.** — Voters shall, in all cases except treason, felony or breach of the peace, be privileged from arrest during their attendance at elections and in going to and returning therefrom.

ARTICLE VII.—EDUCATION—
THE PUBLIC FREE SCHOOLS

Sec. 1. **Public Schools to Be Established.** — A general diffusion of knowledge being essential to the preservation of the liberties and rights of the people, it shall be the duty of the Legislature of the State to establish and make suitable provision for the support and maintenance of an efficient system of public free schools.

Sec. 2. **Provisions Governing the Levy and Collection of Taxes for the Support of the Public Free Schools.** — All funds, lands and other property heretofore set apart and appropriated for the support of public schools, all the alternate sections of land reserved by the State out of grants heretofore made or that may hereafter be made to railroads or other corporations, of any nature whatsoever, one half of the public domain of the State, and all sums of money that may come to the State from the sale of any portion of the same shall constitute a perpetual public school fund.

Sec. 3. **School Taxes.** — One fourth of the revenue derived from the State occupation taxes and a poll tax of one ($1.00) dollar on every inhabitant of this State, between the ages of 21 and 60 years, shall be set apart annually for the benefit of the public free schools; and in addition thereto, there shall be levied and collected an annual ad valorem State tax of such an amount not to exceed 35c on the one hundred ($100.00) dollars valuation, as, with the available school fund arising from all other sources, will be sufficient to maintain and support the public schools of this State for a period of not less than six months in each year, and it shall be the duty of the State Board of Education to set aside a sufficient amount out of the said tax to provide free textbooks for the use of children attending the public free schools of this State; provided, however, that should the limit of taxation herein named be insufficient the deficit may be met by appropriation from the general funds of the State, and the Legislature may also provide for the formation of school districts by general laws, and all such school districts may embrace parts of two or more counties. And the Legislature shall be authorized to pass laws for the assessment and collection of taxes in all said districts and for the management and control of the public school or schools of such districts, whether such districts are composed of territory wholly within a county or in parts of two or more counties. And the Legislature may authorize an additional ad valorem tax to be levied and collected within all school districts heretofore formed or hereafter formed, for the further maintenance of public free schools, and for the erection and equipment of school buildings therein; provided, that a majority of the qualified property taxpaying voters of the district voting at an election to be held for that purpose shall vote such tax not to exceed in any one year $1 on the $100 valuation of the property subject to taxation in such district, but the limitation upon the amount of school district tax herein authorized shall not apply to incorporated cities or towns constituting separate and independent school districts, nor to independent or common school districts created by general or special law.

[Note. — The foregoing Sec. 3 of Art. VII is an amended section, having been altered six times: (1) To authorize a State ad valorem school tax of not more than 20c, and further to authorize creation by Legislature of school districts for local taxation not to exceed 20c. Submitted by Eighteenth Legislature (1883), ratified in election Aug. 14, 1883, and declared adopted Sept. 25, 1883. (2) To authorize maximum tax in school districts of 50c. Submitted by Thirtieth Legislature (1907), ratified in an election Nov. 3, 1908, and declared adopted Feb. 2, 1909. (3) To authorize intercounty school districts and authorizing Legislature to pass laws for management and control of districts. Submitted by Thirty-first Legislature (1909), ratified in election Aug. 3, 1909. See note on 3-a below. (4) To increase maximum tax for State school purposes from 20c to 35c and provide for free textbooks. Submitted by Thirty-fifth Legislature (1917) and adopted at election of Nov. 5, 1918. (5) To remove 50c limit on school district tax submitted by Thirty-sixth Legislature (1919) and adopted at election of Nov. 2, 1920. (6) To eliminate the provision authorizing the Legislature to create districts by special law. Submitted by Thirty-ninth Legislature (1925) and ratified in an election Nov. 2, 1926, and proclaimed Jan. 20, 1927.]

See Sec. 1-e of Art. VIII for provisions to gradually abolish the ad valorem tax as a source for state school support.

[Note. — Sec. 3-a of Art. VII, relating to county line districts, validation, bonds and taxation, was deleted by constitutional amendment in election Aug. 5, 1969.]

Sec. 3-b. **County School Districts.** — No tax for the maintenance of public free schools voted in any independent school district and no tax for the maintenance of a junior college voted by a junior college district, nor any bonds voted in any such district, but unissued, shall be abrogated, canceled or invalidated by change of any kind in the boundaries thereof. After any change in boundaries, the governing body of any such district, without the necessity of an additional election, shall have the power to assess, levy and collect ad valorem taxes on all taxable property within the boundaries of the district as changed, for the purposes of the maintenance of public free schools or the maintenance of a junior college, as the case may be, and the payment of principal of and interest on all bonded indebtedness outstanding against, or attributable, adjusted or allocated to, such district or any territory therein, in the amount, at the rate, or not to exceed the rate, and in the manner authorized in the district prior to the change in its boundaries, and further in accordance with the laws under which all such bonds, respectively, were voted; and such governing body also shall have the power, without the necessity of an additional election, to sell and deliver any unissued bonds voted in the district prior to any such change in boundaries, and to assess, levy and collect ad valorem taxes on all taxable property in the district as changed, for the payment of principal of and interest on such bonds in the manner permitted by the laws under which such bonds were voted. In those instances where the boundaries of any such independent school district are changed by the annexation of, or consolidation with, one or more whole school districts, the taxes to be levied for the purposes herein-above authorized may be in the amount or at not to exceed the rate theretofore voted in the district having at the time of such change the greatest scholastic population according to the latest scholastic census and only the unissued bonds of such district voted prior to such change, may be subsequently sold and delivered and any voted, but unissued, bonds of other school districts involved in such annexation or consolidation shall not thereafter be issued.

[Note. The foregoing Sec. 3-b of Art. VII, an amendment, was added originally for the purpose of allowing independent school districts in Dallas County to work out adjustment of boundaries without abrogating, canceling or invalidating existing tax rates and bonds. Submitted by the Fifty-seventh Legislature (1961) and adopted in election Nov. 6, 1962. Further amended to include school districts in any county of Texas. Submitted by the Fifty-ninth Legislature (1965) and adopted in election Nov. 8, 1966.]

Sec. 4. **Sale of School Lands; No Release to Purchasers; the Investment of Proceeds.** — The lands herein set apart to the public free school fund shall be sold under such regulations, at such times and on such terms as may be prescribed by law; and the Legislature shall not have power to grant any relief to purchasers thereof. The Comptroller shall invest the proceeds of such sales, and of those heretofore made, as may be directed by the Board of Education herein provided for, in the bonds of the United States, the State of Texas, or counties in said State, or in such other securities and under such restrictions as may be prescribed by law; and the State shall be responsible for all investments.

[Note. — The foregoing Sec. 4 of Art. VII is an amended section, the amendment authorizing investment of money from sale of State public school lands in securities other than State and United States bonds, as was required by the original section. The amendment also added the clause making the State responsible for such investments. Submitted by the Eighteenth Legislature (1883), ratified in an election Aug. 14, 1883, and declared adopted Sept. 25, 1883.]

Sec. 4A. **Patents Issued for Free Public School Lands.** — (a) On application to the School Land Board, a natural person is entitled to receive a patent to land from the commissioner of the General Land Office if:

(1) the land is surveyed public free school land, either surveyed or platted according to records of the General Land Office;

(2) the land was not patentable under the law in effect immediately before adoption of this section;

(3) the person acquired the land without knowledge of the title defect out of the State of Texas or Republic of Texas and held the land under color of title, the chain of which dates from at least as early as January 1, 1932; and

(4) the person, in conjunction with his predecessors in interest:

(A) has a recorded deed on file in the respective county courthouse and has claimed the land for a continuous period of at least 50 years as of November 15, 1981; and

(B) for at least 50 years has paid taxes on the land together with all interest and penalties associated with any period of delinquency of said taxes; provided, however, that in the event that public records concerning the tax payments on the land are unavailable for any period within the past 50 years, the tax assessors-collectors of the taxing

Article VII — (Cont'd.)

jurisdictions in which the land is located shall provide the School Land Board with a sworn certificate stating that, to the best of their knowledge, all taxes have been paid for the past 50 years and there are no outstanding taxes nor interest or penalties currently due against the property.

(b) The applicant for the patent must submit to the School Land Board certified copies of his chain of title and a survey of the land for which a patent is sought, if requested to do so by the board. The board shall determine the qualifications of the applicant to receive a patent under this section. Upon a finding by the board that the applicant meets the requirements of Subsection (a) of this section, the commissioner of the General Land Office shall award the applicant a patent. If the applicant is denied a patent, he may file suit against the board in a district court of the county in which the land is situated within 60 days from the date of the denial of the patent under this section. The trial shall be de novo and not subject to the Administrative Procedure and Texas Register Act, and the burden of proof is on the applicant.

(c) This section does not apply to beach land, submerged land, or islands, and may not be used by an applicant to resolve a boundary dispute. This section does not apply to land that, previous to the effective date of this section, was found by a court of competent jurisdiction to be state owned or to land on which the state has given a mineral lease that on the effective date of this section was productive.

(d) Application for a patent under this section must be filed with the School Land Board within five years from the effective date of this section.

(e) This section is self-executing.

(f) This section expires on January 1, 1990.

[Note — The foregoing Sec. 4A of Art. VII, an amendment, was added to authorize the Commissioner of the General Land Office to issue patents for certain public free school fund land held in good faith under color of title for at least 50 years as of Nov. 15, 1981. Submitted by the Sixty-seventh Legislature (1981) and adopted in election Nov. 3, 1981.]

Sec. 5. Permanent School Fund; Interest; Alienation; Sectarian Schools.

— (a) The principal of all bonds and other funds, and the principal arising from the sale of the lands hereinbefore set apart to said school fund, shall be the permanent school fund, and all the interest derivable therefrom and the taxes herein authorized and levied shall be the available school fund. The available school fund shall be applied annually to the support of the public free schools. Except as provided by this section, no law shall ever be enacted appropriating any part of the permanent or available school fund to any other purpose whatever; nor shall the same or any part thereof ever be appropriated to or used for the support of any sectarian school; and the available school fund herein provided shall be distributed to the several counties according to their scholastic population and applied in such manner as may be provided by law.

(b) The Legislature by law may provide for using the permanent school fund and the income from the permanent school fund to guarantee bonds issued by school districts.

(c) The Legislature may appropriate part of the available school fund for administration of the permanent school fund or of a bond guarantee program established under this section.

[Note. — The foregoing Sec. 5 of Art. VII is an amended section. It was first amended to allow Legislature to add not exceeding 1 per cent annually of the total value of the permanent school fund to the available school fund. Submitted by the Twenty-second Legislature (1891), ratified in an election Aug. 11, 1891, and declared adopted Sept. 22, 1891. It was further amended to delete this provision. Submitted by the Fifty-eighth Legislature (1963), and adopted in election Nov. 3, 1964. It was again amended to authorize use of the permanent school fund to guarantee bonds issued by school districts. Submitted by Sixty-eighth Legislature (1983) and adopted in election Nov. 8, 1983.]

Sec. 6. County School Lands; Limitations; Settlers; Proceeds.

— All lands heretofore or hereafter granted to the several counties of this State for educational purposes are of right the property of said counties respectively to which they were granted, and title thereto is vested in said counties, and no adverse possession or limitation shall ever be available against the title of any county. Each county may sell or dispose of its lands in whole or in part in manner to be here provided by the Commissioners' Court of the county. Actual settlers residing on said land shall be protected in the prior right of purchasing the same to the extent of their settlement, not to exceed 160 acres, at the price fixed by said court, which price shall not include the value of existing improvements made thereon by such settlers. Said lands, and the proceeds thereof, when sold, shall be held by said counties alone as a trust for the benefit of public schools therein; said proceeds to be invested in bonds of the

United States, the State of Texas, or counties in said State, or in such other securities and under such restrictions as may be prescribed by law; and the counties shall be responsible for all investments; the interest thereon and other revenue, except principal, shall be available fund.

[Note. — The foregoing Sec. 6 of Art. VII is an amended section, the amendment authorizing the investment of money from sale of county public school lands in securities other than State and United States bonds (as was required in the original section), and making counties responsible for such investments. Submitted by the Eighteenth Legislature (1883), ratified in an election August 14, 1883, and declared adopted Sept. 25, 1883.]

Sec. 6-a. Taxation of County School Lands.

— All agriculture or grazing school land mentioned in Sec. 6 of this article owned by any county shall be subject to taxation except for State purposes to the same extent as lands privately owned.

[Note. — The foregoing Sec. 6-a of Art. VII, an amendment, was added for the stated purpose of providing taxation of lands mentioned in Sec. 6. Submitted by the Thirty-ninth Legislature (1925), ratified in an election Nov. 2, 1926, and proclaimed Jan. 20, 1927.]

Sec. 6-b.

Notwithstanding the provisions of Sec. 6, Art. VII, Constitution of the State of Texas, any county, acting through the commissioners court, may reduce the county permanent school fund of that county and may distribute the amount of the reduction to the independent and common school districts of the county on a per scholastic basis to be used solely for the purpose of reducing bonded indebtedness of those districts or for making permanent improvements. The commissioners court shall, however, retain a sufficient amount of the corpus of the county permanent school fund to pay ad valorem taxes on school lands or royalty interests owned at the time of the distribution. Nothing in this Section affects financial aid to any school district by the State.

[Note. — Sec. 6-b of Art VII is an added amendment to allow a county to reduce its county permanent school fund and distribute the money to independent and common school districts on a per capita basis. Submitted by the Sixty-second Legislature (1971) and adopted in an election Nov. 7, 1972.]

[Note. — Sec. 7 of Art. VII, relating to separate schools for white and colored, was deleted by constitutional amendment in election Aug. 5, 1969.]

Sec. 8. Board of Education; Terms and Duties.

— The Legislature shall provide by law for a State Board of Education, whose members shall be appointed or elected in such manner and by such authority and shall serve for such terms as the Legislature shall prescribe not to exceed six years. The said board shall perform such duties as may be prescribed by law.

[Note. — The foregoing Sec. 8 of Art. VII is an amended section, reconstituting the State Board of Education. The original text provided for a Board of Education consisting of Governor, Comptroller and Secretary of State, serving ex officio. Submitted by the Fortieth Legislature (1927); ratified Nov. 6, 1928; proclaimed Feb. 6, 1929.]

Asylums

Sec. 9. Lands of Asylums; Sale.

All lands heretofore granted for the benefit of the lunatic, blind, deaf and dumb, and orphan asylums, together with such donations as may have been or may hereafter be made to either of them, respectively, as indicated in the several grants, are hereby set apart to provide a permanent fund for the support, maintenance and improvement of said asylums. And the Legislature may provide for the sale of the lands and the investment of the proceeds in the manner as provided for the sale and investment of school lands in Sec. 4 of this article.

University

Sec. 10. University Lands and Funds.

— The Legislature shall, as soon as practicable, establish, organize and provide for the maintenance, support and direction of a University of the first class, to be located by a vote of the people of this State and styled "The University of Texas," for the promotion of literature and the arts and sciences, including an agricultural, and mechanical department.

Sec. 11. University Funds; How Invested.

— In order to enable the Legislature to perform the duties set forth in the foregoing section, it is hereby declared all lands and other property heretofore set apart and appropriated for the establishment and maintenance of the University of Texas, together with all the proceeds of sales of the same, heretofore made or hereafter to be made, and all grants, donations and appropriations that may hereafter be made by the State of Texas, or from any other source, except donations

Article VII — (Cont'd.)

limited to specific purposes, shall constitute and become a permanent university fund. And the same as realized and received into the treasury of the State (together with such sums belonging to the fund, as may now be in the treasury) shall be invested in bonds of the United States, the State of Texas, or counties of said State, or in school bonds of municipalities or in bonds of any city of this State or in bonds issued under and by virtue of the Federal Farm Loan Act approved by the President of the United States July 17, 1916, and amendments thereto; and the interest accruing thereon shall be subject to appropriation by the Legislature to accomplish the purpose declared in the foregoing section; provided, that the one tenth of the alternate sections of the lands granted to railroads reserved by the State, which were set apart and appropriated to the establishment of the University of Texas by an act of the Legislature of Feb. 11, 1858, entitled "An act to establish the University of Texas" shall not be included in or constitute a part of, the permanent university fund.

[Note. — The foregoing Sec. 11 of Art. VII has been twice amended as follows: (1) Adding a clause giving the Board of Regents of the University of Texas latitude in expending part of the permanent fund for buildings. Submitted by the Forty-first Legislature (1929); ratified Nov. 4, 1930. (2) Eliminating this latitude allowed the Board of Regents and restoring the original provisions of the Constitution which limited investments to bonds of the United States, State or civil subdivisions. This last amendment added also the clause "except donations limited to specific purposes." Submitted by the Fortysecond Legislature (1931); adopted Nov. 8, 1932. Proclaimed Jan. 9, 1933.]

Sec. 11-a. In addition to the bonds enumerated in Section 11 of Article VII of the Constitution of the State of Texas, the Board of Regents of The University of Texas may invest the Permanent University Fund in securities, bonds or other obligations issued, insured, or guaranteed in any manner by the United States Government, or any of its agencies, and in such bonds, debentures, or obligations, and preferred and common stocks issued by corporations, associations, and other institutions as the Board of Regents of The University of Texas System may deem to be proper investments for said funds; provided, however, that not more than one per cent (1%) of said fund shall be invested in the securities of any one (1) corporation, nor shall more than five per cent (5%) of the voting stock of any one corporation be owned; provided, further, that stocks eligible for purchase shall be restricted to stocks of companies incorporated within the United States which have paid dividends for five (5) consecutive years or longer immediately prior to the date of purchase and which, except for bank stocks and insurance stocks, are listed upon an exchange registered with the Securities and Exchange Commission or its successors.

In making each and all of such investments said Board of Regents shall exercise the judgment and care under the circumstances then prevailing which men of ordinary prudence, discretion, and intelligence exercise in the management of their own affairs, not in regard to speculation but in regard to the permanent disposition of their funds, considering the probable income therefrom as well as the probable safety of their capital.

The interest, dividends and other income accruing from the investments of the Permanent University Fund, except the portion thereof which is appropriated by the operation of Sec. 18 of Art. VII for the payment of principal and interest on bonds or notes issued thereunder, shall be subject to appropriation by the Legislature to accomplish the purposes declared in Sec. 10 of Article VII of this Constitution.

This amendment shall be self-enacting, and shall become effective upon its adoption, provided, however, that the Legislature shall provide by law for full disclosure of all details concerning the investments in corporate stocks and bonds and other investments authorized herein.

[Note. — Sec.11-a of Art. VII was added to provide for broader investment of the Permanent University Fund in corporate bonds and stocks under certain conditions and limitations. Submitted by the Fifty-fourth Legislature (1955) and adopted in election Nov. 6, 1956. It was further amended to increase the types of securities available for investment to the Permanent University Fund by allowing securities, bonds or other obligations issued, insured or guaranteed in any manner by the federal government. Submitted by the Sixtieth Legislature (1967) and adopted in election Nov.5, 1968.]

Sec. 12. Lands to Be Sold; No Relief of Purchasers. — The land herein set apart to the university fund shall be sold under such regulations at such times.and on such terms as may be provided by law, and the Legislature shall provide for the prompt collection, at maturity, of all debts due on account of university lands heretofore sold, or that may hereafter be sold, and shall in neither event have the power to grant relief to the purchasers.

Sec. 13. Agricultural and Mechanical College; Appropriations. — The Agricultural and Mechanical College of Texas, established by an act of the Legislature passed April 17, 1871, located in the County of Brazos, is hereby made and constituted a branch of the University of Texas, for instruction in agriculture, the mechanic arts and the natural sciences connected therewith. And the Legislature shall at its next session make an appropriation not to exceed $40,000 for the construction and completion of the buildings and improvements, and for providing the furniture necessary to put said college in immediate and successful operation.

Sec. 14. Prairie View A&M. — Prairie View A&M University in Waller County is an institution of the first class under the direction of the same governing board as Texas A&M University referred to in Article VII, Section 13, of this constitution as the Agricultural and Mechanical College of Texas.

[Note. — The foregoing Sec. 14 of Art. VII was substituted for an earlier Sec. 14. It sets out that Prairie View A&M University is an institution of the first class under direction of Texas A&M University governing board. (See also Sections 17 and 18 of Art. VII.) Submitted by the Sixty-eighth Legislature (1983) and adopted in election Nov. 6, 1984.]

Sec. 15. Land Appropriated for University; How Sold. — In addition to the lands heretofore granted to the University of Texas, there is hereby set apart and appropriated, for the endowment, maintenance and support of said university and its branches, 1,000,000 acres of the unappropriated public domain of the State, to be designated and surveyed as may be provided by law; and said lands shall be sold under the same regulations and the proceeds invested in the same manner as is provided for the sale and investment of the permanent university fund; and the Legislature shall not have the power to grant relief to the purchasers of said lands.

Sec. 16. Terms of Office in School Systems. — The Legislature shall fix by law the terms of all offices of the public school system and of the State institutions of higher education, inclusive, and the terms of members of the respective boards, not to exceed six years.

[Note. — The foregoing Sec. 16 of Art. VII is the first of two amendments numbered 16. (See following section and note thereon.) This amendment was added for the stated purpose of providing for fixing of terms of office in public school system. Submitted by the Fortieth Legislature (1927); ratified Nov. 6, 1928; proclaimed Feb. 6, 1929.]

Sec. 16 [a.] Taxation of University Lands. — All land mentioned in Secs. 11, 12 and 15 of Article VII of the Constitution of the State of Texas, now belonging to the University of Texas, shall be subject to the taxation for county purpose to the same extent as lands privately owned; provided, they shall be rendered for taxation upon values fixed by the State Tax Board; and providing, that the State shall remit annually to each of the counties in which said lands are located an amount equal to the tax imposed upon said land for county purposes.

[Note. — The foregoing section, which obviously should have been numbered either 16-a or 17, was designated as No. 16 in H.J.R. No. 11 of the Forty-first Legislature (1929) in which the amendment was submitted. It is customarily printed in legal references as Sec. 16 [a.] This amendment was added for the stated purpose of providing for taxation of University of Texas lands. It was ratified Nov. 4, 1930. Declared adopted Dec. 17, 1930.]

Sec. 17. Support for Higher Education. — (a) In the fiscal year beginning September 1, 1985, and each fiscal year thereafter, there is hereby appropriated out of the first money coming into the state treasury not otherwise appropriated by the constitution $100 million to be used by eligible agencies and institutions of higher education for the purpose of acquiring land either with or without permanent improvements, constructing and equipping buildings or other permanent improvements, major repair or rehabilitation of buildings or other permanent improvements, and acquisition of capital equipment, library books and library materials. During the regular session of the legislature that is nearest, but preceding, the beginning of each fifth fiscal year dating from September 1, 1985, the legislature may by two-thirds vote of the membership of each house adjust the amount of the constitutional appropriation for the ensuing five years but may not adjust the appropriation in such a way as to impair any obligation created by the issuance of bonds or notes in accordance with this section.

(b) The funds appropriated under Subsection (a) of this section shall be for the use of the following eligible agencies and institutions of higher education (even though their names may be changed):

(1) East Texas State University including East Texas State University at Texarkana; (2) Lamar University including Lamar University at Orange and Lamar University at Port Arthur; (3) Midwestern State University; (4) North

Article VII — (Cont'd.)

Texas State University; (5) Pan American University including Pan American University at Brownsville; (6) Stephen F. Austin State University; (7) Texas College of Osteopathic Medicine; (8) Texas State University System Administration and the following component institutions: (9) Angelo State University; (10) Sam Houston State University; (11) Southwest Texas State University; (12) Sul Ross State University including Uvalde Study Center; (13) Texas Southern University; (14) Texas Tech University; (15) Texas Tech University Health Sciences Center; (16) Texas Woman's University; (17) University of Houston System Administration and the following component institutions: (18) University of Houston — University Park; (19) University of Houston — Victoria; (20) University of Houston — Clear Lake; (21) University of Houston — Downtown; (22) University System of South Texas System Administration and the following component institutions: (23) Corpus Christi State University; (24) Laredo State University; (25) Texas A&I University; and (26) West Texas State University.

(c) Pursuant to a two-thirds vote of the membership of each house of the legislature, institutions of higher education may be created at a later date by general law, and, when created, such an institution shall be entitled to participate in the funding provided by this section if it is not created as a part of The University of Texas System or The Texas A&M University System. An institution that is entitled to participate in dedicated funding provided by Article VII, Section 18, of this constitution may not be entitled to participate in the funding provided by this section.

(d) In the year 1985 and every 10 years thereafter, the legislature or an agency designated by the legislature no later than August 31 of such year shall allocate by equitable formula the annual appropriations made under Subsection (a) of this section to the governing boards of eligible agencies and institutions of higher education. The legislature shall review, or provide for a review, of the allocation formula at the end of the fifth year of each 10-year allocation period. At that time adjustments may be made in the allocation formula, but no adjustment that will prevent the payment of outstanding bonds and notes, both principal and interest, may be made.

(e) Each governing board authorized to participate in the distribution of money under this section is authorized to expend all money distributed to it for any of the purposes enumerated in Subsection (a). In addition, unless a single bonding agency is designated as hereinafter provided, such governing board may issue bonds and notes for the purposes of refunding bonds or notes issued under this section or prior law, acquiring land either with or without permanent improvements, constructing and equipping buildings or other permanent improvements, and for major repair and rehabilitation of buildings or other permanent improvements, and may pledge up to 50 percent of the money allocated to such governing board pursuant to this section to secure the payment of the principal and interest of such bonds or notes. Proceeds from the issuance of bonds or notes under this subsection shall be maintained in a local depository selected by the governing board issuing the bonds or notes. The bonds and notes issued under this subsection shall be payable solely out of the money appropriated by this section and shall mature serially or otherwise in not more than 10 years from their respective dates. All bonds issued under this section shall be sold only through competitive bidding and are subject to approval by the attorney general. Bonds approved by the attorney general shall be incontestable. The permanent university fund may be invested in the bonds and notes issued under this section. In lieu of the authority granted to each governing board herein, the legislature by general law may designate a single agency to issue bonds and notes authorized under this section and transfer to that agency the authority to collect and pledge money to the payment of such bonds and notes for the purposes, to the extent, and subject to the restrictions of this section. Provided, that such agency shall be authorized to issue such bonds and notes for the benefit of an eligible institution and pledge money collected hereunder only as directed by the governing board of each eligible institution.

(f) The funds appropriated by this section may not be used for the purpose of constructing, equipping, repairing, or rehabilitating buildings or other permanent improvements that are to be used for student housing, intercollegiate athletics, or auxiliary enterprises.

(g) Except for that portion of the allocated funds that may be required to be transferred to a single bonding agency, if one is created, the comptroller of public accounts shall make annual transfers of the funds allocated pursuant to Subsection (d) directly to the governing boards of the eligible institutions.

(h) To assure efficient use of construction funds and the orderly development of physical plants to accommodate the state's real need, the legislature may provide for the approval or disapproval of all new construction projects at the eligible agencies and institutions entitled to participate in the funding provided by this section.

(i) The legislature by general law may dedicate portions of the state's revenues to the creation of a dedicated fund ("the higher education fund") for the purposes expressed in Subsection (a) of this section. The legislature shall provide for administration of the fund, which shall be invested in the manner provided for investment of the permanent university fund. The income from the investment of the higher education fund shall be credited to the higher education fund until such time as the fund totals $2 billion. The principal of the higher education fund shall never be expended. At the beginning of the fiscal year after the fund reaches $2 billion, as certified by the comptroller of public accounts, the dedication of general revenue funds provided for in Subsection (a) of this section shall cease. At the beginning of the fiscal year after the fund reaches $2 billion, and each year thereafter, 10 percent of the interest, dividends, and other income accruing from the investments of the higher education fund during the previous fiscal year shall be deposited and become part of the principal of the fund, and out of the remainder of the annual income from the investment of the principal of the fund there shall be appropriated an annual sum sufficient to pay the principal and interest due on the bonds and notes issued under this section and the balance of the income shall be allocated, distributed, and expended as provided for the appropriations made under Subsection (a).

(j) The state systems and institutions of higher education designated in this section may not receive any additional funds from the general revenue of the state for acquiring land with or without permanent improvements, for constructing or equipping buildings or other permanent improvements, or for major repair and rehabilitation of buildings or other permanent improvements except that:

(1) In the case of fire or natural disaster the legislature may appropriate from the general revenue an amount sufficient to replace the uninsured loss of any building or other permanent improvement; and

(2) the legislature, by two-thirds vote of each house, may, in cases of demonstrated need, which need must be clearly expressed in the body of the act, appropriate additional general revenue funds for acquiring land with or without permanent improvements, for constructing or equipping buildings or other permanent improvements, or for major repair and rehabilitation of buildings or other permanent improvements.

This subsection does not apply to legislative appropriations made prior to the adoption of this amendment.

(k) Without the prior approval of the legislature, appropriations under this section may not be expended for acquiring land with or without permanent improvements, or for constructing and equipping buildings or other permanent improvements, for a branch campus or educational center that is not a separate degree-granting institution created by general law.

(l) This section is self-enacting upon the issuance of the governor's proclamation declaring the adoption of the amendment, and the state comptroller of public accounts and the state treasurer shall do all things necessary to effectuate this section. This section does not impair any obligation created by the issuance of any bonds and notes in accordance with prior law, and all outstanding bonds and notes shall be paid in full, both principal and interest, in accordance with their terms. If the provisions of this section conflict with any other provisions of this constitution, then the provisions of this section shall prevail, notwithstanding all such conflicting provisions.

[Note. — The foregoing Sec. 17 of Art. VII is an added amendment that supersedes the old Sec. 17 which provided for a confederate pension fund tax, college building fund tax and reduced the ad valorem ceiling for general purposes. That section was deleted in an election Nov. 2, 1982. This added Sec. 17 was proposed to create from general revenue a special higher education assistance fund for construction and related activities, to restructure the permanent university fund and to increase the number of institutions eligible to benefit from the permanent university fund. (See also Sections 14 and 18 of Art. VII.) Submitted by the Sixty-eighth Legislature (1983) and adopted in election Nov. 6, 1984.]

Sec. 18. Building Bonds Authorized for the University of Texas and Texas A&M University; Retired From Income From the Permanent University Fund; Etc. — (a) The Board of Regents of The Texas A&M University System may issue bonds and notes not to exceed a total amount of 10 percent of the cost value of the investments and other assets of the permanent university fund (exclusive of real estate) at the time of the issuance thereof, and may pledge all or any part of its one-third interest in the available university fund to secure the payment of the principal and interest of those bonds and notes, for the purpose of acquiring land either with or without permanent improvements, constructing and equipping buildings or other permanent improvements, major repair and rehabilitation of buildings and

Article VII — (Cont'd.); Article VIII

other permanent improvements, acquiring capital equipment and library books and library materials, and refunding bonds or notes issued under this Section or prior law, at or for The Texas A&M University System administration and the following component institutions of the system:

(1) Texas A&M University, including its medical college which the legislature may authorize as a separate medical institution; (2) Prairie View A&M University, including its nursing school in Houston; (3) Tarleton State University; (4) Texas A&M University at Galveston; (5) Texas Forest Service; (6) Texas Agricultural Experiment Stations; (7) Texas Agricultural Extension Service; (8) Texas Engineering Experiment Stations; (9) Texas Transportation Institute; and (10) Texas Engineering Extension Service.

(b) The Board of Regents of The University of Texas System may issue bonds and notes not to exceed a total amount of 20 percent of the cost value of investments and other assets of the permanent university fund (exclusive of real estate) at the time of issuance thereof, and may pledge all or any part of its two-thirds interest in the available university fund to secure the payment of the principal and interest of those bonds and notes, for the purpose of acquiring land either with or without permanent improvements, constructing and equipping buildings or other permanent improvements, major repair and rehabilitation of buildings and other permanent improvements, acquiring capital equipment and library books and library materials, and refunding bonds or notes issued under this section or prior law, at or for The University of Texas System administration and the following component institutions of the system:

(1) The University of Texas at Arlington; (2) The University of Texas at Austin; (3) The University of Texas at Dallas; (4) The University of Texas at El Paso; (5) The University of Texas of the Permian Basin; (6) The University of Texas at San Antonio; (7) The University of Texas at Tyler; (8) The University of Texas Health Science Center at Dallas; (9) The University of Texas Medical Branch at Galveston; (10) The University of Texas Health Science Center at Houston; (11) The University of Texas Health Science Center at San Antonio; (12) The University of Texas System Cancer Center; (13) The University of Texas Health Center at Tyler; and (14) The University of Texas Institute of Texan Cultures at San Antonio.

(c) Pursuant to a two-thirds vote of the membership of each house of the legislature, institutions of higher education may be created at a later date as a part of The University of Texas System or The Texas A&M University System by general law, and, when created, such an institution shall be entitled to participate in the funding provided by this section for the system in which it is created. An institution that is entitled to participate in dedicated funding provided by Article VII, Section 17, of this constitution may not be entitled to participate in the funding provided by this section.

(d) The proceeds of the bonds or notes issued under Subsection (a) or (b) of this section may not be used for the purpose of constructing, equipping, repairing, or rehabilitating buildings or other permanent improvements that are to be used for student housing, intercollegiate athletics, or auxiliary enterprises.

(e) The available university fund consists of the dividends, interest and other income from the permanent university fund (less administrative expenses) including the net income attributable to the surface of permanent university fund land. Out of one-third of the available university fund, there shall be appropriated an annual sum sufficient to pay the principal and interest due on the bonds and notes issued by the Board of Regents of The Texas A&M University System under this section and prior law, and the remainder of that one-third of the available university fund shall be appropriated to the Board of Regents of The Texas A&M University System which shall have the authority and duty in turn to appropriate an equitable portion of the same for the support and maintenance of The Texas A&M University System administration, Texas A&M University, and Prairie View A&M University. The Board of Regents of The Texas A&M University System, in making just and equitable appropriations to Texas A&M University and Prairie View A&M University, shall exercise its discretion with due regard to such criteria as the board may deem appropriate from year to year, taking into account all amounts appropriated from Subsection (f) into this section. Out of the other two-thirds of the available university fund there shall be appropriated an annual sum sufficient to pay the principal and interest due on the bonds and notes issued by the Board of Regents of The University of Texas System under this section and prior law, and the remainder of such two-thirds of the available university fund, shall be appropriated for the support and maintenance of The University of Texas at Austin and The University of Texas System administration.

(f) It is provided, however, that, for 10 years beginning upon the adoption of this amendment, before any other allocation is made of The University of Texas System's two-thirds share of the available university fund, remaining after payment of principal and interest on its bonds and

notes issued under this section and prior law, $6 million per year shall be appropriated out of that share to the Board of Regents of The Texas A&M University System for said board's use in making appropriations to Prairie View A&M University. This subsection expires and is deleted from this constitution 10 years from the adoption of this amendment.

(g) The bonds and notes issued under this section shall be payable solely out of the available university fund, mature serially or otherwise in not more than 30 years from their respective dates, and, except for refunding bonds, be sold only through competitive bidding. All of these bonds and notes are subject to approval by the attorney general and when so approved are incontestable. The permanent university fund may be invested in these bonds and notes.

(h) To assure efficient use of construction funds and to date the state's real need, the legislature may provide for the approval or disapproval of all new construction projects at the eligible agencies and institutions entitled to participate in the funding provided by this section except The University of Texas at Austin, Texas A&M University in College Station, and Prairie View A&M University.

(i) The state systems and institutions of higher education designated in this section may not receive any funds from the general revenue of the state for acquiring land with or without permanent improvements, for constructing or equipping buildings or other permanent improvements or for major repair and rehabilitation of buildings or other permanent improvements except that:

(1) In the case of fire or natural disaster the legislature may appropriate from the general revenue an amount sufficient to replace the uninsured loss of any building or other permanent improvement; and

(2) the legislature, by two-thirds vote of each house, may, in cases of demonstrated need, which need must be clearly expressed in the body of the act, appropriate general revenue funds for acquiring land with or without permanent improvements, for constructing or equipping buildings or other permanent improvements, or for major repair and rehabilitation of buildings or other permanent improvements.

This subsection does not apply to legislative appropriations made prior to the adoption of this amendment.

(j) This section is self-enacting on the issuance of the governor's proclamation declaring the adoption of this amendment, and the state comptroller of public accounts and the state treasurer shall do all things necessary to effectuate this section. This section does not impair any obligation created by the issuance of bonds or notes in accordance with prior law, and all outstanding bonds and notes shall be paid in full, both principal and interest, in accordance with their terms, and the changes herein made in the allocation of the available university fund shall not affect the pledges thereof made in connection with such bonds or notes heretofore issued. If the provisions of this section conflict with any other provision of this constitution, then the provisions of this section shall prevail, notwithstanding any such conflicting provisions.

[Note. — Sec. 18 and Sec. 17 of Art. VII were originally added to the Constitution as a single amendment to provide for funding of construction at Texas universities and colleges. Submitted by the Fiftieth Legislature (1947) and adopted in election Aug. 23, 1947. It was further amended in election Nov. 6, 1956 and again in an election Nov. 8, 1966. Sec. 17 was repealed in election Nov. 2, 1982. A new Sec. 17 and Sec. 18 were submitted by the Sixty-eighth Legislature (1983) and adopted in election Nov. 6, 1984. (See also note under Sec. 14 and Sec. 17.)]

ARTICLE VIII. — TAXATION AND REVENUE

Sec. 1. Taxation to Be Equal and Uniform; Occupation and Income Taxes; Exemptions; Limitations Upon Counties, Cities, Etc. — Taxation shall be equal and uniform. All real property and tangible personal property in this State whether owned by natural persons or corporations, other than municipal, shall be taxed in proportion to its value which shall be ascertained as may be provided by law. The Legislature may provide for the taxation of intangible property and may also impose occupation taxes, both upon natural persons and upon corporations, other than municipal, doing any business in this State. It may also tax incomes of both natural persons and corporations, other than municipal, except that persons engaged in mechanical and agricultural pursuits shall never be required to pay an occupation tax. The Legislature by general law shall exempt household goods not held or used for production of income and personal effects not held or used for the production of income, and the Legislature by general law may exempt all or part of the personal property homestead of a family or single adult, "personal property homestead" meaning the personal property exempt by law from forced sale for debt from ad valorem taxation. The occupation tax levied by any county, city or town, for any year, on persons or corporations pursuing any profession or business, shall not exceed one half of the tax levied by the State for the same period on such profession or business.

Article VIII — (Cont'd.)

[Note. — Sec. 1 of Art. VIII was amended to provide tax relief for residential homesteads and to provide personal property exemptions. (See also Sec. 1-b, and Sec. 23 of Art. VIII.) Submitted by the Sixty-fifth Legislature, (1977) and adopted in election Nov. 7, 1978.]

Sec. 1-a. Abolishing Ad Valorem Tax for State's General Fund Purposes; Providing Local Tax Rate, Etc. — From and after Jan 1, 1951, no State ad valorem tax shall be levied upon any property within this State for general revenue purposes. From and after January 1, 1951, the several counties of the State are authorized to levy ad valorem taxes upon all property within their respective boundaries for county purposes, except the first three thousand dollars ($3,000) value of residential homesteads of married or unmarried adults, male or female, including those living alone, not to exceed thirty cents (30c) on each one hundred dollars ($100) valuation, in addition to all other ad valorem taxes authorized by the Constitution of this State, provided the revenue derived therefrom shall be used for construction and maintenance of farm-to-market roads or for flood control, except as herein otherwise provided.

Provided that in those counties or political subdivisions or areas of the State from which tax donations have heretofore been granted, the State Automatic Tax Board shall continue to levy the full amount of the State ad valorem tax for the duration of such donation, or until all legal obligations heretofore authorized by the law granting such donation or donations shall have been fully discharged, whichever shall first occur; provided that if such donation to any such county or political subdivision is for less than the full amount of State ad valorem taxes so levied, the portion of such taxes remaining over and above such donation shall be retained by said county or subdivision.

[Note. — Sec. 1-a of Art. VIII was first added and then amended, as follows: (1) Giving homesteads $3,000 exemption from State taxes. Submitted by the Forty-second Legislature (1931), and adopted in an election Nov. 8, 1932. (2) Making more definite the provision for extending the exemption to counties and subdivisions having tax remission as soon as tax remission ceased, whether by expiration of the period designated in the act granting remission or voluntarily by action of local authorities. The original amendment failed to make provision for the latter contingency. Submitted by the Forty-third Legislature (1933), and adopted in an election Aug. 26, 1933. (3) Reducing maximum ad valorem tax for general revenue from 35c to 30c. (4) Abolishing ad valorem tax for state general fund purposes and providing for local taxation as indicated in text of section. (See also Sec. 1-b immediately below and note thereon.) Submitted by the Fiftieth Legislature (1947) and adopted in election Nov. 2, 1948. (5) Extending the $3,000 ad valorem tax exemption to homesteads of unmarried adults. Submitted by the Sixty-third Legislature (1973) and adopted in election Nov. 6, 1973.]

Sec. 1-b. Homestead Exemption Under State Tax. — (a) Three thousand dollars ($3,000) of the assessed taxable value of all residence homesteads of married or unmarried adults, male or female, including those living alone, shall be exempt from all taxation for all State purposes.

(b) From and after January 1, 1973, the governing body of any county, city, town, school district, or other political subdivision of the State may exempt by its own action not less than three thousand dollars ($3,000) of the market value of residence homesteads of persons, married or unmarried, including those living alone, who are under a disability for purposes of payment of disability insurance benefits under Federal Old-Age, Survivors, and Disability Insurance or its successor or of married or unmarried persons sixty-five (65) years of age or older, including those living alone, from all ad valorem taxes thereafter levied by the political subdivision. As an alternative, upon receipt of a petition signed by twenty per cent (20%) of the voters who voted in the last preceding election held by the political subdivision, the governing body of the subdivision shall call an election to determine by majority vote whether an amount not less than three thousand dollars ($3,000) as provided in the petition, of the market value of residence homesteads of disabled persons or of persons sixty-five (65) years of age or over shall be exempt from ad valorem taxes thereafter levied by the political subdivision. An eligible disabled person who is sixty-five (65) years of age or older may not receive both exemptions from the same political subdivision in the same year but may choose either if the subdivision has theretofore adopted both. Where any ad valorem tax has theretofore been pledged for the payment of any debt, the taxing officers of the political subdivision shall have authority to continue to levy and collect the tax against the homestead property at the same rate as the tax so pledged until the debt is discharged, if the cessation of the levy would impair the obligation of the contract by which the debt was created.

An exemption adopted under this subsection based on assessed value is increased, effective January 1, 1979, to an amount that, when converted to market value, provides the same reduction in taxes, except that the market value exemption shall be rounded to the nearest $100.

(c) Five Thousand Dollars ($5,000) of the market value of the residence homestead of a married or unmarried adult, including one living alone, is exempt from ad valorem taxation for general elementary and secondary public school purposes. In addition to this exemption, the legislature by general law may exempt an amount not to exceed Ten Thousand Dollars ($10,000) of the market value of the residence homestead of a person who is disabled as defined in Subsection (b) of this section and of a person sixty-five (65) years of age or older from ad valorem taxation for general elementary and secondary public school purposes. The legislature by general law may base the amount of and condition eligibility for the additional exemption authorized by this subsection for disabled persons and for persons sixty-five (65) years of age or older on economic need. An eligible disabled person who is sixty-five (65) years of age or older may not receive both exemptions from a school district but may choose either. An eligible person is entitled to receive both the exemption required by this subsection for all residence homesteads and any exemption adopted pursuant to Subsection (b) of this section, but the legislature shall provide by general law whether an eligible disabled or elderly person may receive both the additional exemption for the elderly and disabled authorized by this subsection and any exemption for the elderly or disabled adopted pursuant to Subsection (b) of this section. Where ad valorem tax has previously been pledged for the payment of debt, the taxing officers of a school district may continue to levy and collect the tax against the value of homesteads exempted under this subsection until the debt is discharged if the cessation of the levy would impair the obligation of the contract by which the debt was created. The legislature shall provide for formulas to protect school districts against all or part of the revenue loss incurred by the implementation of Article VIII, Sections 1-b(c), 1-b(d), and 1-d-1, of this constitution. The legislature by general law may define residence homestead for purposes of this section.

(d) Except as otherwise provided by this subsection, if a person receives the residence homestead exemption prescribed by Subsection (c) of this section for homesteads of persons sixty-five (65) years of age or older, the total amount of ad valorem taxes imposed on that homestead for general elementary and secondary public school purposes may not be increased while it remains the residence homestead of that person or that person's spouse who receives the exemption. However, those taxes may be increased to the extent the value of the homestead is increased by improvements other than repairs or improvements made to comply with governmental requirements.

(e) The governing body of a political subdivision may exempt from ad valorem taxation a percentage of the market value of the residence homestead of a married or unmarried adult, including one living alone. The percentage may not exceed forty percent (40%) for the years 1982 through 1984, thirty percent (30%) for the years 1985 through 1987, and twenty percent (20%) in 1988 and each subsequent year. However, the amount of an exemption authorized pursuant to this subsection may not be less than Five Thousand Dollars ($5,000) unless the Legislature by general law prescribes other monetary restrictions on the amount of the exemption. An eligible adult is entitled to receive other applicable exemptions provided by law. Where ad valorem tax has previously been pledged for the payment of debt, the governing body of a political subdivision may continue to levy and collect the tax against the value of the homesteads exempted under this subsection until the debt is discharged if the cessation of the levy would impair the obligation of the contract by which the debt was created. The Legislature by general law may prescribe procedures for the administration of residence homestead exemptions.

(e-1) Subsection (e) of this section takes effect January 1, 1982. This subsection expires January 2, 1982.

[Note. — Sec. 1-b of Art. VIII was amended to allow county, city, school district or other political subdivision to exempt not less than $3,000 of the assessed value of residence homesteads of persons 65 years and older from all ad valorem taxes levied by the subdivision. Submitted by Sixty-second Legislature (1971) and adopted in election Nov. 7, 1972. See also note under 1-c below. It was further amended to extend to unmarried persons the $3,000 ad valorem exemption on homesteads. Submitted by Sixty-third Legislature (1973) and adopted in election Nov. 6, 1973. See also Art. XVI, Secs. 50, 51 and 52. It was further amended to give added tax relief to disabled persons and persons over sixty-five and to provide for administration of property tax. It also added Subsections (c) and (d). (See also Sec. 1, Sec. 21, and Sec. 23 of Art. VIII.) Submitted by Sixty-fifth Legislature (1977) and adopted in election Nov. 7, 1978. It was again

Article VIII — (Cont'd.)

amended to add subsection (e) to authorize political subdivisions to provide property tax relief for owners of residence homesteads and changing certain property tax administrative procedures. (See also Sec. 21, Subsection (c) of Art. VIII.) Submitted by Sixty-seventh Legislature (1981) and adopted in election Nov. 3, 1981.]

Sec. 1-c. **Optional Provisions Relating to Sec. 1-a and Sec. 1-b.** — Provided, however, the terms of this resolution shall not be effective unless House Joint Resolution No. 24 is adopted by the people and in no event shall this resolution go into effect until January 1, 1951.

[Note. — Sec. 1-b and Sec. 1-c were added because of an oversight in writing the text of Sec. 1-a (adopted by joint resolution at an earlier date) which would have abolished the $3,000 homestead exemption under the state school tax on adoption of Sec. 1-a by the people. Submitted by the Fiftieth Legislature (1947) and adopted in election Nov. 2, 1948.]

Sec. 1-d. **Taxation of Agricultural Land.** — (a) All land owned by natural persons which is designated for agricultural use in accordance with the provisions of this section shall be assessed for all tax purposes on the consideration of only those factors relative to such agricultural use. "Agricultural use" means the raising of livestock or growing of crops, fruit, flowers, and other products of the soil under natural conditions as a business venture for profit, which business is the primary occupation and source of income of the owner.

(b) For each assessment year the owner wishes to qualify his land under provisions of this section as designated for agricultural use he shall file with the local tax assessor a sworn statement in writing describing the use to which the land is devoted.

(c) Upon receipt of the sworn statement in writing the local tax assessor shall determine whether or not such land qualifies for the designation as to agricultural use as defined herein and in the event it so qualifies he shall designate such land as being for agricultural use and assess the land accordingly.

(d) Such local tax assessor may inspect the land and require such evidence of use and source of income as may be necessary or useful in determining whether or not the agricultural use provision of this article applies.

(e) No land may qualify for the designation provided for in this act unless for at least three (3) successive years immediately preceding the assessment date the land has been devoted exclusively for agricultural use, or unless the land has been continuously developed for agriculture during such time.

(f) Each year during which the land is designated for agricultural use, the local tax assessor shall note on his records the valuation which would have been made had the land not qualified for such designation under this section. If designated land is subsequently diverted to a purpose other than that of agricultural use, or is sold, the land shall be subject to an additional tax. The additional tax shall equal the difference between taxes paid or payable, hereunder, and the amount of tax payable for the preceding three years had the land been otherwise assessed. Until paid, there shall be a lien for additional taxes and interest on land assessed under the provisions of this section.

(g) The valuation and assessment of any minerals or subsurface rights to minerals shall not come within the provisions of this section.

[Note. — The foregoing Sec. 1-d of Art. VIII, an amendment, was added for the stated purpose of providing that all land designated for agricultural use be assessed only as such. Submitted by the Fifty-ninth Legislature (1965) and adopted in an election Nov. 8, 1966.]

Sec. 1-d-1. **Open-Space Land Taxation.** — (a) To promote the preservation of open-space land, the legislature shall provide by general law for taxation of openspace land devoted to farm or ranch purposes on the basis of its productive capacity and may provide by general law for taxation of open-space land devoted to timber production on the basis of its productive capacity. The legislature by general law may provide eligibility limitations under this section and may impose sanctions in furtherance of the taxation policy of this section.

(b) If a property owner qualifies his land for designation for agricultural use under Section 1-d of this article, the land is subject to the provisions of Section 1-d for the year in which the designation is effective and is not subject to a law enacted under this Section 1-d-1 in that year.

[Note. — The foregoing Sec. 1-d-1 of Art. VIII is an added amendment to promote preservation of openspace land and to provide for taxation of production of timber thereon; also redefines use of open land for agricultural purposes and taxation thereon. Submitted by the Sixty-fifth Legislature (1977) and adopted in election Nov. 7, 1978.]

Sec. 1-e. **Gradual Abolition of Ad Valorem Tax.** — (1) No State ad valorem taxes shall be levied upon any property within this State.

(2) All receipts from previously authorized State ad valorem taxes that are collected on or after the effective date of the 1982 amendment to this section shall be deposited to the credit of the general fund of the county collecting the taxes and may be expended for county purposes. Receipts from taxes collected before that date shall be distributed by the Legislature among institutions eligible to receive distributions under prior law. Those receipts and receipts distributed under prior law may be expended for the purposes provided under prior law or for repair and renovation of existing permanent improvements.

[Note. — Sec. 1-e of Art. VIII was added to provide for the gradual abolition of the ad valorem tax for all state purposes except those that were listed under Art. VII, Sec. 17 (which was repealed by constitutional amendment in an election Nov. 2, 1982) for certain institutions of higher education and for pension funds for Confederate veterans and their widows, and for Texas Rangers and their widows. Submitted by the Sixtieth Legislature (1967) and adopted in an election Nov. 5, 1968. Sec. 1-e was amended to abolish the state property tax and to add Subsection (2), which is self-explanatory. Submitted by Called Session of the Sixty-seventh Legislature (1982) and adopted in election Nov. 2, 1982. (See also Art. III, Sec. 51 and Art. XVI, Sec. 66.)]

Sec. 1-f. **Ad Valorem Tax Relief.** — The legislature by law may provide for the preservation of cultural, historical, or natural history resources by:

(1) granting exemptions or other relief from state ad valorem taxes on appropriate property so designated in the manner prescribed by law; and

(2) authorizing political subdivisions to grant exemptions or other relief from ad valorem taxes on appropriate property so designated by the political subdivision in the manner prescribed by general law.

[Note. — Sec. 1-f of Art. VIII was added to authorize tax relief to preserve certain cultural, historical or natural history resources. Submitted by the Sixty-fifth Legislature (1977) and adopted in election Nov. 8, 1977.]

Sec. 1-g. **Tax Relief to Encourage Development and Improvement of Property.** — (a) The legislature by general law may authorize cities, towns, and other taxing units to grant exemptions or other relief from ad valorem taxes on property located in a reinvestment zone for the purpose of encouraging development or redevelopment and improvement of the property.

(b) The Legislature by general law may authorize an incorporated city or town to issue bonds or notes to finance the development or redevelopment of an unproductive, underdeveloped, or blighted area within the city or town and to pledge for repayment of those bonds or notes increases in ad valorem tax revenues imposed on property in the area by the city or town and other political subdivisions.

[Note. — Sec. 1-g of Art. VIII was added to encourage development and improvement of certain areas through tax relief. Submitted by the Sixty-seventh Legislature (1981) and adopted in election Nov. 3, 1981.]

Sec. 1-h — **Validation of Assessment Ratio.** — Sec. 26.03, Tax Code, is validated as of January 1, 1980.

[Note. — Sec. 1-h of Art. VIII, an amendment, was added to give validation of Sec. 26.03 of the Tax Code. Submitted by Called Session of the Sixty-seventh Legislature (1982) and adopted in election Nov. 2, 1982.]

Sec. 2. **Occupation Taxes Equal and Uniform; Exemptions Therefrom.** — (a) All occupation taxes shall be equal and uniform upon the same class of subjects within the limits of the authority levying the tax; but the Legislature may, by general laws, exempt from taxation public property used for public purposes; actual places of religious worship, also any property owned by a church or by a strictly religious society for the exclusive use as a dwelling place for the ministry of such church or religious society, and which yields no revenue whatever to such church or religious society; provided that such exemption shall not extend to more property than is reasonably necessary for a dwelling place and in no event more than one acre of land; places of burial not held for private or corporate profit; solar or wind-powered energy devices; all buildings used exclusively and owned by persons or associations of persons for school purposes and the necessary furniture of all schools and property used exclusively and reasonably necessary in conducting any association engaged in promoting the religious, educational and physical development of boys, girls, young men or young women operating under a State or National organization of like character; also, the endowment funds of such institutions of learning and religion not used with a view to profit; and when the same are invested in bonds or mortgages, or in land or other property which

Article VIII — (Cont'd.)

has been and shall hereafter be bought in by such institutions under foreclosure sales made to satisfy or protect such bonds or mortgages, that such exemption of such land and property shall continue only for two years after the purchase of the same at such sale by such institutions and no longer, and institutions of purely public charity; and all laws exempting property from taxation other than the property mentioned in this Section shall be null and void.

(b) The Legislature may, by general law, exempt property owned by a disabled veteran or by the surviving spouse and surviving minor children of a disabled veteran. A disabled veteran is a veteran of the armed services of the United States who is classified as disabled by the Veterans Administration or by a successor to that agency; or the military service in which he served. A veteran who is certified as having a disability of less than 10 per cent is not entitled to an exemption. A veteran having a disability rating of not less than 10 per cent nor more than 30 per cent may be granted an exemption from taxation for property valued at up to $1,500. A veteran having a disability rating of more than 30 per cent but not more than 50 per cent may be granted an exemption from taxation for property valued at up to $2,000. A veteran having a disability rating of more than 50 per cent but not more than 70 per cent may be granted an exemption from taxation for property valued at up to $2,500. A veteran who has a disability rating of more than 70 per cent, or a veteran who has a disability rating of not less than 10 per cent and has attained the age of 65, or a disabled veteran whose disability consists of the loss or loss of use of one or more limbs, total blindness in one or both eyes, or paraplegia, may be granted an exemption from taxation for property valued at up to $3,000. The spouse and children of any member of the United States Armed Forces who loses his life while on active duty will be granted an exemption from taxation for property valued at up to $2,500. A deceased disabled veteran's surviving spouse and children may be granted an exemption which in the aggregate is equal to the exemption to which the decedent was entitled at the time he died.

[Note. — Sec. 2 of Art. VIII has been amended four times as follows: (1) Adding clause with reference to endowment fund. Submitted by the Twenty-ninth Legislature (1905); ratified Nov. 6, 1906, and proclaimed adopted Jan. 7, 1907. (2) Permitting exemption of ministers' dwellings and certain other property of religious organizations, the original amendment having provided only for exemption for "actual places of worship." Submitted by the Fortieth Legislature (1927); ratified Nov. 6, 1928; proclaimed Feb. 6, 1929. (3) To allow certain tax exemptions to disabled veterans, their surviving spouses and surviving minor children and to survivors of members of the armed forces who lose their life while on active duty. Submitted by the Sixty-second Legislature (1971) and adopted in an election Nov. 7, 1972. (4) Authorizing Legislature to exempt from taxation solar and wind-powered energy devices. Submitted by the Sixty-fifth Legislature (1977) and adopted in election Nov. 7, 1978.]

Sec. 3. **Taxes to Be Collected for Public Purposes Only.** — Taxes shall be levied and collected by general laws and for public purposes only.

Sec. 4. **Power to Tax Corporations Not to Be Surrendered.** — The power to tax corporations and corporate property shall not be surrendered or suspended by act of the Legislature, by any contract or grant to which the State shall be a party.

Sec. 5. **Railroad Taxes Due Cities and Towns.** — All property of railroad companies, of whatever description lying or being with the limits of any city or incorporated town within this State, shall bear its proportionate share of municipal taxation, and if any such property shall not have been heretofore rendered, the authorities of the city or town within which it lies shall have power to require its rendition and collect the usual municipal tax thereon, as on other property lying within said municipality.

Sec. 6. **Appropriations; How Made and for What Period.** — No money shall be drawn from the Treasury but in pursuance of specific appropriations made by law; nor shall any appropriation of money be made for a longer term than two years, except by the First Legislature to assemble under this Constitution, which may make the necessary appropriations to carry on the government until the assembling of the Sixteenth Legislature.

Sec. 7. **Special Funds Not to Be Borrowed or Diverted.** — The Legislature shall not have power to borrow, or in any manner divert from its purpose any special fund that may, or ought to, come into the Treasury; and shall make it penal for any person or persons to borrow, withhold or in any manner to divert from its purpose, any special fund or any part thereof.

Sec. 7-a. **Net Motor License Fees and Motor Fuel Tax Revenues Restricted, Except One Fourth of Fuel Taxes to Schools, to Highway Improvement Policing and Administration.** — Subject to legislative appropriation, allocation and direction, all net revenues remaining after payment of all refunds allowed by law and expenses of collection derived from motor vehicle registration fees, and all taxes, except gross production and ad valorem taxes, on motor fuels and lubricants used to propel motor vehicles over public roadways, shall be used for the sole purpose of acquiring rights of way, constructing, maintaining, and policing such public road ways and for the administration of such laws as may be prescribed by the Legislature pertaining to the supervision of traffic and safety on such roads; and for the payment of the principal and interest on county and road district bonds or warrants voted or issued prior to January 2, 1939, and declared eligible prior to January 2, 1945, for payment out of the County and Road District Highway Fund under existing law, provided, however, that one fourth (¼) of such net revenue from the motor fuel tax shall be allocated to the Available School Fund; and provided, however, that the net revenue derived by counties from motor vehicle registration fees shall never be less than the maximum amounts allowed to be retained by each county and the percentage allowed to be retained by each county under the laws in effect on January 1, 1945. Nothing contained herein shall be construed as authorizing the pledging of the State's credit for any purpose.

[Note. — Sec. 7-a of Art. VIII is an added amendment, restricting revenues from motor vehicle registration and motor fuel taxes to the stated purposes of highway improvement, policing and administration. Submitted by the Forty-ninth Legislature (1945), ratified in an election Nov. 5, 1946.]

Sec. 8. **Railroad Property; How Assessed.** — All property of railroad companies shall be assessed, and the taxes collected in the several counties in which said property is situated, including so much of the roadbed and fixtures as shall be in each county. The rolling stock may be assessed in gross in the county where the principal office of the company is located, and the county tax paid upon it shall be apportioned by the Comptroller, in proportion to the distance such road may run through any such county, among the several counties through which the road passes, as part of their tax assets.

Sec. 9. **Rate of State and Municipal Taxation.** — The State tax on property, exclusive of the tax necessary to pay the public debt, and of the taxes provided for the benefit of the public free school, shall never exceed thirty-five cents (35c) on the One Hundred Dollars ($100) valuation; and no county, city or town shall levy a tax rate in excess of Eighty Cents (80c) on the One Hundred Dollars ($100) valuation in any one (1) year for general fund, permanent improvement fund, road and bridge fund and jury fund purposes; provided further that at the time the Commissioners Court meets to levy the annual tax rate for each county it shall levy whatever tax rate may be needed for the four (4) constitutional purposes; namely, general fund, permanent improvement fund, road and bridge fund and jury fund so long as the Court does not impair any outstanding bonds or other obligations and so long as the total of the foregoing tax levies does not exceed Eighty Cents (80c) on the One Hundred Dollars ($100) valuation in any one (1) year. Once the Court has levied the annual tax rate, the same shall remain in force and effect during that taxable year; and the Legislature may also authorize an additional annual ad valorem tax to be levied and collected for the further maintenance of the public roads; provided that a majority of the qualified property tax-paying voters of the county voting at an election to be held for that purpose shall vote such tax, not to exceed fifteen cents (15c) on the One Hundred Dollars ($100) valuation of the property subject to taxation in such county. Any county may put all tax money collected by the county into one general fund, without regard to the purpose or source of each tax. And the Legislature may pass local laws for the maintenance of the public roads and highways, without the local notice required for special or local laws. This section shall not be construed as a limitation of powers delegated to counties, cities or towns by any other section or sections of this Constitution.

[Note. — The foregoing Sec. 9 of Art. VIII has been amended seven times as follows: (1) To lower State tax rate from 50c to 35c, a separate State school tax having been provided by companion amendment, Sec. 3 of Art. VII. Submitted by Eighteenth Legislature (1883), ratified in an election Aug. 14, 1883, and declared adopted Sept. 25, 1883. (2) To authorize Legislature to provide for a 15c local road tax. Submitted by Twenty-first Legislature (1889), ratified in an election Nov. 3, 1890, and declared adopted Dec. 19, 1890. (3) To authorize 15c tax for jurors. Submitted by Twenty-ninth Legislature (1905), ratified in an election Nov. 6, 1906, and declared adopted Jan. 7, 1907. (4) Providing that County Commissioners "may re-allocate the foregoing county taxes by changing the rates provided for any of the foregoing purposes" if approved by "a majority of the qualified property taxpaying voters," but restricting the period to six years, and restricting total to 80c on the $100 valuation. Submitted by Forty-eighth Legislature and adopted in an elec-

Article VIII — (Cont'd.)

tion Nov. 7, 1944. (5) Abolishing ad valorem tax for State general revenue fund purposes, and making other provisions. (See Sec. 1-a of Art. VIII and note thereon.) Submitted by Fiftieth Legislature (1947) and adopted in election Nov. 2, 1948. (6) Giving Commissioners Court authority to levy whatever sums may be necessary for general fund purposes, permanent improvement fund purposes, road and bridge purposes and jury purposes, so long as total of these tax rates does not exceed 80c on the $100 valuation in any one year. Submitted by Fifty-fourth Legislature (1955) and adopted in election Nov. 6, 1956. (7) To allow counties to put all county taxes into one general fund. Submitted by Sixtieth Legislature (1967) and adopted in election Nov. 14, 1967.]

Sec. 10. **Taxes Not to Be Released Except by Two-Thirds Vote of Each House.** — The Legislature shall have no power to release the inhabitants of, or property in, any county, city or town, from the payment of taxes levied for State or county purposes, unless in case of great public calamity in any such county, city or town, when such release may be made by a vote of two-thirds of each house of the Legislature.

Sec. 11. **Where Property Is to Be Assessed.** — All property, whether owned by persons or corporations, shall be assessed for taxation and the taxes paid in the county where situated, but the Legislature may by a two-thirds vote authorize the payment of taxes of non-residents of counties to be made at the office of the Comptroller of Public Accounts. And all lands and other property not rendered for taxation by the owner thereof shall be assessed at its fair value by the proper officer.

[Note. — Sec. 12 of Art. VIII, relating to unorganized counties, was deleted by constitutional amendment in election Aug. 5, 1969.]

Sec. 13. **Tax Sales; Tax Deeds; Redemptions.** — Provision shall be made by the first Legislature for the speedy sale, without the necessity of a suit in court, of a sufficient portion of all lands and other property for the taxes due thereon, and every year thereafter for the sale, in like manner, of all lands and other property upon which the taxes have not been paid; and the deed of conveyance to the purchaser for all lands and other property thus sold shall be held to vest a good and perfect title in the purchaser thereof, subject to be impeached only for actual fraud; provided, that the former owner shall within two years from date of filing for record of purchaser's deed have the right to redeem the land upon the following basis:

(1) Within the first year of the redemption period upon the payment of the amount of money paid for the land, including one ($1) dollar tax deed recording fee and all taxes, penalties, interest and costs paid plus not exceeding twenty-five (25%) percent of the aggregate total;

(2) Within the last year of the redemption period upon the payment of the amount of money paid for the land, including one ($1) dollar tax deed recording fee and all taxes, penalties, interest and costs paid plus not exceeding fifty (50%) percent of the aggregate total.

[Note. — The foregoing Sec. 13 of Art. VIII was amended to insert the provisions for redemption given above for the original clause, which provided for "double the amount of money paid for the land" to be paid by the original owner for redemption. Submitted by the Forty-second Legislature (1931), and adopted in an election Nov. 8, 1932. Proclaimed July 26, 1933.]

Sec. 14. **County Tax Assessor and Collector.** — Except as provided in Sec. 16 of this Article, there shall be elected by the qualified electors of each county an Assessor and Collector of Taxes, who shall hold his office for four years and until his successor is elected and qualified; and such Assessor and Collector of Taxes shall perform all the duties with respect to assessing property for the purpose of taxation and of collecting taxes as may be prescribed by the Legislature.

[Note. — Sec. 14 of Art. VIII was first amended to consolidate offices of Tax Assessor and Tax Collector. (See also Sec. 16.) Submitted by the Forty-second Legislature (1931), and adopted in an election Nov. 8, 1932. Proclaimed Jan. 9, 1933. It was again amended to change term of office from two to four years. Submitted by the Fifty-third Legislature (1953) and adopted in election Nov. 2, 1954.]

Sec. 15. **Tax Liens and Sales.** — The annual assessment made upon landed property shall be a special lien thereon; and all property, both real and personal, belonging to any delinquent taxpayer shall be liable to seizure and sale for the payment of all the taxes and penalties due by such delinquent, and such property may be sold for the payment of the taxes and penalties due by such delinquent, under such regulations as the Legislature may provide.

Sec. 16. **Sheriff to Be County Tax Assessor-Collector in Some Counties.** — The Sheriff of each county, in addition to his other duties, shall be the Assessor and Collector of Taxes therefor. But in counties having ten thousand (10,000) or more inhabitants, to be determined by the last preceding census of the United States, an Assessor and Collector of Taxes shall be elected, as provided in Sec. 14 of this Article and shall hold office for four years and until his successor shall be elected and qualified.

[Note. — Sec. 16 of Art. VIII was first amended to harmonize with section consolidating offices of Assessor and Collector of Taxes. (See also Sec. 14.) Submitted by the Forty-second Legislature (1931) and adopted in an election Nov. 8, 1932. Proclaimed Jan. 9, 1933. It was again amended to change term of office from two to four years. Submitted by the Fifty-third Legislature (1953) and adopted in election Nov. 2, 1954.]

Sec. 16-a. **Assessor-Collector of Taxes in Counties of Less Than Ten Thousand.** — In any county having a population of less than ten thousand (10,000) inhabitants, as determined by last preceding census of the United States, the Commissioners' Court may submit to the qualified property taxpaying voters of such county at an election the question of adding an Assessor-Collector of Taxes to the list of authorized county officials. If a majority of such voters voting in such election shall approve of adding an Assessor-Collector of Taxes to such list, then such official shall be elected at the next General Election for such Constitutional term of office as is provided for other Tax Assessor-Collectors in this State.

[Note. — The foregoing Sec. 16-a of Art. VIII, an amendment, was added for the stated purpose of providing for a Tax Assessor-Collector in counties of less than 10,000 population. Submitted by the Fifty-third Legislature (1953) and adopted in an election Nov. 2, 1954.]

Sec. 17. **Power of Legislature as to Taxes.** — The specification of the objects and subjects of taxation shall not deprive the Legislature of the power to require other subjects or objects to be taxed, in such manner as may be consistent with the principles of taxation fixed in this Constitution.

Sec. 18. **Equalization of Taxes.** — (a) The Legislature shall provide for equalizing, as near as may be, the valuation of all property subject to or rendered for taxation and may also provide for the classification of all lands with reference to their value in the several counties.

(b) A single appraisal within each county of all property subject to ad valorem taxation by the county and all other taxing units located therein shall be provided by general law. The Legislature, by general law, may authorize appraisals outside a county when political subdivisions are situated in more than one county or when two or more counties elect to consolidate appraisal services.

(c) The Legislature, by general law, shall provide for a single board of equalization for each appraisal entity consisting of qualified persons residing within the territory appraised by that entity. Members of the board of equalization may not be elected officials of the county or of the governing body of a taxing unit.

(d) The Legislature shall prescribe by general law the methods, timing and administrative process for implementing the requirements of this section.

[Note. — Sec. 18 of Art. VIII was amended to provide for a single appraisal and a single board of equalization within each county for ad valorem tax purposes. Submitted by the Sixty-sixth Legislature (1979) and adopted in election Nov. 4, 1980.]

Sec. 19. **Farm Products in the Hands of the Producer Exempt From All Taxation.** — Farm products, livestock, and poultry in the hands of the producer, and family supplies for home and farm use, are exempt from all taxation until otherwise directed by a two-thirds vote of all the members *elect to both houses of the Legislature.

*Explanatory Note. — Expressed thus in official draft of Constitution.

[Note. — The foregoing Sec. 19 of Art. VIII, an amendment, was added for the stated purpose of exempting farm products from taxation. Submitted by the Sixteenth Legislature (1879); ratified in an election Sept. 2, 1879, and declared adopted Oct. 14, 1879. It was amended to change the wording to include livestock and poultry with farm products as exempt from taxation. Submitted by the Sixty-seventh Legislature (1981) and adopted in election Nov. 3, 1981.]

Sec. 19-a. **Farm Implements Exempt From Taxation.** — Implements of husbandry that are used in the production of farm or ranch products are exempt from ad valorem taxation.

[Note. — The foregoing Sec. 19-a of Art. VIII, an amendment, was added to exempt implements of farm husbandry from ad valorem taxation. Submitted by Called Session of

Article VIII — (Cont'd.); Article IX

the Sixty-seventh Legislature (1982) and adopted in election Nov. 2, 1982.]

Sec. 20. Limiting Ad Valorem Tax Assessment; Discount for Prompt Payment of Taxes. —

No property of any kind in this State shall ever be assessed for ad valorem taxes at a greater value than its fair cash market value nor shall any Board of Equalization of any governmental or political subdivision or taxing district within this State fix the value of any property for tax purposes at more than its fair cash market value; provided, that in order to encourage the prompt payment of taxes, the Legislature shall have the power to provide that the taxpayer shall be allowed by the State and all governmental and political subdivisions and taxing districts of the State a three per cent discount on ad valorem taxes due the State or due any governmental or political subdivision or taxing district of the State if such taxes are paid ninety days before the date when they would otherwise become delinquent; and the taxpayer shall be allowed a two per cent discount on said taxes if paid sixty days before said taxes would become delinquent; and the taxpayer shall be allowed a one per cent discount if said taxes are paid thirty days before they would otherwise become delinquent. This amendment shall be effective Jan. 1, 1939. The Legislature shall pass necessary laws for the proper administration of this Section.

[Note. — The foregoing Sec. 20 of Art. VIII, an amendment, was added (1) to restrict assessed value to true market value, and (2) to provide for stated discounts for prepayment of taxes. Adopted in an election Aug. 23, 1937.]

Sec. 21. Limitation on Property Taxes. —

(a) Subject to any exceptions prescribed by general law, the total amount of property taxes imposed by a political subdivision in any year may not exceed the total amount of property taxes imposed by that subdivision in the preceding year unless the governing body of the subdivision gives notice of its intent to consider an increase in taxes and holds a public hearing on the proposed increase before it increases those total taxes. The legislature shall prescribe by law the form, content, timing, and methods of giving the notice and the rules for the conduct of the hearing.

(b) In calculating the total amount of taxes imposed in the current year for the purposes of Subsection (a) of this section, the taxes on property in territory added to the political subdivision since the preceding year and on new improvements that were not taxable in the preceding year are excluded. In calculating the total amount of taxes imposed in the preceding year for the purposes of Subsection (a) of this section, the taxes imposed on real property that is not taxable by the subdivision in the current year are excluded.

(c) The Legislature by general law shall require that, subject to reasonable exceptions, a property owner be given notice of a revaluation of his property and a reasonable estimate of the amount of taxes that would be imposed on his property if the total amount of property taxes for the subdivision were not increased according to any law enacted pursuant to Subsection (a) of this section. The notice must be given before the procedures required in Subsection (a) are instituted.

[Note.—The foregoing Sec. 21 of Art. VIII, an amendment, was added to limit increases in property revaluation and to prescribe method of giving notice before property revaluated. (See also Sec. 1, Sec. 1-b and Sec. 23 of Art. VIII.) Submitted by the Sixty-fifth Legislature (1977) and adopted in election Nov. 7, 1978. It was further amended to change wording of administrative procedures in notifying property owners. (See also Subsection (e) of Section 1-b of Art. VIII.) Submitted by the Sixty-seventh Legislature (1981) and adopted in election Nov. 3, 1981.]

Sec. 22. State Tax Revenues. —

(a) In no biennium shall the rate of growth of appropriations from state tax revenues not dedicated by this constitution exceed the estimated rate of growth of the state's economy. The Legislature shall provide by general law procedures to implement this subsection.

(b) If the Legislature by adoption of a resolution approved by a record vote of a majority of the members of each house finds that an emergency exists and identifies the nature of the emergency, the Legislature may provide for appropriations in excess of the amount authorized by Subsection (a) of this section. The excess authorized under this subsection may not exceed the amount specified in the resolution.

(c) In no case shall appropriations exceed revenues as provided in Article III, Sec. 49-a, of this constitution. Nothing in this section shall be construed to alter, amend, or repeal Article III, Sec. 49-a, of this constitution.

[Note.—The foregoing Sec. 22 of Art. VIII, an amendment, was added to limit the rate of growth of appropriations from state tax revenues; and to provide for emergency spending by state. (See also Sec. 49-a of Art. III.

Submitted by the Sixty-fifth Legislature (1977) and adopted in election Nov. 7, 1978.]

Sec. 23. No Statewide Real Property Appraisal. —

(a) There shall be no statewide appraisal of real property for ad valorem tax purposes; however, this shall not preclude formula distribution of tax revenues to political subdivisions of the state.

(b) Administrative and judicial enforcement of uniform standards and procedures for appraisal of property for ad valorem tax purposes, as prescribed by general law, shall originate in the county where the tax is imposed, except that the Legislature may provide by general law for political subdivisions with boundaries extending outside the county.

[Note. — The foregoing Sec. 23 of Art. VIII, an amendment, was added to prohibit a statewide appraisal of real property for ad valorem tax purposes; but allows local subdivisions to administer tax rate. (See also Sec. 1, Sec. 1-b, Sec. 21 of Art. VIII.) Submitted by the Sixty-fifth Legislature (1977) and adopted in election Nov. 7, 1978.]

ARTICLE IX. — COUNTIES

Sec. 1. Creation and Organization of Counties; Changing of County Lines. —

The Legislature shall have power to create counties for the convenience of the people, subject to the following provisions:

First. In the territory of the State exterior to all counties now existing, no new counties shall be created with a less area than 900 square miles in a square form, unless prevented by pre-existing boundary lines. Should the State lines render this impracticable in border counties, the area may be less. The territory referred to may, at any time, in whole or in part, be divided into counties in advance of population and attached for judicial and land surveying purposes to the most convenient organized county or counties.

Second. Within the territory of any county or counties now existing, no new county shall be created with a less area than 700 square miles, nor shall any such county now existing be reduced to a less area than 700 square miles. No new counties shall be created so as to approach nearer than twelve miles of the county seat of any county from which it may, in whole or in part, be taken. Counties of a less area than 900, but of 700 or more square miles, within counties now existing, may be created by a two-thirds vote of each house of the Legislature, taken by yeas and nays, and entered on the journals. Any county now existing may be reduced to an area of not less than 700 square miles by a like two-thirds vote. When any part of a county is stricken off and attached to or created into another county, the part stricken off shall be holden for and obliged to pay its proportion of all the liabilities then existing of the county from which it was taken, in such manner as may be prescribed by law.

Third. No part of any existing county shall be detached from it and attached to another existing county until the proposition for such change shall have been submitted, in such manner as may be provided by law, to a vote of the electors of both counties, and shall have received a majority of those voting on the question in each.

Sec. 1-a. Regulation of Travel on Gulf Coast Beaches. —

The Legislature may authorize the governing body of any county bordering on the Gulf of Mexico or the tidewater limits thereof to regulate and restrict the speed, parking and travel of motor vehicles on beaches available to the public by virtue of public right and the littering of such beaches.

Nothing in this amendment shall increase the rights of any riparian or littoral landowner with regard to beaches available to the public by virtue of public right or submerged lands.

The Legislature may enact any laws not inconsistent with this Section which it may deem necessary to permit said counties to implement, enforce and administer the provisions contained herein.

[Note. — The foregoing Sec. 1-a of Art. IX, an amendment, was added to authorize regulation of travel on Gulf Coast beaches open to the public. Submitted by the Fifty-seventh Legislature (1961) and adopted in election Nov. 6, 1962.]

County Seats

Sec. 2. How County Seats Are Created and Changed. —

The Legislature shall pass laws regulating the manner of removing county seats, but no county seat situated within five miles of the geographical center of the county shall be removed except by a vote of two-thirds of all electors voting on the subject. A majority of such electors, however, voting at such election, may remove a county seat from a point more than five miles from a geographical center of the county to a point within five miles of such center, in either case the center to be determined by a certificate from the Commissioner of the General Land Office.

[Note. — Sec. 3 of Art. IX, relating to home rule, was

Article IX — (Cont'd.)

deleted by constitutional amendment in election Aug. 5, 1969.]

Sec. 4. County-Wide Hospital Districts.

— The Legislature may by law authorize the creation of county-wide Hospital Districts in counties having a population in excess of 190,000 and in Galveston County, with power to issue bonds for the purchase, acquisition, construction, maintenance and operation of any county-owned hospital, or where the hospital system is jointly operated by a county and city within the county, and to provide for the transfer to the county-wide hospital district of the title to any land, buildings or equipment, jointly or separately owned, and for the assumption by the district of any outstanding bonded indebtedness theretofore issued by any county or city for the establishment of hospitals or hospital facilities; to levy a tax not to exceed seventy-five (75c) cents on the One Hundred ($100.00) Dollars valuation of all taxable property within such district, provided, however, that such district shall be approved at an election held for that purpose, and that only qualified, property taxpaying voters in such county shall vote therein; provided further, that such hospital district shall assume full responsibility for providing medical and hospital care to needy inhabitants of the county, and thereafter such county and cities therein shall not levy any other tax for hospital purposes; and provided further that should such hospital district construct, maintain and support a hospital or hospital system, that the same shall never become a charge against the State of Texas, nor shall any direct appropriation ever be made by the Legislature for the construction, maintenance or improvement of the said hospital or hospitals. Should the Legislature enact enabling laws in anticipation of the adoption of this amendment, such acts shall not be invalid because of their anticipatory character.

[Note. — The foregoing Sec. 4 of Art. IX, an amendment, was added to the Constitution for the purpose of providing for county-wide hospital districts. Submitted by the Fifty-third Legislature (1953) and adopted in election Nov. 2, 1954.]

Sec. 5 (a). The Legislature may by law authorize the creation of two hospital districts, one to be coextensive with and have the same boundaries as the incorporated City of Amarillo, as such boundaries now exist or as they may hereafter be lawfully extended, and the other to be coextensive with Wichita County.

If such district or districts are created, they may be authorized to levy a tax not to exceed Seventy-five Cents (75c) on the One Hundred Dollars ($100.00) valuation of taxable property within the district; provided, however no tax may be levied until approved by a majority vote of the participating resident qualified property taxpaying voters who have duly rendered their property for taxation. The maximum rate of tax may be changed at subsequent elections so long as obligations are not impaired, and not to exceed the maximum limit of Seventy-five Cents (75c) per One Hundred Dollars ($100.00) valuation, and no election shall be required by subsequent changes in the boundaries of the City of Amarillo.

If such tax is authorized, no political subdivision or municipality within or having the same boundaries as the district may levy a tax for medical or hospital care for needy individuals, nor shall they maintain or erect hospital facilities, but the district shall by resolution assume all such responsibilities and shall assume all of the liabilities and obligations (including bonds and warrants) of such subdivisions or municipalities or both. The maximum tax rate submitted shall be sufficient to discharge such obligations, liabilities, and responsibilities, and to maintain and operate the hospital system, and the Legislature may authorize the district to issue tax bonds for the purpose of the purchase, construction, acquisition, repair or renovation of improvements and initially equipping the same, and such bonds shall be payable from said Seventy-five Cents (75c) tax. The Legislature shall provide for transfer of title to properties to the district.

b. The Legislature may by law permit the County of Potter (in which the City of Amarillo is partially located) to render financial aid to that district by paying a part of the expenses of operating and maintaining the system and paying a part of the debts of the district (whether assumed or created by the district) and may authorize the levy of a tax not to exceed Ten Cents (10c) per One Hundred Dollars ($100.00) valuation (in addition to other taxes permitted by this Constitution) upon all property within the county but without the City of Amarillo at the time such levy is made for such purposes. If such tax is authorized, the district shall by resolution assume the responsibilities, obligations, and liabilities of the county in the manner and to the extent hereinabove provided for political subdivisions having boundaries coextensive with the district, and the county shall not thereafter levy taxes (other than herein provided) for hospital purposes nor for providing hospital care for needy individuals of the county.

c. The Legislature may by law authorize the creation of a hospital district within Jefferson County, the boundaries of which shall include only the area comprising the Jefferson County Drainage District No. 7 and the Port Arthur Independent School District, as such boundaries existed on the first day of January, 1957, with the power to issue bonds for the sole purpose of purchasing a site for, and the construction and initial equipping of, a hospital system, and with the power to levy a tax of not to exceed Seventy-five Cents (75c) on the One Hundred Dollars ($100) valuation of property therein for the purpose of paying the principal and interest on such bonds.

The creation of such hospital district shall not be final until approved at an election by a majority of the resident property taxpaying voters voting at said election who have duly rendered their property for taxation upon the tax rolls of either said Drainage or said School District, nor shall such bonds be issued or such tax be levied until so approved by such voters.

The district shall not have the power to levy any tax for maintenance or operation of the hospital or facilities, but shall contract with other political subdivisions of the state or private individuals, associations, or corporations for such purposes.

If the district hereinabove authorized is finally created, no other hospital district may be created embracing any part of the territory within its boundaries, but the Legislature by law may authorize the creation of a hospital district incorporating herein the remainder of Jefferson County, having the powers and duties and with the limitations presently provided by Art. IX, Section 4, of the Constitution of Texas, except that such district shall be confirmed at an election wherein the resident qualified property taxpaying voters who have duly rendered their property within such proposed district for taxation on the county rolls, shall be authorized to vote. A majority of those participating in the election voting in favor of the district shall be necessary for its confirmation and for bonds to be issued.

[Note. — The foregoing Sec. 5 of Art. IX, an amendment, was added to provide for the creation of special hospital districts and authorizing the levying of taxes for their support. Submitted by the Fifty-fifth Legislature (1957) and adopted in an election Nov. 4, 1958.]

Sec. 6. Lamar County Hospital District Abolished.

— On the effective date of this Amendment, the Lamar County Hospital District is abolished. The Commissioners Court of Lamar County may provide for the transfer or for the disposition of the assets of the Lamar County Hospital District.

[Note. — the foregoing Sec. 6 of Art. IX, an amendment, was added to authorize creation of a hospital district in Lamar County and authorizing the levying of taxes for its support. Submitted by the Fifty-sixth Legislature (1959) and adopted in an election Nov. 8, 1960. It was amended to abolish the hospital district. Submitted by the Sixty-second Legislature (1971) and adopted in an election Nov. 7, 1972.]

Sec. 7. Hidalgo County Hospital District; Creation, Tax Rate.

— The Legislature may by law authorize the creation of a Hospital District coextensive with Hidalgo County, having the powers and duties and with the limitations presently provided in Art. IX, Sec. 5 (a), of the Constitution of Texas, as it applies to Hidalgo County, except that the maximum rate of tax that the said Hidalgo County Hospital District may be authorized to levy shall be ten cents (10c) per One Hundred Dollars ($100) valuation of taxable property within the District subject to district taxation.

[Note. — The foregoing Sec. 7 of Art. IX, an amendment, was added to authorize creation of a hospital district in Hidalgo County and authorizing the levying of taxes for its support. Submitted by the Fifty-sixth Legislature (1959) and adopted in an election Nov. 8, 1960.]

Sec. 8. Comanche County Hospital District; Creation, Tax Rate.

— The Legislature may by law authorize the creation of a Hospital District to be coextensive with the limits of County Commissioners Precinct No. 4 of Comanche County, Texas.

If such District is created, it may be authorized to levy a tax not to exceed seventy-five cents (75c) on the One Hundred Dollar ($100) valuation of taxable property within the District; provided, however, no tax may be levied until approved by a majority vote of the participating resident qualified property taxpaying voters who have duly rendered their property for taxation. The maximum rate of tax may be changed at subsequent elections so long as obligations are not impaired, and not to exceed the maximum limit of seventy-five cents (75c) per One Hundred Dollar ($100) valuation, and no election shall be required by subsequent changes in the boundaries of the Commissioners Precinct No. 4 of Comanche County.

If such tax is authorized, no political subdivision or municipality within or having the same boundaries as the District may levy a tax for medical or hospital care for needy

Article IX — (Cont'd.)

individuals, nor shall they maintain or erect hospital facilities, but the District shall by resolution assume all such responsibilities and shall assume all of the liabilities and obligations (including bonds and warrants) of such subdivisions or municipalities or both. The maximum tax rate submitted shall be sufficient to discharge such obligations, liabilities, and responsibilities and to maintain and operate the hospital system, and the Legislature may authorize the District to issue tax bonds for the purpose of the purchase, construction, acquisition, repair or renovation of improvements and initially equipping the same, and such bonds shall be payable from said seventy-five cents (75c) tax. The Legislature shall provide for transfer of title to properties to the District.

(b) The Legislature may by law permit the County of Comanche to render financial aid to that District by paying a part of the expenses of operating and maintaining the system and paying a part of the debts of the District (whether assumed or created by the District) and may authorize the levy of a tax not to exceed ten cents (10c) per One Hundred Dollar ($100) valuation (in addition to other taxes permitted by this Constitution) upon all property within the County but without the County Commissioners Precinct No. 4 of Comanche County at the time such levy is made for such purposes. If such tax is authorized, the District shall by resolution assume the responsibilities, obligations and liabilities of the County in the manner and to the extent hereinabove provided for political subdivisions having boundaries coextensive with the District, and the County shall not hereafter levy taxes (other than herein provided) for hospital purposes nor for providing hospital care for needy individuals of the county.

(c) Should the Legislature enact enabling laws in anticipation of the adoption of this amendment, such Acts shall not be invalid because of their anticipatory character.

[Note. — The foregoing Sec. 8 of Art. IX, an amendment, was added to authorize creation of a hospital district in Comanche County and authorizing the levying of taxes for its support. Submitted by the Fifty-sixth Legislature (1959) and adopted in an election Nov. 8, 1960.]

Sec. 9. The Legislature may by law provide for the creation, establishment, maintenance and operation of hospital districts composed of one or more counties or all or any part of one or more counties with power to issue bonds for the purchase, construction, acquisition, repair or renovation of buildings and improvements and equipping same, for hospital purposes; providing for the transfer to the hospital district of the title to any land, buildings, improvements and equipment located wholly within the district which may be jointly or separately owned by any city, town or county, providing that any district so created shall assume full responsibility for providing medical and hospital care to its needy inhabitants and assume the outstanding indebtedness incurred by cities, towns and counties for hospital purposes prior to the creation of the district, if same are located wholly within its boundaries, and a pro rata portion of such indebtedness based upon the then last approved tax assessment rolls of the included cities, towns and counties if less than all the territory thereof is included within the district boundaries; providing that after its creation no other municipality or political subdivision shall have the power to levy taxes or issue bonds or other obligations for hospital purposes or for providing medical care within the boundaries of the district; providing for the levy of annual taxes at a rate not to exceed seventy-five cents (75c) on the one hundred dollar valuation of all taxable property within such district for the purpose of meeting the requirements of the district's bonds, the indebtedness assumed by it and its maintenance and operating expenses, providing that such district shall not be created or such tax authorized unless approved by a majority of the qualified property taxpaying electors thereof voting at an election called for the purpose; and providing further that the support and maintenance of the district's hospital system shall never become a charge against or obligation of the State of Texas nor shall any direct appropriation be made by the Legislature for the construction, maintenance or improvement of any of the facilities of such district.

Provided, however, that no district shall be created except by act of the Legislature and then only after thirty (30) days' public notice to the district affected, and in no event may the Legislature provide for a district to be created without the affirmative vote of a majority of the taxpaying voters in the district concerned.

The Legislature may also provide for the dissolution of hospital districts provided that a process is afforded by statute for:

(1) Determining the desire of a majority of the qualified voters within the district to dissolve it;

(2). Disposing of or transferring the assets, if any, of the district; and

(3) Satisfying the debts and bond obligations, if any, of the district, in such manner as to protect the interest of the

citizens within the district, including their collective property rights in the assets and property of the district, provided, however, that any grant from federal funds, however dispensed, shall be considered an obligation to be repaid in satisfaction and provided that no election to dissolve shall be held more often than once each year. In such connection, the statute shall provide against disposal or transfer of the assets of the district except for due compensation unless such assets are transferred to another governmental agency, such as a county, embracing such district and using such transferred assets in such a way as to benefit citizens formerly within the district.

[Note.—The foregoing Sec. 9 of Art. IX, an amendment, was added to provide for the creation of special hospital districts and authorizing the levying of taxes for their support. Submitted by the Fifty-seventh Legislature (1961) and adopted in an election Nov. 6, 1962. It was further amended to provide method of dissolution of hospital districts. Submitted by the Fifty-ninth Legislature (1965) and adopted in election Nov. 8, 1966.]

Sec. 11. The Legislature may by law authorize the creation of hospital districts in Ochiltree, Castro, Hansford and Hopkins Counties, each district to be coextensive with the limits of such county.

If any such district is created, it may be authorized to levy a tax not to exceed Seventy-five Cents (75c) on the One Hundred Dollar ($100) valuation of taxable property within the district; provided, however, that no tax may be levied until approved by a majority vote of the participating resident qualified property taxpaying voters who have duly rendered their property for taxation. The maximum rate of tax may be changed at subsequent elections so long as obligations are not impaired, and not to exceed the maximum limit of Seventy-five Cents (75c) per One Hundred Dollar ($100) valuation.

If such tax is authorized, no political subdivision or municipality within or having the same boundaries as the district may levy a tax for medical or hospital care for needy individuals, nor shall they maintain or erect hospital facilities, but the district shall by resolution assume all such responsibilities and shall assume all of the liabilities and obligations (including bonds and warrants) of such subdivisions or municipalities or both. The maximum tax rate submitted shall be sufficient to discharge obligations, liabilities, and responsibilities, and to maintain and operate the hospital system, and the Legislature may authorize the district to issue tax bonds for the purpose of the purchase, construction, acquisition, repair or renovation of improvements and initially equipping the same, and such bonds shall be payable from said Seventy-five Cent (75c) tax. The Legislature shall provide for transfer of title to properties to the district.

[Note.—The foregoing Sec. 11 of Art. IX, an amendment, was added to provide for the creation of special hospital districts and to authorize the levying of taxes for their support. It is obviously misnumbered, as there is no Sec. 10 of Art. IX. Submitted by the Fifty-seventh Legislature (1961) and adopted in an election Nov. 6, 1962.]

Sec. 12. **Establishment of Airport Authorities.** — The Legislature may by law provide for the creation, establishment, maintenance and operation of Airport Authorities composed of one or more counties, with power to issue general obligation bonds, revenue bonds, either or both of them, for the purchase, acquisition by the exercise of the power of eminent domain or otherwise, construction, reconstruction, repair or renovation of any airport or airports, landing fields and runways, airport buildings, hangars, facilities, equipment, fixtures, and any and all property, real or personal, necessary to operate, equip and maintain an airport; shall provide for the option by the governing body of the city or cities whose airport facilities are served by certificated airlines and whose facility or some interest therein, is proposed to be or has been acquired by the authority, to either appoint or elect a board of directors of said authority; if the directors are appointed such appointment shall be made by the County Commissioners Court after consultation with and consent of the governing body or bodies of such city or cities, and if the board of directors is elected they shall be elected by the qualified taxpaying voters of the county which chooses to elect the directors to represent that county, such directors shall serve without compensation for a term fixed by the Legislature not to exceed six (6) years, and shall be selected on the basis of the proportionate population of each county based upon the last preceding federal census, and shall be a resident or residents of such county; provide that no county shall have less than one (1) member on the board of directors; provide for the holding of an election in each county proposing the creation of an authority to be called by the Commissioners Court or Commissioners Courts, as the case may be, upon petition of five percent (5%) of the qualified taxpaying voters within the county or counties, said elections to be held on the same day if more than one county is

Article IX — (Cont'd.); Article X and XI

included, provided that no more than one (1) such election may be called in a county until after the expiration of one (1) year; in the event such an election has failed, and thereafter only upon a petition of ten percent (10%) of the qualified taxpaying voters being presented to the Commissioners Court or Commissioners Courts of the county or counties in which such an election has failed, and in the event that two or more counties vote on the proposition of the creation of an authority therein, the proposition shall not be deemed to carry unless the majority of the qualified taxpaying voters in each county voting thereon vote in favor thereof; provided, however, that an Airport Authority may be created and be composed of the county or counties that vote in favor of its creation if separate propositions are submitted to the voters of each county so that they may vote for a two or more county authority or a single county authority; provide for the appointment by the board of directors of an assessor and collector of taxes in the authority, whether constituted of one or more counties, whose duty it shall be to assess all taxable property, both real and personal, and collect the taxes thereon, based upon the tax rolls approved by the board of directors, the tax to be levied not to exceed seventy-five cents (75c) per one hundred dollars ($100) assessed valuation of the property, provided, however, that the property of state regulated common carriers required by law to pay a tax upon intangible assets shall not be subject to taxation by the authority, said taxable property shall be assessed on a valuation not to exceed the market value and shall be equal and uniform throughout the authority as is otherwise provided by the Constitution; the Legislature shall authorize the purchase or acquisition by the authority of any existing airport facility publicly owned and financed and served by certificated airlines, in fee or of any interest therein, or to enter into any lease agreement therefor, upon such terms and conditions as may be mutually agreeable to the authority and the owner of such facilities, or authorize the acquisition of same through the exercise of the power of eminent domain, and in the event of such acquisition, if there are any general obligation bonds that the owner of the publicly owned airport facility has outstanding, the same shall be fully assumed by the authority and sufficient taxes levied by the authority to discharge said outstanding indebtedness; and likewise any city or owner that has outstanding revenue bonds where the revenues of the airport have been pledged or said bonds constitute a lien against the airport facilities, the authority shall assume and discharge all the obligations of the city under the ordinances and bond indentures under which said revenue bonds have been issued and sold. Any city which owns airport facilities not serving certificated airlines which are not purchased or acquired or taken over as herein provided by such authority, shall have the power to operate the same under the existing laws or as the same may hereafter be amended. Any such authority when created may be granted the power and authority to promulgate, adopt and enforce appropriate zoning regulations to protect the airport from hazards and obstructions which would interfere with the use of the airport and its facilities for landing and takeoff; an additional county or counties may be added to an existing authority if a petition of five percent (5%) of the qualified taxpaying voters is filed with an election is called by the Commissioners Court of the county or counties seeking admission to an authority and the vote is favorable, then admission may be granted to such county or counties by the board of directors of the then existing authority upon such terms and conditions as they may agree upon and evidenced by a resolution approved by two-thirds (⅔) of the then existing board of directors, provided, however, the county or counties that may be so added to the then existing authority shall be given representation on the board of directors by adding additional directors in proportion to their population according to the last preceding federal census.

[Note.—The foregoing Sec. 12 was added to provide by law for the establishment of airport authorities. Submitted by the Fifty-ninth Legislature (1965) and adopted in election Nov. 8, 1966.]

Sec. 13. **Mental Health Services.** — Notwithstanding any other section of this article, the Legislature in providing for the creation, establishment, maintenance, and operation of a hospital district, shall not be required to provide that such district shall assume full responsibility for the establishment, maintenance, support, or operation of mental health services or mental retardation services including the operation of any community mental health centers, community mental retardation centers or community health and mental retardation centers which may exist or be thereafter established within the boundaries of such district, nor shall the Legislature be required to provide that such district shall assume full responsibility of public health department units and clinics and related public health activities or services, and the Legislature shall not be required to restrict the power of any municipality or political subdivision to levy taxes or issue bonds or other obligations or to expend

public moneys for the establishment, maintenance, support, or operation of mental health services, mental retardation services, public health units or clinics or related public health activities or services or the operation of such community mental health or mental retardation centers within the boundaries of the hospital districts; and unless a statute creating a hospital district shall expressly prohibit participation by any entity other than the hospital district in the establishment, maintenance, or support of mental health services, mental retardation services, public health units or clinics or related public health activities within or partly within the boundaries of any hospital district, any municipality or any other political subdivision or state-supported entity within the hospital district may participate in the establishment, maintenance, and support of mental health services, mental retardation services, public health units and clinics and related public health activities and may levy taxes, issue bonds or other obligations, and expend public moneys for such purposes as provided by law.

[Note.—The foregoing Sec. 13 of Art. IX, an amendment, was added to permit municipalities and other political subdivisions within hospital districts to participate in establishment, maintenance, support or operation of mental health, mental retardation or public health services. Submitted by the Sixtieth Legislature (1967) and adopted in election Nov. 11, 1967.]

ARTICLE X. — RAILROADS

[Note.—All of Art. X relating to railroads, except Sec. 2, was deleted by constitutional amendment in election Aug. 5, 1969.]

*Article [Sec.] 2. **Public Highways; Common Carriers; Duty of the Legislature; Fixing Rates.** — Railroads heretofore constructed or which may hereafter be constructed in this State are hereby declared public highways and railroad companies common carriers. The Legislature shall pass laws to regulate railroad freight and passenger tariffs to correct abuses, and prevent unjust discrimination and extortion in the rates of freight and passenger tariffs on the different railroads in this State, and enforce the same by adequate penalties; and to the further accomplishments of these objects and purposes may provide and establish all requisite means and agencies invested with such powers as may be deemed adequate and advisable.

[Note.—The foregoing *"Article Sec. 2" of Art. X is an amended section, the amendment being in the last clause which permitted establishment of the Railroad Commission of Texas. Submitted by the Twenty-first Legislature (1889), ratified in an election Nov. 4, 1890, and declared adopted Dec. 19, 1890.]

*Explanatory Note.—The legislative resolution submitting this amendment erroneously used the word, "Article," instead of the usual abbreviation, "Sec." Order used above is according to official draft of the Constitution.

ARTICLE XI. — MUNICIPAL CORPORATIONS

Sec. 1. **Counties Are Legal Subdivisions of the State.** — The several counties of this State are hereby recognized as legal subdivisions of the State.

Sec. 2. **Public Buildings and Roads.** — The construction of jails, courthouses and bridges and the establishment of county poorhouses and farms and the laying out, construction and repairing of county roads shall be provided for by general laws.

Sec. 3. **No County or Municipal Corporation Shall Become a Subscriber to the Capital Stock of Any Private Corporation or Make Any Donation to the Same.** — No county, city or other municipal corporation shall hereafter become a subscriber to the capital of any private corporation or association, or make any appropriation or donation to the same, or in any wise loan its credit; but this shall not be construed to in any way affect any obligation heretofore undertaken pursuant to law.

Sec. 4. **Cities and Towns Having a Population of 5,000 or Less Inhabitants to Be Chartered by General Laws; Dues to Be Collected in Current Money.** — Cities and towns having a population of 5,000 or less may be chartered alone by general laws. They may levy, assess and collect such taxes as may be authorized by law, but no tax for any purpose shall ever be lawful for any one year which shall exceed 1½ percent of the taxable property of such city; and all taxes shall be collectible only in current money, and all licenses and occupation taxes levied, and all fines, forfeitures and penalties accruing to said cities and towns shall be collectible only in current money.

[Note.—The foregoing Sec. 4 of Art. XI has been twice amended, as follows: (1) To provide that towns of 5,000 or less (instead of 10,000 or less, as provided by the original section) may be chartered alone by general law. Submitted by the Thirty-first Legislature (1909), ratified in an election Aug. 3, 1909, and declared adopted Sept. 24, 1909. (2) To authorize a maximum tax rate, in towns of 5,000 or less, of 1½ percent of taxable values in lieu of the originally spec-

Article XI — (Cont'd.); Article XII, XIII and XIV

fied maximum of one fourth of 1 percent. Submitted by the Thirty-sixth Legislature (1919) and adopted at election of Nov. 2, 1920.]

Sec. 5. **Cities of More Than 5,000 Inhabitants May by a Majority Vote of the Qualified Voters Adopt Their Own Charter; Limitation as to Taxation and Debt.** — Cities having more than five thousand (5,000) inhabitants may, by a majority vote of the qualified voters of said city, at an election held for that purpose, adopt or amend their charters, subject to such limitations as may be prescribed by the Legislature, and providing that no charter or any ordinance passed under said charter shall contain any provision inconsistent with the Constitution of the State or of the general laws enacted by the Legislature of this State; said cities may levy, assess and collect such taxes as may be authorized by law or by their charters; but no tax for any purpose shall ever be lawful for any one year which shall exceed 2½ percent of the taxable property of such city, and no debt shall ever be created by any city unless at the same time provision be made to assess and collect annually a sufficient sum to pay the interest thereon and creating a sinking fund of at least 2 percent thereon; and provided, further, that no city charter shall be altered, amended or repealed oftener than every two years.

[Note.—The foregoing Sec. 5 of Art. XI has been twice amended, as follows: (1) To authorize towns of more than 5,000 population (instead of more than 10,000, as provided in the original section) to be chartered by special act, and allowing in such cities a maximum tax rate of 2½ percent. Submitted by the Thirty-first Legislature (1909), ratified in an election Aug. 3, 1909, and proclaimed Sept. 24, 1909. (2) To grant home rule to cities of more than 5,000 population. Submitted by the Thirty-second Legislature (1911), adopted at election of Nov. 5, 1912, and proclaimed Dec. 30, 1912.]

Sec. 6. **Municipal Taxation.** — Counties, cities, and towns are authorized, in such mode as may now or may hereafter be provided by law, to levy, assess and collect the taxes necessary to pay the interest and provide a sinking fund to satisfy any indebtedness heretofore legally made and undertaken; but all such taxes shall be assessed and collected separately from that levied, assessed and collected for current expenses of municipal government and shall, when levied, specify in the act of levying the purpose therefor; and such taxes may be paid in the coupons, bonds or other indebtedness for the payment of which such tax may have been levied.

Sec. 7. **Taxation of Seawalls, Etc.; Restrictions and Limitations; Eminent Domain.** — All counties and cities bordering on the coast of the Gulf of Mexico are hereby authorized upon a vote of the majority of the resident property taxpayers voting thereon at an election called for such purpose, to levy and collect such tax for construction of seawalls, breakwaters or sanitary purposes, as may now or may hereafter be authorized by law, and may create a debt for such works and issue bonds in evidence thereof. But no debt for any purpose shall ever be incurred in any manner by any city or county unless provision is made at the time of creating the same, for levying and collecting a sufficient tax to pay the interest thereon and provide at least 2 percent as a sinking fund; and the condemnation of the right of way for the erection of such work shall be fully provided for.

[Note.—The foregoing Sec. 7 of Art. XI was amended to simplify language describing electors' qualifications. Submitted by the Forty-second Legislature (1931), adopted in election Nov. 8, 1932. Proclaimed Jan. 9, 1933. Further amended to provide that a majority of resident property taxpayers may vote to issue bonds for construction of seawalls and breakwaters. Submitted by the Sixty-third Legislature (1973) and adopted in election Nov. 6, 1973.]

Sec. 8. **State Aid for Seawalls, Etc.** — The counties and cities on the Gulf Coast being subject to calamitous overflows, and a very large proportion of the general revenue being derived from those otherwise prosperous localities.* The Legislature is specially authorized to aid, by donation of such portion of the public domain as may be deemed proper, and in such mode as may be provided by law, the construction of seawalls or breakwaters, such aid to be proportioned to the extent and value of the works constructed, or to be constructed, in any locality.

*Explanatory Note.—The starting of a new sentence at this point follows the official draft of the Constitution, but it is evident that the foregoing phrase ending with "localities" was meant to modify the following sentence.

Sec. 9. **Public Buildings, Etc.** — The property of counties, cities and towns owned and held only for public purposes, such as public buildings and the sites therefor, fire engines and the furniture thereof, and all property used or intended for extinguishing fires, public grounds and all other property devoted exclusively to the use and benefit of the public, shall be exempt from forced sale and from taxation; pro-

vided, nothing herein shall prevent the enforcement of the vendor's lien, the mechanic's or builder's lien, or other liens now existing.

[Note.—Sec. 10 of Art. XI, relating to special taxes and school districts, was deleted by constitutional amendment in election Aug. 5, 1969.]

Sec. 11. **Term of Office for City Officials.** — A home rule city may provide by charter or charter amendment, and a city, town or village operating under the general laws may provide by majority vote of the qualified voters voting at an election called for that purpose, for a longer term of office than two (2) years for its officers, either elective or appointive, or both, but not to exceed four (4) years; provided, however, that tenure under Civil Service shall not be affected hereby.

Provided, however, if any of such officers, elective or appointive, shall announce their candidacy, or shall in fact become a candidate, in any general, special or primary election, for any office of profit or trust under the laws of this State or the United States other than the office then held, at any time when the unexpired term of the office then held shall exceed one (1) year, such announcement or such candidacy shall constitute an automatic resignation of the office then held, and the vacancy thereby created shall be filled pursuant to law in the same manner as other vacancies for such office are filled.

A municipality so providing a term exceeding two (2) years but not exceeding four (4) years for any of its non-civil service officers must elect all of the members of its governing body by majority vote of the qualified voters in such municipality, and any vacancy or vacancies occurring on such governing body shall not be filled by appointment but must be filled by majority vote of the qualified voters at a special election called for such purpose within one hundred and twenty (120) days after such vacancy or vacancies occur.

[Note.—The foregoing Sec. 11 of Art. XI, an amendment, was added to provide four-year terms for city officials. Submitted by the Fifty-fifth Legislature (1957), adopted in election Nov. 4, 1958.]

Sec. 12. **Sanitation Sewer Lines.** — The Legislature by general law may authorize a city or town to expend public funds for the relocation or replacement of sanitation sewer laterals on private property if the relocation or replacement is done in conjunction with or immediately following the replacement or relocation of sanitation sewer mains serving the property. The law must authorize the city or town to affix, with the consent of the owner of the private property, a lien on the property for the cost of relocating or replacing the sewer laterals on the property and must provide that the cost shall be assessed against the property with repayment by the property owner to be amortized over a period not to exceed five years at a rate of interest to be set as provided by the law. The lien may not be enforced until after five years have expired since the date the lien was affixed.

[Note. — The foregoing Sec. 12 of Art. XI, an amendment, was added to permit a city or town to expend public funds and levy assessments for relocation or replacement of sanitation sewer laterals on private property. Submitted by Sixty-eighth Legislature (1983) and adopted in election Nov. 8, 1983.]

ARTICLE XII. — PRIVATE CORPORATIONS

Sec. 1. **Corporations Created by General Laws.** — No private corporation shall be created except by general laws.

Sec. 2. **General Laws to Be Enacted.** — General laws shall be enacted providing for the creation of private corporations, and shall therein provide fully for the adequate protection of the public and of the individual stockholders.

[Note.—Sections 3, 4, 5 and 7 of Art. XII—relating to franchises, and wharfage and freight tolls—were deleted by constitutional amendment in election Aug. 5, 1969.]

Sec. 6. **The Issuance of Stocks and Bonds by Corporations Prohibited Except for Money Paid and Labor Done, Etc.** — No corporation shall issue stock or bonds except for money paid, labor done, or property actually received, and all fictitious increase of stock or indebtedness shall be void.

ARTICLE XIII. — SPANISH AND MEXICAN LAND TITLES

[Note.—The entire Art. XIII, relating to Spanish and Mexican Land Titles, was deleted by constitutional amendment in election Aug. 5, 1969.]

ARTICLE XIV. — PUBLIC LANDS AND LAND OFFICE

Sec. 1. **General Land Office; Grants to Be Registered in; Land Office to Be Self-Sustaining.** — There shall be one General Land Office in the State, which shall be at the seat of

Article XIV — (Cont'd.); Article XV and XVI

government, where all land titles which have emanated or may hereafter emanate from the State shall be registered, except those titles the registration of which may be prohibited by this Constitution. It shall be the duty of the Legislature at the earliest practicable time to make the Land Office self-sustaining, and from time to time the Legislature may establish such subordinate offices as may be deemed necessary.

[Note.—All of Art. XIV relating to public lands and the Land Office, except Sec. 1, was deleted by constitutional amendment in election Aug. 5, 1969.]

ARTICLE XV. — IMPEACHMENT

Sec. 1. Power of Impeachment Vested in the House of Representatives. — The power of impeachment shall be vested in the House of Representatives.

Sec. 2. Trial by Senate. — Impeachment of the Governor, Lieutenant Governor, Attorney General, Treasurer, Commissioner of the General Land Office, Comptroller, and the Judges of the Supreme Court, Courts of Appeal and District Courts shall be tried by the Senate.

Sec. 3. Oath of Senators. — When the Senate is sitting as a court of impeachment, the Senators shall be on oath, or affirmation, impartially to try the party impeached, and no person shall be convicted without the concurrence of two thirds of the Senators present.

Sec. 4. Judgment; Party Convicted Subject to Indictment Under the Criminal Laws. — Judgment in cases of impeachment shall extend only to removal from office and disqualification from holding any office of honor, trust or profit under this State. A party convicted on impeachment shall also be subject to indictment, trial and punishment, according to law.

Sec. 5. Officers Suspended During Pending Proceedings. — All officers against whom articles of impeachment may be preferred shall be suspended from the exercise of the duties of their office during the pendency of such impeachment. The Governor may make a provisional appointment to fill the vacancy occasioned by the suspension of an officer until the decision on the impeachment.

Sec. 6. Removal of District Judges. — Any Judge of the District Courts of the State who is incompetent to discharge the duties of his office, or who shall be guilty of partiality, or oppression, or other official misconduct, or whose habits and conduct are such as to render him unfit to hold such office or who shall negligently fail to perform his duties as Judge, or who shall fail to execute in a reasonable measure the business in his courts, may be removed by the Supreme Court. The Supreme Court shall have original jurisdiction to hear and determine the causes aforesaid when presented in writing, upon the oaths, taken before some Judge of a court of record, of not less than ten lawyers, practicing in the courts held by such Judge, and licensed to practice in the Supreme Court; said presentment to be founded either upon the knowledge of the persons making it or upon the written oaths as to facts of creditable witnesses. The Supreme Court may issue all needful process and prescribe all needful rules to give effect to this section. Causes of this kind shall have precedence and be tried as soon as practicable.

Sec. 7. Trial and Removal of Other Officers. — The Legislature shall provide by law for the trial and removal from office of all officers of this State, the modes for which have not been provided in this Constitution.

Address

Sec. 8. Removal of Judges of Supreme Court and Courts of Appeals and of District Courts. — The Judges of the Supreme Court, Courts of Appeals and District Courts shall be removed by the Governor on the address of two thirds of each house of the Legislature, for willful neglect of duty, incompetency, habitual drunkenness, oppression in office, or other reasonable cause which shall not be sufficient ground for impeachment; provided, however that the cause or causes for which such removal shall be required shall be stated at length in such address and entered on the journals of each house; and provided, further, that the cause or causes shall be notified to the Judge so intended to be removed, and he shall be admitted to a hearing in his own defense before any vote for such address shall pass; and in all such cases the vote shall be taken by yeas and nays and entered on the journals of each house, respectively.

Sec. 9. Removal of Appointed Officials by Governor; Special Session of Senate for This Purpose. — (a) In addition to the other procedures provided by law for removal of public officers, the governor who appoints an officer may remove the officer with the advice and consent of two-thirds of the members of the senate present.

(b) If the Legislature is not in session when the governor desires to remove an officer, the governor shall call a special session of the senate for consideration of the proposed removal. The session may not exceed two days in duration.

[Note. — The foregoing Sec. 9 of Art. XV, an amendment, was added to authorize the governor to remove ap-

pointed officers with the advice and consent of the senate. Submitted by the Sixty-sixth Legislature (1979) and adopted in election Nov. 4, 1980.]

ARTICLE XVI. — GENERAL PROVISIONS

Sec. 1. Official Oaths. — Members of the Legislature, and all other elected officers, before they enter upon the duties of their offices, shall take the following Oath or Affirmation:

"I, _____, do solemnly swear (or affirm), that I will faithfully execute the duties of the office of _____ of the State of Texas, and will to the best of my ability preserve, protect, and defend the Constitution and laws of the United States and of this State; and I furthermore solemnly swear (or affirm), that I have not, directly nor indirectly paid, offered, or promised to pay, contributed, nor promised to contribute any money, or valuable thing, or promised any public office or employment, as a reward for the giving or withholding a vote at the election at which I was elected. So help me God."

The Secretary of State, and all other appointed officers, before they enter upon the duties of their offices, shall take the following Oath or Affirmation:

"I, _____, do solemnly swear (or affirm), that I will faithfully execute the duties of the office of _____ of the State of Texas, and will to the best of my ability preserve, protect, and defend the Constitution and laws of the United States and of this State; and I furthermore solemnly swear (or affirm), that I have not directly nor indirectly paid, offered, or promised to pay, contributed, or promised to contribute any money, or valuable thing, or promised any public office or employment, as a reward to secure my appointment or the confirmation thereof. So help me God."

[Note.—The foregoing Sec. 1 of Art. XVI was twice amended from the original text to eliminate that part of the oath stating that the incoming official had not fought a duel or sent or accepted a challenge to a duel or acted as a second in a duel. Submitted by the Forty-fifth Legislature (1937) and adopted in an election Nov. 8, 1938. It was further amended to change the form of the oath of office to include appointive officers of the State. Submitted by the Fifty-fourth Legislature (1955) and adopted in an election Nov. 6, 1956.]

Sec. 2. Right of Suffrage to Be Protected; Criminals Disfranchised. — Laws shall be made to exclude from office, serving on juries, and from the right of suffrage, those who may have been or shall hereafter be convicted of bribery, perjury, forgery or other high crimes. The privilege of free suffrage shall be protected by laws, regulating elections and prohibiting, under adequate penalties, all undue influence therein from power, bribery, tumult, or other improper practice.

[Note.—Sections 3 and 4 of Art. XVI—relating to fines, and dueling—were deleted by constitutional amendment in election Aug. 5, 1969.]

Sec. 5. Bribery in Elections Disqualification for Holding Office. — Every person shall be disqualified from holding any office of profit or trust in this State who shall have been convicted of having given or offered a bribe to procure his election or appointment.

Sec. 6. Appropriations for Private Purposes Prohibited; Expenditures to Be Published. — (a) No appropriation for private or individual purposes shall be made, unless authorized by this Constitution. A regular statement, under oath, and an account of the receipts and expenditures of all public money shall be published annually, in such manner as shall be prescribed by law.

(b) State agencies charged with the responsibility of providing services to those who are blind, crippled, or otherwise physically or mentally handicapped may accept money from private or federal sources, designated by the private or federal source as money to be used in and establishing and equipping facilities for assisting those who are blind, crippled, or otherwise physically or mentally handicapped in becoming gainfully employed, in rehabilitating and restoring the handicapped, and in providing other services determined by the state agency to be essential for the better care and treatment of the handicapped. Money accepted under this subsection is state money. State agencies may spend money accepted under this subsection, and no other money, for specific programs and projects to be conducted by local level or other private, nonsectarian associations, groups, and nonprofit organizations, in establishing and equipping facilities for assisting those who are blind, crippled, or otherwise physically or mentally handicapped in becoming gainfully employed, in rehabilitating and restoring the handicapped, and in providing other services determined by the state agency to be essential for the better care or treatment of the handicapped.

The state agencies may deposit money accepted under this subsection either in the state treasury or in other secure depositories. The money may not be expended for any purpose other than the purpose for which it was given. Not-

Article XVI — (Cont'd.)

withstanding any other provision of this Constitution, the state agencies may expend money accepted under this subsection without the necessity of an appropriation, unless the Legislature, by law, requires that the money be expended only on appropriation. The Legislature may prohibit state agencies from accepting money under this subsection or may regulate the amount of money accepted, the way the acceptance and expenditure of the money is administered, and the purposes for which the state agencies may expend the money. Money accepted under this subsection for a purpose prohibited by the Legislature shall be returned to the entity that gave the money.

This subsection does not prohibit state agencies authorized to render services to the handicapped from contracting with privately-owned or local facilities for necessary and essential services, subject to such conditions, standards, and procedures as may be prescribed by law.

[Note.—The foregoing Sec. 6 of Art. XVI was amended to authorize public grants to private groups for assistance to the blind, crippled or otherwise physically and mentally handicapped. Submitted by the Fifty-ninth Legislature (1965) and adopted in election Nov. 8, 1966.]

[Note.—Sec. 7 of Art. XVI, relating to paper money, was deleted by constitutional amendment in election Aug. 5, 1969.]

Sec. 8. **Counties May Provide Workhouses, Poorhouses and Farms.** — Each county in the State may provide, in such manner as may be prescribed by law, a manual labor poorhouse and farm, for taking care of, managing, employing and supplying the wants of its indigent and poor inhabitants.

Sec. 9. **Absence on Business of the State or United States Shall Not Forfeit a Residence Once Obtained.** — Absence on business of the State or of the United States shall not forfeit a residence once obtained, so as to deprive anyone of the right of suffrage, or of being elected or appointed to any office, under the exceptions contained in this Constitution.

Sec. 10. **Deductions From Salaries to be Provided for.** — The Legislature shall provide for deductions from the salaries of public officers who may neglect the performance of any duty that may be assigned them by law.

Sec. 11. **Usurious Interest Prohibited.** — The Legislature shall have authority to classify loans and lenders, license and regulate lenders, define interest and fix maximum rates of interest; provided, however, in the absence of legislation fixing maximum rates of interest all contracts for a greater rate of interest than ten per centum (10%) per annum shall be deemed usurious; provided, further, that in contracts where no rate of interest is agreed upon, the rate shall not exceed six per centum (6%) per annum. Should any regulatory agency, acting under the provisions of this Section, cancel or refuse to grant any permit under any law passed by the Legislature; then such applicant or holder shall have the right of appeal to the courts and granted a trial de novo as that term is used in appealing from the justice of peace court to the county court.

[Note.—The foregoing Sec. 11 of Art. XVI has been twice amended—first setting 10 percent and 6 percent as interest rates, in place of original provision for 12 percent and 8 percent. Submitted by the Twenty-second Legislature (1891), ratified in election Aug. 11, 1891, and declared adopted Sept. 22, 1891. Further amended to grant right of appeal from justice of peace court to county court. Submitted by the Fifty-sixth Legislature (1959) and adopted in election Nov. 8, 1960.]

Sec. 12. **Officers Not Eligible.** — No member of Congress, nor person holding or exercising any office of profit or trust under the United States, or either of them, or under any foreign power, shall be eligible as a member of the Legislature or hold or exercise any office of profit or trust under this State.

[Note.—Sec. 13 of Art. XVI, relating to arbitration laws, was deleted by constitutional amendment in election Aug. 5, 1969.]

Sec. 14. **Residence of Officers.** — All civil officers shall reside within the State, and all district or county officers within their districts or counties, and shall keep their offices at such places as may be required by law; and failure to comply with this condition shall vacate the office so held.

Sec. 15. **Community Property of Husband and Wife; Partition Thereof.** — All Property, both real and personal, of a spouse owned or claimed before marriage, and that acquired afterward by gift, devise or descent, shall be the separate property of that spouse; and laws shall be passed more clearly defining the rights of the spouses, in relation to separate and community property; provided that persons about to marry and spouses, without the intention to defraud pre-existing creditors, may by written instrument from time to time partition between themselves all or part

of their property, then existing or to be acquired, or exchange between themselves the community interest of one spouse or future spouse in any property for the community interest of the other spouse or future spouse in other community property then existing or to be acquired, whereupon the portion or interest set aside to each spouse shall be and constitute a part of the separate property and estate of such spouse or future spouse; and the spouses may from time to time, by written instrument, agree between themselves that the income or property from all or part of the separate property then owned by one of them, or which thereafter might be acquired, shall be the separate property of that spouse; and if one spouse makes a gift of property to the other that gift is presumed to include all the income or property which might arise from that gift of property.

[Note.—Sec. 15 of Art. XVI originally had no provision for partition of community property of husband and wife. Provision for partition was the purpose of the amended section. Submitted by the Fiftieth Legislature (1947) and adopted in election Nov. 2, 1948. It was further amended to allow spouses to agree that income or property arising from separate property is to be separate property. Submitted by the Sixty-sixth Legislature (1979) and adopted in election Nov. 4, 1980.]

Sec. 16. **Banking Corporations.** — (a) The Legislature shall, by general laws, authorize the incorporation of corporate bodies with banking and discounting privileges, and shall provide for a system of state supervision, regulation and control of such bodies which will adequately protect and secure the depositors and creditors thereof.

No such corporate body shall be chartered until all of the authorized capital stock has been subscribed and paid in full in cash. Except as may be permitted by the Legislature pursuant to subsection (b) of this Section 16, such body corporate shall not be authorized to engage in business at more than one place, which shall be designated in its charter.

No foreign corporation, other than the national banks of the United States domiciled in this State, shall be permitted to exercise banking or discounting privileges in this State.

(b) If it finds that the convenience of the public will be served thereby, the Legislature may authorize state and national banks to establish and operate unmanned teller machines within the county or city of their domicile. Such machines may perform all banking functions. Banks which are domiciled within a city lying in two or more counties may be permitted to establish and operate unmanned teller machines within both the city and the county of their domicile. The Legislature shall provide that a bank shall have the right to share in the use of these teller machines, not situated at a banking house, which are located within the county or the city of the bank's domicile, on a reasonable, nondiscriminatory basis, consistent with anti-trust laws. Banks may share the use of such machines within the county or city of their domicile with savings and loan associations and credit unions which are domiciled in the same county or city.

(c) A corporate body created by virtue of the power granted by this section, notwithstanding any other provision of this section, has the same rights and privileges that are or may be granted to national banks of the United States domiciled in this State.

Should the Legislature enact legislation in anticipation of the adoption of this amendment, such law shall not be invalid because of its anticipatory character.

[Note.—The foregoing Sec. 16 of Art. XVI has been amended from the original, as follows: (1) To eliminate the original provision that "No corporate body shall hereafter be created, renewed or extended with banking or discounting privileges," and making possible the establishment of the present state banking system. Submitted by the Twenty-eighth Legislature (1903), ratified in an election Nov. 8, 1904, and declared adopted Dec. 29, 1904. (2) Eliminating a provision, contained in the amendment of 1904, making shareholders of banks liable to the extent of twice the par value of the shares owned. Submitted by the Forty-fifth Legislature (1937), and adopted in an election Aug. 23, 1937. (3) Authorizing banks to use unmanned teller machines within the county or city of their domicile on a shared basis. Submitted by the Sixty-sixth Legislature (1979) and adopted in election Nov. 4, 1980. (4) Adding Subsection (c), providing state banks same rights and privileges as national banks. Submitted by the Sixty-eighth Legislature (1983) and adopted in election Nov. 6, 1984.]

Sec. 17. **Officers to Perform Duties Until Successor Qualified.** — All officers within this State shall continue to perform the duties of their offices until their successors shall be duly qualified.

Sec. 18. **Vested Rights.** — The rights of property and of action, which have been acquired under the Constitution and the laws of the Republic and State, shall not be divested; nor shall any rights or actions, which have been divested, barred or declared null and void by the Constitution of

Article XVI — (Cont'd.)

the Republic and State be reinvested, renewed or reinstated by this Constitution; but the same shall remain precisely in the situation which they were before the adoption of this Constitution, unless otherwise herein provided; and provided, further, that no cause of action heretofore barred shall be revived.

Sec. 19. **Qualifications of Jurors.** — The Legislature shall prescribe by law the qualifications of grand and petit jurors; provided that neither the right nor the duty to serve on grand and petit juries shall be denied or abridged by reason of sex. Whenever in the Constitution the term "men" is used in reference to grand or petit juries, such term shall include persons of the female as well as the male sex.

[Note.—The foregoing Sec. 19 of Art. XVI was amended to include women jurors. Submitted by the Fifty-third Legislature (1953) and adopted in an election Nov. 2, 1954.]

Sec. 20. **Manufacture and Sale of Intoxicants.** — (a) The Legislature shall have the power to enact a Mixed Beverage Law regulating the sale of mixed alcoholic beverages on a local option election basis. The Legislature shall also have the power to regulate the manufacture, sale, possession and transportation of intoxicating liquors, including the power to establish a state monopoly on the sale of distilled liquors.

Should the Legislature enact any enabling laws in anticipation of this amendment, no such law shall be void by reason of its anticipatory nature.

(b) The Legislature shall enact a law or laws whereby the qualified voters of any county, justices precinct or incorporated town or city may, by a majority vote of those voting, determine from time to time whether the sale of intoxicating liquors for beverage purposes shall be prohibited or legalized within the prescribed limits; and such laws shall contain provisions for voting on the sale of intoxicating liquors of various types and various alcoholic content.

(c) In all counties, justices precincts or incorporated towns or cities wherein the sale of intoxicating liquors had been prohibited by local option elections held under the laws of the State of Texas and in force at the time of the taking effect of Section 20, Article XVI of the Constitution of Texas, it shall continue to be unlawful to manufacture, sell, barter or exchange in any such county, justices precinct or incorporated town or city, any spiritous, vinous or malt liquors or medicated bitters capable of producing intoxication or any other intoxicants whatsoever, for beverage purposes, unless and until a majority of the qualified voters in such county or political subdivision thereof voting in an election held for such purposes shall determine such to be lawful; provided that this subsection shall not prohibit the sale of alcoholic beverages containing not more than 3.2 percent alcohol by weight in cities, counties or political subdivisions thereof in which the qualified voters have voted to legalize such sale under the provisions of Chapter 116, Acts of the Regular Session of the Forty-third Legislature.

[Note.—The foregoing Sec. 20 of Art. XVI has been amended from the original (which merely provided for local option elections in "any county, justices precinct, town or city") five times, as follows: (1) To insert a clause in original section "or such subdivision of a county as may be designated by Commissioners' Court of said county," with reference to local option elections. Submitted by Twenty-second Legislature (1891), ratified in an election Aug. 11, 1891, and declared adopted Sept. 22, 1891. (2) To declare state-wide prohibition. Submitted by Thirty-sixth Legislature (1919), and declared adopted May 24, 1919. (3) To legalize sale of vinous and malt liquors of not more than 3.2 percent alcohol. Submitted by Forty-third Legislature (1933), and adopted in an election Aug. 26, 1933. (4) To legalize sale of all liquors, as stated in the section printed above. Submitted by Forty-fourth Legislature (1935), and adopted in an election Aug. 24, 1935. (5) To give Legislature power to enact a Mixed Beverage Law regulating sale of mixed drinks on local option election basis. Submitted by Sixty-first Legislature (1969) and adopted in election Nov. 3, 1970.]

Sec. 21. **Stationery; Public Printing.** — All stationery, printing, fuel used in the Legislature and departments of the government other than the judicial department, printing and binding of the laws, journals, and department reports, and all other printing and binding and the repairing and furnishing of the halls and rooms used during meetings of the Legislature and in committees, except proclamations and such products and services as may be done by handicapped individuals employed in nonprofit rehabilitation facilities providing sheltered employment to the handicapped in Texas, shall be performed under contract, to be given to the lowest responsible bidder, below such maximum price and under such regulations as shall be prescribed by law. No member or officer of any department of the government shall in any way have a financial interest in such contracts, and all such contracts or programs involv-

ing the state use of the products and services of handicapped individuals shall be subject to such requirements as might be established by the Legislature.

[Note.—The foregoing Sec. 21 of Art. XVI was amended to eliminate reference to the Deaf and Dumb Asylum; to allow certain products and services of handicapped persons to be used by agencies of state government; to require other products and services required for operation of state government be acquired under bids by lowest responsible bidder; and to eliminate requirement that Governor, Secretary of State and Comptroller of Public Accounts be personally involved with such transactions. Submitted by the Sixty-fifth Legislature (1977) and adopted in election Nov. 7, 1978.]

Sec. 22. **Fence Laws.** — The Legislature shall have the power to pass such fence laws, applicable to any subdivision of the State or county, as may be needed to meet the wants of the people.

Sec. 23. **Stock Laws.** — The Legislature may pass laws for the regulation of livestock and the protection of stock raisers in the stock raising portion of the State, and exempt from the operation of such laws other portions, sections or counties; and shall have power to pass general and special laws for the inspection of cattle, stock and hides, and for the regulation of brands; provided, that any local law thus passed shall be submitted to the freeholders of the section to be affected thereby, and approved by them before it shall go into effect.

Sec. 24. **Roads; Convict Labor.** — The Legislature shall make provision for laying out and working public roads, for the building of bridges, and for utilizing fines, forfeitures, and convict labor to all these purposes.

Sec. 25. **Drawbacks and Rebates in Freight Insurance, Transportation, Storage, Etc., Prohibited.** — That all drawbacks and rebatement of insurance, freight, transportation, carriage, wharfage, storage, compressing, bailing, repairing, or for any other kind of labor or service of, or to any cotton, grain or any other produce or article of commerce in this State, paid or allowed or contracted for to any common carrier, shipper, merchant, commission merchant, factor, agent or middleman of any kind not the true and absolute owner thereof, are forever prohibited; and it shall be the duty of the Legislature to pass effective laws punishing all persons in this State who pay, receive or contract for or respecting the same.

Sec. 26. **Homicide: Civil Action For.** — Every person, corporation or company that may commit a homicide, through willful act or omission or gross neglect, shall be responsible in exemplary damages to the surviving husband, widow, heirs of his or her body, or such of them as there may be, without regard to any criminal proceeding that may or may not be had in relation to the homicide.

Sec. 27. **Vacancies in Offices Filled for Unexpired Term Only.** — In all elections to fill vacancies of office in this State, it shall be to fill the unexpired term only.

Sec. 28. **Wages Exempt From Garnishment.** — No current wages for personal service shall ever be subject to garnishment, except for the enforcement of court-ordered child support payments.

[Note. — The foregoing Sec. 28 of Art. XVI was amended to allow Legislature to provide for additional remedies to enforce court-ordered child support payments. Submitted by Sixty-eighth Legislature (1983) and adopted in election Nov. 8, 1983.]

[Note.—Sec. 29 of Art. XVI, relating to barratry, was deleted by constitutional amendment in election Aug. 5, 1969.]

Sec. 30. **Duration of Offices; Term of Railroad Commissioner.** — (a) The duration of all offices not fixed by this Constitution shall never exceed two years.

(b) When a Railroad Commission is created by law it shall be composed of three Commissioners, who shall be elected by the people at a general election for state officers, and their term of office shall be six years. Railroad Commissioners first elected after this amendment goes into effect shall hold office as follows: One shall serve two years, and one four years, and one six years; their terms to be decided by lot immediately after they shall have qualified. And one Railroad Commissioner shall be elected every two years thereafter. In case of vacancy in said office the Governor of the State shall fill said vacancy by appointment until the next general election.

(c) The Legislature may provide that members of the governing board of a district or authority created by authority of Art. III, Sec. 52(b) (1) or (2), or Art. XVI, Sec. 59, of this Constitution serve terms not to exceed four years.

[Note. — The foregoing Sec. 30 of Art. XVI was amended from the original to permit six-year terms for the newly created offices of the three-place Railroad Commission of Texas. The original section consisted only of the first clause of the amendment as printed above. Submitted by the Twenty-third Legislature (1893), ratified in an election Nov.

Article XVI — (Cont'd.)

6, 1894, and declared adopted Dec. 21, 1894. It was further amended to provide four-year terms for members of governing boards of certain water districts and conservation and reclamation districts. Submitted by the Sixty-seventh Legislature (1981) and adopted in an election Nov. 2, 1982.]

Sec. 30-a. **Board of Regents, Trustees, Managers, Etc.; Term of Office.** — The Legislature may provide by law that the members of the Board of Regents of the State University and boards of trustees or managers of the educational, eleemosynary and penal institutions of this State, and such boards as have been or may hereafter be established by law, may hold their respective offices for the term of six (6) years, one third of the members of such boards to be elected or appointed every two years in such manner as the Legislature may determine; vacancies in such offices to be filled as may be provided by law, and the Legislature shall enact suitable laws to give effect to this section.

[Note.—The foregoing Sec. 30-a of Art. XVI, an amendment, was added to give the Legislature authority to provide official terms of more than two years. (See Sec. 30 above and note thereunder.) Submitted by the Thirty-second Legislature (1911), ratified at an election Nov. 5, 1912, and declared adopted Dec. 30, 1912.]

Sec. 30-b. **Tenure Under Municipal Civil Service.** — Wherever by virtue of statute or charter provisions appointive officers of any municipality are placed under the terms and provisions of Civil Service and rules are set up governing appointment to and removal from such offices, the provisions of Article 16, Section 30, of the Texas Constitution limiting the duration of all offices not fixed by the Constitution to two (2) years shall not apply, but the duration of such offices shall be governed by the provisions of the Civil Service law or charter provisions applicable thereto.

[Note.—The foregoing Sec. 30-b of Art. XVI, an amendment, was added to extend to local officials terms under the Civil Service exemption from the two-year restriction in the first clause of Sec. 30. (See Secs. 30 and 30-a and notes thereunder.) Submitted by the Forty-sixth Legislature; ratified in an election Nov. 5, 1940.]

Sec. 31. **Qualifications of Physicians to Be Prescribed.** — The Legislature may pass laws prescribing the qualifications of practitioners of medicine in this State, and to punish persons for malpractice, but no preference shall ever be given by law to any schools of medicine.

[Note.—Sec. 32 of Art. XVI, relating to Board of Health and Vital Statistics, was deleted by constitutional amendment in election Aug. 5, 1969.]

Sec. 33. **Condition Under Which a Person Can Not Receive Compensation From the State.** — The accounting officers in this State shall neither draw nor pay a warrant or check on funds of the State of Texas, whether in the treasury or otherwise, to any person for salary or compensation who holds at the same time more than one civil office of emolument, in violation of Sec. 40.

[Note.—The foregoing Sec. 33 of Art. XVI has been amended four times, as follows: (1) To release National Guard of Texas, National Guard Reserve and Officers' Reserve Corps and United States Organized Reserves from the prohibition against holding remunerative office. Submitted by Thirty-ninth Legislature (1925), and adopted in an election Nov. 2, 1926. Proclaimed Jan. 20, 1927. (2) To add to those released from the prohibition against holding remunerative office all retired officers and enlisted men of the United States Army, Navy and Marine Corps. Submitted by Forty-second Legislature (1931), and adopted in an election Nov. 8, 1932. Proclaimed Jan. 9, 1933. (3) To allow nonelective state officers and employees to serve in other nonelective offices under this state or the U.S. until Sept. 1, 1969, and thereafter only if authorized by Legislature, if the offices are of benefit to Texas or are required by state or federal law and there is no conflict of interest; prohibiting elected officers from holding any other office under this state; and adding members of Air National Guard, Air National Guard Reserve, Air Force Reserve and retired members of Air Force to list of persons exempted. Submitted by Sixtieth Legislature (1967) and adopted in election Nov. 11, 1967. (4) It was amended to delete the old Sec. 33 of Art. XVI and substitute the foregoing therefor. (See also note under Sec. 40 of Art. XVI.) Submitted by the Sixty-second Legislature (1971) and adopted in election Nov. 7, 1972.]

[Note.—Sections 34, 35, 36 and 38 of Art. XVI—relating to military forts, laborers on public works, payments to schoolteachers, and a Commissioner of Insurance, Statistics and History—were deleted by constitutional amendment in election Aug. 5, 1969.[1]

Sec. 37. **Mechanic's Liens to Be Enforced.** — Mechanics, artisans and material men of every class shall have a lien upon the buildings and articles made or repaired by them, for the value of their labor done thereon, or material furnished therefor; and the Legislature shall provide by law for the speedy and efficient enforcement of said liens.

Sec. 39. **Memorials of Texas History.** — The Legislature may, from time to time, make appropriations for preserving and perpetuating memorials of the history of Texas, by means of monuments, statues, paintings and documents of historical value.

Sec. 40. **Provision Against Holding More Than One Office; Exceptions.** — No person shall hold or exercise at the same time, more than one civil office of emolument, except that of Justice of the Peace, County Commissioner, Notary Public and Postmaster, Officer of the National Guard, the National Guard Reserve, and the Officers Reserve Corps of the United States and enlisted men of the National Guard, the National Guard Reserve, and the Organized Reserves of the United States, and retired officers of the United States Army, Air Force, Navy, Marine Corps, and Coast Guard, and retired warrant officers, and retired enlisted men of the United States Army, Air Force, Navy, Marine Corps, and Coast Guard, and the officers and directors of soil and water conservation districts, unless otherwise specially provided herein. Provided, that nothing in this Constitution shall be construed to prohibit an officer or enlisted man of the National Guard, and the National Guard Reserve, or an officer in the Officers Reserve Corps of the United States, or an enlisted man in the Organized Reserves of the United States, or retired officers of the United States Army, Air Force, Navy, Marine Corps, and Coast Guard, and retired warrant officers, and retired enlisted men of the United States Army, Air Force, Navy, Marine Corps, and Coast Guard, and officers of the State soil and water conservation districts, from holding at the same time any other office or position of honor, trust or profit, under this State or the United States, or from voting at any election, general, special or primary in this State when otherwise qualified. State employees or other individuals who receive all or part of their compensation either directly or indirectly from funds of the State of Texas and who are not State officers, shall not be barred from serving as members of the governing bodies of school districts, cities, towns, or other local governmental districts; provided, however, that such State employees or other individuals shall receive no salary for serving as members of such governing bodies. It is further provided that a non-elective State officer may hold other non-elective offices under the State or the United States, if the other office is of benefit to the State of Texas or is required by the State or Federal law, and there is no conflict with the original office for which he receives salary or compensation. No member of the Legislature of this State may hold any other office or position of profit under this State, or the United States, except as a notary public if qualified by law.

[Note.—The foregoing Sec. 40 of Art. XVI has been amended three times as follows: (1) To release National Guard, National Guard Reserve and Officers' Reserve Corps and United States Organized Reserves from the prohibition against holding remunerative office. Submitted by Thirty-ninth Legislature (1925), and adopted in an election Nov. 2, 1926. Proclaimed Jan. 20, 1927. (2) To add to those released from the prohibition against holding remunerative office all retired officers and enlisted men of the United States Army, Navy and Marine Corps. Submitted by Forty-second Legislature (1931) and adopted in an election Nov. 8, 1932. Proclaimed Jan. 9, 1933. (3) To add to those released from the prohibition against holding remunerative office retired officers or enlisted men of the Air Force and Coast Guard; and officers and directors of soil and water conservation districts, unless otherwise specially prohibited); also certain other state employees who are not officers of the state. Submitted by Sixty-second Legislature (1971) and adopted in an election Nov. 7, 1972.]

Sec. 41. **Bribery of Certain Officials to Be Prohibited.** — Any person who shall, directly or indirectly, offer, give or promise any money or thing of value, testimonial, privilege or personal advantage to any executive or judicial officer or member of the Legislature, to influence him in the performance of any of his public or official duties, shall be guilty of bribery and be punished in such manner as shall be provided by law. And any member of the Legislature, or executive or judicial officer, who shall solicit, demand or receive, or consent to receive, directly or indirectly, for himself or for another, from any company, corporation or person any money, appointment, employment testimonial, reward, thing of value or employment, or of personal advantage or promise thereof, for his vote or official influence, or for withholding the same, or with any understanding, expressed or implied, that his vote or official action shall be in any way influenced thereby, or who shall solicit, demand and receive any such money or other advantage, matter or thing aforesaid, for another, as the consideration of his vote or official influence, in consideration of the payment or promise of such money, advantage, matter or thing to another, shall be held guilty of bribery within the mean-

Article XVI — (Cont'd.)

ing of the Constitution, and shall incur the disabilities provided for said offenses, with a forfeiture of the office they may hold, and such other additional punishment as is or shall be provided by law.

[Note.—Sec. 42 of Art. XVI, relating to an asylum for inebriates, was deleted by constitutional amendment in election Aug. 5, 1969.]

Sec. 43. **Exemption From Public Service.** — No man or set of men shall ever be exempted, relieved or discharged from the performance of any public duty or service imposed by general law, by any special law. Exemptions from the performance of such public duty or service shall only be made by general law.

Sec. 44. **County Treasurer and Surveyor.** — (a) Except as provided by Subsection (b) and Subsection (b)(1) of this section, the Legislature shall prescribe the duties and provide for the election by the qualified voters of each county in this State, of a County Treasurer and a County Surveyor, who shall have an office at the county seat, and hold their office for four years, and until their successors are qualified; and shall have such compensation as may be provided by law.

(b) The office of County Treasurer in the counties of Tarrant and Bee is abolished and all the powers, duties, and functions of the office in each of these counties are transferred to the County Auditor or to the officer who succeeds to the auditor's functions.

(b)(1) The office of County Treasurer in the counties of Bexar and Collin are abolished and all the powers, duties, and functions of the office in each of these counties are transferred to the County Clerk.

(c) Provided however, that the office of County Treasurer shall be abolished in the above counties only after a local election has been held in each county and the proposition "to abolish the elective office of county treasurer" has passed by a majority of those persons voting in said election.

[Note.—The foregoing Sec. 44 of Art. XVI was amended to raise term of office from two to four years. Submitted by the Fifty-third Legislature (1953) and adopted in election Nov. 2, 1954. It was further amended to abolish the office of County Treasurer in Tarrant and Bee Counties. Submitted by the Sixty-seventh Legislature (1981) and adopted in election Nov. 2, 1982. It was amended again to abolish the office of County Treasurer in Bexar and Collin Counties. Submitted by Sixty-eighth Legislature (1983) and adopted in election Nov. 6, 1984.]

[Note.—Sections 45 and 46 of Art. XVI—relating to records of the history of Texas and organization of a militia — were deleted by constitutional amendment in election Aug. 5, 1969.]

Sec. 47. **Scruples Against Bearing Arms.** — Any person who conscientiously scruples to bear arms shall not be compelled to do so, but shall pay an equivalent for personal service.

Sec. 48. **Laws to Remain in Force.** — All laws and parts of laws now in force in the State of Texas which are not repugnant to the Constitution of the United States or to this Constitution shall continue and remain in force as the laws of this State until they expire by their own limitation or shall be amended or repealed by the Legislature.

Sec. 49. **Exemptions From Forced Sales.** — The Legislature shall have power, and it shall be its duty, to protect by law from forced sale a certain portion of the personal property of all heads of families, and also of unmarried adults, male and female.

Sec. 50. **Homestead Exemptions; Encumbrances, Pretended Sales.** — The homestead of a family, or of a single adult person, shall be, and is hereby protected from forced sale, for the payment of all debts except for the purchase money thereof, or a part of such purchase money, the taxes due thereon, or for work and material used in constructing improvements thereon, and in this last case only when the work and material are contracted for in writing, with the consent of both spouses, in the case of a family homestead, given in the same manner as is required in making a sale and conveyance of the homestead; nor may the owner or claimant of the property claimed as homestead, if married, sell or abandon the homestead without the consent of the other spouse, given in such manner as may be prescribed by law. No mortgage, trust deed, or other lien on the homestead shall ever be valid, except for the purchase money therefor, or improvements made thereon, as hereinbefore provided, whether such mortgage, or trust deed, or other lien, shall have been created by the owner alone, or together with his or her spouse, in case the owner is married. All pretended sales of the homestead involving any condition of defeasance shall be void.

[Note.—The foregoing Sec. 50 of Art. XVI was amended to include single persons under the homestead exemption

provision; and it further made the wife an equal partner under the homestead provision. Submitted by the Sixty-third Legislature (1973) and adopted in election Nov. 6, 1973.]

Sec. 51. **Homestead Defined.** — The homestead, not in a town or city, shall consist of not more than two hundred acres of land, which may be in one or more parcels, with the improvements thereon; the homestead in a city, town or village, shall consist of lot or lots amounting to not more than one acre of land, together with any improvements on the land; provided, that the same shall be used for the purposes of a home, or as a place to exercise the calling or business of the homestead claimant, whether a single adult person, or the head of a family; provided also, that any temporary renting of the homestead shall not change the character of the same, when no other homestead has been acquired.

[Note.—The foregoing Sec. 51 was amended to raise the value of lots, exclusive of improvements, from $5,000 to $10,000 when designated as homesteads. Submitted by the Sixty-first Legislature (1969) and adopted in election Nov. 3, 1970. It was further amended to provide that family homesteads may not be abandoned except with consent of both spouses. Submitted by the Sixty-third Legislature (1973) and adopted in election Nov. 6, 1973. It was again amended to replace the limitation on the value of an urban homestead with a limitation based on size. Submitted by Sixty-eighth Legislature (1983) and adopted in election Nov. 8, 1983.]

Sec. 52. **Descent of Homestead.** — On the death of the husband or wife, or both, the homestead shall descend and vest in like manner as other real property of the deceased, and shall be governed by the same laws of descent and distribution, but it shall not be partitioned among the heirs of the deceased during the lifetime of the surviving husband or wife, or so long as the survivor may elect to use or occupy the same as a homestead, or so long as the guardian of the minor children of the deceased may be permitted, under the order of the proper court having jurisdiction, to use and occupy the same.

Sec. 53. **Declaration Validating Process and Writs.** — That no inconvenience may arise from the adoption of this Constitution, it is declared that all process and writs of all kinds which have been or may be issued and not returned or executed when this Constitution is adopted shall remain valid, and shall not be in any way affected by the adoption of this Constitution.

[Note.—Sections 54 and 55 of Art. XVI—relating to pensions, and the indigent lunatics—were deleted by constitutional amendment in election Aug. 5, 1969.]

Sec. 56. **Advertising Texas' Resources.** — The Legislature of the State of Texas shall have the power to appropriate money and establish the procedure necessary to expend such money for the purpose of developing information about the historical, natural, agricultural, industrial, educational, marketing, recreational and living resources of Texas, and for the purpose of informing persons and corporations of other states through advertising in periodicals having national circulation, and the dissemination of factual information about the advantages and economic resources offered by the State of Texas; providing, however, that neither the name nor the picture of any living state official shall ever be used in any of said advertising, and providing that the Legislature may require that any sum of money appropriated hereunder shall be matched by an equal sum paid into the State Treasury from private sources before any of said money may be expended.

[Note.—The foregoing Sec. 56 of Art. XVI is substituted for the original Section 56 which prohibited the expenditure of state funds for attracting immigrants. Submitted by the Fifty-fifth Legislature (1957) and adopted in an election Nov. 4, 1958.]

[Note.—Sections 57, 58 and 60 of Art. XVI—relating to land for state capitol, management of the prison system and the Texas Centennial—were deleted by constitutional amendment in election Aug. 5, 1969.]

*Sec. 59-a. **Conservation and Development of Natural Resources.** — The conservation and development of all the natural resources of this State, including the control, storing, preservation and distribution of its storm and flood waters, the waters of its rivers and streams, for irrigation, power and all other useful purposes, the reclamation and irrigation of its arid, semi-arid and other lands needing irrigation, the reclamation and drainage of its overflowed lands, and other lands needing drainage, the conservation and development of its forests, water and hydro-electric power, the navigation of its inland and coastal waters, and the preservation and conservation of all such natural resources of the State are each and all hereby declared public rights and duties; and the Legislature shall pass all such laws as may be appropriate thereto.

Article XVI — (Cont'd.)

*The resolution submitting this amendment was headed "Sec. 59-a," followed by paragraphs "(b)" and "(c)." Obviously, the first heading should have been "Sec. 59 (a)," the parenthetical (a) referring only to the first paragraph.

(b) There may be created within the State of Texas or the State may be divided into, such number of conservation and reclamation districts as may be determined to be essential to the accomplishment of the purposes of this amendment to the Constitution, which districts shall be governmental agencies and bodies politic and corporate with such powers of government and with the authority to exercise such rights, privileges and functions concerning the subject matter of this amendment as may be conferred by law.

(c) The Legislature shall authorize all such indebtedness as may be necessary to provide all improvements and the maintenance thereof requisite to the achievement of the purposes of this amendment, and all such indebtedness may be evidenced by bonds of such conservation and reclamation districts, to be issued under such regulations as may be prescribed by law and shall, also, authorize the levy and collection within such districts of all such taxes, equitably distributed, as may be necessary for the payment of the interest and the creation of a sinking fund for payment of such bonds; and also for the maintenance of such districts and improvements, and such indebtedness shall be a lien upon the property assessed for the payment thereof; provided, the Legislature shall not authorize the issuance of any bonds or provide for any indebtedness against any reclamation district unless such proposition shall first be submitted to the qualified property taxpaying voters of such district and the proposition adopted.

(d) No law creating a conservation and reclamation district shall be passed unless notice of the intention to introduce such a bill setting forth the general substance of the contemplated law shall have been published at least thirty (30) days and not more than ninety (90) days prior to the introduction thereof in a newspaper or newspapers having general circulation in the county or counties in which said district or any part thereof is or will be located and by delivering a copy of such notice and such bill to the Governor who shall submit such notice and bill to the Texas Water Commission, or its successor, which shall file its recommendation as to such bill with the Governor, Lieutenant Governor and Speaker of the House of Representatives within thirty (30) days from date notice was received by the Texas Water Commission. Such notice and copy of bill shall also be given of the introduction of any bill amending a law creating or governing a particular conservation and reclamation district if such bill (1) adds additional land to the district, (2) alters the taxing authority of the district, (3) alters the authority of the district with respect to the issuance of bonds, or (4) alters the qualifications or terms of office of the members of the governing body of the district.

(e) No law creating a conservation and reclamation district shall be passed unless, at the time notice of the intention to introduce a bill is published as provided in Subsection (d) of this section, a copy of the proposed bill is delivered to the commissioners court of each county in which said district or any part thereof is or will be located and to the governing body of each incorporated city or town in whose jurisdiction said district or any part thereof is or will be located. Each such commissioners court and governing body may file its written consent or opposition to the creation of the proposed district with the governor, lieutenant governor, and speaker of the house of representatives. Each special law creating a conservation and reclamation district shall comply with the provisions of the general laws then in effect relating to consent by political subdivisions to the creation of conservation and reclamation districts and to the inclusion of land within the district.

(f) A conservation and reclamation district created under this section to perform any or all of the purposes of this section may engage in fire-fighting activities and may issue bonds or other indebtedness for firefighting purposes as provided by law and this constitution.

[Note.—The foregoing Sec. 59-a, obviously meant to be Sec. 59 (see footnote), was added to establish a conservation policy. Submitted by Thirty-fifth Legislature (1917), and adopted in an election of Aug. 21, 1917, and proclaimed Oct. 2, 1917. It was amended by adding paragraph (d) to require notice at both the local level and state level through publication in a newspaper having general circulation in county in which district is to be set up at least 30 days prior to introduction of bill in Legislature. Submitted by Fifty-eighth Legislature (1963) and adopted in election Nov. 3, 1964. It was further amended to establish certain requirements relative to enactment of laws creating certain conservation and reclamation districts. Submitted by Sixty-third Legislature (1973) and adopted in election Nov. 6, 1973. It was further amended by adding Subsection (f), authorizing certain districts to engage in fire-fighting activities and to

issue bonds or otherwise lend their credit for fire-fighting purposes. (See also Subsection (d), Sec. 52, Art. III.) Submitted by Sixty-fifth Legislature (1977) and adopted in election Nov. 7, 1978.]

[Note.—See note after Sec. 56 for Sec. 60.]

Sec. 61. **Compensation of District and County Officials.** — All district officers in the State of Texas and all county officers in counties having a population of twenty thousand (20,000) or more, according to the then last preceding Federal Census, shall be compensated on a salary basis. In all counties in this State, the Commissioners Courts shall be authorized to determine whether precinct officers shall be compensated on a fee basis or on a salary basis, with the exception that it shall be mandatory upon the Commissioners Courts to compensate all justices of the peace, constables, deputy constables and precinct law enforcement officers on a salary basis beginning January 1, 1973; and in counties having a population of less than twenty thousand (20,000), according to the then last preceding Federal Census, the Commissioners Court shall also have the authority to determine whether county officers shall be compensated on a fee basis or on a salary basis, with the exception that it shall be mandatory upon the Commissioners Courts to compensate all sheriffs, deputy sheriffs, county law enforcement officers, including sheriffs who also perform the duties of assessor and collector of taxes, and their deputies, on a salary basis beginning January 1, 1949.

All fees earned by district, county and precinct officers shall be paid into the county treasury where earned for the account of the proper fund, provided that fees incurred by the State, county and any municipality, or in case where a pauper's oath is filed, shall be paid into the county treasury when collected and provided that where any officer is compensated wholly on a fee basis such fees may be retained by such officer or paid into the treasury of the county as the Commissioners Court may direct. All notaries public, county surveyors and public weighers shall continue to be compensated on a fee basis.

[Note.—The foregoing Sec. 61 of Art. XVI has been amended three times, as follows: (1) To put all district and county officials in counties of more than 20,000 population on a salary basis, substituting for fee basis, and making it optional with the Commissioners Courts whether precinct officers in counties of less than 20,000 should be on salary or fee basis and optional with reference to county officers in counties of less than 20,000. Submitted by the Forty-fourth Legislature (1935), and adopted in an election Aug. 24, 1935. (2) To make mandatory a salary basis for constables and precinct enforcement officers in counties of more than 20,000 and making it mandatory, in counties of less than 20,000 population, that all sheriffs, deputy sheriffs and other county enforcement officers, be on salary basis. Submitted by the Fiftieth Legislature (1947) and adopted in election Nov. 2, 1948. (3) To include justices of the peace with those to be compensated on salary basis beginning Jan. 1, 1973. Submitted by the Sixty-second Legislature (1971) and adopted in an election Nov. 7, 1972.]

[Note.—Sec. 62 and Sec. 63 of Art. XVI, pertaining to Retirement, Disability and Death Compensation Funds and Teacher and State Employee Retirement System, respectively, were repealed in a constitutional amendment election April 22, 1975. See also note under Art. III, Sec. 48-a, 48-b, 51-e and 51-f; also see Sec. 67 of Art. XVI, which replaces the foregoing Sections.]

Sec. 64. **Inspector of Hides and Animals; Elective District, County and Precinct Offices; Terms of Office.** — The office of Inspector of Hides and Animals, the elective district, county and precinct offices which have heretofore had terms of two years, shall hereafter have terms of four years; and the holders of such terms shall serve until their successors are qualified.

[Note. — The foregoing Sec. 64 of Art. XVI, an amendment, was added for the purpose of setting term of office for these officials. Submitted by the Fifty-third Legislature (1953) and adopted in election Nov. 2, 1954.]

Sec. 65. **District and County Officials; Terms of Office.** — The following officers elected at the general election in November, 1954, and thereafter, shall serve for the full terms provided in this Constitution.

(a) District Clerks; (b) County Clerks; (c) County Judges; (d) Judges of County Courts-at-Law, County Criminal Courts, County Probate Courts, and County Domestic Relations Courts; (e) County Treasurers; (f) Criminal District Attorneys; (g) County Surveyors; (h) Inspectors of Hides and Animals; (i) County Commissioners for Precincts Two and Four; (j) Justices of the Peace.

Notwithstanding other provisions of this Constitution, the following officers elected at the general election in November, 1954, shall serve only for terms of two years: (a) Sheriffs; (b) Assessors and Collectors of Taxes; (c) District Attorneys; (d) County Attorneys; (e) Public Weighers; (f)

Article XVI — (Cont'd.); Article XVII

County Commissioners for Precincts One and Three; (g) Constables. At subsequent elections, such officers shall be elected for the full terms provided in this Constitution.

In any district, county or precinct where any of the aforementioned offices is of such nature that two or more persons hold such office, with the result that candidates file for "Place No. 1," "Place No. 2," etc., the officers elected at the general election in November, 1954, shall serve for a term of two years if the designation of their office is an uneven number, and for a term of four years, if the designation of their office is an even number. Thereafter, all such officers shall be elected for the term provided in this Constitution.

Provided, however, if any of the officers named herein shall announce their candidacy, or shall in fact become a candidate, in any General, Special or Primary Election, for any office of profit or trust under the laws of this state or the United States other than the office then held, at any time when the unexpired term of the office then held shall exceed one (1) year, such announcement or such candidacy shall constitute an automatic resignation of the office then held, and the vacancy thereby created shall be filled pursuant to law in the same manner as other vacancies for such office are filled.

[Note. — The foregoing Sec. 65 of Art. XVI, an amendment, was added for the purpose of setting the terms of office of the aforementioned officers. Submitted by the Fifty-third Legislature (1953) and adopted in an election Nov. 2, 1954. This section was further amended by adding the provision that a person must resign his present term of office if same has more than a year to run when he becomes a candidate for another office. Submitted by the Fifty-fifth Legislature (1957) and adopted in an election Nov. 4, 1958.]

Sec. 66. **Pensions for Texas Rangers.** — The Legislature shall have authority to provide for a system of retirement and disability pensions for retiring Texas Rangers who have not been eligible at any time for membership in the Employees Retirement System of Texas as that retirement system was established by Chapter 352, Acts of the Fiftieth Legislature, Regular Session, 1947, and who have had as much as two (2) years service as a Texas Ranger, and to their widows; providing that no pension shall exceed Eighty Dollars ($80) per month to any such Texas Ranger or his widow, provided that such widow was legally married prior to January 1, 1957, to a Texas Ranger qualifying for such pension.

These pensions may be paid only from the special fund created by *Sec. 17, Art. VII for a payment of pensions for services in the Confederate army and navy, frontier organizations, and the militia of the State of Texas, and for widows of such soldiers serving in said armies, navies, organizations or militia.

*Sec. 17, Art. VII was repealed by amendment adopted in election Nov. 2, 1982. No provision has been made for deletion of this reference in Art. XVI to Sec. 17, Art. VII. (See Art. VIII, Sec. 1-e.)

[Note. — The foregoing Sec. 66 of Art. XVI, an amendment, was added to provide for retirement pensions for Texas Rangers and their widows. Submitted by the Fifty-fifth Legislature (1957), adopted in an election Nov. 4, 1958. (See also Art. VIII, Sec. 1-e.)]

Sec. 67. **State Retirement Systems.** — (a) General Provisions. (1) The Legislature may enact general laws establishing systems and programs of retirement and related disability and death benefits for public employees and officers. Financing of benefits must be based on sound actuarial principles. The assets of a system are held in trust for the benefit of members and may not be diverted.

(2) A person may not receive benefits from more than one system for the same service, but the Legislature may provide by law that a person with service covered by more than one system or program is entitled to a fractional benefit from each system or program based on service rendered under each system or program calculated as to amount upon the benefit formula used in that system or program. Transfer of service credit between the Employees Retirement System of Texas and the Teacher Retirement System of Texas also may be authorized by law.

(3) Each statewide benefit system must have a board of trustees to administer the system and to invest the funds of the system in such securities as the board may consider prudent investments. In making investments, a board shall exercise the judgment and care under the circumstances then prevailing that persons of ordinary prudence, discretion, and intelligence exercise in the management of their own affairs, not in regard to speculation, but in regard to the permanent disposition of their funds, considering the probable income therefrom as well as the probable safety of their capital. The Legislature by law may further restrict the investment discretion of a board.

(4) General laws establishing retirement systems and

optional retirement programs for public employees and officers in effect at the time of the adoption of this section remain in effect, subject to the general powers of the Legislature established in this subsection.

(b) **State Retirement Systems.** (1) The Legislature shall establish by law a Teacher Retirement System of Texas to provide benefits for persons employed in the public schools, colleges, and universities supported wholly or partly by the state. Other employees may be included under the system by law.

(2) The Legislature shall establish by law an Employees Retirement System of Texas to provide benefits for officers and employees of the state and such state-compensated officers and employees of appellate courts and judicial districts as may be included under the system by law.

(3) The amount contributed by a person participating in the Employees Retirement System of Texas or the Teacher Retirement System of Texas shall be established by the Legislature but may not be less than six percent of current compensation. The amount contributed by the state may not be less than six percent nor more than 10 percent of the aggregate compensation paid to individuals participating in the system. In an emergency, as determined by the governor, the Legislature may appropriate such additional sums as are actuarially determined to be required to fund benefits authorized by law.

(c) **Local Retirement Systems.** (1) The Legislature shall provide by law for:

(A) The creation by any city or county of a system of benefits for its officers and employees;

(B) A statewide system of benefits for the officers and employees of counties or other political subdivisions of the state in which counties or other political subdivisions may voluntarily participate; and

(C) A statewide system of benefits for officers and employees of cities in which cities may voluntarily participate.

(2) Benefits under these systems must be reasonably related to participant tenure and contributions.

(d) **Judicial Retirement System.** (1) Notwithstanding any other provision of this section, the system of retirement, disability, and survivors' benefits heretofore established in the constitution or by law for justices, judges, and commissioners of the appellate courts and judges of the district and criminal district courts is continued in effect. Contributions required and benefits payable are to be as provided by law.

(2) General administration of the Judicial Retirement System of Texas is by the Board of Trustees of the Employees Retirement System of Texas under such regulations as may be provided by law.

(e) **Anticipatory Legislation.** Legislation enacted in anticipation of this amendment is not void because it is anticipatory.

[Note. — The foregoing Sec. 67 of Art. XVI, an amendment, was added to revise and consolidate provisions relating to state and local retirement systems and programs, and providing for a maximum state contribution to state systems of 10 percent of aggregate compensation paid to individuals. Submitted by the Sixty-fourth Legislature (1975) and adopted in an election April 22, 1975. See also notes under Art. III, Sections 48-a, 48-b, 51-e and 51-f; and Art. XVI, Sections 62 and 63.]

Sec. 68. **Promoting, Marketing Agricultural Products.** — The Legislature may provide for the advancement of food and fiber in this state by providing representative associations of agricultural producers with authority to collect such refundable assessments on their product sales as may be approved by referenda of producers. All revenue collected shall be used solely to finance programs of marketing, promotion, research, and education relating to that commodity.

[Note. — The foregoing Sec. 68 of Art. XVI, an amendment, was added to provide for the advancement of food and fiber production and marketing through research, education and promotion, financed by producers of agricultural products. Submitted by Sixty-eighth Legislature (1983) and adopted in election Nov. 8, 1983.]

ARTICLE XVII. — MODE OF AMENDING THE CONSTITUTION OF THIS STATE

Sec. 1. **How the Constitution Is to Be Amended.** — The Legislature, at any regular session, or at any special session when the matter is included within the purposes for which the session is convened, may propose amendments revising the Constitution, to be voted upon by the qualified electors for statewide offices and propositions, as defined in the Constitution and statutes of this State. The date of the elections shall be specified by the Legislature. The proposal for submission must be approved by a vote of two-thirds of all the members elected to each House, entered by yeas and nays on the journals.

A brief explanatory statement of the nature of a proposed amendment, together with the date of the election and the wording of the proposition as it is to appear on the ballot, shall be published twice in each newspaper in the

Article XVII — (Cont'd.)

State which meets requirements set by the Legislature for the publication of official notices of officers and departments of the state government. The explanatory statement shall be prepared by the Secretary of State and shall be approved by the Attorney General. The Secretary of State shall send a full and complete copy of the proposed amendment or amendments to each county clerk who shall post the same in a public place in the courthouse at least 30 days prior to the election on said amendment. The first notice shall be published not more than 60 days nor less than 50 days before the date of the election, and second notice shall be published on the same day in the succeeding week. The Legislature shall fix the standards for the rate of charge for the publication, which may not be higher than the newspaper's published national rate for advertising per column inch.

The election shall be held in accordance with procedures prescribed by the Legislature, and the returning officer in each county shall make returns to the Secretary of State of the number of legal votes cast at the election for and against each amendment. If it appears from the returns that a majority of the votes cast have been cast in favor of an amendment, it shall become a part of this Constitution, and proclamation thereof shall be made by the Governor.

[Note.—Sec. 1 of Art. XVII was amended to revise provisions on time and method of proposing amendments to State Constitution and publishing notice of proposed amendments. Submitted by the Sixty-second Legislature (1971) and adopted in an election Nov. 7, 1972.]

Sec. 2. **Rewriting State Constitution.** — (a) When the Legislature convenes in regular session in January, 1973, it shall provide by concurrent resolution for the establishment of a constitutional revision commission. The Legislature shall appropriate money to provide an adequate staff, office space, equipment, and supplies for the commission.

(b) The commission shall study the need for constitutional change and shall report its recommendations to the members of the Legislature not later than November 1, 1973.

(c) The members of the Sixty-third Legislature shall be convened as a constitutional convention at noon on the second Tuesday in January, 1974. The Lieutenant Governor shall preside until a chairman of the convention is elected.

The convention shall elect other officers it deems necessary, adopt temporary and permanent rules, and publish a journal of its proceedings. A person elected to fill a vacancy in the Sixty-third Legislature before dissolution of the convention becomes a member of the convention on taking office as a member of the Legislature.

(d) Members of the convention shall receive compensation, mileage, per diem as determined by a five-member committee, to be composed of the Governor, Lieutenant Governor, Speaker of the House, Chief Justice of the Supreme Court, and Chief Justice of the Court of Criminal Appeals. This shall not be held in conflict with Art. XVI, Sec. 33 of the Texas Constitution. The convention may provide for the expenses of its members and for the employment of a staff for the convention, and for these purposes may by resolution appropriate money from the general revenue fund of the State Treasury. Warrants shall be drawn pursuant to vouchers signed by the chairman or by a person authorized by him in writing to sign them.

(e) The convention, by resolution adopted on the vote of at least two-thirds of its members, may submit for a vote of the qualified electors of this State a new Constitution which may contain alternative articles or sections, or may submit revisions of the existing Constitution which may contain alternative articles or sections. Each resolution shall specify the date of the election, the form of the ballots, and the method of publicizing the proposals to be voted on. To be adopted, each proposal must receive the favorable vote of the majority of those voting on the proposal. The conduct of the election, the canvassing of the votes, and the reporting of the returns shall be as provided for elections under Sec. 1 of this article.

(f) The convention may be dissolved by resolution adopted on the vote of at least two thirds of its members; but it is automatically dissolved at 11:59 p.m. on May 31, 1974, unless its duration is extended for a period not to exceed 60 days by resolution adopted on the vote of at least two thirds of its members.

(g) The Bill of Rights of the present Texas Constitution shall be retained in full.

[Note.—The foregoing Sec. 2 of Art. XVII is an added amendment, providing for a constitutional convention for the purpose of submitting to the voters a new constitution or revisions of the existing state constitution. Submitted by the Sixty-second Legislature (1971) and adopted in an election Nov. 7, 1972.]

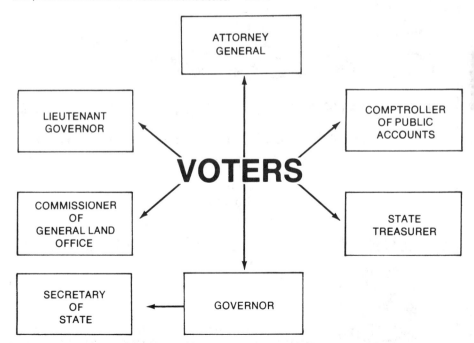

ART. IV, SEC. I of the Constitution makes the governor chief executive officer, but provides for election of other executive officials, which denies him real control of the executive department as shown on this chart. Courtesy of the Texas Advisory Commission on Intergovernmental Relations and the Institute for Urban Studies, University of Houston.

TEXAS
SCIENCE

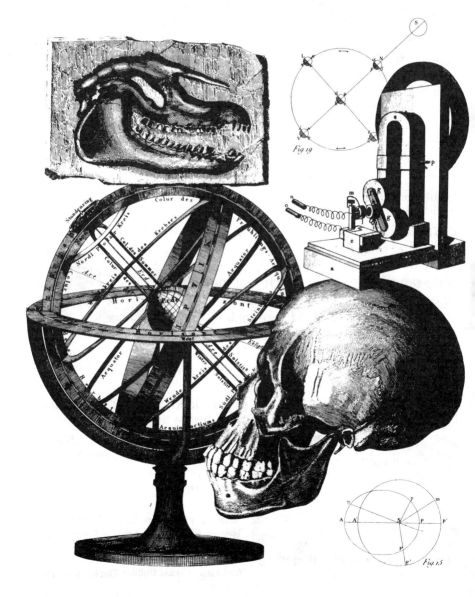

Fig 19

Fig 15

YOU CAN STILL SEE OUR TEXAS PIONEERING SPIRIT AT WORK.

STAYING AT THE LEADING EDGE OF ENERGY TECHNOLOGY.

Trinidad.

From the beginning, Texas Utilities has been a leader when new, better, and more efficient ways of providing electrical energy have been developed.

As early as 1926, we opened the first power plant in Texas to use lignite for fuel. Even in the 1940's, when Texas natural gas was abundant and inexpensive, we were planning for the future by acquiring major supplies of East Texas lignite.

In 1971, at Fairfield, we completed the first lignite generating unit — others followed, and have saved our customers more than $3.5 billion in the last 10 years. And right now we're nearing

Big Brown.

modern-day together they in fuel costs completion of the first nuclear power plant in Texas.

We're still planning for the future in wide-ranging energy research that includes everything from conservation and load management to fusion, solar and wind power. We're using additional energy sources such as cogeneration and combustion turbines. All of these have one aim — to continue to deliver adequate electricity to our customers at a reasonable cost.

The pioneering spirit isn't a list of past deeds or an outline of plans for the future. It's an attitude, a commitment to looking for, finding and developing better ways to do our job. Providing energy today and planning for your energy future.

Comanche Peak.

Dallas Power & Light Company
Texas Electric Service Company
Texas Power & Light Company

Divisions of Texas Utilities Electric Company

Science in Early Texas

This essay on science in Texas was written by Mike Kingston, editor of the Texas Almanac, and was reviewed by Dr. Dan Flores of Texas Tech University and W. Keene Ferguson of Austin, authors of books on science in Texas. Any errors are the author's alone.

Modern civilization is based on the application of scientific discoveries and on technological innovation developed over thousands of years. Human beings have long sought to understand the world in which they live and to control the forces of nature.

Science today is considered the systematic accumulation of knowledge. Experimentation develops a body of knowledge from which general laws of nature can be interpreted. All the world's great societies have included men devoted to the investigation of the mysteries of nature. The Western world traces its scientific heritage to the Greek philosophers who began to make observations and to formulate theories of how the world works as it does. After the fall of the Roman Empire in the fifth century, the Greek tradition was maintained by Moslem and Arab scientists. From their libraries and scientific works, Western scholars began to build today's scientific tradition during the Renaissance.

Science in its most primitive form is simple curiosity. Reasoning human beings have long sought knowledge of their world. Often the curiosity was driven by the survival instinct.

Today scientific investigations range from such esoteric subjects as cosmology and subatomic particles to the more immediately practical splicing of genes to develop pesticides and higher yielding crops.

Only in recent decades has Texas moved to strengthen its scientific standing. Throughout its history, the state's economy was based on plentiful natural resources such as rich land for agriculture and petroleum. As the 20th century draws to a close, however, the state's leadership is determined to make Texas a competitor in the emerging high-technology industries that are expected to dominate the world's economy in the 21st century. To do so, much greater emphasis must be given to excellence in scientific research at state universities.

This essay surveys the development of science in the Texas culture through the 19th century.

Prehistoric "Scientists"

When the ancestors of prehistoric Texans crossed the Bering Strait from Asia to North America 20,000 years or more ago, they brought a body of primitive scientific knowledge. Fire would change the characteristics and form of materials, they knew. Meat and plants could be cooked to improve taste. The points of wooden spears would be hardened by firing.

These early inhabitants knew that certain types of stone made durable tools and weapons. Undoubtedly, they watched for these materials as they moved across the country. Once the best deposits were located, they would be remembered.

A primitive understanding of physics led to the development of the atlatl, or throwing stick, that enhanced the strength of the hunter's arm and broadened the range of his spear. The butchering of animals gave an understanding of anatomy, and experimentation taught which parts of the carcass were the most nutritious. Plants were studied to determine which were edible or poisonous and which had medicinal properties.

Like people elsewhere, these early Texas settlers developed a definitive knowledge of their region. As hunter-gatherers, they became primitive geographers. They learned the migration routes of animals, determined when, where and which plants and nuts would be ripe and noted the location and habits of potential friends or foes.

These early Texans' knowledge of physics expanded about 2,000 years ago when the bow and arrow came into use. Some historians call this man's first "machine."

As groups turned to agriculture, they practiced a rudimentary horticulture. Studies indicate, for example, that Caddo Indians in East Texas were selective in their choice of corn seed, seeking to improve the strains they used. Like many American Indians, these Texas tribes were sophisticated farmers.

All primitive people also studied the sky, for religious observances as well as agricultural pursuits. Some structures on Caddoan temple mounds appear to have their doorways aligned to catch the first rays of the summer and winter solstices. It is not understood if this alignment was for religious services or to determine when to plant crops, or both. Doorways of the huts

of the Antelope Creek peoples on Landergin Mesa in the Panhandle also faced east. The lodges of the Wichitas faced east with the supporting poles set in cardinal and semi-cardinal directions.

Some archaeoastronomers think that pictographs at Hueco Tanks near El Paso and in West Central Texas record the supernova that created the Crab Nebula in 1054 A.D. If this is the case, these early Texans noted an event not observed by European astronomers, although some sky-watchers in the Orient did record the phenomenon.

Though these early Texans exhibited a natural curiosity, their "science" never advanced beyond the observational and experimental stages. They developed no theories concerning the general laws of nature. Their religions and myths were explanation enough for the phenomena at hand.

The European Contact

During the Renaissance, Spain was one of the leading centers of scientific learning in Europe. The final reconquest of the southern peninsula in 1492 gave the Spaniards access to great Moslem scientific libraries. But few scientific specialists accompanied explorers on the early expeditions into Texas. Alvar Nunez Cabeza de Vaca wandered for seven years in the state after being shipwrecked on Galveston Island about 1528. But he and his companions were more interested in survival than exploration. Cabeza de Vaca did gain the distinction of performing the first known surgery in Texas when he removed an arrowhead from an Indian's chest in the 1530s.

Francisco Vasquez de Coronado's expedition, which entered the Texas Panhandle from the west in 1540, was more intent on survival and locating the legendary Seven Cities of Gold and Quivira than in a scientific study of the land. Luis Moscoso de Alvarado, commander of the followers of Hernando de Soto after the leader's death, also performed only topographical observations while traveling through East and North Central Texas in the 1540s.

Not until the late 17th century, when LaSalle established a French colony near the head of Lavaca Bay, did the Spanish take serious interest in their vast domain of Texas. Even then, defense held priority over scientific investigation. Missions were established, but the priests and soldiers concentrated on surviving Indian hostilities and the harshness of the land and climate.

Nicolas de la Fora, a captain of Spanish Royal Engineers, made the first scientific exploration of Texas lands in 1767-68. He described the region of the Balcones Escarpment near San Antonio in his journal and mapped part of the Colorado River during a military survey by the Marquis de Rubi.

Precious metals were always of interest to the Spanish. Legend holds that they discovered silver and worked mines on the San Saba River. But these excavations have never been found.

Between 1762 and 1803, Spanish interest in Texas waned. Texas had been a borderland when the French held the Louisiana Territory. But this region was ceded to Spain in 1762, and the frontier moved from the Sabine River to the Mississippi for four decades. After France regained the region and sold it to the United States, interest in Texas was rekindled on both sides of the Sabine River.

Alexander Von Humbolt, a German scientist, studied the natural history of Mexico between 1799 and 1804, but his map of the country was indefinite about Texas. Anglo-American explorers began to trickle into the region. Early in the 19th century, Philip Nolan, a filibuster who was killed in a gun battle with Spanish authorities, gathered information on Texas that was written up by James Wilkinson. In 1806, Lt. Zebulon Pike, commissioned by President Thomas Jefferson to explore the newly acquired Louisiana Territory, was taken into custody by the Spanish in the Upper Rio Grande Valley and escorted through Texas to the Louisiana border. From that experience, Pike also wrote a description of Texas.

The first published study of geology in Texas was done by Edwin James in 1823. He accompanied the expedition of Maj. Stephen H. Long on a survey of the Rocky Mountains in 1820 and returned along the Canadian River.

Mexico won its independence from Spain in 1821 and stepped up the scientific exploration of Texas. Between 1826 and 1834, Jean Louis Berlandier, who was long regarded as the first scientist to work in Texas, was employed as a botanist and zoologist by the Mexican government. Berlandier also collected plant specimens for scientists in Europe, where interest in the frontier province flourished. Berlandier and Rafael Chovel, a mineralogist, accompanied Gen. Mier y Teran on a survey of Texas' eastern border in 1828. Berlandier also collected specimens around Goliad and Laredo and along the Bexar Road during his career.

As Anglo-American colonization of Texas proceeded, scientific interest in the region grew. Thomas Drummond, a Scottish naturalist, visited the Austin Colony in 1833-34 under the patronage of Sir William James Hooker, Regius Professor of Botany at the University of Glasgow. While touring the settled region of Texas, Drummond collected about 750 species of plants and 150 specimens of birds. The Scotsman planned to settle in Texas, but he died in Cuba during the trip home.

Turbulent times in the mid-1830s slowed scientific work until after Texas won its independence from Mexico. Then natural scientists flocked to the new Republic.

Anglo-American Exploration

The 19th century has been called the heyday of the naturalists. In England and Europe, laymen flocked to the fields, beaches and mountains to collect plant specimens. Religion prompted much of the activity, for it was felt that a study of the wonders of nature brought one closer to God, the creator of it all. In the United States, the study of natural history became a patriotic, as well as scientific, endeavor. European scientists belittled the plants and creatures of the New World, claiming they compared in no way with the wonders of the Old. Thomas Jefferson took offense, going so far on one occasion as to send the skeleton of a huge moose to Comte de Bufon and Baron Georges Cuvier, the leading French naturalist, to prove the superiority of American fauna. To many Americans, natural science offered an opportunity to prove the greatness of the country and its superiority over others.

At the same time that the study of natural science became popular, specialization in the field commenced. Early naturalists both collected and classified their new discoveries. In the early 19th century, these endeavors were separated: Some tramped the wilderness and collected specimens of plants, animals, birds, fish and insects. And others — so-called "closet naturalists" at the universities — devoted themselves to classification of the discoveries and to the systemization of the growing body of knowledge.

Most of the natural scientists in Texas were field collectors who sent their specimens to scientists in the eastern United States and in Europe. Often these field researchers were honored by having species of flora and fauna named for them; these hard workers were usually unsung, while the closet naturalists got credit for the discoveries.

Science in this period also was undergoing a lengthy divorce from religion. From the beginning of the Renaissance, scientific discoveries were measured by their compatibility with religious teachings. One geologic theory was that the surface of the earth was unchanged since the creation, and another held that there was a uniform geologic structure worldwide. "Classical geology" attempted to fit the geology of the New World into these European structural and lithological models.

Edwin James, who studied the Canadian River in the Texas Panhandle, and George W. Featherstonhaugh, after a survey of the geology in Northeast Texas in 1837, were among many American geologists who found that the European models did not apply in America. Their findings helped gain acceptance of the revolution in geological theory that culminated with Charles Lyell's publication of the three-volume "Principles of Geology." The English geologist propounded two major new theories: "uniformitarianism" in which he argued that the physical forces at work on the earth's surface today are the same as those in ages past; and "stratigraphy" in which he held that in a series of strata, the lowest is the oldest. By 1845, when the first formal geological survey was launched in Texas, geologists were practicing modern methods of the science.

Naturalists, however, were by far the largest group of scientists to visit early Texas. Dr. Samuel W. Geiser, a professor of science at Southern Methodist University, compiled a list of 342 men of science who came to the state between 1820-1880 specifically to study its flora and fauna. The opening of Texas coincided with political turbulence in Europe, and Geiser estimated that one-quarter of this total were Germans, many of whom had university training in scientific fields.

Scientists faced a dual hardship in frontier Texas. They were vulnerable to all the dangers faced by other settlers — Indian raids, disease, climate and political instability. Additionally, the scientists often faced hostility from other early Texans. These settlers were of a "practical" mind and did not understand the value of collecting flowers or bugs or poking around river beds looking for fossils. The scientists were considered "idlers" and often were the objects of scorn. Geiser noted it also was a doubly lonely life for the collectors. Usually they were in Texas to stay, and no professional peers were available in the wilderness with whom to discuss their work and compare discoveries.

Ferdinand Jakob Lindheimer was a classic German political refugee. A native of Frankfurt, he attended the University of Bonn, where he developed a love for botany. Lindheimer immigrated to Illinois and later collected in Mexico before coming to Texas during its revolution. For a time in 1839, he collected for another scientist, George Engelmann, before they formed a partnership to provide specimens for Asa Gray of Harvard. Gray, one of the first modern naturalists in the United States, published his first book, "Elements of Botany" in 1832. It was the first American book to break with the Linnaean classification system and to propose a more natural method of classifying specimens. Gray kept up a vast correspondence with naturalists throughout North America, including many in Texas. In his later years, he was one of America's top scientists and was respected in Europe. The Harvard professor also was a long-time correspondent with Charles Darwin and an enthusiastic defender of Darwin's theory of evolution. Specimens gathered in Texas probably were among those evaluated by Darwin while developing his theory, which today is a standard concept in the biological sciences.

For 13 years, Lindheimer was a tireless collector. He collected extensively in a region bounded by Fredricksburg, Houston and San Antonio. A picturesque figure with his two-wheel cart and pair of hunting dogs, the young German often was accompanied by Indians on his forays. More than 1,500 species of plants were collected by Lindheimer, and his collections were sent to England, Switzerland, Germany, Ireland, France and Canada, as well as to collectors in the eastern United States. After his death, the Texas naturalist's collection was shown at the World's Fair in Paris. In 1852, Lindheimer ended his collecting career and became editor of the German community newspaper, "Neu-Braunfelzer Zeitung," which became one of the best foreign language newspapers in America.

In 1839, the internationally known ornithologist John James Audubon visited Texas and collected bird specimens around Galveston and Houston.

Geology also attracted attention. In 1840, Francis Moore Jr., editor of the Houston Telegraph and Texas Register and an amateur geologist, published a description of the state's geology. A year later, William F. Kennedy, the British consul, wrote a book on Texas in which he initiated the myth of the region's rich mineral deposits. Kennedy's contention was not based on scientific evidence.

In Germany, Prince Solms, the first commissioner-general of the Adelsverein, which was colonizing the Fisher-Miller grant in the Texas hill country, became intrigued with the legends of Spanish silver mines in the region. In an attempt to determine the mineral wealth, the Berlin Academy of Sciences was asked to participate in a study of the colony's geology. Ferdinand Roemer of Hildesheim was selected to make the survey.

Roemer arrived in late 1845 and spent 18 months surveying the geology of the region of German colonization. Before leaving Texas in 1847, he accompanied John Meusebach on an expedition to make a treaty with the Comanches on the San Saba River. The German scientist used modern geological methods in his survey. While no precious minerals were discovered, Roemer's work won high praise from contemporaries in Europe. He wrote two books on his experiences in Texas and on the state's geology.

Charles Wright came to Texas in 1837 and stayed 15 years. Wright collected throughout the settled part of the state and accompanied the U.S.-Mexican Boundary Commission in 1849. The young scientist worked with

Gray, and he received the first stipend paid by Smithsonian Institution in exchange for a set of specimens collected while with the boundary commission. Although the U.S. Army agreed to provide transportation for his specimens, Wright had to walk the entire 673 miles from San Antonio to El Paso. Army officers had little more regard for scientists than did Texas' settlers. The Smithsonian published a book in 1853 on the 650 specimens of plants collected by Wright on the expedition. Wright left Texas after the commission finished its work and went on to a distinguished career in his field.

While Roemer and Wright were university-educated scientists, many of the early naturalists in Texas were self-taught. Gideon Lincecum was one of these. Texas was the third frontier upon which Lincecum lived. He developed an early interest in natural history and settled permanently in Texas in 1848. Lincecum corresponded with great scientists on three continents — Louis Agassiz in the United States, Charles Darwin in England and Alexander von Humboldt in Germany. For almost 30 years, Lincecum traveled his adopted state, sending collections of specimens across the nation and the ocean. Many of his papers were published in scientific journals in the United States and Europe. He died in 1874.

Most of these early studies of the geology and natural history of Texas were funded by private sources. After Texas joined the United States in 1845, however, the federal government launched studies of the territory.

Though medicine was far from today's scientific enterprise, interest stirred in the subject in the Republic of Texas. In 1839, Ashbel Smith, a physician and champion of education in early Texas, wrote the state's first scientific paper: a study of a yellow fever epidemic in Galveston in 1839. The following year, Drs. Richardson and Smith of San Luis proposed publication of a medical journal in Texas to deal with "improvements in the science," but it was never published. Other medical treatises also were published within this period. Although they fell far short of scientific standards, their presence reflects an interest in broadening medical knowledge.

The Republic recognized the need for protecting creations and operated a patent office for nine years. All of the 14 existing patents reflected a utilitarian use rather than scientific innovation. The editor of the Matagorda Bulletin counseled that this record should not be judged too harshly: "Our country is yet too young, and our citizens too much engaged in other pursuits to expect much from them in the way of invention or improvement."

Texans of this period did miss one opportunity to gain scientific fame. Samuel F. B. Morse offered to tender "the perpetual use of his Electro Magnetic Telegraph" to the Republic of Texas in 1838. No record exists of the answer of Texas officials to the proposal, but in 1860, Morse formally withdrew the offer in a letter to Gov. Sam Houston.

In general, however, the poor state of the Republic's finances prohibited its ability to aid any type of scientific studies.

Federal Government Surveys

With the purchase of the Louisiana Territory from France in 1803, President Thomas Jefferson launched an era of government surveys of the newly acquired territory. The Lewis and Clark expedition, which covered the Missouri River to the Rocky Mountains and down the Columbia River to the Pacific Ocean, began in 1803. Before it returned, a second expedition was sent into the new territory. Thomas Freedom, a frontier surveyor and civil engineer, was to lead the survey of the Red River from the Mississippi to its source. Dr. Peter Custis was the first academically trained naturalist to accompany one of these government surveys, and his reports on the Red River are the first scientific writings on Texas' flora and fauna, although they have been obscured by others. The expedition was terminated in July 1806 after a confrontation with a superior force of Spaniards on the river. The boundary of the Louisiana Territory was still under negotiation, and Jefferson had instructed Freeman to avoid armed conflict. Custis catalogued nearly 80 birds and animals and almost 190 plants during the four-month survey and is credited with three new biological discoveries. In addition to the biological observations, the scientist also made a mineral collection and took meteorological readings.

Except for Edwin James' survey along part of the Canadian River in 1820, the U.S. government had no occasion to make further explorations of Texas until after annexation in 1845. Thomas Say, a geologist and naturalist, accompanied James.

Between 1845 and 1858, several military surveys were made of western Texas. The goal initially was to develop information for frontier defense, but this later was expanded to include a search for railroad routes and economic development. In 1845, James W. Abert explored along the Canadian River under orders from John C. Fremont. Five years later, Lt. H.C. Whiting first sketched the limits of the Edwards Plateau. And two years later, Randolph B. Marcy led an expedition along the Red River and across the Osage Plains from Fort Belknap, near present-day Graham, to the Llano Estacado. He was accompanied by several scientists including geologist George G. Shumard, paleontologist B. F. Shumard and mineralogist Edward Hitchcock. In 1854, Marcy and George Shumard returned to gather information on the Clear and Double Mountain Forks of the Brazos River. Maj. W. H. Emory's report on the U.S.-Mexican Boundary Survey in 1857 included studies of geology by Arthur Schott and C.C. Parry with a description of the region's fossils by T.A. Conrad.

During this period, Congress developed an interest in building an intercontinental railroad. At the same time, the growing rivalry between the North and South prompted a consideration of several routes, two of which were through Texas. These military surveys also added to the expanding body of knowledge about Texas' geology and ecology. The Pacific Railroad Survey, commanded by Lt. A.W. Whipple, entered Texas in June 1853 and traveled along the 35th parallel near the Canadian River. Jules Marcou, a French geologist, accompanied this party. A second survey team under Capt. John Pope traveled along the southern end of the Llano Estacado from El Paso to present-day Big Spring and then to Preston on the Red River. Marcou wrote a report on the geology of this route from notes kept by Pope. William Blake later wrote reports for both the Whipple and Pope surveys from notes kept by the officers. Dr. J. M. Bigelow published a book on the botany of the area covered by Whipple's survey.

As the 1850s drew to a close, the Army surveys and the work done by Ferdinand Roemer established a scientific heritage of geology in Texas. All natural sciences still were in a descriptive stage in the state. The territory and its flora and fauna were diverse and vast. But for the first time, the state government was to enter the field of scientific exploration, even if in a primitive and misguided way.

The State and Geology

Life in frontier Texas was harsh. Settlers took a no-nonsense approach to spending what little money they had. Science was a frill to Texans — and to most other Americans of the period, too. The Legislature reflected this point of view.

Economic development, however, was another matter. State aid for companies and individuals to stimulate growth had well-established precedents. State geological surveys had been initiated by the Carolinas in 1824, and the federal government financed several explorations into the new western territories. Texas backed geological surveys, not in the interest of science, but to aid farmers and to enhance its economy.

Gov. Peter Bell first proposed a state-financed geological survey in 1851. Supporters argued that a survey would enhance the value of state lands and would allow the state to identify precious minerals and reserve mineral rights on land granted to railroads. The Legislature turned down the proposal.

In 1856, a drought stimulated farmers' demands for state aid. State Sen. Louis Wigfall tied these demands to a geological survey by charging it to locate artesian wells in South Texas. In 1858, Wigfall got legislative approval of his plan, and $20,000 a year was appropriated for the work. B.F. Shumard was appointed the first state geologist, and his brother, George, was named assistant. The first state geological survey began in January 1859, and the state geologist submitted his first report to the governor in December of that year. Shumard concentrated his attention on the overall geology of the state, and his work established a sound basis for a systematic study of Texas' geology.

Unfortunately, the survey soon became embroiled in politics, and the newly elected governor, Sam Houston, replaced Shumard with Francis Moore Jr., an amateur geologist, in 1860. A year later, the Civil War forced the Legislature to suspend funding of the work.

After the Civil War, Reconstruction and the politics of retrenchment stymied serious geological research. The best qualified geologists came from Northern uni-

Mark Francis, a professor of veterinary science at Texas A&M University, was one of Texas' first great research scientists. He developed an inoculation for deadly tick-borne Texas Fever that allowed the cattle industry to improve herds. Francis also developed a dip that would kill the disease-bearing ticks on cattle. Photo courtesy Texas A&M University Archives.

versities, and the former Confederates of Texas would not hire them. When money was available, emphasis was placed on "economic" geology, which was little better than state-funded prospecting, some historians observe. At other times, money was wasted by unqualified officials. Texans' political egalitarianism overlapped into a technical field with the expected results. The main qualification for too many persons associated with state geology was residence in Texas, not scientific expertise. Although money was appropriated for a geological survey in 1866 and 1870, Gov. Richard Coke finally recommended that the effort be canceled in 1875 until adequate funding could be provided.

Perhaps the most competent geologist of the period was Anton R. Roessler, who worked for private firms and drew some of the first small-scale maps of Texas' geological regions. He also wrote pieces on the state's geology for the Texas Almanacs of 1872 and 1873. The Almanac often was the closest thing the state had to a scientific journal at the time.

Improvement in the survey of Texas' geology came in the 1880s. On the recommendation of the National Academy of Sciences, Congress consolidated several surveys in the western states with the creation of the U.S. Geological Survey in 1879. John Wesley Powell, a noted explorer of the American West, was the agency's second director. In 1884, Powell organized a series of cooperative topographic and geologic exploration programs with various states, including Texas. Support developed for a new state survey. Robert T. Hill, a Texan later called "the father of Texas geology," unsuccessfully lobbied for such a bill in 1886. Two years later, in the wake of a state land-reform bill that required the state to make a more diligent classification of lands, a state survey was easily approved by lawmakers. Edwin T. Dumble, a chemist and organizer in 1884 of the Texas State Geological and Scientific Association of Houston, was named state geologist.

The quality and quantity of Dumble's work exceeded that of all previous surveys, but Gov. Hogg vetoed the agency's appropriation in 1894. The retrenchment atmosphere created by the Populist movement and the Depression of 1894 were two major reasons. But the geologic survey also had been centered on soil and water problems in the undeveloped areas west of the 98th meridian. Hogg, an East Texan, saw little value in continuing it.

During the last decade and a half of the 19th century, studies of Texas geology advanced significantly. Both the USGS and the state survey began stratigraphic interpretations of major geologic features. In the 1886-87 USGS report, Powell cited the work of Charles A. White and Robert T. Hill on the Texas Cretaceous as the major geologic event of the year. And out-of-state institutions such as Harvard University and the American Museum of Natural History sponsored studies of aspects of Texas geology.

There also were some colossal mistakes. William Kennedy in the early 1890s discouraged oil exploration after viewing cuttings from a well drilled near where Spindletop was to usher in the Oil Age in 1901. Later, Kennedy tried to dissuade Anthony Lucas from drilling near the salt domes on the Gulf Coast.

Ironically, after Spindletop, the Legislature reactivated the university mineral survey. Its benefits no longer were in doubt.

The Other Sciences

Prior to the Civil War, Texas, even as a frontier state, probably only slightly trailed the rest of the nation in the support of science. In the Post-Civil War decade, about 2,000 people could be included in the circles of American science. Only about 500 of them, concentrated in the universities and federal government agencies in New England and the Middle Atlantic states, were serious researchers.

At this time, Texas did not have any universities, public or private, involved in experimental science. The normal schools concentrated on a classic education, which did not emphasize scientific learning. Early interest in science in Texas was fostered by private organizations.

Soule University opened Texas' first medical school in 1865 in Galveston. It was the forerunner of the University of Texas Medical Branch. The Galveston Medical Journal was published monthly for at least five years beginning in 1866. A year earlier, the Galveston Medical

School opened for eight years, and it was replaced by the Texas Medical College and Hospital in 1873. The quality of medical education in America was not good at this time, but the existence of these schools indicates a desire to improve the training of physicans in the state. All were private schools. Usually the instructors maintained a private practice, and medical research was limited or nonexistent.

Some private organizations interested in aspects of science were established. Most had a "practical" bent. The Texas Agricultural Society, for example, was founded in 1853 to promote improved methods of agriculture, and published at least one journal. But the organization did not last long. Agricultural clubs also existed in the state's German communities. After Reconstruction, the organizational pace quickened. A Texas Archeological Society existed in Austin for a brief time in 1876, and the Texas State Horticultural Society was founded in Houston a year earlier, lasting until 1922. Texas science historian Samuel W. Geiser identified at least 20 horticultural journals, or agricultural journals printing horticultural papers, existing in Texas between 1869 and 1910.

In 1880, the first Texas Academy of Science was organized in Austin by Samuel B. Buckley, Dr. Quintius Cincinnatus Smith and Dr. Franklin L. Yoakum. Several state officials were listed in the initial membership, and Gov. O.M. Roberts was elected the first president. Apparently the founders were seeking to add prestige to the organization, but Dr. Yoakum later wrote, "This was a mistake. The statesmen did nothing for science, and the existence of the Academy was purely nominal."

Two years later, Dr. Yoakum and Buckley moved the Academy to Palestine, where a number of men "interested in natural science were living." The statewide membership grew to 100, and a museum collection to include displays of the state's natural history was begun. The museum was exhibited at the State Fair of Texas at Dallas in 1886. The organization died in 1887 without publishing a journal. The second Texas Academy of Science was organized by members of the University of Texas faculty in Austin in 1892, and it still exists. The second academy published several annual journals, which concentrated more on academic science than on experiment and observation.

Institutionalized science was on the horizon in Texas, but it faced many barriers to acceptance.

Institutions and Science

The value of science was slowly being accepted in the industrializing eastern United States even before the Civil War. Development of a scientific agriculture to improve production was a leading concern. In 1850, educator Johnathan B. Turner proposed that the federal government establish a series of land-grant colleges to make higher education available to the "industrial classes." The schools would be financed by the sale of federal lands. In 1839, a similar idea had been proposed in the Congress of the Republic of Texas, and the Texas State Agricultural Society reiterated the idea for a state-supported school in 1853. U.S. Sen. Justin S. Morrill of Vermont became the champion of Turner's proposal. Morrill was frustrated by opposition from Southern congressmen, for they felt a federally funded school would infringe on states' rights. Even when a bill passed in 1859, President James C. Buchanan vetoed it. Morrill finally was successful in 1862 when Southern opposition was removed from the Congress by the Civil War.

In addition, support also was growing in the industrial East for research in universities, for both expanding scientific knowledge and training young scientists. At the time, ambitious young American scientists had to travel to schools in Europe for post-graduate education. Privately endowed Johns Hopkins University was established as the nation's first research school in 1876.

Texas Agricultural and Mechanical College was established as a federal land-grant school during the turbulent years at the end of Reconstruction and opened its doors in 1876. Its mission was to provide an education in the "agricultural and mechanical" arts. But there was considerable controversy surrounding the early years of the institution.

Like other American farmers, Texans were not convinced that agriculture could be taught in the classroom. This reluctance to embrace scientific farming lingered longer in rural Texas. Indeed, many Texans were not convinced that the government should be involved in higher education at all. At that time, higher education was considered a privilege, not a right. The president of one private school argued that tax dollars should not be spent to train a citizen to be more than a voter, juror or soldier.

Even proponents of a state-financed education disagreed about what curriculum should be offered. Gov. O.M. Roberts saw A&M's role as a vocational school. At one time, the governor asserted that Texas was more in need of skilled laborers than of men "learned in literature and science." The early administrations ignored the vocational training mandate and maintained a classical education curriculum. And there was the ever-present concern with financial frugality in the Legislature.

Slowly, Texas A&M earned respect in the agricultural community. In 1888, the school began publishing the results of experiments in bulletins. The first true experimental substation was opened in Beeville in 1892. Plans also were made to put experiment stations in each congressional district in the state. After the turn of the century, the extension service brought agricultural consultants from the school to every county in Texas. Scientific agriculture was making inroads.

State-supported higher education advanced when the University of Texas opened in Austin in 1883. In its early years, the university offered a classical curriculum. Members of its faculty, however, organized the second Texas Academy of Science in 1892 and began to publish a periodic journal.

In 1891, UT's medical branch was established in Galveston. Research in the institution's early years was limited at best, although there were talented instructors on the faculty. Dr. Allen J. Smith, the first chairman of the department of pathology, for example, published 103 articles on medicine in 30 years, and his work on hookworm was fundamental in establishing it as endemic in this country. A report in 1910, while complimentary of many facets of the medical education being offered, criticized the school's lack of research.

Much of the scientific exploration of Texas still was being done by out-of-staters. In 1885, Dr. V. Harvard published "A Report on the Flora of Western and Southern Texas" in the Proceedings of the U.S. National Museum. And Coulter published "Botany of Western Texas" in Vol. II of the Contributions from the U.S. National Herbarium, 1891-94. With these publications, the descriptive period of botanical research came to an end, and future studies concentrated on the relation of plants to the environment. UT first offered botanical courses in 1897, and two years later, the School of Botany was created by the board of regents. "A Biological Survey of Texas" by Vernon Bailey was published by the U.S. Department of Agriculture in 1905.

By the end of the 19th century, Texas was only gradually testing the concept of the value of science.

Science and "Texas Fever"

After the Civil War, the cattle industry boomed in Texas. Thousands of head of Longhorn were driven to railheads in Kansas and Missouri for shipment to the Midwest and East. Almost as quickly as the industry developed, however, it was shackled by quarantines in many states.

After apparently healthy Texas cattle were driven through an area, the domestic herds often died. The cause of the malady, called "Texas fever," was a mystery. But out-of-state stock owners knew one thing: Texas cattle were unwelcome. Herds from Texas often were forced from an area, and the economic loss caused by the disease, even in Texas, was staggering.

Texas fever also prohibited the improvement of the state's cattle herds. Blooded cattle brought into Texas from other parts of the United States or foreign countries usually contracted the disease and quickly died. Texans were both puzzled and frustrated by the malady.

U.S. Department of Agriculture scientists began studying Texas fever. Experiments in 1879-80 proved that the disease could be transmitted by insects. Further studies indicated that infected regions corresponded with the habitat of a tick, the *Boophilus bovis*. By the 1890s, it was determined that the tick, which could be found on Southern cattle, carried microscopic parasite, a small protozoan, which caused a malarial-type disease. The protozoan, which was traced to the tick, was found in the spleens of cattle that were autopsied after dying of Texas fever.

By tracing the source of the disease to the tiny parasite, scientists found that both propagation and incubation of the disease depended upon the hatching of the tick's eggs. With this information, methods could be developed to identify infected cattle and to set up quarantine zones. In reviewing the successful research,

USDA scientists plugged for public support by emphasizing the role of experimentation.

For Texans, however, this was only half the battle. Forty to 70 percent of the foreign cattle died when brought to the state. In 1889, Mark Francis, a young graduate of Ohio State University, was hired as associate professor of veterinary science and as Extension Service veterinarian. His first assignment: find a cure for Texas fever.

For more than a decade, hampered by a lack of funds and equipment, Francis studied the disease. Working with the cooperation of the Missouri Extension Service, the Texas A&M scientist developed a serum from the blood of resistant Southern cattle for an inoculation of Northern and foreign cattle. As a result of this protection, blooded cattle could be brought into Texas to upgrade existing herds, and the modern Texas cattle industry was born.

Francis provided a further service by developing an economical dip with which to rid cattle of ticks, and Texas fever was almost wiped out within a few years. For his contributions, Francis was called "the father of the modern Texas cattle industry."

While Francis' successes proved the value of scientific research, Texas had to relearn the lesson time and again.

Conclusion

At the end of the 19th century, Texas was behind other parts of the United States in the development of science. Its agrarianism and concomitant suspicion of intellectual pursuits served to keep science at arm's length. Only in cases in which an immediate and recognizable economic impact could be determined was science enlisted. If a geologist turned up precious minerals, a botanist a marketable plant or a Mark Francis a cure for Texas fever, Texans would tolerate the cost. Otherwise, the pursuit of science was a waste of time when there were so many practical endeavors to be pursued.

Such an attitude existed in other parts of the United States, but it did not linger as long as in Texas. Because the state was blessed with rich mineral resources, such as petroleum, which could be had almost for the investment of labor and money, intellectual pursuits had a low priority. It was many decades before the concept of acquiring knowledge for its own sake and for application to problems at a later date took root in the state.

Bibliography

Books

Adler, Mortimer J., and Charles Van Doren, editors, **Great Treasury of Western Thought**; R.R. Bowker Co., New York, 1977.

Alexander, Nancy, **Father of Texas Geology: Robert T. Hill**; Southern Methodist University Press, Dallas, 1976.

Barber, Lynn, **The Heyday of Natural History**; Doubleday & Co., Garden City, N.Y., 1980.

Benton, William, publisher, **Great Issues in American Life: A Conspectus, Vol. 2**; Encyclopaedia Britannica, Inc., Chicago, 1968.

Butterfield, Hubert, **The Origins of Modern Science: Revised Edition**; The Free Press, New York, 1965.

Chapman, John S., **University of Texas Southwestern Medical School: Medical Education in Dallas, 1900-1975**; Southern Methodist University Press, Dallas, 1976.

Coles, James S., editor, **Technological Innovation in the '80s**; Prentice Hall, Inc., Englewood Cliffs, N.J., 1984.

Debus, Allen G., **Man and Nature in the Renaissance**; Cambridge University Press, London and New York, 1978.

Desmond, Adrian, **Archetypes and Ancestors: Palaeontology in Victorian London, 1850-1875**; University of Chicago Press, Chicago, 1982.

Dethloff, Henry C., **A Centennial History of Texas A&M University, 1876-1976, Vols. 1 and 2**; Texas A&M University Press, College Station, 1975.

Faculty and staff, UT Medical Branch at Galveston, **The University of Texas Medical Branch at Galveston: A 75-Year History**; University of Texas Press, Austin, 1967.

Ferguson, W. Keene, **Geology and Politics in Frontier Texas, 1845-1909**; University of Texas Press, Austin, 1969.

Ferguson, W. Keene, **History of the Bureau of Economic Geology, 1909-1960**; Bureau of Economic Geology, University of Texas at Austin, Austin, 1981.

Geiser, Samuel Wood, **Horticulture and Horticulturists in Early Texas**; Southern Methodist University Press, Dallas, 1945.

Geiser, Samuel Wood, **Naturalists of the Frontier**; Southern Methodist University Press, Dallas, revised and enlarged edition, 1948.

Goldstein, Thomas, **Dawn of Modern Science: From the Arabs to Leonardo Da Vinci**; Houghton Mifflin Co., Boston, 1980.

Goldstine, Herman H., **The Computer from Pascal to Von Neumann**; Princeton University Press, Princeton, N.J., 1972.

Greenberg, Daniel S., **The Politics of Pure Science**; World Publishing Co., New York and Cleveland, 1967.

Hutchins, Robert Maynard, **Great Books of the Western World, The Great Ideas II, Vol. 3**; Encyclopaedia Britannica, Chicago, 1952.

Jaffe, Bernard, **Men of Science in America: The Role of Science in the Growth of Our Country**; Simon and Schuster, New York, 1944.

Kastner, Joseph, **A World of Naturalists**; Alfred A. Knopf, Inc., New York, 1977.

Kevles, Daniel J., **The Physicists: A History of a Scientific Community in Modern America**; Alfred A. Knopf, Inc., New York, 1978 (rpt. Vintage Books, New York, 1979).

Kuhn, Thomas S., **The Structure of Scientific Revolutions**; University of Chicago Press, Chicago, 1970.

Lich, Glen E., and Dona B. Reeves, editors, **German Culture in Texas: A Free Earth; Essays from the 1978 Southwestern Symposium**; Twayne Publishers, A Division of G.K. Hall & Co., Boston, 1980.

Newcomb, W.W., Jr., editor, **Indian Tribes of Texas**; Texian Press, Waco, 1971.

Nixon, Pat Ireland, **The Medical Story of Early Texas, 1528-1853**; Mollie Bennett Lupe Memorial Fund, 1946.

Sarton, George, **Ancient Science and Modern Civilization**; University of Nebraska Press, Lincoln, 1954.

Sarton, George, **Six Wings: Men of Science in the Renaissance**; Indiana University Press, Bloomington, 1957.

Sellards, E.H., W.S. Adkins and F.B. Plummer, **The Geology of Texas, Vol. I, Stratigraphy**; University of Texas at Austin Bulletin No. 3232, Aug. 22, 1932 (rpt. UT, Austin, 1966).

Stuik, Dirk J., **Yankee Science in the Making**; Little, Brown and Co., Boston, 1948.

Weniger, Del, **The Explorers' Texas: The Land and Waters**; Eakin Press, Austin, 1984.

Articles

Breeden, James O., "Health of Early Texas: The Military Frontier"; Southwestern Historical Quarterly (SWHQ), Vol. LXXX, No. 4, April 1977.

Flores, Dan L., "The Ecology of the Red River in 1806: Peter Custis and Early Southwestern Natural History"; SWHQ, Vol. LXXXVIII, No. 1, July 1984.

Geiser, Samuel W., "A Century of Scientific Exploration in Texas, Part 1: 1820-1880"; Field & Laboratory, Vol. IV, No. 2, April 1936.

----------------, "A Century of Scientific Exploration in Texas, Part 1b: 1820-1880"; Field & Laboratory, Vol. VII, No. 1, January 1939.

----------------, "The First Texas Academy of Science (1880-1887)"; Field & Laboratory, Vol. XIII, No. 1, January 1939.

Leighton, Morris M., "Natural Resources and Geological Surveys"; Bulletin of the Society of Economic Geologists, Vol. 46, No. 6, Sept.-Oct. 1951.

Muir, Andrew Forest, "Patents and Copyrights in the Republic of Texas"; Journal of Southern History, Vol. XII, No. 2, May 1948.

Ransom, Harry, "Sherman Goodwin - Texas Physician"; SWHQ, Vol. LV, No. 3, January 1952.

Salmon, D.E., "Experiments in Animal Disease: Some Examples of Development of Knowledge Concerning Animal Diseases"; U.S. Department of Agriculture Yearbook of 1899, Washington, 1899.

Winkler, Charles Herman, "The Botany of Texas: An Account of Botanical Investigations in Texas and Adjoining Territory"; Bulletin of the University of Texas, No. 18, Austin, 1915.

Archaeology Beneath The Sea

By Mary Crawford
Editorial Assistant, Texas Almanac

According to one archaeologist, shipwrecks are "windows in time." Some windows are being opened wider by the Institute of Nautical Archaeology, a non-profit, scientific and educational organization with headquarters in College Station. Since its founding in 1973, The institute has applied modern scientific archaeological techniques to underwater archaeology, raising to a science the field once scorned as "mere skin-diving" or treasure hunting by land-based archaeologists, and has vastly increased our understanding of the maritime life of the past 3,000 years.

The Institute, associated with but not part of Texas A&M University, is the brainchild of Dr. George F. Bass. Bass was a graduate archaeology student at the University of Pennsylvania in 1960 when he was chosen to direct a team excavating an ancient shipwreck off Cape Gelidonya in southwest Turkey. Learning to dive in a YMCA pool in six weeks, Bass successfully guided the excavation of the Late Bronze Age shipwreck, the first to be completely excavated using the same scientific standards as are used in land archaeology. For the next several years, Bass, with primary financial backing from the National Geographic Society, the National Science Foundation and the University of Pennsylvania Museum, as well as interested individuals, continued underwater excavations at Cape Gelidonya and at Yassi Ada, also in Turkey. His team further refined undersea archaeological techniques, adapting old equipment for their use or designing new, including a submersible decompression chamber, which allowed for longer dives, and an underwater "telephone booth," a plastic dome on legs which sits on the ocean bottom and allows up to four divers to stand and talk to each other or with people on the surface in comparative comfort. A small research submarine was built for Bass' group, and it was used to test three types of side-scanning sonar for the U.S. Navy.

By 1967, Bass was directing the largest diving project in the world. No one, not even the U.S. Navy, was sending as many divers (25) to as great a depth (140 feet) twice a day, six days a week for months at a time.

After a brief return to land archaeology in 1971, Bass formed the Institute of Nautical Archaeology in 1973, with financial backing from a small but enthusiastic and generous group of supporters. Originally based in Cyprus, the Institute was soon forced to leave because of political instability. After operating out of staff members' houses for several years, the Institute accepted the offer of a permanent home at Texas A&M University in College Station in 1976.

The Institute and the university have a symbiotic relationship: The Institute staff offers a course of study through A&M's anthropology department leading to a masters degree with a specialization in nautical archaeology, and the Institute's internationally acclaimed projects lend prestige to the university. A&M provides office space for the Institute, pays staff salaries for the time devoted to teaching and provides some student fellowships. The Institute pays salaries for the time the staff spends on Institute projects. Bass relinquished the presidency of the Institute in the early 1980s to physics professor Dr. Donald Frey. Bass is now Distinguished Professor of Archaeology at Texas A&M and is archaeological director at the Institute.

There are about 25 masters candidates enrolled in A&M's nautical archaeology program at any one time, studying such topics as classical seafaring, wooden ship construction, patterns of early maritime trade, history of naval warfare, the politics of sea power and the legal aspects of underwater archaeology. They are encouraged to study the foreign language that will be most useful in the part of the world where they expect to be doing their field work: Spanish for the Caribbean and Latin America, French or German for Mediterranean sites. The students gain practical experience working at Institute project sites around the world. In the mid-1980s, these included excavations of a 16th century Spanish mission in the Turks and Caicos Islands, a British Crown Colony in the Caribbean; the city of Port Royal, Jamaica, which sank during an earthquake in 1692; a 3,400-year-old merchant ship near Kas, Turkey, and a 17th century, armed Portuguese merchant ship off the coast of Mombasa, Kenya, and the search for Columbus' last two ships, believed to have sunk in St. Ann's Bay off the north coast of Jamaica in 1503. According to Bass, no other group in the world is doing so much underwater archaeological work in so many different places.

Bass believes that the best preparation for the masters program in nautical archaeology is a good liberal arts education, including history, languages, art history, anthropology and science, but he admits that some of his best students have had engineering backgrounds. Only three other universities in the world offer a similar course of study at present, according to Bass: the University of Haifa in Israel, St. Andrews in Scotland and East Carolina University at Greenville, N. C.

Once the decision is made to excavate a site, the first things to be done are photographing, mapping and taking rough measurements to help the archaeological team decide how to approach the wreck — where to start digging. Much of the divers' time is spent clearing sand away from the site. Merely identifying an object as an artifact is difficult, since anything in the sea accumulates thick deposits of calcium, coral, shells and mud. This buildup, called concretion, starts as soon as an object is placed in the water. "We dropped a hammer at a site in Turkey one year and didn't retrieve it," says Bass. "The following summer we found it completely covered with concretion and almost unidentifiable. Some of the artifacts we're searching for have been in the sea for a couple of thousand years. A mass of concretion as big as a fist may contain something as small as a knife blade. An anchor may weigh half a ton."

Large artifacts are raised to the surface in baskets attached to lifting balloons. Small objects are often retrieved using a large vacuum-cleaner-like suction hose that carries water, sand and objects to the support ship, where they are run through screens, allowing the water and sand to flow back into the sea, leaving small objects behind.

If the wooden hull of the ship has been exposed to sea water, shipworm has usually destroyed it completely. But the hulls of some of the Institute's wrecks have been partially preserved by being buried under silt, mud or cargo. Careful soaking for as much as two years in vats of polyethylene glycol keeps the wood from drying out and crumbling. The preserved hull fragments are pieced back together in the Institute's labs, increasing long-sought knowledge of ancient ship construction.

Once the underwater site is fully excavated, which can take two or more summers, depending on size and difficulty, the real work begins, according to Bass. "Conservation takes much more time than diving. We often do two years of conservation in the lab for every month we spend underwater," he says.

Conservation includes the aforementioned treatment of wooden fragments in polyethylene glycol. Other artifacts must be carefully chipped out of their coat of concretion. Pottery and glass are soaked to leach out salts, then dried slowly for at least a year to keep them from cracking. Metals are treated with caustic solutions and electrolysis to remove concretion and chlorides, then coated with a microcrystalline wax to seal the pores so they can be displayed.

Experts are sometimes brought from outside the Institute to help analyze the finds. One large, archaeologically rich wreck — an 11th century cargo ship near Serce Liman, Turkey, dubbed the "Glass Wreck" because of its large cargo of Islamic glass — required the services of a dozen scholars, some of them borrowed from such prestigious organizations as the Corning Glass Museum, the American Numismatic Society and the Metropolitan Museum of Art, to write the final multivolume publication on it.

Bass' favorite project is the 3,400-year-old ship found near Kas, Turkey. Much of the hull was found intact, having been buried for 34 centuries under layers of silt and cargo, giving the Institute staff valuable information on ship construction at the time King Tut sat on the throne of Egypt. The ship seems to have been a merchant vessel carrying raw materials. Artifacts include three tons of copper and the earliest tin ingots and the earliest glass ingots ever found. There are objects made of gold, silver and faience, and there is raw ivory in the form of an elephant tusk and a hippopotamus tooth. There is Greek pottery, a Canaanite gold medallion and a Mycenaean merchant's seal — such a mix of goods from different cultures that it is, to Bass, "the most exciting and important ancient shipwreck found in the Mediterranean." Excavation of the site, begun in 1985, may take until 1990 to complete. Another decade may be required for conservation and analysis of the finds.

From its landlocked headquarters in College Station, the Institute of Nautical Archaeology plans to continue opening those undersea "windows in time."

Photo Credit
A diver from the Institute of Nautical Archaeology at Texas A&M University takes measurements of the hull of an 11th century Islamic shipwreck at Serce Liman, Turkey. Underwater archaeologists from Texas do work around the world. Institute of Nautical Archaeology Photo.

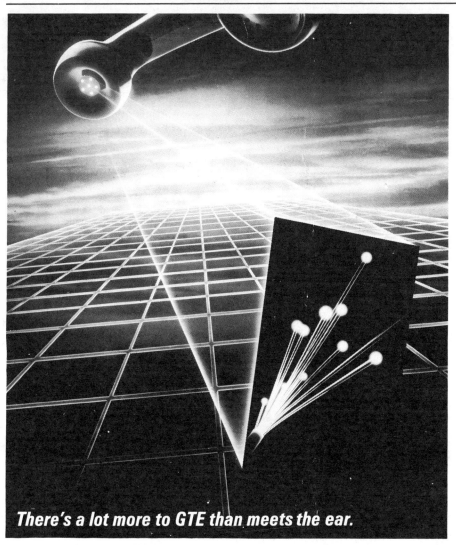

There's a lot more to GTE than meets the ear.

A man in Dallas dials a telephone number in Denton and as he speaks, his voice message — along with thousands more — is transmitted on a light beam finer than a human hair.

Fiber optics. It's the communications technology of tomorrow. And it's at GTE today.

The same GTE that's been providing the Southwest with dependable telephone service since 1926. Whether it's a call from the press box to the sidelines at Texas Stadium. An urgent message to the control tower at D/FW International Airport. Or a check-in call to your babysitter.

The same GTE whose ongoing commitment to research has led to the development of heat shields that protect the space shuttle. Lights that make trees grow inside mountains. A network that helps computers talk to each other no matter what language they speak. And a telephone service that's the most efficient, technologically advanced system available anywhere.

So if you've been thinking we're just another telephone company, you haven't been keeping an eye on us.

There's a lot more to GTE than meets the ear.

FOR INFORMATION ON BUSINESS PHONE SYSTEMS ... PLEASE CALL

DALLAS, TX. 214/258-2000
TULSA, OK. 918/455-2000
HOUSTON, TX. 713/680-9220

Graduate students from Texas A&M University, (l-r) Elizabeth Ham and Cristi Hunter, carefully excavate the tusks of a mammoth found on the Brazos River. The animal's huge tusks measured four and one-half feet from base to tip and six and one-half feet along the curve. Texas A&M University Photo.

The Great Beasts of Texas

From seven million years ago until about 10,000 years ago, huge elephant-like beasts roamed North America. Literally hundreds of fossilized bones and teeth of mammoths and mastodons have turned up to testify to the number of these animals that roamed Texas. Four scientifically significant sites have been excavated in the state in the past decade, revealing much about the animals and, possibly, providing information about when man first came to the region.

Mammoths are related to today's African and Indian elephants; mastodons have no living successors. A mammoth resembled an Indian elephant with its large head, but the prehistoric beasts were larger, standing as much as 12-14 feet tall at the shoulder and weighing a minimum of seven to eight tons. The mammoth had long forelegs, and its back tapered downward to short hind legs, like today's elephant. A mastodon was shorter, but had a stocky body. The beast's legs were of nearly equal length, and it stood between seven and nine feet tall at the shoulder. The body was bulky like a rhinoceros. Both mastodons and mammoths had trunks and tusks.

The animals' eating habits also differed, which becomes an important distinction. Mammoths were herd animals, likely to be found grazing on plains; mastodons were loners, preferring to browse on trees and plants in woodland environments. The teeth of the animals reflect the different eating habits. A mammoth's teeth have rows of ridges, well suited to grinding grass. The enamel on a mammoth's tooth was only about one-sixteenth of an inch thick, while the enamel on the mastodon's heavier, smoother tooth, more suited to chomping, was a quarter inch thick.

Mammoth's and mastodon's relation to man probably is the most intriguing question raised in the excavations of four sites in recent years.

In Brazos County, Dr. D. Gentry Steele, associate professor of anthropology at Texas A&M University, and his research associate, David L. Carlson, advanced the study of *taphonomy* — the study of the disposition of animal bones — through the excavation of a mammoth site.

The remains of the 13-foot tall adult male mammoth were discovered in a Brazos River bank in 1982. About 75 percent of the skeleton was in place. Researchers determined that the animal had been butchered by human beings after it died on a flat river levee sometime in the late Pleistocene age, between 10,000-11,000 years ago.

Natural forces and other animals can break and

Archaeology

scatter bones, so how can it be determined that humans did the work? Researchers pursued the answers to three major questions, Dr. Steele said: What bones were broken? How were they broken? And in what patterns were the bones scattered?

In this case, the only bones broken were the femurs and humeri — hind and foreleg bones. These are the largest bones in the body and took considerable skill and strength to break. So-called "impact points" were identified, indicating that humans had struck the bones with some heavy object.

Why these bones? To open the bone to get at the nutritious, edible marrow or to provide bone blanks for making tools, Dr. Steele said. Additional tests are being conducted to determine if scratches found on the bones were left by stone tools during a butchering process. Researchers have not determined how the animal died, only that humans at some later period used parts of the carcass. This skeleton will be put on display at the Witte Museum in San Antonio, which, along with Texas A&M, financed the excavation.

On a small creek near the Bosque River in Waco, remains of 12 mammoths — six females and six juveniles — have been uncovered. No direct evidence of human involvement with the animals has been found. But Calvin B. Smith, director of the Strecker Museum at Baylor who has supervised recent excavations, said that at least two "indicators" of man have been found.

One of the skeletons was found with the scapulas — the shoulder blades — flip-flopped and none of the other bones out of position. This would occur during butchering, Smith explained. The forelegs would be thrown across the back to begin butchering on the animal's chest.

In addition, Smith said, the animals were found with a separation of the vertebral — or spinal — column that did not appear to be due to water movement or to trampling by other animals. Only one animal had a tail bone, David Lintz, who directed early excavations of the site in 1978 and 1979, pointed out. When an animal is skinned, he said, the tail comes off, too, another "indicator" of human presence.

The Lubbock Lake site offers insight into both the presence of man and mammoth in the late Pleistocene and of the environment at the time. Dr. Eileen Johnson, curator of archaeology and director of the Lubbock Lake Landmark for The Museum at Texas Tech University, has excavated the site since 1973. Remains of three mammoths — one adult and two juveniles — have been found at what appears to be a processing area. Radiocarbon tests date the site at 11,100 years old. Bones of the animals have shown both cut lines made by stone tools during butchering and impact points, indicating that the bones were broken by humans for food or tool blanks. Other scratches indicate the bones were gnawed by anivals as well. No evidence exists to indicate how the animals died, although a Clovis projectile point found in the 1930s drew attention to the site.

Lubbock Lake is one of the most unique archaeological sites in Texas. Excavation through the various strata of remains has found a long-term presence of man in the region. Dr. Johnson said the site has provided the most complete record of the late Pleistocene on the South Plains. During the time in which the mammoths roamed the area, the climate was damper and without the wide temperature fluctuations of today. The region was a lush grassland with scattered trees and occasional deciduous wooded areas, mostly hackberry trees.

Late in 1984, construction workers found the remains of four mastodons and one mammoth while digging the foundation for a new skyscraper in downtown Austin. The Trammell Crow Co. retains contract archaeologist Alton Briggs to study archaeological and paleontological discoveries, like the remains, found during construction of buildings.

Briggs said that preliminary investigations did not indicate the involvement of humans with the animals. The site is significant, however, in providing evidence of mastodons and mammoths in the area between 20,000-25,000 years ago. Scientists at the University of Texas at Austin are studying the remains. The nearby Balcones fault was the dividing line between the forested highlands and the coastal prairie in Texas during the Pleistocene.

The Austin site already is providing information on the region's environment during the period, which was cooler and damper than today. One fossilized plant, an *equisetum*, or horse's tail, still grows, but it's habitat is much farther north. Whole sections of the site were removed to UT's Balcones Research Center, and Briggs expects these deposits to yield information for a decade. The site probably will become a base for comparison when other discoveries are made in the future. With the construction boom under way in Austin, Briggs expects many more sites to be uncovered. Dr. Joel Shiner, a retired professor of anthropology at Southern Methodist University, is pursuing another aspect of the human-mammoth relationship. At a site in San Marcos, Shiner turned up evidence that early humans took parts of the dead mammoths to their camp sites. All the excavations in Texas have been of kill sites where the animals died.

But Shiner found mammoth and mastodon tooth enamel at a camp site, together with Clovis spear points and stone chipping debris. Future excavations are expected to reveal the use humans made of the material.

Shiner thinks it could have been used to make jewelry, since the enamel has the appearance and texture of a fine china.

Man's relation to mammoths and mastodons is a subject of only relatively recent study. While human remains have been found in association with mammoth since the 1930s, it was not until 1952 that the first mammoth determined to have been killed by humans was excavated near Naco, Ariz. Nine Clovis projectile points were found in the skeleton, indicating that hunters had killed the animal. Several kill sites were discovered after the Naco excavation was publicized when people began to report finding large bones.

Several theories have evolved concerning man, mammoth and other megafauna. One holds that man was so skillful that he hunted the megafauna to extinction. Critics claim that a change in climate destroyed the animals' food resources.

Those who support the climate theory question whether early man could have killed the beasts. Dr. David Meltzer, an assistant professor of anthropology at SMU, said there is no evidence that man systematically hunted any animals before the bison. And it is particularly unrealistic to think humans systematically hunted mammoths and mastodons. Foraging groups, Meltzer emphasized, do not specialize in one type prey; that is dangerous, for they have to bring something home.

Meltzer also pointed out that it is very difficult to kill a mammoth. Tests on present-day elephants have determined that it is extremely difficult to penetrate the animal's hide deep enough to cause a mortal wound with a spear. Some of the mammoth kill sites that have been excavated show evidence that the animals were stuck in sink holes. Without the technology to kill them, early humans could have just waited for them to die and scavenged the remains.

Critics of this view argue that we just do not know that much about early man's technology, and they point out that the scavenger theory also ignores the possibility that poison was used to kill the animals.

Whatever the outcome of this debate, however, mammoth and mastodon excavations in Texas will provide fodder for both sides.

David Lintz of Strecker Museum at Baylor University examines a portion of a vertebra of one of the mammoths found in Waco. Lintz performed the early excavations of the site that yielded remains of 12 of the huge animals. Texas Almanac Photo.

Pueblos On the Texas Plains

Texas' Plains Indians usually are thought of as nomadic hunters and gatherers. But during a 250-year period long before Europeans arrived, a culture distinguished by stone pueblos (houses) and an agricultural base thrived in the Canadian River Basin in Oklahoma and Texas. Landergin Mesa in Oldham County is the most spectacular of this series of pueblo-like villages in the Texas Panhandle.

Landergin Mesa, located about 50 miles west of Amarillo, was first recorded in scientific literature in the 1920s. The site was designated a National Historic Landmark and a property on the National Register of Historic Places in 1964. In 1981, the Office of the State Archeologist, Texas Historical Commission, obtained permission from landowner Robert W. Mansfield of Amarillo to carry out the first scientific investigation of the site. Two seasons of archaeological field work were conducted in the fall of 1981 and the spring of 1984 by the Texas Historical Commission with the cooperation of the Panhandle-Plains Historical Museum, West Texas State University, and with major funding from the Texas Historical Foundation and the U.S. Department of Interior, National Park Service. Mansfield received the Texas Historical Commission's Texas Award for Historic Preservation in 1982 for his efforts in protecting the site and promoting scientific studies. In 1984, Landergin Mesa was designated as a State Archeological Landmark and brought under the protection of the Antiquities Code of Texas.

From about 1200 A.D. to between 1450-1500, Landergin Mesa (called Arrowhead Peak by residents of the area) was inhabited by Indians designated by archaeologists as Antelope Creek Focus people. These Plains Indians broke from the traditional hunting-and-gathering practice to maintain agricultural villages. While the climate of the Plains was damper and cooler in the first millennium A.D. than today's, drought-like conditions were advancing during the period of occupation of the mesa. Farming was practiced at this time by the Indians along the eastern limits of the Great Plains. The availability of water was a factor. The Ogallala aquifer fed numerous springs in the Canadian River breaks and along the edge of the Llano Estacado and made agriculture feasible. (Springs disappeared on the Texas plains in the 1930s when commercial irrigation began to deplete the Ogallala aquifer.) Located on a 160-foot high mesa, the Landergin site also is easily defensible.

The 1981 field season, under the direction of State Archeologist Robert J. Mallouf, surveyed the mesa and surrounding area. A permanent grid system was established on the mesa top for all future studies, and the mesa and surrounding terrain were mapped. Controlled collections of artifacts from the surface were made, and two structures were excavated. This work allowed archaeologists to establish a sequence of site occupation and to determine the extent of damage to the site from vandalism and erosion. It was determined that structures once covered the one-acre area on the top of the mesa and that about 50 percent of the site was intact. A THC archaeological team returned in 1984 with Christopher Lintz serving as field director. Another two percent of the mesa top was excavated. Portions of about 10 structures were uncovered, with four proving to be residences and the others small storage or special activity buildings.

Archaeology

The architecture of the Antelope Creek Focus people is varible but has several distinctive features. Only one other group of Plains Indians constructed stone buildings; other groups built stockade or mud daub structures. The residences on Landergin Mesa are single-storied, rectangular in shape and contain up to 400 square feet of living space. Four center poles surrounded a central hearth and supported the roof. Vertical foundation stones were used along the sides of the sunken floors and then stones were set horizontally for the remainder of the walls. The entranceways were actually crawl spaces no more than two to two and one-half feet in height and extending to a maximum of 10 to 12 feet in length. These were always aligned to the east. They may indicate a knowledge of the movements of stars and could have been of religious significance or used to determine when to plant crops.

The buildings were constructed mostly of stone available from the top and sides of the mesa. Cedar, hackberry or cottonwood, probably cut from the banks of nearby Ranch Creek, was used for center posts and crossbeams. The walls were finished with plaster.

Early surveys have not definitely located agricultural fields near the base of the mesa. Many core samples of the soil of the area have been taken for pollen studies that have not yet been completed. However, a large number of grinding stones used to crush corn, probably a major crop, were found on the mesa. A bison bone hoe blade, characteristic of the Plains Indian farming operations, was found during the 1981 field session.

Apparently the Antelope Creek people were part of a widespread trade network. Pieces of many painted ceramics made by other Indians of the Southwest were found. Other exotic materials included a piece of bituminous coal fashioned into an ornament, marine shell beads from the Gulf of Mexico and the Gulf of California and numerous pieces of obsidian, a volcanic glass valued for its extreme sharpness when flaked.

In addition to farming, the inhabitants of the mesa were hunters. During the habitation periods, there was an influx of bison (buffalo) into the region. Meat from these animals was used for food, bones for household and agricultural tools, hides for clothing, sinews for cord. Bones of antelope, terrapin and turkey also were recovered. Evidence also was found on top of the mesa of the breaking and boiling of animal bone to extract the grease, which was used in tanning hides and as a sunburn ointment.

Many questions remain to be answered about the inhabitants of Landergin Mesa. Evidence uncovered in the 1984 excavation revealed that there were at least seven occupation periods between which the mesa may have been abandoned for a time. In addition, it has not been determined how crops were watered. Water could have been carried in containers, of course, but it is possible that diversionary trenches were run from springs to the fields, forming a primitive irrigation system.

Landergin Mesa represents an interesting view of prehistoric Texas. Much archaeological work remains to be done. But the site is one of two (the other is on the banks of the Rio Grande) in Texas at which pueblos were built, and it presents evidence that the Great Plains were successfully farmed long before the influx of farmers in the late 19th and early 20th centuries.

Billy Harrison, curator of archaeology at the Panhandle-Plains Historical Museum at Canyon, points out one of the unique vertical foundation stones at a dwelling on Landergin Mesa. Texas Almanac Photo.

Into the Eye of the Atom

Since 1967, scientists at Texas A&M University have probed the mysteries of the nucleus of the atom with a cyclotron. In the process, they have contributed to the growing field of knowledge about the complex nuclei and have developed practical applications in medicine, agriculture and other fields from the information obtained. By mid-1986 when an $8 million expansion of the machine is completed, the university will become only the second in the nation to possess a superconducting cyclotron that will open even broader vistas in research.

Cyclotrons accelerate subatomic particles to approach the speed of light and then direct the high-energy beams at targets. The results of the collisions of the high-speed particles with those in the target material are recorded and then interpreted to develop insight into the laws of nature that govern the nuclei of atoms.

Until the 1930s, scientists were limited to working with natural radiation to study the structure of the atom. Linear accelerators were first developed to increase the speed of particles. Ernest O. Lawrence of the University of California at Berkeley won the Nobel Prize in 1939 for the invention of the cyclotron, which speeds the particles in a circular path.

Nuclear Physics

Cyclotrons have three basic parts: A large electromagnet, which provides a strong magnetic field; two semicircular hollow shells called "dees" on which a radio frequency alternating voltage is applied; and a device that provides electrically charged nuclear particles. A vacuum is maintained in the cyclotron to keep the charged particles from colliding with air molecules.

The alternating voltage on the dees has a push-pull effect that accelerates the particles to ever higher speeds. The particles gain energy and, true to Einstein's law, $E = mc^2$, mass as they gain speed. The magnetic field forces the particles to follow a circular path, causing them to undergo the acceleration of the dees many times. As the particles accelerate, the circular path grows larger in diameter, and when the high-energy particles reach the outer wall of the cyclotron, they

are directed through an evacuated tube into a "cave" in which targets of various forms of matter are located. Less than one of each one million particles collides with an atomic nucleus in the target, but when they do, major changes in both the target nucleus and the particle can take place. The masses and atomic numbers can be changed and chunks of nuclear material are broken off. The results of these collisions are measured and studied to learn how the nucleus of the atom is structured and how it behaves.

The original cyclotron at Texas A&M University is nine feet in diameter and weighs 400 tons. In the expansion, a companion cyclotron six feet in diameter and weighing 100 tons, but with three times the power, is being constructed. The second unit is being built using the new technology of superconduction. In 1957, it was discovered that when certain alloys (such as niobium-titanium) of wire were cooled to near absolute zero or minus-273 degrees Centigrade, their resistance to flow of electrical current vanished entirely, and the current flowed with no resistance. In recent years, the technology for applying this principle to large magnets has been developed. The magnet of the new cyclotron is wrapped with wires made of an alloy of niobium and titanium embedded in copper and is cooled with liquid helium to within five degrees of absolute zero. At this level, there is no resistance to current flow in the magnet, and much higher currents can be used creating much stronger magnetic fields. The new unit will generate a magnetic field three times stronger than a traditional unit while using less electricity than an electric stove. Operated in tandem, Texas A&M's two units can accelerate particles to an energy of two billion electron volts.

The result of this more efficient unit, Dr. Dave Youngblood, director of the Cyclotron Institute, said, is to allow larger particles to be accelerated to higher speeds. Experiments with the new machine are expected to begin in 1986. Michigan State has the only superconducting cyclotron in the world today.

With the ability to accelerate larger particles, scientists can expand their research into the nature of the nuclei of atoms. Smaller particles tend to penetrate the nuclei, while the larger ones will hit the entire nucleus. "It is like the difference in hitting an automobile with another automobile rather than with a bullet and gives us a different kind of probe," Dr. Youngblood said. The

Graduate students at Texas A&M University's Cyclotron Institute observe the results of experiments in nuclear physics. The school's new superconducting cyclotron is only the second of its type in the nation. Texas A&M University Photo.

collisions with the larger particles will produce a different view of the nature of the atom.

Researchers from 25 foreign countries, as well as scientists from throughout the United States, have used the cyclotron at Texas A&M, which is in use 24 hours a day, seven days a week. The State of Texas provides less than one-third of the institute's $3 million annual budget, with the Robert A. Welch Foundation of Houston providing about one-sixth of the cost. The U.S. Department of Energy provides the rest of the financing. University researchers do not pay for use of the facility, but private industry does.

Texas A&M's research program is conducted by 35 Ph.D. scientists and 22 graduate students with either physics or chemistry backgrounds. A technical staff of 25 engineers, technicians and craftsmen also is employed, and the Institute operates a shop in which much of the equipment for experiments is made. Experiments in a number of areas are being conducted at any one time, Dr. Youngblood explained.

In general, the Texas A&M scientists are investigating the basic strong and weak nuclear forces that bind the nuclei and the atom together, the behavior of the nucleus when struck hard by another particle and left with a great deal of energy, and the behavior of two larger nuclei when they collide.

The practical application of knowledge obtained through experiments has been a major goal of the institute since its founding. In conjunction with the M.D. Anderson Hospital and Tumor Institute, more than 500 cancer patients were treated with beams of neutrons to prove the feasibility of the therapy. As a result, M. D. Anderson has built a cyclotron laboratory in Houston dedicated to neutron therapy. Spinoffs from the research for Anderson provided a number of diagnostic and therapeutic applications in medicine. In addition, new techniques for locating trace elements in materials — important in such applications as increasing the strength of materials, improving the safety of drinking water and identifying potential pollutants in Texas lignite — have been developed at the institute.

Texas A&M's Cyclotron Institute is one of the state's foremost research facilities and keeps its nuclear scientists at the cutting edge of the discipline.

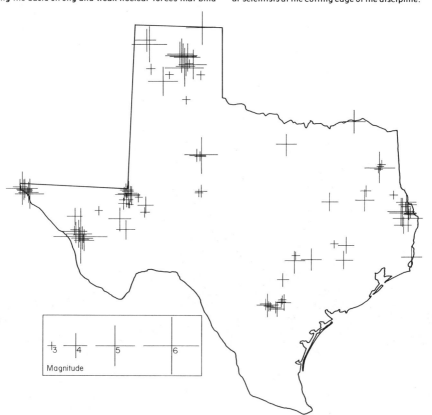

This map shows the location of earthquakes and their intensity since 1847. The size of the cross locating the earthquake indicates the force of the quake on what is commonly called the Richter scale. Map provided by the Department of Geological Sciences, University of Texas at Austin.

Numerous Quakes Shake Texas

This article was prepared by Dr. Wayne D. Pennington and Scott D. Davis. Pennington* was assistant professor of geophysics at the Department of Geological Sciences and the Institute for Geophysics at the University of Texas at Austin, and Davis is a research assistant.

Texas has experienced more than 100 earthquakes of magnitude 3 or greater from February 1847 to December 1984. Eighty-two earthquakes are known to have been felt, and 24 events are associated with reports of damage. One earthquake caused a death. Because the density of both seismographs and people is very low in Texas, knowledge of the state's seismicity is undoubtedly incomplete.

The largest known earthquake in Texas occurred on Aug. 16, 1931, near the town of Valentine in Jeff Davis

County. Magnitude estimates for this earthquake range from 5.6 to 6.4 (on what is commonly called the Richter Scale). The total felt area exceeded one million square kilometers (about 400,000 square miles). Chimneys were knocked down, walls were cracked, and adobe buildings collapsed, resulting in minor injuries. Numerous foreshocks and aftershocks to the Valentine earthquake also were felt.

Ten earthquakes had epicenters near El Paso. Several of these shocks have produced minor damage, such as cracked walls and driveways. One earthquake on March 7, 1923, caused an adobe house to collapse and led to the suffocation of a man in Juarez, Mexico, a few kilometers from the Texas border. This is the only known death caused by a Texas earthquake. Seismic activity in this area of Texas may be related to known faults that have been interpreted as part of the Rio Grande rift zone, a zone of crustal extension.

Geophysics

Notable earthquakes in the Texas Panhandle include the Panhandle and Borger earthquakes of 1917, 1925 and 1936 and the Dalhart event of 1948. All of these shocks produced minor damage to buildings. These earthquakes are probably associated with an ancient zone of crustal weakness that has been reactivated recently. Although the largest known earthquakes in the Panhandle have not exceeded magnitude 5, the potential for very large earthquakes remains uncertain.

Historic earthquakes in East and Central Texas include the 1847 Sequin, 1873 Manor, 1887 Paige, 1902 Creedmore, 1932 Mexia-Wortham and the 1934 Trout Switch events. These earthquakes were all fairly small and probably occurred as a result of sediment loading and resulting flexure in the Gulf of Mexico.

Earthquakes also have been located in Southeast Texas. The 1857 Wellborn, 1910 Hempstead and 1914 Anderson shocks may have been related to salt dome growth or to minor adjustments from sediment loading in the Gulf. The 1891 Rusk and the 1981 Center and Jacksonville earthquakes in Northeast Texas were all located on or near an 80-kilometer segment of the Mount Enterprise fault system.

Fluid withdrawal is usually associated with aseismic subsidence and faulting such as occurs in the Houston area. However, small earthquakes are sometimes reported. In 1925, small shocks were associated with subsidence produced from oil production at the Goose Creek oil field near Houston. Larger earthquakes in East Texas also may have resulted from fluid withdrawal. Tentative relations between withdrawal and seismicity have been proposed for the 1932 Mexia-Wortham and the 1957 Gladewater earthquakes. More convincing evidence exists for the earthquakes in some oil and gas fields in South Texas.

The injection of fluids into the earth's crust for disposal or for secondary recovery of oil also has been known to produce earthquakes in other states. Some earthquakes, none very damaging, may be associated with fluid injection in the Permian Basin of West Texas.

An account of Texas' seismicity would not be complete without considering the effects of earthquakes from neighboring regions. Popular legend holds that the New Madrid, Mo., earthquakes of 1811-1812 were responsible for the formation of Caddo Lake in Northeast Texas. However, there exist accounts of the lake's existence as a swampy area as early as 1722. Whether the shocks deepened the lake is not known. In any case, it is likely that moderately high intensities of shock waves were experienced in Northeast Texas. The Sonora, Mexico, earthquake of 1887 cracked several buildings in El Paso and caused a general panic in the population of that city. Seismic surface waves from the Alaskan earthquake of 1964 damaged a water well in the Texas Panhandle and produced waves, which damaged several boats, in channels along the Gulf Coast.

A fairly large earthquake in 1882 is commonly listed as having an epicenter near Paris, Texas. But this is probably an error; it now appears that the epicenter lay in Oklahoma.

Dr. Pennington's current address is Marathon Oil Co., Denver Research Center, P.O. Box 269, Littleton, CO 80160.

Tinkering With Texas Weather

This article was written by Mike Kingston, Editor of the Texas Almanac.

Everyone talks about the weather, but no one does anything about it. — Mark Twain

If you don't like Texas' weather, stick around a few minutes: It'll change. — An Old Texas Bromide

Not all Texans are content to just talk about the weather or to wait for a change: These are residents of rain-hungry sections of the state that try to give nature encouragement when clouds appear.

Weather modification is not a new concept. Texas Indians tried to coax rain with prayers and dances. Nineteenth-century Anglo-Texans tried to jar rain from clouds with cannon fire and dynamite.

In recent years, weather modification — or rainmaking, as the practice is commonly called — has become more sophisticated. Critics argue, however, that much more data are needed for a truly scientific approach to coaxing rain.

Weather Modification

For 13 years, Bob Riggio, chief of the Weather and Climate Section of the Texas Department of Water Resources in Austin, has overseen attempts to change weather. For several years, state, federal and local agencies were taking an organized approach to weather modification. Between 1974 and 1980, an estimated $4 million were invested in a data-gathering program that would put weather experiments on a sound scientific basis. The research was divided into three phases: Information gathering, experimental design and technology transfer. Only the initial phase was completed before the Reagan administration suspended federal funding for the program. Now officials are limited to analyzing the information that had been gathered. "We now have an experimental design (for modifying weather) and a statistical method to use in evaluation,"

Riggio said. "But we don't have money for the experiments." To complete the research will take a five-year, $1.5 million-per-year program. The Texas Legislature has shown little interest in financing the rest of the research, preferring to fund projects that show a quicker return on investment. Also, weather modification can generate highly emotional opposition.

Some Texas officials are moving ahead with rainmaking programs without state or federal assistance. Three of the seven weather modification projects operating in the state were initiated in 1985.

Weather modification has proved successful in other parts of the country. In the Pacific Northwest, techniques for dissipating cold fog have been developed to clear airport runways. Los Angeles has participated in a modification program to increase snowfall over the Rocky Mountains. Because of the extra spring runoff from the additional snow, the city receives extra water.

In Texas, increased rainfall is the goal, and the modification procedures are tricky.

Even in the middle of August, ice must be present in clouds in Texas to produce rainfall. Rainmaking procedures include "seeding" clouds with silver iodide. The compound has essentially the same crystal structure as ice, and placing these crystals in promising clouds accelerates the rainmaking process. The secret, however, is to know what type of clouds to treat, and when and where to take action. These answers must come from a broad base of knowledge about Texas climate, and then an array of sophisticated equipment and trained personnel is needed to translate this knowledge into action.

Two types of seeding procedures are used in an attempt to enhance rainfall in Texas. The airborne-seeding approach, in which airplanes fly at cloud bases or into clouds to deliver the silver iodide, is the most expensive, but perhaps the most effective. The second procedure is called ground base. In this approach, small generators disperse silver iodide into the atmosphere, where it is caught in wind currents and delivered to the clouds from the ground.

Three ground-base projects are in operation in Tex-

Silver iodide is released from flares on the wing of an airplane in an attempt to stimulate rain production in West Texas. Three airborne-seeding programs now operate in the state to improve rainfall. Texas Department of Water Resources Photo.

as, and each one claims success in increasing rainfall. One is operated by the Red Bluff Water and Power Control District near Pecos in Far West Texas. It was initiated in 1976 and suspended between 1981 to 1983 before resuming operation. This project covers the watershed of the Red Bluff Reservoir, and ground generators are located in four counties.

In the other two ground-base projects — one in the Panhandle and the other around Wichita Falls — the generators are located in Texas, but the target areas for increased rain are in Oklahoma. Both have been in operation since 1971 and claim success.

The oldest airborne-seeding project has headquarters in Big Spring and operates in the watersheds of the J. B. Thomas and E. V. Spence Reservoirs. Operated by the Colorado River Municipal Water District since 1971, this project includes two seeding aircraft and a professional meteorologist.

Cloud development is monitored by radar in Big Spring. When promising clouds appear, the meteorologist dispatches the airplanes, which are equipped with silver iodide flares of various sizes attached to their wings. After reviewing the data, the meteorologist selects the location where the seeding will take place in the cloud and the amount of silver iodide to be used. According to their own evaluation, officials of this project feel rainfall has been increased 20-25 percent.

Airborne-seeding projects for areas around San Angelo, Corpus Christi and San Antonio were started in 1985.

With Texas facing severe water problems as its population and industrial base grow in coming years, some officials think that it is time to take a more serious interest in weather modification. The state is past the time when it can just talk about the weather or wait around for it to change.

Earth to Moon By the Centimeter

This article was written by Diana Hadley, a writer/researcher for McDonald Observatory.

Because spacecraft have traveled to the moon, perhaps the most precisely known position on the surface of the Earth is the location of the University of Texas McDonald Observatory in the Davis Mountains of far West Texas. Such accurate positioning is due to a laser ranging program sponsored by the National Aeronautics and Space Administration at the observatory. A powerful laser shooting through a large telescope projects a beam of light to the moon or to one of several Earth-orbiting satellites, where special mirrors reflect the light back toward that same telescope. The length of time it takes for particles of light, called photons, in the beam to make the round trip is a measure of the exact distance between McDonald Observatory and the object reflecting the laser light.

The accuracy is phenomenal: The distance to the moon, roughly a quarter of a million miles, is measured to within a few centimeters.

McDonald personnel have measured the distance for 16 years, since Apollo 11 astronauts Neil Armstrong and Edwin Aldrin placed the first mirror array, or retroreflector, on the lunar surface in 1969. Prior to 1984, essentially all the world's lunar laser work was accomplished with the McDonald Observatory's 107-inch telescope, the largest and most powerful of the four telescopes atop Mount Locke.

As the space age began in earnest and plans were made for spacecraft to visit other worlds, the need for a source of data on other planetary surfaces and atmospheric conditions spurred the construction of the 107-inch telescope. This great reflector telescope, built as a cooperative project between NASA and the University of Texas, was completed in 1968. At that time, it was the third-largest telescope in existence.

The Korad laser beam, transmitted through the 107-inch telescope, was the world's first high-power, ultra-short-pulse system to range. Generating its light in eight-inch rods of pure ruby, the laser served uniquely well for 16 years. When decommissioned in 1985, the laser was given to the collection of important historical

scientific instruments at the Smithsonian Institution in Washington, D.C.

A more advanced-generation laser system now allows even greater precision in the measurements of the reflected light from the moon. The new laser is coupled to its own special 30-inch telescope to form the permanent McDonald Laser Ranging System (MLRS).

The MLRS not only reaches the moon, but also tracks and beams the laser off several of the artificial satellites placed in orbit around the Earth. The most heavily utilized satellite is LAGEOS, a solid lead "beachball" studded with retroreflectors orbiting about 5,000 miles above the Earth. LAGEOS is a much closer target than the moon and is relatively easy for small telescopes to range on and takes less laser power. The MLRS uses the same Quantel neodymium YAG laser to range both the moon and LAGEOS.

The telescope dedicated to the MLRS is located in a permanently mounted 40-foot equipment van, which also contains the laser and related computer systems.

Astronomy

The laser beam is aimed through the telescope, which also collects the returning photons. These photons are recorded by a photomultiplier, a very sensitive electronic device that converts low-intensity light into electric signals to be read as data by a computer. A second computer processes the data into the needed information.

Ranging is done both during daylight and nighttime. Scheduling must track the very different orbital configurations of the artificial satellite and the moon. Depending on the satellite's position as it passes through the West Texas sky and on whether the moon is also present, LAGEOS can be ranged from one to four times a day.

The lunar laser ranging schedule depends on the monthly cycle of the moon's phases. Presently, the moon is ranged three times a day for about 18 days out of the 29-day lunar month, the period from one new moon to the next. A gap of three days around full moon arises from the lack of contrasting shadows to highlight the mountains and craters that are used to guide the laser. Another gap occurs during new moon, when the lunar hemisphere that always faces the earth is in almost total darkness, making it difficult to aim the telescope precisely at the lunar reflector.

The initial pointing of the telescope is made by a computer, but final laser pinpointing rests on experienced human eyesight. A laser crew member guides the outgoing beam while looking at the image of the moon on a television screen. Two crew members, Windell Williams and Robert Gonzales, have more than 30 years of combined experience at guiding on the lunar surface features. Normally, the lunar laser crew uses the telescope for about an hour at a time for three periods during each 24-hour day. One member of the crew is assigned the outside spotter position, with his hand on a laser override switch, in case an airplane passes overhead. However, the beam is so narrow that someone would have to be looking directly into it for any eye damage to occur.

There were five laser targets placed on the moon. In addition to Apollo 11, the Apollo 14 and 15 missions left retroreflectors in 1971. Two French-made retroreflectors were carried aboard the Soviet's unmanned lunar rovers Lunakhod 1 in 1970 and Lunakhod 2 in 1973. However, no McDonald returns have been received from Lunakhod 1, which apparently failed to leave the reflector pointed at the Earth when it finally shut down.

The Apollo retroreflectors are 18-inch-square arrays containing 100 one-inch corner cubes recessed into square aluminum panels. These reflectors, although of much higher quality, work in the same way as the typical plastic retroreflectors used on highway posts. Their job is to send incoming light directly back toward the source.

The MLRS measures to better than a tenth of a billionth of a second how long it takes the light to go to the reflector and back. In the case of the moon, the light has an average round trip time of 2.5 seconds.

Each pulse of the laser shoots out millions of trillions of photons. The beam is 30 inches across when it leaves the telescope at McDonald, but it spreads out to cover a milewide circle by the time it reaches the moon's surface. The returning beam spreads out even more on its way back to Earth. Only a few photons make it back to the telescope, and only one is timed and recorded. To complicate things, other photons—light "noises" from other sources—also pour into the telescope. A statistical computer program helps indicate which photons came originally from the laser.

Measurement accuracy also depends on the length of the laser pulse. The shorter the pulse, the better the accuracy. The MLRS laser produces a pulse that lasts two tenths of a billionth of a second. It emits such a pulse 10 times a second.

Lunar ranging was originally undertaken to test theories of general relativity on the fundamental nature of space, time and gravity. Early in the project, the results showed that a leading contender, scalar-tensor relativity, was wrong and that Einstein's original 1915 Theory of General Relativity predicts within a few inches the exact shape of the moon's orbit around the Earth.

Data from the laser ranging system have also determined the rotational changes and polar wobbles of both the Earth and the moon far more accurately than the standard optical techniques used for centuries. These studies are basic to timekeeping and inertial navigation, as well as for probing the interior structures of both worlds. The data from the laser ranging system aid astronomers who are probing the question of whether the strength of gravity itself—the glue that holds the universe together—may be weakening as the universe expands.

Laser ranging stations in Hawaii, France, Australia and Germany are joining McDonald Observatory in scientific lunar ranging. As other long-term lunar and satellite laser ranging stations are activated around the globe, the system is providing information on the measurement of continental drift—the movement of tectonic plates over the Earth's surface.

During the early operational stages of the MLRS project, the moon continued to be ranged from both the MLRS and the 107-inch telescope for comparison purposes. Twenty-seven hundred feet, only half a mile, separate the imposing dome of the 107-inch telescope atop Mount Locke and the MLRS telescope. It is a pleasant eight-minute walk down the highest highway in Texas to get to the MLRS site almost hidden from the road in the brush, time enough to allow a visitor to ponder that the light bounced off the moon by these two instruments has aided in the understanding of the geophysical forces that produced the mountains of West Texas.

Mounted in a 40-foot van, the McDonald Laser Ranging System measures the distance between earth and the moon with phenomenal accuracy using a laser beam aimed through a 30-inch telescope.

TEXAS
EDUCATION

TEXAS HIGHER EDUCATION

The following was written for the Texas Almanac by Deborah Bay, director of public information and legislative liaison, Coordinating Board, Texas College and University System.

Seeking a link from its 20th century oil-based economy to a broadly diversified economic base in the 21st century, the State of Texas looked increasingly to its system of higher education to stimulate the transition.

Gov. Mark White in his State of the State address in January 1985 described educated minds and university research as "the oil and gas of our future."

"If our destiny is to be the State of the Future, then our strategy must be to educate our young people to the limits of their abilities. We must never lose sight of the fact that educated minds are the fuel of tomorrow's technology," he said. Calling for a greater state commitment to research, he pointed out that every dollar the state spends on research "will come back to us many fold in terms of greater production, higher productivity and enhanced economic development."

High technology was a major thrust of the state's push toward economic diversification, and a $35 million fund was created by the 69th Texas Legislature in 1985 to promote the development of new technologies in microelectronics, energy, telecommunications, aerospace and biotechnology, among other areas.

Despite early recommendations for severe budget cuts for state colleges and universities, the $6 billion appropriated for the 1986-87 biennium represented a 3.2 percent* increase over the previous two years. As part of the effort to stave off drastic reductions in higher education budgets, lawmakers enacted the first tuition increase to affect resident students in almost 30 years. Nonresident rates also were raised.

Moreover, the state demonstrated its commitment to preserving the quality of the existing system of higher education by holding the line against unnecessary expansion at a time when enrollments were down for the first time in at least two decades.

Proposals to establish four free-standing institutions were defeated as lawmakers turned down bills to convert upper-level centers to universities, a move which would have represented a major draw on state revenues in the future for construction of new campuses and program expansion. The centers, which share campuses with local community colleges, were established during the late sixties and early seventies as a means of expanding opportunities for higher education at low cost to the state. Efforts to create a new technical institute and to convert a marine-science institute into a general-purpose university also were defeated.

In response to continued forecasts of austere state economic conditions for the remainder of the decade, legislators created an interim study committee and directed it to undertake a comprehensive review of higher education. The possible closing or merger of state schools and the efficiency of university operations are among the issues the committee is expected to consider. The 19-member **Select Committee on Higher Education** will include the governor, lieutenant governor, speaker of the house, chairmen of the senate education and house higher education committees and the chairman of the **Coordinating Board, Texas College and University System.**

High Technology

The Legislature clearly expressed its desire to promote policies which would encourage economic development through the enhancement of university research. In addition to the $35 million biennial appropriation for the **Texas Advanced Technology Research Program**, lawmakers funded special technology-related research projects at several institutions of higher education in the 1986-87 funding period.

Some $1.3 million was appropriated for **robotics research** at the **University of Texas at Arlington** and at **Texas Tech University.** A **Center for Applied Quantum Electronics** at **North Texas State University** received $250,000 in funding, and another $200,000 was earmarked for a **Center for Application of Advanced Technology** at **Lamar University.**

A **Geo-Technology Research Institute** was authorized at the **Houston Area Research Center** in The Woodlands to conduct basic and applied research in the discovery of new reserves and the enhancement of oil and gas

---

*Figures for 1986-87 appropriations do not include the 3 percent increase for salaries; those figures were not available at press time.

production potential. To stimulate the transfer of university research findings for private-sector use, the **University of Texas at Austin** received authorization to establish a **Center for Technology Development and Transfer.**

Organized research funds, which provide seed money for attracting federal and private grants, totaled $13.5 million for the biennium at public universities. More than $407.4 million was spent on research activities in public universities and medical schools in fiscal year 1984, with state funds helping to draw $271.8 million in monies from federal and other sources.

In an effort to attract a major federal research project, the state enacted legislation establishing a **Texas National Research Laboratory Commission** to develop a proposal for the **Super-Conducting Super-Collider High-Energy Research Facility.**

Legislators sought to assure, however, that the state's new technological thrust would not be impaired by the weakened Texas economy.

Tuition Increase

In the search for additional sources of revenue without a general tax increase, the Legislature raised tuition for both resident and nonresident students attending state colleges and universities beginning in fall 1985. Resident tuition rates had not been increased since 1957.

Although numerous attempts to increase tuition have been made in recent years, prospects of severe funding cuts in higher education prompted sufficient support in 1985 for the measure. Proponents of the increase pointed out that tuition rates for resident students covered only 3 percent of the actual cost of education, noting that taxpayers have borne the burden for the state's expanding expenditures for higher education.

Opponents agreed to the tuition hike only after provisions were included to assure that additional monies would be available for needy students, in keeping with the state's commitment to promoting broad access to its higher education system.

The higher rates, along with certain other changes in tuition policy, are expected to generate an additional $263.7 million in revenue in the 1986-87 biennium. Legislators also earmarked $45.0 million in new monies for financial assistance through the **Texas Public Educational Grants Program.**

Resident tuition rates were raised from $4 to $12 per semester credit hour in fall 1985, increasing over the next decade to $24 per credit hour by fall 1995. Despite the increases, tuition costs for state residents are expected to remain among the lowest in the nation.

Out-of-state students and foreign students will be paying $120 per semester credit hour in fall 1985. Beginning in fall 1987, nonresident students will pay 100 percent of the cost of their education through a procedure which "indexes" tuition to an average amount appropriated to general academic teaching institutions in a biennium.

Substantial increases in tuition rates for medical and dental students also were enacted.

The added revenue provided by the higher tuition rates, along with careful paring in certain other areas of the budget, allowed legislators to provide a modest increase in overall funding for higher education.

Higher Education Funding

The **Legislative Budget Board** convened in December 1984 to consider its recommendations for funding higher education in the 1986-87 biennium against a gloomy backdrop of deepening state funding shortfalls. When the board completed its recommendations, state colleges and universities were slated for cuts averaging 26 percent of 1985 funding levels.

Under the leadership of Lieut. Gov. William P. Hobby, however, state lawmakers were able to provide a 3.2 percent increase for higher education from the previous biennium.

Particular effort was made to assure that adequate funds were provided to maintain faculty salaries at the same level as in 1985, while appropriations were reduced in such areas as building and grounds maintenance. Legislators also authorized a 3 percent increase in salaries for state employees, including university faculty members. In addition, administrators were given additional flexibility to use appropriated funds in areas of greatest need.

The Legislature for the first time appropriated $100 million each year for a constitutionally dedicated fund to support campus construction and certain other needs at 26 universities outside the University of Texas and Texas A&M University systems. Texas voters in November 1984 ratified a constitutional amendment establishing the higher education assistance fund and broadening participation in the permanent university fund to include all UT and A&M System components.

The table below compares state appropriations (from all funds) for higher education in 1986-87 with 1984-85.

ALL FUNDS COMPARISON OF LEGISLATIVE APPROPRIATIONS FOR THE 1986-87 BIENNIUM WITH THE 1984-85 BIENNIUM
All Agencies of Higher Education

	Appropriated		Increase
	1984-85 Biennium	¶1986-87 Biennium	Amount
*Public Senior Colleges	$2,405,844,457	$2,314,135,392	−$91,709,065
†Public Junior Colleges	880,307,508	889,847,592	9,540,084
‡Health Related Units	1,641,593,657	1,660,478,629	18,884,972
§All Other Agencies	877,965,874	1,125,284,262	247,318,388
Total	$5,805,711,496	$5,989,745,875	$184,034,379

*Includes $15 million appropriated to Texas Southern University for construction in S.B. 9, First Called Session, 68th Legislature.

†Amounts in Appropriations Bill.

‡Includes the Texas A&M University Medical Education Program and funds trusteed to the Coordinating Board for health related purposes.

§Includes Available University Fund and Higher Education Fund.

¶Does not include salary increase funds provided according to Article V, Section 95 of the appropriations bill for the 1986-87 biennium.

Statewide Enrollments

A total of 770,997 students were enrolled in the 139 Texas public and private institutions of higher education in fall 1984, a decline of 0.04 percent from the previous year. Although Texas enrollments have been leveling off for a number of years, the 1984 figures represent the first decline since the Coordinating Board, Texas College and University System, began collecting the data in 1965.

Commenting on the enrollment drop, Texas Higher Education Commissioner Kenneth H. Ashworth said, "The impact of the decline in the number of traditional college-aged people is beginning to show up in Texas, despite the overall population growth. Poor economic conditions during the past couple of years helped buoy enrollments so that the decline was not evident until this fall when more people were in the job market." Studies have shown that more students tend to enroll in higher education during periods of economic recession due to lack of employment opportunities.

The Texas system of public higher education encompasses 24 public 4-year universities, five upper-level universities, five upper-level centers, two lower-division centers, 49 community college districts, one technical institute with four campuses, seven medical schools, two dental schools, a school for marine resources and a special institute for the deaf. Two community college districts have been created in the past two years, the first to be approved by local voters since 1972. The **Northeast Community College District**, established in 1984, covers Camp, Morris and Titus counties; **Collin County Community College District** was authorized in 1985.

In the private sector Texas has 37 independent senior colleges and universities, four junior colleges, one medical school and one dental school. In June 1985 **Gulf Coast Bible College** in Houston moved to Oklahoma City, where it will operate as Mid-America Bible College.

Medical Education

The state continued efforts to improve access to medical services through several programs, including loan cancellations for physicians who practice in certain areas of Texas. Lawmakers appropriated $432,660 for the loan repayment program in the 1986-87 biennium. It allows physicians to cancel a portion of their loans for time employed in economically depressed or rural underserved areas, as well as in certain state agencies such as prisons or mental institutions.

In addition, $14.6 million was authorized to support the family practice residency training program which provides residency training in rural or inner-city areas lacking adequate health-care services.

A biennial total of $78.4 million was appropriated for allocation to the **Baylor Colleges of Medicine and Dentistry** to support the training of additional physicians and dentists.

Financial Aid

Opportunities for financial aid were strengthened by the 69th Legislature to help offset the increase in tuition which will be phased in during the next decade. The amount of funding available through state grants to students attending public universities was increased substantially from the current $5 million annual set aside, and provisions were included allowing institutions to make short-term loans for tuition and fees.

Special efforts continued to increase the participation of disadvantaged students in higher education. For the 1986-87 biennium, legislators appropriated $500,000 in matching funds for scholarships and student recruitment in keeping with the objectives of the **Texas Equal Opportunity Plan for Higher Education**. Another $100,000 was provided as matching funds for recruitment of minority faculty and staff.

During the Second Called Session of the 68th Legislature in June 1984, educators were targeted for special assistance with the enactment of programs to provide additional loan monies for future teachers or for teachers seeking retraining in high-demand fields. Technical problems with the funding were eliminated during the 1985 session, and loans were expected to be made before the beginning of the next academic year.

A **Tuition Equalization Grants Program** helps needy students in meeting the costs of attending independent colleges and universities in Texas. In addition, the state **Hinson-Hazlewood College Student Loan** program extends access to numerous students in both public and private colleges, providing close to 20,000 loans annually. Loans in fiscal year 1984 averaged about $1,200.

Average expenses of attending a Texas public university for a student living on campus in 1984-85 were estimated at $5,359 annually. Comparable costs for a student at an independent institution were about $7,962.

History

While there were earlier efforts toward higher education, the first permanent institutions established were these church-supported schools: **Rutersville University**, established in 1840 by Methodist minister Martin Ruter in Fayette County, predecessor of **Southwestern University**, Georgetown, established in 1843; **Baylor University**, now at Waco, but established in 1845 at Independence, Washington County; and **Austin College**, now at Sherman, but founded in 1849 at Huntsville.

Other historic Texas schools of collegiate rank included: **Larissa College**, 1848, at Larissa, Cherokee County; **McKenzie College**, 1841, Clarksville; **Chappell Hill Male and Female Institute**, 1850, Chappell Hill; **Soule University**, 1855, Chappell Hill; **Johnson Institute**, 1852, Driftwood, Hays County; **Nacogdoches University**, 1845, Nacogdoches; **Salado College**, 1859, Salado, Bell County. **Add-Ran College**, established at Thorp Spring in 1873, was the predecessor of present **Texas Christian University**, Fort Worth.

Texas A&M, authorized by the Legislature in 1871, opened its doors in 1876 to become the first publicly supported institution of higher education. In 1881, Texans voted to establish the **University of Texas** in Austin, with a medical branch in Galveston; the Austin institution opened Sept. 15, 1883, the Galveston school in 1891.

In 1901, the 27th Legislature established the **Girls Industrial College** (forerunner of **Texas Woman's University**), which began classes at its campus in Denton in 1903. A campaign to establish a state industrial college for women was led by the State Grange and Patrons of Husbandry. A bill was signed into law on April 6, 1901, creating the college. It was charged with a dual mission, which continues to guide the university today — to provide a liberal education and to prepare young women with a specialized education ''for the practical industries of the age.'' In 1905 the name of the college was changed to the **College of Industrial Arts**; in 1934, it was changed to **Texas State College for Women**. Since 1957 the name of the institution, which is now the largest university for women in the United States, has been the

Texas Woman's University.

A number of Texas schools were established primarily for **blacks**, although collegiate racial integration is now complete in the state. The black-oriented institutions include state-supported **Prairie View State University**, Prairie View; **Texas Southern University**, Houston; and privately supported **Bishop College**, Dallas; **Huston-Tillotson College**, Austin; **Jarvis Christian College**, Hawkins; **Wiley College**, Marshall; **Paul Quinn College**, Waco; **Mary Allen College**, Crockett; and **Butler** and **Texas Colleges**, Tyler.

Wadley Research Institute, Dallas, and **M. D. Anderson Hospital and Tumor Institute**, Houston, grant graduate degrees although they are not primarily educational institutions.

The following table gives dates of establishment for leading Texas institutions and enrollments, as reported by the schools. In some cases, dates of establishment differ from those given in preceding discussion because schools use the date when authorization was given, rather than actual date of first classwork.

UNIVERSITIES AND COLLEGES OF TEXAS

Table below is from data assembled from these institutions during 1985. Enrollment figures are for the 1984-1985 regular term and the 1984 summer term.

Name of Institution, Location, Ownership, Date of Founding, President —	Number in Faculty	Regular Term 1984-85	Summer Session 1984	*Extension
Abilene Christian University.—Abilene; private; 1906; coed; William J. Teague	250	4,617	1,152	100
Abilene Christian University at Dallas.—Garland. (See **Amber University**.)				
A&M University, Texas.—College Station. (See **Texas A&M University System**.)				
ALAMO COMMUNITY COLLEGE DISTRICT—Byron McClenney, Chancellor				
Palo Alto College.—San Antonio; district; 1985; coed; Terry Dicianna	. . .	. . .	. . .	. . .
St. Philip's College.—San Antonio; state; 1898; coed; Dr. Kay M. Moore, Acting President	462	6,569	4,316	. . .
San Antonio College.—San Antonio; state/local; 1945; coed; Dr. Max Castillo	603	22,397	10,782	. . .
Alvin Community College.—Alvin; state; 1948; coed; Dr. A. Rodney Allbright	192	3,937	3,521	. . .
Amarillo College.—Amarillo; state/local; 1929; coed; Dr. H. D. Yarbrough	300	6,000	1,200	. . .

Name of Institution, Location, Ownership, Date of Founding, President —	Number in Faculty	Enrollment Regular Term 1984-85	Summer Session 1984	*Extension
Amber University.—Garland; independent; (est. 1971 as Dallas branch of **Abilene Christian University;** became fully accredited independent university and name changed to present form in 1982); coed; Dr. Douglas W. Warner	41	868	522	...
American Technological University.—Killeen; private; 1973; coed; Dr. L. Harlan Ford	31	492	403	...
Angelina College.—Lufkin; state; 1967; coed; Dr. Jack W. Hudgins	130	2,400	800	...
Angelo State University.—San Angelo; (1928 as **San Angelo College,** became senior state college and name changed in 1965); coed; Dr. L. D. Vincent	228	6,163	4,375	...
Annunciation College.—Victoria. (Closed in 1971.)				
Arlington Baptist College.—Arlington; Baptist; (1939 as **Bible Baptist Seminary;** changed to present name in 1965); coed; Dr. Wayne Martin	25	244	50	...
Arlington State College.—Arlington. (See **University of Texas at Arlington.**)				
Austin College.—Sherman; Presbyterian, U.S.; 1849; coed; Dr. Harry E. Smith	110	1,174	200	...
Austin Community College.—Austin; public; 1972; coed; Dr. Daniel Angel	727	17,807	12,001	...
Austin Presbyterian Theological Seminary.—Austin; Presbyterian, U.S.; 1902 (successor to **Austin School of Theology** est. 1884); coed; Dr. Jack L. Stotts	15	198	97	...
Baptist Missionary Association Theological Seminary.—Jacksonville; Baptist Missionary; (1955 as **North American Theological Seminary);** coed; Philip R. Bryan	14	76	13	62
Baylor College of Dentistry.—Dallas; private; 1905; coed; Dr. Richard E. Bradley	223	607	344	...
Baylor College of Medicine.—Houston; Baptist until 1969; now private; (Dallas 1903, moved to Houston in 1943); coed; Dr. William T. Butler, president and Dr. Michael E. DeBakey, chancellor	1,182	899	...	
Baylor University.—Waco; Southern Baptist (Baptist Convention of Texas); 1845; coed; Dr. Herbert H. Reynolds	596	10,990	4,601	...
Baylor University School of Nursing.—Waco and Dallas; Southern Baptist (Baptist Convention of Texas); 1909; coed; Dean, Opal S. Hipps	23	156	57	...
Bee County College.—Beeville; state; 1965; coed; Dr. Norman E. Wallace	121	2,240	1,802	...
Bible Baptist Seminary.—Arlington. (See **Arlington Baptist College.**)				
Bishop College.—Dallas; Baptist; (est. in Marshall in 1881; moved to Dallas in 1961); coed; Dr. Wright L. Lassiter	72	1,107	345	...
Blinn College.—Brenham; state-local; (est. as academy in 1883, junior college 1927); coed; Dr. Walter C. Schwartz	176	3,499	1,347	...
Borger City Junior College.—Borger. (See **Frank Phillips College,** new name.)				
Brazosport College.—Lake Jackson; state; 1948; coed; Dr. W. A. Bass	200	3,609	2,453	...
Brownsville Junior College.—Brownsville. (See **Texas Southmost College.**)				
Cedar Valley College.—Lancaster (See **Dallas County Community College District.**)				
Central Texas College.—Killeen; state junior college; 1967; coed; Chancellor, Dr. Luis M. Morton Jr.	223	5,973	5,812	¶

Name of Institution, Location, Ownership, Date of Founding, President —	Number in Faculty	Regular Term 1984-85	Summer Session 1984	*Extension
Christian College of the Southwest.—Garland. (See **Amber University.**)				
Cisco Junior College.—Cisco; state; (1909 as private institution, became state supported in 1939); coed; Dr. Henry E. McCullough	75	1,610	1,523	. . .
Clarendon College.—Clarendon; (1898 as church school, 1927 state); coed; Kenneth D. Vaughan.	33	756	724	. . .
Clifton Junior College.—Clifton. (See **Texas Lutheran College.**).				
College of Marshall, The.—Marshall. (See **East Texas Baptist College.**)				
College of the Mainland.—Texas City; state/local; 1967; coed; Dr. Larry Stanley	147	2,901	1,452	. . .
Concordia Lutheran College.—Austin; Lutheran (Missouri Synod); 1926; coed; Dr. Ray F. Martens	38	463	42	. . .
Connally Technical Institute, James.— Waco. (See **Texas State Technical Institute.**)				
Cooke County College.—Gainesville; state; (1924 as **Gainesville Junior College,** name changed); coed; Dr. Alton Laird.	96	1,687	804	469
Corpus Christi Junior College.—Corpus Christi. (See **Del Mar College.**)				
Corpus Christi State University.—Corpus Christi. (See **University System of South Texas.**). .				
Cypress Basin Community College.—Mount Pleasant. (Ceased operation Sept. 1, 1985.) . .				
Dallas Baptist University.—Dallas; Southern Baptist; (1898 as **Decatur Baptist College;** moved to Dallas in 1965); coed; Dr. W. Marvin Watson.	55	1,551	490	. . .
Dallas Bible College.—Dallas; private; 1940; coed; Rev. U. A. Doiron. (As of Aug. 1, 1985, name changed to **Woodcrest College,** Rt. 1, Box 106, Lindale, Tx. 75771-9723.).	31	209	48	359
Dallas Christian College.—Dallas; Christian; 1949; coed; Thomas M. Marsh, Interim President	20	124	. . .	. . .

DALLAS COUNTY COMMUNITY COLLEGE DISTRICT—Chancellor, R. Jan LeCroy

Brookhaven College.—Farmers Branch; community; 1978; coed; Patsy Fulton	280	6,954	4,909	9,917
Cedar Valley.—Lancaster; community; 1977; coed; Dr. Floyd S. Elkins	82	2,300	1,100	2,000
Eastfield College.—Mesquite; community; 1970; coed; Eleanor Ott	316	8,666	4,020	. . .
El Centro College.—Dallas; community; 1966; coed; Dr. Ruth G. Shaw	495	5,534	3,245	16,653
Mountain View College.—Dallas; community; 1970; coed; Dr. William H. Jordan	221	5,295	2,796	146
North Lake.—Irving; community; 1977; coed; Dr. James F. Horton Jr.	170	5,334	2,461	. . .
Richland College.—Dallas; community; 1972; coed; Dr. Stephen K. Mittelstet.	150	13,500	6,000	. . .

Dallas Theological Seminary.—Dallas; private; 1924; coed; Dr. John F. Walvoord	68	1,471	754	775
Daniel Baker College.—Brownwood. (Merged with **Howard Payne University** in 1953.). . . .				
Decatur Baptist College.—Decatur. (See **Dallas Baptist College.**)				
Del Mar College.—Corpus Christi; state-local; 1935; coed; Dr. Edwin Biggerstaff	273	8,400	3,755	. . .
DeMazenod Scholasticate.—San Antonio. (See **Oblate College of the Southwest.**)				
Dominican College.—Houston. (Closed.)				
Eastfield College.—Mesquite. (See **Dallas County Community College District.**)				
East Texas Baptist College.—Marshall; Baptist; (1913 as **College of Marshall,** changed to present name 1944); coed; Dr. Jerry F. Dawson.	47	718	300	. . .
East Texas State University.—Commerce; state; (1889 as private institution, 1917 as state); coed; Dr. Charles J. Austin	315	7,135	6,998	. . .
East Texas University Metroplex Commuter Facility.—Garland; state; 1976; coed; Dr. Jerry B. Hutton, Director	9	918	715	. . .
East Texas State University Center at Texarkana.—Texarkana; state; 1971; coed; Dr. John F. Moss Jr., Director	45	1,283	1,143	. . .
Edinburg Junior College.—Edinburg. (See **Pan American College.**)				
El Centro College.—Dallas. (See **Dallas County Community College District.**)				
El Paso Community College.—El Paso; state; 1969; coed; three campuses — Rio Grande, TransMountain and Valle Verde; Dr. Robert Shepack.	650	13,930	7,017	. . .
Episcopal Theological Seminary of the Southwest.—Austin; Episcopal; 1951; coed; Very Rev. Durstan R. McDonald, Provost	15	101	39	. . .
Fort Worth Christian College.—Fort Worth. (See **Amber University.**)				
Frank Phillips College.—Borger; state-local; 1948; coed; Dr. Andy Hicks	28	955	276	. . .
Frisco College of Arts and Sciences.—Frisco. (Closed.).				
Gainesville Junior College.—Gainesville. (See **Cooke County College.**)				
Galveston College.—Galveston; state; 1967; coed; Dr. John Pickelman	105	2,014	1,659	1,512
Garland College.—Garland. (Closed.)				
Grayson County College.—Denison; state; 1965; coed; Dr. Jim Williams	200	5,045	3,100	. . .
Gulf Coast Bible College.—Houston. (Moved to Oklahoma in 1985.)				
Hardin College.—Wichita Falls. (Branch of **Midwestern University.**)				
Hardin-Simmons University.—Abilene; Southern Baptist; 1891; coed; Dr. Jesse C. Fletcher	120	1,834	938	. . .
Henderson County Junior College.—Athens; local; 1946; coed; (will change name to **Trinity Valley College** in September, 1986); Dr. William J. Campion.	145	4,229	1,762	. . .
Hill Junior College.—Hillsboro; public; (1922 as **Hillsboro Junior College;** name changed in 1962); coed; Dr. William Auvenshine.	58	1,159	450	. . .
Houston Baptist University.—Houston; Southern Baptist; 1960; coed; Dr. W. H. Hinton. . . .	111	2,962	1,638	. . .
Houston Community College.—Houston; state; 1971; coed; J. B. Whiteley	335	38,177	29,751	. . .
Howard College.—Big Spring; state; 1945; coed; Dr. Bob E. Riley	50	1,040	. . .	. . .
Howard Payne University.—Brownwood; Southern Baptist; 1889; coed; Dr. Ralph A. Phelps Jr.	77	1,165	383	. . .
Huston-Tillotson College.—Austin; United Methodist and United Church of Christ; 1875; coed; Dr. John Q. T. King.	43	569	288	. . .
Incarnate Word College.—San Antonio; Catholic; 1881; coed; Sister Margaret Patrice Slattery	128	1,340	931	. . .
International Bible College.—San Antonio; private; non-sectarian; 1944; coed; Rev. David B. Coote	20	200	. . .	. . .

Name of Institution, Location, Ownership, Date of Founding, President —	Number in Faculty	Enrollment		*Extension
		Regular Term 1984-85	Summer Session 1984	
Jacksonville College.—Jacksonville; Baptist; 1899; coed; Curtis M. Carroll	25	323	100	. . .
James Connally Technical Institute.—Waco. (See **Texas State Technical Institute.**)				
Jarvis Christian College.—Hawkins; Disciples of Christ; 1912; coed; Dr. Charles A. Berry Jr.	51	533	. . .	. . .
Kilgore College.—Kilgore; state; 1935; coed; Dr. Stewart H. McLaurin	150	4,469	1,197	. . .
LAMAR UNIVERSITY SYSTEM—Dr. C. Robert Kemble, Chancellor				
Lamar University at Beaumont.—Beaumont; state; (1923 as junior municipal college, as senior state college Sept., 1951); coed; Dr. Billy J. Franklin	571	15,835	6,200	. . .
Lamar University at Orange.—Orange; state; 1969; coed; Joe Ben Welch.	58	1,065	725	. . .
Lamar University at Port Arthur.—Port Arthur; state; (est. as **Port Arthur College,** 1909, became part of Lamar University 1975); coed; Dr. W. Sam Monroe	75	1,563	950	124
Laredo Junior College.—Laredo; municipal; 1947; coed; Dr. Domingo Arechiga	135	4,038	2,951	. . .
Laredo State University.—Laredo. (See **University System of South Texas.**)				
Lee College.—Baytown; state; 1934; coed; Dr. Robert C. Cloud	105	4,784	2,996	. . .
Le Tourneau College.—Longview; private; (1946 as **LeTourneau Technical Institute;** became 4-year college in 1961); coed; Dr. Richard H. LeTourneau.	65	906	231	. . .
Lon Morris College.—Jacksonville; United Methodist; (1854 as **Danville Academy;** name changed in 1873 to **Alexander Institute** at Kilgore); coed; Dr. W. Faulk Landrum.	33	340	. . .	. . .
Lubbock Christian College.—Lubbock; Church of Christ; 1957; coed; Dr. Steven S. Lemley	82	1,038	146	. . .
Lutheran Concordia College.—Austin. (See **Concordia Lutheran College.**)				
McLennan Community College.—Waco; county; 1965; coed; Dr. Wilbur A. Ball	200	4,427	3,851	. . .
McMurry College.—Abilene; Methodist; 1923; coed; Dr. Thomas K. Kim.	132	1,525	820	. . .
Mary Hardin-Baylor, University of.—Belton; Southern Baptist; 1845; coed; Dr. Bobby E. Parker.	74	1,176	469	. . .
Metrocenter, ACU.—Garland. (See **Amber University.**)				
Midland College.—Midland; state; 1969; coed; Dr. Jess Parrish	181	3,502	2,036	. . .
Midwestern State University.—Wichita Falls; state; (1922 as junior college, 1946 as senior college, 1961 as state college); coed; Dr. Louis J. Rodriguez.	146	4,857	2,009	. . .
Mountain View College.—Dallas. (See **Dallas County Community College District.**)				
Navarro College.—Corsicana; state; 1946; coed; Dr. Kenneth P. Walker	53	2,816	1,560	. . .
North American Theological Seminary.—Jacksonville. (See **Baptist Missionary Assn. Theological Seminary.**)				
Northeast Texas Community College.—Mount Pleasant; state; 1985; coed; Dr. Wayland K. DeWitt (scheduled to open Fall 1985)				
NORTH HARRIS COUNTY COLLEGE DISTRICT—Dr. Joe A. Airola, Chancellor				
East Campus.—Houston; state; 1984; coed; Lester Burks, President.				
‡South Campus.—Houston; state; 1972; coed; Larry Phillips, President	350	10,954	6,966	. . .
North Lake College.—Irving. (See **Dallas County Community College District.**)				
North Texas State University.—Denton; state; (1890 as private institution, 1899 as state college; raised to university status in 1961); coed; Dr. Alfred F. Hurley, Chancellor . . .	1,229	21,414	9,148	267
Northwood Institute.—Cedar Hill; private; 1966; coed; Dean James R. Bromley	10	186	37	15
Oblate School of Theology.—San Antonio; Catholic; (est. in 1903, in present location since 1929; formerly **DeMazenod Scholasticate**); coed; Rev. Patrick Guidon, O.M.I.	20	174	91	. . .
Odessa College.—Odessa; state; 1945; coed; Dr. Philip T. Speegle	250	5,145	1,150	250
Our Lady of the Lake University.—San Antonio; Catholic; (as academy for girls 1896, senior college in 1911, raised to university status in 1975); coed; Sister Elizabeth Anne Sueltenfuss.	86	1,684	1,100	. . .
Pan American University.—Edinburg; (est. as state and county **Edinburg Junior College** in 1927, name changed in 1952; became state senior college in 1965; raised to university status in 1971); coed; Dr. Miguel Nevarez	418	8,594	5,314	. . .
Pan American University at Brownsville.—Brownsville; state; 1973; coed; Dr. Homer J. Pena.	33	1,207	1,360	. . .
Panola Junior College.—Carthage; state; 1947; coed; Dr. Gary McDaniel	58	1,370	1,039	1,626
Paris Junior College.—Paris; district; 1924; coed; Dr. Dennis Michaelis	82	2,199	1,113	7,486

Name of Institution, Location, Ownership, Date of Founding, President —	Number in Faculty	Enrollment Regular Term 1984-85	Enrollment Summer Session 1984	*Extension
Paul Quinn College.—Waco; African Methodist Episcopal; 1872; coed; Dr. Warren W. Morgan	44	355	68	...
Port Arthur College.—Port Arthur. (See **Lamar University at Port Arthur.**)				
Prairie View State University.—Prairie View. (See **Texas A&M University System.**)				
Presbyterian Pan-American School.—Kingsville; Presbyterian U.S.; (1911 as **Texas-Mexican Industrial Institute**; name changed in 1956); coed; Dr. David R. Gifford, Headmaster	20	123	38	...
Ranger Junior College.—Ranger; state; 1926; coed; Dr. Jack Elsom	45	698	330	...
Rice (William Marsh) University.—Houston; private; 1912; coed; Dr. George B. Rupp	441	3,930	400	...
Richland College.—Dallas. (See **Dallas County Community College District.**)				
Rio Grande Bible Institute and Language School.—Edinburg; private; 1946; coed; Dr. Gordon Johnson	50	200	...	...
St. Edwards University.—Austin; Catholic; 1885; coed; Dr. Patricia Hayes.	250	2,355	...	...
St. Mary's University.—San Antonio; Catholic; 1852; coed; Rev. David J. Paul, S.M.	169	3,313	...	...
Sam Houston State University.—Huntsville; state; 1879; coed; Dr. E. T. Bowers	406	10,472	4,509	...
Samuel Huston College.—Austin. (See **Huston-Tillotson College.**)				
San Angelo College.—San Angelo. (See **Angelo State University.**)				
San Antonio Community College District.—San Antonio. (See **Alamo Community College District.**)				
SAN JACINTO COLLEGE DISTRICT—Thomas Sewell, Chancellor				
Central Campus.—Pasadena; state; 1961; coed; Dr. Monte Blue.	406	9,365	3,521	...
North Campus.—Houston; state; 1974; coed; Dr. Edwin E. Lehr	173	3,578	1,500	...
South Campus.—Houston; state; 1979; coed; Dr. Parker Williams.	147	3,791	1,782	...
San Marcos Baptist Academy.—San Marcos; Baptist; 1907; coed; Dr. Jack E. Byrom	44	375	260	...
Schreiner College.—Kerrville; Presbyterian, U.S.; 1923; coed; Dr. Sam M. Junkin.	48	489	108	...
Southern Bible College.—Houston. (Closed; moved to Joplin, Mo. 1984.)				
Southern Methodist University.—Dallas; Methodist; 1910; coed; Dr. L. Donald Shields.	640	9,265	3,596	10,092
South Plains College.—Levelland; state; 1958; coed; Dr. Marvin L. Baker	195	3,672	1,324	75
South Texas College of Law.—Houston; private; 1923; coed; W. J. Williamson	60	1,186	888	...
South Texas Junior College.—Houston. (See **University of Houston Downtown College.**)				
South Texas Medical School of the University of Texas.—San Antonio. (See **University of Texas Medical School at San Antonio.**)				

Name of Institution, Location, Ownership, Date of Founding, President —	Number in Faculty	Enrollment		*Extension
		Regular Term 1984-85	Summer Session 1984	
Southwestern Adventist College.—Keene; Seventh-Day Adventist; (1894 as **Southwestern Junior College**); coed; Dr. Marvin Anderson	67	683	150	. . .
Southwestern Assemblies of God College.—Waxahachie; Assemblies of God; (est. Enid, Okla. in 1927; moved to Waxahachie as **Southwestern Bible Institute** in 1943); coed; James P. Savell, Exec. Vice President	27	511	105	. . .
Southwestern Baptist Theological Seminary.—Fort Worth; Southern Baptist; 1907; coed; Dr. Russell H. Dilday Jr.	128	4,296	1,529	528
Southwestern Christian College.—Terrell; Church of Christ; (est. as **Southern Bible Institute** in Fort Worth, moved and name changed in 1950); coed; Dr. Jack Evans	22	272	. . .	. . .
Southwestern Medical School of the University of Texas.—Dallas. (See **University of Texas Health Science Center at Dallas.**)				
Southwestern University.—Georgetown; United Methodist; 1840; coed; Dr. Roy B. Shilling Jr., President	89	1,001	300	. . .
Southwest Collegiate Institute for the Deaf.—Big Spring; municipal; 1980; coed; Dr. Bob E. Riley	29	113	. . .	. . .
Southwest Texas Junior College.—Uvalde; state; 1946; coed; Dr. Jimmy Goodson	140	2,483	785	1,242
Southwest Texas State University.—San Marcos; state; 1899; coed; Robert L. Hardesty . . .	630	19,207	13,857	21
Stephen F. Austin State University.—Nacogdoches; state; 1923; coed; Dr. William R. Johnson	630	12,658	5,226	50
Sul Ross State University.—Alpine; state; 1920; coed; Dr. Jack Humphries.	122	2,241	1,600	¶
Sul Ross University Uvalde Study Center.—Uvalde; state; 1973; coed; Dr. Frank Abbott, Dean	13	484	450	. . .
Tarleton State University.—Stephenville. (See **Texas A&M University System.**)				
TARRANT COUNTY JUNIOR COLLEGE DISTRICT—Joe B. Rushing, Chancellor				
Northeast Campus.—Hurst-N. Richland Hills; state; 1965; coed; Dr. Herman L. Crow	443	11,010	5,281	. . .
Northwest Campus.—Fort Worth; state; 1975; coed; Dr. Michael Saenz	186	4,753	2,467	. . .
South Campus.—Fort Worth; state; 1965; coed; Dr. Charles L. McKinney.	367	10,606	6,300	. . .
Temple Junior College.—Temple; state; 1926; coed; Dr. Marvin R. Felder.	140	2,432	987	. . .
Texarkana Community College.—Texarkana; state; 1927; coed; Dr. Carl M. Nelson.	124	3,586	1,450	250
Texas A&I University.—Kingsville. (See **University System of South Texas.**)				
TEXAS A&M UNIVERSITY SYSTEM—Arthur G. Hansen, Chancellor				
Moody College of Marine Sciences and Maritime Resources.—Galveston. (See **Texas A&M University at Galveston.**).				

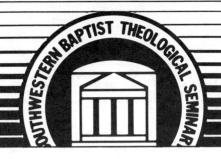

Name of Institution, Location, Ownership, Date of Founding, President —	Number in Faculty	Regular Term 1984-85	Summer Session 1984	*Extension
Prairie View A&M University.—Prairie View; state; (1876 as Alta Vista Agricultural College; name changed to Prairie View State Normal School and then to Prairie View Agricultural and Mechanical College; changed to present name in 1973); coed; Dr. Percy A. Pierre. .	263	4,436	2,482	...
Tarleton State University.—Stephenville; state; (1899; taken over by state in 1917, name changed from John Tarleton Agricultural College in 1949; raised to university in 1973); coed; Dr. Barry B. Thompson	237	4,625	1,659	...
Texas A&M University.—College Station; state; 1876; coed; Dr. Frank E. Vandiver	2,218	36,827	27,520	...
Texas A&M University at Galveston.—Galveston; state; (1962 as Texas Maritime Academy, name changed to Moody College of Marine Sciences and Maritime Resources and raised to 4-yr. college 1971; name changed again to present name); coed; Dr.W. H. Clayton. . .	50	600	650	...
Texas A&M College of Medicine.—College Station; state; 1971; coed; Dr. Robert S. Stone, Dean	71	164	...	...
Texas A&M College of Veterinary Medicine.—College Station; state; 1916; coed; Dr. George C. Shelton, Dean	200	1,600	400	...
Texas Baptist Institute and Seminary.—Henderson; American Baptist Assn.; 1949; coed; Dr. Ray O. Brooks.	12	47	...	40
Texas Christian University.—Fort Worth; Disciples of Christ; 1873; coed; Chancellor, Dr. William E. Tucker.	385	6,747	2,237	...
Texas College.—Tyler; Christian Methodist Episcopal; 1894; coed; Dr. Jimmy Ed Clark . .	43	573	245	...
Texas College of Osteopathic Medicine.—Fort Worth; state; (1966 as private college, became branch of North Texas State in 1975); coed; Dr. David M. Richards, Interim Exec. Vice President	155	395	...	...
Texas Eastern University.—Tyler. (Made part of University of Texas System in 1979.)				
Texas Lutheran College.—Seguin; Lutheran; 1891; coed; Dr. Charles H. Oestreich.	74	1,014	240	362
Texas-Mexican Industrial Institute.—Kingsville. (See Presbyterian Pan-American School.)				
Texas Southern University.—Houston; state; (1926 as Houston College for Negroes; 1947 as Texas State University for Negroes, name changed to present form in 1951); coed; Dr. Leonard H. O. Spearman.	450	8,914	3,638	...
Texas Southmost College.—Brownsville; junior college district; (est. as Brownsville Junior College 1926; name changed in 1949); coed; Dr. Alberto A. Besteiro.	210	4,886	1,966	...
Texas State College for Women.—Denton. (See Texas Woman's University.)				

TEXAS STATE TECHNICAL INSTITUTE—Dr. Jack E. Tompkins, President

Waco Campus.—Waco; state; (1966 as James Connally Technical Institute; name changed in 1969); coed; Dr. Robert D. Krienke, Gen. Mgr.	310	4,561	2,702	...
Amarillo Campus.—Amarillo; state; 1970; coed; Ron DeSpain, Gen. Mgr.	89	1,118	778	...
Harlingen Campus.—Harlingen; state; 1969; coed; J. Gilbert Leal, Gen. Mgr.	164	2,359	1,623	161
Sweetwater Campus.—Sweetwater; state; 1970; coed; Dr. Herbert C. Robbins, Gen. Mgr.	39	502	434	...
Texas Tech University.—Lubbock; state; 1923; coed; Dr. Lauro F. Cavazos	1,647	23,433	9,965	...
Texas Tech University Health Science Center.—Lubbock; state; 1972; coed; Dr. Samuel D. Richards, Vice Pres.	333	660	265	...
Texas Wesleyan College.—Fort Worth; Methodist; 1891; coed; Dr. Jerry G. Bawcom.	86	1,401	847	...
Texas Western College of the University of Texas.—El Paso. (See University of Texas at El Paso.) . .				
Texas Woman's University.—Denton; state; (1901 as College of Industrial Arts; name changed to Texas State College for Women in 1934; changed to present name in 1957); coed some departments; Dr. Mary E. Huey.	673	8,259	5,874	849
Texas Woman's University Institute of Health Sciences.—Denton; Dr. Carolyn Rozier, Provost. Includes Schools of Health Care Services, Occupational Therapy, Physical Therapy and College of Nursing.				
Texas Woman's University Undergraduate General Divisions.—Dr. Wilkes Berry, Provost. Includes Colleges of Humanities and Fine Arts, Natural and Social Sciences, Education, Nutrition, Textiles and Human Development; Health, Physical Education, Recreation and Dance, and School of Library Science.				
Texas Woman's University Graduate School.—Denton; Dr. Leslie Thompson, Dean.				
Tillotson College.—Austin. (See Huston-Tillotson College.)				
Trinity University.—San Antonio; private; 1869; coed; Dr. Ronald Calgaard.	229	2,925	518	...
Trinity Valley College.—Athens. (See Henderson County Junior College.)				
Tyler Junior College.—Tyler; state-community; 1926; coed; Dr. Raymond M. Hawkins . . .	321	8,000	3,000	...
Tyler State College.—Tyler. (See University of Texas at Tyler.))				
U.S. Army-Baylor University Graduate Program in Health Care Administration.—Fort Sam Houston; federal government; 1952; coed; Col. Melvin E. Modderman, D.B.A., Program Director	18	33	33	...
University of Dallas.—Irving; Catholic; 1956; coed; (includes Graduate School of Management); Dr. Robert F. Sasseen.	174	2,466	1,114	...

UNIVERSITY OF HOUSTON SYSTEM—Richard L. Van Horn, Chancellor; Charles E. Bishop, President

University of Houston-University Park.—Houston; state; (1927 as junior college, 1934 as university; made fully state-supported institution of higher education 1963); coed; Dr. Richard L. Vanhorn	1,871	31,114	22,246	...
University of Houston-Downtown.—Houston; state; (1948 as South Texas College, made branch of University of Houston 1974); coed; Dr. Alexander Schilt, Chancellor	125	7,368	2,510	...
University of Houston-Clear Lake.—Clear Lake; state; 1973; coed; Dr. Thomas Stauffer, Chancellor	358	6,392	3,696	...
University of Houston-Victoria.—Victoria; state; 1973; coed; Dr. Martha K. Piper, Chancellor	51	927	941	...
University of Plano.—Plano. (Closed.)				

Name of Institution, Location, Ownership, Date of Founding, President —	Number in Faculty	Enrollment		*Extension
		Regular Term 1984-85	Summer Session 1984	
University of St. Thomas.—Houston; Catholic; 1947; coed; Rev. William J. Young, C.S.B...	196	1,983	810	..
University of San Antonio.—San Antonio. (See **Trinity University.**)				
UNIVERSITY SYSTEM OF SOUTH TEXAS—Dr. Lawrence Pettit, Chancellor (formerly Texas A&I University System).				
Corpus Christi State University.—Corpus Christi; state; 1971; coed; Dr. B. Alan Sugg	182	3,710	2,679	..
Laredo State University.—Laredo; state; 1970; coed; Dr. Manuel T. Pacheco	55	928	1,072	..
Texas A&I University.—Kingsville; state; 1925; (name changed from **South Texas Teachers College** in 1929 to **Texas College of Arts and Industries**); changed to present name in 1967; part of **University of South Texas System** in 1977); coed; Eliseo Torres, Acting President	272	5,512	3,500	2,80(
UNIVERSITY OF TEXAS SYSTEM—Hans Mark, Chancellor				
University of Texas at Arlington.—Arlington; state; (1895 as **Arlington College,** 1917 as state institution; 1923 as **North Texas Agricultural College;** 1949 as **Arlington State;** 1967 to present name); coed; President, Dr. Wendell H. Nedderman..................	850	23,397	11,100	..
University of Texas at Arlington School of Nursing.—Arlington; state; 1976; coed; Dr. Myrna R. Pickard, Dean..	59	635	500	..
University of Texas at Austin.—Austin; state; 1883; coed; President, William H. Cunningham..	5,757	47,973	22,545	..
University of Texas at Austin School of Nursing.—Austin; state; (1890 as **John Sealy Hospital Training School of Nurses;** present name since 1896); coed; Billye J. Brown, Dean	65	935	498	..
University of Texas at Dallas.—Richardson; state; (1969 graduate school only, 1975 university grade); coed; Dr. Robert H. Rutford	400	7,442	4,114	..
University of Texas at El Paso.—El Paso; state; (1913 as **Texas College of Mines,** 1949 as **Texas Western College;** 1967 present name); coed; President, Dr. Haskell M. Monroe ..	640	15,322	8,663	86
University of Texas at El Paso School of Nursing.—El Paso. (Enrollment, faculty included with main university above.)...........................				
University of Texas of the Permian Basin.—Odessa; state; 1969; coed; Dr. Duane M. Leach	67	2,003	1,283	..
University of Texas at San Antonio.—San Antonio; state; 1969; coed; President, Dr. James W. Wagener	484	12,612	...	..
University of Texas at Tyler.—Tyler; (1971 as **Tyler State College;** name changed to **Texas Eastern University** in 1975, made branch of UT System in 1979); coed; Dr. George F. Hamm...	212	3,546	2,048	..

Name of Institution, Location, Ownership, Date of Founding, President —	Number in Faculty	Regular Term 1984-85	Summer Session 1984	*Extension
University of Texas Health Center at Tyler.—Tyler; state; (1947 as **East Texas Chest Hospital,** became branch of UT System Sept., 1977); coed; Dr. George A. Hurst, Director	35	§488	N.A.	N.A.
‡**THE UNIVERSITY OF TEXAS HEALTH SCIENCE CENTER AT DALLAS—** Dr. Charles Sprague, President				
Graduate School of Biomedical Sciences; 1947; coed; Dr. William Neaves, Dean	953	1,398	1,321	. . .
School of Allied Health Sciences; 1968; coed; Dr. John W. Schermerhorn, Dean				
Southwestern Medical School; (est. as private institution in 1943, as branch of University of Texas in 1948); coed; Dean, Dr. Kern Wildenthal				
THE UNIVERSITY OF TEXAS MEDICAL BRANCH AT GALVESTON— Dr. William C. Levin, President				
Graduate School of Biomedical Sciences; 1952; coed; Dr. J. Palmer Saunders, Dean	220	149	119	. . .
Medical School; 1891; coed; Dr. George T. Bryan, Dean	640	800	595	. . .
School of Allied Health Sciences; 1968; coed; Dr. John G. Bruhn, Dean	70	351	365	. . .
School of Nursing; 1890; coed; Dorothy M. Damewood, Dean	44	419	271	. . .
†‡**THE UNIVERSITY OF TEXAS SYSTEM CANCER CENTER—** Dr. Charles A. LeMaistre, President				
M. D. Anderson Hospital and Tumor Institute.—Houston; 1941; coed	422	**1,518		
Science Park.—Bastrop County; 1971; coed				
‡**THE UNIVERSITY OF TEXAS HEALTH SCIENCE CENTER AT HOUSTON—** Dr. Roger Bulger, President				
Dental Branch; 1905; coed; Dr. Don Allen, Dean.	889	2,792	. . .	. . .
Graduate School of Biomedical Sciences; 1963; coed; Dr. R. W. Butcher, Dean				
Medical School; 1970; coed; Dr. Louis A. Faillace, Acting Dean.				
School of Allied Health Sciences; 1973; Judith Craven, Dean				
School of Nursing; 1972; coed; Dr. Patricia L. Starck, Dean				
School of Public Health; 1967; coed; Dr. R. A. Stallones, Dean				
Division of Continuing Education; 1958; coed; Dr. Sam A. Nixon, Director				
‡**THE UNIVERSITY OF TEXAS HEALTH SCIENCE CENTER AT SAN ANTONIO—** Dr. John P. Howe III, President				
Dental School; 1970; coed; Dr. Dominick DePaola, Dean				
Graduate School of Biomedical Sciences; 1970; coed; Dr. Armand J. Guarino, Dean				
School of Allied Health Sciences; 1976; coed; Dr. Armand J. Guarino, Dean				
‡Health Sciences Center; 1972; coed; Dr. John P. Howe III, President	709	2,332	562	. . .
Medical School; (est. 1959 as **South Texas Medical School of University of Texas;** 1966 name changed to present form); coed; Dr. Timothy N. Caris, Acting Dean				
School of Nursing; 1969; coed; Dr. Patty L. Hawken, Dean				
Vernon Regional Junior College.—Vernon; state; 1970; coed; Dr. Joe Mills	125	1,863	965	143
Victoria College.—Victoria; municipal; 1925; coed; Dr. Roland E. Bing	127	2,889	1,000	. . .
Wayland Baptist University.—Plainview; Southern Baptist; 1908; coed; Dr. David L. Jester	123	1,809	1,041	. . .
Weatherford College.—Weatherford; county/state; (1869 as branch of **Southwestern University,** 1922 as denominational junior college; 1949 as municipal junior college); coed; Dr. E. W. Mince.	39	1,850	1,250	. . .
Western Texas College.—Snyder; state; 1971; coed; Dr. Don Newbury	51	1,263	861	. . .
Westminster Junior College and Bible Institute.—Tehuacana. (Closed.)				
West Texas State University.—Canyon; state; 1910; coed; Dr. Ed Roach	224	6,474	4,668	. . .
Wharton County Junior College.—Wharton; state; 1946; coed; Dr. Elbert Hutchins	140	2,526	724	. . .
Wiley College.—Marshall; United Methodist; 1873; coed; Dr. Robert E. Hayes Sr.	38	557	181	. . .
Woodcrest College and Conference Center.—Lindale. (See **Dallas Bible College.**)				

*Extension, or Continuing Education enrollment.
†Teaching Hospital and Research Institute.
‡Includes faculty and enrollment at all branches.
¶Included in on-campus enrollment figures.
§Students from other institutions receiving clinical instruction.
**Enrollment figure is for entire fiscal year.

Public Schools

Public school enrollment in Texas reached a peak of 3,333,820 in 1983-84, according to **Texas Education Agency.**

The seven largest districts (listed alphabetically) which usually have better than one fourth of the total pupil population are: Austin, Dallas, El Paso, Fort Worth, Houston, San Antonio and Ysleta.

History of Public Education

Public education was one of the primary goals of the early settlers of Texas, who listed the failure to provide education as one of their grievances in the Texas Declaration of Independence from Mexico.

As early as 1838, President Mirabeau B. Lamar's message to the Republic of Texas Congress advocated setting aside public domain for public schools. His in-terest caused him to be called the "Father of Education in Texas." In 1839 Congress designated three leagues of land to support public schools for each Texas county and 50 leagues for a state university. In 1840 each county was allocated one more league of land.

The Republic, however, did not establish a public school system or university. The **1845 State Constitution** advocated public education, instructing the Legislature to designate at least 10 per cent of the tax revenue for schools. Further delay occurred until Gov. **Elisha M. Pease,** on Jan. 31, 1854, signed the bill **setting up the Texas public school system.**

The public school system was made possible by setting aside $2 million out of $10 million Texas received for relinquishing its claim to land to the north and west of its present boundaries. (See **Compromise of 1850** in historical section.)

During 1854, legislation provided for state apportionment of funds based upon an annual census and required railroads which were granted land to survey alternate sections that were set aside for public school financing. The first **school census** that year showed **65,463 scholastics; state fund apportionment** was 62c per student.

When adopted in 1876, the present **Texas Constitution** provided: "All funds, lands and other property heretofore set apart and appropriated for the support of public schools; all the alternate sections of land reserved by the state of grants heretofore made or that may hereafter be made to railroads, or other corporations, of any nature whatsoever; one half of the public domain of the state, and all sums of money that may come to the state from the sale of any portion of the same shall constitute a perpetual public school fund."

Over 52,000,000 acres of the Texas public domain were allotted for school purposes. (See table, Public Lands of Texas, in chapter on State Government.)

The Constitution also provided for one fourth of occupation taxes and a poll tax of one dollar for school support, and made provisions for local taxation. No provision was made for direct ad valorem taxation for maintenance of an available school fund, but a maximum 20c state ad valorem school tax was adopted in 1883, and raised to 35c in connection with provision of free textbooks in the amendment of 1918.

In 1949, the **Gilmer-Aikin Laws** reorganized the state system of public schools by making sweeping changes in administration and financing. All schools below college level were, prior to 1984, headed by the **State Board of Education**, whose members were elected from congressional districts as set in 1981. Under the new educational reforms of 1984, a new 15-member board was appointed by the governor to replace the existing 27-member elected panel. This board appoints a **State Commissioner of Education** who is executive head of the **Texas Education Agency**, which administers the public school system. Under the law, TEA consists of (1) the State Board of Education, (2) the State Commissioner of Education, (3) the State Department of Education and (4) the State Board of Vocational Education. The personnel of the State Board of Education and the State Board of Vocational Education is the same, the members of the State Board of Education serving ex officio as members of the State Board of Vocational Education when considering matters relating to vocational education.

The funding of Texas public school education continues to be a major issue before the Texas Legislature in the 1980s. The Sixty-fourth (1975) Legislature made major changes in the state's guaranteed **Foundation School Program** with enactment of HB 1126, which provided increased funding for salaries, operating allowance and transportation. This bill also provided state funds for compensatory education and equalization aid and revised the method for determining state aid received by school districts under the Foundation Program.

Major changes continued with the passage of SB 1 during a called special session of the Sixty-fifth (1977) Texas Legislature. The **School Tax Assessment Practices Board** was created to determine, on a statewide basis, the property wealth of school districts. The board was also charged with upgrading professional standards for appraising and assessing school district property taxes.

The Sixty-sixth (1979) Legislature passed SB 350, which increased most categorical programs, including salaries, and lowered the rate used in calculating the districts' share of the Foundation School Program cost. In addition, SB 621 required the establishment of countywide appraisal districts.

House Bill 1060, which was enacted by the 66th Texas Legislature, implements provisions of the Constitutional Amendment (HJR-1) approved by voters in November, 1978. This bill provides for state payments to school districts to replace taxes lost because of state-mandated reduction of ad valorem tax base due to residential timber and agricultural land.

The Sixty-seventh (1981) Legislature passed HB 656, which increased most categorical programs, including salaries, and lowered the rate used in calculating the district's share of the Foundation School Program cost.

Members of the 68th Texas Legislature, in special session, forged a historic education reform bill in the summer of 1984. Known as House Bill 72, the reform action, with a $2.8 billion price tag, came in response to a growing national and statewide concern over declining test scores and deteriorating general literacy in America's schoolchildren over two decades, a deterioration generally reflected in Texas test scores.

The nationally recognized Texas school reform act was formulated by a Select Committee headed by Dallas computer magnate Ross Perot and appointed by Gov. Mark White at the behest of Lt. Gov. Bill Hobby and Speaker of the House Gib Lewis, following failures by the Legislature — and resistance from the voters — to support teacher pay raises or additional public school funding without education reform.

The result was the reform bill of 1984 that provided equalization formulas for state financial aid for public education, raised teacher salaries but tied those raises to teacher performance, and introduced more stringent teacher certification and initiated competency testing for both entering and existing teachers.

Academic achievement was set as a priority in public education with stricter attendance rules, adoption of a no-pass, no-play rule prohibiting students scoring below 70 in each class from participating in sports and other extracurricular activities, and national norm testing through the grades to assure parents of individual schools' performance through a common frame of reference.

A new 10-member oversight panel, the **Legislative Education Board**, would review all aspects of state education policy and school finance.

Higher academic standards had been enacted by the 67th Legislature under H.B. 246 in 1981, which established a statewide curriculum standard for all grades. The reforms of 1984, however, carried a broader price tag and were supported by legislative vote to increase a host of goods, services, gasoline and business franchise taxes — an action that would not have been possible without the education reforms.

Texas has two types of **school districts**, independent and common, each administering local affairs through a board of trustees. Independent school districts deal

ENROLLMENT BY GRADES

In 1983-84, average daily attendance was 2,745,338; in 1982-83, it was 2,725,009; in 1981-82, it was 2,675,168; in 1980-81, it was 2,639,794; in 1979-80, it was 2,605,174; in 1978-79, it was 2,589,980; in 1977-78, it was 2,576,552; in 1976-77, it was 2,555,294; in 1975-76, it was 2,536,731; in 1974-75, it was 2,546,801; in 1973-74, it was 2,505,496; in 1971-72, it was 2,499,694; in 1970-71, it was 2,487,954; in 1969-70, it was 2,432,420; in 1968-69, it was 2,391,569; in 1967-68, it was 2,340,637; and in 1966-67, it was 2,229,048.

The following table shows enrollment by grades for the school years of 1981-82, 1982-83 and 1983-84.

	1981-82	1982-83	1983-84
Pre-Kindergarten	15,283	15,238	15,651
Kindergarten	212,652	242,184	242,191
Grade One	266,540	289,442	300,795
Grade Two	242,773	268,696	265,660
Grade Three	243,678	259,790	264,080
Grade Four	247,799	260,752	257,556
Grade Five	259,101	265,749	258,866
Grade Six	250,952	278,869	267,560
Grade Seven	251,505	277,845	286,837
Grade Eight	235,213	259,972	269,242
Grade Nine	249,364	273,118	283,619
Grade Ten	222,685	231,740	236,997
Grade Eleven	203,855	202,933	205,018
Grade Twelve	188,388	184,440	179,748
TOTAL	3,089,788	3,310,768	3,333,820

HIGH SCHOOL GRADUATES

Source: Texas Education Agency

1983-84	161,580	1967-68	127,492
1982-83	168,897	1966-67	125,742
1981-82	172,099	1965-66	121,084
1980-81	171,665	1964-65	121,759
1979-80	171,449	1963-64	97,158
1978-79	168,518	1962-63	87,640
1977-78	167,983	1961-62	86,518
1976-77	163,574	1960-61	85,102
1975-76	159,855	1959-60	76,500
1974-75	159,487	1958-59	71,855
1973-74	156,984	1957-58	67,778
1972-73	152,172	1956-57	65,132
1971-72	153,633	1955-56	64,291
1970-71	148,105	1954-55	60,141
1969-70	139,046	1953-54	56,363
1968-69	135,344		

directly with Texas Education Agency; common districts are supervised by elected county school superintendents and county trustees.

Ad valorem taxes provided most of the financial support for schools by school districts until Jan. 1, 1975, when the 5 cents ad valorem tax for the *available school fund* was abolished. This tax also was a significant source of state support, at a rate not to exceed 35c on each $100 in real and personal property but a constitutional amendment adopted in 1968 provided for gradual phasing out of state ad valorem taxes for all purposes except the tax levied by Sec. 17, Art. VII, for certain institutions of higher learning. Sec. 17, Art. VII, was deleted by a Constitutional amendment adopted in an election Nov. 2, 1982. Other state support comes from designated percentages of several taxes and from the **Permanent School Fund.**

TEXAS SCHOOL SALARIES

Year—	Average Annual Salary, Common School Districts	Average Annual Salary, Independent School Districts	Average Annual Salary, State
1872-73	. . .	. . .	$210.00
1886-87	$218.27	$502.09	244.76
1899-1900	219.05	474.84	260.26
1910-11	320.57	514.22	391.21
1920-21	699.48	1,021.76	895.20
1930-31	781.30	1,274.00	1,079.07
*1940-41.	893.00	1,269.00	1,150.00
1950-51	2,967.19	3,250.78	3,215.93
1960-61	. . .	. . .	4,734.00
1970-71	. . .	. . .	8,486.00
1974-75	. . .	. . .	10,257
1975-76	. . .	. . .	11,929
1976-77	. . .	. . .	12,193
1977-78	. . .	. . .	13,266
1978-79	. . .	. . .	13,828
1979-80	. . .	. . .	15,011
1980-81	. . .	. . .	16,724
1981-82	. . .	. . .	18,682
1982-83	. . .	. . .	20,745
1983-84	. . .	. . .	21,418

*Salaries of both white and Negro teachers included beginning with the school year, 1940-41. Only white teachers' salaries included prior to that year.

SCHOOL DISTRICTS

The following Texas Education Agency table shows the change in the types of school districts in Texas, especially the decline in common school districts in recent years.

Year—	Common School Districts*	Independent School Districts	Total
1983-84	10	1,059	1,069
1982-83	10	1,061	1,071
1981-82	12	1,087	1,099
1980-81	12	1,087	1,099
1979-80	12	1,087	1,099
1978-79	13	1,088	1,101
1977-78	104	1,009	1,113
1976-77	115	1,008	1,123
1975-76	118	1,009	1,127
1974-75	132	1,003	1,135
1973-74	144	1,002	1,146
1972-73	162	995	1,157
1971-72	173	994	1,167
1970-71	188	999	1,187
1969-70	216	1,003	1,219
1968-69	237	1,007	1,244
1965-66	322	1,010	1,332
1960-61	530	1,009	1,539
1955-56	849	1,008	1,857
1950-51	1,558	947	2,505
1945-46	4,461	998	5,459
1940-41	5,319	1,090	6,409
1935-36	5,984	1,015	6,999
1930-31	6,425	1,034	7,459
1910-11 (Largest Count) . .	8,053	546	8,599

*Districts in these columns include Rural High School Districts and Independent School Districts with less than 150 scholastics which are under the county superintendent.

PERMANENT SCHOOL FUND

The following table, from the Texas Education Agency, Austin, shows the total value of the **Texas permanent school fund** and the income earned by years since the fund was established.

Year—	*Total Investment Fund	Total Income Earned by P.S.F.
1854	$2,000,000.00	. . .
1880	3,542,126.00	. . .
1898	7,588,712.00	. . .
1899	8,420,588.85	$691,594.85
1900	9,102,872.75	783,142.08
1970	842,217,721.05	34,762,955.32
1971	884,680,139.49	38,107,272.60
1972	927,690,294.64	40,765,514.29
1973	977,970,414.00	44,462,028.00
1974	1,081,492,087.81	50,898,130.46
1975	1,176,441,741.70	61,050,083.01
1976	1,318,313,917.99	67,573,179.43
1977	1,546,151,708.00	84,817,986.33
1978	1,815,364,050.00	104,618,901.41
1979	2,062,710,780.00	130,629,766.02
1980	2,464,579,397.00	163,000,000.00
1981	2,986,784,696.12	217,695,444.70
1982	3,532,013,181.39	270,648,812.76
1983	3,959,923,160.00	698,567,452.76

*Includes cash — bonds at par and stocks at book value.

TEXAS SCHOOL PROFESSIONAL PERSONNEL

This table shows the increase in Texas school professional personnel (teachers, principals, superintendents) from 1872 to 1983-84, according to the Texas Education Agency.

Year—	Number	Year—	Number
1872	1,890	1972-73	145,404
1875	4,030	1973-74	149,139
1891	10,162	1974-75	156,447
1900	15,019	1975-76	164,312
1910	21,277	1976-77	168,857
1920	31,880	1977-78	174,455
1930	45,474	1978-79	179,313
1940	50,015	1979-80	184,278
1950	54,939	1980-81	188,174
1960-61	91,553	1981-82	190,142
1970-71	139,397	1982-83	194,464
1971-72	142,922	1983-84	197,591

SCHOLASTIC POPULATION, APPORTIONMENT, 1854-1984

The Texas public school system was established and the permanent fund set up by the Fifth Legislature, Jan. 31, 1854. The first apportionment by the state to public schools was for the school year 1854-55.

Years—	Scholastic		Apportionment	
	Age	Population	Per Capita	Amount
1854-55	. . .	65,463	$0.62	. . .
1872-73	. . .	229,568	1.81	$405,518
1880-81	. . .	266,439	3.00	679,317
1890-91	8-16	545,616	4.00	2,182,464
1900-01	8-17	706,546	4.25	3,002,820
1910-11	7-17	949,006	6.25	5,931,287
1920-21	7-18	1,271,157	14.50	18,431,716
1930-31	6-17	1,562,427	17.50	27,342,473
1940-41	6-17	1,536,910	22.50	34,580,475
1950-51	6-17	1,566,610	60.00	93,996,600
1960-61	6-17	2,249,157	73.00	164,188,461
1970-71	6-17	2,800,500	119.45	287,159,758
1979-80	6-17	3,012,210	309.00	797,805,344
1980-81	. . .	. . .	397.00	3,042,470
1981-82	. . .	. . .	457.00	3,089,788
1982-83	. . .	. . .	525.00	1,401,767,656
1983-84	. . .	. . .	480.00	1,304,921,553

Scholastic age (6-17 until 1979-80) was determined as follows: A child having attained the age of 6 before Sept 1 was enumerated for the school year beginning on that date. One having attained the age of 18 prior to Sept. was excluded from the school census. There is no longer a school census. Age requirements are generally from to 21, although for special education, ages range from birth through age 22.

TEXAS
BUSINESS & INDUSTRY

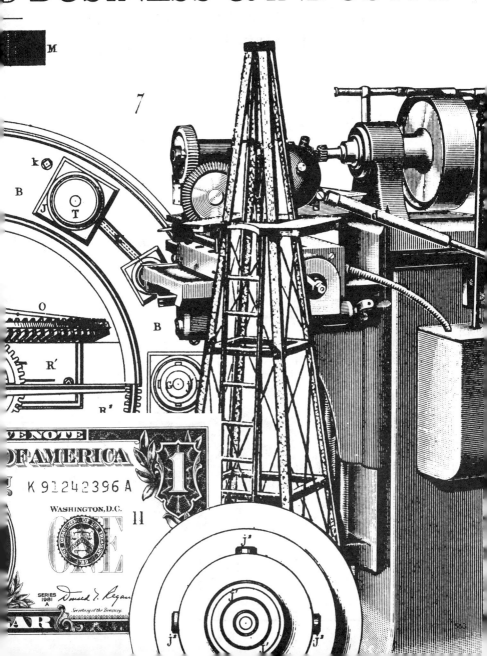

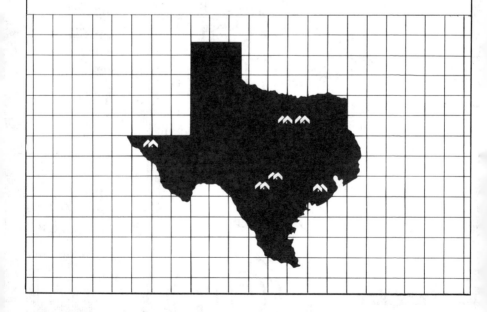

ECONOMIC REGIONS OF TEXAS

Since Texas joined the United States under the condition that it could split into five separate states at any time, various methods for dividing the state have been studied.

Texas' great size, together with the cultural, climatic and geological diversity between its borders, provides ample justification for numerous ways of splitting the state into "regions."

The presence or absence of natural resources has created regional diversity in wealth and economic development across the state with some cities like Midland and Odessa almost totally dependent on petroleum for their recent growth. As in the case of oil production, the use of the land through forestry, farming and ranching has been crucial to development of some regions.

The location of Texas on the Mexican border has added cultural diversity to the natural diversity of the state. The Spanish entered Texas from the south via Mexico, and settled first at San Antonio and Nacogdoches. While San Antonio prospered as a Spanish settlement, Nacogdoches, because it was farther from Mexico with a terrain alien to the Spanish, did not attract as many Spanish settlers. Nacogdoches, therefore, was settled more from neighboring Louisiana and the southern United States than from Mexico and took on a different character than San Antonio. In addition, the plains of North Central Texas received streams of midwestern Americans, while direct immigrants from Europe settled in Central Texas. To this day, these diverse cultures have not completely merged.

Texas lends itself to being divided into economic regions. The natural and cultural characteristics of a region interact and are influenced by external economic events and changes in available technology to determine a particular region's economic base — those products and services which generate income and employment.

Because these economic bases differ from region to region, economic events, such as the oil price decline, peso devaluation or a defense spending increase, can be expected to affect the economy of each region differently.

In order to more accurately assess the implications of such events for Texas, the Comptroller of Public Accounts has divided the state into six economic regions — East Texas, the Metroplex, the Plains, the Central Corridor, the Border and the Gulf Coast — as shown in the accompanying map. The regions are compared on a number of economic and demographic variables in Table 1.

In general, East Texas is primarily a non-metropolitan region, mostly dependent on the production and processing of timber, petroleum and coal. The Metroplex, on the other hand, is almost totally metropolitan with diversified manufacturing and service sectors. The Plains region is the largest and most sparsely populated area of the state with a petroleum and agricultural based economy. The Border area is characterized by its economic dependence on trade with Mexico. The most populous region of Texas, the Gulf Coast, has an economy centered around petroleum and petrochemicals. Finally, the public and private service sectors provide the economic base for the Central Corridor. A more detailed description of each region follows.

EAST TEXAS

The economy of East Texas is based on its natural resources — wood, petroleum and coal. However, agriculture and manufacturing are becoming more important sources of employment as the region grows with the rest of the state.

Almost all of East Texas is covered by the vegetational region of Texas known as the Piney Woods. This area of dense forestation has long been a significant source of lumber and wood products. In 1982, East Texas produced 339 million cubic feet of wood, 76 percent of total Texas production. In addition, employment in lumbering and wood products manufacturing provides about 20,000 jobs regionwide.

Mineral resources, centered around Longview, provide significant income and employment in petroleum, coal mining and in related industries. In 1981, East Texas accounted for 68 percent of the coal. More than 12 percent of the crude oil and 10 percent of the natural gas produced in Texas came from this region, according to 1983 figures. In mid-1984, almost 15,000 East Texans were employed in oil and gas extraction with an additional 10,000 employed in oil field equipment and supplies production. Petroleum-related employment accounted for 8 percent of the East Texas total, well below 1981 when oil prices peaked.

Another important contribution to the East Texas economy is made by agricultural production. As the forests have been cleared in the southern part of the region, the land has been devoted to the production of rice, grain sorghum and peanuts. The northern part of the region produces substantial crops of cotton, soybeans and hay. Poultry production has emerged as a significant contributor to the economy of the region as have cattle and dairy farms.

METROPLEX

Even though it is in an area well-suited to agriculture and with abundant natural resources, the economy of the Metroplex — particularly Dallas and Fort Worth — has grown to be dominated by manufacturing, commerce, services and finance.

The Metroplex is the most diversified of the six regional economies. A healthy durable goods manufacturing sector provides almost 15 percent of the region's total employment, the highest percentage of all the regions. Of particular importance within this broad category of manufacturing is the production of electronics, aerospace and military hardware. Defense outlays alone, primarily for military hardware, totaled $4.1 billion or 40 percent of the defense outlays for the state in 1981.

The role of the Metroplex as a trade and financial center is evident from the employment distribution. The region has a higher percentage of its employment in wholesale trade (8.2 percent of total employment) and finance, insurance and real estate (7.3 percent of total employment) than any of the other regions in Texas.

Significant also is the importance of the tourist industry to the economy of the Metroplex. Dallas is one of the most visited cities in Texas and one of the top five convention and trade show hosts.

THE PLAINS

The economy of the Plains, like that of East Texas, is tied closely to its exhaustible natural resources. The discovery of the West Texas oil fields in the 1930s, the intensive utilization of water from the Ogallala Aquifer for agricultural irrigation and a strong demand for petroleum and agricultural products, have been the determinants of the rapid economic growth of the Plains over the past 40 to 50 years.

The northwestern part of the region, from Lubbock north toward Amarillo, has utilized ground water to produce massive quantities of cotton, grain sorghum, wheat, corn and other feed grains. In addition, this area is the U.S. leader in feedlot cattle production. In 1983, the value of farm production sold from the Plains region was $3.5 billion, 39 percent of the Texas total. In 1982, farm income accounted for 4.4 percent of the total labor and proprietors' income, almost four times the average for other regions of the state.

The recovery of oil and gas dominates the economy of the west central and southwestern areas of the Plains. This area, centered in Midland and Odessa, serves as the focal point of oil and gas production in the Plains. In 1983, about 66 percent of the oil and 41 percent of the gas produced in Texas came from this region. In mid-1984, oil and gas extraction alone accounted for 10 percent of the non-agricultural employment in the Plains region, with many more jobs created by the manufacturing and trade sectors that support the recovery of oil. Falling oil prices eliminated about 15,000 petroleum-related jobs between 1982 and 1984. Total employment fell about 30,000 over the same period. Recently, petroleum industry employment has begun to recover.

In the southeastern part of the Plains, farming becomes smaller scale and less dependent on irrigation. Ranching of cattle, hogs, sheep and goats is more important in this part of the region. In addition, petroleum production has less impact on local economies. San Angelo and Abilene, in particular, are examples of diversified local economies which have withstood the current downturn in oil and agricultural prices.

In general, however, the economy of the Plains region faces not only the short-term problems related to the present soft demand for agricultural and petroleum products. There are also the more serious problems of dependence on petroleum and water, both of which will be in short supply in 40 to 50 years. The development of new techniques in farming and petroleum recovery and the ability to diversify its economy will determine the future economic health of the region.

THE BORDER

The Border is delineated as a separate region because of the severe impact the area continues to experience as a result of the economic turmoil in Mexico. High unemployment and rampant inflation in Mexico led to three devaluations of the peso against the dollar in 1982. This has meant a severe reduction in retail sales to Mexicans all along the border. In addition, the impact on employment has been drastic.

The negative impact of the devaluations has not been equal throughout the Border region. El Paso, with a substantial government payroll, diversified manufacturing, ore smelting and irrigated agriculture, is doing relatively well. The unemployment rate rose from 9.3 percent in January 1982 to 11.4 percent by December — an increase of 23 percent. Laredo, on the other hand, had one of the weaker local economies in the region to start with and was very dependent on trade with Mexico. Its unemployment rate rose from 11.9 percent in January 1982 to 23.7 percent by December 1982 — an increase of almost 100 percent.

Since mid-1983, the situation has improved substantially. Peso devaluations have not kept pace with inflation in Mexico and shoppers from Mexico again are finding bargains by converting pesos to dollars and shopping in Texas. The region's unemployment rate fell from 17.2 percent in March 1983 to 13.4 percent in August 1984.

Sales tax collections in Border cities during the first half of 1984 reflected this growth in commerce. Collections were up 18.8 percent in El Paso, 21.8 percent in Laredo and 18.2 percent in McAllen. Total sales tax collections for the region surged 17.3 percent during the period compared to an 18.1 percent increase for the state as a whole.

Throughout the region, jobs and income are provided by agriculture irrigated from the Rio Grande and underground aquifers. Together, Hidalgo and Cameron Counties, at the southern tip of Texas, contain over a million acres of irrigated cropland.

Although the employment impact is small, oil and gas production contributes substantially to the income of the region. Kleberg County, in the southeastern corner of the region, is a major Texas producer of natural gas. At the time of the 1980 census, agriculture and mining together employed about 6 percent of the workers in the Border region.

The Border is noted also for its high level of local government employment; 24 percent of employment in the region is in the public sector with local government alone providing 14 percent.

CENTRAL CORRIDOR

The Central Corridor, like the Metroplex, has prospered independently of its natural resources and geology. The principal economic centers of the region, with the exception of Bryan-College Station in Brazos County, lie along Interstate Highway 35 between Waco and San Antonio.

Table 1. Selected Economic And Demographic Characteristics For The Economic Regions Of Texas

	The Plains	The Metroplex	East Texas	Gulf Coast	Central Corridor	The Border	*STATE TOTAL
TOTAL POPULATION 1982:	1,819,700	3,492,500	1,141,300	4,647,900	2,682,700	1,494,400	15,278,500
Percent Change 1970-1982	17.6%	31.5%	33.0%	45.8%	35.9%	47.0%	36.0%
Percent Living in Metro Areas	55.2	93.7	33.2	91.5	83.1	78.2	80.5
TOTAL LABOR & PROPRIETORS INCOME 1982 (in billions)	$20.3	$45.1	$11.0	$60.8	$27.0	$10.1	$174.5
Percent Farm	1.4	0.3	2.5	0.3	1.0	1.9	0.8
Percent Nonfarm	98.6	99.7	97.5	99.7	99.0	98.1	99.2
Personal Income Per Capita	11,169	12,925	9,694	13,087	10,072	6,793	11,423
TOTAL EMPLOYMENT 1982:	908,433	1,877,232	469,509	2,363,169	1,250,575	538,276	7,407,194
Percent by Type:							
Proprietors	14.2%	8.3%	16.1%	7.2%	10.5%	9.0%	9.6%
Private usage and salary	69.6	79.6	69.1	80.4	61.6	67.4	74.1
Federal Government - Civilian	1.5	1.9	2.3	1.3	5.0	2.7	2.3
Federal Government - Military	2.7	1.1	0.9	1.0	7.8	5.5	2.7
State and Local Government	12.0	9.0	11.6	10.1	15.1	15.4	11.3
TOTAL WAGE AND SALARY EMPLOYMENT 1982:	779,085	1,721,013	393,718	2,193,875	1,119,237	489,896	6,696,824
Percent Farm	4.4%	0.2%	1.4%	0.5%	0.8%	3.0%	1.2%
Percent Nonfarm	95.6	99.8	98.6	99.5	99.2	97.0	98.8
Nonfarm Employment — Percent by Industry:							
Mining	11.5%	2.2%	4.9%	6.8%	1.4%	3.3%	5.0%
Construction	6.6	6.1	6.7	9.7	6.6	6.2	7.5
Manufacturing - Durable Goods	7.7	14.6	17.0	8.9	8.1	4.9	10.3
Manufacturing - Nondurable Goods	6.0	6.7	8.4	7.4	5.0	11.1	7.0
Transportation, Communications & Public Utilities	7.4	7.5	6.6	7.8	5.8	6.9	7.2
Trade	25.6	27.1	23.2	24.4	25.0	28.4	25.5
Finance, Insurance, Real Estate	4.5	7.3	4.2	5.8	6.1	4.3	5.9
Business & Repair Services	4.7	6.9	3.7	7.1	6.1	4.7	6.3
Personal Services	2.3	2.6	1.8	2.1	2.7	2.1	2.3
Health Services	7.5	5.8	8.5	6.3	8.1	6.3	6.7
Education Services	8.9	6.6	8.7	7.0	11.4	12.9	8.3
Legal Services	0.4	0.6	0.4	0.6	0.6	0.5	0.5
Social Services	1.8	1.2	1.6	1.2	2.6	1.7	1.5
Public Administration	3.7	2.8	3.3	2.5	8.6	5.5	4.1
Other Services	1.4	2.0	1.0	2.4	1.9	1.2	1.9
PERCENT PRODUCTION OF SELECTED COMMODITIES:							
Coal—(1981)	0.3%	0.4%	67.9%	.0%	30.6%	0.8%	100.0%
Crude Oil—(1983)	65.9	1.7	11.5	12.6	5.3	3.0	100.0
Condensate—(1983)	18.0	2.4	12.3	46.0	5.2	16.0	99.9
Natural Gas—(1983)	41.2	3.1	10.0	24.0	4.4	17.2	99.9
Wood—(1982)	0	0	75.9	23.6	0.5	0	100.0
Farm Products—(1983)	38.7	8.1	13.1	12.5	15.3	12.3	100.0
Defense Outlays—(1980)	7.4	40.6	3.1	11.2	30.6	7.1	100.00

*Totals may not add due to rounding.
SOURCES: United States Department of Commerce, Texas Railroad Commission, Community Services Administration and Texas Forest Service.

At Joske's, we're Texas born and bred and proud of it! Wherever you roam -- Big D to Beaumont, El Paso to Austin --you'll find us close by with exciting fashions, home furnishings and lots more. We're a Lone Star tradition, guaranteeing our customers quality merchandise and service since your great great grandmother shopped Joske's for her button top shoes and bustle.
Dallas, Houston, San Antonio, Austin, Corpus Christi, Beaumont and El Paso

JOSKE'S
A UNIT OF ALLIED STORES

The characteristic that unites the economic centers of this region is their ability to weather economic downturns. Two fundamental reasons for the continued economic health of the Central Corridor are the amount spent on public and private services and the operation of military installations in the region.

More than 40 percent of employment in the Central Corridor is in service industries, the greatest percentage of any of the regions of the state. Health services, education services and public administration accounted for 28 percent of total regional employment.

This region received $3.1 billion in defense outlays in 1980, 30.6 percent of the state total and an amount second only to the $4.1 billion received by the Metroplex.

In 1982, total government employment represented 28 percent of total employment in the region. Federal and state government employment is more important to the Central Corridor than to any other region of the state.

The Central Corridor, however, does not rely solely on the service sector or the inflow of government funds but uses these sectors as a base on which to build more diversified economies. For example, manufacturing employment in the Central Corridor grew by more than six percent in 1984, compared to 3.3 percent statewide. This rapid growth in manufacturing is based in fast-growing high technology industries. High-tech employment in the Central Corridor grew by almost 18 percent in 1984, more than any other region.

GULF COAST

From Beaumont to Corpus Christi, the Gulf Coast is united economically by the dominance of the petroleum, petrochemical and related industries. The discovery of oil at **Spindletop**, near Beaumont, in 1901 sparked the first Texas oil boom and the beginning of the oil industry in Texas. Houston, set between the East Texas timber lands and the Gulf of Mexico, became a center for producing oil drilling equipment, refining oil, and transporting petroleum products via rail and sea.

The Gulf Coast accounted for 23 percent of the oil, gas and condensate (a by-product of natural gas production) produced in Texas in 1983. In 1984, 45 percent of the state's mining employment and 63 percent of statewide employment in the petroleum refining and petrochemical production industries were in this region.

About 14 percent of total employment in the Gulf Coast is in industries tied directly to the production of petroleum and petrochemicals. The percentage doubles if one also includes those workers in service industries whose wages are paid indirectly with petro dollars. These percentages have declined since 1982, as the prices of oil fell.

Gulf Coast employment is supplemented by steel production, shipbuilding, fishing, port activity and agriculture. The flat low-lying coastal plain, with its abundant water supply, produces massive quantities of rice, cotton, flax, grain sorghum, soybeans and various grasses for cattle feed.

The Houston metropolitan area, which is the eighth largest in the nation, represents the most diversified local economy in the region, having built on its importance as a petroleum center. Houston is the fourth largest city in the nation. Its economy has diversified into manufacturing, international and domestic trade, banking and as a headquarters for many corporations. Despite diversification, however, Houston's economy and that of the entire Gulf Coast is still dominated by petroleum and petrochemical industries.

Texas Office in Mexico Aids Businessmen

Since 1971, the State of Texas has had an office in Mexico City to aid businessmen from both Texas and Mexico develop trade opportunities. Operated by the Texas Economic Development Commission, the goal of the office staff is to generate more business for the state.

Luis Morales, director of the office, has a staff of two and runs the office for less than $100,000 a year. The office offers a wide range of services, but more than half its time is spent in referring trade leads and counseling businessmen. Morales helps Texas businessmen register with the Mexican government and to comply with the nation's often-changing laws and regulations. In addition, the office aids Texas businessmen in locating Mexican distributors, representatives and suppliers. Other services include trade show assistance, aid in establishing in-bond plants and information on currency.

The state's office also maintains a file of catalogs on Texas products and manufacturers for businessmen to examine, and handles information on agricultural commodities. The office can be contacted by mail at Apartado Postal 5-602, Mexico D.F. 06500. The phone number in Mexico City is 905/525-2217.

SLOWER GROWTH EXPECTED IN TEXAS

This article was prepared by State Comptroller Bob Bullock.

Today, the Texas economy is in a period of transition. An oil-rich state that has lived off its natural resources, Texas' industrial base is shifting away from oil and into a broader base of manufacturing and service industries.

Since 1901, when oil first gushed out of the ground at Spindletop, Texas has been closely identified with the energy industry. During the energy boom of the late 1970s and early 1980s, this relationship served the state well, providing a resource and capital base that spurred the state's rapid growth and made Texas an economic leader among the 50 states.

This close tie also meant that the impact of falling energy prices and the slump in the state petroleum industry, which began to be felt in mid-1982, reverberated through the economy, dulling the sharp upward slant of the state's growth curve.

Today, the Texas economy is growing again, becoming more diverse and less dependent on oil and gas. But while diversification fuels growth, Texas will grow much slower than it did during the energy boom. Low oil prices have hurt the state, but diversification offers a way to help put Texas back in the forefront of the nation's economy.

PERSONAL INCOME: One of the most important measures of a state's economic performance is personal income. This is simply the total of all wages and salaries, business income, investment earnings and other sources of income to a state's citizens. Typically, the personal income total is also divided by state population to arrive at a per-capita income figure.

Texas' personal income totaled $183.7 billion in 1983, accounting for almost 7 percent of the nation's total income. Growth in personal income has slowed since the energy boom, when double-digit growth was the norm. In fact, 1983 income growth in Texas was only 5.3 percent. Falling oil prices meant that the recovery in Texas lagged behind the rest of the nation, as U.S. personal income was up 6.3 percent.

On a per-capita basis, preliminary estimates put Texas' personal income at $11,685 in 1983, up only 3 percent from 1982. This slow growth reflected the effect of lower oil prices on the state. While in 1982, Texas' per-capita income growth easily surpassed the U.S. average by 2.7 percent, in 1983, Texas' income growth equaled the U.S. average.

For 1984, personal income was expected to grow by more than 9 percent from 1983, still less than the double-digits of the energy boom. This slower growth rate reflects the impact of lower oil prices and lower inflation on the Texas economy. This growth should again lag behind the nation, but as the state's economy continues to diversify, Texas' growth should again surpass the nationwide rate.

POPULATION: Another important measure of a state's progress is population growth. With an estimated 15.7 million people in 1983, Texas ranks third among the states in population behind California and New York. Texas has been one of the nation's fastest growing states.

The reasons for Texas' population growth are twofold. First, Texas is a relatively young state and its birthrate is high. Second, while Texas' job growth has slowed, the jobs that are created continue to attract newcomers. While slower economic growth will attract fewer newcomers, Texas is still expected to surpass New York to become the nation's second most populous state by 1990.

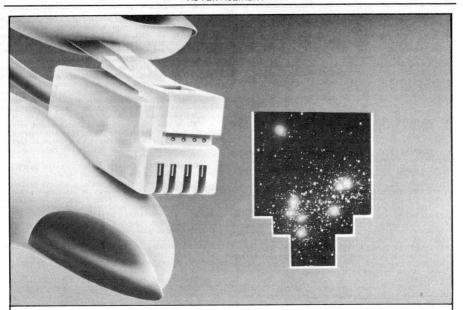

SOUTHWESTERN BELL TELEPHONE. YOUR CONNECTION TO THE FUTURE.

It's just a simple modular jack. But plug it into our network and the future is yours, right at your fingertips. Keeping the benefits of our technology simple and easy to use is important, too. Whatever your communications needs, call your Southwestern Bell Telephone service representative.

Southwestern Bell Telephone

Texans providing telecommunications for a growing state.

Although Texas was predominantly a rural state until 1940, about 80 percent of our population now lives in urban areas. In fact, Texas is more urbanized than the rest of the nation. Only 75 percent of all Americans live in urban areas.

About half of the state's residents can be found in the three urban centers—Houston, Dallas-Fort Worth and San Antonio. Texas has 28 metropolitan areas in all, more than any other state, and each of these cities offers its own unique blend of business and industry, as well as diverse cultures and styles of living.

Texas' population is more ethnically diverse than the United States as a whole. Twenty-one percent of the people in the state are of Spanish origin, compared to 6.4 percent nationwide. Twelve percent of all Texans are black, slightly more than the 11.7 percent nationwide.

EMPLOYMENT: Texas' employment is on the rise again, as new industries lead the state into an era of lower oil prices. In 1984, nonfarm employment was expected to total more than 6.3 million, up about 2.7 percent from 1983. This growth made it the strongest year since 1981, though still far below the 5.9 percent annual rate of growth from 1977 to 1981.

The Texas unemployment rate continues to be below the national standard. Unemployment in 1984 stood at an estimated 6 percent, compared to 7.6 percent nationwide. While this was a substantial improvement from 1983's statewide rate of 8 percent, it was higher than the 5.5 percent average during the energy boom.

The largest employer in Texas is the trade industry. One out of every four Texans works in the trade industry in jobs ranging from store clerks to wholesalers to restaurateurs.

The fastest growing and second largest industry in the state is services. The service industry is a broad range of businesses, including hotels, entertainment, health care, lawyers and many other personal and business services. Employment in service industries has increased much faster than overall employment, a trend that should continue for the next several years. From 1980 to 1983, employment in services increased at an annual rate of 5 percent compared to a 1.8 percent clip for total employment.

Government is the next largest employer in the state, accounting for 16.8 percent of all the state's jobs. The largest government employer is local governments, which include police, fire protection and schools. Local governments employ about 62 percent of all government workers. State employees account for about 21 percent, and federal workers 17 percent.

The state's manufacturers employ 15.6 percent of all working Texans. While overall employment in manufacturing has grown slowly as the energy-related businesses adjust to lower oil prices, some manufacturers have done very well. Employment in high-technology businesses, producing computers and sophisticated electronic equipment, has grown steadily.

While the remaining industries account for less than a quarter of the state's jobs, they are nonetheless very important to the economy as a whole. In fact, oil and gas, construction and agriculture remain keys to the state's economic future.

OIL AND GAS: Despite its decline, the petroleum industry still has a great impact on the state.

Texas is the nation's leading energy-producing state, and trends in the energy industry have profound consequences on the Texas economy. The consequences extend far beyond the process of searching for and producing oil and natural gas. Directly affected are such important industrial sectors as refining, petrochemicals and gasoline marketing. While oil and gas extraction accounts for only 4.3 percent of the state's jobs, the industry touches virtually all other parts of the state economy. Estimates of its direct and indirect impact have ranged from 20 to 50 percent of the state economy.

Texas currently leads the nation in the production of both oil and natural gas, accounting for roughly one-quarter to one-third of the nation's total production of each. Texas also has the largest petroleum refining capacity of any state, accounting for about 27 percent of the nation's total.

Texas also leads the nation in the number of drilling rigs actively searching for oil and gas. However, drilling activity remains well below the peak of 1,404 rigs in operation in January 1982. In 1984, the number of rotary rigs running averaged 850. Uncertainty about oil prices may continue to limit drilling activity.

The current outlook is for the oil and gas industry to remain depressed for some time to come. It is unlikely that oil prices, which have dropped dramatically since early 1982, will rise significantly through 1985. In fact, most industry analysts expect the declines to continue. Because of this, the industry's recovery will be slow and painful, acting as a drag on the state economy in general for many months into the future.

CONSTRUCTION: Building cranes have been a familiar sight across the state in recent years, but recently building activity has slowed substantially. Today, the state has a surplus of both residential and nonresidential buildings.

While 1983 was a record year for housing starts, residential building was off substantially in 1984. Housing starts fell an estimated 17.5 percent from the 282,900 starts in 1983.

On the nonresidential side, 1983 was a down year and 1984 continued the trend. The value of nonresidential construction fell 5 percent in 1983, to $7.4 billion.

Construction employment has declined since 1982. Construction jobs numbered an estimated 404,000 in 1984, down four percent from 1983. Today, the construction industry accounts for about 6.8 percent of the state's jobs.

The outlook for the construction industry is modest. As the state's population growth slows, the number of new families needing housing will decline and limit the number of new housing starts. While the industry should continue to grow over the long term, it is unlikely that 1983's record for starts will be broken in the near future. Lower interest rates will help business over the short term, although the current glut of housing in many areas of the state should limit new building.

Nonresidential construction growth is also likely to be slower over the next few years as the market works to absorb all the building activity that occurred in the late 1970s and early 1980s. However, as the Texas economy regains strength, activity should begin to improve throughout the state.

AGRICULTURE: Employment in Texas agriculture has, of course, not grown as rapidly as other sectors of the state economy. As agricultural methods have become more mechanized, fewer people have been needed to maintain Texas as a national agricultural leader.

In 1983, Texas led—or was among—the nation's most important producers of such basic commodities as cattle, rice, grain sorghum and cotton. The state leads the nation in the number of farms and ranches and in farm and ranch acreage.

However, 1983 was not a good year for agriculture, as Texans and farmers across the nation were plagued

Workers harvest grapes at Ste. Genevieve Vineyards in West Texas. Dallas News Photo by Paula Nelson.

by poor weather and depressed prices. Cash receipts from all Texas farm commodities were an estimated $9 billion in 1983, down from $9.6 billion in 1982.

Texans may expect a general, though slow, improvement in farm conditions in 1984-85, barring a recurrence of unpredictable weather-related crop losses. As the world grows hungrier, the importance of the state's agricultural wealth will only grow more important.

THE OUTLOOK: The Texas economy is in a period of transition. It is leaving a period of extraordinarily rapid growth, which was fueled by the rapid increase in the value of Texas oil and gas production. The economy is entering a period when oil and gas prices will either decline or grow slowly, limiting growth in the energy industry. Because of the state economy's close link with oil and gas, this factor could slow overall state economic growth in coming years. A major challenge for the state will be to deal with this problem and to continue to build an increasingly diversified economic base.

An Old Industry Making A Comeback

This article was prepared by Melissa Gaskill of the Domestic Marketing Program of the Texas Department of Agriculture.

Wineries are returning to Texas. The state has had winemaking since 1662. There were 25 wineries in Texas by 1900, growing grapes from vinifera cuttings brought from Europe. Wild grapes had grown in Texas for centuries, and wine appreciators the world over are, in fact, indebted to the efforts of a Texan, T. V. Munson, who in the late 1800s developed here a vine root stock resistant to a disease that was devastating the vineyards in Europe.

Prohibition nipped Texas' wine industry, and after repeal only one winery remained.

Rejuvenation began in the 1970s. First, drip irrigation proved to be what vines needed to thrive in parts of Texas. Then, the University of Texas began experimental vine planting on its land in West Texas. For decades, the arid lands produced oil and gas, but UT wanted to find other uses for its land. Working with several scientists, it was discovered that a prized European wine grape, Vitus vinifera, did quite well in West Texas. The Texas Grape Growers Association was formed in 1976, and the Texas Department of Agriculture contributed marketing, promotions and legislative support. There are now 16 Texas wineries.

Texas-grown grapes have the same toney names wine lovers the world over know so well — cabernet, chardonnay, riesling, zinfandel. The wines generally take the name of the grape from which they are made. Through hard work, expeience and the help of skilled winemakers from all over the world, Texas vintners are learning the curious blend of science and art that is winemaking.

Wine production increased when those UT wine lands finally went commercial through a lease to a consortium of Texans and French investors (any winery bonded in Texas must be 51 percent Texas-owned). Bottling under the name Ste. Genevieve, this winery may one day rank with the country's largest, since as much as 30,000 acres have been identified as potential vineyards.

The patiarch of the Texas wine industry is 100-year-old Val Verde winery near Del Rio. Owner Thomas Qualia grows primarily Lenoir grapes and some Herbemont in vineyards started by his grandfather. His port wine has earned awards in state competitions.

Most wineries are open at certain times for touring and tasting. Many sell their wine on the premises and through local stores. Shops in Houston, Dallas, Fort Worth, Austin, San Antonio and Midland carry Texas wines, and a number of restaurants are adding them to their wine lists. Each day, more people discover the pleasure of a rediscovered Texas tradition — wine.

The following is a list of the state's wineries as of March 1985:

Chateau Montgolfier, Fort Worth; Cypress Valley Winery, Cypress Mill; Fall Creek Vineyards, Tow; Guadalupe Valley Winery, New Braunfels; Ivanhoe Winery, Ivanhoe; La Buena Vida Vineyards, Springtown; Llano Estacado Winery, Lubbock; Messina Hof Wine Cellars, Bryan; Moyer Texas Champagne Co., New Braunfels; Oberhellman Vineyards, Fredericksburg; Pheasant Ridge Winery, Lubbock; Sanchez Creek Vineyards, Weatherford; Sanuvas Vineyards, El Paso; Ste. Genevieve, Bakersfield; Val Verde Winery, Del Rio; and Wimberley Valley Wines, Driftwood.

Texas a Leader in High Technology

This article was prepared for the Texas Almanac by the Office of the State Comptroller in Austin.

National attention was focused on Texas in 1983 when Austin was selected to be the site of Microelectronics and Computer Technology Corporation (MCC), a high-technology research and development firm. Observers speculated that the MCC headquarters selection would rank Texas high up on the national, if not international, high-technology list. But while high technology is important to the Texas economy, the vast majority of Texans do not work in the industry. Less than four percent of all nonfarm jobs are with high-technology firms.

Texas' reputation for its inexpensive and abundant housing, a willing labor force, quality academic institutions, favorable business and tax climate and quality of living have enabled it to compete vigorously with California's Silicon Valley, Massachusetts' Route 128 and North Carolina's Research Triangle Park to maintain its share of the high-technology market. The number of high-tech businesses, sales volume and employment in the industry have all increased in the last five years, outpacing growth in other sectors of the state's economy.

The Business of High Technology

The number of high-technology businesses in Texas has grown from 1,638 in 1978 to 7,541 in 1984, an average annual increase of 29 percent. Overall, the number of businesses in Texas has only grown by an average of six percent per year. Actually, high technology is not really just one business; it is a combination of many. High-technology firms manufacture everything from hand calculators to sophisticated defense systems. They are linked by their focus on commercial applications of newly developed scientific and engineering technologies, such as computer microchips.

High-technology firms in Texas currently include manufacturers of communication equipment, electronic components, aircraft parts, guided missiles and space vehicles, scientific and research equipment, measuring and controlling instruments, optical instruments and electronic computing equipment. Other businesses, like computer and data processing services, computer equipment stores and research and development laboratories, are also located in Texas.

High Tech Centered in Dallas

The 7,541 firms belonging to the high-technology industry in Texas had more than $2.5 billion in sales taxable business in 1984, up from $1 billion in 1978. (This is an average annual growth rate of 16 percent per year.) The high-tech share of total taxable sales in Texas grew from 2.6 percent to 3.6 percent over the period.

While Austin received much publicity from the coming of MCC, the real heart of Texas high technology is the Dallas-Fort Worth metroplex. More than 37 percent of all high-technology taxable sales in 1984 occurred in the Dallas-Fort Worth area, the largest percentage of any area in Texas.

Dallas' high-tech industry is centered around communication equipment, electronics and aircraft parts. Dallas has 28 percent of all communication equipment businesses in the state. Of all businesses dealing in electronic components, 39 percent are in the Dallas-Fort Worth area, as are 45 percent of firms selling aircraft parts.

Houston ranked second in Texas in high-technology sales with over 19 percent or $483 million of the 1984 total. Houston, like the Dallas-Fort Worth area, has a substantial communication equipment sector. Houston also has a considerable number of businesses making electronic components and measuring and controlling instruments.

Bryan-College Station and Austin have the fastest growing high-technology sales in the state. The average annual sales growth rate for Bryan-College Station was 80 percent and 39 percent for Austin since 1974. (See Table 1.)

Of all the high-technology sectors in Texas, guided missiles and space vehicles and computer equipment stores have had the largest sales growth since 1974, each increasing by over 80 percent annually. Growth in sales of aerospace manufacturing and computer equipment stores is followed by increases in computer and data processing services (48.2 percent).

High-Tech Employment Grows

Employment in the Texas high-tech industry increased by an average 5.1 percent annually, from 176,556 employees in 1979 to 226,060 in 1984. In 1984, 3.6 percent of non-farm employment in the state was in the high-tech field, up from 3.2 percent in 1979.

As in sales, the Dallas-Fort Worth area dominates, employing 57 percent of all high-technology workers in Texas. Houston employs the next largest percentage of high-tech workers — 12.7 percent. (See Table 2.)

Job growth has increased with sales growth, though in a more modest fashion. Employment in the guided missiles and space vehicles manufacturing sector accounted for the largest percentage increase in overall high-tech employment. Between 1979 and 1984, employment in that sector increased by an average of 65.6 percent annually. Dallas-Fort Worth accounted for almost all the growth in that sector — 97 percent.

Jobs increased by 17.3 percent annually in the electronic computing equipment manufacturing sector making it the second largest growth area, with Dallas-Fort Worth experiencing a 45.1 percent growth and Austin having a 29.6 percent increase.

High-Tech Recruitment

Texas may expand its current high-technology base in the coming years. In fierce national competition

Table 1—High-Tech Taxable Sales By Selected MSA (In Millions)

City—	Taxable Sales for 1974	*Taxable Sales for 1984	Percent of 1984 Total	Average Annual Increase
Bryan-College Station . .	$0.0	$7.5	0.3%	79.7%
San Antonio	6.9	92.2	3.7	29.6
Austin.	4.9	134.5	5.4	39.3
Dallas-Fort Worth	192.2	926.4	37.2	17.0
Houston	296.6	483.1	19.4	5.0
Rest of State	74.0	846.7	34.0	27.6
TOTAL	$574.6	$2,491.1	100.0%	15.5%

High-Tech Taxable Sales By Industry (In Millions)

Industry Type—	Taxable Sales for 1974	*Taxable Sales for 1984	Percent of 1984 Total	Average Annual Increase
Guided Missiles and Space Vehicles.	$0.1	$38.2	1.5%	81.2%
Computer Equipment Stores.	0.8	352.9	14.2	83.8
Computer and Data Processing Services	8.7	445.1	17.9	48.2
Electronic Computing Equipment.	12.4	217.7	8.7	33.2
Optical Instruments	0.4	6.5	0.3	32.2
Research and Development Laboratories	4.7	20.3	0.8	15.8
Scientific and Research Equipment.	5.9	39.2	1.6	20.9
Measuring and Controlling Instruments.	25.7	176.3	7.1	21.2
Electronic Components.	69.3	563.6	22.6	23.3
Aircraft Parts.	54.7	156.5	6.3	11.1
Communication Equipment	391.9	474.1	19.0	1.9
TOTAL	$574.6	$2,490.4	100.0%	15.8%

*Estimated.
SOURCE: Comptroller of Public Accounts sales tax records.

among 58 cities, Texas attracted Microelectronics and Computer Technology Corporation (MCC), a joint venture of 18 computer and semiconductor products manufacturers in direct competition with Japanese companies. The consortium eventually expects to employ 400 engineers and scientists and spend about $100 million annually on four programs — the design of a new generation of computers, development of new software technology, component packaging and computer aided design and manufacturing.

Building a High-Tech Base

What factors lure high-tech companies to an area?

High-technology firms are, in a sense, considered "footloose" because they are not bound to a region out of a need for specific raw materials, as are most traditional industries. The lack of dependence upon such basic factors as a large water supply, major waste treatment facilities and massive energy supplies allows high-technology companies extensive freedom in site selection.

Site selection, according to a study by the Congressional Joint Economic Committee, is determined by such factors as costs, availability of skilled labor, access to top-ranked academic institutions, high quality and low cost of living, good transportation systems and a favorable business and tax climate.

Among the main considerations when firms are looking for a new location are costs. Labor is one of the larger cost categories — and wages are generally lower in Texas than in other states.

In addition, land and housing are less expensive and more abundant in Texas, unlike California and Massachusetts where small houses, if available at all, may cost well over $100,000.

A large supply of university graduates with technical skills is also important. Quality academic institutions play an important role in site selection. Not only does close proximity to universities provide a constant supply of skilled personnel, reducing the activities and costs associated with recruitment, but university libraries and laboratories allow for the exchange of ideas and dissemination of recent developments.

A reciprocal relationship between high-technology industry and local universities can expand into an extremely productive venture. This is evident in the alliances that have flourished between high-tech centers like North Carolina's Research Triangle Park and Duke University, North Carolina State University and the University of North Carolina; California's Silicon Valley and Stanford University; and Massachusetts' Route 128 and Harvard University and the Massachusetts Institute of Technology.

In light of Texas' ability to attract high-technology industries, the future of the firms in Texas looks very promising. High technology-related jobs and sales are expected to continue increasing in Texas, outpacing other growth in the state.

It is important to remember, however, that high-tech firms employ 226,060 individuals, less than four percent of the Texas labor force. While Texas will need to continue developing its high-tech base in order to compete with other states for business, such as defense contracts, the majority of Texans will not work in high-tech industries in the foreseeable future.

Table 2—High-Tech Employment By Selected Metropolitan Areas

City—	Total Employed 1979	*Total Employed 1984	Average Annual Change
Austin	11,906	24,909	15.9%
Houston	21,468	28,620	5.9
San Antonio	9,079	11,896	5.6
Dallas-Fort Worth	105,599	129,788	4.2
Bryan-College Station	518	946	12.8
Rest of State	27,987	29,901	1.3
TOTAL	176,557	226,060	5.1%

High-Tech Employment By Industry

Industry Type—	Total Employed 1979	*Total Employed 1984	Average Annual Change
Guided Missiles and Space Vehicles	859	10,692	65.6%
Measuring and Controlling Instruments	5,427	9,151	11.0
Electronic Computing Equipment	12,725	28,197	17.3
Computer and Data Processing Services	20,648	38,306	13.2
Research and Development Laboratories	5,277	9,932	13.5
Scientific and Research Equipment	3,542	3,383	−0.9
Communications Equipment	21,323	23,450	1.9
Electronic Components	57,600	59,795	0.8
Aircraft and Parts	48,279	42,496	−2.5
Optical Instruments	876	658	−5.6
Computer Equipment Stores	NA	NA	—
TOTAL	176,556	226,060	5.1%

*The figures for 1984 are based on average employment during the first three quarters of the year.
SOURCE: Texas Employment Commission and Comptroller of Public Accounts.

Table 3—High-Tech Businesses By Industry Type and Selected MSA*

(Percentage of All Businesses and Each Type Located in the MSA)

Industry Type—	Austin	Bryan-College Station	Dallas-Fort Worth	Houston	San Antonio	Rest of State
Computer and Data Processing Services	7.1%	0.5%	36.2%	20.7%	6.7%	28.6%
Electronic Computing Equipment	4.2	0.7	40.3	22.2	3.5	29.2
Optical Instruments	†	†	34.8	21.7	†	43.5
Research and Development Laboratories	10.3	1.5	17.6	22.1	2.9	45.6
Science and Research Equipment	3.7	0.9	20.2	28.4	3.7	43.1
Measuring and Controlling Instruments	4.9	1.0	18.7	33.0	3.4	38.9
Aircraft Parts	3.4	†	44.9	8.5	16.1	27.1
Communications Equipment	5.4	0.4	27.8	16.6	3.3	46.5
Computer Equipment Stores	7.5	0.8	36.7	28.2	5.3	21.5
Guided Missiles and Space Vehicles	9.1	†	45.5	†	†	45.5
Electronic Components	5.8	0.6	38.9	19.5	2.7	32.5

*Based on sales tax reporting outlets for third quarter of 1984.
†Negligible.

SOURCE: Texas Comptroller of Public Accounts.

Texas Makes Headway in the Movies

This article was written by Mary G. Crawford, Editorial Assistant of the Texas Almanac, based, in part, on research by Bruce Lanier Wright of the State Comptroller's Office, Austin.

A headline in the *New York Times* on Sept. 2, 1984, trumpeted: "Texas Yields a Bumper Crop of Movies." That headline and its accompanying story told the world what many Texans had known for several years: Texas has become one of the most popular places in the country to make movies. Low production costs, a growing local film industry and the Texas mystique drew major TV and film projects with budgets totaling $204 million in 1983-84.

Texas often is touted as the "Third Coast" in filmmaking, the leading center of the film industry after California and New York. By actual numbers of projects filmed, Texas has been vying with Illinois and Florida for the third spot. But after films produced in Texas were awarded seven of the top eight Oscars in 1984, plus being nominated in 14 additional categories, Texas clearly became first among equals. In the 1984 Academy Awards, three of the five pictures nominated for Best Picture — *Silkwood, Tender Mercies* and *Terms of Endearment* — were filmed in Texas, while only one of the five nominees was even partly filmed in Hollywood. Another film, *Paris, Texas*, won the 1984 Palm d'Or Award at the prestigious Cannes Film Festival in France. In 1985, two Oscars were won by *Places in the Heart*, which was shot in Waxahachie.

The number of recent prize-winning films stamped "Made in Texas" reflects the growing tendency of filmmakers to abandon the traditional seat of the industry.

The great increase in the amount of filming in Texas has resulted from demands of today's movie audiences for greater authenticity in the "look" of a film. The portability of modern film equipment has made it possible to film nearly anywhere. Modern filmmakers routinely travel thousands of miles to photograph appropriate settings. And recent public fascination with all things Texan has been lifted to an all-time high by the TV series *Dallas* and movies like *Urban Cowboy*.

But filmmakers are lured to Texas by more than "Texas chic." Compared to California and New York, the state is an inexpensive place to make a movie. On the average, a shot-in-Hollywood movie costs about $11 million; the same movie can be produced in Texas for $2 million or less. Why? First, fees for filming permits are much less expensive. Texas communities have a reputation for being eager to please. Frequently only one or two permits are required to obtain the cooperation of a whole town.

Second, Texas unions are more flexible than those on either of the other coasts, allowing the hiring of only the number of crew members necessary to do the job, rather than the inflated numbers mandated by West and East coast unions. Union scale wage rates in Texas are lower than either coast. A key electrician in Texas is paid about $1,500 a week, contrasted with $2,500 a week paid in New York or Los Angeles. Extras that cost $120 a day or more on the West Coast cost $30 to $50 in Texas. Even with the lower costs, the Screen Actors Guild counts more than 1,000 members in Texas.

Texas actors and technicians are less expensive to employ, but they are no less qualified than their counterparts on the other coasts. The Texas Film Commission's *Production Manual* lists more than 700 companies and individuals involved in every aspect of filmmaking, from writing scripts to making final prints. One intangible, but very real, advantage of using Texas crews is their enthusiasm and cooperation. New York-based producer Michael Hausman said, "I've worked with two Texas crews now, for *Silkwood* and *Places in the Heart*, and they're some of the best I've seen. They're not overexposed, they're eager, and we save all the per diems and other costs of flying in a crew."

Texas actively courts the film industry through the Texas Film Commission and several metropolitan film offices. The film commission, a branch of the governor's office, was created in 1971 by executive order of Gov. Preston Smith, a former theater owner, to attract motion picture production to the state. The film commission assists prospective Texas film projects by acting as a liason with local governments, by scouting film locations and by referring qualified local film personnel.

In recent years, Texas' success in attracting major motion picture productions has been impressive. Of the 308 U.S. feature motion pictures made during 1983-84, 30 were filmed partly or wholly in Texas. And 30 other

major projects — including TV shows and movies-of-the-week — were filmed in Texas during the same period.

In the first four months of 1985, four feature films, five TV movies and a documentary were filmed in Texas.

Texas has long been a major producer of television commercials and "industrials," or corporate and promotional films. Much of this activity is centered in the Dallas-Fort Worth area.

A recent economic survey prepared for the North Dallas Chamber of Commerce indicates that about 11,300 people work full time in the Metroplex film and tape industry (excluding people who show movies).

Dallas-Fort Worth's position as Texas' film center was strengthened by the opening in 1984 of the Dallas Communications Complex. By mid-1985, this $35 millon, 125-acre complex in the suburb of Irving housed over 90 companies serving every facet of the film and tape industry. Its three soundstages represent the largest studio complex between the East and West coasts.

Ground has been broken for an Astrodome-size production studio 22 miles north of Houston. Plans for the $30 million complex include a 140,000-square-foot geodesic dome studio with a 12-foot-deep water tank and an adjacent 100,000-square-foot office building. As of mid-1985, the completion date for the project was still indefinite.

The presence of so much talent and equipment in the state has inspired a new generation of filmmakers to make films entirely in Texas with Texas crews. According to the film commission, seven independent features were produced by Texas companies in 1984, a sharp increase over the three produced in 1983. These films were financed largely by Texas money and manned by Texas crews. At least six more independent Texas projects were scheduled for 1985.

Excitement over Texas films has grown with the number of recognized, bankable filmmakers who have chosen Texas for their base of operations. Producers like Martin Jurow (*Terms of Endearment*) and writers like Horton Foote (*Tender Mercies*) add considerably to the world reputation of Texas films.

All of this film activity is beginning to have a small but definite impact on the state's economy. The Texas Film Commission estimates that of the $204 million spent by makers of the 60 major film projects shot at least partially in Texas in 1983-84, at least 40 percent, or $82 million, went directly into the Texas economy. The ultimate economic impact of this expenditure was undoubtedly much greater.

Precise records of Texas' thriving production of commercials and industrial films are not kept.

Tax records in the State Comptroller's office show that the Texas film/tape production and distribution industry achieved gross sales of $128.8 million in 1984. Gross sales for the industry in Texas have grown an average of 30 percent annually since 1980.

When a film crew begins filming on location, the benefits to the surrounding community are immediate and often highly visible. An official with the San Antonio Convention and Visitors Bureau reports that during a recent six-day location shoot in that city, the cast and crew of TV's *General Hospital* soap opera spent $40,000 on hotels alone.

The Dallas/Fort Worth Metroplex, unofficial capital of the Texas movie industry, probably receives more film revenue than any other city. The North Dallas Chamber of Commerce study estimates that film and tape production and distribution generated $144.2 million in the Metroplex in 1983.

In Houston, from 1980 through March 1985, 107 film and videotape projects requiring 720 production days pumped almost $18.7 million directly into the economy. From 1982 through March 1985, six feature films shot wholly or partly in El Paso spent $24.9 million in the area; 32 commercials added $4.6 million.

The Austin Chamber of Commerce estimates that 1983-84 film projects spent $8 to $12 million in the city. In addition to feature film projects, Austin hosts several TV shows made for cable and public television. One survey indicates that at least 900 local, regional and national commercials were shot in or produced out of Austin during 1983-84.

The barracks set of the award-winning Robert Altman film "Streamers" is shown inside the Dallas Communications Complex in Irving. The entire film was shot inside the 15,000-square-foot Studio A, the largest of the facility's three sound stages.

The arrival of a movie company can have an especially dramatic effect on smaller towns. Waxahachie, a town of 17,000 noted for its finely preserved 19th century architecture, received worldwide publicity following the success of Robert Benton's *Places in the Heart,* which was filmed in the area. The shooting lasted two months in 1983 and poured at least $1 million into the local economy. Since then, three other productions have filmed or plan to film in Waxahachie. Total film benefits to the town's economy are estimated at $2 million-$3 million — plus some priceless publicity. City officials report significant increases in tourism since *Places* "put the town on the map."

Texas is expected to continue to be a popular destination for location photography and a large producer of commercials and industrial films. Whether the state can become a film production center rivaling California and New York remains to be seen.

Competition for runaway Hollywood productions is increasingly vigorous, as more states awaken to the financial potential of what is one of the nation's largest non-polluting industries. Film commissions like Texas' exist in almost every state and in many cities. Some states, like Arkansas, are providing financial incentives to filmmakers who move productions to their states. Texas may find itself involved in bidding wars with other states wishing to attract Hollywood dollars.

Prospects for the development of an all-Texas film industry also seem uncertain. Texas filmmakers still find it much more difficult to finance projects than their Hollywood counterparts, who are backed by the clout of established studios. Many observers of the Texas film industry feel that these difficulties are only the growing pains of an industry beginning to find its way. They point out that Hollywood itself took many years to establish its dominance. Texas filmmakers' financing future appeared brighter with the establishment in 1984 of the FilmDallas Investment Fund by Sam Grogg, Richard Kneipper and Joel Williams III. The $2.4 million limited partnership limits its investment in any one project to $500,000. The partners have held seminars all over the state to teach investors how to analyze a film project before investing.

As long as Texas can offer filmmakers a vast and varied landscape, a rich heritage of history and myth, and quality production at bargain rates, the movie business will continue to be a multimillion dollar industry in Texas.

MANUFACTURING IN TEXAS—1849-1982

Source: U.S. Bureau of Census.

The following data give a summary of manufacturing in Texas. In 1849 when the first Census of Manufacturing was taken, Texas had 309 business establishments. In 1982, date of the last Census of Manufacturing, the number had grown to 20,304. Number of wage earners grew from 1,066 in 1849 to 670,400 in 1982; wages from $322,368 in 1849 to $11,264,200,000 in 1982. Data for non-census years are given where available.

Year—	Estab-lish-ments	All Employees No.	All Employees Salaries and Wages	Wage Earners Only No.	Wage Earners Only Wages	†Cost of Materials Containers Power	‡‡Value Added by Manufacture	Value of Manu-factured Products
1982 . . .	20,304	1,060,900	$21,493,400,000	670,400	$11,264,200,000	$117,223,700,000	§§	$171,456,200,000
1977 . . .	18,107	886,400	11,653,100,000	600,700	6,626,400,000	60,395,800,000	33,080,900,000	92,735,700,000
1972 . . .	14,422	736,100	6,344,600,000	516,600	3,763,300,000	21,355,500,000	15,228,000,000	36,647,900,000
††1976..	†	824,600	9,852,000,000	560,300	5,661,100,000	49,905,000,000	27,600,000,000	. . .
††1975..	†	776,700	8,656,100,000	529,900	4,906,300,000	41,427,000,000	24,786,100,000	. . .
††1974..	†	803,900	8,084,800,000	562,700	4,741,100,000	36,849,000,000	23,398,900,000	. . .
††1973..	†	786,600	7,065,700,000	560,200	4,277,400,000	25,544,900,000	17,688,000,000	. . .
††1971..	12,574	694,000	5,689,800,000	480,300	3,300,500,000	19,289,800,000	13,793,900,000	. . .
††1970..	12,601	722,500	5,584,400,000	503,400	3,286,500,000	18,433,000,000	13,094,800,000	. . .
††1969..	12,471	728,300	5,327,300,000	515,000	3,222,800,000	18,520,000,000	12,922,900,000	. . .
††1968..	12,159	688,080	4,875,400,000	486,000	2,948,500,000	17,515,900,000	11,974,500,000	. . .
1967 . . .	12,722	657,500	4,340,400,000	466,400	2,617,000,000	15,785,000,000	10,922,400,000	26,498,100,000
††1966..	†	607,600	3,773,500,000	430,900	2,313,400,000	14,276,600,000	9,725,400,000	. . .
††1965..	†	566,870	3,365,052,000	400,680	2,065,220,000	12,790,551,000	8,700,197,000	. . .
††1964..	†	535,853	3,130,492,000	375,900	1,894,599,000	11,603,927,000	7,864,759,000	. . .
1963 . . .	11,581	513,802	2,890,500,000	361,471	1,744,187,000	†	7,119,500,000	. . .
††1962..	†	496,200	2,664,100	351,274	1,634,450,000	†	6,360,738,000	. . .
††1961..	†	485,800	2,528,700	344,604	1,558,032,000	†	6,003,580,000	. . .
††1960..	†	485,200	2,455,900	345,593	1,519,513,000	†	5,817,047,000	. . .
††1959..	†	485,400	2,405,600	347,298	1,500,682,000	†	5,614,018,000	. . .
**1958..	10,505	477,591	2,284,871,000	343,092	1,453,915,000	†	5,045,159,000	. . .
††1957..	†	471,509	2,185,230,000	352,395	1,459,327,000	†	5,039,313,000	. . .
††.....	1956	†453,136	2,011,631,000	346,050	1,370,467,000	†	4,736,594,000	. . .
††1955..	†	430,840	1,774,724,000	327,859	1,209,797,000	†	4,155,701,000	. . .
**1954..	8,890	410,364	1,620,344,000	313,938	1,109,061,000	†	3,501,706,000	. . .
††1949..	†	319,599	922,269,000	250,107	651,438,000	†	1,813,914,000	. . .
1947 . . .	7,129	297,054	755,413,000	242,015	558,422,000	†	1,727,476,000	. . .
*1939 . .	5,085	163,978	196,747,000	125,115	126,364,000	†	448,523,000	. . .
*1939 . .	5,376	†	†	126,996	128,138,703	1,075,763,628	453,105,423	1,530,220,676
1937 . . .	4,422	152,055	175,784,853	129,501	132,505,115	1,141,567,954	439,854,447	1,581,422,401
1935 . . .	4,167	117,275	125,069,000	99,124	90,202,214	764,117,512	295,127,739	1,059,245,252
1933 . . .	3,648	†	†	91,374	73,426,730	449,444,996	237,307,351	686,752,347
1931 . . .	4,326	†	†	94,867	99,061,000	†	272,935,000	. . .
1929 . . .	5,198	156,143	201,731,900	134,498	151,827,000	†	460,307,000	. . .
1927 . . .	4,065	†	†	116,763	130,408,661	842,927,286	363,652,676	1,206,579,962
1925 . . .	3,606	†	†	106,792	116,363,302	485,143,862	392,808,607	1,237,952,469
1923 . . .	3,693	†	†	102,358	111,461,949	647,451,774	331,740,283	979,192,057
1921 . . .	3,566	†	†	88,707	103,946,000	569,563,000	272,396,000	841,864,000
*1919 . .	5,390	124,110	146,230,000	106,268	114,935,000	†	295,709,000	. . .
*1919 . .	5,724	124,264	146,438,978	107,522	116,403,800	701,170,898	298,824,898	999,995,796
1914 . . .	5,062	86,232	59,112,000	74,765	44,762,000	253,114,261	108,024,000	361,279,303
1909 . . .	4,588	80,079	48,775,000	70,230	37,907,272	178,178,515	94,717,120	272,895,635
1904 . . .	3,158	54,819	30,587,000	49,066	24,468,942	91,603,630	58,924,759	150,528,389
1899 . . .	3,107	41,465	19,830,000	38,604	16,911,681	54,388,303	38,506,130	92,894,433
1889 . . .	5,268	†	†	34,794	15,148,495	36,152,308	34,281,243	70,433,551
1879 . . .	2,996	†	†	12,159	3,343,087	12,956,269	7,753,659	20,719,928
1869 . . .	2,399	†	†	7,927	1,787,835	6,273,193	5,224,209	11,517,302
1859 . . .	933	†	†	3,449	1,162,756	3,367,372	3,209,930	6,577,202
1849 . . .	309	†	†	1,066	322,368	394,642	773,896	1,168,538

*The years, 1939 and 1919, are given twice with different data. Marked change in the rules for inclusion of industry under "manufactures" in these years makes giving two lines of data advisable for the purpose of making them comparable with both preceding and succeeding years. For example, the top line for 1939 is comparable with the data given for 1947. The lower line for 1939 is comparable with preceding Census year.

†Not reported, or not reported on any comparable basis.

‡This item includes cost of materials, containers for products, fuel and purchased electric energy. There is considerable duplication in these data, caused by the successive processes through which many manufactured products go.

§Total value of products was not given in the printed report of the Bureau of Census after 1939. Actually, this figure is valueless as an indication of the amount of manufacturing done in any given area, or time, because of the great amount of duplication that is involved. The "value added by manufacture" is the net value of the manufactured product, and a much more dependable indication of the volume of manufacturing.

**The 1958 Census of Manufactures figures include ready-mixed concrete and machine shops that were engaged exclusively or almost exclusively in machine shop repair work. The data for such establishments are excluded from the figures for the period 1939-1957, but are included for 1929 and earlier years. The 1954-1958 figures include data for establishments engaged in the processing and distribution of fluid milk.

††The employment and payroll figures for operating manufacturing establishments for these years are estimates derived from a representative sample of manufacturing establishments canvassed in the Annual Survey of Manufactures.

‡‡For the period 1956-1977, value added by manufacture represents adjusted value added, and for earlier years, unadjusted value added. Unadjusted value added is obtained by subtracting the cost of materials, supplies and containers, fuel, purchased electric energy and contract work from the value of shipments for products manufactured plus receipts for services rendered.

§§1982 data not given in preliminary report.

TEXAS UTILITIES

Because of its large size, population and economic activity, Texas ranks high among the states in the scope of its utilities. It was one of the first states to utilize the telegraph and telephone extensively. A history of telephones in Texas appeared in the 1972-73 Texas Almanac, and other editions record much of the development of utilities. The following information was prepared through the cooperation of utility firms and their trade associations.

Telephones

Texas had 7,033,975 telephone lines in service on Dec. 31, 1984, served by 72 local-exchange companies. In addition to local service, those companies also provide approximately one-third of the intrastate long distance service in Texas. AT&T and some 50 other competitive carriers provide most of the intrastate and all of the interstate long distance service enjoyed by Texans.

Southwestern Bell Corporation — which through its telephone company subsidiary also serves Arkansas, Kansas, New Mexico and Oklahoma — became a separate entity Jan. 1, 1984, the date of divestiture of the Bell System, and is no longer associated with AT&T.

The largest subsidiary of the corporation is Southwestern Bell Telphone Company, which provides local telephone access service to some nine million customers in five states, including Texas.

Also in 1984, the Texas Division of Southwestern Bell Telephone was created, with Dallas selected as its headquarters city.

The Texas Division of Southwestern Bell Telephone serves 4.6 million customers in 549 Texas communities. With some 34,000 employees and an annual payroll of about $1.1 billion, it remains one of the largest nongovernmental employers in the state. State and local operating taxes paid by the company in 1984 totalled over $572 million.

Southwestern Bell handles over 75 million local calls, and provides access for an additional 5 million direct-dialed long distance calls each day. The company serves Texas with over 925,000 miles of cable, including 37,500 miles of fiber optics.

By the end of 1984, Southwestern Bell Telephone's investment in Texas telecommunications facilities totalled over $9 billion.

Major independent telephone companies in Texas and their total access lines as of Dec. 31, 1984 were: General Telephone Company of the Southwest, with 862,575 lines; Continental Telephone Co. of Texas, with 148,131 lines; Central Telephone Co. of Texas, with 105,212 lines; and United Telephone Co. of Texas, with 98,962 lines. (Because telephone customers can now own the wiring within their premises, as well as all the equipment inside, the industry no longer counts total telephones they serve. Access lines reflect the number of connections the companies provide, and does not equate to number of customers.)

The 72 independent telephone companies in Texas include 24 telephone cooperatives, subscriber-owned systems serving more than 91,000 access lines through 233 exchanges in the state. The Bell System companies serve four out of every five Texans, while the independent companies serve more than half of the state's 250,000 square miles of certified service territory.

In the Houston metro area, Southwestern Bell and five independent telephone companies cooperate to serve 1,300,000 customers, possibly the largest in the nation. On the other hand, **Big Bend Telephone Co.** in West Texas serves about 2,500 subscribers in a service area of 19,000 square miles — roughly equal to the states of Connecticut, Delaware, Massachusetts and Rhode Island combined.

The following table shows the number of telephone access lines on Dec. 31, 1984, in the calling scope of many of Texas' principal cities. Some of the larger cities and towns not shown are included in the metropolitan exchanges of Dallas, Houston, Fort Worth and San Antonio.

Abilene	50,800
Amarillo	79,200
Arlington	96,000
Austin	237,200
Bay City	11,900
Beaumont	63,100
Brownsville-Harlingen	47,600
Cleburne	15,800
Corpus Christi	111,300
Corsicana	12,100
Dallas	935,700
El Paso	162,900
Fort Worth	486,700
Galveston	37,300
Greenville	12,100
Houston	1,372,700
Laredo	31,800
Longview	46,800
Lubbock	85,300
McAllen-Edinburg	40,200
McKinney	10,700
Midland	49,600
Mineral Wells	8,500
Odessa	44,200
Paris	16,700
Port Arthur	32,000
San Antonio	366,600
Temple	20,700
Texas City	25,100
Tyler	53,500
Vernon	6,700
Victoria	26,000
Waco	49,100
Wichita Falls	50,600
Total	4,696,500
Total Texas (Actuals)	5,958,300

Electric Utilities

On Dec. 31, 1984, Texas had 138 electric power plants with a **total generating capability** of 57,658,400 kilowatts.

Some of the 138 power plants have several units. There were 93 units powered by **steam** and with a total capability of 54,733,500 kilowatts. Fifty-one units were powered by either **internal combustion engines or gas turbines** with a total generating capability of 2,409,700 kilowatts. Twenty were **hydroelectric units** with total capability of 515,200 kilowatts.

Twelve major investor-owned electric utility companies in Texas supply about 70 percent of the state's total generating capability. The remaining 30 percent is supplied by municipally owned systems, rural electric cooperatives and state and federally financed projects.

Major investor-owned electric utility companies operating in Texas are: Central Power & Light, Dallas Power & Light Co., El Paso Electric Co., Gulf States Utilities Co., Houston Lighting and Power Co., Southwestern Electric Power Co., Southwestern Electric Service Co., Southwestern Public Service Co., Texas Electric Service Co., Texas-New Mexico Power Co., Texas Power & Light Co. and West Texas Utilities Co.

As 1985 began, these investor-owned companies had a total investment in Texas plants and facilities of $26,485,498,000. In 1984, they spent $3,682,400,000 for new construction.

In 1970, the **Electric Reliability Council of Texas** was organized by major electric power suppliers to assure ample electric power for the present and future growth of the state.

Location of the **first power plant** in Texas is uncertain. Some authorities believe a plant that began operation on Dec. 17, 1882, in Houston was first; others credit Galveston with the first plant. Either of these would be among the first in the United States, since the initial American plant started in New York City in the summer of 1882.

As late as 1910, Texas electrical operations were mainly limited to isolated municipal and individually owned plants. In 1912 **Texas Power & Light Co.** started building Texas' **first high-voltage transmission line.** It extended from Waco to Fort Worth, with a branch from Hillsboro through Waxahachie to Ferris, where it branched north to Trinity Heights (Dallas) and south to Corsicana.

Rural electrification began after the first transmission lines were constructed. By the early 1930s some 48,000 rural families were receiving service.

Electric Cooperatives

The 77 electric distribution cooperatives operating in Texas were serving over 956,000 rural connections by the end of 1984. The systems, plus two of Texas' three generation and transmission (G&T) cooperatives, were operating more than 242,000 miles of lines extending into all but nine of the 254 counties in Texas. Power produced by the third G&T is relayed through noncooperatively owned lines to the cooperatives' load centers. Average number of consumer units served by the 77 distribution cooperatives, per mile of line: 4.02. Total number of individuals employed by the 80 cooperatives: 5,200.

Gas Utilities

Approximately 280 gas companies in Texas are classified gas utilities and come under the regulatory jurisdiction of the Texas Railroad Commission. These companies reported **gas operating revenue** of $14.7 billion in 1983, with **operating expenses** of $13.8 billion.

In 1983, fixed investment for distribution facilities in Texas was $1.2 billion and for transmission facilities, $3.6 billion. Investment in Texas plants in service totaled $5.9 billion. There were 54 investor-owned and 87 municipally owned distribution systems in operation in 1983 serving approximately 1,035 Texas cities.

The eight largest distribution systems — six private and two municipal — served 96 percent of all residential customers. In 1983, there were approximately 3.1 million residential customers, 269,399 small commercial and industrial users, 530 large industrial customers and 7,350 other gas utility customers. The breakdown of distribution sales to these customers was: 71 Mcf per residential customer, 650.5 Mcf per commercial customer, 504,983 Mcf per industrial customer and 3,606 Mcf for customers in the "other" category. Distribution sales amounted to 688.6 billion cubic feet in 1983.

In addition to industrial sales made by distribution companies, transmission companies reported pipeline-to-industry sales of 1.79 trillion cubic feet and revenue from these sales of $6.05 billion.

In 1983, the average annual residential gas bill in the U.S. was $583. The average annual bill in Texas for the same year was $414, up $30 from the previous year. The State of Texas collected $29.7 million in **gross receipts taxes** from gas utilities in fiscal year 1984.

There were 45,715 producing gas wells in the state at the end of 1984, up 1,604 from the previous year. New gas well completions during 1984 numbered 5,489. That was 462 more than in 1983 but 784 under the 1982 total.

Texas had a total of 127,024 miles of **natural gas pipelines** in operation in 1983, including 18,716 miles of **field and gathering lines**, 44,772 miles of **transmission lines** and 63,586 miles of **distribution lines**.

Estimated proved **gas reserves** in the state amounted to 50.05 trillion cubic feet in 1983. Gross production of natural gas, including **casinghead gas**, in 1984 was 5.81 trillion cubic feet. At year end in 1984, 25 underground storage reservoirs in the state contained 349.19 billion cubic feet of gas.

Telegraphy in Texas

Western Union operates a nationwide microwave system which extends into Texas with terminals at Dallas, Houston, Beaumont, San Antonio, Corpus Christi and Austin. In 1974, Western Union launched the nation's first domestic communications satellite. Dallas has the distinction of having one of the initial ground stations which is located at Cedar Hill. This satellite transmission and receiving station brings a new era to voice and data communications in Texas.

Texas was among the pioneers in use of telegraphy, although the Republic of Texas in 1838 failed to accept an offer of **Samuel F. B. Morse** to give his new invention to the new nation. Morse received no reply to his offer and later withdrew it on Aug. 9, 1860, in a letter to Gov. Sam Houston.

On June 29, 1970, Western Union opened their National Processing Center in Dallas to receive and process accounting and payroll data from Western Union offices nationwide. Additionally, the installation of a major communications computer at Austin, for the General Service Administration in 1973, increased the importance of Texas in the firm's nationwide data transmission system.

Western Union's Dallas Area Headquarters office (one of thirteen) has responsibility for the company's sales, technical and public office operations in Texas and Louisiana.

Western Union's services now include, in addition to telegrams and telegraphic money orders: Mailgrams (Electronic Mail), point-to-point voice data service via Satellite and microwave, high-,medium-and low-speed data communications services such as Telex, TWX, Info-Com, DataCom, Sicom, Broadband and Hot-Line and SpaceTel Telephone Service.

STATE BUILDING AND LOAN ASSOCIATIONS

There were 273 domestic state-chartered savings and loan associations in Texas as of Dec. 31, 1984, the same number that existed in the state as of Dec. 31, 1983, according to report of the State Savings and Loan Department, including both the associations insured within Federal Savings and Loan System and those not insured. (All except two were insured.) There was one foreign association operating in Texas as of Dec. 31, 1984.

Total **assets** of domestic associations as of Dec. 31, 1984, were $67,353,905,292.64; as of Dec. 31, 1983, $47,001,227,395.13; as of Dec 31, 1982, $35,642,705,009.72; as of Dec. 31, 1981, $29,657,222,468.25; as of Dec. 31, 1980, $27,132,151,522.59; as of Dec. 31, 1979, $23,835,730,698.65; as of Dec. 31, 1978, $20,982,698,625.09; as of Dec. 31, 1977, $18,004,995,318.05; as of Dec. 31, 1976, $14,706,563,133.20; as of Dec. 31, 1975, $12,116,927,717.74; as of Dec. 31, 1974, $10,179,240,389.51; as of Dec. 31, 1973, $9,150,774,828.88; as of Dec. 31, 1972, $7,836,999,355.62; as of Dec. 31, 1971, $6,463,498,550.87; as of Dec. 31, 1970, $5,317,862,296.10; as of Dec. 31, 1969, $4,858,004,208.15; as of Dec. 31, 1968, $4,450,943,421.20; as of Dec. 31, 1967, $4,128,632,366.31; as of Dec. 31, 1966, $3,789,724,918.68; as of Dec. 31, 1965, $3,536,011,348.30; as of Dec. 31, 1964, $3,136,916,970.07; as of Dec. 31, 1963, $2,573,364,348.27; as of Dec. 31, 1962, $2,119,697,510.96.

First mortgage and other loans as of Dec. 31, 1984, were $48,779,498,449.09; as of Dec. 31, 1983, $36,001,-319,622.41; as of Dec. 31, 1982, $28,267,050,649.61; as of Dec. 31, 1981, $25,194,505,272.28; as of Dec. 31, 1980, $23,288,239,155.89; as of Dec. 31, 1979, $20,738,503,290.56; as of Dec. 31, 1978, $18,322,524,930.32; as of Dec. 31, 1977, $15,683,368,264.81; as of Dec. 31, 1976, $12,649,549,583.33; as of Dec. 31, 1975, $10,443,368,534.46; as of Dec. 31, 1974, $8,885,417,049.02; as of Dec. 31, 1973, $8,035,741,883.00; as of Dec. 31, 1972, $6,770,574,731.32; as of Dec. 31, 1971, $5,584,494,544.05; as of Dec. 31, 1970, $4,637,282,250.24; as of Dec. 31, 1969, $4,104,156,072.72; as of Dec. 31, 1968, $3,740,532,712.88; as of Dec. 31, 1967, $3,443,482,821.14; as of Dec. 31, 1966, $3,195,605,343.36; as of Dec. 31, 1965, $3,084,074,278.41; as of Dec. 31, 1964, $2,726,486,296.96; as of Dec. 31, 1963, $2,136,336,022.58; as of Dec. 31, 1962, $1,759,951,523.28.

Savings shares capital as of Dec. 31, 1984, was $53,158,688,382.84; as of Dec. 31, 1983, $37,381,969,273.96; as of Dec. 31, 1982, $27,180,035,131.66; as of Dec. 31, 1981, $22,959,660,206.12; as of Dec. 31, 1980, $21,707,038,301.85; as of Dec. 31, 1979, $18,928,190,624.16; as of Dec. 31, 1978, $16,978,272,027.06; as of Dec. 31, 1977, $14,724,713,558.80; as of Dec. 31, 1976, $12,373,667,147.53; as of Dec. 31, 1975, $10,057,119,239.49; as of Dec. 31, 1974, $8,287,819,386.05; as of Dec. 31, 1973, $7,507,013,953.01; as of Dec. 31, 1972, $6,517,681,858.52; as of Dec. 31, 1971, $5,313,072,963.25; as of Dec. 31, 1970, $4,284,160,162.01; as of Dec. 31, 1969, $3,989,750,439.14; as of Dec. 31, 1968, $3,797,518,315.62; as of Dec. 31, 1967, $3,578,794,561.56; as of Dec. 31, 1966, $3,191,103,042.73; as of Dec. 31, 1965, $3,014,382,201.13; as of Dec. 31, 1964, $2,669,270,385.59; as of Dec. 31, 1963, $2,176,306,063.20; as of Dec. 31, 1962, $1,797,178,803.77.

Foreign association assets as of Dec. 31, 1984, were $2,777,705,231.00; as of Dec. 31, 1983, $2,737,183,027.00; as of Dec. 31, 1982, $2,488,987,112.00; as of Dec. 31, 1981, $2,285,379,272.00; as of Dec. 31, 1980, $2,258,968,037.00; as

of Dec. 31, 1979, $2,137,957,286.65; as of Dec. 31, 1978, $1,942,127,639.15; as of Dec. 31, 1977, $1,679,119,277.62; as of Dec. 31, 1976, $1,560,283,246.16; as of Dec. 31, 1975, $1,374,801,661.34; as of Dec. 31, 1974, $1,311,863,804.76; as of Dec. 31, 1973, $1,205,788,912.04; as of Dec. 31, 1972, $1,011,213,010.78; as of Dec. 31, 1971, $812,557,220.81; as of Dec. 31, 1970, $690,900,158.00; as of Dec. 31, 1969, $565,082,478.24; as of Dec. 31, 1968, $501,016,975.31; as of Dec. 31, 1967, $445,993,034.24; as of Dec. 31, 1966, $408,098,520.71; as of Dec. 31, 1965, $380,118,694.48; as of Dec. 31, 1964, $364,625,792.45; as of Dec. 31, 1963, $341,673,381.26; as of Dec. 31, 1962, $329,079,310.95.

SAVINGS AND LOAN, BUILDING AND LOAN ASSOCIATIONS

Texas on Dec. 31, 1984, had 273 insured savings and loan, building and loan associations and savings banks, with total assets of $77,544,202,000. This total included federal- and state-chartered associations, which are members of the Federal Home Loan Bank of Dallas and insured by the Federal Savings and Loan Insurance Corporation.

Details in the following table were supplied by the Federal Home Loan Bank of Dallas, headquarters bank for the district which includes Texas. (In 1983, headquarters were moved to Dallas from Little Rock, Ark.)

TEXAS SAVINGS AND LOAN ASSOCIATIONS
(Thousands of Dollars)

Year—	No. Assns.	Total Assets	‡Mortgage Loans	†Cash	†Investment Securities	Savings Capital	FHLB Advances and other Borrowed Money	*Net Worth
Dec. 31, 1984	273	$77,544,202	$45,859,408	$10,424,113	...	$61,943,815	$10,984,467	$2,938,044
Dec. 31, 1983	273	56,684,508	36,243,290	6,678,808	...	46,224,429	6,317,947	2,386,551
Dec. 31, 1982	288	42,505,924	28,539,378	4,713,742	...	34,526,483	5,168,343	1,631,139
Dec. 31, 1981	311	38,343,703	30,013,805	3,294,327	...	30,075,258	4,846,153	1,493,795
Dec. 31, 1980	318	34,954,129	27,717,383	3,066,791	...	28,439,210	3,187,638	1,711,201
Dec. 31, 1979	310	31,280,006	25,238,483	2,512,797	...	25,197,598	2,969,838	1,640,049
Dec. 31, 1978	318	27,933,526	22,830,872	142,721	1,876,882	22,848,519	2,251,631	1,444,607
Dec. 31, 1977	328	24,186,338	19,765,901	154,027	1,579,440	19,994,347	1,515,045	1,235,096
Dec. 31, 1976	316	19,921,694	16,096,166	196,790	1,344,827	16,908,949	949,231	1,044,611
Dec. 31, 1975	303	16,540,181	13,367,569	167,385	1,000,095	13,876,780	919,404	914,502
Dec. 31, 1974	295	13,944,524	11,452,013	117,097	806,302	11,510,259	1,038,386	834,892
Dec. 31, 1973	288	12,629,928	10,361,847	126,106	795,989	10,483,113	740,725	763,618
Dec. 31, 1972	278	10,914,627	8,919,007	155,901	841,904	9,249,305	459,019	678,086
Dec. 31, 1971	272	9,112,590	7,481,751	140,552	670,622	7,647,906	458,152	589,077
Dec. 31, 1970	271	7,706,639	6,450,730	122,420	509,482	6,335,582	559,953	531,733
Dec. 31, 1969	270	7,055,949	5,998,172	105,604	391,175	5,894,398	473,066	487,308
Dec. 31, 1968	267	6,601,846	5,556,617	131,440	415,958	5,712,331	287,588	429,087
Dec. 31, 1967	268	6,156,108	5,149,689	194,684	359,443	5,402,575	218,569	390,508
Dec. 31, 1966	268	5,693,908	4,816,505	190,820	280,927	4,898,223	331,694	361,697
Dec. 31, 1965	267	5,351,064	4,534,073	228,994	230,628	4,631,999	286,497	333,948
Dec. 31, 1964	262	4,797,085	4,071,044	208,083	218,993	4,145,085	266,242	296,444
Dec. 31, 1963	256	4,192,188	3,517,676	208,698	201,724	3,591,951	257,426	259,169
Dec. 31, 1962	248	3,533,209	2,960,182	173,343	180,192	3,049,144	185,476	230,920
Dec. 31, 1961	240	2,990,527	2,472,648	146,710	183,116	2,647,906	74,762	193,579
Dec. 31, 1960	233	2,508,872	2,083,066	110,028	157,154	2,238,080	48,834	166,927

*Net worth includes permanent stock and paid-in surplus general reserves, surplus and undivided profits.
†Beginning in 1979, cash and investment securities data combined.
‡Beginning in 1982, net of loans in process.

Construction Industry

The construction industry in 1984 faced the same economic problems that other industries faced. Because of the depressed economy, construction awards were down from the high of 1983.

A table below shows the approved Texas construction for 1984. These data were compiled by editors of **Texas Contractor** from official sources.

COMPARISON OF CONSTRUCTION AWARDS BY YEARS
Source: Texas Contractor

Year	Total Awards	Year	Total Awards	Year	Total Awards
1984	$3,424,721,025	1973	1,926,778,365	1962	1,132,607,006
1983	4,074,910,947	1972	1,650,897,233	1961	988,848,239
1982	3,453,784,388	1971	1,751,331,262	1960	1,047,943,630
1981	3,700,112,809	1970	1,458,708,492	1959	1,122,290,957
1980	3,543,117,615	1969	1,477,125,397	1958	1,142,138,674
1979	3,353,243,234	1968	1,363,629,304	1957	1,164,240,546
1978	2,684,743,190	1967	1,316,872,998	1956	1,220,831,984
1977	2,270,788,842	1966	1,421,312,029	1955	949,213,349
1976	1,966,553,804	1965	1,254,638,051	1954	861,623,224
1975	1,737,036,682	1964	1,351,656,302	1953	1,180,320,174
1974	2,396,488,520	1963	1,154,624,634		

Approved Texas Construction, 1985

The following is a recapitulation of all approved Texas construction for 1985. The data were compiled by the editors of **Texas Contractor** from official sources.

FEDERAL

General Services Administration	$ 6,600,000
Federal Aviation Administration	65,797,986
Veterans Administration	15,000,000
Soil Conservation Service	33,323,000
Rural Electrification Administration	461,106,100
Department of Agriculture (Farmers/Home Adm.)	155,000,000
Department of Defense	287,000,000
Federal Highway Aid	850,000,000
Total	**$1,873,827,086**

STATE

Highway Construction Funds	$ 679,723,905
Highway Maintenance Funds	436,379,669
State Building Programs	49,719,572
State Colleges and Universities	210,344,325
Total	**$1,376,167,471**

WATER PROJECTS

Bureau of Reclamation	$ 10,656,000
Corps of Engineers	116,500,000
River Authorities (est.)	200,000,000
Federal Construction Grants	92,500,000
Total	**$ 419,656,000**

CITIES

Schools, Colleges	$ 133,094,980
Streets, Bridges	274,350,000
Waterworks, Sewers	675,862,000
Apartments, Duplexes and Residences	1,630,450,000
Commercial	2,453,875,000
City Buildings	299,676,020
Total	**$5,467,308,000**

COUNTIES

Roads-County Funds	$ 47,733,979
Road Maintenance	109,286,210
Machinery Purchases	22,000,000
County Buildings	20,041,385
Miscellaneous	11,189,131
Total	**$ 210,250,705**
GRAND TOTAL 1985 APPROVED CONSTRUCTION	**$9,347,209,262**

ANALYSIS OF AWARDS

The following table analyzes and classifies awards in Texas for the year 1984, as compared with the corresponding year of 1983, as reported by **Texas Contractor**.

	1984		1983	
	No.	Amount	No.	Amount
Engineering Awards	1,581	$1,278,816,308	1,708	$1,518,996,886
Non-Residential Awards	1,328	2,145,904,717	2,047	2,555,914,061
Total	2,909	$3,424,904,717	3,755	$4,074,910,947

ENGINEERING AWARDS

	1984		1983	
	No.	Amount	No.	Amount
Highways, Streets Airports	885	$917,963,782	974	$1,122,768,859
Waterworks, Sewers, etc.	524	297,902,497	601	339,440,766
Irrigation, Drainage, etc.	86	53,587,601	71	51,669,696
Miscellaneous	86	9,362,428	62	5,117,565
Total	1,581	$1,278,816,308	1,708	$1,518,996,886

NON-RESIDENTIAL CONSTRUCTION AWARDS

	1984		1983	
	No.	Amount	No.	Amount
Educational Bldgs.	309	$554,138,162	392	$531,576,498
Churches, Theaters, etc.	47	42,887,782	111	84,685,834
Hospitals, Hotels, Motels	47	84,383,003	72	232,465,567
Public Bldgs.	320	417,602,269	388	449,750,481
Commercial-Industrial	580	1,037,517,660	1,059	1,253,208,172
Miscellaneous	25	9,375,841	25	4,227,509
Total	1,328	$2,145,904,717	2,047	$2,555,914,061

Insurance in Texas

The State Board of Insurance reported that, on Aug. 31, 1984, there were 2,188 firms licensed to handle insurance business in Texas, including 775 Texas firms and 1,413 out-of-state companies. Annual premium income of firms operating in Texas caused Dallas and some other cities to rank among the nation's major insurance centers.

Additional details are provided in subsequent tables covering the calendar year 1983.

The former **Robertson Law**, enacted in 1907 and repealed in 1963, encouraged the establishment of many Texas insurance firms. It required life insurance companies operating in the state to invest in Texas three-fourths of all reserves held for payment of policies written in the state. Many out-of-state firms withdrew from Texas. Later many companies re-entered Texas and the law was liberalized and then repealed.

The State Board of Insurance administers legislation relating to the insurance business. This agency was established in 1957, following discovery of irregularities in some firms and succeeded two previous regulatory groups, established in 1913 and changed in 1927. The governor appoints the 3-man board, which appoints a State Insurance Commissioner as executive director of the State Insurance Department.

INSURANCE COMPANIES IN TEXAS

The following table shows the number and kinds of insurance companies licensed in Texas on Aug. 31, 1984:

	Texas	Out-of-State	Total		Texas	Out-of-State	Total
Stock Life	302	595	897	Health Maintenance	12	...	12
Mutual Life	4	87	91	Total Legal Reserve	619	1,413	2,032
Stipulated Premium Life	69	...	69				
Non-profit Life	...	1	1	Statewide Mutual Assessment			
Stock Fire	3	7	10	Life, Health and Accident	2	...	2
Stock Fire and Casualty	105	529	634	Local Mutual Aid Associations	63	...	63
Mutual Fire and Casualty	6	76	82	Burial Associations	23	...	23
Stock Casualty	8	49	57	Exempt Associations	16	...	16
Mexican Casualty	...	10	10	Non-profit Hospital Service	1	...	1
Lloyds	78	1	79	County Mutual Fire	25	...	25
Reciprocal Exchanges	13	15	28	Farm Mutual Fire	26	...	26
Fraternal Benefit Societies	12	28	40	Total Mutual Assessment	156	...	156
Titles	6	15	21	Grand Total	775	1,413	2,188
Non-profit Legal Services	1	...	1				

LEGAL RESERVE LIFE INSURANCE COMPANIES
Texas Business Only, for Calendar Year 1983:

	Texas	Out-of-State	Total
*Premium income during 1983.	$1,898,743,848	$4,105,264,452	$6,004,008,300
*Claims and benefits paid during 1983	$1,590,198,273	$3,677,733,415	$5,267,931,688

*Figures include accident and health premiums and claims which were as follows:
Premiums: Texas companies, $1,027,657,262; Out-of-State companies, $1,927,934,435.
Losses: Texas companies, $934,846,128; Out-of-State companies, $1,546,864,081.

MUTUAL FIRE AND CASUALTY INSURANCE COMPANIES
Texas Business Only, for Calendar Year 1983:

	Premiums	Losses
Texas companies	$342,548,728	$399,992,374
Companies of other states	1,033,830,977	675,737,131
Total	$1,376,379,705	$1,075,729,505

LLOYDS INSURANCE
Texas Business Only, for Calendar Year 1983:

	Premiums	Losses
Texas companies	$377,225,574	$322,398,875
Companies of other states	2,568,161	1,465,994
Total	$379,793,735	$323,864,869

RECIPROCAL INSURANCE COMPANIES
Texas Business Only, for Calendar Year 1983:

	Premiums	Losses
Texas companies	$183,431,934	$99,396,886
Companies of other states	100,709,945	105,986,209
Total	$284,141,879	$205,383,095

STOCK FIRE COMPANIES
Texas Business Only, for Calendar Year 1983:

	Premiums	Losses
Texas companies	$1,869,198	$1,399,658
Companies of other states and foreign companies	453,401	276,916
Total	$2,322,599	$1,676,574

FRATERNAL BENEFIT SOCIETIES
Texas Business Only, for Calendar Year 1983:

	Texas	Out-of-State	Total
No. policies issued during 1983.	9,595	27,991	37,586
Amount of insurance issued during 1983.	$99,878,804	$771,151,168	$871,029,972
Amount of Premiums received during 1983 (Life and H&A)	12,939,124	56,118,155	69,057,279
Losses and claims paid during 1983 (Life and H&A)	3,527,628	10,753,733	14,281,361
No. policies in force Dec. 31, 1983.	271,576	319,087	590,663
Amount of insurance in force Dec. 31, 1983.	$728,549,177	$3,265,284,221	$3,993,833,398

STOCK CASUALTY INSURANCE COMPANIES
Texas Business Only, for Calendar Year 1983:

	Premiums	Losses
Texas companies	$5,200,543	$1,682,826
Companies of other states and foreign companies	127,224,593	44,956,996
Total	$132,425,136	$46,639,822

TITLE GUARANTY COMPANIES
Texas Business Only, for Calendar Year 1983:

	Texas	Out-of-State	Total
Premium income	$151,772,553	$249,165,786	$400,938,339
Losses paid.	2,812,559	2,766,844	5,579,403

STOCK FIRE AND CASUALTY INSURANCE COMPANIES
Texas Business Only, for Calendar Year 1983:

	Premiums	Losses
Texas companies	$1,189,402,189	$773,611,116
Companies of other states.	4,637,631,004	3,506,042,169
Total	$5,827,033,193	$4,279,653,285

PER CAPITA PERSONAL INCOME
Source: U.S. Department of Commerce

This table shows the per capita personal income in Texas Metropolitan Statistical Areas as reported in the April 1985 Survey of Current Business. All figures are in dollars. These data are based on MSAs as constituted in 1985.

Per capita personal income for the entire state rose from $1,349 in 1950 to $11,686 in 1983. This compared with the U.S. per capita income which rose from $1,496 in 1950 to $11,685 in 1983, according to U.S. Department of Commerce figures.

Metropolitan Statistical Area	1975	1976	1977	1978	1979	1980	1981	1982	1983
TEXAS.	$5,595	$6,158	$6,714	$7,486	$8,478	$9,439	$10,807	$11,378	$11,686
Abilene	5,406	5,961	6,636	7,242	8,379	9,398	11,076	11,465	11,777
Amarillo.	6,218	6,766	7,541	8,121	8,987	9,545	10,769	11,464	11,924
Austin	5,198	5,644	6,743	7,341	8,067	9,065	10,383	11,174	11,937
Beaumont-Port Arthur	5,676	6,553	7,229	8,109	9,018	9,950	11,184	11,784	12,013
*Brazoria (PMSA)	...	...	...	8,189	9,350	10,188	11,421	12,065	11,860
Brownsville-Harlingen	3,685	3,942	4,375	4,455	4,977	5,506	6,172	6,365	6,654
Bryan-College Station.	4,409	4,700	5,606	5,383	5,956	6,740	8,032	8,524	9,085
Corpus Christi	5,010	5,594	6,176	6,733	7,734	8,518	9,850	10,345	10,503
†Dallas-Fort Worth	6,340	6,928	7,752	...	...	...	...	...	...
†Dallas (PMSA)	...	...	...	8,783	10,000	11,179	12,574	13,415	14,222
Dallas-Fort Worth (CMSA)	...	...	...	8,585	9,755	10,926	12,302	13,070	13,846
El Paso.	4,365	4,692	5,073	5,446	6,051	6,603	7,413	7,753	8,290
†Fort Worth-Arlington (PMSA)	...	...	...	8,183	9,262	10,418	11,755	12,384	13,103
*Galveston-Texas City (PMSA)	6,119	6,670	7,180	8,231	9,233	10,370	11,807	12,575	12,323
*Houston	6,793	7,499	8,361	...	...	...	...	...	...
*Houston-Galveston-Brazoria (CMSA)	...	...	...	9,184	10,348	11,627	13,308	13,755	13,482
Killeen-Temple	5,268	5,578	6,045	6,017	6,373	7,359	8,224	9,187	9,930
Laredo.	3,322	3,526	4,026	4,075	4,605	5,321	6,028	6,174	6,017
Longview-Marshall	5,490	6,241	6,829	7,093	7,968	9,028	10,374	10,886	11,008
Lubbock.	5,162	5,792	6,642	7,011	7,859	8,674	9,690	10,289	11,123
McAllen-Edinburg-Mission.	3,166	3,395	4,003	3,994	4,337	4,939	5,755	5,979	6,012
Midland.	7,130	7,982	9,283	10,128	11,671	13,525	16,149	16,805	15,507
Odessa.	5,917	6,595	7,506	8,147	8,923	10,203	12,264	12,478	11,512
San Angelo.	5,425	6,210	6,927	7,142	7,884	8,899	10,324	11,181	11,580
San Antonio	5,126	5,556	6,035	6,519	7,370	8,346	9,337	9,991	10,569
Sherman-Denison.	5,071	5,615	6,297	7,020	8,035	8,768	9,841	10,521	11,148
Texarkana, Texas-Ark..	4,724	5,273	5,912	6,241	6,994	7,633	8,617	9,139	9,557
Tyler	5,650	6,446	7,294	7,422	8,373	9,404	10,854	11,749	12,188
‡Victoria	...	...	7,000	7,489	8,394	9,498	11,660	12,342	11,928
Waco	5,277	5,854	6,527	6,793	7,495	8,396	9,540	10,252	10,958
Wichita Falls	5,936	6,666	7,186	7,500	8,703	9,857	11,302	11,835	11,970

*In 1983, Brazoria and Galveston/Texas City were added to the old Houston SMSA and made a Consolidated Metropolitan Statistical Area (CMSA). Brazoria and Galveston/Texas City are independent Primary Metropolitan Statistical Areas (PMSA).

†In 1983, the old Dallas/Fort Worth SMSA was reconstituted. Dallas PMSA consists of Collin, Dallas, Denton, Ellis, Kaufman, Rockwall Counties. The Fort Worth/Arlington PMSA consists of Johnson, Parker and Tarrant Counties. Together they constitute the Dallas/Fort Worth CMSA.

‡Victoria County made an MSA in 1981.

Personal Income, 1960-1984

Total personal income in Texas amounted to $18,627,000,000 in 1960, according to revised figures from the Survey of Current Business. According to the April, 1985 issue, it rose to an estimated $202,030,500,000 in 1984, latest data available when this section of the Texas Almanac went to press.

Personal income for the years between 1960 and 1984 are given herewith, all figures in millions (add 000,000): 1961, $19,624; 1962, $20,630; 1963, $21,694; 1964, $23,162; 1965, $25,016; 1966, $27,638; 1967, $30,211; 1968, $33,497; 1969, $36,171; 1970, $39,410; 1971, $42,264; 1972, $47,094; 1973, $53,995; 1974, $60,661; 1975, $68,331; 1976, $77,588; 1977, $88,564; 1978, $101,914; 1979, $118,658; 1980, $136,278; 1981, $158,462; 1982, $173,459; 1983, $183,753; 1984, $202,030.

Revised per capita incomes for the same period are: $1,935 in 1960; $1,998 in 1961; $2,052 in 1962; $2,135 in 1963; $2,255 in 1964; $2,411 in 1965; $2,634 in 1966; $2,850 in 1967; $3,096 in 1968; $3,275 in 1969; $3,507 in 1970; $3,700 in 1971; $4,053 in 1972; $4,564 in 1973; $5,048 in 1974; $5,595 in 1975; $6,158 in 1976; $6,714 in 1977; $7,550 in 1978; $8,477 in 1979; $9,439 in 1980; $10,807 in 1981; $11,380 in 1982; $11,685 in 1983.

An accompanying table shows per capita personal income in the Texas Metropolitan Statistical Areas for nine representative years between 1975 and 1983. In 1975, per capita personal income ranged from a low of $3,166 in McAllen-Edinburg-Mission's MSA to a high of $7,130 in Midland.

By 1983, Midland's per capita income had risen to $15,507, highest in the state as well as the nation. McAllen-Edinburg-Mission's per capita income had risen to $6,012 and was still the state's lowest.

PERSONAL INCOME BY MAJOR SOURCE AND EARNINGS BY MAJOR INDUSTRY

(Thousands of Dollars)

Item—	1978	1979	1980	1981	1982	1983
Income by Place of Residence						
Total Personal Income	101,047,456	117,738,681	135,175,325	159,248,438	174,418,448	183,752,824
Nonfarm Personal Income	99,356,823	115,201,306	133,737,529	156,871,827	172,897,205	181,797,444
Farm Income	1,690,633	2,537,375	1,437,796	2,376,611	1,521,243	1,955,380
Derivation of Total Personal Income:						
Total Earnings by Place of Work	79,922,290	92,681,686	104,663,256	122,670,458	131,744,077	137,938,006
Net Earnings by Place of Residence	75,754,917	87,729,220	98,873,757	115,467,154	123,816,239	129,702,599
Earnings by Place of Work						
Components of Earnings:						
Wages and Salaries	65,767,811	76,239,152	88,591,824	103,840,775	113,059,495	116,754,925
Other Labor Income	6,306,846	7,224,004	8,414,058	9,786,047	11,273,469	12,183,757
¶Proprietors' Income	7,847,633	9,218,530	7,657,374	9,043,636	7,411,113	8,999,324
†Farm	1,193,443	1,968,480	846,056	1,779,359	813,570	1,001,314
Nonfarm	6,654,190	7,250,050	6,811,318	7,264,277	6,597,543	7,998,010
Earnings by Industry:						
Farm	1,690,633	2,537,375	1,437,796	2,376,611	1,521,243	1,955,380
Nonfarm	78,231,657	90,144,311	103,225,460	120,293,847	130,222,834	135,982,626
Private	65,663,821	76,419,191	87,900,884	102,964,349	110,852,520	114,787,156
**Agricultural Services, Forestry, Fisheries and Other	377,884	427,357	441,497	492,583	522,005	558,741
Mining	3,908,636	5,171,048	6,801,634	9,431,146	10,737,971	9,323,146
Construction	6,959,813	8,061,168	8,735,188	9,622,427	10,121,366	10,554,582
Manufacturing	15,894,135	18,532,306	21,405,293	24,961,745	25,296,237	24,584,285
Nondurable Goods	6,802,387	7,641,007	8,566,908	9,682,186	10,218,616	10,550,395
Durable Goods	9,091,748	10,891,299	12,838,385	15,279,559	15,077,621	14,033,890
Transportation and Public Utilities	6,418,421	7,497,009	8,597,177	9,795,132	10,626,036	10,972,308
Wholesale Trade	6,395,034	7,480,832	8,772,510	10,010,141	10,769,809	10,769,464
Retail Trade	8,765,007	9,843,183	10,800,194	12,258,202	13,422,662	14,455,682
Finance, Insurance and Real Estate	4,583,398	5,197,352	5,848,092	6,916,125	7,478,110	9,078,595
Services	12,361,493	14,208,936	16,499,299	19,476,848	21,878,324	24,490,297
Government and Government Enterprises	12,567,836	13,725,120	15,324,576	17,329,498	19,370,314	21,195,470
Federal, Civilian	2,859,893	3,097,357	3,397,403	3,720,221	4,004,024	4,291,767
Federal, Military	1,737,755	1,790,513	1,976,888	2,308,551	2,558,821	2,676,205
State and Local	7,970,188	8,837,250	9,950,285	11,300,726	12,807,469	14,227,498

†Personal contributions for social insurance are included in earnings by type and industry but excluded from personal income.
‡1978-83 farm proprietors and rental income and residence adjustment reflect revisions which have not been made for previous years.
§Includes the capital consumption adjustment for rental income of persons.
¶Includes the inventory valuation and capital consumption adjustments.
**Other—Wages and salaries of U.S. residents working for international organizations in the U.S.

Texas Credit Unions

Membership in Texas' 1,160 credit unions has grown by more than 75 percent during the past decade as credit unions continue to be the fastest growing segment of the financial industry.

Nationally, there are 18,515 credit unions representing more than $113 billion in assets. And Texas remains a leader in the credit union movement. Based on figures compiled by the Texas Credit Union League, Texas credit unions account for more than $8.9 billion and rank second according to asset size. Texas also has the second highest number of credit union members. In the state, there are approximately 3.7 million credit union members — currently, one Texan of every five belongs to a credit union.

In 1984, share (savings) accounts stood at $8.0 billion — up 13.7 percent from the previous year. And

loans amounted to $5.8 billion — an increase of 20.9 percent over 1983 figures.

Deregulation has increased the number of services offered by credit unions, which now include: money market accounts, IRAs, home mortgages, credit cards, share drafts, stock brokerage services, ATM networks and a full line of insurance products through Members Insurance Companies, also based in Dallas.

Credit unions are chartered at federal or state levels. The National Credit Union Administration (NCUA) is the regulatory agency for the 714 federally chartered credit unions in Texas. (Elizabeth Burkhart of Houston is one of the 3-member NCUA Board.) The Texas Credit Union Department, Austin, is the regulatory agency for the 446 state chartered credit unions.

The Texas Credit Union League and Affiliates at 4455 LBJ Freeway, Farmers Branch, Tx. 75244-5998, has been the state association for federal and state chartered credit unions since October 1934.

TOTAL DEPOSITS AND TOTAL ASSETS
OF ALL INSURED COMMERCIAL BANKS IN TEXAS BY COUNTIES
Source: Federal Reserve Bank of Dallas
Dec. 31, 1984
(In thousands of dollars)

County—	No. of Banks	Total Deposits	Total Assets	County—	No. of Banks	Total Deposits	Total Assets
Anderson	6	$251,180	$284,289	Castro	2	66,993	74,275
Andrews	3	102,116	113,130	Chambers	4	101,284	117,275
Angelina	8	422,591	475,344	Cherokee	6	233,971	262,236
Aransas	3	119,309	134,040	Childress	2	36,280	42,016
Archer	1	27,264	29,960	Clay	2	61,946	68,990
Armstrong	1	12,377	13,757	Cochran	1	31,593	34,528
Atascosa	6	137,400	157,509	Coke	2	33,765	36,937
Austin	7	217,665	246,151	Coleman	3	105,640	115,312
Bailey	2	68,257	76,722	Collin	28	1,175,955	1,303,124
Bandera	2	45,400	49,275	Collingsworth	2	46,440	51,891
Bastrop	6	164,989	183,903	Colorado	5	197,048	232,505
Baylor	2	49,451	55,585	Comal	4	208,670	230,314
Bee	3	166,124	193,802	Comanche	4	134,360	148,788
Bell	17	781,721	877,182	Concho	2	26,504	29,610
Bexar	69	7,555,531	8,772,435	Cooke	5	247,854	269,040
Blanco	3	54,288	62,014	Coryell	6	175,473	194,838
Borden	0	0	0	Cottle	1	27,675	34,379
Bosque	6	119,357	138,105	Crane	1	15,915	18,917
Bowie	10	454,955	536,057	Crockett	2	59,236	68,731
Brazoria	23	866,502	982,648	Crosby	3	59,802	68,477
Brazos	10	700,285	778,905	Culberson	1	10,724	12,347
Brewster	1	43,013	49,146	Dallam	3	98,670	110,666
Briscoe	2	37,308	43,958	Dallas	178	27,981,419	42,037,020
Brooks	1	36,780	42,960	Dawson	2	164,071	185,141
Brown	5	233,435	254,720	De Witt	8	246,285	271,417
Burleson	6	129,551	145,054	Deaf Smith	2	156,307	175,928
Burnet	5	252,834	277,654	Delta	3	39,270	43,767
Caldwell	4	129,869	144,754	Denton	17	802,014	882,075
Calhoun	4	160,828	178,737	Dickens	1	18,367	20,549
Callahan	3	75,115	86,107	Dimmit	2	50,772	56,329
Cameron	22	1,592,629	1,752,102	Donley	3	53,905	60,423
Camp	2	71,516	79,260	Duval	2	46,926	50,939
Carson	3	51,572	57,639	Eastland	5	141,173	156,734
Cass	6	147,004	164,511	Ector	9	776,773	868,736

County—	No. of Banks	Total Deposits	Total Assets	County—	No. of Banks	Total Deposits	Total Assets
Edwards	1	13,286	15,856	McMullen	1	13,059	14,830
El Paso	28	2,925,574	3,407,355	Madison	2	111,546	122,492
Ellis	12	439,800	500,488	Marion	2	42,222	45,478
Erath	4	218,579	240,262	Martin	1	37,307	42,188
Falls	6	148,622	166,398	Mason	2	46,862	52,580
Fannin	7	169,144	189,052	Matagorda	4	271,039	307,912
Fayette	8	254,863	282,617	Maverick	2	159,131	172,941
Fisher	2	40,155	44,936	Medina	6	88,524	102,322
Floyd	2	69,462	79,167	Menard	2	24,221	29,194
Foard	1	17,525	19,210	Midland	10	1,037,653	1,132,297
Fort Bend	13	550,755	616,017	Milam	6	178,106	205,221
Franklin	2	55,557	62,477	Mills	2	64,682	73,942
Freestone	6	110,739	123,715	Mitchell	3	69,817	76,927
Frio	2	84,545	95,347	Montague	5	182,687	198,060
Gaines	3	77,384	85,313	Montgomery	14	717,460	801,243
Galveston	20	1,170,790	1,353,865	Moore	3	106,912	121,681
Garza	1	46,906	52,184	Morris	4	100,487	109,045
Gillespie	4	180,450	198,384	Motley	1	6,712	8,243
Glasscock	0	0	0	Nacogdoches	8	409,732	453,755
Goliad	1	29,090	32,980	Navarro	11	1,045,566	1,231,636
Gonzales	5	120,617	140,390	Newton	1	22,218	24,522
Gray	4	272,339	305,351	Nolan	3	164,771	183,059
Grayson	16	742,823	831,858	Nueces	24	2,238,932	2,597,023
Gregg	17	1,117,114	1,263,064	Ochiltree	2	119,624	137,468
Grimes	7	124,554	139,979	Oldham	1	13,178	15,040
Guadalupe	7	305,213	341,967	Orange	6	273,264	312,488
Hale	7	287,301	314,322	Palo Pinto	6	215,113	237,383
Hall	3	52,147	62,893	Panola	4	154,915	177,698
Hamilton	3	85,973	95,702	Parker	6	272,436	301,727
Hansford	2	89,697	102,779	Parmer	3	101,351	115,374
Hardeman	3	63,582	69,390	Pecos	3	122,592	138,132
Hardin	5	121,758	138,174	Polk	4	205,649	232,593
Harris	259	34,435,075	48,680,072	Potter	9	1,876,940	2,266,681
Harrison	6	289,429	321,800	Presidio	2	34,330	39,109
Hartley	0	0	0	Rains	2	43,573	48,288
Haskell	3	71,542	78,388	Randall	3	126,639	137,584
Hays	7	240,403	266,503	Reagan	1	31,817	35,222
Hemphill	2	94,108	103,377	Real	1	10,916	12,382
Henderson	8	274,826	303,659	Red River	2	39,018	42,997
Hidalgo	24	2,054,673	2,302,499	Reeves	2	102,239	116,924
Hill	7	162,069	190,618	Refugio	2	89,331	108,258
Hockley	5	261,097	289,262	Roberts	1	17,298	19,525
Hood	4	144,862	158,052	Robertson	4	91,911	102,765
Hopkins	4	210,303	235,278	Rockwall	4	83,139	91,048
Houston	7	159,504	175,905	Runnels	7	147,493	162,692
Howard	4	302,152	340,250	Rusk	6	305,563	346,654
Hudspeth	1	4,728	5,457	Sabine	2	51,859	57,595
Hunt	10	363,198	407,710	San Augustine	2	54,096	61,131
Hutchinson	4	245,459	279,283	San Jacinto	2	26,408	28,750
Irion	1	33,920	39,094	San Patricio	10	278,405	312,331
Jack	3	94,400	103,838	San Saba	2	42,604	47,918
Jackson	3	134,646	149,305	Schleicher	1	27,303	31,882
Jasper	4	136,897	155,856	Scurry	3	190,991	215,028
Jeff Davis	1	6,321	7,123	Shackelford	2	49,139	56,231
Jefferson	17	1,902,229	2,211,891	Shelby	5	150,298	167,365
Jim Hogg	1	35,224	42,319	Sherman	1	49,760	56,678
Jim Wells	6	277,040	319,985	Smith	16	1,563,425	1,798,039
Johnson	10	490,887	543,628	Somervell	1	20,397	22,801
Jones	4	104,664	117,118	Starr	2	89,190	98,329
Karnes	4	99,688	111,969	Stephens	2	135,359	148,661
Kaufman	9	348,199	382,916	Sterling	1	25,828	28,830
Kendall	3	126,191	138,083	Stonewall	1	19,636	24,164
Kenedy	0	0	0	Sutton	2	51,103	57,748
Kent	1	6,811	7,449	Swisher	4	109,595	127,386
Kerr	5	459,611	512,528	Tarrant	85	8,187,186	10,534,923
Kimble	2	29,244	33,437	Taylor	12	1,613,918	1,886,806
King	0	0	0	Terrell	1	14,638	16,335
Kinney	1	9,850	10,733	Terry	2	105,788	115,233
Kleberg	3	172,068	209,085	Throckmorton	2	23,340	27,044
Knox	2	43,795	48,841	Titus	4	242,833	288,588
La Salle	1	16,827	19,245	Tom Green	8	812,669	934,162
Lamar	6	239,111	268,954	Travis	41	5,411,414	6,775,839
Lamb	6	118,357	134,077	Trinity	2	54,428	62,201
Lampasas	3	117,221	123,935	Tyler	4	63,077	71,190
Lavaca	4	123,720	141,301	Upshur	4	145,551	168,511
Lee	5	178,713	198,280	Upton	2	39,073	44,350
Leon	5	82,039	92,455	Uvalde	4	220,793	244,392
Liberty	8	351,707	390,366	Val Verde	4	214,087	234,904
Limestone	7	138,467	151,604	Van Zandt	8	144,243	158,641
Lipscomb	4	138,244	163,604	Victoria	6	1,073,328	1,251,073
Live Oak	2	85,249	97,158	Walker	6	309,698	346,837
Llano	4	137,421	157,852	Waller	4	84,172	94,207
Loving	0	0	0	Ward	2	113,646	128,660
Lubbock	16	1,953,323	2,242,049	Washington	5	279,438	308,660
Lynn	3	65,611	77,132	Webb	6	1,603,715	1,738,934
McCulloch	2	84,068	93,010	Wharton	8	344,346	388,802
McLennan	18	1,282,831	1,458,958	Wheeler	4	77,238	90,380
				Wichita	10	1,172,342	1,356,598

County—	No. of Banks	Total Deposits	Total Assets
Wilbarger	3	181,701	202,392
Willacy	2	86,750	98,590
Williamson	22	698,396	773,925
Wilson	4	91,345	101,246
Winkler	3	87,514	99,064
Wise	6	167,272	185,158
Wood	7	248,490	275,668
Yoakum	3	70,611	78,903
Young	4	203,007	226,123
Zapata	2	45,398	52,310
Zavala	2	21,696	24,633
TOTAL	1,853	$146,642,174	$188,267,224

The presentation above was derived from the regulatory Report of Condition, consolidating domestic subsidiaries. Therefore, none of the deposits or assets of foreign branches of domestic banks are included in this tabulation. Listed below are the county totals with data from the Call Report consolidating **domestic** and **foreign** subsidiaries. These are:

County—	Total Deposits	Total Assets
Bexar	$7,559,167	$8,776,758
Cameron	1,635,950	1,795,626
Dallas	35,245,372	46,989,633
Harris	38,748,152	53,237,676
Tarrant	8,620,478	10,633,659
Travis	5,427,356	6,775,839
Webb	1,606,560	1,741,779
Total All Counties	$158,718,240	$197,926,869

TEXAS STATE BANKS

Consolidated Statement, Foreign and Domestic
Offices, as of Dec. 31, 1984
Source: Federal Reserve Bank of Dallas

Number of Banks	855

(All figures in thousand dollars)
Assets

Cash and due from banks:	
Noninterest-bearing balances and currency and coin	$4,213,650
Interest-bearing balances	1,758,351
Securities	12,497,655
Fed. funds sold and securities purchased under agreement to resell	4,045,956
Loans and lease financing receivables:	
Loans and leases, net of unearned income	35,543,928
Less: allowance for loan and lease losses	426,553
Loans and leases, net	35,117,375
Assets held in trading accounts	33,629
Premises and fixed assets (including capitalized leases)	1,237,628
Other real estate owned	164,409
Investments in unconsolidated subsidiaries and associated companies	9,415
Customers liability on acceptances outstanding	44,492
Other assets	1,238,451
Total Assets	$60,361,513

Liabilities

Deposits:	
In domestic offices	$52,777,821
Noninterest-bearing	11,520,315
Interest-bearing	41,257,506
In foreign offices, edge & agreement subsidiaries, & IBF's	77,755
Federal funds purchased and securities sold under agreement to repurchase	1,597,549
Demand notes issued to the U.S. Treasury	119,407
Other borrowed money	263,502
Mortgage indebtedness and obligations under capitalized leases	87,682
Banks' liability on acceptances executed and outstanding	44,492
Notes and debentures subordinated to deposits	54,820
Other liabilities	860,502
Total Liabilities	$55,883,530

Equity Capital

Perpetual preferred stock	$725
Common stock	890,068
Surplus	2,002,861
Undivided profits and capital reserves	1,584,321
Total Equity Capital	$4,477,975
Total liabilities, limited preferred stock and equity capital	$60,361,505

TEXAS NATIONAL BANKS

Consolidated Statement, Foreign and Domestic
Offices, as of Dec. 31, 1984
Source: Federal Reserve Bank of Dallas

Number of Banks	999

(All figures in thousand dollars)
Assets

Cash and due from banks:	
Noninterest-bearing balances and currency and coin	$11,303,967
Interest-bearing balances	8,188,303
Securities	18,236,501
Fed. funds sold and securities purchased under agreement to resell	8,828,636
Loans and lease financing receivables:	
Loans and leases, net of unearned income	84,082,031
Less: allowance for loan and lease losses	1,219,643
Loans and leases, net	82,862,388
Assets held in trading accounts	173,016
Premises and fixed assets (including capitalized leases)	2,309,418
Other real estate owned	391,853
Investments in unconsolidated subsidiaries and associated companies	31,668
Customers liability on acceptances outstanding	2,378,965
Intangible assets	156,522
Other assets	2,704,094
Total Assets	$137,565,331

Liabilities

Deposits:	
In domestic offices	$93,864,331
Noninterest-bearing	24,680,607
Interest-bearing	69,183,724
In foreign offices, edge & agreement subsidiaries, & IBF's	11,998,311
Noninterest-bearing	15,244
Interest-bearing	11,983,067
Federal funds purchased and securities sold under agreement to repurchase	15,231,750
Demand notes issued to the U.S. Treasury	779,316
Other borrowed money	2,149,316
Mortgage indebtedness and obligations under capitalized leases	197,046
Banks' liability on acceptances executed and outstanding	2,378,958
Notes and debentures subordinated to deposits	639,681
Other liabilities	1,888,118
Total Liabilities	$129,126,827

Equity Capital

Perpetual preferred stock	$95,120
Common stock	1,567,119
Surplus	2,340,414
Undivided profits and capital reserves	4,436,251
Cumulative foreign currency translation adjustments	−404
Total Equity Capital	$8,438,500
Total liabilities, limited preferred stock and equity capital	$137,565,327

TEXAS BANK RESOURCES AND DEPOSITS—1905-1984

On Dec. 31, 1984, Texas had a total of 1,854 national and state banks with total deposits of $158,718,240,000 and total resources of $197,926,869,000. At one time Texas had many private banks, but the number has declined.

SOURCE: Federal Reserve Bank of Dallas.

(In thousands of dollars)

	National Banks			State Banks			National and State Banks		
Date—	No. Banks	Total Resources	Deposits	No. Banks	Total Resources	Deposits	No. Banks	Total Resources	Deposits
Sept. 30, 1905.	440	$189,484	$101,285	29	$4,341	$2,213	469	$193,825	$103,498
Nov. 10, 1910	516	293,245	145,249	621	88,103	59,766	1,137	381,348	205,015
Dec. 29, 1920	556	780,246	564,135	1,031	391,127	280,429	1,587	1,171,373	844,564
Dec. 31, 1930	560	1,028,420	826,723	655	299,012	231,909	1,215	1,327,432	1,058,632
Dec. 31, 1940	446	1,695,662	1,534,702	393	227,866	179,027	839	1,923,528	1,713,729
Dec. 31, 1950	442	6,467,275	6,076,006	449	1,427,680	1,338,540	891	7,894,955	7,414,546
Dec. 31, 1955	446	8,640,239	7,983,681	472	2,087,066	1,941,706	918	10,727,305	9,925,387
Dec. 31, 1956	452	8,986,456	8,241,159	480	2,231,497	2,067,927	932	11,217,953	10,309,086
Dec. 31, 1957	457	8,975,321	8,170,271	486	2,349,935	2,169,898	943	11,325,256	10,340,169
Dec. 31, 1958	458	9,887,737	9,049,580	499	2,662,270	2,449,474	957	12,550,007	11,499,054
Dec. 31, 1959	466	10,011,949	9,033,495	511	2,813,006	2,581,404	977	12,824,955	11,614,899
Dec. 31, 1960	468	10,520,690	9,560,668	532	2,997,609	2,735,726	1,000	13,518,299	12,296,394
Dec. 30, 1961	473	11,466,767	10,426,812	538	3,297,588	3,009,499	1,011	14,764,355	13,436,311
Dec. 28, 1962	486	12,070,803	10,712,253	551	3,646,404	3,307,714	1,037	15,717,207	14,019,967
Dec. 30, 1963	519	12,682,674	11,193,194	570	4,021,033	3,637,559	1,089	16,703,707	14,830,753
Dec. 31, 1964	539	14,015,957	12,539,142	581	4,495,074	4,099,543	1,120	18,511,031	16,638,685
Dec. 31, 1965	545	14,944,319	13,315,367	585	4,966,947	4,530,675	1,130	19,911,266	17,846,042
Dec. 31, 1966	546	15,647,346	13,864,727	591	5,332,385	4,859,906	1,137	20,979,731	18,724,633
Dec. 31, 1967	542	17,201,752	15,253,496	597	6,112,900	5,574,735	1,139	23,314,652	20,828,231
Dec. 31, 1968	535	19,395,045	16,963,003	609	7,107,310	6,489,357	1,144	26,502,355	23,452,360
Dec. 31, 1969	529	19,937,396	16,687,720	637	7,931,966	7,069,822	1,166	27,869,362	23,757,542
Dec. 31, 1970	530	22,087,890	18,384,922	653	8,907,039	7,958,133	1,183	30,994,929	26,343,055
Dec. 31, 1971	530	25,137,269	20,820,519	677	10,273,200	9,179,451	1,207	35,410,469	29,999,970
Dec. 31, 1972	538	29,106,654	23,892,660	700	12,101,749	10,804,827	1,238	41,208,403	34,697,487
Dec. 31, 1973	550	32,791,219	26,156,659	716	14,092,134	12,417,693	1,266	46,883,353	38,574,352
Dec. 31, 1974	569	35,079,218	28,772,284	744	15,654,983	13,758,147	1,313	50,734,201	42,530,431
Dec. 31, 1975	584	39,138,322	31,631,199	752	17,740,669	15,650,933	1,336	56,878,991	47,282,132
Dec. 31, 1976	596	43,534,570	35,164,285	761	19,846,695	17,835,078	1,357	63,381,265	52,999,363
Dec. 31, 1977	604	49,091,503	39,828,475	773	22,668,498	20,447,012	1,377	71,760,001	60,275,487
Dec. 31, 1978	609	56,489,274	44,749,491	786	25,987,616	23,190,869	1,395	82,476,890	67,940,360
Dec. 31, 1979	615	65,190,891	50,754,782	807	30,408,232	26,975,854	1,422	95,599,123	77,730,636
Dec. 31, 1980	641	75,540,334	58,378,669	825	35,186,113	31,055,648	1,466	110,726,447	89,434,317
Dec. 31, 1981	694	91,811,510	68,750,678	829	42,071,043	36,611,555	1,523	133,882,553	105,362,233
Dec. 31, 1982	758	104,580,333	78,424,478	841	48,336,463	41,940,277	1,599	152,916,796	120,364,755
Dec. 31, 1983	880	126,914,841	98,104,893	848	55,008,329	47,653,797	1,728	181,923,170	145,758,690
Dec. 31, 1984	999	137,565,365	105,862,656	855	60,361,504	52,855,584	1,854	197,926,869	158,718,240

LEADING TEXAS COMMERCIAL BANKS, RANKED BY TOTAL DOMESTIC DEPOSITS

Table below shows the ranking of Texas banks as of Dec. 31, 1984, according to total domestic deposits.

Source: Federal Reserve Bank of Dallas

Rank	Name and Location of Bank—	*Total Deposits (000 dollars)
1	RepublicBank Dallas, Dallas	$6,941,166
2	First City National Bank of Houston, Houston	4,956,114
3	Texas Commerce Bank, Houston	4,680,165
4	MBank Dallas, Dallas	4,320,177
5	InterFirst Bank Dallas, Dallas	3,419,607
6	Allied Bank of Texas, Houston	3,080,358
7	Capital Bank, Houston	2,503,635
8	Texas American Bank/Fort Worth, Fort Worth	1,748,270
9	Frost National Bank of San Antonio, San Antonio	1,482,077
10	InterFirst Bank Austin, Austin	1,357,044
11	RepublicBank Houston, Houston	1,267,870
12	InterFirst Bank Fort Worth, Fort Worth	994,931
13	National Bank of Commerce of San Antonio, San Antonio	991,770
14	Texas Commerce Bank-Austin, Austin	943,830
15	InterFirst Bank Houston, Houston	935,765
16	First City Bank of Dallas, Dallas	828,218
17	Laredo National Bank, Laredo	817,594
18	First National Bank of Amarillo, Amarillo	796,431
19	MBank El Paso, El Paso	779,876
20	RepublicBank First National Midland, Midland	707,981
21	MBank Alamo, San Antonio	706,416
22	First City National Bank of Austin, Austin	699,394
23	El Paso National Bank, El Paso	679,912
24	BancTexas Dallas, Dallas	672,103
25	McAllen State Bank, McAllen	635,350
26	MBank Corpus Christi, Corpus Christi	587,537
27	MBank Preston, Dallas	553,678
28	Victoria Bank & Trust Co., Victoria	527,000
29	Amarillo National Bank, Amarillo	524,305
30	MBank Brownsville, Brownsville	495,214
31	Allied Bank Memorial, Houston	494,811
32	MBank Fort Worth, Fort Worth	493,781
33	MBank Austin, Austin	493,058
34	First National Bank at Lubbock, Lubbock	487,199
35	InterFrst Bank Fannin, Houston	485,637
36	Allied Lakewood Bank, Dallas	456,076
37	First State Bank, Abilene	448,000
38	First City National Bank of Midland, Midland	445,831
39	Cullen Center Bank & Trust, Houston	427,140
40	RepublicBank Lubbock, Lubbock	418,803
41	International Bank of Commerce of Laredo, Laredo	409,081

Rank	Name and Location of Bank—	*Total Deposits (000 dollars)
42	National Bank of Fort Sam Houston, San Antonio	405,695
43	MBank Wichita Falls, Wichita Falls	395,715
44	First City Bank of Corpus Christi, Corpus Christi	394,027
45	InterFirst Bank San Antonio, San Antonio	385,669
46	First City National Bank Beaumont, Beaumont	379,728
47	NorthPark National Bank of Dallas, Dallas	374,110
48	InterFirst Bank Tyler, Tyler	372,443
49	Texas American Bank/Dallas, Dallas	363,657
50	MBank Abilene, Abilene	363,517
51	Texas American Bank/Houston, Houston	361,534
52	Texas Commerce Bank-McAllen, McAllen	358,648
53	InterFirst Bank Wichita Falls, Wichita Falls	352,014
54	Texas Commerce Bank-Dallas, Dallas	341,385
55	RepublicBank Waco, Waco	334,219
56	RepublicBank San Antonio, San Antonio	330,022
57	Western Bank-Westheimer, Houston	326,357
58	First National Bank of Abilene, Abilene	319,684
59	First Victoria National Bank, Victoria	316,947
60	InterFirst Bank Park Cities, Dallas	316,038
61	First City National Bank of El Paso, El Paso	315,317
62	Texas Commerce Bank-Arlington, Arlington	314,220
63	First City National Bank of Tyler, Tyler	312,529
64	Texas Commerce Bank-Reagan, Houston	309,920
65	Texas Commerce Bank-Brownsville, Brownsville	304,220
66	Broadway National Bank, San Antonio	301,134
67	American State Bank, Lubbock	298,352
68	Allied Mercantile Bank, Houston	293,354
69	First State Bank, Denton	287,175
70	RepublicBank Oak Cliff, Dallas	283,796
71	River Oaks Bank, Houston	275,796
72	Texas Commerce Bank-Corpus Christi, Corpus Christi	275,219
73	United Bank of Texas, Austin	274,211
74	MBank Waco, Waco	267,613
75	Heights State Bank, Houston	267,423
76	UnitedBank-Houston, Houston	261,309
77	InterFirst Bank Galveston, Galveston	256,844
78	RepublicBank Tyler, Tyler	255,273
79	Central National Bank of San Angelo, San Angelo	250,827
80	Union National Bank of Laredo, Laredo	250,786
81	Bank of Dallas, Dallas	248,516
82	First City National Bank of Arlington, Arlington	247,339
83	Chas. Schreiner Bank, Kerrville	246,284
84	Texas Commerce Bank-Beaumont, Beaumont	245,867
85	RepublicBank Ridglea, Fort Worth	242,799
86	Allied Champions Bank, Harris County	236,554
87	Charter National Bank-Westheimer, Houston	232,004
88	Texas Commerce Bank-San Angelo, San Angelo	230,308
89	Texas American Bank/Galleria, Houston	226,692
90	Allied American Bank, Houston	223,020
91	MBank Pasadena, Pasadena	221,634
92	Texas American Bank/Amarillo, Amarillo	220,136
93	InterFirst Bank Odessa, Odessa	219,471
94	North Dallas Bank & Trust Co., Dallas	217,816
95	RepublicBank Spring Branch, Houston	214,903
96	RepublicBank Greenville Ave., Dallas	213,922

Rank	Name and Location of Bank—	*Total Deposits (000 dollars)
97	InterFirst Bank Irving, Irving	211,611
98	InterFirst Bank, Abilene, Abilene	211,125
99	Southside State Bank, Tyler	208,893
100	Allied Merchants Bank, Port Arthur	208,532
101	MBank Port Arthur, Port Arthur	207,468
102	Cullen/Frost Bank of Dallas, Dallas	203,361
103	Texas Commerce Bank-San Antonio, San Antonio	197,066
104	RepublicBank Austin, Austin	194,944
105	MBank Odessa, Odessa	194,942
106	Plains National Bank of Lubbock, Lubbock	191,651
107	Grand Bank, R. L. Thornton at Grand, Dallas	191,581
108	First City Bank-Central Park, San Antonio	191,094
109	InterFirst Bank Conroe, Conroe	187,117
110	Texas Commerce Bank-Longview, Longview	186,836
111	Post Oak Bank, Houston	185,341
112	MBank Longview, Longview	184,135
113	InterFirst Bank Harlingen, Harlingen	183,597
114	First City Bank of Richardson, Richardson	183,409
115	First Bank & Trust Bryan Texas, Bryan	182,673
116	Central Bank & Trust, Fort Worth	176,382
117	MBank Sherman, Sherman	175,985
118	Texas American Bank/West Side, Fort Worth	174,800
119	Plano Bank & Trust Co., Plano	174,227
120	First City National Bank of Bryan, Bryan	173,146
121	Longview Bank and Trust Co., Longview	169,900
122	University State Bank, Houston	169,285
123	Allied Northeast Bank, N. Richland Hills	168,704
124	RepublicBank Lufkin, Lufkin	168,379
125	Texas Commerce Medical Bank, Houston	167,846
126	InterFirst Bank Corsicana, Corsicana	167,107
127	Allied Bank of Marble Falls, Marble Falls	165,592
128	Medical Center Bank Houston, Houston	164,359
129	InterFirst Bank San Felipe, Houston	162,678
130	InterFirst Bank Carrollton, Carrollton	161,895
131	InterFirst Bank University Drive, Fort Worth	161,331
132	Texas American Bank/Riverside, Fort Worth	161,241
133	First State Bank & Trust Co., Mission	161,240
134	Texarkana National Bank, Texarkana	159,531
135	BancTexas Houston, Houston	159,096
136	First National Bank in Pampa, Pampa	158,848
137	First State Bank of Uvalde, Uvalde	158,686
138	InterFirst Bank Victoria, Victoria	157,326
139	First City Bank Farmers Branch, Farmers Branch	157,114
140	BancTexas Richardson, Richardson	156,658
141	Texas Commerce Bank of Ft. Worth, Ft. Worth	156,525
142	First National Bank in Big Spring, Big Spring	155,932
143	Texas American Bank/Levelland, Levelland	155,875
144	Texas Commerce Bank-Las Colinas, Irving	154,276
145	Citizens Bank Corpus Christi, Corpus Christi	154,225
146	Texas American Bank/Austin, Austin	154,219
147	South Main Bank, Houston	153,362
148	Texas American Bank/Midland, Midland	151,139
149	InterFirst Bank Southwest-Houston, Bellaire	148,607
150	Allied Bank-West Loop, Houston	148,166

*Total Deposits taken from the Call Report of Condition, Consolidating **Domestic** Subsidiaries only.

TEXAS UNEMPLOYMENT COMPENSATION FUND

This table summarizes the status of the **Texas Unemployment Compensation Fund** on Aug. 31, 1984, and activities during the fiscal year 1983-84, as reported by the Texas Employment Commission.

Fund Balance Sept. 1, 1983	$3,249,345
Receipts	
Gross Payroll Remittances Allocated . . .	859,035,598
Less Refunds and Returned Checks . .	−4,469,558
Less Penalties and Interest	−4,953,314
Less Surtax	−78,385,155
Net Payroll Taxes	771,227,571
Payroll Remittances in Process	4,471,590
Interest on Trust Fund	0
Rent to Amortize State Office Buildings .	745,778
Benefits Reimbursed by Other States . . .	11,052,068
From Federal Funds	
(UCFE, UCX, and ETA-PSE)	13,540,190
Federal Share of Extended Benefits	717,000
Federal Supplemental Compensation . .	138,330,000
Refunds from Reimbursing Employers .	20,033,261
Total Receipts	$960,117,458

Disbursements	
Net Benefits Paid Claimants	
Under State Law (Includes State Share	
Extended Benefits)	$638,205,370
Expenditure of Sec. 903	
Allotment for Buildings	4,845
UCFE, UCX, and ETA-PSE	
Benefits Paid	13,438,117
Federal Supplemental Compensation . .	138,226,346
Extended Benefits Paid	
Federal Share	709,178
Benefits Paid	
Reimbursed by Other States	8,966,119
Reimbursable Benefits Paid	19,426,946
Total Disbursements	$818,976,921
Net Operating Income	141,140,537
Sub-Total	144,389,882
FEDERAL ADVANCES	
Title XII Advances	$412,451,155
Less Title XII Repayments	(−555,433,088)
Net Change in Title XII Advances	$(142,981,933)
Fund Balance Aug. 31, 1984.	$1,407,949

EMPLOYMENT, BY INDUSTRIES AND COUNTIES

This table shows average monthly employment in first quarter of 1984, and total wages paid for the year. (See explanation in footnote at end of table.) Attention is called to the fact that data in this table are limited to employers who are subject to the Texas Unemployment Compensation Act.

Counties—	Total Employment	Mining	Construction	Mfg.	Transp., Comm. and Pub. Util.	Trade	Finance, Ins. and Real Est.	Service	State Govt.	Local Govt.	†Total Wages
Anderson	12,941	1,256	1,165	1,596	360	3,454	598	1,366	1,321	1,759	213,062,948
Andrews	6,803	2,586	611	*	448	1,021	218	884	20	1,015	142,497,216
Angelina	25,325	199	1,982	7,468	1,194	6,060	1,023	3,513	1,219	2,514	413,784,944
Aransas	4,937	323	602	359	332	1,651	163	512	79	583	79,633,824
Archer	2,000	485	241	*	45	506	46	358	20	299	32,101,388
Armstrong	787	*	26	*	4	87	23	557	16	74	22,807,664
Atascosa	5,917	1,149	498	131	357	1,381	230	971	76	994	84,645,028
Austin	6,069	214	965	954	295	1,473	314	938	67	812	94,288,296
Bailey	1,766	*	87	38	161	501	75	300	27	344	22,819,384
Bandera	1,866	*	332	104	*	458	175	444	28	325	28,738,072
Bastrop	4,523	*	296	790	150	1,124	236	518	137	1,226	55,127,272
Baylor	1,519	124	79	*	148	363	77	424	32	272	17,919,376
Bee	6,514	707	472	290	224	1,752	278	1,260	84	1,368	90,004,896
Bell	47,258	67	3,130	7,533	2,148	13,107	2,235	9,851	474	8,571	676,354,228
Bexar	379,720	2,794	30,907	43,113	16,119	111,059	30,393	86,148	9,884	47,205	6,010,117,500
Blanco	1,291	*	86	81	*	276	95	514	41	198	15,234,012
Borden	428	120	*	*	*	*	8	220	10	70	6,469,040
Bosque	3,009	12	110	640	95	840	135	673	41	382	38,971,968
Bowie	22,797	17	1,074	4,017	963	7,269	1,163	4,548	396	3,226	320,815,536
Brazoria	57,441	2,296	6,415	17,241	2,236	10,497	2,104	7,037	1,914	7,249	1,260,328,224
Brazos	45,934	1,547	2,870	3,209	1,641	10,057	1,892	6,485	14,500	3,402	694,985,932
Brewster	2,633	84	81	88	140	583	*	562	693	402	31,123,736
Briscoe	304	*	18	19	26	87	*	44	16	76	3,247,004
Brooks	2,338	388	64	*	96	575	60	368	42	745	30,215,080
Brown	11,256	152	529	2,880	685	2,680	451	2,035	513	1,291	165,202,868
Burleson	3,013	545	166	327	129	719	159	350	50	568	43,081,448
Burnet	4,860	117	434	923	249	1,271	321	652	60	811	65,040,232
Caldwell	5,137	843	256	369	154	1,115	212	1,227	52	874	70,842,448
Calhoun	8,271	268	1,251	3,038	329	1,410	232	583	49	1,111	186,937,608
Callahan	1,471	179	141	65	65	283	78	249	31	380	19,802,476
Cameron	62,059	105	3,306	10,233	3,063	17,584	3,101	10,539	1,848	10,710	776,668,436
Camp	2,638	*	97	631	89	707	141	396	11	287	33,816,808
Carson	3,884	101	181	*	75	318	69	2,770	37	333	85,329,552
Cass	6,445	373	267	1,563	234	1,385	255	985	247	1,126	101,735,008
Castro	2,050	0	68	*	112	463	88	389	27	504	28,646,388
Chambers	6,210	580	574	*	256	1,032	118	2,494	45	1,055	137,146,928
Cherokee	11,941	169	521	2,943	391	2,346	342	1,957	1,634	1,125	160,791,368
Childress	1,963	0	70	*	109	480	75	700	119	367	23,295,540
Clay	1,382	61	90	190	67	342	57	152	26	397	18,865,688
Cochran	1,040	23	12	*	19	201	32	280	19	333	13,376,632
Coke	843	216	*	50	*	101	*	169	16	291	13,473,888
Coleman	2,474	307	106	295	119	632	126	468	33	388	29,769,456
Collin	41,642	*	3,412	7,529	959	12,233	2,505	8,301	164	6,137	722,770,088
Collingsworth . .	1,046	*	97	*	53	207	60	313	26	227	13,001,388
Colorado	5,920	767	498	646	191	1,738	228	923	88	673	87,829,828
Comal	12,403	*	1,027	3,745	434	2,618	584	2,237	100	1,613	178,932,456
Comanche	2,842	13	76	392	117	857	113	402	78	587	33,570,180
Concho	532	*	20	0	*	196	*	141	16	159	6,021,708
Cooke	9,569	927	305	2,382	473	2,651	271	761	299	1,459	140,202,384

Counties—	Total Employment	Mining	Construc- tion	Mfg.	Transp., Comm. and Pub. Util.	Trade	Finance, Ins. and Real Est.	Service	State Govt.	Local Govt.	†Total Wages
Coryell	5,886	0	555	396	83	1,418	366	663	1,019	1,363	75,186,480
Cottle	846	22	24	*	33	322	*	239	33	138	12,796,724
Crane	2,134	875	91	*	163	303	29	281	16	376	47,169,096
Crockett	1,700	301	94	*	171	328	136	278	35	318	27,277,788
Crosby	1,692	*	12	133	62	421	76	375	30	415	21,364,976
Culberson	1,374	*	*	*	*	310	*	788	27	213	21,943,340
Dallam	2,557	*	335	61	135	896	154	555	35	246	37,474,792
Dallas	1,041,617	23,142	66,237	186,548	69,534	286,765	101,600	223,688	8,626	72,042	22,410,460,224
Dawson	3,668	432	136	301	268	1,011	154	386	40	799	51,825,944
Deaf Smith	5,788	*	286	1,277	451	1,387	218	549	42	998	80,558,244
Delta	689	*	*	*	*	166	46	315	31	131	7,519,808
Denton	47,641	57	2,498	10,615	1,577	12,207	1,508	5,997	7,227	5,588	761,277,900
DeWitt	5,724	207	140	1,272	246	1,388	335	871	192	1,073	73,136,520
Dickens	558	*	27	*	78	115	27	102	27	136	6,838,960
Dimmit	2,975	468	223	*	97	465	64	478	58	874	36,895,612
Donley	743	*	6	60	18	142	58	86	21	293	9,461,196
Duval	3,141	892	102	*	65	373	63	440	44	1,162	46,152,792
Eastland	5,254	701	299	847	313	1,072	223	770	80	937	69,119,604
Ector	50,373	9,873	3,307	4,945	2,731	14,191	2,237	6,353	659	5,977	990,619,824
Edwards	364	*	*	*	49	79	14	51	18	153	4,840,324
Ellis	18,177	*	1,004	7,481	754	3,602	644	2,156	146	2,226	274,345,388
El Paso	156,649	345	8,915	35,854	8,508	39,370	7,977	27,682	4,753	22,335	2,208,729,908
Erath	7,548	233	433	939	236	2,278	499	1,180	930	729	99,327,512
Falls	3,356	*	71	480	136	837	264	844	46	615	38,744,116
Fannin	4,911	*	179	1,398	251	1,036	386	604	86	933	65,633,956
Fayette	6,297	784	324	640	195	2,126	267	823	103	1,011	84,374,336
Fisher	1,229	145	*	*	*	217	45	432	20	296	18,967,072
Floyd	1,853	*	52	178	126	406	60	244	33	479	21,931,380
Foard	459	*	*	*	*	77	28	222	7	125	4,560,108
Fort Bend	35,208	1,742	2,555	8,785	1,217	6,826	1,589	4,064	2,230	5,779	694,274,152
Franklin	1,183	*	22	273	16	168	54	316	26	289	12,083,816
Freestone	4,435	502	499	120	924	750	158	710	85	687	75,234,196
Frio	2,763	177	98	79	120	714	93	474	69	689	32,369,024
Gaines	4,756	816	*	257	262	861	143	1,424	23	689	82,709,648
Galveston	68,155	933	4,124	10,194	5,103	13,636	4,485	9,258	10,101	10,085	1,282,567,432
Garza	1,472	556	*	28	57	219	*	175	31	314	22,421,500
Gillespie	4,052	*	314	363	253	1,372	253	936	93	461	46,538,004
Glasscock	226	35	*	*	*	*	*	99	5	87	3,527,820
Goliad	1,120	67	46	14	*	255	41	293	54	350	16,075,200
Gonzales	5,295	214	115	1,052	301	1,311	171	906	73	847	61,050,004
Gray	9,620	1,744	623	1,344	531	2,431	375	1,461	88	938	177,906,976
Grayson	32,874	354	1,109	11,767	1,281	7,451	1,245	5,102	217	4,243	547,149,688
Gregg	46,502	4,073	3,230	7,509	2,658	13,247	2,223	7,903	336	5,102	781,240,700
Grimes	3,868	48	341	888	144	772	205	462	41	862	62,487,944
Guadalupe	12,875	350	948	3,998	271	2,950	478	1,489	119	2,137	180,227,560
Hale	11,420	*	548	1,721	529	3,780	445	1,957	109	1,891	151,712,972
Hall	1,076	0	13	*	*	308	70	298	19	295	12,083,928
Hamilton	1,781	*	61	*	114	473	72	719	32	267	20,370,688
Hansford	1,735	212	55	23	209	394	72	98	15	412	30,139,412
Hardeman	1,839	209	29	*	163	263	73	655	30	377	26,722,212
Hardin	7,301	534	379	1,134	329	1,864	245	1,208	121	1,487	110,391,636
Harris	1,318,891	86,509	111,473	160,957	89,845	343,263	97,877	288,964	31,364	102,042	29,716,422,856
Harrison	18,487	700	1,562	7,540	725	2,935	660	2,235	189	1,919	357,370,408
Hartley	378	*	0	*	*	141	*	76	13	148	4,785,096
Haskell	1,546	151	77	58	111	433	60	191	38	342	20,142,944
Hays	14,287	*	1,112	1,477	458	3,190	578	2,662	3,133	1,625	186,209,204
Hemphill	1,605	397	88	*	120	288	85	249	18	308	30,244,256
Henderson	9,300	351	580	1,787	616	2,420	414	1,325	107	1,561	136,381,800
Hidalgo	83,964	1,588	4,315	9,786	2,623	24,208	3,377	11,072	3,154	15,614	998,861,568
Hill	5,596	0	590	1,145	342	1,171	226	927	80	1,061	72,499,880
Hockley	7,251	2,211	386	229	354	1,451	234	789	34	1,356	126,641,280
Hood	4,263	63	354	227	169	1,356	187	1,080	32	737	70,823,472
Hopkins	8,177	89	234	2,165	539	2,719	321	772	119	1,173	114,695,828
Houston	9,580	265	1,119	1,197	687	2,229	708	1,751	686	867	204,672,804
Howard	11,340	1,197	510	1,425	549	2,920	484	1,681	820	1,646	183,332,848
Hudspeth	529	71	*	*	*	59	*	97	44	170	6,928,960
Hunt	19,290	0	630	7,182	684	3,991	637	1,853	1,987	2,280	309,243,368
Hutchinson	10,998	1,889	1,760	2,540	529	1,763	312	805	56	1,315	253,797,168
Irion	407	107	39	*	*	*	*	171	9	81	8,062,880
Jack	2,036	605	36	*	203	408	80	308	32	364	34,600,480
Jackson	3,192	615	220	70	239	741	163	278	52	761	46,551,568
Jasper	8,541	*	391	2,768	285	1,806	299	1,643	124	1,225	134,285,608
Jeff Davis	387	0	*	0	*	54	*	176	95	62	5,099,768
Jefferson	107,432	1,951	7,935	23,824	8,792	26,567	4,318	20,297	3,380	10,108	2,215,827,068
Jim Hogg	1,289	223	46	*	29	368	*	252	42	329	14,691,712
Jim Wells	11,538	2,839	427	279	578	2,760	507	2,110	96	1,722	178,196,664
Johnson	16,576	49	951	4,432	681	4,269	694	3,047	107	2,346	226,699,796
Jones	4,008	272	122	538	234	1,031	306	458	57	883	57,220,608
Karnes	3,850	664	118	397	216	1,140	152	456	48	618	56,823,844
Kaufman	11,846	89	883	2,779	481	2,338	446	1,639	1,470	1,616	165,197,468
Kendall	2,880	*	365	208	27	767	180	836	37	439	32,783,168

Counties—	Total Employment	Mining	Construction	Mfg.	Transp., Comm. and Pub. Util.	Trade	Finance, Ins. and Real Est.	Service	State Govt.	Local Govt.	†Total Wages
Kenedy	333	*	0	0	0	60	*	247	4	22	4,663,876
Kent	239	19	*	0	*	25	*	42	10	114	2,936,076
Kerr	9,242	*	597	795	384	2,469	529	2,396	933	953	124,430,912
Kimble	1,018	*	36	*	58	366	45	298	44	171	12,233,412
King	218	33	*	0	0	17	*	123	4	41	4,461,764
Kinney	440	0	*	*	*	64	*	198	24	154	4,768,724
Kleberg	9,212	959	409	581	222	2,099	257	1,765	1,185	1,735	124,236,060
Knox	1,142	85	94	*	26	246	56	261	33	298	15,036,960
Lamar	15,157	*	741	5,461	486	3,103	485	2,763	330	1,709	232,709,144
Lamb	4,657	5	*	*	405	1,270	194	1,682	50	754	67,662,972
Lampasas	2,424	*	186	426	46	758	135	405	47	402	28,517,144
LaSalle	991	45	14	0	36	243	64	255	49	285	11,634,268
Lavaca	4,838	340	192	1,551	87	1,238	131	679	75	545	59,172,920
Lee	4,371	830	348	361	282	1,126	184	419	309	486	68,188,528
Leon	2,835	94	398	*	*	672	194	1,026	53	398	48,355,980
Liberty	12,074	2,244	519	1,113	766	3,056	509	1,532	121	2,044	189,717,216
Limestone	7,692	*	2,127	843	154	1,150	256	748	1,719	695	114,095,496
Lipscomb	1,063	242	29	*	34	230	137	145	8	238	17,936,260
Live Oak	2,239	397	151	*	65	592	118	499	51	366	35,061,816
Llano	2,030	12	209	83	33	597	194	486	40	376	24,994,948
Loving	89	65	0	0	*	0	*	14	0	10	1,979,000
Lubbock	85,077	596	4,130	8,738	4,356	26,414	5,186	16,169	10,036	8,693	1,314,983,872
Lynn	1,172	*	*	17	204	222	59	125	26	388	16,273,052
McCulloch	2,465	*	118	*	115	638	102	982	40	446	29,346,920
McLennan	68,645	138	3,595	14,692	3,032	19,636	4,450	13,922	2,288	6,410	1,055,922,860
McMullen	322	64	87	*	*	30	13	46	18	64	5,386,180
Madison	2,749	170	104	*	26	668	166	853	315	447	41,221,988
Marion	1,611	112	34	350	*	383	*	395	33	304	20,503,780
Martin	897	105	*	18	127	186	*	166	21	233	14,894,272
Mason	737	0	22	*	18	291	54	166	24	162	7,015,944
Matagorda	10,696	906	1,509	773	394	2,781	495	1,477	112	1,908	198,673,348
Maverick	6,310	65	175	*	245	1,703	244	1,650	113	1,642	69,647,720
Medina	4,957	103	240	593	186	1,530	166	851	93	1,099	59,221,104
Menard	412	*	6	*	10	108	29	72	16	171	4,550,872
Midland	49,445	11,940	3,115	3,521	2,329	11,923	3,284	8,410	304	4,455	1,084,018,088
Milam	6,555	179	330	*	*	1,074	268	3,584	58	926	135,333,988
Mills	1,248	*	53	*	245	203	*	544	21	182	17,559,460
Mitchell	2,227	230	133	53	151	495	99	317	47	637	30,206,400
Montague	4,460	585	173	1,071	148	943	193	531	58	758	56,961,028
Montgomery	32,193	2,936	2,943	3,009	1,156	8,251	1,732	5,384	251	6,165	565,952,536
Moore	6,219	307	388	*	592	1,237	157	2,394	39	830	118,425,908
Morris	7,188	350	94	*	283	1,028	127	4,701	55	550	138,558,560
Motley	231	0	*	*	*	60	*	62	11	78	2,484,672
Nacogdoches	16,896	100	707	4,087	404	3,790	677	2,159	2,796	1,985	217,248,000
Navarro	11,768	171	464	3,162	512	2,976	472	2,163	244	1,552	177,918,004
Newton	1,908	21	40	603	107	256	*	278	68	535	25,257,420
Nolan	5,741	349	196	1,146	452	1,385	242	685	257	977	85,981,460
Nueces	110,475	6,851	9,696	11,709	6,640	30,018	5,693	22,402	2,585	14,443	1,911,887,248
Ochiltree	4,299	1,546	180	134	326	891	141	467	25	589	80,093,960
Oldham	595	60	*	*	8	112	*	208	17	190	8,009,008
Orange	21,261	342	1,305	6,717	891	4,867	663	2,861	202	3,317	454,473,720
Palo Pinto	7,403	877	248	1,756	500	1,671	302	812	113	1,107	109,575,724
Panola	5,170	604	407	825	231	1,149	169	452	53	1,234	62,431,432
Parker	9,175	300	510	1,983	357	2,561	373	985	91	1,765	122,776,708
Parmer	3,132	0	30	*	97	547	84	1,497	23	525	47,864,140
Pecos	5,403	1,239	397	251	583	1,045	263	397	95	1,022	101,835,656
Polk	6,599	132	332	1,702	284	1,724	288	910	134	1,093	92,237,884
Potter	60,636	2,214	3,364	8,766	4,483	17,898	3,342	10,955	1,301	7,812	1,031,702,636
Presidio	801	*	32	*	53	248	57	128	41	210	9,282,656
Rains	929	*	55	258	*	165	39	204	27	181	11,686,244
Randall	15,303	44	1,103	1,300	383	5,829	654	3,109	1,785	809	220,465,968
Reagan	1,826	931	51	12	210	221	44	87	10	260	35,389,376
Real	314	*	21	*	8	75	*	51	12	147	3,147,164
Red River	3,382	*	11	1,326	116	662	107	410	61	689	36,927,684
Reeves	4,120	485	109	63	494	858	148	641	101	825	61,861,832
Refugio	2,724	684	101	*	201	644	128	310	28	509	44,882,040
Roberts	375	*	*	*	49	56	*	157	4	82	7,083,576
Robertson	2,824	*	135	541	148	753	92	500	66	527	35,886,344
Rockwall	3,517	*	439	666	*	1,084	208	485	40	553	54,582,476
Runnels	3,320	334	107	867	161	731	154	348	33	561	46,398,284
Rusk	12,723	856	1,219	1,905	2,517	2,451	466	1,611	137	1,529	237,763,088
Sabine	1,554	*	40	*	55	327	*	740	25	367	19,794,276
San Augustine	1,439	*	24	166	*	349	95	462	46	297	16,702,924
San Jacinto	1,078	*	65	54	23	206	138	205	30	357	12,856,896
San Patricio	12,312	846	1,324	1,490	722	3,025	461	1,333	133	2,689	202,996,256
San Saba	1,362	*	19	*	28	414	161	481	24	235	15,575,584
Schleicher	894	253	*	*	113	142	32	129	5	220	17,026,832
Scurry	6,756	2,076	232	322	376	1,471	203	718	50	1,244	122,526,748
Shackelford	1,187	571	21	106	23	129	40	119	21	157	20,803,544
Shelby	5,120	35	139	1,750	229	1,080	265	777	68	777	65,414,036
Sherman	1,288	69	140	*	27	336	*	382	14	186	21,989,632

Counties—	Total Employment	Mining	Construction	Mfg.	Transp., Comm. and Pub. Util.	Trade	Finance, Ins. and Real Est.	Service	State Govt.	Local Govt.	†Total Wages
Smith.........	59,761	3,827	2,797	12,086	2,521	15,691	3,273	10,864	2,211	4,995	1,037,516,684
Somervell.....	5,612	*	*	12	*	132	*	5,229	28	211	141,946,492
Starr.........	5,120	436	61	*	114	837	113	381	86	2,274	53,749,400
Stephens......	3,224	686	106	478	184	757	180	346	41	430	47,790,616
Sterling......	386	127	*	0	*	50	*	77	14	118	6,457,036
Stonewall.....	666	191	99	0	33	75	*	87	12	169	10,347,316
Sutton........	1,752	483	85	*	219	333	59	195	53	293	29,977,176
Swisher.......	2,039	0	89	145	128	597	94	197	27	479	25,493,252
Tarrant.......	410,924	4,238	25,978	98,745	20,222	117,823	22,733	77,984	8,026	33,294	7,757,424,888
Taylor........	48,802	4,109	2,893	5,479	2,712	13,373	2,618	10,740	2,376	4,288	776,211,052
Terrell........	371	*	*	*	*	85	*	157	16	113	5,177,020
Terry.........	4,241	890	176	228	348	927	173	414	51	854	71,045,212
Throckmorton..	517	101	19	*	24	88	26	57	14	154	6,826,352
Titus.........	8,328	287	452	1,385	1,736	1,642	326	1,009	109	1,300	148,800,536
Tom Green	36,092	1,020	2,440	5,880	3,825	8,989	1,603	6,484	2,234	3,360	547,891,304
Travis........	263,758	617	18,908	32,582	7,444	60,997	17,794	54,807	46,811	22,909	4,639,132,452
Trinity........	1,643	43	34	247	79	430	130	331	30	319	20,417,092
Tyler.........	2,903	*	123	590	102	582	220	541	41	704	36,178,592
Upshur........	4,385	43	208	484	279	1,240	126	1,023	94	871	52,027,468
Upton.........	1,674	683	19	*	206	209	37	70	22	428	34,690,392
Uvalde........	6,329	288	303	734	262	1,778	315	881	210	1,253	78,400,624
Val Verde.....	7,530	0	402	755	328	2,208	421	1,072	223	2,043	86,260,996
Van Zandt	5,146	456	328	798	184	1,148	212	924	65	930	66,059,100
Victoria.......	27,836	2,972	2,294	2,941	1,380	7,763	1,457	4,929	265	3,689	479,251,400
Walker........	15,887	77	588	1,638	333	3,596	569	1,696	5,889	1,396	240,611,896
Waller	5,571	178	209	147	92	1,308	166	466	1,964	846	72,585,644
Ward	5,104	1,665	161	110	557	1,018	135	345	216	897	101,186,940
Washington ...	9,465	191	735	1,874	212	2,326	572	1,363	980	1,118	143,787,588
Webb.........	29,888	1,590	1,038	1,766	2,905	9,113	1,455	4,736	665	6,149	371,820,792
Wharton	10,913	1,352	454	975	517	3,109	461	1,441	114	1,894	164,150,380
Wheeler.......	1,860	337	96	54	103	391	83	227	27	468	28,070,280
Wichita	47,532	3,880	1,931	8,905	2,384	11,757	2,324	8,813	2,182	5,205	784,641,788
Wilbarger	5,988	312	563	729	165	1,035	313	719	984	898	86,059,204
Willacy	3,289	33	113	*	156	636	95	737	68	928	35,390,876
Williamson.....	20,197	322	2,194	4,182	678	4,447	934	3,301	204	3,787	282,181,232
Wilson	2,340	60	153	110	37	739	111	328	77	669	27,402,144
Winkler	2,595	701	102	74	273	449	91	190	20	695	47,106,044
Wise	5,942	993	127	947	595	1,252	225	657	77	1,041	98,662,728
Wood.........	6,148	609	222	1,012	335	1,428	295	1,213	85	949	83,707,912
Yoakum.......	3,336	1,196	333	78	308	449	85	209	15	575	66,898,912
Young	7,427	1,785	257	1,314	306	1,511	353	809	56	978	122,205,816
Zapata	1,281	265	*	*	22	158	*	266	19	551	16,072,440
Zavala	2,632	35	48	*	*	369	52	1,082	55	674	26,168,296

*Included in Service and Other to avoid disclosing information about individual establishment.
†The figure for total wages, 1984, is an estimate obtained by multiplying by 4 the figure for the first quarter of 1984, as reported by the Texas Employment Commission.

EMPLOYMENT BY INDUSTRIES

This table shows number of employing establishments, employment and wages paid as reported by the Texas Employment Commission for 1984.

Industry Group—	Reporting Units	†Employment	*Total Wages, 1984
All Industries and Federal Agencies....	298,211	6,275,156	117,013,660,916
Industries with Texas UI Coverage only	296,163	6,100,044	113,057,540,552
Agriculture, Forestry, Fisheries	6,091	59,711	650,476,540
Agricultural production—crops	670	17,103	150,591,376
Agricultural prod. —livestock	833	11,808	158,399,384
Agricultural services	4,137	29,109	312,672,880
Forestry	31	795	16,057,224
Fishing, hunting and trapping	420	896	12,755,680
Mining	9,253	266,361	8,619,042,996
Metal mining	36	752	19,862,404
Bituminous coal and lignite mining ...	26	1,322	46,492,796
Oil and gas ext.....	8,941	256,867	8,390,781,120
Nonmetallic min., except fuels	250	7,420	161,906,676
Contract Construction ..	33,985	432,060	8,389,381,280

Industry Group—	Reporting Units	†Employment	*Total Wages, 1984
General building contractors	10,235	103,640	2,092,646,256
Heavy const. contractors	3,346	116,435	2,533,852,416
Special trade contractors	20,404	211,985	3,762,882,604
Manufacturing	17,884	979,618	21,769,683,200
Food and kindred products	1,090	91,658	1,736,465,160
Textile mill products	92	4,881	76,056,840
Apparel and other textile prods.	634	62,723	717,156,124
Lumber and wood products	1,385	41,985	652,801,744
Furniture and fixtures	440	17,960	263,905,268
Paper and allied products	227	23,680	568,224,880
Printing and publishing	3,297	71,600	1,311,477,936
Chemicals and allied products	654	75,895	2,578,028,056	;

Industry Group—	Reporting Units	†Employ- ment	*Total Wages, 1984
Petroleum and coal products	144	42,101	1,480,881,744
Rubber and misc. plastics prods.	672	33,571	654,144,088
Leather and leather products	159	8,135	97,486,668
Stone, clay, and glass products	953	48,371	961,015,380
Primary metal inds.	319	35,520	853,383,096
Fabricated metal products	2,218	81,484	1,642,970,188
Mach. (exc. elec.) . . .	3,245	129,285	3,113,675,072
Electric and electronic equip. . .	820	100,340	2,336,327,444
Transportation equipment	584	74,490	2,025,126,484
Instruments and related prods.	412	22,903	493,386,852
Miscellaneous mfg. industries	539	13,036	207,170,184
Transportation, Communication	10,263	342,665	8,353,370,536
Local, interurban transp.	385	8,279	124,695,908
Trucking and ware- housing	4,748	87,783	1,749,140,900
Water transportation	672	18,802	424,845,200
Transportation, air . .	608	38,135	1,136,100,828
Pipelines (exc. natural gas) . .	55	4,848	171,083,312
Transportation serv.	1,875	16,688	294,753,648
Communication.	1,079	89,572	2,230,783,100
Electric, gas and sanitary serv.	841	78,558	2,221,967,632
Wholesale and Retail Trade	90,476	1,589,184	23,160,469,728
Wholesale trade —durable goods . . .	18,440	269,622	6,648,858,168
Wholesale trade —nondurable	9,861	160,827	3,482,409,972
Building materials and garden supply .	3,753	53,785	779,908,772
Gen. mdse. stores . . .	656	148,331	1,644,868,620
Food stores	7,190	203,932	2,512,828,264
Automotive dealers and serv. stas.	11,363	132,109	2,309,893,204
Apparel and access. stores	5,325	79,317	776,455,956
Furniture and home furns. store . .	5,137	52,268	779,047,184

Industry Group—	Reporting Units	†Employ- ment	*Total Wages, 1984
Eating and drinking places. . . .	14,579	351,180	2,491,590,388
Miscellaneous retail. .	14,172	137,813	1,734,609,196
Finance, Insurance, and Real Estate	27,210	396,205	8,701,642,352
Banking	1,958	103,591	2,021,854,704
Credit agencies other than banks	2,412	53,716	1,147,440,344
Security, commodity brokers and services	797	13,097	791,768,384
Insurance carriers. . .	1,178	75,160	1,588,963,852
Ins. agents, brokers and services	6,233	36,575	758,388,796
Real estate	12,637	99,018	1,867,857,436
Combined real estate, insurance . .	162	579	12,085,384
Holding and other investment offices . .	1,833	14,469	513,283,452
Service Industries	94,764	1,149,673	18,898,710,016
Hotels, and other lodging places	2,097	77,642	727,989,100
Personal services . . .	8,775	77,425	799,876,680
Business services. . . .	16,696	270,462	4,407,395,036
Auto. repair, and garages	7,373	46,619	688,809,112
Miscellaneous repair services	4,044	21,580	364,942,812
Motion pictures	517	8,562	91,857,704
Amusement and recreation services . .	2,618	38,392	436,498,340
Health services	21,764	341,073	6,132,157,280
Legal services	7,078	37,582	1,156,711,628
Educational services . .	848	38,724	576,928,692
Social services.	2,952	54,883	467,467,356
Museums, botanical, zoological gardens	64	1,785	22,394,784
Membership Orgs. . . .	3,716	27,079	395,646,552
Private households . .	7,923	12,090	87,607,480
Misc. services	8,299	95,775	2,542,427,464
Federal Government . . .	2,048	175,112	3,956,120,364
State and Local Government	5,733	881,685	14,475,531,372
Nonclassified Establishments	504	2,882	39,232,536

*The figure for total wages, 1984, is an estimate obtained by multiplying by 4 the figure for the first quarter of 1984. †The March, 1984, figure for employment is used as being representative for the year.

TEXAS CIVILIAN LABOR FORCE

Employment in Texas continued to increase, reaching 6,548,600 in December, 1984, over the 6,323,100 in December, 1983. Average employment for the 1984 year was 6,436,200, an increase over the average for 1983.

The following table shows Texas Employment Commission estimates of the civilian labor force in Texas for December, 1983 and December, 1984, together with annual average employment in 1984.

Employment Status—	Dec. 1983	Dec. 1984	Annual Avg. 1984	Employment Status—	Dec. 1983	Dec. 1984	Annual Avg. 1984
*Total Wage & Salary Employment	6,323,100	6,548,600	6,436,200	Transportation Equipment	72,300	77,100	75,400
Manufacturing Total	977,000	1,005,900	996,500	Aircraft & Parts.	37,300	39,400	38,000
Durable Goods.	560,900	586,100	579,100	Inst. & Related Prods. . .	22,300	22,800	23,000
Lumber, Wood Prod. . .	41,500	41,400	42,500	Misc. Mfg. Ind.	12,800	12,900	12,800
Furniture and Fixtures	17,300	18,200	17,800	Nondurable Goods.	416,100	419,800	417,400
Stone, Clay and Glass Products.	47,400	48,400	48,800	Food, Kindred Prod. . . .	95,600	98,300	94,800
Primary Metal Ind.	34,900	36,200	36,100	Meat Products.	25,100	25,300	25,200
Fabricated Metal Products	81,200	83,300	82,400	Dairy Products	5,000	5,200	5,200
Fabricated Struct. Metal Products	43,300	43,400	43,200	Bakery Products	11,300	12,100	10,800
Machinery, Exc. Elec. . .	128,800	133,900	131,800	Malt Beverages	3,000	2,900	3,100
Oilfield Machinery. . .	38,200	40,700	39,200	Textile Mill Products . .	4,800	4,800	5,000
Electric and Electronic Equipment	102,400	111,900	108,500	Apparel and Other Textile Products	62,000	60,200	62,000
				Paper, Allied Prod.	23,200	24,000	23,800
				Printing, Publishing	70,300	72,400	71,600
				Newsprs, Misc. Publ.	35,500	36,000	35,700

Employment Status—	Dec. 1983	Dec. 1984	Annual Avg. 1984
Chemicals and Allied Products	76,800	77,100	76,700
Pet., Coal Products. . . .	43,000	41,500	41,900
Petroleum Refining. .	39,800	38,300	38,700
Leather and Products . .	8,100	7,700	8,000
Other Nondurable Goods	32,300	33,800	33,600
Nonmanufacturing.	5,346,100	5,542,700	5,439,700
Mining	264,600	273,300	269,900
Oil & Gas Extraction . . .	255,100	263,700	260,300
Metal & Bit. Coal Mining & Nonmet. Mnrls., exc. Fuel. . .	9,500	9,600	9,600
Contract Construction . .	421,600	427,100	430,400
Transportation and Public Utilities. . . .	371,900	373,000	371,300
Interstate Railroads . . .	24,800	24,800	25,100
Other Transportation . .	172,900	180,300	177,700
Transportation, Air . .	35,900	37,800	37,700
Communications exc. U.S. Postal Service. . .	95,500	89,000	89,400
Electric, Gas and Sanitary Services. . . .	78,700	78,900	79,100
Electric Companies . .	43,900	44,400	44,300
Gas Companies	29,600	28,400	28,900
Wholesale & Retail Trade.	1,609,500	1,653,600	1,613,700
Wholesale Trade	428,800	427,900	430,300

Employment Status—	Dec. 1983	Dec. 1984	Annual Avg. 1984
Retail Trade	1,180,700	1,225,700	1,183,400
Finance, Insurance and Real Estate	404,900	421,100	414,900
Banking.	103,100	105,400	104,400
Ins. Carriers, Ins. Agts, Bkrs. & Services.	124,900	128,800	127,300
Other Finance	176,900	186,900	183,200
Services	1,210,400	1,279,300	1,257,500
Hotels & Lodge Places. .	75,700	78,800	78,000
Personal Services.	73,100	81,300	78,200
Business & Repair Services	330,100	361,000	350,100
Amusements, Inc. Motion Pictures.	43,700	52,100	50,600
Medical and Health Services	338,900	341,000	342,300
Educational Services . .	60,400	59,900	57,000
Other Services & Misc.	288,500	305,200	301,300
Government	1,063,200	1,115,300	1,082,000
Federal Government . .	174,400	180,400	176,800
State Government	241,500	264,700	250,100
Local Government	647,300	670,200	655,100

*Number of nonagricultural wage and salary jobs estimated to exist in Texas without reference to place of residence of workers. Estimates by Texas Employment Commission in cooperation with the Bureau of Labor Statistics, U. S. Department of Labor.

*GROSS AVERAGE HOURS AND EARNINGS, 1983 AND 1984

The following table shows average weekly hours and earnings for 1983 and 1984 and average hourly earnings for 1984. Comparable figures for previous years appear in earlier editions of the Texas Almanac.

Source: Texas Employment Commission in cooperation with the Bureau of Labor Statistics.

Industry—	Av. Weekly Earnings 1983	Av. Weekly Earnings 1984	Av. Weekly Hours 1983	Av. Weekly Hours 1984	Av. Hourly Earnings 1984
MANUFACTURING .	$363.19	$376.97	40.9	41.7	$9.04
Durable Goods	356.13	369.09	40.7	41.8	8.83
Lumber and Wood Products. . . .	249.55	258.33	39.8	39.5	6.54
Furniture and Fixtures.	230.50	223.67	39.2	38.3	5.84
Stone, Clay and Glass Products. . . .	353.90	356.83	43.8	43.2	8.26
Primary Metal Industries	404.42	412.84	38.7	41.4	9.96
Fabricated Metal Products	353.42	354.77	39.8	41.3	8.59
Machinery, except Electrical.	351.24	385.24	40.7	42.9	8.98
Oilfield Machinery	432.78	488.70	41.1	45.0	10.86
Electric and Electronic Equip...	361.42	397.74	40.7	42.0	9.47
Transportation Equipment	483.31	500.39	42.1	43.1	11.61
†Aircraft and Parts	. . .	†	. . .	. . .	. . .
Instruments, and Related Prod.	314.03	295.25	39.5	38.9	7.59
Miscellaneous Mfg. Industries . . .	293.87	279.39	41.1	40.2	6.95
Nondurable Goods .	373.27	386.88	41.2	41.6	9.30
Food and Kindred Products	323.17	338.17	42.3	43.3	7.81
Meat Products	288.74	287.98	42.4	43.7	6.59
Malt Beverages . . .	654.28	720.50	44.0	45.4	15.87
Textile Mill Products	$265.02	$277.06	42.2	41.6	$6.66

Industry—	Av. Weekly Earnings 1983	Av. Weekly Earnings 1984	Av. Weekly Hours 1983	Av. Weekly Hours 1984	Av. Hourly Earnings 1984
Apparel and Other Textile Products . .	182.57	188.05	37.8	38.3	4.91
Paper and Allied Products	413.27	427.15	44.2	43.9	9.73
Printing and Publishing	335.56	352.96	39.9	40.2	8.78
Chemicals and Allied Products . . .	567.33	603.08	41.9	42.5	14.19
Petroleum and Coal Products	612.70	604.58	43.3	43.0	14.06
Petroleum Refining.	671.77	626.24	44.4	43.1	14.53
Leather and Leather Products	196.74	204.24	38.5	37.0	5.52
Other Nondurable Goods	353.58	359.96	42.6	42.1	8.55
NONMANU- FACTURING					
Mining	470.93	477.56	45.9	46.5	10.27
Oil and Gas Extraction	475.18	481.38	46.0	46.6	10.33
Metal & Bit. Coal and Nonmet. Mn. . .	387.21	407.69	45.5	45.4	8.98
Comm., exc. U.S.P.O.	401.83	432.69	38.6	39.3	11.01
Elec., Gas and San. Svcs.	416.42	431.07	41.6	40.4	10.67
Whlsle. and Retail Trade	230.50	230.85	34.3	34.2	6.75
Wholesale Trade	354.71	361.70	39.9	40.1	9.02
Retail Trade	185.73	188.31	32.3	32.3	5.83
Banking	244.99	262.13	38.4	39.3	6.67
Gen Mdse. Stores . . .	166.95	166.29	30.3	30.4	5.47

*Figures cover production workers in manufacturing and mining industries only and nonsupervisory employees in other industry divisions. Earnings' averages include premium pay for overtime, holidays, and for lateshift work. †Publication suspended on direction of Bureau of Labor Statistics, Nov. 1983.

Texas Mineral Production

Texas has maintained its role as one of the leading mining states in the nation and as the top petroleum producing state in 1984.

Petroleum products were by far the largest money producers. The comptroller reported crude oil production of 874,079,000 barrels valued at $25,138,520,000. And 5,864,224,000 (5.9 trillion) cubic feet of natural gas brought $13,487,715,000.

Coal production in the state continued its rapid increase. Lignite is by far the most common coal produced, and it is used by Texas Utilities Co. for the production of steam-generated electricity at three plants in East Texas. Three other small bituminous coal operations supply fuel for cement operations near San Antonio and Dallas, but their production is negligible.

Cement was the top-valued construction material, according to the Bureau of Mines, generating $625.6 million in revenue from 11,210,000 short tons produced. Texas also retained its position as a leading **stone** producing state with 79,847,000 short tons produced valued at $266.2 million. **Sand and gravel** shipments of 55,400,000 short tons were valued at $227,600,000.

In addition, Texas was the leading state in the production of Frasch **sulphur**, shipping 2,772,000 metric tons. But the value was not reported to protect producers' proprietary data.

Total **nonfuel mineral production** for the state in 1984 was $1,717,716,000, according to a Bureau of Mines preliminary report.

Oil and Gas in Texas

The 1984 output of crude oil and condensate from wells in Texas, the nation's leading oil producing state, was 874,079,265 barrels, a decline from the 1983 production of 876,205,174 barrels. It was the 12th straight year of decline despite production at or near the maximum effective recovery rate in nearly all of the state's oil fields.

The year's production pushed the state's cumulative production since 1889 to 49.7 billion barrels of oil.

In 1984, 16 counties each produced more than 10 million barrels of crude oil, a decrease of two counties from 1983. The state's five top producing counties during 1984 were: Pecos, 51,318,068 barrels; Yoakum, 40,025,749 barrels; Gaines, 41,793,013 barrels; Ector, 43,934,035 barrels; and Andrews, 39,157,209 barrels.

Gregg County, the first Texas county to produce more than 2 billion barrels of oil in the history of recorded production, remains the all-time leader with a cumulative total through 1984 of 2,887,007,007 barrels. **Ector County,** through 1984, had produced a total of 2,485,875,766 barrels.

The fields with estimated recovery reserves of at least 100 million barrels of oil were the **Fairway Field** in Anderson and Henderson Counties, discovered in 1960, and the **Giddings Field** in Lee, Fayette and Burleson Counties, discovered in 1971.

dition near Sabine Pass.

Melrose, in Nacogdoches County, was the site in 1866 of the first drilled well to produce oil in Texas. The driller was **Lyne T. Barret** (whose name has been spelled several ways by historians). Barret used an auger, fastened to a pipe and rotated by a cogwheel driven by a steam engine—a basic principle of rotary drilling that has been used since, although with much improvement.

In 1867 **Amory (Emory) Starr** and **Peyton F. Edwards** brought in a well at **Oil Springs,** in the same area. Other wells followed and Nacogdoches County was the site of Texas' first commercial oil field, pipeline and effort to refine crude. Several thousand barrels of oil were produced there during these years.

Other oil was found in crudely dug wells in Texas, principally in Bexar County, in the latter years of the 19th century. But it was not until June 9, 1894, that Texas had a major discovery. This occurred in the drilling of a water well for the City of **Corsicana**. Oil caused that well to be abandoned, but a company formed in 1895 drilled several producing wells. The first well-equipped refinery in Texas was built and this plant usually is called the state's first refinery, despite the earlier effort at Nacogdoches. Discovery of the **Powell Field** near Corsicana followed in 1900.

Texas Oil History

Indians found oil seeping from the soils of Texas long before the first Europeans arrived. They told explorers that the fluid had medicinal values. The first record of Europeans using crude oil, however, was the calking of boats in 1543 by survivors of the DeSoto expe-

Spindletop, 1901

Jan. 10, 1901, is the most famous date in Texas petroleum history. This is the date that the great gusher erupted in the oil well being drilled at Spindletop, near Beaumont, by a mining engineer, **Capt. A. F. Lucas.** Thousands of barrels of oil flowed before the well could

NONFUEL MINERAL PRODUCTION AND VALUE, 1982, 1983 and 1984

Source: U.S. Bureau of Mines

(Production measured by mine shipments, sales or marketable production, including consumption by producer.)

Mineral—	1982 Production	1982 Value (add 000)	1983 Production	1983 Value (add 000)	*1984 Production	*1984 Value (add 000)
Cement:						
Masonry, thousand short tons	236	$16,440	276	$19,704	310	$22,360
Portland, thousand short tons	9,732	545,679	9,760	534,298	10,900	603,200
Clays, thousand short tons	4,193	26,497	3,955	22,575	3,971	27,952
Gemstones	†	200	†	225	†	175
Gypsum, thousand short tons	1,954	16,681	2,049	16,357	2,273	18,556
Helium, grade A, million cu. ft.	458	15,572	524	18,340	‡	‡
Lime, thousand short tons	1,125	62,277	1,067	60,193	1,210	66,130
Salt, thousand short tons	7,421	82,805	8,028	65,670	8,142	64,896
Sand and gravel:						
Construction, thousand short tons	45,527	154,515	§58,500	§208,000	53,200	195,200
Industrial, thousand short tons	2,623	45,007	1,788	29,637	2,200	32,400
Stone:						
Crushed, thousand short tons	68,000	205,000	76,453	239,642	79,800	255,000
Dimension, thousand short tons	50	5,822	50	11,071	47	11,226
Sulphur (Frasch), thousand metric tons	2,360	‡	2,468	‡	2,772	‡
Talc and pyrophyllite, thousand short tons	205	3,024	250	3,933	288	5,000
‡Undistributed	...	374,913	...	338,912	...	415,631
Total Texas Values	...	$1,554,432	...	$1,568,557	...	$1,717,716

*Preliminary. †Not available.

‡Includes fluorspar, helium (1984), iron ore, magnesium chloride, magnesium compounds, silver (1983), sodium sulphate and sulphur (Frasch).

§Estimated.

be capped. This was the first salt dome oil discovery. It created a sensation throughout the world, and encouraged exploration and drilling in Texas that has continued since.

Texas oil production increased from 836,039 barrels in 1900 to 4,393,658 in 1901; and in 1902 Spindletop alone produced 17,421,000 barrels, or 94 per cent of the state's production. Prices dropped to 3c a barrel, an all-time low.

A water-well drilling outfit on the **W. T. Waggoner Ranch** in Wichita County hit oil, bringing in the **Electra Field** in 1911. In 1917, came the discovery of the **Ranger Field** in Eastland County. The **Burkburnett Field** in Wichita County was discovered in 1919.

Oil discoveries brought a short era of swindling with oil stock promotion and selling on a nationwide scale. It ended after a series of trials in a federal court.

The **Mexia Field** in Limestone County was discovered in 1920, and the second **Powell Field** in Navarro County in 1924.

Another great area opened in 1921 with discovery of oil in the **Panhandle**, a field which developed rapidly with sensational oil and gas discoveries in Hutchinson and contiguous counties and the booming of Borger.

The **Luling Field** was opened in 1922 and 1925 saw the comeback of **Spindletop** with a production larger than that of the original field. Other fields opened in this period included **Big Lake**, 1923; **Wortham**, 1924-25 and **Yates**, 1926.

In 1925 **Howard County** was opened for production. **Winkler** in West Texas and **Raccoon Bend**, Austin County, were opened in 1927. **Sugar Land** was the most important Texas oil development in 1928. The **Darst Creek Field** was opened in 1929. In the same year, new records were set for the industry at **Van**, Van Zandt County. **Pettus** was another contribution of 1929 in Bee County.

East Texas Field

The East Texas field, biggest of them all, was dis-

This Port Arthur refinery makes a backdrop to the residential area in foreground. David Woo Photo

covered near Turnertown and Joinerville, Rusk County, by veteran wildcatter **C. M. (Dad) Joiner**, in October 1930. The success of this well—drilled on land condemned many times by geologists of the major companies—was followed by the biggest leasing campaign in history. The field soon was extended to Kilgore, Longview and northward.

The East Texas field brought a large overproduction and a rapid sinking of the price. Private attempts were made to prorate production, but without much success. On Aug. 17, 1931, **Gov. Ross S. Sterling** ordered the National Guard into the field, which he placed under martial law. This drastic action was taken after the

RECEIPTS BY TEXAS FROM TIDELANDS
(Source: General Land Office)

The following table shows receipts from tidelands by the Texas General Land Office to Aug. 31, 1984. It does not include revenue from bays and other submerged area owned by Texas.

From	To	Total	Bonus	Rental	Royalty
6- 9-1922	9-28-1945	$924,363.81	$814,055.70	$61,973.75	$48,334.36
9-29-1945	6-23-1947	296,400.30	272,700.00	7,680.00	16,020.30
6-24-1947	6- 5-1950	7,695,552.22	7,231,755.48	377,355.00	86,441.74
6- 6-1950	5-22-1953	55,095.04	—	9,176.00	45,919.04
5-23-1953	6-30-1958	54,264,553.11	49,788,639.03	3,852,726.98	623,187.10
7- 1-1958	8-31-1959	771,064.75	—	143,857.00	627,207.75
9- 1-1959	8-31-1960	983,335.32	257,900.00	98,226.00	627,209.32
9- 1-1960	8-31-1961	3,890,800.15	3,228,639.51	68,578.00	593,582.64
9- 1-1961	8-31-1962	1,121,925.09	297,129.88	127,105.00	697,690.21
9- 1-1962	8-31-1963	3,575,888.64	2,617,057.14	177,174.91	781,656.59
9- 1-1963	8-31-1964	3,656,236.75	2,435,244.36	525,315.00	695,677.39
9- 1-1964	8-31-1965	54,654,576.96	53,114,943.63	755,050.12	784,583.21
9- 1-1965	8-31-1966	22,148,825.44	18,223,357.84	3,163,475.00	761,992.60
9- 1-1966	8-31-1967	8,469,680.86	3,641,414.96	3,711,092.65	1,117,173.25
9- 1-1967	8-31-1968	6,305,851.00	1,251,852.50	2,683,732.50	2,370,266.00
9- 1-1968	8-31-1969	6,372,268.28	1,838,118.33	1,491,592.50	3,042,557.45
9- 1-1969	8-31-1970	10,311,030.48	5,994,666.32	618,362.50	3,698,001.66
9- 1-1970	8-31-1971	9,969,629.17	4,326,120.11	726,294.15	4,917,214.91
9- 1-1971	8-31-1972	7,558,327.21	1,360,212.64	963,367.60	5,234,746.97
9- 1-1972	8-31-1973	9,267,975.68	3,701,737.30	920,121.60	4,646,116.78
9- 1-1973	8-31-1974	41,717,670.04	32,981,619.28	1,065,516.60	7,670,534.16
9- 1-1974	8-31-1975	27,321,536.62	5,319,762.85	2,935,295.60	19,066,478.17
9- 1-1975	8-31-1976	38,747,074.09	6,197,853.00	3,222,535.84	29,326,685.25
9- 1-1976	8-31-1977	84,196,228.27	41,343,114.81	2,404,988.80	40,448,124.66
9- 1-1977	8-31-1978	118,266,812.05	49,807,750.45	4,775,509.92	63,683,551.68
9- 1-1978	8-31-1979	100,410,268.68	34,578,340.94	7,318,748.40	58,513,179.34
9- 1-1979	8-31-1980	200,263,803.03	34,733,270.02	10,293,153.80	155,237,379.21
9- 1-1980	8-31-1981	219,126,876.54	37,467,196.97	13,100,484.25	168,559,195.32
9- 1-1981	8-31-1982	250,824,581.69	27,529,516.33	14,214,478.97	209,080,586.39
9- 1-1982	8-31-1983	165,197,734.83	10,180,696.40	12,007,476.70	143,009,561.73
9- 1-1983	8-31-1984	152,696,065.99	32,839,122.19	8,539,128.57	111,317,815.23
Total		$1,611,062,032.09	$473,373,787.97	$100,359,573.71	$1,037,328,670.41
Recapitulation:					
Inside three-mile line		294,891,678.70	120,074,836.37	28,444,993.28	146,371,849.05
Between three-mile line and three marine-league line		1,313,344,987.81	350,646,867.21	71,741,299.24	890,956,821.36
Outside three marine-league line		2,825,365.58	2,652,084.39	173,281.19	0
Totals		$1,611,062,032.09	$473,373,787.97	$100,359,573.71	$1,037,328,670.41

Texas Railroad Commission had been enjoined from enforcing production restrictions. After the complete shutdown, the Texas Legislature enacted legal prora-tion, the system of regulation still utilized.

The most significant subsequent oil discoveries in Texas were those in West Texas, following a discovery well in Scurry County, Nov. 21, 1948, and later major developments in that region. Many of the leading Texas counties in minerals value are in that section.

MARKETED NATURAL GAS PRODUCTION, TEXAS AND U.S.

This table shows for selected years Texas and United States production of natural gas produced for marketing and Texas percentage of total.

Source: U.S. Department of Energy
(Millions of Cubic Feet)

Year—	Texas	U.S.	% Texas
1935	642,366	1,916,595	33.5
1940	1,063,538	2,660,222	40.0
1945	1,711,401	3,918,686	43.7
1950	3,126,402	6,282,060	49.8
1955	4,730,798	9,405,351	50.3
1960	5,892,704	12,771,038	46.1
1965	6,636,555	16,039,753	41.4
1970	8,357,716	21,920,642	38.1
1971	8,550,705	22,493,012	38.0
1972	8,657,840	22,531,698	38.4
1973	8,513,850	22,647,549	37.6
1974	8,170,798	21,600,522	37.8
1975	7,485,764	20,108,611	37.2
1976	7,191,859	19,952,438	36.0
1977	7,051,027	20,025,463	35.2
1978	6,548,184	19,974,033	32.8
1979	6,620,542	19,723,104	33.6
1980	7,252,879	20,378,787	35.5
1981	7,050,207	20,177,701	34.9
1982	6,468,817	18,519,675	34.9
1983	5,938,561	16,822,144	35.3
1984	6,130,232	18,064,068	33.9

Major Fields

Texas fields with estimated ultimate recovery of 100 million barrels of oil or more are in the following list, which gives the name of the field, county and discovery date. Data furnished by **Oil and Gas Journal.**

Panhandle, Carson-Collingsworth-Gray-Hutchinson-Moore-Potter-Wheeler, 1910; **Thompson** (all fields), Fort Bend, 1921; **Howard-Glasscock,** Howard, 1925; **Iatan East,** Howard, 1926; **Yates,** Pecos, 1926; **Waddell,** Crane, 1927; **Van,** Van Zandt, 1929; **Ward Estes North,** Ward, 1929; **Cowden North,** Ector, 1930; **East Texas,** Gregg-Rusk, 1931; **Sand Hills,** Crane, 1930; **Conroe,** Montgomery, 1931; **Tom O'Connor,** Refugio, 1931; **Cowden South,**

MINERAL VALUES, 1882-1984

Texas total mineral production values for selected years are shown below. (See note at end of table.)

Year—	Value	Year—	Value
1882-86	$4,935,363	1970	6,401,998,000
1890	1,992,806	1971	6,807,955,000
1895	2,856,537	1972	7,211,551,000
1900	5,316,222	1973	8,442,492,000
1905	13,753,346	1974	13,711,144,000
1910	18,383,451	1975	15,529,941,000
1915	29,220,951	1976	18,143,204,000
1920	371,250,979	1977	19,503,244,000
1930	382,676,504	1978	19,644,289,000
1935	528,069,238	*1979	1,407,847,000
1940	714,905,731	*1980	1,735,005,000
1945	1,361,436,346	*1981	1,743,796,000
1950	2,673,949,925	*1982	1,554,432,000
1955	3,993,310,000	*1983	1,568,557,000
1960	4,116,663,000	*1984	1,717,716,000
1965	4,717,036,000		

*Beginning in 1979, only non-petroleum minerals are reported by U.S. Bureau of Mines. (See Table on Nonfuel Mineral Production and Value.)

TEXAS NATURAL GAS RESERVES

Source: Committee on Natural Gas Reserves, American Gas Association and Department of Energy
(Millions of Cubic Feet)

Year—	Proved Reserves	Percent Annual Change	Year—	Proved Reserves	Percent Annual Change	Year—	Proved Reserves	Percent Annual Change
1945	78,306,676	—	1960	119,489,393	−0.8	1975	71,036,854	−9.6
1946	86,363,459	10.3	1961	119,838,711	0.3	1976	64,651,410	−9.0
1947	90,025,566	4.2	1962	119,503,798	−0.3	1977	62,157,836	−3.8
1948	95,708,553	6.3	1963	117,809,376	−1.4	1978	54,600,235	−12.2
1949	99,170,403	3.6	1964	118,855,055	0.9	*1979	53,021,000	−.02
1950	102,404,077	3.3	1965	120,616,760	1.5	*1980	50,287,000	−.05
1951	105,653,229	3.2	1966	123,609,326	2.5	*1981	50,469,000	†
1952	105,732,763	0.1	1967	125,415,064	1.5	1982	49,757,000	†
1953	106,529,626	0.8	1968	119,001,106	−5.1	1983	50,052,000	†
1954	105,129,062	−1.3	1969	112,392,622	−5.6			
1955	108,287,548	3.0	1970	106,352,993	−5.4	*These Department of Energy figures differ from preceding American Petroleum Institute figures.		
1956	112,728,750	4.1	1971	101,472,108	−4.6			
1957	113,084,518	0.3	1972	95,042,043	−6.3			
1958	115,045,743	1.7	1973	84,936,502	−10.6	†Percentage less than one percent.		
1959	120,475,783	4.7	1974	78,540,717	−7.5			

RANK OF REFINING STATES

(Source: The Oil & Gas Journal Survey, March 18, 1985)

Rank	State and Number of Plants	*Crude Oil Capacity	Percent of U.S.	Rank	State and Number of Plants	*Crude Oil Capacity	Percent of U.S.	Rank	State and Number of Plants	*Crude Oil Capacity	Percent of U.S.
1.	Texas (33)	4,145,900	27.39	10.	Oklahoma (5)	374,000	2.47	19.	Alaska (4)	138,930	.91
2.	California (30)	2,265,098	14.96	11.	Mississippi (5)	362,400	2.39	20.	Michigan (4)	119,400	.79
3.	Louisiana (16)	2,188,793	14.46	12.	Kansas (7)	338,000	2.23		All Other States (26)	710,220	4.69
4.	Illinois (8)	946,000	6.24	13.	Kentucky (2)	218,900	1.44				
5.	Pennsylvania (8)	658,700	4.35	14.	Minnesota (2)	204,143	1.34		Total U.S. (161). 15,136,262 †99.91		
6.	Ohio (5)	515,700	3.40	15.	Wyoming (6)	162,778	1.07				
7.	New Jersey (5)	503,000	3.32	16.	Utah (6)	154,950	1.02		*Barrels per calendar day, Jan. 1, 1985.		
8.	Indiana (5)	431,300	2.84	17.	Montana (6)	147,500	.97				
9.	Washington (7)	410,550	2.71	18.	Delaware (1)	140,000	.92		†Does not equal 100% due to rounding.		

TEXAS OIL AND GAS PRODUCTION, AMOUNT AND VALUE

Source: U.S. Bureau of Mines

Year—	Crude Oil Production (thousand bbls.)	Value (Add 000)	Average Price Per Barrel	Natural Gas Production (million cu. ft.)	Value (Add 000)	Average Price (Cents Per MCF)	Year—	Crude Oil Production (thousand bbls.)	Value (Add 000)	Average Price Per Barrel	Natural Gas Production (million cu. ft.)	Value (Add 000)	Average Price (Cents Per MCF)
1915	24,943	$13,027	.52	13,324	$2,594	19.5	1972	1,301,685	4,536,077	3.48	8,657,840	1,419,886	16.4
1920	96,868	313,781	3.24	37,063	7,042	19.0	1973	1,294,671	5,157,623	3.98	8,513,850	1,735,221	20.4
1925	144,648	262,270	1.81	134,872	7,040	5.2	1974	1,262,126	8,773,003	6.95	8,170,798	2,541,118	31.1
1930	290,457	288,410	.99	517,880	18,488	3.6	1975	1,221,929	9,336,570	7.64	7,485,764	3,885,112	51.9
1935	392,666	367,820	.94	642,366	13,233	2.1	1976	1,189,523	10,217,702	8.59	7,191,859	5,163,755	71.8
1940	493,209	494,000	1.00	1,063,538	19,356	1.8	1977	1,137,880	9,986,002	8.78	7,051,027	6,367,077	90.3
1945	754,710	914,410	1.21	1,711,401	44,839	2.6	1978	1,074,050	9,980,333	9.29	6,548,184	6,515,443	99.5
1950	829,874	2,147,160	2.59	3,126,402	146,941	4.7	*1979	1,018,094	12,715,994	12.49	7,174,623	8,509,103	118.6
1955	1,053,297	2,989,330	2.84	4,730,798	378,464	8.0	1980	977,436	21,259,233	21.75	7,115,889	10,673,834	150.0
1960	927,479	2,748,735	2.96	5,892,704	665,876	11.3	1981	945,132	32,692,116	34.59	7,050,207	12,598,712	178.7
1965	1,000,749	2,962,119	2.96	6,636,555	858,396	12.9	1982	923,868	29,074,126	31.47	6,497,678	13,567,151	208.8
1970	1,249,697	4,104,005	3.28	8,357,716	1,203,511	14.4	1983	876,205	22,947,814	26.19	5,643,183	14,672,275	260.0
1971	1,222,926	4,261,775	3.48	8,550,705	1,376,664	16.1	1984	874,079	25,138,520	28.76	5,864,224	13,487,715	230.0

*Beginning in 1979 data are from Department of Energy and Texas State Comptroller of Public Accounts.
Note: The production figures of natural gas differ from those found in table entitled "Ultimate Disposition of Texas Natural Gas," which are provided by the Railroad Commission. DOE figures do nto include gas that is vented or flared or used for pressure maintenance and repressuring, but do include non-hydrocarbon gases.

PETROLEUM INDUSTRY PAYMENTS TO PERMANENT SCHOOL AND UNIVERSITY FUNDS OF TEXAS

Source: Records of State Comptroller

This table shows payments by the petroleum industry into the **Permanent School Fund** and **Permanent University Fund** of Texas. Oil was discovered on university lands in 1923, with the first royalty payments in the 1924 fiscal year. Public school lands were not developed until later, with first payments in fiscal 1932. For related information, see discussion of education.

Fiscal Year Ending 8-31	PERMANENT SCHOOL FUND Lease Rentals & Bonuses	Oil and Gas Royalties	Total	PERMANENT UNIVERSITY FUND Lease Rentals & Bonuses	Oil and Gas Royalties	Total
1924	—	—	—	—	$17,908	$17,908
1930	—	—	—	$1,624,795	2,266,441	3,891,236
1932	$99,556	$354,608	$454,164	23,160	1,115,096	1,138,256
1935	1,326,019	749,086	2,075,105	106,529	776,049	882,578
1940	2,186,029	1,379,206	3,565,235	335,433	678,517	1,013,950
1945	725,842	3,511,318	4,237,160	2,534,732	1,733,930	4,268,662
1950	3,331,486	6,908,900	10,240,386	1,577,060	7,108,814	8,685,874
1955	16,512,435	13,869,157	30,381,592	12,585,425	11,339,497	23,904,922
1960	10,000,203	15,933,295	25,933,498	2,967,946	15,556,247	18,524,193
1965	67,219,624	18,816,010	86,035,634	12,513,346	16,129,182	28,642,528
1970	14,914,526	27,883,617	42,798,143	2,273,950	16,410,890	18,684,840
1971	13,427,333	29,222,953	42,650,286	2,114,172	18,388,045	20,502,217
1972	9,460,851	28,686,754	38,147,605	5,397,221	19,516,591	24,913,812
1973	18,232,579	28,490,081	46,722,660	7,411,074	18,968,522	26,379,596
1974	56,436,191	42,270,655	98,706,846	12,988,408	31,541,165	44,529,573
1975	26,732,550	69,657,438	96,389,988	8,756,314	58,512,449	67,268,763
1976	25,382,860	105,063,124	130,445,984	15,978,211	69,696,569	85,674,780
1977	66,392,028	151,345,761	217,737,789	14,650,500	74,537,623	89,188,123
1978	82,887,813	184,619,219	267,507,032	19,762,747	77,096,802	96,859,549
1979	62,262,606	182,341,161	244,603,767	12,975,781	75,829,944	88,805,725
1980	80,812,873	309,627,046	390,439,919	*2,893,436	114,768,125	117,661,561
1981	112,580,314	378,635,044	491,215,358	101,175,998	153,207,366	254,383,364
1982	89,771,283	397,871,820	487,643,103	22,751,176	174,225,437	196,976,613
1983	40,689,971	331,377,547	372,067,518	2,728,158	154,209,292	156,937,450
1984	66,464,307	311,181,290	377,645,597	9,566,819	145,065,566	154,632,385
Total	$1,141,741,260	$2,936,937,992	$4,078,679,252	$456,623,315	$1,521,189,146	$1,977,812,461

*No bonus lease sale in 1980.

ROTARY RIGS ACTUALLY MAKING HOLE

Source: Hughes Tool Company

Year—	Average	Year—	Average	Year—	Average
1973	376	1978	855.0	1982	989.6
1974	508	1979	770.2	1983	798
1975	637	1980	987.7	1984	850.1
1977	799	1981	1,317.0		

TEXAS NATURAL GAS PRODUCTION AND INITIAL DISPOSITION—1984

Source: Railroad Commission of Texas
(All Gas Volumes in Thousands Cubic Feet)

GAS WELL GAS
Number of Wells, December—46,553

	Volume	Percent of Total
Total Production	4,339,759,400	100.00
Disposition:		
Fuel System & Lease Use	51,374,495	1.18
Gas Lift	9,456,070	.21
Pressure Maintenance and Repressuring	856,583	.01
Transmission Lines	1,355,736,496	31.20
Processing Plants	2,889,935,304	66.59
Carbon Black Plants	1,420,699	.03
Vented or Flared	988,937	.02
Extraction Loss (lease)	29,990,816	.06

CASINGHEAD GAS
Number of Wells, December—207,451

	Volume	Percent of Total
Total Production	1,867,868,870	100.00
Disposition:		
Fuel System and Lease Use	54,363,326	2.91
Pressure Maintenance and Repressuring	7,476,190	.40
Transmission Lines	144,026,992	7.71
Processing Plants	1,642,078,615	87.91
Carbon Black Plants	565,516	.03
Vented or Flared	19,358,231	1.04

ULTIMATE DISPOSITION OF TEXAS NATURAL GAS—1984

Source: Railroad Commission of Texas
(All Gas Volumes in Thousands Cubic Feet)

	Volume	Percent of Total
Total Production	5,813,452,557	100.00
Disposition:		
Plant Fuel & Lease Use	456,756,393	7.85
Pressure Maintenance and Repressuring	271,851,675	4.67
Transmission Lines	4,276,750,706	73.56
Cycled	104,806,080	1.80
Carbon Black	2,456,809	.04
Underground Storage	92,977,688	1.60
Vented or Flared	32,432,385	.56
Plant Meter Difference	22,432,594	.39
Acid Gas H2S & CO2	121,093,764	2.08
*Extraction Loss	431,637,463	7.42

*Shrinkage in volume due to removal of liquified hydrocarbons.

TEXAS LIQUID HYDROCARBON RESERVES 1945-1983

Source: Committee on Petroleum Reserves, American Petroleum Institute
(Thousands of Barrels)

Year—	Crude Oil	Natural Gas Liquids	Total Liquid Hydro-Carbons	Percent Annual Increase
1945	11,470,294	N.A.	N.A.	...
1950	13,581,642	2,496,039	16,077,681	2.7
1955	14,933,502	3,045,361	17,978,863	0.4
1960	14,758,492	3,596,174	18,354,666	0.4
1965	14,303,058	4,059,557	18,362,615	0.6
1970	13,195,476	3,330,159	16,525,635	−1.1
1971	13,023,529	3,100,617	16,124,146	−2.4
1972	12,144,057	2,891,583	15,035,640	−6.7
1973	11,756,613	2,830,143	14,586,756	−3.0
1974	11,001,506	2,796,988	13,798,494	−5.4
1975	10,080,035	2,660,668	12,740,703	−7.7
1976	9,226,250	2,527,837	11,754,087	−7.7
1977	8,467,436	2,398,787	10,866,223	−7.5
1978	7,689,991	2,268,284	9,958,275	−8.4
*1979	8,284,000	2,482,000	10,766,000	8.1
1980	8,206,000	2,453,000	10,659,000	†
1981	8,093,000	2,646,000	10,739,000	†
1982	7,616,000	2,771,000	10,387,000	†
1983	7,539,000	3,038,000	10,577,000	†

*Beginning in 1979 Department of Energy figures are used. This causes percent of annual increase for 1979 not to compare with 1978.
†Less than one percent.
N.A. Not Available.

EXPLORATORY WELLS DRILLED IN TEXAS

Source: The Oil and Gas Journal, AAPG, and API.

	Total	Oil	Gas	Dry	% Dry
1946	1,591	247	34	1,310	82.3
1950	3,443	575	113	2,755	80.0
1955	5,124	883	132	4,109	80.2
1960	3,166	254	64	2,848	89.9
1965	3,012	297	189	2,526	83.9
1970	2,098	256	179	1,663	79.3
1971	1,818	186	172	1,460	80.3
1972	1,973	179	183	1,611	81.7
1973	2,325	207	410	1,708	73.5
1974	2,907	278	562	2,067	71.1
1975	3,203	311	571	2,321	72.5
1976	3,269	386	692	2,191	67.0
1977	3,549	447	672	2,430	68.5
1978	3,884	396	780	2,708	69.7
1979	4,011	414	819	2,778	69.3
1980	4,274	552	971	2,751	64.4
1981	5,102	692	923	3,487	68.3
1982	5,455	689	985	3,781	69.3
1983	4,822	683	824	3,315	68.7
1984	4,883	662	733	3,488	71.4

U.S. ESTIMATED PROVED RESERVES OF NATURAL GAS

Source: Department of Energy, Energy Information Administration, "U.S. Crude Oil, Natural Gas, and Natural Gas Liquids Reserves, 1983 Annual Report."
(Billions of Cubic Feet)

Rank, State	Reserves as of Dec. 31, 1983	% of U.S.	Rank, State	Reserves as of Dec. 31, 1983	% of U.S.	Rank, State	Reserves as of Dec. 31, 1983	% of U.S.
1. Texas	50,052	24.99	9. Colorado	3,148	1.57	18. Alabama Onshore	785	.3
2. *Louisiana	42,561	21.25	10. Utah	2,333	1.16	19. North Dakota	600	.3
3. Alaska	34,283	17.12	11. West Virginia	2,194	1.09	20. Kentucky	554	.2
4. Oklahoma	16,211	8.09	12. Arkansas	2,069	1.03	All Other States	597	.3
5. New Mexico	11,676	5.83	13. Ohio	2,030	1.01	Total U.S.	200,247	†99.9
6. Wyoming	10,227	5.13	14. Pennsylvania	1,882	.94			
7. Kansas	9,553	4.77	15. Mississippi	1,596	.80	*Includes Alabama Offshore.		
8. California	5,781	2.88	16. Michigan	1,219	.61	†Does not equal 100% due to rounding.		
			17. Montana	896	.45			

Ector, 1932; **Greta** (all fields), Refugio, 1933; **Tomball**, Harris, 1933; **Means** (all fields), Andrews-Gaines, 1934; **Anahuac**, Chambers, 1935; **Goldsmith** (all fields), Ector, 1935; **Hastings**, Brazoria, 1935; **Magnet Withers** (all fields), Wharton, 1936; **Seminole** (all fields), Gaines, 1936; **Webster**, Harris, 1936; **Jordan**, Crane-Ector, 1937; **Slaughter**, Cochran, 1937; **Wasson** (all fields), Gaines, 1937; **Dune**, Crane, 1938; **West Ranch**, Jackson, 1938; **Key-**

stone, Winkler, 1939; **Diamond M**, Scurry, 1940; **Hawkins**, Wood, 1940; **Fullerton** (all fields), Andrews, 1941; **McEl-roy**, Crane, 1941; **Oyster Bayou**, Chambers, 1941; **Welch**, Dawson, 1941; **Quitman** (all fields), Wood, 1942; **Anton-Irish**, Hale, 1944; **TXL** (all fields), Ector, 1944; **Block 31**, Crane, 1945; **Levelland**, Cochran-Hockley, 1945; **Midland Farms** (all fields), Andrews; 1945; **Andector**, Ector, 1946; **Dollarhide**, Andrews, 1947; **Kelly-Snyder**, Scurry, 1948; **Cogdell Area**, Scurry, 1949; **Prentice**, Yoakum, 1950; **Salt Creek**, Kent, 1950; **Spraberry Trend**, Glasscock-Midland, 1952; **Lake Pasture**, Refugio, 1953; **Neches**, Anderson-Cherokee, 1953; **Fairway**, Anderson-Henderson, 1960; **Giddings**, Lee-Fayette-Burleson, 1971.

HISTORY OF TEXAS DRILLING
Source: Oil and Gas Journal and American Petroleum Institute.

	Wells Completed	Oil Wells	Gas Wells	Stratigraphic & Core Tests	Service Wells	Dry Holes	Percent Dry
1889-1900*	97	71	2			24	24.7
1901-1910*	692	462	9			221	32.0
1911-1920*	2,451	1,682	66			703	28.7
1921-1930*	6,352	3,745	306			2,301	36.2
1931-1940*	9,915	7,404	288	...	...	2,224	22.9
1941-1950*	9,147	5,767	457	...	44	2,901	32.5
1951-1960*	18,439	10,838	814	...	155	6,632	36.0
1961-1970*	11,595	5,798	1,115	367	393	4,121	35.8
1971	7,728	3,880	810	8	449	2,581	33.4
1972	8,088	3,963	943	8	414	2,760	34.1
1973	8,494	3,686	1,475	34	362	2,937	34.6
1974	9,808	4,402	1,843	19	260	3,284	33.5
1975	12,483	6,074	2,135	36	361	3,877	31.1
1976	12,740	5,779	2,443	45	285	4,188	32.9
1977	14,759	6,533	3,064	37	443	4,682	31.7
1978	15,037	6,086	3,292	26	415	5,218	34.7
1979	16,149	6,765	3,609	35	515	5,225	32.4
1980	19,253	9,668	3,684	10	546	5,345	27.8
1981	23,940	13,052	3,807	2	368	6,711	28.0
1982	26,849	13,851	4,345	4	692	7,957	29.6
1983	24,616	13,102	3,317	...	652	7,545	30.6
1984	26,134	14,591	3,242	17	678	7,606	29.1
Total	872,559	469,232	68,581	1,383	12,140	261,223	29.8

*Annual Averages.

ESTIMATED PROVED RESERVES OF LIQUID HYDROCARBONS IN THE UNITED STATES
Source: "U.S. Crude Oil, Natural Gas, and Natural Gas Liquids Reserves, 1983, Annual Report," published by the Department of Energy, Energy Information Administration.
(Million Bbls. of 42 U.S. Gallons)
(Dec. 31, 1983 — Million Bbls.)

Rank, State	Crude Oil	Natural Gas Liquids	Total Liquid Hydro-carbons	Per-cent of U.S.
1. Texas	7,539,000	3,038,000	10,577,000	29.68
2. Alaska.	7,307,000	8,000	7,315,000	20.51
3. California	5,348,000	151,000	5,499,000	15.43
4. Louisiana	2,707,000	1,332,000	4,039,000	11.33
5. Wyoming.	957,000	*789,000	1,746,000	4.99
6. Oklahoma	931,000	829,000	1,760,000	4.94
7. New Mexico. . .	576,000	551,000	1,127,000	3.16
8. Kansas	344,000	443,000	787,000	2.21
9. North Dakota. .	258,000	69,000	327,000	.92
10. Montana	234,000	19,000	253,000	.71
11. Michigan.	209,000	105,000	314,000	.88
12. Mississippi . . .	205,000	19,000	224,000	.63
13. Utah	187,000	*	187,000	.52
14. Colorado	186,000	183,000	369,000	.10
15. Illinois	135,000	0	135,000	.38
16. Ohio	130,000	0	130,000	.36
17. Arkansas.	120,000	11,000	131,000	.37
18. Florida	78,000	11,000	89,000	.25
19. Alabama	51,000	216,000	267,000	.75
20. West Virginia. .	49,000	91,000	140,000	.39
All Other States. . .	184,000	36,000	220,000	.62
Total U.S.	27,735,000	7,901,000	35,636,000	†99.13

*Utah and Wyoming share the same figure.
†Does not equal 100% due to rounding.

Mineral Fuels Today

Today, the basic mineral fuels, **crude petroleum** and **natural gas**, with their associated products permeate the economy of Texas more than any other activity.

Mineral fuels accounted for most of the state's total mineral value, and associated petrochemical activities have aggregate plant investments and product values measured in billions.

Subsequent discussions and tables tell the history of the discovery of major oil fields and the volume and value of crude oil production in Texas, as well as some data on natural gas. Other information on gas will be found in the business section.

EMPLOYMENT, 1983 TEXAS PETROLEUM INDUSTRY
Source: Texas Employment Commission

Employer—	Average Employment	Total Wages
Crude Petroleum and Natural Gas	114,642	$4,174,226,280
Natural Gas Liquids	3,206	104,858,948
Oil and Gas Field Services	124,645	3,073,687,836
Petroleum Refining	35,755	1,267,403,544
Manufacturers of Asphalt & Tile	1,638	38,417,476
Misc. Production of Petroleum .	882	139,554,720
Pipeline Workers, Exc. Natural Gas	4,335	171,325,844
Gas Production & Distribution. .	25,734	977,263,292
Service Station	35,381	369,417,396
Total	350,553	$10,487,481,180

NATURAL GAS LIQUIDS PRODUCTION, TEXAS AND U.S.
Source: U.S. Department of Energy
(Thousands of Gallons)

Year—	Texas	U.S.	% Texas
1935	516,748	1,651,986	31.3
1940	932,040	2,339,400	39.8
*1945	2,188,305	4,704,173	46.5
1950	3,933,300	7,642,362	51.5
1955	6,697,477	12,918,818	51.8
1960	8,358,497	17,728,581	47.1
1965	11,564,588	23,032,449	50.2
1970	14,381,094	30,739,926	46.8
1971	14,558,628	31,417,386	46.3
1972	15,056,580	32,280,990	46.6
1973	14,942,592	32,392,458	46.1
1974	14,260,008	30,789,864	46.3
1975	13,601,616	29,622,222	45.9
1976	13,445,628	29,650,908	45.3
1977	13,633,830	30,201,822	45.1
1978	12,773,040	29,467,704	43.4
†1979	. . .	. . .	. . .
1980	10,645,278	24,183,054	44.02
1981	11,014,038	24,340,890	45.25
1982	10,010,658	23,821,646	42.02
1983	11,343,990	23,938,656	47.39

*1945 and subsequent years include Natural Gaso-line and LP-Gases. Prior years include Natural Gaso-line only.

†Department of Energy changed publications at end of 1978; data for 1979 not available.

TEXAS OIL PRODUCTION BY COUNTIES

Source: Compiled by Texas Mid-Continent Oil & Gas Association

This table shows the year of oil or gas discovery in each county, total annual and daily crude oil production in 1984 and total crude oil production from date of discovery to Jan. 1, 1985. Counties omitted have not produced oil.

County	Year of Discovery	1984 Crude Production Total Barrels	Barrels Per Day	Total Prdn. to Jan. 1, 1985 (bbls.)
Anderson	1929	3,216,895	8,813	269,744,420
Andrews	1930	39,157,209	107,280	2,131,696,845
Angelina	1936	30,083	82	339,897
Aransas	1936	872,518	2,390	73,750,854
Archer	1911	4,293,036	11,762	448,271,027
Atascosa	1917	2,253,233	6,173	128,634,805
Austin	1915	808,006	2,214	104,791,474
Bastrop	1913	194,467	533	10,198,281
Baylor	1924	459,172	1,258	53,136,538
Bee	1930	1,118,123	3,063	93,546,160
Bell	1980	5	—	446
Bexar	1889	1,183,772	3,243	27,557,034
Borden	1949	7,338,400	20,105	301,394,905
Bowie	1944	54,297	149	1,673,856
Brazoria	1902	7,839,070	21,477	1,190,987,992
Brazos	1942	6,882,864	18,857	33,648,225
Brewster	1969	—	—	56
Briscoe	1982	—	—	3,554
Brooks	1936	1,228,924	3,367	148,095,253
Brown	1917	564,825	1,547	47,406,660
Burleson	1938	9,079,907	24,876	74,075,838
Caldwell	1922	2,845,757	7,797	254,828,755
Calhoun	1935	1,612,580	4,418	84,168,811
Callahan	1923	1,540,735	4,221	72,179,094
Cameron	1944	4,376	12	412,316
Camp	1940	515,983	1,414	19,931,461
Carson	1921	1,591,762	4,361	167,225,543
Cass	1935	1,230,308	3,371	97,832,142
Chambers	1916	7,075,248	19,384	848,582,881
Cherokee	1926	1,527,696	4,185	57,928,799
Childress	1961	9,081	25	1,278,107
Clay	1902	2,803,993	7,682	175,679,087
Cochran	1936	10,588,966	29,011	376,533,023
Coke	1942	2,292,916	6,282	198,091,290
Coleman	1902	1,628,312	4,461	83,303,533
Collin	1963	—	—	53,000
Collingsworth	1936	11,812	32	1,103,582
Colorado	1932	852,418	2,335	26,480,739
Comanche	1918	117,294	321	5,481,344
Concho	1940	300,023	822	5,828,360
Cooke	1926	4,662,128	12,773	341,341,545
Coryell	1964	—	—	1,100
Cottle	1955	110,045	301	2,261,641
Crane	1926	25,836,436	70,785	1,426,343,074
Crockett	1925	4,856,759	13,306	284,370,404
Crosby	1955	1,223,899	3,353	8,822,633
Culberson	1953	642,932	1,761	18,821,214
Dallam	1954	(Gas Only)		(Gas Only)
Dawson	1937	7,783,369	21,324	250,840,367
Delta	1984	28,096	77	28,096
Denton	1937	46,949	129	3,229,518
DeWitt	1930	659,631	1,807	56,881,181
Dickens	1953	43,325	119	4,000,717
Dimmit	1943	3,410,378	9,344	70,760,161
Donley	1967	(Gas Only)		(Gas Only)
Duval	1905	3,879,842	10,630	538,272,599
Eastland	1917	2,754,983	7,548	138,146,478
Ector	1926	43,934,035	120,367	2,485,875,766
Edwards	1946	16,165	44	366,918
Ellis	1953	13,244	36	730,819
Erath	1917	15,490	42	1,851,333
Falls	1937	29,925	82	511,447
Fannin	1980	—	—	13,281
Fayette	1943	6,400,424	17,535	41,028,539
Fisher	1928	3,429,382	9,396	214,021,281
Floyd	1952	2,635	7	90,282
Foard	1929	415,746	1,139	18,557,859
Fort Bend	1919	6,420,568	17,591	615,380,026
Franklin	1936	1,771,620	4,854	158,138,539
Freestone	1916	573,602	1,572	36,784,113
Frio	1934	2,492,517	6,829	86,174,484
Gaines	1936	41,793,013	114,501	1,417,584,567
Galveston	1922	3,849,705	10,547	413,274,896
Garza	1926	7,411,783	20,306	206,710,819
Glasscock	1925	6,220,211	17,042	156,336,516
Goliad	1930	933,998	2,559	67,861,371
Gonzales	1902	2,587,457	7,089	19,989,531
Gray	1925	4,156,420	11,387	622,519,860
Grayson	1930	4,080,103	11,178	213,205,917
Gregg	1931	36,695,427	100,535	2,887,007,007
Grimes	1952	952,744	2,610	3,472,924
Guadalupe	1922	1,667,955	4,570	180,219,047
Hale	1946	3,216,886	8,813	132,706,045
Hamilton	1938	4,122	11	113,823
Hansford	1937	542,393	1,486	31,957,540
Hardeman	1944	2,724,574	7,465	28,338,118
Hardin	1893	4,122,684	11,295	390,197,929
Harris	1905	8,783,454	24,064	1,280,845,508
Harrison	1928	1,368,851	3,750	64,965,528
Hartley	1937	16,623	46	777,940
Haskell	1929	1,465,795	4,016	99,258,891
Hays	1956	—	—	79
Hemphill	1955	1,224,054	3,354	22,758,062
Henderson	1934	3,140,780	8,605	140,290,640
Hidalgo	1934	2,168,738	5,942	47,594,239
Hill	1949	7,609	21	28,298
Hockley	1937	37,809,081	103,587	1,083,561,171
Hood	1958	3,939	11	53,910
Hopkins	1936	1,174,926	3,219	76,827,011
Houston	1934	1,040,666	2,851	40,089,604
Howard	1925	13,872,404	38,007	623,929,346
Hunt	1942	10,169	28	1,835,471
Hutchinson	1923	2,820,890	7,728	497,396,163
Irion	1928	3,550,886	9,728	49,490,829
Jack	1923	3,581,057	9,811	172,156,275
Jackson	1934	6,022,115	16,499	625,959,951
Jasper	1928	712,307	1,952	15,822,351
Jeff Davis	1980	—	—	20,866
Jefferson	1901	4,262,223	11,677	474,570,308
Jim Hogg	1922	805,150	2,206	100,734,065
Jim Wells	1933	1,192,549	3,267	451,007,854
Johnson	1962	—	—	194,000
Jones	1926	2,830,745	7,755	196,422,664
Karnes	1930	783,666	2,147	96,210,774
Kaufman	1948	254,837	698	21,126,894
Kenedy	1947	750,930	2,057	27,440,054
Kent	1946	9,737,998	26,679	383,424,209
Kerr	1982	10,041	28	34,798
Kimble	1939	2,062	6	66,339
King	1943	3,981,888	10,909	73,419,362
Kinney	1960	—	—	402
Kleberg	1926	2,902,322	7,952	314,156,044
Knox	1946	1,552,498	4,253	48,818,451
Lamb	1946	786,786	2,156	24,235,850
La Salle	1940	628,215	1,721	12,844,352
Lavaca	1941	1,193,513	3,270	15,616,178
Lee	1939	7,471,965	20,471	57,746,891
Leon	1936	505,953	1,386	17,135,746
Liberty	1905	3,713,691	10,174	476,886,109
Limestone	1920	279,163	765	114,253,380
Lipscomb	1956	3,000,370	8,220	39,269,577
Live Oak	1931	2,984,832	8,178	58,453,378
Llano	1978	—	—	647
Loving	1925	1,678,036	4,597	78,952,264
Lubbock	1941	2,621,208	7,181	26,614,336
Lynn	1950	567,348	1,554	11,632,520
McCulloch	1938	5,042	14	132,881
McLennan	1902	9,288	25	283,543
McMullen	1919	3,780,131	10,357	49,910,342
Madison	1946	2,293,424	6,283	16,343,827
Marion	1910	426,594	1,169	49,006,893
Martin	1945	8,949,054	24,518	178,230,194
Matagorda	1904	2,502,089	6,855	249,917,584
Maverick	1929	1,481,481	4,059	29,252,939
Medina	1901	291,998	800	7,793,704
Menard	1941	157,683	432	4,729,892
Midland	1945	9,088,316	24,899	399,855,892
Milam	1921	375,192	1,028	9,376,151
Mills	1982	—	—	28,122
Mitchell	1920	7,003,907	19,189	142,285,192
Montague	1924	2,676,481	7,333	252,923,57
Montgomery	1931	7,481,843	20,498	718,317,96
Moore	1936	1,113,487	3,051	19,375,61
Motley	1957	146,557	402	8,155,06
Nacogdoches	1866	225,396	618	2,045,49
Navarro	1895	1,040,093	2,850	207,697,35
Newton	1937	1,099,431	3,012	37,380,19
Nolan	1939	3,380,974	9,263	154,719,68
Nueces	1930	3,541,230	9,702	522,683,60
Ochiltree	1951	3,856,345	10,565	127,020,63
Oldham	1957	1,102,273	3,020	8,546,51

County—	Year of Discovery	1984 Crude Production Total Barrels	1984 Crude Production Barrels Per Day	Total Prdn. to Jan. 1, 1985 (bbls.)
Orange	1913	2,096,329	5,743	117,538,696
Palo Pinto	1902	346,959	951	15,345,433
Panola	1917	1,485,419	4,070	55,658,066
Parker	1942	107,804	295	2,207,484
Parmer	1963	—	—	144,000
Pecos	1926	51,318,068	140,597	1,270,572,950
Polk	1930	998,445	2,735	88,942,663
Potter	1925	228,354	626	4,635,295
Presidio	1980	—	—	1,873
Rains	1955	430	1	148,161
Reagan	1923	9,414,553	25,793	374,932,924
Red River	1951	49,679	136	886,672
Reeves	1939	2,050,238	5,617	55,160,738
Refugio	1928	21,935,955	60,099	1,161,174,956
Roberts	1945	850,892	2,331	36,423,232
Robertson	1944	104,797	287	1,074,322
Runnels	1927	2,628,514	7,201	125,216,686
Rusk	1930	14,093,077	38,611	1,705,099,157
Sabine	1981	134,573	369	239,968
San Augustine	1947	162	.4	17,857
San Jacinto	1940	222,933	611	21,074,422
San Patricio	1930	3,207,548	8,788	454,481,648
San Saba	1982	4,776	13	18,847
Schleicher	1937	1,245,655	3,413	72,178,901
Scurry	1923	27,866,108	76,346	1,713,894,929
Shackelford	1910	2,571,223	7,044	153,426,136
Shelby	1917	59,421	163	897,297
Sherman	1938	147,112	403	1,670,065
Smith	1931	4,788,289	13,119	214,558,758
Somervell	1978	—	—	115
Starr	1929	1,884,796	5,164	253,800,589
Stephens	1916	6,422,289	17,595	246,873,233
Sterling	1947	3,061,470	8,388	50,610,785
Stonewall	1938	3,961,178	10,853	200,735,511
Sutton	1948	190,156	521	5,406,604
Swisher	1981	—	—	6
Tarrant	1969	(Gas Only)	—	(Gas Only)
Taylor	1929	2,173,696	5,955	115,304,521
Terrell	1952	118,872	326	2,931,116
Terry	1940	12,393,206	33,954	305,471,801

County—	Year of Discovery	1984 Crude Production Total Barrels	1984 Crude Production Barrels Per Day	Total Prdn. to Jan. 1, 1985 (bbls.)
Throckmorton	1924	2,167,079	5,937	98,925,000
Titus	1936	2,045,911	5,605	190,462,347
Tom Green	1940	2,158,604	5,914	68,648,551
Travis	1934	5,215	14	691,056
Trinity	1946	3,547	10	66,954
Tyler	1937	533,155	831	31,527,729
Upshur	1931	1,048,644	2,873	273,321,962
Upton	1925	11,461,633	31,402	612,031,318
Uvalde	1950	125	.3	1,807
Val Verde	1935	1,755	5	112,221
Van Zandt	1929	3,310,487	9,070	501,530,731
Victoria	1931	2,322,878	6,364	226,915,229
Walker	1934	12,459	34	336,263
Waller	1934	174,191	477	18,094,667
Ward	1928	9,740,607	26,687	618,364,902
Washington	1915	779,675	2,136	16,562,621
Webb	1921	2,117,224	5,801	109,571,198
Wharton	1925	3,609,729	9,890	277,215,561
Wheeler	1921	917,573	2,514	82,292,776
Wichita	1910	4,839,075	13,258	759,877,284
Wilbarger	1915	1,903,884	5,216	243,174,969
Willacy	1936	1,533,679	4,202	94,404,526
Williamson	1915	13,217	36	9,300,517
Wilson	1941	1,677,485	4,596	26,516,596
Winkler	1926	8,047,328	22,047	968,001,909
Wise	1942	2,191,009	6,003	77,946,292
Wood	1941	16,910,670	46,331	1,013,058,237
Yoakum	1936	40,025,749	109,660	1,454,039,667
Young	1917	4,395,766	12,043	257,859,042
Zapata	1919	377,213	1,033	40,352,906
Zavala	1937	987,415	2,705	16,606,182
TOTAL		**874,079,265**	**2,394,738**	**49,272,783,457**

*Since 1970, production figures have been compiled from records of the Railroad Commission of Texas. In prior years, U.S. Bureau of Mines, and State Comptroller reports were the basis of these compilations. The figures in the final column are cumulative of all previously published figures. The change in sources, due to different techniques, may create some discrepancies in year-to-year comparisons among counties.

Nonpetroleum Minerals

The nonpetroleum minerals that occur in Texas constitute a long list. Some are currently mined; some may have a potential for future development; some are minor occurrences only. Although overshadowed by the petroleum, natural gas and natural gas liquids that are produced in the state, many of the nonpetroleum minerals are, nonetheless, important to the economy.

In 1984, they were valued at approximately $2 billion. Texas is annually among the nation's three leading states in value of nonpetroleum mineral production.

Locations of the resource areas of many nonpetroleum minerals are shown on a "Mineral Resources of Texas" map issued by the Bureau of Economic Geology of the University of Texas at Austin. Also available for purchase from the bureau are an abridged, published directory and a computer-generated, detailed listing of Texas nonpetroleum mineral producers.

The Bureau of Economic Geology, which functions as the state geological survey of Texas, revised the following information about nonpetroleum minerals for this edition of the Texas Almanac. Publications of the bureau, on file in many libraries, contain more detailed information. A catalog of bureau publications also is available free on request from the bureau (University Station, Box X, Austin, Tx. 78712-7508; telephone 512 471-1534).

Texas' nonpetroleum minerals are as follows:

ALUMINUM — No aluminum ores are mined in Texas, but four Texas plants process aluminum materials in one or more ways. A San Patricio County plant produces aluminum oxide (alumina) from imported raw ore (bauxite), and plants in Calhoun, Milam and Anderson Counties are each involved in some way with the production of aluminum.

ASBESTOS — Small occurrences of amphibole-type asbestos have been found in the state. In West Texas, richterite, a white, long-fibered amphibole, is associated with some of the talc deposits northwest of Allamoore in Hudspeth County. Another type, tremolite, has been found in the Llano Uplift of Central Texas where it is associated with serpentinite in eastern Gillespie and western Blanco County. No asbestos is mined in Texas.

ASPHALT (Native) — Asphalt-bearing Cretaceous limestones crop out in Burnet, Kinney, Pecos, Reeves, Uvalde and other counties. The most significant deposit is in southwestern Uvalde County where asphalt occurs naturally in the pore spaces of the Anacacho Limestone. The material is quarried and used extensively as road-paving material. Asphalt-bearing sandstones occur in Anderson, Angelina, Cooke, Jasper, Maverick, Montague, Nacogdoches, Uvalde and Zavala Counties.

BARITE — Deposits of a heavy, nonmetallic mineral, barite (barium sulphate), have been found in many localities, including Baylor, Brown, Brewster, Culberson, Gillespie, Howard, Hudspeth, Jeff Davis, Kinney, Llano, Live Oak, Taylor, Val Verde and Webb Counties. During the 1960s, there was small, intermittent production in the **Seven Heart Gap** area of the **Apache Mountains** in Culberson County, where barite was mined from open pits. Most of the deposits are known to be relatively small, but the Webb County deposit is being evaluated. Grinding plants, which prepare barite mined outside of Texas for use chiefly as a weighting agent in well-drilling muds and as a filler, are located in Brownsville, Corpus Christi, El Paso, Galena Park, Galveston, Houston, Kingsville, Knippa and Pecos, Texas.

BASALT (TRAP ROCK) — Masses of basalt — a hard, dark-colored, fine-grained igneous rock — crop out in Kinney, Travis, Uvalde and several other counties along the Balcones Fault Zone, and also in the Trans-Pecos area of West Texas. Basalt is quarried near Knippa in Uvalde County for use chiefly as road-building material and other aggregate and in the production of mineral (rock) wool.

BENTONITE (see **Clay**).

BRINE (see also **Salt**, **Sodium Sulphate**) — Many wells in Texas produce brine by solution mining of subsurface salt deposits. The annual production of brine has been estimated at over 10 billion gallons, most of which is produced in Andrews, Crane, Ector, Loving, Midland, Pecos, Reeves, Ward and other West Texas counties. These wells in the Permian basin dissolve salt from the Salado Formation, an enormous salt deposit that extends in the subsurface from north of Big Bend northward to Kansas, has an east-west width of 150 to 200 miles, and may have several hundred feet of net salt thickness. The majority of the brine is used in the petroleum industry, but it is also used in water softening, the chemical industry and for other uses.

Three Gulf Coast counties, Fort Bend, Duval and Jefferson, have brine stations that produce from salt domes. Approximately 90 percent of the 10 million tons of salt produced in Texas each year are from brining operations.

BUILDING STONE (DIMENSION STONE) — **Granite** and **limestone** currently are quarried for use as dimension stone. The granite quarries are located in Burnet, Gillespie, Llano and Mason Counties; the limestone quarries are in

Shackelford and Williamson Counties. Past production of limestone for use as dimension stone has been reported in Burnet, Gillespie, Jones, Tarrant, Travis and several other counties. There has also been production of **sandstone** in various counties for use as dimension stone.

CEMENT MATERIALS — Texas is the nation's leading producer and consumer of **portland cement**, which is prepared at 18 plants in Bexar, Comal, Dallas, Ector, Ellis, El Paso, Harris, Hays, McLennan, Nolan, Nueces, Potter and Tarrant Counties. Many of the plants utilize Cretaceous limestones and shales or clays as raw materials for the cement. Such materials occur in the Blacklands, Grand Prairie, Edwards Plateau and Trans-Pecos areas. On the Texas High Plains, a cement plant near Amarillo uses impure **caliche** as the chief raw material. **Iron oxide**, also a constituent of cement, is available from the iron ore deposits of East Texas and from smelter slag. **Gypsum**, added to the cement as a retarder, is found chiefly in North Central Texas, Central Texas and the Trans-Pecos area.

CHROMIUM — Chromite-bearing rock has been found in several small deposits around the margin of the Coal Creek serpentinite mass in northeastern Gillespie County and northwestern Blanco County. Exploration has not revealed significant deposits. Chromium is processed from out-of-state ores in Cameron and El Paso Counties.

CLAYS — Texas has an abundance and variety of ceramic and nonceramic clays and is one of the country's leading producers of clay products.

Almost any kind of clay, ranging from common clay used to make ordinary brick and tile to special clays suitable for manufacture of specialty whitewares, can be used for ceramic purposes. Fire clay suitable for use as refractories occurs chiefly in East and North Central Texas; ball clay, a high-quality plastic ceramic clay, is found locally in East Texas.

Ceramic clay suitable for quality structural clay products such as structural building brick, paving brick and drain tile is especially abundant in East and North Central Texas. Common clay suitable for use in the manufacture of cement and ordinary brick is found in most counties of the state. Many of the Texas clays will expand or bloat upon rapid firing and are suitable for the manufacture of lightweight aggregate, which is used mainly in concrete blocks and highway surfacing.

Nonceramic clays are utilized without firing. They are used primarily as bleaching and adsorbent clays, fillers, coaters, additives, bonding clays, drilling muds, catalysts and potentially as sources of alumina. Most of the nonceramic clays in Texas are **bentonites** and **fuller's earth**. These occur extensively in the Coastal Plain and locally in the High Plains and Big Bend areas. **Kaolin clays** in parts of East Texas are potential sources of such nonceramic products as paper coaters and fillers, rubber fillers and drilling agents. Relatively high in alumina, these clays also are a potential source of metallic aluminum.

COAL (see also **Lignite**) — **Bituminous coal**, which occurs in North Central, South and West Texas, was a significant energy source in Texas prior to the large-scale development of oil and gas. During the period from 1895 through 1943, Texas mines produced more than 25 million tons of coal. The mines were inactive for many years, but the renewed interest in coal as a major energy source prompted a revaluation of Texas' coal deposits. In the late 1970s, bituminous coal production resumed in the state on a limited scale when mines were opened in Coleman, Erath and Webb Counties.

Much of the state's bituminous coal occurs in North Central Texas. Deposits are found there in Pennsylvanian rocks within a large area that includes Coleman, Eastland, Erath, Jack, McCulloch, Montague, Palo Pinto, Parker, Throckmorton, Wise, Young and other counties. Before the general availability of oil and gas, underground coal mines near Thurber, Bridgeport, Newcastle, Strawn and other points annually produced significant coal tonnages. Relatively large amounts of coal remain in the North Central Texas area. The coal seams there are generally no more than 30 inches thick and are commonly covered by well consolidated overburden. Ash and sulphur content are high. In 1979, two bituminous coal mines began operations in North Central Texas — one in southern Coleman County and one in northwestern Erath County. Coal from these mines is used as a fuel by the cement industry.

In South Texas, bituminous coal occurs in the Eagle Pass district of Maverick County, and bituminous **cannel coal** is present in the Santo Tomas district of Webb County. The Eagle Pass area was a leading coal-producing district in Texas during the late 1800s and early 1900s. The bituminous coal in that area, which occurs in the Upper Cretaceous Olmos Formation, has a high ash content and a moderate moisture and sulphur content. Maverick County coal beds range from four to seven feet thick, it is reported.

The cannel coals of western Webb County occur near the Rio Grande in middle Eocene strata. They were mined for more than 50 years and used primarily as a boiler fuel.

Mining ceased from 1939 until 1978, when a surface mine was opened 30 miles northwest of Laredo to produce cannel coal for use as fuel in the cement industry and for export. An additional mine has since been opened in that county. Tests show that the coals of the Webb County Santo Tomas district have a high hydrogen content and yield significant amounts of gas and oil when distilled. They also have a high sulphur content. A potential use might be as a source of various petrochemical products.

Coal deposits in the Trans-Pecos country of West Texas include those in the Cretaceous rocks of the Terlingua area of Brewster County, the Eagle Spring area of Hudspeth County and the San Carlos area of Presidio County. The coal deposits in these areas are believed to have relatively little potential for development in the near term.

COPPER — Copper minerals have been found in the Trans-Pecos area of West Texas, in the Llano Uplift area of Central Texas and in redbed deposits of North Texas. No copper has been mined in Texas during recent years, and the total copper produced in the state has been relatively small. Past attempts to mine the North Texas and Llano Uplift copper deposits resulted in small shipments, but practically all the copper production in the state has been from the Van Horn-Allamoore district of Culberson and Hudspeth Counties in the Trans-Pecos area. Chief output was from the Hazel copper-silver mine of Culberson County, which yielded over 1 million pounds of copper during 1891-1947. Copper ores and concentrates from outside of Texas are processed at smelter's in El Paso and Amarillo.

CRUSHED STONE — Texas is among the leading states in the production of crushed stone. Most production consists of limestone; other kinds of crushed stone produced in the state include basalt (trap rock), dolomite, granite, marble, rhyolite and sandstone. Large tonnages of crushed stone are used as aggregate in concrete, as road material and in the manufacture of cement and lime. Some is used as riprap, terrazzo, roofing chips, filter material, fillers and for other purposes.

DIATOMITE (DIATOMACEOUS EARTH, KIESELGUHR) — Diatomite is a very lightweight siliceous material consisting of the remains of microscopic aquatic plants (diatoms). Its chief use is as a filler; for thermal insulation; as an abrasive, insecticide carrier and a lightweight aggregate, and for other purposes. The diatomite was deposited in shallow fresh-water lakes that were present in the High Plains during portions of the Pliocene and Pleistocene epochs. Deposits have been found in Armstrong, Crosby, Dickens, Ector, Hartley and Lamb Counties. No diatomite is mined in Texas.

DOLOMITE ROCK — Dolomite rock, which consists largely of the mineral dolomite (calcium-magnesium carbonate), commonly is associated with limestone in Texas. Areas in which dolomite rock occurs include Central Texas, the Callahan Divide and parts of the Edwards Plateau, High Plains and West Texas. Some of the principal deposits of dolomite rock are found in Bell, Brown, Burnet, Comanche, Edwards, El Paso, Gillespie, Lampasas, Mills, Nolan, Taylor and Williamson Counties. Dolomite rock can be used as crushed stone (although much of Texas dolomite is soft and not a good aggregate material), in the manufacture of lime and as a source of magnesium.

FELDSPAR — Large crystals and crystalline fragments of feldspar minerals occur in the Precambrian pegmatite rocks that crop out in the Llano Uplift area of Central Texas — including Blanco, Burnet, Gillespie, Llano and Mason Counties — and in the Van Horn area of Culberson and Hudspeth Counties in West Texas. Feldspar has been mined in Llano County for use as roofing granules and as a ceramic material but is not currently mined anywhere within the state.

FLUORSPAR — The mineral fluorite (calcium fluoride), which is known commercially as fluorspar, occurs both in Central and West Texas. In Central Texas, the deposits that have been found in Burnet, Gillespie and Mason Counties are not considered adequate to sustain mining operations. In West Texas, deposits have been found in Brewster, El Paso, Hudspeth, Jeff Davis and Presidio Counties. Fluorspar has been mined in the Christmas Mountains of Brewster County and processed in Marathon. Former West Texas mining activity in the Eagle Mountains district of Hudspeth County resulted in the production of approximately 15,000 short tons of fluorspar during the peak years of 1942-1950. No production has been reported in Hudspeth County since that period. Imported fluorspar is processed in Brownsville, Eagle Pass, El Paso and Marathon. Fluorspar is used in the steel, chemical, aluminum, magnesium, ceramics and glass industries and for various other purposes.

FULLER'S EARTH (see Clay).

GOLD — No major deposits of gold are known in Texas. Small amounts have been found in the Llano Uplift region of Central Texas and in West Texas; minor occurrences have been reported on the Edwards Plateau, the Gulf Coastal Plain and North Central Texas. Nearly all of the gold produced in the state came as a by-product of silver and lead mining at Presidio mine, near Shafter, in Presidio Coun-

ty. Additional small quantities were produced as a by-product of copper mining in Culberson County and from residual soils developed from gold-bearing quartz stringers in metamorphic rocks in Llano County. No gold mining has been reported in Texas since 1952. Total gold production in the state, 1889-1952, amounted to more than 8,419 troy ounces according to U.S. Bureau of Mines figures. Most of the production — at least 73 percent and probably more — came from the Presidio mine.

GRANITE — Granites in shades of red and gray and related intrusive igneous rocks occur in the Llano Uplift of Central Texas and in the Trans-Pecos country of West Texas. Deposits are found in Blanco, Brewster, Burnet, El Paso, Gillespie, Hudspeth, Llano, McCulloch, Mason, Presidio and other counties. Quarries in Burnet, Gillespie, Llano and Mason Counties produce Precambrian granite for a variety of uses as dimension stone and crushed stone.

GRAPHITE — Graphite, a soft, dark-gray mineral, is a form of very high-grade carbon. It occurs in Precambrian schist rocks of the Llano Uplift of Central Texas, notably in Burnet and Llano Counties. Crystalline-flake graphite ore formerly was mined from open pits in the Clear Creek area of western Burnet County and processed at a plant near the mine. The mill now occasionally grinds imported material. Uses of natural crystalline graphite are in refractories, steel production, pencil leads, lubricants, foundry facings and crucibles and for other purposes.

GRINDING PEBBLES (ABRASIVE STONES) — Flint pebbles, suitable for use in tube-mill grinding, are found in the Gulf Coastal Plain where they occur in gravel deposits along rivers and in upland areas. Grinding pebbles are produced from Frio River terrace deposits near the McMullen-Live Oak County line.

GYPSUM — Gypsum is widely distributed in Texas. Chief deposits are bedded gypsum in the area east of the High Plains, in the Trans-Pecos country and in Central Texas. It also occurs in salt dome caprocks of the Gulf Coast. The massive, granular variety known as rock gypsum is the kind most commonly used by industry. Other varieties include alabaster, satin spar and selenite.

Gypsum is one of the important industrial minerals in Texas. Bedded gypsum is produced from surface mines in Culberson, Fisher, Gillespie, Hardeman, Hudspeth, Kimble, Nolan and Stonewall Counties. Gypsum is mined at Gyp Hill salt dome in Brooks County, and was formerly mined at Hockley salt dome in Harris County. Most of the gypsum is calcined and used in the manufacture of gypsum wallboard, plaster, joint compounds and other construction products. Crude gypsum is used chiefly as a retarder in portland cement and as a soil conditioner.

HELIUM — Texas is a leading producer of this very light, nonflammable, chemically inert gas. Helium is extracted from natural gas of the Panhandle area at the U.S. Bureau of Mines Exell plant near Masterson in Moore County and at two privately owned plants in Hansford County. As a conservation measure, the Bureau of Mines injects the helium that is not sold into the Cliffside gas field near Amarillo for storage. Helium is used in cryogenics, welding, pressurizing and purging, leak detection, synthetic breathing mixtures and for other purposes.

IRON — Iron oxide (limonite, goethite and hematite) and iron carbonate (siderite) deposits occur widely in East Texas, notably in Cass, Cherokee, Marion and Morris Counties, and also in Anderson, Camp, Harrison, Henderson, Nacogdoches, Smith, Upshur and other counties. Magnetite (magnetic, black iron oxide) occurs in Central Texas, including a deposit at Iron Mountain in Llano County. Hematite occurs in the Trans-Pecos area and in the Llano Uplift of Central Texas. The extensive deposits of glauconite (a complex silicate containing iron) that occur in East Texas and the hematitic and goethitic Cambrian sandstone that crops out in the northwestern Llano Uplift region are potential sources of low-grade iron ore.

Limonite and other East Texas iron ores are mined from open pits in Cass, Cherokee and Henderson Counties for use in the preparation of portland cement, as a weighting agent in well-drilling fluids, as an animal feed supplement and for other purposes. East Texas iron ores also have been mined for use in the iron-steel industry.

KAOLIN (see Clay).

LEAD AND ZINC — The lead mineral galena (lead sulphide) commonly is associated with zinc and silver. It formerly was produced as a by-product of West Texas silver mining, chiefly from the Presidio mine at Shafter in Presidio County, although lesser amounts were obtained at several other mines and prospects. Deposits of galena also are known to occur in Blanco, Brewster, Burnet, Gillespie and Hudspeth Counties.

Zinc, primarily from the mineral sphalerite (zinc sulphide), was produced chiefly from the Bonanza and Alice Ray mines in the Quitman Mountains of Hudspeth County. In addition, small production was reported from several other areas, including the Chinati and Montezuma mines of Presidio County and the Buck Prospect in the Apache Mountains of Culberson County. Zinc mineralization also occurs in association with the lead deposits in Cambrian rocks of Central Texas.

LIGHTWEIGHT AGGREGATE (see Clay, Diatomite, Perlite, Vermiculite).

LIGNITE — Lignite, a low-rank coal, is found in belts of lower Eocene Tertiary strata that extend across the Texas Gulf Coastal Plain from the Rio Grande in South Texas to the Arkansas and Louisiana borders in East Texas. The largest resources and best grades (approximately 6,500 BTU/pound) of lignite occur in the Wilcox Group of strata north of the Colorado River in East and Central Texas.

The near-surface lignite resources, occurring at depths of less than 200 feet in seams of three feet or thicker, are estimated at 23 billion short tons. Recoverable reserves of strippable lignite — those that can be economically mined under current conditions of price and technology — are estimated to be 9 billion to 11 billion short tons.

Additional lignite resources of the Texas Gulf Coastal Plain, the deep-basin deposits, occur at depths greater than 200 feet below the surface. Approximately 35 billion tons occur at depths of 200 to 2,000 feet in seams of five feet or thicker. The deep-basin lignites are a potential energy resource that conceivably could be utilized by in situ (in place) recovery methods such as underground gasification.

As with bituminous coal, lignite production was significant prior to the general availability of oil and gas. Remnants of old underground mines are common throughout the area of lignite occurrence. Large reserves of strippable lignite have again attracted the attention of energy suppliers, and Texas is now the nation's 6th leading producer of coal, 98.9 percent of it lignite. Seven large strip mines are now producing lignite that is burned for mine-mouth electric power generation, and additional mines are planned. One of the currently operating mines is located in Milam County, where part of the electric power is used for alumina reduction. Other mines are in Atascosa, Freestone, Grimes, Harrison, Hopkins, Panola, Rusk and Titus Counties, where the power generated supplies municipal, domestic and industrial needs. Another Harrison County strip mine produces lignite that is used to make activated carbon.

LIME MATERIAL — Limestones, which are abundant in some areas of Texas, are heated to produce lime (calcium oxide) at a number of plants in the state. High magnesium limestones and **dolomite** are used to prepare lime at plants in Burnet and Comal Counties. The Texas lime plants are located in Bexar, Bosque, Brazoria, Burnet, Calhoun, Comal, Deaf Smith, Harris, Hill, Johnson, Nueces and Travis Counties. Lime is used in soil stabilization, water purification, paper and pulp manufacture, metallurgy, sugar refining, agriculture, construction and for many other purposes.

LIMESTONE (see also **Building Stone**) — Texas is one of the nation's leading producers of limestone, which is quarried in more than 60 counties. Limestone occurs in nearly all areas of the state with the exception of most of the Gulf Coastal Plain and High Plains. Although some of the limestone is quarried for use as **dimension stone**, most of the output is crushed for uses such as bulk building materials (crushed stone base, aggregates), chemical raw materials, fillers or extenders, lime and **portland cement** raw materials, **agricultural limestone** and **sulphur** removal from stack gases.

MAGNESITE — Small deposits of magnesite (natural magnesium carbonate) have been found in Precambrian rocks in Llano and Mason Counties of Central Texas. There formerly was small-scale mining of magnesite in the area — some of the material was used as **agricultural stone** and as **terrazzo chips**. Magnesite also can be calcined to form magnesia, which is used in metallurgical furnace refractories and other products.

MAGNESIUM — On the Texas Gulf Coast in Brazoria County, **magnesium chloride** is extracted from sea water at a plant in Freeport and used to produce magnesium metal. In West Texas, magnesium-bearing brines of the Permian Basin have been used as a raw material for magnesium metal production at a plant in Scurry County. During World War II, high-magnesium Ellenburger **dolomite** rock from Burnet County was used as magnesium ore at a plant near Austin.

MANGANESE — Deposits of manganese minerals, such as braunite, hollandite and pyrolusite, have been found in several areas, including Jeff Davis, Llano, Mason, Presidio and Val Verde Counties. Known deposits are not large. Small shipments have been made from Jeff Davis, Mason and Val Verde Counties, but no manganese mining has been reported in Texas since 1954.

MARBLE — Metamorphic and sedimentary marbles suitable for monument and building stone are found in the Llano Uplift and nearby areas of Central Texas and the Trans-Pecos areas of West Texas. Gray, white, black, greenish black, light green, brown and cream-colored marbles occur in Central Texas in Burnet, Gillespie, Llano and Mason Counties. West Texas metamorphic marbles include the bluish-white and the black marbles found southwest of Alpine in Brewster County and the white marble from **Marble Canyon** north of Van Horn in Culberson County. Marble can be used as **dimension stone** and **terrazzo** and roofing aggregate and for other purposes.

MERCURY (QUICKSILVER) — Mercury minerals, chiefly **cinnabar**, occur in the Terlingua district and nearby districts of southern Brewster and southeastern Presidio Counties. Mining began there about 1894, and from 1905 to 1935, Texas was one of the nation's leading producers of quicksilver. Following World War II, a sharp drop in demand and price, along with depletion of developed ore reserves, caused abandonment of all the Texas mercury mines.

With a rise in the price, sporadic mining took place between 1951-1960, but the mines again became dormant until 1965 when the price of mercury moved to a record high. Interest was renewed in the Texas mercury districts and resulted in the reopening of several mines and the discovery of new ore reserves. By April 1972, however, the price had declined and the mines have reported no production since 1973.

MICA — Large crystals of flexible, transparent mica minerals in igneous pegmatite rocks and mica flakes in metamorphic schist rocks are found in the Llano area of Central Texas and the Van Horn area of West Texas. Most Central Texas deposits do not meet specifications for sheet mica, and although several attempts have been made to produce West Texas sheet mica in Culberson and Hudspeth counties, sustained production has not been achieved. In the early 1980s, a mica quarry began operating in the **Van Horn Mountains** of Culberson and Hudspeth Counties to mine mica schist for use as an additive in rotary drilling fluids.

MOLYBDENUM — Small occurrences of molybdenite have been found in Burnet and Llano Counties, and wulfenite, another molybdenum mineral, has been noted in rocks in the Quitman Mountains of Hudspeth County. Molybdenum minerals also occur at Cave Peak north of Van Horn in Culberson County, in the **Altuda Mountain** area of northwestern Brewster County and in association with **uranium ores** of the Gulf Coastal Plain.

PEAT — This spongy organic substance forms in bogs from plant remains. It has been found in the Gulf Coastal Plain in several localities including Gonzales, Guadalupe, Lee, Milam, Polk and San Jacinto Counties. There has been intermittent, small-scale production of some of the peat for use as a soil conditioner.

PERLITE — Perlite, a glassy igneous rock, expands to a lightweight, porous mass when heated. It can be used as a lightweight aggregate, filter aid, horticultural aggregate and for other purposes. Perlite occurs in Presidio County, where it has been mined in the **Pinto Canyon** area north of the **Chinati Mountains**. No perlite is currently mined in Texas, but perlite mined outside of Texas is expanded at plants in Bexar, Dallas, El Paso, Guadalupe, Harris and Nolan Counties.

PHOSPHATE — In West Texas, rock phosphate is present in Paleozoic rocks in several areas of Brewster and Presidio Counties, but known deposits are not large. In Northeast Texas, sedimentary rock phosphate occurs in thin conglomeratic lenses in Upper Cretaceous and Tertiary rock units; possibly some of these low-grade phosphorites could be processed on a small scale for local use as a fertilizer. Imported phosphate rock is processed at a plant in Brownsville.

POTASH — The potassium mineral **polyhalite** is widely distributed in the subsurface Permian Basin of West Texas and has been found in many wells in that area. During 1927-1931, the federal government drilled a series of potash-test wells in Crane, Crockett, Ector, Glasscock, Loving, Reagan, Upton and Winkler Counties. In addition to polyhalite, these wells revealed the presence of the potassium minerals **carnallite** and **sylvite** in Loving County and carnallite in Winkler County. The known Texas potash deposits are not as rich as those in the New Mexico portion of the Permian Basin and have not been developed.

PUMICITE (VOLCANIC ASH) — Deposits of volcanic ash occur in Brazos, Fayette, Gonzales, Karnes, Polk, Starr and other counties of the Texas Coastal Plain. Deposits also have been found in the Trans-Pecos area, High Plains and in several counties east of the High Plains. Volcanic ash is used to prepare pozzolan cement, cleansing and scouring compounds and soaps and sweeping compounds; as a carrier for insecticides, and for other purposes. It has been mined in Dickens, Lynn, Scurry, Starr and other counties.

QUICKSILVER (see **Mercury**).

SALT (SODIUM CHLORIDE) (see also **BRINES**) — Salt resources of Texas are virtually inexhaustible. Enormous deposits occur in the subsurface Permian Basin of West Texas and in the salt domes of the Gulf Coastal Plain. Salt also is found in the alkali playa lakes of the High Plains, the alkali flats or **salt lakes** in the Salt Basin of Culberson and Hudspeth Counties and along some of the bays and lagoons of the South Texas Gulf Coast.

Texas is one of the leading salt-producing states. **Rock salt** is obtained from underground mines at Grand Saline in Van Zandt County and Hockley in Harris County. Only about 10 percent of the salt produced in the state is from rock salt. Most of the salt, however, is produced — by solution mining — as brines from wells drilled into the underground deposits.

SAND, INDUSTRIAL — Sands used for special purposes, due to high silica content or to unique physical properties, command higher prices than common sand. Industrial sands in Texas occur mainly in the Central Gulf Coastal Plain and in North Central Texas. They include abrasive, blast, chemical, engine, filtration, foundry, glass, hydraulic-fracturing, molding and pottery sands. Recent production of industrial sands has been reported in Atascosa, Colorado, El Paso, Hardin, Harris, Liberty, Limestone, McCulloch, Newton, Smith, Somervell and Wood Counties.

SAND AND GRAVEL (CONSTRUCTIONAL) — Sand and gravel are among the most extensively utilized resources in Texas. Principal occurrence is along the major streams and in stream terraces. Sand and gravel are important bulk construction materials, used as railroad ballast, base materials and for other purposes.

SANDSTONE — Sandstones of a variety of colors and textures are widely distributed in a number of geologic formations in Texas. Some of the sandstones have been quarried for use as dimension stone in El Paso, Parker, Terrell, Ward and other counties. Crushed sandstone is produced in Freestone, Gaines, Jasper, McMullen, Motley and other counties for use as road-building material, **terrazzo stone**, concrete and other aggregate.

SERPENTINITE — Several masses of serpentinite, which formed from the alteration of basic igneous rocks, are associated with other Precambrian metamorphic rocks of the Llano Uplift. The largest deposit is the Coal Creek serpentinite mass in northern Blanco and Gillespie Counties from which **terrazzo chips** have been produced. Other deposits are present in Gillespie and Llano Counties. (The features that are associated with surface and subsurface Cretaceous rocks in several counties in or near the Balcones Fault Zone and that are commonly known as "serpentine plugs" are chiefly necks and pipes and mounds of altered volcanic ash — palagonite — that accumulated around former submarine volcanic pipes.)

SHELL — **Oyster** shells and other shells in shallow coastal waters and in deposits along the Texas Gulf Coast have been produced chiefly by dredging. They were used to a limited extent as raw material in the manufacture of **cement**, as **concrete aggregate** and road base, and for other purposes. No shell has been produced in Texas since 1981.

SILVER — During the period 1885-1952, the production of silver in Texas, as reported by the U.S. Bureau of Mines, totaled about 33 million troy ounces. For about 70 years, silver was the most consistently produced metal in Texas, although always in moderate quantities. All of the production came from the Trans-Pecos country of West Texas, where the silver was mined in Brewster County (**Altuda Mountain**), Culberson and Hudspeth Counties (**Van Horn Mountains** and **Van Horn-Allamoore district**), Hudspeth County (**Quitman Mountains** and **Eagle Mountains**) and Presidio County (**Chinati Mountains** area, **Loma Plata mine** and **Shafter district**). Chief producer was the **Presidio** mine in the Shafter district, which began operations in the late 1800s, and, through September 1942, produced more than 30 million ounces of silver — more than 92 percent of Texas' total silver production. Water in the lower mine levels, lean ores and low price of silver resulted in the closing of the mine in 1942. Another important silver producer was the **Hazel copper-silver mine** in the **Van Horn-Allamoore district** in Culberson County, which accounted for more than 2 million ounces.

An increase in the price of silver in the late 1970s stimulated prospecting for new reserves, and exploration began near the old **Presidio** mine, near the old **Plata Verde mine** in the **Van Horn Mountains** district, at the **Bonanza mine** in the **Quitman Mountains** district and at the old **Hazel** mine. A decline in the price of silver in the early 1980s, however, resulted in reduction of exploration and mine development in the region. There is no current exploration in these areas.

SOAPSTONE (see **Talc** and **Soapstone**).

SODIUM SULPHATE (SALT CAKE) — Sodium sulphate minerals occur in salt beds and brines of the alkali playa lakes of the High Plains in West Texas. In some lakes, the sodium sulphate minerals are present in deposits a few feet beneath the lakebeds. Sodium sulphate also is found in underground brines in the Permian Basin. Current production is from brines and dry salt beds at alkali lakes in Gaines and Terry Counties. Past production was reported in Lynn and Ward Counties. Sodium sulphate is used chiefly by the paper and pulp industry. Other uses are in the preparation of glass, detergents and other products.

STONE (see **Building Stone; Crushed Stone**).

STRONTIUM — Deposits of the mineral **celestite** (strontium sulphate) have been found in a number of places, including localities in Brown, Coke, Comanche, Fisher, Lampasas, Mills, Nolan, Real, Taylor, Travis and Williamson Counties. Most of the occurrences are very minor, and none is currently produced in the state.

SULPHUR — Texas is one of the world's principal sulphur-producing areas. The sulphur is mined from deposits of native sulphur, and it is extracted from sour (sulphur-bearing) natural gas and petroleum. Recovered sulphur is a growing industry and accounted for approximately one-third of all 1984 sulphur production. Native sulphur is found in large deposits in the caprock of some of the salt domes along the Texas Gulf Coast and in some of the surface and subsurface Permian strata of West Texas, notably in Culberson and Pecos Counties. Native sulphur obtained from the underground deposits is known as frasch sulphur, so-called because of Herman Frasch, the chemist who devised the method of drilling wells into the deposits, melting the sulphur with superheated water and forcing the molten sulphur to the surface. Most of the production now goes to the users in molten form.

Frasch sulphur is produced from only one Gulf Coast salt dome in Wharton County and from West Texas underground Permian strata in Culberson and Pecos Counties. Operations at several Gulf Coast domes have been closed in recent years. During the 1940s, acidic sulphur earth was produced in the **Rustler Springs district** in Culberson County for use as a fertilizer and soil conditioner. Sulphur is recovered from sour natural gas and petroleum at plants in numerous Texas counties. Sulphur is used in the preparation of fertilizers and organic and inorganic chemicals, in petroleum refining and for many other purposes.

TALC AND SOAPSTONE — Deposits of talc are found in the Precambrian metamorphic rocks of the **Allamoore area** of eastern Hudspeth and western Culberson Counties. Soapstone, containing **talc**, occurs in the Precambrian metamorphic rocks of the Llano Uplift area, notably in Blanco, Gillespie and Llano Counties. Current production is from surface mines in the Allamoore area. Talc is used in ceramic, roofing, paint, paper, plastic, synthetic rubber and other products.

TIN — Tin minerals have been found in El Paso and Mason Counties. Small quantities were produced during the early 1900s in the **Franklin Mountains** north of El Paso. **Cassiterite** (tin dioxide) occurrences in Mason County are believed to be very minor. The only **tin smelter** in the United States, built at Texas City by the federal government during World War II and later sold to a private company, processes tin concentrates from ores mined outside of Texas, tin residues and secondary tin-bearing materials.

TITANIUM — The titanium mineral rutile has been found in small amounts at the Mueller prospect in Jeff Davis County. Another titanium mineral, ilmenite, occurs in sandstones in Burleson, Fayette, Lee, Starr and several other counties. Deposits that would be considered commercial under present conditions have not been found.

TRAP ROCK (see **Basalt**).

TUNGSTEN — The tungsten mineral scheelite has been found in small deposits in Gillespie and Llano Counties and in the **Quitman Mountains** in Hudspeth County. Small deposits of other tungsten minerals have been prospected in the **Cave Peak** area north of Van Horn in Culberson County.

URANIUM — Uranium deposits were discovered in the Texas Coastal Plain in 1954 when abnormal radioactivity was detected in the Karnes County area. A number of uranium deposits have since been discovered within a belt of strata extending more than 250 miles from the middle Coastal Plain southwestward to the Rio Grande.

Various uranium minerals also have been found in other areas of Texas, including the Trans-Pecos, the Llano Uplift and the High Plains. With the exception of small shipments from the High Plains during the 1950s, all the uranium production in Texas has been from the Coastal Plain. Uranium has been obtained from surface mines extending from northern Live Oak County, southeastern Atascosa County, across northern Karnes County and into southern Gonzales County. All but the Panna Maria Mine (Karnes County) have ceased production and are undergoing reclamation. Uranium-ore processing facilities are located in northern Karnes County. Uranium also has been mined by in situ leaching, brought to the surface through wells, and stripped from the solution at several Coastal Plain recovery operations located in Bee, Duval, Jim Hogg, Karnes, Live Oak and Webb Counties. Because of decreased demand and price, uranium mining declined sharply in the early 1980s.

VERMICULITE — Vermiculite, a mica-like mineral that expands when heated, occurs in Burnet, Gillespie, Llano, Mason and other counties in the Llano region. It has been produced at a surface mine in Llano County. Vermiculite, mined outside of Texas, is exfoliated (expanded) at plants in Dallas, Houston and San Antonio. Exfoliated vermiculite is used for lightweight concrete aggregate, horticulture, insulation and other purposes.

VOLCANIC ASH (see **Pumicite**).

ZEOLITES — The zeolite minerals clinoptilolite and analcime occur in Tertiary lavas and tuffs in Brewster, Jeff Davis and Presidio Counties in West Texas. Clinoptilolite also is found associated with Tertiary tuffs in the southern Texas Coastal Plain, including deposits in Karnes, McMullen and Webb Counties. Production of McMullen County zeolites is expected in 1986. Zeolites sometimes called "molecular sieves," can be used in ion-exchange processes to reduce pollution, as a catalyst in oil cracking, in obtaining high-purity oxygen and nitrogen from air and for many other purposes.

ZINC (see **Lead** and **Zinc**).

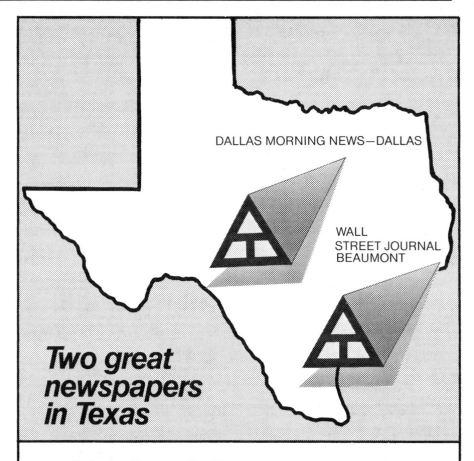

TEXAS
AGRICULTURE

AGRICULTURE IN TEXAS

Agribusiness, the combined phases of food and fiber production, processing, transporting and marketing, is a leading Texas industry. Most of the following discussion is devoted to the phase of production on farms and ranches.

Information was provided by Agricultural Extension Service specialists, Texas and U.S. Departments of Agriculture and U.S. Department of Commerce sources and was coordinated by Carl G. Anderson, Extension Marketing Economist, Texas A&M University. All references are to Texas unless otherwise specified.

Agriculture is one of the most important industries in Texas. Many businesses, financial institutions and individuals are involved in providing supplies, credit and services to farmers and ranchers and in processing and marketing agricultural commodities.

Including all its agribusiness phases, agriculture added about $33 billion to the economic activity of the state in 1984. The estimated **value of farm assets** in Texas — the land, buildings, livestock, machinery, crops, inventory on farms, household goods and farm financial assets — totaled approximately $108 billion in 1984.

Receipts from farm and ranch marketings in 1984 were estimated at $9.5 billion. Ten years earlier this figure was $5.7 billion.

With the increasing demand for food and fiber throughout the world, and because of the importance of agricultural exports to this nation's trade balance, agriculture in Texas is destined to play an even greater role in the future.

The goal of the research and educational efforts of Texas A&M University System is to capitalize on natural advantages that agriculture has in Texas because of the relatively warm climate, productive soils and availability of excellent export and transportation facilities.

The number and nature of Texas farms have changed. The number of farms in Texas has decreased from 418,000 in 1940 to 185,026 by the 1982 Census of Agriculture, and 187,000 in 1984, with an average size of 732 acres. Average value of farm assets, including land and buildings, has increased from $6,196 in 1940 to $481,000 in 1984.

Mechanization of farming continues as new and larger machines replace manpower. Tractors, mechanical harvesters and numerous cropping machines have virtually eliminated menial tasks that for many years were traditional to farming.

Revolutionary agricultural chemicals have appeared along with improved plants and animals and methods of handling them. Hazards of farming and ranching have been reduced by better use of weather information, machinery and other improvements; but rising costs, labor problems and escalating energy costs have added to concerns of farmers and ranchers.

Among the major changes in Texas agriculture since World War II are these:

Farms are fewer, larger, specialized, more expensive to own and operate, but more productive.

Irrigation is a major factor in crop production.

Crops and livestock have changed in production areas as in the concentration of cotton on the High Plains and livestock increases in central and eastern Texas.

Pest and disease control methods are greatly improved. Herbicides are relied upon for weed control.

Ranchmen and farmers are better educated and informed, more science- and business-oriented.

Feedlot finishing, commercial broiler production, artificial insemination, improved pastures and brush control, reduced feed requirements and other changes have greatly increased livestock and poultry efficiency.

Cooperation among farmers in marketing, promotion and other fields has increased.

Agricultural producers are increasingly dependent on off-the-farm services to supply production inputs such as feeds, chemicals, credit and other essentials.

Agribusiness

Texas farmers and ranchers have developed a dependence upon agribusiness. With many producers specializing in the production of certain crops and livestock, they look beyond the farm and ranch for supplies and services. On the input side, they rely on suppliers of production needs and services and on the output side they need assemblers, processors and distributors.

In 1940, about 23 percent of Texans were producers on farms and ranches, and about 17 percent were suppliers or were engaged in assembly, processing and distribution of agricultural products. The agribusiness alignment in 1984 was less than 2.0 percent on farms and

ranches with 20 to 25 percent of the population providing production or marketing supplies and services. The impact of agriculture on the economy of Texas exceeds $33 billion annually.

Cash Receipts

Farm and ranch cash receipts in 1983 totaled $8.970 billion. When estimates of $1,128 million for **government payments**, $912.5 million of non-money income and $132.4 million of other farm income are included, realized **gross farm income** totaled $11.143 billion. With farm production expenses of $9.868 billion and a $281.5 million decrease in farm inventories from the year before, net income totaled $993.6 million or $5,348 per farm. In 1984, cash receipts from farm marketings were estimated at $10.2 billion.

Farm and Ranch Assets

Farm and ranch assets totaled $108 billion on Jan. 1, 1984. This was an increase of 7.0 percent from a year earlier. **Value of real estate** accounted for most of the increase. Liabilities totaled $13.7 billion, .09 percent of the previous year. The value of real estate amounted to $89.3 billion, or 83 percent of total assets.

Percent of Income From Products

Livestock and livestock products accounted for 62 percent of the **cash receipts from farm marketings** in 1983 with the remaining 38 percent from crops.

From **livestock marketings**, meat animals accounted for 43 percent of total receipts received by farmers and ranchers in 1983. Most of these receipts were from **cattle and calf sales.** Dairy products made up 5.7 percent of receipts, **poultry and eggs** 5.0 percent and other livestock 1.0 percent.

From crops, **cotton** accounted for 8.7 percent, **feed crops** 8.4 percent, **food grains** 6.0 percent, **vegetables** 3.8 percent, **oil crops** 2.0 percent, **fruits and nuts** .07 percent, **greenhouse/nursery products** 3.3 percent and other crops 1.2 percent.

Texas' Rank Among States

Measured by cash receipts for farm and ranch marketings, Texas ranked third in 1983, behind California and Iowa.

Texas normally leads all other states in numbers of farms and ranches and farm and ranch land, cattle slaughtered, cattle on feed, calf births, sheep and lambs slaughtered, goats, cash receipts from livestock marketings, cattle and calves, beef cows, sheep and lambs, wool production, mohair production and exports of lard

FARM LABOR

Source: U.S. Department of Agriculture

Year—	*Family Worker Avg. No.	†Hired Worker Avg. No.	‡Total Worker Avg. No.
1955.	323,000	168,000	491,000
1970.	190,000	92,000	282,000
1971.	184,000	84,000	268,000
1972.	187,000	88,000	275,000
1973.	184,000	80,000	264,000
1974.	174,000	84,000	258,000
1975.	173,000	82,000	255,000
1976.	167,000	83,000	250,000
1977.	166,000	83,000	249,000
1978.	155,000	82,000	237,000
1979.	152,000	78,000	230,000
1980.	146,000	77,000	223,000
§1981.	154,000	72,500	226,500
1982.	149,000	70,000	219,000
1983.	120,000	85,000	205,000

*Farm operators or members of their families working 15 hours or more, without pay.

†Persons working one or more hours for pay.

‡Persons employed during the last full calendar week ending at least one day before end of month.

§First and second quarters only; survey discontinued thereafter.

and tallow. The state also usually leads in production of cotton, grain sorghum, watermelons and spinach.

A significant change in ranking for Texas in recent times has been in the number of cattle in feedlots. Texas now ranks ahead of Nebraska, Kansas, Colorado and Iowa as the states with the most cattle on feed in commercial feedlots. Nebraska ranked second and Kansas third.

Texas Agricultural Exports

The value of Texas' share of agricultural exports in fiscal year 1984 was $2.164 billion. Cotton accounted for $746.5 million of the exports; feed grains, $255.1 million; wheat and flour, $356.1 million; rice, $124.2 million; tallow and lard, $110.2 million; cottonseed oil, $34.9 million; hides and skins, $184.4 million; meats and meat products, $125.2 million; fruits, $49.9 million; soybeans, $43.6 million; vegetables, $17.1 million; poultry products, $19.3 million; and miscellaneous and other products, $71.0 million.

Texas exports of $2.164 billion of farm and ranch products compares with $1.680 billion in 1983; $2.569 billion in 1982; $2.660 billion in 1981; $2.976 billion in 1980.

Hunting

The management of wildlife as an economic enterprise through leasing for hunting makes a significant contribution to the economy of many counties. Leasing the right of ingress on a farm or ranch for the purpose of hunting is the service marketed. After the leasing, the consumer — the hunter — goes onto the land to seek the harvest of the wildlife commodity. Hunting lease income to farmers and ranchers in 1984 was an estimated $145 million.

The demand for hunting opportunities is growing while the land capable of producing huntable wildlife is decreasing. As a result, farmers and ranchers are placing more emphasis on wildlife management practices to help meet requests for hunting leases.

Irrigation

Texas farmers irrigated approximately 6.75 million acres of land in 1984. Although some irrigation is practiced in nearly every county of the state, about 68 percent of the total irrigated acreage is in the High Plains of Northwest Texas. Other concentrated areas of irrigation are the Gulf Coast rice producing area, the Lower Rio Grande Valley, the Winter Garden district of South Texas, the Trans-Pecos area of West Texas and the peanut producing area in North Central Texas centered

around Erath, Eastland and Comanche Counties. Sprinkler irrigation was used on about 32 percent of the total irrigated acreage with surface irrigation methods — primarily furrow, border and contour check methods — being used on the remaining 68 percent of the irrigated areas.

Drip, or trickle, irrigation has attracted much attention in recent years for use on tree crops such as citrus, pecans, avocados, peaches and apples. The use of drip irrigation is increasing with present drip irrigated acreage estimated around 29,000 acres.

The use of sprinkler irrigation is also in an upward trend, increasing to 32 percent in 1984, from about 19 percent in 1969.

Approximately 70 percent of the state's irrigated acreage is supplied with water pumped from wells. Sur-

*REALIZED GROSS INCOME AND NET INCOME FROM FARMING, TEXAS, 1958-1983

Year	**Realized Gross Farm Income	Farm Production Expenses	Net Change in Farm Inventories	***Total Net Farm Income	***Total Net Income Per Farm
	Million Dollars				Dollars
1958	$2,666.1	$1,637.5	$17.7	$1,046.3	$3,948.0
1974	6,178.0	5,057.0	−80.3	1,040.7	4,980.0
1975	6,497.4	5,180.3	−106.2	1,210.9	6,407.0
1976	6,897.5	5,926.0	124.8	1,096.3	5,862.0
§1977	7,341.8	6,257.5	−38.4	1,045.8	5,623.0
1978	8,524.7	7,287.7	−87.0	1,149.9	6,216.0
1979	11,063.2	9,011.8	−91.5	1,959.9	10,481.0
1980	10,118.8	8,984.6	−270.1	864.1	4,572.0
1981	11,018.9	9,760.1	591.1	1,849.9	9,788.0
1982	11,321.8	10,114.5	−262.7	994.6	5,025.0
1983	11,143.2	9,868.1	−281.5	993.6	5,313.0

*Details for items may not add to totals because of rounding. Series revised, September, 1981.
**Cash receipts from farm marketings, government payments, value of home consumption and gross rental value of farm dwellings.
***Farm income of farm operators.
§Starting in 1977, farms with production of $1,000 or more used to figure income.

TEXAS' EXPORT SHARES OF AGRICULTURAL COMMODITIES, 1981-84

Source: Foreign Agricultural Trade of the U.S.

Commodity*	1981	1982	1983	1984	1984 Texas Share of U.S. Exports Percent
	Million Dollars				
Rice	261.0	171.2	126.4	124.2	13.8
Cotton	675.9	782.7	387.7	746.5	31.0
Tallow & Lard	92.5	92.5	93.8	110.2	15.7
Hides & Skins	90.3	105.9	133.4	184.4	14.0
Meats other than Poultry	106.9	124.1	104.0	125.2	10.4
Feed Grains	664.4	402.5	206.4	255.1	2.8
Poultry Products . .	35.5	27.6	20.6	19.3	4.7
Fruits	35.2	53.5	53.9	49.9	3.9
Vegetables	25.0	23.7	16.9	17.1	1.7
Wheat & Flour	449.0	544.1	326.7	356.1	5.2
Soybeans.	62.2	44.5	81.7	43.6	0.6
Cottonseed Oil	70.0	91.0	30.4	34.9	0.4
Peanuts.	19.6	24.3	18.7	23.2	11.0
Nuts	.6	1.7	1.5	1.6	0.4
†Dairy Products . .	2.8	1.6	1.4	1.6	0.4
All Other	68.8	77.7	76.0	71.0	—
TOTAL	2,659.7	2,568.6	1,679.5	2,163.9	5.7

*Commodity and related preparations.
†For 1981 and 1982 the USDA changed the variable used to determine export share of dairy products to state fluid milk production.

CASH RECEIPTS FROM FARM MARKETINGS 1936-1983

Source: Texas Crop & Livestock Reporting Service

Year—	Crop	Livestock and Livestock Production	Total Crops and Livestock	*Government Payments	Total Crops, Livestock and Payments
	1,000 dollars				
1936. . . .	$298,361	$186,829	$485,190	$27,121	$512,311
1969. . . .	1,202,150	1,851,386	3,053,536	505,248	3,558,784
1970. . . .	1,264,766	1,956,991	3,221,757	543,156	3,764,913
1971. . . .	1,177,911	2,284,873	3,462,784	468,552	3,931,336
1972. . . .	1,463,123	2,614,518	4,077,641	528,567	4,606,208
1973. . . .	2,811,135	3,686,236	6,497,371	386,554	6,883,925
1974. . . .	2,695,007	2,971,115	5,666,122	80,552	5,746,674
1975. . . .	2,759,514	3,076,782	5,836,296	146,562	5,982,858
1976. . . .	3,091,434	3,201,974	6,293,408	111,735	6,405,143
1977. . . .	3,147,190	3,523,073	6,670,263	157,993	6,828,256
1978. . . .	3,015,882	4,628,470	7,644,352	318,843	7,963,195
1979. . . .	3,991,103	6,059,942	10,051,045	307,099	10,358,144
1980. . . .	3,925,092	5,185,067	9,110,159	231,840	9,341,999
1981. . . .	4,365,995	5,448,215	9,814,210	321,365	10,135,575
1982. . . .	4,228,288	5,421,060	9,649,348	643,598	10,292,946
1983. . . .	3,448,249	5,522,150	8,970,399	1,127,875	10,098,274

*Payments since 1971 were for wheat, cotton, feed grain, sugarbeets, wool, mohair, cropland adjustment, rural environmental assistance and Conservation Programs.

face water sources supply the remaining area. Declining groundwater levels in several of the major aquifers is a serious problem. As the water level declines, well yields decrease and pumping costs increase. Decreasing groundwater supplies and higher fuel prices have contributed to decreasing irrigated acreage. However, recent studies of the availability of water in the Ogallala formation, which supplies water for most of the High Plains irrigation, indicate that a viable irrigated agriculture can be expected to continue in the High Plains area much longer than some predictions in the past have indicated.

Rapidly rising fuel costs pose another serious problem for Texas irrigation farmers. More than half of the irrigation pumps in the state are driven with power units which use natural gas as a fuel. Natural gas prices paid by farmers have increased dramatically in recent years. The cost of other fuels used for pumping irrigation water, primarily electricity and diesel, has also increased significantly. Since fuel costs are a major part of the cost of irrigation water, farmers are facing serious management decisions in the use of irrigation for crop production.

Irrigation is an important factor in the productivity of Texas agriculture. The value of crop production from irrigated acreage is approximately 50 to 60 percent of the total value of all crop production, although only about 30 percent of the state's total harvested cropland acreage is irrigated.

Principal Crops

In most years the value of crop production in Texas is almost half of the total value of the state's agricultural output. Cash receipts from farm sales of crops is less because some grain and roughage is fed to livestock on farms where produced.

In 1983, the **leading Texas counties** in cash receipts from crops were Hidalgo, Gaines, Hale, Wharton and Castro. Receipts from all Texas crops totaled $3.4 billion in 1983; $4.2 billion in 1982; $4.4 billion in 1981; and $4.0 billion in 1980.

Cotton and **wheat** accounted for 22 percent and 15 percent, respectively, of the crop total in 1983. **Grain sorghum, corn, rice, cottonseed, peanuts, hay, vegetables** and **soybeans** are other important cash crops.

Cotton

Cotton has been a major crop in Texas for more than a century. Since 1880, Texas has led all states in cotton production and today the annual Texas cotton harvest amounts to about one-third of total production in the United States. The annual cotton crop has averaged 4.0 million bales since 1976.

Total **value of lint cotton** produced in Texas in 1984 was $1,230,666,000. This compared with $694,800,000 in 1983; and $676,011,000 in 1982. **Cottonseed value** was $177,303,000 in 1984, making the total value of crop $1,407,969,000. This compared with $162,324,000 in 1983, making total value of crop $857,124,000; $90,882,000 in 1982, making total value of crop $766,893,000.

Upland cotton was harvested from 4.8 million acres in 1984, and **American Pima** from 19,300 acres, for a total of 4.819 million acres. This compared with 3.55 million acres of **Upland cotton** and 22,300 acres of **American Pima** in 1983; 4.3 million acres of **Upland** and 19,500 acres of **Pima** in 1982. Cotton acreage harvested in 1983 totaled 3.572 million. Production amounted to 4.03 million bales in 1984 and 2.412 million in 1983. Counties leading in production are Gaines, Dawson, Terry, Cameron and Martin.

Cotton is the raw material for processing operations at gins, oil mills, compresses and a small number of textile mills in Texas.

Cotton in Texas is machine harvested. Growers in 1984 used **stripper harvesters** to gather 85 percent of the crop and **spindle pickers** to harvest the remaining 15 percent. Field storage of harvested seed cotton is gaining in popularity as gins decline in number. In 1984, 57 percent of the cotton was ginned from modules and 43 percent from trailers. Much of the Texas cotton crop is exported. Japan and South Korea are major buyers.

The state's major cotton-producing areas are tied together by an electronic marketing system. This system is a computer network that links producers through terminals that are usually located at gins to a relatively large number of buyers. The network provides farmers with a centralized market that allows many sellers and buyers to trade with each other on a regular basis.

The first high volume instrument cotton classing office in the nation was opened at Lamesa, Texas, in 1980.

CASH RECEIPTS BY COMMODITIES 1981-83

Source: Texas Crop & Livestock Reporting Service

Commodity—	Value 1981	1982	1983	Commodity—	Value 1981	1982	1983
	— 1,000 dollars —				— 1,000 dollars —		
All Commodities	$9,814,210	$9,649,348	$8,970,399	Cucumbers	16,801	14,240	16,474
Livestock and products	5,448,215	5,421,060	5,522,150	Green peppers	25,433	25,171	26,251
Crops	4,365,995	4,228,288	3,448,249	Tomatoes	6,921	13,720	5,897
Livestock and products				Sweet potatoes	10,727	12,155	11,202
Cattle and calves	4,098,218	4,125,911	4,193,111	Oats	14,497	10,138	12,911
Milk, wholesale	529,100	538,740	565,645	Lettuce	10,267	14,380	9,247
Broilers	278,040	258,100	261,498	Honeydew melons	15,912	19,051	15,708
Eggs	190,098	176,813	178,092	Sugarbeets	17,595	20,405	22,887
Hogs	117,164	108,679	93,268	Spinach	19,155	16,635	16,404
Turkeys	56,312	40,560	45,144	Snap beans	1,927	1,152	1,512
Sheep and lambs	58,358	67,058	61,573	Barley	3,361	2,796	3,524
Mohair	34,650	25,500	42,930	Corn, sweet	2,102	2,055	2,363
Wool	24,600	16,212	15,438	Rye	1,138	1,237	815
Milk, retail	11,800	11,330	11,061	Broccoli	14,250	25,569	21,434
*Other	49,875	52,157	54,390	Sunflowers	5,951	14,597	14,984
Crops				Cauliflower	1,820	2,578	4,497
Cotton lint	1,304,792	1,277,696	744,315	Seed crops	8,000	10,000	9,000
Sorghum grain	484,546	587,875	441,400	†Other	51,187	59,331	36,439
Corn	283,731	297,652	252,934	**Fruits and nuts**			
Wheat	657,297	533,234	512,999	Grapefruit	28,358	33,244	14,478
Rice	311,701	224,302	95,947	Pecans	31,429	19,454	33,180
Cottonseed	149,272	80,603	132,654	Oranges	24,894	29,103	17,905
Peanuts	115,697	80,392	90,658	Peaches	5,985	3,900	6,379
Soybeans	83,329	110,253	95,697	**Other products**			
Onions	99,095	74,820	62,112	Greenhouse and nursery	226,000	276,000	333,000
Cabbage	34,834	56,418	34,589	‡Farm forest products	55,000	50,000	54,000
Hay	98,559	78,862	137,932				
Carrots	29,669	28,255	27,458				
Cantaloupes	37,123	36,795	39,378				
Potatoes	21,951	28,351	30,501				
Watermelons	37,022	33,834	35,707				
Sugarcane	18,667	22,035	23,537				

*Includes milkfat, turkey eggs, honey bees, equine, goats, goat milk and other poultry and livestock.

†Miscellaneous vegetables, field crops; other berries, fruits and nuts.

‡Includes only sales from farms.

Grain Sorghum

Grain sorghum usually ranks second in dollar value. Texas **ranked first** in production of grain sorghum in 1982 and 1983. Much of the grain is exported as well as being used in livestock and poultry feed throughout the state.

In 1984, 3.95 million acres of grain sorghum were harvested, yielding an average of 2,968 pounds per acre, for a total production of 117,236,000 cwt. It was valued at $4.61 per cwt., a total value of $540,123,000. In 1983, 3.15 million acres were harvested, yielding 2,800 pounds per acre for a total production of 88,200,000 cwt. It was valued at $459,900,000.

Although grown to some extent in all counties where crops are important, the largest concentrations

COTTONSEED OIL MILLS
1983-84

Number in Each County

Bastrop	1	Hunt	1
Bell	1	Hale	1
Cameron	2	Lubbock	3
Dawson	1	Nolan	1
El Paso	1	Milam	1
Fort Bend	1	Tarrant	2
Hardeman	1	Taylor	1
Hockley	1	Total	19

SELECTED COTTON HARVESTING INFORMATION
Source: Texas Crop and Livestock Reporting Service

Crop Year	Cotton Ginned From:			Wrapping and Ginning Charges Per 480 Lbs. Bale
	Trailers	Modules	Ricks	
	Percent			Dollars
1976	—	—	—	37.29
1977	—	—	—	38.37
1978	75	23	1	39.82
1979	65	33	2	44.65
1980	60	40	0	52.18
1981	40	59	1	46.69
1982	42	57	1	49.01
1983-84	43	57	—	50.20

TEXAS COTTON: METHOD OF HARVESTING COTTON
Source: Texas Crop and Livestock Reporting Service

Crop Year	Hand Picked	Hand Snapped	Machine Picked	Machine Stripped	Machine Scraped
			Percent		
1974	*	*	21	78	1
1975	*	*	7	93	*
1976	*	*	11	89	*
1977	*	*	10	90	*
1978	*	*	14	86	*
1979	*	*	13	86	*
1980	*	*	20	80	*
1981	*	*	9	91	*
1982	*	*	4	96	*

*Less than 0.5 percent.

COTTON GINS BY COUNTIES
Source: Texas Cotton Ginners' Assn. and U.S. Department of Commerce

In the listing below, those counties not reporting number of bales ginned are listed herewith. Those counties with only one gin are: Bastrop, Borden, Caldwell, Clay, Coleman, Deaf Smith, Denton, Eastland, Fannin, Hamilton, King, Kleberg, Live Oak, McCulloch, Matagorda, Medina, Midland, Refugio, Schleicher, Starr, Stonewall, Upton, Uvalde, Van Zandt, Walker and Wichita. Those with two gins are: Baylor, Concho, Culberson, Delta, Frio, Houston, Kent, Lamar, Pecos, Reagan, Taylor, Throckmorton, Travis and Young.

Counties—	Active Gins Operating During 1983-1984 Crop Year	Running Bales Ginned			Counties—	Active Gins Operating During 1983-1984 Crop Year	Running Bales Ginned		
		1983	1982	1981			1983	1982	1981
Bailey	12	28,420	12,889	111,801	Hunt	3	1,957	3,875	6,613
Bell	3	2,180	1,731	3,993	Jones	14	33,442	68,548	98,879
Brazoria	3	3,945	6,586	6,003	Kaufman	3	3,466	2,448	4,460
Brazos	5	14,747	23,031	20,494	Knox	5	10,975	15,453	27,803
Briscoe	5	16,052	10,439	42,927	Lamb	26	77,105	65,523	220,175
Burleson	3	1,628	10,842	11,500	Lubbock	30	132,743	79,588	274,669
Cameron	18	75,334	90,659	109,276	Lynn	21	115,444	93,976	250,308
Castro	10	31,373	22,745	83,618	McLennan	3	4,518	7,609	9,188
Childress	3	6,806	24,011	27,427	Martin	12	24,292	99,673	164,992
Cochran	10	31,124	24,680	88,975	Milam	3	7,083	7,910	9,777
Collin	4	5,855	8,378	12,298	Mitchell	6	16,105	23,634	53,511
Collingsworth	5	16,822	25,917	49,924	Motley	5	7,215	11,831	23,931
Cottle	5	12,240	18,989	32,425	Navarro	4	7,741	9,524	12,050
Crosby	13	74,207	50,740	176,355	Nolan	3	13,228	24,006	50,598
Dawson	23	50,936	153,484	284,111	Nueces	13	57,155	60,135	79,381
Dickens	4	5,059	7,709	23,878	Parmer	9	18,882	19,906	81,010
Donley	3	8,392	10,532	20,619	Reeves	3	13,867	†	26,977
Ellis	7	14,209	14,088	25,678	Robertson	4	20,221	32,430	35,564
El Paso	11	47,392	44,083	48,349	Runnels	7	15,359	30,333	50,972
Falls	4	3,361	2,652	4,967	San Patricio	11	52,604	77,656	70,577
Fisher	7	20,374	47,076	82,842	Scurry	8	30,706	43,508	72,515
Floyd	14	70,922	22,319	163,944	Swisher	10	36,391	25,808	88,189
Foard	3	3,124	7,341	16,008	Terry	19	104,474	119,191	246,388
Fort Bend	10	19,115	21,752	22,964	Tom Green	7	24,350	43,702	58,707
Gaines	23	146,370	151,764	354,121	Wharton	6	18,747	16,184	31,380
Garza	4	6,580	13,144	22,062	Wheeler	3	2,869	4,271	14,126
Glasscock	3	23,308	35,674	48,674	Wilbarger	6	9,863	30,276	50,432
Hale	30	103,227	70,454	263,984	Willacy	7	73,000	72,299	97,344
Hall	11	19,301	48,891	61,096	Williamson	14	37,574	40,052	50,976
Hardeman	4	4,187	17,541	22,695	Yoakum	9	46,435	58,153	91,395
Haskell	11	33,724	43,408	109,088	Zavala	4	28,623	37,975	38,294
Hidalgo	14	58,318	61,694	76,498	All Others	—	105,136	180,134	290,714
Hill	7	10,137	13,097	17,992	Total	657	2,240,874	2,649,165	5,508,519
Hockley	22	92,582	56,239	246,500					
Howard	9	21,953	68,975	124,024	*—None Reported.				
Hudspeth	1	*	†	9,520	†—Included in "All Others."				

are in the High Plains, Rolling Plains, Blackland Prairie, Grand Prairie, Coast Prairie, Coastal Bend, Rio Grande Plain and Lower Rio Grande Valley areas. Counties leading in production are **Hidalgo, Nueces, San Patricio, Wharton, Hockley** and **Hansford.**

Research to develop high-yielding hybrids resistant to diseases and insect damage continues. A leader in this development, **J. Roy Quinby,** is principal author of a history of grain sorghums which appeared in the 1972-73 edition of the Texas Almanac.

Rice

Rice, which is grown in 20 counties on the Coast Prairie of Texas, ranked third in value among Texas crops for a number of years. However, in recent years, cotton, grain sorghum, wheat and corn have outranked rice.

Farms are highly mechanized, producing rice through irrigation and using airplanes for much of the planting, fertilizing and application of insecticides and herbicides.

Texas farmers grow long- and medium-grain rice only. The Texas rice industry, which has grown from 110 acres in 1850 to a high of 642,000 in 1954, has been marked by significant yield increases and improved varieties. Record production was in 1981, with 27,239,000 hundredweights harvested. Highest yield was 5,100 pounds per acre in 1971.

Several different types of rice milling procedures are in use today. The simplest and oldest method produces a product known as **regular milled white rice,** the most prevalent on the market today.

Rice is more valuable if the grains are not broken. In many cases, additional vitamins are added to the grains to produce what is called "enriched rice."

Another process may be used in rice milling to produce a product called **parboiled rice.** After cooking, parboiled rice tends to be fluffy, more separate and plump.

Still another type of rice is **precooked rice,** which is actually milled rice that, after milling, has been cooked. Then the moisture is removed through dehydration process. Precooked rice requires a minimum of

VALUE OF TEXAS COTTON AND COTTONSEED

The following table was compiled by Texas Cottonseed Crushers Association from their historical records and reports of U.S. Department of Commerce and Department of Agriculture.

(All Figures in Thousands)

	Cotton		Cottonseed	
Growth Year—	Production (Bales)	Value	Production (Tons)	Value
1968	3,522	344,142	1,490	75,245
1969	2,859	267,207	1,190	49,742
1970	3,210	332,082	1,242	68,310
*1971	2,614	336,666	1,050	59,325
1972	4,277	476,231	1,642	79,850
1973	4,699	1,041,393	1,788	167,178
1974	2,487	420,479	981	116,739
1975	2,393	527,966	909	81,628
1976	3,314	981,970	1,271	124,558
1977	5,500	1,318,447	2,089	133,696

(All Figures in Thousands)

	Cotton		Cottonseed	
Growth Year—	Production (Bales)	Value	Production (Tons)	Value
1978	3,819	989,441	1,483	166,096
1979	5,539	1,486,010	2,264	262,624
1980	3,345	1,104,576	1,361	161,959
1981	5,663	1,268,863	2,438	207,230
1982	2,723	676,011	1,122	90,882
1983	2,412	694,032	1,002	162,324
1984	4,028	1,230,666	1,689	177,303

*Beginning in 1971, basis for cotton prices was changed from 500 pound gross weight to 480 pound net weight bale; to compute comparable prices for previous years multiply price times 1.04167.

BALANCE SHEET, TEXAS FARMS AND RANCHES
Jan. 1, 1977-84
Source: Economic Indicators of the Farm Sector: State Income and Balance Sheet Statistics, 1983, USDA, ERS.

Table below shows the financial status of Texas farms and ranches as of Jan. 1 of the years 1977 through 1984.

Item	1977	1978	1979	1980	1981	1982	1983	§1984	Net Change 1983-1984 Percent
				Million dollars					
Physical Assets:									
Real estate	41,651	46,843	53,615	62,182	68,142	79,718	82,012	89,342	8.9
Nonreal estate:									
Livestock and poultry	2,839	2,866	5,039	5,571	5,221	4,647	5,112	4,958	—3.2
Machinery and motor vehicles	4,091	4,361	4,821	5,521	5,843	6,253	6,425	6,267	—2.5
*Crops stored on and off farms	804	1,267	1,225	1,409	1,118	1,499	1,720	1,207	—29.8
Household equipment and furnishings	758	764	1,003	1,117	1,252	1,594	1,922	2,261	17.6
Financial assets:									
Deposits and currency	748	949	1,560	1,606	1,631	1,701	1,780	1,864	4.7
U.S. savings bonds	142	226	462	446	420	401	390	400	2.6
Investments in co-ops	864	981	1,157	1,287	1,381	1,481	1,584	1,683	6.3
TOTAL ASSETS	51,897	58,257	68,882	79,139	84,998	97,294	100,953	107,981	7.0
Liabilities:									
†Real estate debt	4,086	4,276	4,480	5,102	5,480	5,783	6,026	6,313	4.8
Nonreal estate debt:									
†Excluding CCC loans	3,325	3,479	4,643	5,274	5,708	6,349	6,501	6,550	.8
‡Commodity Credit Corporation loans	61	431	216	74	66	428	1,147	799	—30.3
TOTAL LIABILITIES	7,472	8,186	9,339	10,451	11,254	12,560	13,674	13,662	—.09
Owners' equities	44,425	50,071	59,543	68,688	73,744	84,734	87,278	94,319	8.1
TOTAL CLAIMS	51,897	58,257	68,882	79,139	84,998	97,294	100,953	107,981	7.0

*Includes all crops held on farms and those crops stored off farms by farmers as security for CCC loans.
†Includes debt owed to institutional lenders and to noninstitutional or miscellaneous lenders.
‡Nonrecourse CCC loans secured by crops owned by farmers. These crops are included as assets in this balance sheet.
§Preliminary.

preparation time since it needs merely to have the moisture restored to it.

The United States produces only a small part of the world's total rice, but it is one of the leading exporters. American rice is popular abroad and is exported to more than 100 foreign countries.

In 1984, 408,000 acres of rice were harvested from 410,000 acres planted, yielding 4,940 cwt. per acre for a total production of 20,160,000 cwt. In 1983, 318,000 acres were harvested from 320,000 acres planted, yielding 4,340 cwt. per acre for a total production of 13,805,000 cwt. At $9.97 per cwt., total value was $137,636,000.

Wheat

Wheat for grain is one of the state's most valuable cash crops, usually exceeded in value only by grain sorghum. Wheat pastures also provide considerable winter forage for cattle, which is reflected in value of livestock produced.

Texas wheat growers planted 7,400,000 acres in 1984 and harvested grain from 5,000,000 acres. The yield was 30 bushels per acre for a total production of 150,000,000 bushels. Valued at $3.35 per bushel, total value was $502,500,000. This compared with 7,750,000 acres planted, 4,600,000 acres harvested in 1983, yielding 35.0 bushels per acre for total production of 161,000,000 bushels. Valued at $3.55 per bushel, total value was $571,550,000.

Leading wheat-producing counties based on acreage planted are Ochiltree, Swisher, Deaf Smith, Hansford, Randall, Dallam, Sherman and Carson.

Wheat was first grown commercially in Texas near Sherman about 1833. The acreage expanded greatly in North Central Texas after 1850 because of rapid settlement of the state and introduction of the well-adapted Mediterranean strain of wheat. A major family flour industry developed in the Fort Worth-Dallas-Sherman area between 1875 and 1900. Now about half of the state acreage is planted on the High Plains and about a third of this is irrigated. Most of the Texas wheat acreage is of the hard red winter class. Because of the recent development of varieties with improved disease resistance and the use of wheat for winter pasture, there has been a sizable expansion of acreage in Central and South Texas.

Most of all wheat harvested for grain is used in some phase of the milling industry. The better quality hard red winter wheat is used in the production of commercial bakery flour. Lower grades and varieties of soft red winter wheat are used in family flours. By-products of milled wheat are used for feed.

Corn

Interest in corn production throughout the state increased during the 1970s. Once the principal grain crop, corn acreage declined as plantings of grain sorghum increased. Only 500,000 acres were being harvested annually in the mid-1970s when development of new hybrids occurred.

Harvested acreage was 1,080,000 acres in 1983 and 1,550,000 acres in 1984. Yields for the corresponding years were 97 and 93 bushels per acre, respectively.

Most of the acreage and yield increase has occurred in the irrigated High Plains. In recent years, corn has ranked fourth in value among the state's crops. It was valued at $439,658,000 in 1984 and $356,136,000 in 1983.

The leading counties in production for 1983 were **Parmer, Castro, Hale, Lamb, Wharton** and **Dallam.**

TEXAS CROP SUMMARY, 1983 and 1984

Source: U.S. Department of Agriculture

Crop—	Year	Acres Harvested (1,000)	Production (1,000 Units)	Av. Price Per Unit (Dollars)	Value of Production (1,000 Dollars)	Crop—	Year	Acres Harvested (1,000)	Production (1,000 Units)	Av. Price Per Unit (Dollars)	Value of Production (1,000 Dollars)
Barley, bu.	1983	45	2,475	$2.52	$6,237	Soybeans, bu. . . .	1983	420	9,450	7.43	70,214
	1984	40	2,000	2.65	5,300		1984	410	11,890	5.65	67,179
Corn, grain, bu. . .	1983	1,080	104,760	3.39	355,136	Sugarbeets, tons .	1983	31.9	622	35.70	22,205
	1984	1,550	144,150	3.05	439,658		1984	37.8	832	—	—
*Cotton, Amer. Pima, bales	1983	22.3	32.0	1.08	16,589	Sugarcane for sugar and seed, tons	1983	35.5	1,122	15.20	17,054
	1984	19.3	28.0	.996	13,386		1984	36.3	1,078	—	—
Cotton Upland, bales. .	1983	3,550	2,380	.593	677,443	¶Sunflowers, lbs. .	1983	34	37,400	10.00	3,740
	1984	4,800	4,000	.634	1,217,280		1984	37	48,100	10.50	5,051
Cottonseed, tons .	1983	—	1,002	162.00	162,324	Sweet potatoes, cwt.	1983	7.1	852	18.40	15,677
	1984	—	1,688.6	105.00	177,303		1984	7.3	803	23.00	18,469
†Grapefruit, boxes	1983	—	11,200	2.16	24,148	§Vegetables, commercial for fresh market, cwt.	1983	64.1	11,430	—	150,045
	1984	—	3,200	2.93	9,385		1984	62.2	9,868	—	172,305
Guar, lbs.	1983	10	6,300	.120	756	**Vegetables, commercial for processing, cwt.	1983	4.1	447	—	2,191
	1984	20	10,000	.115	1,150		1984	6.7	790	—	3,860
Hay, all, tons	1983	3,070	7,486	77.50	580,165	Wheat, winter, bu.	1983	4,600	161,000	3.55	571,550
	1984	3,040	5,415	98.50	533,378		1984	5,000	150,000	3.35	502,500
Oats, bu.	1983	500	24,000	1.78	42,720	Total of Crops listed . . .	1983	17,458.2	—	—	3,508,740
	1984	250	8,750	2.05	17,938		1984	20,229.4	—	—	3,905,552
‡Oranges, boxes .	1983	—	5,680	4.65	26,402						
	1984	—	2,510	4.58	11,492						
††Peaches, lbs. . .	1983	—	23,000	.280	6,440						
	1984	—	21,000	.260	5,460						
Peanuts, lbs.	1983	215	362,275	.253	91,656						
	1984	215	365,500	.256	93,568						
††Pecans, lbs. . . .	1983	—	70,000	.560	39,212						
	1984	—	25,000	.900	22,500						
Potatoes, Irish, cwt.	1983	15.2	3,324	8.50	28,197						
	1984	17.5	4,065	11.70	47,355						
Rice, cwt.	1983	318	13,805	9.97	137,636						
	1984	408	20,160	—	—						
Rye, bu.	1983	25	450	2.45	1,103						
	1984	15	240	3.80	912						
Sorghum, grain, cwt.	1983	3,150	88,200	5.21	459,900						
	1984	3,950	117,236	4.61	540,123						

*Price is cents per pound.
†Grapefruit, Texas 80-lb./box.
‡Oranges, Texas 85-lb./box
¶Dollars per cwt.
§Includes processing total for dual usage crops (broccoli, carrots and cauliflower). Total Texas fresh market vegetables includes: broccoli, carrots, cauliflower, sweet corn, honeydew melons, lettuce, onions and tomatoes.
**Total Texas processing vegetables includes snap beans and tomatoes.
††Utilized production.

Rye

Rye is grown mainly on the Northern and Southern High Plains, the Northern Low Plains, Cross Timbers, Blacklands and East Texas areas. Minor acreages are seeded in South Central Texas, the Edwards Plateau and the Upper Coast. Rye is grown primarily as a cover crop and for grazing during the fall, winter and early spring.

In 1984, 115,000 acres of rye were planted, with 15,000 acres harvested, yielding 16.0 bushels per acre, for a total production of 240,000 bushels, valued at $3.80 per bushel, or $912,000 total value. This compared with 160,000 acres planted in 1983, 25,000 acres harvested, yielding 18 bushels per acre for total production of 450,000 bushels, valued at $2.45 per bushel, or $1,103,000.

Some of the leading rye-producing counties are **Eastland, Henderson, Montague, Briscoe** and **Houston.**

Oats

Oats are grown extensively in Texas for winter pasture, hay, silage, greenchop feeding and some acreage is harvested for grain.

In 1984, farmers planted 1,500,000 acres of oats, harvesting 250,000 acres, which yielded 35 bushels per acre, for a total production of 8,750,000 bushels. This brought $17,938,000, or $2.05 per bushel. Comparable figures for 1983 were 1,400,000 acres planted, 500,000 acres harvested, yielding 48 bushels per acre for total production of 24,000,000 bushels. Valued at $1.78 per bushel, the crop brought total value of $42,720,000.

Almost all oat grain produced in Texas is utilized as feed for livestock within the state. A small acreage is grown exclusively for planting seed.

Leading oat grain-producing counties are **McLennan, Collin, Denton, Falls** and **Cooke.**

Texas ranked eighth in oats production in 1981 and **twelfth** in 1982.

Barley

Texas barley acreage and production falls far below that of wheat and oats. In 1984, 60,000 acres of barley were planted, 40,000 acres were harvested, yielding 50 bushels per acre for total production of 2,000,000 bushels. Valued at $2.65 per bushel, value totaled $5,300,000. Comparable figures for 1983 were 70,000 acres planted, 45,000 acres harvested, yielding 55.0 bushels per acre for total production of 2,475,000 bushels. Valued at $2.52 per bushel, value totaled $6,237,000.

Leading barley-producing counties in 1984 were **Parmer, Deaf Smith, Moore, Dallam** and **Sherman.**

Guar

Guar is a drought-tolerant, summer annual legume adapted to regions of 20-30 inch rainfall. Guar grows well under a wide range of soil types but does best on fertile, deep loam and sandy loam soils.

Guar was first introduced into the U.S. from India in 1903 by the Texas Department of Agriculture. Primary uses at that time were as a vegetable for human consumption, as a cattle feed and as a green manure crop. Where adapted, guar will produce more green manure than any other legume.

Commercial production began in the early 1950s in South Texas, but the center of production quickly moved to the sandy soils in the Rolling Plains of Texas. The leading guar producing counties are Cottle, Hardeman, Haskell, Knox and Wilbarger.

In 1984, guar was harvested from 20,000 acres of the 25,000 acres planted, yielding 500 pounds per acre, for a total production of 10,000,000 pounds. Valued at 11.5 cents a pound, total value was $1,150,000. Comparable figures for 1983 were 10,000 acres harvested from 30,000 acres planted, yielding 630 pounds per acre, for total production of 6,300,000 pounds. Valued at 12 cents per pound, total value was $756,000.

The guar seed (called a bean) has a rather large endosperm, which differs from most other legumes having little or no endosperm. The endosperm contains galactomannan gum which forms a viscous gel in cold water. The bean is processed into food grade gum, industrial gum and meal for livestock feed.

The highly refined food grade gum is used as a stiffener and preservative in many food products such as ice cream, whip and chill puddings and whipped cream substitutes. Industrial grade gum is used in cloth and paper sizing, oil well drilling muds, ore flotation and many cosmetics. The meal remaining is an excellent source of cattle feed, which contains 35 percent protein that is 95 percent digestible. It is equal or superior to cottonseed meal as a protein feed.

Sugarbeets

Sugarbeets have been grown on a commercial scale in Texas since 1964 when the **first beet sugar factory** was built by **Holly Sugar Company** at **Hereford.** The leading counties in production in 1983 were **Castro, Deaf Smith, Parmer** and **Randall.**

In 1984, 37,800 acres of sugarbeets were harvested from 39,000 acres planted, yielding 22 tons per acre for total production of 832,000 tons. In 1983, 31,900 acres were harvested from 33,800 acres planted, yielding 19.5 tons per acre for total production of 622,000 tons. Valued at $35.70 per ton, total value was $22,205,000. Texas **ranked tenth** in sugarbeet production in 1982, eighth in 1983.

Sugarcane

Sugarcane is grown from seed cane planted in late summer or fall. It is harvested 12 months later and milled to produce raw **sugar** and **molasses.** The raw sugar then requires additional refining before it is in final form to be offered to consumers.

The **sugarcane grinding mill** operated at **Santa Rosa,** Cameron County, is considered as one of the most modern mills in the United States. Texas sugarcane-producing counties are **Hidalgo, Cameron** and **Willacy.**

Texas ranked fourth in 1982 and 1983 in sugarcane production.

In 1984, 36,300 acres of sugarcane were harvested for sugar and seed, yielding 29.7 tons per acre for total production of 1,078,000 tons. This compared with 35,500 acres harvested in 1983, yielding 31.6 tons per acre for total production of 1,122,000 tons. Valued at $15.20 per ton, total value was $17,054,000. Sugarcane was not a commercial crop in Texas for about 50 years following its abandonment in 1923 because of adverse markets.

Hay, Silage and Other Forage Crops

A large proportion of Texas' agricultural land is devoted to forage crop production. This acreage produces forage needs and provides essentially the total feed requirements for most of the state's large domestic livestock population as well as game animals.

Approximately 80 million acres of native rangeland, which is primarily in the western half of Texas, provide grazing for beef cattle, sheep, goats, horses and game animals. An additional 20 million acres are devoted to introduced forage species. Of this total, approximately 16 million acres are established to introduced improved **perennial grasses** and **legumes** and are harvested by grazing animals. The average annual acreage of crops grown for hay, silage and other forms of machine harvested forage is over 3 million acres with an estimated value in excess of $500 million.

Hay accounts for the major amount of this production with some **corn** and **sorghum silage** being produced. The most important hay crops are annual and perennial grasses and **alfalfa.**

Hay was harvested from 3,040,000 aces in 1984, yielding 1.78 tons per acre for total production of 5,415,000 tons. Valued at $98.50 per ton, total value was $533,378,000. This compared in 1983 with 3,070,000 acres harvested, yielding 2.44 tons per acre for total production of 7,486,000 tons. Valued at $77.50 per ton, total value was $580,165,000.

Grass hay production is widely distributed with some leading counties being **Lamar, Henderson, Erath, Van Zandt, Hopkins, Wilbarger, Leon, Smith** and **Washington.** Texas ranked seventh in all hay production in 1982, fifth in 1983.

Alfalfa was harvested from 190,000 acres in 1984, yielding 4.5 tons per acre for total production of 855,000 tons. Value for alfalfa hay crop is included with "all hay." Comparable figures for 1983 are 170,000 acres harvested, yielding 4.80 tons per acre for total production of 816,000 tons.

An additional sizable acreage of annual forage crops such as **sudan** and **millet** is grazed, as well as much of the small grain acreage. **Alfalfa, sweetcorn, vetch, arrowleaf clover, grasses** and other forage plants also provide income as seed crops.

Peanuts

Peanuts are grown on approximately 250,000 acres in Texas with some 40 percent of the acreage irrigated. Yet well over half of the crop is annually produced on acreage that is irrigated. **Texas ranked third** nationally in production of peanuts in 1983; fourth in 1982. Among Texas crops, **peanuts** ranked ninth in value.

Until 1973, essentially all of the Texas acreage was planted to the Spanish types, which were favored because of their earlier maturity and better drought tolerance than other types. The Spanish variety is also preferred for some uses due to its distinctive flavor. Florunner, a runner type, is now planted on a sizable proportion of the acreage where soil moisture is favorable. The variety is later maturing but better yielding than Spanish varieties under good growing conditions. Florunner peanuts have acceptable quality to compete with the Spanish in most products.

In 1984, peanuts were harvested from 215,000 acres of the 235,000 acres planted in Texas, yielding 1,700 pounds per acre, for a total production of 365,500,000 pounds. Valued at 25.6 cents per pound, total value amounted to $93,568,000. Comparable figures for 1983 were: 215,000 acres harvested of the 230,000 acres planted, yielding 1,685 pounds per acre, for total production of 362,275,000 pounds, valued at 25.3 cents per pound for total value of $91,656,000.

The leading counties in peanut production are **Comanche, Frio, Atascosa, Gaines** and **Wilson.**

Soybeans

Soybean acreage in Texas increased substantially after 1976. More favorable price levels have stimulated a stronger interest in growing soybeans.

In low rainfall areas, yields have been too low or inconsistent for profitable production under dryland conditions. Soybeans' need for moisture in late summer minimizes economic crop possibilities in the Blacklands and Rolling Plains. In the Blacklands, cotton root rot seriously hinders soybean production. Limited moisture at critical growth stages may occasionally prevent economical yields even in high rainfall areas of Northeast Texas and the Coast Prairie.

Because of day length sensitivity, soybeans should be planted in Texas during the long days of May and June to obtain sufficient vegetative growth for optimum yields. Varieties planted during this period usually cease vegetative development and initiate reproductive processes during the hot, usually dry months of July and August. When moisture is insufficient during the blooming and fruiting period, yields are drastically reduced. In most areas of the state, July and August rainfall is insufficient to permit economical dryland production. The risk of dryland soybean production in the Coast Prairie and Northeast Texas is considerably less when compared to other dryland areas because moisture is available more often during the critical fruiting period.

Soybeans were harvested from 410,000 of the 450,000 acres planted in 1984, yielding 29 bushels per acre for a total production of 11,890,000 bushels. Valued at $5.65 per bushel, total value was $67,179,000. Comparable figures for 1983 were 420,000 acres harvested from 460,000 acres planted, yielding 22.5 bushels per acre for total production of 9,450,000 bushels, valued at $7.43 per bushel, for total value of $70,214,000

Production is largely in the areas of the Upper Coast, irrigated High Plains and Red River Valley of Northeast Texas. Soybeans are adapted to the same general soil climatic conditions as corn, cotton or grain sorghum, provided moisture, disease and insects are not limiting factors. The major counties in soybean production in 1984 were **Hale, Liberty, Chambers, Harris** and **Wharton.**

Sunflowers

Sunflowers constitute one of the most important annual **oilseed crops** in the world. The cultivated types, which are thought to be descendants of the common wild sunflower native to Texas, have been successfully grown in several countries, including Russia, Argentina, Romania, Bulgaria, Uruguay, Western Canada and portions of the northern United States. Extensive trial plantings conducted in the Cotton Belt states since 1968 showed sunflowers have considerable potential as an oilseed crop in much of this area, including Texas. This crop exhibits good cold and drought tolerance, is adapted to a wide range of soil and climatic conditions and tolerates higher levels of hail, wind and sand abrasion than other crops normally grown in the state.

Texas ranked fourth nationally in sunflower seed production in 1982 and 1983.

In 1984, 37,000 acres were harvested from the 40,000 acres planted, yielding 1,300 pounds per acre for a total production of 48,100,000 pounds. Valued at $10.50 per cwt., total value amounted to $5,051,000. Comparable figures for 1983 were 34,000 acres harvested of the 35,000 acres planted, yielding 1,100 pounds per acre for total production of 37,400,000 pounds, valued at $10.00 per

cwt., total value $3,740,000. The leading counties in production in 1983 were **Floyd, Lubbock, Lynn, Bailey** and **Crosby.**

Reasons for growing sunflowers include the need for an additional cash crop with low water and plant nutrient requirements, the recent development of sunflower hybrids and interest by food processors in Texas **sunflower oil,** which has a high oleic acid content. Commercial users have found many advantages in this high oleic oil including excellent cooking stability, particularly for use as a deep fat frying medium for potato chips, corn chips and similar products.

Sunflower meal is a high-quality protein source free of nutritional toxins that can be included in rations for swine, poultry and ruminants. The hulls constitute a source of roughage which can also be included in livestock rations.

Flaxseed

Earliest flax planting was at **Victoria** in 1900. Since the first planting, Texas flax acreage has fluctuated depending on market, winterkill and drought.

Flax acreage has dropped in recent years and estimates were discontinued in 1980.

Forest Products

The non-industrial private forest landowners of Texas, who own two-thirds of the forest land, sold standing timber with an estimated value of $147 million in 1983. Forest industry land had standing timber sales of $135 million with only one-third as much land base as the non-industrial landowners. The delivered value of this timber to the processing plants (such as sawmills, papermills and plywood plants) was over $484 million. In 1983, the volume of pine cut exceeded the growth. Hardwood growth continues to outpace the annual harvest.

Pulpwood, sawlogs, veneer bolts for plywood, utility poles, piling, fence posts and railroad crossties are leading products. Over 210,000 Christmas trees, grown primarily in East Texas but found throughout the state, were sold in the Texas market. In Central Texas some timber is harvested for **fuel wood, lumber, veneer, crossties, posts** and **cedar oil.**

In addition to timber production, the forests of Texas provide a multitude of additional products such as wildlife habitat, watersheds, livestock grazing and opportunities for outdoor recreation. Minor products include **pine straw, edible berries and nuts, wild honey** and **decorative plants** such as mistletoe.

Texas forests face a multitude of problems ranging from urban encroachment to insect and disease control. **Southern pine beetle** threatens many of the poorly managed stands. Regulations restricting control strategies of pine beetle and other pests threaten the existence of East Texas forests for timber products and recreation.

Horticultural Specialty Crops

The trend to increased production of horticulture specialty crops continues to rise as transportation costs on long-distance hauling makes the importation of plants from other growing areas increasingly costly. This has resulted in a marked increase in the production of container-grown plants within the state. This increase is noted especially in the production of **bedding plants, foliage plants,** sod and the woody landscape plants.

Plant rental services have become a multimillion dollar business. This comparative newcomer in the plant industry provides the plants for a fee and maintains them in office buildings, shopping malls, public buildings and even in some homes. The response has been great as evidenced by the growth of companies providing these services.

Extension specialists estimated cash receipts from horticultural specialty crops in Texas to have exceeded $358 million in 1984, making them the **fourth ranking** cash receipts crop. Apparently Texans have decided that they are going to create interesting surroundings by improving their own landscape plantings.

Truck Crops

Some market vegetables are produced in almost all Texas counties, but most of the commercial crop comes from about 200 counties. **Hidalgo County** is the leading Texas county in vegetable acres harvested followed by **Starr** and **Frio Counties.** Other leading producing counties are: **Cameron, Castro, Uvalde, Floyd, Duval** and **Webb.**

Most Texas vegetables are marketed fresh rather than processed.

Nationally, **Texas ranks third** in harvested acreage, and value of fresh market vegetables, being exceeded by California and Florida. Texas had 5.9 percent of the harvested acreage, 4.6 percent of the production and 5.6 percent of the value of fresh market vegetables produced in the United States in 1984.

Vegetables leading in value of production usually are **carrots, onions, watermelons, cantaloupes, cabbage** and **Irish potatoes.** Watermelons led acreage in 1984 and onions accounted for the most value.

Texas growers harvested principal commercial crops valued at $390,563,000 from 186,500 acres in 1984. This compared with $325,545,000 from 162,200 acres in 1983; $368,995,000 from 183,800 acres in 1982; and $382,189,000 from 178,020 acres in 1981.

Onions

Onions were harvested from 24,600 acres in 1984, valued at $87,461,000. This compared with 25,200 acres in 1983, valued at $62,112,000; 25,700 acres in 1982, valued at $74,820,000; and 24,200 acres, valued at $99,095,000 in 1981. Hildago County accounted for almost 50 percent of the acreage in Texas in 1984.

Carrots

Carrot production was valued at $31,716,000 in 1984 from 13,900 acres harvested. This compared with $27,458,000 from 15,300 acres harvested in 1983; $29,461,000 in 1982 from 17,100 acres harvested; and $29,669,000 from 16,500 acres in 1981.

The winter carrot production from South Texas accounts for about three-fourths of the total production during the winter season.

Irish Potatoes

In 1984, Texas harvested 17,500 acres of the 17,900 acres planted in Irish potatoes. Yielding 232 cwt. per acre, total production amounted to 4,065,000 cwt. Valued at $11.70 per cwt., total value was $47,355,000. This compared with 15,200 acres harvested of 15,500 acres planted in 1983, yielding 219 cwt. per acre for total production of 3,324,000 cwt., valued at $8.50 per cwt., total value $28,197,000.

Cantaloupes-Honeydews

Cantaloupes were harvested from 18,000 acres in 1984, valued at $39,965,000. This compared with 19,000 acres, valued at $39,378,000 in 1983; 21,100 acres valued at $36,795,000 in 1982; and 14,800 acres, valued at $37,123,000 in 1981. **Honeydew melons** valued at $14,535,000 were harvested from 5,000 acres in 1984; $15,708,000 from 5,500 acres in 1983; $19,051,000 from 4,900 acres in 1982; and $15,912,000 from 4,000 acres in 1981. Texas ranked second only to California in harvested acreage of cantaloupes and honeydews in 1983.

Cabbage

Texas harvested 14,400 acres of cabbage in 1984, valued at $76,983,000. This compared with 14,600 acres, valued at $34,589,000 in 1983; 16,700 acres valued at $56,418,000 in 1982; and 16,800 acres, valued at $34,834,000 in 1981. Texas was second only to Florida in harvested acreage of cabbage in 1983.

TEXAS VEGETABLE PRODUCTION

Source: Texas Crop and Livestock Reporting Service

	Production		
Crop	1982	1983	1984
	— 1,000 cwt. —		
*Broccoli	625	550	567
*Cabbage.	4,059	4,162	4,088
Cantaloupes.	2,381	2,376	3,154
*Carrots.	2,706	3,201	2,099
*Cauliflower	90	164	147
Sweet Corn.	137	225	192
Cucumbers	961	914	884
Honeydew Melons	784	770	950
Lettuce	907	874	745
*Onions	5,036	5,443	4,908
*Green Peppers	864	888	1,020
Spinach	448	478	369
Tomatoes.	332	293	332
Watermelons	4,360	3,438	6,090
*Total for Fresh Market	23,690	23,776	25,545
†Processed	625	447	790
Total Commercial Vegetables. . .	24,315	24,223	26,335
*Potatoes	3,228	3,324	4,065
*Sweet Potatoes.	792	852	803
Total All Crops	28,335	28,399	31,203

*Includes some quantities processed.

†Snap beans, beets, sweet corn, cucumbers for pickles, spinach and tomatoes.

TEXAS FRUIT-VEGETABLE SHIPMENTS

(Amounts are shown in units of 1,000 hundredweight for rail (RL), truck (TR) and export.)

	1982		1983		1984	
Commodity—	RL	TR	RL	TR	RL	TR
Avocados	0	0	0	5	0	0
Beans	0	0	0	0	0	1
Beets	0	76	0	80	0	28
Broccoli	8	220	8	285	1	133
Broccoli, Expt. . . .	0	0	4	0	1	0
Cabbage	0	3,845	45	4,381	3	3,463
Cabbage, Expt. .	0	0	10	0	0	0
Cantaloupes. . . .	2	1,568	13	2,370	10	2,611
Cantaloupes,						
Expt.	0	0	0	0	0	1
Carrots	0	939	11	1,231	2	790
Cauliflower	0	60	0	77	0	11
Celery	0	108	6	348	1	213
Celery, Expt. . . .	0	0	5	0	0	0
Corn, Sweet	0	28	0	14	0	14
Cucumbers	0	911	1	913	0	741
Eggplant	0	7	0	11	0	7
Grapefruit	0	4,309	51	4,858	0	6
Grapefruit, Expt.	0	807	2	984	0	2
Greens.	0	212	0	236	0	171
Greens, Expt	0	0	1	0	0	0
Honeydews	1	618	10	844	3	944
Honeydews,						
Expt.	0	0	2	0	0	1
Lettuce, Iceberg	0	685	4	750	0	419
Lettuce, Ice.,						
Expt.	0	0	1	0	0	0
Lettuce, other . .	0	1	0	0	0	0
Mixed Citrus . . .	0	0	6	0	0	0
Mixed Misc.						
Melons	0	1	0	7	0	0
Mixed						
Vegetables . . .	0	0	44	0	4	0

	1982		1983		1984	
Commodity—	RL	TR	RL	TR	RL	TR
Mixed Veg.,						
Expt.	0	0	7	0	1	0
Okra	0	4	0	4	0	0
Onions, dry	17	4,365	25	5,229	20	4,096
Onions, dry;						
Expt.	0	0	0	0	0	141
Onions, green. . .	0	20	0	24	0	8
Oranges	0	2,462	39	2,196	0	3
Oranges, Expt. . .	0	4	0	0	0	0
Parsley	0	58	0	58	0	25
Peas, other than						
green	0	1	0	1	0	1
Peppers, bell . . .	0	812	0	786	3	775
Peppers, bell;						
Expt.	0	0	0	0	0	35
Peppers, other . .	0	17	0	5	0	0
Potatoes, table . .	2	2,084	11	1,791	2	2,722
Potatoes, chipper	0	592	0	524	0	467
Radishes	0	0	0	2	0	0
Spinach	8	312	15	389	3	338
Spinach, Expt. . .	10	0	26	0	16	0
Squash.	0	40	0	35	0	29
Tangerines	0	9	0	15	0	0
Tomatoes.	0	177	0	188	0	150
Tomatoes, cherry	0	0	0	0	0	7
Turnips-						
Rutabagas . . .	0	26	0	27	0	9
Watermelons . . .	0	2,123	2	2,186	0	2,478
TOTALS	48	27,501	349	30,854	70	20,840

NOTE: Export data are not complete and should not be interpreted as representing total exports.

Cauliflower

Texas' cauliflower production and value for 1984 were $3,364,000 from 1,800 acres. This compared with $4,497,000 from 1,800 acres in 1983; $3,269,000 from 1,100 acres in 1982; and $1,820,000 from 920 acres in 1981.

Broccoli

Texas' production of broccoli in 1984 was 7,500 acres valued at $19,672,000. This compared with 6,800 acres valued at $21,434,000 in 1983; 7,600 acres valued at $24,421,000 in 1982; and 5,300 acres valued at $14,250,000 in 1981. Broccoli is primarily a South Texas crop.

Watermelons

Watermelons were harvested from 55,000 acres in 1984, valued at $31,569,000. This compared with 32,400 acres, valued at $35,707,000 in 1983; 43,100 acres valued at $33,834,000 in 1982; and 43,900 acres, valued at $37,022,000 in 1981. In 1983, Texas ranked first in harvested acreage of watermelons.

VALUE TEXAS VEGETABLES 1982-1984

Source: U.S. Department of Agriculture
(1,000 Dollars)

Crop	Value		
	1982	1983	1984
For Fresh Market			
*Broccoli, Winter, Fall....	$24,421	$21,434	$19,672
*Cabbage, All	56,418	34,589	76,983
Cantaloupes, All	36,795	39,378	39,965
*Carrots, All	29,461	27,458	31,716
*Cauliflower, Winter, Fall .	3,269	4,497	3,364
Sweet Corn, Early Spring..	2,055	2,068	1,564
Cucumbers, All	14,240	16,474	12,786
Honeydew Melons, Spring .	19,051	15,708	14,535
Lettuce, All	14,200	9,247	6,845
*Onions, All............	74,820	62,112	87,461
*Green Peppers, All......	25,171	26,251	29,401
Spinach, All............	16,635	16,404	14,519
Tomatoes, All	12,388	7,226	6,804
Watermelons, All........	33,834	35,707	31,569
*Total for Fresh Market .	$362,758	$318,553	$377,189
†Total Processed	3,012	2,191	3,860
Commercial Vegetables, Total	$365,770	$320,744	$381,049
*Potatoes, All	29,449	28,197	47,355
*Sweet Potatoes	13,068	15,677	18,469
Total All Crops	$408,287	$364,618	$446,873

*Includes some quantities processed.

†Includes snap beans, beets, sweet corn, cucumbers for pickles, spinach and tomatoes. Excludes values of commodities in fresh market only.

Tomatoes

Commercial production of tomatoes is marketed throughout the year in Texas partly as a result of recent increases in greenhouse production during winter months.

In 1984, tomatoes were harvested from 3,900 acres, valued at $6,804,000. This compared with 3,900 acres valued at $7,226,000 in 1983; 4,200 acres valued at $12,388,000 in 1982; and 4,200 acres valued at $6,443,000 in 1981.

Green Peppers

In 1984, 8,500 acres were harvested for green peppers, valued at $29,406,000. This compared with 9,000 acres valued at $26,251,000 in 1983; 10,400 acres valued at $25,171,000 in 1982; and 7,900 acres valued at $25,433,000 in 1981. Texas ranked second behind Florida in harvested acreage of bell peppers in 1983.

Lettuce

The 3,500 acres of lettuce harvested in 1984 brought $6,845,000. This compared with 3,800 acres valued at $9,247,000 in 1983; 4,600 acres valued at $14,200,000 in 1982; and 4,100 acres valued at $10,267,000 in 1981.

Sweet Potatoes

In 1984, Texas harvested 7,300 acres of sweet potatoes valued at $18,469,000. This compared with 7,100 acres valued at $15,677,000 in 1983; 7,200 acres valued at $12,672,000 in 1982; and 7,800 acres in 1981, valued at $14,227,000.

Spinach

Spinach production is primarily concentrated in the Winter Garden area of South Texas. The 4,300 acres harvested in 1984 brought $14,519,000. This compared with 5,200 acres valued at $16,404,000 in 1983; 6,400 acres valued at $16,635,000 in 1982; and 5,300 acres valued at $18,071,000 in 1981. In 1983, Texas ranked first among states in harvested acreage of spinach.

Cucumbers

Cucumbers were harvested from 6,800 acres in 1984, valued at $12,786,000. This compared with 8,800 acres valued at $16,474,000 in 1983; 9,000 acres valued at $14,240,000 in 1982; and 7,000 acres in 1981, valued at $11,637,000.

Sweet Corn

Sweet corn in Texas was harvested from 3,200 acres in 1984 and was valued at $3,053,000. This compared with 3,000 acres valued at $3,938,000 in 1983; 2,100 acres valued at $2,055,000 in 1982; and 2,100 acres valued at $2,102,000 in 1981.

Other Vegetables

Snap beans, black-eyed peas, beets, okra, garlic, turnips, radishes, rutabagas and many other vegeta-

ACREAGE OF MAJOR VEGETABLES HARVESTED

Source: Texas Crop and Livestock Reporting Service

Crops	CROP YEAR							
	1977	1978	1979	1980	1981	1982	1983	1984
*Broccoli	1,300	2,200	1,150	3,500	5,300	7,600	6,800	7,500
*Cabbage	14,900	20,100	14,400	17,600	16,800	16,700	14,600	14,400
Cantaloupes	17,200	19,300	18,100	16,300	14,800	21,100	19,000	18,000
*Carrots.................	14,200	17,800	16,100	13,600	16,500	17,100	15,300	13,900
*Cauliflower	210	1,000	700	1,020	920	1,100	1,800	1,800
Sweet corn	3,100	1,800	2,500	1,800	2,100	2,100	3,000	3,200
Cucumbers	9,000	9,000	7,300	10,500	7,000	9,000	8,800	6,800
Honeydew melons	5,100	4,000	6,400	4,200	4,000	4,900	5,500	5,000
Lettuce..................	4,600	5,200	5,300	4,800	4,600	4,600	3,800	3,500
*Onions.................	23,700	30,000	29,500	25,500	24,200	25,700	25,200	24,600
*Green peppers...........	8,500	9,100	10,300	8,900	7,900	10,400	9,000	8,500
Spinach	3,400	4,100	6,100	6,400	5,300	6,400	5,200	4,300
Tomatoes	6,600	5,800	6,200	5,400	4,200	4,200	3,900	3,900
Watermelons	58,000	49,000	46,000	36,000	43,900	43,100	32,400	55,000
*Total fresh market........	169,810	178,400	170,050	155,520	157,520	174,000	154,300	170,300
†Total Processed..........	16,800	20,100	20,300	18,400	12,700	...	4,100	6,700
Commercial Veg. Total	186,610	198,500	190,350	173,920	170,220	174,000	158,400	177,000
*Potatoes	15,700	18,500	18,000	13,700	12,700	14,700	15,200	17,500
*Sweet Potatoes	9,500	9,500	7,900	6,500	7,800	7,200	7,100	7,300
Total all Vegetables	211,810	226,500	216,250	194,120	190,720	195,900	180,700	201,800

Includes some quantities processed. †Snap beans, beets, sweet corn, cucumbers for pickles, spinach and tomatoes. Excludes quantities of commodities annotated by footnote.

bles are produced in Texas with the volume and value fluctuating widely from season to season.

Vegetables for Processing

Tomatoes for processing in 1982 were harvested from 2,700 acres valued at $1,860,000. Comparable figures were 1,200 acres valued at $478,000 in 1981.

Data for **cucumbers for pickles, snap beans, beets for canning, sweet corn,** and **spinach** used for processing are not published to avoid individual disclosure.

Fruits and Nuts

Texas is noted for producing a wide variety of fruit. The pecan is the only commercial nut crop in the state. The pecan is native to most of the state's river valleys and is the **Texas state tree.** Citrus, practically all produced in the three southernmost counties in the Lower Rio Grande Valley, is the most valuable fruit crop. Texas pecans and Ruby Red grapefruit are famous for their premium quality throughout the nation. Peaches represent the next most important Texas fruit crop, yet there is considerable amount of interest in growing **apples.**

Citrus

Texas ranks with California and Florida as one of the three leading states in production of citrus. Most of the Texas production is in Cameron, Hidalgo and Willacy Counties of the Lower Rio Grande Valley.

There were 30,600 acres of commercial citrus in Texas in 1985, a 56 percent decrease from the 69,192 acres on Jan. 1, 1983. The severe freeze during 1983 destroyed more than half of the Rio Grande Valley citrus crop.

The number of citrus trees decreased to 3,769,400 on Jan. 1, 1985 from the 8,072,640 on Jan. 1, 1983. **Grapefruit** acreage accounted for 65 percent of the total citrus acreage in Texas; **oranges,** 35 percent; and other citrus, such as **lemons, limes, tangelos** and **tangerines,** less than 1 percent. Hidalgo County continues to rank No. 1 in citrus with 87 percent of the acreage and 88 percent of the trees.

Net acreage of all grapefruit totaled 19,110, down 57 percent from 44,346 acres in 1983. Ruby Red varieties accounted for 87 percent of the grapefruit acreage; Star Ruby, 11 percent; Pink and White, 1 percent each. The total number of grapefruit trees decreased to 2,450,500 from the 5,329,300 on Jan. 1, 1983. Trees per net acre increased from 120 in 1983 to 128 in 1985.

For oranges, net acreage declined to 11,380 in 1985 from the 24,575 in 1983. Early and mid-season varieties accounted for 55 percent of the orange acreage and Valencia 45 percent. The total number of orange trees declined to 1,303,000 from the 2,710,700 in 1983. Trees per net acre rose from 110 to 114.

The 1983-84 citrus crop was estimated at 5.7 million boxes, 66 percent below the 16.9 million boxes reported in 1982-83. It consisted of 3.2 million boxes of grapefruit, valued at $9,385,000 or $2.93 per box, and 2.5 million boxes of oranges, valued at $11,492,000 or $4.58 per box. The 1982-83 crop was estimated at 16.9 million boxes, consisting of 11.2 million boxes of grapefruit, valued at $24,148,000 or $2.16 per box, and 5.7 million boxes of oranges, valued at $26,402,000 or $4.65 per box.

While grapefruit and oranges account for most of the Texas citrus crop, there are some 145 acres and 15,900 trees of **lemons, limes, tangelos** and **tangerines.** Hardy Satsuma oranges grow in home gardens along the Gulf Coast area.

Tangerines and Tangelos

There is some commercial production of tangerines and tangelos (cross between tangerine and grapefruit) in the Lower Rio Grande Valley and other South Texas areas. There are a few small tangerine orchards in the Laredo and Carrizo Springs-Crystal City area of the Winter Garden. Most of the production is for local consumption or gift boxes. Leading varieties of tangerines are the Clementine and Dancy. Most tangelos are of the Orlando variety.

Lemons

A small acreage is grown in the Lower Rio Grande Valley. Major variety of lemon grown in Texas is the Myers; lemons are sold mostly at roadside stands with a few shipped in gift packs.

Peaches

Primary production areas are East Texas, the Hill Country and the West Cross Timbers. Recently peach production has spread to South and West Texas. Low chilling varieties for early marketing are being grown in Atascosa, Frio, Webb, Karnes and Duval Counties.

The 1984 utilized peach crop totaled 438,000 bushels for a value of $5,460,000, or $12.47 per bushel. This compared with 479,000 bushels, valued at $6,440,000, or $13.44 per bushel in 1983; 292,000 bushels, valued at $4,200,000, or $14.38 per bushel in 1982; and 615,000 bushels, valued at $6,195,000, or $10.07 per bushel in 1981.

The demand for high quality Texas peaches greatly exceeds the supply. Texas ranked 11th nationally in peach production in 1984. Leading Texas counties in production during 1984 were Smith, Parker, Montague, Eastland, Comanche, Gillespie and Limestone.

Apples

Small acreages of apples, usually marketed in the state, are grown in a number of counties including Montague and Gillespie. The crop is harvested and marketed from July to October. Most of apples are sold at roadside stands or go to nearby markets.

Pears

Well-adapted for home and small-orchard production, the pear is not commercially significant in Texas. Comanche, Parker, Lampasas, Cooke, McCulloch and Eastland Counties lead in production. Fruit usually goes for home consumption or to nearby markets.

Apricots

Not a commercial crop, apricots are grown chiefly in Comanche, Denton, Wilbarger, Parker and Collingsworth Counties. Others reporting apricots included Martin, Clay, Young, Lampasas, Gillespie, Anderson, Erath, Wichita and Eastland Counties.

Plums

Plum production is scattered over a wide area of the state with the heaviest production in East and Central Texas. The leading counties in production are Smith, Gillespie and Knox. Most of production goes to nearby markets.

Blackberries

Smith County is a blackberry center, with the Tyler-Lindale area having processed the crop since 1890. There are about 1,500 acres in Smith, Wood, Van Zandt and Henderson Counties. The Brazos blackberry is grown as a local market or "pick-your-own" fruit in many sections of the state. **Dewberries** grow wild in Central and East Texas and are gathered for home use and local sale in May and June.

Strawberries

Atascosa County is the leading commercial area, although strawberries are grown for local markets in Wood, Van Zandt and Smith Counties in East Texas. The most concentrated production occurs in the Poteet area below San Antonio.

Avocados

Avocados grow on a small acreage in the Lower Rio Grande Valley. Interest in this crop is increasing and production is expected to expand. Lulu is the principal variety.

Pecans

The pecan, the state tree, is one of the most widely distributed trees in Texas. It is native to 150 counties and is grown commercially in some 30 additional counties. The pecan is also widely used as a dual-purpose yard tree. The commercial plantings of pecans has greatly accelerated in Central and West Texas with many of the new orchards being irrigated. Many new pecan plantings are being established under trickle irrigation systems. Two factors that have greatly helped to increase quality and yields have been the development and use of the new USDA pecan varieties and some 40 county and regional pecan grading demonstrations.

The 1984 utilized production totaled 25,000,000 pounds, valued at $22,500,000, or 90 cents a pound; in 1983, 70,000,000 pounds, valued at $39,200,000, or 56 cents a pound.

Nationally, Texas ranked second in pecan production in 1984. Leading Texas counties in 1984 pecan production were Hood, El Paso, San Saba, Mills, Guadalupe, Comanche, Pecos and Wharton.

Cattle graze in Trinity River bottoms as special treat for the Republican National Convention visitors to Dallas.

Livestock and Their Products

Livestock and their products usually account for more than half of the agricultural cash receipts in Texas. The state ranks first nationally in all cattle, beef cattle, cattle on feed, cattle slaughtered, sheep and lambs, wool, goats and mohair. In 1984, it ranked ninth in dairy cows, seventh in broilers, eighth in eggs and 15th in hogs.

Meat animals normally account for around 80 percent of total cash receipts from marketings of livestock and their products. Sales of livestock and products in 1983 totaled $5.5 billion. This compared with $5.4 billion in 1982; $5.4 billion in 1981; and $5.2 billion in 1980.

Cattle dominates livestock production in Texas, contributing more than 70 percent of cash receipts from livestock and products each year. The Jan. 1, 1985 inventory of all cattle and calves in Texas totaled 14,100,000 head, valued at $4.7 billion. This compared with 14,350,000 head, valued at $4.8 billion in 1984; 15,000,000 head, valued at $5.0 billion in 1983; 13,700,000 head valued at $4.5 billion in 1982, and 13,700,000 head valued at $5.0 billion in 1981.

Texas sheep raisers have reduced their herd because of increasing production costs. On Jan. 1, 1985, the sheep and lamb inventory stood at 1,810,000 head, compared with 1,970,000 in 1984; 3,214,000 in 1983; 2,400,000 in 1982; and 2,360,000 in 1981. **Sheep and lamb production** amounted to 112,735,000 pounds in 1984; 148,295,000 pounds in 1983; and 124,600,000 pounds in 1982. **Wool production** amounted to 17,500,000 pounds in 1984, valued at $16,100,000. This compared with 18,600,000 pounds, valued at $15,438,000 in 1983; 19,300,000 pounds, valued at $16,212,000 in 1982; and 20,500,000 pounds, valued at $24,600,000 in 1981. Price of wool per pound averaged 92 cents in 1984, compared with 83 cents in 1983; 84 cents in 1982; and $1.20 in 1981.

Lamb prices averaged $59.70 per cwt. in 1984, compared with $54.40 per cwt. in 1983, in $53.60 in 1982, and $56.80 in 1981. Average value per head of sheep stock on Jan. 1, 1985, was estimated at $57.50, compared with $39.00 in 1984; $39.00 in 1983; $42.00 in 1982; and $49.50 in 1981.

Mohair production in Texas amounted to 11,200,000 pounds in 1984, compared with 10,600,000 pounds in 1983; 10,000,000 pounds in 1982; 9,900,000 pounds in 1981; and 8,800,000 pounds in 1980. The all-time high production was in 1965 when 31,584,000 pounds were produced, valued at $20,845,000, or 66 cents per pound.

Mohair production was valued at $48,160,000 in 1984, or $4.30 per pound. This compared with $42,930,000, or $4.05 per pound in 1983; $25,500,000, or $2.55 per pound in 1982; and $34,650,000 or $3.50 per pound in 1981.

Beef Cattle

Beef cattle raising is the most extensive agricultural operation in Texas. In 1983, 46.8 percent of the total cash receipts from farm and ranch marketings — $4,193,111,000 of $8,970,339,000 — came from cattle and calves. This compared with $4,125,911,000 of $9,649,348,000 in 1982; $4,098,218,000 of $9,814,210,000 in 1981; and $3,933,393,000 of $9,110,159,000 in 1980. Cotton was the next leading commodity.

Nearly all of the 254 counties in Texas derive more revenue from cattle than from any other agricultural commodity and those that don't usually rank cattle second in importance.

Within the boundaries of Texas are 13 percent of all the cattle in the U.S., as are 16 percent of the beef breeding cows, and 12 percent of the calf crop.

The number of all cattle in Texas on Jan. 1, 1985 totaled 14,100,000. This compared with 14,350,000 in 1984; 15,000,000 in 1983; 13,700,000 in 1982 and 13,700,000 in 1981.

Calves born on Texas farms and ranches in 1984 totaled 5,050,000, compared with 5,450,000 in 1983; 5,650,000 in 1982; and 5,400,000 in 1981.

TEXAS LIVESTOCK NUMBERS AND VALUES

Source: U.S. Department of Agriculture

Class of Livestock	Numbers				Farm Value					
	1983	1984	1985 Preliminary		Value Per Head			Total Value		
			Number	Percent of 1984	1983	1984	1985	1983	1984	1985
	Thousands			Pct.	Dollars			1,000 Dollars		
All Cattle	15,000	14,350	14,100	98	$330.00	$335.00	$335.00	$4,950,000	$4,807,250	$4,723,500
*Milk Cows.	330	333	314	94	1,150	940.00	900.00	385,250	313,020	282,600
*Beef Cows.	6,270	6,067	5,586	92	N.A.	N.A.	N.A.	N.A.	N.A.	N.A.
†Hogs	575	590	415	70	87.00	61.50	78.00	50,025	36,285	32,370
All Sheep	2,225	1,970	1,810	92	39.00	39.00	57.50	86,775	76,830	104,075
Goats.	1,420	1,450	1,550	107	37.50	56.70	48.30	53,250	82,215	74,865
†Chickens	17,200	17,400	17,400	100	1.75	2.00	1.95	30,100	34,800	33,930
†Turkey Hens.	310	155	‡	‡	15.00	17.00	‡	4,650	2,635	‡
Total Value	. . .	. . .	. . .	. . .	. . .	. . .	. . .	$5,560,050	$5,353,035	$5,251,340

*Included in "all cattle." †Figures are as of Dec. 1 of preceding year. ‡Turkey figures not released for 1985 to avoid disclosing individual operations. N.A. Not available.

Receipts of cattle and calves at approximately 157 livestock auctions inspected by Texas Animal Health Commission totaled 7,668,000 head in 1984. This compared with 6,654,000 in 1983; 6,755,000 in 1982; and 5,597,000 in 1981. The number of cattle and calves shipped into Texas totaled 2,498,000 head in 1984; 1,965,000 head in 1983; 1,827,000 head in 1982; and 1,840,782 head in 1981.

There was a total of 152,000 all-cattle operations in Texas in 1984 compared with 156,000 in 1983, 159,000 in 1982, 162,000 in 1981, and 162,000 in 1980.

Livestock Industries

A large portion of Texas livestock is sold through local auction markets.

In 1984, 157 livestock auctions were reported by the Texas Animal Health Commission. Their receipts were 7,668,000 cattle and calves, 455,000 hogs, 868,000 sheep and lambs and 598,000 goats. This compared with 6,654,000 cattle and calves, 440,000 hogs, 840,000 sheep and lambs and 430,000 goats in 1983; in 1982, 6,755,000 cattle and calves, 460,000 hogs, 966,000 sheep and lambs and 366,000 goats; and 5,597,000 cattle and calves, 491,000 hogs, 857,000 sheep and lambs and 335,000 goats in 1981.

During 1984, the commission reported 2,172,000 cattle shipped from Texas to other states and 2,498,000 shipped in, compared with 2,202,000 shipped out and 1,965,000 shipped in during 1983; 2,268,000 shipped out and 1,827,000 shipped in during 1982; and 1,943,000 shipped out and 1,841,000 shipped in during 1981. (Figures exclude cattle shipped direct to slaughter where no health certificates are required.)

During 1984, Texas shipped out 256,000 sheep and lambs and shipped in 222,000. This compared with 154,000 sheep and lambs shipped out and 148,000 shipped in during 1983; 199,000 shipped out and 215,000 shipped in during 1982; and 133,000 shipped out and 227,600 shipped in during 1981.

Feedlot fattening of livestock, mainly cattle, is a major industry in Texas. Texas lots marketed 5,090,000 head of grain-fed cattle in 1984, compared with 4,400,000 head in 1983; 4,075,000 head in 1982; and 3,960,000 head in 1981. In recent years, more cattle have been fed in Texas than any other state in the United States.

During 1984, there were 139 feedlots with a feeding capacity of 1,000 head or more. This compared with 138 in 1983; 149 in 1982; and 145 in 1981.

Federally inspected slaughter plants in Texas numbered 68 in 1985 with 253 state-inspected facilities. This compared with 74 federal and 264 state in 1984; 71 federal and 272 state in 1983; 72 federal and 277 state in 1982; and 73 federal and 289 state in 1981. In 1984, the number

TEXAS CATTLE MARKETED, BY SIZE OF FEEDLOTS

Texas Crop and Livestock Reporting Service

Year—	Under 1,000	1,000-1,999	2,000-3,999	4,000-7,999	8,000-15,999	16,000 & Over	Total
			— Cattle Marketed — 1,000 head —				
1962 ..	105	87	109	194	*261	—	756
1963 ..	120	111	144	205	185	131	896
1964 ..	118	100	174	223	177	179	971
1965 ..	104	108	205	324	107	246	1,094
1966 ..	163	127	268	359	205	290	1,412
1967 ..	138	126	194	372	343	481	1,654
1968 ..	112	91	138	321	439	869	1,970
1969 ..	111	78	133	303	514	1,567	2,706
1970 ..	98	53	112	281	727	1,867	3,138
1971 ..	99	49	117	304	697	2,397	3,663
1972 ..	98	57	112	308	558	3,175	4,308
1973 ..	99	47	74	210	625	3,357	4,412
1974 ..	85	31	48	189	544	3,002	3,899
1975 ..	50	22	51	134	485	2,325	3,067
1976 ..	60	33	62	170	583	3,039	3,947
1977 ..	146	22	38	206	604	3,211	4,227
1978 ..	80	20	50	242	697	3,826	4,915
1979 ..	54	19	46	227	556	3,543	4,445
1980 ..	51	18	47	226	533	3,285	4,160
1981 ..	50	20	50	220	510	3,110	3,960
1982 ..	55	20	60	210	540	3,190	4,075
1983 ..	100	20	80	130	490	3,580	4,400
1984 ..	60	20	180	150	540	4,140	5,090

*Marketing from larger size groups included to avoid disclosing individual operations.

of head slaughtered in Texas totaled 6,767,000 cattle, 271,000 calves, 1,162,000 hogs, 790,000 sheep and lambs and 87,000 goats. This compared with 6,110,000 cattle, 258,000 calves, 1,281,000 hogs, 752,000 sheep and lambs and 66,000 goats in 1983; 5,702,000 cattle, 235,000 calves, 1,286,000 hogs, 904,000 sheep and lambs and 64,000 goats in 1982; and 5,847,000 cattle, 252,000 calves, 1,415,000 hogs, 1,118,000 sheep and lambs and 64,000 goats in 1981.

Increased feeding of cattle in commercial feedlots has been a major economic development during recent years and has stimulated the establishment and expansion of beef slaughtering plants. Most of this development has been in the Panhandle-Plains area of Northwest Texas. This area alone accounts for over 70 percent of the cattle fed in the state.

Feedlots with capacities of 1,000 head or more accounted for more than 98 percent of the cattle fed in Texas. Total feedlot marketings in 1984 represented about 23 percent of total U.S. fed cattle marketings.

Large amounts of capital are required for feedlot operations. This has forced many lots to become custom feeding facilities.

Feedlots are concentrated on the High Plains largely because of extensive supplies of sorghum and other feed. Beef breeding herds have increased most in East Texas, where grazing is abundant.

Dairying

Ninety percent of the state's dairy industry is located east of the line from Wichita Falls to Brownwood, to San Antonio to Corpus Christi. Leading counties in milk production are **Hopkins, Erath** and **Johnson**, which combined produce over 30 percent of the milk in the state with Hopkins producing almost 16 percent of the total.

All the milk sold by Texas dairy farmers is marketed under the terms of Federal Milk Marketing Orders. Most Texas dairymen are members of a cooperative marketing association, with Associated Milk Producers, Inc. representing a majority of the state's producers.

Texas dairy farmers received a gross income of $553,470,000 during 1984, compared with $578,315,000 in 1983; $551,691,000 in 1982; and $542,545,000 in 1981. Price for milk averaged $14.44 per 100 pounds in 1984, compared with $14.50 in 1983; $14.60 in 1982; and $14.95 in 1981. A total of 3.75 billion pounds of milk was sold to plants and dealers in 1984, bringing $536,250,000 of cash receipts, compared with 3.90 billion pounds and $565,645,000 in 1983; 3.69 billion pounds and $538,740,000 in 1982; and 3.58 billion pounds and $529,100,000 in 1981.

The number of milk cows that have calved on Texas farms in 1985 was 314,000 head, compared with 333,000 head in 1984; 335,000 head in 1983; 325,000 head in 1982; and 320,000 head in 1981. Number of cows had declined since the all-time high of 1,594,000 head in 1945. Production per cow averaged 12,031 pounds with 428 pounds of milk fat in 1984; this compared with 11,946 pounds with 426 pounds of milk fat in 1983; 11,489 pounds with 409 pounds of milk fat in 1982. Milk production totaled 3,850 million pounds in 1984, compared with 3,989 million pounds in 1983; 3,780 million pounds in 1982; and 3,665 million pounds in 1981.

There were 9,700 milk cow operations in Texas in 1985, compared with 10,000 in 1984, 10,000 in 1983, 10,000 in 1982; and 11,000 in 1981.

Dairy Manufacturing

The major dairy products manufactured in Texas include creamery butter, cheese and condensed, evaporated and dry milk. No up-to-date data are available for production and value of these products.

Frozen Desserts

Production of **frozen desserts** totaled 108,739,000 gallons in 1984. This compared with 123,742,000 gallons in 1983; 109,364,000 gallons in 1982; and 101,072,000 gallons in 1981. **Ice cream** production in 1984 amounted to 44,898,000 gallons, compared with 57,256,000 gallons in 1983; 50,138,000 gallons in 1982; and 44,507,000 gallons in 1981. **Ice cream mix** produced in Texas in 1984 amounted to 27,750,000 gallons, compared with 29,744,000 gallons in 1983; and 25,235,000 gallons in 1982. **Ice milk** production in Texas amounted to 15,925,000 gallons in 1984, compared with 14,041,000 gallons in 1983; and 13,108,000 gallons in 1982. **Mellorine** in 1984 totaled 3,357,000 gallons. This was 41 percent of the total U.S. production, which makes Texas the largest producer of mellorine in the United States. The 1983 production of mellorine was 5,473,000 gallons, compared with 5,120,000 gallons in 1982; and 8,622,000 gallons in 1981.

Swine

Texas ranked 15th among the states in number of swine on hand Dec. 1, 1984. Swine producers in the state usually produce about 25 to 30 percent of the pork consumed by the state, or about 800,000 head annually marketed.

TEXAS CATTLE FEEDLOTS BY SIZES

Source: **Texas Crop and Livestock Reporting Service**

Year—	Under 1,000	1,000-1,999	2,000-3,999	4,000-7,999	8,000-15,999	16,000 & Over	Total
				Feedlot Capacity (head)			
			— *Number of Lots —				
1962 ..	1,600	98	60	31	†14	—	1,803
1963 ..	1,550	91	65	32	12	3	1,753
1964 ..	1,500	101	73	43	12	5	1,734
1965 ..	1,500	100	77	47	15	6	1,745
1966 ..	1,500	118	79	53	20	8	1,778
1967 ..	1,397	99	66	46	17	12	1,637
1968 ..	1,300	83	50	42	28	19	1,522
1969 ..	1,300	72	54	36	34	37	1,533
1970 ..	1,300	60	44	36	39	48	1,527
1971 ..	1,300	47	49	44	34	51	1,525
1972 ..	1,300	53	38	39	38	62	1,530
1973 ..	1,300	50	37	36	44	66	1,533
1974 ..	1,001	40	21	30	39	69	1,200
1975 ..	921	26	21	27	37	68	1,100
1976 ..	912	25	24	26	35	67	1,089
1977 ..	1,044	18	14	25	35	64	1,200
1978 ..	959	19	13	26	36	67	1,120
1979 ..	886	20	15	26	35	68	1,050
1980 ..	931	21	15	27	35	68	1,097
1981 ..	955	10	16	23	28	68	1,100
1982 ..	951	10	18	23	30	68	1,100
1983 ..	862	9	14	19	30	66	1,000
1984 ..	861	7	17	18	30	67	1,000

*Number of feedlots with 1,000-head capacity or more is number of lots operating at any time during year; number under 1,000-head capacity and total of all feedlots are number at end of year.

†Lots from larger size group included to avoid disclosing individual operations.

NUMBER OF MILK COWS, VALUE AND PRODUCTION FOR TEXAS

Source: **Texas Crop and Livestock Reporting Service**

Year	*No. of Milk Cows	Avg. Per Head	Total Value	Production of Milk	
				†Per Cow	Total
	1,000 head	Dollars	$1,000 Dollars	Pounds	Million Pounds
1925....	985	30	29,550	2,820	2,679
1930....	1,202	56	67,312	3,220	3,655
1935....	1,388	19	26,372	2,950	3,741
1940....	1,430	38	54,340	3,200	4,192
1945....	1,594	65	103,610	3,040	4,068
1950....	1,121	139	155,819	3,390	3,451
1955....	884	94	83,096	3,860	2,988
1960....	649	171	110,979	5,100	2,932
1965....	490	137	67,130	6,930	2,973
1970....	381	230	87,630	8,634	3,065
1971....	355	245	86,975	9,124	3,239
1972....	355	275	97,625	9,330	3,340
1973....	360	350	126,000	9,239	3,280
1974....	350	380	133,000	9,685	3,380
1975....	345	220	75,900	9,634	3,208
1976....	320	270	86,400	10,341	3,309
1977....	318	305	96,990	10,705	3,372
1978....	314	310	97,340	11,039	3,433
1979....	310	548	169,880	10,859	3,377
1980....	315	935	294,525	11,435	3,625
1981....	320	1,150	368,000	11,312	3,665
1982....	325	1,200	390,000	11,489	3,780
1983....	335	1,150	385,250	11,946	3,990
1984....	333	940	313,020	N.A.	N.A.

*Number on farms and value, January 1.
†Average number on farms during year.

HOG PRODUCTION IN TEXAS

Source: Texas A&M—USDA

Year—	Production 1,000 Pounds	Avg. Market Wt. Pounds	Avg. Price Per Cwt. Dollars	Gross Income 1,000 Dollars
1958	262,134	233	$19.50	$44,997
1959	338,343	228	14.40	47,948
1960	288,844	228	14.70	44,634
1961	289,700	229	16.40	49,174
1962	288,815	230	16.30	47,483
1963	282,807	234	15.10	43,685
1964	259,549	240	14.80	43,351
1965	212,404	240	19.80	41,432
1966	234,742	239	22.60	49,992
1967	289,773	240	18.70	51,767
1968	313,515	240	18.10	55,788
1969	325,896	240	21.60	73,027
1970	385,502	241	22.50	75,288
1971	529,986	236	16.60	90,257
1972	449,357	244	24.00	114,730
1973	375,372	242	37.90	148,488
1974	350,811	253	33.30	123,277
1975	271,027	244	43.70	127,323
1976	286,053	247	41.50	117,587
1977	292,290	247	38.00	109,634
1978	303,135	258	43.80	135,006
1979	320,790	261	39.70	125,183
1980	315,827	259	35.90	111,700
1981	264,693	256	41.70	121,054
1982	205,656	256	49.60	112,726
1983	209,621	256	45.20	95,343
1984	189,620	262	45.50	95,657

Production units vary in size from 1 to over 1,100 sows. Although the number of farms producing hogs has steadily decreased, the size of production units has increased. With the trend to larger units, there has been increasing swine production in the Panhandle, South Plains and West Central areas of Texas. The 10 leading counties in number of hogs in 1984 were: **Llano, Lubbock, Wilson, Gillespie, Fayette, Uvalde, Milam, Colorado, Moore, Anderson** and **Brazos.**

Specialization in the swine industry has resulted in a demand for top quality feeder pigs by those farmers who have grain available. To meet this demand, feeder pig marketing associations have been established in the feeder pig producing areas of East and Central Texas. These associations hold feeder pig sales monthly and auction pigs in uniform lots according to grades and weights.

With the establishment of marketing associations capable of shipping slaughter hogs to any point in the United States, and because of the volume of sorghum grain produced in the state, the potential for increased production is tremendous, for both feeder pigs and slaughter hogs.

In 1984, 813,000 head of hogs were marketed in Texas, producing 189,620,000 pounds of pork, valued at $95,657,000 for cash receipts of $93,569,000, or $45.50 per 100 pounds. Comparable figures for 1983 were 818,000 head marketed, 209,621,000 pounds of pork, valued at $95,343,000 with cash receipts of $93,268,000, or $45.20 per 100 pounds; in 1982, 869,000 head marketed, producing 205,656,000 pounds, valued at $115,726,000 for cash receipts of $108,679,000, or $49.60 per 100 pounds; and in 1981, 1,115,000 head marketed, 264,693,000 pounds, valued at $121,054,000 with cash receipts of $117,164,000, or $41.70 per 100 pounds.

There were 15,000 hog operations in Texas in 1983, compared with 19,000 in 1982; 23,000 in 1981 and 27,000 in 1980.

Goats and Mohair

Goats in Texas numbered 1,550,000 on Jan. 1, 1985, compared with 1,450,000 in 1984; 1,420,000 in 1983; 1,410,000 in 1982; and 1,380,000 in 1981. They had a value of $74,865,000 or $48.30 per head in 1985, compared with $82,215,000 or $56.70 per head in 1984; $53,250,000 or $37.50 per head in 1983; $57,810,000 or $41.00 per head in 1982; and $53,130,000 or $38.50 per head in 1981.

The goat herd consists largely of **Angora goats** for mohair production. Angora goats totaled 1,300,000 in 1985, compared with 1,150,000 in 1984; 1,140,000 in 1983; 1,130,000 in 1982; and 1,050,000 in 1981. **Spanish** and others

numbered 250,000 in 1985, compared with 300,000 in 1984; 280,000 in 1983; 280,000 in 1982; and 330,000 in 1981.

Mohair production during 1984 totaled 11,200,000 pounds, compared with 10,600,000 pounds in 1983; 10,000,000 in 1982; and 10,100,000 in 1981. Average price per pound in 1984 was $4.30 from 1,450,000 goats clipped for a total value of $48,160,000. This compared with $4.05 per pound from 1,360,000 goats clipped and total value of $42,930,000 in 1983; $2.55 from 1,330,000 clipped and total value of $25,500,000 in 1982; and $3.50 per pound from 1,300,000 goats clipped and total value of $35,350,000 in 1981.

Nearly half of the world's mohair and 97 percent of the U.S. clip is produced in Texas. The leading Texas counties in Angora goats are: Edwards, Val Verde, Uvalde, Sutton, Kimble, Terrell, Crockett, Mills, Kinney and Mason.

Sheep and Wool

Sheep and lambs in Texas numbered 1,810,000 head on Jan. 1, 1985, compared with 1,970,000 in 1984; 2,225,000 head in 1983; 2,400,000 head in 1982; and 2,360,000 head in 1981.

All sheep were valued at $104,075,000 or $57.50 per head on Jan. 1, 1985, compared with $76,830,000, or $39.00 per head in 1984; $86,775,000, or $39.00 per head in 1983; $100,800,000, or $42.00 per head in 1982; and $116,820,000, or $48.50 per head in 1981.

Breeding ewes one year old and over numbered 1,350,000 in 1985; 1,410,000 in 1984; 1,580,000 in 1983; 1,605,000 in 1982; and 1,700,000 in 1981.

Ewe lambs totaled 160,000 head in 1985; 215,000 in 1984; 265,000 in 1983; 348,000 in 1982; and 270,000 in 1981. Lambs saved numbered 1,120,000 in 1984; 1,150,000 in 1983; 1,200,000 in 1982; and 1,250,000 in 1981. Early lamb crop estimates were discontinued in January, 1983.

ANGORA GOATS AND MOHAIR

Year—	Goats *Number	Goats Farm Value	Mohair Production (lbs.)	Mohair Value
1900	627,333	$923,777	961,328	$267,864
1910	1,135,000	2,514,000	1,998,000	468,000
1920	1,753,000	9,967,000	6,786,000	1,816,000
1930	2,965,000	14,528,000	14,800,000	4,995,000
1940	3,300,000	10,560,000	18,250,000	9,308,000
1950	2,295,000	13,082,000	12,643,000	9,735,000
1951	2,433,000	23,114,000	12,280,000	14,613,000
1952	2,054,000	17,664,000	11,561,000	11,330,000
1953	1,910,000	12,224,000	11,972,000	10,775,000
1954	2,082,000	13,741,000	13,097,000	9,561,000
1955	2,546,000	14,003,000	16,401,000	13,613,000
1956	2,700,000	18,900,000	17,616,000	14,974,000
1957	2,808,000	17,400,000	18,432,000	15,483,000
1958	2,864,000	25,800,000	20,207,000	14,751,000
1959	3,150,000	26,145,000	23,512,000	22,807,000
1960	3,339,000	29,383,000	23,750,000	21,375,000
1961	3,473,000	29,520,000	25,690,000	22,093,000
1962	3,647,000	30,270,000	26,418,000	19,021,000
1963	3,683,000	25,781,000	28,153,000	25,056,000
1964	3,904,000	29,280,000	28,872,000	27,428,000
1965	4,060,000	28,420,000	31,584,000	20,845,000
1966	4,222,000	28,710,000	28,770,000	15,536,000
1967	3,969,000	20,639,000	26,335,000	10,797,000
1968	3,572,000	17,503,000	25,272,000	11,448,000
1969	3,215,000	22,184,000	20,100,000	13,246,000
1970	2,572,000	19,033,000	17,985,000	7,032,000
1971	2,133,000	12,158,000	14,855,000	4,480,000
1972	1,650,000	10,230,000	10,190,000	8,458,000
1973	1,775,000	15,798,000	9,930,000	18,569,000
1974	1,570,000	22,620,000	8,400,000	11,508,000
1975	1,350,000	17,820,000	8,600,000	15,910,000
1976	1,270,000	25,273,000	8,100,000	24,057,000
1977	1,400,000	35,000,000	8,000,000	22,960,000
1978	1,355,000	44,038,000	8,100,000	37,179,000
1979	1,360,000	61,200,000	9,300,000	47,430,000
1980	1,400,000	64,400,000	8,800,000	30,800,000
1981	1,380,000	53,130,000	10,100,000	35,350,000
1982	1,410,000	57,810,000	10,000,000	25,500,000
1983	1,420,000	53,250,000	10,600,000	42,930,000
1984	1,450,000	82,215,000	11,200,000	48,160,000
†1985	1,550,000	74,865,000	N.A.	N.A.

*Number here represents all goats on farms as of Jan. 1; the number of goats clipped will vary each year, but is usually larger because of spring and fall clipping.

†Preliminary.

Sheep operations in Texas were estimated to be 9,000 in 1985, 9,000 in 1984, 9,500 in 1983, 10,000 in 1982 and 9,500 in 1981.

Texas **wool production** in 1984 was 17,500,000 pounds from 2,500,000 sheep. Value totaled $16,100,000 or 92 cents a pound. This compared with 18,600,000 pounds from 2,550,000 sheep valued at $15,438,000 or 83 cents a pound in 1983; 19,300,000 pounds from 2,650,000 sheep valued at $16,212,000 or 84 cents a pound in 1982; and 20,500,000 pounds from 2,750,000 sheep valued at $24,600,000 or 1.20 cents a pound in 1981.

Most sheep in Texas are concentrated in the Edwards Plateau area of West Central Texas and nearby counties. The ten leading counties are: Crockett, Concho, Val Verde, Tom Green, Terrell, Kinney, Menard, Gillespie, Schleicher and Pecos. Sheep production is largely dual purpose, for both wool and lamb production.

San Angelo long has been the largest sheep and wool market in the nation and the center for wool and mohair warehouses, scouring plants and slaughterhouses.

Bees and Honey

There were an estimated 190,000 colonies of bees in Texas in 1981, compared with 198,000 colonies in 1980, 190,000 colonies in 1979 and 185,000 in 1978. Estimates were discontinued in 1982. They produced 11,400,000 pounds of honey valued at $6,657,600 in 1981. This compared with 6,930,000 pounds valued at $3,880,800 in 1980; 11,400,000 pounds valued at $5,791,200 in 1979 and 8,695,000 pounds valued at $4,139,000 in 1978.

Texas bees produced 239,000 pounds of beeswax in 1981, valued at $442,400. This compared with 125,000 pounds valued at $228,200 in 1980; 194,000 pounds valued at $360,800 in 1979 and 148,000 pounds valued at $252,000 in 1978. Total value of honey and beeswax produced in 1981 was $7,100,000, compared with $4,109,000 in 1980; $6,152,000 in 1979 and $4,391,000 in 1978.

Texas ranked 4th nationally in the number of colonies of bees in 1981. The states with more colonies of bees were: California, Florida and North Dakota.

Bees added additionally to the agricultural production of the state through cross pollinating many vegetable, fruit, nut and legume crops requiring or benefiting from cross pollination. The direct value of this pollination to Texas agricultural producers and the Texas consumer is substantial. Particular interest has been observed in the pollination of cucumbers, cantaloupes and alfalfa.

Poultry and Eggs

Poultry and eggs annually contribute about 5 percent of the average yearly cash receipts of Texas farmers. In 1983, Texas ranked 7th among the states in broilers produced, 8th in hens and pullets of laying age and eggs produced.

In 1983, **cash receipts** to producers from production of broilers, eggs, chickens and turkeys totaled $500,274,000, compared with $492,835,000 in 1982; and $545,244,000 in 1981.

Gross income from eggs was $217,437,000 in 1984, compared with $180,192,000 in 1983; $178,998,000 in 1982; and $192,365,000 in 1981. Eggs produced in 1984 totaled 3.2 billion, compared with 3.1 billion in 1983; 3.1 billion in 1982; and 3.2 billion in 1981. Average price received per dozen in 1984 was 82 cents, compared with 70 cents in 1983; 69 cents in 1982; and 71.6 cents in 1981. Leading egg-producing counties are: **Gonzales, Camp, Fayette, Denton, Caldwell, Shelby, Nacogdoches, Garza, Wharton** and **Lubbock.**

Broiler production in 1984 totaled 200,500,000 birds, compared with 212,600,000 in 1983; 222,500,000 in 1982; and 231,700,000 in 1981. Gross income from broilers in 1984 amounted to $294,735,000, compared with $261,498,000 in 1983; $258,100,000 in 1982; and $278,040,000 in 1981. Price per pound averaged 35 cents in 1984; 30 cents in 1983; 29 cents in 1982; and 30 cents in 1981. Leading broiler producing counties are: **Nacogdoches, Gonzales, Shelby, Panola, San Augustine, Camp, Sabine, Wood, Titus** and **Upshur.**

No inventory figures were released for 1984 on turkey production to avoid disclosing individual operation. Turkey production grossed $45,144,000 from 5,400,000 turkeys in 1983, compared with $40,560,000 from 5,200,000 turkeys in 1982; $56,312,000 from 7,300,000 turkeys in 1981; and $57,428,000 from 7,750,000 turkeys in 1980. Leading counties in turkey production are: **Gonzales, McLennan, Hill, Coryell, Gillespie, Bosque, Lee, Bell, Falls, Brown** and **Williamson.**

Gross income from farm chickens in 1984 totaled $7,011,000, compared with $5,285,000 in 1983; $4,983,000 in 1982; and $4,755,000 in 1981.

An estimated $10,000,000 to $15,000,000 is grossed from sales of turkey hatching eggs, ducks, geese, quail, pigeons and other poultry items.

Horses

Nationally, Texas ranks as the leading state in horse numbers and is the headquarters for many national horse organizations. The largest single horse breed registry in America, the **American Quarter Horse Association,** has its headquarters in Amarillo. The **National Cutting Horse Association** and the **American Paint Horse Association** are both located in Fort Worth. The central office of the **American Association of Sheriff Posses and Riding Clubs** is in Fort Worth and the **Galiceno Horse Breeders Association** is in Tyler. In addition to these national associations, Texas also has active state associations that include **Arabians, Thoroughbreds, Appaloosa and Ponies.**

The largest increase in horse numbers within the state can be found in the urban and suburban areas. Horses are most abundant in the heavily populated areas of the state. State participation activities consist of horse shows, trail rides, play days, rodeos, polo and horse racing. Residential subdivisions have been developed within the state to provide facilities for urban and suburban horse owners.

TEXAS SHEEP AND WOOL PRODUCTION

Year—	Sheep		Wool	
	*Number	Value	Production (lbs.)	Value
1850	100,530	N. A.	131,917	N. A.
1860	753,363	N. A.	1,493,363	N. A.
1870	1,223,000	$2,079,000	N. A.	N. A.
1880	6,024,000	12,048,000	N. A.	N. A.
1890	4,752,000	7,128,000	N. A.	N. A.
1900	2,416,000	4,590,000	9,630,000	N. A.
1910	1,909,000	5,536,000	8,943,000	$1,699,170
1920	3,360,000	33,600,000	22,813,000	5,019,000
1930	6,304,000	44,758,000	48,262,000	10,135,000
1940	10,069,000	49,413,000	79,900,000	23,171,000
1950	6,756,000	103,877,000	51,480,000	32,947,000
1951	7,119,000	154,962,000	48,712,000	48,225,000
1952	6,188,000	114,910,000	46,277,000	26,841,000
1953	5,574,000	56,833,000	42,511,000	26,782,000
1954	5,331,000	53,829,000	44,220,000	26,090,000
1955	5,659,000	57,125,000	45,137,000	19,409,000
1956	5,376,000	58,337,000	42,653,000	18,767,000
1957	4,749,000	46,769,000	39,409,000	22,069,000
1958	4,891,000	85,306,000	38,716,000	15,099,000
1959	5,458,000	95,154,000	46,726,000	20,559,000
1960	5,938,000	85,801,000	51,980,000	21,832,000
1961	6,140,000	72,859,000	52,225,000	23,501,000
1962	5,854,000	58,300,000	49,752,000	23,881,000
1963	5,538,000	55,175,000	46,602,000	23,767,000
1964	5,185,000	47,668,000	38,836,000	20,195,000
1965	4,539,000	50,811,000	41,109,000	18,499,000
1966	4,795,000	69,587,000	38,777,000	19,001,000
1967	4,802,000	67,686,000	36,998,000	15,169,000
1968	4,419,000	56,800,000	33,363,000	15,347,000
1969	4,029,000	67,284,000	29,717,000	14,561,000
1970	3,708,000	73,602,000	30,784,000	11,082,000
1971	3,789,000	66,308,000	30,397,000	4,864,000
1972	3,524,000	65,194,000	29,430,000	14,126,000
1973	3,214,000	64,280,000	26,352,000	23,190,000
1974	3,090,000	80,340,000	23,900,000	15,535,000
1975	2,715,000	63,803,000	23,600,000	14,868,000
1976	2,600,000	81,900,000	22,000,000	17,380,000
1977	2,520,000	93,240,000	21,000,000	17,220,000
1978	2,460,000	111,930,000	18,500,000	15,355,000
1979	2,415,000	152,145,000	19,075,000	18,503,000
1980	2,400,000	138,000,000	18,300,000	17,751,000
1981	2,360,000	116,820,000	20,500,000	24,600,000
1982	2,400,000	100,800,000	19,300,000	16,212,000
1983	2,225,000	86,775,000	18,600,000	15,438,000
1984	1,970,000	76,830,000	17,500,000	16,100,000
†1985	1,810,000	104,075,000	N. A.	N. A.

*Number given here represents all sheep on farms as of Jan. 1; number clipped will vary because of spring and fall clipping.

†Preliminary.

HEALTH CARE

Even though population and knowledge of medicine and health care are increasing, and this field of essential services has greatly expanded in Texas, many small communities of the state have no doctor and must rely upon other places for hospitalization. Houston, Dallas and some other cities are internationally known for their medical centers.

Health care has become the number one concern of Texans, as evidenced by the coverage of health care issues by the Texas media. Rural parts of the state have continued to expand their health care capabilities to care for the growing populations in those areas.

The following information has been supplied chiefly by the **Texas Hospital Association** and state agencies concerned with vital statistics.

Hospitals

Texas hospitals employed 224,532 persons in 1983 at a record payroll of more than $3.8 billion. These employees were reported by the 562 hospitals with 84,935 beds registered with the American Hospital Association. One of every 12 U.S. hospitals is located in Texas.

The average length of stay in the 495 short-term, general hospitals was 6.6 days in 1983, compared to 6.8 days in 1975. The length of stay in Texas hospitals was one day less than the U.S. average and the average cost per admission was $2,319, which was 17 percent less than the U.S. average of $2,789. Admissions to short-term, general hospitals totaled 2,523,640 or 92 percent of the total admissions to all Texas hospitals. There were 42,570 RNs, 21,058 LVNs and 4,031 health care professions trainees working in Texas hospitals in 1983.

Allied Health Training

Hospitals are the leading source of allied health education in Texas with over 90 percent of all allied health personnel either completely or partially educated in a clinical, internship or residency situation within the hospital.

The University of Texas system, as well as Texas Woman's University with campuses in all of the major urban areas, are Texas' major providers of health care professionals.

Texas continues to experience a shortage of allied health manpower. Student enrollments and the number of graduates have increased steadily over the past five years. However, there is still a great demand for physical therapists, occupational therapists, respiratory therapists, medical records technicians, medical technologists, radiologic technologists, pharmacists and registered nurses. In the forseeable future, these demands for manpower will continue to exist due largely to the population growth and the expanding requirements for health services.

The Texas Health Careers Program, P.O. Box 15587, Austin, Texas 78761, has free information available for anyone interested in a career in the health field.

Schools of Nursing

There are currently **64** schools of nursing in Texas accredited by the **Board of Nurse Examiners** for the State of Texas. Forty offer associate degree programs, 21 offer baccalaureate degree programs and 3 have hospital diploma programs.

CAUSES OF DEATH

The 10 leading causes of death in Texas in 1983, and the rate per 100,000 population were:

Cause	Deaths	*Rate	% of Total Deaths
All Causes	114,714	729.5	100.0
Heart Disease	39,849	253.4	34.7
Malignant Neoplasms. . .	23,358	148.5	20.4
Cerebrovascular Diseases	8,914	56.7	7.8
Accidents and Adverse Effects.	7,275	46.3	6.3
Bronchitis, Emphysema, Asthma, and Allied Conditions	3,535	22.5	3.1
Pneumonia, Influenza . .	2,919	18.6	2.5
Homicide	2,322	14.8	2.0
Suicide	2,066	13.1	1.8
Diabetes Mellitus.	1,954	12.4	1.7
Certain Conditions Originating in the Perinatal Period	1,545	9.8	1.3
All Other Causes.	20,977	133.4	18.3

*Rates per 100,000 estimated population

The associate degree programs include: **Alvin Junior College** Department of Nursing, Alvin; **Amarillo College** Associate Degree Nursing Program, Amarillo; **Austin Community College**, Austin; **Lee College** Associate Degree Nursing Program, Baytown; **Lamar University** Associate Degree Nursing Program, Beaumont; **Howard County Junior College** Associate Degree Nursing Program, Big Spring; **Texas Southmost College** School of Nursing, Brownsville; **Del Mar College** Department of Registered Nurse Education, Corpus Christi; **Navarro College** School of Nursing, Corsicana; **El Centro College** Division of Associate Degree Nursing, Dallas; **Grayson County College** Associate Degree of Nursing Program, Denison; **Pan American University** Department of Nursing, Edinburg; **El Paso Community College** Department of Nursing, El Paso; **Tarrant County Junior College** Department of Nursing, Fort Worth; **Cooke County Junior College** Department of Nursing, Gainesville; **Galveston College**, Galveston; **Henderson Community College** School of Nursing, Henderson; **Houston Community College** Department of Nursing, Houston; **North Harris County College** Associate Degree Nursing Program, Houston; **Southwestern Adventist College** Department of Nursing, Keene; **Kilgore College** Department of Nursing, Kilgore; **Central Texas College** School of Nursing, Killeen; **Laredo Junior College** Department of Nursing, Laredo; **Angelina College** Division of Nursing, Lufkin; **Midland College** School of Nursing, Midland; **Odessa College** Associate Degree Nursing Program, Odessa; **Paris Junior College** Department of Nursing, Paris; **San Jacinto College** Department of Nursing Education, Pasadena; **Angelo State University** Department of Nursing, San Angelo; **San Antonio College** Department of Nursing, San Antonio; **Tarleton State University**

LIVE BIRTHS AND DEATHS
(Rates per 1,000 Estimated Population)

Year—	Live Births No.	Live Births Rate	Deaths No.	Deaths Rate
1967	203,790	19.2	86,193	8.1
1968	207,191	19.2	92,098	8.5
1969	220,647	20.0	93,336	8.5
1970	230,624	20.6	94,287	8.4
1971	228,983	20.0	94,724	8.3
1972	214,613	18.4	99,275	8.5
1973	209,651	17.8	101,487	8.6
1974	210,787	17.5	99,426	8.3
1975	215,426	17.6	98,354	8.0
1976	218,447	17.5	100,620	8.1
1977	228,871	17.8	100,077	7.8
1978	236,612	18.2	103,670	8.0
1979	254,263	19.0	104,745	7.8
1980	273,433	19.2	108,018	7.6
1981	281,558	19.1	110,498	7.5
1982	297,683	19.5	111,263	7.3
1983	295,178	18.8	114,714	7.3

MENTAL HEALTH ORGANIZATIONS

Below is a compilation of mental health organizations providing inpatient and/or residential treatment care, by type of organization, in January 1982, latest data available.

Total expenditures for state and county mental hospitals, 1981, were: Current dollars, $157,635; constant dollars, $54,545.

Per capita total expenditures were: Current dollars, $10.78; constant dollars, $3.73.

Source: **U.S. Department of Health and Human Services**

	No. Hospitals	No. Beds
All organizations.	92	12,545
State and county hospitals	10	6,754
Private psychiatric hospitals	13	1,067
Veterans Administration psych. services	7	1,425
Non-federal general hospitals	34	1,671
Residential centers for emotionally disturbed children	14	1,102
Multi-service health organizations. .	14	526

School of Nursing, Stephenville; **Texarkana Community College** William Buchanan Department of Nursing, Texarkana; **College of the Mainland** Nursing Department, Texas City; **Tyler Junior College,** Tyler; **Victoria College** Associate Degree Nursing Program, Victoria; **McLennan Community College** Department of Nursing, Waco; **Wharton County Junior** College School of Nursing, Wharton; **Midwestern University** Department of Nursing, Wichita Falls.

Baccalaureate degree programs include: **Abilene Intercollegiate** School of Nursing, Abilene; **University of Texas** School of Nursing at Arlington, Arlington; **The University of Texas** School of Nursing at Austin, Austin; **Lamar University** School of Nursing, Beaumont; **Mary Hardin-Baylor University** Department of Nursing, Belton; **West Texas State University** School of Nursing, Canyon; **Baylor University** School of Nursing, Dallas; **Dallas Baptist College** Division of Nursing, Dallas; **Texas Woman's University** College of Nursing (which also offers the master's and doctoral degrees in nursing), Denton; **The University of Texas** School of Nursing at El Paso, El Paso; **Texas Christian University** Harris College of Nursing, Fort Worth; **The University of Texas** School of Nursing at Galveston, Galveston; **Houston Baptist University** School of Nursing, Houston; **University of St. Thomas** School of Nursing, Houston; **The University of Texas** School of Nursing at Houston, Houston; **Prairie View A&M University** College of Nursing, Houston; **Incarnate Word College** Department of Nursing, San Antonio; **The University of Texas** School of Nursing at San Antonio, San Antonio; **Texas Tech University** School of Nursing, Lubbock; **Stephen F. Austin University** School of Nursing, Nacogdoches; **University of Texas at Tyler** School of Nursing, Tyler.

The hospital diploma programs are: Northwest Texas Hospital School of Nursing, Amarillo; Methodist Hospital School of Nursing, Lubbock; Baptist Memorial Hospital School of Nursing, San Antonio.

Church Membership, 1980

Below is given the number of churches, number of full members (confirmed communicants) and number of total adherents of the different denominations in Texas in 1980 (latest year for which data available). These data are taken from "Churches and Church Membership in the United States 1980," authors Bernard Quinn, Herman Anderson, Martin Bradley, Paul Goetting and Peggy Shriver. This is an enumeration by region, state and county based on data reported by 111 church bodies with 112,538,310 adherents. It was copyrighted in 1982 by the National Council of the Churches of Christ in the U.S.A. It was published by the Glenmary Research Center, Atlanta, Ga. and is reprinted here with their written permission. Further use not sanctioned without written permission from the above-named source. For various reasons, some small groups did not participate.

Church Name—	No. of Churches	Full Members (Confirmed Communicants)	No. Total Adherents	Church Name—	No. of Churches	Full Members (Confirmed Communicants)	No. Total Adherents
Advent Christian....	4	299	*364	Evan. Lutheran Assn.	4	657	925
A.M.E. Zion	7	1,752	2,095	Evan. Lutheran Synod	2	39	157
American Baptist				Evan. Methodist	17	1,686	*2,050
Assn.	340	45,361	45,361	Free Methodist	18	564	1,857
Am. Baptist U.S.A. ...	59	17.787	*21,770	Friends-U.S.A.	15	1,525	*1,867
American Lutheran. .	257	85,286	106,657	Gen. Conf. Mennonite			
Assemblies of God ...	1,134	117,957	162,232	Brethren	9	358	*461
Baptist Missionary				Grace Brethren.....	1	13	*16
Assn.	517	97,351	*118,643	Internatl. Foursquare			
Brethren in Christ...	1	57	86	Gospel..........	49	5,674	*6,988
Catholic	1,227	N.A.	2,340,162	Conservative Judaism	16	6,136	*7,557
Ch. & Missionary				Reformed Judaism ..	30	18,592	*22,857
Alliance	23	1,160	2,239	Luth. Ch. America...	106	27,934	36,670
Chris. Ch. (Disciples				Lutheran-Missouri			
of Christ)	448	84,295	120,296	Synod	311	88,377	117,074
Chr. Churches & Chs.				Mennonite	10	564	*712
of Christ.........	149	22,090	*27,255	Mennonite Gen.			
C.M.E.	312	68,825	*83,932	Conference	1	60	84
Christian Reformed .	3	105	165	Metro Community...	7	1,004	2,008
Church God (ABR) ..	3	86	*107	N. Am. Baptist Conf. .	11	798	*981
Church God				Orthodox			
(Anderson)	84	5,550	16,650	Presbyterian	2	244	*299
Church God				Pentecostal Holiness .	70	3,353	*4,190
(Cleveland)	192	12,824	*15,708	Christian Brethren ..	32	2,015	3,520
Church God (7th Day)				Presbyterian Ch. Am.	15	1,309	1,543
(Denver)........	20	644	*804	†Presbyterian Ch.,			
Ch. God in Christ				U.S.	519	106,566	*130,895
(Mennonite)	4	207	207	Protestant Reformed	1	10	26
Ch. of Jes. Christ				Ref. Presbyterian-			
(Bickertonite)....	1	13	13	Evan.	3	355	454
Latter-Day Saints ...	212	N.A.	68,375	Salvation Army.....	44	4,379	14,720
Church of Brethren ..	4	310	*377	Seventh Day			
Ch. Lutheran				Adventists	178	18,974	*23,354
Confession.....	3	147	201	S-D Baptist Gen. Conf.	2	18	*22
Church of Nazarene..	309	24,670	39,479	Southern Baptist Con.	3,896	2,172,997	*2,659,894
Churches of Christ...	2,222	278,820	355,396	Southern Methodist..	6	229	315
Congregational				Syrian Antioch	2	800	*976
Christian	3	633	*782	Unitarian-Universal .	34	3,838	*4,701
Congregational				United Ch. of Christ..	71	16,889	*20,626
Holiness.........	2	60	*73	United Methodist ...	2,257	761,290	*932,488
Conservative				†United Presby. Ch.,			
Congregational ...	1	74	*92	U.S.A.	348	53,278	*65,150
Cumberland				Wisconsin Evan.			
Presbyterian	51	4,969	8,408	Lutheran........	19	1,701	2,453
Episcopal	395	136,416	174,581	Total.	16,111	4,311,259	*7,781,967
Evangelical Ch.							
of N.A..........	1	46	46				
Evangelical							
Congregational ...	1	38	*50				
Evangelical Covenant							
Ch. Am..........	1	59	*77				
Evangelical Free							
Church	15	1,142	*1,394				

N.A. Not applicable. *Total adherents estimated from known number of communicant, confirmed, full members. †Presbyterian Church, U.S. (Southern) and United Presbyterian Church, U.S.A., united after this census was taken and are now known as Presbyterian Church, (U.S.A.).

TRANSPORTATION

Much of the information on Transportation was provided to the **Texas Almanac** by Edward Kasparik, Railroad Commission of Texas; the Texas Department of Highways and Public Transportation, and the U.S. Army Corps of Engineers.

Texas leads all other states in a number of transportation indicators, including total road and street mileage, total railroad mileage and total number of airports. **Texas ranks** second behind California in motor vehicle registrations and in number of general aviation aircraft.

The Texas transportation system includes over **250,000 miles of municipal and rural highways**, over **13,000 miles of railroad line**, approximately **1,330 airports and 13 major Gulf Coast ports.** Texans own and operate over **12 million motor vehicles** and about **15,000 aircraft**.

The transportation industry is a major employer in Texas. Statistics compiled by the Texas Employment Commission indicate that approximately 169,559 Texans are **employed** in the transportation industry. The largest group — 87,783 — is employed in trucking and warehousing. Railroads employ 24,839, air transportation 38,135 and water transportation 18,802.

The largest state government agency involved in transportation is the **Texas State Department of Highways and Public Transportation**, formed by the merger of the Texas Highway Department and the Texas Mass Transportation Commission in 1975. The **Railroad Commission of Texas** has intrastate regulatory authority over railroads, truck lines, buses and pipelines. Another state agency with a major role in transportation is the **Texas Aeronautics Commission**.

DEVELOPMENT OF TEXAS RAILROADS, REPUBLIC OF TEXAS TO PRESENT

The following history of railroading in Texas during the Republic was written for the 1956-57 edition of the Texas Almanac by the late **Arthur L. Carnahan**, Chief Statistician of the Railroad Commission of Texas at that time. From many years of handling railroad data, Mr. Carnahan gained a wide knowledge of railroad history and operation. It has been revised and brought up to date by the current State Rail Planner, **Edward Kasparik**.

With great resources for the production of freight tonnage, yet with no navigable rivers of consequence, Texas was faced from the beginning of its economic development with the problem of transportation. Early Texas leaders were quick to appreciate this problem and, throughout the early history of Texas, beginning during the days of the Republic, there was great enthusiasm for railroad construction. The Republic and State of Texas, first and last, subsidized early railroad building by land grants totaling 32,153,878 acres. There were some, although inconsequential, local subsidies aimed at obtaining rail connections.

Because of the instability of the Republic, the War Between the States and Reconstruction, however, railroad building was slow until the 1870s, when the boom began. Construction continued with alternating booms and slow developments until a peak of 17,078.29 miles was reached in 1932.

Earliest Texas Railroad Projects

Within six years after steam railroads began operating in the United States, the Republic of Texas made a first gesture toward building one within its own boundaries. But not until seven years after the Republic had become a state of the Union was this effort accomplished. The Republic during its lifetime issued **four railroad charters**, the first charter on Dec. 16, 1836, to the **Texas Rail-Road, Navigation and Banking Company.** The TRRN&B was authorized to construct a continuous transport route from the Rio Grande to the Sabine, using some combination of railroad and canal.

This was the first railroad charter west of the Mississippi River. Its incorporators included two senators of the Republic, four representatives, a founder of the city of Houston, a merchant-banker and Stephen F. Austin, the "Father of Texas," all men of the highest integrity. The charter passed the House almost without debate, the Senate without a recorded vote and was signed by President Houston two days later.

Then unpopularity caught up with it. A letter dated Dec. 26 from one congressman to another became public, boasting privileges in the charter "beyond arithmetical calculation." Newspaper opposition developed, a candidate was elected to Congress on his pledge to get rid of the company; and, as a final stroke, the prospective sale in the United States of $1,025,000 in company stock was blocked by the financial panic of May, 1837. When this stock was offered in Houston only $86,000 in Texas paper money was raised.

Banking-Railroading

The railroad provisions of the charter were not unusual or irregular. Free transportation of soldiers and war munitions was required, and a tax of 2½ percent on the net profit. Any citizen could buy public land at the same price that was asked for its right of way. A paid-in specie capital of $1,000,000 was required for the bank, and discounts and charges upon paper were limited to 10 percent. Branch banks were authorized.

Construction was to begin after the bank went into operation, and to establish the bank a bonus of $25,000 in gold or silver was required to be paid to the Republic within 18 months. This limitation would end June 16, 1838, and when the bonus was proffered on June 5 in Texas paper money it was refused by the Treasurer of the Republic, with the support of the attorney general.

Thus the charter was violated, and so ended the first effort to build a railroad in Texas. Many bitter words were exchanged, but history does not support any record of dishonorable acts. Public opinion was troubled by the pitiful outcome, and fervor was dampened by the continued financial depression in the United States. But hope for a railroad, stimulated by its need and by the rivalry between the three young towns of Galveston, Harrisburg and Houston, did not die.

Second Railroad Project

The Republic issued its **second railroad** charter on May 24, 1838, to the **Brazos and Galveston Rail-road Company**, to connect Galveston Bay with the rich agriculture of the Brazos River Valley by means of railroads, turnpikes and later, through charter amendments, by canals. Bank privileges were prohibited. A 150-foot right of way was granted across the public domain at the minimum land price. Rates were limited to 2½ cents per hundredweight-mile; soldiers and war munitions were to be carried free; the charter would forfeit upon failure to build 10 miles within four years. A down payment of $20 per share was required for capital stock sales, with $80 callable, in installments not exceeding $10, on 60-day notice.

The financing was never accomplished but it stimulated action in the rival town of Houston, now itself a seaport through navigation on the Buffalo Bayou. To its citizens, including some promoters of the demised TRRN&B, the Republic issued its third railroad charter Jan. 26, 1839, under title of the **Houston and Brazos Rail Road Company**. Its provisions resembled those of the B&G RR Co., but without canals; allowed a 300-foot right of way at no cost; provided no freight rates or free army transportation; permitted tolls after 10 miles of turnpike were finished; required work to start within 18 months and be finished within seven years; and called for a down payment of $5 per share for capital stock, and a stockholders' meeting to elect officers after 1,000 shares were sold.

The stockholders' meeting was on Dec. 29, 1839, directors and officers were elected, a 10-mile contract was let on May 6, 1840, advertisements for laborers were published, and on July 25 elaborate ceremonies were held for the breaking of ground, with a parade of Masons, Odd-Fellows, the Milam Guards and the citizenry. But S. G. Reed in his "History of Texas Railroads" said no record could be found of any actual grading. The abandonment of the project was attributed to the threat of a Mexican invasion.

Andrew Briscoe's Project

The fourth charter issued by the Republic was based on a realistic foundation. Andrew Briscoe of Harrisburg in the spring of 1840 did the first railroad grading in Texas. He was a signer of the Texas Declaration of Independence, a veteran of the War of Independence, and in 1836 the Congress of the Republic appointed him chief justice of the municipality of Harrisburg. This town was a strong business rival of its close neighbor Houston on the north and more remote neighbor

Galveston on the south. Navigation on the Buffalo Bay-ou reached it before it reached Houston, and Briscoe planned to go after the Brazos River Valley trade by means of a railroad in competition with both his neigh-bors. He used the unincorporated name of Harrisburg & Brazos Railroad, and on Feb. 28, 1840, signed a con-tract for 3,000 post oak or cedar ties, and later for grad-ing the railroad.

Harrisburg had been burned by Santa Anna and his Mexican army in 1836, during the War of Independence, and Briscoe's contract provided that "should the coun-try be invaded by a foreign foe all obligations shall be suspended and shall commence again on the departure of the enemy." This reflected an uneasiness that affect-ed all similar enterprises. To carry forward his plan Briscoe advertised the sale of town lots on April 10 and 11 for the benefit of the railroad, and for 50 Negro men to work on the grading. His full plan was to build to the Pacific coast by way of El Paso, financing the work by town-lot sales along the route.

"Railroad and Trading Company"

The Republic issued its **fifth railroad charter** on Jan. 9, 1841, to incorporate Briscoe's project as the **Harris-burg Railroad and Trading Company** (the word "trad-ing" presumably to allow for the sale of town lots). Similar to its two predecessors, it provided for a rail-road to the Brazos River Valley. Imported engines and supplies for the railroad were to be duty-free. It was given no right of way, freight rates and capital stock sales were unregulated, railroad transportation only was authorized, work was required to commence within 18 months, and 30 miles to be completed within five years. The issuing of exchange bills or promissory notes for general circulation was prohibited.

About two miles of grading were completed, but the deadly stagnation of business because of Mexican threats, accented by the 2-day and 4-day occupations of San Antonio by the Mexican army in September, 1842,

and the financial depression reflected from the United States, forced work to stop. It was not resumed until after Texas had entered the Union. Although Briscoe did not live to see the outcome, his project was carried through much as planned, even the transcontinental railroad, which grew out of the Buffalo Bayou, Brazos and Colorado, successor to the Harrisburg Railroad and Trading Company.

The two first railroad charters issued by the State of Texas, to the **La Vaca, Guadalupe & San Saba** and the **Colorado & Wilson Creek** in 1846, developed nothing. But the third, to the **Galveston and Red River Railway Com-pany** on March 11, 1848, developed into the second rail-road built in Texas.

First Railroad

The first railroad built was the successor to the project of Andrew Briscoe. Gen. Sidney Sherman, vet-eran of the War of Independence, associated himself with Briscoe, bought his 1,272 unsold town lots and 3,617 acres adjoining on March 30, 1847, took the idea to Bos-ton, Mass., his earlier home, secured financial support, and on Oct. 31, 1847, made an agreement which was incorporated in Massachusetts as the Harrisburg City Company.

The Texas Legislature issued a charter to the **Buffa-lo Bayou, Brazos and Colorado Railway Company** on Feb. 11, 1850, to implement the project developed in Boston. The same legislative act authorized the City of Houston to build a branch railway to connect with the BBB&C. No provision was made for use of the public domain. Passenger fare was limited to 5 cents per mile, freight rates to 50 cents per hundredweight for every 100 miles, and the price for carrying the mails was to be regulated by the state. The sale of town lots was not binding unless 20 miles of railroad were completed within three years.

By amendment on Jan. 29, 1853, a grant was given of eight sections of land for every mile of railroad com-

RAILROAD NAMES

Railroads operating in Texas and the initials used to designate them on this map are:

AMTK—Amtrak.
A&NR—Angelina & Neches River.
AT&SF—Atchison, Topeka & Santa Fe Railway Co.
BN—Burlington Northern.
BRR—Belton Railroad.
GH&H—Galveston, Houston & Henderson.
GRR—Georgetown Railroad.
KCS—Kansas City Southern.
MKT—Missouri-Kansas-Texas.
MP—Missouri Pacific.
MC&SA—Moscow, Camden & San Augustine.
OK&T—Oklahoma, Kansas & Texas Railroad Company
PVS—Pecos Valley Southern.

TEXAS RAILROAD MAP
1985

Railroad Names (Con.)

PC&N—Point Comfort & Northern.
RS&S—Rockdale, Sandow & Southern.
RS&P—Roscoe, Snyder & Pacific.
SLSW—St. Louis Southwestern.
SP—Southern Pacific.
TC—Texas Central.
TM—Texas Mexican.
T&N—Texas & Northern.
TNW—Texas North Western Railway Company.
TSE—Texas South-Eastern.
WMW&NW—Weatherford, Mineral Wells & Northwestern.

INSET 1

INSET 2

pleted, the **first railroad land grant** in Texas. Grading began in June, 1851, a locomotive, the "General Sherman," arrived in Galveston by boat in November, 1852 and 20 miles were completed and in operation to Stafford's Point on Aug. 22, 1853. It reached the Brazos River in December, 1855, and Alleyton, 80 miles from Harrisburg and 2½ miles short of the Colorado River, in April, 1861. This gap was completed by the Columbus Tap Railway Company which sold it to the BBB&C Sept. 21, 1866. The name of the BBB&C was changed on July 27, 1870, to the Galveston, Harrisburg and San Antonio. Building was completed to San Antonio in April, 1873, and to El Paso in July, 1881. It was consolidated with the Texas & New Orleans, June 30, 1934, and is today a part of the Southern Pacific system.

The **Galveston & Red River**, begun in 1853, was **Texas' second railroad**. Originally promoted by Galveston men it was taken over by Houston interests and the named changed on Sept. 1, 1856, to Houston and Texas Central Railway Company. Before the outbreak of the war 80 miles had been completed northward to Millican, near the Brazos River.

Another railroad, the **Washington County Rail Road Company**, chartered Feb. 2, 1856, later a part of the H&TC, was built by Washington County farmers and merchants from Hempstead to Brenham and completed in 1861.

San Antonio Project

These projects threatened the trade of San Antonio, whose citizens, led by S. A. Maverick, on Sept. 5, 1850, secured a charter for the **San Antonio and Mexican Gulf Railroad** to run from Port Lavaca or any point on the Gulf to San Antonio, with bonds of $100,000, which were paid, although the road never reached there. Twenty-seven miles were completed to Victoria, early in 1861. It was practically destroyed in December, 1862, by Confederate Gen. Magruder to prevent the federal army, then threatening the coast near Port Lavaca, from using it. It was rebuilt by the U.S. Army in 1865-66, and sold in 1870 to satisfy a claim of the United States government for this expense.

Galveston became concerned over Houston's activity in railroad projects and on Feb. 7, 1853, secured a charter for the **Galveston, Houston and Henderson Railroad Company**, began work in 1856, completed 40 miles from the mainland to the outskirts of Houston by Oct. 22, 1859, and built the bridge across the bay the next year. But it was never extended through to Henderson and the Red River as projected. It was used effectively by Gen. Magruder, especially in the successful attack on the federal army at Galveston on Jan. 1, 1863.

Sugar Bowl Road

None of these projects helped the planters of Brazoria County, then the richest in the state, nor Matagorda, Colorado and Wharton Counties, known as the "sugar bowl." They decided to build a railroad from Columbia to Houston, the **Houston Tap & Brazoria**. It was chartered on Sept. 1, 1856, and completed by Dec. 1, 1859. The charter provided for a line to the Rio Grande, and 50 miles to Wharton had been graded when the war broke out. After the war the road became the property of the International & Great Northern.

It embraced the Houston Tap Railroad, built in 1857 by a bond issue voted by Houston, to connect that city with the BBB&C at Pierce Junction. A year after completion it was sold to the planters at a $42,000 profit.

"Defense" Road

The Sabine & Galveston Railroad & Lumber Company was chartered Sept. 1, 1856. But no work had been done up to 1859 and probably none would have been done then but for a resolution adopted on Sept. 1 of that year by the Louisiana Legislature addressed to the Legislature of Texas calling attention to this project, stressing its strategic importance in the event of civil war, then impending, authorizing the road to build from the Sabine to the Mississippi under the name of the Texas & New Orleans Railroad Company, Louisiana division. The Texas Legislature acted promptly and favorably. The company had no trouble raising funds and the road was completed from Houston to Orange, 106 miles, by Jan. 1, 1861. But only 45 miles were built in Louisiana. The gap was not filled until after the war.

Coast Road

The next road along the coast built before the war was the **Eastern Texas Railroad**. Sabine Pass in those days was a thriving port. Beaumont was also becoming a city. Since 1852 both had been trying to get a railroad through the East Texas Piney Woods to the Red River. Finally on Jan. 21, 1858, this road was chartered, 25 miles between the two cities built and 25 miles graded

north of Beaumont by 1861. It was never operated. Dick Dowling used the rails in September, 1863, to erect a fort at Sabine Pass which enabled his little band of 41 Confederates to withstand a federal bombardment and to disperse a strong fleet with heavy loss. The road was not rebuilt after the war.

Early North Texas Roads

The other two railroads constructed before the war were in North Texas, which by 1852 had attracted much immigration. Many new towns had sprung up. Among them Dallas, Jefferson and Clarksville were the largest. They were the centers of heavy "freighting" and river shipping. All of this section clamored for railroads and wanted to be on the route of the Transcontinental Road which all Texas then thought would be built through this state.

Two roads were projected as parts of the plan. The first was the **Texas Western**, chartered Feb. 16, 1852. It built 20 miles of railroad from the head of navigation on Caddo Lake, directed toward Marshall. In 1856, the Legislature renewed the charter and changed the name to the Southern Pacific Railroad. This had no connection with the present Southern Pacific. This company built a little more line and had 25 miles graded when the war broke out. Gen. Magruder took up about 15 miles of the rails and relaid it toward Shreveport, using it for transporting war materials.

The other road was the **Memphis, El Paso & Pacific**, chartered Feb. 7, 1853, to build across the state. Before the war began they had graded 57 miles but had only five miles in operation from Caddo Lake to Jefferson. Later the two charters were amended so as to serve different portions of North Texas and to authorize them to operate jointly west of Dallas. In 1872 the Texas Legislature, after a bitter fight, approved the sale of the Southern Pacific and the Memphis, El Paso & Pacific, with "all rights, benefits and privileges granted or intended to be granted," to the Texas & Pacific, which was operating under a federal charter. Dallas was reached in 1873 when the panic stopped work.

Indianola Railroad

The Indianola Railroad was chartered Jan. 21, 1858, to build 15 miles to connect with the SA&MG. The grading was done and ties on hand, but they were destroyed in 1862 to prevent the federal military forces then threatening the coast from using them. The road was actually built in 1871. Indianola was visited by a tropical hurricane in 1875 and destroyed by another in 1886. The track was then taken up.

At the breaking out of the war in 1861 there were 10 roads in operation with a total mileage of 469.

When the war ended in 1865 all of the 10 roads were financially bankrupt with roadbed and equipment sadly deteriorated. It was five years before any of them were able to begin rebuilding and before any new ones were undertaken except one — the H&TC — which was able to resume construction in 1867, reached Dallas in 1872 and Denison in 1873.

Railroad Boom Begins

In 1871, however, it looked as if Texas were in for an era of railroad building. Money was plentiful; the BBB&C, reorganized as the Galveston, Harrisburg & San Antonio, was preparing for extension westward; the T&P was on its way to El Paso, the H&TC was pushing northward and the International & Great Northern was about to begin construction. These lines did build nearly a thousand miles before the panic of 1873. This retarded work until 1876. During this and the next six years over 4,000 miles were built. Then building practically ceased, for several causes. One was the reduction of passenger fare from 5 cents to 3 cents; another the repeal of the land grant act, both in 1882.

There were many roads then being built that had been financed in part by grants of lands. There was, however, no alternative for the state but to repeal the land grant act, because it had already outstanding certificates calling for about 8,000,000 acres more than there were left of unappropriated state lands.

Beginning of Railroad Regulation

Still another deterrent to railroad building was the rising tide of feeling over the abuses by the railroad managements and the demand for more effective regulation. In the second railroad charter, that for the Brazos & Galveston in 1838, the Republic reserved the right to fix rates, or "tolls," as they called them. In all of the later charters maximum rates for freight and passengers were fixed. In 1853 the state passed a comprehensive law **regulating railroads**, the first of its kind in the United States, although Texas at that time had no railroad operating. This was supplemented later. But this did not deal with rates. Prior to the war, there were no complaints about rail rates because even the maximum, when charged, was so much less than the cost of "freighting."

After the war, the roads came in for much criticism for excessive and discriminating rates and other abuses but were powerful enough in the legislative halls to prevent any punitive laws or stricter rate regulation. The **Grange**, which in 1872 had over 40,000 members in Texas, forced a constitutional convention in 1875 which required the Legislature to pass laws "to correct abuses and prevent unjust discriminations and extortion in rates of freight and passenger tariffs and to enforce all such laws by adequate penalties."

Establishment of Railroad Commisson

The leader of this agitation was **James Stephen Hogg**. It was an active issue in state politics during these years and was the leading issue in 1890 when Hogg was elected governor on a platform calling for a constitutional amendment to authorize the creation of a **Railroad Commission**, which was approved by the people and the commission created April 3, 1891. It was patterned after the Interstate Commerce Act of 1887 and **John H. Reagan**, then United States Senator, who had long been an advocate of both state and interstate commissions and had had much to do with the framing of both plans, resigned his seat in the senate to accept the chairmanship, which he held until his death on March 6, 1905. At first it was appointive, but by constitutional amendment in 1894 it was made elective.

Except for a few years after the repeal of the land grant act and for a few years after the creation of the Railroad Commission and the panic of 1893, railroad building continued at the rate of 300 or 400 miles a year until the First World War. After 1914 there was little building until 1925, when the Santa Fe, Rock Island and Fort Worth & Denver roads began building into the South Plains, and the Southern Pacific into the Rio Grande Valley. At the end of 1932 **the peak was reached** with **17,078.29 miles** of main line in Texas.

Current Operations

Track mileage continues to decline as large Class 1 railroads abandon little-used segments of certain branch lines. In 1984, the Roscoe, Snyder & Pacific Railway (RS&P), an independent short line 30 miles in length, ceased operations on 27 miles between Roscoe and Snyder. While 3 miles of track will be retained by the company at Roscoe, the RS&P is essentially defunct, a victim of railroad deregulation and changing economic conditions.

Even though track mileage is falling, freight tonnage hauled by railroads in Texas continues at high levels. After the all-time peak tonnage year of 1981 the national economy went into recession. The latest years of which official statistics are available (1982 and 1983) reflect somewhat lessened rail traffic in Texas but the long-term trends are generally progressive insofar as tonnage and net revenue are concerned. Incomplete

Amtrak Passengers On/Off at Texas Stations

Station	FY84	FY83	FY82	FY81
San Antonio	30,919	29,522	30,816	41,663
Dallas	26,296	24,850	22,644	47,673
Houston	16,940	16,843	17,715	47,406
El Paso	15,748	15,203	15,029	16,994
Ft. Worth	12,551	12,708	12,206	30,396
Austin	13,213	12,851	11,936	17,849
Longview	5,574	5,740	5,654	8,540
Temple	5,609	5,254	5,597	17,807
Beaumont	3,699	4,377	4,437	3,647
Texarkana	4,318	4,184	4,085	6,903
Marshall	4,497	4,052	3,747	4,919
Taylor	3,697	3,151	2,841	3,970
Cleburne	2,669	2,694	2,333	5,163
San Marcos	2,330	2,132	2,091	1,821
Alpine	1,894	1,810	1,899	2,104
McGregor	1,852	1,750	1,810	3,591
Del Rio	1,295	1,701	1,385	1,480
Sanderson	573	642	650	511
Laredo	— Service Discontinued —			8,688
Brenham	— Service Discontinued —			7,138
Rosenberg	— Service Discontinued —			4,090
Gainesville	— Service Discontinued —			. . .
Totals	153,674	149,464	146,875	282,353

Source: Amtrak Office of State & Local Services Analysis, Washington, D.C.

RAIL LINE ABANDONMENTS 1983-1984

Carrier	End Points or Common Name	Official Mileage	Counties
AT&SF. .	Whiteface-Bledsoe	24.2	Cochran
AT&SF. .	Winnie-Whites Ranch	12.0	Chambers
MP	Sugarland-Pryor	0.95	Fort Bend
MP	Swan-Thedford	3.2	Smith
RS&P. . .	Roscoe-Snyder	27.4	Nolan, Mitchell, Scurry
SP	Athens Branch	2.8	Dallas
SP	Gregory-Portland	3.9	San Patricio
SP	Alice-Falfurrias	39.3	Jim Wells and Brooks
Total. .		113.75	

RAILROAD MILEAGE OPERATED BY CARRIER IN TEXAS, 1983

Railroad	Miles Operated
Class 1 Railroads*	
Atchison, Topeka & Santa Fe Railway Company	3,388
Burlington Northern Railroad Company	1,350
Kansas City Southern Railway Company	293
Missouri-Kansas-Texas Railroad Company	1,176
Missouri Pacific Railroad Company	3,310
St. Louis-Southwestern Railway Company	637
Southern Pacific Transportation Company	2,788
Total Class 1	12,942
Class 2 Railroads	
Texas Mexican Railway Company	157
Total Class 2	157
Class 3 Railroads	
Angelina & Neches River Railroad Company .	22
Belton Railroad Company	6
Galveston, Houston & Henderson Railroad Company	48
Galveston Wharves, Board of Trustees of the .	46
Georgetown Railroad Company, Inc.	16
Great Southwest Railroad, Inc.	20
Houston Belt and Terminal Railway Company	56
Moscow, Camden & San Augustine Railroad Company	7
Pecos Valley Southern Railway Company	34
Point Comfort & Northern Railway Company	13
Port Terminal Railroad Association	32
Rockdale, Sandow & Southern Railroad Company	6
Roscoe, Snyder & Pacific Railway Company. .	30
Sabine River & Northern Railroad Company. .	30
Texas & Northern Railway Company	8
Texas Central Railroad Company	25
Texas City Terminal Railway Company	6
Texas North Western Railway Company	71
Texas South-Eastern Railroad Company	18
Texas Transportation Company	1
Weatherford, Mineral Wells & Northwestern Railway Company	23
Western Railroad Company	4
Total Class 3	522
Total Class 1, 2 and 3	13,621

*Class 1 railroads are those having annual operating revenues of $50,000,000 or more. Class 2 railroads are those having annual operating revenues of less than $50,000,000 but more than $10,000,000. Class 3 railroads are those having annual operating revenues of $10,000,000 or less.

returns for 1984 show advances beyond the 1982 and 1983 figures.

Amtrak continues to provide some inter-city railroad passenger service in Texas. The Sunset Limited and the Eagle each operate every-other-day to a total of 18 communities. Ridership is slowly increasing. The only other scheduled rail passenger trains in Texas are those of the Texas State Railroad (TSR) running between Palestine and Rusk. TSR is owned by the State of Texas and operated as a state historical park. Steam locomotive-powered trains haul tourists through the beautiful woods of East Texas (toll free telephone reservation number 1-800-442-8951).

Mergers of major rail carriers into mega-railroad continue. On Dec. 22, 1982, the Missouri Pacific Railroad and Union Pacific Railroad merged. The Missouri Pacific Railroad is now part of the Union Pacific System. When this section went to press, the U.S. Interstate Commerce Commission had not made a final decision as to the merger application of the Atchison, Topeka and Santa Fe Railway Company (AT&SF) and the Southern Pacific Transportation Company (SPT) (including the St. Louis-Southwestern Railway Company). If approved, the consolidated carrier would control more than 50 percent of all track mileage in Texas, easily becoming the single largest railroad in the state.

STATISTICAL HISTORY OF RAILROAD OPERATION IN TEXAS, 1891-1983

The table below shows development and trends of railroad line operations, freight tonnage, operating revenues and expenses in Texas since the Railroad Commission's first report.

							Amounts per Mile Operated			
Year	Average Miles Operated Including Trackage Rights	Tons Revenue Freight	Railway Operating Revenues	Railway Operating Expenses	Operating Ratio	*Net Revenue From Railway Operations	Freight Revenue	Passenger Revenue	Net From Operations	Freight Revenue Per Ton-Mile
1983	12,942.00	245,502,145	$2,032,792,000	$1,705,625,000	83.8	$327,167,000	$147,548.00	...	$25,824.00	$.029
1982	13,017.00	242,451,128	2,138,768,000	1,883,375,000	85.2	225,393,000	145,147.00	...	23,178.00	.032
1981	13,051.00	274,576,260	2,400,252,000	2,055,057,000	81.78	345,195,000	169,528.00	...	32,585.00	.032
1980	13,075.00	268,445,039	2,064,108,000	1,761,650,000	85.34	304,742,000	151,918.00	...	23,310.00	.026
†1979	13,075.00	239,943,773	1,718,912,000	1,469,238,000	85.47	249,674,000	126,819.00	...	19,096.00	.024
‡1978	13,923.00	241,386,721	1,445,104,000	1,265,949,000	87.60	166,937,000	100,110.00	...	11,990.00	.021
1977	14,554.00	242,267,810	1,314,952,036	993,342,280	75.54	321,609,756	86,994.26	...	22,097.69	.021
1976	14,679.00	206,130,425	1,158,004,603	874,250,182	75.50	283,754,421	75,737.76	...	19,330.64	.022
1975	14,717.00	230,120,781	1,073,029,254	792,786,773	73.88	280,242,481	69,982.79	...	19,042.09	.019
1974	14,712.00	247,320,696	1,048,980,920	794,249,941	75.72	254,730,979	67,805.72	...	17,314.50	.017
1973	14,830.00	253,365,741	928,419,976	699,019,572	75.29	229,400,404	59,512.05	0.15	15,468.67	.014
1972	14,800.00	222,303,703	784,815,674	614,035,456	78.24	170,780,218	50,884.46	0.20	11,539.20	.014
1971	14,909.00	208,878,010	725,469,372	554,790,694	76.46	170,786,678	46,429.13	38.81	11,455.27	.014
1970	14,683.00	211,069,076	655,638,834	504,146,691	76.89	151,492,143	42,245.42	170.71	10,317.52	.013
1969	15,019.00	201,455,133	599,461,296	465,795,906	77.70	133,665,390	37,570.23	206.72	8,899.75	.013
1968	15,039.00	193,822,546	560,178,714	446,936,382	79.78	113,242,332	34,672.47	291.82	7,529.91	.013
1967	15,128.00	183,742,685	517,617,077	411,306,768	79.46	106,310,309	31,432.83	400.93	7,027.39	.013
1966	15,295.00	197,208,761	543,803,770	408,281,725	75.08	135,522,045	32,349.45	522.48	8,860.55	.013
1965	15,214.00	181,553,163	502,191,485	380,412,080	75.75	121,779,405	29,754.73	605.40	8,004.43	.013
1964	15,254.00	173,074,704	462,053,638	366,103,656	79.23	95,949,982	26,875.78	712.94	6,290.15	.013
1963	15,279.00	158,750,736	445,048,337	348,210,665	78.24	96,837,672	25,635.01	791.81	6,337.96	.013
1962	15,389.00	155,728,821	439,606,758	351,277,249	79.91	88,329,509	24,948.34	871.95	5,739.78	.013
1961	15,622.00	157,700,142	429,983,796	344,217,323	80.05	85,766,473	23,915.32	892.94	5,490.11	.013
1960	15,445.00	149,360,161	438,531,081	347,353,628	79.21	91,177,453	26,149.41	937.69	5,903.36	.013
1959	15,600.00	162,985,000	460,813,237	355,981,564	77.25	104,831,673	25,889.59	924.41	6,719.98	.013
1958	15,853.00	152,687,265	449,909,607	338,708,662	75.28	111,200,945	24,908.93	904.14	7,014.50	.013
1957	16,003.00	156,218,472	455,449,879	349,842,282	76.81	105,607,597	24,923.21	1,002.17	6,599.24	.013
1956	16,078.00	163,448,004	451,785,741	354,734,911	78.52	97,050,830	24,502.50	1,089.91	6,036.25	.013
1955	16,151.00	166,742,660	450,865,455	341,963,345	75.85	108,902,110	24,482.83	1,085.84	6,742.75	.013
1954	16,254.00	151,639,475	426,223,548	326,373,490	76.57	99,850,058	22,758.67	1,161.88	6,143.11	.013
1953	16,248.00	163,120,436	474,112,360	359,553,092	75.84	114,559,268	25,489.81	1,238.52	7,050.67	.013
1952	16,249.00	171,536,799	480,598,102	353,835,324	73.62	126,762,778	25,554.16	1,471.58	7,801.27	.013
1951	16,268.00	171,974,878	458,070,697	351,407,963	76.71	106,662,734	24,025.44	1,582.08	6,556.60	.013
1950	16,296.00	155,970,914	520,804,968	310,731,697	73.83	210,133,271	22,021.66	1,366.76	6,758.30	.013
1949	16,326.67	147,769,627	389,948,675	298,378,439	76.52	91,570,236	20,461.53	1,390.79	5,608.63	.013
1948	16,344.72	172,717,282	436,136,267	330,029,402	75.67	106,106,865	22,907.44	1,626.45	6,491.81	.013
1947	16,345.71	163,222,681	372,282,426	280,421,729	75.32	91,860,697	19,005.06	1,727.19	5,619.86	.003
1946	16,365.62	140,735,375	321,208,561	261,245,259	81.33	59,963,302	15,183.86	2,634.56	3,663.98	.003
1945	16,375.97	159,795,571	390,672,459	263,883,854	67.54	126,788,605	17,635.26	4,370.32	7,742.36	.010
1944	16,413.17	165,921,126	412,831,093	251,675,821	60.96	161,155,272	18,411.51	4,933.33	9,818.66	.010
1943	16,524.09	164,970,686	379,659,061	222,135,959	58.51	157,523,102	16,671.20	4,615.05	9,532.94	.010
1942	16,774.93	141,223,552	283,433,884	169,494,082	59.80	113,939,802	13,187.93	2,440.20	6,792.27	.010
1941	17,016.00	91,780,832	180,368,515	127,218,178	70.53	53,150,337	8,859.09	1,205.19	3,123.55	.011
1940	17,057.38	69,107,695	144,124,269	110,626,057	76.76	33,498,212	7,028.74	944.72	1,963.85	.011
1935	17,295.66	61,452,202	117,611,146	93,681,088	79.65	23,930,058	5,579.27	802.07	1,383.58	.011
1930	17,569.02	88,942,552	204,371,667	152,169,952	74.46	52,201,715	9,557.06	1,739.55	2,971.24	.011
1925	16,646.53	90,338,397	227,252,064	169,382,692	74.54	57,869,372	10,653.42	2,673.33	3,476.36	.011
1920	16,382.99	77,803,926	235,353,895	234,718,643	99.73	635,252	9,714.47	4,291.77	38.77	.011
1915	16,294.10	54,354,684	107,414,011	85,900,985	79.97	21,513,026	4,504.81	1,809.82	1,320.29	.011
1910	14,339.21	47,084,828	94,731,430	72,524,020	76.56	22,207,410	4,601.92	1,981.27	1,548.72	.011
1905	11,670.65	30,653,070	68,145,132	52,411,748	76.91	15,733,384	4,044.88	1,493.65	1,348.12	.011
1900	9,971.21	22,380,607	47,062,868	35,626,922	75.70	11,435,946	3,537.81	1,106.78	1,167.98	.009
1895	9,353.80	15,591,262	39,387,869	28,864,994	73.28	10,522,875	3,159.04	984.73	1,124.98	.011
1891	8,718.65	10,944,195	35,666,498	28,762,836	80.64	6,903,662	2,956.58	1,081.59	791.83	.011

*Net revenue before interest and taxes.
†No data available for Rock Island in 1979 and 1980.
‡Beginning in 1978, data no longer reported for Class II and III carriers.

AVIATION IN TEXAS

The following was prepared for the Texas Almanac by George B. Dresser, Program Manager, and his staff, Texas Transportation Institute, Texas A&M University, College Station.

Air transportation is a vital and vigorous part of the Texas economy. Texans are major users of air transportation and the state airport system ranks as one of the busiest and largest in the nation. Texas has more than 50 airlines which serve 35 airports and enplane over 30 million passengers annually. The more than 23,000 registered aircraft are being flown by a resident pilot population of nearly 60,000, utilizing over 1,500 landing facilities.

The **Texas Aeronautics Commission** (TAC) is the state agency with major responsibility for aeronautics. The TAC was created in 1945 and was directed by the Legislature to encourage, foster and assist in the development of aeronautics within the state, and to encourage the establishment of airports and air navigational facilities. The commission's first annual report of Dec. 31, 1946, stated that Texas had 592 designated airports and 7,756 civilian aircraft.

Today the TAC is organized into three operational divisions. The **Aviation Facilities Development Division** has statutory authority to provide engineering and technical services and financial assistance through matching state grants and loans to state agencies authorized to operate airports, and to any governmental entity in this state for the establishment, construction, reconstruction, enlargement or repair of airports, airstrips or air navigational facilities.

The **Air Carrier Administration Division** conducts the commuter carrier certification program which involves a determination of the applicant's financial, managerial and equipment fitness, traffic pro-forma statements and revenues and expenses. Upon determination of fitness the applicant is issued a certificate to provide scheduled service within Texas.

The **Aviation Services and Information Division** provides specialized training programs, aeronautical publications and safety information to individuals and groups involved or interested in aviation throughout the state.

Commercial air carriers have experienced strong growth during 1983 and 1984. Nationwide enplanements on commercial air carriers (carriers holding a certificate issued by the Civil Aeronautics Board) increased 7.2 percent from 1982 to 1983 and 8.7 percent from 1983 to 1984. Commercial air carriers operate transport aircraft with more than 60 passenger seats. Commercial air carrier enplanements in Texas increased 4 percent from 1982 to 1983 reflecting a lower rate of growth than the nation as a whole; however, Texas with 6.5 percent of the nation's population accounted for 11.3 percent of the nation's enplanements. One of every 10 air travelers in the United States boarded at a Texas airport.

In 1983 30,853,297 passengers were enplaned by U.S. commercial air carriers in Texas. As of January 1985 there were 27 U.S. and 12 foreign flag air carriers serving Texas airports.

Texas **ranked first** in the United States in aircraft departures and second after California in enplaned passengers by commercial air carriers. Over 93 percent of the state's population lives within 50 miles of an airport with scheduled air passenger service.

Ten cities accounted for the major portion of the enplanements. **Dallas/Fort Worth International Airport, Dallas Love Field, Houston Intercontinental** and **Houston's William P. Hobby** together accounted for 79 percent of the enplaned passengers on commercial air carriers.

Texas also was served by 19 commuter airlines as of January 1985. Commuter airlines operate small aircraft of 60 seats or less and perform at least five scheduled round trips per week between two or more cities. Commuters provided service from 31 cities and provided the only scheduled service from 19 of these cities. In 1983 commuter airlines enplaned approximately 1.5 million passengers at Texas airports. Since passage of the federal Airline Deregulation Act of 1978 route development activity by commuter airlines has been vigorous in Texas and throughout the nation. Development of success-

RANKING OF TOP 10 STATES, 1983

Source: CAB-FAA

Rank	State	Enplaned Passengers	Rank	State	Aircraft Departures
1	California	37,302,600	1	Texas	456,491
2	Texas	30,853,297	2	California	444,409
3	New York	23,150,072	3	Florida	348,203
4	Florida	22,896,084	4	New York	300,785
5	Illinois	19,343,558	5	Illinois	271,186
6	Georgia	19,328,539	6	Georgia	258,195
7	Colorado	11,801,822	7	Missouri	197,250
8	Pennsylvania	10,044,645	8	Pennsylvania	161,679
9	Missouri	10,461,660	9	Colorado	160,149
10	New Jersey	8,634,168	10	Ohio	152,783

TEXAS ENPLANED PASSENGERS—1983

This table shows total passenger traffic enplaned at all Texas cities having scheduled air carrier or commuter service during calendar year 1983.

City	Enplanements	City	Enplanements
Abilene	57,137	Laredo	22,296
Amarillo	425,135	Longview	17,891
Austin	1,253,500	Lubbock	529,674
Beaumont-Port Arthur	80,618	*Lufkin	421
Brownsville	58,382	McAllen	137,978
Brownwood	1,087	Midland-Odessa	621,601
Clear Lake City	33,499	Paris	1,508
College Station	30,761	San Angelo	42,287
Corpus Christi	403,277	San Antonio	1,837,601
Dallas-Fort Worth	16,101,636	†Sugar Land	5,721
El Paso	1,035,185	Temple	6,311
Fort Worth	914	Texarkana	22,433
Harlingen	352,711	Tyler	28,096
Houston	8,639,390	Victoria	13,999
Killeen	32,005	Waco	21,276
Lake Jackson	6,646	Wichita Falls	49,413

NOTE: Data obtained from a variety of sources including CAB, TAC, airlines and airports.
*—Service terminated in 1983.
†—Service initiated in 1983.

ful new commuter markets in Texas has proved to be difficult and numerous routes have been initiated only to be subsequently abandoned. A recent development has been the initiation of scheduled service from **Hull Field** and **Lakeside** airports located on the western side of the Houston metropolitan area. In 1983 new commuter service was initiated from eight airports and terminated at seven airports. In 1984 new commuter service was initiated from 18 airports and terminated at three airports.

The Texas general aviation fleet, all aircraft except the military and the commercial airlines, consisted of 23,469 registered aircraft as of Jan. 1, 1983. The proportion of the general aviation fleet consisting of single engine airplanes, planes associated with personal or pleasure flying, is decreasing while the proportion consisting of multiengine airplanes, planes associated with business and executive transportation, is increasing. Business is continuing to increase its use of general aviation aircraft. In 1983, 32 percent of the aircraft hours flown was for business and business transportation, 24 percent was for personal transportation, 14 percent for instructional flying, 12 percent for commuter and air taxi, 5 percent for aerial application and 13 percent for other purposes. Texas, with 7 percent of the

nation's population, has 9 percent of the nation's registered aircraft including 15 percent of the turbin powered aircraft. The state's 58,752 pilots in 1983 represented 8 percent of the nation's pilots.

Texas leads the nation in the number of aircraft landing facilities, 1,543 as of December 1983, followed by Illinois with 909. These include 1,212 airports, 325 heliports, 5 stolports and 1 seaplane base. The **Texas Aeronautical Facilities Plan** published by the TAC contains a total of 308 airports — 285 existing facilities and 23 proposed new and replacement airports. These airports are needed to meet the forecast aviation demand for the state to the year 2000 and to maximize access by business aircraft to the state's population, business activity, agricultural production value and mineral production value.

TEXAS AIR TRAFFIC

Airline passenger traffic enplaned in Texas by scheduled certificated carriers.

Source: CAB-FAA

Year—	Domestic	International	Total
1957	2,699,393	109,165	2,808,55
1958	2,658,897	83,870	2,742,76
1959*	2,750,391	78,150	2,828,54
1960	3,045,391	68,191	3,113,58
1961	3,431,788	72,680	3,505,27
1962*	3,599,658	83,325	3,682,98
1963*	3,914,309	105,150	4,019,45
1964*	4,514,200	108,257	4,622,45
1965	5,635,179	122,510	5,757,68
1966	6,991,148	178,464	7,169,61
1967	7,983,634	189,251	8,172,88
1968	9,286,973	220,026	9,506,99
1969	9,923,696	218,352	10,142,04
1970*	10,039,886	216,805	10,256,69
1971	9,936,887	225,024	10,161,91
1972	11,022,538	232,875	11,255,41
1973	11,954,536	276,325	12,230,86
1974	12,934,999	274,569	13,209,56
1975	12,918,709	264,248	13,182,95
1976	14,218,189	267,151	14,485,34
1977	15,595,237	275,910	15,871,14
1978	17,805,693	435,336	18,241,02
1979	20,966,571	580,223	21,546,79
1980	24,693,080	610,134	25,303,21
1981	26,853,393	596,087	27,449,48
1982	29,031,114	510,674	29,541,78
1983	30,291,548	561,749	30,853,29

*Fiscal year July 1 through June 30, all other year calendar.

TOP TEN TEXAS CITIES—1983
Source: CAB-FAA

City—	Aircraft Departures Performed	Percent of Total	Enplaned Passengers	Percent of Total
Dallas-Fort Worth	207,279	45	15,682,626	51
Houston	129,993	29	8,504,411	28
San Antonio	29,833	7	1,823,971	6
Austin	22,618	5	1,248,759	4
El Paso	18,142	4	1,035,185	3
Midland/Odessa	12,016	3	621,185	2
Lubbock	9,920	2	529,674	2
Amarillo	8,269	2	425,135	1
Brownsville-Harlingen-San Benito	6,476	1	411,093	1
Corpus Christi	7,782	2	403,277	1

**Total Texas
Aircraft Departures Performed** 456,491

**Total Texas
Enplaned Passengers** 30,853,297

TEXAS ENPLANED TRAFFIC—1983
CAB CERTIFIED CARRIERS

This table shows domestic airline traffic at Texas cities during calendar year 1983, as reported by the Civil Aeronautics Board and the Federal Aviation Administration. In addition, U.S. carriers' traffic to foreign destinations is shown.

City—	Aircraft Departures	Enplaned Passengers	Air Mail (Tons)	Cargo (Tons)	City—	Aircraft Departures	Enplaned Passengers	Air Mail (Tons)	Cargo (Tons)
DOMESTIC					Mission-McAllen-Edinburg	2,796	135,485	18	1
Abilene	80	1,824	...	8	San Antonio	29,470	1,786,910	4,402	3,2
Amarillo	8,269	425,135	297	291	**Total Domestic**	450,092	30,291,548	75,142	126,8
Austin	22,618	1,248,759	2,204	1,267	**INTERNATIONAL**				
Beaumont-Port Arthur	704	18,702	3	12	Dallas-Fort Worth	2,890	292,057	659	2,2
Brownsville-Harlingen-San Benito	6,476	411,093	...	2,342	Houston	3,094	230,138	148	6
Corpus Christi	7,782	403,277	247	489	Mission-McAllen-Edinburg	52	2,493	...	
Dallas-Fort Worth	204,389	15,390,569	51,093	76,571	San Antonio	363	37,061	4	
El Paso	18,142	1,035,185	1,339	3,621	**Total Intl.**	6,399	561,749	811	2,9
Houston	126,899	8,274,273	15,161	37,588					
Laredo	531	9,477	...	142	**TOTAL**	456,491	30,853,297	75,953	129,8
Lubbock	9,920	529,674	288	649					
Midland-Odessa	12,016	621,185	90	497					

PRINCIPAL TEXAS PORTS

During 1983, Texas ports showed a 1 percent decrease in waterborne commerce, according to the Galveston District Corps of Engineers.

Total tonnage handled by Texas ports was 260,698,551 in 1982, compared with 257,934,340 in 1983.

The Texas portion of the **Gulf Intracoastal Waterway** showed an increase from 59,838,458 tons in 1982 to 61,288,406 tons in 1983.

Orange and **Port Mansfield** tied for first place in greatest percentage increase, 43 percent, during 1983, Orange tonnage increasing from 279,728 in 1982 to 399,092 in 1983. Port Mansfield increased from 1,431 in 1982 to 62,871 tons in 1983. **Long Mott** increased 22 percent, up from 2,744,633 in 1982 to 3,242,181 in 1983.

Palacios showed the greatest decline in tonnage, down 99.9 percent from 54,545 in 1982 to only 86 tons in 1983. **Aransas Pass** was second in declining tonnage, down 92 percent from 12,243 tons in 1982 to 959 tons in 1983. **Sabine Pass** was down 48 percent, from 1,164,632 in 1982 to 605,108 in 1983. **Brownsville** showed a 39 percent decrease, down to 1,338,550 in 1983 from the 2,200,132 tons in 1982.

Houston, Texas' leading port, showed a loss of 6 percent, down in 1983 to 88,706,519 from 94,649,549 tons in 1982.

Commerce through the **Freeport jetties**, serving the port of Freeport, showed the largest increase, up to

13,766,730 tons in 1983 over the 13,012,765 tons in 1982. Most of the jetties showed a loss in 1983. Total tonnage was down to 177,325,123 tons in 1983 from 185,058,928 tons in 1982.

Dry cargo handled through the deepwater ports amounted to 43,210,420 tons in 1983; **liquid cargo** amounted to 206,363,640 tons, for a total tonnage of 249,574,060.

1983 RECEIPTS AND SHIPMENTS

(All figures in short tons.)

SABINE PASS HARBOR: **Coastwise Receipts:** Lubricating oils and greases, 300. **Internal Receipts:** Crude petroleum, 76,095; distillate fuel oil, 59,360. **Internal Shipments:** Crude petroleum, 338,429; distillate fuel oil, 43,525; water, 42,372.

ORANGE HARBOR: **Imports:** Fabricated metal prod., 760. **Internal Receipts:** Building cement, 161,905; basic chemicals, nec, 64,720; sand and gravel, 52,750; residual fuel oil, 23,522. **Internal Shipments:** Building cement, 33,302; basic chemicals, nec, 19,493; crude petroleum, 14,712. **Local:** Residual fuel oil, 1,954.

BEAUMONT HARBOR: **Imports:** Crude petroleum, 13,564,380; basic chemicals, nec, 212,102; liquefied gases, 124,671; naphtha, 104,115; residual fuel oil, 60,192. **Exports:** Wheat, 2,795,937; wheat flour, 502,531; lubricating oils and greases, 138,298; coke, pet. coke, 138,113; basic chemicals, nec, 106,977; soybeans, 91,621; distillate fuel

FOREIGN TRADE, 1920-1983, BY CUSTOMS DISTRICTS

Source: Bureau of Business Research, University of Texas; and U.S. Department of Commerce

(All figures in millions of dollars)

Year—	Exports							Imports						
	Total Texas	‡Houston	†Port Arthur	Galveston	Laredo	El Paso	§Dallas/Fort Worth	Total Texas	***Houston	†Port Arthur	**Galveston	Laredo	El Paso	§Dallas/Fort Worth
1920...	$832		$113	$649	$56	$14		$55		$9	$31	$10	$5	
1930...	555		66	397	82	10		33		2	22	4	5	
1940...	290		52	191	39	8		41		2	29	6	4	
1950...	1,420		97	992	300	31		312		3	209	76	25	
1951...	1,834		117	1,213	456	48		417		4	337	47	25	
1952...	1,745.8		141.7	1,167.9	385.4	50.8		509.7		4.8	350.3	91.8	62.8	
1953...	1,295.0		146.4	706.9	395.0	46.7		437.6		3.9	337.6	67.3	28.8	
1954...	1,321.6		116.4	770.2	393.3	41.7		362.2		5.8	303.5	46.3	40.6	
1955...	1,419.1		129.8	835.4	397.7	56.2		430.4		5.7	314.5	69.8	40.4	
1956...	2,003.3		230.9	1,192.9	516.3	63.2		489.8		4.6	373.4	70.0	41.8	
1957...	2,383.5		255.6	1,503.3	554.8	69.5		494.5		4.8	332.9	88.9	67.9	
1958...	2,052.4		224.4	1,214.6	544.4	69.0		574.8		9.4	397.7	102.4	65.3	
1959...	2,074.9		252.2	1,306.7	466.3	38.7		642.9		8.3	489.9	100.3	44.5	
1960...	2,593.5		318.2	1,715.7	514.2	45.4		618.1		11.0	472.5	93.1	41.5	
1961...	2,598.9		321.0	1,729.1	512.2	36.6		626.2		11.1	422.5	135.5	57.1	
1962...	2,308.0		364.5	1,425.8	486.0	31.7		676.0		11.1	461.6	146.8	56.5	
1963...	2,333.7		346.4	1,428.3	521.4	37.6		731.1		14.1	491.9	174.2	50.9	
1964...	3,030.8		462.6	1,822.8	698.2	47.2		815.9		23.6	569.9	174.8	47.6	
1965...	3,137.1		452.6	1,857.0	765.5	62.0		858.2		21.7	590.6	188.8	57.1	
1966...	3,420.5	1,315.2	535.0	705.9	806.5	57.9		1,073.7	586.5	39.4	136.2	227.1	84.5	
1967...	3,325.5	1,363.0	431.5	633.1	828.9	69.2		1,116.8	592.4	57.6	168.8	219.7	78.2	
1968...	3,640.1	1,522.0	404.3	707.7	930.3	75.8		1,423.9	781.8	47.8	187.1	289.3	117.9	
1969...	3,251.1	1,243.1	355.3	603.1	962.7	86.9		1,462.2	763.1	51.5	181.4	321.1	145.1	
1970...	4,028.4	1,698.0	458.6	695.2	1,065.2	111.4		1,748.8	956.0	59.6	184.1	369.5	179.6	
1971...	4,209.8	2,046.2	388.2	654.7	1,006.6	114.1		2,206.4	1,258.5	85.1	251.2	405.6	206.0	
1972...	4,631.3	2,166.3	454.2	700.8	1,155.0	154.9		2,666.3	1,480.3	108.2	254.4	548.9	283.5	
1973...	7,926.0	3,694.7	747.5	1,533.1	1,677.4	273.3		3,834.3	1,919.1	344.1	444.2	753.1	373.7	
1974...	11,278.0	4,937.8	1,098.6	2,112.4	2,680.9	448.3		7,958.0	3,400.1	1,362.1	1,583.6	1,110.7	501.6	
1975...	12,885.3	6,092.5	1,141.3	1,971.3	3,091.5	588.7		8,853.1	3,492.8	1,551.2	2,199.2	1,096.9	513.0	
1976...	12,455.2	5,623.5	1,049.0	2,242.9	2,960.1	579.7		12,748.6	4,503.9	3,142.2	3,016.4	1,419.2	666.9	
1977...	12,179.5	5,810.7	923.6	2,298.0	2,659.0	488.3		17,523.8	5,742.4	4,424.9	4,826.7	1,746.6	783.2	
1978...	15,365.0	7,766.4	1,132.4	2,315.3	3,520.1	630.8		20,680.7	7,539.6	4,594.0	5,452.4	2,035.2	1,059.6	
1979...	21,298.3	10,358.4	1,539.4	3,038.7	5,649.8	712.1		28,254.4	9,397.6	7,580.9	7,569.1	2,463.7	1,243.1	
1980...	28,320.9	12,148.6	2,013.6	3,627.1	8,301.5	1,753.8	476.3	34,912.0	10,064.5	9,359.2	10,148.0	2,668.2	1,497.2	1,174.9
1981...	31,477.2	13,531.9	2,014.5	3,679.0	9,877.2	1,813.2	561.4	36,371.4	12,518.2	7,584.3	10,224.0	1,660.6	1,355.0
¶1982...	27,322.3	...	...	...	...	...	...	30,340.2	19,800.8	4,256.2	...	3,210.6	1,751.0	1,321.7
1983...	22,532.0	...	...	...	...	...	...	28,115.7	15,744.4	4,910.4	...	4,048.0	1,901.0	1,511.8

*Waterborne trade only. †In 1966, Sabine District changed to Port Arthur. ‡Houston District added in 1966. §Dallas/Fort Worth added in 1980.
¶Beginning in 1982, export trade not listed by individual Customs Districts. Total for Texas only given.
**Beginning in 1982, Galveston imports included with Houston as Galveston/Houston Custom District.

oil, 72,216; plastic materials, 54,891. **Coastwise Receipts:** Crude petroleum, 3,029,013; distillate fuel oil, 202,060; residual fuel oil, 118,012; petroleum and coal prod., nec, 117,643; lubricating oils and greases, 112,590. **Coastwise Shipments:** Gasoline, 1,377,131; liquid sulphur, 774,579; distillate fuel oil, 500,132; residual fuel oil, 372,731; crude petroleum, 345,907; jet fuel, 342,058; naphtha, 321,044; alcohols, 189,834; lubricating oils and greases, 159,514. **Internal Receipts:** Crude petroleum, 2,379,629; residual fuel oil, 551,262; distillate fuel oil, 474,801; iron and steel scrap, 385,644; naphtha, 291,396; gasoline, 260,936; basic chemicals, nec, 214,588; petroleum and coal prod., nec, 115,738; benzene and toluene, 101,369; lubricating oils and greases, 73,148; unmanufactured marine shell, 61,040. **Internal Shipments:** Residual fuel oil, 1,205,091; alcohols, 606,162; distillate fuel oil, 420,036; basic chemicals, nec, 367,704; benzene and toluene, 275,450; lubricating oils and greases, 237,992; jet fuel, 234,562; naphtha, 206,646; asphalt tar, 156,538; gasoline, 135,751; crude petroleum, 103,781. **Local:** Crude petroleum, 76,179; benzene and toluene, 51,910.

PORT ARTHUR HARBOR: Imports: Crude petroleum, 3,837,045; basic chemicals, nec., 341,425; residual fuel oil, 245,401; distillate fuel oil, 128,373; naphtha, 77,984. **Exports:** Coke, pet. coke, 2,370,186; residual fuel oil, 632,834; basic chemicals, nec., 265,275; lubricating oils and greases, 165,641; distillate fuel oil, 96,295; wheat, 80,966; paper and paperboard, 76,318; rice, 51,642. **Coastwise Receipts:** Crude petroleum, 547,616; residual fuel oil, 145,520; gasoline, 102,453. **Coastwise Shipments:** Gasoline, 2,131,853; residual fuel oil, 932,728; distillate fuel oil, 790,587; jet fuel, 471,085; lubricating oils and greases, 211,086. **Internal receipts:** Residual fuel oil, 172,508; gasoline, 148,168; crude petroleum, 109,510; benzene and toluene, 103,708; distillate fuel oil, 77,494; lubricating oils and greases, 63,184. **Internal Shipments:** Residual fuel oil, 1,622,089; basic chemicals, nec 462,990; distillate fuel oil, 331,947; petroleum and coal prod., nec, 265,464; gasoline, 154,120; kerosene, 145,228; lubricating oils and greases, 103,860; crude petroleum, 101,444; coke, pet. coke, 97,709; benzene and toluene, 71,389. **Local:** Jet fuel, 17,838.

HOUSTON HARBOR: Imports: Crude petroleum, 7,319,564; residual fuel oil, 1,373,626; basic chemicals, nec, 1,257,615; iron, steel shapes, 1,250,711; distillate fuel oil, 1,020,927; iron and steel pipe, 798,550; naphtha, 736,669; liquefied gases, 642,443; misc. chemical prod., 525,420; molasses, 399,729; motor vehicles, parts, 307,840; benzene and toluene, 286,023; gasoline, 264,525; building cement, 254,851; gypsum, 182,829; alcohols, 174,714; clay, 168,519; fabricated metal products, 156,086; alcoholic beverages, 131,615; jet fuel, 107,779. **Exports:** Wheat, 8,366,308; basic chemicals, nec, 2,441,202; residual fuel oil, 1,377,959; corn, 1,176,698; grain sorghum, 1,083,351; plastic materials, 708,146; liquefied gases, 572,705; alco-

hols, 547,500; coke, pet. coke, 521,519; rice, 502,663; lubricating oils and greases, 443,065; potassic chem. fertilizers, 390,202; misc. chemical prod., 370,974; tallow and animal fats, 365,322; soybeans, 351,905; machinery, exc. electrical, 269,002; crude tar prod., 200,507; gasoline, 181,513; fertilizer and materials, nec, 177,848; cotton, 150,056; distillate fuel oil, 146,417; vegetable oils, 127,565; iron and steel pipe, 127,284; electrical machinery and equip., 116,098; nitrogenous chem. fertilizers, 111,874. **Coastwise Receipts:** Crude petroleum, 6,157,673; phosphate rock, 746,030; residual fuel oil, 321,377; distillate fuel oil, 303,293; commodities, nec, 172,370; naphtha, 135,008; lubricating oils and greases, 111,915. **Coastwise Shipments:** Residual fuel oil, 2,536,050; gasoline, 1,608,708; distillate fuel oil, 1,101,759; lubricating oils and greases, 623,855; naphtha, 495,072; crude petroleum, 442,687; jet fuel, 278,634; alcohols, 237,574; commodities, nec, 200,692; basic chemicals, nec 172,687; potassic chem. fertilizers, 163,218; sodium hydroxide, 139,633. **Internal Receipts:** Residual fuel oil, 4,167,813; gasoline, 2,211,555; basic chemicals, nec, 1,121,720; crude petroleum, 1,006,641; distillate fuel oil, 957,038; alcohols, 606,829; jet fuel, 578,723; sand and gravel, 538,691; building cement, 369,591; benzene and toluene, 323,436; waste and scrap, 310,653; sodium hydroxide, 256,987; naphtha, 247,712; petroleum and coal prod., nec, 231,613; asphalt, 169,409; iron and steel plates, 160,976; lubricating oils and greases, 143,766; sulphuric acid, 143,593; iron and steel pipe, 136,184; coke, pet. coke, 100,472. **Internal Shipments:** Residual fuel oil, 2,940,464; basic chemicals, nec, 2,344,935; crude petroleum, 810,168; waste and scrap, 718,224; lubricating oils and greases, 589,645; gasoline, 563,683; sulphuric acid, 526,101; distillate fuel oil, 466,618; alcohols, 319,894; potassic chem. fertilizers, 309,121; naphtha, 297,107; benzene and toluene, 291,688; sodium hydroxide, 274,815; petroleum and coal prod., nec, 188,296; liquid sulphur, 165,168; crude tar prod., 163,751; liquefied gases, 114,344. **Local:** Residual fuel oil, 1,449,309; gasoline, 809,480; basic chemicals, nec, 637,647; alcohols, 564,759; benzene and toluene, 408,811; sand and gravel, 373,286; distillate fuel oil, 206,334; waste and scrap, 190,040; crude petroleum, 137,431.

TEXAS CITY HARBOR: Imports: Crude petroleum, 14,328,418; basic chemicals, nec, 880,564. **Exports:** Basic chemicals, nec, 366,224; coke, pet. coke, 240,371; alcohols, 161,967; residual fuel oil, 140,128. **Coastwise Receipts:** Crude petroleum, 4,981,763; basic chemicals, nec, 221,568; residual fuel oil, 155,793; alcohols, 49,562. **Coastwise Shipments:** Gasoline, 1,290,536; basic chemicals, nec, 769,765; residual fuel oil, 583,170; distillate fuel oil, 447,809; alcohols, 126,606; kerosene, 75,521; petroleum and coal prod., nec, 63,436. **Internal Receipts:** Crude petroleum, 2,900,544; basic chemicals, nec, 1,139,725; naphtha, 449,194; benzene and toluene, 387,118; residual fuel oil, 322,627; distillate fuel oil, 310,733; gasoline, 198,755;

FOREIGN AND DOMESTIC COMMERCE THROUGH MAJOR TEXAS PORTS

Data in table below represent receipts and shipments for only the 13 major Texas ports in 1983. Total receipts and shipments for these 13 ports amounted to 246,246,483 tons. Total receipts and shipments for all Texas ports amounted to 257,934,340.

Source: U.S. Army Corps of Engineers
(All figures in short tons)

| | | Foreign | | Domestic | | | | |
| | | | | Coastwise | | Internal | | |
	Total	Imports	Exports	Receipts	Shipments	Receipts	Shipments	Local
Sabine Pass	605,108	. . .	. . .	300	. . .	151,908	452,900	. . .
Orange	399,092	760	. . .	. . .	. . .	310,688	85,690	1,954
Beaumont	36,001,675	14,154,281	4,066,847	3,645,872	4,457,481	5,125,802	4,266,043	285,349
Port Arthur	18,338,237	4,663,797	3,928,765	911,192	4,601,766	727,642	3,468,721	36,354
Houston	88,706,519	18,501,446	22,129,954	8,240,794	8,169,220	14,668,007	11,757,055	5,240,043
Texas City	35,496,241	15,271,314	982,445	5,408,686	3,373,211	6,147,555	4,180,030	133,000
Galveston.	10,177,718	1,308,137	7,265,472	202,119	835,162	458,167	90,192	18,469
Freeport	15,671,990	8,441,081	680,638	4,117,324	527,687	1,191,638	701,214	12,408
†Corpus Christi	37,455,132	13,249,124	3,035,764	3,471,265	7,047,690	1,965,277	6,385,098	2,300,914
‡Port Isabel	284,758	. . .	. . .	. . .	. . .	95,160	189,598	. . .
‡Brownsville	1,338,550	283,107	317,972	3,459	49,720	464,677	219,615	. . .
†Port Aransas								
(Harbor Island) . . .	1,708,592	926,354	646	157,811	. . .	584,291	39,490	. . .
Port Mansfield	62,871	. . .	. . .	. . .	. . .	15,525	47,346	. . .
Total	246,246,483	76,799,401	42,408,503	26,158,822	29,061,937	31,906,337	31,882,992	8,028,491

†Combined total for Corpus Christi given in other tables in this chapter; these two totals will not add to the combined total given in other tables, due to duplication in some instances.

‡Combined total for Brownsville given in other tables in this chapter.

crude tar prod., 187,702; alcohols, 148,397; sulphuric acid, 52,772. **Internal Shipments:** Basic chemicals, nec, 1,015,210; residual fuel oil, 1,010,368; gasoline, 562,624; distillate fuel oil, 543,601; naphtha, 324,633; alcohols, 268,869; benzene and toluene, 215,047; crude petroleum, 73,990; sulphuric acid, 59,599. **Local:** Residual fuel oil 70,527; basic chemicals, nec, 26,287; benzene and toluene, 20,305.

GALVESTON HARBOR: **Imports:** Bananas and plantains, 339,673; sugar, 237,681; crude petroleum, 202,517; veneer and plywood, 75,211; iron and steel shapes, 53,114. **Exports:** Wheat, 5,147,195; dry sulphur, 579,566; grain sorghum, 355,533; rice, 330,794; wheat flour, 202,906; plastic materials, 188,303. **Coastwise Receipts:** Sugar, 124,082; residual fuel oil, 64,109. **Coastwise Shipments:** Liquid sulphur, 764,099; residual fuel oil, 37,262; crude petroleum, 33,751. **Internal Receipts:** Residual fuel oil, 275,626; distillate fuel oil, 97,964; gasoline, 34,032. **Internal Shipments:** Residual fuel oil, 36,679; limestone, 16,337. **Local:** Residual fuel oil, 18,469.

FREEPORT HARBOR: **Imports:** Crude petroleum, 8,233,302; basic chemicals, nec, 143,210; benzene and toluene, 21,782. **Exports:** Basic chemicals, nec, 548,791; plastic materials, 50,251; crude tar prod., 36,358; rice, 32,525. **Coastwise Receipts:** Crude petroleum, 3,975,321; basic chemicals, nec, 124,602; benzene and toluene,

17,207. **Coastwise Shipments:** Basic chemicals, nec, 345,151; gasoline, 80,773; sodium hydroxide, 44,919; distillate fuel oil, 32,494. **Internal Receipts:** Benzene and toluene, 271,278; sulphuric acid, 253,781; basic chemicals, nec, 238,923; sand and gravel, 160,654; crude petroleum, 122,827; residual fuel oil, 42,030; sodium hydroxide, 29,990; alcohols, 28,175. **Internal Shipments:** Basic chemicals, nec, 436,355; sodium hydroxide, 80,912; gasoline, 47,042; residual fuel oil, 30,234; benzene and toluene, 27,600. **Local:** Crude petroleum, 9,756; basic chemicals, nec, 2,652.

CORPUS CHRISTI HARBOR: **Imports:** Crude petroleum, 8,259,795; residual fuel oil, 2,561,479; aluminium ores, 1,100,842; distillate fuel oil, 897,605; basic chemicals, nec, 731,695; naphtha, 270,855; clay, 225,874; nonferrous ores, 76,004. **Exports:** Grain sorghum, 692,851; basic chemicals, nec, 616,710; distillate fuel oil, 536,448; coke, pet. coke, 310,709; wheat, 283,991; residual fuel oil, 229,069; gasoline, 147,006; liquefied gases, 60,401; coal and lignite, 55,131. **Coastwise Receipts:** Crude petroleum, 3,406,676; residual fuel oil, 86,141; distillate fuel oil, 70,565; gasoline, 65,469. **Coastwise Shipments:** Gasoline, 3,280,681; distillate fuel oil, 1,720,468; residual fuel oil, 664,675; jet fuel, 498,643; crude petroleum, 413,488; basic chemicals, nec, 286,716; petroleum and coal prod., nec, 139,257. **Internal Receipts:** Crude petroleum, 1,385,945; re-

TONNAGE HANDLED BY TEXAS PORTS, 1974-1983

Source: U.S. Army Corps of Engineers

Table below gives consolidated tonnage handled by ports and moving through Gulf Intracoastal Waterway. All figures are in short tons.

Ports	1983	1982	1981	1980	1979	1978	1977	1976	1975	1974
Brwnsvle	1,338,550	2,200,132	2,810,018	2,569,697	2,508,076	2,163,590	2,130,440	2,584,916	2,829,009	2,836,664
Port Isabel	284,758	307,856	313,036	304,964	308,021	245,151	203,702	208,287	255,938	233,216
Corpus Christi .	39,131,318	37,974,192	41,980,354	45,001,096	55,597,104	54,678,296	56,041,113	43,492,959	41,290,771	35,645,004
Freeport .	15,671,990	14,989,683	23,357,106	20,131,067	19,983,837	21,712,480	15,332,518	9,710,609	8,194,136	8,898,947
Galveston	10,177,718	9,349,856	11,268,337	9,631,091	8,982,285	7,786,146	9,563,626	7,302,900	5,971,160	7,171,226
Houston .	88,706,519	94,649,549	100,966,741	108,937,268	117,550,908	111,936,099	104,291,267	89,897,598	83,674,039	89,106,389
Texas City	35,496,241	33,370,791	27,852,242	25,948,936	35,954,301	34,656,219	33,583,596	28,516,499	23,863,770	20,151,777
Sabine. . .	605,108	1,164,632	1,063,238	949,404	867,813	531,491	882,692	677,425	513,062	390,370
Port Arthur .	18,338,237	19,945,958	26,037,529	29,796,633	32,773,346	33,474,523	30,753,732	30,687,203	26,597,557	27,799,593
Beaumont	36,001,675	33,286,791	40,358,920	52,260,728	58,136,896	52,770,276	48,918,843	43,939,073	30,582,512	33,503,880
Orange .	399,092	279,728	484,942	567,157	631,694	513,009	1,003,331	981,626	912,014	1,331,360
Port Lavaca	3,422,854	4,308,436	4,148,664	3,991,089	4,562,702	4,677,509	3,894,810	4,256,320	4,342,515	4,930,654
Anahuac .	0	31,122	25,276	41,665	14,900	16,219	18,050	31,024	48,159	27,070
Moss Bluff	0	128,747	196,402	207,471	290,493	296,833	379,680	279,813	275,105	356,990
Clear Creek. .	0	0	0	20,700	103,280	148,182	154,611	195,266	182,500	216,560
Double Bayou .	12,915	11,843	26,136	48,554	49,618	48,957	72,731	43,131	23,764	25,885
Cedar Bayou .	454,993	404,816	231,485	328,513	361,179	431,047	430,322	570,889	815,963	920,728
Sweeny . .	629,816	726,684	660,291	673,740	601,435	321,305	414,142	578,986	536,503	506,177
Palacios .	86	54,545	100,293	85,862	88,804	48,080	97,555	42,232	74,582	72,110
Dickinson Bayou .	16,055	17,921	23,275	19,275	105,573	220,258	93,413	150,776	110,294	118,853
Aransas Pass. . .	959	12,243	9,953	9,113	21,559	6,323	8,359	5,856	7,922	16,612
Port Mansfld	62,871	1,431	115,874	13,432	11,000	10,863	8,969	35,008	29,438	40,348
Rio Hndo-Harlngn	702,242	862,969	655,127	623,292	666,223	716,122	709,354	586,380	642,879	584,414
Long Mott	3,342,181	2,744,633	2,930,820	3,303,122	2,807,135	2,819,807	2,564,684	3,238,520	3,030,897	3,135,921
Choc. Byu	2,608,300	3,043,107	4,301,199	2,934,850	3,040,894	3,057,207	2,566,214	2,975,438	2,450,062	2,876,161
Colo. Riv.	380,744	392,933	403,016	436,585	458,681	455,448	. . .	. . .	. . .	. . .
*Other Ports . .	149,118	437,953	848,517	772,349	556,931	520,657	1,198,070	1,046,842	410,344	297,915
Total	1983, 257,934,340; 1982, 260,698,551; 1981, 291,168,791; 1980, 309,607,653; 1979, 347,034,688; 1978, 334,262,097; 1977, 315,315,824; 1976, 272,035,576; 1975, 237,664,895; 1974, 241,194,824									

Intracoastal Canal (Through Traffic)

	1983	1982	1981	1980	1979	1978	1977	1976	1975	1974
Sabine R. to Galv. . .	40,165,385	38,796,688	43,092,704	41,976,730	42,920,273	43,703,545	45,486,574	41,868,705	37,638,364	40,062,686
Galv. to Corpus Christi	19,340,594	18,975,500	22,692,629	21,142,516	22,436,774	20,433,301	18,796,671	18,159,321	19,467,870	23,311,153
Corpus Christi to Mexico	1,782,427	2,066,270	2,231,646	2,388,221	2,488,372	2,106,132	1,993,577	1,949,616	2,230,313	2,711,310
Total	61,288,406	59,838,458	68,016,979	65,507,467	67,845,419	66,242,978	66,276,822	61,977,642	59,336,547	66,085,149

*Other ports include Rockport, Johnsons Bayou and Channel to Liberty.

sidual fuel oil, 354,755; crude tar prod., 149,863; gasoline, 139,798; sodium hydroxide, 63,277. **Internal Shipments:** Gasoline, 1,595,805; residual fuel oil, 1,519,180; distillate fuel oil, 866,287; naphtha, 632,076; basic chemicals, nec, 571,643; jet fuel, 335,102; benzene and toluene, 200,982; sodium hydroxide, 119,291; alcohols, 115,579; crude petroleum, 111,614; coke, pet. coke, 77,412. **Local:** Residual fuel oil, 1,162,658; distillate fuel oil, 282,648; benzene and toluene, 245,832; crude petroleum, 238,519; gasoline, 117,539; naphtha, 92,329; jet fuel, 72,306; petroleum and coal prod., nec, 45,073.

PORT MANSFIELD HARBOR: Internal Receipts: Misc. mfr. products, 7,336; sand and gravel, 4,403; iron and steel pipe, 1,213. **Internal Shipments:** Misc. mfr. products, 23,267; water, 10,849; sand and gravel, 3,600; limestone, 2,568.

BROWNSVILLE HARBOR: Imports: Lubricating oils and greases, 156,657; basic chemicals, nec, 65,787; clay, 24,680; nonferrous ores, 15,237. **Exports:** Grain sorghum, 222,632; basic chemicals, nec, 47,751; fresh fruits, 25,124. **Coastwise Receipts:** Petroleum and coal prod., nec, 3,159. **Coastwise Shipments:** Residual fuel oil, 49,720. **Internal Receipts:** Gasoline, 240,621; lubricating oils and greases, 119,164; sand and gravel, 92,792; petroleum and coal prod., nec, 25,324; distillate fuel oil, 25,157. **Internal Shipments:** Crude petroleum, 200,084; basic chemicals, nec, 103,934; nonmetallic minerals, nec, 36,300.

INTRACOASTAL CANAL TRAFFIC

From the Sabine River to Brownsville, the **Gulf Intracoastal Waterway** parallels the Texas Gulf Coast for 423 miles. Dimension of the main channel is 12 feet deep by 125 feet wide at bottom. The channel from the Gulf of Mexico through Padre Island and Laguna Madre to the turning basin at Port Mansfield is 14 feet deep, 100 feet wide.

During 1983, the Texas section showed a slight increase over the 1982 tonnage, up from 59,838,458 in 1982 to 61,288,406 in 1983. (These figures include some duplications, total amount of which is not available.)

Principal commodities for 1983 were as follows, with all figures in short tons: Residual fuel oil, 10,722,693; crude petroleum, 10,683,437; basic chemicals, nec., 10,243,950; gasoline, 4,985,572; distillate fuel oil, 3,834,357; naphtha, 1,970,174; sand and gravel, 1,954,331; benzene and toluene, 1,657,569; alcohols, 1,385,190; lubricating oils and greases, 1,378,517; unmanufactured shell, 1,169,027; waste and scrap, 1,032,151; jet fuel, 988,499; sodium hydroxide, 925,156; petroleum and coal, 834,485; sulphuric acid, 722,706; crude tar, 622,520; iron and steel scrap, 581,594; nitrogenous fertilizers, 562,196; building cement, 562,088; asphalt tar, 467,954; coke, pet. coke, 443,829; potassic fertilizers, 310,580; kerosene, 286,290; iron and steel plates, 252,219; liquefied gases, 247,247; liquid sulphur, 224,173; fertilizers, nec., 217,454; iron and steel pipe, 163,963; nonmetallic minerals, nec., 146,831; iron and steel products, 125,505; water, 103,099; rice, 100,382.

COMMERCE THROUGH TEXAS PORTS
BY COMMODITIES
1983

Source: U.S. Army Corps of Engineers
(All figures in short tons)

Product	Foreign Imports	Exports	Domestic Receipts	Shipmts.
Alcoholic beverages ..	166,780	12,039	64	22
Alcohols	247,866	791,043	886,260	2,497,836
Aluminum ores	1,114,530	291	5,976	2,709
Asphalt, tars .	2,690	25,652	201,009	253,461
Basic chemicals, nec......	3,645,488	4,424,092	3,216,287	7,595,957
Bananas, plantains ..	340,596	35	...	...
Benzene and toluene....	333,947	101,321	1,300,915	1,906,533
Building cement....	266,855	3,199	568,966	86,558
Clay	445,710	20,195	4,608	25,953
Coke, pet. coke...	73	3,581,144	111,042	222,040
Commodities, nec...	34,279	26,431	177,720	255,673
Corn	29	1,208,231	6,193	4,575
Cotton......	...	201,781	...	...
Crude petroleum .	55,745,021	...	30,085,045	3,460,678
Crude tars ...	91,204	286,297	445,708	393,750
Distillate fuel oil	2,051,356	859,464	2,634,398	7,792,624
Electrical Machinery	30,430	129,716	319	3,873
Fabricated metal products...	190,868	68,011	6,521	5,324
Fertilizers, nec......	75	183,505	94,309	62,058
Gasoline	321,066	330,190	3,538,195	13,759,254
Grain sorghum...	...	2,370,042	...	...
Gypsum.....	182,829	5,862	4,646	23
Iron and steel pipe ..	839,636	139,530	148,049	32,100
Iron and steel plates .	7,739	10,904	170,945	71,443
Iron and steel scrap .	8,192	104,543	481,499	12,112
Iron and steel shapes	1,309,377	7,120	34,234	63,944

Product	Foreign Imports	Exports	Domestic Receipts	Shipmts.
Jet fuel	107,779	33,328	659,437	2,341,957
Kerosene....	90,928	39,196	66,540	396,040
Liquefied gases	802,798	635,715	75,714	206,891
Lubricating oils, greases ...	208,075	760,255	649,722	2,089,036
Machinery, exc. elec. ..	106,845	307,704	10,910	28,634
Misc. chemicals..	544,547	402,115	57,380	85,234
Molasses ..	413,495	...	56,903	...
Motor vehs...	313,476	37,768	3,385	3,377
Naphtha	1,195,381	44,456	1,172,991	2,482,493
Nitrogenous fertilizer...	443	115,871	83,628	11,986
Petroleum and coal ...	7,076	16,811	545,634	888,968
Phosphate rock......	...	2,345	746,030	...
Plastics	41,892	1,004,946	3,761	6,556
Potassic fertilizer...	20	400,369	1,459	475,342
Residual fuel oil	4,244,210	2,413,734	6,809,862	16,260,174
Rice	400	931,628	64,340	28,753
Sand, gravel	369	18,144	884,334	386,973
Sodium hydroxide..	...	...	418,094	686,667
Soybeans ..	...	443,552	...	...
Sugar	237,681	...	148,347	...
Sulphur, dry......	...	612,288	747	...
Sulphur, liquid	...	...	7,284	1,731,846
Sulphuric acid	...	...	517,749	696,951
Tallow, animal fat..	...	375,096	...	...
Vegetable oils	12,206	132,372	4,749	11,968
Waste	...	...	314,750	982,581
Water	...	...	32,987	114,505
Wheat	...	16,690,767	34,827	...
Wheat flour ..	...	829,893	...	9,499

TEXAS HIGHWAYS

Texas has the largest road network in the nation. There are 273,981 miles of roadways in the state, of which 71,592 are maintained by the Texas Department of Highways and Public Transportation. The state-maintained system, however, includes practically all the freeways and other high traffic-carrying highways. With less than three-tenths of the total center-line miles, the state-maintained system carries almost three-fourths of all the miles driven in Texas. In the 1986-87 biennium, the state will spend $5,001,223,519 for maintenance and new construction.

HIGHWAY DEPARTMENT RECEIPTS, DISBURSEMENTS, 1984

Summary statement showing all cash receipts and expenditures of the Texas Department of Highways and Public Transportation for the fiscal year Sept. 1, 1983 through Aug. 31, 1984:

Revenues

State's General Revenue Fund

Allocations	$259,650,558
Transfers	38,300,000
Legislative Appropriations	59,327

Reimbursed Construction, Right-of-Way, and Research Costs—

Federal Highway Administration	568,416,608
Cities and other Political Subdivisions	23,144,000
Counties	12,839,187
National Highway Traffic Safety Administration	5,425,019
Federal Urban Mass Transportation Administration	528,870

Dedicated Revenue—

Motor Fuel Taxes	379,725,787
Vehicle License Fees	290,453,595
Sales Tax on Lubricants	23,229,000
Interest on Deposits	21,489,134
Vehicle Title Fees	20,778,853
Permits for Oversize and Overweight Vehicles	9,736,606
Sale of "Texas Highways" Magazine	2,741,590

Reimbursements for Damages to

Property	2,324,019
Sale of Land and Equipment	2,308,643
Work Outside Department	945,038
Sale of Maps and Documents	565,555
Outdoor Advertising Fees	38,017
Miscellaneous	2,391,373
Total Revenues	**$1,665,090,779**

Expenditures

Current Operating—Personnel Costs

Salaries	$314,114,473
Social Security Payments by State	32,977,540
Retirement Fund Contributions	25,451,108

Insurance Premiums for Employees and Retirees—

State's Portion	16,809,450
Workers' Compensation	1,426,548
Miscellaneous Personnel Costs	715,499
Contracted Highway Construction and Maintenance	782,313,977
Construction Materials	116,811,025
Right-of-Way Costs	62,312,324

Other Contracted Maintenance—

Highways	29,622,208
Highway Equipment Supplies	27,088,857
Professional Fees and Services	23,412,424
Grants to Cities, Counties and Other Public Entities	16,262,101

MOTOR VEHICLE ACCIDENTS, LOSSES

The following statistics for motor vehicle accidents, deaths and injuries, miles traveled and economic losses are from the Texas Department of Public Safety, Austin.

Year—	No. Killed	†No. Injured	Accidents by Kinds				Vehicle Miles Traveled			§Economic Loss
			No. Fatal	†No. Involving Injury	†No. Non-Injury	†Total	*Number	Deaths per 100 million miles	
1970	3,560	223,000	2,965	124,000	886,000	1,012,965	‡68,031,000,000	5.2	$1,042,200,000
1971	3,594	224,000	2,993	124,000	890,000	1,016,993	70,709,000,000	5.1	1,045,000,000
1972	3,688	128,158	3,099	83,607	346,292	432,998	76,690,000,000	4.8	1,035,000,000
1973	3,692	132,635	3,074	87,631	373,521	464,226	80,615,000,000	4.6	1,035,000,000
1974	3,046	123,611	2,626	83,341	348,227	434,194	78,290,000,000	3.9	1,095,000,000
1975	3,429	138,962	2,945	92,510	373,141	468,596	84,575,000,000	4.1	1,440,000,000
1976	3,230	145,282	2,780	96,348	380,075	479,203	91,279,000,000	3.5	1,485,000,000
1977	3,698	161,635	3,230	106,923	393,848	504,001	96,998,000,000	3.8	1,960,000,000
1978	**3,980	178,228	3,468	117,998	††304,830	††426,296	102,624,000,000	3.9	2,430,000,000
1979	4,229	184,550	3,685	122,793	322,336	448,814	101,909,000,000	4.1	2,580,000,000
1980	4,424	185,964	3,863	123,577	305,500	432,940	103,255,000,000	4.3	3,010,000,000
1981	4,701	206,196	4,137	136,396	317,484	458,017	111,036,000,000	4.2	3,430,000,000
1982	4,271	204,666	3,752	135,859	312,159	451,770	‡‡124,910,000,000	3.4	3,375,000,000
§§1983	3,823	208,157	3,328	137,695	302,876	443,899	129,309,000,000	3.0	3,440,000,000
1984	3,913	220,720	3,466	145,543	293,285	442,294	137,280,000,000	2.9	3,795,000,000

*Vehicle miles traveled since 1964 were estimated on the basis of new data furnished by U.S. Bureau of Public Roads through National Safety Council. Vehicle miles and deaths per 100 million vehicle miles after 1964 cannot, therefore, be compared with previous years.

†In August 1967, amended estimating formula received from National Safety Council. Starting with 1972, actual reported injuries are listed rather than estimates.

‡Vehicle miles traveled estimated by Texas Highway Department starting with 1970. Method of calculation varies from that used for prior years. Vehicle miles and deaths per 100,000,000 vehicle miles for 1969 and before cannot be compared to subsequent years.

§Economic loss formula last changed 1984.

**Change in counting fatalities. Counted when injury results in death within 90 days of vehicle accident in which the injury occurred.

††Total accidents and non-injury accidents for 1978-84 cannot be compared with years prior to 1978 due to changes in reporting laws.

‡‡Method of calculating vehicle miles traveled revised for 1982 by the Texas State Department of Highways and Public Transportation. Vehicle miles and deaths per 100,000,000 miles cannot be compared to prior years.

§§Change in counting fatalities. Counted when injury results in death within 30 days of vehicle accident in which the injury occurred.

Utilities	11,898,914
General Supplies	8,208,227
Rent or Lease of Equipment and Facilities	6,213,056
Interagency Contracts	4,643,063
Travel	4,569,768
Repairs of Equipment	4,379,563
Equipment Acquisition and Land Improvements, Noncapitalized	4,258,996
Postage	4,218,215
Vehicle License Plates and Validation Stickers	3,938,243
Photowork, Publications and Reproduction	3,338,487
Telephone, Teletype and Telegraph	2,648,692
Repairs to Buildings	1,992,454
Freight and Delivery Charges	1,465,228
Janitorial Services and Supplies	1,333,734
Insurance Premiums	960,564
Railroad Crossing Maintenance	809,648
Judgements and Court Costs	386,179
Advertising	304,619
Sign and Junkyard Control	14,467
Miscellaneous	386,611
Total Current Operating Expenditures	**$1,515,286,262**

MOTOR VEHICLE REGISTRATION, LICENSE FEES, BY COUNTIES

The following State Department of Highways and Public Transportation table shows, for Sept. 1, 1983, through Aug. 31, 1984, by counties, motor vehicle registrations and license fees. These figures include all types of motor vehicles.

County—	Total Vehicles Registered	Total Gross License Fees (Dollars)	Net to County (Dollars)	Net to State (Dollars)	County—	Total Vehicles Registered	Total Gross License Fees (Dollars)	Net to County (Dollars)	Net to State (Dollars)
Anderson...	34,910	$1,060,312	$350,000	$643,259	Donley.....	4,938	119,629	107,529	2,642
Andrews	16,057	593,578	296,278	265,721	Duval......	8,479	259,652	238,703	5,625
Angelina ...	57,153	1,734,357	350,000	1,273,493	Eastland ...	20,207	616,816	361,296	215,744
Aransas ...	13,935	329,105	204,954	98,172	Ector......	128,299	4,379,695	350,000	3,788,459
Archer.....	8,251	279,756	232,269	32,983	Edwards ...	2,113	64,129	59,207	1,072
Armstrong..	2,774	88,321	82,219	1,266	Ellis......	63,081	1,915,366	350,000	1,441,434
Atascosa ...	21,323	692,551	350,000	302,332	El Paso	317,799	7,911,276	350,000	6,872,048
Austin	19,515	683,092	349,999	296,197	Erath......	23,512	682,047	365,126	271,688
Bailey	7,802	251,217	231,681	4,160	Falls	15,596	992,442	350,000	613,956
Bandera....	8,908	232,306	210,466	5,410	Fannin.....	17,374	432,263	280,766	119,467
Bastrop	25,841	676,719	385,288	243,217	Fayette	20,618	649,113	365,887	245,878
Baylor.....	6,125	193,657	179,018	3,057	Fisher	5,775	188,234	175,686	2,647
Bee	19,263	598,878	346,783	215,287	Floyd......	9,006	255,809	229,429	9,947
Bell	140,884	3,479,718	350,000	2,827,170	Foard	2,005	60,780	56,288	951
Bexar......	816,600	21,467,530	350,000	19,462,189	Fort Bend ..	121,230	3,173,130	350,000	2,585,798
Blanco.....	6,232	234,258	172,019	49,998	Franklin ...	6,206	152,744	137,527	3,465
Borden	1,181	56,617	54,221	484	Freestone ..	15,271	402,916	295,023	78,592
Bosque.....	15,090	428,146	307,247	90,924	Frio.......	8,753	301,456	239,546	45,110
Bowie	72,038	1,741,954	350,000	1,259,063	Gaines.....	12,728	451,865	323,278	104,951
Brazoria....	156,957	4,154,339	350,000	3,512,500	Galveston ..	164,062	3,926,019	287,700	3,312,427
Brazos	82,090	2,329,345	333,900	1,829,615	Garza......	4,960	173,245	161,698	2,551
Brewster ...	6,225	161,127	146,388	3,359	Gillespie ..	16,524	477,830	331,634	115,103
Briscoe ...	2,694	78,944	72,788	1,380	Glasscock ..	1,945	68,092	63,964	853
Brooks.....	5,184	151,139	118,051	22,561	Goliad	4,942	123,778	112,871	2,432
Brown	35,198	945,395	350,000	526,408	Gonzales ..	15,198	495,468	341,761	125,040
Burleson ...	13,276	451,632	316,783	110,715	Gray	31,413	1,033,847	350,000	625,979
Burnet.....	23,528	610,465	342,706	220,258	Grayson ...	79,575	1,992,493	350,000	1,491,547
Caldwell....	17,807	634,758	321,685	279,124	Gregg	118,079	3,711,785	272,650	3,215,237
Calhoun....	18,348	453,119	271,820	145,901	Grimes	14,129	399,867	294,657	77,355
Callahan ...	14,632	412,162	300,626	83,357	Guadalupe..	44,368	1,324,051	350,000	888,873
Cameron ...	136,541	3,705,216	350,000	3,089,823	Hale.......	33,597	1,015,632	350,000	602,221
Camp......	8,645	285,544	199,419	69,838	Hall.......	4,947	119,001	107,889	2,431
Carson.....	7,614	212,632	195,348	3,714	Hamilton ..	8,152	241,134	221,224	4,613
Cass.......	24,504	624,181	360,962	220,207	Hansford ...	8,327	283,497	240,462	28,154
Castro	9,896	345,962	279,840	46,869	Hardeman ..	5,916	223,053	209,276	3,018
Chambers ..	20,362	636,654	325,977	273,750	Hardin.....	37,415	945,670	350,000	522,051
Cherokee...	33,127	911,072	350,000	497,511	Harris	2,160,725	59,854,893	350,000	55,330,783
Childress ...	6,775	173,404	156,830	3,887	Harrison ...	42,648	1,163,901	350,000	737,603
Clay.......	8,826	251,727	230,680	4,531	Hartley	4,132	135,980	126,401	2,217
Cochran....	4,598	140,393	129,478	2,447	Haskell	8,771	239,419	219,793	4,030
Coke	4,817	141,064	129,626	2,517	Hays	37,766	960,357	350,000	534,990
Coleman ...	11,232	328,356	266,380	41,772	Hemphill ...	5,847	203,866	171,521	20,530
Collin......	140,230	3,264,980	350,000	2,642,512	Henderson ..	48,407	1,209,096	350,000	768,664
Collingsworth	4,542	129,594	119,054	2,283	Hidalgo	195,042	6,120,189	350,000	5,350,751
Colorado ...	20,398	983,522	350,000	595,609	Hill	26,140	679,035	377,139	252,601
Comal	41,435	1,151,692	350,000	725,612	Hockley	23,510	806,484	350,000	413,106
Comanche ..	13,104	385,448	288,996	71,530	Hood	24,303	574,813	313,618	210,129
Concho	3,425	82,369	74,369	1,745	Hopkins....	24,454	748,366	350,000	348,039
Cooke	28,753	817,655	350,000	413,855	Houston....	18,587	531,239	355,529	140,774
Coryell.....	30,591	698,249	367,196	270,545	Howard	35,455	1,059,837	350,000	642,500
Cottle......	2,782	84,188	77,552	1,431	Hudspeth...	1,993	56,442	51,417	1,298
Crane	5,719	274,831	186,972	78,086	Hunt	49,586	1,188,920	350,000	735,911
Crockett ...	4,773	163,889	153,075	2,247	Hutchinson .	34,516	1,094,534	350,000	683,290
Crosby.....	7,223	187,884	171,038	3,630	Irion	1,936	77,182	72,567	1,076
Culberson ..	2,625	108,649	101,797	1,499	Jack	8,393	345,714	270,800	59,245
Dallam.....	7,306	262,342	240,629	8,399	Jackson....	14,414	451,830	320,818	103,475
Dallas	1,476,794	41,137,236	37,537,579	37,530,880	Jasper	28,650	775,895	350,000	372,387
Dawson	13,459	445,159	319,618	101,293	Jeff Davis ..	1,778	54,823	50,844	843
Deaf Smith..	18,866	764,077	350,000	378,255	Jefferson...	204,291	5,226,987	306,600	4,481,844
Delta	4,611	117,375	105,809	2,814	Jim Hogg...	4,182	141,736	108,644	24,995
Denton.....	154,489	3,794,022	350,000	3,100,706	Jim Wells...	28,922	1,173,446	349,999	767,915
De Witt	18,232	518,710	349,416	134,811	Johnson....	79,361	2,070,879	350,000	1,555,634
Dickens....	2,933	76,327	69,222	1,646	Jones......	17,330	562,116	354,201	175,712
Dimmit	7,545	354,220	237,880	102,530					

County—	Total Vehicles Registered	Total Gross License Fees (Dollars)	Net to County (Dollars)	Net to State (Dollars)
Karnes.....	11,816	368,217	282,287	63,407
Kaufman ...	37,411	991,397	350,000	571,395
Kendall	14,923	384,159	255,642	99,668
Kenedy	331	7,267	6,565	130
Kent	1,465	35,977	32,766	660
Kerr	31,019	826,717	349,999	416,232
Kimble	4,599	157,676	146,074	2,682
King	449	15,923	14,994	179
Kinney.....	2,115	53,699	48,636	1,243
Kleberg....	23,805	681,276	233,450	401,965
Knox......	5,385	150,502	138,232	2,440
Lamar.....	40,053	1,130,289	350,000	703,064
Lamb......	17,070	489,385	337,457	120,957
Lampasas ..	11,867	321,589	261,633	37,205
La Salle	3,527	94,981	86,882	1,755
Lavaca	17,756	486,541	336,561	119,620
Lee	13,647	481,757	333,614	122,469
Leon	11,623	314,242	260,834	31,646
Liberty	46,766	1,551,959	350,000	1,111,186
Limestone ..	17,612	547,943	364,091	149,766
Lipscomb...	5,125	164,918	153,115	2,654
Live Oak ...	9,952	435,779	318,350	98,668
Llano......	12,928	323,416	262,291	36,723
Loving.....	285	13,728	13,148	107
Lubbock ...	182,600	5,079,712	350,000	4,362,218
Lynn	7,134	189,686	173,566	3,485
McCulloch ..	9,201	311,092	266,220	27,320
McLennan ..	157,230	4,707,495	350,000	4,061,253
McMullen ..	1,128	38,790	36,287	519
Madison....	9,498	301,980	211,767	73,099
Marion	8,557	231,004	208,101	7,872
Martin.....	5,569	199,817	187,678	2,569
Mason	4,022	107,256	98,374	1,902
Matagorda..	33,948	1,029,744	350,000	613,326
Maverick ...	15,525	448,875	216,984	201,631
Medina	22,330	620,388	359,979	219,398
Menard	5,092	606,612	219,100	379,365
Midland....	103,469	3,280,899	350,000	2,730,403
Milam	20,873	545,168	360,298	146,519
Mills	4,924	133,817	122,674	2,456
Mitchell....	9,407	296,963	245,148	34,912
Montague ..	19,462	563,963	351,911	174,959
Montgomery	131,232	3,385,915	350,000	2,764,480
Moore	18,435	594,832	320,551	238,980
Morris.....	17,481	647,378	276,500	338,212
Motley.....	1,935	46,448	42,050	992
Nacogdoches	37,692	1,024,380	350,000	604,482
Navarro....	32,072	984,611	350,000	571,724
Newton	8,806	257,508	234,491	6,621
Nolan......	17,410	511,713	345,898	130,924
Nueces.....	223,360	6,680,440	350,000	5,870,087
Ochiltree ...	13,168	499,989	346,678	129,040
Oldham	2,574	82,360	76,509	1,239
Orange	73,957	1,725,802	337,050	1,249,484
Palo Pinto ..	26,699	731,885	364,407	314,882
Panola.....	19,276	532,987	356,520	141,796
Parker.....	47,287	1,271,987	350,000	831,440
Parmer....	11,009	351,415	275,893	55,838
Pecos......	14,408	493,639	337,326	130,553
Polk.......	27,332	754,300	374,980	327,140
Potter	102,894	3,334,877	325,850	2,792,292
Presidio....	4,145	105,630	96,331	1,998
Rains......	6,025	143,504	128,451	3,520
Randall	80,300	1,987,125	350,000	1,477,868
Reagan	4,584	217,623	187,803	21,204
Real.......	2,575	80,593	73,903	1,643
Red River ..	12,924	319,057	259,710	35,343
Reeves.....	12,023	410,776	303,611	85,092
Refugio	8,249	258,204	173,295	69,769
Roberts	1,750	53,377	49,447	862
Robertson ..	13,178	340,525	281,086	35,435
Rockwall ...	17,578	558,816	214,200	311,903
Runnels	13,833	483,967	338,664	120,745
Rusk	35,593	1,060,466	350,000	644,654
Sabine	9,658	236,286	210,796	8,191
SanAugustine	7,899	219,609	201,516	4,187
San Jacinto .	11,381	306,681	251,262	33,647
San Patricio .	48,499	1,378,419	350,000	936,459
San Saba ...	5,514	161,190	148,218	2,866
Schleicher ..	3,513	111,483	103,459	1,798
Scurry	20,932	755,369	350,000	368,410
Shackelford .	4,620	180,796	169,882	2,606
Shelby	21,927	762,024	350,000	371,995
Sherman ...	3,997	141,908	131,738	1,964

County—	Total Vehicles Registered	Total Gross License Fees (Dollars)	Net to County (Dollars)	Net to State (Dollars)
Smith......	128,864	3,471,053	350,000	2,848,547
Somervell ..	4,943	133,579	109,956	14,710
Starr	16,022	516,830	347,649	132,180
Stephens ...	11,809	410,128	295,838	91,071
Sterling	1,668	46,416	42,507	887
Stonewall...	3,009	104,003	97,252	1,479
Sutton	5,901	284,589	236,666	37,355
Swisher	9,136	262,260	239,521	6,306
Tarrant	912,222	24,321,714	350,000	22,195,106
Taylor	117,066	3,636,564	350,000	3,047,001
Terrell......	1,485	40,281	37,137	625
Terry......	14,161	455,801	323,855	106,182
Throckmortn	2,650	82,499	76,545	1,217
Titus	20,318	558,066	328,004	190,680
Tom Green..	88,505	2,446,281	350,000	1,922,551
Travis......	404,437	10,039,602	350,000	8,818,678
Trinity.....	10,892	319,270	235,066	63,857
Tyler	14,821	404,270	296,539	79,971
Upshur.....	24,329	609,243	352,535	211,965
Upton	5,092	262,447	246,782	6,575
Uvalde.....	18,213	638,804	297,500	307,796
Val Verde...	28,306	694,480	279,297	361,507
Van Zandt ..	35,280	857,018	350,000	444,358
Victoria	68,920	2,001,002	350,000	1,519,457
Walker.....	28,660	824,196	350,000	418,507
Waller	28,913	789,584	388,666	348,087
Ward	14,582	593,003	344,948	222,597
Washington .	23,568	772,414	350,000	377,508
Webb......	60,791	2,065,592	303,100	1,631,162
Wharton....	38,902	1,325,515	350,000	899,836
Wheeler....	7,681	243,505	226,636	3,453
Wichita	118,837	3,227,472	329,000	2,676,611
Wilbarger ..	15,431	424,049	304,534	88,539
Willacy	11,587	375,323	285,642	66,849
Williamson..	75,415	1,931,405	350,000	1,438,515
Wilson	14,355	370,933	281,660	63,826
Winkler	10,232	341,307	224,828	97,906
Wise	32,599	1,212,719	350,000	803,972
Wood	27,998	723,814	360,802	311,383
Yoakum....	9,620	367,680	285,308	65,310
Young	23,520	812,973	350,000	416,390
Zapata	5,709	148,154	102,934	34,174
Zavala	6,861	207,273	173,237	21,015
County Totals	13,126,933	368,096,644	65,969,886	275,965,266
State Collections		17,599,547		17,599,547
Grand Totals	13,126,933	385,696,191	65,969,886	293,564,813

Truck, Bus Transportation

The following information was provided to the Texas Almanac by the Texas Motor Transportation Association, Austin:

The Texas truck and bus industry operates 3,330,285 vehicles and **employs** 632,090 persons. In 1983, the industry had a **payroll** totaling more than $11 billion.

In 1982 the industry paid more than $767 million in state and federal **highway user taxes**, which amounts to almost $2.1 million daily. With these highway user taxes, the industry pays for almost 1 out of every 2 miles of highways constructed.

Trucks serve every one of the 2,795 populated cities and towns in Texas and almost 70 percent depend entirely on trucks because they have no other kind of shipping service.

In 1983 trucks transported almost all — 98.7 percent — of fresh fruits and vegetables produced by Texas farmers to the nation's principal markets. Besides the 340,000 trucks operated in the field of **agriculture** in 1982, the **construction industry** operated 320,000, **wholesale businesses** operated 142,400, **services** operated 172,600, **retail businesses** operated 90,900 and **utility companies** operated 81,800. Other types of businesses each operated fewer than 70,000.

The industry paid more than $3.6 billion for new trucks and buses to the state's truck and bus dealers and paid almost $5.4 billion for fuel in 1983.

TEXAS MOTOR VEHICLES, 1917-1984

Motor vehicles registered in Texas during the period April 1 through March 31 of the following year are given for the period 1917-1976. In 1978, the State Department of Highways and Public Transportation went to an annual registration procedure whereby expiration of license plates occurs at staggered intervals throughout the year. Therefore, figures for 1977 and after are for the calendar year ending Dec. 31.

Registration Year	Vehicles Registration	*Percentage of Increase or Decrease	Registration Year	Vehicles Registration	*Percentage of Increase or Decrease	Registration Year	Vehicles Registration	*Percentage of Increase or Decrease
1917.	194,720	...	1940.	1,802,063	5.85	1963.	5,721,773	4.85
1918.	250,201	28.49	1941.	1,830,821	.60	1964.	5,985,986	4.62
1919.	331,721	32.58	1942.	1,704,295	−6.91	1965.	6,168,649	3.05
1920.	430,377	29.74	1943.	1,624,593	−4.68	1966.	6,395,770	3.68
1921.	470,575	9.34	1944.	1,625,428	.05	1967.	6,651,767	4.00
1922.	531,608	12.97	1945.	1,713,944	5.45	1968.	7,016,402	5.48
1923.	695,822	30.89	1946.	1,943,716	11.82	1969.	7,351,437	4.77
1924.	840,560	20.80	1947.	2,192,654	12.81	1970.	7,642,221	3.96
1925.	983,420	17.00	1948.	2,441,158	11.34	1971.	8,086,061	5.81
1926.	1,060,716	7.86	1949.	2,784,480	14.06	1972.	8,564,582	5.92
1927.	1,126,982	6.25	1950.	3,132,577	12.50	1973.	9,070,160	5.90
1928.	1,235,162	9.60	1951.	3,285,693	4.89	1974.	9,386,063	3.48
1929.	1,376,427	11.44	1952.	3,373,053	2.66	1975.	9,878,896	5.25
1930.	1,401,748	1.84	1953.	3,551,004	5.28	1976.	10,432,636	5.61
1931.	1,345,436	−4.02	1954.	3,781,235	6.48	1977.	11,152,302	9.66
1932.	1,237,850	−7.99	1955.	4,089,718	8.16	1978.	11,297,938	1.31
1933.	1,241,848	.32	1956.	4,220,702	3.20	1979.	10,085,254	−10.73
1934.	1,358,882	9.42	1957.	4,396,714	4.17	1980.	11,989,419	18.88
1935.	1,426,949	5.01	1958.	4,531,010	3.05	1981.	12,418,020	3.06
1936.	1,537,947	7.78	1959.	4,744,005	4.70	1982.	12,765,555	2.80
1937.	1,612,533	4.85	1960.	4,885,300	2.98	1983.	13,853,020	8.52
1938.	1,630,040	1.09	1961.	5,206,543	6.58	1984.	13,491,236	−2.61
1939.	1,702,507	4.45	1962.	5,456,913	4.81			

*Decrease indicated by minus (−) sign.

HIGHWAY MILEAGE AND EXPENDITURES—1918-1984

Selected years of operation of the State Highway Department, which was established in 1917 and made its first report for fiscal year ended Aug. 31, 1918, is covered by this table:

Fiscal Year	Paved Roads	Total Mileage Maintained	Total Expenditures All Purposes	Fiscal Year	Paved Roads	Total Mileage Maintained	Total Expenditures All Purposes
1918.	†	†	$ 1,268,284.82	1981.	70,764	70,804	1,675,356,011.20
1920.	†	†	2,411,285.26	1982.	70,926	70,933	1,469,004,766.17
1925.	†	†	20,602,264.66	1983.	71,060	71,065	1,570,521,630
1930.	7,317	18,528	47,331,977.54	1984.	71,165	71,172	1,515,286,262
1935.	13,285	20,359	35,796,704.45	Total.			$23,920,934,197.94
1940.	19,440	23,434	40,210,347.86				
1945.	23,562	25,705	26,955,618.80				
1946.	24,544	26,327	43,315,184.94				
1947.	26,248	27,626	81,318,630.32				
1948.	29,004	30,146	106,629,214.23				
1949.	31,639	32,555	106,335,219.90				
1950.	34,200	34,929	115,282,344.55				
1951.	39,741	40,368	133,412,463.68				
1952.	41,846	42,288	135,668,281.48				
1953.	43,877	44,179	160,887,682.32				
1954.	46,399	46,676	166,378,588.36				
1955.	48,678	48,840	192,826,643.81				
1956.	50,697	50,839	212,863,034.52				
1957.	52,849	52,977	246,009,210.04				
1958.	54,166	54,367	317,371,972.63				
1959.	55,750	55,932	411,743,735.10				
1960.	56,941	57,015	397,185,292.27				
1961.	58,194	58,286	381,611,493.03				
1962.	59,305	59,434	384,345,117.70				
1963.	60,387	60,520	410,897,834.26				
1964.	61,493	61,604	466,357,175.67				
1965.	62,421	62,618	451,909,168.85				
1966.	63,640	63,718	470,945,064.73				
1967.	64,486	64,580	562,358,008.43				
1968.	65,241	65,335	547,505,442.17				
1969.	66,017	66,091	593,923,831.27				
1970.	67,139	67,272	674,031,313.81				
1971.	67,536	67,651	701,124,133.89				
1972.	68,125	68,204	669,939,862.44				
1973.	68,463	68,564	646,024,497.30				
1974.	69,169	69,268	730,767,580.05				
1975.	69,392	69,470	905,008,667.20				
1976.	69,613	69,685	820,634,135.48				
1977.	69,990	70,020	784,044,000.00				
1978.	70,233	70,389	1,013,975,000.00				
1979.	71,132	71,212	1,097,793,290.91				
1980.	70,605	70,605	1,720,255,170.65				

Fiscal Year ended Aug. 31.
†Not reported definitely for these years.

DRIVERS' LICENSES

The following report from Texas Department of Public Safety shows the number of drivers' licenses issued during the fiscal year and number of valid licenses at the end of each fiscal year.

Fiscal Year Ending—	*Licenses Issued During Year	Valid Licenses at Year's End
Aug. 31, 1984	4,498,902	11,009,567
Aug. 31, 1983	4,090,602	10,805,539
Aug. 31, 1982	4,281,652	10,463,962
Aug. 31, 1981	3,818,303	9,909,721
Aug. 31, 1980	3,699,543	9,551,683
Aug. 31, 1979	3,616,754	9,189,198
Aug. 31, 1978	3,529,926	8,805,604
Aug. 31, 1977	3,418,606	8,420,678
Aug. 31, 1976	3,233,610	8,127,188
Aug. 31, 1975	2,980,024	7,806,703
Aug. 31, 1974	2,887,456	7,588,372
Aug. 31, 1973	2,807,828	7,334,913
Aug. 31, 1972	2,573,010	7,098,425
Aug. 31, 1971	2,418,170	6,768,319
Aug. 31, 1970	2,321,416	6,420,602
Aug. 31, 1969	3,403,122	6,035,944
Aug. 31, 1968	3,603,082	5,849,126
Aug. 31, 1967	3,516,794	5,772,852
Aug. 31, 1966	3,505,108	5,587,709
Aug. 31, 1965	3,325,010	5,454,476

*Includes renewals during year.

TEXAS
POLITICS & GOVERNMENT

President Reagan and Vice President George Bush are shown at the Republican National Convention in Dallas in August of 1984. This was the first time the Republican Party had held its convention in Texas. The Democrats held their convention in Houston in 1928. Associated Press Photo

Politics In Texas

1984 can be characterized as the Year of Ronald Reagan in Texas. The popular conservative Republican president swept the state in the general election, and, in the process, carried record numbers of GOP candidates into office on his coattails.

The most stunning upsets occurred in the state's congressional delegation in which Republicans gained four seats and now hold 10 of 27 positions. Three Democratic incumbents lost to GOP challengers. Tom Vandergriff of Arlington lost to Richard Armey of Lewisville in the 26th district; Jack Hightower of Vernon, a five-term veteran of Congress, fell to Beau Boulter of Amarillo in the 13th district; and William Patman, a four-year incumbent, was defeated by Mac Sweeney of Wharton in the 14th district. In addition, Larry Combest of Lubbock won the 19th district seat that was vacated by Democrat Kent Hance, who ran for the U.S. Senate. Republicans Joe Barton of Ennis in the 6th district and Tom DeLay of Sugerland in the 22nd district won seats vacated by Republicans Phil Gramm and Ron Paul, both of whom ran for the U.S. Senate.

Republican Gramm easily defeated Lloyd Doggett for the U.S. Senate seat vacated by John Tower. Republicans have held this seat since Tower defeated a field of more than 70 candidates in a special election in 1961 to become the first popularly elected Republican senator from Texas.

Republican legislative candidates also benefitted from the president's popularity. In the Texas Legislature, Republicans now hold 51 of 150 House seats, up from 37 in 1983, and six of 31 Senate seats, a gain of one. Both represent the party's high since Reconstruction more than a century ago.

Former Texas Atty. Gen. John Hill, a Democrat who lost a close gubernatorial race to Republican William P. Clements Jr. in 1978, was elected chief justice of the Texas Supreme Court. Clements was the state's only Republican governor since Reconstruction.

Reagan's coattails proved long for Republicans running for local offices, too. In 1984, 434 Texas Republicans were elected to public offices ranging down to constable. That was a 56 percent increase over the 278 elected in 1982, according to the party's state headquarters in Austin.

In urban areas like Houston, Dallas, San Antonio and Fort Worth, there is evidence of widespread lever-pulling in Republican districts, indicating to some officials that there is a basic party realignment taking place in traditionally Democratic Texas. One gauge is the straight-ticket voting that cost several incumbent Democratic judges their seats in Dallas and Harris Counties. Some longtime Democrats complain that the national party has become too liberal and too irresponsive to conservative opinion. The realignment theory will be put to the test in future elections.

Primaries' Results

Republicans had spirited primaries across the state as the party fielded more candidates than ever for local offices. In the party's major statewide race, Phil Gramm, a Democrat-turned-Republican congressman from College Station, easily defeated three challengers for the nomination. The conservative Republican in turn rode the Reagan tide to victory over Democrat Lloyd Doggett, a liberal, in the fall.

The major upsets came in the Democratic primary. Former congressman Bob Krueger of New Braunfels had run former Sen. Tower a close race in 1978 and was the odds-on favorite to get the Democratic nomination in 1984. Facing five challengers, however, the moderate

Krueger finished third in the first primary. Doggett, a liberal state senator from Austin, edged conservative congressman Kent Hance of Lubbock in the runoff for the nomination. Many conservative Democrats crossed party lines to vote against Doggett in the general election. Hance changed his political affiliation to the Republican Party in May 1985.

In the second upset in the Democratic primary, Albert G. Bustamante of San Antonio defeated nine-term incumbent Abraham "Chick" Kazen Jr. of Laredo and also won the general election.

Party Primaries

Texas political parties have held primaries since passage of the **Terrell Election Law** in 1905. It mandates primaries for parties whose gubernatorial candidates received more than 200,000 votes in the previous general election. Democrats have held primaries each election since enactment of the law. Republicans have held 17 primaries in 1926, 1930, 1934, 1954, 1958, 1962, 1964, 1966, 1968, 1970, 1972, 1974, 1976, 1978, 1980, 1982 and 1984.

Both parties held presidential primaries for the first time in 1976 and continued the practice thereafter, although in slightly different forms. Republican results are translated directly into delegate votes at the national convention, while Democrats used a combination primary-convention system to elect delegates. Reagan won the GOP primary in 1984, and Walter Mondale won under the Democrats' system.

Voter Registration

A total of 7,900,167 Texans registered to vote in the general election of 1984 and 68.3 percent of them participated in the presidential election.

Texas abandoned use of the **poll tax** as a voter qualification when the system was declared unconstitutional in 1966. The largest number of poll taxes paid under the system was 2,411,679 in 1966, when it was estimated that exemptions for the elderly increased the number of eligible voters to 3,014,597.

Additional information on Texas' political parties and primary and general election results for selected races appear on the following pages.

DEMOCRATIC STATE EXECUTIVE COMMITTEE

Chairman, Bob Slagle, Box 1244, Sherman 75090; **Vice Chairman**, Dr. Judith Zaffirini, 305 Century Dr., Laredo 78043; **Vice Chairman For Financial Affairs**, Perry Bradley, Box 533, Sulphur Springs 75482; **Secretary**, Ronald Luna, 1383 Old Lockhart Rd., Buda 78610; **Treasurer**, Frank Thompson, 6937 Peyton, Houston 77028. **Office Address:** 815 Brazos, Ste. 200, Austin 78701.

National Committee Members: Millie Bruner, Grand Prairie; Billie Carr, Houston; Sue Pate, Bridge City; Gene Rodriquez Jr., San Antonio; Paul G. Gray, Austin; Al Edwards, Houston; Dora Olivo, Rosenberg; Steve Carriker, Roby; Hazel Obey, Austin.

District—Member and Address:

1. — Dr. Jeanie Stanley, 1225 Oak Dr., Kilgore; Lamar Yarborough, Rt. 2, Box 225, Beckville.
2. — Mary Elizabeth Jackson, Rt. 1, Box 291F, Tyler; Bob H. Fickett, Box 469, Kaufman.
3. — Jeanette Coffield, Box 6057, Jasper; Rodney Conwell, 409 Nursery Ln., Wells.
4. — Bettye R. Smith, 3380 Worcester, Beaumont; Dewey Updegraff, 402 Bilbo, Orange.
5. — Alta K. Rickett, 36911 Susan, Magnolia; Jim Carter, 1724 18th, Huntsville.
6. — Cora L. Johnson, 10126 Alfred Ln., Houston; Terry Bonds, 13000 Woodforest, #212, Houston.
7. — Dianne Richards, 5850 San Felipe, Ste. 480, Houston; Stewart W. Gagnon, 2303 Lexford Lane, Houston.
8. — Dr. Louise Young, 8261 Clearsprings Rd., Dallas; Richard Johnston, 4208 Hockaday, Dallas.
9. — Margaret Mills, 4821 Ridgeview, Waco; Troy M. Thomason, 113 Meadow Ln., Groesbeck.
10. — Martha Mewhirter, 1221 Wentwood Dr., Irving; Gary Horton, 1815 Briar Meadow, Arlington.
11. — F.G. (Jean) Martin, 3707 Longwood, Pasadena; Richard Kirkpatrick, Galveston County Courthouse, Room A-135, Galveston.
12. — Martha Singleton, 3029 Gardenia Dr., Fort Worth; Lloyd Scurlock, 3717 Kelvin, Fort Worth.

13. — Janie Reyes, 502 Highland, Houston; Anthony Hall, 3709 Rio Vista, Houston.
14. — Mary Benavides, 1805 Running Brook, Austin; Jim Boyle, 7509 Step Down Cove, Austin.
15. — Franacis Frazier, 650 F.M. 1959, Houston; David Patronella, 2215 Droxford, Houston.
16. — Nora A. Linares, 6001 Village Glen Dr., #3106, Dallas; Ken Molberg, 5640 Swiss, Dallas.
17. — Blanche Darley, 1602 El Camino Real, #302, Houston; Edmund L. Cogburn, 5002 Doliver, Houston.
18. — Diane Rhodes, Box 37, Nursery; Dan Buie, 1005 N. Main, Elgin.
19. — Ruth Jones, 3811 Willowood, San Antonio; Gilbert Kissling, 418 E. Huisache, San Antonio.
20. — Esperanza Torres, Rt. 1, Box 321-A, Kingsville; Santiago Cantu, 1010 Weber Pkwy., Corpus Christi.
21. — Ninfa Moncada, 809 E. Kinney, Crystal City; Adolfo Alvarez, Box 281, Pearsall.
22. — Nancy Brannon, 1503 Carnation, Lewisville; Harris Worcester, Rt. 2, Box 61, Aledo.
23. — Joan Jackson Bouldin, 3507 Alaska Ave., Dallas; Fred Tinsley, 6770 Keswick, Dallas.
24. — Vada Sutton, Box 702, Belton; Charles Scarborough, 1617 Woodridge, Abilene.
25. — Maxine Molberg, 143 E. Main, Fredericksburg; Gerald Ratliff, 635 S. Jefferson, San Angelo.
26. — Christine Hernandez, 822 Hoover Ave., San Antonio; Jim Bode, 315 Lively, San Antonio.
27. — Rachel G. Perelman, 1860 Price Rd., Brownsville; Samuel Sanchez, 120 Frost Proof, Weslaco.
28. — Natalie Rothstein, 4230 E. Everglade, Odessa; Madison Sowder, 1703 Ave. K, Lubbock.
29. — Patricia R. Sutton, 3501 Mountain, El Paso; Stanley B. Roberts, 3420 McLean, El Paso.
30. — Dorthy Wise, 1308 Sunnyside Ln., Wichita Falls; Calvin Gambill, 711 W. California, Seymour.
31. — Angela Lamb, Rt. 1, Box 505, Amarillo; Doug Seal, 1701 Corsicana, Wellington.

YOUNG DEMOCRATS

Roy L. Brooks, 4900 Littlepage, Fort Worth; Steve McDonald, Box 12345, Austin.

COUNTY CHAIRMAN'S ASSOCIATION

H. D. Pate, Box 261, Bridge City; Karen McLeaish, 4656 Lemonwood, Odessa.

YOUNG DEMOCRATIC CLUBS OF TEXAS

Tom Eisenberg, Box 12345, Austin 78711.

REPUBLICAN STATE EXECUTIVE COMMITTEE

Chairman, George W. Strake Jr., 811 Rusk, Ste. 1360, Houston 77002; **Vice Chairman**, Diana Denman, 503 Terrell Rd., San Antonio 78209; **Secretary**, Holly Decherd, 4204 Tallowood, Austin 78731; **Treasurer**, Henry Santamaria, 801 Somerset, El Paso 79912. **Office Address:** 1300 Guadalupe, Ste. 205, Austin 78701.

National Committeeman, Ernest Angelo Jr., 410 N. Main, Midland 79701; **National Committeewoman**, Mrs. Fran Chiles, Box 26162, Fort Worth 76116.

District, Member and Address:

1. — William Osborn, 1320 Colgate Dr., Longview; Nancy Gordon, Box 175, Avinger.
2. — Dr. Gene Hightower, Rt. 1, Box 316, Van; Jane Yancey, 1921 Palo Alto Cr., Plano.
3. — Steve Lilly, Rt. 10, Box 7440, Nacogdoches; Marguerete Graves, Box 127, Kirbyville.
4. — Dr. Ray Benski, 927 30th, Nederland; Marguerite Foulk, 3670 Crestwood Dr., Beaumont.
5. — Don Redd, 76 S. Wavy Oak, The Woodlands; Katye Kowierschke, 2950 I-45, Ste. 7, Huntsville.
6. — Gary Jones, 3710 Fox Dr., Baytown; Wilda Lindstrom, 12843 Eastbrook, Houston.
7. — Carol Belton, 5411 Pebble Springs Dr., Houston; Patricia Vanoni, 10726 Holly Springs, Houston.
8. — Bob Driegert, 3 Shadywood Pl., Richardson; Virginia Steenson, 602 Vernet, Richardson.
9. — Bruce McDougal, 102 Roma, Duncanville; Joan Wood, 8901 Raven, Waco.
10. — James Cribbs, Box 13060, Arlington; Pat Jacobson, 5113 Jennings Dr., Ft. Worth.
11. — Dr. Paul Cunningham, 200 University Blvd., Ste. 922, Galveston; Gayle West, 4030 Fox Meadow, Pasadena.
12. — Joseph D. Ambrose, 909 Throckmorton, Ft. Worth; Darla Mortensen, 7012 Falling Springs Rd., Ft. Worth.

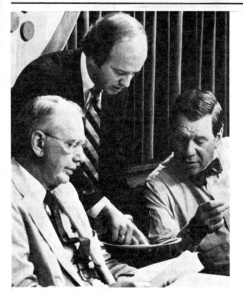

State Sen. Grant Jones, Sen. Kent Caperton and Lt. Gov. Bill Hobby (from left) discuss possible nominees for new State Board of Education. Associated Press Photo

13.—Jerry Smith, Box 13608, Houston; Iris Manes, 4939 Glenmeadow, Houston.
14.—Mark Lehman, 1510 W. North Loop, Ste. 1121, Austin; Kay Danks, 7200 West Rim, Austin.
15.—Earl Lairson, Box 500017, Houston; Nelda Eppes, 5426 Poinciana, Houston.
16.—Tom Carter, 513 Blanco, Mesquite; Martha Weisend, 8238 San Benito Way, Dallas.
17.—Steve Munisteri, 4214 Swarthmore, Houston; Vicki Hapke, 18206 Blanchmont, Houston.
18.—E. V. Blissard, Rt. 2, Box 61-L, Richmond; Anne Ashy, 204 Leisure, Victoria.
19.—Van Henry Archer Jr., 218 West Lynwood, San Antonio; Katy Evans, 621 Weatherly Dr., San Antonio.
20.—Eugene J. Seaman, 525 S. Shoreline, Corpus Christi; Leona Knight, 1202 Southbay Dr., Corpus Christi.
21.—H. Pulse Martinez, Box 21, San Antonio; Robbie Borchers, 1355 Hueco Springs Rd., New Braunfels.
22.—Dunman Perry Jr., Box 640, Mineral Wells; Vivian Millirons, 1016 Stuckert Dr., Burleson.
23.—Dr. Jimmy Morgan, Box 61204, DFW Airport; Patricia Taylor, 4577 Lynnacre Cr., Dallas.
24.—Marcus Anderson, Box 353, Abilene; Amelia Dixon, 171 Park Ln., Sunrise Beach.
25.—David Godfrey, Box 994, Midland; Ann Peden, 1118 18th, Hondo.
26.—Jess Young, 4241 Piedras Dr. E., Ste. 115, San Antonio; Diane Rath, 227 Springwood Ln., San Antonio.
27.—Frank Yturria, 54 Calle Cenizo, Brownsville; Becki Olivares, 2445 Iris, McAllen.
28.—Ron Fleming, 1804 Albany, Lubbock; Janelle Evans, Box 3, Brownfield.
29.—Ronald Ederer, 709 Walpham, El Paso; Bette Hervey, 3920 Hillcrest Dr., El Paso.
30.—Paul Brown, 1608 Crescent, Sherman; Jacque Allen, 2206 Clarinda, Wichita Falls.
31.—Meryl Barnett, 1517 Balin Rd., Borger; Lottie Eller, Box 984, Panhandle.

Electing Texas' U.S. Senators

U.S. Senators were selected by the legislatures of the states until the U.S. Constitution was amended in 1913 to require popular elections. In Texas, the first senator chosen by voters in a general election was Charles A. Culberson in 1916.

Because of political pressures, however, the rules of the Democratic Party of Texas were changed in 1904 to require that all candidates for office stand before voters in the primary. Consequently, Texas' senators faced voters in 1906, 1910 and 1912 before the U.S. Constitution was changed.

The 1912 Democratic primary saw the first contested senatorial election. Sen. Joseph W. Bailey declined to seek another term in office, and Morris Sheppard received a plurality of the votes cast in the primary. The following year, the Legislature named F. W. Johnson, a friend of Gov. Oscar Colquitt and long-time party supporter, to replace Bailey in February. Sheppard's supporters complained that the selection of Johnson cost their candidate valuable seniority in the U.S. Senate. The Legislature relented, and Johnson left the office. Sheppard took the seat on Feb. 13, 1913. Sheppard authored the constitutional amendment that brought prohibition to the United States. He was re-elected four times and died in office in 1941.

ELECTIONS OF TEXAS SENATORS

Below is given a compilation of past U.S. senatorial elections in Texas insofar as information is available to the Texas Almanac.

1906 ELECTION	
J. W. Bailey (unopp.). . . .	283,315

1910 ELECTION **DEMOCRATIC PRIMARY**	
C. A. Culberson (unopp.) .	359,939

1912 ELECTION **DEMOCRATIC PRIMARY**	
Morris Sheppard	178,281
Jacob F. Wolters	142,050
Choice B. Randall	40,349
Matthew Zollner	3,868
Total vote.	364,548

1916 ELECTION **1st DEMOCRATIC PRIMARY**	
Charles A. Culberson. . . .	87,421
Robert L. Henry	37,726
O. B. Colquitt.	119,598
S. P. Brooks.	78,641
T. M. Campbell	65,721
John Davis	9,924
*G. W. Riddle	335
Total vote.	399,366
*Had withdrawn	

2nd DEMOCRATIC PRIMARY	
Charles A. Culberson. . . .	163,182
O. B. Colquitt.	94,098
Total vote.	257,280

*GENERAL ELECTION	
Charles A. Culberson (Dem.)	301,905
Alex W. Atcheson (Rep.) .	48,775
E. H. Conibear (Proh.). . .	2,313
T. A. Hickey (Soc.).	18,616
Total Vote	371,609

*First general election for U.S. Senator. Prior to 1916, Legislature appointed Senators.

1918 ELECTION **DEMOCRATIC PRIMARY**	
Morris Sheppard (unopp.)	649,876

GENERAL ELECTION	
Morris Sheppard (Dem.).	155,158
J. Webster Flanagan (Rep.)	22,183
M. A. Smith (Soc.)	1,587
Total vote.	178,928

1922 ELECTION **1st DEMOCRATIC PRIMARY**	
C. A. Culberson	99,635
Earle B. Mayfield	153,538
Cullen F. Thomas	88,026
James E. Ferguson	127,071
Clarence Ousley	62,451
R. L. Henry	41,567
Sterling P. Strong	1,085
Total vote.	573,373

2nd DEMOCRATIC PRIMARY	
Earle B. Mayfield	273,308
James E. Ferguson	228,701
Total vote.	502,009

GENERAL ELECTION	
Earle B. Mayfield (Dem.)	264,260
George E. B. Peddy (Rep.).	130,744
Total vote.	395,004

Election of Texas Senators, 1906-1984 (Continued)

1924 ELECTION
1st DEMOCRATIC PRIMARY

Morris Sheppard	440,511
Fred W. Davis	159,663
John F. Maddox	80,070
Total vote	680,244

GENERAL ELECTION

Morris Sheppard (Dem.)	579,208
T. M. Kennerly (Rep.)	98,207
Total vote	677,415

1928 ELECTION
1st DEMOCRATIC PRIMARY

Thomas L. Blanton	126,758
Tom Connally	178,091
Minnie Fisher Cunningham	28,944
Earle B. Mayfield	200,246
Jeff McLemore	9,244
Alvin Owsley	131,755
Total vote	675,038

2nd DEMOCRATIC PRIMARY

Tom Connally	320,071
Earle B. Mayfield	257,747
Total vote	577,818

GENERAL ELECTION

Tom Connally (Dem.)	566,139
T. M. Kennerly (Rep.)	129,910
David Curran (Soc.)	690
John Rust (Com.)	114
Total vote	696,853

1930 ELECTION
1st DEMOCRATIC PRIMARY

Morris Sheppard	526,293
C. A. Mitchner	40,130
Robert L. Henry	174,260
Total vote	740,683

1st REPUBLICAN PRIMARY
(158 Counties Reporting)

Doran John Haesly	3,645
*Harve H. Haines	2,568
*C. O. Harris	2,784
Total vote	8,997

*No runoff; candidates withdrew

GENERAL ELECTION

Morris Sheppard (Dem.)	258,929
D. J. Haesley (Rep.)	35,357
Guy L. Smith (Soc.)	790
W. A. Berry (Com.)	282
Total vote	295,358

1934 ELECTION
1st DEMOCRATIC PRIMARY

Joseph W. Bailey	355,963
Tom Connally	567,139
Guy B. Fisher	41,421
Total vote	964,523

GENERAL ELECTION

Tom Connally (Dem.)	439,375
U.S. Goen (Rep.)	12,895
W. B. Starr (Soc.)	1,828
L. C. Keel (Com.)	310
Total vote	454,408

1936 ELECTION
1st DEMOCRATIC PRIMARY

Morris Sheppard	616,293
Guy B. Fisher	89,215
Richard C. Bush	37,842
Joseph H. Price	45,919
Joe H. Eagle	136,718
J. Edward Glenn	28,641
Total vote	954,628

GENERAL ELECTION

Morris Sheppard (Dem.)	774,975
Carlos G. Watson (Rep.)	59,491
W. B. Starr (Soc.)	958
Gertrude Wilson (Union)	1,836
Total vote	837,260

1940 ELECTION
1st DEMOCRATIC PRIMARY

Tom Connally	923,219
A. P. Belcher	66,962
Guy B. Fisher	98,125
Total vote	1,088,306

GENERAL ELECTION

Tom Connally (Dem.)	978,095
George Shannon (Rep.)	59,340
Homer Brooks (Const.)	408
Total vote	1,037,843

1941 Special Election
June 28, 1941
(24 Dems., 1 Rep., 1 Ind. and 1 Communist)

W. Lee O'Daniel	175,590
Lyndon B. Johnson	174,279
Gerald C. Mann	140,807
Martin Dies	80,653
*Total vote	571,329

*Above candidates only; votes for others not available.

1942 ELECTION
1st DEMOCRATIC PRIMARY

James V. Allred	317,501
Dan Moody	178,471
W. Lee O'Daniel	475,541
Floyd E. Ryan	12,213
Total vote	983,726

2nd DEMOCRATIC PRIMARY

James V. Allred	433,203
W. Lee O'Daniel	451,359
Total vote	884,562

GENERAL ELECTION

W. Lee O'Daniel (Dem.)	260,629
Dudley Lawson (Rep.)	12,064
Charles L. Somerville (P.U.P.)	1,934
Total vote	274,627

1946 ELECTION
1st DEMOCRATIC PRIMARY

Tom Connally	823,818
Cyclone Davis	74,252
Floyd E. Ryan	85,292
Terrell Sledge	66,947
Laverne Somerville	42,290
Total vote	1,092,599

GENERAL ELECTION

Tom Connally (Dem.)	336,931
Murray C. Sells (Rep.)	43,750
Write-in	5
Total vote	380,686

1948 ELECTION
1st DEMOCRATIC PRIMARY

Otis C. Myers	15,330
F. B. Clark	7,420
Roscoe H. Collier	12,327
Coke R. Stevenson	477,077
Cyclone Davis	10,871
Frank G. Cortez	13,344
Jesse C. Saunders	7,401
George E. B. Peddy	237,195
Lyndon B. Johnson	405,617
Terrell Sledge	6,692
James F. Alford	9,117
Write-in	1
Total vote	1,202,392

2nd DEMOCRATIC PRIMARY

Lyndon B. Johnson	494,191
Coke R. Stevenson	494,104
Total vote	988,295

GENERAL ELECTION

Lyndon B. Johnson (Dem.)	702,985
Jack Porter (Rep.)	349,665
Sam Morris (Proh.)	8,913
Total vote	1,061,563

1952 ELECTION
1st DEMOCRATIC PRIMARY

Price Daniel	940,770
Lindley Beckworth	285,842
E. W. Napier	70,132
Total vote	1,296,744

GENERAL ELECTION

Price Daniel (Dem.)	1,425,007
Price Daniel (Rep.)	469,594
Price Daniel (No Party)	591
Total vote	1,895,192

1954 ELECTION
1st DEMOCRATIC PRIMARY

Lyndon B. Johnson	883,264
Dudley T. Dougherty	354,188
Total vote	1,237,452

GENERAL ELECTION

Lyndon B. Johnson (Dem.)	538,417
Carlos G. Watson (Rep.)	95,033
Fred T. Spangler (Const.)	3,025
Total vote	636,475

Special Senatorial Election

Following are results in the special senatorial election held April 2, 1957, to fill the unexpired term of former Sen. Price Daniel who resigned to make the race for Governor in the Democratic primaries and who was elected in the general election Nov. 6, 1956. Official vote is given below as determined by the State Board of Canvassers:

Elmer Adams	2,228
H. J. Antoine Sr.	576
M. T. Banks	2,153
Jacob Bergolofsky	890
Searcy Bracewell	33,384
John C. Burns Sr.	600
*H. Frank Connally Jr.	514
Frank G. Cortez	1,350
*J. Cal Courtney	879
*R. W. (Waire) Currin	646
Martin Dies	290,803
C. O. Foerster Jr.	776
Curtis Ford	767
Ralph W. Hammonds	2,372
James P. Hart	19,739
*Charles W. (Jack) Hill	1,025
Thad Hutcheson	219,591
Walter Scott McNutt	500
Clyde R. Orms	356
John C. White	11,876
J. Perrin Wills	817
Hugh Wilson	851
Ralph W. Yarborough	364,605
Total	957,298

*Withdrew from race before election day, but after their names had been placed on printed ballot.

1958 ELECTION
1st DEMOCRATIC PRIMARY

William A. Blakley	536,073
Ralph W. Yarborough	760,856
Write-in	4
Total vote	1,296,933

Election of Texas Senators, 1906-1984 (Continued)

GENERAL ELECTION

Ralph W. Yarborough (Dem.)	587,030
Ray Whittenburg (Rep.) .	185,926
Bard A. Logan (Const.) . .	14,172
Total vote.	787,128

1960 ELECTION
1st DEMOCRATIC PRIMARY

Lyndon B. Johnson	1,407,109
Write-in	145
Total vote.	1,407,254

GENERAL ELECTION

Lyndon B. Johnson (Dem.)	1,306,625
John G. Tower (Rep.) . . .	926,653
Bard A. Logan (Const.) . .	20,506
Total vote.	2,253,784

1961 SPECIAL ELECTION

Dr. G. H. Allen, 849; Jim W. Amos, 527; Dale Baker, 612; Dr. Mali Jean Rauch Barraco, 434; Tom E. Barton, 395; R. G. Becker, 462; Jacob Bergolofsky, 377; Dr. Ted Bisland, 831; William A. Blakley, 190,818; G. E. Blewett, 474; Lawrence S. Bosworth Jr., 410; Joyce J. Bradshaw, 352; Chester D. Brooks, 711; W. L. Burlison, 1,695; Ronald J. Byers, 175; Joseph M. Carter, 185; George A. Davisson, 897; Mrs. Winnie K. Derrick, 327; Harry R. Diehl, 293; Harvill O. Eaton, 178; Rev. Jonnie Mae Eckman, 342; Paul F. Eix, 317; Ben H. Faber, 363; Dr. H.E. Fanning, 293; Charles Otto Foerster Jr., 133; Harold Franklin, 196; George N. Gallagher Jr., 985; Richard J. Gay, 939; Van T. George Jr., 307; Arthur Glover, 1,528; Henry B. Gonzalez, 97,659; Delbert E. Grandstaff, 2,959; Curtis E. Hill, 389; Willard Park Holland, 669; John N. Hopkins, 490; Mary Hazel Houston, 726; Ben M. Johnson, 681; Guy Johnson, 748; Morgan H. Johnson, 334; C. B. Kennedy, 770; H. Springer Knoblauch, 186.

Hugh O. Lea, 651; V. C. Logan, 314; Frank A. Matera, 599; Maury Maverick Jr., 104,992; Brown McCallum, 323; James E. McKee, 762; Steve Nemecek, 1,017; George E. Noyes, 174; Floyd Payne, 227; Cecil D. Perkins, 773; W. H. Posey, 592; George Red, 99; Wesley Roberts, 386; D. T. Sampson, 417; Eristus Sams, 4,490; A. Dale Savage, 400; Carl A. Schrade, 283; Albert Roy Smith, 341; Homer Hyrim Stalarow, 735; Frank Stanford, 240; John B. Sypert, 252; John G. Tower, 327,308; Mrs. Martha Tredway, 1,227; S. S. Vela, 241; Bill Whitten; 350; Hoyt G. Wilson, 2,165; Hugh Wilson, 2,997; Will Wilson, 121,961; Jim Wright, 171,328; Marcos Zertuche, 422; Write-ins, 42.

Total vote.	1,058,124

1961 RUN-OFF OF
SPECIAL ELECTION

William A. Blakley.	437,874
John G. Tower.	448,217
Total vote.	886,091

1964 ELECTION
1st DEMOCRATIC PRIMARY

Ralph Yarborough	905,011
Gordon McLendon	672,573
Write-in	23
Total vote.	1,577,607

1st REPUBLICAN PRIMARY

George Bush	62,985
Jack Cox.	45,561
Milton V. Davis	6,067
Robert Morris.	28,279
Total vote.	142,892

2nd REPUBLICAN PRIMARY

George Bush	49,751
Jack Cox.	30,333
Total vote.	80,084

GENERAL ELECTION

Ralph Yarborough (Dem.).	1,463,958
George Bush (Rep.)	1,134,337
Jack Carswell (Const.) . .	5,542
Write-in	19
Total vote.	2,603,856

1966 ELECTION
1st DEMOCRATIC PRIMARY

John R. Willoughby	226,598
Waggoner Carr	899,523
Total vote.	1,126,121

GENERAL ELECTION

Waggoner Carr (Dem.) . .	643,855
John G. Tower (Rep.) . . .	842,501
Jas. Barker Holland (Const.)	6,778
Total vote.	1,493,134

1970 ELECTION
1st DEMOCRATIC PRIMARY

Lloyd Bensen	814,316
Ralph Yarborough	726,447
Total vote.	1,540,763

REPUBLICAN PRIMARY

George Bush	96,806
Robert Morris.	13,659
Total vote.	110,465

GENERAL ELECTION

Lloyd Bentsen (Dem.) . . .	1,226,568
George Bush (Rep.)	1,071,234
Other	1,808
Total vote.	2,299,610

1972 ELECTION
1st DEMOCRATIC PRIMARY

Thomas M. Cartlidge. . . .	66,240
Barefoot Sanders	787,504
Alfonso Veloz	53,938
Hugh Wilson	125,460
Ralph Yarborough	1,032,606
Total vote.	2,065,748

2nd DEMOCRATIC PRIMARY

Barefoot Sanders	1,008,499
Ralph Yarborough	928,087
Total vote.	1,936,586

REPUBLICAN PRIMARY

John G. Tower (unopp.). .	107,648

GENERAL ELECTION

Barefoot Sanders (Dem.)	1,511,985
John G. Tower (Rep.) . .	1,822,877
Flores Amaya (Raza) . . .	63,543
Tom Leonard (Soc.)	14,464
Other	1,034
Total vote.	3,413,903

1976 ELECTION
1st DEMOCRATIC PRIMARY

Lloyd Bentsen	970,983
Leon Dugi.	19,870
Phil Gramm	427,597
Hugh Wilson	109,715
Other	1,003
Total vote.	1,529,168

REPUBLICAN PRIMARY

Louis Leman.	40,651
Alan Steelman.	251,252
Hugh Sweeney.	64,404
Total vote.	356,307

GENERAL ELECTION

Lloyd Bentsen (Dem.) . . .	2,199,956
Alan Steelman, (Rep.) . . .	1,636,370
Marjorie P. Gallion (Am.)	17,355
Pedro Vasques (Soc. Worker)	20,549
Total vote.	3,874,230

1978 ELECTION
1st DEMOCRATIC PRIMARY

Joe Christie.	701,892
Robert Krueger	853,485
Total vote.	1,555,377

REPUBLICAN PRIMARY

John G. Tower (Unopp.) .	142,202

GENERAL ELECTION

Robert Krueger (Dem.). .	1,139,149
John G. Tower (Rep.) . . .	1,151,376
Luis A. Diaz de Leon (Raza Unida)	17,869
Miguel Pendas (Soc. Worker)	4,018
Other	128
Total vote.	2,312,540

1982 ELECTION
1st DEMOCRATIC PRIMARY

Lloyd Bentsen	987,985
Joe Sullivan	276,453
Total vote.	1,264,438

REPUBLICAN PRIMARY

Don L. Richardson	18,616
Jim Collins	152,469
Walter H. Mengden Jr. . .	91,780
Total vote.	262,865

GENERAL ELECTION

Jim Collins (Rep.)	1,256,759
Lloyd Bentsen (Dem.) . . .	1,818,223
John E. Ford (Lib.)	23,494
Lineaus H. Lorette (Const.)	4,564
Darryl Anderson (W-I). . .	39
Other	88
Total vote.	3,103,167

1984 ELECTION
1st DEMOCRATIC PRIMARY

Lloyd Doggett	456,173
Kent Hance.	456,446
Robert Krueger	454,886
Harley Schlanger	14,149
Robert Sullivan	34,733
David Young.	47,062
Total vote.	1,463,449

2nd DEMOCRATIC PRIMARY

Lloyd Doggett	491,251
Kent Hance	489,906
Total vote.	981,157

REPUBLICAN PRIMARY

Phil Gramm	246,716
Henry Grover	8,388
Robert Mosbacher	26,279
Ron Paul.	55,431
Total vote.	336,814

GENERAL ELECTION

Lloyd Doggett (Dem.) . . .	2,202,557
Phil Gramm (Rep.)	3,111,348
Other	273
Total Vote	5,314,178

1984 PRIMARIES

Below are totals for contests in the Democratic primaries, held May 5, 1984, and June 2, 1984, respectively. Included are statewide races; and district races for Congress, State Senate, State Board of Education and Courts of Appeals in contested races only. Following these results are given results of the Republican primaries, held on the same dates.

United States Senate

Lloyd Doggett	456,173
Kent Hance	456,446
Robert Krueger	454,886
Harley Schlanger	14,149
Robert Sullivan	34,733
David Young	47,062
Total vote	1,463,449

Railroad Commissioner

Mack Wallace	972,122

Chief Justice, Supreme Court

John Hill	1,074,508
Sears McGee	236,429
Total vote	1,310,937

Associate Justice, Supreme Court, Place 1

Franklin Spears	960,819

Associate Justice, Supreme Court, Place 2

C. R. Ray	668,981
Shelby Sharpe	360,290
Texas Ward	192,917
Total vote	1,222,188

Associate Justice, Court Criminal Appeals, Place 1

Sam Clinton	739,000
Oliver Kitzman	342,699
Total vote	1,081,699

Associate Justice, Court Criminal Appeals, Place 2

W. C. Davis	445,023
Roy E. Greenwood	275,809
George Martinez	265,760
Buddy Stevens	169,032
Total vote	1,155,624

Associate Justice, Court Criminal Appeals, Place 3

Walter Boyd	102,589
George Ellis	115,581
Kerry P. Fitzgerald	159,481
Harry R. Heard	66,014
William B. Phillips	111,525
Thomas B. Thorpe	177,259
Bill White	381,823
Total vote	1,114,272

COURTS OF APPEALS

Below are results of contested races only in the race for justices of the Courts of Appeals in the First Democratic Primary, May 5, 1984:

Associate Justice, District 1, Place 2

F. Briscoe	60,366
J. Mims	23,588
Michol O'Connor	44,834
F. Price	29,559
Total vote	158,347

Associate Justice, District 13

H. Salinas	56,953
Horace S. Young	75,083
Total vote	132,036

Associate Justice, District 14

R. Behrens	9,080
Warren Hancock	36,362
Q. Hodges	25,295
T. Ingversen	19,594
E. Lindsay	45,155
Total vote	135,486

CONGRESS

Below are results of contested races only in the race for Congress in the First Democratic Primary, May 5, 1984:

District 2

Lloyd Dickens	9,045
William Duncan	4,373
Mitchell Hickman	4,245
Jerry Johnson	32,438
Charles Wilson	61,684
Total vote	111,785

District 3

James McNees	4,928
James Westbrook	6,889
Total vote	11,817

District 6

Dan Kubiak	38,143
Hugh Parmer	26,770
Jesse Van Winkle	5,279
Total vote	70,192

District 8

Donald Buford	11,083
Jay Hill	10,621
Total vote	21,704

District 17

Noel Cowling	10,867
Charles W. Stenholm	81,312
Total vote	92,179

District 18

Mickey Leland	33,072
Frank Saulsberry	3,421
Total vote	36,493

District 19

Gary D. Condra	4,779
Delwin Jones	7,987
Don Richards	18,411
Thomas Richards	17,481
John Selby	10,808
Total vote	59,466

District 21

Bobby Locke	18,582
Joe Sullivan	24,431
Total vote	43,013

District 22

Nick Benton	4,873
Jim Mooney	6,507
Douglas Williams	10,256
Total vote	21,636

District 23

Albert Bustamante	40,855
Stanley Green	3,286
Abraham Kazen	25,588
Total vote	69,729

District 24

Martin Frost	25,248
Dan Leach	2,185
Total vote	27,433

District 25

Mike Andrews	28,513
Bruce Director	1,737
Total vote	30,250

STATE SENATE

Below are results in contested races only for State Senate in the First Democratic Primary, May 5, 1984:

District 1

Jim Chapman	36,253
Ed Howard	49,397
Total vote	85,650

District 3

Roy Blake	54,251
John McDonald	40,373
Total vote	94,624

District 4

J. Liston	13,847
Carl Parker	50,187
Total vote	64,034

District 14

Gonzalo Barrientos	32,247
C. Bonner	7,900
M. Moore	15,401
E. Small	14,337
Total vote	69,885

District 24

Grant Jones	33,824
C. White	13,683
Total vote	47,507

STATE BOARD OF EDUCATION

Below are results in contested races only for State Board of Education in the First Democratic Primary

May 5, 1984. The State Board was revamped by the special legislative session in 1984 and the Governor has appointed a 15-member board to serve until 1989. (See State Boards and Commissions.) Voters will elect board members again in primary and general elections in 1988. These results are printed to serve only as a record.

District 2
Wayne Frederick	51,691
B. Packard	38,829
Total vote	90,520

District 5
Don H. Cook	9,749
Charles Hardt	5,203
Total vote	14,952

District 12
J. Carpenter	17,112
G. Kroh	7,471
Total vote	24,583

District 20
Mike Fernandez Jr.	22,064
L. Lowther	10,389
Total vote	32,453

District 24
Jim Hollingsworth	6,389
Ruthe Jackson	16,394
Total vote	22,783

REPUBLICAN PRIMARIES

Below are totals for contests in the Republican primaries, held May 5, 1984, and June 2, 1984, respectively. Included are statewide races; and district races for Congress, State Senate, State Board of Education and Courts of Appeals in contested races only.

U.S. Senate
Phil Gramm	246,716
Henry Grover	8,388
Robert Mosbacher	26,279
Ron Paul	55,431
Total vote	336,814

Railroad Commissioner
John T. Henderson	262,726

Chief Justice, State Supreme Court
John L. Bates	264,999

Associate Justice, Court Criminal Appeals, Place 1
Virgil E. Mulanax	252,357

Congress
Below are results in contested races only for Congress in the Republican primary, May 5, 1984:

District 6
Joe Barton	7,563
Pat Friedrichs	2,014
Bob Harris	2,857
Max Hoyt	5,590
Total vote	18,024

District 9
Lisa Duperier	3,675
Jim Mahan	4,227
Total vote	7,902

District 14
Chris Mealy	3,346
Wayne Pryor	1,167
Mac Sweeney	4,455
Total vote	8,968

District 19
Larry Combest	5,562
Ron Fleming	3,881
Tom Schaefer	1,624
Richard Wilder	421
Total vote	11,488

District 22
Joe Agris	279
Tom DeLay	11,580
Gary Engebretson	1,006
Ellen Heath	2,135
J. C. Helms	5,711
Don Richardson	1,029
Total vote	21,740

District 24
Jack Bower	3,598
Bob Burk	5,570
Total vote	9,168

Courts of Appeals
Below are results of the only contested race for Courts of Appeals in the Republican primary, May 5, 1984:

Associate Justice, Court of Appeals, Fifth District, Place 2
Pat McClung	34,393
Gordon Rowe	22,034
Total vote	56,427

State Senate
Below are results of the only contested race for State Senate in the Republican primary, May 5, 1984:

District 8
O.A. Ike Harris	19,232
Jeff Moseley	11,287
Total vote	30,519

State Board of Education
Below are results in the only contested race for State Board of Education in the Republican primary, May 5, 1984. See note under Democratic primaries.

District 7
M. Bishop	14,960
J. Butler	11,505
Total vote	26,465

SECOND DEMOCRATIC PRIMARY
Below are results in the Second Democratic primary, June 2, 1984:

United States Senator
Lloyd Doggett	491,251
Kent Hance	489,906
Total vote	981,157

Associate Justice, Court Criminal Appeals, Place 2
W. C. Davis	480,660
Roy E. Greenwood	301,444
Total vote	782,104

Associate Justice, Court Criminal Appeals, Place 3
Thomas B. Thorpe	279,514
Bill White	498,446
Total vote	777,960

Courts of Appeals
Below are results in races for Courts of Appeals in the Second Democratic primary, June 2, 1984:

Associate Justice, District 1, Place 2
F. Briscoe	48,909
Michol O'Connor	61,502
Total vote	110,411

Associate Justice, District 14
Warren Hancock	46,778
E. Lindsay	44,085
Total vote	90,863

Congress
Below are results in races for Congress in the Second Democratic primary, June 2, 1984:

District 19
Don Richards	29,144
Thomas Richards	28,429
Total vote	57,573

District 22
Jim Mooney	5,398
Douglas Williams	8,717
Total vote	14,115

State Senate
Below are results of the only race in the Second Democratic primary, June 2, 1984, for state senate:

District 14
Gonzalo Barrientos	38,344
M. Moore	29,110
Total vote	67,454

Second Republican Primary
Below are results in the races in the Second Republican primary, June 2, 1984:

Congress
District 6
Joe Barton	4,632
Max Hoyt	4,622
Total vote	9,254

District 14		
Chris Mealy		1,944
Mac Sweeney		2,887
Total vote		**4,831**

District 19		
Larry Combest		4,255
Ron Fleming		3,143
Total vote		**7,398**

GENERAL ELECTION, 1984

Below are given results of the general election held Nov. 6, 1984, for all statewide races, and for those contested congressional, state senate, Courts of Appeals and state board of education races. These are official returns as canvassed by the **State Canvassing Board.** Abbreviations used are: (Dem.) Democrat, (Rep.) Republican, (Ind.) Independent.

President

Walter Mondale (Dem.)	1,949,276
Ronald Reagan (Rep.)	3,433,428
Lyndon Larouche (Ind.)	14,613
Other	254
Total vote	5,397,571

U.S. Senator

Lloyd Doggett (Dem.)	2,202,557
Phil Gramm (Rep.)	3,111,348
Other	273
Total vote	5,314,178

Railroad Commissioner

Mack Wallace (Dem.)	2,476,793
John T. Henderson (Rep.)	2,443,835
Total vote	4,920,628

Chief Justice, Supreme Court

John L. Hill (Dem.)	2,733,318
John L. Bates (Rep.)	2,309,293
Total vote	5,042,611

Associate Justice, Supreme Court, Place 1

Franklin S. Spears (Dem.)	2,983,152

Associate Justice, Supreme Court, Place 2

C. L. Ray (Dem.)	2,929,888

Judge, Court Criminal Appeals, Place 1

Sam H. Clinton (Dem.)	2,437,924
Virgil E. Mulanax (Rep.)	2,338,528
Total vote	4,776,452

Judge, Court Criminal Appeals, Place 2

W. C. Davis (Dem.)	2,954,461

Judge, Court Criminal Appeals, Place 3

Bill White (Dem.)	2,976,004

CONGRESS

Below are results in contested races only for U.S. Congress in the general election, Nov. 6, 1984:

District 2

Charles Wilson (Dem.)	113,225
Louis Dugas Jr. (Rep.)	77,842
Total vote	191,067

District 3

James Westbrook (Dem.)	46,890
Steve Bartlett (Rep.)	228,819
Total vote	275,709

District 4

Ralph Hall (Dem.)	120,749
Thomas Blow (Rep.)	87,553
Other	39
Total vote	208,341

District 6

Dan Kubiak (Dem.)	100,799
Joe Barton (Rep.)	131,482
Total vote	232,281

District 7

Billy Willibey (Dem.)	32,835
Bill Archer (Rep.)	213,480
Total vote	246,315

District 8

Donald Buford (Dem.)	62,072
Jack Fields (Rep.)	113,031
Total vote	175,103

District 9

Jack Brooks (Dem.)	120,559
Jim Mahan (Rep.)	84,306
Total vote	204,865

District 10

J. J. Pickle (Dem.)	186,447
Other	338
Total vote	186,785

District 12

Jim Wright (Dem.)	106,299
Other	3
Total vote	106,302

District 13

Jack Hightower (Dem.)	95,367
Beau Boulter (Rep.)	107,600
Total vote	202,967

District 14

William N. Patman (Dem.)	98,885
Mac Sweeney (Rep.)	104,181
Total vote	203,066

District 16

Ron Coleman (Dem.)	76,375
Jack Hammond (Rep.)	56,589
Total vote	132,964

District 18

Mickey Leland (Dem.)	109,626
Glen R. Beaman (Rep.)	26,400
Jose Alvarado (Ind.)	3,064
Other	20
Total vote	139,110

District 19

Don Richards (Dem.)	74,044
Larry Combest (Rep.)	102,805
Total vote	176,849

District 21

Joe Sullivan (Dem.)	48,039
Tom Loeffler (Rep.)	199,909
Other	32
Total vote	247,980

District 22

Douglas Williams (Dem.)	66,495
Tom DeLay (Rep.)	125,225
Other	31
Total vote	191,751

District 24

Martin Frost (Dem.)	105,210
Bob Burk (Rep.)	71,703
Other	5
Total vote	176,918

District 25

Mike Andrews (Dem.)	113,946
Jerry Patterson (Rep.)	63,974
Total vote	177,920

District 26

Tom Vandergriff (Dem.)	120,451
Richard Armey (Rep.)	126,641
Other	2
Total vote	247,094

District 27

Solomon Ortiz (Dem.)	105,516
Richard Moore (Rep.)	60,283
Total vote	165,799

STATE SENATE

Below are results in contested races only for state senate in the general election, Nov. 6, 1984:

District 2

Ted Lyon (Dem.)	87,233
Richard Harvey (Rep.)	85,171
Total vote	172,404

District 14

Gonzalo Barrientos (Dem.)	136,373
Patrick McNamara (Rep.)	93,132
Total vote	229,505

District 26

Bob Vale (Dem.)	60,077
Cynthia T. Krier (Rep.)	94,945
Total vote	155,022

District 28

John T. Montford (Dem.)	99,672
Sol O. Thomas (Rep.)	55,816
Total vote	155,488

STATE BOARD OF EDUCATION

Below are results in contested races only for State Board of Education in the general election, Nov. 6, 1984. These results are given as a matter of record, as this board was abolished by legislative action in 1984 and a new board was appointed.

District 7

Mary Bishop (Rep.)	187,443
Other	9
Total vote	187,452

District 12

Johnnie C. Carpenter (Dem.)	90,811
Elaine Klos (Rep.)	81,371
Total vote	172,182

COURTS OF APPEALS

Below are results in contested races only for Courts of Appeals in the general election, Nov. 6, 1984:

Associate Justice, First District, Place 1

Freeman Bullock (Dem.)	517,119
D. Camille Dunn (Rep.)	534,727
Total vote	1,051,846

Associate Justice, First District, Place 2

Michol O'Connor (Dem.)	502,799
Ken Hoyt (Rep.)	549,789
Total vote	1,052,588

Associate Justice, Fifth District, Place 1

Charles Storey (Dem.)	297,667
Charles Ben Howell (Rep.)	394,278
Total vote	691,945

Associate Justice, Fifth District, Place 2

Howard G. Wilson (Dem.)	264,846
Pat McClung (Rep.)	423,811
Total vote	688,657

Associate Justice, Fifth District, Place 3 (unexpired term)

Annette Stewart (Dem.)	311,800
Joe Devany (Rep.)	383,482
Total vote	695,282

Associate Justice, Fifth District, Place 4

Floyd A. Shumpert (Dem.)	259,499
Robert Maloney (Rep.)	424,777
Total vote	684,276

Associate Justice, Fourteenth District

Warren E. Hancock (Dem.)	474,699
Paul C. Murphy (Rep.)	566,201
Total vote	1,040,900

GENERAL ELECTION, 1984

Below are results of the presidential and U.S. Senate races, Nov. 6, 1984. The first column gives the percent of voter turnout in the race for President.

County—	Voter Turnout	President Walter Mondale (Dem.)	Ronald Reagan (Rep.)	U.S. Senator Lloyd Doggett (Dem.)	Phil Gramm (Rep.)
Anderson	64.6	4,747	8,634	5,570	7,747
Andrews	69.9	420	3,918	1,058	3,660
Angelina	66.2	9,054	14,685	10,381	13,462
Aransas	74.3	1,698	4,352	1,948	4,008
Archer	75.2	1,089	2,467	1,371	2,173
Armstrong	77.5	238	791	299	725
Atascosa	62.8	3,547	5,279	3,981	4,710
Austin	70.9	1,941	4,872	2,247	4,467
Bailey	70.3	684	1,888	838	1,562
Bandera	74.9	771	3,152	1,019	2,866
Bastrop	64.5	4,744	6,439	5,534	5,547
Baylor	68.3	1,019	1,314	1,142	1,158
Bee	62.8	3,659	5,377	3,955	4,899
Bell	70.1	13,322	31,117	15,754	27,911
Bexar	68.9	136,947	203,319	151,535	178,958
Blanco	75.1	700	1,957	921	1,706
Borden	81.8	140	325	148	310
Bosque	75.0	2,046	3,923	2,395	3,583
Bowie	65.2	10,077	18,244	12,098	16,350
Brazoria	69.3	18,609	39,166	22,343	36,487
Brazos	75.5	12,348	34,733	13,595	33,786
Brewster	71.3	1,462	2,066	1,587	1,835
Briscoe	66.4	471	538	542	477
Brooks	59.5	2,702	896	2,760	684
Brown	71.3	4,070	8,468	4,461	8,031
Burleson	68.9	7,578	3,076	2,829	2,786
Burnet	71.8	2,983	5,895	3,558	4,817
Caldwell	64.8	3,401	4,315	3,901	3,741
Calhoun	64.6	2,586	4,434	3,116	3,884
Callahan	69.0	1,305	3,538	1,554	3,275
Cameron	58.6	26,394	29,545	27,781	26,010
Camp	73.9	1,917	2,238	2,094	2,006
Carson	74.6	826	2,412	998	2,229
Cass	65.4	5,053	6,677	5,402	5,938
Castro	64.5	1,009	2,026	1,153	1,824
Chambers	64.7	2,632	4,322	3,168	4,000
Cherokee	63.4	4,494	8,187	5,143	7,165
Childress	68.3	900	1,574	997	1,449
Clay	68.9	1,844	2,569	2,106	2,281
Cochran	67.9	557	1,117	648	957
Coke	69.7	532	1,060	611	965
Coleman	66.9	1,420	2,790	1,659	2,509
Collin	75.9	13,604	61,095	17,673	56,349
Collingsworth	85.2	742	1,396	810	1,219
Colorado	68.4	2,428	4,528	2,639	3,966
Comal	73.5	4,179	13,452	5,146	12,478
Comanche	63.8	2,248	2,678	2,480	2,504
Concho	70.2	580	821	679	702
Cooke	72.6	3,278	8,260	3,794	7,592
Coryell	71.1	3,113	9,056	4,130	2,920
Cottle	62.8	623	507	661	466
Crane	65.0	392	1,473	501	1,338
Crockett	61.1	589	1,094	566	1,051
Crosby	62.1	1,212	1,376	1,319	1,242
Culberson	53.7	407	509	400	457
Dallam	66.8	496	1,594	596	1,455
Dallas	69.0	203,592	405,444	229,649	371,128
Dawson	64.9	1,761	3,685	1,855	3,465
Deaf Smith	63.5	1,485	4,762	1,751	4,379
Delta	64.9	773	1,024	1,070	888
Denton	71.4	16,772	52,865	20,915	48,325
De Witt	67.1	1,882	4,401	2,093	4,063
Dickens	62.2	692	594	749	508
Dimmit	56.3	2,546	1,338	2,598	1,171
Donley	74.9	529	1,297	608	1,179
Duval	57.0	3,748	1,201	3,756	1,037
Eastland	65.5	2,522	4,841	2,808	4,518
Ector	69.6	8,913	31,228	10,644	29,352
Edwards	63.1	159	626	209	545
Ellis	69.1	8,029	16,873	8,983	15,832
El Paso	61.9	51,917	66,114	59,741	57,696
Erath	69.2	3,234	6,122	3,785	5,574
Falls	59.3	2,834	3,133	3,117	2,733
Fannin	60.1	4,399	4,692	4,895	4,130
Fayette	69.2	2,379	5,711	2,906	4,934
Fisher	71.4	1,384	965	1,427	903
Floyd	62.7	1,023	2,092	1,158	1,922
Foard	65.5	448	472	492	398
Fort Bend	73.0	18,729	41,370	21,704	37,425
Franklin	69.8	1,104	1,836	1,207	1,703
Freestone	67.8	2,489	3,624	2,697	3,407
Frio	60.4	2,656	2,003	2,673	1,800
Gaines	60.9	797	2,714	1,047	2,453
Galveston	68.3	36,092	40,262	38,525	36,266
Garza	65.0	521	1,219	597	1,097
Gillespie	74.8	1,137	5,496	1,457	5,239
Glasscock	75.0	128	403	153	392
Goliad	67.9	836	1,540	891	1,402
Gonzales	60.2	2,196	3,962	2,420	3,541
Gray	74.2	2,003	8,955	2,454	8,408
Grayson	68.9	11,803	22,564	13,886	20,327

County	Voter Turnout	President — Walter Mondale (Dem.)	President — Ronald Reagan (Rep.)	U.S. Senator — Lloyd Doggett (Dem.)	U.S. Senator — Phil Gramm (Rep.)
Gregg	69.9	10,700	29,697	12,346	27,004
Grimes	66.2	2,370	3,365	2,502	3,148
Guadalupe	72.6	5,060	14,362	6,191	12,961
Hale	68.4	3,202	7,670	3,292	7,150
Hall	66.5	984	1,058	1,044	894
Hamilton	68.7	1,130	2,118	1,354	1,882
Hansford	75.3	259	2,213	365	2,073
Hardeman	64.9	927	1,238	960	1,034
Hardin	57.9	6,782	8,380	7,453	7,706
Harris	67.3	334,135	536,029	367,293	493,518
Harrison	63.0	7,773	12,619	8,161	11,566
Hartley	77.8	356	1,419	424	1,341
Haskell	66.7	1,434	1,701	1,528	1,540
Hays	70.8	6,663	12,467	8,684	10,435
Hemphill	75.2	413	1,650	496	1,498
Henderson	67.3	7,302	12,725	8,492	11,380
Hidalgo	57.9	44,141	35,059	44,702	31,792
Hill	62.7	3,420	5,344	3,690	5,095
Hockley	63.5	2,044	5,462	2,535	4,980
Hood	72.6	3,063	6,817	3,489	6,398
Hopkins	69.1	3,707	5,772	3,975	5,416
Houston	64.3	3,275	4,542	3,593	4,065
Howard	67.9	4,115	7,519	4,676	6,944
Hudspeth	72.6	362	557	387	439
Hunt	66.7	6,971	14,303	8,293	12,795
Hutchinson	73.0	2,052	9,078	2,633	8,400
Irion	81.5	199	619	266	544
Jack	63.4	945	1,825	1,097	1,653
Jackson	69.9	1,804	3,661	2,085	3,230
Jasper	62.1	5,787	5,965	6,363	5,228
Jeff Davis	72.1	299	511	306	409
Jefferson	69.0	54,846	45,124	58,903	41,322
Jim Hogg	57.8	1,703	608	1,791	442
Jim Wells	61.0	7,795	5,896	8,124	5,233
Johnson	70.5	9,148	18,254	10,335	17,114
Jones	64.2	2,343	4,017	2,636	3,687
Karnes	66.2	1,802	3,068	1,960	2,771
Kaufman	65.2	5,554	9,343	6,456	8,329
Kendall	77.5	938	4,568	1,196	4,367
Kenedy	62.9	110	96	110	83
Kent	66.1	253	332	273	309
Kerr	77.2	3,102	11,829	3,701	10,897
Kimble	70.4	442	1,333	474	1,271
King	68.8	53	141	69	124
Kinney	69.7	486	774	569	616
Kleberg	71.4	4,924	5,712	5,014	5,218
Knox	62.9	921	1,027	1,055	875
Lamar	66.2	5,504	9,273	6,650	7,979
Lamb	62.9	1,919	3,892	2,163	3,533
Lampasas	68.7	1,356	3,285	1,624	2,994
La Salle	68.2	1,504	1,007	1,526	827
Lavaca	69.2	2,464	5,058	2,891	4,488
Lee	68.5	1,659	2,967	2,004	2,582
Leon	65.7	1,821	3,207	1,992	2,957
Liberty	67.3	6,292	10,504	7,071	9,490
Limestone	57.2	3,228	4,063	3,393	3,861
Lipscomb	76.0	241	1,461	346	1,321
Live Oak	55.4	1,260	2,481	1,404	2,280
Llano	72.1	1,894	4,042	2,270	3,628
Loving	76.0	16	57	15	55
Lubbock	72.2	18,793	57,151	22,779	53,612
Lynn	61.4	1,009	1,617	1,167	1,446
McCulloch	68.6	1,433	2,060	1,519	1,959
McLennan	67.9	23,206	42,232	26,289	39,067
McMullen	64.0	61	337	67	325
Madison	66.9	1,384	2,158	1,532	1,954
Marion	63.4	2,111	2,336	2,248	2,066
Martin	66.3	512	1,218	569	1,142
Mason	73.2	570	1,168	629	1,097
Matagorda	67.8	5,201	8,452	5,792	7,752
Maverick	45.5	3,063	1,783	3,117	1,495
Medina	66.9	3,053	5,737	3,416	5,223
Menard	67.3	394	725	454	504
Midland	75.1	7,214	33,706	8,281	32,078
Milam	66.2	3,734	4,384	4,251	3,798
Mills	65.8	688	1,262	730	1,016
Mitchell	70.2	1,332	2,007	1,506	1,788
Montague	66.0	2,602	4,406	2,855	4,117
Montgomery	74.9	13,293	41,230	15,704	38,188
Moore	70.6	1,129	4,649	1,419	4,303
Morris	63.3	2,925	2,778	3,086	2,545
Motley	68.9	282	533	324	475
Nacogdoches	66.9	5,594	13,063	6,705	12,079
Navarro	65.3	5,672	7,816	6,177	7,231
Newton	65.6	3,296	2,123	3,538	1,791
Nolan	69.4	2,524	3,608	2,664	3,319
Nueces	67.9	46,721	54,333	49,232	49,784
Ochiltree	74.6	419	3,492	558	3,304
Oldham	73.8	226	762	295	662
Orange	71.9	16,816	15,386	18,156	13,647
Palo Pinto	66.6	3,349	5,701	3,865	5,161
Panola	69.3	3,179	5,676	3,689	4,995
Parker	73.4	6,050	13,647	7,274	12,309
Parmer	71.4	567	2,524	723	2,340
Pecos	65.2	1,596	3,451	1,934	3,034
Polk	65.3	3,898	5,987	4,457	5,416
Potter	71.2	8,365	20,396	9,824	19,273
Presidio	66.6	992	837	963	737
Rains	70.5	1,027	1,560	1,235	1,316
Randall	78.2	6,044	30,249	7,774	28,578
Reagan	63.9	243	1,079	322	989
Real	66.0	360	1,004	462	847
Red River	61.8	2,518	2,979	2,756	2,559
Reeves	58.2	2,396	2,461	2,504	2,228
Refugio	70.0	1,559	2,421	1,738	2,147
Roberts	80.7	106	539	138	498
Robertson	64.6	3,339	2,663	3,470	2,489
Rockwall	72.9	1,639	6,688	2,090	6,172
Runnels	64.0	1,179	2,968	1,464	2,653
Rusk	59.0	4,599	11,081	5,481	10,042
Sabine	44.3	1,940	2,045	2,106	1,816
San Augustine	55.8	1,583	1,937	1,764	1,667
San Jacinto	65.0	2,466	3,174	2,605	2,852
San Patricio	62.8	8,838	11,074	9,160	10,327
San Saba	76.3	1,070	1,566	1,195	1,406
Schleicher	73.8	326	854	394	771
Scurry	71.1	1,564	5,028	1,753	4,829
Shackelford	65.1	415	1,181	496	1,087
Shelby	61.9	3,610	4,863	4,023	4,278
Sherman	79.0	246	1,269	333	1,148
Smith	72.6	15,227	40,740	18,261	37,613
Somervell	72.8	535	1,422	826	1,159
Starr	42.8	5,047	1,658	5,194	1,290
Stephens	65.1	1,046	2,898	1,164	2,750
Sterling	79.2	129	577	185	488
Stonewall	73.1	643	599	695	519
Sutton	65.1	465	1,251	503	1,195
Swisher	68.1	1,642	1,611	1,817	1,370
Tarrant	72.5	120,147	248,050	135,541	228,117
Taylor	72.8	9,528	34,444	11,771	32,290
Terrell	71.4	289	407	315	357
Terry	59.9	1,535	3,181	1,551	3,056
Throckmorton	69.0	388	586	421	557
Titus	70.5	3,631	5,069	4,143	4,466
Tom Green	69.8	8,981	23,847	11,111	21,840
Travis	73.5	44,124	124,944	117,518	101,337
Trinity	58.6	2,115	2,599	2,380	2,238
Tyler	64.7	3,119	3,638	3,398	3,286
Upshur	66.5	4,614	7,325	5,315	6,473
Upton	70.4	380	1,603	522	1,361
Uvalde	60.3	2,482	4,790	2,778	4,309
Val Verde	68.1	3,857	5,909	4,405	5,065
Van Zandt	64.8	4,506	8,474	5,307	7,564
Victoria	67.3	7,037	18,787	7,579	17,241
Walker	69.2	4,263	8,809	4,964	7,998
Waller	57.1	3,828	4,116	4,133	3,843
Ward	69.4	1,168	3,474	1,478	3,257
Washington	68.7	2,483	6,506	2,970	5,964
Webb	51.0	12,308	8,582	15,032	6,370
Wharton	64.5	5,072	8,495	5,876	7,630
Wheeler	66.7	805	2,251	954	2,024
Wichita	72.2	16,009	28,932	18,986	25,856
Wilbarger	69.9	2,011	3,644	2,287	3,264
Willacy	58.9	3,037	2,340	3,128	2,077
Williamson	70.7	9,911	25,774	13,434	21,931
Wilson	63.8	2,829	4,588	3,150	4,044
Winkler	63.1	752	2,213	860	2,083
Wise	68.4	3,856	6,958	4,523	6,260
Wood	70.6	3,449	7,144	4,026	6,454
Yoakum	69.9	456	2,204	656	1,996
Young	70.9	2,203	5,282	2,627	4,823
Zapata	57.0	1,577	1,214	1,723	962
Zavala	53.6	2,937	924	2,889	712
Total	68.3	1,949,276	3,433,428	2,202,557	3,111,348

Other vote in presidential race, 14,826; other vote in senatorial race, 273.
Total presidential vote, 5,397,571.
Total senatorial vote, 5,314,178.

LOCAL GOVERNMENTS

Texas has 254 counties, a number which has not changed since 1931 when Loving County was organized. Loving had 91 population in the 1980 Census, compared with 164 in 1970 and its peak of 285 in 1940. It is the least-populous county in Texas. In contrast, Harris County is the most-populous in Texas and was fifth in the U.S. in 1980 with 2,409,547 population.

Counties range in area from Rockwall's 128 square miles to the 6,169 square miles in Brewster, which is equal to the combined area of the states of Connecticut and Rhode Island.

The Texas Constitution makes a county a legal subdivision of the state. Each county has a commissioners court. It consists of four commissioners, each elected from a commissioner's precinct, and a county judge elected from the entire county. In smaller counties, the county judge retains judicial responsibilities in probate and insanity cases.

Eleven hundred Texas municipalities range in size from fewer than 10 residents to Houston's 1,595,138 in the 1980 Census. More than 80 per cent of the state's population lives in cities and towns meeting the U.S. Census Bureau definition of urban areas.

Texas had 237 municipalities with more than 5,000 population in the 1980 Census. Under law, these cities may adopt their own charters by a majority vote. Cities of less than 5,000 population may be chartered only under the general law.

There were 249 home-rule cities on June 1, 1985, most of them cities with over 5,000 residents. Some of these cities now show fewer than 5,000 residents, because population has declined since they adopted their home-rule charters.

MAYORS AND CITY MANAGERS OF TEXAS CITIES

List below was compiled from questionnaires sent out immediately after the municipal elections in April 1985. Name of city manager is included for those municipalities having that form of government.

Authority by which managers hold their positions is explained by footnotes to which the symbols *, †, ‡ and § refer. If no symbol precedes name of City Manager, it denotes that none was given by Texas Municipal League.

City—	Mayor
Abbott	Ronald E. Kaska
Abernathy	J. Pete Thompson
†City Mgr.,	Frank Russell
Abilene	David Stubbeman
*City Mgr.,	Jim C. Blagg
Ackerly	J. D. Hall
Addison	Jerry Redding
*City Mgr.,	Ronald Whitehead
Adrian	Robt. A. Gruhlkey
Agua Dulce	Robert Sablatura
Alamo	Rodolfo Villarreal
City Mgr.,	Mario A. Espinosa
Alamo Heights (6616 Broadway,	
San Antonio) .	Wm. D. Balthrope
Alba	Wm. H. Cranford
Albany	Wayne Hogan
City Mgr.,	Liston F. Todd
Aledo	Dwight Wilkins
Alice.	Octavio Figueroa Jr.
*City Mgr.,	Roel Valadez
Allen.	Donald Rodenbaugh
*City Mgr.,	Jon McCarty
Alma (Rt. 1, Box 109,	
Ennis)	W. L. Hammonds
Alpine.	Delbert A. Dyke
‡City Mgr.,	T. A. Longman
Alto	Douglas Bradford
Alton (P.O. Drawer 9004,	
Mission)	Rogelio Reyes
Alvarado	Amon T. Adcock
Alvin	Ted Hartman
*City Mgr.,	Donald R. Birkner
Alvord	Tim Coffee
Amarillo	R. P. Klein
*City Mgr.,	John Q. Ward
Ames (Box 1904, Liberty	
75575). .	Malcolm J. Goudeau Sr.
Amherst	Joe A. Miller
Anahuac. . . .	Monroe Krevzer Jr.
City Mgr.,	J. R. Nelson
Andrews	Dr. E. W. Harper
*City Mgr.,	Len L. Wilson
Angleton	B. G. Peck
*City Mgr.,	Clifford Hicks
Angus	
(Rt. 3, Corsicana) .	Tom Keating
Anna	Jon Hendricks
Annetta South	
(Parker Co.)	Carl Robbins
Annona	Bobby L. Brem
City Mgr.,	Carl Wilcox
Anson	Gene Rodgers
Anthony	James J. Stewart
Anton	Louis E. Boothe
City Mgr.,	Larry Conkin
Appleby	N. F. Burt
Aransas Pass	Tommy Knight
*City Mgr.,	Rick Ewaniszyk
Archer City.	Jack Mueller
City Mgr.,	L. B. Boren Jr.

City—	Mayor
Arcola (Fort Bend	
Co.).	Mike R. Saenz
Argyle	Larry D. Alderson
Arlington . . .	Harold E. Patterson
*City Mgr.,	William E. Kirchhoff
Arp.	Vaughn Lowry
Asherton. .	Ramon de la Fuente Jr.
Aspermont	Jack McGough
Athens	E. Herbert Gatlin
*City Mgr.,	Kevin P. Evans
Atlanta	Elston R. Law
*City Mgr.,	Sidney R. Davis
Aubrey	Tim Leslie
Aurora (Rt. 1,	
Rhome)	O. W. McCarty
Austin.	Frank Cooksey
*City Mgr.,	Jorge Carrasco
Austwell	Albert J. Covey
Avery	Walter E. Stinson
Avinger	M. A. Parvino
Azle	C. Y. Rone
*City Mgr.,	Harry H. Dulin Jr.
Bailey	Jewel A. Mims
Baileys Prairie (Box 71,	
Angleton) . . .	Dr. W. D. Reed Jr.
Baird	F. A. Payne
Balch Springs (3117 Hickory Tree,	
Mesquite)	Brent Erickson
City Mgr.,	Mozell Strain
Balcones Heights (123 Altgelt,	
San Antonio) . . .	Kirk K. Colyer
Ballinger	Wayne Irby
*City Mgr.,	Dennis Jones
Balmorhea	Pearl Blakemore
Bandera	Robert W. Cowan
Bangs	Arnett Weeks
City Mgr.,	Frank Starling
Bardwell.	George Grammer
Barry	John W. Braly Sr.
Barstow	Angel Abila
Bartlett.	Wilson Franz
Bastrop	David Lock
‡City Mgr.,	Marvin Patterson
Bay City	Wm. M. Bell
Bayside	T. D. Buchanan
Baytown	Emmett Hutto
*City Mgr.,	Fritz Lanham
Bayview (Box 1640, Los	
Fresnos 78566) .	Gregory Warren
Beach City (Drawer 1345,	
Mont Belvieu) . .	Jim Ainsworth
Beasley. . .	Ervin Randermann Jr.
Beaumont. . . .	William E. Neild
*City Mgr.,	Karl Nollenberger
Beckville	Thomas R. Adams
Bedford	L. Don Dodson
*City Mgr.,	Jim Walker
Beeville	Jesse T. DeRusse
*City Mgr.,	Joe B. Montez
Bellaire	Sam McKinney
*City Mgr.,	William K. Cole
Bellevue	J. W. Horton

City—	Mayor
Bellmead (3015 Bellmead,	
Bellmead 76705) . . .	James Wyatt
*City Mgr.,	Harold Baker
Bells	A. L. Isom
Bellville	Abner E. Jackson
City Mgr.,	John Mumme
Belton.	Barry Couch
*City Mgr.,	Jeff Holberg
Benavides .	Fernando A. Caballero
Benbrook	Jerry Dunn
‡City Mgr.,	Ken Neystel
Benjamin	Vernon McCanlies
§City Mgr.,	Ernie Eaton
Berryville (Rt. 1, Frankston	
75763).	Glenda Kindle
Bertram . . .	Johnnie Mae Wheeler
Beverly Hills (3418 Memorial,	
Waco 76711)	Kenneth Boen
Bevil Oaks (Rt. 1, Box 293,	
Beaumont) . . .	H. C. Davidson
Big Lake.	H. F. Ritchie
City Mgr.,	Tony Willie
Big Sandy	Joe Woodard
Big Spring	Clyde Angel
*City Mgr.,	Donald B. Davis
Big Wells.	Alvaro Escobedo
City Mgr.,	Carol Cottle
Bishop	Joe A. Cisneros
Blackwell	Richard Bell
Blanco	Marge Waxler
Blanket.	Royce Rodgers
Bloomburg	Olan Lundy
Blooming Grove	Don von Hoffman
Blossom	Jerry L. Williams
Blue Mound (1600 Bell,	
Fort Worth)	Dale Jensen
Blue Ridge	Jimmie Hopper
Blum	Homer D. Waller Sr.
Boerne	A. E. Howell Jr.
§City Mgr.,	Ronald C. Bowman
Bogata	John W. Hood
Bonham	Roy Floyd
*City Mgr.,	Tom Taylor
Bonney (Rt. 2, Rosharon	
77584).	Mary M. Coleman
Booker	Neal Flathers
§City Mgr.,	James E. Blankenship
Borger	Frank Selfridge
*City Mgr.,	A. C. Spears
Bovina	James D. Roach
Bowie	John Middleton
§City Mgr.,	H. H. Cunningham Jr.
Boyd	Ronnie T. White
Brackettville. .	William Mendeke
City Mgr.,	Charles Olsen
Brady	John Bucy
§City Mgr.,	Joe C. Benton
Brazoria	Joe Ann Miller
City Mgr.,	K. C. Timmermann
Breckenridge . . .	Roger Wootton
*City Mgr.,	Dwain Tolle
Bremond	Billy Lee Stellbauer

City—	Mayor
Brenham	Dorothy Flisowski
*City Mgr., Leonard Addicks	
Briar Oaks (Box 568,	
Burleson 76028)	Alan W. Myers
Bridge City	John Banken
‡City Mgr., C. R. Nash	
Bridgeport	Walter Hales
Broaddus	W. E. Sheffield
¶Bronson	Eugenia Driskell
Bronte	J. T. Henry
Brookshire	Harry K. Searle
Brookside Village (Box 3008,	
Pearland)	Phillip W. Rutter
Browndell (P.O.	
Jasper)	Madie Williams
Brownfield	T. A. Hicks
*City Mgr., R. C. Fletcher	
Brownsboro	Thomas A. Crow
Brownsville . Emilio A. Hernandez	
*City Mgr., Kenneth Lieck	
Brownwood	Bert V. Massey II
*City Mgr., Virgil Gray	
Bruceville-Eddy	E. B. Firquin
Bryan	Marvin Tate
*City Mgr., E. R. Clark	
Bryson	Willard Schlittler
Buckholts	Frances Fuchs
Buckingham (Box 75,	
Richardson)	E. O. Jackson Jr.
Buda	Peter A. Stone
Buffalo	H. L. Burke
Buffalo Gap	C. D. Anderson
Bullard	Jack Studdard
Bunker Hill (Box 19404,	
Houston)	Shirley T. Inman
City Mgr., Harry E. Uhlig	
Burkburnett	Bill Bonnell
*City Mgr., Gary B. Bean	
Burke (Rt. 1, Box 81	
Diboll)	Tom Treadwell
Burleson	Jerry Boone
*City Mgr., Ron Crabtree	
Burnet	Howard R. Benton
†City Mgr., K. A. Taylor	
Burton	James Powell
Byers	Billy Ray Jones
Bynum	Rosco E. Waller
Cactus	Leon W. Graham
Caddo Mills	Boyd Johnson
Caldwell	William L. Broaddus
‡City Mgr., J. D. Teague	
Callisburg (Rt. 2	
Gainesville)	Bobby McDaniel
Calvert	Cooper Wiese
Cameron	Milton J. Schiller
City Mgr., Lanny C. French	
Campbell	Jack White
Camp Wood	Austin Dean
Canadian . Mrs. Therese Abraham	
†City Mgr., Jody Butler	
Caney City (Rt. 1,	
Malakoff)	Wm. H. Rodgers
Canton	Dr. Dennis Teal
City Mgr., Gerald Turner	
Canyon	Phil Langen
*City Mgr., Glen R. Metcalf	
Carbon	Ted Hamilton
Carmine	Jerry Dean Jacob
Carrizo Springs. Marcelino Costilla	
*City Mgr., Gilbert T. Perales	
Carrollton	Kenny Marchant
*City Mgr., Mike Eastland	
Carthage	Carson C. Joines
*City Mgr., Charles Thomas	
Castle Hills (6915 West Ave., San	
Antonio)	Dr. H. P. Lundblade
‡City Mgr., David R. Seyfarth	
Castroville	Virginia Suehs
City Mgr., Stevan R. Gallegos	
Cedar Hill	Kenneth Lander
‡City Mgr., Gregory T. Vick	
Cedar Park	George B. Bowling
‡City Mgr., Dennis Connelly	
Celeste	J. S. Milton
Celina	Paul W. Duke
City Mgr., Frank Svoboda Jr.	
Center	George W. Ihlo
‡City Mgr., Jeff Ellington	
Centerville . . . Robt. D. Sherbrook	
Chandler	Joy Clark
Channing	Alan Dillingham

City—	Mayor
Charlotte	Ray W. Roby
Chateau Woods (Montgomery	
Co.)	Arnold Farias
Chester	James G. Casper
Chico	Nobie Tucker
Childress	J. B. Holland
‡City Mgr., David Galligan	
Chillicothe	Frank E. Berngen
China	Ronald Kuebodeaux
China Grove (Rt. 1, Box 142,	
Adkins 78101)	John D. Passano
Chireno	Orland Strickland
City Mgr., W. Percy Wilson	
Christine	Adelee Bowen
Cibolo	Bill Little
City Mgr., David Harp	
Cisco	Eris Ritchie
§City Mgr., M. D. Moore	
Clarendon	James Kuhn
Clarksville	L. D. Williamson
†City Mgr., James L. Pryor	
Clarksville City (Box 1209,	
Gladewater) . Harvey G. Griffin	
City Mgr., Billy F. Silvertooth Jr.	
Claude	J. D. Pepper
Clear Lake Shores (Box 75,	
Kemah 77565)	R. S. Larrabee
Cleburne	George W. Marti
*City Mgr., Lloyd E. Moss	
Cleveland	Ronnie McWaters
‡City Mgr., Bill Petropolis	
Clifton	Kent Westley
Clint	G. Michael Goodwin
Clute	Jerry Adkins
*City Mgr., Wm. Pennington	
Clyde	J. G. Bennett
Coahoma	Eleanor Garrett
Cockrell Hill (4125 W. Clarendon,	
Dallas)	H. W. Jakubec
Coffee City (Box 216,	
Frankston 75763)	Wayne Phillips
Coldspring	James H. Sewell
Coleman	J. Hugh Stempel
*City Mgr., Roy McCorkle	
College Station Dr. Gary M. Halter	
*City Mgr., North Bardell	
Colleyville	J. R. Hubbard
City Mgr., C. R. Ballenger	
Collinsville	Cecil D. Miller
Colmesneil	Jonathan Sears
Colorado City	Elmer Martin
*City Mgr., Brenda Tarter	
Columbus	Richard Heffley
†City Mgr., George Purefoy	
Comanche	Johnny Livingston
City Mgr., Wade Pyburn	
Combes	Mrs. Alvice Tucker
Combine (Rt. 2, Box 34, Seagoville	
75159)	Robert Yates
Commerce	W. J. Bell
*City Mgr., Edward Badgett	
Como	Bob Butler
Conroe	Carl Barton Jr.
‡City Mgr., Olen R. Petty	
Converse	Bruce Fricsahahn
‡City Mgr., Kent A. Myers	
Cool (R. Rt., Box 150-FM 113 South,	
Weatherford 76086) Billy C. Page	
Coolidge	Kathy Washburn
Cooper	Richard C. Huie
Coppell	Lou Duggan
‡City Mgr., (vacancy)	
Copperas Cove	Jim French
§City Mgr., Mark Roath	
Copper Canyon (400 Woodland	
Dr., Rt. 2, Lewisville	
75067)	Hugh Meilinger
Corinth (Rt. 3, 2003 S. Corinth,	
Denton, 76201)	
Mrs. Shirley Spellerberg	
Corpus Christi	Luther Jones
*City Mgr., Edward A. Martin	
Corral City (Rt. 2, Box 52,	
Argyle 76226)	Gary Hulstein
Corrigan	M. G. Reily
‡City Mgr., Pee Wee Drake	
Corsicana	Jim Gill
*City Mgr., Craig Lonon	
Cotulla	W. L. Cotulla
¶Cove (Rt. 2, Box 198A,	
Baytown 77520)	Judy Leggett

City—	Mayor
Covington	John H. Milburn
Crandall	Jerry Fields
Crane	Jack Atkinson
§City Mgr., Bill Sanders	
Cranfills Gap	B. T. Hamby
Crawford	Frank Golson
Crockett	Howard Edmiston
*City Mgr., Philip Cook	
Crosbyton	Gary N. Mitchell
§City Mgr., Norton Barrett	
Cross Plains . . . Frank Robertson	
City Mgr., Billy D. Dillard Sr.	
Cross Roads (Rt. 3, Box 435,	
Aubrey)	Mark Coats
Crowell	Robert Kincaid
Crowley	Walton G. Eller
Crystal Beach (Galveston	
Co.)	John R. Stewart
Crystal City. . . Eliseo Sanchez Jr.	
*City Mgr., Jose L. Balderas	
Cuero	Ben E. Prause
*City Mgr., James Pratt	
Cumby	James Strickland
Cushing	R. C. Pace
City Mgr., Jerry L. Bowers	
Cut and Shoot (Rt. 3, Box 440,	
Conroe)	Gene Douget
Daingerfield	Jerry Grainger
§City Mgr., (vacancy)	
Daisetta	Pat Abshier
Dalhart. . . Mrs. Lorraine Wardell	
*City Mgr., Warren K. Driver	
Dallas	A. Starke Taylor
*City Mgr., Charles S. Anderson	
Dalworthington Gardens (2600	
Roosevelt Dr., Arlington	
76016)	Billy Bob Burdette
Danbury	Orvill Hatthorn
Darrouzett	Jack Webster
City Mgr., George H. Pratt	
Dawson	Bobby Nesmith
Dayton	W. M. Moreau
§City Mgr., Louis N. Neumeyer	
Decatur	Bobby Wilson
Deer Park	Jimmy Burke
*City Mgr., Floyd O. Socia	
DeKalb	Billy D. Eubanks
DeLeon	Scottie Campbell
City Mgr., James Minor	
Dell City	Frank D. Gomez
Del Rio	Roger S. Cerny
*City Mgr., Jim Miceli	
Denison	Ronnie Cole
*City Mgr., Jim Stiff	
Denton	Richard O. Stewart
*City Mgr., (vacancy)	
Denver City	Kenneth Brown
City Mgr., Paul Grohman	
Deport	Charles Foster
De Soto	Ernest E. Roberts
*City Mgr., (vacancy)	
Detroit	Dale Miller
City Mgr., Pete D. Wright	
Devers	I. E. Wiser
Devine (3035 S. Teel Dr.,	
78016)	S. R. Malone
Diboll	C. H. Shepherd Jr.
‡City Mgr., Vernon Cupit	
Dickens	Bill Scott
Dickinson	Joseph F. Molloy
City Mgr., Luther Morgan	
Dilley	Mrs. Inez Asher
Dimmitt	Wayne Collins
City Mgr., Paul Catoe	
Dodd City	Johnnie Mills
Dodson . . . . Thurman Crownover	
Domino (Rt. 1, Queen	
City 75572)	Frank Propps
Donna	Jose M. Yanez
*City Mgr., Luciano Ozuna Jr.	
Dorchester	James W. Stewart
Double Oak (Box 1396,	
Lewisville)	Jay Wood
Douglassville	W. A. McCoy
Driscoll	Dan Capehart
Dublin	Jack Pratt
‡City Mgr., David Johnson	
Dumas	Mike Salim
*City Mgr., Larry A. Smith	
Duncanville	Cliff Boyd
*City Mgr., Dan Dodson	

City—	Mayor
Eagle Lake	Elmer A. Struss
‡City Mgr., Robert Klockman	
Eagle Pass	Enrique Montalvo
City Mgr., E. P. Rodrigues	
Early (Rt. 2, Box 360,	
Brownwood)	Earl Rhea
City Mgr., Gordon N. Beck	
Earth	Larry Tunnell
Eastland	C. P. Marshall
*City Mgr., Roy D. Underwood	
East Mountain (Rt. 1, Box	
500, Gilmer)	Ralph B. Collins
Easton	E. T. Bell
East Tawakoni (Rt. 1,	
Lone Oak)	Allen Blair
Eastvale (Rt. 3, Box 358,	
Lewisville 75067)	Bert Eubank
Ector	Linwood Hugue
Edcouch	E. Jackson
City Mgr., Antonio Barco	
Eddy (See Bruceville-Eddy)	
Eden	James C. Schumann
Edgecliff Village (1605 Edgecliff	
Rd., Fort Worth)	J. H. LaFaver
City Mgr., Charles Talbot	
Edgewood	Fred Hutchins
Edinburg	Richard R. Alamia
*City Mgr., A. Brent Branham	
Edmonson	Don Ketchum
Edna	Richard E. Browning
*City Mgr., Larry Keesler	
Edom (Rt. 2, Box 298C, Ben	
Wheeler 75754)D. Morris Brantley	
El Campo	R. Cecil Davis
*City Mgr., Robert R. Lundy	
Eldorado	Bob Lester
Electra	Ray B. Dickey Sr.
*City Mgr., Roger L. Dunlap	
Elgin	Marvin Carter
§City Mgr., Al McDonald	
Elkhart	Bessie M. Durnell
El Lago (P.O. Box 284,	
Seabrook)	Sharon M. Ewen
Elmendorf (Box 247,	
78112)	Simon R. Tarin
El Paso	Jonathan W. Rogers
§City Mgr., K. E. Beasley	
Elsa	Antonio Barco
City Mgr., Ernesto Briones	
Emhouse	Bud Whitehead
Emory	James E. Graham
Enchanted Oaks (Box 517, Mabank	
75147)	Blair Whitelaw
Encinal	John Harvey
Ennis	W. D. Murff
*City Mgr., Steve Howerton	
Estelline	Melvin Long
City Mgr., David Galligan	
Euless	Harold Samuels
*City Mgr., W. M. Sustaire	
Eustace	F. Douglas Barker
¶Evant	Byron L. Standard
Everman	Troy Daffron
Fairfield	W. F. Daniel
Fairview (Box 551,	
McKinney)	F. D. Carvajal
Falfurrias	E. Villarreal Jr.
City Mgr., A. C. Rodriguez	
Falls City	Lonnie N. Tracy
Farmers Branch	John D. Dodd
*City Mgr., Paul M. West	
Farmersville	B. J. Harrison
City Mgr., Ron Holifield	
Farwell	Walter Kaltwasser
Fate	W. E. Crawford
Fayetteville	William Graeter
Ferris	Jimmie Birdwell
Flatonia	Ernest Mica
Florence	Lee Roy Knauth
Floresville	Roy G. Sanchez
§City Mgr., Jack Chaney	
Flower Mound	Andy Bukaty
‡City Mgr., Steven Lewis	
Floydada	Parnell Powell
§City Mgr., Wm. A. Feuerbacher	
Follett	Betty Redelsperger
City Mgr., Kenneth V. Sharpe	
Forest Hill (6800 Forest Hill Dr.,	
Fort Worth)	Donald Walker
City Mgr., Rebecca Stark	

City—	Mayor
Forney	Don T. Cates
Forsan	O. W. Scudday
Fort Gates (Box 127, Gatesville	
76528)	Johnny Williams
City Mgr., Margie Waters	
Fort Stockton	Joe Shuster
†City Mgr., Jessie Garcia	
Fort Worth	Bob Bolen
*City Mgr., Douglas Harman	
Franklin	Carroll McCauley
Frankston	Ronald A. Smith
Fredericksburg	Boyd K. Harper
Freeport	Mark X. Vandaveer
*City Mgr., Earl Heath	
Freer	Malloy A. Hamilton
Friendswood	Ralph L. Lowe
*City Mgr., James C. Morgan	
Friona	Clarence Monroe
†City Mgr., Beelee Goodwin	
Frisco	John Clanton
Fritch	Dane Welch
‡City Mgr., Dan Graves	
Frost	J. O. Williams
Fruitvale	Mrs. Hallie Randall
Fulshear	Edward Dozier
Fulton	Leslie Cole Sr.
Gainesville	Harry M. Roark
*City Mgr., William A. Gaither	
Galena Park	Alvin D. Baggett
Galveston	Janice R. Coggeshall
*City Mgr., Douglas Matthews	
Ganado	James Johnson
Garden Ridge (Rt. 3,	
Box 922, Garden Ridge	
78218)	Paul A. Davis
Garland	Charles R. Matthews
*City Mgr., James K. Spore	
Garrett	J. R. Davenel
Garrison	M. H. Stoddard
Gary	Joe Latham
Gatesville	Creston Brazzil
*City Mgr., Bob Stevens	
Georgetown	Carl Doering
*City Mgr., Leo Wood	
George West	Gene Riser
City Mgr., Brad Arvin	
Gholson (Rt. 5, Box 590,	
Waco)	H. T. Sexton
Giddings	Robert Placke
§City Mgr., Larry Pippen	
Gilmer	Orear Watson
‡City Mgr., T. E. Brymer	
Gladewater	James N. Walker
*City Mgr., H. R. Macomber	
Glenn Heights (Rt. 1, Box 418A,	
De Soto)	Mo Craddock
Glen Rose	Mrs. Charlie J. West
Godley	Jim Roberts
Goldsmith	H. D. Timmons
Goldthwaite	Jesse D. Harper
†City Mgr., Dale Allen	
Goliad	Shirley A. Young
Golinda (Rt. 2, Box 684	
Lorena)	George W. Zinn
Gonzales	Carroll E. Wiley
*City Mgr., Calvin E. Spacek	
Goodrich	Miller Moffett
Gordon	Harold W. Burgett
Goree	George K. Cotton
City Mgr., Jim Cooke	
Gorman	Charles Garrett
Graford	Audrey Altum
Graham	Edwin S. Graham III
*City Mgr., Larry M. Fields	
Granbury	Charles E. Baker
†City Mgr., Robt. D. Brockman	
Grandfalls	J. D. Stocks
Grand Prairie	Jerry Debo
*City Mgr., Bob Blodgett	
Grand Saline	M. P. Pugh Sr.
Grandview	Rudolph C. McDuff
Granger	Dollie Hajda
Granite Shoals (Rt. 1, Box 304E,	
Marble Falls) Clifton E. Anderson	
Grapeland	George M. Bartee
Grapevine	Tom Powers
*City Mgr., James L. Hancock	
Grayburg	Johnie Floyd
Grays Prairie (Rt. 2, Box 627,	
Scurry)	W. G. Cubley

City—	Mayor
Greenville	Bill F. Morgan
*City Mgr., William R. Cook	
Gregory	Celestino Zambrano
Grey Forest (Rt. 15, Box 212, San	
Antonio 78238)	Matt Vyverman
Groesbeck	Jim Longbotham
Groom	Alfred A. Homer
Groves	Sylvester Moore
*City Mgr., A. R. Kimler	
Groveton (Mayor	
Pro Tem)	Melburn Minter
Gruver	J. C. Harris
‡City Mgr., A. J. Ratliff	
Gun Barrel City (P.O.	
Mabank)	Wilson Tippit
Gunter	Foy Wallace
Gustine	Roger L. Oliver
Hale Center	Bob W. Brown
Hallettsville	Troy H. Deavers
City Mgr., Maxine Mikulenka	
Hallsburg (Rt. 7, Box 428, Waco	
76705)	Mrs. Margie Wilbanks
Hallsville	T. Bynum Hatley
Haltom City (Box 14246,	
Fort Worth)	Jack O. Lewis
*City Mgr., Mike Groomer	
Hamilton	J. L. Hamilton
§City Mgr., Cad W. Berry	
Hamlin	Robert Fowler
Happy	Mrs. Mary S. Eakes
Hardin	Arley J. Finley
Harker Heights (120 Harley Dr.,	
Harker Heights)	Danny Hurd
City Mgr., Harold Weiler	
Harlingen	Samuel C. Lozano
*City Mgr., Gavino D. Sotelo	
Hart	Joe D. Bailey
Haskell	Abe Turner
City Mgr., Robert Baker	
Haslet	Odie M. Cowart
Hawkins	Douglas Sexton
Hawley	W. D. Williams
Hays (12631 Red Bud Trail,	
Buda)	Lamont Ramage
Hearne	Baylor Carrington
*City Mgr., Jay Williams	
Heath (200 Laurence Dr., Heath	
75087)	L. Newton Burns
Hebron (Rt. 3, Box 190,	
Lewisville 75056)	Stanley Dozier
City Mgr., C. W. Morris	
Hedley	Jon L. Leggitt
Hedwig Village (955 Piney	
Point, Houston	
77024)	Thomas W. Bartlett
Hemphill	Ronnie L. Felts
City Mgr., Tommy Neal	
Hempstead	Leroy Singleton
Henderson	Lester Brown
‡City Mgr., Jack Dickerson	
Henrietta	Melvin D. Adams
‡City Mgr., George W. Hicks	
Hereford	Wesley S. Fisher
*City Mgr., C. Dudley Bayne	
Hewitt	Tom C. Burke
City Mgr., Doug Henderson	
Hickory Creek (Box 453,	
Lake Dallas)	Lon Brown
Hico	W. W. Rutledge Jr.
Hidalgo	Eduardo C. Vela
City Mgr., Eudocio Garcia	
Higgins	Billy B. Cornett
Highland Park (4700 Drexel Dr.,	
Dallas)	John L. Lancaster III
‡City Mgr., George Patterson	
Highland Village (Rt. 2,	
Lewisville)	Arthur L. Newman
City Mgr., Joseph Gambill Jr.	
Hill Country Village (116 Aspen	
Ln., San Antonio	
78232)	P. Otis Hibler
Hillcrest Village (Box 1172,	
Alvin)	Mrs. Joe B. Jansen
Hillsboro	Ronald Rhoads
*City Mgr., Joe Ed Ward	
Hilshire Village (1206 Pine Chase Dr.,	
Houston 77055)	Ronnie Ralston
Hitchcock	C. E. Clifford
Holiday Lakes (Brazoria	
Co.)	Claude Hunter

City—	Mayor
Holland	G. L. Brisbin
Holliday	Don H. Duke
City Mgr., Gary W. Jones	
Hollywood Park (2 Mecca Dr., San Antonio)	Ruby M. Weinholt
Hondo	Andrew Patterson
Honey Grove	Theo Avery
Hooks	James B. Earnest
Houston	Kathryn J. Whitmire
Howardwick (Box 1143, Clarendon)	Freland D. Davis
Howe	Jerry M. Kirby
City Mgr., Richard M. Britton	
Hubbard	David McClinton
§City Mgr., Harvey H. Schronk	
Hudson (Rt. 5, Box 129, Lufkin)	Lloyd W. Bonner
Hudson Oaks (3211 B Fort Worth Hwy., Weatherford)	J. Y. McClure
Hughes Springs Dr. G. W. Brackeen	
City Mgr., James W. Dean	
Humble	H. E. McKay
‡City Mgr., James P. Baker	
Hunters Creek Village (8433 Katy Fwy., Suite 203, Houston)	Cebe Sue Barnett
Huntington	Don Black
Huntsville	Jane Monday
*City Mgr., Gene Pipes	
Hurst	Bill Souder
*City Mgr., Jim Starr	
Hutchins	Billy Rogers
Hutto	Edmund G. Schmidt
Huxley (Rt. 1, Box 156, Shelbyville)	Billy Ray Jones
Idalou	Curtis Cook
City Mgr., Russell Hamilton	
Impact (Box 1271, Abilene)	Dallas Perkins
Indian Lake (Box 6992, San Benito)	Helen Wilson
Ingleside	J. G. Herrington
City Mgr., Del Lewis	
Iowa Colony (Rt. 1, Box 218, Rosharon)	Maurice Bright
Iowa Park	T. W. Hunter
‡City Mgr., James Barrington	
Iraan	Rick Rylander
City Mgr., Howard Floyd	
Iredell	Mrs. Ellen L. Bishop
Irving	Bobby Joe Raper
*City Mgr., Jack D. Huffman	
Italy	John P. Goodman
Itasca	Rodney Adams
City Mgr., David Bowman	
Jacinto City (10301 Market, Houston)	Mike Blasingame
§City Mgr., Joann Griggs	
Jacksboro	F. C. Heard
‡City Mgr., Jerry R. Lewis	
Jacksonville	R. L. Nichols
*City Mgr., Gordon C. Pierce	
Jamaica Beach (Galveston County)	Jack Westbrook
City Mgr., Joan Walstad	
Jasper	F. R. Lindsey Jr.
*City Mgr., Wayne DuBose	
Jayton	T. R. Smith
Jefferson	Ruel D. Young Sr.
Jersey Village (16501 Jersey Dr., Houston)	Carl A. Norman Jr.
Jewett	C. R. Beddingfield
Joaquin	Steve Hughes
Johnson City	Kermit Roeder
Jones Creek (Brazoria Co.)	Lawrence A. Willis
Josephine	John T. Lemley
City Mgr., Jane Daugherty	
Joshua	Opal Brawner
Jourdanton	Austin Teutsch
§City Mgr., Louis C. Tarazon	
Junction	W. K. Blackburn
‡City Mgr., Raymond M. Litton	
Justin	Louis F. Tate
Karnes City	Benhardt Ahrens
Katy	Johnny Nelson
Kaufman	Harry H. Holcomb
City Mgr., Norman Smith	

City—	Mayor
Keene	Roger L. Ackermann
Keller	Larry Bowman
‡City Mgr., Johnny Sartain	
Kemah	Ben Blackledge
Kemp	Clyde Morton
Kendleton	W. M. McNeil
City Mgr., Glenn Dillard Sr.	
Kenedy	R. C. Franklin
Kenefick (Box 596, Dayton)	Verlon I. Moore Sr.
Kennard	Glenn Westbrook
Kennedale	Danny G. Taylor
‡City Mgr., Ted Rowe	
Kerens	James Kelley
Kermit	O. L. Marshall
‡City Mgr., Randall E. Holly	
Kerrville	A. J. Brough
*City Mgr., J. Louis Odle	
Kilgore	Mickey Smith
*City Mgr., Ronald E. Cox	
Killeen	Allen C. Cloud
*City Mgr., Robert M. Hopkins	
Kingsville	Billie G. Gunter
*City Mgr., George K. Noe	
Kirby (112 Baumann, San Antonio 78219)	J. Thomas Webb
City Mgr., Robert Perez	
Kirbyville	Victor Hamilton
Kirvin	Billie Walthall
Kleberg (Consolidated with Dallas)	
Knox City	Greg Kuehler
City Mgr., Teri Anderson	
Kosse	W. C. Graeber
Kountze	Robert Fife
Kress	Kenneth Hughes
Krugerville (Rt. 1, Box 615 Aubrey 76227)	Bill LaBarr
City Mgr., Marilyn Carrigan	
Krum	Joe D. Cates
Kyle	J. W. Dwyer
City Mgr., Merle D. Wilkins	
Lacoste	George T. Lagleder
Lacy-Lakeview (302 E. Craven, Waco)	Glover Laird
Ladonia	Elgin Fowler
LaFeria	Scott Sloane
City Mgr., Thos. V. Kolterman	
Lago Vista (Travis County)	W. H. Laseter
LaGrange	Charlie Jungmichel
‡City Mgr., J. D. Legler	
LaGrulla	Hector Lozano
Laguna Vista (122 Fernandez, Laguna Vista 78578)	Edna Maye Heinze
La Joya	William Leo
City Mgr., Lucrecio Flores	
Lake Barbara (Consolidated with Clute)	
Lake Bridgeport (Rt. 2, Box 244F, Bridgeport)	Jeanita Carney
Lake City (Box 178, Mathis)	Joe Veit
Lake Dallas	Ronald E. Honse
Lake Jackson	Vick Vickers
*City Mgr., A. A. MacLean	
Lakeport (Box 7728, Longview)	Virgil Miller
Lakeside (Rt. 8, Box 539, Fort Worth) (Mayor Pro Tem)	John Shen
Lakeside City (112 Land's End, Lakeside City 76308)	Joseph H. White
Lake Tanglewood (Rt. 7, Box 35-15, Amarillo)	John C. Ricketts
Lakeview (Merged with Port Arthur)	
Lakeview	Russell J. Payne
Lakeway (104 Cross Creek, Austin)	Kenneth Shepherd
Lake Worth (6720 Telephone Rd., Fort Worth)	Richard W. Trimble
City Mgr., Bob Turner	
La Marque	Jack W. Nash
*City Mgr., Ivan Langford	
Lamesa	D. R. Bethel
*City Mgr., Paul Feazelle	
Lampasas	H. V. Campbell Jr.
§City Mgr., Robert K. Coffelt	

City—	Mayor
Lancaster	Don Welch
*City Mgr., Carl Tomerlin	
La Porte	Norman Malone
*City Mgr., Jack Owen	
Laredo	Aldo Tatangelo
*City Mgr., R. Marvin Townsend	
Latexo	Winfred E. Alexander
La Vernia	Charles Malloy
La Villa	Hector Elizondo
City Mgr., Roberto Garcia	
Lavon	William H. Morrow
La Ward	Thelma Deyton
Lawn	Johnny B. Hudson
League City	Joe L. Lamb
City Mgr., Paul Nutting	
Leakey	J. H. Chisum
Leander	Mrs. Pat Bryson
City Mgr., R. Kimball	
Lefors	R. B. White
Leona	F. L. Thompson
Leonard	Tom Hymer
Leon Valley (6400 El Verde Rd., San Antonio 78238)	Irene Baldridge
§City Mgr., Donald R. Manning	
Leroy	W. H. Janes
Levelland	Kenny Willmon
*City Mgr., M. G. Ingham	
Lewisville	Ann Pomykal
*City Mgr., Bettye Harris	
Lexington	Larry W. Nichols
Liberty	C. Scott Parker
*City Mgr., Roy Bennett	
Lincoln Park (Rt. 1, Box 105, Aubrey)	Roger Pock
Lindale	Hurchal Duncan
City Mgr., Johnny Mallory	
Linden	Ted H. Elders
City Mgr., Sammy C. Wells	
Lindsay	Joe Bezner
Lipan	Ottis Privitt
Little Elm	Charles Boatright
Littlefield	Paul D. Bennett
*City Mgr., George T. Shackelford	
Little River-Academy (Box 521, Little River 76554)	Vernie May
Live Oak (7906 Village Oak Dr., San Antonio)	Ralph E. Cullip
*City Mgr., Charles W. Pinto	
Liverpool	Marjorie Glassford
Livingston	Joe Pedigo
†City Mgr., Tom Nevinger	
Llano	John Landon
City Mgr., George Rogers	
Lockhart	Maxine R. Goodman
‡City Mgr., Cecil Massey	
Lockney	J. D. Copeland
Lomax (Merged with La Porte)	
Lometa	Mary E. McAnelly
City Mgr., Levi Cash III	
Lone Oak	Luther South
Lone Star	C. E. Nichols
Longview	Lou Galosy
*City Mgr., C. Ray Jackson	
Loraine	Tommy Green
Lorena	S. B. Collins
Lorenzo	Don C. Nickson
City Mgr., Leon Moore	
Los Fresnos	Richard Sparks
City Mgr., Tom Brooks	
Lott	Gordon Broome
Lovelady	Troy R. Driskell
Lowry Crossing (360 Bridgefarmer Rd., McKinney 75069)	J. Douglas Roper
Lubbock	Alan Henry
*City Mgr., Larry Cunningham	
Lucas (Rt. 7 McKinney)	Waymon Rose
Lueders	James Neal Shepherd
Lufkin	Pitser H. Garrison
*City Mgr., Harvey Westerholm	
Luling	W. S. Hooper
*City Mgr., T. H. Caffall	
Lumberton (Hardin Co.)	Charles E. Taylor
Lyford	Morris Dodd
Lytle	Joe M. Carter
McAllen	Othal E. Brand
‡City Mgr., Jose Escamilla	
McCamey	John Tucker

City—	Mayor
McGregor	Felix A. Morris
*City Mgr., Kyle H. McCain	
McKinney	Jim Ledbetter
*City Mgr., D. E. Paschal Jr.	
McLean	George W. Terry
McLendon-Chisholm (Rockwall Co.)	Choice Smith
City Mgr., Kay Morse	
Mabank	B. G. Autry
Madisonville	Joe H. Drew
§City Mgr., Joe C. Manning	
Magnolia	D. W. Cloyd
Malakoff	T. D. Morriss
City Mgr., A. M. Thompson	
Malone (Mayor Pro Tem)	Harold Hollifield
Manor	Douglas R. Parker
Mansfield	Wayne Wilshire
§City Mgr., Clayton W. Chandler	
Manvel	R. L. Kitchens
City Mgr., Frank Levoy	
Marble Falls	Kenneth McKinney
‡City Mgr., C. W. Alton	
Marfa	Jane B. Shurley
Marietta	Delton W. Miller
Marion	Clarence Jackson
Marlin	H. B. Stallworth Jr.
‡City Mgr., Harold Underwood	
Marquez	John Madden
Marshall	Lane Strahan
*City Mgr., Tony Williams	
Mart	Mrs. Babe Aycock
Mason	W. B. Aubrey
Matador	Gary L. Lancaster
Mathis	James T. Knight
Maud	Edward M. Holley
Maypearl	James S. Waller
Meadow	Dale Wylie
Megargel	Charlie J. Kulhanek
Melissa	Haley Harlow
Melvin	Tommy Dan Turner
Memphis	Kenneth Dale
Menard	W. A. Wilkinson
City Mgr., James F. Cannon	
Mercedes	Gilberto Dominguez
*City Mgr., Alan Kamasaki	
Meridian	Hugh Trotter
Merkel	Kent Satterwhite
City Mgr., J. A. Sadler	
Mertens	Robert M. Lindloff
Mertzon	John D. Nicholson
Mesquite Mrs. Brunhilde Nystrom	
*City Mgr., C. K. Duggins	
Mexia	Sidney Johnston
*City Mgr., Gerald Yarbrough	
Miami	Tom Stribling
Midland	G. Thane Akins
‡City Mgr., James W. Brown	
Midlothian	George H. Kent
*City Mgr., Howard F. Brown	
Milano	Roger Hashem
Miles	W. A. Smith
Milford	Bobby D. Cooper
Millers Cove (Rt. 3, Mt. Pleasant)	Wayne Miller
Millsap	Alton B. Parker
Mineola	E. M. Bradshaw
Mineral Wells Dr. H. Arthur Zappe	
*City Mgr., Sam Phelps	
Mingus	Joe Bielinski
Mission	Pat Townsend
*City Mgr., Benito Lopez	
Missouri City	John B. Knox
‡City Mgr., David A. Harner	
Mobeetie	Mrs. Leona House
Monahans	Richard J. Hoyer
*City Mgr., Jack Forga	
Mont Belvieu	Fred R. Miller
§City Mgr., Jay Jorden	
Montgomery	Donald E. Duncan
Monticello (Box 369, Mt. Pleasant)	Harold J. Smith
Moody	Bennie Hargrove
§City Mgr., Charleen Dowell	
Moore Station (Rt. 1, Larue 75770)	Matthew Wallace
Moran	Marie Smith
§City Mgr., H. D. Connally	
Morgan	Harold E. Vandiver Jr.
Morgan's Point (P.O. Box 2389, La Porte)	John A. Grimes

City—	Mayor
Morgan's Point Resort (Rt. 1, Box 373, Belton)	Carl P. Brown
†City Mgr., Bill L. Senkel	
Morton	Howell R. Luper
§City Mgr., Albert L. Field	
Moulton	Harry Meyer
Mount Calm	Jack Hawkins
Mount Enterprise	Norman Self
Mount Pleasant	Jerry Boatner
*City Mgr., Van James	
Mount Vernon	Mike Edwards
City Mgr., Jack N. Perrin	
Muenster	Richard Grewing
City Mgr., Joe Fenton	
Muleshoe	Darrell E. Turner
*City Mgr., Dave Marr Jr.	
Mullin	A. C. Spinks
Munday	Doris Dickerson
§City Mgr., W. M. Hertle	
Murchison	Larry Everett
Murphy (205 N. Murphy Rd., Plano 75074)	J. Cyril Poindexter
Mustang (Rt. 3, Corsicana)	E. E. Hobdy Jr.
Nacogdoches	A. L. Mangham Jr.
*City Mgr., Jarvis Ammons	
Naples	Howard Belville
Nash	Montie Williams
Nassau Bay (18100 Upper Bay Rd., Houston 77058)	Gerald Allen
*City Mgr., Howard L. Ward	
Natalia	John L. Hill
Navasota	H. LaVearne Backhus
*City Mgr., Ed Thatcher	
Nazareth	Thomas E. Hoelting
Nederland	H. E. Nagel
*City Mgr., Howard McDaniel	
Needville	John A. Stern
¶Nesbitt (Rt. 5, Box 93, Marshall)	Roy A. Nesbitt
Newark	Robert W. Fowler
New Boston	John H. McCoy
New Braunfels	Barbara Tieken
*City Mgr., Joe A. Michie	
Newcastle	R. B. Maxwell Jr.
New Deal	H. G. Lorenz
New Home	Clifton Clem
City Mgr., Betsy Pridmore	
New Hope (Rt. 10, Box 10, McKinney 75069) Harold J. Dowell	
New London . . Charlie McConnico	
New Summerfield	Bill Poteet
Newton	Charles M. Glover
New Waverly	Danny E. Brown
¶Neylandville, (Rt. 1, Box 242, Greenville 75401)	Robert L. Lee
Nixon	Dr. W. G. Millington
City Mgr., James E. Talley	
Nocona	Lynn Roberts
‡City Mgr., Tommy Sparks	
Nolanville	Warren Broadstreet
Nome	Hugh R. Ferguson
Noonday (Smith Co.) Bennie Smith	
Nordheim	H. R. Mutschler
Normangee	R. G. Grimes
North Cleveland (Box 1191, Cleveland)	Woodrow Squier
Northcrest (613 N. Lacy Dr., Waco)	L. D. Pettey Jr.
Northlake (Rt. 2, Justin 76247)	Bert H. Gibbs
North Richland Hills (4101 Morgan Cir., Fort Worth)	Dan Echols
*City Mgr., Rodger Line	
Novice	J. O. Casey
Oak Grove (Kaufman County)	Richard H. Harris Jr.
Oak Point (Rt. 1, Box 180H, Frisco)	R. W. Hartman
Oak Ridge (Box 1085, Terrell 75160)	O. W. Wurdeman
Oak Ridge North (Montgomery Co.)	Fred Wagner
Oakwood	Gale Brice
O'Brien	Charlene Brothers
Odem	Jessie Rodriguez Sr.
Odessa	John B. Minor
*City Mgr., John D. Harrison	
O'Donnell	Truett Hodnett
Oglesby	Savoy Lawrence

City—	Mayor
Old River-Winfree (Box 1169, Mont Belvieu)	Arthur LaFour
Olmos Park (119 El Prado Dr., San Antonio)	W. W. Altgelt Jr.
†City Mgr., E. Gene Sprague	
Olney	David H. Penn
‡City Mgr., Jack R. Northrup	
Olton	C. J. Givens
Omaha	B. B. Brown
Onalaska	Robert C. Goodson
Orange	James R. Dunaway
*City Mgr., Charles L. Curry	
Orange Grove	Truett L. Thomas
City Mgr., Fred H. Hilmer	
Orchard	Eugene L. Demny
Ore City	Albert J. Hiles
Overton	Leon Bridges
City Mgr., (Vacant)	
Ovilla	Albert Phillips
Oyster Creek (Brazoria Co.)	Clifford L. Guidry
City Mgr., Max Pitts	
Paducah	Leon Fletcher
§City Mgr., Bill Cartwright Sr.	
Paint Rock	Gary Broz
Palacios	Leonard L. Lamar
Palestine	Jack K. Selden Jr.
*City Mgr., Kenneth N. Berry	
Palmer	Michael Greenlee
Palmhurst (Rt. 1, Box 358, Mission)	Sandford E. Orme
City Mgr., Gary Toothaker	
Palm Valley (Cameron Co.)	Bliss Clark
Palmview (Rt. 7, Box 598B, Mission 78572)	Ramiro Vela
Pampa	Sherman Cowan
*City Mgr., Bob Hart	
Panhandle	Leslie L. McNeill
‡City Mgr., Larry D. Gilley	
Panorama Village (98 Hiwon Dr., Conroe 77304) Donald R. Branham	
Pantego (1614 S. Bowen Rd., Pantego 76013)	Hank Bloom
‡City Mgr., Robert T. McDaniel	
Paris	George Fisher
*City Mgr., David H. Doty	
Parker (Rt. 1, Box 36, Allen 75002)	Jack Albritton
Pasadena	John R. Harrison
Pattison	C. Truett Bell
Patton (Rt. 1, Box 500, Splendora 77372)	Charles G. Bailey
Payne Springs (Rt. 2, Box 96, Mabank 75147)	Gary Walsh
Pearland	Tom Reid
*City Mgr., Ronald J. Wicker	
Pear Ridge (Merged with Port Arthur 1977.)	
Pearsall	Ruben Leal
§City Mgr., Andres Garza Jr.	
Pecan Gap	John Reid
Pecos	Frank Sanchez
‡City Mgr., William E. Hopper	
Pelican Bay (Tarrant Co.)	Daniel L. Howard
¶Penelope	Malcolm Svacina
Perryton	Mike R. Richardson
†City Mgr., J. B. Whigham Jr.	
Petersburg	Jim Fox
§City Mgr., Jesse J. Nave	
Petrolia	Paul Ridinger
Pflugerville	Ben H. Boyd
Pharr	Fidencio R. Barrera
‡City Mgr., Victor M. Alonzo	
Pilot Point	Tom W. Porter
City Mgr., Thomas L. Mattis	
Pinehurst (3640 Mockingbird, Orange)	Grady L. Johnson
City Mgr., Curtis F. Jeanis	
Pineland	John O. Booker Jr.
Piney Point Village (7745 San Felipe, #101, Houston)	A. Lee Smith
Pittsburg	D. H. Abernathy
†City Mgr., Winfred T. Newsome	
Plains	T. J. Miller
Plainview	E. V. Ridlehuber
*City Mgr., Jim Jeffers	
Plano	Jack Harvard
*City Mgr., Robert Woodruff Jr.	

City—	Mayor
Pleasanton (Box 209, 78064)	Danny Qualls
‡Acting City Mgr., Cindy Kimball	
Pleasant Valley (Rt. 2, Box 129, Iowa Park)	Leon T. Little
¶Plum Grove (Rt. 4, Box 322, Cleveland 77327)	L. Morrow
Point	W. C. Garrett
Pointblank	C. C. McDougle
Point Comfort.	Trinidad Rocha Jr.
Ponder	Jo Montague
Port Aransas	Dale Bietendorf
‡City Mgr., Joyce Pulich	
Port Arthur	Malcolm Clark
*City Mgr., George E. Dibrell	
Port Isabel	Baldemar U. Alaniz
City Mgr., James R. Elium III	
Portland	Bobby Whittington
*City Mgr., William H. Lewis	
Port Lavaca	Kenneth D. Lester
*City Mgr., M. H. Gildon	
Port Neches	Gary C. Graham Sr.
*City Mgr., Charles E. Norwood	
Post	Giles C. McCrary
§City Mgr., W. G. Pool Jr.	
Post Oak Bend (Rt 4, Box 32, Kaufman)	Floyd Kirby
Poteet	Salvador Almanza Jr.
Poth	Ronald W. Eckel
Pottsboro	Van Davis
Powell	Paul J. Sloan
Poynor	C. C. Morton
Prairie View	Ronald Leverett
Premont	F. Tino Perez
Primera (Box 8445, Primera 78550)	Ronald D. Harwell
Princeton	James S. Funsch
Progreso Lakes (Box 511, Progreso 78579)	William Cain
Prosper	John Cockrell
Putnam	Winford Fry
Pyote	Bob Siekman
Quanah	Charles E. Hurt
Queen City	Charles E. Lawrence
Quinlan	Lois Cagle
Quintana (Rt. 1, 314 Holly, Freeport 77541)	Linde Lowry
Quitaque	Jake Merrell
Quitman	M. T. Shamburger
Ralls	Kirk A. McLaughlin
Rancho Viejo (Cameron Co.)	Walter F. Halleman Jr.
Ranger	Raymond Hart
¶Rangerville (Rt. 4, Box 77, San Benito 78586)	Wayne Halbert
Rankin	W. R. Stafford
Ransom Canyon (Lubbock Co.)	Scott Bolton
Raymondville	Joe Alexandre
City Mgr., C. M. Crowell	
Red Oak	Jean Sheley
Refugio	C. M. Barnhart Sr.
Reklaw	Harlan Crawford
Reno (Lamar Co.)	Myra J. Blount
Reno (Rt. 1, Box 270, Azle 76020)	D. A. Creamer
Retreat (Rt. 3, Corsicana)	Mrs. Frances Robinson
Rhome	David E. Wilson
Rice	Jean Foust
Richardson	Martha E. Ritter
*City Mgr., Bob Hughey	
Richland	Guy Lansford
Richland Hills (3201 Diana Dr., Fort Worth)	David L. Ragan
‡City Mgr., Dennis Woodard	
Richland Springs	Dean Atchison
Richmond	Hilmar G. Moore
§City Mgr., Keith Crawford	
Richwood (215 Halbert, Clute)	Thomas W. Jones
Riesel	Burney B. Mullens
Rio Hondo	Sarah Tatum
Rio Vista	Harold Slaughter
Rising Star	H. V. Burk
River Oaks (4900 River Oaks Blvd., Fort Worth)	Thomas M. Holland
City Mgr., W. C. Ray	
Riverside	Verla S. Cook
Roanoke	John Tidwell

City—	Mayor
Roaring Springs	Eugene H. Watson
Robert Lee	R. D. Vaughan
Robinson (104 W. Lyndale, Waco)	Arthur E. Kackley
Robstown	Julio Garcia Jr.
Roby	W. C. Matthies
City Mgr., Jimmy C. Price	
Rochester	Alton L. Byrd
Rockdale	Bill T. Avrett
‡City Mgr., Elizabeth Fenter	
Rockport	C. H. Mills Jr.
City Mgr., Herman C. Johnson	
Rocksprings	Charles W. Bonham
Rockwall	Leon Tuttle
‡City Mgr., Bill Eisen	
Rocky Mound (Box 795, Pittsburg)	Noble T. Smith
Rogers	W. A. Persky
Rollingwood (3202 Gentry, Austin)	Harry Rogers
§City Mgr., Cindy Selman	
Roma-Los Saenz	Jose C. Saenz
§City Mgr., Andy Canales	
Roman Forest (Box 397, New Caney 77357)	A. D. Davis
Ropesville	Bill Odom
Roscoe	Jean Zetzman
City Mgr., Don Allen	
Rosebud	Ellen Roberts
†City Mgr., Wanda Fischer	
Rose City (370 Rose City Dr., Vidor 77662)	Mary Ann Hargraves
Rose Hill Acres (Box 8285, Lumberton)	David Littleton
City Mgr., Carol Littleton	
Rosenberg	Ben S. Babovec
Ross	K. P. Bryant
Rotan	Jerry A. Marshall
§City Mgr., Kenneth R. Vann	
Round Rock	Mike Robinson
‡City Mgr., Jack A. Harzke	
Round Top	Robert P. Sterk
Rowlett	Bill Payne
*City Mgr., John R. Milford	
Roxton	Lloyd M. Moore
Royse City	Gary Earl Elliott
City Mgr., Erby Campbell	
Rule	R. C. Langford
Runaway Bay	Horace L. McQuiston
Runge	Daniel L. Esparza
City Mgr., Mike Castro	
Rusk	James B. Long
‡City Mgr., Doug Driggers	
Sabinal	John H. Ilse
Sachse (Rt. 2, Box 153C, Garland)	Jim Anderson
City Mgr., Joel Larkin	
¶Sadler	O. L. Woods
Saginaw	J. D. Johnson
Saint Hedwig	Albert Strzelczyk
Saint Jo	Westall Williams
Saint Paul (Rt. 1, Wylie 75098)	Dennis Allen
San Angelo	Burt Terrill
*City Mgr., Stephen Brown	
San Antonio	Henry Cisneros
*City Mgr., Louis J. Fox	
San Augustine	J. W. Richey
‡City Mgr., Alton B. Shaw	
San Benito	Cesar Gonzalez
*City Mgr., Domingo Ramirez	
San Diego	Rupert Canales Jr.
San Felipe	E. N. Baxley
Sanford	Douglas Whipkey
Sanger	Nel Armstrong
§City Mgr., Lloyd Henderson	
San Juan	Hector Palacios
*City Mgr., Ricardo Gomez	
San Leanna (Box 86, Manchaca 78652)	R. W. Kidd
San Marcos	Emmie Craddock
*City Mgr., A. C. Gonzalez	
San Perlita	Pete Murphy
City Mgr., Marjorie Champagne	
San Saba	Joe Ragsdale
City Mgr., James Reavis	
Sansom Park Village (5500 Buchanan, Fort Worth 76114)	George Worley
Santa Anna	Joe Guerrero

City—	Mayor
Santa Fe (Box 950, Alta Loma 77510)	John A. Roberts
Santa Rosa	James E. Cameron
Savoy	Thomas A. DeBerry
Schertz	Earl W. Sawyer
‡City Mgr., Jimmy G. Gilmore	
Schulenburg	Leo Kopecky
†City Mgr., Sam Barrington	
Scotland	Albert Hilbers
Scottsville	John P. Verhalen
Seabrook	L. W. Dickerson
*City Mgr., Al Holguin	
Seadrift	Donald G. Holder
Seagoville	Lonnie Hopkins
§City Mgr., Don Hamon	
Seagraves	Glenn Lewis
Sealy	Jim Walters
‡City Mgr., Chas. Hinze Jr.	
Seguin	Betty Jean Jones
Selma (Rt. 20, Box 181B, San Antonio)	Steve Gose
Seminole	Jamiel Aryain
‡City Mgr., Lanny S. Lambert	
¶Seven Oaks (Rt. 1, Leggett 77350)	Viola Jones
Seven Points (Rt. 5, Kemp)	W. V. Taliaferro
Seymour	Charles T. Sessions
Shady Shores (Box 362, Lake Dallas)	Mrs. Olive Stephens
Shallowater	Bill Burgett
Shamrock	Douglas O. V. Rives
†City Mgr., Johnny Rhodes	
Shavano Park (101 Saddletree Rd., San Antonio)	Earl M. McCrary
Shenandoah	Joe McGlaun
Shepherd	Victor A. Schrubb
Sherman	Dean Gilbert
*City Mgr., T. N. Buie	
Shiner	Arthur T. Ward
Shoreacres (619 Shoreacres Blvd., La Porte)	Chas. L. Ritterhouse
Silsbee	E. W. Gilchriest
*City Mgr., Ronald M. Hickerson	
Silverton	A. R. Martin
City Mgr., Jerry Patton	
Simonton	Maurice Berkman
Sinton	Jose A. Gutierrez
*City Mgr., Walter W. Hill Jr.	
Skellytown	Wesley L. Russell
Slaton	Donald R. Sikes
§City Mgr., Jim Estes	
Smiley	L. F. Poehler
Smithville	Bill Davison
¶Smyer	Edmond R. Krizan
Snook	Kim Janke
Snyder	Rod Waller
*City Mgr., John Gayle	
Somerset	K. Dale Hicks
Somerville	Michael A. Rhodes
City Mgr., David Lozano	
Sonora	Billy C. Gosney
†City Mgr., James E. Dover	
Sour Lake	Charlie Lyons Jr.
City Mgr., Gerald Greak	
South Houston (Box 238, Houston)	Al Thiel
Southlake	Lloyd Latta
Southmayd	Betty Perez
South Padre Island (Box 2072, Port Isabel 78578)	Minnie Solomonson
‡City Mgr., John P. Smith	
South Side Place (6309 Edloe, Houston)	David Bellamy
City Mgr., L. L. Hill	
Spearman	C. Ralph Blodgett
†City Mgr., Jim Murray	
Splendora	Jack E. Lucas
¶Spofford	J. B. Herndon
Springlake	Harlon Watson
Springtown	E. L. Lockhart
Spring Valley (1025 Campbell Rd., Houston, 77055)	Diane D. Tate
City Mgr., George R. Parker	
Spur	Dusty Cranford
Stafford	Leonard Scarcella
Stagecoach (Montgomery County)	Barbara Bray
Stamford	Robert Prichard
*City Mgr., Mark S. Watson	

City—	Mayor
Stanton	Danny Fryar
§City Mgr., Jimmy Mathis	
Star Harbor (P.O. Box A.W.,	
Malakoff 75148)	Joe C. Gerard
Stephenville	David Clayton
‡City Mgr., Kurt J. Ackermann	
Sterling City	John Copeland Jr.
City Mgr., Sherry Gartman	
Stinnett	Ronnie E. Griffin
City Mgr., Bruce Titus	
Stockdale	Willard Jordan
§City Mgr., Carl R. Lambeck	
Stratford	John M. Wilson
Strawn	J. C. Chesnut
¶Streetman	J. E. Sims
Sudan	Kenneth Wiseman
Sugar Land	Walter S. McMeans
Sulphur Springs	David Baucom
*City Mgr., David R. Tooley	
Sundown	Randy Winfrey
‡City Mgr., Thomas Adams	
Sunnyvale (Rt. 2, Box 612,	
Mesquite)	Milford Therrell
City Mgr., Robert J. Ewalt	
Sunray	John Humphreys
§City Mgr., Darce Foshee	
Sunrise Beach	
(Llano Co.)	Edward Houy
Sunset Valley (2 Lone Oak Trail,	
Austin)	Larry Hada
Sun Valley (Rt. 2, Box 800, Paris	
75460)	Harley E. Wagnon
Surfside Beach (Brazoria	
Co.)	Robert E. Caraway
Sweeny	A. M. Anderson
Sweetwater	Rick Rhodes
*City Mgr., David Maddox	
Taft	Herbert O. Grebe Jr.
‡City Mgr., Zachary Z. Zoul	
Tahoka	Jim Solomon
‡City Mgr., Carl Reynolds	
Talco	Joe B. Morse
Tatum	M. E. Adams
Taylor	George Ruzicka
*City Mgr., Dan Mize	
Taylor Lake Village	
(113 Cedar Lane Cir., Seabrook	
77586)	James E. Cumming
Teague	Clydell R. Webb
‡City Mgr., Emory Partin	
Tehuacana	E. B. Trotter
Temple	John F. Sammons Jr.
*City Mgr., Jack Parker	
Tenaha	George N. Bowers
Terrell	J. R. Briggs Jr.
*City Mgr., Michael H. Talbot	
Terrell Hills (5100 N. New	
Braunfels, San Antonio	
78209)	George C. Mead
*City Mgr., M. E. Murphy	
Texarkana	Durwood Swanger
*City Mgr., H. Russell Crider	
Texas City	Emmett F. Lowry
Texhoma	Mark Freeman
Texline	John Burns
City Mgr., Bernard Eads	
The Colony	Larry D. Sample
*City Mgr., Janice Carroll	
Thompsons	G. W. Longserre
Thorndale	A. J. Lehman
§City Mgr., Roscoe Conoley	
Thornton	Charles M. Peery
Thorntonville (2414 W. 2nd,	
Monahans)	Bob J. Meek
Thrall	Charles F. Becker
Three Rivers	E. L. Evans
City Mgr., Tom Nance III	
Throckmorton	D. K. Weaver
Tiki Island Village (Galveston	
Co.)	Phillip C. Lipoma
Timpson	Ross Graves
Tioga	Robert E. Adams
Tira (Rt. 3, Sulphur Springs	
75482)	Coy O. Vicars

City—	Mayor
Toco (2103 Chestnut, Brookston	
75421)	Hugh D. Thompson
Todd Mission (Rt. 2, Box 650,	
Plantersville)	George Coulam
Tolar	A. D. Haddock
City Mgr., Howard Nance	
Tomball	Lee Tipton
§City Mgr., Don R. Badeaux	
Tom Bean	Fern Hamm
Tool (Rt. 3,	
Kemp 75143)	G. K. Gustafson
Toyah	Marcus Chaddick
Trent	Randy Hunt
City Mgr., Bruce McGlothlin	
Trenton	William E. Dodson
Trinidad	E. L. Jenkins
Trinity	Dr. Sam R. Barnes
Troup	Zack Taylor
Troy	Robert L. McKee
Tulia	T. A. Hayhurst
*City Mgr., Marshall Shelton	
Turkey	Hubert Price
City Mgr., Jerry Landery	
Tuscola	Robert Knott
Tye	Violet E. Law
Tyler	Charles R. Halstead
*City Mgr., Gary Gwyn	
Uncertain (Rt. 2, Karnack	
75661)	James E. Delmar
Union Grove (Box 1326,	
Gladewater) Mrs. Jessie Boshear	
Universal City (Box 3008, Universal	
City 78148)	Bruce A. Barnard
*City Mgr., Mike Tanner	
University Park (3800 Univ. Blvd.,	
Dallas)	Ed Drake
‡City Mgr., Leland Nelson	
Uvalde	J. D. Goode Jr.
*City Mgr., James Thurmond	
Valentine	Jesus Calderon
Valley Mills	Howard Hillin
Valley View	Mary Bierschenk
Van	V. M. Camper
Van Alstyne	Sherman Taylor
Van Horn	Okey D. Lucas
Vega	Mark Groneman
Venus	James Flatt
Vernon	George E. Maxon Jr.
*City Mgr., Fred H. Hays	
Victoria	Ted B. Reed
*City Mgr., James J. Miller	
Vidor	Dru Stephenson
Waco	Ruben Santos
*City Mgr., David F. Smith	
Waelder	Joe B. Parr
Wake Village (611 Burma Rd.,	
Texarkana)	John J. Forte
Waller	Danny L. Marburger
Wallis	August D. Zurek
Walnut Springs	Robert Shipman
Warren City (Rt. 2, Box 72C,	
Gladewater	
75647)	Claude R. Smith
Waskom	Billy R. Randolph
Watauga (5633 Linda Dr.,	
Keller)	Virgil R. Anthony
Waxahachie	John Snider
*City Mgr., Robert W. Sokoll	
Weatherford	Tom Vick
*City Mgr., Kenneth Reneau	
Webster	Dennis Waggett
‡City Mgr., Frank A. Proctor Jr.	
Weimar	Tommy Brasher
†City Mgr., F. E. Parks	
¶Weinert (Box 245,	
Haskell 76388)	J. E. Jetton
City Mgr., R. M. Walker	
Wellington	Ralph D. Owens
§City Mgr., Glen Taylor	
Wellman	Homer E. Jones
Wells	Homer S. Gibson
Weslaco	Hector Farias
*City Mgr., Hilda R. Adame	
West	William F. Pareya

City—	Mayor
Westbrook	A. G. Board
West	
Columbia	M. A. Brooks
City Mgr., Vicki S. Knight	
Westlake	
(Roanoke P.O.)	Dale L. White
West Lake Hills (1107 West	
Lake Dr., Austin)	Tom H. Taylor
§City Mgr., Richard A. Hargarten	
Westminster	Richard J. Davis
Weston (Rt. 2, Box A58A,	
Celina)	Kennith R. Cowan
West Orange	J. D. Alford
‡City Mgr., Walter Schexnyder	
Westover Hills	
(5834 Merrymount Rd., Fort	
Worth)	Raymond B. Kelly Jr.
West Tawakoni	
(Rt. 1 Quinlan) Helen M. Munday	
West University Place	
(3800 Univ. Blvd.,	
Houston)	Michael L. Parks
‡City Mgr., R. R. Rockenbaugh	
Westworth (311 Burton Hill Rd.,	
Fort Worth 76114)	Jodie Colvard
Wharton	Donald R. Carlson
*City Mgr., Vacancy	
Wheeler	Louis C. Stas
¶White Deer	Virgil D. James
Whiteface	H. J. Harrison
City Mgr., Mary Lou Martin	
Whitehouse	Dale E. Reel
White Oak	Marshall Cline
Whitesboro	Chas. W. Winchester
‡City Mgr., Faye Lynn Anderson	
White Settlement (214 Meadow	
Park Dr., White Settlement	
76108)	James M. Herring
*City Mgr., J. E. Keaton	
Whitewright	Clarence Tillett Jr.
Whitney	Harry Sims Jr.
Wichita Falls	Gary D. Cook
*City Mgr., James P. Berzina	
Wickett	Alvie Pardue
Willis	Carl H. Kleimann
Willow Park	Carl T. Heath Jr.
Wills Point	Richard E. Herrin
City Mgr., Wilson Read	
Wilmer	Billy Wickliffe
Wilson	Jackie Bishop
Windcrest (8601 Midcrown,	
San Antonio	
78239)	Robert O. Whitmore
Windom	Frank Howell
Windthorst	Henry J. Ostermann
Winfield	Jack Gandy
Wink	Maxie Watts
Winnsboro	Lee Ray
City Mgr., L. E. Guess Jr.	
Winona	Virgil R. Hussey
Winters	Randy M. Springer
Wolfe City	Ronald H. Wensel
Wolfforth	Don Bell
Woodbranch (Rt. 1, Box 267, New	
Caney 77357)	W. D. Sumrall Jr.
¶Woodloch (Montgomery	
County)	Mary E. Gilbert
Woodsboro	
Mrs. Marguerite Copeland-Luce	
Woodson	Bobby Mathiews
Woodville	John A. Gilchrist
City Mgr., Walton Davis	
Woodway (P.O. Box 7485,	
Waco)	Paul Hubbard
*City Mgr., Carl S. Dossey	
Wortham	F. B. Covert
Wylie	John W. Akin
‡City Mgr., Gus H. Pappas	
Yantis	Julius Mapes
Yoakum	M. W. Harbus Jr.
*City Mgr., Terry K. Roberts	
Yorktown	George F. Klein
City Mgr., Milton Ledwig	
¶Zavalla	William B. Weeks

*Cities having charter provision for city manager.
†General law cities adopting plan by election.
‡Cities adopting manager plan by ordinance.
§Cities having officer performing duties of manager. These are city secretaries and other paid officials, who are city managers in fact, though not by strict definition of the term. All are places operating under general law.
¶No answer to 1985 questionnaire; data repeated from 1983 listing.

HOME-RULE CITIES

The 249 home-rule cities of Texas are listed below, as reported by the **Texas Municipal League**, Austin, June 1, 1985.

City—	Present Form of Government	Present Form Adopted	*First Charter	City—	Present Form of Government	Present Form Adopted	*First Charter
Abilene	Council-Mgr.	1946	1916	Edinburg	Commission-Mgr.	1949	1949
‡§Addison	…	…	…	Edna	Council-Mgr.	1966	1966
Alamo	Mayor-Council	1978	1978	El Campo	Council-Mgr.	1954	1954
Alamo Heights	Council	1954	1954	Electra	Council	1917	1917
Alice	Council-Mgr.	1949	1949	El Paso	Council	1907	1873
‡Allen	Council-Mgr.			‡§Elsa	…	…	…
Alvin	Council-Mgr.	1963	1963	Ennis	Commission-Mgr.	1956	1913
Amarillo	Commission-Mgr.	1913	1913	Euless	Council-Mgr.	1962	1962
Andrews	Council-Mgr.	1959	1959	Farmers Branch	Council-Mgr.	1956	1956
Angleton	Council-Adm.	1967	1967	Flower Mound	Council-Mgr.	1981	1981
Anson	Council	1920	1913	Forest Hill	Council-Mgr.	1976	1976
Aransas Pass	Council-Mgr.	1951	1951	Fort Worth	Council-Mgr.	1925	1919
Arlington	Council-Mgr.	1949	1920	Freeport	Council-Mgr.	1960	1949
Athens	Council-Mgr.	1966	1960	Friendswood	Council-Mgr.	1971	1971
Atlanta	Council-Mgr.	1968	1968	Gainesville	Council-Mgr.	1950	1920
Austin	Council-Mgr.	1924	1919	Galena Park	Commission	1946	1946
Azle	Council-Mgr.	1971	1971	Galveston	Council-Mgr.	1960	1913
Ballinger	Commission-Mgr.	1963	1963	Garland	Council-Mgr.	1951	1951
Baytown	Council-Mgr.	1948	1948	Gatesville	Council-Mgr.	1966	1966
Beaumont	Council-Mgr.	1919	1913	Georgetown	Council-Mgr.	1970	1970
Bedford	Council-Mgr.	1967	1967	‡George West	Council-Mgr.		
Beeville	Council-Mgr.	1951	1951	Giddings	Council-Mgr.	1981	1981
Bellaire	Council-Mgr.	1949	1949	Gladewater	Council-Mgr.	1955	1955
Bellmead	Council-Mgr.	1961	1955	Gonzales	Council-Mgr.	1957	1957
Belton	Council-Mgr.	1931	1914	Gorman	Commission	1920	1920
‡§Benbrook	…	…	…	Graham	Council-Mgr.	1920	1920
Big Spring	Council-Mgr.	1972	1926	Grand Prairie	Council-Mgr.	1972	1948
Bonham	Commission-Mgr.	1947	1914	Grapevine	Council-Mgr.	1965	1965
Borger	Commission-Mgr.	1930	1927	Greenville	Council-Mgr.	1953	1921
Breckenridge	Commission-Mgr.	1954	1954	Groves	Council-Mgr.	1959	1953
Brenham	Commission-Mgr.	1920	1920	Haltom City	Council-Mgr.	1955	1955
†Bridge City	Council-Mgr.	1974	1974	Harker Heights	Council-Mgr.	1971	1971
Brownfield	Council-Mgr.	1954	1954	Harlingen	Commission-Mgr.	1927	1927
Brownsville	Commission-Mgr.	1915	1915	Hearne	Council-Mgr.	1964	1964
Brownwood	Council-Mgr.	1916	1914	Henderson	Council-Mgr.	1974	1947
Bryan	Council-Mgr.	1917	1917	Hereford	Council-Mgr.	1952	1952
Burkburnett	Commission-Mgr.	1923	1923	‡§Hewitt	…	…	…
Burleson	Council-Mgr.	1969	1969	Highland Park	Council-Mgr.	1975	1975
Cameron	Council	1956	1956	Hillsboro	Council-Mgr.	1962	1915
Canyon	Commission-Mgr.	1959	1959	Hitchcock	Commission	1960	1960
Carrizo Springs	Council-Mgr.	1959	1959	Houston	Council	1946	1913
Carrollton	Council-Mgr.	1961	1961	Humble	Mayor-Ald.	1970	1970
Carthage	Commission-Mgr.	1948	1948	Huntsville	Council-Mgr.	1972	1968
Cedar Hill	Council-Mgr.	1975	1975	Hurst	Council-Mgr.	1956	1956
‡§Center	…	…	…	‡Ingleside	Council-Mgr.		
†Childress	Council-Mgr.	1917	1917	Irving	Council-Mgr.	1952	1952
Cisco	Council-Mgr.	1974	1919	Jacinto City	Council-Mgr.	1980	1980
Cleburne	Council-Mgr.	1950	1914	Jacksonville	Council-Mgr.	1931	1931
‡§Cleveland	…	…	…	Jasper	Council-Mgr.	1967	1964
Clute	Council-Mgr.	1967	1957	Katy	Council-Mgr.	1981	1981
Coleman	Council-Mgr.	1949	1949	Keller	Council-Mgr.	1982	1982
College Station	Council-Mgr.	1952	1952	Kerrville	Council-Mgr.	1942	1942
Colleyville	Council-Mgr.	1977	1977	Kilgore	Commission-Mgr.	1960	1960
Colorado City	Council-Mgr.	1948	1948	Killeen	Council-Mgr.	1949	1949
Commerce	Commission-Mgr.	1954	1954	Kingsville	Commission-Mgr.	1951	1916
Conroe	Mayor-Council	1965	1965	‡§La Grange	…	…	…
Converse	Council-Mgr.	1981	1981	Lake Jackson	Council-Mgr.	1954	1954
Copperas Cove	Council-Mgr.	1979	1979	Lake Worth	Council	1965	1965
Corpus Christi	Council-Mgr.	1945	1926	La Marque	Council-Mgr.	1975	1957
Corsicana	Commission-Mgr.	1956	1913	Lamesa	Council-Mgr.	1945	1945
Crockett	Council-Adm.	1964	1964	Lancaster	Council-Mgr.	1956	1956
Crystal City	Council-Mgr.	1958	1958	La Porte	Council-Mgr.	1967	1949
Cuero	Council-Mgr.	1969	1944	Laredo	Council	1921	1921
†Daingerfield	Council-Mgr.			League City	Council	1962	1962
Dalhart	Council-Mgr.	1960	1960	Levelland	Council-Mgr.	1949	1949
Dallas	Council-Mgr.	1931	1889	Lewisville	Council-Mgr.	1963	1963
Dayton	Council-Mgr.	1976	1976	Liberty	Council-Mgr.	1958	1958
Deer Park	Council-Adm.	1960	1960	Littlefield	Council-Mgr.	1959	1959
De Leon	Commission	1919	1919	‡Live Oak	Council-Mgr.		
Del Rio	Council-Mgr.	1967	1918	Lockhart	Council-Mgr.	1973	1973
Denison	Council-Mgr.	1956	1925	Longview	Council-Mgr.	1923	1923
Denton	Council-Mgr.	1959	1914	Lubbock	Council-Mgr.	1917	1917
De Soto	Council-Mgr.	1969	1969	Lufkin	Commission-Mgr.	1919	1919
Donna	Council-Mgr.	1957	1957	Luling	Council-Mgr.	1977	1977
Dumas	Commission-Mgr.	1969	1955	†McAllen	Commission-Mgr.	1927	1927
Duncanville	Council-Mgr.	1962	1962	McKinney	Council-Mgr.	1959	1913
Eagle Pass	Council-Mgr.	1964	1918	Mansfield	Council-Mgr.	1975	1975
Eastland	Commission-Mgr.	1919	1919	†Marlin	Council-Mgr.	1915	1915

City—	Present Form of Government	Present Form Adopted	*First Charter
Marshall	Commission-Mgr.	1927	1913
Mercedes	Commission-Mgr.	1973	1931
Mesquite	Council-Mgr.	1953	1953
Mexia	Commission-Mgr.	1924	1924
†Midland	Council-Mgr.	1940	1940
‡Midlothian	Council-Mgr.		
Mineral Wells	Council-Mgr.	1966	1913
Mission	Commission-Mgr.	1961	1928
‡Missouri City	Council-Mgr.		
Monahans	Council-Mgr.	1954	1954
Mount Pleasant	Council-Mgr.	1948	1948
Muleshoe	Council-Mgr.	1960	1960
Nacogdoches	Commission-Mgr.	1929	1929
Nassau Bay	Council-Mgr.	1973	1973
Navasota	Commission-Mgr.	1947	1922
Nederland	Council-Mgr.	1955	1955
New Braunfels	Council-Mgr.	1966	1964
North Richland Hills	Council-Mgr.	1964	1964
Odessa	Council-Mgr.	1969	1945
‡§Olney	...	...	...
Orange	Council-Mgr.	1954	1914
Palestine	Commission	1917	1917
Pampa	Commission-Mgr.	1927	1927
Paris	Council-Mgr.	1948	1919
Pasadena	Mayor-Council	1964	1943
Pearland	Council-Mgr.	1971	1971
‡§Pecos	...	...	...
Pharr	Council-Mgr.	1971	1949
Plainview	Council-Mgr.	1964	1920
Plano	Council-Mgr.	1961	1961
‡§Pleasanton	...	...	...
†Port Aransas	Council-Mgr.		
Port Arthur	Council-Mgr.	1932	1915
Portland	Council-Mgr.	1967	1967
Port Lavaca	Council-Mgr.	1956	1956
Port Neches	Council-Mgr.	1967	1955
Quanah	Council	1919	1919
Ranger	Commission-Mgr.	1919	1919
Raymondville	Commission-Mgr.	1955	1955
Richardson	Council-Mgr.	1956	1956
River Oaks	Council	1949	1949
Robstown	Council	1948	1948
Rockdale	Mayor-Council	1978	1978
‡§Rockport	...	...	...
‡§Rockwall	...	...	...
Rosenberg	Council	1960	1956
‡Round Rock	Council-Mgr.		
Rowlett	Council-Mgr.	1979	1979
San Angelo	Council-Mgr.	1915	1915
San Antonio	Council-Mgr.	1951	1914
San Benito	Commission-Mgr.	1920	1920
San Juan	Commission-Mgr.	1975	1975
San Marcos	Council-Mgr.	1967	1967
Santa Fe	Council-Mgr.	1981	1981
Schertz	Council-Mgr.	1974	1974
Seabrook	Council-Mgr.	1979	1979
Seagoville	Council-Mgr.	1969	1969
Seguin	Mayor-Council	1971	1971
Sherman	Council-Mgr.	1915	1915
Silsbee	Council-Mgr.	1956	1956
Sinton	Council-Mgr.	1966	1966
Slaton	Commission	1929	1929
Snyder	Council-Mgr.	1952	1952
Stamford	Council-Mgr.	1918	1918
Stephenville	Council-Mgr.	1961	1961
Sugar Land	Council-Mgr.	1981	1981
Sulphur Springs	Commission-Mgr.	1947	1917
Sweetwater	Commission-Mgr.	1927	1913
Taylor	Commission-Mgr.	1914	1914
Temple	Commission-Mgr.	1922	1922
Terrell	Council-Mgr.	1973	1913
Terrell Hills	Council-Mgr.	1957	1957
Texarkana	Council-Mgr.	1960	1917
Texas City	Commission	1946	1946
The Colony	Council-Mgr.	1978	1978
Tulia	Council-Mgr.	1972	1972
Tyler	Council-Mgr.	1915	1915
Universal City	Council-Mgr.	1972	1972
†Uvalde	Council-Mgr.	1951	1934
Vernon	Commission-Mgr.	1962	1916
Victoria	Council-Mgr.	1957	1915
Vidor	Mayor-Council	1969	1969
Waco	Council-Mgr.	1948	1913

City—	Present Form of Government	Present Form Adopted	*First Charter
Waxahachie	Council-Mgr.	1946	1916
Weatherford	Commission-Mgr.	1956	1918
Weslaco	Commission-Mgr.	1927	1927
West Orange	Council	1956	1956
†West University Place	Commission-Mgr.	1940	1940
Wharton	Council-Mgr.	1970	1970
White Settlement	Council-Mgr.	1968	1954
Wichita Falls	Council-Mgr.	1920	1913
‡Woodway	Council-Mgr.		
Yoakum	Commission-Mgr.	1915	1915

*Present (1985) home-rule amendment (Art. XI, Sec. 5) ratified Nov. 5, 1912.

†Has city manager by ordinance.

‡Date present form of charter adopted and date of first charter adoption not available.

§Data on form of government not available.

Councils of Government

The concept of regional planning and cooperation, fostered by enabling legislation in 1965, has spread across Texas since organization of the **North Central Texas Council of Governments** in 1966.

Legal responsibilities of regional councils include making studies and plans to guide the unified development of their areas, elimination of duplication and promotion of economy and efficiency in coordinated area development. They make recommendations to their member governments and may, upon request, assist in implementation of those plans.

Financing is provided by the local governments, the state and the federal government.

A list of the 24 regional councils, the counties served and the executive director as of June, 1985, follows:

Alamo Area Council of Governments: Counties — Atascosa, Bandera, Bexar, Comal, Frio, Gillespie, Guadalupe, Kendall, Kerr, Medina and Wilson. Executive director, Al Notzon III, 118 Broadway, Ste. 400, San Antonio 78205.

Ark-Tex Council of Governments: Counties — Bowie, Cass, Delta, Franklin, Hopkins, Lamar, Morris, Red River and Titus. Executive director, James D. Goerke, P.O. Box 5307, Texarkana, Texas 75505.

Brazos Valley Development Council: Counties — Brazos, Burleson, Grimes, Leon, Madison, Robertson and Washington. Executive director, Glenn J. Cook, P.O. Box 4128, Bryan 77805-4128.

Capital Area Planning Council: Counties — Bastrop, Burnet, Caldwell, Fayette, Hays, Lee, Llano, Travis and Williamson. Executive director, Richard G. Bean, 2520 IH 35 South, Suite 100, Austin 78704.

Central Texas Council of Governments: Counties — Bell, Coryell, Hamilton, Lampasas, Milam, Mills and San Saba. Executive director, Walton B. Reedy, P.O. Box 729, Belton 76513-0729.

Coastal Bend Council of Governments: Counties — Aransas, Bee, Brooks, Duval, Jim Wells, Karnes, Kleberg, Live Oak, McMullen, Nueces, Refugio and San Patricio. Executive director, John Buckner, P.O. Box 9909, Corpus Christi 78469.

Concho Valley Council of Governments: Counties — Coke, Concho, Irion, Kimble, McCulloch, Menard, Reagan, Sterling, Tom Green and Mason. Executive director, Bob Weaver, P.O. Box 60050, San Angelo 76906.

Deep East Texas Council of Governments: Counties — Angelina, Hardin, Houston, Jasper, Nacogdoches, Newton, Polk, Sabine, San Augustine, San Jacinto, Shelby, Trinity and Tyler. Executive director, E. Ray Hill, P.O. Drawer 1170, Jasper 75951.

East Texas Council of Governments: Counties — Anderson, Camp, Cherokee, Gregg, Harrison, Henderson, Marion, Panola, Rains, Rusk, Smith, Upshur, Van Zandt and Wood. Executive director, Glynn Knight, Stoneridge Plaza Office Bldg., 3800 Stone Rd., Kilgore 75662.

Golden Crescent Regional Planning Commission: Counties — Calhoun, De Witt, Goliad, Gonzales, Jackson, Lavaca and Victoria. Executive director, Patrick J. Kennedy, P.O. Box 2028, Victoria 77902.

Heart of Texas Council of Governments: Counties — Bosque, Falls, Freestone, Hill, Limestone and McLennan. Executive director, Hugh Davis, 320 Franklin Ave., Waco 76701.

Houston-Galveston Area Council: Counties — Austin, Brazoria, Chambers, Colorado, Fort Bend, Galveston, Harris, Liberty, Matagorda, Montgomery, Walker, Waller and Wharton. Executive director, Jack Steele, P.O. Box 22777, Houston 77227.

Lower Rio Grande Valley Development Council: Counties — Cameron, Hidalgo and Willacy. Executive director, Robert A. Chandler, 207 Commerce Bank Bldg., McAllen 78501.

Middle Rio Grande Development Council: Counties — Dimmit, Edwards, Kinney, La Salle, Maverick, Real, Uvalde, Val Verde and Zavala. Executive director, Mike M. Patterson, P.O. Box 702, Carrizo Springs 78834.

North Central Texas Council of Governments: Counties — Collin, Dallas, Denton, Ellis, Erath, Hood, Hunt, Johnson, Kaufman, Navarro, Palo Pinto, Parker, Rockwall, Somervell, Tarrant and Wise. Executive director, William J. Pitstick, P.O. Drawer COG, Arlington 76005-5888.

Nortex Regional Planning Commission: Counties — Archer, Baylor, Childress, Clay, Cottle, Foard, Hardeman, Jack, Montague, Wichita, Wilbarger and Young. Executive director, Edwin B. Daniel, P.O. Box 5144, Wichita Falls 76307.

Panhandle Regional Planning Commission: Counties — Armstrong, Briscoe, Carson, Castro, Collingsworth, Deaf Smith, Donley, Gray, Hall, Hartley, Hemphill, Lipscomb, Moore, Oldham, Parmer, Potter, Randall,

Swisher and Wheeler. Executive director, Jerry S. McGuire, P.O. Box 9257, Amarillo 79105.

Permian Basin Regional Planning Commission: Counties — Andrews, Borden, Dawson, Ector, Gaines, Glasscock, Howard, Martin, Midland, Pecos, Reeves, Terrell, Upton and Ward. Executive director, Ernest W. Crawford, P.O. Box 6391 ATS, Midland 79711.

South East Texas Regional Planning Commission: Counties — Jefferson and Orange. Executive director, Don Kelly, P.O. Drawer 1387, Nederland 77627.

South Plains Association of Governments: Counties — Bailey, Cochran, Crosby, Dickens, Garza, King, Lubbock, Lynn, Motley and Terry. Executive director, Jerry D. Casstevens, P.O. Box 2787, Lubbock 79408.

South Texas Development Council: Counties — Jim Hogg, Starr, Webb and Zapata. Executive director, Amando Garza Jr., P.O. Box 2187, Laredo 78044-2187.

Texoma Regional Planning Commission: Counties — Cooke, Fannin and Grayson. Executive director, Larry Cruise, 10000 Grayson Dr., Denison 75020.

West Central Texas Council of Governments: Counties — Brown, Callahan, Coleman, Eastland, Fisher, Haskell, Jones, Kent, Knox, Mitchell, Nolan, Runnels, Scurry, Shackelford, Stephens, Stonewall, Taylor and Throckmorton. Executive director, Brad Helbert, P.O. Box 3195, Abilene 79604.

West Texas Council of Governments: Counties — Brewster, Culberson, El Paso, Hudspeth and Presidio. Executive director, Justin R. Ormsby, 5th Floor, Two Civic Center Plaza, El Paso 79999.

COUNTY APPRAISERS

The following list of Chief Appraisers for Texas counties was furnished by Ms. Christine Clore, Executive Coordinator, Texas Association of Appraisal Districts, P.O. Box 15997, Austin 78761. It includes the mailing address for each appraiser and is current to June 1, 1985.

Anderson—Elaine Huddleston, Box 279, Palestine 75801
Andrews—David Robinson, 405 N.W. 3rd, Andrews 79714
Angelina—Guy F. Emanis, Box 2357, Lufkin 75901
Aransas—Robert Springer, Box 1786, Rockport 78382
Archer—A. G. Reis, Box 1141, Archer City 76351
Armstrong—Ron Patterson, Drawer D, Claude 79019
Atascosa—Vernon A. Warren, 1010 Zanderson, Jourdanton 78026
Austin—Bart Townsend, 5 E. Main, Bellville 77418
Bailey—vacancy, 104 E. Ave. C, Muleshoe 79347
Bandera—Larry Reagan, Box 1119, Bandera 78003
Bastrop—Lorraine Perry (Interim), Drawer 578, Bastrop 78602
Baylor—Grady Hicks, 101 S. Washington, Seymour 76380
Bee—Blaine Luthringer, Box 1262, Beeville 78102
Bell—Tolly Moore, Box 390, Belton 76513
Bexar—Bill Burnette, 535 S. Main, San Antonio 78204
Blanco—Mrs. Hollis Petri, Box 338, Johnson City 78636
Borden—R. D. Lewis, Box 298, Gail 79738
Bosque—David Cooper, Box 393, Meridian 76665
Bowie—Wayne Hawkins, Box 6527, Texarkana 75505
Brazoria—J. R. Gayle, 500 N. Chenango St., Angleton 77515
Brazos—Buddy Winn, 1121 Villa Maria Rd., Bryan 77801
Brewster—Jerry Ratcliff, Box 1231, Alpine 79831
Briscoe—Carlye Hill, Box 728, Silverton 79257
Brooks—Humberto Rivera, Drawer A, Falfurrias 78355
Brown—Alvis Sewalt, 403 Fisk, Brownwood 76801
Burleson—Elizabeth Plagens, Box 1000, Caldwell 77836
Burnet—Alvin C. Williams, Drawer E, Burnet 78611
Caldwell—Joe Rector, Box 59, Lockhart 78644
Calhoun—Keith Matlock, Drawer CC, Port Lavaca 77979
Callahan—Albert Lovell, Box 1055, Baird 79504
Cameron—Ken Monroe, Box 1945, San Benito 78586
Camp—Vaudene Bennett, Box 739, Pittsburg 75686
Carson—Dianne B. Lavake, P.O. Box 970, Panhandle 79068-0970
Cass—Janelle Clements, Box 16, Linden 75563
Castro—Jerry Heller, 204 S.E. 3rd (Rear), Dimmitt 79027
Chambers—Sherwood Blair, Box 1520, Anahuac 77514
Cherokee—S. R. Danner, Box 494, Rusk 75785
Childress—Nadine Parr, Courthouse Box 13, Childress 79201
Clay—Ross Fry, 101 E. Omega, Henrietta 76365
Cochran—Glen McDaniel, 109 S.E. 1st, Morton 79346
Coke—Patsy N. Dunn, P.O. Box 2, Robert Lee 76945
Coleman—John Skelton, Box 914, Coleman 76834
Collin—D. W. Pauling (Acting), 1201 W. 15th St., Rm. 136, Plano 75075
Collingsworth—Ann Wauer, Courthouse 1st Floor, Rm. 1, Wellington 79095
Colorado—William Youens, P.O. Box 10, Columbus 78934
Comal—Glenn Brucks, Box 1222, New Braunfels 78130
Comanche—Nan Owen, Box 6, Comanche 76442

Concho—Eugene Dillard, Box 68, Paint Rock 76866
Cooke—W. C. Mowell (Acting), 200 W. California, Gainesville 76240
Coryell—Darrell Lisenbe, Box 142, Gatesville 76528
Cottle—Rue Young, Box 459, Paducah 79248
Crane—Mary Lauderbach, 511 West 8th St., Crane 79731
Crockett—W. Tommy Stokes, Drawer H, Ozona 76943
Crosby—Arlice Wittie, Box 479, Crosbyton 79322
Culberson—Sally Floyd, Box 550, Van Horn 79855
Dallam—H. V. Stanley, Box 592, Dalhart 79022
Dallas—Foy Mitchell, 2601 Live Oak, Dallas 75204
Dawson—Tom Anderson, Box 797, Lamesa 79331
Deaf Smith—Fred E. Fox, Box 2298, Hereford 79045
Delta—Mike Shelton, Box 47, Cooper 75432
Denton—Joe Rogers, Box 2816, Denton 76201
DeWitt—Wayne Woolsey, Box 4, Cuero 77954
Dickens—Jerrie Ballard, Box 57, Dickens 79229
Dimmit—Allen Dockery, 409 W. Houston St., Carrizo Springs 78834
Donley—Charles SoRelle, Box 1220, Clarendon 79226
Duval—Ernesto Molina Jr., Box 809, San Diego 78384
Eastland—Steve Thomas, Box 914, Eastland 76448
Ector—James A. Goodwin, Box 4956, Odessa 79760-4956
Edwards—Sondra Madden, Box 378, Rocksprings 78880
Ellis—Gray Chamberlain, Box 878, Waxahachie 75165
El Paso—Cora Viescas, 100 N. Ochoa, El Paso 79901
Erath—Jim Bachus, Box 94, Stephenville 76401
Falls—Charles Belson, Drawer 430, Marlin 76661
Fannin—Ms. Pat Pickett, 401 N. Main, Bonham 75418
Fayette—James Parker, Box 836, LaGrange 78945
Fisher—Teddy Kral, Box 516, Roby 79543
Floyd—Sheila Faulkenberry, County Courthouse Rm. 107, Floydada 79235
Foard—J. H. Gillespie, Box 419, Crowell 79227
Fort Bend—Gene Brewer, Drawer A, Rosenburg 77471
Franklin—Edward Morrow, Box 720, Mt. Vernon 75457
Freestone—Sherrill Minze, Box 675, Fairfield 75840
Frio—Irma Gonzalez, Box 1129, Pearsall 78061
Gaines—Pam Owens, Box 490, Seminole 79360
Galveston—Chuck Wilson, Box 1169, Galveston 77553
Garza—Jean Westfall, Drawer F, Post 79356
Gillespie—Olan Tisdale, Box 168, Fredericksburg 78624
Glasscock—Royce Pruit, Box 89, Garden City 79739
Goliad—E. J. Bammert, Box 34, Goliad 77963
Gonzales—Nancy Seitz, Box 867, Gonzales 78629
Gray—Charles Buzzard, Box 836, Pampa 79065
Grayson—Robert H. Tollison, 124 S. Crockett, Sherman 75090
Gregg—Bill Carroll, Box 6700, Longview 75608
Grimes—Bill Sullivan, Box 489, Anderson 77830
Guadalupe—J. Michael Morris, Box 1226, Seguin 78155
Hale—Linda Jaynes, Box 29, Plainview 79072
Hall—Jim McMorries, 721 Robertson St., Memphis 79245
Hamilton—Doyle Roberts, Box 446, Hamilton 76531

Hansford—Alice Peddy, Box 567, Spearman 79081-0567
Hardeman—Helen Wood, Box 388, Quanah 79252
Hardin—Edwin Barry, Box 670, Kountze 77625
Harris—K. E. Graeber, Box 920975, Houston 77292
Harrison—Donald Duncan, Box 818, Marshall 75670
Hartley—Troy Sloan, Box 405, Hartley 79044
Haskell—John L. Grissom, Box 467, Haskell 79521
Hays—Jesse Click, Courthouse Annex 102 LBJ, Blair Rm., San Marcos 78666
Hemphill—James McCarley, Box 65, Canadian 79014
Henderson—Ron Groom, Box 430, Athens 75751
Hidalgo—Daniel Boone, Box 632, Pharr 78577
Hill—William L. Brown, Box 416, Hillsboro 76645
Hockley—Keith Toomire, Box 1090, Levelland 79336
Hood—Ben Griffin, Box 819, Granbury 76048
Hopkins—Tom Witt, Box 753, Sulphur Springs 75482
Houston—Katherine Keith, Box 1125, Crockett 75835
Howard—F. E. Pereira, Box 1441, Big Spring 79721
Hudspeth—John L. Ferrell, Box 186, Ft. Hancock 79851
Hunt—Henry Popp, Box 1339, Greenville 75401
Hutchinson—William Hodge, Box 1177, Borger 79007
Irion—Frances Grice, Box 980, Mertzon 76941
Jack—Doris Ray, Box 850, Jacksboro 76056
Jackson—James Surratt, 303 N. Wells, Edna 77957
Jasper—David Luther, Co. Courthouse, Jasper 75951
Jeff Davis—John L. Ferrell, Box 373, Fort Davis 79734
Jefferson—Roland Bieber, Drawer 1176, Nederland 77627
Jim Hogg—Ovidio Garza, Box 459, Hebbronville 78361
Jim Wells—Hector Flores, Box 607, Alice 78332
Johnson—Don Gilmore, 109 N. Main, Cleburne 76031
Jones—John Steele, Box 348, Anson 79501
Karnes—Doris Ahrens, 120 W. Calvert, Karnes City 78118
Kaufman—Jackie Self, 116 E. Mulberry, Kaufman 75142
Kendall—Sue Wiedenfeld, Box 788, Boerne 78006
Kenedy—Carl Maultsby, Box 26510, Austin 78755
Kent—Jarri Parker, Box 167, Jayton 79528
Kerr—Juanita Maples, Box 1885, Kerrville 78028
Kimble—Paul Bierschwale, Box 307, Junction 76849
King—Bama Nell Oliver, Box 1007, Guthrie 79236
Kinney—Marcus Tidwell, Box 1377, Brackettville 78832
Kleberg—Adelia Arnold, Box 1027, Kingsville 78363
Knox—Oscar Mangis, Box 2, Benjamin 79505
Lamar—Rodney Anderson (Acting), 1523 Lamar Ave., Paris 75460
Lamb—Jackie F. Samford, Box 552, Littlefield 79339
Lampasas—Dana Ripley, Box 175, Lampasas 76550
La Salle—Juanita Lozano, Drawer 0, Cotulla 78014
Lavaca—Joe Pat Davis, Box 386, Hallettsville 77964
Lee—James L. Dunham, 218 E. Richmond, Giddings 78942
Leon—Tom G. Holmes, Box 536, Centerville 75833
Liberty—L. E. Robinson Jr., Box 712, Liberty 77575
Limestone—Clydene Hyden, P.O. Drawer 831, Groesbeck 76642
Lipscomb—Cecil Gooch, Box 128, Darrouzett 79024
Live Oak—Gayland Wofford, Box MM, George West 78022
Llano—Margie Jung, Box 307, Llano 78643
Loving—Mary Belle Jones, Box 170, Mentone 79754
Lubbock—Dave Kimbrough, Box 10542, Lubbock 79408
Lynn—Dovie Miller, Box 789, Tahoka 79373
McCulloch—Marjorie D. Neal, 104 N. College, Brady 76825
McLennan—Charles Gauer, Box 2297, Waco 76703
McMullen—Mary K. Edwards, Box 38, Tilden 78072
Madison—Dan Singletary, Box 1328, Madisonville 77864
Marion—Linda Rodriguez, Box 690, Jefferson 75657
Martin—Delbert Dickenson, Box 1349, Stanton 79782
Mason—Ann Stapp, Drawer 1119, Mason 76856
Matagorda—Kyle Wilfong, Box 268, Bay City 77414
Maverick—Victor Perry, Box 2628, Eagle Pass 78852
Medina—Leon Mangold, 1102 15th St., Hondo 78861
Menard—Peggy Decker, Box 1058, Menard 76859
Midland—Roland Wilkinson, Dellwood Mall, Suite 160, Midland 79703
Milam—Lynn Gillen, Box 769, Cameron 76520
Mills—Doran Lemke, Box 565, Goldthwaite 76844
Mitchell—Clarence Burt, Box 358, Colorado City 79512
Montague—Wanda Russell, Box 121, Montague 76251
Montgomery—Harold J. Hagan, Box 2233, Conroe 77301
Moore—Joyce Jones, Box 717, Dumas 79029
Morris—B. W. Skipper, Box 563, Daingerfield 75638
Motley—Forrest Campbell, Box 400, Matador 79244
Nacogdoches—Gary Woods, Box 1893, Nacogdoches 75961
Navarro—Harry Hudson, Box 3118, Corsicana 75110
Newton—Linda Crombie, Drawer X, Newton 75966
Nolan—Patricia Davis, Box 1256, Sweetwater 79556
Nueces—George Moff, Co. Courthouse, Suite 302, Corpus Christi 78401

Ochiltree—Terry Symons, 415 S. Ash, Perryton 79070
Oldham—Jen Carter, Drawer 449, Vega 79092
Orange—Faye Gillet, Box 457, Orange 77630
Palo Pinto—John Winters, P.O. Box 250, Palo Pinto 76072
Panola—Jewell Ellis, 1122 West Panola, Carthage 75633
Parker—Larry Hammonds, 118 W. Columbia, Weatherford 76086
Parmer—Ron Procter, Box 56, Bovina 79009
Pecos—Earnestine Smith, Box 237, Ft. Stockton 79735
Polk—J. V. Snook, Box 305, Livingston 77351
Potter—Jim Nugent, Box 7190, Amarillo 79114-7190
Presidio—John Ferrell, Box 879, Marfa 79843
Rains—Charles D. Nugent, Box 71, Emory 75440
Randall—Jim Nugent, Box 7190, Amarillo 79114-7190
Reagan—Christine Gardner, Reagan Co. Courthouse, Big Lake 76932
Real—Fred Thurmond, Box 158, Leakey 78873
Red River—Harold Quillen, P.O. Box R, Clarksville 75426
Reeves—Carol K. Markham, Box 1229, Pecos 79772
Refugio—Bettye Kret, Box 156, Refugio 78377
Roberts—Debbie Stribling, Box 476, Miami 79059
Robertson—Sue Sims, P.O. Box 818, Calvert 77837
Rockwall—Ray Helm, 106 N. San Jacinto, Rockwall 75087
Runnels—Clayton Brazelton, Box 524, Ballinger 76821
Rusk—Melvin Cooper, Box 7, Henderson 75653-0007
Sabine—Jim Nethery, Box 137, Hemphill 75948
San Augustine—Jamie Doherty, 122 N. Harrison, San Augustine 75972
San Jacinto—Ruth Morrison, Box 117, Coldspring 77331
San Patricio—Bennie Stewart, Box 938, Sinton 78387
San Saba—G. P. Adams, Courthouse, San Saba 76877
Schleicher—Ray Ballew, Box 936, El Dorado 76936
Scurry—L. R. Peveler, 2612 College Ave., Snyder 79549
Shackelford—Betty Viertel, Box 565, Albany 76430
Shelby—Harold Robertson, Rt. 5, Box 66, Center 75935
Sherman—Marillyn Albert, Box 239, Stratford 79084
Smith—Michael D. Barnett, 245 South S.E. Loop 323, Tyler 75702
Somervell—Sandra Montgomery, Box 699, Glen Rose 76043
Starr—Heberto Barrera, Box 137, Rio Grande City 78582
Stephens—Mary Sorrells, Box 351, Breckenridge 76024
Sterling—Linda Low, P.O. Box 28, Sterling City 76951
Stonewall—Oscar E. Dickerson, Box 308, Aspermont 79502
Sutton—Rex Ann Fries, 222 N.E. Main St., Sonora 76950
Swisher—Rose Lee Powell, Box 8, Tulia 79088
Tarrant—Dr. Nelson F. Eichman, 1701 River Run, Suite 200, Fort Worth 76107
Taylor—Richard Petree, Box 1800, Abilene 79604
Terrell—E. E. Harkins Jr., Box 747, Sanderson 79848
Terry—J. O. Burnett Jr., Box 426, Brownfield 79316
Throckmorton—Ruby Dunlap, Box 759, Throckmorton 76083
Titus—John Jennings, Box 528, Mt. Pleasant 75455
Tom Green—Elvin W. Field, Box 3307, San Angelo 76902
Travis—James Archer, Box 15997, Austin 78761
Trinity—Mark W. Whitmire, Box 950, Groveton 75845
Tyler—Mary F. Mann, Drawer X, Woodville 75979
Upshur—Louise Stracener, Box 280, Gilmer 75644
Upton—W. J. Campbell Jr., Box 1110, McCamey 79752
Uvalde—Brownie J. Jones, Uvalde County Courthouse, Uvalde 78801
Val Verde—Lillie Sue Stout, Box 1059, Del Rio 78841
Van Zandt—Lady Wright, Box 926, Canton 75103
Victoria—Jim Williams, 1611-A E. North, Victoria 77901
Walker—Grover Cook, Box 1798, Huntsville 77340
Waller—Preston Kelly, Box 159, Katy 77492
Ward—Everette H. Hewett, Box 905, Monahans 79756
Washington—Charles Gaskamp, Box 681, Brenham 77833
Webb—Ezequiel P. Laurel, Box 719, Laredo 78040
Wharton—Kenneth Wright, Box 1068, Wharton 77488
Wheeler—Marilyn Copeland, Box 349, Wheeler 79096
Wichita—Lanier Wilson, Box 5172, Wichita Falls 76307
Wilbarger—Russell A. Garrison, Box 1519, Vernon 76385-1519
Willacy—Agustin Colchado, Rt. 2, Box 256, Raymondville 78580
Williamson—Clendon Thames, Box 1085, Georgetown 78626-1085
Wilson—Leon Stoeltje, Box 849, Floresville 78114
Winkler—John R. Oglesby, Box 1219, Kermit 79745
Wise—Harold Chestnut, Box 509, Decatur 76234
Wood—Carson Wages, Box 951, Quitman 75783
Yoakum—J. D. Brown, Box 748, Plains 79355
Young—Pat Butler, Box 337, Graham 76046
Zapata—Rosalva Villarreal, Box 2315, Zapata 78076
Zavala—Richard Diaz, 101 E. Dimmit, Crystal City 78839

TEXAS COUNTY AND DISTRICT OFFICIALS—TABLE NO. 1

County Seats, County Judges, County Clerks, County Attorneys, County Treasurers, Tax Assessors-Collectors and Sheriffs.

See following pages for another table of county and district officials. The officials listed in this table are elected by popular vote.

County—	County Seat	County Judge	County Clerk	County Attorney	County Treasurer	Assessor-Collector	Sheriff
Anderson	Palestine	*Edward A. Copeland	Mrs. Jo Huddleston	S. D. Carroll	Virginia Salmon	Betty Broyles	Gary Thomas
Andrews	Andrews	Les Brown	James Craddock	James L. Rex	Reeder Price	Louise Williams	Wayne Farmer
Angelina	Lufkin	†Dan Jones	Pauline Grisham	Ed C. Jones	Frona Lee	Douglas Allen	Michael P. Lawrence
Aransas	Rockport	John D. Wendell	Val Jean Eaton	James Anderson Jr.	Marvine D. Wix	Allena Jones	Robert O. Hewes
Archer	Archer City	B. G. Holder	Mrs. Jane Adams	Gary Southard	Betty Tarno	Charles McDaniel	James J. Harney
Armstrong	Claude	Gladys Posey	Betty Parker		Bernice Stephenson	Ronald Patterson	Charles Strange
Atascosa	Jourdanton	O. B. Gates	Elidia Segura	R. T. Franklin	John N. Self	Beth Statler	Tommy Williams
Austin	Bellville	LeRoy H. Grebe	Dorothy Himly	C. L. Smith	Betty Krueger	Eddie Richter	T. A. Maddox
Bailey	Muleshoe	Gordon H. Green	Barbara McCamish	Linda Elder	Dorothy Turner	Kathleen Hayes	Bobby Henderson
Bandera	Bandera	Tommy W. Curbo	Vera King	Sam L. Darden	Mrs. Elizabeth James	Mrs. M. Stevens	Guy V. Pickett
Bastrop	Bastrop	Jack A. Griesenbeck	Joyce Schaefer		Doris Oldfield	Barbara Brinkmeyer	I. R. Hoskins
Baylor	Seymour	Joe Dickson	Amy Hayley	W. E. Liebel	Patricia Coker	Grady Hicks	Wes Hollar
Bee	Beeville	Kinkler Handly	Julia V. Torres	J. T. Kimbrough		Lulan Fraser	Robt. L. Horn
Bell	Belton	‡John Garth	Mrs. Ruby McKee	Pat Ridley	Charles Jones	Tolly Moore	Dan Smith
Bexar	San Antonio	§Tom Vickers	Robert D. Green		Bill Finck	Rudy A. Garza	Harland Compeland
Blanco	Johnson City	Charles Scott	Dorothy Uecker	D. C. Myane	Sandra Danz	Joyce Koch	Holton Burleson
Borden	Gail	Van L. York	Dorothy Browne		Melissa Ludecke	Norman Sneed	Norman Sneed
Bosque	Meridian	Earl W. Page	Patsy O. Mize	David B. Christian	Hugh H. Trotter	Elva Seidel	Denny Proffitt
Bowie	Boston	¶Edward Miller	Mrs. Marylene Megason		Margaret Yates	Aleatha Lyle	Thomas Hodge
Brazoria	Angleton	**E. E. Brewer	Dolly Bailey		Susan Neighbours	Ray Cornett	E. J. King
Brazos	Bryan	††R. J. Holmgreen	F. J. Boriskie	Jim Kuboviak	B. V. Elkins	G. L. Winn	Ronnie Miller
Brewster	Alpine	Tom Connor	Mrs. Shirley A. Scholl	Mrs. Val Beard	Hortencia Ramos	Jerry Ratcliff	George Jones
Briscoe	Silverton	Fred W. Mercer	Bess McWilliams	J. W. Lyon Jr.	Mrs. Mildred J. Reid	Fairy L. McWilliams	Richard Roehr
Brooks	Falfurrias	Joe B. Garcia	Calixto Mora	David T. Garcia	Sulema Garza	R. Castellano	R. Castellano
Brown	Brownwood	Ernest Cadenhead	Nita Bailey	Tanya Cooper	Connie Cline	Mrs. R. McInnis	W. B. Donahoo
Burleson	Caldwell	Woods A. Caperton	Evelyn M. Henry	J. J. Skrivanek III	Katherine Bravenec	Floy Stephens	A. G. Wilhelm
Burnet	Burnet	D. C. Kincheloe	Millie Williams	Jim M. Cross	Katy Gilmore	J. B. Baker	Weldon Buck
Caldwell	Lockhart	‡‡Leonard W. Scott	Kathleen Royal	J. L. Van Horn	Amelia Rizzuto	Mrs. Mattie Robuck	Elvin Hoskins
Calhoun	Port Lavaca	Ralph Wyatt	Mrs. L. McMahan		Sharron Marek	Jo Ann Evins	A. P. Lacy
Callahan	Baird	Mack Kniffen	Darlene Walker	Robert E. McCool	Dora Hounshell	Albert Lovell	Bill Skinner
Cameron	Brownsville	§§M. V. Vela	Mike Sheldon	Benjamin Euresti	Katherine Bravenec	Hugh Riley	Alex F. Perez
Camp	Pittsburg	Larry McCasland	Lollis Irby	Paul Mayben	Virginia Zachary	Brenda Irby	Charles Elwonger
Carson	Panhandle	J. R. Roselius	Mrs. Sue Persons	Ed Hinshaw	Mrs. Peggy Butler	Lloyd Sterling	Connie Reed
Cass	Linden	C. W. Johnson	Wilma O'Rand		Jo Ellen Whatley	Fay Glover	Paul W. Boone
Castro	Dimmitt	Mrs. M. Simpson Jr.	Joy Jones	Jimmy Davis	Oleta Raper	Billy Hackleman	Lonny Rhynes
Chambers	Anahuac	Alma L. Turner	Norma Rowland	E. T. Jenson	Jimmie Moorhead	Irene Clore	C. E. Morris
Cherokee	Rusk	Robert McNatt	Fairy H. Crutshaw	Leland Sutton	Diann Norton	Linda Beard	Allen Horton
Childress	Childress	C. L. Darter	Winona Furr	Ann Musgrove	Tom Newberry	Elton Howard	C. B. Lane
Clay	Henrietta	Bill Nobles	John J. McGee	R. F. Mitchell	Sue S. Brock	Tom Whitley	Jake Bogard
Cochran	Morton	Daniel Keith	Mrs. D. Richardson	J. C. Adams Jr.	Betty Hudson	Betty Akin	C. G. Richards
Coke	Robert Lee	Aubrey Denman	Ettie Hubbard	Bill J. Helwig	Mrs. Jerry Thomason	Maurine D. Vosburg	Marshall Millican
Coleman	Coleman	W. W. Skelton	Glenn Thomas	Joe D. LeMay	Barbara Freeman	Billie Baker	H. F. Fenton
Collin	McKinney	¶¶Wm. J. Roberts	Helen Starnes	H. Owenby	Nathan E. White Jr.	Kenneth L. Maun	Terry Box
Collingsworth	Wellington	Zook Thomas	Helen Gollihugh	Charles Darter	Yvonne Brewer	Ann Wauer	John Rainey
Colorado	Columbus	L. J. Cranek	Annie L. Franta	E. Woolery-Price	Mrs. Martha Bodungen	Evelyn Thomas	Jim Broussard

*Anderson County Court at Law, Bascom W. Bentley III. †Angelina County Court at Law, David M. Cook. ‡Bell County Courts at Law: No. 1, James H. Russell; No. 2, Wayne Bachus. §Bexar County Courts at Law: No. 1, Anthony J. Ferro; No. 2, Charles A. Gonzalez; No. 3, Ray Wietzel; No. 4, Jay Miller; No. 5, Benjamin Samples; No. 6, Robert Lozano; No. 7, Antonio Jimenez; No. 8, Michael Peden; No. 9, Bonnie Reed. Bexar County Probate Courts: No. 1, Keith Burris; No. 2, T. Armour Ball. ¶Bowie County Juvenile Court, Ben Grigson. **Brazoria County Courts at Law: No. 1, Anthony Willy; No. 2, A. R. Mason. ††Brazos County Court at Law, (vacancy). ‡‡Caldwell County Court at Law, E. P. Slater. §§Cameron County Courts at Law: No. 1, Roy Valdez; No. 2, Gilberto Hinojosa. ¶¶Collin County Courts at Law: No. 1, Richard Schell; No. 2, Robert Harkins.

County Officials.—Table No. 1: Judges, Clerks, Attorneys, Treasurers, Tax Assessors, Sheriffs.—(Continued.)

County—	County Seat	County Judge	County Clerk	County Attorney	County Treasurer	Assessor-Collector	Sheriff
Comal	New Braunfels	*Fred Clark	Rosie Bosenbury	Bill M. Reimer	Betty J. Engelhardt	Gloria K. Clennan	Walter Fellers
Comanche	Comanche	Mrs. Bobbye Allen	Mrs. Betty Conway	James L. Edwards	Hazel Carouth	Gay Horton	W. G. Garmon
Concho	Paint Rock	C. J. Dankworth	Margaret T. Taylor	John M. Harrod	Mrs. D. Kirkpatrick	Ernest L. Skeen	Ernest L. Skeen
Cooke	Gainesville	Jim A. Robertson	Frank Scoggin	Janelle Haverkamp	Mrs. Irene Bryant	Joyce Zwinggi	John S. Aston
Coryell	Gatesville	Douglas H. Smith	Mrs. Tribble Shepherd	E. E. Powell Jr.	Mrs. Vesta Leonard	Mrs. Joan Blanchard	Gerald Kitchens
Cottle	Paducah	Vana Tobias	Geneva Bragg	Roy A. Jones	Mrs. Atha Prater	Rue Young	Frank Taylor
Crane	Crane	Charles Blue	Mrs. Doris Bond	Gene Clack	Lena M. Simmons	Raymond Weatherby	Raymond Weatherby
Crockett	Ozona	A. O. Fields	Debbi Puckett	Tom Cameron	Jim Dudley	Tom Stokes	Billy Mills
Crosby	Crosbyton	Robert Work	Floyd McGinnes	John L. Barnhill	Joyce Whitehead	Buran House	Lavoice Riley
Culberson	Van Horn	John Conoly	Rosalinda Abreo	Stephen L. Mitchell	Lola B. McAfee	Mildred Straley	R. E. Upchurch
Dallam	Dalhart	George Briant	Betty Steele		F. E. Payne	Patricia Radford	E. H. Little
Dallas	Dallas	†David Fox	Earl Bullock		Bill Melton	John Childs	Jim Bowles
Dawson	Lamesa	Glenn R. White	Mrs. Billie Bingham	Roland Saul	Mrs. Barbara Stone	Diane Hogg	Bill Horton
Deaf Smith	Hereford	W. Glen Nelson	David Ruland	C. M. Ederer	Vesta M. Nunley	Nell Miller	Joe C. Brown Jr.
Delta	Cooper	Fred Potts	Patsy Barton		Martha Jones	Pauline St. Clair	L. C. Talley
Denton	Denton	‡Buddy Cole	Mary Jo Hill		Claudia Mulkey	H. A. Barnhart	Randy Kaisner
De Witt	Cuero	Robt. B. Sheppard	Ann Drehr	Robert W. Post	Walter Wolf	Ken Wiggins	Bobby McMahan
Dickens	Dickens	H. L. Young	Helen Arrington	David Cave	Mrs. Druline Rape	Mrs. Jerrie Ballard	Doyle King
Dimmit	Carrizo Springs	R. L. Guerra	Mario Z. Garcia	Frank Ponce	Arturo S. Juarez	Esther Z. Perez	Ben Murray
Donley	Clarendon	W. R. Christal	P. C. Messer	Patrick Slavin	Frieda Gray	Sandra Eads	W. J. Thompson
Duval	San Diego	Gilberto Uresti	Oscar Garcia Jr.	Abelardo Garza	Z. Gutierrez III	Arnoldo Cuellar	Raul S. Serna
Eastland	Eastland	Scott Bailey	Joann Johnson		Edith McCullough	Mrs. Nancy Trout	Don Underwood
Ector	Odessa	§Jan Fisher	Lucille Wolz	Gary Garrison	Susie Rippy	Lea Taylor	Bob Brookshire
Edwards	Rocksprings	Neville G. Smart Jr.	Dorothy R. Hatley	Gary C. Gilmer	Mrs. Jewell V. Merritt	Connie Gonzales	Robert Bates
Ellis	Waxahachie	¶Constance McGuire	Mrs. F. Washington	W. G. Knize	Frances Phillips	Bettye Meador	Barney Boyd
El Paso	El Paso	**Pat F. O'Rourke	Hector Enriquez Jr.	Luther Jones	Marshall Finley	James S. Hicks	Leo Samaniego
Erath	Stephenville	Randy Thomas	Mrs. Pauline Chandler	Gale Warren	Mrs. Edith Carr	Jennifer Schlicke	David O. Coffee
Falls	Marlin	Burke Kirkpatrick	Ruth H. Wood	Tom Sehon	Marilyn Ejem	Randy Chandler	Larry Pamplin
Fannin	Bonham	Wm. C. Terry	Margaret Gilbert	Dan Meehan	Florence Keahey	C. W. Bond Jr.	Sam Patton
Fayette	La Grange	Dan R. Beck	Irene Pratka	John W. Wied	Carol Johnson	Gordon F. Baker	Vastine Koopmann
Fisher	Roby	Marshal Bennett	Bettie Rivers	Rudy V. Hamric	Ilene Hale	Teddy Kral	Mickey A. Counts
Floyd	Floydada	Choise Smith	Margaret Collier	Kenneth Bain Jr.	Mrs. G. Orman	Jonelle Fawver	Fred A. Cardinal
Foard	Crowell	Charlie Bell	Cornelia McDaniel	Marshall Capps	Jeannette Bond	Mark Ford	Mark Ford
Fort Bend	Richmond	††J. E. Stavinoha	Dianne Wilson	B. F. Hicks	Kathy Hynson	Marsha P. Gaines	Gus George
Franklin	Mount Vernon	W. B. Meek	Wanda Johnson		Jeanette O'Neal	Shirley Johnson	W. W. Foster
Freestone	Fairfield	H. D. Black Jr.	Mrs. Doris Welch	Robert W. Gage	Mrs. Pat Robinson	Patsy Stroud	James R. Sessions Jr.
Frio	Pearsall	Sid Williams III	Mona Hoyle	J. W. Smith Jr.	Elizabeth Sifuentes	Ysabela Pena	Benny C. Sanders
Gaines	Seminole	Max Townsend	Freida Nichols	Joe McGill	Linda Clark	Johnnie Stanley	Ed Welch
Galveston	Galveston	‡‡Ray Holbrook	Mary J. Christensen	Wm. D. Decker	Richard Kirkpatrick	Charles E. Wilson	Joe M. Taylor
Garza	Post	Giles Dalby	Carl Cederholm	Preston Poole	Mrs. V. B. Gradine	Mrs. Ruth Reno	J. F. Pippin
Gillespie	Fredericksburg	Mark B. Wieser	Mrs. Doris Lange	Gerald W. Schmidt	Reuben Herbort	Leola Brodbeck	David Nehr
Glasscock	Garden City	John E. Robinson	Betty Pate	Rick Hamby	Judy Kingston	Royce Pruitt	Royce Pruitt
Goliad	Goliad	John R. Barnhill	Gail M. Turley	W. B. Davis	LaNell Oehlke	Mrs. Neva Thigpen	F. B. Byrne
Gonzales	Gonzales	H. H. Vollentine	B. J. Fullilove	R. B. Scheske	Kaye Brzozowski	Norma J. DuBose	J. C. Parsley
Gray	Pampa	Carl Kennedy	Mrs. Wanda Carter	R. D. McPherson	Mrs. Jean Scott	Mrs. Margie Gray	R. H. Jordan

*Comal County Court at Law: Ronald D. Zipp. †Dallas County Courts at Law: No. 1, B. F. Coker; No. 2, Candace G. Tyson; No. 3, Mark Whittington; No. 4, Robert Day; No. 5, Bob White. County Criminal Courts: Ben F. Ellis; No. 2, John J. Orvis; No. 3, Michael E. Schwille; No. 4, F. Harold Entz; No. 5, Tom Price; No. 6, Berlaind Brashear; No. 7, John P. McCall; No. 8, John C. Hendrick; No. 9, George B. Shepherd Jr.; No. 10, Bob Moss. County Probate Courts: No. 1, Nikki De Shazo; No. 2, David D. Jackson; No. 3, Joseph E. Ashmore Jr. County Criminal Courts of Appeal: Kenneth Vaughan; No. 2, Tom Fuller. ‡Denton County Courts at Law: No. 1, J. Ray Martin; No. 2, Lon Darley. §Ector County Court at Law: Carol Gregg. ¶Ellis County Court at Law: Roy A. Scoggins Jr. **El Paso County Courts at Law: No. 1, Robert J. Galvan; No. 2, John L. Fashing; No. 3, Jack Ferguson; No. 4, D. Clark Hughes; No. 5, Herbert Cooper. ††Fort Bend County Court at Law: Thomas R. Culver III. ‡‡Galveston County Courts at Law: No. 1, John Thoma; No. 2, Ronald L. Wilson. County Probate Court: Jerome Jones.

County Officials. — Table No. 1: Judges, Clerks, Attorneys, Treasurers, Tax Assessors, Sheriffs. — (Continued.)

County—	County Seat	County Judge	County Clerk	County Attorney	County Treasurer	Assessor-Collector	Sheriff
Grayson	Sherman	*Horace Groff	Paul E. Lee	Steve Davidchik	Dorothy Stroud	John Ramsey	Jack Driscoll
Gregg	Longview	†Henry Atkinson Jr.	Janice Hancock	Phil Brin	James Fuller	Bobby Crawford	Bobby Weaver
Grimes	Anderson	Ben F. Swank Jr.	Trinston Harris	Ben Curd Jr.	Mrs. Lena M. Jarvis	Claude Jolly Jr.	Bill Foster
Guadalupe	Seguin	‡Jas. E. Sagebiel	Cecil Schulze	Elizabeth C. Jandt	Margie Reinhardt	Betty Boyd	Melvin Harborth
Hale	Plainview	Bill Hollars	Mildred Tucker	R. J. Thornton	Harold N. Martin	Mrs. C. Vinson	Charles Tue
Hall	Memphis	J. E. Chappell	Phyllis Dunn	John E. Chamberlain	Sandra Braddock	Patsy R. Jarrell	T. W. Tippett
Hamilton	Hamilton	Betty S. Jenkins	Virginia Lovell	Thos. E. White	Karen S. Tyson	Alvin Kautzsch	Cecil Proctor
Hansford	Spearman	Roy L. McClellan	Amelia C. Johnson	J. L. Hutchison	Verna G. Keim	Helen Dry	R. L. McFarlin
Hardeman	Quanah	Ross Greene	Loraine White	S. R. Watson	Lucille Jobe	Pauline Moore	Chester L. Ingram
Hardin	Kountze	Milton McKinney	Geraldine Collins	B. B. Wright	Henry E. Donelson	J. McCreight	H. R. Holzapfel
Harris	Houston	§Jon Lindsay	Anita Rodeheaver	Mike Driscoll	Henry Kriegel	Carl S. Smith	Johnny Klevenhagen
Harrison	Marshall	¶R. M. Anderson	Glenn Link		Betty Anderson	Marie Noland	Bill Oldham
Hartley	Channing	Joe N. Thomas	Grady Belew	Homer A. Davis	Betty Edwards	J. E. Williams Jr.	J. E. Williams Jr.
Haskell	Haskell	B. O. Roberson	Woodrow Frazier	Charles Chapman	Willie Tidrow	Bobbye Collins	Johnny Mills
Hays	San Marcos	**Walter Burnett	Mrs. L. B. Clayton		Mrs. Dorothy Sims	Ruth Clayton	Alfard Hohman
Hemphill	Canadian	Bob W. Gober	Mrs. G. Vandiver	Charles L. Kessie	Lorene Burton	Gladene Woodside	Billy V. Bowen
Henderson	Athens	Winston Reagan	Joe Dan Fowler	Allen B. Boswell	Carolyn Sorrell	Betty Smith	Charlie Fields
Hidalgo	Edinburg	††Santos Saldana	J. E. Ruiz	O. T. Beaty	Arturo Soliz	Ciro Trevino	Brig Marmolejo
Hill	Hillsboro	Charles R. Herd	Ruth Pelham	Jim Weems	Jewel Burton	Tommy Jo Davis	Brent Button
Hockley	Levelland	R. L. Bowman	Raymond O. Dennis		Jo Beth Hittson	C. Clevenger	Leroy Schulle
Hood	Granbury	Milton Meyer	Anjanette Ables	John Hughes	Buster Damron	Ann Smith	Edwin Tomlinson
Hopkins	Sulphur Springs	H. W. Scott	Mary Attlesey	John F. Perry	Mrs. Betty Green	Jeff Taylor	C. W. Grayson
Houston	Crockett	‡‡H. L. Morgan	Dorothy English	Chester V. Hines	Mrs. Faye Hiroms	Mrs. Odessa Brown	Morris Minter
Howard	Big Spring	Milton L. Kirby	Margaret Ray	Timothy Yeats	Bonnie Franklin	Dorothy W. Moore	A. N. Standard
Hudspeth	Sierra Blanca	Doyle L. Ziler	Patricia Bramblett	Roger L. Moore	Pilar West	Stella C. Kelcy	Richard I. Love
Hunt	Greenville	§§J. W. Green	Jimmy P. Hamilton	Russell Brooks	Allie C. Pearce	Joyce Barrow	Bobby G. Young
Hutchinson	Stinnett	Tom Wicker	Janice Knowles	Wm. D. Smith	June Christian	Mary L. Henderson	Lon Blackmon
Irion	Mertzon	Vic Lindley	Jane Ethridge	Tom Davidson	Mrs. Mildred James	Joyce Gray	Delmon West
Jack	Jacksboro	Bobbie A. Owen	Patsy Ramzy	M. G. Mask	Mrs. R. Abernathie	Betty Cleveland	W. B. Mathis
Jackson	Edna	Sam D. Seale	Mrs. Martha Knapp		Toni Reckaway	Mrs. La Verne Ellison	Harvey Reynolds
Jasper	Jasper	H. E. Kennedy	Evelyn Stott	Guy J. Gray	Reba Galloway	Robert Pace Jr.	Aubrey E. Cole
Jeff Davis	Fort Davis	Ann Scudday	Peggy Robertson			Harvey Adams	Harvey Adams
Jefferson	Beaumont	¶¶R. P. LeBlanc Jr.	R. L. Barnes	E. A. Garza	N. Palmarozzi Jr.	Nick Lampson	R. E. Culbertson
Jim Hogg	Hebbronville	R. J. Vasquez	Lilla Pena	J. Sanchez-Vera	Linda Jo Soliz	Margarita R. Alaniz	Gilberto Ybanez
Jim Wells	Alice	Roberto Guerra	Arnoldo Gonzalez		Adan Valadez Jr.	A. Lozano Jr.	Oscar Lopez
Johnson	Cleburne	Tommy Altaras	Robby G. Goodnight	Dale Hanna	Mildred Honea	W. E. Carroll	Eddy Boggs
Jones	Anson	Roy Thorn	Mrs. Buryl Rye	Joe E. Boaz	L. R. Winkels Jr.	Lucille Higgs	Mike Middleton
Karnes	Karnes City	Kenneth Pearce	Mrs. E. Swize	J. W. Berry	Mrs. C. Blaschke	Ruth Lindsey	R. R. Mutz
Kaufman	Kaufman	Maxine Darst	Jimmy Graham		Mrs. Mildred Becker	Donna Sprague	Robert Harris
Kendall	Boerne	K. D. Muller	Darlene Herrin	Frank Y. Hill Jr.	Joyce F. George	Betty J. Asher	Lee H. D'Spain Jr.
Kenedy	Sarita	J. A. Garcia Jr.	Mrs. Faye Chandler	R. C. Johnston	John W. Turcotte	L. G. Weiss	Jas. M. Chandler Jr.
Kent	Jayton	Mark A. Geeslin	Cornelia Cheyne	Howard Freemyer	Laverna Harrison	Purvis Sorelle	Purvis Sorelle
Kerr	Kerrville	Gordon S. Morriss	Mrs. Patricia Dye	Gary E. Kersey	Dorothy Hilburn	Doris L. Smith	C. A. Greeson
Kimble	Junction	Wilbur R. Dunk	Louise P. Oliver	Donnie J. Coleman	Sue Gibbs	Pat Davis	Pat Davis
King	Guthrie	Herman Oliver	Evelyn Sursa		Kay Criswell	Jim R. Waller	Jim R. Waller

*Grayson County Courts at Law: No. 1, Richard Perkins; No. 2, Lloyd Perkins. †Gregg County Court at Law: Larry Starr. ‡Guadalupe County Court at Law: Fred J. Moore. §Harris County Courts at Law: No. 1, Ed Landry; No. 2, Tom Sullivan; No. 3, Jon Allen Hughes; No. 4, Charles Coussons. County Criminal Courts at Law: No. 1, Bill Ragan; No. 2, Don L. Hendrix; No. 3, Jimmie Duncan; No. 4, Jack Treadway; No. 5, Neil McKay; No. 6, Bob Musslewhite; No. 7, Shelly P. Hancock; No. 8, Neel Richardson; No. 9, Alfred G. Leal; No. 10, Sherman A. Ross; No. 11, Jack Pickren; No. 12, Joe Terracina. Probate Courts: No. 1, William Bear; No. 2, Pat Gregor; No. 3, Jim Scanlan. ¶Harrison County Court at Law: Ray F. Kirkpatrick. **Hays County Court at Law: Howard S. Warner II. ††Hidalgo County Courts at Law: No. 1, Manuel Trejo Jr.; No. 2, G. Jaime Garza; No. 3, Richard H. Garcia. ‡‡Houston County Court at Law: Lynn E. Markham. §§Hunt County Court at Law: Joe Leonard. ¶¶Jefferson County Courts at Law: No. 1, Alfred S. Gerson; No. 2, Tom Maness; No. 3, Donald J. Floyd.

County Officials. — Table No. 1: Judges, Clerks, Attorneys, Treasurers, Tax Assessors, Sheriffs. — (Continued.)

County—	County Seat	County Judge	County Clerk	County Attorney	County Treasurer	Assessor-Collector	Sheriff
Kinney	Brackettville	A. A. Postell	Dolores Raney	Tully Shahan	C. De La Rosa	Norman H. Hooten	Norman H. Hooten
Kleberg	Kingsville	W. C. McDaniel	Ura Dean Ware	W. A. Ewert Jr.	Sopha N. Fitch	Juanita R. Lara	J. S. Scarborough III
Knox	Benjamin	David N. Perdue	Gloria L. West	B. D. Burnett	J. T. Cypert	Oscar Mangis	Morris E. Nix
Lamar	Paris	Brady Fisher	Margaret Coplin	Tom Wells III	Latricia Miller	Theda Corbin	James W. Parker
Lamb	Littlefield	Wayne Whiteaker	Bill Johnson	C. R. Wilkinson	Lucy M. Moreland	Linda Charlton	Elson McNeese
Lampasas	Lampasas	Dorothye Harper	Connie Hartmann	Larry W. Allison	Leona Hurst	Glenda Henderson	Gordon Morris
La Salle	Cotulla	L. Martinez Jr.	Nora M. Tyler	Edward Hargrove	Jimmy P. Patterson	Nora G. Martinez	Darwin D. Avant
Lavaca	Hallettsville	W. D. Roznovsky	Charles Strauss	James W. Carr	T. M. Grahmann	Mary Lee Supak	Robert E. Wurm
Lee	Giddings	E. W. Kraus	Carol Dismukes	Steven W. Keng	Rose M. Fritsche	Arlene D. Kasper	Joe G. Goodson
Leon	Centerville	Robert L. Gresham	Fonsein Gresham	Gary J. Taylor	Wm. D. Lemons	Louise Wilson	R. G. Wilson
Liberty	Liberty	Dempsie Henley	Wanda Barker	A. J. Hartel	Mrs. Vivian Terrell	Laverne Zbranek	E. W. Applebe
Limestone	Groesbeck	Howard Smith	Sue Lown	Pat Simmons	Imogene Arney	Barbara Rader	Dennis J. Walker
Lipscomb	Lipscomb	James P. Shearer	Coeta Sperry	Dana Ehrlich	Louise Mingus	Mary W. Gunn	C. J. Babitzke
Live Oak	George West	Bill Kendall	Mildred James	W. L. Hardwick	Mrs. L. Stainthorpe	Larry Busby	Larry Busby
Llano	Llano	W. R. Miller	H. A. Raesener	L. T. DesChamps	Margaret Hardin	Margie Jung	Gale Ligon
Loving	Mentone	Donald C. Creager	Mrs. Edna Dewees		Faye Busby	Elgin R. Jones	Elgin R. Jones
Lubbock	Lubbock	*Rodrick L. Shaw	Ann Davidson	J. B. Wright	Connie Nicholson	F. A. Stuart	D. L. Keesee
Lynn	Tahoka	J. F. Brandon	C. W. Roberts		Cynthia Bryan	George D. McCracken	Stan Krause
McCulloch	Brady	Boyd Hunt	Rose M. Luttrell	Jacqueline O'Quin	Norma G. Holloway	F. V. Waddill Jr.	Bill Strickland
McLennan	Waco	†Stanley Reniz	Frank Denny	Vic Feazell	Odessa Wells	Gene Prickett	Jack Harwell
McMullen	Tilden	Claude Franklin Jr.	William K. Hodgin	John Oxley	J. R. White	Mary E. Edwards	Eddie M. Reeves
Madison	Madisonville	Jimmy Fite	Joyce M. Coleman	James T. Hileman	Mrs. Inez Bates	Guslyn Hairston	Ed Fannin
Marion	Jefferson	Sonny Haggard	Mrs. Clairece Ford	Robert S. Morris	Mrs. Peggy McLendon	Sarah Wirt	Walter Thomas
Martin	Stanton	Bob Deavenport	Mrs. Doris Stephenson	Harold Schmidt	H. D. Howard	Leona Louder	Dan Saunders
Mason	Mason	Fritz E. Landers	Beatrice Langehennig		Mrs. Jane Hoerster	Don K. Grote	Don K. Grote
Matagorda	Bay City	Burt O'Connell	Sarah Vaughn	John Dickerson III	Suzanne Kucera	James Humphries	S. L. Hurta
Maverick	Eagle Pass	Rudolph Bowles Jr.	E. Sumpter	Rolando Menchaca	M. Reyes Jr.	Esteban Luna	Tom Bowles
Medina	Hondo	‡Jerome H. Decker	Anna Van DeWalle	Hunter Schuehle	Mrs. D. Hartman	Leon Mangold	Alvin Santleben
Menard	Menard	O. H. Lyckman	Kay Kennemer	B. K. Neel	Mickey Crowell	Madelon Highsmith	Floyd Rendon
Midland	Midland	§Wm. B. Ahders	Rosenelle Cherry	Mark Dettman	Dee Thompson	Frances Shuffield	Gary Painter
Milam	Cameron	Gene F. Blake	Willie Mae Wieser	Charles E. Lance	Charlie J. Maddox	Porter Young	Leroy Broadus
Mills	Goldthwaite	T. W. Johnson	Walter A. Bryant		Gloria Marler	Mack Casbeer	Mack Casbeer
Mitchell	Colorado City	Bill F. Carter	Joan Beach	R. L. McKinney	Ann Hallmark	C. C. Burt	Wendell Bryant
Montague	Montague	Thomas W. Brown	Christine Cook	Brian E. Powers	Shirley Lanier	Christine Patterson	Harry J. Walker
Montgomery	Conroe	¶J. C. Edwards III	Roy Harris	D. C. Dozier	Margaret Caskey	John P. Neece Jr.	Joe Corley
Moore	Dumas	Jack D. Powell	Rhonnie Mayer	R. A. Ratliff	Phyllis Holmes	Mrs. Billie Donnell	M. R. Weaver
Morris	Daingerfield	Ronald M. Cowan	Doris McNatt	O. G. Stanley	Ann G. Clevenger	Jerry L. Chambliss	Joe Skipper
Motley	Matador	B. J. Whitaker	Mrs. L. Campbell	Howard Traweek	Mrs. Wilna Hobbs	Alton Marshall	Alton Marshall
Nacogdoches	Nacogdoches	**O. L. Westmoreland	Mrs. Hope Skipper	B. H. Davis Jr.	Kay Watkins	Mrs. Patsy Cates	Joe Evans
Navarro	Corsicana	Gary Bennett	James F. Doolen		E. L. Parrish	Freddy L. Nutt	Jim Hodge
Newton	Newton	Lee Roy Fillyaw	Mrs. Melba Canty	Edward J. Tracy	Ruth Dickerson	Geraldine A. Kerr	Robert C. Woods
Nolan	Sweetwater	††Terry Julian	Judy Brazelton	Carl M. Anderson	Naurvelle Rogers	Betty Bryant	Jim Blackley
Nueces	Corpus Christi	‡‡Robert N. Barnes	Marion Uehlinger	Carlos Valdez	David S. Chappell	Richard D. Magee	James Hickey
Ochiltree	Perryton	Howard E. Stone	Mrs. Mabel McLarty	Bruce Roberson	Ginger Hays	Mrs. Ruby Malaney	Joe Hataway
Oldham	Vega	John P. Glitter	Martha Thompson	R. W. Brainerd	Modean Erwin	Carolyn Slutz	David Medlin
Orange	Orange	§§James D. Stringer	Molly Theriot	Stephen C. Howard	Earlene Hilliard	L. Hryhorchuk	James Wade
Palo Pinto	Palo Pinto	Norman Porter	Bobbie Smith	N. A. Irsfeld	Wilson Unkart	John R. Winters	John L. Turpin
Panola	Carthage	¶¶Ruff Wall	Roy Cadenhead Jr.	Morris Samford Jr.	Mrs. Sue Parker	W. E. Blair	Tommy Harris

*Lubbock County Courts at Law: No. 1, Cecil G. Puryear; No. 2, Mackey K. Hancock. †McLennan County Courts at Law: No. 1, David L. Hodges; No. 2, Mike Gassaway. ‡Medina County Court at Law: Joe E. Briscoe. §Midland County Court at Law: Willie B. DuBose. ¶Montgomery County Courts at Law: No. 1, E. P. Oualline; No. 2, Jerry Winfree. **Nacogdoches County Court at Law: J. J. Yarbrough. ††Nolan County Court at Law: Robert M. Faver. ‡‡Nueces County Courts at Law: No. 1, Robert M. Blackmon; No. 2, Hector DePena; No. 3, Hilda Tagle; No. 4, James E. Klager. §§Orange County Court at Law: Michael W. Shuff. ¶¶Panola County Court at Law: Crawford Parker Jr.

County Officials.—Table No. 1: Judges, Clerks, Attorneys, Treasurers, Tax Assessors, Sheriffs.—(Continued.)

County—	County Seat	County Judge	County Clerk	County Attorney	County Treasurer	Assessor-Collector	Sheriff
Parker	Weatherford	Gerald Birdwell	Carrie Reed	Fred Barker	Geneva Carter	Judy Spradlin	Billy R. Cain
Parmer	Farwell	Porter Roberts	Mrs. Bonnie Warren	Charles Aycock	Mrs. Benna Felts	Hugh Moseley	M. C. Morgan Jr.
Pecos	Fort Stockton	Charles Warnock	Paul W. Yeager	W. C. McDonald Jr.	Garnett McCallister	E. F. Triplett	Bruce Wilson
Polk	Livingston	Wayne R. Baker	Aline Stephenson	Stephen Phillips	Sally R. Kessler	Robt. C. Willis	Ted Everitt
Potter	Amarillo	*Edward L. Poole	Mrs. Sue Daniel	Bill Baumann	Lawrence Youngblood	Maxine Pickett	Jimmy D. Boydston
Presidio	Marfa	C. W. Henderson Jr.	Ramona Lara	John Calhoun	Mario S. Rivera	R. D. Thompson	R. D. Thompson
Rains	Emory	B. D. Chism	Mary Sheppard	L. M. Braziel	Mrs. Allie R. Harris	Andrew Roberts	Andrew Roberts
Randall	Canyon	†Charlie Purcell	Le Roy Hutton		Judy Monk	Carol Autry	W. C. Longest
Reagan	Big Lake	Frank Sandel	Mrs. Hazel S. Carr	Jack P. Schulze	Mrs. Flora McIntyre	Christine Gardner	Paul Weatherby
Real	Leakey	G. W. Twilligear Jr.	Marjorie Kellner		Bonnie Crider	Pearl Brice	Buck Miller
Red River	Clarksville	Wm. S. Whiteman	Mary Hausler	Thos. H. Fowler	Donna Townes	J. Benningfield	Bob Storey
Reeves	Pecos	‡W. O. Pigman	Catherine Ashley	Scott Johnson	Nina Abila	Mrs. J. C. Preslar	Raul Florez
Refugio	Refugio	Ginger Fagan	Rebekah Scott	Robt. P. McGuill	Betty Greebon	Margie Gregorcyk	Jim Hodges
Roberts	Miami	Newton M. Cox	Jackie M. Jackson		Sarah E. Gill	Carol Billingsley	Eddie D. Brines
Robertson	Franklin	Wesley E. Peyton	Mary B. Reagan	Jim McCullough	Virginia Turner	Charlene Bush	Lee S. Hurley
Rockwall	Rockwall	Harold Crawford	Paulette Burks		Harless Dudley	Doris H. Willess	John McWhorter
Runnels	Ballinger	M. B. Murchison	L. Bruchmiller	Kendal Granzin	Nora Halfmann	Va Rue McWilliams	Bill Baird
Rusk	Henderson	James B. Porter	Helen Sillick	W. L. Ferguson	Virgil Cole	Tommy Haskins	M. J. Strong
Sabine	Hemphill	Royce C. Smith	Minnie Gooch		Ollie F. Sparks	Diane Husband	Blan Greer
San Augustine	San Augustine	Jack B. Nichols	Geraldine Smith	James A. Doherty	Carol W. Vaughn	Mary Lou Alford	N. L. Tindall
San Jacinto	Coldspring	Joe McMurrey	Lois Cooksey	Robt. H. Trapp	Charlene Everitt	Ruth G. Morrison	Robert E. Brumley
San Patricio	Sinton	J. M. Edmondson Jr.	Dottie Maley	David Aken	J. J. McWhorter	Davis Vickers	Wayne Hitt
San Saba	San Saba	Thomas Bowden	Nila R. Barker	David M. Williams	Mrs. Mada L. Smith	Billy C. Williams	Billy C. Williams
Schleicher	Eldorado	Johnny Griffin	Helen Blakeway	T. Giovannitti	A. G. McCormack	Dorothy M. Evans	O. N. Edmiston
Scurry	Snyder	Preston Wilson	Mrs. Beverly Ainsworth	Gary Terrell	Billy W. Thompson	Rona Sikes	Keith Collier
Shackelford	Albany	E. D. Fincher	Bobbie L. Cox	Jack Willingham	Mrs. Alma Maxwell	Ben Jack Riley	Ben Jack Riley
Shelby	Center	Johnie Johnson	C. R. Ramsey	Karren Kirkley	LaMerle Davis	Harlon Eakin	Paul Ross
Sherman	Stratford	W. S. Frizzell Jr.	Mary Lou Albert		Linda Keener	Zelda Pickens	Tom Wade
Smith	Tyler	§R. H. Hayes	Mrs. Mary Morris		Joyce W. Smith	Harris Oswalt	J. B. Smith
Somervell	Glen Rose	George Crump	Dorothy McFall	Tim Rudolph	Mrs. Wynell Whitt	Janet Boren	Frank J. Laramore
Starr	Rio Grande City	Blas Chapa	Juan J. Mills	Alex W. Gabert	Jose D. Villarreal	Maria O. Saenz	Gene Falcon Jr.
Stephens	Breckenridge	Miller Tuttle	Helen Haddock	Jimmy Browning	Nancy Clary	Allena Dover	James N. Cain
Sterling	Sterling City	Roland L. Lowe	Mrs. Sandra Peel	Drew T. Durham	Beth Kilpatrick	Lloyd J. Brown	Lloyd J. Brown
Stonewall	Aspermont	George Frazier	Betty L. Smith	Isaac Castro	Linda Messick	Joyce Y. McNutt	Leroy Morrow
Sutton	Sonora	Karla Fields	Erma Lee Turner	David Wallace	Joyce H. Chalk	Ann Hill	W. W. Webster
Swisher	Tulia	Jay V. Johnson	Pat Wesley		Lanelle Dovel	Shirley Whitehead	John Gayler
Tarrant	Fort Worth	¶Mike Moncrief	Madrin Huffman	Terry McEachern	§§	June Garrison	Don Carpenter
Taylor	Abilene	**J. A. Holloway	Janice Lyons		Mrs. Hayden Thomas	Lavena Cheek	John Middleton
Terrell	Sanderson	Charles Staveley	Patty Phillips	Marsha Monroe	Mrs. G. Litton	Dalton Hogg	Dalton Hogg
Terry	Brownfield	Herbert Chesshir	Frank T. Gray	G. D. Pruitt	Mrs. B. Montgomery	Paul E. Brock	Ralph Murry
Throckmorton	Throckmorton	Patricia Harrington	Cathey Mitchell	Clyde Boose	Margaret Lilly	Greg Dunlap	Greg Dunlap
Titus	Mount Pleasant	Bill Harper	Eugenia Roach	Tim Taylor	Cynthia Agan	June Roach	John A. Moss
Tom Green	San Angelo	††Edd B. Keyes	Marie Russell	William R. Moore	Billie McDaniel	Evelyn A. Vordick	Ernest Haynes
Travis	Austin	‡‡Mike Renfro	Mrs. Doris Shropshire	Ken Oden	Johnny Crow	Bill Aleshire	Doyne Bailey
Trinity	Groveton	Jimmie Thornton	Elaine Lockhart	Joe W. Bell II	Linda O'Neal	Clara Hathorn	Kenneth Moore
Tyler	Woodville	Allen Sturrock	Grace Bostick		Austin Fuller	Mrs. Barbara Tolbert	Leon Fowler
Upshur	Gilmer	Everett Dean	J. B. Hill Jr.		Vernon Vick	M. L. Smith	Dale Jewkes

*Potter County Courts at Law: No. 1, David L. Gleason; No. 2, Richard Dambold. †Randall County Court at Law: Richard L. Wilcox. ‡Reeves County Court at Law: Lee S. Green. §Smith County Courts at Law: No. 1, Milton G. Mell; No. 2, Cynthia Kent. ¶Tarrant County Courts at Law: No. 1, Bill Brigham; No. 2, Doyle Willis Jr. County Criminal Courts at Law: No. 1, Frank Coffey; No. 2, George McManus; No. 3, Billy Mills; No. 4, Pete Perez; No. 5, Jake Cook. Probate Courts: Robert M. Burnett and Patrick Ferchill. **Taylor County Court at Law: John Saringer. ††Tom Green County Court at Law: R. L. Blann. ‡‡Travis County Courts at Law: No. 1, Leslie Taylor; No. 2, Steve Russell; No. 3, Michael L. Schless; No. 4, Guy Herman. §§Office of County Treasurer in Tarrant County abolished in election April 2, 1983.

County Officials.—Table No. 1: Judges, Clerks, Attorneys, Treasurers, Tax Assessors, Sheriffs.—(Continued.)

County—	County Seat	County Judge	County Clerk	County Attorney	County Treasurer	Assessor-Collector	Sheriff
Upton	Rankin	Mrs. Peggy Garner	Buena R. Coffee	R. E. Motsenbocker	Doris L. Speed	Glenn Willeford	Glenn Willeford
Uvalde	Uvalde	J. R. White	Eileen Carlisle	David R. White	Josephine Noble	Helen Angermiller	Kenneth Kelley
Val Verde	Del Rio	*Sergio Gonzalez Jr.	Mildred Hildreth	V. R. Garcia	Cecil T. Adams	Mrs. E. Monzingo	James R. Koog
Van Zandt	Canton	Sam Hilliard	Elizabeth Everitt	Tommy Wallace	Mrs. Shirley Morgan	J. D. Floyd	Travis Shafer
Victoria	Victoria	†Norman D. Jones	Val D. Huvar		Helen R. Walker	Bessie Lassmann	D. G. Meyer
Walker	Huntsville	‡Ralph A. Davis Jr.	James D. Patton	L. C. Eakin Jr.	Barbara R. McGilberry	O. L. Thorne	W. D. White
Waller	Hempstead	§A. M. McCaig	Elva D. Mathis	Randy Cleveland	Patricia S. Sneed	Chrystal Weaver	R. L. Sitton
Ward	Monahans	Richard Sitz	Mrs. Pat V. Finley	L. J. Lacina Jr.	Mrs. Audrey Harris	Mrs. Edith Porter	D. Hall
Washington	Brenham	Gus Mutscher	Gertrude Lehrmann	Richard G. Morales	Rosa Lee Fuchs	Vennie Herzog	Elwood Goldberg
Webb	Laredo	‖C. Y. Benavides	Henry Flores		Hector Farias Jr.	Ezequiel Laurel	Mario Santos Jr.
Wharton	Wharton	I. J. Irvin Jr.	Delfin Marek	Scott Cline	Gus Wessels Jr.	F. H. Konvicka	R. R. Machala
Wheeler	Wheeler	Wendell Morgan	T. J. Daughtry	N. K. Sims	Jerrie Moore	Jerry D. Helley	Lonnie Miller
Wichita	Wichita Falls	¶Tom Bacus	Vernon Cannon	James Rasmussen	Mary L. Welborn	Miles Graham	W. L. Burrow
Wilbarger	Vernon	Bob Arnold	Frances McGee	Kelly Wright	Janice King	JoAnn Bourland	Gerald King
Willacy	Raymondville	Bill Rapp	Lalo Gomez	Lee P. Fernon	O. O. Loya	Mrs. Emma Ross	Larry G. Spence
Williamson	Georgetown	††Don Wilson	James N. Boydston	Billy R. Stubblefield	Irvin Leschber	Dorothy E. Jones	Jim Boutwell
Wilson	Floresville	W. D. Cox	Richard Bolf	Howard C. Berger	Peggy Jaeggli	Anna D. Gonzales	M. H. Baumann
Winkler	Kermit	Mrs. Frances Clark	Ruth Godwin	S. Tallaferro	John W. Stout	Mae Barnes	Wm. H. Sage
Wise	Decatur	‡‡R. L. Holloway Jr.	La Verne Forman	Patrick Morris	Mrs. Emma Ray	J. C. Stockton	C. L. Aaron Jr.
Wood	Quitman	Lee E. Williams	Mrs. Martha R. Bridges		Frankie Flournoy	Fred Morrow	Frank White
Yoakum	Plains	Paul Cobb	Ruby Bruton	Warren New	Genice Logan	Wanda Smith	Jimmie Rice
Young	Graham	Hugh G. Grubbs	LaFonda Taack	Stanley D. Curbo	Wanda Primrose	Jean Hester	Ed Shields
Zapata	Zapata	Jacob G. Rathmell	Arnoldo Flores	A. A. Figueroa	Jose L. Guevara	Jaime A. Gonzalez	G. Villarreal
Zavala	Crystal City	Ron Carr	Teresa P. Flores	Pablo Avila	Susie Perez	Martha P. Cruz	Alberto Sanchez

*Val Verde County Court at Law: James M. Simmonds. †Victoria County Courts at Law: Jerry J. Garrett; No. 2, Juan Velasquez III. ‡Walker County Court at Law: Ann P. Baker.
§Waller County Court at Law: Karl N. Micklitz. ‖Webb County Court at Law: Manuel R. Flores. **Wichita County Court at Law: Jim Hogan. ††Williamson County Court at Law: T. G.
Maresh. ‡‡Wise County Court at Law: W. H. Turner.

Dallas' growth is shown in this photo looking north from a Trinity River bridge from the Oak Cliff suburb of Dallas. Dallas News Photo

District Judges, District Clerks, District Attorneys and County Commissioners. See also Table 1.

County—	Dist.	District Judge	District Clerk	District Attorney	Comm. Precinct 1	Comm. Precinct 2	Comm. Precinct 3	Comm. Precinct 4
Anderson	3 87 349	Wayne Lawrence Sam B. Bournias Melvin D. Whitaker	Mrs. Lulu F. Nation	Richard Handorf	Truman Starr	R. O. Browne Sr.	T. L. Beard	B. G. Lambright
Andrews	109	James H. Clack	Imogene Tate	James L. Rex	Bill Chesney	W. G. Hathcock	J. W. Moxley	Willard Snow
Angelina	159 217	David Walker David V. Wilson	Jimmie F. Robinson	Gerald Goodwin	Joe Berry	I. D. Henderson Jr.	Monroe Nerren	Robert Colwell
Aransas	36 156 343	R. M. Yeager Rachel Littlejohn A. T. Rodriquez	Agnes Harden	Thos. L. Bridges	Owen H. Booher	Ray Longino	Pete Sanders	Mike Womack
Archer	97	F. J. Douthitt	Jane Adams	Jack McGaughey	Evon Carter	James Berend	Ben Buerger	D. W. Stone
Armstrong	47	Bryan Poff Jr.	Betty Parker	Danny Hill	Leo Oles	C. A. Brewer	Bill Heisler	David Irons
Atascosa	81 218	Olin B. Strauss R. L. Eschenburg II	Mary Guerra	A. H. Kendall	Victor Holguin	E. Mikolajczyk	Buford Wilson	D. D. Hoover
Austin	155	Oliver S. Kitzman	Mrs. Lorri Coody	Charles D. Houston	J. E. Grawunder	Hilbert L. Galle	Everett Tomlinson	L. L. Melnar
Bailey	287	Jack D. Young	Nelda Merriott	Johnny Ackinson	R. L. Scott	Roy Whitt	Joey R. Kindle	Rudolph Moraw
Bandera	216	Robert R. Barton	Vera King	E. Bruce Curry	Jim Russell	Dan C. Alanis III	A. A. Reed	N. P. Thompson
Bastrop	21 335	John L. Placke Harold R. Towslee	Peggy Walicek	Chas. D. Penick	Tom Adams	Billy Davis	Jerry Alexander	Marvin Markert
Baylor	50	David W. Hajek	Amy Hayley	Wm. H. Heatly	G. C. Landy Jr.	James Smajastrala	Jim Richardson	Tom McMorris
Bee	36 156 343	R. M. Yeager Rachel Littlejohn A. T. Rodriquez	Margie P. Carter	C. F. Moore	Adam V. Gonzales	Julius R. Helm	Santiago Martinez	Henry C. Lohse
Bell	27 146 169 264	C. W. Duncan Jr. Wm. C. Black J. F. Clawson Jr. Jack W. Prescott	Mrs. D. Carpenter	Arthur Eads Jr.	Cliff Jones	R. L. Peters	Roy Goad	John Oliver
Bexar	37 45 57 73 131 144 150	John Cornyn III Carol R. Haberman John G. Yates James C. Onion Rose Spector Roy Barrera Jr. Fred Biery	David J. Garcia **Bexar County Dist. Judges (Cont'd.)** 166 Peter Michael Curry 175 P. G. Chavarria Jr. 186 James E. Barlow 187 Patrick Priest	Sam Millsap **Bexar County Dist. Judges (Cont'd.)**	John A. Longoria **Bexar County Dist. Judges (Cont'd.)** 224 Carolyn Spears 225 Alfonso Chapa 226 M. Ted Butler 227 Mike M. Machado	Andy Casias **Bexar County Dist. Judges (Cont'd.)** 285 David Peeples 288 Raul Rivera 289 Tom Rickhoff 290 David Berchelmann	Lamar Smith **Bexar County Dist. Judges (Cont'd.)**	Bob Lee
Blanco	33 132 220	Clayton E. Evans Gene L. Dulaney James E. Morgan	Dorothy Uecker	Sam Oatman	Reuben W. Cage	Robert Riddell	E. Bergman	Alton Koch
Borden	132	Gene L. Dulaney	Dorothy Browne	Ernie Armstrong	Frank Currey	Larry D. Smith	Vernon Wolf	Ed Rinehart
Bosque	220	James E. Morgan	Diana Wellborn	Andy J. McMullen	Glen Thompson	H. J. Morrison	Calvin Rueter	J. Paul Howard
Bowie	5 102 202	Jack E. Carter Leon F. Pesek Guy E. Jones	Mrs. Winnie Stone	Louis Raffaelli	Dexter Henry	L. B. Grimes	Dale Barrett	Paul Fannin
Brazoria	23 149 239 300	Neil Caldwell Paul E. Ferguson J. R. Gayle III Thomas Kenyon	Mrs. Frances G. Bennett	Jim Mapel	Ronnie Broaddus	G. L. Rouse	Billy J. Plaster	John P. Gayle Jr.
Brazos	85 272 361	W. T. McDonald Jr. Carolyn Ruffino John Delaney	W. D. Burley	Bill Turner	Bill J. Cooley	Walter Wilcox	Billy Beard	Milton Turner
Brewster	83	Alex R. Gonzalez	Mrs. Shirley A. Scholl	Phil Pollan	Wm. B. Ward	Roberto Valadez	E. B. Salmon	Ernesto Gallego
Briscoe	110	George W. Miller	Bess McWilliams	John R. Hollums	Shafe Weaver	Paul A. Ramsey	B. L. Long	Bryant Eddleman
Brooks	79	Romeo Flores	Pete Martinez	Rolando Ramirez	J. M. Alaniz	Gustavo Barrera	Jose Garcia	L. E. Wilder
Brown	35	Ernest Cadenhead Jr.	Janice Brown	Steve Ellis	Kenneth Boyd	J. D. Chastain	Chester Damron	B. N. Levisay
Burleson	21 335	John L. Placke Harold R. Towslee	Doris H. Brewer	Charles Sebesta Jr.	F. J. Beran	Don L. Groce	W. J. Stracener	B. E. Schoppe
Burnet	33	Clayton E. Evans	Modena R. Curington	Sam Oatman	Mac Hammond	Hardy Willis	Kenny Baker	John E. Mead
Caldwell	22 207 274	Charles R. Ramsay R. T. Pfeuffer Fred A. Moore	Emma J. Schulle	J. L. Van Horn	Jack Schneider	Ray B. Hall	Ronnie Duesterheft	Lester Taylor

District Judges, District Clerks, District Attorneys and County Commissioners. See also Table 1. (Continued)

County—	Dist.	District Judge	District Clerk	District Attorney	Comm. Precinct 1	Comm. Precinct 2	Comm. Precinct 3	Comm. Precinct 4
Calhoun	24	C. N. Stevenson	Ollie H. Cuellar	Dan Heard	Leroy Belk	S. L. Mikula	Roy Smith	Oscar F. Hahn
	135	Frank H. Crain						
	267	W. W. Kilgore						
Callahan	42	Don Lane	Cubelle L. Harris	Robert E. McCool	Eugene Kitchens	Lowell Johnson	F. P. Shackelford	E. F. Odom
Cameron	103	Diego Leal	Aurora de la Garza	Benjamin Euresti	D. J. Lerma	Mike Cortinas Jr.	Adolph Thomae Jr.	Tony Gutierrez
	107	Melchor Chavez						
	138	Robert Garza						
	197	Darrell Hester						
	357	Menton Murray Jr.						
Camp	76	B. D. Moye	Deloria Bradshaw	Chas. MacCobb	Jack Efurd	M. F. King	O. C. Taylor	Horace Peek
	276	Wm. R. Porter						
	100	John T. Forbis						
Carson			Mrs. Sue Persons	David M. McCoy	R. J. Britten	E. L. Jones	Jerry Strawn	Pleasant Meadows
Cass	5	Jack E. Carter	W. A. Watson Jr.	Neal Birmingham	T. E. Kessler	Nolan Moore	Robt. J. Buzbee	Olon Endsley
Castro	64	Jack R. Miller	Joy Jones	J. F. Davis	Curtis Snitker	Edd Wilson Jr.	Jeff Robertson	V. Guggemos
	242	Marvin F. Marshall						
Chambers	253	W. G. Woods	R. B. Scherer Jr.	Michael R. Little	Kenneth Bettis	S. Desormeaux Jr.	Earl Porter	Carolyn Adair
	344	Carroll E. Wilborn Jr.						
Cherokee	2	Morris Hassell	Mavis Parrott	Charles Holcomb	R. J. Underwood	O. B. Sartain	Joe Henderson	Frank R. Ross
Childress	100	John T. Forbis	Winona Furr	David M. McCoy	Stanley Terry	Charles Mock	Irby Teague	H. H. Wilson
Clay	97	F. J. Douthitt	J. Dan Slagle	Jack McGaughey	G. E. Liggett	Les Lyde	C. F. Copeland	Elmer R. Allison
Cochran	286	James K. Walker	Mrs. D. Richardson	W. G. Tabor Jr.	Billy D. Carter	E. J. McKissack	A. W. Coffman	Kenneth Burke
Coke	51	Royal Hart	Effie Hubbard	Gerald Fohn	George Newby	Billy Joe Luckett	Finis Millican	J. A. Tidwell
Coleman	42	Don Lane	Louise Thompson	Jorge Solis	Jack Strickland	Jake McCreary	Vernon Slate	Max Horne
Collin	199	John Roach	Bernice M. Fraze	H. Ownby	Howard Thornton	Jerry Hoagland	Wallace Webb	R. E. May
	219	John L. McCraw Jr.						
	296	Verla Sue Holland						
Collingsworth	100	John T. Forbis	Helen Gollihugh	David M. McCoy	Dan Langford	Joe F. Knoll	Bill Lowe	Dudley Coleman
Colorado	25	B. B. Schraub	Harvey Vornsand	W. C. Kirkendall	Otto Loessin	Rafael Veselka	Jerome Wicke	L. W. Stiles Jr.
	2D25	Gus J. Strauss						
Comal	22	Charles R. Ramsay	Mrs. Hazel K. Kuhn	Wm. L. Schroeder	J. L. Evans	Monroe Wetz	Lorenzo Camarillo	W. N. George
	207	R. T. Pfeuffer						
	274	Fred A. Moore						
Comanche	220	James E. Morgan	LaNell Shaw Williams	Andy J. McMullen	Wade Davis	Murlin Elliott	Brent Daniel	Clyde Brinson
Concho	119	Curt F. Steib	Margaret T. Taylor	Dick Alcala	Elmo Grounds	O. D. Hight	Dewey Bingham Jr.	John B. Williams
	198	V. Murray Jordan		Ronald L. Sutton				
Cooke	235	Larry B. Sullivant	Bobbie Calhoun	Phil L. Adams	Danny Knight	K. D. Alexander	Jerry Lewis	R. J. Bayer
Coryell	52	Bobby L. Cummings	Carolyn Pollard	Phillip H. Zeigler	Donald K. Fisher	Cloyce Duncan	H. A. Davidson	John A. Hull
Cottle	50	David W. Hajek	Geneva Bragg	Wm. H. Heatly	Paul Whitener	John Shavor	Lester Moss	Terry Brooks
Crane	109	James H. Clack	Mrs. Doris Bond	Michael L. Fostel	Gordon Hooper	Billy I. Butler	D. F. Tipton	Marvin Dacy
Crockett	112	M. Brock Jones Jr.	Debbi Puckett	J. W. Johnson Jr.	S. DeHoyos	B. W. Stuart	J. F. Williams	Jesus Castro
Crosby	72	John D. Bevers	Mrs. B. J. Freeman	John L. Barnhill	Nelton Chote	R. W. Self	Herschel Bird	J. S. Williams
Culberson	34	Jerry Woodard	Rosalinda Abreo	Steve W. Simmons	I. M. Navarrette	Oscar Espinoza	John T. Jones	I. V. Espudo
	205	Sam Callan						
	210	Sam M. Paxson						
Dallam	69	Bill Sheehan	Betty Steele	B. E. Blackwell	George G. Reeves	Robert Lockhart	Don J. Bowers	Eulan Sheets
Dallas	14	John M. Marshall	Bill Long	Henry Wade	Jim Jackson	Mrs. Nancy Judy	John Wiley Price	Chris Semos
	44	H. Dee Johnson Jr.						
	68	Gary Hall						
	95	Nathan L. Hecht						
	101	Craig T. Enoch						
	116	Fred Harless						
	134	Joe Burnett						
	160	Leonard Hoffman						
	162	Catherine J. Crier						

Dallas County Dist. Judges (Cont'd.)

Dist.	Judge	Dist.	Judge
191	James B. Zimmermann	254	Dee Miller
192	Harlan Martin	255	Don Koons
193	John Whittington	256	Linda Thomas
194	James Ed Kinkeade	265	John Ovard
195	R. T. Scales	282	Kelly Loving
203	Thomas B. Thorpe	283	Jack Hampton
204	Richard D. Mays	291	Gerry H. Meier

Dallas County Dist. Judges (Cont'd.)

Dist.	Judge	Dist.	Judge
292	M. E. Keasler	330	Theo Bedard
298	S. A. Fitzwater	Cr. 1	Ron Chapman
301	Bob O'Donnell	Cr. 2	Larry W. Baraka
302	Frances Harris	Cr. 3	Gary R. Stephens
303	Merrill Hartman	Cr. 4	Frances Maloney
304	Craig Penfold	Cr. 5	Pat McDowell
305	Annette Stewart		

District Judges, District Clerks, District Attorneys and County Commissioners. See also Table 1. (Continued)

County—	Dist.	District Judge	District Clerk	District Attorney	Comm. Precinct 1	Comm. Precinct 2	Comm. Precinct 3	Comm. Precinct 4
Dawson	106	George Hansard	R. E. L. Smith	Ricky Smith	Rudy Arredondo	Kenneth Pearson	Gene Hendon	Dalton Myers
Deaf Smith	222	David W. Gulley	Lola Faye Veazy	Roland Saul	William L. Bradly	Austin C. Rose	Troy Don Moore	James L. Voyles
Delta	8	Lanny Ramsay	Patsy P. Barton	Frank Long	C. D. Goforth	Charles Allen	Ardell Allison	Tommy Maddox
Denton	62 / 16 / 158 / 211	Jim N. Thompson / John K. Narsutis / Jack Gray / Sam Houston	Mrs. Gladys Whitten	Gerald Cobb	Ruth Tansey	Sandy Jacobs	Lee Walker	B. E. Switzer
DeWitt	24 / 135 / 267	C. N. Stevenson / Frank H. Crain / W. W. Kilgore	Mrs. Gerry Smith	Wiley L. Cheatham	Harold Heyer	P. G. Schaffner	Gilbert Pargmann	Odell White
Dickens	110	George W. Miller	Helen Arrington	John R. Hollums	E. L. Williams	R. J. Bell	Vernon Wright	Darrell Thomason
Dimmit	293	Ben A. Martinez	A. G. Martinez Jr.	Amado Abascal III	Don Urban	Joaquin Salgado	Oscar Alvarado	Ramon B. Jaime
Donley	100	John T. Forbis	P. C. Messer	David M. McCoy	Steve Reynolds	Clarence Cornell	Buford Holland	Wm. Chamberlain
Duval	229	R. H. Garcia	Antonio Salinas	F. A. Cerda	A. C. Garcia	Carolina T. Saenz	R. M. Barton	W. E. Wiederkehr.
Eastland	91	Jim R. Wright	Mary J. Rowch-Brown	E. C. Walton	R. A. Robinson	O. E. Blackwell	L. T. Owen	C. B. Dill
Ector	70 / 161 / 244	Gene Ater / Tryon Lewis / Joe Connally	Jackie Sue Barnes	Eric Augesen	Bill Tolbert	B. N. Henderson	Gerrid Bowen	Willie Hammond.
Edwards	63	George M. Thurmond	Dorothy R. Hatley	Thomas F. Lee	Tony Villarreal	Gene Borchardt	Mrs. S. Bonham	Bill Mitchell
Ellis	40	Milton Hartsfield.	Gayle Simpson	Gene Knize	David Jones	Don Johnson	J. B. Sims	Albert Baucum.
El Paso	34 / 41	Jerry Woodard / John McKellips	Edie Rubalcaba	S. W. Simmons	Charles C. Hooten	Miguel Solis	Rogelio Sanchez	Mary Haynes

El Paso County Dist. Judges (Cont'd.)

	Dist.	District Judge	District Clerk	District Attorney	Comm. Precinct 1	Comm. Precinct 2	Comm. Precinct 3	Comm. Precinct 4
	65	Eduardo S. Marquez	205 Sam Callan.		243 Herb Marsh Jr.		346 Jose J. Baca	
	120	Brunson Moore	210 Sam M. Paxson.		327 E. H. Pena.			
	168	Ward L. Koehler						
	171	Edwin F. Berliner						

County—	Dist.	District Judge	District Clerk	District Attorney	Comm. Precinct 1	Comm. Precinct 2	Comm. Precinct 3	Comm. Precinct 4
Erath	266	Donald R. Jones	Thomas Pack	John Terrill	Kenneth Robertson	Don Stone.	Duane Oakes	C. T. Fulfer
Falls	82	Robert Stem	L. R. Hoelscher	Tom Sehon	J. S. Williams	James Lynn	T. L. Hoelscher.	Elmer Albright
Fannin	6	Henry Braswell.	Eva Lindsey	Dan Meehan	Derrell Hall	Billy Grimes	A. D. McBurnett	Choice Wilson
Fayette	336 / 155	Ray F. Grisham. / Oliver S. Kitzman	Virginia Wied	Charles D. Houston	Arno L. Ruether	Jack Littlejohn.	Wilbert L. Gross	R. O. Brauner,
Fisher	32	Weldon Kirk	Bettie Hargrove	Norman Arnett	Tommie J. Stuart	B. M. Henderson.	Jay R. Hendon	Jimmy Wright
Floyd	110	George W. Miller	Mary L. McPherson	John R. Hollums	Sam A. Spence	Bob Jarrett.	Thomas Warren	Jack Lackey,
Foard	46	Leslie L. Thomas.	Cornelia McDaniel	Gene Heatly	Thomas S. Haney	Beverly Gray	Wilson Myers	T. R. Cates
Fort Bend	240 / 268 / 328	Chas. A. Dickerson / A. Reagan Clark / Tom O. Stansbury	Irene Wleczyk	W. A. Meltzen	John Pustka	Ben Denham	A. B. Pressley	Bob S. Lutts
Franklin	8 / 62	Lanny Ramsay / Jim N. Thompson	Wanda Johnson	Frank Long	Jerald Cooper.	Charles Broach.	B. F. Ingram.	A. W. Jones Jr.
Freestone	77	P. K. Reiter.	Sue Gregory		Danny T. Willard	W. R. McSwane	Don Nesbitt	John J. Stubbs
Frio	81 / 218	Olin B. Strauss. / R. L. Eschenburg II	Jack M. Sorrell	A. H. Kendall	Antonio Moreno Jr.	Alvin Mann	Adolfo Alvarez	Noel Perez
Gaines	106	George Hansard	Wilma McNew.	Ricky Smith	Travis Bagley	Robert Matthews	Otis Johnson.	Gail Barnett
Galveston	10 / 56 / 122 / 212 / 306	Ed J. Harris / I. Allan Lerner / H. G. Dalehite Jr. / Don B. Morgan / Andrew Z. Baker	V. J. Beninati Jr.	Mike Guarino III	Earl Llewellyn	Frank T. Carmona	Ron Crowder	Billy J. Pegues
Garza	106	George Hansard	Carl Cederholm	Ricky Smith	T. D. Craft	Ted Aten	Tommy Young	Herbert Walls
Gillespie	216	Robert R. Barton	Alberta Gaddy	E. Bruce Curry.	D. F. Herber.	J. T. McMahon	L. E. Kusenberger	A. L. Hahn
Glasscock	118	James W. Gregg	Betty Pate.	Rick Hamby.	Wayne Halfmann	Alex Fry.	Randell Sherrod.	Michael Hoch

District Judges, District Clerks, District Attorneys and County Commissioners. See also Table 1. (Continued)

County—	Dist.	District Judge	District Clerk	District Attorney	Comm. Precinct 1	Comm. Precinct 2	Comm. Precinct 3	Comm. Precinct 4
Goliad	24	C. N. Stevenson	Gail M. Turley	Wiley L. Cheatham	W. T. Barnhill	James R. Farley	Edwin Lude	F. F. Post Jr.
	135	Frank H. Crain						
	267	W. W. Kilgore						
Gonzales	25	B. B. Schraub	Patricia Heinemeyer	W. C. Kirkendall	E. R. Breitschopf	J. V. Ochs	Royce Towns	W. M. Gibson
	2D25	Gus J. Strauss						
Gray	31	Grainger McIlhany	Mary Clark	Guy Hardin	O. L. Presley	Ronnie Rice	Gerald Wright	Ted Simmons
Grayson	223	Don E. Cain	Cyndi Mathis		Carl Thompson	Johnnie McGraw	C. E. Kretsinger	Carlos Brady Jr.
	15	Jim Fry						
	59	Joseph M. Joiner						
	336	Ray F. Grisham						
Gregg	124	Alvin Khoury	Mrs. Ruby Cooper	Carter Beckworth	Elmer Ferguson	Jim Gray	C. B. Young	Jack Bean
	188	Marcus Vascocu						
	307	Wm. C. Martin III						
Grimes	12	E. G. Ernst	Wayne Rucker	Latham Boone III	J. P. Brown	W. V. Borski	Albin Finke	Fred Voelter
	278	Jerry Sandel						
Guadalupe	25	B. B. Schraub	James Behrandt	W. C. Kirkendall	Bobby J. Bulgerin	Monroe Schubert	James E. Brannon	George Grein
	2D25	Gus J. Strauss						
	274	Fred A. Moore						
Hale	64	Jack R. Miller	Mrs. Dorothy Sinclair	T. D. McEachern	Ronald Morris	Homer Roberson	Henry Rieff	James A. Belk
	242	Marvin F. Marshall						
Hall	100	John T. Forbis	Phyllis Dunn	David M. McCoy	Jerry D. Smith	Bobby H. Barbee	Troy Phillips	Dale Garner
Hamilton	220	James E. Morgan	La Juan Mizell	Andy J. McMullen	W. O. McCollum Jr.	Bolding Cole Jr.	George Kilgo	Raymond Wenzel
Hansford	84	J. E. Blackburn	Amelia C. Johnson	Gene Compton	Garland Head	Joe T. Venneman	B. J. Renner	Val Winger
Hardeman	46	Leslie L. Thomas	Mrs. Loraine White	Gene Heatly	Charles McSpadden	James Rine	Charles Taylor	Van Foster
Hardin	88	Earl B. Stover	Aline Harper	R. F. Horka	Andrew Redkey	J. H. McGallion	R. P. Douglas	J. D. Brown
	356	Britton Plunk						
Harris	11	W. N. Blanton Jr.	Ray Hardy	John B. Holmes Jr.	El Franco Lee	James Fonteno	Bob Eckels	E. A. Lyons Jr.
	55	Reagan Cartwright						
	61	R. Shearn Smith						
	80	William R. Powell						
	113	Geraldine Tennant						
	125	Mike O'Brien						
	127	Sharolyn Wood						
	129	Hugo Touchy						
	133	David Hittner						
	151	A. J. P. Farris						
	152	Jack O'Neill						
	157	Felix Salazar Jr.						
	164	Peter S. Solito						
	165	R. L. Smith						

Harris County Dist. Judges (Cont'd.)

Dist.	District Judge	Dist.	District Judge	Dist.	District Judge	Dist.	District Judge
174	Jon N. Hughes	190	Wyatt H. Heard	248	Woody R. Densen	310	Allen J. Daggett
176	W. M. Hatten	208	Thomas H. Routt	257	Norman R. Lee	311	Bill Elliott
177	Miron A. Love	209	Michael T. McSpadden	262	Doug Shaver	312	Robert S. Webb III
178	William T. Harmon	215	Eugene Chambers	263	Charles J. Hearn	313	Robert L. Lowry
179	I. D. McMaster	228	Ted Poe	269	David West	314	Robert B. Baum
180	Patricia R. Lykos	230	Joe Kegans	270	Ann Cochran	315	Eric G. Andell
182	Donald K. Shipley	232	A. D. Azios	280	Thomas R. Phillips	333	Davie Wilson
183	Joseph M. Guarino	234	Ruby Sondock	281	Louis M. Moore	334	Marsha Anthony
184	Carroll Weaver	245	Henry G. Schuble III	295	Frank O. White	337	Johnny R. Kolenda
185	George L. Walker	246	John W. Peavy Jr.	308	Bob Robertson	338	Mary Bacon
189	Lynn N. Hughes	247	Charles D. Huckabee	309	Herman Gordon	339	Norman Lanford
						351	Albert Pruett

County—	Dist.	District Judge	District Clerk	District Attorney	Comm. Precinct 1	Comm. Precinct 2	Comm. Precinct 3	Comm. Precinct 4
Harrison	71	Ben Z. Grant	Mrs. Betty Cawood	Sam F. Baxter	James Mooney	Wm. D. Power	George K. Brumble	Telly H. Miller
Hartley	69	Bill Sheehan	Grady Belew	B. E. Blackwell	J. R. Frantz II	Bob Hunnicutt	James A. Yoder	Ray Snead II.
Haskell	39	Charles Chapman	Carolyn Reynolds	John Fouts	T. C. Burson	Ronnie Chapman	J. R. Perry	C. A. Turnbow
Hays	22	Charles R. Ramsay	W. H. Moore	Wm. M. Rugeley	Rafael Gonzales	Dan Campos	Craig Payne	L. C. McCarty
	207	R. T. Pfeuffer						
	274	Fred A. Moore						
Hemphill	31	Grainger McIlhany	Mrs. Gerry Vandiver	Guy Hardin	Kenneth Osborne	Don Thomason	L. F. Powledge	Robert Forrest
Henderson	3	Wayne Lawrence	Mrs. Lela M. Garner	Billy Bandy	Jim Blakeney	Jack Stegall	W. E. McLean	Leland Tarrant
	173	Jack Holland						
Hidalgo	92	Homero Salinas	Pauline G. Gonzalez	Rene Guerra	Samuel Sanchez	Lalo Arcaute	N. Salinas	Leonard Camarillo
	93	John F. Dominguez						
	139	Raul L. Longoria						
	206	Joe Evins						
	275	Arturo E. Guerra Jr.						
	332	Mario Ramirez						
				Glen Thomas		Kenneth Reid	Jim Carmichall	Kenneth R. Davis

...Judge, District Clerk, District Attorneys and County Commissioners. see also Table 1. (Continued)

County—	Dist.	District Judge	District Clerk	District Attorney	Comm. Precinct 1	Comm. Precinct 2	Comm. Precinct 3	Comm. Precinct 4
Hood	355	Ralph H. Walton Jr.	Joyce Beckworth	Dan Grissom	Joe C. Brown	Melvin Gifford	David Cleveland	Albert W. Hall
Hopkins	8	Lanny Ramsay	Ola Beckham	Frank Long	Elton Stewart	H. W. Halcomb	Delbert Tully	Wayne Mobley
	62	Jim N. Thompson						
Houston	3	Wayne Lawrence	Glen Welch	Richard Handorf	George H. Bush	Randal McCullar	Otis C. Wooten	A. A. McKinney
	349	Melvin D. Whitaker		Donald J. Gordon				
Howard	118	James W. Gregg	Peggy Crittenden	Rick Hamby	O. L. Brown	Paul H. Allen	W. B. Crooker Jr.	David Barr
Hudspeth	34	Jerry Woodard	Patricia Bramblett	Steve W. Simmons	Leon Snyder	L. R. Talley	Larry Karr	Ray Collier
	205	Sam Callan						
	210	Sam M. Paxson						
Hunt	196	E. Paul Banner	Mrs. J. E. Prince	F. Duncan Thomas	J. H. Lyon	H. L. Grimes	John Mizell	Mike Crowell
	354	Richard Bosworth						
Hutchinson	84	J. E. Blackburn	Rena G. Dorsett	Gene Compton	Murry Jennings	Wade Gillespie	W. D. Shipley	Blaine Scott
	316	Guy Hazlett						
Irion	51	Royal Hart	Jane Ethridge	Gerald Fohn	Mike Dolan	Robert Molina	Steve Elkins	Clyde Harris
Jack	271	John R. Lindsey	Mrs. L. V. Cozart	B. R. Smith	Clide Ogle	T. N. Cranford	Raymond Matlock	J. T. Rumage
Jackson	24	C. N. Stevenson	Mrs. Edna Stanford	Robert E. Bell	Miller Rutledge	Lifford Weidner	Edwin E. Hurta Jr.	W. O. Walker
	135	Frank H. Crain						
	267	W. W. Kilgore						
Jasper	1	O'Neal Bacon	Nell Powers	Guy J. Gray	E. W. Lewis	A. J. Byerly	Holbert H. Jones	Corbit Whitehead
	1-A	Monte D. Lawlis						
Jeff Davis	83	Alex R. Gonzalez	Peggy Robertson	Phil Pollan	J. R. Prude	Chris Lacy	H. L. Kokernot Jr.	Ben F. Gearhart Jr.
Jefferson	58	Ronald L. Walker	John S. Appleman	James S. McGrath	N. J. Troy	James A. Smith Jr.	Dave Smith Jr.	Rolfe Christopher
	60	Gary Sanderson						
	136	Jack R. King						
	172	Thomas A. Thomas						
	252	Leonard J. Giblin Jr.						
	279	Robert P. Walker						
	317	James M. Farris						
	Cr.	Lawrence J. Gist						
Jim Hogg	229	R. H. Garcia	Lilla Pena	F. A. Cerda	Raymundo Farias	A. Molina Jr.	Jaime Gomez	F. G. Garza
Jim Wells	79	Romeo Flores	Manuel M. Perez	Rolando Ramirez	Lucilla DeLeon	Hubert Adami	J. B. Freiley Jr.	W. M. Laughlin
Johnson	18	E. Byron Crosier	Mrs. Betty Cooke	Dan Boulware	Billy F. Roe	Davis Russell	Jimmie W. York	B. B. Aldridge
	249	John R. MacLean						
Jones	259	H. G. Andrews Jr.	W. L. McDonald	Jack G. Willingham	W. L. Moore	Jerry Manske	H. R. Hay	J. G. Heald
Karnes	81	Olin B. Strauss	F. A. Enlinger	A. H. Kendall	L. B. Hailey Jr.	Tom Dworaczyk	Albert Banduch	Claude Osburn Jr.
	218	R. L. Eschenburg II						
Kaufman	86	Glen M. Ashworth	Mrs. Ray Vick	L. W. Conradt Jr.	George A. Mayfield	John Darden	B. H. Wyatt	Carl Lee Hall
Kendall	216	Robert R. Barton	Shirley Stehling	E. Bruce Curry	David Masters	Marsha Beckett	Victor Phillip	L. Klemstein
Kenedy	28	Walter Dunham Jr.	Mrs. Faye Chandler	Grant Jones	J. E. Errington	L. E. Turcotte Jr.	T. R. Armstrong	Ed Durham
	105	Vernon Harville						
Kent	39	Charles Chapman	Cornelia Cheyne	John Fouts	W. H. Parks	Troy E. Hagar	Roy H. Parker	Don Trammel
Kerr	198	V. Murray Jordan	Mrs. Mary Brooks	Ronald L. Sutton	Fred Holland	Edward Higgins	Victor Lich	B. J. Guthrie Jr.
	216	Robert R. Barton		E. Bruce Curry				
Kimble	198	V. Murray Jordan	Louise P. Oliver	Ronald L. Sutton	Luke Hagood	Gene Simon	Frank Goodman	Archie K. Lennon
King	50	David W. Hajek	Evelyn Sursa	Wm. H. Heatly	Jordan Rogers	Roy B. Keith	B. J. Tidmore	Owen Brazee
Kinney	63	George M. Thurmond	Dolores Raney	Thomas F. Lee	Joe N. Garza	A. J. Sheedy III	Tim Ward	Joe York Jr.
Kleberg	28	Walter Dunham Jr.	Anita Kisiah	Grant Jones	Doyle Dreyer	E. S. Roberts	Earl Hubert	Romeo Lomas
	105	Vernon Harville						
Knox	50	David W. Hajek	Gloria L. West	Wm. H. Heatly	Billy G. Johnston	Bobby Roberson	Philip Homer	Lee G. Patterson
Lamar	6	Henry Braswell	Tommie Duke	Tom Wells	Jimmie Sparks	Maxie Wofford	Gene Buster	James Wheeler
	62	Jim N. Thompson						
Lamb	154	Pat Boone Jr.	Ray L. Britt	C. R. Wilkinson	A. J. Spain	T. H. Lewis	Emil Macha	Leonard Pierce
Lampasas	27	C. W. Duncan Jr.	Margy Jones	Arthur Eads Jr.	D. C. Herring	J. B. Ferguson	Willard Potts	C. N. Lancaster
LaSalle	81	Olin B. Strauss	Nora Mae Tyler	A. H. Kendall	James R. Black	Marie R. Villarreal	A. A. Garcia	Carlos B. Gonzalez
	218	R. L. Eschenburg II						

District Judges, District Clerks, District Attorneys and County Commissioners. See also Table 1. (Continued)

County—	Dist.	District Judge	District Clerk	District Attorney	Comm. Precinct 1	Comm. Precinct 2	Comm. Precinct 3	Comm. Precinct 4
Lavaca	25 / 2D25	B. B. Schraub / Gus J. Strauss	E. S. Kelly	W. C. Kirkendall	Jimmie J. Steffek	Eddie Vrana	Daniel Peters	Edward Hermes
Lee	21 / 335	John L. Placke / Harold R. Towslee	Adeline Melcher	Charles Sebesta Jr.	Elsie Rose	Otto Becker Jr.	W. G. Boyd	Monroe Markert
Leon	12 / 87 / 278	E. G. Ernst / Sam B. Bournias / Jerry Sandel	Mrs. Audrey Blake	Latham Boone III	Julian Wakefield	Lloyd Richmond	Craig Graham	Curtis Neyland
Liberty	75 / 253	C. D. Cain / W. G. Woods	Mrs. Joy McManus	Michael R. Little	Bobby D. Blake	D. E. Emanuel	Melvin Hunt	Bob Martin
Limestone	77 / 87	P. K. Reiter / Sam B. Bournias	Mary D. Budde	Pat Simmons	Grady Rasco	Billy G. Waldrop	Wilmer Little	Jeff Stuver
Lipscomb	31	Grainger McIlhany	Coeta Sperry	Guy Hardin	John W. Floyd	Verle Woods	Cecil Wynn	Ross G. Zenor
Live Oak	36 / 156 / 343	R. M. Yeager / Rachel Littlejohn / A. T. Rodriguez	Ellen J. McCarley	C. F. Moore	Clem McKinney	Hilbert Kopplin	Bill Goodwin	Loyd Miller
Llano	33	Clayton E. Evans	Wanda Osbourn	Sam Oatman	W. R. Bauman	Walter Overstreet	Rex King	Leonard Grenweige
Loving	143	Lawrence Fuller	Mrs. Edna Dewees	Jack McGowen	C. G. Ely	J. J. Wheat	J. E. Wilkinson	JeriAnn Blair
Lubbock	72 / 99 / 137 / 140 / 237	John D. Bevers / Thomas L. Clinton / Robert C. Wright / Wm. R. Shaver / John R. McFall	Wayne LeCroy	Jim B. Darnell	Boyd O. Roberts	Coy Biggs	Eliseo Solis	Alton Brazell
Lynn	106 / 198	George Hansard / V. Murray Jordan	Joy Laws	Ricky Smith	Eldon Gattis	Boyd Barnes	Bart Anderson	J. T. Miller
McCulloch	198	V. Murray Jordan	Mrs. Fayrene Williams	Ronald L. Sutton	Paul Willis	Jerry Bratton	Zane Carroll	Glenn A. Smith
McLennan	19 / 54 / 74 / 170	Bill Logue / George Allen / Derwood Johnson / R. R. Mormino	Joe Johnson	Vic Feazell	Wayne Davis	Jim Lewis	Vince Incardona	Don Cantrell
McMullen	36 / 156 / 343	R. M. Yeager / Rachel Littlejohn / A. T. Rodriguez	Wm. K. Hodgin	C. F. Moore	T. A. Goff	Rodney Swaim Jr.	Herman Smith	D. W. Atkinson
Madison	278 / 12	Jerry Sandel / E. G. Ernst	Joyce Batson	Latham Boone III	Billy Wilson	Walton Reynolds	Alvin Martin	Clifton Marks
Marion	115 / 276	Virgil E. Mulanax / Wm. R. Porter	Mrs. Syble Blackburn	Tony Hileman	H. H. Johnson	Odis A. Powell	J. B. McNeely	George Wolaver
Martin	118	James W. Gregg	Doris Stephenson	Rick Hamby	James Biggs	D. L. Tollison	Ronnie Deatherage	E. D. Holcomb
Mason	33	Clayton E. Evans	Beatrice Langehennig	Sam Oatman	Carl Martin	T. J. Webster	Jesse Dobbs	Calvin Leifeste
Matagorda	23 / 130	Neil Caldwell / W. Jack Salyer	Paul Hatchett	Danny Shindler	O. W. Birkner	J. D. Sutherland	F. P. Brhlik	A. W. Hurta
Maverick	293	Ben A. Martinez	D. Trevino	Amado Abascal III	Felix M. Cerna	Salvador Flores	Edwardo Trevino	Luis S. Minton
Medina	38	Mickey R. Pennington	Jean Marty	Earle Caddel	David Montgomery	Leon Tschirhart	Enrique Santos	H. B. Briscoe
Menard	198	V. Murray Jordan	Kay Kennemer	Ronald L. Sutton	Harvey Carriger	Banner Swindall	Ray McGuffin	Tim Childers
Midland	142 / 238 / 318	Pat M. Baskin / Vann Culp / Barbara Culver	Vivian Wood	Al Schorre	Durward Wright	C. Wallace Craig	Scott Welch	W. L. Brown
Milam	20	Don G. Humble	Leola Komar	Charles E. Lance	V. W. Hauk	L. C. McKinney	Gerald Vinton	Walter Stolte
Mills	35	Ernest Cadenhead Jr.	Walter A. Bryant	Steve Ellis	Marvin Lindsay	Lewis D. Watson	Lee Roy Schwartz	H. B. Jernigan
Mitchell	32	Weldon Kirk	B. H. Erwin	Norman Arnett	Edward B. Roach	Johnny Shackelford	Paul B. Hunter	Billy H. Preston
Montague	97	F. J. Douthitt	Starr Johnson	J. A. McGaughey	Dwight Whitaker	Milton L. Hopkins	Glenn Seay	Gene Parker
Montgomery	9 / 2D9 / 221 / 284 / 359	Lynn Coker / John Martin / Lee G. Alworth / Olen Underwood / James H. Keeshan	Peggy Stevens	J. H. Keeshan	Oliver H. Hance	Mrs. C. G. Shelton	Weldon Locke	A. V. Sallas
Moore	69	Bill Sheehan	June Mills	Jess Starkey	B. E. Blackwell	E. O. Hanna	J. C. Williams	M. O. Bain
Morris	76	R. D. Moye	Reynolds Taylor	O. G. Stanley	Robert L. McCain	R. W. Bass	Forrest A. Clair	W. G. Smith

...Commissioners. See also Table 1. (Continued)

County	Dist.	District Judge	District Clerk	District Attorney	Comm. Precinct 1	Comm. Precinct 2	Comm. Precinct 3	Comm. Precinct 4
Motley	110	George W. Hall	Mrs. L. Campbell	John R. Hollums	J. M. Russell	Bill D. Washington	Joseph E. Simpson	Billy Hand
Nacogdoches	145	Jack Pierce	Shelby Solomon	Herbert Hancock	Billy Reneau	E. Whitaker	Charles Simmons	John Hill
Navarro	13	Kenneth A. Douglas	C. O. Curington	P. C. Batchelor	Betty Armstrong	Jimmie Spencer	Thomas Dyer	Billy Hargrove
Newton	1-A	Monte D. Lawlis	Abbie N. Stark	Bill A. Martin	Joe C. Powell	Ottis Lewis	M. G. Jarrell	Gaylord Wood
	1	O'Neal Bacon						
Nolan	32	Weldon Kirk	Vera Holloman	Norman Arnett	J. T. Johnson	Ernest Shuler	Adrian Barton	Billy Muncy
Nueces	28	Walter Dunham Jr.	Oscar Soliz	Grant Jones	Wm. McKinzie	Carl Bluntzer	R. M. Borchard	J. P. Luby
	94	Rene Haas						
	105	Vernon Harville						
	117	Jack R. Blackmon						
	148	Margarito Garza						
	214	Mike Westergren						
	319	Max Bennett						
	347	Joaquin Villarreal III						
Ochiltree	84	J. E. Blackburn	Wilma Srof	Bruce Roberson	Jack Kile	Richard Haley	J. L. Luthi	Myron McCartor
Oldham	222	David W. Gulley	Martha Thompson	Richard Brainerd	Herb Schroeder	Ben Moore	Roger Morris Jr.	R. H. Brown
Orange	128	Patrick Clark	Billye Minter	Stephen C. Howard	Forrest E. Hudson	C. A. McQuhae Jr.	Donald E. Cole	Archie B. Smith
	163	David A. Dunn						
	260	Buddie J. Hahn						
Palo Pinto	29	David Cleveland	Mrs. Helen Slemmons	Jimmy A. Ashby	David Lee	George Berry	George Nowak	Charles Kitchens
Panola	123	Bennie Boles	Marie Seale	John Walker	Carl Hendrickson	L. O. Nail	Leonard Jones	Roland Davis
Parker	43	James O. Mullin	Lana Tibbitts	Mac Smith	Waymon Wright	Chandler Sanders	Harold Anderson	P. M. Cardwell Jr.
Parmer	287	Jack D. Young	Marjorie Watkins	Johnny Actkinson	Ernest Anthony	Tommy Williams	Robert White	Raymond McGehee
Pecos	83	Alex R. Gonzalez	Peggy Young	Phil Pollan	Gregg McKenzie	M. R. Gonzalez Jr.	Neal Sconiers	Truman Grove
	112	M. Brock Jones Jr.		J. W. Johnson Jr.				
Polk	9	Lynn Coker	Nell Lowe	J. H. Keeshan	H. N. Denham	R. D. Cunningham	J. J. Purvis	Paul Harrell
	2D9	John Martin		Joe L. Price				
	258	Joe Ned Dean						
Potter	47	Bryan Poff Jr.	Mrs. Billie N. Hill	Danny Hill	Pat Cunningham	Phil Haynes	Ray Berry	Elisha Demerson
	108	Edward B. Nobles						
	181	George E. Dowlen						
	251	Naomi Harney						
	320	Don R. Emerson						
Presidio	83	Alex R. Gonzalez	Ramona Lara	Phil Pollan	Felipe A. Cordero	Daniel T. Estrada	Ben Benavidez	Frances E. Howard
Rains	8	Lanny Ramsay	Mary Sheppard	Frank Long	Doris Cochran	J. T. Kirkpatrick	Ralph Middleton	W. D. Fenter
	354	Richard Bosworth						
Randall	47	Bryan Poff Jr.	Mrs. L. Polvadore	Randall Sherrod	Walter L. Simms	Bill Thomas	Fred Begert	Paul Roberts
	181	George E. Dowlen						
	251	Naomi Harney						
Reagan	83	Alex R. Gonzalez	Mrs. Hazel S. Carr	Phil Pollan	Lester Ratliff	Mike Elkins	Bill Schneemann	Thomas Strube
	112	M. Brock Jones Jr.						
Real	38	Mickey R. Pennington	Marjorie Kellner	J. W. Johnson Jr.	Lanny Leinweber	Wade Reagor	C. San Miquel	M. Wooldridge
				Earle Caddel				
Red River	6	Henry Braswell	Clara Gaddis	Thos. H. Fowler	Drue Pirtle	Jackie R. Barton	Ben B. Storey	Lane Duncan
	102	Leon F. Pesek						
Reeves	143	Lawrence Fuller	Annis Rasberry	Jack McGowen	Felipe Arredondo	Howard W. Davis	I. Dutchover	Bernardo Martinez
Refugio	24	C. N. Stevenson	Mrs. Marilou English	Wiley L. Cheatham	James R. Henry	Clara M. Geistman	Joe D. McGuill	Freddy Fagan
	135	Frank H. Crain						
	267	W. W. Kilgore						
Roberts	31	Grainger McIlhany	Jackie M. Jackson	Guy Hardin	Wm. H. Clark	Ronnie Gill	Don Morrison	Sam Condo
Robertson	82	Robert Stem	Mrs. M. D. Hicks	Jimmie McCullough	Tommy C. Singleton	Alvis Bishop	O. A. Cargill	Sam Abraham
Rockwall	86	Glen M. Ashworth	Margie Hooker	Nick Woodall	Bob Jolly	Gerald Burgamy	D. V. Brooks	Wayne Krider
Runnels	119	Curt F. Steib	L. Michalewicz	Dick Alcala	Robert Virden	J. D. Wilson	Gilbert Smith	Marvin Salling
Rusk	4	Donald R. Ross	Pat Endsley	Wm. L. Ferguson	Talmadge Mercer	Harold Kuykendall	Dan Dickeson	Kenneth Ashby
	1	O'Neal Bacon		R. E. Smith	R. E. Smith	Billy Joe McGee	Eldridge Ellison	Chester Cox
Sabine	273	John L. Smith	Minnie Gooch	Bill A. Martin				
San Augustine	273	John L. Smith	Jo Anna Johnson	Bill A. Martin	Tommy Jackson	Herbert Jackson	James J. Craig	Harlon Hall

District Judges, District Clerks, District Attorneys and County Commissioners. See also Table 1. (Continued)

County—	Dist.	District Judge	District Clerk	District Attorney	Comm. Precinct 1	Comm. Precinct 2	Comm. Precinct 3	Comm. Precinct 4
San Jacinto	9	Lynn Coker	Edna M. Cox	J. H. Keeshan	Norman J. Street	Roy Lewis	Donald Cox	Curtis B. Cain
	2D9	John Martin						
	258	Joe Ned Dean						
San Patricio	36	R. M. Yeager	Patricia Norton	Joe L. Price	Joe Zapata	Carl Duncan	Glenn Dorris	Hazel Edwards
	156	Rachel Littlejohn		Thos. L. Bridges				
	343	A. T. Rodriguez						
San Saba	33	Clayton E. Evans	Nila Ruth Barker	Sam Oatman	Ronald G. McBride	Calvin Bush	W. Kuykendall	B. L. Lively
Schleicher	51	Royal Hart	Helen Blakeway	Gerald Fohn	J. F. Mayo Jr.	Kerry Joy	P. Paxton	Ross Whitten
Scurry	132	Gene L. Dulaney	Mrs. P. Underwood	Ernie Armstrong	Ted Billingsley	Eldon Perry	Earl Sneed	C. D. Gray Jr.
Shackelford	259	H. G. Andrews Jr.	Bobbie L. Cox	Jack G. Willingham	Fred J. Coulter	W. S. Jones	H. D. Connally	W. O. McKeever
Shelby	123	Bennie Boles	Marsha Singletary	John Walker	Charles Williams	Edward Risinger	R. D. Green	V. L. Wedgeworth
	273	John L. Smith						
Sherman	69	Bill Sheehan	Mary Lou Albert	B. E. Blackwell	Wayne Cummings	Boyd Spurlock	Dale Hamilton	Mike O'Brien
Smith	7	Don Carroll	R. Brad Burger	Jack M. Skeen Jr.	B. J. Payne	G. T. Shamburger	Gene Chandler	A. R. Melontree
	114	Galloway Calhoun Jr.						
	241	Joe Tunnell						
	321	Ruth Blake						
Somervell	18	E. Byron Crosier	Dorothy McFall	Dan Boulware	Elizabeth Hammond	Joe G. Whitworth	Billy C. Miller	Earl Cromeans
	249	John R. MacLean						
Starr	229	R. H. Garcia	Juan E. Saenz	F. A. Cerda	J. M. Alvarez	Amando Pena	Eloy Garza	R. Alaniz
Stephens	90	R. E. Thornton	Juanita Speake	Tim D. Eyssen	F. J. Copeland	D. C. Sikes	O. Devenport	Carroll Williams
Sterling	51	Royal Hart	Sandra Peel	Gerald Fohn	Johnny Hughes	Russell Noletubby	B. R. Bynum	Melvin Foster
Stonewall	39	Charles Chapman	Betty L. Smith	John Fouts	John A. Smith	T. R. Cumbie	J. D. Parker	Dean Clark
Sutton	112	M. Brock Jones Jr.	Erma Lee Turner	J. W. Johnson Jr.	M. Villanueva	Bill Wade	Bill Keel	J. C. Gonzales
Swisher	64	Jack R. Miller	Pat Wesley	T. D. McEachern	F. L. McGavock	A. G. House	Roma Boggs	James Vineyard
	242	Marvin F. Marshall						
Tarrant	17	Charles Murray	J. W. Boorman	Tim Curry	Dick Andersen	O. L. Watson	Bob Hampton	B. D. Griffin
	48	Wm. L. Hughes Jr.	**Tarrant County Dist. Judges (Cont'd.)**	**Tarrant County Dist. Judges (Cont'd.)**	**Tarrant County Dist. Judges (Cont'd.)**			
	67	George A. Crowley	233 Harold L. Valderas	324 Brian A. Carper	360 Catherine Adamski			
	96	Hal M. Lattimore	236 Albert L. White Jr.	325 Robert L. Wright	Cr. 1 E. L. Goldsmith			
	141	James E. Wright	297 Charles Dickens	342 Joe Cunningham	Cr. 2 L. Clifford Davis			
	153	S. C. Farrar Jr.	322 Frank Sullivan	348 M. D. Schattman	Cr. 3 Don Leonard			
	213	Tom Cave	323 Scott Moore	352 John Street	Cr. 4 Joe Drago III			
	231	Maryellen W. Hicks						
Taylor	42	Don Lane	Rilla Mahoney	Jorge Solis	D. A. Bolls	Don Dudley	John G. Thompson	J. T. McMillon
	104	Billy J. Edwards						
	326	Henry J. Strauss						
	350	William A. Thomas Jr.						
Terrell	63	George M. Thurmond	Patty Phillips	Thomas F. Lee	Robert M. Salazar	A. R. Escamilla	W. L. Babb	Graham Childress
Terry	121	Ray D. Anderson	Betty Frazier	G. D. Pruitt	Harvey Smith	Bill Keesee	Delton Gregg	James G. Martin
Throckmorton	39	Charles Chapman	Cathey Mitchell	John Fouts	H. L. Martin	Max Coalson	Carlton Sullivan	George Seedig
Titus	76	B. D. Moye	Bobby LaPrade	Chas. Mac Cobb	Dempsey Johnson	James C. Thomas	J. W. Terrell Jr.	Loyd Clark
	276	Wm. R. Porter						
Tom Green	51	Royal Hart	Sue Bramhall	Gerald Fohn	B. C. Dominguez	Mary Burk	E. W. Wilson	E. S. Newman
	119	Curt F. Steib		Dick Alcala				
	340	Marilyn Aboussie						
Travis	53	Mary P. Williams	John Dickson	Ronald Earle	Jimmy Snell	Bob Honts	Pam Reed	Richard Moya
	98	Hume Cofer	**Travis County Dist. Judges (Cont'd.)**	**Travis County Dist. Judges (Cont'd.)**	**Travis County Dist. Judges (Cont'd.)**			
	126	Joe H. Hart	167 Robert Jones	250 Harley Clark	331 Robert A. Perkins			
	147	Mace B. Thurman Jr.	200 Paul R. Davis Jr.	261 Peter Lowry	345 Juan Gallardo			
			201 Jerry Dellana	299 Jon N. Wisser	353 Joe Dibrell Jr.			
Trinity	2D9	John Martin	Jorene Legg	Joe L. Price	Lynn Reynolds	Dean Price	Cecil Webb	Joe Don Davis
	258	Joe Ned Dean						

District Judges, District Clerks, District Attorneys and County Commissioners. See also Table 1. (Continued)

County	Dist.	District Judge	District Clerk	District Attorney	Comm. Precinct 1	Comm. Precinct 2	Comm. Precinct 3	Comm. Precinct 4
Tyler	88	Earl B. Stover	Patricia Brown	Pat Hardy	Maxie Riley	H. K. Lowe	Willis Graham	James Jordan
	1-A	Monte D. Lawlis						
Upshur	115	Virgil E. Mulanax	Horace A. Ray	Lowell Holt	Gadis Lindsey	J. W. Meadows	David Loyd	Paul Davis
Upton	83	Alex R. Gonzalez	Buena R. Coffee	Phil Pollan	M. E. McKenzie	T. D. Workman Jr.	Jack Carr	Chas. T. Fletcher
	112	M. Brock Jones Jr.		J. W. Johnson Jr.				
Uvalde	38	Mickey R. Pennington	June Richardson	Earle Caddel	A. E. McKinley	Gilbert Torres	Austin Schaffer	Amaro Cardona
Val Verde	63	George M. Thurmond	Martha Germany	Thomas F. Lee	R. G. Padilla	Bob Rodriquez	J. L. Leonard	Martin Wardlaw
Van Zandt	294	Richard D. Davis	Veta Burns	Tommy W. Wallace	A. L. Herron	Bill Freeman	Bruce Wilemon	Carbon Smith
Victoria	24	C. N. Stevenson	Alton F. Spoerl	G. J. Filley III	N. Hinojosa	Jerry Nobles	John J. Hammack	Rex L. Easley
	135	Frank H. Crain						
	267	W. W. Kilgore						
Walker	12	E. G. Ernst	Betty Tackett	Frank Blazek	Sam Park	James Burnett	Curtis Ellisor	Joe Malak Jr.
	278	Jerry Sandel						
Waller	9	Lynn Coker	R. R. Foster	J. H. Keeshan	F. R. Zach	James R. Muse	Richard Frey	W. C. Taylor
	155	Oliver S. Kitzman		Charles D. Houston				
Ward	143	Lawrence Fuller	Betty Love	Jack McGowen	H. A. Collins	Bill Middlebrooks	J. H. Raglin	Milbert Helm
Washington	21	John L. Placke	Blondean Kuecker	Charles Sebesta Jr.	Joe Renn	Alois Bilski	Gilbert Janner	Weldon Matthies
	335	Harold R. Towslee						
Webb	49	Ruben Garcia	Manuel Gutierrez	Julio Garcia	R. C. Centeno	J. R. Esparza	Jose L. Rodriguez	Arnulfo Santos
	111	A. A. Zardenetta						
	341	Elma T. Salinas						
Wharton	23	Neil Caldwell	Roland J. Carlson	Daniel Shindler	Carl Nichols	J. J. Grigar Jr.	A. Schoeneberg	C. F. Drapela Jr.
	329	Daniel R. Sklar						
Wheeler	31	Grainger McIlhany	Paul Topper	Guy Hardin	E. R. Harrison	B. V. Atherton	Clois Hanner	E. E. Henderson
Wichita	30	Calvin Ashley	Wayne Wiggins	Barry L. Macha	Dod Wiley	Weldon Nix	Gordon Griffith	H. C. Greer Jr.
	78	Keith Nelson						
	89	Temple Driver						
Wilbarger	46	Leslie L. Thomas	Mrs. Ann Minyard	Gene Healy	O. J. Walker	Bill Box	Glen Turner	Lenville Morris
Willacy	103	Diego Leal	Conrado Garcia	Edna Cisneros	E. Gonzales	Fred Stone	Alfredo Serrato	Simon Salinas
	107	Melchor Chavez						
	138	Robert Garza						
	197	Darrell Hester						
	357	Menton Murray Jr.						
Williamson	26	Wm. S. Lott	Bonnie Wolbrueck	E. J. Walsh	Ron Wood	W. O. Foust	Raymond Rister	J. L. Mehevec
	277	John R. Carter						
	368	Olin B. Strauss						
Wilson	218	R. L. Eschenburg II	Jody Gregory	A. H. Kendall	B. L. Talamantez	Albert Pruski	Billy Deagen	C. W. Daniels
Winkler	109	James H. Clack	Mrs. Virginia Healy	Michael L. Fostel	D. L. Nutt	Henry Jones	J. M. Dawson	C. W. Wright
Wise	271	John R. Lindsey	Doris Claborn	B. R. Smith	Max I. Weaver	H. N. Nikirk Jr.	Chas. F. Wolfe Jr.	B. G. Newton
Wood	114	Galloway Calhoun Jr.	Jo Anna Nelson	M. D. Taylor	Glenn Bevil	Sid Cox	Roger Pace	W. B. Woodard
	294	Richard D. Davis						
Yoakum	121	Ray D. Anderson	Mae Barnett	Warren New	John Avara	R. W. Thurston	Jim Barron	J. L. Fitzgerald
Young	90	R. E. Thornton	George C. Birdwell	Tim D. Eyssen	G. R. Denny	D. W. Sloan	A. D. Bishop	C. H. Prater
Zapata	49	Ruben Garcia	Arnoldo Flores	Julio Garcia	Romeo Flores	Angel Garza	David Morales	D. Villarreal
Zavala	293	Ben A. Martinez	Rosa E. Mata	Amado Abascall III	Hector Gomez	Frank Guerrero	Abelardo Marquez	Matthew McHazlett

STATE GOVERNMENT

State government is divided into **executive, legislative** and **judicial branches** under the Texas Constitution, adopted in 1876. The chief executive is the **Governor** whose term, effective in 1975, is for 4 years, according to a constitutional amendment approved by Texas voters in 1972. Other elected state officials with executive responsibilities include the **Lieutenant Governor, Attorney General, Comptroller of Public Accounts, Treasurer, Commissioner of the General Land Office** and **Commissioner of Agriculture.** The terms of these officials also were increased from 2 to 4 years by the constitutional amendment. Three members of the **Railroad Commis-**sion are elected for 6-year terms.

Except for making numerous appointments, the governor's powers are limited in comparison with those in most states.

The legislative branch is comprised of 31 members of the Senate and 150 members of the House of Representatives.

The judiciary consists of the **Supreme Court** and its co-ordinate **State Court of Criminal Appeals, 14 Courts of Appeals** and more than 330 district courts. Members are elected.

State and Federal Courts

The following lists include U.S. district courts in Texas, Texas district courts, Texas higher courts and administrative judicial districts. The lists were compiled from reports of the Texas Judicial Council and other sources.

The section — Counties, Cities and Towns — shows, alphabetically by counties, judicial districts to which each county is assigned.

Table No. 2 of District and County Officials also shows the district judges by counties.

U.S. District Courts In Texas

Texas is divided into four federal judicial districts, and each district is composed of several divisions. Appeal from all Texas federal district courts is to the **Fifth Circuit Court of Appeals,** New Orleans. Judges are appointed for life and receive a salary of $76,000 annually.

NORTHERN TEXAS DISTRICT

District Judges. — Chief Judge, Halbert O. Woodward, Lubbock. Temporary **Emergency Court of Appeals** Judge and Senior Judge, Joe E. Estes, Dallas. **Judges:** Eldon B. Mahon, and David Belew Jr., Fort Worth; Mary Lou Robinson, Amarillo; Robert W. Porter, Jerry Buchmeyer, Barefoot Sanders, A. Joe Fish and Robert B. Maloney, Dallas. **Clerk of District Court:** Nancy Hall Doherty, Dallas. **U.S. Attorney:** Marvin Collins, Dallas (Fort Worth). **U.S. Marshal:** Clint J. Peoples, Dallas. Court is in continuous session in each division of the Northern Texas District. Following are the different divisions of the Northern District and the counties in each division:

Dallas Division
Dallas, Ellis, Hunt, Johnson, Kaufman, Navarro and Rockwall. **Magistrates:** William F. Sanderson Jr. and John B. Tolle, Dallas. **Bankruptcy Judges:** Robert C. McGuire and John C. Ford, Dallas. **Chief Deputy Clerk:** Julian F. Schonter Jr.

Fort Worth Division
Comanche, Erath, Hood, Jack, Palo Pinto, Parker, Tarrant and Wise. **Magistrate:** Alex H. McGlinchey, Fort Worth. **Bankruptcy Judge:** Michael A. McConnell, Fort Worth. **Deputy Clerk in charge:** Faye Ray.

Amarillo Division
Armstrong, Briscoe, Carson, Castro, Childress, Collingsworth, Dallam, Deaf Smith, Donley, Gray, Hall, Hansford, Hartley, Hemphill, Hutchinson, Lipscomb, Moore, Ochiltree, Oldham, Parmer, Potter, Randall, Roberts, Sherman, Swisher and Wheeler. **Magistrate:** Robert R. Sanders, Amarillo. **Bankruptcy Judge:** Bill H. Brister, Lubbock. **Deputy Clerk in charge:** May Harris.

Abilene Division
Callahan, Eastland, Fisher, Haskell, Howard, Jones, Mitchell, Nolan, Shackelford, Stephens, Stonewall, Taylor and Throckmorton. **Magistrate:** John Weeks, Abilene. **Bankruptcy Judge:** Michael A. McConnell, Fort Worth. **Deputy Clerk in charge:** Georgia Sanders.

San Angelo Division
Brown, Coke, Coleman, Concho, Crockett, Glasscock, Irion, Menard, Mills, Reagan, Runnels, Schleicher, Sterling, Sutton and Tom Green. **Magistrate:** Philip R. Lane, San Angelo. **Bankruptcy Judge:** Michael A. McConnell, Fort Worth. **Deputy Clerk in charge:** Anne Loyd.

Wichita Falls Division
Archer, Baylor, Clay, Cottle, Foard, Hardeman, King, Knox, Montague, Wichita, Wilbarger and Young. **Magistrate:** Robert K. Roach, Wichita Falls. **Bankruptcy Judge:** John C. Ford, Dallas. **Deputy Clerk in charge:** Nina Hatcher.

Lubbock Division
Bailey, Borden, Cochran, Crosby, Dawson, Dickens, Floyd, Gaines, Garza, Hale, Hockley, Kent, Lamb, Lubbock, Lynn, Motley, Scurry, Terry and Yoakum.

Magistrate: J. Q. Warnick Jr., Lubbock. **Bankruptcy Judge:** Bill H. Brister, Lubbock. **Deputy Clerk in charge:** Kristy Chandler.

WESTERN TEXAS DISTRICT

District Judges: Chief Judge, William S. Sessions, San Antonio. **Judges:** Edward C. Prado, San Antonio; H. F. Garcia, San Antonio; Lucius D. Bunton III, Midland; Harry Lee Hudspeth, El Paso; James R. Nowlin, Austin; Walter S. Smith Jr., Waco. **Senior Judges:** D. W. Suttle, San Antonio; Jack Roberts, Austin. **Clerk of District Court:** Charles W. Vagner, San Antonio. **U.S. Attorney:** Helen Eversburg, San Antonio. **U.S. Marshal:** William J. Jonas Jr., San Antonio. Following are the different divisions of the Western District, and the counties in each division.

San Antonio Division
Atascosa, Bandera, Bexar, Comal, Dimmit, Frio, Gonzales, Guadalupe, Karnes, Kendall, Kerr, Medina, Real and Wilson. Court is in continuous session at San Antonio. **Magistrates:** Robert B. O'Connor, Jamie C. Boyd and Dan A. Naranjo, San Antonio. **Bankruptcy Judges:** Bert W. Thompson and Joseph C. Elliott, San Antonio.

Austin Division
Bastrop, Blanco, Burleson, Burnet, Caldwell, Gillespie, Hays, Kimble, Lampasas, Lee, Llano, Mason, McCulloch, San Saba, Travis, Washington and Williamson. Court for the Austin division shall be held at Austin. **Magistrate:** Philip E. Sanders, Austin. **Bankruptcy Judge:** Joseph C. Elliott, San Antonio. **Deputy in charge:** Barry Edwards.

El Paso Division
El Paso County only. Court is in continuous session in El Paso. **Magistrates:** Janet Ruesch and Philip T. Cole, El Paso. **Bankruptcy Judge:** Bert W. Thompson, San Antonio. **Deputy in charge:** Lupe E. Martinez.

Waco Division
Bell, Bosque, Coryell, Falls, Freestone, Hamilton, Hill, Leon, Limestone, McLennan, Milam, Robertson and Somervell. Court for the Waco division shall be held at Waco. **Magistrate:** Dennis Green, Waco. **Bankruptcy Judge:** Bert W. Thompson, San Antonio. **Deputy in charge:** Linda D. Wollard.

Del Rio Division
Edwards, Kinney, Maverick, Terrell, Uvalde, Val Verde and Zavala. Court for the Del Rio division shall be held at Del Rio. **Magistrate:** Durwood Edwards, Del Rio. **Bankruptcy Judge:** Bert W. Thompson, San Antonio. **Deputy In charge:** Katherine K. West.

Pecos Division
Brewster, Culberson, Hudspeth, Jeff Davis, Loving, Reeves, Pecos, Presidio, Ward and Winkler. Court for the Pecos division shall be held at Pecos. **Magistrate:** John M. Preston, Pecos. **Bankruptcy Judge:** Joseph C. Elliott, San Antonio. **Deputy in charge:** Linda B. Zeman.

Midland-Odessa Division
Andrews, Crane, Ector, Martin, Midland and Upton. Court for the Midland-Odessa Division shall be held at Midland. Court may be held, in the discretion of the court, in Odessa, when courtroom facilities are made available at no expense to the government. **Magistrate:** Darrell F. Smith, Midland. **Bankruptcy Judge:** Joseph C.

Elliott, San Antonio. **Deputy in charge:** Larry Bick, Midland.

EASTERN TEXAS DISTRICT

District Judges.—Chief Judge, William Wayne Justice, Tyler. **Judges:** Joe J. Fisher, Beaumont; William M. Steger, Tyler; Robert M. Parker, Marshall; Howell Cobb, Beaumont; Sam Hall, Texarkana. **Clerk of District Court:** Murray L. Harris, Tyler. **U.S. Attorney:** Robert J. Wortham, Beaumont. **U.S. Marshal:** James G. Barton, Tyler. **Chief U.S. Probation Officer:** Wade E. French, Tyler. **Judge in Bankruptcy for all divisions of the Eastern District:** Joe D. Huffstutler, Tyler. Following are the different divisions of the Eastern District, and the counties in each division:

Tyler Division

Anderson, Cherokee, Gregg, Henderson, Panola, Rains, Rusk, Smith, Van Zandt and Wood. Court in continuous session. **Magistrates:** C. Houston Abel, Tyler; Harry W. McKee, Tyler. **Chief Deputy:** Frank Monges. **Deputy Clerk:** Myra L. Barton.

Beaumont Division

Hardin, Jasper, Jefferson, Liberty, Newton, Orange. Court in continuous session. **Magistrate:** Earl Hines, Beaumont. **Deputy Clerk:** Vacancy.

Marshall Division

Camp, Cass, Harrison, Marion, Morris, Upshur. Sessions held as business dictates and as announced by the court. **Deputy Clerk:** Peggy Anderson.

Sherman Division

Collin, Cooke, Denton and Grayson. Sessions held as business dictates and as announced by the court. **Magistrate:** Roger Sanders. **Deputy Clerk:** Shirley Davis.

Texarkana Division

Bowie, Franklin and Titus. Sessions held as business dictates and as announced by the court. **Magistrate:** Vacancy. **Deputy Clerk:** Anita Thomason.

Paris Division

Delta, Fannin, Lamar, Red River and Hopkins. Sessions held as business dictates and as announced by the court.

Lufkin Division

Angelina, Houston, Nacogdoches, Polk, Sabine, San Augustine, Shelby, Trinity, Tyler.

SOUTHERN TEXAS DISTRICT

District Judges.—Chief Judge, John V. Singleton Jr., Houston. **Judges:** Carl O. Bue Jr., Ross N. Sterling, George Cire, Gabrielle McDonald, Norman Black and James DeAnda, Houston; Hayden W. Head Jr., Corpus Christi; Hugh Gibson, Galveston; Filemon B. Vela, Brownsville; George Kazen, Laredo; Ricardo H. Hinojosa, Brownsville. **Senior Judges:** Woodrow B. Seals, Houston; Owen D. Cox, Corpus Christi. **Clerk of District Court:** Jesse E. Clark, Houston. **U. S. Attorney:** Henry K. Oncken, Houston. **U.S. Marshal:** Basil S. Baker, Houston. **Bankruptcy Judges:** Randolph F. Wheless Jr., Manuel D. Leal and Letitia Z. Taitle, Houston. Following are the different divisions of the Southern District and the counties in each division:

Houston Division

Austin, Brazos, Colorado, Fayette, Fort Bend, Grimes, Harris, Madison, Montgomery, San Jacinto, Walker, Waller and Wharton. **Magistrates:** Calvin Botley, H. Lingo Platter, Karen K. Brown and George A. Kett Jr., Houston. **Clerk:** Jesse E. Clark.

Brownsville Division

Cameron, Hidalgo, Starr and Willacy. **Magistrates:** William Mallett and F. G. Garza (part-time), Brownsville. **Deputy Clerk:** Mrs. Sofia Anderson.

McAllen Operation: **Part-time Magistrate,** Susan R. Williams. (Operation served out of Brownsville Clerk's office.)

Corpus Christi Division

Aransas, Bee, Brooks, Duval, Jim Wells, Kenedy, Kleberg, Live Oak, Nueces and San Patricio. **Magistrate:** Eduardo E. deAses, Corpus Christi. **Deputy Clerk:** Mrs. Sue F. McCall.

Galveston Division

Brazoria, Chambers, Galveston and Matagorda. **Deputy Clerk:** Wilfred H. Bartlett.

Laredo Division

Jim Hogg, LaSalle, McMullen, Webb and Zapata. **Magistrate:** Marcel C. Notzon, Laredo. **Deputy Clerk:** Beatriz Garcia.

Victoria Division

Calhoun, DeWitt, Goliad, Jackson, Lavaca, Refugio and Victoria. **Deputy Clerk:** Thelma Maxine Gammon.

State Higher Courts

The state's higher courts are listed below with corrections to July 1, 1985. Notations in parentheses indicate dates of expiration of **terms of office.** Judges of the Supreme Court, Court of Criminal Appeals and Courts of Appeals are elected to 6-year, overlapping terms. District Court judges are elected to 4-year terms. As of Sept. 1, 1985, the Chief Justice of the Supreme Court and the Presiding Judge of the Court of Criminal Appeals each received $79,310; Justices each received $78,795; Chief Justices of the Courts of Appeals received $71,379; justices received $70,915 from the state. In addition a supplemental amount may be paid by counties but total salary must be at least $1,000 less than that received by Supreme Court justices. District Court judges received $56,135 from the state, plus supplemental pay from various subdivisions. Their total salary must be $1,000 less than that received by Courts of Appeals justices.

The judiciary of the state consists of nine members of the **State Supreme Court;** nine of the **Court of Criminal Appeals;** 80 of the **Courts of Appeals;** 361 of the **State District Courts;** 10 of the **Criminal District Courts;** 133 of the **County Courts at Law;** 11 of the **Probate Courts;** 254 of the **County Courts;** 940 **Justice of the Peace Courts;** and 832 **Municipal Courts.**

Below is given information on only the Supreme Court, Court of Criminal Appeals, Courts of Appeals and state District Courts. Names of county court judges, as well as names of the various district court judges, are given by counties in two tables beginning on page 667.

Supreme Court

Chief Justice, John L. Hill Jr. (1-1-91). **Justices,** Sears McGee (1-1-87); Robert M. Campbell (1-1-87); Franklin S. Spears (1-1-91); C. L. Ray (1-1-91); James P. Wallace (1-1-87); Ted Z. Robertson (1-1-89); William W. Kilgarlin (1-1-89); Raul A. Gonzalez (1-1-89). **Clerk of Court,** Mary M. Wakefield. **Location of court,** Austin.

Court of Criminal Appeals

Presiding Judge, John F. Onion Jr. (1-1-89). **Justices:** Tom G. Davis (1-1-87); W. C. Davis (1-1-91); Sam Houston Clinton (1-1-91); Michael J. McCormick (1-1-87); Marvin O. Teague (1-1-87); Chuck Miller (1-1-89); Charles F. Campbell (1-1-89); Bill White

(1-1-91). In 1971, the 62nd Legislature authorized the appointment of two Commissioners to assist the Court of Criminal Appeals. In 1977, a constitutional amendment raised the number of judges to eight, doing away with the office of Commissioner, effective Jan. 1, 1978. **State's Attorney,** Robert Huttash. **Clerk of Court,** Thomas F. Lowe. **Location of court,** Austin.

Courts of Appeals

These courts have jurisdiction within their respective supreme judicial districts. A constitutional amendment approved in 1978 raised the number of associate justices for Courts of Appeals where needed. Another amendment adopted in 1980 changed the name of the old **Courts of Civil Appeals** to the **Courts of Appeals** and changed the jurisdiction of the courts. See Art. V, Sec. 6 of the State Constitution.

First District.—*Houston. Chief Justice, Frank Evans III (1-1-87). Associate Justices: James F. Warren (1-1-87); Jack Smith (1-1-89); Sam H. Bass Jr. (1-1-89); F. Lee Duggan Jr. (1-1-89); M. B. Cohen (1-1-89); Ben G. Levy (1-1-89); Kenneth M. Hoyt (1-1-91) and D. Camille Dunn (1-1-91). Clerk of court, Kathryn Cox. Counties in the First District are as follows: Austin, Brazoria, Brazos, Burleson, Chambers, Colorado, Fort Bend, Galveston, Grimes, Harris, Trinity, Walker, Waller, Washington.

Second District.—Fort Worth: Chief Justice, Howard M. Fender (1-1-89). Associate Justices: Walter E. Jordan (1-1-89); Clyde R. Ashworth (1-1-89); William E. Burdock (1-1-89); Joe Spurlock II (1-1-87); John Hill (1-1-91) and Harry Hopkins (1-1-87). Clerk of court, Mrs. Yvonne Palmer. Counties in Second District are as follows: Archer, Clay, Cooke, Denton, Hood, Jack, Montague, Parker, Tarrant, Wichita, Wise, Young.

Third District.—Austin: Chief Justice, Bob Shannon (1-1-91). Associate Justices: John Powers (1-1-87); James L. Carroll (1-1-87); Jim Brady (1-1-89); Robert A. Gammage (1-1-89) and Earl W. Smith (1-1-89). Clerk of court, Mrs. Margie Love. Counties in the Third District are as follows: Bastrop, Bell, Blanco, Burnet, Caldwell, Coke, Comal, Concho, Fayette, Hays, Irion, Lampasas, Lee, Llano, McCulloch, Milam, Mills, Runnels, San Saba, Schleicher, Sterling, Tom Green, Travis, Williamson.

Fourth District.—San Antonio: Chief Justice, Carlos C. Cadena (1-1-91). Associate Justices: Rudolf Esquivel

(1-1-87); Shirley W. Butts (1-1-89); Antonio G. Cantu (1-1-89); Blair Reeves (1-1-89); Pete Tijerina (1-1-89) and Preston H. Dial Jr. (1-1-89). Clerk of court, Herb Schaefer. Counties in the Fourth District are as follows: Atascosa, Bandera, Bexar, Brooks, Dimmit, Duval, Edwards, Frio, Gillespie, Guadalupe, Jim Hogg, Jim Wells, Karnes, Kendall, Kerr, Kimble, Kinney, LaSalle, McMullen, Mason, Maverick, Medina, Menard, Real, Starr, Sutton, Uvalde, Val Verde, Webb, Wilson, Zapata, Zavala.

Fifth District.—Dallas: Chief Justice, Clarence A. Guittard (1-1-89). Associate Justices: Ted M. Akin (1-1-87); Spencer Carver (1-1-87); Charles Ben Howell (1-1-91); Bill J. Stephens (1-1-89); Jon Sparling (1-1-89); John C. Vance (1-1-89); James K. Allen (1-1-89); Warren Whitham (1-1-89); Patrick C. Guillot (1-1-89); Joe Devany (1-1-91); Pat McClung (1-1-91); one vacancy. Clerk of Court, Kenneth P. Stripling. Counties in the Fifth District are as follows: Collin, Dallas, Grayson, Hunt, Kaufman, Rockwall, Van Zandt.

Sixth District.—Texarkana: Chief Justice, William J. Cornelius (1-1-87). Associate Justices: Charles M. Bleil (1-1-89) and Bun L. Hutchinson (1-1-91). Clerk of court, Louise Waldrop Lohse. Counties in the Sixth District are as follows: Bowie, Camp, Cass, Delta, Fannin, Franklin, Gregg, Harrison, Hopkins, Hunt, Lamar, Marion, Morris, Panola, Red River, Rusk, Titus, Upshur, Wood.

Seventh District.—Amarillo: Chief Justice, Charles L. Reynolds (1-1-89). Associate Justices: Carlton B. Dodson (1-1-87); Richard N. Countiss (1-1-89) and John T. Boyd (1-1-89). Clerk of court, Peggy Culp. Counties in the Seventh District are as follows: Armstrong, Bailey, Briscoe, Carson, Castro, Childress, Cochran, Collingsworth, Cottle, Crosby, Dallam, Deaf Smith, Dickens, Donley, Floyd, Foard, Garza, Gray, Hale, Hall, Hansford, Hardeman, Hartley, Hemphill, Hockley, Hutchinson, Kent, King, Lamb, Lipscomb, Lubbock, Lynn, Moore, Motley, Ochiltree, Oldham, Parmer, Potter, Randall, Roberts, Sherman, Swisher, Terry, Wheeler, Wilbarger, Yoakum.

Eighth District.—El Paso: Chief Justice, Stephen F. Preslar (1-1-91). Associate Justices: William E. Ward (1-1-87); Max N. Osborn (1-1-89) and Charles R. Schulte (1-1-89). Clerk of court, Martha S. Diaz. Counties in the Eighth District are as follows: Andrews, Brewster, Crane, Crockett, Culberson, Ector, El Paso, Gaines, Glasscock, Hudspeth, Jeff Davis, Loving, Martin, Midland, Pecos, Presidio, Reagan, Reeves, Terrell, Upton, Ward, Winkler.

Ninth District.—Beaumont: Chief Justice, Martin Dies Jr. (1-1-91). Associate Justices: Jack Brookshire (1-1-89) and Don Burgess (1-1-87). Clerk of court, Joe A. Hulgan. Counties in the Ninth District are as follows: Angelina, Hardin, Jasper, Jefferson, Liberty, Montgomery, Newton, Orange, Polk, San Jacinto, Tyler.

Tenth District.—Waco: Chief Justice, Frank G. McDonald (1-1-89). Associate Justices: Vic Hall (1-1-87) and Bob L. Thomas (1-1-91). Clerk of court, Robert G. Watts. Counties in the Tenth District are as follows: Bosque, Brazos, Coryell, Ellis, Falls, Freestone, Hamilton, Hill, Johnson, Leon, Limestone, McLennan, Madison, Navarro, Robertson, Somervell.

Eleventh District.—Eastland: Chief Justice, Austin O. McCloud (1-1-89). Associate Justices: Raleigh Brown (1-1-91) and Charles R. Dickenson (1-1-87). Clerk of court, Mrs. Oleta Moseley. Counties in the Eleventh District are as follows: Baylor, Borden, Brown, Callahan, Coleman, Comanche, Dawson, Eastland, Erath, Fisher, Haskell, Howard, Jones, Knox, Mitchell, Nolan, Palo Pinto, Scurry, Shackelford, Stephens, Stonewall, Taylor, Throckmorton.

Twelfth District.—Tyler: Chief Justice, J. W. Summers (1-1-91). Associate Justices: James W. Bass Jr. (1-1-87) and Paul S. Colley (1-1-87). Clerk of court, Barbara A. Holman. Counties in the Twelfth District are as follows: Anderson, Cherokee, Gregg, Henderson, Hopkins, Houston, Kaufman, Nacogdoches, Panola, Rains, Rusk, Sabine, Smith, San Augustine, Shelby, Upshur, Van Zandt, Wood.

Thirteenth District.—Corpus Christi: Chief Justice, Paul W. Nye (1-1-89). Associate Justices: Noah O. Kennedy (1-1-89); Norman L. Utter (1-1-89); Robert J. Seerden (1-1-87); Fortunato P. Benavides (1-1-87) and J. Bonner Dorsey (1-1-87). Clerk of court, Beth Gray. Counties in the Thirteenth District are as follows: Aransas, Bee, Calhoun, Cameron, DeWitt, Goliad, Gonzales, Hidalgo, Jackson, Kenedy, Kleberg, Lavaca, Live Oak, Matagorda, Nueces, Refugio, San Patricio, Victoria, Wharton, Willacy.

Fourteenth District.—†Houston: Chief Justice, J. Curtiss Brown (1-1-91). Associate Justices: Paul Pressler (1-1-87); William E. Junell (1-1-87); Paul C. Murphy (1-1-91); Ross A. Sears (1-1-89); George T. Ellis (1-1-89); Joe L. Draughn (1-1-89); Bill Cannon (1-1-89) and Samuel H. Robertson Jr. (1-1-89). Clerk of court, Mary Jane Smart. Counties in the Fourteenth District are as follows: Austin, Brazoria, Brazos, Burleson, Chambers, Colorado, Fort Bend, Galveston, Grimes, Harris, Trinity, Walker, Waller, Washington.

*The location of the First Court of Appeals was changed from Galveston to Houston by the Fifty-fifth Legislature, with the provision that all cases originated in Galveston County be tried in that city and with the further provision that any case may, at the discretion of the court, be tried in either city.

†Because of the heavy workload of the Houston area Court of Appeals, the Sixtieth Legislature, in 1967, provided for the establishment of a Fourteenth Appeals Court at Houston.

Administrative Judicial Districts of Texas

There are nine administrative judicial districts in the state for administrative purposes. An active or retired district judge or an active or retired appellate judge with judicial experience in a district court serves as the Presiding Judge upon appointment by the Governor. They receive extra compensation of $5,000 paid by counties in the respective administrative districts.

The Presiding Judge convenes an annual conference of the judges in the administrative district to consult on the state of business in the courts. This conference is empowered to adopt rules for the administration of cases in the district. The Presiding Judge may assign active or retired district judges residing within the administrative district to any of the district courts within the administrative district. The Presiding Judge of one administrative district may request the Presiding Judge of another administrative district to assign a judge from that district to sit in a district court located in the administrative district of the Presiding Judge making the request.

The Chief Justice of the Supreme Court of Texas convenes an annual conference of the nine Presiding Judges to determine the need for assignment of judges and to promote the uniform administration of the assignment of judges. The Chief Justice is empowered to assign judges of one administrative district for service in another whenever such assignments are necessary for the prompt and efficient administration of justice.

First District. — Presiding Judge, John D. Ovard, Dallas: Anderson, Bowie, Camp, Cass, Cherokee, Collin, Dallas, Delta, Ellis, Fannin, Franklin, Grayson, Gregg, Harrison, Henderson, Hopkins, Houston, Hunt, Kaufman, Lamar, Marion, Morris, Nacogdoches, Panola, Rains, Red River, Rockwall, Rusk, Shelby, Smith, Titus, Upshur, Van Zandt and Wood.

Second District. — Thomas J. Stovall Jr., Huntsville: Angelina, Bastrop, Brazoria, Brazos, Burleson, Chambers, Fort Bend, Freestone, Galveston, Grimes, Hardin, Harris, Jasper, Jefferson, Lee, Leon, Liberty, Limestone, Madison, Matagorda, Montgomery, Newton, Orange, Polk, Robertson, Sabine, San Augustine, San Jacinto, Trinity, Tyler, Walker, Waller, Washington and Wharton.

Third District. — James F. Clawson Jr., Belton: Austin, Bell, Blanco, Bosque, Burnet, Caldwell, Colorado, Comal, Comanche, Coryell, Falls, Fayette, Gonzales, Guadalupe, Hamilton, Hays, Hill, Johnson, Lampasas, Lavaca, Llano, McLennan, Mason, Menard, Milam, Navarro, San Saba, Somervell, Travis and Williamson.

Fourth District. — Joe E. Kelly, Victoria: Aransas, Atascosa, Bee, Bexar, Calhoun, DeWitt, Dimmit, Frio, Goliad, Jackson, Karnes, LaSalle, Live Oak, McMullen, Refugio, San Patricio, Victoria, Webb, Wilson and Zapata.

Fifth District. — Joe B. Evins, Edinburg: Brooks, Cameron, Duval, Hidalgo, Jim Hogg, Jim Wells, Kenedy, Kleberg, Nueces, Starr and Willacy.

Sixth District. — George M. Thurmond, Del Rio: Bandera, Brewster, Crockett, Culberson, Edwards, El Paso, Gillespie, Hudspeth, Jeff Davis, Kendall, Kerr, Kimble, Kinney, Maverick, Medina, Pecos, Presidio, Reagan, Real, Sutton, Terrell, Upton, Uvalde, Val Verde and Zavala.

Seventh District. — Ray L. McKim, Odessa: Andrews, Borden, Brown, Callahan, Coke, Coleman, Concho, Crane, Dawson, Ector, Fisher, Gaines, Garza, Glasscock, Haskell, Howard, Irion, Jones, Kent, Loving, Lynn, McCulloch, Martin, Midland, Mills, Mitchell, Nolan, Reeves, Runnels, Schleicher, Scurry, Shackelford, Sterling, Stonewall, Taylor, Throckmorton, Tom Green, Ward and Winkler.

Eighth District. — Charles J. Murray, Fort Worth: Archer, Clay, Cooke, Denton, Eastland, Erath, Hood, Jack, Montague, Palo Pinto, Parker, Stephens, Tarrant, Wichita, Wise and Young.

Ninth District. — Eugene E. Jordan, Amarillo: Armstrong, Bailey, Baylor, Briscoe, Carson, Castro, Childress, Cochran, Collingsworth, Cottle, Crosby, Dallam, Deaf Smith, Dickens, Donley, Floyd, Foard, Gray, Hale, Hall, Hansford, Hardeman, Hartley, Hemphill, Hockley, Hutchinson, King, Knox, Lamb, Lipscomb, Lubbock, Moore, Motley, Ochiltree, Oldham, Parmer, Potter, Randall, Roberts, Sherman, Swisher, Terry, Wheeler, Wilbarger and Yoakum.

State District Courts

There are over 360 district and 10 criminal district courts, each having its own judge and statutory geographical jurisdiction. In metropolitan areas and some others, the geographical jurisdiction of two or more District Courts is overlapping or identical. In the latter case, several courts operate to considerable degree as if they were one court of several judges, although sitting separately. Term of office is four years. Basic salary (paid by the state) is $56,135, plus supplemental pay may be paid by various subdivisions. Total salary must be $1,000 less than that received by Courts of Appeals justices.

A constitutional amendment adopted in 1980 made extensive changes in the state courts. See Art. V, Sections 1, 2, 3, 5, 6 and 16.

Dist. No., Name of Judge, Counties Within Jurisdiction

1—O'Neal Bacon: Jasper, Newton, Sabine, San Augustine.
1-A—Monte D. Lawlis: Jasper, Newton, Tyler.
2—Morris W. Hassell: Cherokee.
3—R. Wayne Lawrence: Anderson, Henderson, Houston.
4—Donald R. Ross: Rusk.
5—Jack E. Carter: Bowie, Cass.
6—Henry G. Braswell: Fannin, Lamar, Red River.
7—Don Carroll: Smith.
8—Lanny R. Ramsay: Delta, Franklin, Hopkins, Rains.
9—Lynn J. Coker: Montgomery, Polk, San Jacinto, Waller.
2D9—John C. Martin: Montgomery, Polk, San Jacinto, Trinity.
10—Ed J. Harris: Galveston.
11—William N. Blanton Jr.: Harris.
12—E. G. Ernst: Grimes, Leon, Madison, Walker.
13—Kenneth A. Douglas: Navarro.
14—John M. Marshall: Dallas.
15—Jim Fry: Grayson.
16—John K. Narsutis: Denton.
17—Charles J. Murray: Tarrant.
18—E. Byron Crosier: Johnson, Somervell.
19—Bill Logue: McLennan.
20—Don G. Humble: Milam.
21—John L. Placke: Bastrop, Burleson, Lee, Washington.
22—Charles R. Ramsay: Caldwell, Comal, Hays.
23—Neil Caldwell: Brazoria, Matagorda, Wharton.
24—C. N. Stevenson: Calhoun, De Witt, Goliad, Jackson, Refugio, Victoria.
25—B. B. Schraub: Colorado, Gonzales, Guadalupe, Lavaca.
2D25—Gus J. Strauss: Colorado, Gonzales, Guadalupe, Lavaca.
26—William S. Lott: Williamson.
27—C. W. Duncan Jr.: Bell, Lampasas.
28—Walter Dunham Jr.: Kenedy, Kleberg, Nueces.
29—David Cleveland: Palo Pinto.
30—Calvin Ashley: Wichita.
31—Grainger W. McIlhany: Gray, Hemphill, Lipscomb, Roberts, Wheeler.

Dist. No., Name of Judge, Counties Within Jurisdiction

32—Weldon Kirk: Fisher, Mitchell, Nolan.
33—Clayton E. Evans: Blanco, Burnet, Llano, Mason, San Saba.
34— Jerry Woodard: Culberson, El Paso, Hudspeth.
35—Ernest Cadenhead Jr.: Brown, Mills.
36—R. M. Yeager: Aransas, Bee, Live Oak, McMullen, San Patricio.
37— John Cornyn III: Bexar.
38—Mickey R. Pennington: Medina, Real, Uvalde.
39—Charles Chapman: Haskell, Kent, Stonewall, Throckmorton.
40—Milton A. Hartsfield: Ellis.
41—John L. McKellips: El Paso.
42—Don H. Lane: Callahan, Coleman, Taylor.
43—James O. Mullin: Parker.
44—Hubert D. Johnson Jr.: Dallas.
45—Carol R. Haberman: Bexar.
46—Leslie L. Thomas: Foard, Hardeman, Wilbarger.
47—H. Bryan Poff Jr.: Armstrong, Potter, Randall.
48—Wm. L. Hughes Jr.: Tarrant.
49—Ruben Garcia: Webb, Zapata.
50—David W. Hajek: Baylor, Cottle, King, Knox.
51—I. Royal Hart: Coke, Irion, Schleicher, Sterling, Tom Green.
52—Bobby L. Cummings: Coryell.
53—Mary P. Williams: Travis.
54—George H. Allen: McLennan.
55—Reagan Cartwright: Harris.
56—I. A. Lerner: Galveston.
57—John G. Yates: Bexar.
58—Ronald L. Walker: Jefferson.
59—Joseph M. Joiner: Grayson.
60—J. Gary Sanderson: Jefferson.
61—R. Shearn Smith: Harris.
62—Jim N. Thompson: Delta, Franklin, Hopkins, Lamar.
63—George M. Thurmond: Edwards, Kinney, Terrell, Val Verde.
64—Jack R. Miller: Castro, Hale, Swisher.
65—Eduardo S. Marquez: El Paso.
66—Robert G. Dohoney: Hill.
67—George A. Crowley: Tarrant.
68—Gary Hall: Dallas.
69—Bill H. Sheehan: Dallam, Hartley, Moore, Sherman.
70—Gene Ater: Ector.
71—Ben Z. Grant: Harrison.
72—John D. Bevers: Crosby, Lubbock.
73—James C. Onion: Bexar.
74—Derwood Johnson: McLennan.
75—C. D. Cain: Liberty.
76—B. D. Moye: Camp, Morris, Titus.
77—P. K. Reiter: Freestone, Limestone.
78—J. Keith Nelson: Wichita.
79—Romeo M. Flores: Brooks, Jim Wells.
80—William R. Powell: Harris.
81—Olin B. Strauss: Atascosa, Frio, Karnes, La Salle, Wilson.
82—Robert Stem: Falls, Robertson.
83—Alex R. Gonzalez: Brewster, Jeff Davis, Pecos, Presidio, Reagan, Upton.
84—Juan E. Blackburn: Hansford, Hutchinson, Ochiltree.
85—W. T. McDonald Jr.: Brazos.
86—Glen M. Ashworth: Kaufman, Rockwall.
87—Sam B. Bournias: Anderson, Freestone, Leon, Limestone.
88—Earl B. Stover: Hardin, Tyler.
89—R. Temple Driver: Wichita.
90—R. E. Thornton: Stephens, Young.
91—Jim R. Wright: Eastland.
92—Homer Salinas: Hidalgo.
93—John F. Dominguez: Hidalgo.
94—Rene Haas: Nueces.
95—Nathan L. Hecht: Dallas.
96—Hal M. Lattimore: Tarrant.
97—F. J. Douthitt: Archer, Clay, Montague.
98—Hume Cofer: Travis.
99—Thomas L. Clinton: Lubbock.
100—John T. Forbis: Carson, Childress, Collingsworth, Donley, Hall.
101—Craig T. Enoch: Dallas.
102—Leon F. Pesek: Bowie, Red River.
103—Diego Leal: Cameron, Willacy.
104—Billy J. Edwards: Taylor.

Dist. No., Name of Judge, Counties Within Jurisdiction

105—Vernon D. Harville: Kenedy, Kleberg, Nueces.
106—George H. Hansard: Dawson, Gaines, Garza, Lynn.
107—Melchor Chavez: Cameron, Willacy.
108—Edward B. Nobles: Potter.
109—James H. Clack: Andrews, Crane, Winkler.
110—George W. Miller: Briscoe, Dickens, Floyd, Motley.
111—Antonio A. Zardenetta: Webb.
112—M. Brock Jones Jr.: Crockett, Pecos, Reagan, Sutton, Upton.
113—Geraldine B. Tennant: Harris.
114—Galloway Calhoun Jr.: Smith, Wood.
115—Virgil E. Mulanax: Marion, Upshur.
116—Fred S. Harless: Dallas.
117—Jack R. Blackmon: Nueces.
118—James W. Gregg: Glasscock, Howard, Martin.
119—Curt F. Steib: Concho, Runnels, Tom Green.
120—Brunson D. Moore: El Paso.
121—Ray D. Anderson: Terry, Yoakum.
122—H. G. Dalehite Jr.: Galveston.
123—Bennie C. Boles: Panola, Shelby.
124—Alvin G. Khoury: Gregg.
125—Mike O'Brien: Harris.
126—Joseph H. Hart: Travis.
127—Sharolyn P. Wood: Harris.
128—Patrick A. Clark: Orange.
129—Hugo A. Touchy: Harris.
130—W. Jack Salyer: Matagorda.
131—Rose Spector: Bexar.
132—Gene L. Dulaney: Borden, Scurry.
133—David Hittner: Harris.
134—Joe Burnett: Dallas.
135—Frank H. Crain: Calhoun, De Witt, Goliad, Jackson, Refugio, Victoria.
136—Jack R. King: Jefferson.
137—Robert C. Wright: Lubbock.
138—Robert Garza: Cameron, Willacy.
139—Raul L. Longoria: Hidalgo.
140—Wm. R. Shaver: Lubbock.
141—James E. Wright: Tarrant.
142—Pat M. Baskin: Midland.
143—Lawrence Fuller: Loving, Reeves, Ward.
144—Roy R. Barrera Jr.: Bexar.
145—Jack Pierce: Nacogdoches.
146—Wm. C. Black: Bell.
147—Mace B. Thurman Jr.: Travis.
148—Margarito C. Garza: Nueces.
149—Paul F. Ferguson: Brazoria.
150—Fred Biery: Bexar.
151—A. J. P. Farris: Harris.
152—Jack O'Neill: Harris.
153—Sidney C. Farrar Jr.: Tarrant.
154—Pat H. Boone Jr.: Lamb.
155—Oliver S. Kitzman: Austin, Fayette, Waller.
156—W. Rachel Littlejohn: Aransas, Bee, Live Oak, McMullen, San Patricio.
157—Felix Salazar Jr.: Harris.
158—Jack Gray: Denton.
159—David Walker: Angelina.
160—Leonard E. Hoffman Jr.: Dallas.
161—Tryon D. Lewis: Ector.
162—Catherine Crier: Dallas.
163—David A. Dunn: Orange.
164—Peter S. Solito: Harris.
165—R. L. Smith: Harris.
166—Peter Michael Curry: Bexar.
167—Robert Jones: Travis.
168—Ward L. Koehler: El Paso.
169—J. F. Clawson Jr.: Bell.
170—R. R. Mormino: McLennan.
171—Edwin F. Berliner: El Paso.
172—Thomas A. Thomas: Jefferson.
173—Jack H. Holland: Henderson.
174—Jon N. Hughes: Harris.
175—Phil G. Chavarria Jr.: Bexar.
176—Wm. M. Hatten: Harris.
177—Miron A. Love: Harris.
178—William T. Harmon: Harris.
179—I. D. McMaster: Harris.
180—Patricia R. Lykos: Harris.
181—George E. Dowlen: Potter, Randall.
182—Donald K. Shipley: Harris.
183—J. M. Guarino: Harris.
184—Carroll Weaver: Harris.
185—George L. Walker: Harris.
186—James E. Barlow: Bexar.

Dist. No., Name of Judge, Counties Within Jurisdiction

187—Patrick Priest: Bexar.
188—Marcus F. Vascocu: Gregg.
189—Lynn N. Hughes: Harris.
190—Wyatt H. Heard: Harris.
191—James B. Zimmermann: Dallas.
192—Harlan A. Martin: Dallas.
193—John H. Whittington Jr.: Dallas.
194—James E. Kinkeade: Dallas.
195—R. T. Scales: Dallas.
196—E. Paul Banner: Hunt.
197—Darrell B. Hester: Cameron, Willacy.
198—V. Murray Jordan: Concho, Kerr, Kimble, McCulloch, Menard.
199—John R. Roach: Collin.
200—Paul R. Davis Jr.: Travis.
201—Jerry Dellana: Travis.
202—Guy E. Jones: Bowie.
203—Thomas B. Thorpe: Dallas.
204—Richard D. Mays: Dallas.
205—Sam W. Callan: El Paso, Culberson, Hudspeth.
206—Joe B. Evins: Hidalgo.
207—R. T. Pfeuffer: Caldwell, Comal, Hays.
208—Thomas H. Routt: Harris.
209—M. T. Mc Spadden: Harris.
210—Sam M. Paxson: El Paso, Culberson, Hudspeth.
211—I. Sam Houston: Denton.
212—Don B. Morgan: Galveston.
213—Tom Cave: Tarrant.
214—Mike Westergren: Nueces.
215—Eugene Chambers: Harris.
216—Robert R. Barton: Bandera, Gillespie, Kendall, Kerr.
217—David V. Wilson: Angelina.
218—R. L. Eschenburg II: Atascosa, Frio, Karnes, La Salle, Wilson.
219—John L. McCraw Jr.: Collin.
220—James E. Morgan: Bosque, Comanche, Hamilton.
221—Lee G. Alworth: Montgomery.
222—David W. Gulley: Deaf Smith, Oldham.
223—Don E. Cain: Gray.
224—Carolyn H. Spears: Bexar.
225—Alfonso Chapa: Bexar.
226—M. Ted Butler: Bexar.
227—Mike M. Machado: Bexar.
228—Ted Poe: Harris.
229—R. H. Garcia: Duval, Jim Hogg, Starr.
230—N. Joe Kegans: Harris.
231—Maryellen W. Hicks: Tarrant.
232—A.D. Azios: Harris.
233—Harold L. Valderas: Tarrant.
234—Ruby K. Sondock: Harris.
235—Larry B. Sullivant: Cooke.
236—Albert L. White Jr.: Tarrant.
237—John R. McFall: Lubbock.
238—Vann Culp: Midland.
239—J. R. Gayle III: Brazoria.
240—Chas. A. Dickerson: Fort Bend.
241—Joe Tunnell: Smith.
242—Marvin F. Marshall: Castro, Hale, Swisher.
243—Herb Marsh Jr.: El Paso.
244—H. Joseph Connally: Ector.
245—H. G. Schuble III: Harris.
246—J. W. Peavy Jr.: Harris.
247—Charles D. Huckabee: Harris.
248—Woody R. Densen: Harris.
249—John R. MacLean: Johnson, Somervell.
250—Harley R. Clark Jr.: Travis.
251—Naomi Harney: Potter, Randall.
252—L. J. Giblin Jr.: Jefferson.
253—W. G. Woods Jr.: Chambers, Liberty.
254—Dee Miller: Dallas.
255—Don D. Koons: Dallas.
256—Linda B. Thomas: Dallas.
257—Norman R. Lee: Harris.
258—Joe Ned Dean: Polk, San Jacinto, Trinity.
259—H. G. Andrews Jr.: Jones, Shackelford.
260—Buddie J.Hahn: Orange.
261—Peter M. Lowry: Travis.
262—Lloyd D. Shaver: Harris.
263—Charles J. Hearn: Harris.
264—Jack W. Prescott: Bell.
265—John D. Ovard: Dallas.
266—Donald R. Jones: Erath.
267—W. W. Kilgore: Calhoun, De Witt, Goliad, Jackson, Refugio, Victoria.

Dist. No., Name of Judge, Counties Within Jurisdiction

268—A. Reagan Clark: Fort Bend.
269—W. David West: Harris.
270—Ann Cochran: Harris.
271—John R. Lindsey: Jack, Wise.
272—John M. Delaney: Brazos.
273—John L. Smith: Sabine, San Augustine, Shelby.
274—Fred A. Moore: Caldwell, Comal, Guadalupe, Hays.
275—Arturo E. Guerra Jr.: Hidalgo.
276—William R. Porter: Camp, Marion, Morris, Titus.
277—John R. Carter: Williamson.
278—Jerry A. Sandel: Grimes, Leon, Madison, Walker.
279—Robert P. Walker: Jefferson.
280—Thomas R. Phillips: Harris.
281—Louis M. Moore: Harris.
282—Kelly W. Loving: Dallas.
283—M. Jack Hampton: Dallas.
284—Olen Underwood: Montgomery.
285—Homer D. Peeples: Bexar.
286—James K. Walker: Cochran, Hockley.
287—Jack D. Young: Bailey, Parmer.
288—Raul Rivera: Bexar.
289—Tom Rickhoff: Bexar.
290—David A. Berchelmann: Bexar.
291—Gerry H. Meier: Dallas.
292—Michael E. Keasler: Dallas.
293—Benjamin A. Martinez: Dimmit, Maverick, Zavala.
294—Richard D. Davis: Van Zandt, Wood.
295—Frank O. White: Harris.
296—Verla S. Holland: Collin.
297—Charles Dickens: Tarrant.
298—Sidney A. Fitzwater: Dallas.
299—Jon Neil Wisser: Travis.
300—Thomas Kenyon: Brazoria.
301—Bob O'Donnell: Dallas.
302—Frances Ann Harris: Dallas.
303—Merrill Hartman: Dallas.
304—Craig Penfold: Dallas.
305—Annette Stewart: Dallas.
306—Andrew Z. Baker: Galveston.
307—Wm. C. Martin III: Gregg.
308—Bob W. Robertson: Harris.
309—Herman Gordon: Harris.
310—Allen J. Daggett: Harris.
311—Bill Elliott: Harris.
312—Robert S. Webb III: Harris.
313—R. L. Lowry: Harris.
314—Robert B. Baum: Harris.
315—Eric G. Andell: Harris.
316—Guy Hazlett: Hutchinson.
317—James M. Farris: Jefferson.
318—Barbara G. Culver: Midland.
319—Max L. Bennett: Nueces.
320—Don R. Emerson: Potter.

Dist. No., Name of Judge, Counties Within Jurisdiction

321—Ruth Blake: Smith.
322—Frank W. Sullivan III: Tarrant.
323—Scott D. Moore: Tarrant.
324—Brian A. Carper: Tarrant.
325—R. L. Wright: Tarrant.
326—Henry J. Strauss: Taylor.
327—E. H. Pena: El Paso.
328—Thomas O. Stansbury: Fort Bend.
329—Daniel R. Sklar: Wharton.
330—Theo Bedard: Dallas.
331—Robert A. Perkins: Travis.
332—Mario E. Ramirez Jr.: Hidalgo.
333—Davie L. Wilson: Harris.
334—Marsha D. Anthony: Harris.
335—Harold R. Towslee: Bastrop, Burleson, Lee, Washington.
336—Ray F. Grisham: Fannin, Grayson.
337—Johnny R. Kolenda: Harris.
338—Mary Bacon: Harris.
339—Norman Lanford: Harris.
340—Marilyn Aboussie: Tom Green.
341—Elma T. Salinas: Webb.
342—Joe B. Cunningham: Tarrant.
343—Alonzo T. Rodriguez: Aransas, Bee, Live Oak, McMullen, San Patricio.
344—Carroll E. Wilborn Jr.: Chambers.
345—Juan F. Gallardo: Travis.
346—Jose J. Baca: El Paso.
347—Joaquin Villarreal III: Nueces.
348—Michael D. Schattman: Tarrant.
349—Melvin D. Whitaker: Anderson, Houston.
350—William A. Thomas Jr.: Taylor.
351—Albert Pruett: Harris.
352—John Street: Tarrant.
353—Joe B. Dibrell Jr.: Travis.
354—Richard Bosworth: Hunt, Rains.
355—Ralph H. Walton Jr.: Hood.
356—Britton E. Plunk: Hardin.
357—Menton J. Murray Jr.: Cameron, Willacy
358—Effective Sept. 1, 1985: Ector
359—James H. Keeshan: Montgomery.
360—Catherine H. Adamski: Tarrant.
361—Carolyn Ruffino: Brazos.

Dallas County Criminal District Courts:
Cr. 1—Ron Chapman.
Cr. 2—Larry W. Baraka.
Cr. 3—Gary R. Stephens.
Cr. 4—Frances Maloney.
Cr. 5—Pat McDowell.

Jefferson County Criminal District Court:
Lawrence J. Gist.

Tarrant County Criminal District Courts:
Cr. 1—E. L. Goldsmith.
Cr. 2—L. Clifford Davis.
Cr. 3—Don Leonard.
Cr. 4—Joe Drago III.

TEXAS DEPARTMENT OF CORRECTIONS

The Texas Department of Corrections operates the state prison system for adult felony offenders. The headquarters is in Huntsville, with O. Lane Cotter as director. The system maintains more than 100,000 acres of land on 27 units, and houses in excess of 36,000 inmates.

Since 1982, TDC has been under a federal court order to relieve overcrowding and to upgrade various services.

The following summary of current operations deals only with the Texas Department of Corrections. Juvenile offenders are under the jurisdiction of a separate state agency, administered as the **Texas Youth Council.**

The **Texas Board of Corrections** guides the administration and operation of the department in the areas of policy, planning and budgetary matters; the nine board members are nonsalaried and appointed for 6-year terms by the governor. Cotter has served as director since June 18, 1985.

The average number of inmates during fiscal year 1984 was 35,619. Prison population has grown from 18,151 on Aug. 31, 1975, to 20,976 on Aug. 31, 1976, to 20,862 on Aug. 31, 1977, to 24,615 on Aug. 31, 1978 to 25,164 on Aug. 31, 1979, to 28,543 on Aug. 31, 1980, to 30,315 on Aug. 31, 1981, to 34,393 on Aug 31, 1982, to 36,769 on Aug 31, 1983,

and to 35,772 on Aug. 31, 1984. Currently, the recidivism rate is approximately 42 percent.

On Aug. 31, 1984, fixed assets of the department were $611,628,526.44, including land, buildings and equipment. Total monies appropriated to the department by the Texas Legislature for the 1985 fiscal year amounted to $298,692,882 (this includes $21,068,304 for building programs).

Agriculture and livestock operations are under efficient management and provide a savings to taxpayers. Combined with prison industries and construction projects utilizing inmate labor, this financial effort gives Texas one of the lowest per capita inmate costs to taxpayers in the nation. **Costs daily** per inmate were: 1984 - $17.70; 1983 - $14.57; 1982 - $12.11; 1981 - $9.80; - 1980 - $8.61; 1979 - $7.34; 1978 - $7.15; 1977 - $7.32; 1976 - $5.97; 1975 - $5.20; 1974 - $4.59; 1973 - $3.89 and 1972 - $3.31.

Most treatment programs in the areas of education, recreation, medicine and worship are funded by legislative appropriations, or other state funds. Supplemental monies to extend these programs are derived from prison commissary operations and through the famed annual **Texas Prison Rodeo**, held each Sunday in October.

Cooperative programs in **higher education** are being carried out on all units. Junior college programs leading to Associate of Arts degrees are in effect with **Lee College, Brazosport College, Alvin College, Central Texas College, Blinn College** and **Henderson County Junior College.** Bachelors degrees can be earned through **Sam Houston State University,** the **University of Houston at Clear Lake City, Tarleton State University** or **Stephen F. Austin State University.** During the 1983-1984 school year, 13,146 inmates participated in college programs. In addition, 2,587 inmates participated in Apprenticeships, Related Training and **Texas A&M University Extension Programs** to qualify for craft certificates.

In 1969, an independent school (**Windham School District**) was created within the department to offer education in grades 1-12 and special education leading to a G.E.D., or high school diploma. A total of 27,570 inmates have received certificates or diplomas from 1969 to 1984, and 1984 average monthly enrollment involved approximately 15,330 of the inmate population.

Approximately 90 courses are offered in various vocational skills through the Windham School District and college programs. Participants in the college and secondary level vocational courses numbered 7,117 students during fiscal year 1984.

Rehabilitative programs are also available in the fields of physiological and psychiatric health care, varied recreational programs, legal services, religious activities, inmate self-help groups, work-release programs, job placement services, pre-release programs and support programs in conjunction with other state agencies.

Units

Beto Units, Tennessee Colony, Anderson County: Agriculture operations include livestock, field crops, rabbits, hog feeder slab, fence building, hot house and dog kennels. Industrial operations include a highway sign factory, records conversion and bus repair. Beto is divided into Beto I and Beto II.

Central Unit, Sugar Land, Fort Bend County: Agriculture operations include field and edible crops, livestock, central agriculture commissary, agriculture administrative offices, canning plant, veterinary clinic and a combine operation. Industrial operations include a soap and detergent factory and a transportation warehouse. Other operations include the industrial distribution warehouse and the headquarters for southern area construction activities.

Clemens Unit, Brazoria, Brazoria County: Agriculture operations include field and edible crops, livestock and grain dryer.

Coffield Unit, Tennessee Colony, Anderson County: Agriculture operations include livestock, field and edible crops, feedlot, feed mill, meat packing plant, hog feeder slabs, sawmill and a poultry house. Industrial operations include records conversion, metal fabrication and dump truck bed factory. Other operations include the headquarters for northern area maintenance, asphalt plant and a rock crusher.

Darrington Unit, Rosharon, Brazoria County: Agriculture operations include field and edible crops, livestock and poultry layers. Other operations include tire recapping and a concrete batch plant.

Diagnostic Unit, Huntsville, Walker County: Special operations include testing and classifying of all newly received male inmates in order to assign them to a permanent unit.

Eastham Unit, Lovelady, Houston County: Agriculture operations include field and edible crops, livestock, dairy, gin, feedmill, poultry house, hogs, feeder slab and a brooder slab. Other operations include a garment factory.

Ellis Units, Huntsville, Walker County: Agriculture operations include field and edible crops, livestock, dairy, gin, farrowing barn, stocker cattle and land clearing. Industrial operations include a dental lab, woodworking shop, shoe factory and bus repair. Other operations include the headquarters for central area maintenance and the central area region fire and safety office. Ellis is divided into Ellis I and Elis II.

Ferguson Unit, Midway, Madison County: Agriculture operations include field and edible crops, livestock, swine farrowing and a feeder slab. Other operations include a mop and broom factory and the headquarters for the central area construction program.

Gatesville Unit, Gatesville, Coryell County (Women's Unit): Special operations include a garment factory, and the testing and classifying of all newly received female inmates in order to assign them to a permanent unit.

Goree Unit, Huntsville, Walker County: Agriculture operations include a horse breeding program.

Hilltop Unit, Gatesville, Coryell County: Agriculture operations include field and edible crops and a horse breeding program. Industrial operations include records conversion and bus repair. Other operations include a satellite headquarters for northern area maintenance.

Mountain View Unit, Gatesville, Coryell County (Women's Unit): Special operations include a braille facility, psychological treatment center and pre-release for female inmates.

Pack Units, Navasota, Grimes County: Agriculture operations include field and edible crops and livestock. Other operations include a stainless steel products factory. Pack is divided into Pack I and Pack II.

Ramsey Units, Rosharon, Brazoria County: Agriculture operations include field and edible crops, livestock, dairy, dehydrator and gin. Other operations include furniture refinishing, operations center for portable buildings crew and the headquarters for southern area maintenance. Ramsey is divided into Ramsey I, Ramsey II and Ramsey III.

Retrieve Unit, Angleton, Brazoria County: Agriculture operations include field and edible crops, livestock and a dairy.

Wynne Unit, Huntsville, Walker County: Agriculture operations include field and edible crops, livestock, dairy and dog kennel program. Industrial operations include a license plate plant, validation sticker plant, mattress factory, corrugated box factory, plastic sign shop, records conversion, transportation department, prison store and laundries. Other operations include the **Windham School District's** administrative offices and warehouse and headquarters for in-house construction.

Texas Department of Corrections Hospital, Galveston, Galveston County: Special operations include facilities for major surgery, acute care and unique treatment.

History of Texas Public Lands

The History of Texas Public Lands was revised for the Texas Almanac by **Commissioner Garry Mauro** and the staff of the General Land Office of Texas. It is a summary of a longer history of the Texas **public domain** in the General Land Office.

The **Texas General Land Office** is one of the oldest governmental entities in the state, dating back to the Republic. The practice of having a commissioner to administer public lands reaches even farther back into Texas history when proprietors of Spanish and Mexican land grants "commissioned" representatives to handle land transactions.

Before the American Revolution, proprietors of the colonies along the eastern seaboard established land offices under the supervision of the commissioned representative to sell land and control squatting or trespassing. Later in Texas, when the Mexican government began issuing land grants for colonization, each empresario colony had a land commissioner to issue individual land titles and settle disputes.

The first General Land Office was established in the **constitution of the Republic of Texas** in 1836, and the first Texas Congress enacted the provision into law in 1837. However, President Sam Houston vetoed the act on the grounds that the office would not be able to function properly until the records of the various empresario colonies, Spanish and Mexican land grants, and the appropriate archives could be properly gathered together. But the new Congress was so anxious to settle land questions that it overrode his veto.

The sale of public lands had been temporarily suspended during the War for Texas Independence from Mexico, and there was a great clamor to open up the public lands again. New settlers were arriving every day and the demand for free or cheap land was tremendous.

Because the new Texas government needed to become stable and productive, it sought to attract and keep these settlers. The Texas Congress enacted generous laws offering large tracts of land to just about anyone who wanted them. For example, all heads of households in Texas as of March 2, 1836, were entitled to a league and a labor of land (about 4,605 acres). Single men could claim a third of a league. In the 10 years Texas existed as a Republic, it alloted 41,570,733 acres to encourage settlement, to reward veterans of the War for Independence, to pay the Republic's debts and to finance its operations.

In 1844, as negotiations proceeded for Texas to join the Union, the resulting treaty stipulated that the U.S. would pay $10 million of the Republic's debts and acquire 175 million acres of the public domain. Opponents to statehood in the U.S. Congress felt that Texas' lands were not worth the assumption of the $10 million debt and refused to make the trade. In the final resolution for annexation, Texas was to keep its public domain and the U.S. was to disclaim any responsibility for Texas' debt. Texas officially came into the Union Dec. 29, 1845, keeping both its debt and its public lands.

When the first **state constitution** was drawn up in July, 1845, it provided no major change in the administration of the Texas public domain. All land titles issued under the laws of Spain, Mexico and the Republic of Texas were recognized. The Commissioner of the General Land Office became one of the elected constitutional officials of the state government.

In the early years of statehood, Texas established the precedent of using its vast public domain for public benefit. The first use was to sell or trade off land to eliminate the huge debt remaining from the War for Independence and early years of the Republic. A western area of 67 million acres, now part of New Mexico, Colorado, Oklahoma, Kansas and Wyoming, was transferred to the United States by the Texas Legislature on Nov. 25, 1850. Texas received $10 million in government bonds. The state had shed all its debts by 1855 and still had over 98 million acres of open domain. Texas gave away land for **internal improvements, homesteads, veterans grants, capitol construction,** and for settlement of **boundary disputes.** More than 32 million acres were given away to promote **railroad construction.** And 50 million acres were set aside as an **endowment to public schools and colleges.**

By 1898, there was very little remaining unappropriated public land in Texas. The **homestead policy,** which had seen 4.8 million acres of land given away to settlers, was finally abandoned in 1899. The Legislature in 1900 determined that the public schools and the **Permanent School Fund** would receive all unsurveyed land and the few remaining unappropriated public lands. Finally in 1939, all lakes, bays, islands and the submerged areas off the Texas coast accrued to the School Fund.

The end of the vast unappropriated public domain might have signaled the end of the use of public land for the benefit of all Texans. But when oil was discovered in 1921 on state lands under lease, this remaining public land became a most valuable economic asset to the state. After selling off 91.4 percent of its surface land without reserving mineral rights, Texas finally had established the right to its subsurface minerals in 1895. And the Relinquishment Act of 1919 gave the surface owners of the land rights to participate in the mineral wealth as "agents" of the state. The economic value of the public lands of Texas in the 20th Century thus resulted from the belated development of its mineral ownership.

Today, 22.5 million acres are considered to be in the **public domain.** This includes 4,045,000 acres from the Texas shoreline out to the three marine league line. More than one million acres make up the state's riverbeds and vacant areas. The University of Texas System holds title to 2,109,000 fee acres, and other state agencies or special schools hold title to between 2 to 3 million acres. Texas owns mineral rights alone in another 7 to 8 million acres covered under the Relinquishment Act, and has outright ownership to 872,000 upland acres, mostly west of the Pecos River.

Perhaps the most valuable segment of the Texas public domain is its **coastal submerged land.** And for some time, there was serious question about the state's ownership. The Republic of Texas had proclaimed its Gulf boundaries as three marine leagues, recognized by international law as traditional national boundaries. These boundaries were never seriously questioned when Texas joined the Union in 1845, and Texas continued to claim jurisdiction. A congressional resolution in 1930 authorized the U.S. Attorney General to file suit to establish the offshore lands as properties of the federal government.

The legal question was more important to Texas in the 20th Century than it would have been upon entering the Union, since offshore oil and gas production had become a source of tremendous income to the state.

Public Lands of Texas

Taken from the records of the General Land Office of Texas, the following summary shows the disposition of the public domain. The total area given here differs from the U.S. Census Bureau figure of 171,096,320 given elsewhere in this volume.

	Acres.	Subtotals.
Total area to tidewater		172,366,000
Total area to 3-league (10.36-mile) limit		3,900,000
		176,266,000
Grants to promote citizenship and to induce immigration—		
By governments of Spain and Mexico	26,280,000	
Headrights and bounties	36,876,492	
Colonies—(Peter's, Mercer's et al.)	4,494,806	
Homestead donations (pre-emptions)	4,847,136—	72,498,434
Donations to veterans—		
San Jacinto veterans—Act of 1879 and 1881	1,169,382	
Confederate veterans—Act of 1881	1,979,852—	3,149,234
Sold to pay public debts by Republic	1,329,200	
50c Sales scrip act of 1879 and $2 sales scrip act of 1887	1,660,936—	2,990,136
Internal improvements—		
State Capitol Building	3,025,000	
Irrigation, drainage, iron works, Kiamasha Road and sundry	4,088,640—	7,113,640
To acquire transportation facilities—		
Grants to railroads	32,153,878—	32,153,878
For education—		
State University and A&M	2,329,168	
County school purposes	4,229,166	
Eleemosynary institutions	410,600	
Public free school	44,443,744	
Unsold public school land	872,000—	52,284,678
Total surveyed land		170,341,000
Less conflicts (estimated at one half of 1 percent)		840,000
Net as per original surveys		169,501,000
Excess (estimated at approximately 1.1 percent)		1,865,000
River beds and vacancies (estimated)		1,000,000
Submerged coastal areas to three-league limit		3,900,000
Total		176,266,000

Gulf of Mexico leases between the three mile and the three marine league limit (the area claimed by the federal government) have brought the state more than $1.8 billion in revenue since the first oil lease there in 1922. Congress returned the disputed lands to Texas in 1953, and the Supreme Court finally confirmed Texas' ownership to the 1,878,394 acres in 1960. (See Tidelands History in 1972-73 Texas Almanac.)

The General Land Office handles leases and revenue accounting on all lands dedicated to the **Permanent School Fund** and on land owned by various state agencies. The Land Commissioner, two members of the University of Texas Board of Regents and one A&M University Board of Regents member make up the Board for Lease of lands dedicated to the Permanent University Fund. Revenue accounting for income from Permanent University Lands is processed by the University of Texas; investment income from the fund is divided approximately two-thirds to one-third between the University of Texas and Texas A&M University, respectively. The **Permanent University Fund** totals more than $2 billion; the **Permanent School Fund** totals more than $4.5 billion.

All activities on state lands are reviewed for their environmental impact, and restrictions are placed in offshore drilling leases where needed to protect resources.

VETERANS LAND PROGRAM

In 1946, the Legislature created a bond program to aid veterans in purchasing farm land. $1.2 billion in bonds have been authorized over the years in a series of constitutional amendments; as of Dec. 24, 1984, $875 million of the bonds had been sold to fund loans.

Loans cannot exceed $20,000 and tracts purchased through the program must be at least 10 acres. To date, 84,000 veterans have participated in the land program, purchasing more than 4.3 million acres of land.

VETERANS HOUSING ASSISTANCE PROGRAM

The Sixty-Eighth Legislature created the **Veterans Housing Assistance Program**, which is also funded through bond proceeds. The first $500 million in bonds was approved in a constitutional amendment in November 1983.

Eligible veterans may borrow up to $20,000 toward the purchase of a home; the balance of the purchase price is financed through private sector lending institutions. When the low interest veterans loan is combined with private sector interest rates, monthly payments are significantly reduced.

Since the housing program began operation in January 1984, 250-300 veterans have applied for loans each week. An additional $500 million in bonds will be submitted to the voters for approval in November 1985.

Both veterans programs are administered by the **Veterans Land Board** which is headed by the **Texas Land Commissioner**. The bond debt for the programs and all administrative costs are completely financed by the veterans who use the programs; there is no cost to Texas taxpayers.

Details about the programs may be obtained from the Veterans Land Board by calling toll free 1-800-252-VETS.

STATE INSTITUTIONS FOR HUMAN SERVICES

Texas Department of Mental Health and Mental Retardation, Austin, is responsible for conserving and helping the mentally retarded achieve maximum potential. The department administers state mental hospitals, schools for the mentally retarded, research facilities and human development centers. The department's address is Box 12668, Capitol Station, Austin 78711.

MENTAL HEALTH SERVICES

Austin State Hospital.—Austin; 1857; Kenny Dudley, acting superintendent; 711 patients.

Big Spring State Hospital.—Big Spring; 1939; A. K. Smith, superintendent; 380 patients.

Kerrville State Hospital.—Kerrville; 1950; Dr. Luther W. Ross, superintendent; 549 patients.

Rusk State Hospital.—Rusk; 1919; Dr. John V. White, superintendent; (including Skyview Maximum Security Unit), 750 patients.

San Antonio State Hospital.—San Antonio; 1892; Dr. R. M. Inglis, superintendent; 670 patients.

Terrell State Hospital.—Terrell; 1885; Don A. Gilbert, superintendent; 715 patients.

Vernon State Hospital.—Vernon; 1969; Dr. Frankie E. Williams, superintendent; 400 patients.

Wichita Falls State Hospital.—Wichita Falls; 1920; Richard M. Bruner, superintendent; 500 patients.

STATE SCHOOLS FOR MENTALLY RETARDED

Abilene State School.—Abilene; 1899; Bill Waddill, superintendent; 1,167 residents.

Austin State School.—Austin; 1917; Dr. B. R. Walker, superintendent; 700 students.

Brenham State School.—Brenham; 1974; Dr. Jimmy R. Haskins, superintendent; 650 clients.

Corpus Christi State School.—Corpus Christi; 1970; Dr. James G. Armstrong, superintendent; 498 students.

Denton State School.—Denton; 1960; Burtis R. Hollis, superintendent; 930 students.

Fort Worth State School.—Fort Worth; 1976; Mel Hughes, superintendent; 484 students.

Lubbock State School.—Lubbock; 1969; Lonnie H. Willis, superintendent; 520 students.

Lufkin State School.—Lufkin; 1962; W. W. Beaver, superintendent; 652 students.

Mexia State School.—Mexia; 1946; W. H. Lowry, superintendent; 1,935 students.

Richmond State School.—Richmond; 1968; Joseph H. Emerson, superintendent; 1,000 students.

San Angelo State School.—Carlsbad; 1969; R. Allen Williams, superintendent; 700 residents.

San Antonio State School.—San Antonio; 1978; Dr. Tom Deliganis, superintendent; 405 residents.

Travis State School.—Austin; 1934; Dr. Victor Hinojosa, superintendent; 932 students.

STATE CENTERS FOR HUMAN DEVELOPMENT

Amarillo State Center.—Amarillo; 1968; Harry G. Heyman, director; 350 clients.

Beaumont State Center.—Beaumont; 1968; Martin T. Woodard, director; 582 patients.

El Paso State Center.—El Paso; 1973; Dr. James D. Hooker, director; 190 patients.

Laredo State Center.—Laredo; 1969; Delores V. Rodriguez, director; 830 patients.

Rio Grande State Center.—Harlingen; 1962; Blas Cantu Jr., superintendent; 190 in-patients. Also operates three mental health centers: Kingsville Community M. H. Center; Laredo Mental Health Center and Cameron-Willacy County MH Center. Also includes Harlingen residential facility and school for mentally retarded.

Texas Research Institute of Mental Sciences.—Houston; 1957; Dr. Joseph C. Schoolar, director; 6,000 patients.

Waco Center for Youth.—Waco; (1922 as Waco State Home, transferred 1979 to Texas Department of Mental Health and name changed); Charles Locklin, director; 90 patients.

COMMUNITY MENTAL HEALTH AND MENTAL RETARDATION CENTERS

Abilene Regional MHMR Center.—Abilene; 1971; Russell B. Evans, administrative director; 2,300 patients.

Amarillo MHMR Regional Center.—Amarillo; 1966; Claire Rigler, executive director; 3,807 clients.

Austin-Travis County MHMR Center.—Austin; 1967; John E. Brubaker, administrative director; 7,100 patients.

MHMR of Southeast Texas (formerly Southeast Texas Regional MHMR Center).—Beaumont; 1973; Dr. Roger Pricer, executive director; 6,000 clients.

MHMR Center for Central Texas.—Brownwood; 1974; Roy A. Cronenberg, executive director; N.A.

MHMR Authority of Brazos Valley.—Bryan-College Station; 1974; Dr. Ann Pye-Shively, executive director; 3,303 clients.

Nueces County MHMR Community Center.—Corpus Christi; 1969; Wallace E. Whitworth Jr., executive director; 3,400 patients.

Navarro County MHMR Center.—Corsicana; 1979; Julia W. Lang, executive director; 900 patients.

Dallas County MHMR Center.—Dallas; 1966; James E. Craft, executive director; 12,255 clients.

MHMR Services of Texoma.—Denison; 1974; Carl Kelly, executive director; 2,682 clients.

Tropical Texas Center for MHMR.—Edinburg; 1967; Marion G. Shirah, executive director; 6,000 patients.

El Paso Center for MHMR Services.—El Paso; 1966; Lee W. Yudin, executive director; 5,249 patients.

Tarrant County MHMR Services.—Fort Worth; 1969; Loyd Kilpatrick, executive director; 14,000 patients.

Gulf Coast Regional MHMR Center.—Galveston; 1973; G. Michael Winburn, executive director; 2,408 patients.

MHMR Authority of Harris County.—Houston; 1965; Eugene Williams, executive director; 14,000 patients.

Sabine Valley Regional MHMR Center (formerly Gregg-Harrison MHMR Center).—Longview; 1970; Ronald R. Cookston, executive director; 4,573 clients.

Lubbock Regional MHMR Center.—Lubbock; 1966; Gene Menefee, executive director; 4,000 clients.

Deep East Texas Regional MHMR Services.—Lufkin; 1974; Jim McDermott, executive director; 3,000 clients.

North Central Texas MHMR Services.—McKinney; 1978; Albert L. Jackson Jr., board chairman; 4,237 clients.

Permian Basin Community Center for MHMR.—Midland/Odessa; 1973; Bob Dickson, executive director; 4,000 clients.

Central Plains Comprehensive Community MHMR Center.—Plainview; 1970; Rick Van Hersh, executive director; 2,700 patients.

Concho Valley Center for Human Advancement (formerly MHMR Center for Greater West Texas).—San Angelo; 1966; James M. Young, executive director; 1,615 clients.

Bexar County MHMR Center.—San Antonio; 1966; George Farias, executive director; 9,546 clients.

Pecan Valley MHMR Center.—Stephenville; 1977; Theresa Mulloy, executive director; 2,300 patients.

Central Counties Center for MHMR Services.—Temple; 1967; Dr. Steven B. Schnee, executive director; 5,200 clients.

Northeast Texas MHMR Center.—Texarkana; 1968; Joe Bob Hall, executive director; 1,400 patients.

MHMR Regional Center of East Texas.—Tyler; 1968; Richard J. DeSanto, executive director; 4,850 patients.

Gulf Bend MHMR Center.—Victoria; 1970; T. G. Kelliher Jr., executive director; 2,973 patients.

Heart of Texas MHMR Center.—Waco; 1968; Dean Maberry, executive director; 2,500 patients.

Wichita Falls Community Center for MHMR Services.—Wichita Falls; 1969; James E. Snowden, executive director; 2,400 patients.

Leander Rehabilitation Center.—Leander; 1973; Calvin C. Evans, director; recreational center serving residents of other department and community MHMR facilities.

YOUTH INSTITUTIONS AND CHEST HOSPITALS

The following institutions are under the direction of the **Texas Youth Council**, in instances relating to children; and the **State Board of Health** in the case of the chest hospitals.

HOMES FOR DEPENDENT AND NEGLECTED CHILDREN

Corsicana State Home.—Corsicana; 1897; Sandra L. Burnam, superintendent; 66 students.

CORRECTIONAL INSTITUTIONS FOR CHILDREN

Brownwood State School.—Brownwood; 1970; Steve Robinson, superintendent; 235 students.

Crockett State School and Wilderness Program.—Crockett; 1947 as Brady State School for Colored Girls; changed to Crockett State School for Girls; and in 1975 name changed to present form; Robert Drake, superintendent; 112 students.

Gainesville State School.—Gainesville; 1916; T. G. Riddle, superintendent; 252 students.

Gatesville State School for Boys.—Gatesville. (Transferred to Texas Department of Corrections in 1979.)

Giddings State Home and School.—Giddings; 1972; Calvin Crenshaw, superintendent; 290 students.

Mountainview School for Boys.—Gatesville. (Transferred to Texas Department of Corrections in 1975.)

West Texas Children's Home.—Pyote; 1966; Allan B. Spearman, superintendent; 192 students. (Formerly a home for dependent and neglected children.)

In addition, the Texas Youth Council maintains the

Reception Center for Delinquent Girls at Brownwood, under administration of the superintendent of the Brownwood State Home and School for Girls. Also, the **Reception Center for Delinquent Boys**, maintained under administration of the superintendent of the Gatesville State Schools for Boys.

CHEST HOSPITALS

East Texas Chest Hospital.—Tyler. (Transferred in Sept. 1979, to University of Texas System.)

San Antonio State Chest Hospital.—San Antonio; 1953; Dr. Andre J. Ognibene, director; 150 patients.

South Texas Hospital (formerly Harlingen State Chest Hospital).—Harlingen; 1954; Dr. Albert L. Gore, director; 125 patients.

WET AND DRY COUNTIES

When approved in local option elections in "wet" precincts of counties, sale of **liquor by the drink** is permitted in Texas. This resulted from adoption of an amendment to the Texas Constitution in 1970 and subsequent legislation, followed by local option elections. For the first time in more than 50 years liquor by the drink was made legal in Texas.

Below are compilations showing the status of wet and dry counties in Texas as of Aug. 31, 1984. A dagger (†) indicates counties in which the sale of mixed beverages is legal in all or part of the county (89). An asterisk (*) indicates counties wholly wet (36). All others are dry in part (76).

Counties in Which Distilled Spirits Are Legal (174): Anderson, †*Aransas, Archer, Atascosa, †*Austin, †Bandera, *Bastrop, †*Bee, †Bell, †*Bexar, †Blanco, Bosque, †Brazoria, †*Brazos, †*Brewster, Brooks, Brown, Burleson, †Burnet, †Calhoun, Callahan, †*Cameron, †Camp, Carson, Cass, Castro, Chambers, Childress, Clay, Coleman, Collin, †*Colorado, †*Comal, Comanche, Cooke, Crane, *Culberson, Dallam, †Dallas, Deaf Smith, †Denton, †De Witt, Dickens, †Dimmit, †Donley, †*Duval, Eastland, †Ector, Edwards, Ellis, †*El Paso, †Falls, Fannin, †Fayette, †*Fort Bend, †Frio, †Galveston, Garza, †Gillespie, †Goliad, Gonzales, Gray, Grayson, Gregg, †Grimes, †Guadalupe, Hall, Hamilton, Hardin, †Harris, Harrison, Haskell, †Hays, †Henderson, †*Hidalgo, Hill, Hood, Howard, †*Hudspeth, Hunt, Hutchinson, †Jackson, Jasper, Jeff Davis, †Jefferson, †*Jim Hogg, †Jim Wells, *Karnes, Kaufman, †*Kendall, Kenedy, †Kerr, Kimble, King, †*Kinney, †Kleberg, †Lamar, †La Salle, †Lavaca, †Lee, Leon, Liberty, Lipscomb, Live Oak, †Llano, †*Loving, †Lubbock, Marion, †Matagorda, †Maverick, †McCulloch, †McLennan, †Medina, Menard, †Midland, Milam, Mills, Mitchell, †Montgomery, †*Moore, Nacogdoches, †Navarro, Newton, Nolan, †Nueces, †Orange, Palo Pinto, Pecos, †Polk, †Potter, †*Presidio, Rains, †Randall, *Reagan, Red River, †Reeves, Refugio, Robertson, Runnels, San Augustine, San Jacinto, †San Patricio, San Saba, *Schleicher, Shelby, †*Starr, Stonewall, †*Sutton, †Tarrant, †Taylor, *Terrell, †Titus, †Tom Green, †*Travis, *Trinity, Upshur, *Upton, Uvalde, Val Verde, †Victoria, †Walker, †Waller, Ward, †*Washington, †*Webb, †Wharton, Wichita, Wilbarger, †Willacy, †Williamson, †*Wilson, *Winkler, †*Zapata, †Zavala.

Counties in Which Only 4 Per Cent Beer Is Legal (14): Baylor, Caldwell, Cherokee, Concho, Dawson, Glasscock, Hartley, Irion, Mason, McMullen, Oldham, Sabine, Stephens, Wise.

Counties in Which 14 Per Cent Beverages Are Legal (2): Limestone, Somervell.

Counties Wholly Dry (64): Andrews, Angelina, Armstrong, Bailey, Borden, Bowie, Briscoe, Cochran, Coke, Collingsworth, Coryell, Cottle, Crockett, Crosby, Delta, Erath, Fisher, Floyd, Foard, Franklin, Freestone, Gaines, Hale, Hansford, Hardeman, Hemphill, Hockley, Hopkins, Houston, Jack, Johnson, Jones, Kent, Knox, Lamb, Lampasas, Lynn, Madison, Martin, Montague, Morris, Motley, Ochiltree, Panola, Parker, Parmer, Real, Roberts, Rockwall, Rusk, Scurry, Schackelford, Sherman, Smith, Sterling, Swisher, Terry, Throckmorton, Tyler, Van Zandt, Wheeler, Wood, Yoakum, Young.

The Great Depression brought an expansion of welfare programs in Texas. Destitute families, like the one pictured above, often had nowhere to turn for aid but to state and local agencies, which distributed federal funds. Photo courtesy of the Library of Congress.

Aiding Texas' Disadvantaged

This article was written by Bluford B. Hestir, former administrator of the media services division of the Texas Department of Human Services.

In 1939, Texas created a State Department of Public Welfare (DPW) to "provide necessary and prompt assistance to citizens, especially the poor, the aged, and the needy or abused children." Today the old welfare department is called the Department of Human Services (DHS). By either name, it has for nearly 50 years administered financial assistance programs using both state and federal funds and offered social services for families and children and for the aged and disabled.

The department grew out of three agencies created in the Depression years as part of the national effort to help citizens hardest hit by the social and economic disasters of that time: the Division of Child Welfare in the Board of Control (1932), the Texas Relief Commission (1933) and the Old Age Assistance Commission (1936). Some aspects of the work of each continue in today's department.

The Division of Child Welfare (DCW), earliest direct ancestor of DHS, was authorized by the 42nd Legislature in 1931 and was organized in 1932, with Mrs. Violet Greenhill of Houston as director. With an initial budget of $18,000, she and her five-person unit began educating county officials about the needs and care of children. Nolan County was the first to set up a county child welfare board in 1932. Other counties followed, and today, 185 counties have such boards.

The Child Welfare Division was one of the earliest supporters of Aid to Dependent Children (ADC) funds, which helped prevent the removal of children from their homes for purely financial reasons. As these funds were not available in Texas until 1941 and many children could not remain at home, the division was responsible for making sure that the institutions and homes that cared for children were run according to certain minimum standards. Herein lies the beginning of the child care licensing program.

When the Social Security Act of 1935 made matching federal funds available to help establish local child welfare units in predominantly rural areas, Nolan County was again the first to respond, establishing its Child Welfare Unit in the spring of 1936.

The state's first relief or "welfare" agency in modern times (there were some set up after the Civil War) was created as the direct result of the Great Depression. Initially, the principal federal agency providing funds for state relief efforts was the Reconstruction Finance Corporation, begun under President Herbert Hoover's administration. Texas received its first RFC money in October 1932, distributing the funds to approved projects through the three regional chambers of commerce.

So that Texas could continue to receive RFC funds, Gov. Miriam "Ma" Ferguson created the Texas Relief Commission by proclamation March 1, 1933. Shortly afterward, the 43rd Legislature formally authorized the establishment of the commission and empowered it to administer relief through county welfare boards that it named.

Among the flood of agencies set up to confront Depression problems, the New Deal created the Federal Emergency Relief Administration (FERA) headed by Harry Hopkins. To get FERA funds, Texas had to match federal money dollar for dollar. Gov. Ferguson pushed through the Legislature a constitutional amendment providing for the issuance of $20 million in state bonds, known as "Bread Bonds." By early 1934, millions of dollars in direct relief grants and work relief funds began reaching people who needed them most.

Direct relief went to people who couldn't work. Work relief, directed by the county boards, put the employable needy, both men and women, to work sewing, canning and building bridges, courthouses, latrines, parks and roads. Conditions improved in Texas.

Col. Lawrence Westbrook of San Angelo, a staunch Ferguson backer, was the first director of TRC. Adam R. Johnson, city manager of Austin, succeeded Westbrook, and, when the Department of Public Welfare was created by the 46th Legislature in 1939, Johnson became its first executive director.

The third unit comprising the original DPW, the Old Age Assistance Commission, sprang from the Social Security Act of 1935 and its provisions for financial assistance for needy per-

Directors of the Texas Department of Human Services and its predecessor agencies have included (l-r on this and the following page) John H. Winters, Burton Hackney, Raymond Vowell, Jerome Chapman and Marlin W. Johnston. Photos courtesy the Texas Department of Human Services.

sons 65 or older. By the time Congress passed the Social Security Act in 1935, Texas had amended its constitution to provide matching money, voted a maximum $30 "pension" to needy persons over 65, and created a commission to administer the funds. In voting for the pension, most Texans ignored the needs basis and misunderstood it to mean any person over 65 would be entitled to the $30. The Old Age Assistance Commission was set up in February 1936, and it began distributing application blanks within a few weeks. Rich and poor Texans alike flooded the small, inexperienced staff with applications. Since every application had to be investigated, many deserving poor found help woefully slow in coming. Urgent needs fueled wide complaints about OAA, and many applicants moderately or very well off were dismayed to learn they failed to qualify for grants and would get no pension.

Turmoil engulfed the new agency almost from the start, and public and political shock waves hit OAAC. Almost from the start, Director Orville Carpenter recognized that the standards for eligibility were too lenient, and he began calling for the Legislature to adopt tighter criteria.

This was done through House Bill 8, effective Oct. 31, 1936, that noted "it is impracticable to pay benefits to persons over 65 except those who are in necessitous circumstances," and declared, "the number of persons receiving old age assistance benefits must be decreased."

The act abolished the commission as it existed, transferring its name, assets, functions and staff to the Board of Control. The three members of the Board of Control sat as the commission when dealing with old age assistance matters and appointed W. A. "Jack" Little to succeed Carpenter as director of OAAC.

In Texas, as in the rest of the nation, early efforts to ensure the welfare of individuals in society began on the local level. Many communities in frontier Texas were fairly self-sufficient when it came to providing for their own needy. Neighbors and kinfolk stepped in to help when help was needed. As towns got bigger, efforts to collect food and money to meet a crisis became common, but there were few attempts to organize and coordinate services for the needy.

Change began in the 19th century when organizations and agencies began to form to serve the needs of specialized groups. In Texas, one of the first such steps was the establishment of the state Deaf and Dumb Asylum in 1856. Institutions for the blind, lunatic and orphaned opened during the next few years. Other states had evolved a similar pattern, and by 1873, there were many people throughout the nation interested in welfare reform. A united body of welfare advocates, called the Texas Conference of Social Welfare (TCSW) was set up in 1909 to "address welfare issues and to promote social improvement." Members came from all over the state, but the largest and most influential groups were from Houston and Dallas. Some of these people were soon to become involved in such public and private social welfare efforts as creation of the Dallas Public Welfare Dept., organized by Elmer Scott in 1916, the Dallas Civic Federation, formed by Scott in 1917, and the DePelchin Faith Home in Houston, a child-care institution organized around a home founded by Kezia DePelchin.

From its first days, the TCSW urged creation of a state agency to aid children and the poor. In 1911 and each succeeding year, TCSW lobbied for a state board of charities and corrections, pointing out that Texas was one of the few states without such an agency. A bill to establish a welfare department failed to pass in 1919, slowing the TCSW campaign until 1927. It then found more support for a child welfare board than for a welfare board as such. Changing focus, TCSW won passage in 1931 of a bill authorizing a Child Welfare Division in the Board of Control. When it began work in 1932, it was the earliest direct ancestor of DPW.

The Legislature finally passed the Public Welfare Act of 1937, creating not a department, but a division under the Board of Control. The final step to department status came on May 31, 1939, crowning more than 20 years of effort to win this level of state government attention to the needs of the poor.

The act brought together the functions and staff of the old Child Welfare Division, TRC and OAAC. These units saw little immediate change. The new board elected TRC head Adam R. Johnson the first director of DPW, continued Violet Greenhill as head of the Child Welfare Division, and Jack Little as head of OAA. The Old Age Assistance problems remained as intractable as before.

Gov. W. Lee O'Daniel wanted his own man as DPW director, and in September 1940, the board replaced Johnson with John S. Murchison of Corsicana. Murchison found the going no easier than Johnson had, with angry legislators and investigations on the way assistance was being handled making him so unhappy that he soon asked the DPW board to find a replacement.

On Aug. 16, 1943, the board named John H. Winters, an Amarillo businessman and Potter County commissioner, the third executive director of the DPW. He was immediate past president of the County Judges and Commissioners Association and retained close ties to this body throughout his tenure. Under Winters the OAA dragon was subdued, the department achieved respect for its work, and Winters remained as director, and later commissioner, for 23 years. It is a record unlikely to be broken.

Since its beginning, the DPW board has been comprised of three members appointed by the governor and confirmed by the senate. The first board members were Judge Beeman Strong of Beaumont, chairman, Marvin Leonard of Fort Worth and Dr. M. E. Sadler of Austin.

Including these first members, 27 men and three women have served as board members. Fifteen men and one woman, Mrs. Richard Turrentine of Denton, have served as chairman. All of these men and women have served without pay.

When the first board was organized, it found that almost all of the Bread Bond money had been spent, and through the Social Security Act of 1935, the Roosevelt administration had changed the emphasis from direct relief through grants to work relief. The federal government was pouring millions through the Works Progress Administration to put people back to work. The Old Age Assistance program was to take care of the needs of older Americans, and Aid to Dependent Children was to take care of the younger.

The DPW worked with WPA and the Civilian Conservation Corps (CCC) to determine the eligibility of people for employment under these programs, handled commodities and cooperated with counties in a growing variety of efforts to help the poor.

With the change from direct relief to work relief, the new department was handling grants only to old age recipients. OAA rolls continued to grow steadily until the United States entered World War II in 1941. Then, as young men went into service, many made allotments to their parents, and fewer new applications came to DPW for help for older citizens.

When John Winters was named director in 1943, the department's responsibilities had expanded to encompass not only Old Age Assistance and Child Welfare, but also Aid to the Blind, Aid to Dependent Children and several smaller assign-

ments. The budget for all of it, Winters found, was $50 million for his first fiscal year, Sept. 1, 1943 to Aug. 31, 1944. The staff numbered 1,059.

During Winters' first years, DPW was handed several unusual tasks. War-time assignments included caring for sailors cast up on Texas' shores when rescued from ships torpedoed in the Gulf, creating and funding day-care centers for children whose mothers worked at defense jobs, and looking after dependents of enemy aliens who had been imprisoned by the United States. In 1949, DPW was given the job of managing the state's three juvenile training schools, and, in 1951, the state orphans' home. This assignment ended in 1957 with the creation of the Texas Youth Council.

The 52nd Legislature asked the DPW to administer the Social Security program for the state, county and municipal employees from 1951 to 1975.

A program called Aid to Permanently and Totally Disabled Persons (APTD) was added to the DPW's responsibilities in 1957, bringing the agency's major welfare grant programs to four: OAA, ADC, ANB and APTD.

When each program began, a limit was placed by the Legislature on spending. For many years, the lawmakers had to raise the welfare spending ceiling almost every session by the awkward method of amending the constitution. Finally, the Legislature of 1981 found a formula that places a flexible cap on the welfare budget by providing that the amount spent on welfare grants cannot exceed one percent of the state budget. Since the Legislature establishes actual spending budgets each biennium for the welfare programs, the amount appropriated is well below this ceiling. This amendment went into effect in 1982.

Medical assistance was provided in the early welfare programs in very limited amounts almost as an afterthought. Slight increases were made over the years, but not until Congress adopted the Kerr-Mills Act in 1960, sharply increasing the amount of federal funds available to the states for medical care programs for recipients of old age assistance, was there a comprehensive program to fund medical costs of the elderly.

Texas used a unique funding plan under Kerr-Mills, employing insurance contracts to pay part of its medical program costs through Group Hospital Services (Blue Cross-Blue Shield). The plan, a concept of Commissioner John Winters, saved the state untold millions of dollars. In 1964, Congress amended Kerr-Mills to include medical assistance to the blind, the disabled and dependent children. Texas signed new contracts with Group Hospital Services to include the new recipients.

Kerr-Mills was followed in 1965 by President Lyndon Johnson's Medicare and Medicaid programs. The Medical Assistance Act of 1967 provided for the state's role in administering the two programs. Medicaid covered all classes of needy and provided not only hospitalization and nursing home payments, but also help with doctor and drug bills. Medicare provided similar coverage for those over 65 years of age.

Even as the Department of Public Welfare was moving through the maze of laws, regulations and budgets of blossoming medical programs, it was beginning yet another program that would grow to major importance: food stamps. As early as the first relief efforts by the Texas Relief Commission, food was an important part of helping Texans. Commodities were made available as soon as Washington began to comprehend the magnitude of the Depression.

The Roosevelt administration began buying food in bulk, helping both the farmer and the poor. In addition, county relief boards at first, and later the Texas Relief Commission, began to hire unemployed people to work in canneries, putting up

produce from farms and gardens on shares. The TRC equipped the canneries and paid the workers, and the growers provided the produce free, receiving half the canned goods. The government's half then went to the welfare recipients. Men and women who had been out of work had income, the growers had a market and the poor had food.

A variation of this approach was applied in West Texas during the terrible drought of the 1930s, when sheep, cattle and goats were purchased by the United States Department of Agriculture to keep ranchers from going broke and to feed the poor. USDA put up the money, but Texas welfare workers found themselves hiring and supervising cowboys. The animals were driven to railheads and shipped first to slaughter houses and then to canneries. The meat was then distributed from welfare offices.

With the passage of the National School Lunch Act of 1946, the USDA was required to work with public and private school systems to make nutritious meals available to all children. Managing the distribution program by working directly with thousands of county judges and school superintendents was too difficult for the USDA to continue indefinitely. It ruled that a state could participate in the commodity distribution program only if a state agency managed the detail work. In 1953, the Legislature named the DPW to handle the program in Texas and to set up a Commodities Division. Although some counties were too poor to pay administrative costs and others resented the competition with local grocers, the program grew statewide. The amounts of food distributed were immense: 300 boxcar loads in 1958-59; 99 million pounds of food in 1964; 161 million pounds in 1969, by which time the value of the food provided had reached $45.5 million.

As effective as the commodity distribution system was, it still had to depend on finding a public or private agency to handle the food locally, and it gave recipients little choice of foods. Though 25 or 30 varieties of foods were provided each month, they were dry or canned, might not suit the palates of some recipients and certainly didn't meet the nutritional needs of the very young or the very old. The USDA responded to these problems by testing a food stamp program. Texas participation began in October 1965 with a pilot project in Tarrant County.

Tests in Tarrant County went well, and during Fiscal Year 1967 (September 1966 to August 1967) the food stamp program expanded to include the Trans-Pecos counties plus Red River and Terrell counties, a total of 10 counties. Coupons valued at $235,174 were distributed the first year. The following fiscal year, Bexar County joined the program, and coupon values for the 11 counties shot up to $4 million.

In 1969, stamps were in use in 25 counties, and the stamp value had risen to $7 million; another 139 counties had Commodity Distribution Programs. In December 1969, the Federal District Court in Dallas, ruling on a class action suit against DPW and USDA, directed that a food assistance program had to be established in all counties in the state. The program could be either commodity distribution or food stamps, but USDA food had to be made available to the needy. At that time, 99 counties in Texas had no program of either sort. By June 1970 through strenuous efforts by DPW, USDA and county officials, all counties but two had the program, and those two were served from adjacent counties.

The reluctance of counties to manage and pay for their share of the program was solved two years later. In July 1972 the third called session of the 62nd Legislature voted to assume the counties' costs and management of the food stamp program and assigned the job to DPW. The department soon be-

Hard times during the depression forced many Texans to improvise their housing. This shack near Corpus Christi is but one example of the shelter that was used. Photo courtesy of the Library of Congress.

gan issuing Authorization to Purchase cards to welfare recipients. The cards indicated the number of stamps each recipient was entitled to get when the card was presented each month at a distribution office. The system remains little changed today.

With the development of the food stamp program, the commodity distribution program shrank but did not disappear. School lunches, lunches for day care centers, food for nursing homes and for all manner of public and non-profit institutions that could help feed needy people received commodities through USDA by way of DPW.

In addition, commodities in DPW warehouses became a part of the state's disaster relief plan. Not only could bulk packages of food be distributed, but centers could be set up in schools and churches for feeding disaster victims.

As commodity distribution waned, the food stamp program grew. Some idea of that growth is seen by comparing the $235,174 worth of coupons distributed in 1967 with the $680 million worth distributed in 1983.

The statewide implementation of the food stamp program in 1973 completed the list of DPW's truly major welfare programs. No program of similar size has been added since.

In 1977, the DPW was renamed the Texas Department of Human Resources, reflecting the shift from cash welfare grants to health and social services, brought about primarily by creation in 1972 of the Supplementary Security Income Program within the Social Security Administration. Under SSI, the federal government relieved the states of financial responsibility for the three adult welfare programs formerly state-administered and partially state-financed. Old Age Assistance, Aid to the Blind and Aid to the Permanently and Totally Disabled had become federal programs on Jan. 1, 1974, closing the books on more than 36 years of aid to Texas' older citizens, 31 years of help to blind and 16 to assist the disabled. The three programs together had provided $4.1 billion of state and federal aid to the poor.

With SSI in place, DPW was left with only one direct assistance grant program: Aid to Families with Dependent Children. But SSI did not free DPW completely from responsibility for the aged, the blind or the disabled. Although it no longer provided direct grants, DPW continued to serve recipients through its responsibility for Medicaid, food stamps, commodities, long-term care in nursing homes and other institutions, and an array of social services. Transfer of the three categories of needy to SSI ended some of the eligibility determination DPW had had to make for decades, and in its place came a monthly computer tape from SSI headquarters in Baltimore listing SSI eligibles. These Texans automatically became eligible for Medicaid cards and often for food stamps and other programs.

In 1973, the Legislature passed a strong law making reporting of child abuse compulsory, and its effects were immediate. The number of cases of abuse and neglect reported nearly quadrupled within a year, and the size of the Child Protective Services staff doubled.

The Child Support Enforcement program received new legal foundations, and millions of dollars of enforced support from absent parents began reaching children who otherwise were almost entirely dependent upon welfare money. The financial load on the AFDC program was eased a little, and some mothers and their dependent children were able to get off welfare rolls. This program, launched by DPW, was transferred to the state Attorney General's office in 1983.

Still another effort in support of child welfare has centered around the Child Development Program, through which DPW has provided guidance to licensed and registered day care facilities. The quality of care available has been raised by consultation, how-to publications and training provided through DPW.

Even though their financial support was now coming from SSI, the elderly were served by the DPW's strong programs of social services, many of them designed to help old people live more comfortably and remain in their own homes longer. Beginning in 1974, a matrix of services was created under the initial title of Alternate Care — alternate to nursing homes. Later expanded and renamed Community Care, the program offered home care, home medical care, day activities, congregate and home-delivered meals, supervised living arrangements and adult foster care. These services help the older clients to avoid premature entry into nursing homes, keeps them happier and usually healthier, and results in savings to the old and to the state averaging about $130 per person per month.

Family Self-Support Services supplement the AFDC program. Broadly speaking, Medicaid and food stamps for AFDC families are part of the Family Self-Support Program, but the Self-Support Program goes much further. Several job-training programs have helped many welfare clients break away from the cycle of dependence on government aid. Particularly important has been Work Incentive, which provides training, income while training and child day care to AFDC mothers while they learn a marketable skill. Family Planning Services have reduced the number of teen-age births among AFDC children and have helped welfare mothers avoid having unwanted children.

As with so many aspects of modern life, the change in welfare efforts has accelerated during the last 20 years. Presiding over those changes since the death of Commissioner John Winters on Dec. 1, 1966, have been four commissioners. Each faced major changes, and each had to guide an increasingly complex department through decisions that touched the lives of most people in the state.

A month after Winters' death, Burton Hackney of Brownfield was sworn in as commissioner. He had been a member of the board of DPW for 10 years and served as chairman during the final portion of Winters' 23 years of work. He brought to the job knowledge of the programs and understanding of the difficulties facing the department as it launched Medicaid. He also presided over the first significant expansions of the DPW staff. When Winters died, the staff numbered 3,143. When Hackney resigned on June 30, 1971, the total was 4,929, nearly a thousand of whom were added in 1969-70. This was the year in which the staffing impact of Medicaid became apparent, and the department was trying at the same time to adjust to the growing commodity distribution and food stamp programs.

Medicaid posed a tremendous administrative challenge to Hackney, and with it came a growing realization of the impact of the other aspects of the Great Society legislation and its huge increases in federal spending. It was a tough time to be running the department.

By 1971, Commissioner Hackney wanted out of the job. Gov. Preston Smith arranged a four-way swap of jobs within the top administrative positions of the state. Coming into the commissioner's post was Raymond Vowell, an experienced administrator who had headed the Austin State School. He was also executive director of the Board for State Hospitals and Special Schools and was Vice Chancellor of the University of Texas.

Vowell began July 1, 1971, and he served six years and two months, second only to Winters in length of tenure to this time. He presided over the period of most rapid growth in the department, in both staff and budget, and led the planning for a 14 percent reduction in staff during his last year, Fiscal Year 1977. The biggest challenges of Commissioner Vowell's years were the difficult adjustment to changes brought by the passage of SSI in 1972, the beginning of department-wide computerization of all case records and payments and the redirecting of the emphasis of the department from administering welfare grants to providing health and social services. Vowell pushed for the change in the department's name from Welfare to Human Resources as a means of signaling the change in focus.

Between July 1, 1971, and March 1, 1977, the staff ballooned from 4,929 to 15,000. Fueling this growth was federal money, in larger amounts than available earlier and with better federal-state match, as a result of Great Society legislation. New ways of tapping those funds were being developed in other states and applied in Texas also. For example, states saw that Old Age Assistance recipients being cared for in nursing homes under Title XIX could also be helped with social services funded under Title XX. Since Title XX matching funds were generally more favorable than the slowly decreasing Medicaid match, new money became available from federal sources with much smaller increases in state funds.

The larger staff and bigger budgets enabled the department to expand existing programs and undertake new ones. Significant among these were intensive emphasis, beginning in 1974, on Child Protective Services, the beginning of the Community Care Program for the aged, statewide implementation of food stamps, creation of an Investigation Division to tackle problems of welfare fraud, expansion of the Child Development Program, launching a statewide Volunteer Services Program to assist the work of the paid staff, and conducting a broad study of department management and organization.

With the results of the management study in hand, and prodded by the first cutbacks in federal funding, the department in 1977 began consolidating some of the new programs, combining some functions and reducing staff. The process was to continue for four years.

Raymond Vowell retired as reductions in force were beginning, and Jerome C. Chapman took over Sept. 1, 1977. He served precisely three years, during which he guided the staff reduction from 14,000 to 11,928 and designed one of the most sweeping reorganizations in the department's history. Commissioner Chapman was the first home-grown commissioner to serve the department. He came up through the ranks from field worker in the Child Welfare Division to become Vowell's deputy during most of his tenure.

Traditionally, DHS had been organized according to federal funding sources. If Congress enacted and the Texas Legislature authorized a new program, say food stamps, then the food stamp program became a new DPW organizational unit, with separate staff and budget. The result of this approach was that a welfare recipient might have to deal with several different staff offices and sets of paperwork. An AFDC family entitled to a grant, to Medicaid and to food stamps might have to go to three locations to get things set up or changed. Chapman proposed that the focus be placed on people, not programs. The goal was to fit program to needs, not the other way around, and the new DPW organizational networks reflected this fact. Two main divisions were created: Services to Families and Children and Services to Aged and Disabled. The same AFDC family could now deal with just one staff and office.

This broad reorganization affected every level of the department. Beginning in 1980, it was not fully operative at the end of August when Commissioner Chapman retired after 30 years' service. Succeeding him on Sept. 1, 1980, was Marlin W Johnston, another who came up through the department from field worker to executive deputy commissioner under Chapman.

Throughout its history, the welfare effort in Texas has been aimed at improving the fortunes of the unfortunate, the disabled and the aged. By most standards, it has been a successful effort.

Department of Human Services

The **Texas Department of Human Services** administers programs which provide financial and medical assistance and social services to those who are eligible. It also is responsible for licensing child care facilities and child placing agencies. The department's headquarters is in Austin but its services are available in all 254 Texas counties.

The **Texas Board of Human Services** is responsible for adoption of all policies, rules and regulations of the department. (See **State Boards and Commissions** for membership.)

Department services are provided through 10 administrative regions with two subregions, which correspond to the boundaries of the state's 12 former Health Service Areas. Each region is supervised by a regional administrator. The department's Austin headquarters maintains staff for the development of program policy and provides support functions such as legal, personnel, data processing and fiscal services, which serve all programs.

The department is organized according to client needs. The structure centers around the networks of services — one for families and children and the other for aged and disabled persons.

FAMILIES AND CHILDREN — Services include aid to families with dependent children (AFDC), food stamps, home energy assistance, disaster relief, temporary emergency relief, family self-support services, health screening, day care, family planning, employment services, family violence, protective services for children, licensing, refugee assistance, repatriate services and food services.

Licensing — During fiscal year 1984, the department's Licensing Branch regulated 27,626 child day-care facilities and 4,423 residential 24-hour-care facilities. These facilities had a combined capacity to care for more than 600,000 children. The department also licenses 273 administrators of child care institutions and certified over 8,000 social workers as meeting educational and experience qualifications.

AGED AND DISABLED — Community care services are provided to enable aged and disabled individuals to live in their own homes. Institutional care services are available for persons who need continuous medical attention and require professional care in nursing homes. The department also provides protective services for aged or disabled adults.

Medical Services — The department purchases health insurance for eligible dependent children, and the aged and disabled persons served by the department.

In addition to providing for inpatient and outpatient hospital care, physician services, lab and x-ray services, the department also pays for up to three prescriptions per month for those same recipient groups. Other medical services are health screening, diagnosis and treatment for children receiving Medicaid, transportation to and from medical services, and hearing aids for eligible adults. The department also provides certain dental services, eyeglasses, podiatric services, home health services, chiropractic services and in-home support services.

COSTS/SERVICES

Costs of most programs are shared by the state and federal governments. Expenditures and services for fiscal year 1984 are as follows:

FINANCIAL ASSISTANCE: AFDC, $188,470,698; 337,396 recipients per month. Food stamp value, $664.9 million 1,304,853 recipients per month. Commodities distributed $84 million; 1,731,068 clients per day. Refugee assistance payments (100% federal funds), $10.2 million, 2,291 clients per month. Energy assistance payments $39.2 million; 304,203 households received heating assistance, 310,753 households received cooling assistance Temporary emergency relief, $1,000,441; 28,144 clients.

MEDICAL PROGRAMS: Purchased health services $656,727,916; 611,738 Medicaid eligibles. Vendor drugs $96,337,054; 6,442,249 prescriptions. Medical transportation, $4,808,629; 718,872 one-way trips.

FAMILIES & CHILDREN SERVICES: Protective services for abused and neglected children, $94,690,473; 61,576 investigations; 156,600 clients. Family planning services $25,277,373; 284,997 clients. Child day care services $36,251,753; 15,201 children per day. Early periodic screening, diagnosis and treatment, $15,276,659; 71,628 medical screenings; 83,022 dental treatments. Family violence services, $2,186,087; 13,650 residents. Family support services, $17,492,421; 53,054 employment registrants. Licensing of child care facilities, $6,925,400; 32,049 facilities registered or regulated.

AGED & DISABLED SERVICES: Long-term institutional care, $499,869,091; 59,487 clients per month. Medical assistance in state institutions, $229,308,447; 9,035 clients. Community care, $103,734,577; 39,896 clients per month. Adult protective services, $2,163,982; 8,364 investigations; 1,49 clients per month.

CHIEF TEXAS ADMINISTRATIVE OFFICIALS

On this and following pages are lists of the principal administrative officials who have served the Republic and State of Texas with dates of their tenures of office. In a few instances there are disputes as to the exact beginning and ending of these tenures. Dates given in these lists are those that appear to be most authentic.

*Spanish Royal Governors

Domingo Teran de los Rios	1691-1692
Gregorio de Salinas	1692-1697
Francisco Cuerbo y Valdez	1698-1702
Mathias de Aguirre	1703-1705
Martin de Alarcon	1705-1708
Simon Padilla y Cordova	1708-1712
Pedro Fermin de Echevers y Subisa	1712-1714
Juan Valdez	1714-1716
Martin de Alarcon	1716-1719
Marquis de San Miguel de Aguayo	1719-1722
Fernando Perez de Almazan	1722-1727
Melchor de Media Villa y Ascona	1727-1730
Juan Bustillo Zevallos	1730-1734
Manuel de Sandoval	1734-1736
Carlos Benites Franquis de Lugo	1736-1737
Prudencio de Orobio y Bazterra	1737-1741
Tomas Felipe Wintuisen	1741-1743
Justo Boneo y Morales	1743-1744
Francisco Garcia Larios	1744-1748
Pedro del Barrio Junco y Espriella	1748-1751
Jacinto de Barrios y Jauregui	1751-1759
Angel Martos y Navarrete	1759-1766
Hugo Oconor	1767-1770
Baron de Ripperda	1770-1778
Domingo Cabello	1778-1786
Bernardo Bonavia	1786-1786
Rafael Martinez Pacheco	1787-1788

The office of Governor was ordered suppressed and the province put under a presidial captain for a period in 1788-1789

Manuel Munoz	1790-1798
Josef Irigoyen	1798-1800
Juan Bautista de Elguezabal	1800-1805
Antonio Cordero y Bustamante	1805-1810
Juan Bautista Casas	1811-1811
Manuel de Salcedo	1811-1813
Cristobal Dominguez	1814-1817
Ignacio Perez	1817-1817
Manuel Pardo	1817-1817
Antonio Martinez	1817-1822

Governors Under Mexican Rule

The first two Governors under Mexican rule, Trespalacios and Garcia, were of Texas only as Texas was then constituted. Beginning with Gonzales, 1824, the Governors were for the joint State of Coahuila-Texas.

Jose Felix Trespalacios	1822-1823
Luciano Garcia	1823-1824
Rafael Gonzales	1824-1826
Victor Blanco	1826-1827
Jose Maria Viesca	1827-1830
Ramon Eca y Musquiz	1830-1831
Jose Maria Letona	1831-1832
Ramon Eca y Musquiz	1832-1832
Juan Martin de Beramendi	1832-1833
Juan Jose de Vidauri y Villasenor	1833-1834
Juan Jose Elguezabal	1834-1835
Jose Maria Cantu	1835-1835
Agustin M. Viesca	1835-1835
Marciel Borrego	1835-1835
Ramon Eca y Musquiz	1835-1835

Provisional Colonial Governor, Before Independence

†Henry Smith (Impeached)	1835
‡James W. Robinson	

Presidents of the Republic of Texas

David G. Burnet	Mar. 16, 1836-Oct. 22, 1836
Sam Houston	Oct. 22, 1836-Dec. 10, 1838
Mirabeau B. Lamar	Dec. 10, 1838-Dec. 13, 1841
Sam Houston	Dec. 13, 1841-Dec. 9, 1844
Anson Jones	Dec. 9, 1844-Feb. 19, 1846

Governors Since Annexation

J. Pinckney Henderson	Feb. 19, 1846-Dec. 21, 1847
‡Albert C. Horton	
George T. Wood	Dec. 21, 1847-Dec. 21, 1849
P. Hansbrough Bell	Dec. 21, 1849-Nov. 23, 1853
J. W. Henderson	Nov. 23, 1853-Dec. 21, 1853
Elisha M. Pease	Dec. 21, 1853-Dec. 21, 1857
Hardin R. Runnels	Dec. 21, 1857-Dec. 21, 1859
Sam Houston (resigned because of state's secession)	Dec. 21, 1859-Mar. 16, 1861
Edward Clark	Mar. 16, 1861-Nov. 7, 1861
Francis R. Lubbock (resigned to enter Confederate Army)	Nov. 7, 1861-Nov. 5, 1863

Pendleton Murrah (administration terminated by fall of Confederacy) ...... Nov. 5, 1863-June 17, 1865 Fletcher S. Stockdale (Lt. Gov. performed some duties of office on Murrah's departure, but is sometimes included in list of Governors. Hamilton's appointment was for immediate succession as shown by dates.)

Andrew J. Hamilton (Provisional, appointed by President Johnson)	June 17, 1865-Aug. 9, 1866
Jas. W. Throckmorton	Aug. 9, 1866-Aug. 8, 1867
Elisha M. Pease (appointed July 30, 1867, under martial law)	Aug. 8, 1867-Sept. 30, 1869

Interregnum

Pease resigned and vacated office Sept. 30, 1869; no successor was named until Jan. 8, 1870. Some historians extend Pease's term until Jan. 8, 1870, but in reality Texas was without a head of its civil government from Sept. 30, 1869 until Jan. 8, 1870. Republican Edmund J. Davis (appointed provisional Governor after being elected) .... Jan. 8, 1870-Jan. 15, 1874

Richard Coke (resigned to enter United States Senate)	Jan. 15, 1874-Dec. 1, 1876
Richard B. Hubbard	Dec. 1, 1876-Jan. 21, 1879
Oran M. Roberts	Jan. 21, 1879-Jan. 16, 1883
John Ireland	Jan. 16, 1883-Jan. 18, 1887
Lawrence Sullivan Ross	Jan. 18, 1887-Jan. 20, 1891
James Stephen Hogg	Jan. 20, 1891-Jan. 15, 1895
Charles A. Culberson	Jan. 15, 1895-Jan. 17, 1899
Joseph D. Sayers	Jan. 17, 1899-Jan. 20, 1903
S. W. T. Lanham	Jan. 20, 1903-Jan. 15, 1907
Thos. Mitchell Campbell	Jan. 15, 1907-Jan. 17, 1911
Oscar Branch Colquitt	Jan. 17, 1911-Jan. 19, 1915
James E. Ferguson (impeached)	Jan. 19, 1915-Aug. 25, 1917
William Pettus Hobby	Aug. 25, 1917-Jan. 18, 1921
Pat Morris Neff	Jan. 18, 1921-Jan. 20, 1925
Miriam A. Ferguson	Jan. 20, 1925-Jan. 17, 1927
Dan Moody	Jan. 17, 1927-Jan. 20, 1931
Ross S. Sterling	Jan. 20, 1931-Jan. 17, 1933
Miriam A. Ferguson	Jan. 17, 1933-Jan. 15, 1935
James V. Allred	Jan. 15, 1935-Jan. 17, 1939
W. Lee O'Daniel (resigned to enter United States Senate)	Jan. 17, 1939-Aug. 4, 1941
Coke R. Stevenson	Aug. 4, 1941-Jan. 21, 1947
Beauford H. Jester	Jan. 21, 1947-July 11, 1949
Allan Shivers (Lt. Governor succeeded on death of Governor Jester. Elected in 1950 and re-elected in 1952 and 1954)	July 11, 1949-Jan. 15, 1957
Price Daniel	Jan. 15, 1957-Jan. 15, 1963
John Connally	Jan. 15, 1963-Jan. 21, 1969
Preston Smith	Jan. 21, 1969 to Jan. 16, 1973
**Dolph Briscoe	Jan. 16, 1973 to Jan. 16, 1979
William Clements	Jan. 16, 1979 to Jan. 18, 1983
Mark White	Jan. 18, 1983 to Present

*Some authorities would include Texas under administrations of several earlier Spanish Royal Governors. The late Dr. C. E. Castaneda, Latin-American librarian of University of Texas and authority on history of Texas and Southwestern region, would include the following four: Francisco de Garay, 1523-26; Panfilo de Narvaez, 1526-28; Nuno de Guzman, 1528-30; Hernando de Soto, 1538.

†Served as acting Governor just prior to March 2, 1836, after Smith was impeached.

‡Acting Governor while Henderson away in Mexican War.

**Effective in 1975, term of office was raised to 4 years, according to a constitutional amendment approved by Texas voters in 1972. See lead to State Government chapter in this edition for other state officials whose terms were raised to 4 years.

TEXAS VICE PRESIDENTS AND LIEUTENANT GOVERNORS
Vice Presidents of Republic

	Date Elected.
Lorenzo de Zavala (provisional Vice President.)	
M. B. Lamar	Sept. 5, 1836
David G. Burnet	Sept. 3, 1838
Edward Burleson	Sept. 6, 1841
Kenneth L. Anderson	Sept. 2, 1844

Lieutenant Governors

Albert C. Horton	1846-1847
John A. Greer	1847-1851

J. W. Henderson, Aug. 4, 1851 (Served as Governor of Texas from Nov. 23, 1853, to Dec. 21, 1853.)

D. C. Dickson	1853-1855
H. R. Runnels	Aug. 6, 1855

(Runnels became Governor of Texas in 1857.)

F. R. Lubbock	Aug. 4, 1857

(Became Governor of Texas during Confederacy.)

Edward Clark	Aug. 1, 1859

(Became Governor of Texas during Confederacy.)

John M. Crockett	1861-1863
Fletcher S. Stockdale	1863-1866
George W. Jones	1866

(Jones was removed by General Sheridan.)

J. W. Flanagan	1869

(Flanagan was elected a U.S. Senator and was never inaugurated as Lt. Gov.)

R. B. Hubbard	1873-1876

(Became Governor of Texas in 1876.)

J. D. Sayers	1878-1880
L. J. Storey	1880-1882
Marion Martin	1882-1884
Barnett Gibbs	1884-1886
T. B. Wheeler	1886-1888
T. B. Wheeler	1888-1890
George C. Pendleton	1890-1892
M. M. Crane	Jan. 17, 1893-Jan. 25, 1895
George T. Jester	1895-1896
George T. Jester	1896-1898
J. N. Browning	1898-1902
George D. Neal	1902-1906
A. B. Davidson	1906-1912
Will H. Mayes	1912-1914
W. P. Hobby	1914-1917

(Became Governor of Texas in September, 1917.)

W. A. Johnson (succeeded Hobby as Lieutenant Governor, serving his unexpired term and until January, 1920).

Lynch Davidson	1920-1922
T. W. Davidson	1922-1924
Barry Miller	1924-1931
Edgar E. Witt	1931-1935
Walter Woodul	1935-1939
Coke R. Stevenson	1939-1941

(Became Governor of Texas Aug. 4, 1941.)

John Lee Smith	1943-Jan. 21, 1947
Allan Shivers	Jan. 21, 1947-July 11, 1949

(Shivers succeeded to the governorship on death of Governor Beauford H. Jester, July 11, 1949.)

Ben Ramsey	1951-Sept. 18, 1961

(Ben Ramsey resigned to become a member of the State Railroad Commission, Sept. 18, 1961.)

Preston Smith	1963-1969
Ben Barnes	1969-1973
William P. Hobby	1973 to Present

SECRETARIES OF STATE
Republic of Texas

Raines Yearbook for Texas, 1901, gives the following record of Secretaries of State during the era of the Republic of Texas:

Under President ad interim David G. Burnet—Samuel P. Carson, James Collingsworth and W. H. Jack.

Under Sam Houston (first term)—Stephen F. Austin, 1836. J. Pinckney Henderson and Dr. Robert A. Irion, 1837-38.

Under Mirabeau B. Lamar—Bernard Bee appointed Dec. 16, 1838; James Webb appointed Feb. 6, 1839; D. G. Burnet appointed Acting Secretary of State, May 31, 1839; N. Amory appointed Acting Secretary of State, July 23, 1839; D. G. Burnet appointed Acting Secretary of State, Aug. 5, 1839; Abner S. Lipscomb appointed Secretary of State, Jan. 31, 1840, and resigned Jan. 22, 1841; Joseph Waples appointed Acting Secretary of State, Jan. 23, 1841, and served until Feb. 8, 1841; James S. Mayfield appointed Feb. 8, 1841; Joseph Waples appointed April 30, 1841, and served until May 25, 1841; Samuel A. Roberts appointed May 25, 1841, and reappointed Sept. 7, 1841.

Under President Sam Houston (second term)—E. Lawrence Stickney, Acting Secretary of State until Anson Jones appointed Dec. 13, 1841. Jones served as Secretary of State throughout this term except during the summer and part of this term of 1842, when Joseph Wa-

ples filled the position as Acting Secretary of State.

Under President Anson Jones—Ebenezer Allen served from Dec. 10, 1844, until Feb. 5, 1845, when Ashbel Smith became Secretary of State. Allen was again named Acting Secretary of State, March 31, 1845, and later named Secretary of State.

State Secretaries of State

Charles Mariner	Feb. 20, 1846-May 4, 1846
David G. Burnet	May 4, 1846-Jan. 1, 1848
Washington D. Miller	Jan. 1, 1848-Jan. 2, 1850
James Webb	Jan. 2, 1850-Nov. 14, 1851
Thomas H. Duval	Nov. 14, 1851-Dec. 22, 1853
Edward Clark	Dec. 22, 1853-Dec., 1857
T. S. Anderson	Dec. 1857-Dec. 27, 1859
E. W. Cave	Dec. 27, 1859-Mar. 16, 1861
Bird Holland	Mar. 16, 1861-Nov., 1861
Charles West	Nov., 1861-Sept., 1862
Robert J. Townes	Sept., 1862-May 2, 1865
Charles R. Pryor	May 2, 1865-Aug., 1865
James H. Bell	Aug., 1865-Aug., 1866
John A. Green	Aug., 1866-Aug., 1867
D. W. C. Phillips	Aug., 1867-Jan., 1870
J. P. Newcomb	Jan. 1, 1870-Jan. 17, 1874
George Clark	Jan. 17, 1874-Jan. 27, 1874
A. W. DeBerry	Jan. 27, 1874-Dec. 1, 1876
Isham G. Searcy	Dec. 1, 1876-Jan. 23, 1879
J. D. Templeton	Jan. 23, 1879-Jan. 22, 1881
T. H. Bowman	Jan. 22, 1881-Jan. 18, 1883
J. W. Baines	Jan. 18, 1883-Jan. 21, 1887
John M. Moore	Jan. 21, 1887-Jan. 22, 1891
George W. Smith	Jan. 22, 1891-Jan. 17, 1895
Allison Mayfield	Jan. 17, 1895-Jan. 5, 1897
J. W. Madden	Jan. 5, 1897-Jan. 18, 1899
D. H. Hardy	Jan. 18, 1899-Jan. 19, 1901
John G. Tod	Jan. 19, 1901-Jan., 1903
J. R. Curl	Jan., 1903-April, 1905
O. K. Shannon	April, 1905-Jan., 1907
L. T. Dashiel	Jan., 1907-Feb., 1908
W. R. Davie	Feb., 1908-Jan., 1909
W. B. Townsend	Jan., 1909-Jan., 1911
C. C. McDonald	Jan., 1911-Dec., 1912
J. T. Bowman	Dec., 1912-Jan., 1913
John L. Wortham	Jan., 1913-June, 1913
F. C. Weinert	June, 1913-Nov., 1914
D. A. Gregg	Nov., 1914-Jan., 1915
John G. McKay	Jan., 1915-Dec., 1916
C. J. Bartlett	Dec., 1916-Nov., 1917
George F. Howard	Nov., 1917-Nov., 1920
C. D. Mims	Nov., 1920-Jan., 1921
S. L. Staples	Jan., 1921-Aug., 1924
J. D. Strickland	Sept., 1924-Jan. 1, 1925
Henry Hutchings	Jan. 1, 1925-Jan. 20, 1925
Mrs. Emma G. Meharg	Jan. 20, 1925-Jan., 1927
Mrs. Jane Y. McCallum	Jan., 1927-Jan., 1933
W. W. Heath	Jan., 1933-Jan., 1935
Gerald C. Mann	Jan., 1935-Aug. 31, 1935
R. B. Stanford	Aug. 31, 1935-Aug. 25, 1936
B. P. Matocha	Aug. 25, 1936-Jan. 18, 1937
Edward Clark	Jan. 18, 1937-Jan., 1939
Tom L. Beauchamp	Jan., 1939-Oct., 1939
M. O. Flowers	Oct. 26, 1939-Feb. 25, 1941
William J. Lawson	Feb. 25, 1941-Jan., 1943
Sidney Latham	Jan., 1943-Feb., 1945
Claude Isbell	Feb., 1945-Jan., 1947
Paul H. Brown	Jan., 1947-Jan. 19, 1949
Ben Ramsey	Jan. 19, 1949-Feb. 9, 1950
John Ben Shepperd	Feb. 9, 1950-April 30, 1952
Jack Ross	April 30, 1952-Jan. 9, 1953
Howard A. Carney	Jan. 9, 1953-Apr. 30, 1954
C. E. Fulgham	May 1, 1954-Feb. 15, 1955
Al Muldrow	Feb. 16, 1955-Nov. 1, 1955
Tom Reavley	Nov. 1, 1955-Jan. 16, 1957
Zollie Steakley	Jan. 16, 1957-Jan. 2, 1962
P. Frank Lake	Jan. 2, 1962-Jan. 15, 1963
Crawford C. Martin	Jan. 15, 1963-March 12, 1966
John L. Hill	March 12, 1966-Jan. 22, 1968
Roy Barrera	March 7, 1968-Jan. 23, 1969
Martin Dies Jr.	Jan. 23, 1969-Sept. 1, 1971
Robert D. Bullock	Sept. 1, 1971-Jan. 2, 1973
V. Larry Teaver Jr.	Jan. 2, 1973-Jan. 19, 1973
Mark W. White Jr.	Jan. 19, 1973-Oct. 27, 1977
Steven C. Oaks	Oct. 27, 1977-Jan. 16, 1979
George W. Strake Jr.	Jan. 16, 1979 to Oct. 6, 1981
David A. Dean	Oct. 22, 1981-Jan. 18, 1983
John Fainter	Jan. 18, 1983-July 31, 1984
Myra A. McDaniel	Sept. 6, 1984 to Present

ATTORNEYS GENERAL
Attorneys General Under Republic

David Thomas and

Peter W. Grayson	Mar. 2-Oct. 22, 1836

J. Pinckney Henderson, Peter W. Grayson,
John Birdsall, A. S. Thurston. 1836-1838
J. C. Watrous . . . . Dec., 1838-June 1, 1840
Joseph Webb and F. A. Morris 1840-1841
George W. Terrell, Ebenezer Allen. 1841-1844
Ebenezer Allen 1844-1846

*Attorneys General, State

Volney E. Howard . . . . Feb. 21, 1846-May 7, 1846
John W. Harris . . . . May 7, 1846-Oct. 31, 1849
Henry P. Brewster. . . . . Oct. 31, 1849-Jan. 15, 1850
A. J. Hamilton. . . . . Jan. 15, 1850-Aug. 5, 1850
Ebenezer Allen . . . . Aug. 5, 1850-Aug. 2, 1852
Thomas J. Jennings . . . . Aug. 2, 1852-Aug. 4, 1856
James Willie . . . . Aug. 4, 1856-Aug. 2, 1858
Malcolm D. Graham . . . . Aug. 2, 1858-Aug. 6, 1860
George M. Flournoy . . . . Aug. 6, 1860-Jan. 15, 1862
N. G. Shelley . . . . Feb. 3, 1862-Aug. 1, 1864
B. E. Tarver . . . . Aug. 1, 1864-Dec. 11, 1865
Wm. Alexander. . . . . Dec. 11, 1865-June 25, 1866
W. M. Walton . . . . June 25, 1866-Aug. 27, 1867
Wm. Alexander. . . . . Aug. 27, 1867-Nov. 5, 1867
Ezekiel B. Turner . . . . Nov. 5, 1867-July 11, 1870
Wm. Alexander. . . . . July 11, 1870-Jan. 27, 1874
George Clark . . . . Jan. 27, 1874-Apr. 25, 1876
H. H. Boone. . . . . Apr. 25, 1876-Nov. 5, 1878
George McCormick. . . . . Nov. 5, 1878-Nov. 2, 1880
J. H. McLeary. . . . . Nov. 2, 1880-Nov. 7, 1882
John D. Templeton . . . . Nov. 7, 1882-Nov. 2, 1886
James S. Hogg . . . . Nov. 2, 1886-Nov. 4, 1890
C. A. Culberson . . . . Nov. 4, 1890-Nov. 6, 1894
M. M. Crane . . . . Nov. 6, 1894-Nov. 8, 1898
Thomas S. Smith . . . . Nov. 8, 1898-Mar. 15, 1901
C. K. Bell. . . . . Mar. 20, 1901-Jan., 1904
R. V. Davidson . . . . Jan., 1904-Dec. 31, 1909
Jewel P. Lightfoot . . . . Jan. 1, 1910-Aug. 31, 1912
James D. Walthall . . . . Sept. 1, 1912-Jan. 1, 1913
B. F. Looney . . . . Jan. 1, 1913-Jan., 1919
C. M. Cureton . . . . Jan., 1919-Dec., 1921
N. A. Keeling . . . . Dec., 1921-Jan., 1925
Dan Moody . . . . Jan., 1925-Jan., 1927
Claude Pollard . . . . Jan., 1927-Sept., 1929
R. L. Bobbitt (Apptd.) . . . . Sept., 1929-Jan., 1931
James V. Allred . . . . Jan., 1931-Jan., 1935
William McCraw. . . . . Jan., 1935-Jan., 1939
Gerald C. Mann (resigned) . . . . . Jan., 1939-Jan., 1944
Grover Sellers. . . . . Jan., 1944-Jan., 1947
Price Daniel . . . . Jan., 1947-Jan., 1953
John Ben Shepperd . . . . Jan., 1953-Jan. 1, 1957
Will Wilson . . . . Jan. 1, 1957-Jan. 15, 1963
Waggoner Carr . . . . Jan. 15, 1963-Jan. 1, 1967
Crawford C. Martin. . . . . Jan. 1, 1967-Dec. 29, 1972
John Hill . . . . Jan. 1, 1973-Jan. 16, 1979
Mark White. . . . . Jan. 16, 1979 to Jan. 18, 1983
Jim Mattox . . . . Jan. 18, 1983 to Present

*The first few Attorneys General held office by ap-
pointment of the Governor. The office was made elective in 1850 by constitutional amendment and Ebenezer
Allen was first elected Attorney General.

TREASURERS
Treasurers Under Republic

Asa Brigham. 1838-1840
James W. Simmons 1840-1841
Asa Brigham. 1841-1844
Moses Johnson 1844-1846

Treasurers Under State

James H. Raymond . . . . Feb. 24, 1846-Aug. 2, 1858
C. H. Randolph . . . . Aug. 2, 1858-June, 1865
Samuel Harris . . . . Oct. 2, 1865-June 25, 1866
N. M. Royston. . . . . June 25, 1866-Sept. 1, 1867
John Y. Allen . . . . Sept. 1, 1867-Jan., 1869
George W. Honey . . . . Jan., 1869-Jan., 1874
B. Graham . . . . . (short term) beginning May 27, 1872
A. J. Dorn . . . . Jan., 1874-Jan., 1879
F. R. Lubbock . . . . Jan., 1879-Jan., 1891
W. B. Wortham . . . . Jan., 1891-Jan., 1899
John W. Robbins. . . . . Jan., 1899-Jan., 1907
Sam Sparks. . . . . Jan., 1907-Jan., 1912
J. M. Edwards. . . . . Jan., 1912-Jan., 1919
John W. Baker. . . . . Jan., 1919-Jan., 1921
G. N. Holton . . . . July, 1921-Nov. 21, 1921
C. V. Terrell . . . . Nov. 21, 1921-Aug. 15, 1924
L. Staples . . . . Aug. 16, 1924-Jan. 16, 1925
W. Gregory Hatcher . . . . Jan. 16, 1925-Jan. 1, 1931
Charley Lockhart . . . . Jan. 1, 1931-Oct. 25, 1941
Jesse James . . . . Oct. 25, 1941-Sept. 29, 1977
Warren G. Harding . . . . Oct. 7, 1977-Jan. 3, 1983
Ann Richards . . . . Jan. 3, 1983 to Present

*Honey was removed from office for a short period
in 1872 and B. Graham served in his place.
†Randolph fled to Mexico upon collapse of Confederacy. No exact date available for his departure
from office or for Harris' succession to the post. It is
believed Harris took office Oct. 2, 1865.

RAILROAD COMMISSION OF TEXAS

John H. Reagan, June 10, 1891-Jan. 20, 1903.
L. L. Foster, June 10, 1891-April 30, 1895.
W. P. McLean, June 10, 1891-Nov. 20, 1894.
L. J. Storey (succeeding W. P. McLean), Nov. 21,
1894-Mar. 28, 1909.
N. A. Stedman (succeeding L. L. Foster), May 1,
1895-Jan. 4, 1897.
Allison Mayfield (succeeding N. A. Stedman), Jan.
5, 1897-Jan. 23, 1923.
O. B. Colquitt (succeeding John H. Reagan), Jan.
21, 1903-Jan. 17, 1911.
William D. Williams (succeeding L. J. Storey),
April 28, 1909-Oct. 1, 1916.
John L. Wortham (succeeding O. B. Colquitt), Jan.
21, 1911-Jan. 1, 1913.
Earle B. Mayfield (succeeding John L. Wortham),
Jan. 2, 1913-March 1, 1923.
Charles H. Hurdleston (succeeding William D. Wil-
liams), Oct. 10, 1916-Dec. 31, 1918.
Clarence E. Gilmore (succeeding Charles H. Hur-
dleston), Jan. 1, 1919-Jan. 1, 1929.
W. A. Nabors (succeeding Allison Mayfield), March
1, 1923-Jan. 18, 1925.
W. M. W. Splawn (succeeding Earle B. Mayfield),
March 1, 1923-Aug. 1, 1924.
C. V. Terrell (succeeding W. M. W. Splawn), Aug.
15, 1924-Jan. 1, 1939.
Lon A. Smith (succeeding W. A. Nabors), Jan. 19,
1925-Jan. 1, 1941.
Pat M. Neff (succeeding Clarence E. Gilmore),
Jan. 1, 1929-Jan. 1, 1933.
Ernest O. Thompson (succeeding Pat M. Neff),
Jan. 1, 1933-Jan. 8, 1965.
G. A. Sadler (succeeding C. V. Terrell), Jan. 1,
1939-Jan. 1, 1943.
Olin Culberson (succeeding Lon A. Smith), Jan. 1,
1941-June 22, 1961.
Beauford Jester (succeeding G. A. Sadler), Jan. 1,
1943-Jan. 21, 1947.
William J. Murray Jr. (succeeding Beauford Jes-
ter), Jan. 21, 1947-Apr. 10, 1963.
Jim C. Langdon (succeeding William J. Murray
Jr.), May 28, 1963-Jan. 3, 1978.
Ben Ramsey (succeeding Olin Culberson), Sept. 18,
1961-Jan. 1, 1977.
Jon Newton (succeeding Ben Ramsey), Jan. 1,
1977-Jan. 1, 1979.
Byron Tunnell (succeeding Ernest O. Thompson),
Jan. 8, 1965-Sept. 15, 1973.
Mack Wallace (succeeding Byron Tunnell), Sept.
15, 1973 to Present.
John H. Poerner (succeeding Jim C. Langdon),
Jan. 3, 1978 to Jan. 1, 1981.
James E. Nugent (succeeding Jon Newton), Jan. 1,
1979 to Present.
Buddy Temple (succeeding John H. Poerner),
Jan. 1, 1981 to Present.

COMPTROLLER OF PUBLIC ACCOUNTS
Comptrollers Under Republic

John H. Money . . . . Dec. 30, 1835-Jan. 17, 1836
H. C. Hudson . . . . Jan. 17, 1836-Oct. 22, 1836
E. M. Pease. . . . . June, 1837-Dec., 1837
F. R. Lubbock . . . . Dec., 1837-Jan., 1839
Jas. W. Simmons . . . . Jan. 15, 1839-Sept. 30, 1840
Jas. B. Shaw . . . . Sept. 30, 1840-Dec. 24, 1841
F. R. Lubbock . . . . Dec. 24, 1841-Jan. 1, 1842
Jas. B. Shaw . . . . Jan. 1, 1842-Jan. 1, 1846

State Comptrollers

Jas. B. Shaw . . . . Feb. 24, 1846-Aug. 2, 1858
Clement R. Johns . . . . Aug. 2, 1858-Aug. 1, 1864
Willis L. Robards. . . . . Aug. 1, 1864-Oct. 12, 1865
Albert H. Latimer . . . . Oct. 12, 1865-Mar. 27, 1866
Robert H. Taylor. . . . . Mar. 27, 1866-June 25, 1866
Willis L. Robards. . . . . June 25, 1866-Aug. 27, 1867
Morgan C. Hamilton . . . . . . Aug. 27, 1867-Jan. 8, 1870
A. Bledsoe. . . . . Jan. 8, 1870-Jan. 20, 1874
Stephen H. Darden . . . . . . Jan. 20, 1974-Nov. 2, 1880
W. M. Brown . . . . Nov. 2, 1880-Jan. 16, 1883
W. J. Swain . . . . Jan. 16, 1883-Jan. 18, 1887
John D. McCall . . . . Jan. 18, 1887-Jan. 15, 1895
R. W. Finley . . . . Jan. 15, 1895-Jan. 15, 1901
R. M. Love . . . . Jan. 15, 1901-Jan., 1903

J. W. Stephen	Jan., 1903-Jan., 1911
W. P. Lane	Jan., 1911-Jan., 1915
H. B. Terrell	Jan., 1915-Jan., 1920
M. L. Wiginton	Jan., 1920-Jan., 1921
Lon A. Smith	Jan., 1921-Jan., 1925
S. H. Terrell	Jan., 1925-Jan., 1931
Geo. H. Sheppard	Jan., 1931-Jan. 17, 1949
Robert S. Calvert	Jan. 17, 1949-Jan., 1975
Robert D. Bullock	Jan., 1975 to Present

TEXAS SENATORIAL SUCCESSION

Following is the succession of Texas representatives in the United States Senate since the annexation of Texas to the Union in 1845:

Houston Succession

Sam Houston	Feb. 21, 1846-Mar. 4, 1859
John Hemphill	Mar. 4, 1859-July 11, 1861

Louis T. Wigfall and W. S. Oldham took their seats in the Confederate Senate, Nov. 16, 1861, and served in that body until fall of Confederacy. After collapse of the Confederacy the State Legislature on Aug. 21, 1866, elected David G. Burnet and Oran M. Roberts to the United States Senate, anticipating immediate readmission to the Union, but they were not allowed to take their seats.

*Morgan C. Hamilton	Feb. 22, 1870-Mar. 3, 1877
Richard Coke	Mar. 4, 1877-Mar. 3, 1895
Horace Chilton	Mar. 3, 1895-Mar. 3, 1901
Joseph W. Bailey	Mar. 3, 1901-Jan. 8, 1913
R. M. Johnson	Jan. 8, 1913-Feb. 3, 1913
Morris Sheppard (died)	Feb. 13, 1913-Apr. 9, 1941
Andrew J. Houston	June 2-26, 1941
W. Lee O'Daniel	Aug. 4, 1941-Jan. 3, 1949
Lyndon B. Johnson	Jan. 3, 1949-Jan. 20, 1961
William A. Blakley	Jan. 20, 1961-June 15, 1961
*John G. Tower	June 15, 1961-Jan. 21, 1985
Phil Gramm	Jan. 21, 1985-Present

Rusk Succession

Thomas J. Rusk (died)	Feb 21, 1846-July 29, 1857
J. Pinckney Henderson (died)	Nov. 9, 1857-June 4, 1858
Matthias Ward (appointed interim)	Sept. 29, 1858-Dec. 5, 1859

Note.—Succession broken by expulsion of Texas Senators following secession of Texas from Union. See note above under "Houston Succession" on Louis T. Wigfall and W. S. Oldham and Burnet and Roberts.

*James W. Flanagan	Feb. 22, 1870-Mar. 3, 1875
Samuel B. Maxey	Mar. 3, 1875-Mar. 3, 1887
John H. Reagan (resigned)	Mar. 3, 1887-June 10, 1891
Horace Chilton (filled vacancy on appointment)	Dec. 7, 1891-Mar. 30, 1892
Roger Q. Mills	Mar. 30, 1892-Mar. 3, 1899
†Charles A. Culberson	Mar. 3, 1899-Mar. 4, 1923
Earle B. Mayfield	Mar. 4, 1923-Mar. 4, 1929
Tom Connally	Mar. 4, 1929-Jan. 3, 1953
Price Daniel	Jan. 3, 1953-Jan. 15, 1957
William A. Blakley	Jan. 15, 1957-Apr. 27, 1957
Ralph W. Yarborough	Apr. 27, 1957-Jan. 12, 1971
Lloyd Bentsen	Jan. 12, 1971 to Present

*Republican members.

†First election to U.S. Senate held in 1916. Prior to that time, senators were appointed by the Legislature.

COMMISSIONERS OF THE GENERAL LAND OFFICE

Commissioners Under Republic

John P. Borden	Aug. 23, 1837-Dec. 12, 1840
H. W. Raglin	Dec. 12, 1840-Jan. 4, 1841
*Thomas William Ward	Jan. 4, 1841-Mar. 20, 1848

Commissioners Under State

George W. Smyth	Mar. 20, 1848-Aug. 4, 1851
Stephen Crosby	Aug. 4, 1851-Mar. 1, 1858
Francis M. White	Mar. 1, 1858-Mar. 1, 1862
Stephen Crosby	Mar. 1, 1862-Sept. 1, 1865
Francis M. White	Sept. 1, 1865-Aug. 7, 1866
Stephen Crosby	Aug. 7, 1866-Aug. 27, 1867
Joseph Spence	Aug. 27, 1867-Jan. 19, 1870
Jacob Kuechler	Jan. 19, 1870-Jan. 20, 1874
J. J. Groos	Jan. 20, 1874-June 15, 1878
W. C. Walsh	July 30, 1878, Jan. 10, 1887
R. M. Hall	Jan. 10, 1887-Jan. 16, 1891
W. L. McGaughey	Jan. 16, 1891-Jan. 26, 1895
A. J. Baker	Jan. 26, 1895-Jan. 16, 1899
George W. Finger	Jan. 16, 1899-May 4, 1899
Charles Rogan	May 11, 1899-Jan. 10, 1903
John J. Terrell	Jan. 10, 1903-Jan. 11, 1909
J. T. Robison	Jan, 1909-Sept. 11, 1929
J. H. Walker	Sept. 11, 1929-Jan., 1937
William H. McDonald	Jan, 1937-Jan., 1939
Bascom Giles	Jan., 1939-Jan. 5, 1955
J. Earl Rudder	Jan. 5, 1955-Feb. 1, 1958

Bill Allcorn	Feb. 1, 1958-Jan. 1, 1961
Jerry Sadler	Jan. 1, 1961-Jan. 1, 1971
Bob Armstrong	Jan. 1, 1971-Jan. 1, 1983
Garry Mauro	Jan. 1, 1983 to Present

*Part of term after annexation.

FIRST LADIES OF TEXAS

Martha Evans Gindratt Wood	1847-49
*Bell Administration	1849-53
Lucadia Christiana Niles Pease	1853-57; 1867-69
†Runnels Administration	1857-59
Margaret Moffette Lea Houston	1859-61
Martha Evans Clark	1861
Adele Barron Lubbock	1861-63
Susie Ellen Taylor Murrah	1863-65
Mary Jane Bowen Hamilton	1865-66
Annie Rattan Throckmorton	1866-67
Ann Elizabeth Britton Davis	1870-74
Mary Home Coke	1874-76
Janie Roberts Hubbard	1876-79
Frances Wickliff Edwards Roberts	1879-83
Anne Maria Penn Ireland	1883-87
Elizabeth Dorothy Tinsley Ross	1887-91
Sarah Stinson Hogg	1891-95
Sally Harrison Culberson	1895-99
Orlene Walton Sayers	1899-1903
Sarah Beona Meng Lanham	1903-07
Fannie Brunner Campbell	1907-11
Alice Fuller Murrell Colquitt	1911-15
‡Miriam A. Wallace Ferguson	1915-17; 1925-27; 1933-35
Willie Cooper Hobby	1917-21
Myrtle Mainer Neff	1921-25
Mildred Paxton Moody	1927-31
Maud Gage Sterling	1931-33
Jo Betsy Miller Allred	1935-39
Merle Estella Butcher O'Daniel	1939-41
**Fay Wright Stevenson	1941-42
**Stevenson Administration	1942-46
Mabel Buchanan Jester	1946-49
Marialice Shary Shivers	1949-57
Jean Houston Baldwin Daniel	1957-63
Idanell Brill Connally	1963-69
Ima Mae Smith	1969-73
Betty Jane Slaughter Briscoe	1973-1979
Rita Clements	1979-1983
Linda Gale White	1983 to Present

*Gov. Peter Hansbrough Bell was married at expiration of his term of office, March 3, 1857, to Mrs. Ella Reeves Eaton Dickens.

†Gov. Hardin R. Runnels never married.

‡Mistress of the Mansion while her husband, James E. Ferguson, was Governor, 1915-17; both Mansion Mistress and Governor of Texas, 1925-27 and 1933-35.

**Mrs. Coke R. (Fay Wright) Stevenson died in the Governor's Mansion Jan. 3, 1942. Governor Stevenson's mother and daughter-in-law served as Mistresses of the Mansion during the remainder of his term. He was married to Mrs. Marguerite King Heap Jan. 16, 1954.

SUPERINTENDENTS OF PUBLIC INSTRUCTION

Pryor Lea	Nov. 10, 1866-Sept. 12, 1867
Edwin M. Wheelock	Sept. 12, 1867-May 6, 1871
Jacob C. DeGress	May 6, 1871-Jan. 20, 1874
O. H. Hollingsworth	Jan. 20, 1874-May 6, 1884
B. M. Baker	May 6, 1884-Jan. 18, 1887
O. H. Cooper	Jan 18, 1887-Sept. 1, 1890
H. C. Pritchett	Sept. 1, 1890-Sept. 15, 1891
J. M. Carlisle	Sept. 15, 1891-Jan. 10, 1899
J. S. Kendall	Jan. 10, 1899-July 2, 1901
Arthur Lefevre	July 2, 1901-Jan. 12, 1905
R. B. Cousins	Jan. 12, 1905-Jan. 1, 1910
F. M. Bralley	Jan. 1, 1910-Sept. 1, 1913
W. F. Doughty	Sept. 1, 1913-Jan. 1, 1919
Annie Webb Blanton	Jan. 1, 1919-Jan. 16, 1923
S. M. N. Marrs	Jan. 16, 1923-April 28, 1932
C. N. Shaver	April 28, 1932-Oct. 1, 1932
L. W. Rogers	Oct. 1, 1932-Jan. 16, 1933
L. A. Woods	Jan. 16, 1933-*1950

State Commissioner of Education

J. W. Edgar	May 31, 1951-June 30, 1974
Marlin L. Brockette	July 1, 1974-Sept. 1, 1979
Alton O. Bowen	Sept. 1, 1979-June 1, 1981
Raymon Bynum	June 1, 1981-Oct. 31, 1984
W. N. Kirby	April 13, 1985 to Present

*The office of State Superintendent of Public Instruction was abolished by the Gilmer-Aikin act of 1949 and the office of Commissioner of Education created, appointed by a new State Board of Education elected by the people.

Former Speakers of the Texas House attended ceremonies at capitol honoring House Speaker Gib Lewis. They are front row, from left: Robert W. Calvert, Billy Clayton, Byron Tunnell and Waggoner Carr. Back row, from left: Jim Lindsey, Gib Lewis, Rayford Price and Price Daniel Sr. Associated Press Photo

Speaker of the Texas House

The Speaker of the Texas House of Representatives is the presiding officer of the lower chamber of the state Legislature. The official is elected at the beginning of each regular session by a vote of the members of the House. (This list is taken from a 1981 publication of the Texas Legislative Council entitled, "Presiding Officers of the Texas Legislature 1846-1982.")

Speaker, Residence —	Elected	Legislature
William E. Crump, Bellville	1846	1st
William H. Bourland, Paris	1846	1st
James W. Henderson, Houston	1847	2nd
Charles G. Keenan, Huntsville	1849	3rd
David C. Dickson, Anderson	1851	4th
Hardin R. Runnels, Boston	1853	5th
Hamilton P. Bee, Laredo	1855	6th
William S. Taylor, Larissa	1857	7th
Matt F. Locke, Lafayette	1858	7th
Marion DeKalb Taylor, Jefferson	1859	8th
Constantine W. Buckley, Richmond	1861	9th
Nicholas H. Darnell, Dallas	1861	9th
Constantine W. Buckley, Richmond	1863	9th
Marion DeKalb Taylor, Jefferson	1863	10th
Nathaniel M. Burford, Dallas	1866	11th
Ira H. Evans, Corpus Christi	1870	12th
William H. Sinclair, Galveston	1871	12th
Marion DeKalb Taylor, Jefferson	1873	13th

Speaker, Residence —	Elected	Legislature
Guy M. Bryan, Galveston	1874	14th
Thomas R. Bonner, Tyler	1876	15th
John H. Cochran, Dallas	1879	16th
George R. Reeves, Pottsboro	1881	17th
Charles R. Gibson, Waxahachie	1883	18th
Lafayette L. Foster, Groesbeck	1885	19th
George C. Pendleton, Belton	1887	20th
Frank P. Alexander, Greenville	1889	21st
Robert T. Milner, Henderson	1891	22nd
John H. Cochran, Dallas	1893	23rd
Thomas Slater Smith, Hillsboro	1895	24th
L. Travis Dashiell, Jewett	1897	25th
J. S. Sherrill, Greenville	1899	26th
Robert E. Prince, Corsicana	1901	27th
Pat M. Neff, Waco	1903	28th
Francis W. Seabury, Rio Grande City	1905	29th
Thomas B. Love, Lancaster	1907	30th
Austin M. Kennedy, Waco	1909	31st
John W. Marshall, Whitesboro	1909	31st
Sam Rayburn, Bonham	1911	32nd
Chester H. Terrell, San Antonio	1913	33rd
John W. Woods, Rotan	1915	34th
Franklin O. Fuller, Coldspring	1917	35th
R. Ewing Thomason, El Paso	1919	36th
Charles G. Thomas, Lewisville	1921	37th
Richard E. Seagler, Palestine	1923	38th
Lee Satterwhite, Amarillo	1925	39th
Robert L. Bobbitt, Laredo	1927	40th
W. S. Barron, Bryan	1929	41st

Speaker, Residence —	Elected	Legislature
Fred H. Minor, Denton	1931	42nd
Coke R. Stevenson, Junction	1933	43rd
''	1935	44th
Robert W. Calvert, Hillsboro	1937	45th
R. Emmett Morse, Houston	1939	46th
Homer L. Leonard, McAllen	1941	47th
Price Daniel, Liberty	1943	48th
Claud H. Gilmer, Rocksprings	1945	49th
William O. Reed, Dallas	1947	50th
Durwood Manford, Smiley	1949	51st
Reuben Senterfitt, San Saba	1951	52nd
''	1953	53rd
Jim T. Lindsey, Texarkana	1955	54th
Waggoner Carr, Lubbock	1957	55th
''	1959	56th
James A. Turman, Gober	1961	57th
Byron M. Tunnell, Tyler	1963	58th
Ben Barnes, DeLeon	1965	59th
''	1967	60th
Gus F. Mutscher, Brenham	1969	61st
''	1971	62nd
Rayford Price, Palestine	1972	62nd
Price Daniel Jr., Liberty	1973	63rd
Bill Clayton, Springlake	1975	64th
''	1977	65th
''	1979	66th
''	1981	67th
Gibson D. Lewis, Fort Worth	1983	68th

CHIEF JUSTICE OF SUPREME COURT
Republic of Texas
James Collinsworth. . . . . . . Dec. 16, 1836-July 23, 1838
John Birdsall . . . . Nov. 19-Dec. 12, 1838
Thomas J. Rusk . . . . Dec. 12, 1838-Dec. 5, 1840
John Hemphill . . . . Dec. 5, 1840-Dec. 29, 1845
Constitutions of 1845 and 1861
John Hemphill . . . . Mar. 2, 1846-Oct. 10, 1858
Royall T. Wheeler . . . . Oct. 11, 1858-April 1864
Oran M. Roberts . . . . Nov. 1, 1864-June 30, 1866

Constitution of 1866 (Presidential Reconstruction)
*George F. Moore . . . . Aug. 16, 1866-Sept. 10, 186
*Removed under Congressional Reconstruction b
military authorities who appointed members of th
next court.
Constitution of 1866 (Congressional Reconstruction)
†Amos Morrill. . . . . Sept. 10, 1867-July 5, 187
†Court on which he sat is generally referred to a
the "Military Court" and its decisions have little or n
precedential value.
Constitution of 1869
Lemuel D. Evans. . . . . July 5, 1870-Aug. 31, 187
Wesley Ogden. . . . . Aug. 31, 1873-Jan. 29, 187
Oran M. Roberts. . . . . Jan. 29, 1874-Apr. 18, 187
Constitution of 1876
Oran M. Roberts. . . . . Apr. 18, 1876-Oct. 1, 187
George F. Moore. . . . . Nov. 5, 1878-Nov. 1, 188
Robert S. Gould. . . . . Nov. 1, 1881-Dec. 23, 188
Asa H. Willie . . . . Dec. 23, 1882-Mar. 3, 188
John W. Stayton . . . . Mar. 3, 1888-July 5, 189
Reuben R. Gaines . . . . July 10, 1894-Jan. 5, 191
Thomas J. Brown . . . . Jan. 7, 1911-May 26, 191
Nelson Phillips . . . . June 1, 1915-Nov. 16, 192
C. M. Cureton . . . . Dec. 2, 1921-Apr. 8, 194
W. F. Moore . . . . Apr. 17, 1940-Jan. 1, 194
James P. Alexander . . . . Jan. 1, 1941-Jan. 1, 194
J. E. Hickman . . . . Jan. 5, 1948-Jan. 3, 196
Robert W. Calvert . . . . Jan. 3, 1961-Oct. 4, 197
Joe R. Greenhill . . . . Oct. 4, 1972-Oct. 25, 198
Jack Pope. . . . . Nov. 23, 1982-Presen
PRESIDING JUDGES, COURT OF APPEALS (1876-1891) and COURT OF CRIMINAL APPEALS (1891-Present)
Mat D. Ector. . . . . May 6, 1876-Oct. 29, 187
John P. White . . . . Nov. 9, 1879-Apr. 26, 189
James M. Hurt . . . . May 4, 1892-Dec. 31, 189
W. L. Davidson . . . . Jan. 2, 1899-June 27, 191
A. C. Prendergast . . . . June 27, 1913-Dec. 31, 191
W. L. Davidson . . . . Jan. 1, 1917-Jan. 25, 192
Wright C. Morrow . . . . Feb. 8, 1921-Oct. 16, 193
Frank Lee Hawkins . . . . Oct. 16, 1939-Jan. 2, 195
Harry N. Graves . . . . Jan. 2, 1951-Dec. 31, 195
W. A. Morrison . . . . Jan. 1, 1955-Jan. 2, 196
Kenneth K. Woodley . . . . Jan. 3, 1961-Jan. 4, 196
W. T. McDonald . . . . Jan. 4, 1965-June 25, 196
W. A. Morrison . . . . June 25, 1966-Jan. 1, 196
Kenneth K. Woodley . . . . Jan. 1, 1967-Jan. 1, 197
John F. Onion Jr. . . . . Jan. 1, 1971-Presen

Members of Texas Legislature

The Texas Legislature has 31 members in the Senate and 150 in the House of Representatives. Regular session convene on the second Tuesday of January in odd-numbered years, but the governor may call special sessions Article III of the Texas Constitution deals with the legislative branch.

The following lists are of members of the 69th Legislature which convened on Jan. 8, 1985, following the Nov. 1984, election.

STATE SENATE

Thirty-one members of the State Senate are elected for four-year, **overlapping terms.** Date in parentheses after each name below indicates expiration of **term of office. Salary:** The salary of all members of the Legislature, including both Senators and Representatives, was set by a constitutional amendment, adopted April 22, 1975, as follows: $600 per month and $30 per diem during legislative sessions; **mileage allowance** at same rate provided by law for state employees. The old provision limited salary to $4,800 a year and the per diem of $12 for the first 120 days of a regular session and the first 30 days of a special session. A mileage allowance of $2.50 was provided for each 25 miles traveled to and from seat of government, provided that no mileage be paid for any session called within one day after the close of the next preceding regular or special session. This provision was removed. The new rate of pay of $30 per diem applies during each regular and special session of the Legislature. The address of senators is Texas Senate, P.O. Box 12068, Capitol Station, Austin, Texas 78711.

Senatorial Districts include one or more whole counties and some counties have more than one Senator.

President of the Senate is Lt. Gov. William P. Hobby, Houston. Other officers are: **President Pro Tempore,** Ray Farabee, Wichita Falls. **Secretary of the Senate,** Mrs. Betty King, Austin. **Sergeant at Arms,** Steve Guest, Austin.

Dist., Name, Address, Term of Office, Occupation.

14—Barrientos, Gonzalo, Austin (1-1-89); businessman.

3—Blake, Roy, Nacogdoches (1-1-89); insurance-real estate.

*17—Brown, James E., Lake Jackson (1-1-89); attorney.

5—Caperton, Kent, Bryan (1-1-87); attorney.

9—Edwards, Chet, Duncanville (1-1-89); businessman.

30—Farabee, Ray, Wichita Falls (1-1-89); attorney.

22—Glasgow, Bob, Stephenville (1-1-89); attorney.

6—Green, Gene, Houston (1-1-87); printer-attorney.

*8—Harris, Ike, Dallas (1-1-89); attorney.

*7—Henderson, Don, Houston (1-1-87); attorney.

1—Howard, Ed, Texarkana (1-1-89); businessman.

24—Jones, Grant, Abilene (1-1-89); insurance.

19—Kothmann, Glenn, San Antonio (1-1-87); real estate-cattle.

*26—Krier, Cynthia T., San Antonio (1-1-89); attorney.

*16—Leedom, John, Dallas (1-1-87); businessman.

2—Lyon, Ted, Mesquite (1-1-89); attorney.

*10—McFarland, Bob, Arlington (1-1-87); attorney.

23—Mauzy, Oscar, Grand Prairie (1-1-87); attorney

28—Montford, John, Lubbock (1-1-89); attorney.

4—Parker, Carl, Port Arthur (1-1-89); attorney.

12—Parmer, Hugh, Fort Worth (1-1-87); businessman.

29—Santiesteban, H. Tati, El Paso (1-1-87); attorney.

31—Sarpalius, Bill, Hereford (1-1-89); educator-businessman.

18—Sharp, John, Victoria (1-1-87); real estate.

25—Sims, Bill, San Angelo (1-1-87); businessman-rancher.

21—Traeger, John, Seguin (1-1-87); businessman.
20—Truan, Carlos, Corpus Christi (1-1-89); insurance.
27—Uribe, Hector, Brownsville (1-1-87); attorney.
13—Washington, Craig, Houston (1-1-87); attorney.
15—Whitmire, John, Houston (1-1-87); attorney.
*Republican members; all others are Democrats.

HOUSE OF REPRESENTATIVES

This list shows 150 members of the House of Representatives in the 69th Legislature. They were elected on Nov. 6, 1984, from districts shown in the list below. Members are elected for 2-year terms. Representatives and Senators receive the same salary; see State Senate. Numbers before names denote district. The address of representatives is House of Representatives, P. O. Box 2910, Austin, Texas 78769.

Speaker, Gib Lewis. **Chief Clerk,** Betty Murray. **Sergeant at Arms,** Ron Hinkle.

Dist., Name, Address, Term of Office, Occupation.
119—Adkisson, Tommy, San Antonio; attorney.
*114—Agnich, Fred, Dallas; businessman.
32—Armbrister, Kenneth, Victoria; real estate.
4—Arnold, Gordon Jr., Terrell; attorney.
144—Barton, Erwin W., Pasadena; businessman.
34—Berlanga, Hugo, Corpus Christi; businessman.
*105—Blackwood, Bill, Mesquite; engineer.
*99—Blanton, William W., Carrollton; businessman.
88—Buchanan, J. W., Dumas; legislator.
66—Burnett, Richardson J., San Angelo; retired FBI.
62—Bush, Robert, Sherman; attorney.
107—Cain, David H., Dallas; attorney.
*61—Campbell, Ben, Flower Mound; real estate.
78—Carriker, S. A., Roby; farmer-rancher.
*91—Carter, Bill G., Fort Worth; insurance.
35—Cavazos, Eddie, Corpus Christi; real estate.
*112—Ceverha, Bill, Richardson; businessman.
20—Clark, Jerry, Buna; farmer-businessman.
17—Clemons, Billy, Pollok; railroad clerk.
132—Colbert, Paul, Houston; consultant.
23—Collazo, Frank Jr., Port Arthur; businessman.
*126—Connelly, E. Barry, Houston; businessman.
*47—Cooper, Anne, San Marcos; housewife.
*76—Craddick, Tom, Midland; businessman.
25—Criss, Lloyd W. Jr., LaMarque; businessman.
137—Danburg, Debra, Houston; attorney.
50—Delco, Mrs. Exalton, Austin; legislator.
56—Denton, Mrs. Lane, Waco; attorney.
142—Dutton, Harold V., Houston; businessman.
33—Earley, Robert, Portland; legislator.
*133—Eckels, Robert, Houston; public relations.
45.—Edge, Eldon, Poth; retired schoolman.
146—Edwards, Al, Houston; public relations.
*127—Emmett, Ed, Kingwood; businessman.
92—Evans, Charles, Hurst; attorney.
147—Evans, Larry, Houston; attorney.
80—Finnell, Charles, Holliday; attorney.
*125—Fox, Milton E., Houston; investor.
115—Garcia, Orlando, San Antonio; attorney.
42—Garcia, Tony, Pharr; attorney.
81—Gavin, John, Wichita Falls; insurance.
*67—Geisweidt, Gerald, Mason; rancher-attorney.
58—Gibson, Bruce, Cleburne; attorney-farmer.
3—Gilley, Smith, Greenville; attorney.
*83—Givens, Ron, Lubbock; real estate.
44—Glossbrenner, Ernestine, Alice; teacher.
*75—Godwin, Kelly, Odessa; consultant.
108—Granoff, Al, Dallas; attorney.
51—Guerrero, Lena, Austin; advertising.
139—Hackney, Clint, Houston; attorney.
10—Haley, Bill, Center; teacher.
43—Hall, W. N. Jr., Laredo; rancher-investments.
*109—Hammond, Bill, Dallas; businessman.
*93—Harris, Chris, Arlington; attorney.
*27—Harris, Jack, Pearland; dentist.
68—Harrison, Dudley, Sanderson; car dealer.
*149—Heflin, Talmadge, Houston; businessman.
18—Hightower, Allen R., Huntsville; car salesman.
*150—Hilbert, Paul J., Spring; attorney.
*101—Hill, Anita, Garland; legislator.
*102—Hill, Patricia, Dallas; attorney.
41—Hinojosa, Juan, McAllen; attorney.
5—Hollowell, Bill, Grand Saline; attorney.
*59—Horn, Jim N., Denton; businessman.
6—Hudson, David, Tyler; legislator.
100—Hudson, Samuel W. III, Dallas; attorney.
24—Hury, James, Galveston; attorney.

Dist., Name, Address, Term of Office, Occupation.
*113—Jackson, Lee F., Dallas; businessman.
11—Johnson, Cliff, Palestine; real estate.
*60—Johnson, Sam, Plano; home builder.
*71—Jones, Arves E., El Paso; investments.
*104—Keller, Ray, Duncanville; construction.
13—Kubiak, Dan, Rockdale; veterinarian
*46—Kuempel, Edmund, Seguin; businessman.
85—Laney, James E., Hale Center; farmer.
38—Lee, Don, Harlingen; insurance.
*97—Leonard, Bob Jr., Fort Worth; investments.
89—Lewis, Gibson D., Fort Worth; businessman.
19—Lewis, Ron E., Mauriceville; real estate.
143—Luna, Albert III, Houston; businessman.
116—Luna, Gregory, San Antonio; attorney.
73—McDonald, Nancy, El Paso; nurse.
*94—McKenna, Jan, Arlington; businesswoman.
15—McKinney, Mike, Centerville; doctor.
9—McWilliams, Jim, Hallsville; rancher-businessman.
117—Madla, Frank, San Antonio; insurance.
148—Martinez, Roman, Houston; investments.
57—Melton, Bob, Gatesville; businessman.
53—Messer, Bill, Belton; attorney.
96—Millsap, Mike, Fort Worth; insurance.
124—Morales, Dan, San Antonio; attorney.
40—Moreno, Alejandro Jr., Edinburg; attorney.
72—Moreno, Paul, El Paso; attorney.
39—Oliveira, Rene O., Brownsville; attorney.
111—Oliver, Jesse Dean, Dallas; attorney.
65—Parker, Jim, Comanche; rancher-attorney.
*123—Patrick, Kae T., San Antonio; businessman.
138—Patronella, David, Houston; attorney.
2—Patterson, L. P., Brookston; farmer-rancher.
*130—Pennington, Randy, Houston; businessman.
74—Perez, Nicholas J., El Paso; attorney.
64—Perry, Rick, Haskell; farmer-rancher.
*122—Pierce, George, San Antonio; public relations.
128—Polumbo, Tony, Houston; real estate.
22—Price, Albert J., Beaumont; pilot.
110—Ragsdale, Paul, Dallas; legislator.
37—Rangel, Irma, Kingsville; attorney.
*49—Richardson, Bob, Austin; attorney.
*52—Riley, Randall, Round Rock; self-employed.
*36—Roberts, Ted, Corpus Christi; attorney.
31—Robinson, Phyllis, Gonzales; housewife.
*82—Robnett, Nolan J., Lubbock; real estate-investments.
77—Rudd, Jim D., Brownfield; attorney.
8—Russell, Sam, Mt. Pleasant; attorney.
30—Saunders, Robert, La Grange; businessman.
54—Schlueter, Stan, Salado; real estate.
*121—Schoolcraft, Alan, Universal City; attorney.
69—Shaw, Larry D., Big Spring; farmer-real estate.
*98—Shea, Gwyn C., Irving; businesswoman.
1—Short, Alex Jr., Texarkana; real estate.
*136—Smith, Ashley, Houston; attorney.
106—Smith, Carlyle, Grand Prairie; architect.
*14—Smith, Richard, Bryan; real estate.
*48—Smith, Terral R., Austin; attorney.
*86—Smithee, John T., Amarillo; attorney.
*87—Staniswalis, Charles J., Amarillo; real estate.
21—Stiles, Mark, Beaumont; businessman.
120—Sutton, Mrs. Lou Nelle, San Antonio; businesswoman.
*26—Tallas, Jim, Sugarland; insurance.
*55—Taylor, M.A., Waco; businessman.
118—Tejeda, Frank M., San Antonio; attorney.
95—Thompson, Garfield, Fort Worth; retired.
79—Thompson, Gary, Abilene; educator.
141—Thompson, Mrs. Senfronia, Houston; attorney.
*135—Toomey, Mike, Houston; attorney.
29—Uher, Donald R., Bay City; attorney.
*16—Valiqura, Keith W., Conroe; attorney.
*70—Vowell, Jack, El Paso; investments.
12—Waldrop, Tom C., Corsicana; businessman-rancher.
145—Wallace, Ralph III, Houston; businessman.
129—Watson, Ed R., Deer Park; oil operator.
84—Whaley, Foster, Pampa; rancher.
63—Williamson, Richard, Weatherford; businessman.
90—Willis, Doyle, Fort Worth; attorney-rancher.
*28—Willy, John, Angleton; real estate.
131—Wilson, Ron, Houston; businessman.
103—Wolens, Steve, Dallas; attorney.
*134—Wright, Brad, Houston; attorney.
*7—Yost, Gerald V., Longview; advertising.

*Republicans; all others are Democrats.

Texas State Officials, Boards, Commissions

A list of Texas State officialdom is given on this and following pages, revised to Aug. 1, 1985. Information is given in following order: (1) Date of creation of office. (2) Whether elective or appointive. (3) Length of term. (4) Number of members, if a board or commission. (5) Name of official (or officials). Dates in parentheses indicate termination of appointment. Names of towns in parentheses indicate home of official whose residence is officially in Austin. In some instances the dates of expiration are prior to issuance of this volume; in such instances a holdover term is indicated, no new appointment having been made at time of publication of the Texas Almanac. Most positions marked "apptv." are appointive by the Governor. Where otherwise, appointing authority is designated. Most Advisory Boards are not listed. Salaries given were furnished by the Legislative Budget Board and are those effective Sept. 1, 1985, for the 1986 year. Add 1.0 percent for 1987 salary.

Accident Board, Industrial. — (See **Industrial Accident Board.**)

Accountancy, State Board of Public. — (1945 with 2-year terms; reorganized 1959 as nine-member board with 6-yr. overlapping terms; number of members increased to twelve in 1979); expenses paid from fees collected by board; twelve members: Walter D. Davis, Missouri City (1-31-89); James F. Dunn Jr., Houston (1-31-89); Mrs. Barbara Shimaitis, Katy (1-31-89); Oscar C. Mascorro, San Antonio (1-31-89); Frank T. Rea, Houston (1-31-87); S. J. Scott, Dallas (1-31-87); R. S. Driegert, Richardson (1-31-87); William H. Quimby, Dallas (1-31-87); Jarman Bass, Dallas (1-31-91); Dwight L. Kinard, Abilene (1-31-91); R. D. Pattillo, Waco (1-31-91); Mrs. Nancy Brannon, Lewisville (1-31-91). Executive Director, Bob E. Bradley, 1033 La Posada Dr., Suite 340, Austin 78752-3894 (nonmember) ($47,380).

Adjutant General. — (1836 by Republic of Texas; 1905 present office established); apptv.: Maj. Gen. James T. Dennis, Box 5218, Austin 78763 (2-1-87) ($55,826, plus house and utilities).

Adjutant General for Army, Assistant. — Brig. Gen. Willard D. Hill Jr., Austin (2-1-87) ($52,324, plus house and utilities).

Adjutant General for Air, Assistant. — Brig. Gen. Belisario D. J. Flores, Austin (2-1-87) ($52,324, plus house and utilities).

Administrative Judicial Districts of Texas, Presiding Judges of. — (Apptv. by Governor); serve terms concurrent with term as District Judge, subject to reappointment if re-elected to bench. No extra compensation: No. 1, John D. Ovard, Dallas; No. 2, Thomas J. Stovall Jr., Seabrook; No. 3, James F. Clawson Jr., Belton; No. 4, Joe E. Kelly, Victoria; No. 5, Joe B. Evins, Edinburg; No. 6, George M. Thurmond, Del Rio; No. 7, Ray L. McKim, Odessa; No. 8, Charles J. Murray, Fort Worth; No. 9, Eugene E. Jordan, Amarillo.

Adult Probation Commission, Texas. — (1977); apptv. as designated; expenses; 6-yr.; nine members: Three judges of district courts and two citizens not employed in criminal justice system to be apptd. by Chief Justice of Texas Supreme Court as follows: B. B. Schraub, 25th District Court, Seguin (6-10-89); Sam W. Callan, 205th District Court, El Paso (6-10-89); Donald Carroll, 7th District Court, Tyler (6-10-85); Max Sherman, Austin (6-10-85); Vice Chairman, Mrs. Diana S. Clark, Dallas (6-10-87). Three judges of district courts and one citizen not employed in the criminal justice system to be apptd. by presiding judge of Texas Court of Criminal Appeals as follows: Chairman, Clarence N. Stevenson, 24th District Court, Victoria (6-10-87); Joe N. Kegans, 230th District Court, Houston (6-10-89); John C. Vance, Associate Justice, 5th Court of Appeals, Dallas (6-10-85); Rev. D. N. Brosnan, San Antonio (6-10-89). Executive Director, Don R. Stiles (nonmember), Box 12427, Austin 78711 ($49,749).

Ad Valorem Tax Rate, Board to Calculate the. — (1907); ex officio; term in other office; three members: Gov. Mark White; State Comptroller Robert D. Bullock and State Treasurer Ann Richards.

Aeronautics Commission, Texas. — (1945); apptv.; 6-yr.; per diem and expenses; six members: George M. Underwood Jr., Dallas (12-31-86); Stephen E. Cone Jr., Lubbock (2-1-91); Walther Umphrey, Port Arthur (2-1-91); Warren C. Harmon, Bryan (12-31-88); Jack H. McCreary, Austin (12-31-86). Executive Director, C. A. Wilkins, Box 12607, Capitol Station, Austin 78711 (nonmember) ($49,208).

Aging, Texas Department on. — (1965 as **Governor's Committee on Aging;** name changed in 1981 to present form; due to go out of existence 9-1-97 unless continued operation needed); apptv.; expenses; nine apptv. members: Chairman, R. H. Gibbons, Fort Worth serves at pleasure of Governor; George W. Arrington, Canadian (8-30-85); Tony G. Wakin, Houston (8-30-85); Mrs. Evelyn Porter, San Antonio (8-30-85); James Roberts, Andrews (8-30-87); Mrs. Willie Lee Glass, Tyler (8-30-87); Mrs. Rose R. Duvall, Dripping Springs (8-30-87); Eustolio Gonzales, Raymondville (8-30-89); Bert Scheinbrum, Waco (8-30-89); Floyd C. Burnett, Ladonia (8-30-89). Executive Director, O. P. Bobbitt, Box 12786, Capitol Station, Austin 78711 (nonmember) ($42,200).

A&M University System, Board of Regents of Texas. — (1875); apptv.; 6-yr.; expenses; nine members: John Mobley, Austin (2-1-91); L. Lowry Mays, San Antonio (2-1-91); Royce Wisenbaker, Tyler (2-1-91); Dr. John B. Coleman, Houston (1-10-89); Chairman, David G. Eller, Houston (1-10-89); Joe Reynolds, Houston (1-10-89); Henry Cisneros, San Antonio (1-10-87); William A. McKenzie, Dallas (1-10-87); Joe C. Richardson Jr., Amarillo (1-10-87). Chancellor, Arthur Hansen; Secretary, Valerie P. Nelson, College Station 77843-1123 (nonmembers).

Air Control Board, Texas. — (1965 as six-member board; membership increased to nine in 1967); apptv.; 6-yr.; per diem and expenses; nine members: Dr. D. Jack Killian, Lake Jackson (9-1-85); Vittorio K. Argento, Duncanville (9-1-85); Chairman John L. Blair, Kountze (9-1-85); Charles R. Jaynes, Waco (9-1-83); Hubert Oxford III, Beaumont (9-1-89); Dr. Otto Kunze, College Station (9-1-89); Richard H. Moorman IV, Brenham (9-1-87); Bob G. Bailey, Abilene (9-1-87); Fred Hartman, Baytown (9-1-87). Executive Director, Bill Stewart, 6330 Highway 290 E., Austin 78723 (nonmember) ($55,517).

Aircraft Pooling Board, State. — (1979); apptv.; five members — two ex officio: representative of State Auditor's Office and representative of State Purchasing and General Services Commission; three apptv. — one by Governor, one by Speaker of House of Representatives and one by Lieutenant Governor. Governor's appointee: James L. Nelson, Austin (1-31-89). Executive Director Fred R. Spies, Box 12224, Austin 78711 (nonmember) ($50,985).

Alcoholic Beverage Commission, Texas. — (1935 as **Liquor Control Board;** name changed 1970); apptv.; 6-yr.; per diem and expenses; administrator appointed by commission; three members: Chairman, Louis M. Pearce Jr., Houston (11-15-85); Morris Atlas, McAllen (11-15-89); J. A. Whittenburg III, Amarillo (11-15-87). Administrator, Sherman McBeath, Box 13127, Capitol Station, Austin 78711 (nonmember) ($57,474).

Alcoholism, Texas on. — (1953); apptv.; 6-yr.; per diem and expenses; six members: Dr. David Wade, Austin (6-8-85); Jerry P. Cunningham, Dallas (6-8-85); Mrs. Margaret E. B. Sharpe, Dallas (6-8-87); Chairman, Jim Clipson Jr., Eagle Lake (6-8-87); Mrs. Tom Kritser, Amarillo (6-8-89); Robert W. Harrell, Austin (6-8-89). Executive Director, Ross Newby, 1705 Guadalupe, Austin 78701 (nonmember) ($44,702).

Amusement Machine Commission. — (1971 as **Vending Commission;** name changed in 1973); apptv.; per diem; 6-yr.; six members — three ex officio: Attorney General Jim Mattox; James B. Adams, Director Department of Public Safety; Sam Kelley, Consumer Credit Commissioner. Three apptv. members: Chairman, Hall E. Timanus Sr., Houston (1-31-85); Perry O. Chrisman, Dallas (1-31-89); Jose M. Blanco Jr., Victoria (1-31-87). Executive Director, Jim Lusk, 1606 Headway Circle, Ste. 201, Austin 78754 (nonmember) ($43,157).

Angelina and Neches River Authority. — (Est. 1935 as **Sabine-Neches Conservation District;** reorganized 1950 and name changed to **Neches River Conservation District;** changed to present name in 1977); apptv.; expenses; 6-yr.; nine members: Richard Baldwin, Camden (9-5-85); Steve Lilly, Nacogdoches (9-5-85); Salah Craig, Henderson (9-5-89); Chester H. Moore, Lufkin (9-5-83); Mrs. Joyce Swearingen, Nacogdoches (9-5-87); S. D. Griffin, Lufkin (9-5-87); Warner A. Dunn, Nacogdoches (9-5-83); Don T. Forse, Houston (9-5-85); Horace F. McQueen, Whitehouse (9-5-87). Executive Director, William A. Elmore, Box 387, Lufkin 75901 (nonmember).

Animal Health Commission, Texas. — (1893 as **Texas Livestock Sanitary Commission;** reorganized 1955; name changed in 1959; membership increased to nine in 1973; raised to twelve in 1983); apptv.; per diem and expenses; 6-yr.; twelve members: James D. Sartwell, Houston (9-6-85); James B. Owen, Tyler (9-6-85); Bobby Baros, Gonzales (9-6-85); Chairman, Robert F. Bartlett, Canton (9-6-85); Charles Koontz, Olton (9-6-87); C. E. Knolle, Sandia (9-6-87); Dr. Marten Botard, Kingsville (9-6-87); Laurence H. Bostick, Brookshire (9-6-87); James Eller, Bryan (9-6-89); Mrs. Florence Rieck, Roosevelt (9-6-89); James L. Snyder, Baird (9-6-89); Mrs. Mary Nan West, Batesville (9-6-89). Executive Director, Dr. John W. Holcombe, 210 Barton Springs Rd., Austin 78704 (nonmember) ($53,251).

Antiquities Committee, State. — (1969 as seven-member board; membership increased to nine in 1983 with addition of one ex officio and one apptv. member); apptv.; per diem and expenses; 2-yr.; nine members—six ex officio, term in other office: Chairman Texas Historical Commission; Director State Parks and Wildlife Department; Commissioner of General Land Office; State Archeologist; State Engineer Director State Department of Highways and Public Transportation; and Executive Director Texas Department Wa...

ter Resources. Three apptv. members: Dr. William C. Griggs, Houston (1-31-87); Dr. William G. Reeder, Austin (1-31-85); Anne A. Fox, San Antonio (1-31-87).

Architectural Examiners, Texas Board of. — (1937 as three member board; raised to six members in 1951; membership increased to nine in 1977); apptv.; 6-yr.; per diem and expenses; nine members: Raymond A. Gill, Round Rock (6-21-85); Chairman, Paul A. Hesson, San Antonio (6-21-85); Trammell S. Crow, Dallas (6-21-85); Ned R. Rosario, Fort Worth (1-31-87); O. E. Schrickel, Arlington (1-31-87); Ralph B. Perkins, Wichita Falls (1-31-87); James E. Buie, Longview (1-31-89); Benjamin J. Lednicky, Houston (1-31-89); Mrs. Nolanda S. Hill, Dallas (1-31-89). Executive Director, Philip D. Creer, 8213 Shoal Creek Blvd., Suite 107, Austin 78751 (nonmember) ($45,320).

Arts, Texas Commission on the. — (1965 as Texas Fine Arts Commission; name changed to Texas Commission on the Arts and Humanities and membership increased to 18 in 1971; name changed to present form in 1979); apptv.; 6-yr.; expenses; eighteen members: Walter Mathis, San Antonio (8-31-85); Manuel A. Sanchez III, Houston (8-31-85); Edith O'Donnell, Dallas (8-31-85); Mrs. Mary Moody Northen, Galveston (8-31-85); Dr. Francis A. Morris Jr., Austin (8-31-85); Jocelyn L. Straus, San Antonio (8-31-85); Margaret C. B. Brown, Waco (8-31-87); Chairman, Hugo V. Neuhaus Jr., Houston (8-31-87); Camilla D. Trammell, Houston (8-31-87); Mrs. Carla Jo C. Francis, Dallas (8-31-87); Beatrice C. Pickens, Amarillo (8-31-87); Edward L. Protz, Galveston (8-31-87); Mrs. Nancy H. Nelson, Dallas (8-31-89); Mrs. Louann Temple, Austin (8-31-89); Mrs. Terrylin G. Neale, Houston (8-31-89); Adan Medrano, San Antonio (8-31-89); E. J. Grivetti, Houston (8-31-89); Mrs. Nancy Ann Davis, Fort Worth (8-31-89). Executive Director, Richard E. Huff, 5th Floor, 920 Colorado, Austin 78711 (nonmember) ($44,496).

Arts and Industries, Texas College of. — (See University System of South Texas.)

Athletic Trainers, Advisory Board of. — (1971 as Texas Board of Athletic Trainers; name changed and membership increased to six in 1975); expenses; 6-yr.: Spanky Stephens, Austin (1-31-85); W. F. Pickard Jr., Bryan (1-31-91); Cash Birdwell, Dallas (1-31-87); Al Wilson, Killeen (1-31-87); Samuel M. Russell, Lewisville (1-31-89); Louis K. Grevelle, Lubbock (1-31-83).

Attorney General, State. — (1836 by original Constitution of Republic of Texas, 1876 by present Constitution); elective; (2-yr. by original Constitution; term raised to 4-yr. in 1972, effective 1975): Jim Mattox, Box 12548, Capitol Sta., Austin 78711 (1-1-87) ($73,233).

Attorney, State's. — Apptv.: Robert Huttash, Box 12405, Austin 78711 ($56,135).

Auditor, State. — (1929); apptv. by Legislative Audit Committee, a joint Senate-House committee; 2-yr.: Lawrence F. Alwin, (Houston), Box 12067, Capitol Sta., Austin 8711 ($66,950).

Automated Information Systems Advisory Council. — 1981); apptv.; 2-yr.; expenses; seven members: Three pptd. by governor; two apptd. by Lieutenant Governor nd two apptd. by Speaker of House. Governor's appointees: Dr. Charles H. Warlick, Austin (1-31-86); Chairman, James A. Patterson, San Antonio (2-1-85); Mrs. Nancy Nor-s, Austin (2-1-85). Executive Director, Charles K. Winston r., P. O. Box 13564, Capitol Sta., Austin 78711 (nonmember) $49,337).

Bandera County River Authority. — (1971); apptv.; 6-yr.; ine members; expenses: M. R. Sandidge (1-31-85); Mrs. armen Hicks (1-31-85); J. B. Edwards, Pipecreek (1-31-85); aymond Hicks (1-31-87); T. S. Tobin (1-31-87); Paul Garri-n Jr. (1-31-87); Eldon Boltinghouse (1-31-83); Henry Fisher 1-31-83); R. E. Adams (1-31-83).

Banking Board, State. — (1909); two ex officio members, erm in other office; one apptd. by Governor for 2 years; ree members: Ex officio members — Commissioner of anking and State Treasurer. Apptv. member: R. E. Ream-r, Houston (1-31-85).

Banking Commissioner, State. — (1923); apptv. by State inance Commission; 2-yr.: James L. Sexton, 2601 N. La-ar, Austin 78705 ($79,310). (See also Finance Commission of exas.)

Bar of Texas, State. — (1939 as administrative arm of upreme Court); 30 members elected by membership; 3-yr. rms; expenses paid from dues collected from member-ip. President, president-elect, vice president and imme-ate past president serve as ex officio members. Executive rector, Edward O. Coultas, P.O. Box 12487, Austin 78711 onmember).

Barber Examiners, State Board of. — (1929 as three-mem-er board; membership increased in 1975); apptv.; 6-yr.; $30 er diem and expenses while on duty; six members: Bill asson, Corpus Christi (5-19-85); Mrs. Doris Frazier, Dallas -19-85); Ken Gjemre, Dallas (1-31-87); Mrs. Vera LeBlanc, ederland (1-31-87); President, Mrs. Helen Spears, Dallas -31-89); Edward N. Borkland, Austin (1-31-89). Executive rector, Jo King McCrorey, 1300 E. Anderson Lane, Bldg. , Suite 275, Austin 78752 (nonmember) ($31,518).

Battleship Texas Advisory Board. — (1983; supersedes

Battleship Texas Commission); apptv.; 6-yr.; nine members: Chairman, Denny G. Hair, Houston (2-1-89); Mrs. Rosalie L. Kuntz, Pasadena (2-1-89); Frank E. Tritico, Houston (2-1-89); Steven Lunsford, Galveston (2-1-87); Joe S. Cathey, Deer Park (2-1-87); Philip L. Chumlea, Houston (2-1-87); Mrs. Caroline K. Gregory, Houston (2-1-89); Robert M. Ewing, Dallas (2-1-85); one vacancy.

Blind, Governing Board of the Texas School for the. — (1979); apptv.; 6-yr.; nine members; expenses: Dr. Virginia Sowell, Lubbock (1-31-85); Chairman, William P. Gibson, Houston (1-31-85); Thomas Cue Baird, Temple (1-31-85); Mrs. Wandene Coughran, Abilene (1-31-87); Dr. M. Ray Harrington, Dallas (1-31-87); Mrs. Olivia C. Blundell, El Paso (1-31-87); Robert D. Tindle, Austin (1-31-87); Crispin E. Sanchez, Laredo (1-31-89); Dr. Sue Tullos, Austin (1-31-89). Executive Director, William H. Miller, 1100 W. 45th, Austin 78756 (nonmember).

Blind and Severely Disabled Persons, Texas Committee on Purchases of Products and Services of. — (1979); apptv.; 2-yr.; ten members: Robert E. Flaherty, Austin (1-31-85); Ray Vaughn, Austin (1-31-85); Mrs. Jane D. Pieper, San Antonio (1-31-85); Chairman, Gibson Duterroil, Houston (1-31-85); Marion Truitt, Abilene (1-31-85); Billy J. Killion, Austin (1-31-85); Robert Vassallo, Austin (1-31-85); Dr. Thomas R. Irons, Lubbock (1-31-85); Robert Crieder, Kingswood (1-31-85); Gordon Richardson, Caldwell (1-31-85).

Blind, Texas Commission for the. — (1931 as six-member State Commission for the Blind; raised to nine members in 1979; name changed in 1985); apptv.; 6-yr.; expenses; nine members: Chairman, William C. Conner, Fort Worth (1-1-87); John M. Turner, Dallas (1-1-87); Mrs. Susan Fischer, Dallas (1-1-87); Walter Musler, San Antonio (1-1-91); Lewis Timberlake, Austin (1-1-91); Dr. Robert Peters, Tyler (1-1-91); John W. Longley, Stamford (1-1-89); Don L. Steelman, Marshall (1-1-89); Mrs. Ann Masterson, Houston (1-1-89). Executive Director, John C. Wilson, Box 12866, Austin 78711 (nonmember) ($55,105).

Board of. — (Note: In most instances, state boards are alphabetized under specific reference word, as Accountancy, State Board of Public.)

Board of Control, State. — (This board, established originally in 1919, consisted of three members, appointed by the Governor, serving 6-yr. terms but functioning only as policy makers at nominal salaries. Administration of affairs of the board was in the hands of an executive director, appointed by the board. In 1979, name changed to State Purchasing and General Services Commission.)

Brazos River Authority, Directors of. — (Organized in 1929 by legislature act as Brazos River Conservation and Reclamation District; name changed to Brazos River Authority by Legislature in 1953); apptv.; 6-yr.; expenses; twenty-one members: Chester R. Upham III, Mineral Wells (2-1-87); William A. Prewitt III, Temple (2-1-87); J. C. Chambers, Lubbock (2-1-87); A. L. Brooks Jr., Bellville (2-1-87); James C. Atkins Jr., Lake Jackson (2-1-87); Roland Adamson, Richmond (2-1-87); Nelson Durst, Bryan (2-1-87); John M. Wehby, Taylor (2-1-91); Charles Moser, Brenham (2-1-91); Don T. Kearby, Mineral Wells (2-1-91); J. J. Gibson, Guthrie (2-1-91); James H. Mills, Round Rock (2-1-91); Lyndon Olson Sr., Waco (2-1-91); Sidney E. Niblo, Abilene (2-1-91); Paul H. Harvey Jr., Hillsboro (2-1-89); Henry J. Boehm Sr., Brenham (2-1-89); Walter C. Wiese Jr., Calvert (2-1-89); Douglas A. Strain, W. Columbia (2-1-89); President, Glynn A. Williams, Bryan (2-1-89); R. E. Chambers, Wichita Falls (2-1-89); Vice President, Bruce Campbell Jr., Knox City (2-1-89). General Manager, Carson H. Hoge, Box 7555, Waco 76710 (nonmember); Asst. Gen. Manager-Treasurer, Jack Wooley.

Budget Board, Legislative. — (1949); ten members; Ex officio members — Lt. Gov. William P. Hobby; Speaker of House of Representatives; Chairman of Senate Finance and Public Affairs Committees; Chairmen of Appropriations and Revenue, and Ways and Means Committees; and four other members of Legislature. Director, James P. Oliver, Box 12666, Capitol Station, Austin 78711-2666 (nonmember).

Caddo Lake Compact Commission. — (1979); apptv.; 2-yr.; expenses; two ex officio members—Red River Compact Commissioner and Exec. Dir. of Texas Department of Water Resources. (Apptv. member's function is to negotiate with other states respecting waters of Caddo Lake. See also Interstate Compact Commission and Canadian River Compact Commissioner.): Nathan Irving Reiter Jr., Texarkana.

Canadian River Compact Commissioner. — (1951); apptv.; salary and expenses; (his function is to negotiate with other states respecting waters of the Canadian. See also Interstate Compact Commission and Caddo Lake Compact Commission): John C. Sims, Lubbock (12-31-85).

Cancer Council, Texas. — (1985); 16 members as follows: two ex officio: chairman of Texas Board of Human Services, chairman of Texas Board of Health; seven each apptd. by Speaker of House of Representatives and Lieutenant Governor; 6-yr., except legislators and representatives of state agencies; expenses. (No appointments made when this section printed.)

Canvassers, State Board of. — (1897); two ex officio members, term in other office; one apptd. by Governor for 2-yr. term: Gov. Mark White and Secretary of State Myra McDaniel, ex officio members. Apptv. member: E. C. Green, Denison (8-23-85).

Central Colorado River Authority. — (See Colorado River.)

Chemist, State. — (1911); ex officio, indefinite term: Dr. L. R. Richardson, Texas Agricultural Experiment Station, College Station.

Childhood Intervention Services, Interagency Council on Early. — (1981); apptv.; 2-yr.; five members — one apptd. by Governor, one each by Department of Health, Department of Mental Health and Mental Retardation, Department of Human Services and Central Education Agency. Gov.'s apptee: Patricia S. Bizzell, Austin (2-1-85). Acting Administrator, Louise Iscoe, Department of Health, 1100 W. 49th, Austin 78756 (nonmember).

Child Abuse and Neglect Prevention, Council on. — (1985); apptv.; 2-yr.; expenses; nine members. (No appointments made at time this section printed.)

Children and Youth, Texas Commission on Services to. — No longer in existence.

Chiropractic Examiners, State Board of. — (1949); apptv.; 6-yr.; expenses; nine members: Dr. T. A. Baker, Lake Jackson (8-3-87); Dr. R. E. Hartong, San Antonio (8-3-87); Dr. Jack Christie, Houston (8-3-87); Dr. Bill G. Williams, Waco (8-3-85); Dr. Jerry E. Whitehead, Perryton (8-3-85); Dr. R. L. Matkin, Mt. Pleasant (8-3-85); Dr. Sterling H. Pruitt Sr., Fort Worth (8-3-89); Dr. Edmund E. Lacy, Dallas (8-3-89); Dr. Jay H. Perreten, Houston (8-3-89). Executive Secretary, Edna A. Parsons, 1300 E. Anderson Lane, Bldg. C., Suite 245, Austin 78752 (nonmember) ($25,338).

Civil Air Patrol, Commission for the Texas. — Not renewed by Sunset Commission. Civil Air Patrol now agency under Texas Dept. of Public Safety.

Civil Judicial Council, Texas. — (See Judicial Council, Texas.)

Coastal Water Authority, Board of Directors of. — (1967 as Coastal Industrial Water Authority, Board of Directors of; name changed in 1985); seven members — four to be appointed by mayor of Houston with advice and consent of governing body of Houston; three apptd. by Governor; per diem and expenses; 2-yr. Governor's appointees: Wallace Claypool, Houston (3-31-87); Johnnie G. Jennings, Baytown (3-31-83); Buster E. French, Dayton (3-31-84). Acting Executive Director, Sam B. Dixon, Citicorp Center, 1200 Smith, Suite 2260, Houston 77002 (nonmember).

College and University System, Coordinating Board, Texas. — (1953 as temporary board; 1955 as permanent 15-member Texas Commission on Higher Education; changed to 18-member board in 1965); apptv; 6-yr; expenses; eighteen members: Preston Smith, Lubbock (9-1-85); Dr. Mario E. Ramirez, Rio Grande City (9-1-85); H. M. Daugherty Jr., El Paso (9-1-85); R. F. Juedeman, Odessa (9-1-85); Herbert Schiff, Dallas (9-1-85); George Bramblett, Dallas (9-1-85); C. F. Guerra Jr., San Antonio (9-1-87); Harlan R. Crow, Dallas (9-1-87); Mrs. Chandler Lindsley, Dallas (9-1-87); Dr. William R. Patterson, Texarkana (9-1-87); Gary L. Watkins, Odessa (9-1-87); William J. Caraway, Houston (9-1-87); Vice Chairman, Harvey Weil, Corpus Christi (9-1-89); John S. Carroll III, El Campo (9-1-89); Mrs. Eleanor N. Conrad, Dallas (9-1-89); Ray Clymer, Wichita Falls (9-1-89); Mrs. Lee H. Jamail, Houston (9-1-89); Chairman, Larry E. Temple, Austin (9-1-89). Commissioner of Higher Education, Dr. Kenneth H. Ashworth, Box 12788, Austin 78711 (nonmember) ($65,920).

Colorado River Authority, Central, Board of Directors. — (1935); apptv.; 6-yr.; per diem on duty; nine members: Louis Pittard, Gouldbusk (1-1-85); Bill Sneed, Coleman (1-1-85); Jim Bob Thweatt, Coleman (1-1-91); Ross L. Jones, Coleman (1-1-89); Roy D. Young, Burkett (1-1-89); Baker Rudolph, Coleman (1-1-89); Nick Knox, Coleman (1-1-87); Isaac S. Pate, Voss (1-1-87); Robert J. Cheaney, Santa Anna (1-1-87). Secretary, Jerri Ann Chambers, Box 964, Coleman 76834 (nonmember).

Colorado River Authority, Lower, Directors of. — (1934 as 9-member board; membership increased in 1951 and 1975); apptv.; 6-yr.; $50 per diem on duty; fifteen members: John K. Dixon, Sunrise Beach (1-1-87); John W. Hancock, El Campo (1-1-87); John W. Jones, Brady (1-1-87); Merritt Schumann, New Braunfels (1-1-87); Milton J. Anderson, Eagle Lake (1-1-87); Marvin Selig, Seguin (1-1-87); Martin E. McLean, Marble Falls (1-1-87); James A. Martin, Austin (1-1-89); Mrs. John Wilson, La Grange (1-1-89); Charles Matus, Johnson City (1-1-89); John M. Scanlan, Austin (1-1-89); Jack Littlejohn, Carmine (1-1-91); Jack B. Miller, San Saba (1-1-91); Cecil Long, Bastrop (1-1-91); Burton B. Letulle, Bay City (1-1-91). General Manager, Elof H. Soderberg, Box 220, Austin 78767 (nonmember).

Colorado River Authority, Upper. — (1935 as nine-member board; reorganized in 1965); apptv.; 6-yr.; $50 a day and expenses on duty; indefinite number of members: Harvey D. Glass Jr., Sterling City (1-1-87); Bruce H. Fisher, San Angelo (1-1-87); Brian Richards, Bronte (1-1-87); William H. Allen, Robert Lee (1-1-85); Homer J. Hodge, Winters (1-1-85); Victor W. Choate, San Angelo (1-1-85); J. R. Salmon, San Angelo (1-1-89); Cumbie Ivey, Robert Lee

(1-1-89); Everett J. Grindstaff, Box 576, Ballinger 76821 (1-1-89).

Commissioner of Agriculture. — (1907); elective; (2-yr. by original constitutional provision, term raised to 4-yr. in 1972, effective in 1975): Jim Hightower, Box 12847, Capitol Sta., Austin 78711-2847 (1-1-87) ($73,233).

Commissioner of Education. — (1866 as Superintendent of Public Instruction; 1949 changed to Commissioner of Education by Gilmer-Aikin Law); apptv. by State Board of Education; 4-yr.: W. N. Kirby, 201 E. 11th, Austin 78701 ($67,362 plus supplement from private sources). See also Education, State Board of.

Commissioner of General Land Office. — (1836 by Constitution of Republic of Texas; 1876 by present Constitution); elective; (2-yr. by original Constitutional provision; term raised to 4-yr. in 1972, effective 1975): Garry Mauro, S. F. Austin Bldg., Room 835, Austin 78701 (1-1-87) ($72,233).

Commissioner of Health. — (1879 as State Health Officer; 1955 changed to Commissioner of Health; 1975 changed to Director, Texas Department of Health Resources; 1977 changed to Commissioner, Texas Department of Health); apptv.; 2-yr: Dr. Robert Bernstein, Austin (1-1-87); ($66,641).

Community Affairs, Advisory Council on. — (1971); apptv.; 2-yr.; expenses; twelve members: Raymond Ovalle, Corpus Christi (1-31-85); Sam D. Seale, Edna (1-31-87); Phyllis Kittinger, Sweeny (1-31-85); Ivory E. Moore, Commerce (1-31-85); Cathleen A. Oxford, Texarkana (1-31-85); Gary O. Boren, Lubbock (1-31-85); Maria A. Berriozabal, San Antonio (1-31-86); Linda Bridges, Corpus Christi (1-31-86); Richard Borchard, Robstown (1-31-86); Telly H. Miller, Marshall (1-31-86); David Ojeda Jr., Carrizo Springs (1-31-86); Vick Gomez, Odessa (1-31-86). Executive Director, Rafael Quintanilla, Box 13166, Capitol Station, Austin 78711 (Chairman ex officio) ($52,221).

Comptroller of Public Accounts. — (1835 by Provisional Government of Texas; 1876 by present Constitution); elective; (2-yr. by original Constitution; term raised to 4-yr. in 1972, effective 1975): Robert D. Bullock, LBJ State Office Bldg., Austin 78774 (1-1-87) ($73,233).

Concho River Water and Soil Conservation Authority, Lower, Directors of. — (1939); 6-yr.; nine members: Howard Loveless, Eden (1-1-87); Leroy Beach, Millersview (1-1-87); Bill J. Mikeska, Eola (1-1-87); Scott L. Hartgrove, Paint Rock (1-1-85); Benjamin O. Sims, Paint Rock (1-1-85); E. H. Brosig Jr., Paint Rock (1-1-85); Harvey P. Williams, Eola (1-1-89); Edwin T. Tickle, Paint Rock (1-1-89); N. A. Taylor, Eden (1-1-89).

Conservation Foundation, Texas. — (1969 as 12-member board; membership reduced to six in 1979); apptv.; expenses; 6-yr.; six members—three ex officio, term in other office; one apptd. by Governor and one each apptd. by Speaker of House of Representatives and Lieutenant Governor. Governor's appointee: Chairman, George Bristol, Austin (6-13-87), Ex officio members: Executive Director, Parks and Wildlife Department; Commissioner of General Land Office and Executive Director of Texas Historical Commission. Executive Director, John Hamilton, 611 S. F. Austin Bldg., Austin 78701 (nonmember) ($35,947).

Conservatorship Board, State. — (1979); apptv.; expenses; 6-yr.; three members: Chairman, Jack N. Roper, Dallas (1-31-85); William M. Noble, Victoria (1-31-83); Frank Junell, San Angelo (1-31-87).

Corrections, Texas Board of. — (1885 as Texas Prison Board; superseded Superintendent of Penitentiaries est. in 1849; name changed to present form 1957); apptv.; per diem and expenses; 6-yr.; nine members: Chmn., Robert H. Gunn, Wichita Falls (2-15-87); Lindsley Waters Jr., Dallas (2-15-87); James Parsons, Palestine (2-15-87); Alfred Hughes, Austin (2-15-91); Dennis R. Hendrix, Dallas (2-15-91); Robert Lane, Austin (2-15-91); Thomas R. McDade, Houston (2-15-89); Deralyn R. Davis, Fort Worth (2-15-89), Vice Chmn., Joe LaMantia, Weslaco (2-15-89). Director, O. Lane Cotter, Box 99, Huntsville 77340 (nonmember) ($68,265 and emoluments).

Corrections, Texas Department of. — Apptv.; indefinite term: Director, O. Lane Cotter, Huntsville 77340.

Cosmetology Commission, Texas. — (1935 as three-member State Board of Hairdressers and Cosmetologists; name changed and membership increased to six apptv. and one ex officio in 1971); apptv.; per diem and expenses; 6-yr.: Larry L. Steinman, Austin (12-31-85); Vice Chmn., Evelyn Hunter, Dallas (12-31-85); Betty Sue Bird, Austin (12-31-87); Sec.-Treasurer, Hope T. Scott, San Antonio (12-31-87); Chairman, Dr. James R. Tarter, Odessa (12-31-89); Rona B. Jemison, Houston (12-31-89). Ex officio member: Dr. Pat W. Lindsey, Austin. Executive Director, Herbert E. Cohen, 1111 Rio Grande, Austin 78701 (nonmember) ($34,814).

Counselors, Texas State Board of Examiners of Professional. — (1981); apptv.; 6-yr.; expenses; nine members: Chairman, Louis S. Parker Jr., Austin (2-1-87); Vice Chairman, Dr. Jeanie Stanley, Kilgore (2-1-89); Yvonne L. Kohutek, San Antonio (2-1-87); Stephen A. Haberman, Cleveland (2-1-85); Bettye Whitney, Dallas (2-1-87); Julian Biggers Jr., Lubbock (2-1-85); Edward C. Bonk, Denton (2-1-85); Raul Castillo, Houston (2-1-83); Ann Karen Barlow, Fort Worth (2-1-89). Executive Secretary, Daniel L. Boone, 1100 W. 49, Austin 78756-3183 (nonmember).

Court Reporters Certification Board. — (1977 as nine-member Texas Reporters Committee; name changed to present form and membership increased to twelve with addition of three citizen members in 1983); apptv. by State Supreme Court; 6-yr.; expenses; twelve members: Ronald C. Bird, San Antonio (12-31-86); Linda Hyde, Austin (12-31-86); Jack B. Moorhead, Houston (12-31-86); Chairman, Joseph H. Hart, Austin (12-31-88); Louise Morse, Austin (12-31-88); Jerry Spence, Big Spring (12-31-88); Charles Griggs, Sweetwater (12-31-90); Judy Kulhanek, Houston (12-31-90); David B. Jackson, Dallas (12-31-90). Citizen members: John M. Keel, Austin (12-31-88); Tom Prentice, Austin (12-31-86); Jean Nipper, Austin (12-31-90). Executive Director, C. Raymond Judice, Box 12066, Capitol Station, Austin 78711 (nonmember).

Credit Commissioner, Consumer. — (1969); apptv. by State Finance Commission; 2-yr.: Sam Kelley, Box 2107, Austin 78768 ($66,360).

Credit Union Commission of Texas. — (1949 as 3-member Credit Union Advisory Commission; name changed and number members increased to six in 1969; number members increased to nine in 1981 with addition of three public members); apptv.; 6-yr.; expenses; nine members: Walter V. Duncan, Richardson (2-15-87); Jimmy Sasser, Edinburg (2-15-87); Calvin Phillips, Dallas (2-15-85); Clarence T. Howell, Amarillo (2-15-85); B. L. Cockrell, San Antonio (2-15-89); Ada Williams, Dallas (2-15-89). Public members: Miguel San Juan, Sugar Land (2-15-87); Dennis Morgan, El Campo (2-15-85). Acting Commissioner, John Hale, 914 E. Anderson Lane, Austin 78752-1699 (nonmember) ($77,250).

Crime Stoppers Advisory Council. — (1981); apptv.; 2-yr.; five members: Mrs. Peggy J. Pickle, Austin (9-1-85); Frank L. Breedlove, Dallas (9-1-85); Richard W. Carter, Arlington (9-1-85); Cary O. Fox, Conroe (9-1-85); Rogelio Martinez, McAllen (9-1-85).

Criminal Justice Coordinating Council. — (1983); eleven ex officio members: Director Department Corrections; Executive Director Adult Probation Commission; Executive Director Board of Pardons and Paroles; Executive Director Prosecutors Coordinating Council; Executive Director Judicial Council; Executive Director Commission on Jail Standards; Director Department Public Safety; Executive Director Criminal Justice Division of Governor's office; Executive Director Texas Youth Commission; Executive Director Juvenile Probation Commission; Executive Director Texas Commission on Law Enforcement; Executive Director State Bar of Texas. Three apptv. members — one each by Governor, Speaker and Lieutenant Governor: Gov.'s apptee: Anita Ashton, Austin.

Criminal Justice Division Advisory Board. — (1981); twenty-one members — seven apptd. by Governor; seven apptd. by Lieut. Governor, and seven apptd. by Speaker of House; 2-yr.; expenses. Gov.'s apptees.: Chairman, Omar Harvey, Dallas (9-1-83); Vice Chmn., Joe Greenhill, Austin (9-1-83); James B. Adams, Austin (9-1-83); John B. Holmes Jr., Houston (9-1-83); Barbara G. Culver, Midland (9-1-83); Henry Wade, Dallas (9-1-83); Leonard Hancock, Temple (9-1-83); Director, Gilbert J. Pena, Box 12428, Austin 78711 (nonmember).

Criminal Justice Policy Council. — (1983); three ex officio members; eight apptv. — two each by Lieutenant Governor and Speaker of House; four apptd. by Governor. Ex officio members: Governor, Lieutenant Governor and Speaker of House. Gov.'s apptees: Victor Strecher, Huntsville; Cappy Eads, Belton; Mario Santos, Laredo; Mrs. Myra McDaniel, Austin. (All have indefinite terms.) Executive Director, Donald D. Champion, Rm. 410, Sam Houston Bldg., 201 E. 14th, Austin 78701 (nonmember) ($53,045).

Deaf, Texas Commission for the. — (1971 as six-member board; membership raised to nine in 1979); apptv.; 6-yr.; nine members—three deaf persons, two parents of deaf, two professionals serving deaf and two from general public; expenses: Deaf members: Betsy Stanley, Fort Worth (1-31-87); William A. Floerke, Taft (1-31-87); Rudolph D. Lamblin, Amarillo (1-31-85). Parents of deaf: George R. Dean, Houston (1-31-87); Mrs. John White Sr., San Antonio (1-31-85). Professionals serving deaf: Mrs. Beatrice Groninski, Houston (1-31-87); Jerry G. Hassell, Austin (1-31-89). General public members: Jerry A. McCutchin, Coppell (1-31-89); Chairman, Stanley E. Neely, Dallas (1-31-85). Executive Director, Fred Tammen, Box 12904, Capitol Station, Austin 78711 (nonmember) ($36,462).

Deaf, Governing Board of Texas School for the. — (1979); 6-yr.; expenses; nine members—three each from workers with deaf, parent of a deaf person and deaf persons: Deaf members: Glynn Whittemore, Houston (1-31-87); Larry Evans, Big Spring (1-31-85); Robert E. Bevill, Pasadena (1-31-89). Workers with deaf: Marjorie Moore, Brackettville (1-31-87); Ernest R. Fuentes, Austin (1-31-89); Polly P. Walton, Beaumont (1-31-85). Parent of deaf person: Jack W. Prescott, Temple (1-31-87); Avril Thompson, Houston (1-31-89); Gayle Lindsey, Austin (1-31-85). Executive Director, Victor Galloway, P.O. Box 3538, Austin 78764 (nonmember) ($46,000).

Dental Examiners, State Board of. — (1919 as six-member board; increased to nine members in 1971; increased to twelve members in 1981 with addition of three public members); apptv.; 6-yr.; per diem while on duty; twelve members: Dr. Jack T. Clark, Fort Worth (5-10-87); Dr. Brian Babin, Woodville (5-10-87); Dr. Will F. Graham, Borger (5-10-87); Dr. William J. Kemp, Haskell (5-10-91); Dr. Sam H. Rabon, Kingsville (5-10-91); Dr. Terry D. Dickinson, Houston (5-10-91); Dr. L. Jack Bolton, Dallas (5-10-89); Dr. Frank Santos Jr., San Antonio (5-10-89); Dr. R. D. Minatra, Houston (5-10-89). Public members: Joseph E. Gardner Jr., Corpus Christi (5-10-85); Mrs. Evelynne Vick, Waco (5-10-89); Lydia E. Torres, Midland (5-10-87). Executive Director, William S. Nail, 411 W. 13th, Suite 503, Austin 78701 (nonmember) ($48,204).

Depository Board, State. — (1905); three ex officio; term in other office; one apptd. by Governor for 2-yr. term; four members: Ex officio members — Treasurer Ann Richards, Banking Commissioner James L. Sexton, Comptroller Bob Bullock. Apptv. member: W. R. Vance, Austin (Bryan) (8-22-85).

Developmental Disabilities Planning Council. — (1971); twenty-six members; apptv.; 6-yr.; nineteen apptv. members, seven ex officio. Ex officio members: Representatives from Department of Mental Health and Mental Retardation; Rehabilitation Commission; Department of Health; Department of Human Services; Texas Education Agency; Texas Commission for the Blind; Texas Commission for the Deaf. Apptv. members: Mrs. Opal H. Washington, Austin (2-1-89); Ward R. Burke, Lufkin (2-1-89); Mrs. Patricia McCallum, Seagoville (2-1-89); Diana Fricke, Fort Worth (2-1-89); Dr. James W. Cooper, Corpus Christi (2-1-87); Mary C. Knott, El Paso (2-1-86); Jann E. Steed, Schertz (2-1-91); James McBryde, Abilene (2-1-89); Mary Jane Clark, Pharr (2-1-91); Ronnie N. Alexander, San Antonio (2-1-85); Angela K. Lamb, Amarillo (2-1-91); Jerry G. Hassell, Austin (2-1-91); Mrs. Debbie Francis, Dallas (2-1-87); Laura R. Guerra, Mercedes (2-1-91); Gary Shreve, Monahans (2-1-87); Gloria Drass, Fort Worth (2-1-91); Mrs. Lee Veenker, Irving (2-1-87); Cathryn D. Bebee, Austin (2-1-91); Dr. Tom Deliganis, San Antonio (2-1-89). Executive Director, Joellen Simmons, 118 E. Riverside Dr., Austin 78704 (nonmember).

Diabetes Council, Texas. — (1983); 2-yr.; eleven members — six from public and five ex officio. Ex officio members: One each from Texas Department of Health, Texas Education Agency, Texas Department of Human Services, Texas Commission for the Blind and Texas Rehabilitation Commission. Public members: David C. Warner, Austin (2-1-85); Wendell Mayes Jr., Austin (2-1-85); Dr. Luther B. Travis, Galveston (2-1-85); Carolyn Grubb, Austin (2-1-86); Mrs. Jacqueline Colvill, Houston (2-1-86); Dr. Maria Luisa Urdanetta, San Antonio (2-1-84).

Dieticians, Texas State Board of Examiners of. — (1983); apptv.; nine members — three from general public and six licensed dieticians; 6-yr.; per diem and expenses: Gracie Specks, Temple (9-1-85); James T. Moore, Austin (9-1-85); Dr. Johnnie Ruth Stripling, Tyler (9-1-85); Mrs. Mary Adams, Lubbock (9-1-87); Mrs. Rosario P. Hamilton, San Antonio (9-1-87); Madgelean Bush, Houston (9-1-87); Irma Gutierrez, Laredo (9-1-89); Ronnie A. Nutt, Paris (9-1-89); Dale Smith, DeLeon (9-1-89).

Disabilities, Council on. — (1983); apptv. as indicated; 2-yr.; twenty-one members: Four apptd. by Governor, four by Lieutenant Governor, four by Speaker; one member each from Department Human Services, Department Mental Health and Mental Retardation, Department Health, Texas Education Agency, Texas Rehabilitation Commission, Texas Commission for the Deaf, State Commission for the Blind, Texas Department on Aging, Texas Commission on Alcoholism. Gov.'s apptees: Reed Martin, Austin (1-31-85); Judy Cantu, Austin (1-31-85); Joann Mata, Midland (1-31-85); Bob L. Thomas, Waco (1-31-85).

District Review Committee. — (See Medical District Review Committee.)

East Texas State University, Board of Regents of. — (1969); apptv.; 6-yr.; nine members: Leon J. Coker Jr., Texarkana (2-15-89); Herman Furlough Jr., Terrell (2-15-89); James L. Toler, Garland (2-15-89); Larry D. Franklin, San Antonio (2-15-91); Raymond B. Cameron, Rockwall (2-15-91); Ted H. Peters, Greenville (2-15-91); W. Ben Munson III, Denison (2-15-87); Peggy M. Wilson, Dallas (2-15-87); Gene W. Hightower, Van (2-15-87). President, Charles J. Austin, ETSU, Commerce 75428 (nonmember).

Economic Development Commission, Texas. — (1920 as 5-member Texas Industrial Commission; expanded by Legislature in 1959 to 9-member board; increased to 12 members in 1973 by addition of three rural members; name changed to present form and three members added in 1983); apptv.; 6-yr.; expenses; fifteen members: Hector Gutierrez Jr., Fort Worth (2-15-87); Barbara Chaney, El Paso (2-15-87); J.A. Koesel Jr., Midland (2-15-87); John F. Sammons Jr., Temple (2-15-87); Edd Hargett, Douglasville (2-15-87); Ed Smith, Houston (2-15-89); William H. Crook, San Marcos (2-15-89); Bob L. Herchert, Fort Worth (2-15-89); Dan Petty, Dallas (2-15-89); Hugh G. Robinson, Dallas (2-15-91); Joe E. Russo, Houston (2-15-91); George McLaughlin, Beaumont (2-15-91); Clyde H. Alexander II, Athens (2-15-91); James H. Simms, Amarillo (2-15-85). (One vacancy.) Executive Director, Charles B. Wood, Box 12728, Capitol Station, Austin 78711 (nonmember) ($55,929).

Education, Advisory Council for Technical-Vocational. — (1969 as 25-member board; made 13-member board in 1984); expenses and per diem; appointed by Governor with advice and consent of Senate; all terms expire Jan. 1, 1989: Donna Price, Houston; Jane S. Lack, Victoria; Shirlene Cook, Beaumont; Joe Pentony, Houston; William E. Zinsmeyer, San Antonio; Gary O. Boren, Lubbock; John Cox, Houston; Jim Hutchins, Estelline; Talmadge D. Steinke, Waco; Hank Brown, San Antonio; George F. Matott, Austin; Ted Martinez, Dallas; Filomena Leo, La Joya. Executive Director, Will Reece, Box 1886, Austin 78767 (nonmember) ($48,101).

Education Agency, Texas. — Legal name of group of educational agencies, including **State Board of Education, State Commissioner of Education and Advisory Council for Technical-Vocational Education.** See these separate agencies.

Education, State Board of. — (1866; re-created 1928 and reformed by Gilmer-Aikin Act, 1949, to consist of 21 elective members, from districts co-extensive with 21 congressional districts at that time; membership increased to 24 with congressional redistricting in 1971, effective 1973; membership increased to 27 with congressional redistricting in 1981, effective 1983; reorganized by special legislative session as 15-member apptv. board in 1984 to become elective board again in 1988); expenses; 15 members; 4-yr.; all terms expire (1-1-89). Figures before names indicate district numbers: (1) Maria Elena Flood, El Paso; (2) Mary Helen Berlanga, Corpus Christi; (3) Pete J. Morales Jr., Devine; (4) Volly C. Bastine Jr., Houston; (5) William V. McBride, San Antonio; (6) Charles Duncan, Houston; (7) Carolyn Crawford, Beaumont; (8) Jack Strong, Longview; (9) Vice-chairman, Rebecca D. Canning, Waco; (10) John Prescott, College Station; (11) Chairman, Jon Brumley, Fort Worth; (12) Geraldine Miller, Dallas; (13) Dr. Emmett Conrad, Dallas; (14) Katherine P. Raines, Cleburne; (15) Paul C. Dunn, Levelland. (See also **Commissioner of Education** who is appointed by this board.)

Education Board of Control, Southern Regional. — (1969); apptv.; 4-yr.; four apptv. members and Governor as ex officio member. Apptv. members: Carl Parker, Port Arthur (6-30-84); Wilhelmina Delco, Austin (6-30-85); Dr. C. Robert Kemble, Beaumont (6-30-86); Becky Brooks, Jefferson (6-30-87). Dr. Winfred L. Godwin, President, Southern Regional Education Board, 130 6th St. N. W., Atlanta, Ga. 30313.

Education Board, Legislative. — Est. 1984 as temporary advisory board; to expire Jan. 1, 1989; ten members, all ex officio as follows: Lieutenant Governor; Speaker House of Representatives; chairman House Public Education Committee; chairman Senate Education Committee; chairman House Appropriations Committee; chairman Senate Finance Committee; two representatives apptd. by Speaker; two senators apptd. by Lieutenant Governor.

Egg Marketing Advisory Board. — (1957); apptv.; 6-yr.; eleven members — two ex officio, nine apptv. Commissioner of Agriculture serves as chairman; one apptd. by head of Poultry Science Department, A&M University. Gov.'s apptees: Ernest A. Mahard Jr., Prosper (9-27-83); Hobart H. Joe, Houston (9-27-83); T. P. Metcalfe, Franklin (9-27-83); D. R. Barrett, Bryan (9-27-85); Kervin E. Jacob, Houston (9-27-85); Edgar H. Burton, Lufkin (9-27-85); James O. Lipscomb, Lockhart (9-27-87); Richard Doty, Corpus Christi (9-27-87); Carl Smith, Flatonia (9-27-87).

Elderly, Coordinating Council on Long-Term Care for the. — (1983); apptv. as indicated; 2-yr.; indefinite number of members: Four apptd. by Governor; four by Lieutenant Governor, four by Speaker; one each from Texas Department on Aging, Texas Department of Human Services, Texas Department of Health and Texas Department of Mental Health and Mental Retardation. Gov.'s apptees: A. R. Arriola, Alice (1-31-85); Mrs. Johnnie Cavanaugh, Austin (1-31-85); Rev. Bob Greene, Austin (1-31-85); Dr. David Maldonado, Arlington (1-31-85).

Election Commission, State. — (1973); nine members apptv. as indicated: Chairman Democratic State Executive Committee; Chairman Republican State Executive Committee; Chief Justice of Supreme Court; Presiding Judge Court of Criminal Appeals; two persons to be named — one a justice of the Court of Appeals appointed by Chief Justice of Supreme Court; one District Judge appointed by Presiding Judge of Court of Criminal Appeals; two county chairmen — one each from Democratic and Republican parties — named by the parties; Secretary of State.

Employment Commission, Texas. — (1936); apptv.; $60,461; 6-yr.; three members: Mrs. Mary S. Nabers (management), Austin (Brownwood) (2-1-91); Ronald E. Luna (labor), Austin (Buda) (11-21-86); Chairman, Ed W. Grisham (public), Austin (11-21-88). Administrator, William Grossenbacher, 638 TEC Bldg., 101 E. 15th, Austin 78778 (nonmember) ($57,628).

Engineers, State Board of Registration for Professional. — (1937 as six-member board; membership increased to nine in 1981 with addition of three members from general public); apptv.; per diem and expenses; 6-yr.; nine members: Frank B. Harrell, Dallas (9-26-85); Edwin H. Blaschke, Houston (9-26-85); D. S. Hammett, Dallas (9-26-87); Bill W. Klotz,

Houston (9-26-87); Robert Navarro, El Paso (9-26-89); Clay Roming, Eddy (9-26-89). Public members: James K. Newman, Denton (9-26-85); Ron Garrett, Waco (9-26-87); Jack M. Webb, Houston (9-26-89). Executive Director, Woodrow W. Mize, Drawer 18329, Austin 78760 (nonmember) ($50,676).

Enterprise Zone Board. — (1983); apptv.; expenses; 6-yr.; nine members as follows: One member each from Industrial Commission, Texas Employment Commission, Texas Dept. of Community Affairs, one municipal government, one county government, one independent school district, one from small business, one employee and one from general public: Ralph Quintanilla, Austin (2-1-85); Kenyon Clapp, Austin (2-1-85); Henry Cisneros, San Antonio (2-1-85); R. H. Lackner, Brownsville (2-1-87); Santos Saldana, Edinburg (2-1-87); Carlos Carrasco, El Paso (2-1-87); Homer Scott, Mission (2-1-87); Vidal Trevino, Laredo (2-1-89); Karin Richmond, McAllen (2-1-89).

Entomologist, State. — (1900); ex officio: Paul W. Jackson, Entomologist at Texas Agricultural Experiment Station, College Station.

Evergreen Underground Water Conservation District Board of Directors. — (1965); five members—four elected (two each from Wilson and Atascosa Counties) and one apptd. by Governor; 2-yr.: Mark Connally, Floresville (1-13-85).

Family Farm and Ranch Security Program Advisory Council. — (1979); apptv.; expenses; 6-yr.; nine members: Eristus Sams, Waller (1-31-87); Kenneth Irwin, Gruver (1-31-87), Mrs. Virginia Ann Armstrong, Dimmitt (1-31-87); Randal C. Dixon, Groesbeck (1-31-89); Harold R. Pruitt, Slidell (1-31-89); Alfred L. Parks, Cypress (1-31-89); Jerry H. Jones, Lubbock (1-31-85); Charles Wilson, Quanah (1-31-85); J. T. Garrett, Danbury (1-31-85).

Family Practice Residency Advisory Committee. — (1977), apptv. as indicated; expenses; 3-yr.; 12 members as follows: One practicing physician apptd. by Texas Osteopathic Medical Assn.; two apptd. by Association of Directors of Family Practice Training Programs; one apptd. by Texas Medical Assn.; two apptd. by Texas Academy of Family Physicians; two administrators of hospitals apptd. by Gov.; three public members apptd. by Gov.; and the president of the Texas Academy of Family Physicians. Gov.'s apptees: Chairman, Dr. Exalton A. Delco Jr., Austin (8-29-85); Dr. E. J. Mason, Dallas (8-29-84); (One vacancy.)

Finance Commission of Texas. — (1923 as Banking Commission; reorganized as **Finance Commission** 1943 with nine members: membership increased to twelve in 1983 with addition of three consumer credit members from general public); apptv.; 6-yr.; per diem and traveling expenses. Six members of banking section of commission as follows: Richard H. Skinner, Houston (2-1-91); Carroll N. Sullivan Jr., Georgetown (2-1-85); Gerald H. Smith, Houston (2-1-87); Cullen R. Looney, Edinburg (2-1-87); Ruben H. Johnson Austin (2-1-89); Phillip G. Newsom, Ennis (2-1-89). Three members of savings and loan section of commission as follows: D. Gene Phelps, Tomball (2-1-91); Henry Sauer Jr. Houston (2-1-87); Ralph D. Reed, College Station (2-1-89). Three members from general public: Alan Lerner, Dallas (2-1-85); Leopoldo Palacios, Pharr (2-1-87); Richard H. Skinner, Houston (2-1-89). Banking Commissioner, James L. Sexton, 2601 N. Lamar, Austin 78705, appointee of Finance Commission. (See also **Banking Commissioner, State.**)

Firemen's Pension Commissioner. — (1937); apptv.; 2-yr. Hal H. Hood, 503-F Sam Houston Bldg., Austin 78701 (7-1-85) ($31,518).

Fire Fighters' Relief and Retirement Fund, Board of Trustees of the. — (1977); apptv.; expenses; 6-yr.; six members: W. Harold Brodt, Seguin (9-1-87); Jimmy Lynn Dugger, Dalhart (9-1-89); Marvin R. Setzer Sr., Brazoria (9-1-89); Bobby Joe Looney, Mansfield (9-1-85); J. J. Pruitt, Huffman (9-9-87); E. L. Taylor, McKinney (9-1-85).

Fire Protection Personnel Standards and Education, Commission on. — (1969); apptv.; expenses; 6-yr.; nine apptv. members and two ex-officio members: Ex officio members — Commissioner of Higher Education of the Coordinating Board, Texas College and University System, and the Commissioner of the Texas Education Agency. Apptv. members: Ernest A. Emerson, Austin (6-11-89); P. E. Adams, El Paso (6-11-89); Lt. A. J. Bostick Sr., Fort Worth (6-11-89); Mike B. Perez Jr., Laredo (6-11-85); Alcus Greer, Houston (6-11-85); E. E. Spillman, Irving (6-11-85); Dodd Miller, Dallas (6-11-87); Chairman, Henry D. Smith, College Station (6-11-87); Rae M. Eastland, Waco (6-11-87). Executive Director, Garland W. Fulbright, 510 S. Congress, Suite 406, Austin 78704 (nonmember) ($31,518).

Forester, State. — (1915); apptv. by board of directors of A&M University: Bruce R. Miles, College Station.

Good Neighbor Commission. — (1943); apptv.; 6-yr.; expenses; nine members: Haygood Gulley, Del Rio (6-18-85); Manuel Jara, Fort Worth (6-18-85); Rosemary Cervantes, Houston (6-18-85); Nathan Safir, San Antonio (6-18-87); Ste A. Lillard III, Zapata (6-18-87); Dr. Richard Rubottom, Dallas (6-18-87); David L. Garza Jr., Houston (6-18-89); Jo Alvarado Jr., Corpus Christi (6-18-89); Travis Johnson, Paso (6-18-89). Executive Director, Bob Watson, Box 120 Capitol Station, Austin 78711 (nonmember) ($43,260).

Governor. — (1845 by original Constitution, 1876 by present Constitution); elective; (2-yr. by original constitutional provision, term raised to 4-yr. in 1972, effective 1975): Mark White, Austin (1-1-87) ($94,348).

Guadalupe-Blanco River Authority. — (1935); apptv.; per diem and expenses on duty; 6-yr.; nine members: H. E. Knox, New Braunfels (2-1-87); Sec.-Treas., Preston A. Stofer, Long Mott (2-1-87); A. C. Schwethelm, Comfort (2-1-87); E. T. Summers Jr., Cuero (2-18-89); Harry E. Gumbert Jr., Wimberley (2-1-89); Mrs. Kathryn Chenault, Gonzales (2-1-89); Joseph P. Kelly, Victoria (2-1-91); John C. Taylor, McQueeney (2-1-91); Warren P. Kirksey, Lockhart (2-1-91). General Manager, John H. Specht, Box 271, Seguin 78155 (nonmember).

Guadalupe River Authority, Upper. — (1939); apptv.; 6-yr.; nine members: E. C. Parker Jr., Kerrville (11-1-86); Betty Strohacker, Kerrville (11-1-86); President, Darrell G. Lochte, Kerrville (11-1-86); Frank Harrison, Hunt (11-1-84); Harry Schwethelm, Kerrville (11-1-84); Charles Schreiner IV, Mountain Home (11-1-88); L. F. E. Koehler, Hunt (11-1-88); Raymond Mosty, Center Point (11-1-88); Dr. R. H. Holekamp, Kerrville (11-1-84). General Manager, B. W. Bruns, Box 1278, Kerrville 78029-1278.

Gulf Coast Waste Disposal Authority. — (1969); apptv.; 2-yr.; $50 a day and expenses on duty; nine members—three apptv. by Governor, three by County Commissioners Courts of counties in district, and three by Municipalities Waste Disposal Councils of counties in district. Governor's appointees: Rick Ferguson, Winnie (8-31-86); Clyde R. Bickham, Houston (8-31-85); John Unbehagen, Galveston (8-31-86). Gen. Mgr., L. Jack Davis (nonmember), 910 Bay Area Blvd., Houston 77058.

Gulf States Marine Fisheries Commission. — (1949); apptv.; 3-yr.; three members: Charles Travis, Executive Director Parks and Wildlife Commission, Austin; Rep. Leroy Wieting, Portland; Leslie E. Casterline Jr., Fulton (3-17-87). Executive Director, Charles H. Lyles, Box 726, Ocean Springs, Ms. 39564.

Hairdressers and Cosmetologists, State Board of. — (Name changed; see Cosmetology Commission.)

Health Coordinating Council, Statewide. — (1975); apptv.; 2-yr.; 27 apptv., one ex officio member: Betsy Attel, El Paso (10-21-85); Max Brown, Dallas (10-21-85); Lynda Calcote, Abilene (10-21-85); Jose L. Gonzalez, Laredo (10-21-85); Richard Barajas, Fort Stockton (10-21-85); Father Robert J. Brooks, Houston (10-21-85); Hon. Lester Cranek, Columbus (10-21-85); James Easter, Houston (10-21-85); James L. Grey, Austin (10-21-85); Hon. Giles Dalby, Post (10-21-85); Marjorie Daniels, Hereford (10-21-85); Dr. Robert B. Stell, San Angelo (10-21-85); Doris M. Watson, College Station (10-21-85); Chairman, Dr. Marion R. Zetzman, Dallas (indefinite term); Dr. Edward A. R. Lord Jr., Houston (10-21-86); Jarmese Morris, Houston (10-21-86); Gilbert Ochoa, San Antonio (10-21-86); Jack L. Campbell, Austin (10-21-86); Lynda Fant Hill, Fort Worth (10-21-86); Dolores Lawless, Beaumont (10-26-86); Hon. Frank Madla, San Antonio (10-21-86); Shirley K. Price, Houston (10-21-86); Margarethe M. T. Rosales, El Paso (10-21-86); Adrian Arriaga, McAllen (10-21-86); Hon. Buddy Cole, Pilot Point (10-21-86); Melinda Gonzales, Corpus Christi (10-21-86); M. Madesta Smith, Clarksville (10-21-86).

Health and Human Services Coordinating Council. — (1975 as nine-member board; membership increased to nineteen in 1983); 6-yr.; nineteen members. Ex officio members: Governor, Lieutenant Governor, Speaker of House, Chairman Texas Board of Human Services, Chairman Texas Board of Health, Chairman Texas Board of Mental Health and Mental Retardation, Chairman State Board of Education. Two board members of State agencies appointed by Governor: Rafael Quintanilla, Austin (9-1-85); Marshall W. Cooper, Whiteface (9-1-85). Two senators appointed by Lieutenant Governor; two representatives appointed by Speaker; two general public members appointed by Governor: Judith L. Craven, Houston (9-1-85); Sid Stahl, Dallas (9-1-85). Two general public members appointed by Lieutenant Governor: Rebecca Canning, Waco (9-1-85); Helen Farabee, Wichita Falls (9-1-85). Two general public members appointed by Speaker: Sharon Flippen, Austin (9-1-85); Louise Maberry, Orange (9-1-85). Executive Director, Dr. Lynn H. Leverty, P. O. Box 12428, Austin 78711 (nonmember) ($50,882); Administrative Assistant, Joe Ann Stoker (nonmember).

Health Facilities Commission, Texas. — (Ceased functioning Aug. 31, 1985.)

Health Services Advisory Council, Home. — (1979); apptv.; 2-yr.; nine members: Chairman, Dr. Ruth L. Constant, Victoria (health agencies) (1-31-87); Essie L. Bellfield, Orange (home health agency services consumer) (1-31-87); Mrs. Eddie Bernice Johnson, Dallas (voluntary nonprofit agencies) (1-31-87); Rev. C. E. Means, San Antonio (home health agency services consumer) (1-31-85); Mrs. Joyce Snead, El Paso (health agencies) (1-31-86); Maurice B. Shaw, Austin (Department of Health) (1-31-86); Mrs. Bettie J. Girling, Austin (proprietary agencies) (1-31-86); Kenneth Lemke, Victoria (home health agencies) (1-31-86); Dr. Hilary Connor, Austin (Department Human Services) (1-31-86).

Health, Dental Advisory Committee to the Texas Board of. — Abolished by Legislature in 1985.

Health, Texas Board of. — (1903 as State Board of Health; superseded similar department created in 1891; name changed in 1975 to Texas Board of Health Resources and membership increased to eighteen; name changed in 1977 to present form); apptv.; per diem and expenses on duty; 6-yr.; eighteen members: Chmn., Dr. Ron J. Anderson, Dallas (2-1-89); Dr. Arthur L. Raines, Cleburne (2-1-89); Dr. Max M. Stettner, Lubbock (2-1-89); Dr. Barry D. Cunningham, Round Rock (2-1-89); William J. Foran, Amarillo (2-1-83); Dennis K. McIntosh, Seguin (2-1-89); Mrs. Johnnie M. Benson, Fort Worth (2-1-87); Dr. Joaquin G. Cigarroa Jr., Laredo (2-1-87); Ben M. Durr, Humble (2-1-87); Mrs. Barbara T. Slover, Fort Worth (2-1-87); Dr. Bob D. Glaze, Gilmer (2-1-87); Dr. Frank Bryant Jr., San Antonio (2-1-87); Isadore Roosth, Tyler (2-1-85); Sister Bernard Marie Borgmeyer, San Antonio (2-1-85); Dr. Robert D. Moreton, Houston (2-1-85); Joe N. Pyle, San Antonio (2-1-85); Dr. Edward H. Zunker, Seguin (2-1-91); Vice Chmn., Dr. L. N. Nickey, El Paso (2-1-85). Commissioner of Health, Dr. Robert Bernstein, 1100 W. 49th, Austin 78756 (nonmember) ($62,800).

Hearing Aids, Texas Board of Examiners in the Fitting and Dispensing of. — (1969); apptv.; 6-yr.; expenses; nine members: William E. Keim, Sugar Land (12-31-87); Richard C. Durbin, Rowlett (12-31-89); Mrs. Alice Scruggs, El Paso (12-31-85); Rev. H. E. Myrick, El Paso (12-31-87); Thomas R. Jones, Fort Worth (12-31-87); George Holland Jr., Lubbock (12-31-85); Dr. Henry M. Carder, Dallas (12-31-89); Carl McGovern, Commerce (12-31-89); President, Mrs. Thomas B. Brennan, Houston (12-31-85). Executive Director, Wanda F. Stewart, 105 W. Riverside Dr., Suite 124, Austin 78704 (nonmember) ($23,175).

Higher Education, State Commission on. — (See College and University System, Coordinating Board.)

Highways and Public Transportation Commission, State. — (1917 as State Highway Commission; merged with Mass Transportation Commission and name changed to present form in 1975); apptv.; 6-yr.; ($35,123); three members: Thomas Dunning, Dallas (2-15-87); Chairman, Robert C. Lanier, Houston (2-15-89); Ray C. Stoker Jr., Odessa (2-15-91).

Highways and Public Transportation, State Engineer-Director for. — (1917 as State Highway Engineer; name changed to present form in 1975); apptv. by State Highways and Public Transportation Commission; indefinite term: M. G. Goode, 11th and Brazos, Austin 78701 ($68,701).

Historical Commission, Texas. — (1953); apptv.; expenses; 6-yr.; eighteen members: Richard H. Collins, Dallas (1-1-87); Duncan Boeckman, Dallas (1-1-87); Louis P. Terrazas, San Antonio (1-1-87); Mrs. Albert G. Hill, Dallas (1-1-87); Barney M. Davis, Somerville (1-1-85); George Christian, Austin (1-1-85); Woodrow Glasscock Jr., Hondo (1-1-85); Dr. Dan Willis, Fort Worth (1-1-85); Mrs. James F. Biggart Jr., Dallas (1-1-85); Mrs Virginia Long, Kilgore (1-1-85); T. R. Fehrenbach, San Antonio (1-1-89); Dr. Robert D. Hunter, Abilene (1-1-89); James S. Nabors, Lake Jackson (1-1-87); John M. Bennett, San Antonio (1-1-89); Mrs. Maxine Flournoy, Alice (1-1-89); Chairman, Harry A. Golemon, Houston (1-1-87); Mrs. Martha Gay Ratliff, Austin (1-1-89); Mrs. Evangeline L. Whorton, Galveston (1-1-89). Executive Director, Curtis Tunnell, Box 12276, Capitol Sta., Austin 78711 (nonmember) ($46,968).

Historical Records Advisory Board, State. — (1976); apptv.; 3-yr.; nine members: John W. Crain, Dallas (1-23-85); Dr. David B. Gracy II, Austin (1-23-85); Dorman H. Winfrey, Austin (1-23-85); Kent Keeth, Waco (1-23-87); Dr. David J. Murrah, Lubbock (1-23-86); Betty Kissler, San Marcos (1-23-86); A. Jean Shepherd, Baytown (1-23-86); Don Carleton, Austin (1-23-87); Michael Q. Hooks, Austin (1-23-87). State Historical Records Coordinator, Dr. David B. Gracy II, State Library, Austin.

Hospital Council, Advisory — (1947); twelve members; State Health Commissioner as ex officio member; expenses; apptv. members serve 6-yr. terms: Dr. Joseph T. Ainsworth, Houston (7-17-85); Mrs. Jessica Harden, Houston (7-17-85); Dr. J. R. Maxfield, Dallas (7-17-85); Dr. James A. Hallmark, Fort Worth (7-17-85); Margaret Read, Dallas (7-17-87); James E. Bullard, Hereford (7-17-87); Mrs. Terrie Lynn Brown, Houston (7-17-87); W. B. Lipes, Corpus Christi (7-17-87); O. Ray Hurst, Houston (7-17-89); A. J. Gallerano, Houston (7-17-89); Dora Olivo, Rosenberg (7-17-89); Elizabeth L. Kimmel, Houston (7-17-89). Ex officio member, State Commissioner of Health, 1100 W. 49th, Austin.

Hospital Licensing Advisory Council. — (1959); apptv.; per diem and expenses; 6-yr.; nine members — three each representing physicians, hospital administrators and general public, as follows: Physicians: Dr. Van D. Goodall, Clifton (12-7-83); Dr. Jim Bob Brame, Eldorado (12-7-87); Dr. C. R. Stasney, Houston (12-7-85). Three hospital administrators: Mrs. Marcella V. Hinsky, Hallettsville (12-7-83); Guy H. Dalrymple, Beaumont (12-7-85); Joe M. Stevens, Gonzales (12-7-87). Three from general public: Fred Farner, Houston (12-7-89); J. T. Palmer, Roby (12-7-87); Mrs. Dorothea Ann Mather, Houston (12-7-85).

Housing Agency, Board of Directors of the Texas. — (1979); apptv.; expenses; 6-yr.; nine apptv. members: Executive Director Texas Dept. of Community Affairs ex officio member and Chairman of Board. Apptv. members: Kenneth J. Fuqua, Houston (1-31-87); Salvador Canchola, El Paso (1-31-87); Ray P. Moudy, Midland (1-31-87); J. Stanley Stephen, Bryan (1-31-89); Melva W. Becnel, Houston (1-31-89); Fred E. Rizk, Houston (1-31-89); Richard Jordan, Austin (1-31-91); W. E. Daniels, Houston (1-31-91); Arthur Navarro, Austin (1-31-91). Executive Administrator, Earline Jewett, Box 13941, Capitol Station, Austin 78711 (nonmember).

Humanities, Texas Commission on the Arts and. — (See **Arts, Texas Commission on the.**)

Humanities, Texas Committee for the. — (1972); apptv. and elective by the Committee; 2-yr. for apptv. members; 4-yr. for elective; twenty-two members — four apptv. by Governor as follows: Mrs. Carol McKay, Fort Worth (12-31-86); Dr. Phyllis Bridges, Denton (12-31-85); Mrs. Ellena Stone Huckaby, Houston (12-31-85); William P. Wright Jr., Abilene (12-31-85). Executive Director, James F. Veninga, 1604 Nueces, Austin 78701 (nonmember).

Human Rights Commission, State. — (1983); apptv.; 6-yr.; expenses; six members: Mrs. Mallory Robinson, Houston (9-24-85); Mrs. Maxine Lee, Austin (9-24-85); Alberto H. Magnon Jr., Laredo (9-24-87); Ramiro Casso, McAllen (9-24-87); Chairman, Frank Thompson Jr., Houston (9-24-89); Helen Giddings, Dallas (9-24-89). Executive Director, Bill Hale, Box 13493, Capitol Station, Austin 78711 (nonmember) ($48,204).

Human Services, Texas Board of. — (1941 as State Board of Public Welfare; name changed to present form in 1985); apptv.; 6-yr.; per diem and expenses; three members and a commissioner: J. L. Kosberg, Houston (1-20-91); Vicki Garza, Corpus Christi (1-20-89). (One vacancy.) **Commissioner,** Marlin W. Johnston, Box 2960, Austin 78769 ($68,289).

Indebtedness, Board of County and District Road Bond. — (1932); ex officio; term in other office; three members: Comptroller Robert D. Bullock, Treasurer Ann Richards and State Highway Engineer, M. G. Goode, LBJ State Office Bldg., Austin 78701.

Indian Commission, Texas. — (1965); apptv.; 6-yr.; per diem and expenses; three members: W. E. Fifer Jr., El Paso (1-31-87); Mrs. Owanah P. Anderson, Wichita Falls (1-31-85); Don E. Ellyson, Waxahachie (1-31-89). Executive Director, Raymond D. Apodaca, 9434 Viscount, Suite 122, El Paso 79925. (Office will be moved to Austin by Dec. 1, 1985. Address not available at press time.) (nonmember) ($39,346).

Industrial Accident Board. — (1913); apptv.; (Chairman, $56,495, others $55,774); 6-yr.; three members: Chairman, Mrs. Margaret M. Maisel, San Antonio (attorney) (9-1-85); Bobby J. Barnes, Baytown (employee) (9-1-89); N. J. Huestis, Corpus Christi (employer) (9-1-87). Executive Director, William Treacy, Bevington A. Reed Bldg., 200 E. Riverside Dr., Austin 78704 (nonmember apptd. by board) ($52,015).

Industrial Commission, Texas. — (See **Economic Development Commission** to which name changed in 1983.)

Insurance, State Board of. — (Originally created as State Board of Insurance Commissioners in 1927; superseded similar commission of 1913; re-created 1957 to form **State Board of Insurance**); apptv.; 6-yr.; three members at $63,345 each and **State Insurance Commissioner** at $60,873, who serves 2-yr. term and is appointed by board members: David H. Thornberry, Austin (1-31-91); Chairman, Lyndon Olson Jr., Austin (Waco) (1-31-87); Carole K. McClellan, Austin (1-31-89). **Commissioner,** Tom Bond, State Insurance Bldg., Austin 78786.

Intergovernmental Relations, Texas Advisory Commission on. — (1971); apptv.; 6-yr.; 24 apptd. and 2 ex officio members. Appointed members: Four city officials: Rosalie Brown, Sinton (9-1-87); Anthony Hall, Houston (9-1-89); Two vacancies. Four county officials: Tom Vickers, San Antonio (9-1-85); Bill Bailey, Pasadena (9-1-85); Joe B. Garcia, Falfurrias (9-1-87); Norman Troy, Beaumont (9-1-89). Two school officials: M. Eli Douglass, Garland (9-1-85); Victor Rodriguez, San Antonio (9-1-87). Two federal officials: Dick Whittington, Dallas (9-1-89); J. Lynn Futch, Temple (9-1-87). Four private citizens: Edward J. Drake, Dallas (9-1-85); Yvonne M. Van Dyke, Austin (9-1-87); Jim D. Dannenbaum, Houston (9-1-89); Mrs. Pic Rivers, Houston (9-1-89). Two from other political subdivisions: Chairman, Fred N. Pfeiffer, San Antonio (9-1-87); Sam Collins, Orange (9-1-89). Three senators appointed by Lt. Governor. Three representatives appointed by Speaker of the House of Representatives. Two ex officio members: Lt. Gov. William P. Hobby and Speaker of the House of Representatives Gib Lewis. Executive Director, Jay G. Stanford, Box 13206, Austin 78711 (nonmember) ($42,848).

Interstate Compact for Supervision of Parolees and Probationers, Texas Administrator. — (1951); ex officio: Atty. Gen. Jim Mattox, Austin.

Interstate Co-operation, Texas Commission on. — (1941); originally set up as commission with fifteen voting and three non-voting members; membership increased to nineteen in 1973, as follows: Governor, Lieutenant Governor and

Speaker of the House. Sixteen apptd. as follows: Five each apptd. by Lieutenant Governor and Speaker of the House; six apptd. by Governor.

Interstate Indian Council, Governor's (Texas Representatives). — (1965); designated: Raymond D. Apodaca, El Paso and W. E. Fifer, El Paso.

Interstate Oil Compact Commission, Texas Representative. — (1935); ex officio or apptv. according to Governor's choice; per diem and expenses. Ex officio member: Garry Mauro, Land Commissioner, Austin. Apptv. members: John E. Robertson, Austin (Houston); John R. Brose, Austin (Midland); John Newman Jr., Austin (San Antonio); Kenneth Loep, Austin (Houston).

Interstate Parole Compact Administrator. — (1951); apptv.: Tom W. Bullington, Austin.

Irrigators, Texas Board of. — (1979); apptv.; 6-yr.; expenses; six members as follows: Two from general public, four licensed irrigators. General public members: Weldon Pool, Tyler (1-31-85); Douglas Hawthorne, Dallas (1-31-87). Licensed irrigators: Robert I. Goehrs, Houston (1-31-85); Samuel D. Ousley, Dallas (1-31-89); Herman R. Johnson Sr., Corpus Christi (1-31-89); Hugh Rushing Jr., Austin (1-31-87). Executive Secretary, Joyce Watson, P.O. Box 12337, Capitol Station, Austin 78711 (nonmember) ($27,192).

Jail Standards, Commission on. — (1975); apptv.; 6-yr.; expenses; nine members as follows: Two sheriffs — Joe A. Corley, Conroe (1-31-91); John Klevenhagen, Houston (1-31-91). One county judge — Pat F. O'Rourke, El Paso (1-1-89). One doctor — Dr. Hanes H. Brindley, Temple (1-31-87) and five private citizens — Ronald L. Ramey, Houston (1-31-85); Chairman, Mrs. William R. Cree, Abilene (1-31-87); Vice Chairman, Robert J. Uhr, New Braunfels (1-31-89); Fred L. Tinsley, Dallas (1-31-89); Pat Newhouse, Honey Grove (1-31-87). Executive Director, Robert O. Viterna, Box 12985, Austin 78711 (nonmember) ($40,376).

Judicial Conduct, State Commission on. — (1965 as nine-member **Judicial Qualifications Commission**; name changed in 1977 to present form and membership raised to eleven); expenses; 6-yr.; eleven members appointed as follows: Five apptd. by Supreme Court — Chairman, John T. Boyd, Amarillo, Associate Justice, 7th Court of Appeals (11-19-87); William E. Junell, Houston, Associate Justice, 14th Court of Appeals (11-19-89); Raul Longoria, Edinburg, Judge 139th Judicial District Court (11-19-87); S. J. Richburg, Dallas, Justice of the Peace (11-19-85); Elinor Walters, Municipal Court Judge, Seabrook (11-19-89); J. Ray Kirkpatrick, Judge, County Court at Law, Marshall, (11-19-89). Two board members appointed by State Bar — Vice Chairman Robert H. Parsley, Houston (11-19-87); J. H. Clements, Temple (11-19-87). Four appointed by Governor — Max Emmert III, Odessa (11-19-89); Secretary, Nathan I. Reiter Jr., Texarkana (11-19-87); Scott Taliaferro, Abilene (11-19-85); Robert D. Rogers, Dallas (11-19-85). Executive Director, Robert C. Flowers, Box 12265, Capitol Station, Austin 78711 (nonmember) ($56,135).

Judicial Council, Texas. — (1929 as Texas Civil Judicial Council; name changed in 1975); ex officio terms vary; apptv. 6-yr.; expenses; nineteen members as follows: Six ex officio members: President, Ben Z. Grant, past chairman of House Judiciary Committee; Vice President, John L. Hill Jr., Austin, Chief Justice of Texas Supreme Court; Secretary, Tom G. Davis, Judge, Court of Criminal Appeals, Austin; Rep. Robert Bush, chairman of House Judiciary Committee; Sen. Ray Farabee, past chairman of Senate Jurisprudence Committee; Sen. Oscar Mauzy, chairman of Senate Jurisprudence Committee. Four apptv. members with ex officio qualifications: Sam H. Bass Jr., Associate Justice, First Court of Appeals, Houston; Ray L. McKim, Presiding Judge, Seventh Administrative Judicial District, Odessa; Paul C. Murphy III, Associate Justice, Fourteenth Court of Appeals, Houston; Charles J. Murray, Presiding Judge, Eighth Administrative Judicial District, Fort Worth. Nine apptv. members: John L. McCraw Jr., McKinney (7-1-89); Robert O. Smith, Austin (7-1-85); Mark Martin, Dallas (7-1-85); J. Wm. Hartman, Rosenberg (7-1-89); Gene McLaughlin, Ralls (7-1-89); Charles W. Barrow, Waco (7-1-87); A. W. McNeill, Beaumont (7-1-87); L. E. Frazier, Houston (7-1-87); One vacancy. Executive Director, C. Raymond Judice (nonmember), Box 12066, Capitol Sta., Austin 78711.

Judicial Districts of Texas, Administrative, Presiding Judges of. — (See **Administrative Judicial Districts.**)

Judicial Qualifications Commission, State — (See **State Commission on Judicial Conduct.**)

Juvenile Probation Commission, Texas. — (1981); apptv. 6-yr.; expenses; nine members — three judges of District Courts and six private citizens: Judges: Scott D. Moore, Fort Worth (8-31-91); William C. Martin III, Longview (8-31-87); F. P. Benavides, Mission (8-31-85). Citizen members: Vice Chmn., Jerrell S. Reed Jr., Winnsboro (8-31-85); Carol H. Lane, Houston (8-31-85); Mrs. Clara P. Willoughby, San Angelo (8-31-87); Lois Carpenter, Midland (8-31-87); Chairman, Marshall W. Cooper, Whiteface (8-31-89); Amos Landry, Beaumont (8-31-89). Executive Director, Bill Anderson, Box 13547, Austin 78711 (nonmember) ($49,749).

Labor and Standards, Commissioner of. — (1909); apptv.; 2-yr.: Allen R. Parker Sr., Box 12157, Capitol Station, Austin 78711 (2-1-87) ($55,002).

Lamar University, Board of Regents of. — (1949); apptv.; 6-yr.; expenses; nine members: Regina Rogers, Houston (10-4-85); B. A. Steinhagen, Beaumont (10-4-85); Otho Plummer, Beaumont (10-4-85); Joseph D. Deshotel, Beaumont (10-4-87); George Dishman Jr., Beaumont (10-4-87); Merlin Breaux, Sour Lake (10-4-87); Lloyd L. Hayes, Port Arthur (10-4-89); H. D. Pate, Bridge City (10-4-89); Thomas M. Maes II, Beaumont (10-4-89). President, C. Robert Kemble, Lamar Sta. Box 10002, Beaumont 77110 (nonmember).

Land Board, School. — (1939); one ex officio, term in other office; two apptd. — one by Governor and one by Attorney General for 2-yr. term; per diem and expenses; three members: Commissioner of General Land Office Garry Mauro. Gov.'s apptee: Lola L. Bonner, Rockport (8-29-85).

Land Board, Veterans. — (Est. 1949 as three-member ex officio board; reorganized 1956); 4-yr.; per diem and expenses; three members, one of whom is chairman and ex officio member as Commissioner of General Land Office. Commissioner Garry Mauro; Jack M. Rains, Houston (finance member) (12-29-86); Karl M. May, Waco (veterans affairs) (12-29-88). Executive Secretary, Richard Keahey, Land Office Bldg., Austin 78701 (nonmember) ($57,474).

Land Office. — (See **Commissioner of General Land Office.**)

Land Surveyors, Board of Examiners of Licensed State. — (In 1979, this board and the State Board of Registration for Public Surveyors were consolidated. See State Board of Land Surveying, which follows.)

Land Surveying, Texas Board of. — (1979; formed from consolidation of membership of Board of Examiners of Licensed Land Surveyors, est. 1977, and State Board of Registration for Public Surveyors, est. 1955); apptv.; 6-yr.; 10 members — Commissioner of General Land Office serving by statute; three members of general public; two licensed land surveyors; four registered public surveyors, as follows: William C. Wilson Jr., San Angelo (1-31-85); Calvin Dudley, San Antonio (1-31-85); Robert Spears, Midland (1-31-85); Byron L. Simpson, San Antonio (1-31-85); Milton Hanks, Deer Park (1-31-89); C. B. Thomson, Junction (1-31-89); D. D. Shine, Silsbee (1-31-87); G. W. Gilley, Fort Worth (1-31-87); Chairman, W. T. Satterwhite, Rockwall (1-31-87). Executive Secretary, Mrs. Betty J. Pope, 1106 Clayton, Suite 210W Twin Towers Bldg., Austin 78723 (nonmember) ($31,209).

Lands, State Board for Lease of State Park. — (1965); 2-yr.; three members — two ex officio and one apptd. by Attorney General. Ex Officio members are Commissioner of General Land Office Garry Mauro and Chairman of Parks and Wildlife Commission; apptv. member is Mrs. Judy Sauer, Houston.

Lands, Board for Lease of University. — (1929 as three-member board; membership increased to four in 1985); ex officio; term in other office; four members: Commissioner of General Land Office Garry Mauro, Chairman; two members of Board of Regents of University of Texas; one member Board of Regents of A&M University.

Lavaca County Flood Control District. — (1960); apptv.; 2-yr.; seven members (2 ex officio). Apptv. members: Chairman, Bryant J. Pesek, Hallettsville (1-1-83); Reynold Veselka, Hallettsville (1-1-83); Leon Kahanek Jr., Hallettsville (1-1-84); Alfred Neumeyer Jr., Hallettsville (1-1-84); Robert Gindler, Hallettsville (1-1-84).

Lavaca-Navidad River Authority, Directors of. — (1954 as seven-member Jackson County Flood Control District; reorganized as nine-member board in 1959; name changed to present form in 1969); apptv.; 6-yr.; per diem and expenses; nine members: M. H. Brock, Edna (5-1-87); Gene A. Ratliff, Edna (5-1-87); Joe Bonnot, Lolita (5-1-87); Cecil D. Fenner, Edna (5-1-89); Carl W. Swenson, Ganado (5-1-89); Hans Wittenburg, Edna (5-1-89); Harrison Stafford, Edna (5-1-85); S. B. Allen, Edna (5-1-85); Ed Duenow, Lolita (5-1-85). General Manager, W. R. Farquhar Jr., Box 429, Edna 77957 (nonmember).

Law Enforcement Officer Standards and Education, Commission on. — (1965); expenses; nine apptv. and five ex officio members. Ex officio members: Atty. Gen. Jim Mattox, Director of Public Safety James M. Adams, Commissioner of Education, Executive Director Criminal Justice Division-Governor's Office and Commissioner of Higher Education. Apptv. members: David L. Collier, Houston (8-30-85); Louise H. Wing, Houston (8-30-85); W. H. Gardner, Dallas (8-30-85); Mrs. Suzanne Hildebrand, San Antonio (8-30-87); Barto Watson, Humble (8-30-87); Sammy Leach Jr., Lufkin (8-30-87); Walter H. Rankin, Houston (8-30-89); Robert J. Thomas, Tomball (8-30-89); Ruben B. Cisneros, Corpus Christi (8-30-89). Executive Director, Fred Toler, 1606 Headway Circle, Suite 101, Austin 78754 (nonmember) ($47,380).

Law Examiners, State Board of. — (1919 as five-member board; revised 1977 to increase membership to nine); apptd. by Supreme Court; 2-yr.; expenses; nine members: Chairman, William E. Collins, Dallas; vice chairman, Mrs. Beverly Tarpley, Abilene; G. R. Garza Jr., Corpus Christi; War-

lick Carr, Lubbock; Warren W. Shipman III, Fort Worth; Ralph W. Brite, San Antonio; Raymon Jordan, Houston; Robert M. Roller, Austin; Artie G. Giotes, Waco. Executive Director, Wayne E. Denton, Box 12248, Austin 78711 (nonmember).

Law Library Board, State. — (1971); ex officio; expenses; three members: Chief Justice State Supreme Court, Presiding Judge Court of Criminal Appeals and Attorney General. Director, Marian Boner (nonmember), Box 12367, Austin 78711 ($35,226).

Laws, Commission on Uniform State. — (1941 as five-member Commissioners to the National Conference on Uniform State Laws; name changed to present form, membership increased to six and term of office raised to six years in 1977); apptv.; 6-yr.; six members: Millard H. Ruud, Austin (9-30-85); E. R. Wood, Dallas (9-30-85); R. F. Dole Jr., Houston (9-30-87); Patrick C. Guillot, Dallas (9-30-87); Stanley Plettman, Beaumont (9-30-89); Peter K. Munson, Sherman (9-30-90).

Legislative Council, Texas. — (1949); seventeen members — four senators named by President of Senate; nine representatives named by Speaker; Chairman House Administration Committee; Chairman Senate Administration Committee; President of Senate and Speaker. Executive Director, Robert I. Kelly, Box 12128, Austin 78711 (nonmember).

Legislative Redistricting Board. — (1948); five members; ex officio, term in other office: Lt. Gov. William P. Hobby, Speaker of House Gib Lewis, Attorney General Jim Mattox, Comptroller Robert D. Bullock and Commissioner of Land Office Garry Mauro.

Librarian, State. — (Originally established in 1839; present office established 1909); apptv.; indefinite term: Dorman H. Winfrey, Lorenzo de Zavala Archives and Library Bldg., Austin ($48,410).

Library and Archives Commission, Texas State. — (1909 as five-member Library and State Historical Commission; number of members increased to six by Fifty-Third Legislature, 1953; name changed to present form in 1979); apptv.; per diem and expenses on duty; 6-yr.; six members: Chairman, Mrs. Ed Palm, Fort Worth (9-28-85); Price Daniel Sr., Liberty (9-28-85); Ralph W. Yarborough, Austin (9-28-89); T. Frank Glass Jr., Houston (9-28-89); John Ben Shepperd, Odessa (9-28-87); Vice Chairman, Mrs. Anne W. Cragg, McAllen (9-28-87). Director, Dorman H. Winfrey, State Librarian, Box 12927, Capitol Station, Austin 78711 ($48,410).

Library, State Legislative Reference. — (1909); indefinite term: Director, James R. Sanders, Box 12488, Austin 78711.

Lieutenant Governor, State. — (1836 by original Constitution of the Republic of Texas; 1876 by present Constitution); elective; salary same as Senators when acting as President of Senate, Governor's salary when acting as Governor; (2-yr. by original Constitution, term raised to 4-yr. in 1972, effective 1975): William P. Hobby, Box 12068, Capitol Station, Austin 78711 (1-1-87).

Liquor Control Board. — (See **Alcoholic Beverage Commission.**)

Lower Colorado River Authority. — (See **Colorado River Authority, Lower.**)

Marine Council, Texas Coastal and. — (Abolished by Sunset Commission Sept. 1, 1985.)

Medical Education Board, State Rural. — (1973); apptv.; 6-yr.; per diem and expenses; six members: Dr. Joel H. Johnson, Brenham (2-27-86); Leo L. Westerholm, Port Lavaca (2-27-86); Mrs. Billie Marie Veach, Burnet (2-27-90); Dr. Richard M. Hall, Eden (2-27-90); Chairman, Dr. Sam A. Nixon, Floresville (2-27-88); Lawrence Harmel, Seymour (2-27-88). Executive Director, Duane C. Keeran, Room 310, Southwest Tower Bldg., 211 E. 7th, Austin 78701 (nonmember).

Medical Examiners, State Board of. — (1907 as twelve-member board; membership raised to fifteen in 1981 with addition of three public members); apptv.; 6-yr.; $30 a day on duty; nine members: Dr. Jesse D. Ibarra Jr., Temple (4-13-87); Vice Pres., Dr. James D. Holliday, Mesquite (4-13-87); Dr. M. A. Calabrese, El Paso (4-13-87); Dr. John A. Welty, Harlingen (4-13-85); Dr. James K. Peden, Dallas (4-13-85); President, Dr. Carlos D. Godinez, McAllen (4-13-85); Dr. James W. Lively, Corpus Christi (4-13-85); Sec. Treas., Dr. D. D. Williams, Baytown (4-13-89); Dr. Sol Forman, Galveston (4-13-89); Dr. Susanne Ahn, Dallas (4-13-89); Dr. Robert L. M. Hilliard, San Antonio (4-13-89). Public members: Cindy Jenkins, Stowell (4-13-85); Adele Lucas, Cuero (4-13-87); Bob Crouch, Greenville (4-13-89). Executive Director, Dr. G. V. Brindley, Box 13562, Capitol Sta., Austin 78711 ($47,586). One vacancy.

Medical District Review Committee. — (1977); apptv.; 6-yr.; expenses; twelve members: Dist. 1: Dr. Thomas P. Clarke, Houston (1-15-86); Dr. Herman R. Goehrs, Austin (1-15-86); Dr. Arthur M. Jansa, Houston (1-15-88). Dist. 2: Dr. John W. Nichols, Galena Park (1-15-88). Dist. 2: Dr. Phillip E. Williams Jr., Houston (1-15-86); Dr. Robert G. Haman, Irving (1-15-86); Dr. Clyde Caperton, Bryan (1-15-82). Dist. 3: Dr. Grant F. Begley, Fort Worth (1-15-84); Dr. Wm. G. McGee,

El Paso (1-15-86); Dr. Jesse D. Cone, 318 W. Alleghaney, Odessa 79761 (1-15-88). Dist. 4: Dr. Armando Cuellar, Weslaco (1-15-84); Dr. Harold R. High, Cuero (1-15-88).

Mental Health and Mental Retardation, Texas Department of. — (1965, superseded Board of Texas State Hospitals and Special Schools); apptv.; 6-yr.; per diem and expenses; nine members: Sam F. Rhodes, Dallas (1-31-87); Roger Bateman, Corpus Christi (1-31-87); David M. Shannon, Odessa (1-31-87); Rush H. Record, Houston (1-31-85); Mrs. Marvin Selig, Seguin (1-31-85); L. Gray Beck, San Angelo (1-31-85); Chairman, Richard C. Mills, Waco (1-31-89); Dr. Roberto L. Jimenez, San Antonio (1-31-89); Dr. Grace K. Jameson, Galveston (1-31-89). One vacancy. Commissioner of Mental Health, Gary Miller, Box 12668, Capitol Sta., Austin 78711-2668 (nonmember) ($72,615, plus other emoluments).

Merit System Council. — Abolished as of 9-1-85.

Metric System Council. — Not renewed by Sunset Commission.

Midwestern University, Board of Regents of. — (1959); apptv.; 6-yr.; nine members: Dr. David G. Allen, Wichita Falls (2-25-86); Mrs. Aurora S. Bolin, Wichita Falls (2-25-86); Joe B. Meissner Jr., Wichita Falls (2-25-86); Edward W. Moran Jr., Wichita Falls (2-25-88); Jack L. Russell, Midland (2-25-88); Harold D. Rogers, Wichita Falls (2-25-88); Larry L. Lambert, Wichita Falls (2-25-90); Mrs. Margaret Darden, Dallas (2-25-90); Tom Blakeney Jr., Alvin (2-25-90). President, Louis J. Rodriguez, 3400 Taft, Wichita Falls 76308 (nonmember).

Mining Council, Texas. — (1975); apptv.; 2-yr.; eleven members, as follows: Three representing state commissions, four mining industry and four general public. State commission members: Mack Wallace, Austin (5-8-83); Robert L. Armstrong, Austin (5-8-83); Dr. H. M. Rollins, Austin (5-8-83). Mining industry members: John H. Montgomery, Fairfield (5-8-83); William R. Kelly, El Paso (5-8-83); Franklin W. Daugherty, Alpine (5-8-83); one vacancy. General public members: James Earl Kellum, Arlington (5-8-83); Ed O. Vetter, Dallas (5-8-83); Linton Barbee, Dallas (5-8-83); George M. Hail Jr., Houston (5-8-83).

Morticians, State Board of. — (1903 as State Board of Embalming; 1935 as State Board of Funeral Directors and Embalmers; 1953 as six-member board; membership increased to nine in 1979); apptv.; per diem and expenses; 6-yr.; nine members: James P. Hunter III, Lufkin (5-31-91); Donald H. Taft, Beaumont (5-31-91); T. Grady Baskin Jr., Tyler (1-31-85); James B. Broussard, Beaumont (1-31-87); Dr. Michael Kearl, San Antonio (1-31-87); Mrs. Margaret Ward, Houston (1-31-87); Rev. William T. Stephenson, Dallas (1-31-89); Henry Thomae Sr., San Benito (1-31-89); John W. Amey, Austin (1-31-89). Executive Secretary, John W. Shocklee, 1513 S. IH-35, Austin 78741 (nonmember) ($35,123).

Music Commission, Texas. — (1985); apptv.; 6-yr.; expenses; nine members. (No appointments made when this section printed.)

Motor Vehicle Commission, Texas. — (1971 as six-member board; membership increased to nine in 1979); apptv.; 6-yr.; $25 plus expenses; nine members: Ted D. Treadaway, Richardson (1-31-85); Rudy T. Garza Sr., Corpus Christi (1-31-85); George C. Miller, Lubbock (1-31-85); Mrs. Selma A. Hermann, Alvin (1-31-87); Robert H. Hoy Jr., El Paso (1-31-87); T. M. Demarest Jr., Arlington (1-31-87); John W. Dalton, Houston (1-31-89); Ramsay Gillman, Houston (1-31-89); Bennie W. Bock II, New Braunfels (1-31-89). Executive Director, Russell Harding, Box 2293, Austin 78768 (nonmember) ($46,350).

National Guard Commander, Texas. — (1947); apptv.: Maj. Gen. Willie L. Scott, Austin.

National Guard Armory Board, Texas. — (1935 as three-member board; reorganized as six-member board in 1981); 6-yr.; six members — three from general public and three ex officio members of National Guard. Ex officio members: Brig. Gen. Robert W. McDonald, Allen (4-30-91); Brig. Gen. James B. McGoodwin, Fort Worth (4-30-87); Maj. Gen. Charles H. Kone, La Pryor (4-30-89). Public members: V. C. Eissler, Houston (4-30-89); Hal Boyd, Big Spring (4-30-91); Tom E. Chapoton Jr., Austin (4-30-87). Director, Donald J. Kerr, Box 5218, Austin 78763 (nonmember) ($45,011).

Natural Fibers and Food Protein Commission. — (1941 as Cotton Research Committee; name changed in 1971 and again in 1975); four ex officio members and seven members apptd. to executive advisory committee by chairman with approval of commission members, to serve 2-yr. terms. Ex officio members serve indefinite term. Dr. Mary Evelyn Huey, President, Texas Woman's University, Denton; Dr. Lauro F. Cavazos, President, Texas Tech University, Lubbock; Arthur G. Hansen, Chancellor, A&M University System, College Station; President, University of Texas at Austin. Executive Director, Carl Cox, Box 17360 Coit Rd., Dallas 75252 (nonmember) ($49,543).

Neches River Conservation District, Directors of. — (See Angelina and Neches River Authority.)

Neches River (Upper) Municipal Water Authority, Board of Directors of. — (Est. 1953 as nine-member board; made three-member board in 1959); apptv.; 6-yr.; three members:

President, Gordon B. Broyles, Palestine (1-1-87); Lester Hamilton, Palestine (1-1-85); Ben Swinney, Palestine (1-1-89). General Manager, Roy Douglas, Drawer Y, Palestine 75801 (nonmember).

Neches Valley Authority, Lower, Directors of. — (1933); apptv.; per diem and expenses on duty; 6-yr.; nine members: Joe Broussard II, Beaumont (7-28-89); Dr. William S. Nichols, Woodville (7-28-89); William Doornbos, Nederland (7-28-87); Clyde E. Cole, Silsbee (7-28-87); Ralph A. Leaf, Beaumont (7-28-87); Lee Moore, Port Arthur (7-28-83); F. M. Archer, Woodville (7-28-85); Jack Scott, Port Arthur (7-28-85); Paul Georges, Silsbee (7-28-85). General Manager, J. D. Nixon, Drawer 3464, Beaumont 77704 (nonmember). General Counsel, Josiah Wheat, Box 156, Woodville (nonmember).

Nimitz Memorial Naval Museum Commission, Fleet Adm. Chester W. — (No longer a commission; transferred to State Parks and Wildlife Dept. and known as Adm. Nimitz State Historical Park.)

Nonresident Violator Compact Administrator. — (1981); apptv.; 2-yr.; George Griffin, Austin (2-1-85).

North Texas State University, Board of Regents of. — (1949); apptv.; 6-yr.; nine members: Charles E. Greene, Duncanville (5-22-87); Wayne O. Stockseth, Corpus Christi (5-22-87); Lucille G. Murchison, Dallas (5-22-87); Mrs. Becky Ann Garth, Temple (5-22-89); J. Jack Hays, Dallas (5-22-89); C. Dean Davis, Austin (5-22-89); Mrs. Topsy R. Wright, Grand Prairie (5-22-91); B. Craig Raupe, Granbury (5-22-91); E. Bruce Street Sr., Graham (5-22-91). President, Alfred F. Hurley; Board Secretary, Jan Dobbs, Box 13737, NT Station, Denton 76203-3737 (nonmember).

Nueces River Authority. — (1935 as Nueces River Conservation and Reclamation District; name changed in 1971); apptv.; 6-yr.; per diem and expenses; twenty-one members: Gus T. Canales, Premont (2-1-87); Joseph W. Taylor, Crystal City (2-1-87); William A. Beinhorn Jr., San Antonio (2-1-87); Stevan R. Gallegos, Castroville (2-1-87); Leslie H. Laffere, Uvalde (2-1-87); Harry J. Schulz, Three Rivers (2-1-87); George A. Finley III, Corpus Christi (2-1-87); Charles S. Carr, Crystal City (2-1-89); George Morrill Jr., Beeville (2-1-89); Salvador Almanza, Poteet (2-1-89); Allen Wood, Corpus Christi (2-1-89); William R. Edwards, Corpus Christi (2-1-89); Edward M. Jones, Corpus Christi (2-1-89); Jesse Lockhart Jr., Barksdale (2-1-89); Bob Mullen, Alice (2-1-91); James L. Donnell, Fowlerton (2-1-91); George T. Jambers Jr., Whitsett (2-1-91); S. N. Flores, Mathis (2-1-91); Carl Duncan, Portland (2-1-85); Albert A. Ivy, Carrizo Springs (2-1-91); Roy Martin, Cotulla (2-1-91). Executive Director, Con Mims III, Box 349, Uvalde 78801.

Nurse Examiners, State Board of. — (1909 as six-member board; reorganized and membership increased to nine in 1981 with addition of three public members); apptv.; per diem and expenses; 6-yr.; nine members: Karen G. Barnes-Cure, Temple (1-31-89); Mrs. Claud B. Jacobs, Yoakum (1-31-89); Elizabeth J. Pryor, Fort Worth (1-31-87); Marlene A. Hudgins, Amarillo (1-31-87); Dr. Eileen Jacobi, El Paso (1-31-85); Mrs. Pauline Barnes, Texarkana (1-31-85). Public members: Mrs. Leo Evelyn Johnson, Corpus Christi (1-31-85); Mary E. Jackson, Tyler (1-31-89); Dr. Ruby Lee Morris, Midland (1-31-87). Executive Secretary, Mrs. Margaret L. Rowland, 1300 E. Anderson Lane, Bldg. C., Suite 225, Austin 78752 (nonmember) ($45,423).

Nurse Examiners, State Board of Vocational. — (1951 as nine-member board; membership increased to twelve in 1981); apptv.; 6-yr.; twelve members — one doctor, one registered nurse, one hospital adminstrator, seven licensed vocational nurses and two from general public. Doctor — Dr. Max E. Johnson, San Antonio (9-6-85). Hospital administrator — Ben M. McKibbens, Harlingen (9-6-85). Registered nurse — Mrs. Adelia D. Miller, Whitehouse (9-6-89). Vocational Nurses: Mrs. Linda R. Gambill, Seymour (9-6-89); Mrs. Linda Savannah, Fort Worth (9-6-89); Mrs. Dorothy S. Harris, Victoria (9-6-87); Mrs. E. Kathleen Franklin, Port Arthur (9-6-87); Mrs. Lola Marie Mills, San Angelo (9-6-87); Mrs. Bobbie Jo Haney, Fort Worth (9-6-85); Mrs. Elizabeth Cooper, Wichita Falls (9-6-85). Two from general public — Rafael Acosta, Houston (9-6-89); Lucille Behar, San Antonio (9-6-87). Executive Secretary, Waldeen D. Wilson, 1300 Anderson Lane, Bldg. C., Suite 285, Austin 78752 (nonmember) ($33,166).

Nursing Home Administrators, Texas State Board of Licensure for. — (1969 as six-member board; membership raised to eleven members in 1979); apptv.; per diem and expenses; 6-yr.; eleven members — nine apptv. and two ex officio. Ex officio members: Commissioner of Human Services and Commissioner of Health. Apptv. members: Lillo. Hagan, Tyler (1-31-89); Chairman, Dr. Ed Lefeber, Galveston (1-31-89); Mrs. John E. Watson, Houston (1-31-87); Dr. Clint M. Hines, Newton (1-31-85); Rev. E. Stanley Branch, Houston (1-31-89); Guy E. Shuttlesworth, Smithville (1-31-85); Mrs. Virginia Atkinson, Waco (1-31-89); Mrs. Velda Phelps-Wasson, Pasadena (1-31-89); Mrs. Jean Trebert, Dallas (1-31-89). Executive Director, Dr. Karl E. Bishop, 3407 N. Interregional, Austin 78722 (nonmember) ($29,870).

Occupational Safety Board. — (1967); three members, two ex officio and one apptv. by governor: Ex officio members — Director, Department of Health and Commissioner of Labor and Standards. Apptv. member: 2-year term, $25 per diem plus travel expense: H. L. Kusnetz, Houston (7-17-83). **State Safety Engineer,** Walter G. Martin, Austin (nonmember).

Occupational Therapy, Texas Advisory Board of. — (1983); apptv.; six members — three occupational therapists, one assistant occupational therapist and two from general public; 6-yr.; per diem and expenses: Arthur H. Dilley, Austin (2-1-89); Heidi B. Schoenfield, San Antonio (2-1-89); Mrs. Marianne L. Punchard, Mart (2-1-91); Mrs. Peggy Pickens, Houston (2-1-91); Linda Veale, Abilene (2-1-87); Donald S. Thomas, Austin (2-1-87).

Optometry Board, Texas. — (1921 as six-member State Board of Examiners in Optometry; revised in 1969 and name changed to present form; again revised in 1981 to increase membership to nine with addition of three from general public); apptv.; per diem; 6-yr.; nine members: Dr. Stanley C. Pearle, Dallas (1-31-91); Dr. William D. Pittman, Mexia (1-31-91); Dr. Gene B. Blackwell, Childress (1-31-89); Dr. James B. Thomas, Galveston (1-31-89); Dr. Barry J. Davis, Port Arthur (1-31-89); Dr. John W. Davis, Dallas (1-31-87); Dr. Salvador S. Mora, Laredo (1-31-87). Public members: Marilyn Kay Walls, Cleburne (1-31-85); Gary E. Griffith, Dallas (1-31-87). Executive Director, Mrs. Lois Ewald, 1300 E. Anderson Lane, Suite C-240, Austin 78752 (nonmember) ($32,651).

Pan American University, Board of Regents of. — (1965); apptv.; 6-yr.; nine members: Dr. Rodolfo E. Margo, Weslaco (8-31-85); Ramon Garcia, Edinburg (8-31-85); Robert Shepard, Harlingen (8-31-85); K. E. Schaefer, Brownsville (8-31-87); Eddie R. Cano, McAllen (8-31-87); Melvin J. Hill, Houston (8-31-87); Mrs. Lauryn G. White, Dallas (8-31-89); Mrs. Margaret L. McAllen, Weslaco (8-31-89); Natividad Lopez, Harlingen (8-31-89). President, Miguel A. Nevarez, 1201 W. University, Edinburg 78539 (nonmember).

Pardons and Paroles, Board of. — (1893 as Board of Pardon Advisers; changed in 1936 to present name with three members; membership increased to six in 1983); apptv.; 6-yr.; six members at $52,633: Chairman, Albert Neal Pfeiffer, Austin (Elgin) (1-31-89); Wendell A. Odom, Austin (Pasadena) (1-31-91); Connie Jackson, Austin (Dallas) (1-31-87); Ruben Torres, Austin (Brownsville) (1-31-83); Winona W. Miles, Austin (1-31-91); Antonio Gil Morales, Austin (Fort Worth) (1-31-87). Executive Director, John W. Byrd, Box 13401, Capitol Station, Austin 78711 (nonmember) ($48,719).

Parks and Wildlife Commission, State. — (1963 as three member board; membership increased to six in 1971 and increased to nine in 1983); apptv.; expenses; 6-yr.; nine members: Wm. O. Braecklein, Dallas (2-1-87); Wm. M. Wheless III, Houston (2-1-87); Dr. Ray E. Santos, Lubbock (2-1-87); William L. Graham, Amarillo (2-1-89); Richard R. Morrison III, Houston (2-1-89); George R. Bolin, Houston (2-1-89); Chairman, Edwin L. Cox Jr., Dallas (2-1-91); Robert L. Armstrong, Austin (2-1-91); Antonio R. Sanchez Jr., Laredo (2-1-91). Executive Director, Charles Travis, 4200 Smith School Rd., Austin 78744 (nonmember) ($60,461).

Pecos River Compact Commissioner for Texas. — (1942); apptv.; 2-yr.; expenses: Billy L. Moody, Fort Stockton (1-23-87) ($16,800).

Pension Boards. — For old age, blind and dependent children's assistance, see **Human Services, State Board of.** For unemployment compensation, **Employment Commission, Texas.** For retirement pay to state and municipal employees, see **Retirement.** For teacher retirement, see **Teachers.**

Pension Review Board, State. — (1979); apptv.; 6-yr.; nine members — seven apptd. by Governor; one Representative apptd. by Speaker of House; one Senator apptd. by Lieutenant Governor. Governor's apptees.: Dean Gorham, Austin (1-31-87); Chairman, Norman W. Parrish, Houston (1-31-89); Dr. Robert L. Rouse, Lubbock (1-31-89); Frank Eikenburg, Plano (1-31-89); Robert Parker, Houston (1-31-91); Vice Chmn., James M. Brelsford, Houston (1-31-91); Peggy S. McAdams, Huntsville (1-31-91). Executive Director, Rita Horwitz, Box 13498, Austin 78711 (nonmember) ($36,668).

Pest Control Board, Structural. — (1971 as seven-member board; membership raised to nine in 1979); apptv.; 2-yr.; expenses; nine members — six apptd. by Governor and three ex officio. Ex officio members: Commissioner of Agriculture, Commissioner of Health and head of Entomology Dept., Texas A&M University, College Station. Six apptv. members: Larry A. Esparza, Brownsville (8-30-84); Tommy L. Brown, Fort Worth (8-31-84); Maxine R. Goodman, Lockhart (8-30-84); John P. Mercer, Corpus Christi (8-30-85); Roger P. Maddox, Duncanville (8-30-85); Jim Burns, Houston (8-31-85). Executive Director, David A. Ivie, 1300 E. Anderson Lane, Bldg. C, Ste. 250, Austin 78752 (nonmember) ($45,320).

Pharmacy, State Board of. — (1907 as six-member board; membership increased to nine in 1981); apptv.; 6-yr.; nine

members: Jerry H. Hodge, Amarillo (8-31-87); R. E. Post Jr., Houston (8-31-87); Virginia M. Bauman, Irving (8-31-87); Judy Taylor, Yorktown (8-31-85); Albert Hopkins, Houston (8-31-85); William C. Pittman, Amarillo (8-31-85); William H. Pieratt Jr., Giddings (8-31-89); Mrs. Renee Solis, El Paso (8-31-89); H. Craig Darby, Burleson (8-31-89). Executive Director-Secretary, Fred S. Brinkley Jr., Southwest Tower, Suite 1121, 211 E. 7th, Austin 78701 (nonmember) ($56,238).

Physical Fitness, Governor's Commission on. — (1971); apptv.; 6-yr.; fifteen members: Dr. Richard L. Shorkey, Beaumont (6-13-87); Cissy Woomer, Austin (6-13-87); Dr. Ted L. Edwards, Austin (6-13-87); Chairman, Rollin A. Sininger, Denton (6-13-87); Amanda Bullard, Austin (6-13-87); Vice Chmn., J. Terry Townsend, Austin (6-13-89); Dr. Kenneth H. Cooper, Dallas (6-13-89); A. D. Gearner Jr., Dallas (6-13-89); Dr. William G. Squires Jr., Seguin (6-13-89); Mrs. Patrice McKinney, Colorado City (6-13-89); Neal Spelce, Austin (6-13-85); Diego M. Vacca, San Antonio (6-13-85); Robert P. Higley, Austin (6-13-85); Wm. R. Smith, Houston (6-13-85); Dr. James W. Simmons, San Antonio (6-13-85). Executive Director, A. A. Rooker, 4200 N. Lamar, Suite 110, Austin 78756 (nonmember) ($42,127).

Physical Therapy Examiners, Board of. — (1971); apptv.; 6-yr.; nine members; expenses: Cecilia G. Akers, San Antonio (1-31-91); Richard Tinsley, Houston (1-31-91); Patricia K. Winchester, Midlothian (1-31-91); David A. Hardison, Fredericksburg (1-31-87); Barbara Barton, Manchaca (1-31-87); Henry L. Laird, Amarillo (1-31-87); Betty M. Schocke, Galveston (1-31-89); Vernon Wilson Jr., Houston (1-31-89); Robert Hawkins, Bellmead (1-31-89). Executive Director, Lois M. Smith, 1300 E. Anderson Lane, Bldg. C., Suite 260, Austin 78752 (nonmember) ($25,956).

Plumbing Examiners, State Board of. — (1947 as six-member board; membership increased to nine in 1981 with provision that one member each must be a master plumber, journeyman plumber, plumbing contractor, licensed sanitary engineer and plumbing inspector; two must be building contractors and two from general public); apptv.; expenses; 6-yr.; nine members: William D. Pickens, Houston (journeyman plumber) (9-4-85); Jay Lee Drymalia, Columbus (contractor-commercial) (9-4-89); Edward A. Tschoepe, San Antonio (sanitary engineer) (9-4-87); Vice Chmn., Edward Lee Smith, San Antonio (master plumber) (9-4-87); William G. Wheeler, Victoria (plumbing inspector) (9-4-87); Chairman, Stanley J. Briers, Seabrook (plumbing contractor) (9-4-85); Ronald Gene Goodnight, Killeen (home building contractor) (9-4-89). Two from general public: Mario Estrada, San Antonio (9-4-89); Mervin Phlegm, Houston (9-4-85). Administrator, Lynn Brown, Box 4200, Austin 78765 (nonmember) ($54,487).

Podiatry Examiners, State Board of. — (1923 as six-member State Board of Chiropody Examiners; name changed in 1967, made nine-member board in 1981); apptv.; 6-yr.; expenses; nine members: Dr. Ruth Y. Ackers, Abilene (7-10-85); Dr. Isaac Willis Jr., Longview (7-10-85); Pres., Dr. Jerry W. Patterson, San Antonio (7-10-89); Dr. Ben Clark Jr., Dallas (7-10-89); Dr. R. E. Sciolo, Lubbock (7-10-87); Dr. Marion J. Filippone, Houston (7-10-87). Three public members: Mrs. Johnnie Davis, Odessa (7-10-87); Dr. John T. Donohoo, San Antonio (7-10-85); Perry O. Chrisman, Dallas (7-10-89). Executive Director, J. C. Littrell, 411 W. 13th, Suite 504, Austin 78701 (nonmember) (part-time $15,862).

Polygraph Examiners Board. — (1965); apptv.; 6-yr.; six members: Wm. R. Knight, Midland (6-18-85); William W. Fisher, Houston (6-18-85); William J. Taylor, Round Rock (6-18-87); Charles M. Nelson, Gonzales (6-18-87); Vern L. Thrower, Houston (6-18-89); James E. Hood III, Richardson (6-18-89). System Administrator, Eddie R. Day, Box 4143, Austin 78765 (nonmember) ($28,016).

Preservation Board, State. — (1983); 2-yr.; six members: Three ex officio members: Governor, Lieutenant Governor and Speaker of House; three apptv. members — one apptd. by Governor, one senator apptd. by Lieutenant Governor and one representative apptd. by Speaker. Gov.'s apptee: Lowell Lebermann, Austin (2-1-85). Office Address: Box 13286, Austin 78711.

Printing Board to Approve Contracts for Fuel and Public. — (1876); ex officio; term in other office: Gov. Mark White, Secretary of State Mrs. Myra McDaniel and Comptroller Robert D. Bullock.

Prison Board, Texas. — (See **Corrections, Texas Board of.**)

Private Investigators and Private Security Agencies, Texas Board of. — (1969); apptv.; expenses; 6-yr.; eight members — two ex officio and six apptv. Ex officio members: Director, Department of Public Safety and the Attorney General. Apptv. members: Rev. Harold R. King, Fort Worth (1-31-85); Robert D. Sanders, Dallas (1-31-91); Dale O. Simpson, Dallas (1-31-87); Vice Chmn., George A. Smith Jr., Dallas (1-31-87); John W. Snelson, Houston (1-31-89); Chmn., Roland M. Searcy, Bryan (1-31-89). Executive Director, Mrs. Clema D. Sanders, Box 13509, Capitol Sta., Austin 78711 (nonmember) ($39,140).

Produce Recovery Fund Board. — (1977 as three-member board; membership increased to six in 1981); apptv.; expenses; 6-yr.; six members — two each from commission merchants, general public and producer representative.

Commission merchants: Curt Cargil, Uvalde (1-31-85); N. J. Martino, Houston (1-31-87). Public members: Ronald Osborn, Hereford (1-31-87); Dr. John C. Boling, Raymondville (1-31-83). Producers: Chairman, Wayne A. Showers, McAllen (1-31-83); G. E. Glassford, Laredo (1-31-85).

Prosecutors Council, The. — (1977 as 4-yr., nine-member **Texas Prosecutors' Coordinating Council;** name changed to present form, membership makeup changed and terms raised to 6-yr. in 1981); apptv.; expenses; 6-yr.; nine members: Four apptd. by Governor and five prosecutors elected by their peers. Gov.'s apptees: Ken Epley, San Angelo (12-31-89); Dick W. Hicks, Bandera (12-31-85); Claude J. Kelley Jr., Fredericksburg (12-31-87); Joe L. Schott, Castroville (12-31-85). Executive Director, Andy Shuval, Box 13555, Austin 78711 (nonmember) ($54,500).

Psychologists, Texas State Board of Examiners of. — (1969 as six-member board; membership increased to nine in 1981 with addition of one psychologist's assistant and two members from general public); apptv.; 6-yr.; per diem and expenses; nine members: Dr. Joseph Siegel, Dallas (10-31-87); Dr. J. C. Kobos, San Antonio (10-31-87); Dr. Van Carter Secrest, Fort Worth (10-31-89); Dr. Laurence Abrams, Houston (10-31-89); Dr. Joan S. Anderson, Houston (10-31-85); Dr. Robert P. Anderson, Canyon (10-31-85). Psychological Associate: Macy Kinzel, Corpus Christi (10-31-87). Public members: Mrs. Sidney S. Smith, Austin (10-31-89); Joe D. Robbins, Texarkana (10-31-85). Executive Director, Patricia S. Bizzell, 1300 E. Anderson Lane, Bldg. C, Ste. 270, Austin 78752 ($37,595).

Public Building Authority, the Texas. — (1983); apptv.; 6-yr.; three members; $50 per diem and expenses: Marilyn Jones, San Antonio (2-1-87); Glen Hefner, Houston (2-1-89); Gerald Goff, Austin (2-1-85).

Public Safety Commission. — (1935); apptv.; expenses; 6-yr.; three members: W. C. Perryman, Athens (12-31-85); Ruben R. Cardenas, McAllen (12-31-89); John Fainter Jr., Austin (12-31-87). Director, James B. Adams, Box 4087, Austin 78773 (nonmember) ($66,641).

Public Utility Commission of Texas. — (1975); apptv.; 6-yr.; three members at $60,976: Chairman, Philip F. Ricketts, Austin (8-31-85); Peggy Rosson, El Paso (8-31-87); Dennis L. Thomas, Austin (8-31-89). Executive Director, Jay H. Stewart, 7800 Shoal Creek Blvd., Exchange Park Bldg., Suite 400 N, Austin 78757 (nonmember) ($55,620).

Public Utility Counsel. — (1983); apptv.; 2-yr.: James G. Boyle, Austin (2-1-87) ($60,976).

Public Welfare, State Board of. — (Name changed, see **Human Services, Texas Board of.**)

Purchasing and General Services Commission, State. — (Established 1919 as **Board of Control;** name changed 1979); apptv.; 6-yr.; expenses; three members: Chairman, James R. Collier, Houston (1-31-89); Richard C. Strauss, Dallas (1-31-87); One vacancy. Executive Director, H. A. Foerster, Box 13047, Capitol Station, Austin 78711-3047 (nonmember) ($56,856).

Radiation Advisory Board. — (1961 as 9-member board; membership increased to 18 in 1981); apptv.; 6-yr.; expenses; eighteen members: Dr. Gordon L. Black, El Paso (4-16-85); Ralph L. Buell, Lake Jackson (4-16-85); Dr. Ben DuBilier, Seguin (4-16-85); Russell F. Cash, Pasadena (4-16-89); Douglas B. Owen, Dallas (4-16-89); Dr. Philip C. Johnson Jr., Houston (4-16-89); Dr. Wm. G. McGee, El Paso (4-16-87); Dr. Dan Hightower, Bryan (4-16-87); Howard Drew, Fort Worth (4-16-85); Chairman, Dr. Ed Griffin, Dallas (4-16-87); Dr. John A. Burdine, Houston (4-16-85); George Riddle, Houston (4-16-89); Dr. E. Linn Draper, Beaumont (4-16-89); Robert C. Dunlap Jr., Dallas (4-16-87); Vice Chairman, Mrs. Laura Keever, Houston (4-16-83); William A. Hendrick, Austin (4-16-85); Two vacancies.

Radioactive Waste Disposal Authority, Texas Low-Level. — (1981); apptv.; 6-yr.; six members; expenses. Membership composed of one medical doctor, one health physicist, one attorney, one geologist and two from general public: Vice Chmn., John E. Simek, Bryan (health physicist) (2-1-89); Dr. Robert L. Clement, Austin (doctor) (2-1-89); Chairman, Dr. William L. Fisher, Austin (geologist) (2-1-87); James P. Allison, Austin (attorney) (2-1-91); Dr. Elbert Wharton, Galveston (public member) (2-1-91); Jim R. Phillips, El Paso (public member) (2-1-87). General Manager, Lawrence R. Jacobi Jr., 1300-C E. Anderson Lane, Ste. 175, Austin 78752 (nonmember) ($58,504).

Railroad Commission of Texas. — (1891); elective; 6-yr.; ($72,233); three members: James E. Nugent, Austin (Kerrville) (12-31-88); Mack Wallace, Austin (Athens) (12-31-90); Chairman, Buddy Temple, Austin (Lufkin) (12-31-86). Drawer 12967, Austin 78711 (nonmember).

Real Estate Commission, Texas. — (1949 as six member board; membership increased to nine in 1979) apptv.; per diem and expenses; 6-yr.; nine members: Michael N. Wieland, El Paso (1-31-91); Billie Heffner, Burleson (1-31-91); Joshua Morriss Jr., Texarkana (1-31-85); W. N. Moseley, Houston (1-31-87); Frank Tompkins, Corpus Christi (1-31-87); Gene Stimmel, Bedford (1-31-87); Mrs. Rachel Perelman, Brownsville (1-31-89); David Cook, Houston (1-31-89);

Robert H. Bliss, Dallas (1-31-89). Administrator, Wallace Collins, Box 12188, Capitol Station, Austin 78711 (nonmember) ($48,925).

Real Estate Research Advisory Committee. — (1971); apptv.; 6-yr.; nine apptv. and one ex-officio member: Ex officio member represents **Texas Real Estate Commission.** Apptv. members: Bill Jennings, Fort Worth (1-31-91); David Stirton, Houston (1-31-91); Frederick D. McClure, San Augustine (1-31-91); Lawrence Miller Jr., Dallas (1-31-87); David L. Fair, Dallas (1-31-87); Benny McMahan, Dallas (1-31-87); Patsy Bohannan, Midland (1-31-89); Mrs. Doris Farmer, Longview (1-31-89); James Fatheree, Richmond (1-31-89). Director, Richard L. Floyd, Texas Real Estate Research Center, Texas A&M, College Station 77843.

Records Preservation Advisory Committee. — (1965); apptv.; ex officio term in other office; eight members: Chairman, Dorman H. Winfrey, Texas State Librarian; Robert B. Fitzgerald, Texas State Library; Sec. of State Mrs. Myra McDaniel; State Auditor Lawrence F. Alwin; State Comptroller Robert D. Bullock; Atty. Gen. Jim Mattox; Sec. of the Senate, Betty King; Chief Clerk of the House, Betty Murray.

Redistricting Board, Legislative. — (See **Legislative.**)

Red River Authority of Texas. — (1959); apptv.; 6-yr.; per diem and expenses; nine members: Robert L. Bliss, Friona (8-11-85); J. W. Campbell, Pampa (8-11-85); Albert B. Wharton III, Vernon (8-11-85); William H. Summers, Whitewright (8-11-83); Charles Moorehead, Canadian (8-11-89); Alvin L. Barnes, Wichita Falls (8-11-89); John R. Armstrong, Bonham (8-11-87); Austin T. Guest, Clarksville (8-11-87); Wales Madden III, Amarillo (8-11-87). General Manager, Fred Parkey, 302 Hamilton Bldg., Wichita Falls 76301 (nonmember).

Red River Compact Commissioner. — (1949); apptv.; 4-yr.; (his functions are to negotiate with other states respecting waters of the Red. See also **Canadian River Compact Commission** and **Caddo Lake Compact Commission**): Kenneth E. Nelson, 231 Leda Dr. Dallas (2-1-85) ($22,400).

Rehabilitation Commission, Texas. — (1969); apptv.; expenses; 6-yr.; six members: Wendell D. Faulkner, Pecos (8-31-89); Ernestine Washington, Beaumont (8-31-89); Dr. Anne R. Race, Dallas (8-31-85); Dr. George H. McCullough, Fort Worth (8-31-85); William C. Morrow, Midland (8-31-87); Chairman, Jerry Kane, Corpus Christi (8-31-87). **Commissioner,** Vernon M. Arrell, 118 E. Riverside Dr., Austin 78704 (nonmember) ($65,199).

Retirement System, Municipal, Board of Trustees. — (1947); apptv.; 6-yr.; expenses; six members: Three executive trustees — Leland D. Nelson, Dallas (1-31-87); Don Cates, Amarillo (1-31-91); Virgil C. Gray, Brownwood (1-31-89); David B. Brinson, Port Arthur (1-31-87); Ernest M. Briones, Corpus Christi (1-31-89); Charles E. Wilson, Waco (1-31-91). Executive Director, Jimmie L. Mormon, Box 2225, Austin 78768 (nonmember).

Retirement System, Texas County and District, Board of Trustees. — (1967); apptv.; 6-yr.; nine members: Norment Foley, Uvalde (12-31-83); Carl Smith, Houston (12-31-85); Wilburn C. Rust, Austin (12-31-85); Bill D. Hicks, Odessa (12-31-85); Joan H. Cason, Nacogdoches (12-31-87); Winston C. Reagan, Athens (12-31-87); David Chappell, Corpus Christi (12-31-87); John P. Gayle Jr., West Columbia (12-13-89); Jack Treadway, Houston (12-31-89). Executive Director, J. Robert Brown, 400 W. 14th, Austin 78701 (nonmember).

Retirement System of Texas, Employees. — (1947); apptv.; 6-yr.; six members; one is apptd. by the Governor, one by the Chief Justice of State Supreme Court and one by Speaker of the House; and three are employee members of the system serving 6-yr. overlapping terms. Apptd. by Governor: Gary R. Rodgers, Austin (8-31-88). Apptd. by Speaker of House: B. L. Parker, Austin (8-31-90). Apptd. by Chief Justice Supreme Court: Jack D. Kyle, Huntsville (8-31-86). Three elected members: Chairman, Marcus L. Yancey Jr., State Highway Department, Austin (8-31-87); Maurice Beckham, Austin (8-31-89); Pamela A. Carley, Austin (8-31-87). Executive Director, Clayton T. Garrison, Box 13207, Capitol Sta., Austin 78711 (nonmember).

Retirement System, Teachers, Board of. — (See **Teachers Retirement System, Board of.**)

Rio Grande Compact Commissioner for Texas. — (1929); apptv.; 2-yr.: Jesse B. Gilmer, El Paso (6-9-85) ($34,200).

Rio Grande Valley Municipal Water Authority. — (1969); apptv.; 2-yr.; nine members: Paul G. Veale, McAllen (4-30-84); W. W. Scurlock, McAllen (4-30-84); William F. Powell, Weslaco (4-30-84); I. G. Gutierrez, Rio Grande City (4-30-83); Juan Garcia, Lyford (4-30-81); Reynaldo L. Lopez, Brownsville (4-30-85); Dr. Joseph B. Coutler, Brownsville (4-30-85); Sam Risica, Edinburg (4-30-83). (One vacancy.)

Road Bond Indebtedness, Board of County and District. — (See **Indebtedness, Board of County and District Road Bond.**)

Runnels County Water Authority. — (1955); apptv.; 6-yr.; nine members: President, Arnold Frerich, Rowena (1-1-87); Vice President, Ray Alderman, Winters (1-1-87); Secretary-Treasurer, James J. Mueller, Ballinger (1-1-85); Barney C. Puckett, Winters (1-1-85); George A. Ruppert, Rowena (1-1-85); Charles T. Boecking, Ballinger (1-1-89); E. E. Thormeyer, Winters (1-1-89); Elliott J. Kemp, Ballinger (1-1-87); Wesley M. Hays, Winters (1-1-89).

Sabine River Authority. — (1949); apptv.; per diem and expenses; 6-yr.; nine members: O. V. Joffrion, Carthage (7-6-85); L. E. Davis, Hemphill (7-6-85); John H. Butts, San Augustine, (7-6-85); James E. Campbell, Center (7-6-89); C. C. Rice, Hemphill (7-6-89); Juan D. Nichols, Quitman (7-6-89); William J. Butler, Orange (7-6-87); H. M. Smotherman, Tyler (7-6-87); William Y. Rice, Longview (7-6-87). Executive Vice President and General Manager, John W. Simmons, Box 579, Orange 77630 (nonmember).

Sabine River Compact Commission. — (1953); apptv.; five members: One member and chairman apptd. by President of United States without a vote; two from Texas and two from Louisiana. Texas members: David Cardner, Orange (7-12-86); Jim Tom McMahon, Newton (7-12-89) ($3,700).

San Antonio River Authority. — (1937); elected; $100 a meeting and expenses; six from Bexar County and two each from Wilson, Karnes and Goliad Counties; 6-yr.; 12 members: Paul K. Herder, San Antonio (2-1-91); Chmn., Cecil W. Bain, San Antonio (2-1-91); David Evans, San Antonio (2-1-87); Allan B. Polunsky, San Antonio (2-1-87); Walter W. McAllister III, San Antonio (2-1-89); Martha C. McNeel, San Antonio (2-1-89); R. H. Ramsey Jr., Goliad (2-1-89); Vice Chmn., Truett Hunt, Kenedy (2-1-89); Hugh B. Ruckman Jr., Karnes City (2-1-91); J. C. Turner, Floresville (2-1-91); W. W. Lorenz, Stockdale (2-1-91); Mrs. William G. McCampbell Jr., Goliad (2-1-91). General Manager, Fred N. Pfeiffer, Box 9284, San Antonio 78204 (nonmember) ($68,250).

San Jacinto Historical Advisory Board. — (1907 as San Jacinto State Park Commission; changed to San Jacinto Battleground Commission and changed again in 1965 to present name); apptv.; 6-yr.; five members — two ex officio: Director, Parks Division, Parks and Wildlife Department and president of San Jacinto Museum of History Assn. Three apptd. by Governor: Mrs. Ward N. Adkins, Houston (9-1-85); Miss Lennie E. Hunt, Houston (9-1-87); Frank W. Calhoun, Houston (9-1-89).

San Jacinto River Authority, Board of Directors of. — (1937); apptv.; expenses while on duty; 6-yr.; six members: Vice President, E. Davis Hailey, Conroe (10-16-87); Frank E. Nadolney, Houston (10-16-89); President, D. F. McAdams Jr., Huntsville (10-16-85); Secretary, Oliver Kneisley, Conroe (10-16-87); Varreece Berry, Pasadena (10-16-85); Treasurer, Gilbert M. Turner, Houston (10-16-89). General Manager, Jack K. Ayer, Box 329, Conroe 77305 (nonmember).

Savings and Loan Commissioner. — Apptv. by State Finance Commission: Linton Bowman III, Box 1089, Austin 78767 ($77,250).

Secretary of State. — (1836 by Constitution of Republic of Texas, 1876 by present Constitution); apptv.: Mrs. Myra McDaniel, Box 12887, Capitol Station, Austin 78711-2887 ($64,890).

Securities Board, State. — (Est. 1957, the outgrowth of several amendments to the Texas Securities Act, originally passed in 1913); act is administered by the **Securities Commissioner** who is appointed by the board members who have six-year terms; expenses; Chairman, Alan D. Feld, Austin (Dallas) (1-15-91); Robert K. Uttley III, Temple (1-15-89); Hal M. Bateman, Lubbock (1-15-87). **Securities Commissioner,** Richard D. Latham, Box 13167, Capitol Station, Austin 78711 ($55,929).

Seed and Plant Board, State. — (1959); apptv.; 2-yr.; six members: J. Owen Gilbreath, Gladewater (10-6-84); Eddie Lee Thompson, Waco (10-6-84); Kenneth W. Boatwright, Austin (10-6-84); Ray Joe Riley, Hart (10-6-85); Vice Chmn., Dr. David Koeppe, Lubbock (10-6-85); Chairman, Dr. E. C. A. Runge, College Station (10-6-85).

Sex Offender Treatment, Interagency Council on. — (1983); ex officio and apptv.; twelve members — nine ex officio; three apptv. by Governor. Ex officio members: One each from Texas Department of Corrections, Board of Pardons and Paroles, Texas Adult Probation Commission, Texas Juvenile Probation Commission, Texas Department of Mental Health and Mental Retardation, Texas Youth Council, Sam Houston State University, Texas Department of Human Services and one member of Governor's office administering criminal justice planning; three apptv. from general public; 6-yr.; expenses. Apptv. members: Collier M. Cole, Dickinson (2-1-91); Michael Cox, Houston (2-1-87); Mrs. Jan Marie Delipsey, Dallas (2-1-89).

Soil and Water Conservation Board, Texas State. — (1939); elected by convention in each of five state districts created by State Soil Conservation Act; 2-yr.; per diem and expenses; five members: Dist. 1, J. Frank Gray, Lubbock; Dist. 2, Joe Antilley, Abilene; Dist. 3, C. F. Schendel, Goliad; Dist. 4, Albert Roach, Paris; Dist. 5, Hermon L. Petty, Mineral Wells. Executive Director, Harvey D. Davis, 311 N. 5th, Temple 76503 (nonmember) ($44,908).

Speech Pathology and Audiology, State Committee of Examiners on. — (1983); apptv.; nine members — three audiologists, three speech-language pathologists and three from general public; 6-yr.; per diem and expenses: Karen Jones Howard, Abilene (8-31-89); Steven D. Schaefer, Dallas (8-31-89); Dr. Kathryn S. Stream, Denton (8-31-89); Dr. Mary Lovey Wood, Austin (8-31-87); Susan G. N. Dorsett, Stephenville (8-31-87); Sue D. Rosenzweig, Houston (8-31-87); Harold G. Beaver, Holland (8-31-85); Mrs. Vatra Solomon, Mt. Vernon (8-31-85); One vacancy.

State Board (Commission, Bureau) of. — (Note: in most instances state agencies are alphabetized under key reference word, as, Accountancy, State Board of.)

State-Federal Relations, Division of. — (1965); apptv.; term same as Governor's. Director, John Hanson, Room 207, Sam Houston Bldg., Austin 78701 ($51,191).

State Property Tax Board. — (1977 as School Tax Assessment Practices Board; name changed in 1980); apptv.; 6-yr.; six members; expenses: Stephen T. Jordan, Farmers Branch (3-1-85); Chairman, Wm. B. Munson IV, San Antonio (3-1-85); Marvin L. Jones, Spearman (3-1-87); William J. Burnett, San Antonio (3-1-87); Ciro Trevino, Edinburg (3-1-89); Nicholas V. Lampson, Beaumont (3-1-89). Executive Director, Ron Patterson, Box 15900, Austin 78761 (nonmember) ($59,122).

State Railroad, Board of Managers of. — (1921; revised 1953); apptv. by Governor; expenses; 6-yr.; three members: Wayne C. Sellers, Palestine; O. V. Mullins, Henderson; Chairman, N. S. Petty, Garland.

State Senior Colleges, Board of Regents of. — (See Texas State University System, Board of Regents of.)

Stephen F. Austin University, Board of Regents of. — (1969); apptv.; expenses; 6-yr.; nine members: Homer Bryce, Henderson (1-31-87); David L. Jackson, Plano (1-31-87); William F. Garner Jr., Bridge City (1-31-87); John O. Sutton, Nacogdoches (1-31-91); Dan Haynes, Burnet, (1-31-91); Richard C. Hile, Jasper (1-31-91); Phil Simpson, Dallas (1-31-89); Mrs. Willia B. Murphy, Crockett (1-31-89); Luke S. Honea, Wildwood (1-31-89).

Student Loan Corporation, Texas Guaranteed. — (1979); apptv. and ex officio; 6-yr.; eleven members — eight apptd. by Governor; one ex officio, Comptroller of Public Accounts; one apptd. by Commissioner of Higher Education and one apptd. by Chairman of Coordinating Board. Gov.'s. apptees: Gary W. Bruner, Dallas (1-31-87); Mrs. Shirley Binder, Austin (1-31-87); Wm. H. Schroeder Jr., Lockhart (1-31-89); Hulen M. Davis Sr., Prairie View (1-31-89); John R. Schott, San Marcos (1-31-89); Dr. Lawrence K. Pettit, Kingsville (1-31-91); George M. Crews, Bedford (1-31-91); George Verduzco, Laredo (1-31-91). Executive Director, Joe L. McCormick, Box 15996, Austin 78761 (nonmember).

Surplus Property Agency, Texas. — (1945 as Texas State Educational Agency for Surplus Property; name changed to present form 1949); apptv.; 6-yr.; expenses; nine members: William C. English, Kingsville (3-19-87); Garland P. Ferguson, Gladewater (3-19-87); Raymond R. Brimble, Houston (3-19-89); Charles L. Slaton, Lubbock (3-19-89); Robert A. Lansford, Austin (3-19-89); Chairman, Wm. H. Borchers, New Braunfels (3-19-85); Gerald D. Irons, The Woodlands (3-19-85); A. Max Scheid, Garland (3-19-85); One vacancy. Executive Director, Marvin J. Titzman, Box 8120, Wainwright Station, San Antonio 78208-0120 (nonmember).

Tax Professional Examiners, Board of. — (1977 as **Board of Tax Assessor Examiners;** name changed to present form 1983); apptv.; expenses; 6-yr.; six members: Frances Shuffield, Midland (3-1-87); Joel D. Whitmire, Richmond (3-1-87); E. P. Laurel, Laredo (3-1-89); Ray M. Cornett, Angleton (3-1-89); Roy B. Sinclair, Lufkin (3-1-85); Robert C. Willis, Livingston (3-1-85). Executive Director, Sam H. Smith, Box 15920, Austin 78761 (nonmember) ($38,213).

Tax Board, State. — (1905); ex officio; term in other office; no compensation; three members: Comptroller Robert D. Bullock, Secretary of State Mrs. Myra McDaniel and State Treasurer Ann Richards.

Teachers College, State Board of Regents of. — (See Texas State University System.)

Teachers' Professional Practices Commission. — (1969); apptv.; expenses; 2-yr.; fifteen members: Ms. Jeretta Thompson, Carthage (8-31-86); Dr. Andy Nutt, Beckville (8-31-86); Jose Salgado, El Paso (8-31-85); Yolanda Villarreal, Robstown (8-31-85); Mrs. Kathryn White, Arlington (8-31-85); Pete DeHoyos, Del Rio (8-31-85); Jeff Sanders, Uvalde (8-31-85); Thomas J. Cleaver, Prairie View (8-31-85); Mrs. Verma Russell, Fort Worth (8-31-85); Louise Daniel, Amarillo (8-31-85); Mrs. Marva Miller, Houston (8-31-85); Jack Davidson, Tyler (8-31-85); Edward Wilson, Abilene (8-31-85); Ron Reaves, San Antonio (8-31-85); Bernard Jackson, Houston (8-31-85).

Teacher Retirement System of Texas, Board of Trustees to Administer. — (1937 as six-member board; membership increased to nine in 1973); expenses; 6-yr.; nine members — two apptd. by State Board of Education, three apptd. by Governor and four TRS members apptd. by Governor after being nominated by popular ballot of the members of the retirement system, one of these four to be a retired member and another to be a member from higher education. Apptd. by Governor from nominees of Retirement System: C. A. Roberson, Fort Worth (8-31-87); Mary W. Kasting, Copperas Cove (8-31-89); Mrs. Sheila J. Payne, Arlington (8-31-85); Frank Monroe, Dallas (8-31-87) retired member. Apptd. by State Board of Education: Robert R. Ashworth, Amarillo (8-31-87); Dr. George M. Crowson, Houston (8-31-89). Apptd. by Governor: Edward H. Wicker, Beeville (8-31-85); Henry M. Bell Jr., Tyler (8-31-89); Don Houseman, Dallas (8-31-87). Executive Secretary, Bruce Hineman, 1001 Trinity, Austin 78701 (nonmember) ($65,000).

Technology Training Board. — (1985); apptv. by respective organizations; 2-yr.; eight members: three members of Texas Economic Development Commission; two members of State Job Training Coordinating Council; one member of board of regents of Texas State Technical Institute; one member of Coordinating Board of Texas College and University System; one member of State Board of Education.

Texas A&I University at Kingsville, Board of Directors of. — (See University System of South Texas.)

Texas Development Board. — (1959); three members: Gov. Mark White, Austin; Chairman Texas Industrial Commission and Chairman of Texas Highways and Public Transportation Commission.

Texas 1986 Sesquicentennial Commission. — (1979; Will dissolve on 8-31-87; unexpired terms will also end on that date); apptv.; 6-yr.; 26 members as follows: Nine apptd. by Governor, three each by Speaker of House of Representatives and Lieutenant Governor, and eleven ex officio. Ex officio members: Executive Director of Texas Tourist Development Agency; Executive Director Texas Historical Commission; Executive Director Texas Commission on the Arts and Humanities; Executive Director Texas Film Commission; Executive Director Texas State Library and Archives Commission; Executive Director Texas State Historical Association; Director of Travel Division of Texas Department Highways and Public Transportation; Executive Director Institute of Texan Cultures; Executive Vice President General Manager State Fair of Texas; executive head East Texas Historical Association; and Panhandle-Plains Historical Museum. Governor's appointees: Dr. Robert H. Wilson, Dallas (1-31-87); Ann Quirk, San Antonio (1-31-87); Calvin Guest, Bryan (1-31-91); Jim D. Bowmer, Killeen (1-31-91); Mrs. Omar Harvey, Dallas (1-31-87); Bob Bowman, Tyler (1-31-91); Chris Semos, Dallas (1-31-87); Beverly Cummings, Houston (1-31-89); Chairwoman Mrs. Emmie Craddock, San Marcos (1-31-89). Apptd. by Speaker of House: Gib Lewis, Fort Worth (1-31-87); Rep. Al Luna, Houston (1-31-87); and Rep. Wilhelmina Delco, Austin (1-31-87). Apptd. by Lieutenant Governor: Sen. Tati Santiesteban, El Paso (1-31-85); Sen. O. H. "Ike" Harris, Dallas (1-31-83); Sen. Craig Washington, Houston (1-31-87). Executive Director, Lynn Nabers, P.O. Box 1986, Austin 78767 (nonmember) ($34,299).

Texas Sesquicentennial Museum Board. — Abolished by Legislature in 1983.

Texas Southern University, Board of Regents of. — (1947); expenses; 6-yr.; nine members: Percy P. Creuzot, Houston (2-1-87); Randal B. McDonald, Houston (2-1-87); Mrs. Naomi Andrews, Houston (2-1-87); James C. Belt Jr., Dallas (2-1-91); Milton Carroll, Missouri City (2-1-91); Andrew R. Melontree, Tyler (2-1-89); Arthur Gaines Jr., Houston (2-1-89); Dr. Larry Greenfield, Houston (2-1-89); Larry R. Veselka, Houston (2-1-91). President, Dr. Leonard Spearman, 3100 Cleburne, Houston 77004 (nonmember).

Texas State Board, Commission, Bureau of. — (In most instances, agencies are alphabetized under key reference word, as Pharmacy, State Board of.)

Texas State Technical Institute, Board of Regents for. — (1969); apptv.; expenses; 6-yr.; nine members: Gerald D. Phariss, Seagoville (8-31-89); Ed Aiken Jr., Sweetwater (8-31-89); H. Gene Evans, Waco (8-31-89); Chairman, L. Hinojosa, Mercedes (8-31-85); Jesse S. Harris, Dallas (8-31-85); Ralph A. Lowenfield, El Paso (8-31-85); F. Herman Coleman, Waco (8-31-87); J. A. Besselman, Amarillo (8-31-87); R. T. Dosher Jr., Dallas (8-31-87). President, Jack Tompkins, TSTI System, Waco 76705 (nonmember).

Texas State University System, Board of Regents of the. — (1911 as Board of Regents of State Teachers Colleges; name changed in 1965 to Board of Regents of State Senior Colleges; changed again to present form in 1975); apptv.; per diem and expenses; 6-yr.; nine members: John S. Cargile, San Angelo (2-1-87); W. C. Perry, Waco (2-1-87); Bernard G. Johnson, Houston (2-1-87); Philip G. Warner, Houston (2-1-91); Jack L. Martin, Austin (2-1-91); Edmund M. Longcope, San Marcos (2-1-91); Ruben M. Escobedo, San Antonio (2-1-89); Katherine S. Lowry, Austin (2-1-89); Lee Drain, Dallas (2-1-89). Executive Director, Lamar G. Urbanovsky, 505 Sam Houston Bldg., Austin 78701 (nonmember).

Texas Tech University, Board of Regents of. — (1923); apptv.; expenses; 6-yr.; nine members: Gerald Ford, Dallas (1-31-89); Wesley Masters, Amarillo (1-3-89); Larry Johnson, Houston (1-31-89); Wendell Mayes Jr., Austin (1-31-91); Dr. Wm. G. McGee, El Paso (1-31-91); J. Fred Bucy Jr., Dallas (1-31-91); Anne W. Sowell, Fort Worth (1-31-87); Rex P. Fuller, Lubbock (1-31-87); John E. Birdwell Jr., Lubbock (1-31-87). President, Lauro F. Cavazos, Box 4349, Lubbock 79409 (nonmember).

Texas Tourist Development Agency. — (1963 as 6-member board of advisers; made independent board and membership increased to nine members in 1969; apptv.; expenses; 6-yr.; nine members: Gordon Wynne Jr., Wills Point (8-23-87); Mrs. Virginia M. Eggers, Dallas (8-23-87); Mrs. Margaret M. Martin, Austin (8-23-87); D. J. Bernardi Jr., El Paso (8-23-85); Wm. E. Ochse, San Antonio (8-23-85); Susan S. Richardson, Amarillo (8-23-85); Paul E. Pendergast, Ir-

ving (8-23-89); Richard E. Phillips, San Marcos (8-23-89); R. C. Richards Jr., McAllen (8-23-89). Executive Director, Larry Todd, 1032 Stephen F. Austin State Office Bldg., Austin 78711 (nonmember) ($45,732).

Texas Woman's University, Board of Regents of. — (1901); apptv.; expenses; 6-yr.; nine members: Mrs. Frances H. Chiles, Fort Worth (1-10-87); Chairman, Margaret E. Davis, Irving (1-10-87); Mrs. June Page Johnson, Austin (2-1-87); Elizabeth B. Sellers, Houston (1-10-89); LaVonne P. Mason, Austin (1-10-89); Roland Boyd, McKinney (1-10-89); Mrs. Lavonne Unsell, Fort Worth (2-1-91); Richard White Jr., Houston (2-1-91); Mrs. Mary Beth Scull, Lubbock (2-1-91). President, Mary Evelyn Huey, Box 23925, TWU Station, Denton 76204 (nonmember).

Textbook Committee, State. — (1929 as Textbook Advisory Committee; under Gilmer-Aikin Act of 1949 name changed to present form); apptd. by State Board of Education and is recommended by Commissioner of Education; 1-yr.; fifteen members: Margaret A. Anderson, El Paso; Anita C. Arnold, San Antonio; Cathy A. Beicker, Seguin; Lou A. Davis, Klein; Billie J. Love, Amarillo; Carol A. Greaney, Galveston; Shirley Heard, Terrell; Georgeann V. Johnston, Hallsville; Carla J. Parrish, Irving; S. Don Rogers, Austin; Arlene H. Ruffin, Dallas; Susan C. Smith, Edinburg; Bill R. Tittle, Abilene; Edwyna Wheadon, Houston; James D. White, Denton.

Trade Council, Texas World. — (1985); expenses; 15 members — four ex officio; term in other office; 11 apptd. by Governor to 2-yr. terms: one from small export business, two from institutions of higher education, six from international commerce, one chairman of North Texas District Export Council, one chairman of South Texas District Export Council. (No appointments made at press time).

Treasurer, State. — (1835 by Provisional Government of Texas, 1876 by present Constitution); elective; (2-yr. by original constitutional provision; raised to 4-yr. in 1972, effective 1975: Ann Richards, Box 12608, Capitol Station, Austin 78711 (1-1-87) ($72,233).

Tri-County Municipal Water District. — (1955); 2-yr.; apptv.: W. W. Siddons Jr., Hillsboro, director-at-large apptd. by Governor.

Trinity River Authority of Texas. — (1955); apptv.; twenty-four directors — three from Tarrant County, four from Dallas County, two from area-at-large and one each from fifteen other districts; per diem and expenses; 6-yr.: Roger Hunsaker, Fort Worth (3-15-87); T. W. Erwin III, Ennis (3-15-87); F. L. Thompson, Leona (3-15-87); John W. Rhea Jr., Dallas (3-15-87); Tommy W. Hollis, Coldspring (3-15-87); Edward Nash, Kaufman (3-15-87); Joe Scott Evans, Groveton (3-15-87); John R. Parten, Madisonville (3-15-87); Vice Pres., Blake Gillen, Corsicana (3-15-85); A. W. Cullum III, Dallas (3-15-85); J. C. Payton, Euless (3-15-85); B. C. Lively, Livingston (3-15-85); R. E. Palm, Fort Worth (3-15-85); Robert T. Maddox, Crockett (3-15-85); John G. Middleton, Wallisville (3-15-85); Vice President, B. Michael Cummings, Fort Worth (3-15-85); J. L. Conner, Dayton (3-15-89); Mrs. Helen M. Hooper, Palestine (3-15-89); Charles A. Hunter, Dallas (3-15-89); Donald R. Cutler, Duncanville (3-15-89); Howard C. Brants Jr., Fort Worth (3-15-89); Thomas C. Letts, Huntsville (3-15-89); Suel Hill, Fairfield (3-15-89); Bruce Smith, Kemp (3-15-89). General Manager, Danny F. Vance, Box 60, Arlington 76010 (nonmember).

Turnpike (Toll Road) Authority, Texas. — (1953 as nine-member board; increased to twelve members in 1971); 6-yr.; twelve members — nine apptv. and three ex officio; ex officio members are three members of the State Highway and Public Transportation Commission (see Highway Commission in this list); apptv. members: S. Frank Holt III, Dallas (2-15-87); Chairman, John P. Thompson, Dallas (2-15-87); Jerry H. Deutser, Houston (2-15-87); Jack Dulworth, Houston (2-15-85); Clive Runnels, Houston (2-15-85); Walter M. Mischer Sr., Houston (2-15-85); C. C. Smitherman, Houston (2-15-89); R. J. Lindley Jr., Houston (2-15-89); Royce B. West, Dallas (2-15-89). Engineer-Manager, H. M. Reily (nonmember); Secretary-Treasurer, Harry Kabler, Box 190369, Dallas 75219 (nonmember).

University of Houston, Board of Regents of. — (1963); apptv.; expenses; 6-yr.; nine members: Charles B. Marino, Houston (9-1-85); Wm. A. Kistler Jr., Houston (9-1-85); Xavier C. Lemond, Katy (9-1-85); Chester B. Benge Jr., Houston (9-1-87); Chairman, James E. Kolb, Houston (9-1-87); Leonard Rauch, Houston (9-1-87); Mrs. Debbie Hanna, Austin (9-1-89); Jose Molina, Houston (9-1-89); Don A. Sanders, Houston (9-1-89). President, Charles E. Bishop, 4600 Gulf Fwy., Suite 500, Houston 77023 (nonmember).

University of Texas System, Board of Regents of the. — (1881); apptv.; expenses; 6-yr.; nine members: Tom B. Rhodes, Dallas (1-10-87); Mrs. Dolph Briscoe, Uvalde (1-10-87); Mr. Beryl E. Milburn, Austin (1-10-87); Shannon Ratliff, Austin (1-10-91); Jack Blanton, Houston (1-10-91); W. F. Roden, Midland (1-10-91); Chairman, Jess Hay, Dallas (1-10-89); Mario Yzaguirre, Brownsville (1-10-89); Robert B. Baldwin III, Austin (1-10-89). Chancellor, E. D. Walker; Secretary, Betty Anne Thedford, 601 Colorado, Austin 78701 (nonmembers).

Gov. Mark White administers oath of office to Paul Hopkins as his wife, Jerri, looks on. Hopkins is a member of the Texas Water Commission. Associated Press Photo

University of Texas at Tyler, Board of Regents of. — (1971 as Tyler State College Board of Regents; name changed in 1975 to Texas Eastern University; changed in 1979 to present form and is now administered by the University of Texas Board of Regents.)

University System of South Texas, Board of Directors of the. — (1929 as College of Arts & Industries; name changed in 1967 to Texas A&I University of Kingsville; changed to present name in 1977); apptv.; 6-yr.; nine members: Wm. M. Pena, Houston (8-31-85); Mrs. Radcliffe Killam, Laredo (8-31-85) ; President, Ricardo Gutierrez, Rio Grande City (8-31-85); Blas M. Martinez, Laredo (8-31-89); Gilbert Acuna, Kingsville (8-31-89); Wayne H. King, San Antonio (8-31-89); Mrs. Paul R. Haas, Corpus Christi (8-31-87); Clemente Garcia, Corpus Christi (8-31-87); Mrs. Richard M. Kleberg Jr., Kingsville (8-31-87); Chancellor, Lawrence K. Pettit, Box 1238, Kingsville 78363 (nonmember).

Vehicle Equipment Safety Commissioner. — (1965); apptv.: George W. Busby, Department of Public Safety, Austin.

Veterans Commission, Texas. — (1927 as Veterans State Service Office; reorganized as Veterans Affairs Commission 1947 with five members; membership increased to six in 1981 with addition of one disabled veteran as a member; name changed to Texas Veterans Commission in 1985); apptv.; 6-yr.; per diem while on duty and expenses; six members: Jack W. Flynt, Dimmitt (12-31-85); Arturo T. Benavides, Bruni (12-31-83); Robert J. Lyons, Vidor (12-31-87); John E. McKelvey, Electra (12-31-87); Samuel Bier, Austin (disabled veteran member) (12-31-85); One vacancy. Executive Director, Aubrey L. Bullard, Box 12277, Capitol Station, Austin 78711 (nonmember) ($46,041).

Veterinary Medical Examiners, State Board of. — (1911; revised 1953; made nine-member board in 1981); apptv.; expenses on duty; 6-yr.; nine members: Dr. Edward S. Murray, Spur (8-26-87); Jay Pumphrey, Fort Worth (8-26-85); Dr. Frank E. Mann Jr., Wharton (8-26-89); Dr. Ed B. Avery, Pearsall (8-26-87); Dr. D. L. K. Frey, Corpus Christi (8-26-85); Dr. Billy R. Trimmier, San Antonio (8-26-85); Jim Humphrey, Henrietta (8-26-89); Dr. William L. Anderson, Addison (8-26-89); Dr. Kenneth Dorris, Stephenville (8-26-89). Executive Secretary, Roger D. Shipman, 3810 Medical Pkwy., Ste. 119, Austin 78756 (nonmember) ($42,436).

Water Development Board, Texas. — (1957; legislative function for the Texas Department of Water Resources 1977); apptv.; per diem and expenses; 6-yr.; six members: Chairman, Louis A. Beecherl Jr., Dallas (12-31-85); Louie Welch, Houston (12-31-87); L. A. Pilgrim, Pittsburg (12-31-85); George McCleskey, Lubbock (12-31-87); Glen E. Roney, McAllen (12-31-89); Stuart S. Coleman, Brownwood (12-31-89). Executive Director, TDWR, Charles E. Nemir, P.O. Box 13087, Capitol Station, Austin 78711 (nonmember) ($62,200).

Water Commission, Texas. — (1913 as State Board of Water Engineers; name changed in 1962 to Texas Water Commission, reorganized and name again changed in 1965 to Water Rights Commission; reorganized and name changed to present form in 1977 to perform the judicial function for the Texas Department of Water Resources); apptv.; 6-yr.; three members full-time at $51,100: Chairman, Paul Hopkins, Aus-

tin (LaMarque) (8-31-89); Ralph Roming, Bovina (8-31-87); Lee B. M. Biggart, Austin (8-31-85). Executive Director, Larry Soward ($44,700); Chief Clerk, Mary Ann Hefner (nonmembers), P.O. Box 13087, Capitol Station, Austin 78711.

Water Resources Planning Commission, Multi-State. — (1985); apptv.; 6 yr.; six members. (No appointments made at press time.)

Water Well Drillers Board. — (1965 as eight-member board; reorganized 1981 and made nine-member board); apptv.; per diem and expenses; 6-yr.; nine members — six to be water well drillers and three members from general public. Drillers: James Frank Grimes, Dallas (9-15-87); Tommy C. Bussell, Houston (9-15-85); W. L. Rehkop, Athens (9-15-85); Walton O'Neil Loftis, Midland (9-15-87); M. Don McKinley, Pearsall (9-15-89); Gary D. Grant, Abernathy (9-15-89). Public members: James L. Shawn, III, Austin (9-15-87); Mrs. Mary Lou Parsons, Odessa (9-15-85); Nestor Perez, Melvin (9-15-83). James L. Dyess Jr., TDWR, Box 13087, Capitol Station, Austin 78711 (nonmember).

West Texas State University, Board of Regents of. — (1969); apptv.; 6-yr.; nine members: Francis E. Barrett, Hereford (8-31-85); Stanley K. Davis, Amarillo (8-31-85); Mrs. Lee T. Bivins, Amarillo (8-31-85); Chairman, T. Boone Pickens Jr., Amarillo (8-31-87); Tom Christian, Claude (8-31-87); J. R. Walsh Jr., Borger (8-31-87); Nolon Henson Jr., Happy (8-31-89); Mrs. Lennie C. Sims, Wellington (8-31-89); Leo Forrest, Amarillo (8-31-89). President, Ed D. Roach, Box 997, Canyon 79016 (nonmember).

Work Furlough Program Advisory Board, Texas. — (1977 as Texas Work Release Program Advisory Board; name changed in 1985); apptv.; expenses; 6-yr.; nine members—three labor union members; six general public, as follows: Labor Union members: B. M. Devora, Houston (1-31-85); Dewey L. Upshaw, Pasadena (1-31-81); Raymond Scott, Port Arthur (1-31-83). General public members: Dr. William A. Lufburrow, Houston (1-31-85); G. Keith Jenkins, Conroe (1-31-85); Frank Sepulveda, San Antonio (1-31-81); Fred L. Blair, Dallas (1-31-81); James F. Johnson, Fort Worth (1-31-83); Nathan J. Bell IV, Paris (1-31-83).

Youth Camp Safety, Advisory Council on. — (1973); apptv.; 2-yr.; expenses; eleven members: Ex officio member and chairman, Commissioner of Health Dr. Robert Bernstein. Apptv. members: Mrs. Thomas P. Hubbard, Dallas (12-1-85); Carl Hawkins, Ingram (12-1-85); Mrs. Cordie R. Hines, Dallas (12-1-85); Raymond B. Bean, Dallas (12-1-85); Ann Cunningham, Arlington (12-1-85); Ron Anderson, Kerrville (12-1-85); B. Michael Adams, Henderson (12-1-85); Silas B. Ragsdale Jr., Hunt (12-1-85); Dr. H. Phillip Hook, Tyler (12-1-85); C. Joseph Nelson, Irving (12-1-85); One vacancy.

Youth Commission, Texas. — (1949 as nine-member board; reorganized 1957 and again in 1975); six apptv. members; 6-yr.; per diem on duty: Dr. William M. Shamburger, Tyler (9-1-87); Chairman, Dr. George Beto, Huntsville (9-1-87); James S. Bowie, Houston (9-1-85); Floyd Williams, Houston (8-31-89); Richard Abalos, Odessa (8-31-89); Mrs. Susan E. Bush, Athens (8-31-89). Executive Director, Ron Jackson, Box 9999, Austin 78766 (nonmember) ($58,916).

Texas State Finances

State government spending in the 1986-87 biennium increased by 19.6 percent over spending in the 1984-85 biennium, which was only 15 percent higher than the previous biennium.

Executive and administrative departments had the largest percent increase, up 27 percent in the 1986-87 biennium over the 1984-85 biennium. The next largest increase was in the Legislature, at 20 percent, followed by education, 18.5 percent; health, hospitals and youth institutions, 12.6 percent; and the judiciary, less than 4 percent.

The largest dollar increase was in education, from $16,160,115,176 to $19,154,870,039, an increase of $2,994,754,863.

STATE GOVERNMENT BUDGET, 1985-86 and 1986-87

The state budget as adopted by the 69th Legislature and certified by the State Comptroller of Public Accounts for fiscal years Sept. 1, 1985 to Aug. 31, 1986, and Sept. 1, 1986 to Aug. 31, 1987.

Fiscal 1986	General Revenue	Other	Total
Article I—Executive and Administrative Departments and Agencies	$1,609,622,966	$3,680,603,703	$5,290,226,669
Article II — Public Health, Hospitals and Youth Institutions	1,768,887,305	1,685,227,002	3,454,114,307
Article III—Education	7,990,055,660	1,472,437,759	9,462,493,419
Article IV—Judiciary	52,173,902	492,026	52,665,928
Article VI—Legislature	50,066,388	. . .	50,066,388
Total, Fiscal Year 1986	$11,470,806,221	$6,838,760,490	$18,309,566,711

Fiscal 1987	General Revenue	Other	Total
Article I—Executive and Administrative Departments and Agencies	$1,534,525,337	$3,729,760,104	$5,264,285,441
Article II — Public Health, Hospitals and Youth Institutions	1,754,796,129	1,703,554,029	3,458,350,158
Article III—Education	8,155,272,086	1,537,104,534	9,692,376,620
Article IV—Judiciary	51,938,544	492,026	52,430,570
Article VI—Legislature	55,795,625	. . .	55,795,625
Total, Fiscal Year 1987	$11,552,327,721	$6,970,910,693	$18,523,238,414
Grand total, 1986-87 Biennium	$23,023,133,942	$13,809,671,183	$36,832,805,125

STATEMENT OF CASH CONDITION, Aug. 31, 1984

Beginning Cash Balance, Sept. 1, 1983	$2,684,518,446	
Cash in Petty Cash	3,291,982	$2,687,810,428
RECEIPTS		
Net Revenues		16,198,554,754
Other Net Receipts		
Sale/Redemption of Investments	$7,387,396,568	
Repayment of Loans	457,595,727	
Departmental Transfers	315,565,657	
Operating Fund Transfers	2,839,670,543	
Bond Sale Proceeds	325,000,000	
School Bus Repayments	39,025,961	
Residual Equity Transfers	126,321	
Net Deposits & Clearances from		
Trust & Suspense Funds	5,686,352,410	
Direct Deposit Transfers	388,799,331	
TOTAL RECEIPTS		$17,439,532,518
TOTAL RECEIPTS AND BEGINNING CASH BALANCE		$33,638,087,272
DISBURSEMENTS		
Net Expenditures		$ 14,940,809,858
Other Net Disbursements:		
Purchase of Securities	$10,096,208,031	
Repayment of Loans	23,256,849	
Departmental Transfers	311,252,499	
Operating Fund Transfers	2,244,762,159	
Misc. Non-Governmental Expenditures	39,063,069	
Land and Merchandise Purchases for Resale	142,818,253	
Trust and Suspense Payment	4,934,419,124	
Teachers and Employees Retirement Payments	622,394,161	
Direct Deposit Transfers	388,799,331	
Total, Other Disbursements		18,802,973,476
TOTAL DISBURSEMENTS		$33,743,783,334
ENDING CASH BALANCE, Aug. 31, 1984		$2,582,403,332
Cash in State Treasury		$2,578,822,384
Petty Cash Accounts Held Outside the State Treasury		3,580,948

STATE GOVERNMENT INCOME, 1984

Sources from which cash was received by the state, and amounts for the fiscal year ended Aug. 31, 1984, as reported by the State Comptroller of Public Accounts, Austin, are given below. Due to rounding, totals differ from Comptroller's report of $33,638,087,271.56 for total revenue.

TAXES

Ad Valorem tax.	$21,558
Bedding tax	155,679
Inheritance tax.	97,543,483
Oil production tax.	1,120,162,034
Natural and casinghead gas tax.	1,095,485,322
Sulphur tax.	3,383,040
Gas utility administration tax	20,246,746
Cement tax.	6,326,153
Utilities tax.	190,726,103
Telephone tax.	84,756,554
Oil and gas well servicing tax	11,017,724
Carline companies tax	−218,907
Telegraph tax.	382,848
Miscellaneous occupation taxes	−370
Motor vehicle sales and rental tax	717,523,433
Hotel, motel and miscellaneous excise taxes.	44,899,925
Cigarette tax	330,085,413
Tobacco products tax	10,186,037
Mixed beverage tax	157,317,140
Liquor tax	47,170,562
Wine tax.	5,367,250
Ale tax.	2,302,725
Beer tax.	72,346,506
Airline Beverage Tax	299,485
Special motor fuels tax	108,862,161
Motor fuel gasoline tax	422,867,992
Franchise tax.	606,792,949
Insurance companies occupation tax.	362,459,870
Admission tax.	24,077
Coin device machine tax	2,581,446
Limited sales and use tax	3,784,765,414
Total taxes	**$9,305,840,352**

LICENSES, PERMITS, REGISTRATIONS, FEES, INSPECTIONS AND CERTIFICATIONS

Motorboat registration, title fees	$5,414,037
Cigarette and tobacco tax permit fees	444,918
Motor vehicle registration fees	310,122,943
Liquor permit fees	16,046,708
Wine and beer permit fees.	4,908,515
Coin machine business license fees	1,070,834
Misc. business fees	849,045
Manufactured housing fees.	2,974,240
Bingo licenses and fees	1,414,886
Veterans Land Board fees.	2,197,976
Oil and gas well servicing permits, fees	4,198,253
Waste treatment inspection fees	2,076,980
Expedited handling charges	541,180
Air pollution control fees.	427,993
Agriculture Department license fees	417,493

Commercial transportation fees	4,109,971
Drivers record information fees	3,982,888
Bedding permit fees	42,110
Land Office fees	1,692,646
Insurance companies, agents fees	5,612,984
Prepaid funeral contract audits	243,241
Water use permits	347,671
Teacher certification fees	396,272
Trucker lease agreement act fees	219,736
Health care facilities fees	2,551,099
Local MTA sales tax service fees	5,122,465
Turnpike policing fees	681,445
Medical examination, registration fees	3,513,456
Health related professional fees	2,112,705
Vital statistics fees	1,607,628
Social worker regulation.	194,448
Fees for copies or filing of records.	1,028,067
Fees for examinations and audits	110,689
Insurance Dept. license and reg. fees.	8,213,590
Motor vehicle safety violations	3,583,889
Motor carrier act fines	833,400
Professional examination and reg. fees	31,224,201
Higher education reg. fees	58,115,609
Motor vehicle inspection and certification fees.	44,137,943
Agriculture Department inspection and certification fees	2,108,493
Boiler inspection fees	522,493
State parks fees	6,730,096
Welfare/MHR fees	750,774
Higher education administration fees	1,442,635
Higher education student fees.	5,339,915
Food and drug fees	325,581
City sales tax service fees	16,108,882
General business filing fees	23,332,758
Game and fish license fees	24,557,730
Driver license fees	32,815,984
Miscellaneous licenses, permits, reg. fees	1,234,944
Total licenses, permits, registrations, fees, inspections and certifications	**$648,054,439**

SALES, ROYALTIES AND RENTALS

Principal on land sales	$1,244,754
Oil and gas royalties	475,283,734
Sand, shell and gravel	716,955
Building sales.	313,271
Machinery and equipment sales	5,575,473
Sale of textbooks.	3,016,177
Parks and wildlife publication sales.	1,443,845
Care, treatment of outpatients	1,051,031
Publication and advertising sales	5,988,666

STATE GOVERNMENTAL EXPENDITURES

(1940, 1950, 1960, 1970, 1980 and 1984)
Figures below on the cost of Texas Government are from reports of the State Comptroller of Public Accounts.

	Total Expenditures, Years Ended Aug. 31					
	1940	1950	1960	1970	1980	1984
Legislative	$32,047	$404,544	$442,856	$5,231,303	$23,135,137	$44,383,237
Judicial.	2,317,504	2,842,943	4,728,480	8,369,957	25,480,076	45,513,218
Executive and administrative	2,236,914	4,792,638	12,219,958	32,681,107	179,497,147	377,666,690
Protection to persons, property	1,649,597	6,065,887	14,260,868	38,950,552	103,404,512	160,192,231
Regulation of business, industry	2,464,036	4,127,122	6,825,038	16,311,447	59,296,627	106,431,943
Conservation of health and sanitation	1,299,250	9,428,794	11,792,269	34,367,133	153,682,641	210,728,355
Development and conservation of natural resources	2,269,438	8,143,140	13,462,581	28,114,854	94,303,991	138,424,731
Highways	53,720,158	123,486,034	386,700,411	633,234,063	1,580,922,041	1,437,715,827
Mental Health, correctional.	8,091,871	23,560,113	60,798,551	140,971,864	513,621,785	864,077,111
Educational	58,579,342	211,820,152	425,968,532	1,208,871,794	4,627,655,693	6,697,513,717
Parks and monuments.	169,276	450,822	519,450	21,137,827	59,355,849	84,381,828
Public welfare (pensions and benefits)	29,460,943	132,036,789	187,914,672	695,013,203	1,601,321,095	2,315,713,094
Payment on public debt	3,384,725	33,136	6,175,497	41,627,195	108,948,644	743,997,551
Miscellaneous government cost.	42,504	60,334	299,959	49,863,487	1,080,282,276	1,714,070,224
Total	**$165,717,612**	**$527,252,453**	**$1,184,384,436**	**$2,954,745,786**	**$10,210,907,514**	**$14,940,809,757**

Dormitory, cafeteria and merchandise sales	7,788,753	Unemployment benefit repaid	1,404,819
Other sales	3,327,895	Other misc. governmental revenue.	11,081,016
Mineral lease bonus and prospect rental	77,958,846	Telecommunications service	1,873,606
Land easements	1,966,745	Medical assistance cost recovery	2,074,042
Grazing lease rentals	1,876,998	Child support collections.	12,216,905
Other rentals, leases and easements . . .	2,283,366	Supplies/equipment/services	50,912,253
Total sales, royalties and rentals . . .	$589,836,509	Criminal offenses fees	4,486,910
		Misdemeanor, felony cases fees	26,637,302
INTEREST AND DIVIDENDS		Unemployment compensation penalties	4,778,552
		Gain/Loss on investments.	301,273,955
Interest on state deposits.	$195,179,171	Miscellaneous revenues	1,164,757
Interest on local deposits.	3,537,724	Local account balances.	1,340,643
Interest on securities owned	1,761,632,191	Total miscellaneous governmental revenues	$501,389,308
Interest on land sales	28,579,252	
Other interest.	2,575,775	
Interest on loans to college students. . . .	10,225,879	**FEDERAL, COUNTY AND OTHER AID**	
Support and maintenance of patients fees	32,202,052	
Total interest and dividends	$2,033,932,044	Federal grants to highways.	$564,699,259
		Federal grants to public health	212,164,659
MISCELLANEOUS GOVERNMENTAL REVENUE		Federal child support collections.	5,045,556
		Federal grants to public welfare	1,298,853,968
Prison industries sales	$8,417,225	Federal grants to public education	600,410,460
Arrest fees, game and fish.	1,404,200	Federal grants, miscellaneous	380,457,878
Alcoholic beverage code money	1,281,550	Federal grants, Parks and Wildlife	14,359,485
Judgments.	2,681,133	Land reclamation fees	21,598
Judicial fees.	197,485	Federal receipts-earned credits	38,991,933
Teachers retirement reimbursement funds.	31,800,026	County and city grants	38,629
Escheated estates.	11,269,775	Other political subdivision grants	682,447
Insurance damages	2,621,119	Other donations and grants.	3,776,142
Warrants voided by statute of limitation	2,115,607	Total federal, county and other aid	$3,119,502,014
Judges retirement contribution	1,412,802	Total net receipts	$16,198,554,666
Reimbursements-third party	8,218,630	Interfund transfers.	17,439,532,517
Reimbursements-intra-agency	10,724,996	Total receipts	$33,638,087,183

STATE GOVERNMENT EXPENDITURES, 1984

The following table shows the expenditures by the Texas State Government, giving agencies and purposes of expenditures for the fiscal year ended Aug. 31, 1984, as reported by the State Comptroller of Public Accounts. Due to rounding, total in this compilation differs from the $33,743,783,331.76 reported by the Comptroller's office.

Legislative:		**Executive and Administrative:**	
Senate	$12,884,276	Governor's Office	$10,556,660
House of Representatives	13,096,886	Attorney General	35,014,041
Legislative Council	9,091,011	Purchasing and General Services Comm.	74,350,584
Legislative Budget Board	1,857,394	Comptroller of Public Accounts	96,006,215
Legislative Reference Library.	334,903	General Land Office	13,522,053
Commission on Uniform State Laws. . .	27,627	Library and Archives Commission	5,260,085
Sunset Advisory Commission.	679,497	Secretary of State	7,833,324
Legislative Information System Committee.	232,804	Texas Department on Aging	1,464,482
Auditor.	6,012,786	Treasurer	4,688,387
Automated Information System Adv. Council	166,053	Securities Board	1,889,097
Total Legislative.	$44,383,237	Commission for the Blind.	4,768,324
		Good Neighbor Commission	185,452
Judicial:		Employees' Retirement System.	100,756,570
Supreme Court	$2,069,441	Veterans Land Board	1,356,097
Court of Criminal Appeals	2,104,640	Dept. of Community Affairs.	8,927,756
Office of Court Administration.	908,308	Office of State-Federal Relations	899,962
State Attorney before Court of Criminal Appeals	288,203	Advisory Commission Intergovernmental Relations	416,759
District Courts (Comptroller's Judiciary Section)	26,115,521	Commission for Deaf.	1,048,564
Comm. Jud. Conduct.	202,291	State Ethics Advisory Commission. . . .	2,341
Law Library	520,372	Public Building Authority	35,082
Texas Prosecutors Coordinating Council	538,564	Commission on Human Rights.	279,861
		Department of Highways & Public Transportation	1,561,117
Courts of Appeals:		State Property Tax Bd.	4,030,479
First District.	$1,445,998	Bd. of Tax Professional Examiners . . .	86,057
Second District	1,117,514	State Pension Review Board	127,220
Third District	1,021,580	Texas Merit System Council.	869,877
Fourth District	1,026,128	State Aircraft Pooling Board	1,730,244
Fifth District.	2,059,273	Total Executive and Administrative	$377,666,690
Sixth District.	465,288	
Seventh District	634,305	**Protection of Persons and Property:**	
Eighth District	674,788	Adjutant General	$9,037,485
Ninth District	468,204	Veterans Affairs Commission	1,843,340
Tenth District	377,446	Department of Public Safety	144,528,998
Eleventh District.	507,176	National Guard Armory Board.	1,988,911
Twelfth District.	551,838	Law Enforcement Officer Standards and Education	2,127,164
Thirteenth District	995,802	Commission on Fire Protection Personnel Standards and Education	132,009
Fourteenth District	1,420,538	Commission on Jail Standards.	393,784
Total Judicial	$45,513,218	Criminal Justice Policy Council	140,540
		Total Protection of Persons and Property	$160,192,231

Regulation of Business and Industry:

Real Estate Commission	$2,603,354
Department of Banking	137,006
Department of Labor Statistics	5,525,439
Industrial Accident Board	8,761,937
Board of Insurance	19,899,010
Railroad Commission	29,257,180
Board of Plumbing Examiners	766,121
Alcoholic Beverage Commission	20,501,712
Board of Architectural Examiners	337,686
Board of Registration for Professional Engineers	673,219
Aeronautics Commission	1,387,141
Economic Development Commission . .	2,188,933
Board of Private Investigators	1,090,349
Polygraph Examiners Board	71,051
Motor Vehicle Commission	285,713
Amusement Machine Commission	785,817
Texas Structural Pest Control Board . .	351,061
Public Utilities Commission	9,086,045
Board of Public Accountancy	1,926,536
Texas Bd. of Land Surveying	136,372
Texas Bd. of Irrigators	74,560
Public Utility Counsel	585,701
Total Regulation of Business and Industry	$106,431,943

Conservation of Health and Sanitation:

Department of Health	$111,712,061
Board of Barber Examiners	397,867
Board of Medical Examiners	969,784
Board of Dental Examiners	546,503
Cosmetology Commission	1,096,204
University of Texas — M.D. Anderson Hospital and Tumor Institute	74,865,071
Board of Nurse Examiners	894,139
Board of Chiropractic Examiners	101,197
Board of Examiners for Hearing Aids . .	63,029
Board of Podiatry Examiners	50,188
Board of Vocational Nurse Examiners	602,567
Optometry Board	126,734
Board of Pharmacy	1,057,034
Low-Level Waste Disposal Authority . .	1,266,313
Commission on Alcoholism	2,064,586
Board of Morticians	222,462
Air Control Board	12,988,461
Board of Examiners of Psychologists . .	192,703
Governor's Commission on Physical Fitness	136,447
Board of Physical Therapy Examiners	109,856
Board of Nursing Home Administrators	195,394
Health Facilities Commission	1,129,755
Total Conservation of Health and Sanitation	$210,728,355

Development and Conservation of Natural Resources:

Texas Energy Advisory Council	$663,043
Department of Agriculture	18,940,732
Texas Animal Health Commission	13,185,368
Agricultural Extension Service	29,180,646
Agricultural Experiment Station	31,252,388
Veterinary Medical Diagnostic Laboratory	1,676,132
Forest Service	8,195,303
Rodent and Predatory Animal Control	2,188,483
Board of Veterinary Examiners	242,138
Rio Grande Compact Commission	104,882
Department Water Resources	29,377,327
Water Well Drillers Board	9,456
Sabine River Compact Commission . . .	26,820
Texas Coastal and Marine Council	212,483
Soil and Water Conservation Board . . .	1,482,343
Red River Compact Commission	25,546
Canadian River Commission	15,242
Pecos River Compact Commission	48,935
Natural Fibers and Food Protein Committee	1,597,464
Total Development and Conservation of Natural Resources	$138,424,731

Highway Maintenance and Construction $1,437,715,827

Mental Health and Correctional:

Dept. of Mental Health	$46,864,768
Commission for Indian Affairs	539,473
Youth Council	40,719,556

Texas Adult Probation Commission . . .	1,975,455
Texas Juvenile Probation Commission	812,387
Department of Corrections	297,743,870
Board of Pardons and Paroles	20,444,459
Miscellaneous Eleemosynary	454,977,143
Total Mental Health and Correctional	$864,077,111

Educational:

Governor's Fund	$2,563,371
Commission for the Blind	6,625,751
Department of Community Affairs	2,309,071
Department of Public Safety	84,387
Department of Highways and Public Transportation	1,432,464
Texas Education Agency	4,587,681,852
A&M University System Administration	49,533,415
A&M University Main University	151,077,205
Engineering Experiment Station	4,780,553
Tarleton College	11,588,371
University of Texas—Arlington	57,102,131
Prairie View A&M University	19,247,538
Texas Transportation Institute	1,050,805
Engineering Extension Service	2,898,464
Texas Southern University	29,510,106
A&M University at Galveston	5,321,916
Texas State Technical Institute	44,136,080
University of Texas System	69,150,719
University of Texas—Austin	196,542,150
University of Texas Medical Branch—Galveston	154,275,206
University of Texas—El Paso	34,377,067
University of Texas Science Center —Dallas	57,687,704
University of Houston	107,207,014
Texas Woman's University	35,261,887
Texas A&I University	16,953,384
Texas Technological University	84,985,046
Lamar University	41,814,267
Midwestern University	11,881,768
Pan American University	20,911,594
Angelo State University	15,070,342
University of Texas—Tyler	7,613,018
Texas Energy and Natural Resources Advisory Council	690,122
Texas Department on Aging	25,289
Texas Department of Health	1,290,180
Public Utilities Commission	1,004,005
Commission on Alcoholism	188,449
University of Texas—Dallas	23,668,020
Texas Tech Univ. Health Sciences Center	40,398,756
Advisory Council for Technical/ Vocational Education	163,015
University of Texas— Permian Basin	7,098,156
University of Texas—San Antonio	24,299,605
University of Texas Health Science Center—Houston	81,895,778
University of Texas Health Science Center—San Antonio	70,359,192
Pan American Univ. at Brownsville . . .	2,782,299
University of Houston— Clear Lake	14,843,225
Corpus Christi University	9,559,200
Laredo University	3,259,103
University of South Texas Administration	332,328
East Texas State University	24,621,135
North Texas State University	62,895,272
Sam Houston State University	32,921,090
Southwest Texas State University	47,577,911
S. F. Austin State University	33,476,861
Sul Ross State University	7,801,129
School for the Blind	7,647,737
School for the Deaf	11,209,996
West Texas State University	17,789,946
Board of Regents State University System	276,563
Coordinating Bd. College and Univ. System	276,853,379
Texas College of Osteopathic Medicine	21,179,470
East Texas State University— Texarkana	3,511,784
University of Houston-Victoria Center	2,622,507
State Rural Medical Education Board .	50,685
University of Houston System	6,330,227

University of Houston—Downtown....	12,681,941
UT Health Center—Tyler...........	11,520,937
UT Institute of Texan Cultures......	2,139,261
Texas Commission on the Arts.......	313,233
Southwest Collegiate Institute for Deaf	1,548,785
Comptroller—State Fiscal.........	12,500
Total Education	**$6,697,513,717**
Parks and Monuments	**$84,381,828**
Public Welfare	**2,315,713,094**
Payment of Public Debt	**743,997,551**
State Cost, Employees Retirement	**152,853,145**
State Cost, O.A.S.I.	**362,640,772**
Grants to Political Subdivisions	
and Others	**581,695,371**
State Cost, Teacher Retirement	**596,829,309**
Miscellaneous	**20,051,627**
Total governmental	
expenditures...............	$14,940,809,757
Total nongovernmental	
expenditures and transfer	
between funds..............	18,802,973,474
Total expenditures............	**$33,743,783,231**

STATE BONDED INDEBTEDNESS

Bonded indebtedness of the State of Texas on Aug. 31, 1984 was $1,699,266,000, according to records of the State Comptroller of Public Accounts. Issuance of bonds requires amendment of the Constitution of Texas, authorized in a statewide election.

Outstanding bonded indebtedness, Aug. 31, 1984, consisted of the following:

University of Texas and A&M	..
Permanent University Fund Bonds..	$408,605,000.00
Veterans Land Fund Bonds.........	892,296,000.00
Texas Water Development Bonds.....	251,190,000.00
Texas Student Loan Bonds..........	132,325,000.00
Texas Park Development Bonds	4,850,000.00
Farm, Ranch Loan Securities Bonds ..	10,000,000.00
Total All Bonds	**$1,699,266,000.00**

STATE GOVERNMENT COSTS

The yearly cost of state government is shown here. Costs have risen from $127,677 in 1847 to $14,940,809,857 in 1984. Figures have been rounded out, hence may vary slightly from those in other tables.

Fiscal Year Ended	Expenditures	Fiscal Year Ended	Expenditures
1984	$14,940,809,857	1947	319,988,101
1983	13,642,028,057	1946	238,616,434
1982	12,074,205,469	1945	186,493,191
1981	11,367,553,831	1944	142,234,249
1980	10,210,907,514	1943	181,795,949
1979	8,600,168,100	1942	205,741,882
1978	7,864,096,032	1941	166,073,023
1977	6,606,979,386	1940	165,717,612
1976	6,203,503,772	1939	164,323,500
1975	5,377,326,615	1938	157,747,878
1974	4,492,958,989	1937	144,770,274
1973	4,041,620,277	1936	125,693,992
1972	3,810,046,333	1935	111,001,067
1971	3,453,207,618	1934	111,866,296
1970	2,954,745,796	1933	107,922,451
1969	2,514,507,766	1932	95,800,981
1968	2,339,869,601	1931	101,164,453
1967	2,060,881,279	1930	103,137,982
1966	1,860,633,769	1929	84,478,447
1965	1,610,278,049	1928	84,358,918
1964	1,574,959,268	1927	73,563,721
1963	1,467,683,645	1926	66,381,069
1962	1,305,846,369	1925	67,210,128
1961	1,200,374,164	1924	50,919,819
1960	1,184,384,437	1923	66,041,795
1959	1,163,593,583	1922	60,484,232
1958	1,027,389,546	1921	67,223,838
1957	872,680,662	1920	34,750,685
1956	805,686,551	1910	10,868,388
1955	777,243,167	1900	5,754,218
1954	706,121,196	1890	4,162,960
1953	662,495,496	1880	2,922,342
1952	617,210,793	1870	660,215
1951	568,153,444	1860	828,726
1950	527,252,453	1850	148,055
1949	443,776,824	1847	127,677
1948	403,983,966		

STATE TAX RATES, VALUES

For many years an ad valorem tax was set at a maximum of 35c on the $100 for the general revenue fund, 35c for the school fund and 7 cents for the Confederate pension fund. In 1947 the Confederate pension was reduced to 2 cents, and 5 cents transferred to state colleges. In 1954, an amendment provided that unused Confederate pension money be transferred to the state building fund. The ad valorem tax for general revenue fund was abolished in 1951. Table shows ad valorem tax rates and assessed valuations to 1980.

According to the **State Property Tax Board**, in 1982, Sec. 1-e, Art. VIII of the State Constitution was amended to provide that no state ad valorem taxes shall be levied upon any property within the state. It was further amended to provide that all receipts from previously authorized state ad valorem taxes collected on or after Nov. 23, 1982, shall be deposited to the credit of the general fund of the county collecting the taxes and may be expended for county purposes. Previously authorized state ad valorem taxes collected **before** Nov. 23, 1982, shall be deposited to the **College Building Fund**.

Year	General Fund	Available School Fund	Confederate Pension Fund	College Building Fund	Total Assessed Valuation	*Net Assessed Valuation
1921...	$.22	$.35	$.05	...	$3,455,360,089	...
1925...	.35	.35	.07	...	3,526,581,523	...
1930...	.27	.35	.07	...	4,328,212,712	...
1932...	.27	.35	.07	...	3,962,841,346	$3,962,841,346
1935...	.35	.20	.07	...	3,800,046,096	3,191,608,321
1940...	.35	.27	.07	...	4,273,321,619	3,580,407,685
1945...	.35	.35	.02	...	4,983,270,005	4,168,149,237
1950...	.30	.35	.02	.05	7,160,058,064	6,005,732,164
1955...		.35	.02	.05	9,897,990,815	8,325,513,414
1956...		.35	.02	.05	10,552,725,749	8,825,384,812
1957...		.35	.02	.05	11,212,159,527	9,369,108,943
1958...		.35	.02	.05	11,594,947,559	9,647,017,566
1959...		.35	.02	.05	12,234,911,034	10,197,023,739
1960...		.35	.02	.05	12,720,008,069	10,563,099,590
1961...		.35	.02	.05	13,317,144,302	11,055,640,559
1962...		.35	.02	.05	13,754,874,050	11,434,362,559
1963...		.35	.02	.05	14,363,518,161	11,921,849,991
1964...		.35	.02	.05	14,958,609,244	12,400,698,531
1965...		.35	.02	.05	15,646,432,902	13,009,003,922
1966...		.35	.02	.10	16,365,714,599	13,635,331,663
1967...		.35	.02	.10	17,239,779,973	14,226,623,993
1968...		.35	.02	.10	18,227,316,006	15,196,120,248
1969...		.30	.02	.10	19,607,556,461	16,424,856,807
1970...		.25	.02	.10	21,492,870,651	18,220,192,600
1971...		.20	.02	.10	23,781,357,155	20,350,280,394
1972...		.15	.02	.10	25,878,905,388	22,266,497,713
1973...		.10	.02	.10	28,219,142,903	24,468,238,082
1974...		.05	.02	.10	31,925,713,114	27,988,105,590
1975...		†	.02	.10	36,570,253,331	32,418,585,233
1976...			‡.02	.10	41,183,111,257	36,752,240,417
1977...				.10	51,333,983,515	46,589,819,473
§1978...				.10	55,244,068,932	50,819,868,63
1979...				.10	57,421,272,578	52,522,602,22
**1980...						

*Net assessed valuation includes only property subject to state taxes (less **homestead exemption**). Prior to the homestead exemption amendment (beginning in 1933), the state used the total value of the county rolls.

†Ad valorem tax for the Available School Fund was abolished by Constitutional Amendment (see Sec. 1-e Art. VIII) effective Jan. 1, 1975.

‡Effective Dec. 31, 1976, the 2 cents ad valorem tax for support of Confederate veterans and their widows was abolished. (See Sec. 1-e, Art. VIII and footnote thereunder.)

§Valuations for 1978 exclude Bexar and Fort Bend as values are not available.

**Sec. 26.03, Property Tax Code, which provided a assessment ratio for state ad valorem taxes of .0001 percent, was validated as of Jan. 1, 1980. As a result of the .0001 percent assessment ratio, the total assessed value for state purposes for 1980 was approximately $147,040.

FEDERAL GOVERNMENT IN TEXAS

Below and on following pages are brief accounts of activities of the federal government in Texas. Federal tax collections are given in table below. On immediately following pages are brief accounts of military activities in Texas.

Texans in Congress

Texas is entitled to 27 members of the House of Representatives, plus two senators, in Congress.

The **salary** of both senators and representatives was raised to $72,200 with the provision that they could not receive more than $20,940 from lectures and other outside activities.

Term of office is two years for members of the House of Representatives and six years for senators. Dates in parentheses after names of senators indicate year term will expire. All representatives' terms will expire Jan. 1, 1987. Representatives may be addressed at the room numbers given after their names. The abbreviations stand for the following buildings: CHOB, Cannon House Office Building; LHOB, Longworth House Office Building; RHOB, Rayburn House Office Building. The zip code for the House is 20515; for the Senate 20510.

Senators
Lloyd Bentsen, D-Houston, 703 Hart Bldg., (1989).
Phil Gramm, R-College Station, 179 Russell Bldg., (1991).

Representatives
1. Jim Chapman, D-Sulphur Springs. (No address available when this section went to press.)
2. Charles Wilson, D-Lufkin, 2265 RHOB.
3. Steve Bartlett, R-Dallas, 1709 LHOB.
4. Ralph Hall, D-Rockwall, 1728 LHOB.
5. John Bryant, D-Dallas, 412 CHOB.
6. Joe Barton, R-Ennis, 1017 LHOB.
7. Bill Archer, R-Houston, 1135 LHOB.
8. Jack Fields, R-Houston, 413 CHOB.
9. Jack Brooks, D-Beaumont, 2449 RHOB.
10. J. J. Pickle, D-Austin, 242 CHOB.
11. Marvin Leath, D-Marlin, 336 CHOB.
12. James C. Wright Jr., D-Fort Worth, 1236 LHOB.
13. Beau Boulter, R-Amarillo, 1427 LHOB.
14. Mac Sweeney, R-Wharton, 1713 LHOB.
15. Eligio De La Garza, D-Mission, 1401 LHOB.
16. Ron Coleman, D-El Paso, 416 CHOB.
17. Charles W. Stenholm, D-Stamford, 1232 LHOB.
18. George Leland, D-Houston, 419 CHOB.
19. Larry Combest, R-Lubbock, 1529 LHOB.
20. Henry B. Gonzalez, D-San Antonio, 2413 RHOB.
21. Tom Loeffler, R-Hunt, 1212 LHOB.
22. Tom DeLay, R-Sugrland, 1234 LHOB.
23. Albert G. Bustamante, D-San Antonio, 1116 LHOB.
24. Martin Frost, D-Dallas, 1238 LHOB.
25. Mike Andrews, D-Houston, 1039 LHOB.
26. Richard Armey, R-Lewisville, 514 CHOB.
27. Solomon Ortiz, D-Corpus Christi, 1524 LHOB.

U.S. EXPENDITURES IN TEXAS

Below are federal expenditures in Texas for fiscal year 1983, as furnished by the U.S. Bureau of the Census for the Office of Management and Budget. Direct federal expenditures or obligations amounted to $37,636,164,000. In addition, $1,151,021,000 was spent for direct loans and $22,054,353,000 for guaranteed loans and insurance. See also the section on Counties and Cities for federal expenditures by counties.

Item—	Expenditure (add 000)
TOTAL EXPENDITURES	$60,841,538
Direct federal expenditures or obligations:	
Total direct expenditures:	
Total expenditures	37,636,164
Defense Department	12,309,917
All other agencies	25,326,247
Grant awards	4,736,154
Salaries and wages:	
Total	6,369,833
Defense Department	3,799,484
Direct payment for individuals:	
Total	17,413,022
Retirement and disability	12,476,403
All other	4,936,619
Procurement contract awards:	
Total	8,155,561
Defense Department	6,995,633
Other federal expenditures or obligations . .	961,594
Other federal assistance:	
Direct loans	1,151,021
Guaranteed loans and insurance	22,054,353

Army and Air Force Exchange Service

Dallas is headquarters for the worldwide **Army and Air Force Exchange Service**, which directs both domestic

U.S. TAX COLLECTIONS IN TEXAS

*Fiscal Year	Individual Income And Employment Taxes	Corporation Income Taxes	Estate Taxes	Gift Taxes	Excise Taxes	Total U.S. Taxes Collected in Texas
†1983	$37,416,203,000	$4,750,079,000	$494,431,000	$19,844,000	$5,553,491,000	$48,234,048,000
1982	36,072,975,000	6,574,940,000	624,559,000	6,789,000	6,880,102,000	50,159,365,000
1981	31,692,219,000	7,526,687,000	526,420,000	31,473,000	8,623,799,000	48,400,598,000
1980	25,707,514,000	7,232,486,000	453,830,000	23,722,000	4,122,538,000	37,540,089,000
1979	22,754,959,000	5,011,334,000	397,810,000	18,267,000	1,680,118,000	29,862,488,000
1978	17,876,628,000	5,128,609,000	337,883,000	19,189,000	1,757,045,000	25,119,354,000
1977	16,318,652,000	4,135,046,000	422,984,000	182,623,000	1,324,989,000	22,384,294,000
1976	11,908,546,000	2,736,374,000	350,326,000	48,804,000	1,320,496,000	16,364,546,000
1975	11,512,883,000	2,882,776,000	269,185,000	44,425,000	1,338,713,000	16,047,982,000
1974	9,884,442,000	1,989,710,000	259,306,000	43,109,000	1,338,656,000	13,515,223,000
1973	8,353,841,000	1,614,204,000	240,470,000	53,329,000	1,511,754,000	11,773,598,000
1972	7,125,930,000	1,485,559,000	288,674,000	24,792,000	1,478,340,000	10,403,295,000
1971	6,277,877,000	1,229,479,000	179,694,000	31,817,000	1,056,540,000	8,775,407,000
1970	6,096,961,000	1,184,342,000	135,694,000	20,667,000	843,724,000	8,281,389,000
1969	5,444,372,000	1,180,047,000	158,028,000	23,024,000	810,061,000	7,615,532,000
1968	4,721,316,000	935,302,000	138,102,000	24,878,000	821,576,000	6,707,952,000
1967	3,616,869,000	1,133,126,000	124,052,000	20,764,000	691,156,000	5,651,336,000
1966	3,063,000,000	847,000,000	130,000,000	17,000,000	717,000,000	4,774,000,000
1965	2,705,318,000	786,916,000	115,733,000	15,771,000	710,940,000	4,334,678,000
1964	2,745,342,000	716,288,000	93,497,000	14,773,000	670,309,000	4,240,209,000
1963	2,582,821,000	654,888,000	83,013,000	12,840,000	638,525,000	3,972,087,000
1962	2,361,614,000	675,035,000	101,263,000	13,095,000	444,279,000	3,595,287,000
1961	2,131,707,000	622,076,000	80,001,000	9,550,000	266,714,000	3,110,047,000
1960	2,059,075,000	622,822,000	70,578,000	10,583,000	209,653,000	2,972,712,000
1959	1,868,515,000	545,334,000	63,138,000	7,205,000	198,285,000	2,682,478,000
1958	1,786,686,000	625,267,000	68,379,000	10,672,000	206,307,000	2,697,309,000
1957	1,696,288,000	615,527,000	55,592,000	7,918,000	192,413,000	2,567,739,000

*Beginning in 1976, the fiscal year ending date was changed to Sept. 30, from June 30.
†Latest year for which data were available when this section went to press.

Color guard from Texas National Guard unit at nearby Camp Mabry presents the U.S. and Texas flags at a ceremony in House chamber to call attention to Armed Forces Day. Associated Press Photo

and overseas operations of the military retail-food-service organization. The Exchange Service is a self-sustaining organization, with minimal tax-dollar support, which employs nearly 70,000 people, including 7,452 in Texas.

Approximately 2,400 employees work in the Dallas headquarters, which had operating expenses of $52.7 million in 1984. Through regional offices, the Exchange Service operates Exchange outlets in Texas at Bergstrom AFB (Austin), Fort Bliss (El Paso), Brooks AFB (San Antonio), Carswell AFB (Fort Worth), Dyess AFB (Abilene), Goodfellow AFB (San Angelo), Fort Hood (Killeen), Fort Sam Houston (San Antonio), Kelly AFB (San Antonio), Lackland AFB (San Antonio), Laughlin AFB (Del Rio), Randolph AFB (Universal City), Reese AFB (Lubbock) and Sheppard AFB (Wichita Falls). In 1984, $2.4 million in exchange funds was expended in

Texas for AAFES construction projects, while more than $804 million was spent in Texas for procurement of goods and services.

The Exchange Service operates nearly 16,000 retail, food, personal services and automotive activities, movie theaters and vending outlets in the United States and foreign areas. These activities generated $4.9 billion in sales during 1984. Earnings from those sales are contributed to the Army and Air Force morale and welfare programs worldwide. AAFES supplies more than 7 million servicemen and women, dependents and retired military personnel with a variety of services and merchandise.

The Exchange Service headquarters moved from New York to Dallas in January, 1967. Employees moved into the $3.5 million office building in Southwest Oak Cliff in late 1967.

MILITARY ACTIVITIES

Since 1845 Texas has been one of the leading states in military activities, with its strategic location on the Gulf of Mexico midway between the East and West Coasts, its generally mild climate and its varied terrain. Back in 1845, however, it was the **Mexican War**, precipitated by the annexation of Texas by the United States, that made Texas the center of operations. Between then and the outbreak of the **Civil War** in 1861, U.S. Army forts were established to protect settlers from Indians and to maintain peace in areas still claimed by Mexico.

Fifth U.S. Army headquarters, a 3-star command, has been located in the historic **Quadrangle** at **Fort Sam Houston, San Antonio,** since July 1, 1971, when Fourth and Fifth Armies merged. With "Readiness" its watchword and mission, Fifth Army commands **U.S. Army Reserve (USAR)** units and supervises training and readiness of **Army National Guard (ARNG)** units in its 8-state area of responsibility — Arkansas, Louisiana, Missouri, Oklahoma, Texas, New Mexico, Kansas and Nebraska. Together, the Guard and Reserve form the **Reserve Components.**

The ARNG is the only Army resource with dual status as federal and state military force (a unit is never on both duties at the same time). The governor is commander in chief of the Texas National and State Guards, while the command function is exercised through an **adjutant general** appointed by the governor and approved by both federal and state legislative authorities. Training is conducted under supervision of the Fifth Army commander. Office of the adjutant general, state of Texas, is in Austin. Located there under his jurisdiction is the **Command and Control Headquarters,** also headquarters of the **49th Armored Division,** one of nine major ARNG commands in the Fifth Army area subordinate to the state adjutants general. For Texas Army/Air/State Guard, see **Texas Guard** listing.

USAR units in the Fifth Army area fall within nine major commands, with the following headquartered in

Texas: 75th Maneuver Area Command, Houston; 90th U.S. Army Reserve Command, San Antonio; 420th Engineer Brigade, Bryan; and 807th Medical Brigade, Seagoville. Other units range from small detachments to brigades. Seven USAR schools, under jurisdiction of the 90th, are located in Austin, Beaumont, Dallas, Fort Worth, Houston, Lubbock and San Antonio (Fort Sam Houston).

A Readiness Group at Fort Sam Houston, one of three in the Army area, provides on-the-spot assistance to ARNG/USAR commanders, and reports directly to the Fifth Army commander. Groups provide combat, combat support, combat service support and maintenance and administrative teams.

One of five continental Armies, Fifth Army is an executive agent for **U.S. Army Forces Command, Fort McPherson, Ga.,** for domestic emergency plans and operations and for specified civil-military programs within in the Army area. It also has command responsibility over some 450 civilian employees (including 12 student aides) and about 2,900 USAR unit technicians.

U.S. ARMY RESERVE

The U.S. Army Reserve (USAR), a vital ingredient in the total Army's national defense role, is well represented throughout Texas. Army reservists from a walks of civilian life devote, usually, one weekend a month and two weeks for annual training a year to make themselves and their units ready for mobilization should the need arise.

These citizen-soldiers of Texas are members of 186 separate units which are authorized over 12,500 people and are subordinate to four major Army Reserve commands. These major commands are the **90th U.S. Army Reserve Command (ARCOM)**, Fort Sam Houston, San Antonio; **75th Maneuver Area Command (MAC)**, Houston; **420th Engineer Brigade**, Bryan; and the **807th Medical Brigade**, Seagoville.

Except for the 75th MAC, which is located entirely in Houston, these major commands have units in virtually all major metropolitan areas of the state. The Dallas-Fort Worth metroplex has one of the largest concentrations with 28 units stationed in the area.

There are 28 units in San Antonio and others in Amarillo, Austin, Beaumont-Port Arthur, Corpus Christi, El Paso, Houston, Laredo, Lubbock, Texarkana and Wichita Falls. Also, smaller communities such as Abilene, Bay City, Bryan, Harlingen, Huntsville, Paris, Pleasanton, San Marcos, Sinton, Tomball, Tyler, Victoria, Waco and Yoakum are represented with units.

Texas units vary in size and missions, ranging from a 3-person military history detachment to combat engineer brigades to a 1,000-bed hospital unit. There are engineer, supply and service, medical, aviation, transportation, chemical, military police, maintenance, military intelligence, Army Security Agency and judge advocate general units, as well as Army Reserve schools.

Texas Guard

Tracing its history to early frontier days, the Texas Guard is composed of three separate, yet coordinated, entities: The **Texas Army National Guard**, the **Texas Air National Guard** and the **Texas State Guard**.

The Texas State Guard, an all-volunteer backup force, was originally created by the Texas Legislature in 1941. It became an active element of the state military forces in 1965 with a mission of reinforcing the National Guard in state emergencies, and of replacing National Guard units called into federal service. The Texas State Guard, which has a membership of approximately 1,670 personnel, also participates in local emergencies.

When the Guard was reorganized following World War II, the Texas Air National Guard was added. Texas Air National Guard units serve as augmentation units to major Air Force commands, including the Air Defense Command, the Tactical Air Command and the Strategic Air Command.

The Army Guard is available for either national or state emergencies and has been used extensively during hurricanes, tornadoes and floods. Army guardsmen are members of 194 units distributed in 120 cities of Texas.

When called into active federal service, National Guard units come within the chain of command of the Army, Air Force or theater in which they serve. When not in federal service, Camp Mabry, in Austin, is the main storage, maintenance and administrative headquarters for the Texas Guard.

The governor of Texas is commander-in-chief of the Texas National and State Guards. This command function is exercized through an **adjutant general** appointed by the governor and approved by both federal and state legislative authority.

The adjutant general is active administrative head of the Guard, and head of the Adjutant General's Department, a state agency, working in conjunction with the National Guard Bureau, a federal agency.

Fort Bliss

Located at El Paso in the vast expanse of West Texas, Fort Bliss is the home of the **U.S. Army Air Defense Center**, largest air defense center in the Free World. Its primary mission is to train individual missilemen and air defense artillery units, which also include foreign military students from as many as 25 countries at one time. Here at Fort Bliss are the key training, development and support activities for the Army's vital guided missile and air defense artillery programs.

Fort Bliss is home of the **U.S. Army Air Defense Artillery School**, the 11th Air Defense Artillery Brigade, U.S. Army Air Defense Board, Range Command 3d Armored Cavalry Regiment and the 70th Ordnance Battalion's 2d Platoon, 507th Medical Company (Air Ambulance). As part of the **Military Assistance to Safety and Traffic**

(MAST), the 507th provides emergency air transportation for residents of West Texas and New Mexico to medical facilities in El Paso.

Tenant activities include the **U.S. Army Sergeants Major Academy**, an element of the **U.S. Army Materiel Development and Readiness Command, Army Research Institute, U.S. Army Audit Agency, U.S. Army Special Security Detachment**, and a **Nuclear Weapons Support Detachment**. In addition, the **German Air Force Training Command** and the **German Air Force Air Defense School** are on post through an agreement between the U.S. Government and the Federal Republic of Germany.

Fort Bliss and its ranges comprise over 1,125,000 acres extending from Texas' Upper Rio Grande Valley into New Mexico — an area greater than that of Rhode Island. The post's almost 20,000 military personnel and some 8,000 civilian employees receive an annual payroll of about $404 million.

Fort Hood

Fort Hood, named for colorful **Confederate Gen. John Bell Hood**, covers 339 square miles in Central Texas just west of Killeen, midway between Waco and Austin.

Originally home of the **Army Tank Destroyer Center** throughout World War II, Fort Hood today is the only post in the United States that accommodates two armored divisions. In addition to the **1st Cavalry Division** and the **2nd Armored Division**, the **6th Cavalry Brigade (Air Combat)**, the **13th Support Command (Corps)**, the **3rd Signal Brigade, 89th Military Police Brigade, 504th Military Intelligence Group**, the **TRADOC Combined Arms Testing Activity (TCATA)**, the **Medical Support Activity (MEDDAC)**, the **Dental Activity (DENTACO)**, and various other units and tenant organizations are an integral part of Fort Hood.

A product of World War II, the original site was purchased in 1941 and activated in 1942 as **South Camp Hood**. Soon, **North Camp Hood** was established 17 miles north near Gatesville. In 1950, South Camp Hood became a permanent installation, redesignated **Fort Hood**, while North Camp Hood became **North Fort Hood**.

To the west, **Gray Air Force Base** was built by the Air Force in 1949, on **Killeen Base** which had been established in 1947 as a function of the Defense Atomic Support Agency. Both were manned by Air Force personnel until the Army assumed operation of Killeen Base in 1952. Fort Hood took charge of the airfield in 1963 and the name was changed to **Robert Gray Army Airfield**. In 1969 when the Department of Defense closed Killeen Base, it officially became a subordinate element of Fort Hood, designated **West Fort Hood**.

Fort Hood supports more than 180,000 active and retired military, their dependents and Department of the Army civilians. It maintains more than 4,600 buildings, housing facilities for some 24,000 bachelor enlisted service members and 5,200 family units.

Visitors are welcome at this open post. On July Fourth there are special activities for the public, including displays and demonstrations. The **1st Cavalry Division** and **2d Armored Division** museums are open daily.

Fort Sam Houston

Headquarters Fort Sam Houston is the hub of support to many tenant commands and activities on the post. They range from a major burn center at Brooke Army Medical Center to the U.S. Modern Pentathlon Training Center for athletes who represent the United States in international competition.

Fort Sam Houston hosts **Headquarters Fifth U.S. Army, Headquarters U.S. Army Health Services Command**, (a major Department of the Army Command), the **Academy of Health Sciences, U.S. Army Dental Activity** and the **U.S. Army Area Dental Laboratory** and **Headquarters U.S Army Fifth Recruiting Brigade (Southwest)**.

Other tenants include the San Antonio field office of the Defense Mapping Agency Topographic Center; the Defense Mapping Agency Inter-American Geodetic Survey; Fort Sam Houston National Cemetery; and the real estate projects office of the Fort Worth District Corps of Engineers.

National Guard and Reserve units and high school and college ROTC elements throughout South Texas are also among the functions supported by the post commander.

As part of its support, the command manages Camp Bullis, a 28,000-acre sub-post 20 miles northwest. Numerous government agencies, including FBI and Air Force personnel, train there on a year-round basis.

Fort Sam Houston is the birthplace of military aviation, and that legacy is carried on today by the post's 507th Medical Company, a helicopter ambulance unit which transports patients in need of immediate medical care. The 507th spearheaded the Defense Department's part in establishing **Military Assistance to Safety and Traffic (MAST)** in 1970. Working with civil authorities, the pilots and medical aid personnel respond to medical emergencies to evacuate patients much the same as wounded soldiers were "MEDEVACed" in Vietnam.

Fort Sam Houston is located in the center of the country's 11th largest city. With a 3-county population of 1,071,952, San Antonio's community calendar is a record of year-round civic activities which involve the post.

Health Services Command

The **U.S. Army Health Services Command (HSC)**, headquartered at Fort Sam Houston, is one of the Army's largest major commands. HSC directs the operations of eight Army medical centers, 30 Army community hospitals, 41 dental activities and laboratories, the **Academy of Health Sciences** and numerous health clinics throughout the continental United States, Alaska, Hawaii, Panama, Puerto Rico, Guam, Johnston Island and the Trust Territory of the Pacific Islands.

The command's primary mission is readiness to support an Army committed to combat. This preparedness is achieved by providing complete health care services to the Army in peacetime. These services include hospitalization, outpatient care, environmental hygiene, dental care, optometric care, veterinary services, nursing care, physical and occupational therapy and dietetic services.

HSC's veterinary role covers an even larger scope than its health and dental care operations. HSC veterinary personnel are located in all but two states and extend throughout the Pacific to include the Philippines and Hong Kong. HSC provides veterinary support for all the military services in its area of responsibility. Services include preventive medicine, food inspection, medical research and development and care of government owned animals.

The command employs approximately 54,000 military and civilian personnel working as a team to provide total health care. About half of the work force is civilian.

Academy of Health Sciences

The **Academy of Health Sciences (AHS)**, at Fort Sam Houston, is an organizational element of U.S. Army Health Services Command. AHS is the largest and probably the most diverse school of allied health sciences in the Free World, with between 25,000 and 35,000 officers, enlisted men and women and civilians enrolled in correspondence courses. The programs of study range from one week to more than two years, and in complexity from apprentice-level medical technical training to graduate programs in health care administration, physical therapy and anesthesiology for Nurse Corps officers.

Qualified students who successfully complete selected programs of study are eligible for award of college credit from the Academy of Health Sciences. Of the programs which are affiliated with civilian colleges and universities, one program results in a bachelor of science degree for warrant officers and three result in a master's degree for officer students. AHS maintains graduate-level affiliations with **Baylor** and **Tulane Universities, Texas Wesleyan College,** and undergraduate-level affiliations with **Regis College** and the **University of Oklahoma.**

As the principal medical education and training institution for the Army, AHS also includes the **U.S. Army Medical Equipment and Optical School** in Aurora, Colo., and the **U.S. Army School of Aviation Medicine,** Fort Rucker, Ala.

Historically, the academy dates back to 1920 when it was founded as the **Medical Department Field School** at Carlisle Barracks, Pa. In 1946 it was moved to Fort Sam Houston, where it was known first as **Army Medical Service School** and then as **Medical Field Service School.** In 1972 it moved to its present location at Fort Sam Houston and was redesignated Academy of Health Sciences, U.S. Army.

Brooke Army Medical Center

Brooke Army Medical Center (BAMC) at Fort Sam

Houston, is the successor to Brooke General Hospital which was established as a post hospital in April 1881. The second largest of the U.S. Army Health Services Command's eight medical centers, it has a worldwide mission of responsibility in every phase of medical education, patient care and medical research.

BAMC operates 692 hospital beds for definitive inpatient treatment, including all phases of surgical, medical, neuropsychiatric and dental care. It also provides an emergency room, walk-in general medical/surgical clinic, and clinics in all medical specialties.

Besides an annual inpatient load of 18,600 and outpatient visits of one million, the Center conducts a vast postgraduate medical education program including internship and resident training in 22 medical specialties. Graduate resident training is conducted in health care administration, pharmacy, dietetics, specialized nursing and clinical pastoral education.

The **U.S. Army Institute of Surgical Research,** attached for administrative and logistical support, has an international reputation for its outstanding work in research and treatment of burns. Procedures developed here are used throughout the world. Teams flown to scenes of burn cases in the continental U.S. return patients to the Institute for care in a matter of hours.

U.S. Army Area Dental Laboratory

The **U.S. Army Area Dental Laboratory** at Fort Sam Houston is one of four throughout HSC providing fixed and removable dental prosthetic appliances for eligible beneficiaries in an 8-state area and Panama. It also provides consultation service to Directors of Dental Services at designated Army installations.

The **Fort Sam Houston Dental Activity (DENTAC)** was organized in May 1978. The DENTAC operates three dental clinics with 56 dental treatment rooms to support over 12,000 active military personnel in the Fort Sam Houston area. In addition to dental care, the DENTAC at Fort Sam Houston offers three residency programs. There are 38 DENTACS located throughout the Health Services Command.

William Beaumont Army Medical Center

William Beaumont Army Medical Center in El Paso symbolizes the latest developments in military medicine in the Southwest.

The striking glass and concrete tower standing at the base of the Franklin Mountains serves the medical needs of all military services in the tri-state area of Arizona, New Mexico and West Texas.

The 12-story medical center was dedicated in 1972. Encompassing over a half-million square feet, the structure houses departments and clinics providing a full range of treatment capabilities and physician training in virtually every medical specialty.

The Beaumont mission also includes operation of the Army's first Residential Treatment Facility for alcoholism and a regional trauma unit. Other activities include medical clinical investigations, alcohol and drug abuse prevention and control programs, preventive medicine and mental health.

William Beaumont Army Medical Center is one of eight major medical centers under the Army's Health Services Command.

Darnall Army Community Hospital

Opened in 1965, **Darnall Army Hospital** (as it was originally named) at **Fort Hood** was the Army's first permanent 200-300 bed hospital and was known as one of the most modern in the military. However, the $12-million, fully equipped hospital was designed only to provide primary care to 40,000 people, and as Fort Hood grew and the retiree population increased, the need for expansion became evident. In 1979, a massive wraparound reconstruction and addition project began and five years later the hospital had doubled its size.

Darnall is the only Army Medical Department Activity under the U.S. Army Health Services Command with a newborn intensive care unit, nuclear medicine and a computerized axial tomography (CAT) scanner.

Although not a medical center, Darnall does have an emergency medicine residency program. Additionally, there are training programs in nursing anesthesiology, nursing education training and military occupational specialty training.

Darnall presently supports 39,000 active duty, 45,000 family members, and 88,000 retired personnel and their families.

Military Aviation

The birth of military aviation took place at San Antonio in 1910, although some earlier flights were made elsewhere. On Feb. 5, 1910, Benjamin D. Foulois arrived at Fort Sam Houston and was instructed to teach himself to fly. His first flight was made March 8, 1910. (See Page 654, 1970-71 Texas Almanac, for more details.)

In 1917, during World War I, San Antonio's **Kelly Field** was activated and became one of the world's largest air training fields. It remained open after the war and **Randolph Field** was activated in 1930. During World War II, thousands of pilots, navigators and bombardiers trained at Texas fields.

Present Activities

Air Force bases in Texas in 1985 included:

Bergstrom AFB—7 miles southeast of Austin. 67th Tactical Reconnaissance Wing (host); HQ, 12th Air Force, (Tactical Air Command); 924th Tactical Fighter Group, HQ, 10th Air Force (Reserve).

Brooks AFB—7 miles southeast of San Antonio. Medical research, education and training, (Air Force Systems Command), **Aerospace Medical Division**. Occupational and Environmental Lab, USAF School of Aerospace Medicine and Air Force Medical Service Center.

Carswell AFB—7 miles west-northwest of Fort Worth. Bomber and tanker base, (**Strategic Air Command**); Tactical Fighter Wing (Air Force Reserve).

Dyess AFB—6 miles west-southwest of Abilene. Bomber and tanker base, Hq., 19th Air Division (Strategic Air Command); 301st TF Wing (Military Airlift Command).

Goodfellow AFB—2 miles southeast of San Angelo. USAF Technical Training School; Air Training Command Base.

Kelly AFB—5 miles southwest of San Antonio. HQ, San Antonio Air Logistics Center (Air Force Logistics Command). USAF Service Information and News Center. HQ, Electronic Security Command; A. F. Commissary Service; A. F. Cryptologic Support Center; Joint Electronic Warfare Center; A. F. Electronic Warfare Center; 149th Tactical Fighter Group (Air National Guard); 433d Military Airlift Wing (A. F. Reserves).

Lackland AFB—8 miles west-southwest of San Antonio. Air Training Command base. Includes: Basic military training for airmen; precommissioning training for officers; technical training for security police and law-enforcement personnel, patrol dog handlers, instructors, recruiters and social action/drug abuse counselors. Also site of Wilford Hall Medical Center, and Defense Language Institute-English Language Center.

Laughlin AFB—6 miles east of Del Rio. Undergraduate pilot training (Air Training Command).

Randolph AFB—20 miles east-northeast of San Antonio. HQ, Air Training Command instructor-pilot training, Air Force Manpower and Personnel Center, HQ USAF Recruiting Service.

Reese AFB—6 miles west of Lubbock. Undergraduate pilot training (Air Training Command).

Sheppard AFB—4 miles north of Wichita Falls. Technical and pilot training (Air Training Command); School of Health Care Sciences.

There is also an ANG Tactical Airlift Wing at Dallas Naval Air Station that flies the C-130 and an ANG Fighter Interceptor Group at Ellington ANGB.

The Air Force Reserve in Texas

The major **U.S. Air Force Reserve** units in Texas are located in San Antonio, Austin and Fort Worth. The units are HQ 10th Air Force (R), Bergstrom AFB (Austin), 433d Military Airlift Wing, Kelly AFB (San Antonio) and the 301st Tactical Fighter Wing, Carswell AFB (Fort Worth). The 924th Tactical Fighter Group is located at Bergstrom AFB.

HQ 10th Air Force (R) is an administrative organization supervising five subordinate wings throughout the United States. The 433d's mission aircraft is the C-5. The 924th flies the F-4. Their primary mission is to maintain a constant state of readiness to be able to augment the tactical forces in the active duty Air Force on a worldwide basis. The 301st mission aircraft is the F-4.

The Air Force Reserve plays a vital role in helping the active duty Air Force accomplish its mission. With better equipment, more front-line missions and professional people, the Air Force Reserve is making a significant contribution to the defense of our country.

Civil Air Patrol

The Civil Air Patrol (CAP) is a volunteer civilian auxiliary of the Air Force. Southwest Regional headquarters, located at Dallas Naval Air Station, Building 1239, directs CAP activities in Texas, Arizona, Arkansas, Louisiana, Oklahoma and New Mexico. There are 2,711 members of the Texas Wing of the CAP, with headquarters at Grand Prairie. Its membership includes 985 cadet members (ages 13 to 18) and 1,726 senior members, over 18, from many Texas communities. Mailing address of the Texas Wing is P.O. Box 530957, Grand Prairie 75053.

Red River Army Depot

Red River Army Depot at Texarkana was activated in August 1941 following a government purchase of 116 farms and ranches, plus wooded acreage. Occupying 50 square miles, it has approximately 1,400 buildings and structures.

Red River's primary mission is to receive, store, recondition and issue all types Army ordnance general supplies and ammunition. It is a major Army maintenance point for rebuilding combat and general purpose vehicles and other types Army ordnance. It has a limited number of military personnel and about 6,000 Civil Service employees.

Corpus Christi Army Depot

Corpus Christi Army Depot (CCAD), activated in 1961, on the site of the **Corpus Christi Naval Air Station**, covers 140 acres mostly under roof. The Army's main overhaul and repair facility for UH-1 Huey, AH-1G Huey Cobra and other helicopters, CCAD also overhauls other U.S. armed forces helicopters for use worldwide.

Utilizing about 130 job skills in the wage grade series and 80 in the general classification series, CCAD has some 4,279 civilians and about 44 assigned military. It is the largest single employer in South Texas, with an annual budget of about $285.9 million and an annual payroll of about $118.4 million.

U.S. Navy and Marines

Naval service activities in Texas include regular and reserve components.

Naval air training installations at Corpus Christi, Beeville and Kingsville are commanded by the Chief of Naval Air Training located at the **Naval Air Station** in Corpus Christi.

The Texas group of the Navy's "mothball fleet" is located at the **Inactive Ships Maintenance Facility**, Orange.

Headquarters for the Seventh Naval Recruiting District is in Dallas.

Naval Reserve

More than 5,500 Naval reservists residing in Texas, or affiliated with Reserve units in Texas, are in a drill-pay status and attend drills for professional and military training.

There are three **Naval Reserve Officer Training Corps** units in Texas; at the University of Texas in Austin, at Prairie View A&M, Prairie View, and at Rice University, Houston. A department of naval science is located at the Merchant Marine and State Marine Academy in Galveston.

Navy and Marine Corps Reserve Centers are located in Abilene, Amarillo, Austin, Corpus Christi, Dallas, El Paso, Harlingen, Houston, Lubbock, Orange, San Antonio, Waco and Wichita Falls. Other reservists drill at Naval Reserve Facilities in Laredo, Midland and Tyler. The **Naval Air Station** in Dallas trains Naval air reservists.

The Naval Air Station at Dallas, under the administrative control of the Commander Naval Reserve Force, headquartered in New Orleans, trains Naval reservists who are members of various base and support groups. Additionally, three Reserve Force Squadrons (two fighter squadrons and a transport squadron) are stationed aboard NAS Dallas to provide further training to Naval reservists.

ADVERTISERS' INDEX
Page

INDEX